PETERSON'S PRIVATE SECONDARY SCHOOLS 2014–15

 PETERSON'S

© 2014 Peterson's, a Nelnet company

Previous editions published as *Peterson's Guide to Independent Secondary Schools* © 1980, 1981, 1982, 1983, 1984, 1985, 1986, 1987, 1988, 1989, 1990, 1991, 1992 and as *Peterson's Private Secondary Schools* © 1993, 1994, 1995, 1996, 1997, 1998, 1999, 2000, 2001, 2002, 2003, 2004, 2005, 2006, 2007, 2008, 2009, 2010, 2011, 2012, 2013

ISSN 1544-2330
ISBN-13: 978-0-7689-3776-3

Printed in the United States of America

10 9 8 7 6 5 4 3 2 1   16 15 14

Thirty-fifth Edition

Sustainability—Its Importance to Peterson's

What does sustainability mean to Peterson's? As a leading publisher, we are aware that our business has a direct impact on vital resources—most especially the trees that are used to make our books. Peterson's Publishing is proud that its products are certified by the Sustainable Forestry Initiative (SFI) chain-of-custody standard and that all of its books are printed on paper that is 40% post-consumer waste using vegetable-based ink.

Being a part of the Sustainable Forestry Initiative (SFI) means that all of our vendors—from paper suppliers to printers—have undergone rigorous audits to demonstrate that they are maintaining a sustainable environment.

Peterson's continuously strives to find new ways to incorporate sustainability throughout all aspects of its business.

Contents

Contents

A Note from Peterson's Editors

Peterson's Private Secondary Schools 2014–15 is the authoritative source of information for parents and students who are exploring the alternative of privately provided education. In this edition, you will find information for more than 1,000 schools worldwide. The data published in this guide are obtained directly from the schools themselves to help you make a fully informed decision.

If you've decided to look into private schooling for your son or daughter but aren't sure how to begin, relax. You won't have to go it alone. **What You Should Know About Private Education** can help you plan your search and demystify the admission process. In the articles that follow, you'll find valuable advice from admission experts about applying to private secondary schools and choosing the school that's right for your child.

In "Why Choose an Independent School?" Dr. John E. Chubb, President of the National Association of Independent Schools (NAIS), describes the reasons why an increasing number of families are considering private schooling.

If you want a private education for your child but are hesitant about sending him or her away to a boarding school, read "Another Option: Independent Day Schools" where Lila Lohr, former Head of School at Princeton Day School in Princeton, New Jersey, discusses the benefits of day schools.

If you are considering attending a boarding school, you will want to read our new article, "Why Boarding School: Reasons I Chose This Path and Why You Might Too," by Justin Muchnick, a boarding school student at Phillips Academy Andover. Or check out the article, "Study Confirms Benefits of Boarding School," with valuable data from The Association of Boarding Schools (TABS).

Mark Meyer-Braun, Former Head of School at the Outdoor Academy, offers "Semester Schools: Great Opportunities," which explores various options for

Schools will be pleased to know that Peterson's helped you in your private secondary school selection.

students to spend an exciting semester in a new "school-away-from-school."

If you are considering a special needs or therapeutic school for your child, you will want to read "Why a Therapeutic or Special Needs School?" by Diederik van Renesse, an educational consultant who specializes in this area.

To help you compare private schools and make the best choice for your child, check out "Finding the Perfect Match" by Helene Reynolds, a former educational planning and placement counselor.

"Plan a Successful School Search" gives you an overview of the admission process.

If the admission application forms have you baffled and confused, read "Understanding the Admission Application Form," by Gregg W. M. Maloberti, former Dean of Admission at The Lawrenceville School.

For the lowdown on standardized testing, Heather Hoerle, Executive Director of the Secondary School Admission Test Board (SSATB), describes the two tests most often required by private schools and the role that tests play in admission decisions in "About Admission Tests and the SSAT." In addition, you can read about another private schools admissions test in "The Independent School Entrance Exam (ISEE)" article.

In "Paying for a Private Education," Mark Mitchell, Vice President, School and Student Services at NAIS, shares some thoughts on financing options.

Finally, "How to Use This Guide" gives you all the information you need on how to make *Peterson's Private Secondary Schools 2014–15* work for you!

Next up, the **Quick-Reference Chart**, "Private Secondary Schools At-a-Glance," lists schools by state, U.S. territory, or country and provides essential information about a school's students, range of grade levels, enrollment figures, faculty, and special offerings.

The **School Profiles** follow, and it's here you can learn more about particular schools. *Peterson's Private Secondary Schools 2014–15* contains three **School Profiles** sections—one for traditional college-preparatory and general academic schools, one for special needs schools that serve students with a variety of special learning and social needs, and one for junior boarding schools that serve students in middle school grades. Many schools have chosen to submit a display ad, which appears near their profile and offers specific information the school wants you to know.

Close-Ups follow each **School Profiles** section and feature expanded two-page school descriptions written exclusively for this guide. There is a reference at the end of a profile directing you to that school's **Close-Up.**

Summer programs are more important than ever for teens. Aside from looking good on a college application, they can be extremely transformative— helping students develop leadership skills, gain greater self-knowledge, and cultivate friendships with peers from across the country or around the world. Finding meaningful summer programs for teens can often be challenging. *Peterson's Private Secondary Schools* guide offers a Summer Programs section that includes two-page descriptions, complete with photos, of exciting opportunities taking place at private schools in the United States and abroad during the summer months.

You'll find great information about program offerings, facilities, staff, costs, and much more.

The **Specialized Directories** are generated from responses to Peterson's annual school survey. These directories group schools by the categories considered most important when choosing a private school, including type, entrance requirements, curricula, financial aid data, and special programs.

Finally, in the **Index** you'll find the "Alphabetical Listing of Schools" for the page references of schools that have already piqued your interest.

Peterson's publishes a full line of resources to help guide you and your family through the private secondary school admission process. Peterson's publications can be found at your local bookstore and library and your school guidance office, and you can access us online at www.petersonsbooks.com. Peterson's books are also available as ebooks.

We welcome any comments or suggestions you may have about this publication. Please send us an e-mail at custsvc@petersons.com. Your feedback will help us make your educational dreams possible.

Schools will be pleased to know that Peterson's helped you in your private secondary school selection. Admission staff members are more than happy to answer questions, address specific problems, and help in any way they can. The editors at Peterson's wish you great success in your search!

What You Should Know About Private Education

Why Choose an Independent School?

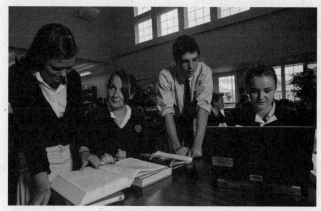

Dr. John E. Chubb
President of the National Association of Independent Schools (NAIS)

More than half a million families each year choose independent private schools. Each independent school has a unique mission that guides its offerings. At an independent school, you can choose a school where the philosophy, values, and teaching approach are right for your child.

Independent schools nurture not just students' intellectual ability and curiosity but also their personal and social growth and civic conscience. Opportunities extend well beyond the classroom to athletic competitions, artistic pursuits, and school leadership experiences.

If you're interested in personal attention for your child, independent private schools have low student-teacher ratios, which help teachers to get to know students well. More than twice as many students at the schools belonging to the National Association of Independent Schools (NAIS) reported that they received helpful feedback from teachers on assignments compared to students at all other types of schools, according to *The High*

> *Independent schools nurture not just students' intellectual ability and curiosity but also their personal and social growth and civic conscience.*

School Survey of Student Engagement (http://ceep.indiana.edu/hssse/index.html). In addition, students who attended NAIS schools were more than twice as likely as students at other schools to say that the school contributed "very much" to their growth in critical thinking.

The Freshman Survey Trends Report, an annual study conducted by the Higher Education Research Institute, found that graduates of NAIS schools felt more prepared for the academic demands of college than their public school counterparts. As college freshmen, NAIS graduates reported that they were more likely to ask questions in class and explore topics on their own, even though it was not required for a class.

Independent schools offer dynamic communities in which parents are invested in their children's education and participate actively in the life of the school. These schools promote regular communication among students, parents, and teachers to ensure everyone is working toward the same goals for the student.

Visit the http://parents.nais.org today to learn more about independent private schools.

Another Option: Independent Day Schools

Lila Lohr

For those of us who are fortunate enough to be able to send our children to an independent day school, it seems to offer the best of both worlds. Our children are able to reap the enormous benefits of an independent school education and we, as parents, are able to continue to play a vital, daily role in the education of our children. Parents enjoy being seen as partners with day schools in educating their children.

As more and more independent day schools have sprung up in communities across the country, more and more parents are choosing to send their children to them, even when it might involve a lengthy daily commute. Contrary to some old stereotypes, parents of independent school students are not all cut from the same mold, living in the same neighborhood with identical dreams and aspirations for their children. Independent school parents represent a wide range of interests, attitudes, and parenting styles.

They also have several things in common. Most parents send their children to independent day schools because they think their children will get a better education in a safe, value-laden environment. Many parents are willing to pay substantial annual tuition because they believe their children will be held to certain standards, challenged academically, and thoroughly prepared for college.

This willingness to make what are, for many, substantial financial sacrifices reflects the recognition that much of one's character is formed in school. Concerned parents want their children to go to schools where values are discussed and reinforced. They seek schools that have clear expectations and limits. The nonpublic status allows independent schools to establish specific standards of behavior and performance and to suspend or expel students who don't conform to those expectations.

Understanding the power of adolescent peer pressure, parents are eager to have their children go to school with other teens who are academically ambitious and required to behave. They seek an environment where it is "cool" to be smart, to work hard, and to be involved in the school community. In independent day schools, students spend their evenings doing homework, expect to be called on in class, and participate in sports or clubs.

Successful independent schools, whether elementary or high school, large or small, single-sex or coed, recognize the importance of a school-parent partnership in educating each child. Experienced faculty members and administrators readily acknowledge that, while they are experts on education, parents are the experts on their own children. Gone are the days when parents simply dropped their children off in the morning, picked them up at the end of the day, and assumed the school would do the educating. Clearly, children benefit enormously when their parents and teachers work together, sharing their observations and concerns openly and frequently.

Most independent schools welcome and encourage parental involvement and support.

Independent schools encourage this two-way give-and-take and are committed to taking it well beyond the public school model. Annual back-to-school nights are attended by more than 90 percent of parents. Teacher-parent and student-teacherparent conferences, extensive written comments as part of the report cards, and adviser systems that encourage close faculty-student relationships are all structures that facilitate this parent-school partnership. Although more and more independent school parents work full-time, they make time for these critical opportunities to sit down and discuss their children's progress.

Most independent schools welcome and encourage parental involvement and support. Although the individual structures vary from school to school, most include opportunities beyond making cookies and chaperoning dances. Many parents enjoy being involved in community service projects, working on school fund raisers, participating in admission activities, sharing their expertise in appropriate academic classes, and even offering student internships. Most schools have made a concerted effort to structure specific opportunities for working parents to participate in the life of the school.

Independent day schools recognize the benefits of parent volunteers and of extending themselves so that parents feel that they are an important part of the school family. Buddy systems that pair new parents with families who have been at the school for several years help ease the transition for families who are new to the independent school sector.

Independent schools have also responded to increased parental interest in programs focusing on parenting skills. Recognizing the inherent difficulties of raising children, independent day schools have provided forums for discussing and learning about drugs, depression, stress management, peer pressure, and the like. Book groups, panel discussions, and workshops provide important opportunities for parents to share their concerns and to get to know the parents of their children's classmates. Schools recognize that this parent-to-parent communication and networking strengthens the entire school community.

Many current day school parents would contend that when you choose an independent day school for your child you are really choosing a school for the entire family. The students become so involved in their academic and extracurricular activities and the parents spend so much time at school supporting those activities that it does become the entire family's school.

_____

Lila Lohr is a former Head of School at Princeton Day School in Princeton, New Jersey, and the Friends School of Baltimore in Baltimore, Maryland. She has been a teacher and an administrator in independent day schools for more than thirty years and is the mother of 3 independent day school graduates.

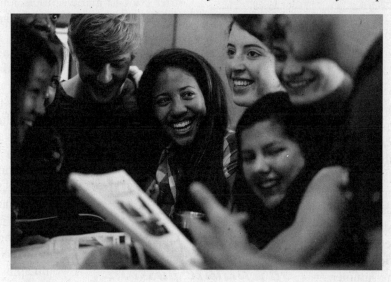

Why Boarding School: Reasons I Chose This Path and Why You Might, Too

Justin Muchnick

My seventh-grade literature class changed my life. To be more exact, Mr. Rogers, my seventh-grade literature teacher, changed my life. Only a temporary substitute teacher (the regular faculty member took the year off for maternity leave), Mr. Rogers entered the classroom on the first day of school and did something remarkable: he asked his students to have a conversation about a book we had read over the summer. My school's traditional "raise your hand and wait to be called on" style of learning had left me completely unprepared for a teacher who *wanted* me to talk. Nevertheless, I relished the opportunity to learn in this interesting and dynamic classroom environment, and I certainly jumped at a chance to voice my opinions without fear of being chastised for speaking out of turn.

Within a few weeks, active participation had fully cemented its reputation as the primary way of learning in Mr. Rogers' class. Instead of employing a standard row-and-column classroom seating pattern, Mr. Rogers positioned our seats in a large circle. This "Harkness" method encouraged free-flowing conversations in which Mr. Rogers would serve only as a mediator and participant. Rather than writing bland responses to even blander study questions, my class honed its public speaking skills by participating in spur-of-the-moment debates about these topics. Mr. Rogers' classroom, remi-niscent of a scene out of *Dead Poets Society*, allowed the act of learning to intellectually stretch and stimulate me.

As Mr. Rogers became my friend and mentor as well as my teacher, I learned that he had previously worked as the Writer in Residence at Phillips Exeter Academy, a boarding school in New England. At that time, I thought that boarding school meant a place where disobedient children were sent to resolve their behavioral issues. Mr. Rogers, though, spoke glowingly of the East Coast boarding school system and told me that schools like Exeter utilize an active, discussion-based, Mr. Rogers-esque style of teaching. Soon, I started dreaming of a school full of teachers like Mr. Rogers, full of intellectually curious students, and full of eager learners. I did some research about Exeter and other New England schools, and in the spring of my seventh-grade year, I presented the boarding school idea to my mom and dad.

At first, my parents commended me on the excellent joke I had pulled on them; however, they quickly realized that I was serious. They began to think that I wanted to get away from them or that I disliked my family. But after extensive negoti-ations, I was able to convince them that this was not the case, and by midway through the summer after seventh grade, they fully backed my decision. Once my family agreed that I was in fact going to pursue the boarding school idea, we made it our mission to select the schools to which I would apply. I devised a list of qual-ities I was looking for in a boarding school. At this point in the application process, you, too, should create a list of criteria—you can save yourself the wasted time and effort of applying to the "wrong" schools by knowing what kinds of schools best suit you. Though your personal list may be very different, mine was as follows:

Size: I tried to find a relatively big school. At my primary school, the average grade size was about 50 students, and, as time wore on, my desire to expand beyond my small group of classmates grew stronger. By applying to larger schools, I felt that I could both broaden my social experience and avoid another "small school burnout."

Uniform Policy: My former school enforced a strict dress code. Since collared shirts and I never really hit if off, I had definitely worn a uniform for long enough. Thus, I did not want to spend my high school years wearing a blazer and slacks.

> *For me, the process of applying to and selecting boarding schools was fueled by my innate passion for learning: I simply wanted to find a place where it was "cool to be smart."*

Single-Sex or Coed: I didn't really want to spend my high school years at an all-boys school.

Location: For me, the East Coast seemed like the best place to find a boarding school. After all, that's what Mr. Rogers had recommended.

Academics: I have an unquenchable thirst for knowledge. I did not wish to "dehydrate" myself at a school with a less-than-excellent academic reputation.

Proximity to an Airport: My mom thought of this one. She suggested that I should apply to schools located near a major airport that offered nonstop flights from Los Angeles. Cross-country flights are tough enough; complicating matters with a connecting flight seemed unnecessary.

Here are some other things that you might want to consider:

Religious Affiliation: Do you want religion to play a large part in your high school experience, or would you rather go to a nondenominational school?

Specialty Schools: Do you want to apply to schools that focus on a specific aspect or method of learning? Are you particularly talented in a certain field? If so, look into arts, math and sciences, or military schools.

Athletics: If you play a sport, you might try to look for schools with strong teams and exceptional athletic facilities. One good way to do this is to contact a school's coach or athletic director. As both a soccer player and a wrestler, I talked to many coaches from a number of different boarding schools to get a sense of each school's athletic program.

Cost/Financial Aid Policy: Obviously, some schools are more expensive than others. In addition to looking at the tuition, you may want to find out which schools offer need-based financial aid or any merit-based scholarships.

By comparing various schools to my personal list of attributes, I was able to find four schools that really matched my requirements. I sent applications to Choate Rosemary Hall, The Lawrenceville School, Phillips Exeter Academy, and Phillips Academy Andover, and I was fortunate enough to have been accepted by all four schools. After taking the SSAT, writing applications, and interviewing with admission officers, little did I realize that I would still have one last, equally significant hurdle to jump. The choice that I was about to make would directly impact the next four years of my life, so my parents and I did everything in our power to ensure that my decision was the correct one. By obtaining contact information from admission offices as well as school counselors and friends of friends, we sought out current students who lived locally and attended each of the schools. We scheduled face-to-face meetings with as

many of them as we could, during which we "grilled" them on the pros and cons of their schools. We spent hours reading websites, blogs, and Facebook pages in hopes of getting students' unsolicited perspectives of their schools. Most importantly, however, we attended the revisit days for each of the schools. For those at this stage of the boarding school process, I would highly recommend going to the admitted students events if you have the financial means and your schedule permits. At any given revisit day, I was truly able to get a feel for the campus and environment and see if I could envision myself as a student at that school next year—sometimes my gut instinct would tell me "yes," and other times it would tell me "no." While on campus, I also had the opportunity to ask countless current students about their high school experiences. Don't be afraid to ask tough questions. By doing so, you can better understand the general campus vibe. After the revisit days, I was able to make my decision with confidence. I was going to Andover!

You might choose to apply to boarding schools for different reasons than I did. No two cases are exactly alike, but many applicants fall into these categories.

Ready to Leave Home: Whether it's a desire for independence, friction within the household, or any other reason, waiting until college to live on your own isn't the best option for you.

Family Tradition: As a baby, you wore a boarding school bib around your neck. Your favorite shirt is one emblazoned with a particular school's emblem. A few older family members have paved the way, or, perhaps, generations of relatives have attended. Boarding school is in your blood.

Diversity: You have grown up in a homogenous community, or you yearn for difference in both tradition and mindset. Today's boarding schools afford you interaction with peers of all racial, financial, geographical, and religious backgrounds—conducive to a multicultural educational experience.

Love of Learning: Is your nose perpetually stuck in a book? Do you stay after class to delve deeper into a conversation with your teacher? Is your idea of a fun weekend activity reading up on political affairs or the latest scientific breakthrough? Do you love learning for learning's sake? If so, boarding school is undoubtedly worth exploring.

For me, the process of applying to and selecting boarding schools was fueled by my innate passion for learning: I simply wanted to find a place where it was "cool to be smart." When I look back at this initial notion, I realize that it was certainly idealistic and a bit naïve, but Andover has come about as close as possible. Though busy work and uninteresting conversations bog me down from time to time, they are more than made up for by engaging writing prompts, stimulating discussions, and inspirational teachers that would make even Mr. Rogers proud.

To learn more about boarding schools, look for Peterson's *The Boarding School Survival Guide*, by Justin Muchnick, available in stores, online, and as an eBook in June 2014.

Justin Muchnick is a student at Phillips Academy Andover in Massachusetts. He is a varsity wrestler, plays soccer, participates on the Mock Trial team, and works as a campus tour guide. A passionate learner, Justin enjoys reading, writing, Latin, and modern American history. He co-authored Straight-A Study Skills (Adams Media, January 2013). He is the youngest journalist for The Bootleg® (http://stanford.scout.com), Stanford University's sports news website, where he writes articles about college football. When he is not at boarding school, Justin resides in Newport Beach, California, with his parents and three younger siblings.

Study Confirms Benefits of Boarding School

Many people have long sung the praises of the boarding school experience. The high-level academics, the friendships, and the life lessons learned are without rival at private day or public schools, they say.

A study released by The Association of Boarding Schools (TABS), a nonprofit organization of independent, college-preparatory schools, validates these claims. Not only do boarding school students spend more time studying (and less time watching TV), they are also better prepared for college and progress more quickly in their careers than their counterparts who attended private day or public schools.

The survey, which was conducted by the Baltimore-based research firm the Art & Science Group, involved interviews with 1,000 students and alumni from boarding schools, 1,100 from public schools, and 600 from private day schools (including independent day and parochial schools).

The results not only affirm the benefits enjoyed by boarding school graduates but those bestowed upon current boarding school students as well. "The study helps us better understand how the opportunities for interaction and learning beyond the classroom found at boarding schools impact a student's life at school and into adulthood," explained Steve Ruzicka, former TABS executive director. Ruzicka said the survey also provides boarding school alumni with empirical data to help when considering their children's educational options.

Rigorous Academics Prevail

Why do students apply to boarding schools? The TABS study found that the primary motivation for both applicants and their parents is the promise of a better education. And, happily, the vast majority of current and past students surveyed reported that their schools deliver on this promise. Current students indicated sig-

nificantly higher levels of satisfaction with their academic experience at boarding schools than their peers at public and private day schools by more than ten percentage points (54 percent of boarding students versus 42 percent of private day students and 40 percent of public school students). Boarders reported in greater relative percentages that they find their schools academically challenging, that their peers are more motivated, and the quality of teaching is very high.

But the boarding environment is valued just as much for the opportunities for interaction and learning beyond the classroom. Interactions in the dining room, the dormitory, and on the playing field both complement and supplement academics, exposing students to a broad geographic and socioeconomic spectrum, challenging their boundaries, and broadening their vision of the world.

The Boarding School Boost

The 24/7 life at boarding schools also gives students a significant leg up when they attend college, the survey documents.

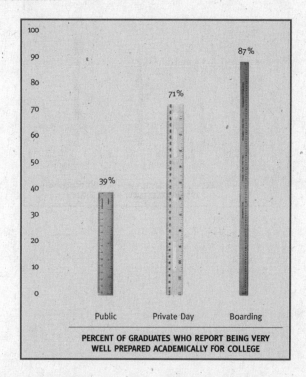

PERCENT OF GRADUATES WHO REPORT BEING VERY
WELL PREPARED ACADEMICALLY FOR COLLEGE

Some 87 percent of boarding school graduates said they were very well prepared academically for college, with only 71 percent of private day and just 39 percent of public school alumni saying the same. And 78 percent of boarders reported that their schools also helped better prepare them to face the nonacademic aspects of college life, such as independence, social life, and time management. Only 36 percent of private day graduates and 23 percent of public school graduates said the same.

9

Study Confirms Benefits of Boarding School

The TABS survey also documented that a larger percentage of boarding school graduates go on to earn advanced degrees once they finish college: 50 percent, versus 36 percent of private day and 21 percent of public school alumni.

Beyond college, boarding school graduates also reap greater benefits from their on-campus experiences, advancing faster and further in their careers comparatively. The study scrutinized former boarders versus private day and public school graduates in terms of achieving positions in top management and found that by midcareer, 44 percent of boarding school graduates had reached positions in top management versus 33 percent of private day school graduates and 27 percent of public school graduates.

By late in their careers, more than half of the surveyed boarding school sample, 52 percent, held positions in top management as opposed to 39 percent of private day and 27 percent of public school graduates.

But perhaps the most compelling statistic that the study produced is the extremely high percentage—some 90 percent—of boarding school alumni who say they would, if given the opportunity, repeat their boarding school experience. This alone is a strong argument that validates the enduring value of the boarding school model. It is hoped that the study will help dispel many of the myths and stereotypes that have dogged the image of boarding schools over the last century and spread the good news that boarding schools today are diverse, exciting places for bright, well-adjusted students who are looking for success in their academic lives—and beyond.

For more information on TABS visit the Web site at www.schools.com.

Used by permission of The Association of Boarding Schools.

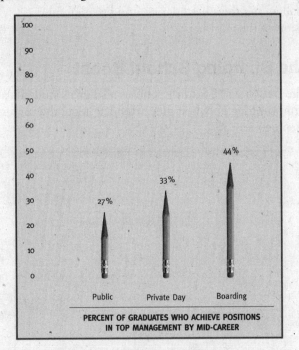

PERCENT OF GRADUATES WHO ACHIEVE POSITIONS IN TOP MANAGEMENT BY MID-CAREER

Semester Schools: Great Opportunities

Mark Meyer-Braun
Former Head of School, The Outdoor Academy

Over the last twenty years, there has been tremendous growth in the range of educational opportunities available to young Americans. The advent of semester schools has played no small part in this trend. Similar in many ways to semester-abroad programs, semester schools provide secondary school students the opportunity to leave their home school for half an academic year to have a very different kind of experience—the experience of living and learning within a small community, among diverse students, and in a new and different place. The curricula of such schools tend to be thematic, interdisciplinary, rigorous, and experiential.

What Are the Benefits?

As a starting point for their programs, semester schools have embraced many of the qualities typical of independent schools. In fact, a number of semester schools were developed as extension programs by existing independent schools, providing unusual opportunities to their own students and those from other schools. Other semester schools have grown from independent educational organizations or foundations that bring their own educational interests and expertise to their semester programs. In both cases, semester schools provide the kind of challenging environment for which independent schools are known.

Across the board, semester school programs provide students with exceptional opportunities for contact with their teachers. Individual instruction and intimate classes are common, as is contact with teachers outside the classroom. At semester schools, students have a full-immersion experience in a tightly knit learning community. In such a setting, teachers are able to challenge each student in his or her own area of need, mentoring students to both academic and personal fulfillment.

Semester schools have developed around specialized curricular interests, often involving unique offerings or nontraditional subjects. In almost every case, these specialized curricula are related to the school's location. Indeed, place-based learning is a common thread in semester school education. Whether in New York City or the Appalachian Mountains, semester schools enable students to cultivate a sense of place and develop greater sensitivity to their surroundings. This is often accomplished through a combination of experiential education and traditional instruction. Students develop academic knowledge and practical skills in tandem through active participation in intellectual discourse, creative projects, hands-on exercises, and service learning opportunities. Throughout, emphasis is placed on the importance of combining intellectual exploration with thoughtful self-reflection, often facilitated by journaling exercises or group processing activities.

At semester schools, students inevitably learn their most important lessons through their membership in the school community. Living closely with peers and teachers and working together for the benefit of the group enables students to develop extraordinary communication skills and high levels of interpersonal accountability. Through this experience, students gain invaluable leadership and cooperation skills.

Ultimately, semester schools seek to impart translatable skills to their students. The common goal is for students to return to their schools and families with greater motivation, empathy, self-knowledge, and self-determination. These skills help to prepare students for the college experience and beyond. In addition, semester school participants report that their experiences helped to distinguish them in the college application process. Semester school programs are certainly not for everybody, but they serve an important role for students who are seeking something beyond the ordinary—students who wish to know themselves and the world in a profound way. All of the following semester school programs manifest these same values in their own distinctive way.

CITYterm

CITYterm, founded in 1996, is an interdisciplinary, experience-based program that takes 30 juniors and seniors from across the country and engages them in a

> *At semester schools, students have a full-immersion experience in a tightly knit learning community.*

semester-long study of New York City. CITYterm students typically spend three days a week in the classroom, reading, writing, and thinking about New York City, and three days a week in the city working on projects, studying diverse neighborhoods, or meeting with politicians, urban historians, authors, artists, actors, and various city experts. Much of the excitement of CITYterm comes from experiencing firsthand in the city what has been studied in the classroom. Many of the projects are done in collaborative teams where the groups engage not only in formal academic research at the city's libraries but also use the resources of New York City's residents and institutions to gather the information necessary for presentations. Students come to see themselves as the active creators of their own learning both in the classroom and in the world. Learn more about CITYterm by visiting www.cityterm.org.

Conserve School

Conserve School is a semester school for high school juniors that is focused on the theme of environmental stewardship. Attending Conserve School gives high school students a one-semester opportunity to step out of their regular school and into a unique educational setting, while still continuing their required academic studies. Conserve School's challenging, college-prep curriculum immerses high school juniors in environmental history, nature literature, and the science of conservation. Because Conserve School is located on a 1,200-acre wilderness campus, a significant portion of the curriculum is delivered via outdoors, hands-on, active learning. Conserve School is located just west of Land O' Lakes, Wisconsin, near the border of Michigan's Upper Peninsula. Learn more about the Conserve School at www.conserveschool.org/.

The Island School

The Island School, founded in 1999 by The Lawrenceville School, is an independent academic program in the Bahamas for high school sophomores or juniors. The fourteen-week academic course of study includes honors classes in science, field research (a laboratory science), history, math, art, English literature, and physical/outdoor education and a weekly community service component. All courses are place-based and explicitly linked, taking advantage of the school's surroundings to both deepen understandings of complex academic and social issues and to make those understandings lasting by connecting course content with experience. Students apply their investigative, interpretive, and problem-solving skills during four- and eight-day kayaking expeditions, SCUBA diving opportunities, teaching environmental issues to local students, and in daily life at the school. In addition to traditional

classroom assessments, students conduct research on mangrove communities, coastal management, artificial reefs, permaculture, and marine protected areas. These projects support national research and are conducted under the auspices of the Bahamian government. At the conclusion of the semester, students present their work to a panel of visiting scientists and educators, including local and national government officials from the Bahamas. The opportunity to interact with the local community through research, outreach, and the rigorous physical and academic schedule creates a transformative experience for students. The admissions process is competitive, and selected students demonstrate solid academic performance, leadership potential, and a high degree of self-motivation. Contact The Island School for more information at www.islandschool.org.

Chewonki Semester School

The Chewonki Semester School (formerly Maine Coast Semester) offers a small group of eleventh-grade students the chance to live and work on a 400-acre saltwater peninsula with the goal of exploring the natural world through courses in natural science, environmental issues, literature and writing, art, history, mathematics, and foreign language. Since 1988, this semester school has welcomed students from more than 230 public and private schools across the country and in Canada. The Chewonki community is small—39 students and 20 faculty members—and the application process is competitive. In addition to their studies, students work for several hours each afternoon on an organic farm, in a wood lot, or on maintenance and construction projects. Students who attend are highly motivated, capable, and willing to take the risk of leaving friends and family for a portion of their high school career. They enjoy hard work, both intellectual and physical, and they demonstrate a tangible desire to contribute to the world. Chewonki students return to their schools with self-confidence, an appreciation for the struggles and rewards of community living, and an increased sense of ownership of their education. For information on the Chewonki Semester School, go to www.chewonki.org.

The High Mountain Institute Semester

The High Mountain Institute (HMI) Semester is a unique opportunity for juniors and some seniors in high school to spend a semester living, traveling, and studying in the mountains of central Colorado and the canyons of southeastern Utah. The school combines some of the best qualities of an academic program at a rigorous boarding school with the adventure of a summer backpacking expedition. The HMI Semester offers an honors and AP-level curriculum to prepare students to thrive during their senior year and in college. Courses are designed to match the content and rigor of the sending schools to ensure smooth transitions for HMI graduates. The High Mountain Institute is accredited by the Association of Colorado Independent Schools.

Interested students can learn more about The High Mountain Institute Semester at http://www.hminet.org/HMIsemester.

The Mountain School

The Mountain School of Milton Academy, founded in 1984, hosts 45 high school juniors from private and public schools throughout the United States who have chosen to spend four months on a working organic farm in Vermont. Courses provide a demanding and integrated learning experience, taking full advantage of the school's small size and mountain campus. Students and adults develop a social contract of mutual trust that expects individual and communal responsibility, models the values of simplicity and sustainability, and challenges teenagers to engage in meaningful work. Students live with teachers in small houses and help make important decisions concerning how to live together and manage the farm. Courses offered include English, environmental science, U.S. history, and all levels of math, physics, chemistry, Spanish, French, Latin, studio art, and humanities. To learn more, please visit the Web site at www. mountainschool.org.

The Outdoor Academy of the Southern Appalachians

The Outdoor Academy offers tenth-grade and select eleventh-grade students from across the country a semester away in the mountains of North Carolina. Arising from more than eighty years of experiential education at Eagle's Nest Foundation, this school-away-from-school provides a college-preparatory curriculum

along with special offerings in environmental education, outdoor leadership, the arts, and community service. Each semester, up to 35 students embrace the Southern Appalachians as a unique ecological, historical, and cultural American region. In this setting, students and teachers live as a close-knit community, and lessons of cooperation and responsibility abound. Students develop a healthy work ethic as course work and projects are pursued both in and out of the classroom. Courses in English, mathematics, science, history, foreign language, visual and performing arts, and music emphasize hands-on and cooperative learning. Classes often meet outside on the 180-acre wooded campus or in nearby national wilderness areas, where the natural world enhances intellectual pursuits. On weekends and extended trips, the outdoor leadership program teaches hiking, backpacking, caving, canoeing, and rock-climbing skills. The Outdoor Academy is open to students from both public and private secondary schools and is accredited by the Southern Association of Colleges and Schools. Learn more about The Outdoor Academy at www.enf.org/outdoor_academy/academic_program.

The Oxbow School

The Oxbow School in Napa, California, is a one-semester visual arts program for high school juniors and seniors from public and private schools nationwide. Oxbow offers students a unique educational experience focused on in-depth study in sculpture, printmaking, drawing and painting, and photography and digital media, including animation. The interdisciplinary, project-based curriculum emphasizes experiential learning, critical thinking, and the development of research skills as a means of focused artistic inquiry. Each semester, 2 Visiting Artists are invited to work collaboratively with students and teachers. By engaging students in the creative process, Oxbow fosters a deep appreciation for creativity in all areas of life beyond the classroom. Since its founding in 1998, students who have spent a semester at The Oxbow School have matriculated to leading universities, colleges, and independent colleges of art and design around the country. Learn more at www.oxbowschool.org.

The Woolman Semester School

The Woolman Semester School is a progressive academic school for young people who want to make a difference in the world. Students in their junior, senior, or gap year come for a "semester away" to take charge of their education and study the issues that matter most to them. Woolman students earn transferable high school credits while taking an active role in their learning experience through community work, organic gardening and cooking, permaculture, art, wilderness exploration, service work, and by doing advocacy and activism work with real issues of peace, justice, and sustainability in the world.

The academic foundation of the semester school consists of three core academic classes: Peace Studies, Environmental Science, and Global Issues as well as two academic electives, math (Algebra II and Pre-Calculus), and Spanish II and III. All students take Art, Nonviolent Communication, and Farm to Table classes. In addition, students who do not need math or Spanish may choose from nonacdemic electives, which are offered each semester. In the past, these courses have included Art as Activism, Wilderness Training, Permaculture, the History of American Music and others.

Four times a semester, Woolman learning goes on the road. The backpacking trip along the wild and scenic Yuba River orients students to the natural world that is Woolman's backyard. During the Food Intensive, students and teachers travel to the San Francisco Bay area and California's Central Valley for a week-long exploration of food systems as part of the Environmental Science curriculum. The Peace Studies trip explores different forms of story-telling in the Bay area and

empowers the students to tell their own stories that will contribute to a culture of peace. Finally, the Global Issues Great Turning trip integrates peace with social and environmental justice by traveling to the Bay area to connect with and learn from activists living what they believe.

Students at Woolman live and learn with their classmates and teachers exploring the 230 acres and the nearby Yuba River. They connect with environmental and peace organizations in the local communities of Grass Valley and Nevada City. Through their experience at Woolman, students become activists that engage issues of peace, social justice, and sustainability on a local and global scale.

For more information on The Woolman Semester School, visit http://semester.woolman.org/.

The author wishes to acknowledge and thank all the semester school programs for contributing their school profiles and collaborating in order to spread the word about semester school education.

Why a Therapeutic or Special Needs School?

Diederik van Renesse

Families contact me when a son or daughter is experiencing increased difficulties in school or has shown a real change in attitude at home. Upon further discussion, parents often share the fact that they have spoken with their child's teachers and have held meetings to establish support systems in the school and at home. Evaluations, medications, therapists, and motivational counseling are but a few of the multiple approaches that parents and educators take—yet in some cases, the downward spiral continues. Anxiety builds in the student and family members; school avoidance and increased family turmoil reach a point where the situation is intolerable, and alternatives must be explored—be it a special needs school, a therapeutic school, or a combination of both.

But should that school be a day or residential school, and how do parents decide which will best meet their child's needs? Resources such as *Peterson's Private Secondary Schools*, the Internet, guidance/school counselors, and therapists are valuable; however, the subtle nuances involved in determining the environment that will best serve the child are difficult to ascertain. Some families seek the help of an independent education consultant to identify the most appropriate setting. Many independent education consultants specialize in working with children who have special needs such as learning differences, anxiety disorders, emotional issues, ADHD, opposition, defiance, school phobia, drug or alcohol abuse, Asperger Syndrome, autism, and more. Consultants have frequent contact with the schools, and they work closely with parents during the enrollment process.

Some families seek the help of an independent education consultant to identify the most appropriate setting.

Given the broad spectrum of needs presented by individual students, many parents question whether there is indeed a day school that can meet the needs of their child. The answer often depends on location, space availability, willingness to relocate, and appropriateness of the options. While there are many day school options throughout the United States, there are even more residential or boarding options. Clearly the decision to have your child attend a residential school is not made easily. As a family you may feel as though you do not have a choice—but you should undertake a thorough assessment of all the day options and how they might meet the majority of your child's needs.

When the primary concerns are learning differences, many local options (though often small and issue-specific) are available to families. Local counselors are often valuable resources as are local chapters of national LD organizations. If you come up with a variety of options, carefully compare them by visiting the schools and meeting with the specialists at each school—those individuals who will work directly with your child.

With the day options, it is important to keep the following factors in mind: program and staff credentials, transportation time to and from the school, availability of additional resources (support services) in or outside the school setting, sports and extracurricular offerings, facilities and accessibility, and your child's potential peer group. You will also need to assess many of these factors when considering residential schools, although most residential schools are more self-contained than day schools. Also significant is whether the school has been approved by and accepts funding from its state and/or school district.

For families who cannot avail themselves of local day options or whose child is best served in a residential setting, an even greater spectrum of options is available. These range from traditional boarding schools with built-in academic support services to therapeutic boarding schools, wilderness or outdoor therapeutic programs, emotional growth or behavior modification schools, transitional or independent living programs, and even residential treatment centers, hospitals, or other health facilities.

Given the breadth of the residential schools or programs, most families are best served by a team that includes not only the parents (and at times the student), but also the professionals who have taught, counseled, and worked closely with the child. Together, the team can identify the specific needs, deficits, or behavioral issues that must be addressed, and they can work together to match those with the appropriate schools. As with day schools, you should arrange to visit the facilities so that you are well-informed about each option and will be comfortable with your final decision. These visits are not only opportunities for you to meet the staff and students, but also for you and your child to begin a relationship that will continue when your child is enrolled.

There is no question that seeking alternative options, whether they are special needs or therapeutic, is a daunting task. However, with the help of expert resources and reliable professionals, the right school can make a significant and lasting impact on your child's health and well-being.

Diederik van Renesse is a Senior Partner at Steinbrecher & Partners Educational Consulting Services in Westport, Connecticut. A former teacher, admission director, and private school counselor, he now specializes in helping families throughout the United States and abroad with youngsters who require special needs or alternative schools or who need interventions and therapeutic settings.

Finding the Perfect Match

Helene Reynolds

One of the real benefits of independent education is that it allows you to deliberately seek out and choose a school community for your child. If you are like most parents, you want your child's school years to reflect an appropriate balance of academic challenge, social development, and exploration into athletics and the arts. You hope that through exposure to new ideas and sound mentoring your child will develop an awareness of individual social responsibility, as well as the study skills and work ethic to make a contribution to his or her world. It is every parent's fondest wish to have the school experience spark those areas of competence that can be pursued toward excellence and distinction.

An increasing number of parents realize that this ideal education is found outside their public school system, that shrinking budgets, divisive school boards, and overcrowded classrooms have resulted in schools where other agendas vie with education for attention and money. In this environment there is less time and energy for teachers to focus on individual needs.

The decision to choose a private school can be made for as many different reasons as there are families making the choice. Perhaps your child would benefit from smaller classes or accelerated instruction. Perhaps your child has needs or abilities that can be more appropriately addressed in a specialized environment. Perhaps you are concerned about the academic quality of your local public school and the impact it may have on your child's academic future. Or perhaps you feel that a private school education is a gift you can give your child to guide him or her toward a more successful future.

Every child is an individual, and this makes school choice a process unique to each family. The fact that your father attended a top-flight Eastern boarding school to prepare for the Ivy League does not necessarily make this educational course suitable for all of his grandchildren. In addition to determining the school's overall quality, you must explore the appropriateness of philosophy, curriculum, level of academic difficulty, and style before making your selection. The right school is the school where your child will thrive, and a famous name and a hallowed reputation are not necessarily the factors that define the right environment. The challenge is in discovering what the factors are that make the match between your child and his or her school the right one.

No matter how good its quality and reputation, a single school is unlikely to be able to meet the needs of all children. The question remains: How do families begin their search with confidence so they will find what they are looking for? How do they make the right connection?

As a parent, there are a number of steps you can follow to establish a reasoned and objective course of information gathering that will lead to a subjective discussion of this information and the way it applies to the student in question. This can only occur if the first step is done thoroughly and in an orderly manner. Ultimately, targeting a small group of schools, any of which could be an excellent choice, is only possible after information gathering and discussion have taken place. With work and a little luck, the result of this process is a school with an academically sound and challenging program based on an educational philosophy that is an extension of the family's views and which will provide an emotionally and socially supportive milieu for the child.

Step 1: Identify Student Needs

Often the decision to change schools seems to come out of the blue, but, in retrospect, it can be seen as a decision the family has been leading up to for some time. I would urge parents to decide on their own goals for the search first and to make sure, if possible, that they can work in concert toward meeting these goals before introducing the idea to their child. These goals are as different as the parents who hold them. For one parent, finding a school with a state-of-the-art computer program is a high priority. For another, finding a school with a full dance and music program is important. Others will be most concerned about finding a school that has the best record of college acceptances and highest SAT or ACT scores.

Once you have decided your own goals for the search, bring the child into the discussion. I often say to parents that the decision to explore is *not* the decision to change schools but only the decision to gather information and consider options. It is important to be aware that everyone has an individual style of decision making and that the decision to make a change is loaded with concerns, many of which will not be discovered until the process has begun.

If you have already made the decision to change your child's school, it is important to let your child know that this aspect of the decision is open to discussion but not to negotiation. It is equally important that you let your child know that he or she will have responsibility in choosing the specific school. Without that knowledge, your son or daughter may feel that he or she has no control over the course of his or her own life.

Some students are responsible enough to take the lead in the exploration; some are too young to do so. But in all cases, children need reassurance about their future and clarity about the reasons for considering other school settings. Sometimes the situation is fraught with disparate opinions that can turn school choice into a family battleground, one in which the child is the ultimate casualty. It is always important to keep in mind that the welfare of the child is the primary goal.

The knowledge that each individual has his or her own agenda and way of making decisions should be warning enough to pursue some preliminary discussion so that you, as parents, can avoid the pitfall of conflicting goals and maintain a united front and a reasonably directed course of action. The family discussion should be energetic, and differences of opinion should be encouraged as healthy and necessary and expressed in a climate of trust and respect.

There are many reasons why you may, at this point, decide to involve a professional educational consultant. Often this choice is made to provide a neutral ground where you and your child can both speak and be heard. Another reason is to make sure that you have established a sound course of exploration that takes both your own and your child's needs into consideration. Consultants who are up-to-date on school information, who have visited each campus, and who are familiar with the situations of their clients can add immeasurably to the process. They can provide a reality check, rein-

forcement of personal impressions, and experience-based information support for people who are doing a search of this type for the first time. All the research in the world cannot replace the experience and industry knowledge of a seasoned professional. In addition, if the specific circumstances of the placement are delicate, the educational consultant is in a position to advocate for your child during the placement process. There are also situations in which a family in crisis doesn't have the time or the ability to approach school choice in a deliberate and objective manner.

These are some of the many reasons to engage the services of a consultant, but it is the family guidance aspect that most families overlook at the start of the process and value most highly after they have completed it. A good consultant provides neutral ground and information backup that are invaluable.

If you have already made the decision to change your child's school, it is important to let your child know that this aspect of the decision is open to discussion but not to negotiation.

Step 2: Evaluate Your Child's Academic Profile

If your child's academic profile raises questions about his or her ability, learning style, or emotional profile, get a professional evaluation to make sure that your expectations for your child are congruent with the child's actual abilities and needs.

Start gathering information about your child from the current school. Ask guidance counselors and teachers for their observations, and request a formal meeting to review the standardized testing that virtually every school administers. Question their views of your child's behavior, attentiveness, and areas of strength and weakness. Make sure you fully understand the reasons behind their recommendations. Do not feel shy about calling back to ask questions at a later date, after you have had time to think and consider this important information. Your child's future may depend on the decisions you are making; don't hesitate to keep asking until you have the information you need.

If a picture of concern emerges, ask the guidance counselor, other parents, or your pediatrician for suggestions regarding learning specialists or psychologists in the community who work with children and can provide an evaluation of their academic ability, academic achievement, and learning style. The evaluation should be reviewed in-depth with the specialist, who should be asked about specific recommendations for changes in the youngster's schooling.

Remember, as the parent, it is ultimately your responsibility to weigh the ideas of others and to decide if the difficulty lies with your child or the environment, either of which could indicate a need for a change of school.

Step 3: Review the Goals of Placement

Discuss your differences of opinion about making a change. Identify a list of schools that creates a ballpark of educational possibilities. (An educational consultant can also be helpful at this stage.)

It is important that both you and your child take the time to consider what characteristics, large and small, you would like in the new school and which you would like to avoid. As you each make lists of priorities and discuss them, the process of school choice enters the subjective arena. The impersonal descriptions of school environments transform into very personal visualizations of the ways you and your child view the child in a new setting.

A chance to play ice hockey, a series of courses in Mandarin Chinese, the opportunity to take private flute lessons, or a desire to meet others from all over the world may sound like a bizarre mix of criteria, but the desire to explore and find all of these options in a single environment expresses the expansiveness of the student's mind and the areas he or she wants to perfect, try out, or explore. Don't expect perfectly logical thinking from your child as he or she considers options; don't take everything he or she says literally or too seriously. Open and respectful discussion will allow a child to embrace a new possibility one day and reject it the next—this is part of the process of decision making and affirmation and part of the fun of exploration.

Step 4: Set an Itinerary

Set an itinerary for visits and interviews so that you and your child can compare campuses and test your preconceived ideas of the schools you have researched against the reality of the campus community; forward standardized testing scores and transcripts to the schools prior to visits so that the admission office has pertinent information in advance of your meeting.

In order to allow your child the freedom to form opinions about the schools you visit, you may want to keep these pointers in mind:

- Parents should allow their child to be front and center during the visits and interviews—allow your child to answer questions, even if they leave out details you think are important.

- Parents should stay in the background and have confidence that the admission officers know how to engage kids in conversation.
- This may be the first time your child has been treated by a school as an individual and responsible person—enjoy watching him or her adjust to this as an observer, not as a protector or participant.
- Don't let your own anxiety ruin your child's experience.
- Discuss dress in advance so it doesn't become the issue and focus of the trip.

Keep your ideas and impressions to yourself and allow your child first shot at verbalizing opinions. Remember that immediate reactions are not final decisions; often the first response is only an attempt to process the experience.

Step 5: Use the Application Process for Personal Guidance

Make sure your child uses the application process not only to satisfy the school's need for information but also to continue the personal guidance process of working through and truly understanding his or her goals and expectations.

Application questions demand your child's personal insight and exploration. Addressing questions about significant experiences, people who have influenced his or her life, or selecting four words that best describe him or her are ways of coming to grips with who your child is and what he or she wants to accomplish both at the new school and in life. Although parents want their children to complete seamless and perfect applications, it is important to remember that the application must be the work of the child and that the parent has an excellent opportunity to discuss the questions and answers to help guide the student in a positive and objective self-review.

It is more important that the application essays accurately reflect the personality and values of the student than that they be technically flawless. Since the school is basing part of its acceptance decision on the contents of the application, the school needs to meet the real student in the application. The child's own determination of what it is important for the school to know about them is crucial to this process. That being said, parents can play an important role in helping the child understand the difference between unnecessarily brutal honesty and putting his or her best foot forward.

Step 6: Trust Your Observations

Although the process of school exploration depends on objectivity, it is rare that a family will embrace a school solely because of its computer labs, endowment, library, SAT or ACT scores, or football team. These objective criteria frame the search, but it tends to be the intangibles that determine the decision. It is the subjective—instinctive responses to events on campus, people met, quality of interview, unfathomable vibes—that makes the match.

It is important to review what aspects of the school environment made you feel at home. These questions apply equally to parent and child. Did you like the people you met on campus? Was the tour informational but informal, with students stopping to greet you or the tour guide? Was the tone of the campus (austere or homey, modern or traditional) consistent with the kind of educational atmosphere you are looking for? Are the sports facilities beyond your wildest expectation? Does the college-sending record give you confidence that your child will find an intellectually comfortable peer group? How long do the teachers tend to stay with the school, and do they send their own children there? If it is a boarding school, do teachers live on campus? How homey is the dorm setup?

The most fundamental questions are: Do people in the school community like where they are, trust each other, have respect for each other, and feel comfortable there? Is it a family you would care to join? These subjective responses will help you recognize which schools will make your child feel he or she is part of the community, where he or she will fit in and be respected for who he or she is and wants to become.

Helene Reynolds is a former educational consultant from Princeton, New Jersey.

Plan a Successful School Search

Application deadlines, entrance exams, interviews, and acceptance or rejection letters—these are some of the challenges you can expect to encounter when applying to private schools. The school search may seem daunting, but it doesn't have to be. Here are some tips to help get you on your way.

The first step is to gather information, preferably in the spring before you plan on applying. *Peterson's Private Secondary Schools*, with vital statistics on more than 1,000 leading private schools in the United States and abroad, can help you evaluate schools, clarify your choices, and hone your search.

If you're considering boarding schools, you may also want to obtain a free copy of the *Boarding Schools Directory* from The Association of Boarding Schools (TABS) by calling 828-258-5354 or by going online to www.tabs.org/Directory_Request.pdf.

Visiting Schools

The next step is to start a list of schools that pique your or your child's interest. You'll want to call, fax, e-mail, or write to admission offices for catalogs and applications. At this stage, don't let cost rule out choices. You'll learn more about the school later—the financing resources it makes available to students and its policies of awarding aid.

With school brochures and catalogs in hand, start planning fall visits and interviews. Review your school calendar, noting Saturdays, holidays, and vacations. Try to plan interviews for these days off. Each interview could last about 3 hours, as campus tours and other activities are often included.

Once you have determined which schools you want to see, where they are, and in what order you want to see them, call each school to set the interview date and time.

Keep in mind that there is no "magic number" of schools to see. Some students interview at and apply to only one school, feeling that if they are not accepted, they will stay at their current school. Some students

interview at many, thinking that considering a large number and a variety of schools will help them focus on real needs and desires.

After you've made an appointment to visit the school, reread the school's catalog and, if possible, its description in this guide, and check out its Web site so that facts about the school will be fresh in your mind when you visit.

The Application Process

Once the fact-finding is completed, your child will need to work on applications. Most schools have January or February deadlines, so it pays to begin filling out forms in November.

Applications may ask for all or some of the following: school records, references from teachers, a student statement, a writing sample or essay, an application fee, and medical history form.

If you are working with a hard-copy form, make photocopies of all application pages before your child begins to complete them. That way, he or she will have at least one copy for use as a rough draft. Also make copies of each completed application for your records.

References are usually written on specific school forms and are considered confidential. To ensure confidentiality, people providing references mail their comments directly to the school. A school may require four or five references—three academic references, usually from an English teacher, a math teacher, and one other teacher, and one or two references from other evaluators who know your child's strengths in areas other than academics. Ask these people in advance if they will write on your child's behalf. Give reference-writers appropriate forms with any special instructions and stamped envelopes addressed to the school; be sure to provide as much lead time before the deadline as possible.

The student application is completed on a special form and consists of factual family information, as well as some long or short essay questions. As tempting as it may be to help, let your child do the writing. The schools need to see the student's style, mechanical skills, and the way he or she looks at life and education. Some schools require a corrected writing sample from an English assignment. In this case, have your child ask his or her English teacher to help choose his or her best work.

For additional information on applications, including the common application forms, check out the next article, "Understanding the Admission Application Form."

Most schools have January or February deadlines, so it pays to begin filling out forms in November.

Once the applications are mailed or submitted online, the hard part is done. Ask admission officers when you can expect to hear their decisions. Most schools will let you know in early March. While you wait, you may want to remind your son or daughter that being turned down by a school is not a statement about his or her worth. Schools have many different objectives in putting a class together. And that's a lesson that will come in handy when you face the college application process.

Understanding the Admission Application Form

Gregg W. M. Maloberti
Former Dean of Admission
The Lawrenceville School
Lawrenceville, New Jersey

Students applying to independent schools are presented with a myriad of options when it comes time to choose the method of completing the application process. Where once each school issued and required its own paper application, many schools now accept common applications such as the Secondary Schools Application from SSAT (Secondary School Admission Test), the Admission Application Form from TABS (The Association of Boarding Schools), or various other online application forms sponsored by individual schools and placement programs. With so many options, many applicants and parents are perplexed as to which method to employ, and others worry that the choice of one method over another may have a negative effect on their chances of admission. Understanding more about why these changes came about and how they save applicants and schools time and money may help applicants and their parents make an informed choice about which method to use.

The recent developments and innovations in independent school applications mirror the changes that have occurred at the college level. The College Board's Common Application is accepted at over 300 colleges and is available online. The Internet has accelerated the interest in online applications. At the same time, students are much more accustomed to writing on a computer than they once were with pen and paper. Concerns about the financial and environmental costs of a paper-based application that travels from the printer to the school, to the candidate, to the candidate's school, and back to the admission office by mail or courier contribute to the idea that the time of an online commonly accepted application has come.

The Standard Application Online (SAO) is available on the SSAT Web site at http://www.ssat.org/admission/the-sao. The Boarding Schools Admission Application Form is available in the TABS Boarding Schools Directory and in electronic form from the TABS Web site: http://www.boardingschools.com/how-to-apply/application.aspx.

There are a few schools that accept only the recommendation forms from the Admission Application Form. It's best to check with each school to find out which forms are preferred. The list of schools accepting the Secondary Schools Application from SSAT is available at this SSAT Web site: http://www.ssat.org/member-search.

Common Applications Make Sense

Anxious parents' lingering doubts about the use of one of the common application forms are hard to ignore: Will the substitution of the common application for the individual school's application cause the admission committee to be offended and compromise my child's chances for admission? Parents should rest assured that schools agreeing to accept the common application forms believe that a fair and effective admission decision can be made on the basis of the common form and that its use in no way erodes the quality of their selection process.

How Does the Common Application Differ?

All applications begin with a biographical sketch of the candidate: name, address, birth date, mailing address, parents' names, and schools attended. Information regarding sibling or legacy relationships, interest in financial aid, citizenship, language spoken, and even racial and ethnic diversity is collected as well. Except for the order in which these questions appear, there is little variation in these question types from one school's application to another. The common application forms certainly relieve candidates of the burden of providing the very same biographical information over and over again.

The second section of an application generally reveals a candidate's accomplishments and ambitions. Often, the applicants are asked to catalog their interests and activities in list or narrative form. Schools want to know what the candidate has done, for how long, with whom, and to what distinction, if any. In a few cases, some schools ask for a series of short answers to a combination of questions or look for the applicant to complete a sentence. There are generally no "right" answers to these questions—but honest answers can help the school begin to characterize the applicant's curiosity, maturity, ambition, and self-esteem. Here again, great similarity exists in the manner and style with which this information is gathered. While the common application forms ask these question types in a more direct manner, they are no less effective than the individual school's application, and their use affords a candidate a genuine measure of efficiency without compromising individuality.

Schools that advocate the use of their own applications over that of the common application forms often bitterly defend the third and final portion of their applications since it generally includes essay questions. With few exceptions, these questions, while occasionally posed in a unique or original manner, seek to probe much the same territory covered by the three choices listed in the essay section of the common application forms:

1. Describe a person you admire or who has influenced you a great deal.
2. What makes you the interesting person that you are?
3. Explain the impact of an event or activity that has created a change in your life or in your way of thinking.

Many schools that use the common applications require a supplement that affords an opportunity for candidates to provide information that is not requested by the common applications.

While the candidate's ability to write well is certainly under review in the essay question, the exercise investigates a candidate's values and explores the individual experiences that have shaped his or her character. These questions give candidates a chance to reveal such qualities as independence, self-reliance, creativity, originality, humility, generosity, curiosity, and genius. Viewed in this light, answering these questions becomes a tall order. The best advice may be to just answer them. In addition, candidates should recognize that although the content of their essays is always of interest, grammar, spelling, punctuation, organization, and the inclusion of evidence or examples are of equal importance.

Candidates who come from disadvantaged backgrounds often find this section of the application the most challenging and occasionally exclusionary. Some schools assume that all applicants have access to opportunities such as summer camps, music instruction, and periodicals and newspapers. Whatever the case, the common application forms attempt to be more inclusive of a broader set of experiences. In fact, many outreach agencies who seek to identify and place disadvantaged

students in independent schools have either used one of the existing common application forms or have developed their own applications in lieu of individual school application forms.

If a student fears that using one of the common applications will somehow fail to convey a unique aspect of his or her individuality or that the essay question answers will not speak to the unique qualities of why a particular school might be a good match, he or she may want to think about including an extra essay. Just because a candidate uses a common application does not mean that he or she must use a common approach to completing it. Imagine how welcome a splash of creativity might be to an individual reader or committee of admission officers who may read hundreds or even thousands of applications each admission season. An application that parrots the list of school courses, sports, and activities offers little insight into the candidate. A well-written application will be as unique as the individual who wrote it.

Using a common application makes the process of applying to multiple schools a much more manageable endeavor.

Applicants and their parents are not the only winners when a common application form is used. The teachers who dutifully complete countless recommendation forms enjoy the convenience of having to complete only one form for each of their students applying to independent schools. Practically speaking, if there is ever a time that a student wants to be in good favor with his or her teacher, it is the moment at which a reference is being given. Using a common application makes the process of applying to multiple schools a much more manageable endeavor. When there is only one form to complete, most teachers will provide longer and more informative answers that are far more helpful to admission officers. Common applications are a great remedy for the fatigue and frustration endured by teachers who have been overwhelmed by a barrage of recommendation forms. Currently, there are even more schools accepting common recommendation forms than there are schools accepting the entire Secondary School Application or the Admission Application Form. Before discounting the benefits of a common application, be sure to consider at least the use of the recommendation forms.

Counselors and Consultants Speak Out

Lee Carey, Director of Admissions and Secondary School Counseling at Shore Country Day School in Beverly, Massachusetts, has been advising eighth-graders for many years and finds the workload associated with the application process unreasonable for most of her students. "It is inconceivable to expect a 14-year-old student to write upwards of eight individual essays, all of top quality. From taking time for school visits, making up missed schoolwork, organizing forms, completing paperwork, and polishing writing, the act of applying to secondary schools becomes a whole second job for eighth- and ninth-grade students." Considering that the average application includes up to ten documents, some of which must pass between the applicant, the sending school, and back to the applicant or the receiving school, an eighth grader and his or her parents are now looking at completing more than eighty documents! On top of the testing process and applying for financial aid, this amounts to an enormous administrative challenge.

Karl Koenigsbauer, Director of Secondary School Placement, Eaglebrook School in Deerfield, Massachusetts, agrees that the common application forms make the process more efficient, but he worries about how they might erode the process as well. "My goal is to help students find the school that will be the best match for their abilities and interests. The essay questions from some schools really help the candidate to understand more about what qualities of mind and spirit a school values. When a candidate comes to me and says a particular question is too difficult, too simplistic, or just plain confusing, it gives me an opportunity to help him or her see how that question represents the identity of that particular school and why it may or may not be a good match. I worry that the common application forms will homogenize the application process to the point where I lose this opportunity to fine-tune the placement process."

Faith Howland, an independent educational consultant in Boston, Massachusetts, and a member of the Independent Educational Consultants Association (IECA), works with families to find the right school and is also often contacted for help when a student's first round of applications has not been successful. "The application process can be near overwhelming for 13- and 14-year-olds. To write as many as eight different applications, each with different essays, just when you are expected to get great grades and continue your sports commitments and other extracurricular activities—not to mention working to prepare for entrance tests. This is high stress! Use of a common application form would be supportive to students and would be extremely helpful in streamlining the teacher recommendations. For those kids who need to submit a second round of applications, the common application forms could be invaluable. These youngsters are coping with disappointment while needing to research new possibilities. If schools were willing to share the common

application forms, it's conceivable that many more students who might simply give up if not successful on their first applications could be placed."

Many Schools, One Application

Increased acceptance of the Secondary Schools Application and the Admission Application Form could lead to a marked increase in applications. Common applications are especially helpful to the candidate who fails to earn any acceptance letters at the end of the application process. Traditionally, if a candidate wants to apply to a new list of schools, he or she must start from scratch and complete a new set of forms. Common applications certainly speed up this process, and in the case of the Secondary School Application from SSAT, sending an application to an additional school is as easy as sending the test scores. Candidates simply sign in to their accounts and select another school.

More than half of the candidates who apply to independent schools come from public schools and may not enjoy the benefit of placement counselors at their schools nor do they seek the advice of independent counselors. Regardless, most candidates are well served in using one of the common application forms when applying to multiple schools. One strategy may be to complete a few individual applications and then submit one of the common application forms to a few other schools—identifying some additional options and increasing the likelihood of having meaningful choices after the decision letters are mailed. Many candidates find it much easier to figure out which school they want once they know which school wants them.

Few schools realize how difficult the application process can be for families who are applying to more than one school. Common application forms make the process of applying to multiple schools a much more manageable endeavor. The use of a common application form affords families much more time and energy to devote to other aspects of the application and interview process. By reducing the duplicated paperwork of recommendations and the need to complete so many essays, applicants and their parents are granted a greater opportunity to discuss the real issues surrounding school selection, such as the compatibility of curriculum, style of teaching, and program offerings. Rather than creating folders for each school and chasing down multiple letters of recommendation, applicants and their parents can focus on just a few essays and remove the stress associated with sorting and tracking multiple documents.

Candidates and their families can be assured of the professionalism of admission officers and feel free to use one of the common applications. The Secondary School Application and the Admission Application Form represent the efforts of the very best admission officers who have put the interests of the applicant at the fore—shifting the focus away from the school and back to the candidate. Candidates can be confident that the

common application form will more than adequately allow them to make a strong case for their own admission at any school accepting the form.

About Admission Tests and the SSAT

Heather Hoerle
Executive Director
Secondary School Admission Test Board (SSATB)

Mention the word "testing" to even the most capable student, and he or she is likely to become anxious. It's no wonder, then, that testing in the independent school admission process causes nail-biting among students and parents alike.

It is important to remember, though, that results of admission testing, while integral to an application, are just one of many factors considered by admission officers when determining if your child and their schools make a great match. The degree of emphasis placed on scores depends on the school and on other information, such as the transcript and teacher recommendations. For the vast majority of schools, students with a wide range of SSAT scores are admitted.

The most important thing to remember about admission tests is that they are different from other kinds of tests. Admission tests, while "standardized," are different from aptitude and achievement tests. A classroom math test, for example, is an achievement test: The teacher specifically designed it to evaluate how much you know about what has been covered in class. The SSAT, on the other hand, is designed to measure the verbal, quantitative, and reading skills you have acquired over time, instead of focusing on your mastery of particular course materials. The SSAT provides independent school admission professionals with meaningful information about the possible academic success of potential students like you at their institutions, regardless of students' background or experience.

Admission tests are also different from classroom and achievement tests, because they are "norm-referenced." This means that your child's score is interpreted relative to the group of students taking the test (the *norm group*). For example, if you are a boy in the sixth grade, and your percentile rank on the SSAT verbal section is 70 percent, it means that 70 percent of all the other sixth grade boys' (who have taken the test for the first time on one of the Standard Saturday or Sunday SSAT administrations in the USA and Canada between 2008 and 2011) scores fall below your scale score. Therefore, the same scale score on the SSAT may have a different percentile rank from year to year. In contrast, your percent correct from a classroom math test is 90 percent because you answered 90 percent of the questions correctly. Your score is not referenced to the performance of anyone else in your class.

Finally, admission tests are constructed so that only 50 percent of the examinees will get the average test question correct. This is so that the test will effectively differentiate among test-takers, who vary in their level of skills. Therefore, "average" on the SSAT (50 percent) is different than "average" on your child's math test (which may be something more like 80 percent). Many parents express concern that their child's SSAT Percentile is lower than they typically score on other tests such as standardized achievement tests and school exams. It is important to remember that SSAT test-takers are members of a small and highly competitive group of students who plan to attend some of the world's best private/independent schools. Being in the middle of this group is still impressive!

> *It's important to remember that results of admission testing, while integral to an application, are just one of many factors considered by admission officers.*

Taking the SSAT

There are three levels of the SSAT administered. The Upper Level is administered to students in grades 8–11. The Middle Level is administered in grades 5–7, and the Elementary Level is administered in grades 3 and 4. The Middle and Upper Level exams are both approximately 3 hours in length, while the Elementary test is just short of 2 hours. Each test has verbal, reading, and quantitative sections that are constructed in a multiple choice format, along with an unscored writing sample.

The two mathematics sections of the Middle and Upper Level SSAT measures a student's knowledge of algebra, geometry, and other quantitative concepts and consists of two 25-question sections. The Elementary Level SSAT tests measures knowledge of elementary arithmetic, algebra, and geometry in one 30-minute, 30-question section.

The reading comprehension section of the test measures a student's ability to understand what they have read. After reading a passage, the student will be asked questions about its content or about the author's style, intent, or point of view. The goals are to discern the main idea of the piece, identify the important details that move the narrative along or create a mood or tone, or to identify the details that support the writer's opinion. The Upper and Middle level tests contain 40 questions, while the Elementary test consists of 28 reading comprehension questions.

The verbal section asks students to identify synonyms and interpret analogies. The synonym questions test the strength of the student's vocabulary, while the analogy questions measure a student's ability to relate ideas to each other logically. The Upper and Middle Level SSATs consist of 60 verbal questions, while the Elementary test has just 30 verbal section questions.

In addition, the exam contains an unscored writing sample that is not scored but is provided to schools to offer a sense of the student's writing skills. The writing sample section varies based on the level of test. The Upper and Middle Level SSATs offer a choice of two writing prompts. In the Upper Level SSAT, one prompt is a creative prompt and the other an essay prompt. On the Middle Level exam, both are creative prompt choices. The Elementary Level exam offers a picture, and the student must write a story about what is happening in the picture.

There are two types of SSAT test administrations: Standard and Flex. The Standard administrations are given eight Saturdays during the academic year (October, November, December, January, February, March, April, and June) at various test locations throughout the United States, Canada, and other locations around the world. Students also have the option of "on demand" Flex testing through select educational consultants or placement directors at some independent schools. Students can take up to all eight of the Standard Tests, but they can only take the Flex test once.

Test-takers can arrange to have SSAT scores sent to different schools and have the option to select school score recipients either during test registration or after receiving their scores. Students can research schools, register for the test, find a test center, order score services, and fees online at ssat.org or by calling 609-683-

4440. In addition, students can order the *Official Guide to the SSAT* for the Middle and Upper Level tests. *The Official Guide to the SSAT* is the only study guide written by the SSAT test development team. *The Official Guide to the Elementary Level SSAT* is available for free download on ssat.org.

SSAT.org also offers a variety of sources on the independent school application process; it also offers family webinars on the test, understanding score reports, and more.

> *When taking the SSAT, if a student cannot eliminate one or more of the answer choices as wrong, it is best to skip the question to maintain a higher score.*

How is the SSAT Scored?

The SSAT is a formula scored test, meaning students earn one point for every correct answer, zero points for omitted questions, and they lose ¼ point for each incorrect answer. Each student's score report includes the number of correct and incorrect answers, as well as the number of questions omitted.

Understanding formula scoring is critical to a student's test-taking strategy. When taking the SSAT, if a student cannot eliminate one or more of the answer choices as wrong, it is best to skip the question to maintain a higher score.

How Important Are the Tests?

The SSAT norm group is a highly competitive group. Your child is being compared to all the other students (same grade/gender) who are taking this test for admission into independent schools—some of which can be the most selective schools in the country. I can assure you, though, that in 100 percent of independent schools, the test is just one part of the selection process. This is vital for students and families to remember as it relieves the "test-taking pressure" we've read so much about in the media and heard from families, teachers, and the educational community. Admission officers are tasked with finding the right students that not only fit the academic piece of their school, but the culture and community found unique to each independent school environment. The SSAT is not designed to measure other characteristics such as motivation, persistence, or creativity that a student may contribute to in a particular school community environment.

That said, parents should be partners in the test-preparation process, both as a tutor and reassuring voice for the student. This same relationship should extend to partnering with your student to submit an application that highlights a student's school work portfolios and other academic achievements, recommendations, and other elements that are just as critical to the selection process. Remember, admission officers must find applicants that are the right academic AND social/cultural fit for their school. The SSAT can only assist in determining one element of this process.

Heather Hoerle's career in independent schools began as an administrator, student advisor, and teacher at George School (PA) and Westtown School (PA). She then embarked on a successful 23-year tenure in leadership roles with two of the world's largest nonprofit independent school organizations: first as Associate Director of The Association of Boarding Schools (TABS), then as Director of Admission and Marketing Services for The National Association of Independent Schools (NAIS), leading to her most recent position as NAIS' Vice President of Member Relations. Heather emphasizes, "I believe passionately in the power of education (and especially independent private schools) to open minds and create better human beings. I have seen through my own experiences as a student, admission officer, teacher, trustee, and parent in independent schools, that our community regularly transforms children helping them to become thoughtful contributors in this interconnected, global society."

Heather holds a B.A. in Art History from Mount Holyoke College and a M.Ed. from Harvard University. She is a Board Member of the Westtown School and the Friends Council on Education. Heather currently resides in Hopewell, New Jersey, with her husband and daughter, and is an avid fan of the theater.

10 Tips for Doing Your Best on the SSAT

1. Practice, practice, practice—early!

For the SSAT, just like other standardized tests, if you practice, you will feel more confident that you'll do well. Purchase the *Official Guide to the SSAT* a couple of months before you plan to take the test, if possible.

2. Read—a lot!

The best way to build your vocabulary and to get a better sense for the meanings of unfamiliar words is to see them in the context of other words.

3. If you know you're weak in a particular subject, get help before you take the test.

If you know that math is your weakest subject, make sure you address it as soon as you can. Begin early and practice every day if possible until your skills improve. Look to teachers, tutors, or your parents for advice and assistance.

4. Be prepared.

The night before the test, gather everything you need: your admission ticket, pencils, a snack, and so on. This will allow you time in the morning to eat a healthy breakfast and review, if necessary.

5. Get a good night's rest.

We can't stress enough the importance of trying to relax and get plenty of sleep the night before your exam.

6. Arrive at the test center early on test day and come prepared.

Arrive 30 minutes early. Be sure to have your admission ticket, three #2 pencils, a snack in a clear plastic bag, and water. Leave your cell phones and backpacks at home!

7. Relax!

Your attitude and outlook will be reflected in the outcome of the test. Stay confident and calm throughout your exam. If you start to feel nervous or anxious, take a few deep breaths to collect yourself.

8. Set a pace.

Don't spend too much time on one question, and don't speed through carelessly. If you get stuck on a question, skip it, and return to it later if you have time—be sure to leave the bubble unmarked on your answer sheet for this question! Read each question carefully, and answer accurately.

9. Remember your test-taking strategy!

You receive one point for every correct answer and lose ¼ of a point for each wrong answer on a question. You don't lose points by skipping a question. If you can't eliminate at least one or two of the choices in a question and take an "educated guess," it's better to leave the question unanswered. This strategy can help you receive the highest possible score:

10. Remember: The SSAT is one piece of the admission picture!

The SSAT is just one piece of your admission application. Schools will look at your grades, recommendations, test scores, your interview, and more to decide if you are a fit for their school.

Good luck!

About the Independent School Entrance Exam (ISEE)

The ISEE is an admission test that has three levels: A Lower Level, Middle Level, and Upper Level. The Lower Level is for students currently in grades 4 and 5 who are candidates for admission to grades 5 and 6. The Middle Level is for students in grades 6 and 7 who are candidates for grades 7 and 8. The Upper Level is for students in grades 8 through 11 who are candidates for grades 9 through 12. The ISEE has different forms at each level for security purposes.

At all levels, the ISEE consists of three parts:

1. Carefully constructed and standardized verbal and quantitative reasoning tests that measure a student's capability for learning

2. Reading comprehension and mathematics achievement tests that provide specific information about a student's strengths and weakness in those areas

3. An essay section

The ISEE essay is timed and written in response to a prompt. The essay is not scored; it is photocopied and sent only to the schools the student requested.

Test Sections and Timing

The Middle Level and Upper Level tests are 2 hours 40 minutes in length. Students receive a 5-minute warning before the end of each test section. In the essay section, the students receive both a 15-minute warning and a 5-minute warning before time is called. Once time is called, students may not return to a completed test section.

Testing Policy

Practice administrations of the ISEE are not allowed. Students may test only when making a formal application to a school. Students may be tested only once within a six-month period. If a student takes the test a second time during that six-month period, results of the second administration cannot be reported, and the test fee will not be returned.

Raw Score vs. Scaled Score

A raw score is the number of questions a student answered correctly. There is no penalty for incorrect answers on the ISEE.

The scaled score is a common scale, derived from the raw score, which has the same meaning for all students regardless of the edition or form taken. The scaled score is used to control for slight variations among different forms of a test. It enables the test-maker, ERB, to report a score on a common scale that has the same meaning for all students. The scaled score range for all sections and levels of the ISEE falls between 760 and 940.

What to Expect on the ISEE

Educational Records Bureau (ERB) provides "What to Expect on the ISEE" preparation materials at no cost when viewed or downloaded from its website at http://erblearn.org. These materials offer parents and students the opportunity to review the types of questions presented on each level of the ISEE test.

Each "What to Expect on the ISEE" guide includes level-specific background information about the ISEE testing experience, including sample questions, a full-length practice test (for Lower, Middle, and Upper levels only), an actual answer sheet, a sample writing prompt, scoring information, and a section on understanding the Individual Student Report (ISR).

ISEE's Role in the Admission Process

Schools use the ISEE scores as one piece of the overall student profile for applicant consideration. The ISEE offers a standardized assessment comparing a student's reasoning and achievement skills to those of other students applying to the same grade from different schools.

The standards on the ISEE align with those of the National Council of Teachers of English (NCTE), the International Reading Association (IRA), and the National Council of Teachers of Mathematics (NCTM).

Paper-Pencil and Online Tests Available

The ISEE is offered in both a paper-pencil and online format for the Lower, Middle, and Upper levels. Both modalities have the same number of questions, the same timing, and the same opportunity for students to change their answers during the test section. For the essay, however, the online option requires a student to type his or her essay, while a student taking the paper-pencil test will need to handwrite his or her essay.

The online ISEE is available through a partnership with Prometric, a subsidiary of ETS, which has testing offices in more than 400 cities in both the United States and abroad. For more information, visit http://erblearn.org/parents/admission/isee/testing_at_prometric.

_____

Source: http://erblearn.org/parents/admission/isee/isee-test-overview

Paying for a Private School Education

Mark J. Mitchell

Vice President, School and Student Services
National Association of Independent
Schools (NAIS)

Imagine being able to buy a $23,000 car for $12,000 because that is all you can afford. When you buy a car, you know that you will be paying more than it cost to design, build, ship, and sell the car. The sales staff will not offer you a price based on your income. At best, you may receive discounts, rebates, or other incentives that allow you to pay the lowest price the dealer is willing to accept. No matter how you look at it, you pay more than the car cost to make.

Tuition at many private schools can approach the cost of a new car, but paying for a private school education is not the same as buying a car. One difference is the availability of financial aid at thousands of schools in the United States and abroad. Financial aid helps offset the cost of tuition. Learning about the financing options and procedures available can make private school a reality for many families.

Need-Based Financial Aid

Many private schools offer assistance to families who demonstrate financial need. In fact, for a recent academic year, schools that belonged to the National Association of Independent Schools (NAIS) provided more than $1.5 trillion in need-based financial aid to nearly 23 percent of their students. For 2012–13, the median grant for boarding school students was $22,053 and the median grant for day school students was $10,574. These need-based grants do not need to be repaid and are used to offset the school's tuition. Schools make this substantial commitment as one way of ensuring a socio-economically diverse student body and to help ensure that every student qualified for admission has the best chance to enroll, regardless of his or her financial circumstances.

How Financial Need Is Determined

Many schools use a process of determining financial need that requires the completion of applications and the submission of tax forms and other documentation to help them decide how much help each family needs. Currently, more than 2,100 schools nationwide ask families to complete The School and Student Services (SSS by NAIS) Parents' Financial Statement (PFS) online at http://SSSbyNAIS.org to determine eligibility for aid. The Parents' Financial Statement gathers information about family size, income and expenses, parents' assets and indebtedness, and the child's assets. From this and other information, schools are provided with an estimate of the amount of discretionary income (after several allowances are made for basic necessities) available for education costs. Schools review each case individually and use this estimate, along with such supporting documentation as most recent income tax forms, to make a final decision on a family's need for a financial aid grant. For more information, please visit http://sssbynais.org.

The amount of a need-based financial aid award varies from person to person and school to school. Just as individuals have different financial resources and obligations that dictate their need for assistance, schools have different resources and policies that dictate their ability to meet your financial need. Tuition costs, endowment incomes, and the school's philosophy about financial aid are a few of the things that can affect how much aid a school can offer. If your decision to send your child to a private school depends heavily on getting financial help, you would benefit from applying for aid at more than one school.

Merit-Based Awards

While the majority of aid offered is based on a family's financial situation, not everyone who receives financial assistance must demonstrate financial need. Private schools offer millions of dollars in merit-based scholarships to thousands of students. In the 2012–13 academic year, 313 NAIS-member schools granted an average annual merit award worth $6,180 to students, totaling more than $55.4 million. Even with this level of commitment, such awards are rare (just 5.6 percent of all enrolled students receive this type of aid) and, therefore, highly competitive. They may serve to reward demonstrated talents or achievements in areas ranging from academics to athletics to the arts.

Some additional resources may be available from organizations and agencies in your community. Civic and religious groups, foundations, and even your employer may sponsor scholarships for students at private schools. Unfortunately, these options tend to be few and far between, and limited in number and size of award. Be sure to ask a financial aid officer at the school(s) in which you are interested if he or she is aware of such organizations and opportunities. Whether it is offered by the school or a local organization, understanding the requirements or conditions on which a merit-based scholarship is based is critical. Ask if the award is renewable and, if so, under what conditions. Often, certain criteria must be met (such as minimum GPA, community service, or participation in activities) to ensure renewal of the award in subsequent years, and some merit awards are available for just one year.

The financial aid officer at the school is the best source of information about your options.

Tuition Financing Options

Whether or not you qualify for grants or scholarships, another way to get financial help involves finding ways to make tuition payments easier on your family's monthly budget. One common option is the tuition payment plan. These plans allow you to spread tuition payments (less any forms of financial aid you receive) over a period of eight to ten months. In most cases, payments start before the school year begins, but this method can be more feasible than coming up with one or two lump sum payments before the beginning of the school year. Payment plans may be administered by the schools themselves or by a private company approved by the school. They do not normally require credit checks or charge interest; however, they typically charge an application or service fee, which may include tuition insurance. Additional information about tuition payment plans is available on the NAIS Web site at http://sssbynais.org.

Since a high-quality education is one of the best investments they can make in their child's future, many parents finance the cost just as they would any other important expense. A number of schools, banks, and other agencies offer tuition loan programs specifically for elementary and secondary school expenses. While such loans are subject to credit checks and must be repaid with interest, they tend to offer rates and terms that are more favorable than those of other consumer loans. It pays to compare the details of more than one type of loan program to find the best one for your needs. Although they should always be regarded as an option of last resort, tuition loan programs can be helpful. Of course, every family must consider both the short- and long-term costs of borrowing and make its decision part of a larger plan for education financing.

A Final Word

Although the primary responsibility to pay for school costs rests with the family, there are options available if you need help. As you can see, financing a private school education can result in a partnership between the family, the school, and sometimes outside agencies or companies, with each making an effort to provide ways to meet the costs. The financial aid officer at the school is the best source of information about your options and is willing to help you in every way he or she can. Always go to the financial aid officer at a school in which you are interested whenever you have any questions or concerns about programs or the application process. Understanding your responsibilities, meeting deadlines, and learning about the full range of options are your best strategies for obtaining assistance. Although there are no guarantees, with proper planning and by asking the right questions, your family just might get the high-quality private education for less.

How to Use This Guide

Quick-Reference Chart

"Private Secondary Schools At-a-Glance" presents data listed in alphabetical order by state and U.S. territories; schools in Canada and other countries follow state listings. If your search is limited to a specific state, turn to the appropriate section and scan the chart for quick information about each school in that state: Are students boarding, day, or both? Is it coeducational? What grade levels are offered? How many students are enrolled? What is the student/faculty ratio? How many sports are offered? Does the school offer Advanced Placement test preparation?

School Profiles and Displays

The **School Profiles** and **Displays** contain basic information about the schools and are listed alphabetically in each section. An outline of a **School Profile** follows. The items of information found under each section heading are defined and displayed. Any item discussed below that is omitted from a **School Profile** either does not apply to that particular school or is one for which no information was supplied.

Heading Name and address of school, along with the name of the Head of School.

General Information Type (boys', girls', coeducational, boarding/day, distance learning) and academic emphasis, religious affiliation, grades, founding date, campus setting, nearest major city, housing, campus size, total number of buildings, accreditation and memberships, languages of instruction, endowment, enrollment, upper school average class size, upper school faculty-student ratio, number of required school days per year (Upper School), number of days per week Upper School students typically attend, and length of the average school day.

Upper School Student Profile Breakdown by grade, gender, boarding/day, geography, and religion.

Faculty Total number; breakdown by gender, number with advanced degrees, and number who reside on campus.

Subjects Offered Academic and general subjects.

Graduation Requirements Subjects and other requirements, including community service.

Special Academic Programs Honors and Advanced Placement courses, accelerated programs, study at local college for college credit, study abroad, independent study, ESL programs, programs for gifted/remedial students and students with learning disabilities.

College Admission Counseling Number of recent graduates, representative list of colleges attended. May include mean or median SAT/ACT scores and percentage of students scoring over 600 on each section of the SAT, over 1800 on the combined SAT, or over 26 on the composite ACT.

Student Life Dress code, student council, discipline, and religious service attendance requirements.

Summer Programs Programs offered and focus; location; open to boys, girls, or both and availability to students from other schools; usual enrollment; program dates and application deadlines.

Tuition and Aid Costs, available financial aid.

Admissions New-student figures, admissions requirements, application deadlines, fees.

Athletics Sports, levels, and gender; number of PE instructors, coaches, and athletic trainers.

Computers List of classes that use computers, campus technology, and availability of student e-mail accounts, online student grades, and a published electronic and media policy.

Contact Person to whom inquiries should be addressed.

Displays, provided by school administrators, present information designed to complement the data already appearing in the **School Profile.**

Close-Ups

Close-Ups, written expressly for Peterson's by school administrators, provide in-depth information about the schools that have chosen to submit them. These descriptions are all in the same format to provide maximum comparability. **Close-Ups** follow each **School Profile** section; there is a page reference at the end of a **School Profile** directing you to that school's **Close-Up** as well as its **Summer Program Close-Up,** if one was provided. Schools are listed alphabetically in each section.

Special Needs Schools

One of the great strengths of private schools is their variety. This section is dedicated to the belief that there is an appropriate school setting for every child, one in which he or she will thrive academically, socially, and emotionally. The task for parents, counselors, and educators is to know the child's needs and the schools' resources well enough to make the right match.

Schools in this section serve those students who may have special challenges, including learning differences, dyslexia, language delay, attention deficit disorders, social maladjustment to family and surroundings, or emotional disturbances; these students may need individual attention or are underachieving for some other reason. Parents of children who lag significantly behind their grade level in basic academic skills or who have little or no motivation for schoolwork will also want to consult this section. (For easy reference, schools that offer extra help for students are identified in two directories: "Schools Reporting Programs for Students with Special Needs" and "Schools Reporting That They Accommodate Underachievers.") The schools included here chose to be in this section because they consider special needs education to be their primary focus. It is the mission of these schools, whose curricula and methodologies vary widely, to uncover a student's strengths and, with appropriate academic, social, and psychological counseling, enable him or her to succeed.

Junior Boarding Schools

As parents know, the early adolescent years are ones of tremendous physical and emotional change. Junior boarding schools specialize in this crucial period by taking advantage of children's natural curiosity, zest for learning, and growing self-awareness. While junior boarding schools enroll students with a wide range of academic abilities and levels of emotional self-assurance, their goal is to meet each youngster's individual needs within a supportive community. They accomplish this through low student-teacher ratios and enrollment numbers deliberately kept low.

The boarding schools featured in this section serve students in the middle school grades (6–9); some offer primary programs as well. For more information about junior boarding schools, visit the Junior Boarding Schools Association Web site at www.jbsa.org.

Summer Programs

The Summer Programs section offers Close-Ups of exciting summer programs that are taking place at private schools throughout the United States and abroad. These two-page in-depth descriptions provide details on the summer program's background and philosophy, program offerings, location, staff, facilities, daily schedule, extra opportunities and activities, medical care, transportation, costs, financial aid, application timetable, and contact information. The photos included in the Summer Program Close-Ups offer a glimpse of the facilities, surroundings, and faces of program participants. Those schools whose summer program descriptions are included in this section have paid a fee to Peterson's to provide this information to you.

Specialized Directories

These directories are compiled from the information gathered in *Peterson's Annual Survey of Private Secondary Schools*. The schools that did not return a survey or provided incomplete data are not fully represented in these directories. For ease of reference, the directories are grouped by category: type, curricula, financial data, special programs, and special needs.

Index

The "Alphabetical Listing of Schools" shows page numbers for School Profiles in regular type, page numbers for Displays in italics, and page numbers for Close-Ups in boldface type.

Data Collection Procedures

The data contained in *Peterson's Private Secondary Schools 2014–15* **School Profiles, Quick-Reference Chart, Specialized Directories,** and **Index** were collected through *Peterson's Annual Survey of Private Secondary Schools* during summer and fall 2013. Also included were schools that submitted information for the 2012–13 data collection effort but did not submit updates in the summer/fall of 2013. Questionnaires were posted online. With minor exceptions, data for those schools that responded to the questionnaire were submitted by officials at the schools themselves. All usable information received in time for publication has been included. The omission of a particular item from a **School Profile** means that it is either not applicable to that school or not available or usable. Because of Peterson's extensive system of checking data, we believe that the information presented in this guide is accurate. However, errors and omissions are possible in a data collection and processing endeavor of this scope. Therefore, students and parents should check with a specific school at the time of application to verify all pertinent information.

Criteria for Inclusion in This Book

Most schools in this book have curricula that are primarily college preparatory. If a school is accredited or is a candidate for accreditation by a regional accrediting group, including the European Council of International Schools, and/or is approved by a state Department of Education, and/or is a member of the National Association of Independent Schools or the European Council of International Schools, then such accreditation, approval, or membership is stated. Schools appearing in the **Special Needs Schools** section may not have such accreditation or approval.

Quick-Reference Chart

Private Secondary Schools At-a-Glance

| | STUDENTS ACCEPTED | | | | GRADES | | | STUDENT/FACULTY | | | SCHOOL OFFERINGS | |
| | BOARDING | | DAY | | | | | | | | | |
	Boys	Girls	Boys	Girls	Lower	Middle	Upper	Total	Upper	Student/Faculty Ratio	Advanced Placement Preparation	Sports
UNITED STATES												
Alabama												
Briarwood Christian High School, Birmingham			X	X	K–6	7–8	9–12	1,971	591	23:1	X	18
The Donoho School, Anniston			X	X	PS–6	7–8	9–12	344	120	12:1	X	11
Edgewood Academy, Elmore			X	X	PK–5	6–8	9–12	314	100	11:1	X	12
The Ellis Academy, Toney		X	X	X	K–5	6–10	11–PG	9	2	5:1	X	18
John T. Morgan Academy, Selma			X	X	PK–6	7–9	10–12	500	122	22:1		28
Madison Academy, Madison			X	X	PS–6	–	7–12	900	450	15:1		9
Mars Hill Bible School, Florence			X	X	K4–4	5–8	9–12	540	198	14:1	X	11
McGill-Toolen Catholic High School, Mobile			X	X	–	–	9–12	1,170	1,170	14:1	X	14
The Westminster School at Oak Mountain, Birmingham					K–6	–	7–12	508	178			6
Alaska												
Grace Christian School, Anchorage			X	X	K–6	7–8	9–12	617	205	15:1	X	8
Arizona												
Blueprint Education, Glendale					–							
Bourgade Catholic High School, Phoenix			X	X	–	–	9–12	401	401	20:1	X	16
Brophy College Preparatory, Phoenix			X		–	6–8	9–12	1,362	1,284	14:1	X	44
The Orme School, Mayer	X	X	X	X	–	–	8–PG	110	110	6:1	X	40
Phoenix Christian Unified Schools, Phoenix			X	X	PS–5	6–8	9–12	424	231	20:1	X	16
Pusch Ridge Christian Academy, Tucson			X	X	–	6–8	9–12	962	481	16:1	X	12
Saint Mary's High School, Phoenix			X	X	–	–	9–12	503	503	15:1	X	17
Salpointe Catholic High School, Tucson			X	X	–	–	9–12	1,041	1,041	15:1	X	23
Scottsdale Christian Academy, Phoenix			X	X	PK–5	6–8	9–12	851	295	15:1	X	15
Seton Catholic High School, Chandler			X	X	–	–	9–12	580	580	12:1	X	22
Southwestern Academy, Rimrock	X	X	X	X	–	–	9–PG	17	17	3:1		53
Tri-City Christian Academy, Chandler			X	X	K4–6	7–8	9–12	304	92	16:1		4
Xavier College Preparatory, Phoenix				X	–	–	9–12	1,173	1,173	22:1	X	30
Arkansas												
Episcopal Collegiate School, Little Rock			X	X	PK–5	6–8	9–12	780	224	10:1	X	16
Subiaco Academy, Subiaco	X		X		–	7–8	9–12	182	154	9:1	X	46
California												
Academy of Our Lady of Peace, San Diego				X	–	–	9–12	725	725	14:1	X	11
Alma Heights Christian High School, Pacifica			X	X	K–4	5–8	9–12	303	147	10:1	X	9
Archbishop Mitty High School, San Jose			X	X	–	–	9–12	1,725	1,725	17:1	X	27
Army and Navy Academy, Carlsbad	X		X		7–9	–	10–12	302	224	15:1	X	28
The Athenian School, Danville	X	X	X	X	–	6–8	9–12	476	311	10:1	X	15
The Bay School of San Francisco, San Francisco			X	X	–	–	9–12	324	324	8:1		18
Besant Hill School, Ojai	X	X	X	X	–	–	9–12	100	100	4:1	X	44
Bishop Montgomery High School, Torrance			X	X	–	–	9–12	938	938	22:1	X	17
Bishop O'Dowd High School, Oakland			X	X	–	–	9–12	1,151	1,151	15:1	X	35
Brentwood School, Los Angeles			X	X	K–6	7–8	9–12	996	467	7:1	X	41
Bridges Academy, Studio City			X	X	–	5–8	9–12	138	74	8:1		3
Campbell Hall (Episcopal), North Hollywood			X	X	K–6	7–8	9–12	1,117	547	8:1	X	20
Capistrano Valley Christian Schools, San Juan Capistrano			X	X	JK–6	7–8	9–12	396	162	13:1	X	16
Carondelet High School, Concord				X	–	–	9–12	800	800	15:1	X	22
Castilleja School, Palo Alto				X	–	6–8	9–12	445	258	6:1	X	14
Central Catholic High School, Modesto			X	X	–	–	9–12	385	385	14:1	X	15
Chadwick School, Palos Verdes Peninsula			X	X	K–6	7–8	9–12	831	352	5:1	X	20
Chaminade College Preparatory, West Hills			X	X	–	6–8	9–12	2,011	1,328	16:1	X	25
Children's Creative and Performing Arts Academy of San Diego, San Diego	X	X	X	X	K–5	6–8	9–12	262	100	18:1		31
Chinese Christian Schools, Alameda	X	X	X	X	–	–	9–12	220	220	8:1		17
Crespi Carmelite High School, Encino			X		–	–	9–12	517	517	14:1	X	17
Crossroads School for Arts & Sciences, Santa Monica			X	X	K–5	6–8	9–12	1,159	510	11:1		21
Crystal Springs Uplands School, Hillsborough			X	X	–	6–8	9–12	350	250	9:1		24
Damien High School, La Verne			X		–	–	9–12	923	923	18:1	X	27
De La Salle High School, Concord			X		–	–	9–12	1,042	1,042	28:1	X	19
Delphi Academy of Los Angeles, Lake View Terrace			X	X	K–3	4–8	9–12	144	35	15:1		20
Eldorado Emerson Private School, Orange			X	X	K–6	–	7–12	150	80	18:1	X	7
Faith Christian High School, Yuba City			X	X	–	–	9–12	100	100	12:1	X	8
Flintridge Preparatory School, La Canada Flintridge			X	X	–	7–8	9–12	500	400	8:1	X	17

Private Secondary Schools At-a-Glance

	STUDENTS ACCEPTED				GRADES			STUDENT/FACULTY			SCHOOL OFFERINGS	
	BOARDING		DAY									
	Boys	Girls	Boys	Girls	Lower	Middle	Upper	Total	Upper	Student/Faculty Ratio	Advanced Placement Preparation	Sports
Fresno Christian Schools, Fresno			X	X	K–6	7–8	9–12	465	188	11:1	X	16
The Frostig School, Pasadena			X	X	1–5	6–8	9–12	90	52	6:1		4
Grace Brethren School, Simi Valley			X	X	K–6	7–8	9–12	830	300	11:1	X	17
The Grauer School, Encinitas			X	X	–	6–8	9–12	161	100	6:1	X	54
Harvard-Westlake School, Studio City			X	X	–	7–8	9–12	1,597	1,157	8:1	X	21
Head-Royce School, Oakland			X	X	K–5	6–8	9–12	876	370	9:1	X	20
Hebrew Academy, Huntington Beach		X	X	X	N–5	6–8	9–12	247	36	4:1	X	14
Heritage Christian School, North Hills			X	X	–	7–8	9–12	794	643	22:1	X	11
Highland Hall Waldorf School, Northridge			X	X	N–6	7–8	9–12	241	86	6:1		6
Immaculate Heart High School and Middle School, Los Angeles				X	–	6–8	9–12	520	520	15:1	X	
International High School, San Francisco			X	X	PK–5	6–8	9–12	1,046	339	10:1		24
Junipero Serra High School, San Mateo			X		–	–	9–12	860	860	27:1	X	29
Kings Christian School, Lemoore			X	X	PK–6	7–8	9–12	294	88	11:1	X	17
La Jolla Country Day School, La Jolla			X	X	N–4	5–8	9–12	1,131	472	16:1	X	31
Lick-Wilmerding High School, San Francisco			X	X			9–12	460	460	9:1	X	18
Linfield Christian School, Temecula			X	X	JK–5	6–8	9–12	757	320	12:1	X	13
Lodi Academy, Lodi			X	X	–	–	9–12	90	90	9:1	X	6
Louisville High School, Woodland Hills				X	–	–	9–12	430	430	25:1	X	15
Lycee International de Los Angeles, Burbank			X	X	PK–5	6–8	9–12	1,004	115	9:1	X	13
Maranatha High School, Pasadena			X	X	–	–	9–12	670	670	14:1	X	20
Marin Academy, San Rafael			X	X	–	–	9–12	406	406	9:1	X	35
Marymount High School, Los Angeles				X	–	–	9–12	374	374	7:1	X	20
Mercy High School College Preparatory, San Francisco				X	–	–	9–12	391	391	14:1	X	11
Mesa Grande Seventh-Day Academy, Calimesa			X	X	K–6	7–8	9–12	265	119	10:1		9
Midland School, Los Olivos	X	X			–	–	9–12	77	77	5:1		13
Mid-Peninsula High School, Menlo Park			X	X	–	–	9–12	117	117	8:1		7
Modesto Christian School, Modesto			X	X	K–5	6–8	9–12	580	280	10:1	X	13
Notre Dame Academy, Los Angeles				X	–	–	9–12	380	380	12:1	X	10
Notre Dame High School, San Jose				X			9–12	628	628	16:1	X	12
Oak Grove School, Ojai	X	X	X	X	PK–6	7–8	9–12	209	53	7:1	X	15
Orinda Academy, Orinda			X	X	–	7–8	9–12	90	81	9:1	X	4
Palma School, Salinas			X		–	7–8	9–12	534	402	15:1	X	22
Palo Alto Preparatory School, Mountain View			X	X	–	–	8–12	65	65	8:1	X	
Paradise Adventist Academy, Paradise			X	X	K–4	5–8	9–12	180	76	8:1		5
Providence High School, Burbank			X	X	–	–	9–12	419	419	9:1	X	17
Redwood Christian Schools, Castro Valley			X	X	K–5	6–8	9–12	692	299	10:1	X	8
Rolling Hills Preparatory School, San Pedro			X	X	–	6–8	9–12	225	130	9:1	X	21
Sacramento Country Day School, Sacramento			X	X	PK–5	6–8	9–12	481	115	9:1	X	15
Sage Hill School, Newport Coast			X	X	–	–	9–12	479	479	10:1	X	13
St. Augustine High School, San Diego			X		–	–	9–12	700	700	25:1	X	44
St. Catherine's Academy, Anaheim	X		X		K–6	7–8		157		14:1		24
Saint Elizabeth High School, Oakland			X	X	–	–	9–12	143	143	15:1	X	7
Saint Francis Girls High School, Sacramento				X	–	–	9–12	1,078	1,078	15:1	X	15
Saint Francis High School, La Canada Flintridge			X		–	–	9–12	678	678	15:1	X	10
Saint Francis High School, Mountain View			X	X	–	–	9–12	1,753	1,753	29:1	X	29
Saint Lawrence Academy, Santa Clara			X	X	–	–	9–12	250	250	15:1		12
St. Michael's Preparatory School of the Norbertine Fathers, Silverado	X				–	–	9–12	67	67	3:1	X	11
San Diego Jewish Academy, San Diego			X	X	K–5	6–8	9–12	485	181	18:1	X	26
San Domenico School, San Anselmo		X	X	X	PK–5	6–8	9–12	598	163	5:1	X	12
Santa Catalina School, Monterey		X		X	–	–	9–12	259	259	8:1	X	31
Sonoma Academy, Santa Rosa			X	X	–	–	9–12	268	268	12:1	X	28
Southwestern Academy, San Marino	X	X	X	X	–				124	6:1	X	34
Squaw Valley Academy, Olympic Valley	X	X	X	X	–	–	9–12	100	100	8:1	X	68
Stevenson School, Pebble Beach	X	X	X	X	PK–5	6–8	9–12	747	520	10:1	X	34
Summerfield Waldorf School, Santa Rosa			X	X	K–6	7–8	9–12	409	106	7:1		4
The Thacher School, Ojai	X	X	X	X	–	–	9–12	252	252	6:1		46
Valley Christian High School, San Jose			X	X	K–5	6–8	9–12	2,475	1,415	17:1	X	20
Victor Valley Christian School, Victorville			X	X	K–6	7–8	9–12	300	120	15:1	X	10
Viewpoint School, Calabasas			X	X	K–5	6–8	9–12	1,212	505	10:1	X	33
The Webb Schools, Claremont	X	X	X	X	–	–	9–12	405	405	8:1	X	19
Westridge School, Pasadena				X	4–6	7–8	9–12	482	264	6:1	X	19
Westview School, Los Angeles			X	X	–	5–8	9–12	134	101	8:1		4
Colorado												
Denver Academy, Denver			X	X	1–6	7–8	9–12	331	175	8:1		28
Denver Christian High School, Denver			X	X	–	–	9–12	142	142	19:1		12
Fountain Valley School of Colorado, Colorado Springs	X	X	X	X	–	–	9–12	244	244	6:1	X	42
Front Range Christian High School, Littleton			X	X	PK–6	7–8	9–12	435	167	8:1	X	25

Private Secondary Schools At-a-Glance

	STUDENTS ACCEPTED				GRADES			STUDENT/FACULTY			SCHOOL OFFERINGS	
	BOARDING		DAY									
	Boys	Girls	Boys	Girls	Lower	Middle	Upper	Total	Upper	Student/Faculty Ratio	Advanced Placement Preparation	Sports
Humanex Academy, Englewood			X	X	–	6–8	9–12	30	18	8:1		21
Kent Denver School, Englewood			X	X	–	6–8	9–12	692	471	7:1	X	28
The Lowell Whiteman School, Steamboat Springs	X	X	X	X	–	–	9–12	5,360	53	7:1	X	70
Telluride Mountain School, Telluride			X	X	PK–4	5–8	9–12	88	14	5:1		27
Temple Grandin School, Boulder			X	X	–	6–8	8–12	24	14	3:1		
Connecticut												
Brunswick School, Greenwich			X		PK–4	5–8	9–12	939	357	5:1	X	20
Chase Collegiate School, Waterbury			X	X	PK–5	6–8	9–12	402	185	7:1	X	32
Convent of the Sacred Heart, Greenwich			X	X	PS–4	5–8	9–12	737	295	7:1	X	22
Eagle Hill School, Greenwich	X	X	X	X	1–6	–	6–9	255	120	4:1		33
Fairfield College Preparatory School, Fairfield			X		–	–	9–12	901	901	18:1	X	31
The Glenholme School, Devereux Connecticut, Washington	X	X	X	X	5–6	7–8	9–PG	95	79	10:1		44
The Gunnery, Washington	X	X	X	X	–	–	9–PG	298	298	6:1	X	22
Holy Cross High School, Waterbury			X	X	–	–	9–12	630	630	15:1	X	24
Hopkins School, New Haven			X	X	–	7–8	9–12	711	560	6:1	X	37
King Low Heywood Thomas, Stamford			X	X	PK–5	6–8	9–12	692	326	8:1	X	21
Kingswood-Oxford School, West Hartford			X	X	–	6–8	9–12	511	366	8:1	X	19
Lauralton Hall, Milford				X	–	–	9–12	477	477	12:1		18
Miss Porter's School, Farmington		X		X	–	–	9–12	311	311	7:1	X	45
Northwest Catholic High School, West Hartford			X	X	–	–	9–12	601	601	12:1	X	36
The Norwich Free Academy, Norwich			X	X	–	–	9–12	2,300		22:1	X	36
The Rectory School, Pomfret	X	X	X	X	1–4	5–9		251		4:1		38
Rumsey Hall School, Washington Depot	X	X	X	X	K–5	6–9		333	221	8:1		48
St. Joseph High School, Trumbull			X	X	–	–	9–12	830	830	20:1	X	17
The Taft School, Watertown	X	X	X	X	–	–	9–PG	579	579	5:1	X	46
Watkinson School, Hartford			X	X	–	6–8	9–PG	266	192	6:1		30
Wellspring Foundation, Bethlehem	X	X	X	X	1–6	–	7–12	51				
Westminster School, Simsbury	X	X	X	X	–	–	9–PG	390	390	6:1	X	34
Westover School, Middlebury		X		X	–	–	9–12	204	204	7:1	X	48
The Woodhall School, Bethlehem	X		X		–	–	9–PG	43	43	4:1	X	26
Delaware												
Tower Hill School, Wilmington			X	X	PS–4	5–8	9–12	747	252	6:1	X	23
Wilmington Christian School, Hockessin			X	X	PK–5	6–8	9–12	517	231	15:1	X	12
Wilmington Friends School, Wilmington			X	X	PS–5	6–8	9–12	765	270	10:1	X	15
District of Columbia												
Georgetown Day School, Washington			X	X	PK–5	6–8	9–12	1,075	500	7:1	X	9
Georgetown Visitation Preparatory School, Washington				X	–	–	9–12	490	490	11:1	X	20
Gonzaga College High School, Washington			X		–	–	9–12	958	958	15:1	X	33
The Lab School of Washington, Washington			X	X	1–6	7–8	9–12	356	125	8:1		10
Maret School, Washington			X	X	K–4	5–8	9–12	635	305	6:1	X	23
National Cathedral School, Washington				X	4–6	7–8	9–12	581	315	7:1	X	43
St. Albans School, Washington	X		X		4–8	–	9–12	593	323	7:1	X	35
Washington International School, Washington			X	X	PK–5	6–8	9–12	899	270	7:1		10
Florida												
Academy at the Lakes, Land O'Lakes			X	X	PK–4	5–8	9–12	428	141	5:1	X	17
American Heritage School, Delray Beach			X	X	PK–5	6–8	9–12	1,130	609	10:1	X	26
American Heritage School, Plantation			X	X	PK–6	–	7–12	2,395	1,686	15:1	X	22
Belen Jesuit Preparatory School, Miami			X		–	6–8	9–12	1,488	890	13:1	X	19
The Benjamin School, North Palm Beach			X	X	PK–5	6–8	9–12	1,081	420	8:1	X	22
Berkeley Preparatory School, Tampa			X	X	PK–5	6–8	9–12	1,290	565	9:1	X	28
Bishop John J. Snyder High School, Jacksonville			X	X	–	–	9–12	472	472	15:1	X	17
The Bolles School, Jacksonville	X	X	X	X	PK–5	6–8	9–12	1,670	787	11:1	X	18
Canterbury School, Fort Myers			X	X	PK–6	7–8	9–12	580	199	10:1	X	13
The Canterbury School of Florida, St. Petersburg			X	X	PK–4	5–8	9–12	450	175	7:1	X	35
Cardinal Mooney Catholic High School, Sarasota			X	X	–	–	9–12	474	474	13:1	X	20
Cardinal Newman High School, West Palm Beach			X	X	–	–	9–12	540	540	25:1	X	18
Chaminade-Madonna College Preparatory, Hollywood			X	X	–	–	9–12	552	552	19:1	X	16
Clearwater Central Catholic High School, Clearwater			X	X	–	–				13:1	X	19
The Community School of Naples, Naples			X	X	PK–5	6–8	9–12	706	286	8:1		17
The Crenshaw School, Gotha			X	X	PK–5	6–8	9–12	102	50	10:1		
Father Lopez High School, Daytona Beach			X	X	–	–	9–12	438	438	13:1	X	18
The First Academy, Orlando			X	X	K4–6	7–8	9–12	990	410	17:1	X	22
Forest Lake Academy, Apopka	X	X	X	X	–	–	9–12	357	357	12:1		13
Foundation Academy, Winter Garden			X	X	K–5	6–8	9–12	585	175	5:1	X	14
Glades Day School, Belle Glade			X	X	PK–6	7–8	9–12	307	123	15:1	X	10
Gulliver Preparatory School, Miami			X	X	PK–4	5–8	9–12	1,834	754	8:1	X	38
Immaculata-La Salle High School, Miami			X	X	–	–	9–12	804	804	15:1	X	17

Private Secondary Schools At-a-Glance

| | STUDENTS ACCEPTED | | | | GRADES | | | STUDENT/FACULTY | | | SCHOOL OFFERINGS | |
| | BOARDING | | DAY | | | | | | | | | |
	Boys	Girls	Boys	Girls	Lower	Middle	Upper	Total	Upper	Student/Faculty Ratio	Advanced Placement Preparation	Sports
Jesuit High School of Tampa, Tampa			X		–	–	9–12	758	758	13:1	X	19
Lake Mary Preparatory School, Lake Mary	X	X	X	X	PK–5	6–8	9–12	640	275	22:1	X	21
Montverde Academy, Montverde	X	X	X	X	PK–5	6–8	9–PG	1,010	558	12:1	X	37
The North Broward Preparatory Upper School, Coconut Creek	X	X	X	X	PK–5	6–8	9–12	1,375	696	18:1	X	28
Out-Of-Door-Academy, Sarasota			X	X	PK–5	6–8	9–12	680	247	7:1	X	20
Pensacola Catholic High School, Pensacola			X	X	–	–	9–12	611	611	18:1	X	9
Ransom Everglades School, Miami			X	X	–	6–8	9–12	1,064	608	10:1	X	22
Saddlebrook Preparatory School, Wesley Chapel	X	X	X	X	3–5	6–8	9–12	80	63	8:1		1
Saint Edward's School, Vero Beach			X	X	PK–5	6–8	9–12	500	225	8:1	X	20
St. Joseph Academy, St. Augustine			X	X	–	–	9–12	260	260	11:1	X	17
St. Thomas Aquinas High School, Fort Lauderdale			X	X	–	–	9–12	2,194	2,194	18:1	X	30
Tampa Preparatory School, Tampa			X	X	–	6–8	9–12	576	403	10:1	X	32
Trinity Preparatory School, Winter Park			X	X	–	6–8	9–12	865	520	10:1	X	21
University School of Nova Southeastern University, Fort Lauderdale			X	X	PK–5	6–8	9–12	1,845	720	18:1		19
The Vanguard School, Lake Wales	X	X	X	X	–	5–8	9–PG	109	99	7:1		26
Westminster Christian School, Palmetto Bay			X	X	PK–5	6–8	9–12	1,068	473	15:1		13
Windermere Preparatory School, Windermere	X		X	X	PK–5	6–8	9–12	1,193	432	11:1	X	22
Georgia												
Athens Academy, Athens			X	X	N–4	5–8	9–12	949	287	8:1	X	11
Augusta Christian School, Martinez			X	X	K–5	6–8	9–12	634	275	10:1	X	13
Augusta Preparatory Day School, Martinez			X	X	PS–4	5–8	9–12	552	212	9:1		15
Blessed Trinity High School, Roswell			X	X	–	–	9–12	965	965	14:1	X	17
Eaton Academy, Roswell			X	X	K–5	6–8	9–12	80	40	5:1		34
First Presbyterian Day School, Macon			X	X	PK–5	6–8	9–12	1,008	355	12:1	X	17
The Galloway School, Atlanta			X	X	P3–4	5–8	9–12	769	270	11:1	X	11
The Heritage School, Newnan			X	X	PK–4	5–8	9–12	428	170	8:1	X	28
The Howard School, Atlanta			X	X	K–5	6–8	9–12	256	80	8:1		6
Landmark Christian School, Fairburn			X	X	K4–5	6–8	9–12	862	274	8:1		16
The Lovett School, Atlanta			X	X	K–5	6–8	9–12	1,649	629	8:1	X	45
Marist School, Atlanta			X	X	–	–	7–12	1,085	1,085	12:1	X	17
Mt. De Sales Academy, Macon			X	X	–	6–8	9–12	641	422	9:1		19
Mount Paran Christian School, Kennesaw			X	X	K–5	6–8	9–12	1,105	406		X	19
Mount Vernon Presbyterian School, Atlanta			X	X	K–4	5–8	9–12	891	242	10:1		19
The Paideia School, Atlanta			X	X	PK–6	7–8	9–12	987	420	10:1	X	23
Piedmont Academy, Monticello			X	X	1–5	6–8	9–12	277	109	13:1		10
Pinecrest Academy, Cumming			X	X	PK–5	6–8	9–12	790	275	9:1	X	15
Rabun Gap-Nacoochee School, Rabun Gap	X	X	X	X	–	5–8	9–12	404	306	10:1	X	37
St. Pius X Catholic High School, Atlanta			X	X	–	–	9–12	1,100	1,100	12:1	X	23
Woodward Academy, College Park			X	X	PK–6	7–8	9–12	2,738	1,101		X	20
Guam												
Academy of Our Lady of Guam, Agana			X		–	–	9–12	413	413	25:1	X	10
Hawaii												
Hanalani Schools, Mililani			X	X	PK–6	–	7–12	700	337	16:1	X	25
Hawaii Baptist Academy, Honolulu			X	X	K–6	7–8	9–12	1,106	472	17:1	X	22
Hawai'i Preparatory Academy, Kamuela	X	X	X	X	K–5	6–8	9–12	620	397	13:1	X	24
Ho'Ala School, Wahiawa			X	X	K–6	7–8	9–12	73	15	5:1	X	4
Lutheran High School of Hawaii, Honolulu			X	X	–	7–8	9–12	55	51	7:1	X	23
Mid-Pacific Institute, Honolulu			X	X	K–5	6–8	9–12	1,550	840	20:1	X	31
Punahou School, Honolulu			X	X	K–5	6–8	9–12	3,771	1,738	10:1	X	21
Idaho												
Bishop Kelly High School, Boise			X	X	–	–	9–12	723	723	15:1	X	22
Cole Valley Christian High School, Meridian			X	X	PK–6	7–8	9–12	813	260	10:1	X	10
Riverstone International School, Boise			X	X	PS–5	6–8	9–12	314	107	6:1		29
Illinois												
Acacia Academy, Lagrange Highlands			X	X	1–6	7–8	9–12	100	60	3:1		4
Alleman High School, Rock Island					–	–	9–12	465	465			
Benet Academy, Lisle			X	X	–	–	9–12	1,357	1,357	18:1	X	23
Boylan Central Catholic High School, Rockford			X	X	–	–	9–12	1,025	1,025	12:1	X	27
Brehm Preparatory School, Carbondale	X	X	X	X	–	6–8	9–PG	85	75	4:1		19
Carmel High School, Mundelein			X	X	–	–	9–12	1,350	1,350	16:1	X	19
The Chicago Academy for the Arts, Chicago			X	X	–	–	9–12	143	143	10:1	X	
Elgin Academy, Elgin			X	X	PS–4	5–8	9–12	387	140	7:1	X	9
The Governor French Academy, Belleville	X	X	X	X	K–8	–	9–12	157	51	7:1	X	6
IC Catholic Prep, Elmhurst			X	X	–	–	9–12	308	308	9:1	X	21
Josephinum Academy, Chicago				X	–	–	9–12	199	199	10:1	X	7

Private Secondary Schools At-a-Glance

| | STUDENTS ACCEPTED | | | | GRADES | | | STUDENT/FACULTY | | | SCHOOL OFFERINGS | |
| | BOARDING | | DAY | | | | | | | | | |
	Boys	Girls	Boys	Girls	Lower	Middle	Upper	Total	Upper	Student/Faculty Ratio	Advanced Placement Preparation	Sports
The Latin School of Chicago, Chicago			X	X	JK–4	5–8	9–12	1,124	444	8:1	X	25
Marian Central Catholic High School, Woodstock			X	X	–	–	9–12	716	716	17:1	X	16
Mooseheart High School, Mooseheart	X	X	X	X	K–5	6–8	9–12	212	117	6:1		12
Mother McAuley High School, Chicago				X	–	–	9–12	1,215	1,215	17:1	X	21
Nazareth Academy, LaGrange Park			X	X	–	–	9–12	802	802	18:1	X	16
North Shore Country Day School, Winnetka			X	X	PK–5	6–8	9–12	510	210	8:1	X	15
Notre Dame College Prep, Niles			X		–	–	9–12	834	834	17:1	X	27
Saint Anthony High School, Effingham			X	X	–	–	9–12	190	190	10:1	X	13
Saint Joseph High School, Westchester			X	X	–	–	9–12	476	476	16:1	X	20
Saint Viator High School, Arlington Heights			X	X	–	–	9–12	990	990	13:1		18
Timothy Christian High School, Elmhurst			X	X	K–6	7–8	9–12	1,030	375	13:1	X	12
University of Chicago Laboratory Schools, Chicago			X	X	N–5	6–8	9–12	1,888	515	10:1	X	15
Walther Christian Academy, Melrose Park					–	–				12:1	X	13
Wheaton Academy, West Chicago			X	X	–	–	9–12	640	640	15:1	X	35
Yeshiva High School, Skokie	X		X		–	–	9–12	145	145	13:1	X	9
Indiana												
Concordia Lutheran High School, Fort Wayne			X	X	–	–	9–12	708	708	16:1	X	21
The Culver Academies, Culver	X	X	X	X	–	–	9–PG	802	802	9:1	X	95
International School of Indiana, Indianapolis			X	X	–5	6–8	9–12					64
Oldenburg Academy, Oldenburg			X	X	–	–	9–12	198	198	12:1	X	15
Shawe Memorial Junior/Senior High School, Madison			X	X	K–6	7–8	9–12	342	111	8.5:1	X	12
Iowa												
Alpha Omega Academy, Rock Rapids			X	X	K–5	6–8	9–12	2,350	1,600			
Dowling Catholic High School, West Des Moines			X	X	–	–	9–12	1,400	1,400	18:1	X	20
Maharishi School of the Age of Enlightenment, Fairfield	X	X	X	X	PS–6	7–8	9–12	213	91	12:1		33
Regina Junior-Senior High School, Iowa City					PK–6	–	7–12	902	383		X	13
Saint Albert Junior-Senior High School, Council Bluffs					PK–6	7–8	9–12	740	207	10:1	X	16
Scattergood Friends School, West Branch	X	X	X	X	–	–	9–PG	40	40	2:1		22
Kansas												
Hyman Brand Hebrew Academy of Greater Kansas City, Overland Park			X	X	K–5	6–8	9–12	224	39	5:1	X	4
Independent School, Wichita			X	X	PK–5	6–8	9–12	520	220	9:1	X	16
Maur Hill-Mount Academy, Atchison	X	X	X	X	–	–	9–12	195	195	9:1	X	35
Saint Thomas Aquinas High School, Overland Park			X	X	–	–	9–12	937	937	15:1	X	20
Kentucky												
Beth Haven Christian School, Louisville			X	X	K4–5	6–8	9–12	211	60	9:1		7
Landmark Christian Academy, Louisville			X	X	K4–6	7–8	9–12	140	24	6:1		4
Lexington Catholic High School, Lexington			X	X	–	–	9–12	810	810	13:1	X	21
Oneida Baptist Institute, Oneida	X	X	X	X	–	6–8	9–12	275	210	11:1	X	10
St. Francis High School, Louisville			X	X	–	–	9–12	150	150	9:1	X	26
Trinity High School, Louisville			X		–	–	9–12	1,320	1,320	12:1	X	51
Villa Madonna Academy, Covington			X	X	K–6	7–8	9–12	426	136	8:1		10
Whitefield Academy, Louisville			X	X	PS–5	6–8	9–12	778	187	20:1	X	17
Louisiana												
Academy of the Sacred Heart, New Orleans				X	1–4	5–8	9–12	618	213	16:1		26
Archbishop Shaw High School, Marrero			X		–	8–9	10–12	655	415	24:1	X	14
Holy Cross School, New Orleans			X		–	5–7	8–12	1,020	729	13:1	X	28
Holy Savior Menard Catholic High School, Alexandria			X	X	–	7–8	9–12	494	329	12:1	X	15
St. Joseph's Academy, Baton Rouge				X	–	–	9–12	1,048	1,048	15:1	X	25
St. Martin's Episcopal School, Metairie			X	X	PK–5	6–8	9–12	483	205	6:1	X	16
Saint Thomas More Catholic High School, Lafayette			X	X	–	–	9–12	1,085	1,085	25:1	X	27
Teurlings Catholic High School, Lafayette			X	X	–	–	9–12	681	681	21:1		22
Vandebilt Catholic High School, Houma			X	X	–	–	8–12	921	921	25:1		18
Westminster Christian Academy, Opelousas			X	X	PK–6	7–8	9–12	1,143	248	13:1	X	13
Maine												
Bangor Christian School, Bangor			X	X	K4–5	6–8	9–12	310	80	10:1		10
Fryeburg Academy, Fryeburg	X	X	X	X	–	–	9–PG	599	599	10:1	X	63
Gould Academy, Bethel	X	X	X	X	–	–	9–PG	232	232	6:1	X	12
Lee Academy, Lee	X	X	X	X	–	–	9–PG	260	260	15:1	X	51
Maine Central Institute, Pittsfield	X	X	X	X	–	–	9–PG	455	455	14:1	X	29
Saint Dominic Academy, Auburn			X	X	PK–6	7–8	9–12	571	203	12:1	X	15
Thornton Academy, Saco	X	X	X	X	–	6–8	9–12	1,503	1,338	14:1	X	29
Waynflete School, Portland			X	X	PK–5	6–8	9–12	575	261	12:1	X	23
Maryland												
Academy of the Holy Cross, Kensington				X	–	–	9–12	520	520		X	21
Archbishop Curley High School, Baltimore			X		–	–	9–12	526	526	14:1	X	20

Private Secondary Schools At-a-Glance

| | STUDENTS ACCEPTED | | | | GRADES | | | STUDENT/FACULTY | | | SCHOOL OFFERINGS | |
| | BOARDING | | DAY | | | | | | | | | |
Private Secondary Schools At-a-Glance	Boys	Girls	Boys	Girls	Lower	Middle	Upper	Total	Upper	Student/Faculty Ratio	Advanced Placement Preparation	Sports
The Bryn Mawr School for Girls, Baltimore			X	X	K–5	6–8	9–12	685	289	7:1	X	41
Calvert Hall College High School, Baltimore			X		–	–	9–12	1,196	1,196	12:1	X	35
The Catholic High School of Baltimore, Baltimore				X	–	–	9–12	320	320	17:1	X	17
Chelsea School, Hyattsville			X	X	–	5–8	9–12	61	44	8:1	X	4
DeMatha Catholic High School, Hyattsville			X		–	–	9–12	795	795	13:1	X	24
Elizabeth Seton High School, Bladensburg				X	–	–	9–12	565	565	11:1	X	29
Garrison Forest School, Owings Mills		X	X	X	N–5	6–8	9–12	628	291	8:1	X	28
Georgetown Preparatory School, North Bethesda	X		X		–	–	9–12	490	490	8:1	X	51
Gilman School, Baltimore			X		K–5	6–8	9–12	1,033	461	8:1	X	26
The Heights School, Potomac			X		3–5	6–8	9–12	460	240	7:1	X	17
Indian Creek School, Crownsville					–	–					X	15
Institute of Notre Dame, Baltimore				X	–	–	9–12	367	367	11:1	X	32
The Key School, Annapolis			X	X	PK–4	5–8	9–12	652	209	7:1	X	27
Landon School, Bethesda			X		3–5	6–8	9–12	675	330	6:1	X	25
Loyola-Blakefield, Baltimore			X		–	6–8	9–12	983	744	10:1	X	24
McDonogh School, Owings Mills	X	X	X	X	K–4	5–8	9–12	1,299	585	9:1	X	28
The Nora School, Silver Spring			X	X	–	–	9–12	60	60	5:1		27
Our Lady of Mount Carmel High School, Baltimore			X	X	PK–5	6–8	9–12			16:1	X	12
The Park School of Baltimore, Baltimore			X	X	PK–5	6–8	9–12	833	331	7:1	X	17
Roland Park Country School, Baltimore			X	X	PS–5	6–8	9–12	676	316	7:1	X	25
St. Andrew's Episcopal School, Potomac			X	X	PS–3	4–8	9–12	506	248	7:1	X	17
Saint Mary's High School, Annapolis			X	X	–	–	9–12	500	500	15:1	X	20
St. Timothy's School, Stevenson		X		X	–	–	9–12	165	165	6:1		23
Sandy Spring Friends School, Sandy Spring	X	X	X	X	PK–5	6–8	9–12	572	263	8:1	X	43
Worcester Preparatory School, Berlin			X	X	PK–5	6–8	9–12	525	201	9:1	X	13
Massachusetts												
The Academy at Charlemont, Charlemont			X	X	–	7–8	9–PG	97	64	9:1		20
Berkshire School, Sheffield	X	X	X	X	–	–	9–PG		386	5:1	X	36
Bishop Connolly High School, Fall River			X	X	–	–	9–12	280	280	16:1	X	17
Bishop Stang High School, North Dartmouth			X	X	–	–	9–12	644	644	13:1	X	30
Boston University Academy, Boston			X	X	–	–	9–12	163	163	8:1		13
Brimmer and May School, Chestnut Hill			X	X	PK–5	6–8	9–12	400	135	6:1	X	20
The British School of Boston, Boston			X	X	PK–5	6–8	9–12	417	59	3:1		20
Brooks School, North Andover	X	X	X	X	–	–	9–12	376	376	5:1	X	19
Buxton School, Williamstown	X	X	X	X	–	–	9–12	89	89	4:1		25
Cape Cod Academy, Osterville			X	X	PK–5	6–8	9–12	317	155	4:1	X	18
Central Catholic High School, Lawrence			X	X	–	–	9–12	1,327	1,327	24:1	X	32
Commonwealth School, Boston			X	X	–	–	9–12	145	145	4:1	X	16
Concord Academy, Concord	X	X	X	X	–	–	9–12	378	378	6:1		35
Deerfield Academy, Deerfield	X	X	X	X	–	–	9–PG	630	630	6:1		46
Dexter Southfield, Brookline			X		PK–5	6–8	9–12	424	136	7:1	X	16
Dexter Southfield, Brookline				X	PK–5	6–8	9–12	330	74	7:1	X	18
Eaglebrook School, Deerfield	X		X		–	6–9		254		4:1		64
Falmouth Academy, Falmouth			X	X	–	7–8	9–12	195	116	4:1	X	3
Fay School, Southborough	X	X	X	X	PK–2	3–6	7–9	473	223	8:1		21
Gann Academy (The New Jewish High School of Greater Boston), Waltham			X	X	–	–	9–12	309	309	5:1	X	16
Hillside School, Marlborough	X		X		–	5–9		135		7:1		48
The Judge Rotenberg Educational Center, Canton	X	X			–	–			130			3
Landmark School, Prides Crossing	X	X	X	X	1–5	6–8	9–12	449	301	3:1		19
Lawrence Academy, Groton	X	X	X	X	–	–	9–12	399	399	5:1	X	30
Matignon High School, Cambridge			X	X	–	–	9–12	458	458	18:1	X	25
Middlesex School, Concord	X	X	X	X	–	–	9–12	378	378	6:1	X	23
Miss Hall's School, Pittsfield		X		X	–	–	9–PG	206	206	6:1	X	33
Noble and Greenough School, Dedham	X	X	X	X	–	7–8	9–12	613	490	7:1	X	8
Northfield Mount Hermon School, Mount Hermon	X	X	X	X	–	–	9–PG	650	650	6:1	X	51
Notre Dame Academy, Hingham				X	–	–	7–12	568	568	11:1	X	24
The Pingree School, South Hamilton			X	X	–	–	9–12	330	330	7:1	X	32
Pioneer Valley Christian School, Springfield			X	X	PS–5	6–8	9–12	270	71	4:1	X	10
The Rivers School, Weston			X	X	–	6–8	9–12	479	359	6:1	X	18
The Roxbury Latin School, West Roxbury			X		–	–	7–12	299	299	7:1	X	10
St. John's Preparatory School, Danvers			X		–	–	9–12	1,200	1,200	11:1	X	47
The Sudbury Valley School, Framingham			X	X	–	–		160		16:1		
Valley View School, North Brookfield	X		X		–	5–8	9–12	56	26	6:1		50
Waldorf High School of Massachusetts Bay, Belmont			X	X	–	–	9–12	55	55	7:1		3
Whitinsville Christian School, Whitinsville			X	X	K–5	6–8	9–12	499	180	8:1	X	10
Wilbraham & Monson Academy, Wilbraham	X	X	X	X	–	6–8	9–PG	431	357	6:1	X	44
The Williston Northampton School, Easthampton	X	X	X	X	–	7–8	9–PG	544	469	6:1	X	39
The Woodward School, Quincy				X	–	6–8	9–12	125	81	8:1	X	4
Worcester Academy, Worcester	X	X	X	X	–	6–8	9–PG	625	510	8:1	X	20

Private Secondary Schools At-a-Glance

| | STUDENTS ACCEPTED | | | | GRADES | | | STUDENT/FACULTY | | | SCHOOL OFFERINGS | |
| | BOARDING | | DAY | | | | | | | | | |
	Boys	Girls	Boys	Girls	Lower	Middle	Upper	Total	Upper	Student/Faculty Ratio	Advanced Placement Preparation	Sports
Michigan												
Detroit Country Day School, Beverly Hills			X	X	PK–5	6–8	9–12	1,600	698	8:1	X	32
Gabriel Richard Catholic High School, Riverview			X	X	–	–	9–12	289	289	17:1	X	17
Greenhills School, Ann Arbor			X	X	–	6–8	9–12	569	330	8:1	X	15
Jean and Samuel Frankel Jewish Academy of Metropolitan Detroit, West Bloomfield			X	X	–	–	9–12	230	230		X	
Kalamazoo Christian High School, Kalamazoo			X	X	K–4	5–8	9–12	773	149	12:1	X	17
The Leelanau School, Glen Arbor	X	X	X	X	–	–	9–12	50	50	5:1	X	49
Lutheran High School Northwest, Rochester Hills			X	X	–	–	9–12	289	289	15:1	X	20
Powers Catholic High School, Flint			X	X	–	–	9–12	545*	545	18:1	X	29
Southfield Christian High School, Southfield			X	X	PK–5	6–8	9–12	577	209	20:1	X	12
University Liggett School, Grosse Pointe Woods			X	X	PK–5	6–8	9–12	616	282	8:1		16
The Valley School, Swartz Creek			X	X	PK–4	5–8	9–12	58	14	8:1		8
Minnesota												
Cotter Schools, Winona	X	X	X	X	–	7–8	9–12	343	259	11:1	X	30
Cretin-Derham Hall, Saint Paul			X	X	–	–	9–12	1,317	1,317	17:1	X	34
DeLaSalle High School, Minneapolis			X	X	–	–	9–12	731	731	14:1	X	22
Marshall School, Duluth			X	X	–	4–8	9–12	451	253	11:1	X	18
Providence Academy, Plymouth			X	X	PK–5	6–8	9–12	867	335	11:1	X	16
St. Croix Schools, West St. Paul	X	X	X	X	–	6–8	9–12	500	440	15:1	X	38
Saint John's Preparatory School, Collegeville	X	X	X	X	6–6	7–8	9–PG	295	220	10:1	X	50
St. Paul Academy and Summit School, St. Paul			X	X	K–5	6–8	9–12	901	390	7:1	X	25
St. Paul Preparatory School, Saint Paul			X	X	–	–	9–12	203	203	12:1	X	2
Shattuck-St. Mary's School, Faribault	X	X	X	X	–	6–9	9–PG	443	338	9:1	X	27
Mississippi												
Brookhaven Academy, Brookhaven			X	X	–6	–	7–12	506	209	13:1		13
St. Stanislaus College, Bay St. Louis	X		X		–	7–8	9–12	352	250	12:1	X	34
Vicksburg Catholic School, Vicksburg			X	X	PK–6	–	7–12	577	270	11:1	X	13
Missouri												
John Burroughs School, St. Louis			X	X	–	7–8	9–12	600	409	7:1	X	27
Kansas City Academy, Kansas City			X	X	–	6–8	9–12	45	32	6:1		
Lutheran High School North, St. Louis			X	X	–	–	9–12	310	310	10:1	X	13
Mary Institute and St. Louis Country Day School (MICDS), St. Louis			X	X	JK–4	5–8	9–12	1,247	628	8:1	X	27
Missouri Military Academy, Mexico	X		X		–	6–8	9–PG	210	178	11:1	X	42
MU High School, Columbia			X	X	–	–					X	
Nerinx Hall, Webster Groves				X	–	–	9–12	593	593	10:1	X	13
New Covenant Academy, Springfield			X	X	JK–6	7–8	9–12	397	82			6
Rockhurst High School, Kansas City			X		–	–	9–12		1,100	12:1	X	23
Saint Teresa's Academy, Kansas City				X	–	–	9–12	607	607	12:1	X	25
Thomas Jefferson School, St. Louis	X	X	X	X	–	7–8	9–PG	91	68	6:1	X	9
Valle Catholic High School, Ste. Genevieve			X	X	–	–	9–12	152	152	9:1		14
Visitation Academy, St. Louis			X	X	PK–6	–	7–12	642	478	9:1	X	15
Whitfield School, St. Louis			X	X	–	–	6–12	379	379	8:1	X	14
Montana												
Butte Central Catholic High School, Butte	X		X	X	–	–	9–12	141	141	10:1	X	11
Lustre Christian High School, Lustre	X	X	X	X	–	–	9–12	40	40	4:1		4
Manhattan Christian High School, Manhattan			X	X	PK–5	6–8	9–12	266	65	8:1	X	12
Summit Preparatory School, Kalispell	X	X			–	–	9–12	46	46	5:1	X	61
Nebraska												
Mount Michael Benedictine School, Elkhorn	X		X		–	–	9–12	221	221	8:1	X	22
Nebraska Christian Schools, Central City	X	X	X	X	K–6	7–8	9–12	204	121	10:1	X	6
Scotus Central Catholic High School, Columbus			X	X	–	7–8	9–12	396	257	14:1	X	13
Nevada												
The Dr. Miriam and Sheldon G. Adelson Educational Campus, The Adelson Upper School, Las Vegas			X	X	PS–4	5–8	9–12	618	132	10:1	X	15
Faith Lutheran High School, Las Vegas			X	X	–	6–8	9–12	1,390	749	17:1	X	22
The Meadows School, Las Vegas			X	X	PK–5	6–8	9–12	895	273	11:1	X	14
New Hampshire												
Bishop Brady High School, Concord			X	X	–	–	9–12	344	344	16:1	X	30
Bishop Guertin High School, Nashua			X	X	–	–	9–12	900	900			35
Cardigan Mountain School, Canaan	X		X		–	6–9		215	192	4:1		41
The Derryfield School, Manchester			X	X	–	6–8	9–12	387	271	8:1	X	26
Hampshire Country School, Rindge	X		X		3–6	–	7–12	21	16	2:1		23
High Mowing School, Wilton	X	X	X	X	–	–	9–12	109	109	5:1	X	41
Kimball Union Academy, Meriden	X	X	X	X	–	–	9–PG	338	338	6:1	X	38

Private Secondary Schools At-a-Glance

| | STUDENTS ACCEPTED | | | | GRADES | | | STUDENT/FACULTY | | | SCHOOL OFFERINGS | |
| | BOARDING | | DAY | | | | | | | | | |
	Boys	Girls	Boys	Girls	Lower	Middle	Upper	Total	Upper	Student/Faculty Ratio	Advanced Placement Preparation	Sports
Portsmouth Christian Academy, Dover			X	X	PK–5	6–8	9–12	617	181	13:1	X	16
Proctor Academy, Andover	X	X	X	X	–	–	9–12	360	360	5:1	X	58
St. Thomas Aquinas High School, Dover			X	X	–	–	9–12	585	585	14:1	X	18
Tilton School, Tilton	X	X	X	X	–	–	9–PG	222	222	5:1	X	28
Trinity High School, Manchester			X	X	–	–	9–12	442	442	12:1	X	22
The White Mountain School, Bethlehem	X	X	X	X	–	–	9–PG	112	112	5:1	X	45
New Jersey												
The American Boychoir School, Princeton	X		X		4–5	6–8		51		5:1		2
Barnstable Academy, Oakland			X	X	–	5–8	9–12	120	90	8:1	X	16
Bishop Eustace Preparatory School, Pennsauken			X	X	–	–	9–12	661	661	12:1	X	20
Christian Brothers Academy, Lincroft			X		–	–	9–12	1,007	1,007	14:1	X	16
Delbarton School, Morristown			X		–	7–8	9–12	558	491	13:1	X	28
DePaul Catholic High School, Wayne			X	X	–			650		19:1	X	38
Hawthorne Christian Academy, Hawthorne			X	X	PS–5	6–8	9–12	496	147	7:1	X	9
The Hudson School, Hoboken			X	X	–	5–8	9–12	185	85	4:1	X	15
The Hun School of Princeton, Princeton	X	X	X	X	–	6–8	9–PG	630	535	8:1	X	35
Kent Place School, Summit			X	X	N–5	6–8	9–12	636	277	7:1	X	17
The Lawrenceville School, Lawrenceville	X	X	X	X	–	–	9–PG	819	819	8:1		51
Moorestown Friends School, Moorestown			X	X	PS–4	5–8	9–12	722	303	7:1	X	18
Newark Academy, Livingston			X	X	–	6–8	9–12	582	406	12:1	X	32
Our Lady of Mercy Academy, Newfield				X	–	–	9–12	150	150	11:1		17
The Pennington School, Pennington	X	X	X	X	–	6–8	9–12	487	406	8:1	X	24
The Pingry School, Basking Ridge			X	X	K–5	6–8	9–12	1,084	558	8:1	X	25
Pope John XXIII Regional High School, Sparta			X	X	–	–	8–12	943	943	13:1	X	19
Ranney School, Tinton Falls			X	X	N–5	6–8	9–12	820	303	9:1	X	25
Saint Augustine Preparatory School, Richland			X		–	–	9–12	680	680	12:1	X	25
Villa Victoria Academy, Ewing				X	PK–6	7–8	9–12	168	55	8:1	X	10
Villa Walsh Academy, Morristown				X	–	7–8	9–12	252	222	8:1	X	11
New Mexico												
Albuquerque Academy, Albuquerque			X	X	–	6–7	8–12	1,110	813	9:1	X	28
Sandia Preparatory School, Albuquerque			X	X	–	6–8	9–12	612	348	7:1		33
New York												
Allendale Columbia School, Rochester			X	X	N–5	6–8	9–12	375	141		X	11
All Hallows High School, Bronx			X		–	–	9–12	640	640	15:1		14
Bay Ridge Preparatory School, Brooklyn			X	X	K–5	6–8	9–12			7:1	X	13
The Beekman School, New York			X	X	–	–	9–PG	80	80	8:1	X	
Berkeley Carroll School, Brooklyn			X	X	N–4	5–8	9–12	900	270	8:1		15
The Birch Wathen Lenox School, New York			X	X	K–5	6–8	9–12	570	170	15:1	X	26
Cascadilla School, Ithaca	X	X	X	X	–	–	9–PG		50	6:1	X	51
Cathedral High School, New York				X	–	–	9–12	550	550	17:1	X	6
Catholic Central High School, Troy			X	X	–	7–8	9–12	520	415	15:1	X	17
Christian Brothers Academy, Syracuse			X	X	–	–	7–12	750	750		X	18
Christian Central Academy, Williamsville			X	X	K–5	6–8	9–12	355	110	10:1	X	12
Collegiate School, New York			X		K–4	5–8	9–12	650	227	4:1	X	13
Convent of the Sacred Heart, New York				X	PK–4	5–8	9–12	700	210	10:1	X	23
Darrow School, New Lebanon	X	X	X	X	–	–	9–12	120	120	4:1	X	27
Dominican Academy, New York				X	–	–	9–12	208	208	8:1	X	9
Fordham Preparatory School, Bronx			X		–	–	9–12	936	936	11:1	X	23
French-American School of New York, Mamaroneck			X	X	N–5	6–8	9–12	842	208	6:1	X	8
Friends Academy, Locust Valley			X	X	N–5	6–8	9–12	780	376	8:1	X	18
The Harley School, Rochester			X	X	N–4	5–8	9–12	537	186	8:1	X	15
Hebrew Academy of the Five Towns & Rockaway, Cedarhurst			X	X	–	–	9–12	388	388		X	7
Houghton Academy, Houghton	X	X	X	X	–	6–8	9–PG	130	107	8:1	X	15
The Kew-Forest School, Forest Hills			X	X	N–6	7–8	9–12	238	100	8:1	X	17
Kildonan School, Amenia	X	X	X	X	2–6	7–8	9–PG	91	50	2:1		39
La Scuola D'Italia Guglielmo Marconi, New York			X	X	PK–5	6–8	9–12	261	44		X	4
Little Red School House and Elisabeth Irwin High School, New York			X	X	N–4	5–8	9–12	650	240	7:1		28
Long Island Lutheran Middle and High School, Brookville			X	X	–	6–8	9–12	590	413	9:1	X	23
Loyola School, New York			X	X	–	–	9–12	202	202	9:1		15
Maplebrook School, Amenia	X	X	X	X				75	62	8:1		41
The Mary Louis Academy, Jamaica Estates				X	–	–	9–12	855	855	13:1	X	27
The Masters School, Dobbs Ferry	X	X	X	X	–	5–8	9–12	650	475	7:1	X	32
Millbrook School, Millbrook	X	X	X	X	–	–	9–12	283	283	5:1	X	30
Norman Howard School, Rochester			X	X	4–4	5–8	9–12	123	82	3:1		7
The Park School of Buffalo, Snyder	X	X	X	X	PK–4	5–8	9–12	290	133	8:1	X	31

Private Secondary Schools At-a-Glance

| | STUDENTS ACCEPTED | | | | GRADES | | | STUDENT/FACULTY | | | SCHOOL OFFERINGS | |
| | BOARDING | | DAY | | | | | | | | | |
Private Secondary Schools At-a-Glance	Boys	Girls	Boys	Girls	Lower	Middle	Upper	Total	Upper	Student/Faculty Ratio	Advanced Placement Preparation	Sports
Poughkeepsie Day School, Poughkeepsie			X	X	PK–5	6–8	9–12	280	115	7:1	X	27
Preston High School, Bronx				X	–	–	9–12	600	600	25:1	X	7
Professional Children's School, New York			X	X	–	6–8	9–12	195	160	8:1		
Regis High School, New York			X		–	–	9–12	530	530	15:1	X	8
Riverdale Country School, Bronx			X	X	PK–5	6–8	9–12	1,125	500	8:1		23
Ross School, East Hampton	X	X	X	X	N–6	–	7–12	521	370	7:1	X	21
Smith School, New York			X	X	–	7–8	9–12	57	42	4:1		7
Soundview Preparatory School, Yorktown Heights			X	X	–	6–8	9–12	68	56	5:1	X	4
The Spence School, New York				X	K–4	5–8	9–12	725	234	7:1	X	13
The Storm King School, Cornwall-on-Hudson	X	X	X	X	–	8–8	9–12	139	132	6:1	X	65
Trevor Day School, New York			X	X	N–5	6–8	9–12	800	248	6:1	X	14
Trinity-Pawling School, Pawling	X		X		–	7–8	9–PG	283	260	8:1	X	40
The Waldorf School of Garden City, Garden City			X	X	N–5	6–8	9–12	350	105	5:1		14
The Waldorf School of Saratoga Springs, Saratoga Springs			X	X	PK–8	–	9–12	241	45	13:1		15
The Windsor School, Flushing			X	X		6–8	9–13	180	170	14:1	X	11
Winston Preparatory School, New York			X	X	–	4–8	9–12	180	124	3:1		14
York Preparatory School, New York			X	X	–	6–8	9–12	358	262	6:1		26
North Carolina												
Arthur Morgan School, Burnsville	X	X	X	X	–	7–9		27		2:1		26
Cape Fear Academy, Wilmington			X	X	PK–5	6–8	9–12	573	222	7:1	X	13
Cardinal Gibbons High School, Raleigh			X	X	–	–	9–12	1,294	1,294	14:1	X	34
Charlotte Country Day School, Charlotte			X	X	PK–4	5–8	9–12	1,631	506	12:1		21
Charlotte Latin School, Charlotte			X	X	K–5	6–8	9–12	1,401	500	8:1	X	20
Durham Academy, Durham			X	X	PK–4	5–8	9–12	1,165	411	8:1	X	25
Fayetteville Academy, Fayetteville			X	X	PK–5	6–8	9–12	370	140	14:1	X	13
Gaston Day School, Gastonia			X	X	PS–4	5–8	9–12	512	158	7:1	X	11
Harrells Christian Academy, Harrells			X	X	K–5	6–8	9–12	412	163	11:1	X	9
The O'Neal School, Southern Pines			X	X	PK–5	6–8	9–12	415	158	12:1	X	10
Providence Day School, Charlotte			X	X	PK–5	6–8	9–12	1,580	570	9:1	X	24
Salem Academy, Winston-Salem		X		X	–	–	9–12	160	160	7:1	X	22
Westchester Country Day School, High Point			X	X	PK–5	6–8	9–12	355	126	6:1	X	15
North Dakota												
Shanley High School, Fargo			X	X			9–12	313	313	18:1	X	11
Ohio												
Archbishop Alter High School, Kettering			X	X	–		9–12	673	673	12:1	X	20
Archbishop Hoban High School, Akron			X	X			9–12	861	861	15:1	X	22
The Columbus Academy, Gahanna			X	X	PK–4	5–8	9–12	1,085	372	8:1	X	15
Columbus School for Girls, Columbus				X	PK–5	6–8	9–12	561	195	9:1	X	16
The Grand River Academy, Austinburg	X				–	–	9–12	111	111	6:1	X	62
Lawrence School, Sagamore Hills			X	X	K–6	7–8	9–12	280	136	11:1		11
Padua Franciscan High School, Parma			X	X	–		9–12	755	755	19:1	X	43
St. Francis de Sales High School, Toledo			X		–		9–12	612	612	14:1	X	17
Saint Ursula Academy, Toledo				X	–	7–8	9–12	549	522	12:1	X	31
The Seven Hills School, Cincinnati			X	X	PK–5	6–8	9–12	1,028	315	9:1	X	13
The Summit Country Day School, Cincinnati			X	X	PK–4	5–8	9–12	1,020	369	9:1	X	19
Trinity High School, Garfield Heights			X	X	–		9–12	352	352	12:1	X	15
Villa Angela-St. Joseph High School, Cleveland			X	X	–	–	9–12	375	375	12:1	X	21
Oklahoma												
Bishop McGuinness Catholic High School, Oklahoma City			X	X	9–10	–	11–12	701	341	13:1	X	18
Oregon												
Blanchet School, Salem			X	X	–	6–8	9–12	357	231	17:1	X	15
The Catlin Gabel School, Portland			X	X	PS–5	6–8	9–12	753	309	8:1		50
De La Salle North Catholic High School, Portland			X	X	–	–	9–12	322	322	17:1	X	7
Northwest Academy, Portland			X	X	–	6–8	9–12	182	80	4:1		10
Oregon Episcopal School, Portland	X	X	X	X	PK–5	6–8	9–12	858	316	7:1	X	21
Pacific Crest Community School, Portland			X	X	–	6–8	9–12	85	55	9:1		12
St. Mary's School, Medford	X	X	X	X	–	6–8	9–12	461	312	11:1	X	30
Salem Academy, Salem			X	X	K–5	6–8	9–12	631	258	9:1	X	12
Wellsprings Friends School, Eugene			X	X	–	–	9–12	45	45	8:1		7
Pennsylvania												
Academy of the New Church Boys' School, Bryn Athyn	X		X		–	–	9–12	124	124	8:1	X	6
Academy of the New Church Girls' School, Bryn Athyn		X		X	–	–	9–12	101	101	8:1	X	9
The Agnes Irwin School, Rosemont				X	PK–4	5–8	9–12	703	289	5:1	X	23
Bishop Shanahan High School, Downingtown			X	X	–		9–12	1,125	1,125		X	16
Camphill Special School, Glenmoore	X	X	X	X	K–5	6–8	9–13	118	59	5:1		

Private Secondary Schools At-a-Glance

	STUDENTS ACCEPTED				GRADES			STUDENT/FACULTY			SCHOOL OFFERINGS	
	BOARDING		DAY									
	Boys	Girls	Boys	Girls	Lower	Middle	Upper	Total	Upper	Student/Faculty Ratio	Advanced Placement Preparation	Sports
Cardinal O'Hara High School, Springfield			X	X	–	–	9–12		1,289	21:1	X	21
Christopher Dock Mennonite High School, Lansdale	X	X	X	X	–	–	9–12	351	351	11:1	X	12
The Concept School, Westtown			X	X	–	5–8	9–12	24	16	5:1		13
Country Day School of the Sacred Heart, Bryn Mawr				X	PK–4	5–8	9–12	314	165	8:1	X	11
Devon Preparatory School, Devon			X		–	6–8	9–12	253	199	10:1	X	10
The Episcopal Academy, Newtown Square			X	X	PK–5	6–8	9–12	1,216	528	7:1	X	37
Father Judge High School, Philadelphia			X		–	–	9–12	986	986	28:1	X	24
Friends' Central School, Wynnewood			X	X	N–5	5–8	9–12	812	377	8:1		25
George School, Newtown	X	X	X	X	–	–	9–12	545	545	7:1	X	25
Germantown Friends School, Philadelphia			X	X	K–5	6–8	9–12	861	353	9:1		17
Girard College, Philadelphia	X	X			1–6	–	7–12	331	201	16:1	X	32
Grier School, Tyrone		X			–	7–8	9–PG	306	262	7:1	X	46
The Hill Top Preparatory School, Rosemont			X	X	–	5–9	10–12	73	34	6:1		27
Lancaster Country Day School, Lancaster			X	X	PS–5	6–8	9–12	615	213	6:1	X	20
Lancaster Mennonite High School, Lancaster	X	X	X	X	PK–5	6–8	9–12	1,412	638	15:1	X	14
Lansdale Catholic High School, Lansdale			X	X	–	–	9–12	763	763	21:1	X	25
Lehigh Valley Christian High School, Catasauqua			X	X	–	–	9–12	122	122	9:1	X	8
Marian Catholic High School, Tamaqua			X	X	–	–	9–12	378	378	11:1	X	8
Mercersburg Academy, Mercersburg	X	X	X	X	–	–	9–PG	430	430	5:1	X	58
MMI Preparatory School, Freeland			X	X	–	6–8	9–12	247	157	11:1	X	11
Moravian Academy, Bethlehem			X	X	PK–5	6–8	9–12	750	300	7:1	X	14
Nazareth Academy High School for Girls, Philadelphia				X	–	–	9–12	378	378	9:1	X	14
Notre Dame Junior/Senior High School, East Stroudsburg			X	X	–	–	7–12	270	270	15:1	X	14
The Oakland School, Pittsburgh			X	X	–	–	8–12	40	40	6:1		32
The Pathway School, Norristown			X	X	–	–	–	120	46	6:1		5
The Phelps School, Malvern	X		X		–	–	7–PG	110	110	4:1	X	24
Philadelphia-Montgomery Christian Academy, Erdenheim			X	X	K–5	6–8	9–12	309	140	10:1	X	8
St. Joseph's Preparatory School, Philadelphia			X		–	–	9–12	968	968	16:1	X	32
Sewickley Academy, Sewickley			X	X	PK–5	6–8	9–12	708	289	7:1	X	15
Shady Side Academy, Pittsburgh	X	X	X	X	PK–5	6–8	9–12	935	492	8:1	X	25
The Shipley School, Bryn Mawr			X	X	PK–5	6–8	9–12	823	352	7:1	X	25
Springside Chestnut Hill Academy, Philadelphia			X	X	PK–4	5–8	9–12	1,102	472	7:1	X	18
Villa Joseph Marie High School, Holland				X	–	–	9–12	363	363	9:1	X	15
Westtown School, West Chester	X	X	X	X	PK–5	6–8	9–12	632	381	8:1	X	36
William Penn Charter School, Philadelphia			X	X	PK–5	6–8	9–12	966	458	9:1	X	19
Woodlynde School, Strafford			X	X	K–5	6–8	9–12	262	100	5:1	X	11
Puerto Rico												
Baldwin School of Puerto Rico, Bayamón			X	X	PK–5	6–8	9–12	812	216	8:1	X	14
Colegio San Jose, San Juan			X		–	7–8	9–12	515	351	15:1	X	13
Fowlers Academy, Guaynabo			X		–	7–8	9–12	64	44	15:1		8
Guamani Private School, Guayama			X	X	1–6	7–8	9–12	606	164	13:1	X	6
Wesleyan Academy, Guaynabo			X	X	PK–6	7–8	9–12	959	161	23:1	X	8
Rhode Island												
Bishop Hendricken High School, Warwick			X		–	–	9–12	948	948	14:1	X	34
Mount Saint Charles Academy, Woonsocket			X	X	–	–	7–12	699	699	14:1	X	27
Providence Country Day School, East Providence			X	X	–	6–8	9–12	200	160	7:1	X	19
St. Andrew's School, Barrington	X	X	X	X	–	6–8	9–PG	205	175	5:1	X	32
St. George's School, Middletown	X	X	X	X	–	–	9–12	365	365	6:1	X	22
The Wheeler School, Providence			X	X	N–5	6–8	9–12	817	350	7:1	X	15
South Carolina												
Ashley Hall, Charleston			X	X	PS–4	5–6	7–12	677	299	8:1	X	41
Christ Church Episcopal School, Greenville			X	X	K–4	5–8	9–12	1,151	409	10:1		16
Hank Haney International Junior Golf Academy, Hilton Head Island	X	X	X	X	–	–	5–PG	140	140	10:1	X	1
Porter-Gaud School, Charleston			X	X	1–5	6–8	9–12	886	359	12:1	X	26
St. Joseph's Catholic School, Greenville			X	X	–	6–8	9–12	669	405	13:1	X	18
Wilson Hall, Sumter			X	X	PS–5	6–8	9–12	778	242	13:1	X	34
South Dakota												
Freeman Academy, Freeman	X	X	X	X	1–4	5–8	9–12	68	34	5:1		7
Sunshine Bible Academy, Miller	X	X	X	X	K–5	6–8	9–12	94	65	9:1		12
Tennessee												
Bachman Academy, McDonald	X	X	X	X	–	6–8	9–PG	39	28	3:1		40
Battle Ground Academy, Franklin			X	X	K–4	5–8	9–12	809	324	8:1	X	30
Briarcrest Christian High School, Eads			X	X	PK–5	6–8	9–12	1,640	535	12:1	X	20
Chattanooga Christian School, Chattanooga			X	X	K–5	6–8	9–12	1,179	449	17:1	X	18

Private Secondary Schools At-a-Glance

| | STUDENTS ACCEPTED | | | | GRADES | | | STUDENT/FACULTY | | | SCHOOL OFFERINGS | |
| | BOARDING | | DAY | | | | | | | | | |
	Boys	Girls	Boys	Girls	Lower	Middle	Upper	Total	Upper	Student/Faculty Ratio	Advanced Placement Preparation	Sports
Clarksville Academy, Clarksville			X	X	PK–5	6–8	9–12	576	183	12:1	X	12
Columbia Academy, Columbia			X	X	K–6	–	7–12	765	326	10:1	X	15
Currey Ingram Academy, Brentwood			X	X	K–4	5–8	9–12	301	77	4:1		8
Davidson Academy, Nashville			X	X	PK–6	7–8	9–12	750		17:1	X	16
Donelson Christian Academy, Nashville			X	X	K4–5	6–8	9–12	701	219	16:1	X	19
Ezell-Harding Christian School, Antioch			X	X	PK–4	5–8	9–12	543	198	14:1	X	14
Father Ryan High School, Nashville			X	X	–	–	9–12	948	948	12:1	X	30
Franklin Road Academy, Nashville			X	X	PK–4	5–8	9–12	720	264	8:1	X	23
Girls Preparatory School, Chattanooga				X	–	6–8	9–12	584	347	8:1	X	45
Grace Baptist Academy, Chattanooga			X	X	K4–5	6–8	9–12	572	161	12:1	X	16
The Harpeth Hall School, Nashville				X	–	5–8	9–12	671	400	8:1	X	38
Lipscomb Academy, Nashville			X	X	PK–4	5–8	9–12	1,318	523	15:1	X	14
Middle Tennessee Christian School, Murfreesboro			X	X	PK–6	7–8	9–12	665	200	18:1	X	13
Montgomery Bell Academy, Nashville			X		–	7–8	9–12	718	495	7:1	X	38
St. Benedict at Auburndale, Cordova			X	X	–	–	9–12	945	945	16:1	X	24
St. George's Independent School, Collierville			X	X	PK–5	6–8	9–12	1,213	394	7:1	X	16
St. Mary's Episcopal School, Memphis				X	PK–4	5–8	9–12	849	246	13:1	X	12
Trinity Christian Academy, Jackson			X	X	PS–5	6–8	9–12	772	241	7:1		13
University School of Jackson, Jackson			X	X	PK–5	6–8	9–12	1,150	315	13:1	X	16
Webb School of Knoxville, Knoxville			X	X	K–5	6–8	9–12	1,034	471	10:1	X	19
Texas												
The Brook Hill School, Bullard	X	X	X	X	PK–5	6–8	9–12	519	191	9:1	X	24
Carrollton Christian Academy, Carrollton			X	X	PK–6	7–8	9–12	252				14
Central Catholic High School, San Antonio			X		–	–	9–12	520	520	17:1	X	12
Cistercian Preparatory School, Irving			X		–	5–8	9–12	352	178	5:1	X	14
Duchesne Academy of the Sacred Heart, Houston				X	PK–4	5–8	9–12	680	236	7:1	X	14
The Emery/Weiner School, Houston			X	X	–	6–8	9–12			7:1	X	15
Episcopal High School, Bellaire			X	X	–	–	9–12	676	676	9:1	X	23
First Baptist Academy, Dallas			X	X	PK–5	6–8	9–12	207	89	8:1	X	14
Fort Worth Christian School, North Richland Hills			X	X	PK–5	6–8	9–12	850	356	14:1	X	16
Gateway School, Arlington			X	X	–	5–8	9–12			5:1		6
Greenhill School, Addison			X	X	PK–4	5–8	9–12	1,276	476	7:1	X	29
The Hockaday School, Dallas		X		X	PK–4	5–8	9–12	1,086	478	15:1	X	42
Huntington-Surrey School, Austin			X	X	–	–	9–12	48	48	4:1		1
Hyde Park Baptist School, Austin			X	X	PK–5	6–8	9–12	599	286	12:1	X	14
Jesuit College Preparatory School, Dallas			X		–	–	9–12	1,095	1,095	11:1	X	28
Keystone School, San Antonio			X	X	K–4	5–8	9–12	431	128	10:1	X	8
Lakehill Preparatory School, Dallas			X	X	K–4	5–8	9–12	400	115	10:1	X	17
Marine Military Academy, Harlingen	X				–	–	8–12	250	250	13:1	X	40
North Central Texas Academy, Granbury	X	X	X	X	K–5	6–8	9–12	194	70	7:1		17
Parish Episcopal School, Dallas			X	X	PK–4	5–8	9–12	1,100				22
Presbyterian Pan American School, Kingsville	X	X	X	X	–	–	9–12	160	160	10:1		19
Providence Catholic School, The College Preparatory School for Girls Grades 6-12, San Antonio				X	–	6–8	9–12	315	193	11:1	X	20
St. Agnes Academy, Houston				X	–	–	9–12	899	899	12:1	X	20
St. Mark's School of Texas, Dallas			X		1–4	5–8	9–12	851	364	8:1	X	41
Saint Mary's Hall, San Antonio			X	X	PK–5	6–8	9–PG	1,008	397	6:1	X	21
St. Pius X High School, Houston			X	X	–	–	9–12	670	670	12:1	X	17
St. Stephen's Episcopal School, Austin	X	X	X	X	–	6–8	9–12	689	487	8:1	X	39
San Marcos Baptist Academy, San Marcos	X	X	X	X	–	7–8	9–12	286	237	7:1	X	24
Shelton School and Evaluation Center, Dallas			X	X	PS–4	5–8	9–12	827	262	8:1		12
The Tenney School, Houston			X	X	–	6–8	9–12	57	37	2:1		
TMI - The Episcopal School of Texas, San Antonio	X	X	X	X	–	6–8	9–12	470	340	10:1	X	23
Trinity School of Texas, Longview			X	X	PK–5	6–8	9–12	275	60	8:1	X	12
Trinity Valley School, Fort Worth			X	X	K–4	5–8	9–12	970	348	5:1	X	12
Tyler Street Christian Academy, Dallas			X	X	P3–6	7–8	9–12	198	47	13:1	X	16
The Ursuline Academy of Dallas, Dallas				X	–	–	9–12	800	800	10:1	X	14
Westbury Christian School, Houston			X	X	PK–4	5–8	9–12	480	225	10:1	X	13
The Winston School, Dallas			X	X	1–6	7–8	9–12	166	80	5:1		21
The Winston School San Antonio, San Antonio			X	X	K–6	7–8	9–12	206	95	8:1		14
Utah												
Intermountain Christian School, Salt Lake City			X	X	PK–5	6–8	9–12	285	59	9:1	X	5
Realms of Inquiry, Murray			X	X	–	6–8	9–12	14	10	7:1		62
Rowland Hall, Salt Lake City			X	X	PK–5	6–8	9–12	927	300	7:1	X	30
Wasatch Academy, Mt. Pleasant	X	X	X	X	–	7–8	9–PG	304	290	10:1	X	65
The Waterford School, Sandy			X	X	PK–5	6–8	9–12	875	251	4:1	X	33
Vermont												
Burr and Burton Academy, Manchester	X	X	X	X	–	–	9–12	667	667	12:1	X	26
Long Trail School, Dorset			X	X	–	6–8	9–12	155	93	8:1		26
The Sharon Academy, Sharon			X	X	–	7–8	9–12	165	129	16:1		

Private Secondary Schools At-a-Glance

	STUDENTS ACCEPTED				GRADES			STUDENT/FACULTY			SCHOOL OFFERINGS	
	BOARDING		DAY									
	Boys	Girls	Boys	Girls	Lower	Middle	Upper	Total	Upper	Student/Faculty Ratio	Advanced Placement Preparation	Sports
Virgin Islands												
Good Hope Country Day School, Kingshill			X	X	N–6	7–8	9–12	440	150	12:1	X	12
Virginia												
Bishop Denis J. O'Connell High School, Arlington			X	X	–	–		1,221	1,221	12:1	X	24
Bishop Ireton High School, Alexandria			X	X	–	–	9–12	785	785	14:1	X	25
Cape Henry Collegiate School, Virginia Beach			X	X	PK–5	6–8	9–12	863	382	10:1	X	45
Carlisle School, Axton	X	X	X	X	PK–5	6–8	9–12	453	138	8:1	X	17
Eastern Mennonite High School, Harrisonburg			X	X	K–5	6–8	9–12	385	194	12:1	X	11
Episcopal High School, Alexandria	X	X			–	–	9–12	439	439	6:1	X	44
Fishburne Military School, Waynesboro	X		X		–	7–8	9–12	170	155	9:1	X	12
Foxcroft School, Middleburg		X		X	–	–	9–12	165	165	7:1	X	34
Fredericksburg Academy, Fredericksburg			X	X	PK–5	6–8	9–12	552	135	6:1	X	11
Fuqua School, Farmville			X	X	PK–5	6–8	9–12	382	143	7:1	X	13
Hampton Roads Academy, Newport News			X	X	PK–4	5–8	9–12	588	248	10:1	X	32
Hargrave Military Academy, Chatham	X		X		–	7–9	10–PG	310	260	12:1	X	49
Little Keswick School, Keswick	X				–	–		34		3:1		13
The Madeira School, McLean		X		X	–	–	9–12	310	310	10:1	X	18
Norfolk Academy, Norfolk			X	X	1–6	7–9	10–12	1,248	379	10:1	X	22
Oakland School, Keswick	X	X	X	X						5:1		43
The Potomac School, McLean			X	X	K–3	4–8	9–12	1,024	423	6:1	X	29
Randolph-Macon Academy, Front Royal	X	X	X	X	–	6–8	9–PG	330	264	14:1	X	27
Saint Gertrude High School, Richmond		X			–	–	9–12	266	266	9:1	X	12
St. Stephen's & St. Agnes School, Alexandria			X	X	JK–5	6–8	9–12	1,144	456	9:1	X	28
Wakefield School, The Plains			X	X	PS–5	6–8	9–12	397	152	11:1	X	17
Washington												
Annie Wright School, Tacoma		X	X	X	PS–5	6–8	9–12	467	180	5:1		8
Archbishop Thomas J. Murphy High School, Everett			X	X	–	–				14:1	X	14
Chrysalis School, Woodinville			X	X	K–6	7–8	9–12	165	108	3:1		
Explorations Academy, Bellingham			X	X	–	–		41	41	7:1	X	
Holy Names Academy, Seattle				X	–	–	9–12	690	690			
The Overlake School, Redmond			X	X	–	5–8	9–12	534	304	9:1	X	36
Seattle Academy of Arts and Sciences, Seattle			X	X	–	6–8	9–12	720	458	9:1		26
Shoreline Christian, Shoreline			X	X	PS–6	7–8	9–12	212	76	7:1		5
West Sound Academy, Poulsbo	X	X	X	X	–	6–8	9–12	95	61	7:1	X	15
West Virginia												
The Linsly School, Wheeling	X	X	X	X	5–8	–	9–12	443	298	10:1	X	47
Wisconsin												
Catholic Central High School, Burlington			X	X	–	–	9–12	180	180	9:1	X	23
Madison Country Day School, Waunakee			X	X	PK–4	5–8	9–12	366	62	6:1		5
St. Lawrence Seminary High School, Mount Calvary	X				–	–	9–12	195	195	9:1		26
University School of Milwaukee, Milwaukee			X	X	PK–4	5–8	9–12	1,120	376	9:1		16
CANADA												
The Academy for Gifted Children (PACE), Richmond Hill, ON			X	X	1–3	4–7	8–12	306	113	15:1	X	43
Balmoral Hall School, Winnipeg, MB		X		X	N–5	6–8	9–12	474	154	7:1	X	67
Branksome Hall, Toronto, ON		X		X	JK–6	7–8	9–12	885	445	9:1		42
Central Alberta Christian High School, Lacombe, AB			X	X	–	–	10–12	103	103	13:1		22
Columbia International College of Canada, Hamilton, ON	X	X	X	X	–	7–9	10–12	1,804	1,600	20:1	X	50
Community Hebrew Academy, Toronto, ON			X	X	–	–	9–12	1,300	1,300	8:1		17
The Country Day School, King City, ON			X	X	JK–6	7–8	9–12	700	300	9:1	X	32
Covenant Canadian Reformed School, Neerlandia, AB			X	X	K–6	7–9	10–12	221	28	10:1		17
Crawford Adventist Academy, Willowdale, ON			X	X	JK–6	7–8	9–12	354	151	16:1	X	13
De La Salle College, Toronto, ON			X	X	5–6	7–8	9–12	627	434	15:1	X	21
Glenlyon Norfolk School, Victoria, BC			X	X	JK–5	6–8	9–12	685	280	8:1		27
Great Lakes Christian High School, Beamsville, ON	X	X	X	X	–	–	9–12	94	94			19
Heritage Christian School, Jordan, ON			X	X	K–8	–	9–12	630	181	15:1		5
Highroad Academy, Chilliwack, BC			X	X	K–6	7–8	9–12	390	114	10:1		
Holy Trinity School, Richmond Hill, ON			X	X	JK–6	7–8	9–12	750	400	17:1	X	15
King's-Edgehill School, Windsor, NS	X	X	X	X	–	6–9	10–12	290	200	10:1		33
Kingsway College, Oshawa, ON	X	X	X	X	–	–	9–12	187	187	12:1		17
Lakefield College School, Lakefield, ON	X	X	X	X	–	–	9–12	366	366	7:1	X	43
The Laureate Academy, Winnipeg, MB			X	X	1–5	6–8	9–12	80	30	6:1		36
Luther College High School, Regina, SK	X	X	X	X	–	–	9–12	430	430	17:1		21

Private Secondary Schools At-a-Glance

	STUDENTS ACCEPTED				GRADES			STUDENT/FACULTY			SCHOOL OFFERINGS	
	BOARDING		DAY							Student/Faculty	Advanced Placement	
	Boys	Girls	Boys	Girls	Lower	Middle	Upper	Total	Upper	Ratio	Preparation	Sports
Meadowridge School, Maple Ridge, BC			X	X	JK–5	–	6–12	540	290	12:1		12
Mennonite Collegiate Institute, Gretna, MB	X	X	X	X	–	7–8	9–12	140	122	13:1	X	14
Miss Edgar's and Miss Cramp's School, Montreal, QC				X	K–5	6–8	9–11	335	115	9:1	X	26
Newton's Grove School, Toronto, ON			X	X	JK–6	7–8	9–12	255	120	18:1		27
Niagara Christian Community of Schools, Fort Erie, ON	X	X	X	X	–	6–8	9–12	178	165	16:1		18
North Toronto Christian School, Toronto, ON			X	X	JK–6	7–8	9–12	438	182	15:1		27
Queen Margaret's School, Duncan, BC		X	X	X	PS–3	4–8	9–12	317	128	8:1	X	63
Redeemer Christian High School, Ottawa, ON			X	X	–		9–12	167	167	9:1		
Ridley College, St. Catharines, ON	X	X	X	X	JK–8	–	9–PG	651	470	7:1		78
Rosseau Lake College, Rosseau, ON	X	X	X	X	–	7–8	9–12	84	74	6:1		82
Royal Canadian College, Vancouver, BC			X	X	–	9–10	11–12	110	91	20:1		7
Sacred Heart School of Halifax, Halifax, NS			X	X	K–6	–	7–12	461	258	10:1	X	17
St. Andrew's College, Aurora, ON	X		X		–	5–8	9–12	613	446	8:1	X	62
St. Andrew's Regional High School, Victoria, BC			X	X	–	8–9	10–12			14:1		8
St. George's School, Vancouver, BC	X		X		1–7	–	8–12	1,157	778	8:1	X	33
St. George's School of Montreal, Montreal, QC			X	X	K–6	–	7–11	426	236	15:1	X	41
St. Michael's College School, Toronto, ON			X		–	7–8	9–12	1,067	870	16:1	X	32
St. Patrick's Regional Secondary, Vancouver, BC			X	X	–	–	8–12	500	500		X	6
St. Paul's High School, Winnipeg, MB			X		–	–	9–12	596	596	14:1	X	22
Shawnigan Lake School, Shawnigan Lake, BC	X	X	X	X	–	–	8–12	457	457	8:1	X	52
Signet Christian School, North York, ON			X	X	JK–8	–	9–12	37	16	5:1		9
The Study, Westmount, QC				X	K–3	4–6	7–11	316	125	8:1	X	30
Trafalgar Castle School, Whitby, ON		X		X	–	5–8	9–12	191	134	9:1	X	29
Trinity College School, Port Hope, ON	X	X	X	X	–	5–8	9–12	554	450	8:1	X	37
United Mennonite Educational Institute, Leamington, ON			X	X	–		9–12	48	48	15:1		18
Upper Canada College, Toronto, ON	X		X		K–7	8–9	9–12	1,190	650	8:1		59
Venta Preparatory School, Ottawa, ON	X	X	X	X	JK–7	–	8–10	74	20	6:1		14
The York School, Toronto, ON			X	X	JK–5	6–8	9–12	600	235	16:1		26

INTERNATIONAL

	STUDENTS ACCEPTED				GRADES			STUDENT/FACULTY			SCHOOL OFFERINGS	
	Boys	Girls	Boys	Girls	Lower	Middle	Upper	Total	Upper	Ratio	Preparation	Sports
Colombia												
Colegio Bolivar, Cali			X	X	PK–5	6–8	9–12	1,258	365	9:1	X	13
Greece												
American Community Schools of Athens, Athens			X	X	JK–5	6–8	9–12	859	342	20:1	X	11
Italy												
St. Stephen's School, Rome, Rome	X	X	X	X	–	–	9–PG	278	278	7:1	X	7
Japan												
Saint Maur International School, Yokohama			X	X	PK–5	6–8	9–12	436	128	4:1	X	6
Seisen International School, Tokyo			X	X	K–6	7–8	9–12	634	198	6:1		12
Malaysia												
Mont'Kiara International School, Kuala Lumpur			X	X	1–5	6–8	9–12	1,005	250	10:1		18
Mexico												
The American School Foundation, Mexico City, D.F.			X	X	1–5	6–8	9–12	2,571	743	11:1	X	7
Philippines												
International School Manila, 1634 Taguig City			X	X	PK–4	5–8	9–12	2,200	780	9:1	X	18
Spain												
The American School of Madrid, Madrid			X	X	PK–5	6–8	9–12	868	284	8:1		8
Switzerland												
Institut Monte Rosa, Montreux	X	X	X	X	–	–				5:1	X	39
Thailand												
International School Bangkok, Pakkret			X	X	PK–5	6–8	9–12	1,896	709	10:1	X	15
Turkey												
Istanbul International Community School, Istanbul			X	X	1–6	–	7–12	578	269	9:1		12
United Kingdom												
Merchiston Castle School, Edinburgh	X		X		–				174	9:1		46

Traditional Day and Boarding Schools

ACACIA ACADEMY

Lagrange Highlands, Illinois
See Special Needs Schools section.

THE ACADEMY AT CHARLEMONT

1359 Route 2
The Mohawk Trail
Charlemont, Massachusetts 01339

Head of School: Ms. Nell Todd

General Information Coeducational day college-preparatory and arts school. Grades 7–PG. Founded: 1981. Setting: rural. Nearest major city is Northampton. 52-acre campus. 3 buildings on campus. Approved or accredited by Association of Independent Schools in New England, New England Association of Schools and Colleges, and Massachusetts Department of Education. Member of National Association of Independent Schools and Secondary School Admission Test Board. Endowment: $425,000. Total enrollment: 97. Upper school average class size: 16. Upper school faculty-student ratio: 1:9. There are 160 required school days per year for Upper School students. Upper School students typically attend 5 days per week. The average school day consists of 7 hours and 15 minutes.

Upper School Student Profile Grade 9: 13 students (8 boys, 5 girls); Grade 10: 17 students (7 boys, 10 girls); Grade 11: 16 students (7 boys, 9 girls); Grade 12: 17 students (10 boys, 7 girls).

Faculty School total: 25. In upper school: 9 men, 9 women; 12 have advanced degrees.

Subjects Offered 3-dimensional art, 3-dimensional design, algebra, American legal systems, American literature, art, art history, biology, calculus, ceramics, chemistry, choral music, computer programming, creative writing, dance, drama, drawing, earth science, ecology, English, English literature, environmental science, ethics, European history, expository writing, fine arts, French, geography, geometry, government/civics, grammar, health, history, jazz band, Latin, mathematics, music, music appreciation, philosophy, photography, physical education, physics, pre-algebra, publishing, religion, Russian, science, senior humanities, senior project, social studies, Spanish, speech, theater, trigonometry, world history, world literature.

Graduation Requirements Algebra, American government, American literature, American studies, arts and fine arts (art, music, dance, drama), biology, calculus, chemistry, civics, computer literacy, English, foreign language, four units of summer reading, geography, geometry, Latin, mathematics, physics, pre-calculus, science, senior project, social studies (includes history), year-long independent senior project equal to one full course, requiring outside evaluation and a presentation.

Special Academic Programs Independent study; term-away projects; study abroad.

College Admission Counseling 21 students graduated in 2013; 20 went to college, including Barnard College; Middlebury College; Oberlin College; Tufts University; University of Chicago; Wesleyan University. Other: 1 went to work. Mean SAT critical reading: 673, mean SAT math: 640, mean SAT writing: 678, mean combined SAT: 1992, mean composite ACT: 30.

Student Life Upper grades have specified standards of dress, student council, honor system. Discipline rests primarily with faculty.

Summer Programs Sports, art/fine arts programs offered; session focuses on drama, music, soccer, visual arts; held on campus; accepts boys and girls; open to students from other schools. 2014 schedule: July 8 to August 16. Application deadline: June 15.

Tuition and Aid Day student tuition: $24,500. Tuition installment plan (monthly payment plans, individually arranged payment plans). Need-based scholarship grants available. In 2013–14, 77% of upper-school students received aid. Total amount of financial aid awarded in 2013–14: $593,000.

Admissions Traditional secondary-level entrance grade is 9. For fall 2013, 21 students applied for upper-level admission, 18 were accepted, 7 enrolled. SSAT required. Deadline for receipt of application materials: February 15. Application fee required: $40. On-campus interview required.

Athletics Interscholastic: alpine skiing (boys, girls), baseball (b,g), basketball (b,g), cross-country running (b,g), lacrosse (g), skiing (downhill) (b,g), soccer (b,g), ultimate Frisbee (b,g); intramural: independent competitive sports (b,g), indoor soccer (b,g); coed interscholastic: baseball, cross-country running, soccer, tennis, ultimate Frisbee; coed intramural: alpine skiing, basketball, canoeing/kayaking, cooperative games, hiking/backpacking, kayaking, outdoor activities, outdoor recreation, rafting, skiing (cross-country), skiing (downhill), soccer, tennis, yoga. 7 coaches.

Computers Computers are regularly used in all classes. Computer network features include on-campus library services, Internet access, wireless campus network, Internet filtering or blocking technology, school Web site for schedules and other administrative information. Student e-mail accounts and computer access in designated common areas are available to students. Students grades are available online. The school has a published electronic and media policy.

Contact Martha Tirk, Director of Admissions and Advancement. 413-339-4912 Ext. 113. Fax: 413-339-4324. E-mail: mtirk@charlemont.org. Website: www.charlemont.org

ACADEMY AT THE LAKES

2331 Collier Parkway
Land O'Lakes, Florida 34639

Head of School: Mr. Mark Heller

General Information Coeducational day college-preparatory, arts, and technology school. Grades PK–12. Founded: 1992. Setting: suburban. Nearest major city is Tampa. 11-acre campus. 10 buildings on campus. Approved or accredited by Southern Association of Colleges and Schools and Florida Department of Education. Member of National Association of Independent Schools and Secondary School Admission Test Board. Total enrollment: 428. Upper school average class size: 14. Upper school faculty-student ratio: 1:5. There are 175 required school days per year for Upper School students. Upper School students typically attend 5 days per week. The average school day consists of 7 hours and 15 minutes.

Faculty School total: 60. In upper school: 9 men, 15 women; 18 have advanced degrees.

Graduation Requirements Standard curriculum.

Special Academic Programs 11 Advanced Placement exams for which test preparation is offered; honors section; ESL.

College Admission Counseling 30 students graduated in 2013; 29 went to college.

Student Life Upper grades have specified standards of dress, student council, honor system. Discipline rests primarily with faculty.

Summer Programs Enrichment, sports, art/fine arts, computer instruction programs offered; held on campus; accepts boys and girls; open to students from other schools. 2014 schedule: June to August.

Tuition and Aid Day student tuition: $9240–$18,470. Tuition installment plan (monthly payment plans). Need-based scholarship grants available.

Admissions Traditional secondary-level entrance grade is 9. For fall 2013, 58 students applied for upper-level admission, 42 were accepted, 32 enrolled. SSAT required. Deadline for receipt of application materials: none. Application fee required: $75. Interview required.

Athletics Interscholastic: baseball (boys), basketball (b,g), cheering (g), cross-country running (b,g), football (b), golf (b,g), physical fitness (b,g), physical training (b,g), soccer (b,g), softball (g), strength & conditioning (b,g), swimming and diving (b,g), tennis (b,g), track and field (b,g), volleyball (g), weight training (b,g), winter soccer (b,g); coed interscholastic: physical fitness, physical training, soccer, strength & conditioning, weight training. 3 PE instructors, 11 coaches, 1 athletic trainer.

Computers Computer network features include on-campus library services, Internet access, wireless campus network, Internet filtering or blocking technology. Student e-mail accounts are available to students. Students grades are available online. The school has a published electronic and media policy.

Contact Mrs. Melissa Starkey, Associate Director of Admissions. 813-909-7919. Fax: 813-949-0563. E-mail: mstarkey@academyatthelakes.org. Website: www.academyatthelakes.org/

THE ACADEMY FOR GIFTED CHILDREN (PACE)

12 Bond Crescent
Richmond Hill, Ontario L4E 3K2, Canada

Head of School: Barbara Rosenberg

General Information Coeducational day college-preparatory and differentiated curriculum for Intellectually gifted students school. Grades 1–12. Founded: 1993. Setting: suburban. Nearest major city is Toronto, Canada. 3-acre campus. 2 buildings on campus. Approved or accredited by Ontario Ministry of Education and Ontario Department of Education. Language of instruction: English. Total enrollment: 306. Upper school average class size: 17. Upper school faculty-student ratio: 1:15. There are 187 required school days per year for Upper School students. Upper School students typically attend 5 days per week. The average school day consists of 6 hours.

Upper School Student Profile Grade 8: 35 students (20 boys, 15 girls); Grade 9: 18 students (11 boys, 7 girls); Grade 10: 16 students (12 boys, 4 girls); Grade 11: 21 students (10 boys, 11 girls); Grade 12: 23 students (18 boys, 5 girls).

Faculty School total: 27. In upper school: 5 men, 7 women; 4 have advanced degrees.

Subjects Offered 20th century world history, Advanced Placement courses, algebra, analytic geometry, biology, calculus, calculus-AP, Canadian geography, Canadian history, Canadian law, career education, chemistry, chemistry-AP, civics, computer programming, computer science, computer science-AP, computer studies, dramatic arts, English, finite math, French, French as a second language, geometry, health education, language, law, literature, mathematics, modern Western civilization, music, philosophy, physical education, physics, science, sociology, visual arts, world civilizations, writing.

Graduation Requirements Advanced chemistry, advanced math, algebra, analytic geometry, biology, calculus, Canadian geography, Canadian history, Canadian literature, career education, chemistry, civics, English literature, French as a second language, healthful living, law, music, philosophy, pre-algebra, pre-calculus, science, scuba diving, senior humanities, social sciences, sociology, theater arts, visual arts, minimum of 40 hours of community service, OSSLT.

Special Academic Programs 5 Advanced Placement exams for which test preparation is offered; honors section; independent study; academic accommodation for the gifted.

College Admission Counseling 22 students graduated in 2013; all went to college, including Harvard University; McMaster University; Queen's University at Kingston; The University of Western Ontario; University of Toronto; University of Waterloo. Median SAT critical reading: 780, median SAT math: 800, median SAT writing: 780, median combined SAT: 2360. 100% scored over 600 on SAT critical reading, 100% scored over 600 on SAT math, 100% scored over 600 on SAT writing, 100% scored over 1800 on combined SAT.

Student Life Upper grades have specified standards of dress, student council, honor system. Discipline rests primarily with faculty.

Tuition and Aid Day student tuition: CAN$11,500. Tuition installment plan (monthly payment plans).

Admissions Traditional secondary-level entrance grade is 8. For fall 2013, 10 students applied for upper-level admission, 6 were accepted, 6 enrolled. Psychoeducational evaluation, Wechsler Individual Achievement Test, WISC III or other aptitude measures; standardized achievement test and WISC-R required. Deadline for receipt of application materials: none. No application fee required. On-campus interview required.

Athletics Interscholastic: badminton (boys, girls), ball hockey (b), baseball (b,g), basketball (b,g), flag football (b), floor hockey (b), golf (b,g), independent competitive sports (b,g), indoor soccer (b,g), sailboarding (b,g), soccer (b,g), softball (b,g), tennis (b,g), track and field (b,g), volleyball (b,g), winter soccer (b,g); intramural: badminton (b,g), basketball (b,g), soccer (b,g), softball (b,g); coed interscholastic: badminton, baseball, bowling, cross-country running, flag football, indoor soccer, sailboarding, tennis, track and field, ultimate Frisbee; coed intramural: alpine skiing, badminton, ball hockey, baseball, basketball, blading, climbing, cooperative games, cross-country running, curling, dance, fitness, floor hockey, handball, ice skating, indoor soccer, jogging, jump rope, life saving, outdoor activities, outdoor education, outdoor skills, physical fitness, rock climbing, ropes courses, scuba diving, skiing (cross-country), skiing (downhill), snowboarding, snowshoeing, track and field, ultimate Frisbee, volleyball, wall climbing. 2 PE instructors, 10 coaches.

Computers Computers are regularly used in career exploration, desktop publishing, digital applications, English, information technology, keyboarding, news writing, newspaper, programming, science, technology, theater, writing, yearbook classes. Computer network features include Internet access, wireless campus network, Internet filtering or blocking technology. Computer access in designated common areas is available to students. The school has a published electronic and media policy.

Contact Barbara Rosenberg, Director. 905-773-3997. Fax: 905-773-4722. Website: www.pace.on.ca

ACADEMY OF NOTRE DAME DE NAMUR

560 Sproul Road
Villanova, Pennsylvania 19085-1220

Head of School: Mrs. Veronica Collins Harrington

General Information Girls' day college-preparatory, arts, and religious studies school, affiliated with Roman Catholic Church. Grades 6–12. Founded: 1856. Setting: suburban. Nearest major city is Philadelphia. 38-acre campus. 9 buildings on campus. Approved or accredited by Middle States Association of Colleges and Schools, National Catholic Education Association, Pennsylvania Association of Independent Schools, and Pennsylvania Department of Education. Member of National Association of Independent Schools. Endowment: $5 million. Total enrollment: 519. Upper school average class size: 15. Upper school faculty-student ratio: 1:8. There are 170 required school days per year for Upper School students. Upper School students typically attend 5 days per week. The average school day consists of 6 hours and 45 minutes.

Upper School Student Profile Grade 9: 99 students (99 girls); Grade 10: 98 students (98 girls); Grade 11: 89 students (89 girls); Grade 12: 106 students (106 girls). 88% of students are Roman Catholic.

Faculty School total: 62. In upper school: 9 men, 45 women; 39 have advanced degrees.

Subjects Offered Advanced biology, American history-AP, Bible, biology, biology-AP, calculus, calculus-AP, ceramics, chemistry, chemistry-AP, choral music, Christian and Hebrew scripture, Christian ethics, comparative government and politics-AP, computer skills, contemporary history, dance, economics, English, English literature, English literature and composition-AP, environmental science, French, French language-AP, geometry, government and politics-AP, health, health education, Hebrew scripture, instrumental music, journalism, Latin, Latin-AP, literature, literature and composition-AP, mathematics, multimedia design, music, music performance, music theory, music theory-AP, music-AP, physical education, physics-AP, pre-algebra, pre-calculus, psychology, SAT/ACT preparation, Spanish, Spanish language-AP, Spanish-AP, studio art-AP, U.S. government and politics-AP, U.S. history-AP, United States government-AP, visual and performing arts, world cultures.

Graduation Requirements Art, English, foreign language, guidance, mathematics, music, physical education (includes health), religion (includes Bible studies and theology), science, social studies (includes history), 40 hours of social service.

Special Academic Programs Honors section; independent study; study at local college for college credit; study abroad; academic accommodation for the gifted, the musically talented, and the artistically talented.

College Admission Counseling 100 students graduated in 2012; all went to college, including Boston College; Georgetown University; Penn State University Park; Saint Joseph's University; University of Delaware; Villanova University. Median SAT critical reading: 600, median SAT math: 600, median SAT writing: 630, median combined SAT: 1820, median composite ACT: 26. 51% scored over 600 on SAT critical reading, 56% scored over 600 on SAT math, 64% scored over 600 on SAT writing, 55% scored over 1800 on combined SAT, 37% scored over 26 on composite ACT.

Student Life Upper grades have uniform requirement, student council, honor system. Discipline rests primarily with faculty. Attendance at religious services is required.

Tuition and Aid Day student tuition: $16,932–$19,646. Tuition installment plan (Insured Tuition Payment Plan, monthly payment plans, quarterly and semi-annual payment plans). Merit scholarship grants, need-based scholarship grants available. In 2012–13, 32% of upper-school students received aid; total upper-school merit-scholarship money awarded: $370,500. Total amount of financial aid awarded in 2012–13: $449,500.

Admissions Traditional secondary-level entrance grade is 9. For fall 2012, 351 students applied for upper-level admission, 268 were accepted, 170 enrolled. High School Placement Test required. Deadline for receipt of application materials: December 17. Application fee required: $40. Interview required.

Athletics Interscholastic: basketball, crew, cross-country running, dance, diving, field hockey, golf, lacrosse, rowing, soccer, softball, swimming and diving, tennis, track and field, volleyball, winter (indoor) track; intramural: dance, kickball, modern dance. 2 PE instructors, 31 coaches, 1 athletic trainer.

Computers Computers are regularly used in all classes. Computer network features include on-campus library services, online commercial services, Internet access, wireless campus network, Internet filtering or blocking technology, Smart Boards in classrooms. Student e-mail accounts are available to students. Students grades are available online. The school has a published electronic and media policy.

Contact Mrs. Diane Sander, Director of Admissions. 610-971-0498. Fax: 610-687-1912. E-mail: dsander@ndapa.org. Website: www.ndapa.org

ACADEMY OF OUR LADY OF GUAM

233 Archbishop F.C. Flores Street
Agana, Guam 96910

Head of School: Sr. Francis Jerome Cruz

General Information Girls' day college-preparatory, arts, business, and religious studies school, affiliated with Roman Catholic Church; primarily serves Parentally placed learning disable students. Grades 9–12. Founded: 1949. Setting: urban. Nearest major city is Hagatna. 1-acre campus. 3 buildings on campus. Approved or accredited by Western Catholic Education Association and Guam Department of Education. Endowment: $207,295. Total enrollment: 413. Upper school average class size: 23. Upper school faculty-student ratio: 1:25. There are 180 required school days per year for Upper School students. Upper School students typically attend 5 days per week. The average school day consists of 7 hours and 10 minutes.

Upper School Student Profile Grade 9: 125 students (125 girls); Grade 10: 104 students (104 girls); Grade 11: 95 students (95 girls); Grade 12: 89 students (89 girls). 90% of students are Roman Catholic.

Faculty School total: 31. In upper school: 7 men, 24 women; 15 have advanced degrees.

Subjects Offered Accounting, advanced biology, advanced chemistry, advanced math, Advanced Placement courses, algebra, American government, American history, American history-AP, American literature, anatomy and physiology, ancient world history, art, biology, British literature, business, calculus, calculus-AP, chemistry, Christian and Hebrew scripture, Christian doctrine, Christian ethics, church history, English, English language and composition-AP, English language-AP, English literature, English literature and composition-AP, entrepreneurship, ESL, European history-AP, fine arts, general business, general science, geography, geometry, government, government-AP, health, honors algebra, honors English, honors geometry, Japanese, library assistant, Life of Christ, math analysis, math applications, music, New Testament, physical education, physical fitness, physics, pre-algebra, pre-calculus, psychology, psychology-AP, senior composition, Spanish, swimming, tennis, theology, trigonometry, U.S. government, U.S. government and politics-AP, U.S. history, U.S. history-AP, work experience, world geography, world history, world history-AP, yearbook.

Graduation Requirements Algebra, all academic, American government, American history, American literature, ancient world history, British literature, calculus, Catholic belief and practice, chemistry, Christian and Hebrew scripture, Christian doctrine, church history, English, English composition, English literature, foreign language, general science, geography, geometry, government, health education, history of the Catholic Church, modern world history, physical education (includes health), pre-calculus, senior composition, social sciences, swimming, theology, U.S. government, U.S. history, world geography, world history, world literature.

Special Academic Programs 8 Advanced Placement exams for which test preparation is offered; honors section; ESL (2 students enrolled).

College Admission Counseling 111 students graduated in 2013; 100 went to college, including Saint Mary's College of California; San Diego State University; Seattle University; University of Guam; University of Portland; University of San Diego. Other: 10 went to work, 1 had other specific plans. Median SAT critical reading: 490, median SAT math: 470, median SAT writing: 500, median combined SAT: 1460. 15% scored over 600 on SAT critical reading, 14% scored over 600 on SAT math, 22% scored over 600 on SAT writing, 51% scored over 1800 on combined SAT.

Student Life Upper grades have uniform requirement, student council, honor system. Discipline rests primarily with faculty. Attendance at religious services is required.

Summer Programs Remediation, enrichment programs offered; session focuses on make up credits or tutorial for incoming students; held on campus; accepts girls; not open to students from other schools. 25 students usually enrolled. 2014 schedule: June 1 to June 30. Application deadline: June 1.

Tuition and Aid Day student tuition: $4650. Guaranteed tuition plan. Tuition installment plan (The Tuition Plan, monthly payment plans, individually arranged payment plans, extended payment dates, Quarterly payment plan, full year payment plan). Need-based scholarship grants available. In 2013–14, 9% of upper-school students received aid. Total amount of financial aid awarded in 2013–14: $63,705.

Admissions Traditional secondary-level entrance grade is 9. For fall 2013, 413 students applied for upper-level admission, 413 were accepted, 413 enrolled. Deadline for receipt of application materials: July 31. Application fee required: $45. On-campus interview recommended.

Athletics Interscholastic: basketball, cross-country running, golf, paddling, rugby, soccer, softball, tennis, track and field, volleyball. 3 PE instructors, 14 coaches, 4 athletic trainers.

Computers Computers are regularly used in accounting, all academic, Bible studies, business, English, foreign language, geography, health, history, library, mathematics, music, psychology, religion, social sciences, social studies, Spanish, theology, yearbook classes. Computer network features include Internet access, Internet filtering or blocking technology, Resource Technology Lab, Technology Labs 1, 2, and 3. Computer access in designated common areas is available to students. Students grades are available online. The school has a published electronic and media policy.

Contact Mrs. Mary A.T. Meeks, Principal. 671-477-8203 Ext. 204. Fax: 671-477-8555. E-mail: maryaolg@gmail.com. Website: www.aolg.edu.gu

ACADEMY OF OUR LADY OF PEACE

4860 Oregon Street
San Diego, California 92116-1393

Head of School: Mrs. Lauren Lek

General Information Girls' day college-preparatory, arts, religious studies, and technology school, affiliated with Roman Catholic Church. Grades 9–12. Founded: 1882. Setting: urban. 20-acre campus. 7 buildings on campus. Approved or accredited by National Catholic Education Association, Western Association of Schools and Colleges, Western Catholic Education Association, and California Department of Education. Endowment: $250,000. Total enrollment: 725. Upper school average class size: 28. Upper school faculty-student ratio: 1:14. There are 180 required school days per year for Upper School students. Upper School students typically attend 5 days per week. The average school day consists of 6 hours and 45 minutes.

Upper School Student Profile Grade 9: 200 students (200 girls); Grade 10: 194 students (194 girls); Grade 11: 162 students (162 girls); Grade 12: 169 students (169 girls). 91% of students are Roman Catholic.

Faculty School total: 56. In upper school: 11 men, 45 women; 35 have advanced degrees.

Subjects Offered Algebra, American literature, art, Bible studies, biology, biology-AP, British literature, calculus, calculus-AP, campus ministry, ceramics, chemistry, chemistry-AP, dance, drama, economics, English, English language and composition-AP, English literature and composition-AP, ethics, fitness, French, French language-AP, French-AP, genetics, geometry, government, graphic arts, health, marine science, music appreciation, music theory-AP, painting, physical education, physics, pre-calculus, psychology, Spanish, Spanish language-AP, Spanish literature-AP, speech, studio art-AP, study skills, U.S. government and politics-AP, U.S. history, U.S. history-AP, video film production, Western civilization, yearbook, yoga.

Graduation Requirements Arts and fine arts (art, music, dance, drama), English, foreign language, mathematics, physical education (includes health), religion (includes Bible studies and theology), science, social sciences, social studies (includes history), speech, 75 hours of community service, 9-11 reflection paper required for seniors.

Special Academic Programs 13 Advanced Placement exams for which test preparation is offered; honors section.

College Admission Counseling 187 students graduated in 2013; 186 went to college, including Creighton University; Gonzaga University; Grossmont College; Loyola Marymount University; San Diego State University; University of San Diego. Other: 1 had other specific plans. Median SAT critical reading: 540, median SAT math: 520, median SAT writing: 550, median combined SAT: 1610. 34% scored over 600 on SAT critical reading, 22% scored over 600 on SAT math, 37% scored over 600 on SAT writing, 50% scored over 1800 on combined SAT, 10% scored over 26 on composite ACT.

Student Life Upper grades have uniform requirement, student council, honor system. Discipline rests equally with students and faculty. Attendance at religious services is required.

Summer Programs Enrichment, advancement programs offered; session focuses on advancement and remediation/make-up; held on campus; accepts girls; open to students from other schools. 200 students usually enrolled. 2014 schedule: June 9 to July 18. Application deadline: May 1.

Tuition and Aid Day student tuition: $14,580. Tuition installment plan (FACTS Tuition Payment Plan). Need-based scholarship grants available. In 2013–14, 50% of upper-school students received aid. Total amount of financial aid awarded in 2013–14: $2,500,000.

Admissions Traditional secondary-level entrance grade is 9. For fall 2013, 245 students applied for upper-level admission, 225 were accepted, 200 enrolled. High School Placement Test required. Deadline for receipt of application materials: January 10. Application fee required: $50. On-campus interview required.

Athletics Interscholastic: basketball, cheering, cross-country running, golf, gymnastics, soccer, softball, swimming and diving, tennis, track and field, volleyball. 4 PE instructors, 16 coaches.

Computers Computers are regularly used in computer applications, media production, music, music technology, photography, Web site design, word processing classes. Computer network features include on-campus library services, online commercial services, Internet access, wireless campus network, Internet filtering or blocking technology. Campus intranet, student e-mail accounts, and computer access in designated common areas are available to students. Students grades are available online. The school has a published electronic and media policy.

Contact Mrs. Melissa Acosta, Registrar and Admissions Assistant. 619-725-9118. Fax: 619-297-2473. E-mail: admissions@aolp.org. Website: www.aolp.org

ACADEMY OF THE HOLY CROSS

4920 Strathmore Avenue
Kensington, Maryland 20895-1299

Head of School: Ms. Kathleen R. Prebble

General Information Girls' day college-preparatory, arts, and religious studies school, affiliated with Roman Catholic Church. Grades 9–12. Founded: 1868. Setting: suburban. Nearest major city is Rockville. 28-acre campus. 2 buildings on campus. Approved or accredited by Association of Independent Schools of Greater Washington, International Baccalaureate Organization, Middle States Association of Colleges and Schools, National Catholic Education Association, The College Board, and Maryland Department of Education. There are 175 required school days per year for Upper School students. Upper School students typically attend 5 days per week. The average school day consists of 7 hours.

Upper School Student Profile Grade 9: 114 students (114 girls); Grade 10: 122 students (122 girls); Grade 11: 135 students (135 girls); Grade 12: 149 students (149 girls).

Faculty School total: 51. In upper school: 9 men, 42 women.

Subjects Offered Acting, Advanced Placement courses, African studies, algebra, American history, American literature, Arabic, art, art history-AP, Asian studies, biology, biology-AP, calculus, calculus-AP, ceramics, chemistry, chemistry-AP, Christian scripture, computer science, concert choir, creative writing, design, drama, drawing, earth science, economics, English, English language and composition-AP, English literature, English literature and composition-AP, environmental science, ethnic studies, expository writing, fine arts, forensics, French, genetics, geography, geometry, government/civics, grammar, health, Hebrew scripture, history, history of the Catholic Church, honors English, honors geometry, humanities, instrumental music, jazz dance, Latin, Latin American studies, madrigals, mathematics, moral theology, music, music appreciation, musical theater, musical theater dance, painting, peace studies, personal finance, photography, physical education, physical science, physics, physiology, pre-calculus, psychology, public speaking, religion, religious studies, science, sculpture, Shakespeare, social sciences, social studies, Spanish, sports medicine, statistics, studio art, studio art-AP, tap dance, technology, theater, theater design and production, theology, trigonometry, U.S. government, U.S. government and politics-AP, U.S. history, U.S. history-AP, Web site design, world history, world studies.

Graduation Requirements Art, electives, English, foreign language, mathematics, performing arts, physical education (includes health), science, senior project, social sciences, social studies (includes history), theology, Christian service commitment, senior project internship.

Special Academic Programs International Baccalaureate program; Advanced Placement exam preparation; honors section; independent study; academic accommodation for the gifted and the artistically talented.

College Admission Counseling 113 students graduated in 2013; all went to college, including Boston University; University of Delaware; University of Maryland, Baltimore County; University of Maryland, College Park; University of South Carolina; University of Virginia. Mean SAT critical reading: 577, mean SAT math: 561, mean SAT writing: 586, mean combined SAT: 1725, mean composite ACT: 25. 40% scored over 600 on SAT critical reading, 38% scored over 600 on SAT math, 37% scored over 600 on SAT writing, 44% scored over 1800 on combined SAT, 42% scored over 26 on composite ACT.

Student Life Upper grades have uniform requirement, student council, honor system. Discipline rests equally with students and faculty. Attendance at religious services is required.

Summer Programs Enrichment, advancement, sports, art/fine arts, computer instruction programs offered; session focuses on enrichment and athletic skill-building; held on campus; accepts girls; open to students from other schools. 200 students usually enrolled.

Tuition and Aid Day student tuition: $19,550. Tuition installment plan (individually arranged payment plans). Tuition reduction for siblings, merit scholarship grants, need-based scholarship grants, alumnae stipends available. In 2013–14, 72% of upper-school students received aid.

Admissions Traditional secondary-level entrance grade is 9. High School Placement Test required. Deadline for receipt of application materials: December 6. Application fee required: $60.

Athletics Interscholastic: archery, basketball, crew, cross-country running, diving, equestrian sports, field hockey, golf, ice hockey, lacrosse, rugby, soccer, softball, swimming and diving, tennis, track and field, volleyball; intramural: basketball, cheering, dance, dance team, kayaking, lacrosse, soccer. 2 PE instructors, 35 coaches, 1 athletic trainer.

Computers Computers are regularly used in art, foreign language, mathematics, science, social sciences classes. Computer network features include on-campus library services, online commercial services, Internet access, wireless campus network, Internet filtering or blocking technology. Campus intranet, student e-mail accounts, and computer access in designated common areas are available to students. Students grades are available online. The school has a published electronic and media policy.

Contact Mrs. Gracie Smith, Director of Admissions. 301-929-6442. Fax: 301-929-6440. E-mail: admissions@ahctartans.org. Website: www.ahctartans.org

ACADEMY OF THE NEW CHURCH BOYS' SCHOOL

2815 Benade Circle
Box 707
Bryn Athyn, Pennsylvania 19009

Head of School: Mr. Jeremy T. Irwin

General Information Boys' boarding and day college-preparatory, arts, and religious studies school, affiliated with Church of the New Jerusalem. Grades 9–12. Founded: 1887. Setting: suburban. Nearest major city is Philadelphia. Students are housed in single-sex dormitories. 200-acre campus. 8 buildings on campus. Approved or accredited by Middle States Association of Colleges and Schools and Pennsylvania Department of Education. Member of National Association of Independent Schools. Endowment: $200 million. Total enrollment: 124. Upper school average class size: 15. Upper school faculty-student ratio: 1:8. There are 180 required school days per year for Upper School students. Upper School students typically attend 5 days per week. The average school day consists of 7 hours and 15 minutes.

Upper School Student Profile Grade 9: 27 students (27 boys); Grade 10: 29 students (29 boys); Grade 11: 40 students (40 boys); Grade 12: 28 students (28 boys). 36% of students are boarding students. 75% are state residents. 18 states are represented in upper school student body. 5% are international students. International students from Canada, China, and Republic of Korea. 85% of students are Church of the New Jerusalem.

Faculty School total: 40. In upper school: 18 men, 18 women; 32 have advanced degrees; 10 reside on campus.

Subjects Offered Advanced chemistry, Advanced Placement courses, African-American literature, algebra, American history, American history-AP, American literature, American literature-AP, anatomy, anatomy and physiology, ancient world history, art, art history, Bible studies, biology, British literature, calculus, calculus-AP, ceramics, chemistry, civics, computer programming, computer science, creative writing, dance, drama, ecology, English, English literature, English literature-AP, environmental science, European history, expository writing, fine arts, French, geometry, German, government/civics, grammar, health, history, honors U.S. history, industrial arts, journalism, Latin, mathematics, music, music theater, musical theater, philosophy, photography, physical education, physical science, physics, physiology, portfolio art, pre-calculus, printmaking, probability and statistics, religion, religious education, religious studies, science, sculpture, senior project, social sciences, social studies, sociology, Spanish, speech, statistics, studio art, theater, theater arts, theater design and production, theater production, theology, trigonometry, U.S. history-AP, vocal ensemble, vocal music, women in literature, world history, world literature.

Graduation Requirements Arts and fine arts (art, music, dance, drama), English, foreign language, mathematics, physical education (includes health), religion (includes Bible studies and theology), science, social sciences, social studies (includes history).

Special Academic Programs Advanced Placement exam preparation; honors section; independent study; study at local college for college credit; academic accommodation for the gifted, the musically talented, and the artistically talented; remedial reading and/or remedial writing; remedial math; programs in English, mathematics, general development for dyslexic students; ESL (6 students enrolled).

College Admission Counseling 34 students graduated in 2013; 33 went to college, including Arcadia University; Bryn Athyn College of the New Church;

Gettysburg College; Penn State University Park; Virginia Polytechnic Institute and State University; West Chester University of Pennsylvania. Other: 1 entered military service. Median SAT critical reading: 540, median SAT math: 560, median SAT writing: 530, median combined SAT: 1630. 28% scored over 600 on SAT critical reading, 33% scored over 600 on SAT math, 31% scored over 600 on SAT writing, 31% scored over 1800 on combined SAT.

Student Life Upper grades have specified standards of dress, student council. Discipline rests primarily with faculty. Attendance at religious services is required.

Summer Programs Sports programs offered; held on campus; accepts boys and girls; open to students from other schools. 110 students usually enrolled. 2014 schedule: July 11 to August 1. Application deadline: June 1.

Tuition and Aid Day student tuition: $14,600; 7-day tuition and room/board: $21,350. Tuition installment plan (monthly payment plans, individually arranged payment plans, term payment plan). Need-based scholarship grants available. In 2013–14, 60% of upper-school students received aid. Total amount of financial aid awarded in 2013–14: $750,000.

Admissions Traditional secondary-level entrance grade is 9. For fall 2013, 50 students applied for upper-level admission, 39 were accepted, 34 enrolled. Iowa Subtests, PSAT, SAT or SSAT required. Deadline for receipt of application materials: none. Application fee required: $50. Interview required.

Athletics Interscholastic: baseball, basketball, football, ice hockey, lacrosse, wrestling. 1 PE instructor, 6 coaches, 1 athletic trainer.

Computers Computers are regularly used in English, foreign language, history, mathematics, science classes. Computer network features include on-campus library services, online commercial services, Internet access, wireless campus network, Internet filtering or blocking technology. Campus intranet, student e-mail accounts, and computer access in designated common areas are available to students. Students grades are available online. The school has a published electronic and media policy.

Contact Denise DiFiglia, Director of Admissions. 267-502-4855. Website: www.ancss.org

ACADEMY OF THE NEW CHURCH GIRLS' SCHOOL

2815 Benade Circle
Box 707
Bryn Athyn, Pennsylvania 19009

Head of School: Susan O. Odhner

General Information Girls' boarding and day college-preparatory, general academic, arts, and religious studies school, affiliated with Church of the New Jerusalem, Christian faith. Grades 9–12. Founded: 1884. Setting: suburban. Nearest major city is Philadelphia. Students are housed in single-sex dormitories. 200-acre campus. 8 buildings on campus. Approved or accredited by Middle States Association of Colleges and Schools and Pennsylvania Department of Education. Member of National Association of Independent Schools. Endowment: $200 million. Total enrollment: 101. Upper school average class size: 15. Upper school faculty-student ratio: 1:8. There are 180 required school days per year for Upper School students. Upper School students typically attend 5 days per week. The average school day consists of 7 hours and 15 minutes.

Upper School Student Profile Grade 9: 24 students (24 girls); Grade 10: 24 students (24 girls); Grade 11: 25 students (25 girls); Grade 12: 27 students (27 girls). 31% of students are boarding students. 75% are state residents. 13 states are represented in upper school student body. 13% are international students. International students from Canada, China, and Republic of Korea. 85% of students are Church of the New Jerusalem, Christian.

Faculty School total: 40. In upper school: 18 men, 18 women; 32 have advanced degrees; 10 reside on campus.

Subjects Offered Advanced chemistry, Advanced Placement courses, African-American literature, algebra, American history, American history-AP, American literature, anatomy, ancient history, ancient world history, art, art history, Bible studies, biology, British literature, calculus, calculus-AP, chemistry, civics, computer science, creative writing, drafting, drama, dramatic arts, drawing, ecology, ecology, environmental systems, economics, English, English literature, English literature-AP, English-AP, European history, expository writing, film studies, fine arts, French, geometry, government/civics, grammar, health, history, honors algebra, honors English, honors geometry, honors U.S. history, human anatomy, Latin, mathematics, medieval history, music, painting, philosophy, photography, physical education, physical science, physics, physiology, pre-calculus, printmaking, religion, science, sculpture, senior project, social sciences, social studies, Spanish, speech, stained glass, statistics-AP, theater, theology, trigonometry, women in literature, world history, world literature.

Graduation Requirements Arts and fine arts (art, music, dance, drama), English, foreign language, mathematics, physical education (includes health), religion (includes Bible studies and theology), science, social sciences, social studies (includes history).

Special Academic Programs Advanced Placement exam preparation; honors section; independent study; study at local college for college credit; academic accommodation for the gifted, the musically talented, and the artistically talented; remedial reading and/or remedial writing; remedial math; special instructional classes for students with Attention Deficit Disorder and learning-disabled children; ESL (8 students enrolled).

College Admission Counseling 24 students graduated in 2013; all went to college, including Arcadia University; Bryn Athyn College of the New Church; Gettysburg College; Penn State University Park; Virginia Polytechnic Institute and State University; West Chester University of Pennsylvania. Median SAT critical reading: 540, median SAT math: 560, median SAT writing: 530, median combined SAT: 1630. 28% scored over 600 on SAT critical reading, 33% scored over 600 on SAT math, 31% scored over 600 on SAT writing, 31% scored over 1800 on combined SAT.

Student Life Upper grades have uniform requirement, student council. Discipline rests primarily with faculty. Attendance at religious services is required.

Summer Programs Sports programs offered; held on campus; accepts boys and girls; open to students from other schools. 130 students usually enrolled. 2014 schedule: July 11 to August 1. Application deadline: June 1.

Tuition and Aid Day student tuition: $14,600; 7-day tuition and room/board: $21,350. Tuition installment plan (monthly payment plans, individually arranged payment plans, term payment plan). Need-based scholarship grants, need-based loans, middle-income loans available. In 2013–14, 60% of upper-school students received aid. Total amount of financial aid awarded in 2013–14: $750,000.

Admissions Traditional secondary-level entrance grade is 9. For fall 2013, 50 students applied for upper-level admission, 42 were accepted, 35 enrolled. Iowa Subtests, PSAT, SAT or SSAT required. Deadline for receipt of application materials: none. Application fee required: $50. Interview required.

Athletics Interscholastic: basketball, dance team, field hockey, ice hockey, lacrosse, soccer, softball, tennis, volleyball. 1 PE instructor, 6 coaches, 1 athletic trainer.

Computers Computers are regularly used in English, foreign language, history, Latin, mathematics, science classes. Computer network features include on-campus library services, online commercial services, Internet access, wireless campus network, Internet filtering or blocking technology. Campus intranet and student e-mail accounts are available to students. Students grades are available online.

Contact Denise DiFiglia, Director of Admissions. 267-502-4855. Fax: 267-502-2617. E-mail: denise.difiglia@ancss.org. Website: www.ancss.org

ACADEMY OF THE SACRED HEART

4521 St. Charles Avenue
New Orleans, Louisiana 70115-4831

Head of School: Dr. Timothy Matthew Burns

General Information Girls' day college-preparatory, arts, religious studies, bilingual studies, and technology school, affiliated with Roman Catholic Church. Grades PK–12. Founded: 1887. Setting: urban. 7-acre campus. 3 buildings on campus. Approved or accredited by Independent Schools Association of the Southwest, National Catholic Education Association, Network of Sacred Heart Schools, Southern Association of Colleges and Schools, and Louisiana Department of Education. Member of National Association of Independent Schools. Endowment: $7.7 million. Total enrollment: 618. Upper school average class size: 16. Upper school faculty-student ratio: 1:16. There are 178 required school days per year for Upper School students. Upper School students typically attend 5 days per week. The average school day consists of 6 hours and 30 minutes.

Upper School Student Profile Grade 9: 58 students (58 girls); Grade 10: 48 students (48 girls); Grade 11: 51 students (51 girls); Grade 12: 56 students (56 girls). 88% of students are Roman Catholic.

Faculty School total: 102. In upper school: 7 men, 21 women; 18 have advanced degrees.

Subjects Offered Advanced chemistry, algebra, American government, American history, American history-AP, American literature, American literature-AP, anatomy and physiology, art, astronomy, athletics, baseball, basketball, biology, biology-AP, British literature, British literature-AP, broadcasting, calculus, calculus-AP, campus ministry, Catholic belief and practice, ceramics, cheerleading, chemistry, chemistry-AP, clayworking, college admission preparation, college awareness, college counseling, college planning, computer applications, computer education, computer processing, computer resources, computer science, computer skills, computer studies, creative writing, drama, drawing, electives, English, English literature, English literature-AP, English-AP, fine arts, foreign language, French, French-AP, geometry, government, government-AP, guidance, handbells, history of the Catholic Church, honors algebra, honors English, honors geometry, honors U.S. history, honors world history, painting, peer counseling, physics, physics-AP, physiology, pre-calculus, religion, robotics, social justice, Spanish, Spanish-AP, statistics, statistics-AP, television, U.S. government, U.S. government and politics, U.S. government and politics-AP, U.S. history, U.S. history-AP, U.S. literature, video communication, Web site design, world history, world history-AP, world religions.

Graduation Requirements 1 1/2 elective credits, Advanced Placement courses, algebra, American government, American history, American literature, arts, arts and fine arts (art, music, dance, drama), athletics, Basic programming, biology, British literature, calculus, campus ministry, career/college preparation, ceramics, chemistry, church history, civics, computer applications, computer literacy, computers, drawing, electives, English, foreign language, French, geometry, government/civics, guidance, health and wellness, history of the Catholic Church, moral theology, painting, peer counseling, physical education (includes health), physics, pre-calculus, religion

(includes Bible studies and theology), science, scripture, senior project, social justice, social studies (includes history), Spanish, statistics, U.S. government, U.S. government and politics, U.S. history, United States government-AP, world geography, world history, world literature, world religions, senior project, 50 hours of required community service.

Special Academic Programs Advanced Placement exam preparation; honors section; study at local college for college credit; domestic exchange program (with Network of Sacred Heart Schools).

College Admission Counseling 44 students graduated in 2013; all went to college, including Harvard University; Louisiana State University and Agricultural and Mechanical College; Spring Hill College; University of Georgia; University of Pennsylvania.

Student Life Upper grades have uniform requirement, student council, honor system. Discipline rests equally with students and faculty. Attendance at religious services is required.

Summer Programs Enrichment, sports, art/fine arts programs offered; session focuses on arts, creative writing, robotics, strength and conditioning; held both on and off campus; held at Upper School campus, gym, area tracks; accepts girls; not open to students from other schools. 18 students usually enrolled. 2014 schedule: June to August.

Tuition and Aid Day student tuition: $14,800. Tuition installment plan (The Tuition Plan, individually arranged payment plans, bank loan). Merit scholarship grants, need-based scholarship grants available. In 2013–14, 28% of upper-school students received aid; total upper-school merit-scholarship money awarded: $20,650. Total amount of financial aid awarded in 2013–14: $265,000.

Admissions Traditional secondary-level entrance grade is 9. Achievement tests, admissions testing, ERB, OLSAT/Stanford or PSAT or SAT for applicants to grade 11 and 12 required. Deadline for receipt of application materials: none. Application fee required: $50. Interview required.

Athletics Interscholastic: aerobics, ballet, baseball, basketball, cheering, cross-country running, fitness, golf, indoor track & field, physical fitness, soccer, softball, strength & conditioning, swimming and diving, tennis, track and field, volleyball; intramural: aerobics, cooperative games, fitness, jogging, jump rope, kickball, modern dance, outdoor activities, outdoor recreation, physical fitness, volleyball, walking, yoga. 5 PE instructors, 14 coaches, 1 athletic trainer.

Computers Computers are regularly used in all classes. Computer network features include on-campus library services, online commercial services, Internet access, wireless campus network, Internet filtering or blocking technology. Campus intranet, student e-mail accounts, and computer access in designated common areas are available to students. Students grades are available online. The school has a published electronic and media policy.

Contact Ms. Christy Sevante, Admission Director. 504-269-1214. Fax: 504-896-7880. E-mail: csevante@ashrosary.org. Website: www.ashrosary.org

ACADÉMIE STE CÉCILE INTERNATIONAL SCHOOL

925 Cousineau Road
Windsor, Ontario N9G 1V8, Canada

Head of School: Mlle. Thérèse H. Gadoury

General Information Coeducational boarding and day college-preparatory, arts, and bilingual studies school, affiliated with Roman Catholic Church. Boarding grades 6–12, day grades JK–12. Founded: 1993. Setting: suburban. Nearest major city is Toronto, Canada. Students are housed in single-sex by floor dormitories. 30-acre campus. 2 buildings on campus. Approved or accredited by International Baccalaureate Organization, Ontario Ministry of Education, The Association of Boarding Schools, and Ontario Department of Education. Languages of instruction: English and French. Total enrollment: 236. Upper school average class size: 15. Upper school faculty-student ratio: 1:15. There are 180 required school days per year for Upper School students. Upper School students typically attend 5 days per week. The average school day consists of 6 hours and 15 minutes.

Upper School Student Profile Grade 9: 19 students (10 boys, 9 girls); Grade 10: 29 students (10 boys, 19 girls); Grade 11: 38 students (15 boys, 23 girls); Grade 12: 34 students (24 boys, 10 girls). 45% of students are boarding students. 2% are province residents. 2 provinces are represented in upper school student body. 45% are international students. International students from China, Hong Kong, Mexico, Taiwan, and United States; 2 other countries represented in student body. 70% of students are Roman Catholic.

Faculty School total: 50. In upper school: 13 men, 11 women; 10 have advanced degrees; 4 reside on campus.

Subjects Offered Accounting, advanced chemistry, advanced computer applications, advanced math, algebra, art, art education, art history, audio visual/media, ballet, basketball, biology, business technology, calculus, campus ministry, career education, careers, Catholic belief and practice, chemistry, choir, choral music, civics, classical music, computer information systems, computer programming, computer science, concert band, concert bell choir, concert choir, creative dance, creative drama, creative thinking, creative writing, critical thinking, critical writing, dance, dance performance, decision making skills, desktop publishing, desktop publishing, ESL, discrete mathematics, drama performance, drama workshop, dramatic arts, drawing,

drawing and design, driver education, earth science, economics, English, English literature, environmental studies, ethics, expository writing, family living, French, French studies, geography, geometry, German, golf, handbells, health and wellness, health education, history, history of dance, history of music, history of religion, history of the Catholic Church, honors algebra, honors English, honors geometry, honors world history, instrumental music, International Baccalaureate courses, Internet, Internet research, intro to computers, Italian, jazz band, jazz dance, journalism, keyboarding, Latin, leadership, library skills, Life of Christ, literature, literature and composition-AP, mathematics, media studies, music, music appreciation, music composition, music history, music performance, music theory, organ, painting, philosophy, photography, physical education, physics, piano, poetry, prayer/spirituality, pre-algebra, pre-calculus, probability and statistics, public speaking, reading, reading/study skills, religion, research skills, SAT preparation, science, sculpture, Shakespeare, social studies, softball, Spanish, stage and body movement, stained glass, strings, student government, swimming, tennis, TOEFL preparation, track and field, values and decisions, visual arts, vocal ensemble, voice, volleyball, wind ensemble, wind instruments, world religions, writing, yearbook.

Graduation Requirements Ontario Ministry of Education requirements.

Special Academic Programs International Baccalaureate program; Advanced Placement exam preparation; honors section; accelerated programs; academic accommodation for the gifted, the musically talented, and the artistically talented; remedial reading and/or remedial writing; remedial math; ESL (40 students enrolled).

College Admission Counseling 35 students graduated in 2012; they went to McMaster University; The University of British Columbia; The University of Western Ontario; University of Toronto; University of Waterloo; University of Windsor. Other: 35 entered a postgraduate year. Mean SAT critical reading: 593, mean SAT math: 724, mean SAT writing: 615. 67% scored over 600 on SAT critical reading, 83% scored over 600 on SAT math, 67% scored over 600 on SAT writing.

Student Life Upper grades have uniform requirement, student council, honor system. Discipline rests primarily with faculty.

Tuition and Aid Day student tuition: CAN$13,850; 7-day tuition and room/board: CAN$45,500. Tuition installment plan (Insured Tuition Payment Plan). Tuition reduction for siblings, merit scholarship grants available. In 2012–13, 5% of upper-school students received aid; total upper-school merit-scholarship money awarded: CAN$4500. Total amount of financial aid awarded in 2012–13: CAN$15,000.

Admissions Traditional secondary-level entrance grade is 9. For fall 2012, 25 students applied for upper-level admission, 21 were accepted, 18 enrolled. Deadline for receipt of application materials: none. Application fee required: CAN$300. Interview recommended.

Athletics Interscholastic: aquatics (boys, girls), badminton (b,g), basketball (b,g), equestrian sports (b,g), golf (b,g), horseback riding (b,g), ice hockey (g), independent competitive sports (b,g), modern dance (b,g), physical fitness (b,g), soccer (b,g), softball (b,g), swimming and diving (b,g), tennis (b,g), volleyball (b,g); intramural: aquatics (b,g), badminton (b,g), ballet (g), basketball (b,g), bowling (b,g), cross-country running (b,g), dance (b,g), dressage (b,g), equestrian sports (b,g), golf (b,g), horseback riding (b,g), paddle tennis (b,g), soccer (b,g), softball (b,g), swimming and diving (b,g), table tennis (b,g), tennis (b,g), volleyball (b,g); coed interscholastic: aquatics, badminton, basketball, dressage, equestrian sports, fitness, golf, horseback riding, indoor track & field, modern dance, physical fitness, soccer, softball, swimming and diving, tennis, volleyball; coed intramural: aquatics, badminton, basketball, bowling, cross-country running, dance, dressage, equestrian sports, floor hockey, golf, horseback riding, modern dance, soccer, softball, swimming and diving, tennis, volleyball. 2 PE instructors, 8 coaches.

Computers Computers are regularly used in accounting, business, desktop publishing, ESL, information technology, mathematics classes. Computer network features include Internet access, wireless campus network.

Contact Ms. Gwen A. Gatt, Admissions Clerk. 519-969-1291. Fax: 519-969-7953. E-mail: info@stececile.ca. Website: www.stececile.ca

THE AGNES IRWIN SCHOOL

Ithan Avenue and Conestoga Road
Rosemont, Pennsylvania 19010

Head of School: Dr. Mary F. Seppala

General Information Girls' day college-preparatory school. Grades PK–12. Founded: 1869. Setting: suburban. Nearest major city is Philadelphia. 18-acre campus. 5 buildings on campus. Approved or accredited by Middle States Association of Colleges and Schools and Pennsylvania Department of Education. Member of National Association of Independent Schools, Secondary School Admission Test Board, and National Coalition of Girls' Schools. Endowment: $20.8 million. Total enrollment: 703. Upper school average class size: 15. Upper school faculty-student ratio: 1:5. There are 162 required school days per year for Upper School students. Upper School students typically attend 5 days per week. The average school day consists of 6 hours and 45 minutes.

Upper School Student Profile Grade 9: 66 students (66 girls); Grade 10: 73 students (73 girls); Grade 11: 83 students (83 girls); Grade 12: 67 students (67 girls).

Faculty School total: 112. In upper school: 20 men, 41 women; 42 have advanced degrees.

Subjects Offered 20th century world history, advanced studio art-AP, African-American history, algebra, American history, American history-AP, Ancient Greek, art history, Asian studies, bioethics, bioethics, DNA and culture, biology, biology-AP, calculus, calculus-AP, chemistry, chemistry-AP, choreography, computer programming, dance, drama, English, English language and composition-AP, English language-AP, English literature, English literature and composition-AP, English-AP, environmental science-AP, European history, European history-AP, film history, French, French-AP, geometry, Greek, health, history, honors algebra, honors English, honors geometry, honors U.S. history, honors world history, independent study, Innovation in the Arts, international relations, Latin, mathematics-AP, media arts, Middle East, Middle Eastern history, music theory, photography, physical education, physics, physics-AP, pre-calculus, public speaking, robotics, Spanish, Spanish-AP, statistics, studio art, theater arts, trigonometry.

Graduation Requirements Arts and fine arts (art, music, dance, drama), English, foreign language, history, mathematics, media literacy, physical education (includes health), science, Senior assembly given by each girl before graduation. Community service is required.

Special Academic Programs 12 Advanced Placement exams for which test preparation is offered; honors section; independent study; term-away projects; study abroad; academic accommodation for the gifted.

College Admission Counseling 66 students graduated in 2013; all went to college, including Boston College; Bucknell University; Georgetown University; University of Pennsylvania; University of Virginia. Middle 50% SAT critical reading: 570-710, middle 50% SAT math: 590-720, middle 50% SAT writing: 600-740, middle 50% SAT combined: 1800-2140, middle 50% ACT composite: 25-31.

Student Life Upper grades have uniform requirement, student council, honor system. Discipline rests equally with students and faculty.

Summer Programs Remediation, enrichment, advancement, sports, art/fine arts, computer instruction programs offered; session focuses on arts, academics, and athletics; held on campus; accepts boys and girls; open to students from other schools. 500 students usually enrolled. 2014 schedule: June 15 to July 31. Application deadline: none.

Tuition and Aid Day student tuition: $31,600. Tuition installment plan (monthly payment plans). Need-based scholarship grants available. In 2013–14, 26% of upper-school students received aid. Total amount of financial aid awarded in 2013–14: $1,457,924.

Admissions Traditional secondary-level entrance grade is 9. For fall 2013, 79 students applied for upper-level admission, 37 were accepted, 20 enrolled. ISEE, SSAT or WISC-R or WISC-III required. Deadline for receipt of application materials: December 13. Application fee required: $50. Interview required.

Athletics Interscholastic: basketball, crew, cross-country running, diving, field hockey, golf, independent competitive sports, lacrosse, running, soccer, softball, squash, swimming and diving, tennis, track and field, volleyball; intramural: crew, dance, fitness, modern dance, physical fitness, physical training, strength & conditioning, weight training. 4 PE instructors, 27 coaches, 1 athletic trainer.

Computers Computers are regularly used in art, English, foreign language, history, mathematics, media arts, photography, science, yearbook classes. Computer network features include on-campus library services, online commercial services, Internet access, wireless campus network, online databases. Campus intranet, student e-mail accounts, and computer access in designated common areas are available to students. The school has a published electronic and media policy.

Contact Mrs. Sally B. Keidel, Assistant Head of School for Enrollment and External Relations. 610-525-8400. Fax: 610-525-8908. E-mail: skeidel@agnesirwin.org. Website: www.agnesirwin.org

ALBUQUERQUE ACADEMY

6400 Wyoming Boulevard NE
Albuquerque, New Mexico 87109

Head of School: Andrew Watson

General Information Coeducational day college-preparatory, arts, technology, experiential education, and global languages school. Grades 6–12. Founded: 1955. Setting: suburban. 312-acre campus. 9 buildings on campus. Approved or accredited by Independent Schools Association of the Southwest and New Mexico Department of Education. Member of National Association of Independent Schools and Secondary School Admission Test Board. Endowment: $94.3 million. Total enrollment: 1,110. Upper school average class size: 15. Upper school faculty-student ratio: 1:9. There are 171 required school days per year for Upper School students. Upper School students typically attend 5 days per week. The average school day consists of 7 hours and 30 minutes.

Upper School Student Profile Grade 8: 158 students (74 boys, 84 girls); Grade 9: 169 students (77 boys, 92 girls); Grade 10: 170 students (80 boys, 90 girls); Grade 11: 165 students (78 boys, 87 girls); Grade 12: 151 students (74 boys, 77 girls).

Faculty School total: 180. In upper school: 66 men, 61 women; 100 have advanced degrees.

Subjects Offered Advanced Placement courses, algebra, American history, anatomy, Arabic, art, art history, astronomy, band, biochemistry, biology, calculus, chemistry, chemistry-AP, computer science, creative writing, dance, drama, drawing, earth science, economics, electronics, English, English-AP, European history, fine arts,

French, French language-AP, genetics, geometry, German, government/civics, history, history-AP, horticulture, Japanese, jazz, Latin American history, law, library studies, Mandarin, mathematics, media, music, outdoor education, painting, philosophy, photography, physical education, physics, physiology, printmaking, psychology, religion, robotics, Russian, science, social studies, Spanish, speech, swimming, theater, trigonometry, weight training, women's studies, world history, writing.

Graduation Requirements English, experiential education, foreign language, mathematics, physical education (includes health), science, social studies (includes history), experiential education (environmental and outdoor activities).

Special Academic Programs 18 Advanced Placement exams for which test preparation is offered; independent study; term-away projects; study abroad.

College Admission Counseling 169 students graduated in 2013; all went to college, including Arizona State University; The University of Texas at Austin; University of New Mexico; Washington University in St. Louis. Mean SAT critical reading: 663, mean SAT math: 660, mean SAT writing: 650, mean combined SAT: 1973, mean composite ACT: 29.

Student Life Upper grades have specified standards of dress, student council, honor system. Discipline rests primarily with faculty.

Summer Programs Remediation, enrichment, advancement, sports, art/fine arts, computer instruction programs offered; session focuses on enrichment; held on campus; accepts boys and girls; open to students from other schools. 1,900 students usually enrolled. 2014 schedule: June 2 to July 11. Application deadline: none.

Tuition and Aid Day student tuition: $20,946. Tuition installment plan (FACTS Tuition Payment Plan, monthly payment plans, individually arranged payment plans, 1- and 2-payment plans). Need-based scholarship grants available. In 2013–14, 29% of upper-school students received aid. Total amount of financial aid awarded in 2013–14: $3,526,266.

Admissions Traditional secondary-level entrance grade is 9. For fall 2013, 147 students applied for upper-level admission, 64 were accepted, 40 enrolled. ISEE, school's own exam or SSAT required. Deadline for receipt of application materials: February 10. Application fee required: $55. Interview required.

Athletics Interscholastic: baseball (boys), basketball (b,g), bowling (b,g), cross-country running (b,g), dance (b,g), diving (b,g), football (b), golf (b,g), hiking/backpacking (b,g), life saving (b,g), modern dance (b,g), outdoor education (b,g), outdoor skills (b,g), physical training (b,g), rafting (b,g), rappelling (b,g), rock climbing (b,g), soccer (b,g), softball (g), swimming and diving (b,g), tennis (b,g), track and field (b,g), volleyball (g), wrestling (b,g); coed intramural: ballet, basketball, canoeing/kayaking, wilderness, wilderness survival. 9 PE instructors, 84 coaches, 3 athletic trainers.

Computers Computers are regularly used in foreign language, history, library science, mathematics classes. Computer network features include on-campus library services, online commercial services, Internet access, wireless campus network, Internet filtering or blocking technology. Campus intranet and student e-mail accounts are available to students. The school has a published electronic and media policy.

Contact Amy Eglinton Keller, Director of Admission. 505-828-3208. Fax: 505-828-3128. E-mail: keller@aa.edu. Website: www.aa.edu

ALEXANDER DAWSON SCHOOL

10455 Dawson Drive
Lafayette, Colorado 80026

Head of School: Mr. George Moore

General Information Coeducational day college-preparatory, arts, technology, and engineering, global studies school. Grades K–12. Founded: 1970. Setting: rural. Nearest major city is Boulder. 113-acre campus. 11 buildings on campus. Approved or accredited by Association of Colorado Independent Schools and Colorado Department of Education. Member of National Association of Independent Schools and Secondary School Admission Test Board. Total enrollment: 453. Upper school average class size: 15. Upper school faculty-student ratio: 1:7. There are 172 required school days per year for Upper School students. Upper School students typically attend 5 days per week. The average school day consists of 9 hours and 30 minutes.

Upper School Student Profile Grade 9: 62 students (27 boys, 35 girls); Grade 10: 43 students (23 boys, 20 girls); Grade 11: 44 students (25 boys, 19 girls); Grade 12: 44 students (17 boys, 27 girls).

Faculty School total: 53. In upper school: 17 men, 10 women; 23 have advanced degrees.

Subjects Offered Algebra, American history, American literature, art, art history, biology, calculus, ceramics, chemistry, Chinese, computer math, computer multimedia, computer programming, computer science, creative writing, dance, drafting, drama, earth science, economics, English, English literature, European history, expository writing, fine arts, French, geography, geometry, government-AP, government/civics, grammar, health, history, industrial arts, journalism, Latin, mathematics, mechanical drawing, music, photography, physical education, physics, science, social sciences, social studies, Spanish, speech, theater, trigonometry, world history, world literature, writing.

Graduation Requirements Arts and fine arts (art, music, dance, drama), computer science, English, foreign language, history, mathematics, science, sports.

Special Academic Programs 15 Advanced Placement exams for which test preparation is offered; honors section; independent study; term-away projects; study at local college for college credit; study abroad; academic accommodation for the gifted, the musically talented, and the artistically talented; remedial reading and/or remedial writing; remedial math; special instructional classes for deaf students.

College Admission Counseling 38 students graduated in 2012; all went to college, including Middlebury College; Pomona College; University of Denver; Wellesley College. Mean SAT critical reading: 616, mean SAT math: 620, mean composite ACT: 27.

Student Life Upper grades have specified standards of dress, student council, honor system. Discipline rests equally with students and faculty.

Tuition and Aid Day student tuition: $20,550. Tuition installment plan (Insured Tuition Payment Plan, monthly payment plans, individually arranged payment plans). Need-based scholarship grants, need-based loans available. In 2012–13, 18% of upper-school students received aid. Total amount of financial aid awarded in 2012–13: $1,300,000.

Admissions Traditional secondary-level entrance grade is 9. For fall 2012, 45 students applied for upper-level admission, 31 were accepted, 24 enrolled. Deadline for receipt of application materials: none. Application fee required: $75. Interview required.

Athletics Interscholastic: baseball (boys), basketball (b,g), lacrosse (b), soccer (b,g), swimming and diving (b,g), synchronized swimming (g), tennis (b,g), track and field (b,g), volleyball (g); intramural: lacrosse (b); coed interscholastic: bicycling, canoeing/kayaking, cross-country running, equestrian sports, golf, kayaking, martial arts, paddling, skiing (downhill), Special Olympics; coed intramural: aerobics, aerobics/dance, backpacking, Circus, climbing, dance, equestrian sports, fitness, flag football, football, Frisbee, golf, hiking/backpacking, indoor soccer, martial arts, modern dance, outdoor activities, outdoor education, outdoor recreation, outdoor skills, physical fitness, rafting, rock climbing, ropes courses, running, strength & conditioning, weight lifting. 3 PE instructors, 22 coaches, 1 athletic trainer.

Computers Computers are regularly used in art, engineering, mathematics, science classes. Computer network features include on-campus library services, online commercial services, Internet access, wireless campus network, Internet filtering or blocking technology. Student e-mail accounts and computer access in designated common areas are available to students. Students grades are available online. The school has a published electronic and media policy.

Contact Ms. Denise LaRusch, Assistant to the Director of Admissions. 303-665-6679. Fax: 303-381-0415. E-mail: dlarusch@dawsonschool.org. Website: www.dawsonschool.org

ALLEMAN HIGH SCHOOL

1103 40th Street
Rock Island, Illinois 61201-3114

Head of School: Mr. Colin Letendre

General Information college-preparatory school, affiliated with Roman Catholic Church. Founded: 1949. Approved or accredited by Illinois Department of Education. Total enrollment: 465. Upper school average class size: 18.

Upper School Student Profile 94.5% of students are Roman Catholic.

Student Life Upper grades have specified standards of dress, student council. Attendance at religious services is required.

Admissions Application fee required: $25.

Contact Mr. Colin Letendre, Principal. 309-786-7793. Fax: 309-786-7834. E-mail: allemanhs@mchsi.com. Website: www.allemanhighschool.org

ALLENDALE COLUMBIA SCHOOL

519 Allens Creek Road
Rochester, New York 14618

Head of School: Mick Gee

General Information Coeducational day college-preparatory school. Grades N–12. Founded: 1890. Setting: suburban. 33-acre campus. 5 buildings on campus. Approved or accredited by New York State Association of Independent Schools. Member of National Association of Independent Schools. Endowment: $15 million. Total enrollment: 375. There are 165 required school days per year for Upper School students. Upper School students typically attend 5 days per week. The average school day consists of 6 hours and 30 minutes.

Upper School Student Profile Grade 9: 25 students (11 boys, 14 girls); Grade 10: 41 students (18 boys, 23 girls); Grade 11: 44 students (21 boys, 23 girls); Grade 12: 31 students (15 boys, 16 girls).

Faculty School total: 57. In upper school: 11 men, 17 women; 23 have advanced degrees.

Subjects Offered Advanced Placement courses, advanced studio art-AP, algebra, American history, American history-AP, American literature, American literature-AP, art, art-AP, astronomy, bioethics, biology, biology-AP, calculus, calculus-AP, chemistry, chemistry-AP, composition-AP, computer science, digital art, discrete mathematics, earth science, economics, English, English language and composition-AP, English literature, environmental science, environmental science-AP, European history, European history-AP, expository writing, French, French-AP, genetics, geology, geometry, government/civics, grammar, health, history, history of China and Japan, jazz ensemble, Latin, Latin-AP, mathematics, mathematics-AP, music, photography, physical education, physics, physics-AP, pre-calculus, probability and statistics, science, social studies, Spanish, Spanish-AP, statistics-AP, U.S. history, U.S. history-AP, world history, writing.

Graduation Requirements Art, arts, computer science, English, foreign language, history, mathematics, physical education (includes health), science, participation in at least one team sport in both 9th and 10th grade.

Special Academic Programs 19 Advanced Placement exams for which test preparation is offered; independent study.

College Admission Counseling 29 students graduated in 2013; 27 went to college, including Columbia University; Cornell University; Embry-Riddle Aeronautical University–Daytona; Rochester Institute of Technology; University of Michigan; University of Rochester. Other: 1 entered military service, 1 had other specific plans. Mean SAT critical reading: 600, mean SAT math: 636, mean SAT writing: 608, mean combined SAT: 1844.

Student Life Upper grades have specified standards of dress, student council. Discipline rests primarily with faculty.

Summer Programs Enrichment, sports, art/fine arts, computer instruction programs offered; held on campus; accepts boys and girls; open to students from other schools. 750 students usually enrolled. 2014 schedule: June 10 to August 16. Application deadline: none.

Tuition and Aid Day student tuition: $8310–$20,960. Tuition installment plan (FACTS Tuition Payment Plan). Need-based scholarship grants available. In 2013–14, 48% of upper-school students received aid. Total amount of financial aid awarded in 2013–14: $873,130.

Admissions Traditional secondary-level entrance grade is 9. For fall 2013, 76 students applied for upper-level admission, 40 were accepted, 25 enrolled. ERB - verbal abilities, reading comprehension, quantitative abilities (level F, form 1), essay, math and English placement tests, school's own exam or writing sample required. Deadline for receipt of application materials: none. Application fee required: $50. Interview required.

Athletics Interscholastic: baseball (boys), basketball (b,g), cross-country running (b,g), soccer (b,g), softball (g), tennis (b,g), volleyball (g); coed interscholastic: bowling, golf, swimming and diving, track and field. 4 PE instructors.

Computers Computers are regularly used in all academic classes. Computer network features include on-campus library services, Internet access, wireless campus network, Internet filtering or blocking technology, county-wide library services. Student e-mail accounts and computer access in designated common areas are available to students. Students grades are available online. The school has a published electronic and media policy.

Contact Karyn Vella, Director of Admissions. 585-641-5344. Fax: 585-383-1191. E-mail: admissions@allendalecolumbia.org. Website: www.allendalecolumbia.org

ALL HALLOWS HIGH SCHOOL

111 All Hallows Way
Bronx, New York 10452-9402

Head of School: Mr. Paul P. Krebbs

General Information Boys' day college-preparatory, general academic, business, and religious studies school, affiliated with Roman Catholic Church. Grades 9–12. Founded: 1909. Setting: urban. 1 building on campus. Approved or accredited by Christian Brothers Association, Middle States Association of Colleges and Schools, and New York Department of Education. Total enrollment: 640. Upper school average class size: 27. Upper school faculty-student ratio: 1:15. There are 180 required school days per year for Upper School students. Upper School students typically attend 5 days per week. The average school day consists of 6 hours and 8 minutes.

Upper School Student Profile 85% of students are Roman Catholic.

Faculty School total: 42. In upper school: 37 men, 5 women; 33 have advanced degrees.

Subjects Offered Algebra, American history, art, Bible studies, biology, calculus, chemistry, computer science, economics, English, English literature, environmental science, geometry, government/civics, grammar, history, humanities, Latin, mathematics, media studies, physical education, physics, political science, religion, science, social studies, Spanish, speech, trigonometry.

Graduation Requirements Arts and fine arts (art, music, dance, drama), business skills (includes word processing), computer science, English, foreign language, mathematics, physical education (includes health), religion (includes Bible studies and theology), science, social sciences, social studies (includes history). Community service is required.

Special Academic Programs Remedial reading and/or remedial writing; remedial math.

College Admission Counseling 154 students graduated in 2013; all went to college.

Student Life Upper grades have specified standards of dress, student council, honor system. Discipline rests primarily with faculty. Attendance at religious services is required.

Tuition and Aid Merit scholarship grants available.

Admissions School's own exam required. Deadline for receipt of application materials: none. No application fee required. On-campus interview required.

Athletics Interscholastic: baseball, basketball, bowling, cross-country running, fencing, golf, indoor track & field, soccer, track and field, winter (indoor) track; intramural: field hockey, flag football, indoor soccer, lacrosse. 1 PE instructor, 4 coaches.

Computers Computers are regularly used in English, history, mathematics, media studies, science classes. Computer resources include on-campus library services, Internet access.

Contact Mr. Sean Sullivan, Principal. 718-293-4545. Fax: 718-293-8634. E-mail: alhallow@aol.com. Website: www.allhallows.org

ALLIANCE ACADEMY

Casilla 17-11-06186
Quito, Ecuador

Head of School: Dr. David Wells

General Information Coeducational boarding and day and distance learning college-preparatory, arts, and religious studies school, affiliated with Christian faith. Boarding grades 7–12, day grades PK–12. Distance learning grades 10–12. Founded: 1929. Setting: urban. Students are housed in single-sex by floor dormitories and mission agency dormitories. 8-acre campus. 6 buildings on campus. Approved or accredited by Association of American Schools in South America, Association of Christian Schools International, and Southern Association of Colleges and Schools. Language of instruction: English. Total enrollment: 604. Upper school average class size: 15. Upper school faculty-student ratio: 1:7. There are 200 required school days per year for Upper School students. Upper School students typically attend 5 days per week. The average school day consists of 6 hours and 30 minutes.

Upper School Student Profile Grade 9: 51 students (27 boys, 24 girls); Grade 10: 60 students (26 boys, 34 girls); Grade 11: 44 students (14 boys, 30 girls); Grade 12: 53 students (27 boys, 26 girls). 1% of students are boarding students. 34% are international students. International students from Canada, China, Japan, Republic of Korea, Taiwan, and United States; 9 other countries represented in student body. 40% of students are Christian faith.

Faculty School total: 91. In upper school: 21 men, 24 women; 14 have advanced degrees; 3 reside on campus.

Subjects Offered Algebra, American history, American literature, art, auto mechanics, band, Bible, Bible as literature, Bible studies, biology, biology-AP, business, calculus, calculus-AP, chemistry, choir, Christian doctrine, Christian ethics, Christian studies, church history, computer applications, computer art, computer programming, computer science, concert band, creative writing, debate, desktop publishing, drama, earth science, economics, English, English as a foreign language, English language-AP, English literature, English literature-AP, ESL, family and consumer science, fine arts, French, French as a second language, geography, geometry, government/civics, grammar, health, health education, history, home economics, industrial arts, journalism, keyboarding, Life of Christ, marching band, mathematics, music, novels, photography, physical education, physics, pre-algebra, pre-calculus, public speaking, religion, religion and culture, science, senior seminar, small engine repair, social sciences, social studies, Spanish, Spanish literature, Spanish literature-AP, speech, speech and debate, theater, trigonometry, video communication, vocal ensemble, woodworking, world geography, world history, world religions, writing, yearbook.

Graduation Requirements 1 1/2 elective credits, algebra, arts and fine arts (art, music, dance, drama), comparative government and politics, computer applications, English, foreign language, health education, mathematics, physical education (includes health), religion (includes Bible studies and theology), science, social sciences, social studies (includes history), U.S. government and politics, U.S. history.

Special Academic Programs 12 Advanced Placement exams for which test preparation is offered; independent study; study at local college for college credit; academic accommodation for the gifted; remedial reading and/or remedial writing; remedial math; programs in English, mathematics, general development for dyslexic students; special instructional classes for students with developmental and/or learning disabilities; ESL (52 students enrolled).

College Admission Counseling 52 students graduated in 2012; 39 went to college, including Azusa Pacific University; Calvin College; John Brown University; Simpson University; Worcester Polytechnic Institute. Other: 4 went to work, 2 entered military service, 7 had other specific plans. Median SAT critical reading: 495, median SAT math: 517, median SAT writing: 496, median combined SAT: 1508, median composite ACT: 22. 36% scored over 600 on SAT critical reading, 29% scored over 600 on SAT math, 30% scored over 600 on SAT writing, 32% scored over 1800 on combined SAT, 26% scored over 26 on composite ACT.

Student Life Upper grades have specified standards of dress, student council, honor system. Discipline rests primarily with faculty. Attendance at religious services is required.

Tuition and Aid Day student tuition: $9900. Tuition installment plan (monthly payment plans, individually arranged payment plans). Tuition reduction for siblings, need-based scholarship grants, paying campus jobs, tuition reduction for children of missionaries, two full scholarships for children of Ecuadorian military personnel available. In 2012–13, 30% of upper-school students received aid. Total amount of financial aid awarded in 2012–13: $800,000.

Admissions Traditional secondary-level entrance grade is 9. For fall 2012, 46 students applied for upper-level admission, 28 were accepted, 26 enrolled. English entrance exam, English proficiency, WRAT or writing sample required. Deadline for receipt of application materials: none. Application fee required: $100. On-campus interview required.

Athletics Interscholastic: basketball (boys, girls), soccer (b,g), volleyball (b,g); intramural: badminton (b,g), ball hockey (b), horseshoes (b), in-line hockey (b), modern dance (g), table tennis (b,g); coed intramural: backpacking, basketball, bocce, climbing, croquet, field hockey, flag football, floor hockey, football, hiking/backpacking, indoor soccer, kickball, martial arts, outdoor adventure, paddle tennis, running, soccer, softball, strength & conditioning, table tennis, volleyball, wall climbing. 2 PE instructors, 1 coach.

Computers Computers are regularly used in basic skills, business education, career exploration, college planning, computer applications, design, desktop publishing, desktop publishing, ESL, digital applications, graphic design, independent study, information technology, introduction to technology, keyboarding, lab/keyboard, language development, media arts, media production, media services, photography, photojournalism, programming, publications, technology, video film production, word processing, writing, yearbook classes. Computer network features include on-campus library services, online commercial services, Internet access, wireless campus network, Internet filtering or blocking technology. Campus intranet, student e-mail accounts, and computer access in designated common areas are available to students. Students grades are available online. The school has a published electronic and media policy.

Contact Mrs. Alexandra Chavez, Director of Admissions. 593-2-226-6985. Fax: 593-2-226-4350. E-mail: achavez@alliance.k12.ec. Website: www.alliance.k12.ec

ALMA HEIGHTS CHRISTIAN HIGH SCHOOL

1030 Linda Mar Boulevard
Pacifica, California 94044
Head of School: David Gross

General Information Coeducational day college-preparatory, general academic, arts, religious studies, and technology school, affiliated with Christian faith. Grades K–12. Founded: 1955. Setting: suburban. Nearest major city is San Francisco. 36-acre campus. 5 buildings on campus. Approved or accredited by Association of Christian Schools International, Western Association of Schools and Colleges, and California Department of Education. Total enrollment: 303. Upper school average class size: 22. Upper school faculty-student ratio: 1:10. There are 176 required school days per year for Upper School students. Upper School students typically attend 5 days per week. The average school day consists of 7 hours and 25 minutes.

Upper School Student Profile Grade 6: 18 students (13 boys, 5 girls); Grade 7: 21 students (5 boys, 16 girls); Grade 8: 14 students (9 boys, 5 girls); Grade 9: 25 students (11 boys, 14 girls); Grade 10: 29 students (14 boys, 15 girls); Grade 11: 45 students (21 boys, 24 girls); Grade 12: 44 students (28 boys, 16 girls). 80% of students are Christian.

Faculty School total: 20. In upper school: 10 men, 9 women; 7 have advanced degrees.

Special Academic Programs International Baccalaureate program; 6 Advanced Placement exams for which test preparation is offered; honors section; accelerated programs; special instructional classes for students with ADD and dyslexia; ESL (19 students enrolled).

College Admission Counseling 40 students graduated in 2013; 35 went to college, including Azusa Pacific University; Biola University; University of California, Berkeley; University of California, Davis; University of California, Irvine; Whitworth University. Other: 5 went to work. Mean SAT critical reading: 494, mean SAT math: 529, mean SAT writing: 503.

Student Life Upper grades have uniform requirement, student council, honor system. Discipline rests primarily with faculty. Attendance at religious services is required.

Summer Programs Sports, art/fine arts, rigorous outdoor training programs offered; held on campus; accepts boys and girls; open to students from other schools.

Tuition and Aid Day student tuition: $9400. Tuition installment plan (monthly payment plans, individually arranged payment plans). Tuition reduction for siblings, merit scholarship grants, need-based scholarship grants, paying campus jobs available. In 2013–14, 5% of upper-school students received aid.

Admissions Traditional secondary-level entrance grade is 9. Placement test required. Deadline for receipt of application materials: none. Application fee required: $75. Interview required.

Athletics Interscholastic: baseball (boys), basketball (b,g), football (b), soccer (b), softball (g), volleyball (b,g); intramural: flag football (b), indoor soccer (b); coed interscholastic: cross-country running, soccer. 3 PE instructors, 6 coaches.

Computers Computer resources include on-campus library services, online commercial services, Internet access, wireless campus network, Internet filtering or blocking technology. Campus intranet, student e-mail accounts, and computer access in designated common areas are available to students. Students grades are available online. The school has a published electronic and media policy.

Contact Anna Valladares, High School Admissions Coordinator. 650-355-1935 Ext. 106. Fax: 650-355-3488. E-mail: avalladares@almaheights.ort. Website: www.almaheights.org

ALPHA OMEGA ACADEMY

804 North Second Avenue East
Rock Rapids, Iowa 51246
Head of School: Mr. Joseph A. Bakker

General Information Coeducational day and distance learning college-preparatory, general academic, and distance learning school, affiliated with Christian faith. Grades K–12. Distance learning grades K–12. Founded: 1992. Setting: small town. Approved or accredited by CITA (Commission on International and Trans-Regional Accreditation) and North Central Association of Colleges and Schools. Total enrollment: 2,350. Upper School students typically attend 5 days per week.

Faculty School total: 36. In upper school: 14 men, 19 women; 6 have advanced degrees.

Subjects Offered 20th century history, accounting, algebra, American government, American history, American literature, art, Bible, biology, British literature, calculus, career planning, chemistry, civics, consumer mathematics, earth science, English, English composition, English literature, French, general math, general science, geography, geometry, health, history, home economics, language arts, mathematics, music appreciation, music theory, physical fitness, science, Spanish, state history, Vietnam War, world geography, world history.

Graduation Requirements 1 1/2 elective credits, algebra, biology, chemistry, language arts, mathematics, physical education (includes health), science, social studies (includes history), one credit of Bible.

Special Academic Programs Accelerated programs; independent study; remedial math.

College Admission Counseling 250 students graduated in 2013.

Student Life Upper grades have honor system. Discipline rests primarily with faculty.

Summer Programs Remediation, advancement programs offered; session focuses on credit recovery; accepts boys and girls; open to students from other schools.

Tuition and Aid Day student tuition: $600–$3000. Tuition installment plan (Six Month Payment Plan, Two Payment Plan). Tuition reduction for siblings available.

Admissions Math and English placement tests or placement test required. Deadline for receipt of application materials: none. Application fee required: $185. Interview required.

Athletics 2 PE instructors.

Computers Computers are regularly used in accounting, Bible studies, business skills, career technology, college planning, English, foreign language, French, geography, health, history, mathematics, music, science, social sciences, social studies, Spanish classes. Students grades are available online. The school has a published electronic and media policy.

Contact Mrs. Robin Inlow, Continuous Improvement Coordinator. 800-682-7396 Ext. 6253. Fax: 712-472-6830. E-mail: rinlow@aoacademy.com. Website: www.aoacademy.com

ALVERNO HIGH SCHOOL

200 North Michillinda Avenue
Sierra Madre, California 91024
Head of School: Ms. Ann M. Gillick

General Information Girls' day college-preparatory, arts, religious studies, and technology school, affiliated with Roman Catholic Church. Grades 9–12. Founded: 1960. Setting: suburban. Nearest major city is Pasadena. 13-acre campus. 8 buildings on campus. Approved or accredited by California Association of Independent Schools, National Catholic Education Association, Western Association of Schools and Colleges, and California Department of Education. Upper school average class size: 18. Upper school faculty-student ratio: 1:12. There are 181 required school days per year for Upper School students. Upper School students typically attend 5 days per week. The average school day consists of 7 hours and 45 minutes.

Upper School Student Profile Grade 9: 53 students (53 girls); Grade 10: 39 students (39 girls); Grade 11: 37 students (37 girls); Grade 12: 45 students (45 girls). 65% of students are Roman Catholic.

Faculty School total: 17. In upper school: 4 men, 13 women; 11 have advanced degrees.

Subjects Offered ACT preparation, advanced biology, advanced chemistry, advanced studio art-AP, algebra, American literature, band, biology-AP, British literature (honors), calculus-AP, Catholic belief and practice, ceramics, choir, college counseling, conceptual physics, dance, dramatic arts, driver education, earth science, English language-AP, English literature-AP, European history-AP, finite math, fitness, freshman seminar, geometry, health, history of the Catholic Church, honors algebra, honors English, honors geometry, honors U.S. history, honors world history, human geography - AP, improvisation, language-AP, leadership and service, literature and composition-AP, literature-AP, Mandarin, modern European history-AP, multicultural studies, musical theater, photography, pre-calculus, religion, SAT preparation, science, senior project, Shakespeare, social studies, softball, Spanish-AP, sports conditioning, stagecraft, student government, studio art-AP, technology/design, theater arts, theater design and production, track and field, trigonometry, U.S. history-AP, United States government-AP, video film production, visual and performing arts, world literature, world religions, writing, yearbook, zoology.

Graduation Requirements Completion of 140 service hours.

Special Academic Programs 11 Advanced Placement exams for which test preparation is offered; honors section; independent study; academic accommodation for the gifted; remedial reading and/or remedial writing; remedial math; programs in English, mathematics, general development for dyslexic students.

College Admission Counseling 45 students graduated in 2012; 44 went to college, including California State Polytechnic University, Pomona; Marymount College, Palos Verdes, California; University of California, Davis; University of California, Riverside; University of La Verne. Other: 1 entered military service.

Student Life Upper grades have uniform requirement, student council, honor system. Discipline rests primarily with faculty. Attendance at religious services is required.

Tuition and Aid Day student tuition: $13,500. Tuition installment plan (FACTS Tuition Payment Plan, monthly payment plans). Tuition reduction for siblings, merit scholarship grants, need-based scholarship grants available. In 2012–13, 40% of upper-school students received aid; total upper-school merit-scholarship money awarded: $172,198. Total amount of financial aid awarded in 2012–13: $253,313.

Admissions Traditional secondary-level entrance grade is 9. For fall 2012, 118 students applied for upper-level admission, 116 were accepted, 53 enrolled. High School Placement Test (closed version) from Scholastic Testing Service required. Deadline for receipt of application materials: January 18. Application fee required: $75. On-campus interview required.

Athletics Interscholastic: aquatics, basketball, cross-country running, soccer, softball, volleyball; intramural: aerobics/dance, dance, modern dance, self defense. 1 PE instructor, 4 coaches.

Computers Computers are regularly used in all academic classes. Computer network features include on-campus library services, Internet access, wireless campus network, Internet filtering or blocking technology. Students grades are available online. The school has a published electronic and media policy.

Contact Ms. Sara McCarthy, Director of Admissions and Public Relations. 626-355-3463 Ext. 235. Fax: 626-355-3153. E-mail: smccarthy@alverno-hs.org. Website: myalverno.org/

AMERICAN ACADEMY

Plantation, Florida
See Special Needs Schools section.

THE AMERICAN BOYCHOIR SCHOOL

Princeton, New Jersey
See Junior Boarding Schools section.

AMERICAN COMMUNITY SCHOOLS OF ATHENS

129 Aghias Paraskevis Street
Halandri
Athens 152 34, Greece

Head of School: Dr. Stefanos Gialamas

General Information Coeducational day college-preparatory, arts, and technology school. Grades JK–12. Founded: 1945. Setting: suburban. 3-hectare campus. 4 buildings on campus. Approved or accredited by CITA (Commission on International and Trans-Regional Accreditation) and Middle States Association of Colleges and Schools. Affiliate member of National Association of Independent Schools; member of European Council of International Schools. Language of instruction: English. Total enrollment: 859. Upper school average class size: 20. Upper school faculty-student ratio: 1:20. There are 180 required school days per year for Upper School students. Upper School students typically attend 5 days per week. The average school day consists of 6 hours and 30 minutes.

Upper School Student Profile Grade 9: 77 students (35 boys, 42 girls); Grade 10: 87 students (43 boys, 44 girls); Grade 11: 96 students (41 boys, 55 girls); Grade 12: 82 students (43 boys, 39 girls).

Faculty School total: 95. In upper school: 15 men, 37 women; 40 have advanced degrees.

Subjects Offered Algebra, American history, American literature, analysis, Arabic, art, art history, band, biology, business skills, calculus, chemistry, Chinese, computer programming, computer science, dance, drama, earth science, economics, English, English literature, environmental science, ESL, European history, expository writing, fine arts, French, geometry, German, government/civics, grammar, Greek, history, humanities, information technology, journalism, mathematics, music, peer counseling, photography, physical education, physical science, physics, psychology, science, social sciences, social studies, sociology, Spanish, speech, statistics, theater, theory of knowledge, trigonometry, writing.

Graduation Requirements Arts and fine arts (art, music, dance, drama), computer science, English, foreign language, mathematics, physical education (includes health), science, social sciences, social studies (includes history).

Special Academic Programs International Baccalaureate program; 4 Advanced Placement exams for which test preparation is offered; honors section; accelerated

programs; independent study; study at local college for college credit; academic accommodation for the gifted; remedial reading and/or remedial writing; remedial math; programs in English, mathematics, general development for dyslexic students; special instructional classes for deaf students, blind students, students with mild learning disabilities; ESL (17 students enrolled).

College Admission Counseling 97 students graduated in 2013; 96 went to college, including Boston College; Boston University; Columbia University; Georgetown University; New York University; Tufts University. Other: 1 had other specific plans. Mean SAT critical reading: 543, mean SAT math: 550, mean SAT writing: 579. 27% scored over 600 on SAT critical reading, 25% scored over 600 on SAT math, 26% scored over 600 on SAT writing.

Student Life Upper grades have specified standards of dress, student council, honor system. Discipline rests primarily with faculty.

Summer Programs Enrichment, advancement, ESL, sports, art/fine arts, computer instruction programs offered; session focuses on recreational and international leadership, and Summer Scholar's Academy; held both on and off campus; held at various museums and historical sites (for the leadership program) and Summer Leadership Institute in cooperation with St. Louis Univ. at their campus; accepts boys and girls; open to students from other schools. 365 students usually enrolled. 2014 schedule: June 23 to July 6. Application deadline: May 15.

Tuition and Aid Day student tuition: €11,994. Tuition installment plan (individually arranged payment plans, semester and quarterly payment plans). Tuition reduction for siblings, need-based scholarship grants available. In 2013–14, 1% of upper-school students received aid. Total amount of financial aid awarded in 2013–14: €60,000.

Admissions Traditional secondary-level entrance grade is 9. For fall 2013, 340 students applied for upper-level admission, 307 were accepted, 219 enrolled. English for Non-native Speakers or math and English placement tests required. Deadline for receipt of application materials: none. No application fee required. Interview required.

Athletics Interscholastic: basketball (boys, girls), cross-country running (b,g), soccer (b,g), softball (b,g), swimming and diving (b,g), tennis (b,g), track and field (b,g), volleyball (b,g), wrestling (b); coed interscholastic: gymnastics; coed intramural: martial arts. 2 PE instructors, 3 coaches.

Computers Computers are regularly used in all academic classes. Computer network features include on-campus library services, Internet access. Campus intranet, student e-mail accounts, and computer access in designated common areas are available to students. Students grades are available online.

Contact John G. Papadakis, Director of Enrollment, Communications, and Technology. 30-210-639-3200. Fax: 30-210-639-0051. E-mail: papadakisj@acs.gr. Website: www.acs.gr

AMERICAN HERITAGE SCHOOL

6200 Linton Boulevard
Delray Beach, Florida 33484

Head of School: Robert Stone

General Information Coeducational day college-preparatory, arts, technology, and pre-medical, pre-law, pre-engineering school. Grades PK–12. Founded: 1994. Setting: suburban. Nearest major city is Fort Lauderdale. 40-acre campus. 9 buildings on campus. Approved or accredited by Association of Independent Schools of Florida, Southern Association of Colleges and Schools, Southern Association of Independent Schools, and Florida Department of Education. Member of National Association of Independent Schools. Total enrollment: 1,130. Upper school average class size: 17. Upper school faculty-student ratio: 1:10. There are 175 required school days per year for Upper School students. Upper School students typically attend 5 days per week. The average school day consists of 6 hours and 30 minutes.

Upper School Student Profile Grade 6: 79 students (42 boys, 37 girls); Grade 7: 86 students (46 boys, 40 girls); Grade 8: 99 students (50 boys, 49 girls); Grade 9: 153 students (95 boys, 58 girls); Grade 10: 168 students (97 boys, 71 girls); Grade 11: 160 students (82 boys, 78 girls); Grade 12: 128 students (70 boys, 58 girls).

Faculty School total: 124. In upper school: 24 men, 52 women; 55 have advanced degrees.

Subjects Offered Acting, algebra, American government, American history, American history-AP, American legal systems, American literature, American literature-AP, anatomy and physiology, architectural drawing, art, band, biology, biology-AP, calculus-AP, ceramics, chemistry, chemistry-AP, Chinese, chorus, community service, computer graphics, computer science, computer science-AP, constitutional law, costumes and make-up, creative writing, dance, digital photography, drama, drawing, economics, engineering, English, English language and composition-AP, English literature, English literature and composition-AP, environmental science, environmental science-AP, ESL, film and literature, fine arts, forensics, French, French-AP, geometry, graphic design, guitar, honors algebra, honors English, honors geometry, honors U.S. history, honors world history, journalism, law studies, Mandarin, mathematics, multimedia, multimedia design, music theory-AP, oceanography, orchestra, painting, photography, physical education, physics, physics-AP, portfolio art, pre-algebra, pre-calculus, probability and statistics, psychology, psychology-AP, public policy, research skills, SAT/ACT preparation, science, sculpture, set design, Spanish, Spanish-AP, speech and debate, stagecraft, statistics-AP, studio art, theater, U.S.

government and politics-AP, vocal music, Web site design, weight training, world history, world history-AP, world literature, writing, writing, yearbook.

Graduation Requirements Arts and fine arts (art, music, dance, drama), English, foreign language, mathematics, physical education (includes health), science, social studies (includes history), acceptance to a 4-year college, community service requirement. Community service is required.

Special Academic Programs 19 Advanced Placement exams for which test preparation is offered; academic accommodation for the gifted, the musically talented, and the artistically talented; remedial reading and/or remedial writing; remedial math; programs in English, mathematics, general development for dyslexic students; special instructional classes for deaf students, blind students; ESL (43 students enrolled).

College Admission Counseling 147 students graduated in 2013; 145 went to college, including Florida Atlantic University; Florida Gulf Coast University; Florida State University; Palm Beach Atlantic University; University of Central Florida; University of Florida. Other: 1 entered military service, 1 had other specific plans. Median SAT critical reading: 530, median SAT math: 550, median SAT writing: 540. 23% scored over 600 on SAT critical reading, 33% scored over 600 on SAT math, 32% scored over 600 on SAT writing, 25% scored over 1800 on combined SAT.

Student Life Upper grades have uniform requirement, student council. Discipline rests primarily with faculty.

Summer Programs Remediation, enrichment, advancement, ESL programs offered; session focuses on academics; held on campus; accepts boys and girls; open to students from other schools. 130 students usually enrolled. 2014 schedule: June 6 to August 9. Application deadline: none.

Tuition and Aid Day student tuition: $20,000. Tuition installment plan (monthly payment plans, semester payment plan, yearly). Tuition reduction for siblings, merit scholarship grants, need-based scholarship grants available. In 2013–14, 22% of upper-school students received aid; total upper-school merit-scholarship money awarded: $2,789,928. Total amount of financial aid awarded in 2013–14: $4,623,928.

Admissions Traditional secondary-level entrance grade is 9. For fall 2013, 650 students applied for upper-level admission, 275 were accepted, 138 enrolled. Slossen Intelligence and Stanford Achievement Test required. Deadline for receipt of application materials: none. Application fee required: $100. Interview required.

Athletics Interscholastic: baseball (boys), basketball (b,g), broomball (g), cheering (b), cross-country running (b,g), dance (b,g), dance squad (g), dance team (g), diving (b,g), football (b), golf (b,g), lacrosse (b), polo (b), soccer (b,g), softball (g), volleyball (g), water polo (b), weight training (b,g), winter soccer (b,g), wrestling (b); coed interscholastic: equestrian sports, physical fitness, swimming and diving, tennis, track and field, yoga. 2 PE instructors, 40 coaches, 1 athletic trainer.

Computers Computers are regularly used in all academic, college planning, computer applications, desktop publishing, digital applications, drawing and design, economics, English, ESL, foreign language, French, geography, graphic design, history,

human geography - AP, journalism, keyboarding, library, literary magazine, mathematics, media arts, media production, multimedia, music, music technology, newspaper, photography, programming, psychology, reading, SAT preparation, science, social sciences, social studies, Spanish, speech, video film production, Web site design, writing, yearbook classes. Computer network features include on-campus library services, online commercial services, Internet access, wireless campus network, Internet filtering or blocking technology, Questia, Noodle Tools, Naviance, Lexis-Nexus, Quia, ProQuest/SIRS, Turnitin, Cengage Learning Gale, Learning Today, Nettrekker, EBSCOhost, Accelerated Reader. Student e-mail accounts and computer access in designated common areas are available to students. Students grades are available online. The school has a published electronic and media policy.

Contact Mr. Harold Bailey, DD, Director of Admissions. 561-495-7272 Ext. 236. Fax: 561-495-4192. E-mail: harold.bailey@ahschool.com. Website: www.ahschool.com

See Display below and Close-Up on page 512.

AMERICAN HERITAGE SCHOOL

12200 West Broward Boulevard
Plantation, Florida 33325

Head of School: William R. Laurie

General Information Coeducational day college-preparatory, arts, technology, pre-medical, pre-law, pre-engineering, bio-medical, arts, and journalism, broadcasting school. Grades PK–12. Founded: 1969. Setting: suburban. Nearest major city is Fort Lauderdale. 40-acre campus. 5 buildings on campus. Approved or accredited by Association of Independent Schools of Florida, CITA (Commission on International and Trans-Regional Accreditation), Southern Association of Colleges and Schools, and Florida Department of Education. Total enrollment: 2,395. Upper school average class size: 19. Upper school faculty-student ratio: 1:15. There are 175 required school days per year for Upper School students. Upper School students typically attend 5 days per week. The average school day consists of 7 hours and 15 minutes.

Upper School Student Profile Grade 7: 181 students (90 boys, 91 girls); Grade 8: 163 students (78 boys, 85 girls); Grade 9: 337 students (178 boys, 159 girls); Grade 10: 352 students (189 boys, 163 girls); Grade 11: 331 students (194 boys, 137 girls); Grade 12: 322 students (158 boys, 164 girls).

Faculty School total: 188. In upper school: 45 men, 83 women; 64 have advanced degrees.

Subjects Offered Acting, algebra, American government, American history, American history-AP, American legal systems, American literature, American literature-AP, anatomy and physiology, architectural drawing, architecture, art, band, biology, biology-AP, business law, calculus-AP, ceramics, chemistry, chemistry-AP,

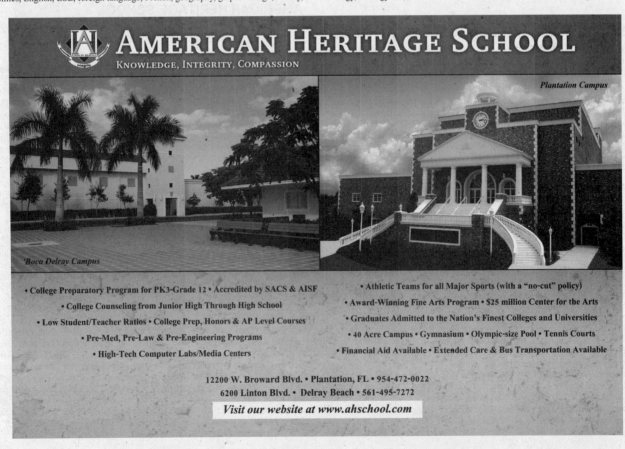

Chinese, chorus, community service, computer graphics, computer science, computer science-AP, constitutional law, costumes and make-up, creative writing, dance, drama, drawing, economics, economics-AP, engineering, English, English language and composition-AP, English literature, English literature and composition-AP, environmental science, environmental science-AP, ESL, European history-AP, fine arts, forensics, French, French language-AP, French-AP, geometry, government-AP, graphic design, guitar, honors algebra, honors English, honors geometry, honors U.S. history, honors world history, human geography - AP, journalism, law studies, literary magazine, mathematics, music theory, music theory-AP, oceanography, orchestra, organic chemistry, painting, photography, physical education, physics, physics-AP, portfolio art, pre-algebra, pre-calculus, probability and statistics, psychology, psychology-AP, public speaking, research, research skills, SAT preparation, SAT/ACT preparation, science, sculpture, set design, sociology, Spanish, Spanish-AP, speech and debate, stage design, stagecraft, statistics-AP, studio art, technical theater, theater, U.S. government and politics-AP, video film production, visual arts, vocal music, Web site design, weight training, world history, world history-AP, world literature, writing, writing, yearbook.

Graduation Requirements Arts and fine arts (art, music, dance, drama), English, foreign language, mathematics, physical education (includes health), science, social studies (includes history), acceptance to a 4-year college. Community service is required.

Special Academic Programs Advanced Placement exam preparation; honors section; academic accommodation for the gifted, the musically talented, and the artistically talented; ESL (59 students enrolled).

College Admission Counseling 291 students graduated in 2013; all went to college, including Florida International University; Florida State University; Nova Southeastern University; University of Central Florida; University of Florida; University of Miami. Mean SAT critical reading: 559, mean SAT math: 580, mean SAT writing: 595, mean composite ACT: 27. 43% scored over 600 on SAT critical reading, 49% scored over 600 on SAT math, 49% scored over 600 on SAT writing, 48% scored over 26 on composite ACT.

Student Life Upper grades have uniform requirement, student council. Discipline rests primarily with faculty.

Summer Programs Remediation, enrichment, advancement, ESL, art/fine arts, computer instruction programs offered; session focuses on academics; held on campus; accepts boys and girls; open to students from other schools. 500 students usually enrolled. 2014 schedule: June 9 to August 8. Application deadline: none.

Tuition and Aid Day student tuition: $22,173–$23,930. Tuition installment plan (monthly payment plans, Semester payment plan, yearly). Tuition reduction for siblings, merit scholarship grants, need-based scholarship grants available. In 2013–14, 22% of upper-school students received aid; total upper-school merit-scholarship money awarded: $3,800,000. Total amount of financial aid awarded in 2013–14: $3,800,000.

Admissions Traditional secondary-level entrance grade is 9. Slossen Intelligence and Stanford Achievement Test required. Deadline for receipt of application materials: none. Application fee required: $100. On-campus interview required.

Athletics Interscholastic: baseball (boys), basketball (b,g), cross-country running (b,g), diving (b,g), football (b), golf (b,g), ice hockey (b), lacrosse (b,g), soccer (b,g), softball (g), swimming and diving (b,g), tennis (b,g), track and field (b,g), volleyball (b,g), weight training (b,g), winter soccer (b,g), wrestling (b); coed interscholastic: cheering, dance team, physical fitness, physical training, strength & conditioning. 4 PE instructors, 6 coaches.

Computers Computers are regularly used in all academic classes. Computer network features include on-campus library services, online commercial services, Internet access, wireless campus network, Internet filtering or blocking technology, Questia, iPads used by students and teachers on school Intranet. Campus intranet, student e-mail accounts, and computer access in designated common areas are available to students. Students grades are available online. The school has a published electronic and media policy.

Contact William R. Laurie, President. 954-472-0022 Ext. 3062. Fax: 954-472-3088. E-mail: admissions@ahschool.com. Website: www.ahschool.com

See Display on previous page and Close-Up on page 512.

AMERICAN INTERNATIONAL SCHOOL, LUSAKA

PO Box 320176
Lusaka, Zambia

Head of School: Mr. Thomas J. Pado

General Information Coeducational day college-preparatory school. Grades 6–12. Founded: 1986. Setting: suburban. 12-acre campus. 11 buildings on campus. Approved or accredited by Council of International Schools, International Baccalaureate Organization, and Middle States Association of Colleges and Schools. Member of European Council of International Schools. Language of instruction: English. Total enrollment: 257. Upper school average class size: 18. Upper school faculty-student ratio: 1:7. There are 180 required school days per year for Upper School students. Upper School students typically attend 5 days per week. The average school day consists of 5 hours and 50 minutes.

Upper School Student Profile Grade 9: 33 students (20 boys, 13 girls); Grade 10: 33 students (21 boys, 12 girls); Grade 11: 39 students (23 boys, 16 girls); Grade 12: 33 students (18 boys, 15 girls).

Faculty School total: 39. In upper school: 15 men, 21 women; 19 have advanced degrees.

Subjects Offered International Baccalaureate courses.

Graduation Requirements International Baccalaureate courses.

Special Academic Programs International Baccalaureate program; ESL (16 students enrolled).

College Admission Counseling 35 students graduated in 2012; 31 went to college. Other: 1 entered military service, 3 had other specific plans. Median SAT critical reading: 530, median SAT math: 520, median SAT writing: 540, median combined SAT: 1610, median composite ACT: 23. 26.7% scored over 600 on SAT critical reading, 26.7% scored over 600 on SAT math, 40% scored over 600 on SAT writing, 33.3% scored over 1800 on combined SAT, 27.8% scored over 26 on composite ACT.

Student Life Upper grades have student council, honor system. Discipline rests primarily with faculty.

Tuition and Aid Day student tuition: $17,100.

Admissions Traditional secondary-level entrance grade is 11. For fall 2012, 12 students applied for upper-level admission, 11 were accepted, 10 enrolled. English Composition Test for ESL students required. Deadline for receipt of application materials: none. No application fee required.

Athletics Intramural: badminton (boys, girls), basketball (b,g), climbing (b,g), cross-country running (b,g), dance (b,g), field hockey (b,g), fitness (b,g), floor hockey (b,g), Frisbee (b,g), handball (b,g), indoor soccer (b,g), rugby (b), soccer (b,g), swimming and diving (b,g), tennis (b,g), triathlon (b,g), ultimate Frisbee (b,g), volleyball (b,g), wall climbing (b,g), water polo (b,g), weight training (b,g); coed intramural: badminton, basketball, climbing, cross-country running, dance, field hockey, fitness, floor hockey, Frisbee, handball, indoor soccer, soccer, swimming and diving, tennis, triathlon, ultimate Frisbee, volleyball, wall climbing, water polo, weight training. 3 PE instructors, 14 coaches.

Computers Computers are regularly used in all classes. Computer network features include on-campus library services, Internet access, wireless campus network, Internet filtering or blocking technology. Campus intranet is available to students. Students grades are available online. The school has a published electronic and media policy.

THE AMERICAN SCHOOL FOUNDATION

Bondojito 215
Colonia Las Americas
Mexico City, D.F. 01120, Mexico

Head of School: Mr. Paul Williams

General Information Coeducational day college-preparatory, Mexican Program Curriculum, and U.S. program curriculum school. Grades PK–12. Founded: 1888. Setting: urban. Nearest major city is Mexico City, Mexico. 17-acre campus. 4 buildings on campus. Approved or accredited by International Baccalaureate Organization and Southern Association of Colleges and Schools. Affiliate member of National Association of Independent Schools; member of Secondary School Admission Test Board. Languages of instruction: English and Spanish. Endowment: 149.1 million Mexican pesos. Total enrollment: 2,571. Upper school average class size: 18. Upper school faculty-student ratio: 1:11. There are 182 required school days per year for Upper School students. Upper School students typically attend 5 days per week. The average school day consists of 6 hours and 45 minutes.

Upper School Student Profile Grade 9: 173 students (96 boys, 77 girls); Grade 10: 189 students (104 boys, 85 girls); Grade 11: 192 students (85 boys, 107 girls); Grade 12: 182 students (84 boys, 98 girls).

Faculty School total: 262. In upper school: 44 men, 43 women; 54 have advanced degrees.

Subjects Offered Advanced Placement courses, algebra, American history, American literature, anatomy, art, art history, biology, calculus, ceramics, chemistry, computer programming, computer science, drafting, drama, earth science, ecology, economics, English, English literature, European history, expository writing, film, fine arts, French, geography, geometry, government/civics, grammar, health, history, humanities, journalism, mathematics, Mexican history, music, philosophy, photography, physical education, physics, physiology, psychology, science, social sciences, social studies, Spanish, speech, statistics, trigonometry, world history, world literature, writing.

Graduation Requirements English, foreign language, health, humanities, mathematics, physical education (includes health), science, social studies (includes history), technology, IB Personal Project (10th grade), Week Without Walls (9th grade).

Special Academic Programs International Baccalaureate program; 12 Advanced Placement exams for which test preparation is offered; independent study; remedial reading and/or remedial writing; programs in English, mathematics, general development for dyslexic students; special instructional classes for deaf students, blind students, learning disabilities (LD), Attention Deficit Hyperactivity Disorder (ADHD), and speech and language disorders.

College Admission Counseling 176 students graduated in 2013; 148 went to college, including Lynn University. Other: 28 had other specific plans. Median SAT critical reading: 580, median SAT math: 600, median SAT writing: 570, median combined SAT: 1760, median composite ACT: 26. 39% scored over 600 on SAT critical reading, 48.7% scored over 600 on SAT math, 35.4% scored over 600 on SAT writing, 43.6% scored over 1800 on combined SAT, 27% scored over 26 on composite ACT.

Student Life Upper grades have specified standards of dress, student council. Discipline rests primarily with faculty.

Tuition and Aid Day student tuition: 169,000 Mexican pesos. Tuition installment plan (monthly payment plans, Tuition Insurance). Need-based scholarship grants available. In 2013–14, 14% of upper-school students received aid. Total amount of financial aid awarded in 2013–14: 8,300,000 Mexican pesos.

Admissions Traditional secondary-level entrance grade is 10. For fall 2013, 242 students applied for upper-level admission, 80 were accepted, 79 enrolled. Essay required. Deadline for receipt of application materials: none. Application fee required: 1000 Mexican pesos. On-campus interview required.

Athletics Interscholastic: basketball (boys, girls), dance team (g), football (b), soccer (b,g), swimming and diving (b,g), volleyball (g); coed interscholastic: running. 12 PE instructors, 36 coaches, 1 athletic trainer.

Computers Computers are regularly used in all classes. Computer network features include on-campus library services, online commercial services, Internet access, wireless campus network, Internet filtering or blocking technology. Campus intranet, student e-mail accounts, and computer access in designated common areas are available to students. Students grades are available online. The school has a published electronic and media policy.

Contact Patricia Hubp, Director of Admission. 52-555-227-4900. Fax: 52-55273-4357. E-mail: martindehubp@asf.edu.mx. Website: www.asf.edu.mx

THE AMERICAN SCHOOL IN EL SALVADOR

VIPSAL 1352
Miami, Florida 33102-5364

Head of School: Mr. Ken Templeton

General Information Coeducational day college-preparatory school. Grades PK–12. Founded: 1946. Setting: urban. Nearest major city is San Salvador, El Salvador. 15-acre campus. 5 buildings on campus. Approved or accredited by Florida Department of Education. Member of National Association of Independent Schools. Total enrollment: 1,605. Upper school average class size: 21. Upper school faculty-student ratio: 1:18. There are 185 required school days per year for Upper School students. Upper School students typically attend 5 days per week. The average school day consists of 5 hours and 55 minutes.

Faculty School total: 170. In upper school: 22 men, 24 women; 15 have advanced degrees.

Subjects Offered Advanced Placement courses, advanced studio art-AP, algebra, American government, American history-AP, American literature-AP, ancient world history, art, art-AP, biology, biology-AP, calculus, calculus-AP, chemistry, chemistry-AP, college counseling, comparative government and politics-AP, Eastern world civilizations, English, English language and composition-AP, English language-AP, English literature, English literature and composition-AP, environmental science, French, French language-AP, geometry, health, honors algebra, honors English, honors U.S. history, honors world history, Italian, Latin American history, life science, life skills, philosophy, photography, physical education, physical science, physics, physics-AP, pre-calculus, pre-calculus, psychology, psychology-AP, SAT preparation, service learning/internship, Spanish, Spanish language-AP, Spanish literature-AP, study skills, U.S. history-AP.

Special Academic Programs Advanced Placement exam preparation.

College Admission Counseling 103 students graduated in 2012; 102 went to college, including Florida International University; Loyola University New Orleans; Savannah College of Art and Design; Texas Christian University; Trinity University.

Student Life Upper grades have uniform requirement, student council, honor system. Discipline rests primarily with faculty.

Tuition and Aid Day student tuition: $7937. Tuition installment plan (monthly payment plans).

Admissions Traditional secondary-level entrance grade is 9. Academic Profile Tests, admissions testing, any standardized test or Iowa Test, CTBS, or TAP required. Deadline for receipt of application materials: none. Application fee required: $50. On-campus interview required.

Athletics Interscholastic: basketball (boys, girls), cross-country running (b,g), handball (b,g), soccer (b,g), table tennis (b,g), volleyball (b,g), wall climbing (b,g); intramural: basketball (b,g), handball (b,g), soccer (b,g), table tennis (b,g), volleyball (b,g); coed interscholastic: cross-country running; coed intramural: basketball, soccer, table tennis, volleyball. 10 PE instructors, 30 coaches.

Computers Computer resources include on-campus library services, Internet access, wireless campus network, Internet filtering or blocking technology. Student e-mail accounts and computer access in designated common areas are available to students. Students grades are available online.

Contact Mrs. Yolanda Lopez, Director of Admissions. 503-252-8822 Ext. 0. Fax: 503-252-8822 Ext. 2. E-mail: lopez.yolanda@amschool.edu.sv. Website: www.amschool.edu.sv

THE AMERICAN SCHOOL OF MADRID

Apartado 80
Madrid 28080, Spain

Head of School: Mr. William D. O'Hale

General Information Coeducational day college-preparatory, arts, and technology school. Grades PK–12. Founded: 1961. Setting: suburban. 4-hectare campus. 3 buildings on campus. Approved or accredited by International Baccalaureate Organization and Middle States Association of Colleges and Schools. Affiliate member of National Association of Independent Schools; member of European Council of International Schools. Language of instruction: English. Total enrollment: 868. Upper school average class size: 20. Upper school faculty-student ratio: 1:8. There are 175 required school days per year for Upper School students. Upper School students typically attend 5 days per week. The average school day consists of 6 hours and 45 minutes.

Upper School Student Profile Grade 9: 67 students (37 boys, 30 girls); Grade 10: 72 students (38 boys, 34 girls); Grade 11: 73 students (38 boys, 35 girls); Grade 12: 72 students (31 boys, 41 girls).

Faculty School total: 103. In upper school: 20 men, 15 women; 30 have advanced degrees.

Subjects Offered 3-dimensional art, algebra, American history, American literature, art, biology, business studies, calculus, chemistry, choir, computer math, computer science, computer skills, computer-aided design, creative writing, debate, earth science, English, English literature, environmental science, European history, expository writing, French, geography, geometry, government/civics, health, history, instrumental music, jazz band, journalism, mathematics, music, orchestra, philosophy, physical education, physics, psychology, science, social studies, Spanish, speech, U.S. history, world history, world literature, world wide web design, yearbook.

Graduation Requirements Electives, English, foreign language, information technology, mathematics, physical education (includes health), science, social studies (includes history).

Special Academic Programs International Baccalaureate program; independent study; ESL (50 students enrolled).

College Admission Counseling 65 students graduated in 2013; 63 went to college, including Georgetown University; New York University; Saint Louis University; Suffolk University; The University of Tampa. Other: 2 entered military service. Mean SAT critical reading: 551, mean SAT math: 566, mean SAT writing: 558.

Student Life Upper grades have specified standards of dress, student council, honor system. Discipline rests equally with students and faculty.

Summer Programs ESL, sports, art/fine arts, computer instruction programs offered; session focuses on ESL, soccer; held on campus; accepts boys and girls; open to students from other schools. 275 students usually enrolled. 2014 schedule: July 1 to July 31. Application deadline: June.

Tuition and Aid Day student tuition: €17,415. Tuition installment plan (monthly payment plans, individually arranged payment plans, semester payment plan). Tuition reduction for siblings, need-based scholarship grants, scholarships for children of employees available. In 2013–14, 5% of upper-school students received aid.

Admissions Traditional secondary-level entrance grade is 11. For fall 2013, 83 students applied for upper-level admission, 50 were accepted, 50 enrolled. Achievement/Aptitude/Writing, Comprehensive Test of Basic Skills, ERB, independent norms, Iowa Tests of Basic Skills, PSAT or TAP required. Deadline for receipt of application materials: none. Application fee required: €140. On-campus interview required.

Athletics Interscholastic: basketball (boys, girls), soccer (b,g), volleyball (b,g); coed interscholastic: golf, gymnastics, martial arts, tennis; coed intramural: weight lifting. 2 PE instructors, 7 coaches.

Computers Computers are regularly used in all classes. Computer network features include on-campus library services, Internet access, wireless campus network, Internet filtering or blocking technology. Campus intranet is available to students. The school has a published electronic and media policy.

Contact Ms. Sholeh Farpour, Admissions Head. 34-91 740 1904. Fax: 34-91 357 2678. E-mail: admissions@asmadrid.org. Website: www.asmadrid.org

ANACAPA SCHOOL

814 Santa Barbara Street
Santa Barbara, California 93101

Head of School: Mr. Gordon Sichi

General Information Coeducational day college-preparatory and arts school. Grades 7–12. Founded: 1981. Setting: urban. 2 buildings on campus. Approved or accredited by Western Association of Schools and Colleges and California Department of Education. Total enrollment: 49. Upper school average class size: 12. Upper school faculty-student ratio: 1:9. Upper School students typically attend 5 days per week. The average school day consists of 7 hours and 10 minutes.

Upper School Student Profile Grade 9: 13 students (6 boys, 7 girls); Grade 10: 4 students (2 boys, 2 girls); Grade 11: 8 students (6 boys, 2 girls); Grade 12: 12 students (4 boys, 8 girls).

Faculty School total: 12. In upper school: 5 men, 5 women; 4 have advanced degrees.

Special Academic Programs Advanced Placement exam preparation.

College Admission Counseling 11 students graduated in 2012; all went to college, including Santa Barbara City College; University of California, Los Angeles; Westmont College.

Student Life Upper grades have specified standards of dress, student council, honor system. Discipline rests primarily with faculty.

Tuition and Aid Tuition installment plan (individually arranged payment plans). Merit scholarship grants, need-based scholarship grants, paying campus jobs available. In 2012–13, 69% of upper-school students received aid.

Admissions Traditional secondary-level entrance grade is 9. For fall 2012, 6 students applied for upper-level admission, 6 were accepted, 5 enrolled. Deadline for receipt of application materials: none. Application fee required: $100. Interview required.

Athletics Coed Intramural: aquatics, backpacking, basketball, canoeing/kayaking, dance, fitness, flag football, hiking/backpacking, jogging, kayaking, outdoor activities, outdoor adventure, running, sailing, scuba diving, skiing (downhill), soccer, softball, squash, surfing, swimming and diving, table tennis, yoga.

Computers Computers are regularly used in all academic classes. Computer resources include Internet access, wireless campus network. Computer access in designated common areas is available to students. The school has a published electronic and media policy.

Contact Ms. Sheryn Sears, Executive Administrator. 805-965-0228. Fax: 805-899-2758. E-mail: anacapa@anacapaschool.org. Website: www.anacapaschool.org

ANNIE WRIGHT SCHOOL

827 North Tacoma Avenue
Tacoma, Washington 98403

Head of School: Mr. Christian Sullivan

General Information Girls' boarding and coeducational day college-preparatory, arts, bilingual studies, technology, and mathematics, science and music school, affiliated with Episcopal Church. Boarding girls grades 9–12, day boys grades PS–8, day girls grades PS–12. Founded: 1884. Setting: suburban. Nearest major city is Seattle. Students are housed in single-sex dormitories. 10-acre campus. 3 buildings on campus. Approved or accredited by International Baccalaureate Organization, National Association of Episcopal Schools, Northwest Accreditation Commission, Northwest Association of Independent Schools, Northwest Association of Schools and Colleges, The Association of Boarding Schools, and Washington Department of Education. Member of National Association of Independent Schools and Secondary School Admission Test Board. Endowment: $15 million. Total enrollment: 467. Upper school average class size: 12. Upper school faculty-student ratio: 1:5. There are 180 required school days per year for Upper School students. Upper School students typically attend 5 days per week. The average school day consists of 7 hours and 10 minutes.

Upper School Student Profile Grade 9: 44 students (44 girls); Grade 10: 40 students (40 girls); Grade 11: 52 students (52 girls); Grade 12: 44 students (44 girls). 55% of students are boarding students. 45% are state residents. 12 states are represented in upper school student body. 37% are international students. International students from China, Japan, Republic of Korea, Taiwan, and Thailand; 9 other countries represented in student body. 10% of students are members of Episcopal Church.

Faculty School total: 85. In upper school: 15 men, 20 women; 15 have advanced degrees; 6 reside on campus.

Subjects Offered Algebra, American history, American literature, anatomy, art, art history, biology, calculus, ceramics, chemistry, computer programming, computer science, creative writing, dance, drama, earth science, economics, English, English literature, ESL, fine arts, French, geometry, government/civics, health, history, Japanese, mathematics, music, music history, physical education, physics, religion, science, social studies, Spanish, theater, world history, world literature.

Graduation Requirements Arts and fine arts (art, music, dance, drama), English, history, mathematics, modern languages, physical education (includes health), religion (includes Bible studies and theology), science, social studies (includes history), swim safety test.

Special Academic Programs International Baccalaureate program; independent study; term-away projects; study abroad; ESL (47 students enrolled).

College Admission Counseling 31 students graduated in 2013; all went to college, including The George Washington University; University of San Francisco; University of Washington. Mean SAT critical reading: 584, mean SAT math: 649, mean SAT writing: 614.

Student Life Upper grades have uniform requirement, student council, honor system. Discipline rests equally with students and faculty.

Tuition and Aid Day student tuition: $22,900; 5-day tuition and room/board: $35,700; 7-day tuition and room/board: $45,950. Tuition installment plan (monthly payment plans, individually arranged payment plans). Merit scholarship grants, need-based scholarship grants available. In 2013–14, 8% of upper-school students received aid; total upper-school merit-scholarship money awarded: $1,093,935. Total amount of financial aid awarded in 2013–14: $1,093,935.

Admissions Traditional secondary-level entrance grade is 9. International English Language Test or TOEFL required. Deadline for receipt of application materials: February 8. Application fee required: $100. Interview required.

Athletics Interscholastic: basketball, cross-country running, golf, running, soccer, tennis, track and field, volleyball. 5 PE instructors, 10 coaches, 1 athletic trainer.

Computers Computers are regularly used in all academic classes. Computer network features include on-campus library services, Internet access, wireless campus network. Student e-mail accounts are available to students. Students grades are available online. The school has a published electronic and media policy.

Contact Ms. Trisha Fintel, Enrollment Assistant. 253-284-8600. Fax: 253-572-3616. E-mail: Trisha_Fintel@aw.org. Website: www.awschools.org/

ARCHBISHOP ALTER HIGH SCHOOL

940 East David Road
Kettering, Ohio 45429-5512

Head of School: Mrs. Lourdes Lambert

General Information Coeducational day college-preparatory, general academic, arts, and religious studies school, affiliated with Roman Catholic Church. Grades 9–12. Founded: 1962. Setting: suburban. Nearest major city is Dayton. 3 buildings on campus. Approved or accredited by National Catholic Education Association, North Central Association of Colleges and Schools, Ohio Catholic Schools Accreditation Association (OCSAA), and Ohio Department of Education. Total enrollment: 673. Upper school average class size: 22. Upper school faculty-student ratio: 1:12. There are 185 required school days per year for Upper School students.

Upper School Student Profile Grade 9: 174 students (103 boys, 71 girls); Grade 10: 174 students (78 boys, 96 girls); Grade 11: 168 students (94 boys, 74 girls); Grade 12: 157 students (86 boys, 71 girls). 90% of students are Roman Catholic.

Faculty School total: 57. In upper school: 22 men, 33 women; 37 have advanced degrees.

Subjects Offered Accounting, advanced chemistry, advanced math, Advanced Placement courses, algebra, American Civil War, American government, American history, American history-AP, American literature, American literature-AP, analysis and differential calculus, analytic geometry, anatomy and physiology, band, Basic programming, biology-AP, British literature, business, business law, calculus, calculus-AP, Catholic belief and practice, chemistry, chemistry-AP, choir, choral music, Christian and Hebrew scripture, church history, Civil War, civil war history, costumes and make-up, ecology, environmental systems, economics, English, English literature, French, health, history, history of the Catholic Church, honors algebra, honors English, honors geometry, honors U.S. history, integrated mathematics, introduction to theater, keyboarding, Latin, marching band, mechanical drawing, music appreciation, personal finance, physical fitness, physics, physics-AP, pre-calculus, public speaking, reading/study skills, Spanish, speech, theater arts, U.S. government and politics-AP, U.S. history, U.S. history-AP.

Graduation Requirements Arts and fine arts (art, music, dance, drama), English, health, keyboarding, mathematics, physical education (includes health), science, social studies (includes history), speech, theology, word processing, additional requirements for students enrolled in the Alter Scholars Program or Conservatory for the Arts.

Special Academic Programs Advanced Placement exam preparation; honors section; study at local college for college credit.

College Admission Counseling 156 students graduated in 2013; 153 went to college, including Miami University; Ohio University; The Ohio State University; University of Cincinnati; University of Dayton; Wright State University. Other: 2 went to work, 1 had other specific plans. Mean SAT critical reading: 571, mean SAT math: 589, mean SAT writing: 573, mean combined SAT: 1733, mean composite ACT: 25.

Student Life Upper grades have uniform requirement, student council, honor system. Discipline rests equally with students and faculty. Attendance at religious services is required.

Tuition and Aid Day student tuition: $5960–$8690. Tuition installment plan (FACTS Tuition Payment Plan). Tuition reduction for siblings, merit scholarship grants, need-based scholarship grants available. In 2013–14, 15% of upper-school students received aid; total upper-school merit-scholarship money awarded: $32,000. Total amount of financial aid awarded in 2013–14: $150,000.

Admissions Traditional secondary-level entrance grade is 9. For fall 2013, 190 students applied for upper-level admission, 185 were accepted, 174 enrolled. Scholastic Testing Service High School Placement Test (open version) or STS required. Deadline for receipt of application materials: December 1. Application fee required: $100.

Athletics Interscholastic: baseball (boys), basketball (b,g), bowling (b,g), cheering (g), cross-country running (b,g), dance team (g), diving (b,g), football (b), golf (b,g), gymnastics (g), ice hockey (b,g), lacrosse (b), soccer (b,g), softball (g), strength & conditioning (b,g), swimming and diving (b,g), tennis (b,g), track and field (b,g), volleyball (b,g), wrestling (b). 1 PE instructor, 3 coaches, 1 athletic trainer.

Computers Computers are regularly used in all classes. Computer network features include on-campus library services, online commercial services, Internet access, wireless campus network, Internet filtering or blocking technology, 1:1 laptop program. Campus intranet, student e-mail accounts, and computer access in designated common areas are available to students. Students grades are available online. The school has a published electronic and media policy.

Contact Mrs. Mary Ruth Shearer, Director of Enrollment Management. 937-428-5394. Fax: 937-434-0507. E-mail: maryruth.shearer@alterhs.org. Website: www.alterhighschool.org

ARCHBISHOP CURLEY HIGH SCHOOL

3701 Sinclair Lane
Baltimore, Maryland 21213

Head of School: Fr. Joseph Benicewicz

General Information Boys' day college-preparatory school, affiliated with Roman Catholic Church. Grades 9–12. Founded: 1961. Setting: urban. 33-acre campus. 3 buildings on campus. Approved or accredited by Middle States Association of Colleges and Schools and Maryland Department of Education. Endowment: $3.2 million. Total enrollment: 526. Upper school average class size: 22. Upper school faculty-student ratio: 1:14. Upper School students typically attend 5 days per week. The average school day consists of 6 hours and 30 minutes.

Upper School Student Profile Grade 9: 154 students (154 boys); Grade 10: 127 students (127 boys); Grade 11: 124 students (124 boys); Grade 12: 128 students (128 boys). 65% of students are Roman Catholic.

Faculty School total: 54. In upper school: 42 men, 12 women; 24 have advanced degrees.

Subjects Offered 20th century world history, 3-dimensional design, advanced chemistry, advanced computer applications, advanced math, algebra, American government, American history, American history-AP, American literature, analytic geometry, art, art appreciation, astronomy, band, Basic programming, biology, biology-AP, British literature, British literature (honors), business law, business mathematics, calculus, calculus-AP, campus ministry, Catholic belief and practice, chemistry, chemistry-AP, choral music, Christian and Hebrew scripture, Christian doctrine, Christian ethics, computer applications, computer studies, concert band, consumer law, consumer mathematics, earth science, English, English literature and composition-AP, environmental science, ethical decision making, European history, fine arts, French, freshman seminar, geography, geometry, government, government-AP, health, history of the Catholic Church, HTML design, instrumental music, jazz band, journalism, keyboarding, Latin, Life of Christ, music theory, photography, physical science, physics, physics-AP, pre-algebra, pre-calculus, probability and statistics, psychology, psychology-AP, reading/study skills, SAT/ACT preparation, Spanish, Spanish language-AP, U.S. government and politics-AP.

Graduation Requirements Algebra, American government, American history, art appreciation, biology, British literature, chemistry, church history, computer applications, English, foreign language, geometry, keyboarding, Life of Christ, physical fitness, physics, world history, world religions, 30 hours of community service with a written paper.

Special Academic Programs Advanced Placement exam preparation; honors section; independent study; study at local college for college credit; remedial reading and/or remedial writing; remedial math; programs in English, mathematics for dyslexic students.

College Admission Counseling 128 students graduated in 2013; they went to Loyola University Maryland; Mount St. Mary's University; Stevenson University; Towson University; University of Maryland, College Park; York College of Pennsylvania.

Student Life Upper grades have specified standards of dress, student council, honor system. Discipline rests primarily with faculty. Attendance at religious services is required.

Summer Programs Remediation, enrichment, advancement, sports, art/fine arts, computer instruction programs offered; held on campus; accepts boys and girls; open to students from other schools. 2014 schedule: June 15 to August 9. Application deadline: June 15.

Tuition and Aid Day student tuition: $11,800. Tuition installment plan (FACTS Tuition Payment Plan, monthly payment plans, individually arranged payment plans). Tuition reduction for siblings, merit scholarship grants, need-based scholarship grants, paying campus jobs available.

Admissions Traditional secondary-level entrance grade is 9. For fall 2013, 300 students applied for upper-level admission, 154 enrolled. High School Placement Test (closed version) from Scholastic Testing Service required. Deadline for receipt of application materials: December 17. Application fee required: $25. Interview required.

Athletics Interscholastic: baseball, basketball, cross-country running, football, golf, indoor track & field, lacrosse, soccer, swimming and diving, tennis, track and field, volleyball, wrestling; intramural: basketball, flag football, Frisbee, handball, martial arts, touch football, weight lifting, weight training. 2 PE instructors, 32 coaches, 1 athletic trainer.

Computers Computers are regularly used in creative writing, English, graphic arts, journalism, library, photography, SAT preparation, science, technology classes. Computer network features include on-campus library services, Internet access, wireless campus network, Internet filtering or blocking technology. Student e-mail accounts are available to students. Students grades are available online. The school has a published electronic and media policy.

Contact Mr. Nick Brownlee, Admissions Director. 410-485-5000 Ext. 289. Fax: 410-485-1090. E-mail: nbrownlee@archbishopcurley.org. Website: www.archbishopcurley.org

ARCHBISHOP HOBAN HIGH SCHOOL

1 Holy Cross Boulevard
Akron, Ohio 44306

Head of School: Dr. Todd R. Sweda, EdD

General Information Coeducational day college-preparatory, arts, business, religious studies, and technology school, affiliated with Roman Catholic Church. Grades 9–12. Founded: 1953. Setting: urban. 75-acre campus. 3 buildings on campus. Approved or accredited by National Catholic Education Association, North Central Association of Colleges and Schools, Ohio Catholic Schools Accreditation Association (OCSAA), and Ohio Department of Education. Endowment: $7 million. Total enrollment: 861. Upper school average class size: 23. Upper school faculty-student ratio: 1:15. There are 178 required school days per year for Upper School students. Upper School students typically attend 5 days per week. The average school day consists of 6 hours and 55 minutes.

Upper School Student Profile Grade 9: 240 students (126 boys, 114 girls); Grade 10: 214 students (103 boys, 111 girls); Grade 11: 207 students (100 boys, 107 girls); Grade 12: 200 students (102 boys, 98 girls). 80% of students are Roman Catholic.

Faculty School total: 58. In upper school: 26 men, 32 women; 41 have advanced degrees.

Subjects Offered Advanced chemistry, advanced math, Advanced Placement courses, advanced studio art-AP, algebra, American literature, anatomy and physiology, art, art history-AP, astronomy, biology, biology-AP, British literature, calculus-AP, Catholic belief and practice, ceramics, chemistry, chemistry-AP, Chinese, Christian and Hebrew scripture, church history, clayworking, computer applications, computer graphics, conceptual physics, concert choir, desktop publishing, digital imaging, digital music, drawing, earth science, economics, electronic music, engineering, English, English language and composition-AP, English literature and composition-AP, ensembles, environmental science, environmental studies, European history-AP, fine arts, French, French language-AP, geometry, guitar, health education, history of the Catholic Church, honors algebra, honors English, honors geometry, honors world history, human anatomy, Italian, Latin, learning strategies, moral and social development, newspaper, orchestra, painting, philosophy, physical education, physics, physics-AP, pre-algebra, pre-calculus, printmaking, psychology, psychology-AP, social justice, Spanish, statistics-AP, studio art, television, trigonometry, U.S. government, U.S. history, U.S. history-AP, values and decisions, Web site design, world cultures, world literature, yearbook.

Graduation Requirements Algebra, arts and fine arts (art, music, dance, drama), biology, economics, electives, English, health education, mathematics, physical education (includes health), religious studies, science, social studies (includes history), U.S. government, U.S. government and politics-AP, Christian service totaling 75 hours over four years.

Special Academic Programs 15 Advanced Placement exams for which test preparation is offered; honors section; academic accommodation for the gifted; remedial reading and/or remedial writing; remedial math.

College Admission Counseling 198 students graduated in 2013; 196 went to college, including Kent State University; Ohio University; The Ohio State University; The University of Akron; The University of Toledo; University of Dayton. Other: 1 went to work, 1 entered military service. Median SAT critical reading: 550, median SAT math: 560, median SAT writing: 560, median combined SAT: 1670, median composite ACT: 23. 31% scored over 600 on SAT critical reading, 32% scored over 600 on SAT math, 32% scored over 600 on SAT writing, 31% scored over 1800 on combined SAT, 23% scored over 26 on composite ACT.

Student Life Upper grades have specified standards of dress, student council, honor system. Discipline rests primarily with faculty. Attendance at religious services is required.

Tuition and Aid Day student tuition: $9400. Tuition installment plan (FACTS Tuition Payment Plan, individually arranged payment plans, semester payment plan, quarterly payment plan). Tuition reduction for siblings, merit scholarship grants, need-based scholarship grants, paying campus jobs available. In 2013–14, 66% of upper-school students received aid; total upper-school merit-scholarship money awarded: $250,000. Total amount of financial aid awarded in 2013–14: $2,200,000.

Admissions Traditional secondary-level entrance grade is 9. For fall 2013, 324 students applied for upper-level admission, 276 were accepted, 254 enrolled. High School Placement Test required. Deadline for receipt of application materials: none. No application fee required. Interview recommended.

Athletics Interscholastic: baseball (boys), basketball (b,g), bowling (b,g), cross-country running (b,g), dance team (g), football (b), golf (b,g), gymnastics (g), indoor track & field (b,g), lacrosse (b,g), soccer (b,g), softball (g), swimming and diving (b,g), tennis (b,g), track and field (b,g), volleyball (b,g), wrestling (b); intramural: flag football (g); coed interscholastic: cheering; coed intramural: basketball, strength & conditioning, ultimate Frisbee, weight training. 1 PE instructor, 1 athletic trainer.

Computers Computers are regularly used in graphic design, newspaper, science, video film production, Web site design, yearbook classes. Computer network features include on-campus library services, Internet access, wireless campus network, Internet filtering or blocking technology. Campus intranet, student e-mail accounts, and computer access in designated common areas are available to students. Students grades are available online. The school has a published electronic and media policy.

Contact Mr. Christopher Fahey, Admissions Counselor. 330-773-6658 Ext. 215. Fax: 330-773-9100. E-mail: Faheyc@hoban.org. Website: www.hoban.org

ARCHBISHOP MITTY HIGH SCHOOL

5000 Mitty Avenue
San Jose, California 95129

Head of School: Mr. Tim Brosnan

General Information Coeducational day college-preparatory, arts, religious studies, and technology school, affiliated with Roman Catholic Church. Grades 9–12. Founded: 1964. Setting: suburban. 24-acre campus. 11 buildings on campus. Approved or accredited by National Catholic Education Association, Western Association of Schools and Colleges, and California Department of Education. Endowment: $11.5 million. Total enrollment: 1,725. Upper school average class size: 27. Upper school faculty-student ratio: 1:17. There are 180 required school days per year for Upper School students. Upper School students typically attend 5 days per week. The average school day consists of 6 hours and 45 minutes.

Upper School Student Profile Grade 9: 434 students (218 boys, 216 girls); Grade 10: 443 students (230 boys, 213 girls); Grade 11: 451 students (207 boys, 244 girls); Grade 12: 397 students (183 boys, 214 girls). 75% of students are Roman Catholic.

Faculty School total: 110. In upper school: 55 men, 55 women; 75 have advanced degrees.

Subjects Offered 3-dimensional art, acting, American history-AP, American literature-AP, ancient world history, art, biology, biology-AP, British literature, calculus, calculus-AP, Catholic belief and practice, chemistry, chemistry-AP, choral music, chorus, church history, college placement, college writing, community service, computer graphics, computer multimedia, concert band, concert choir, drawing, economics and history, English, English language and composition-AP, English literature, English literature-AP, French, French language-AP, French literature-AP, French studies, French-AP, geometry, history-AP, honors algebra, honors English, honors geometry, honors U.S. history, honors world history, music, music appreciation, music theory-AP, philosophy, physics, physics-AP, political science, religion, social sciences, Spanish, Spanish language-AP, Spanish literature, Spanish literature-AP, student government, theater arts, U.S. government and politics, U.S. government and politics-AP, U.S. history, U.S. history-AP, U.S. literature, visual and performing arts, visual arts, world history.

Graduation Requirements Art, English, foreign language, mathematics, philosophy, physical education (includes health), religious studies, science, social sciences, 80 hours of Christian service.

Special Academic Programs 18 Advanced Placement exams for which test preparation is offered; honors section; study at local college for college credit; academic accommodation for the gifted, the musically talented, and the artistically talented.

College Admission Counseling 389 students graduated in 2013; all went to college, including California Polytechnic State University, San Luis Obispo; Santa Clara University; Stanford University; University of California, Berkeley; University of California, Davis; University of California, Los Angeles. Mean SAT critical reading: 600, mean SAT math: 608, mean SAT writing: 623, mean combined SAT: 1831, mean composite ACT: 27.

Student Life Upper grades have specified standards of dress, student council, honor system. Discipline rests primarily with faculty. Attendance at religious services is required.

Summer Programs Remediation, enrichment, advancement, sports, art/fine arts, computer instruction programs offered; session focuses on academics and athletics; held on campus; accepts boys and girls; open to students from other schools. 500 students usually enrolled. 2014 schedule: June 12 to July 17. Application deadline: May 31.

Tuition and Aid Day student tuition: $16,350. Tuition installment plan (SMART Tuition Payment Plan). Need-based scholarship grants, paying campus jobs available. In 2013–14, 25% of upper-school students received aid. Total amount of financial aid awarded in 2013–14: $3,300,000.

Admissions Traditional secondary-level entrance grade is 9. For fall 2013, 1,400 students applied for upper-level admission, 434 were accepted, 434 enrolled. High School Placement Test required. Deadline for receipt of application materials: December 13. Application fee required: $75.

Athletics Interscholastic: aquatics (boys, girls), badminton (b,g), baseball (b), basketball (b,g), cross-country running (b,g), dance team (g), diving (b,g), field hockey (g), football (b), golf (b,g), lacrosse (b,g), soccer (b,g), softball (g), swimming and diving (b,g), tennis (b,g), track and field (b,g), volleyball (b,g), water polo (b,g), weight training (b,g), winter soccer (b,g); intramural: roller hockey (b,g); coed interscholastic: physical fitness, strength & conditioning, wrestling; coed intramural: basketball, ice hockey, in-line hockey, table tennis. 4 PE instructors, 110 coaches, 2 athletic trainers.

Computers Computers are regularly used in all classes. Computer network features include on-campus library services, online commercial services, Internet access, wireless campus network, Internet filtering or blocking technology. Campus intranet, student e-mail accounts, and computer access in designated common areas are available to students. Students grades are available online. The school has a published electronic and media policy.

Contact Mrs. Lori Robowski, Assistant for Admissions. 408-342-4300. Fax: 408-342-4308. E-mail: admissions@mitty.com. Website: www.mitty.com/

ARCHBISHOP SHAW HIGH SCHOOL

1000 Barataria Boulevard
Marrero, Louisiana 70072-3052

Head of School: Mr. George Hebert Jr.

General Information Boys' day college-preparatory, arts, religious studies, and technology school, affiliated with Roman Catholic Church. Grades 8–12. Founded: 1962. Setting: suburban. Nearest major city is New Orleans. 71-acre campus. 5 buildings on campus. Approved or accredited by National Catholic Education Association, Southern Association of Colleges and Schools, and Louisiana Department of Education. Total enrollment: 655. Upper school average class size: 24. Upper school faculty-student ratio: 1:24.

Upper School Student Profile Grade 10: 158 students (158 boys); Grade 11: 119 students (119 boys); Grade 12: 138 students (138 boys). 85% of students are Roman Catholic.

Faculty School total: 47. In upper school: 24 men, 18 women; 30 have advanced degrees.

Subjects Offered 20th century history, accounting, advanced math, algebra, art, band, Bible studies, biology, British literature, business law, calculus, calculus-AP, Catholic belief and practice, chemistry, Christian and Hebrew scripture, Christian doctrine, Christian ethics, Christian testament, Christianity, civics, civics/free enterprise, college counseling, college writing, community service, composition, computer applications, computer literacy, computer science-AP, concert band, driver education, earth science, economics, English, English composition, English literature, ethical decision making, fitness, French, geometry, guidance, health, history, history of the Catholic Church, history-AP, honors algebra, honors English, honors geometry, honors world history, human sexuality, instrumental music, Internet, jazz band, keyboarding, lab science, marching band, moral theology, music, physical education, pre-algebra, pre-calculus, psychology, religious studies, SAT/ACT preparation, Spanish, symphonic band, U.S. history, U.S. history-AP, wind instruments, world geography, world history.

Graduation Requirements Algebra, American history, biology, chemistry, civics/free enterprise, earth science, English composition, English literature, foreign language, geometry, health, mathematics, physical fitness, physical science, religious studies, world geography, world history, 50 service hours.

Special Academic Programs Advanced Placement exam preparation; honors section; study at local college for college credit.

College Admission Counseling 110 students graduated in 2013; 95 went to college, including Louisiana State University and Agricultural and Mechanical College; Louisiana Tech University; University of Louisiana at Lafayette; University of New Orleans. Other: 10 went to work, 5 had other specific plans. Median composite ACT: 21. 15% scored over 26 on composite ACT.

Student Life Upper grades have uniform requirement, student council, honor system. Discipline rests primarily with faculty. Attendance at religious services is required.

Tuition and Aid Day student tuition: $5380. Tuition installment plan (monthly payment plans, individually arranged payment plans, Local Bank). Merit scholarship grants, need-based scholarship grants, paying campus jobs, educational bank loan financing available. In 2013–14, 10% of upper-school students received aid.

Admissions Traditional secondary-level entrance grade is 10. For fall 2013, 190 students applied for upper-level admission, 180 were accepted, 176 enrolled. High School Placement Test (closed version) from Scholastic Testing Service required. Deadline for receipt of application materials: none. Application fee required: $20. On-campus interview required.

Athletics Interscholastic: baseball, basketball, bowling, cross-country running, football, golf, running, soccer, tennis, track and field, wrestling; intramural: basketball, flag football, football, rugby, volleyball. 3 PE instructors, 9 coaches, 1 athletic trainer.

Computers Computers are regularly used in all academic classes. Computer network features include on-campus library services, online commercial services, Internet access, wireless campus network, Internet filtering or blocking technology. Students grades are available online. The school has a published electronic and media policy.

Contact Mr. Matthew Ducote, Admissions Director. 504-340-6727 Ext. 52. Fax: 504-347-9883. E-mail: shawadm@archdiocese-no.org. Website: www.archbishopshaw.org

ARCHBISHOP THOMAS J. MURPHY HIGH SCHOOL

12911 39th Avenue SE
Everett, Washington 98208

Head of School: Steve Schmutz

General Information Coeducational day college-preparatory, arts, and religious studies school, affiliated with Roman Catholic Church. Grades 9–12. Founded: 1988. Setting: suburban. 4-acre campus. 3 buildings on campus. Approved or accredited by Northwest Association of Schools and Colleges and Washington Department of

Education. Upper school average class size: 21. Upper school faculty-student ratio: 1:14. The average school day consists of 6 hours.

Faculty School total: 42. In upper school: 28 have advanced degrees.

Subjects Offered Acting, algebra, art, biology, calculus, chemistry, civics, computer applications, creative writing, design, economics, English, environmental science, geometry, graphic design, health, math analysis, physical education, physics, psychology, social sciences, Spanish, theology, trigonometry, U.S. history, vocal music, Washington State and Northwest History, world history, yearbook.

Graduation Requirements Arts and fine arts (art, music, dance, drama), business skills (includes word processing), English, foreign language, mathematics, physical education (includes health), religion (includes Bible studies and theology), science, social sciences. Community service is required.

Special Academic Programs Advanced Placement exam preparation; honors section; independent study; study at local college for college credit; ESL (20 students enrolled).

College Admission Counseling 122 students graduated in 2013; 120 went to college, including Gonzaga University; Seattle University; University of Portland; University of Washington; Washington State University; Western Washington University. Other: 2 went to work.

Student Life Upper grades have specified standards of dress, student council, honor system. Discipline rests primarily with faculty. Attendance at religious services is required.

Tuition and Aid Day student tuition: $13,395. Tuition installment plan (monthly payment plans). Tuition reduction for siblings, need-based scholarship grants available. In 2013–14, 34% of upper-school students received aid. Total amount of financial aid awarded in 2013–14: $800,000.

Admissions ISEE required. Deadline for receipt of application materials: none. Application fee required: $25.

Athletics Interscholastic: baseball (boys), basketball (b,g), cheering (g), cross-country running (b,g), diving (b,g), football (b), golf (b,g), lacrosse (b,g), soccer (b,g), softball (g), tennis (b,g), volleyball (g), wrestling (b); coed interscholastic: basketball, cross-country running, diving, golf, tennis, track and field. 2 PE instructors.

Computers Computer network features include Internet access.

Contact Mary Thompson, Admissions Assistant. 425-379-6363. Fax: 425-385-2875. E-mail: mthompson@am-hs.org. Website: www.am-hs.org

ARMY AND NAVY ACADEMY

2605 Carlsbad Boulevard
PO Box 3000
Carlsbad, California 92018-3000

Head of School: Brig. Gen. Stephen M. Bliss, Retd.

General Information Boys' boarding and day college-preparatory, Junior ROTC, and military school. Grades 7–12. Founded: 1910. Setting: small town. Nearest major city is San Diego. Students are housed in single-sex dormitories. 16-acre campus. 34 buildings on campus. Approved or accredited by California Association of Independent Schools and Western Association of Schools and Colleges. Member of National Association of Independent Schools and Secondary School Admission Test Board. Endowment: $560,414. Total enrollment: 302. Upper school average class size: 15. Upper school faculty-student ratio: 1:15. There are 180 required school days per year for Upper School students. Upper School students typically attend 5 days per week. The average school day consists of 7 hours.

Upper School Student Profile Grade 10: 69 students (69 boys); Grade 11: 86 students (86 boys); Grade 12: 69 students (69 boys). 90% of students are boarding students. 55% are state residents. 12 states are represented in upper school student body. 45% are international students. International students from China, Malaysia, Mexico, Russian Federation, Taiwan, and Viet Nam; 15 other countries represented in student body.

Faculty School total: 32. In upper school: 14 men, 18 women; 15 have advanced degrees; 1 resides on campus.

Subjects Offered Algebra, art, biology, biology-AP, calculus-AP, chemistry, chemistry-AP, composition-AP, drama, economics, English, English literature-AP, English-AP, ESL, European history-AP, French, geography, geometry, German, guitar, independent study, JROTC, Mandarin, marching band, music technology, photography, physical education, physics, physics-AP, pre-calculus, psychology-AP, Spanish, Spanish-AP, sports psychology, studio art-AP, study skills, U.S. government, U.S. history, U.S. history-AP, video film production, weight training, world history, yearbook.

Graduation Requirements Arts and fine arts (art, music, dance, drama), electives, English, foreign language, lab science, leadership education training, mathematics, physical education (includes health), social studies (includes history).

Special Academic Programs 8 Advanced Placement exams for which test preparation is offered; honors section; independent study; special instructional classes for students with Attention Deficit Disorder and learning disabilities; ESL (37 students enrolled).

College Admission Counseling 83 students graduated in 2013; 76 went to college, including Arizona State University; University of California, Irvine; University of California, Los Angeles; University of California, Riverside; University of California, San Diego; University of Illinois at Urbana–Champaign. Other: 5 entered military service, 2 had other specific plans. Median SAT critical reading: 470, median SAT math: 540, median SAT writing: 470.

Student Life Upper grades have uniform requirement, student council, honor system. Discipline rests primarily with faculty.

Summer Programs Remediation, enrichment, ESL, sports, art/fine arts, rigorous outdoor training, computer instruction programs offered; session focuses on academic, JROTC leadership, and recreation; held on campus; accepts boys and girls; open to students from other schools. 300 students usually enrolled. 2014 schedule: June 30 to August 4. Application deadline: none.

Tuition and Aid Day student tuition: $20,400; 7-day tuition and room/board: $34,500. Tuition installment plan (individually arranged payment plans). Tuition reduction for siblings, need-based scholarship grants, military discount available. In 2013–14, 16% of upper-school students received aid. Total amount of financial aid awarded in 2013–14: $329,175.

Admissions Traditional secondary-level entrance grade is 10. For fall 2013, 121 students applied for upper-level admission, 62 were accepted, 59 enrolled. ISEE, Otis-Lennon School Ability Test, SSAT, Star-9 or TOEFL required. Deadline for receipt of application materials: none. Application fee required: $100. Interview required.

Athletics Interscholastic: aquatics, baseball, basketball, cross-country running, drill team, football, golf, in-line hockey, marksmanship, riflery, soccer, surfing, swimming and diving, tennis, track and field, water polo, weight lifting, wrestling; intramural: aquatics, combined training, fitness, hockey, independent competitive sports, JROTC drill, outdoor activities, outdoor recreation, physical fitness, physical training, strength & conditioning, surfing. 15 coaches, 1 athletic trainer.

Computers Computers are regularly used in media, music technology, video film production, yearbook classes. Computer network features include on-campus library services, Internet access, wireless campus network, Internet filtering or blocking technology. Computer access in designated common areas is available to students. Students grades are available online. The school has a published electronic and media policy.

Contact Candice Heidenrich, Director of Admissions. 888-762-2338. Fax: 760-434-5948. E-mail: admissions@armyandnavyacademy.org. Website: www.armyandnavyacademy.org

ARROWSMITH SCHOOL

Toronto, Ontario, Canada
See Special Needs Schools section.

ARROYO PACIFIC ACADEMY

41 West Santa Clara Street
Arcadia, California 91007-0661

Head of School: Philip Clarke

General Information Coeducational day college-preparatory and arts school. Grades 9–12. Founded: 1998. Setting: suburban. 2 buildings on campus. Approved or accredited by Western Association of Schools and Colleges and California Department of Education. Upper school average class size: 12. Upper school faculty-student ratio: 1:8. There are 160 required school days per year for Upper School students. Upper School students typically attend 5 days per week. The average school day consists of 6 hours.

Faculty School total: 22. In upper school: 13 men, 9 women.

Subjects Offered Acting, advanced biology, advanced chemistry, advanced math, Advanced Placement courses, algebra, American government, American history, American history-AP, American literature, American literature-AP, American sign language, applied arts, applied music, art, ASB Leadership, athletics, basketball, biology-AP, British literature, broadcast journalism, broadcasting, business, business mathematics, calculus-AP, career and personal planning, career/college preparation, chemistry, chemistry-AP, China/Japan history, Chinese, Chinese history, Chinese literature, Chinese studies, choir, chorus, cinematography, classical music, college admission preparation, college counseling, college planning, college writing, computer art, computer education, computer graphics, computer music, computer skills, computer technologies, conceptual physics, creative arts, creative dance, creative drama, creative thinking, creative writing, culinary arts, dance, dance performance, digital art, digital music, drama, drama performance, dramatic arts, drawing, earth science, economics-AP, English, English language and composition-AP, English language-AP, English literature and composition-AP, English literature-AP, English-AP, environmental science, environmental science-AP, film, filmmaking, fine arts, fitness, food and nutrition, foreign language, forensics, geometry, government-AP, graphic design, health education, history, history of music, history-AP, instrumental music, instruments, intro to computers, introduction to digital multitrack recording techniques, introduction to technology, introduction to theater, jazz, jazz band, jazz ensemble, lab science, lab/keyboard, literature and composition-AP, macro/microeconomics-AP, Mandarin, mathematics-AP, media, media arts, media communications, media production, microeconomics-AP, modern Chinese history, music, music appreciation, music composition, music history, music performance, music technology, music theater, musical productions, musical theater, musical theater dance, nutrition, orchestra, outdoor education, participation in sports, personal finance, personal fitness, personal money management, photo shop, photography, photojournalism, physical education, physical fitness, physics, physics-AP, play production, play/screen writing, playwriting, playwriting and directing, poetry, pre-algebra, pre-calculus, psychology, SAT preparation, scene study, science, science and technology, sign language, Spanish, Spanish language-AP, Spanish-AP, stage and body movement, stage design, statistics, statistics-AP, student government, theater, theater arts, theater design and production, theater production, trigonometry, U.S. government, U.S. government and politics, U.S. government and politics-AP, U.S. history, U.S. history-AP, United States government-AP, video film production, visual and performing arts, visual arts, vocal ensemble, vocal music, voice, volleyball, world history, world history-AP.

Special Academic Programs 11 Advanced Placement exams for which test preparation is offered; independent study.

College Admission Counseling 50 students graduated in 2012; they went to Kent State University; University of California, Irvine; University of Southern California.

Student Life Upper grades have specified standards of dress, student council, honor system. Discipline rests primarily with faculty.

Tuition and Aid Day student tuition: $14,500. Tuition installment plan (FACTS Tuition Payment Plan).

Admissions Deadline for receipt of application materials: none. Application fee required: $150. Interview required.

Athletics Interscholastic: basketball (boys), flag football (b), rugby (b); intramural: cheering (g); coed interscholastic: soccer, tennis, track and field; coed intramural: aerobics, aerobics/dance, backpacking, dance, dance squad, dance team, fitness, hiking/backpacking, outdoor skills, outdoors, physical fitness.

Computers Computers are regularly used in all classes. Computer resources include Internet access, advanced photo/video design software. Campus intranet and computer access in designated common areas are available to students.

Contact Aling Zhang, Admissions Coordinator. 626-294-0661. E-mail: azhang@arroyopacific.org. Website: www.arroyopacific.org/

ARTHUR MORGAN SCHOOL

Burnsville, North Carolina
See Junior Boarding Schools section.

ASHLEY HALL

172 Rutledge Avenue
Charleston, South Carolina 29403-5877

Head of School: Jill Swisher Muti

General Information Coeducational day (boys' only in lower grades) college-preparatory, arts, technology, and science, mathematics school. Boys grades PS–K, girls grades PS–12. Founded: 1909. Setting: urban. 16-acre campus. 4 buildings on campus. Approved or accredited by South Carolina Independent School Association, Southern Association of Colleges and Schools, and Southern Association of Independent Schools. Member of National Association of Independent Schools. Endowment: $12 million. Total enrollment: 677. Upper school average class size: 16. Upper school faculty-student ratio: 1:8.

Upper School Student Profile Grade 7: 55 students (55 girls); Grade 8: 49 students (49 girls); Grade 9: 50 students (50 girls); Grade 10: 58 students (58 girls); Grade 11: 42 students (42 girls); Grade 12: 50 students (50 girls).

Faculty School total: 85. In upper school: 8 men, 20 women; 18 have advanced degrees.

Subjects Offered 3-dimensional design, algebra, American history, American history-AP, American literature, art, art history, art history-AP, bioethics, biology, biology-AP, calculus, calculus-AP, ceramics, chemistry, chemistry-AP, choir, computer science, creative writing, desktop publishing, drama, economics, economics and history, English, English literature, English-AP, European history, European history-AP, forensics, foundations of civilization, French, French-AP, geography, geometry, government/civics, history, Internet, keyboarding, Latin, Latin-AP, marine biology, mathematics, microeconomics-AP, music, photo shop, photography, physical education, physical science, physics, physics-AP, pre-calculus, programming, psychology, social studies, Spanish, Spanish-AP, speech, statistics, statistics-AP, studio art, studio art-AP, technology, trigonometry, U.S. government and politics-AP, Web site design, world history.

Graduation Requirements Advanced Placement courses, arts and fine arts (art, music, dance, drama), English, foreign language, history, mathematics, physical education (includes health), science.

Special Academic Programs Advanced Placement exam preparation; honors section; independent study; term-away projects; study at local college for college credit; study abroad; academic accommodation for the gifted, the musically talented, and the artistically talented.

College Admission Counseling 36 students graduated in 2013; all went to college, including Clemson University; College of Charleston; Dartmouth College; Sewanee: The University of the South; The University of North Carolina at Chapel Hill; University of South Carolina.

Student Life Upper grades have uniform requirement, student council, honor system. Discipline rests equally with students and faculty.

Summer Programs Enrichment, sports, art/fine arts, computer instruction programs offered; session focuses on enrichment, athletics, adventure, and day camps; held on campus; accepts boys and girls; open to students from other schools. 900 students usually enrolled. 2014 schedule: June 1 to July 28. Application deadline: none.

Tuition and Aid Day student tuition: $13,565–$20,735; 7-day tuition and room/board: $48,230. Tuition installment plan (FACTS Tuition Payment Plan). Need-based scholarship grants, paying campus jobs available. In 2013–14, 23% of upper-school students received aid. Total amount of financial aid awarded in 2013–14: $1,215,000.

Admissions Traditional secondary-level entrance grade is 9. For fall 2013, 47 students applied for upper-level admission, 45 were accepted, 24 enrolled. ISEE, Kaufman Test of Educational Achievement or SSAT required. Deadline for receipt of application materials: February 1. Application fee required: $75. Interview required.

Athletics Interscholastic: basketball, cross-country running, running, sailing, soccer, softball, strength & conditioning, swimming and diving, tennis, track and field, volleyball; intramural: aerobics/dance, aquatics, backpacking; basketball, canoeing/kayaking, climbing, cross-country running, dance, dance squad, dance team, equestrian sports, fitness, golf, hiking/backpacking, horseback riding, jogging, judo, jump rope, kayaking, kickball, life saving, martial arts, mountain biking, mountaineering, outdoor adventure, outdoor education, outdoor skills, physical fitness, physical training, rock climbing, running, soccer, softball, strength & conditioning, swimming and diving, tennis, track and field, volleyball, walking, weight training. 2 PE instructors, 4 coaches, 1 athletic trainer.

Computers Computers are regularly used in animation, art, career exploration, college planning, desktop publishing, graphic design, independent study, introduction to technology, library skills, newspaper, photography, research skills, SAT preparation, video film production, Web site design, yearbook classes. Computer network features include on-campus library services, online commercial services, Internet access, wireless campus network, Internet filtering or blocking technology. The school has a published electronic and media policy.

Contact Katie Ozburn, Associate Director of Admissions. 843-965-8501. Fax: 843-720-2868. E-mail: ozburnk@ashleyhall.org. Website: www.ashleyhall.org

ASSETS SCHOOL

Honolulu, Hawaii
See Special Needs Schools section.

THE ATHENIAN SCHOOL

2100 Mount Diablo Scenic Boulevard
Danville, California 94506

Head of School: Eric Feron Niles

General Information Coeducational boarding and day college-preparatory school. Boarding grades 9–12, day grades 6–12. Founded: 1965. Setting: suburban. Nearest major city is San Francisco. Students are housed in single-sex dormitories. 75-acre campus. 25 buildings on campus. Approved or accredited by The Association of Boarding Schools, The College Board, Western Association of Schools and Colleges, and California Department of Education. Member of National Association of Independent Schools and Secondary School Admission Test Board. Endowment: $9 million. Total enrollment: 476. Upper school average class size: 15. Upper school faculty-student ratio: 1:10. Upper School students typically attend 5 days per week. The average school day consists of 5 hours and 35 minutes.

Upper School Student Profile Grade 9: 72 students (33 boys, 39 girls); Grade 10: 82 students (42 boys, 40 girls); Grade 11: 81 students (37 boys, 44 girls); Grade 12: 76 students (41 boys, 35 girls). 14% of students are boarding students. 90% are state residents. 3 states are represented in upper school student body. 13% are international students. International students from China, Japan, Republic of Korea, Russian Federation, Taiwan, and Viet Nam; 7 other countries represented in student body.

Faculty School total: 55. In upper school: 27 men, 24 women; 37 have advanced degrees; 25 reside on campus.

Subjects Offered African-American studies, algebra, American history, American literature, American literature-AP, anatomy, art, art history, Asian history, Asian literature, biology, calculus-AP, ceramics, chemistry, classical studies, college writing, community service, comparative cultures, comparative religion, computer programming, computer science, computer skills, contemporary history, creative writing, dance, dance performance, debate, drama, drama performance, drama workshop, drawing, earth science, ecology, economics, economics and history, English, English as a foreign language, English literature, English-AP, environmental studies, ESL, ethics, European history, European history-AP, expository writing, fencing, fine arts, French, French-AP, geography, geology, geometry, government/civics, graphic design, health, history, humanities, introduction to technology, jazz band, jewelry making, literary magazine, literature seminar, literature-AP, mathematics, modern European history-AP, music, music history, music performance, musical theater, painting, philosophy, photography, physical education, physics, science, science project, sculpture, sociology, Spanish, Spanish literature-AP, Spanish-AP, stained glass, statistics, statistics-AP, theater, theater design and production, trigonometry, U.S.

history-AP, wilderness experience, world cultures, world history, world literature, writing, yearbook, yoga.

Graduation Requirements American history, arts and fine arts (art, music, dance, drama), English, foreign language, history, literature, mathematics, physical education (includes health), science, wilderness experience, world history, The Athenian Wilderness Experience, community service. Community service is required.

Special Academic Programs Advanced Placement exam preparation; honors section; independent study; term-away projects; study at local college for college credit; domestic exchange program; study abroad; ESL (8 students enrolled).

College Admission Counseling 76 students graduated in 2013; 75 went to college, including California State University, Chico; Duke University; New York University; Occidental College; University of California, Berkeley; University of Pennsylvania. Other: 1 had other specific plans. Median SAT critical reading: 650, median SAT math: 650, median SAT writing: 640, median combined SAT: 1940. 66% scored over 600 on SAT critical reading, 76% scored over 600 on SAT math, 63% scored over 600 on SAT writing, 72% scored over 1800 on combined SAT.

Student Life Upper grades have specified standards of dress, student council. Discipline rests equally with students and faculty.

Summer Programs Enrichment, advancement, ESL, sports, art/fine arts, computer instruction programs offered; session focuses on academic enrichment, sports, and ESL; held on campus; accepts boys and girls; open to students from other schools. 200 students usually enrolled. 2014 schedule: June 13 to August 3. Application deadline: none.

Tuition and Aid Day student tuition: $33,516; 5-day tuition and room/board: $53,650; 7-day tuition and room/board: $53,650. Tuition installment plan (Insured Tuition Payment Plan, monthly payment plans). Need-based scholarship grants available. In 2013–14, 22% of upper-school students received aid. Total amount of financial aid awarded in 2013–14: $2,100,000.

Admissions Traditional secondary-level entrance grade is 9. For fall 2013, 451 students applied for upper-level admission, 103 were accepted, 49 enrolled. International English Language Test, ISEE, SSAT or TOEFL required. Deadline for receipt of application materials: January 16. Application fee required: $75. Interview required.

Athletics Interscholastic: baseball (boys), basketball (b,g), cross-country running (b,g), golf (b), soccer (b,g), softball (g), swimming and diving (b,g), tennis (b,g); coed interscholastic: volleyball, wrestling; coed intramural: basketball, climbing, cross-country running, dance, fencing, weight training, yoga. 12 coaches.

Computers Computers are regularly used in English, foreign language, graphic design, history, humanities, information technology, library science, literary magazine, mathematics, publications, science, yearbook classes. Computer network features include on-campus library services, online commercial services, Internet access, wireless campus network, Internet filtering or blocking technology. Campus intranet, student e-mail accounts, and computer access in designated common areas are available to students. Students grades are available online. The school has a published electronic and media policy.

Contact Beverly Gomer, Associate Director of Admission. 925-362-7223. Fax: 925-362-7228. E-mail: bgomer@athenian.org. Website: www.athenian.org

See Display below and Close-Up on page 514.

ATHENS ACADEMY

1281 Spartan Lane
PO Box 6548
Athens, Georgia 30604

Head of School: Kay Chambers

General Information Coeducational day college-preparatory and technology school. Grades N–12. Founded: 1967. Setting: suburban. Nearest major city is Atlanta. 154-acre campus. 11 buildings on campus. Approved or accredited by Georgia Independent School Association, Southern Association of Colleges and Schools, Southern Association of Independent Schools, and Georgia Department of Education. Member of National Association of Independent Schools and Secondary School Admission Test Board. Endowment: $6.5 million. Total enrollment: 949. Upper school average class size: 18. Upper school faculty-student ratio: 1:8.

Upper School Student Profile Grade 9: 76 students (37 boys, 39 girls); Grade 10: 77 students (40 boys, 37 girls); Grade 11: 66 students (36 boys, 30 girls); Grade 12: 68 students (37 boys, 31 girls).

Faculty School total: 102. In upper school: 22 men, 20 women; 31 have advanced degrees.

Subjects Offered Algebra, American history, American literature, anatomy, art, art history, biology, calculus, chemistry, chemistry-AP, computer math, creative writing, drama, ecology, economics, English, English literature, European history, expository writing, fine arts, French, geography, geometry, government/civics, grammar, health, history, Latin, mathematics, music, photography, physical education, physical science, physics, physiology, robotics, science, social studies, Spanish, statistics, theater, trigonometry, world history, world literature.

Graduation Requirements Arts and fine arts (art, music, dance, drama), English, foreign language, mathematics, physical education (includes health), science, social studies (includes history).

Special Academic Programs 13 Advanced Placement exams for which test preparation is offered; honors section; independent study.

College Admission Counseling 79 students graduated in 2013; all went to college, including Georgia Institute of Technology; University of Georgia. Median SAT critical reading: 623, median SAT math: 629, median SAT writing: 606, median combined SAT: 1858, median composite ACT: 27.

Student Life Upper grades have specified standards of dress, student council, honor system. Discipline rests primarily with faculty.

Summer Programs Remediation, enrichment, computer instruction programs offered; session focuses on enrichment and review; held on campus; accepts boys and girls; open to students from other schools. 80 students usually enrolled. 2014 schedule: June 15 to August 13. Application deadline: none.

Tuition and Aid Day student tuition: $7800–$15,900. Tuition installment plan (Insured Tuition Payment Plan, monthly payment plans). Tuition reduction for siblings, need-based scholarship grants available. In 2013–14, 20% of upper-school students received aid. Total amount of financial aid awarded in 2013–14: $400,000.

Admissions Traditional secondary-level entrance grade is 9. For fall 2013, 37 students applied for upper-level admission, 28 were accepted, 23 enrolled. CTP III and Otis-Lennon School Ability Test, ERB CPT III required. Deadline for receipt of application materials: February 12. Application fee required: $85. On-campus interview required.

Athletics Interscholastic: baseball (boys), basketball (b,g), cheering (g), cross-country running (b,g), football (b), soccer (b,g), swimming and diving (b,g), tennis (b,g), track and field (b,g), volleyball (g); coed interscholastic: cross-country running, golf, swimming and diving, tennis, track and field. 6 PE instructors, 5 coaches.

Computers Computers are regularly used in English, French, history, Latin, mathematics, science, Spanish classes. Computer network features include on-campus library services, online commercial services, Internet access, wireless campus network. Student e-mail accounts are available to students. The school has a published electronic and media policy.

Contact Mr. Stuart A. Todd, Director of Admissions. 706-549-9225. Fax: 706-354-3775. E-mail: stodd@athensacademy.org. Website: www.athensacademy.org/

AUGUSTA CHRISTIAN SCHOOL

313 Baston Road
Martinez, Georgia 30907

Head of School: Dr. David M. Piccolo

General Information Coeducational day college-preparatory, arts, religious studies, and technology school. Grades K–12. Founded: 1958. Setting: suburban. Nearest major city is Augusta. 26-acre campus. 10 buildings on campus. Approved or accredited by Association of Christian Schools International, Southern Association of Colleges and Schools, and Georgia Department of Education. Total enrollment: 634. Upper school average class size: 18. Upper school faculty-student ratio: 1:10. There are 180 required school days per year for Upper School students. Upper School students typically attend 5 days per week. The average school day consists of 7 hours and 5 minutes.

Upper School Student Profile Grade 9: 58 students (33 boys, 25 girls); Grade 10: 69 students (27 boys, 42 girls); Grade 11: 74 students (35 boys, 39 girls); Grade 12: 74 students (32 boys, 42 girls).

Faculty School total: 56. In upper school: 10 men, 16 women; 10 have advanced degrees.

Subjects Offered Advanced chemistry, advanced computer applications, advanced math, Advanced Placement courses, algebra, American government, American history, American history-AP, American literature, anatomy and physiology, art, athletic training, athletics, band, baseball, basketball, Bible, Bible studies, biology, biology-AP, British literature, British literature-AP, calculus-AP, ceramics, cheerleading, chemistry, choir, choral music, chorus, Christian education, Christian studies, college counseling, comparative religion, computer education, computer skills, drama, drama performance, earth science, ecology, economics and history, electives, English, English composition, English literature, English literature-AP, English-AP, European history, French, general science, geography, geometry, government, grammar, health, health science, history, instrumental music, keyboarding, life skills, mathematics, mathematics-AP, music appreciation, musical productions, New Testament, physics, piano, pre-algebra, pre-calculus, public speaking, reading, remedial/makeup course work, SAT preparation, science, social studies, Spanish, speech, sports, state history, student government, swimming, U.S. government, U.S. history, U.S. history-AP, U.S. literature, volleyball, weight training, weightlifting, world history, wrestling, yearbook.

Graduation Requirements Bible, computers, electives, English, foreign language, mathematics, physical education (includes health), science, social studies (includes history), speech.

Special Academic Programs Advanced Placement exam preparation; honors section; study at local college for college credit; programs in English, mathematics for dyslexic students; ESL (15 students enrolled).

College Admission Counseling 59 students graduated in 2013; all went to college, including Augusta State University; Georgia Institute of Technology; Georgia Southern University; University of Georgia.

Student Life Upper grades have specified standards of dress, student council. Discipline rests primarily with faculty. Attendance at religious services is required.

Summer Programs Remediation, enrichment, advancement programs offered; session focuses on academics; held on campus; accepts boys and girls; open to students from other schools.

Tuition and Aid Day student tuition: $1000–$12,300. Tuition installment plan (Insured Tuition Payment Plan, monthly payment plans, individually arranged payment plans). Tuition reduction for siblings, need-based scholarship grants available.

Admissions Traditional secondary-level entrance grade is 9. Stanford Achievement Test required. Deadline for receipt of application materials: none. Application fee required: $100. Interview required.

Athletics Interscholastic: baseball (boys), basketball (b,g), cross-country running (b,g), football (b), soccer (b,g), softball (g), swimming and diving (b,g), tennis (b,g), track and field (b,g), volleyball (g), wrestling (b); coed interscholastic: cheering, golf. 3 PE instructors.

Computers Computers are regularly used in computer applications, keyboarding, yearbook classes. Computer network features include on-campus library services, Internet access, wireless campus network, Internet filtering or blocking technology. Campus intranet is available to students. Students grades are available online. The school has a published electronic and media policy.

Contact Mr. Cary Rivers, Director of Admissions. 706-863-2905 Ext. 106. Fax: 706-860-6618. E-mail: CaryRivers@augustachristian.org. Website: www.augustachristian.org

AUGUSTA PREPARATORY DAY SCHOOL

285 Flowing Wells Road
Martinez, Georgia 30907

Head of School: Becky Gilmore

General Information Coeducational day college-preparatory school. Grades PS–12. Founded: 1960. Setting: suburban. Nearest major city is Augusta. 52-acre campus. 6 buildings on campus. Approved or accredited by Georgia Independent School Association, Southern Association of Colleges and Schools, and Southern Association of Independent Schools. Member of National Association of Independent Schools and Secondary School Admission Test Board. Endowment: $6 million. Total enrollment: 552. Upper school average class size: 11. Upper school faculty-student ratio: 1:9. There are 180 required school days per year for Upper School students. Upper School students typically attend 5 days per week. The average school day consists of 7 hours and 15 minutes.

Upper School Student Profile Grade 9: 58 students (27 boys, 31 girls); Grade 10: 46 students (24 boys, 22 girls); Grade 11: 61 students (31 boys, 30 girls); Grade 12: 47 students (24 boys, 23 girls).

Faculty School total: 65. In upper school: 15 men, 10 women; 18 have advanced degrees.

Subjects Offered Advanced Placement courses, advanced studio art-AP, algebra, American history, American literature, art, biology, biology-AP, calculus, calculus-AP, chemistry, chemistry-AP, computer programming, drama, ecology, economics, English, English literature, English literature-AP, European history-AP, French, French-AP, geometry, government, government/civics, Latin, Latin-AP, marine science, physics, pre-calculus, Russian, senior project, Spanish, Spanish-AP, statistics-AP, studio art-AP, theater design and production, U.S. history-AP, world history, zoology.

Graduation Requirements American government, American history, arts and fine arts (art, music, dance, drama), English, foreign language, mathematics, physical education (includes health), science, social studies (includes history), Wellness Requirement.

Special Academic Programs Honors section; independent study; term-away projects; academic accommodation for the gifted.

College Admission Counseling 54 students graduated in 2013; all went to college, including Augusta State University; College of Charleston; Furman University; Georgia Institute of Technology; Mercer University; University of Georgia. Median SAT critical reading: 602, median SAT math: 602, median SAT writing: 603, median combined SAT: 1807, median composite ACT: 27. 50% scored over 600 on SAT critical reading, 50% scored over 600 on SAT math, 50% scored over 600 on SAT writing, 50% scored over 1800 on combined SAT, 50% scored over 26 on composite ACT.

Student Life Upper grades have specified standards of dress, student council, honor system. Discipline rests equally with students and faculty.

Summer Programs Enrichment, sports, art/fine arts programs offered; session focuses on enrichment/sports; held on campus; accepts boys and girls; open to students from other schools. 2014 schedule: June 6 to August 1.

Tuition and Aid Day student tuition: $14,635. Tuition installment plan (Insured Tuition Payment Plan). Tuition reduction for siblings, need-based scholarship grants available. In 2013–14, 25% of upper-school students received aid. Total amount of financial aid awarded in 2013–14: $250,000.

Admissions Traditional secondary-level entrance grade is 9. For fall 2013, 25 students applied for upper-level admission, 24 were accepted, 20 enrolled. ERB CTP III required. Deadline for receipt of application materials: none. No application fee required. Interview required.

Athletics Interscholastic: aquatics (boys, girls), baseball (b), basketball (b,g), cheering (g), cross-country running (b,g), fitness (b,g), football (b), golf (b), physical training (b,g), swimming and diving (b,g), track and field (b,g), volleyball (g), weight lifting (b,g), weight training (b,g), yoga (b,g). 3 PE instructors, 1 athletic trainer.

Computers Computers are regularly used in data processing classes. Computer network features include on-campus library services, online commercial services, Internet access, wireless campus network, Internet filtering or blocking technology.

Campus intranet, student e-mail accounts, and computer access in designated common areas are available to students. Students grades are available online. The school has a published electronic and media policy.

Contact Rosie Herrmann, Director of Admission. 706-863-1906 Ext. 201. Fax: 706-863-6198. E-mail: admissions@augustaprep.org. Website: www.augustaprep.org

THE AWTY INTERNATIONAL SCHOOL

7455 Awty School Lane
Houston, Texas 77055

Head of School: Dr. Stephen Codrington

General Information Coeducational day college-preparatory and bilingual studies school. Grades PK–12. Founded: 1956. Setting: urban. 25-acre campus. 16 buildings on campus. Approved or accredited by French Ministry of Education, Independent Schools Association of the Southwest, International Baccalaureate Organization, and Texas Department of Education. Member of National Association of Independent Schools, Secondary School Admission Test Board, and European Council of International Schools. Languages of instruction: English, French, and Spanish. Endowment: $3.9 million. Total enrollment: 1,489. Upper school average class size: 17. Upper school faculty-student ratio: 1:18. Upper School students typically attend 5 days per week.

Faculty School total: 186. In upper school: 24 men, 57 women; 63 have advanced degrees.

Subjects Offered Algebra, American history, Arabic, art, biology, calculus, chemistry, community service, computer programming, computer science, computer studies, drama, Dutch, English, ESL, fine arts, French, geography, geometry, German, grammar, history, Italian, Mandarin, mathematics, music, Norwegian, philosophy, physical education, physics, science, social sciences, social studies, Spanish, theater, theory of knowledge, trigonometry, world history, world literature, writing.

Graduation Requirements Arts and fine arts (art, music, dance, drama), computer science, English, foreign language, mathematics, physical education (includes health), science, social sciences, social studies (includes history), 4000-word extended essay. Community service is required.

Special Academic Programs International Baccalaureate program; ESL.

College Admission Counseling 92 students graduated in 2012; all went to college, including Georgetown University; McGill University; Princeton University; Rice University; University of Houston. Median SAT critical reading: 620, median SAT math: 640, median SAT writing: 640, median combined SAT: 1880, median composite ACT: 30. 69% scored over 600 on SAT critical reading, 81% scored over 600 on SAT math, 82% scored over 600 on SAT writing, 77% scored over 1800 on combined SAT, 83% scored over 26 on composite ACT.

Student Life Upper grades have uniform requirement, student council, honor system. Discipline rests primarily with faculty.

Tuition and Aid Day student tuition: $20,472. Tuition installment plan (monthly payment plans, individually arranged payment plans, semi-annual payment plan, Dewar Tuition Refund Plan). Need-based scholarship grants, need-based financial aid available. In 2012–13, 8% of upper-school students received aid. Total amount of financial aid awarded in 2012–13: $407,857.

Admissions Traditional secondary-level entrance grade is 9. For fall 2012, 222 students applied for upper-level admission, 131 were accepted, 89 enrolled. ISEE, OLSAT, ERB and writing sample required. Deadline for receipt of application materials: January 31. Application fee required: $100. On-campus interview required.

Athletics Interscholastic: cheering (girls), dance squad (g), dance team (g); coed interscholastic: basketball, cross-country running, golf, running, soccer, tennis, track and field, volleyball, winter soccer; coed intramural: aerobics/dance, badminton, bicycling, fitness, table tennis, triathlon. 5 PE instructors, 7 coaches, 1 athletic trainer.

Computers Computers are regularly used in all academic classes. Computer network features include on-campus library services, online commercial services, Internet access, wireless campus network, Internet filtering or blocking technology. Computer access in designated common areas is available to students. Students grades are available online. The school has a published electronic and media policy.

Contact Mrs. Erika Benavente, Co-Director of Admissions. 713-328-5804. Fax: 713-686-4956. E-mail: ebenavente@awty.org. Website: www.awty.org

BACHMAN ACADEMY

McDonald, Tennessee
See Special Needs Schools section.

BAKERSFIELD CHRISTIAN HIGH SCHOOL

12775 Stockdale Highway
Bakersfield, California 93314

Head of School: Mr. Stephen Dinger

General Information Coeducational day college-preparatory and religious studies school, affiliated with Christian faith. Grades 9–12. Founded: 1979. Setting: suburban. 47-acre campus. 9 buildings on campus. Approved or accredited by Association of Christian Schools International, Western Association of Schools and Colleges, and California Department of Education. Endowment: $500,000. Total enrollment: 436. Upper school average class size: 22. Upper school faculty-student ratio: 1:17. There are 180 required school days per year for Upper School students. Upper School students typically attend 5 days per week. The average school day consists of 7 hours.

Faculty School total: 44. In upper school: 21 men, 23 women; 7 have advanced degrees.

Subjects Offered Advanced Placement courses, advanced studio art-AP, agriculture, American literature, American literature-AP, Bible, biology, biology-AP, British literature, British literature-AP, calculus, calculus-AP, chemistry, chemistry-AP, choir, Christian ethics, comparative religion, computer animation, contemporary issues, digital photography, drama, economics, economics-AP, English, English literature, English literature-AP, English-AP, European history, European history-AP, foreign language, forensics, French, history-AP, human anatomy, introduction to literature, jazz band, performing arts, photography, physical science, physics, physics-AP, pre-calculus, Spanish, Spanish-AP, statistics, statistics-AP, studio art, studio art-AP, U.S. history, U.S. history-AP, video and animation, world history, world literature.

Graduation Requirements 40 hours community service.

Special Academic Programs Advanced Placement exam preparation; independent study.

Student Life Upper grades have specified standards of dress, student council, honor system. Discipline rests primarily with faculty. Attendance at religious services is required.

Tuition and Aid Day student tuition: $11,090. Tuition installment plan (FACTS Tuition Payment Plan, monthly payment plans, individually arranged payment plans). Tuition reduction for siblings, need-based financial aid available. In 2012–13, 33% of upper-school students received aid. Total amount of financial aid awarded in 2012–13: $170,000.

Admissions Traditional secondary-level entrance grade is 9. Deadline for receipt of application materials: none. Application fee required: $75. On-campus interview required.

Athletics Interscholastic: baseball (boys), basketball (b,g), cheering (g), football (b), golf (b,g), soccer (b,g), softball (g); tennis (b,g), volleyball (g), weight lifting (b), weight training (b,g), wrestling (b); coed interscholastic: cross-country running, swimming and diving, track and field. 10 coaches, 1 athletic trainer.

Computers Computer network features include on-campus library services, Internet access, Internet filtering or blocking technology. Computer access in designated common areas is available to students. Students grades are available online. The school has a published electronic and media policy.

Contact Mrs. Alice E. Abril, Director of Admissions. 661-410-7000. Fax: 661-410-7007. E-mail: aabril@bakersfieldchristian.com. Website: www.bakersfieldchristian.com

BALDWIN SCHOOL OF PUERTO RICO

PO Box 1827
Bayamn, Puerto Rico 00960-1827

Head of School: Mr. James Nelligan

General Information Coeducational day college-preparatory school. Grades PK–12. Founded: 1968. Setting: suburban. Nearest major city is San Juan. 23-acre campus. 7 buildings on campus. Approved or accredited by Middle States Association of Colleges and Schools and Puerto Rico Department of Education. Member of National Association of Independent Schools. Languages of instruction: English and Spanish. Total enrollment: 812. Upper school average class size: 20. Upper school faculty-student ratio: 1:8. There are 173 required school days per year for Upper School students. Upper School students typically attend 5 days per week. The average school day consists of 6 hours and 40 minutes.

Upper School Student Profile Grade 9: 71 students (30 boys, 41 girls); Grade 10: 64 students (23 boys, 41 girls); Grade 11: 56 students (28 boys, 28 girls); Grade 12: 45 students (22 boys, 23 girls).

Faculty School total: 90. In upper school: 7 men, 31 women; 20 have advanced degrees.

Subjects Offered Algebra, American history, American literature, art, biology, biology-AP, British literature, calculus, calculus-AP, chemistry, chemistry-AP, computer information systems, computer literacy, computer programming, computer science, computers, English, English literature, English literature-AP, environmental science, European history-AP, fine arts, French, French-AP, geography, geometry, grammar, history, mathematics, music, physical education, physics, pre-calculus, psychology, Puerto Rican history, science, social studies, Spanish, Spanish language-AP, Spanish literature-AP, study skills, visual arts, world literature, writing.

Graduation Requirements Algebra, American history, American literature, arts and fine arts (art, music, dance, drama), biology, British literature, chemistry, computer science, English, English literature, geometry, mathematics, physical education (includes health), Puerto Rican history, science, social studies (includes history), Spanish, Spanish literature, U.S. history, Western civilization, Spanish as a Second Language, Spanish.

Special Academic Programs Advanced Placement exam preparation.

College Admission Counseling 40 students graduated in 2013; all went to college, including Boston University; Harvard University; Massachusetts Institute of

Technology; The George Washington University; Tufts University; University of Puerto Rico, Río Piedras. Median SAT critical reading: 597, median SAT math: 613, median SAT writing: 630.

Student Life Upper grades have uniform requirement, student council, honor system. Discipline rests equally with students and faculty.

Summer Programs Remediation, enrichment, ESL programs offered; session focuses on remediation; held on campus; accepts boys and girls; open to students from other schools. 160 students usually enrolled. 2014 schedule: June 1 to June 30. Application deadline: May 14.

Tuition and Aid Day student tuition: $11,361–$12,015. Guaranteed tuition plan. Tuition installment plan (annual payment plan, biannual payment plan, quarterly payment plan). Tuition reduction for siblings, need-based scholarship grants, tuition reduction for children of staff, full scholarship program for eligible students, financial assistance for elegible students available. In 2013–14, 1% of upper-school students received aid. Total amount of financial aid awarded in 2013–14: $50,000.

Admissions Traditional secondary-level entrance grade is 9. For fall 2013, 32 students applied for upper-level admission, 27 were accepted, 22 enrolled. Brigance Test of Basic Skills and Stanford Achievement Test, Otis-Lennon required. Deadline for receipt of application materials: none. Application fee required: $150. On-campus interview recommended.

Athletics Interscholastic: baseball (boys), basketball (b,g), cheering (g), indoor soccer (b,g), soccer (b,g), swimming and diving (b,g), tennis (b,g), track and field (b,g), volleyball (b,g), water polo (b); intramural: flag football (b,g), touch football (b,g), track and field (b,g); coed interscholastic: golf, physical fitness. 6 PE instructors, 17 coaches, 1 athletic trainer.

Computers Computers are regularly used in English, history, mathematics, psychology, science, Spanish, technology classes. Computer network features include on-campus library services, Internet access, wireless campus network, Internet filtering or blocking technology. Student e-mail accounts and computer access in designated common areas are available to students. Students grades are available online. The school has a published electronic and media policy.

Contact Mrs. Ely Mejas, Director of Admissions. 787-720-2421 Ext. 239. Fax: 787-790-0619. E-mail: emejias@baldwin-school.org. Website: www.baldwin-school.org

BALMORAL HALL SCHOOL

630 Westminster Avenue
Winnipeg, Manitoba R3C 3S1, Canada

Head of School: Mrs. Joanne Kamins

General Information Girls' boarding and day college-preparatory, arts, technology, and athletics/prep hockey school. Boarding grades 6–12, day grades N–12. Founded: 1901. Setting: urban. Students are housed in apartment-style residence. 12-acre campus. 2 buildings on campus. Approved or accredited by Canadian Association of Independent Schools, Canadian Educational Standards Institute, International Baccalaureate Organization, The Association of Boarding Schools, and Manitoba Department of Education. Affiliate member of National Association of Independent Schools; member of Secondary School Admission Test Board. Language of instruction: English. Endowment: CAN$1 million. Total enrollment: 474. Upper school average class size: 18. Upper school faculty-student ratio: 1:7. There are 183 required school days per year for Upper School students. Upper School students typically attend 5 days per week. The average school day consists of 5 hours.

Upper School Student Profile Grade 9: 32 students (32 girls); Grade 10: 38 students (38 girls); Grade 11: 40 students (40 girls); Grade 12: 44 students (44 girls). 24% of students are boarding students. 80% are province residents. 4 provinces are represented in upper school student body. 18% are international students. International students from China, Hong Kong, Mexico, Republic of Korea, Taiwan, and United States; 1 other country represented in student body.

Faculty School total: 47. In upper school: 5 men, 14 women; 7 have advanced degrees; 4 reside on campus.

Subjects Offered Acting, advanced math, Advanced Placement courses, advanced studio art-AP, advanced TOEFL/grammar, art, biology, biology-AP, calculus, calculus-AP, career and personal planning, career/college preparation, chemistry, chemistry-AP, choir, college planning, communications, community service, computer science, consumer mathematics, dance performance, debate, desktop publishing, digital art, digital photography, drama, driver education, English, English language and composition-AP, English literature, English literature and composition-AP, English literature-AP, English/composition-AP, ESL, ethics, French, French language-AP, French literature-AP, general science, geography, health, history, history-AP, jazz ensemble, mathematics, mathematics-AP, media arts, modern Western civilization, multimedia, music, musical theater, performing arts, personal development, physical education, physics, physics-AP, pre-calculus, psychology-AP, SAT/ACT preparation, science, social studies, Spanish, Spanish-AP, studio art-AP, technology, vocal ensemble, world affairs, world history.

Graduation Requirements Minimum of 10 hours per year of Service Learning participation in grades 9 through 12.

Special Academic Programs Advanced Placement exam preparation; honors section; accelerated programs; study at local college for college credit; academic accommodation for the gifted; ESL (37 students enrolled).

College Admission Counseling 46 students graduated in 2013; all went to college, including McGill University; The University of British Columbia; The University of Western Ontario; The University of Winnipeg; University of Manitoba; University of Toronto.

Student Life Upper grades have uniform requirement, student council, honor system. Discipline rests primarily with faculty.

Tuition and Aid Day student tuition: CAN$14,700; 5-day tuition and room/board: CAN$30,400. Tuition installment plan (The Tuition Plan). Tuition reduction for siblings, bursaries, merit scholarship grants available. In 2013–14, 23% of upper-school students received aid; total upper-school merit-scholarship money awarded: CAN$14,000. Total amount of financial aid awarded in 2013–14: CAN$253,096.

Admissions Traditional secondary-level entrance grade is 9. School's own exam required. Deadline for receipt of application materials: none. Application fee required: CAN$150. Interview required.

Athletics Interscholastic: badminton, basketball, cross-country running, curling, Frisbee, golf, ice hockey, indoor track & field, outdoor skills, running, soccer, speedskating, track and field, ultimate Frisbee, volleyball; intramural: aerobics, aerobics/dance, aerobics/Nautilus, alpine skiing, backpacking, badminton, ballet, baseball, basketball, bicycling, bowling, broomball, cooperative games, Cosom hockey, cross-country running, curling, dance, dance team, fencing, field hockey, figure skating, fitness, fitness walking, flag football, floor hockey, Frisbee, golf, gymnastics, handball, hiking/backpacking, hockey, ice hockey, ice skating, in-line skating, indoor hockey, indoor track & field, jogging, jump rope, modern dance, netball, outdoor activities, outdoor education, outdoor skills, physical fitness, physical training, roller blading, rowing, rugby, running, skiing (cross-country), skiing (downhill), snowboarding, snowshoeing, soccer, softball, speedskating, strength & conditioning, swimming and diving, table tennis, tennis, track and field, ultimate Frisbee, volleyball, walking, wall climbing, weight training, yoga. 2 PE instructors, 4 coaches.

Computers Computers are regularly used in all classes. Computer network features include on-campus library services, Internet access, wireless campus network, Internet filtering or blocking technology. Campus intranet, student e-mail accounts, and computer access in designated common areas are available to students. Students grades are available online. The school has a published electronic and media policy.

Contact Ms. Bin Dong Jiang, Admissions Officer. 204-784-1608. Fax: 204-774-5534. E-mail: bdjiang@balmoralhall.com. Website: www.balmoralhall.com

THE BALTIMORE ACTORS' THEATRE CONSERVATORY

The Dumbarton House
300 Dumbarton Road
Baltimore, Maryland 21212-1532

Head of School: Walter E. Anderson

General Information Coeducational day and distance learning college-preparatory and arts school. Grades K–12. Distance learning grades 9–12. Founded: 1979. Setting: suburban. 35-acre campus. 3 buildings on campus. Approved or accredited by Association of Independent Maryland Schools, Middle States Association of Colleges and Schools, and Maryland Department of Education. Endowment: $200,000. Total enrollment: 24. Upper school average class size: 6. Upper school faculty-student ratio: 1:3. There are 175 required school days per year for Upper School students. Upper School students typically attend 5 days per week. The average school day consists of 7 hours and 30 minutes.

Upper School Student Profile Grade 9: 3 students (2 boys, 1 girl); Grade 11: 4 students (4 girls); Grade 12: 1 student (1 girl); Postgraduate: 2 students (1 boy, 1 girl).

Faculty School total: 12. In upper school: 2 men, 8 women; 9 have advanced degrees.

Subjects Offered Acting, algebra, American history-AP, ballet, biology-AP, British literature, chemistry, English language-AP, environmental science-AP, French, geometry, health science, music history, music theory-AP, novels, physics, pre-calculus, psychology, sociology, theater history, trigonometry, world history, world history-AP.

Graduation Requirements Algebra, American history, ballet, chemistry, English, French, geometry, modern dance, music history, music theory, physical science, psychology, sociology, theater history, world history, students are required to complete graduation requirements in the three performing arts areas of music, drama, and dance.

Special Academic Programs Advanced Placement exam preparation; honors section; accelerated programs; independent study; study at local college for college credit; academic accommodation for the gifted, the musically talented, and the artistically talented.

College Admission Counseling Colleges students went to include Nazareth College of Rochester. Median SAT critical reading: 600, median SAT math: 570, median composite ACT: 26.

Student Life Upper grades have uniform requirement, student council, honor system. Discipline rests primarily with faculty.

Tuition and Aid Day student tuition: $10,000. Tuition installment plan (SMART Tuition Payment Plan, FACTS Tuition Payment Plan, individually arranged payment plans). Need-based scholarship grants available. In 2012–13, 10% of upper-school students received aid. Total amount of financial aid awarded in 2012–13: $12,000.

Admissions Traditional secondary-level entrance grade is 9. For fall 2012, 50 students applied for upper-level admission, 15 were accepted, 7 enrolled. Any standardized test, English, French, and math proficiency and writing sample required. Deadline for receipt of application materials: April 3. Application fee required: $50. On-campus interview required.

Computers Computers are regularly used in college planning, creative writing, dance, desktop publishing, English, historical foundations for arts, history, independent study, introduction to technology, keyboarding, music, music technology, psychology, senior seminar, theater, theater arts, word processing, writing classes. Computer network features include Internet access, wireless campus network, Internet filtering or blocking technology. Student e-mail accounts are available to students. The school has a published electronic and media policy.

Contact Mr. Walter E. Anderson, Headmaster. 410-337-8519. Fax: 410-337-8582. E-mail: batpro@baltimoreactorstheatre.org. Website: www.baltimoreactorstheatre.org

BALTIMORE LUTHERAN SCHOOL

1145 Concordia Drive
Towson, Maryland 21286-1796

Head of School: Mr. Alan Freeman

General Information Coeducational day and distance learning college-preparatory, arts, religious studies, and technology school, affiliated with Lutheran Church–Missouri Synod. Grades 6–12. Distance learning grades 9–12. Founded: 1965. Setting: suburban. Nearest major city is Baltimore. 25-acre campus. 5 buildings on campus. Approved or accredited by Association of Independent Maryland Schools, Middle States Association of Colleges and Schools, and Maryland Department of Education. Endowment: $1.3 million. Total enrollment: 240. Upper school average class size: 16. Upper school faculty-student ratio: 1:12. There are 174 required school days per year for Upper School students. Upper School students typically attend 5 days per week. The average school day consists of 6 hours and 45 minutes.

Upper School Student Profile 30% of students are Lutheran Church–Missouri Synod.

Faculty School total: 36. In upper school: 14 men, 15 women; 16 have advanced degrees.

Subjects Offered 20th century history, 3-dimensional art, acting, advanced biology, Advanced Placement courses, algebra, American government, American history, American literature, analytic geometry, anatomy, art, Bible studies, biology, biology-AP, brass choir, British literature, British literature (honors), calculus, chemistry, Chesapeake Bay studies, Christian doctrine, Christian scripture, church history, college counseling, college planning, computer education, computer graphics, computer programming, computers, concert band, concert choir, creative writing, digital photography, drama, drama performance, dramatic arts, drawing, drawing and design, earth science, ecology, economics, economics and history, English, English literature, English literature-AP, expository writing, French, geometry, German, government/civics, grammar, graphic arts, graphic design, health, honors English, independent study, intro to computers, jazz band, journalism, keyboarding, Latin, law, mathematics, music, painting, photography, physical education, physics, pre-algebra, psychology, religion, SAT/ACT preparation, science, social studies, Spanish, Spanish-AP, speech, studio art, theater, theology, trigonometry, Web site design, word processing, world history, world history-AP, world literature, writing, yearbook.

Graduation Requirements Arts and fine arts (art, music, dance, drama), English, foreign language, mathematics, physical education (includes health), religion (includes Bible studies and theology), science, social studies (includes history), technology.

Special Academic Programs 5 Advanced Placement exams for which test preparation is offered; honors section; independent study; study at local college for college credit; academic accommodation for the gifted; programs in English, mathematics for dyslexic students.

College Admission Counseling 79 students graduated in 2012; 78 went to college, including Brown University; Loyola University Maryland; The Johns Hopkins University; Towson University; University of Maryland, Baltimore County; University of Maryland, College Park. Other: 1 went to work. Mean SAT critical reading: 539, mean SAT math: 522, mean SAT writing: 545.

Student Life Upper grades have uniform requirement, student council, honor system. Discipline rests primarily with faculty. Attendance at religious services is required.

Tuition and Aid Day student tuition: $10,950. Tuition installment plan (FACTS Tuition Payment Plan). Tuition reduction for siblings, merit scholarship grants, need-based scholarship grants, academic merit scholarships for students from Christian schools available. In 2012–13, 25% of upper-school students received aid; total upper-school merit-scholarship money awarded: $18,000. Total amount of financial aid awarded in 2012–13: $70,000.

Admissions Traditional secondary-level entrance grade is 9. For fall 2012, 85 students applied for upper-level admission, 70 were accepted, 40 enrolled. ISEE, school placement exam, TOEFL or SLEP and writing sample required. Deadline for receipt of application materials: none. Application fee required: $50. On-campus interview required.

Athletics Interscholastic: baseball (boys), basketball (b,g), cheering (g), cross-country running (b,g), field hockey (g), football (b), golf (b), indoor soccer (g), lacrosse (b,g), soccer (b,g), softball (g), tennis (b,g), track and field (b,g), volleyball (g), winter soccer (g), wrestling (b); coed intramural: skiing (downhill), snowboarding. 2 PE instructors, 5 coaches, 1 athletic trainer.

Computers Computers are regularly used in English, graphic design, history, independent study, journalism, library, mathematics, newspaper, photography, SAT preparation, social sciences, technology, writing, yearbook classes. Computer network features include on-campus library services, online commercial services, Internet access, wireless campus network, Internet filtering or blocking technology. Student e-mail accounts are available to students. Students grades are available online. The school has a published electronic and media policy.

Contact Mr. Jim Carter, Director of Admissions. 410-825-2323 Ext. 272. Fax: 410-825-2506. E-mail: jcarter@baltimorelutheran.org. Website: www.baltimorelutheran.org

BANGOR CHRISTIAN SCHOOL

1476 Broadway
Bangor, Maine 04401

Head of School: Mr. James Frost

General Information Coeducational day college-preparatory, arts, business, vocational, religious studies, bilingual studies, and technology school, affiliated with Baptist Church. Grades K4–12. Founded: 1970. Setting: suburban. 35-acre campus. 3 buildings on campus. Approved or accredited by New England Association of Schools and Colleges and Maine Department of Education. Languages of instruction: English and Spanish. Total enrollment: 310. Upper school average class size: 20. Upper school faculty-student ratio: 1:10. There are 175 required school days per year for Upper School students. Upper School students typically attend 5 days per week. The average school day consists of 6 hours and 45 minutes.

Upper School Student Profile Grade 6: 15 students (6 boys, 9 girls); Grade 7: 22 students (11 boys, 11 girls); Grade 8: 29 students (12 boys, 17 girls); Grade 9: 20 students (7 boys, 13 girls); Grade 10: 20 students (4 boys, 16 girls); Grade 11: 17 students (4 boys, 13 girls); Grade 12: 23 students (14 boys, 9 girls). 55% of students are Baptist.

Faculty School total: 23. In upper school: 5 men, 8 women; 5 have advanced degrees.

Special Academic Programs ESL (3 students enrolled).

College Admission Counseling 27 students graduated in 2013; 20 went to college, including Rensselaer Polytechnic Institute; University of Maine. Other: 2 went to work, 3 entered military service, 2 had other specific plans.

Student Life Upper grades have specified standards of dress, student council, honor system. Discipline rests primarily with faculty. Attendance at religious services is required.

Tuition and Aid Day student tuition: $4700. Guaranteed tuition plan. Tuition installment plan (monthly payment plans). Tuition reduction for siblings, need-based scholarship grants available.

Admissions Traditional secondary-level entrance grade is 9. Deadline for receipt of application materials: none. Application fee required: $100. Interview required.

Athletics Interscholastic: baseball (boys), basketball (b,g), cheering (b,g), cross-country running (b,g), indoor track & field (b,g), soccer (b,g), softball (g), swimming and diving (b,g), track and field (b,g), winter (indoor) track (b,g); intramural: basketball (b,g), cheering (b,g), soccer (b,g), softball (g); coed interscholastic: cheering. 2 PE instructors, 12 coaches.

Computers Computers are regularly used in introduction to technology, keyboarding, lab/keyboard, research skills, typing, word processing, yearbook classes. Computer network features include on-campus library services, Internet access, wireless campus network, Internet filtering or blocking technology. Student e-mail accounts are available to students. Students grades are available online. The school has a published electronic and media policy.

Contact Mrs. Terri L. Conley, Main Office Secretary. 207-947-7356 Ext. 331. Fax: 207-262-9528. E-mail: tconley@bangorchristian.org. Website: www.bangorchristian.com

BARNSTABLE ACADEMY

8 Wright Way
Oakland, New Jersey 07436

Head of School: Ms. Lizanne M. Coyne

General Information Coeducational day college-preparatory, general academic, arts, and technology school; primarily serves individuals with Attention Deficit Disorder. Grades 5–12. Founded: 1978. Setting: suburban. Nearest major city is New York, NY. 4-acre campus. 1 building on campus. Approved or accredited by Middle States Association of Colleges and Schools, National Independent Private Schools Association, and New Jersey Department of Education. Total enrollment: 120. Upper school average class size: 10. Upper school faculty-student ratio: 1:8. There are 174 required school days per year for Upper School students. The average school day consists of 6 hours.

Upper School Student Profile Grade 7: 2 students (2 girls); Grade 9: 20 students (12 boys, 8 girls); Grade 10: 23 students (15 boys, 8 girls); Grade 11: 23 students (15 boys, 8 girls); Grade 12: 19 students (13 boys, 6 girls).

Faculty School total: 20. In upper school: 6 men, 11 women; 12 have advanced degrees.

Subjects Offered Advanced math, algebra, American culture, American government, American legal systems, biology, business mathematics, calculus, chemistry, computer applications, contemporary issues, economics, English literature, English-AP, French, geometry, Latin, physical education, physics, psychology, Spanish, U.S. history, world history.

Special Academic Programs Advanced Placement exam preparation; honors section; accelerated programs; independent study; study at local college for college credit; academic accommodation for the gifted, the musically talented, and the artistically talented; remedial reading and/or remedial writing; remedial math; programs in English, general development for dyslexic students; special instructional classes for students with learning disabilities and Attention Deficit Disorder, the fragile emotionally disturbed; ESL (8 students enrolled).

College Admission Counseling 20 students graduated in 2013; 17 went to college, including Drew University; The College of New Jersey. Other: 1 went to work, 1 entered a postgraduate year, 1 had other specific plans. Median SAT critical reading: 520, median SAT math: 530, median SAT writing: 560, median composite ACT: 26. 25% scored over 600 on SAT critical reading, 25% scored over 600 on SAT math, 25% scored over 600 on SAT writing, 25% scored over 1800 on combined SAT.

Student Life Upper grades have specified standards of dress, student council. Discipline rests primarily with faculty.

Summer Programs Remediation, enrichment, advancement programs offered; held on campus; accepts boys and girls; open to students from other schools. 25 students usually enrolled. 2014 schedule: June 29 to July 31. Application deadline: June 28.

Tuition and Aid Day student tuition: $22,750–$29,975. Tuition installment plan (monthly payment plans, individually arranged payment plans). Merit scholarship grants, need-based scholarship grants available. In 2013–14, 30% of upper-school students received aid; total upper-school merit-scholarship money awarded: $150,000. Total amount of financial aid awarded in 2013–14: $200,000.

Admissions Traditional secondary-level entrance grade is 9. For fall 2013, 200 students applied for upper-level admission, 100 were accepted, 48 enrolled. Deadline for receipt of application materials: none. No application fee required. On-campus interview required.

Athletics Interscholastic: baseball (boys), cheering (g), softball (g); coed interscholastic: aerobics/Nautilus, basketball, bowling, dance, horseback riding, Nautilus, physical training, soccer, tennis, walking; coed intramural: aerobics, aerobics/dance, aerobics/Nautilus, alpine skiing. 2 PE instructors, 3 coaches.

Computers Computers are regularly used in computer applications, reading classes. Computer network features include Internet access, Internet filtering or blocking technology. Campus intranet and student e-mail accounts are available to students.

Contact Dr. Laura Merkle, Head of School. 201-651-0200 Ext. 108. Fax: 201-337-9797. E-mail: lmerkle@barnstableacademy.com. Website: www.barnstableacademy.com

BARRIE SCHOOL

13500 Layhill Road
Silver Spring, Maryland 20906

Head of School: Mr. Charles Abelmann

General Information Coeducational day college-preparatory school. Grades N–12. Founded: 1932. Setting: suburban. Nearest major city is Washington, DC. 45-acre campus. 8 buildings on campus. Approved or accredited by Middle States Association of Colleges and Schools and Maryland Department of Education. Member of National Association of Independent Schools and Secondary School Admission Test Board. Endowment: $320,000. Total enrollment: 293. Upper school average class size: 15. Upper school faculty-student ratio: 1:8. There are 175 required school days per year for Upper School students. Upper School students typically attend 5 days per week. The average school day consists of 7 hours and 20 minutes.

Upper School Student Profile Grade 9: 14 students (12 boys, 2 girls); Grade 10: 11 students (8 boys, 3 girls); Grade 11: 11 students (5 boys, 6 girls); Grade 12: 18 students (7 boys, 11 girls).

Faculty School total: 34. In upper school: 10 men, 9 women; 13 have advanced degrees.

Subjects Offered Algebra, art, biology, calculus, calculus-AP, ceramics, chemistry, community service, drama, drawing, environmental science-AP, fitness, French, French-AP, geometry, health, health and wellness, history, humanities, illustration, instrumental music, music, painting, performing arts, physics, pre-calculus, sculpture, service learning/internship, Spanish, statistics-AP, studio art, world geography, world history, writing, yearbook.

Graduation Requirements Algebra, art, biology, chemistry, English, foreign language, health, history, humanities, mathematics, physics, pre-algebra, science, sports, U.S. history, 96 hours of community service.

Special Academic Programs 13 Advanced Placement exams for which test preparation is offered; independent study.

College Admission Counseling 22 students graduated in 2012; 21 went to college, including Babson College; Earlham College; St. Mary's College of Maryland; The College of Wooster; University of Maryland, Baltimore County; University of Maryland, College Park. Other: 1 had other specific plans. Mean SAT critical reading: 536, mean SAT math: 525, mean SAT writing: 541, mean combined SAT: 1602, mean

composite ACT: 25. 21% scored over 600 on SAT critical reading, 26% scored over 600 on SAT math, 21% scored over 600 on SAT writing, 21% scored over 1800 on combined SAT, 17% scored over 26 on composite ACT.

Student Life Upper grades have student council. Discipline rests primarily with faculty.

Tuition and Aid Day student tuition: $26,100. Tuition installment plan (FACTS Tuition Payment Plan, monthly payment plans, The Tuition Refund Plan). Need-based scholarship grants, need-based financial aid grants available. In 2012–13, 47% of upper-school students received aid. Total amount of financial aid awarded in 2012–13: $539,950.

Admissions Traditional secondary-level entrance grade is 9. For fall 2012, 28 students applied for upper-level admission, 9 were accepted, 7 enrolled. ISEE, SSAT or TOEFL or SLEP required. Deadline for receipt of application materials: January 18. Application fee required: $50. Interview required.

Athletics Interscholastic: basketball (boys, girls), soccer (b); coed interscholastic: cross-country running, equestrian sports, horseback riding, outdoor activities, physical fitness, running, tennis, track and field, ultimate Frisbee. 4 coaches.

Computers Computers are regularly used in all classes. Computer network features include Internet access, wireless campus network, Internet filtering or blocking technology. Campus intranet, student e-mail accounts, and computer access in designated common areas are available to students. The school has a published electronic and media policy.

Contact Ms. Alyssa Jahn, Director of Admission. 301-576-2839. Fax: 301-576-2803. E-mail: ajahn@barrie.org. Website: www.barrie.org

BATTLE GROUND ACADEMY

PO Box 1889
Franklin, Tennessee 37065-1889

Head of School: Mr. Stanley R. Tucker Jr.

General Information Coeducational day college-preparatory, arts, and technology school. Grades K–12. Founded: 1889. Setting: suburban. Nearest major city is Nashville. 55-acre campus. 13 buildings on campus. Approved or accredited by Southern Association of Colleges and Schools, Southern Association of Independent Schools, and Tennessee Department of Education. Member of National Association of Independent Schools. Endowment: $8.3 million. Total enrollment: 809. Upper school average class size: 16. Upper school faculty-student ratio: 1:8. There are 180 required school days per year for Upper School students. Upper School students typically attend 5 days per week. The average school day consists of 7 hours and 15 minutes.

Upper School Student Profile Grade 6: 69 students (45 boys, 24 girls); Grade 7: 76 students (38 boys, 38 girls); Grade 8: 90 students (42 boys, 48 girls); Grade 9: 85 students (47 boys, 38 girls); Grade 10: 79 students (45 boys, 34 girls); Grade 11: 79 students (35 boys, 44 girls); Grade 12: 81 students (50 boys, 31 girls).

Faculty School total: 88. In upper school: 19 men, 19 women; 33 have advanced degrees.

Subjects Offered Accounting, algebra, American history, American literature, art, art history, biology, calculus, chemistry, chorus, computer applications, computer programming, computer science, drama, early childhood, economics, English, English literature, English literature and composition-AP, European history, fine arts, French, French-AP, geography, geometry, government/civics, grammar, health, history, Latin, mathematics, modern European history-AP, music, music history, physical education, physics, science, social studies, Spanish, speech, technical theater, theater, trigonometry, U.S. history, U.S. history-AP, world history, world history-AP, world literature, writing.

Graduation Requirements Arts and fine arts (art, music, dance, drama), computer science, English, foreign language, mathematics, physical education (includes health), science, social studies (includes history). Community service is required.

Special Academic Programs Advanced Placement exam preparation; honors section.

College Admission Counseling 90 students graduated in 2013; 88 went to college. Other: 1 entered military service, 1 had other specific plans. Mean SAT critical reading: 631, mean SAT math: 618, mean SAT writing: 604, mean combined SAT: 1853, mean composite ACT: 27.

Student Life Upper grades have uniform requirement, student council, honor system. Discipline rests primarily with faculty.

Summer Programs Remediation, enrichment, sports, art/fine arts, computer instruction programs offered; session focuses on remediation, enrichment, and sports; held both on and off campus; held at Local Farm; accepts boys and girls; open to students from other schools. 550 students usually enrolled. 2014 schedule: June 3 to July 27. Application deadline: none.

Tuition and Aid Day student tuition: $18,750. Tuition installment plan (The Tuition Plan, FACTS Tuition Payment Plan, individually arranged payment plans). Merit scholarship grants, need-based scholarship grants, paying campus jobs available. In 2013–14, 21% of upper-school students received aid. Total amount of financial aid awarded in 2013–14: $530,941.

Admissions Traditional secondary-level entrance grade is 9. ISEE required. Deadline for receipt of application materials: none. Application fee required: $50. Interview required.

Athletics Interscholastic: baseball (boys), basketball (b,g), cheering (g), cross-country running (b,g), dance team (g), fitness (b,g), football (b), golf (b,g), physical fitness (b,g), physical training (b,g), soccer (b,g), softball (g), strength & conditioning (b,g), swimming and diving (b,g), tennis (b,g), track and field (b,g), volleyball (g), weight training (b,g), wrestling (b); intramural: baseball (b,g), basketball (b,g), fitness (b,g), football (b), softball (g); coed interscholastic: bowling, fitness, marksmanship, riflery, trap and skeet; coed intramural: fitness, flag football, hiking/backpacking, mountain biking, outdoor activities, outdoor adventure, physical training, rock climbing, ropes courses, soccer. 1 PE instructor, 4 coaches, 1 athletic trainer.

Computers Computers are regularly used in art, college planning, desktop publishing, English, foreign language, geography, history, library, literary magazine, mathematics, newspaper, photography, SAT preparation, science, social studies, Spanish, study skills, technology, theater, writing classes. Computer network features include on-campus library services, online commercial services, Internet access, wireless campus network, Internet filtering or blocking technology. Campus intranet, student e-mail accounts, and computer access in designated common areas are available to students. Students grades are available online. The school has a published electronic and media policy.

Contact Robin Goertz, Director of Admissions. 615-567-9014. E-mail: robin.goertz@mybga.org. Website: www.battlegroundacademy.org

BAY RIDGE PREPARATORY SCHOOL

7420 Fourth Avenue
Brooklyn, New York 11209
Head of School: Dr. Michael T. Dealy

General Information Coeducational day college-preparatory, general academic, and arts school. Grades K–12. Founded: 1998. Setting: urban. 1 building on campus. Approved or accredited by New York State Board of Regents and New York Department of Education. Member of National Association of Independent Schools. Upper school average class size: 17. Upper school faculty-student ratio: 1:7. Upper School students typically attend 5 days per week. The average school day consists of 6 hours and 15 minutes.

Faculty School total: 30. In upper school: 25 have advanced degrees.

Subjects Offered Algebra, American government, American history, American literature, ancient world history, art, art history, biology, calculus, chemistry, college admission preparation, college counseling, college writing, computer science, creative writing, earth science, economics, English, English literature, European history, European literature, geometry, health education, journalism, microbiology, modern history, music composition, physics, SAT preparation, Shakespeare, Spanish, statistics, U.S. government and politics.

Special Academic Programs Advanced Placement exam preparation; honors section; independent study; study at local college for college credit; academic accommodation for the gifted, the musically talented, and the artistically talented; remedial reading and/or remedial writing; remedial math; programs in English, mathematics, general development for dyslexic students.

College Admission Counseling 56 students graduated in 2013; 55 went to college. Other: 1 entered military service.

Student Life Upper grades have specified standards of dress, honor system. Discipline rests primarily with faculty.

Tuition and Aid Tuition installment plan (FACTS Tuition Payment Plan, monthly payment plans). Tuition reduction for siblings, merit scholarship grants available.

Admissions Traditional secondary-level entrance grade is 9. For fall 2013, 75 students applied for upper-level admission, 20 were accepted, 15 enrolled. Deadline for receipt of application materials: none. Application fee required: $60. Interview required.

Athletics Interscholastic: baseball (boys), basketball (b,g), soccer (b,g); intramural: baseball (b), basketball (g), cheering (g), hockey (b), soccer (b,g), softball (g); coed interscholastic: squash; coed intramural: cross-country running, dance, dance squad, martial arts, squash, track and field, yoga. 4 PE instructors, 7 coaches.

Computers Computer network features include Internet access, wireless campus network. Student e-mail accounts and computer access in designated common areas are available to students. Students grades are available online.

Contact Ms. Wendy Freeburn, Admissions Coordinator. 718-833-9090 Ext. 305. Fax: 718-833-6680. E-mail: admissions@bayridgeprep.org. Website: www.bayridgeprep.org

THE BAY SCHOOL OF SAN FRANCISCO

35 Keyes Avenue, The Presidio of San Francisco
San Francisco, California 94129
Head of School: Mr. Timothy Johnson

General Information Coeducational day college-preparatory school. Grades 9–12. Founded: 2004. Setting: urban. 2 buildings on campus. Approved or accredited by Western Association of Schools and Colleges and California Department of Education. Member of National Association of Independent Schools and Secondary School Admission Test Board. Total enrollment: 324. Upper school average class size: 14. Upper school faculty-student ratio: 1:8. The average school day consists of 6 hours and 40 minutes.

Upper School Student Profile Grade 9: 90 students (90 girls); Grade 10: 82 students (82 girls); Grade 11: 78 students (78 girls); Grade 12: 74 students (74 girls).

Faculty School total: 38. In upper school: 17 men, 21 women; 27 have advanced degrees.

Graduation Requirements Senior Signature Project.

Student Life Upper grades have student council. Discipline rests equally with students and faculty.

Tuition and Aid Day student tuition: $39,000. Tuition installment plan (Insured Tuition Payment Plan, monthly payment plans). Need-based scholarship grants available. In 2013–14, 30% of upper-school students received aid.

Admissions Traditional secondary-level entrance grade is 9. ISEE, PSAT or SAT for applicants to grade 11 and 12 or SSAT required. Deadline for receipt of application materials: January 16. Application fee required: $90. Interview required.

Athletics Interscholastic: baseball (boys), basketball (b), climbing (b), golf (b), lacrosse (b), tennis (b); coed interscholastic: cross-country running, sailing, track and field, volleyball; coed intramural: aerobics, aerobics/dance, backpacking, dance, dance squad, hiking/backpacking, rock climbing, yoga.

Computers Computer network features include on-campus library services, Internet access, wireless campus network, Internet filtering or blocking technology. Student e-mail accounts are available to students.

Contact Ms. Brooke Wilson, Admission Associate. 415-684-8949. Fax: 415-561-5808. E-mail: admission@bayschoolsf.org. Website: www.bayschoolsf.org/

BAYSIDE ACADEMY

303 Dryer Avenue
Daphne, Alabama 36526
Head of School: Mr. Peter B. Huestis

General Information Coeducational day college-preparatory, arts, and technology school. Grades PK–12. Founded: 1970. Setting: small town. Nearest major city is Mobile. 44-acre campus. 9 buildings on campus. Approved or accredited by Southern Association of Colleges and Schools, Southern Association of Independent Schools, and Alabama Department of Education. Total enrollment: 727. Upper school average class size: 18. Upper school faculty-student ratio: 1:9. There are 177 required school days per year for Upper School students. The average school day consists of 7 hours.

Faculty School total: 72. In upper school: 11 men, 15 women; 22 have advanced degrees.

Subjects Offered Advanced Placement courses, algebra, American history, American literature, art, art history, biology, biology-AP, calculus, chemistry, chemistry-AP, computer programming, computer science, creative writing, drama, economics, English, English literature, environmental science, European history, film, fine arts, French, genetics, geography, geometry, government/civics, grammar, histology, history, Latin, marine biology, mathematics, multimedia, music, photography, physical education, physics, science, social studies, Spanish, speech, theater, trigonometry, world history, world literature, writing.

Graduation Requirements Arts and fine arts (art, music, dance, drama), computer science, English, foreign language, mathematics, physical education (includes health), science, social studies (includes history).

Special Academic Programs 15 Advanced Placement exams for which test preparation is offered; honors section; independent study; study abroad; programs in English, mathematics, general development for dyslexic students.

College Admission Counseling 73 students graduated in 2012; 72 went to college, including Auburn University; College of Charleston; Rhodes College; The University of Alabama; Tulane University; Vanderbilt University. Other: 1 entered military service. 80% scored over 26 on composite ACT.

Student Life Upper grades have uniform requirement, student council, honor system. Discipline rests primarily with faculty.

Tuition and Aid Day student tuition: $10,300. Tuition installment plan (monthly payment plans, individually arranged payment plans). Need-based scholarship grants available. In 2012–13, 15% of upper-school students received aid.

Admissions Traditional secondary-level entrance grade is 9. For fall 2012, 23 students applied for upper-level admission, 18 were accepted, 14 enrolled. Otis-Lennon School Ability Test, Stanford Achievement Test and Stanford Achievement Test, Otis-Lennon School Ability Test required. Deadline for receipt of application materials: none. Application fee required: $100. Interview required.

Athletics Interscholastic: aerobics/dance (girls), aquatics (b,g), baseball (b), basketball (b,g), cheering (g), cross-country running (b,g), dance (g), dance squad (g), dance team (g), football (b), golf (b,g), indoor track (b,g), indoor track & field (b,g), soccer (b,g), softball (g), swimming and diving (b,g), tennis (b,g), track and field (b,g), volleyball (g); intramural: ballet (g), dance (g), dance team (g), football (b), soccer (b,g); coed intramural: ballet, basketball, bicycling, canoeing/kayaking, dance, equestrian sports, physical training, sailing, scuba diving, soccer, strength & conditioning, track and field, weight training, yoga. 6 PE instructors, 11 coaches, 1 athletic trainer.

Computers Computer network features include on-campus library services, online commercial services, Internet access, wireless campus network, Internet filtering or blocking technology. Campus intranet is available to students. Students grades are available online.

Contact Alan M. Foster, Director of Admissions. 251-338-6415. Fax: 251-338-6310. E-mail: afoster@baysideacademy.org. Website: www.baysideacademy.org

BAYVIEW GLEN SCHOOL

275 Duncan Mill Road
Toronto, Ontario M3B 3H9, Canada

Head of School: Mrs. Eileen Daunt

General Information Coeducational day college-preparatory, general academic, arts, business, technology, and athletics school. Grades PK–12. Founded: 1962. Setting: urban. 40-acre campus. 1 building on campus. Approved or accredited by Canadian Association of Independent Schools, Conference of Independent Schools of Ontario, and Ontario Department of Education. Language of instruction: English. Upper school average class size: 22. Upper school faculty-student ratio: 1:22. Upper School students typically attend 5 days per week. The average school day consists of 7 hours.

Faculty School total: 100. In upper school: 18 men, 14 women.

Subjects Offered Advanced Placement courses, all academic.

Special Academic Programs Advanced Placement exam preparation.

Student Life Upper grades have uniform requirement, student council. Discipline rests primarily with faculty.

Tuition and Aid Day student tuition: CAN$21,200. Guaranteed tuition plan. Tuition installment plan (monthly payment plans, individually arranged payment plans). Bursaries, need-based scholarship grants available.

Admissions Admissions testing required. Application fee required. On-campus interview required.

Computers Computers are regularly used in all academic classes. Computer network features include on-campus library services, Internet access, wireless campus network, Internet filtering or blocking technology. Campus intranet, student e-mail accounts, and computer access in designated common areas are available to students. Students grades are available online. The school has a published electronic and media policy.

Contact Mrs. Judy Maxwell, Director of Admissions. 416-443-1030 Ext. 605. Fax: 416-443-1032. E-mail: jmaxwell@bayviewglen.ca. Website:

BEARSPAW CHRISTIAN SCHOOL

15001 69 Street NW
Calgary, Alberta T3R 1C5, Canada

Head of School: Mr. Kelly Blake

General Information Coeducational day and distance learning college-preparatory, general academic, business, and religious studies school, affiliated with Christian faith. Grades K–12. Distance learning grades 1–12. Founded: 1991. Setting: rural. 40-acre campus. 3 buildings on campus. Approved or accredited by Association of Christian Schools International, Association of Independent Schools and Colleges of Alberta, and Alberta Department of Education. Language of instruction: English. Total enrollment: 559. Upper school average class size: 20. Upper school faculty-student ratio: 1:10. There are 177 required school days per year for Upper School students. The average school day consists of 6 hours and 45 minutes.

Upper School Student Profile Grade 10: 41 students (15 boys, 26 girls); Grade 11: 35 students (11 boys, 24 girls); Grade 12: 40 students (12 boys, 28 girls). 95% of students are Christian faith.

Faculty School total: 24. In upper school: 7 men, 17 women; 2 have advanced degrees.

Subjects Offered 20th century history, 20th century world history, acting, advanced chemistry, advanced math, algebra, applied music, art, athletic training, athletics, Bible studies, biology, business, business communications, business education, business law, calculus, Canadian history, Canadian law, career and personal planning, career education, chemistry, Christian education, Christianity, communication skills, computer applications, English composition, food and nutrition, foreign language, French as a second language, general math, health and wellness, keyboarding, media arts, physical education, physics, science, social studies, Spanish, world history.

Graduation Requirements Bible, English, mathematics, science, social studies (includes history).

Special Academic Programs Honors section; independent study; remedial math; special instructional classes for students with learning disabilities, Attention Deficit Disorder, emotional problems, and dyslexia.

College Admission Counseling 34 students graduated in 2012; they went to Trinity Western University; University of Alberta; University of Calgary; University of Victoria.

Student Life Upper grades have uniform requirement, student council, honor system. Discipline rests primarily with faculty. Attendance at religious services is required.

Tuition and Aid Day student tuition: CAN$5765. Tuition installment plan (monthly payment plans, individually arranged payment plans). Tuition reduction for siblings, need-based scholarship grants available. In 2012–13, 16% of upper-school students received aid. Total amount of financial aid awarded in 2012–13: CAN$125,245.

Admissions Traditional secondary-level entrance grade is 10. For fall 2012, 11 students applied for upper-level admission, 7 were accepted, 7 enrolled. Achievement

tests, admissions testing, CTB/McGraw-Hill/Macmillan Co-op Test, WAIS, WICS, Woodcock-Johnson and writing sample required. Deadline for receipt of application materials: September 30. Application fee required: CAN$400. Interview required.

Athletics Interscholastic: badminton (boys, girls), basketball (b,g), cross-country running (b,g), floor hockey (b,g), golf (b,g), indoor soccer (b,g), track and field (b,g), volleyball (b,g), wrestling (b); intramural: aerobics/dance (b,g), badminton (b,g), basketball (b,g), cross-country running (b,g), flag football (b,g), floor hockey (b,g), track and field (b,g), volleyball (b,g), wrestling (b,g); coed interscholastic: badminton, indoor soccer, soccer; coed intramural: aerobics/dance, badminton, ball hockey, basketball, flag football, floor hockey, handball, indoor soccer, strength & conditioning, volleyball. 2 PE instructors, 1 athletic trainer.

Computers Computers are regularly used in all academic classes. Computer network features include Internet access, wireless campus network, Internet filtering or blocking technology. Student e-mail accounts and computer access in designated common areas are available to students. Students grades are available online. The school has a published electronic and media policy.

Contact Mrs. Amie Lee, Registrar. 403-295-2566 Ext. 1102. Fax: 403-275-8170. E-mail: alee@bearspawschool.com. Website: www.bearspawschool.com

BEAVER COUNTRY DAY SCHOOL

791 Hammond Street
Chestnut Hill, Massachusetts 02467

Head of School: Peter R. Hutton

General Information Coeducational day college-preparatory and arts school. Grades 6–12. Founded: 1920. Setting: suburban. Nearest major city is Boston. 17-acre campus. 3 buildings on campus. Approved or accredited by Association of Independent Schools in New England, New England Association of Schools and Colleges, The College Board, and Massachusetts Department of Education. Member of National Association of Independent Schools and Secondary School Admission Test Board. Endowment: $10 million. Total enrollment: 451. Upper school average class size: 15. Upper school faculty-student ratio: 1:8. Upper School students typically attend 5 days per week. The average school day consists of 7 hours and 40 minutes.

Upper School Student Profile Grade 9: 70 students (41 boys, 29 girls); Grade 10: 90 students (48 boys, 42 girls); Grade 11: 80 students (40 boys, 40 girls); Grade 12: 86 students (40 boys, 46 girls).

Faculty School total: 71. In upper school: 24 men, 34 women; 41 have advanced degrees.

Subjects Offered 20th century American writers, 20th century history, 20th century world history, 3-dimensional art, 3-dimensional design, acting, advanced biology, advanced chemistry, advanced math, algebra, American Civil War, American democracy, American foreign policy, American government, American history, American literature, American studies, anatomy and physiology, art, art history, arts, astronomy, athletics, bioethics, bioethics, DNA and culture, biology, biotechnology, business communications, business skills, calculus, career education internship, cell biology, ceramics, chamber groups, chemistry, child development, Chinese history, chorus, civil rights, Civil War, civil war history, classical music, college counseling, college placement, college writing, community service, comparative civilizations, comparative cultures, comparative government and politics, comparative politics, comparative religion, computer graphics, computer math, computer programming, computer skills, constitutional history of U.S., contemporary history, contemporary issues in science, costumes and make-up, creative writing, current history, dance, decision making skills, digital photography, diversity studies, DNA, drama, drawing and design, driver education, economics, English, English literature, equality and freedom, European civilization, European history, expository writing, fine arts, foreign language, foreign policy, French, French as a second language, French studies, functions, gender and religion, gender issues, general math, geography, geometry, geometry with art applications, government, government/civics, grammar, great books, health, history, Holocaust and other genocides, Holocaust studies, honors algebra, honors English, honors geometry, honors U.S. history, human biology, human sexuality, independent study, integrated mathematics, international affairs, jazz, jazz band, journalism, junior and senior seminars, Latin American history, Latin American studies, marketing, mathematics, Middle Eastern history, modern European history, music, musical theater, painting, peer counseling, philosophy, photography, physical education, physics, play production, poetry, pre-calculus, programming, psychology, science, Shakespeare, social justice, social studies, society, politics and law, Spanish, Spanish literature, squash, statistics, studio art, study skills, theater, trigonometry, typing, U.S. history, world history, writing.

Graduation Requirements Arts, English, foreign language, history, interdisciplinary studies, mathematics, science, 40 hours of community service.

Special Academic Programs Honors section; independent study.

College Admission Counseling 78 students graduated in 2012; all went to college, including Harvard University; Occidental College; Skidmore College; Smith College; Stanford University; University of Southern California.

Student Life Upper grades have student council, honor system. Discipline rests equally with students and faculty.

Tuition and Aid Day student tuition: $38,590. Tuition installment plan (Academic Management Services Plan, Key Tuition Payment Plan, monthly payment plans, individually arranged payment plans). Need-based scholarship grants available. In

2012–13, 26% of upper-school students received aid. Total amount of financial aid awarded in 2012–13: $3,335,098.

Admissions Traditional secondary-level entrance grade is 9. For fall 2012, 433 students applied for upper-level admission, 326 were accepted, 97 enrolled. ISEE or SSAT required. Deadline for receipt of application materials: January 15. Application fee required: $45. Interview required.

Athletics Interscholastic: baseball (boys), basketball (b,g), cross-country running (b,g), field hockey (g), ice hockey (g), lacrosse (b,g), soccer (b,g), softball (g), tennis (b,g), volleyball (b); wrestling (b); coed interscholastic: cross-country running, fencing, fitness, Frisbee, golf, squash, ultimate Frisbee; coed intramural: dance team, flag football, floor hockey, physical fitness, strength & conditioning, yoga. 2 PE instructors, 108 coaches, 1 athletic trainer.

Computers Computers are regularly used in art, English, foreign language, history, mathematics, science classes. Computer network features include on-campus library services, online commercial services, Internet access, wireless campus network, Internet filtering or blocking technology. Student e-mail accounts are available to students. Students grades are available online. The school has a published electronic and media policy.

Contact Nedda Bonassera, Admission Office Manager. 617-738-2725. Fax: 617-738-2767. E-mail: admission@bcdschool.org. Website: www.bcdschool.org

THE BEEKMAN SCHOOL

220 East 50th Street
New York, New York 10022

Head of School: George Higgins

General Information Coeducational day and distance learning college-preparatory, general academic, arts, and technology school. Grades 9–PG. Distance learning grades 9–12. Founded: 1925. Setting: urban. 1 building on campus. Approved or accredited by New York State Board of Regents and New York Department of Education. Total enrollment: 80. Upper school average class size: 8. Upper school faculty-student ratio: 1:8. There are 165 required school days per year for Upper School students. Upper School students typically attend 5 days per week. The average school day consists of 6 hours and 15 minutes.

Upper School Student Profile Grade 9: 15 students (8 boys, 7 girls); Grade 10: 19 students (11 boys, 8 girls); Grade 11: 21 students (12 boys, 9 girls); Grade 12: 25 students (13 boys, 12 girls); Postgraduate: 2 students (1 boy, 1 girl).

Faculty School total: 12. In upper school: 4 men, 8 women; 10 have advanced degrees.

Subjects Offered Advanced Placement courses, algebra, American history, anatomy and physiology, ancient world history, art, astronomy, bioethics, biology, business mathematics, calculus, calculus-AP, chemistry, computer animation, computer art, computer science, conceptual physics, creative writing, drama, drawing, Eastern religion and philosophy, ecology, economics, English, environmental science, ESL, European history, film, French, geometry, government, health, modern politics, modern world history, photography, physical education, physical science, physics, poetry, pre-calculus, psychology, SAT preparation, sculpture, Spanish, TOEFL preparation, trigonometry, U.S. history, video film production, Web site design, Western philosophy.

Graduation Requirements Art, computer technologies, electives, English, foreign language, health education, mathematics, physical education (includes health), science, social studies (includes history).

Special Academic Programs Advanced Placement exam preparation; honors section; accelerated programs; independent study; academic accommodation for the gifted, the musically talented, and the artistically talented; remedial reading and/or remedial writing; remedial math; programs in English, mathematics, general development for dyslexic students; ESL (4 students enrolled).

College Admission Counseling 28 students graduated in 2013; 27 went to college, including Arizona State University; Boston University; Fordham University; New York University; Sarah Lawrence College; University of Vermont. Other: 1 had other specific plans. Mean SAT critical reading: 556, mean SAT math: 519, mean SAT writing: 543. 33% scored over 600 on SAT critical reading, 27% scored over 600 on SAT math, 30% scored over 600 on SAT writing.

Student Life Upper grades have student council, honor system. Discipline rests primarily with faculty.

Summer Programs Remediation, enrichment, advancement, ESL programs offered; session focuses on academics; held on campus; accepts boys and girls; open to students from other schools. 35 students usually enrolled. 2014 schedule: July 7 to August 14. Application deadline: June 27.

Tuition and Aid Day student tuition: $35,000. Tuition installment plan (monthly payment plans, individually arranged payment plans). Merit scholarship grants available.

Admissions Traditional secondary-level entrance grade is 9. For fall 2013, 39 students applied for upper-level admission, 38 were accepted, 33 enrolled. Deadline for receipt of application materials: none. No application fee required. On-campus interview required.

Athletics 1 PE instructor.

Computers Computer resources include online commercial services, Internet access.

Contact George Higgins, Headmaster. 212-755-6666. Fax: 212-888-6085. E-mail: georgeh@beekmanschool.org. Website: www.BeekmanSchool.org

BELEN JESUIT PREPARATORY SCHOOL

500 Southwest 127th Avenue
Miami, Florida 33184

Head of School: Fr. Pedro A. Suarez, SJ

General Information Boys' day college-preparatory and religious studies school, affiliated with Roman Catholic Church. Grades 6–12. Founded: 1854. Setting: urban. 32-acre campus. 3 buildings on campus. Approved or accredited by CITA (Commission on International and Trans-Regional Accreditation), Jesuit Secondary Education Association, National Catholic Education Association, Southern Association of Colleges and Schools, and Florida Department of Education. Endowment: $8 million. Total enrollment: 1,488. Upper school average class size: 25. Upper school faculty-student ratio: 1:13. There are 175 required school days per year for Upper School students. Upper School students typically attend 5 days per week. The average school day consists of 8 hours.

Upper School Student Profile Grade 9: 201 students (201 boys); Grade 10: 233 students (233 boys); Grade 11: 236 students (236 boys); Grade 12: 220 students (220 boys). 98% of students are Roman Catholic.

Faculty School total: 120. In upper school: 43 men, 34 women; 67 have advanced degrees.

Subjects Offered Advanced Placement courses, art, art history, biology, chemistry, composition, computers, English, English literature, French, history, mathematics, music, philosophy, physical education, physics, religion, science, social studies, Spanish.

Graduation Requirements Arts and fine arts (art, music, dance, drama), electives, English, foreign language, mathematics, philosophy, physical education (includes health), religion (includes Bible studies and theology), science, social sciences, social studies (includes history). Community service is required.

Special Academic Programs Advanced Placement exam preparation; honors section; study at local college for college credit.

College Admission Counseling 201 students graduated in 2013; all went to college, including Florida International University; Florida State University; Miami Dade College; Tallahassee Community College; University of Florida; University of Miami. Mean SAT critical reading: 587, mean SAT math: 597, mean SAT writing: 571, mean combined SAT: 1755, mean composite ACT: 25. 36% scored over 1800 on combined SAT, 40% scored over 26 on composite ACT.

Student Life Upper grades have uniform requirement, student council. Discipline rests primarily with faculty.

Summer Programs Remediation, enrichment programs offered; session focuses on make-up courses; held on campus; accepts boys; not open to students from other schools. 200 students usually enrolled. 2014 schedule: June 18 to July 18.

Tuition and Aid Day student tuition: $13,500. Tuition installment plan (monthly payment plans). Need-based scholarship grants available. In 2013–14, 35% of upper-school students received aid. Total amount of financial aid awarded in 2013–14: $400,000.

Admissions Traditional secondary-level entrance grade is 9. For fall 2013, 123 students applied for upper-level admission, 44 were accepted, 32 enrolled. School's own exam required. Deadline for receipt of application materials: January 30. Application fee required: $60.

Athletics Interscholastic: baseball, basketball, bowling, crew, cross-country running, football, golf, lacrosse, soccer, swimming and diving, tennis, track and field, volleyball, water polo, wrestling; intramural: fencing, fishing, in-line hockey, weight training. 6 PE instructors, 22 coaches, 1 athletic trainer.

Computers Computers are regularly used in art, English, foreign language, history, mathematics, music, science classes. Computer network features include on-campus library services, online commercial services, Internet access, wireless campus network, Internet filtering or blocking technology. Campus intranet and student e-mail accounts are available to students. Students grades are available online. The school has a published electronic and media policy.

Contact Mrs. Chris Besil, Admissions Secretary. 786-621-4032. Fax: 786-621-4033. E-mail: admissions@belenjesuit.org. Website: www.belenjesuit.org

BELLARMINE COLLEGE PREPARATORY

960 West Hedding Street
San Jose, California 95126

Head of School: Mr. Chris Meyercord

General Information Boys' day college-preparatory, arts, religious studies, and technology school, affiliated with Roman Catholic Church. Grades 9–12. Founded: 1851. Setting: suburban. 26-acre campus. 14 buildings on campus. Approved or accredited by National Catholic Education Association and Western Association of Schools and Colleges. Endowment: $57 million. Total enrollment: 1,600. Upper school average class size: 25. Upper school faculty-student ratio: 1:13. There are 170 required school days per year for Upper School students. Upper School students typically attend 5 days per week. The average school day consists of 6 hours and 25 minutes.

Upper School Student Profile Grade 9: 415 students (415 boys); Grade 10: 410 students (410 boys); Grade 11: 390 students (390 boys); Grade 12: 385 students (385 boys). 75% of students are Roman Catholic.

Faculty School total: 90. In upper school: 60 men, 30 women; 65 have advanced degrees.

Subjects Offered Algebra, American history, American literature, anatomy, art, arts, biology, calculus, ceramics, chemistry, community service, computer science, drama, English, English literature, ethics, European history, expository writing, fine arts, French, geography, geometry, government/civics, history, international relations, Latin, Mandarin, mathematics, music, physical education, physics, psychology, religion, science, social sciences, social studies, Spanish, speech, theater, theology, trigonometry, world history, world literature, writing.

Graduation Requirements Arts and fine arts (art, music, dance, drama), English, foreign language, mathematics, physical education (includes health), religion (includes Bible studies and theology), science, social sciences, social studies (includes history), 75 hours of Christian service.

Special Academic Programs Advanced Placement exam preparation; honors section; independent study; special instructional classes for students with learning disabilities and Attention Deficit Disorder.

College Admission Counseling 392 students graduated in 2012; 390 went to college, including California Polytechnic State University, San Luis Obispo; San Jose State University; Santa Clara University; University of California, Berkeley; University of California, Davis; University of Southern California. Other: 2 had other specific plans. Mean combined SAT: 1884, mean composite ACT: 27.

Student Life Upper grades have specified standards of dress, student council, honor system. Discipline rests primarily with faculty. Attendance at religious services is required.

Tuition and Aid Day student tuition: $16,770. Tuition installment plan (FACTS Tuition Payment Plan, semester payment plan, 11 installment plan). Need-based scholarship grants available. In 2012–13, 24% of upper-school students received aid. Total amount of financial aid awarded in 2012–13: $3,700,000.

Admissions Traditional secondary-level entrance grade is 9. For fall 2012, 950 students applied for upper-level admission, 500 were accepted, 415 enrolled. High School Placement Test required. Deadline for receipt of application materials: December 15. Application fee required: $70.

Athletics Interscholastic: aquatics, baseball, basketball, cross-country running, diving, football, golf, ice hockey, lacrosse, soccer, swimming and diving, tennis, track and field, volleyball, water polo, wrestling; intramural: basketball, flag football, Frisbee, in-line hockey, indoor hockey, soccer, tai chi, touch football, yoga. 4 PE instructors, 15 coaches, 2 athletic trainers.

Computers Computers are regularly used in art, English, foreign language, mathematics, music, science classes. Computer network features include on-campus library services, online commercial services, Internet access, wireless campus network. Student e-mail accounts are available to students. Students grades are available online. The school has a published electronic and media policy.

Contact Terry Council, Admissions Assistant. 408-294-9224. Fax: 408-294-1894. E-mail: admissions@bcp.org. Website: www.bcp.org

BENET ACADEMY

2200 Maple Avenue
Lisle, Illinois 60532

Head of School: Mr. Stephen A. Marth

General Information Coeducational day college-preparatory, arts, and religious studies school, affiliated with Roman Catholic Church. Grades 9–12. Founded: 1887. Setting: suburban. Nearest major city is Chicago. 54-acre campus. 8 buildings on campus. Approved or accredited by North Central Association of Colleges and Schools and Illinois Department of Education. Total enrollment: 1,357. Upper school average class size: 27. Upper school faculty-student ratio: 1:18. There are 177 required school days per year for Upper School students. Upper School students typically attend 5 days per week. The average school day consists of 6 hours and 59 minutes.

Upper School Student Profile Grade 9: 358 students (184 boys, 174 girls); Grade 10: 327 students (159 boys, 168 girls); Grade 11: 342 students (178 boys, 164 girls); Grade 12: 330 students (165 boys, 165 girls). 97% of students are Roman Catholic.

Faculty School total: 76. In upper school: 45 men, 31 women; 67 have advanced degrees.

Subjects Offered Algebra, American history, American literature, art history, biology, business, calculus, chemistry, computer programming, computer science, creative writing, drama, driver education, economics, English, European history, French, geography, geometry, German, government/civics, health, history, Latin, mathematics, music, physical education, physics, religion, science, Spanish, speech, statistics, trigonometry, U.S. history-AP, world history, world literature, writing.

Graduation Requirements Computer science, English, foreign language, mathematics, physical education (includes health), religion (includes Bible studies and theology), science, social studies (includes history).

Special Academic Programs 21 Advanced Placement exams for which test preparation is offered; honors section; study at local college for college credit; academic accommodation for the gifted.

College Admission Counseling 324 students graduated in 2013; 323 went to college, including Indiana University–Purdue University Fort Wayne; Miami University; University of Dayton; University of Illinois; University of Missouri;

University of Notre Dame. Other: 1 had other specific plans. Mean SAT critical reading: 652, mean SAT math: 653, mean SAT writing: 650, mean composite ACT: 28.

Student Life Upper grades have uniform requirement, student council. Discipline rests primarily with faculty. Attendance at religious services is required.

Summer Programs Computer instruction programs offered; session focuses on computer literacy skills for incoming freshmen; held on campus; accepts boys and girls; not open to students from other schools. 320 students usually enrolled. 2014 schedule: June 9 to July 25.

Tuition and Aid Day student tuition: $9950. Tuition installment plan (monthly payment plans). Tuition reduction for siblings, need-based scholarship grants available. In 2013–14, 5% of upper-school students received aid. Total amount of financial aid awarded in 2013–14: $150,000.

Admissions Traditional secondary-level entrance grade is 9. For fall 2013, 550 students applied for upper-level admission, 430 were accepted, 358 enrolled. High School Placement Test required. Deadline for receipt of application materials: January 11. Application fee required: $35. On-campus interview required.

Athletics Interscholastic: baseball (boys), basketball (b,g), cheering (g), cross-country running (b,g), dance team (g), fishing (b), football (b), golf (b,g), lacrosse (b,g), pom squad (g), soccer (b,g), softball (g), strength & conditioning (b), swimming and diving (b,g), tennis (b,g), track and field (b,g), volleyball (b,g); intramural: weight training (b,g), yoga (g); coed interscholastic: ice hockey; coed intramural: bowling, flag football, Frisbee. 4 PE instructors, 30 coaches, 1 athletic trainer.

Computers Computers are regularly used in English, history, mathematics, science, Spanish classes. Computer network features include on-campus library services, online commercial services, Internet access, wireless campus network, Internet filtering or blocking technology. Campus intranet and student e-mail accounts are available to students. Students grades are available online. The school has a published electronic and media policy.

Contact Mr. James E. Brown, Assistant Principal. 630-719-2782. Fax: 630-719-2849. E-mail: jbrown@benet.org. Website: www.benet.org/

THE BENJAMIN SCHOOL

11000 Ellison Wilson Road
North Palm Beach, Florida 33408

Head of School: Mr. Robert S. Goldberg

General Information Coeducational day college-preparatory and arts school. Grades PK–12. Founded: 1960. Setting: suburban. Nearest major city is West Palm Beach. 50-acre campus. 5 buildings on campus. Approved or accredited by Southern Association of Colleges and Schools and Florida Department of Education. Member of National Association of Independent Schools and Secondary School Admission Test Board. Endowment: $5.6 million. Total enrollment: 1,081. Upper school average class size: 16. Upper school faculty-student ratio: 1:8. There are 175 required school days per year for Upper School students. Upper School students typically attend 5 days per week. The average school day consists of 5 hours and 30 minutes.

Upper School Student Profile Grade 9: 102 students (47 boys, 55 girls); Grade 10: 105 students (55 boys, 50 girls); Grade 11: 113 students (64 boys, 49 girls); Grade 12: 100 students (52 boys, 48 girls).

Faculty School total: 141. In upper school: 18 men, 21 women; 35 have advanced degrees.

Subjects Offered 3-dimensional art, acting, African studies, algebra, American history, anatomy and physiology, art, art history, Asian studies, band, Basic programming, biology, biology-AP, calculus, calculus-AP, Caribbean history, cartooning/animation, ceramics, chemistry, chemistry-AP, choral music, chorus, comparative government and politics-AP, comparative religion, composition-AP, computer animation, computer programming, computer science, computer science-AP, current events, dance, debate, drama, earth science, ecology, economics, economics-AP, English, English language and composition-AP, English literature, English literature and composition-AP, environmental science, European history, expository writing, film studies, French, French language-AP, genetics, geometry, government-AP, government/civics, grammar, honors English, honors geometry, human geography - AP, literature and composition-AP, marine biology, modern European history-AP, mythology, physical education, physics, piano, pre-calculus, psychology, SAT preparation, Spanish, Spanish language-AP, Spanish literature-AP, speech, statistics-AP, theater, trigonometry, U.S. government, U.S. government and politics-AP, U.S. history-AP, video film production, world history.

Graduation Requirements Arts and fine arts (art, music, dance, drama), computer science, English, foreign language, mathematics, physical education (includes health), science, social sciences, social studies (includes history), work program for seniors.

Special Academic Programs 22 Advanced Placement exams for which test preparation is offered; honors section; academic accommodation for the gifted, the musically talented, and the artistically talented.

College Admission Counseling 113 students graduated in 2013; 112 went to college, including Florida State University; Harvard University; The University of Alabama; University of Florida; University of Miami; Wake Forest University. Mean SAT critical reading: 574, mean SAT math: 579, mean SAT writing: 598, mean composite ACT: 26.

Student Life Upper grades have uniform requirement, student council, honor system. Discipline rests primarily with faculty.

Summer Programs Enrichment, advancement, sports, computer instruction programs offered; session focuses on academic advancement; held on campus; accepts boys and girls; open to students from other schools. 40 students usually enrolled. 2014 schedule: June 1 to August 15. Application deadline: May 1.

Tuition and Aid Day student tuition: $24,500. Tuition installment plan (monthly payment plans, The Tuition Solution). Merit scholarship grants, need-based scholarship grants, need-based loans available. In 2013–14, 24% of upper-school students received aid; total upper-school merit-scholarship money awarded: $24,500. Total amount of financial aid awarded in 2013–14: $1,388,838.

Admissions Traditional secondary-level entrance grade is 9. For fall 2013, 83 students applied for upper-level admission, 76 were accepted, 42 enrolled. ERB or SSAT required. Deadline for receipt of application materials: February 1. Application fee required: $100. On-campus interview required.

Athletics Interscholastic: ballet (girls), baseball (b), basketball (b,g), bowling (b,g), cross-country running (b,g), dance (g), dance team (g), diving (b,g), football (b), golf (b,g), lacrosse (b,g), modern dance (g), soccer (b,g), softball (g), tennis (b,g), track and field (b,g), volleyball (g), wrestling (b); coed interscholastic: aerobics/dance, cheering, swimming and diving; coed intramural: sailing. 1 PE instructor, 1 coach, 1 athletic trainer.

Computers Computers are regularly used in art, computer applications, English, foreign language, history, mathematics, science classes. Computer network features include on-campus library services, Internet access, wireless campus network, Internet filtering or blocking technology, tablet laptop program for grades 9 to 12. Student e-mail accounts are available to students. The school has a published electronic and media policy.

Contact Mrs. Mary Lou Primm, Director of Admission. 561-472-3451. Fax: 561-472-3410. E-mail: marylou.primm@thebenjaminschool.org. Website: www.thebenjaminschool.org

BERKELEY CARROLL SCHOOL

181 Lincoln Place
Brooklyn, New York 11217

Head of School: Mr. Robert D. Vitalo

General Information Coeducational day college-preparatory school. Grades N–12. Founded: 1886. Setting: urban. Nearest major city is New York. 3 buildings on campus. Approved or accredited by New York Department of Education. Member of National Association of Independent Schools. Endowment: $2.5 million. Total enrollment: 900. Upper school average class size: 15. Upper school faculty-student ratio: 1:8. There are 174 required school days per year for Upper School students. Upper School students typically attend 5 days per week. The average school day consists of 6 hours and 30 minutes.

Upper School Student Profile Grade 9: 68 students (34 boys, 34 girls); Grade 10: 68 students (34 boys, 34 girls); Grade 11: 68 students (34 boys, 34 girls); Grade 12: 68 students (34 boys, 34 girls).

Faculty School total: 132. In upper school: 28 men, 27 women; 47 have advanced degrees.

Subjects Offered Algebra, American history, American literature, art, art history, astronomy, biology, calculus, ceramics, chemistry, community service, computer applications, conceptual physics, creative writing, dance, drama, economics, engineering, English, environmental science, European history, fine arts, French, geometry, health, history, humanities, Latin, music, photography, physical education, physics, science, Shakespeare, Spanish, statistics, theater, trigonometry, video and animation, world history, writing.

Graduation Requirements Arts and fine arts (art, music, dance, drama), computer science, English, foreign language, mathematics, physical education (includes health), science, social sciences, 2-week Spring Intensives, Senior Speaker Program. Community service is required.

Special Academic Programs Independent study; study abroad.

College Admission Counseling 50 students graduated in 2013; all went to college, including Oberlin College; Rochester Institute of Technology.

Student Life Upper grades have student council, honor system. Discipline rests equally with students and faculty.

Summer Programs Enrichment, sports, art/fine arts programs offered; session focuses on creative arts, athletics, math; held on campus; accepts boys and girls; open to students from other schools. 250 students usually enrolled. 2014 schedule: July 1 to August 1. Application deadline: none.

Tuition and Aid Day student tuition: $35,365. Tuition installment plan (Insured Tuition Payment Plan, Academic Management Services Plan, monthly payment plans, individually arranged payment plans). Need-based scholarship grants available. In 2013–14, 53% of upper-school students received aid. Total amount of financial aid awarded in 2013–14: $2,513,655.

Admissions Traditional secondary-level entrance grade is 9. For fall 2013, 110 students applied for upper-level admission, 40 were accepted, 15 enrolled. ISEE, PSAT and SAT for applicants to grade 11 and 12, SSAT, TOEFL or SLEP or writing sample required. Deadline for receipt of application materials: December 1. Application fee required: $100. On-campus interview required.

Athletics Interscholastic: baseball (boys), basketball (b,g), cross-country running (b,g), indoor track & field (b,g), soccer (b,g), track and field (b,g), volleyball (b,g); intramural: fencing (b,g), yoga (b,g); coed interscholastic: aquatics, dance, judo, swimming and diving, tennis; coed intramural: aquatics, fitness, swimming and diving. 2 PE instructors, 10 coaches.

Computers Computers are regularly used in art, English, foreign language, history, mathematics, music, science classes. Computer network features include on-campus library services, online commercial services, Internet access, Internet filtering or blocking technology. The school has a published electronic and media policy.

Contact Ms. Vanessa Prescott, Director of Admissions. 718-789-6060 Ext. 6527. Fax: 718-398-3640. E-mail: vprescott@berkeleycarroll.org. Website: www.berkeleycarroll.org

BERKELEY PREPARATORY SCHOOL

4811 Kelly Road
Tampa, Florida 33615

Head of School: Joseph W. Seivold

General Information Coeducational day college-preparatory, arts, religious studies, bilingual studies, and technology school, affiliated with Episcopal Church. Grades PK–12. Founded: 1960. Setting: suburban. 80-acre campus. 8 buildings on campus. Approved or accredited by Florida Council of Independent Schools, National Association of Episcopal Schools, Southern Association of Colleges and Schools, Southern Association of Independent Schools, The College Board, and Florida Department of Education. Member of National Association of Independent Schools and Secondary School Admission Test Board. Total enrollment: 1,290. Upper school average class size: 15. Upper school faculty-student ratio: 1:9. Upper School students typically attend 5 days per week. The average school day consists of 7 hours.

Faculty School total: 175. In upper school: 30 men, 38 women; 45 have advanced degrees.

Subjects Offered African history, algebra, American government, American history, American literature, art, art history, biology, biology-AP, calculus, calculus-AP, ceramics, chemistry, chemistry-AP, China/Japan history, community service, computer math, computer programming, computer science, creative writing, dance, drama, drama performance, drama workshop, early childhood, economics, English, English literature, English-AP, environmental science-AP, etymology, European history, expository writing, fine arts, French, French-AP, freshman seminar, geography, geometry, government/civics, grammar, guitar, health, history, history of China and Japan, honors algebra, honors English, honors geometry, instruments, Latin, Latin American history, Latin-AP, logic, Mandarin, math analysis, mathematics, media arts, microbiology, modern European history, modern European history-AP, music, performing arts, philosophy, physical education, physics, physics-AP, pre-calculus, psychology, religious studies, SAT preparation, science, social studies, Spanish, Spanish-AP, speech, stage design, statistics, statistics-AP, technical theater, television, theater, theater production, U.S. history, U.S. history-AP, video, video film production, Western civilization, world history, world literature, writing.

Graduation Requirements Arts and fine arts (art, music, dance, drama), computer science, English, foreign language, mathematics, physical education (includes health), religious studies, science, social studies (includes history). Community service is required.

Special Academic Programs Advanced Placement exam preparation; honors section; independent study; study abroad.

College Admission Counseling 150 students graduated in 2012; all went to college, including Boston College; Duke University; Harvard University; University of Florida; University of Michigan; Wake Forest University. Mean SAT critical reading: 616, mean SAT math: 633, mean SAT writing: 632, mean combined SAT: 1881, mean composite ACT: 28.

Student Life Upper grades have specified standards of dress, student council, honor system. Discipline rests equally with students and faculty.

Tuition and Aid Day student tuition: $20,110. Tuition installment plan (8-installment plan). Merit scholarship grants, need-based scholarship grants available. Total upper-school merit-scholarship money awarded for 2012–13: $8,600,000.

Admissions Traditional secondary-level entrance grade is 9. Otis-Lennon Mental Ability Test and SSAT required. Deadline for receipt of application materials: January 30. Application fee required: $75. On-campus interview required.

Athletics Interscholastic: baseball (b,g), basketball (b,g), cheering (g), crew (b,g), cross-country running (b,g), dance squad (g), dance team (g), diving (b,g), football (b), golf (b,g), ice hockey (b), lacrosse (b), rowing (b,g), soccer (b,g), softball (g), swimming and diving (b,g), tennis (b,g), track and field (b,g), volleyball (b,g); coed interscholastic: weight lifting, wrestling; coed intramural: physical fitness, physical training, power lifting, project adventure, strength & conditioning, wall climbing, weight training. 14 PE instructors, 74 coaches, 2 athletic trainers.

Computers Computers are regularly used in art, English, foreign language, history, mathematics, music, science classes. Computer network features include on-campus library services, online commercial services, Internet access, wireless campus network, Internet filtering or blocking technology. Student e-mail accounts are available to students. Students grades are available online. The school has a published electronic and media policy.

Contact Janie McIlvaine, Director of Admissions. 813-885-1673. Fax: 813-886-6933. E-mail: mcilvjan@berkeleyprep.org. Website: www.berkeleyprep.org

See Display below and Close-Up on page 516.

BERKSHIRE SCHOOL

245 North Undermountain Road
Sheffield, Massachusetts 01257

Head of School: Michael J. Maher

General Information Coeducational boarding and day college-preparatory, arts, and technology school. Grades 9–PG. Founded: 1907. Setting: rural. Nearest major city is Hartford, CT. Students are housed in single-sex dormitories. 400-acre campus. 37 buildings on campus. Approved or accredited by Association of Independent Schools in New England, New England Association of Schools and Colleges, and The Association of Boarding Schools. Member of National Association of Independent Schools and Secondary School Admission Test Board. Endowment: $91 million. Upper school average class size: 12. Upper school faculty-student ratio: 1:5. Upper School students typically attend 6 days per week. The average school day consists of 6 hours and 45 minutes.

Upper School Student Profile Grade 9: 63 students (35 boys, 28 girls); Grade 10: 109 students (66 boys, 43 girls); Grade 11: 102 students (56 boys, 46 girls); Grade 12: 96 students (54 boys, 42 girls); Postgraduate: 16 students (14 boys, 2 girls). 92% of students are boarding students. 8% are state residents. 27 states are represented in upper school student body. 18% are international students. International students from Canada, China, Mexico, Republic of Korea, Venezuela, and Viet Nam; 21 other countries represented in student body.

Faculty School total: 67. In upper school: 42 men, 25 women; 42 have advanced degrees; 49 reside on campus.

Subjects Offered 3-dimensional design, acting, Advanced Placement courses, algebra, American government, American history, American literature, anatomy, ancient history, animal behavior, art, art history, aviation, biology, calculus, ceramics, chemistry, Chinese, choral music, chorus, comparative government and politics, comparative religion, computer programming, constitutional law, creative writing, dance, digital art, drama, drawing and design, economics, English, English literature, environmental science, ESL, ethics, European history, expository writing, French, geology, geometry, health, history, instrumental music, Latin, mathematics, music, music technology, painting, philosophy, photography, physics, pre-calculus, psychology, science, Spanish, studio art, theater, trigonometry, world religions, writing.

Graduation Requirements Arts and fine arts (art, music, dance, drama), English, foreign language, history, mathematics, science. Community service is required.

Special Academic Programs 16 Advanced Placement exams for which test preparation is offered; honors section; independent study; study abroad; ESL (8 students enrolled).

College Admission Counseling 113 students graduated in 2012; all went to college, including Bates College; Colgate University; Connecticut College; Emory University; Hamilton College; Union College.

Student Life Upper grades have specified standards of dress, student council, honor system. Discipline rests equally with students and faculty.

Tuition and Aid Day student tuition: $39,900; 7-day tuition and room/board: $49,900. Tuition installment plan (Key Tuition Payment Plan, monthly payment plans). Need-based scholarship grants available. In 2012–13, 30% of upper-school students received aid. Total amount of financial aid awarded in 2012–13: $4,955,292.

Admissions Traditional secondary-level entrance grade is 9. For fall 2012, 1,012 students applied for upper-level admission, 374 were accepted, 149 enrolled. ACT, PSAT, SAT, SSAT or TOEFL required. Deadline for receipt of application materials: January 15. Application fee required: $75. Interview required.

Athletics Interscholastic: baseball (boys), basketball (b,g), crew (b,g), cross-country running (b,g), field hockey (g), football (b), ice hockey (b,g), lacrosse (b,g), soccer (b,g), softball (g), squash (b,g), tennis (b,g), track and field (b,g), volleyball (g); coed interscholastic: alpine skiing, golf, mountain biking; coed intramural: alpine skiing, canoeing/kayaking, climbing, dance, fly fishing, hiking/backpacking, kayaking, modern dance, mountaineering, outdoor adventure, outdoor education, outdoor skills, rappelling, rock climbing, ropes courses, skiing (cross-country), skiing (downhill), snowboarding, wilderness, wilderness survival. 2 athletic trainers.

Computers Computers are regularly used in art, English, foreign language, mathematics, music, science, technology classes. Computer network features include on-campus library services, online commercial services, Internet access, wireless campus network, Internet filtering or blocking technology, network printing, interactive Polyvision white boards (smart boards). Campus intranet and student e-mail accounts are available to students. Students grades are available online. The school has a published electronic and media policy.

Contact Ms. Karin Tucker, Assistant to Director of Admission. 413-229-1003. Fax: 413-229-1016. E-mail: admission@berkshireschool.org. Website: www.berkshireschool.org

See Display on next page and Close-Up on page 518.

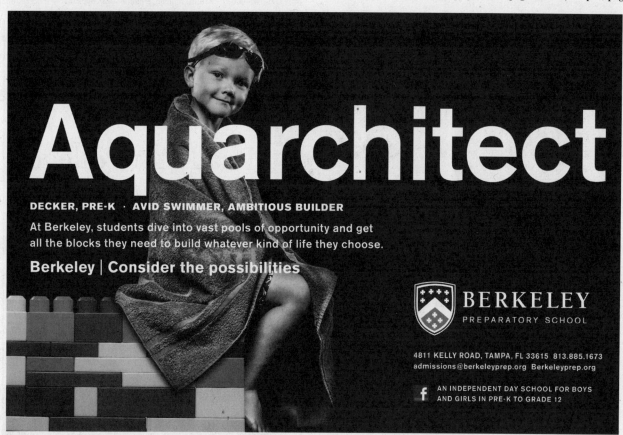

BESANT HILL SCHOOL

8585 Ojai Santa Paula Road
PO Box 850
Ojai, California 93024

Head of School: Mr. Randy Bertin

General Information Coeducational boarding and day college-preparatory and arts school; primarily serves individuals with Attention Deficit Disorder. Grades 9–12. Founded: 1946. Setting: small town. Nearest major city is Los Angeles. Students are housed in single-sex dormitories. 500-acre campus. 14 buildings on campus. Approved or accredited by The Association of Boarding Schools, Western Association of Schools and Colleges, and California Department of Education. Member of National Association of Independent Schools and Secondary School Admission Test Board. Endowment: $1 million. Total enrollment: 100. Upper school average class size: 10. Upper school faculty-student ratio: 1:4. Upper School students typically attend 5 days per week. The average school day consists of 8 hours and 15 minutes.

Upper School Student Profile Grade 9: 17 students (9 boys, 8 girls); Grade 10: 26 students (14 boys, 12 girls); Grade 11: 29 students (16 boys, 13 girls); Grade 12: 28 students (14 boys, 14 girls). 84% of students are boarding students. 40% are state residents. 12 states are represented in upper school student body. 40% are international students. International students from Cameroon, China, Germany, Japan, Mexico, and Taiwan; 5 other countries represented in student body.

Faculty School total: 25. In upper school: 12 men, 13 women; 12 have advanced degrees; 22 reside on campus.

Subjects Offered Acting, adolescent issues, algebra, American history, art, art history, astronomy, biology, calculus, calculus-AP, ceramics, chemistry, computer science, digital art, drama, English, English as a foreign language, English language and composition-AP, English literature, English-AP, environmental science, ESL, ethics, expository writing, film, fine arts, geography, geometry, government/civics, history, mathematics, music, music history, music theory, music theory-AP, philosophy, photography, physical education, physics, psychology, scene study, science, social sciences, social studies, Spanish, theater, world history.

Graduation Requirements Arts and fine arts (art, music, dance, drama), English, foreign language, mathematics, physical education (includes health), science, social sciences, social studies (includes history).

Special Academic Programs 4 Advanced Placement exams for which test preparation is offered; honors section; independent study; study at local college for college credit; academic accommodation for the musically talented and the artistically talented; programs in English, mathematics, general development for dyslexic students; ESL (25 students enrolled).

College Admission Counseling 27 students graduated in 2013; 26 went to college, including San Diego State University; Sarah Lawrence College; University of California, Santa Barbara; University of California, Santa Cruz; University of Colorado Boulder. Other: 1 had other specific plans. Median SAT critical reading: 580, median SAT math: 550, median SAT writing: 500. 18% scored over 600 on SAT critical reading, 10% scored over 600 on SAT math, 15% scored over 600 on SAT writing.

Student Life Upper grades have student council, honor system. Discipline rests equally with students and faculty.

Summer Programs ESL programs offered; session focuses on ESL; held on campus; accepts boys and girls; open to students from other schools. 30 students usually enrolled. 2014 schedule: June 29 to August 2. Application deadline: May 1.

Tuition and Aid Day student tuition: $21,500; 7-day tuition and room/board: $45,886. Tuition installment plan (Academic Management Services Plan, Key Tuition Payment Plan). Tuition reduction for siblings, need-based scholarship grants available. In 2013–14, 25% of upper-school students received aid. Total amount of financial aid awarded in 2013–14: $450,000.

Admissions Traditional secondary-level entrance grade is 9. For fall 2013, 245 students applied for upper-level admission, 86 were accepted, 37 enrolled. Deadline for receipt of application materials: February 1. Application fee required: $75. Interview required.

Athletics Interscholastic: basketball (boys), soccer (b,g), volleyball (g); intramural: baseball (b), basketball (b), soccer (b,g), softball (b), wrestling (b); coed interscholastic: aerobics/dance, backpacking, cross-country running, dance, fitness, fitness walking, Frisbee, golf, hiking/backpacking, modern dance, mountain biking, outdoor activities, outdoor adventure, outdoor education, outdoor skills, paddle tennis, physical training, ropes courses, skeet shooting; coed intramural: bicycling, billiards, climbing, jogging, kayaking, running, skateboarding, skiing (downhill), surfing, swimming and diving, table tennis, tennis, track and field, ultimate Frisbee, walking, wall climbing, weight lifting, wilderness, yoga. 2 coaches, 1 athletic trainer.

Computers Computers are regularly used in desktop publishing, graphic arts, graphic design, mathematics, media arts, publications, video film production classes. Computer network features include on-campus library services, online commercial services, Internet access, wireless campus network, Internet filtering or blocking technology. Campus intranet, student e-mail accounts, and computer access in designated common areas are available to students. Students grades are available online.

Contact Terra Furguiel, Associate Director of Admissions. 805-646-4343 Ext. 111. Fax: 805-646-4371. E-mail: tfurguiel@besanthill.org. Website: www.besanthill.org

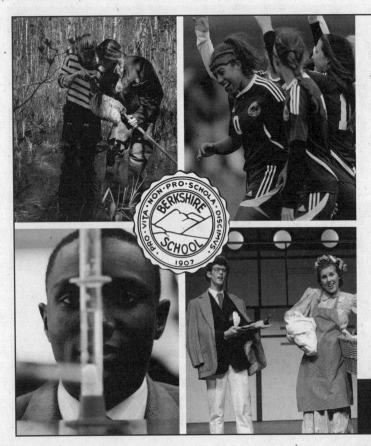

BETH HAVEN CHRISTIAN SCHOOL

5515 Johnsontown Road
Louisville, Kentucky 40272

Head of School: Mr. Jeff Bailey

General Information Coeducational day college-preparatory and religious studies school, affiliated with Baptist Church. Grades K4–12. Founded: 1971. Setting: suburban. 2-acre campus. 1 building on campus. Approved or accredited by Association of Christian Schools International, Association of Independent Schools of Greater Washington, and Kentucky Department of Education. Total enrollment: 211. Upper school average class size: 12. Upper school faculty-student ratio: 1:9. There are 177 required school days per year for Upper School students. Upper School students typically attend 5 days per week. The average school day consists of 7 hours.

Upper School Student Profile Grade 9: 9 students (5 boys, 4 girls); Grade 10: 12 students (8 boys, 4 girls); Grade 11: 18 students (10 boys, 8 girls); Grade 12: 21 students (13 boys, 8 girls). 65% of students are Baptist.

Faculty School total: 15. In upper school: 6 men, 2 women; 3 have advanced degrees.

Subjects Offered ACT preparation, Advanced Placement courses, algebra, American history, American literature, analytic geometry, Bible studies, biology, British literature (honors), business mathematics, chemistry, computer applications, drama, dramatic arts, earth science, economics, English, English composition, English language and composition-AP, health, honors algebra, honors English, honors geometry, honors U.S. history, honors world history, independent study, journalism, keyboarding, lab science, psychology, senior seminar, Spanish, speech, trigonometry, U.S. government and politics-AP, world geography, world history, yearbook.

Graduation Requirements ACT preparation, algebra, American government, American history, American literature, analytic geometry, arts appreciation, Bible, biology, British literature, chemistry, earth science, economics, English, language, physical education (includes health), world geography, world history.

Special Academic Programs Honors section; independent study; study at local college for college credit.

College Admission Counseling 26 students graduated in 2013; 24 went to college, including Abilene Christian University; Asbury University; Bellarmine University; Indiana University Bloomington; Jefferson Community and Technical College; University of Louisville. Other: 1 entered military service, 1 had other specific plans. Median composite ACT: 22. 5% scored over 26 on composite ACT.

Student Life Upper grades have uniform requirement, student council, honor system. Discipline rests primarily with faculty.

Summer Programs Remediation, sports programs offered; held on campus; accepts boys and girls; not open to students from other schools. 50 students usually enrolled. 2014 schedule: June 3 to August 16. Application deadline: June 3.

Tuition and Aid Day student tuition: $4575. Tuition installment plan (FACTS Tuition Payment Plan). Tuition reduction for siblings, need-based scholarship grants, two full-tuition memorial scholarships are awarded each year based on a combination of merit and need available. In 2013–14, 5% of upper-school students received aid. Total amount of financial aid awarded in 2013–14: $8000.

Admissions Traditional secondary-level entrance grade is 9. Stanford Test of Academic Skills required. Deadline for receipt of application materials: none. Application fee required: $250. Interview required.

Athletics Interscholastic: baseball (boys), basketball (b,g), cheering (g), football (b), softball (g), volleyball (g); coed interscholastic: cross-country running. 1 PE instructor, 6 coaches.

Computers Computers are regularly used in computer applications, journalism, yearbook classes. Computer network features include Internet access, Internet filtering or blocking technology. Computer access in designated common areas is available to students. Students grades are available online. The school has a published electronic and media policy.

Contact Ms. Denise Lamkin. 502-937-3516. Fax: 502-937-3364. E-mail: dlamkin@bethhaven.com. Website: www.bethhaven.com/

THE BIRCH WATHEN LENOX SCHOOL

210 East 77th Street
New York, New York 10075

Head of School: Mr. Frank J. Carnabuci III

General Information Coeducational day college-preparatory school. Grades K–12. Founded: 1916. Setting: urban. 1 building on campus. Approved or accredited by New York Department of Education. Member of National Association of Independent Schools. Endowment: $7.2 million. Total enrollment: 570. Upper school average class size: 15. Upper school faculty-student ratio: 1:15. Upper School students typically attend 5 days per week. The average school day consists of 7 hours.

Upper School Student Profile Grade 9: 46 students (24 boys, 22 girls); Grade 10: 45 students (25 boys, 20 girls); Grade 11: 46 students (23 boys, 23 girls); Grade 12: 48 students (22 boys, 26 girls).

Faculty School total: 120. In upper school: 30 men, 85 women; 115 have advanced degrees.

Subjects Offered Algebra, American history, American history-AP, American literature, American literature-AP, art, art history, biology, calculus, ceramics, chemistry, community service, computer math, computer science, creative writing, dance, drama, driver education, economics, English, English literature, environmental science, European history, expository writing, fine arts, French, geography, geology, geometry, government/civics, grammar, industrial arts, Japanese, journalism, mathematics, music, philosophy, photography, physical education, physics, science, Shakespeare, social studies, Spanish, speech, swimming, theater, trigonometry, typing, world history, writing.

Graduation Requirements 20th century world history, arts and fine arts (art, music, dance, drama), computer science, English, foreign language, mathematics, physical education (includes health), science, social studies (includes history). Community service is required.

Special Academic Programs Advanced Placement exam preparation; honors section; independent study; study abroad; academic accommodation for the gifted, the musically talented, and the artistically talented.

College Admission Counseling 44 students graduated in 2013; all went to college, including Columbia University; Princeton University; Trinity College; University of Pennsylvania; Vanderbilt University; Wesleyan University. Mean SAT critical reading: 650, mean SAT math: 650, mean SAT writing: 700.

Student Life Upper grades have uniform requirement, student council, honor system. Discipline rests equally with students and faculty.

Summer Programs Enrichment programs offered; session focuses on math and science; not open to students from other schools.

Tuition and Aid Day student tuition: $40,898. Tuition installment plan (Key Tuition Payment Plan, monthly payment plans, individually arranged payment plans). Merit scholarship grants, need-based scholarship grants available. In 2013–14, 15% of upper-school students received aid; total upper-school merit-scholarship money awarded: $100,000. Total amount of financial aid awarded in 2013–14: $1,200,000.

Admissions Traditional secondary-level entrance grade is 9. For fall 2013, 100 students applied for upper-level admission, 30 were accepted, 20 enrolled. ERB, ISEE, Math Placement Exam or writing sample required. Deadline for receipt of application materials: none. Application fee required: $50. On-campus interview required.

Athletics Interscholastic: baseball (boys), basketball (b,g), cross-country running (b,g), field hockey (g), hockey (b), ice hockey (b), lacrosse (b), soccer (b,g), softball (g), squash (b,g), swimming and diving (b,g), tennis (b,g), track and field (b,g), volleyball (g); intramural: aerobics (b,g), badminton (g), baseball (b), basketball (b,g), dance (b), ice hockey (b), indoor soccer (b), running (b,g), skiing (downhill) (b,g), soccer (b,g), softball (g), swimming and diving (b,g), tennis (b,g), track and field (b,g), volleyball (b,g); coed interscholastic: cross-country running, Frisbee, golf, ice hockey, indoor track & field, lacrosse, squash; coed intramural: bicycling, dance, golf, gymnastics, indoor track & field, skiing (cross-country), skiing (downhill). 5 PE instructors, 8 coaches.

Computers Computers are regularly used in all academic classes. Computer network features include on-campus library services, Internet access, wireless campus network, MOBY, Smartboard. Student e-mail accounts are available to students.

Contact Billie Williams, Admissions Coordinator. 212-861-0404. Fax: 212-879-3388. E-mail: bwilliams@bwl.org. Website: www.bwl.org

BISHOP BRADY HIGH SCHOOL

25 Columbus Avenue
Concord, New Hampshire 03301

Head of School: Mr. Trevor Bonat

General Information Coeducational day college-preparatory school, affiliated with Roman Catholic Church. Grades 9–12. Founded: 1963. Setting: suburban. 8-acre campus. 1 building on campus. Approved or accredited by National Catholic Education Association, New England Association of Schools and Colleges, and New Hampshire Department of Education. Total enrollment: 344. Upper school average class size: 17. Upper school faculty-student ratio: 1:16. There are 180 required school days per year for Upper School students. Upper School students typically attend 5 days per week. The average school day consists of 6 hours and 30 minutes.

Upper School Student Profile Grade 9: 94 students (59 boys, 35 girls); Grade 10: 81 students (44 boys, 37 girls); Grade 11: 81 students (34 boys, 47 girls); Grade 12: 88 students (47 boys, 41 girls). 70% of students are Roman Catholic.

Faculty School total: 31. In upper school: 13 men, 18 women; 25 have advanced degrees.

Subjects Offered Advanced chemistry, advanced math, algebra, anatomy and physiology, art appreciation, arts, biology, biology-AP, calculus-AP, career/college preparation, chemistry, chemistry-AP, Christian scripture, civics, college awareness, college counseling, computer education, conceptual physics, drama, English, English literature-AP, English-AP, film studies, French-AP, freshman seminar, geometry, guidance, health education, history, history-AP, honors English, Latin, moral theology, music appreciation, musical theater, physical education, physics-AP, pre-calculus, probability and statistics, psychology, religious studies, research and reference, SAT preparation, social justice, Spanish-AP, theology, trigonometry, U.S. history-AP, world religions, writing.

Graduation Requirements Algebra, American literature, arts and fine arts (art, music, dance, drama), biology, chemistry, computer education, English, geometry, languages, physical education (includes health), science, social studies (includes history), theology, 90 hours of community service.

Special Academic Programs 8 Advanced Placement exams for which test preparation is offered; honors section; independent study; study at local college for college credit; academic accommodation for the gifted; ESL (25 students enrolled).

College Admission Counseling 95 students graduated in 2013; 90 went to college, including Rensselaer Polytechnic Institute; Saint Anselm College; University of New Hampshire. Other: 1 entered military service, 4 had other specific plans. Mean SAT critical reading: 556, mean SAT math: 544, mean SAT writing: 552, mean composite ACT: 25. 30% scored over 600 on SAT critical reading, 30% scored over 600 on SAT math.

Student Life Upper grades have specified standards of dress, student council, honor system. Discipline rests primarily with faculty. Attendance at religious services is required.

Summer Programs Remediation, enrichment, advancement, sports programs offered; session focuses on football and conditioning, mathematics, study skills; held on campus; accepts boys and girls; open to students from other schools. 60 students usually enrolled. 2014 schedule: June 20 to August 15.

Tuition and Aid Day student tuition: $9800. Tuition installment plan (Insured Tuition Payment Plan, monthly payment plans, individually arranged payment plans). Tuition reduction for siblings, merit scholarship grants, need-based scholarship grants available. In 2013–14, 35% of upper-school students received aid.

Admissions Traditional secondary-level entrance grade is 9. For fall 2013, 157 students applied for upper-level admission, 145 were accepted, 94 enrolled. SSAT required. Deadline for receipt of application materials: June 15. Application fee required: $45. Interview required.

Athletics Interscholastic: alpine skiing (boys, girls), baseball (b), basketball (b,g), cheering (g), cross-country running (b,g), field hockey (g), football (b), golf (b,g), hockey (b), ice hockey (b), indoor track (b,g), lacrosse (b,g), skiing (downhill) (b,g), soccer (b,g), softball (g), swimming and diving (b,g), tennis (b,g), track and field (b,g); intramural: basketball (b,g); coed interscholastic: equestrian sports, juggling, outdoor activities, outdoor adventure; coed intramural: basketball, indoor track, outdoor activities, outdoor adventure, rock climbing, skiing (cross-country), skiing (downhill), snowboarding, strength & conditioning, table tennis, volleyball, weight lifting, weight training. 1 PE instructor.

Computers Computers are regularly used in business applications, college planning, journalism, literary magazine, newspaper classes. Computer network features include on-campus library services, online commercial services, Internet access, wireless campus network, Internet filtering or blocking technology. Student e-mail accounts and computer access in designated common areas are available to students. Students grades are available online. The school has a published electronic and media policy.

Contact Mrs. Lonna J. Abbott, Director of Admissions and Enrollment. 603-224-7419. Fax: 603-228-6664. E-mail: labbott@bishopbrady.edu. Website: www.bishopbrady.edu

BISHOP CONATY-OUR LADY OF LORETTO HIGH SCHOOL

2900 West Pico Boulevard
Los Angeles, California 90006

Head of School: Mr. Richard A. Spicer

General Information Girls' day college-preparatory, general academic, arts, religious studies, and technology school, affiliated with Roman Catholic Church. Grades 9–12. Founded: 1923. Setting: urban. 3-acre campus. 2 buildings on campus. Approved or accredited by National Catholic Education Association, The College Board, Western Association of Schools and Colleges, Western Catholic Education Association, and California Department of Education. Endowment: $579,607. Total enrollment: 326. Upper school average class size: 21. Upper school faculty-student ratio: 1:12. There are 182 required school days per year for Upper School students. Upper School students typically attend 5 days per week. The average school day consists of 5 hours and 15 minutes.

Upper School Student Profile Grade 9: 62 students (62 girls); Grade 10: 108 students (108 girls); Grade 11: 77 students (77 girls); Grade 12: 79 students (79 girls). 91% of students are Roman Catholic.

Faculty School total: 22. In upper school: 7 men, 14 women; 16 have advanced degrees.

Subjects Offered Aerobics, algebra, American literature, anatomy and physiology, ASB Leadership, athletics, biology, British literature, Catholic belief and practice, ceramics, chemistry, Christian and Hebrew scripture, computer literacy, dance, dance performance, drama, drawing, drawing and design, economics, English, English language and composition-AP, European history-AP, French, geometry, government, government and politics-AP, health, honors algebra, honors English, honors geometry, integrated science, linear algebra, moral reasoning, painting, physical education, physics, pre-calculus, religion, senior project, social justice, Spanish, Spanish language-AP, statistics, trigonometry, U.S. government, U.S. history, U.S. history-AP, visual arts, Web site design, world history, world religions, yearbook.

Graduation Requirements Arts and fine arts (art, music, dance, drama), computer science, English, foreign language, mathematics, physical education (includes health), religion (includes Bible studies and theology), science, social studies (includes history), 100 hours of community service, senior project.

Special Academic Programs 6 Advanced Placement exams for which test preparation is offered; honors section; remedial reading and/or remedial writing; remedial math.

College Admission Counseling 68 students graduated in 2012; all went to college, including California State University, Northridge; Loyola Marymount University; Marymount College, Palos Verdes, California; Mount St. Mary's College; Santa Monica College; University of California, Riverside. Median SAT critical reading: 440, median SAT math: 390, median SAT writing: 440, median combined SAT: 1300, median composite ACT: 19. 6% scored over 600 on SAT critical reading, 2% scored over 600 on SAT math, 6% scored over 600 on SAT writing, 4% scored over 1800 on combined SAT, 11% scored over 26 on composite ACT.

Student Life Upper grades have uniform requirement, student council, honor system. Discipline rests primarily with faculty. Attendance at religious services is required.

Tuition and Aid Day student tuition: $6325–$8350. Tuition installment plan (monthly payment plans, individually arranged payment plans). Tuition reduction for siblings, need-based scholarship grants, paying campus jobs available. In 2012–13, 91% of upper-school students received aid. Total amount of financial aid awarded in 2012–13: $593,619.

Admissions Traditional secondary-level entrance grade is 9. For fall 2012, 110 students applied for upper-level admission, 82 were accepted, 62 enrolled. High School Placement Test required. Deadline for receipt of application materials: August 15. Application fee required: $55. On-campus interview required.

Athletics Interscholastic: basketball, cross-country running, soccer, softball, volleyball. 3 coaches.

Computers Computers are regularly used in computer applications, Web site design, yearbook classes. Computer network features include on-campus library services, Internet access, wireless campus network, Internet filtering or blocking technology. Computer access in designated common areas is available to students. Students grades are available online. The school has a published electronic and media policy.

Contact Sr. Harriet Stellern, Director of Admissions. 323-737-0012 Ext. 103. Fax: 323-737-1749. E-mail: hstellern@bishopconatyloretto.org. Website: www.bishopconatyloretto.org

BISHOP CONNOLLY HIGH SCHOOL

373 Elsbree Street
Fall River, Massachusetts 02720

Head of School: Mr. Christopher Myron

General Information Coeducational day college-preparatory and religious studies school, affiliated with Roman Catholic Church. Grades 9–12. Founded: 1966. Setting: suburban. Nearest major city is Providence, RI. 72-acre campus. 1 building on campus. Approved or accredited by New England Association of Schools and Colleges and Massachusetts Department of Education. Total enrollment: 280. Upper school average class size: 18. Upper school faculty-student ratio: 1:16. There are 185 required school days per year for Upper School students. Upper School students typically attend 5 days per week. The average school day consists of 6 hours and 30 minutes.

Upper School Student Profile 90% of students are Roman Catholic.

Faculty School total: 30. In upper school: 18 men, 12 women; 22 have advanced degrees.

Subjects Offered Advanced Placement courses, algebra, American literature, American studies, anatomy and physiology, art, art history, Bible studies, biology, biology-AP, British literature, British literature (honors), calculus, calculus-AP, campus ministry, chemistry, chemistry-AP, choir, chorus, community service, computer programming, creative writing, desktop publishing, drama, English, English literature, English-AP, environmental science, European history-AP, French, French-AP, geometry, health, history, honors algebra, honors English, honors geometry, honors U.S. history, honors world history, human biology, instrumental music, keyboarding, math analysis, mathematics, music, music history, music theory, physical education, physics, Portuguese, psychology, religion, science, social studies, Spanish, theology, trigonometry, U.S. history-AP, world history, world literature.

Graduation Requirements English, foreign language, mathematics, religion (includes Bible studies and theology), science, social studies (includes history). Community service is required.

Special Academic Programs Advanced Placement exam preparation; honors section; independent study; study at local college for college credit.

College Admission Counseling 72 students graduated in 2013; 70 went to college, including Bridgewater State University; Northeastern University; Providence College; Quinnipiac University; University of Massachusetts Dartmouth; University of Rhode Island. Other: 2 entered military service. Mean SAT critical reading: 525, mean SAT math: 471. 13% scored over 600 on SAT critical reading, 11% scored over 600 on SAT math.

Student Life Upper grades have uniform requirement, student council. Discipline rests primarily with faculty. Attendance at religious services is required.

Tuition and Aid Day student tuition: $8550. Tuition installment plan (FACTS Tuition Payment Plan, monthly payment plans). Merit scholarship grants, need-based scholarship grants available.

Admissions Traditional secondary-level entrance grade is 9. High School Placement Test required. Deadline for receipt of application materials: none. No application fee required. Interview recommended.

Athletics Interscholastic: baseball (boys), basketball (b,g), cheering (g), cross-country running (b,g), field hockey (g), football (b), ice hockey (b), lacrosse (b), soccer (b,g), softball (g), tennis (b,g), track and field (b,g), volleyball (g), winter (indoor) track (b,g); intramural: field hockey (g); coed interscholastic: golf, indoor soccer, indoor track & field. 1 PE instructor, 18 coaches, 1 athletic trainer.

Computers Computers are regularly used in all classes. Computer network features include online commercial services, Internet access, wireless campus network, Internet filtering or blocking technology. Computer access in designated common areas is available to students. The school has a published electronic and media policy.

Contact Mr. Anthony C. Ciampanelli, Director of Admissions/Alumni. 508-676-1071 Ext. 333. Fax: 508-676-8594. E-mail: aciampanelli@bishopconnolly.com. Website: www.bishopconnolly.com

BISHOP DENIS J. O'CONNELL HIGH SCHOOL

6600 Little Falls Road
Arlington, Virginia 22213

Head of School: Dr. Joseph Vorbach III

General Information Coeducational day college-preparatory, arts, business, religious studies, bilingual studies, and technology school, affiliated with Roman Catholic Church. Grades 9–12. Founded: 1957. Setting: suburban. Nearest major city is Washington, DC. 28-acre campus. 1 building on campus. Approved or accredited by National Catholic Education Association, Southern Association of Colleges and Schools, Southern Association of Independent Schools, and Virginia Department of Education. Member of Secondary School Admission Test Board. Total enrollment: 1,221. Upper school average class size: 19. Upper school faculty-student ratio: 1:12. There are 180 required school days per year for Upper School students. Upper School students typically attend 5 days per week. The average school day consists of 7 hours and 15 minutes.

Upper School Student Profile 83% of students are Roman Catholic.

Faculty School total: 110. In upper school: 73 have advanced degrees.

Subjects Offered Accounting, African American history, African-American history, algebra, American history, American history-AP, American literature, analysis, art, art history, athletic training, Basic programming, Bible studies, biology, biology-AP, business, business technology, calculus, calculus-AP, chemistry, chemistry-AP, choir, choral music, chorus, church history, comparative government and politics-AP, comparative political systems-AP, computer graphics, computer multimedia, computer music, computer programming, computer science, computer science-AP, computer skills, creative writing, digital art, dramatic arts, driver education, earth science, East Asian history, ecology, economics, economics-AP, English, English language-AP, English literature, English literature-AP, environmental science-AP, European history, European history-AP, fine arts, forensics, French, French language-AP, French-AP, geography, geometry, German, German-AP, government and politics-AP, government-AP, government/civics, guitar, health, history, history of the Catholic Church, honors English, honors geometry, honors U.S. history, honors world history, introduction to theater, Italian, jazz band, journalism, Latin, Latin-AP, literature-AP, macro/microeconomics-AP, macroeconomics-AP, marketing, mathematics, media arts, microeconomics-AP, modern European history-AP, music, music theory-AP, music-AP, New Testament, newspaper, orchestra, painting, personal finance, personal fitness, photo shop, photography, photojournalism, physical education, physical fitness, physics, physics-AP, piano, play production, pre-calculus, probability, psychology, psychology-AP, public speaking, religion, remedial study skills, science, science research, social sciences, social studies, sociology, Spanish, Spanish language-AP, Spanish literature-AP, Spanish-AP, speech, speech and debate, sports conditioning, sports psychology, statistics, statistics-AP, student government, studio art-AP, theater arts, theater design and production, theology, trigonometry, U.S. and Virginia government-AP, U.S. and Virginia history, U.S. government, U.S. government and politics-AP, U.S. history, U.S. history-AP, United States government-AP, video film production, voice ensemble, Web site design, weight training, weightlifting, world history, world literature.

Graduation Requirements Arts and fine arts (art, music, dance, drama), computer science, English, foreign language, mathematics, physical education (includes health), religion (includes Bible studies and theology), science, social sciences, social studies (includes history), community service program incorporated into graduation requirements.

Special Academic Programs 26 Advanced Placement exams for which test preparation is offered; honors section; independent study; study at local college for college credit; academic accommodation for the gifted; remedial math; programs in general development for dyslexic students; ESL (20 students enrolled).

College Admission Counseling 304 students graduated in 2013; 300 went to college, including George Mason University; James Madison University; The College of William and Mary; University of Virginia; Virginia Commonwealth University; Virginia Polytechnic Institute and State University. Other: 4 entered military service. Median SAT critical reading: 563, median SAT math: 549, median SAT writing: 555, median combined SAT: 1667, median composite ACT: 29.

Student Life Upper grades have uniform requirement, student council, honor system. Discipline rests equally with students and faculty. Attendance at religious services is required.

Summer Programs Remediation, enrichment, advancement, sports, art/fine arts, computer instruction programs offered; held on campus; accepts boys and girls; open to students from other schools. 200 students usually enrolled. 2014 schedule: June 15 to August 15. Application deadline: none.

Tuition and Aid Day student tuition: $12,585–$15,350. Tuition installment plan (FACTS Tuition Payment Plan). Tuition reduction for siblings, merit scholarship grants, need-based scholarship grants, scholarship competition only for eighth graders currently enrolled in a Diocese of Arlington Catholic school available. In 2013–14, 30% of upper-school students received aid; total upper-school merit-scholarship money awarded: $50,000. Total amount of financial aid awarded in 2013–14: $1,800,000.

Admissions High School Placement Test required. Deadline for receipt of application materials: January 27. Application fee required: $50.

Athletics Interscholastic: baseball (boys), basketball (b,g), crew (b,g), cross-country running (b,g), dance team (g), diving (b,g), field hockey (g), football (b), ice hockey (b), lacrosse (b,g), soccer (b,g), softball (g), swimming and diving (b,g), tennis (b,g), track and field (b,g), volleyball (g), weight lifting (b,g), weight training (b,g), winter (indoor) track (b,g), wrestling (b); intramural: basketball (b,g), weight lifting (b,g); coed interscholastic: golf, ice hockey, sailing; coed intramural: crew, flag football, softball, ultimate Frisbee, volleyball. 7 PE instructors, 7 coaches, 1 athletic trainer.

Computers Computers are regularly used in accounting, all academic, art, business, computer applications, English, foreign language, health, history, mathematics, science, social sciences classes. Computer network features include on-campus library services, online commercial services, Internet access, wireless campus network, Internet filtering or blocking technology. Campus intranet, student e-mail accounts, and computer access in designated common areas are available to students. Students grades are available online. The school has a published electronic and media policy.

Contact Mr. Michael Cresson, Director of Admissions. 703-237-1433. Fax: 703-241-9066. E-mail: mcresson@bishopoconnell.org. Website: www.bishopoconnell.org

BISHOP EUSTACE PREPARATORY SCHOOL

5552 Route 70
Pennsauken, New Jersey 08109-4798

Head of School: Br. James Beamesderfer, SAC

General Information Coeducational day college-preparatory, arts, religious studies, and technology school, affiliated with Roman Catholic Church. Grades 9–12. Founded: 1954. Setting: suburban. Nearest major city is Philadelphia, PA. 32-acre campus. 7 buildings on campus. Approved or accredited by Middle States Association of Colleges and Schools and New Jersey Department of Education. Endowment: $4.5 million. Total enrollment: 661. Upper school average class size: 19. Upper school faculty-student ratio: 1:12. There are 165 required school days per year for Upper School students. Upper School students typically attend 5 days per week. The average school day consists of 6 hours and 20 minutes.

Upper School Student Profile 88% of students are Roman Catholic.

Faculty School total: 57. In upper school: 24 men, 31 women; 43 have advanced degrees.

Subjects Offered Advanced chemistry, advanced computer applications, Advanced Placement courses, algebra, American history, American history-AP, American literature, anatomy, anatomy and physiology, applied music, art and culture, art history, band, Bible studies, biology, biology-AP, British literature, British literature (honors), calculus, calculus-AP, campus ministry, career education, career exploration, career/college preparation, chemistry, chemistry-AP, choir, Christian doctrine, Christian education, Christian ethics, Christian scripture, clinical chemistry, college counseling, college placement, college planning, comparative religion, computer education, computer science, creative writing, driver education, economics and history, electives, English, English literature, English literature and composition-AP, environmental science, environmental science-AP, ethics, European history-AP, film, film and literature, fine arts, French, French as a second language, gender issues, genetics, geometry, German, government and politics-AP, government/civics, grammar, health, history, honors algebra, honors English, honors geometry, honors U.S. history, honors world history, instrumental music, journalism, Latin, law, law studies, macroeconomics-AP, mathematics, mathematics-AP, music, music composition, music history, music theory, music theory-AP, physical education, physical science, physics, physics-AP, physiology, pre-calculus, psychology, psychology-AP, science, sex education, social studies, sociology, Spanish, Spanish-AP, statistics-AP, theology, trigonometry, U.S. government and politics-AP, U.S. history, U.S. history-AP, vocal music, women's studies, world affairs, world history, world religions.

Graduation Requirements Art history, arts and fine arts (art, music, dance, drama), career exploration, computer science, English, foreign language, mathematics, physical education (includes health), religion (includes Bible studies and theology), science, social studies (includes history). Community service is required.

Special Academic Programs 16 Advanced Placement exams for which test preparation is offered; honors section; independent study; study at local college for college credit; academic accommodation for the gifted and the musically talented.

College Admission Counseling 180 students graduated in 2013; 178 went to college, including Drexel University; Loyola University Maryland; Penn State University Park; Saint Joseph's University; University of Delaware; Villanova University. Other: 1 entered a postgraduate year, 1 had other specific plans. 36% scored over 600 on SAT critical reading, 43% scored over 600 on SAT math, 36% scored over 600 on SAT writing.

Student Life Upper grades have uniform requirement, student council, honor system. Discipline rests primarily with faculty. Attendance at religious services is required.

Summer Programs Enrichment, advancement, sports programs offered; session focuses on student recruitment and enrichment for middle school students; advancement in math for current students; held on campus; accepts boys and girls; open to students from other schools. 150 students usually enrolled. 2014 schedule: June 16 to July 24. Application deadline: June 15.

Tuition and Aid Day student tuition: $15,600. Tuition installment plan (FACTS Tuition Payment Plan). Merit scholarship grants, need-based scholarship grants available. In 2013–14, 35% of upper-school students received aid; total upper-school merit-scholarship money awarded: $280,800. Total amount of financial aid awarded in 2013–14: $800,000.

Admissions Traditional secondary-level entrance grade is 9. High School Placement Test, math and English placement tests or placement test required. Deadline for receipt of application materials: none. Application fee required: $60.

Athletics Interscholastic: baseball (boys), basketball (b,g), bowling (b,g), cheering (g), crew (b,g), cross-country running (b,g), field hockey (g), football (b), ice hockey (b), indoor track & field (b,g), lacrosse (b,g), running (b,g), soccer (b,g), softball (g), swimming and diving (b,g), tennis (b,g), track and field (b,g); coed interscholastic: aquatics, diving, golf. 3 PE instructors, 61 coaches, 1 athletic trainer.

Computers Computers are regularly used in all academic classes. Computer network features include on-campus library services, online commercial services, Internet access, wireless campus network, Internet filtering or blocking technology. Campus intranet and computer access in designated common areas are available to students. Students grades are available online. The school has a published electronic and media policy.

Contact Mr. Nicholas Italiano, Director of Admissions. 856-662-2160 Ext. 240. Fax: 856-662-0025. E-mail: admissions@eustace.org. Website: www.eustace.org

BISHOP FENWICK HIGH SCHOOL

4855 State Route 122
Franklin, Ohio 45005

Head of School: Mr. Trevor Block

General Information Coeducational day college-preparatory, arts, and religious studies school, affiliated with Roman Catholic Church. Grades 9–12. Founded: 1952. Setting: small town. Nearest major city is Cincinnati. 66-acre campus. 1 building on campus. Approved or accredited by National Catholic Education Association, North Central Association of Colleges and Schools, Ohio Catholic Schools Accreditation Association (OCSAA), and Ohio Department of Education. Upper school average class size: 24. Upper school faculty-student ratio: 1:14. There are 184 required school days per year for Upper School students. Upper School students typically attend 5 days per week. The average school day consists of 6 hours and 35 minutes.

Upper School Student Profile Grade 9: 145 students (80 boys, 65 girls); Grade 10: 130 students (73 boys, 57 girls); Grade 11: 160 students (98 boys, 62 girls); Grade 12: 118 students (61 boys, 57 girls). 88% of students are Roman Catholic.

Faculty School total: 40. In upper school: 18 men, 22 women; 23 have advanced degrees.

Subjects Offered Accounting, ACT preparation, algebra, American democracy, art, art-AP, athletic training, biology, botany, calculus-AP, career planning, cell biology, chemistry, choir, chorus, church history, college admission preparation, computer graphics, computer programming, concert band, creative writing, economics, engineering, English, English-AP, ensembles, film and literature, fine arts, French, functions, general business, geometry, government, government/civics-AP, health, honors algebra, honors English, honors geometry, integrated mathematics, jazz band, Latin, Latin-AP, leadership, marching band, mathematics, multimedia, music appreciation, mythology, physical education, physical science, physics, physiology, portfolio art, pre-algebra, psychology, publications, religion, science, social studies, Spanish, statistics, study skills, technology, theater, theater arts, trigonometry, U.S. history, U.S. history-AP, Web site design, world geography, world history, writing, yearbook, zoology.

Graduation Requirements Arts and fine arts (art, music, dance, drama), English, foreign language, mathematics, physical education (includes health), religion (includes Bible studies and theology), science, social studies (includes history), technology, community service, retreats, pass the Ohio Graduation Test.

Special Academic Programs Advanced Placement exam preparation; honors section; study at local college for college credit; academic accommodation for the gifted; special instructional classes for deaf students.

College Admission Counseling 124 students graduated in 2012; 122 went to college, including Miami University; Ohio University; The Ohio State University; University of Cincinnati; University of Dayton; Xavier University. Other: 1 went to work, 1 entered military service. Median SAT critical reading: 550, median SAT math: 560, median SAT writing: 530, median combined SAT: 1640. Mean composite ACT: 24. 37% scored over 600 on SAT critical reading, 39% scored over 600 on SAT math, 26% scored over 600 on SAT writing, 33% scored over 1800 on combined SAT, 38% scored over 26 on composite ACT.

Student Life Upper grades have uniform requirement, student council, honor system. Discipline rests primarily with faculty. Attendance at religious services is required.

Tuition and Aid Day student tuition: $8400. Tuition installment plan (FACTS Tuition Payment Plan). Tuition reduction for siblings, merit scholarship grants, need-based scholarship grants, paying campus jobs available. In 2012–13, 19% of upper-school students received aid.

Admissions Traditional secondary-level entrance grade is 9. High School Placement Test required. Deadline for receipt of application materials: December 1. No application fee required.

Athletics Interscholastic: baseball (boys), basketball (b,g), bowling (b,g), cheering (g), cross-country running (b,g), dance team (g), football (b), golf (b,g), lacrosse (b,g), soccer (b,g), softball (g), tennis (b,g), volleyball (b,g), weight training (b,g), wrestling (b); intramural: basketball (b), weight training (b,g); coed interscholastic: in-line hockey, roller hockey, swimming and diving, track and field; coed intramural: freestyle skiing, paint ball, skiing (downhill), snowboarding, strength & conditioning. 1 PE instructor, 62 coaches, 1 athletic trainer.

Computers Computers are regularly used in career exploration, career technology, college planning, engineering, graphic arts, graphic design, introduction to technology, multimedia, photography, publications, technology, video film production, Web site design, yearbook classes. Computer network features include on-campus library services, Internet access, wireless campus network, Internet filtering or blocking technology, laptop carts, iPad cart. Campus intranet and computer access in designated common areas are available to students. Students grades are available online. The school has a published electronic and media policy.

Contact Mrs. Betty Turvy, Director of Admissions. 513-428-0525. Fax: 513-727-1501. E-mail: bturvy@fenwickfalcons.org. Website: www.fenwickfalcons.org

BISHOP GUERTIN HIGH SCHOOL

194 Lund Road
Nashua, New Hampshire 03060-4398

Head of School: Br. Mark Hilton, SC

General Information Coeducational day college-preparatory and religious studies school, affiliated with Roman Catholic Church. Grades 9–12. Founded: 1963. Setting: suburban. Nearest major city is Boston, MA. 1 building on campus. Approved or accredited by New England Association of Schools and Colleges and New Hampshire Department of Education. Total enrollment: 900. Upper school average class size: 20. Upper School students typically attend 5 days per week. The average school day consists of 6 hours and 30 minutes.

Upper School Student Profile 70% of students are Roman Catholic.

Subjects Offered 20th century history, 20th century world history, acting, advanced biology, advanced chemistry, advanced computer applications, advanced math, Advanced Placement courses, algebra, American history-AP, American literature, American literature-AP, analysis and differential calculus, anatomy and physiology, ancient world history, art appreciation, art history, band, Bible studies, biology, biology-AP, British history, British literature, British literature (honors), business law, calculus, calculus-AP, campus ministry, career/college preparation, chemistry, chemistry-AP, chorus, Christian and Hebrew scripture, Christian doctrine, Christian education, Christian ethics, Christianity, church history, civics, college admission preparation, college counseling, college writing, community service, comparative government and politics, comparative government and politics-AP, comparative religion, computer applications, computer art, computer education, computer literacy, computer multimedia, computer processing, computer programming, computer programming-AP, computer science, computer science-AP, computer technologies, computer-aided design, concert band, concert choir, constitutional history of U.S., consumer economics, contemporary history, CPR, creative writing, death and loss, debate, desktop publishing, digital photography, discrete mathematics, dramatic arts, drawing, driver education, economics, emergency medicine, English, English composition, English literature, English literature and composition-AP, English literature-AP, English-AP, environmental science, environmental science-AP, ethics, European history, film studies, fine arts, foreign language, French, French-AP, geography, geometry, government and politics-AP, government/civics, grammar, Greek, health, health and wellness, health education, health enhancement, healthful living, history, Holocaust and other genocides, honors geometry, honors U.S. history, honors world history, human anatomy, human biology, human sexuality, instrumental music, introduction to literature, jazz band, journalism, Latin, Latin-AP, law, literary magazine, marching band, mechanics of writing, moral reasoning, moral theology, music, music appreciation, philosophy, photography, physical education, physics, physics-AP, pre-calculus, psychology, religion, religious studies, science, senior seminar, Shakespeare, social justice, social studies, Spanish, Spanish-AP, statistics, studio art, studio art-AP, The 20th Century, theater, trigonometry, U.S. government and politics, U.S. government and politics-AP, U.S. history, U.S. history-AP, U.S. literature, world history, world literature, yearbook.

Graduation Requirements Arts and fine arts (art, music, dance, drama), computer science, English, foreign language, mathematics, physical education (includes health), religion (includes Bible studies and theology), science, social studies (includes history).

Special Academic Programs 13 Advanced Placement exams for which test preparation is offered; honors section; study at local college for college credit; academic accommodation for the gifted.

College Admission Counseling 211 students graduated in 2013; 208 went to college. Other: 2 entered military service, 1 entered a postgraduate year. Median combined SAT: 1702, median composite ACT: 26.

Student Life Upper grades have uniform requirement, student council, honor system. Discipline rests primarily with faculty. Attendance at religious services is required.

Summer Programs Enrichment programs offered; held on campus; accepts boys and girls; not open to students from other schools. 40 students usually enrolled. 2014 schedule: July 1 to July 31. Application deadline: May 1.

Tuition and Aid Day student tuition: $12,550. Tuition installment plan (FACTS Tuition Payment Plan, individually arranged payment plans). Merit scholarship grants, need-based scholarship grants available. In 2013–14, 10% of upper-school students received aid. Total amount of financial aid awarded in 2013–14: $600,000.

Admissions Traditional secondary-level entrance grade is 9. High School Placement Test required. Deadline for receipt of application materials: January 6. Application fee required: $35.

Athletics Interscholastic: baseball (boys), basketball (b,g), cheering (b,g), cross-country running (b,g), field hockey (g), football (b), gymnastics (g), hockey (b,g), ice hockey (b,g), lacrosse (b), skiing (downhill) (b,g), soccer (b,g), softball (g), swimming and diving (b,g), tennis (b,g), track and field (b,g), volleyball (g), wrestling (b); intramural: crew (b,g); coed interscholastic: aquatics, cheering, golf, ice hockey, indoor track, nordic skiing, paint ball, skiing (downhill); coed intramural: aerobics/dance, basketball, bowling, crew, dance, fishing, freestyle skiing, golf, mountain biking, outdoor education, strength & conditioning, swimming and diving, table tennis, tennis, volleyball, weight lifting, weight training. 4 PE instructors, 55 coaches, 2 athletic trainers.

Computers Computers are regularly used in career education, career exploration, career technology, college planning, data processing, desktop publishing, independent study, information technology, introduction to technology, library, library science, library skills, literary magazine, multimedia, music, news writing, newspaper, programming, publications, publishing, research skills, stock market, technology, Web site design, word processing, yearbook classes. Computer network features include on-campus library services, online commercial services, Internet access, wireless campus network, Internet filtering or blocking technology. The school has a published electronic and media policy.

Contact Mrs. Alison Mueller '03, Director of Admissions. 603-889-4107 Ext. 4304. Fax: 603-889-0701. E-mail: admit@bghs.org. Website: www.bghs.org

BISHOP HENDRICKEN HIGH SCHOOL

2615 Warwick Avenue
Warwick, Rhode Island 02889

Head of School: Mr. John A. Jackson

General Information Boys' day college-preparatory, arts, business, religious studies, and technology school, affiliated with Roman Catholic Church. Grades 9–12. Founded: 1959. Setting: suburban. Nearest major city is Providence. 34-acre campus. 1 building on campus. Approved or accredited by National Catholic Education Association, New England Association of Schools and Colleges, and Rhode Island Department of Education. Total enrollment: 948. Upper school average class size: 24. Upper school faculty-student ratio: 1:14. There are 180 required school days per year for Upper School students. Upper School students typically attend 5 days per week. The average school day consists of 6 hours.

Upper School Student Profile Grade 9: 228 students (228 boys); Grade 10: 258 students (258 boys); Grade 11: 264 students (264 boys); Grade 12: 201 students (201 boys). 90% of students are Roman Catholic.

Faculty School total: 77. In upper school: 57 men, 20 women; 32 have advanced degrees.

Subjects Offered Accounting, advanced biology, advanced chemistry, advanced computer applications, advanced math, Advanced Placement courses, algebra, American history, American history-AP, American literature, American literature-AP, analysis, art, Basic programming, biochemistry, biology, biology-AP, British history, British literature, British literature (honors), British literature-AP, business, calculus, calculus-AP, cell biology, chemistry, chemistry-AP, college writing, communications, computer programming, computer programming-AP, computer-aided design, drama, drama performance, drama workshop, drawing, drawing and design, economics, English, English language and composition-AP, English literature, English literature and composition-AP, European history, European history-AP, film and new technologies, filmmaking, finance, fine arts, foreign language, French, French language-AP, French-AP, geometry, graphic arts, graphic design, health, history, history of rock and roll, history-AP, honors algebra, honors English, honors geometry, honors U.S. history, honors world history, instrumental music, introduction to technology, introduction to theater, Italian, jazz, jazz ensemble, linear algebra, media arts, music, music theory-AP, physics-AP, psychology, SAT preparation, Spanish, Spanish-AP, theater arts, theology, U.S. history-AP, video film production, visual and performing arts, visual arts, world civilizations.

Graduation Requirements Senior Experience—a work internship required in the second semester of the senior year.

Special Academic Programs 15 Advanced Placement exams for which test preparation is offered; honors section; special instructional classes for deaf students, blind students.

College Admission Counseling 218 students graduated in 2013; 208 went to college, including Boston College; Bryant University; Johnson & Wales University; Providence College; Quinnipiac University; University of Rhode Island. Other: 3 went to work, 2 entered military service, 2 entered a postgraduate year, 3 had other specific plans. Mean SAT critical reading: 532, mean SAT math: 543, mean SAT writing: 537.

Student Life Upper grades have specified standards of dress, student council, honor system. Discipline rests primarily with faculty. Attendance at religious services is required.

Summer Programs Enrichment, sports, art/fine arts, computer instruction programs offered; session focuses on enrichment and developmental training; held on campus; accepts boys and girls; open to students from other schools.

Tuition and Aid Day student tuition: $12,750. Tuition installment plan (monthly payment plans, individually arranged payment plans). Merit scholarship grants, need-based scholarship grants available. In 2013–14, 52% of upper-school students received aid; total upper-school merit-scholarship money awarded: $74,000. Total amount of financial aid awarded in 2013–14: $1,600,000.

Admissions Traditional secondary-level entrance grade is 9. For fall 2013, 426 students applied for upper-level admission, 387 were accepted, 228 enrolled. Catholic High School Entrance Examination or High School Placement Test (closed version) from Scholastic Testing Service required. Deadline for receipt of application materials: January 1. Application fee required: $50.

Athletics Interscholastic: baseball, basketball, cross-country running, diving, football, golf, ice hockey, indoor track, indoor track & field, lacrosse, rugby, sailing, soccer, Special Olympics, swimming and diving, tennis, track and field, volleyball, winter (indoor) track, wrestling; intramural: archery, badminton, billiards, bocce, bowling, flag football, fly fishing, golf, handball, paddle tennis, physical training, rugby, skiing (downhill), surfing, table tennis, weight training. 5 PE instructors, 14 coaches, 2 athletic trainers.

Computers Computers are regularly used in computer applications, desktop publishing, digital applications, drafting, graphic design, introduction to technology, media arts, music technology, programming, technology, video film production, Web site design classes. Computer resources include on-campus library services, Internet access, wireless campus network, Internet filtering or blocking technology. Campus intranet and computer access in designated common areas are available to students. Students grades are available online. The school has a published electronic and media policy.

Contact Mrs. Catherine A. Solomon, Director of Admissions. 401-739-3450 Ext. 163. Fax: 401-732-8261. E-mail: csolomon@hendricken.com. Website: www.hendricken.com

BISHOP IRETON HIGH SCHOOL

201 Cambridge Road
Alexandria, Virginia 22314-4899

Head of School: Dr. Thomas J. Curry

General Information Coeducational day college-preparatory, arts, religious studies, and technology school, affiliated with Roman Catholic Church. Grades 9–12. Founded: 1964. Setting: suburban. 12-acre campus. 1 building on campus. Approved or accredited by National Catholic Education Association and Southern Association of Colleges and Schools. Total enrollment: 785. Upper school average class size: 24. Upper school faculty-student ratio: 1:14. There are 180 required school days per year for Upper School students. Upper School students typically attend 5 days per week. The average school day consists of 6 hours.

Upper School Student Profile Grade 9: 197 students (87 boys, 110 girls); Grade 10: 208 students (98 boys, 110 girls); Grade 11: 199 students (83 boys, 116 girls); Grade 12: 181 students (90 boys, 91 girls). 85% of students are Roman Catholic.

Faculty School total: 63. In upper school: 30 men, 33 women; 50 have advanced degrees.

Subjects Offered Advanced Placement courses, Catholic belief and practice, computer science, driver education, English, film, fine arts, foreign language, health, mathematics, physical education, religion, science, social studies.

Graduation Requirements Arts and fine arts (art, music, dance, drama), computer science, English, foreign language, mathematics, physical education (includes health), religion (includes Bible studies and theology), science, social studies (includes history), 60 hours of community service. Community service is required.

Special Academic Programs 16 Advanced Placement exams for which test preparation is offered; honors section; academic accommodation for the musically talented; special instructional classes for students with Attention Deficit Disorder.

College Admission Counseling 213 students graduated in 2013; all went to college, including Christopher Newport University; George Mason University; James Madison University; University of Virginia; Virginia Commonwealth University; Virginia Polytechnic Institute and State University. Mean SAT critical reading: 585, mean SAT math: 565, mean SAT writing: 591, mean combined SAT: 1741, mean composite ACT: 25.

Student Life Upper grades have uniform requirement, honor system. Discipline rests primarily with faculty. Attendance at religious services is required.

Summer Programs Remediation, enrichment, art/fine arts, computer instruction programs offered; session focuses on remediation; held on campus; accepts boys and girls; open to students from other schools. 50 students usually enrolled. 2014 schedule: June to July.

Tuition and Aid Day student tuition: $12,900–$17,711. Tuition installment plan (FACTS Tuition Payment Plan, monthly payment plans). Tuition reduction for siblings, merit scholarship grants, need-based scholarship grants available. In 2013–14, 15% of upper-school students received aid; total upper-school merit-scholarship money awarded: $143,000. Total amount of financial aid awarded in 2013–14: $592,000.

Admissions Traditional secondary-level entrance grade is 9. For fall 2013, 436 students applied for upper-level admission, 392 were accepted, 220 enrolled. High School Placement Test (closed version) from Scholastic Testing Service required. Deadline for receipt of application materials: January 27. Application fee required: $50.

Athletics Interscholastic: baseball (boys), basketball (b,g), field hockey (g), football (b), lacrosse (b,g), soccer (b,g), softball (g), swimming and diving (b,g), tennis (b,g), track and field (b,g), volleyball (g), water polo (b), winter (indoor) track (b,g), wrestling (b); intramural: weight training (b,g); coed interscholastic: cheering, crew, cross-country running, diving, golf, ice hockey, indoor track, water polo, weight training; coed intramural: Frisbee, skiing (downhill), table tennis. 4 PE instructors, 2 athletic trainers.

Computers Computers are regularly used in all academic classes. Computer network features include on-campus library services, online commercial services, Internet access, wireless campus network, Internet filtering or blocking technology. Student e-mail accounts and computer access in designated common areas are available to students. Students grades are available online. The school has a published electronic and media policy.

Contact Mr. Peter J. Hamer, Director of Admissions and Financial Aid. 703-212-5190. Fax: 703-212-8173. E-mail: hamerp@bishopireton.org. Website: www.bishopireton.org

BISHOP JOHN J. SNYDER HIGH SCHOOL

5001 Samaritan Way
Jacksonville, Florida 32210

Head of School: Deacon David Yazdiya

General Information Coeducational day college-preparatory school, affiliated with Roman Catholic Church. Grades 9–12. Founded: 2002. Setting: suburban. 50-acre campus. 15 buildings on campus. Approved or accredited by Council of Accreditation and School Improvement, National Catholic Education Association, Southern Association of Colleges and Schools, and Florida Department of Education. Upper school average class size: 21. Upper school faculty-student ratio: 1:15. There are 180 required school days per year for Upper School students. Upper School students typically attend 5 days per week. The average school day consists of 6 hours and 47 minutes.

Upper School Student Profile Grade 9: 119 students (60 boys, 59 girls); Grade 10: 129 students (64 boys, 65 girls); Grade 11: 115 students (67 boys, 48 girls); Grade 12: 109 students (51 boys, 58 girls). 80% of students are Roman Catholic.

Faculty School total: 32. In upper school: 16 men, 16 women; 15 have advanced degrees.

Subjects Offered Advanced biology, advanced chemistry, Advanced Placement courses, algebra, American government, American history, American history-AP, American literature, American literature-AP, anatomy and physiology, applied skills, art, athletics, Basic programming, Bible, biology, biology-AP, British literature, British literature (honors), calculus-AP, campus ministry, chemistry-AP, Chinese, choir, choral music, Christian doctrine, church history, college admission preparation, college awareness, college counseling, college planning, composition-AP, computer skills, creative writing, debate, economics, economics-AP, English, English composition, English language and composition-AP, English literature and composition-AP, French, geography, geometry, government, government-AP, guidance, healthful living, history of the Catholic Church, honors algebra, honors English, honors geometry, honors U.S. history, honors world history, Latin, marine science, physics, religious education, Spanish, speech and debate, statistics, studio art, the Web, U.S. history, U.S. history-AP, world history, world history-AP.

Graduation Requirements 20th century world history, American government, American history, world history.

Special Academic Programs 9 Advanced Placement exams for which test preparation is offered.

College Admission Counseling 103 students graduated in 2013; 101 went to college, including Florida Gulf Coast University; Florida State University; University of Central Florida; University of Florida; University of North Florida; University of South Florida. Other: 1 went to work, 1 entered military service.

Student Life Upper grades have uniform requirement, student council, honor system. Discipline rests primarily with faculty. Attendance at religious services is required.

Summer Programs Remediation programs offered; held on campus; accepts boys and girls; not open to students from other schools. 15 students usually enrolled. 2014 schedule: June to July.

Tuition and Aid Day student tuition: $7015. Tuition installment plan (FACTS Tuition Payment Plan). Tuition reduction for siblings, need-based scholarship grants

available. In 2013–14, 35% of upper-school students received aid. Total amount of financial aid awarded in 2013–14: $300,000.

Admissions Traditional secondary-level entrance grade is 9. For fall 2013, 475 students applied for upper-level admission, 472 were accepted, 472 enrolled. Explore required. Deadline for receipt of application materials: none. Application fee required: $375. Interview recommended.

Athletics Interscholastic: baseball (boys), basketball (b,g), cheering (b,g), cross-country running (b,g), diving (b,g), drill team (b,g), football (b), golf (b,g), lacrosse (b), soccer (b,g), softball (g), swimming and diving (b,g), tennis (b,g), track and field (b,g), volleyball (g), weight lifting (b), wrestling (b). 3 PE instructors, 23 coaches, 1 athletic trainer.

Computers Computers are regularly used in all academic classes. Computer network features include on-campus library services, Internet access, wireless campus network, Internet filtering or blocking technology. Computer access in designated common areas is available to students. Students grades are available online.

Contact Mrs. Mary Anne Briggs, Assistant to the Principal. 904-771-1029. Fax: 904-908-8988. E-mail: maryannebriggs@bishopsnyder.org. Website: www.bishopsnyder.org

BISHOP KELLY HIGH SCHOOL

7009 Franklin Road
Boise, Idaho 83709-0922

Head of School: Mr. Robert R. Wehde

General Information Coeducational day college-preparatory and religious studies school, affiliated with Roman Catholic Church. Grades 9–12. Founded: 1964. Setting: urban. 68-acre campus. 2 buildings on campus. Approved or accredited by National Catholic Education Association, Northwest Accreditation Commission, Western Catholic Education Association, and Idaho Department of Education. Endowment: $9.7 million. Total enrollment: 723. Upper school average class size: 21. Upper school faculty-student ratio: 1:15. There are 178 required school days per year for Upper School students. Upper School students typically attend 5 days per week. The average school day consists of 7 hours.

Upper School Student Profile Grade 9: 201 students (107 boys, 94 girls); Grade 10: 182 students (98 boys, 84 girls); Grade 11: 186 students (91 boys, 95 girls); Grade 12: 151 students (80 boys, 71 girls); Grade 13: 3 students (3 boys). 78% of students are Roman Catholic.

Faculty School total: 49. In upper school: 22 men, 27 women; 35 have advanced degrees.

Subjects Offered Advanced Placement courses, algebra, American government, American history-AP, art, art appreciation, art-AP, band, biology, biology-AP, calculus-AP, campus ministry, Catholic belief and practice, chemistry, chemistry-AP, choir, Christianity, comparative religion, computer applications, computer science-AP, conceptual physics, creative writing, drawing, economics, English, English language and composition-AP, English-AP, fitness, French, geometry, health, history of the Catholic Church, horticulture, instrumental music, literature, moral reasoning, painting, physical education, physics, physics-AP, pottery, pre-algebra, pre-calculus, psychology, reading/study skills, religious education, religious studies, senior seminar, service learning/internship, social justice, Spanish, Spanish-AP, speech, speech and debate, sports medicine, statistics-AP, theater, theater arts, theology, U.S. history, weight training, world history, yearbook.

Graduation Requirements Computer science, English, foreign language, mathematics, physical education (includes health), religion (includes Bible studies and theology), science, social studies (includes history), 30 hours of community service.

Special Academic Programs Advanced Placement exam preparation; honors section; independent study; study at local college for college credit.

College Admission Counseling 142 students graduated in 2013; 141 went to college, including Boise State University; Carroll College; Gonzaga University; Northern Arizona University; The College of Idaho; University of Idaho. Other: 1 had other specific plans. Mean SAT critical reading: 550, mean SAT math: 588, mean SAT writing: 539, mean combined SAT: 1677.

Student Life Upper grades have specified standards of dress, student council, honor system. Discipline rests primarily with faculty. Attendance at religious services is required.

Tuition and Aid Day student tuition: $7290. Tuition installment plan (The Tuition Plan, monthly payment plans, individually arranged payment plans). Need-based scholarship grants available. In 2013–14, 80% of upper-school students received aid. Total amount of financial aid awarded in 2013–14: $1,166,804.

Admissions Traditional secondary-level entrance grade is 9. For fall 2013, 723 students applied for upper-level admission, 723 were accepted, 723 enrolled. Deadline for receipt of application materials: none. Application fee required: $205.

Athletics Interscholastic: baseball (boys), basketball (b,g), cheering (g), cross-country running (b,g), fitness (b,g), football (b), golf (b,g), lacrosse (b,g), physical fitness (b,g), skiing (downhill) (b,g), snowboarding (b,g), soccer (b,g), softball (g), swimming and diving (b,g), tennis (b,g), track and field (b,g), volleyball (g), weight lifting (b,g), weight training (b,g), wrestling (b); coed interscholastic: ice hockey, water polo. 3 PE instructors, 11 coaches, 1 athletic trainer.

Computers Computers are regularly used in economics, English, foreign language, history, journalism, mathematics, science classes. Computer network features include on-campus library services, Internet access, wireless campus network, Internet filtering or blocking technology, Blackboard, 1:1 Technology-Bring Your Own Device. Student e-mail accounts and computer access in designated common areas are available to students. Students grades are available online. The school has a published electronic and media policy.

Contact Mrs. Kelly Shockey, Director of Admissions. 208-375-6010. Fax: 208-375-3626. E-mail: kshockey@bk.org. Website: www.bk.org

BISHOP KENNY HIGH SCHOOL

1055 Kingman Avenue
Jacksonville, Florida 32207

Head of School: Rev. Michael R. Houle

General Information Coeducational day college-preparatory school, affiliated with Roman Catholic Church. Grades 9–12. Founded: 1952. Setting: urban. 55-acre campus. 10 buildings on campus. Approved or accredited by Southern Association of Colleges and Schools. Total enrollment: 1,210. Upper school average class size: 22. Upper school faculty-student ratio: 1:17. There are 180 required school days per year for Upper School students. Upper School students typically attend 5 days per week. The average school day consists of 6 hours and 30 minutes.

Upper School Student Profile Grade 9: 308 students (147 boys, 161 girls); Grade 10: 323 students (162 boys, 161 girls); Grade 11: 283 students (127 boys, 156 girls); Grade 12: 293 students (143 boys, 150 girls). 85% of students are Roman Catholic.

Faculty School total: 71. In upper school: 23 men, 48 women; 49 have advanced degrees.

Subjects Offered Accounting, desktop publishing, technology, word processing.

Graduation Requirements Electives, English, foreign language, health, mathematics, performing arts, personal fitness, practical arts, religion (includes Bible studies and theology), science, social studies (includes history), service hour requirements.

Special Academic Programs Advanced Placement exam preparation; honors section.

College Admission Counseling 323 students graduated in 2012; all went to college, including Auburn University; Florida State University; Jacksonville University; University of Central Florida; University of Florida; University of North Florida. Median SAT critical reading: 540, median SAT math: 530, median SAT writing: 520; median combined SAT: 1600, median composite ACT: 24. 22% scored over 600 on SAT critical reading, 18% scored over 600 on SAT math, 15% scored over 600 on SAT writing, 17% scored over 1800 on combined SAT, 28% scored over 26 on composite ACT.

Student Life Upper grades have uniform requirement, student council, honor system. Discipline rests primarily with faculty. Attendance at religious services is required.

Tuition and Aid Day student tuition: $7020–$9900. Tuition installment plan (FACTS Tuition Payment Plan, individually arranged payment plans). Tuition reduction for siblings, need-based scholarship grants available. In 2012–13, 20% of upper-school students received aid.

Admissions Traditional secondary-level entrance grade is 9. ACT-Explore or Explore required. Deadline for receipt of application materials: none. Application fee required. On-campus interview required.

Athletics Interscholastic: baseball (boys), basketball (b,g), cheering (g), cross-country running (b,g), diving (b,g), drill team (g), football (b), golf (b,g), JROTC drill (b,g), riflery (b,g), soccer (b,g), softball (g), swimming and diving (b,g), tennis (b,g), track and field (b,g), volleyball (g), weight lifting (b), wrestling (b). 1 athletic trainer.

Computers Computers are regularly used in computer applications, journalism, keyboarding, newspaper, yearbook classes. Computer resources include on-campus library services, Internet access, Internet filtering or blocking technology, design software for Journalism and MultiMedia, CS4 Suite, 5 computer labs. The school has a published electronic and media policy.

Contact Mr. Caleb Kitchings, Director of Admissions. 904-398-7545. Fax: 904-398-5728. E-mail: admissions@bishopkenny.org. Website: www.bishopkenny.org

BISHOP LUERS HIGH SCHOOL

333 East Paulding Road
Fort Wayne, Indiana 46816

Head of School: Mrs. Mary T. Keefer

General Information Coeducational day college-preparatory and religious studies school, affiliated with Roman Catholic Church; primarily serves individuals with Attention Deficit Disorder. Grades 9–12. Founded: 1958. Setting: urban. 5-acre campus. 1 building on campus. Approved or accredited by National Catholic Education Association, North Central Association of Colleges and Schools, and Indiana Department of Education. Total enrollment: 596. Upper school average class size: 25. Upper school faculty-student ratio: 1:17. There are 180 required school days per year for Upper School students. Upper School students typically attend 5 days per week. The average school day consists of 6 hours and 35 minutes.

Upper School Student Profile Grade 9: 181 students (93 boys, 88 girls); Grade 10: 148 students (91 boys, 57 girls); Grade 11: 125 students (60 boys, 65 girls); Grade 12: 142 students (77 boys, 65 girls). 89% of students are Roman Catholic.

Faculty School total: 31. In upper school: 10 men, 21 women; 18 have advanced degrees.

Subjects Offered 3-dimensional art, accounting, algebra, Bible, biology, biology-AP, business, business law, calculus-AP, chamber groups, chemistry, chemistry-AP, chorus, church history, computer applications, computer programming, concert band, creative writing, drawing, economics, English, French, geometry, government, health education, honors algebra, honors English, honors geometry, honors U.S. history, honors world history, Latin, music appreciation, music theory, painting, physical education, physics, physiology, pre-calculus, probability and statistics, psychology, sculpture, sociology, Spanish, speech communications, student government, student publications, study skills, theater arts, theater production, theology, trigonometry, U.S. history, world civilizations, world geography, world history.

Graduation Requirements Computers, English, mathematics, physical education (includes health), religion (includes Bible studies and theology), science, social studies (includes history).

Special Academic Programs Advanced Placement exam preparation; honors section; study at local college for college credit; academic accommodation for the gifted and the musically talented; remedial reading and/or remedial writing; remedial math.

College Admission Counseling 128 students graduated in 2012; 119 went to college, including Ball State University; Indiana University–Purdue University Fort Wayne; Indiana University Bloomington; Purdue University. Other: 5 went to work, 4 entered military service. Mean SAT critical reading: 483, mean SAT math: 486, mean SAT writing: 461, mean composite ACT: 22. 13.8% scored over 600 on SAT critical reading, 11.5% scored over 600 on SAT math, 6.9% scored over 600 on SAT writing.

Student Life Upper grades have specified standards of dress, student council. Discipline rests equally with students and faculty. Attendance at religious services is required.

Tuition and Aid Day student tuition: $4725. Tuition installment plan (FACTS Tuition Payment Plan). Tuition reduction for siblings, merit scholarship grants, need-based scholarship grants, paying campus jobs available. In 2012–13, 61% of upper-school students received aid.

Admissions Traditional secondary-level entrance grade is 9. Admissions testing required. Deadline for receipt of application materials: none. Application fee required: $120.

Athletics Interscholastic: baseball (boys), basketball (b,g), bowling (b,g), cheering (g), cross-country running (b,g), dance (g), dance team (g), diving (b,g), football (b), golf (b,g), lacrosse (b), riflery (b,g), running (b,g), soccer (b,g), softball (g), swimming and diving (b,g), tennis (b,g), track and field (b,g), volleyball (g), wrestling (g); intramural: lacrosse (b,g); coed intramural: lacrosse, riflery, weight training. 2 PE instructors, 25 coaches, 2 athletic trainers.

Computers Computers are regularly used in all academic, business, yearbook classes. Computer network features include on-campus library services, Internet access, Internet filtering or blocking technology. Students grades are available online. The school has a published electronic and media policy.

Contact Mrs. Jennifer Andorfer, Co-Director of Admissions and Public Relations. 260-456-1261 Ext. 3141. Fax: 260-456-1262. E-mail: jandorfer@bishopluers.org. Website: www.bishopluers.org/

BISHOP MCGUINNESS CATHOLIC HIGH SCHOOL

1725 NC Highway 66 South
Kernersville, North Carolina 27284

Head of School: Mr. George L. Repass

General Information Coeducational day college-preparatory, arts, and religious studies school, affiliated with Roman Catholic Church. Grades 9–12. Founded: 1959. Setting: small town. Nearest major city is Winston-Salem. 42-acre campus. 2 buildings on campus. Approved or accredited by National Catholic Education Association, Southern Association of Colleges and Schools, The College Board, and North Carolina Department of Education. Member of National Association of Independent Schools. Endowment: $100,000. Total enrollment: 549. Upper school average class size: 18. Upper school faculty-student ratio: 1:15. There are 180 required school days per year for Upper School students. Upper School students typically attend 5 days per week. The average school day consists of 6 hours and 50 minutes.

Upper School Student Profile Grade 9: 142 students (87 boys, 55 girls); Grade 10: 152 students (81 boys, 71 girls); Grade 11: 111 students (69 boys, 42 girls); Grade 12: 144 students (76 boys, 68 girls). 75% of students are Roman Catholic.

Faculty School total: 36. In upper school: 20 men, 16 women; 31 have advanced degrees.

Subjects Offered Algebra, American history, anatomy, art history, arts, biology, biology-AP, calculus, calculus-AP, chemistry, chemistry-AP, community service, computer science, computer science-AP, creative writing, earth science, English, English language-AP, English literature and composition-AP, environmental science, European history-AP, fine arts, French, French language-AP, French-AP, geometry, health, Latin, Latin-AP, mathematics, music, music theory-AP, photography, physical education, physical science, physics, political science, religion, science, social studies, Spanish, Spanish-AP, statistics-AP, trigonometry, U.S. history-AP, world history.

Graduation Requirements 1 1/2 elective credits, arts and fine arts (art, music, dance, drama), English, foreign language, mathematics, physical education (includes health), religion (includes Bible studies and theology), science, social studies (includes history), all students must attend the retreat for their grade level; all seniors must complete the senior career project. Community service is required.

Special Academic Programs 16 Advanced Placement exams for which test preparation is offered; honors section; independent study; term-away projects; study at local college for college credit.

College Admission Counseling Colleges students went to include Appalachian State University; East Carolina University; North Carolina State University; The University of North Carolina at Chapel Hill; The University of North Carolina at Charlotte; The University of North Carolina Wilmington. Mean SAT critical reading: 553, mean SAT math: 539, mean SAT writing: 534, mean combined SAT: 1626, mean composite ACT: 24. 30% scored over 600 on SAT critical reading, 29% scored over 600 on SAT math, 20% scored over 600 on SAT writing, 27% scored over 1800 on combined SAT, 29% scored over 26 on composite ACT.

Student Life Upper grades have specified standards of dress, student council, honor system. Discipline rests primarily with faculty. Attendance at religious services is required.

Tuition and Aid Tuition installment plan (monthly payment plans, yearly, semester, and quarterly payment plans). Tuition reduction for siblings, need-based scholarship grants available. In 2012–13, 19% of upper-school students received aid. Total amount of financial aid awarded in 2012–13: $288,550.

Admissions Traditional secondary-level entrance grade is 9. For fall 2012, 182 students applied for upper-level admission, 172 were accepted, 154 enrolled. Achievement/Aptitude/Writing or High School Placement Test required. Deadline for receipt of application materials: none. Application fee required: $75. On-campus interview required.

Athletics Interscholastic: baseball (boys), basketball (b,g), cheering (g), fencing (b), football (b), lacrosse (b), soccer (b,g), softball (g), tennis (b,g), volleyball (g), wrestling (b); coed interscholastic: cross-country running, golf, swimming and diving, track and field, weight training. 3 PE instructors, 40 coaches, 1 athletic trainer.

Computers Computers are regularly used in accounting classes. Computer resources include on-campus library services, Internet access, Internet filtering or blocking technology. Student e-mail accounts and computer access in designated common areas are available to students. Students grades are available online. The school has a published electronic and media policy.

Contact Mr. Robert Belcher, Admissions Director. 336-564-1011. Fax: 336-564-1060. E-mail: rb@bmhs.us. Website: www.bmhs.us

BISHOP MCGUINNESS CATHOLIC HIGH SCHOOL

801 Northwest 50th Street
Oklahoma City, Oklahoma 73118-6001

Head of School: Mr. David L. Morton

General Information Coeducational day college-preparatory, arts, business, religious studies, bilingual studies, and technology school, affiliated with Roman Catholic Church. Grades 9–12. Founded: 1950. Setting: urban. 20-acre campus. 4 buildings on campus. Approved or accredited by North Central Association of Colleges and Schools, Oklahoma Private Schools Accreditation Commission, and Oklahoma Department of Education. Total enrollment: 701. Upper school average class size: 15. Upper school faculty-student ratio: 1:13. There are 177 required school days per year for Upper School students. Upper School students typically attend 5 days per week. The average school day consists of 6 hours and 10 minutes.

Upper School Student Profile Grade 11: 167 students (75 boys, 92 girls); Grade 12: 174 students (97 boys, 77 girls). 74% of students are Roman Catholic.

Faculty School total: 58. In upper school: 12 men, 15 women; 11 have advanced degrees.

Subjects Offered Algebra, American literature, art, band, Bible, biology, biology-AP, broadcasting, business, business law, calculus-AP, Catholic belief and practice, ceramics, chemistry, chemistry-AP, Chinese studies, chorus, church history, computer technologies, creative writing, culinary arts, current events, dance, debate, digital photography, drama, drawing, drawing and design, economics, electives, English, English language and composition-AP, English literature, English literature and composition-AP, ethics, French, geometry, German, government, health and wellness, history of the Catholic Church, honors algebra, honors English, honors geometry, human geography - AP, introduction to theater, Latin, Latin-AP, leadership, learning lab, Life of Christ, macroeconomics-AP, media production, music appreciation, newspaper, painting, personal finance, photography, physical education, physical science, physics, physics-AP, physiology, practical arts, prayer/spirituality, pre-calculus, psychology, psychology-AP, scripture, social justice, sociology, Spanish, Spanish-AP, speech, stagecraft, state history, statistics-AP, strategies for success, theater, trigonometry, U.S. government and politics-AP, U.S. history, U.S. history-AP, weight training, world history, world history-AP, world religions, writing workshop, yearbook.

Graduation Requirements Arts and fine arts (art, music, dance, drama), electives, English, foreign language, mathematics, physical education (includes health), practical arts, science, social studies (includes history), theology, 90 hours of Christian service.

Special Academic Programs 16 Advanced Placement exams for which test preparation is offered; honors section; academic accommodation for the gifted and the artistically talented; programs in English, mathematics for dyslexic students; special instructional classes for students with learning differences.

College Admission Counseling 178 students graduated in 2013; 169 went to college, including Oklahoma City University; Oklahoma State University; University of Oklahoma; University of San Diego. Other: 2 went to work, 1 entered military service, 3 entered a postgraduate year, 3 had other specific plans. Median SAT critical reading: 590, median SAT math: 550, median SAT writing: 600. Mean composite ACT: 25.

Student Life Upper grades have uniform requirement, student council, honor system. Discipline rests primarily with faculty. Attendance at religious services is required.

Summer Programs Remediation, enrichment, sports programs offered; session focuses on science enrichment, PE enrichment, math enrichment and remediation; held on campus; accepts boys and girls; not open to students from other schools. 20 students usually enrolled. 2014 schedule: June 7 to August 1. Application deadline: May.

Tuition and Aid Day student tuition: $8350. Tuition installment plan (FACTS Tuition Payment Plan). Need-based scholarship grants, paying campus jobs available. In 2013–14, 16% of upper-school students received aid. Total amount of financial aid awarded in 2013–14: $163,200.

Admissions Traditional secondary-level entrance grade is 11. For fall 2013, 7 students applied for upper-level admission, 7 were accepted, 7 enrolled. STS or writing sample required. Deadline for receipt of application materials: May 1. Application fee required: $400. On-campus interview required.

Athletics Interscholastic: baseball (boys), basketball (b,g), bowling (b,g), cheering (g), cross-country running (b,g), football (b), golf (b,g), soccer (b,g), softball (g), swimming and diving (b,g), tennis (b,g), track and field (b,g), volleyball (g), weight training (b,g), winter (indoor) track (b,g), wrestling (b); coed interscholastic: dance team, physical fitness. 28 coaches, 1 athletic trainer.

Computers Computers are regularly used in all academic classes. Computer network features include on-campus library services, online commercial services, Internet access, wireless campus network, Internet filtering or blocking technology, laptop classroom carts, wireless printing, eBooks, and My Road, Digital Citizenship classes, iPad classroom carts. Student e-mail accounts and computer access in designated common areas are available to students. Students grades are available online. The school has a published electronic and media policy.

Contact Ms. Amy Hanson, 9th Grade Counselor. 405-842-6638 Ext. 225. Fax: 405-858-9550. E-mail: ahanson@bmchs.org. Website: www.bmchs.org

BISHOP MONTGOMERY HIGH SCHOOL

5430 Torrance Boulevard
Torrance, California 90503

Head of School: Ms. Rosemary Distaso-Libbon

General Information Coeducational day college-preparatory, arts, religious studies, and technology school, affiliated with Roman Catholic Church. Grades 9–12. Founded: 1957. Setting: suburban. Nearest major city is Los Angeles. 27-acre campus. 9 buildings on campus. Approved or accredited by National Catholic Education Association, Western Association of Schools and Colleges, Western Catholic Education Association, and California Department of Education. Total enrollment: 938. Upper school average class size: 22. Upper school faculty-student ratio: 1:22. There are 180 required school days per year for Upper School students. Upper School students typically attend 5 days per week. The average school day consists of 6 hours and 10 minutes.

Upper School Student Profile Grade 9: 236 students (104 boys, 132 girls); Grade 10: 218 students (112 boys, 106 girls); Grade 11: 243 students (114 boys, 129 girls); Grade 12: 241 students (112 boys, 129 girls). 75% of students are Roman Catholic.

Faculty School total: 60. In upper school: 25 men, 33 women; 22 have advanced degrees.

Subjects Offered Advanced Placement courses, algebra, American history, American history-AP, American literature, anatomy, art, Bible studies, biology, calculus, chemistry, chorus, composition, computer science, drama, economics, English, English literature, English literature-AP, fine arts, French, geometry, government/civics, health, history, languages, literature, mathematics, physical education, physics, physics-AP, physiology, religion, science, social studies, Spanish, statistics, theater, weight training, world history, yearbook.

Graduation Requirements Arts and fine arts (art, music, dance, drama), business skills (includes word processing), computer science, English, mathematics, physical education (includes health), religion (includes Bible studies and theology), science, social studies (includes history).

Special Academic Programs Advanced Placement exam preparation; honors section.

College Admission Counseling 246 students graduated in 2013; 243 went to college, including California State University, Dominguez Hills; California State University, Long Beach; Loyola Marymount University; University of California, Irvine; University of California, Los Angeles; University of California, Riverside. Other: 1 entered military service, 2 had other specific plans. Mean SAT critical reading: 527, mean SAT math: 527, mean SAT writing: 526.

Student Life Upper grades have uniform requirement, student council, honor system. Discipline rests primarily with faculty. Attendance at religious services is required.

Summer Programs Remediation, enrichment, advancement, sports, art/fine arts, computer instruction programs offered; session focuses on academic enrichment/remediation and athletic conditioning; held on campus; accepts boys and girls; not open to students from other schools. 900 students usually enrolled. 2014 schedule: June 18 to July 22. Application deadline: June 20.

Tuition and Aid Day student tuition: $8400. Tuition installment plan (monthly payment plans). Tuition reduction for siblings, merit scholarship grants, need-based scholarship grants, financial need available. In 2013–14, 4% of upper-school students received aid; total upper-school merit-scholarship money awarded: $38,000. Total amount of financial aid awarded in 2013–14: $68,000.

Admissions Traditional secondary-level entrance grade is 9. High School Placement Test, Iowa Tests of Basic Skills and Stanford 9 required. Deadline for receipt of application materials: January 16. Application fee required: $100.

Athletics Interscholastic: baseball (boys), basketball (b,g), cheering (g), cross-country running (b,g), dance (g), dance team (g), football (b), golf (b,g), soccer (b,g), softball (g), strength & conditioning (b,g), tennis (b,g), volleyball (b,g); coed interscholastic: aerobics, surfing, swimming and diving, track and field. 3 PE instructors, 32 coaches, 2 athletic trainers.

Computers Computers are regularly used in library, newspaper, programming, publications, technology, Web site design classes. Computer network features include on-campus library services, Internet access, wireless campus network. Students grades are available online. The school has a published electronic and media policy.

Contact Mrs. Casey Dunn, Director of Admissions. 310-540-2021 Ext. 227. Fax: 310-543-5102. E-mail: cdunn@bmhs-la.org. Website: www.bmhs-la.org

BISHOP O'DOWD HIGH SCHOOL

9500 Stearns Avenue
Oakland, California 94605-4799

Head of School: Dr. Stephen Phelps

General Information Coeducational day college-preparatory, arts, religious studies, technology, and Environmental Science school, affiliated with Roman Catholic Church. Grades 9–12. Founded: 1951. Setting: urban. 8-acre campus. 13 buildings on campus. Approved or accredited by Western Association of Schools and Colleges, Western Catholic Education Association, and California Department of Education. Endowment: $1 million. Total enrollment: 1,151. Upper school average class size: 25. Upper school faculty-student ratio: 1:15. Upper School students typically attend 5 days per week. The average school day consists of 6 hours and 30 minutes.

Upper School Student Profile Grade 9: 308 students (155 boys, 153 girls); Grade 10: 290 students (139 boys, 151 girls); Grade 11: 309 students (152 boys, 157 girls); Grade 12: 245 students (122 boys, 123 girls). 55% of students are Roman Catholic.

Faculty School total: 79. In upper school: 41 men, 38 women; 55 have advanced degrees.

Subjects Offered Art, computer science, English, fine arts, foreign language, mathematics, physical education, religion, science, social studies.

Graduation Requirements Arts and fine arts (art, music, dance, drama), English, foreign language, mathematics, physical education (includes health), religion (includes Bible studies and theology), religious studies, science, social studies (includes history), 100 hour service learning project to be completed over all four years.

Special Academic Programs Advanced Placement exam preparation; honors section; academic accommodation for the gifted, the musically talented, and the artistically talented; remedial reading and/or remedial writing; remedial math; special instructional classes for students with ADD and dyslexia.

College Admission Counseling 296 students graduated in 2013; 294 went to college, including California Polytechnic State University, San Luis Obispo; San Francisco State University; University of California, Berkeley; University of California, Davis; University of California, Santa Cruz; University of Oregon. Other: 2 had other specific plans. Mean SAT critical reading: 566, mean SAT math: 565, mean SAT writing: 575.

Student Life Upper grades have specified standards of dress, student council. Discipline rests equally with students and faculty.

Summer Programs Remediation, computer instruction programs offered; session focuses on review; held on campus; accepts boys and girls; open to students from other schools. 120 students usually enrolled. 2014 schedule: June 13 to July 20. Application deadline: June 1.

Tuition and Aid Day student tuition: $14,700. Tuition installment plan (monthly payment plans, individually arranged payment plans). Tuition reduction for siblings, merit scholarship grants, need-based scholarship grants available. In 2013–14, 30% of upper-school students received aid; total upper-school merit-scholarship money awarded: $150,000. Total amount of financial aid awarded in 2013–14: $2,300,000.

Admissions Traditional secondary-level entrance grade is 9. For fall 2013, 760 students applied for upper-level admission, 475 were accepted, 310 enrolled. High School Placement Test and High School Placement Test (closed version) from Scholastic Testing Service required. Deadline for receipt of application materials: none. Application fee required: $90.

Athletics Interscholastic: aquatics (boys, girls), baseball (b), basketball (b,g), cross-country running (b,g), diving (b,g), football (b), golf (b,g), lacrosse (b,g), rugby (b,g), soccer (b,g), softball (g), strength & conditioning (b,g), swimming and diving (b,g), tennis (b,g), track and field (b,g), volleyball (g), water polo (b,g); intramural: basketball (b,g), dance squad (g), physical training (b,g), soccer (b,g), weight training (b,g); coed interscholastic: cheering, cross-country running, strength & conditioning; coed intramural: aerobics, aerobics/dance, alpine skiing, backpacking, bicycling, bowling, combined training, fitness, flag football, Frisbee, hiking/backpacking, mountain biking, skiing (downhill), snowboarding, weight training. 5 PE instructors, 36 coaches, 1 athletic trainer.

Computers Computers are regularly used in all academic, career exploration, library, library skills, mathematics, media arts, media production, newspaper, programming, research skills, science, video film production, yearbook classes. Computer network features include on-campus library services, online commercial services, Internet access, wireless campus network, Internet filtering or blocking technology, one-to-one laptop program—every student has a laptop on campus. Student e-mail accounts are available to students. Students grades are available online. The school has a published electronic and media policy.

Contact Mr. Tyler Kreitz, Director of Admissions. 510-577-9100. Fax: 510-638-3259. E-mail: tkreitz@bishopodowd.org. Website: www.bishopodowd.org

BISHOP'S COLLEGE SCHOOL

80 Moulton Hill Road
PO Box 5001, Succ. Lennoxville
Sherbrooke, Quebec J1M 1Z8, Canada

Head of School: Mr. William Mitchell

General Information Coeducational boarding and day college-preparatory, arts, and bilingual studies school. Grades 7–12. Founded: 1836. Setting: small town. Nearest major city is Montreal, Canada. Students are housed in single-sex dormitories. 270-acre campus. 30 buildings on campus. Approved or accredited by Canadian Association of Independent Schools, Canadian Educational Standards Institute, Quebec Association of Independent Schools, The Association of Boarding Schools, and Quebec Department of Education. Affiliate member of National Association of Independent Schools. Languages of instruction: English and French. Endowment: CAN$15.6 million. Total enrollment: 216. Upper school average class size: 18. Upper school faculty-student ratio: 1:7. There are 180 required school days per year for Upper School students. Upper School students typically attend 6 days per week. The average school day consists of 8 hours.

Upper School Student Profile Grade 10: 32 students (18 boys, 14 girls); Grade 11: 64 students (37 boys, 27 girls); Grade 12: 42 students (27 boys, 15 girls). 75% of students are boarding students. 44% are province residents. 11 provinces are represented in upper school student body. 49% are international students. International students from Bahamas, China, France, Mexico, Saudi Arabia, and United States; 17 other countries represented in student body.

Faculty School total: 30. In upper school: 17 men, 13 women; 15 reside on campus.

Subjects Offered Algebra, art, biology, calculus, chemistry, computer science, creative writing, dance, drama, economics, English, environmental science, ESL, ethics, finite math, French, French as a second language, geography, geometry, history, mathematics, music, philosophy, physical education, physical science, physics, political science, religion, science, sociology, study skills, technology, theater, trigonometry, world history.

Graduation Requirements Follow Ministry of Quebec guidelines, follow Ministry of Ontario guidelines.

Special Academic Programs Advanced Placement exam preparation; term-away projects; study at local college for college credit; study abroad; academic accommodation for the gifted, the musically talented, and the artistically talented; remedial reading and/or remedial writing; remedial math; ESL (31 students enrolled).

College Admission Counseling 44 students graduated in 2012; 42 went to college, including Carleton University; Ryerson University; University of Guelph; University of Toronto. Other: 2 had other specific plans.

Student Life Upper grades have uniform requirement, student council, honor system. Discipline rests equally with students and faculty.

Tuition and Aid Day student tuition: CAN$17,200; 7-day tuition and room/board: CAN$44,500. Tuition installment plan (monthly payment plans, individually arranged payment plans, single payment plan). Tuition reduction for siblings, bursaries, merit scholarship grants, need-based scholarship grants, need-based loans available.

Admissions Admissions testing or English for Non-native Speakers required. Deadline for receipt of application materials: none. Application fee required: CAN$100. Interview required.

Athletics Interscholastic: baseball (boys), football (b,g), gymnastics (g), hockey (b), ice hockey (b), softball (g); coed interscholastic: alpine skiing, aquatics, basketball, bicycling, climbing, cross-country running, equestrian sports, golf, horseback riding, independent competitive sports, nordic skiing, outdoor adventure, rugby, skiing (cross-country), skiing (downhill), soccer, swimming and diving, track and field; coed intramural: aerobics, alpine skiing, backpacking, badminton, basketball, climbing, Cosom hockey, curling, dance, figure skating, fitness, fitness walking, floor hockey, hiking/backpacking, hockey, horseback riding, ice hockey, ice skating, indoor hockey, jogging, mountain biking, outdoor activities, outdoor education, physical fitness, rock climbing, snowshoeing, squash, strength & conditioning, yoga. 1 PE instructor, 10 coaches, 1 athletic trainer.

Computers Computer network features include on-campus library services, Internet access, wireless campus network, Internet filtering or blocking technology, school-wide laptop initiative (included in tuition), fiber optic network. Student e-mail accounts are available to students. The school has a published electronic and media policy.

Contact Mrs. Ashli MacInnis, Director of Recruitment and Admissions. 819-566-0227 Ext. 296. Fax: 819-566-8123. E-mail: amacinnis@bishopscollegeschool.com. Website: www.bishopscollegeschool.com

BISHOP SHANAHAN HIGH SCHOOL

220 Woodbine Road
Downingtown, Pennsylvania 19335

Head of School: Sr. Regina Plunkett, IHM

General Information Coeducational day college-preparatory and general academic school, affiliated with Roman Catholic Church. Grades 9–12. Founded: 1957. Setting: suburban. Nearest major city is Philadelphia. 80-acre campus. 1 building on campus. Approved or accredited by Pennsylvania Department of Education. Total enrollment: 1,125. Upper School students typically attend 5 days per week. The average school day consists of 5 hours and 10 minutes.

Upper School Student Profile Grade 9: 247 students (115 boys, 132 girls); Grade 10: 286 students (138 boys, 148 girls); Grade 11: 298 students (142 boys, 156 girls); Grade 12: 294 students (141 boys, 153 girls).

Subjects Offered Algebra, American history, American history-AP, American literature, chemistry-AP.

Graduation Requirements World history.

Special Academic Programs 17 Advanced Placement exams for which test preparation is offered; honors section; study at local college for college credit.

Student Life Upper grades have uniform requirement, student council. Discipline rests primarily with faculty.

Tuition and Aid Day student tuition: $6850. Tuition installment plan (monthly payment plans). Tuition reduction for siblings, need-based scholarship grants available.

Admissions Deadline for receipt of application materials: none. Application fee required: $400. Interview recommended.

Athletics Interscholastic: baseball (boys), basketball (b,g), cheering (g), cross-country running (b,g), field hockey (g), football (b), golf (b), ice hockey (b,g), lacrosse (b,g), rugby (b), soccer (b,g), softball (g), swimming and diving (b,g), tennis (b,g), track and field (b,g), volleyball (g).

Computers Computer network features include Internet filtering or blocking technology. The school has a published electronic and media policy.

Contact Mrs. Carol S. Dale, Enrollment Manager. 610-343-6206. Fax: 610-343-6220. E-mail: cdale@shanahan.org. Website: www.shanahan.org

THE BISHOP'S SCHOOL

7607 La Jolla Boulevard
La Jolla, California 92037

Head of School: Aimeclaire Roche

General Information Coeducational day college-preparatory, arts, religious studies, and technology school, affiliated with Episcopal Church. Grades 6–12. Founded: 1909. Setting: suburban. Nearest major city is San Diego. 11-acre campus. 8 buildings on campus. Approved or accredited by California Association of Independent Schools, National Association of Episcopal Schools, Western Association of Schools and Colleges, and California Department of Education. Member of National Association of Independent Schools. Endowment: $27 million. Total enrollment: 800. Upper school average class size: 14. Upper school faculty-student ratio: 1:14. Upper School students typically attend 5 days per week. The average school day consists of 7 hours.

Upper School Student Profile Grade 9: 138 students (62 boys, 76 girls); Grade 10: 143 students (82 boys, 61 girls); Grade 11: 136 students (69 boys, 67 girls); Grade 12: 141 students (69 boys, 72 girls).

Faculty School total: 93. In upper school: 38 men, 45 women; 71 have advanced degrees.

Subjects Offered Acting, Advanced Placement courses, advanced studio art-AP, algebra, American history, American literature, art history, art history-AP, arts, ASB Leadership, biology, biology-AP, calculus, calculus-AP, ceramics, chemistry, chemistry-AP, Chinese, Chinese studies, chorus, community service, comparative government and politics-AP, comparative religion, computer programming, computer science, creative writing, dance, discrete mathematics, drama, drawing, earth science, ecology, economics, economics and history, economics-AP, English, English literature, environmental science, ethics, European history, European history-AP, forensics, French, French language-AP, French literature-AP, genetics, geography, geometry, government/civics, health, history, human anatomy, humanities, integrated mathematics, Internet, jazz band, journalism, Latin, Latin American studies, Latin-AP, literature and composition-AP, literature-AP, macro/microeconomics-AP, marine biology, mathematics, music, painting, philosophy, photography, physical education,

physical science, physics, physics-AP, physiology, pre-algebra, pre-calculus, probability, programming, religious studies, Shakespeare, social studies, Spanish, Spanish language-AP, Spanish literature-AP, speech, speech and debate, stained glass, statistics, statistics-AP, studio art-AP, tap dance, theater, theater design and production, typing, U.S. government and politics-AP, U.S. history, U.S. history-AP, visual reality, world history, yearbook.

Graduation Requirements Arts and fine arts (art, music, dance, drama), computer science, English, foreign language, mathematics, physical education (includes health), religion (includes Bible studies and theology), science, social sciences, social studies (includes history), swimming test, computer proficiency. Community service is required.

Special Academic Programs Advanced Placement exam preparation; honors section; independent study; study abroad.

College Admission Counseling 133 students graduated in 2012; 129 went to college, including Boston College; Brown University; New York University; Stanford University; University of California, Berkeley; University of Southern California. Other: 4 had other specific plans. Median SAT critical reading: 670, median SAT math: 680, median SAT writing: 700, median combined SAT: 2080, median composite ACT: 31. 79% scored over 600 on SAT critical reading, 86% scored over 600 on SAT math, 83% scored over 600 on SAT writing, 83% scored over 1800 on combined SAT, 85% scored over 26 on composite ACT.

Student Life Upper grades have uniform requirement, student council, honor system. Discipline rests equally with students and faculty. Attendance at religious services is required.

Tuition and Aid Day student tuition: $28,000. Tuition installment plan (FACTS Tuition Payment Plan, semester payment plans, Key Resources Achiever Loan). Need-based scholarship grants available. In 2012–13, 20% of upper-school students received aid. Total amount of financial aid awarded in 2012–13: $2,900,000.

Admissions Traditional secondary-level entrance grade is 9. For fall 2012, 390 students applied for upper-level admission, 226 were accepted, 175 enrolled. ISEE required. Deadline for receipt of application materials: February 1. Application fee required: $100. On-campus interview required.

Athletics Interscholastic: baseball (boys), basketball (b,g), cross-country running (b,g), equestrian sports (b,g), field hockey (g), football (b), golf (b,g), gymnastics (g), lacrosse (b,g), soccer (b,g), softball (g), swimming and diving (b,g), tennis (b,g), track and field (b,g), volleyball (b,g), water polo (b,g); intramural: weight training (b,g); coed interscholastic: sailing. 5 PE instructors, 38 coaches, 1 athletic trainer.

Computers Computers are regularly used in English, foreign language, history, journalism, library, music, science, yearbook classes. Computer network features include on-campus library services, online commercial services, Internet access.

Contact Kim Peckham, Director of Admissions and Financial Aid. 858-875-0809. Fax: 858-459-2990. E-mail: peckhamk@bishops.com. Website: www.bishops.com

BISHOP STANG HIGH SCHOOL

500 Slocum Road
North Dartmouth, Massachusetts 02747-2999

Head of School: Mr. Peter V. Shaughnessy

General Information Coeducational day college-preparatory, arts, business, religious studies, technology, science, and arts school, affiliated with Roman Catholic Church. Grades 9–12. Founded: 1959. Setting: suburban. Nearest major city is New Bedford. 8-acre campus. 1 building on campus. Approved or accredited by New England Association of Schools and Colleges and Massachusetts Department of Education. Endowment: $2 million. Total enrollment: 644. Upper school average class size: 19. Upper school faculty-student ratio: 1:13. There are 180 required school days per year for Upper School students. Upper School students typically attend 5 days per week. The average school day consists of 6 hours and 30 minutes.

Upper School Student Profile Grade 9: 149 students (55 boys, 94 girls); Grade 10: 166 students (79 boys, 87 girls); Grade 11: 173 students (84 boys, 89 girls); Grade 12: 156 students (69 boys, 87 girls). 85% of students are Roman Catholic.

Faculty School total: 61. In upper school: 19 men, 32 women; 29 have advanced degrees.

Subjects Offered 20th century American writers, 20th century world history, 3-dimensional art, 3-dimensional design, advanced biology, advanced chemistry, advanced math, Advanced Placement courses, algebra, alternative physical education, American history, American history-AP, American literature, American literature-AP, anatomy and physiology, art, athletics, biochemistry, bioethics, biology, biology-AP, business law, calculus, calculus-AP, campus ministry, career and personal planning, career/college preparation, Catholic belief and practice, chemistry, chemistry-AP, chorus, church history, clayworking, collage and assemblage, college admission preparation, college awareness, college counseling, college placement, college planning, college writing, communications, community service, comparative religion, computer education, computer literacy, computer science, computer technologies, concert band, criminal justice, criminology, death and loss, drama, drama performance, dramatic arts, drawing, drawing and design, driver education, ecology, English, English language and composition-AP, English literature, English literature-AP, English-AP, environmental science, fine arts, French, geometry, government/civics, health, health science, history, history of the Catholic Church, honors algebra, honors English, honors geometry, honors U.S. history, honors world history, human biology, human development, instrumental music, introduction to theater, jazz band, lab science, Latin, leadership and service, Life of Christ, marine biology, marketing, mathematics, mechanical drawing, media production, modern European history, modern European history-AP, moral theology, music, oceanography, painting, photography, physical education, physics, physics-AP, physiology, Portuguese, prayer/spirituality, psychology, psychology-AP, public service, public speaking, religion, religious studies, SAT/ACT preparation, science, social sciences, social studies, sociology, Spanish, study skills, technical drawing, theater arts, trigonometry, U.S. history-AP, Web authoring, Web site design, world history, world literature, writing, yearbook.

Graduation Requirements Arts and fine arts (art, music, dance, drama), business skills (includes word processing), computer science, English, foreign language, mathematics, physical education (includes health), religion (includes Bible studies and theology), science, social sciences, social studies (includes history), service project. Community service is required.

Special Academic Programs 9 Advanced Placement exams for which test preparation is offered; honors section; remedial reading and/or remedial writing; remedial math; programs in English, mathematics, general development for dyslexic students.

College Admission Counseling Colleges students went to include Providence College; Roger Williams University; Stonehill College; University of Massachusetts Amherst; University of Massachusetts Dartmouth; University of Rhode Island. Mean SAT critical reading: 563, mean SAT math: 536, mean SAT writing: 549, mean combined SAT: 1648.

Student Life Upper grades have uniform requirement, student council, honor system. Discipline rests primarily with faculty. Attendance at religious services is required.

Summer Programs Enrichment, advancement, sports, art/fine arts, computer instruction programs offered; session focuses on sport and activity camps; held on campus; accepts boys and girls; open to students from other schools. 200 students usually enrolled. 2014 schedule: July 1 to August 19. Application deadline: June.

Tuition and Aid Day student tuition: $8650. Tuition installment plan (FACTS Tuition Payment Plan, monthly payment plans). Merit scholarship grants, need-based scholarship grants available. In 2013–14, 26% of upper-school students received aid; total upper-school merit-scholarship money awarded: $12,500. Total amount of financial aid awarded in 2013–14: $500,000.

Admissions Traditional secondary-level entrance grade is 9. For fall 2013, 230 students applied for upper-level admission, 225 were accepted, 149 enrolled. Scholastic Testing Service High School Placement Test or SSAT required. Deadline for receipt of application materials: none. No application fee required. On-campus interview recommended.

Athletics Interscholastic: aquatics (boys, girls), baseball (b), basketball (b,g), cheering (g), cross-country running (b,g), diving (b,g), field hockey (g), fitness (b,g), football (b), ice hockey (b,g), indoor track (b,g), lacrosse (b,g), soccer (b,g), softball (g), swimming and diving (b,g), tennis (b,g), track and field (b,g), volleyball (b,g), winter (indoor) track (b,g); coed interscholastic: golf, sailing, strength & conditioning; coed intramural: climbing, crew, Frisbee, physical training, rowing, sailing, strength & conditioning, ultimate Frisbee, weight lifting, weight training. 1 PE instructor, 13 coaches, 1 athletic trainer.

Computers Computers are regularly used in all classes. Computer network features include on-campus library services, online commercial services, Internet access, wireless campus network, Internet filtering or blocking technology. Campus intranet, student e-mail accounts, and computer access in designated common areas are available to students. Students grades are available online. The school has a published electronic and media policy.

Contact Mrs. Christine Payette, Admissions Director. 508-996-5602 Ext. 424. Fax: 508-994-6756. E-mail: admits@bishopstang.com. Website: www.bishopstang.com

BLAIR ACADEMY

2 Park Street
Blairstown, New Jersey 07825

Head of School: T. Chandler Hardwick III

General Information Coeducational boarding and day college-preparatory, arts, and technology school, affiliated with Presbyterian Church. Boarding grades 9–PG, day grades 9–12. Founded: 1848. Setting: rural. Nearest major city is New York, NY. Students are housed in single-sex dormitories. 425-acre campus. 42 buildings on campus. Approved or accredited by Middle States Association of Colleges and Schools, The Association of Boarding Schools, and New Jersey Department of Education. Member of National Association of Independent Schools and Secondary School Admission Test Board. Endowment: $67 million. Total enrollment: 450. Upper school average class size: 11. Upper school faculty-student ratio: 1:6. Upper School students typically attend 6 days per week. The average school day consists of 6 hours and 45 minutes.

Upper School Student Profile Grade 9: 88 students (44 boys, 44 girls); Grade 10: 115 students (64 boys, 51 girls); Grade 11: 115 students (66 boys, 49 girls); Grade 12: 124 students (68 boys, 56 girls); Postgraduate: 7 students (5 boys, 2 girls). 80% of students are boarding students. 22 states are represented in upper school student body. 17% are international students. International students from China, Hong Kong, Republic of Korea, Spain, Thailand, and United Kingdom; 17 other countries represented in student body.

Faculty School total: 80. In upper school: 40 men, 27 women; 57 have advanced degrees; 78 reside on campus.

Subjects Offered 3-dimensional art, 3-dimensional design, advanced math, Advanced Placement courses, advanced studio art-AP, African history, algebra, American government, American history, American history-AP, American literature, anatomy, architectural drawing, architecture, art, art history-AP, art-AP, Asian studies, biochemistry, biology, biology-AP, biotechnology, calculus, calculus-AP, ceramics, chemistry, chemistry-AP, Chinese, comparative government and politics-AP, computer programming, computer science, computer science-AP, creative writing, dance, drafting, drama, drawing, drawing and design, driver education, economics, economics and history, economics-AP, English, English language-AP, English literature, English literature-AP, environmental science, environmental science-AP, ethics, European history, European history-AP, filmmaking, fine arts, French, French language-AP, geometry, government/civics, health, history, Japanese history, jazz band, Latin, marine biology, marine science, mathematics, mechanical drawing, music, music theory-AP, painting, philosophy, photography, physics, pre-calculus, psychology, religion, robotics, science, social studies, Spanish, Spanish language-AP, statistics-AP, theater, theology, world history, world history-AP, world literature, writing.

Graduation Requirements Arts and fine arts (art, music, dance, drama), biology, English, foreign language, mathematics, performing arts, religion (includes Bible studies and theology), science, social studies (includes history), U.S. history, athletic requirement.

Special Academic Programs 23 Advanced Placement exams for which test preparation is offered; honors section; independent study; study abroad.

College Admission Counseling 134 students graduated in 2012; 133 went to college, including Boston College; Cornell University; Lehigh University; New York University; Syracuse University; University of Pennsylvania. Other: 1 entered a postgraduate year. Mean SAT critical reading: 610, mean SAT math: 620, mean SAT writing: 630.

Student Life Upper grades have specified standards of dress, student council, honor system. Discipline rests equally with students and faculty.

Tuition and Aid Day student tuition: $35,600; 7-day tuition and room/board: $49,500. Tuition installment plan (Key Tuition Payment Plan, monthly payment plans). Need-based scholarship grants, need-based loans available. In 2012–13, 32% of upper-school students received aid. Total amount of financial aid awarded in 2012–13: $5,100,000.

Admissions Traditional secondary-level entrance grade is 9. For fall 2012, 789 students applied for upper-level admission, 241 were accepted, 145 enrolled. SSAT or TOEFL required. Deadline for receipt of application materials: January 15. Application fee required: $50. On-campus interview required.

Athletics Interscholastic: alpine skiing (boys, girls), baseball (b), basketball (b,g), crew (b,g), cross-country running (b,g), field hockey (g), football (b), golf (b,g), indoor track (b,g), lacrosse (b,g), rowing (b,g), running (b,g), skiing (downhill) (b,g), soccer (b,g), softball (g), squash (b,g), swimming and diving (b,g), tennis (b,g), track and field (b,g), volleyball (g), winter (indoor) track (b,g), wrestling (b); intramural: basketball (b,g), crew (b,g), ice hockey (b,g), rowing (b,g), volleyball (g); coed intramural: alpine skiing, bicycling, canoeing/kayaking, dance, equestrian sports, fitness, flag football, golf, horseback riding, kayaking, life saving, modern dance, mountaineering, outdoor activities, outdoor adventure, outdoor education, outdoor skills, physical fitness, skiing (downhill), snowboarding, squash, swimming and diving, tennis, weight lifting, weight training, wrestling, yoga. 3 athletic trainers.

Computers Computers are regularly used in architecture, drawing and design, English, foreign language, graphic arts, graphic design, history, information technology, mathematics, media production, science, video film production, writing classes. Computer network features include on-campus library services, online commercial services, Internet access, Internet filtering or blocking technology. Campus intranet, student e-mail accounts, and computer access in designated common areas are available to students. The school has a published electronic and media policy.

Contact Nancy Klein, Administrative. 800-462-5247. Fax: 908-362-7975. E-mail: admissions@blair.edu. Website: www.blair.edu

THE BLAKE SCHOOL

110 Blake Road South
Hopkins, Minnesota 55343

Head of School: Dr. Anne E. Stavney

General Information Coeducational day college-preparatory school. Grades PK–12. Founded: 1900. Setting: urban. Nearest major city is Minneapolis. 5-acre campus. 1 building on campus. Approved or accredited by Independent Schools Association of the Central States. Member of National Association of Independent Schools. Endowment: $52 million. Total enrollment: 1,372. Upper school average class size: 16. Upper school faculty-student ratio: 1:8. There are 176 required school days per year for Upper School students. Upper School students typically attend 5 days per week. The average school day consists of 7 hours and 30 minutes.

Upper School Student Profile Grade 9: 130 students (66 boys, 64 girls); Grade 10: 134 students (68 boys, 66 girls); Grade 11: 136 students (71 boys, 65 girls); Grade 12: 129 students (63 boys, 66 girls).

Faculty School total: 136. In upper school: 30 men, 24 women; 36 have advanced degrees.

Subjects Offered Advanced chemistry, African-American literature, algebra, American history, American literature, art, Asian studies, astronomy, band, biology, biology-AP, calculus, calculus-AP, ceramics, chemistry, chemistry-AP, Chinese, choir, chorus, communication arts, communications, computer math, creative writing, debate, design, drama, drawing, economics, English, English literature, English-AP, ethics, European history, European history-AP, fine arts, French, French language-AP, French literature-AP, geology, geometry, German-AP, government/civics, history, instrumental music, jazz ensemble, journalism, Latin, mathematics, multicultural studies, music, painting, performing arts, photography, physical education, physics, physics-AP, policy and value, political science, printmaking, psychology, religion, science, sculpture, senior project, social psychology, social studies, Spanish, Spanish language-AP, speech, statistics, statistics-AP, studio art, studio art-AP, theater, theater arts, trigonometry, visual and performing arts, vocal ensemble, women's studies, world cultures, world history, world literature, writing.

Graduation Requirements Arts and fine arts (art, music, dance, drama), communications, English, foreign language, mathematics, physical education (includes health), science, social studies (includes history), assembly speech.

Special Academic Programs 14 Advanced Placement exams for which test preparation is offered; honors section; term-away projects; study at local college for college credit; study abroad.

College Admission Counseling 133 students graduated in 2012; 128 went to college, including Boston College; Colby College; Dartmouth College; Northwestern University; Wellesley College. Other: 1 entered military service, 4 had other specific plans. Median SAT critical reading: 650, median SAT math: 650, median SAT writing: 650, median combined SAT: 1950, median composite ACT: 29. 68% scored over 600 on SAT critical reading, 64% scored over 600 on SAT math, 69% scored over 600 on SAT writing, 75% scored over 26 on composite ACT.

Student Life Upper grades have specified standards of dress, student council, honor system. Discipline rests primarily with faculty.

Tuition and Aid Day student tuition: $23,525. Tuition installment plan (local bank-arranged plan). Need-based scholarship grants, need-based loans, academic year low-interest loans, tuition remission for children of faculty available. In 2012–13, 20% of upper-school students received aid. Total amount of financial aid awarded in 2012–13: $1,912,893.

Admissions Traditional secondary-level entrance grade is 9. For fall 2012, 90 students applied for upper-level admission, 59 were accepted, 34 enrolled. ERB or WISC/Woodcock-Johnson required. Deadline for receipt of application materials: January 31. Application fee required: $100. On-campus interview required.

Athletics Interscholastic: alpine skiing (boys, girls), baseball (b), basketball (b,g), cross-country running (b,g), diving (b,g), football (b), golf (b,g), ice hockey (b,g), lacrosse (b,g), skiing (cross-country) (b,g), skiing (downhill) (b,g), soccer (b,g), softball (g), swimming and diving (b,g); coed interscholastic: fencing. 1 PE instructor, 45 coaches, 1 athletic trainer.

Computers Computers are regularly used in all classes. Computer network features include on-campus library services, online commercial services, Internet access, wireless campus network, Internet filtering or blocking technology, laptops. Campus intranet, student e-mail accounts, and computer access in designated common areas are available to students. Students grades are available online. The school has a published electronic and media policy.

Contact Bryan Fleming, Director of Admissions. 952-988-3420. Fax: 952-988-3455. E-mail: bfleming@blakeschool.org. Website: www.blakeschool.org

BLANCHET SCHOOL

4373 Market Street NE
Salem, Oregon 97305

Head of School: Mr. Anthony Guevara

General Information Coeducational day college-preparatory, arts, and religious studies school, affiliated with Roman Catholic Church. Grades 6–12. Founded: 1995. Setting: suburban. 22-acre campus. 2 buildings on campus. Approved or accredited by National Catholic Education Association, Northwest Association of Schools and Colleges, and Oregon Department of Education. Endowment: $265,400. Total enrollment: 357. Upper school average class size: 18. Upper school faculty-student ratio: 1:17. There are 175 required school days per year for Upper School students. Upper School students typically attend 5 days per week. The average school day consists of 7 hours.

Upper School Student Profile 70% of students are Roman Catholic.

Faculty School total: 22. In upper school: 7 men, 15 women; 12 have advanced degrees.

Subjects Offered Advanced Placement courses, algebra, American government, American history-AP, American literature, anatomy, anatomy and physiology, art, art education, band, Bible studies, biology, calculus, campus ministry, career and personal planning, Catholic belief and practice, chemistry, chemistry-AP, choir, civics, college counseling, college placement, comparative religion, composition, critical thinking, critical writing, debate, digital photography, drama, economics, economics and history, English literature, English literature and composition-AP, first aid, fitness, French, geometry, global studies, government, great books, health, health and safety, health and wellness, health education, history of the Catholic Church, history-AP, lab science, leadership, literature and composition-AP, mathematics, media production, music,

personal finance, physical education, physical fitness, physical science, physics, pre-algebra, pre-calculus, psychology, publications, religion, religion and culture, SAT/ACT preparation, sociology, Spanish, speech and debate, U.S. government, U.S. history, U.S. history-AP, weight training, world history, world religions, World War II.

Graduation Requirements Applied arts, arts and fine arts (art, music, dance, drama), electives, English, foreign language, mathematics, physical education (includes health), religion (includes Bible studies and theology), science, social studies (includes history), 20 hours of community service for each year in attendance.

Special Academic Programs 2 Advanced Placement exams for which test preparation is offered; honors section; study at local college for college credit; special instructional classes for deaf students; ESL (6 students enrolled).

College Admission Counseling 65 students graduated in 2013; 62 went to college, including Chemeketa Community College; Gonzaga University; Oregon State University; University of Oregon; University of Portland; Willamette University. Other: 1 went to work, 2 entered military service. Mean SAT critical reading: 553, mean SAT math: 535, mean SAT writing: 534, mean composite ACT: 25.

Student Life Upper grades have specified standards of dress, student council. Discipline rests primarily with faculty. Attendance at religious services is required.

Summer Programs Remediation, enrichment, sports programs offered; session focuses on preparation for the next academic year, athletic training; held on campus; accepts boys and girls; open to students from other schools. 75 students usually enrolled. 2014 schedule: June 13 to August 31.

Tuition and Aid Day student tuition: $7675. Tuition installment plan (FACTS Tuition Payment Plan). Tuition reduction for siblings, merit scholarship grants, need-based scholarship grants available. In 2013–14, 35% of upper-school students received aid; total upper-school merit-scholarship money awarded: $8500. Total amount of financial aid awarded in 2013–14: $250,000.

Admissions Traditional secondary-level entrance grade is 9. For fall 2013, 100 students applied for upper-level admission, 97 were accepted, 95 enrolled. Math Placement Exam required. Deadline for receipt of application materials: none. Application fee required: $100. Interview recommended.

Athletics Interscholastic: baseball (boys), basketball (b,g), cheering (g), cross-country running (b,g), fencing (b,g), football (b), golf (b,g), physical fitness (b,g), soccer (b,g), softball (g), swimming and diving (b,g), tennis (b,g), track and field (b,g), volleyball (g), weight training (b,g); intramural: weight training (b,g). 4 PE instructors, 60 coaches.

Computers Computers are regularly used in business, media production, photography, science, social studies classes. Computer network features include online commercial services, Internet access, wireless campus network, Internet filtering or blocking technology. Computer access in designated common areas is available to students. Students grades are available online. The school has a published electronic and media policy.

Contact Mrs. Cathy McClaughry, Admissions Office. 503-485-4491. Fax: 503-399-1259. E-mail: cathy@blanchetcatholicschool.com. Website: www.blanchetcatholicschool.com

BLESSED TRINITY HIGH SCHOOL

11320 Woodstock Road
Roswell, Georgia 30075

Head of School: Mr. Frank Moore

General Information Coeducational day college-preparatory and religious studies school, affiliated with Roman Catholic Church. Grades 9–12. Founded: 2000. Setting: suburban. Nearest major city is Atlanta. 68-acre campus. 2 buildings on campus. Approved or accredited by Georgia Independent School Association, Southern Association of Colleges and Schools, Southern Association of Independent Schools, and Georgia Department of Education. Member of National Association of Independent Schools and Secondary School Admission Test Board. Upper school average class size: 20. Upper school faculty-student ratio: 1:14. Upper School students typically attend 5 days per week. The average school day consists of 6 hours.

Upper School Student Profile 87% of students are Roman Catholic.

Faculty School total: 80. In upper school: 40 men, 40 women; 45 have advanced degrees.

Graduation Requirements American government, American history, American literature, ancient world history, theology.

Special Academic Programs 23 Advanced Placement exams for which test preparation is offered.

College Admission Counseling 227 students graduated in 2013; all went to college, including Auburn University; Georgia College & State University; Georgia Institute of Technology; Georgia Southern University; The University of Alabama; University of Georgia.

Student Life Upper grades have uniform requirement, student council. Discipline rests primarily with faculty. Attendance at religious services is required.

Tuition and Aid Day student tuition: $11,100. Tuition installment plan (FACTS Tuition Payment Plan). Need-based scholarship grants available. In 2013–14, 18% of upper-school students received aid.

Admissions Traditional secondary-level entrance grade is 9. SSAT required. Deadline for receipt of application materials: February 1. Application fee required: $100.

Athletics Interscholastic: baseball (boys), basketball (b,g), cheering (g), cross-country running (b,g), dance (b,g), dance team (g), football (b), golf (b,g), lacrosse (b,g), soccer (b,g), softball (g), strength & conditioning (b,g), swimming and diving (b,g), tennis (b,g), track and field (b,g), volleyball (g), wrestling (b). 5 PE instructors, 2 athletic trainers.

Contact Mr. Brian Marks, Director of Admissions. 678-277-0983 Ext. 502. Fax: 678-277-9756. E-mail: bmarks@btcatholic.org. Website: www.btcatholic.org

BLUEPRINT EDUCATION

5651 West Talavi Boulevard
Suite 170
Glendale, Arizona 85306
Head of School: Mr. Doug Covey

General Information Distance learning only college-preparatory, general academic, technology, and distance learning school. Distance learning grades 7–12. Founded: 1969. Approved or accredited by CITA (Commission on International and Trans-Regional Accreditation), North Central Association of Colleges and Schools, and Arizona Department of Education.

Faculty School total: 4. In upper school: 1 man, 3 women; all have advanced degrees.

Subjects Offered Algebra, American government, American history, art, art history, auto mechanics, biology, British literature, calculus, career experience, career exploration, career planning, careers, chemistry, child development, computer applications, computer education, earth science, economics, English, English composition, entrepreneurship, foreign language, geometry, government, health and wellness, health education, independent study, interpersonal skills, mathematics, parenting, personal development, physical education, physical fitness, physics, pre-algebra, psychology, reading, remedial/makeup course work, service learning/internship, sociology, Spanish, speech, speech communications, statistics, travel, trigonometry, U.S. government, wellness, wilderness education, work experience, world geography, world history.

Graduation Requirements Arts and fine arts (art, music, dance, drama), computers, economics, English, foreign language, geography, health, mathematics, science, social studies (includes history), speech.

Special Academic Programs Honors section; accelerated programs; independent study; academic accommodation for the musically talented and the artistically talented; remedial reading and/or remedial writing; remedial math.

College Admission Counseling Colleges students went to include Arizona State University; Northern Arizona University; Pima Community College; The University of Arizona.

Student Life Upper grades have honor system.

Summer Programs Remediation, advancement programs offered; session focuses on remediation and advancement; held off campus; held at various locations for independent study; accepts boys and girls; open to students from other schools.

Tuition and Aid Need-based scholarship grants available.

Admissions Deadline for receipt of application materials: none. Application fee required: $39.

Computers Computers are regularly used in all academic classes. Computer resources include Internet access. Students grades are available online. The school has a published electronic and media policy.

Contact Mrs. Jeanne Lind, Coordinator. 800-426-4952 Ext. 4832. Fax: 602-943-9700. E-mail: jeannel@blueprinteducation.org. Website: www.blueprinteducation.org

THE BOLLES SCHOOL

7400 San Jose Boulevard
Jacksonville, Florida 32217-3499
Head of School: Bradley R Johnson

General Information Coeducational boarding and day college-preparatory and arts school. Boarding grades 7–PG, day grades PK–PG. Founded: 1933. Setting: suburban. Students are housed in single-sex dormitories. 52-acre campus. 12 buildings on campus. Approved or accredited by Southern Association of Colleges and Schools, Southern Association of Independent Schools, The Association of Boarding Schools, and Florida Department of Education. Member of National Association of Independent Schools and Secondary School Admission Test Board. Endowment: $10.7 million. Total enrollment: 1,670. Upper school average class size: 17. Upper school faculty-student ratio: 1:11. There are 175 required school days per year for Upper School students. Upper School students typically attend 5 days per week. The average school day consists of 6 hours.

Upper School Student Profile 10% of students are boarding students. 92% are state residents. 11 states are represented in upper school student body. 8% are international students. International students from Brazil, China, Colombia, Democratic People's Republic of Korea, Germany, and Mexico; 23 other countries represented in student body.

Faculty School total: 145. In upper school: 40 men, 51 women; 76 have advanced degrees; 9 reside on campus.

Subjects Offered Acting, algebra, American Civil War, American government, American history, American literature, anatomy, art, art history, art history-AP, art-AP, band, biology, biology-AP, British literature, calculus, calculus-AP, ceramics, chemistry, chemistry-AP, Chinese, chorus, comparative government and politics-AP, composition, computer applications, computer science, computer science-AP, contemporary history, creative writing, dance, data analysis, design, directing, drama, drawing, driver education, earth science, ecology, economics, English, English literature-AP, environmental science, ESL, European history, fine arts, French, French-AP, geography, geometry, government/civics, health, history, history-AP, humanities, Japanese, journalism, Latin, Latin-AP, life management skills, life skills, literature, marine science, mathematics, Middle Eastern history, modern European history-AP, multimedia, music, mythology, neurobiology, painting, performing arts, photography, physical education, physics, physics-AP, portfolio art, pre-algebra, pre-calculus, programming, psychology, public speaking, publications, science, sculpture, social sciences, social studies, Spanish, Spanish-AP, statistics, statistics-AP, studio art, theater, U.S. government and politics-AP, visual arts, Web site design, weight training, world cultures, world history.

Graduation Requirements Arts and fine arts (art, music, dance, drama), English, foreign language, mathematics, physical education (includes health), science, social studies (includes history).

Special Academic Programs Advanced Placement exam preparation; honors section; independent study; term-away projects; study at local college for college credit; ESL (45 students enrolled).

College Admission Counseling 196 students graduated in 2013; 194 went to college, including Florida State University; The University of Alabama; The University of Alabama at Birmingham; University of Central Florida; University of Florida; University of North Florida. Other: 1 entered a postgraduate year, 1 had other specific plans. 50% scored over 600 on SAT critical reading, 50% scored over 600 on SAT math, 49% scored over 600 on SAT writing, 47% scored over 1800 on combined SAT, 50% scored over 26 on composite ACT.

Student Life Upper grades have specified standards of dress, student council, honor system. Discipline rests equally with students and faculty.

Summer Programs Enrichment, ESL, art/fine arts, computer instruction programs offered; held on campus; accepts boys and girls; open to students from other schools. 150 students usually enrolled. 2014 schedule: June 6 to July 22.

Tuition and Aid Day student tuition: $21,200; 7-day tuition and room/board: $43,300. Tuition installment plan (major increment payment plan, 10-month plan, June payment plan). Need-based scholarship grants, faculty tuition remission available. In 2013–14, 22% of upper-school students received aid.

Admissions Traditional secondary-level entrance grade is 9. For fall 2013, 378 students applied for upper-level admission, 164 were accepted, 94 enrolled. ISEE required. Deadline for receipt of application materials: none. Application fee required: $45. Interview required.

Athletics Interscholastic: baseball (boys), basketball (b,g), cheering (g), crew (b,g), cross-country running (b,g), dance (b,g), diving (b,g), football (b), golf (b,g), lacrosse (b,g), soccer (b,g), softball (g), swimming and diving (b,g), tennis (b,g), track and field (b,g), volleyball (g), weight lifting (b), wrestling (b). 2 PE instructors, 5 coaches, 1 athletic trainer.

Computers Computers are regularly used in all academic classes. Computer network features include on-campus library services, online commercial services, Internet access, wireless campus network, Internet filtering or blocking technology. Computer access in designated common areas is available to students. Students grades are available online. The school has a published electronic and media policy.

Contact Mark I. Frampton, Director of Upper School and Boarding Admission. 904-256-5032. Fax: 904-739-9929. E-mail: framptonm@bolles.org. Website: www.bolles.org

See Display on next page and Close-Up on page 520.

BOSTON TRINITY ACADEMY

17 Hale Street
Boston, Massachusetts 02136
Head of School: Mr. Frank Guerra

General Information Coeducational day college-preparatory school, affiliated with Christian faith. Grades 6–12. Founded: 2002. Setting: urban. 5-acre campus. 1 building on campus. Approved or accredited by Association of Independent Schools in New England, New England Association of Schools and Colleges, and Massachusetts Department of Education. Member of National Association of Independent Schools and Secondary School Admission Test Board. Total enrollment: 213. Upper school average class size: 14. Upper school faculty-student ratio: 1:8. There are 169 required school days per year for Upper School students. Upper School students typically attend 5 days per week. The average school day consists of 6 hours and 30 minutes.

Upper School Student Profile 70% of students are Christian faith.

Faculty School total: 29. In upper school: 13 men, 16 women; 18 have advanced degrees.

Special Academic Programs 9 Advanced Placement exams for which test preparation is offered; ESL (19 students enrolled).

College Admission Counseling 39 students graduated in 2012; 38 went to college. Other: 1 had other specific plans.

Student Life Upper grades have uniform requirement, student council, honor system. Discipline rests primarily with faculty. Attendance at religious services is required.

Tuition and Aid Day student tuition: $15,200. Tuition installment plan (FACTS Tuition Payment Plan). Need-based scholarship grants available. In 2012–13, 61% of upper-school students received aid. Total amount of financial aid awarded in 2012–13: $1,223,000.

Admissions Traditional secondary-level entrance grade is 9. ISEE or SSAT required. Deadline for receipt of application materials: January 31. Application fee required: $50. Interview required.

Athletics Interscholastic: baseball (boys), basketball (b,g), cross-country running (b,g), lacrosse (b,g), soccer (b,g), tennis (b,g), wrestling (b); intramural: physical fitness (b,g), table tennis (b,g).

Computers Computer network features include on-campus library services, Internet access, wireless campus network, Internet filtering or blocking technology. Campus intranet and computer access in designated common areas are available to students. Students grades are available online. The school has a published electronic and media policy.

Contact Mrs. Elaine Carroll, Associate Director of Admission. 617-364-3700 Ext. 219. Fax: 617-364-3800. E-mail: ecarroll@bostontrinity.org. Website: www.bostontrinity.org

BOSTON UNIVERSITY ACADEMY

One University Road
Boston, Massachusetts 02215

Head of School: Mr. James Berkman

General Information Coeducational day college-preparatory and arts school. Grades 9–12. Founded: 1993. Setting: urban. 132-acre campus. 1 building on campus. Approved or accredited by Association of Independent Schools in New England, New England Association of Schools and Colleges, and Massachusetts Department of Education. Member of National Association of Independent Schools and Secondary School Admission Test Board. Total enrollment: 163. Upper school average class size: 11. Upper school faculty-student ratio: 1:8. There are 164 required school days per year for Upper School students. Upper School students typically attend 5 days per week. The average school day consists of 7 hours.

Upper School Student Profile Grade 9: 38 students (20 boys, 18 girls); Grade 10: 45 students (25 boys, 20 girls); Grade 11: 43 students (22 boys, 21 girls); Grade 12: 37 students (21 boys, 16 girls).

Faculty School total: 21. In upper school: 12 men, 9 women; 18 have advanced degrees.

Subjects Offered Advanced math, African American studies, algebra, American history, American literature, Ancient Greek, ancient history, anthropology, Arabic, archaeology, art, art history, astronomy, biochemistry, biology, calculus, chemistry, Chinese, classical studies, college counseling, community service, computer programming, drama, English, English literature, European history, French, geometry, German, Hebrew, history, Italian, Japanese, Latin, music, physical education, physics, robotics, Russian, sculpture, senior project, Spanish, statistics, theater, trigonometry, women's studies, writing.

Graduation Requirements Ancient Greek, arts and fine arts (art, music, dance, drama), chemistry, English, history, Latin, mathematics, physical education (includes health), physics, two-semester senior thesis project, coursework at Boston University. Community service is required.

Special Academic Programs Honors section; accelerated programs; independent study; study at local college for college credit; academic accommodation for the gifted.

College Admission Counseling 38 students graduated in 2013; all went to college, including Boston University; Brown University; Harvard University; Northeastern University; The Johns Hopkins University. Median SAT critical reading: 740, median SAT math: 740, median SAT writing: 750, median combined SAT: 2230. 94.7% scored over 600 on SAT critical reading, 100% scored over 600 on SAT math, 94.7% scored over 600 on SAT writing, 94.7% scored over 1800 on combined SAT.

Student Life Upper grades have student council, honor system. Discipline rests equally with students and faculty.

Tuition and Aid Day student tuition: $34,582. Tuition installment plan (Insured Tuition Payment Plan, monthly payment plans, individually arranged payment plans, Tuition Management Systems). Need-based scholarship grants available. In 2013–14, 38% of upper-school students received aid. Total amount of financial aid awarded in 2013–14: $1,243,223.

Admissions Traditional secondary-level entrance grade is 9. For fall 2013, 144 students applied for upper-level admission, 88 were accepted, 42 enrolled. SSAT required. Deadline for receipt of application materials: January 31. Application fee required: $50. On-campus interview required.

Athletics Interscholastic: basketball (boys, girls), crew (b,g); intramural: volleyball (g); coed interscholastic: cross-country running, fencing, soccer, tennis, ultimate Frisbee; coed intramural: climbing, dance, hiking/backpacking, sailing, softball, volleyball. 10 PE instructors, 7 coaches.

Computers Computers are regularly used in art, English, foreign language, history, mathematics, science classes. Computer network features include on-campus library services, online commercial services, Internet access, Internet filtering or blocking technology, internal electronic bulletin board system. Campus intranet and student e-

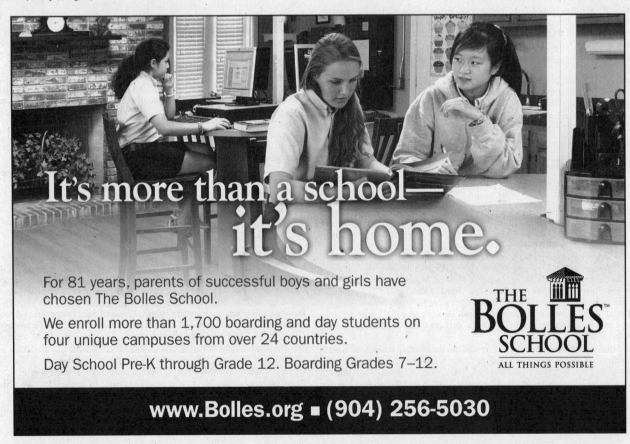

mail accounts are available to students. Students grades are available online. The school has a published electronic and media policy.

Contact Ms. Anna Ziering, Admission Receptionist. 617-358-2493. Fax: 617-353-8999. E-mail: anna_ziering@buacademy.org. Website: www.buacademy.org

BOURGADE CATHOLIC HIGH SCHOOL

4602 North 31st Avenue
Phoenix, Arizona 85017

Head of School: Ms. Kathryn Rother

General Information Coeducational day college-preparatory, arts, religious studies, and English Pre-AP curriculum for 9th and 10th grade students school, affiliated with Roman Catholic Church. Grades 9–12. Founded: 1962. Setting: urban. 27-acre campus. 6 buildings on campus. Approved or accredited by North Central Association of Colleges and Schools, Western Catholic Education Association, and Arizona Department of Education. Total enrollment: 401. Upper school average class size: 32. Upper school faculty-student ratio: 1:20. There are 184 required school days per year for Upper School students. Upper School students typically attend 5 days per week. The average school day consists of 6 hours.

Upper School Student Profile Grade 9: 106 students (55 boys, 51 girls); Grade 10: 103 students (54 boys, 49 girls); Grade 11: 88 students (43 boys, 45 girls); Grade 12: 104 students (49 boys, 55 girls). 94% of students are Roman Catholic.

Faculty School total: 27. In upper school: 12 men, 15 women; 22 have advanced degrees.

Subjects Offered Acting, advanced biology, advanced chemistry, algebra, American government, American history, American history-AP, ancient world history, art, band, bell choir, biology, calculus, calculus-AP, Catholic belief and practice, chemistry, chemistry-AP, choir, Christian and Hebrew scripture, Christian doctrine, Christian ethics, church history, college admission preparation, computer graphics, constitutional history of U.S., creative dance, dance, desktop publishing, digital photography, drama performance, earth science, economics, English, English composition, foreign language, general science, geography, government, graphic design, health education, Hebrew scripture, honors algebra, honors English, honors geometry, honors U.S. history, honors world history, leadership and service, modern dance, New Testament, photography, pre-algebra, psychology, reading, social justice, Spanish, Spanish-AP, speech, study skills, theater arts, U.S. government, U.S. history, U.S. history-AP, world religions, yearbook.

Graduation Requirements Advanced Placement courses, arts and fine arts (art, music, dance, drama), English, foreign language, mathematics, physical education (includes health), religion (includes Bible studies and theology), science.

Special Academic Programs Advanced Placement exam preparation; honors section; study at local college for college credit; ESL (8 students enrolled).

College Admission Counseling 83 students graduated in 2013; all went to college, including Arizona State University; Grand Canyon University; Northern Arizona University; The University of Arizona.

Student Life Upper grades have uniform requirement, student council, honor system. Discipline rests primarily with faculty. Attendance at religious services is required.

Summer Programs Remediation, enrichment programs offered; held on campus; accepts boys and girls; not open to students from other schools. 45 students usually enrolled. 2014 schedule: June to July.

Tuition and Aid Day student tuition: $11,700. Tuition installment plan (FACTS Tuition Payment Plan, monthly payment plans). Merit scholarship grants, need-based scholarship grants, paying campus jobs, Catholic Education Arizona (CEA) available. In 2013–14, 85% of upper-school students received aid. Total amount of financial aid awarded in 2013–14: $1,600,000.

Admissions Traditional secondary-level entrance grade is 9. For fall 2013, 410 students applied for upper-level admission, 410 were accepted, 401 enrolled. ETS high school placement exam or Stanford 9 required. Deadline for receipt of application materials: January 31. Application fee required: $40. On-campus interview required.

Athletics Interscholastic: baseball (boys), basketball (b,g), cheering (g), dance (g), danceline (g), football (b), golf (b), soccer (b), softball (g), strength & conditioning (b,g), swimming and diving (b,g), tennis (b,g), track and field (b,g), volleyball (g), wrestling (b); intramural: weight training (b,g). 2 PE instructors, 2 coaches, 1 athletic trainer.

Computers Computers are regularly used in all academic, art, college planning, design, foreign language, French, graphic arts, media, newspaper, photography, publications, SAT preparation classes. Computer network features include on-campus library services, Internet access, wireless campus network, Internet filtering or blocking technology. Campus intranet and student e-mail accounts are available to students. Students grades are available online. The school has a published electronic and media policy.

Contact Ms. Mary Ann Burns, Admissions Coordinator. 602-973-4000 Ext. 116. Fax: 602-973-5854. E-mail: maburns@bourgadecatholic.org. Website: www.bourgadecatholic.org

BOYLAN CENTRAL CATHOLIC HIGH SCHOOL

4000 Saint Francis Drive
Rockford, Illinois 61103-1699

Head of School: Mr. Jerry Kerrigan

General Information Coeducational day and distance learning college-preparatory, general academic, arts, business, vocational, religious studies, bilingual studies, and technology school, affiliated with Roman Catholic Church. Grades 9–12. Distance learning grades 9–12. Founded: 1960. Setting: urban. Nearest major city is Chicago. 60-acre campus. 3 buildings on campus. Approved or accredited by North Central Association of Colleges and Schools and Illinois Department of Education. Endowment: $3 million. Total enrollment: 1,025. Upper school average class size: 24. Upper school faculty-student ratio: 1:12. There are 176 required school days per year for Upper School students. Upper School students typically attend 5 days per week. The average school day consists of 7 hours.

Upper School Student Profile Grade 9: 249 students (120 boys, 129 girls); Grade 10: 260 students (133 boys, 127 girls); Grade 11: 262 students (126 boys, 136 girls); Grade 12: 254 students (120 boys, 134 girls). 90% of students are Roman Catholic.

Faculty School total: 85. In upper school: 36 men, 49 women; 57 have advanced degrees.

Subjects Offered 20th century history, 3-dimensional art, accounting, ACT preparation, acting, advanced computer applications, Advanced Placement courses, advanced studio art-AP, algebra, American history, American history-AP, American literature-AP, analysis and differential calculus, analytic geometry, anatomy and physiology, architectural drawing, architecture, art, art history, art history-AP, art-AP, athletics, band, biology, biology-AP, botany, British literature, British literature (honors), broadcasting, business, business education, business law, calculus, calculus-AP, career education, career exploration, career planning, Catholic belief and practice, cheerleading, chemistry, chemistry-AP, child development, Chinese, choir, chorus, Christian and Hebrew scripture, Christian doctrine, Christian ethics, church history, college counseling, communications, comparative religion, composition-AP, computer multimedia, computer-aided design, concert band, concert choir, consumer economics, consumer education, consumer mathematics, contemporary history, contemporary issues, contemporary studies, creative writing, critical thinking, culinary arts, debate, drafting, drama, dramatic arts, earth and space science, earth science, economics-AP, English, English language-AP, English literature-AP, English/composition-AP, environmental science, European history, European history-AP, family and consumer science, family living, fashion, fiction, finite math, foods, French, French as a second language, French literature-AP, French-AP, general math, geography, geometry, German, government, government and politics-AP, government-AP, graphics, guitar, health, health education, history of music, illustration, industrial technology, information processing, integrated science, jazz band, keyboarding, library assistant, marketing, music appreciation, music composition, music history, music technology, music theory, music theory-AP, physical science, physics, physics-AP, pre-algebra, pre-calculus, psychology, psychology-AP, religion, senior composition, Spanish, Spanish-AP, statistics, studio art, swimming, technological applications, technology/design, trigonometry, U.S. history, vocal music, Web authoring, Web site design, world geography, world history, world literature, writing, yearbook, zoology.

Graduation Requirements Consumer education, English, mathematics, physical education (includes health), religious studies, science, social studies (includes history), fine and applied arts, community service.

Special Academic Programs 14 Advanced Placement exams for which test preparation is offered; honors section; independent study; academic accommodation for the gifted, the musically talented, and the artistically talented; remedial reading and/or remedial writing; remedial math; programs in general development for dyslexic students; special instructional classes for deaf students, blind students.

College Admission Counseling 251 students graduated in 2013; 231 went to college, including Illinois State University; Loyola University Chicago; Marquette University; Northern Illinois University; The University of Iowa; University of Illinois at Urbana–Champaign. Other: 10 went to work, 2 entered military service. 36% scored over 26 on composite ACT.

Student Life Upper grades have uniform requirement, student council. Discipline rests primarily with faculty. Attendance at religious services is required.

Summer Programs Enrichment, sports, art/fine arts, rigorous outdoor training programs offered; session focuses on enrichment; held on campus; accepts boys and girls; open to students from other schools. 150 students usually enrolled. 2014 schedule: June 9 to July 31.

Tuition and Aid Day student tuition: $5400. Tuition installment plan (monthly payment plans, individually arranged payment plans, full-year or semester payment plan). Tuition reduction for siblings, need-based scholarship grants, paying campus jobs available. In 2013–14, 30% of upper-school students received aid. Total amount of financial aid awarded in 2013–14: $583,264.

Admissions Traditional secondary-level entrance grade is 9. For fall 2013, 270 students applied for upper-level admission, 270 were accepted, 249 enrolled. ETS HSPT (closed) required. Deadline for receipt of application materials: none. Application fee required: $100. Interview required.

Athletics Interscholastic: aerobics/dance (girls), baseball (b), basketball (b,g), bowling (b,g), cheering (g), cross-country running (b,g), dance (g), dance team (g), diving (b,g), fishing (b,g), football (b), golf (b,g), soccer (b,g), softball (g), swimming and diving (b,g), tennis (b,g), track and field (b,g), volleyball (g), wrestling (b); intramural: outdoor education (b,g), physical fitness (b,g), physical training (b,g), running (b,g), strength & conditioning (b,g), volleyball (b), weight training (b,g); coed intramural: Frisbee, ultimate Frisbee. 4 PE instructors, 1 athletic trainer.

Computers Computers are regularly used in all academic, architecture, business applications, computer applications, desktop publishing, drawing and design, keyboarding, music technology, photography, publications, technical drawing, technology, video film production, Web site design, word processing, yearbook classes. Computer network features include on-campus library services, online commercial services, Internet access, wireless campus network, Internet filtering or blocking technology. Campus intranet, student e-mail accounts, and computer access in designated common areas are available to students. Students grades are available online. The school has a published electronic and media policy.

Contact Mr. Chris Rozanski, Assistant Principal. 815-877-0531 Ext. 227. Fax: 815-877-2544. E-mail: crozanski@boylan.org. Website: www.boylan.org

BRADENTON CHRISTIAN SCHOOL

3304 43rd Street West
Bradenton, Florida 34209

Head of School: Mr. Dan van der Kooy

General Information Coeducational day college-preparatory, arts, business, religious studies, and technology school, affiliated with Christian faith. Grades PK–12. Founded: 1960. Setting: suburban. Nearest major city is Tampa. 24-acre campus. 5 buildings on campus. Approved or accredited by Christian Schools International, Christian Schools of Florida, Southern Association of Colleges and Schools, and Florida Department of Education. Member of National Association of Independent Schools. Total enrollment: 542. Upper school average class size: 18. Upper school faculty-student ratio: 1:14. Upper School students typically attend 5 days per week. The average school day consists of 7 hours.

Upper School Student Profile 100% of students are Christian faith.

Faculty School total: 51. In upper school: 13 men, 9 women; 12 have advanced degrees.

Graduation Requirements 3 1/2 credits of Bible.

Special Academic Programs Advanced Placement exam preparation; honors section; study at local college for college credit.

College Admission Counseling 39 went to college, including University of South Florida. Mean SAT critical reading: 565, mean SAT math: 545, mean composite ACT: 25. 43% scored over 600 on SAT critical reading, 25% scored over 600 on SAT math.

Student Life Upper grades have specified standards of dress, student council, honor system. Discipline rests primarily with faculty. Attendance at religious services is required.

Tuition and Aid Day student tuition: $9990. Tuition installment plan (monthly payment plans, individually arranged payment plans). Tuition reduction for siblings, need-based scholarship grants available.

Admissions Traditional secondary-level entrance grade is 9. Academic Profile Tests or Woodcock-Johnson required. Deadline for receipt of application materials: none. Application fee required: $200. On-campus interview required.

Athletics Interscholastic: baseball (boys), basketball (b,g), cheering (b,g), football (b), soccer (b,g), softball (g), swimming and diving (g), tennis (b,g), track and field (b,g), volleyball (g); intramural: dance (g), flag football (b), touch football (b); coed interscholastic: golf, physical fitness; coed intramural: kickball. 2 PE instructors, 25 coaches.

Computers Computers are regularly used in art, Bible studies, business, business applications, business skills, career exploration, Christian doctrine, creative writing, design, desktop publishing, ESL, drawing and design, economics, English, ethics, foreign language classes. Computer network features include on-campus library services, Internet access, wireless campus network, Internet filtering or blocking technology. Student e-mail accounts and computer access in designated common areas are available to students. Students grades are available online. The school has a published electronic and media policy.

Contact Darcy Leahy, Director of Admissions. 941-792-5454 Ext. 104. Fax: 941-795-7190. E-mail: dleahy@bcspanthers.org. Website: www.bcspanthers.org

BRANKSOME HALL

10 Elm Avenue
Toronto, Ontario M4W 1N4, Canada

Head of School: Karen Jurjevich

General Information Girls' boarding and day college-preparatory and arts school. Boarding grades 8–12, day grades JK–12. Founded: 1903. Setting: urban. Students are housed in single-sex dormitories. 13-acre campus. 6 buildings on campus. Approved or accredited by Canadian Association of Independent Schools, Canadian Educational Standards Institute, International Baccalaureate Organization, Ontario Ministry of Education, The Association of Boarding Schools, and Ontario Department of Education. Affiliate member of National Association of Independent Schools; member of Secondary School Admission Test Board. Language of instruction: English. Endowment: CAN$15 million. Total enrollment: 885. Upper school average class size: 18. Upper school faculty-student ratio: 1:9. There are 180 required school days per year for Upper School students. Upper School students typically attend 5 days per week. The average school day consists of 8 hours.

Upper School Student Profile Grade 9: 105 students (105 girls); Grade 10: 104 students (104 girls); Grade 11: 115 students (115 girls); Grade 12: 121 students (121 girls). 13% of students are boarding students. 87% are province residents. 3 provinces are represented in upper school student body. 13% are international students. International students from China, Germany, India, Mexico, Nigeria, and United States; 16 other countries represented in student body.

Faculty School total: 115. In upper school: 13 men, 79 women; 25 have advanced degrees; 3 reside on campus.

Subjects Offered Accounting, acting, advanced math, algebra, all academic, American history, American literature, ancient history, ancient world history, Arabic, art, art and culture, art history, arts, athletics, band, biology, British history, British literature, business, calculus, Canadian geography, Canadian history, Canadian law, Canadian literature, Cantonese, career and personal planning, career exploration, career/college preparation, chemistry, Chinese, Chinese studies, classical civilization, classical Greek literature, computer multimedia, computer programming, computer science, critical thinking, critical writing, drama, drawing, economics, economics and history, English, English literature, environmental science, environmental systems, ethics, European history, European literature, expository writing, film studies, fine arts, food science, French, French studies, geography, geometry, German, government/civics, health, history, home economics, independent study, interdisciplinary studies, Latin, Mandarin, mathematics, music, physical education, physics, science, social sciences, social studies, Spanish, theater, theory of knowledge, trigonometry, typing, vocal ensemble, vocal music, world affairs, world arts, world civilizations, world cultures, world geography, world governments, world history, world issues, world literature, world religions, world studies, writing, writing workshop, yearbook.

Graduation Requirements Arts and fine arts (art, music, dance, drama), business skills (includes word processing), English, International Baccalaureate courses, language, mathematics, physical education (includes health), science, social sciences, social studies (includes history), IB diploma or certificate requirements.

Special Academic Programs International Baccalaureate program; honors section; academic accommodation for the gifted, the musically talented, and the artistically talented; ESL (38 students enrolled).

College Admission Counseling 111 students graduated in 2013; 109 went to college, including Dalhousie University; McGill University; Queen's University at Kingston; The University of Western Ontario; University of Toronto; University of Waterloo. Other: 2 had other specific plans.

Student Life Upper grades have uniform requirement, student council, honor system. Discipline rests primarily with faculty.

Summer Programs Remediation, enrichment programs offered; session focuses on two-week summer academy in courses including math and English; held on campus; accepts boys and girls; open to students from other schools. 2014 schedule: August to September.

Tuition and Aid Day student tuition: CAN$27,620; 7-day tuition and room/board: CAN$51,500. Tuition installment plan (monthly payment plans, tri-annual payment, early payment option ($500 savings)). Bursaries, merit scholarship grants available. In 2013–14, 10% of upper-school students received aid. Total amount of financial aid awarded in 2013–14: CAN$675,000.

Admissions Traditional secondary-level entrance grade is 9. For fall 2013, 350 students applied for upper-level admission, 220 were accepted, 157 enrolled. SSAT required. Deadline for receipt of application materials: December 16. Application fee required: CAN$200. Interview required.

Athletics Interscholastic: alpine skiing, aquatics, badminton, baseball, basketball, crew, cross-country running, field hockey, golf, hockey, ice hockey, indoor track, indoor track & field, rowing, rugby, skiing (downhill), soccer, softball, swimming and diving, synchronized swimming, tennis, track and field, volleyball; intramural: aerobics, aerobics/dance, aquatics, badminton, ball hockey, ballet, baseball, basketball, cheering, climbing, cooperative games, cross-country running, dance, dance squad, field hockey, fitness, gymnastics, outdoor activities, paddle tennis, physical fitness, physical training, rugby, soccer, softball, squash, strength & conditioning, swimming and diving, table tennis, tennis, track and field, volleyball, yoga. 6 PE instructors, 2 coaches, 1 athletic trainer.

Computers Computers are regularly used in art, geography, mathematics, music, science classes. Computer network features include on-campus library services, Internet access, wireless campus network, Internet filtering or blocking technology. Campus intranet, student e-mail accounts, and computer access in designated common areas are available to students. The school has a published electronic and media policy.

Contact Kimberly Carter, Director of Admissions. 416-920-9741 Ext. 136. Fax: 416-920-5390. E-mail: admissions@branksome.on.ca. Website: www.branksome.on.ca

THE BREARLEY SCHOOL

610 East 83rd Street
New York, New York 10028

Head of School: Mrs. Jane Foley. Fried

General Information Girls' day college-preparatory school. Grades K–12. Founded: 1884. Setting: urban. 2 buildings on campus. Approved or accredited by New York State Association of Independent Schools. Member of National Association of Independent Schools. Endowment: $107 million. Total enrollment: 688. Upper school average class size: 12. Upper school faculty-student ratio: 1:6. There are 169 required school days per year for Upper School students. Upper School students typically attend 5 days per week. The average school day consists of 7 hours.

Upper School Student Profile Grade 9: 56 students (56 girls); Grade 10: 54 students (54 girls); Grade 11: 57 students (57 girls); Grade 12: 47 students (47 girls).

Faculty School total: 134. In upper school: 21 men, 53 women; 56 have advanced degrees.

Subjects Offered 20th century world history, advanced biology, advanced chemistry, African history, algebra, American history, American literature, applied music, art, art history, biology, calculus, calculus-AP, chamber groups, chemistry, computer science, critical writing, drama, drama performance, drawing, English, English literature, environmental science, equality and freedom, expository writing, fiction, finite math, French, French studies, geometry, history, history of China and Japan, Homeric Greek, independent study, Latin, Mandarin, mathematics, modern European history, multimedia design, music, music history, oil painting, painting, physical education, physics, political thought, pre-calculus, senior project, Shakespeare, Spanish, Spanish literature, statistics, trigonometry, vocal music, water color painting, Web site design, world history.

Graduation Requirements Arts and fine arts (art, music, dance, drama), English, foreign language, history, mathematics, physical education (includes health), science.

Special Academic Programs 12 Advanced Placement exams for which test preparation is offered; independent study; term-away projects; study abroad.

College Admission Counseling 46 students graduated in 2012; all went to college, including Columbia University; Dartmouth College; Harvard University; Princeton University; University of Pennsylvania. Median SAT critical reading: 730, median SAT math: 690. 99% scored over 600 on SAT critical reading, 92% scored over 600 on SAT math.

Student Life Upper grades have specified standards of dress, student council. Discipline rests equally with students and faculty.

Tuition and Aid Day student tuition: $36,800. Tuition installment plan (Key Tuition Payment Plan, individually arranged payment plans). Need-based scholarship grants, need-based loans available. In 2012–13, 22% of upper-school students received aid. Total amount of financial aid awarded in 2012–13: $4,245,080.

Admissions Traditional secondary-level entrance grade is 9. For fall 2012, 121 students applied for upper-level admission, 21 were accepted, 13 enrolled. ISEE and school's own exam required. Deadline for receipt of application materials: December 1. Application fee required: $60. On-campus interview required.

Athletics Interscholastic: aquatics, badminton, basketball, cross-country running, field hockey, gymnastics, lacrosse, soccer, softball, squash, swimming and diving, tennis, track and field, volleyball; intramural: aquatics, badminton, basketball, cooperative games, dance, dance team, field hockey, fitness, gymnastics, jogging, lacrosse, modern dance, outdoor adventure, physical fitness, soccer, softball, strength & conditioning, swimming and diving, tai chi, team handball, track and field, volleyball, yoga. 12 PE instructors, 3 coaches, 2 athletic trainers.

Computers Computers are regularly used in classics, computer applications, foreign language, history, mathematics, multimedia, music, photography, science, theater arts, Web site design classes. Computer network features include on-campus library services, Internet access, wireless campus network, Internet filtering or blocking technology, Britannica Online, EBSCO, SIRS Researcher, ProQuest, JSTOR, ArtStor, AtomicLearning.com (software tutorials), a file server. Student e-mail accounts and computer access in designated common areas are available to students. The school has a published electronic and media policy.

Contact Ms. Joan Kaplan, Director of Middle and Upper School Admission. 212-744-8582. Fax: 212-472-8020. E-mail: admission@brearley.org. Website: www.brearley.org

BRECK SCHOOL

123 Ottawa Avenue North
Minneapolis, Minnesota 55422

Head of School: Edward Kim

General Information Coeducational day college-preparatory, arts, and religious studies school, affiliated with Episcopal Church. Grades PK–12. Founded: 1886. Setting: suburban. 53-acre campus. 1 building on campus. Approved or accredited by Independent Schools Association of the Central States. Member of National Association of Independent Schools and Secondary School Admission Test Board. Endowment: $49 million. Total enrollment: 1,127. Upper school average class size: 16. Upper school faculty-student ratio: 1:11.

Upper School Student Profile 10% of students are members of Episcopal Church.

Faculty School total: 145. In upper school: 12 men, 17 women; 22 have advanced degrees.

Subjects Offered Algebra, American history, American literature, art, astronomy, biology, calculus, ceramics, chemistry, Chinese, chorus, community service, computer math, computer programming, creative writing, dance, drama, ecology, economics, English, English literature, environmental science, ethics, European history, expository writing, fine arts, French, geometry, health, history, mathematics, music, orchestra, physical education, physics, religion, science, social studies, Spanish, statistics, theater, theology, trigonometry, world history, world literature, writing.

Graduation Requirements Arts and fine arts (art, music, dance, drama), English, foreign language, mathematics, physical education (includes health), religion (includes Bible studies and theology), science, social studies (includes history), senior speech, May Program. Community service is required.

Special Academic Programs Advanced Placement exam preparation; honors section; independent study; term-away projects; academic accommodation for the gifted, the musically talented, and the artistically talented.

College Admission Counseling 94 students graduated in 2012; all went to college, including Boston College; Colby College; Miami University; Middlebury College; University of Denver; University of Minnesota, Twin Cities Campus. Mean SAT critical reading: 634, mean SAT math: 626, mean SAT writing: 644, mean combined SAT: 1904, mean composite ACT: 27.

Student Life Upper grades have specified standards of dress, student council, honor system. Discipline rests equally with students and faculty. Attendance at religious services is required.

Tuition and Aid Day student tuition: $24,995. Tuition installment plan (Key Tuition Payment Plan). Need-based scholarship grants available. In 2012–13, 23% of upper-school students received aid.

Admissions Traditional secondary-level entrance grade is 9. CTP III required. Deadline for receipt of application materials: February 1. Application fee required: $75. On-campus interview required.

Athletics Interscholastic: alpine skiing (boys, girls), baseball (b), basketball (b,g), cross-country running (b,g), diving (b,g), football (b), golf (b,g), gymnastics (g), ice hockey (b,g), lacrosse (b,g), nordic skiing (b,g), skiing (cross-country) (b,g), skiing (downhill) (b,g), soccer (b,g), softball (g), swimming and diving (b,g), tennis (b,g), track and field (b,g), volleyball (g). 6 PE instructors, 82 coaches, 1 athletic trainer.

Computers Computers are regularly used in all classes. Computer network features include on-campus library services, online commercial services, Internet access, wireless campus network, Internet filtering or blocking technology, multimedia imaging, video presentation, student laptop program. Campus intranet and student e-mail accounts are available to students. The school has a published electronic and media policy.

Contact Scott D. Wade, Director of Admissions. 763-381-8200. Fax: 763-381-8288. E-mail: scott.wade@breckschool.org. Website: www.breckschool.org

BREHM PREPARATORY SCHOOL

Carbondale, Illinois
See Special Needs Schools section.

BRENTWOOD COLLEGE SCHOOL

2735 Mount Baker Road
Mill Bay, British Columbia V0R 2P1, Canada

Head of School: Mr. Bud Patel

General Information Coeducational boarding and day college-preparatory, arts, and athletics, leadership, and citizenship school. Grades 9–12. Founded: 1923. Setting: rural. Nearest major city is Victoria, Canada. Students are housed in single-sex dormitories. 49-acre campus. 16 buildings on campus. Approved or accredited by British Columbia Independent Schools Association, Canadian Association of Independent Schools, The Association of Boarding Schools, Western Boarding Schools Association, and British Columbia Department of Education. Affiliate member of National Association of Independent Schools. Language of instruction: English. Total enrollment: 435. Upper school average class size: 16. Upper school faculty-student ratio: 1:9.

Upper School Student Profile Grade 9: 83 students (53 boys, 30 girls); Grade 10: 115 students (61 boys, 54 girls); Grade 11: 124 students (62 boys, 62 girls); Grade 12: 113 students (62 boys, 51 girls). 81% of students are boarding students. 58% are province residents. 20 provinces are represented in upper school student body. 27% are international students. International students from Germany, Hong Kong, Mexico, Republic of Korea, Saudi Arabia, and United States; 12 other countries represented in student body.

Faculty School total: 50. In upper school: 24 men, 17 women; 13 have advanced degrees; 30 reside on campus.

Subjects Offered Advanced Placement courses, algebra, art history-AP, athletics, audio visual/media, band, basketball, biology, biology-AP, business, calculus, calculus-AP, Canadian geography, Canadian history, Canadian law, career and personal planning, ceramics, chemistry, chemistry-AP, choir, choreography, computer graphics, computer science, dance, dance performance, debate, design, drafting, drama, dramatic arts, drawing, economics, economics-AP, English, English literature, English literature-AP, French, French language-AP, geography, geometry, golf, government and politics-AP, health and wellness, history, human geography - AP, information technology, instrumental music, international studies, jazz band, jazz ensemble, marketing, mathematics, musical productions, musical theater, orchestra, outdoor education, painting, photography, physics, physics-AP, pottery, psychology, psychology-AP, public speaking, science, sculpture, sex education, social studies, Spanish, Spanish-AP, stagecraft, technical theater, tennis, theater design and production, video film production, visual and performing arts, vocal jazz, volleyball, yearbook.

Graduation Requirements Arts and fine arts (art, music, dance, drama), career and personal planning, English, foreign language, mathematics, physical education (includes health), science, social studies (includes history).

Special Academic Programs Advanced Placement exam preparation.

College Admission Counseling 112 students graduated in 2012; all went to college, including Duke University; McGill University; Queen's University at Kingston; The University of British Columbia; University of California, Berkeley; University of California, Los Angeles.

Student Life Upper grades have uniform requirement, student council, honor system. Discipline rests primarily with faculty.

Tuition and Aid Day student tuition: CAN$18,300; 7-day tuition and room/board: CAN$39,900–CAN$51,500. Tuition installment plan (The Tuition Plan). Tuition reduction for siblings available.

Admissions Traditional secondary-level entrance grade is 9. Henmon-Nelson or SSAT required. Deadline for receipt of application materials: none. Application fee required: CAN$2500. Interview required.

Athletics Interscholastic: basketball (boys, girls), crew (b,g), cross-country running (b,g), field hockey (g), hockey (g), rowing (b,g), rugby (b,g), running (b,g), soccer (b,g), squash (b,g), tennis (b,g), volleyball (g); intramural: crew (b,g), cross-country running (b,g), field hockey (g), indoor hockey (g), soccer (b,g), squash (b,g), tennis (b,g), track and field (b,g), volleyball (g), weight training (g); coed interscholastic: badminton, ballet, canoeing/kayaking, fitness, golf, ice hockey, judo, kayaking, modern dance, ocean paddling, outdoor activities, rock climbing, sailing; coed intramural: aerobics, aerobics/dance, badminton, canoeing/kayaking, cooperative games, dance, fitness, floor hockey, hiking/backpacking, indoor soccer, kayaking, outdoor activities, physical fitness, physical training, rowing, rugby, running, skiing (downhill), snowboarding, strength & conditioning, table tennis, touch football, weight lifting, weight training. 6 PE instructors, 36 coaches.

Computers Computers are regularly used in photojournalism, video film production classes. Computer network features include on-campus library services, Internet access, wireless campus network, Internet filtering or blocking technology. Campus intranet and student e-mail accounts are available to students. The school has a published electronic and media policy.

Contact Mr. Clayton Johnston, Director of Admissions. 250-743-5521. Fax: 250-743-2911. E-mail: admissions@brentwood.bc.ca. Website: www.brentwood.bc.ca

BRENTWOOD SCHOOL

100 South Barrington Place
Los Angeles, California 90049

Head of School: Dr. Michael Riera

General Information Coeducational day college-preparatory school. Grades K–12. Founded: 1972. Setting: suburban. 30-acre campus. 12 buildings on campus. Approved or accredited by California Association of Independent Schools and Western Association of Schools and Colleges. Member of National Association of Independent Schools and Secondary School Admission Test Board. Endowment: $7 million. Total enrollment: 996. Upper school average class size: 17. Upper school faculty-student ratio: 1:7. Upper School students typically attend 5 days per week. The average school day consists of 8 hours.

Upper School Student Profile Grade 9: 121 students (61 boys, 60 girls); Grade 10: 116 students (63 boys, 53 girls); Grade 11: 108 students (55 boys, 53 girls); Grade 12: 122 students (64 boys, 58 girls).

Faculty School total: 130. In upper school: 45 men, 49 women; 70 have advanced degrees.

Subjects Offered Acting, Advanced Placement courses, advanced studio art-AP, algebra, American history, American literature, Ancient Greek, anthropology, art, art history, art history-AP, art-AP, astronomy, biology, biology-AP, calculus, calculus-AP, ceramics, chemistry, chemistry-AP, Chinese, choir, choral music, chorus, community service, comparative government and politics-AP, computer programming, computer programming-AP, computer science, computer science-AP, concert choir, creative writing, dance, digital photography, directing, drama, drawing, ecology, economics, economics-AP, English, English literature, environmental science-AP, European history, filmmaking, fine arts, French, French-AP, geometry, global studies, government and politics-AP, government-AP, history, honors algebra, honors English, honors geometry, human development, human geography - AP, Japanese, jazz band, jazz dance, journalism, language-AP, Latin, Latin-AP, literature-AP, math analysis, mathematics, music, music theater, music theory-AP, orchestra, organic chemistry, philosophy, photography, physical education, physics, physics-AP, probability and

statistics, robotics, science, senior seminar, senior thesis, social sciences, social studies, Spanish, Spanish-AP, speech, speech and debate, stagecraft, stained glass, statistics-AP, studio art-AP, theater, U.S. government and politics-AP, U.S. history-AP, video, word processing, world history, world literature.

Graduation Requirements Arts and fine arts (art, music, dance, drama), English, foreign language, mathematics, physical education (includes health), science, senior seminar, social sciences, social studies (includes history). Community service is required.

Special Academic Programs 26 Advanced Placement exams for which test preparation is offered; honors section; independent study; study at local college for college credit; academic accommodation for the gifted and the artistically talented.

College Admission Counseling 108 students graduated in 2013; all went to college, including Georgetown University; University of Pennsylvania; University of Southern California. Mean SAT critical reading: 660, mean SAT math: 670, mean SAT writing: 680, mean combined SAT: 2010.

Student Life Upper grades have specified standards of dress, student council, honor system. Discipline rests primarily with faculty.

Summer Programs Remediation, enrichment, advancement, sports, art/fine arts, computer instruction programs offered; session focuses on academic enrichment and sports; held on campus; accepts boys and girls; open to students from other schools. 350 students usually enrolled. 2014 schedule: June 25 to July 27. Application deadline: none.

Tuition and Aid Day student tuition: $34,450. Tuition installment plan (Insured Tuition Payment Plan, monthly payment plans, individually arranged payment plans). Need-based scholarship grants available. In 2013–14, 15% of upper-school students received aid. Total amount of financial aid awarded in 2013–14: $3,500,000.

Admissions Traditional secondary-level entrance grade is 9. For fall 2013, 220 students applied for upper-level admission, 19 were accepted, 16 enrolled. ISEE required. Deadline for receipt of application materials: January 13. Application fee required: $125. On-campus interview required.

Athletics Interscholastic: baseball (boys), basketball (b,g), cheering (g), cross-country running (b,g), dance squad (g), dance team (g), football (b), independent competitive sports (b,g), lacrosse (b,g), soccer (b,g), softball (g), swimming and diving (b,g), tennis (b,g), track and field (b,g), volleyball (b,g), water polo (b), wrestling (b); intramural: modern dance (g), ultimate Frisbee (b); coed interscholastic: dance, diving, drill team, equestrian sports, fencing, football, golf, swimming and diving, water polo; coed intramural: bicycling, fitness, Frisbee, jogging, mountain biking, outdoor activities, physical fitness, physical training, running, sailing, surfing, table tennis, ultimate Frisbee, weight lifting, weight training, wilderness, yoga. 6 PE instructors, 40 coaches, 2 athletic trainers.

Computers Computers are regularly used in college planning, computer applications, desktop publishing, digital applications, foreign language, graphic design, introduction to technology, journalism, literary magazine, mathematics, media arts, media production, photojournalism, programming, publications, research skills, science, technical drawing, technology, video film production, Web site design classes. Computer network features include on-campus library services, online commercial services, Internet access, wireless campus network, Internet filtering or blocking technology, Schoology (learning management system). Campus intranet, student e-mail accounts, and computer access in designated common areas are available to students. Students grades are available online. The school has a published electronic and media policy.

Contact Ms. Sarah Wallace, Admissions Assistant. 310-889-2657. Fax: 310-476-4087. E-mail: ecadmissions@bwscampus.com. Website: www.bwscampus.com

BRIARCREST CHRISTIAN HIGH SCHOOL

76 S. Houston Levee Road
Eads, Tennessee 38028

Head of School: Mr. Eric Sullivan

General Information Coeducational day college-preparatory, arts, religious studies, and technology school, affiliated with Christian faith. Grades 9–12. Founded: 1973. Setting: suburban. Nearest major city is Memphis. 100-acre campus. 1 building on campus. Approved or accredited by Association of Christian Schools International, Southern Association of Colleges and Schools, Southern Association of Independent Schools, and Tennessee Association of Independent Schools. Member of National Association of Independent Schools. Total enrollment: 1,640. Upper school average class size: 18. Upper school faculty-student ratio: 1:12. There are 176 required school days per year for Upper School students. Upper School students typically attend 5 days per week. The average school day consists of 7 hours and 30 minutes.

Upper School Student Profile Grade 9: 131 students (75 boys, 56 girls); Grade 10: 131 students (64 boys, 67 girls); Grade 11: 128 students (67 boys, 61 girls); Grade 12: 145 students (63 boys, 82 girls). 91% of students are Christian.

Faculty School total: 44. In upper school: 19 men, 25 women; 26 have advanced degrees.

Subjects Offered Algebra, American history, American literature, anatomy, art, Bible studies, biology, business, calculus, chemistry, computer math, computer programming, computer science, creative writing, drama, driver education, English, English literature, environmental science, European history, expository writing, French, geography, geometry, government/civics, grammar, health, history, Latin, mathematics, music, physical education, physics, physiology, psychology, religion, science, social sciences, social studies, sociology, Spanish, speech, theater, trigonometry, typing, world history, writing.

Graduation Requirements Arts and fine arts (art, music, dance, drama), business skills (includes word processing), English, foreign language, mathematics, physical education (includes health), religion (includes Bible studies and theology), science, social sciences, social studies (includes history).

Special Academic Programs Advanced Placement exam preparation; honors section; study at local college for college credit; academic accommodation for the gifted, the musically talented, and the artistically talented; programs in English, mathematics, general development for dyslexic students.

College Admission Counseling 147 students graduated in 2013; 144 went to college, including Christian Brothers University; Mississippi State University; The University of Tennessee; University of Arkansas; University of Memphis; University of Mississippi. Other: 1 entered military service, 2 had other specific plans. Median composite ACT: 25. 31% scored over 26 on composite ACT.

Student Life Upper grades have uniform requirement, student council, honor system. Discipline rests primarily with faculty. Attendance at religious services is required.

Tuition and Aid Day student tuition: $13,395. Tuition installment plan (Insured Tuition Payment Plan, monthly payment plans, individually arranged payment plans, 2-payment plan). Tuition reduction for siblings, need-based tuition assistance available. In 2013–14, 12% of upper-school students received aid.

Admissions Traditional secondary-level entrance grade is 9. ISEE required. Deadline for receipt of application materials: none. Application fee required: $50. On-campus interview required.

Athletics Interscholastic: baseball (boys), basketball (b,g), cheering (g), cross-country running (b,g), drill team (g), football (b), golf (b,g), lacrosse (b,g), pom squad (g), soccer (b,g), softball (g), strength & conditioning (b), swimming and diving (b,g), tennis (b,g), track and field (b,g), trap and skeet (b,g), volleyball (g), weight lifting (b), wrestling (b); coed interscholastic: bowling, cross-country running, swimming and diving. 2 PE instructors.

Computers Computers are regularly used in accounting, art, English, history, journalism, keyboarding, lab/keyboard, language development, mathematics, newspaper, science, social sciences, social studies, Spanish, speech, yearbook classes. Computer network features include on-campus library services, Internet access, wireless campus network, Internet filtering or blocking technology. Campus intranet, student e-mail accounts, and computer access in designated common areas are available to students. Students grades are available online. The school has a published electronic and media policy.

Contact Mrs. Claire Foster, Admissions Coordinator. 901-765-4605. Fax: 901-765-4614. E-mail: cofoster@briarcrest.com. Website: www.briarcrest.com

BRIARWOOD CHRISTIAN HIGH SCHOOL

6255 Cahaba Valley Road
Birmingham, Alabama 35242

Head of School: Dr. Barrett Mosbacker

General Information Coeducational day college-preparatory, arts, and religious studies school, affiliated with Presbyterian Church in America. Grades K4–12. Founded: 1964. Setting: suburban. 85-acre campus. 5 buildings on campus. Approved or accredited by Association of Christian Schools International, Southern Association of Colleges and Schools, and Alabama Department of Education. Endowment: $500,000. Total enrollment: 1,971. Upper school average class size: 23. Upper school faculty-student ratio: 1:23. There are 177 required school days per year for Upper School students. Upper School students typically attend 5 days per week. The average school day consists of 6 hours and 10 minutes.

Upper School Student Profile Grade 9: 146 students (81 boys, 65 girls); Grade 10: 153 students (75 boys, 78 girls); Grade 11: 150 students (76 boys, 74 girls); Grade 12: 142 students (72 boys, 70 girls). 25% of students are Presbyterian Church in America.

Faculty School total: 125. In upper school: 30 men, 25 women; 35 have advanced degrees.

Subjects Offered Accounting, algebra, American history, American literature, art, band, Bible studies, biology, calculus, chemistry, community service, computer science, creative writing, debate, drama, driver education, economics, English, English literature, ethics, European history, French, geometry, government, grammar, health, history, Latin, Mandarin, mathematics, music, philosophy, photo shop, physical education, physics, psychology, religion, science, social sciences, social studies, Spanish, speech, trigonometry, world history, world literature.

Graduation Requirements 20th century history, business skills (includes word processing), computer science, English, foreign language, mathematics, physical education (includes health), religion (includes Bible studies and theology), science, social sciences, social studies (includes history). Community service is required.

Special Academic Programs Advanced Placement exam preparation; honors section; academic accommodation for the gifted; special instructional classes for students with learning disabilities, Attention Deficit Disorder.

College Admission Counseling 144 students graduated in 2013; 142 went to college, including Auburn University; Mississippi State University; Samford

University; The University of Alabama; Troy University; University of Mississippi. Other: 2 went to work. Mean combined SAT: 1200, mean composite ACT: 26.

Student Life Upper grades have specified standards of dress, student council. Discipline rests primarily with faculty. Attendance at religious services is required.

Summer Programs Remediation, advancement programs offered; session focuses on social studies and mathematics; held on campus; accepts boys and girls; not open to students from other schools. 50 students usually enrolled. 2014 schedule: June 11 to July 28. Application deadline: March 1.

Tuition and Aid Day student tuition: $6970. Tuition installment plan (monthly payment plans). Tuition reduction for siblings available. In 2013–14, 3% of upper-school students received aid. Total amount of financial aid awarded in 2013–14: $5000.

Admissions Traditional secondary-level entrance grade is 9. For fall 2013, 63 students applied for upper-level admission, 28 were accepted, 27 enrolled. SSAT required. Deadline for receipt of application materials: none. Application fee required: $75. On-campus interview required.

Athletics Interscholastic: baseball (boys), basketball (b,g), cheering (g), cross-country running (b,g), dance team (g), football (b), golf (b,g), indoor track (b,g), indoor track & field (b,g), outdoor activities (b,g), physical fitness (b,g), soccer (b,g), softball (g), strength & conditioning (b), swimming and diving (b,g), tennis (b,g), track and field (b,g), volleyball (g). 5 PE instructors, 15 coaches, 1 athletic trainer.

Computers Computers are regularly used in computer applications classes. Computer network features include on-campus library services, online commercial services, Internet access. Students grades are available online.

Contact Mrs. Kelly McCarthy Mooney, Director of Admissions. 205-776-5812. Fax: 205-776-5816. E-mail: kmooney@bcsk12.org. Website: www.bcsk12.org

BRIDGES ACADEMY

Studio City, California
See Special Needs Schools section.

BRIMMER AND MAY SCHOOL

69 Middlesex Road
Chestnut Hill, Massachusetts 02467

Head of School: Mrs. Judy Guild

General Information Coeducational day college-preparatory, arts, technology, Creative Arts Diploma Program, and Global Studies Diploma Program school. Grades PK–12. Founded: 1880. Setting: suburban. Nearest major city is Boston. 7-acre campus. 7 buildings on campus. Approved or accredited by Association of Independent Schools in New England and New England Association of Schools and Colleges. Member of National Association of Independent Schools and Secondary School Admission Test Board. Total enrollment: 400. Upper school average class size: 12. Upper school faculty-student ratio: 1:6. There are 175 required school days per year for Upper School students. Upper School students typically attend 5 days per week. The average school day consists of 7 hours and 20 minutes.

Upper School Student Profile Grade 9: 27 students (15 boys, 12 girls); Grade 10: 34 students (17 boys, 17 girls); Grade 11: 37 students (22 boys, 15 girls); Grade 12: 37 students (16 boys, 21 girls).

Faculty School total: 70. In upper school: 14 men, 21 women; 22 have advanced degrees.

Subjects Offered Acting, adolescent issues, Advanced Placement courses, advanced studio art-AP, algebra, American history, American literature, art, biology, biology-AP, calculus, ceramics, chamber groups, chemistry, chorus, college counseling, community service, computer education, creative arts, creative writing, desktop publishing, drama, economics, economics-AP, English, English literature, English literature-AP, ESL, European history, expository writing, fine arts, French, geometry, grammar, health, health education, history, humanities, Internet research, mathematics, music, music theory, newspaper, participation in sports, performing arts, photography, physical education, physical science, physics, psychology, social studies, Spanish, statistics-AP, theater, trigonometry, typing, U.S. history, video film production, world history, world literature, writing, yearbook.

Graduation Requirements Creative arts, English, foreign language, history, mathematics, physical education (includes health), science, technology, Senior Independent project, senior thesis defense, Creative Art Diploma Program (optional). Community service is required.

Special Academic Programs 15 Advanced Placement exams for which test preparation is offered; honors section; independent study; study at local college for college credit; ESL (18 students enrolled).

College Admission Counseling 32 students graduated in 2013; all went to college, including Boston University; Connecticut College; Hobart and William Smith Colleges; Tufts University; Vassar College.

Student Life Upper grades have specified standards of dress, student council, honor system. Discipline rests equally with students and faculty.

Tuition and Aid Day student tuition: $39,975. Tuition installment plan (monthly payment plans, Tuition Management Systems). Need-based scholarship grants available. In 2013–14, 43% of upper-school students received aid. Total amount of financial aid awarded in 2013–14: $1,118,270.

Admissions Traditional secondary-level entrance grade is 9. For fall 2013, 89 students applied for upper-level admission, 45 were accepted, 22 enrolled. ISEE, SSAT or TOEFL or SLEP required. Deadline for receipt of application materials: January 17. Application fee required: $50. Interview required.

Athletics Interscholastic: baseball (boys), basketball (b,g), field hockey (g), lacrosse (b,g), soccer (b,g), softball (g), tennis (b,g); coed interscholastic: cross-country running, curling, golf; coed intramural: alpine skiing, fitness, outdoor education, physical fitness, rowing, running, skiing (downhill), snowboarding, strength & conditioning, tennis, weight training. 3 PE instructors, 20 coaches, 2 athletic trainers.

Computers Computers are regularly used in architecture, desktop publishing, foreign language, graphic design, humanities, journalism, media production, technology, typing, video film production, Web site design, yearbook classes. Computer network features include on-campus library services, online commercial services, Internet access, wireless campus network, Internet filtering or blocking technology. Campus intranet, student e-mail accounts, and computer access in designated common areas are available to students. Students grades are available online. The school has a published electronic and media policy.

Contact Myra Korin, Admissions Coordinator. 617-738-8695. Fax: 617-734-5147. E-mail: admissions@brimmer.org. Website: www.brimmerandmay.org

THE BRITISH SCHOOL OF BOSTON

416 Pond Street
Boston, Massachusetts 02130

Head of School: Mr. Paul Wiseman, OBE

General Information Coeducational day college-preparatory, International Baccalaureate Diploma Programme, and International Primary Curriculum/International Middle Years school. Grades PK–12. Founded: 2000. Setting: suburban. 40-acre campus. 2 buildings on campus. Approved or accredited by Council of International Schools and Massachusetts Department of Education. Candidate for accreditation by New England Association of Schools and Colleges. Member of National Association of Independent Schools and Secondary School Admission Test Board. Total enrollment: 417. Upper school average class size: 10. Upper school faculty-student ratio: 1:3. There are 180 required school days per year for Upper School students. Upper School students typically attend 5 days per week. The average school day consists of 7 hours.

Faculty School total: 65. In upper school: 4 men, 17 women.

Subjects Offered ACT preparation, International Baccalaureate courses.

Graduation Requirements International Baccalaureate courses.

Special Academic Programs International Baccalaureate program; academic accommodation for the gifted; ESL.

Student Life Upper grades have specified standards of dress, student council, honor system. Discipline rests equally with students and faculty.

Tuition and Aid Day student tuition: $29,800. Tuition reduction for siblings, merit scholarship grants available.

Admissions ISEE or SSAT required. Deadline for receipt of application materials: February 1. Application fee required: $150. Interview required.

Athletics Interscholastic: basketball (boys, girls), cross-country running (b,g), independent competitive sports (b), soccer (b,g), swimming and diving (b,g), tennis (b,g); intramural: basketball (b,g); coed interscholastic: curling, rugby, soccer; coed intramural: alpine skiing, backpacking, combined training, cross-country running, fitness, golf, hiking/backpacking, life saving, outdoor activities, outdoor education, outdoors, sailing, strength & conditioning. 2 PE instructors.

Computers Computers are regularly used in all classes. Computer network features include Internet access, wireless campus network. Computer access in designated common areas is available to students. Students grades are available online. The school has a published electronic and media policy.

Contact Ms. Lisa van Horne, Director of Admissions and Marketing. 617-522-2261 Ext. 141. Fax: 617-522-0385. E-mail: l.vanhorne@wclschools.org. Website: www.britishschoolofboston.org/

BROCKWOOD PARK SCHOOL

Brockwood Park
Bramdean
Hampshire
Alresford SO24 0LQ, United Kingdom

Head of School: Mr. Bill Taylor

General Information Coeducational boarding college-preparatory, general academic, arts, business, vocational, religious studies, bilingual studies, and technology school. Ungraded, ages 14–19. Founded: 1969. Setting: rural. Nearest major city is Winchester, United Kingdom. Students are housed in individual rooms, single-sex compound. 40-acre campus. 8 buildings on campus. Approved or accredited by Office for Standards in Education (OFSTED). Language of instruction: English. Total enrollment: 65. Upper school average class size: 7. Upper school faculty-student ratio: 1:7. Upper School students typically attend 5 days per week. The average school day consists of 8 hours.

Upper School Student Profile 100% of students are boarding students. 75% are international students. International students from France, Germany, Italy, Netherlands, Spain, and United States; 10 other countries represented in student body.

Faculty School total: 30. In upper school: 12 men, 18 women; all reside on campus.

Subjects Offered Advanced biology, advanced chemistry, advanced math, area studies, art, band, biology, body human, bookbinding, business studies, career and personal planning, career education, carpentry, cartooning/animation, chamber groups, chemistry, choir, choral music, cinematography, classical music, communication skills, computers, design, desktop publishing, diversity studies, drama, drama performance, drama workshop, English, English literature, environmental education, ESL, ethics, ethics and responsibility, fabric arts, filmmaking, fine arts, folk dance, food and nutrition, French, gardening, gender issues, geography, graphic design, history, mathematics, music, physics, pottery, psychology, science, social studies, Spanish, statistics.

Graduation Requirements Graduation requirements determined on an individual basis.

Special Academic Programs Independent study; term-away projects; study abroad; academic accommodation for the gifted, the musically talented, and the artistically talented; remedial reading and/or remedial writing; remedial math; programs in English, mathematics, general development for dyslexic students; special instructional classes for deaf students, blind students; ESL (30 students enrolled).

College Admission Counseling 29 students graduated in 2012; 25 went to college, including University of London. Other: 2 went to work, 2 had other specific plans.

Student Life Upper grades have specified standards of dress, student council. Discipline rests equally with students and faculty.

Tuition and Aid 7-day tuition and room/board: £17,960. Tuition installment plan (individually arranged payment plans). Bursaries available. In 2012–13, 10% of upper-school students received aid.

Admissions Traditional secondary-level entrance age is 14. 3-R Achievement Test, any standardized test or ESL required. Deadline for receipt of application materials: none. Application fee required: £20. On-campus interview required.

Athletics 1 coach, 2 athletic trainers.

Computers Computer network features include Internet access, Internet filtering or blocking technology.

Contact Mrs. Victoria Lewin, Admissions Officer. 44-1962 771744. Fax: 44-1962 771875. E-mail: enquiry@brockwood.org.uk. Website: www.brockwood.org.uk

BROOKHAVEN ACADEMY

943 Brookway Boulevard Extension
Brookhaven, Mississippi 39601

Head of School: Mrs. Julie Wright

General Information Coeducational day college-preparatory and general academic school, affiliated with Christian faith. Grades PK–12. Founded: 1970. Setting: small town. Nearest major city is Jackson. 25-acre campus. 5 buildings on campus. Approved or accredited by Southern Association of Colleges and Schools, Southern Association of Independent Schools, and Mississippi Department of Education. Total enrollment: 506. Upper school average class size: 13. Upper school faculty-student ratio: 1:13. There are 175 required school days per year for Upper School students. Upper School students typically attend 5 days per week. The average school day consists of 7 hours and 15 minutes.

Upper School Student Profile Grade 7: 23 students (13 boys, 10 girls); Grade 8: 32 students (17 boys, 15 girls); Grade 9: 41 students (19 boys, 22 girls); Grade 10: 35 students (20 boys, 15 girls); Grade 11: 42 students (23 boys, 19 girls); Grade 12: 36 students (23 boys, 13 girls). 100% of students are Christian faith.

Faculty School total: 20. In upper school: 5 men, 14 women; 9 have advanced degrees.

Subjects Offered Accounting, algebra, American history, anatomy, art, astronomy, Bible studies, biology, business law, calculus, career education, chemistry, choral music, composition, computer applications, creative writing, economics, English, English composition, finance, geography, geology, geometry, government, health, honors English, keyboarding, physical education, physics, physiology, reading, Spanish, speech, speech communications, state history, statistics, world history.

Graduation Requirements Advanced math, business skills (includes word processing), computer science, English, foreign language, mathematics, science, social studies (includes history), 20 hours of community service.

Special Academic Programs Honors section; study at local college for college credit.

College Admission Counseling 35 students graduated in 2013; 34 went to college, including Millsaps College; Mississippi College; Mississippi State University; University of Mississippi; University of Southern Mississippi. Other: 1 went to work. Median composite ACT: 22. 10% scored over 26 on composite ACT.

Student Life Upper grades have specified standards of dress, student council, honor system. Discipline rests primarily with faculty.

Summer Programs Remediation, sports programs offered; session focuses on remediation; held on campus; accepts boys and girls; open to students from other schools. 14 students usually enrolled. 2014 schedule: June 2 to June 30. Application deadline: June 2.

Tuition and Aid Day student tuition: $4344. Tuition installment plan (monthly payment plans, individually arranged payment plans). Tuition reduction for siblings, need-based scholarship grants available. Total amount of financial aid awarded in 2013–14: $13,000.

Admissions Traditional secondary-level entrance grade is 9. For fall 2013, 15 students applied for upper-level admission, 15 were accepted, 15 enrolled. Admissions testing required. Deadline for receipt of application materials: none. Application fee required: $100. On-campus interview required.

Athletics Interscholastic: baseball (boys), basketball (b,g), cheering (g), cross-country running (b,g), dance team (g), football (b), golf (b), soccer (b,g), softball (g), strength & conditioning (b,g), tennis (b,g), track and field (b,g), weight training (b,g). 1 PE instructor, 3 coaches.

Computers Computers are regularly used in all academic, yearbook classes. Computer network features include on-campus library services, Internet access, wireless campus network, Internet filtering or blocking technology. Campus intranet, student e-mail accounts, and computer access in designated common areas are available to students. Students grades are available online. The school has a published electronic and media policy.

Contact Daisy Arnold, Counselor. 601-833-4041. Fax: 601-833-1846. E-mail: bacounselor@cableone.net. Website: www.brookhavenacademy.org

THE BROOK HILL SCHOOL

1051 N. Houston
Bullard, Texas 75757

Head of School: Rod Fletcher

General Information Coeducational boarding and day college-preparatory and arts school, affiliated with Christian faith. Boarding grades 8–12, day grades PK–12. Founded: 1997. Setting: small town. Nearest major city is Dallas. Students are housed in single-sex dormitories. 280-acre campus. 9 buildings on campus. Approved or accredited by Association of Christian Schools International, Southern Association of Colleges and Schools, The Association of Boarding Schools, and The College Board. Member of National Association of Independent Schools. Endowment: $1 million. Total enrollment: 519. Upper school average class size: 10. Upper school faculty-student ratio: 1:9. There are 176 required school days per year for Upper School students. Upper School students typically attend 5 days per week. The average school day consists of 6 hours and 30 minutes.

Upper School Student Profile Grade 9: 48 students (22 boys, 26 girls); Grade 10: 53 students (30 boys, 23 girls); Grade 11: 51 students (28 boys, 23 girls); Grade 12: 39 students (26 boys, 13 girls). 25% of students are boarding students. 65% are state residents. 4 states are represented in upper school student body. 20% are international students. International students from China, Nigeria, Republic of Korea, Saudi Arabia, South Africa, and Viet Nam; 20 other countries represented in student body. 70% of students are Christian faith.

Faculty School total: 50. In upper school: 14 men, 17 women; 19 have advanced degrees; 6 reside on campus.

Subjects Offered Accounting, ACT preparation, advanced biology, advanced chemistry, advanced math, Advanced Placement courses, advanced studio art-AP, advanced TOEFL/grammar, algebra, American government, American history, American history-AP, American literature, American literature-AP, analysis and differential calculus, anatomy and physiology, ancient history, ancient world history, art, art-AP, athletics, baseball, basketball, Bible as literature, Bible studies, biology, British literature, British literature-AP, business, calculus, calculus-AP, career/college preparation, chemistry, chemistry-AP, choir, choral music, Christian ethics, Christian studies, Christianity, church history, civics/free enterprise, classics, college admission preparation, college awareness, college writing, communication skills, communications, community service, comparative religion, composition, composition-AP, computer applications, computer art, computer education, conceptual physics, concert choir, creation science, dance, dance performance, digital art, digital photography, drama, drama performance, dramatic arts, drawing, economics, economics-AP, English, English composition, English language and composition-AP, English language-AP, English literature, English literature and composition-AP, English literature-AP, English/composition-AP, ensembles, environmental science, epic literature, ESL, European history, European history-AP, European literature, finance, fine arts, foreign language, four units of summer reading, French, French as a second language, geometry, government, government and politics-AP, government-AP, great books, health, history-AP, honors algebra, honors English, honors geometry, human biology, lab science, Latin, leadership and service, literary genres, literature and composition-AP, literature-AP, logic, logic, rhetoric, and debate, macro/microeconomics-AP, macroeconomics-AP, mathematics-AP, microeconomics-AP, modern European history-AP, modern languages, orchestra, painting, physical education, physics, physics-AP, pre-calculus, public speaking, religion, rhetoric, SAT preparation, SAT/ACT preparation, senior project, Spanish, Spanish language-AP, Spanish literature-AP, Spanish-AP, speech communications, stagecraft, statistics-AP, strings, student government, student publications, studio art-AP, theater arts, TOEFL preparation, U.S. government and politics, U.S. government and politics-AP, U.S. history, U.S. history-AP, volleyball, yearbook.

Graduation Requirements Arts and fine arts (art, music, dance, drama), Bible, college admission preparation, economics, electives, English, foreign language,

government, history, lab science, leadership, mathematics, physical education (includes health). Community service is required.

Special Academic Programs 12 Advanced Placement exams for which test preparation is offered; honors section; study at local college for college credit; ESL (3 students enrolled).

College Admission Counseling 50 students graduated in 2013; all went to college, including Baylor University; Texas A&M University; Texas Tech University; The University of Texas at Austin; University of Mississippi; Wheaton College. Median SAT critical reading: 630, median SAT math: 632, median SAT writing: 611, median combined SAT: 1873, median composite ACT: 28. 67% scored over 600 on SAT critical reading, 67% scored over 600 on SAT math, 65% scored over 600 on SAT writing, 65% scored over 1800 on combined SAT.

Student Life Upper grades have uniform requirement, student council, honor system. Discipline rests primarily with faculty. Attendance at religious services is required.

Summer Programs Remediation, enrichment, advancement, ESL, sports, art/fine arts programs offered; session focuses on enrichment; held on campus; accepts boys and girls; open to students from other schools. 125 students usually enrolled. 2014 schedule: June 1 to August 10. Application deadline: none.

Tuition and Aid Day student tuition: $9570; 7-day tuition and room/board: $34,285. Tuition installment plan (FACTS Tuition Payment Plan, individually arranged payment plans). Tuition reduction for siblings, need-based scholarship grants available. In 2013–14, 40% of upper-school students received aid. Total amount of financial aid awarded in 2013–14: $850,000.

Admissions Traditional secondary-level entrance grade is 10. For fall 2013, 89 students applied for upper-level admission, 33 were accepted, 30 enrolled. International English Language Test, Iowa Test, CTBS, or TAP, Iowa Tests of Basic Skills, SSAT, Stanford Achievement Test, Otis-Lennon School Ability Test, TOEFL or TOEFL or SLEP required. Deadline for receipt of application materials: none. Application fee required: $75. Interview recommended.

Athletics Interscholastic: baseball (boys, girls), basketball (b,g), cheering (g), cross-country running (b,g), dance (g), dance squad (g), dance team (g), football (b), golf (b,g), independent competitive sports (b,g), physical fitness (b,g), physical training (b,g), soccer (b,g), softball (g), strength & conditioning (b,g), swimming and diving (b,g), tennis (b,g), track and field (b,g), volleyball (b,g), weight training (b,g); intramural: baseball (b,g), basketball (b,g), fishing (b,g), flag football (b,g), Frisbee (b,g), ultimate Frisbee (b,g); coed interscholastic: cheering, dance, dance squad, dance team, tennis; coed intramural: fishing, flag football, Frisbee. 1 PE instructor, 2 coaches, 1 athletic trainer.

Computers Computers are regularly used in all academic classes. Computer network features include on-campus library services, Internet access, wireless campus network, Internet filtering or blocking technology. Computer access in designated common areas is available to students. Students grades are available online. The school has a published electronic and media policy.

Contact Mr. Landry Humphries, Associate Director of Admissions, Boarding. 903-894-5000 Ext. 1042. Fax: 903-894-6332. E-mail: Landry.humphries@brookhill.org. Website: www.brookhill.org/

BROOKS SCHOOL

1160 Great Pond Road
North Andover, Massachusetts 01845-1298

Head of School: Mr. John R. Packard

General Information Coeducational boarding and day college-preparatory school, affiliated with Episcopal Church. Grades 9–12. Founded: 1926. Setting: suburban. Nearest major city is Boston. Students are housed in single-sex dormitories. 251-acre campus. 40 buildings on campus. Approved or accredited by Association of Independent Schools in New England, National Association of Episcopal Schools, New England Association of Schools and Colleges, The Association of Boarding Schools, and Massachusetts Department of Education. Member of National Association of Independent Schools and Secondary School Admission Test Board. Endowment: $67.2 million. Total enrollment: 376. Upper school average class size: 12. Upper school faculty-student ratio: 1:5. There are 180 required school days per year for Upper School students. Upper School students typically attend 5 days per week. The average school day consists of 7 hours.

Upper School Student Profile Grade 9: 78 students (43 boys, 35 girls); Grade 10: 89 students (52 boys, 37 girls); Grade 11: 105 students (62 boys, 43 girls); Grade 12: 104 students (53 boys, 51 girls). 67% of students are boarding students. 62% are state residents. 25 states are represented in upper school student body. 11% are international students. International students from Canada, China, Egypt, Japan, Philippines, and Republic of Korea; 10 other countries represented in student body.

Faculty School total: 87. In upper school: 30 men, 32 women; 47 have advanced degrees; 47 reside on campus.

Subjects Offered Algebra, American history, American history-AP, American literature, art history, art history-AP, astronomy, Bible studies, biology, biology-AP, calculus, calculus-AP, ceramics, chemistry, chemistry-AP, Chinese, chorus, computer math, creative writing, drama, driver education, earth science, English, English literature, English-AP, environmental science-AP, ethics, European history, expository writing, film, fine arts, French, French language-AP, French literature-AP, French-AP, geometry, government and politics-AP, grammar, Greek, health, history, history-AP, honors algebra, honors geometry, honors world history, integrated arts, journalism, Latin, Latin-AP, life skills, Mandarin, mathematics, Middle East, music, music theory, painting, photography, physics, physics-AP, playwriting, poetry, psychology, public speaking, religion, rhetoric, robotics, senior project, senior seminar, Southern literature, Spanish, Spanish language-AP, Spanish literature, Spanish literature-AP, Spanish-AP, statistics, studio art, theater, theater design and production, theology, trigonometry, U.S. government and politics-AP, visual arts, world history, world history-AP, world literature, writing.

Graduation Requirements Arts and fine arts (art, music, dance, drama), English, foreign language, health, history, mathematics, religion (includes Bible studies and theology), science. Community service is required.

Special Academic Programs 14 Advanced Placement exams for which test preparation is offered; honors section; independent study; term-away projects; study abroad.

College Admission Counseling 99 students graduated in 2013; all went to college, including Bates College; Colby College; Cornell University; Trinity College; University of Colorado Boulder; University of Southern California. Mean SAT critical reading: 600, mean SAT math: 631, mean SAT writing: 607, mean combined SAT: 1838.

Student Life Upper grades have specified standards of dress, student council. Discipline rests primarily with faculty. Attendance at religious services is required.

Summer Programs Enrichment, advancement, sports, computer instruction programs offered; session focuses on English, mathematics, and SAT preparation; held on campus; accepts boys and girls; open to students from other schools. 70 students usually enrolled. 2014 schedule: June 28 to August 20. Application deadline: none.

Tuition and Aid Day student tuition: $38,780; 7-day tuition and room/board: $51,240. Tuition installment plan (Academic Management Services Plan, FACTS Tuition Payment Plan, individually arranged payment plans). Need-based scholarship grants available. In 2013–14, 22% of upper-school students received aid. Total amount of financial aid awarded in 2013–14: $3,300,000.

Admissions Traditional secondary-level entrance grade is 9. For fall 2013, 1,016 students applied for upper-level admission, 269 were accepted, 113 enrolled. ISEE, SSAT, ERB, PSAT, SAT, PLAN or ACT or TOEFL required. Deadline for receipt of application materials: January 15. Application fee required: $50. Interview required.

Athletics Interscholastic: baseball (boys), basketball (b,g), crew (b,g), cross-country running (b,g), field hockey (g), football (b), ice hockey (b,g), lacrosse (b,g), soccer (b,g), softball (g), squash (b,g), tennis (b,g), wrestling (b); coed interscholastic: golf; coed intramural: dance, fitness, sailing, skiing (downhill), yoga. 2 athletic trainers.

Computers Computers are regularly used in all academic classes. Computer network features include on-campus library services, online commercial services, Internet access, wireless campus network, Internet filtering or blocking technology. Campus intranet, student e-mail accounts, and computer access in designated common areas are available to students. Students grades are available online. The school has a published electronic and media policy.

Contact Mrs. Bini Egertson, Interim Director of Admission. 978-725-6272. Fax: 978-725-6298. E-mail: admission@brooksschool.org. Website: www.brooksschool.org

BROOKSTONE SCHOOL

440 Bradley Park Drive
Columbus, Georgia 31904

Head of School: Brian D. Kennerly

General Information Coeducational day college-preparatory school. Grades PK–12. Founded: 1951. Setting: suburban. Nearest major city is Atlanta. 112-acre campus. 11 buildings on campus. Approved or accredited by Georgia Independent School Association, Southern Association of Colleges and Schools, Southern Association of Independent Schools, and Georgia Department of Education. Member of National Association of Independent Schools. Endowment: $20.4 million. Total enrollment: 799. Upper school average class size: 14. Upper school faculty-student ratio: 1:10. There are 176 required school days per year for Upper School students. Upper School students typically attend 5 days per week. The average school day consists of 5 hours and 20 minutes.

Upper School Student Profile Grade 9: 82 students (42 boys, 40 girls); Grade 10: 84 students (43 boys, 41 girls); Grade 11: 74 students (40 boys, 34 girls); Grade 12: 67 students (34 boys, 33 girls).

Faculty School total: 82. In upper school: 13 men, 16 women; 23 have advanced degrees.

Subjects Offered Advanced computer applications, Advanced Placement courses, algebra, American Civil War, American government, American history, American history-AP, American literature, anatomy and physiology, art, art-AP, band, biology, biology-AP, calculus, calculus-AP, chemistry, chemistry-AP, choral music, chorus, Civil War, communications, comparative government and politics-AP, comparative religion, computer applications, computer multimedia, computer programming, computer science, computers, concert band, concert choir, constitutional law, creative writing, drama, ecology, economics, economics-AP, English, English composition, English literature, English literature and composition-AP, European history, European history-AP, fine arts, French, French language-AP, French-AP, geometry, government and politics-AP, graphic design, health, history-AP, honors algebra, honors English, honors geometry, human geography - AP, humanities, Latin, Latin-AP, law, literature-AP,

macro/microeconomics-AP, marine biology, mathematics, mythology, neuroanatomy, ornithology, physical education, physics, pre-calculus, psychology, science, social sciences, social studies, Spanish, Spanish language-AP, Spanish-AP, statistics, statistics-AP, studio art-AP, theater, trigonometry, U.S. government, U.S. government and politics-AP, U.S. history, U.S. history-AP, weight training, world history, yearbook, zoology.

Graduation Requirements Algebra, American government, American history, arts and fine arts (art, music, dance, drama), biology, chemistry, computer science, economics, electives, English, foreign language, geometry, mathematics, physical education (includes health), science, social sciences, social studies (includes history), world history, senior year speech.

Special Academic Programs 18 Advanced Placement exams for which test preparation is offered; honors section.

College Admission Counseling 49 students graduated in 2012; all went to college, including Auburn University; Georgia Institute of Technology; Georgia Southern University; The University of Alabama; University of Georgia; University of Mississippi. Mean SAT critical reading: 582, mean SAT math: 594, mean SAT writing: 610, mean combined SAT: 1786, mean composite ACT: 25. 47% scored over 600 on SAT critical reading, 47% scored over 600 on SAT math, 49% scored over 600 on SAT writing, 45% scored over 1800 on combined SAT, 46% scored over 26 on composite ACT.

Student Life Upper grades have specified standards of dress, student council, honor system. Discipline rests equally with students and faculty.

Tuition and Aid Day student tuition: $14,545. Tuition installment plan (monthly payment plans, individually arranged payment plans, 3 payments in months July, September and November (no interest)). Tuition reduction for siblings, merit scholarship grants, need-based scholarship grants, need-based loans, middle-income loans available. In 2012–13, 37% of upper-school students received aid; total upper-school merit-scholarship money awarded: $427,145. Total amount of financial aid awarded in 2012–13: $812,545.

Admissions Traditional secondary-level entrance grade is 9. For fall 2012, 68 students applied for upper-level admission, 56 were accepted, 31 enrolled. Otis-Lennon IQ Test or SSAT, ERB, PSAT, SAT, PLAN or ACT required. Deadline for receipt of application materials: none. Application fee required: $50. Interview required.

Athletics Interscholastic: baseball (boys), basketball (b,g), cheering (g), cross-country running (b,g), football (b), golf (b,g), soccer (b,g), softball (g), tennis (b,g), track and field (b,g), volleyball (g), wrestling (b); intramural: basketball (b,g). 6 PE instructors.

Computers Computers are regularly used in college planning, computer applications, creative writing, English, foreign language, French, geography, graphic arts, graphic design, history, human geography - AP, information technology, mathematics, media production, programming, publications, science, social studies, Spanish, video film production, Web site design, yearbook classes. Computer network features include on-campus library services, online commercial services, Internet access, wireless campus network, Internet filtering or blocking technology. Campus intranet and student e-mail accounts are available to students. Students grades are available online. The school has a published electronic and media policy.

Contact Mary S. Snyder, Enrollment Director. 706-324-1392. Fax: 706-571-0178. E-mail: msnyder@brookstoneschool.org. Website: www.brookstoneschool.org

BROPHY COLLEGE PREPARATORY

4701 North Central Avenue
Phoenix, Arizona 85012-1797

Head of School: Mr. Robert E. Ryan III

General Information Boys' day college-preparatory, arts, religious studies, and technology school, affiliated with Roman Catholic Church (Jesuit order). Grades 6–12. Founded: 1928. Setting: urban. 38-acre campus. 8 buildings on campus. Approved or accredited by Jesuit Secondary Education Association, National Catholic Education Association, and Western Catholic Education Association. Endowment: $19 million. Total enrollment: 1,362. Upper school average class size: 24. Upper school faculty-student ratio: 1:14. There are 180 required school days per year for Upper School students. Upper School students typically attend 5 days per week. The average school day consists of 6 hours and 40 minutes.

Upper School Student Profile Grade 9: 341 students (341 boys); Grade 10: 325 students (325 boys); Grade 11: 323 students (323 boys); Grade 12: 295 students (295 boys). 66% of students are Roman Catholic Church (Jesuit order).

Faculty School total: 94. In upper school: 62 men, 22 women; 70 have advanced degrees.

Subjects Offered Advanced Placement courses, advanced studio art-AP, algebra, American history, American literature, anatomy, art, Bible studies, biology, business, calculus, chemistry, community service, computer math, computer programming, computer science, creative writing, drama, earth science, economics, engineering, English, English literature, ethics, European history, expository writing, fine arts, French, geography, geometry, government/civics, health, history, Latin, mathematics, mechanical drawing, music, physical education, physics, probability and statistics, psychology, religion, science, social sciences, social studies, sociology, Spanish, speech, theater, theology, trigonometry, video film production, world history, world literature.

Graduation Requirements Arts and fine arts (art, music, dance, drama), English, foreign language, mathematics, physical education (includes health), religion (includes Bible studies and theology), science, social studies (includes history). Community service is required.

Special Academic Programs Advanced Placement exam preparation; honors section; study at local college for college credit; study abroad.

College Admission Counseling 309 students graduated in 2013; all went to college, including Arizona State University; Creighton University; Gonzaga University; Northern Arizona University; Santa Clara University; The University of Arizona. Median SAT critical reading: 600, median SAT math: 607, median SAT writing: 589, median combined SAT: 1796, median composite ACT: 26.

Student Life Upper grades have specified standards of dress, student council, honor system. Discipline rests primarily with faculty. Attendance at religious services is required.

Summer Programs Enrichment, advancement, sports, art/fine arts, computer instruction programs offered; session focuses on academic skills and sports; held both on and off campus; held at Manresa Retreat (Sedona, AZ), Brophy East Campus, and Brophy Sports Campus; accepts boys and girls; open to students from other schools. 1,300 students usually enrolled. 2014 schedule: June 2 to July 3. Application deadline: May 31.

Tuition and Aid Day student tuition: $13,500. Tuition installment plan (The Tuition Plan, monthly payment plans, individually arranged payment plans). Need-based scholarship grants, paying campus jobs available. In 2013–14, 29% of upper-school students received aid. Total amount of financial aid awarded in 2013–14: $2,098,895.

Admissions Traditional secondary-level entrance grade is 9. For fall 2013, 650 students applied for upper-level admission, 390 were accepted, 341 enrolled. STS required. Deadline for receipt of application materials: January 31. Application fee required: $50. On-campus interview required.

Athletics Interscholastic: aquatics, baseball, basketball, cross-country running, diving, flagball, football, golf, ice hockey, lacrosse, soccer, swimming and diving, tennis, track and field, volleyball, wrestling; intramural: aquatics, badminton, baseball, basketball, bicycling, bowling, cheering, climbing, crew, cricket, fishing, fitness, flag football, Frisbee, golf, handball, hockey, ice hockey, lacrosse, mountain biking, outdoor activities, physical fitness, physical training, rock climbing, skiing (downhill), softball, strength & conditioning, table tennis, touch football, ultimate Frisbee, volleyball, wall climbing, water polo, weight lifting, weight training. 2 PE instructors, 15 coaches, 2 athletic trainers.

Computers Computers are regularly used in all academic classes. Computer network features include on-campus library services, online commercial services, Internet access, wireless campus network, Blackboard, computer tablets, iPads. Student e-mail accounts are available to students. Students grades are available online. The school has a published electronic and media policy.

Contact Ms. Shelly Scheuring, Assistant to Director of Admissions. 602-264-5291 Ext. 6233. Fax: 602-234-1669. E-mail: sscheuring@brophyprep.org. Website: www.brophyprep.org/

BROTHER RICE HIGH SCHOOL

7101 Lahser Road
Bloomfield Hills, Michigan 48301

Head of School: Mr. John Birney

General Information Boys' day college-preparatory, arts, business, religious studies, and technology school, affiliated with Roman Catholic Church. Grades 9–12. Founded: 1960. Setting: suburban. Nearest major city is Detroit. 20-acre campus. 1 building on campus. Approved or accredited by North Central Association of Colleges and Schools and Michigan Department of Education. Endowment: $2 million. Total enrollment: 675. Upper school average class size: 22. Upper school faculty-student ratio: 1:13. Upper School students typically attend 5 days per week. The average school day consists of 6 hours and 51 minutes.

Upper School Student Profile Grade 9: 163 students (163 boys); Grade 10: 182 students (182 boys); Grade 11: 161 students (161 boys); Grade 12: 163 students (163 boys). 75% of students are Roman Catholic.

Faculty School total: 60. In upper school: 32 men, 10 women; 36 have advanced degrees.

Subjects Offered 20th century world history, accounting, algebra, American government, anatomy, anthropology, architectural drawing, art, band, biology, biology-AP, business law, calculus, calculus-AP, chemistry, Chinese, choir, church history, computer science, computer science-AP, computers, concert band, creative writing, death and loss, debate, drama, earth science, economics, electronics, engineering, English, English composition, English language-AP, ensembles, European history, family living, forensics, French, French-AP, geometry, German, global science, health, jazz band, Latin, library science, literature, mathematics, mechanical drawing, music, music history, music theory, organic chemistry, photography, photojournalism, physical education, physics, physiology, pre-calculus, probability and statistics, psychology, social justice, Spanish, Spanish-AP, speech, studio art-AP, theology, trigonometry, U.S. government and politics-AP, U.S. history, U.S. history-AP, Western civilization, world geography, world religions.

Graduation Requirements Computer science, electives, English, foreign language, mathematics, physical education (includes health), science, social studies (includes history), speech, theology.

Special Academic Programs Advanced Placement exam preparation; honors section; remedial reading and/or remedial writing; remedial math.

College Admission Counseling 145 students graduated in 2012; 144 went to college, including Central Michigan University; Michigan State University; University of Michigan. Other: 1 entered military service. Median combined SAT: 1838, median composite ACT: 25.

Student Life Upper grades have specified standards of dress, student council, honor system. Discipline rests primarily with faculty. Attendance at religious services is required.

Tuition and Aid Day student tuition: $11,050. Tuition installment plan (The Tuition Plan, monthly payment plans, individually arranged payment plans). Tuition reduction for siblings, merit scholarship grants, need-based scholarship grants available. In 2012–13, 40% of upper-school students received aid; total upper-school merit-scholarship money awarded: $600,000. Total amount of financial aid awarded in 2012–13: $900,000.

Admissions Traditional secondary-level entrance grade is 9. For fall 2012, 425 students applied for upper-level admission, 295 were accepted, 163 enrolled. SAS, STS-HSPT required. Deadline for receipt of application materials: none. No application fee required. Interview required.

Athletics Interscholastic: alpine skiing, baseball, basketball, bowling, cross-country running, diving, football, golf, hockey, ice hockey, lacrosse, skiing (downhill), soccer, swimming and diving, tennis, track and field, wrestling; intramural: basketball, bowling, drill team, fitness, football, golf, ice hockey, paint ball, rugby, skiing (downhill), snowboarding, strength & conditioning, touch football, ultimate Frisbee, winter (indoor) track. 50 coaches, 1 athletic trainer.

Computers Computer resources include online commercial services, Internet access. The school has a published electronic and media policy.

Contact Mr. David D. Sofran, Director of Admissions. 248-833-2022. Fax: 248-833-2011. E-mail: sofran@brrice.edu. Website: www.brrice.edu

BRUNSWICK SCHOOL

100 Maher Avenue
Greenwich, Connecticut 06830

Head of School: Thomas W. Philip

General Information Boys' day college-preparatory school. Grades PK–12. Founded: 1902. Setting: suburban. Nearest major city is New York, NY. 118-acre campus. 4 buildings on campus. Approved or accredited by New England Association of Schools and Colleges and Connecticut Department of Education. Member of National Association of Independent Schools. Endowment: $85 million. Total enrollment: 939. Upper school average class size: 15. Upper school faculty-student ratio: 1:5. The average school day consists of 9 hours and 30 minutes.

Upper School Student Profile Grade 9: 87 students (87 boys); Grade 10: 92 students (92 boys); Grade 11: 89 students (89 boys); Grade 12: 89 students (89 boys).

Faculty School total: 171. In upper school: 42 men, 14 women; 46 have advanced degrees.

Subjects Offered 20th century history, 3-dimensional design, acting, advanced chemistry, African-American literature, algebra, American history, American history-AP, American literature, anthropology, Arabic, architecture, art, art history, art history-AP, astronomy, biology, biology-AP, calculus, calculus-AP, ceramics, chemistry, chemistry-AP, Chinese, choir, community service, computer graphics, computer programming, computer programming-AP, creative writing, digital art, digital music, drama, earth science, economics, economics-AP, English, environmental science-AP, ethics, European history, European history-AP, film and literature, fine arts, French, French language-AP, French literature-AP, geometry, government-AP, Greek, Greek culture, health, history, honors algebra, honors geometry, human geography - AP, Italian, Japanese history, jazz, jazz band, jazz ensemble, Latin, Latin American literature, Latin-AP, mathematics, media studies, microeconomics, military history, music, oceanography, philosophy, photography, physical education, physics, physics-AP, poetry, pre-calculus, psychology, psychology-AP, science, senior seminar, Shakespeare, short story, social studies, Spanish, Spanish language-AP, Spanish literature-AP, speech and debate, statistics-AP, studio art, studio art-AP, theater, trigonometry, U.S. government and politics-AP, U.S. history-AP, world cultures, world history-AP, writing.

Graduation Requirements Arts and fine arts (art, music, dance, drama), English, foreign language, mathematics, physical education (includes health), science, social studies (includes history). Community service is required.

Special Academic Programs Advanced Placement exam preparation; honors section; independent study; term-away projects; academic accommodation for the gifted, the musically talented, and the artistically talented.

College Admission Counseling 81 students graduated in 2013; all went to college, including Cornell University; Dartmouth College; Duke University; Georgetown University; University of Virginia; Yale University. Mean SAT critical reading: 660, mean SAT math: 665, mean SAT writing: 670, mean combined SAT: 1985. 75% scored over 600 on SAT critical reading, 87% scored over 600 on SAT math, 88% scored over 600 on SAT writing, 85% scored over 1800 on combined SAT.

Student Life Upper grades have specified standards of dress, student council, honor system. Discipline rests equally with students and faculty.

Summer Programs Enrichment programs offered; session focuses on academic enrichment; held on campus; accepts boys and girls; open to students from other schools. 2014 schedule: June 13 to July 8. Application deadline: April 1.

Tuition and Aid Day student tuition: $34,500. Tuition installment plan (Key Tuition Payment Plan, monthly payment plans). Need-based scholarship grants available. In 2013–14, 11% of upper-school students received aid. Total amount of financial aid awarded in 2013–14: $1,250,000.

Admissions Traditional secondary-level entrance grade is 9. For fall 2013, 162 students applied for upper-level admission, 38 were accepted, 33 enrolled. ISEE, PSAT or SSAT required. Deadline for receipt of application materials: December 15. Application fee required: $75. On-campus interview required.

Athletics Interscholastic: baseball, basketball, crew, cross-country running, fencing, fitness, football, golf, ice hockey, lacrosse, sailing, soccer, squash, tennis, track and field, water polo, wrestling; intramural: basketball, softball, squash, touch football, ultimate Frisbee. 4 PE instructors, 2 athletic trainers.

Computers Computers are regularly used in career technology classes. Computer network features include online commercial services, Internet access, wireless campus network, Internet filtering or blocking technology. Campus intranet and student e-mail accounts are available to students. The school has a published electronic and media policy.

Contact Stephen Garnett, Director, Upper School Admission. 203-625-5842. Fax: 203-625-5863. E-mail: sgarnett@brunswickschool.org. Website: www.brunswickschool.org

THE BRYN MAWR SCHOOL FOR GIRLS

109 West Melrose Avenue
Baltimore, Maryland 21210

Head of School: Maureen E. Walsh

General Information Coeducational day (boys' only in lower grades) college-preparatory and arts school. Boys grade PK, girls grades PK–12. Founded: 1885. Setting: suburban. 26-acre campus. 9 buildings on campus. Approved or accredited by Association of Independent Maryland Schools and Maryland Department of Education. Member of National Association of Independent Schools. Endowment: $29.9 million. Total enrollment: 685. Upper school average class size: 14. Upper school faculty-student ratio: 1:7. There are 180 required school days per year for Upper School students. Upper School students typically attend 5 days per week. The average school day consists of 7 hours.

Upper School Student Profile Grade 9: 78 students (78 girls); Grade 10: 73 students (73 girls); Grade 11: 67 students (67 girls); Grade 12: 72 students (72 girls).

Faculty School total: 129. In upper school: 10 men, 33 women; 23 have advanced degrees.

Subjects Offered Accounting, acting, African studies, African-American history, African-American literature, algebra, American history, American literature, anatomy, anatomy and physiology, Arabic, architectural drawing, art, art history, art history-AP, astronomy, biology, biology-AP, British literature, calculus, ceramics, chemistry, chemistry-AP, Chinese, comparative religion, computer programming, computer science, computer science-AP, creative writing, dance, design, digital art, digital photography, drama, drawing, ecology, economics, emerging technology, English, English literature, English-AP, environmental science-AP, ethics, European history, fine arts, forensics, French, French literature-AP, genetics, geography, geology, geometry, German, grammar, Greek, health, Holocaust studies, Irish literature, Latin, Latin American history, mathematics, mechanical drawing, moral theology, music, music theory, mythology, Native American studies, orchestra, painting, personal finance, photography, physical education, physics, physics-AP, poetry, pre-calculus, public speaking, rite of passage, Russian, science, Shakespearean histories, short story, social studies, Spanish, statistics, strings, technology, theater, trigonometry, U.S. government and politics-AP, U.S. history, U.S. history-AP, urban studies, Vietnam War, world history, world history-AP, world literature, World War I, World War II, writing.

Graduation Requirements Arts and fine arts (art, music, dance, drama), emerging technology, English, foreign language, history, mathematics, physical education (includes health), public speaking, science, 50 hours of community service, convocation speech.

Special Academic Programs Advanced Placement exam preparation; honors section; independent study; term-away projects; study abroad; academic accommodation for the gifted, the musically talented, and the artistically talented.

College Admission Counseling 73 students graduated in 2013; all went to college, including Columbia University; Duke University; University of Denver; University of Maryland, College Park; University of Pennsylvania; Wesleyan University. Median SAT critical reading: 640, median SAT math: 630, median SAT writing: 650, median combined SAT: 1900, median composite ACT: 28. 72.2% scored over 600 on SAT critical reading, 59.7% scored over 600 on SAT math, 86.1% scored over 600 on SAT writing, 72.2% scored over 1800 on combined SAT, 74.3% scored over 26 on composite ACT.

Student Life Upper grades have uniform requirement, student council, honor system. Discipline rests equally with students and faculty.

Summer Programs Enrichment, sports, art/fine arts programs offered; session focuses on arts, crafts, language, culture, and sports; held on campus; accepts boys and girls; open to students from other schools. 350 students usually enrolled. 2014 schedule: June 16 to August 1. Application deadline: none.

Tuition and Aid Day student tuition: $26,390. Tuition installment plan (FACTS Tuition Payment Plan, individually arranged payment plans, Tuition Management Services, Semi-monthly Payroll Deduction (for employees only)). Need-based scholarship grants, need-based loans, middle-income loans available. In 2013–14, 31% of upper-school students received aid. Total amount of financial aid awarded in 2013–14: $1,359,941.

Admissions Traditional secondary-level entrance grade is 9. For fall 2013, 101 students applied for upper-level admission, 53 were accepted, 30 enrolled. ISEE or OLSAT/Stanford required. Deadline for receipt of application materials: December 2. Application fee required: $60. On-campus interview required.

Athletics Interscholastic: badminton, ballet, basketball, crew, cross-country running, dance, field hockey, hockey, indoor soccer, indoor track & field, lacrosse, rowing, running, soccer, softball, squash, tennis, track and field, volleyball, winter (indoor) track, winter soccer; intramural: aerobics, aerobics/dance, aerobics/Nautilus, archery, badminton, ball hockey, basketball, bowling, cooperative games, croquet, cross-country running, dance, fitness, flag football, floor hockey, ice hockey, jogging, outdoor activities, physical training, pillo polo, ropes courses, running, strength & conditioning, tennis, touch football, weight training. 5 PE instructors, 27 coaches, 2 athletic trainers.

Computers Computers are regularly used in all academic, animation, art, computer applications, Web site design classes. Computer network features include on-campus library services, online commercial services, Internet access, off-campus email. Campus intranet and student e-mail accounts are available to students. Students grades are available online. The school has a published electronic and media policy.

Contact Talia Titus, Director of Admission and Financial Aid. 410-323-8800 Ext. 1237. Fax: 410-435-4678. E-mail: titust@brynmawrschool.org. Website: www.brynmawrschool.org

BUFFALO ACADEMY OF THE SACRED HEART

3860 Main Street
Buffalo, New York 14226-3398

Head of School: Ms. Jennifer M. Demert, Esq.

General Information Girls' day college-preparatory, arts, religious studies, technology, and music school, affiliated with Roman Catholic Church. Grades 9–12. Founded: 1877. Setting: suburban. 2-acre campus. 2 buildings on campus. Approved or accredited by Middle States Association of Colleges and Schools, New York State Board of Regents, and New York Department of Education. Total enrollment: 407. Upper school average class size: 20. Upper school faculty-student ratio: 1:10. Upper School students typically attend 5 days per week. The average school day consists of 7 hours.

Upper School Student Profile Grade 9: 110 students (110 girls); Grade 10: 106 students (106 girls); Grade 11: 100 students (100 girls); Grade 12: 91 students (91 girls). 87% of students are Roman Catholic.

Faculty School total: 41. In upper school: 9 men, 32 women; 31 have advanced degrees.

Subjects Offered Advanced Placement courses, aerobics, algebra, American history, American literature, art, biology, business, business skills, calculus, chemistry, Chinese, community service, computer math, computer programming, computer science, creative writing, desktop publishing, drama, driver education, earth science, economics, English, English literature, environmental science, European history, fine arts, French, geography, geometry, government/civics, grammar, health, history, home economics, instrumental music, journalism, Latin, mathematics, music, physical education, physics, psychology, religion, science, social studies, sociology, Spanish, theater, theology, vocal music, world history.

Graduation Requirements Arts and fine arts (art, music, dance, drama), business skills (includes word processing), computer science, English, foreign language, mathematics, physical education (includes health), religion (includes Bible studies and theology), science, social studies (includes history), 20 hours of community service per year, 4 years of leadership studies. Community service is required.

Special Academic Programs 13 Advanced Placement exams for which test preparation is offered; honors section; accelerated programs; study at local college for college credit; academic accommodation for the gifted, the musically talented, and the artistically talented; remedial math.

College Admission Counseling 90 students graduated in 2012; 89 went to college, including Boston College; Canisius College; St. Bonaventure University; State University of New York College at Geneseo; Syracuse University; University at Buffalo, the State University of New York. Other: 1 had other specific plans. Median SAT critical reading: 567, median SAT math: 550, median SAT writing: 569.

Student Life Upper grades have uniform requirement, student council, honor system. Discipline rests primarily with faculty. Attendance at religious services is required.

Tuition and Aid Day student tuition: $9565. Tuition installment plan (FACTS Tuition Payment Plan). Tuition reduction for siblings, merit scholarship grants, need-based scholarship grants, paying campus jobs, discounts for children of employees, emergency tuition assistance available. In 2012–13, 31% of upper-school students received aid. Total amount of financial aid awarded in 2012–13: $275,000.

Admissions Traditional secondary-level entrance grade is 9. For fall 2012, 155 students applied for upper-level admission, 135 were accepted, 110 enrolled. High School Placement Test required. Deadline for receipt of application materials: none. Application fee required: $20. Interview recommended.

Athletics Interscholastic: basketball, bowling, cheering, crew, cross-country running, dance, field hockey, fitness walking, golf, ice hockey, indoor track & field, lacrosse, rowing, running, sailing, soccer, softball, swimming and diving, tennis, track and field, volleyball; intramural: crew, drill team, jogging, skiing (downhill), yoga. 2 PE instructors, 9 coaches.

Computers Computers are regularly used in business applications, English, foreign language, mathematics, music, science classes. Computer network features include on-campus library services, online commercial services, Internet access, wireless campus network, Internet filtering or blocking technology. Student e-mail accounts are available to students. Students grades are available online. The school has a published electronic and media policy.

Contact Ms. Mary Ganey Cochrane, Director of Admissions. 716-834-2101 Ext. 311. Fax: 716-834-2944. E-mail: mcochrane@sacredheartacademy.org. Website: www.sacredheartacademy.org

BULLOCH ACADEMY

873 Westside Road
Statesboro, Georgia 30458

Head of School: Mrs. Leisa Houghton

General Information Coeducational day college-preparatory, arts, and technology school, affiliated with Protestant faith, Baptist Church. Grades PK–12. Founded: 1971. Setting: small town. Nearest major city is Savannah. 35-acre campus. 4 buildings on campus. Approved or accredited by Georgia Accrediting Commission, Georgia Independent School Association, Southern Association of Colleges and Schools, and Southern Association of Independent Schools. Member of National Association of Independent Schools. Total enrollment: 498. Upper school average class size: 17. Upper school faculty-student ratio: 1:17. There are 180 required school days per year for Upper School students. Upper School students typically attend 5 days per week. The average school day consists of 8 hours.

Upper School Student Profile Grade 9: 35 students (19 boys, 16 girls); Grade 10: 36 students (20 boys, 16 girls); Grade 11: 42 students (19 boys, 23 girls); Grade 12: 45 students (20 boys, 25 girls). 90% of students are Protestant, Baptist.

Faculty School total: 31. In upper school: 4 men, 11 women; 4 have advanced degrees.

Subjects Offered Advanced Placement courses, American government, American history, anatomy and physiology, art, art education, biology, calculus, chemistry, computer applications, computer science, earth science, economics, economics and history, English, ethics, geometry, government, government-AP, government/civics, health education, journalism, language and composition, language arts, literature-AP, mathematics-AP, music, performing arts, physical education, physics, pre-algebra, pre-calculus, research skills, science, social sciences, Spanish, speech and debate, technology, U.S. government and politics-AP, U.S. history, Web site design, world geography, world history.

Graduation Requirements Computer science, English, foreign language, mathematics, physical education (includes health), science, social sciences, social studies (includes history).

Special Academic Programs 6 Advanced Placement exams for which test preparation is offered; honors section; independent study; study at local college for college credit; academic accommodation for the gifted, the musically talented, and the artistically talented.

College Admission Counseling 30 students graduated in 2012; 29 went to college, including Furman University; Georgia Institute of Technology; Georgia Southern University; The University of Alabama; University of Georgia; University of Oklahoma. Other: 1 went to work. Median SAT critical reading: 518, median SAT math: 530, median SAT writing: 508, median combined SAT: 1556, median composite ACT: 20.

Student Life Upper grades have specified standards of dress, student council, honor system. Discipline rests primarily with faculty.

Tuition and Aid Day student tuition: $6710. Tuition installment plan (monthly payment plans, individually arranged payment plans). Tuition reduction for siblings, need-based scholarship grants, tuition assistance available. In 2012–13, 10% of upper-school students received aid. Total amount of financial aid awarded in 2012–13: $50,000.

Admissions Traditional secondary-level entrance grade is 9. For fall 2012, 25 students applied for upper-level admission, 24 were accepted, 24 enrolled. Any standardized test required. Deadline for receipt of application materials: none. Application fee required: $375. Interview recommended.

Athletics Interscholastic: baseball (boys), basketball (b,g), cheering (g), cross-country running (b,g), dance team (g), football (b), golf (b,g), physical fitness (b,g), running (b,g), soccer (b,g), softball (g), strength & conditioning (b,g), tennis (b,g), track and field (b,g), weight lifting (b,g), weight training (b,g), wrestling (b); intramural: cheering (g), cross-country running (b,g), football (b), physical fitness (b,g); coed interscholastic: physical fitness; coed intramural: basketball, football, physical fitness. 3 PE instructors, 7 coaches, 3 athletic trainers.

Computers Computers are regularly used in art, career education, career exploration, computer applications, creative writing, desktop publishing, economics, geography, history, independent study, keyboarding, technology classes. Computer network features include on-campus library services, online commercial services, Internet access, wireless campus network, Internet filtering or blocking technology. Student e-mail accounts are available to students. Students grades are available online. The school has a published electronic and media policy.

Contact Mr. Leisa Houghton, Head of School. 912-764-6297. Fax: 912-764-3165. E-mail: lhoughton@bullochacademy.com. Website: www.bullochacademy.com

BURR AND BURTON ACADEMY

57 Seminary Avenue
Manchester, Vermont 05254

Head of School: Mr. Mark Tashjian

General Information Coeducational boarding and day college-preparatory, general academic, arts, and technology school. Grades 9–12. Founded: 1829. Setting: small town. Nearest major city is Albany, NY. Students are housed in single-sex dormitories and homes of host families. 49-acre campus. 7 buildings on campus. Approved or accredited by New England Association of Schools and Colleges and Vermont Department of Education. Member of National Association of Independent Schools. Total enrollment: 667. Upper school average class size: 19. Upper school faculty-student ratio: 1:12. There are 175 required school days per year for Upper School students. Upper School students typically attend 5 days per week. The average school day consists of 6 hours and 40 minutes.

Upper School Student Profile Grade 9: 142 students (69 boys, 73 girls); Grade 10: 162 students (73 boys, 89 girls); Grade 11: 187 students (99 boys, 88 girls); Grade 12: 176 students (88 boys, 88 girls). 8% are international students.

Faculty School total: 60. In upper school: 35 men, 25 women; 30 have advanced degrees.

Subjects Offered 1968, algebra, American history, American literature, anatomy, art, art history, biology, business, calculus, chemistry, computer math, computer programming, computer science, drafting, drama, driver education, earth science, ecology, English, English literature, environmental science, expository writing, French, geometry, German, government/civics, health, history, industrial arts, mathematics, music, photography, physical education, physics, psychology, science, social studies, Spanish, theater, trigonometry, typing, world history, world literature.

Graduation Requirements Arts, computer literacy, English, mathematics, physical education (includes health), science, social studies (includes history), U.S. history. Community service is required.

Special Academic Programs 14 Advanced Placement exams for which test preparation is offered; honors section; independent study; term-away projects; study abroad; remedial reading and/or remedial writing; remedial math; programs in English, mathematics, general development for dyslexic students; special instructional classes for deaf students, blind students; ESL (20 students enrolled).

College Admission Counseling 157 students graduated in 2013; 130 went to college, including Michigan State University; University of Vermont. Other: 22 went to work, 3 entered military service, 2 had other specific plans.

Student Life Upper grades have specified standards of dress, student council. Discipline rests primarily with faculty.

Tuition and Aid Day student tuition: $15,875; 7-day tuition and room/board: $39,960. Tuition installment plan (individually arranged payment plans). Financial aid available to upper-school students. In 2013–14, 2% of upper-school students received aid.

Admissions Traditional secondary-level entrance grade is 9. School's own test, SLEP for foreign students and TOEFL or SLEP required. Deadline for receipt of application materials: none. No application fee required. Interview required.

Athletics Interscholastic: alpine skiing (boys, girls), baseball (b), basketball (b,g), cross-country running (b,g), dance team (g), field hockey (g), football (b), golf (b,g), hockey (b,g), ice hockey (b,g), lacrosse (b,g), nordic skiing (b,g), skiing (cross-country) (b,g), skiing (downhill) (b,g), snowboarding (b,g), soccer (b,g), softball (g), tennis (b,g), track and field (b,g), wrestling (b,g); coed intramural: equestrian sports, floor hockey, outdoor adventure, outdoor education, volleyball, weight training. 4 PE instructors, 1 athletic trainer.

Computers Computers are regularly used in drafting, drawing and design, English, foreign language, graphic design, history, information technology, mathematics, science, video film production, Web site design, yearbook classes. Computer network features include on-campus library services, online commercial services, Internet access, wireless campus network, Internet filtering or blocking technology. Campus intranet, student e-mail accounts, and computer access in designated common areas are available to students.

Contact Mr. Philip G. Anton, Director of Admission and School Counseling. 802-362-1775 Ext. 125. Fax: 802-362-0574. E-mail: panton@burrburton.org. Website: www.burrburton.org

BUTTE CENTRAL CATHOLIC HIGH SCHOOL

9 South Idaho Street
Butte, Montana 59701

Head of School: Mr. Kevin St. John

General Information Boys' boarding and coeducational day college-preparatory, arts, business, vocational, religious studies, and technology school, affiliated with Roman Catholic Church. Boarding boys grades 9–12, day boys grades 9–12, day girls grades 9–12. Founded: 1892. Setting: small town. Nearest major city is Bozeman. 6-acre campus. 1 building on campus. Approved or accredited by National Catholic Education Association, Northwest Accreditation Commission, Northwest Association of Schools and Colleges, Western Catholic Education Association, and Montana Department of Education. Endowment: $300,000. Total enrollment: 141. Upper school average class size: 17. Upper school faculty-student ratio: 1:10. There are 180 required school days per year for Upper School students. Upper School students typically attend 5 days per week. The average school day consists of 7 hours.

Upper School Student Profile Grade 9: 35 students (16 boys, 19 girls); Grade 10: 43 students (17 boys, 26 girls); Grade 11: 30 students (22 boys, 8 girls); Grade 12: 33 students (19 boys, 14 girls). 4% of students are boarding students. 93% are state residents. 1 state is represented in upper school student body. 7% are international students. International students from Brazil, China, Germany, Portugal, and Taiwan. 75% of students are Roman Catholic.

Faculty School total: 17. In upper school: 6 men, 11 women; 3 have advanced degrees.

Subjects Offered Accounting, advanced math, Advanced Placement courses, algebra, American literature-AP, animal behavior, art, athletic training, biology, calculus, calculus-AP, career education, chemistry, choir, college counseling, college placement, college planning, college writing, community service, computer science, computers, debate, desktop publishing, drama, English, English literature and composition-AP, foreign language, French, French as a second language, geometry, government/civics, health, history, honors algebra, honors English, honors geometry, human biology, integrated mathematics, keyboarding, mathematics, model United Nations, physical education, physics, pre-calculus, public speaking, reading, religion, science, social studies, Spanish, student government, trigonometry, Web site design, weightlifting, world history, writing, yearbook.

Graduation Requirements American government, American history, arts and fine arts (art, music, dance, drama), electives, English, foreign language, global studies, health education, keyboarding, mathematics, physical education (includes health), religion (includes Bible studies and theology), science, social studies (includes history), writing. Community service is required.

Special Academic Programs 2 Advanced Placement exams for which test preparation is offered; honors section; independent study; study at local college for college credit; remedial reading and/or remedial writing; remedial math.

College Admission Counseling 42 students graduated in 2013; 39 went to college, including Carroll University; Division of Technology of Montana Tech of The University of Montana; Gonzaga University; Montana State University; The University of Montana Western. Other: 1 went to work, 2 entered military service. Median composite ACT: 20. 7% scored over 26 on composite ACT.

Student Life Upper grades have specified standards of dress, student council, honor system. Discipline rests primarily with faculty. Attendance at religious services is required.

Tuition and Aid Day student tuition: $4000–$8000; 7-day tuition and room/board: $10,000–$15,000. Guaranteed tuition plan. Tuition installment plan (FACTS Tuition Payment Plan, monthly payment plans, individually arranged payment plans). Tuition reduction for siblings, need-based scholarship grants available. In 2013–14, 25% of upper-school students received aid. Total amount of financial aid awarded in 2013–14: $68,000.

Admissions For fall 2013, 141 students applied for upper-level admission, 141 were accepted, 141 enrolled. Admissions testing required. Deadline for receipt of application materials: none. Application fee required: $150. Interview required.

Athletics Interscholastic: basketball (boys, girls), cheering (g), cross-country running (b,g), football (b), golf (b,g), softball (g), strength & conditioning (b,g), tennis (b,g), track and field (b,g), volleyball (g), wrestling (b). 1 PE instructor, 30 coaches, 1 athletic trainer.

Computers Computer network features include on-campus library services, Internet access, Internet filtering or blocking technology. The school has a published electronic and media policy.

Contact Mr. Timothy Norbeck, Principal. 406-782-6761. Fax: 406-723-3873. E-mail: tim.norbeck@buttecentralschools.org. Website: www.buttecentralschools.org

BUXTON SCHOOL

291 South Street
Williamstown, Massachusetts 01267

Head of School: Peter Smith '74

General Information Coeducational boarding and day college-preparatory and arts school. Grades 9–12. Founded: 1928. Setting: small town. Nearest major city is Boston. Students are housed in single-sex dormitories. 120-acre campus. 18 buildings on campus. Approved or accredited by Association of Independent Schools in New England, New England Association of Schools and Colleges, The Association of Boarding Schools, and Massachusetts Department of Education. Member of National Association of Independent Schools and Secondary School Admission Test Board. Endowment: $2.9 million. Total enrollment: 89. Upper school average class size: 9. Upper school faculty-student ratio: 1:4. There are 222 required school days per year for Upper School students. Upper School students typically attend 7 days per week. The average school day consists of 5 hours and 15 minutes.

Upper School Student Profile Grade 9: 13 students (6 boys, 7 girls); Grade 10: 26 students (11 boys, 15 girls); Grade 11: 20 students (7 boys, 13 girls); Grade 12: 30 students (10 boys, 20 girls). 91% of students are boarding students. 26% are state residents. 12 states are represented in upper school student body. 17% are international students. International students from Cameroon, China, Japan, Mexico, and Spain.

Faculty School total: 22. In upper school: 12 men, 10 women; 7 have advanced degrees; 12 reside on campus.

Subjects Offered Advanced math, African dance, African drumming, African studies, algebra, American history, American literature, anatomy and physiology, anthropology, architecture, astronomy, biology, British literature, calculus, cell biology, ceramics, chemistry, civil rights, costumes and make-up, creative writing, critical writing, dance performance, drama, drama performance, drawing, economics, education, English, English literature, ensembles, ESL, European history, expository writing, fiction, film history, French, geometry, grammar, history, improvisation, independent study, instruments, lab science, linear algebra, literary genres, literature, Mandarin, marine biology, medieval/Renaissance history, music, music composition, music performance, music theory, mythology, oceanography, painting, performing arts, philosophy, photography, physics, poetry, pre-calculus, printmaking, psychology, religion, set design, social sciences, Spanish, studio art, technical theater, TOEFL preparation, trigonometry, video film production, voice, Western civilization, writing workshop.

Graduation Requirements American history, English, foreign language, lab science, mathematics, social sciences.

Special Academic Programs Honors section; independent study; study at local college for college credit; academic accommodation for the gifted, the musically talented, and the artistically talented; ESL (14 students enrolled).

College Admission Counseling 19 students graduated in 2013; 18 went to college, including Bard College; Ithaca College; Mount Holyoke College; Pitzer College; Reed College; Sarah Lawrence College. Other: 1 entered a postgraduate year.

Student Life Discipline rests primarily with faculty.

Tuition and Aid Day student tuition: $29,000; 7-day tuition and room/board: $48,500. Tuition installment plan (individually arranged payment plans, Tuition Management Systems). Need-based scholarship grants, need-based loans with limited in-house financing available. In 2013–14, 49% of upper-school students received aid. Total amount of financial aid awarded in 2013–14: $1,600,000.

Admissions Traditional secondary-level entrance grade is 9. SSAT or TOEFL or SLEP required. Deadline for receipt of application materials: February 1. Application fee required: $50. Interview required.

Athletics Interscholastic: soccer (boys, girls); intramural: cheering (g), soccer (b,g); coed interscholastic: basketball, ultimate Frisbee; coed intramural: basketball, bicycling, dance, fitness, hiking/backpacking, horseback riding, ice skating, indoor soccer, jogging, martial arts, mountain biking, outdoor activities, running, skateboarding, skiing (cross-country), skiing (downhill), snowboarding, soccer, table tennis, ultimate Frisbee, volleyball, walking, weight lifting, yoga.

Computers Computers are regularly used in architecture, ESL, language development, mathematics, media production, multimedia, music, photography, science, Spanish, video film production, writing, yearbook classes. Computer network features include Internet access, wireless campus network, Internet filtering or blocking technology. Campus intranet and computer access in designated common areas are available to students. The school has a published electronic and media policy.

Contact Admissions Office. 413-458-3919. Fax: 413-458-9428. E-mail: Admissions@BuxtonSchool.org. Website: www.BuxtonSchool.org

CALVARY CHRISTIAN SCHOOL

5955 Taylor Mill Road
Covington, Kentucky 41015

Head of School: Dr. Bill Dickens

General Information Coeducational day college-preparatory, arts, religious studies, and technology school, affiliated with Baptist Church. Grades K4–12. Founded: 1974. Setting: suburban. Nearest major city is Cincinnati, OH. 64-acre campus. 1 building on campus. Approved or accredited by Association of Christian Schools International, CITA (Commission on International and Trans-Regional Accreditation), Southern Association of Colleges and Schools, and Kentucky Department of Education. Total enrollment: 359. Upper school average class size: 17. Upper school faculty-student ratio: 1:8. There are 177 required school days per year for Upper School students. Upper School students typically attend 5 days per week. The average school day consists of 7 hours.

Upper School Student Profile Grade 9: 26 students (12 boys, 14 girls); Grade 10: 32 students (11 boys, 21 girls); Grade 11: 22 students (12 boys, 10 girls); Grade 12: 28 students (12 boys, 16 girls). 30% of students are Baptist.

Faculty School total: 30. In upper school: 9 men, 11 women; 6 have advanced degrees.

Subjects Offered Advanced math, algebra, American history-AP, American literature-AP, Ancient Greek, ancient history, art, art appreciation, Bible, biology, calculus, chemistry, chemistry-AP, choir, chorus, Christian doctrine, Christian ethics, communication arts, computer applications, computer multimedia, computer science, concert band, concert choir, consumer mathematics, creative writing, cultural geography, drama, drama performance, earth science, economics, English, English composition, English language and composition-AP, English language-AP, English literature, English literature and composition-AP, English literature-AP, English-AP, ethics, European history-AP, fitness, food and nutrition, general math, general science, geography, geometry, government-AP, grammar, health education, home economics, honors algebra, independent study, journalism, Kentucky history, keyboarding, lab science, language arts, library assistant, literature-AP, logic, music theory, newspaper, physical education, physical science, physics-AP, pre-algebra, pre-calculus, rhetoric, Spanish, Spanish-AP, speech and debate, state history, student government, student publications, student teaching, U.S. government, U.S. government and politics-AP, U.S. history, U.S. history-AP, world governments, world history, yearbook.

Graduation Requirements Algebra, art appreciation, Bible, biology, chemistry, Christian doctrine, church history, civics, economics, English, English composition, English literature, European history, foreign language, geometry, health, physical science, U.S. government, U.S. history, world history, 4 years of high school Bible required for graduation.

Special Academic Programs Advanced Placement exam preparation; honors section; independent study; study at local college for college credit.

College Admission Counseling 26 students graduated in 2012; 25 went to college, including Eastern Kentucky University; Northern Kentucky University; University of Cincinnati; University of Kentucky; University of Louisville. Other: 1 went to work. Median composite ACT: 27. 25% scored over 26 on composite ACT.

Student Life Upper grades have uniform requirement, student council. Discipline rests primarily with faculty. Attendance at religious services is required.

Tuition and Aid Day student tuition: $6050. Tuition installment plan (FACTS Tuition Payment Plan, monthly payment plans, individually arranged payment plans). Tuition reduction for siblings, need-based scholarship grants, paying campus jobs available. In 2012–13, 9% of upper-school students received aid. Total amount of financial aid awarded in 2012–13: $23,000.

Admissions Traditional secondary-level entrance grade is 9. For fall 2012, 14 students applied for upper-level admission, 14 were accepted, 14 enrolled. Terra Nova-CTB required. Deadline for receipt of application materials: none. Application fee required: $285. Interview required.

Athletics Interscholastic: baseball (boys), basketball (b,g), bowling (b,g), cheering (g), cross-country running (b,g), diving (b,g), golf (b), physical fitness (b,g), soccer (b,g), softball (g), swimming and diving (b,g), tennis (b,g), track and field (b,g), volleyball (g), weight lifting (b), weight training (b); intramural: indoor soccer (b,g), martial arts (b,g), skiing (downhill) (b,g), strength & conditioning (b,g), weight training (b); coed intramural: bowling, gymnastics, physical fitness, running. 2 PE instructors, 15 coaches.

Computers Computers are regularly used in architecture, art, computer applications, design, desktop publishing, drafting, graphics, information technology, journalism, keyboarding, lab/keyboard, library, photography, photojournalism, science, Spanish, technical drawing, Web site design, yearbook classes. Computer network features include on-campus library services, Internet access, wireless campus network, Internet filtering or blocking technology. Campus intranet is available to students. Students grades are available online. The school has a published electronic and media policy.

Contact Mrs. Laurie Switzer, Registrar. 859-356-9201. Fax: 859-359-8962. E-mail: laurie.switzer@ccsky.org. Website: www.ccsky.org

CALVERT HALL COLLEGE HIGH SCHOOL

8102 LaSalle Road
Baltimore, Maryland 21286

Head of School: Mr. Frank Bramble

General Information Boys' day college-preparatory, arts, religious studies, and technology school, affiliated with Roman Catholic Church. Grades 9–12. Founded: 1845. Setting: suburban. 32-acre campus. 6 buildings on campus. Approved or accredited by Christian Brothers Association, Middle States Association of Colleges and Schools, National Catholic Education Association, and Maryland Department of Education. Endowment: $7.8 million. Total enrollment: 1,196. Upper school average class size: 21. Upper school faculty-student ratio: 1:12. There are 174 required school days per year for Upper School students. Upper School students typically attend 5 days per week. The average school day consists of 6 hours and 20 minutes.

Upper School Student Profile Grade 9: 306 students (306 boys); Grade 10: 310 students (310 boys); Grade 11: 305 students (305 boys); Grade 12: 275 students (275 boys). 71% of students are Roman Catholic.

Faculty School total: 100. In upper school: 74 men, 26 women; 72 have advanced degrees.

Subjects Offered Algebra, American history, American literature, art, art history, band, Bible studies, biology, business, business skills, calculus, chemistry, chorus, computer programming, computer science, creative writing, drama, earth science, economics, engineering, English, English literature, ethics, European history, fine arts, French, geography, geometry, German, government/civics, graphic arts, history, journalism, Latin, leadership, mathematics, music, painting, philosophy, physical education, physics, psychology, religion, science, sculpture, social sciences, social studies, Spanish, speech, statistics, theater, theology, typing, world history, world literature, writing.

Graduation Requirements Arts and fine arts (art, music, dance, drama), English, foreign language, mathematics, physical education (includes health), religion (includes Bible studies and theology), science, social sciences, social studies (includes history).

Special Academic Programs 22 Advanced Placement exams for which test preparation is offered; honors section; academic accommodation for the gifted, the musically talented, and the artistically talented; programs in English, mathematics, general development for dyslexic students.

College Admission Counseling 297 students graduated in 2013; 290 went to college, including Loyola University Maryland; Stevenson University; Towson University; University of Maryland, Baltimore County; University of Maryland, College Park. Other: 1 went to work, 2 entered military service. Median SAT critical reading: 555, median SAT math: 558, median SAT writing: 538.

Student Life Upper grades have specified standards of dress, student council, honor system. Discipline rests primarily with faculty. Attendance at religious services is required.

Summer Programs Remediation, enrichment, sports, art/fine arts, computer instruction programs offered; session focuses on remediation and make-up courses; held on campus; accepts boys and girls; open to students from other schools. 250 students usually enrolled. 2014 schedule: June 24 to July 26. Application deadline: June 15.

Tuition and Aid Day student tuition: $13,300. Tuition installment plan (monthly payment plans, individually arranged payment plans). Merit scholarship grants, need-based scholarship grants available. In 2013–14, 53% of upper-school students received aid; total upper-school merit-scholarship money awarded: $711,000. Total amount of financial aid awarded in 2013–14: $2,582,782.

Admissions Traditional secondary-level entrance grade is 9. For fall 2013, 652 students applied for upper-level admission, 564 were accepted, 313 enrolled. High School Placement Test (closed version) from Scholastic Testing Service required. Deadline for receipt of application materials: none. Application fee required: $25.

Athletics Interscholastic: aquatics, baseball, basketball, cross-country running, football, golf, hockey, ice hockey, indoor track & field, lacrosse, rugby, soccer, squash, swimming and diving, tennis, track and field, volleyball, water polo, winter (indoor) track, wrestling; intramural: basketball, bicycling, billiards, bocce, bowling, fitness, flag football, freestyle skiing, martial arts, outdoor adventure, rock climbing, rugby, sailing, skiing (downhill), table tennis, ultimate Frisbee, weight lifting. 2 PE instructors, 11 coaches, 1 athletic trainer.

Computers Computers are regularly used in accounting, business, college planning, computer applications, digital applications, economics, English, foreign language, graphic design, history, independent study, journalism, keyboarding, library, literary magazine, mathematics, music, programming, religion, SAT preparation, science, social sciences, stock market, video film production, writing, yearbook classes. Computer network features include on-campus library services, Internet access, wireless campus network, Internet filtering or blocking technology. Campus intranet, student e-mail accounts, and computer access in designated common areas are available to students. Students grades are available online. The school has a published electronic and media policy.

Contact Chris Bengel, Director of Admissions. 410-825-4266 Ext. 126. Fax: 410-825-6826. E-mail: bengelc@calverthall.com. Website: www.calverthall.com

CALVIN CHRISTIAN HIGH SCHOOL

2000 North Broadway
Escondido, California 92026

Head of School: Mr. Terry D. Kok

General Information Coeducational day college-preparatory, arts, and religious studies school, affiliated with Reformed Church, Presbyterian Church. Grades PK–12. Founded: 1980. Setting: suburban. Nearest major city is San Diego. 24-acre campus. 2 buildings on campus. Approved or accredited by Christian Schools International, Western Association of Schools and Colleges, and California Department of Education. Endowment: $830,000. Total enrollment: 491. Upper school average class size: 18. Upper school faculty-student ratio: 1:17. There are 175 required school days per year for Upper School students. Upper School students typically attend 5 days per week. The average school day consists of 6 hours and 25 minutes.

Upper School Student Profile Grade 9: 51 students (27 boys, 24 girls); Grade 10: 44 students (28 boys, 16 girls); Grade 11: 43 students (24 boys, 19 girls); Grade 12: 24 students (11 boys, 13 girls). 35% of students are Reformed, Presbyterian.

Faculty School total: 15. In upper school: 8 men, 7 women; 8 have advanced degrees.

Subjects Offered Advanced Placement courses, algebra, American government, art, band, Bible, biology, biology-AP, business mathematics, calculus-AP, chemistry, choir, Christian doctrine, Christian ethics, Christian studies, church history, computer applications, computer programming, computers, dramatic arts, economics, electives, English, English literature-AP, geometry, health, instrumental music, intro to computers, media, modern history, photography, physical education, physical science, physics, pre-calculus, psychology, robotics, Spanish, Spanish-AP, speech, U.S. history, U.S. history-AP, world history, World War II, yearbook.

Graduation Requirements Advanced Placement courses, arts and fine arts (art, music, dance, drama), English, foreign language, mathematics, media, physical education (includes health), religion (includes Bible studies and theology), science, social studies (includes history), technology, service-learning requirements.

Special Academic Programs 6 Advanced Placement exams for which test preparation is offered; remedial reading and/or remedial writing.

College Admission Counseling 31 students graduated in 2012; all went to college, including California State University, San Marcos; Calvin College; Dordt College; Point Loma Nazarene University; Trinity Christian College; University of California, San Diego. Mean SAT critical reading: 568, mean SAT math: 570, mean SAT writing: 549, mean composite ACT: 24. 43% scored over 600 on SAT critical reading, 36% scored over 600 on SAT math, 29% scored over 600 on SAT writing.

Student Life Upper grades have specified standards of dress, student council, honor system. Discipline rests primarily with faculty. Attendance at religious services is required.

Tuition and Aid Day student tuition: $8834. Tuition installment plan (monthly payment plans, individually arranged payment plans). Need-based scholarship grants, need-based loans available. In 2012–13, 30% of upper-school students received aid. Total amount of financial aid awarded in 2012–13: $228,000.

Admissions Traditional secondary-level entrance grade is 9. For fall 2012, 31 students applied for upper-level admission, 29 were accepted, 24 enrolled. Deadline for receipt of application materials: none. Application fee required: $300. Interview required.

Athletics Interscholastic: baseball (boys), basketball (b,g), cross-country running (b,g), football (b), soccer (b,g), softball (g), track and field (b,g), volleyball (g); coed interscholastic: golf, in-line hockey; coed intramural: weight training. 2 PE instructors, 16 coaches.

Computers Computers are regularly used in computer applications, keyboarding, photography, programming, science, yearbook classes. Computer network features include on-campus library services, Internet access, wireless campus network, Internet filtering or blocking technology. Student e-mail accounts are available to students. Students grades are available online. The school has a published electronic and media policy.

Contact Mr. Frank Steidl, Principal. 760-489-6430. Fax: 760-489-7055. E-mail: franksteidl@calvinchristianescondido.org. Website: www.calvinchristianescondido.org

CAMPBELL HALL (EPISCOPAL)

4533 Laurel Canyon Boulevard
North Hollywood, California 91607

Head of School: Rev. Julian Bull

General Information Coeducational day college-preparatory, arts, and technology school, affiliated with Episcopal Church. Grades K–12. Founded: 1944. Setting: suburban. Nearest major city is Los Angeles. 15-acre campus. 12 buildings on campus. Approved or accredited by The College Board, Western Association of Schools and Colleges, and California Department of Education. Member of National Association of Independent Schools. Endowment: $5 million. Total enrollment: 1,117. Upper school average class size: 15. Upper school faculty-student ratio: 1:8. There are 140 required school days per year for Upper School students. Upper School students typically attend 5 days per week. The average school day consists of 7 hours and 15 minutes.

Upper School Student Profile Grade 7: 116 students (61 boys, 55 girls); Grade 8: 114 students (58 boys, 56 girls); Grade 9: 135 students (72 boys, 63 girls); Grade 10: 153 students (84 boys, 69 girls); Grade 11: 127 students (61 boys, 66 girls); Grade 12: 132 students (65 boys, 67 girls). 7% of students are members of Episcopal Church.

Faculty School total: 110. In upper school: 23 men, 32 women; 30 have advanced degrees.

Subjects Offered Algebra, American history, American literature, American studies, ancient history, art, art history, astronomy, band, biology, calculus, ceramics, chemistry, Chinese, community service, computer programming, computer science, creative writing, dance, drama, drawing, earth science, ecology, economics, English, English literature, environmental science, ethics, European history, filmmaking, fine arts, French, geography, geometry, government/civics, history, human development, humanities, instrumental music, Japanese, law, mathematics, music, orchestra, painting, philosophy, photography, physical education, physics, physiology, pre-calculus, printmaking, psychology, science, sculpture, senior seminar, social studies, sociology, Spanish, speech, statistics, theater, theater arts, trigonometry, voice, yearbook.

Graduation Requirements Arts and fine arts (art, music, dance, drama), computer science, English, foreign language, mathematics, physical education (includes health), science, social studies (includes history). Community service is required.

Special Academic Programs Advanced Placement exam preparation; honors section; independent study; study at local college for college credit.

College Admission Counseling 129 students graduated in 2013; all went to college, including Boston University; Indiana University Bloomington; New York University; University of California, Los Angeles; University of Michigan; University of Southern California.

Student Life Upper grades have uniform requirement, student council, honor system. Discipline rests equally with students and faculty. Attendance at religious services is required.

Summer Programs Enrichment, advancement, sports, art/fine arts, computer instruction programs offered; session focuses on creative arts and sports; held on campus; accepts boys and girls; open to students from other schools. 200 students usually enrolled. 2014 schedule: June 16 to August 1. Application deadline: June 1.

Tuition and Aid Day student tuition: $26,980–$33,100. Tuition installment plan (Insured Tuition Payment Plan, monthly payment plans, individually arranged payment plans). Need-based scholarship grants, Episcopal Credit Union tuition loans available. In 2013–14, 25% of upper-school students received aid. Total amount of financial aid awarded in 2013–14: $4,000,000.

Admissions Traditional secondary-level entrance grade is 9. ISEE required. Deadline for receipt of application materials: December 18. Application fee required: $135. Interview required.

Athletics Interscholastic: aerobics/dance (boys, girls), ballet (b,g), baseball (b), basketball (b,g), cheering (b,g), cross-country running (b,g), dance (b,g), dance squad (b,g), equestrian sports (b,g), flag football (b,g), football (b), golf (b,g), horseback riding (b,g), modern dance (b,g), soccer (b,g), softball (g), tennis (b,g), track and field (b,g), volleyball (b,g); intramural: weight lifting (b,g); coed interscholastic: aerobics/dance, ballet, cheering, cross-country running, dance, dance squad, golf, horseback riding, modern dance, track and field. 5 PE instructors, 13 coaches, 2 athletic trainers.

Computers Computers are regularly used in art, English, foreign language, history, humanities, mathematics, science, theater arts classes. Computer network features include on-campus library services, online commercial services, Internet access, wireless campus network, Internet filtering or blocking technology. Campus intranet, student e-mail accounts, and computer access in designated common areas are available to students. The school has a published electronic and media policy.

Contact Ms. Alice Fleming, Director of Admissions. 818-980-7280. Fax: 818-762-3269. Website: www.campbellhall.org

See Display on next page and Close-Up on page 522.

CAMPHILL SPECIAL SCHOOL

Glenmoore, Pennsylvania
See Special Needs Schools section.

CANNON SCHOOL

5801 Poplar Tent Road
Concord, North Carolina 28027

Head of School: Mr. Matthew Gossage

General Information Coeducational day college-preparatory school. Grades PK–12. Founded: 1969. Setting: suburban. Nearest major city is Charlotte. 65-acre campus. 3 buildings on campus. Approved or accredited by Southern Association of Colleges and Schools, Southern Association of Independent Schools, and North Carolina Department of Education. Member of National Association of Independent Schools. Endowment: $2.8 million. Total enrollment: 905. Upper school average class size: 17. Upper school faculty-student ratio: 1:9.

Faculty School total: 97. In upper school: 18 men, 28 women; 27 have advanced degrees.

Subjects Offered Acting, advanced math, algebra, American history, American history-AP, American literature, anatomy and physiology, biology, biology-AP, British literature, calculus-AP, character education, chemistry, chemistry-AP, Chinese, chorus, college counseling, computer programming-AP, creative writing, dance, directing, discrete mathematics, drawing, English, English language-AP, English literature-AP, environmental science-AP, ethics, film and literature, film history, finance, French, French-AP, functions, geometry, jazz band, law and the legal system, marine science, mathematical modeling, painting, physics, physics-AP, playwriting, poetry, pre-calculus, psychology-AP, publications, sculpture, senior project, Spanish, Spanish language-AP, statistics-AP, strings, studio art-AP, theater design and production, trigonometry, U.S. government and politics-AP, visual arts, weight training, wind ensemble, world history, world literature, world religions, yearbook.

Graduation Requirements Arts and fine arts (art, music, dance, drama), biology, chemistry, computer literacy, English, foreign language, history, mathematics, physical education (includes health), science, senior project, trigonometry, U.S. history. Community service is required.

Special Academic Programs Advanced Placement exam preparation; honors section; independent study.

College Admission Counseling 87 students graduated in 2012; all went to college, including Appalachian State University; Clemson University; Emory University; Furman University; North Carolina State University; The University of North Carolina at Chapel Hill. Mean SAT critical reading: 610, mean SAT math: 624, mean SAT writing: 623, mean combined SAT: 1857, mean composite ACT: 27.

Student Life Upper grades have specified standards of dress, student council, honor system. Discipline rests equally with students and faculty.

Tuition and Aid Day student tuition: $18,170. Tuition installment plan (Insured Tuition Payment Plan, monthly payment plans). Need-based scholarship grants available. In 2012–13, 10% of upper-school students received aid. Total amount of financial aid awarded in 2012–13: $310,000.

Admissions Traditional secondary-level entrance grade is 9. For fall 2012, 79 students applied for upper-level admission, 33 were accepted, 24 enrolled. Admissions testing and ISEE required. Deadline for receipt of application materials: none. Application fee required: $90. On-campus interview required.

Athletics Interscholastic: baseball (boys), basketball (b,g), cheering (g), cross-country running (b,g), dance (g), dance team (g), football (b), golf (b,g), lacrosse (b), physical fitness (b,g), running (b,g), soccer (b,g), softball (g), strength & conditioning (b,g), swimming and diving (b,g), tennis (b,g), track and field (b,g), volleyball (g), weight training (b,g); coed interscholastic: fitness, golf, running, strength & conditioning, track and field, weight training; coed intramural: yoga. 6 PE instructors, 28 coaches, 1 athletic trainer.

Computers Computers are regularly used in all academic, art, music classes. Computer network features include on-campus library services, online commercial services, Internet access, wireless campus network, Internet filtering or blocking technology, productivity software. Campus intranet, student e-mail accounts, and computer access in designated common areas are available to students. Students grades are available online. The school has a published electronic and media policy.

Contact Mr. William D. Diskin, Director of Admission. 704-721-7164. Fax: 704-788-7779. E-mail: wdiskin@cannonschool.org. Website: www.cannonschool.org

THE CANTERBURY EPISCOPAL SCHOOL

1708 North Westmoreland Road
DeSoto, Texas 75115

Head of School: Mr. Sandy Doerge

General Information Coeducational day college-preparatory school, affiliated with Episcopal Church. Grades K–12. Founded: 1992. Setting: suburban. Nearest major city is Dallas. 36-acre campus. 2 buildings on campus. Approved or accredited by Southwest Association of Episcopal Schools, Tennessee Association of Independent Schools, and Texas Department of Education. Member of National Association of Independent Schools. Total enrollment: 251. Upper school average class size: 11. Upper school faculty-student ratio: 1:11. There are 173 required school days per year for Upper School students. Upper School students typically attend 5 days per week. The average school day consists of 6 hours and 50 minutes.

Upper School Student Profile Grade 9: 28 students (16 boys, 12 girls); Grade 10: 20 students (11 boys, 9 girls); Grade 11: 22 students (15 boys, 7 girls); Grade 12: 10 students (1 boy, 9 girls). 5% of students are members of Episcopal Church.

Faculty School total: 36. In upper school: 8 men, 11 women; 9 have advanced degrees.

Subjects Offered 1 1/2 elective credits, advanced chemistry, Advanced Placement courses, algebra, American government, American literature, anatomy and physiology, art history-AP, athletics, basketball, biology, biology-AP, calculus, calculus-AP, cheerleading, chemistry, chemistry-AP, college counseling, comparative religion, computer applications, debate, economics, English composition, English language and composition-AP, English literature, English literature and composition-AP, environmental science-AP, European history-AP, fine arts, foreign language, geometry, government, health, math applications, music, personal money management, physics-AP, psychology-AP, Spanish, speech, studio art, theology, U.S. history, U.S. history-AP, visual and performing arts, world geography, world history, yearbook.

Graduation Requirements 1 1/2 elective credits, algebra, anatomy and physiology, arts and fine arts (art, music, dance, drama), biology, calculus, chemistry, computer applications, economics, English, English composition, English language and composition-AP, English literature, European history, foreign language, geometry, government, health, math applications, physical education (includes health), physics, pre-calculus, religion (includes Bible studies and theology), speech, trigonometry, U.S. history, world geography, Senior Thesis in English IV.

Special Academic Programs 9 Advanced Placement exams for which test preparation is offered; honors section; independent study; study at local college for college credit.

College Admission Counseling 23 students graduated in 2012; all went to college. Median SAT critical reading: 574, median SAT math: 553, median SAT writing: 574, median combined SAT: 1686, median composite ACT: 25. 35% scored over 600 on SAT critical reading, 18% scored over 600 on SAT math, 41% scored over 600 on SAT writing, 29% scored over 1800 on combined SAT, 33% scored over 26 on composite ACT.

Student Life Upper grades have uniform requirement, student council, honor system. Discipline rests primarily with faculty. Attendance at religious services is required.

Tuition and Aid Day student tuition: $14,932. Tuition installment plan (FACTS Tuition Payment Plan, individually arranged payment plans). Tuition reduction for siblings, need-based scholarship grants available. In 2012–13, 45% of upper-school students received aid.

Admissions Traditional secondary-level entrance grade is 9. For fall 2012, 15 students applied for upper-level admission, 12 were accepted, 9 enrolled. OLSAT, Stanford Achievement Test required. Deadline for receipt of application materials: none. Application fee required: $150. Interview required.

Athletics Interscholastic: baseball (boys), basketball (b,g), cheering (g), golf (b), softball (g), volleyball (g); intramural: flag football (b); coed interscholastic: soccer, swimming and diving, tennis, track and field. 1 PE instructor, 1 coach, 1 athletic trainer.

Campbell Hall
EPISCOPAL

Coeducational, K-12, College Preparatory

Campbell Hall, founded in 1944, is an independent, co-educational, college preparatory, Episcopal day school for students in kindergarten through grade 12. *The school is a community of inquiry committed to academic excellence and to the nurturing of decent, loving, and responsible human beings.* The school provides a climate where the values of community, self-worth, compassion, respect, service, and responsibility are taught as part of the school's Judeo-Christian tradition.

The mission of Campbell Hall is to nurture the soul and character of all students entrusted to its care. Themes of faith and reason are central to the school's philosophy. Campbell Hall honors its Episcopal tradition as a place of open inquiry and of spiritual formation through its chapel, community service, counseling, human development, and environmental education programs. Campbell Hall seeks students willing to accept the challenge of a rigorous academic program and who will be contributing members of the school community by actively participating in a wide variety of school activities.

The college preparatory curriculum at the secondary level readies our students for the subject mastery and learning processes necessary for advanced study in all disciplines: English, mathematics, science, world languages, history, the visual arts, the performing arts, computer science, human development, experiential education, and physical education. Supporting and enriching this core curriculum is a variety of studies and experiences both within and beyond the classroom walls. The school and its faculty endeavor to explore and build a knowledge base of both intellectual and personal skills for our students, which nurture the development of reasoning and independent critical thinking throughout their lives.

4533 Laurel Canyon Blvd., North Hollywood 91607   (818) 980-7280   www.campbellhall.org

Campbell Hall admits students of any religion, race, sexual orientation, national or ethnic origin to all rights, privileges, programs, and activities generally accorded or made available to students at the school. It does not discriminate on the basis of any of the aforementioned facets of diversity or any other legally protected status in administration of its educational policies, admission policies, financial aid and loan programs, and athletic and other school-administered programs.

Computers Computers are regularly used in computer applications, yearbook classes. Computer resources include Internet access, Internet filtering or blocking technology. Computer access in designated common areas is available to students. Students grades are available online.

Contact Mrs. Libby Conder, Director of Admissions and Development. 972-572-7200 Ext. 106. Fax: 972-572-2470. E-mail: ConderL@TheCanterburySchool.org. Website: www.thecanterburyschool.org/

CANTERBURY SCHOOL

8141 College Parkway
Fort Myers, Florida 33919

Head of School: Mr. John Anthony (Tony) Paulus II

General Information Coeducational day college-preparatory and liberal arts school. Grades PK–12. Founded: 1964. Setting: suburban. Nearest major city is Fort Myers-Sarasota. 33-acre campus. 7 buildings on campus. Approved or accredited by Council of Accreditation and School Improvement, Southern Association of Colleges and Schools, Southern Association of Independent Schools, The College Board, and Florida Department of Education. Member of National Association of Independent Schools and Secondary School Admission Test Board. Endowment: $7.1 million. Total enrollment: 580. Upper school average class size: 18. Upper school faculty-student ratio: 1:10. There are 181 required school days per year for Upper School students. Upper School students typically attend 5 days per week. The average school day consists of 7 hours and 10 minutes.

Upper School Student Profile Grade 9: 62 students (36 boys, 26 girls); Grade 10: 54 students (23 boys, 31 girls); Grade 11: 46 students (21 boys, 25 girls); Grade 12: 37 students (18 boys, 19 girls).

Faculty School total: 95. In upper school: 21 men, 19 women; 22 have advanced degrees.

Subjects Offered Advanced Placement courses, algebra, American history, American history-AP, American literature, anatomy, art, art history, biology, biology-AP, British literature, calculus, calculus-AP, ceramics, chemistry, chemistry-AP, comparative government and politics-AP, computer programming, constitutional law, creative writing, critical writing, drama, earth science, ecology, economics, English, English literature, English literature-AP, environmental science-AP, European history, fine arts, French, French language-AP, geography, geometry, government-AP, government/civics, grammar, health, history, Latin, leadership, macroeconomics-AP, marine biology, mathematics, music, nationalism and ethnic conflict, photography, physical education, physics, physics-AP, physiology, SAT preparation, science, social studies, sociology, Spanish, Spanish language-AP, speech, statistics, theater, U.S. government and politics-AP, U.S. history, United Nations and international issues, world history, world literature, writing, yearbook.

Graduation Requirements Arts and fine arts (art, music, dance, drama), English, foreign language, mathematics, physical education (includes health), science, social studies (includes history), speech. Community service is required.

Special Academic Programs 15 Advanced Placement exams for which test preparation is offered; independent study; study at local college for college credit.

College Admission Counseling 37 students graduated in 2013; all went to college, including Boston College; Harvard University; University of Florida; University of Miami; University of Pennsylvania; University of South Florida. Mean SAT critical reading: 630, mean SAT math: 620, mean SAT writing: 630, mean combined SAT: 1850, mean composite ACT: 27.

Student Life Upper grades have specified standards of dress, student council, honor system. Discipline rests primarily with faculty.

Summer Programs Remediation, enrichment, advancement, sports, art/fine arts programs offered; session focuses on academic enrichment; held on campus; accepts boys and girls; open to students from other schools. 125 students usually enrolled. 2014 schedule: June 14 to July 30. Application deadline: none.

Tuition and Aid Day student tuition: $19,155. Tuition installment plan (Insured Tuition Payment Plan, monthly payment plans, individually arranged payment plans, quarterly payment plan). Merit scholarship grants, need-based scholarship grants available. In 2013–14, 25% of upper-school students received aid; total upper-school merit-scholarship money awarded: $274,100. Total amount of financial aid awarded in 2013–14: $782,050.

Admissions Traditional secondary-level entrance grade is 9. For fall 2013, 35 students applied for upper-level admission, 24 were accepted, 17 enrolled. ERB CTP IV or SSAT required. Deadline for receipt of application materials: none. Application fee required: $100. Interview required.

Athletics Interscholastic: baseball (boys), basketball (b,g), cheering (g), football (b), lacrosse (b,g), soccer (b,g), volleyball (g), winter soccer (b,g); intramural: volleyball (b); coed interscholastic: cross-country running, golf, swimming and diving, tennis, track and field. 6 PE instructors, 26 coaches.

Computers Computers are regularly used in art, college planning, English, foreign language, French, history, independent study, journalism, Latin, library, mathematics, science, social sciences, Spanish, speech, theater arts, yearbook classes. Computer network features include on-campus library services, Internet access, wireless campus network, Internet filtering or blocking technology. Campus intranet, student e-mail accounts, and computer access in designated common areas are available to students.

Students grades are available online. The school has a published electronic and media policy.

Contact Ms. Julie A. Peters, Director of Admission. 239-415-8945. Fax: 239-481-8339. E-mail: jpeters@canterburyfortmyers.org. Website: www.canterburyfortmyers.org

See Display on next page and Close-Up on page 524.

THE CANTERBURY SCHOOL OF FLORIDA

990 62nd Avenue NE
St. Petersburg, Florida 33702

Head of School: Mr. Mac H. Hall

General Information Coeducational day college-preparatory, arts, and marine studies, international program school, affiliated with Episcopal Church. Grades PK–12. Founded: 1968. Setting: suburban. 20-acre campus. 5 buildings on campus. Approved or accredited by The College Board and Florida Department of Education. Member of National Association of Independent Schools. Total enrollment: 450. Upper school average class size: 15. Upper school faculty-student ratio: 1:7. There are 180 required school days per year for Upper School students. Upper School students typically attend 5 days per week. The average school day consists of 7 hours and 23 minutes.

Upper School Student Profile Grade 9: 44 students (19 boys, 25 girls); Grade 10: 41 students (20 boys, 21 girls); Grade 11: 43 students (27 boys, 16 girls); Grade 12: 48 students (21 boys, 27 girls). 20% of students are members of Episcopal Church.

Faculty School total: 80. In upper school: 7 men, 17 women; 15 have advanced degrees.

Subjects Offered 20th century world history, advanced computer applications, Advanced Placement courses, advanced studio art-AP, algebra, American government, American history-AP, American literature, anatomy, Ancient Greek, ancient world history, art, art history, art history-AP, astronomy, athletics, band, Basic programming, biology, biology-AP, British literature, British literature (honors), calculus, calculus-AP, career exploration, ceramics, character education, chemistry, chemistry-AP, choir, choral music, chorus, classical language, classical studies, college counseling, college placement, communication skills, community service, comparative government and politics-AP, competitive science projects, computer multimedia, computer science, computer science-AP, computer skills, contemporary issues, creative writing, critical thinking, dance, dance performance, digital imaging, drama, earth science, economics, economics-AP, English, English composition, English language and composition-AP, English literature, English literature and composition-AP, English literature-AP, environmental science, environmental science-AP, environmental studies, ethics, European history, expository writing, film studies, fine arts, finite math, foreign language, French, French-AP, freshman seminar, geography, geometry, golf, government and politics-AP, government/civics, grammar, Greek culture, guitar, health, history, history of music, history-AP, honors algebra, honors geometry, honors U.S. history, honors world history, human geography - AP, independent living, interdisciplinary studies, journalism, keyboarding, Latin, Latin-AP, leadership, leadership and service, library, library research, library skills, life management skills, life science, life skills, macro/microeconomics-AP, macroeconomics-AP, Mandarin, marine biology, marine ecology, marine science, marine studies, mathematics, mathematics-AP, mechanical drawing, mentorship program, modern world history, multimedia, music, musical productions, musical theater, oceanography, outdoor education, personal and social education, personal fitness, photojournalism, physical education, physical science, physics, physics-AP, play production, portfolio art, pottery, prayer/spirituality, pre-algebra, pre-calculus, pre-college orientation, psychology, psychology-AP, reading/study skills, robotics, SAT preparation, SAT/ACT preparation, science, senior composition, senior seminar, senior thesis, Shakespeare, social sciences, social studies, Spanish, Spanish language-AP, Spanish literature-AP, Spanish-AP, speech, speech and debate, sports conditioning, stagecraft, statistics-AP, student government, student publications, student teaching, studio art-AP, swimming, technical theater, tennis, theater arts, theater design and production, theater history, theater production, track and field, typing, U.S. history, U.S. history-AP, values and decisions, visual and performing arts, volleyball, weight fitness, weight training, Western philosophy, world history, world literature, world religions, yearbook, yoga.

Graduation Requirements Arts and fine arts (art, music, dance, drama), career/college preparation, electives, English, ethics, foreign language, history, mathematics, physical education (includes health), research, science, senior seminar, writing, research and writing, mini-term, character education. Community service is required.

Special Academic Programs 23 Advanced Placement exams for which test preparation is offered; honors section; independent study; term-away projects; study at local college for college credit; study abroad; ESL (6 students enrolled).

College Admission Counseling 36 students graduated in 2013; all went to college, including Columbia University; Southern Methodist University; University of Florida; University of South Florida; Washington and Lee University. Mean combined SAT: 1638, mean composite ACT: 23.

Student Life Upper grades have specified standards of dress, student council, honor system. Discipline rests equally with students and faculty. Attendance at religious services is required.

Summer Programs Remediation, enrichment, advancement, sports, art/fine arts, computer instruction programs offered; session focuses on multi-discipline skills and abilities; held on campus; accepts boys and girls; open to students from other schools. 50 students usually enrolled. 2014 schedule: June 9 to August 8. Application deadline: March 15.

Tuition and Aid Day student tuition: $16,975. Tuition installment plan (Insured Tuition Payment Plan, monthly payment plans, individually arranged payment plans). Tuition reduction for siblings, need-based scholarship grants available. In 2013–14, 15% of upper-school students received aid.

Admissions Traditional secondary-level entrance grade is 9. For fall 2013, 50 students applied for upper-level admission, 32 were accepted, 25 enrolled. 3-R Achievement Test, any standardized test, ERB, SSAT or TOEFL required. Deadline for receipt of application materials: none. Application fee required: $75. On-campus interview required.

Athletics Interscholastic: baseball (boys), basketball (b,g), cross-country running (b,g), dance (g), dance team (g), diving (b,g), football (b), golf (b,g), soccer (b,g), softball (g), swimming and diving (b,g), tennis (b,g), track and field (b,g), volleyball (g); intramural: yoga (g); coed interscholastic: cheering, soccer; coed intramural: canoeing/kayaking, fitness, flag football, floor hockey, hiking/backpacking, kayaking, kickball, modern dance, outdoor activities, outdoor adventure, outdoor education, paddle tennis, physical fitness, ropes courses, running, scuba diving, strength & conditioning, ultimate Frisbee, weight training. 2 PE instructors, 21 coaches, 1 athletic trainer.

Computers Computers are regularly used in all academic classes. Computer network features include on-campus library services, online commercial services, Internet access, wireless campus network, Internet filtering or blocking technology, iPad program for grades 3, 4 and 6 (each child receives an iPad). Computer access in designated common areas is available to students. Students grades are available online. The school has a published electronic and media policy.

Contact Mrs. Michelle Robinson, Director of Advancement and Admission. 727-521-5903. Fax: 727-525-2545. E-mail: mrobinson@canterburyflorida.org. Website: www.canterburyflorida.org

CANTON ACADEMY

Post Office Box 116
One Nancy Drive
Canton, Mississippi 39046

Head of School: Mr. Phil Hannon

General Information Coeducational day college-preparatory, arts, and religious studies school; primarily serves individuals with Attention Deficit Disorder and dyslexic students. Grades 6–12. Founded: 1965. Setting: small town. Nearest major city is Jackson. 1 building on campus. Approved or accredited by Mississippi Private School Association, Southern Association of Independent Schools, and Mississippi Department of Education. Total enrollment: 333. Upper school average class size: 17. Upper school faculty-student ratio: 1:17. There are 175 required school days per year for Upper School students. Upper School students typically attend 5 days per week. The average school day consists of 7 hours and 20 minutes.

Faculty School total: 60. In upper school: 6 men, 7 women.

Graduation Requirements Accounting, advanced biology, community service hours.

Special Academic Programs Honors section; independent study; study at local college for college credit; academic accommodation for the gifted; remedial reading and/or remedial writing; remedial math; programs in English, mathematics for dyslexic students.

College Admission Counseling 32 students graduated in 2012; all went to college, including Delta State University; Millsaps College; Mississippi College; Mississippi State University; University of Mississippi; University of Southern Mississippi.

Student Life Upper grades have specified standards of dress, student council, honor system. Discipline rests primarily with faculty. Attendance at religious services is required.

Tuition and Aid Tuition installment plan (monthly payment plans, individually arranged payment plans). Tuition reduction for siblings, need-based scholarship grants, paying campus jobs available. In 2012–13, 18% of upper-school students received aid. Total amount of financial aid awarded in 2012–13: $64,000.

Admissions Traditional secondary-level entrance grade is 10. For fall 2012, 15 students applied for upper-level admission, 13 were accepted, 13 enrolled. Comprehensive Test of Basic Skills required. Deadline for receipt of application materials: January 26. Application fee required: $35. Interview recommended.

Athletics Interscholastic: aerobics/dance (girls), archery (b,g), baseball (b,g), basketball (b,g), cheering (g), combined training (b,g), cross-country running (b,g), dance team (g), equestrian sports (b,g), football (b), golf (b), horseback riding (b,g), jogging (b,g), power lifting (b), running (b,g), soccer (b,g), softball (g), swimming and diving (b,g), tennis (b,g), track and field (b,g), weight training (b,g). 2 PE instructors, 8 coaches, 2 athletic trainers.

Computers Computer resources include Internet access. Campus intranet and student e-mail accounts are available to students. Students grades are available online. The school has a published electronic and media policy.

Contact Ms. Laura Pitre, Admissions. 601-859-5231. Fax: 601-859-5232. E-mail: lpitre@cantonacademy.org. Website: www.cantonacademy.org

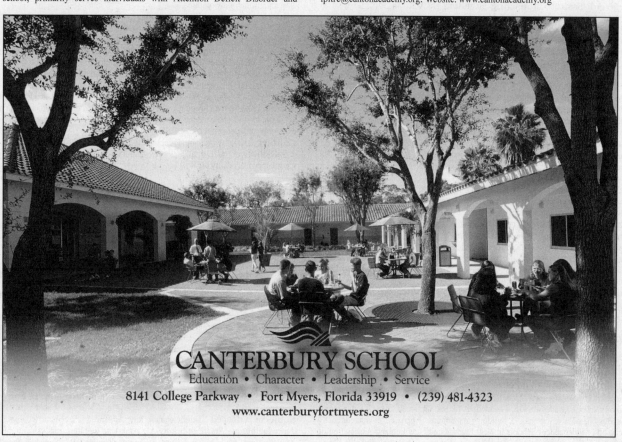

CANYONVILLE CHRISTIAN ACADEMY

PO Box 1100
Canyonville, Oregon 97417-1100
Head of School: Mrs. Cathy Lovato

General Information Coeducational boarding and day college-preparatory, general academic, religious studies, and English for Speakers of Other Languages school, affiliated with Christian faith. Grades 9–12. Founded: 1924. Setting: rural. Nearest major city is Medford. Students are housed in single-sex dormitories. 10-acre campus. 11 buildings on campus. Approved or accredited by Association of Christian Schools International, Northwest Accreditation Commission, The Association of Boarding Schools, and Oregon Department of Education. Upper school average class size: 20. Upper school faculty-student ratio: 1:9. There are 180 required school days per year for Upper School students. Upper School students typically attend 5 days per week. The average school day consists of 7 hours.

Upper School Student Profile Grade 9: 13 students (8 boys, 5 girls); Grade 10: 33 students (16 boys, 17 girls); Grade 11: 43 students (27 boys, 16 girls); Grade 12: 35 students (25 boys, 10 girls). 90% of students are boarding students. 10% are state residents. 4 states are represented in upper school student body. 85% are international students. International students from China, Colombia, Hong Kong, Russian Federation, Rwanda, and Taiwan; 6 other countries represented in student body. 70% of students are Christian faith.

Faculty School total: 14. In upper school: 6 men, 8 women; 3 have advanced degrees; 4 reside on campus.

Subjects Offered Advanced Placement courses, aerobics, algebra, American culture, American history, art, Bible, biology, calculus, calculus-AP, career/college preparation, chemistry, choir, Christian doctrine, composition, computer education, computer technologies, computers, consumer economics, desktop publishing, digital art, economics, English, English literature, ESL, foreign language, French as a second language, general science, government, grammar, health, integrative seminar, keyboarding, language and composition, library assistant, Life of Christ, mathematics, New Testament, physical education, physical science, physics, pre-calculus, religious education, Spanish, speech and debate, theology, U.S. government, U.S. history, United States government-AP, world history.

Graduation Requirements 1 1/2 elective credits, algebra, arts and fine arts (art, music, dance, drama), Bible, biology, economics, English, foreign language, government, health and wellness, mathematics, physical education (includes health), physical science, speech and debate, U.S. history, world history.

Special Academic Programs Advanced Placement exam preparation; honors section; accelerated programs; independent study; study at local college for college credit; ESL (50 students enrolled).

College Admission Counseling 30 students graduated in 2012; 25 went to college, including Oregon State University; Sarah Lawrence College; University of Illinois at Urbana–Champaign; University of Oregon; Washington State University. Other: 1 entered military service, 2 had other specific plans. Mean SAT critical reading: 421, mean SAT math: 571, mean SAT writing: 411, mean combined SAT: 1403.

Student Life Upper grades have specified standards of dress, student council, honor system. Discipline rests primarily with faculty. Attendance at religious services is required.

Tuition and Aid Day student tuition: $4600; 7-day tuition and room/board: $24,500. Tuition installment plan (monthly payment plans, individually arranged payment plans). Tuition reduction for siblings, merit scholarship grants, need-based scholarship grants, paying campus jobs available. In 2012–13, 15% of upper-school students received aid. Total amount of financial aid awarded in 2012–13: $390,000.

Admissions Traditional secondary-level entrance grade is 9. TOEFL or SLEP required. Deadline for receipt of application materials: none. Application fee required: $100. Interview recommended.

Athletics Interscholastic: basketball (boys, girls), cheering (g), cross-country running (b,g), soccer (b), tennis (b,g), track and field (b,g), volleyball (g); intramural: aerobics (g), soccer (b); coed interscholastic: soccer, tennis; coed intramural: badminton, basketball, billiards, table tennis, tennis, volleyball. 3 PE instructors, 9 coaches.

Computers Computers are regularly used in business applications, drawing and design, technology, yearbook classes. Computer network features include Internet access, wireless campus network, Internet filtering or blocking technology. Student e-mail accounts and computer access in designated common areas are available to students. Students grades are available online.

Contact Mr. Ed Lovato, Director of Admissions. 541-839-4401. Fax: 541-839-6228. E-mail: admissions@canyonville.net. Website: www.canyonville.net

CAPE COD ACADEMY

50 Osterville-West Barnstable Road
Osterville, Massachusetts 02655
Head of School: Mr. Philip Petru

General Information Coeducational day college-preparatory, arts, and technology school. Grades PK–12. Founded: 1976. Setting: small town. Nearest major city is Boston. 47-acre campus. 5 buildings on campus. Approved or accredited by Association of Independent Schools in New England and New England Association of Schools and Colleges. Member of National Association of Independent Schools and

Secondary School Admission Test Board. Endowment: $2.2 million. Total enrollment: 317. Upper school average class size: 13. Upper school faculty-student ratio: 1:4. There are 172 required school days per year for Upper School students. Upper School students typically attend 5 days per week. The average school day consists of 6 hours and 30 minutes.

Upper School Student Profile Grade 9: 25 students (12 boys, 13 girls); Grade 10: 30 students (14 boys, 16 girls); Grade 11: 56 students (30 boys, 26 girls); Grade 12: 44 students (25 boys, 19 girls).

Faculty School total: 52. In upper school: 19 men, 20 women; 28 have advanced degrees.

Subjects Offered Advanced biology, advanced chemistry, advanced math, Advanced Placement courses, advanced studio art-AP, algebra, American history, American literature, art, art history, art history-AP, art-AP, biology, calculus, calculus-AP, ceramics, chemistry, chemistry-AP, community service, computer math, computer programming, computer science, digital photography, drama, earth science, English, English literature, English-AP, environmental science, ethics, European history, expository writing, fine arts, French, French-AP, geography, geometry, health, history, history-AP, honors algebra, honors geometry, Latin, mathematics, music, music composition, music history, music theory, philosophy, photography, physical education, physics, SAT preparation, science, senior internship, social sciences, social studies, Spanish, Spanish-AP, statistics-AP, studio art-AP, theater, trigonometry, world history, world literature.

Graduation Requirements Arts and fine arts (art, music, dance, drama), computer science, English, foreign language, history, independent study, mathematics, physical education (includes health), science. Community service is required.

Special Academic Programs 10 Advanced Placement exams for which test preparation is offered; honors section; independent study; term-away projects; study abroad.

College Admission Counseling 27 students graduated in 2013; all went to college, including Boston College; Boston University; Roger Williams University; University of Massachusetts Amherst; University of Pennsylvania; Wheaton College. Mean SAT critical reading: 600, mean SAT math: 620.

Student Life Upper grades have specified standards of dress, student council, honor system. Discipline rests primarily with faculty.

Tuition and Aid Day student tuition: $21,150–$25,290. Tuition installment plan (Academic Management Services Plan, SMART Tuition Payment Plan, monthly payment plans, individually arranged payment plans). Need-based scholarship grants available. In 2013–14, 40% of upper-school students received aid. Total amount of financial aid awarded in 2013–14: $1,600,000.

Admissions Traditional secondary-level entrance grade is 9. ISEE or SSAT required. Deadline for receipt of application materials: February 1. Application fee required: $95. On-campus interview required.

Athletics Interscholastic: baseball (boys), basketball (b,g), lacrosse (b,g), soccer (b,g), tennis (b,g); coed interscholastic: cross-country running, golf, ice hockey, sailing; coed intramural: aerobics, aerobics/Nautilus, archery, basketball, combined training, fitness, floor hockey, physical training, sailing, soccer, strength & conditioning, weight training. 1 PE instructor, 11 coaches, 1 athletic trainer.

Computers Computers are regularly used in all academic classes. Computer network features include on-campus library services, online commercial services, Internet access, wireless campus network, Internet filtering or blocking technology. Campus intranet, student e-mail accounts, and computer access in designated common areas are available to students. Students grades are available online. The school has a published electronic and media policy.

Contact Laurie Wyndham, Director of Admissions. 508-428-5400 Ext. 226. Fax: 508-428-0701. E-mail: lwyndham@capecodacademy.org. Website: www.capecodacademy.org

CAPE FEAR ACADEMY

3900 South College Road
Wilmington, North Carolina 28412
Head of School: Mr. Donald Berger

General Information Coeducational day college-preparatory and arts school. Grades PK–12. Founded: 1967. Setting: suburban. 27-acre campus. 4 buildings on campus. Approved or accredited by Southern Association of Colleges and Schools, Southern Association of Independent Schools, and North Carolina Department of Education. Member of National Association of Independent Schools. Endowment: $733,149. Total enrollment: 573. Upper school average class size: 17. Upper school faculty-student ratio: 1:7. There are 177 required school days per year for Upper School students. Upper School students typically attend 5 days per week. The average school day consists of 7 hours and 20 minutes.

Upper School Student Profile Grade 9: 39 students (21 boys, 18 girls); Grade 10: 57 students (29 boys, 28 girls); Grade 11: 60 students (26 boys, 34 girls); Grade 12: 66 students (30 boys, 36 girls).

Faculty School total: 70. In upper school: 11 men, 19 women; 13 have advanced degrees.

Subjects Offered 3-dimensional art, Advanced Placement courses, algebra, American history, American history-AP, American literature, analysis, art, art history, band, biology, biology-AP, British literature, calculus-AP, chemistry, choral music, comparative government and politics-AP, computer science, conceptual physics, critical studies in film, discrete mathematics, drama, earth and space science, English, English language-AP, English literature, English literature-AP, environmental science, environmental science-AP, European history, European history-AP, film studies, finance, fine arts, fitness, geometry, global studies, government and politics-AP, government-AP, history, honors geometry, human anatomy, independent study, journalism, language, literature, marine science, mathematics, music, music theory-AP, musical theater, newspaper, organizational studies, photography, physical education, physics, pre-calculus, psychology, publications, religion, SAT preparation, science, sculpture, social studies, Spanish, student publications, theater, video film production, vocal ensemble, weight training, world history.

Graduation Requirements Arts and fine arts (art, music, dance, drama), biology, English, foreign language, mathematics, physical education (includes health), science, social studies (includes history), U.S. government, U.S. history, 72 hours of community service over 4 years. Community service is required.

Special Academic Programs 11 Advanced Placement exams for which test preparation is offered; honors section; independent study; study at local college for college credit; study abroad.

College Admission Counseling 65 students graduated in 2013; all went to college, including East Carolina University; North Carolina State University; The University of North Carolina at Chapel Hill; The University of North Carolina Wilmington. Mean combined SAT: 1768, mean composite ACT: 26.

Student Life Upper grades have specified standards of dress, student council, honor system. Discipline rests primarily with faculty.

Summer Programs Enrichment, advancement, sports, art/fine arts, computer instruction programs offered; session focuses on enrichment and sports; held on campus; accepts boys and girls; open to students from other schools. 250 students usually enrolled. 2014 schedule: June 12 to August 8. Application deadline: none.

Tuition and Aid Day student tuition: $15,443. Tuition installment plan (Insured Tuition Payment Plan, FACTS Tuition Payment Plan, monthly payment plans). Merit scholarship grants, need-based scholarship grants available. In 2013–14, 14% of upper-school students received aid; total upper-school merit-scholarship money awarded: $40,490. Total amount of financial aid awarded in 2013–14: $223,729.

Admissions Traditional secondary-level entrance grade is 9. ERB, ISEE, PSAT or SAT or SSAT required. Deadline for receipt of application materials: none. Application fee required: $75. On-campus interview recommended.

Athletics Interscholastic: basketball (boys, girls), cheering (g), field hockey (g), lacrosse (b,g), soccer (b,g), tennis (b,g), volleyball (g); coed interscholastic: cross-country running, golf, outdoor education, outdoor recreation, surfing, swimming and diving. 2 PE instructors, 11 coaches, 1 athletic trainer.

Computers Computers are regularly used in all academic classes. Computer network features include on-campus library services, online commercial services, Internet access, wireless campus network, Internet filtering or blocking technology. Campus intranet, student e-mail accounts, and computer access in designated common areas are available to students. Students grades are available online. The school has a published electronic and media policy.

Contact Mrs. Carla Whitwell, Director of Admission. 910-791-0287 Ext. 1015. Fax: 910-791-0290. E-mail: cwhitwell@capefearacademy.org. Website: www.capefearacademy.org

CAPE HENRY COLLEGIATE SCHOOL

1320 Mill Dam Road
Virginia Beach, Virginia 23454-2306

Head of School: Dr. John P. Lewis

General Information Coeducational day college-preparatory, arts, technology, and global education school. Grades PK–12. Founded: 1924. Setting: suburban. 30-acre campus. 9 buildings on campus. Approved or accredited by Southern Association of Independent Schools and Virginia Association of Independent Schools. Member of National Association of Independent Schools. Endowment: $6 million. Total enrollment: 863. Upper school average class size: 14. Upper school faculty-student ratio: 1:10. There are 176 required school days per year for Upper School students. Upper School students typically attend 5 days per week. The average school day consists of 7 hours and 20 minutes.

Upper School Student Profile Grade 9: 68 students (42 boys, 26 girls); Grade 10: 106 students (59 boys, 47 girls); Grade 11: 106 students (51 boys, 55 girls); Grade 12: 102 students (61 boys, 41 girls).

Faculty School total: 107. In upper school: 19 men, 23 women; 28 have advanced degrees.

Subjects Offered Algebra, American history, American literature, art, art history, biology, botany, business skills, calculus, ceramics, chemistry, community service, computer programming, computer science, creative writing, drama, driver education, earth science, ecology, economics, English, English literature, environmental science, European history, expository writing, fine arts, French, geography, geology, geometry, government/civics, health, history, journalism, Latin, law, marine biology, mathematics, music, oceanography, photography, physical education, physics, science, social sciences, social studies, sociology, Spanish, speech, statistics, theater, trigonometry, world history, world literature, writing.

Graduation Requirements Arts and fine arts (art, music, dance, drama), computer science, English, foreign language, mathematics, physical education (includes health), science, social sciences, social studies (includes history). Community service is required.

Special Academic Programs Advanced Placement exam preparation; honors section; independent study; academic accommodation for the gifted, the musically talented, and the artistically talented; ESL (10 students enrolled).

College Admission Counseling 92 students graduated in 2013; all went to college, including Hampden-Sydney College; James Madison University; The College of William and Mary; University of Virginia; Virginia Polytechnic Institute and State University; Washington and Lee University.

Student Life Upper grades have specified standards of dress, student council, honor system. Discipline rests equally with students and faculty.

Summer Programs Enrichment, advancement, ESL, sports, art/fine arts, computer instruction programs offered; session focuses on academics and enrichment; held on campus; accepts boys and girls; open to students from other schools. 1,200 students usually enrolled. 2014 schedule: June 9 to August 15. Application deadline: none.

Tuition and Aid Day student tuition: $18,445. Tuition installment plan (The Tuition Plan, Insured Tuition Payment Plan, monthly payment plans, individually arranged payment plans, 3-payment plan). Merit scholarship grants, need-based scholarship grants available. In 2013–14, 20% of upper-school students received aid.

Admissions Traditional secondary-level entrance grade is 9. For fall 2013, 108 students applied for upper-level admission, 83 were accepted, 51 enrolled. Brigance Test of Basic Skills, ERB CTP, ISEE or writing sample required. Deadline for receipt of application materials: none. Application fee required: $50. On-campus interview required.

Athletics Interscholastic: baseball (boys), basketball (b,g), crew (b,g), cross-country running (b,g), field hockey (g), fitness (b,g), golf (b,g), lacrosse (b,g), physical fitness (b,g), soccer (b,g), softball (g), tennis (b,g), volleyball (b,g), wrestling (b); intramural: baseball (b), basketball (b,g), crew (b,g), cross-country running (b,g), field hockey (g), floor hockey (b,g), wrestling (b); coed interscholastic: cheering, dance, swimming and diving, track and field; coed intramural: aerobics, aerobics/dance, aerobics/Nautilus, archery, backpacking, badminton, ballet, cheering, dance, fishing, fitness, fitness walking, golf, hiking/backpacking, jogging, kayaking, lacrosse, modern dance, ocean paddling, outdoor activities, outdoor adventure, physical fitness, physical training, skiing (downhill), snowboarding, soccer, strength & conditioning, surfing, swimming and diving, table tennis, tennis, volleyball, weight lifting, weight training, wilderness, yoga. 3 PE instructors, 25 coaches, 1 athletic trainer.

Computers Computers are regularly used in computer applications, desktop publishing, graphic arts, information technology, literary magazine, newspaper, publications, technology, video film production, Web site design, word processing, yearbook classes. Computer network features include on-campus library services, online commercial services, Internet access, wireless campus network, Internet filtering or blocking technology. Student e-mail accounts and computer access in designated common areas are available to students. Students grades are available online. The school has a published electronic and media policy.

Contact Mrs. Angie Finley, Admissions Associate. 757-963-8234. Fax: 757-481-9194. E-mail: angiefinley@capehenry.org. Website: www.capehenrycollegiate.org

CAPISTRANO VALLEY CHRISTIAN SCHOOLS

32032 Del Obispo Street
San Juan Capistrano, California 92675

Head of School: Dr. Ron Sipus

General Information Coeducational day college-preparatory, arts, business, vocational, religious studies, bilingual studies, and technology school, affiliated with Christian faith. Grades JK–12. Founded: 1972. Setting: suburban. 8-acre campus. 3 buildings on campus. Approved or accredited by American Association of Christian Schools, Western Association of Schools and Colleges, and California Department of Education. Total enrollment: 396. Upper school average class size: 18. Upper school faculty-student ratio: 1:13. There are 180 required school days per year for Upper School students. Upper School students typically attend 5 days per week. The average school day consists of 6 hours.

Upper School Student Profile Grade 9: 35 students (17 boys, 18 girls); Grade 10: 35 students (24 boys, 11 girls); Grade 11: 43 students (23 boys, 20 girls); Grade 12: 50 students (24 boys, 26 girls). 80% of students are Christian faith.

Faculty School total: 52. In upper school: 15 men, 18 women; 11 have advanced degrees.

Subjects Offered Advanced biology, advanced chemistry, advanced computer applications, advanced math, Advanced Placement courses, advanced TOEFL/grammar, algebra, American government, American history, American history-AP, American literature, American literature-AP, anatomy, art, ASB Leadership, athletic training, athletics, Bible, Bible studies, biology, biology-AP, business, business applications, business communications, business education, business law, business skills, business studies, calculus, calculus-AP, career planning, chemistry, choir, chorus, Christian doctrine, Christian ethics, Christian scripture, Christian studies, Christian testament, Christianity, church history, college admission preparation, college counseling, college placement, college planning, comparative government and politics-AP, competitive science projects, composition, composition-AP, computer applications, computer education, computer information systems, computer literacy, computer multimedia, computer skills, computer technologies, dance, desktop publishing, drama performance, economics, English, English literature-AP, English-AP, ESL, European history, geometry, government, health, history, honors algebra, honors English, independent study, Internet, intro to computers, journalism, keyboarding, kinesiology, lab science, leadership, physical education, physical science, physics, public speaking, research skills, Spanish, sports medicine, sports nutrition, statistics, statistics-AP, student government, TOEFL preparation, U.S. government and politics-AP, U.S. history-AP, Web site design, world cultures, yearbook.

Graduation Requirements Algebra, American government, American history, American literature, arts and fine arts (art, music, dance, drama), Bible, biology, composition, computer skills, economics, electives, English, European history, foreign language, freshman foundations, geometry, physical education (includes health), research skills, speech, graduation requirements meet UC and CSU entrance requirements.

Special Academic Programs 9 Advanced Placement exams for which test preparation is offered; honors section; independent study; study at local college for college credit; special instructional classes for Oportunity School Program; ESL (18 students enrolled).

College Admission Counseling 40 students graduated in 2013; 39 went to college, including Biola University; Concordia University; Point Loma Nazarene University; University of California, Irvine; Westmont College. Other: 1 went to work. Median SAT critical reading: 544, median SAT math: 609, median SAT writing: 539, median combined SAT: 1692.

Student Life Upper grades have uniform requirement, student council, honor system. Discipline rests primarily with faculty. Attendance at religious services is required.

Summer Programs Remediation, enrichment, advancement, sports, art/fine arts programs offered; session focuses on credit recovery; held on campus; accepts boys and girls; open to students from other schools. 35 students usually enrolled. 2014 schedule: July 11 to August 5. Application deadline: May 1.

Tuition and Aid Day student tuition: $12,490. Tuition installment plan (FACTS Tuition Payment Plan, monthly payment plans, individually arranged payment plans, Payroll deductions). Tuition reduction for siblings, need-based scholarship grants available. In 2013–14, 30% of upper-school students received aid. Total amount of financial aid awarded in 2013–14: $250,000.

Admissions Traditional secondary-level entrance grade is 9. For fall 2013, 45 students applied for upper-level admission, 39 were accepted, 35 enrolled. Admissions testing, ESOL English Proficiency Test, High School Placement Test, Stanford Test of Academic Skills or TOEFL required. Deadline for receipt of application materials: none. Application fee required: $100. On-campus interview required.

Athletics Interscholastic: baseball (boys); basketball (b,g); cheering (g); combined training (b,g); cross-country running (b,g); football (b); soccer (b,g); softball (g); tennis (g); volleyball (b,g); coed interscholastic: equestrian sports, golf, physical training, strength & conditioning, track and field, weight training. 2 PE instructors, 13 coaches, 2 athletic trainers.

Computers Computers are regularly used in all academic, Bible studies, data processing, design, journalism, yearbook classes. Computer network features include on-campus library services, Internet access, wireless campus network, Internet filtering or blocking technology, 1 to 1 tablet PC program. Campus intranet, student e-mail accounts, and computer access in designated common areas are available to students. Students grades are available online. The school has a published electronic and media policy.

Contact Mrs. Jo Beveridge, Director of Admissions/Development. 949-493-5683 Ext. 109. Fax: 949-493-6057. E-mail: jbeveridge@cvcs.org. Website: www.cvcs.org

CARDIGAN MOUNTAIN SCHOOL

Canaan, New Hampshire
See Junior Boarding Schools section.

CARDINAL GIBBONS HIGH SCHOOL

1401 Edwards Mill Road
Raleigh, North Carolina 27607

Head of School: Mr. Jason Curtis

General Information Coeducational day college-preparatory, arts, business, religious studies, and technology school, affiliated with Roman Catholic Church. Grades 9–12. Founded: 1909. Setting: suburban. 36-acre campus. 1 building on campus. Approved or accredited by Southern Association of Colleges and Schools and Southern Association of Independent Schools. Endowment: $750,000. Total enrollment: 1,294. Upper school average class size: 14. Upper school faculty-student ratio: 1:14. Upper School students typically attend 5 days per week. The average school day consists of 7 hours.

Upper School Student Profile Grade 9: 349 students (185 boys, 164 girls); Grade 10: 331 students (173 boys, 158 girls); Grade 11: 311 students (144 boys, 167 girls); Grade 12: 303 students (160 boys, 143 girls). 86% of students are Roman Catholic.

Faculty School total: 95. In upper school: 45 men, 49 women; 62 have advanced degrees.

Special Academic Programs Advanced Placement exam preparation; honors section; accelerated programs; independent study.

College Admission Counseling 311 students graduated in 2013; 306 went to college, including Appalachian State University; University of Notre Dame. Other: 5 had other specific plans.

Student Life Upper grades have uniform requirement, student council. Discipline rests primarily with faculty. Attendance at religious services is required.

Summer Programs Sports, art/fine arts programs offered; session focuses on sports; held on campus; accepts boys and girls; open to students from other schools. 2014 schedule: June to August.

Tuition and Aid Day student tuition: $9475–$13,380. Tuition installment plan (FACTS Tuition Payment Plan). Need-based scholarship grants available.

Admissions Traditional secondary-level entrance grade is 9. Application fee required: $100. On-campus interview required.

Athletics Interscholastic: aerobics/dance (boys, girls); ballet (g); baseball (b,g); basketball (b,g); cheering (g); cross-country running (b,g); dance (g); dance squad (g); dance team (g); diving (b,g); field hockey (g); football (b); golf (b,g); kickball (b,g); lacrosse (b,g); modern dance (g); mountain biking (b,g); outdoor education (b,g); physical fitness (b,g); physical training (b,g); roller hockey (b); running (b,g); soccer (b,g); softball (g); strength & conditioning (b); surfing (b,g); swimming and diving (b,g); tennis (b,g); track and field (b,g); ultimate Frisbee (b,g); volleyball (g); weight lifting (b,g); weight training (g); wrestling (b).

Computers Computer network features include Internet access, wireless campus network, Internet filtering or blocking technology. Campus intranet, student e-mail accounts, and computer access in designated common areas are available to students.

Contact Mrs. Marianne McCarty, Admissions Director. 919-834-1625 Ext. 209. Fax: 919-834-9771. E-mail: mmccarty@cghsnc.org. Website: www.cghsnc.org

CARDINAL MOONEY CATHOLIC HIGH SCHOOL

4171 Fruitville Road
Sarasota, Florida 34232

Head of School: Mr. Stephen J. Christie

General Information Coeducational day college-preparatory, arts, religious studies, and technology school, affiliated with Roman Catholic Church. Grades 9–12. Founded: 1959. Setting: suburban. Nearest major city is Tampa. 36-acre campus. 5 buildings on campus. Approved or accredited by Southern Association of Colleges and Schools. Endowment: $1.8 million. Total enrollment: 474. Upper school average class size: 18. Upper school faculty-student ratio: 1:13. There are 180 required school days per year for Upper School students. Upper School students typically attend 5 days per week. The average school day consists of 6 hours and 35 minutes.

Upper School Student Profile Grade 9: 126 students (76 boys, 50 girls); Grade 10: 121 students (61 boys, 60 girls); Grade 11: 132 students (69 boys, 63 girls); Grade 12: 95 students (45 boys, 50 girls). 80% of students are Roman Catholic.

Faculty School total: 45. In upper school: 12 men, 26 women; 25 have advanced degrees.

Subjects Offered Algebra, American government, American history, anatomy, art, biology, business, calculus, ceramics, chemistry, chorus, Christian and Hebrew scripture, community service, computer applications, computer graphics, contemporary history, creative writing, drama, earth science, economics, economics and history, English, English literature, environmental science, fine arts, French, geometry, guitar, health, history, instrumental music, integrated mathematics, journalism, keyboarding, learning strategies, marine biology, mathematics, music, physical education, physics, psychology, science, social justice, social studies, sociology, Spanish, speech, theology, trigonometry, U.S. government and politics-AP, world history, world literature, world religions.

Graduation Requirements Arts and fine arts (art, music, dance, drama), electives, English, foreign language, mathematics, physical education (includes health), religion (includes Bible studies and theology), science, social studies (includes history), 100 hours of community service.

Special Academic Programs 8 Advanced Placement exams for which test preparation is offered; honors section; remedial reading and/or remedial writing; remedial math; programs in English, mathematics for dyslexic students.

College Admission Counseling 123 students graduated in 2013; all went to college, including Florida Gulf Coast University; Florida State University; University of Central Florida; University of Florida; University of North Florida; University of South Florida. Median SAT critical reading: 512, median SAT math: 507, median SAT writing: 506, median composite ACT: 23. 31% scored over 600 on SAT critical reading, 41% scored over 600 on SAT math, 35% scored over 600 on SAT writing, 38% scored over 26 on composite ACT.

Student Life Upper grades have specified standards of dress, student council. Discipline rests primarily with faculty. Attendance at religious services is required.

Tuition and Aid Tuition installment plan (monthly payment plans, semester payment plan). Tuition reduction for siblings, merit scholarship grants, need-based scholarship grants available. In 2013–14, 25% of upper-school students received aid. Total amount of financial aid awarded in 2013–14: $200,000.

Admissions Traditional secondary-level entrance grade is 9. For fall 2013, 180 students applied for upper-level admission, 180 were accepted, 133 enrolled. Placement test required. Deadline for receipt of application materials: none. No application fee required. On-campus interview required.

Athletics Interscholastic: baseball (boys), basketball (b,g), cheering (g), cross-country running (b,g), dance team (g), diving (b,g), football (b), golf (b,g), lacrosse (b,g), modern dance (g), physical fitness (b,g), soccer (b,g), softball (g), strength & conditioning (b,g), swimming and diving (b,g), track and field (b,g), volleyball (g), weight lifting (b,g), weight training (b,g); intramural: basketball (b,g), volleyball (b,g); coed interscholastic: aquatics; coed intramural: volleyball. 4 PE instructors, 66 coaches, 4 athletic trainers.

Computers Computers are regularly used in art, basic skills, Christian doctrine, computer applications, creative writing, English, foreign language, French, history, mathematics, religious studies, remedial study skills, science, social sciences, social studies, Spanish, technology, theater arts, video film production, writing, yearbook classes. Computer network features include on-campus library services, Internet access, wireless campus network. Student e-mail accounts are available to students. Students grades are available online. The school has a published electronic and media policy.

Contact Mrs. Joanne Mades, Registrar. 941-371-4917. Fax: 941-371-6924 Ext. 135. E-mail: jmades@cmhs-sarasota.org. Website: www.cmhs-sarasota.org

CARDINAL NEWMAN HIGH SCHOOL

512 Spencer Drive
West Palm Beach, Florida 33409-3699

Head of School: Fr. David W. Carr

General Information Coeducational day college-preparatory and International Baccalaureate school, affiliated with Roman Catholic Church. Grades 9–12. Founded: 1961. Setting: suburban. Nearest major city is Miami. 50-acre campus. 5 buildings on campus. Approved or accredited by National Catholic Education Association, Southern Association of Colleges and Schools, and Florida Department of Education. Total enrollment: 540. Upper school average class size: 25. Upper school faculty-student ratio: 1:25. There are 180 required school days per year for Upper School students. Upper School students typically attend 5 days per week. The average school day consists of 6 hours and 40 minutes.

Upper School Student Profile Grade 9: 154 students (84 boys, 70 girls); Grade 10: 130 students (67 boys, 63 girls); Grade 11: 117 students (61 boys, 56 girls); Grade 12: 139 students (63 boys, 76 girls). 80% of students are Roman Catholic.

Faculty School total: 38. In upper school: 15 men, 23 women; 25 have advanced degrees.

Subjects Offered Algebra, American government, American history, American literature, anatomy and physiology, art, band, Bible studies, biology, biology-AP, calculus, calculus-AP, chemistry, chorus, church history, computer applications, computer science, desktop publishing, drama, economics, English, English literature, English-AP, ethics, European history, fine arts, French, French-AP, geometry, government/civics, health, history, honors algebra, honors English, honors geometry, integrated science, International Baccalaureate courses, journalism, leadership, marine biology, mathematics, physical education, physics, political science, pre-calculus, probability and statistics, religion, social justice, social studies, Spanish, speech, world history, world literature, writing, yearbook.

Graduation Requirements Arts and fine arts (art, music, dance, drama), English, foreign language, mathematics, physical education (includes health), religion (includes Bible studies and theology), science, social studies (includes history), 100-hour community service requirement.

Special Academic Programs International Baccalaureate program; Advanced Placement exam preparation; honors section; study at local college for college credit; academic accommodation for the gifted; remedial reading and/or remedial writing; remedial math.

College Admission Counseling 121 students graduated in 2013; 118 went to college, including Florida Atlantic University; Florida Gulf Coast University; Florida State University; Palm Beach State College; University of Central Florida; University of Florida. Other: 2 entered military service, 1 had other specific plans.

Student Life Upper grades have uniform requirement, student council, honor system. Discipline rests primarily with faculty. Attendance at religious services is required.

Summer Programs Remediation, enrichment, sports programs offered; session focuses on freshman preparation; held on campus; accepts boys and girls; not open to students from other schools. 75 students usually enrolled. 2014 schedule: June 15 to June 30.

Tuition and Aid Day student tuition: $11,050–$12,050. Tuition installment plan (FACTS Tuition Payment Plan). Need-based scholarship grants available. In 2013–14, 18% of upper-school students received aid.

Admissions Traditional secondary-level entrance grade is 9. STS required. Deadline for receipt of application materials: none. Application fee required: $50. On-campus interview recommended.

Athletics Interscholastic: baseball (boys), basketball (b,g), bowling (b,g), cheering (g), cross-country running (b,g), dance team (g), diving (b,g), football (b), golf (b,g), lacrosse (b,g), physical fitness (b,g), soccer (b,g), softball (g), swimming and diving (b,g), tennis (b,g), track and field (b,g), volleyball (g), wrestling (b). 2 PE instructors, 1 athletic trainer.

Computers Computers are regularly used in all academic, Bible studies, yearbook classes. Computer network features include on-campus library services, online

commercial services, Internet access, wireless campus network, Internet filtering or blocking technology. Student e-mail accounts are available to students. Students grades are available online. The school has a published electronic and media policy.

Contact Mrs. Carol Throop, Admissions Director. 561-242-2268. Fax: 561-683-7307. E-mail: cthroop@cardinalnewman.com. Website: www.cardinalnewman.com

CARDINAL O'HARA HIGH SCHOOL

1701 South Sproul Road
Springfield, Pennsylvania 19064-1199

Head of School: Mrs. Marie Rogai

General Information Coeducational day college-preparatory school, affiliated with Roman Catholic Church. Grades 9–12. Founded: 1963. Setting: suburban. Nearest major city is Philadelphia. 1 building on campus. Approved or accredited by Pennsylvania Department of Education. Upper school average class size: 30. Upper school faculty-student ratio: 1:21. There are 180 required school days per year for Upper School students. Upper School students typically attend 5 days per week. The average school day consists of 6 hours and 35 minutes.

Upper School Student Profile Grade 9: 287 students (125 boys, 162 girls); Grade 10: 332 students (140 boys, 192 girls); Grade 11: 362 students (156 boys, 206 girls); Grade 12: 308 students (134 boys, 174 girls). 83% of students are Roman Catholic.

Faculty School total: 76. In upper school: 42 men, 34 women; 31 have advanced degrees.

Special Academic Programs Advanced Placement exam preparation; academic accommodation for the musically talented.

Student Life Upper grades have uniform requirement, student council, honor system. Discipline rests primarily with faculty. Attendance at religious services is required.

Summer Programs Enrichment programs offered; held on campus; accepts boys and girls; not open to students from other schools. 75 students usually enrolled.

Tuition and Aid Day student tuition: $5600. Tuition installment plan (monthly payment plans). Need-based scholarship grants available.

Admissions Traditional secondary-level entrance grade is 9. Application fee required: $250.

Athletics Interscholastic: baseball (boys), basketball (b,g), bowling (b,g), cheering (g), cross-country running (b,g), field hockey (g), football (b), Frisbee (b,g), golf (b), ice hockey (b), indoor track (b,g), indoor track & field (b,g), lacrosse (b,g), rugby (b), soccer (b,g), softball (g), tennis (b,g), track and field (b,g), ultimate Frisbee (b,g), volleyball (g), wrestling (b).

Computers Computer resources include on-campus library services, Internet access, wireless campus network, Internet filtering or blocking technology. Students grades are available online. The school has a published electronic and media policy.

Contact Mrs. Patti Arnold, Admissions Director. 610-544-3800 Ext. 70. Fax: 610-544-1189. E-mail: pattiarnold@cohs.com. Website: www.cohs.com

CARLISLE SCHOOL

300 Carlisle Road
Axton, Virginia 24054

Head of School: Mr. Thomas P. Hudgins Jr.

General Information Coeducational boarding and day college-preparatory, International Baccalaureate (IB), and IB Middle Years program and Primary Years program school. Boarding grades 9–12, day grades PK–12. Founded: 1968. Setting: rural. Nearest major city is Danville. Students are housed in single-sex dormitories and hosted by local families. 50-acre campus. 5 buildings on campus. Approved or accredited by International Baccalaureate Organization, Southern Association of Colleges and Schools, and Virginia Department of Education. Member of National Association of Independent Schools. Endowment: $1.5 million. Total enrollment: 453. Upper school average class size: 15. Upper school faculty-student ratio: 1:8. There are 171 required school days per year for Upper School students. Upper School students typically attend 5 days per week. The average school day consists of 6 hours and 45 minutes.

Upper School Student Profile Grade 9: 35 students (14 boys, 21 girls); Grade 10: 30 students (19 boys, 11 girls); Grade 11: 40 students (22 boys, 18 girls); Grade 12: 38 students (22 boys, 16 girls). 11% of students are boarding students. 74% are state residents. 2 states are represented in upper school student body. 26% are international students. International students from Australia, China, Finland, Japan, Republic of Korea, and Uganda; 3 other countries represented in student body.

Faculty School total: 30. In upper school: 5 men, 18 women; 11 have advanced degrees; 3 reside on campus.

Subjects Offered Advanced computer applications, advanced math, Advanced Placement courses, algebra, American government, American history, American history-AP, American literature, art, arts, band, biology, biology-AP, calculus, calculus-AP, chemistry, chemistry-AP, choir, composition-AP, computer information systems, computer programming, computer science, computer science-AP, concert band, creative dance, creative drama, creative writing, dance, drama, earth science, economics, economics-AP, English, English language and composition-AP, English literature,

English literature and composition-AP, English literature-AP, ESL, film studies, fine arts, geometry, government, government/civics, health, health and wellness, history, history of the Americas, honors algebra, honors English, honors geometry, HTML design, independent study, International Baccalaureate courses, intro to computers, jazz band, jazz ensemble, journalism, lab science, madrigals, mathematics, mathematics-AP, music, physical education, physics, play production, pre-algebra, pre-calculus, psychology, psychology-AP, publications, robotics, science, senior project, social studies, Spanish, statistics, statistics-AP, studio art, theater, theory of knowledge, U.S. government and politics-AP, U.S. history-AP, wind ensemble, world civilizations, world history, world history-AP, world wide web design, yearbook.

Graduation Requirements Advanced math, algebra, arts and fine arts (art, music, dance, drama), computer science, electives, English, foreign language, mathematics, physical education (includes health), science, social studies (includes history), U.S. and Virginia history, U.S. government, community and service, senior project, IB MYP Personal Project.

Special Academic Programs International Baccalaureate program; Advanced Placement exam preparation; honors section; independent study; term-away projects; study at local college for college credit; ESL (17 students enrolled).

College Admission Counseling 49 students graduated in 2013; all went to college, including James Madison University; The University of North Carolina at Chapel Hill; The University of North Carolina at Greensboro; University of Virginia; Virginia Commonwealth University; Wake Forest University. Median SAT critical reading: 546, median SAT math: 540, median SAT writing: 526. 33% scored over 600 on SAT critical reading, 37% scored over 600 on SAT math, 33% scored over 600 on SAT writing.

Student Life Upper grades have specified standards of dress, student council, honor system. Discipline rests equally with students and faculty.

Summer Programs Remediation, enrichment, advancement, ESL, sports, art/fine arts, computer instruction programs offered; session focuses on enrichment, academics, sports, fun; held on campus; accepts boys and girls; open to students from other schools. 60 students usually enrolled. 2014 schedule: June 15 to August 15. Application deadline: June 1.

Tuition and Aid Day student tuition: $9975; 5-day tuition and room/board: $14,975; 7-day tuition and room/board: $35,000. Tuition installment plan (Insured Tuition Payment Plan, FACTS Tuition Payment Plan). Need-based scholarship grants available. In 2013–14, 50% of upper-school students received aid. Total amount of financial aid awarded in 2013–14: $250,000.

Admissions Traditional secondary-level entrance grade is 9. Nelson-Denny Reading Test, Woodcock-Johnson or writing sample required. Deadline for receipt of application materials: none. Application fee required: $65. Interview required.

Athletics Interscholastic: basketball (boys, girls), cheering (g), field hockey (g), soccer (b,g), softball (g), tennis (b,g), volleyball (g); intramural: basketball (b,g), cheering (g), softball (g); coed interscholastic: baseball, cross-country running, dance, fencing, golf; coed intramural: aerobics/Nautilus, archery, basketball, Frisbee, table tennis, weight lifting. 2 PE instructors, 10 coaches.

Computers Computers are regularly used in all academic classes. Computer network features include on-campus library services, online commercial services, Internet access, wireless campus network, Internet filtering or blocking technology. Campus intranet and computer access in designated common areas are available to students. Students grades are available online. The school has a published electronic and media policy.

Contact Mrs. Jenna Martin, International Student Affairs Coordinator, Admissions Assistant. 276-632-7288 Ext. 221. Fax: 276-632-9545. E-mail: jmartin@carlisleschool.org. Website: www.carlisleschool.org

CARMEL HIGH SCHOOL

One Carmel Parkway
Mundelein, Illinois 60060-2499

Head of School: Judith Mucheck, PhD

General Information Coeducational day college-preparatory, arts, business, religious studies, and technology school, affiliated with Roman Catholic Church. Grades 9–12. Founded: 1962. Setting: suburban. Nearest major city is Libertyville. 45-acre campus. 1 building on campus. Approved or accredited by National Catholic Education Association, North Central Association of Colleges and Schools, and Illinois Department of Education. Total enrollment: 1,350. Upper school average class size: 25. Upper school faculty-student ratio: 1:16.

Upper School Student Profile 85% of students are Roman Catholic.

Faculty School total: 90. In upper school: 33 men, 57 women; 63 have advanced degrees.

Subjects Offered 20th century world history, accounting, advanced chemistry, advanced math, Advanced Placement courses, advanced studio art-AP, algebra, American government, American history, American literature, American literature-AP, anatomy and physiology, art, athletic training, band, biology, biology-AP, biotechnology, botany, British literature, British literature (honors), business, calculus, calculus-AP, chemistry, chemistry-AP, choir, choral music, chorus, community service, computer applications, computer programming, computer programming-AP, concert band, drama, drama performance, drawing, economics, English, English composition, English language and composition-AP, English literature, English literature-AP,

European history-AP, French, French language-AP, French-AP, geography, geometry, government, government-AP, history of religion, honors algebra, honors English, honors geometry, honors U.S. history, honors world history, instrumental music, Internet research, intro to computers, jazz band, journalism, Latin, Latin-AP, Mandarin, marching band, music, music composition, music theory-AP, orchestra, performing arts, physical education, physical science, physics, physics-AP, pre-algebra, pre-calculus, probability and statistics, psychology, reading/study skills, religion, religious education, scripture, sociology, Spanish, strings, student government, student publications, student teaching, studio art, studio art-AP, theater arts, trigonometry, U.S. government and politics-AP, U.S. history, U.S. history-AP, Web site design, wind ensemble, women spirituality and faith, world history, world history-AP, world literature, yearbook, zoology.

Graduation Requirements Ministry requirement, 20 hours of ministry service per semester.

Special Academic Programs 19 Advanced Placement exams for which test preparation is offered; honors section; special instructional classes for deaf students, blind students.

College Admission Counseling 320 students graduated in 2013; 316 went to college, including Marquette University; Purdue University; The University of Iowa; University of Illinois at Urbana–Champaign. Other: 1 went to work, 3 entered military service. Mean composite ACT: 25.

Student Life Upper grades have uniform requirement, student council. Discipline rests primarily with faculty. Attendance at religious services is required.

Summer Programs Enrichment, advancement, sports, art/fine arts, computer instruction programs offered; session focuses on courses for enrolled students; held on campus; accepts boys and girls; not open to students from other schools. 200 students usually enrolled. 2014 schedule: June 9 to July 2. Application deadline: May 8.

Tuition and Aid Day student tuition: $9950. Tuition installment plan (FACTS Tuition Payment Plan). Merit scholarship grants, need-based scholarship grants available. In 2013–14, 13% of upper-school students received aid; total upper-school merit-scholarship money awarded: $16,000. Total amount of financial aid awarded in 2013–14: $1,300,000.

Admissions Traditional secondary-level entrance grade is 9. Explore required. Deadline for receipt of application materials: January 24. Application fee required: $400.

Athletics Interscholastic: baseball (boys), basketball (b,g), cheering (g), cross-country running (b,g), football (b), golf (b,g), gymnastics (g), ice hockey (b), lacrosse (b,g), pom squad (g), soccer (b,g), softball (g), tennis (b,g), track and field (b,g), volleyball (b,g), wrestling (b); intramural; basketball (b,g); coed intramural: Frisbee, volleyball, winter soccer, yoga.

Computers Computers are regularly used in all classes. Computer resources include on-campus library services, Internet access. Students grades are available online. The school has a published electronic and media policy.

Contact Mr. Brian Stith, Director of Admissions. 847-388-3320. Fax: 847-566-8465. E-mail: bstith@carmelhs.org. Website: www.carmelhs.org

CAROLINA DAY SCHOOL

1345 Hendersonville Road
Asheville, North Carolina 28803

Head of School: Thomas F. H. Trigg

General Information Coeducational day college-preparatory school. Grades PK–12. Founded: 1987. Setting: suburban. 60-acre campus. 9 buildings on campus. Approved or accredited by Southern Association of Colleges and Schools, Southern Association of Independent Schools, and North Carolina Department of Education. Member of National Association of Independent Schools. Endowment: $3.4 million. Total enrollment: 610. Upper school average class size: 12. Upper school faculty-student ratio: 1:6. There are 180 required school days per year for Upper School students. Upper School students typically attend 5 days per week. The average school day consists of 6 hours and 25 minutes.

Upper School Student Profile Grade 9: 44 students (18 boys, 26 girls); Grade 10: 45 students (28 boys, 17 girls); Grade 11: 37 students (19 boys, 18 girls); Grade 12: 44 students (19 boys, 25 girls).

Faculty School total: 114. In upper school: 11 men, 12 women; 17 have advanced degrees.

Subjects Offered 3-dimensional art, 3-dimensional design, acting, advanced biology, advanced chemistry, advanced studio art-AP, algebra, American literature, art history, art history-AP, biology, biology-AP, calculus, calculus-AP, ceramics, chemistry, chemistry-AP, chorus, CPR, creative writing, debate, ecology, English language and composition-AP, English literature, environmental science-AP, European history-AP, fiction, French, geometry, global studies, history, industrial arts, language and composition, linear algebra, linguistics, literature, literature and composition-AP, martial arts, music theory, music theory-AP, photography, physical education, physics, physics-AP, pre-calculus, psychology-AP, reading/study skills, research, science, Spanish, Spanish-AP, speech, statistics-AP, studio art, theater, U.S. government and politics-AP, U.S. history, U.S. history-AP, world literature.

Graduation Requirements Algebra, arts and fine arts (art, music, dance, drama), biology, chemistry, electives, English, geometry, global studies, modern languages, physical education (includes health), public speaking, social studies (includes history), U.S. history, CPR/First Aid (non-credit class).

Special Academic Programs 14 Advanced Placement exams for which test preparation is offered; honors section; independent study.

College Admission Counseling 54 students graduated in 2012; 52 went to college, including Amherst College; Duke University; High Point University; The University of North Carolina Wilmington; University of North Carolina at Asheville; University of South Carolina. Other: 2 had other specific plans. Median SAT critical reading: 570, median SAT math: 600, median SAT writing: 560, median combined SAT: 1740, median composite ACT: 26.

Student Life Upper grades have specified standards of dress, student council, honor system. Discipline rests equally with students and faculty.

Tuition and Aid Day student tuition: $19,500–$20,700. Tuition installment plan (Insured Tuition Payment Plan, FACTS Tuition Payment Plan, monthly payment plans, individually arranged payment plans, 1-payment plan or 2-installments plan (August and January)). Merit scholarship grants, need-based scholarship grants available. In 2012–13, 47% of upper-school students received aid; total upper-school merit-scholarship money awarded: $152,459. Total amount of financial aid awarded in 2012–13: $553,447.

Admissions Traditional secondary-level entrance grade is 9. For fall 2012, 33 students applied for upper-level admission, 23 were accepted, 16 enrolled. ERB, ISEE, PSAT or SAT or SSAT required. Deadline for receipt of application materials: none. Application fee required: $100. On-campus interview required.

Athletics Interscholastic: baseball (boys), basketball (b,g), cross-country running (b,g), field hockey (g), swimming and diving (b,g), tennis (b,g), track and field (b,g), volleyball (g); coed interscholastic: golf; coed intramural: basketball, lacrosse, skiing (downhill), snowboarding, table tennis. 2 PE instructors, 11 coaches, 1 athletic trainer.

Computers Computers are regularly used in all academic classes. Computer network features include on-campus library services, online commercial services, Internet access, wireless campus network, Internet filtering or blocking technology. Campus intranet, student e-mail accounts, and computer access in designated common areas are available to students. The school has a published electronic and media policy.

Contact Michelle Nailen, Assistant Director of Admissions. 828-274-0757 Ext. 318. Fax: 828-274-0756. E-mail: mnailen@carolinaday.org. Website: www.carolinaday.org

CARONDELET HIGH SCHOOL

1133 Winton Drive
Concord, California 94518

Head of School: Nancy Libby

General Information Girls' day college-preparatory, arts, religious studies, and technology school, affiliated with Roman Catholic Church. Grades 9–12. Founded: 1965. Setting: suburban. Nearest major city is Oakland. 9-acre campus. 5 buildings on campus. Approved or accredited by Western Association of Schools and Colleges. Total enrollment: 800. Upper school average class size: 30. Upper school faculty-student ratio: 1:15. Upper School students typically attend 5 days per week. The average school day consists of 7 hours and 30 minutes.

Upper School Student Profile Grade 9: 200 students (200 girls); Grade 10: 200 students (200 girls); Grade 11: 200 students (200 girls); Grade 12: 200 students (200 girls). 90% of students are Roman Catholic.

Faculty School total: 65. In upper school: 13 men, 48 women; 30 have advanced degrees.

Subjects Offered Algebra, American studies, animation, architectural drawing, art, band, biology, calculus, calculus-AP, cartooning/animation, chemistry, chorus, church history, civics, community service, computer applications, concert band, concert choir, creative writing, criminal justice, dance, design, drafting, drawing, economics, English, English-AP, ethics, finite math, fitness, French, geometry, government-AP, health, honors algebra, honors English, honors geometry, Italian, jazz band, journalism, Latin, marching band, marine biology, music history, music theory, musical theater, orchestra, painting, physical education, physics, physics-AP, physiology, pre-algebra, pre-calculus, psychology, psychology-AP, relationships, sculpture, Spanish, Spanish-AP, sports medicine, statistics, studio art-AP, technical drawing, transition mathematics, U.S. history, U.S. history-AP, water color painting, Web site design, women's health, world arts, world civilizations, world religions, writing, yearbook.

Graduation Requirements Computer literacy, English, mathematics, modern languages, physical education (includes health), religious studies, science, social studies (includes history), visual and performing arts.

Special Academic Programs 12 Advanced Placement exams for which test preparation is offered; honors section; independent study; academic accommodation for the gifted.

College Admission Counseling 199 students graduated in 2013; all went to college, including California Polytechnic State University, San Luis Obispo; California State University, Chico; University of California, Berkeley. Mean SAT critical reading: 548, mean SAT math: 538, mean SAT writing: 556, mean composite ACT: 24.

Student Life Upper grades have uniform requirement, honor system. Discipline rests primarily with faculty. Attendance at religious services is required.

Tuition and Aid Day student tuition: $15,100. Tuition installment plan (SMART Tuition Payment Plan, monthly payment plans, prepayment plan, semester or quarterly payment plans). Need-based scholarship grants available. In 2013–14, 25% of upper-

school students received aid. Total amount of financial aid awarded in 2013–14: $1,300,000.

Admissions Traditional secondary-level entrance grade is 9. For fall 2013, 380 students applied for upper-level admission, 240 were accepted, 220 enrolled. ACT-Explore required. Deadline for receipt of application materials: December 2. Application fee required: $100. On-campus interview recommended.

Athletics Interscholastic: aquatics, basketball, cheering, combined training, cross-country running, dance squad, dance team, diving, golf, lacrosse, soccer, softball, swimming and diving, tennis, volleyball, water polo; intramural: badminton, basketball, broomball, flag football, physical fitness, physical training, touch football, volleyball. 3 PE instructors, 40 coaches, 1 athletic trainer.

Computers Computers are regularly used in computer applications classes. Computer network features include on-campus library services, Internet access, wireless campus network, Internet filtering or blocking technology. Student e-mail accounts are available to students. Students grades are available online. The school has a published electronic and media policy.

Contact Ms. Kathy Harris, Director of Admissions. 925-686-5353 Ext. 161. Fax: 925-671-9429. E-mail: kharris@carondeleths.org. Website: www.carondelet.net

CARROLLTON CHRISTIAN ACADEMY

2205 East Hebron Parkway
Carrollton, Texas 75010

Head of School: Mr. David Culpepper

General Information Coeducational day college-preparatory, arts, religious studies, and technology school, affiliated with United Methodist Church. Grades PK–12. Founded: 1980. Setting: suburban. Nearest major city is Dallas/Fort Worth. 25-acre campus. 2 buildings on campus. Approved or accredited by Association of Christian Schools International, Southern Association of Colleges and Schools, University Senate of United Methodist Church, and Texas Department of Education. Language of instruction: Spanish. Total enrollment: 252. Upper school average class size: 20. The average school day consists of 7 hours.

College Admission Counseling 100 went to college.

Student Life Upper grades have uniform requirement, student council, honor system. Discipline rests primarily with faculty. Attendance at religious services is required.

Summer Programs Session focuses on Strength/Agility/Conditioning; accepts boys and girls.

Tuition and Aid Day student tuition: $11,800. Tuition installment plan (FACTS Tuition Payment Plan). Tuition reduction for siblings, need-based scholarship grants available.

Admissions Stanford Achievement Test required. Application fee required: $125. Interview required.

Athletics Interscholastic: baseball (boys), basketball (b,g), cheering (g), cross-country running (b,g), dance team (g), football (b), golf (b,g), soccer (b,g), softball (g), strength & conditioning (b,g), tennis (b,g), track and field (b,g), volleyball (g), winter soccer (b,g).

Contact Ms. Jane Funk, Admissions Coordinator. 972-242-6688 Ext. 1360. Fax: 469-568-1396. E-mail: jane.funk@ccasaints.org. Website: www.ccasaints.org

CASCADES ACADEMY OF CENTRAL OREGON

2150 NE Studio Road
Suite 2
Bend, Oregon 97701

Head of School: Blair Jenkins

General Information Distance learning only college-preparatory and experiential education school. Distance learning grades K–12. Founded: 2003. Setting: suburban. 4-acre campus. 1 building on campus. Approved or accredited by Northwest Accreditation Commission, Northwest Association of Independent Schools, and Oregon Department of Education. Total enrollment: 143. Upper school average class size: 10. Upper school faculty-student ratio: 1:6. There are 168 required school days per year for Upper School students. Upper School students typically attend 5 days per week. The average school day consists of 7 hours and 15 minutes.

Upper School Student Profile Grade 9: 13 students (5 boys, 8 girls); Grade 10: 3 students (2 boys, 1 girl); Grade 11: 6 students (5 boys, 1 girl); Grade 12: 1 student (1 boy).

Faculty School total: 21. In upper school: 1 man, 3 women; 3 have advanced degrees.

Graduation Requirements Internship.

College Admission Counseling 6 students graduated in 2012; all went to college, including Rensselaer Polytechnic Institute; University of Oregon; Willamette University.

Student Life Upper grades have honor system. Discipline rests primarily with faculty.

Tuition and Aid Day student tuition: $10,950. Tuition installment plan (monthly payment plans, individually arranged payment plans). Merit scholarship grants, need-based scholarship grants available. In 2012–13, 48% of upper-school students received aid.

Admissions Traditional secondary-level entrance grade is 9. For fall 2012, 7 students applied for upper-level admission, 6 were accepted, 5 enrolled. Deadline for receipt of application materials: none. Application fee required: $50. On-campus interview required.

Computers Computer network features include Internet access, wireless campus network, Internet filtering or blocking technology. Student e-mail accounts and computer access in designated common areas are available to students. Students grades are available online. The school has a published electronic and media policy.

Contact 541-382-0699. Fax: 541-382-0225. Website: www.cascadesacademy.org/

CASCADILLA SCHOOL

116 Summit Street
Ithaca, New York 14850

Head of School: Patricia T. Kendall

General Information Coeducational boarding and day college-preparatory, arts, bilingual studies, English/language arts (The Cascadilla Seminar/Cornell Univ.), and mathematics school. Grades 9–PG. Founded: 1870. Setting: urban. Nearest major city is Syracuse. Students are housed in single-sex dormitories. 2-acre campus. 3 buildings on campus. Approved or accredited by New York State Board of Regents, New York State University, The College Board, US Department of State, and New York Department of Education. Endowment: $1.5 million. Upper school average class size: 7. Upper school faculty-student ratio: 1:6. There are 185 required school days per year for Upper School students. Upper School students typically attend 5 days per week. The average school day consists of 8 hours and 40 minutes.

Upper School Student Profile Grade 9: 10 students (5 boys, 5 girls); Grade 10: 14 students (8 boys, 6 girls); Grade 11: 13 students (7 boys, 6 girls); Grade 12: 13 students (6 boys, 7 girls). 30% of students are boarding students. 45% are state residents. 4 states are represented in upper school student body. 55% are international students. International students from Angola, China, Portugal, Republic of Korea, and United Kingdom; 3 other countries represented in student body.

Faculty School total: 16. In upper school: 7 men, 9 women; 15 have advanced degrees; 4 reside on campus.

Subjects Offered Advanced chemistry, Advanced Placement courses, advanced TOEFL/grammar, African literature, algebra, alternative physical education, American history, American literature, analysis and differential calculus, analytic geometry, anatomy and physiology, art, biochemistry, biology, biology-AP, calculus, calculus-AP, career/college preparation, chemistry, chemistry-AP, college admission preparation, college awareness, college counseling, college placement, college planning, college writing, computer programming, computer science, creative writing, decision making skills, earth science, economics, English, English composition, English literature, English literature and composition-AP, English literature-AP, environmental education, environmental science, ethics, European history, expository writing, fabric arts, French, French as a second language, geometry, government/civics, health, health and wellness, health education, history, honors algebra, honors English, honors geometry, honors U.S. history, honors world history, lab science, Latin, leadership, mathematics, philosophy, photography, physical education, physics, psychology, public speaking, reading, reading/study skills, SAT preparation, SAT/ACT preparation, science, Shakespeare, social studies, Spanish, trigonometry, typing, video film production, world history, world history-AP, world literature, writing.

Graduation Requirements Alternative physical education, arts, arts and fine arts (art, music, dance, drama), computer science, current events, debate, economics, economics and history, English, European history, foreign language, government, health education, international affairs, mathematics, physical education (includes health), political science, public speaking, research, research and reference, research seminar, science, senior seminar, social studies (includes history), study skills, U.S. government and politics, English V-The Cascadilla Seminar (for college research preparation). Community service is required.

Special Academic Programs 5 Advanced Placement exams for which test preparation is offered; honors section; accelerated programs; independent study; term-away projects; study at local college for college credit; academic accommodation for the gifted, the musically talented, and the artistically talented; remedial reading and/or remedial writing; remedial math; programs in English, mathematics for dyslexic students; special instructional classes for students with learning disabilities and Attention Deficit Disorder.

College Admission Counseling 10 students graduated in 2013; 8 went to college, including Le Moyne College; Miami University; Northeastern University; Pace University; Quinnipiac University; St. John's University. Other: 2 entered a postgraduate year. Median SAT critical reading: 600, median SAT math: 650, median SAT writing: 550. 50% scored over 600 on SAT critical reading, 50% scored over 600 on SAT math, 15% scored over 600 on SAT writing.

Student Life Upper grades have specified standards of dress, student council, honor system. Discipline rests equally with students and faculty.

Summer Programs Remediation, enrichment, advancement, art/fine arts programs offered; session focuses on academics; held on campus; accepts boys and girls; open to students from other schools. 10 students usually enrolled. 2014 schedule: July 1 to August 17. Application deadline: June 30.

Tuition and Aid Day student tuition: $18,000; 7-day tuition and room/board: $39,500. Tuition installment plan (monthly payment plans, individually arranged payment plans). Tuition reduction for siblings, merit scholarship grants, need-based scholarship grants available. In 2013–14, 40% of upper-school students received aid; total upper-school merit-scholarship money awarded: $50,000. Total amount of financial aid awarded in 2013–14: $60,000.

Admissions Traditional secondary-level entrance grade is 10. For fall 2013, 70 students applied for upper-level admission, 16 were accepted, 15 enrolled. English Composition Test for ESL students, English entrance exam, English for Non-native Speakers, English language, English proficiency, High School Placement Test, math and English placement tests, mathematics proficiency exam, non-standardized placement tests, Reading for Understanding, school's own exam or writing sample required. Deadline for receipt of application materials: none. Application fee required: $75. Interview recommended.

Athletics Interscholastic: crew (boys, girls), modern dance (g); intramural: crew (b,g), fencing (b), independent competitive sports (b,g), rowing (b,g), sailing (b,g), skiing (cross-country) (b,g), skiing (downhill) (b,g), soccer (b,g), tennis (b,g); coed interscholastic: aerobics, aerobics/Nautilus, alpine skiing, aquatics, backpacking, badminton, ballet, basketball, billiards, blading, bowling, climbing, combined training, fencing, fitness, fitness walking, Frisbee, hiking/backpacking, jogging, kayaking, nordic skiing, outdoor activities, outdoor adventure, outdoor education, physical fitness, physical training, swimming and diving, table tennis, weight lifting, yoga; coed intramural: aerobics, aerobics/dance, badminton, basketball, blading, bowling, horseback riding, independent competitive sports, jogging, Nautilus, nordic skiing, outdoor activities, outdoor adventure, physical fitness, physical training, pillo polo, racquetball, rowing, sailboarding, skiing (cross-country), skiing (downhill), snowboarding, soccer, strength & conditioning, tennis, volleyball, walking, wall climbing, windsurfing. 3 PE instructors.

Computers Computers are regularly used in career exploration, college planning, creative writing, desktop publishing, English, foreign language, language development, literary magazine, mathematics, media arts, newspaper, photography, photojournalism, publishing, research skills, SAT preparation, senior seminar, Spanish, stock market, theater, theater arts, video film production, Web site design, word processing, writing, yearbook classes. Computer network features include on-campus library services, online commercial services, Internet access, wireless campus network, Internet filtering or blocking technology, dormitories are fitted for high speed internet: Student e-mail accounts and computer access in designated common areas are available to students. Students grades are available online.

Contact Donna W. Collins, Administrative Assistant. 607-272-3110. Fax: 607-272-0747. E-mail: admissions@cascadillaschool.org. Website: www.cascadillaschool.org

See Display on next page and Close-Up on page 526.

CASTILLEJA SCHOOL

1310 Bryant Street
Palo Alto, California 94301

Head of School: Nanci Z. Kauffman

General Information Girls' day college-preparatory, arts, and technology school. Grades 6–12. Founded: 1907. Setting: suburban. Nearest major city is San Francisco/San Jose. 5-acre campus. 7 buildings on campus. Approved or accredited by California Association of Independent Schools, National Council for Private School Accreditation, and Western Association of Schools and Colleges. Member of National Association of Independent Schools and Secondary School Admission Test Board. Endowment: $35 million. Total enrollment: 445. Upper school average class size: 14. Upper school faculty-student ratio: 1:6. Upper School students typically attend 5 days per week. The average school day consists of 7 hours.

Upper School Student Profile Grade 9: 65 students (65 girls); Grade 10: 68 students (68 girls); Grade 11: 63 students (63 girls); Grade 12: 62 students (62 girls).

Faculty School total: 75. In upper school: 12 men, 34 women; 40 have advanced degrees.

Subjects Offered Advanced Placement courses, African studies, algebra, American history, American literature, art, art history, biology, calculus, ceramics, chemistry, computer math, computer science, creative writing, drama, economics, English, English literature, environmental science, European history, expository writing, fine arts, French, geometry, global issues, government/civics, grammar, health, history, journalism, Latin, marine biology, mathematics, music, philosophy, physical education, physics, psychology, Russian history, science, social studies, Spanish, speech, statistics, theater, trigonometry, world history, writing.

Graduation Requirements Arts and fine arts (art, music, dance, drama), English, foreign language, health and wellness, mathematics, science, social studies (includes history).

Special Academic Programs 13 Advanced Placement exams for which test preparation is offered; honors section; independent study; academic accommodation for the gifted.

College Admission Counseling 63 students graduated in 2013; all went to college, including Brown University; Dartmouth College; Northwestern University; Stanford University; University of Southern California. Mean SAT critical reading: 708, mean SAT math: 693, mean SAT writing: 731.

Student Life Upper grades have uniform requirement, student council, honor system. Discipline rests equally with students and faculty.

Tuition and Aid Day student tuition: $36,800. Tuition installment plan (monthly payment plans, individually arranged payment plans). Need-based scholarship grants available. In 2013–14, 20% of upper-school students received aid. Total amount of financial aid awarded in 2013–14: $2,200,000.

Admissions Traditional secondary-level entrance grade is 9. ISEE, SSAT or TOEFL required. Deadline for receipt of application materials: January 16. Application fee required: $75. On-campus interview required.

Athletics Interscholastic: basketball, cross-country running, golf, lacrosse, soccer, softball, swimming and diving, tennis, track and field, volleyball, water polo; intramural: climbing, fitness, rock climbing. 6 PE instructors, 15 coaches, 1 athletic trainer.

Computers Computers are regularly used in art, English, foreign language, history, mathematics, science classes. Computer network features include on-campus library services, online commercial services, Internet access, wireless campus network, Internet filtering or blocking technology, one-to-one laptop program. Campus intranet and student e-mail accounts are available to students. Students grades are available online. The school has a published electronic and media policy.

Contact Jill V.W. Lee, Director of Admission. 650-470-7731. Fax: 650-326-8036. E-mail: jlee@castilleja.org. Website: www.castilleja.org

CATHEDRAL HIGH SCHOOL

5225 East 56th Street
Indianapolis, Indiana 46226

Head of School: Mr. Stephen J. Helmich

General Information Coeducational day college-preparatory, arts, religious studies, technology, International Baccalaureate, and AP/honors school, affiliated with Roman Catholic Church. Grades 9–12. Founded: 1918. Setting: urban. 40-acre campus. 5 buildings on campus. Approved or accredited by Independent Schools Association of the Central States, National Catholic Education Association, National Council for Private School Accreditation, North Central Association of Colleges and Schools, and Indiana Department of Education. Endowment: $4 million. Total enrollment: 1,255. Upper school average class size: 19. Upper school faculty-student ratio: 1:13. There are 185 required school days per year for Upper School students. Upper School students typically attend 5 days per week. The average school day consists of 7 hours and 40 minutes.

Upper School Student Profile Grade 9: 349 students (178 boys, 171 girls); Grade 10: 314 students (156 boys, 158 girls); Grade 11: 298 students (155 boys, 143 girls); Grade 12: 295 students (162 boys, 133 girls). 75% of students are Roman Catholic.

Faculty School total: 100. In upper school: 47 men, 53 women; 54 have advanced degrees.

Subjects Offered Advanced biology, advanced chemistry, advanced math, Advanced Placement courses, algebra, American history, American history-AP, American literature-AP, American studies, anatomy, anatomy and physiology, art and culture, art history, arts, Bible, Bible studies, biology, botany, business, business communications, business education, business law, calculus, calculus-AP, career and personal planning, Catholic belief and practice, ceramics, chemistry, chemistry-AP, choir, choral music, chorus, Christianity, civics, civil war history, college counseling, composition-AP, computer science, debate, drama, driver education, earth science, economics, economics-AP, English, English literature, English literature and composition-AP, English literature-AP, English-AP, English/composition-AP, environmental science, fine arts, French, French language-AP, geography, geology, geometry, German, German-AP, government and politics-AP, government-AP, history, history-AP, independent study, journalism, lab science, language development, Latin, life science, macro/microeconomics-AP, mathematics, mathematics-AP, microbiology, music, music appreciation, news writing, newspaper, organic chemistry, photography, photojournalism, physical education, physical fitness, physics, physiology, psychology, religion, SAT/ACT preparation, science, social sciences, social studies, sociology, Spanish, speech, textiles, theater, theater design and production, theater production, theory of knowledge, trigonometry, U.S. government and politics-AP, U.S. history, U.S. history-AP, vocal music, world history, world literature.

Graduation Requirements Arts and fine arts (art, music, dance, drama), biology, composition, economics, English, foreign language, government, mathematics, modern world history, physical education (includes health), religious studies, science, social studies (includes history), speech and debate, technology, U.S. history, 30 hours annually of community service.

Special Academic Programs International Baccalaureate program; Advanced Placement exam preparation; honors section; independent study; academic accommodation for the gifted, the musically talented, and the artistically talented; remedial reading and/or remedial writing; remedial math; programs in English, mathematics for dyslexic students; special instructional classes for deaf students, blind students, students with learning disabilities, Attention Deficit Disorder, and dyslexia.

College Admission Counseling 314 students graduated in 2012; 312 went to college, including Ball State University; Indiana University Bloomington; Loyola University Chicago; Purdue University; University of Dayton; Xavier University. Other: 2 entered military service. Mean SAT critical reading: 541, mean SAT math: 548, mean SAT writing: 536, mean composite ACT: 25.

Student Life Upper grades have uniform requirement, student council, honor system. Discipline rests primarily with faculty. Attendance at religious services is required.

Tuition and Aid Day student tuition: $11,750. Tuition installment plan (Key Tuition Payment Plan, monthly payment plans). Merit scholarship grants, need-based scholarship grants, paying campus jobs available. In 2012–13, 42% of upper-school students received aid; total upper-school merit-scholarship money awarded: $566,000. Total amount of financial aid awarded in 2012–13: $2,300,000.

Admissions Traditional secondary-level entrance grade is 9. For fall 2012, 627 students applied for upper-level admission, 491 were accepted, 349 enrolled. High School Placement Test and High School Placement Test (closed version) from Scholastic Testing Service required. Deadline for receipt of application materials: none. No application fee required. On-campus interview required.

Athletics Interscholastic: baseball (boys), basketball (b,g), cheering (g), cross-country running (b,g), football (b), golf (b,g), soccer (b,g), softball (g), swimming and diving (b,g), tennis (b,g), track and field (b,g), volleyball (g), wrestling (b); intramural: dance squad (g), dance team (g), field hockey (g), kickball (g), lacrosse (b,g), rugby (b,g), volleyball (b), weight lifting (b,g); coed interscholastic: bowling, diving, ice hockey; coed intramural: badminton, bicycling, crew, fencing, Frisbee, martial arts, skiing (downhill), ultimate Frisbee. 6 PE instructors, 1 athletic trainer.

Computers Computers are regularly used in business, business skills, creative writing, desktop publishing, English, foreign language, history, information technology, journalism, mathematics, newspaper, photography, photojournalism, SAT preparation, science, writing, writing, yearbook classes. Computer network features include on-campus library services, online commercial services, Internet access, wireless campus network, Internet filtering or blocking technology. Student e-mail accounts are available to students. Students grades are available online. The school has a published electronic and media policy.

Contact Mr. Duane Emery, Vice President for Enrollment Management. 317-968-7360. Fax: 317-968-7395. E-mail: demery@gocathedral.com. Website: www.cathedral-irish.org/

CATHEDRAL HIGH SCHOOL

350 East 56th Street
New York, New York 10022-4199

Head of School: Ms. Maria Spagnuolo

General Information Girls' day college-preparatory, arts, business, religious studies, and technology school, affiliated with Roman Catholic Church. Grades 9–12. Founded: 1905. Setting: urban. 1 building on campus. Approved or accredited by Middle States Association of Colleges and Schools, National Catholic Education Association, New York Department of Education, New York State Board of Regents, The College Board, and New York Department of Education. Total enrollment: 550. Upper school average class size: 30. Upper school faculty-student ratio: 1:17. Upper School students typically attend 5 days per week. The average school day consists of 7 hours.

Upper School Student Profile 75% of students are Roman Catholic.

Subjects Offered Advanced Placement courses, algebra, art, band, biology, biology-AP, business law, business skills, business studies, calculus, calculus-AP, campus ministry, career education internship, career exploration, Catholic belief and practice, chemistry, chemistry-AP, choir, chorus, Christian doctrine, college admission preparation, college counseling, computer education, computer graphics, computers, constitutional history of U.S., crafts, drama, earth science, economics, electives, English composition, English literature, English-AP, English/composition-AP, fashion, fitness, foreign language, French, general math, geometry, government, guidance, health, health education, honors algebra, honors English, honors geometry, honors U.S. history, honors world history, HTML design, integrated mathematics, internship, lab science, law and the legal system, literature, mathematics-AP, physics, physics-AP, physiology, portfolio art, pre-algebra, pre-calculus, psychology, psychology-AP, religion, science, social education, sociology, Spanish literature, Spanish-AP, studio art, U.S. government, U.S. history, U.S. history-AP, world history, world wide web design.

Graduation Requirements Art, electives, English, foreign language, mathematics, music, physical education (includes health), religion (includes Bible studies and theology), science, social studies (includes history), New York State Regents.

Special Academic Programs 7 Advanced Placement exams for which test preparation is offered; honors section; study at local college for college credit.

College Admission Counseling Colleges students went to include College of the Holy Cross; Fordham University; New York University; Quinnipiac University; Vassar College; Villanova University.

Student Life Upper grades have uniform requirement, student council, honor system. Discipline rests primarily with faculty. Attendance at religious services is required.

Summer Programs Remediation programs offered; held on campus; accepts boys and girls; open to students from other schools. 2014 schedule: July to August. Application deadline: July.

Tuition and Aid Day student tuition: $6990. Tuition installment plan (FACTS Tuition Payment Plan). Tuition reduction for siblings, merit scholarship grants, need-based scholarship grants available.

Admissions Traditional secondary-level entrance grade is 9. Catholic High School Entrance Examination required. Deadline for receipt of application materials: none. No application fee required.

Athletics Interscholastic: basketball, lacrosse, soccer, softball, volleyball; intramural: basketball, swimming and diving. 1 PE instructor, 3 coaches.

Computers Computers are regularly used in all academic classes. Computer network features include on-campus library services, Internet access, Internet filtering or blocking technology. Campus intranet, student e-mail accounts, and computer access in designated common areas are available to students. Students grades are available online.

Contact Mrs. Johanna Velez, Director of Admissions & Recruitment. 212-688-1545 Ext. 224. Fax: 212-754-2024. E-mail: jcastex@cathedralhs.org. Website: www.cathedralhs.org

CATHEDRAL PREPARATORY SCHOOL

225 West 9th Street
Erie, Pennsylvania 16501

Head of School: Rev. Scott William Jabo

General Information Boys' day college-preparatory, arts, religious studies, and technology school, affiliated with Roman Catholic Church. Grades 9–12. Founded: 1921. Setting: urban. 16-acre campus. 1 building on campus. Approved or accredited by Middle States Association of Colleges and Schools and Pennsylvania Department of Education. Endowment: $31 million. Total enrollment: 581. Upper school average class size: 22. Upper school faculty-student ratio: 1:13. There are 180 required school days per year for Upper School students. Upper School students typically attend 5 days per week. The average school day consists of 6 hours and 47 minutes.

Upper School Student Profile Grade 9: 153 students (153 boys); Grade 10: 134 students (134 boys); Grade 11: 151 students (151 boys); Grade 12: 143 students (143 boys). 85% of students are Roman Catholic.

Faculty School total: 48. In upper school: 35 men, 13 women; 23 have advanced degrees.

Subjects Offered Aerospace science, algebra, American history, American history-AP, anatomy and physiology, aviation, Basic programming, biology, biology-AP, calculus, ceramics, chemistry, chemistry-AP, church history, computer literacy, computer programming, creative writing, critical thinking, death and loss, debate, desktop publishing, discrete mathematics, drawing, driver education, English, expository writing, finance, first aid, flight instruction, French, geometry, German, health, history of the Catholic Church, history-AP, human anatomy, integrated science, interpersonal skills, introduction to theater, jazz band, keyboarding, Latin, leadership, Mandarin, mechanical drawing, men's studies, Microsoft, moral theology, newspaper, physical education, physics, pre-calculus, probability and statistics, public speaking, reading, ROTC, sexuality, social justice, Spanish, studio art, theater, trigonometry, U.S. government and politics-AP, video communication, video film production, Vietnam War, world geography, world history, writing, yearbook.

Graduation Requirements American government, biology, chemistry, economics, English, English composition, English literature, geography, government, language, mathematics, physical education (includes health), physics, psychology, social studies (includes history), theology, U.S. government, 100 hours of community service (school, church and community).

Special Academic Programs 13 Advanced Placement exams for which test preparation is offered; honors section; study at local college for college credit.

College Admission Counseling 115 students graduated in 2012; 111 went to college, including Edinboro University of Pennsylvania; Gannon University; John Carroll University; Penn State Erie, The Behrend College; Penn State University Park; University of Pittsburgh. Other: 4 went to work.

Student Life Upper grades have uniform requirement, student council, honor system. Discipline rests primarily with faculty. Attendance at religious services is required.

Tuition and Aid Day student tuition: $7345. Tuition installment plan (FACTS Tuition Payment Plan). Tuition reduction for siblings, merit scholarship grants, need-based scholarship grants available. In 2012–13, 51% of upper-school students received aid; total upper-school merit-scholarship money awarded: $10,000. Total amount of financial aid awarded in 2012–13: $550,000.

Admissions Traditional secondary-level entrance grade is 9. For fall 2012, 212 students applied for upper-level admission, 195 were accepted, 153 enrolled. High School Placement Test required. Deadline for receipt of application materials: March 1. No application fee required. Interview recommended.

Athletics Interscholastic: baseball, basketball, cross-country running, football, golf, hockey, independent competitive sports, JROTC drill, lacrosse, outdoor recreation, power lifting, skiing (cross-country), skiing (downhill), soccer, swimming and diving, tennis, track and field, water polo, weight lifting, weight training, wrestling; intramural: bowling, table tennis, weight lifting. 2 PE instructors, 1 athletic trainer.

Computers Computers are regularly used in all academic classes. Computer network features include on-campus library services, Internet access, wireless campus network, Internet filtering or blocking technology, all students receive an Apple iPad upon admission. Campus intranet and student e-mail accounts are available to students. Students grades are available online. The school has a published electronic and media policy.

Contact Mr. Timothy Dougherty, Director of Admissions. 814-453-7737 Ext. 2242. Fax: 814-455-5462. E-mail: Timothy.Dougherty@prep-villa.com. Website: www.prep-villa.com

CATHOLIC CENTRAL HIGH SCHOOL

625 Seventh Avenue
Troy, New York 12182-2595

Head of School: Mr. Christopher Bott

General Information Coeducational day college-preparatory, arts, business, and religious studies school, affiliated with Roman Catholic Church. Grades 7–12. Founded: 1924. Setting: suburban. 4-acre campus. 2 buildings on campus. Approved or accredited by National Catholic Education Association and New York State Board of Regents. Endowment: $50,000. Total enrollment: 520. Upper school average class size: 16. Upper school faculty-student ratio: 1:15. There are 168 required school days per year for Upper School students. Upper School students typically attend 5 days per week. The average school day consists of 6 hours and 40 minutes.

Upper School Student Profile Grade 9: 102 students (47 boys, 55 girls); Grade 10: 101 students (46 boys, 55 girls); Grade 11: 96 students (33 boys, 63 girls); Grade 12: 110 students (46 boys, 64 girls). 85% of students are Roman Catholic.

Faculty School total: 39. In upper school: 15 men, 22 women; 26 have advanced degrees.

Subjects Offered Accounting, algebra, anatomy and physiology, art, band, biology, business communications, business law, calculus, Catholic belief and practice, chemistry, chorus, computer art, computer programming, computer science, drama, drawing and design, driver education, earth science, economics, English, English language-AP, global studies, government, health, history, honors English, honors U.S. history, Internet, keyboarding, library skills, mathematics, physics, pre-calculus, religion, social studies, Spanish, technology, U.S. history.

Graduation Requirements Art, English, mathematics, physical education (includes health), science, social studies (includes history), theology.

Special Academic Programs Advanced Placement exam preparation; remedial reading and/or remedial writing; remedial math; ESL (12 students enrolled).

College Admission Counseling 108 students graduated in 2013; 107 went to college, including Binghamton University, State University of New York; Le Moyne College; Siena College; State University of New York at New Paltz; University at Albany, State University of New York. Other: 1 went to work.

Student Life Upper grades have uniform requirement, student council. Discipline rests primarily with faculty. Attendance at religious services is required.

Tuition and Aid Day student tuition: $6600. Tuition installment plan (FACTS Tuition Payment Plan). Need-based scholarship grants, paying campus jobs available. In 2013–14, 26% of upper-school students received aid. Total amount of financial aid awarded in 2013–14: $240,000.

Admissions Traditional secondary-level entrance grade is 9. Scholastic Testing Service High School Placement Test required. Deadline for receipt of application materials: none. Application fee required: $100. Interview recommended.

Athletics Interscholastic: baseball (boys), basketball (b,g), bowling (b,g), cross-country running (b,g), dance squad (g), football (b), golf (b), indoor track & field (b,g), soccer (b,g), softball (g), tennis (b,g), track and field (b,g), volleyball (g); intramural: figure skating (g), lacrosse (g); coed interscholastic: cheering; coed intramural: Frisbee. 2 PE instructors, 8 coaches, 1 athletic trainer.

Computers Computers are regularly used in accounting, art, business applications, graphic design, programming classes. Computer network features include on-campus library services, Internet access, Internet filtering or blocking technology.

Contact Mrs. Teresa Mainello, Publicity Director. 518-235-7100 Ext. 224. Fax: 518-237-1796. E-mail: tmainello@cchstroy.org. Website: www.cchstroy.org

CATHOLIC CENTRAL HIGH SCHOOL

148 McHenry Street
Burlington, Wisconsin 53105

Head of School: Mr. Eric Henderson

General Information Coeducational day college-preparatory, arts, business, religious studies, bilingual studies, and technology school, affiliated with Roman Catholic Church. Grades 9–12. Founded: 1924. Setting: small town. Nearest major city is Milwaukee. 25-acre campus. 2 buildings on campus. Approved or accredited by North Central Association of Colleges and Schools and Wisconsin Department of Education. Endowment: $1.4 million. Total enrollment: 180. Upper school average class size: 14. Upper school faculty-student ratio: 1:9. There are 180 required school days per year for Upper School students. Upper School students typically attend 5 days per week. The average school day consists of 7 hours.

Upper School Student Profile Grade 9: 47 students (22 boys, 25 girls); Grade 10: 55 students (25 boys, 30 girls); Grade 11: 45 students (19 boys, 26 girls); Grade 12: 33 students (20 boys, 13 girls). 86% of students are Roman Catholic.

Faculty School total: 19. In upper school: 9 men, 10 women; 9 have advanced degrees.

Subjects Offered 20th century history, 3-dimensional art, 3-dimensional design, accounting, advanced biology, advanced chemistry, advanced computer applications, advanced math, Advanced Placement courses, African-American history, algebra, American government, American history, American literature, American literature-AP, analytic geometry, anatomy, anatomy and physiology, animation, Arabic, art, band, Bible, Bible studies, biology, biology-AP, biotechnology, botany, business, business education, business technology, calculus, calculus-AP, cartooning/animation, Catholic

belief and practice, ceramics, chemistry, Chinese, choir, church history, college admission preparation, college planning, composition, composition-AP, computer animation, computer graphics, computer skills, consumer education, digital photography, diversity studies, drawing, earth science, economics, English, English literature-AP, environmental science, finance, forensics, French, geography, geometry, government, health, history of religion, history of the Catholic Church, human anatomy, human biology, integrated science, intro to computers, Italian, journalism, language-AP, marketing, mathematics-AP, music theory, New Testament, painting, personal finance, personal fitness, photography, physical fitness, physics, physiology, pre-calculus, probability and statistics, psychology, psychology-AP, religion, religious studies, skills for success, social justice, sociology, Spanish, speech, statistics, study skills, theology, trigonometry, U.S. history, video and animation, world religions, zoology.

Graduation Requirements 20th century history, American government, health, personal finance, physical education (includes health), religious education, speech.

Special Academic Programs 3 Advanced Placement exams for which test preparation is offered; honors section; independent study; study at local college for college credit; study abroad; academic accommodation for the gifted and the artistically talented.

College Admission Counseling 37 students graduated in 2013; 34 went to college, including Marquette University; Milwaukee Area Technical College; University of Wisconsin–La Crosse; University of Wisconsin–Madison; University of Wisconsin–Milwaukee. Other: 1 went to work, 2 entered military service. Median composite ACT: 22. 6% scored over 26 on composite ACT.

Student Life Upper grades have specified standards of dress, student council, honor system. Discipline rests primarily with faculty. Attendance at religious services is required.

Summer Programs Sports programs offered; session focuses on basketball; held on campus; accepts boys and girls; open to students from other schools. 150 students usually enrolled. 2014 schedule: June 15 to July 31. Application deadline: June 15.

Tuition and Aid Day student tuition: $6950–$7600. Tuition installment plan (FACTS Tuition Payment Plan, individually arranged payment plans). Tuition reduction for siblings, need-based scholarship grants available. In 2013–14, 60% of upper-school students received aid. Total amount of financial aid awarded in 2013–14: $120,000.

Admissions For fall 2013, 185 students applied for upper-level admission, 182 were accepted, 180 enrolled. ACT-Explore required. Deadline for receipt of application materials: none. Application fee required: $100. On-campus interview required.

Athletics Interscholastic: baseball (boys), basketball (b,g), dance team (g), football (b), golf (b), softball (g), tennis (g), volleyball (g), wrestling (b); coed interscholastic: bowling, cheering, cross-country running, fitness, gymnastics, physical fitness, track and field; coed intramural: bicycling, dance, dance squad, strength & conditioning, table tennis, ultimate Frisbee, weight training. 1 PE instructor, 31 coaches, 1 athletic trainer.

Computers Computers are regularly used in accounting, business, economics, graphic design, journalism, multimedia, newspaper, photography, typing, video film production, Web site design, writing classes. Computer network features include Internet access, wireless campus network, Internet filtering or blocking technology. Student e-mail accounts and computer access in designated common areas are available to students. Students grades are available online. The school has a published electronic and media policy.

Contact Mr. Kyle Scott, Admissions Director. 262-763-1510 Ext. 225. Fax: 262-763-1509. E-mail: kscott@cchsnet.org. Website: www.cchsnet.org

THE CATHOLIC HIGH SCHOOL OF BALTIMORE

2800 Edison Highway
Baltimore, Maryland 21213

Head of School: Dr. Barbara D. Nazelrod

General Information Girls' day and distance learning college-preparatory, general academic, arts, religious studies, and technology school, affiliated with Roman Catholic Church. Grades 9–12. Distance learning grades 9–12. Founded: 1939. Setting: urban. 6-acre campus. 1 building on campus. Approved or accredited by Association of Independent Maryland Schools, Middle States Association of Colleges and Schools, National Catholic Education Association, and Maryland Department of Education. Endowment: $3.3 million. Total enrollment: 320. Upper school average class size: 17. Upper school faculty-student ratio: 1:17. There are 174 required school days per year for Upper School students. Upper School students typically attend 5 days per week. The average school day consists of 6 hours and 45 minutes.

Upper School Student Profile Grade 9: 92 students (92 girls); Grade 10: 89 students (89 girls); Grade 11: 83 students (83 girls); Grade 12: 56 students (56 girls). 76% of students are Roman Catholic.

Faculty School total: 31. In upper school: 13 men, 18 women; 20 have advanced degrees.

Subjects Offered Algebra, American history, American literature, anatomy, art, band, biology, calculus, chemistry, community service, computer programming, computer science, creative writing, dance, drama, earth science, English, English literature, expository writing, fine arts, French, geometry, government/civics, grammar, health, history, instrumental music, journalism, keyboarding, literature, mathematics, music, photography, physical education, physics, physiology, psychology, reading, religion, science, social studies, Spanish, speech, study skills, technology, theater, theology, Web site design, world history, world literature.

Graduation Requirements Arts and fine arts (art, music, dance, drama), computer science, English, foreign language, mathematics, physical education (includes health), science, social studies (includes history), theology. Community service is required.

Special Academic Programs Advanced Placement exam preparation; honors section; independent study; study at local college for college credit; remedial reading and/or remedial writing; remedial math; programs in English, mathematics, general development for dyslexic students.

College Admission Counseling 57 students graduated in 2013; all went to college, including Neumann University; Towson University; University of Maryland, Baltimore County. Median SAT critical reading: 475, median SAT math: 440, median SAT writing: 500, median combined SAT: 1415. 13% scored over 600 on SAT critical reading, 11% scored over 600 on SAT math, 15% scored over 600 on SAT writing, 11% scored over 1800 on combined SAT.

Student Life Upper grades have uniform requirement, student council, honor system. Discipline rests primarily with faculty. Attendance at religious services is required.

Summer Programs Enrichment, sports, computer instruction programs offered; session focuses on enrichment; held both on and off campus; held at sports field; accepts girls; not open to students from other schools. 100 students usually enrolled. 2014 schedule: June 16 to July 30. Application deadline: none.

Tuition and Aid Day student tuition: $12,300. Guaranteed tuition plan. Tuition installment plan (Insured Tuition Payment Plan, FACTS Tuition Payment Plan, biannual payment plan, annual payment plan). Tuition reduction for siblings, merit scholarship grants, need-based scholarship grants available. In 2013–14, 33% of upper-school students received aid; total upper-school merit-scholarship money awarded: $389,025. Total amount of financial aid awarded in 2013–14: $589,525.

Admissions Traditional secondary-level entrance grade is 9. For fall 2013, 212 students applied for upper-level admission, 199 were accepted, 95 enrolled. High School Placement Test required. Deadline for receipt of application materials: December 18. Application fee required: $50. On-campus interview required.

Athletics Interscholastic: basketball, cheering, cross-country running, dance team, field hockey, golf, indoor track & field, lacrosse, soccer, softball, swimming and diving, tennis, track and field, volleyball; intramural: aerobics, aerobics/dance, cooperative games. 1 PE instructor, 20 coaches, 1 athletic trainer.

Computers Computers are regularly used in art, English, foreign language, history, mathematics, music, science, theology classes. Computer network features include on-campus library services, online commercial services, Internet access, wireless campus network, Internet filtering or blocking technology. Campus intranet and student e-mail accounts are available to students. Students grades are available online. The school has a published electronic and media policy.

Contact Ms. Michelle Illar, Assistant Director of Enrollment. 410-732-6200 Ext. 213. Fax: 410-732-7639. E-mail: millar@thecatholichighschool.org. Website: www.thecatholichighschool.org

THE CATLIN GABEL SCHOOL

8825 SW Barnes Road
Portland, Oregon 97225

Head of School: Dr. Lark P. Palma

General Information Coeducational day college-preparatory, arts, technology, and sciences school. Grades PK–12. Founded: 1957. Setting: suburban. 60-acre campus. 13 buildings on campus. Approved or accredited by Northwest Association of Schools and Colleges. Member of National Association of Independent Schools and Secondary School Admission Test Board. Endowment: $19.5 million. Total enrollment: 753. Upper school average class size: 15. Upper school faculty-student ratio: 1:8. There are 170 required school days per year for Upper School students. Upper School students typically attend 5 days per week. The average school day consists of 7 hours and 10 minutes.

Upper School Student Profile Grade 6: 56 students (27 boys, 29 girls); Grade 7: 64 students (30 boys, 34 girls); Grade 8: 65 students (29 boys, 36 girls); Grade 9: 79 students (39 boys, 40 girls); Grade 10: 77 students (40 boys, 37 girls); Grade 11: 76 students (44 boys, 32 girls); Grade 12: 77 students (38 boys, 39 girls).

Faculty School total: 92. In upper school: 28 men, 22 women; 34 have advanced degrees.

Subjects Offered Acting, advanced chemistry, advanced computer applications, advanced math, algebra, American democracy, American history, American literature, ancient world history, art, art history, arts, astronomy, athletics, baseball, Basic programming, basketball, biology, bookmaking, bowling, calculus, ceramics, chemistry, Chinese, college admission preparation, college counseling, comedy, computer art, computer graphics, computer programming, computer resources, computer science, computer skills, computer studies, concert choir, creative writing, critical studies in film, critical thinking, debate, digital imaging, digital photography, drama, drama performance, dramatic arts, drawing and design, ecology, economics, English, English literature, ensembles, ethics and responsibility, European history, expository writing, fiber arts, film studies, fine arts, foreign language, foreign policy, French, geometry, golf, government/civics, graphic arts, graphic design, health, history, human sexuality, jazz band, mathematics, model United Nations, music, musical productions, ornithology, outdoor education, peer counseling, performing arts, photo shop, photography, physical education, physical fitness, physics, playwriting and directing, pre-calculus, probability and statistics, robotics, science, set design, Shakespeare, social studies, Spanish, Spanish literature, speech and debate, stage design, stagecraft, statistics, studio art, study skills, technical theater, tennis, theater, theater arts, theater design and production, track and field, trigonometry, U.S. history, visual and performing arts, vocal ensemble, voice, voice ensemble, volleyball, weight fitness, weight training, woodworking, world affairs, world history, world literature, world wide web design, writing, writing workshop, yearbook.

Graduation Requirements Arts and fine arts (art, music, dance, drama), English, foreign language, mathematics, physical education (includes health), science, social studies (includes history). Community service is required.

Special Academic Programs Honors section; independent study; term-away projects; study at local college for college credit; study abroad; academic accommodation for the gifted, the musically talented, and the artistically talented; special instructional classes for deaf students.

College Admission Counseling 77 students graduated in 2013; all went to college, including Brown University; Colgate University; Oberlin College; Stanford University; The George Washington University; Tulane University. Mean SAT critical reading: 655, mean SAT math: 644, mean SAT writing: 644, mean combined SAT: 1943, mean composite ACT: 29. 89% scored over 600 on SAT critical reading, 87% scored over 600 on SAT math, 80% scored over 600 on SAT writing, 86% scored over 1800 on combined SAT, 96% scored over 26 on composite ACT.

Student Life Upper grades have student council, honor system. Discipline rests equally with students and faculty.

Summer Programs Enrichment, sports, art/fine arts, computer instruction programs offered; session focuses on arts and enrichment; held both on and off campus; held at various outdoor areas—hiking, climbing, etc.; accepts boys and girls; open to students from other schools. 85 students usually enrolled. 2014 schedule: June 24 to August 2.

Tuition and Aid Day student tuition: $19,200–$25,850. Tuition installment plan (Insured Tuition Payment Plan, monthly payment plans, individually arranged payment plans). Merit scholarship grants, need-based scholarship grants available. In 2013–14, 29% of upper-school students received aid. Total amount of financial aid awarded in 2013–14: $1,323,000.

Admissions Traditional secondary-level entrance grade is 9. For fall 2013, 64 students applied for upper-level admission, 50 were accepted, 29 enrolled. SSAT required. Deadline for receipt of application materials: February 4. Application fee required: $75. Interview required.

Athletics Interscholastic: baseball (boys, girls), basketball (b,g), cross-country running (b,g), golf (b,g), racquetball (b,g), soccer (b,g), tennis (b,g), track and field (b,g), volleyball (g); coed interscholastic: racquetball; coed intramural: aerobics/dance, alpine skiing, backpacking, bicycling, bowling, canoeing/kayaking, climbing, fishing, fitness, Frisbee, hiking/backpacking, jogging, kayaking, mountain biking, mountaineering, nordic skiing, ocean paddling, outdoor activities, outdoor adventure, outdoor education, outdoor recreation, outdoors, physical fitness, physical training, rafting, rock climbing, ropes courses, running, skiing (cross-country), skiing (downhill), snowshoeing, strength & conditioning, telemark skiing, ultimate Frisbee, walking, wall climbing, weight lifting, weight training, wilderness, wilderness survival, yoga. 6 PE instructors, 20 coaches.

Computers Computers are regularly used in animation, art, English, foreign language, graphic design, mathematics, science, theater, writing classes. Computer network features include on-campus library services, online commercial services, Internet access, wireless campus network, laptop requirement for all upper school students, videoconferencing, SmartBoards. Campus intranet and student e-mail accounts are available to students. The school has a published electronic and media policy.

Contact Ms. Sara Nordhoff, Director of Admission and Financial Aid. 503-297-1894 Ext. 345. Fax: 503-297-0139. E-mail: nordhoffs@catlin.edu. Website: www.catlin.edu

CENTRAL ALBERTA CHRISTIAN HIGH SCHOOL

22 Eagle Road
Lacombe, Alberta T4L 1G7, Canada

Head of School: Mr. Mel Brandsma

General Information Coeducational day college-preparatory, general academic, religious studies, and bilingual studies school, affiliated with Christian Reformed Church. Grades 10–12. Founded: 1989. Setting: rural. Nearest major city is Red Deer, Canada. 12.5-acre campus. 1 building on campus. Approved or accredited by Association of Independent Schools and Colleges of Alberta, Christian Schools International, and Alberta Department of Education. Language of instruction: English. Total enrollment: 103. Upper school average class size: 103. Upper school faculty-student ratio: 1:13. There are 181 required school days per year for Upper School students. Upper School students typically attend 5 days per week. The average school day consists of 6 hours and 25 minutes.

Upper School Student Profile Grade 10: 35 students (19 boys, 16 girls); Grade 11: 30 students (15 boys, 15 girls); Grade 12: 38 students (17 boys, 21 girls). 75% of students are members of Christian Reformed Church.

Faculty School total: 8. In upper school: 4 men, 4 women; 2 have advanced degrees.

Subjects Offered Accounting, agriculture, all academic, art, career education, Christian ethics, computer education, drafting, foods, French as a second language, photography, physical education, work experience.

Graduation Requirements All academic, French.

College Admission Counseling 34 students graduated in 2013; they went to Redeemer University College.

Student Life Upper grades have student council, honor system. Discipline rests primarily with faculty. Attendance at religious services is required.

Tuition and Aid Day student tuition: CAN$5450. Tuition installment plan (monthly payment plans, individually arranged payment plans). Tuition reduction for siblings available.

Admissions Traditional secondary-level entrance grade is 10. Deadline for receipt of application materials: none. No application fee required. Interview recommended.

Athletics Coed Interscholastic: badminton, basketball, bowling, climbing, cross-country running, fitness, ice skating, jogging, outdoor activities, physical fitness, physical training, running, soccer, softball, swimming and diving, track and field, volleyball, wall climbing, weight training, whiffle ball; coed intramural: basketball, broomball, cooperative games. 1 PE instructor, 1 coach.

Computers Computers are regularly used in all classes. Computer network features include Internet access, wireless campus network, Internet filtering or blocking technology. Campus intranet is available to students.

Contact Office. 403-782-4535. Fax: 403-782-5425. E-mail: office@cachs.ca. Website: www.cachs.ca/

CENTRAL CATHOLIC HIGH SCHOOL

200 South Carpenter Road
Modesto, California 95351

Head of School: Jim Pecchenino

General Information Coeducational day college-preparatory, arts, religious studies, and bilingual studies school, affiliated with Roman Catholic Church. Grades 9–12. Founded: 1966. Setting: urban. Nearest major city is Sacramento. 21-acre campus. 13 buildings on campus. Approved or accredited by National Catholic Education Association, Western Association of Schools and Colleges, and Western Catholic Education Association. Endowment: $2.2 million. Total enrollment: 385. Upper school average class size: 22. Upper school faculty-student ratio: 1:14. There are 180 required school days per year for Upper School students. Upper School students typically attend 5 days per week. The average school day consists of 6 hours and 50 minutes.

Upper School Student Profile Grade 9: 103 students (59 boys, 44 girls); Grade 10: 96 students (55 boys, 41 girls); Grade 11: 100 students (52 boys, 48 girls); Grade 12: 99 students (51 boys, 48 girls). 81% of students are Roman Catholic.

Faculty School total: 26. In upper school: 8 men, 18 women; 11 have advanced degrees.

Subjects Offered Algebra, American history, American literature, art, Bible studies, biology, broadcast journalism, calculus, chemistry, dance, drama, drawing and design, economics, English, English literature, environmental science, ethics, European history, geometry, government/civics, health, mathematics, music, physical education, physical science, physics, pre-calculus, Spanish, speech, theology, vocal ensemble, world history, world literature, yearbook.

Graduation Requirements Arts and fine arts (art, music, dance, drama), English, mathematics, physical education (includes health), religion (includes Bible studies and theology), science, social studies (includes history), speech, 100 Christian service hours.

Special Academic Programs Advanced Placement exam preparation; honors section; study at local college for college credit; remedial reading and/or remedial writing; remedial math; programs in English, mathematics, general development for dyslexic students.

College Admission Counseling 102 students graduated in 2013; 101 went to college, including California Polytechnic State University, San Luis Obispo; California State University, Stanislaus; Saint Mary's College of California; University of California, Berkeley; University of California, Davis; University of California, Los Angeles. Other: 1 entered a postgraduate year. Median SAT critical reading: 540, median SAT math: 520, median SAT writing: 500, median combined SAT: 1560. 18.2% scored over 600 on SAT critical reading, 22.7% scored over 600 on SAT math, 11.7% scored over 600 on SAT writing, 15.6% scored over 1800 on combined SAT.

Student Life Upper grades have specified standards of dress, student council. Discipline rests primarily with faculty. Attendance at religious services is required.

Summer Programs Remediation programs offered; session focuses on remediation and SAT Prep; held on campus; accepts boys and girls; open to students from other schools. 105 students usually enrolled. 2014 schedule: June 4 to July 6. Application deadline: May 11.

Tuition and Aid Day student tuition: $9542–$9948. Tuition installment plan (FACTS Tuition Payment Plan, monthly payment plans, individually arranged payment plans, quarterly and semiannual payment plans). Tuition reduction for siblings, merit scholarship grants, need-based scholarship grants, paying campus jobs available. In 2013–14, 36% of upper-school students received aid; total upper-school merit-scholarship money awarded: $16,450. Total amount of financial aid awarded in 2013–14: $488,434.

Admissions Traditional secondary-level entrance grade is 9. For fall 2013, 123 students applied for upper-level admission, 94 were accepted, 94 enrolled. Otis-Lennon School Ability Test required. Deadline for receipt of application materials: none. Application fee required: $45. On-campus interview required.

Athletics Interscholastic: baseball (boys), basketball (b,g), cross-country running (b,g), football (b), golf (b,g), soccer (b,g), softball (g), tennis (b,g), track and field (b,g), volleyball (g), water polo (b,g), wrestling (b,g); intramural: cheering (g); coed interscholastic: swimming and diving; coed intramural: dance. 2 PE instructors, 91 coaches.

Computers Computers are regularly used in literacy, yearbook classes. Computer network features include on-campus library services, Internet access, Internet filtering or blocking technology. Computer access in designated common areas is available to students. Students grades are available online. The school has a published electronic and media policy.

Contact Jodi Tybor, Admissions Coordinator/Registrar. 209-524-9611 Ext. 104. Fax: 209-524-4913. E-mail: tybor@cchsca.org. Website: www.cchsca.org

CENTRAL CATHOLIC HIGH SCHOOL

300 Hampshire Street
Lawrence, Massachusetts 01841

Head of School: Mrs. Doreen A. Keller

General Information Coeducational day college-preparatory, arts, business, religious studies, and technology school, affiliated with Roman Catholic Church. Grades 9–12. Founded: 1935. Setting: urban. Nearest major city is Boston. 1 building on campus. Approved or accredited by Commission on Independent Schools, New England Association of Schools and Colleges, and Massachusetts Department of Education. Member of National Association of Independent Schools. Total enrollment: 1,327. Upper school average class size: 25. Upper school faculty-student ratio: 1:24. There are 165 required school days per year for Upper School students. Upper School students typically attend 5 days per week. The average school day consists of 6 hours and 15 minutes.

Upper School Student Profile Grade 9: 348 students (151 boys, 197 girls); Grade 10: 358 students (176 boys, 182 girls); Grade 11: 317 students (170 boys, 147 girls); Grade 12: 304 students (151 boys, 153 girls). 80% of students are Roman Catholic.

Faculty School total: 101. In upper school: 42 men, 48 women; 59 have advanced degrees.

Subjects Offered Art, arts, computer science, English, fine arts, French, health, mathematics, physical education, religion, science, social studies, Spanish.

Graduation Requirements Arts and fine arts (art, music, dance, drama), computer science, English, foreign language, mathematics, religion (includes Bible studies and theology), science, social studies (includes history).

Special Academic Programs International Baccalaureate program; Advanced Placement exam preparation; honors section; study at local college for college credit.

College Admission Counseling 314 students graduated in 2013; 296 went to college. Other: 1 went to work, 1 entered military service. Mean SAT critical reading: 553, mean SAT math: 545, mean SAT writing: 537, mean combined SAT: 1615, mean composite ACT: 24. 24% scored over 600 on SAT critical reading, 31% scored over 600 on SAT math, 24% scored over 600 on SAT writing, 36.7% scored over 26 on composite ACT.

Student Life Upper grades have uniform requirement, student council, honor system. Discipline rests primarily with faculty. Attendance at religious services is required.

Tuition and Aid Day student tuition: $11,860. Tuition installment plan (FACTS Tuition Payment Plan, monthly payment plans). Merit scholarship grants, need-based scholarship grants available. In 2013–14, 28% of upper-school students received aid; total upper-school merit-scholarship money awarded: $102,571. Total amount of financial aid awarded in 2013–14: $1,460,044.

Admissions Traditional secondary-level entrance grade is 9. For fall 2013, 733 students applied for upper-level admission, 698 were accepted, 348 enrolled. Archdiocese of Boston High School entrance exam provided by STS, High School Placement Test and High School Placement Test (closed version) from Scholastic Testing Service required. Deadline for receipt of application materials: none. No application fee required. Interview required.

Athletics Interscholastic: baseball (boys), basketball (b,g), bowling (b,g), cheering (g), cross-country running (b,g), dance squad (b,g), diving (b,g), field hockey (g), figure skating (g), fishing (b,g), football (b), golf (b), gymnastics (g), hockey (b), ice hockey (b), ice skating (g), indoor hockey (g), indoor track (b,g), indoor track & field (b,g), lacrosse (b,g), martial arts (b,g), modern dance (b,g), soccer (b,g), softball (g), swimming and diving (b,g), tennis (b,g), track and field (b,g), volleyball (b,g), wall climbing (b,g), winter (indoor) track (b,g), wrestling (b); intramural: basketball (b,g); coed interscholastic: dance team. 3 PE instructors, 80 coaches, 1 athletic trainer.

Computers Computer network features include on-campus library services, Internet access, wireless campus network, Internet filtering or blocking technology. Campus intranet, student e-mail accounts, and computer access in designated common areas are available to students. The school has a published electronic and media policy.

Contact Mr. Thomas Sipsey, Assistant Director of Admissions. 978-682-0260 Ext. 623. Fax: 978-685-2707. E-mail: tsipsey@centralcatholic.net. Website: www.centralcatholic.net

CENTRAL CATHOLIC HIGH SCHOOL

1403 North St. Mary's Street
San Antonio, Texas 78215-1785

Head of School: Rev. Richard G.T. Wosman, S.M.

General Information Boys' day college-preparatory school, affiliated with Roman Catholic Church. Grades 9–12. Founded: 1852. Setting: urban. 10-acre campus. 3 buildings on campus. Approved or accredited by National Catholic Education Association, Southern Association of Colleges and Schools, Texas Catholic Conference, and Texas Department of Education. Endowment: $4 million. Total enrollment: 520. Upper school average class size: 23. Upper school faculty-student ratio: 1:17. There are 180 required school days per year for Upper School students. Upper School students typically attend 5 days per week. The average school day consists of 6 hours and 30 minutes.

Upper School Student Profile Grade 9: 136 students (136 boys); Grade 10: 127 students (127 boys); Grade 11: 127 students (127 boys); Grade 12: 130 students (130 boys). 90% of students are Roman Catholic.

Faculty School total: 46. In upper school: 33 men, 13 women; 33 have advanced degrees.

Subjects Offered Algebra, American government, American history-AP, anatomy, art, biology, calculus-AP, ceramics, chemistry, chemistry-AP, chorus, Christian and Hebrew scripture, church history, community service, computer science, concert band, economics, English, English language and composition-AP, English language-AP, English literature and composition-AP, English literature-AP, environmental science, fine arts, geometry, health, honors algebra, honors English, honors geometry, honors world history, humanities, information technology, jazz band, journalism, JROTC, languages, Latin, marching band, physics, pre-calculus, probability and statistics, psychology, religion, science, social studies, Spanish, Spanish literature-AP, speech, trigonometry, world geography, world history.

Graduation Requirements Algebra, American government, American history, arts and fine arts (art, music, dance, drama), biology, chemistry, Christian and Hebrew scripture, Christian doctrine, computer information systems, computer science, economics, English, foreign language, geometry, health, JROTC, moral reasoning, religion (includes Bible studies and theology), religious education, social justice, speech, trigonometry, world civilizations, world geography, world history, world religions, different requirements for Marianist Honors Diploma. Community service is required.

Special Academic Programs 8 Advanced Placement exams for which test preparation is offered; honors section; study at local college for college credit.

College Admission Counseling 135 students graduated in 2013; 134 went to college, including Saint Mary's University; Texas A&M University; Texas Tech University; The University of Texas at Austin; The University of Texas at San Antonio; University of the Incarnate Word. Other: 1 entered military service. Mean SAT critical reading: 541, mean SAT math: 537, mean SAT writing: 528, mean combined SAT: 1606, mean composite ACT: 25.

Student Life Upper grades have specified standards of dress, student council, honor system. Discipline rests primarily with faculty. Attendance at religious services is required.

Tuition and Aid Day student tuition: $1040. Tuition installment plan (FACTS Tuition Payment Plan, monthly payment plans, individually arranged payment plans, semester payment plan, Tuition Management Systems). Tuition reduction for siblings, merit scholarship grants, need-based scholarship grants, paying campus jobs available. In 2013–14, 45% of upper-school students received aid; total upper-school merit-scholarship money awarded: $125,000. Total amount of financial aid awarded in 2013–14: $285,000.

Admissions Traditional secondary-level entrance grade is 9. Essay, Scholastic Testing Service High School Placement Test and writing sample required. Deadline for receipt of application materials: none. No application fee required. On-campus interview required.

Athletics Interscholastic: baseball, basketball, cheering (g), cross-country running, drill team, football, golf, JROTC drill, lacrosse, physical training, riflery; intramural: basketball, bowling, football. 1 PE instructor, 21 coaches, 1 athletic trainer.

Computers Computers are regularly used in college planning, computer applications, drawing and design, engineering, English, information technology, journalism, newspaper, science, yearbook classes. Computer network features include on-campus library services, Internet access, Internet filtering or blocking technology, access to other libraries through Texas Library Connection. Students grades are available online. The school has a published electronic and media policy.

Contact Mrs. Veronica Beck, Director of Admissions and Tuition Assistance. 210-225-6794 Ext. 209. Fax: 210-227-9353. E-mail: admissions@cchs-satx.org. Website: www.cchs-satx.org

CHADWICK SCHOOL

26800 South Academy Drive
Palos Verdes Peninsula, California 90274

Head of School: Frederick T. Hill

General Information Coeducational day college-preparatory, arts, and technology school. Grades K–12. Founded: 1935. Setting: suburban. Nearest major city

is Los Angeles. 45-acre campus. 5 buildings on campus. Approved or accredited by Association for Experiential Education, The College Board, Western Association of Schools and Colleges, and California Department of Education. Member of National Association of Independent Schools. Endowment: $20 million. Total enrollment: 831. Upper school average class size: 17. Upper school faculty-student ratio: 1:5. There are 170 required school days per year for Upper School students. Upper School students typically attend 5 days per week. The average school day consists of 7 hours and 45 minutes.

Upper School Student Profile Grade 9: 101 students (42 boys, 59 girls); Grade 10: 88 students (37 boys, 51 girls); Grade 11: 81 students (35 boys, 46 girls); Grade 12: 82 students (39 boys, 43 girls).

Faculty School total: 76. In upper school: 34 men, 42 women; 53 have advanced degrees.

Subjects Offered 3-dimensional art, Advanced Placement courses, African history, algebra, American history, American literature, American studies, art, art history-AP, art-AP, Asian history, biology, calculus, calculus-AP, ceramics, chemistry, chemistry-AP, choral music, comparative government and politics-AP, computer math, computer programming, computer science-AP, constitutional law, creative writing, dance, drama, economics, English, English literature, English literature-AP, environmental science, environmental science-AP, European history, expository writing, fine arts, forensics, French, French-AP, geometry, grammar, health, history, honors algebra, honors geometry, instrumental music, integrated science, Latin, Latin American history, Latin American studies, life science, Mandarin, marine biology, Middle East, Middle Eastern history, music, music theory-AP, outdoor education, photography, physical education, physics, pre-calculus, probability, robotics, science, social studies, South African history, Spanish, Spanish-AP, speech, statistics, statistics-AP, theater, trigonometry, U.S. history-AP, wilderness education, world history, world literature, writing, yearbook.

Graduation Requirements Arts and fine arts (art, music, dance, drama), English, foreign language, history, mathematics, outdoor education, performing arts, physical education (includes health), science.

Special Academic Programs Advanced Placement exam preparation; honors section; independent study; term-away projects; study abroad; academic accommodation for the gifted, the musically talented, and the artistically talented.

College Admission Counseling 94 students graduated in 2013; all went to college, including Cornell University; Georgetown University; New York University; Santa Clara University; University of Chicago; University of Southern California. Mean SAT critical reading: 646, mean SAT math: 682, mean SAT writing: 684, mean combined SAT: 2014, mean composite ACT: 29.

Student Life Upper grades have specified standards of dress, student council, honor system. Discipline rests equally with students and faculty.

Summer Programs Sports, art/fine arts, computer instruction programs offered; session focuses on visual and performing arts, academics, athletics, enrichment; held on campus; accepts boys and girls; open to students from other schools. 500 students usually enrolled. 2014 schedule: June 23 to July 25. Application deadline: April.

Tuition and Aid Day student tuition: $30,640. Tuition installment plan (Key Tuition Payment Plan, individually arranged payment plans). Need-based scholarship grants, paying campus jobs, Malone Scholarship (need/merit-based), MacFarlane Scholarship (need/merit-based) available. In 2013–14, 17% of upper-school students received aid. Total amount of financial aid awarded in 2013–14: $1,841,675.

Admissions Traditional secondary-level entrance grade is 9. ISEE required. Deadline for receipt of application materials: January 17. Application fee required: $125. On-campus interview required.

Athletics Interscholastic: baseball (boys), basketball (b,g), cheering (g), cross-country running (b,g), diving (b,g), football (b), golf (b,g), lacrosse (b,g), soccer (b,g), softball (g), swimming and diving (b,g), tennis (b,g), track and field (b,g), volleyball (b,g), water polo (b,g); intramural: aerobics/dance (g), dance (g), horseback riding (g); coed interscholastic: cheering, equestrian sports; coed intramural: fencing. 11 coaches, 3 athletic trainers.

Computers Computers are regularly used in art, college planning, computer applications, creative writing, drawing and design, economics, engineering, English, foreign language, geography, graphic arts, health, history, humanities, journalism, mathematics, music, newspaper, photography, photojournalism, programming, publications, research skills, science, social studies, theater arts, Web site design, wilderness education, writing, yearbook classes. Computer network features include on-campus library services, Internet access, wireless campus network, Internet filtering or blocking technology. Campus intranet, student e-mail accounts, and computer access in designated common areas are available to students. Students grades are available online. The school has a published electronic and media policy.

Contact Admission Manager. 310-377-1543 Ext. 4025. Fax: 310-377-0380. E-mail: admissions@chadwickschool.org. Website: www.chadwickschool.org

CHAMBERLAIN-HUNT ACADEMY

124 McComb Avenue
Port Gibson, Mississippi 39150

Head of School: Col. Jack Gardner West

General Information Boys' boarding and coeducational day college-preparatory, arts, religious studies, and military school, affiliated with Presbyterian Church,

Reformed Church. Boarding boys grades 7–12, day boys grades 7–12, day girls grades 7–12. Founded: 1879. Setting: small town. Nearest major city is Vicksburg. Students are housed in single-sex dormitories. 230-acre campus. 11 buildings on campus. Approved or accredited by Assocaition of Classical Christian Schools, Mississippi Private School Association, Southern Association of Colleges and Schools, and Mississippi Department of Education. Endowment: $29 million. Total enrollment: 90. Upper school average class size: 5. Upper school faculty-student ratio: 1:5. There are 180 required school days per year for Upper School students. Upper School students typically attend 5 days per week. The average school day consists of 7 hours and 45 minutes.

Upper School Student Profile Grade 10: 19 students (19 boys); Grade 11: 25 students (25 boys); Grade 12: 17 students (17 boys). 95% of students are boarding students. 27% are state residents. 20 states are represented in upper school student body. 2% are international students. International students from Costa Rica, India, Kenya, Singapore, and Venezuela. 16% of students are Presbyterian, Reformed.

Faculty School total: 19. In upper school: 12 men, 2 women; 11 have advanced degrees; 11 reside on campus.

Subjects Offered ACT preparation, advanced math, Advanced Placement courses, algebra, American Civil War, American government, American history, American literature-AP, ancient history, art, Bible, biology, British literature, business, calculus, chemistry, choir, Christian doctrine, Christian ethics, church history, classical Greek literature, computer programming, computer skills, CPR, earth science, economics, English, English literature, English literature-AP, ethics, French, geometry, government, keyboarding, Latin, logic, men's studies, military history, physics, pre-algebra, rhetoric, Spanish, theology, U.S. government, U.S. history, vocal ensemble, wilderness experience, world history, world wide web design.

Graduation Requirements Algebra, American literature, anatomy and physiology, Bible, biology, British literature, chemistry, classical Greek literature, economics, electives, geometry, intro to computers, languages, medieval literature, rhetoric, state history, Talmud, U.S. government, U.S. history, world geography, world history, oral comprehensive exams, senior speech, worldview class.

Special Academic Programs International Baccalaureate program; honors section; accelerated programs; independent study; academic accommodation for the gifted, the musically talented, and the artistically talented; remedial reading and/or remedial writing; remedial math; ESL.

College Admission Counseling 10 students graduated in 2012; 7 went to college, including Auburn University; Hinds Community College; Louisiana State University and Agricultural and Mechanical College; Mississippi College; Palm Beach Atlantic University; University of the Ozarks. Other: 2 went to work, 1 entered military service. Median composite ACT: 22. 20% scored over 26 on composite ACT.

Student Life Upper grades have uniform requirement, student council, honor system. Discipline rests primarily with faculty. Attendance at religious services is required.

Tuition and Aid Day student tuition: $14,500; 7-day tuition and room/board: $25,000. Guaranteed tuition plan. Tuition installment plan (The Tuition Plan, monthly payment plans, individually arranged payment plans). Tuition reduction for siblings, merit scholarship grants, need-based scholarship grants available. In 2012–13, 33% of upper-school students received aid; total upper-school merit-scholarship money awarded: $10,000. Total amount of financial aid awarded in 2012–13: $250,000.

Admissions Traditional secondary-level entrance grade is 10. For fall 2012, 39 students applied for upper-level admission, 35 were accepted, 30 enrolled. Math and English placement tests required. Deadline for receipt of application materials: none. Application fee required: $50. Interview required.

Athletics Interscholastic: basketball, cross-country running, football, golf, independent competitive sports, soccer, track and field, winter soccer; intramural: archery, baseball, basketball, canoeing/kayaking, climbing, cross-country running, field hockey, fishing, fitness, flag football, jogging, life saving, marksmanship, outdoor activities, outdoor adventure, outdoor education, outdoor recreation, outdoor skills, paint ball, physical fitness, physical training, pistol, rappelling, riflery, rock climbing, ropes courses, running, soccer, softball, strength & conditioning, table tennis, tennis, track and field, volleyball, wall climbing, weight lifting, weight training, wilderness, wilderness survival, wildernessways. 6 PE instructors, 4 coaches, 1 athletic trainer.

Computers Computers are regularly used in library skills, programming, typing, Web site design classes. Computer network features include on-campus library services, online commercial services, Internet access, wireless campus network, Internet filtering or blocking technology. Students grades are available online. The school has a published electronic and media policy.

Contact Mr. Wesley McClure, Admissions Counselor. 601-437-8855 Ext. 225. Fax: 601-437-3212. E-mail: wes.mcclure@chamberlain-hunt.com. Website: www.chamberlain-hunt.com/

CHAMINADE COLLEGE PREPARATORY

7500 Chaminade Avenue
West Hills, California 91304

Head of School: Mr. Stephen Lepire

General Information Coeducational day college-preparatory, arts, business, religious studies, and technology school, affiliated with Roman Catholic Church. Grades 9–12. Founded: 1952. Setting: suburban. Nearest major city is Los Angeles. 21-acre campus. 15 buildings on campus. Approved or accredited by Western Association of Schools and Colleges, Western Catholic Education Association, and California Department of Education. Endowment: $5.6 million. Total enrollment: 2,011. Upper school average class size: 26. Upper school faculty-student ratio: 1:16. There are 180 required school days per year for Upper School students. Upper School students typically attend 5 days per week. The average school day consists of 6 hours and 25 minutes.

Upper School Student Profile Grade 9: 339 students (180 boys, 159 girls); Grade 10: 337 students (181 boys, 156 girls); Grade 11: 341 students (172 boys, 169 girls); Grade 12: 311 students (157 boys, 154 girls). 50% of students are Roman Catholic.

Faculty School total: 90. In upper school: 40 men, 50 women; 66 have advanced degrees.

Subjects Offered Algebra, American history, American literature, anatomy, art, art history, athletic training, band, baseball, basketball, biology, biology-AP, British literature, British literature (honors), calculus, calculus-AP, chemistry, chemistry-AP, Chinese, Christian and Hebrew scripture, community service, comparative government and politics-AP, composition, computer programming, computer programming-AP, computer science, creative writing, dance, dance performance, debate, drama, drawing, driver education, economics, economics and history, English, English language-AP, English literature and composition-AP, environmental science-AP, ethics, European history, expository writing, film studies, finance, fine arts, finite math, French, French language-AP, French literature-AP, geography, geometry, government-AP, government/civics, guitar, human geography - AP, jazz ensemble, journalism, Latin, Latin-AP, literature and composition-AP, macroeconomics-AP, marching band, mathematics, modern European history-AP, music, music appreciation, music performance, physical education, physical science, physics, physics-AP, physiology, play/screen writing, probability and statistics, psychology, psychology-AP, religion, science, science fiction, scripture, Shakespeare, social studies, Spanish, Spanish language-AP, Spanish literature-AP, speech, speech and debate, sports medicine, statistics-AP, studio art, theater, trigonometry, U.S. government, U.S. history, U.S. history-AP, United States government-AP, visual and performing arts, visual arts, Western philosophy, Western religions, women's studies, world history, world history-AP, world literature, writing.

Graduation Requirements Arts and fine arts (art, music, dance, drama), college writing, computer science, English, foreign language, mathematics, physical education (includes health), religious studies, science, social studies (includes history), speech. Community service is required.

Special Academic Programs 15 Advanced Placement exams for which test preparation is offered; honors section.

College Admission Counseling 337 students graduated in 2013; 331 went to college, including California Polytechnic State University, San Luis Obispo; California State University, Northridge; University of California, Santa Barbara; University of Colorado Boulder; University of Southern California. Other: 1 entered military service, 3 had other specific plans. Mean SAT critical reading: 568, mean SAT math: 571, mean SAT writing: 581, mean combined SAT: 1720, mean composite ACT: 25. 38% scored over 600 on SAT critical reading, 40% scored over 600 on SAT math, 45% scored over 600 on SAT writing, 41% scored over 1800 on combined SAT, 38% scored over 26 on composite ACT.

Student Life Upper grades have uniform requirement, student council, honor system. Discipline rests primarily with faculty. Attendance at religious services is required.

Summer Programs Remediation, enrichment, advancement, sports, art/fine arts, computer instruction programs offered; session focuses on Remediation; held on campus; accepts boys and girls; open to students from other schools. 450 students usually enrolled. 2014 schedule: June 16 to July 23. Application deadline: none.

Tuition and Aid Day student tuition: $13,600. Tuition installment plan (monthly payment plans, 2-payment plan, discounted one-payment plan). Merit scholarship grants, need-based scholarship grants available. In 2013–14, 26% of upper-school students received aid; total upper-school merit-scholarship money awarded: $18,000. Total amount of financial aid awarded in 2013–14: $2,290,865.

Admissions Traditional secondary-level entrance grade is 9. For fall 2013, 389 students applied for upper-level admission, 365 were accepted, 205 enrolled. Non-standardized placement tests required. Deadline for receipt of application materials: January 11. Application fee required: $100. On-campus interview required.

Athletics Interscholastic: aquatics (boys, girls), baseball (b), basketball (b,g), cross-country running (b,g), equestrian sports (b,g), fencing (b,g), field hockey (g), football (b), golf (b,g), lacrosse (b,g), soccer (b,g), softball (g), strength & conditioning (b,g), swimming and diving (b,g), tennis (b,g), track and field (b,g), volleyball (b,g), weight training (b,g), wrestling (b); coed interscholastic: cheering, dance, equestrian sports, physical fitness, strength & conditioning, weight training; coed intramural: dance team, hiking/backpacking, table tennis. 3 PE instructors, 85 coaches, 2 athletic trainers.

Computers Computers are regularly used in all classes. Computer network features include on-campus library services, online commercial services, Internet access, wireless campus network, Internet filtering or blocking technology, Laptops are issued to students in grades 9-12, Blackboard online learning system, Dyno. Student e-mail accounts are available to students. Students grades are available online. The school has a published electronic and media policy.

Contact Mrs. Yolanda Uramoto, Assistant to Admissions and Registrar. 818-347-8300 Ext. 355. Fax: 818-348-8374. E-mail: yuramoto@chaminade.org. Website: www.chaminade.org

CHAMINADE COLLEGE PREPARATORY SCHOOL

425 South Lindbergh Boulevard
St. Louis, Missouri 63131-2799

Head of School: Rev. Ralph A. Siefert, SM

General Information Boys' boarding and day college-preparatory, arts, business, religious studies, bilingual studies, and technology school, affiliated with Roman Catholic Church. Grades 6–12. Founded: 1910. Setting: suburban. Students are housed in single-sex dormitories. 55-acre campus. 12 buildings on campus. Approved or accredited by Independent Schools Association of the Central States, Midwest Association of Boarding Schools, National Catholic Education Association, North Central Association of Colleges and Schools, The Association of Boarding Schools, The College Board, and Missouri Department of Education. Member of National Association of Independent Schools and Secondary School Admission Test Board. Endowment: $11 million. Total enrollment: 775. Upper school average class size: 17. Upper school faculty-student ratio: 1:10. There are 174 required school days per year for Upper School students. Upper School students typically attend 5 days per week. The average school day consists of 7 hours.

Upper School Student Profile Grade 9: 134 students (134 boys); Grade 10: 131 students (131 boys); Grade 11: 117 students (117 boys); Grade 12: 117 students (117 boys). 8% of students are boarding students. 92% are state residents. 3 states are represented in upper school student body. 8% are international students. International students from China, Japan, Mexico, Republic of Korea, Taiwan, and Viet Nam; 3 other countries represented in student body. 81% of students are Roman Catholic.

Faculty School total: 89. In upper school: 68 men, 16 women; 67 have advanced degrees; 6 reside on campus.

Subjects Offered Accounting, algebra, American government, American history, American history-AP, American literature, anatomy and physiology, architecture, art, art history, band, Bible studies, biology, biology-AP, botany, broadcasting, business, business law, business skills, calculus, calculus-AP, campus ministry, Catholic belief and practice, chemistry, chemistry-AP, Chinese, church history, civics, communication skills, communications, community service, comparative government and politics-AP, comparative political systems-AP, computer literacy, computer processing, computer programming, computer programming-AP, computer science, computer science-AP, concert band, creative writing, drama, dramatic arts, earth science, ecology, economics, economics-AP, engineering, English, English composition, English literature, English literature-AP, English/composition-AP, ESL, European history, European history-AP, expository writing, fine arts, French, French-AP, geography, geology, geometry, government/civics, grammar, health, history, industrial arts, keyboarding, Latin, Latin-AP, mathematics, music theory-AP, physical education, physics, physics-AP, psychology, psychology-AP, religion, science, social studies, sociology, Spanish, Spanish-AP, speech, statistics, statistics-AP, studio art-AP, theater, theology, trigonometry, weight training, world affairs, world history, world literature, writing.

Graduation Requirements Arts and fine arts (art, music, dance, drama), computer science, English, foreign language, mathematics, physical education (includes health), practical arts, religion (includes Bible studies and theology), science, social studies (includes history). Community service is required.

Special Academic Programs 23 Advanced Placement exams for which test preparation is offered; honors section; study at local college for college credit; academic accommodation for the gifted; ESL (32 students enrolled).

College Admission Counseling 118 students graduated in 2012; 117 went to college, including Purdue University; Saint Louis University; University of Dayton; University of Illinois at Urbana–Champaign; University of Missouri; Vanderbilt University. Other: 1 entered military service. Mean composite ACT: 26. 42% scored over 26 on composite ACT.

Student Life Upper grades have specified standards of dress, honor system. Discipline rests primarily with faculty. Attendance at religious services is required.

Tuition and Aid Day student tuition: $15,765; 5-day tuition and room/board: $31,991; 7-day tuition and room/board: $33,091. Tuition installment plan (FACTS Tuition Payment Plan). Merit scholarship grants, need-based scholarship grants, paying campus jobs available. In 2012–13, 32% of upper-school students received aid; total upper-school merit-scholarship money awarded: $95,000. Total amount of financial aid awarded in 2012–13: $1,600,000.

Admissions Traditional secondary-level entrance grade is 9. For fall 2012, 78 students applied for upper-level admission, 66 were accepted, 53 enrolled. SSAT required. Deadline for receipt of application materials: none. Application fee required: $50. Interview required.

Athletics Interscholastic: baseball, basketball, bowling, cross-country running, football, golf, ice hockey, lacrosse, racquetball, soccer, swimming and diving, tennis, track and field, ultimate Frisbee, volleyball, water polo, wrestling; intramural: in-line hockey, rugby, table tennis, weight training. 5 PE instructors, 30 coaches, 1 athletic trainer.

Computers Computers are regularly used in all academic classes. Computer network features include on-campus library services, online commercial services, Internet access, wireless campus network, Internet filtering or blocking technology. Campus intranet and student e-mail accounts are available to students. Students grades are available online. The school has a published electronic and media policy.

Contact Ms. Dianne Dunning-Gill, Associate Director of Admissions. 314-692-6640. Fax: 314-993-5732. E-mail: ddunning-gill@chaminade-stl.com. Website: www.chaminade-stl.org

CHAMINADE-MADONNA COLLEGE PREPARATORY

500 Chaminade Drive
Hollywood, Florida 33021-5800

Head of School: Fr. Larry Doersching, SM

General Information Coeducational day college-preparatory, arts, business, and religious studies school, affiliated with Roman Catholic Church. Grades 9–12. Founded: 1960. Setting: suburban. Nearest major city is Fort Lauderdale. 13-acre campus. 10 buildings on campus. Approved or accredited by Southern Association of Colleges and Schools and Florida Department of Education. Total enrollment: 552. Upper school average class size: 26. Upper school faculty-student ratio: 1:19. There are 180 required school days per year for Upper School students. Upper School students typically attend 5 days per week. The average school day consists of 6 hours and 45 minutes.

Upper School Student Profile Grade 9: 134 students (84 boys, 50 girls); Grade 10: 108 students (64 boys, 44 girls); Grade 11: 172 students (102 boys, 70 girls); Grade 12: 137 students (84 boys, 53 girls). 70% of students are Roman Catholic.

Faculty School total: 36. In upper school: 14 men, 22 women.

Subjects Offered Advanced chemistry, advanced computer applications, advanced math, Advanced Placement courses, advanced studio art-AP, algebra, American government, American history, American history-AP, American literature, American literature-AP, anatomy, art, art history, athletic training, band, biology, business skills, calculus, calculus-AP, campus ministry, Catholic belief and practice, ceramics, chemistry, chemistry-AP, choir, chorus, college placement, community service, computer applications, computer graphics, computer skills, creative writing, dance, dance performance, design, directing, drama, drama performance, dramatic arts, economics, English, English composition, English language and composition-AP, English literature and composition-AP, ethics, European history-AP, film studies, fine arts, foreign language, French, French-AP, geography, geometry, government/civics, health, health and wellness, history, history of the Catholic Church, history-AP, honors algebra, honors English, honors geometry, honors U.S. history, honors world history, international relations, journalism, keyboarding, leadership, macro/microeconomics-AP, marine biology, mathematics, model United Nations, music, music history, music theater, musical productions, New Testament, newspaper, peace and justice, philosophy, physical education, physics, physics-AP, physiology, play production, practical arts, pre-calculus, psychology, public speaking, reading, religion, SAT/ACT preparation, science, Shakespeare, social studies, sociology, Spanish, Spanish language-AP, Spanish literature-AP, speech, sports medicine, stagecraft, theater, trigonometry, U.S. history-AP, weight training, word processing, world history, writing, yearbook.

Graduation Requirements Arts and fine arts (art, music, dance, drama), business skills (includes word processing), English, foreign language, mathematics, physical education (includes health), practical arts, religion (includes Bible studies and theology), science, social studies (includes history), 80 community service hours.

Special Academic Programs 10 Advanced Placement exams for which test preparation is offered; honors section; study at local college for college credit; academic accommodation for the gifted, the musically talented, and the artistically talented; remedial reading and/or remedial writing; remedial math; programs in general development for dyslexic students; special instructional classes for students with learning disabilities, Attention Deficit Disorder, and dyslexia.

College Admission Counseling 138 students graduated in 2013; all went to college, including Florida Atlantic University; Florida Gulf Coast University; Florida International University; Florida State University; University of Central Florida; University of Florida. Mean composite ACT: 22.

Student Life Upper grades have uniform requirement, student council, honor system. Discipline rests primarily with faculty. Attendance at religious services is required.

Summer Programs Remediation, enrichment programs offered; session focuses on remediation/make-up; held on campus; accepts boys and girls; not open to students from other schools.

Tuition and Aid Day student tuition: $10,450. Tuition installment plan (FACTS Tuition Payment Plan). Merit scholarship grants, need-based scholarship grants, need-based loans available. In 2013–14, 33% of upper-school students received aid. Total amount of financial aid awarded in 2013–14: $400,000.

Admissions Traditional secondary-level entrance grade is 9. For fall 2013, 250 students applied for upper-level admission, 200 were accepted, 174 enrolled. High School Placement Test (closed version) from Scholastic Testing Service required. Deadline for receipt of application materials: none. Application fee required: $50. Interview required.

Athletics Interscholastic: baseball (boys), basketball (b,g), cheering (g), cross-country running (b,g), dance (g), dance team (g), football (b), golf (b,g), hockey (b,g), ice hockey (b,g), soccer (b,g), softball (g), swimming and diving (b,g), track and field (b,g), volleyball (b,g), wrestling (b). 2 PE instructors, 1 athletic trainer.

Computers Computers are regularly used in all classes. Computer network features include on-campus library services, online commercial services, Internet access, wireless campus network, Internet filtering or blocking technology. Student e-mail accounts are available to students. The school has a published electronic and media policy.

Contact Mrs. Carol Manzella, Director of Admissions. 954-989-5150 Ext. 136. Fax: 954-983-4663. E-mail: cmanzella@cmlions.org. Website: www.cmlions.org

CHARLOTTE COUNTRY DAY SCHOOL

1440 Carmel Road
Charlotte, North Carolina 28226

Head of School: Mr. Mark Reed

General Information Coeducational day college-preparatory school. Grades JK–12. Founded: 1941. Setting: suburban. 60-acre campus. 10 buildings on campus. Approved or accredited by Southern Association of Colleges and Schools, Southern Association of Independent Schools, and North Carolina Department of Education. Member of National Association of Independent Schools and Secondary School Admission Test Board. Endowment: $39 million. Total enrollment: 1,631. Upper school average class size: 12. Upper school faculty-student ratio: 1:12. There are 170 required school days per year for Upper School students. Upper School students typically attend 5 days per week. The average school day consists of 7 hours and 15 minutes.

Upper School Student Profile Grade 9: 128 students (57 boys, 71 girls); Grade 10: 117 students (57 boys, 60 girls); Grade 11: 132 students (70 boys, 62 girls); Grade 12: 129 students (68 boys, 61 girls).

Faculty School total: 214. In upper school: 35 men, 32 women; 46 have advanced degrees.

Subjects Offered Algebra, American history, American history-AP, anatomy, art, art history-AP, astronomy, biology, biology-AP, biotechnology, calculus-AP, ceramics, chemistry, chemistry-AP, Chinese, computer graphics, computer science, computer science-AP, creative writing, dance, debate, discrete mathematics, drama, ecology, economics, English, English literature, English-AP, environmental science-AP, ESL, European history, European history-AP, French, French-AP, geography, geometry, German, German-AP, Japanese, journalism, Latin, Latin-AP, library studies, music, novels, photography, physical education, physics, physics-AP, physiology, poetry, political science, pre-calculus, probability and statistics, psychology-AP, sculpture, Shakespeare, short story, Spanish, Spanish-AP, studio art-AP, theater, theory of knowledge, trigonometry, visual arts, yearbook.

Graduation Requirements Arts and fine arts (art, music, dance, drama), computer science, English, foreign language, mathematics, physical education (includes health), science, social sciences, social studies (includes history). Community service is required.

Special Academic Programs International Baccalaureate program; honors section; independent study; term-away projects; study abroad; academic accommodation for the gifted; ESL (14 students enrolled).

College Admission Counseling 116 students graduated in 2013; all went to college, including Elon University; North Carolina State University; The University of North Carolina at Chapel Hill; University of Georgia; Vanderbilt University; Wake Forest University. Median SAT critical reading: 620, median SAT math: 635, median SAT writing: 625, median combined SAT: 1880, median composite ACT: 28. 60% scored over 600 on SAT critical reading, 74% scored over 600 on SAT math, 65% scored over 600 on SAT writing, 66% scored over 1800 on combined SAT, 72% scored over 26 on composite ACT.

Student Life Upper grades have specified standards of dress, student council, honor system. Discipline rests primarily with faculty.

Summer Programs Remediation, enrichment, advancement, ESL, sports, art/fine arts, computer instruction programs offered; session focuses on enrichment classes, academic courses, and sports camps; held on campus; accepts boys and girls; open to students from other schools. 200 students usually enrolled. 2014 schedule: June 9 to July 25. Application deadline: none.

Tuition and Aid Day student tuition: $21,440. Tuition installment plan (The Tuition Plan, Insured Tuition Payment Plan, monthly payment plans). Need-based scholarship grants available. In 2013–14, 16% of upper-school students received aid. Total amount of financial aid awarded in 2013–14: $1,250,457.

Admissions Traditional secondary-level entrance grade is 9. For fall 2013, 145 students applied for upper-level admission, 76 were accepted, 45 enrolled. CTP III, ERB or ISEE required. Deadline for receipt of application materials: January 15. Application fee required: $90. On-campus interview required.

Athletics Interscholastic: baseball (boys), basketball (b,g), cheering (g), crew (g), cross-country running (b,g), dance (g), dance team (g), field hockey (g), fitness (b,g), football (b), golf (b,g), lacrosse (b,g), soccer (b,g), softball (g), strength & conditioning (b,g), swimming and diving (b,g), tennis (b,g), track and field (b,g), volleyball (g), weight training (b,g), wrestling (b). 1 PE instructor, 38 coaches, 3 athletic trainers.

Computers Computers are regularly used in art, computer applications, English, foreign language, mathematics, photography, science, yearbook classes. Computer network features include on-campus library services, Internet access, wireless campus network, Internet filtering or blocking technology. Campus intranet and student e-mail accounts are available to students. Students grades are available online. The school has a published electronic and media policy.

Contact Nancy R. Ehringhaus, Director of Admissions. 704-943-4530 Ext. 4531. Fax: 704-943-4536. E-mail: nancy.ehringhaus@charlottecountryday.org. Website: www.charlottecountryday.org

CHARLOTTE LATIN SCHOOL

9502 Providence Road
Charlotte, North Carolina 28277-8695

Head of School: Mr. Arch N. McIntosh Jr.

General Information Coeducational day college-preparatory school. Grades K–12. Founded: 1970. Setting: suburban. 122-acre campus. 7 buildings on campus. Approved or accredited by Southern Association of Colleges and Schools, Southern Association of Independent Schools, and North Carolina Department of Education. Member of National Association of Independent Schools and Secondary School Admission Test Board. Endowment: $26 million. Total enrollment: 1,401. Upper school average class size: 15. Upper school faculty-student ratio: 1:8. There are 173 required school days per year for Upper School students. Upper School students typically attend 5 days per week. The average school day consists of 7 hours and 5 minutes.

Upper School Student Profile Grade 9: 125 students (67 boys, 58 girls); Grade 10: 121 students (61 boys, 60 girls); Grade 11: 129 students (66 boys, 63 girls); Grade 12: 125 students (64 boys, 61 girls).

Faculty School total: 153. In upper school: 35 men, 24 women; 41 have advanced degrees.

Subjects Offered 20th century American writers, 20th century history, 20th century physics, 20th century world history, 3-dimensional art, acting, advanced chemistry, Advanced Placement courses, algebra, American culture, American government, American history, American history-AP, American literature, anatomy, anatomy and physiology, art, biology, biology-AP, British literature, calculus, calculus-AP, ceramics, chemistry, chemistry-AP, college counseling, computer applications, computer math, computer programming, computer science, computer science-AP, conceptual physics, concert band, concert choir, creative writing, debate, discrete mathematics, drama, dramatic arts, earth science, ecology, economics, economics and history, engineering, English, English literature, English-AP, environmental science, European history, European history-AP, expository writing, finite math, French, French-AP, geography, geology, geometry, government/civics, grammar, Greek, health, history, Holocaust and other genocides, honors algebra, honors English, honors geometry, human rights, international relations, international studies, journalism, Latin, Latin-AP, leadership and service, mathematics, media literacy, music, music theory, music theory-AP, physical education, physics, physics-AP, pre-calculus, programming, psychology, science, social studies, Southern literature, Spanish, Spanish language-AP, Spanish-AP, speech, sports medicine, statistics-AP, studio art, technical theater, theater, trigonometry, U.S. government and politics-AP, Web site design, world history, world literature, world religions, writing, yearbook.

Graduation Requirements Electives, English, foreign language, history, mathematics, physical education (includes health), science.

Special Academic Programs 14 Advanced Placement exams for which test preparation is offered; honors section; study abroad; academic accommodation for the gifted.

College Admission Counseling 123 students graduated in 2013; 122 went to college, including Davidson College; North Carolina State University; The University of Alabama; The University of North Carolina at Chapel Hill; University of South Carolina; Washington University in St. Louis. Other: 1 entered a postgraduate year. 60% scored over 600 on SAT critical reading, 79% scored over 600 on SAT math, 79% scored over 600 on SAT writing, 75% scored over 1800 on combined SAT, 73% scored over 26 on composite ACT.

Student Life Upper grades have specified standards of dress, student council, honor system. Discipline rests primarily with faculty.

Summer Programs Enrichment, sports, art/fine arts, computer instruction programs offered; session focuses on enrichment, sports camps; held both on and off campus; held at N.C. coast (offered for Charlotte Latin students only); accepts boys and girls; open to students from other schools. 850 students usually enrolled. 2014 schedule: June 9 to August 1. Application deadline: none.

Tuition and Aid Day student tuition: $20,250. Tuition installment plan (monthly payment plans, individually arranged payment plans). Merit scholarship grants, need-based scholarship grants available. In 2013–14, 16% of upper-school students received aid; total upper-school merit-scholarship money awarded: $214,438. Total amount of financial aid awarded in 2013–14: $887,525.

Admissions Traditional secondary-level entrance grade is 9. For fall 2013, 124 students applied for upper-level admission, 56 were accepted, 38 enrolled. ERB, ISEE, Wechsler Intelligence Scale for Children or Woodcock-Johnson required. Deadline for receipt of application materials: none. Application fee required: $90. On-campus interview required.

Athletics Interscholastic: aquatics (boys, girls), baseball (b), basketball (b,g), cross-country running (b,g), dance team (g), field hockey (g), football (b), golf (b,g), independent competitive sports (b,g), indoor track (b,g), lacrosse (b,g), soccer (b,g), softball (g), swimming and diving (b,g), tennis (b,g), track and field (b,g), volleyball (g), wrestling (b); intramural: basketball (b,g), outdoor activities (b,g); coed interscholastic: ultimate Frisbee; coed intramural: outdoor activities. 6 PE instructors, 54 coaches, 3 athletic trainers.

Computers Computers are regularly used in all academic classes. Computer network features include on-campus library services, online commercial services, Internet access, wireless campus network. Student e-mail accounts and computer access in designated common areas are available to students. The school has a published electronic and media policy.

Contact Mr. Peter C. Egan, Director of Admissions. 704-846-7207. Fax: 704-847-8776. E-mail: pegan@charlottelatin.org. Website: www.charlottelatin.org

See Display below and Close-Up on page 528.

CHASE COLLEGIATE SCHOOL

565 Chase Parkway
Waterbury, Connecticut 06708-3394

Head of School: Joseph A. Hadam

General Information Coeducational day college-preparatory and arts school. Grades PK–12. Founded: 1865. Setting: suburban. 47-acre campus. 8 buildings on campus. Approved or accredited by New England Association of Schools and Colleges and Connecticut Department of Education. Member of National Association of Independent Schools and Secondary School Admission Test Board. Endowment: $12 million. Total enrollment: 402. Upper school average class size: 11. Upper school faculty-student ratio: 1:7. There are 173 required school days per year for Upper School students. Upper School students typically attend 5 days per week. The average school day consists of 6 hours and 45 minutes.

Upper School Student Profile Grade 9: 41 students (21 boys, 20 girls); Grade 10: 45 students (24 boys, 21 girls); Grade 11: 47 students (25 boys, 22 girls); Grade 12: 52 students (25 boys, 27 girls).

Faculty School total: 54. In upper school: 11 men, 15 women; 23 have advanced degrees.

Subjects Offered 20th century American writers, 20th century history, 3-dimensional art, acting, Advanced Placement courses, African-American literature, algebra, American foreign policy, ancient world history, animation, archaeology, art, art history-AP, astronomy, band, biology, biology-AP, calculus, calculus-AP, ceramics, chamber groups, chemistry, chemistry-AP, China/Japan history, chorus, classical Greek literature, classical language, college writing, computer animation, computer graphics, computer programming, computer science-AP, concert band, concert bell choir, current events, digital photography, directing, drama, drawing, ecology, economics, economics-AP, English, English language-AP, English literature and composition-AP, environmental science, environmental science-AP, ethics, film studies, filmmaking, fine arts, foreign policy, French, French language-AP, French literature-AP, freshman seminar, geometry, Greek, handbells, health and wellness, history of China and Japan, honors algebra, honors geometry, humanities, independent study, introduction to theater, jazz band, jazz ensemble, journalism, Latin, Latin-AP, macro/microeconomics-AP, model United Nations, modern European history, music, music technology, natural history, oceanography, oil painting, photography, physics, physics-AP, play production, playwriting and directing, pre-calculus, probability and statistics, public speaking, sculpture, senior project, society and culture, socioeconomic problems, sociology, Spanish, Spanish literature-AP, Spanish-AP, statistics, technical theater, technology, theater, U.S. government and politics-AP, U.S. history, U.S. history-AP, visual arts, water color painting, Web site design, woodworking, world cultures, world history-AP, yearbook.

Graduation Requirements Arts and fine arts (art, music, dance, drama), athletics, computer literacy, electives, English, ethics, foreign language, history, lab science, mathematics, music appreciation, psychology, public speaking, science, technology, theater arts, senior speech.

Special Academic Programs 18 Advanced Placement exams for which test preparation is offered; honors section; accelerated programs; independent study; study abroad; academic accommodation for the gifted.

College Admission Counseling 45 students graduated in 2013; all went to college, including Boston University; Loyola University Maryland; Providence College; Quinnipiac University; Tufts University; University of Connecticut. Mean SAT critical reading: 592, mean SAT math: 591, mean SAT writing: 598, mean combined SAT: 1781.

Student Life Upper grades have specified standards of dress, student council, honor system. Discipline rests equally with students and faculty.

Summer Programs Enrichment, advancement, sports, art/fine arts, computer instruction programs offered; session focuses on enrichment and advancement; held on campus; accepts boys and girls; open to students from other schools. 300 students usually enrolled. 2014 schedule: June to August. Application deadline: none.

Tuition and Aid Day student tuition: $33,325. Tuition installment plan (monthly payment plans). Tuition reduction for siblings, merit scholarship grants, need-based scholarship grants, Founders' Scholarships (for students entering 9th grade) available. In 2013–14, 50% of upper-school students received aid; total upper-school merit-scholarship money awarded: $399,900. Total amount of financial aid awarded in 2013–14: $2,716,560.

Admissions Traditional secondary-level entrance grade is 9. For fall 2013, 107 students applied for upper-level admission, 71 were accepted, 26 enrolled. SSAT required. Deadline for receipt of application materials: none. Application fee required: $60. On-campus interview required.

Athletics Interscholastic: baseball (boys), basketball (b,g), cross-country running (b,g), independent competitive sports (b,g), lacrosse (b,g), soccer (b,g), softball (g), tennis (b,g), volleyball (g), wrestling (b,g); intramural: ice hockey (b,g), strength & conditioning (b,g); coed interscholastic: crew, Frisbee, golf, independent competitive sports, rowing, swimming and diving, ultimate Frisbee, wrestling; coed intramural: aerobics/dance, aerobics/Nautilus, curling, dance, equestrian sports, figure skating, fitness, ice skating, modern dance, outdoor education, physical fitness, skiing (downhill), snowboarding, weight training. 2 PE instructors, 20 coaches, 1 athletic trainer.

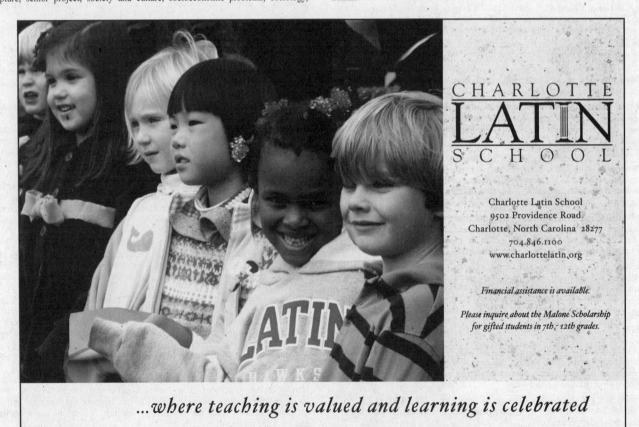

Computers Computers are regularly used in art, college planning, creative writing, English, foreign language, history, humanities, library, literary magazine, mathematics, music, newspaper, photography, research skills, SAT preparation, science, social sciences, study skills, technology, yearbook classes. Computer network features include on-campus library services, online commercial services, Internet access, wireless campus network, Internet filtering or blocking technology. Campus intranet, student e-mail accounts, and computer access in designated common areas are available to students. Students grades are available online. The school has a published electronic and media policy.

Contact Ruth Teague, Director of Admissions. 203-236-9560. Fax: 203-236-9503. E-mail: rteague@chasemail.org. Website: www.chasecollegiate.org

CHATTANOOGA CHRISTIAN SCHOOL

3354 Charger Drive
Chattanooga, Tennessee 37409

Head of School: Mr. Chad Dirkse

General Information Coeducational day college-preparatory, arts, religious studies, technology, college-level (AP) courses, and dual enrollment courses school, affiliated with Christian faith. Grades K–12. Founded: 1970. Setting: urban. Nearest major city is Atlanta, GA. 60-acre campus. 6 buildings on campus. Approved or accredited by Christian Schools International, Southern Association of Colleges and Schools, Southern Association of Independent Schools, and Tennessee Department of Education. Endowment: $8 million. Total enrollment: 1,179. Upper school average class size: 20. Upper school faculty-student ratio: 1:17. There are 175 required school days per year for Upper School students. Upper School students typically attend 5 days per week. The average school day consists of 7 hours.

Upper School Student Profile Grade 6: 112 students (51 boys, 61 girls); Grade 7: 118 students (68 boys, 50 girls); Grade 8: 112 students (55 boys, 57 girls); Grade 9: 114 students (52 boys, 62 girls); Grade 10: 117 students (57 boys, 60 girls); Grade 11: 113 students (57 boys, 56 girls); Grade 12: 105 students (39 boys, 66 girls). 100% of students are Christian faith.

Faculty School total: 104. In upper school: 32 men, 35 women; 19 have advanced degrees.

Subjects Offered Advanced biology, advanced chemistry, advanced studio art-AP, algebra, American government, American history, American literature, anatomy, ancient history, art, art and culture, art appreciation, art history, art-AP, astronomy, band, Bible, Bible studies, biology, biology-AP, calculus, calculus-AP, chemistry, choir, civil rights, community service, computer applications, computer programming, computer-aided design, concert band, concert choir, creative writing, current events, dance, drama, drama performance, earth science, Eastern world civilizations, economics, English, English literature, English-AP, entrepreneurship, environmental science, environmental studies, ethics, European history, European history-AP, fine arts, foreign language, French, geometry, German, government, health, honors geometry, industrial arts, introduction to theater, Latin, leadership education training, life science, mathematics, mathematics-AP, mechanical drawing, Microsoft, modern dance, modern European history-AP, music, music theory, New Testament, personal finance, physical education, physical science, physics, physics-AP, physiology, psychology, religion, science, shop, Spanish, statistics-AP, studio art-AP, theater, trigonometry, U.S. history-AP, Web site design, weight training, wellness, world literature, writing.

Graduation Requirements Arts and fine arts (art, music, dance, drama), computer science, English, foreign language, mathematics, physical education (includes health), religion (includes Bible studies and theology), science, social sciences, social studies (includes history). Community service is required.

Special Academic Programs Advanced Placement exam preparation; honors section; independent study; study at local college for college credit; academic accommodation for the gifted and the artistically talented; remedial reading and/or remedial writing; remedial math.

College Admission Counseling 104 students graduated in 2013; 98 went to college, including Chattanooga State Community College; Covenant College; Samford University; Tennessee Technological University; The University of Tennessee; The University of Tennessee at Chattanooga. Other: 1 went to work, 5 had other specific plans. Mean SAT critical reading: 560, mean SAT math: 536, mean SAT writing: 542, mean combined SAT: 1639, mean composite ACT: 24. 32% scored over 600 on SAT critical reading, 24% scored over 600 on SAT math, 29% scored over 600 on SAT writing, 26% scored over 1800 on combined SAT, 35% scored over 26 on composite ACT.

Student Life Upper grades have specified standards of dress, student council, honor system. Discipline rests primarily with faculty. Attendance at religious services is required.

Summer Programs Remediation, enrichment, sports, art/fine arts programs offered; session focuses on sports camps and arts camps; held on campus; accepts boys and girls; open to students from other schools. 100 students usually enrolled. 2014 schedule: June 4 to June 29. Application deadline: May 31.

Tuition and Aid Day student tuition: $9331. Tuition installment plan (monthly payment plans, individually arranged payment plans). Tuition reduction for siblings, need-based scholarship grants, paying campus jobs available. In 2013–14, 20% of upper-school students received aid. Total amount of financial aid awarded in 2013–14: $500,000.

Admissions For fall 2013, 155 students applied for upper-level admission, 124 were accepted, 96 enrolled. Deadline for receipt of application materials: none. Application fee required: $100. Interview required.

Athletics Interscholastic: baseball (boys), basketball (b,g), bowling (b,g), cheering (g), cross-country running (b,g), football (b), golf (b,g), soccer (b,g), softball (g), strength & conditioning (b,g), swimming and diving (b,g), tennis (b,g), track and field (b,g), volleyball (b,g), weight lifting (b,g), weight training (b,g), wrestling (b); intramural: basketball (b,g); coed intramural: aerobics/dance, swimming and diving. 4 PE instructors, 15 coaches, 2 athletic trainers.

Computers Computers are regularly used in all academic, drawing and design, English, foreign language, history, lab/keyboard, library, mathematics, psychology, science, technology classes. Computer network features include on-campus library services, Internet access, wireless campus network, Internet filtering or blocking technology. Students grades are available online. The school has a published electronic and media policy.

Contact Mrs. Charlene Wolfe, Admission Director. 423-265-6411 Ext. 209. Fax: 423-756-4044. E-mail: cwolfe@ccsk12.com. Website: www.ccsk12.com

CHELSEA SCHOOL

Hyattsville, Maryland
See Special Needs Schools section.

CHEVERUS HIGH SCHOOL

267 Ocean Avenue
Portland, Maine 04103

Head of School: Mr. John H.R. Mullen

General Information Coeducational day college-preparatory, religious studies, technology, Honors, and AP courses school, affiliated with Roman Catholic Church (Jesuit order). Grades 9–12. Founded: 1917. Setting: suburban. 32-acre campus. 2 buildings on campus. Approved or accredited by Association of Independent Schools in New England, Independent Schools of Northern New England, Jesuit Secondary Education Association, New England Association of Schools and Colleges, The College Board, and Maine Department of Education. Endowment: $3 million. Total enrollment: 504. Upper school average class size: 22. Upper school faculty-student ratio: 1:12. There are 173 required school days per year for Upper School students. Upper School students typically attend 5 days per week. The average school day consists of 6 hours and 30 minutes.

Upper School Student Profile Grade 9: 120 students (77 boys, 43 girls); Grade 10: 133 students (83 boys, 50 girls); Grade 11: 128 students (63 boys, 65 girls); Grade 12: 123 students (75 boys, 48 girls). 65% of students are Roman Catholic Church (Jesuit order).

Faculty School total: 50. In upper school: 26 men, 20 women; 28 have advanced degrees.

Subjects Offered Advanced Placement courses, algebra, American history, art, biology, calculus, chemistry, college counseling, creative writing, economics, English, European history, fine arts, French, geography, geometry, government/civics, history, journalism, Latin, library skills, mathematics, music, physics, religion, science, social studies, Spanish, statistics, trigonometry, world history, yearbook.

Graduation Requirements Arts and fine arts (art, music, dance, drama), computer science, English, foreign language, health, mathematics, science, social studies (includes history), theology, all seniors are required to fill a community service requirement. Community service is required.

Special Academic Programs Advanced Placement exam preparation; honors section; study at local college for college credit; programs in general development for dyslexic students.

College Admission Counseling 119 students graduated in 2012; 113 went to college, including Endicott College; Maine Maritime Academy; Saint Anselm College; Stonehill College; University of Maine; University of Southern Maine. Other: 1 had other specific plans. Median SAT critical reading: 555, median SAT math: 573, median SAT writing: 549.

Student Life Upper grades have specified standards of dress, student council, honor system. Discipline rests primarily with faculty. Attendance at religious services is required.

Tuition and Aid Day student tuition: $15,835. Tuition installment plan (FACTS Tuition Payment Plan, monthly payment plans, individually arranged payment plans). Tuition reduction for siblings, merit scholarship grants, need-based scholarship grants, paying campus jobs available. In 2012–13, 66% of upper-school students received aid; total upper-school merit-scholarship money awarded: $12,500. Total amount of financial aid awarded in 2012–13: $1,919,108.

Admissions Traditional secondary-level entrance grade is 9. For fall 2012, 193 students applied for upper-level admission, 173 were accepted, 143 enrolled. English language and Math Placement Exam required. Deadline for receipt of application materials: none. Application fee required: $50. On-campus interview required.

Athletics Interscholastic: baseball (boys), basketball (b,g), cross-country running (b,g), diving (b,g), field hockey (g), football (b), golf (b,g), ice hockey (b,g), indoor track & field (b,g), lacrosse (b,g), sailing (b,g), skiing (downhill) (b,g), soccer (b,g), softball (g), swimming and diving (b,g), tennis (b,g), track and field (b,g), volleyball (g), winter (indoor) track (b,g), wrestling (b); intramural: basketball (b,g), flag football (b,g); coed interscholastic: alpine skiing, outdoor adventure; coed intramural: basketball, bicycling, flag football, hiking/backpacking, table tennis, volleyball. 82 coaches, 2 athletic trainers.

Computers Computers are regularly used in creative writing, economics, history, information technology, journalism, mathematics, SAT preparation, science, word processing, yearbook classes. Computer network features include on-campus library services, online commercial services, Internet access, wireless campus network. Student e-mail accounts and computer access in designated common areas are available to students. Students grades are available online. The school has a published electronic and media policy.

Contact Ms. Kate Luke-Jenkins, Admissions Assistant. 207-774-6238 Ext. 35. Fax: 207-321-0004. E-mail: luke-jenkins@cheverus.org. Website: www.cheverus.org

THE CHICAGO ACADEMY FOR THE ARTS

1010 West Chicago Avenue
Chicago, Illinois 60642

Head of School: Ms. Pamela Jordan

General Information Coeducational day college-preparatory and arts school. Grades 9–12. Founded: 1981. Setting: urban. 1-acre campus. 1 building on campus. Approved or accredited by Independent Schools Association of the Central States, North Central Association of Colleges and Schools, and Illinois Department of Education. Member of National Association of Independent Schools. Total enrollment: 143. Upper school average class size: 13. Upper school faculty-student ratio: 1:10. There are 163 required school days per year for Upper School students. Upper School students typically attend 5 days per week. The average school day consists of 8 hours.

Upper School Student Profile Grade 9: 35 students (11 boys, 24 girls); Grade 10: 25 students (7 boys, 18 girls); Grade 11: 40 students (17 boys, 23 girls); Grade 12: 43 students (16 boys, 27 girls).

Faculty School total: 43. In upper school: 21 men, 21 women; 21 have advanced degrees.

Subjects Offered Advanced math, Advanced Placement courses, African-American literature, algebra, American history, American literature, anatomy, anatomy and physiology, art, art history, art history-AP, arts, ballet, ballet technique, biology, biology-AP, Broadway dance, business law, calculus, calculus-AP, chemistry, choreography, cinematography, classical music, college counseling, consumer law, creative writing, critical studies in film, dance, dance performance, digital art, digital music, discrete mathematics, drama, drawing, drawing and design, English, English literature and composition-AP, European history-AP, film, film history, film studies, filmmaking, fine arts, French, French language-AP, geometry, geometry with art applications, global issues, global studies, graphic arts, guitar, historical foundations for arts, history of dance, history of drama, history of music, honors English, honors geometry, humanities, instrumental music, jazz, jazz band, jazz theory, keyboarding, Latin American literature, mathematics, mathematics-AP, media arts, modern dance, music, music composition, music for dance, music history, music performance, music theater, music theory, physics, play production, play/screen writing, playwriting and directing, poetry, printmaking, public speaking, scene study, science, sculpture, senior internship, set design, Shakespeare, shop, social sciences, Spanish, Spanish language-AP, speech, stage design, stagecraft, statistics-AP, studio art, study skills, theater, theater design and production, theater history, U.S. history, U.S. literature, urban design, video, video and animation, video film production, visual and performing arts, visual arts, vocal ensemble, vocal jazz, vocal music, voice, wind ensemble, wind instruments, world affairs, world history, world religions, World War I.

Graduation Requirements Arts and fine arts (art, music, dance, drama), English, foreign language, mathematics, science, social sciences, U.S. history, requirements vary according to arts discipline.

Special Academic Programs Advanced Placement exam preparation; honors section; academic accommodation for the musically talented and the artistically talented; programs in general development for dyslexic students.

College Admission Counseling 24 students graduated in 2013; 23 went to college, including Berklee College of Music; California Institute of the Arts; Rhode Island School of Design; The Boston Conservatory; University of Cincinnati; University of Southern California. Other: 1 had other specific plans.

Student Life Upper grades have honor system. Discipline rests equally with students and faculty.

Tuition and Aid Day student tuition: $23,100. Tuition installment plan (FACTS Tuition Payment Plan, monthly payment plans). Merit scholarship grants, need-based scholarship grants available. In 2013–14, 55% of upper-school students received aid; total upper-school merit-scholarship money awarded: $240,000. Total amount of financial aid awarded in 2013–14: $765,690.

Admissions Traditional secondary-level entrance grade is 9. For fall 2013, 150 students applied for upper-level admission, 75 were accepted, 42 enrolled. ISEE required. Deadline for receipt of application materials: December 2. Application fee required: $65. On-campus interview required.

Computers Computers are regularly used in animation, college planning, commercial art, English, graphic arts, graphics, historical foundations for arts, media arts, media production, music technology, video film production classes. Computer

resources include online commercial services, Internet access, graphic design and production, Animation, Film Making and production.

Contact Ms. Mollie Kolosky, Admissions Assistant. 312-421-0202 Ext. 32. Fax: 312-421-3816. E-mail: mkolosky@chicagoartsacademy.org. Website: www.chicagoartsacademy.org

CHICAGO WALDORF SCHOOL

1300 West Loyola Avenue
Chicago, Illinois 60626

Head of School: Mr. Leukos Goodwin

General Information Coeducational day college-preparatory, arts, vocational, service learning, and arts integrated school. Grades 1–12. Founded: 1974. Setting: urban. 2 buildings on campus. Approved or accredited by Association of Waldorf Schools of North America, Independent Schools Association of the Central States, and Illinois Department of Education. Member of National Association of Independent Schools. Total enrollment: 279. Upper school average class size: 25. There are 166 required school days per year for Upper School students. Upper School students typically attend 5 days per week. The average school day consists of 7 hours and 30 minutes.

Upper School Student Profile Grade 9: 26 students (14 boys, 12 girls); Grade 10: 19 students (11 boys, 8 girls); Grade 11: 15 students (8 boys, 7 girls); Grade 12: 11 students (1 boy, 10 girls).

Faculty School total: 50. In upper school: 12 men, 12 women.

Subjects Offered All academic.

Special Academic Programs Independent study; study abroad.

College Admission Counseling 21 students graduated in 2012; all went to college, including DePaul University; Grinnell College; Knox College; Skidmore College; University of Illinois at Urbana–Champaign; Vassar College.

Student Life Upper grades have specified standards of dress, student council. Discipline rests primarily with faculty.

Tuition and Aid Day student tuition: $17,480. Tuition installment plan (SMART Tuition Payment Plan, monthly payment plans, individually arranged payment plans). Tuition reduction for siblings, need-based scholarship grants available. In 2012–13, 55% of upper-school students received aid. Total amount of financial aid awarded in 2012–13: $361,783.

Admissions Traditional secondary-level entrance grade is 9. For fall 2012, 18 students applied for upper-level admission, 13 were accepted, 9 enrolled. Deadline for receipt of application materials: none. Application fee required: $75. Interview required.

Athletics Interscholastic: basketball (boys, girls), soccer (b,g), touch football (b), volleyball (b,g); coed interscholastic: Circus, cross-country running. 2 PE instructors, 4 coaches.

Computers Computers are regularly used in all academic classes. Computer network features include Internet access, wireless campus network. The school has a published electronic and media policy.

Contact Ms. Lisa Payton, Admissions Director. 773-465-2371. Fax: 773-465-6648. E-mail: lpayton@chicagowaldorf.org. Website: www.chicagowaldorf.org/

CHILDREN'S CREATIVE AND PERFORMING ARTS ACADEMY OF SAN DIEGO

3051 El Cajon Boulevard
San Diego, California 92104

Head of School: Mrs. Janet M. Cherif

General Information Coeducational boarding and day college-preparatory, arts, mathematics, and science school. Boarding grades 6–12, day grades K–12. Founded: 1981. Setting: urban. Students are housed in homestay families. 1-acre campus. 1 building on campus. Approved or accredited by Western Association of Schools and Colleges and California Department of Education. Total enrollment: 262. Upper school average class size: 18. Upper school faculty-student ratio: 1:18. There are 186 required school days per year for Upper School students. Upper School students typically attend 5 days per week. The average school day consists of 7 hours and 30 minutes.

Upper School Student Profile Grade 6: 18 students (8 boys, 10 girls); Grade 7: 18 students (9 boys, 9 girls); Grade 8: 18 students (8 boys, 10 girls); Grade 9: 25 students (10 boys, 15 girls); Grade 10: 27 students (12 boys, 15 girls); Grade 11: 23 students (11 boys, 12 girls); Grade 12: 25 students (13 boys, 12 girls). 20% of students are boarding students. 70% are state residents. 1 state is represented in upper school student body. 30% are international students. International students from China, Mexico, Republic of Korea, Taiwan, Thailand, and Viet Nam; 3 other countries represented in student body.

Faculty School total: 30. In upper school: 3 men, 14 women; 10 have advanced degrees.

Subjects Offered 3-dimensional art, 3-dimensional design, algebra, American government, anatomy and physiology, art, art history, art history-AP, art-AP, audition methods, ballet, band, biology, business skills, calculus, calculus-AP, ceramics, chamber groups, cheerleading, chemistry, Chinese, choir, choreography, chorus, communications, comparative government and politics-AP, computer applications, computer literacy, computer programming-AP, concert band, concert choir, creative writing, dance performance, digital photography, drama, drama performance, earth science, English, English literature-AP, English-AP, English/composition-AP, ensembles, environmental science-AP, ESL, European history-AP, film, fitness, French, French language-AP, geometry, government and politics-AP, government/civics, government/civics-AP, graphic design, gymnastics, health, history of music, history-AP, honors algebra, honors English, honors geometry, honors U.S. history, honors world history, HTML design, human anatomy, instrumental music, Japanese, jazz band, jazz dance, jazz ensemble, journalism, Latin, mathematics, mathematics-AP, modern dance, music history, music performance, music theory-AP, orchestra, performing arts, physical education, physics, physics-AP, playwriting and directing, political science, portfolio art, pottery, pre-algebra, pre-calculus, reading/study skills, SAT preparation, SAT/ACT preparation, science, senior seminar, social sciences, social studies, Spanish, Spanish language-AP, Spanish literature-AP, speech, sports, stage design, statistics, studio art-AP, tap dance, tennis, theater design and production, TOEFL preparation, track and field, trigonometry, U.S. government and politics-AP, U.S. history, U.S. history-AP, vocal ensemble, vocal jazz, voice ensemble, volleyball, Web site design, Western civilization, world history, world history-AP, writing, writing workshop, yearbook.

Graduation Requirements Algebra, arts, biology, business skills (includes word processing), chemistry, choir, chorus, computer applications, computer skills, English, English composition, English literature, foreign language, government/civics, history, mathematics, modern world history, music, physical education (includes health), physics, science, social sciences, Spanish, sports, TOEFL preparation, trigonometry, U.S. government, U.S. history, visual and performing arts, senior recital or project, 30 hours of community service per year of attendance. Community service is required.

Special Academic Programs 14 Advanced Placement exams for which test preparation is offered; honors section; accelerated programs; independent study; academic accommodation for the gifted, the musically talented, and the artistically talented; remedial reading and/or remedial writing; remedial math; ESL (20 students enrolled).

College Admission Counseling 24 students graduated in 2013; all went to college, including California Polytechnic State University, San Luis Obispo; California State University, San Marcos; San Diego State University; University of California, Berkeley; University of California, Davis; University of California, San Diego. Median SAT critical reading: 520, median SAT math: 600, median SAT writing: 590, median combined SAT: 1710. 8.3% scored over 600 on SAT critical reading, 57.1% scored over 600 on SAT math, 16.7% scored over 600 on SAT writing, 16.7% scored over 1800 on combined SAT.

Student Life Upper grades have uniform requirement, student council, honor system. Discipline rests primarily with faculty.

Summer Programs Remediation, enrichment, advancement, ESL, art/fine arts, computer instruction programs offered; session focuses on academic advancement; held on campus; accepts boys and girls; open to students from other schools. 40 students usually enrolled. 2014 schedule: June 16 to August 1. Application deadline: none.

Tuition and Aid Day student tuition: $10,000; 7-day tuition and room/board: $18,400. Tuition installment plan (individually arranged payment plans, Pay by semester). Tuition reduction for siblings, merit scholarship grants, need-based scholarship grants, paying campus jobs, music scholarships available. In 2013–14, 20% of upper-school students received aid; total upper-school merit-scholarship money awarded: $10,000. Total amount of financial aid awarded in 2013–14: $25,000.

Admissions Traditional secondary-level entrance grade is 10. For fall 2013, 20 students applied for upper-level admission, 17 were accepted, 17 enrolled. Admissions testing, any standardized test, audition, math and English placement tests, Math Placement Exam, TOEFL or SLEP or writing sample required. Deadline for receipt of application materials: none. Application fee required: $300. Interview recommended.

Athletics Interscholastic: badminton (boys, girls), baseball (b,g), basketball (b,g), cross-country running (b,g), flag football (b), indoor soccer (b,g), soccer (b,g), softball (g), track and field (b,g), volleyball (b,g); intramural: aerobics/dance (b,g), badminton (b,g), ballet (b,g), baseball (b,g), basketball (b,g), bowling (b,g), cheering (g), dance (b,g), dance squad (b,g), dance team (b,g), field hockey (b,g), fitness (b,g), flag football (b,g), gymnastics (b,g), hiking/backpacking (b,g), horseback riding (b,g), indoor soccer (b,g), jump rope (b,g), modern dance (b,g), outdoor activities (b,g), outdoor education (b,g), physical fitness (b,g), soccer (b,g), softball (b,g), surfing (b,g), swimming and diving (b,g), table tennis (b,g), tennis (b,g), track and field (b,g), volleyball (b,g); coed interscholastic: indoor soccer; coed intramural: aerobics/dance, badminton, ballet, baseball, bowling, dance, dance squad, dance team, fitness, flag football, hiking/backpacking, indoor soccer, jump rope, modern dance, outdoor activities, outdoor education, physical fitness, softball, surfing, swimming and diving, table tennis, track and field. 2 PE instructors, 2 coaches.

Computers Computers are regularly used in architecture, business skills, creative writing, desktop publishing, drawing and design, journalism, keyboarding, media arts, music, programming, SAT preparation, typing, video film production, Web site design, word processing, yearbook classes. Computer network features include Internet access, college credit classes online.

Contact Karen Peterson, Admissions Department. 619-584-2454. Fax: 619-584-2422. E-mail: jmcherif@yahoo.com. Website: www.ccpaasd.com

CHINESE CHRISTIAN SCHOOLS
1501 Harbor Bay Parkway
Alameda, California 94502
Head of School: Mr. Robin S. Hom

General Information Coeducational boarding and day college-preparatory and religious studies school, affiliated with Bible Fellowship Church, Evangelical/Fundamental faith. Grades 9–12. Founded: 1979. Setting: suburban. Nearest major city is Oakland. Students are housed in student residences. 10-acre campus. 3 buildings on campus. Approved or accredited by Association of Christian Schools International, The College Board, US Department of State, Western Association of Schools and Colleges, and California Department of Education. Endowment: $20,000. Total enrollment: 220. Upper school average class size: 20. Upper school faculty-student ratio: 1:8. There are 173 required school days per year for Upper School students. Upper School students typically attend 5 days per week. The average school day consists of 7 hours and 5 minutes.

Upper School Student Profile Grade 9: 55 students (29 boys, 26 girls); Grade 10: 55 students (22 boys, 33 girls); Grade 11: 55 students (28 boys, 27 girls); Grade 12: 55 students (22 boys, 33 girls). 20% of students are Bible Fellowship Church, Evangelical/Fundamental faith.

Faculty School total: 38. In upper school: 15 men, 20 women; 12 have advanced degrees.

Subjects Offered Advanced computer applications, Advanced Placement courses, aerobics, algebra, American government, American history, American history-AP, American literature, American literature-AP, applied music, art, art-AP, audio visual/media, Basic programming, basketball, Bible, Bible studies, biology, biology-AP, British literature, calculus, calculus-AP, career/college preparation, chemistry, Chinese, Chinese studies, choir, choral music, Christian doctrine, Christian ethics, Christian studies, civics, civics/free enterprise, college counseling, college placement, college planning, communications, community service, comparative religion, computer applications, computer graphics, computer science, computer science-AP, CPR, debate, drama, driver education, economics, economics-AP, electives, English, English language-AP, English literature, English literature-AP, ESL, European history-AP, first aid, foreign language, general science, geometry, government, government and politics-AP, government-AP, graphic arts, honors English, intro to computers, language arts, leadership and service, learning strategies, library assistant, literature and composition-AP, literature-AP, macro/microeconomics-AP, Mandarin, marching band, marine science, martial arts, mathematics-AP, microeconomics, microeconomics-AP, music, newspaper, participation in sports, physical education, physics, physics-AP, pre-algebra, pre-calculus, probability and statistics, psychology-AP, public speaking, religious education, religious studies, ROTC (for boys), SAT preparation, SAT/ACT preparation, science, science research, Spanish, speech, speech and debate, speech communications, sports, state history, statistics, student government, theater, theater arts, trigonometry, U.S. government, U.S. government and politics-AP, U.S. history, U.S. history-AP, visual and performing arts, volleyball, Web authoring, world history, world wide web design, yearbook.

Graduation Requirements Algebra, American government, American history, Bible, Chinese, CPR, driver education, economics, English, first aid, foreign language, geometry, history, lab science, Life of Christ, mathematics, physical education (includes health), physics, pre-algebra, science, visual and performing arts, world history, Mandarin I or Chinese Culture class.

Special Academic Programs 14 Advanced Placement exams for which test preparation is offered; honors section; term-away projects; study at local college for college credit; study abroad; academic accommodation for the gifted; remedial reading and/or remedial writing; ESL (30 students enrolled).

College Admission Counseling 68 students graduated in 2013; all went to college, including California Polytechnic State University, San Luis Obispo; California State Polytechnic University, Pomona; San Jose State University; University of California, Davis; University of California, Riverside; University of the Pacific. Mean SAT critical reading: 601, mean SAT math: 657, mean SAT writing: 607, mean combined SAT: 1865. 55% scored over 600 on SAT critical reading, 71% scored over 600 on SAT math, 55% scored over 600 on SAT writing, 60% scored over 1800 on combined SAT.

Student Life Upper grades have uniform requirement, student council. Discipline rests primarily with faculty. Attendance at religious services is required.

Summer Programs Remediation, enrichment, advancement, ESL, sports programs offered; session focuses on academic enrichment or remediation; held on campus; accepts boys and girls; open to students from other schools. 40 students usually enrolled. 2014 schedule: June 18 to July 18. Application deadline: May 15.

Tuition and Aid Day student tuition: $9800–$10,700. Tuition installment plan (monthly payment plans, individually arranged payment plans, eTuition automatic electronic deposit). Tuition reduction for siblings, merit scholarship grants, need-based scholarship grants, paying campus jobs, tuition reduction for staff children, tuition reduction for children of full-time Christian ministers of like faith available. In 2013–14, 10% of upper-school students received aid; total upper-school merit-scholarship money awarded: $10,000. Total amount of financial aid awarded in 2013–14: $120,000.

Admissions Traditional secondary-level entrance grade is 9. For fall 2013, 55 students applied for upper-level admission, 53 were accepted, 47 enrolled. Achievement/Aptitude/Writing, admissions testing, California Achievement Test, CTBS (or similar from their school), Math Placement Exam, Stanford Achievement

Test or writing sample required. Deadline for receipt of application materials: none. No application fee required. Interview required.

Athletics Interscholastic: badminton (boys, girls), baseball (b), basketball (b,g), cross-country running (b,g), drill team (b,g), golf (b,g), JROTC drill (b,g), soccer (b,g), tennis (b,g), track and field (b,g), volleyball (b,g); intramural: basketball (b,g), drill team (b,g), martial arts (b,g), outdoor education (b,g), outdoor recreation (b,g), soccer (b,g), softball (b,g), table tennis (b,g), volleyball (b,g); coed interscholastic: badminton, golf, swimming and diving; coed intramural: outdoor education, outdoor recreation, softball, table tennis, volleyball. 2 PE instructors, 1 coach.

Computers Computers are regularly used in lab/keyboard, programming, science, senior seminar, Web site design classes. Computer network features include on-campus library services, Internet access, wireless campus network, Internet filtering or blocking technology. Student e-mail accounts are available to students. Students grades are available online. The school has a published electronic and media policy.

Contact Mrs. Christine Hom, Admissions Director. 510-522-0200. Fax: 510-522-0204. E-mail: ChristineHom@cchsrams.org. Website: www.ccs-rams.org

CHOATE ROSEMARY HALL

333 Christian Street
Wallingford, Connecticut 06492-3800

Head of School: Alex D. Curtis, PhD

General Information Coeducational boarding and day college-preparatory school. Grades 9–PG. Founded: 1890. Setting: small town. Nearest major city is New Haven. Students are housed in single-sex dormitories. 458-acre campus. 121 buildings on campus. Approved or accredited by Connecticut Association of Independent Schools, New England Association of Schools and Colleges, The Association of Boarding Schools, and Connecticut Department of Education. Member of National Association of Independent Schools and Secondary School Admission Test Board. Endowment: $283 million. Total enrollment: 864. Upper school average class size: 12. Upper school faculty-student ratio: 1:6. There are 166 required school days per year for Upper School students. Upper School students typically attend 5 days per week. The average school day consists of 5 hours.

Upper School Student Profile Grade 9: 143 students (70 boys, 73 girls); Grade 10: 230 students (118 boys, 112 girls); Grade 11: 228 students (113 boys, 115 girls); Grade 12: 240 students (119 boys, 121 girls); Postgraduate: 23 students (17 boys, 6 girls). 74% of students are boarding students. 41% are state residents. 37 states are represented in upper school student body. 15% are international students. International students from Canada, China, Hong Kong, Republic of Korea, Saudi Arabia, and Thailand; 38 other countries represented in student body.

Faculty School total: 139. In upper school: 72 men, 59 women; 125 have advanced degrees; 110 reside on campus.

Subjects Offered Algebra, American history, American literature, anatomy, Arabic, architecture, art, astronomy, biology, British history, calculus, calculus-AP, ceramics, chemistry, chemistry-AP, child development, Chinese, computer programming, computer science, computer science-AP, creative writing, dance, drama, ecology, economics, English, English literature, environmental science, environmental science-AP, European history-AP, fine arts, French, French language-AP, French studies, geometry, government and politics-AP, history, history-AP, Holocaust, interdisciplinary studies, international studies, Italian, language, Latin, Latin-AP, linear algebra, macroeconomics-AP, marine biology, mathematics, microbiology, microeconomics-AP, music, music composition, music history, music performance, music technology, music theater, music theory-AP, music-AP, musical productions, musical theater, musical theater dance, musicianship, philosophy, photography, physics, physics-AP, psychology, psychology-AP, public speaking, religion, Spanish, Spanish language-AP, Spanish literature, Spanish literature-AP, Spanish-AP, statistics, statistics-AP, studio art, theater, trigonometry, U.S. history, U.S. history-AP, visual arts, world history, world literature, world religions, world studies, wrestling, writing, writing, writing workshop.

Graduation Requirements Art, English, foreign language, global studies, history, mathematics, philosophy, physical education (includes health), science, 30 hours of community service.

Special Academic Programs 25 Advanced Placement exams for which test preparation is offered; honors section; independent study; term-away projects; study abroad; academic accommodation for the gifted, the musically talented, and the artistically talented.

College Admission Counseling 240 students graduated in 2012; 235 went to college, including Boston University; Columbia University; Georgetown University; New York University; Wesleyan University; Yale University. Other: 1 entered a postgraduate year, 4 had other specific plans. Mean SAT critical reading: 664, mean SAT math: 674, mean SAT writing: 680, mean combined SAT: 2018, mean composite ACT: 29.

Student Life Upper grades have specified standards of dress, student council, honor system. Discipline rests primarily with faculty.

Tuition and Aid Day student tuition: $37,000; 7-day tuition and room/board: $48,000. Tuition installment plan (Smart Tuition Payment Plan). Need-based scholarship grants, need-based loans available. In 2012–13, 33% of upper-school students received aid. Total amount of financial aid awarded in 2012–13: $10,000,000.

Admissions Traditional secondary-level entrance grade is 9. For fall 2012, 2,018 students applied for upper-level admission, 447 were accepted, 269 enrolled. ACT,

ISEE, PSAT or SAT for applicants to grade 11 and 12, SSAT or TOEFL required. Deadline for receipt of application materials: January 10. Application fee required: $60. Interview required.

Athletics Interscholastic: baseball (boys), basketball (b,g), crew (b,g), cross-country running (b,g), diving (b,g), field hockey (g), football (b), golf (b,g), ice hockey (b,g), lacrosse (b,g), soccer (b,g), softball (g), squash (b,g), swimming and diving (b,g), tennis (b,g), track and field (b,g), volleyball (b,g), water polo (b,g); intramural: crew (b,g), squash (b,g); coed interscholastic: archery, ultimate Frisbee, wrestling; coed intramural: aerobics, aerobics/dance, aerobics/Nautilus, ballet, basketball, dance, dance squad, fitness, martial arts, modern dance, Nautilus, outdoor activities, physical fitness, physical training, rock climbing, running, soccer, softball, strength & conditioning, swimming and diving, tennis, ultimate Frisbee, volleyball, wall climbing, weight training, winter (indoor) track, yoga. 10 coaches, 3 athletic trainers.

Computers Computers are regularly used in all academic, art, college planning, computer applications, desktop publishing, drawing and design, graphic design, information technology, library skills, literary magazine, media production, music, newspaper, photography, programming, stock market, study skills, theater arts, video film production, word processing, yearbook classes. Computer network features include on-campus library services, online commercial services, Internet access, wireless campus network, Internet filtering or blocking technology. Campus intranet, student e-mail accounts, and computer access in designated common areas are available to students. Students grades are available online. The school has a published electronic and media policy.

Contact Raymond M. Diffley III, Director of Admission. 203-697-2239. Fax: 203-697-2629. E-mail: admission@choate.edu. Website: www.choate.edu

CHRISTA MCAULIFFE ACADEMY SCHOOL OF ARTS AND SCIENCES

5200 SW Meadows Road, Ste 150
Lake Oswego, Oregon 97035

Head of School: Christopher M. Geis

General Information Coeducational day and distance learning college-preparatory, general academic, vocational, technology, and advanced placement, honors, credit recovery school. Grades K–12. Distance learning grades K–12. Founded: 2009. Setting: small town. Nearest major city is Portland. 1 building on campus. Approved or accredited by CITA (Commission on International and Trans-Regional Accreditation), Northwest Accreditation Commission, and Oregon Department of Education. Total enrollment: 108. Upper school average class size: 25. Upper school faculty-student ratio: 1:25. There are 195 required school days per year for Upper School students. Upper School students typically attend 5 days per week. The average school day consists of 5 hours.

Faculty School total: 18. In upper school: 1 man, 12 women; 4 have advanced degrees.

Subjects Offered ACT preparation, alternative physical education, American government, American history, American literature, American sign language, art, art appreciation, art history, astronomy, Bible studies, British literature, British literature (honors), career education, chemistry, child development, Chinese, civics, computer literacy, economics, electives, English, English composition, environmental science, foreign language, forensics, French, geography, geometry, German, government, health, Japanese, keyboarding, Latin, mathematics, music, occupational education, physical education, science, social studies, standard curriculum, technology.

Graduation Requirements Art, career exploration, computer applications, English, mathematics, music, pre-vocational education, science, social studies (includes history).

Special Academic Programs Advanced Placement exam preparation; honors section; accelerated programs; independent study; academic accommodation for the gifted, the musically talented, and the artistically talented; remedial reading and/or remedial writing; remedial math; programs in general development for dyslexic students.

College Admission Counseling 20 students graduated in 2012; 12 went to college, including Florida State University; Massachusetts Institute of Technology; Penn State University Park; University of Illinois at Chicago; University of Washington; Washington State University.

Student Life Upper grades have student council, honor system. Discipline rests equally with students and faculty.

Tuition and Aid Day student tuition: $5295. Guaranteed tuition plan. Tuition installment plan (monthly payment plans, individually arranged payment plans). Tuition reduction for siblings available.

Admissions Traditional secondary-level entrance grade is 9. Achievement/Aptitude/Writing required. Deadline for receipt of application materials: none. Application fee required: $250.

Computers Computer resources include Internet access. The school has a published electronic and media policy.

Contact Kimberly Fowler, Director of Administrative Services. 888-832-9437 Ext. 3. Fax: 866-920-1619. E-mail: kfowler@personalizededucation.org. Website: www.personalizededucation.org/schools/sas

CHRIST CHURCH EPISCOPAL SCHOOL

245 Cavalier Drive
Greenville, South Carolina 29607

Head of School: Dr. Leonard Kupersmith

General Information Coeducational day college-preparatory, arts, religious studies, and technology school, affiliated with Episcopal Church. Grades K–12. Founded: 1959. Setting: suburban. Nearest major city is Charlotte, NC. 72-acre campus. 8 buildings on campus. Approved or accredited by International Baccalaureate Organization, National Association of Episcopal Schools, South Carolina Independent School Association, Southern Association of Colleges and Schools, Southern Association of Independent Schools, and The College Board. Member of National Association of Independent Schools. Endowment: $12.2 million. Total enrollment: 1,151. Upper school average class size: 13. Upper school faculty-student ratio: 1:10. There are 175 required school days per year for Upper School students. Upper School students typically attend 5 days per week. The average school day consists of 7 hours.

Upper School Student Profile Grade 9: 108 students (56 boys, 52 girls); Grade 10: 107 students (47 boys, 60 girls); Grade 11: 102 students (56 boys, 46 girls); Grade 12: 93 students (49 boys, 44 girls). 23% of students are members of Episcopal Church.

Faculty School total: 128. In upper school: 20 men, 25 women; 32 have advanced degrees.

Subjects Offered 20th century world history, algebra, Ancient Greek, ancient history, archaeology, art, art-AP, band, Bible studies, biology, biology-AP, calculus, calculus-AP, ceramics, chemistry, chemistry-AP, China/Japan history, comparative government and politics-AP, computer applications, computer graphics, computer programming, computer science, computer science-AP, contemporary issues, creative writing, digital applications, digital art, digital photography, economics, English, environmental science, environmental science-AP, environmental systems, ESL, ethics, European history, European history-AP, film appreciation, French, French-AP, geometry, German, government and politics-AP, government/civics, graphic arts, honors English, instrumental music, International Baccalaureate courses, journalism, Latin, Latin-AP, literature-AP, Mandarin, mathematics, military history, modern European history, music, music history, music theory, music theory-AP, orchestra, physical education, physical fitness, physics, physics-AP, pre-calculus, probability and statistics, psychology, psychology-AP, religion, sculpture, senior thesis, service learning/internship, Southern literature, Spanish, Spanish-AP, sports conditioning, statistics, statistics-AP, theater, theater design and production, theology, theory of knowledge, U.S. history, U.S. history-AP, video communication, visual and performing arts, visual arts, voice, voice ensemble, Web authoring, world religions, World War II, yearbook.

Graduation Requirements American history, arts and fine arts (art, music, dance, drama), electives, English, foreign language, mathematics, physical education (includes health), religion (includes Bible studies and theology), science, senior thesis, service learning/internship, extended essay (for IB diploma candidates), sophomore project (all students), senior thesis (for non-IB diploma candidates).

Special Academic Programs International Baccalaureate program; honors section; independent study; academic accommodation for the gifted; remedial reading and/or remedial writing; remedial math; ESL (40 students enrolled).

College Admission Counseling 90 students graduated in 2013; all went to college, including Clemson University; College of Charleston; Furman University; The University of Alabama; University of South Carolina; Wofford College. Mean SAT critical reading: 603, mean SAT math: 606, mean SAT writing: 605, mean combined SAT: 1815, mean composite ACT: 27.

Student Life Upper grades have specified standards of dress, student council, honor system. Discipline rests equally with students and faculty. Attendance at religious services is required.

Summer Programs Enrichment, advancement, sports programs offered; session focuses on enrichment, athletics, academics; held both on and off campus; held at field trips to other locations; accepts boys and girls; open to students from other schools. 98 students usually enrolled. 2014 schedule: June 2 to August 25.

Tuition and Aid Day student tuition: $17,450. Tuition installment plan (Insured Tuition Payment Plan, FACTS Tuition Payment Plan, monthly payment plans). Merit scholarship grants, need-based scholarship grants available. In 2013–14, 22% of upper-school students received aid; total upper-school merit-scholarship money awarded: $195,098. Total amount of financial aid awarded in 2013–14: $519,018.

Admissions Traditional secondary-level entrance grade is 9. For fall 2013, 57 students applied for upper-level admission, 49 were accepted, 33 enrolled. ERB or PSAT required. Deadline for receipt of application materials: December 2. Application fee required: $150. On-campus interview required.

Athletics Interscholastic: baseball (boys), basketball (b,g), cheering (g), cross-country running (b,g), dance team (g), field hockey (g), football (b), golf (b,g), lacrosse (b,g), soccer (b,g), softball (g), swimming and diving (b,g), tennis (b,g), track and field (b,g), volleyball (g), wrestling (b); intramural: dance team (g). 2 PE instructors, 53 coaches, 1 athletic trainer.

Computers Computers are regularly used in all academic classes. Computer network features include on-campus library services, online commercial services, Internet access, wireless campus network, Internet filtering or blocking technology, classroom computers, 6-8th grade 1 to 1 iPad program. Student e-mail accounts and computer access in designated common areas are available to students. Students grades are available online. The school has a published electronic and media policy.

Contact Mrs. Kathy Jones, Director of Admission. 864-299-1522 Ext. 1208. Fax: 864-299-8861. E-mail: jonesk@cces.org. Website: www.cces.org

CHRISTCHURCH SCHOOL

49 Seahorse Lane
Christchurch, Virginia 23031

Head of School: Mr. John E. Byers

General Information Coeducational boarding and day college-preparatory, marine and environmental sciences, and ESL school, affiliated with Episcopal Church. Grades 9–12. Founded: 1921. Setting: rural. Nearest major city is Richmond. Students are housed in single-sex dormitories. 125-acre campus. 14 buildings on campus. Approved or accredited by National Association of Episcopal Schools, The Association of Boarding Schools, The College Board, Virginia Association of Independent Schools, and Virginia Department of Education. Member of National Association of Independent Schools and Secondary School Admission Test Board. Endowment: $3 million. Total enrollment: 221. Upper school average class size: 12. Upper school faculty-student ratio: 1:6. There are 165 required school days per year for Upper School students. Upper School students typically attend 5 days per week. The average school day consists of 9 hours.

Upper School Student Profile Grade 9: 30 students (18 boys, 12 girls); Grade 10: 62 students (47 boys, 15 girls); Grade 11: 72 students (52 boys, 20 girls); Grade 12: 57 students (54 boys, 3 girls). 60% of students are boarding students. 65% are state residents. 14 states are represented in upper school student body. 21% are international students. International students from Bahamas, China, Germany, Ghana, Guatemala, and Republic of Korea; 5 other countries represented in student body. 17% of students are members of Episcopal Church.

Faculty School total: 42. In upper school: 27 men, 15 women; 26 have advanced degrees; 25 reside on campus.

Subjects Offered Advanced biology, advanced chemistry, algebra, ancient world history, art, biology, calculus, chemistry, Chesapeake Bay studies, Chinese, computer art, computer-aided design, conceptual physics, digital art, drawing and design, economics, English, English language and composition-AP, English literature and composition-AP, environmental science, environmental science-AP, ESL, fine arts, finite math, geography, geometry, health and wellness, honors U.S. history, honors world history, marine biology, modern world history, Native American history, physical education, physics, pre-calculus, probability and statistics, SAT/ACT preparation, Spanish, Spanish-AP, technology/design, theology, U.S. government, U.S. government and politics-AP, U.S. history, U.S. history-AP, world geography, world history.

Graduation Requirements Arts and fine arts (art, music, dance, drama), English, foreign language, health and wellness, mathematics, physical education (includes health), religion (includes Bible studies and theology), science, social studies (includes history), theology, Great Journeys Integrated Work.

Special Academic Programs 11 Advanced Placement exams for which test preparation is offered; honors section; independent study; academic accommodation for the gifted; ESL (18 students enrolled).

College Admission Counseling 58 students graduated in 2012; all went to college, including James Madison University; Randolph-Macon College; Roanoke College; University of Mary Washington; University of Virginia; Virginia Polytechnic Institute and State University. Mean SAT critical reading: 521, mean SAT math: 554, mean SAT writing: 516, mean combined SAT: 1591. 25% scored over 600 on SAT critical reading, 25% scored over 600 on SAT math.

Student Life Upper grades have specified standards of dress, student council, honor system. Discipline rests equally with students and faculty. Attendance at religious services is required.

Tuition and Aid Day student tuition: $18,700; 7-day tuition and room/board: $43,900. Tuition installment plan (monthly payment plans, individually arranged payment plans, 10 month plan, 1st payment due 6/15, 4-payment plan, first payment due 6/15, 2-payment plan, first payment due 6/15). Need-based scholarship grants available. In 2012–13, 46% of upper-school students received aid. Total amount of financial aid awarded in 2012–13: $1,957,070.

Admissions Traditional secondary-level entrance grade is 9. For fall 2012, 228 students applied for upper-level admission, 169 were accepted, 78 enrolled. PSAT or SAT, SSAT, TOEFL or WISC/Woodcock-Johnson required. Deadline for receipt of application materials: none. Application fee required: $50. Interview required.

Athletics Interscholastic: baseball (boys), basketball (b,g), crew (b,g), field hockey (g), football (b), golf (b), lacrosse (b), sailing (b,g), soccer (b,g), tennis (b,g), volleyball (g); intramural: basketball (b), weight training (b,g); coed interscholastic: cross-country running, golf, sailing; coed intramural: backpacking, canoeing/kayaking, fishing, fitness, fly fishing, Frisbee, hiking/backpacking, indoor soccer, kayaking, mountain biking, outdoor activities, outdoor adventure, outdoor education, outdoor recreation, outdoor skills, outdoors, paint ball, physical training, rock climbing, sailing, skateboarding, skeet shooting, snowboarding, soccer, strength & conditioning, tennis, winter soccer. 1 athletic trainer.

Computers Computers are regularly used in all academic classes. Computer network features include on-campus library services, online commercial services, Internet access, wireless campus network, Internet filtering or blocking technology. Campus intranet, student e-mail accounts, and computer access in designated common areas are

available to students. Students grades are available online. The school has a published electronic and media policy.

Contact Mr. Lawrence J. Jensen, Director of Admission. 804-758-2306. Fax: 804-758-0721. E-mail: admission@christchurchschool.org. Website: www.christchurchschool.org

CHRISTIAN ACADEMY OF KNOXVILLE

529 Academy Way
Knoxville, Tennessee 37923

Head of School: Mr. Scott Sandie

General Information Coeducational day college-preparatory, arts, religious studies, and technology school, affiliated with Christian faith. Grades PK–12. Founded: 1977. Setting: suburban. 77-acre campus. 1 building on campus. Approved or accredited by Association of Christian Schools International, Southern Association of Colleges and Schools, Tennessee Association of Independent Schools, and Tennessee Department of Education. Total enrollment: 1,158. Upper school average class size: 20. Upper school faculty-student ratio: 1:17. There are 180 required school days per year for Upper School students. Upper School students typically attend 5 days per week. The average school day consists of 7 hours and 25 minutes.

Upper School Student Profile 100% of students are Christian faith.

Faculty School total: 98. In upper school: 15 men, 20 women; 26 have advanced degrees.

Subjects Offered U.S. government and politics-AP.

Student Life Upper grades have specified standards of dress, student council, honor system. Discipline rests primarily with faculty. Attendance at religious services is required.

Tuition and Aid Guaranteed tuition plan. Tuition installment plan (The Tuition Plan, monthly payment plans). Need-based scholarship grants available.

Admissions Traditional secondary-level entrance grade is 9. Admissions testing required. Application fee required: $250. On-campus interview required.

Athletics Interscholastic: baseball (boys), cheering (g), dance team (g), football (b), softball (g), volleyball (g), wrestling (b); coed interscholastic: aquatics, basketball, cross-country running, golf, hiking/backpacking, soccer, strength & conditioning, swimming and diving. 4 PE instructors, 14 coaches, 5 athletic trainers.

Computers Computer resources include on-campus library services, Internet access, wireless campus network, Internet filtering or blocking technology. Campus intranet, student e-mail accounts, and computer access in designated common areas are available to students. Students grades are available online. The school has a published electronic and media policy.

Contact Mrs. Amy Williams, Admissions Director. 865-690-4721 Ext. 190. Fax: 865-690-4752. E-mail: awilliams@cakmail.org. Website:

CHRISTIAN BROTHERS ACADEMY

850 Newman Springs Road
Lincroft, New Jersey 07738

Head of School: Mr. Peter Santanello

General Information Boys' day college-preparatory, religious studies, Math, English, French, Spanish, Latin, Arabic, Science, Hist, and Geography, Environmental Sci, Computer Sci school, affiliated with Roman Catholic Church. Grades 9–12. Founded: 1959. Setting: suburban. Nearest major city is New York, NY. 157-acre campus. 3 buildings on campus. Approved or accredited by Middle States Association of Colleges and Schools. Total enrollment: 1,007. Upper school average class size: 18. Upper school faculty-student ratio: 1:14. There are 180 required school days per year for Upper School students. Upper School students typically attend 5 days per week. The average school day consists of 6 hours and 15 minutes.

Upper School Student Profile Grade 9: 264 students (264 boys); Grade 10: 291 students (291 boys); Grade 11: 230 students (230 boys); Grade 12: 222 students (222 boys). 86% of students are Roman Catholic.

Faculty School total: 70. In upper school: 46 men, 24 women; 44 have advanced degrees.

Subjects Offered 20th century history, algebra, American government, American history, anatomy and physiology, Arabic, Bible studies, biology, biology-AP, business, business skills, calculus, calculus-AP, chemistry, chemistry-AP, computer science, computer science-AP, creative writing, driver education, economics, economics-AP, English, English language-AP, English literature-AP, environmental science, environmental science-AP, European history, European history-AP, French, French-AP, geometry, health, history, honors algebra, honors English, honors geometry, honors U.S. history, journalism, Latin, Latin-AP, linear algebra, mathematics, physical education, physics, physics-AP, psychology, psychology-AP, religion, science, social sciences, social studies, Spanish, Spanish-AP, theology, trigonometry, U.S. history, world history, world literature, writing.

Graduation Requirements Business skills (includes word processing), computer science, English, foreign language, mathematics, physical education (includes health), religion (includes Bible studies and theology), science, social sciences, social studies (includes history).

Special Academic Programs Advanced Placement exam preparation; honors section.

College Admission Counseling 222 students graduated in 2013; 219 went to college, including Boston College; La Salle University; Loyola University Maryland; Penn State University Park; Rutgers, The State University of New Jersey, New Brunswick; Villanova University. Other: 3 had other specific plans. Median SAT critical reading: 590, median SAT math: 620, median SAT writing: 590, median combined SAT: 1800.

Student Life Upper grades have specified standards of dress, student council. Discipline rests primarily with faculty. Attendance at religious services is required.

Tuition and Aid Day student tuition: $14,150. Tuition installment plan (FACTS Tuition Payment Plan, individually arranged payment plans). Merit scholarship grants, need-based scholarship grants available. In 2013–14, 19% of upper-school students received aid; total upper-school merit-scholarship money awarded: $216,000. Total amount of financial aid awarded in 2013–14: $1,152,500.

Admissions Traditional secondary-level entrance grade is 9. For fall 2013, 530 students applied for upper-level admission, 350 were accepted, 301 enrolled. School's own test required. Deadline for receipt of application materials: none. Application fee required: $75.

Athletics Interscholastic: baseball, basketball, bowling, cross-country running, fencing, golf, ice hockey, lacrosse, soccer, swimming and diving, tennis, track and field, winter (indoor) track, wrestling; intramural: baseball, basketball, bowling, Frisbee, soccer, tennis, volleyball. 3 PE instructors, 21 coaches, 1 athletic trainer.

Computers Computers are regularly used in mathematics, science classes. Computer network features include on-campus library services, Internet access. Computer access in designated common areas is available to students. Students grades are available online.

Contact Mr. Peter Santanello, Principal. 732-747-1959 Ext. 100. Fax: 732-747-1643. Website: www.cbalincroftnj.org

CHRISTIAN BROTHERS ACADEMY

6245 Randall Road
Syracuse, New York 13214

Head of School: Br. Joseph Jozwiak, FSC

General Information Coeducational day college-preparatory and religious studies school, affiliated with Roman Catholic Church. Grades 7–12. Founded: 1900. Setting: suburban. 40-acre campus. 1 building on campus. Approved or accredited by Christian Brothers Association, Middle States Association of Colleges and Schools, and New York State Board of Regents. Endowment: $800,000. Total enrollment: 750. Upper school average class size: 25.

Upper School Student Profile 85% of students are Roman Catholic.

Faculty School total: 62. In upper school: 32 men, 30 women; 58 have advanced degrees.

Subjects Offered Advanced Placement courses, American history, American literature, art, biology, business, calculus, chemistry, chemistry-AP, earth science, economics, English, English literature, European history, expository writing, fine arts, French, government/civics, grammar, health, history, mathematics, music, physical education, physics, pre-calculus, psychology, religion, science, social sciences, social studies, Spanish, theology, world history, world literature.

Graduation Requirements Arts and fine arts (art, music, dance, drama), English, foreign language, mathematics, physical education (includes health), religion (includes Bible studies and theology), science, social sciences, social studies (includes history), community service for seniors.

Special Academic Programs Advanced Placement exam preparation; honors section.

College Admission Counseling 122 students graduated in 2013; 121 went to college, including Le Moyne College; Loyola University Maryland; New York University; Saint Joseph's University; Syracuse University. Other: 1 entered a postgraduate year. Mean SAT critical reading: 567, mean SAT math: 573, mean SAT writing: 547, mean combined SAT: 1687, mean composite ACT: 25.

Student Life Upper grades have specified standards of dress, student council. Discipline rests primarily with faculty. Attendance at religious services is required.

Tuition and Aid Day student tuition: $9405. Tuition installment plan (SMART Tuition Payment Plan, individually arranged payment plans). Merit scholarship grants, need-based scholarship grants available. In 2013–14, 95% of upper-school students received aid; total upper-school merit-scholarship money awarded: $650,000.

Admissions Traditional secondary-level entrance grade is 9. For fall 2013, 50 students applied for upper-level admission, 38 were accepted, 38 enrolled. Admissions testing required. Deadline for receipt of application materials: February 1. Application fee required: $40. Interview recommended.

Athletics Interscholastic: baseball (boys), basketball (b,g), cheering (g), cross-country running (b,g), diving (b,g), football (b), golf (b,g), gymnastics (b), ice hockey (b), lacrosse (b,g), soccer (b,g), softball (g), swimming and diving (b,g), tennis (b,g), track and field (b,g), volleyball (g), wrestling (b); coed interscholastic: bowling. 3 PE instructors, 1 athletic trainer.

Computers Computer network features include on-campus library services, Internet access, Internet filtering or blocking technology. Students grades are available online. The school has a published electronic and media policy.

Contact Mr. Mark Person, Assistant Principal for Student Affairs. 315-446-5960 Ext. 1227. Fax: 315-446-3393. E-mail: mperson@cbasyracuse.org. Website: www.cbasyracuse.org

CHRISTIAN CENTRAL ACADEMY

39 Academy Street
Williamsville, New York 14221

Head of School: Mrs. Nurline Lawrence

General Information Coeducational day college-preparatory, arts, and religious studies school, affiliated with Christian faith. Grades K–12. Founded: 1949. Setting: suburban. Nearest major city is Buffalo. 5-acre campus. 4 buildings on campus. Approved or accredited by Association of Christian Schools International, Middle States Association of Colleges and Schools, New York State Board of Regents, and New York Department of Education. Member of Secondary School Admission Test Board. Endowment: $900,000. Total enrollment: 355. Upper school average class size: 20. Upper school faculty-student ratio: 1:10. There are 180 required school days per year for Upper School students. Upper School students typically attend 5 days per week. The average school day consists of 6 hours and 36 minutes.

Upper School Student Profile Grade 9: 27 students (11 boys, 16 girls); Grade 10: 31 students (18 boys, 13 girls); Grade 11: 29 students (12 boys, 17 girls); Grade 12: 23 students (12 boys, 11 girls). 100% of students are Christian faith.

Faculty School total: 46. In upper school: 8 men, 15 women; 13 have advanced degrees.

Subjects Offered Advanced computer applications, advertising design, algebra, art, band, Bible, biology, biology-AP, business mathematics, calculus-AP, career/college preparation, chemistry, chorus, communications, computer skills, drawing, driver education, earth science, economics, English, English language-AP, English literature-AP, European history-AP, geometry, global studies, government, health, honors English, independent study, journalism, mathematics, music, music theory, orchestra, painting, physical education, physics, physics-AP, pre-calculus, Spanish, studio art, trigonometry, U.S. history, U.S. history-AP, yearbook.

Graduation Requirements Algebra, American government, American history, American literature, arts and fine arts (art, music, dance, drama), Bible, biology, chemistry, earth science, economics, English, geometry, global studies, keyboarding, physical education (includes health), physics, pre-calculus, Spanish, trigonometry, writing, community service hours for all four years, completion of standardized NYS Regents exams, honors and high honors diplomas have more rigorous requirements.

Special Academic Programs 7 Advanced Placement exams for which test preparation is offered; honors section; independent study.

College Admission Counseling 24 students graduated in 2013; all went to college, including Canisius College; Hillsdale College; Liberty University; University at Buffalo, the State University of New York. Median SAT critical reading: 567, median SAT math: 554, median SAT writing: 585, median combined SAT: 1706. 26% scored over 600 on SAT critical reading, 39% scored over 600 on SAT math, 39% scored over 600 on SAT writing, 26% scored over 1800 on combined SAT.

Student Life Upper grades have specified standards of dress, student council, honor system. Discipline rests primarily with faculty. Attendance at religious services is required.

Summer Programs Sports programs offered; session focuses on basketball camp, soccer camp; held on campus; accepts boys and girls; open to students from other schools. 45 students usually enrolled. 2014 schedule: July 1 to July 1. Application deadline: June 1.

Tuition and Aid Day student tuition: $8465. Tuition installment plan (FACTS Tuition Payment Plan, monthly payment plans, prepayment discount plans, multiple-student discounts, pastors/full-time Christian service discounts). Tuition reduction for siblings, merit scholarship grants available. In 2013–14, 45% of upper-school students received aid; total upper-school merit-scholarship money awarded: $5000. Total amount of financial aid awarded in 2013–14: $108,875.

Admissions Traditional secondary-level entrance grade is 9. For fall 2013, 78 students applied for upper-level admission, 78 were accepted, 67 enrolled. Admissions testing, Brigance Test of Basic Skills, essay, Iowa Subtests, school's own test or writing sample required. Deadline for receipt of application materials: none. Application fee required: $50. Interview recommended.

Athletics Interscholastic: baseball (boys), basketball (b,g), bowling (b), cheering (g), cross-country running (b,g), flag football (b), golf (b), soccer (b,g), softball (g); intramural: basketball (b,g), physical fitness (b,g), soccer (b,g); coed interscholastic: cross-country running, soccer; coed intramural: basketball, track and field, volleyball. 2 PE instructors, 17 coaches.

Computers Computers are regularly used in college planning, computer applications, desktop publishing, drawing and design, English, journalism, library skills, photojournalism, yearbook classes. Computer network features include on-campus library services, Internet access, wireless campus network, Internet filtering or blocking technology, teacher-guided use of programs in various subject areas. Computer access in designated common areas is available to students. Students grades are available online. The school has a published electronic and media policy.

Contact Lisa A. Woodard, Director of Admissions. 716-634-4821 Ext. 107. Fax: 716-634-5851. E-mail: lwoodard@christianca.com. Website: www.christianca.com

CHRISTOPHER COLUMBUS HIGH SCHOOL

3000 Southwest 87th Avenue
Miami, Florida 33165-3293

Head of School: Br. Michael Brady, FMS

General Information Boys' day college-preparatory school, affiliated with Roman Catholic Church. Grades 9–12. Founded: 1958. Setting: suburban. 19-acre campus. 10 buildings on campus. Approved or accredited by National Catholic Education Association, Southern Association of Colleges and Schools, and Florida Department of Education. Total enrollment: 1,357. Upper school average class size: 25. Upper school faculty-student ratio: 1:17. There are 180 required school days per year for Upper School students. Upper School students typically attend 5 days per week. The average school day consists of 6 hours and 25 minutes.

Upper School Student Profile Grade 9: 347 students (347 boys); Grade 10: 363 students (363 boys); Grade 11: 302 students (302 boys); Grade 12: 345 students (345 boys). 95% of students are Roman Catholic.

Faculty School total: 82. In upper school: 56 men, 26 women; 35 have advanced degrees.

Subjects Offered 3-dimensional art, accounting, acting, advanced biology, advanced chemistry, advanced computer applications, advanced math, Advanced Placement courses, algebra, American government, American history, American history-AP, American literature, analysis, anatomy, ancient world history, architectural drawing, art, athletic training, athletics, band, Basic programming, Bible, biology, biology-AP, British literature (honors), business law, business skills, calculus, calculus-AP, campus ministry, Catholic belief and practice, chemistry, chemistry-AP, Christian and Hebrew scripture, Christian doctrine, Christian ethics, church history, college counseling, composition-AP, computer applications, computer information systems, computer programming, computer science, computer science-AP, computer-aided design, contemporary history, debate, drama, economics, economics-AP, English, English language and composition-AP, English literature, English literature-AP, English-AP, ethics, European history, European history-AP, French, French language-AP, French-AP, geometry, global studies, government, government and politics-AP, health, history of the Catholic Church, Holocaust studies, keyboarding, library assistant, marine biology, physical education, physical fitness, physics, physics-AP, pre-algebra, pre-calculus, psychology, Spanish, Spanish language-AP, Spanish literature, Spanish literature-AP, speech, U.S. government, U.S. government and politics, U.S. government and politics-AP, U.S. history, U.S. history-AP, Vietnam War, word processing, world governments, yearbook.

Graduation Requirements Algebra, arts and fine arts (art, music, dance, drama), computer applications, English, lab science, language, mathematics, personal fitness, physical education (includes health), practical arts, religion (includes Bible studies and theology), science, social studies (includes history), students must earn a Florida scale GPA of 2.0, students must complete 75 hours of community service during their four years of high school.

Special Academic Programs Advanced Placement exam preparation; honors section; study at local college for college credit; academic accommodation for the gifted; remedial reading and/or remedial writing.

College Admission Counseling Colleges students went to include Florida International University; The University of Alabama; University of Florida; University of Miami; University of Notre Dame; University of Pennsylvania.

Student Life Upper grades have uniform requirement, student council, honor system. Discipline rests primarily with faculty. Attendance at religious services is required.

Tuition and Aid Tuition installment plan (monthly payment plans, individually arranged payment plans). Bursaries available.

Admissions Traditional secondary-level entrance grade is 9. For fall 2012, 494 students applied for upper-level admission, 347 were accepted, 347 enrolled. High School Placement Test required. Deadline for receipt of application materials: none. Application fee required: $50. Interview required.

Athletics Interscholastic: baseball, basketball, bowling, cross-country running, football, golf, lacrosse, soccer, swimming and diving, tennis, track and field, volleyball, water polo, wrestling; intramural: basketball, flag football, power lifting, roller hockey, weight training. 2 PE instructors, 25 coaches, 2 athletic trainers.

Computers Computers are regularly used in architecture, computer applications, history, journalism, keyboarding, media production, science, yearbook classes. Computer network features include on-campus library services, online commercial services, Internet access, wireless campus network, Internet filtering or blocking technology. Campus intranet and computer access in designated common areas are available to students. Students grades are available online. The school has a published electronic and media policy.

Contact Mrs. Rebecca Rafuls, Registrar. 305-223-5650 Ext. 2239. Fax: 305-559-4306. E-mail: rrafuls@columbushs.com. Website: www.columbushs.com

CHRISTOPHER DOCK MENNONITE HIGH SCHOOL

1000 Forty Foot Road
Lansdale, Pennsylvania 19446

Head of School: Dr. Conrad J. Swartzentruber

General Information Coeducational boarding and day college-preparatory, general academic, arts, business, vocational, religious studies, and technology school, affiliated with Christian faith, Mennonite Church. Grades 9–12. Founded: 1954. Setting: suburban. Nearest major city is Philadelphia. Students are housed in homes. 75-acre campus. 6 buildings on campus. Approved or accredited by Mennonite Education Agency, Mennonite Schools Council, Middle States Association of Colleges and Schools, and Pennsylvania Department of Education. Endowment: $2.2 million. Total enrollment: 351. Upper school average class size: 21. Upper school faculty-student ratio: 1:11. There are 180 required school days per year for Upper School students. Upper School students typically attend 5 days per week. The average school day consists of 6 hours and 55 minutes.

Upper School Student Profile Grade 9: 70 students (33 boys, 37 girls); Grade 10: 89 students (49 boys, 40 girls); Grade 11: 86 students (35 boys, 51 girls); Grade 12: 106 students (52 boys, 54 girls). 2% of students are boarding students. 84% are state residents. 2 states are represented in upper school student body. 11% are international students. International students from China, Comoros, Indonesia, Kenya, and Republic of Korea. 49% of students are Christian, Mennonite.

Faculty School total: 33. In upper school: 19 men, 14 women; 24 have advanced degrees.

Subjects Offered Accounting, advanced biology, advanced chemistry, advanced math, Advanced Placement courses, algebra, all , American government, American history, American literature, anatomy, anatomy and physiology, art, art history, arts, arts appreciation, athletic training, athletics, Basic programming, Bible, Bible studies, biology, British literature, business, business mathematics, business skills, calculus, calculus-AP, career education internship, career technology, ceramics, chemistry, child development, choir, choral music, chorus, Christian and Hebrew scripture, Christian doctrine, Christian education, Christian ethics, Christian scripture, Christian studies, Christian testament, Christianity, church history, communication skills, communications, composition-AP, computer graphics, computer information systems, computer literacy, computer programming, computer science, computer skills, computer technologies, computers, concert choir, consumer economics, creative writing, design, digital art, digital imaging, digital music, digital photography, drama, driver education, early childhood, earth science, ecology, environmental systems, economics, economics and history, economics-AP, English, English language and composition-AP, English literature, environmental science, European history, family and consumer science, family living, family studies, fine arts, food science, foreign language, forensics, genetics, geography, geology, geometry, global studies, government-AP, government/civics, grammar, graphic design, guitar, health, health and wellness, health education, history, honors English, honors geometry, instrumental music, instruments, international foods, jazz band, journalism, keyboarding, language and composition, Life of Christ, life saving, life science, mathematics, mathematics-AP, music, New Testament, oral communications, parent/child development, peace and justice, peace education, peace studies, personal finance, photography, physical education, physics, religion, religion and culture, religious education, religious studies, research and reference, rhetoric, science, science research, scripture, sculpture, senior internship, service learning/internship, social sciences, social studies, Spanish, Spanish language-AP, Spanish literature-AP, Spanish-AP, speech, speech communications, sports team management, stage and body movement, statistics, student government, student publications, theater, trigonometry, U.S. government, U.S. history, U.S. literature, Vietnam, vocal ensemble, vocal music, vocational skills, vocational-technical courses, Web site design, word processing, work-study, world cultures, world history, world literature.

Graduation Requirements Arts and fine arts (art, music, dance, drama), business skills (includes word processing), computer science, English, family and consumer science, mathematics, physical education (includes health), religion (includes Bible studies and theology), science, social sciences, social studies (includes history), three-day urban experience, senior independent study/service experience (one week), senior presentation.

Special Academic Programs 16 Advanced Placement exams for which test preparation is offered; honors section; term-away projects; study at local college for college credit; remedial reading and/or remedial writing; programs in English for dyslexic students.

College Admission Counseling 84 students graduated in 2013; 77 went to college, including Cairn University; Eastern Mennonite University; Eastern University; Messiah College; Montgomery County Community College. Other: 4 went to work, 1 entered military service, 2 had other specific plans. Mean SAT critical reading: 531, mean SAT math: 560, mean SAT writing: 531, mean combined SAT: 1622. 28% scored over 600 on SAT critical reading, 45% scored over 600 on SAT math, 27% scored over 600 on SAT writing, 33% scored over 1800 on combined SAT.

Student Life Upper grades have specified standards of dress, student council, honor system. Discipline rests primarily with faculty. Attendance at religious services is required.

Tuition and Aid Day student tuition: $14,895; 7-day tuition and room/board: $27,895. Tuition installment plan (monthly payment plans). Tuition reduction for siblings, need-based scholarship grants available. In 2013–14, 66% of upper-school students received aid. Total amount of financial aid awarded in 2013–14: $500,000.

Admissions Traditional secondary-level entrance grade is 9. For fall 2013, 136 students applied for upper-level admission, 131 were accepted, 94 enrolled. Deadline for receipt of application materials: none. Application fee required: $50. Interview required.

Athletics Interscholastic: baseball (boys), basketball (b,g), bowling (b,g), cheering (g), cross-country running (b,g), field hockey (g), golf (b), soccer (b,g), softball (g), tennis (b,g), track and field (b,g), volleyball (b,g); coed interscholastic: bowling, track and field. 3 PE instructors, 37 coaches, 1 athletic trainer.

Computers Computers are regularly used in accounting, art, computer applications, design, digital applications, graphic design, journalism, keyboarding, lab/keyboard, library, library skills, mathematics, music, music technology, programming, research skills, SAT preparation, science, technology, Web site design, word processing, yearbook classes. Computer network features include on-campus library services, online commercial services, Internet access, wireless campus network, Internet filtering or blocking technology, PowerSchool, WinSNAP, 1:1 iPad program. Computer access in designated common areas is available to students. Students grades are available online. The school has a published electronic and media policy.

Contact Doug Hackman, Admissions Director. 215-362-2675 Ext. 106. Fax: 215-362-2943. E-mail: dhackman@dockhs.org. Website: www.dockhs.org

CHRYSALIS SCHOOL

14241 North East Woodinville-Duvall Road
PMB 243
Woodinville, Washington 98072

Head of School: Karen Fogle

General Information Coeducational day college-preparatory, general academic, arts, and technology school. Grades 1–12. Founded: 1983. Setting: suburban. Nearest major city is Seattle. 1 building on campus. Approved or accredited by Northwest Accreditation Commission, Northwest Association of Schools and Colleges, and Washington Department of Education. Total enrollment: 165. Upper school average class size: 8. Upper school faculty-student ratio: 1:3. Upper School students typically attend 4 days per week. The average school day consists of 5 hours.

Upper School Student Profile Grade 9: 19 students (11 boys, 8 girls); Grade 10: 28 students (18 boys, 10 girls); Grade 11: 41 students (31 boys, 10 girls); Grade 12: 29 students (19 boys, 10 girls).

Faculty School total: 36. In upper school: 13 men, 23 women; 15 have advanced degrees.

Subjects Offered Advanced biology, advanced chemistry, advanced computer applications, advanced math, art, audio visual/media, career planning, college counseling, computer technologies, drama, English, filmmaking, French, geography, German, graphics, history, Japanese, mathematics, physical education, SAT preparation, science, social sciences, Spanish.

Graduation Requirements Career and personal planning, computer literacy, English, foreign language, history, mathematics, physical education (includes health), science, portfolio.

Special Academic Programs Honors section; accelerated programs; study at local college for college credit; academic accommodation for the gifted; programs in English, mathematics, general development for dyslexic students; special instructional classes for students with learning challenges.

College Admission Counseling 33 students graduated in 2013; 27 went to college, including Bellevue College; Central Washington University; University of Washington; Washington State University; Western Washington University. Other: 4 went to work, 2 had other specific plans.

Student Life Upper grades have specified standards of dress, honor system. Discipline rests primarily with faculty.

Summer Programs Remediation, enrichment, advancement, computer instruction programs offered; session focuses on enrichment; held on campus; accepts boys and girls; open to students from other schools. 35 students usually enrolled. 2014 schedule: July 10 to August 23. Application deadline: June 1.

Tuition and Aid Tuition installment plan (monthly payment plans).

Admissions Traditional secondary-level entrance grade is 9. For fall 2013, 100 students applied for upper-level admission, 60 were accepted, 60 enrolled. Deadline for receipt of application materials: none. Application fee required: $750. On-campus interview required.

Computers Computers are regularly used in computer applications, English, foreign language, graphic arts, history, information technology, introduction to technology, keyboarding, mathematics, media, science, video film production, Web site design, word processing, yearbook classes. Computer resources include on-campus library services, online commercial services, Internet access, wireless campus network, Internet filtering or blocking technology. Computer access in designated common areas is available to students. The school has a published electronic and media policy.

Contact Wanda Metcalfe, Director of Student Services. 425-481-2228. Fax: 425-486-8107. E-mail: wanda@chrysalis-school.com. Website: www.chrysalis-school.com

THE CHURCH FARM SCHOOL

1001 East Lincoln Highway
Exton, Pennsylvania 19341

Head of School: Rev. Edmund K. Sherrill II

General Information Boys' boarding and day college-preparatory, arts, and technology school, affiliated with Episcopal Church. Grades 7–12. Founded: 1918. Setting: suburban. Nearest major city is Philadelphia. Students are housed in single-sex dormitories. 150-acre campus. 19 buildings on campus. Approved or accredited by

Middle States Association of Colleges and Schools, National Association of Episcopal Schools, The Association of Boarding Schools, and Pennsylvania Department of Education. Member of National Association of Independent Schools and Secondary School Admission Test Board. Endowment: $135 million. Total enrollment: 193. Upper school average class size: 12. Upper school faculty-student ratio: 1:6. There are 180 required school days per year for Upper School students. Upper School students typically attend 5 days per week. The average school day consists of 7 hours and 5 minutes.

Upper School Student Profile Grade 9: 42 students (42 boys); Grade 10: 47 students (47 boys); Grade 11: 40 students (40 boys); Grade 12: 33 students (33 boys). 90% of students are boarding students. 35% are state residents. 15 states are represented in upper school student body. 16% are international students. International students from British Virgin Islands, China, Mexico, Nigeria, Republic of Korea, and Thailand; 4 other countries represented in student body. 10% of students are members of Episcopal Church.

Faculty School total: 33. In upper school: 22 men, 11 women; 17 have advanced degrees; 24 reside on campus.

Subjects Offered 20th century history, 3-dimensional design, African-American history, algebra, American government, American history, American history-AP, American literature, American studies, anatomy and physiology, art, art history, biology, biology-AP, British literature, calculus-AP, ceramics, chemistry, chemistry-AP, choir, choral music, clayworking, college writing, composition, computer science, construction, creative writing, design, drama, driver education, earth science, ecology, economics, English, English-AP, environmental science, ethics, European history, expository writing, film and literature, fine arts, French, geometry, government/civics, grammar, health, history, history of jazz, industrial arts, instrumental music, journalism, leadership, mathematics, medieval history, music, music history, music technology, musicianship, mythology, photography, physical education, physics, poetry, pre-calculus, psychology, public speaking, Russian history, science, Shakespeare, Shakespearean histories, social studies, sociology, Spanish, speech, statistics, technology, theater, trigonometry, Vietnam history, Vietnam War, weaving, Web site design, woodworking, world history, world literature, world religions, World War II, writing.

Graduation Requirements Arts and fine arts (art, music, dance, drama), English, foreign language, mathematics, physical education (includes health), religion (includes Bible studies and theology), science, social studies (includes history), technology, Challenge of Required Experience (combination of community service and outdoor educational experience).

Special Academic Programs 5 Advanced Placement exams for which test preparation is offered; honors section; accelerated programs; independent study; study at local college for college credit; study abroad; academic accommodation for the gifted, the musically talented, and the artistically talented.

College Admission Counseling 35 students graduated in 2012; 32 went to college, including Bard College; Brandeis University; Emory University; Northwestern University; University of California, San Diego; University of Southern California. Other: 1 went to work, 2 had other specific plans. Median SAT critical reading: 540, median SAT math: 570, median SAT writing: 520, median combined SAT: 1660. 29% scored over 600 on SAT critical reading, 43% scored over 600 on SAT math, 29% scored over 600 on SAT writing, 30% scored over 1800 on combined SAT.

Student Life Upper grades have specified standards of dress, student council, honor system. Discipline rests primarily with faculty. Attendance at religious services is required.

Tuition and Aid Day student tuition: $17,172; 5-day tuition and room/board: $30,000; 7-day tuition and room/board: $30,000. Tuition installment plan (monthly payment plans, individually arranged payment plans). Tuition reduction for siblings, need-based scholarship grants, paying campus jobs available. In 2012–13, 90% of upper-school students received aid. Total amount of financial aid awarded in 2012–13: $3,881,717.

Admissions Traditional secondary-level entrance grade is 9. For fall 2012, 264 students applied for upper-level admission, 94 were accepted, 60 enrolled. 3-R Achievement Test, ISEE, SSAT or TOEFL required. Deadline for receipt of application materials: none. Application fee required: $25. Interview required.

Athletics Interscholastic: baseball, basketball, cross-country running, golf, indoor track, soccer, tennis, track and field, wrestling; intramural: fitness, floor hockey, indoor soccer, physical fitness, strength & conditioning, touch football, weight lifting. 2 coaches, 1 athletic trainer.

Computers Computers are regularly used in art, English, foreign language, history, mathematics, music, science, technology classes. Computer network features include on-campus library services, online commercial services, Internet access, wireless campus network, Internet filtering or blocking technology, 1:1 MacBook program. Campus intranet and student e-mail accounts are available to students. Students grades are available online. The school has a published electronic and media policy.

Contact Mr. Bart Bronk, Director of Admissions. 610-363-5346. Fax: 610-280-6746. E-mail: bbronk@gocfs.net. Website: www.gocfs.net

CINCINNATI COUNTRY DAY SCHOOL

6905 Given Road
Cincinnati, Ohio 45243-2898

Head of School: Dr. Robert P. Macrae

General Information Coeducational day college-preparatory, arts, and technology school. Grades PK–12. Founded: 1926. Setting: suburban. 62-acre campus. 8 buildings on campus. Approved or accredited by Independent Schools Association of the Central States and Ohio Department of Education. Member of National Association of Independent Schools and Secondary School Admission Test Board. Endowment: $18 million. Total enrollment: 830. Upper school average class size: 15. Upper school faculty-student ratio: 1:9. There are 180 required school days per year for Upper School students. Upper School students typically attend 5 days per week. The average school day consists of 7 hours.

Upper School Student Profile Grade 9: 72 students (33 boys, 39 girls); Grade 10: 78 students (38 boys, 40 girls); Grade 11: 65 students (32 boys, 33 girls); Grade 12: 57 students (25 boys, 32 girls).

Faculty School total: 110. In upper school: 24 men, 16 women; 32 have advanced degrees.

Subjects Offered Acting, algebra, American history, American history-AP, American literature, analysis, art, art history, biology, biology-AP, calculus, calculus-AP, ceramics, chemistry, chemistry-AP, choir, computer graphics, computer programming, computer science, CPR, creative writing, dance, drama, earth science, English, English literature, European history, fine arts, French, French language-AP, French literature-AP, genetics, geometry, health, humanities, music, photography, physical education, physics, psychology, public speaking, Spanish, Spanish language-AP, Spanish literature-AP, speech, statistics, theater, trigonometry, world history.

Graduation Requirements Arts and fine arts (art, music, dance, drama), computer science, English, foreign language, history, mathematics, physical education (includes health), science, senior project. Community service is required.

Special Academic Programs Advanced Placement exam preparation; honors section; independent study; study abroad.

College Admission Counseling 70 students graduated in 2012; all went to college, including Denison University; Indiana University Bloomington; The Ohio State University; Vanderbilt University; Williams College. Mean SAT critical reading: 630, mean SAT math: 630, mean SAT writing: 640, mean combined SAT: 1900, mean composite ACT: 27.

Student Life Upper grades have specified standards of dress, student council, honor system. Discipline rests equally with students and faculty.

Tuition and Aid Day student tuition: $21,920. Tuition installment plan (Insured Tuition Payment Plan, FACTS Tuition Payment Plan, monthly payment plans, individually arranged payment plans). Merit scholarship grants, need-based scholarship grants, parent loans, Sallie Mae loans available. In 2012–13, 40% of upper-school students received aid; total upper-school merit-scholarship money awarded: $520,000. Total amount of financial aid awarded in 2012–13: $1,400,000.

Admissions Traditional secondary-level entrance grade is 9. For fall 2012, 63 students applied for upper-level admission, 41 were accepted, 28 enrolled. ISEE, Otis-Lennon Ability or Stanford Achievement Test or SSAT, ERB, PSAT, SAT, PLAN or ACT required. Deadline for receipt of application materials: February 15. Application fee required: $25. Interview recommended.

Athletics Interscholastic: baseball (boys), basketball (b,g), crew (b,g), cross-country running (b,g), football (b), golf (b,g), gymnastics (g), lacrosse (b,g), softball (g), swimming and diving (b,g), tennis (b,g), track and field (b,g); intramural: dance team (g); coed interscholastic: crew, dance squad. 4 PE instructors, 1 athletic trainer.

Computers Computers are regularly used in all academic classes. Computer network features include on-campus library services, online commercial services, Internet access, wireless campus network, Internet filtering or blocking technology. Campus intranet, student e-mail accounts, and computer access in designated common areas are available to students. Students grades are available online. The school has a published electronic and media policy.

Contact Mr. Aaron B. Kellenberger, Director of Admission. 513-979-0220. Fax: 513-527-7614. E-mail: kellenbea@countryday.net. Website: www.countryday.net

CISTERCIAN PREPARATORY SCHOOL

3660 Cistercian Road
Irving, Texas 75039

Head of School: Fr. Paul McCormick

General Information Boys' day college-preparatory, arts, and religious studies school, affiliated with Roman Catholic Church. Grades 5–12. Founded: 1962. Setting: suburban. Nearest major city is Dallas. 80-acre campus. 7 buildings on campus. Approved or accredited by Independent Schools Association of the Southwest, Texas Catholic Conference, and Texas Department of Education. Member of National Association of Independent Schools. Endowment: $6.9 million. Total enrollment: 352. Upper school average class size: 22. Upper school faculty-student ratio: 1:5. There are 180 required school days per year for Upper School students. Upper School students typically attend 5 days per week. The average school day consists of 8 hours.

Upper School Student Profile Grade 9: 46 students (46 boys); Grade 10: 45 students (45 boys); Grade 11: 44 students (44 boys); Grade 12: 43 students (43 boys). 82% of students are Roman Catholic.

Faculty School total: 50. In upper school: 32 men, 5 women; 31 have advanced degrees.

Subjects Offered Advanced biology, advanced chemistry, algebra, American history, American literature, art, athletics, baseball, basketball, biology, calculus, chemistry, computer science, creative writing, digital applications, drama, earth science, ecology, economics, English, English composition, English literature, epic literature, ethics, European history, expository writing, fine arts, French, geometry, government/civics, grammar, health, history, history of the Catholic Church, Latin, modern world history, music, performing arts, photography, physical education, physics, pre-algebra, pre-calculus, religion, science, senior project, social studies, Spanish, speech, studio art, swimming, tennis, Texas history, theology, trigonometry, world history, world literature.

Graduation Requirements Arts and fine arts (art, music, dance, drama), electives, English, foreign language, mathematics, physical education (includes health), science, senior project, social studies (includes history), theology, completion of an independent senior project during fourth quarter of senior year.

Special Academic Programs 18 Advanced Placement exams for which test preparation is offered; independent study; study at local college for college credit.

College Admission Counseling 41 students graduated in 2013; all went to college, including Harvard University; Texas A&M University; Texas Christian University; The University of Texas at Austin; University of Tulsa; Washington University in St. Louis. Median SAT critical reading: 700, median SAT math: 700, median SAT writing: 690, median combined SAT: 2070, median composite ACT: 30. 92% scored over 600 on SAT critical reading, 97% scored over 600 on SAT math, 95% scored over 600 on SAT writing, 97% scored over 1800 on combined SAT, 93% scored over 26 on composite ACT.

Student Life Upper grades have uniform requirement, student council. Discipline rests primarily with faculty. Attendance at religious services is required.

Summer Programs Remediation, enrichment, sports, art/fine arts, computer instruction programs offered; session focuses on remediation and enrichment in mathematics and English, arts and fine arts, computers, and sports camp; held on campus; accepts boys; open to students from other schools. 125 students usually enrolled. 2014 schedule: June 9 to July 3. Application deadline: May 30.

Tuition and Aid Day student tuition: $16,995–$17,295. Tuition installment plan (FACTS Tuition Payment Plan). Need-based scholarship grants available. In 2013–14, 48% of upper-school students received aid. Total amount of financial aid awarded in 2013–14: $319,485.

Admissions Traditional secondary-level entrance grade is 9. For fall 2013, 13 students applied for upper-level admission, 5 were accepted, 5 enrolled. English language, High School Placement Test, Iowa Tests of Basic Skills, ITBS achievement test, Kuhlmann-Anderson, mathematics proficiency exam or writing sample required. Deadline for receipt of application materials: January 10. Application fee required: $100.

Athletics Interscholastic: baseball, basketball, cross-country running, football, physical training, soccer, swimming and diving, tennis, track and field; intramural: basketball, physical training, soccer, strength & conditioning, ultimate Frisbee, volleyball, weight lifting, weight training. 5 coaches, 1 athletic trainer.

Computers Computers are regularly used in college planning, computer applications, digital applications, library, literary magazine, newspaper, photography, programming, publications, yearbook classes. Computer network features include on-campus library services, Internet access, Internet filtering or blocking technology, online college applications, numerous online databases, reference sources, Moodle. Student e-mail accounts and computer access in designated common areas are available to students. The school has a published electronic and media policy.

Contact Mrs. Lisa Richard, Assistant to Headmaster/Registrar. 469-499-5402. Fax: 469-499-5440. E-mail: lrichard@cistercian.org. Website: www.cistercian.org

CLARKSVILLE ACADEMY

710 North Second Street
Clarksville, Tennessee 37040-2998

Head of School: Mrs. Kay D. Drew

General Information Coeducational day college-preparatory and 1:1 Apple Program school. Grades PK–12. Founded: 1970. Setting: urban. 31-acre campus. 7 buildings on campus. Approved or accredited by Southern Association of Colleges and Schools and Tennessee Department of Education. Member of National Association of Independent Schools. Endowment: $1 million. Total enrollment: 576. Upper school average class size: 15. Upper school faculty-student ratio: 1:12. There are 175 required school days per year for Upper School students. Upper School students typically attend 5 days per week. The average school day consists of 7 hours.

Upper School Student Profile Grade 9: 54 students (22 boys, 32 girls); Grade 10: 47 students (24 boys, 23 girls); Grade 11: 39 students (20 boys, 19 girls); Grade 12: 43 students (24 boys, 19 girls).

Faculty School total: 60. In upper school: 11 men, 15 women; 12 have advanced degrees.

Subjects Offered ACT preparation, American history, anatomy and physiology, art, art appreciation, art history, Bible as literature, biology, biology-AP, botany, broadcasting, calculus, calculus-AP, calligraphy, ceramics, chemistry, chemistry-AP, choir, chorus, college writing, computer education, computer science, debate, drama, driver education, economics, economics and history, English language and composition-AP, English literature and composition-AP, fitness, French, geometry, government, graphic design, guitar, health, health education, honors algebra, honors English, honors geometry, honors U.S. history, honors world history, Latin, literature, media arts, modern history, multimedia design, music, music theory-AP, mythology, personal finance, physical education, physical fitness, physics, physics-AP, piano, political science, pre-calculus, printmaking, psychology, publications, sculpture, Spanish, speech, statistics, studio art, study skills, trigonometry, U.S. history, U.S. history-AP, weight training, wellness, women's health, world history, writing, yearbook, zoology.

Graduation Requirements 24 credit, 4 years of high school math required.

Special Academic Programs 7 Advanced Placement exams for which test preparation is offered; honors section; independent study; study at local college for college credit.

College Admission Counseling 56 students graduated in 2013; all went to college, including Austin Peay State University; Lipscomb University; Samford University; The University of Tennessee; The University of Tennessee at Chattanooga.

Student Life Upper grades have specified standards of dress, student council, honor system. Discipline rests primarily with faculty.

Summer Programs Remediation, enrichment, sports, art/fine arts, computer instruction programs offered; session focuses on enrichment and remediation; held both on and off campus; held at sports complex; accepts boys and girls; open to students from other schools. 2014 schedule: June 1 to August 13. Application deadline: May 20.

Tuition and Aid Tuition installment plan (monthly payment plans). Tuition reduction for siblings, paying campus jobs available.

Admissions Otis-Lennon School Ability Test required. Deadline for receipt of application materials: none. Application fee required: $75. On-campus interview required.

Athletics Interscholastic: baseball (boys), basketball (b,g), cheering (g), dance team (g), football (b), soccer (b,g), softball (g), volleyball (g); coed interscholastic: bowling, cross-country running, golf, tennis. 5 coaches.

Computers Computers are regularly used in art classes. Computer network features include on-campus library services, Internet access, wireless campus network, Internet filtering or blocking technology, 1:1 Apple MacBook program, 1:1 Apple iPad program, 1:1 Apple iPad mini program. Campus intranet, student e-mail accounts, and computer access in designated common areas are available to students. Students grades are available online. The school has a published electronic and media policy.

Contact Mrs. Angie Henson, Business Office and Admissions. 931-647-6311. Fax: 931-906-0610. E-mail: ahenson@clarksvilleacademy.com. Website: www.clarksvilleacademy.com

CLEARWATER CENTRAL CATHOLIC HIGH SCHOOL

2750 Haines Bayshore Road
Clearwater, Florida 33760

Head of School: Dr. John A. Venturella

General Information Coeducational day college-preparatory, arts, religious studies, technology, and International Baccalaureate diploma program school, affiliated with Roman Catholic Church. Grades 9–12. Founded: 1962. Setting: suburban. Nearest major city is Tampa. 40-acre campus. 8 buildings on campus. Approved or accredited by International Baccalaureate Organization, National Catholic Education Association, Southern Association of Colleges and Schools, The College Board, and Florida Department of Education. Upper school average class size: 25. Upper school faculty-student ratio: 1:13. There are 190 required school days per year for Upper School students. Upper School students typically attend 5 days per week. The average school day consists of 6 hours and 13 minutes.

Upper School Student Profile 80% of students are Roman Catholic.

Faculty School total: 41. In upper school: 14 men, 27 women; 32 have advanced degrees.

Subjects Offered Acting, advanced chemistry, Advanced Placement courses, aerobics, algebra, American government, American history, American history-AP, American literature, American literature-AP, American sign language, anatomy, architecture, Bible studies, biology, biology-AP, British literature, British literature (honors), calculus, calculus-AP, campus ministry, chemistry, chemistry-AP, choral music, chorus, church history, composition, computer processing, creative writing, desktop publishing, discrete mathematics, drama, drawing, drawing and design, ecology, economics, English, English literature and composition-AP, foreign language, French, general science, geometry, health, honors algebra, honors English, honors geometry, honors U.S. history, honors world history, information technology, journalism, keyboarding, language arts, law, law studies, leadership, learning strategies, life management skills, marine biology, music appreciation, oral communications, painting, personal fitness, philosophy, physical education, physics, pre-algebra, probability and statistics, psychology, sociology, Spanish, Spanish language-AP, speech, speech and debate, theater, theology, trigonometry, U.S. government, U.S.

government and politics-AP, U.S. history, U.S. history-AP, video, volleyball, Web site design, wellness, world history.

Graduation Requirements Algebra, biology, ceramics, chemistry, comparative government and politics-AP, economics, English, general science, geometry, global studies, physical education (includes health), physical fitness, physical science, physics, Spanish, theology, U.S. government, U.S. history, United States government-AP, visual and performing arts, world geography, world history, world religions, yearbook.

Special Academic Programs International Baccalaureate program; Advanced Placement exam preparation; honors section; study at local college for college credit; programs in English, mathematics, general development for dyslexic students.

College Admission Counseling 130 students graduated in 2013; all went to college, including Florida State University; University of Central Florida; University of Florida; University of South Florida.

Student Life Upper grades have uniform requirement, student council, honor system. Discipline rests primarily with faculty. Attendance at religious services is required.

Summer Programs Remediation, enrichment, advancement, sports, computer instruction programs offered; session focuses on work-ahead classes for credit; held on campus; accepts boys and girls; open to students from other schools. 225 students usually enrolled. 2014 schedule: June 9 to June 27. Application deadline: May 15.

Tuition and Aid Day student tuition: $10,600–$12,500. Tuition installment plan (SMART Tuition Payment Plan). Tuition reduction for siblings, merit scholarship grants, need-based scholarship grants available. In 2013–14, 20% of upper-school students received aid.

Admissions Traditional secondary-level entrance grade is 9. For fall 2013, 230 students applied for upper-level admission, 200 were accepted, 170 enrolled. Explore required. Deadline for receipt of application materials: none. Application fee required: $100. Interview recommended.

Athletics Interscholastic: baseball (boys), basketball (b,g), cheering (g), cross-country running (b,g), diving (b,g), football (b), golf (b,g), physical fitness (b,g), running (b,g), soccer (b,g), softball (g), swimming and diving (b,g), tennis (b,g), track and field (b,g), volleyball (g), weight lifting (b,g), weight training (b,g), winter soccer (b,g), wrestling (b). 1 PE instructor, 43 coaches, 1 athletic trainer.

Computers Computer network features include on-campus library services, online commercial services, Internet access, wireless campus network, all students utilize iPad Technology. Campus intranet and student e-mail accounts are available to students. Students grades are available online. The school has a published electronic and media policy.

Contact Mrs. Tara Shea McLaughlin, Director of Admissions. 727-531-1449 Ext. 304. Fax: 727-451-0003. E-mail: tsheamclaughlin@ccchs.org. Website: www.ccchs.org

COLEGIO BOLIVAR

Calle 5 # 122-21 Via a Pance
Cali, Colombia

Head of School: Dr. Joseph Nagy

General Information Coeducational day college-preparatory, bilingual studies, and technology school. Grades PK–12. Founded: 1947. Setting: suburban. 14-hectare campus. 7 buildings on campus. Approved or accredited by Association of American Schools in South America, Colombian Ministry of Education, and Southern Association of Colleges and Schools. Languages of instruction: English and Spanish. Total enrollment: 1,258. Upper school average class size: 18. Upper school faculty-student ratio: 1:9. There are 180 required school days per year for Upper School students. The average school day consists of 7 hours.

Upper School Student Profile Grade 9: 85 students (40 boys, 45 girls); Grade 10: 100 students (45 boys, 55 girls); Grade 11: 86 students (44 boys, 42 girls); Grade 12: 94 students (44 boys, 50 girls).

Faculty School total: 159. In upper school: 20 men, 21 women; 23 have advanced degrees.

Subjects Offered Advanced chemistry, Advanced Placement courses, algebra, American history, American literature, art, art history, biology, business, calculus, chemistry, computer science, dance, drama, English, English literature, environmental science, ESL, ethics, French, geology, government/civics, graphic design, history, journalism, mathematics, music, philosophy, photography, physical education, physics, programming, psychology, religion, robotics, social studies, Spanish, theater, trigonometry, world literature.

Graduation Requirements Algebra, American history, American literature, art, biology, calculus, chemistry, computer education, economics, electives, geography, geometry, history of the Americas, music, physical education (includes health), physics, political science, pre-calculus, senior project, Spanish, Spanish literature, trigonometry, world history, world literature, writing, social service hours, senior project.

Special Academic Programs Advanced Placement exam preparation; independent study; remedial reading and/or remedial writing; remedial math; ESL.

College Admission Counseling 86 students graduated in 2013; 62 went to college, including Georgetown University; Georgia Institute of Technology; Northwestern State University of Louisiana; Trinity University; University of Pittsburgh. Other: 24 had other specific plans. Median SAT critical reading: 548, median SAT math: 558, median SAT writing: 524, median combined SAT: 1631, median composite ACT: 22. 33% scored over 600 on SAT critical reading, 36% scored

over 600 on SAT math, 26% scored over 600 on SAT writing, 28% scored over 1800 on combined SAT, 25% scored over 26 on composite ACT.

Student Life Upper grades have specified standards of dress, student council, honor system. Discipline rests equally with students and faculty.

Tuition and Aid Day student tuition: 16,717,825 Colombian pesos–23,774,188 Colombian pesos. Tuition installment plan (monthly payment plans, annual payment plan). Need-based scholarship grants available.

Admissions Traditional secondary-level entrance grade is 9. School's own exam required. Deadline for receipt of application materials: none. Application fee required: 80,000 Colombian pesos. On-campus interview required.

Athletics Interscholastic: aerobics/dance (girls), baseball (b), basketball (b,g), dance (g), equestrian sports (b,g), gymnastics (b,g), horseback riding (b,g), running (b,g), soccer (b,g), swimming and diving (b,g), track and field (b,g), volleyball (b,g); intramural: gymnastics (b,g), soccer (b,g), softball (b), swimming and diving (b,g), track and field (b,g), volleyball (b,g). 11 PE instructors, 23 coaches.

Computers Computers are regularly used in graphic design, photography, Web site design, yearbook classes. Computer network features include Internet access, Internet filtering or blocking technology. The school has a published electronic and media policy.

Contact Mrs. Patricia Nasser, Admissions Assistant. 57-2-485-5050 Ext. 274. Fax: 57-2-4850453. E-mail: pnasser@colegiobolivar.edu.co. Website: www.colegiobolivar.edu.co

COLEGIO SAN JOSE

PO Box 21300
San Juan, Puerto Rico 00928-1300

Head of School: Br. Francisco T. Gonzalez, DMD

General Information Boys' day college-preparatory, arts, business, religious studies, bilingual studies, technology, science, anatomy, and environmental science, and psychology, humanities, health, economy, political science school, affiliated with Roman Catholic Church. Grades 7–12. Founded: 1938. Setting: urban. 6-acre campus. 2 buildings on campus. Approved or accredited by Middle States Association of Colleges and Schools, National Catholic Education Association, The College Board, and Puerto Rico Department of Education. Languages of instruction: English and Spanish. Endowment: $293,000. Total enrollment: 515. Upper school average class size: 22. Upper School students typically attend 5 days per week. The average school day consists of 6 hours and 50 minutes.

Upper School Student Profile Grade 9: 88 students (88 boys); Grade 10: 63 students (63 boys); Grade 11: 92 students (92 boys); Grade 12: 108 students (108 boys). 90% of students are Roman Catholic.

Faculty School total: 45. In upper school: 24 men, 21 women; 24 have advanced degrees.

Subjects Offered Accounting, algebra, American history, American literature, anatomy, art, art history, biology, biology-AP, broadcasting, business skills, calculus, chemistry, choir, Christian ethics, computer education, computer science, ecology, English, English literature, ethics, European history, French, French as a second language, geography, geometry, government/civics, grammar, health, history, instrumental music, keyboarding, mathematics, music, physical education, physics, pre-calculus, psychology, religion, science, social studies, Spanish, world history.

Graduation Requirements Business skills (includes word processing), computer science, English, foreign language, history, mathematics, physical education (includes health), religion (includes Bible studies and theology), science, social studies (includes history), Spanish, 40 hours of Christian community service.

Special Academic Programs International Baccalaureate program; Advanced Placement exam preparation; honors section.

College Admission Counseling 72 students graduated in 2013; all went to college, including University of Dayton; University of Puerto Rico, Mayagüez Campus; University of Puerto Rico, Río Piedras.

Student Life Upper grades have uniform requirement, student council, honor system. Discipline rests equally with students and faculty. Attendance at religious services is required.

Summer Programs Remediation programs offered; session focuses on remediation/make-up; held on campus; accepts boys and girls; open to students from other schools. 150 students usually enrolled. 2014 schedule: June 1 to June 30. Application deadline: May 30.

Tuition and Aid Day student tuition: $7050. Tuition installment plan (The Tuition Plan, individually arranged payment plans). Need-based scholarship grants available. In 2013–14, 13% of upper-school students received aid. Total amount of financial aid awarded in 2013–14: $293,000.

Admissions Traditional secondary-level entrance grade is 9. Catholic High School Entrance Examination required. Deadline for receipt of application materials: February 28. Application fee required: $10. On-campus interview required.

Athletics Interscholastic: baseball, basketball, bowling, cross-country running, fitness, golf, indoor soccer, physical fitness, soccer, swimming and diving, tennis, track and field, volleyball; intramural: cross-country running, indoor soccer, soccer, swimming and diving, tennis, track and field, volleyball. 4 PE instructors, 6 coaches, 1 athletic trainer.

Computers Computers are regularly used in accounting, art, data processing, English, foreign language, keyboarding, mathematics, music, psychology, science, Spanish, yearbook classes. Computer network features include on-campus library services, online commercial services, Internet access, wireless campus network, Internet filtering or blocking technology, Edline, Rediker. Campus intranet and student e-mail accounts are available to students. Students grades are available online. The school has a published electronic and media policy.

Contact Mrs. Mara E. Guzmn, Guidance Advisor. 787-751-8177 Ext. 229. Fax: 866-955-7646. E-mail: mguzman@csj-rpi.org. Website: www.csj-rpi.org

COLE VALLEY CHRISTIAN HIGH SCHOOL

200 East Carlton Avenue
Meridian, Idaho 83642

Head of School: Mr. Bradley Carr

General Information Coeducational day college-preparatory, general academic, arts, religious studies, bilingual studies, and technology school, affiliated with Christian faith. Grades PK–12. Founded: 1990. Setting: suburban. Nearest major city is Boise. 5-acre campus. 2 buildings on campus. Approved or accredited by Association of Christian Schools International and Idaho Department of Education. Total enrollment: 813. Upper school average class size: 24. Upper school faculty-student ratio: 1:10. There are 180 required school days per year for Upper School students. Upper School students typically attend 5 days per week. The average school day consists of 5 hours and 50 minutes.

Upper School Student Profile 95% of students are Christian.

Faculty School total: 29. In upper school: 11 men, 18 women; 5 have advanced degrees.

Subjects Offered 20th century history, acting, algebra, American government, American literature, art, Bible, biology, British literature, business mathematics, calculus-AP, chemistry, choral music, computer literacy, ecology, economics, English, English literature, French, geometry, honors English, physical education, physical science, physics, pre-algebra, pre-calculus, Spanish, speech, U.S. history, world history, yearbook.

Graduation Requirements 20th century history, American government, economics, English, mathematics, physical education (includes health), religion (includes Bible studies and theology), science, social studies (includes history), speech, Bible classes.

Special Academic Programs Advanced Placement exam preparation; honors section; independent study; study at local college for college credit.

College Admission Counseling 56 students graduated in 2013; 49 went to college, including Boise State University; Grand Canyon University; Northwest Nazarene University; The College of Idaho; University of Idaho. Other: 6 went to work, 1 entered military service.

Student Life Upper grades have specified standards of dress, student council, honor system. Discipline rests primarily with faculty. Attendance at religious services is required.

Tuition and Aid Day student tuition: $6000. Tuition installment plan (monthly payment plans, individually arranged payment plans). Tuition reduction for siblings, need-based scholarship grants available. In 2013–14, 20% of upper-school students received aid.

Admissions Traditional secondary-level entrance grade is 9. Deadline for receipt of application materials: none. Application fee required: $175. Interview required.

Athletics Interscholastic: basketball (boys, girls), cheering (g), cross-country running (b,g), football (b), track and field (b,g), volleyball (g), wrestling (b); intramural: skiing (cross-country) (b,g), skiing (downhill) (b,g), snowboarding (b,g). 3 PE instructors, 12 coaches.

Computers Computers are regularly used in all academic classes. Computer network features include on-campus library services, Internet access, wireless campus network, Internet filtering or blocking technology. Student e-mail accounts are available to students. Students grades are available online.

Contact Mrs. Robin Didriksen, Administrative Assistant to the Guidance Counselor/Registrar. 208-947-1212 Ext. 1210. Fax: 208-898-9016. E-mail: rdidriksen@cvcsonline.org. Website: www.colevalleychristian.org

COLLEGIATE SCHOOL

260 West 78th Street
New York, New York 10024

Head of School: Dr. Lee M. Levison

General Information Boys' day college-preparatory and arts school. Grades K–12. Founded: 1628. Setting: urban. 4 buildings on campus. Approved or accredited by New York State Association of Independent Schools. Member of National Association of Independent Schools. Endowment: $70 million. Total enrollment: 650. Upper school average class size: 14. Upper school faculty-student ratio: 1:4. There are 164 required school days per year for Upper School students. Upper School students typically attend 5 days per week. The average school day consists of 6 hours and 45 minutes.

Upper School Student Profile Grade 9: 59 students (59 boys); Grade 10: 54 students (54 boys); Grade 11: 56 students (56 boys); Grade 12: 58 students (58 boys).

Faculty School total: 115. In upper school: 39 men, 22 women; 56 have advanced degrees.

Subjects Offered African drumming, African history, algebra, American history, Ancient Greek, applied music, architecture, art, art appreciation, art history, Asian history, athletics, biology, calculus, ceramics, chemistry, Chinese, chorus, contemporary issues in science, digital photography, drama, dramatic arts, drawing, drawing and design, East Asian history, economics, English, environmental science, European history, film, film appreciation, film studies, foreign policy, French, geometry, health and wellness, history, Latin, Latin American history, linear algebra, literature, logic, Mandarin, mathematics, Middle Eastern history, music, music composition, music theory, orchestra, painting, philosophy, photography, physical education, physics, play production, poetry, pre-calculus, religion, sculpture, senior project, Shakespeare, social studies, Spanish, technical theater, theater, U.S. history, Web site design, world history, world literature, world religions.

Graduation Requirements Drama, English, foreign language, history, mathematics, music, physical education (includes health), religion (includes Bible studies and theology), science, visual arts. Community service is required.

Special Academic Programs 15 Advanced Placement exams for which test preparation is offered; honors section; independent study; term-away projects; study abroad.

College Admission Counseling 55 students graduated in 2013; all went to college, including Bowdoin College; Brown University; Harvard University; Princeton University; University of Pennsylvania; Yale University.

Student Life Upper grades have specified standards of dress, student council, honor system. Discipline rests equally with students and faculty.

Tuition and Aid Day student tuition: $41,200. Tuition installment plan (SMART Tuition Payment Plan). Need-based scholarship grants available. In 2013–14, 20% of upper-school students received aid. Total amount of financial aid awarded in 2013–14: $150,000.

Admissions Traditional secondary-level entrance grade is 9. ERB or ISEE required. Deadline for receipt of application materials: December 1. Application fee required: $60. On-campus interview required.

Athletics Interscholastic: baseball, basketball, cross-country running, indoor track & field, lacrosse, soccer, tennis, track and field, winter (indoor) track, wrestling; intramural: physical fitness, weight training, yoga. 3 PE instructors, 8 coaches, 2 athletic trainers.

Computers Computers are regularly used in all academic classes. Computer network features include on-campus library services, online commercial services, Internet access, wireless campus network, Internet filtering or blocking technology. Campus intranet, student e-mail accounts, and computer access in designated common areas are available to students. The school has a published electronic and media policy.

Contact Joanne P. Heyman, Director of Admissions and Financial Aid. 212-812-8552. Fax: 212-812-8547. E-mail: jheyman@collegiateschool.org. Website: www.collegiateschool.org

THE COLLEGIATE SCHOOL

103 North Mooreland Road
Richmond, Virginia 23229

Head of School: Keith A. Evans

General Information Coeducational day college-preparatory, arts, and technology school. Grades K–12. Founded: 1915. Setting: suburban. 211-acre campus. 13 buildings on campus. Approved or accredited by Southern Association of Colleges and Schools and Virginia Department of Education. Member of National Association of Independent Schools and Secondary School Admission Test Board. Endowment: $45.4 million. Total enrollment: 1,602. Upper school average class size: 15. Upper school faculty-student ratio: 1:15. There are 174 required school days per year for Upper School students. Upper School students typically attend 5 days per week. The average school day consists of 7 hours.

Upper School Student Profile Grade 9: 133 students (66 boys, 67 girls); Grade 10: 139 students (71 boys, 68 girls); Grade 11: 124 students (61 boys, 63 girls); Grade 12: 125 students (62 boys, 63 girls).

Faculty School total: 193. In upper school: 31 men, 39 women; 46 have advanced degrees.

Subjects Offered 20th century history, acting, advanced chemistry, African studies, algebra, American Civil War, American history, American history-AP, American literature, art, Asian literature, Bible as literature, biology, biology-AP, calculus-AP, ceramics, chemistry, chemistry-AP, community service, computer applications, creative writing, drama, driver education, earth science, economics, economics-AP, English, English literature, ethics, European history, film and literature, fine arts, French, French-AP, geometry, government and politics-AP, government/civics, health, journalism, Latin, music, photography, physics, physics-AP, religion, robotics, Russian literature, senior project, senior seminar, Spanish, Spanish language-AP, statistics, theater, trigonometry, world history, World War II.

Graduation Requirements Arts and fine arts (art, music, dance, drama), English, ethics, foreign language, government, history, mathematics, physical education (includes health), religion (includes Bible studies and theology), science, sports, senior speech. Community service is required.

Special Academic Programs 16 Advanced Placement exams for which test preparation is offered; honors section; independent study; study at local college for college credit; programs in general development for dyslexic students.

College Admission Counseling 125 students graduated in 2012; all went to college, including Elon University; James Madison University; The College of William and Mary; University of South Carolina; University of Virginia; Virginia Polytechnic Institute and State University.

Student Life Upper grades have specified standards of dress, student council, honor system. Discipline rests equally with students and faculty.

Tuition and Aid Day student tuition: $20,690. Tuition installment plan (Insured Tuition Payment Plan, monthly payment plans). Need-based scholarship grants available.

Admissions Traditional secondary-level entrance grade is 9. For fall 2012, 108 students applied for upper-level admission, 44 were accepted, 25 enrolled. PSAT and SAT for applicants to grade 11 and 12, SSAT or writing sample required. Deadline for receipt of application materials: none. Application fee required: $50. Interview required.

Athletics Interscholastic: baseball (boys), basketball (b,g), cross-country running (b,g), diving (b,g), field hockey (g), football (b), indoor track & field (b,g), lacrosse (b,g), soccer (b,g), softball (g), swimming and diving (b,g), tennis (b,g), track and field (b,g), volleyball (g), winter (indoor) track (b,g), wrestling (b); coed interscholastic: golf, indoor soccer; coed intramural: combined training, dance, dance squad, dance team, fitness, modern dance. 3 PE instructors, 50 coaches, 2 athletic trainers.

Computers Computers are regularly used in all academic classes. Computer network features include on-campus library services, Internet access, wireless campus network, Internet filtering or blocking technology. Student e-mail accounts are available to students. The school has a published electronic and media policy.

Contact Amanda L. Surgner, Vice President for Advancement. 804-741-9722. Fax: 804-741-9128. E-mail: asurgner@collegiate-va.org. Website: www.collegiate-va.org/

THE COLORADO SPRINGS SCHOOL

21 Broadmoor Avenue
Colorado Springs, Colorado 80906

Head of School: Mr. Kevin Reel

General Information Coeducational day college-preparatory, arts, experiential learning, and global perspectives school. Grades PK–12. Founded: 1962. Setting: suburban. 30-acre campus. 6 buildings on campus. Approved or accredited by Association of Colorado Independent Schools. Member of National Association of Independent Schools, Secondary School Admission Test Board, and National Association for College Admission Counseling. Endowment: $3.1 million. Total enrollment: 302. Upper school average class size: 16. Upper school faculty-student ratio: 1:6. There are 160 required school days per year for Upper School students. Upper School students typically attend 5 days per week. The average school day consists of 6 hours and 30 minutes.

Upper School Student Profile Grade 9: 22 students (12 boys, 10 girls); Grade 10: 26 students (9 boys, 17 girls); Grade 11: 25 students (19 boys, 6 girls); Grade 12: 31 students (11 boys, 20 girls).

Faculty School total: 46. In upper school: 11 men, 13 women; 18 have advanced degrees.

Subjects Offered 20th century history, 3-dimensional art, 3-dimensional design, ACT preparation, acting, adolescent issues, advanced chemistry, advanced math, Advanced Placement courses, advanced studio art-AP, African history, African studies, algebra, American government, American history, American history-AP, American literature, American literature-AP, American studies, analysis and differential calculus, anatomy and physiology, art history, art-AP, athletics, band, biology, biology-AP, botany, British literature-AP, calculus, calculus-AP, career education internship, career/college preparation, ceramics, chemistry, choir, choral music, clayworking, college admission preparation, college counseling, community service, comparative government and politics, comparative government and politics-AP, composition, computer applications, concert band, costumes and make-up, creative arts, digital art, digital photography, directing, discrete mathematics, drama, drawing, economics, economics-AP, English, English literature, English literature and composition-AP, English literature-AP, environmental science, environmental science-AP, environmental studies, equality and freedom, ethics, European history-AP, European literature, experiential education, filmmaking, fine arts, French, French language-AP, French literature-AP, French-AP, functions, gardening, geography, geology, geometry, glassblowing, global studies, government and politics-AP, grammar, health and wellness, history, history-AP, Latin American history, literature, macro/microeconomics-AP, microeconomics, music, music appreciation, musical productions, painting, philosophy, photography, photojournalism, physical education, physics, physics-AP, playwriting, post-calculus, pottery, pre-algebra, pre-calculus, printmaking, SAT/ACT preparation, science, sculpture, Spanish, Spanish literature, Spanish literature-AP, speech, statistics, statistics-AP, stone carving, studio art, studio art-AP, textiles, theater, theater arts, theater production, trigonometry, U.S. history, U.S. history-AP, welding, Western civilization, world geography, world history, world literature, writing, writing workshop, yearbook.

Graduation Requirements Arts and fine arts (art, music, dance, drama), athletics, college admission preparation, English, experiential education, foreign language, mathematics, science, social studies (includes history), speech and oral interpretations, experience-centered seminar each year, college overview course, 24 hours of community service per each year of high school.

Special Academic Programs Advanced Placement exam preparation; honors section; independent study; term-away projects; academic accommodation for the gifted; programs in general development for dyslexic students; special instructional classes for deaf students.

College Admission Counseling 30 students graduated in 2012; all went to college, including Vanderbilt University. Mean combined SAT: 1952, mean composite ACT: 27.

Student Life Upper grades have specified standards of dress, student council, honor system. Discipline rests equally with students and faculty.

Tuition and Aid Day student tuition: $18,275. Tuition installment plan (Insured Tuition Payment Plan, monthly payment plans, individually arranged payment plans). Merit scholarship grants, need-based scholarship grants available. In 2012–13, 51% of upper-school students received aid; total upper-school merit-scholarship money awarded: $54,237. Total amount of financial aid awarded in 2012–13: $224,825.

Admissions Traditional secondary-level entrance grade is 9. For fall 2012, 16 students applied for upper-level admission, 14 were accepted, 12 enrolled. Otis-Lennon School Ability Test or SLEP for foreign students required. Deadline for receipt of application materials: none. Application fee required: $50. Interview required.

Athletics Interscholastic: basketball (boys, girls), cross-country running (b,g), golf (b), ice hockey (b), lacrosse (b), soccer (b,g), tennis (b,g), volleyball (g); intramural: archery (b,g), climbing (b,g), physical fitness (b,g), physical training (b,g); coed intramural: fly-fishing, golf, mountaineering, outdoor activities, outdoor education, paddle tennis, rock climbing, skiing (cross-country), skiing (downhill), wilderness, yoga. 2 PE instructors, 8 coaches.

Computers Computer network features include on-campus library services, online commercial services, Internet access, wireless campus network, Internet filtering or blocking technology. Campus intranet, student e-mail accounts, and computer access in designated common areas are available to students. Students grades are available online. The school has a published electronic and media policy.

Contact Mrs. Nori Madrigal, Director of Admission and Financial Assistance. 719-475-9747 Ext. 524. Fax: 719-475-9864. E-mail: nmadrigal@css.org. Website: www.css.org

COLUMBIA ACADEMY

1101 West 7th Street
Columbia, Tennessee 38401

Head of School: Dr. James Thomas

General Information Coeducational day college-preparatory, arts, business, religious studies, and technology school, affiliated with Church of Christ. Grades K–12. Founded: 1978. Setting: small town. Nearest major city is Nashville. 67-acre campus. 6 buildings on campus. Approved or accredited by National Christian School Association, Southern Association of Colleges and Schools, and Tennessee Department of Education. Endowment: $2.4 million. Total enrollment: 765. Upper school average class size: 17. Upper school faculty-student ratio: 1:10. There are 175 required school days per year for Upper School students. Upper School students typically attend 5 days per week. The average school day consists of 7 hours.

Upper School Student Profile Grade 7: 77 students (39 boys, 38 girls); Grade 8: 63 students (31 boys, 32 girls); Grade 9: 51 students (20 boys, 31 girls); Grade 10: 45 students (26 boys, 19 girls); Grade 11: 52 students (23 boys, 29 girls); Grade 12: 47 students (24 boys, 23 girls). 60% of students are members of Church of Christ.

Faculty School total: 25. In upper school: 14 men, 11 women; 13 have advanced degrees.

Subjects Offered Advanced math, algebra, American history, American literature, anatomy and physiology, art, band, Bible, biology, British literature, calculus, chemistry, computer applications, economics, English, English literature and composition-AP, environmental science, fine arts, geometry, government/civics, grammar, health, keyboarding, math review, music, personal finance, physical education, physics, pre-calculus, psychology, religion, Spanish, speech, U.S. history-AP, world geography, world history.

Graduation Requirements Arts and fine arts (art, music, dance, drama), computer applications, economics, electives, English, foreign language, mathematics, physical education (includes health), religion (includes Bible studies and theology), science, social sciences, social studies (includes history), speech, four hours of approved service required for each quarter enrolled.

Special Academic Programs Advanced Placement exam preparation; honors section; independent study; study at local college for college credit.

College Admission Counseling 27 students graduated in 2013; 26 went to college, including Columbia State Community College; Freed-Hardeman University; Lipscomb University; The University of Tennessee at Chattanooga; The University of Tennessee at Martin; University of North Alabama. Other: 1 entered military service. Median composite ACT: 23. 19% scored over 26 on composite ACT.

Student Life Upper grades have specified standards of dress, student council, honor system. Discipline rests primarily with faculty.

Summer Programs Remediation programs offered; session focuses on make-up or credit recovery for failing grades during the semesters; held on campus; accepts boys and girls; not open to students from other schools. 5 students usually enrolled. 2014 schedule: May 29. Application deadline: May 11.

Tuition and Aid Day student tuition: $6600. Tuition installment plan (monthly payment plans, individually arranged payment plans). Tuition reduction for siblings, need-based scholarship grants, paying campus jobs available. In 2013–14, 10% of upper-school students received aid. Total amount of financial aid awarded in 2013–14: $55,000.

Admissions Traditional secondary-level entrance grade is 9. For fall 2013, 45 students applied for upper-level admission, 44 were accepted, 39 enrolled. Otis-Lennon School Ability Test required. Deadline for receipt of application materials: none. Application fee required: $50. On-campus interview recommended.

Athletics Interscholastic: baseball (boys), basketball (b,g), cheering (g), football (b), golf (b,g), soccer (b,g), softball (g), strength & conditioning (b), tennis (b,g), trap and skeet (b,g), volleyball (g); intramural: flag football (g); coed interscholastic: bowling, cross-country running, marksmanship. 1 coach.

Computers Computers are regularly used in all academic, computer applications, keyboarding, library, yearbook classes. Computer network features include on-campus library services, Internet access, wireless campus network, Internet filtering or blocking technology, students in grades 7-12 are issued iPads. Campus intranet, student e-mail accounts, and computer access in designated common areas are available to students. Students grades are available online. The school has a published electronic and media policy.

Contact Mrs. Emily Lansdell, Director of Admissions. 931-398-5355. Fax: 931-380-8506. E-mail: emily.lansdell@cabulldogs.org. Website: www.columbia-academy.net

COLUMBIA INTERNATIONAL COLLEGE OF CANADA

1003 Main Street West
Hamilton, Ontario L8S 4P3, Canada

Head of School: Mr. Ron Rambarran

General Information Coeducational boarding and day college-preparatory, general academic, arts, business, technology, science, and mathematics school. Grades 7–12. Founded: 1979. Setting: urban. Nearest major city is Toronto, Canada. Students are housed in single-sex dormitories. 12-acre campus. 7 buildings on campus. Approved or accredited by Ontario Ministry of Education and Ontario Department of Education. Language of instruction: English. Endowment: CAN$1 million. Total enrollment: 1,804. Upper school average class size: 20. Upper school faculty-student ratio: 1:20. There are 208 required school days per year for Upper School students. Upper School students typically attend 5 days per week. The average school day consists of 7 hours and 15 minutes.

Upper School Student Profile 80% of students are boarding students. 5% are province residents. 5 provinces are represented in upper school student body. 95% are international students. International students from China, Indonesia, Mexico, Nigeria, Russian Federation, and Viet Nam; 70 other countries represented in student body.

Faculty School total: 125. In upper school: 38 men, 57 women; 35 have advanced degrees.

Subjects Offered 20th century world history, accounting, advanced TOEFL/grammar, algebra, analytic geometry, anthropology, applied arts, art, band, biology, business, calculus, calculus-AP, Canadian geography, Canadian history, career education, character education, chemistry, Chinese, choir, civics, computer programming, computer science, computer technologies, dance, discrete mathematics, dramatic arts, economics, English, English composition, English literature, ESL, family studies, food and nutrition, French, French as a second language, general business, general math, general science, geography, geometry, history, intro to computers, kinesiology, Korean, lab science, language arts, law, leadership, leadership and service, life skills, Mandarin, marketing, math applications, mathematics, mathematics-AP, music, outdoor education, physical education, physics, psychology, society challenge and change, sociology, Spanish, visual arts.

Graduation Requirements Arts, business, English, mathematics, science, social studies (includes history), community volunteer hours, Ontario Secondary School Literacy Test.

Special Academic Programs 4 Advanced Placement exams for which test preparation is offered; accelerated programs; study at local college for college credit; academic accommodation for the gifted; ESL.

College Admission Counseling Colleges students went to include Brock University; McMaster University; The University of Western Ontario; University of Toronto; University of Waterloo; York University.

Student Life Upper grades have uniform requirement, student council. Discipline rests primarily with faculty.

Summer Programs Remediation, advancement, ESL, sports, art/fine arts, computer instruction programs offered; session focuses on academics, ESL, and leadership education; held both on and off campus; held at Bark Lake Outdoor Education and Leadership Centre; accepts boys and girls; open to students from other schools. 700 students usually enrolled. 2014 schedule: July 2 to August 12. Application deadline: May 31.

Tuition and Aid Day student tuition: CAN$17,896–CAN$29,791; 7-day tuition and room/board: CAN$21,435–CAN$36,871. Tuition reduction for siblings, merit

scholarship grants, tuition reduction for Canadian citizens and permanent residents available.

Admissions Traditional secondary-level entrance grade is 11. Math Placement Exam and SLEP required. Deadline for receipt of application materials: none. Application fee required: CAN$200. Interview recommended.

Athletics Interscholastic: badminton (boys, girls), basketball (b), indoor soccer (b), soccer (b); intramural: aerobics (g), aerobics/dance (g), aquatics (b,g), badminton (b,g), ball hockey (b,g), basketball (b,g), cheering (g), dance (g), field hockey (b,g), fitness (b,g), floor hockey (b), football (b), hockey (b,g), indoor hockey (b,g), indoor soccer (b,g), jump rope (b,g), martial arts (b), outdoor activities (b,g), outdoor adventure (b,g), outdoor education (b,g), physical fitness (b,g), soccer (b,g), squash (b), strength & conditioning (b), swimming and diving (b,g), table tennis (b,g), track and field (b,g), volleyball (b,g), weight training (b,g), winter walking (b,g); coed interscholastic: badminton, indoor track & field; coed intramural: aquatics, badminton, ball hockey, canoeing/kayaking, cooperative games, cross-country running, fitness, floor hockey, golf, hiking/backpacking, hockey, in-line skating, indoor hockey, indoor track & field, jogging, jump rope, kayaking, martial arts, outdoor activities, outdoor adventure, outdoor education, physical fitness, physical training, roller blading, ropes courses, running, self defense, skiing (cross-country), snowshoeing, squash, strength & conditioning, swimming and diving, table tennis, track and field, volleyball, wallyball, weight training, wilderness, wilderness survival, winter walking, yoga. 3 PE instructors, 4 coaches.

Computers Computers are regularly used in accounting, business, business applications, career education, economics, English, ESL, geography, information technology, music, SAT preparation, science classes. Computer network features include Internet access, wireless campus network. Computer access in designated common areas is available to students. Students grades are available online.

Contact Ms. Marina Rosas, Admissions Officer. 905-572-7883 Ext. 2835. Fax: 905-572-9332. E-mail: admissions02@cic-totalcare.com. Website: www.cic-TotalCare.com

COLUMBIA INTERNATIONAL SCHOOL

153 Matsugo
Tokorozawa, Saitama 359-0027, Japan

Head of School: Mr. Barrie McCliggott

General Information Coeducational boarding and day and distance learning college-preparatory, business, bilingual studies, and technology school. Boarding grades 7–12, day grades 1–12. Distance learning grade X. Founded: 1988. Setting: suburban. Nearest major city is Tokyo, Japan. Students are housed in coed dormitories. 2-acre campus. 3 buildings on campus. Approved or accredited by Ontario Ministry of Education, Western Association of Schools and Colleges, and state department of education. Language of instruction: English. Endowment: ¥100 million. Total enrollment: 278. Upper school average class size: 14. Upper school faculty-student ratio: 1:12. There are 180 required school days per year for Upper School students. Upper School students typically attend 5 days per week. The average school day consists of 5 hours and 30 minutes.

Upper School Student Profile Grade 10: 25 students (13 boys, 12 girls); Grade 11: 23 students (10 boys, 13 girls); Grade 12: 25 students (14 boys, 11 girls). 5% of students are boarding students. 10% are international students. International students from Canada, China, Philippines, Republic of Korea, United Kingdom, and United States; 10 other countries represented in student body.

Faculty School total: 24. In upper school: 12 men, 2 women; 7 have advanced degrees; 4 reside on campus.

Subjects Offered 1 1/2 elective credits, 20th century world history, advanced TOEFL/grammar, algebra, ancient world history, art, Asian history, biology, business, calculus, Canadian geography, Canadian history, chemistry, communications, community service, computer science, computers, economics, English, ESL, foreign language, geography, geometry, global issues, history, Internet, keyboarding, literacy, mathematics, media studies, physical education, reading, TOEFL preparation, world issues, yearbook.

Graduation Requirements 20th century history, arts, Asian history, biology, chemistry, economics, English, geography, humanities, law, mathematics, physical education (includes health), science, social sciences, Ontario Literacy Test, 40 hours of community involvement activities.

Special Academic Programs Advanced Placement exam preparation; honors section; accelerated programs; independent study; study abroad; remedial reading and/or remedial writing; remedial math; ESL (70 students enrolled).

College Admission Counseling 21 students graduated in 2012; 19 went to college, including Queen's University at Kingston; Temple University; The University of British Columbia; University of Saskatchewan; University of Victoria; Western Michigan University. Other: 2 had other specific plans.

Student Life Upper grades have uniform requirement, student council, honor system. Discipline rests primarily with faculty.

Tuition and Aid Day student tuition: ¥1,575,000; 7-day tuition and room/board: ¥2,805,000. Tuition installment plan (individually arranged payment plans, term payment plans). Tuition reduction for siblings, merit scholarship grants available. In 2012–13, 5% of upper-school students received aid; total upper-school merit-scholarship money awarded: ¥2,735,000. Total amount of financial aid awarded in 2012–13: ¥3,360,000.

Admissions Traditional secondary-level entrance grade is 10. For fall 2012, 53 students applied for upper-level admission, 30 were accepted, 26 enrolled. Any standardized test required. Deadline for receipt of application materials: none. Application fee required: ¥25,000. Interview required.

Athletics Coed Interscholastic: basketball, dance, football, soccer; coed intramural: aerobics, alpine skiing, artistic gym, badminton, ball hockey, baseball, bicycling, bowling, climbing, cooperative games, dance team, field hockey, fitness, flag football, floor hockey, freestyle skiing, Frisbee, golf, hiking/backpacking, hockey, horseback riding, indoor hockey, indoor soccer, juggling, kickball, life saving, mountain biking, outdoor activities, physical fitness, power lifting, rock climbing, self defense, ski jumping, skiing (downhill), snowboarding, softball, table tennis, team handball, tennis, volleyball, wall climbing, weight lifting, weight training, yoga. 2 PE instructors.

Computers Computers are regularly used in all classes. Computer network features include Internet access, wireless campus network, Internet filtering or blocking technology, repair service. Campus intranet and student e-mail accounts are available to students. The school has a published electronic and media policy.

Contact Mr. Christopher Holland, Administrator. 81-4-2946-1911. Fax: 81-4-2946-1955. E-mail: holland@columbia-ca.co.jp. Website: www.columbia-ca.co.jp

THE COLUMBUS ACADEMY

4300 Cherry Bottom Road
Gahanna, Ohio 43230

Head of School: Melissa B. Soderberg

General Information Coeducational day college-preparatory school. Grades PK–12. Founded: 1911. Setting: suburban. Nearest major city is Columbus. 231-acre campus. 16 buildings on campus. Approved or accredited by Independent Schools Association of the Central States and Ohio Department of Education. Member of National Association of Independent Schools and Secondary School Admission Test Board. Endowment: $30 million. Total enrollment: 1,085. Upper school average class size: 14. Upper school faculty-student ratio: 1:8. The average school day consists of 7 hours and 5 minutes.

Upper School Student Profile Grade 9: 95 students (52 boys, 43 girls); Grade 10: 94 students (48 boys, 46 girls); Grade 11: 93 students (43 boys, 50 girls); Grade 12: 94 students (54 boys, 40 girls).

Faculty School total: 148. In upper school: 25 men, 22 women; 36 have advanced degrees.

Subjects Offered Advanced chemistry, advanced computer applications, advanced math, Advanced Placement courses, advanced studio art-AP, algebra, American history, American history-AP, American literature, analysis and differential calculus, art history, biology, biology-AP, British literature, calculus, calculus-AP, career/college preparation, ceramics, chemistry, chemistry-AP, Chinese, choir, choral music, chorus, college counseling, comparative government and politics-AP, comparative political systems-AP, computer applications, computer education, computer science, computer science-AP, concert band, concert choir, creative writing, drawing and design, economics, economics-AP, English, European history, fine arts, French-AP, geology, geometry, government and politics-AP, government-AP, health education, history of China and Japan, instrumental music, Latin, Latin-AP, military history, photography, physical education, physics, physics-AP, pre-calculus, robotics, senior career experience, South African history, Spanish, Spanish language-AP, Spanish literature-AP, speech, statistics-AP, strings, theater, trigonometry, U.S. government and politics-AP, U.S. history-AP, United States government-AP, weight training, world history, world religions.

Graduation Requirements Arts and fine arts (art, music, dance, drama), English, foreign language, mathematics, science, social studies (includes history), formal speech delivered to the students and faculty of the upper school during junior year, community service requirement.

Special Academic Programs 21 Advanced Placement exams for which test preparation is offered; honors section; independent study; academic accommodation for the gifted.

College Admission Counseling 93 students graduated in 2013; all went to college, including Columbia University; Harvard University; Miami University; The George Washington University; The Ohio State University; Yale University. Mean SAT critical reading: 643, mean SAT math: 656, mean SAT writing: 639, mean combined SAT: 1974, mean composite ACT: 29.

Student Life Upper grades have specified standards of dress, student council. Discipline rests equally with students and faculty.

Summer Programs Remediation, enrichment, advancement, art/fine arts, computer instruction programs offered; session focuses on academic enrichment, fine arts, fun and games; held on campus; accepts boys and girls; open to students from other schools. 400 students usually enrolled. 2014 schedule: June 15 to August 22.

Tuition and Aid Day student tuition: $21,600. Tuition installment plan (The Tuition Plan, Academic Management Services Plan, Tuition Management Systems Plan). Merit scholarship grants, need-based scholarship grants available. In 2013–14, 20% of upper-school students received aid. Total amount of financial aid awarded in 2013–14: $99,190.

Admissions Traditional secondary-level entrance grade is 9. For fall 2013, 63 students applied for upper-level admission, 30 were accepted, 23 enrolled. ISEE or

SSAT required. Deadline for receipt of application materials: February 10. Application fee required: $50. On-campus interview required.

Athletics Interscholastic: baseball (boys), basketball (b,g), bowling (b,g), cross-country running (b,g), diving (b,g), field hockey (g), football (b), lacrosse (b,g), soccer (b,g), swimming and diving (b,g), tennis (b,g), track and field (b,g), volleyball (g), wrestling (b); coed intramural: bicycling. 3 PE instructors, 2 athletic trainers.

Computers Computers are regularly used in college planning, current events, economics, English, foreign language, humanities, journalism, Latin, learning cognition, library skills, mathematics, media production, multimedia, music, photography, publications, reading, research skills, SAT preparation, science, technology, theater, writing, yearbook classes. Computer network features include on-campus library services, online commercial services, Internet access, wireless campus network. Campus intranet, student e-mail accounts, and computer access in designated common areas are available to students. The school has a published electronic and media policy.

Contact John Wuorinen, Director of Admissions and Financial Aid. 614-509-2220. Fax: 614-475-0396. E-mail: admissions@columbusacademy.org. Website: www.ColumbusAcademy.org

COLUMBUS SCHOOL FOR GIRLS

56 South Columbia Avenue
Columbus, Ohio 43209

Head of School: Mrs. Elizabeth M. Lee

General Information Girls' day college-preparatory, arts, technology, and STEM school. Grades PK–12. Founded: 1898. Setting: urban. 80-acre campus. 1 building on campus. Approved or accredited by Independent Schools Association of the Central States and Ohio Association of Independent Schools. Member of National Association of Independent Schools. Endowment: $24 million. Total enrollment: 561. Upper school average class size: 13. Upper school faculty-student ratio: 1:9. There are 182 required school days per year for Upper School students. Upper School students typically attend 5 days per week. The average school day consists of 7 hours and 30 minutes.

Upper School Student Profile Grade 9: 44 students (44 girls); Grade 10: 55 students (55 girls); Grade 11: 43 students (43 girls); Grade 12: 53 students (53 girls).

Faculty School total: 77. In upper school: 7 men, 19 women; 20 have advanced degrees.

Subjects Offered Acting, Advanced Placement courses, algebra, American literature, astronomy, band, biology, biology-AP, British literature, calculus, calculus-AP, ceramics, chemistry, chemistry-AP, civics, college admission preparation, comparative government and politics-AP, computer science, concert choir, digital photography, discrete mathematics, drawing, economics, English, English language and composition-AP, English literature and composition-AP, European history-AP, fine arts, geometry, German, health, lab science, Latin, Latin-AP, Mandarin, modern European history-AP, music theory-AP, newspaper, philosophy, photography, physical education, physics, physics-AP, pre-calculus, public speaking, robotics, senior seminar, Spanish, Spanish language-AP, statistics, strings, studio art-AP, theater, trigonometry, U.S. government and politics-AP, U.S. history, visual arts, vocal ensemble, world history, world literature, world religions, yearbook.

Graduation Requirements Algebra, arts and fine arts (art, music, dance, drama), biology, chemistry, civics, college planning, electives, English, foreign language, geometry, health, physical education (includes health), physics, public speaking, self-defense, technology, U.S. history, world history, Senior May program, service hours, water safety.

Special Academic Programs Advanced Placement exam preparation; honors section; independent study; study at local college for college credit.

College Admission Counseling 60 students graduated in 2013; all went to college, including Kenyon College; Miami University; Michigan State University; Northeastern University; The Ohio State University; Xavier University. Median SAT critical reading: 610, median SAT math: 630, median SAT writing: 610, median combined SAT: 1860, median composite ACT: 29. 59% scored over 600 on SAT critical reading, 71% scored over 600 on SAT math, 55% scored over 600 on SAT writing, 61% scored over 1800 on combined SAT, 73% scored over 26 on composite ACT.

Student Life Upper grades have uniform requirement, student council, honor system. Discipline rests primarily with faculty.

Summer Programs Remediation, enrichment, advancement, sports, art/fine arts, rigorous outdoor training, computer instruction programs offered; session focuses on academic areas; held both on and off campus; held at various sites in community and CSG's Kirk Athletic Campus; accepts boys and girls; open to students from other schools. 500 students usually enrolled. 2014 schedule: June 9 to August 8. Application deadline: June 1.

Tuition and Aid Day student tuition: $18,500–$21,300. Tuition installment plan (Tuition Management Systems Plan). Tuition reduction for siblings, need-based scholarship grants, tuition reduction for three or more siblings available. In 2013–14, 31% of upper-school students received aid. Total amount of financial aid awarded in 2013–14: $669,770.

Admissions Traditional secondary-level entrance grade is 9. For fall 2013, 31 students applied for upper-level admission, 16 were accepted, 12 enrolled. CTP, ISEE or school's own test required. Deadline for receipt of application materials: February 14. Application fee required: $50. On-campus interview required.

Athletics Interscholastic: basketball, cross-country running, diving, field hockey, golf, independent competitive sports, lacrosse, running, soccer, swimming and diving, tennis, track and field, volleyball; intramural: aquatics, basketball, field hockey, golf, lacrosse, martial arts, running, self defense, soccer, swimming and diving, tennis, track and field, volleyball. 1 PE instructor, 26 coaches, 1 athletic trainer.

Computers Computers are regularly used in art, English, foreign language, freshman foundations, health, history, mathematics, music, publications, science, technology, theater, yearbook classes. Computer network features include on-campus library services, online commercial services, Internet access, wireless campus network, Internet filtering or blocking technology. Campus intranet, student e-mail accounts, and computer access in designated common areas are available to students. Students grades are available online. The school has a published electronic and media policy.

Contact Jenni Biehn, Director of Admission and Financial Aid. 614-252-0781 Ext. 104. Fax: 614-252-0571. E-mail: jbiehn@columbusschoolforgirls.org. Website: www.columbusschoolforgirls.org

COMMONWEALTH PARKVILLE SCHOOL

PO Box 70177
San Juan, Puerto Rico 00936-8177

Head of School: Mr. F. Richard Marracino

General Information Coeducational day college-preparatory, arts, and technology school. Grades PS–12. Founded: 1952. Setting: urban. 1-acre campus. 1 building on campus. Approved or accredited by Middle States Association of Colleges and Schools and Puerto Rico Department of Education. Member of National Association of Independent Schools. Endowment: $502,005. Total enrollment: 672. Upper school average class size: 13. Upper school faculty-student ratio: 1:7. There are 180 required school days per year for Upper School students. Upper School students typically attend 5 days per week. The average school day consists of 5 hours and 8 minutes.

Upper School Student Profile Grade 9: 41 students (20 boys, 21 girls); Grade 10: 38 students (19 boys, 19 girls); Grade 11: 41 students (19 boys, 22 girls); Grade 12: 54 students (36 boys, 18 girls).

Faculty School total: 27. In upper school: 11 men, 16 women; 13 have advanced degrees.

Subjects Offered 3-dimensional art, Advanced Placement courses, algebra, American history, American literature, American literature-AP, art, art history-AP, band, biology, business mathematics, calculus, ceramics, chemistry, chemistry-AP, civics, computer science, computer technologies, creative writing, drama, drawing, ecology, English, English language and composition-AP, English literature, ethics, European history, forensics, French, geometry, health, journalism, mathematics, modern world history, music, music appreciation, music history, painting, physical education, physics, play production, pre-calculus, sculpture, Spanish, Spanish-AP, stained glass, theater, trigonometry, world history.

Graduation Requirements Art, computer science, English, ethics, health, mathematics, music, physical education (includes health), Puerto Rican history, science, social studies (includes history), Spanish, community service hours.

Special Academic Programs 8 Advanced Placement exams for which test preparation is offered; honors section; independent study; domestic exchange program (with The Network Program Schools); study abroad; programs in English, mathematics, general development for dyslexic students; special instructional classes for students with mild learning disabilities and Attention Deficit Disorder.

College Admission Counseling 46 students graduated in 2012; all went to college, including Bentley University; Boston College; Massachusetts Institute of Technology; New York University; Syracuse University; University of Puerto Rico, Río Piedras. Mean SAT critical reading: 560, mean SAT math: 570, mean SAT writing: 575.

Student Life Upper grades have uniform requirement, student council, honor system. Discipline rests primarily with faculty.

Tuition and Aid Day student tuition: $10,350–$12,810. Tuition installment plan (monthly payment plans, individually arranged payment plans, annual and semester payment plans). Tuition reduction for siblings, merit scholarship grants, need-based scholarship grants available. In 2012–13, 12% of upper-school students received aid; total upper-school merit-scholarship money awarded: $47,818. Total amount of financial aid awarded in 2012–13: $82,318.

Admissions Traditional secondary-level entrance grade is 9. For fall 2012, 34 students applied for upper-level admission, 32 were accepted, 26 enrolled. Math and English placement tests, Stanford Achievement Test and writing sample required. Deadline for receipt of application materials: none. Application fee required: $85. Interview required.

Athletics Interscholastic: baseball (boys), basketball (b), bowling (b,g), cross-country running (b,g), fitness (b,g), football (b), indoor soccer (b,g), physical fitness (b,g), soccer (b,g), softball (g), table tennis (b,g), tennis (b,g), track and field (b,g), volleyball (b,g), weight training (b,g); intramural: soccer (b,g), softball (b,g), volleyball (b,g); coed interscholastic: swimming and diving; coed intramural: badminton, basketball, cooperative games, field hockey, fitness, flag football, Frisbee, indoor soccer, jogging, outdoor activities, outdoor education, outdoor recreation, physical fitness, physical training, soccer, softball, strength & conditioning, table tennis, tennis, track and field, volleyball, walking. 3 PE instructors, 9 coaches.

Computers Computers are regularly used in all academic, music, yearbook classes. Computer network features include on-campus library services, Internet access, wireless campus network, Internet filtering or blocking technology. Campus intranet, student e-mail accounts, and computer access in designated common areas are available to students. Students grades are available online. The school has a published electronic and media policy.

Contact Mrs. Jo-Ann Aranguren, Director of Admissions and Alumni. 787-765-4411 Ext. 232. Fax: 787-764-3809. E-mail: jaranguren@cpspr.org. Website: www.cpspr.org

COMMONWEALTH SCHOOL

151 Commonwealth Avenue
Boston, Massachusetts 02116

Head of School: Mr. William D. Wharton

General Information Coeducational day college-preparatory school. Grades 9–12. Founded: 1957. Setting: urban. 1 building on campus. Approved or accredited by Association of Independent Schools in New England, New England Association of Schools and Colleges, and Massachusetts Department of Education. Member of National Association of Independent Schools and Secondary School Admission Test Board. Endowment: $15.5 million. Total enrollment: 145. Upper school average class size: 12. Upper school faculty-student ratio: 1:4. Upper School students typically attend 5 days per week. The average school day consists of 6 hours and 30 minutes.

Upper School Student Profile Grade 9: 30 students (10 boys, 20 girls); Grade 10: 41 students (20 boys, 21 girls); Grade 11: 39 students (16 boys, 23 girls); Grade 12: 36 students (17 boys, 19 girls).

Faculty School total: 36. In upper school: 14 men, 22 women; 28 have advanced degrees.

Subjects Offered 20th century American writers, 20th century history, acting, advanced biology, advanced chemistry, advanced computer applications, advanced math, Advanced Placement courses, African-American literature, algebra, American history, American history-AP, American literature, analysis and differential calculus, analysis of data, analytic geometry, ancient history, ancient world history, art, art history, biology, biology-AP, calculus, calculus-AP, ceramics, chamber groups, chemistry, chemistry-AP, choral music, chorus, classics, computer programming, computer science, creative writing, current events, dance, drama, drawing, economics, economics-AP, English, English literature, English-AP, environmental science, environmental studies, ethics, European history, European history-AP, expository writing, film series, film studies, fine arts, foreign language, French, French language-AP, French literature-AP, French studies, French-AP, geometry, Greek, health and safety, Hispanic literature, history of the Americas, history-AP, honors algebra, honors English, honors geometry, honors U.S. history, Japanese history, jazz, jazz band, jazz ensemble, jazz theory, Latin, Latin American history, Latin-AP, mathematics, mathematics-AP, medieval history, medieval/Renaissance history, modern European history-AP, music, music theory, music theory-AP, orchestra, organic chemistry, painting, performing arts, philosophy, photography, physical education, physics, physics-AP, poetry, pottery, pre-calculus, printmaking, probability and statistics, psychology, Russian literature, science, short story, society, politics and law, Spanish, Spanish language-AP, Spanish literature, Spanish literature-AP, Spanish-AP, studio art, theater, U.S. history-AP, visual and performing arts, visual arts, voice, voice ensemble, writing.

Graduation Requirements Algebra, ancient history, art, biology, calculus, chemistry, English, ethics, foreign language, geometry, medieval history, physical education (includes health), physics, U.S. history, City of Boston course, completion of a one- to three-week project each year (with report), Health and Community. Community service is required.

Special Academic Programs Advanced Placement exam preparation; honors section; independent study; term-away projects; study abroad; academic accommodation for the gifted, the musically talented, and the artistically talented.

College Admission Counseling 38 students graduated in 2013; all went to college, including Harvard University; Middlebury College; Smith College; Tufts University; University of Chicago. Mean SAT critical reading: 742, mean SAT math: 718, mean SAT writing: 719.

Student Life Discipline rests primarily with faculty.

Tuition and Aid Day student tuition: $35,970. Tuition installment plan (Key Tuition Payment Plan). Need-based scholarship grants, need-based loans available. In 2013–14, 30% of upper-school students received aid. Total amount of financial aid awarded in 2013–14: $1,146,990.

Admissions Traditional secondary-level entrance grade is 9. For fall 2013, 167 students applied for upper-level admission, 81 were accepted, 36 enrolled. ISEE or SSAT required. Deadline for receipt of application materials: February 1. Application fee required: $50. On-campus interview required.

Athletics Interscholastic: basketball (boys, girls), independent competitive sports (b,g), soccer (b,g); coed interscholastic: baseball, cross-country running, fencing, squash, ultimate Frisbee; coed intramural: aerobics/Nautilus, ballet, cross-country running, dance, fencing, fitness, martial arts, sailing, squash, tai chi, yoga. 12 coaches.

Computers Computers are regularly used in computer applications, photography, programming classes. Computer network features include on-campus library services, online commercial services, Internet access, wireless campus network, Internet filtering or blocking technology. Campus intranet, student e-mail accounts, and computer access in designated common areas are available to students. The school has a published electronic and media policy.

Contact Ms. Estefania Torres, Assistant Director of Admissions. 617-266-7525 Ext. 239. Fax: 617-266-5769. E-mail: admissions@commschool.org. Website: www.commschool.org

COMMUNITY CHRISTIAN ACADEMY

11875 Taylor Mill Road
Independence, Kentucky 41051

Head of School: Tara Montez Bates

General Information Coeducational day college-preparatory and religious studies school, affiliated with Pentecostal Church. Grades PS–12. Founded: 1983. Setting: rural. Nearest major city is Cincinnati, OH. 112-acre campus. 2 buildings on campus. Approved or accredited by International Christian Accrediting Association and Kentucky Department of Education. Total enrollment: 268. Upper school average class size: 15. Upper school faculty-student ratio: 1:15. There are 175 required school days per year for Upper School students. Upper School students typically attend 5 days per week. The average school day consists of 6 hours.

Upper School Student Profile Grade 9: 20 students (9 boys, 11 girls); Grade 10: 11 students (5 boys, 6 girls); Grade 11: 10 students (7 boys, 3 girls); Grade 12: 20 students (11 boys, 9 girls). 50% of students are Pentecostal.

Faculty School total: 14. In upper school: 1 man, 5 women; 2 have advanced degrees.

Subjects Offered Advanced biology, advanced math, algebra, American history, art appreciation, Bible, biology, business skills, calculus, chemistry, choral music, computer applications, cultural geography, English, geography, health, integrated science, life skills, literature, pre-algebra, pre-calculus, Spanish.

Graduation Requirements Bible, electives, English, foreign language, mathematics, physical education (includes health), science, social studies (includes history), statistics, visual and performing arts.

College Admission Counseling 15 students graduated in 2012; 12 went to college, including Cincinnati State Technical and Community College; Northern Kentucky University; University of Cincinnati. Other: 2 went to work, 1 entered military service. Mean composite ACT: 21. 20% scored over 26 on composite ACT.

Student Life Upper grades have uniform requirement, student council, honor system. Discipline rests primarily with faculty. Attendance at religious services is required.

Tuition and Aid Day student tuition: $3349. Guaranteed tuition plan. Tuition installment plan (The Tuition Plan, monthly payment plans). Financial aid available to upper-school students. In 2012–13, 5% of upper-school students received aid. Total amount of financial aid awarded in 2012–13: $9000.

Admissions Traditional secondary-level entrance grade is 9. For fall 2012, 20 students applied for upper-level admission, 15 were accepted, 15 enrolled. Admissions testing required. Deadline for receipt of application materials: none. Application fee required: $50. Interview required.

Athletics Interscholastic: baseball (boys), basketball (b,g), cheering (g), golf (b), volleyball (g); coed interscholastic: archery. 2 PE instructors, 13 coaches.

Computers Computers are regularly used in foreign language classes. Computer network features include Internet access.

Contact Edie Carkeek, Secretary. 859-356-7990 Ext. 112. Fax: 859-356-7991. E-mail: edie.carkeek@ccaky.org. Website: www.ccaky.org

COMMUNITY HEBREW ACADEMY

200 Wilmington Avenue
Toronto, Ontario M3H 5J8, Canada

Head of School: Rabbi Lee Buckman

General Information Coeducational day college-preparatory, general academic, arts, religious studies, and technology school, affiliated with Jewish faith. Grades 9–12. Founded: 1964. Setting: urban. 6-acre campus. 2 buildings on campus. Approved or accredited by Ontario Department of Education. Language of instruction: English. Endowment: CAN$250,000. Total enrollment: 1,300. Upper school average class size: 22. Upper school faculty-student ratio: 1:8. There are 185 required school days per year for Upper School students. Upper School students typically attend 5 days per week. The average school day consists of 8 hours.

Upper School Student Profile 100% of students are Jewish.

Faculty School total: 195. In upper school: 85 men, 110 women; 40 have advanced degrees.

Subjects Offered Accounting, American history, art, athletics, biology, business, calculus, Canadian history, Canadian law, careers, chemistry, communications, computer information systems, computer technologies, creative writing, discrete mathematics, drama, economics, English, entrepreneurship, exercise science, first aid, French, general math, geography, health education, Hebrew, Hebrew scripture, Holocaust, information technology, interdisciplinary studies, Jewish history, mathematics, media studies, modern Western civilization, peer counseling, personal fitness, physical education, physics, Rabbinic literature, remedial study skills, social studies, Spanish, Talmud.

Graduation Requirements English, 72 hours of community service over 4 years.

Special Academic Programs ESL (2 students enrolled).

College Admission Counseling 353 students graduated in 2013; 300 went to college, including McGill University; Queen's University at Kingston; The University of Western Ontario; University of Guelph; University of Toronto; York University. Other: 53 had other specific plans.

Student Life Upper grades have specified standards of dress, student council. Discipline rests primarily with faculty.

Tuition and Aid Day student tuition: CAN$20,100. Tuition installment plan (monthly payment plans, individually arranged payment plans, individual payment plans). Need-based scholarship grants, need-based loans available. In 2013–14, 25% of upper-school students received aid. Total amount of financial aid awarded in 2013–14: 2,000,000 .

Admissions Traditional secondary-level entrance grade is 9. For fall 2013, 400 students applied for upper-level admission, 357 enrolled. Math and English placement tests and writing sample required. Deadline for receipt of application materials: January 14. Application fee required: CAN$150. On-campus interview required.

Athletics Interscholastic: baseball (boys), basketball (b,g), field hockey (g), flag football (b), ice hockey (b,g), rugby (b), soccer (b,g), softball (b), tennis (b,g), volleyball (b,g); coed interscholastic: alpine skiing, cross-country running, curling, golf, skiing (cross-country), skiing (downhill), snowboarding. 10 PE instructors.

Computers Computers are regularly used in business applications, information technology, media classes. Computer resources include on-campus library services, Internet access. Computer access in designated common areas is available to students. Students grades are available online.

Contact Ms. Jill Garazi, Admissions Coordinator. 905-787-8772 Ext. 2509. Fax: 905-787-8773. E-mail: jgarazi@tanenbaumchat.org. Website: www.tanenbaumchat.org

THE COMMUNITY SCHOOL OF NAPLES

13275 Livingston Road
Naples, Florida 34109

Head of School: Dr. David Watson

General Information Coeducational day college-preparatory and arts school. Grades PK–12. Founded: 1982. Setting: suburban. Nearest major city is Miami. 77-acre campus. 4 buildings on campus. Approved or accredited by Florida Council of Independent Schools. Member of National Association of Independent Schools and Secondary School Admission Test Board. Endowment: $9.4 million. Total enrollment: 706. Upper school average class size: 12. Upper school faculty-student ratio: 1:8. There are 173 required school days per year for Upper School students. Upper School students typically attend 5 days per week. The average school day consists of 6 hours.

Upper School Student Profile Grade 9: 76 students (29 boys, 47 girls); Grade 10: 84 students (50 boys, 34 girls); Grade 11: 69 students (27 boys, 42 girls); Grade 12: 57 students (34 boys, 23 girls).

Faculty School total: 90. In upper school: 19 men, 23 women; 27 have advanced degrees.

Subjects Offered 3-dimensional art, 3-dimensional design, advanced computer applications, advanced math, Advanced Placement courses, advanced studio art-AP, algebra, American government, American history, American literature, American literature-AP, American sign language, anatomy and physiology, art, art history, art history-AP, art-AP, band, biology, biology-AP, biotechnology, calculus, calculus-AP, chemistry, chemistry-AP, chorus, clayworking, comparative government and politics-AP, composition, composition-AP, computer graphics, computer programming, computer programming-AP, computer science, computer science-AP, creative writing, digital photography, drama performance, dramatic arts, drawing, drawing and design, economics, economics-AP, electives, English, English composition, English language and composition-AP, English language-AP, English literature, English literature and composition-AP, English literature-AP, English-AP, English/composition-AP, environmental science, environmental science-AP, fine arts, French, French language-AP, French literature-AP, French-AP, geometry, government, government and politics-AP, government-AP, government/civics, government/civics-AP, graphic design, health, history, history-AP, honors algebra, honors English, honors geometry, honors U.S. history, honors world history, human geography - AP, jazz band, Latin, literature, literature and composition-AP, literature-AP, macro/microeconomics-AP, macroeconomics-AP, marine biology, marine science, mathematics, mathematics-AP, microeconomics, microeconomics-AP, modern European history-AP, music, music theory-AP, oceanography, painting, performing arts, personal fitness, photography, physical education, physical fitness, physics, physics-AP, portfolio art, pre-algebra, pre-calculus, psychology, psychology-AP, robotics, science, senior project, Spanish, Spanish language-AP, Spanish literature-AP, Spanish-AP, statistics-AP, strings, studio art-AP, theater, U.S. government and politics, U.S. government and politics-AP, U.S. history, U.S. history-AP, United States government-AP, visual and performing arts, visual arts, vocal music, Web site design, world history, world history-AP, world literature.

Graduation Requirements Arts and fine arts (art, music, dance, drama), computer science, electives, English, foreign language, history, mathematics, physical education (includes health), science, community service hours (25 per year).

Special Academic Programs 26 Advanced Placement exams for which test preparation is offered; honors section; independent study; study at local college for college credit; study abroad.

College Admission Counseling 56 students graduated in 2013; all went to college, including Chapman University; Florida Gulf Coast University; Florida State University; The University of Alabama; University of Florida; University of Mississippi. Median SAT critical reading: 600, median SAT math: 630, median SAT writing: 620, median combined SAT: 1820, median composite ACT: 27. 59% scored over 600 on SAT critical reading, 67% scored over 600 on SAT math, 57% scored over 600 on SAT writing, 53% scored over 1800 on combined SAT, 59% scored over 26 on composite ACT.

Student Life Upper grades have specified standards of dress, student council, honor system. Discipline rests equally with students and faculty.

Summer Programs Enrichment programs offered; session focuses on mathematics, English, and SAT preparation, sports; held on campus; accepts boys and girls; open to students from other schools. 25 students usually enrolled. 2014 schedule: June 9 to August 8. Application deadline: June 1.

Tuition and Aid Day student tuition: $23,050. Tuition installment plan (Insured Tuition Payment Plan, monthly payment plans, individually arranged payment plans). Merit scholarship grants, need-based scholarship grants available. In 2013–14, 31% of upper-school students received aid; total upper-school merit-scholarship money awarded: $55,000. Total amount of financial aid awarded in 2013–14: $1,042,686.

Admissions Traditional secondary-level entrance grade is 9. For fall 2013, 65 students applied for upper-level admission, 50 were accepted, 34 enrolled. Math, reading, and mental ability tests or SSAT required. Deadline for receipt of application materials: February 1. Application fee required: $100.

Athletics Interscholastic: baseball (boys), basketball (b,g), cross-country running (b,g), diving (b,g), football (b), golf (b,g), lacrosse (b,g), soccer (b,g), softball (g), swimming and diving (b,g), tennis (b,g), track and field (b,g), volleyball (g), winter soccer (b,g); coed intramural: cheering, rock climbing, sailing. 4 PE instructors, 67 coaches, 1 athletic trainer.

Computers Computers are regularly used in art, computer applications, creative writing, design, desktop publishing, digital applications, English, foreign language, history, mathematics, music, science, Web site design, writing, writing, yearbook classes. Computer network features include on-campus library services, online commercial services, Internet access, wireless campus network, Internet filtering or blocking technology. Campus intranet, student e-mail accounts, and computer access in designated common areas are available to students. The school has a published electronic and media policy.

Contact Mrs. Wynnie Hathaway, Administrative Assistant, Admissions. 239-597-7575 Ext. 133. Fax: 239-598-2973. E-mail: WHathawayt@communityschoolnaples.org. Website: www.communityschoolnaples.org

THE CONCEPT SCHOOL

1120 E. Street Rd
PO Box 54
Westtown, Pennsylvania 19395

Head of School: Mr. James Symonds

General Information Coeducational day college-preparatory, general academic, arts, technology, and The Arts school. Grades 5–12. Founded: 1972. Setting: suburban. Nearest major city is Philadelphia. 10-acre campus. 1 building on campus. Approved or accredited by Pennsylvania Department of Education. Endowment: $250,000. Total enrollment: 24. Upper school average class size: 8. Upper school faculty-student ratio: 1:5. There are 180 required school days per year for Upper School students. Upper School students typically attend 5 days per week. The average school day consists of 6 hours and 30 minutes.

Upper School Student Profile Grade 6: 1 student (1 girl); Grade 8: 7 students (2 boys, 5 girls); Grade 9: 5 students (4 boys, 1 girl); Grade 10: 3 students (2 boys, 1 girl); Grade 11: 3 students (3 boys); Grade 12: 5 students (5 boys).

Faculty School total: 7. In upper school: 2 men, 5 women; 4 have advanced degrees.

Subjects Offered 20th century world history, acting, algebra, American history, art, biology, career and personal planning, consumer mathematics, cultural arts, English, environmental science, foreign language, general science, geometry, government/civics, health, history, independent study, lab science, language arts, mathematics, physical education, pre-algebra, pre-calculus, science, Shakespeare, social sciences, social studies, U.S. government, visual arts.

Graduation Requirements Arts and fine arts (art, music, dance, drama), computer science, English, foreign language, mathematics, physical education (includes health), science, social sciences, social studies (includes history).

Special Academic Programs Accelerated programs; independent study; remedial reading and/or remedial writing; remedial math.

College Admission Counseling 3 students graduated in 2013; all went to college, including Barry University. Mean SAT critical reading: 510, mean SAT math: 490, mean SAT writing: 480.

Student Life Upper grades have specified standards of dress, honor system. Discipline rests primarily with faculty.

Tuition and Aid Day student tuition: $19,750. Tuition installment plan (monthly payment plans, individually arranged payment plans). Tuition reduction for siblings available.

Admissions Traditional secondary-level entrance grade is 9. For fall 2013, 19 students applied for upper-level admission, 8 were accepted, 6 enrolled. Stanford Binet, Wechsler Individual Achievement Test or WISC or WAIS required. Deadline for receipt of application materials: none. Application fee required: $75. On-campus interview required.

Athletics Coed Intramural: aerobics, basketball, bowling, ice skating, in-line skating, kickball, outdoor activities, physical fitness, physical training, roller skating, skiing (downhill), snowboarding, yoga. 1 PE instructor.

Computers Computers are regularly used in all academic classes. Computer network features include on-campus library services, Internet access, wireless campus network, Internet filtering or blocking technology, all students are issued Chrome Books. Campus intranet and student e-mail accounts are available to students. Students grades are available online. The school has a published electronic and media policy.

Contact Mrs. Carol McAdam, School Secretary. 610-399-1135. Fax: 610-399-0767. E-mail: cmcadam@theconceptschool.org. Website: www.theconceptschool.org

CONCORD ACADEMY

166 Main Street
Concord, Massachusetts 01742

Head of School: Rick Hardy

General Information Coeducational boarding and day college-preparatory and arts school. Grades 9–12. Founded: 1922. Setting: suburban. Nearest major city is Boston. Students are housed in single-sex dormitories. 39-acre campus. 29 buildings on campus. Approved or accredited by New England Association of Schools and Colleges, The Association of Boarding Schools, and Massachusetts Department of Education. Member of National Association of Independent Schools and Secondary School Admission Test Board. Endowment: $56 million. Total enrollment: 378. Upper school average class size: 12. Upper school faculty-student ratio: 1:6. Upper School students typically attend 5 days per week. The average school day consists of 6 hours and 30 minutes.

Upper School Student Profile Grade 9: 89 students (45 boys, 44 girls); Grade 10: 96 students (44 boys, 52 girls); Grade 11: 92 students (43 boys, 49 girls); Grade 12: 100 students (48 boys, 52 girls). 42% of students are boarding students. 71% are state residents. 18 states are represented in upper school student body. 11% are international students. International students from Canada, China, Hong Kong, Republic of Korea, Taiwan, and Thailand; 6 other countries represented in student body.

Faculty School total: 63. In upper school: 27 men, 36 women; 55 have advanced degrees; 26 reside on campus.

Subjects Offered 20th century American writers, 3-dimensional art, advanced chemistry, advanced math, African history, African-American literature, algebra, American history, American literature, ancient history, ancient world history, anthropology, applied music, architecture, art, art history, Asian history, astronomy, astrophysics, batik, Bible as literature, biochemistry, biology, bookmaking, British literature, calculus, ceramics, chamber groups, chemistry, Chinese history, choreography, chorus, classical civilization, classical Greek literature, classical language, computer multimedia, computer programming, computer science, computer studies, creative writing, critical studies in film, dance, dance performance, digital imaging, directing, drama, drama performance, drawing, earth science, economics, English, English literature, environmental science, environmental studies, European history, experimental science, expository writing, fiber arts, fiction, film, film history, filmmaking, forensics, French, freshman seminar, geology, geometry, German, German literature, guitar, health and wellness, history, history of China and Japan, history of music, Holocaust, HTML design, improvisation, instruments, introduction to digital multitrack recording techniques, Irish literature, Islamic history, jazz ensemble, journalism, Latin, Latin American history, Latin American literature, life management skills, literature seminar, math analysis, mathematics, medieval/Renaissance history, Middle East, Middle Eastern history, model United Nations, modern dance, modern European history, modern languages, music, music composition, music history, music technology, music theory, musical productions, neuroscience, newspaper, novels, oceanography, orchestra, painting, performing arts, philosophy, photography, physical education, physics, piano, play/screen writing, poetry, post-calculus, pre-calculus, printmaking, probability and statistics, Roman civilization, science, science fiction, sculpture, senior project, sex education, Shakespeare, Spanish, Spanish literature, statistics, student publications, studio art, technical theater, theater, theater design and production, theater history, trigonometry, U.S. history, urban studies, visual arts, voice, Web site design, wind ensemble, writing.

Graduation Requirements Computer science, English, foreign language, history, mathematics, performing arts, physical education (includes health), science, visual arts.

Special Academic Programs Honors section; independent study; term-away projects; study abroad; academic accommodation for the gifted, the musically talented, and the artistically talented.

College Admission Counseling 93 students graduated in 2013; all went to college, including Bates College; Brown University; New York University; The

Colorado College; Tufts University; Yale University. Mean SAT critical reading: 659, mean SAT math: 685, mean SAT writing: 656, mean combined SAT: 2000.

Student Life Upper grades have student council, honor system. Discipline rests equally with students and faculty.

Tuition and Aid Day student tuition: $42,200; 7-day tuition and room/board: $52,200. Tuition installment plan (Key Tuition Payment Plan, monthly payment plans). Need-based scholarship grants, need-based loans available. In 2013–14, 24% of upper-school students received aid. Total amount of financial aid awarded in 2013–14: $3,830,370.

Admissions Traditional secondary-level entrance grade is 9. For fall 2013, 822 students applied for upper-level admission, 249 were accepted, 112 enrolled. ISEE, SSAT or TOEFL required. Deadline for receipt of application materials: January 15. Application fee required: $50. Interview recommended.

Athletics Interscholastic: baseball (boys), basketball (b,g), cross-country running (b,g), field hockey (g), lacrosse (g), skiing (downhill) (b,g), soccer (b,g), squash (g), tennis (b,g), volleyball (g), wrestling (b); intramural: softball (g), squash (b); coed interscholastic: alpine skiing, golf, lacrosse, ultimate Frisbee; coed intramural: aerobics, aerobics/dance, ballet, canoeing/kayaking, combined training, cross-country running, dance, fencing, fitness, jogging, martial arts, modern dance, outdoor activities, physical fitness, physical training, sailing, self defense, skiing (downhill), strength & conditioning, track and field, ultimate Frisbee, weight training, yoga. 8 PE instructors, 35 coaches, 2 athletic trainers.

Computers Computers are regularly used in English, foreign language, history, library skills, mathematics, music, newspaper, science, social studies, technology, video film production, Web site design, yearbook classes. Computer network features include on-campus library services, online commercial services, Internet access, wireless campus network, Internet filtering or blocking technology. Campus intranet, student e-mail accounts, and computer access in designated common areas are available to students. Students grades are available online. The school has a published electronic and media policy.

Contact Marie D. Myers, Director of Admissions. 978-402-2250. Fax: 978-402-2345. E-mail: admissions@concordacademy.org. Website: www.concordacademy.org

CONCORDIA LUTHERAN HIGH SCHOOL

1601 Saint Joe River Drive
Fort Wayne, Indiana 46805

Head of School: Mr. Terry Breininger

General Information Coeducational day college-preparatory and religious studies school, affiliated with Lutheran Church–Missouri Synod. Grades 9–12. Founded: 1935. Setting: urban. Nearest major city is Indianapolis. 3 buildings on campus. Approved or accredited by National Lutheran School Accreditation, North Central Association of Colleges and Schools, and Indiana Department of Education. Total enrollment: 708. Upper school average class size: 25. Upper school faculty-student ratio: 1:16. There are 180 required school days per year for Upper School students. Upper School students typically attend 5 days per week. The average school day consists of 7 hours and 5 minutes.

Upper School Student Profile Grade 9: 218 students (105 boys, 113 girls); Grade 10: 170 students (81 boys, 89 girls); Grade 11: 171 students (84 boys, 87 girls); Grade 12: 149 students (75 boys, 74 girls). 76% of students are Lutheran Church–Missouri Synod.

Faculty School total: 45. In upper school: 24 men, 20 women; 23 have advanced degrees.

Subjects Offered 3-dimensional art, Advanced Placement courses, algebra, American history, American literature, anatomy and physiology, art, band, Bible studies, biology, biology-AP, broadcasting, business, calculus, calculus-AP, ceramics, chemistry, chemistry-AP, choir, computer science, creative writing, discrete mathematics, driver education, earth science, economics, English, English literature, English literature and composition-AP, entrepreneurship, environmental science, ethics, expository writing, family and consumer science, food and nutrition, French, geography, geometry, German, government/civics, grammar, health, health and safety, history, home economics, honors algebra, honors English, honors geometry, internship, journalism, JROTC, JROTC or LEAD (Leadership Education and Development), keyboarding, Latin, marching band, mathematics, media arts, media communications, microeconomics-AP, music, newspaper, painting, physical education, physics, physics-AP, psychology, religion, science, social sciences, social studies, sociology, Spanish, speech, statistics-AP, theater, theater arts, theology, typing, U.S. government, U.S. history, U.S. history-AP, video film production, weight training, world history, world literature, writing, yearbook.

Graduation Requirements English, foreign language, mathematics, physical education (includes health), religion (includes Bible studies and theology), science, social sciences, social studies (includes history). Community service is required.

Special Academic Programs Advanced Placement exam preparation; honors section; independent study; study at local college for college credit; programs in English, mathematics, general development for dyslexic students.

College Admission Counseling 168 students graduated in 2013; 157 went to college, including Ball State University; Indiana University–Purdue University Fort Wayne; Indiana University Bloomington; Purdue University; Valparaiso University.

Other: 10 went to work, 1 entered military service. Mean SAT critical reading: 519, mean SAT math: 538, mean SAT writing: 502, mean composite ACT: 29.

Student Life Upper grades have uniform requirement, student council. Discipline rests primarily with faculty. Attendance at religious services is required.

Summer Programs Remediation, advancement, sports, art/fine arts, computer instruction programs offered; session focuses on summer classes, drivers education, summer conditioning and sports camps; held both on and off campus; held at various locations based on sport; accepts boys and girls; open to students from other schools. 700 students usually enrolled.

Tuition and Aid Day student tuition: $7225–$8675. Tuition installment plan (FACTS Tuition Payment Plan, monthly payment plans, individually arranged payment plans, Bank loan). Tuition reduction for siblings, merit scholarship grants, need-based scholarship grants available.

Admissions Traditional secondary-level entrance grade is 9. Deadline for receipt of application materials: none. Application fee required: $35. On-campus interview recommended.

Athletics Interscholastic: baseball (boys), basketball (b,g), cheering (g), cross-country running (b,g), football (b), golf (b,g), gymnastics (g), lacrosse (b), soccer (b,g), softball (g), swimming and diving (b,g), tennis (b,g), track and field (b,g), volleyball (g), wrestling (b); coed interscholastic: bowling, crew, dance team, JROTC drill, rappelling, riflery; coed intramural: volleyball. 3 PE instructors, 70 coaches, 2 athletic trainers.

Computers Computers are regularly used in all academic, newspaper, religion, yearbook classes. Computer resources include on-campus library services, online commercial services, Internet access, wireless campus network, Internet filtering or blocking technology. Student e-mail accounts and computer access in designated common areas are available to students. Students grades are available online.

Contact Mrs. Krista Friend, Director of Enrollment and Retention. 260-483-1102. Fax: 260-471-0180. E-mail: kfriend@clhscadets.com. Website: www.clhscadets.com

CONCORDIA PREPARATORY SCHOOL

12723 S Park Ave
Riverton, Utah 84065

Head of School: Mr. Darren Morrison

General Information Coeducational day and distance learning college-preparatory, general academic, and religious studies school, affiliated with Lutheran Church. Grades 9–12. Distance learning grades 10–12. Founded: 1984. Setting: suburban. 10-acre campus. 1 building on campus. Approved or accredited by National Lutheran School Accreditation, Northwest Accreditation Commission, and Utah Department of Education. Total enrollment: 58. Upper school average class size: 10. Upper school faculty-student ratio: 1:3. There are 180 required school days per year for Upper School students. Upper School students typically attend 5 days per week. The average school day consists of 6 hours and 45 minutes.

Upper School Student Profile Grade 9: 9 students (6 boys, 3 girls); Grade 10: 7 students (5 boys, 2 girls); Grade 11: 7 students (3 boys, 4 girls); Grade 12: 8 students (3 boys, 5 girls). 25% of students are Lutheran.

Faculty School total: 9. In upper school: 4 men, 5 women; 5 have advanced degrees.

Subjects Offered Advanced biology, advanced chemistry, advanced computer applications, advanced math, Advanced Placement courses, algebra, American history, American literature, art, band, bell choir, Bible studies, biology, calculus, chemistry, chorus, computer science, drama, English, general science, geography, geometry, government/civics, health, journalism, keyboarding, literature, mathematics, novels, physical education, physics, psychology, religion, science, social sciences, sociology, Spanish, speech, vocal music, word processing, world history, world literature.

Graduation Requirements Arts and fine arts (art, music, dance, drama), business skills (includes word processing), computer science, English, mathematics, physical education (includes health), religion (includes Bible studies and theology), science, social sciences.

Special Academic Programs Advanced Placement exam preparation; honors section; accelerated programs; independent study; study at local college for college credit; academic accommodation for the gifted; remedial reading and/or remedial writing.

College Admission Counseling 10 students graduated in 2012; all went to college, including Concordia College Alabama; Salt Lake Community College; Southern Utah University; University of Utah; Utah State University; Westminster College. Median composite ACT: 24. 23% scored over 26 on composite ACT.

Student Life Upper grades have uniform requirement, student council, honor system. Discipline rests equally with students and faculty. Attendance at religious services is required.

Tuition and Aid Day student tuition: $9000. Tuition installment plan (SMART Tuition Payment Plan). Tuition reduction for siblings, merit scholarship grants, need-based scholarship grants available. In 2012–13, 40% of upper-school students received aid; total upper-school merit-scholarship money awarded: $16,000. Total amount of financial aid awarded in 2012–13: $33,700.

Admissions Traditional secondary-level entrance grade is 9. For fall 2012, 35 students applied for upper-level admission, 33 were accepted, 32 enrolled. School placement exam, SLEP for foreign students, TOEFL or SLEP or writing sample required. Deadline for receipt of application materials: none. Application fee required: $250. Interview required.

Athletics Interscholastic: baseball (boys), basketball (b,g), cross-country running (b,g), golf (b,g), soccer (b,g), swimming and diving (b,g), track and field (b,g), volleyball (g); coed interscholastic: cross-country running, golf, swimming and diving, track and field; coed intramural: badminton, basketball, cross-country running, fencing, golf, outdoors, physical fitness, physical training, soccer, track and field, volleyball, weight training. 3 coaches.

Computers Computers are regularly used in all classes. Computer network features include online commercial services, Internet access, wireless campus network, Internet filtering or blocking technology. Campus intranet, student e-mail accounts, and computer access in designated common areas are available to students. Students grades are available online. The school has a published electronic and media policy.

Contact Mrs. Tia Donohoe, Director of Admissions. 801-878-1515. Fax: 801-878-1730. E-mail: tdonohoe@concordiautah.org. Website: concordiautah.org

CONTRA COSTA CHRISTIAN HIGH SCHOOL

2721 Larkey Lane
Walnut Creek, California 94596

Head of School: Mr. Darren Price

General Information Coeducational day and distance learning college-preparatory and religious studies school. Grades PK–12. Distance learning grades K–12. Founded: 1978. Setting: suburban. 2 buildings on campus. Approved or accredited by Western Association of Schools and Colleges and California Department of Education. Total enrollment: 230. Upper school average class size: 15. Upper school faculty-student ratio: 1:10. Upper School students typically attend 5 days per week. The average school day consists of 7 hours.

Upper School Student Profile Grade 9: 16 students (8 boys, 8 girls); Grade 10: 19 students (8 boys, 11 girls); Grade 11: 22 students (12 boys, 10 girls); Grade 12: 29 students (16 boys, 13 girls).

Faculty In upper school: 4 men, 6 women.

Subjects Offered 1968, 20th century ethnic conflicts, 20th century history, 20th century world history, 3-dimensional design, accounting, ACT preparation, acting, addiction, ADL skills, adolescent issues, advanced biology, advanced chemistry, advanced computer applications, advanced math, Advanced Placement courses, advanced studio art-AP, advanced TOEFL/grammar, advertising design, aerobics, aerospace education, aerospace science, aesthetics, African American history, African American studies, African dance, African drumming, African history, African literature, African studies, African-American history, African-American literature, African-American studies, agriculture, agroecology, Alabama history and geography, algebra, all , all academic, alternative physical education, American biography, American Civil War, American culture, American democracy, American foreign policy, American government, American history, American history-AP, American legal systems, American literature, American literature-AP, American minority experience, American politics in film, American sign language, American studies, analysis, analysis and differential calculus, analysis of data, analytic geometry, anatomy and physiology, Ancient Greek, ancient history, ancient world history, ancient/medieval philosophy, animal behavior, animal husbandry, animal science, animation, anthropology, applied arts, applied music, applied skills, aquatics, Arabic, Arabic studies, archaeology, architectural drawing, architecture, area studies, art, art and culture, art appreciation, art education, art history, art history-AP, art in New York, art-AP, arts, arts and crafts, arts appreciation, ASB Leadership, Asian history, Asian literature, Asian studies, astronomy, astrophysics, athletic training, athletics, atomic theory, audio visual/media, audition methods, auto mechanics, automated accounting, aviation, backpacking, bacteriology, ballet, ballet technique, band, banking, baseball, basic imaging, basic language skills, Basic programming, basic skills, basketball, batik, bell choir, Bible, Bible as literature, Bible studies, biochemistry, bioethics, bioethics, DNA and culture, biology, biology-AP, biotechnology, bivouac, Black history, boat building, boating, body human, Bolivian history, Bolivian social studies, bookbinding, bookkeeping, bookmaking, botany, bowling, brass choir, Brazilian history, Brazilian social studies, Brazilian studies, British history, British literature, British literature (honors), British literature-AP, British National Curriculum, broadcast journalism, broadcasting, Broadway dance, Buddhism, business, business applications, business communications, business education, business law, business mathematics, business skills, business studies, business technology, cabinet making, calculus, calculus-AP, California writers, calligraphy, campus ministry, Canadian geography, Canadian history, Canadian law, Canadian literature, Cantonese, career and personal planning, career and technology systems, career education, career education internship, career experience, career exploration, Career Passport, career planning, career technology, career/college preparation, careers, Caribbean history, carpentry, cartography, cartooning/animation, Catholic belief and practice, celestial navigation, cell biology, Central and Eastern European history, ceramics, ceremonies of life, chamber groups, chaplaincy, character education, cheerleading, chemistry, chemistry-AP, Cherokee, Chesapeake Bay studies, Cheyenne history, Cheyenne language, child development, China/Japan history, Chinese, Chinese history, Chinese literature, Chinese studies, choir, choral music, choreography, chorus, Christian and Hebrew scripture, Christian doctrine, Christian education, Christian ethics, Christian scripture, Christian studies, Christian testament, Christianity, church history, cinematography, circus acts, civics,

civics/free enterprise, civil rights, Civil War, civil war history, classical civilization, classical Greek literature, classical language, classical music, classical studies, classics, clayworking, clinical chemistry, collage and assemblage, college admission preparation, college awareness, college counseling, college placement, college planning, college writing, Colorado ecology, comedy, Coming of Age in the 20th Century, commercial art, communication arts, communication skills, communications, community garden, community service, comparative civilizations, comparative cultures, comparative government and politics, comparative government and politics-AP, comparative political systems-AP, comparative politics, comparative religion, competitive science projects, composition, composition-AP, computer animation, computer applications, computer art, computer education, computer graphics, computer information systems, computer literacy, computer math, computer multimedia, computer music, computer processing, computer programming, computer programming-AP, computer resources, computer science, computer science-AP, computer skills, computer studies, computer technologies, computer technology certification, computer tools, computer-aided design, computers, conceptual physics, concert band, concert bell choir, concert choir, conflict resolution, conservation, constitutional history of U.S., constitutional law, construction, consumer economics, consumer education, consumer law, consumer mathematics, contemporary art, contemporary history, contemporary issues, contemporary issues in science, contemporary math, contemporary problems, contemporary studies, contemporary technique, contemporary women writers, costumes and make-up, CPR, crafts, creation science, creative arts, creative dance, creative drama, creative thinking, creative writing, criminal justice, criminology, critical studies in film, critical thinking, critical writing, culinary arts, cultural arts, cultural criticism, cultural geography, current events, current history, dance, dance performance, Danish, data analysis, data processing, death and loss, debate, decision making skills, democracy in America, design, desktop publishing, desktop publishing, ESL, developmental language skills, developmental math, digital applications, digital art, digital imaging, digital music, digital photography, directing, discrete mathematics, diversity studies, DNA, DNA research, DNA science lab, drafting, drama, drama performance, drama workshop, dramatic arts, drawing, drawing and design, driver education, Dutch, early childhood, earth and space science, earth science, earth systems analysis, East Asian history, East European studies, Eastern religion and philosophy, Eastern world civilizations, Easterner in the West, ecology, ecology, environmental systems, economics, economics and history, economics-AP, education, Egyptian history, electives, electronic imagery, electronic music, electronic publishing, electronic research, electronics, emergency medicine, emerging technology, engineering, English, English as a foreign language, English composition, English language and composition-AP, English language-AP, English literature, English literature and composition-AP, English literature-AP, English-AP, English/composition-AP, ensembles, entomology, entrepreneurship, environmental education, environmental geography, environmental science, environmental science-AP, environmental studies, environmental systems, epic literature, equality and freedom, equestrian sports, equine management, equine science, equitation, ESL, ESL, essential learning systems, ethical decision making, ethics, ethics and responsibility, ethnic literature, ethnic studies, ethology, etymology, European civilization, European history, European history-AP, European literature, eurythmics (guard), eurythmy, evolution, exercise science, existentialism, experiential education, experimental science, expository writing, expressive arts, fabric arts, family and consumer science, family living, family studies, Far Eastern history, Farsi, fashion, female experience in America, fencing, fiber arts, fiction, field ecology, Filipino, film, film and literature, film and new technologies, film appreciation, film history, film series, film studies, filmmaking, finance, fine arts, finite math, Finnish, first aid, fitness, flight instruction, folk art, folk dance, folk music, food and nutrition, food science, foods, foreign language, foreign policy, forensics, forest resources, forestry, foundations of civilization, four team activities, four units of summer reading, fractal geometry, French, French as a second language, French language-AP, French literature-AP, French studies, French-AP, freshman foundations, freshman seminar, functions, gardening, gender and religion, gender issues, general, general business, general math, general science, genetics, geography, geology, geometry, geometry with art applications, geopolitics, German, German literature, German-AP, gerontology, glassblowing, global issues, global science, global studies, golf, government, government and politics-AP, government-AP, government/civics, government/civics-AP, grammar, graphic arts, graphic design, graphics, great books, great issues, Greek, Greek culture, Greek drama, guidance, guitar, gymnastics, Haitian studies, handbells, Harlem Renaissance, Hausa, Hawaiian history, Hawaiian language, health, health and safety, health and wellness, health education, health enhancement, health immersion, health science, healthful living, Hebrew, Hebrew scripture, heritage of American Women, high adventure outdoor program, Hindi, Hispanic literature, histology, historical foundations for arts, historical research, historiography, history, history and culture of Portugal, history of architecture, history of China and Japan, history of computing, history of dance, history of drama, history of England, history of ideas, history of jazz, history of mathematics, history of music, history of religion, history of rock and roll, history of science, history of the Americas, history of the Catholic Church, history-AP, Holocaust, Holocaust and other genocides, Holocaust legacy, Holocaust seminar, Holocaust studies, holography, home economics, Homeric Greek, Honduran history, honors algebra, honors English, honors geometry, honors U.S. history, honors world history, horticulture, HTML design, human anatomy, human biology, human development, human geography - AP, human issues, human movement and its application to health, human relations, human rights, human sexuality, humanities, hydrology, ideas, illustration, immunology, improvisation, independent living, independent study, Indian studies, Indonesian, Indonesian studies, industrial arts, industrial technology, information design technology, information processing, information technology, inorganic chemistry, inquiry into relationship, instrumental music, instruments, integrated arts, integrated mathematics, integrated physics, integrated science, integrated technology fundamentals, integrative seminar, interactive media, interdisciplinary studies, interior design, international affairs, International Baccalaureate courses, international foods, international relations, international studies, Internet, Internet research, internship, interpersonal skills, intro to computers, introduction to digital multitrack recording techniques, introduction to liberal studies, introduction to literature, introduction to technology, introduction to theater, Irish literature, Irish studies, Islamic history, Islamic studies, Israeli studies, issues of the 90's, Italian, Italian history, Japanese, Japanese and American values compared, Japanese as Second Language, Japanese history, Japanese literature, Japanese studies, jazz, jazz band, jazz dance, jazz ensemble, jazz theory, jewelry making, Jewish history, Jewish studies, John F. Kennedy, journalism, JROTC, JROTC or LEAD (Leadership Education and Development), Judaic studies, junior and senior seminars, justice seminar, Kentucky history, keyboarding, kinesiology, Korean, Korean culture, Korean literature, lab science, lab/keyboard, land and ranch management, land management, language, language and composition, language arts, language development, language enhancement and development, language of the theater, language structure, language-AP, languages, Latin, Latin American history, Latin American literature, Latin American studies, Latin History, Latin-AP, law, law and the legal system, law studies, leadership, leadership and service, leadership education training, learning cognition, learning lab, learning strategies, leatherworking, lettering, library, library assistant, library research, library science, library skills, library studies, life issues, life management skills, Life of Christ, life saving, life science, life skills, limnology, linear algebra, linguistics, literacy, literary genres, literary magazine, literature, literature and composition-AP, literature by women, literature seminar, literature-AP, logarithms, logic, logic, rhetoric, and debate, macro/microeconomics-AP, macroeconomics-AP, madrigals, Malay, Malay culture, management information systems, Mandarin, marching band, marine biology, marine ecology, marine science, marine studies, maritime history, marketing, martial arts, math analysis, math applications, math methods, math review, mathematical modeling, mathematics, mathematics-AP, mechanical drawing, mechanics, mechanics of writing, media, media arts, media communications, media literacy, media production, media services, media studies, mediator, medieval history, medieval literature, medieval/Renaissance history, meditation, men's studies, mentorship program, metal fabrication technology, metalworking, meteorology, methods of research, Mexican history, Mexican literature, microbiology, microcomputer technology applications, microeconomics, microeconomics-AP, Microsoft, Middle East, Middle Eastern history, military history, military science, minority studies, model United Nations, modeling, modern Chinese history, modern civilization, modern dance, modern European history, modern European history-AP, modern history, modern languages, modern political theory, modern politics, modern problems, modern Western civilization, modern world history, money management, Montana history, moral and social development, moral reasoning, moral theology, Moroccan studies, multicultural literature, multicultural studies, multimedia, multimedia design, museum science, music, music appreciation, music composition, music for dance, music history, music performance, music technology, music theater, music theory, music theory-AP, music-AP, musical productions, musical theater, musical theater dance, musicianship, mythology, nationalism and ethnic conflict, Native American arts and crafts, Native American history, Native American studies, natural history, natural resources management, nature study, nature writers, Navajo, naval science, navigation, neuroanatomy, neurobiology, neuroscience, New Testament, news writing, newspaper, NJROTC, non-Western literature, non-Western societies, North American literature, North Carolina history, Norwegian, novels, nuclear science, nutrition, occupational education, oceanography, official social customs, oil painting, opera, optics, oral communications, oral expression, orchestra, organ, organic biochemistry, organic chemistry, organic gardening, organizational studies, ornithology, outdoor education, Pacific art, Pacific Island studies, Pacific Northwest seminar, pack animal trips, painting, paleontology, parent/child development, parenting, participation in sports, peace and justice, peace education, peace studies, peer counseling, peer ministry, performing arts, permaculture, Persian, personal and social education, personal development, personal finance, personal fitness, personal growth, personal money management, Philippine culture, philosophy, philosophy of government, photo shop, photography, photojournalism, physical education, physical fitness, physical science, physics, physics-AP, physiology, piano, piloting, play production, play/screen writing, playwriting, playwriting and directing, poetry, policy and value, Polish, political economy, political science, political systems, political thought, politics, Polynesian dance, portfolio art, portfolio writing, Portuguese, Portuguese literature, post-calculus, pottery, practical arts, practical living, practicum, pragmatics, prayer/spirituality, pre-algebra, pre-calculus, pre-college orientation, pre-vocational education, printmaking, probability, probability and statistics, production, programming, projective geometry, psychology, psychology-AP, public policy, public policy issues and action, public service, public speaking, publications, publicity, publishing, Puerto Rican history, Quakerism and ethics, qualitative analysis, Rabbinic literature, radio broadcasting, reading, reading/study skills, reconstructive language, regional studies, relationships, religion, religion and culture, religious education, religious studies, remedial study skills, remedial/makeup course work, research, research and reference, research in consciousness, research seminar, research skills, rhetoric, rhetoric of war, rite of passage, robotics, Roman civilization, Roman culture,

Roman historiography, Romantic period literature, ROTC, ROTC (for boys), Russia and contemporary Europe, Russian, Russian history, Russian literature, Russian studies, Sanskrit, SAT, SAT preparation, SAT/ACT preparation, scene study, science, science and technology, science fiction, science project, science research, scripture, scuba diving, sculpture, self-defense, senior career experience, senior composition, senior humanities, senior internship, senior project, senior science survey, senior seminar, senior thesis, Serbo-Croatian, service learning/internship, set design, sewing, sex education, sexuality, Shakespeare, Shakespearean histories, shop, short story, sign language, silk screening, single survival, Sinhalese, siSwati, skills for success, small engine repair, social doctrine, social education, social issues, social justice, social psychology, social sciences, social skills, social studies, society, society and culture, society challenge and change, society, politics and law, socioeconomic problems, sociology, softball, software design, sophomore skills, South African history, Southern literature, space and physical sciences, Spanish, Spanish language-AP, Spanish literature, Spanish literature-AP, Spanish-AP, speech, speech and debate, speech and oral interpretations, speech communications, speech origins of English, speech therapy, sports, sports conditioning, sports medicine, sports nutrition, sports performance development, sports psychology, sports science, sports team management, squash, stage and body movement, stage design, stagecraft, stained glass, standard curriculum, state government, state history, statistics, statistics-AP, stock market, stone carving, strategies for success, street law, strings, student government, student publications, student teaching, studio art, studio art-AP, study skills, substance abuse, surfing, survival training, Swahili, Swedish, swimming, swimming competency, swimming test, Swiss culture, symphonic band, synchronized swimming, Talmud, Tamil, tap dance, taxonomy, technical arts, technical drawing, technical education, technical skills, technical studies, technical theater, technical writing, techniques of living and coping, technological applications, technology, technology/design, telecommunications, telecommunications and the Internet, television, tennis, Texas history, textiles, Thai, Thailand and Southeast Asia, The 20th Century, the comic tradition, the Presidency, the Sixties, the Web, theater, theater arts, theater design and production, theater history, theater production, theology, theology and the arts, theory of knowledge, therapeutic horseback riding, TOEFL preparation, Tok Pisin, topics in dramatic literature, track and field, traditional camping, training, transition mathematics, transportation technology, travel, trigonometry, tropical biology, tropical ecology, Turkish history, twentieth century ethnic conflicts, typing, U.S. and Virginia government, U.S. and Virginia government-AP, U.S. and Virginia history, U.S. constitutional history, U.S. government, U.S. government and politics, U.S. government and politics-AP, U.S. history, U.S. history-AP, U.S. literature, U.S. Presidents, Ukolelc, Ukrainian, unified math, United Nations and international issues, United States government-AP, urban design, urban studies, Urdu, utopia, values and decisions, Vedic science, veterinary science, video, video and animation, video communication, video film production, Vietnam, Vietnam history, Vietnam War, Virginia government, visual and performing arts, visual arts, visual literacy, visual reality, vocal ensemble, vocal jazz, vocal music, vocational arts, vocational skills, vocational-technical courses, voice, voice and diction, voice ensemble, volleyball, Washington State and Northwest History, water color painting, water polo, waterskiing, weaving, Web authoring, Web site design, weight fitness, weight reduction, weight training, weightlifting, welding, wellness, Western civilization, Western literature, Western philosophy, Western religions, white-water trips, wilderness education, wilderness experience, wind ensemble, wind instruments, windsurfing, women in literature, women in society, women in the classical world, women in world history, women spirituality and faith, women's health, women's literature, women's studies, wood lab, wood processing, woodworking, word processing, work camp program, work experience, work-study, world affairs, world arts, world civilizations, world cultures, world geography, world governments, world history, world history-AP, world issues, world literature, world religions, world religions, world studies, World War I, World War II, world wide web design, World-Wide-Web publishing, wrestling, writing, writing, writing workshop, yearbook, Yiddish, yoga, youth culture, Zen Buddhism, zoology.

Graduation Requirements Community service is required.

Special Academic Programs 4 Advanced Placement exams for which test preparation is offered; ESL (15 students enrolled).

College Admission Counseling 28 students graduated in 2012.

Student Life Upper grades have specified standards of dress. Discipline rests primarily with faculty. Attendance at religious services is required.

Tuition and Aid Tuition installment plan (FACTS Tuition Payment Plan).

Admissions Deadline for receipt of application materials: none. Application fee required.

Athletics Interscholastic: aquatics (boys, girls), basketball (b,g), cross-country running (b,g), soccer (b,g), volleyball (b,g). 2 PE instructors, 12 coaches.

Computers Computers are regularly used in accounting, aerospace science, all academic, animation, architecture, art, aviation, basic skills, Bible studies, business, business applications, business education, business skills, business studies, cabinet making, career education, career exploration, career technology, Christian doctrine, classics, college planning, commercial art, computer applications, construction, creative writing, current events, dance, data processing, design, desktop publishing, desktop publishing, ESL, digital applications, drafting, drawing and design, economics, engineering, English, ESL, ethics, foreign language, French, French as a second language, freshman foundations, geography, graphic arts, graphic design, graphics, health, historical foundations for arts, history, human geography - AP, humanities, independent study, industrial technology, information technology, introduction to technology, journalism, JROTC, keyboarding, lab/keyboard, language development, Latin, learning cognition, library, library science, library skills, life skills, literacy, literary magazine, mathematics, media, media arts, media production, media services, mentorship program, multimedia, music, music technology, news writing, newspaper, NJROTC, occupational education, philosophy, photography, photojournalism, programming, psychology, publications, publishing, reading, religion, religious studies, remedial study skills, research skills, SAT preparation, science, senior seminar, social sciences, social studies, Spanish, speech, stock market, study skills, technical drawing, technology, theater, theater arts, theology, typing, video film production, vocational-technical courses, Web site design, wilderness education, woodworking, word processing, writing, writing, yearbook classes. Computer network features include wireless campus network, Internet filtering or blocking technology. Student e-mail accounts and computer access in designated common areas are available to students. Students grades are available online. The school has a published electronic and media policy.

Contact Ms. Lisa Asher. 925-934-4964. E-mail: lasher@cccss.org. Website: www.cccss.org

CONVENT OF THE SACRED HEART

1177 King Street
Greenwich, Connecticut 06831

Head of School: Mrs. Pamela Juan Hayes

General Information Coeducational day (boys only in lower grades) and distance learning college-preparatory, arts, religious studies, and technology school, affiliated with Roman Catholic Church. Boys grades PS–PK, girls grades PS–12. Distance learning grades 9–12. Founded: 1848. Setting: suburban. Nearest major city is New York, NY. 118-acre campus. 10 buildings on campus. Approved or accredited by Network of Sacred Heart Schools, New England Association of Schools and Colleges, and Connecticut Department of Education. Member of National Association of Independent Schools and Secondary School Admission Test Board. Endowment: $29.9 million. Total enrollment: 737. Upper school average class size: 13. Upper school faculty-student ratio: 1:7. There are 163 required school days per year for Upper School students. Upper School students typically attend 5 days per week. The average school day consists of 7 hours and 15 minutes.

Upper School Student Profile Grade 9: 77 students (77 girls); Grade 10: 77 students (77 girls); Grade 11: 81 students (81 girls); Grade 12: 60 students (60 girls). 70% of students are Roman Catholic.

Faculty School total: 125. In upper school: 11 men, 39 women; 39 have advanced degrees.

Subjects Offered 20th century world history, advanced biology, advanced chemistry, advanced math, Advanced Placement courses, advanced studio art-AP, algebra, American literature, American literature-AP, Arabic, biology, biology-AP, broadcast journalism, calculus, calculus-AP, Catholic belief and practice, chemistry, chemistry-AP, Chinese, choir, choral music, Christian and Hebrew scripture, Christian education, Christian ethics, Christianity, college counseling, community service, comparative government and politics-AP, computer science, concert bell choir, design, drama, drawing, English language and composition-AP, English literature, English literature and composition-AP, environmental science-AP, ethics, European history, European history-AP, fine arts, French, French language-AP, geometry, health, honors algebra, honors geometry, honors U.S. history, HTML design, instrumental music, journalism, Latin, literary magazine, photography, physical education, physics, physics-AP, pre-calculus, SAT/ACT preparation, Spanish, Spanish language-AP, Spanish literature-AP, statistics, theology, trigonometry, U.S. history, U.S. history-AP, world cultures, world literature.

Graduation Requirements Arts and fine arts (art, music, dance, drama), electives, English, foreign language, mathematics, physical education (includes health), religion (includes Bible studies and theology), science, social studies (includes history), 100 hours of community service by graduation. Community service is required.

Special Academic Programs 19 Advanced Placement exams for which test preparation is offered; honors section; independent study; term-away projects; domestic exchange program (with Network of Sacred Heart Schools); study abroad; academic accommodation for the gifted and the artistically talented.

College Admission Counseling 82 students graduated in 2013; all went to college, including Boston College; Brown University; Colgate University; Cornell University; Georgetown University; Northwestern University.

Student Life Upper grades have uniform requirement, student council, honor system. Discipline rests primarily with faculty. Attendance at religious services is required.

Summer Programs Enrichment programs offered; session focuses on enrichment; held on campus; accepts girls; not open to students from other schools. 2014 schedule: June to June.

Tuition and Aid Day student tuition: $35,900. Tuition installment plan (Sallie May Payment Plan). Need-based scholarship grants available. In 2013–14, 17% of upper-school students received aid. Total amount of financial aid awarded in 2013–14: $2,500,000.

Admissions Traditional secondary-level entrance grade is 9. For fall 2013, 99 students applied for upper-level admission, 42 were accepted, 32 enrolled. ISEE or SSAT required. Deadline for receipt of application materials: February 1. Application fee required: $50. On-campus interview required.

Athletics Interscholastic: basketball, cooperative games, crew, cross-country running, dance, diving, field hockey, fitness, golf, jogging, lacrosse, physical fitness, running, soccer, softball, squash, swimming and diving, tennis, volleyball; intramural: fitness, independent competitive sports, physical training, strength & conditioning. 4 PE instructors, 34 coaches, 1 athletic trainer.

Computers Computers are regularly used in all academic classes. Computer network features include on-campus library services, online commercial services, Internet access, wireless campus network, Internet filtering or blocking technology, course selection online; grades online; CSH is a member of the Online School for Girls, laptops mandatory for students in grades 6 to 12. Campus intranet, student e-mail accounts, and computer access in designated common areas are available to students. Students grades are available online. The school has a published electronic and media policy.

Contact Mrs. Catherine Cullinane, Director of Admission. 203-532-3534. Fax: 203-532-3301. E-mail: admission@cshct.org. Website: www.cshgreenwich.org

See Display on next page and Close-Up on page 530.

CONVENT OF THE SACRED HEART

1 East 91st Street
New York, New York 10128-0689

Head of School: Dr. Joseph J. Ciancaglini

General Information Girls' day college-preparatory, arts, religious studies, bilingual studies, and technology school, affiliated with Roman Catholic Church. Grades PK–12. Founded: 1881. Setting: urban. 2 buildings on campus. Approved or accredited by Network of Sacred Heart Schools, New York State Board of Regents, and New York Department of Education. Member of National Association of Independent Schools and Secondary School Admission Test Board. Endowment: $33.8 million. Total enrollment: 700. Upper school average class size: 14. Upper school faculty-student ratio: 1:10. Upper School students typically attend 5 days per week.

Upper School Student Profile Grade 9: 56 students (56 girls); Grade 10: 57 students (57 girls); Grade 11: 45 students (45 girls); Grade 12: 45 students (45 girls). 65% of students are Roman Catholic.

Faculty School total: 110. In upper school: 10 men, 30 women; 38 have advanced degrees.

Subjects Offered Advanced studio art-AP, algebra, American history, American literature, art, audio visual/media, biology, biology-AP, calculus, calculus-AP, campus ministry, ceramics, chemistry, chemistry-AP, chorus, computer applications, computer multimedia, creative writing, dance, desktop publishing, digital photography, drama, earth science, East European studies, English, English-literature, English literature-AP, environmental science, ethics, European history, expository writing, film history, fine arts, finite math, forensics, French, French-AP, functions, geography, geometry, government/civics, handbells, health, history, journalism, Latin, madrigals, mathematics, model United Nations, multicultural literature, multimedia design, music, musical theater, performing arts, photography, physical education, physical science, physics, physics-AP, portfolio art, pottery, pre-calculus, religion, science, science research, social studies, Spanish, Spanish-AP, speech, statistics, statistics-AP, theater, theology, trigonometry, U.S. history-AP, visual arts, women's literature, world history, world issues, world literature, world religions, writing.

Graduation Requirements Arts and fine arts (art, music, dance, drama), computer science, English, foreign language, history, mathematics, physical education (includes health), religion (includes Bible studies and theology), science, social studies (includes history).

Special Academic Programs 18 Advanced Placement exams for which test preparation is offered; honors section; independent study; term-away projects; domestic exchange program (with Network of Sacred Heart Schools); study abroad.

College Admission Counseling 48 students graduated in 2013; all went to college, including Colgate University; Cornell University; Dartmouth College; Georgetown University; Stanford University; Wake Forest University. Mean SAT critical reading: 698, mean SAT math: 669.

Student Life Upper grades have uniform requirement, student council. Discipline rests primarily with faculty. Attendance at religious services is required.

Summer Programs Sports, art/fine arts, computer instruction programs offered; session focuses on visual and performing arts; held on campus; accepts boys and girls; open to students from other schools. 200 students usually enrolled. 2014 schedule: June 25 to July 25. Application deadline: April 15.

Tuition and Aid Day student tuition: $41,040. Tuition installment plan (monthly payment plans). Need-based scholarship grants available. In 2013–14, 38% of upper-school students received aid. Total amount of financial aid awarded in 2013–14: $2,300,000.

Admissions Traditional secondary-level entrance grade is 9. For fall 2013, 200 students applied for upper-level admission, 35 were accepted, 16 enrolled. ERB or ISEE required. Deadline for receipt of application materials: December 1. Application fee required: $65. On-campus interview required.

Athletics Interscholastic: basketball, cross-country running, indoor track & field, lacrosse, soccer, softball, swimming and diving, tennis, track and field, volleyball, winter (indoor) track; intramural: aerobics/dance, aquatics, ballet, basketball, dance, fitness, gymnastics, jogging, physical training, roller blading, running, soccer, softball, swimming and diving, tennis, track and field, volleyball, weight lifting, weight training. 8 PE instructors, 8 coaches, 1 athletic trainer.

Computers Computers are regularly used in all academic classes. Computer network features include on-campus library services, online commercial services, Internet access, wireless campus network, Internet filtering or blocking technology. Campus intranet, student e-mail accounts, and computer access in designated common areas are available to students. The school has a published electronic and media policy.

Contact Amanda Rosenthal, Admissions Office Coordinator. 212-722-4745 Ext. 105. Fax: 212-996-1784. E-mail: arosenthal@cshnyc.org. Website: www.cshnyc.org

COPPER CANYON ACADEMY

Rimrock, Arizona
See Special Needs Schools section.

COTTER SCHOOLS

1115 West Broadway
Winona, Minnesota 55987-1399

Head of School: Sr. Judith Schaefer, OP

General Information Coeducational boarding and day college-preparatory, general academic, arts, religious studies, technology, and ESL school, affiliated with Roman Catholic Church. Boarding grades 9–12, day grades 7–12. Founded: 1911. Setting: small town. Nearest major city is Minneapolis. Students are housed in single-sex by floor dormitories. 75-acre campus. 7 buildings on campus. Approved or accredited by Midwest Association of Boarding Schools, National Catholic Education Association, North Central Association of Colleges and Schools, The Association of Boarding Schools, and Minnesota Department of Education. Endowment: $15 million. Total enrollment: 343. Upper school average class size: 18. Upper school faculty-student ratio: 1:11. There are 176 required school days per year for Upper School students. Upper School students typically attend 5 days per week. The average school day consists of 5 hours and 55 minutes.

Upper School Student Profile Grade 9: 61 students (31 boys, 30 girls); Grade 10: 55 students (30 boys, 25 girls); Grade 11: 78 students (35 boys, 43 girls); Grade 12: 65 students (31 boys, 34 girls). 31% of students are boarding students. 65% are state residents. 4 states are represented in upper school student body. 30% are international students. International students from China, Japan, Mexico, Republic of Korea, Taiwan, and Viet Nam; 7 other countries represented in student body. 66% of students are Roman Catholic.

Faculty School total: 36. In upper school: 17 men, 19 women; 32 have advanced degrees; 3 reside on campus.

Subjects Offered Algebra, American history, anatomy, art, band, Bible, biology, calculus, calculus-AP, campus ministry, chemistry, chorus, Christian and Hebrew scripture, Christian ethics, community service, computer science, death and loss, economics, English, environmental science, ESL, German, health, Hebrew scripture, honors English, learning lab, linear algebra, literature and composition-AP, math analysis, mathematics, media, painting, physical education, physical science, physics, psychology, science, Spanish, statistics, U.S. history, U.S. history-AP, visual arts, world geography, world religions.

Graduation Requirements English, foreign language, mathematics, performing arts, physical education (includes health), religion (includes Bible studies and theology), science, social studies (includes history), visual arts, 80 hours of community service.

Special Academic Programs 13 Advanced Placement exams for which test preparation is offered; honors section; accelerated programs; independent study; term-away projects; study at local college for college credit; study abroad; academic accommodation for the gifted, the musically talented, and the artistically talented; remedial reading and/or remedial writing; remedial math; programs in English, mathematics for dyslexic students; ESL (25 students enrolled).

College Admission Counseling 85 students graduated in 2013; 84 went to college, including Saint John's University; Saint Mary's University of Minnesota; University of Illinois at Urbana–Champaign; University of Minnesota, Twin Cities Campus; University of St. Thomas; University of Wisconsin–Madison. Other: 1 had other specific plans. Median combined SAT: 1722, median composite ACT: 24. 50% scored over 26 on composite ACT.

Student Life Upper grades have specified standards of dress, student council. Discipline rests primarily with faculty. Attendance at religious services is required.

Summer Programs Remediation, enrichment, advancement, sports, art/fine arts programs offered; held on campus; accepts boys and girls; open to students from other schools. 150 students usually enrolled. 2014 schedule: June 5 to July 25.

Tuition and Aid Day student tuition: $6075; 5-day tuition and room/board: $25,850; 7-day tuition and room/board: $31,800. Tuition installment plan (FACTS Tuition Payment Plan, monthly payment plans, individually arranged payment plans). Tuition reduction for siblings, merit scholarship grants, need-based scholarship grants available. In 2013–14, 60% of upper-school students received aid.

Admissions Traditional secondary-level entrance grade is 9. For fall 2013, 81 students applied for upper-level admission, 56 were accepted, 36 enrolled. SLEP for foreign students or TOEFL required. Deadline for receipt of application materials: none. Application fee required: $100. Interview required.

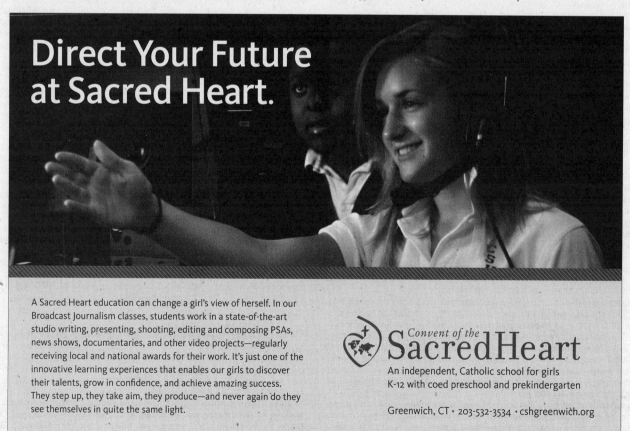

Athletics Interscholastic: aerobics/dance (girls), baseball (b), basketball (b,g), cheering (g), cross-country running (b,g), dance (g), dance team (g), danceline (g), football (g), gymnastics (g), hockey (b,g), ice hockey (b,g), skiing (cross-country) (b,g), soccer (b,g), softball (g), swimming and diving (b,g), tennis (b,g), track and field (b,g), volleyball (g), weight lifting (b,g), weight training (b,g), wrestling (b); intramural: basketball (b,g), indoor soccer (b), skiing (downhill) (b,g), snowboarding (b,g), yoga (b,g); coed interscholastic: weight lifting, weight training; coed intramural: alpine skiing, badminton, basketball, canoeing/kayaking, curling, indoor soccer, skiing (downhill), snowboarding, yoga. 2 PE instructors, 66 coaches, 1 athletic trainer.

Computers Computers are regularly used in art, freshman foundations, graphic arts, graphic design, introduction to technology, journalism, photography, technology, video film production classes. Computer network features include on-campus library services, Internet access, wireless campus network, Internet filtering or blocking technology. Campus intranet, student e-mail accounts, and computer access in designated common areas are available to students. Students grades are available online. The school has a published electronic and media policy.

Contact Mr. Will Gibson, Director of Admissions. 507-453-5403. Fax: 507-453-5006. E-mail: wgibson@cotterschools.org. Website: www.cotterschools.org

THE COUNTRY DAY SCHOOL

13415 Dufferin Street
King City, Ontario L7B 1K5, Canada
Head of School: Mr. John Liggett

General Information Coeducational day college-preparatory, arts, business, and technology school. Grades JK–12. Founded: 1972. Setting: rural. Nearest major city is Toronto, Canada. 100-acre campus. 2 buildings on campus. Approved or accredited by Canadian Association of Independent Schools, Canadian Educational Standards Institute, Conference of Independent Schools of Ontario, and Ontario Department of Education. Affiliate member of National Association of Independent Schools. Language of instruction: English. Total enrollment: 700. Upper school average class size: 17. Upper school faculty-student ratio: 1:9. Upper School students typically attend 5 days per week. The average school day consists of 6 hours and 25 minutes.

Upper School Student Profile Grade 9: 75 students (30 boys, 45 girls); Grade 10: 75 students (30 boys, 45 girls); Grade 11: 75 students (30 boys, 45 girls); Grade 12: 75 students (30 boys, 45 girls).

Faculty School total: 81. In upper school: 28 men, 20 women.

Subjects Offered Advanced chemistry, advanced computer applications, advanced math, algebra, American history, anatomy and physiology, ancient history, ancient/medieval philosophy, art and culture, art history, athletics, band, biology, business studies, Canadian geography, Canadian history, Canadian literature, career education, career/college preparation, choir, comparative politics, computer programming, creative writing, English, environmental geography, European history, French, government/civics, history, languages, mathematics, modern Western civilization, performing arts, philosophy, physical education, physics, politics, science, society, world history.

Graduation Requirements Ministry Grade 10 Literacy Test (Government of Ontario).

Special Academic Programs Advanced Placement exam preparation; study abroad.

College Admission Counseling 74 students graduated in 2013; 72 went to college, including McGill University; McMaster University; Queen's University at Kingston; The University of Western Ontario; University of Toronto; Wilfrid Laurier University. Other: 2 had other specific plans.

Student Life Upper grades have uniform requirement, student council, honor system. Discipline rests primarily with faculty.

Summer Programs Advancement, sports, art/fine arts programs offered; session focuses on advancement; held both on and off campus; held at Costa Rica, England, and Greece & Italy; accepts boys and girls; open to students from other schools. 20 students usually enrolled. 2014 schedule: July 2 to July 31. Application deadline: March 1.

Tuition and Aid Day student tuition: CAN$25,300. Bursaries, need-based scholarship grants available.

Admissions Traditional secondary-level entrance grade is 9. For fall 2013, 97 students applied for upper-level admission, 58 were accepted, 37 enrolled. CAT 5 or SSAT required. Deadline for receipt of application materials: none. Application fee required: CAN$125. On-campus interview required.

Athletics Interscholastic: baseball (girls), basketball (b,g), cross-country running (b,g), golf (b,g), hockey (b,g), ice hockey (b,g), rugby (b,g), running (b,g), soccer (b,g), softball (b,g), tennis (b,g), track and field (b,g), volleyball (b,g); intramural: badminton (b,g), basketball (b,g), bowling (b,g), ice hockey (b), ice skating (b,g), physical fitness (b,g), skiing (downhill) (b,g), snowboarding (b,g), soccer (b,g), softball (b,g), volleyball (b,g); coed interscholastic: skiing (cross-country); coed intramural: curling, Frisbee, mountain biking, nordic skiing, outdoor activities, outdoor education, physical fitness, physical training, strength & conditioning, swimming and diving, table tennis, weight training, yoga. 5 PE instructors.

Computers Computers are regularly used in accounting, business, career education, English, geography, history, mathematics, media, music, writing, yearbook classes. Computer network features include on-campus library services, Internet access, wireless campus network, Internet filtering or blocking technology, access to online library resources from home, access to homework online via Blackboard Software. Campus intranet is available to students.

Contact Mr. David Huckvale, Director of Admission. 905-833-1220. Fax: 905-833-1350. E-mail: admissions@cds.on.ca. Website: www.cds.on.ca/

COUNTRY DAY SCHOOL OF THE SACRED HEART

480 Bryn Mawr Avenue
Bryn Mawr, Pennsylvania 19010
Head of School: Sr. Matthew Anita MacDonald, SSJ

General Information Girls' day college-preparatory, arts, religious studies, and technology school, affiliated with Roman Catholic Church. Grades PK–12. Founded: 1865. Setting: suburban. Nearest major city is Philadelphia. 16-acre campus. 3 buildings on campus. Approved or accredited by Middle States Association of Colleges and Schools, Network of Sacred Heart Schools, and Pennsylvania Department of Education. Member of National Association of Independent Schools. Total enrollment: 314. Upper school average class size: 15. Upper school faculty-student ratio: 1:8. There are 180 required school days per year for Upper School students. The average school day consists of 7 hours.

Upper School Student Profile Grade 9: 41 students (41 girls); Grade 10: 48 students (48 girls); Grade 11: 40 students (40 girls); Grade 12: 36 students (36 girls). 75% of students are Roman Catholic.

Faculty School total: 44. In upper school: 4 men, 30 women; 23 have advanced degrees.

Subjects Offered Algebra, American history, American history-AP, American literature, art, arts, Bible studies, biology, calculus, chemistry, composition, computer science, economics, English, English literature, environmental science, ethics, European history, film, fine arts, French, geometry, government/civics, health, Latin, mathematics, media studies, physical education, physics, pre-calculus, religion, science, social sciences, social studies, Spanish, trigonometry, word processing, world history, world literature.

Graduation Requirements Arts and fine arts (art, music, dance, drama), English, foreign language, mathematics, physical education (includes health), religion (includes Bible studies and theology), science, social studies (includes history), two weeks of senior independent study with a working professional, 25 hours of community service per year.

Special Academic Programs 7 Advanced Placement exams for which test preparation is offered; honors section; independent study; term-away projects; study at local college for college credit; domestic exchange program (with Network of Sacred Heart Schools); study abroad; academic accommodation for the musically talented.

College Admission Counseling 35 students graduated in 2013; all went to college, including Drexel University; Fordham University; Georgetown University; Saint Joseph's University; The Catholic University of America; University of Pittsburgh. Mean SAT critical reading: 620, mean SAT math: 580, mean SAT writing: 650. 45% scored over 600 on SAT critical reading, 40% scored over 600 on SAT math, 50% scored over 600 on SAT writing.

Student Life Upper grades have uniform requirement, student council. Discipline rests equally with students and faculty. Attendance at religious services is required.

Tuition and Aid Day student tuition: $16,900. Tuition installment plan (SMART Tuition Payment Plan). Tuition reduction for siblings, merit scholarship grants, need-based scholarship grants available. In 2013–14, 72% of upper-school students received aid; total upper-school merit-scholarship money awarded: $415,900. Total amount of financial aid awarded in 2013–14: $424,500.

Admissions Traditional secondary-level entrance grade is 9. For fall 2013, 90 students applied for upper-level admission, 65 were accepted, 32 enrolled. High School Placement Test required. Deadline for receipt of application materials: none. Application fee required: $35. Interview required.

Athletics Interscholastic: basketball, crew, cross-country running, field hockey, golf, lacrosse, softball, tennis, track and field, volleyball; intramural: fitness walking. 2 PE instructors, 12 coaches, 1 athletic trainer.

Computers Computers are regularly used in English, foreign language, history, mathematics, science, technology classes. Computer network features include on-campus library services, online commercial services, Internet access, wireless campus network. Student e-mail accounts are available to students. Students grades are available online. The school has a published electronic and media policy.

Contact Mrs. Mary Lee FitzPatrick, Director of Admissions. 610-527-3915 Ext. 214. Fax: 610-527-0942. E-mail: mfitzpatrick@cdssh.org. Website: www.cdssh.org

COVENANT CANADIAN REFORMED SCHOOL

3030 TWP Road 615A
PO Box 67
Neerlandia, Alberta T0G 1R0, Canada
Head of School: Mr. James Meinen

General Information Coeducational day college-preparatory, general academic, business, religious studies, and technology school, affiliated with Reformed Church. Grades K–12. Founded: 1977. Setting: rural. Nearest major city is Edmonton, Canada. 5-acre campus. 2 buildings on campus. Approved or accredited by Association of

Independent Schools and Colleges of Alberta and Alberta Department of Education. Language of instruction: English. Total enrollment: 221. Upper school average class size: 10. Upper school faculty-student ratio: 1:10. There are 167 required school days per year for Upper School students. Upper School students typically attend 4 days per week. The average school day consists of 6 hours and 10 minutes.

Upper School Student Profile Grade 10: 11 students (7 boys, 4 girls); Grade 11: 8 students (3 boys, 5 girls); Grade 12: 9 students (6 boys, 3 girls). 100% of students are Reformed.

Faculty School total: 16. In upper school: 6 men, 3 women.

Subjects Offered Accounting, architectural drawing, Bible studies, biology, Canadian geography, career and personal planning, career technology, chemistry, child development, Christian education, computer information systems, computer skills, computer studies, consumer law, desktop publishing, digital photography, drama, drawing and design, early childhood, electronic publishing, English, ESL, French as a second language, geology, health education, history, HTML design, information processing, intro to computers, introduction to technology, keyboarding, mathematics, physical education, physics, prayer/spirituality, religious studies, science, sewing, social studies, theology and the arts, Web site design, Western religions, work experience, world geography, world religions, yearbook.

Graduation Requirements Must pass religious studies courses offered in grades 10, 11, and 12 for years attended.

Special Academic Programs Independent study; remedial reading and/or remedial writing; remedial math.

College Admission Counseling 10 students graduated in 2013; 3 went to college, including University of Alberta; University of Calgary; University of Lethbridge. Other: 7 went to work.

Student Life Upper grades have specified standards of dress, student council. Discipline rests primarily with faculty.

Tuition and Aid Day student tuition: CAN$6900. Tuition installment plan (monthly payment plans, individually arranged payment plans). Tuition rates per family available.

Admissions Traditional secondary-level entrance grade is 10. Achievement tests or CTBS or ERB required. Deadline for receipt of application materials: none. No application fee required. Interview required.

Athletics Interscholastic: track and field (boys, girls), volleyball (b,g); coed intramural: badminton, ball hockey, baseball, basketball, flag football, floor hockey, football, Frisbee, hockey, ice hockey, indoor hockey, indoor soccer, lacrosse, soccer, softball, volleyball. 4 PE instructors, 6 coaches.

Computers Computers are regularly used in all classes. Computer network features include on-campus library services, Internet access, Internet filtering or blocking technology. Computer access in designated common areas is available to students. The school has a published electronic and media policy.

Contact Mr. James Meinen, Principal. 780-674-4774. Fax: 780-401-3295. E-mail: principal@covenantschool.ca. Website: www.covenantschool.ca/

CRAWFORD ADVENTIST ACADEMY

531 Finch Avenue West
Willowdale, Ontario M2R 3X2, Canada

Head of School: Mr. Norman Brown

General Information Coeducational day college-preparatory, arts, business, religious studies, bilingual studies, and technology school, affiliated with Seventh-day Adventist Church. Grades JK–12. Founded: 1954. Setting: urban. Nearest major city is Toronto, Canada. 5-acre campus. 1 building on campus. Approved or accredited by National Council for Private School Accreditation, Ontario Ministry of Education, and Ontario Department of Education. Language of instruction: English. Total enrollment: 354. Upper school average class size: 25. Upper school faculty-student ratio: 1:16. There are 196 required school days per year for Upper School students. Upper School students typically attend 5 days per week. The average school day consists of 7 hours and 15 minutes.

Upper School Student Profile Grade 9: 32 students (18 boys, 14 girls); Grade 10: 35 students (16 boys, 19 girls); Grade 11: 39 students (19 boys, 20 girls); Grade 12: 43 students (21 boys, 22 girls). 90% of students are Seventh-day Adventists.

Faculty School total: 18. In upper school: 12 men, 6 women; 12 have advanced degrees.

Subjects Offered Advanced computer applications, band, Bible, biology, business, business technology, calculus, Canadian geography, Canadian history, chemistry, choir, civics, community service, computer applications, computer information systems, drama, dramatic arts, earth and space science, English, English composition, French, French as a second language, geography, guidance, independent study, information technology, marketing, mathematics, physical education, physics, religion, science, writing, yearbook.

Graduation Requirements French as a second language, complete 40 Community Service hours, pass the Ontario Secondary School Literacy Test.

Special Academic Programs 3 Advanced Placement exams for which test preparation is offered; remedial reading and/or remedial writing; programs in English for dyslexic students; ESL.

College Admission Counseling 32 students graduated in 2013; 4 went to college, including Andrews University; Oakwood University; Ryerson University;

University of Toronto; University of Waterloo; York University. Other: 28 entered a postgraduate year. Median composite ACT: 20. 22% scored over 26 on composite ACT.

Student Life Upper grades have uniform requirement, student council, honor system. Discipline rests primarily with faculty. Attendance at religious services is required.

Tuition and Aid Day student tuition: CAN$8500. Tuition installment plan (monthly payment plans, individually arranged payment plans). Tuition reduction for siblings, need-based scholarship grants, paying campus jobs available. In 2013–14, 25% of upper-school students received aid. Total amount of financial aid awarded in 2013–14: CAN$40,000.

Admissions Traditional secondary-level entrance grade is 11. For fall 2013, 5 students applied for upper-level admission, 5 were accepted, 5 enrolled. CAT, CAT 2, CCAT, CTBS (or similar from their school) or Learn Aid Aptitude Test required. Deadline for receipt of application materials: none. Application fee required: CAN$50. On-campus interview required.

Athletics Interscholastic: basketball (boys, girls), weight lifting (b,g); intramural: basketball (b,g); coed interscholastic: cooperative games, outdoor recreation; coed intramural: basketball, flag football, floor hockey, indoor soccer, outdoor education, outdoor recreation, physical fitness, physical training, snowboarding, soccer, volleyball. 1 PE instructor, 2 coaches.

Computers Computers are regularly used in accounting, business, computer applications, yearbook classes. Computer network features include Internet access, wireless campus network, Internet filtering or blocking technology. Student e-mail accounts and computer access in designated common areas are available to students. Students grades are available online. The school has a published electronic and media policy.

Contact Mr. Andrew Mark Thomas, Principal, 9-12. 416-633-0090 Ext. 223. Fax: 416-633-0467. E-mail: athomas@caasda.com. Website: www.tadsb.com/

THE CRENSHAW SCHOOL

2342 Hempel Ave.
Gotha, Florida 34734

Head of School: Mrs. Brenda Crenshaw

General Information Coeducational day college-preparatory school. Grades PK–12. Founded: 1999. Setting: suburban. Nearest major city is Orlando. 1 building on campus. Approved or accredited by Association of Independent Schools of Florida, National Council for Private School Accreditation, and Florida Department of Education. Total enrollment: 102. Upper school average class size: 10. Upper school faculty-student ratio: 1:10. There are 180 required school days per year for Upper School students. Upper School students typically attend 5 days per week. The average school day consists of 6 hours.

Faculty School total: 18. In upper school: 2 men, 6 women; 3 have advanced degrees.

Subjects Offered 1968.

Special Academic Programs ESL (10 students enrolled).

College Admission Counseling Colleges students went to include University of Central Florida.

Student Life Upper grades have specified standards of dress, student council, honor system. Discipline rests equally with students and faculty.

Admissions Application fee required: $250. Interview required.

Computers Computer resources include wireless campus network. Students grades are available online.

Contact Mrs. Brenda Crenshaw, Director. 407-877-7412. Fax: 407-877-0541. E-mail: bcrenshaw@crenshawschool.com. Website: www.crenshawschool.com/

CRESPI CARMELITE HIGH SCHOOL

5031 Alonzo Avenue
Encino, California 91316-3699

Head of School: Dr. Jonathan Schild, EdD

General Information Boys' day college-preparatory, arts, and religious studies school, affiliated with Roman Catholic Church. Grades 9–12. Founded: 1959. Setting: suburban. Nearest major city is Los Angeles. 3-acre campus. 3 buildings on campus. Approved or accredited by Western Association of Schools and Colleges, Western Catholic Education Association, and California Department of Education. Total enrollment: 517. Upper school average class size: 23. Upper school faculty-student ratio: 1:14. There are 182 required school days per year for Upper School students. Upper School students typically attend 5 days per week. The average school day consists of 6 hours.

Upper School Student Profile Grade 9: 128 students (128 boys); Grade 10: 132 students (132 boys); Grade 11: 123 students (123 boys); Grade 12: 134 students (134 boys). 59% of students are Roman Catholic.

Faculty School total: 37. In upper school: 33 men, 4 women; 29 have advanced degrees.

Subjects Offered Advanced Placement courses, advanced studio art-AP, algebra, American history-AP, American literature-AP, anatomy and physiology, Ancient Greek, ancient world history, applied music, ASB Leadership, astronomy, athletic training, audio visual/media, baseball, Basic programming, basketball, biology, biology-AP,

British literature, British literature-AP, business mathematics, calculus, calculus-AP, chemistry, Christian scripture, church history, classical Greek literature, computer graphics, constitutional law, drama performance, driver education, earth science, economics and history, economics-AP, English composition, English literature and composition-AP, environmental science, ethics, European history-AP, film studies, French language-AP, French-AP, geometry, golf, government, government and politics-AP, Greek, Greek culture, health, history of the Catholic Church, Holocaust, Holocaust studies, honors English, honors geometry, international studies, journalism, language and composition, Latin-AP, law, media arts, men's studies, model United Nations, moral and social development, music appreciation, music composition, photography, physical science, physics-AP, prayer/spirituality, pre-calculus, probability and statistics, psychology, Shakespeare, social justice, Spanish, Spanish language-AP, Spanish literature-AP, Spanish-AP, speech, sports, sports conditioning, statistics-AP, student government, student publications, U.S. history, U.S. history-AP, video film production, Vietnam War, visual arts, Web site design, weight training, Western civilization, Western religions, world cultures, world geography, world religions, yearbook, zoology.

Graduation Requirements Arts and fine arts (art, music, dance, drama), English, foreign language, mathematics, physical education (includes health), religion (includes Bible studies and theology), science, social sciences, social studies (includes history). Community service is required.

Special Academic Programs 13 Advanced Placement exams for which test preparation is offered; honors section.

College Admission Counseling 129 students graduated in 2013; 122 went to college, including California Polytechnic State University, San Luis Obispo; California State University, Northridge; University of California, Los Angeles; University of California, Santa Barbara; University of San Diego. Other: 1 entered military service, 6 had other specific plans. Mean SAT critical reading: 530, mean SAT math: 540, mean SAT writing: 534.

Student Life Upper grades have specified standards of dress, student council, honor system. Discipline rests primarily with faculty. Attendance at religious services is required.

Summer Programs Remediation, enrichment, advancement, sports, art/fine arts programs offered; session focuses on remediation and/or enrichment in math, science, language, and social studies; held on campus; accepts boys and girls; open to students from other schools. 250 students usually enrolled. 2014 schedule: June 23 to July 25. Application deadline: June 20.

Tuition and Aid Day student tuition: $12,000. Tuition installment plan (FACTS Tuition Payment Plan, Tuition Management Systems Plan). Merit scholarship grants, need-based scholarship grants available. In 2013–14, 32% of upper-school students received aid; total upper-school merit-scholarship money awarded: $48,600.

Admissions Traditional secondary-level entrance grade is 9. For fall 2013, 295 students applied for upper-level admission, 286 were accepted, 128 enrolled. High School Placement Test required. Deadline for receipt of application materials: January 24. Application fee required: $95. On-campus interview required.

Athletics Interscholastic: aquatics, baseball, basketball, cross-country running, football, golf, lacrosse, soccer, swimming and diving, tennis, track and field, volleyball, water polo, wrestling; intramural: basketball, floor hockey, Frisbee, table tennis.

Computers Computers are regularly used in business applications, business studies, economics, English, foreign language, history, mathematics, media production, science, video film production, yearbook classes. Computer network features include on-campus library services, online commercial services, Internet access, wireless campus network. Students grades are available online. The school has a published electronic and media policy.

Contact Ms. Michele Enich, Assistant Admissions Director. 818-345-1672 Ext. 329. Fax: 818-705-0209. E-mail: menich@crespi.org. Website: www.crespi.org

CRETIN-DERHAM HALL

550 South Albert Street
Saint Paul, Minnesota 55116

Head of School: Mr. Richard Engler

General Information Coeducational day college-preparatory, general academic, arts, business, religious studies, technology, and Junior ROTC school, affiliated with Roman Catholic Church. Grades 9–12. Founded: 1987. Setting: urban. Nearest major city is St. Paul. 15-acre campus. 5 buildings on campus. Approved or accredited by Academy of Orton-Gillingham Practitioners and Educators and North Central Association of Colleges and Schools. Total enrollment: 1,317. Upper school average class size: 22. Upper school faculty-student ratio: 1:17. The average school day consists of 5 hours and 25 minutes.

Upper School Student Profile Grade 9: 331 students (174 boys, 157 girls); Grade 10: 337 students (180 boys, 157 girls); Grade 11: 324 students (170 boys, 154 girls); Grade 12: 326 students (159 boys, 167 girls). 89% of students are Roman Catholic.

Faculty School total: 120. In upper school: 56 men, 64 women; 61 have advanced degrees.

Subjects Offered 3-dimensional art, aerobics, algebra, American history, American literature, analysis, art history, arts, audio visual/media, biology, business, chemistry, computer math, computer programming, computer science, drama, economics, English,

environmental science, ethics, fine arts, French, geography, geometry, German, government/civics, history, JROTC, Latin, mathematics, music, physical education, physics, religion, science, social studies, Spanish, speech, theater, theology, trigonometry, U.S. government and politics-AP, yearbook.

Graduation Requirements Arts and fine arts (art, music, dance, drama), English, foreign language, health science, mathematics, physical education (includes health), religion (includes Bible studies and theology), science, social studies (includes history).

Special Academic Programs 11 Advanced Placement exams for which test preparation is offered; honors section; accelerated programs; independent study; study at local college for college credit; academic accommodation for the gifted; remedial reading and/or remedial writing; remedial math; programs in English, mathematics, general development for dyslexic students; special instructional classes for deaf students, blind students.

College Admission Counseling 329 students graduated in 2013; 320 went to college, including College of Saint Benedict; University of Minnesota, Twin Cities Campus; University of St. Thomas; University of Wisconsin–Madison. Other: 1 entered military service, 8 had other specific plans.

Student Life Upper grades have uniform requirement, student council. Discipline rests primarily with faculty. Attendance at religious services is required.

Summer Programs Remediation, enrichment, sports, art/fine arts, rigorous outdoor training, computer instruction programs offered; session focuses on enrichment; held on campus; accepts boys and girls; open to students from other schools. 500 students usually enrolled. 2014 schedule: June 7 to August 13. Application deadline: none.

Tuition and Aid Day student tuition: $11,000. Tuition installment plan (monthly payment plans, individually arranged payment plans, 2- and 3-payment plans). Need-based scholarship grants, paying campus jobs available. In 2013–14, 55% of upper-school students received aid. Total amount of financial aid awarded in 2013–14: $2,500,000.

Admissions Traditional secondary-level entrance grade is 9. For fall 2013, 475 students applied for upper-level admission, 425 were accepted, 330 enrolled. STS required. Deadline for receipt of application materials: none. No application fee required.

Athletics Interscholastic: baseball (boys), basketball (b,g), cross-country running (b,g), dance team (g), diving (b,g), figure skating (g), football (b), golf (b,g), gymnastics (g), ice hockey (b,g), lacrosse (b,g), riflery (b,g), skiing (downhill) (b,g), soccer (b,g), softball (g), swimming and diving (b,g), tennis (b,g), track and field (b,g), ultimate Frisbee (b,g), volleyball (g), yoga (b); intramural: dance team (g); coed interscholastic: alpine skiing, badminton, cheering, fencing, JROTC drill; coed intramural: basketball, bowling, drill team, fencing, Frisbee, physical training, snowboarding, strength & conditioning, table tennis, ultimate Frisbee, volleyball, weight lifting. 5 PE instructors, 50 coaches, 1 athletic trainer.

Computers Computers are regularly used in all academic, data processing, publications, yearbook classes. Computer network features include on-campus library services, online commercial services, Internet access, wireless campus network, Internet filtering or blocking technology, check assignments and contact faculty. Campus intranet and student e-mail accounts are available to students. Students grades are available online. The school has a published electronic and media policy.

Contact Tony Leseman, Admissions Director. 651-690-2443 Ext. 302. Fax: 651-696-3394. E-mail: tleseman@c-dh.org. Website: www.c-dh.org

CROSSPOINT ACADEMY

4012 Chico Way NW
Bremerton, Washington 98312-1397

Head of School: Mr. Nick Sweeney

General Information Coeducational day college-preparatory, arts, religious studies, and technology school, affiliated with Christian faith. Grades K–12. Founded: 1991. Setting: small town. Nearest major city is Silverdale. 7-acre campus. 7 buildings on campus. Approved or accredited by Washington Department of Education. Member of National Association of Independent Schools. Total enrollment: 253. Upper school average class size: 24. Upper school faculty-student ratio: 1:8. There are 171 required school days per year for Upper School students. Upper School students typically attend 5 days per week. The average school day consists of 6 hours and 45 minutes.

Upper School Student Profile 70% of students are Christian faith.

Faculty School total: 30. In upper school: 6 men, 10 women; 8 have advanced degrees.

Subjects Offered Algebra, American literature, art, band, Bible, biology, calculus-AP, chemistry, choir, computer animation, computers, creative writing, desktop publishing, digital photography, drama, drama performance, earth science, English, geography, geometry, health, introduction to theater, keyboarding, leadership, life science, life skills, physical fitness, physical science, physics, practical living, pre-algebra, pre-calculus, programming, religion, science, senior project, Spanish, speech, student government, technology, U.S. government and politics-AP, U.S. history, U.S. history-AP, video, vocal ensemble, Washington State and Northwest History, weight training, world history, world literature, world religions, world wide web design, yearbook.

Graduation Requirements Arts and fine arts (art, music, dance, drama), Bible, computer science, English, foreign language, mathematics, physical education (includes health), practical living, science, social studies (includes history), speech.

Special Academic Programs Honors section; study at local college for college credit.

College Admission Counseling 23 students graduated in 2012; all went to college, including Baylor University; Central Washington University; Georgia Institute of Technology; Olympic College; Seattle Pacific University; University of Washington. Mean SAT critical reading: 578, mean SAT math: 569, mean SAT writing: 557, mean combined SAT: 1704, mean composite ACT: 24. 36% scored over 600 on SAT critical reading, 24% scored over 600 on SAT math, 36% scored over 600 on SAT writing, 36% scored over 1800 on combined SAT, 14% scored over 26 on composite ACT.

Student Life Upper grades have specified standards of dress, student council, honor system. Discipline rests primarily with faculty. Attendance at religious services is required.

Tuition and Aid Day student tuition: $9430. Tuition installment plan (monthly payment plans, prepayment discount plan, active military discount, Pastor, church employee, and Christian school employee discounts). Tuition reduction for siblings, need-based scholarship grants available. In 2012–13, 28% of upper-school students received aid. Total amount of financial aid awarded in 2012–13: $171,000.

Admissions Traditional secondary-level entrance grade is 9. Comprehensive educational evaluation required. Deadline for receipt of application materials: none. Application fee required: $50. Interview required.

Athletics Interscholastic: basketball (boys, girls), cross-country running (b,g), golf (b), soccer (b,g), softball (g), track and field (b,g), volleyball (g), weight training (b,g). 2 PE instructors, 8 coaches.

Computers Computers are regularly used in animation, computer applications, desktop publishing, digital applications, graphics, keyboarding, photography, publications, technology, video film production, Web site design, yearbook classes. Computer network features include Internet access, wireless campus network, Internet filtering or blocking technology. Student e-mail accounts are available to students. Students grades are available online. The school has a published electronic and media policy.

Contact Ms. Sherri M. Miller, Admissions and Marketing Coordinator. 360-377-7700 Ext. 5004. Fax: 360-377-7795. E-mail: sherri.miller@gatewaychristianschools.org. Website: www.gatewaychristianschools.org/

CROSSROADS SCHOOL FOR ARTS & SCIENCES

1714 21st Street
Santa Monica, California 90404-3917

Head of School: Bob Riddle

General Information Coeducational day college-preparatory, arts, and technology school. Grades K–12. Founded: 1971. Setting: urban. Nearest major city is Los Angeles. 3-acre campus. 19 buildings on campus. Approved or accredited by Western Association of Schools and Colleges and California Department of Education. Member of National Association of Independent Schools. Endowment: $16.5 million. Total enrollment: 1,159. Upper school average class size: 15. Upper school faculty-student ratio: 1:11. There are 164 required school days per year for Upper School students. Upper School students typically attend 5 days per week. The average school day consists of 7 hours.

Upper School Student Profile Grade 9: 132 students (68 boys, 64 girls); Grade 10: 133 students (65 boys, 68 girls); Grade 11: 123 students (65 boys, 58 girls); Grade 12: 122 students (52 boys, 70 girls).

Faculty School total: 156. In upper school: 34 men, 37 women; 42 have advanced degrees.

Subjects Offered Algebra, American history, American studies, art history, biology, calculus, ceramics, chemistry, community service, computer programming, computer science, creative writing, critical studies in film, cultural arts, dance, earth and space science, English, environmental education, film studies, French, gender issues, geometry, graphic design, great books, Greek, human development, Japanese, jazz ensemble, jazz theory, journalism, Latin, marine biology, marine ecology, music appreciation, music theory, orchestra, photography, physical education, physics, physiology, pre-calculus, sculpture, Spanish, statistics, studio art, theater, trigonometry, video film production, world civilizations, yoga.

Graduation Requirements Arts and fine arts (art, music, dance, drama), English, foreign language, human development, mathematics, physical education (includes health), science, social studies (includes history), community service hours, Senior Project. Community service is required.

Special Academic Programs Honors section; term-away projects; academic accommodation for the gifted, the musically talented, and the artistically talented.

College Admission Counseling 130 students graduated in 2013; 125 went to college, including Boston University; New York University; Stanford University; University of Michigan; University of Southern California; Yale University. Mean SAT critical reading: 638, mean SAT math: 619, mean SAT writing: 657, mean combined SAT: 1914, mean composite ACT: 27. 67% scored over 600 on SAT critical reading, 54% scored over 600 on SAT math, 77% scored over 600 on SAT writing, 69% scored over 1800 on combined SAT, 55% scored over 26 on composite ACT.

Student Life Upper grades have student council. Discipline rests primarily with faculty.

Summer Programs Remediation, enrichment, advancement, sports, art/fine arts, computer instruction programs offered; session focuses on enrichment, academics, day care, aquatics, arts, musical productions, jazz camp; held on campus; accepts boys and girls; open to students from other schools. 1,000 students usually enrolled. 2014 schedule: June 23 to August 1. Application deadline: March 1.

Tuition and Aid Day student tuition: $33,527. Tuition installment plan (individually arranged payment plans, In-House only - 2 payment plan for full pay students and 10, payment plan exclusively for financial aid students only). Need-based scholarship grants, tuition reduction fund, need-based financial aid available. In 2013–14, 42% of upper-school students received aid. Total amount of financial aid awarded in 2013–14: $2,896,320.

Admissions Traditional secondary-level entrance grade is 9. For fall 2013, 182 students applied for upper-level admission, 60 were accepted, 37 enrolled. ISEE required. Deadline for receipt of application materials: December 4. Application fee required: $150. On-campus interview required.

Athletics Interscholastic: baseball (boys), basketball (b,g), cross-country running (b,g), soccer (b,g), softball (g), tennis (b,g), track and field (b,g), volleyball (b,g); coed interscholastic: flag football, golf, swimming and diving; coed intramural: canoeing/kayaking, climbing, hiking/backpacking, kayaking, outdoor activities, outdoor education, rock climbing, ropes courses, snowshoeing, table tennis. 9 PE instructors, 60 coaches, 2 athletic trainers.

Computers Computers are regularly used in college planning, creative writing, foreign language, graphic design, journalism, Latin, mathematics, music, newspaper, programming, science classes. Computer network features include on-campus library services, online commercial services, Internet access, wireless campus network. Student e-mail accounts and computer access in designated common areas are available to students. Students grades are available online. The school has a published electronic and media policy.

Contact Celia Lee, Director of Admissions. 310-829-7391 Ext. 104. Fax: 310-392-9011. E-mail: clee@xrds.org. Website: www.xrds.org

CRYSTAL SPRINGS UPLANDS SCHOOL

400 Uplands Drive
Hillsborough, California 94010

Head of School: Ms. Amy Richards

General Information Coeducational day college-preparatory school. Grades 6–12. Founded: 1952. Setting: suburban. Nearest major city is San Francisco. 10-acre campus. 4 buildings on campus. Approved or accredited by American Association of Christian Schools, Western Association of Schools and Colleges, and California Department of Education. Member of National Association of Independent Schools and Secondary School Admission Test Board. Endowment: $15 million. Total enrollment: 350. Upper school average class size: 14. Upper school faculty-student ratio: 1:9. Upper School students typically attend 5 days per week. The average school day consists of 7 hours.

Faculty School total: 44. In upper school: 18 men, 26 women; 24 have advanced degrees.

Subjects Offered Acting, advanced computer applications, algebra, American history, American literature, art, astronomy, biology, calculus, ceramics, chamber groups, chemistry, chorus, comparative cultures, computer math, computer programming, computer science, concert bell choir, creative writing, dance, dance performance, drama, English, English literature, ensembles, European history, fine arts, French, geometry, graphic design, health, history, mathematics, multicultural literature, music, photography, physical education, physics, poetry, post-calculus, pre-calculus, science, Shakespeare, Spanish, statistics, theater, video film production, wellness, world history, world literature, writing.

Graduation Requirements Arts and fine arts (art, music, dance, drama), English, foreign language, history, mathematics, physical education (includes health), science, senior project.

Special Academic Programs Honors section; independent study; term-away projects; domestic exchange program; study abroad.

College Admission Counseling 61 students graduated in 2013; all went to college, including Stanford University; University of California, Los Angeles; University of California, San Diego; University of Pennsylvania; University of Southern California. Mean SAT critical reading: 674, mean SAT math: 703, mean SAT writing: 688, mean combined SAT: 2067, mean composite ACT: 29.

Student Life Upper grades have specified standards of dress, student council, honor system. Discipline rests equally with students and faculty.

Tuition and Aid Day student tuition: $37,485. Tuition installment plan (Insured Tuition Payment Plan, monthly payment plans, Tuition Management Systems Plan). Need-based scholarship grants available. In 2013–14, 20% of upper-school students received aid. Total amount of financial aid awarded in 2013–14: $2,200,000.

Admissions Traditional secondary-level entrance grade is 9. For fall 2013, 477 students applied for upper-level admission, 137 were accepted, 77 enrolled. ISEE or SSAT required. Deadline for receipt of application materials: January 16. Application fee required: $85. On-campus interview required.

Athletics Interscholastic: baseball (boys), basketball (b,g), cross-country running (b,g), football (b), soccer (b,g), softball (g), swimming and diving (b,g), tennis (b,g), track and field (b,g), volleyball (g); coed interscholastic: badminton, dance, golf, running, strength & conditioning; coed intramural: dance, fitness, Frisbee, hiking/backpacking, outdoors, rock climbing, table tennis, ultimate Frisbee, weight lifting, weight training. 3 PE instructors, 14 coaches, 1 athletic trainer.

Computers Computers are regularly used in all academic classes. Computer network features include on-campus library services, online commercial services, Internet access, wireless campus network, Internet filtering or blocking technology. Campus intranet, student e-mail accounts, and computer access in designated common areas are available to students. Students grades are available online. The school has a published electronic and media policy.

Contact Admission Office, Admission Office. 650-342-4175. Fax: 650-342-7611. E-mail: admission@csus.org. Website: www.csus.org

THE CULVER ACADEMIES

1300 Academy Road
Culver, Indiana 46511

Head of School: Mr. John N. Buxton

General Information Coeducational boarding and day college-preparatory, arts, and business school. Grades 9–PG. Founded: 1894. Setting: small town. Nearest major city is South Bend. Students are housed in single-sex dormitories. 1,700-acre campus. 38 buildings on campus. Approved or accredited by Independent Schools Association of the Central States, North Central Association of Colleges and Schools, and Indiana Department of Education. Member of National Association of Independent Schools and Secondary School Admission Test Board. Endowment: $305 million. Total enrollment: 802. Upper school average class size: 13. Upper school faculty-student ratio: 1:9. There are 185 required school days per year for Upper School students. Upper School students typically attend 5 days per week. The average school day consists of 6 hours.

Upper School Student Profile Grade 9: 150 students (86 boys, 64 girls); Grade 10: 215 students (123 boys, 92 girls); Grade 11: 225 students (118 boys, 107 girls); Grade 12: 212 students (121 boys, 91 girls). 92% of students are boarding students. 30% are state residents. 41 states are represented in upper school student body. 32% are international students. International students from Canada, China, Mexico, Republic of Korea, Saudi Arabia, and Taiwan; 26 other countries represented in student body.

Faculty School total: 97. In upper school: 53 men, 44 women; 83 have advanced degrees; 16 reside on campus.

Subjects Offered Acting, advanced math, African-American history, algebra, American government, American history, American history-AP, American literature, anatomy, anatomy and physiology, art, art history, arts, ballet, Basic programming, biology, biology-AP, calculus, calculus-AP, career/college preparation, ceramics, character education, chemistry, chemistry-AP, Chinese, choir, church history, college admission preparation, college placement, college planning, comparative government and politics-AP, comparative religion, computer math, computer programming, computer science, computer science-AP, dance, drama, dramatic arts, driver education, economics, economics-AP, English, English language-AP, English literature, entrepreneurship, equestrian sports, equine science, equitation, ESL, ethics and responsibility, European history, film studies, fine arts, fitness, French, French-AP, geology, geometry, German, German literature, German-AP, global studies, government, government-AP, government/civics, health and wellness, honors English, honors geometry, humanities, instrumental music, integrated mathematics, integrated science, jazz band, Latin, Latin-AP, leadership, library research, macro/microeconomics-AP, mathematics, mentorship program, music, music theory, music theory-AP, photography, physical education, physics, physics-AP, physiology, piano, play production, pottery, pre-algebra, pre-calculus, science, science research, Shakespeare, social studies, Spanish, Spanish language-AP, Spanish-AP, speech, statistics-AP, strings, theater, trigonometry, U.S. government and politics-AP, U.S. history-AP, world history, world religions.

Graduation Requirements Arts and fine arts (art, music, dance, drama), English, foreign language, health education, history, leadership, mathematics, science, senior community service project.

Special Academic Programs 25 Advanced Placement exams for which test preparation is offered; honors section; study abroad; academic accommodation for the gifted, the musically talented, and the artistically talented; ESL (24 students enrolled).

College Admission Counseling 204 students graduated in 2013; 197 went to college, including Indiana University Bloomington; Princeton University; Purdue University; The University of North Carolina at Chapel Hill; United States Military Academy. Other: 1 entered military service, 4 entered a postgraduate year, 2 had other specific plans.

Student Life Upper grades have uniform requirement, student council, honor system. Discipline rests equally with students and faculty. Attendance at religious services is required.

Summer Programs Enrichment, advancement, ESL, sports, art/fine arts, rigorous outdoor training, computer instruction programs offered; session focuses on leadership training, citizenship, lifetime interests and skills development; held on campus; accepts boys and girls; open to students from other schools. 1,385 students usually enrolled. 2014 schedule: June 21 to August 1. Application deadline: April 1.

Tuition and Aid Day student tuition: $31,000; 7-day tuition and room/board: $41,000. Tuition installment plan (Key Tuition Payment Plan). Merit scholarship grants, need-based scholarship grants available. In 2013–14, 33% of upper-school students received aid; total upper-school merit-scholarship money awarded: $7,850,000. Total amount of financial aid awarded in 2013–14: $8,900,000.

Admissions Traditional secondary-level entrance grade is 9. For fall 2013, 2,500 students applied for upper-level admission, 528 were accepted, 261 enrolled. SSAT or TOEFL required. Deadline for receipt of application materials: June 1. Application fee required: $30. Interview required.

Athletics Interscholastic: baseball (boys), basketball (b,g), crew (b,g), cross-country running (b,g), diving (b,g), equestrian sports (b,g), fencing (b,g), football (b), golf (b,g), hockey (b,g), horseback riding (b,g), ice hockey (b,g), indoor hockey (b,g), indoor track & field (b,g), lacrosse (b,g), polo (b,g), rugby (b,g), soccer (b,g), softball (g), swimming and diving (b,g), tennis (b,g), track and field (b,g), volleyball (g), winter (indoor) track (b,g), wrestling (b,g); intramural: aerobics (b,g), basketball (b,g), dance (b,g), dance squad (g), dance team (g), danceline (g), drill team (b,g), flag football (b,g), ice hockey (b,g), indoor soccer (b,g), marksmanship (b,g), modern dance (b,g), paint ball (b,g), soccer (b,g); coed interscholastic: cheering, dressage, sailing, trap and skeet; coed intramural: aerobics, aerobics/dance, aerobics/Nautilus, alpine skiing, aquatics, archery, backpacking, badminton, ballet, bicycling, broomball, canoeing/kayaking, climbing, combined training, cooperative games, cross-country running, figure skating, fitness, fitness walking, Frisbee, handball, hiking/backpacking, horseback riding, ice skating, independent competitive sports, indoor track & field, jogging, life saving, Nautilus, outdoor activities, outdoor adventure, outdoor education, outdoor recreation, outdoor skills, outdoors, paddling, physical fitness, physical training, power lifting, project adventure, racquetball, ropes courses, rowing, running, scuba diving, skeet shooting, skiing (downhill), snowboarding, strength & conditioning, swimming and diving, table tennis, tai chi, ultimate Frisbee, volleyball, walking, wall climbing, weight lifting, weight training, wilderness, winter walking, yoga. 8 PE instructors, 4 athletic trainers.

Computers Computers are regularly used in all classes. Computer network features include on-campus library services, online commercial services, Internet access, wireless campus network, Internet filtering or blocking technology, each student is issued a laptop. Campus intranet, student e-mail accounts, and computer access in designated common areas are available to students. Students grades are available online. The school has a published electronic and media policy.

Contact Mr. Michael Turnbull, Director of Admissions. 574-842-7100. Fax: 574-842-8066. E-mail: Michael.Turnbull@culver.org. Website: www.culver.org

CURREY INGRAM ACADEMY

6544 Murray Lane
Brentwood, Tennessee 37027

Head of School: Mr. Paul Wenninger

General Information Coeducational day college-preparatory, arts, technology, ethics and character education, and service learning school; primarily serves students with learning disabilities, individuals with Attention Deficit Disorder, dyslexic students, non-verbal learning disabilities, and speech and language disabilities. Grades K–12. Founded: 1968. Setting: suburban. Nearest major city is Nashville. 83-acre campus. 2 buildings on campus. Approved or accredited by Council of Accreditation and School Improvement, Southern Association of Colleges and Schools, Southern Association of Independent Schools, and Tennessee Department of Education. Member of National Association of Independent Schools. Total enrollment: 301. Upper school average class size: 7. Upper school faculty-student ratio: 1:4. There are 175 required school days per year for Upper School students. Upper School students typically attend 5 days per week. The average school day consists of 7 hours and 30 minutes.

Faculty School total: 122.

Subjects Offered Algebra, American government, art, basic language skills, biology, British literature, character education, chemistry, cinematography, college admission preparation, college awareness, college counseling, college planning, community service, digital music, digital photography, drama performance, earth science, economics, electives, English composition, English literature, environmental science, ethics and responsibility, government, health, history, integrated technology fundamentals, learning strategies, life skills, literature, modern world history, music, newspaper, physical education, physics, pragmatics, pre-calculus, reading/study skills, social studies, sports, studio art, technology, video film production, vocal music, writing, writing workshop, yearbook.

Graduation Requirements Arts and fine arts (art, music, dance, drama), electives, English, ethics, foreign language, mathematics, physical education (includes health), science, social studies (includes history), students who need remediation in reading/writing take reading/writing workshop instead of foreign language, seniors must complete Service Learning credit plus 30 hours of community service.

Special Academic Programs Honors section; independent study; academic accommodation for the gifted, the musically talented, and the artistically talented; remedial reading and/or remedial writing; programs in English, mathematics, general development for dyslexic students.

College Admission Counseling 13 students graduated in 2013; all went to college.

Student Life Upper grades have uniform requirement, student council, honor system. Discipline rests primarily with faculty.

Summer Programs Enrichment, art/fine arts programs offered; session focuses on camp for theatre and music; held on campus; accepts boys and girls; open to students from other schools. 2014 schedule: June.

Tuition and Aid Day student tuition: $34,498–$36,690. Tuition installment plan (Insured Tuition Payment Plan, monthly payment plans). Need-based scholarship grants available. In 2013–14, 35% of upper-school students received aid. Total amount of financial aid awarded in 2013–14: $1,500,000.

Admissions Traditional secondary-level entrance grade is 9. Psychoeducational evaluation required. Deadline for receipt of application materials: none. Application fee required: $250. Interview required.

Athletics Interscholastic: basketball (boys, girls), cheering (g), cross-country running (b,g), dance (b,g), golf (b,g), volleyball (g); intramural: fitness (b,g); coed interscholastic: soccer.

Computers Computers are regularly used in all academic classes. Computer network features include on-campus library services, Internet access, wireless campus network, Internet filtering or blocking technology, iPods for instructional use in classrooms, 1:1 laptop program, assistive technology. Students grades are available online. The school has a published electronic and media policy.

Contact Ms. Amber Cathey, Director of Admission. 615-507-3173 Ext. 244. Fax: 615-507-3170. E-mail: amber.cathey@curreyingram.org. Website: www.curreyingram.org

DAKAR ACADEMY

Rue des Peres Maristes, #69
Dakar, Senegal

Head of School: Joseph M. Rosa

General Information Coeducational boarding and day college-preparatory and general academic school, affiliated with Christian faith. Boarding grades 6–12, day grades K–12. Founded: 1961. Setting: suburban. Students are housed in single-sex dormitories. 6-acre campus. 5 buildings on campus. Approved or accredited by Association of Christian Schools International. Language of instruction: English. Upper school average class size: 20. Upper school faculty-student ratio: 1:6. There are 174 required school days per year for Upper School students. Upper School students typically attend 5 days per week. The average school day consists of 7 hours and 15 minutes.

Upper School Student Profile Grade 6: 10 students (4 boys, 6 girls); Grade 7: 17 students (8 boys, 9 girls); Grade 8: 20 students (8 boys, 12 girls); Grade 9: 15 students (10 boys, 5 girls); Grade 10: 24 students (12 boys, 12 girls); Grade 11: 28 students (20 boys, 8 girls); Grade 12: 36 students (23 boys, 13 girls). 46% of students are boarding students. 75% of students are Christian faith.

Faculty School total: 36. In upper school: 10 men, 14 women; 11 reside on campus.

Special Academic Programs Advanced Placement exam preparation; honors section; accelerated programs; independent study.

College Admission Counseling 42 students graduated in 2012.

Student Life Upper grades have specified standards of dress, honor system. Discipline rests primarily with faculty. Attendance at religious services is required.

Admissions For fall 2012, 24 students applied for upper-level admission, 21 were accepted, 18 enrolled. Deadline for receipt of application materials: none. Application fee required: $300.

Athletics Interscholastic: basketball (boys, girls), soccer (b,g), softball (b), volleyball (b,g); intramural: basketball (b,g), handball (b,g), soccer (b,g), softball (b), volleyball (b,g); coed interscholastic: softball; coed intramural: ultimate Frisbee.

Contact Office Manager. 221-33 832 0682. Fax: 221-33 832 1721. E-mail: office@dakar-academy.org. Website: www.dakar-academy.org

DALLAS CHRISTIAN SCHOOL

1515 Republic Parkway
Mesquite, Texas 75150

Head of School: Mr. Chris King

General Information Coeducational day college-preparatory and religious studies school, affiliated with Church of Christ. Grades PK–12. Founded: 1957. Setting: suburban. Nearest major city is Dallas. 60-acre campus. 7 buildings on campus. Approved or accredited by National Christian School Association, Southern Association of Colleges and Schools, and Texas Department of Education. Total enrollment: 585. Upper school average class size: 25. Upper school faculty-student ratio: 1:12. There are 178 required school days per year for Upper School students. Upper School students typically attend 5 days per week. The average school day consists of 7 hours and 15 minutes.

Upper School Student Profile Grade 6: 45 students (20 boys, 25 girls); Grade 7: 43 students (16 boys, 27 girls); Grade 8: 53 students (31 boys, 22 girls); Grade 9: 51 students (29 boys, 22 girls); Grade 10: 51 students (19 boys, 32 girls); Grade 11: 57 students (31 boys, 26 girls); Grade 12: 63 students (43 boys, 20 girls). 36% of students are members of Church of Christ.

Faculty School total: 56. In upper school: 13 men, 17 women; 14 have advanced degrees.

Subjects Offered Algebra, American history, American literature, art, band, Bible studies, biology, calculus, cheerleading, chemistry, chorus, computer math, computer science, creative writing, drama, economics, English, English literature, fine arts, French, geography, geometry, government/civics, health, history, humanities, journalism, mathematics, newspaper, physical education, physics, religion, science, sign language, social studies, Spanish, speech, speech origins of English, theater, world history, world literature, yearbook.

Graduation Requirements Arts and fine arts (art, music, dance, drama), computer science, English, foreign language, mathematics, physical education (includes health), religion (includes Bible studies and theology), science, social studies (includes history), speech origins of English, seniors must take SAT or ACT.

Special Academic Programs Study at local college for college credit.

College Admission Counseling 71 students graduated in 2012; 70 went to college, including Abilene Christian University; Austin College; Baylor University; Dallas Baptist University; Pepperdine University; Texas A&M University.

Student Life Upper grades have uniform requirement, student council, honor system. Discipline rests primarily with faculty. Attendance at religious services is required.

Tuition and Aid Day student tuition: $12,450. Tuition installment plan (FACTS Tuition Payment Plan). Tuition reduction for siblings, need-based scholarship grants available. In 2012–13, 18% of upper-school students received aid. Total amount of financial aid awarded in 2012–13: $180,000.

Admissions ERB IF, ERB Mathematics, ERB Reading and Math and Woodcock-Johnson Revised Achievement Test required. Deadline for receipt of application materials: none. Application fee required: $400. On-campus interview required.

Athletics Interscholastic: baseball (boys), basketball (b,g), cheering (g), cross-country running (b,g), drill team (g), football (b), golf (b,g), soccer (b,g), softball (g), tennis (b,g), track and field (b,g), volleyball (g). 2 PE instructors.

Computers Computers are regularly used in computer applications, newspaper, Web site design, yearbook classes. Computer network features include on-campus library services, Internet access, Internet filtering or blocking technology. Student e-mail accounts are available to students. Students grades are available online.

Contact Mrs. Katie Neuroth, Admissions Assistant. 972-270-5495 Ext. 266. Fax: 972-686-9436. E-mail: kneuroth@dallaschristian.com. Website: www.dallaschristian.com

DAMIEN HIGH SCHOOL

2280 Damien Avenue
La Verne, California 91750

Head of School: Dr. Merritt Hemenway

General Information Boys' day college-preparatory school, affiliated with Roman Catholic Church. Grades 9–12. Founded: 1959. Setting: suburban. Nearest major city is Los Angeles. 28-acre campus. 9 buildings on campus. Approved or accredited by Western Association of Schools and Colleges, Western Catholic Education Association, and California Department of Education. Member of National Association of Independent Schools. Endowment: $2 million. Total enrollment: 923. Upper school average class size: 22. Upper school faculty-student ratio: 1:18. There are 180 required school days per year for Upper School students. Upper School students typically attend 5 days per week. The average school day consists of 7 hours.

Upper School Student Profile Grade 9: 225 students (225 boys); Grade 10: 252 students (252 boys); Grade 11: 235 students (235 boys); Grade 12: 211 students (211 boys). 75% of students are Roman Catholic.

Faculty School total: 60. In upper school: 42 men, 12 women; 25 have advanced degrees.

Subjects Offered Advanced Placement courses, algebra, American history, art history, biology, chemistry, choir, computer applications, debate, economics, English composition, English literature, French, German, government, health, history, mathematics, music, physics, pre-calculus, Spanish, theater arts, theology, U.S. government and politics, U.S. history, visual arts, Western civilization, world history.

Graduation Requirements 20th century American writers, algebra, American government, American history, ancient world history, art, biology, chemistry, Christian and Hebrew scripture, Christian doctrine, Christian ethics, Christian scripture, computer applications, economics, English, English composition, foreign language, geometry, government, health and wellness, world history, world literature.

Special Academic Programs 22 Advanced Placement exams for which test preparation is offered; honors section; study at local college for college credit; remedial reading and/or remedial writing; remedial math; ESL (30 students enrolled).

College Admission Counseling 223 students graduated in 2013; 215 went to college, including Azusa Pacific University; California State Polytechnic University, Pomona; Mt. San Antonio College; Northern Arizona University; University of California, Riverside; University of La Verne. Other: 1 went to work, 4 entered military service. Mean SAT critical reading: 524, mean SAT math: 529, mean SAT writing: 521, mean combined SAT: 1574, mean composite ACT: 23.

Student Life Upper grades have uniform requirement, student council. Discipline rests primarily with faculty.

Summer Programs Remediation, enrichment, advancement, sports, art/fine arts, computer instruction programs offered; session focuses on Academic Advancement; held on campus; accepts boys and girls; open to students from other schools. 600

students usually enrolled. 2014 schedule: June 18 to July 18. Application deadline: June 1.

Tuition and Aid Day student tuition: $7700. Guaranteed tuition plan. Tuition installment plan (The Tuition Plan, FACTS Tuition Payment Plan). Tuition reduction for siblings, merit scholarship grants, need-based scholarship grants available. In 2013–14; 25% of upper-school students received aid; total upper-school merit-scholarship money awarded: $600,000. Total amount of financial aid awarded in 2013–14: $600,000.

Admissions Traditional secondary-level entrance grade is 9. For fall 2013, 330 students applied for upper-level admission, 320 were accepted, 245 enrolled. Scholastic Testing Service required. Deadline for receipt of application materials: none. Application fee required: $75. On-campus interview required.

Athletics Interscholastic: baseball, basketball, billiards, cross-country running, diving, field hockey, fishing, football, golf, hockey, ice hockey, in-line hockey, indoor hockey, lacrosse, physical fitness, racquetball, roller hockey, running, soccer, surfing, swimming and diving, tennis, track and field, water polo, weight lifting, wrestling; intramural: bowling. 2 PE instructors, 30 coaches, 2 athletic trainers.

Computers Computers are regularly used in all academic classes. Computer network features include on-campus library services, online commercial services, Internet access, wireless campus network, Internet filtering or blocking technology. Campus intranet, student e-mail accounts, and computer access in designated common areas are available to students. Students grades are available online. The school has a published electronic and media policy.

Contact Mrs. Christina Provenzano, Admissions Coordinator. 909-596-1946 Ext. 247. Fax: 909-596-6112. E-mail: christina@damien-hs.edu. Website: www.damien-hs.edu

DANA HALL SCHOOL

45 Dana Road
Wellesley, Massachusetts 02482

Head of School: Ms. Caroline Erisman, JD

General Information Girls' boarding and day college-preparatory and Forum-Life Skills school. Boarding grades 9–12, day grades 6–12. Founded: 1881. Setting: suburban. Nearest major city is Boston. Students are housed in single-sex dormitories. 55-acre campus. 34 buildings on campus. Approved or accredited by Association of Independent Schools in New England, Massachusetts Department of Education, New England Association of Schools and Colleges, The Association of Boarding Schools, and Massachusetts Department of Education. Member of National Association of Independent Schools and Secondary School Admission Test Board. Endowment: $29 million. Total enrollment: 475. Upper school average class size: 12. Upper school faculty-student ratio: 1:9. There are 180 required school days per year for Upper School students. Upper School students typically attend 5 days per week. The average school day consists of 7 hours and 30 minutes.

Upper School Student Profile Grade 9: 84 students (84 girls); Grade 10: 86 students (86 girls); Grade 11: 98 students (98 girls); Grade 12: 88 students (88 girls). 40% of students are boarding students. 90% are state residents. 15 states are represented in upper school student body. 25% are international students. International students from China, Hong Kong, Mexico, Republic of Korea, Taiwan, and Thailand; 14 other countries represented in student body.

Faculty School total: 64. In upper school: 18 men, 33 women; 39 have advanced degrees; 36 reside on campus.

Subjects Offered 20th century history, acting, African history, African studies, algebra, American history, American literature, architecture, art, art history, art-AP, astronomy, biology, calculus, ceramics, chemistry, chorus, community service, computer programming, computer science, computer science-AP, creative writing, dance, dance performance, drama, drama workshop, drawing, East Asian history, economics, electives, English, English composition, English language and composition-AP, English/composition-AP, European history, European history-AP, fitness, French, French language-AP, French literature-AP, freshman foundations, geometry, government, government/civics, health, journalism, Latin, Latin American history, Latin-AP, leadership education training, library, Mandarin, marine biology, mathematics-AP, Middle Eastern history, music, music composition, music performance, music theory, photography, physics, physics-AP, public speaking, Russian studies, Spanish, Spanish-AP, statistics-AP, trigonometry, U.S. history-AP, U.S. literature, weight training, Western civilization, women in the classical world.

Graduation Requirements American history, area studies, computer science, English, fitness, foreign language, mathematics, performing arts, science, social studies (includes history), visual arts, 20 hours of community service.

Special Academic Programs 17 Advanced Placement exams for which test preparation is offered; honors section; independent study; term-away projects; study abroad.

College Admission Counseling 90 students graduated in 2012; all went to college, including New York University; Syracuse University; Tufts University; Tulane University; University of Richmond; Wellesley College. Mean SAT critical reading: 613, mean SAT math: 639, mean SAT writing: 633, mean combined SAT: 1885, mean composite ACT: 28.

Student Life Upper grades have specified standards of dress, student council, honor system. Discipline rests equally with students and faculty.

Tuition and Aid Day student tuition: $39,266; 7-day tuition and room/board: $52,131. Tuition installment plan (monthly payment plans, K-12 Family Education Loan, AchieverLoan). Need-based scholarship grants, need-based loans available. In 2012–13, 20% of upper-school students received aid. Total amount of financial aid awarded in 2012–13: $3,395,219.

Admissions Traditional secondary-level entrance grade is 9. For fall 2012, 555 students applied for upper-level admission, 260 were accepted, 116 enrolled. ISEE, SSAT or TOEFL required. Deadline for receipt of application materials: January 15. Application fee required: $50. Interview required.

Athletics Interscholastic: basketball, cross-country running, equestrian sports, fencing, field hockey, golf, horseback riding, ice hockey, lacrosse, modern dance, soccer, softball, squash, swimming and diving, tennis, volleyball; intramural: aerobics, aerobics/dance, aquatics, ballet, crew, dance, equestrian sports, fitness, Frisbee, golf, hiking/backpacking, horseback riding, indoor track; life saving, martial arts, modern dance, Nautilus, outdoor activities, physical fitness, physical training, rock climbing, scuba diving, self defense, skiing (downhill), squash, strength & conditioning, swimming and diving, tennis, ultimate Frisbee, weight lifting, weight training, yoga. 5 PE instructors, 20 coaches, 1 athletic trainer.

Computers Computers are regularly used in art, English, French, history, Latin, mathematics, science, Spanish, Web site design, yearbook classes. Computer network features include on-campus library services, online commercial services, Internet access, wireless campus network, Internet filtering or blocking technology. Campus intranet, student e-mail accounts, and computer access in designated common areas are available to students.

Contact Mrs. Brenda Dowdell, Admission Office Manager. 781-235-3010 Ext. 2531. Fax: 781-239-1383. E-mail: admission@danahall.org. Website: www.danahall.org

DARLINGTON SCHOOL

1014 Cave Spring Road
Rome, Georgia 30161

Head of School: Thomas C. Whitworth III

General Information Coeducational boarding and day college-preparatory, arts, and technology school. Boarding grades 9–PG, day grades PK–PG. Founded: 1905. Setting: small town. Nearest major city is Atlanta. Students are housed in single-sex dormitories. 500-acre campus. 15 buildings on campus. Approved or accredited by Georgia Independent School Association, Southern Association of Colleges and Schools, Southern Association of Independent Schools, The Association of Boarding Schools, The College Board, and Georgia Department of Education. Member of National Association of Independent Schools and Secondary School Admission Test Board. Endowment: $29.2 million. Total enrollment: 848. Upper school average class size: 13. Upper school faculty-student ratio: 1:13. There are 176 required school days per year for Upper School students. Upper School students typically attend 5 days per week. The average school day consists of 7 hours and 30 minutes.

Upper School Student Profile Grade 9: 98 students (57 boys, 41 girls); Grade 10: 111 students (59 boys, 52 girls); Grade 11: 138 students (78 boys, 60 girls); Grade 12: 130 students (69 boys, 61 girls). 38% of students are boarding students. 72% are state residents. 22 states are represented in upper school student body. 31% are international students. International students from Bahamas, Bermuda, China, Germany, Mexico, and Republic of Korea; 16 other countries represented in student body.

Faculty School total: 98. In upper school: 45 men, 53 women; 47 have advanced degrees; 57 reside on campus.

Subjects Offered Advanced biology, advanced chemistry, Advanced Placement courses, advanced studio art-AP, algebra, ancient world history, art, art history, art history-AP, band, biology, biology-AP, calculus, calculus-AP, chemistry, chemistry-AP, choir, chorus, college counseling, computer programming, computer science, concert choir, creative writing, drama, drawing, economics, economics-AP, English, English language and composition-AP, English language-AP, English literature, English literature-AP, English-AP, ensembles, environmental science, environmental science-AP, ESL, fine arts, French, geometry, government-AP, graphic arts, graphic design, health, honors algebra, honors English, honors geometry, honors world history, humanities, jazz ensemble, journalism, lab science, macro/microeconomics-AP, macroeconomics-AP, modern European history-AP, music, music theory-AP, musical theater, newspaper, personal fitness, physical education, physics, physics-AP, pre-calculus, probability and statistics, psychology-AP, robotics, Spanish, Spanish language-AP, Spanish literature-AP, Spanish-AP, statistics-AP, studio art-AP, trigonometry, U.S. history, U.S. history-AP, video, video film production, vocal ensemble, wind ensemble, world cultures, world history, world history-AP, yearbook.

Graduation Requirements Arts and fine arts (art, music, dance, drama), English, foreign language, information technology, mathematics, physical education (includes health), science, social studies (includes history), community service/servant leadership program, after school activity.

Special Academic Programs 21 Advanced Placement exams for which test preparation is offered; honors section; academic accommodation for the musically talented; ESL (18 students enrolled).

College Admission Counseling 135 students graduated in 2012; all went to college, including Furman University; Georgia Institute of Technology; The University of Alabama; University of Georgia; University of Mississippi; University of

Washington. Median SAT critical reading: 547, median SAT math: 574, median SAT writing: 557, median combined SAT: 1678.

Student Life Upper grades have uniform requirement, student council, honor system. Discipline rests equally with students and faculty.

Tuition and Aid Day student tuition: $18,200; 7-day tuition and room/board: $42,300–$47,300. Tuition installment plan (FACTS Tuition Payment Plan, monthly payment plans, individually arranged payment plans). Merit scholarship grants, need-based scholarship grants available. In 2012–13, 44% of upper-school students received aid; total upper-school merit-scholarship money awarded: $486,600. Total amount of financial aid awarded in 2012–13: $3,405,880.

Admissions Traditional secondary-level entrance grade is 9. For fall 2012, 265 students applied for upper-level admission, 195 were accepted, 113 enrolled. PSAT and SAT for applicants to grade 11 and 12, SSAT or WISC III or TOEFL required. Deadline for receipt of application materials: February 1. Application fee required: $50. Interview required.

Athletics Interscholastic: baseball (boys), basketball (b,g), cheering (g), crew (b,g), cross-country running (b,g), diving (b,g), football (b), golf (b,g), lacrosse (b,g), rowing (b,g), soccer (b,g), softball (g), swimming and diving (b,g), tennis (b,g), track and field (b,g), volleyball (g), wrestling (b); intramural: aerobics/dance (g), aquatics (b,g), basketball (b,g), cheering (g), dance squad (g), fitness (b,g), flag football (b,g), flagball (b,g), running (b,g), tennis (b,g), volleyball (b,g); coed intramural: aerobics, fishing, fly fishing, Frisbee, independent competitive sports, outdoor activities, outdoor education, outdoor recreation, physical fitness, physical training, skeet shooting, soccer, speleology, strength & conditioning, table tennis, ultimate Frisbee, water volleyball, weight lifting, weight training. 2 PE instructors, 11 coaches, 2 athletic trainers.

Computers Computers are regularly used in computer applications, English, foreign language, history, mathematics, science, Web site design classes. Computer network features include on-campus library services, Internet access, wireless campus network, Internet filtering or blocking technology. Campus intranet, student e-mail accounts, and computer access in designated common areas are available to students. Students grades are available online. The school has a published electronic and media policy.

Contact Mrs. Kila McCann, Director of Boarding Admission. 706-236-0447. Fax: 706-232-3600. E-mail: kmccann@darlingtonschool.org. Website: www.darlingtonschool.org

DARROW SCHOOL

110 Darrow Road
New Lebanon, New York 12125

Head of School: Mr. Simon Holzapfel

General Information Coeducational boarding and day college-preparatory, arts, hands-on learning, and sustainability school. Grades 9–12. Founded: 1932. Setting: rural. Nearest major city is Pittsfield, MA. Students are housed in single-sex dormitories. 365-acre campus. 26 buildings on campus. Approved or accredited by Middle States Association of Colleges and Schools, The Association of Boarding Schools, and New York Department of Education. Member of National Association of Independent Schools and Secondary School Admission Test Board. Endowment: $3.1 million. Upper school average class size: 9. Upper school faculty-student ratio: 1:4. There are 220 required school days per year for Upper School students. Upper School students typically attend 6 days per week. The average school day consists of 6 hours.

Upper School Student Profile 80% of students are boarding students. 52% are state residents. 13 states are represented in upper school student body. 25% are international students. International students from Bahamas, China, Jamaica, Japan, Republic of Korea, and Russian Federation; 5 other countries represented in student body.

Faculty School total: 33. In upper school: 17 men, 16 women; 15 have advanced degrees; 30 reside on campus.

Subjects Offered 3-dimensional art, advanced math, African drumming, African-American literature, algebra, American literature, art, art history, athletics, biology, calculus, ceramics, chemistry, civil rights, clayworking, computer graphics, creative writing, critical writing, culinary arts, design, digital art, drama, drawing, drawing and design, ecology, economics, English, English literature, ensembles, environmental education, environmental science, environmental studies, ESL, ethics, experiential education, fine arts, French, geometry, health and wellness, history, independent study, Latin American literature, leadership, literature, mathematics, microeconomics, multicultural studies, music appreciation, music theory, oil painting, ornithology, photo shop, photography, physics, play production, poetry, portfolio art, pottery, pre-calculus, reading/study skills, Russian literature, science, social studies, Spanish, Spanish literature, sports, studio art, study skills, theater, U.S. history, Western civilization, women's literature, woodworking, writing, yearbook.

Graduation Requirements Arts, arts and fine arts (art, music, dance, drama), electives, English, foreign language, history, mathematics, physical education (includes health), science.

Special Academic Programs Advanced Placement exam preparation; independent study; term-away projects; academic accommodation for the musically talented and the artistically talented; ESL (10 students enrolled).

College Admission Counseling 30 students graduated in 2013; 29 went to college, including Brandeis University; Clarkson University; Hartwick College; Hobart

and William Smith Colleges; Suffolk University; Wheaton College. Other: 1 went to work.

Student Life Upper grades have specified standards of dress, student council, honor system. Discipline rests equally with students and faculty.

Summer Programs ESL programs offered; session focuses on ESOL immersion; held both on and off campus; held at home stays, day trips; accepts boys and girls; not open to students from other schools. 8 students usually enrolled. 2014 schedule: August 15 to August 30.

Tuition and Aid Day student tuition: $29,200; 7-day tuition and room/board: $51,200. Tuition installment plan (Academic Management Services Plan, SMART Tuition Payment Plan, individually arranged payment plans). Need-based scholarship grants available. In 2013–14, 32% of upper-school students received aid. Total amount of financial aid awarded in 2013–14: $1,100,000.

Admissions Traditional secondary-level entrance grade is 9. For fall 2013, 170 students applied for upper-level admission, 109 were accepted, 52 enrolled. SLEP for foreign students or TOEFL or SLEP required. Deadline for receipt of application materials: none. Application fee required: $50. On-campus interview required.

Athletics Interscholastic: basketball (boys, girls), cross-country running (b,g), soccer (b,g), softball (g), tennis (b,g); coed interscholastic: cross-country running, Frisbee, lacrosse, tennis, ultimate Frisbee; coed intramural: aerobics/dance, alpine skiing, backpacking, dance, equestrian sports, fitness, freestyle skiing, hiking/backpacking, horseback riding, lacrosse, outdoor activities, outdoor education, physical fitness, rock climbing, skiing (cross-country), skiing (downhill), snowboarding, telemark skiing, weight lifting, yoga. 1 coach.

Computers Computers are regularly used in graphic design, photography, video film production classes. Computer network features include on-campus library services, Internet access, wireless campus network, Internet filtering or blocking technology. Campus intranet, student e-mail accounts, and computer access in designated common areas are available to students. The school has a published electronic and media policy.

Contact Ms. Betsy Strickler, Director of Admission. 518-794-6008. Fax: 518-794-7065. E-mail: stricklerb@darrowschool.org. Website: www.darrowschool.org

DAVIDSON ACADEMY

1414 W. Old Hickory Boulevard
Nashville, Tennessee 37207-1098

Head of School: Dr. Bill Chaney

General Information Coeducational day college-preparatory, arts, religious studies, technology, and science, mathematics school, affiliated with Christian faith. Grades PK–12. Founded: 1980. Setting: suburban. 67-acre campus. 1 building on campus. Approved or accredited by Association of Christian Schools International, Southern Association of Colleges and Schools, and Tennessee Department of Education. Endowment: $25,000. Total enrollment: 750. Upper school average class size: 17. Upper school faculty-student ratio: 1:17. There are 180 required school days per year for Upper School students. Upper School students typically attend 5 days per week. The average school day consists of 5 hours.

Upper School Student Profile 99.9% of students are Christian faith.

Faculty School total: 34. In upper school: 16 men, 18 women.

Subjects Offered 3-dimensional art, ACT preparation, advanced math, Advanced Placement courses, algebra, American government, American history, American history-AP, art, art appreciation, audio visual/media, band, Bible, Bible studies, biology, calculus, calculus-AP, cheerleading, chemistry, choral music, chorus, church history, college admission preparation, college counseling, college placement, composition-AP, computer applications, computer skills, conceptual physics, concert band, concert choir, consumer economics, creative writing, drama, drama performance, dramatic arts, earth science, economics, English, English literature-AP, English-AP, English/composition-AP, European history-AP, film and new technologies, geography, geometry, government-AP, health and wellness, history, honors algebra, honors English, honors geometry, human anatomy, independent study, Latin, leadership and service, Life of Christ, literature, marching band, mathematics, mathematics-AP, music, musical productions, New Testament, newspaper, physical education, physical fitness, physical science, physics, physics-AP, poetry, pre-algebra, pre-calculus, pre-college orientation, probability and statistics, psychology, reading, religious studies, science, senior project, Spanish, speech, speech communications, trigonometry, U.S. history, U.S. history-AP, video film production, wellness, world geography, world history, writing, yearbook.

Graduation Requirements Algebra, art, biology, calculus, chemistry, computer technologies, drama, economics, electives, English, English composition, English literature, foreign language, geometry, government, literature, physical science, physics, senior project, trigonometry, U.S. history, wellness, world history, Senior Research Project, Bible.

Special Academic Programs 3 Advanced Placement exams for which test preparation is offered; honors section; independent study; study at local college for college credit; programs in general development for dyslexic students; ESL (6 students enrolled).

College Admission Counseling 54 students graduated in 2013; all went to college, including Lipscomb University; Tennessee Technological University; The University of Tennessee at Chattanooga.

Student Life Upper grades have uniform requirement, student council, honor system. Discipline rests primarily with faculty.

Summer Programs Enrichment, advancement, sports, art/fine arts programs offered; session focuses on physical and mental growth through a caring, Christian, and learning-enriched environment; held on campus; accepts boys and girls; open to students from other schools. 250 students usually enrolled. 2014 schedule: May 30 to July 30. Application deadline: April 15.

Tuition and Aid Day student tuition: $9300. Tuition installment plan (monthly payment plans, individually arranged payment plans). Tuition reduction for siblings, need-based scholarship grants, need-based financial aid, tuition reduction for children of faculty and staff available. In 2013–14, 10% of upper-school students received aid.

Admissions Traditional secondary-level entrance grade is 9. Admissions testing, any standardized test and WRAT required. Deadline for receipt of application materials: none. Application fee required: $125.

Athletics Interscholastic: baseball (boys), basketball (b,g), cheering (g), cross-country running (b,g), dance team (g), football (b), golf (b,g), soccer (b,g), softball (g), tennis (b,g), track and field (b,g), volleyball (g); intramural: ballet (g), dance (g), weight training (b); coed interscholastic: bowling. 1 athletic trainer.

Computers Computers are regularly used in computer applications, English, graphic arts, history, mathematics, media production, yearbook classes. Computer network features include on-campus library services, Internet access, wireless campus network, Internet filtering or blocking technology, RenWeb, Accelerated Reader, CollegeView. Computer access in designated common areas is available to students. Students grades are available online. The school has a published electronic and media policy.

Contact Mr. Jason McGehee, Admission Counselor. 615-860-5317. Fax: 615-860-7631. E-mail: jason.mcgehee@davidsonacademy.com. Website: www.davidsonacademy.com

DEERFIELD ACADEMY

7 Boyden Lane
Deerfield, Massachusetts 01342

Head of School: Dr. Margarita O'Byrne Curtis

General Information Coeducational boarding and day college-preparatory school. Grades 9–PG. Founded: 1797. Setting: rural. Nearest major city is Hartford, CT. Students are housed in single-sex dormitories. 280-acre campus. 81 buildings on campus. Approved or accredited by Association of Independent Schools in New England, National Independent Private Schools Association, New England Association of Schools and Colleges, and Massachusetts Department of Education. Member of National Association of Independent Schools and Secondary School Admission Test Board. Endowment: $398 million. Total enrollment: 630. Upper school average class size: 12. Upper school faculty-student ratio: 1:6. There are 150 required school days per year for Upper School students. Upper School students typically attend 5 days per week. The average school day consists of 5 hours and 25 minutes.

Upper School Student Profile Grade 9: 101 students (52 boys, 49 girls); Grade 10: 150 students (73 boys, 77 girls); Grade 11: 180 students (86 boys, 94 girls); Grade 12: 179 students (90 boys, 89 girls); Postgraduate: 26 students (20 boys, 6 girls). 88% of students are boarding students. 23% are state residents. 39 states are represented in upper school student body. 18% are international students. International students from Canada, China, Jamaica, Republic of Korea, Singapore, and Thailand; 32 other countries represented in student body.

Faculty School total: 124. In upper school: 67 men, 57 women; 89 have advanced degrees; 115 reside on campus.

Subjects Offered Advanced chemistry, advanced computer applications, advanced math, advanced studio art-AP, algebra, American government, American history-AP, American studies, analytic geometry, anatomy, applied arts, applied music, Arabic, architectural drawing, architecture, art, art history, art history-AP, Asian history, Asian literature, Asian studies, astronomy, Basic programming, biochemistry, biology, biology-AP, Black history, calculus, calculus-AP, chemistry, chemistry-AP, Chinese, computer applications, computer math, computer programming, computer science, computer science-AP, concert band, creative writing, dance, dance performance, discrete mathematics, drama, drama performance, drama workshop, drawing and design, earth science, Eastern religion and philosophy, economics, economics-AP, English, English literature, English literature-AP, English-AP, environmental science, ethics, European history, expository writing, fine arts, French, geology, geometry, Greek, health, health education, history, instrumental music, journalism, Latin, literature, mathematics, modern European history, music, philosophy, photography, physics, physics-AP, physiology, probability and statistics, religion, science, social studies, Spanish, Spanish literature, studio art, studio art-AP, theater, theater arts, trigonometry, U.S. history, U.S. literature, video, vocal music, Western civilization, world civilizations, world governments, world history, world literature, world religions, writing.

Graduation Requirements Arts and fine arts (art, music, dance, drama), English, foreign language, history, mathematics, philosophy, science.

Special Academic Programs Advanced Placement exam preparation; honors section; independent study; term-away projects; study abroad; academic accommodation for the gifted, the musically talented, and the artistically talented; ESL (6 students enrolled).

College Admission Counseling 197 students graduated in 2013; 190 went to college, including Brown University; Dartmouth College; Georgetown University;

Harvard University; Middlebury College; Yale University. Other: 7 had other specific plans. Mean SAT critical reading: 653, mean SAT math: 662, mean SAT writing: 661.

Student Life Upper grades have specified standards of dress, student council, honor system. Discipline rests equally with students and faculty.

Tuition and Aid Day student tuition: $37,850; 7-day tuition and room/board: $52,300. Tuition installment plan (Educational Data Systems, Inc.). Need-based scholarship grants available. In 2013–14, 35% of upper-school students received aid. Total amount of financial aid awarded in 2013–14: $7,800,000.

Admissions Traditional secondary-level entrance grade is 9. For fall 2013, 2,090 students applied for upper-level admission, 365 were accepted, 236 enrolled. ACT, ISEE, PSAT, SAT, SSAT or TOEFL required. Deadline for receipt of application materials: January 15. Application fee required: $60. Interview required.

Athletics Interscholastic: alpine skiing (boys, girls), baseball (b), basketball (b,g), crew (b,g), cross-country running (b,g), diving (b,g), field hockey (g), football (b), golf (b), ice hockey (b,g), lacrosse (b,g), rowing (b,g), skiing (downhill) (b,g), soccer (b,g), softball (g), squash (b,g), swimming and diving (b,g), tennis (b,g), track and field (b,g), volleyball (g), water polo (b,g), wrestling (b); intramural: dance (b,g), fitness (b,g), modern dance (b,g); coed interscholastic: bicycling, diving, golf, indoor track & field, swimming and diving; coed intramural: aerobics/dance, aerobics/Nautilus, alpine skiing, aquatics, ballet, canoeing/kayaking, combined training, dance, dance team, fitness, hiking/backpacking, life saving, modern dance, nordic skiing, outdoor recreation, outdoor skills, paddle tennis, sailing, skiing (cross-country), skiing (downhill), snowboarding, soccer, squash, strength & conditioning, swimming and diving, tennis, volleyball, weight lifting, weight training. 1 coach, 2 athletic trainers.

Computers Computers are regularly used in architecture, mathematics, programming, science classes. Computer network features include on-campus library services, online commercial services, Internet access, wireless campus network, Internet filtering or blocking technology. Campus intranet, student e-mail accounts, and computer access in designated common areas are available to students. Students grades are available online. The school has a published electronic and media policy.

Contact Pam Safford, Dean of Admission and Financial Aid. 413-774-1400. Fax: 413-772-1100. E-mail: admission@deerfield.edu. Website: www.deerfield.edu

See Display on next page and Close-Up on page 532.

DE LA SALLE COLLEGE

131 Farnham Avenue
Toronto, Ontario M4V 1H7, Canada

Head of School: Br. Domenic Viggiani, FSC

General Information Coeducational day college-preparatory, arts, business, religious studies, bilingual studies, technology, and Advanced Placement Courses school, affiliated with Roman Catholic Church. Grades 5–12. Founded: 1851. Setting: urban. 12-acre campus. 4 buildings on campus. Approved or accredited by Conference of Independent Schools of Ontario, Western Catholic Education Association, and Ontario Department of Education. Language of instruction: English. Total enrollment: 627. Upper school average class size: 22. Upper school faculty-student ratio: 1:15. The average school day consists of 5 hours and 40 minutes.

Upper School Student Profile 89% of students are Roman Catholic.

Faculty School total: 44. In upper school: 33 men, 11 women.

Special Academic Programs Advanced Placement exam preparation; accelerated programs.

College Admission Counseling 100 students graduated in 2013; all went to college, including McGill University; McMaster University; Queen's University at Kingston; The University of Western Ontario; University of Toronto; York University.

Student Life Upper grades have uniform requirement, student council, honor system. Discipline rests primarily with faculty. Attendance at religious services is required.

Summer Programs Enrichment, advancement programs offered; held on campus; accepts boys and girls; open to students from other schools. 50 students usually enrolled. 2014 schedule: July 1 to July 31. Application deadline: June 15.

Tuition and Aid Day student tuition: CAN$12,600. Tuition installment plan (monthly payment plans). Bursaries, merit scholarship grants, need-based scholarship grants available. In 2013–14, 12% of upper-school students received aid.

Admissions Traditional secondary-level entrance grade is 9. For fall 2013, 150 students applied for upper-level admission, 75 were accepted, 50 enrolled. School's own test and SSAT required. Deadline for receipt of application materials: December 6. Application fee required: CAN$100. Interview required.

Athletics Interscholastic: baseball (boys), basketball (b,g), field hockey (g), ice hockey (b,g), rugby (g), soccer (b,g), softball (b,g), volleyball (b); coed interscholastic: alpine skiing, aquatics, badminton, cross-country running, golf, skiing (downhill), swimming and diving, track and field, ultimate Frisbee; coed intramural: ball hockey, physical fitness, physical training, strength & conditioning. 4 PE instructors.

Computers Computer network features include on-campus library services, Internet access, wireless campus network, Internet filtering or blocking technology. Student e-mail accounts are available to students.

Contact Ms. Anna Di Benedetto, Head Secretary. 416-969-8771 Ext. 222. Fax: 416-969-9175. E-mail: adib@delasalleoaklands.org. Website: www.delasalleoaklands.org

DE LA SALLE HIGH SCHOOL

1130 Winton Drive
Concord, California 94518-3528

Head of School: Br. Robert J. Wickman, FSC

General Information Boys' day college-preparatory, arts, and religious studies school, affiliated with Roman Catholic Church. Grades 9–12. Founded: 1965. Setting: suburban. Nearest major city is Oakland. 25-acre campus. 11 buildings on campus. Approved or accredited by Western Association of Schools and Colleges and Western Catholic Education Association. Endowment: $3.7 million. Total enrollment: 1,042. Upper school average class size: 30. Upper school faculty-student ratio: 1:28. There are 172 required school days per year for Upper School students. Upper School students typically attend 5 days per week. The average school day consists of 6 hours and 5 minutes.

Upper School Student Profile Grade 9: 285 students (285 boys); Grade 10: 266 students (266 boys); Grade 11: 250 students (250 boys); Grade 12: 241 students (241 boys). 80% of students are Roman Catholic.

Faculty School total: 73. In upper school: 50 men, 23 women; 41 have advanced degrees.

Subjects Offered Advanced studio art-AP, algebra, American history, anatomy, art, band, Bible studies, biology, calculus, chemistry, chorus, design, drafting, drawing, economics, English, English-AP, ethics, fine arts, first aid, French, geometry, government/civics, health, history, Italian, jazz, Latin, literature, marine biology, mathematics, music theory, painting, physical education, physics, physiology, pre-calculus, psychology, religion, science, sculpture, social studies, Spanish, Spanish-AP, sports medicine, statistics, statistics-AP, trigonometry, world history, world religions, writing.

Graduation Requirements Arts and fine arts (art, music, dance, drama), English, foreign language, mathematics, physical education (includes health), religion (includes Bible studies and theology), science, social studies (includes history).

Special Academic Programs Advanced Placement exam preparation; honors section; independent study; remedial math.

College Admission Counseling 251 students graduated in 2013; 250 went to college, including California Polytechnic State University, San Luis Obispo; Saint Mary's College of California; San Jose State University; The University of Arizona; University of California, Berkeley; University of Portland. Other: 1 entered military service. Mean SAT critical reading: 559, mean SAT math: 565, mean SAT writing: 542, mean combined SAT: 1666, mean composite ACT: 25. 31% scored over 600 on SAT critical reading, 35% scored over 600 on SAT math, 27% scored over 600 on SAT writing, 28% scored over 1800 on combined SAT, 35% scored over 26 on composite ACT.

Student Life Upper grades have specified standards of dress, student council, honor system. Discipline rests primarily with faculty. Attendance at religious services is required.

Summer Programs Remediation programs offered; session focuses on remediation for incoming and/or conditionally accepted freshmen only; held on campus; accepts boys; not open to students from other schools. 40 students usually enrolled. 2014 schedule: July 7 to August 1. Application deadline: May 30.

Tuition and Aid Day student tuition: $15,650. Tuition installment plan (individually arranged payment plans, 10-month). Need-based scholarship grants, need-based grants available. In 2013–14, 33% of upper-school students received aid. Total amount of financial aid awarded in 2013–14: $2,250,000.

Admissions Traditional secondary-level entrance grade is 9. For fall 2013, 400 students applied for upper-level admission, 286 were accepted, 286 enrolled. High School Placement Test required. Deadline for receipt of application materials: November 30. Application fee required: $75. On-campus interview required.

Athletics Interscholastic: baseball, basketball, cross-country running, diving, football, golf, lacrosse, rugby, soccer, swimming and diving, tennis, track and field, volleyball, water polo, wrestling; intramural: bowling, flag football, floor hockey, football, ultimate Frisbee. 3 PE instructors, 85 coaches, 3 athletic trainers.

Computers Computers are regularly used in animation, Web site design, yearbook classes. Computer network features include on-campus library services, Internet access, wireless campus network, Internet filtering or blocking technology. Student e-mail accounts and computer access in designated common areas are available to students. Students grades are available online. The school has a published electronic and media policy.

Contact Mr. Joseph Grantham, Director of Admissions. 925-288-8102. Fax: 925-686-3474. E-mail: granthamj@dlshs.org. Website: www.dlshs.org

DELASALLE HIGH SCHOOL

One DeLaSalle Drive
Minneapolis, Minnesota 55401-1597

Head of School: Mr. Barry Lieske

General Information Coeducational day college-preparatory, arts, business, religious studies, and technology school, affiliated with Roman Catholic Church. Grades 9–12. Founded: 1900. Setting: urban. 10-acre campus. 3 buildings on campus. Approved or accredited by National Catholic Education Association, North Central Association of Colleges and Schools, and Minnesota Department of Education.

Endowment: $3 million. Total enrollment: 731. Upper school average class size: 23. Upper school faculty-student ratio: 1:14. There are 175 required school days per year for Upper School students. Upper School students typically attend 5 days per week. The average school day consists of 6 hours and 30 minutes.

Upper School Student Profile Grade 9: 223 students (101 boys, 122 girls); Grade 10: 163 students (79 boys, 84 girls); Grade 11: 207 students (95 boys, 112 girls); Grade 12: 137 students (61 boys, 76 girls). 70% of students are Roman Catholic.

Faculty School total: 53. In upper school: 25 men, 28 women; 46 have advanced degrees.

Subjects Offered 20th century history, 20th century world history, advanced computer applications, advanced studio art-AP, African literature, algebra, American government, American history, American history-AP, ancient world history, anthropology, art, band, Bible, biology, biology-AP, business applications, calculus, calculus-AP, campus ministry, Catholic belief and practice, chamber groups, chemistry, chemistry-AP, Chinese, choir, Christian and Hebrew scripture, Christian ethics, comparative religion, computer graphics, concert band, concert choir, creative writing, economics, English, English language and composition-AP, English language-AP, English literature-AP, environmental studies, ethics, European history, European history-AP, first aid, fitness, forensics, French, geography, geometry, government, graphic arts, graphic design, health and wellness, history of the Catholic Church, history-AP, honors algebra, honors English, honors geometry, honors U.S. history, honors world history, instrumental music, journalism, mathematics, mathematics-AP, moral and social development, personal finance, philosophy, physical education, physical science, physics, physics-AP, pre-calculus, psychology, psychology-AP, social justice, Spanish, Spanish language-AP, speech, street law, studio art-AP, U.S. government and politics-AP, Western civilization, world geography, world religions, World War II, writing.

Graduation Requirements Arts and fine arts (art, music, dance, drama), English, foreign language, mathematics, physical education (includes health), religious studies, science, social studies (includes history), 60 hours of documented Christian service.

Special Academic Programs Advanced Placement exam preparation; honors section; independent study; study at local college for college credit.

College Admission Counseling 154 students graduated in 2013; 152 went to college, including College of Saint Benedict; Marquette University; Saint John's University; Saint Mary's University of Minnesota; University of Minnesota, Twin Cities Campus; University of St. Thomas. Other: 1 went to work, 1 entered military service. Mean composite ACT: 25. 61% scored over 26 on composite ACT.

Student Life Upper grades have uniform requirement, student council, honor system. Discipline rests primarily with faculty. Attendance at religious services is required.

Summer Programs Enrichment, advancement programs offered; held on campus; accepts boys and girls; open to students from other schools. 350 students usually enrolled. 2014 schedule: June 8 to July 30. Application deadline: June 1.

Tuition and Aid Day student tuition: $11,495. Tuition installment plan (monthly payment plans). Merit scholarship grants, need-based scholarship grants, off-campus work programs for tuition benefit available. In 2013–14, 53% of upper-school students received aid; total upper-school merit-scholarship money awarded: $383,000. Total amount of financial aid awarded in 2013–14: $2,530,000.

Admissions Traditional secondary-level entrance grade is 9. For fall 2013, 437 students applied for upper-level admission, 291 were accepted, 223 enrolled. Academic Profile Tests or High School Placement Test required. Deadline for receipt of application materials: none. No application fee required. Interview required.

Athletics Interscholastic: baseball (boys), basketball (b,g), cross-country running (b,g), football (b), golf (b,g), hockey (b,g), soccer (b,g), softball (g), swimming and diving (g), tennis (b,g), track and field (b,g), volleyball (g), wrestling (b); coed interscholastic: cheering, rowing, weight training; coed intramural: aerobics, archery, bowling, dance, dance team, strength & conditioning. 2 PE instructors, 63 coaches, 1 athletic trainer.

Computers Computers are regularly used in all academic, art, business, English, French, graphic design, independent study, journalism, media, media production, music, science, social studies, Spanish, writing classes. Computer network features include on-campus library services, online commercial services, Internet access, wireless campus network, Internet filtering or blocking technology, one-to-one iPad technology for all students. Student e-mail accounts are available to students. Students grades are available online. The school has a published electronic and media policy.

Contact Mr. Patrick Felicetta, Director of Admission. 612-676-7605. Fax: 612-676-7699. E-mail: patrick.felicetta@delasalle.com. Website: www.delasalle.com

DE LA SALLE NORTH CATHOLIC HIGH SCHOOL

7528 N. Fenwick Avenue
Portland, Oregon 97217

Head of School: Mr. Tim Joy

General Information Coeducational day college-preparatory and business school, affiliated with Roman Catholic Church. Grades 9–12. Founded: 2000. Setting: urban. 1 building on campus. Approved or accredited by Northwest Accreditation Commission and Oregon Department of Education. Total enrollment: 322. Upper school average class size: 81. Upper school faculty-student ratio: 1:17. There are 180 required school days per year for Upper School students. Upper School students

typically attend 4 days per week. The average school day consists of 7 hours and 30 minutes.

Upper School Student Profile Grade 9: 80 students (36 boys, 44 girls); Grade 10: 79 students (35 boys, 44 girls); Grade 11: 80 students (36 boys, 44 girls); Grade 12: 79 students (35 boys, 44 girls). 40% of students are Roman Catholic.

Faculty School total: 19. In upper school: 10 men, 9 women; 16 have advanced degrees.

Special Academic Programs 2 Advanced Placement exams for which test preparation is offered; honors section; independent study; remedial reading and/or remedial writing; remedial math.

College Admission Counseling 46 students graduated in 2013; 44 went to college, including College of Saint Benedict; Georgetown University; Oregon State University; Pacific University; Portland Community College. Other: 1 went to work, 1 entered military service.

Student Life Upper grades have uniform requirement, student council, honor system. Discipline rests primarily with faculty. Attendance at religious services is required.

Summer Programs Remediation, enrichment programs offered; session focuses on academic preparation and work-study training program; held on campus; accepts boys and girls; not open to students from other schools. 120 students usually enrolled.

Tuition and Aid Day student tuition: $2995. Tuition installment plan (monthly payment plans, individually arranged payment plans). Need-based scholarship grants, paying campus jobs available. In 2013–14, 83% of upper-school students received aid.

Admissions Traditional secondary-level entrance grade is 9. Catholic High School Entrance Examination required. Deadline for receipt of application materials: none. No application fee required. On-campus interview required.

Athletics Interscholastic: basketball (boys, girls), cross-country running (b,g), golf (b,g), soccer (b,g), track and field (b,g), volleyball (g), wrestling (b,g). 1 PE instructor, 5 coaches.

Computers Computers are regularly used in business education classes. Computer network features include on-campus library services, Internet access, wireless campus network, Internet filtering or blocking technology. Campus intranet, student e-mail accounts, and computer access in designated common areas are available to students. Students grades are available online. The school has a published electronic and media policy.

Contact Mariana Parra, Admissions Assistant. 503-285-9385 Ext. 135. Fax: 503-285-9546. E-mail: mparra@dlsnc.org. Website: www.delasallenorth.org/

DELBARTON SCHOOL

230 Mendham Road
Morristown, New Jersey 07960

Head of School: Br. Paul Diveny, OSB

General Information Boys' day college-preparatory, arts, religious studies, and technology school, affiliated with Roman Catholic Church. Grades 7–12. Founded: 1939. Setting: suburban. Nearest major city is New York, NY. 200-acre campus. 7 buildings on campus. Approved or accredited by Middle States Association of Colleges and Schools, National Catholic Education Association, New Jersey Association of Independent Schools, and New Jersey Department of Education. Member of National Association of Independent Schools and Secondary School Admission Test Board. Endowment: $26 million. Total enrollment: 558. Upper school average class size: 15. Upper school faculty-student ratio: 1:13. There are 160 required school days per year for Upper School students. Upper School students typically attend 5 days per week. The average school day consists of 6 hours and 15 minutes.

Upper School Student Profile Grade 9: 128 students (128 boys); Grade 10: 117 students (117 boys); Grade 11: 117 students (117 boys); Grade 12: 129 students (129 boys). 80% of students are Roman Catholic.

Faculty School total: 88. In upper school: 72 men, 14 women; 57 have advanced degrees.

Subjects Offered Accounting, advanced chemistry, algebra, American history, American literature, art, art history, astronomy, biology, calculus, chemistry, computer math, computer programming, computer science, creative writing, driver education, economics, English, English literature, environmental science, ethics, European history, fine arts, French, geography, geometry, German, grammar, health, history, international relations, Latin, mathematics, music, philosophy, physical education, physics, religion, Russian, social studies, Spanish, speech, trigonometry, world history.

Graduation Requirements Arts and fine arts (art, music, dance, drama), computer science, English, foreign language, mathematics, physical education (includes health), religion (includes Bible studies and theology), science, social studies (includes history), speech.

Special Academic Programs Advanced Placement exam preparation; independent study.

College Admission Counseling 119 students graduated in 2013; 117 went to college, including Boston College; Columbia University; Georgetown University; Loyola University Maryland; Princeton University; Villanova University.

Student Life Upper grades have specified standards of dress, student council, honor system. Discipline rests primarily with faculty. Attendance at religious services is required.

Summer Programs Enrichment, advancement, sports, computer instruction programs offered; session focuses on summer school (coed) and summer sports (boys);

held on campus; accepts boys and girls; open to students from other schools. 1,200 students usually enrolled. 2014 schedule: June 25 to August 1. Application deadline: June 1.

Tuition and Aid Day student tuition: $32,200. Tuition installment plan (monthly payment plans, individually arranged payment plans). Need-based scholarship grants available. In 2013–14, 18% of upper-school students received aid. Total amount of financial aid awarded in 2013–14: $1,700,000.

Admissions Traditional secondary-level entrance grade is 9. For fall 2013, 384 students applied for upper-level admission, 153 were accepted, 133 enrolled. Stanford Achievement Test, Otis-Lennon School Ability Test, school's own exam required. Deadline for receipt of application materials: November 28. Application fee required: $65. On-campus interview required.

Athletics Interscholastic: baseball, basketball, bowling, cross-country running, football, golf, ice hockey, indoor track, lacrosse, soccer, squash, swimming and diving, tennis, track and field, winter (indoor) track, wrestling; intramural: bicycling, combined training, fitness, flag football, Frisbee, independent competitive sports, mountain biking, skiing (downhill), strength & conditioning, ultimate Frisbee, weight lifting, weight training. 3 PE instructors, 2 athletic trainers.

Computers Computers are regularly used in computer applications, music, science, word processing classes. Computer network features include on-campus library services, online commercial services, Internet access, wireless campus network. Student e-mail accounts are available to students. Students grades are available online.

Contact Mrs. Connie Curnow, Administrative Assistant, Office of Admissions. 973-538-3231 Ext. 3019. Fax: 973-538-8836. E-mail: ccurnow@delbarton.org. Website: www.delbarton.org

See Display on this page and Close-Up on page 534.

DELPHI ACADEMY OF LOS ANGELES

11341 Brainard Avenue
Lake View Terrace, California 91342

Head of School: Mrs. Karen Dale

General Information Coeducational day college-preparatory, general academic, arts, business, and technology school. Grades K–12. Founded: 1984. Setting: suburban. Nearest major city is Los Angeles. 10-acre campus. 4 buildings on campus. Approved or accredited by California Department of Education. Total enrollment: 144. Upper school average class size: 15. Upper school faculty-student ratio: 1:15. There are 176 required school days per year for Upper School students. Upper School students typically attend 5 days per week. The average school day consists of 7 hours and 45 minutes.

Upper School Student Profile Grade 9: 20 students (11 boys, 9 girls); Grade 10: 7 students (4 boys, 3 girls); Grade 11: 7 students (3 boys, 4 girls); Grade 12: 2 students (1 boy, 1 girl).

Faculty School total: 20. In upper school: 2 men, 1 woman.

Subjects Offered Acting, advanced chemistry, advanced computer applications, advanced math, algebra, American literature, anatomy and physiology, art, art history, ASB Leadership, Basic programming, biology, business skills, calculus, calligraphy, career and personal planning, career education internship, career/college preparation, ceramics, chemistry, choir, college counseling, communication skills, community service, comparative religion, competitive science projects, composition, computer applications, consumer economics, consumer mathematics, current events, decision making skills, drama, drawing, economics, education, electronics, English, English literature, ethical decision making, ethics and responsibility, expository writing, family living, fine arts, first aid, fitness, French, geography, geometry, government, grammar, health, history, intro to computers, language arts, leadership, literature seminar, logic, math applications, mathematics, music, nutrition, personal money management, philosophy, physical education, physical science, physics, pre-algebra, pre-calculus, public speaking, religion, research skills, SAT preparation, science, science project, senior career experience, Shakespeare, social studies, Spanish, student government, study skills, trigonometry, U.S. constitutional history, U.S. government, Western civilization, world history.

Graduation Requirements Advanced chemistry, advanced computer applications, calculus, communication skills, comparative religion, constitutional history of U.S., current events, economics, English literature, foreign language, government/civics, health, physics, public speaking, Shakespeare, student government.

Special Academic Programs Accelerated programs; independent study; term-away projects; academic accommodation for the gifted; remedial reading and/or remedial writing; remedial math.

College Admission Counseling 10 students graduated in 2013; 5 went to college, including California State Polytechnic University, Pomona; California State University, Northridge; Occidental College. Other: 5 went to work. Mean SAT critical reading: 660, mean SAT math: 680, mean SAT writing: 670. 100% scored over 600 on SAT critical reading, 100% scored over 600 on SAT math, 100% scored over 600 on SAT writing.

Student Life Upper grades have specified standards of dress, student council, honor system. Discipline rests primarily with faculty.

Summer Programs Remediation, enrichment, advancement, ESL, sports, art/fine arts, computer instruction programs offered; session focuses on study skills and outdoor fun; held on campus; accepts boys and girls; open to students from other schools. 150 students usually enrolled. 2014 schedule: June 20 to August 20. Application deadline: none.

Tuition and Aid Day student tuition: $16,500. Tuition installment plan (monthly payment plans, individually arranged payment plans). Tuition reduction for siblings, need-based scholarship grants available. In 2013–14, 50% of upper-school students received aid. Total amount of financial aid awarded in 2013–14: $50,000.

Admissions Traditional secondary-level entrance grade is 9. For fall 2013, 4 students applied for upper-level admission, 4 were accepted, 4 enrolled. Admissions testing, OLSAT, Stanford Achievement Test and writing sample required. Deadline for receipt of application materials: none. Application fee required: $100. On-campus interview required.

Athletics Interscholastic: softball (boys, girls), volleyball (g); intramural: basketball (b,g), softball (b,g), volleyball (b,g); coed interscholastic: baseball, basketball, equestrian sports, flag football, football, soccer, softball; coed intramural: aerobics, aerobics/dance, cooperative games, dance, field hockey, fitness, flag football, football, Frisbee, jogging, outdoor activities, outdoor recreation, physical fitness, soccer, ultimate Frisbee. 3 PE instructors, 3 coaches.

Computers Computers are regularly used in all academic, business, business applications, career exploration, college planning, data processing, desktop publishing, engineering, library skills, newspaper, photography, research skills, yearbook classes. Computer network features include Internet access, wireless campus network, Internet filtering or blocking technology.

Contact Mrs. Virginia Lindskog, Admissions Registrar. 818-583-1070 Ext. 111. Fax: 818-583-1082. E-mail: virginia_lindskog@delphila.org. Website: www.delphila.org

DEMATHA CATHOLIC HIGH SCHOOL

4313 Madison Street
Hyattsville, Maryland 20781

Head of School: Daniel J. McMahon, PhD

General Information Boys' day college-preparatory, arts, business, religious studies, technology, and music (instrumental and choral) school, affiliated with Roman Catholic Church. Grades 9–12. Founded: 1946. Setting: suburban. Nearest major city is Washington, DC. 6-acre campus. 5 buildings on campus. Approved or accredited by Middle States Association of Colleges and Schools, National Catholic Education Association, and Maryland Department of Education. Endowment: $3 million. Total enrollment: 795. Upper school average class size: 17. Upper school faculty-student ratio: 1:13. There are 178 required school days per year for Upper School students. Upper School students typically attend 5 days per week. The average school day consists of 6 hours.

Upper School Student Profile Grade 9: 191 students (191 boys); Grade 10: 200 students (200 boys); Grade 11: 190 students (190 boys); Grade 12: 214 students (214 boys). 59% of students are Roman Catholic.

Faculty School total: 68. In upper school: 53 men, 15 women; 43 have advanced degrees.

Subjects Offered Accounting, Advanced Placement courses, algebra, American government, American history, American history-AP, anatomy and physiology, art, art history, art-AP, astronomy, band, biology, biology-AP, British literature, British literature-AP, business, business law, calculus, calculus-AP, campus ministry, chemistry, chemistry-AP, Chinese, choral music, chorus, Christian ethics, church history, college admission preparation, community service, computer applications, computer programming, computer science, computer science-AP, computer skills, computer studies, contemporary art, digital photography, English, English composition, English literature, environmental science, film studies, French, French language-AP, geology, geometry, German, German-AP, government, government-AP, Greek, health, health education, history, history of religion, history of rock and roll, honors algebra, honors English, honors geometry, honors U.S. history, honors world history, instrumental music, jazz, journalism, Latin, Latin American studies, Latin-AP, literature-AP, mathematics, modern languages, music, music performance, mythology, newspaper, photography, photojournalism, physical education, physical science, physics, physics-AP, pre-calculus, psychology, SAT preparation, science, science research, social studies, Spanish, Spanish-AP, speech, sports medicine, statistics, studio art, studio art-AP, study skills, symphonic band, theology, trigonometry, U.S. government, U.S. government and politics-AP, U.S. history, U.S. literature, vocal music, world history, writing, yearbook.

Graduation Requirements Arts, computer science, English, foreign language, mathematics, physical education (includes health), science, social studies (includes history), theology, 55 hours of Christian service, service reflection paper.

Special Academic Programs 17 Advanced Placement exams for which test preparation is offered; honors section; independent study; academic accommodation for the gifted, the musically talented, and the artistically talented; remedial reading and/or remedial writing.

College Admission Counseling 185 students graduated in 2013; 180 went to college, including Howard University; Salisbury University; The Catholic University of America; Towson University; University of Maryland, Baltimore County; University of Maryland, College Park. Other: 2 went to work, 3 entered military service. Mean SAT critical reading: 530, mean SAT math: 530, mean SAT writing: 506. 26% scored over

600 on SAT critical reading, 26% scored over 600 on SAT math, 15% scored over 600 on SAT writing.

Student Life Upper grades have uniform requirement, student council, honor system. Discipline rests primarily with faculty. Attendance at religious services is required.

Summer Programs Remediation, enrichment, sports, art/fine arts, computer instruction programs offered; session focuses on remediation/enrichment; held on campus; accepts boys and girls; open to students from other schools. 400 students usually enrolled. 2014 schedule: June 23 to July 25. Application deadline: June 20.

Tuition and Aid Day student tuition: $14,750. Tuition installment plan (FACTS Tuition Payment Plan). Tuition-reduction for siblings, merit scholarship grants, need-based scholarship grants, paying campus jobs available. In 2013–14, 58% of upper-school students received aid; total upper-school merit-scholarship money awarded: $551,950. Total amount of financial aid awarded in 2013–14: $1,454,688.

Admissions Traditional secondary-level entrance grade is 9. For fall 2013, 450 students applied for upper-level admission, 350 were accepted, 197 enrolled. Archdiocese of Washington Entrance Exam, High School Placement Test or High School Placement Test (closed version) from Scholastic Testing Service required. Deadline for receipt of application materials: December 15. Application fee required: $50.

Athletics Interscholastic: baseball, basketball, crew, cross-country running, diving, football, golf, hockey, ice hockey, indoor track, indoor track & field, lacrosse, rugby, soccer, swimming and diving, tennis, track and field, ultimate Frisbee, water polo, winter (indoor) track, wrestling; intramural: basketball, paddle tennis, strength & conditioning, table tennis. 2 PE instructors, 1 coach, 2 athletic trainers.

Computers Computers are regularly used in computer applications, digital applications, English, independent study, lab/keyboard, library, newspaper, publishing, science, technology, Web site design, word processing, yearbook classes. Computer network features include on-campus library services, Internet access, wireless campus network, Internet filtering or blocking technology, ProQuest, SIRS, World Book. Computer access in designated common areas is available to students. Students grades are available online. The school has a published electronic and media policy.

Contact Mrs. Christine Thomas, Assistant Director of Admissions. 240-764-2210. Fax: 240-764-2277. E-mail: cthomas@dematha.org. Website: www.dematha.org

DENVER ACADEMY

Denver, Colorado
See Special Needs Schools section.

DENVER CHRISTIAN HIGH SCHOOL

2135 South Pearl Street
Denver, Colorado 80210

Head of School: Mr. Steve Kortenhoeven

General Information Coeducational day college-preparatory, general academic, arts, business, religious studies, bilingual studies, and technology school, affiliated with Christian Reformed Church. Grades 9–12. Founded: 1950. Setting: urban. 4-acre campus. 1 building on campus. Approved or accredited by Association of Christian Schools International, Christian Schools International, North Central Association of Colleges and Schools, and Colorado Department of Education. Endowment: $1.5 million. Total enrollment: 142. Upper school average class size: 20. Upper school faculty-student ratio: 1:19. There are 180 required school days per year for Upper School students. Upper School students typically attend 5 days per week. The average school day consists of 6 hours and 45 minutes.

Upper School Student Profile Grade 9: 45 students (26 boys, 19 girls); Grade 10: 38 students (16 boys, 22 girls); Grade 11: 29 students (18 boys, 11 girls); Grade 12: 30 students (18 boys, 12 girls). 20% of students are members of Christian Reformed Church.

Faculty School total: 17. In upper school: 8 men, 9 women; 16 have advanced degrees.

Subjects Offered Acting, advanced biology, advanced chemistry, advanced computer applications, advanced math, algebra, American government, American history, American literature, art, band, Bible, biology, British literature, calculus, chamber groups, chemistry, choir, Christian doctrine, Christian scripture, church history, composition, computer applications, concert band, concert choir, consumer economics, drama, driver education, earth science, European history, general math, government, grammar, health, introduction to literature, jazz band, keyboarding, personal fitness, physical education, physical fitness, physics, poetry, pre-algebra, pre-calculus, psychology, research, senior seminar, Shakespeare, Spanish, speech, studio art, symphonic band, the Web, trigonometry, U.S. government, U.S. history, Web site design, weight fitness, Western civilization, world geography, world history, yearbook.

Graduation Requirements Bible studies.

Special Academic Programs Honors section; independent study; special instructional classes for deaf students.

College Admission Counseling 40 students graduated in 2013; 32 went to college, including Baylor University; Calvin College; Colorado State University; Dordt College; University of Northern Colorado. Other: 4 went to work, 1 entered military service, 3 had other specific plans. Mean SAT critical reading: 560, mean SAT math: 545, mean composite ACT: 24.

Student Life Upper grades have specified standards of dress, student council. Discipline rests primarily with faculty. Attendance at religious services is required.

Tuition and Aid Day student tuition: $10,340. Tuition installment plan (FACTS Tuition Payment Plan, monthly payment plans). Tuition reduction for siblings, merit scholarship grants, need-based scholarship grants available. In 2013–14, 45% of upper-school students received aid; total upper-school merit-scholarship money awarded: $1200. Total amount of financial aid awarded in 2013–14: $35,000.

Admissions Traditional secondary-level entrance grade is 9. For fall 2013, 18 students applied for upper-level admission, 15 were accepted, 13 enrolled. WISC-III and Woodcock-Johnson, WISC/Woodcock-Johnson or Woodcock-Johnson Educational Evaluation, WISC III required. Deadline for receipt of application materials: none. Application fee required: $260. Interview required.

Athletics Interscholastic: baseball (boys), basketball (b,g), cheering (g), cross-country running (b,g), football (b), golf (b), soccer (b,g), track and field (b,g), volleyball (g); coed interscholastic: physical training, strength & conditioning, weight training. 3 PE instructors, 24 coaches, 1 athletic trainer.

Computers Computer network features include on-campus library services, Internet access, wireless campus network, Internet filtering or blocking technology. Student e-mail accounts are available to students. Students grades are available online. The school has a published electronic and media policy.

Contact Mrs. Sandie Posthumus, Administrative Assistant. 303-733-1804 Ext. 110. Fax: 303-733-7734. E-mail: sposthumus@denverchristian.org. Website: www.denverchristian.org

DEPAUL CATHOLIC HIGH SCHOOL

1512 Alps Road
Wayne, New Jersey 07470

Head of School: Mr. Joseph Tweed

General Information Coeducational day college-preparatory, arts, religious studies, and technology school, affiliated with Roman Catholic Church. Grades 8–12. Founded: 1956. Setting: suburban. Nearest major city is New York, NY. 5-acre campus. 2 buildings on campus. Approved or accredited by National Catholic Education Association and New Jersey Department of Education. Total enrollment: 650. Upper school average class size: 22. Upper school faculty-student ratio: 1:19. There are 185 required school days per year for Upper School students. Upper School students typically attend 5 days per week. The average school day consists of 7 hours.

Upper School Student Profile 90% of students are Roman Catholic.

Faculty School total: 65. In upper school: 25 men, 40 women; 40 have advanced degrees.

Special Academic Programs International Baccalaureate program; Advanced Placement exam preparation; honors section; accelerated programs; remedial reading and/or remedial writing; remedial math; programs in general development for dyslexic students; special instructional classes for deaf students, blind students.

College Admission Counseling 175 students graduated in 2013; 174 went to college. Other: 1 entered military service.

Student Life Upper grades have uniform requirement, student council, honor system. Discipline rests equally with students and faculty. Attendance at religious services is required.

Summer Programs Enrichment, advancement, sports, computer instruction programs offered; session focuses on academics and physical fitness; held on campus; accepts boys and girls; open to students from other schools. 300 students usually enrolled. 2014 schedule: June 20 to August 29.

Tuition and Aid Day student tuition: $11,100. Tuition installment plan (SMART Tuition Payment Plan, monthly payment plans, individually arranged payment plans). Tuition reduction for siblings, merit scholarship grants, need-based scholarship grants available.

Admissions Traditional secondary-level entrance grade is 9. For fall 2013, 550 students applied for upper-level admission, 350 were accepted, 150 enrolled. Deadline for receipt of application materials: none. No application fee required. Interview recommended.

Athletics Interscholastic: baseball (boys), basketball (b,g), cheering (g), cross-country running (b,g), dance (g), dance squad (g), dance team (g), danceline (g), figure skating (g), football (b), gymnastics (g), ice skating (g), independent competitive sports (b,g), indoor track (b,g), indoor track & field (b,g), lacrosse (b,g), modern dance (g), soccer (b,g), softball (b), swimming and diving (b,g), tennis (b,g), track and field (b,g), volleyball (b,g), weight lifting (b,g), weight training (b,g), winter (indoor) track (b,g), wrestling (b); intramural: aerobics/dance (g), equestrian sports (g), strength & conditioning (b,g); coed interscholastic: alpine skiing, bowling, drill team, golf, ice hockey, skiing (downhill); coed intramural: backpacking, hiking/backpacking. 5 PE instructors, 40 coaches, 1 athletic trainer.

Computers Computer network features include on-campus library services, Internet access, wireless campus network, Internet filtering or blocking technology. Campus intranet, student e-mail accounts, and computer access in designated common areas are available to students. Students grades are available online. The school has a published electronic and media policy.

Contact Mr. John W. Merritt, Director of Admissions. 973-694-3702 Ext. 410. Fax: 973-694-3525. E-mail: merrittj@dpchs.org. Website: www.depaulcatholic.org

THE DERRYFIELD SCHOOL

2108 River Road
Manchester, New Hampshire 03104-1302

Head of School: Mrs. Mary Halpin Carter, PhD

General Information Coeducational day college-preparatory school. Grades 6–12. Founded: 1964. Setting: suburban. Nearest major city is Boston, MA. 84-acre campus. 4 buildings on campus. Approved or accredited by Association of Independent Schools in New England, Independent Schools of Northern New England, New England Association of Schools and Colleges, and New Hampshire Department of Education. Member of National Association of Independent Schools and Secondary School Admission Test Board. Endowment: $5 million. Total enrollment: 387. Upper school average class size: 14. Upper school faculty-student ratio: 1:8. There are 160 required school days per year for Upper School students. Upper School students typically attend 5 days per week. The average school day consists of 6 hours and 45 minutes.

Upper School Student Profile Grade 9: 75 students (35 boys, 40 girls); Grade 10: 59 students (37 boys, 22 girls); Grade 11: 70 students (35 boys, 35 girls); Grade 12: 67 students (35 boys, 32 girls).

Faculty School total: 46. In upper school: 18 men, 16 women; 23 have advanced degrees.

Subjects Offered 20th century history, 3-dimensional art, algebra, American literature, anatomy and physiology, ancient world history, art, biology, British literature, calculus, calculus-AP, chemistry, chemistry-AP, China/Japan history, Chinese, chorus, computer science, contemporary issues, creative writing, drafting, drama, driver education, earth science, economics, economics and history, engineering, English, English composition, English literature, English-AP, European history, expository writing, film, fine arts, freshman foundations, geography, geometry, global issues, government/civics, graphics, Greek, health, history, Holocaust, independent study, Latin, Latin-AP, mathematics, media, music, music theory, mythology, organic chemistry, philosophy, physical education, physics, physics-AP, pre-calculus, public speaking, robotics, science, sculpture, senior project, social studies, Spanish, Spanish language-AP, speech, statistics, statistics-AP, studio art, theater, trigonometry, U.S. history-AP, Western civilization, world history, world literature, writing.

Graduation Requirements Arts and fine arts (art, music, dance, drama), athletics, English, foreign language, health and wellness, history, mathematics, science.

Special Academic Programs Advanced Placement exam preparation; honors section; independent study; term-away projects.

College Admission Counseling 57 students graduated in 2013; 56 went to college, including Dartmouth College; Elon University; The Johns Hopkins University; University of Michigan; University of New Hampshire; University of Vermont. Other: 1 entered a postgraduate year. Mean SAT critical reading: 607, mean SAT math: 613, mean SAT writing: 616, mean combined SAT: 1836, mean composite ACT: 26.

Student Life Upper grades have specified standards of dress, student council. Discipline rests equally with students and faculty.

Summer Programs Enrichment, art/fine arts programs offered; session focuses on multi-camp program: theater, robotics, math, writing; held on campus; accepts boys and girls; open to students from other schools. 175 students usually enrolled. 2014 schedule: July to August. Application deadline: June.

Tuition and Aid Day student tuition: $28,535. Tuition installment plan (SMART Tuition Payment Plan). Merit scholarship grants, need-based scholarship grants, Malone Family Foundation grants available. In 2013–14, 24% of upper-school students received aid; total upper-school merit-scholarship money awarded: $195,730. Total amount of financial aid awarded in 2013–14: $1,595,407.

Admissions Traditional secondary-level entrance grade is 9. SSAT required. Deadline for receipt of application materials: January 31. Application fee required: $50. On-campus interview required.

Athletics Interscholastic: alpine skiing (boys, girls), baseball (b), basketball (b,g), crew (b,g), cross-country running (b,g), diving (b), field hockey (g), independent competitive sports (b,g), lacrosse (b,g), skiing (cross-country) (b,g), skiing (downhill) (b,g), soccer (b,g), softball (g), tennis (b,g); coed interscholastic: equestrian sports, golf, swimming and diving; coed intramural: aerobics, cooperative games, dance, flag football, physical training, ropes courses, strength & conditioning, weight training, yoga. 1 PE instructor, 10 coaches, 1 athletic trainer.

Computers Computers are regularly used in all academic, college planning classes. Computer network features include on-campus library services, online commercial services, Internet access, wireless campus network, online computer linked to New Hampshire State Library. Campus intranet, student e-mail accounts, and computer access in designated common areas are available to students. Students grades are available online. The school has a published electronic and media policy.

Contact Ms. Kathleen Rutty-Fey, Director of Admission. 603-669-4524. Fax: 603-641-9521. E-mail: krutty@derryfield.org. Website: www.derryfield.org

See Display on next page and Close-Up on page 536.

DETROIT COUNTRY DAY SCHOOL

22305 West Thirteen Mile Road
Beverly Hills, Michigan 48025-4435

Head of School: Glen P. Shilling

General Information Coeducational day college-preparatory and arts school. Grades PK–12. Founded: 1914. Setting: suburban. Nearest major city is Detroit. Students are housed in on-campus homes. 100-acre campus. 1 building on campus. Approved or accredited by Independent Schools Association of the Central States and Michigan Department of Education. Member of National Association of Independent Schools. Endowment: $32 million. Total enrollment: 1,600. Upper school average class size: 15. Upper school faculty-student ratio: 1:8.

Upper School Student Profile Grade 9: 141 students (78 boys, 63 girls); Grade 10: 170 students (99 boys, 71 girls); Grade 11: 175 students (106 boys, 69 girls); Grade 12: 169 students (99 boys, 70 girls).

Faculty School total: 202. In upper school: 35 men, 37 women; 60 have advanced degrees.

Subjects Offered African-American studies, algebra, American history, American literature, American studies, analytic geometry, anatomy, anatomy and physiology, ancient history, art, art and culture, art appreciation, art-AP, astronomy, band, biology, botany, calculus, ceramics, chemistry, Chinese, chorus, college counseling, community service, composition, computer programming, computer science, current events, design, drama, drawing, ecology, economics, economics and history, English, English literature, environmental science, European history, fine arts, finite math, French, genetics, geometry, German, government/civics, grammar, graphic arts, health, history, humanities, Japanese, Latin, literature, mathematics, media, metalworking, microbiology, music, music history, music theory, natural history, orchestra, painting, photography, physical education, physical science, physics, physiology, poetry, pre-calculus, printmaking, science, sculpture, social studies, Spanish, speech, statistics, study skills, theater, theory of knowledge, Western civilization, world literature, zoology.

Graduation Requirements American government, American history, arts and fine arts (art, music, dance, drama), English, foreign language, mathematics, science, speech, athletic participation, skill-oriented activities, service-oriented activities.

Special Academic Programs International Baccalaureate program; Advanced Placement exam preparation; honors section; academic accommodation for the gifted, the musically talented, and the artistically talented.

College Admission Counseling 166 students graduated in 2013; all went to college, including Michigan State University; University of Chicago; University of Michigan. Mean SAT critical reading: 652, mean SAT math: 693, mean SAT writing: 665, mean combined SAT: 2010, mean composite ACT: 27.

Student Life Upper grades have uniform requirement, student council, honor system. Discipline rests primarily with faculty.

Summer Programs Enrichment, advancement, sports, art/fine arts, computer instruction programs offered; session focuses on academic enrichment and sports camps; held on campus; accepts boys and girls; open to students from other schools. 2014 schedule: June 18 to August 3.

Tuition and Aid Day student tuition: $27,700. Tuition installment plan (The Tuition Plan, Insured Tuition Payment Plan, Academic Management Services Plan, Key Tuition Payment Plan, SMART Tuition Payment Plan, FACTS Tuition Payment Plan, Dewars Tuition Refund Plan). Need-based scholarship grants available.

Admissions Traditional secondary-level entrance grade is 9. ISEE and Otis-Lennon School Ability Test required. Deadline for receipt of application materials: none. Application fee required: $50. Interview required.

Athletics Interscholastic: alpine skiing (boys, girls), ball hockey (g), baseball (b), basketball (b,g), bicycling (b,g), bowling (b,g), cross-country running (b,g), dance squad (g), dance team (g), diving (b,g), field hockey (g), football (b), golf (b,g), hockey (b), ice hockey (b,g), lacrosse (b,g), skiing (downhill) (b,g), soccer (b,g), softball (g), swimming and diving (b,g), tennis (b,g), track and field (b,g), volleyball (g), wrestling (b); intramural: weight lifting (b,g); coed interscholastic: cheering, mountain biking, outdoor adventure, sailing, snowboarding; coed intramural: basketball, project adventure, strength & conditioning. 4 coaches, 2 athletic trainers.

Computers Computers are regularly used in all classes. Computer network features include on-campus library services, online commercial services, Internet access, wireless campus network, Internet filtering or blocking technology. Campus intranet and student e-mail accounts are available to students. Students grades are available online. The school has a published electronic and media policy.

Contact Michele Reimer, Enrollment and Admissions Manager. 248-430-3587. Fax: 248-203-2184. E-mail: mreimer@dcds.edu. Website: www.dcds.edu

DEVON PREPARATORY SCHOOL

363 North Valley Forge Road
Devon, Pennsylvania 19333-1299

Head of School: Rev. James J. Shea, Sch.P

General Information Boys' day college-preparatory and religious studies school, affiliated with Roman Catholic Church. Grades 6–12. Founded: 1956. Setting: suburban. Nearest major city is Philadelphia. 20-acre campus. 7 buildings on campus. Approved or accredited by Middle States Association of Colleges and Schools, National Catholic Education Association, and Pennsylvania Department of Education. Member of National Association of Independent Schools. Endowment: $600,000. Total enrollment: 253. Upper school average class size: 15. Upper school faculty-student ratio: 1:10. There are 180 required school days per year for Upper School students. Upper School students typically attend 5 days per week. The average school day consists of 6 hours.

Upper School Student Profile Grade 9: 53 students (53 boys); Grade 10: 54 students (54 boys); Grade 11: 52 students (52 boys); Grade 12: 40 students (40 boys). 84% of students are Roman Catholic.

Faculty School total: 32. In upper school: 23 men, 9 women; 15 have advanced degrees.

Subjects Offered Accounting, ACT preparation, Advanced Placement courses, algebra, American history, American literature, anatomy and physiology, art, biology, biology-AP, British literature, calculus, calculus-AP, chemistry, chemistry-AP, community service, computer science, computer science-AP, economics, English, environmental science, environmental science-AP, European history, forensics, French, French language-AP, geography, geometry, German, German-AP, health, human geography - AP, language-AP, Latin, literature and composition-AP, mathematics, modern European history, physical education, physics, physics-AP, political science, pre-calculus, religion, science, social studies, Spanish, Spanish-AP, trigonometry, U.S. history-AP, world cultures, world literature.

Graduation Requirements Computer science, English, foreign language, geography, Latin, mathematics, physical education (includes health), political science, religion (includes Bible studies and theology), science, social studies (includes history). Community service is required.

Special Academic Programs 21 Advanced Placement exams for which test preparation is offered.

College Admission Counseling 39 students graduated in 2013; all went to college, including Drexel University; Loyola University Maryland; Penn State University Park; Rochester Institute of Technology; Saint Joseph's University; University of Pennsylvania. Median SAT critical reading: 613, median SAT math: 623, median SAT writing: 587, median combined SAT: 1823.

Student Life Upper grades have specified standards of dress, student council. Discipline rests primarily with faculty. Attendance at religious services is required.

Tuition and Aid Day student tuition: $20,800. Tuition installment plan (monthly payment plans). Tuition reduction for siblings, merit scholarship grants, need-based scholarship grants available. In 2013–14, 65% of upper-school students received aid; total upper-school merit-scholarship money awarded: $660,000. Total amount of financial aid awarded in 2013–14: $1,030,000.

Admissions Traditional secondary-level entrance grade is 9. For fall 2013, 200 students applied for upper-level admission, 75 were accepted, 32 enrolled. Math and English placement tests required. Deadline for receipt of application materials: none. Application fee required: $50. On-campus interview recommended.

Athletics Interscholastic: baseball, basketball, cross-country running, golf, indoor track & field, lacrosse, soccer, swimming and diving, tennis, track and field. 2 PE instructors, 9 coaches, 1 athletic trainer.

Computers Computers are regularly used in all academic, newspaper, technology, writing, yearbook classes. Computer network features include on-campus library services, Internet access, wireless campus network, Internet filtering or blocking technology. Student e-mail accounts and computer access in designated common areas are available to students. Students grades are available online. The school has a published electronic and media policy.

Contact Mr. Patrick Kane, Director of Admissions. 610-688-7337 Ext. 129. Fax: 610-688-2409. E-mail: pkane@devonprep.com. Website: www.devonprep.com

DEXTER SOUTHFIELD

20 Newton Street
Brookline, Massachusetts 02445

Head of School: Mr. Todd A. Vincent

General Information Boys' day college-preparatory and arts school. Grades 1–12. Founded: 1926. Setting: suburban. Nearest major city is Boston. 36-acre campus. 4 buildings on campus. Approved or accredited by Association of Independent Schools in New England and Massachusetts Department of Education. Candidate for accreditation by New England Association of Schools and Colleges. Member of National Association of Independent Schools and Secondary School Admission Test Board. Endowment: $24 million. Total enrollment: 424. Upper school average class size: 16. Upper school faculty-student ratio: 1:7. There are 172 required school days per year for Upper School students. Upper School students typically attend 5 days per week. The average school day consists of 6 hours and 45 minutes.

Upper School Student Profile Grade 9: 31 students (31 boys); Grade 10: 25 students (25 boys); Grade 11: 38 students (38 boys); Grade 12: 42 students (42 boys).

Faculty School total: 110. In upper school: 26 men, 23 women; 31 have advanced degrees.

Subjects Offered Acting, advanced studio art-AP, algebra, American government, American history-AP, American literature, American literature-AP, analysis and differential calculus, Ancient Greek, ancient history, art, art history, art history-AP, art-AP, astronomy, biology, biology-AP, British literature, British literature-AP, calculus, calculus-AP, Central and Eastern European history, ceramics, character education, chemistry, chemistry-AP, Chinese history, choral music, community service, computer graphics, computer music, conceptual physics, constitutional law, digital photography, drama workshop, earth and space science, economics, electronic music, engineering,

English, English language-AP, English literature-AP, environmental science, ethics, European history, European history-AP, European literature, Far Eastern history, French, French language-AP, French literature-AP, French-AP, geometry, grammar, graphic arts, history of China and Japan, history of England, history of music, honors algebra, honors English, honors geometry, honors U.S. history, independent study, instrumental music, jazz ensemble, Latin, Latin-AP, marine biology, medieval history, Middle Eastern history, modern European history, music, music composition, music history, music technology, music theory, music theory-AP, music-AP, photography, physics, physics-AP, probability and statistics, public speaking, robotics, Russian history, SAT preparation, Spanish, Spanish language-AP, Spanish literature-AP, Spanish-AP, statistics, studio art, studio art-AP, U.S. history, U.S. history-AP, vocal music, woodworking, writing workshop.

Special Academic Programs 11 Advanced Placement exams for which test preparation is offered; honors section; independent study.

College Admission Counseling 40 students graduated in 2013; 39 went to college, including Boston College; Bowdoin College; Colgate University; Harvard University; Middlebury College; Trinity College. Other: 1 entered a postgraduate year.

Student Life Upper grades have specified standards of dress, student council, honor system. Discipline rests equally with students and faculty. Attendance at religious services is required.

Tuition and Aid Day student tuition: $40,795. Tuition installment plan (monthly payment plans). Need-based scholarship grants available. In 2013–14, 25% of upper-school students received aid. Total amount of financial aid awarded in 2013–14: $3,000,000.

Admissions Traditional secondary-level entrance grade is 9. For fall 2013, 71 students applied for upper-level admission, 38 were accepted, 15 enrolled. ISEE, PSAT and SAT for applicants to grade 11 and 12 or SSAT required. Deadline for receipt of application materials: February 1. Application fee required: $50. Interview required.

Athletics Interscholastic: baseball, basketball, crew, cross-country running, curling, fitness, football, golf, ice hockey, lacrosse, rowing, soccer, squash, strength & conditioning, swimming and diving, tennis. 6 coaches, 2 athletic trainers.

Computers Computers are regularly used in all classes. Computer network features include on-campus library services, online commercial services, Internet access, wireless campus network, Internet filtering or blocking technology, one-to-one laptop program. Campus intranet and student e-mail accounts are available to students. The school has a published electronic and media policy.

Contact Mrs. Jennifer DaPonte, Admissions Office Manager. 617-454-2721. Fax: 617-928-7691. E-mail: admissions@dextersouthfield.org. Website: www.dextersouthfield.org

DEXTER SOUTHFIELD

20 Newton Street
Brookline, Massachusetts 02445

Head of School: Mr. Todd A. Vincent

General Information Girls' day college-preparatory and arts school. Grades PK–12. Founded: 1992. Setting: suburban. Nearest major city is Boston. 36-acre campus. 4 buildings on campus. Approved or accredited by Association of Independent Schools in New England and Massachusetts Department of Education. Candidate for accreditation by New England Association of Schools and Colleges. Endowment: $8 million. Total enrollment: 330. Upper school average class size: 14. Upper school faculty-student ratio: 1:7. There are 172 required school days per year for Upper School students. Upper School students typically attend 5 days per week. The average school day consists of 6 hours and 45 minutes.

Upper School Student Profile Grade 9: 19 students (19 girls); Grade 10: 22 students (22 girls); Grade 11: 23 students (23 girls); Grade 12: 10 students (10 girls).

Faculty School total: 110. In upper school: 26 men, 23 women; 31 have advanced degrees.

Subjects Offered Advanced studio art-AP, algebra, American government, American history, American history-AP, American literature, anatomy and physiology, Ancient Greek, ancient world history, art, art history, astronomy, biology, biology-AP, British history, British literature, British literature (honors), calculus-AP, chemistry, chemistry-AP, Chinese history, choir, college counseling, community service, computer music, constitutional history of U.S., digital imaging, digital photography, drama performance, drama workshop, earth and space science, English, English language-AP, English literature-AP, environmental science, equality and freedom, ethics, European history, European history-AP, French, French-AP, geometry, grammar, health and wellness, honors algebra, honors English, honors geometry, human anatomy, jazz ensemble, Latin, Latin-AP, marine biology, music technology, music theory-AP, painting, physics, physics-AP, physiology, pre-calculus, probability and statistics, public speaking, SAT preparation, senior project, shop, space and physical sciences, Spanish, Spanish language-AP, statistics-AP, studio art, studio art-AP, The 20th Century, U.S. history, U.S. history-AP, world history, world history-AP.

Graduation Requirements All academic.

Special Academic Programs 13 Advanced Placement exams for which test preparation is offered; honors section; independent study.

College Admission Counseling 19 students graduated in 2013; 18 went to college, including Columbia University; Dartmouth College; Harvard University;

Massachusetts Institute of Technology; The George Washington University; Trinity College. Other: 1 entered a postgraduate year.

Student Life Upper grades have specified standards of dress, student council, honor system. Discipline rests equally with students and faculty. Attendance at religious services is required.

Tuition and Aid Day student tuition: $40,795. Tuition installment plan (monthly payment plans). Need-based scholarship grants available. In 2013–14, 27% of upper-school students received aid. Total amount of financial aid awarded in 2013–14: $3,000,000.

Admissions Traditional secondary-level entrance grade is 9. For fall 2013, 39 students applied for upper-level admission, 29 were accepted, 8 enrolled. ISEE, PSAT and SAT for applicants to grade 11 and 12, SSAT or TOEFL required. Deadline for receipt of application materials: February 1. Application fee required: $50. Interview required.

Athletics Interscholastic: basketball, crew, cross-country running, curling, field hockey, ice hockey, independent competitive sports, lacrosse, physical fitness, rowing, soccer, softball, squash, tennis, weight training; intramural: dance, hiking/backpacking, life saving. 4 coaches, 2 athletic trainers.

Computers Computers are regularly used in all classes. Computer network features include on-campus library services, online commercial services, Internet access, wireless campus network, Internet filtering or blocking technology, one-to-one device program. Campus intranet and student e-mail accounts are available to students. The school has a published electronic and media policy.

Contact Mrs. Jennifer DaPonte, Admissions Office Manager. 617-454-2721. Fax: 617-928-7691. E-mail: admissions@dextersouthfield.org. Website: www.dextersouthfield.org

DOANE STUART SCHOOL

199 Washington Avenue
Rensselaer, New York 12144

Head of School: Mrs. Lisa F. Brown

General Information Coeducational day college-preparatory, arts, religious studies, Irish and peace studies, and bioethics school, affiliated with Episcopal Church. Grades N–12. Founded: 1852. Setting: urban. Nearest major city is Albany. 27-acre campus. 3 buildings on campus. Approved or accredited by National Association of Episcopal Schools and New York Department of Education. Member of National Association of Independent Schools. Endowment: $1 million. Total enrollment: 302. Upper school average class size: 14. Upper school faculty-student ratio: 1:7. Upper School students typically attend 5 days per week. The average school day consists of 7 hours and 30 minutes.

Upper School Student Profile Grade 9: 36 students (15 boys, 21 girls); Grade 10: 49 students (23 boys, 26 girls); Grade 11: 36 students (18 boys, 18 girls); Grade 12: 33 students (13 boys, 20 girls). 10% of students are members of Episcopal Church.

Faculty School total: 50. In upper school: 13 men, 10 women; 13 have advanced degrees.

Subjects Offered 3-dimensional art, 3-dimensional design, accounting, advanced biology, advanced chemistry, advanced math, advanced studio art-AP, African-American literature, algebra, American history, American literature, art, bioethics, biology, Buddhism, calculus, campus ministry, ceramics, chemistry, choral music, college admission preparation, college counseling, college placement, college planning, college writing, community service, computer science, creative writing, earth science, economics, English, English literature, environmental science, ethics, fencing, fine arts, French, geometry, government/civics, health, history, independent study, instrumental music, instruments, international studies, internship, Irish literature, Irish studies, jazz band, jazz ensemble, journalism, literature, mathematics, mechanical drawing, media arts, medieval/Renaissance history, mentorship program, microeconomics, Middle Eastern history, music, music composition, music performance, music theory, newspaper, oil painting, opera, oral communications, oral expression, organ, painting, peace and justice, peace education, peace studies, performing arts, photography, physical education, physical fitness, physical science, physics, play production, play/screen writing, playwriting, playwriting and directing, poetry, policy and value, political economy, political science, politics, portfolio art, portfolio writing, pre-algebra, pre-calculus, psychology, psychology-AP, public service, public speaking, religion, SAT preparation, science, senior humanities, senior seminar, Shakespeare, social studies, Spanish, theater, trigonometry, world history, writing.

Special Academic Programs 30 Advanced Placement exams for which test preparation is offered; independent study; term-away projects; study at local college for college credit; domestic exchange program; study abroad; academic accommodation for the gifted, the musically talented, and the artistically talented.

College Admission Counseling 29 students graduated in 2012; all went to college, including Emory University; Northwestern University; The Juilliard School; Tufts University; University of California, Berkeley; Vassar College.

Student Life Upper grades have uniform requirement, student council. Discipline rests primarily with faculty. Attendance at religious services is required.

Tuition and Aid Day student tuition: $20,105–$22,255. Tuition installment plan (Academic Management Services Plan). Need-based scholarship grants available. In 2012–13, 50% of upper-school students received aid. Total amount of financial aid awarded in 2012–13: $844,207.

Admissions Traditional secondary-level entrance grade is 9. For fall 2012, 121 students applied for upper-level admission, 70 were accepted, 40 enrolled. School's own test required. Deadline for receipt of application materials: none. Application fee required: $75. On-campus interview required.

Athletics Interscholastic: baseball (boys), basketball (b,g), crew (b,g), soccer (b,g), softball (g), volleyball (g); intramural: backpacking (b,g), independent competitive sports (b,g); coed interscholastic: crew, cross-country running, independent competitive sports, tennis; coed intramural: backpacking, crew, cross-country running, fencing, Frisbee, hiking/backpacking, independent competitive sports, jogging, outdoor adventure, outdoors, physical fitness, sailing, soccer, strength & conditioning, tai chi, ultimate Frisbee, walking, yoga. 2 PE instructors, 8 coaches.

Computers Computers are regularly used in accounting, architecture, art, basic skills, business, career exploration, college planning, creative writing, current events, data processing, desktop publishing, drawing and design, economics, English, ethics, foreign language, freshman foundations, geography, graphic arts, graphic design, graphics, health, historical foundations for arts, history, humanities, independent study, introduction to technology, journalism, keyboarding, language development, learning cognition, library science, library skills, literary magazine, mathematics, media arts, media production, mentorship program, multimedia, music, music technology, news writing, newspaper, philosophy, photography, programming, psychology, publications, publishing, reading, religion, religious studies, remedial study skills, research skills, SAT preparation, science, senior seminar, social sciences, social studies, study skills, technology, theater, theater arts, video film production, Web site design, writing, writing, yearbook classes. Computer resources include on-campus library services, online commercial services, Internet access, wireless campus network. Computer access in designated common areas is available to students. The school has a published electronic and media policy.

Contact Mr. Michael Green, Director of Admission. 518-465-5222 Ext. 241. Fax: 518-465-5230. E-mail: mgreen@doanestuart.org. Website: www.doanestuart.org

THE DR. MIRIAM AND SHELDON G. ADELSON EDUCATIONAL CAMPUS, THE ADELSON UPPER SCHOOL

9700 West Hillpoint Road
Las Vegas, Nevada 89134

Head of School: Mr. Paul Schiffman

General Information Coeducational day college-preparatory, arts, religious studies, and bilingual studies school, affiliated with Jewish faith. Grades PS–12. Founded: 1979. Setting: suburban. 30-acre campus. 1 building on campus. Approved or accredited by Nevada Department of Education. Member of National Association of Independent Schools. Languages of instruction: English, Hebrew, and Spanish. Endowment: $8 million. Total enrollment: 618. Upper school average class size: 16. Upper school faculty-student ratio: 1:10. There are 185 required school days per year for Upper School students. Upper School students typically attend 5 days per week. The average school day consists of 8 hours and 15 minutes.

Upper School Student Profile Grade 9: 44 students (25 boys, 19 girls); Grade 10: 28 students (12 boys, 16 girls); Grade 11: 31 students (14 boys, 17 girls); Grade 12: 29 students (15 boys, 14 girls). 80% of students are Jewish.

Faculty School total: 20. In upper school: 8 men, 12 women; all have advanced degrees.

Subjects Offered Yoga.

Graduation Requirements Jewish studies.

Special Academic Programs 8 Advanced Placement exams for which test preparation is offered; honors section; study at local college for college credit; academic accommodation for the gifted; programs in English, mathematics for dyslexic students; ESL (5 students enrolled).

College Admission Counseling Colleges students went to include University of Colorado Boulder.

Student Life Upper grades have uniform requirement, student council, honor system. Discipline rests primarily with faculty. Attendance at religious services is required.

Tuition and Aid Day student tuition: $19,950. Tuition installment plan (monthly payment plans). Tuition reduction for siblings, need-based scholarship grants available. In 2013–14, 30% of upper-school students received aid. Total amount of financial aid awarded in 2013–14: $1,000,000.

Admissions Traditional secondary-level entrance grade is 9. For fall 2013, 48 students applied for upper-level admission, 41 were accepted, 38 enrolled. Admissions testing and ERB (CTP-Verbal, Quantitative) required. Deadline for receipt of application materials: none. No application fee required. Interview required.

Athletics Interscholastic: aerobics/dance (girls), baseball (b), basketball (b,g), cheering (g), cross-country running (b,g), dance (b,g), dance team (b,g), fencing (b,g), modern dance (b,g), soccer (b,g), swimming and diving (b,g), tennis (b,g), volleyball (b,g); coed interscholastic: aquatics, golf. 12 PE instructors, 10 coaches.

Computers Computer network features include on-campus library services, Internet access, wireless campus network, Internet filtering or blocking technology. Student e-mail accounts are available to students. Students grades are available online. The school has a published electronic and media policy.

Contact 702-255-4500. Fax: 702-255-7232. Website: www.adelsoncampus.org

DOMINICAN ACADEMY

44 East 68th Street
New York, New York 10065

Head of School: Sr. Barbara Kane, OP

General Information Girls' day college-preparatory, arts, religious studies, and technology school, affiliated with Roman Catholic Church. Grades 9–12. Founded: 1897. Setting: urban. 1 building on campus. Approved or accredited by Middle States Association of Colleges and Schools, National Catholic Education Association, New York State Board of Regents, and New York Department of Education. Member of National Association of Independent Schools and Secondary School Admission Test Board. Total enrollment: 208. Upper school average class size: 20. Upper school faculty-student ratio: 1:8. There are 180 required school days per year for Upper School students. Upper School students typically attend 5 days per week. The average school day consists of 6 hours and 30 minutes.

Upper School Student Profile Grade 9: 53 students (53 girls); Grade 10: 55 students (55 girls); Grade 11: 40 students (40 girls); Grade 12: 60 students (60 girls). 85% of students are Roman Catholic.

Faculty School total: 27. In upper school: 3 men, 24 women; 20 have advanced degrees.

Subjects Offered Algebra, American history, American history-AP, American literature, art history-AP, biology, biology-AP, calculus, calculus-AP, chemistry, chemistry-AP, Chinese, chorus, communications, computer science, creative writing, dance, debate, drama, economics, economics-AP, English, English literature, English-AP, European history-AP, forensics, French, French-AP, geometry, global studies, government and politics-AP, government/civics, health, history, Latin, Latin-AP, library studies, logic, mathematics, music, music theory, physical education, physics, physics-AP, pre-calculus, psychology, religion, science, social studies, Spanish, Spanish-AP, world history.

Graduation Requirements Alternative physical education, arts and fine arts (art, music, dance, drama), English, foreign language, Latin, mathematics, religion (includes Bible studies and theology), science, social studies (includes history).

Special Academic Programs 11 Advanced Placement exams for which test preparation is offered; honors section.

College Admission Counseling 55 students graduated in 2013; all went to college, including Binghamton University, State University of New York; Boston University; Fordham University; Loyola University Maryland; New York University; Smith College.

Student Life Upper grades have uniform requirement, student council. Discipline rests primarily with faculty. Attendance at religious services is required.

Summer Programs Remediation, enrichment, advancement programs offered; session focuses on integrated Algebra Regents prep; held on campus; accepts girls; open to students from other schools. 8 students usually enrolled. 2014 schedule: June 27 to August 14. Application deadline: May 15.

Tuition and Aid Day student tuition: $11,750. Tuition installment plan (FACTS Tuition Payment Plan, individually arranged payment plans, quarterly payment plan, semester payment plan). Tuition reduction for siblings, merit scholarship grants, need-based scholarship grants, paying campus jobs available. In 2013–14, 33% of upper-school students received aid; total upper-school merit-scholarship money awarded: $45,000.

Admissions Traditional secondary-level entrance grade is 9. For fall 2013, 390 students applied for upper-level admission, 215 were accepted, 53 enrolled. Catholic High School Entrance Examination required. Deadline for receipt of application materials: December 20. No application fee required.

Athletics Interscholastic: basketball, cross-country running, soccer, softball, tennis, track and field, volleyball; intramural: billiards, dance, soccer, track and field, volleyball. 1 PE instructor.

Computers Computers are regularly used in economics, health, history, Latin, library science, library studies, mathematics, religious studies, science, technology classes. Computer network features include on-campus library services, online commercial services, Internet access, wireless campus network, Internet filtering or blocking technology, T1 fiber optic network. Campus intranet, student e-mail accounts, and computer access in designated common areas are available to students. The school has a published electronic and media policy.

Contact Ms. Olivia Soriano, Director of Admissions. 212-744-0195 Ext. 31. Fax: 212-744-0375. E-mail: osoriano@dominicanacademy.org. Website: www.dominicanacademy.org

DONELSON CHRISTIAN ACADEMY

300 Danyacrest Drive
Nashville, Tennessee 37214

Head of School: Mr. Keith M. Singer

General Information Coeducational day college-preparatory, arts, religious studies, and technology school, affiliated with Christian faith. Grades K4–12. Founded: 1971. Setting: suburban. 50-acre campus. 1 building on campus. Approved or accredited by Association of Christian Schools International, Southern Association of Colleges and Schools, and Tennessee Department of Education. Endowment: $78,000. Total enrollment: 701. Upper school average class size: 16. Upper school faculty-

student ratio: 1:16. There are 175 required school days per year for Upper School students. Upper School students typically attend 5 days per week. The average school day consists of 6 hours and 50 minutes.

Upper School Student Profile Grade 9: 48 students (26 boys, 22 girls); Grade 10: 41 students (20 boys, 21 girls); Grade 11: 66 students (33 boys, 33 girls); Grade 12: 64 students (29 boys, 35 girls). 95% of students are Christian faith.

Faculty School total: 66. In upper school: 10 men, 17 women; 19 have advanced degrees.

Subjects Offered 3-dimensional art, ACT preparation, Advanced Placement courses, advanced studio art-AP, algebra, American history, American history-AP, American literature, American literature-AP, anatomy, art, athletic training, Bible studies, biology, biology-AP, business, business skills, calculus, calculus-AP, chemistry, chemistry-AP, Chinese, choir, community service, computer science, creative writing, drama, earth science, ecology, economics, English, English language and composition-AP, English literature, English literature and composition-AP, environmental science, ESL, European history-AP, fine arts, French, geography, geometry, government/civics, grammar, health, history, honors algebra, honors English, honors geometry, honors U.S. history, journalism, keyboarding, Latin, Latin-AP, mathematics, music, personal finance, physical education, physics, physiology, psychology, religion, science, social sciences, social studies, sociology, Spanish, speech, theater, U.S. history-AP, world history, world literature, yearbook.

Graduation Requirements Arts and fine arts (art, music, dance, drama), Bible, chemistry, electives, English, foreign language, mathematics, physical education (includes health), science, social sciences, social studies (includes history), wellness, senior service (community service for 12th grade students).

Special Academic Programs 6 Advanced Placement exams for which test preparation is offered; honors section; independent study; study at local college for college credit; academic accommodation for the gifted; ESL (12 students enrolled).

College Admission Counseling 74 students graduated in 2013; 72 went to college, including Lipscomb University; Middle Tennessee State University; Tennessee Technological University; The University of Tennessee System; Trevecca Nazarene University; Union University. Other: 2 went to work. Median SAT critical reading: 670, median SAT math: 670, median SAT writing: 700, median combined SAT: 2040, median composite ACT: 23. 60% scored over 600 on SAT critical reading, 80% scored over 600 on SAT math, 60% scored over 600 on SAT writing, 60% scored over 1800 on combined SAT, 18% scored over 26 on composite ACT.

Student Life Upper grades have uniform requirement, student council, honor system. Discipline rests primarily with faculty. Attendance at religious services is required.

Summer Programs Sports, art/fine arts programs offered; session focuses on skill development; held on campus; accepts boys and girls; not open to students from other schools. 230 students usually enrolled. 2014 schedule: June 1 to August 1. Application deadline: none.

Tuition and Aid Day student tuition: $9995. Tuition installment plan (FACTS Tuition Payment Plan). Need-based scholarship grants available. In 2013–14, 24% of upper-school students received aid. Total amount of financial aid awarded in 2013–14: $142,580.

Admissions Traditional secondary-level entrance grade is 9. For fall 2013, 25 students applied for upper-level admission, 17 were accepted, 13 enrolled. Admissions testing required. Deadline for receipt of application materials: none. Application fee required: $40. On-campus interview required.

Athletics Interscholastic: baseball (boys), basketball (b,g), bowling (b,g), cheering (g), cross-country running (b,g), football (b), golf (b,g), soccer (b,g), softball (g), tennis (b,g), track and field (b,g), volleyball (g), wrestling (b); intramural: basketball (b,g), football (b); coed interscholastic: fitness, physical fitness, swimming and diving, weight training; coed intramural: fitness, kickball, rappelling. 1 PE instructor, 2 coaches, 1 athletic trainer.

Computers Computers are regularly used in all academic, career exploration, college planning, creative writing, English, French, history, journalism, library, mathematics, newspaper, science, social sciences, Spanish, technology, yearbook classes. Computer network features include on-campus library services, Internet access, wireless campus network, Internet filtering or blocking technology. Campus intranet and student e-mail accounts are available to students. Students grades are available online. The school has a published electronic and media policy.

Contact Mrs. Nicole Schierling, Assistant to Advancement and Admissions. 615-577-1215. Fax: 615-883-2998. E-mail: nschierling@dcawildcats.org. Website: www.dcawildcats.org

DONNA KLEIN JEWISH ACADEMY

9801 Donna Klein Boulevard
Boca Raton, Florida 33428-1524

Head of School: Helena Levine

General Information Coeducational day college-preparatory, arts, religious studies, and bilingual studies school, affiliated with Jewish faith. Grades PK–12. Founded: 1979. Setting: suburban. 32-acre campus. 1 building on campus. Approved or accredited by Florida Council of Independent Schools, Southern Association of Colleges and Schools, and Florida Department of Education. Member of National Association of Independent Schools. Languages of instruction: English and Hebrew. Upper school average class size: 15. Upper school faculty-student ratio: 1:6. There are

172 required school days per year for Upper School students. Upper School students typically attend 5 days per week. The average school day consists of 7 hours and 30 minutes.

Upper School Student Profile Grade 9: 49 students (22 boys, 27 girls); Grade 10: 41 students (18 boys, 23 girls); Grade 11: 26 students (12 boys, 14 girls); Grade 12: 23 students (6 boys, 17 girls). 100% of students are Jewish.

Faculty School total: 24. In upper school: 11 men, 13 women; 11 have advanced degrees.

Subjects Offered Advanced biology, advanced chemistry, advanced math, Advanced Placement courses, advanced studio art-AP, anatomy and physiology, art, band, basketball, Bible studies, biology, calculus, calculus-AP, chemistry, college counseling, computer programming, computer skills, computer tools, dance, debate, drama, economics, English, English language and composition-AP, English literature and composition-AP, environmental science, environmental science-AP, French studies, geometry, government, government-AP, guidance, health, Hebrew, honors English, honors geometry, honors U.S. history, honors world history, Jewish history, journalism, Judaic studies, literature and composition-AP, model United Nations, physical education, pre-calculus, psychology-AP, SAT/ACT preparation, softball, Spanish, statistics, statistics-AP, student government, studio art-AP, theater production, U.S. government and politics, U.S. history-AP, visual arts, volleyball, world history, world history-AP, writing, yearbook.

Graduation Requirements Electives, English, foreign language, history, Judaic studies, mathematics, physical education (includes health), science, writing, completion of 225 hours of community service.

Special Academic Programs 15 Advanced Placement exams for which test preparation is offered; honors section; independent study; study at local college for college credit; study abroad.

College Admission Counseling 25 students graduated in 2012; 23 went to college, including Boston University; Florida Atlantic University; Florida State University; University of Central Florida; University of Florida; University of Miami. Other: 2 went to work. Median combined SAT: 1090, median composite ACT: 25.

Student Life Upper grades have specified standards of dress, student council, honor system. Discipline rests primarily with faculty. Attendance at religious services is required.

Tuition and Aid Tuition installment plan (Key Tuition Payment Plan, monthly payment plans, individually arranged payment plans). Need-based scholarship grants available. In 2012–13, 52% of upper-school students received aid.

Admissions Traditional secondary-level entrance grade is 9. For fall 2012, 30 students applied for upper-level admission, 14 were accepted, 14 enrolled. SSAT required. Deadline for receipt of application materials: none. Application fee required: $100. On-campus interview required.

Athletics Interscholastic: baseball (boys), basketball (b,g), dance team (g), golf (b), soccer (b,g), softball (g), volleyball (g); coed interscholastic: cross-country running, tennis; coed intramural: dance team, fitness, scuba diving, self defense, swimming and diving, tennis, weight lifting, weight training. 1 PE instructor, 6 coaches.

Computers Computers are regularly used in all classes. Computer network features include Internet access, wireless campus network, Internet filtering or blocking technology. Campus intranet and student e-mail accounts are available to students. Students grades are available online. The school has a published electronic and media policy.

Contact Mrs. Jodi Orshan, Assistant Director of Admissions, High School. 561-558-2583. Fax: 561-558-2581. E-mail: orshanj@dkja.org. Website: www.dkja.org

THE DONOHO SCHOOL

2501 Henry Road
Anniston, Alabama 36207

Head of School: Mrs. Janice Hurd

General Information Coeducational day college-preparatory and arts school. Grades PS–12. Founded: 1963. Setting: suburban. Nearest major city is Birmingham. 73-acre campus. 4 buildings on campus. Approved or accredited by Southern Association of Colleges and Schools and Alabama Department of Education. Member of National Association of Independent Schools. Total enrollment: 344. Upper school average class size: 12. Upper school faculty-student ratio: 1:12. There are 180 required school days per year for Upper School students. Upper School students typically attend 5 days per week. The average school day consists of 5 hours and 25 minutes.

Upper School Student Profile Grade 9: 37 students (18 boys, 19 girls); Grade 10: 36 students (14 boys, 22 girls); Grade 11: 24 students (15 boys, 9 girls); Grade 12: 23 students (9 boys, 14 girls).

Faculty School total: 32. In upper school: 5 men, 7 women; 11 have advanced degrees.

Subjects Offered Algebra, American history, American literature, anatomy, art, arts, band, biology, calculus, chemistry, chorus, computer science, drama, economics, English, English literature, European history, fine arts, French, geography, geometry, government/civics, grammar, health, history, journalism, Latin, mathematics, music, physical education, physics, physiology, public speaking, science, social studies, Spanish, speech, theater, world history.

Graduation Requirements Arts and fine arts (art, music, dance, drama), English, foreign language, mathematics, physical education (includes health), public speaking, science, social sciences, social studies (includes history).

Special Academic Programs Advanced Placement exam preparation; honors section; term-away projects; study at local college for college credit; ESL (8 students enrolled).

College Admission Counseling 32 students graduated in 2013; all went to college, including Auburn University; Birmingham-Southern College; Samford University; University of Montevallo; Vanderbilt University.

Student Life Upper grades have specified standards of dress, student council, honor system. Discipline rests primarily with faculty.

Summer Programs Remediation, enrichment programs offered; session focuses on enrichment; held on campus; accepts boys and girls; open to students from other schools. 50 students usually enrolled. 2014 schedule: June 3 to July 19. Application deadline: May 18.

Tuition and Aid Day student tuition: $4305–$8975. Tuition installment plan (FACTS Tuition Payment Plan, monthly payment plans). Need-based scholarship grants available. In 2013–14, 18% of upper-school students received aid.

Admissions Traditional secondary-level entrance grade is 10. For fall 2013, 13 students applied for upper-level admission, 13 were accepted, 12 enrolled. Admissions testing, Woodcock-Johnson and writing sample required. Deadline for receipt of application materials: none. Application fee required: $50. Interview required.

Athletics Interscholastic: baseball (boys), basketball (b,g), cheering (g), cross-country running (b,g), football (b), golf (b,g), soccer (b,g), swimming and diving (b,g), tennis (b,g), track and field (b,g), volleyball (g). 2 coaches.

Computers Computers are regularly used in English, foreign language, mathematics, science classes. Computer network features include on-campus library services, online commercial services, Internet access, wireless campus network, Internet filtering or blocking technology, laptop and Ipad use welcomed on campus. Student e-mail accounts and computer access in designated common areas are available to students. Students grades are available online. The school has a published electronic and media policy.

Contact Mrs. Laura Phillips, Lower School Principal/Dean of Academics. 256-236-4459 Ext. 108. Fax: 256-237-6474. E-mail: lphillips@donohoschool.com. Website: www.donohoschool.com/

DOWLING CATHOLIC HIGH SCHOOL

1400 Buffalo Road
West Des Moines, Iowa 50265

Head of School: Dr. Jerry M. Deegan

General Information Coeducational day college-preparatory, general academic, arts, business, religious studies, bilingual studies, technology, performing arts, and Advanced Placement school, affiliated with Roman Catholic Church. Grades 9–12. Founded: 1918. Setting: suburban. 60-acre campus. 1 building on campus. Approved or accredited by North Central Association of Colleges and Schools and Iowa Department of Education. Endowment: $9 million. Total enrollment: 1,400. Upper school average class size: 25. Upper school faculty-student ratio: 1:18. The average school day consists of 6 hours and 30 minutes.

Upper School Student Profile 95% of students are Roman Catholic.

Faculty School total: 79. In upper school: 39 men, 40 women; 40 have advanced degrees.

Subjects Offered 20th century world history, accounting, ACT preparation, acting, advanced chemistry, advanced computer applications, advanced math, Advanced Placement courses, advertising design, algebra, American government, American history, American history-AP, American literature, American literature-AP, applied arts, aquatics, art, art history, athletics, band, baseball, Basic programming, biology, biology-AP, brass choir, British literature, business, business communications, business law, calculus, calculus-AP, career and personal planning, career planning, career/college preparation, ceramics, chamber groups, cheerleading, chemistry, chemistry-AP, choir, choral music, chorus, church history, college counseling, college planning, composition, composition-AP, computer applications, computer information systems, computer processing, computer programming, computers, concert band, concert choir, creative writing, digital photography, drama, economics, economics-AP, engineering, English, English composition, English language and composition-AP, English literature, environmental science, European history, European history-AP, finance, fine arts, foreign language, French, general business, general science, geography, geometry, German, government, government-AP, health, health education, history, history-AP, honors algebra, honors English, honors geometry, honors U.S. history, honors world history, humanities, information processing, integrated mathematics, jazz band, journalism, keyboarding, Latin, life saving, literature, literature-AP, marching band, metalworking, modern European history, newspaper, painting, personal finance, physical education, physics, physics-AP, play production, poetry, pottery, pre-algebra, pre-calculus, probability and statistics, programming, religion, SAT/ACT preparation, scuba diving, social justice, sociology, Spanish, Spanish language-AP, speech and debate, swimming, tennis, theater production, theology, U.S. government, U.S. government and politics-AP, U.S. history, U.S. history-AP, visual arts, vocal jazz, weight training, world religions, yearbook.

Graduation Requirements Arts, business, electives, English, mathematics, reading, science, social studies (includes history), theology, Reading Across the Curriculum (RAC), 10 service hours per semester/20 per year, 10.5 credits of electives. Community service is required.

Special Academic Programs Advanced Placement exam preparation; study at local college for college credit; academic accommodation for the gifted, the musically talented, and the artistically talented; remedial reading and/or remedial writing; remedial math; special instructional classes for blind students.

College Admission Counseling 320 students graduated in 2013; 318 went to college, including Creighton University; Iowa State University of Science and Technology; Loras College; The University of Iowa; University of Northern Iowa. Other: 1 went to work, 1 entered military service. Median SAT critical reading: 663, median SAT math: 640, median SAT writing: 623, median combined SAT: 648, median composite ACT: 24.

Student Life Upper grades have uniform requirement, student council, honor system. Discipline rests primarily with faculty. Attendance at religious services is required.

Summer Programs Enrichment, advancement, sports, art/fine arts, computer instruction programs offered; session focuses on advancement for the purpose of freeing up a slot in the schedule to take an elective; held on campus; accepts boys and girls; not open to students from other schools. 450 students usually enrolled. 2014 schedule: June 5 to July 1.

Tuition and Aid Day student tuition: $6674. Tuition installment plan (monthly payment plans, individually arranged payment plans). Need-based scholarship grants available. In 2013–14, 46% of upper-school students received aid. Total amount of financial aid awarded in 2013–14: $1,000,000.

Admissions Traditional secondary-level entrance grade is 9. Placement test required. Deadline for receipt of application materials: none. Application fee required: $95.

Athletics Interscholastic: aerobics/dance (girls), aquatics (b,g), baseball (b), basketball (b,g), bowling (b,g), cheering (g), cross-country running (b,g), dance team (g), diving (g), drill team (g), football (b), golf (b,g), soccer (b,g), softball (g), swimming and diving (b,g), tennis (b,g), track and field (b,g), volleyball (g), wrestling (b); coed interscholastic: cheering; coed intramural: ultimate Frisbee.

Computers Computers are regularly used in keyboarding classes. Computer network features include on-campus library services, Internet access, wireless campus network, Internet filtering or blocking technology. Computer access in designated common areas is available to students. Students grades are available online.

Contact Mrs. Lynn Wampler, Admissions Assistant. 515-222-1047. Fax: 515-222-1056. E-mail: lwampler@dowlingcatholic.org. Website: www.dowlingcatholic.org

DUBLIN CHRISTIAN ACADEMY

106 Page Road
Dublin, New Hampshire 03444

Head of School: Mr. Kevin E. Moody

General Information Coeducational boarding and day college-preparatory, arts, business, and religious studies school, affiliated with Christian faith, Christian faith. Boarding grades 7–12, day grades K–12. Founded: 1964. Setting: rural. Nearest major city is Boston, MA. Students are housed in single-sex dormitories. 200-acre campus. 5 buildings on campus. Approved or accredited by American Association of Christian Schools and New Hampshire Department of Education. Total enrollment: 88. Upper school average class size: 15. Upper school faculty-student ratio: 1:8. There are 170 required school days per year for Upper School students. Upper School students typically attend 5 days per week. The average school day consists of 5 hours and 45 minutes.

Upper School Student Profile Grade 9: 10 students (5 boys, 5 girls); Grade 10: 15 students (9 boys, 6 girls); Grade 11: 7 students (2 boys, 5 girls); Grade 12: 18 students (8 boys, 10 girls). 33% of students are boarding students. 57% are state residents. 5 states are represented in upper school student body. 25% are international students. International students from China and Republic of Korea. 80% of students are Christian faith, Christian.

Faculty School total: 22. In upper school: 7 men, 7 women; 7 have advanced degrees; 17 reside on campus.

Subjects Offered Accounting, algebra, art, Bible studies, biology, business, calculus, ceramics, chemistry, chorus, computer literacy, consumer mathematics, economics, English, geometry, history, home economics, instrumental music, law, mathematics, music, physics, piano, religion, science, social studies, Spanish, speech, studio art, study skills, U.S. history, voice, word processing, world history.

Graduation Requirements English, foreign language, mathematics, religion (includes Bible studies and theology), science, social studies (includes history), speech.

Special Academic Programs Advanced Placement exam preparation; academic accommodation for the musically talented and the artistically talented; remedial reading and/or remedial writing; remedial math.

College Admission Counseling 16 students graduated in 2012; 14 went to college, including Bob Jones University; Clearwater Christian College; Grove City College; Johnson & Wales University; Liberty University; The Master's College and Seminary. Other: 2 entered military service. Mean SAT critical reading: 620, mean SAT math: 560, mean SAT writing: 510, mean composite ACT: 23.

Student Life Upper grades have uniform requirement, student council, honor system. Discipline rests primarily with faculty. Attendance at religious services is required.

Tuition and Aid Day student tuition: $6500; 7-day tuition and room/board: $12,500. Tuition installment plan (FACTS Tuition Payment Plan). Need-based scholarship grants available. In 2012–13, 20% of upper-school students received aid. Total amount of financial aid awarded in 2012–13: $45,000.

Admissions Traditional secondary-level entrance grade is 9. SLEP for foreign students or Stanford Diagnostic Test required. Deadline for receipt of application materials: June 1. Application fee required: $35. Interview recommended.

Athletics Interscholastic: basketball (boys, girls), soccer (b), volleyball (g); intramural: cheering (g), flag football (b); coed intramural: alpine skiing, ice skating, snowboarding, softball, table tennis. 1 PE instructor, 4 coaches.

Computers Computers are regularly used in accounting, business, English, foreign language, history, mathematics, music, science classes. Computer network features include on-campus library services, Internet access, Internet filtering or blocking technology.

Contact Mrs. Jenn Lawton, Admissions Secretary. 603-563-8505. Fax: 603-563-8008. E-mail: jlawton@dublinchristian.org. Website: www.dublinchristian.org

DUBLIN SCHOOL

Box 522
18 Lehmann Way
Dublin, New Hampshire 03444-0522

Head of School: Bradford D. Bates

General Information Coeducational boarding and day college-preparatory, arts, and technology school; primarily serves students with learning disabilities and individuals with Attention Deficit Disorder. Grades 9–12. Founded: 1935. Setting: rural. Nearest major city is Boston, MA. Students are housed in single-sex dormitories. 300-acre campus. 22 buildings on campus. Approved or accredited by Independent Schools of Northern New England, New England Association of Schools and Colleges, and The Association of Boarding Schools. Member of National Association of Independent Schools and Secondary School Admission Test Board. Endowment: $2.2 million. Total enrollment: 140. Upper school average class size: 8. Upper school faculty-student ratio: 1:4. Upper School students typically attend 5 days per week. The average school day consists of 4 hours and 30 minutes.

Upper School Student Profile Grade 9: 26 students (16 boys, 10 girls); Grade 10: 31 students (19 boys, 12 girls); Grade 11: 39 students (22 boys, 17 girls); Grade 12: 44 students (22 boys, 22 girls). 75% of students are boarding students. 30% are state residents. 16 states are represented in upper school student body. 28% are international students. International students from China, Egypt, France, Republic of Korea, Russian Federation, and Spain; 8 other countries represented in student body.

Faculty School total: 42. In upper school: 15 men, 20 women; 35 have advanced degrees; 28 reside on campus.

Subjects Offered Acting, advanced biology, advanced math, algebra, American foreign policy, American literature, anatomy and physiology, ancient world history, art, arts, biology, biology-AP, calculus, calculus-AP, carpentry, ceramics, chemistry, choir, chorus, college counseling, college placement, community service, computer education, computer literacy, computer programming, costumes and make-up, creative arts, creative dance, creative drama, cultural arts, dance performance, digital music, drama, drama performance, dramatic arts, drawing and design, electronic music, English, English composition, English literature, ESL, European civilization, European history, film history, fine arts, foreign policy, French, geology, geometry, guitar, honors U.S. history, instrumental music, Latin, library research, library skills, literature, marine biology, mathematics, modern dance, modern European history, music, music composition, music performance, music technology, music theory, musical productions, musical theater, musical theater dance, painting, personal and social education, personal development, philosophy, photography, physics, poetry, pre-calculus, psychology, research, science, senior project, Shakespeare, social studies, Spanish, stagecraft, statistics, student government, studio art, study skills, theater, theater arts, U.S. government and politics, U.S. history, U.S. history-AP, video film production, vocal ensemble, voice, voice ensemble, Web site design, weight training, white-water trips, wilderness experience, women's studies, woodworking, world literature, writing, writing workshop, yearbook.

Graduation Requirements Art, computer skills, English, general science, history, languages, mathematics, Senior Presentation, graduation requirements for honors diploma different.

Special Academic Programs 12 Advanced Placement exams for which test preparation is offered; honors section; independent study; term-away projects; study at local college for college credit; domestic exchange program (with The Network Program Schools); academic accommodation for the gifted; programs in general development for dyslexic students; ESL (10 students enrolled).

College Admission Counseling 35 students graduated in 2012; all went to college, including Barnard College; New York University; Smith College; University of New Hampshire; University of Pennsylvania; University of Washington. Median SAT critical reading: 480, median SAT math: 605, median SAT writing: 525, median combined SAT: 1610, median composite ACT: 24.

Student Life Upper grades have specified standards of dress, student council, honor system. Discipline rests equally with students and faculty.

Tuition and Aid Day student tuition: $28,000; 7-day tuition and room/board: $48,200. Tuition installment plan (monthly payment plans). Need-based scholarship grants, loans and payment plans are through a third party available. In 2012–13, 32% of upper-school students received aid. Total amount of financial aid awarded in 2012–13: $1,200,000.

Admissions Traditional secondary-level entrance grade is 9. For fall 2012, 143 students applied for upper-level admission, 97 were accepted, 48 enrolled. SSAT, SSAT, ERB, PSAT, SAT, PLAN or ACT or TOEFL or SLEP required. Deadline for receipt of application materials: January 31. Application fee required: $50. Interview required.

Athletics Interscholastic: basketball (boys, girls), crew (b,g), cross-country running (b,g), lacrosse (b,g), mountain biking (b), nordic skiing (b,g), rowing (b,g), running (b,g), sailing (b,g), skiing (cross-country) (b,g), skiing (downhill) (b,g), snowboarding (b,g), soccer (b,g), tennis (b,g); coed interscholastic: aerobics/dance, alpine skiing, ballet, crew, cross-country running, dance, dance team, equestrian sports, golf, modern dance, mountain biking, nordic skiing, rowing, running, sailing, skiing (cross-country), skiing (downhill), snowboarding; coed intramural: aerobics/dance, alpine skiing, archery, backpacking, badminton, basketball, biathlon, bicycling, billiards, bowling, canoeing/kayaking, climbing, cooperative games, equestrian sports, fencing, fishing, fitness, flag football, flagball, fly fishing, freestyle skiing, Frisbee, golf, hiking/backpacking, horseback riding, ice hockey, indoor soccer, kayaking, martial arts, outdoor activities, outdoor adventure, outdoor education, outdoor recreation, paddle tennis, physical fitness, physical training, rafting, rock climbing, ropes courses, rowing, sailing, skateboarding, skiing (cross-country), skiing (downhill), snowshoeing, softball, strength & conditioning, table tennis, telemark skiing, tennis, ultimate Frisbee, volleyball, wall climbing, weight lifting, weight training, whiffle ball, wrestling, yoga. 20 coaches, 1 athletic trainer.

Computers Computers are regularly used in all academic classes. Computer network features include on-campus library services, online commercial services, Internet access, wireless campus network, Internet filtering or blocking technology. Campus intranet and student e-mail accounts are available to students. The school has a published electronic and media policy.

Contact Jill Hutchins, Director of Admission and Financial Aid. 603-563-1233. Fax: 603-563-8671. E-mail: admission@dublinschool.org. Website: www.dublinschool.org/

DUBOIS CENTRAL CATHOLIC HIGH SCHOOL/MIDDLE SCHOOL

PO Box 567
200 Central Christian Road
DuBois, Pennsylvania 15801

Head of School: Mrs. Dawn Bressler

General Information Coeducational day college-preparatory and general academic school, affiliated with Roman Catholic Church. Grades 6–12. Founded: 1961. Setting: small town. Nearest major city is Pittsburgh. 51-acre campus. 1 building on campus. Approved or accredited by Middle States Association of Colleges and Schools, National Catholic Education Association, Western Catholic Education Association, and Pennsylvania Department of Education. Endowment: $500,000. Total enrollment: 241. Upper school average class size: 20. Upper school faculty-student ratio: 1:14. There are 180 required school days per year for Upper School students. Upper School students typically attend 5 days per week. The average school day consists of 6 hours and 20 minutes.

Upper School Student Profile Grade 9: 35 students (18 boys, 17 girls); Grade 10: 39 students (12 boys, 27 girls); Grade 11: 42 students (22 boys, 20 girls); Grade 12: 45 students (17 boys, 28 girls). 86% of students are Roman Catholic.

Faculty School total: 30. In upper school: 9 men, 21 women; 13 have advanced degrees.

Subjects Offered 20th century American writers, 20th century history, 20th century physics, 20th century world history, 3-dimensional art, accounting, advanced biology, advanced chemistry, advanced computer applications, advanced math, Advanced Placement courses, algebra, American government, American history, American legal systems, American literature, analysis and differential calculus, anatomy and physiology, ancient world history, biology, biology-AP, British literature, calculus, calculus-AP, calligraphy, career and personal planning, career planning, career/college preparation, Catholic belief and practice, chemistry, chemistry-AP, Christian doctrine, Christian ethics, Christian scripture, Christian testament, civil war history, college admission preparation, college counseling, college placement, college planning, college writing, communications, computer applications, computer graphics, constitutional law, contemporary art, creative drama, creative writing, critical writing, debate, digital applications, digital imaging, drama, drama performance, driver education, earth science, ecology, ecology, environmental systems, economics, electives, English, English composition, English literature, English/composition-AP, environmental education, ethics and responsibility, expository writing, fitness, foreign language, forensics, French, general math, general science, geography, geometry, German, government, grammar, graphic arts, graphic design, guidance, health and wellness, health education, history of the Catholic Church, honors algebra, honors English, honors geometry, humanities, information technology, Internet, Internet research, journalism, keyboarding, lab science, language and composition, language arts, law,

leadership and service, library, library assistant, library science, library skills, life management skills, Life of Christ, literature, marketing, mathematics, media communications, medieval/Renaissance history, methods of research, Microsoft, minority studies, moral and social development, moral theology, multicultural literature, music, music appreciation, music composition, music performance, music theater, musical productions, musical theater dance, mythology, Native American history, nature study, New Testament, news writing, newspaper, nutrition, oral communications, participation in sports, peer ministry, performing arts, personal fitness, philosophy, physical education, physical fitness, physical science, physics, piano, poetry, political systems, prayer/spirituality, pre-algebra, pre-calculus, probability and statistics, psychology, public speaking, publications, reading, reading/study skills, religion and culture, research, research seminar, research skills, Roman culture, SAT preparation, science, science and technology, science project, science research, scripture, senior career experience, senior humanities, senior project, senior seminar, Shakespeare, Shakespearean histories, short story, skills for success, social issues, social justice, sociology, sophomore skills, Spanish, speech, speech and debate, speech communications, sports, standard curriculum, student government, student publications, student teaching, study skills, substance abuse, technology, telecommunications and the Internet, theater, trigonometry, U.S. government, U.S. history, U.S. literature, values and decisions, visual and performing arts, vocal ensemble, Web site design, wellness, Western religions, word processing, world cultures, world history, world literature, world religions, writing, writing workshop, yearbook.

Graduation Requirements Seniors must take an exit exam, service hours are mandated for each grade level from 6th through 12th.

Special Academic Programs International Baccalaureate program; honors section; independent study; study at local college for college credit.

College Admission Counseling 44 students graduated in 2012; 41 went to college, including Gannon University; Penn State University Park. Other: 1 entered military service, 2 had other specific plans.

Student Life Upper grades have uniform requirement, student council. Discipline rests primarily with faculty.

Tuition and Aid Tuition installment plan (FACTS Tuition Payment Plan, monthly payment plans, individually arranged payment plans). Tuition reduction for siblings, merit scholarship grants, need-based scholarship grants, Rotary Rebate Program uses 'scrips' both national and local, tuition aid based on criteria selected by the donor (certain parish, town, etc) available. In 2012–13, 46% of upper-school students received aid; total upper-school merit-scholarship money awarded: $448,000. Total amount of financial aid awarded in 2012–13: $448,000.

Admissions Traditional secondary-level entrance grade is 9. For fall 2012, 26 students applied for upper-level admission, 26 were accepted, 26 enrolled. ACT-Explore, Math Placement Exam, school's own exam or writing sample required. Application fee required: $25. On-campus interview required.

Athletics 2 PE instructors, 17 coaches.

Computers Computer network features include on-campus library services, Internet access, wireless campus network, Internet filtering or blocking technology, personal laptops or notebooks mandated in 2011-12 for all 8th, 9th, and 10th graders, soon all students in grades 6th through 12th will be required for curricular instruction. Campus intranet, student e-mail accounts, and computer access in designated common areas are available to students. Students grades are available online. The school has a published electronic and media policy.

Contact Mrs. Joyce Taylor, Director of Development. 814-371-3060 Ext. 606. Fax: 814-371-3215. E-mail: jtaylor@duboiscatholic.com. Website: www.duboiscatholic.com

DUCHESNE ACADEMY OF THE SACRED HEART

10202 Memorial Drive
Houston, Texas 77024

Head of School: Ms. Patricia Swenson

General Information Girls' day college-preparatory, arts, religious studies, and technology school, affiliated with Roman Catholic Church. Grades PK–12. Founded: 1960. Setting: suburban. 14-acre campus. 2 buildings on campus. Approved or accredited by Independent Schools Association of the Southwest, National Catholic Education Association, Network of Sacred Heart Schools, Texas Catholic Conference, and Texas Department of Education. Endowment: $7 million. Total enrollment: 680. Upper school average class size: 14. Upper school faculty-student ratio: 1:7. There are 180 required school days per year for Upper School students. Upper School students typically attend 5 days per week. The average school day consists of 7 hours and 25 minutes.

Upper School Student Profile Grade 9: 70 students (70 girls); Grade 10: 67 students (67 girls); Grade 11: 42 students (42 girls); Grade 12: 57 students (57 girls). 64% of students are Roman Catholic.

Faculty School total: 93. In upper school: 2 men, 36 women; 28 have advanced degrees.

Subjects Offered Algebra, American literature, art history, arts, band, Bible studies, bioethics, biology, British literature, calculus, calculus-AP, ceramics, chemistry, chemistry-AP, community service, composition, computer graphics, computer programming, creative writing, desktop publishing, drawing, economics, English, English literature, European history, fine arts, French, French-AP, geometry, government/civics, health, human sexuality, Internet, Latin, mathematics, music, photography, physical education, physical fitness, physics, prayer/spirituality, precalculus, psychology, religious studies, science, scripture, sexuality, Shakespeare, social justice, social studies, Spanish, Spanish-AP, speech, statistics, statistics-AP, studio art, theater, theater production, theology, U.S. government and politics-AP, U.S. history, U.S. history-AP, Western literature, women's studies, world history, world literature, world religions, writing.

Graduation Requirements Arts and fine arts (art, music, dance, drama), computer science, English, foreign language, history, mathematics, physical education (includes health), religion (includes Bible studies and theology.), science, completion of social awareness program. Community service is required.

Special Academic Programs 15 Advanced Placement exams for which test preparation is offered; honors section; independent study; domestic exchange program (with Network of Sacred Heart Schools); academic accommodation for the musically talented and the artistically talented.

College Admission Counseling 63 students graduated in 2013; all went to college, including Georgia Institute of Technology; Purdue University; Rice University; Texas A&M University; The University of Texas at Austin. Median SAT critical reading: 600, median SAT math: 585, median SAT writing: 640, median combined SAT: 1845, median composite ACT: 27. 61% scored over 600 on SAT critical reading, 48% scored over 600 on SAT math, 78% scored over 600 on SAT writing, 59% scored over 1800 on combined SAT, 54% scored over 26 on composite ACT.

Student Life Upper grades have uniform requirement, student council, honor system. Discipline rests primarily with faculty. Attendance at religious services is required.

Summer Programs Enrichment, art/fine arts, computer instruction programs offered; session focuses on high school credit, and math review, enrichment; held on campus; accepts boys and girls; open to students from other schools. 225 students usually enrolled. 2014 schedule: June 9 to August 1.

Tuition and Aid Tuition installment plan (monthly payment plans). Merit scholarship grants, need-based scholarship grants available. In 2013–14, 21% of upper-school students received aid; total upper-school merit-scholarship money awarded: $46,300. Total amount of financial aid awarded in 2013–14: $641,530.

Admissions Traditional secondary-level entrance grade is 9. For fall 2013, 95 students applied for upper-level admission, 70 were accepted, 27 enrolled. ISEE required. Deadline for receipt of application materials: January 15. Application fee required: $80. On-campus interview required.

Athletics Interscholastic: basketball, combined training, cross-country running, dance team, diving, field hockey, golf, soccer, softball, swimming and diving, tennis, track and field, volleyball, winter soccer. 5 PE instructors, 25 coaches, 2 athletic trainers.

Computers Computers are regularly used in all academic classes. Computer network features include on-campus library services, online commercial services, Internet access, wireless campus network, Internet filtering or blocking technology. Student e-mail accounts are available to students. Students grades are available online. The school has a published electronic and media policy.

Contact Mrs. Tahra Edwards Peterson, Admissions Associate. 713-468-8211 Ext. 139. Fax: 713-465-9809. E-mail: tahra.peterson@duchesne.org. Website: www.duchesne.org

DURHAM ACADEMY
3601 Ridge Road
Durham, North Carolina 27705
Head of School: Mr. Michael Ulku-Steiner

General Information Coeducational day college-preparatory, arts, and technology school. Grades PK–12. Founded: 1933. Setting: suburban. 75-acre campus. 10 buildings on campus. Approved or accredited by Southern Association of Colleges and Schools, Southern Association of Independent Schools, and North Carolina Department of Education. Member of National Association of Independent Schools and Secondary School Admission Test Board. Endowment: $10.5 million. Total enrollment: 1,165. Upper school average class size: 15. Upper school faculty-student ratio: 1:8. There are 179 required school days per year for Upper School students. Upper School students typically attend 5 days per week. The average school day consists of 6 hours.

Upper School Student Profile Grade 9: 108 students (50 boys, 58 girls); Grade 10: 103 students (48 boys, 55 girls); Grade 11: 99 students (42 boys, 57 girls); Grade 12: 101 students (49 boys, 52 girls).

Faculty School total: 196. In upper school: 26 men, 30 women; 47 have advanced degrees.

Subjects Offered 3-dimensional art, accounting, acting, advanced biology, advanced chemistry, advanced computer applications, advanced math, Advanced Placement courses, advanced studio art-AP, algebra, American history, American literature, art, art history, art history-AP, astronomy, biology, calculus, ceramics, chemistry, chemistry-AP, Chinese, Chinese studies, chorus, community service, computer graphics, computer programming, computer science, computer science-AP, concert band, creative writing, dance, drama, ecology, economics, engineering, English, English language and composition-AP, English literature, English literature and composition-AP, environmental science, environmental science-AP, fine arts, finite math, forensics, French, French language-AP, French-AP, geometry, German, history, Latin, literature and composition-AP, mathematics, mathematics-AP, modern European history-AP, music, outdoor education, physical education, physics, psychology,

robotics, science, social studies, Spanish, statistics, studio art-AP, theater, U.S. government and politics-AP, U.S. history-AP.

Graduation Requirements Arts and fine arts (art, music, dance, drama), computer science, English, foreign language, mathematics, outdoor education, physical education (includes health), science, senior project, social studies (includes history), community service hours required for graduation, senior project required for graduation.

Special Academic Programs Advanced Placement exam preparation; honors section; independent study; special instructional classes for students with learning disabilities and Attention Deficit Disorder.

College Admission Counseling 103 students graduated in 2013; 101 went to college, including Duke University; Elon University; Furman University; North Carolina State University; Stanford University; The University of North Carolina at Chapel Hill. Other: 2 had other specific plans. Mean SAT critical reading: 655, mean SAT math: 660, mean SAT writing: 656.

Student Life Upper grades have specified standards of dress, student council, honor system. Discipline rests equally with students and faculty.

Summer Programs Remediation, enrichment, sports, art/fine arts, computer instruction programs offered; session focuses on academic enrichment, non-academic activities; held on campus; accepts boys and girls; open to students from other schools. 847 students usually enrolled. 2014 schedule: June 9 to July 25. Application deadline: none.

Tuition and Aid Day student tuition: $21,610. Tuition installment plan (FACTS Tuition Payment Plan). Need-based scholarship grants available. In 2013–14, 14% of upper-school students received aid. Total amount of financial aid awarded in 2013–14: $896,508.

Admissions Traditional secondary-level entrance grade is 9. For fall 2013, 104 students applied for upper-level admission, 51 were accepted, 42 enrolled. ISEE required. Deadline for receipt of application materials: January 17. Application fee required: $55. Interview required.

Athletics Interscholastic: aquatics (boys, girls), baseball (b), basketball (b,g), cross-country running (b,g), dance team (g), field hockey (g), golf (b,g), lacrosse (b,g), soccer (b,g), softball (g), swimming and diving (b,g), tennis (b,g), track and field (b,g), volleyball (g), weight training (b,g); coed interscholastic: outdoor adventure, outdoor education, ultimate Frisbee, weight training; coed intramural: indoor soccer, judo, martial arts, modern dance, physical fitness, physical training, winter soccer. 1 PE instructor, 3 coaches, 2 athletic trainers.

Computers Computers are regularly used in all academic, animation, computer applications, graphic arts, graphic design, introduction to technology, video film production, Web site design classes. Computer network features include on-campus library services, online commercial services, Internet access, wireless campus network, Internet filtering or blocking technology. Student e-mail accounts and computer access in designated common areas are available to students. Students grades are available online. The school has a published electronic and media policy.

Contact Ms. S. Victoria Muradi, Director of Admission and Financial Aid. 919-493-5787. Fax: 919-489-4893. E-mail: admissions@da.org. Website: www.da.org

EAGLEBROOK SCHOOL
Deerfield, Massachusetts
See Junior Boarding Schools section.

EAGLE HILL SCHOOL
Greenwich, Connecticut
See Special Needs Schools section.

EAGLE HILL SCHOOL
Hardwick, Massachusetts
See Special Needs Schools section.

EASTERN MENNONITE HIGH SCHOOL
801 Parkwood Drive
Harrisonburg, Virginia 22802
Head of School: Mr. Paul G. Leaman

General Information Coeducational day college-preparatory, general academic, arts, religious studies, and technology school, affiliated with Mennonite Church. Grades K–12. Founded: 1917. Setting: small town. Nearest major city is Washington, DC. 24-acre campus. 1 building on campus. Approved or accredited by Mennonite Education Agency, Southern Association of Colleges and Schools, and Virginia Department of Education. Member of National Association of Independent Schools. Endowment: $3 million. Total enrollment: 385. Upper school average class size: 20. Upper school faculty-student ratio: 1:12. There are 180 required school days per year for Upper School students. Upper School students typically attend 5 days per week. The average school day consists of 7 hours.

Upper School Student Profile Grade 6: 30 students (18 boys, 12 girls); Grade 7: 39 students (20 boys, 19 girls); Grade 8: 35 students (23 boys, 12 girls); Grade 9: 33 students (20 boys, 13 girls); Grade 10: 51 students (26 boys, 25 girls); Grade 11: 53 students (24 boys, 29 girls); Grade 12: 57 students (29 boys, 28 girls). 60% of students are Mennonite.

Faculty School total: 50. In upper school: 21 men, 14 women; 24 have advanced degrees.

Subjects Offered Acting, advanced math, algebra, American government, American history, American literature, analysis, applied music, art, art history, band, bell choir, Bible studies, biology, British literature, British literature (honors), business, business skills, ceramics, chemistry, Chinese, Chinese studies, choir, choral music, chorus, Christian and Hebrew scripture, Christian doctrine, Christian ethics, Christian studies, Christian testament, Christianity, church history, community service, computer education, computer science, concert choir, consumer mathematics, creative writing, desktop publishing, drama, drawing, driver education, earth science, economics, engineering, English, English composition, English literature, family and consumer science, fiction, fine arts, food and nutrition, food science, French, general science, geography, geometry, government, grammar, guitar, handbells, health, health education, history, home economics, honors English, human development, industrial arts, industrial technology, instrumental music, interior design, keyboarding, Latin, mathematics, mechanical drawing, music, music composition, music theory, novels, oil painting, orchestra, outdoor education, painting, photography, physical education, physical science, physics, poetry, pottery, pre-algebra, religion, religious education, research skills, science, sculpture, sewing, shop, social sciences, social studies, sociology, Spanish, speech, speech communications, stained glass, study skills, theater, typing, U.S. government, U.S. history, vocal music, voice, water color painting, woodworking, world cultures, world history, writing.

Graduation Requirements Arts and fine arts (art, music, dance, drama), electives, English, foreign language, history, home economics, keyboarding, mathematics, physical education (includes health), religion (includes Bible studies and theology), science, social studies (includes history), technical arts.

Special Academic Programs 5 Advanced Placement exams for which test preparation is offered; honors section; independent study; term-away projects; study at local college for college credit; study abroad; academic accommodation for the gifted; remedial reading and/or remedial writing; remedial math; ESL (6 students enrolled).

College Admission Counseling 53 students graduated in 2013; 50 went to college, including Boston University; Eastern Mennonite University; James Madison University; University of Virginia; Vassar College; West Virginia University. Other: 3 went to work. Median SAT critical reading: 585, median SAT math: 606, median SAT writing: 567, median combined SAT: 1758. 47% scored over 600 on SAT critical reading, 43% scored over 600 on SAT math, 46% scored over 600 on SAT writing, 60% scored over 1800 on combined SAT.

Student Life Upper grades have specified standards of dress, student council. Discipline rests primarily with faculty. Attendance at religious services is required.

Tuition and Aid Day student tuition: $6277–$13,207. Tuition installment plan (monthly payment plans, individually arranged payment plans). Need-based scholarship grants available. In 2013–14, 50% of upper-school students received aid. Total amount of financial aid awarded in 2013–14: $150,000.

Admissions Traditional secondary-level entrance grade is 9. For fall 2013, 29 students applied for upper-level admission, 28 were accepted, 25 enrolled. Any standardized test required. Deadline for receipt of application materials: none. Application fee required: $50. Interview recommended.

Athletics Interscholastic: basketball (boys, girls), cheering (g), cross-country running (b,g), golf (b), soccer (b,g), softball (g), tennis (b,g), track and field (b,g), volleyball (g); intramural: baseball (b), basketball (b,g), soccer (g), wrestling (b); coed interscholastic: baseball; coed intramural: volleyball. 3 PE instructors, 9 coaches, 2 athletic trainers.

Computers Computers are regularly used in business skills, foreign language, French, graphic design, industrial technology, library, literary magazine, mathematics, music, publications, research skills, science, social sciences, social studies, Web site design, word processing, yearbook classes. Computer resources include on-campus library services, Internet access, wireless campus network, Internet filtering or blocking technology. Campus intranet, student e-mail accounts, and computer access in designated common areas are available to students. Students grades are available online. The school has a published electronic and media policy.

Contact Mrs. Kate Bergy, Admissions Counselor. 540-236-6021. Fax: 540-236-6028. E-mail: bergeyk@emhs.net. Website: www.emhs.net

EATON ACADEMY

1000 Old Roswell Lakes Parkway
Roswell, Georgia 30076

Head of School: Ms. Bridgit Eaton-Partalis

General Information Coeducational day and distance learning college-preparatory school. Grades K–12. Distance learning grades 5–12. Founded: 1995. Setting: suburban. Nearest major city is Atlanta. 12-acre campus. 1 building on campus. Approved or accredited by Southern Association of Colleges and Schools, Southern Association of Independent Schools, and Georgia Department of Education. Total enrollment: 80. Upper school average class size: 5. Upper school faculty-student ratio: 1:5. There are 180 required school days per year for Upper School students. Upper

School students typically attend 5 days per week. The average school day consists of 6 hours and 45 minutes.

Upper School Student Profile Grade 9: 8 students (7 boys, 1 girl); Grade 10: 8 students (6 boys, 2 girls); Grade 11: 8 students (8 boys); Grade 12: 8 students (6 boys, 2 girls).

Faculty School total: 33. In upper school: 3 men, 6 women; 6 have advanced degrees.

Subjects Offered All academic.

Graduation Requirements All academic.

Special Academic Programs Honors section; accelerated programs; independent study; academic accommodation for the gifted, the musically talented, and the artistically talented; remedial reading and/or remedial writing; remedial math; special instructional classes for deaf students.

College Admission Counseling 22 students graduated in 2013; all went to college, including Georgia College & State University; Georgia Institute of Technology; Georgia Perimeter College; Georgia Southern University; Kennesaw State University; University of Georgia.

Student Life Upper grades have specified standards of dress. Discipline rests primarily with faculty.

Summer Programs Remediation, enrichment, advancement, ESL, sports, art/fine arts, computer instruction programs offered; session focuses on academic acceleration and remediation; held both on and off campus; held at local sports facilities; accepts boys and girls; open to students from other schools. 35 students usually enrolled. 2014 schedule: June 3 to July 26. Application deadline: none.

Tuition and Aid Day student tuition: $19,400.

Admissions For fall 2013, 50 students applied for upper-level admission, 25 were accepted, 20 enrolled. Deadline for receipt of application materials: none. Application fee required: $250. Interview required.

Athletics Coed Intramural: aquatics, artistic gym, basketball, bowling, canoeing/kayaking, crew, cross-country running, equestrian sports, field hockey, fitness walking, flag football, floor hockey, Frisbee, golf, gymnastics, hockey, horseback riding, ice hockey, ice skating, jogging, kayaking, martial arts, modern dance, outdoor activities, physical fitness, racquetball, rock climbing, ropes courses, running, scuba diving, strength & conditioning, tennis, volleyball, weight training. 2 PE instructors.

Computers Computers are regularly used in all academic classes. Computer network features include Internet access, wireless campus network, Internet filtering or blocking technology. Student e-mail accounts are available to students. Students grades are available online. The school has a published electronic and media policy.

Contact Ms. Margie Cohan, Admissions Director. 770-645-2673 Ext. 242. Fax: 770-645-2711. E-mail: mcohan@eatonacademy.org. Website: www.eatonacademy.org

EDGEWOOD ACADEMY

5475 Elmore Road
PO Box 160
Elmore, Alabama 36025

Head of School: Mr. Clint Welch

General Information Coeducational day college-preparatory, arts, business, religious studies, bilingual studies, and technology school. Boys grades PK–12, girls grades K–12. Founded: 1967. Setting: small town. Nearest major city is Montgomery. 30-acre campus. 4 buildings on campus. Approved or accredited by CITA (Commission on International and Trans-Regional Accreditation), National Council for Private School Accreditation, Southern Association of Colleges and Schools, and Alabama Department of Education. Total enrollment: 314. Upper school average class size: 18. Upper school faculty-student ratio: 1:11. There are 177 required school days per year for Upper School students. Upper School students typically attend 5 days per week. The average school day consists of 5 hours and 45 minutes.

Upper School Student Profile Grade 9: 22 students (15 boys, 7 girls); Grade 10: 20 students (11 boys, 9 girls); Grade 11: 33 students (16 boys, 17 girls); Grade 12: 25 students (17 boys, 8 girls).

Faculty School total: 21. In upper school: 3 men, 7 women; 7 have advanced degrees.

Graduation Requirements Advanced diploma requires 100 hours of community service, standard diplomas requires 50 hours of community service.

Special Academic Programs Advanced Placement exam preparation; study at local college for college credit.

College Admission Counseling 32 students graduated in 2013; they went to Auburn University; Auburn University at Montgomery; The University of Alabama. Median composite ACT: 25.

Student Life Upper grades have specified standards of dress, student council.

Summer Programs Session focuses on driver education; held both on and off campus; held at on the road/street/highway; accepts boys and girls; open to students from other schools. 15 students usually enrolled. 2014 schedule: June to July. Application deadline: May.

Tuition and Aid Day student tuition: $6400. Tuition installment plan (SMART Tuition Payment Plan). Tuition reduction for siblings available.

Admissions Admissions testing required. Deadline for receipt of application materials: none. No application fee required. Interview required.

Athletics Interscholastic: baseball (boys), basketball (b,g), cheering (g), football (b), physical fitness (b,g), physical training (b,g), softball (g), volleyball (g), weight lifting (b), weight training (b,g); coed interscholastic: fishing, track and field. 2 PE instructors, 4 coaches.

Computers Computers are regularly used in lab/keyboard, yearbook classes. Computer network features include on-campus library services, Internet access, wireless campus network, Internet filtering or blocking technology, Smart Board Technology. Students grades are available online. The school has a published electronic and media policy.

Contact Carole Angus, Office Manager. 334-567-5102 Ext. 201. Fax: 334-567-8316. E-mail: cangus@edgewoodacademy.org. Website: www.edgewoodacademy.org/pages/Edgewood_Academy

EDMUND BURKE SCHOOL

4101 Connecticut Avenue NW

Washington, District of Columbia 20008

Head of School: Andrew Slater

General Information Coeducational day college-preparatory and arts school. Grades 6–12. Founded: 1968. Setting: urban. 2 buildings on campus. Approved or accredited by Association of Independent Schools of Greater Washington, Middle States Association of Colleges and Schools, and District of Columbia Department of Education. Member of National Association of Independent Schools and Secondary School Admission Test Board. Endowment: $829,556. Total enrollment: 297. Upper school average class size: 12. Upper school faculty-student ratio: 1:6. There are 180 required school days per year for Upper School students. Upper School students typically attend 5 days per week. The average school day consists of 5 hours.

Upper School Student Profile Grade 9: 42 students (19 boys, 23 girls); Grade 10: 52 students (29 boys, 23 girls); Grade 11: 53 students (30 boys, 23 girls); Grade 12: 60 students (29 boys, 31 girls).

Faculty School total: 50. In upper school: 19 men, 19 women; 25 have advanced degrees.

Subjects Offered African-American literature, algebra, American history, American literature, anatomy, anthropology, biology, calculus, ceramics, chemistry, computer science, creative writing, economics, English, English literature, European history, French, geography, geometry, health, history, journalism, Latin, linguistics, music, performing arts, philosophy, photography, physical education, physics, senior seminar, Spanish, theater, trigonometry, values and decisions, visual arts, women's studies, world history, writing.

Graduation Requirements English, foreign language, history, mathematics, physical education (includes health), science, social sciences, values and decisions, visual and performing arts, senior research seminar. Community service is required.

Special Academic Programs Advanced Placement exam preparation; independent study; term-away projects.

College Admission Counseling 65 students graduated in 2012; all went to college, including New York University; University of New Hampshire; University of Pittsburgh; University of Rhode Island; Wesleyan University. Median SAT critical reading: 651, median SAT math: 641, median SAT writing: 648.

Student Life Upper grades have student council, honor system. Discipline rests primarily with faculty.

Tuition and Aid Day student tuition: $31,820. Tuition installment plan (The Tuition Plan, Insured Tuition Payment Plan, Academic Management Services Plan, individually arranged payment plans). Need-based scholarship grants available. In 2012–13, 29% of upper-school students received aid. Total amount of financial aid awarded in 2012–13: $978,185.

Admissions Traditional secondary-level entrance grade is 9. For fall 2012, 130 students applied for upper-level admission, 86 were accepted, 45 enrolled. ISEE or SSAT required. Deadline for receipt of application materials: January 7. Application fee required: $60. Interview required.

Athletics Interscholastic: aquatics (boys, girls), basketball (b,g), cross-country running (b,g), golf (b,g), soccer (b,g), softball (g), swimming and diving (g), track and field (b,g), volleyball (b,g), wrestling (b,g); intramural: dance team (b,g), Frisbee (b,g), martial arts (b,g), physical fitness (b,g), weight lifting (b,g); coed interscholastic: swimming and diving; coed intramural: indoor soccer, jogging. 2 PE instructors, 2 coaches.

Computers Computers are regularly used in creative writing, English, foreign language, French, graphic arts, history, journalism, mathematics, science classes. Computer network features include on-campus library services, online commercial services, Internet access. Students grades are available online. The school has a published electronic and media policy.

Contact Admissions Office. 202-362-8882 Ext. 670. Fax: 202-362-1914. E-mail: admissions@burkeschool.org. Website: www.burkeschool.org

ELDORADO EMERSON PRIVATE SCHOOL

4100 East Walnut Street
Orange, California 92869

Head of School: Dr. Glory Ludwick

General Information Coeducational day college-preparatory, general academic, and arts school. Grades K–12. Founded: 1958. Setting: suburban. Nearest major city is Los Angeles. 5-acre campus. 8 buildings on campus. Approved or accredited by Western Association of Schools and Colleges and California Department of Education. Total enrollment: 150. Upper school average class size: 18. Upper school faculty-student ratio: 1:18. There are 180 required school days per year for Upper School students. Upper School students typically attend 5 days per week. The average school day consists of 6 hours.

Upper School Student Profile Grade 7: 7 students (3 boys, 4 girls); Grade 8: 6 students (3 boys, 3 girls); Grade 9: 7 students (3 boys, 4 girls); Grade 10: 17 students (7 boys, 10 girls); Grade 11: 17 students (6 boys, 11 girls); Grade 12: 25 students (9 boys, 16 girls).

Faculty School total: 25. In upper school: 7 men, 6 women; 11 have advanced degrees.

Subjects Offered Acting, advanced chemistry, advanced math, advanced TOEFL/grammar, algebra, American government, American history-AP, analysis and differential calculus, anatomy, ancient world history, applied arts, applied music, Arabic, art, art and culture, art appreciation, art education, art history, Basic programming, biology, biology-AP, calculus, calculus-AP, cell biology, ceramics, chemistry, chemistry-AP, Chinese, civil war history, classical civilization, classical Greek literature, classical music, classics, clayworking, computer processing, computer programming, computer skills, concert band, contemporary art, contemporary history, creative drama, creative writing, cultural geography, current events, current history, drama workshop, drawing, earth science, economics and history, Egyptian history, English, English literature, ESL, fine arts, gardening, general math, geography, geometry, grammar, jazz band, keyboarding, library skills, Mandarin, math analysis, physics, physics-AP, pre-algebra, pre-calculus, reading, SAT preparation, science, Shakespeare, Spanish, TOEFL preparation, U.S. government and politics-AP, U.S. history, world history.

Graduation Requirements Art, English, foreign language, mathematics, music, physical education (includes health), science, social studies (includes history). Community service is required.

Special Academic Programs Advanced Placement exam preparation; honors section; accelerated programs; independent study; study at local college for college credit; academic accommodation for the gifted, the musically talented, and the artistically talented; ESL (50 students enrolled).

College Admission Counseling 25 students graduated in 2013; they went to California State University, Fullerton; Chapman University; Occidental College; Purdue University; The Johns Hopkins University; University of California, Santa Cruz.

Student Life Upper grades have specified standards of dress, honor system. Discipline rests equally with students and faculty.

Summer Programs Enrichment, sports, art/fine arts programs offered. 2014 schedule: July 1 to July 31. Application deadline: June 1.

Tuition and Aid Day student tuition: $12,150; 7-day tuition and room/board: $20,000–$30,000. Tuition installment plan (monthly payment plans, individually arranged payment plans). Tuition reduction for siblings, need-based scholarship grants available. In 2013–14, 10% of upper-school students received aid. Total amount of financial aid awarded in 2013–14: $50,000.

Admissions Traditional secondary-level entrance grade is 10. For fall 2013, 95 students applied for upper-level admission, 70 were accepted, 70 enrolled. Achievement tests or any standardized test required. Deadline for receipt of application materials: none. Application fee required: $250. Interview required.

Athletics Interscholastic: baseball (boys), flag football (b), soccer (b); coed interscholastic: baseball, cross-country running, fitness, flag football, physical fitness, physical training, soccer. 1 PE instructor, 4 coaches.

Computers Computers are regularly used in desktop publishing, graphic design, keyboarding, Web site design, word processing, yearbook classes. Computer resources include Internet access, Internet filtering or blocking technology.

Contact Mrs. Venessa Marquez, Administration. 714-633-4774. Fax: 714-744-3304. E-mail: mbently@eldoradoemerson.org. Website: www.eldorado-emerson.org

ELGIN ACADEMY

350 Park Street
Elgin, Illinois 60120

Head of School: Mr. Seth L. Hanford

General Information Coeducational day college-preparatory, arts, and technology school. Grades PS–12. Founded: 1839. Setting: suburban. Nearest major city is Chicago. 20-acre campus. 8 buildings on campus. Approved or accredited by Independent Schools Association of the Central States. Member of National Association of Independent Schools and Secondary School Admission Test Board. Endowment: $10 million. Total enrollment: 387. Upper school average class size: 12. Upper school faculty-student ratio: 1:7. There are 183 required school days per year for

Upper School students. Upper School students typically attend 5 days per week. The average school day consists of 6 hours and 30 minutes.

Upper School Student Profile Grade 9: 40 students (20 boys, 20 girls); Grade 10: 37 students (17 boys, 20 girls); Grade 11: 30 students (17 boys, 13 girls); Grade 12: 33 students (12 boys, 21 girls).

Faculty In upper school: 12 men, 13 women; 23 have advanced degrees.

Subjects Offered Algebra, American history, American literature, anatomy and physiology, art, art history, biology, calculus, ceramics, chemistry, computer programming, computer science, creative writing, drama, English, English literature, environmental science, European history, expository writing, fine arts, finite math, French, geometry, government/civics, grammar, history, Latin, Latin-AP, mathematics, music, painting, photography, physical education, psychology, psychology-AP, science, social studies, Spanish, statistics, theater, trigonometry, world history, world literature, writing.

Graduation Requirements 20th century history, arts and fine arts (art, music, dance, drama), English, foreign language, mathematics, science, social studies (includes history).

Special Academic Programs 16 Advanced Placement exams for which test preparation is offered; honors section; independent study.

College Admission Counseling 41 students graduated in 2013; all went to college, including Boston University; Duke University; New York University; Pepperdine University; Tufts University; University of California, Berkeley. Median SAT critical reading: 610, median SAT math: 600, median SAT writing: 600, median combined SAT: 1660, median composite ACT: 29.

Student Life Upper grades have specified standards of dress, student council, honor system. Discipline rests primarily with faculty.

Summer Programs Enrichment, sports, art/fine arts programs offered; session focuses on college prep work, academics, athletics, art, music; held on campus; accepts boys and girls; open to students from other schools. 120 students usually enrolled. 2014 schedule: June 1 to August 30.

Tuition and Aid Day student tuition: $23,810. Tuition installment plan (FACTS Tuition Payment Plan, 10-month payment plan). Tuition reduction for siblings, merit scholarship grants, need-based scholarship grants available. In 2013–14, 40% of upper-school students received aid; total upper-school merit-scholarship money awarded: $50,000. Total amount of financial aid awarded in 2013–14: $600,000.

Admissions Traditional secondary-level entrance grade is 9. For fall 2013, 44 students applied for upper-level admission, 20 were accepted, 15 enrolled. ERB - verbal abilities, reading comprehension, quantitative abilities (level F, form 1) required. Deadline for receipt of application materials: none. Application fee required: $50. Interview required.

Athletics Interscholastic: baseball (boys), field hockey (g), golf (b), volleyball (g); coed interscholastic: basketball, cross-country running, soccer, tennis, track and field. 2 PE instructors.

Computers Computers are regularly used in art, English, foreign language, mathematics, science, social studies classes. Computer network features include on-campus library services, online commercial services, Internet access, wireless campus network. Campus intranet is available to students. Students grades are available online. The school has a published electronic and media policy.

Contact Mr. Shannon D. Howell, Assistant Head of School for 'Institutional Advancement. 847-695-0303. Fax: 847-695-5017. E-mail: showell@elginacademy.org. Website: www.elginacademy.org

ELIZABETH SETON HIGH SCHOOL

5715 Emerson Street
Bladensburg, Maryland 20710-1844

Head of School: Sr. Ellen Marie Hagar

General Information Girls' day college-preparatory, arts, religious studies, bilingual studies, technology, Enngineering, and music school, affiliated with Roman Catholic Church. Grades 9–12. Founded: 1959. Setting: suburban. Nearest major city is Washington, DC. 24-acre campus. 2 buildings on campus. Approved or accredited by Middle States Association of Colleges and Schools, National Catholic Education Association, and Maryland Department of Education. Total enrollment: 565. Upper school average class size: 16. Upper school faculty-student ratio: 1:11. There are 180 required school days per year for Upper School students. Upper School students typically attend 5 days per week. The average school day consists of 6 hours and 30 minutes.

Upper School Student Profile Grade 9: 166 students (166 girls); Grade 10: 122 students (122 girls); Grade 11: 149 students (149 girls); Grade 12: 147 students (147 girls). 55% of students are Roman Catholic.

Faculty School total: 55. In upper school: 3 men, 52 women; 35 have advanced degrees.

Subjects Offered Advanced chemistry, advanced math, advanced studio art-AP, algebra, American history, American history-AP, American literature, analytic geometry, anatomy, art, art-AP, band, bioethics, biology, biology-AP, British literature-AP, calculus, calculus-AP, ceramics, chemistry, chemistry-AP, choir, choral music, chorus, Christian and Hebrew scripture, Christianity, church history, computer multimedia, computer programming, computer science, concert band, concert choir,

dance, earth science, economics, English, English literature, English literature and composition-AP, English literature-AP, environmental science, environmental science-AP, ethics, European history, film and literature, fine arts, French, French-AP, geography, geometry, government-AP, government/civics, government/civics-AP, grammar, health, history, honors algebra, honors English, honors geometry, HTML design, journalism, keyboarding, Latin, mathematics, music, newspaper, orchestra, philosophy, photography, physical education, physics, physiology, pre-calculus, probability and statistics, psychology, psychology-AP, religion, robotics, science, social studies, sociology, Spanish, speech, statistics-AP, symphonic band, theology, trigonometry, U.S. government and politics-AP, U.S. history-AP, Web site design, weightlifting, wind ensemble, women in literature, world history, world history-AP, world literature, writing.

Graduation Requirements 1 1/2 elective credits, arts and fine arts (art, music, dance, drama), English, foreign language, health education, mathematics, physical education (includes health), religion (includes Bible studies and theology), science, social studies (includes history), technology. Community service is required.

Special Academic Programs Advanced Placement exam preparation; honors section; independent study; academic accommodation for the gifted, the musically talented, and the artistically talented; programs in general development for dyslexic students; special instructional classes for students with mild learning disabilities, organizational deficiencies, Attention Deficit Disorder, and dyslexia.

College Admission Counseling 179 students graduated in 2013; all went to college, including Frostburg State University; Salisbury University; Temple University; Towson University; University of Maryland, Baltimore County; University of Maryland, College Park. Mean SAT critical reading: 533, mean SAT math: 502, mean SAT writing: 550.

Student Life Upper grades have uniform requirement, student council, honor system. Discipline rests equally with students and faculty. Attendance at religious services is required.

Summer Programs Remediation, enrichment, sports, art/fine arts, computer instruction programs offered; held on campus; accepts girls; open to students from other schools. 2014 schedule: June to August.

Tuition and Aid Day student tuition: $11,850. Tuition installment plan (FACTS Tuition Payment Plan, monthly payment plans, individually arranged payment plans, quarterly payment plan). Tuition reduction for siblings, merit scholarship grants, need-based scholarship grants, paying campus jobs available. In 2013–14, 40% of upper-school students received aid; total upper-school merit-scholarship money awarded: $104,000. Total amount of financial aid awarded in 2013–14: $500,000.

Admissions Traditional secondary-level entrance grade is 9. High School Placement Test required. Deadline for receipt of application materials: December 5. Application fee required: $50, On-campus interview required.

Athletics Interscholastic: basketball, cheering, crew, cross-country running, dance squad, dance team, equestrian sports, field hockey, golf, horseback riding, indoor track, indoor track & field, lacrosse, rowing, running, soccer, softball, swimming and diving, tennis, volleyball, winter (indoor) track; intramural: dance, flag football, martial arts, outdoor recreation, physical fitness, strength & conditioning, weight lifting, weight training. 5 PE instructors, 32 coaches, 1 athletic trainer.

Computers Computers are regularly used in computer applications, desktop publishing, English, graphic design, independent study, keyboarding, lab/keyboard, literary magazine, multimedia, photojournalism, programming, research skills, science, typing, Web site design, word processing, yearbook classes. Computer network features include on-campus library services, online commercial services, Internet access, wireless campus network, Internet filtering or blocking technology. Campus intranet and student e-mail accounts are available to students. Students grades are available online. The school has a published electronic and media policy.

Contact Ms. Melissa Davey, Director of Admissions. 301-864-4532 Ext. 7015. Fax: 301-864-8946. E-mail: mdavey@setonhs.org. Website: www.setonhs.org

THE ELLIS ACADEMY

347 Jade Road
Toney, Alabama 35773

Head of School: Dr. Diane Ellis Miles

General Information Girls' boarding and coeducational day and distance learning college-preparatory, arts, business, technology, family and consumer sciences, and Ecology and Environment school. Boarding girls grades 9–PG, day boys grades K–8, day girls grades K–8. Distance learning grades K–PG. Founded: 2009. Setting: rural. Nearest major city is Huntsville. 10-acre campus. 2 buildings on campus. Approved or accredited by United Private Schools Association of Pennsylvania. Total enrollment: 9. Upper school average class size: 5. Upper school faculty-student ratio: 1:5. There are 175 required school days per year for Upper School students. Upper School students typically attend 5 days per week. The average school day consists of 7 hours.

Upper School Student Profile Grade 6: 1 student (1 girl); Grade 7: 1 student (1 girl); Grade 8: 1 student (1 girl). 90% are state residents. 2 states are represented in upper school student body.

Faculty School total: 6. In upper school: 1 man, 3 women; 3 have advanced degrees.

Subjects Offered Addiction, all academic.

Graduation Requirements 20th century world history, graduation standards.

Special Academic Programs 5 Advanced Placement exams for which test preparation is offered; academic accommodation for the gifted; programs in English, mathematics for dyslexic students; ESL.

Student Life Upper grades have uniform requirement, honor system. Discipline rests equally with students and faculty. Attendance at religious services is required.

Summer Programs Remediation, enrichment, ESL, sports, art/fine arts, computer instruction programs offered; session focuses on art and academics; held on campus; accepts boys and girls; open to students from other schools. 7 students usually enrolled. 2014 schedule: June 15 to July 15. Application deadline: June 1.

Tuition and Aid Day student tuition: $7500. Tuition installment plan (monthly payment plans, individually arranged payment plans). Tuition reduction for siblings, merit scholarship grants, need-based scholarship grants, need-based loans, textbook scholarships available. Total upper-school merit-scholarship money awarded for 2013–14: $3500.

Admissions For fall 2013, 7 students applied for upper-level admission, 7 were accepted, 3 enrolled. Stanford Achievement Test, Otis-Lennon School Ability Test, school's own exam and writing sample required. Deadline for receipt of application materials: January 14. Application fee required: $50. On-campus interview required.

Athletics Intramural: outdoor recreation; coed intramural: baseball, cross-country running, dance, fitness, fitness walking, flag football, golf, jogging, jump rope, kickball, physical fitness, running, strength & conditioning, touch football, walking, whiffle ball, winter walking. 1 coach, 1 athletic trainer.

Computers Computer network features include Internet access, wireless campus network, Internet filtering or blocking technology. Campus intranet and computer access in designated common areas are available to students. The school has a published electronic and media policy.

Contact Dr. Diane Ellis Miles, President/Head of School. 256-420-8312. E-mail: info@TheEllisAcademy.com. Website: www.theellisacademy.com/

ELYRIA CATHOLIC HIGH SCHOOL

725 Gulf Road
Elyria, Ohio 44035-3697

Head of School: Mrs. Amy Butler

General Information Coeducational day college-preparatory, arts, business, and religious studies school, affiliated with Roman Catholic Church. Grades 9–12. Founded: 1948. Setting: suburban. Nearest major city is Cleveland. 16-acre campus. 1 building on campus. Approved or accredited by North Central Association of Colleges and Schools and Ohio Department of Education. Endowment: $3 million. Total enrollment: 486. Upper school average class size: 24. Upper school faculty-student ratio: 1:14. There are 180 required school days per year for Upper School students. Upper School students typically attend 5 days per week. The average school day consists of 6 hours and 42 minutes.

Upper School Student Profile Grade 9: 131 students (67 boys, 64 girls); Grade 10: 94 students (48 boys, 46 girls); Grade 11: 121 students (67 boys, 54 girls); Grade 12: 101 students (51 boys, 50 girls). 90% of students are Roman Catholic.

Faculty School total: 40. In upper school: 18 men, 15 women; 19 have advanced degrees.

Subjects Offered Accounting, advanced math, algebra, American government, American history, American history-AP, analysis of data, anatomy and physiology, art, band, biology, business, calculus, calculus-AP, campus ministry, Catholic belief and practice, chamber groups, chemistry, child development, choir, Christian and Hebrew scripture, Christian doctrine, Christian ethics, church history, computer applications, concert band, concert choir, current events, data analysis, drama, drama performance, earth science, English, fine arts, food and nutrition, French, French language-AP, geometry, German, health, history, honors English, industrial arts, introduction to theater, journalism, leadership, life issues, marching band, music appreciation, parent/child development, peer ministry, physical fitness, physics, prayer/spirituality, pre-calculus, psychology, reading/study skills, social justice, Spanish, Spanish language-AP, theater, world religions, yearbook.

Graduation Requirements Arts and fine arts (art, music, dance, drama), computers, English, mathematics, physical education (includes health), religion (includes Bible studies and theology), science, social studies (includes history), school and community service hours, Ohio Proficiency Test.

Special Academic Programs Advanced Placement exam preparation; honors section; study at local college for college credit; remedial reading and/or remedial writing; remedial math; special instructional classes for students with learning disabilities and Attention Deficit Disorder.

College Admission Counseling 105 students graduated in 2012; 103 went to college. Other: 2 entered military service. Mean SAT critical reading: 570, mean SAT math: 557.

Student Life Upper grades have specified standards of dress, student council, honor system. Discipline rests primarily with faculty. Attendance at religious services is required.

Tuition and Aid Day student tuition: $7050. Tuition installment plan (monthly payment plans). Tuition reduction for siblings, merit scholarship grants, need-based scholarship grants, paying campus jobs available. In 2012–13, 24% of upper-school students received aid; total upper-school merit-scholarship money awarded: $20,000. Total amount of financial aid awarded in 2012–13: $200,000.

Admissions Traditional secondary-level entrance grade is 9. For fall 2012, 152 students applied for upper-level admission, 139 were accepted, 131 enrolled. High School Placement Test (closed version) from Scholastic Testing Service required. Deadline for receipt of application materials: January 14. No application fee required. Interview recommended.

Athletics Interscholastic: baseball (boys), basketball (b,g), cross-country running (b,g), football (b), golf (b), ice hockey (b), rugby (b), soccer (b,g), softball (g), tennis (b,g), volleyball (g), wrestling (b); coed interscholastic: bowling, cheering, swimming and diving, track and field. 2 PE instructors, 47 coaches, 1 athletic trainer.

Computers Computers are regularly used in business studies, journalism, newspaper, typing, word processing, yearbook classes. Computer network features include on-campus library services, Internet access, Internet filtering or blocking technology. Students grades are available online. The school has a published electronic and media policy.

Contact Mr. Michael Polevacik, Director of Admissions. 440-365-1821 Ext. 16. Fax: 440-365-7536. E-mail: polevacik@elyriacatholic.com. Website: www.elyriacatholic.com

THE EMERY/WEINER SCHOOL

9825 Stella Link
Houston, Texas 77025

Head of School: Mr. Stuart J Dow

General Information Coeducational day college-preparatory, general academic, arts, religious studies, bilingual studies, and technology school, affiliated with Jewish faith. Grades 6–12. Founded: 1978. Setting: urban. 12-acre campus. 2 buildings on campus. Approved or accredited by Independent Schools Association of the Southwest, Southern Association of Colleges and Schools, and Texas Department of Education. Upper school average class size: 15. Upper school faculty-student ratio: 1:7. There are 167 required school days per year for Upper School students. Upper School students typically attend 5 days per week. The average school day consists of 8 hours.

Faculty School total: 62. In upper school: 15 men, 16 women; 13 have advanced degrees.

Subjects Offered Acting, advanced chemistry, advanced math, algebra, art, biology, biology-AP, calculus, calculus-AP, ceramics, chemistry, chemistry-AP, civil war history, clayworking, composition, composition-AP, computer graphics, computer science, drama, drama performance, drawing, English, English-AP, foreign language, geometry, Hebrew, Hebrew scripture, history, history of religion, history-AP, honors English, honors U.S. history, Judaic studies, lab science, mathematics, mathematics-AP, newspaper, painting, physics, play production, play/screen writing, religion and culture, religious education, religious studies, Spanish, Spanish-AP, study skills, theater arts, theater design and production, U.S. history, U.S. history-AP, yearbook.

Graduation Requirements Arts, English, foreign language, history, Judaic studies, mathematics, physical education (includes health), science, one year Hebrew requirement for Upper School. Community service is required.

Special Academic Programs Advanced Placement exam preparation; honors section; independent study; academic accommodation for the gifted.

College Admission Counseling Colleges students went to include American University; Emory University; Indiana University Bloomington; The University of Texas at Austin; Trinity University; University of Michigan.

Student Life Upper grades have specified standards of dress, student council, honor system. Discipline rests primarily with faculty. Attendance at religious services is required.

Tuition and Aid Day student tuition: $22,308. Tuition installment plan (monthly payment plans). Need-based scholarship grants available. In 2013–14, 33% of upper-school students received aid. Total amount of financial aid awarded in 2013–14: $1,200,000.

Admissions Traditional secondary-level entrance grade is 9. ISEE required. Deadline for receipt of application materials: January 10. Application fee required: $105. On-campus interview required.

Athletics Interscholastic: baseball (boys), basketball (b,g), cross-country running (b,g), football (b), golf (b,g), lacrosse (b,g), soccer (b,g), softball (g), tennis (b,g), track and field (b,g), volleyball (g); intramural: aerobics/dance (g), dance (g), yoga (g); coed intramural: outdoor activities.

Computers Computers are regularly used in computer applications, graphic design, programming, Web site design classes. Computer network features include on-campus library services, online commercial services, Internet access, wireless campus network, Internet filtering or blocking technology, Adobe Creative Suite, Microsoft Publisher, Word, Excel, PowerPoint. Campus intranet, student e-mail accounts, and computer access in designated common areas are available to students. Students grades are available online. The school has a published electronic and media policy.

Contact Ms. Caroline Sarnoff, Director of Admissions. 832-204-5900 Ext. 201. Fax: 832-204-5910. E-mail: csarnoff@emeryweiner.org. Website: www.emeryweiner.org

EMMA WILLARD SCHOOL

285 Pawling Avenue
Troy, New York 12180

Head of School: Ms. Trudy E. Hall

General Information Girls' boarding and day college-preparatory and arts school. Grades 9–PG. Founded: 1814. Setting: suburban. Nearest major city is Albany. Students are housed in single-sex dormitories. 137-acre campus. 23 buildings on campus. Approved or accredited by The Association of Boarding Schools and New York Department of Education. Member of National Association of Independent Schools and Secondary School Admission Test Board. Endowment: $86.1 million. Total enrollment: 329. Upper school average class size: 12. Upper school faculty-student ratio: 1:6. There are 167 required school days per year for Upper School students. Upper School students typically attend 5 days per week. The average school day consists of 7 hours and 20 minutes.

Upper School Student Profile Grade 9: 77 students (77 girls); Grade 10: 73 students (73 girls); Grade 11: 89 students (89 girls); Grade 12: 89 students (89 girls); Postgraduate: 3 students (3 girls). 63% of students are boarding students. 53% are state residents. 22 states are represented in upper school student body. 27% are international students. International students from China, Hong Kong, Japan, Mexico, Republic of Korea, and Taiwan; 22 other countries represented in student body.

Faculty School total: 60. In upper school: 13 men, 46 women; 39 have advanced degrees; 43 reside on campus.

Subjects Offered Advanced Placement courses, advanced studio art-AP, algebra, American history, American literature, ancient world history, art, art history, art history-AP, art-AP, ballet, bioethics, biology, biology-AP, calculus, calculus-AP, ceramics, chemistry, chemistry-AP, chorus, comparative government and politics-AP, computer programming, computer science, computer science-AP, conceptual physics, creative writing, dance, digital imaging, drama, drawing and design, economics, English, English literature, English literature and composition-AP, ESL, European history, expository writing, fiber arts, fine arts, forensics, French, French language-AP, geometry, government and politics-AP, government-AP, government/civics, health and wellness, history, internship, Latin, Latin-AP, mathematics, medieval/Renaissance history, music, neuroscience, orchestra, photography, physical education, physics, physics-AP, poetry, practicum, pre-calculus, SAT preparation, science, social sciences, Spanish, Spanish language-AP, Spanish-AP, statistics, statistics-AP, studio art-AP, theater, trigonometry, U.S. history-AP, weaving, world history, world literature.

Graduation Requirements Arts and fine arts (art, music, dance, drama), computer science, English, foreign language, mathematics, physical education (includes health), science, social studies (includes history). Community service is required.

Special Academic Programs 14 Advanced Placement exams for which test preparation is offered; independent study; term-away projects; domestic exchange program (with The Masters School); study abroad; academic accommodation for the gifted, the musically talented, and the artistically talented.

College Admission Counseling 84 students graduated in 2012; 82 went to college, including Cornell University; Hamilton College; Ithaca College; New York University; St. Lawrence University; Wellesley College. Other: 2 had other specific plans. Median SAT critical reading: 630, median SAT math: 630, median SAT writing: 650, median combined SAT: 1930, median composite ACT: 24. 58% scored over 600 on SAT critical reading, 61% scored over 600 on SAT math, 67% scored over 600 on SAT writing, 67% scored over 1800 on combined SAT, 32% scored over 26 on composite ACT.

Student Life Upper grades have specified standards of dress, student council, honor system. Discipline rests equally with students and faculty.

Tuition and Aid Day student tuition: $29,690; 7-day tuition and room/board: $48,480. Tuition installment plan (Key Tuition Payment Plan, monthly payment plans). Merit scholarship grants, need-based scholarship grants, Davis Scholars Program, Day Student /Capital District Scholarships available. In 2012–13, 54% of upper-school students received aid; total upper-school merit-scholarship money awarded: $44,535. Total amount of financial aid awarded in 2012–13: $4,408,666.

Admissions Traditional secondary-level entrance grade is 9. For fall 2012, 467 students applied for upper-level admission, 167 were accepted, 112 enrolled. ISEE, PSAT, SAT, or ACT for applicants to grade 11 and 12, psychoeducational evaluation, SSAT or TOEFL required. Deadline for receipt of application materials: February 1. Application fee required: $50. Interview required.

Athletics Interscholastic: aquatics, basketball, crew, cross-country running, diving, field hockey, lacrosse, rowing, soccer, softball, swimming and diving, tennis, track and field, volleyball; intramural: aerobics, aerobics/dance, ballet, basketball, dance, fencing, fitness, fitness walking, floor hockey, hiking/backpacking, jogging, martial arts, modern dance, outdoor activities, physical fitness, physical training, riflery, running, skiing (downhill), snowboarding, soccer, softball, strength & conditioning, swimming and diving, tennis, ultimate Frisbee, volleyball, water polo, weight training. 3 PE instructors, 3 coaches, 1 athletic trainer.

Computers Computers are regularly used in all classes. Computer network features include on-campus library services, online commercial services, Internet access, wireless campus network, Internet filtering or blocking technology. Campus intranet, student e-mail accounts, and computer access in designated common areas are available to students. Students grades are available online. The school has a published electronic and media policy.

Contact Ms. Sharon Busone, Officer Manager. 518-883-1327. Fax: 518-883-1805. E-mail: sbusone@emmawillard.org. Website: www.emmawillard.org

THE ENGLISH COLLEGE IN PRAGUE

Sokolovska 320
Prague 190 00, Czech Republic

Head of School: Mr. Mark A. Waldron

General Information Coeducational day college-preparatory and arts school. Grades 8–13. Founded: 1994. Setting: urban. 1-acre campus. 2 buildings on campus. Approved or accredited by Department of Education and Employment, United Kingdom, Headmasters' Conference, Independent Schools Council (UK), and International Baccalaureate Organization. Language of instruction: English. Total enrollment: 360. Upper school average class size: 13. Upper school faculty-student ratio: 1:11. The average school day consists of 7 hours and 30 minutes.

Faculty School total: 40. In upper school: 22 men, 18 women.

Subjects Offered Independent study, International Baccalaureate courses.

Graduation Requirements International Baccalaureate courses, Czech maturita for Czech students.

Special Academic Programs International Baccalaureate program; independent study; academic accommodation for the gifted, the musically talented, and the artistically talented; programs in English for dyslexic students; ESL (30 students enrolled).

College Admission Counseling 67 students graduated in 2012; 64 went to college. Other: 1 went to work, 2 had other specific plans.

Student Life Upper grades have student council, honor system. Discipline rests primarily with faculty.

Tuition and Aid Tuition reduction for siblings, bursaries, merit scholarship grants, need-based scholarship grants available. In 2012–13, 30% of upper-school students received aid.

Admissions Traditional secondary-level entrance grade is 12. For fall 2012, 15 students applied for upper-level admission, 6 were accepted, 6 enrolled. English entrance exam and mathematics proficiency exam required. Deadline for receipt of application materials: May 1. Application fee required: 500 Czech korun. Interview required.

Athletics 2 PE instructors.

Computers Computers are regularly used in all academic classes. Computer network features include on-campus library services, online commercial services, Internet access, wireless campus network, Internet filtering or blocking technology. Campus intranet, student e-mail accounts, and computer access in designated common areas are available to students. Students grades are available online.

Contact Mrs. Iva Rozkosna, Admissions Registrar. 420-283893113. Fax: 420-283890118. E-mail: office@englishcollege.cz. Website: www.englishcollege.cz

THE EPISCOPAL ACADEMY

1785 Bishop White Drive
Newtown Square, Pennsylvania 19073-1300

Head of School: Dr. Thomas John Locke

General Information Coeducational day college-preparatory, arts, religious studies, and technology school, affiliated with Episcopal Church. Grades PK–12. Founded: 1785. Setting: suburban. Nearest major city is Philadelphia. 123-acre campus. 12 buildings on campus. Approved or accredited by National Association of Episcopal Schools and Pennsylvania Department of Education. Member of National Association of Independent Schools. Endowment: $42.1 million. Total enrollment: 1,216. Upper school average class size: 15. Upper school faculty-student ratio: 1:7. There are 172 required school days per year for Upper School students. Upper School students typically attend 5 days per week. The average school day consists of 8 hours.

Upper School Student Profile Grade 6: 90 students (50 boys, 40 girls); Grade 7: 91 students (47 boys, 44 girls); Grade 8: 93 students (48 boys, 45 girls); Grade 9: 135 students (73 boys, 62 girls); Grade 10: 137 students (68 boys, 69 girls); Grade 11: 131 students (67 boys, 64 girls); Grade 12: 125 students (72 boys, 53 girls).

Faculty School total: 157. In upper school: 42 men, 37 women; 70 have advanced degrees.

Subjects Offered Algebra, American history, American history-AP, American literature, art, art history, biology, calculus, ceramics, chemistry, classical language, college counseling, computer art, computer graphics, computer information systems, computer programming, computer programming-AP, creative writing, drama, drawing, earth science, ecology, economics, English, English-AP, environmental science, ethics, European history, fine arts, French, French language-AP, French literature-AP, French studies, French-AP, geometry, government and politics-AP, Greek, health and safety, history, Latin, Latin-AP, mathematics, mechanical drawing, modern world history, music, painting, photography, physical education, physics, physics-AP, pre-calculus, psychology, religion, science, senior project, social studies, Spanish, Spanish language-AP, Spanish literature, Spanish literature-AP, Spanish-AP, statistics-AP, studio art, studio art-AP, theater history, theater production, theology, U.S. government and politics-AP, U.S. history, U.S. history-AP, Vietnam history, visual and performing arts, vocal ensemble, vocal music, water polo, weight training, woodworking, world cultures, world history, writing.

Graduation Requirements Arts and fine arts (art, music, dance, drama), English, foreign language, mathematics, physical education (includes health), religion (includes Bible studies and theology), science, senior project, social studies (includes history), participation in Outward Bound Program.

Special Academic Programs Advanced Placement exam preparation; honors section; independent study; study abroad.

College Admission Counseling 127 students graduated in 2013; all went to college, including Boston College; Cornell University; Georgetown University; Harvard University; Penn State University Park; University of Pennsylvania. Mean SAT critical reading: 646, mean SAT math: 655, mean SAT writing: 667, mean combined SAT: 1968, mean composite ACT: 28.

Student Life Upper grades have uniform requirement, student council, honor system. Discipline rests primarily with faculty. Attendance at religious services is required.

Summer Programs Remediation, enrichment, advancement, art/fine arts, computer instruction programs offered; session focuses on acceleration, athletics, camp fun; held on campus; accepts boys and girls; open to students from other schools. 700 students usually enrolled.

Tuition and Aid Day student tuition: $30,130. Tuition installment plan (monthly payment plans, individually arranged payment plans, Tuition Management Systems. 60% due July 1, remainder by December 1). Need-based scholarship grants available. In 2013–14, 29% of upper-school students received aid. Total amount of financial aid awarded in 2013–14: $3,456,893.

Admissions Traditional secondary-level entrance grade is 9. For fall 2013, 213 students applied for upper-level admission, 118 were accepted, 65 enrolled. ISEE or SSAT required. Deadline for receipt of application materials: December 15. Application fee required: $50. On-campus interview required.

Athletics Interscholastic: aquatics (boys, girls), baseball (b), basketball (b,g), crew (b,g), cross-country running (b,g), diving (b,g), field hockey (g), football (b), golf (b,g), indoor track (b,g), lacrosse (b,g), rowing (b,g), soccer (b,g), softball (g), squash (b,g), swimming and diving (b,g), tennis (b,g), track and field (b,g), water polo (b,g), winter (indoor) track (b,g), wrestling (b); intramural: aerobics (g), floor hockey (b); coed interscholastic: ice hockey, paddle tennis; coed intramural: aerobics/dance, aerobics/Nautilus, basketball, dance, dance squad, dance team, fencing, fitness, fitness walking, Frisbee, physical training, weight lifting, weight training. 1 PE instructor, 14 coaches, 2 athletic trainers.

Computers Computers are regularly used in art, English, foreign language, history, mathematics, science, technology classes. Computer network features include on-campus library services, Internet access, wireless campus network, Internet filtering or blocking technology. Campus intranet, student e-mail accounts, and computer access in designated common areas are available to students. Students grades are available online. The school has a published electronic and media policy.

Contact Ms. Rachel G. Tilney, Director of Admission and Enrollment. 484-424-1400 Ext. 1444. Fax: 484-424-1604. E-mail: rtilney@episcopalacademy.org. Website: www.episcopalacademy.org

EPISCOPAL COLLEGIATE SCHOOL

Jackson T. Stephens Campus
1701 Cantrell Road
Little Rock, Arkansas 72201

Head of School: Mr. Steve Hickman

General Information Coeducational day college-preparatory, arts, and technology school, affiliated with Episcopal Church. Grades PK–12. Founded: 2000. Setting: suburban. Nearest major city is Memphis, TN. 34-acre campus. 3 buildings on campus. Approved or accredited by National Association of Episcopal Schools and Southwest Association of Episcopal Schools. Member of National Association of Independent Schools. Endowment: $70 million. Total enrollment: 780. Upper school average class size: 15. Upper school faculty-student ratio: 1:10. There are 179 required school days per year for Upper School students. Upper School students typically attend 5 days per week. The average school day consists of 7 hours and 30 minutes.

Upper School Student Profile Grade 9: 53 students (22 boys, 31 girls); Grade 10: 63 students (26 boys, 37 girls); Grade 11: 50 students (29 boys, 21 girls); Grade 12: 60 students (27 boys, 33 girls). 20% of students are members of Episcopal Church.

Faculty School total: 96. In upper school: 15 men, 25 women; 33 have advanced degrees.

Graduation Requirements Senior chapel talk.

Special Academic Programs 16 Advanced Placement exams for which test preparation is offered; honors section; independent study.

College Admission Counseling 53 students graduated in 2013; all went to college, including Hendrix College; Rhodes College; Sewanee: The University of the South; The University of Texas at Austin; Tulane University; University of Arkansas. Mean SAT critical reading: 637, mean SAT math: 610, mean SAT writing: 633, mean combined SAT: 1879, mean composite ACT: 27. 66% scored over 600 on SAT critical reading, 47% scored over 600 on SAT math, 63% scored over 600 on SAT writing, 63% scored over 1800 on combined SAT, 43% scored over 26 on composite ACT.

Student Life Upper grades have uniform requirement, student council, honor system. Discipline rests primarily with faculty. Attendance at religious services is required.

Summer Programs Enrichment, sports, art/fine arts, computer instruction programs offered; session focuses on enrichment; held on campus; accepts boys and girls; open to students from other schools. 150 students usually enrolled. 2014 schedule: June 1 to July 31. Application deadline: May 30.

Tuition and Aid Day student tuition: $11,400. Tuition installment plan (FACTS Tuition Payment Plan). Need-based scholarship grants available. In 2013–14, 19% of upper-school students received aid. Total amount of financial aid awarded in 2013–14: $482,000.

Admissions Traditional secondary-level entrance grade is 9. For fall 2013, 21 students applied for upper-level admission, 11 were accepted, 9 enrolled. Stanford 9 required. Deadline for receipt of application materials: none. Application fee required: $50. Interview required.

Athletics Interscholastic: baseball (boys), basketball (b,g), cross-country running (b,g), fishing (b,g), fitness (b,g), football (b), golf (b,g), physical fitness (b,g), physical training (b,g), soccer (b,g), tennis (b,g), track and field (b,g), volleyball (g), weight training (b,g), wrestling (b,g); coed interscholastic: cheering. 4 PE instructors, 9 coaches, 2 athletic trainers.

Computers Computers are regularly used in all academic classes. Computer network features include on-campus library services, online commercial services, Internet access, wireless campus network, Internet filtering or blocking technology. Campus intranet, student e-mail accounts, and computer access in designated common areas are available to students. Students grades are available online. The school has a published electronic and media policy.

Contact Ms. Ashley Honeywell, Director of Admission. 501-372-1194 Ext. 2406. Fax: 501-372-2160. E-mail: ahoneywell@episcopalcollegiate.org. Website: www.episcopalcollegiate.org

EPISCOPAL HIGH SCHOOL

4650 Bissonnet
Bellaire, Texas 77401

Head of School: Mr. C. Edward Smith

General Information Coeducational day college-preparatory, arts, religious studies, and technology school, affiliated with Episcopal Church. Grades 9–12. Founded: 1984. Setting: urban. Nearest major city is Houston. 35-acre campus. 7 buildings on campus. Approved or accredited by Independent Schools Association of the Southwest, National Association of Episcopal Schools, The College Board, and Texas Department of Education. Member of National Association of Independent Schools and Secondary School Admission Test Board. Total enrollment: 676. Upper school average class size: 15. Upper school faculty-student ratio: 1:9. Upper School students typically attend 5 days per week. The average school day consists of 8 hours.

Upper School Student Profile Grade 9: 167 students (87 boys, 80 girls); Grade 10: 174 students (100 boys, 74 girls); Grade 11: 167 students (78 boys, 89 girls); Grade 12: 168 students (73 boys, 95 girls). 22.9% of students are members of Episcopal Church.

Faculty School total: 87. In upper school: 44 men, 43 women; 60 have advanced degrees.

Subjects Offered Acting, algebra, anatomy, ancient history, art appreciation, art history, band, Bible studies, biology, biology-AP, calculus-AP, ceramics, chemistry, choir, civil rights, dance, debate, design, drawing, English, English-AP, ethics, European history, French, French-AP, geography, geology, geometry, government, government-AP, graphic design, health, history of science, instrumental music, journalism, Latin, Latin American studies, music theory, newspaper, oceanography, orchestra, painting, photography, physical education, physics, physics-AP, physiology, pre-calculus, sculpture, Spanish, Spanish-AP, speech, stagecraft, statistics, theater, theology, U.S. history, U.S. history-AP, video film production, Vietnam War, world religions, World War II, writing, yearbook.

Graduation Requirements Arts and fine arts (art, music, dance, drama), English, foreign language, mathematics, physical education (includes health), religion (includes Bible studies and theology), religious studies, science, social studies (includes history).

Special Academic Programs 14 Advanced Placement exams for which test preparation is offered; honors section; independent study; study at local college for college credit.

College Admission Counseling 171 students graduated in 2013; all went to college, including Southern Methodist University; Texas A&M University; Texas Christian University; The University of Texas at Austin; Washington and Lee University. Mean SAT critical reading: 630, mean SAT math: 650, mean SAT writing: 630, mean combined SAT: 1910.

Student Life Upper grades have uniform requirement, student council, honor system. Discipline rests equally with students and faculty. Attendance at religious services is required.

Summer Programs Remediation, enrichment, advancement, art/fine arts programs offered; session focuses on remediation, advancement, enrichment; held on campus; accepts boys and girls; open to students from other schools. 250 students usually enrolled. 2014 schedule: June 2 to July 12. Application deadline: May 15.

Tuition and Aid Day student tuition: $23,850. Tuition installment plan (Insured Tuition Payment Plan, SMART Tuition Payment Plan, monthly payment plans). Need-based scholarship grants, middle-income loans available. In 2013–14, 19% of upper-school students received aid. Total amount of financial aid awarded in 2013–14: $1,700,000.

Admissions Traditional secondary-level entrance grade is 9. For fall 2013, 745 students applied for upper-level admission, 498 were accepted, 196 enrolled. ERB, ISEE and Otis-Lennon Ability or Stanford Achievement Test required. Deadline for receipt of application materials: December 16. Application fee required: $75. On-campus interview required.

Athletics Interscholastic: ballet (boys, girls), baseball (b), basketball (b,g), cheering (b,g), cross-country running (b,g), dance (b,g), drill team (g), field hockey (b,g), fitness (b,g), football (b), golf (b,g), lacrosse (b,g), physical fitness (b,g), running (b,g), soccer (b,g), softball (g), strength & conditioning (b,g), swimming and diving (b,g), tennis (b,g), track and field (b,g), volleyball (b,g), weight training (b,g), wrestling (b). 7 PE instructors, 8 coaches, 1 athletic trainer.

Computers Computers are regularly used in art, English, foreign language, history, mathematics, music, religion, science classes. Computer network features include on-campus library services, online commercial services, Internet access, wireless campus network, CollegeView. Student e-mail accounts are available to students. Students grades are available online. The school has a published electronic and media policy.

Contact Audrey Koehler, Director of Admission. 713-512-3400. Fax: 713-512-3603. E-mail: kpiper@ehshouston.org. Website: www.ehshouston.org/

EPISCOPAL HIGH SCHOOL

1200 North Quaker Lane
Alexandria, Virginia 22302

Head of School: Mr. F. Robertson Hershey

General Information Coeducational boarding college-preparatory, arts, religious studies, and technology school, affiliated with Episcopal Church. Grades 9–12. Founded: 1839. Setting: urban. Nearest major city is Washington, DC. Students are housed in single-sex dormitories. 130-acre campus. 26 buildings on campus. Approved or accredited by Southern Association of Colleges and Schools and Virginia Department of Education. Member of National Association of Independent Schools and Secondary School Admission Test Board. Endowment: $189 million. Total enrollment: 439. Upper school average class size: 11. Upper school faculty-student ratio: 1:6. The average school day consists of 7 hours.

Upper School Student Profile Grade 9: 73 students (36 boys, 37 girls); Grade 10: 121 students (61 boys, 60 girls); Grade 11: 126 students (59 boys, 67 girls); Grade 12: 119 students (67 boys, 52 girls). 100% of students are boarding students. 28% are state residents. 33 states are represented in upper school student body. 11% are international students. International students from Bermuda, Canada, China, Republic of Korea, and United Kingdom; 13 other countries represented in student body. 40% of students are members of Episcopal Church.

Faculty School total: 68. In upper school: 44 men, 24 women; 60 have advanced degrees; 58 reside on campus.

Subjects Offered 3-dimensional art, 3-dimensional design, acting, advanced biology, advanced chemistry, advanced computer applications, advanced math, aesthetics, algebra, all academic, American history, anatomy and physiology, art history, astronomy, Bible studies, biology, biotechnology, calculus, ceramics, chemistry, Chinese, Chinese history, Chinese literature, Chinese studies, choir, Christian education, comparative religion, computer programming, computer science, computer studies, conceptual physics, dance, digital photography, drama, drawing, drawing and design, ecology, ecology, environmental systems, economics, electives, engineering, English, English composition, English literature, equality and freedom, forensics, French, French studies, genetics, geology, geometry, German, German literature, global studies, government, government/civics, Greek, guitar, health and wellness, honors algebra, honors English, honors geometry, independent study, intro to computers, introduction to digital multitrack recording techniques, Latin, linear algebra, modern politics, music theory, orchestra, painting, photography, physics, portfolio art, pre-calculus, Shakespeare, Spanish, Spanish literature, statistics, studio art, technology, theater, theater arts, theater design and production, theater production, theology, U.S. history.

Graduation Requirements Arts and fine arts (art, music, dance, drama), computer studies, English, foreign language, mathematics, physical education (includes health), science, social studies (includes history), theology.

Special Academic Programs Advanced Placement exam preparation; honors section; independent study; term-away projects; study abroad; academic accommodation for the gifted, the musically talented, and the artistically talented.

College Admission Counseling 96 students graduated in 2013; all went to college, including The University of North Carolina at Chapel Hill; University of Virginia; Washington and Lee University. Mean SAT critical reading: 626, mean SAT math: 622, mean SAT writing: 633, mean combined SAT: 1880.

Student Life Upper grades have specified standards of dress, student council, honor system. Discipline rests primarily with faculty. Attendance at religious services is required.

Summer Programs Enrichment, advancement, sports, art/fine arts programs offered; session focuses on academic enrichment and athletic skills; held on campus; accepts boys and girls; open to students from other schools.

Tuition and Aid 7-day tuition and room/board: $47,850. Tuition installment plan (Insured Tuition Payment Plan, monthly payment plans). Merit scholarship grants, need-based scholarship grants, paying campus jobs available. In 2013–14, 30% of upper-school students received aid; total upper-school merit-scholarship money awarded: $189,500. Total amount of financial aid awarded in 2013–14: $5,000,000.

Admissions Traditional secondary-level entrance grade is 9. For fall 2013, 586 students applied for upper-level admission, 229 were accepted, 124 enrolled. ISEE, PSAT or SAT or SSAT required. Deadline for receipt of application materials: January 15. Application fee required: $60. Interview required.

Athletics Interscholastic: baseball (boys), basketball (b,g), crew (g), cross-country running (b,g), field hockey (g), football (b), golf (b), indoor track (b,g), indoor track & field (b,g), lacrosse (b,g), rowing (g), soccer (b,g), softball (g), squash (b,g), tennis (b,g), track and field (b,g), volleyball (g), winter (indoor) track (b,g), wrestling (b); intramural: soccer (b), strength & conditioning (b,g); coed interscholastic: climbing, fitness, outdoor education, outdoor recreation, outdoors, physical fitness, physical training, rock climbing, strength & conditioning, weight lifting, weight training; coed intramural: aerobics, aerobics/dance, aerobics/Nautilus, backpacking, ballet, canoeing/kayaking, climbing, dance, fitness, hiking/backpacking, kayaking, modern dance, outdoor activities, outdoor adventure, physical fitness, physical training, power lifting, rock climbing, wall climbing, weight lifting, weight training. 4 coaches, 2 athletic trainers.

Computers Computers are regularly used in all academic classes. Computer network features include on-campus library services, online commercial services, Internet access, wireless campus network, Internet filtering or blocking technology. Campus intranet and student e-mail accounts are available to students. Students grades are available online. The school has a published electronic and media policy.

Contact Mr. Scott Conklin, Director of Admission. 703-933-4062. Fax: 703-933-3016. E-mail: admissions@episcopalhighschool.org. Website: www.episcopalhighschool.org

EPISCOPAL HIGH SCHOOL OF JACKSONVILLE

Episcopal School of Jacksonville
4455 Atlantic Boulevard
Jacksonville, Florida 32207

Head of School: Charles F. Zimmer

General Information Coeducational day college-preparatory, arts, religious studies, and technology school, affiliated with Episcopal Church. Grades 6–12. Founded: 1966. Setting: urban. 88-acre campus. 25 buildings on campus. Approved or accredited by Florida Council of Independent Schools, National Association of Episcopal Schools, Southern Association of Colleges and Schools, and Southern Association of Independent Schools. Member of National Association of Independent Schools. Endowment: $15.4 million. Total enrollment: 857. Upper school average class size: 17. Upper school faculty-student ratio: 1:10. There are 175 required school days per year for Upper School students. Upper School students typically attend 5 days per week. The average school day consists of 6 hours and 50 minutes.

Upper School Student Profile Grade 9: 140 students (76 boys, 64 girls); Grade 10: 142 students (73 boys, 69 girls); Grade 11: 140 students (73 boys, 67 girls); Grade 12: 144 students (77 boys, 67 girls). 33% of students are members of Episcopal Church.

Faculty School total: 93. In upper school: 35 men, 58 women; 53 have advanced degrees.

Subjects Offered Advanced studio art-AP, algebra, American history, American history-AP, American literature, ancient history, art, art history, art history-AP, band, Basic programming, biology, biology-AP, calculus, calculus-AP, ceramics, chemistry, chemistry-AP, Chinese, computer programming, computer science, computer science-AP, dance, drama, earth science, economics, electronic publishing, English, English language and composition-AP, English literature and composition-AP, English/composition-AP, environmental science-AP, European history-AP, fine arts, French, French language-AP, geography, geometry, German, German-AP, government and politics-AP, government/civics, health, history, journalism, Latin, Latin-AP, marine biology, mathematics, music, music history, music theory, music theory-AP, photography, physical education, physics, physics-AP, public speaking, religion, religious studies, science, social studies, Spanish, Spanish language-AP, statistics, statistics-AP, studio art-AP, technical theater, theater, theology, trigonometry, U.S. government and politics-AP, U.S. history-AP, world history, writing, yearbook.

Graduation Requirements Arts and fine arts (art, music, dance, drama), computer science, English, foreign language, leadership, library skills, mathematics, physical education (includes health), religion (includes Bible studies and theology), science, social studies (includes history), 75 community service hours. Community service is required.

Special Academic Programs Advanced Placement exam preparation; honors section; independent study; study abroad; academic accommodation for the gifted.

College Admission Counseling 156 students graduated in 2012; all went to college, including Florida State University; University of Florida; University of North Florida. Median SAT critical reading: 579, median SAT math: 584, median SAT writing: 567, median combined SAT: 1729, median composite ACT: 26.

Student Life Upper grades have uniform requirement, student council, honor system. Discipline rests equally with students and faculty. Attendance at religious services is required.

Tuition and Aid Day student tuition: $18,500. Tuition installment plan (Insured Tuition Payment Plan, monthly payment plans). Need-based scholarship grants available. In 2012–13, 23% of upper-school students received aid. Total amount of financial aid awarded in 2012–13: $2,000,000.

Admissions Traditional secondary-level entrance grade is 9. For fall 2012, 89 students applied for upper-level admission, 58 were accepted, 38 enrolled. ISEE required. Deadline for receipt of application materials: January 11. Application fee required: $50. On-campus interview required.

Athletics Interscholastic: baseball (boys), basketball (b,g), crew (b,g), cross-country running (b,g), football (b), golf (b,g), lacrosse (b,g), modern dance (b,g), soccer (b,g), softball (g), swimming and diving (b,g), tennis (b,g), track and field (b,g), volleyball (g), weight lifting (b), weight training (b), wrestling (b); intramural: dance (g); coed interscholastic: cheering, dance, dance squad, dance team, wrestling; coed intramural: fencing. 7 PE instructors, 100 coaches, 4 athletic trainers.

Computers Computers are regularly used in all classes. Computer network features include on-campus library services, online commercial services, Internet access, wireless campus network, Internet filtering or blocking technology, Senior Systems: My BackPack online grading and student accounts, online parent portals, RSS feeds. Campus intranet, student e-mail accounts, and computer access in designated common areas are available to students. Students grades are available online. The school has a published electronic and media policy.

Contact Peggy P. Fox, Director of Admissions. 904-396-7104. Fax: 904-396-0981. E-mail: foxp@episcopalhigh.org. Website: www.episcopalhigh.org

ESCOLA AMERICANA DE CAMPINAS

Rua Cajamar, 35
Chcara da Barra
Campinas-SP 13090-860, Brazil

Head of School: Stephen A. Herrera

General Information Coeducational day college-preparatory, arts, bilingual studies, and technology school. Grades PK–12. Founded: 1956. Setting: urban. Nearest major city is So Paulo, Brazil. 4-acre campus. 4 buildings on campus. Approved or accredited by Association of American Schools in South America and Southern Association of Colleges and Schools. Affiliate member of National Association of Independent Schools; member of European Council of International Schools. Languages of instruction: English and Portuguese. Endowment: $350,000. Total enrollment: 300. Upper school average class size: 20. Upper school faculty-student ratio: 1:7.

Upper School Student Profile Grade 6: 46 students (26 boys, 20 girls); Grade 7: 39 students (15 boys, 24 girls); Grade 8: 53 students (28 boys, 25 girls); Grade 9: 42 students (19 boys, 23 girls); Grade 10: 41 students (19 boys, 22 girls); Grade 11: 45 students (21 boys, 24 girls); Grade 12: 34 students (17 boys, 17 girls).

Faculty School total: 76. In upper school: 11 men, 24 women; 30 have advanced degrees.

Subjects Offered Algebra, American history, American literature, art, biology, calculus, chemistry, computer science, creative writing, drama, economics, English, English literature, fine arts, geography, geometry, government/civics, grammar, history, journalism, mathematics, music, physical education, physics, Portuguese, psychology, science, social studies, speech, trigonometry, world history, world literature, writing.

Graduation Requirements Arts and fine arts (art, music, dance, drama), computer science, English, foreign language, mathematics, physical education (includes health), science, social studies (includes history). Community service is required.

Special Academic Programs Advanced Placement exam preparation; honors section; term-away projects; study at local college for college credit; study abroad; special instructional classes for students with mild learning differences; ESL (5 students enrolled).

College Admission Counseling 17 students graduated in 2012; 16 went to college, including Emerson College; Northwestern University; Southwestern University; The University of Tampa. Other: 1 entered a postgraduate year. Median SAT critical reading: 610, median SAT math: 640, median SAT writing: 540, median combined SAT: 1790.

Student Life Upper grades have student council, honor system. Discipline rests equally with students and faculty.

Tuition and Aid Day student tuition: 57,594 Brazilian reals. Tuition installment plan (monthly payment plans). Need-based scholarship grants available. In 2012–13, 10% of upper-school students received aid. Total amount of financial aid awarded in 2012–13: $51,000.

Admissions Traditional secondary-level entrance grade is 9. For fall 2012, 57 students applied for upper-level admission, 33 were accepted, 28 enrolled. Admissions testing, English Composition Test for ESL students, ERB CTP IV, Iowa Test, CTBS, or TAP, SAT and writing sample required. Deadline for receipt of application materials: September 3. No application fee required. On-campus interview required.

Athletics Interscholastic: basketball (boys, girls), canoeing/kayaking (g), cheering (g), indoor soccer (b,g), soccer (b,g), volleyball (g); intramural: ballet (g), basketball (b,g), canoeing/kayaking (g), cheering (g), climbing (b,g), indoor soccer (b,g), soccer (b,g); coed intramural: aerobics, baseball, basketball, climbing, cooperative games, fitness, flag football, Frisbee, gymnastics, handball, indoor soccer, jogging, judo, kickball, martial arts, physical fitness, self defense, soccer, softball, strength & conditioning, table tennis, track and field, ultimate Frisbee, volleyball. 6 PE instructors, 11 coaches.

Computers Computers are regularly used in art, English, history, independent study, mathematics, science, yearbook classes. Computer network features include on-campus library services, online commercial services, Internet access. Campus intranet is available to students.

Contact Davi Sanchez, High School Principal. 55-19-2102-1006. Fax: 55-19-2102-1016. E-mail: davi.sanchez@eac.com.br. Website: www.eac.com.br

THE ETHEL WALKER SCHOOL

230 Bushy Hill Road
Simsbury, Connecticut 06070

Head of School: Mrs. Elizabeth Cromwell Speers

General Information Girls' boarding and day college-preparatory and arts school. Boarding grades 9–12, day grades 6–12. Founded: 1911. Setting: suburban. Nearest major city is Hartford. Students are housed in single-sex dormitories. 300-acre campus. 9 buildings on campus. Approved or accredited by Connecticut Association of Independent Schools, New England Association of Schools and Colleges, The Association of Boarding Schools, and Connecticut Department of Education. Member of National Association of Independent Schools and Secondary School Admission Test Board. Endowment: $15.9 million. Total enrollment: 260. Upper school average class size: 12. Upper school faculty-student ratio: 1:6. There are 180 required school days per year for Upper School students. Upper School students typically attend 5 days per week. The average school day consists of 7 hours.

Upper School Student Profile Grade 9: 42 students (42 girls); Grade 10: 63 students (63 girls); Grade 11: 64 students (64 girls); Grade 12: 52 students (52 girls). 62% of students are boarding students. 43% are state residents. 23 states are represented in upper school student body. 19% are international students. International students from Afghanistan, China, Germany, Republic of Korea, Somalia, and Spain; 9 other countries represented in student body.

Faculty School total: 45. In upper school: 12 men, 31 women; 27 have advanced degrees; 30 reside on campus.

Subjects Offered 3-dimensional art, acting, advanced studio art-AP, African history, African literature, African studies, algebra, American government, American history, American history-AP, American literature, anatomy and physiology, Ancient Greek, ancient world history, art, art history, art-AP, Asian history, astronomy, bell choir, biology, biology-AP, calculus, calculus-AP, Caribbean history, ceramics, chemistry, chemistry-AP, Chinese, choir, choral music, choreography, civil rights, computer literacy, computer science, computer science-AP, conceptual physics, concert bell choir, concert choir, creative writing, digital photography, directing, diversity studies, drama, drama performance, dramatic arts, drawing, drawing and design, East Asian history, economics, economics-AP, English, English composition, English literature, English literature and composition-AP, English literature-AP, environmental science, environmental science-AP, environmental studies, equine science, ethics, European history, European history-AP, fiber arts, fiction, fine arts, forensics, French language-AP, geography, geometry, graphic design, health and wellness, history, history-AP, honors algebra, honors English, honors geometry, honors U.S. history, honors world history, independent study, instrumental music, Islamic studies, justice seminar, Latin, Latin American history, Latin-AP, leadership, macro/microeconomics-AP, Mandarin, Middle Eastern history, modern civilization, modern European history, modern European history-AP, music, music theory, musical theater, mythology, newspaper, painting, peace and justice, philosophy of government, photography, physics, physics-AP, playwriting, poetry, pre-calculus, psychology, psychology-AP, public speaking, religion and culture, Russian studies, sculpture, senior project, set design, Shakespeare, social justice, Spanish, Spanish language-AP, Spanish literature-AP, statistics-AP, student publications, studio art-AP, the Web, theater, trigonometry, U.S. history, U.S. history-AP, visual and performing arts, voice, Western civilization, women in literature, women's health, world history, world literature, world religions, writing, yearbook.

Graduation Requirements Arts and fine arts (art, music, dance, drama), English, ethics, foreign language, history, leadership, mathematics, performing arts, science, women's health, Junior/Senior project, community service hours. Community service is required.

Special Academic Programs 19 Advanced Placement exams for which test preparation is offered; honors section; independent study; term-away projects; study at local college for college credit; study abroad; academic accommodation for the gifted, the musically talented, and the artistically talented; ESL (12 students enrolled).

College Admission Counseling 41 students graduated in 2012; 39 went to college, including Barnard College; Bates College; Boston University; Carnegie Mellon University; Colgate University; Harvard University. Other: 2 entered a postgraduate year. Mean SAT critical reading: 545, mean SAT math: 552, mean SAT writing: 579, mean composite ACT: 24.

Student Life Upper grades have specified standards of dress, student council, honor system. Discipline rests equally with students and faculty.

Tuition and Aid Day student tuition: $36,350; 7-day tuition and room/board: $49,925. Tuition installment plan (monthly payment plans, individually arranged payment plans, 1-, 2-, and 10-payment plans). Need-based scholarship grants available. In 2012–13, 42% of upper-school students received aid. Total amount of financial aid awarded in 2012–13: $3,058,789.

Admissions Traditional secondary-level entrance grade is 9. For fall 2012, 321 students applied for upper-level admission, 171 were accepted, 88 enrolled. SSAT and TOEFL required. Deadline for receipt of application materials: February 1. Application fee required: $60. Interview required.

Athletics Interscholastic: alpine skiing, basketball, dance, dressage, equestrian sports, field hockey, golf, horseback riding, independent competitive sports, lacrosse, modern dance, nordic skiing, skiing (downhill), soccer, softball, squash, swimming and diving, tennis, volleyball; intramural: ballet, climbing, combined training, cross-country running, dance, dance team, equestrian sports, fitness, hiking/backpacking, jogging, kayaking, mountain biking, mountaineering, Nautilus, outdoor activities, outdoor adventure, physical fitness, physical training, rock climbing, ropes courses, running, strength & conditioning, wall climbing, weight lifting, weight training, yoga. 5 coaches, 1 athletic trainer.

Computers Computer network features include on-campus library services, online commercial services, Internet access, wireless campus network, Internet filtering or blocking technology. Student e-mail accounts and computer access in designated common areas are available to students. Students grades are available online. The school has a published electronic and media policy.

Contact Ms. Missy Shea, Director of Admission. 860-408-4200. Fax: 860-408-4201. E-mail: mshea@ethelwalker.org. Website: www.ethelwalker.org

EXPLORATIONS ACADEMY

PO Box 3014
Bellingham, Washington 98227

Head of School: Daniel Kirkpatrick

General Information Coeducational day and distance learning college-preparatory, experiential education, and international field study expeditions school. Ungraded, ages 11–18. Distance learning grades 9–12. Founded: 1995. Setting: urban. Nearest major city is Vancouver, BC, Canada. 1-acre campus. 1 building on campus. Approved or accredited by Northwest Accreditation Commission, Northwest Association of Independent Schools, Northwest Association of Schools and Colleges, and Washington Department of Education. Total enrollment: 41. Upper school average class size: 10. Upper school faculty-student ratio: 1:7. There are 177 required school days per year for Upper School students. Upper School students typically attend 5 days per week. The average school day consists of 6 hours.

Faculty School total: 10. In upper school: 5 men, 5 women; 7 have advanced degrees.

Subjects Offered Agriculture, American literature, anatomy and physiology, anthropology, archaeology, art, boat building, botany, calculus, carpentry, chemistry, Chinese, computer graphics, computer programming, conflict resolution, construction, creative writing, desktop publishing, drawing, earth science, ecology, environmental science, first aid, gardening, gender issues, geology, government, health, horticulture, human relations, journalism, Latin American studies, leadership, marine biology, media, meteorology, microbiology, music, music history, painting, philosophy, photography, physical education, physics, poetry, political science, psychology, sculpture, sexuality, short story, Spanish, technology, theater design and production, video film production, world cultures, world geography, world history, world literature, writing.

Graduation Requirements Arts and fine arts (art, music, dance, drama), computer science, English, foreign language, human relations, lab science, mathematics, occupational education, physical education (includes health), science, social sciences, social studies (includes history), U.S. government and politics, Washington State and Northwest History, world history, one term of self-designed interdisciplinary studies, one month-long international study/service expedition. Community service is required.

Special Academic Programs Advanced Placement exam preparation; honors section; accelerated programs; independent study; term-away projects; academic accommodation for the gifted.

College Admission Counseling 6 students graduated in 2013; 5 went to college, including The Evergreen State College; University of Washington; Western Washington University. Other: 1 went to work.

Student Life Upper grades have honor system. Discipline rests primarily with faculty.

Summer Programs Enrichment, advancement, art/fine arts, rigorous outdoor training programs offered; session focuses on experiential learning; held both on and off campus; held at local urban and wilderness areas; accepts boys and girls; open to students from other schools. 12 students usually enrolled. 2014 schedule: July 8 to August 16. Application deadline: none.

Tuition and Aid Day student tuition: $13,600. Tuition installment plan (monthly payment plans, individually arranged payment plans, school's own payment plan). Merit scholarship grants, need-based scholarship grants, need-based loans, low-interest loans with deferred payment available. In 2013–14, 48% of upper-school students received aid; total upper-school merit-scholarship money awarded: $35,000. Total amount of financial aid awarded in 2013–14: $200,000.

Admissions Traditional secondary-level entrance age is 14. For fall 2013, 44 students applied for upper-level admission, 43 were accepted, 41 enrolled. Non-standardized placement tests required. Deadline for receipt of application materials: none. Application fee required: $60. Interview required.

Computers Computers are regularly used in animation, art, English, French, graphics, mathematics, media production, publications, SAT preparation, science, writing, yearbook classes. Computer network features include online commercial services, Internet access, wireless campus network. Computer access in designated common areas is available to students. The school has a published electronic and media policy.

Contact Bethany Denton, Volunteer and Outreach Coordinator. 360-671-8085. Fax: 360-671-2521. E-mail: info@explorationsacademy.org. Website: www.ExplorationsAcademy.org

EZELL-HARDING CHRISTIAN SCHOOL

574 Bell Road
Antioch, Tennessee 37013

Head of School: Mrs. Belvia Pruitt

General Information Coeducational day college-preparatory and religious studies school, affiliated with Church of Christ. Grades K–12. Founded: 1973. Setting: suburban. Nearest major city is Nashville. 30-acre campus. 1 building on campus. Approved or accredited by National Christian School Association, Southern Association of Colleges and Schools, and Tennessee Association of Independent Schools. Endowment: $100,000. Total enrollment: 543. Upper school average class size: 17. Upper school faculty-student ratio: 1:14. There are 176 required school days per year for Upper School students. Upper School students typically attend 5 days per week. The average school day consists of 7 hours.

Upper School Student Profile Grade 9: 54 students (28 boys, 26 girls); Grade 10: 46 students (21 boys, 25 girls); Grade 11: 50 students (25 boys, 25 girls); Grade 12: 48 students (15 boys, 33 girls). 31% of students are members of Church of Christ.

Faculty School total: 57. In upper school: 10 men, 10 women; 12 have advanced degrees.

Subjects Offered ACT preparation, advanced math, Advanced Placement courses, algebra, American history, American history-AP, anatomy and physiology, art, band, Bible, biology, broadcasting, calculus, calculus-AP, chemistry, chorus, computer applications, computer technologies, economics, English literature and composition-AP, European history, European history-AP, fitness, geography, geometry, government, grammar, keyboarding, microcomputer technology applications, physical science, psychology, sociology, Spanish, statistics-AP, trigonometry, weight training, wellness, world history.

Graduation Requirements American history, Bible, computers, economics, English, government, lab science, physical education (includes health), wellness, world history.

Special Academic Programs 5 Advanced Placement exams for which test preparation is offered; honors section; independent study; study at local college for college credit; remedial math.

College Admission Counseling 63 students graduated in 2013; 60 went to college, including Harding University; Lipscomb University; Middle Tennessee State University; Tennessee Technological University; The University of Tennessee at Chattanooga. Other: 1 went to work, 2 had other specific plans. Median composite ACT: 26. 48.4% scored over 26 on composite ACT.

Student Life Upper grades have uniform requirement, student council. Discipline rests primarily with faculty.

Tuition and Aid Day student tuition: $8200. Tuition installment plan (The Tuition Plan, monthly payment plans). Need-based scholarship grants available. In 2013–14, 27% of upper-school students received aid.

Admissions Traditional secondary-level entrance grade is 9. For fall 2013, 24 students applied for upper-level admission, 18 were accepted, 18 enrolled. MAT 7 Metropolitan Achievement Test, TOEFL or SLEP or writing sample required. Deadline for receipt of application materials: none. Application fee required: $75. Interview required.

Athletics Interscholastic: baseball (boys), basketball (b,g), bowling (b,g), cheering (g), cross-country running (b,g), drill team (g), football (b), golf (b,g), soccer (b,g), softball (g), tennis (b,g), track and field (b,g), volleyball (g), weight training (b,g). 1 PE instructor, 6 coaches, 1 athletic trainer.

Computers Computers are regularly used in all academic classes. Computer network features include on-campus library services, Internet access, wireless campus network, Internet filtering or blocking technology. Student e-mail accounts are available to students. Students grades are available online. The school has a published electronic and media policy.

Contact Mrs. Deborah Chapman, Admissions Officer. 615-367-0532 Ext. 109. Fax: 615-399-8747. E-mail: dchapman@ezellharding.com. Website: www.ezellharding.com

FAIRFIELD COLLEGE PREPARATORY SCHOOL

1073 North Benson Road

Fairfield, Connecticut 06824-5157

Head of School: Rev. John J. Hanwell, SJ

General Information Boys' day college-preparatory, arts, religious studies, and technology school, affiliated with Roman Catholic Church. Grades 9–12. Founded: 1942. Setting: suburban. Nearest major city is Bridgeport. 220-acre campus. 4 buildings on campus. Approved or accredited by Jesuit Secondary Education Association, New England Association of Schools and Colleges, and Connecticut Department of Education. Member of National Association of Independent Schools. Endowment: $17 million. Total enrollment: 901. Upper school average class size: 21. Upper school faculty-student ratio: 1:18. There are 182 required school days per year for Upper School students. Upper School students typically attend 5 days per week. The average school day consists of 5 hours and 50 minutes.

Upper School Student Profile Grade 9: 249 students (249 boys); Grade 10: 211 students (211 boys); Grade 11: 222 students (222 boys); Grade 12: 219 students (219 boys). 68% of students are Roman Catholic.

Faculty School total: 55. In upper school: 33 men, 22 women; 49 have advanced degrees.

Subjects Offered Advanced Placement courses, algebra, American Civil War, American government, American history, American history-AP, American literature, American literature-AP, art, Asian studies, band, biology, biology-AP, British literature, British literature-AP, calculus, calculus-AP, career exploration, chemistry, chemistry-AP, choir, chorus, Christian education, Christian ethics, Christian scripture, Christian studies, Christianity, civil rights, Civil War, college admission preparation, college planning, community service, computer education, computer literacy, computer science, constitutional history of U.S., constitutional law, creative writing, drama, drama workshop, drawing and design, driver education, economics, English, English literature, English literature and composition-AP, English literature-AP, English-AP, environmental science, ethical decision making, ethics and responsibility, European history, European history-AP, expository writing, fine arts, French, French language-AP, French literature-AP, French-AP, geometry, government-AP, grammar, graphics, guidance, history, history of religion, history of the Catholic Church, honors algebra, honors English, honors geometry, honors U.S. history, introduction to theater, jazz band, journalism, language and composition, language arts, language structure, Latin, Latin-AP, Life of Christ, literary magazine, mathematics, Middle East, modern European history-AP, moral theology, music, musical productions, musical theater, physics, physics-AP, pre-calculus, religion, remedial study skills, SAT preparation, science, social justice, social studies, sociology, Spanish, Spanish language-AP, Spanish-AP, student government, studio art, symphonic band, technical drawing, theater, theater arts, theology, trigonometry, U.S. constitutional history, U.S. history-AP, United States government-AP, values and decisions, visual and performing arts, visual arts, Web site design, Western civilization, wind ensemble, word processing, world history, world literature, world religions, world religions, world studies, World War I, World War II, writing.

Graduation Requirements Arts and fine arts (art, music, dance, drama), computer science, English, foreign language, mathematics, religion (includes Bible studies and theology), science, social studies (includes history), senior comprehensive exercises. Community service is required.

Special Academic Programs Advanced Placement exam preparation; honors section; study at local college for college credit.

College Admission Counseling 201 students graduated in 2013; 193 went to college, including College of the Holy Cross; Loyola University Maryland; Saint Joseph's University; University of Connecticut; University of Notre Dame; Villanova University. Other: 8 entered a postgraduate year. Mean SAT critical reading: 588, mean SAT math: 604, mean SAT writing: 594, mean combined SAT: 1786.

Student Life Upper grades have specified standards of dress, student council. Discipline rests primarily with faculty. Attendance at religious services is required.

Summer Programs Remediation, enrichment, sports, computer instruction programs offered; session focuses on enrichment; held on campus; accepts boys and girls; open to students from other schools. 160 students usually enrolled. 2014 schedule: June 30 to July 25.

Tuition and Aid Day student tuition: $17,700. Tuition installment plan (FACTS Tuition Payment Plan). Need-based scholarship grants available. In 2013–14, 29% of upper-school students received aid. Total amount of financial aid awarded in 2013–14: $2,163,000.

Admissions Traditional secondary-level entrance grade is 9. For fall 2013, 481 students applied for upper-level admission, 249 enrolled. High School Placement Test required. Deadline for receipt of application materials: December 1. Application fee required: $60.

Athletics Interscholastic: baseball, basketball, bowling, crew, cross-country running, diving, fencing, football, golf, ice hockey, indoor track & field, lacrosse, rugby, sailing, skiing (downhill), soccer, strength & conditioning, swimming and diving, tennis, track and field, weight training, winter (indoor) track, wrestling; intramural: alpine skiing, basketball, bicycling, fitness, flag football, mountain biking, skiing (downhill), strength & conditioning, table tennis, weight lifting, weight training, whiffle ball. 33 coaches, 2 athletic trainers.

Computers Computers are regularly used in art, English, foreign language, history, mathematics, science, technology, theology classes. Computer network features include on-campus library services, online commercial services, Internet access, Internet filtering or blocking technology. Student e-mail accounts are available to students. Students grades are available online. The school has a published electronic and media policy.

Contact Mrs. Colleen H. Adams, Director of Communications. 203-254-4200 Ext. 2487. Fax: 203-254-4071. E-mail: cadams@fairfieldprep.org. Website: www.fairfieldprep.org

FAIRHILL SCHOOL

Dallas, Texas

See Special Needs Schools section.

FAITH CHRISTIAN HIGH SCHOOL

3105 Colusa Highway

Yuba City, California 95993

Head of School: Mr. Stephen Finlay

General Information Coeducational day college-preparatory, arts, religious studies, and technology school, affiliated with Christian faith. Grades 9–12. Founded: 1975. Setting: small town. Nearest major city is Sacramento. 10-acre campus. 4 buildings on campus. Approved or accredited by Association of Christian Schools International, Western Association of Schools and Colleges, and California Department of Education. Total enrollment: 100. Upper school average class size: 25. Upper school faculty-student ratio: 1:12. There are 175 required school days per year for Upper School students. Upper School students typically attend 5 days per week. The average school day consists of 5 hours and 30 minutes.

Upper School Student Profile Grade 9: 22 students (9 boys, 13 girls); Grade 10: 25 students (12 boys, 13 girls); Grade 11: 18 students (10 boys, 8 girls); Grade 12: 23 students (15 boys, 8 girls). 85% of students are Christian.

Faculty School total: 16. In upper school: 10 men, 6 women; 4 have advanced degrees.

Subjects Offered Algebra, arts, Bible, biology, biology-AP, British literature, calculus-AP, chemistry, civics, computer science, computer studies, concert band, drama, economics, English, English composition, English literature, English-AP, geography, geometry, government, health, honors English, physical education, physical science, pre-calculus, senior project, Spanish, U.S. history, world geography, world history, yearbook.

Graduation Requirements Algebra, Bible, biology, civics, economics, English, geometry, health, physical science, senior project, U.S. history, world geography, world history.

Special Academic Programs Advanced Placement exam preparation; study at local college for college credit.

College Admission Counseling 28 students graduated in 2013; 25 went to college, including Azusa Pacific University; Point Loma Nazarene University; Simpson University; University of California, Davis; University of Nevada, Reno; University of the Pacific. Other: 3 entered military service. Median SAT critical reading: 580, median SAT math: 540, median SAT writing: 550, median combined SAT: 1640, median composite ACT: 20. 30% scored over 600 on SAT critical reading, 20% scored over 600 on SAT math, 30% scored over 600 on SAT writing, 30% scored over 1800 on combined SAT, 25% scored over 26 on composite ACT.

Student Life Upper grades have specified standards of dress, student council, honor system. Discipline rests primarily with faculty. Attendance at religious services is required.

Tuition and Aid Day student tuition: $7460. Tuition installment plan (monthly payment plans). Tuition reduction for siblings, need-based scholarship grants available. In 2013–14, 20% of upper-school students received aid. Total amount of financial aid awarded in 2013–14: $50,000.

Admissions Traditional secondary-level entrance grade is 9. For fall 2013, 18 students applied for upper-level admission, 17 were accepted, 17 enrolled. Achievement tests required. Deadline for receipt of application materials: none. Application fee required: $50. Interview required.

Athletics Interscholastic: baseball (boys), basketball (b,g), cheering (g), cross-country running (b,g), soccer (b), softball (g), volleyball (g); coed interscholastic: golf. 1 PE instructor, 8 coaches.

Computers Computers are regularly used in all academic classes. Computer network features include on-campus library services, Internet access, Internet filtering or blocking technology. Students grades are available online. The school has a published electronic and media policy.

Contact Mrs. Sue Shorey, Secretary. 530-674-5474. Fax: 530-674-0194. E-mail: sshorey@fcs-k12.org. Website: www.fcs-k12.org

FAITH LUTHERAN HIGH SCHOOL

2015 South Hualapai Way
Las Vegas, Nevada 89117-6949

Head of School: Dr. Steve J. Buuck

General Information Coeducational day college-preparatory and religious studies school, affiliated with Lutheran Church–Missouri Synod, Evangelical Lutheran Church in America. Grades 6–12. Founded: 1979. Setting: suburban. 39-acre campus. 4 buildings on campus. Approved or accredited by Lutheran School Accreditation Commission, National Lutheran School Accreditation, Northwest Accreditation Commission, Northwest Association of Schools and Colleges, and Nevada Department of Education. Endowment: $1 million. Total enrollment: 1,390. Upper school average class size: 25. Upper school faculty-student ratio: 1:17. There are 180 required school days per year for Upper School students. Upper School students typically attend 5 days per week. The average school day consists of 7 hours.

Upper School Student Profile 25% of students are Lutheran Church–Missouri Synod, Evangelical Lutheran Church in America.

Faculty School total: 92. In upper school: 32 men, 54 women; 48 have advanced degrees.

Subjects Offered Algebra, American history, art, biology, chemistry, computer science, earth science, English, fine arts, fitness, geometry, German, health, mathematics, music, physical education, physical science, religion, SAT/ACT preparation, science, social studies, Spanish.

Graduation Requirements American history, arts and fine arts (art, music, dance, drama), computer science, English, foreign language, mathematics, physical education (includes health), religion (includes Bible studies and theology), science, social studies (includes history).

Special Academic Programs 7 Advanced Placement exams for which test preparation is offered; honors section; independent study; study at local college for college credit; academic accommodation for the musically talented.

College Admission Counseling 156 students graduated in 2013; 154 went to college, including Concordia University; University of Nevada, Las Vegas; University of Nevada, Reno. Other: 1 went to work, 1 had other specific plans. Median SAT critical reading: 540, median SAT math: 520, median SAT writing: 510, median combined SAT: 1570, median composite ACT: 23. 25% scored over 600 on SAT critical reading, 25% scored over 600 on SAT math, 20% scored over 600 on SAT writing, 23% scored over 1800 on combined SAT, 30% scored over 26 on composite ACT.

Student Life Upper grades have uniform requirement, student council. Discipline rests primarily with faculty. Attendance at religious services is required.

Summer Programs Remediation programs offered; held on campus; accepts boys and girls; not open to students from other schools.

Tuition and Aid Day student tuition: $10,100. Tuition installment plan (monthly payment plans, individually arranged payment plans). Tuition reduction for siblings, need-based scholarship grants available. In 2013–14, 12% of upper-school students received aid. Total amount of financial aid awarded in 2013–14: $512,000.

Admissions Traditional secondary-level entrance grade is 9. For fall 2013, 110 students applied for upper-level admission, 100 were accepted, 90 enrolled. High School Placement Test and Stanford 9 required. Deadline for receipt of application materials: none. Application fee required: $350. On-campus interview required.

Athletics Interscholastic: aerobics/dance (girls), aquatics (b,g), baseball (b), basketball (b,g), cheering (g), cross-country running (b,g), dance team (g), football (b), golf (b,g), lacrosse (b,g), soccer (b,g), softball (g), swimming and diving (b,g), tennis (b,g), track and field (b,g), volleyball (g), wrestling (b); intramural: strength & conditioning (b,g), weight training (b,g); coed interscholastic: strength & conditioning; coed intramural: skiing (downhill), snowboarding, ultimate Frisbee. 7 PE instructors, 26 coaches, 2 athletic trainers.

Computers Computers are regularly used in keyboarding, yearbook classes. Computer network features include on-campus library services, online commercial services, Internet access, wireless campus network, Internet filtering or blocking technology. Student e-mail accounts and computer access in designated common areas are available to students. Students grades are available online. The school has a published electronic and media policy.

Contact Mr. Joel Arnold, Director of Admissions. 702-804-4413. Fax: 702-562-7728. E-mail: arnoldj@flhsemail.org. Website: www.faithlutheranlv.org

FALMOUTH ACADEMY

7 Highfield Drive
Falmouth, Massachusetts 02540

Head of School: Mr. Mark W. Segar

General Information Coeducational day college-preparatory and arts school. Grades 7–12. Founded: 1976. Setting: small town. Nearest major city is Boston. 34-acre campus. 2 buildings on campus. Approved or accredited by Association of Independent Schools in New England and New England Association of Schools and Colleges. Member of National Association of Independent Schools and Secondary School Admission Test Board. Endowment: $5 million. Total enrollment: 195. Upper school average class size: 12. Upper school faculty-student ratio: 1:4. There are 163 required school days per year for Upper School students. Upper School students typically attend 5 days per week. The average school day consists of 6 hours and 20 minutes.

Upper School Student Profile Grade 9: 32 students (18 boys, 14 girls); Grade 10: 28 students (15 boys, 13 girls); Grade 11: 34 students (15 boys, 19 girls); Grade 12: 22 students (11 boys, 11 girls).

Faculty School total: 43. In upper school: 15 men, 28 women; 27 have advanced degrees.

Subjects Offered Algebra, American history, American literature, art, biology, calculus, ceramics, chemistry, creative writing, drama, earth science, ecology, English, English literature, environmental science, European history, expository writing, fine arts, French, geography, geology, geometry, German, grammar, health, history, journalism, mathematics, music, photography, physical education, physics, science, sculpture, social studies, statistics, theater, trigonometry, woodworking, world history, world literature, writing.

Graduation Requirements Arts and fine arts (art, music, dance, drama), English, foreign language, history, mathematics, science.

Special Academic Programs 5 Advanced Placement exams for which test preparation is offered; independent study; term-away projects; study abroad; ESL (4 students enrolled).

College Admission Counseling 28 students graduated in 2013; all went to college, including New York University; Ohio Wesleyan University; University of Vermont. Mean SAT critical reading: 657, mean SAT math: 611, mean SAT writing: 658.

Student Life Upper grades have specified standards of dress, student council, honor system. Discipline rests primarily with faculty.

Summer Programs Enrichment, sports, art/fine arts programs offered; session focuses on arts enrichment; held on campus; accepts boys and girls; open to students from other schools. 150 students usually enrolled. 2014 schedule: July 1 to August 15.

Tuition and Aid Day student tuition: $25,295. Merit scholarship grants, need-based scholarship grants, need-based loans available. In 2013–14, 45% of upper-school students received aid; total upper-school merit-scholarship money awarded: $6000. Total amount of financial aid awarded in 2013–14: $928,000.

Admissions Traditional secondary-level entrance grade is 9. For fall 2013, 24 students applied for upper-level admission, 23 were accepted, 12 enrolled. SSAT required. Deadline for receipt of application materials: March 1. Application fee required: $50. On-campus interview required.

Athletics Interscholastic: basketball (boys, girls), lacrosse (b,g), soccer (b,g). 1 PE instructor, 1 athletic trainer.

Computers Computers are regularly used in design, English, foreign language, humanities, mathematics, science classes. Computer resources include on-campus library services, Internet access, Internet filtering or blocking technology. The school has a published electronic and media policy.

Contact Mr. Michael J. Earley, Assistant Head of School/Director of Admissions. 508-457-9696 Ext. 224. Fax: 508-457-4112. E-mail: mearley@falmouthacademy.org. Website: www.falmouthacademy.org

FATHER JUDGE HIGH SCHOOL

3301 Solly Avenue
Philadelphia, Pennsylvania 19136

Head of School: Rev. James Dalton, OSFS

General Information Boys' day college-preparatory, arts, business, religious studies, and technology school, affiliated with Roman Catholic Church. Grades 9–12. Founded: 1954. Setting: suburban. 3 buildings on campus. Approved or accredited by Middle States Association of Colleges and Schools, National Catholic Education Association, and Pennsylvania Department of Education. Total enrollment: 986. Upper school average class size: 28. Upper school faculty-student ratio: 1:28. There are 180 required school days per year for Upper School students. Upper School students typically attend 5 days per week. The average school day consists of 7 hours.

Upper School Student Profile Grade 9: 274 students (274 boys); Grade 10: 246 students (246 boys); Grade 11: 220 students (220 boys); Grade 12: 246 students (246 boys). 98% of students are Roman Catholic.

Faculty School total: 65. In upper school: 46 men, 19 women.

Subjects Offered Acting.

Graduation Requirements Biology, electives, English, foreign language, health education, mathematics, physical education (includes health), physical science, religion (includes Bible studies and theology), science, theology, U.S. government, world history, Christian Service Project each school year.

Special Academic Programs 5 Advanced Placement exams for which test preparation is offered; honors section; study at local college for college credit.

College Admission Counseling 247 students graduated in 2013; 222 went to college, including Bloomsburg University of Pennsylvania; Community College of Philadelphia; Holy Family University; La Salle University; Penn State University Park; Temple University. Other: 5 went to work, 10 entered military service, 10 entered a postgraduate year.

Student Life Upper grades have uniform requirement, student council, honor system. Discipline rests primarily with faculty. Attendance at religious services is required.

Summer Programs Enrichment programs offered; session focuses on enrichment; held on campus; accepts boys; not open to students from other schools. 20 students usually enrolled.

Tuition and Aid Day student tuition: $6150. Tuition installment plan (monthly payment plans). Tuition reduction for siblings, merit scholarship grants, need-based scholarship grants available. In 2013–14, 80% of upper-school students received aid; total upper-school merit-scholarship money awarded: $148,000. Total amount of financial aid awarded in 2013–14: $740,000.

Admissions Traditional secondary-level entrance grade is 9. For fall 2013, 300 students applied for upper-level admission, 274 were accepted, 274 enrolled. Any standardized test or TerraNova required. Deadline for receipt of application materials: none. Application fee required: $170. Interview recommended.

Athletics Interscholastic: baseball, basketball, bowling, cheering (g), crew, cross-country running, dance (g), dance squad (g), dance team (g), danceline (g), football, golf, ice hockey, indoor track, lacrosse, rugby, soccer, swimming and diving, tennis, track and field, winter (indoor) track, wrestling; intramural: flag football, touch football. 1 PE instructor, 30 coaches, 1 athletic trainer.

Computers Computers are regularly used in all classes. Computer network features include on-campus library services, Internet access, wireless campus network, Internet filtering or blocking technology. Student e-mail accounts are available to students. Students grades are available online. The school has a published electronic and media policy.

Contact Ms. Jennifer Russell, Admissions Director. 215-338-9494 Ext. 1132. Fax: 215-338-0250. E-mail: jrussell@fatherjudge.com. Website: www.fatherjudge.com

FATHER LOPEZ HIGH SCHOOL

3918 LPGA Boulevard
Daytona Beach, Florida 32124

Head of School: Dr. Michael J. Coury

General Information Coeducational day college-preparatory and religious studies school, affiliated with Roman Catholic Church. Grades 9–12. Founded: 1959. Setting: urban. 90-acre campus. 7 buildings on campus. Approved or accredited by National Catholic Education Association, Southern Association of Colleges and Schools, and Florida Department of Education. Total enrollment: 438. Upper school average class size: 16. Upper school faculty-student ratio: 1:13. There are 181 required school days per year for Upper School students. Upper School students typically attend 5 days per week. The average school day consists of 7 hours and 16 minutes.

Upper School Student Profile Grade 9: 125 students (57 boys, 68 girls); Grade 10: 109 students (62 boys, 47 girls); Grade 11: 130 students (73 boys, 57 girls); Grade 12: 74 students (40 boys, 34 girls). 59% of students are Roman Catholic.

Faculty School total: 33. In upper school: 14 men, 19 women; 16 have advanced degrees.

Subjects Offered Advanced biology, advanced chemistry, advanced math, Advanced Placement courses, algebra, American history, American history-AP, American literature, anatomy and physiology, applied skills, art, art-AP, audio visual/media, basketball, biology, biology-AP, British literature, calculus, calculus-AP, Catholic belief and practice, chemistry, chemistry-AP, Chinese, Christian and Hebrew scripture, Christian studies, church history, classical Greek literature, college writing, communication skills, computer applications, computer art, computer graphics, consumer mathematics, critical writing, culinary arts, dance, dance performance, death and loss, design, digital photography, drama, drama performance, dramatic arts, drawing, economics, English, English as a foreign language, English literature, English literature and composition-AP, film, film and literature, filmmaking, French, French-AP, geometry, government, grammar, graphic design, health education, honors algebra, honors English, honors geometry, honors U.S. history, honors world history, human geography - AP, journalism, Latin, marine science, mathematics, moral and social development, philosophy, photography, physical education, physical science, physics, physics-AP, pre-calculus, psychology, psychology-AP, senior science survey, senior seminar, senior thesis, social justice, sociology, Spanish, speech, statistics, statistics-AP, studio art-AP, television, tennis, trigonometry, U.S. government and politics-AP, U.S. history, U.S. history-AP, video film production, Web authoring, Web site design, weight training, weightlifting, world geography, world history, world history-AP, world religions, writing, yearbook.

Graduation Requirements Algebra, American history, American literature, arts and fine arts (art, music, dance, drama), biology, British literature, chemistry, economics, electives, English, English literature, foreign language, geometry, health and wellness, physical education (includes health), physics, theology, U.S. government, world history, 100 hours of community service.

Special Academic Programs 13 Advanced Placement exams for which test preparation is offered; honors section; study at local college for college credit; ESL (16 students enrolled).

College Admission Counseling 92 students graduated in 2013; all went to college, including Florida State University; Stetson University; University of Central Florida; University of Florida; University of North Florida. Mean SAT critical reading: 498, mean SAT math: 521, mean SAT writing: 494, mean composite ACT: 22.

Student Life Upper grades have uniform requirement, student council, honor system. Discipline rests primarily with faculty. Attendance at religious services is required.

Tuition and Aid Day student tuition: $10,100. Tuition installment plan (FACTS Tuition Payment Plan). Tuition reduction for siblings, merit scholarship grants, need-based scholarship grants, tiered tuition rate based on income available. In 2013–14,

62% of upper-school students received aid. Total amount of financial aid awarded in 2013–14: $1,023,796.

Admissions Traditional secondary-level entrance grade is 9. For fall 2013, 178 students applied for upper-level admission, 176 were accepted, 141 enrolled. High School Placement Test required. Deadline for receipt of application materials: none. Application fee required: $50. Interview required.

Athletics Interscholastic: baseball (boys), basketball (b,g), cross-country running (b,g), football (b), golf (b,g), lacrosse (b), softball (g), swimming and diving (b,g), tennis (b,g), track and field (b,g), volleyball (g), winter soccer (b,g); coed intramural: cheering, dance team, pom squad, table tennis, weight lifting, weight training. 2 PE instructors, 25 coaches, 1 athletic trainer.

Computers Computers are regularly used in all academic, art, computer applications, graphic design, media production, photography, video film production, yearbook classes. Computer network features include Internet access, wireless campus network, Internet filtering or blocking technology. Student e-mail accounts and computer access in designated common areas are available to students. Students grades are available online. The school has a published electronic and media policy.

Contact Mrs. Carmen Rivera, Admissions Coordinator. 386-253-5213 Ext. 325. Fax: 386-252-6101. E-mail: crivera@fatherlopez.org. Website: www.fatherlopez.org

FATHER RYAN HIGH SCHOOL

700 Norwood Drive
Nashville, Tennessee 37204

Head of School: Mr. Jim McIntyre

General Information Coeducational day college-preparatory, arts, and religious studies school, affiliated with Roman Catholic Church. Grades 9–12. Founded: 1925. Setting: suburban. 40-acre campus. 9 buildings on campus. Approved or accredited by National Catholic Education Association, Southern Association of Colleges and Schools, Southern Association of Independent Schools, Tennessee Association of Independent Schools, and The College Board. Endowment: $5 million. Total enrollment: 948. Upper school average class size: 20. Upper school faculty-student ratio: 1:12. There are 180 required school days per year for Upper School students. Upper School students typically attend 5 days per week. The average school day consists of 7 hours and 10 minutes.

Upper School Student Profile Grade 9: 254 students (149 boys, 105 girls); Grade 10: 240 students (141 boys, 99 girls); Grade 11: 227 students (134 boys, 93 girls); Grade 12: 227 students (132 boys, 95 girls). 90% of students are Roman Catholic.

Faculty School total: 84. In upper school: 43 men, 41 women; 48 have advanced degrees.

Subjects Offered 3-dimensional design, Advanced Placement courses, aerobics, algebra, American government, American history, American history-AP, American literature, anatomy, art, art history, art-AP, Bible studies, biology, British literature, calculus, calculus-AP, Catholic belief and practice, chemistry, chemistry-AP, Chinese, Chinese studies, chorus, church history, college counseling, college planning, college writing, computer programming, computer science, computer studies, dance, dance performance, drama, drama performance, driver education, economics, English, English literature, English-AP, European history, European history-AP, film studies, French, French-AP, geography, geometry, government-AP, government/civics, grammar, health, history, honors geometry, honors U.S. history, journalism, Latin, mathematics, music, physical education, physics, physics-AP, physiology, psychology, psychology-AP, religion, SAT preparation, science, Shakespeare, social studies, Spanish, Spanish-AP, speech, statistics-AP, theater, theater production, theology, trigonometry, U.S. government and politics-AP, Web site design, wind ensemble, world history, world literature, world religions, writing.

Graduation Requirements Arts and fine arts (art, music, dance, drama), computer science, English, foreign language, health education, mathematics, physical education (includes health), religion (includes Bible studies and theology), science, social studies (includes history), service hours required each year.

Special Academic Programs 27 Advanced Placement exams for which test preparation is offered; honors section; academic accommodation for the gifted, the musically talented, and the artistically talented; programs in English, mathematics for dyslexic students.

College Admission Counseling 211 students graduated in 2013; all went to college, including Belmont University; Middle Tennessee State University; Tennessee Technological University; The University of Tennessee; Western Kentucky University. Median SAT critical reading: 553, median SAT math: 524, median composite ACT: 24. 20% scored over 26 on composite ACT.

Student Life Upper grades have uniform requirement, student council. Discipline rests primarily with faculty. Attendance at religious services is required.

Summer Programs Remediation, enrichment, advancement, sports, art/fine arts, computer instruction programs offered; held on campus; accepts boys and girls; open to students from other schools. 240 students usually enrolled. 2014 schedule: June 1 to June 30. Application deadline: none.

Tuition and Aid Day student tuition: $11,440. Tuition installment plan (FACTS Tuition Payment Plan, individually arranged payment plans). Tuition reduction for siblings, need-based scholarship grants available. In 2013–14, 13% of upper-school students received aid. Total amount of financial aid awarded in 2013–14: $550,000.

Admissions Traditional secondary-level entrance grade is 9. For fall 2013, 347 students applied for upper-level admission, 278 were accepted, 251 enrolled. High School Placement Test required. Deadline for receipt of application materials: none. Application fee required: $80. On-campus interview required.

Athletics Interscholastic: aquatics (boys, girls), baseball (b), basketball (b,g), bowling (b,g), cheering (g), cross-country running (b,g), dance (b,g), dance squad (b), dance team (g), diving (b,g), football (b), golf (b,g), ice hockey (b), lacrosse (b,g), modern dance (g), power lifting (b), soccer (b,g), softball (g), Special Olympics (b,g), strength & conditioning (b,g), swimming and diving (b,g), tennis (b,g), track and field (b,g), volleyball (g), weight lifting (b,g), weight training (b,g), wrestling (b); intramural: fishing (b,g), indoor soccer (b,g), physical fitness (b,g). 1 athletic trainer.

Computers Computers are regularly used in all classes. Computer network features include on-campus library services, online commercial services, Internet access, wireless campus network, Internet filtering or blocking technology. Computer access in designated common areas is available to students. Students grades are available online. The school has a published electronic and media policy.

Contact Ms. Kate Goetzinger, Director of Admissions. 615-383-4200. Fax: 615-783-0264. E-mail: goetzinferk@fatherryan.org. Website: www.fatherryan.org

FAYETTEVILLE ACADEMY

3200 Cliffdale Road
Fayetteville, North Carolina 28303

Head of School: Mr. Ray J. Quesnel

General Information Coeducational day college-preparatory, arts, and technology school. Grades PK–12. Founded: 1970. Setting: suburban. 30-acre campus. 10 buildings on campus. Approved or accredited by Southern Association of Colleges and Schools, Southern Association of Independent Schools, The College Board, and North Carolina Department of Education. Member of National Association of Independent Schools. Endowment: $416,700. Total enrollment: 370. Upper school average class size: 14. Upper school faculty-student ratio: 1:14. There are 175 required school days per year for Upper School students. Upper School students typically attend 5 days per week. The average school day consists of 6 hours and 55 minutes.

Upper School Student Profile Grade 9: 35 students (12 boys, 23 girls); Grade 10: 33 students (17 boys, 16 girls); Grade 11: 42 students (23 boys, 19 girls); Grade 12: 30 students (15 boys, 15 girls).

Faculty School total: 62. In upper school: 5 men, 15 women; 11 have advanced degrees.

Subjects Offered Algebra, American history, American literature, anatomy, art, band, biology, biology-AP, calculus, calculus-AP, chemistry, chemistry-AP, chorus, communications, ecology, English, English language and composition-AP, English literature, English literature-AP, European history, European history-AP, geography, geometry, government/civics, history, honors geometry, mathematics, music, physical education, physics, physiology, pre-calculus, psychology, science, social studies, Spanish, Spanish-AP, statistics-AP, trigonometry, typing, U.S. history-AP, weight training, world history, world history-AP, yearbook.

Graduation Requirements Arts and fine arts (art, music, dance, drama), English, foreign language, history, lab science, mathematics, physical education (includes health), senior projects.

Special Academic Programs Advanced Placement exam preparation; honors section; independent study.

College Admission Counseling 34 students graduated in 2013; all went to college, including East Carolina University; North Carolina State University; The University of North Carolina at Chapel Hill; The University of North Carolina at Charlotte; The University of North Carolina at Greensboro; Wake Forest University. Mean SAT critical reading: 579, mean SAT math: 569, mean SAT writing: 563, mean combined SAT: 1711, mean composite ACT: 25.

Student Life Upper grades have specified standards of dress, student council, honor system. Discipline rests primarily with faculty.

Summer Programs Enrichment, sports, art/fine arts, computer instruction programs offered; session focuses on enrichment; held on campus; accepts boys and girls; open to students from other schools. 200 students usually enrolled. 2014 schedule: June 12 to August 1.

Tuition and Aid Day student tuition: $8784–$13,757. Tuition installment plan (monthly payment plans, payment in full, 3-payment plan). Need-based scholarship grants available. In 2013–14, 25% of upper-school students received aid. Total amount of financial aid awarded in 2013–14: $465,212.

Admissions Traditional secondary-level entrance grade is 9. For fall 2013, 32 students applied for upper-level admission, 28 were accepted, 20 enrolled. ERB, SSAT and TOEFL or SLEP required. Deadline for receipt of application materials: none. Application fee required: $75. On-campus interview recommended.

Athletics Interscholastic: baseball (boys), basketball (b,g), cheering (g), cross-country running (b,g), fitness (b,g), soccer (b,g), softball (g), tennis (b,g), track and field (b,g), volleyball (g); intramural: weight training (g); coed interscholastic: golf, swimming and diving. 4 PE instructors, 10 coaches, 1 athletic trainer.

Computers Computers are regularly used in all classes. Computer network features include on-campus library services, online commercial services, Internet access, wireless campus network. Computer access in designated common areas is available to

students. Students grades are available online. The school has a published electronic and media policy.

Contact Ms. Barbara E. Lambert, Director of Admissions. 910-868-5131 Ext. 3311. Fax: 910-868-7351. E-mail: blambert@fayettevilleacademy.com. Website: www.fayettevilleacademy.com

FAY SCHOOL

Southborough, Massachusetts
See Junior Boarding Schools section.

THE FIRST ACADEMY

2667 Bruton Boulevard
Orlando, Florida 32805

Head of School: Dr. Steve D. Whitaker

General Information Coeducational day college-preparatory, arts, religious studies, and technology school, affiliated with Christian faith. Grades K4–12. Founded: 1986. Setting: suburban. 140-acre campus. 1 building on campus. Approved or accredited by Association of Christian Schools International, Association of Independent Schools of Florida, Southern Association of Colleges and Schools, Southern Association of Independent Schools, and Florida Department of Education. Endowment: $2.5 million. Total enrollment: 990. Upper school average class size: 17. Upper school faculty-student ratio: 1:17. There are 180 required school days per year for Upper School students. Upper School students typically attend 5 days per week. The average school day consists of 6 hours and 30 minutes.

Upper School Student Profile Grade 9: 94 students (41 boys, 53 girls); Grade 10: 111 students (50 boys, 61 girls); Grade 11: 110 students (64 boys, 46 girls); Grade 12: 95 students (48 boys, 47 girls). 100% of students are Christian.

Faculty School total: 90. In upper school: 17 men, 17 women; 14 have advanced degrees.

Subjects Offered Advanced chemistry, advanced computer applications, advanced math, Advanced Placement courses, advanced studio art-AP, algebra, American government, American history, American history-AP, American literature, American literature-AP, analytic geometry, anatomy, ancient world history, art, art-AP, athletics, audio visual/media, band, Bible, Bible studies, biology, biology-AP, broadcasting, calculus, calculus-AP, chemistry, chemistry-AP, choir, Christian doctrine, Christian ethics, Christian testament, comparative government and politics, composition, computer programming, computer science, creative writing, drama, economics, economics and history, electives, English, English composition, English literature, English literature-AP, English-AP, ethics, European history, European history-AP, expository writing, fine arts, genetics, geometry, government, grammar, health, history, history-AP, honors algebra, honors English, honors geometry, honors U.S. history, honors world history, integrated mathematics, journalism, keyboarding, Latin, life skills, literature, literature-AP, marine biology, mathematics, media communications, music, newspaper, physical education, physical science, physics, politics, pottery, pre-algebra, pre-calculus, psychology, psychology-AP, religion, SAT/ACT preparation, science, social sciences, social studies, Spanish, Spanish-AP, speech, speech and debate, theater, trigonometry, U.S. government, U.S. government and politics-AP, world history, world history-AP, world literature, writing, yearbook.

Graduation Requirements Arts and fine arts (art, music, dance, drama), computer science, English, foreign language, mathematics, physical education (includes health), religion (includes Bible studies and theology), science, social sciences, social studies (includes history).

Special Academic Programs Advanced Placement exam preparation; honors section; study at local college for college credit.

College Admission Counseling 86 students graduated in 2013; all went to college, including Auburn University at Montgomery; Clemson University; Florida State University; Samford University; University of Central Florida; University of Florida.

Student Life Upper grades have uniform requirement, student council, honor system. Discipline rests primarily with faculty. Attendance at religious services is required.

Summer Programs Enrichment, advancement, sports, art/fine arts programs offered; session focuses on academics and athletic camps; held on campus; accepts boys and girls; open to students from other schools. 200 students usually enrolled. 2014 schedule: June 1 to July 31. Application deadline: March 1.

Tuition and Aid Day student tuition: $14,000. Tuition installment plan (SMART Tuition Payment Plan). Need-based scholarship grants available.

Admissions Traditional secondary-level entrance grade is 9. TerraNova required. Deadline for receipt of application materials: none. Application fee required: $125. On-campus interview required.

Athletics Interscholastic: baseball (boys), basketball (b,g), cheering (g), cross-country running (b,g), diving (b,g), flag football (b), football (b), golf (b,g), lacrosse (b), physical fitness (b,g), physical training (b,g), power lifting (b), running (b,g), soccer (b,g), softball (g), strength & conditioning (b,g), swimming and diving (b,g), tennis (b,g), track and field (b,g), volleyball (g), weight lifting (b), wrestling (b). 6 PE instructors, 18 coaches, 1 athletic trainer.

Computers Computers are regularly used in all classes. Computer network features include on-campus library services, Internet access, wireless campus network, Internet filtering or blocking technology. Campus intranet and student e-mail accounts are available to students. Students grades are available online. The school has a published electronic and media policy.

Contact Kristi Summers, Admission Coordinator. 407-206-8818. Fax: 407-206-8700. E-mail: kristisummers@thefirstacademy.org. Website: www.TheFirstAcademy.org

FIRST BAPTIST ACADEMY

PO Box 868
Dallas, Texas 75221
Head of School: Mr. Brian Littlefield

General Information Coeducational day college-preparatory, arts, religious studies, and technology school, affiliated with Baptist Church, Southern Baptist Convention. Grades PK–12. Founded: 1972. Setting: urban. 1 building on campus. Approved or accredited by Accreditation Commission of the Texas Association of Baptist Schools, Association of Christian Schools International, Southern Association of Colleges and Schools, Texas Private School Accreditation Commission, and Texas Department of Education. Endowment: $1 million. Total enrollment: 207. Upper school average class size: 15. Upper school faculty-student ratio: 1:8. There are 176 required school days per year for Upper School students. Upper School students typically attend 5 days per week. The average school day consists of 7 hours.

Upper School Student Profile 50% of students are Baptist, Southern Baptist Convention.

Faculty School total: 49. In upper school: 6 men, 8 women; 11 have advanced degrees.

Subjects Offered Algebra, American history, architecture, Bible, biology, calculus, calculus-AP, chemistry, choir, computer skills, concert band, desktop publishing, drawing, economics, English, English literature-AP, English-AP, fine arts, geometry, government-AP, health, history, math analysis, photography, physics, pre-calculus, Spanish, speech and debate, theater arts, world history.

Graduation Requirements Algebra, American history, arts and fine arts (art, music, dance, drama), Basic programming, Bible studies, biology, chemistry, economics, electives, English, foreign language, government, history, keyboarding, mathematics, physical education (includes health), physics, science, U.S. history, world geography, service hours are required for graduation. Community service is required.

Special Academic Programs 4 Advanced Placement exams for which test preparation is offered; honors section.

College Admission Counseling 25 students graduated in 2013; all went to college, including Baylor University; Texas A&M University; Texas Tech University; The University of Texas at Austin; University of Mississippi; University of Oklahoma.

Student Life Upper grades have uniform requirement, student council, honor system. Discipline rests primarily with faculty. Attendance at religious services is required.

Tuition and Aid Day student tuition: $13,700. Tuition installment plan (FACTS Tuition Payment Plan). Need-based scholarship grants available. In 2013–14, 22% of upper-school students received aid.

Admissions Traditional secondary-level entrance grade is 9. ERB (grade level), ISEE or Stanford Achievement Test required. Deadline for receipt of application materials: none. Application fee required: $75. Interview required.

Athletics Interscholastic: aquatics (boys, girls), baseball (b), basketball (b,g), cheering (g), diving (b,g), football (b), golf (b,g), softball (g), strength & conditioning (b,g), swimming and diving (b,g), tennis (b,g), track and field (b,g), volleyball (g), wrestling (b). 1 PE instructor, 25 coaches.

Computers Computers are regularly used in computer applications, desktop publishing, yearbook classes. Computer resources include on-campus library services, Internet access. Students grades are available online. The school has a published electronic and media policy.

Contact Elizabeth Gore, Director of Admissions and Marketing. 214-969-7861. Fax: 214-969-7797. E-mail: egore@firstdallas.org. Website: www.fbacademy.com

FIRST PRESBYTERIAN DAY SCHOOL

5671 Calvin Drive
Macon, Georgia 31210
Head of School: Mr. Gregg E. Thompson

General Information Coeducational day college-preparatory, arts, religious studies, and technology school, affiliated with Christian faith, Presbyterian Church in America. Grades PK–12. Founded: 1970. Setting: suburban. Nearest major city is Atlanta. 104-acre campus. 7 buildings on campus. Approved or accredited by Christian Schools International, Georgia Independent School Association, Southern Association of Colleges and Schools, Southern Association of Independent Schools, and Georgia Department of Education. Endowment: $3.8 million. Total enrollment: 1,008. Upper school average class size: 18. Upper school faculty-student ratio: 1:12. There are 180 required school days per year for Upper School students. Upper School students typically attend 5 days per week. The average school day consists of 7 hours.

Upper School Student Profile Grade 9: 93 students (46 boys, 47 girls); Grade 10: 98 students (47 boys, 51 girls); Grade 11: 94 students (49 boys, 45 girls); Grade 12: 92 students (44 boys, 48 girls). 89% of students are Christian, Presbyterian Church in America.

Faculty School total: 73. In upper school: 26 men, 33 women; 45 have advanced degrees.

Subjects Offered 3-dimensional design, accounting, advanced biology, advanced chemistry, Advanced Placement courses, advanced studio art-AP, algebra, American literature, anatomy and physiology, art, art appreciation, art-AP, band, Bible, biology, biology-AP, British literature, calculus-AP, chemistry, chemistry-AP, chorus, comparative religion, computer applications, debate, economics, English, English language and composition-AP, English literature and composition-AP, family living, French, geometry, government, government-AP, honors algebra, honors English, honors geometry, journalism, Latin, Latin-AP, logic, model United Nations, modern European history, music appreciation, physical science, physics, physics-AP, pre-calculus, psychology, Spanish, statistics, studio art-AP, theater, U.S. government and politics-AP, U.S. history, U.S. history-AP, world history.

Graduation Requirements Arts and fine arts (art, music, dance, drama), Bible, computer skills, electives, English, foreign language, mathematics, physical education (includes health), science, social studies (includes history), service to distressed populations.

Special Academic Programs 17 Advanced Placement exams for which test preparation is offered; honors section; ESL (10 students enrolled).

College Admission Counseling 86 students graduated in 2013; all went to college, including Auburn University; Georgia College & State University; Georgia Institute of Technology; Mercer University; Samford University; University of Georgia. 35% scored over 600 on SAT critical reading, 47% scored over 600 on SAT math, 38% scored over 600 on SAT writing, 43% scored over 1800 on combined SAT.

Student Life Upper grades have uniform requirement, student council, honor system. Discipline rests primarily with faculty. Attendance at religious services is required.

Summer Programs Remediation, enrichment, sports, art/fine arts programs offered; session focuses on reading and study skills, mathematics enrichment, science, sports; held on campus; accepts boys and girls; open to students from other schools. 200 students usually enrolled. 2014 schedule: June 10 to July 30. Application deadline: May 15.

Tuition and Aid Day student tuition: $12,440. Tuition installment plan (monthly payment plans). Tuition reduction for siblings, merit scholarship grants, need-based scholarship grants available. In 2013–14, 40% of upper-school students received aid; total upper-school merit-scholarship money awarded: $28,000. Total amount of financial aid awarded in 2013–14: $874,000.

Admissions Traditional secondary-level entrance grade is 9. CTP, Math Placement Exam or writing sample required. Deadline for receipt of application materials: February 1. Application fee required: $50. Interview recommended.

Athletics Interscholastic: baseball (boys), basketball (b,g), cheering (g), cross-country running (b,g), dance team (g), football (b), golf (b,g), soccer (b,g), softball (g), swimming and diving (b,g), tennis (b,g), track and field (b,g), volleyball (g), wrestling (b,g); intramural: football (b), indoor soccer (b,g), soccer (b,g), strength & conditioning (b,g), weight training (b,g). 3 PE instructors, 6 coaches, 1 athletic trainer.

Computers Computers are regularly used in all classes. Computer network features include on-campus library services, online commercial services, Internet access, wireless campus network, Internet filtering or blocking technology, students issued convertible tablet PC. Campus intranet, student e-mail accounts, and computer access in designated common areas are available to students. Students grades are available online. The school has a published electronic and media policy.

Contact Mrs. Cheri Frame, Director of Admissions. 478-477-6505 Ext. 107. Fax: 478-477-2804. E-mail: admissions@fpdmacon.org. Website: www.fpdmacon.org

FISHBURNE MILITARY SCHOOL

225 South Wayne Avenue
Waynesboro, Virginia 22980
Head of School: Col. Gary R. Morrison

General Information Boys' boarding and day college-preparatory, Army Junior ROTC, and military school. Grades 7–PG. Founded: 1879. Setting: small town. Nearest major city is Washington, DC. Students are housed in single-sex dormitories. 10-acre campus. 4 buildings on campus. Approved or accredited by Southern Association of Colleges and Schools and Virginia Department of Education. Endowment: $1.3 million. Total enrollment: 170. Upper school average class size: 9. Upper school faculty-student ratio: 1:9. Upper School students typically attend 5 days per week. The average school day consists of 6 hours.

Upper School Student Profile Grade 9: 35 students (35 boys); Grade 10: 45 students (45 boys); Grade 11: 50 students (50 boys); Grade 12: 45 students (45 boys); Postgraduate: 15 students (15 boys). 90% of students are boarding students. 53% are state residents. 17 states are represented in upper school student body. 5% are international students. International students from Aruba, Mexico, Republic of Korea, Russian Federation, Saudi Arabia, and Taiwan; 5 other countries represented in student body.

Faculty School total: 20. In upper school: 14 men, 6 women; 5 have advanced degrees; 6 reside on campus.

Subjects Offered Algebra, American history, American literature, biology, calculus, chemistry, computer programming, computer science, computer technologies, creative writing, driver education, earth science, English, English literature, environmental science, French, geography, geology, geometry, government/civics, grammar, health, history, JROTC, mathematics, military science, music, physical education, physics, science, social studies, Spanish, speech, trigonometry, world history.

Graduation Requirements Computer science, English, foreign language, JROTC, mathematics, physical education (includes health), science, social studies (includes history).

Special Academic Programs Advanced Placement exam preparation; honors section; study at local college for college credit; remedial reading and/or remedial writing; remedial math.

College Admission Counseling 47 students graduated in 2013; 45 went to college, including Miami University; Penn State University Park; United States Military Academy; University of Virginia; Virginia Military Institute; Virginia Polytechnic Institute and State University. Other: 2 entered military service. Median SAT critical reading: 470, median SAT math: 530, median SAT writing: 540, median combined SAT: 1535. 4.5% scored over 600 on SAT critical reading, 11.4% scored over 600 on SAT math, 4.5% scored over 600 on SAT writing, 2.3% scored over 1800 on combined SAT.

Student Life Upper grades have uniform requirement, student council, honor system. Discipline rests equally with students and faculty.

Summer Programs Remediation, advancement, sports programs offered; session focuses on academic; held on campus; accepts boys; open to students from other schools. 80 students usually enrolled. 2014 schedule: June 28 to July 30. Application deadline: June 20.

Tuition and Aid Day student tuition: $12,250; 7-day tuition and room/board: $28,000. Tuition installment plan (FACTS Tuition Payment Plan, monthly payment plans, individually arranged payment plans). Tuition reduction for siblings, merit scholarship grants, need-based scholarship grants available.

Admissions Traditional secondary-level entrance grade is 10. For fall 2013, 200 students applied for upper-level admission, 180 were accepted, 65 enrolled. Deadline for receipt of application materials: none. Application fee required: $50. Interview required.

Athletics Interscholastic: aquatics, baseball, basketball, canoeing/kayaking, cooperative games, cross-country running, drill team, football, JROTC drill, marksmanship, wrestling; intramural: baseball, basketball, fitness. 1 PE instructor, 15 coaches, 1 athletic trainer.

Computers Computers are regularly used in English, foreign language, history, mathematics, science classes. Computer network features include on-campus library services, Internet access, Internet filtering or blocking technology. Campus intranet and student e-mail accounts are available to students. The school has a published electronic and media policy.

Contact Mr. Cedrick Broadhurst, Director of Admissions. 800-946-7773. Fax: 540-946-7738. E-mail: cbroadhurst@fishburne.org. Website: www.fishburne.org

FLINT HILL SCHOOL

3320 Jermantown Road
Oakton, Virginia 22124

Head of School: Mr. John Thomas

General Information Coeducational day college-preparatory, arts, technology, and athletics, community service school. Grades JK–12. Founded: 1956. Setting: suburban. Nearest major city is Washington, DC. 45-acre campus. 1 building on campus. Approved or accredited by Virginia Association of Independent Schools and Virginia Department of Education. Member of National Association of Independent Schools and Secondary School Admission Test Board. Endowment: $1.9 million. Total enrollment: 1,099. Upper school average class size: 12. Upper school faculty-student ratio: 1:7. There are 168 required school days per year for Upper School students. Upper School students typically attend 5 days per week. The average school day consists of 6 hours and 30 minutes.

Upper School Student Profile Grade 9: 129 students (65 boys, 64 girls); Grade 10: 135 students (69 boys, 66 girls); Grade 11: 124 students (63 boys, 61 girls); Grade 12: 125 students (75 boys, 50 girls).

Faculty School total: 163. In upper school: 28 men, 44 women; 52 have advanced degrees.

Subjects Offered 20th century history, advanced chemistry, algebra, anatomy, art, ballet, biology, biology-AP, British literature, calculus, calculus-AP, ceramics, chemistry, chemistry-AP, Chinese, choir, choral music, chorus, civil rights, community service, computer animation, computer graphics, computer programming, computer science-AP, concert band, concert choir, creative writing, digital imaging, discrete mathematics, drama, drawing, drawing and design, earth science, economics-AP, English, English literature, English literature and composition-AP, English-AP, environmental science, environmental science-AP, environmental studies, European civilization, European history, fine arts, French, French language-AP, French literature-AP, geometry, government-AP, history, history of music, honors English, improvisation, jazz band, jazz dance, Latin, Latin American studies, Latin-AP, macro/microeconomics-AP, marine science, modern European history-AP, music, music history, music theory, music theory-AP, orchestra, ornithology, photography, physical education, physics, physics-AP, physiology, playwriting, pre-calculus, psychology, psychology-AP, science, sculpture, senior project, Shakespeare, short story, Spanish, Spanish-AP,

statistics-AP, studio art, study skills, symphonic band, theater, trigonometry, U.S. history, U.S. history-AP, world religions.

Graduation Requirements Arts and fine arts (art, music, dance, drama), athletics, English, foreign language, history, mathematics, physical education (includes health), science, senior project. Community service is required.

Special Academic Programs 23 Advanced Placement exams for which test preparation is offered; honors section; academic accommodation for the musically talented and the artistically talented.

College Admission Counseling 119 students graduated in 2012; 116 went to college, including Christopher Newport University; James Madison University; The College of William and Mary; University of Colorado Boulder; University of Virginia; Virginia Polytechnic Institute and State University. Other: 1 entered military service, 1 entered a postgraduate year, 1 had other specific plans. Median SAT critical reading: 590, median SAT math: 610, median SAT writing: 590, median combined SAT: 1790, median composite ACT: 26. 48% scored over 600 on SAT critical reading, 60% scored over 600 on SAT math, 52% scored over 600 on SAT writing, 54% scored over 1800 on combined SAT, 55% scored over 26 on composite ACT.

Student Life Upper grades have specified standards of dress, student council, honor system. Discipline rests primarily with faculty.

Tuition and Aid Day student tuition: $30,950. Tuition installment plan (Insured Tuition Payment Plan, FACTS Tuition Payment Plan, monthly payment plans, one payment, two payments, or ten payments). Need-based scholarship grants available. In 2012–13, 19% of upper-school students received aid. Total amount of financial aid awarded in 2012–13: $2,027,705.

Admissions Traditional secondary-level entrance grade is 9. For fall 2012, 269 students applied for upper-level admission, 145 were accepted, 73 enrolled. ISEE, PSAT, SAT or SSAT required. Deadline for receipt of application materials: January 16. Application fee required: $50. On-campus interview required.

Athletics Interscholastic: aerobics/dance (girls), baseball (b), basketball (b,g), cross-country running (b,g), dance (g), dance team (g), diving (b,g), football (b), lacrosse (b,g), self defense (g), soccer (b,g), softball (g), swimming and diving (b,g), tennis (b,g), track and field (b,g), volleyball (g); coed interscholastic: golf, hockey, ice hockey, independent competitive sports, physical fitness, running, strength & conditioning, yoga; coed intramural: aerobics/dance, canoeing/kayaking, climbing, dance, fitness, modern dance, mountaineering, outdoor activities, outdoor education, physical fitness, physical training, strength & conditioning, wall climbing, weight training, winter soccer. 16 coaches, 2 athletic trainers.

Computers Computers are regularly used in all academic classes. Computer network features include on-campus library services, online commercial services, Internet access, wireless campus network, Internet filtering or blocking technology. Campus intranet, student e-mail accounts, and computer access in designated common areas are available to students. Students grades are available online. The school has a published electronic and media policy.

Contact Mr. Chris Pryor, Director of Admission. 703-584-2300. Fax: 703-242-0718. E-mail: cpryor@flinthill.org. Website: www.flinthill.org

FLINTRIDGE PREPARATORY SCHOOL

4543 Crown Avenue
La Canada Flintridge, California 91011

Head of School: Mr. Peter H. Bachmann

General Information Coeducational day college-preparatory school. Grades 7–12. Founded: 1933. Setting: suburban. Nearest major city is Los Angeles. 7-acre campus. 8 buildings on campus. Approved or accredited by California Association of Independent Schools, The College Board, and Western Association of Schools and Colleges. Member of National Association of Independent Schools. Total enrollment: 500. Upper school average class size: 12. Upper school faculty-student ratio: 1:8. Upper School students typically attend 5 days per week. The average school day consists of 6 hours and 20 minutes.

Upper School Student Profile Grade 9: 98 students (47 boys, 51 girls); Grade 10: 99 students (47 boys, 52 girls); Grade 11: 101 students (51 boys, 50 girls); Grade 12: 102 students (49 boys, 53 girls).

Faculty School total: 69. In upper school: 37 men, 32 women; 44 have advanced degrees.

Subjects Offered Algebra, American history, American literature, analysis and differential calculus, anatomy and physiology, art, art history, art history-AP, art-AP, Basic programming, Bible as literature, biology, biology-AP, British literature-AP, business applications, calculus, calculus-AP, ceramics, chemistry, chemistry-AP, choral music, college counseling, computer literacy, computer programming, creative writing, dance, drama, earth science, economics, English, English literature-AP, environmental studies, European history, expository writing, fine arts, French, French language-AP, geography, geometry, government/civics, grammar, great books, history, jazz band, Latin, mathematics, music, photography, physical education, physics, physics-AP, psychology, science, social studies, Spanish, Spanish literature-AP, Spanish-AP, statistics, statistics-AP, theater, trigonometry, U.S. government and politics-AP, U.S. history-AP, world history, world literature, writing.

Graduation Requirements Arts and fine arts (art, music, dance, drama), English, foreign language, mathematics, science, social studies (includes history), community service.

Special Academic Programs 18 Advanced Placement exams for which test preparation is offered; honors section; independent study; study abroad.

College Admission Counseling 96 students graduated in 2013; all went to college, including Boston University; Tulane University; University of California, Berkeley; University of Southern California; University of Washington. Mean SAT critical reading: 690, mean SAT math: 700, mean SAT writing: 700, mean combined SAT: 2090.

Student Life Upper grades have specified standards of dress, student council, honor system. Discipline rests equally with students and faculty.

Summer Programs Remediation, enrichment, advancement, sports, art/fine arts, rigorous outdoor training, computer instruction programs offered; session focuses on academic enrichment/advancement, fine arts, and athletics; held on campus; accepts boys and girls; open to students from other schools. 300 students usually enrolled. 2014 schedule: June 23 to August 1. Application deadline: June 23.

Tuition and Aid Day student tuition: $30,000. Tuition installment plan (SMART Tuition Payment Plan, Tuition Management Systems). Need-based scholarship grants available. In 2013–14, 29% of upper-school students received aid. Total amount of financial aid awarded in 2013–14: $2,047,000.

Admissions Traditional secondary-level entrance grade is 9. ISEE required. Deadline for receipt of application materials: January 17. Application fee required: $95. On-campus interview required.

Athletics Interscholastic: aquatics (boys, girls), baseball (b), basketball (b,g), cheering (g), cross-country running (b,g), diving (b,g), football (b), soccer (b,g), softball (g), swimming and diving (b,g), tennis (b,g), track and field (b,g), volleyball (b,g), water polo (b,g), winter soccer (b,g); coed interscholastic: equestrian sports, golf. 4 PE instructors, 41 coaches, 1 athletic trainer.

Computers Computers are regularly used in all academic, foreign language, mathematics, photography, science classes. Computer network features include on-campus library services, online commercial services, Internet access, wireless campus network. Campus intranet, student e-mail accounts, and computer access in designated common areas are available to students. The school has a published electronic and media policy.

Contact Ms. Dana Valentino, Admissions Assistant. 818-949-5514. Fax: 818-952-6247. E-mail: dvalentino@flintridgeprep.org. Website: www.flintridgeprep.org

FLINT RIVER ACADEMY

11556 East Highway 85
Woodbury, Georgia 30293

Head of School: Mrs. Michele Purvis

General Information Coeducational day college-preparatory, arts, and technology school. Grades PK–12. Founded: 1967. Setting: rural. Nearest major city is Atlanta. 8-acre campus. 1 building on campus. Approved or accredited by Georgia Accrediting Commission and Southern Association of Colleges and Schools. Total enrollment: 312. Upper school average class size: 18. Upper school faculty-student ratio: 1:14. There are 180 required school days per year for Upper School students. Upper School students typically attend 5 days per week. The average school day consists of 6 hours and 23 minutes.

Upper School Student Profile Grade 9: 28 students (16 boys, 12 girls); Grade 10: 21 students (13 boys, 8 girls); Grade 11: 24 students (14 boys, 10 girls); Grade 12: 18 students (9 boys, 9 girls).

Faculty School total: 45. In upper school: 2 men, 12 women; 10 have advanced degrees.

Subjects Offered Algebra, American history, American literature, art, biology, calculus, chemistry, creative writing, drama, earth science, economics, English, fine arts, geography, geometry, government/civics, grammar, health, history, mathematics, music, physical education, physics, physiology, science, social studies, Spanish, theater, trigonometry, typing, world history, world literature.

Graduation Requirements Arts and fine arts (art, music, dance, drama), business skills (includes word processing), computer science, English, foreign language, mathematics, physical education (includes health), science, social sciences, social studies (includes history).

Special Academic Programs Advanced Placement exam preparation; honors section; study at local college for college credit; academic accommodation for the musically talented and the artistically talented; remedial math.

College Admission Counseling 28 students graduated in 2012; all went to college, including Columbus State University; Georgia Institute of Technology; Georgia Southern University; Kennesaw State University; University of Georgia; Valdosta State University. Median SAT critical reading: 210, median SAT math: 527, median SAT writing: 513, median combined SAT: 1544, median composite ACT: 20.

Student Life Upper grades have specified standards of dress, student council, honor system. Discipline rests primarily with faculty.

Tuition and Aid Day student tuition: $6555. Tuition installment plan (monthly payment plans). Tuition reduction for third sibling available.

Admissions Traditional secondary-level entrance grade is 9. For fall 2012, 4 students applied for upper-level admission, 4 were accepted, 4 enrolled. ACT-Explore required. Deadline for receipt of application materials: none. Application fee required: $50. On-campus interview required.

Athletics Interscholastic: baseball (boys), basketball (b,g), cheering (g), cross-country running (b,g), football (b), golf (b,g), softball (g), tennis (b,g), track and field (b,g); intramural: baseball (b), basketball (b,g), cheering (g), dance team (g), golf (g), soccer (b), softball (g), tennis (b,g), volleyball (b,g), weight lifting (b,g), weight training (b); coed intramural: ropes courses. 2 PE instructors, 2 coaches.

Computers Computer network features include on-campus library services, Internet access.

Contact Ms. Ida Ann Dunn, Guidance Counselor. 706-553-2541. Fax: 706-553-9777. E-mail: counselor@flintriveracademy.com. Website: www.flintriveracademy.com

FONTBONNE HALL ACADEMY

9901 Shore Road
Brooklyn, New York 11209

Head of School: Sr. Dolores F. Crepeau, CSJ

General Information Girls' day college-preparatory, arts, religious studies, and technology school, affiliated with Roman Catholic Church. Grades 9–12. Founded: 1937. Setting: urban. Nearest major city is New York. 5 buildings on campus. Approved or accredited by Middle States Association of Colleges and Schools, New York State Board of Regents, and New York Department of Education. Total enrollment: 486. Upper school average class size: 18. Upper school faculty-student ratio: 1:13. There are 180 required school days per year for Upper School students. Upper School students typically attend 5 days per week. The average school day consists of 6 hours and 30 minutes.

Upper School Student Profile Grade 9: 101 students (101 girls); Grade 10: 132 students (132 girls); Grade 11: 125 students (125 girls); Grade 12: 128 students (128 girls). 90% of students are Roman Catholic.

Faculty School total: 39. In upper school: 3 men, 36 women; 37 have advanced degrees.

Subjects Offered Advanced chemistry, algebra, American literature-AP, anatomy and physiology, anthropology, art, biology-AP, calculus, calculus-AP, chemistry, chorus, computer multimedia, computers, earth science, economics, English, forensics, genetics, government, health, history-AP, Italian, Latin, marine science, mathematics, music, photography, physical education, physics, religion, Spanish, Spanish language-AP, U.S. history, world geography, world history.

Graduation Requirements Algebra, American government, American history, American literature, art, biology, British literature, chemistry, college counseling, college writing, computer applications, economics, electives, English, European civilization, foreign language, geometry, government, guidance, Internet research, lab science, music, physical education (includes health), religion (includes Bible studies and theology), science, world civilizations, Board of Regents requirements, 60 hours of service.

Special Academic Programs Advanced Placement exam preparation; honors section; study at local college for college credit.

College Admission Counseling 132 students graduated in 2012; all went to college, including Columbia University; Fordham University; Georgetown University; Manhattan College; New York University; The Catholic University of America. Median SAT critical reading: 560, median SAT math: 550, median SAT writing: 640, median combined SAT: 1750.

Student Life Upper grades have uniform requirement, student council. Discipline rests primarily with faculty. Attendance at religious services is required.

Tuition and Aid Day student tuition: $8100. Tuition installment plan (monthly payment plans, 3 payments per year). Tuition reduction for siblings, merit scholarship grants, Service Scholarships available. In 2012–13, 20% of upper-school students received aid; total upper-school merit-scholarship money awarded: $100,000. Total amount of financial aid awarded in 2012–13: $121,500.

Admissions Traditional secondary-level entrance grade is 9. For fall 2012, 437 students applied for upper-level admission, 356 were accepted, 214 enrolled. Diocesan Entrance Exam required. Deadline for receipt of application materials: February 4. Application fee required: $250.

Athletics Interscholastic: aquatics, baseball, basketball, cheering, cross-country running, dance, dance squad, drill team, fishing, golf, running, soccer, softball, swimming and diving, tennis, track and field, volleyball. 2 PE instructors, 23 coaches.

Computers Computers are regularly used in all academic classes. Computer network features include on-campus library services, Internet access, wireless campus network, Internet filtering or blocking technology. Campus intranet and computer access in designated common areas are available to students. The school has a published electronic and media policy.

Contact Sr. Dolores F. Crepeau, CSJ, Principal. 718-748-2244. Fax: 718-745-3841. E-mail: crepeau@fontbonne.org. Website: www.fontbonne.org

FOOTHILLS ACADEMY

Calgary, Alberta, Canada
See Special Needs Schools section.

FORDHAM PREPARATORY SCHOOL

441 E. Fordham Road
Bronx, New York 10458-5175

Head of School: Rev. Christopher Devron, SJ

General Information Boys' day college-preparatory school, affiliated with Roman Catholic Church. Grades 9–12. Founded: 1841. Setting: urban. Nearest major city is New York. 5-acre campus. 2 buildings on campus. Approved or accredited by Jesuit Secondary Education Association, Middle States Association of Colleges and Schools, National Catholic Education Association, and New York Department of Education. Member of National Association of Independent Schools. Endowment: $1.8 million. Total enrollment: 936. Upper school average class size: 24. Upper school faculty-student ratio: 1:11.

Upper School Student Profile Grade 9: 230 students (230 boys); Grade 10: 219 students (219 boys); Grade 11: 248 students (248 boys); Grade 12: 239 students (239 boys). 75% of students are Roman Catholic.

Faculty School total: 88. In upper school: 62 men, 26 women; 79 have advanced degrees.

Subjects Offered Advanced chemistry, American history, American history-AP, American literature, Ancient Greek, architectural drawing, art history-AP, biochemistry, biology, biology-AP, calculus, calculus-AP, chemistry, chemistry-AP, Chinese, computer graphics, computer programming, constitutional history of U.S., creative writing, drama, economics, emerging technology, English, English language and composition-AP, English literature-AP, European history-AP, forensics, French, geometry, German, global studies, government and politics-AP, health, Italian, Latin, Latin-AP, macroeconomics-AP, media communications, modern history, modern world history, music, physical education, physics, physics-AP, pre-calculus, religious studies, short story, Spanish, Spanish language-AP, Spanish literature-AP, statistics-AP, studio art, studio art-AP, trigonometry, world history-AP.

Graduation Requirements Arts and fine arts (art, music, dance, drama), English, foreign language, mathematics, physical education (includes health), religious studies, science, social studies (includes history), senior service project.

Special Academic Programs Advanced Placement exam preparation; honors section; study at local college for college credit.

College Admission Counseling 242 students graduated in 2013; 240 went to college, including Binghamton University; State University of New York; Boston College; Fairfield University; Fordham University; Loyola University Maryland; Manhattan College. Other: 1 went to work, 1 had other specific plans. Mean SAT critical reading: 597, mean SAT math: 600, mean SAT writing: 592, mean combined SAT: 1789.

Student Life Upper grades have specified standards of dress. Discipline rests primarily with faculty. Attendance at religious services is required.

Tuition and Aid Day student tuition: $17,560. Tuition installment plan (monthly payment plans). Merit scholarship grants, need-based scholarship grants available. In 2013–14, 35% of upper-school students received aid; total upper-school merit-scholarship money awarded: $400,000. Total amount of financial aid awarded in 2013–14: $2,600,000.

Admissions Traditional secondary-level entrance grade is 9. For fall 2013, 1,153 students applied for upper-level admission, 600 were accepted, 236 enrolled. Cooperative Entrance Exam (McGraw-Hill), Diocesan Entrance Exam, ISEE, SSAT or STS required. Deadline for receipt of application materials: December 15. No application fee required.

Athletics Interscholastic: baseball, basketball, bowling, crew, cross-country running, diving, football, golf, ice hockey, indoor track, lacrosse, rugby, soccer, swimming and diving, tennis, track and field, volleyball, winter (indoor) track, wrestling; intramural: basketball, fitness, Frisbee, rock climbing, weight training. 2 PE instructors, 16 coaches.

Computers Computers are regularly used in art, English, foreign language, history, mathematics, science classes. Computer network features include on-campus library services, online commercial services, Internet access, wireless campus network, Internet filtering or blocking technology, Rosetta Stone. Student e-mail accounts are available to students. The school has a published electronic and media policy.

Contact Christopher Lauber, Director of Admissions. 718-584-8367. Fax: 718-367-7598. E-mail: lauberc@fordhamprep.org. Website: www.fordhamprep.org

FOREST LAKE ACADEMY

500 Education Loop
Apopka, Florida 32703

Head of School: Mr. David Denton

General Information Coeducational boarding and day and distance learning college-preparatory, arts, religious studies, and bilingual studies school, affiliated with Seventh-day Adventists. Grades 9–12. Distance learning grades 9–12. Founded: 1918. Setting: suburban. Nearest major city is Orlando. Students are housed in single-sex dormitories. 6 buildings on campus. Approved or accredited by CITA (Commission on International and Trans-Regional Accreditation), Middle States Association of Colleges and Schools, National Council for Private School Accreditation, and Florida Department of Education. Total enrollment: 357. Upper school average class size: 22. Upper school faculty-student ratio: 1:12. There are 179 required school days per year for Upper School students. Upper School students typically attend 5 days per week. The average school day consists of 6 hours.

Upper School Student Profile Grade 9: 86 students (40 boys, 46 girls); Grade 10: 79 students (40 boys, 39 girls); Grade 11: 105 students (50 boys, 55 girls); Grade 12: 87 students (45 boys, 42 girls). 8% of students are boarding students. 84% are state residents. 13 states are represented in upper school student body. 1% are international students. International students from Argentina, Bermuda, Brazil, China, Italy, and Spain; 3 other countries represented in student body. 95% of students are Seventh-day Adventists.

Faculty School total: 32. In upper school: 20 men, 12 women; 15 have advanced degrees; 4 reside on campus.

Subjects Offered Algebra, American government, American literature, art, band, bell choir, Bible studies, biology, calculus, chemistry, choir, church history, computer applications, desktop publishing, digital photography, economics, English, environmental science, geometry, health, honors algebra, honors English, honors geometry, honors world history, integrated mathematics, life management skills, physical science, physics, play production, pre-calculus, psychology, SAT preparation, senior project, Spanish, statistics, strings, swimming, tennis, U.S. history, video film production, world geography, world history, world literature, writing, yearbook.

Graduation Requirements Algebra, American government, American literature, arts and fine arts (art, music, dance, drama), Bible studies, biology, chemistry, computer applications, computer science, economics, English, environmental science, fitness, foreign language, geometry, health education, life management skills, physical education (includes health), physical science, pre-calculus, religion (includes Bible studies and theology), science, social studies (includes history), Spanish, statistics, U.S. history, world history, world literature, writing, 20 hours of community service activity for each year enrolled.

Special Academic Programs Honors section; study at local college for college credit; ESL (22 students enrolled).

College Admission Counseling 94 students graduated in 2013; 92 went to college, including Adventist University of Health Sciences; Andrews University; Oakwood University; Seminole State College of Florida; Southern Adventist University; University of Central Florida.

Student Life Upper grades have uniform requirement, student council, honor system. Discipline rests primarily with faculty.

Tuition and Aid Day student tuition: $11,905; 7-day tuition and room/board: $22,995. Tuition installment plan (FACTS Tuition Payment Plan, monthly payment plans, individually arranged payment plans). Merit scholarship grants, need-based scholarship grants, paying campus jobs available. In 2013–14, 37% of upper-school students received aid; total upper-school merit-scholarship money awarded: $75,000. Total amount of financial aid awarded in 2013–14: $347,000.

Admissions Traditional secondary-level entrance grade is 9. For fall 2013, 380 students applied for upper-level admission, 360 were accepted, 357 enrolled. WRAT required. Deadline for receipt of application materials: none. Application fee required: $60. Interview recommended.

Athletics Interscholastic: basketball (boys, girls), golf (b), volleyball (g); intramural: golf (b); coed interscholastic: aquatics, life saving, physical fitness, strength & conditioning, tennis; coed intramural: basketball, flag football, floor hockey, indoor hockey, indoor soccer, soccer, tennis, volleyball. 2 PE instructors, 1 coach.

Computers Computers are regularly used in desktop publishing, photography, Web site design, writing, yearbook classes. Computer resources include on-campus library services, Internet access, wireless campus network, Internet filtering or blocking technology, financial aid and grant search programs for college. Campus intranet, student e-mail accounts, and computer access in designated common areas are available to students. Students grades are available online. The school has a published electronic and media policy.

Contact Mrs. Claudia Dure C. Osorio, Director of Student Records. 407-862-8411 Ext. 743. Fax: 407-862-7050. E-mail: osorioc@forestlake.org. Website: www.forestlakeacademy.org

FORSYTH COUNTRY DAY SCHOOL

5501 Shallowford Road
PO Box 549
Lewisville, North Carolina 27023-0549

Head of School: Mrs. Joyce Henson

General Information Coeducational day college-preparatory school. Grades PK–12. Founded: 1970. Setting: suburban. Nearest major city is Winston-Salem. 80-acre campus. 7 buildings on campus. Approved or accredited by Southern Association of Colleges and Schools, Southern Association of Independent Schools, The College Board, and North Carolina Department of Education. Member of National Association of Independent Schools. Endowment: $13 million. Total enrollment: 776. Upper school average class size: 15. Upper school faculty-student ratio: 1:12. There are 175 required school days per year for Upper School students. Upper School students typically attend 5 days per week. The average school day consists of 5 hours and 45 minutes.

Upper School Student Profile Grade 9: 70 students (41 boys, 29 girls); Grade 10: 80 students (44 boys, 36 girls); Grade 11: 92 students (55 boys, 37 girls); Grade 12: 77 students (44 boys, 33 girls).

Faculty School total: 175. In upper school: 18 men, 29 women; 24 have advanced degrees.

Subjects Offered Advanced Placement courses, advanced studio art-AP, algebra, American history, American history-AP, American literature, art, astronomy, biology, calculus, calculus-AP, ceramics, chemistry, Chinese studies, community service, computer math, computer programming, computer science, creative writing, digital art, drama, English, English literature, European history, fine arts, foreign policy, French, freshman seminar, geometry, grammar, health, history, history of science, humanities, international relations, Japanese studies, journalism, Latin, Mandarin, mathematics, Middle Eastern history, music, photography, physical education, physics, psychology, SAT/ACT preparation, science, social studies, Spanish, statistics-AP, theater, yearbook.

Graduation Requirements Arts and fine arts (art, music, dance, drama), English, foreign language, history, mathematics, physical education (includes health), physical fitness, science. Community service is required.

Special Academic Programs 18 Advanced Placement exams for which test preparation is offered; honors section; academic accommodation for the gifted; programs in English, general development for dyslexic students; ESL (2 students enrolled).

College Admission Counseling 106 students graduated in 2012; all went to college, including Duke University; Elon University; North Carolina State University; The University of North Carolina at Chapel Hill; The University of North Carolina Wilmington; Wake Forest University. Median SAT critical reading: 600, median SAT math: 615. 70% scored over 600 on SAT critical reading, 68% scored over 600 on SAT math.

Student Life Upper grades have specified standards of dress, student council, honor system. Discipline rests equally with students and faculty.

Tuition and Aid Day student tuition: $19,910. Tuition installment plan (Insured Tuition Payment Plan, monthly payment plans, individually arranged payment plans). Need-based scholarship grants available. In 2012–13, 23% of upper-school students received aid. Total amount of financial aid awarded in 2012–13: $846,329.

Admissions Traditional secondary-level entrance grade is 9. For fall 2012, 61 students applied for upper-level admission, 51 were accepted, 41 enrolled. ERB CTP IV, WRAT and writing sample required. Deadline for receipt of application materials: none. Application fee required: $100. On-campus interview recommended.

Athletics Interscholastic: baseball (boys), basketball (b,g), cheering (g), cross-country running (b,g), field hockey (g), football (b), golf (b,g), lacrosse (b,g), physical fitness (b,g), soccer (b,g), softball (g), tennis (b,g), track and field (b,g), volleyball (g), wrestling (b); coed interscholastic: swimming and diving; coed intramural: sailing. 4 PE instructors, 4 coaches, 2 athletic trainers.

Computers Computers are regularly used in art, English, foreign language, history, mathematics, music, science classes. Computer network features include on-campus library services, online commercial services, Internet access, wireless campus network, Internet filtering or blocking technology. Campus intranet, student e-mail accounts, and computer access in designated common areas are available to students. Students grades are available online. The school has a published electronic and media policy.

Contact Cindy C. Kluttz, Director of Admission. 336-945-3151 Ext. 340. Fax: 336-945-2907. E-mail: cindykluttz@fcds.org. Website: www.fcds.org

FORT WORTH CHRISTIAN SCHOOL

6200 Holiday Lane
North Richland Hills, Texas 76180

Head of School: Mr. Kelly Moore

General Information Coeducational day college-preparatory, arts, religious studies, and technology school, affiliated with Christian faith, Christian faith. Grades PK–12. Founded: 1958. Setting: suburban. 40-acre campus. 6 buildings on campus. Approved or accredited by National Christian School Association, Southern Association of Colleges and Schools, Texas Private School Accreditation Commission, and Texas Department of Education. Endowment: $600,000. Total enrollment: 850. Upper school average class size: 17. Upper school faculty-student ratio: 1:14. There are 175 required school days per year for Upper School students. Upper School students typically attend 5 days per week. The average school day consists of 6 hours and 40 minutes.

Upper School Student Profile Grade 9: 71 students (35 boys, 36 girls); Grade 10: 74 students (36 boys, 38 girls); Grade 11: 97 students (53 boys, 44 girls); Grade 12: 90 students (48 boys, 42 girls). 80% of students are Christian faith, Christian.

Faculty School total: 108. In upper school: 12 men, 21 women; 12 have advanced degrees.

Subjects Offered Advanced Placement courses, African drumming, algebra, anatomy and physiology, art, band, Bible studies, biology, biology-AP, calculus, calculus-AP, chemistry, chemistry-AP, chorus, computer applications, computer information systems, computer science-AP, drama, economics, economics and history, economics-AP, English, English language and composition-AP, English literature and composition-AP, ethics, family studies, geometry, golf, government, government/civics,

Latin, physical education, physics, pre-calculus, robotics, SAT/ACT preparation, Spanish, strings, theater arts, U.S. history, U.S. history-AP, video, world geography, world history, world history-AP, yearbook.

Graduation Requirements Arts and fine arts (art, music, dance, drama), business skills (includes word processing), computer science, electives, English, foreign language, mathematics, physical education (includes health), religion (includes Bible studies and theology), science, social sciences, social studies (includes history), world geography, community service hours.

Special Academic Programs Advanced Placement exam preparation; honors section; independent study; study at local college for college credit.

College Admission Counseling 104 students graduated in 2013; all went to college, including Abilene Christian University; Baylor University; Harding University; Texas A&M University; Texas Christian University; University of North Texas. Mean SAT critical reading: 537, mean SAT math: 543, mean SAT writing: 520, mean combined SAT: 1600, mean composite ACT: 24. 49% scored over 600 on SAT critical reading, 59% scored over 600 on SAT math, 46% scored over 600 on SAT writing, 21% scored over 1800 on combined SAT, 37% scored over 26 on composite ACT.

Student Life Upper grades have uniform requirement, student council, honor system. Discipline rests primarily with faculty. Attendance at religious services is required.

Tuition and Aid Day student tuition: $11,600. Tuition installment plan (FACTS Tuition Payment Plan, monthly payment plans). Tuition reduction for siblings, need-based scholarship grants, tuition reduction for children of faculty and staff available. In 2013–14, 13% of upper-school students received aid. Total amount of financial aid awarded in 2013–14: $111,000.

Admissions Traditional secondary-level entrance grade is 9. For fall 2013, 58 students applied for upper-level admission, 52 were accepted, 52 enrolled. Wechsler Individual Achievement Test required. Deadline for receipt of application materials: none. Application fee required: $75. On-campus interview required.

Athletics Interscholastic: baseball (boys), basketball (b,g), cheering (g), cross-country running (b,g), football (b), golf (b,g), physical fitness (b,g), physical training (b,g), rodeo (b,g), running (b,g), soccer (b,g), softball (g), strength & conditioning (b,g), tennis (b,g), track and field (b,g), volleyball (g). 8 coaches, 1 athletic trainer.

Computers Computers are regularly used in computer applications, desktop publishing, independent study, media production, newspaper, technology, word processing, yearbook classes. Computer network features include on-campus library services, Internet access, wireless campus network, Internet filtering or blocking technology, online courses. Student e-mail accounts and computer access in designated common areas are available to students. Students grades are available online. The school has a published electronic and media policy.

Contact Mrs. Shirley Atkinson, Director of Admissions. 817-520-6561. Fax: 817-281-7063. E-mail: satkinson@fwc.org. Website: www.fwc.org

FORT WORTH COUNTRY DAY SCHOOL

4200 Country Day Lane
Fort Worth, Texas 76109-4299

Head of School: Evan D. Peterson

General Information Coeducational day college-preparatory, arts, and technology school. Grades K–12. Founded: 1962. Setting: suburban. 100-acre campus. 13 buildings on campus. Approved or accredited by Independent Schools Association of the Southwest. Member of National Association of Independent Schools. Endowment: $42 million. Total enrollment: 1,110. Upper school average class size: 14. Upper school faculty-student ratio: 1:10. There are 174 required school days per year for Upper School students. Upper School students typically attend 5 days per week. The average school day consists of 8 hours.

Upper School Student Profile Grade 9: 90 students (46 boys, 44 girls); Grade 10: 104 students (50 boys, 54 girls); Grade 11: 110 students (53 boys, 57 girls); Grade 12: 99 students (50 boys, 49 girls).

Faculty School total: 137. In upper school: 16 men, 21 women; 12 have advanced degrees.

Subjects Offered 3-dimensional art, algebra, American history, American literature, art, art history, biology, calculus, ceramics, chemistry, comparative religion, computer math, computer programming, computer science, computer technologies, creative writing, dance, drama, earth science, ecology, economics, English, English literature, European history, fine arts, French, geography, geology, geometry, government/civics, health, history, journalism, Latin, mathematics, modern problems, music, music history, photography, physical education, physics, psychology, science, social studies, Spanish, technology, theater, trigonometry, word processing, world history, writing.

Graduation Requirements Algebra, American government, arts and fine arts (art, music, dance, drama), biology, English, foreign language, lab science, mathematics, physical education (includes health), science, social studies (includes history), participation in athletics, completion of a two year College Counseling Course. Community service is required.

Special Academic Programs 22 Advanced Placement exams for which test preparation is offered; study at local college for college credit; academic accommodation for the gifted, the musically talented, and the artistically talented.

College Admission Counseling 96 students graduated in 2012; all went to college, including Southern Methodist University; Texas A&M University; Texas Christian University; The University of Texas at Austin; University of Georgia; University of Oklahoma.

Student Life Upper grades have uniform requirement, student council, honor system. Discipline rests equally with students and faculty.

Tuition and Aid Day student tuition: $19,505. Tuition installment plan (monthly payment plans, individually arranged payment plans). Merit scholarship grants, need-based scholarship grants, Malone Scholars Program, Betty Reese Memorial, Vicki and Edward P. Bass Scholarship, Reilly Breakthrough Scholarship, Joey Pollard Memorial Scholarship, Joann Chandler Thompson Memorial Scholarship available. In 2012–13, 22% of upper-school students received aid; total upper-school merit-scholarship money awarded: $176,482. Total amount of financial aid awarded in 2012–13: $980,225.

Admissions Traditional secondary-level entrance grade is 9. For fall 2012, 65 students applied for upper-level admission, 38 were accepted, 27 enrolled. ERB or ISEE required. Deadline for receipt of application materials: March 3. Application fee required: $75. Interview required.

Athletics Interscholastic: ballet (boys, girls); baseball (b), basketball (b,g), cheering (g), field hockey (g), football (b), lacrosse (b), track and field (b,g), volleyball (b,g), winter soccer (b,g), wrestling (b); intramural: lacrosse (b); coed interscholastic: ballet, cross-country running, dance, dance team, fitness, golf, independent competitive sports, outdoor education, outdoor recreation, physical fitness, physical training, ropes courses, strength & conditioning, swimming and diving, tennis, weight training. 12 PE instructors, 45 coaches, 2 athletic trainers.

Computers Computers are regularly used in architecture, college planning, computer applications, creative writing, desktop publishing, English, foreign language, history, humanities, introduction to technology, journalism, library skills, life skills, mathematics, music, newspaper, publications, reading, science, Web site design, writing, yearbook classes. Computer network features include on-campus library services, online commercial services, Internet access, wireless campus network, Internet filtering or blocking technology. Campus intranet, student e-mail accounts, and computer access in designated common areas are available to students. Students grades are available online. The school has a published electronic and media policy.

Contact Yolanda Espinoza, Admission Associate. 817-302-3209. Fax: 817-377-3425. E-mail: yolanda.espinoza@fwcd.org. Website: www.fwcd.org

FOUNDATION ACADEMY

15304 Tilden Road
Winter Garden, Florida 34787

Head of School: Dr. Lorne Wenzel

General Information Coeducational day college-preparatory, general academic, and arts school, affiliated with Baptist Church. Grades 6–12. Founded: 1958. Setting: suburban. Nearest major city is Orlando. 75-acre campus. 3 buildings on campus. Approved or accredited by Association of Christian Schools International, Southern Association of Colleges and Schools, and Florida Department of Education. Total enrollment: 585. Upper school average class size: 16. Upper school faculty-student ratio: 1:5. There are 180 required school days per year for Upper School students. Upper School students typically attend 5 days per week. The average school day consists of 6 hours and 20 minutes.

Upper School Student Profile Grade 9: 60 students (33 boys, 27 girls); Grade 10: 39 students (18 boys, 21 girls); Grade 11: 32 students (16 boys, 16 girls); Grade 12: 44 students (30 boys, 14 girls). 20% of students are Baptist.

Faculty School total: 34. In upper school: 11 men, 23 women; 10 have advanced degrees.

Subjects Offered Advanced math, Advanced Placement courses, algebra, American government, American literature, anatomy and physiology, art, band, Bible, biology, biology-AP, business law, business mathematics, calculus, calculus-AP, career/college preparation, chemistry, choir, Christian education, college admission preparation, communication skills, computer processing, drama, ecology, economics and history, English, English composition, English language-AP, English literature, English literature-AP, geometry, government, health and wellness, health education, history-AP, honors algebra, honors English, honors geometry, honors U.S. history, honors world history, human anatomy, human biology, journalism, life science, marine biology, personal fitness, physical education, physical fitness, pre-algebra, pre-calculus, SAT preparation, SAT/ACT preparation, science, science project, Spanish, speech, speech and debate, speech communications, sports conditioning, studio art-AP, U.S. government and politics-AP, U.S. history, weight training, weightlifting, yearbook.

Graduation Requirements Algebra, American government, American history, American literature, anatomy and physiology, art, arts and fine arts (art, music, dance, drama), Bible, Bible studies, biology, chemistry, college admission preparation, economics and history, English, English composition, English literature, geography, geometry, government, health and wellness, history, human anatomy, languages, pre-calculus, SAT preparation, science, U.S. history, 4 credits of Bible.

Special Academic Programs Advanced Placement exam preparation; honors section; independent study; study at local college for college credit; remedial reading and/or remedial writing; remedial math; programs in English, mathematics for dyslexic students; special instructional classes for deaf students.

College Admission Counseling 29 students graduated in 2013; 28 went to college, including Cornell University; Florida Gulf Coast University; Florida State University; University of Central Florida; University of Florida; Valencia College. Other: 1 entered military service.

Student Life Upper grades have uniform requirement, student council. Discipline rests primarily with faculty. Attendance at religious services is required.

Summer Programs Remediation, enrichment, sports, art/fine arts programs offered; session focuses on sports camps, art, drama, academic; held on campus; accepts boys and girls; open to students from other schools. 100 students usually enrolled. 2014 schedule: June 1 to July 31.

Tuition and Aid Day student tuition: $10,498–$10,941. Tuition installment plan (SMART Tuition Payment Plan). Tuition reduction for siblings, need-based scholarship grants available. In 2013–14, 10% of upper-school students received aid. Total amount of financial aid awarded in 2013–14: $300,000.

Admissions Traditional secondary-level entrance grade is 9. For fall 2013, 106 students applied for upper-level admission, 90 were accepted, 80 enrolled. Admissions testing, Gates MacGinite Reading Tests, Math Placement Exam and Wide Range Achievement Test required. Deadline for receipt of application materials: none. Application fee required: $150. Interview required.

Athletics Interscholastic: baseball (boys), basketball (b,g), bowling (b,g), boxing (b,g), cheering (g), cross-country running (b,g), football (b), golf (b,g), soccer (b,g), softball (g), tennis (b,g), track and field (b,g), volleyball (g); coed intramural: archery. 2 PE instructors, 2 athletic trainers.

Computers Computers are regularly used in career exploration, college planning, computer applications, economics, English, geography, health, history, independent study, keyboarding, library skills, mathematics, music, SAT preparation, word processing, writing, yearbook classes. Computer network features include on-campus library services, Internet access, wireless campus network, Internet filtering or blocking technology. Campus intranet and student e-mail accounts are available to students. Students grades are available online.

Contact Mrs. Michelle Campbell, Admissions Director. 407-877-2744 Ext. 223. Fax: 407-877-1985. E-mail: mcampbell@foundationacademy.net. Website: www.foundationacademy.net

FOUNTAIN VALLEY SCHOOL OF COLORADO

6155 Fountain Valley School Road
Colorado Springs, Colorado 80911

Head of School: William V. Webb

General Information Coeducational boarding and day college-preparatory, arts, technology, and Global Education school. Grades 9–12. Founded: 1930. Setting: suburban. Students are housed in single-sex dormitories. 1,100-acre campus. 42 buildings on campus. Approved or accredited by Association of Colorado Independent Schools, The Association of Boarding Schools, and Colorado Department of Education. Member of National Association of Independent Schools and Secondary School Admission Test Board. Endowment: $31 million. Total enrollment: 244. Upper school average class size: 12. Upper school faculty-student ratio: 1:6. Upper School students typically attend 5 days per week. The average school day consists of 9 hours and 15 minutes.

Upper School Student Profile Grade 9: 42 students (14 boys, 28 girls); Grade 10: 61 students (34 boys, 27 girls); Grade 11: 74 students (35 boys, 39 girls); Grade 12: 67 students (27 boys, 40 girls). 68% of students are boarding students. 51% are state residents. 27 states are represented in upper school student body. 27% are international students. International students from China, Germany, Japan, Mexico, Republic of Korea, and Saudi Arabia; 12 other countries represented in student body.

Faculty School total: 40. In upper school: 16 men, 14 women; 24 have advanced degrees; 22 reside on campus.

Subjects Offered 3-dimensional art, 3-dimensional design, ACT preparation, advanced chemistry, Advanced Placement courses, advanced studio art-AP, algebra, American history, American history-AP, American literature, band, biology, biology-AP, British literature, calculus, calculus-AP, ceramics, chamber groups, chemistry, chemistry-AP, college counseling, Colorado ecology, composition, computer applications, computer multimedia, computer programming, creative writing, drama, English, English literature and composition-AP, environmental science-AP, ESL, fiction, film and literature, French, French language-AP, geology, geometry, global issues, honors algebra, honors English, honors geometry, instrumental music, jewelry making, literature, Mandarin, music theory, musical productions, outdoor education, photography, physics, physics-AP, pre-calculus, probability and statistics, robotics, senior project, senior seminar, Shakespeare, Shakespearean histories, short story, Spanish, Spanish language-AP, statistics-AP, strings, student government, student publications, studio art, studio art-AP, U.S. government and politics-AP, visual and performing arts, vocal ensemble, wilderness education, wind ensemble, world history, world history-AP, world literature, writing.

Graduation Requirements Arts and fine arts (art, music, dance, drama), computer science, English, foreign language, history, mathematics, physical education (includes health), science, social studies (includes history), Senior Seminar. Community service is required.

Special Academic Programs 20 Advanced Placement exams for which test preparation is offered; honors section; independent study; ESL (17 students enrolled).

College Admission Counseling 52 students graduated in 2013; 44 went to college, including Occidental College; Syracuse University; The Colorado College; University of Colorado Boulder; University of Denver. Other: 1 entered military service, 1 entered a postgraduate year, 6 had other specific plans. Mean SAT critical reading: 592, mean SAT math: 626, mean SAT writing: 608, mean composite ACT: 28.

Student Life Upper grades have specified standards of dress, student council, honor system. Discipline rests equally with students and faculty.

Summer Programs Enrichment, ESL programs offered; session focuses on outdoor education, natural sciences, leadership, sports camps, international student enrichment; held both on and off campus; held at FVS' 40-acre Mountain Campus and surrounding Mount Princeton region; accepts boys and girls; not open to students from other schools. 11 students usually enrolled. 2014 schedule: June 5 to August 15. Application deadline: none.

Tuition and Aid Day student tuition: $26,400; 7-day tuition and room/board: $48,600. Tuition installment plan (Key Tuition Payment Plan, monthly payment plans, individually arranged payment plans). Merit scholarship grants, need-based scholarship grants available. In 2013–14, 41% of upper-school students received aid. Total amount of financial aid awarded in 2013–14: $2,387,900.

Admissions Traditional secondary-level entrance grade is 9. For fall 2013, 209 students applied for upper-level admission, 147 were accepted, 81 enrolled. SSAT or TOEFL required. Deadline for receipt of application materials: February 1. Application fee required: $50. Interview required.

Athletics Interscholastic: basketball (boys, girls), cross-country running (b,g), diving (g), hockey (b), ice hockey (b), lacrosse (b,g), soccer (b,g), swimming and diving (g), tennis (b,g), track and field (b,g), volleyball (b,g); coed interscholastic: climbing, equestrian sports, golf, horseback riding, independent competitive sports, mountain biking, rock climbing, rodeo, skiing (downhill), snowboarding, telemark skiing, wall climbing; coed intramural: aerobics/dance, alpine skiing, backpacking, climbing, equestrian sports, fitness, Frisbee, hiking/backpacking, horseback riding, modern dance, mountain biking, mountaineering, outdoor activities, outdoor adventure, outdoor education, outdoor recreation, outdoor skills, physical fitness, rock climbing, skiing (downhill), snowboarding, strength & conditioning, table tennis, telemark skiing, tennis, ultimate Frisbee, wall climbing, weight training, wilderness. 2 coaches, 1 athletic trainer.

Computers Computers are regularly used in all academic, college planning, multimedia, news writing, newspaper, photography, publications, Web site design, yearbook classes. Computer network features include on-campus library services, online commercial services, Internet access, wireless campus network, Internet filtering or blocking technology, live webcasts of select athletic events. Campus intranet, student e-mail accounts, and computer access in designated common areas are available to students. Students grades are available online. The school has a published electronic and media policy.

Contact Kila McCann, Director of Admission. 719-390-7035 Ext. 297. Fax: 719-390-7762. E-mail: kmccan@fvs.edu. Website: www.fvs.edu

FOWLERS ACADEMY

PO Box 921
Guaynabo, Puerto Rico 00970-0921

Head of School: Mr. Jared Ramos

General Information Coeducational day general academic, arts, religious studies, technology, music, and graphic art design school, affiliated with Christian faith; primarily serves underachievers. Grades 7–12. Founded: 1986. Setting: suburban. 2-acre campus. 2 buildings on campus. Approved or accredited by Comisión Acreditadora de Instituciones Educativas, The College Board, and Puerto Rico Department of Education. Languages of instruction: English and Spanish. Total enrollment: 64. Upper school average class size: 15. Upper school faculty-student ratio: 1:15. There are 160 required school days per year for Upper School students. Upper School students typically attend 5 days per week. The average school day consists of 6 hours and 50 minutes.

Upper School Student Profile Grade 9: 11 students (9 boys, 2 girls); Grade 10: 14 students (11 boys, 3 girls); Grade 11: 10 students (8 boys, 2 girls); Grade 12: 9 students (7 boys, 2 girls).

Faculty School total: 7. In upper school: 5 men, 2 women; 4 have advanced degrees.

Subjects Offered Algebra, American history, ancient world history, art, athletics, basketball, Bible, character education, chemistry, Christian education, Christian ethics, Christian scripture, computer applications, computer art, computer education, computer graphics, computer literacy, computer skills, drama, drawing, earth science, electives, English, film appreciation, geometry, history, instrumental music, keyboarding, leadership, leadership and service, martial arts, mathematics, music, physical education, physics, pre-algebra, pre-college orientation, Puerto Rican history, science, sex education, Spanish, Spanish literature, theater, U.S. history, world history.

Graduation Requirements Algebra, ancient world history, biology, chemistry, Christian education, electives, English, geometry, physical education (includes health), physical science, physics, pre-college orientation, Puerto Rican history, Spanish, U.S. history, world history.

Special Academic Programs Accelerated programs; special instructional classes for students with ADD and LD.

College Admission Counseling 13 students graduated in 2013; 10 went to college, including University of Puerto Rico, Río Piedras; University of Puerto Rico at Carolina. Other: 3 entered a postgraduate year.

Student Life Upper grades have uniform requirement, student council, honor system. Discipline rests primarily with faculty.

Summer Programs Remediation, enrichment, advancement programs offered; session focuses on academic courses and remediation; held on campus; accepts boys and girls; open to students from other schools. 35 students usually enrolled. 2014 schedule: June 1 to June 28. Application deadline: May 31.

Tuition and Aid Day student tuition: $6000. Tuition installment plan (monthly payment plans, individually arranged payment plans). Tuition reduction for siblings, need-based scholarship grants available. In 2013–14, 5% of upper-school students received aid. Total amount of financial aid awarded in 2013–14: $27,000.

Admissions Psychoeducational evaluation required. Deadline for receipt of application materials: none. No application fee required. On-campus interview required.

Athletics Interscholastic: basketball (boys); intramural: basketball (b); coed interscholastic: archery, cooperative games, physical fitness; coed intramural: archery, fitness, physical fitness, soccer, table tennis, volleyball. 1 PE instructor.

Computers Computers are regularly used in English, graphic arts, graphic design, keyboarding, mathematics, religious studies, science, Spanish classes. Computer resources include Internet access, Internet filtering or blocking technology. Computer access in designated common areas is available to students.

Contact Mr. Lynette Montes, Registrar. 787-787-1350. Fax: 787-789-0055. E-mail: fowlersacademy@gmail.com. Website:

FOXCROFT SCHOOL

22407 Foxhound Lane
P.O. Box 5555
Middleburg, Virginia 20118

Head of School: Mary Louise Leipheimer

General Information Girls' boarding and day college-preparatory school. Grades 9–12. Founded: 1914. Setting: rural. Nearest major city is Washington, DC. Students are housed in single-sex dormitories. 500-acre campus. 32 buildings on campus. Approved or accredited by The Association of Boarding Schools and Virginia Department of Education. Member of National Association of Independent Schools and Secondary School Admission Test Board. Endowment: $22.8 million. Total enrollment: 165. Upper school average class size: 12. Upper school faculty-student ratio: 1:7. There are 160 required school days per year for Upper School students. Upper School students typically attend 5 days per week. The average school day consists of 7 hours and 15 minutes.

Upper School Student Profile Grade 9: 31 students (31 girls); Grade 10: 46 students (46 girls); Grade 11: 38 students (38 girls); Grade 12: 50 students (50 girls). 71% of students are boarding students. 48% are state residents. 21 states are represented in upper school student body. 20% are international students. International students from China, Jamaica, Mexico, Republic of Korea, Spain, and United Kingdom; 1 other country represented in student body.

Faculty School total: 23. In upper school: 6 men, 17 women; 17 have advanced degrees; 17 reside on campus.

Subjects Offered 3-dimensional art, acting, advanced chemistry, algebra, American literature, anatomy and physiology, ancient world history, architecture, art, art history, astronomy, biology, British literature, calculus, calculus-AP, cell biology, ceramics, chemistry, chemistry-AP, choir, chorus, college counseling, community service, comparative religion, computer graphics, computer science, conceptual physics, constitutional law, creative dance, creative drama, creative writing, current events, dance, debate, digital photography, discrete mathematics, drama, drawing and design, economics, economics-AP, electives, English, English composition, English literature, English literature-AP, environmental science, European civilization, European history, European literature, expository writing, fine arts, fitness, French, French language-AP, general science, geology, geometry, grammar, health education, history, human anatomy, independent study, leadership, library, macroeconomics-AP, mathematics, microbiology, music, music theory, music theory-AP, painting, performing arts, photography, physical education, physics, piano, poetry, pottery, pre-calculus, probability and statistics, production, public speaking, SAT preparation, sculpture, senior project, social studies, Spanish, Spanish language-AP, Spanish literature, Spanish literature-AP, studio art, studio art-AP, technology, The 20th Century, trigonometry, U.S. history, U.S. history-AP, vocal ensemble, world cultures, world literature, writing, yearbook, yoga.

Graduation Requirements Arts and fine arts (art, music, dance, drama), English, foreign language, history, mathematics, physical education (includes health), science, senior thesis if student is not enrolled in AP English.

Special Academic Programs 11 Advanced Placement exams for which test preparation is offered; independent study; term-away projects; study abroad; academic accommodation for the gifted, the musically talented, and the artistically talented; ESL (25 students enrolled).

College Admission Counseling 38 students graduated in 2013; all went to college, including Barnard College; Cornell University; St. Lawrence University;

University of Virginia; Virginia Polytechnic Institute and State University; Washington and Lee University.

Student Life Upper grades have specified standards of dress, student council, honor system. Discipline rests equally with students and faculty.

Summer Programs Sports, art/fine arts programs offered; session focuses on traditional summer camp activities; held on campus; accepts boys and girls; open to students from other schools. 100 students usually enrolled. 2014 schedule: July 9 to August 10.

Tuition and Aid Day student tuition: $41,580; 7-day tuition and room/board: $49,400. Tuition installment plan (Insured Tuition Payment Plan, Tuition Management Systems Plan (Monthly Payment Plan)). Merit scholarship grants, need-based scholarship grants, merit-based scholarship grants are offered to prospective 9th grade students available. In 2013–14, 30% of upper-school students received aid; total upper-school merit-scholarship money awarded: $31,000. Total amount of financial aid awarded in 2013–14: $1,200,000.

Admissions Traditional secondary-level entrance grade is 9. For fall 2013, 180 students applied for upper-level admission, 121 were accepted, 57 enrolled. SSAT or TOEFL required. Deadline for receipt of application materials: February 1. Application fee required: $75. Interview required.

Athletics Interscholastic: basketball, cross-country running, dressage, equestrian sports, field hockey, horseback riding, lacrosse, running, soccer, softball, tennis, volleyball; intramural: aerobics, aerobics/dance, basketball, climbing, combined training, dance, dance team, dressage, equestrian sports, field hockey, fitness, horseback riding, indoor soccer, indoor track, lacrosse, modern dance, outdoor activities, physical fitness, physical training, rock climbing, ropes courses, running, squash, strength & conditioning, swimming and diving, tennis, volleyball, walking, weight lifting, weight training, yoga. 3 coaches, 1 athletic trainer.

Computers Computers are regularly used in all classes. Computer resources include on-campus library services, online commercial services, Internet access, wireless campus network, Internet filtering or blocking technology. Campus intranet, student e-mail accounts, and computer access in designated common areas are available to students. The school has a published electronic and media policy.

Contact Gina B. Finn, Director of Admission and Financial Aid. 540-687-4340. Fax: 540-687-3627. E-mail: gina.finn@foxcroft.org. Website: www.foxcroft.org

FOX VALLEY LUTHERAN HIGH SCHOOL

5300 North Meade Street
Appleton, Wisconsin 54913-8383

Head of School: Mr. Paul Hartwig

General Information Coeducational day college-preparatory, general academic, arts, business, vocational, religious studies, and technology school, affiliated with Wisconsin Evangelical Lutheran Synod. Grades 9–12. Founded: 1953. Setting: suburban. 63-acre campus. 1 building on campus. Approved or accredited by National Council for Private School Accreditation and Wisconsin Department of Education. Endowment: $4.1 million. Total enrollment: 542. Upper school average class size: 22. Upper school faculty-student ratio: 1:14. There are 180 required school days per year for Upper School students. Upper School students typically attend 5 days per week. The average school day consists of 6 hours and 30 minutes.

Upper School Student Profile Grade 9: 121 students (62 boys, 59 girls); Grade 10: 144 students (74 boys, 70 girls); Grade 11: 135 students (59 boys, 76 girls); Grade 12: 142 students (74 boys, 68 girls). 85% of students are Wisconsin Evangelical Lutheran Synod.

Faculty School total: 42. In upper school: 28 men, 14 women; 18 have advanced degrees.

Subjects Offered Accounting, advanced chemistry, advanced computer applications, advanced math, algebra, American government, American history, American literature, art, athletics, band, basic language skills, Basic programming, Bible, Bible studies, biology, British literature, British literature (honors), British literature-AP, business, business law, calculus, calculus-AP, choir, Christian doctrine, church history, communication skills, comparative religion, composition, computer applications, computer programming, computer skills, computer-aided design, concert band, concert choir, construction, critical writing, digital applications, digital photography, earth science, economics, economics-AP, engineering, English, English composition, foods, general science, geometry, German, government, graphic arts, health and wellness, honors English, keyboarding, language and composition, Latin, Life of Christ, modern Western civilization, modern world history, personal fitness, physical fitness, physics, piano, psychology, reading/study skills, religion, remedial/makeup course work, sewing, Spanish, statistics, symphonic band, woodworking, world geography, world history.

Graduation Requirements 1 1/2 elective credits, arts and fine arts (art, music, dance, drama), English, mathematics, physical education (includes health), religion (includes Bible studies and theology), science.

Special Academic Programs 1 Advanced Placement exam for which test preparation is offered; honors section; accelerated programs; study at local college for college credit; academic accommodation for the gifted; remedial reading and/or remedial writing; remedial math.

College Admission Counseling 154 students graduated in 2012; 144 went to college, including Martin Luther College; University of Wisconsin–Fox Valley;

University of Wisconsin–Madison; University of Wisconsin–Oshkosh. Other: 4 went to work, 2 entered military service, 1 had other specific plans. Median composite ACT: 24.

Student Life Upper grades have specified standards of dress, student council, honor system. Discipline rests primarily with faculty. Attendance at religious services is required.

Tuition and Aid Day student tuition: $5100–$7700. Tuition installment plan (FACTS Tuition Payment Plan). Tuition reduction for siblings, need-based scholarship grants available. In 2012–13, 25% of upper-school students received aid. Total amount of financial aid awarded in 2012–13: $325,000.

Admissions Traditional secondary-level entrance grade is 9. ACT-Explore or Explore required. Deadline for receipt of application materials: none. Application fee required: $25. Interview required.

Athletics Interscholastic: baseball (boys), basketball (b,g), cheering (g), cross-country running (b,g), dance team (g), football (b), golf (b,g), hockey (b,g), ice hockey (b,g), soccer (b,g), softball (g), track and field (b,g), volleyball (g), wrestling (b). 2 PE instructors, 1 athletic trainer.

Computers Computers are regularly used in business, current events, drafting, economics, engineering, English, foreign language, graphic arts, keyboarding, science classes. Computer network features include on-campus library services, Internet access, Internet filtering or blocking technology. Campus intranet and student e-mail accounts are available to students. Students grades are available online. The school has a published electronic and media policy.

Contact Mrs. Heather Knoll, Guidance Assistant. 920-739-4441. Fax: 920-739-4418. E-mail: hknoll@fvlhs.org. Website: www.fvlhs.org

FRANKLIN ROAD ACADEMY

4700 Franklin Road
Nashville, Tennessee 37220

Head of School: Dr. Margaret Wade

General Information Coeducational day college-preparatory, arts, religious studies, and technology school; primarily serves students with learning disabilities and ASPIRE—Student Learning Services Program. Grades PK–12. Founded: 1971. Setting: suburban. 57-acre campus. 5 buildings on campus. Approved or accredited by Southern Association of Colleges and Schools, Southern Association of Independent Schools, and Tennessee Department of Education. Member of National Association of Independent Schools. Endowment: $10.4 million. Total enrollment: 720. Upper school average class size: 8. Upper school faculty-student ratio: 1:8. There are 185 required school days per year for Upper School students. Upper School students typically attend 5 days per week. The average school day consists of 6 hours and 30 minutes.

Upper School Student Profile Grade 9: 67 students (33 boys, 34 girls); Grade 10: 67 students (34 boys, 33 girls); Grade 11: 63 students (31 boys, 32 girls); Grade 12: 67 students (33 boys, 34 girls).

Faculty School total: 100. In upper school: 20 men, 14 women; 20 have advanced degrees.

Subjects Offered Advanced chemistry, Advanced Placement courses, algebra, American history, American literature, anatomy and physiology, art, art-AP, band, baseball, basketball, Bible, Bible studies, biology, biology-AP, calculus, calculus-AP, chemistry, chemistry-AP, choral music, Civil War, college counseling, computer education, computer music, computer programming, computer science, current events, dance, drama, dramatic arts, economics, economics and history, electronic music, English, English language-AP, English literature, English literature-AP, environmental science, European history, European history-AP, fine arts, French, French language-AP, French literature-AP, geometry, government/civics, grammar, history, history-AP, honors algebra, honors English, honors geometry, honors U.S. history, human anatomy, jazz band, keyboarding, Latin, Latin-AP, Life of Christ, mathematics, mathematics-AP, model United Nations, music, music theory, personal development, physical education, physics, physics-AP, pottery, pre-calculus, SAT preparation, SAT/ACT preparation, science, social sciences, social studies, Spanish, Spanish language-AP, Spanish literature-AP, speech, statistics, statistics-AP, student government, student publications, technical theater, theater, theater production, track and field, trigonometry, U.S. government, U.S. history, U.S. history-AP, vocal music, volleyball, weight training, world history, world literature, wrestling, writing.

Graduation Requirements Algebra, arts and fine arts (art, music, dance, drama), computer science, English, foreign language, mathematics, physical education (includes health), religion (includes Bible studies and theology), science, social studies (includes history), community service hours required for graduation. Community service is required.

Special Academic Programs Advanced Placement exam preparation; honors section; independent study; term-away projects; academic accommodation for the gifted, the musically talented, and the artistically talented; programs in general development for dyslexic students.

College Admission Counseling 67 students graduated in 2013; all went to college, including Auburn University; Belmont University; Texas Christian University; The University of Tennessee; University of Georgia. 45% scored over 600 on SAT critical reading, 55% scored over 600 on SAT math, 55% scored over 26 on composite ACT.

Student Life Upper grades have uniform requirement, student council, honor system. Discipline rests primarily with faculty.

Summer Programs Enrichment, sports, art/fine arts, computer instruction programs offered; session focuses on day camps, the arts, technology, and sports; held both on and off campus; held at area swimming pool; accepts boys and girls; open to students from other schools. 400 students usually enrolled. 2014 schedule: June 2 to July 19.

Tuition and Aid Day student tuition: $18,435. Tuition installment plan (Insured Tuition Payment Plan, FACTS Tuition Payment Plan, individually arranged payment plans). Need-based scholarship grants available. In 2013–14, 20% of upper-school students received aid. Total amount of financial aid awarded in 2013–14: $500,000.

Admissions Traditional secondary-level entrance grade is 9. For fall 2013, 76 students applied for upper-level admission, 47 were accepted, 26 enrolled. Admissions testing, ISEE and writing sample required. Deadline for receipt of application materials: none. Application fee required: $40. On-campus interview required.

Athletics Interscholastic: baseball (boys), basketball (b,g), bowling (b,g), cheering (g), cross-country running (b,g), dance (g), diving (b,g), football (b), golf (b,g), hockey (b), ice hockey (b), soccer (b,g), softball (g), swimming and diving (b,g), tennis (b,g), track and field (b,g), volleyball (g), wrestling (b); intramural: aerobics/dance (g), physical fitness (b,g), physical training (b,g), power lifting (b), strength & conditioning (b,g); coed intramural: aerobics/dance. 2 PE instructors, 2 coaches, 1 athletic trainer.

Computers Computers are regularly used in art, Bible studies, college planning, creative writing, economics, English, foreign language, French, history, journalism, keyboarding, Latin, library skills, literary magazine, mathematics, music, religious studies, science, social sciences, Spanish, technology, theater, theater arts, Web site design, writing, yearbook classes. Computer network features include on-campus library services, online commercial services, Internet access, wireless campus network, Internet filtering or blocking technology, networked instructional software. Campus intranet, student e-mail accounts, and computer access in designated common areas are available to students. Students grades are available online. The school has a published electronic and media policy.

Contact Mrs. Courtney Williamson, Director of Admissions. 615-832-8845. Fax: 615-834-8845. E-mail: williamsonc@franklinroadacademy.com. Website: www.franklinroadacademy.com

FREDERICA ACADEMY

200 Murray Way
St. Simons Island, Georgia 31522

Head of School: Mr. Greg F. Griffeth

General Information Coeducational day college-preparatory, arts, and technology school. Grades PK–12. Founded: 1970. Setting: small town. Nearest major city is Jacksonville, FL. 40-acre campus. 7 buildings on campus. Approved or accredited by Georgia Independent School Association, Southern Association of Colleges and Schools, and Georgia Department of Education. Member of National Association of Independent Schools. Endowment: $2 million. Total enrollment: 412. Upper school average class size: 18. Upper school faculty-student ratio: 1:9. There are 180 required school days per year for Upper School students. Upper School students typically attend 5 days per week. The average school day consists of 8 hours and 5 minutes.

Upper School Student Profile Grade 9: 36 students (20 boys, 16 girls); Grade 10: 40 students (20 boys, 20 girls); Grade 11: 41 students (23 boys, 18 girls); Grade 12: 29 students (14 boys, 15 girls).

Faculty School total: 50. In upper school: 8 men, 9 women; 10 have advanced degrees.

Subjects Offered Algebra, American history, American literature, anatomy, ancient history, art, biology, biology-AP, calculus-AP, chemistry, choral music, computer applications, drama, economics, English, English literature, environmental science, geometry, government/civics, grammar, keyboarding, literature-AP, photography, physical education, physical science, physics, pre-calculus, psychology, public speaking, science, Spanish, U.S. history-AP, world history, world literature, writing, yearbook.

Graduation Requirements Algebra, American government, American history, arts and fine arts (art, music, dance, drama), biology, chemistry, computer applications, economics, English literature, foreign language, geometry, physical education (includes health), world history.

Special Academic Programs Advanced Placement exam preparation; honors section.

College Admission Counseling 23 students graduated in 2012; all went to college, including Georgia Institute of Technology; Georgia Southern University; University of Georgia. Mean SAT critical reading: 591, mean SAT math: 583, mean SAT writing: 584, mean combined SAT: 1758.

Student Life Upper grades have specified standards of dress, student council, honor system. Discipline rests primarily with faculty.

Tuition and Aid Day student tuition: $15,900. Tuition installment plan (The Tuition Plan, Insured Tuition Payment Plan). Need-based scholarship grants, local bank financing available. In 2012–13, 30% of upper-school students received aid. Total amount of financial aid awarded in 2012–13: $500,000.

Admissions Traditional secondary-level entrance grade is 9. Admissions testing, any standardized test, Cognitive Abilities Test, OLSAT/Stanford and writing sample

required. Deadline for receipt of application materials: none. Application fee required: $75. On-campus interview required.

Athletics Interscholastic: aquatics (boys, girls), baseball (b), basketball (b,g), cheering (g), cross-country running (b,g), equestrian sports (b,g), fitness (b,g), football (b), golf (b,g), lacrosse (b), outdoor education (b,g), physical fitness (b,g), sailing (b,g), soccer (b,g), tennis (b,g), track and field (b,g), volleyball (g), weight training (b,g); coed interscholastic: cross-country running, fitness, golf, sailing, swimming and diving. 2 PE instructors, 5 coaches, 1 athletic trainer.

Computers Computers are regularly used in all academic, English, library skills, photography, yearbook classes. Computer network features include on-campus library services, online commercial services, Internet access, wireless campus network, Internet filtering or blocking technology. Campus intranet and student e-mail accounts are available to students. Students grades are available online. The school has a published electronic and media policy.

Contact Mrs. Julie J. Ackerman, Director of Admission. 912-638-9981 Ext. 106. Fax: 912-638-1442. E-mail: julieackerman@fredericaacademy.org. Website: www.fredericaacademy.org

FREDERICKSBURG ACADEMY

10800 Academy Drive
Fredericksburg, Virginia 22408-1931

Head of School: Ms. Karen A. Moschetto

General Information Coeducational day college-preparatory and technology school. Grades PK–12. Founded: 1992. Setting: suburban. Nearest major city is Washington, DC. 45-acre campus. 3 buildings on campus. Approved or accredited by Virginia Association of Independent Specialized Education Facilities and Virginia Department of Education. Member of National Association of Independent Schools. Endowment: $2 million. Total enrollment: 552. Upper school average class size: 13. Upper school faculty-student ratio: 1:6. There are 175 required school days per year for Upper School students. The average school day consists of 7 hours and 10 minutes.

Upper School Student Profile Grade 9: 38 students (14 boys, 24 girls); Grade 10: 34 students (17 boys, 17 girls); Grade 11: 31 students (18 boys, 13 girls); Grade 12: 32 students (14 boys, 18 girls).

Faculty School total: 75. In upper school: 9 men, 15 women; 15 have advanced degrees.

Subjects Offered Algebra, American history, American history-AP, art, biology, biology-AP, British literature, calculus-AP, chemistry, choral music, classical civilization, classics, computer science, computer science-AP, creative writing, critical thinking, cultural arts, drama, earth science, English, English-AP, expository writing, film history, fine arts, foreign language, French, geometry, health, history, history-AP, instrumental music, jazz band, journalism, language arts, Latin, Latin History, life science, mathematics, music, music history, newspaper, oral communications, physical education, physics, probability and statistics, programming, reading, science, Shakespeare, social studies, Spanish, studio art, studio art-AP, technical writing, technology, trigonometry, U.S. history, U.S. history-AP, world geography, world history, world literature, writing, writing workshop, yearbook.

Graduation Requirements Algebra, American government, American history, American literature, arts, biology, British literature, English literature, foreign language, government, mathematics, science, world cultures, world history, senior exhibit-research and presentation.

Special Academic Programs Advanced Placement exam preparation; independent study.

College Admission Counseling 30 students graduated in 2013; all went to college, including George Mason University; James Madison University; Radford University; University of Mary Washington; University of Virginia; Virginia Polytechnic Institute and State University. Median SAT critical reading: 586, median SAT math: 600, median SAT writing: 574.

Student Life Upper grades have specified standards of dress, student council, honor system. Discipline rests equally with students and faculty.

Summer Programs Enrichment programs offered; session focuses on enrichment and athletic opportunities; held on campus; accepts boys and girls; open to students from other schools. 100 students usually enrolled. 2014 schedule: June 16 to August 15. Application deadline: June 1.

Tuition and Aid Day student tuition: $18,975. Tuition installment plan (FACTS Tuition Payment Plan, monthly payment plans). Merit scholarship grants, need-based scholarship grants available. In 2013–14, 34% of upper-school students received aid; total upper-school merit-scholarship money awarded: $141,824. Total amount of financial aid awarded in 2013–14: $750,000.

Admissions Traditional secondary-level entrance grade is 9. For fall 2013, 20 students applied for upper-level admission, 12 were accepted, 8 enrolled. Admissions testing required. Deadline for receipt of application materials: January 31. Application fee required: $50. On-campus interview required.

Athletics Interscholastic: basketball (boys, girls), cross-country running (b,g), dance team (g), field hockey (g), lacrosse (b,g), soccer (b,g), swimming and diving (b,g), tennis (b,g); intramural: aerobics/dance (g); coed interscholastic: aquatics, golf. 3 PE instructors, 15 coaches, 1 athletic trainer.

Computers Computers are regularly used in English, foreign language, French, history, journalism, Latin, mathematics, newspaper, programming, publications, science, Spanish, writing, yearbook classes. Computer network features include on-campus library services, online commercial services, Internet access, wireless campus network, Internet filtering or blocking technology. Student e-mail accounts are available to students. The school has a published electronic and media policy.

Contact Mr. Brandon L. Perry, Admission Assistant. 540-898-0020 Ext. 249. Fax: 540-898-8951. E-mail: bperry@fredericksburgacademy.org. Website: www.fredericksburgacademy.org

FREEMAN ACADEMY

748 South Main Street
PO Box 1000
Freeman, South Dakota 57029

Head of School: Ms. Pam Tieszen

General Information Coeducational boarding and day college-preparatory, arts, and religious studies school, affiliated with Mennonite Church. Boarding grades 9–12, day grades 5–12. Founded: 1900. Setting: rural. Nearest major city is Sioux Falls. Students are housed in coed dormitories and host family homes. 80-acre campus. 6 buildings on campus. Approved or accredited by Mennonite Schools Council, North Central Association of Colleges and Schools, and South Dakota Department of Education. Endowment: $450,000. Total enrollment: 68. Upper school average class size: 9. Upper school faculty-student ratio: 1:5. There are 180 required school days per year for Upper School students. Upper School students typically attend 5 days per week. The average school day consists of 8 hours.

Upper School Student Profile Grade 9: 8 students (6 boys, 2 girls); Grade 10: 9 students (4 boys, 5 girls); Grade 11: 11 students (4 boys, 7 girls); Grade 12: 6 students (4 boys, 2 girls). 29% of students are boarding students. 71% are state residents. 3 states are represented in upper school student body. 21% are international students. International students from China, Gambia, Paraguay, Republic of Korea, and Uganda. 55% of students are Mennonite.

Faculty School total: 10. In upper school: 4 men, 6 women; 3 have advanced degrees.

Subjects Offered Computer science, English, fine arts, humanities, mathematics, music, religion, science, social sciences.

Graduation Requirements Arts and fine arts (art, music, dance, drama), computer science, English, foreign language, mathematics, religion (includes Bible studies and theology), science, social studies (includes history), humanities.

Special Academic Programs Independent study; academic accommodation for the musically talented and the artistically talented.

College Admission Counseling 15 students graduated in 2013; all went to college, including Bethel College; Dordt College; Eastern Mennonite University; Hesston College; University of Minnesota, Twin Cities Campus; University of Sioux Falls. Median composite ACT: 25. 31% scored over 26 on composite ACT.

Student Life Upper grades have specified standards of dress, honor system. Discipline rests primarily with faculty. Attendance at religious services is required.

Tuition and Aid Day student tuition: $6310; 7-day tuition and room/board: $21,550. Tuition installment plan (FACTS Tuition Payment Plan, monthly payment plans, individually arranged payment plans, semester payment plan). Tuition reduction for siblings, merit scholarship grants, need-based scholarship grants available. In 2013–14, 28% of upper-school students received aid; total upper-school merit-scholarship money awarded: $500. Total amount of financial aid awarded in 2013–14: $32,000.

Admissions Traditional secondary-level entrance grade is 9. For fall 2013, 4 students applied for upper-level admission, 4 were accepted, 4 enrolled. Secondary Level English Proficiency required. Deadline for receipt of application materials: none. No application fee required. Interview recommended.

Athletics Interscholastic: basketball (boys, girls), cheering (g), cross-country running (b,g), golf (b,g), soccer (b,g), track and field (b,g), volleyball (g); coed interscholastic: soccer. 4 coaches.

Computers Computers are regularly used in English, keyboarding, mathematics, religion, science, social studies, speech, yearbook classes. Computer network features include on-campus library services, Internet access, wireless campus network, Internet filtering or blocking technology. Student e-mail accounts and computer access in designated common areas are available to students. Students grades are available online. The school has a published electronic and media policy.

Contact Ms. Bonnie Young, Enrollment Director. 605-925-4237 Ext. 225. Fax: 605-925-4271. E-mail: byoung@freemanacademy.org. Website: www.freemanacademy.org

FRENCH-AMERICAN SCHOOL OF NEW YORK

525 Fenimore Road
Mamaroneck, New York 10543

Head of School: Mr. Jol Peinado

General Information Coeducational day college-preparatory and bilingual studies school. Grades N–12. Founded: 1980. Setting: suburban. Nearest major city is White Plains. 1 building on campus. Approved or accredited by Middle States Association of Colleges and Schools and New York Department of Education. Member of National Association of Independent Schools. Languages of instruction: English and French. Total enrollment: 842. Upper school average class size: 17. Upper school faculty-student ratio: 1:6. There are 169 required school days per year for Upper School

students. Upper School students typically attend 5 days per week. The average school day consists of 7 hours and 45 minutes.

Upper School Student Profile Grade 9: 69 students (40 boys, 29 girls); Grade 10: 38 students (22 boys, 16 girls); Grade 11: 54 students (22 boys, 32 girls); Grade 12: 47 students (16 boys, 31 girls).

Faculty School total: 72. In upper school: 17 men, 21 women; 29 have advanced degrees.

Subjects Offered Algebra, American history, American literature, art, biology, choir, civics, computer applications, computer multimedia, current events, earth science, ecology, economics, English, ESL, European history, expository writing, French, French language-AP, French literature-AP, French studies, geometry, German, government, health, Latin, mathematics, multimedia, music, newspaper, philosophy, physical education, physics, physics-AP, public speaking, science, social studies, Spanish, Spanish language-AP, world history, world literature, writing, yearbook.

Graduation Requirements 20th century history, algebra, American history, biology, calculus, chemistry, civics, computer studies, current events, English, European history, foreign language, French, geography, geology, geometry, mathematics, music, philosophy, physical education (includes health), physics, pre-algebra, pre-calculus, research seminar, social studies (includes history). Community service is required.

Special Academic Programs Advanced Placement exam preparation; honors section; ESL (38 students enrolled).

College Admission Counseling 44 students graduated in 2013; all went to college, including Columbia University; Hampshire College; McGill University; University of Michigan. Mean SAT critical reading: 626, mean SAT math: 624, mean SAT writing: 634.

Student Life Upper grades have specified standards of dress, student council. Discipline rests primarily with faculty.

Tuition and Aid Day student tuition: $26,100–$27,120. Tuition installment plan (Academic Management Services Plan). Need-based scholarship grants available. In 2013–14, 8% of upper-school students received aid. Total amount of financial aid awarded in 2013–14: $223,276.

Admissions Traditional secondary-level entrance grade is 9. For fall 2013, 53 students applied for upper-level admission, 36 were accepted, 23 enrolled. English, French, and math proficiency required. Deadline for receipt of application materials: none. Application fee required: $150. Interview recommended.

Athletics Interscholastic: baseball (boys), basketball (b,g), cross-country running (b,g), rugby (b,g), soccer (b,g), softball (g), tennis (b,g); coed intramural: fencing. 4 PE instructors, 4 coaches.

Computers Computers are regularly used in art, English, foreign language, French, history, mathematics, music, publications, science classes. Computer network features include on-campus library services, Internet access, Internet filtering or blocking technology, laptop use (in certain classes), new iPad program in seventh grade. Student e-mail accounts are available to students. The school has a published electronic and media policy.

Contact Mr. Antoine Agopian, Director of Admissions. 914-250-0400. Fax: 914-940-2214. E-mail: aagopian@fasny.org. Website: www.fasny.org

FRESNO CHRISTIAN SCHOOLS

7280 North Cedar Avenue
Fresno, California 93720

Head of School: Mrs. Debbie Siebert

General Information Coeducational day college-preparatory, arts, religious studies, and technology school, affiliated with Protestant-Evangelical faith. Grades K–12. Founded: 1977. Setting: suburban. 27-acre campus. 4 buildings on campus. Approved or accredited by Association of Christian Schools International, Western Association of Schools and Colleges, and California Department of Education. Endowment: $161,867. Total enrollment: 465. Upper school average class size: 20. Upper school faculty-student ratio: 1:11. There are 176 required school days per year for Upper School students. Upper School students typically attend 5 days per week. The average school day consists of 5 hours and 50 minutes.

Upper School Student Profile Grade 9: 42 students (26 boys, 16 girls); Grade 10: 55 students (23 boys, 32 girls); Grade 11: 43 students (22 boys, 21 girls); Grade 12: 48 students (28 boys, 20 girls). 90% of students are Protestant-Evangelical faith.

Faculty School total: 26. In upper school: 11 men, 7 women; 5 have advanced degrees.

Subjects Offered Advanced Placement courses, algebra, alternative physical education, American government, American history, American history-AP, art, athletics, band, baseball, basketball, Bible, Bible studies, biology, biology-AP, British literature, calculus-AP, cheerleading, chemistry, Chinese, choir, choral music, Christian education, civics, composition-AP, concert band, concert choir, drama, drama performance, economics, economics and history, English, English language and composition-AP, English literature and composition-AP, English-AP, ensembles, European history-AP, geometry, golf, home economics, honors algebra, honors English, honors geometry, humanities, jazz band, journalism, leadership, marching band, mathematics, mathematics-AP, physical education, physical science, physics, pre-calculus, softball, Spanish, sports, statistics-AP, student government, tennis, track and field, trigonometry, U.S. history, video film production, vocal music, volleyball, woodworking, work experience, world history, yearbook.

Graduation Requirements Arts and fine arts (art, music, dance, drama), electives, English, mathematics, physical education (includes health), religion (includes Bible studies and theology), science, social studies (includes history), 4 years of Biblical Studies classes.

Special Academic Programs 7 Advanced Placement exams for which test preparation is offered; honors section; independent study; study at local college for college credit; remedial reading and/or remedial writing; remedial math; special instructional classes for students with learning disabilities.

College Admission Counseling 41 students graduated in 2013; 38 went to college, including Azusa Pacific University; Biola University; California State University, Fresno; Fresno City College; University of California, Santa Barbara; Westmont College. Other: 2 went to work, 1 had other specific plans. Mean SAT critical reading: 553, mean SAT math: 543, mean SAT writing: 533, mean combined SAT: 1538.

Student Life Upper grades have specified standards of dress, student council, honor system. Discipline rests primarily with faculty. Attendance at religious services is required.

Tuition and Aid Day student tuition: $8275. Tuition installment plan (monthly payment plans, individually arranged payment plans). Tuition reduction for siblings, merit scholarship grants, need-based scholarship grants available. In 2013–14, 25% of upper-school students received aid. Total amount of financial aid awarded in 2013–14: $163,537.

Admissions Traditional secondary-level entrance grade is 9. Stanford Achievement Test required. Deadline for receipt of application materials: none. Application fee required: $100. Interview required.

Athletics Interscholastic: baseball (boys), basketball (b,g), cheering (g), cross-country running (b,g), drill team (g), football (b), soccer (b,g), softball (g), strength & conditioning (b,g), tennis (b,g), track and field (b,g), volleyball (g), weight training (b,g); coed interscholastic: golf, physical training; coed intramural: outdoor recreation, volleyball. 1 PE instructor, 16 coaches.

Computers Computers are regularly used in media production, publications, yearbook classes. Computer network features include on-campus library services, online commercial services, Internet access, wireless campus network, Internet filtering or blocking technology. Computer access in designated common areas is available to students. Students grades are available online. The school has a published electronic and media policy.

Contact Mrs. Kerry Roberts, Registrar. 559-299-1695 Ext. 102. Fax: 559-299-1051. E-mail: kroberts@fresnochristian.com. Website: www.fresnochristian.com

FRIENDS ACADEMY

270 Duck Pond Road
Locust Valley, New York 11560

Head of School: William Morris

General Information Coeducational day college-preparatory school, affiliated with Society of Friends. Grades N–12. Founded: 1876. Setting: suburban. Nearest major city is New York. 65-acre campus. 8 buildings on campus. Approved or accredited by New York Department of Education. Member of National Association of Independent Schools and Secondary School Admission Test Board. Endowment: $30 million. Total enrollment: 780. Upper school average class size: 15. Upper school faculty-student ratio: 1:8. There are 165 required school days per year for Upper School students. Upper School students typically attend 5 days per week. The average school day consists of 7 hours.

Upper School Student Profile Grade 9: 95 students (55 boys, 40 girls); Grade 10: 97 students (41 boys, 56 girls); Grade 11: 98 students (41 boys, 57 girls); Grade 12: 86 students (46 boys, 40 girls). 1% of students are members of Society of Friends.

Faculty School total: 117. In upper school: 30 men, 37 women; 40 have advanced degrees.

Subjects Offered Advanced Placement courses, African studies, algebra, American history, American literature, art, art history, Bible studies, biology, calculus, ceramics, chemistry, community service, computer literacy, computer programming, computer science, creative writing, drama, driver education, English, English literature, environmental science, ethics, European history, expository writing, fine arts, French, geography, geometry, grammar, Greek, health, history, Italian, Latin, logic, mathematics, mechanical drawing, music, outdoor education, photography, physical education, physics, psychology, religion, science, social sciences, social studies, Spanish, speech, theater, trigonometry, Western civilization, world literature, writing.

Graduation Requirements Arts and fine arts (art, music, dance, drama), computer literacy, English, foreign language, mathematics, outdoor education, physical education (includes health), religion (includes Bible studies and theology), science, social sciences, social studies (includes history), speech, participation in on-campus work crew program, independent service program. Community service is required.

Special Academic Programs 18 Advanced Placement exams for which test preparation is offered; honors section; independent study; remedial reading and/or remedial writing; remedial math.

College Admission Counseling 96 students graduated in 2013; all went to college, including Boston College; Brown University; Dartmouth College; Michigan State University; New York University; The George Washington University.

Student Life Upper grades have specified standards of dress, student council. Discipline rests primarily with faculty. Attendance at religious services is required.

Summer Programs Art/fine arts programs offered; session focuses on arts and sports; held both on and off campus; held at Off-campus for golf, sailing and riding. and off-campus field trips; accepts boys and girls; open to students from other schools. 250 students usually enrolled. 2014 schedule: June 30 to August 22.

Tuition and Aid Day student tuition: $29,000. Tuition installment plan (Insured Tuition Payment Plan, monthly payment plans). Need-based scholarship grants, Quaker grants, tuition remission for children of faculty and staff available. In 2013–14, 20% of upper-school students received aid. Total amount of financial aid awarded in 2013–14: $1,699,000.

Admissions Traditional secondary-level entrance grade is 9. For fall 2013, 118 students applied for upper-level admission, 52 were accepted, 43 enrolled. SSAT required. Deadline for receipt of application materials: January 15. Application fee required: $55. Interview required.

Athletics Interscholastic: baseball (boys), basketball (b,g), crew (b,g), cross-country running (b,g), field hockey (g), fitness (b,g), football (b), golf (b,g), ice hockey (b), indoor track & field (b,g), lacrosse (b,g), soccer (b,g), softball (g), tennis (b,g), track and field (b,g), winter (indoor) track (b,g); coed intramural: dance, volleyball. 9 PE instructors, 1 athletic trainer.

Computers Computers are regularly used in English, mathematics, science, technology classes. Computer network features include on-campus library services, online commercial services, Internet access, wireless campus network, Internet filtering or blocking technology, iPad Program for Middle School students. Campus intranet, student e-mail accounts, and computer access in designated common areas are available to students. Students grades are available online. The school has a published electronic and media policy.

Contact Joanna Kim, Admissions Associate. 516-393-4244. Fax: 516-465-1718. E-mail: joanna_kim@fa.org. Website: www.fa.org

FRIENDS' CENTRAL SCHOOL

1101 City Avenue
Wynnewood, Pennsylvania 19096

Head of School: Craig N. Sellers

General Information Coeducational day college-preparatory school, affiliated with Society of Friends. Grades N–12. Founded: 1845. Setting: suburban. Nearest major city is Philadelphia. 23-acre campus. 7 buildings on campus. Approved or accredited by Pennsylvania Department of Education. Member of National Association of Independent Schools and Secondary School Admission Test Board. Endowment: $22 million. Total enrollment: 812. Upper school average class size: 18. Upper school faculty-student ratio: 1:8. There are 170 required school days per year for Upper School students. Upper School students typically attend 5 days per week. The average school day consists of 6 hours and 40 minutes.

Upper School Student Profile Grade 9: 88 students (43 boys, 45 girls); Grade 10: 97 students (50 boys, 47 girls); Grade 11: 96 students (48 boys, 48 girls); Grade 12: 96 students (50 boys, 46 girls). 3% of students are members of Society of Friends.

Faculty School total: 130. In upper school: 26 men, 26 women; 38 have advanced degrees.

Subjects Offered Advanced biology, advanced chemistry, advanced math, algebra, American history, American literature, Bible, biology, calculus, ceramics, chemistry, chorus, computer applications, computer programming, conflict resolution, drama, English, French, geometry, instrumental music, Latin, life skills, media studies, modern European history, music history, music theory, philosophy, photography, physical education, physical science, physics, pre-calculus, psychology, sexuality, Spanish, studio art, study skills, Western literature, women in world history, woodworking, world history, writing workshop.

Graduation Requirements Arts and fine arts (art, music, dance, drama), English, foreign language, mathematics, science, service learning/internship, U.S. history, world cultures.

Special Academic Programs Honors section; independent study; term-away projects.

College Admission Counseling 105 students graduated in 2013; all went to college, including Bryn Mawr College; Emory University; Syracuse University; The George Washington University; University of Pennsylvania; Yale University. Mean SAT critical reading: 642, mean SAT math: 638, mean SAT writing: 640.

Student Life Upper grades have specified standards of dress, student council, honor system. Discipline rests primarily with faculty. Attendance at religious services is required.

Summer Programs Remediation, advancement programs offered; held on campus; accepts boys and girls; open to students from other schools. 37 students usually enrolled. 2014 schedule: June 23 to August 1.

Tuition and Aid Day student tuition: $14,250–$29,200. Tuition installment plan (monthly payment plans, Higher Education Service, Inc). Need-based scholarship grants available. In 2013–14, 36% of upper-school students received aid. Total amount of financial aid awarded in 2013–14: $2,928,646.

Admissions Traditional secondary-level entrance grade is 9. For fall 2013, 154 students applied for upper-level admission, 80 were accepted, 37 enrolled. ISEE, SSAT or Wechsler Intelligence Scale for Children required. Deadline for receipt of application materials: January 15. Application fee required: $50. On-campus interview required.

Athletics Interscholastic: aquatics (boys, girls), baseball (b), basketball (b,g), cross-country running (b,g), field hockey (g), indoor track (b,g), lacrosse (b,g), soccer (b,g), softball (g), tennis (b,g), track and field (b,g), winter (indoor) track (b,g), wrestling (b,g); coed interscholastic: golf, squash, water polo; coed intramural: aerobics, aerobics/dance, aerobics/Nautilus, cheering, dance, fitness, flag football, life saving, table tennis. 8 PE instructors, 10 coaches, 1 athletic trainer.

Computers Computers are regularly used in college planning, foreign language, French, health, information technology, introduction to technology, Latin, mathematics, publishing, science, Spanish, technology, Web site design, yearbook classes. Computer network features include on-campus library services, online commercial services, Internet access, wireless campus network, Internet filtering or blocking technology, Intranet collaboration. Campus intranet, student e-mail accounts, and computer access in designated common areas are available to students. Students grades are available online. The school has a published electronic and media policy.

Contact Randy Roach, Director of Enrollment Management. 610-645-5032. Fax: 610-658-5644. E-mail: admission@friendscentral.org. Website: www.friendscentral.org

FRONT RANGE CHRISTIAN HIGH SCHOOL

6637 West Ottawa Avenue
Littleton, Colorado 80128

Head of School: David Cooper

General Information Coeducational day college-preparatory, general academic, arts, business, vocational, religious studies, bilingual studies, technology, and science, math, language arts, media, Spanish school, affiliated with Christian faith. Grades PK–12. Founded: 1994. Setting: suburban. Nearest major city is Denver. 20-acre campus. 3 buildings on campus. Approved or accredited by Association of Christian Schools International, North Central Association of Colleges and Schools, and Colorado Department of Education. Total enrollment: 435. Upper school average class size: 25. Upper school faculty-student ratio: 1:8. There are 175 required school days per year for Upper School students. Upper School students typically attend 5 days per week. The average school day consists of 6 hours and 30 minutes.

Upper School Student Profile Grade 9: 39 students (15 boys, 24 girls); Grade 10: 46 students (21 boys, 25 girls); Grade 11: 47 students (19 boys, 28 girls); Grade 12: 45 students (22 boys, 23 girls). 95% of students are Christian faith.

Faculty School total: 45. In upper school: 12 men, 21 women; 16 have advanced degrees.

Subjects Offered ACT preparation, acting, advanced biology, advanced math, Advanced Placement courses, algebra, American history, American literature, anatomy and physiology, ancient world history, art, athletics, band, baseball, basketball, Bible, biology, biology-AP, British literature, calculus, career and personal planning, career/college preparation, cheerleading, chemistry, choir, Christian and Hebrew scripture, Christian doctrine, Christian scripture, composition, dance, digital photography, drama, drama performance, earth science, electives, foreign language, forensics, geometry, golf, grammar, guitar, health education, home economics, honors algebra, honors English, honors U.S. history, honors world history, horticulture, junior and senior seminars, lab science, language arts, leadership and service, Life of Christ, literature and composition-AP, modern dance, music, music theory, musical productions, participation in sports, performing arts, photography, photojournalism, physical education, physical fitness, physics, pre-calculus, probability and statistics, psychology, Spanish, speech, speech and oral interpretations, sports, statistics, trigonometry, video and animation, video film production, visual arts, vocal ensemble, volleyball, world religions, yearbook.

Graduation Requirements Algebra, career planning, college planning, history, language arts, science, Spanish, speech, participation in annual Spring Practicum, participation in monthly service projects (called Go! Wednesdays).

Special Academic Programs 4 Advanced Placement exams for which test preparation is offered; honors section; study at local college for college credit; academic accommodation for the gifted; remedial reading and/or remedial writing; remedial math; programs in English, mathematics, general development for dyslexic students; special instructional classes for deaf students, blind students.

College Admission Counseling 44 students graduated in 2013; 33 went to college, including Colorado Christian University; Colorado State University; Grand Canyon University; John Brown University; University of Colorado Denver. Other: 1 had other specific plans. Median SAT critical reading: 570, median SAT math: 590, median SAT writing: 570, median combined SAT: 1650, median composite ACT: 24. 33% scored over 26 on composite ACT.

Student Life Upper grades have specified standards of dress, student council, honor system. Discipline rests equally with students and faculty. Attendance at religious services is required.

Summer Programs Enrichment, sports, art/fine arts programs offered; session focuses on grades K-12 summer camps; held on campus; accepts boys and girls; open to students from other schools. 50 students usually enrolled. 2014 schedule: June to August.

Tuition and Aid Day student tuition: $9050. Tuition installment plan (FACTS Tuition Payment Plan, monthly payment plans). Merit scholarship grants, need-based scholarship grants, employee discounts for parents with students who attend available. In 2013–14, 22% of upper-school students received aid; total upper-school merit-scholarship money awarded: $3000. Total amount of financial aid awarded in 2013–14: $176,880.

Admissions Traditional secondary-level entrance grade is 9. For fall 2013, 28 students applied for upper-level admission, 28 were accepted, 26 enrolled. English proficiency, essay and Math Placement Exam required. Deadline for receipt of application materials: April 1. Application fee required: $50. Interview required.

Athletics Interscholastic: baseball (boys), basketball (b,g), cheering (g), football (b), golf (b), soccer (g), volleyball (g); intramural: basketball (b,g), rugby (b), volleyball (g); coed interscholastic: cross-country running, track and field; coed intramural: aerobics, combined training, dance, fitness, martial arts, modern dance, mountain biking, outdoor recreation, outdoor skills, physical fitness, physical training, rock climbing, skiing (downhill), snowboarding, weight training. 5 coaches.

Computers Computers are regularly used in all academic, basic skills, computer applications, introduction to technology, media arts, multimedia, yearbook classes. Computer network features include Internet access, wireless campus network, Internet filtering or blocking technology, RenWeb Parents and Student access, 1 to 1 iPad program, My Big Campus access. Student e-mail accounts and computer access in designated common areas are available to students. Students grades are available online. The school has a published electronic and media policy.

Contact Sarah Lloyd, Admissions Coordinator. 720-922-3269 Ext. 4597. Fax: 720-922-3296. E-mail: admissions@frcs.org. Website: www.frcs.org

THE FROSTIG SCHOOL

Pasadena, California
See Special Needs Schools section.

FRYEBURG ACADEMY

745 Main Street
Fryeburg, Maine 04037-1329

Head of School: Ms. Erin P. Mayo

General Information Coeducational boarding and day college-preparatory, general academic, and arts school. Grades 9–PG. Founded: 1792. Setting: rural. Nearest major city is Portland. Students are housed in single-sex dormitories. 35-acre campus. 17 buildings on campus. Approved or accredited by Association of Independent Schools in New England, Independent Schools of Northern New England, New England Association of Schools and Colleges, The Association of Boarding Schools, The College Board, and Maine Department of Education. Member of National Association of Independent Schools and Secondary School Admission Test Board. Endowment: $18.5 million. Total enrollment: 599. Upper school average class size: 14. Upper school faculty-student ratio: 1:10. There are 170 required school days per year for Upper School students. Upper School students typically attend 5 days per week. The average school day consists of 6 hours and 30 minutes.

Upper School Student Profile Grade 9: 126 students (60 boys, 66 girls); Grade 10: 139 students (67 boys, 72 girls); Grade 11: 140 students (76 boys, 64 girls); Grade 12: 165 students (95 boys, 70 girls). 25% of students are boarding students. 83% are state residents. 9 states are represented in upper school student body. 17% are international students. International students from China, Democratic People's Republic of Korea, Germany, Serbia and Montenegro, Spain, and Viet Nam; 12 other countries represented in student body.

Faculty School total: 67. In upper school: 29 men, 30 women; 34 have advanced degrees; 25 reside on campus.

Subjects Offered Algebra, American literature, anatomy, art, art history, biology, botany, business, calculus, chemistry, computer math, computer programming, computer science, creative writing, drafting, drama, driver education, earth science, ecology, economics, English, English literature, ethics, European history, expository writing, fine arts, French, geography, geometry, government/civics, grammar, health, history, industrial arts, journalism, Latin, linear algebra, marine biology, mathematics, mechanical drawing, music, photography, physical education, physics, physiology, psychology, science, social studies, sociology, Spanish, speech, theater, trigonometry, typing, world history, world literature, writing.

Graduation Requirements Arts and fine arts (art, music, dance, drama), computer science, English, foreign language, mathematics, physical education (includes health), science, social studies (includes history). Community service is required.

Special Academic Programs 16 Advanced Placement exams for which test preparation is offered; honors section; independent study; study at local college for college credit; academic accommodation for the musically talented; remedial reading and/or remedial writing; remedial math; programs in English, mathematics, general development for dyslexic students; special instructional classes for students with learning disabilities, Attention Deficit Disorder, and dyslexia; ESL (38 students enrolled).

College Admission Counseling 187 students graduated in 2013; 163 went to college, including Boston University; Colby College; Massachusetts Institute of

Technology; Northeastern University; University of Maine; University of New Hampshire. Other: 20 went to work, 4 had other specific plans.

Student Life Upper grades have specified standards of dress, student council. Discipline rests primarily with faculty.

Tuition and Aid Day student tuition: $20,800; 5-day tuition and room/board: $34,800; 7-day tuition and room/board: $43,600. Tuition installment plan (monthly payment plans, individually arranged payment plans). Need-based scholarship grants available. In 2013–14, 42% of upper-school students received aid. Total amount of financial aid awarded in 2013–14: $2,100,000.

Admissions Traditional secondary-level entrance grade is 10. For fall 2013, 158 students applied for upper-level admission, 108 were accepted, 47 enrolled. Writing sample required. Deadline for receipt of application materials: February 1. Application fee required: $50. Interview required.

Athletics Interscholastic: baseball (boys), basketball (b,g), cross-country running (b,g), field hockey (g), football (b), golf (b), hockey (b,g), ice hockey (b), lacrosse (b,g), skiing (cross-country) (b,g), skiing (downhill) (b,g), soccer (b,g), softball (g), tennis (b,g), track and field (b,g), wrestling (b); intramural: ice hockey (g), strength & conditioning (b,g), table tennis (b,g); coed interscholastic: alpine skiing, cheering, mountain biking, nordic skiing; coed intramural: alpine skiing, archery, backpacking, badminton, ball hockey, basketball, bicycling, billiards, bowling, canoeing/kayaking, climbing, figure skating, fishing, fitness, fitness walking, flag football, floor hockey, fly fishing, freestyle skiing, Frisbee, golf, hiking/backpacking, ice skating, jogging, kayaking, mountain biking, mountaineering, paint ball, physical fitness, physical training, pistol, rock climbing, roller blading, skiing (downhill), snowboarding, snowshoeing, swimming and diving, table tennis, tai chi, telemark skiing, tennis, ultimate Frisbee, volleyball, walking, wall climbing, weight lifting, whiffle ball, winter walking. 2 PE instructors, 3 coaches, 1 athletic trainer.

Computers Computers are regularly used in all classes. Computer network features include on-campus library services, Internet access, wireless campus network. Student e-mail accounts and computer access in designated common areas are available to students. Students grades are available online. The school has a published electronic and media policy.

Contact Stephanie S. Morin, Director of Enrollment Management and Marketing. 207-935-2013. Fax: 207-935-4292. E-mail: smorin@fryeburgacademy.org. Website: www.fryeburgacademy.org

FUQUA SCHOOL

605 Fuqua Drive
PO Box 328
Farmville, Virginia 23901

Head of School: Ms. Ruth S. Murphy

General Information Coeducational day college-preparatory, arts, and business school. Grades PK–12. Founded: 1959. Setting: small town. Nearest major city is Richmond. 65-acre campus. 19 buildings on campus. Approved or accredited by Southern Association of Colleges and Schools and Virginia Department of Education. Member of National Association of Independent Schools and Secondary School Admission Test Board. Endowment: $5.1 million. Total enrollment: 382. Upper school average class size: 15. Upper school faculty-student ratio: 1:7. There are 180 required school days per year for Upper School students. Upper School students typically attend 5 days per week. The average school day consists of 6 hours.

Upper School Student Profile Grade 9: 37 students (23 boys, 14 girls); Grade 10: 31 students (16 boys, 15 girls); Grade 11: 36 students (20 boys, 16 girls); Grade 12: 41 students (19 boys, 22 girls).

Faculty School total: 42. In upper school: 9 men, 12 women; 6 have advanced degrees.

Subjects Offered Agriculture, algebra, art, band, biology-AP, calculus-AP, chemistry, chemistry-AP, communications, composition, computer information systems, driver education, economics, English composition, English literature-AP, English-AP, environmental science, environmental studies, ethics, fitness, general business, geometry, government-AP, grammar, health, history-AP, industrial technology, personal finance, physics, pre-calculus, psychology, Spanish, theater, U.S. government, U.S. history-AP, United States government-AP, weight training, world religions, yearbook, zoology.

Graduation Requirements Arts and fine arts (art, music, dance, drama), communications, composition, computer information systems, driver education, English, fitness, foreign language, grammar, health education, mathematics, physical education (includes health), science, social studies (includes history). Community service is required.

Special Academic Programs Advanced Placement exam preparation; honors section; accelerated programs; independent study; study at local college for college credit; ESL (6 students enrolled).

College Admission Counseling 39 students graduated in 2013; all went to college, including James Madison University; Longwood University; Lynchburg College; University of Virginia; Virginia Polytechnic Institute and State University; Washington and Lee University. Median SAT critical reading: 570, median SAT math: 540, median SAT writing: 550, median composite ACT: 26. 42% scored over 600 on

SAT critical reading, 41% scored over 600 on SAT math, 40% scored over 600 on SAT writing, 57% scored over 26 on composite ACT.

Student Life Upper grades have specified standards of dress, student council, honor system. Discipline rests primarily with faculty.

Summer Programs Enrichment, sports, art/fine arts programs offered; session focuses on sports and sport skills, arts, enrichment; held on campus; accepts boys and girls; open to students from other schools. 75 students usually enrolled. 2014 schedule: June 15 to July 31. Application deadline: May 15.

Tuition and Aid Day student tuition: $7750. Tuition installment plan (The Tuition Plan, Insured Tuition Payment Plan, monthly payment plans, individually arranged payment plans). Tuition reduction for siblings, merit scholarship grants, need-based scholarship grants available. In 2013–14, 44% of upper-school students received aid; total upper-school merit-scholarship money awarded: $7000. Total amount of financial aid awarded in 2013–14: $44,000.

Admissions Traditional secondary-level entrance grade is 9. For fall 2013, 23 students applied for upper-level admission, 23 were accepted, 23 enrolled. Placement test required. Deadline for receipt of application materials: none. Application fee required: $100. On-campus interview required.

Athletics Interscholastic: baseball (boys), basketball (b,g), cheering (g), football (b), lacrosse (b,g), softball (g), tennis (g), volleyball (g); coed interscholastic: cross-country running, golf, soccer, swimming and diving, track and field; coed intramural: basketball. 4 PE instructors, 38 coaches, 1 athletic trainer.

Computers Computers are regularly used in desktop publishing classes. Computer network features include on-campus library services, online commercial services, Internet access, wireless campus network, Internet filtering or blocking technology. Student e-mail accounts and computer access in designated common areas are available to students. The school has a published electronic and media policy.

Contact Mrs. Christy M. Murphy, Director of Admissions. 434-392-4131 Ext. 273. Fax: 434-392-5062. E-mail: murphycm@fuquaschool.com. Website: www.fuquaschool.com

GABRIEL RICHARD CATHOLIC HIGH SCHOOL

15325 Pennsylvania Road
Riverview, Michigan 48193

Head of School: Mr. Joseph J. Whalen

General Information Coeducational day college-preparatory school, affiliated with Roman Catholic Church. Grades 9–12. Founded: 1965. Setting: suburban. Nearest major city is Detroit. 23-acre campus. 1 building on campus. Approved or accredited by North Central Association of Colleges and Schools and Michigan Department of Education. Total enrollment: 289. Upper school average class size: 17. Upper school faculty-student ratio: 1:17. There are 180 required school days per year for Upper School students. Upper School students typically attend 5 days per week. The average school day consists of 7 hours and 5 minutes.

Upper School Student Profile Grade 9: 71 students (34 boys, 37 girls); Grade 10: 78 students (44 boys, 34 girls); Grade 11: 60 students (30 boys, 30 girls); Grade 12: 80 students (39 boys, 41 girls); Postgraduate: 289 students (147 boys, 142 girls). 90% of students are Roman Catholic.

Faculty School total: 18. In upper school: 4 men, 14 women; 13 have advanced degrees.

Subjects Offered 1 1/2 elective credits, 20th century American writers, 20th century history, 20th century world history, accounting, acting, advanced chemistry, advanced math, Advanced Placement courses, advanced studio art-AP, algebra, American Civil War, American democracy, American government, American history, American history-AP, American literature, American literature-AP, anatomy, anatomy and physiology, ancient history, ancient world history, animal science, art, band, basic language skills, biology, biology-AP, British literature (honors), business law, calculus, calculus-AP, campus ministry, Catholic belief and practice, ceramics, chemistry, chemistry-AP, Christian doctrine, Christian education, Christian scripture, Christian testament, Christianity, church history, Civil War, civil war history, clayworking, college planning, communications, comparative politics, comparative religion, constitutional history of U.S., constitutional law, digital art, digital photography, drama, drawing, earth science, economics, English literature, English-AP, environmental science, European history-AP, family living, forensics, French, general science, geography, geometry, government, government-AP, health, history, history of the Catholic Church, history-AP, honors algebra, honors English, human anatomy, humanities, lab science, logic, New Testament, participation in sports, peace and justice, peer ministry, photography, physical fitness, physics, physics-AP, portfolio art, psychology-AP, publications, research, senior composition, sociology, Spanish, speech, sports, studio art-AP, theater arts, U.S. government and politics-AP, U.S. history, U.S. history-AP, United States government-AP, weight training, zoology.

Graduation Requirements Arts and fine arts (art, music, dance, drama), English, mathematics, physical education (includes health), science, social studies (includes history), speech, theology.

Special Academic Programs Advanced Placement exam preparation; honors section; independent study.

College Admission Counseling 85 students graduated in 2013; all went to college. Median composite ACT: 24. 32% scored over 26 on composite ACT.

Student Life Upper grades have uniform requirement, student council, honor system. Discipline rests primarily with faculty. Attendance at religious services is required.

Tuition and Aid Tuition installment plan (The Tuition Plan, Academic Management Services Plan). Tuition reduction for siblings, merit scholarship grants, need-based scholarship grants available.

Admissions Traditional secondary-level entrance grade is 9. For fall 2013, 79 students applied for upper-level admission, 79 were accepted, 79 enrolled. High School Placement Test required. Deadline for receipt of application materials: none. Application fee required: $100. Interview required.

Athletics Interscholastic: baseball (boys), basketball (b,g), cheering (g), cross-country running (b,g), football (b), ice hockey (b), pom squad (g), soccer (b,g), softball (g), tennis (b,g), track and field (b,g), volleyball (g), wrestling (b); coed interscholastic: bowling, equestrian sports, figure skating, golf. 1 PE instructor.

Computers Computers are regularly used in digital applications, research skills, speech classes. Computer network features include on-campus library services, Internet access, Internet filtering or blocking technology. Computer access in designated common areas is available to students. Students grades are available online.

Contact Mr. Joseph J. Whalen, Principal. 734-284-1875. Fax: 734-284-9304. E-mail: whalenj@gabrielrichard.org. Website: www.gabrielrichard.org

THE GALLOWAY SCHOOL

215 West Wieuca Road NW
Atlanta, Georgia 30342

Head of School: Mrs. Suzanna Jemsby

General Information Coeducational day college-preparatory, arts, and technology school. Grades P3–12. Founded: 1969. Setting: suburban. 8-acre campus. 4 buildings on campus. Approved or accredited by Academy of Orton-Gillingham Practitioners and Educators, Georgia Independent School Association, Southern Association of Colleges and Schools, Southern Association of Independent Schools, and Georgia Department of Education. Member of National Association of Independent Schools and Secondary School Admission Test Board. Endowment: $14 million. Total enrollment: 769. Upper school average class size: 15. Upper school faculty-student ratio: 1:11. There are 171 required school days per year for Upper School students. Upper School students typically attend 5 days per week. The average school day consists of 7 hours.

Upper School Student Profile Grade 6: 63 students (31 boys, 32 girls); Grade 7: 66 students (36 boys, 30 girls); Grade 8: 60 students (32 boys, 28 girls); Grade 9: 81 students (37 boys, 44 girls); Grade 10: 63 students (24 boys, 39 girls); Grade 11: 57 students (32 boys, 25 girls); Grade 12: 69 students (34 boys, 35 girls).

Faculty School total: 39. In upper school: 13 men, 13 women; 26 have advanced degrees.

Subjects Offered 20th century American writers, 20th century history, 20th century world history, 3-dimensional design, acting, advanced biology, advanced chemistry, advanced computer applications, advanced math, Advanced Placement courses, advanced studio art-AP, algebra, American Civil War, American culture, American government, American history, American history-AP, American literature, American literature-AP, analytic geometry, animation, art history, audio visual/media, band, biology, biology-AP, British literature, British literature-AP, calculus, calculus-AP, ceramics, chemistry, chemistry-AP, chorus, comparative government and politics-AP, composition-AP, computer animation, computer applications, computer graphics, concert band, desktop publishing, digital art, digital music, digital photography, drama, economics, electives, English, English-AP, filmmaking, fine arts, French, geometry, guidance, history, integrated physics, language arts, Latin, library, mathematics, music, physical education, physical science, political science, pre-calculus, public speaking, science, senior composition, social studies, Spanish, technology, U.S. government and politics-AP, visual arts, world geography, world history, world literature.

Graduation Requirements Arts and fine arts (art, music, dance, drama), computers, electives, English, foreign language, health and wellness, mathematics, science, social studies (includes history).

Special Academic Programs Advanced Placement exam preparation; accelerated programs; independent study; term-away projects; study at local college for college credit; academic accommodation for the gifted, the musically talented, and the artistically talented.

College Admission Counseling 62 students graduated in 2013; all went to college, including College of Charleston; Emory University; New York University; University of Dayton; University of Georgia. Median SAT critical reading: 660, median SAT math: 620, median SAT writing: 660, median combined SAT: 1970, median composite ACT: 28. 74% scored over 600 on SAT critical reading, 61% scored over 600 on SAT math, 81% scored over 600 on SAT writing, 82% scored over 1800 on combined SAT, 67% scored over 26 on composite ACT.

Student Life Upper grades have student council, honor system. Discipline rests primarily with faculty.

Summer Programs Remediation, enrichment, advancement, sports, art/fine arts programs offered; held both on and off campus; held at Athletics Complex; accepts boys and girls; open to students from other schools. 55 students usually enrolled. 2014 schedule: June 10 to July 26. Application deadline: June 3.

Tuition and Aid Day student tuition: $21,370. Tuition installment plan (FACTS Tuition Payment Plan, 50/50 - twice a year paymements, Payroll deductions, Special

arrangements provided to families based upon their circumstances). Need-based scholarship grants available. In 2013–14, 25% of upper-school students received aid. Total amount of financial aid awarded in 2013–14: $1,033,485.

Admissions Traditional secondary-level entrance grade is 9. For fall 2013, 123 students applied for upper-level admission, 53 were accepted, 36 enrolled. Admissions testing and SSAT required. Deadline for receipt of application materials: February 4. Application fee required: $100. On-campus interview required.

Athletics Interscholastic: baseball (boys), basketball (b,g), golf (b,g), soccer (b,g), softball (g), swimming and diving (b,g), tennis (b,g), track and field (b,g), volleyball (g); coed interscholastic: cross-country running, ultimate Frisbee. 1 PE instructor, 3 coaches, 1 athletic trainer.

Computers Computers are regularly used in art, desktop publishing, drawing and design, English, graphic arts, information technology, introduction to technology, journalism, keyboarding, literary magazine, mathematics, multimedia, music, newspaper, photography, publishing, research skills, science, technology, theater, Web site design, yearbook classes. Computer network features include on-campus library services, online commercial services, Internet access, wireless campus network, Internet filtering or blocking technology, print sharing. Campus intranet, student e-mail accounts, and computer access in designated common areas are available to students. Students grades are available online. The school has a published electronic and media policy.

Contact Elizabeth King, Director of Admissions. 404-252-8389 Ext. 106. Fax: 404-252-7770. E-mail: e.king@gallowayschool.org. Website: www.gallowayschool.org

GANN ACADEMY (THE NEW JEWISH HIGH SCHOOL OF GREATER BOSTON)

333 Forest Street
Waltham, Massachusetts 02452

Head of School: Rabbi Marc A. Baker

General Information Coeducational day college-preparatory, arts, and religious studies school, affiliated with Jewish faith. Grades 9–12. Founded: 1997. Setting: suburban. Nearest major city is Boston. 20-acre campus. 2 buildings on campus. Approved or accredited by Association of Independent Schools in New England, New England Association of Schools and Colleges, and Massachusetts Department of Education. Member of National Association of Independent Schools. Endowment: $9 million. Total enrollment: 309. Upper school average class size: 14. Upper school faculty-student ratio: 1:5. There are 165 required school days per year for Upper School students. Upper School students typically attend 5 days per week. The average school day consists of 8 hours.

Upper School Student Profile Grade 9: 59 students (30 boys, 29 girls); Grade 10: 72 students (36 boys, 36 girls); Grade 11: 85 students (36 boys, 49 girls); Grade 12: 93 students (45 boys, 48 girls). 100% of students are Jewish.

Faculty School total: 69. In upper school: 29 men, 40 women; 52 have advanced degrees.

Subjects Offered Advanced Placement courses, algebra, American history-AP, American literature-AP, art history, arts, Bible as literature, biology, calculus, calculus-AP, chemistry, computer science, creative arts, creative writing, drama, English, French, geometry, health and wellness, Hebrew, history, Holocaust, Jewish history, Judaic studies, Mandarin, modern dance, music, photography, physics, pre-calculus, Rabbinic literature, robotics, Spanish.

Graduation Requirements Arts, athletics, Bible as literature, English, health, Hebrew, history, mathematics, Rabbinic literature, science.

Special Academic Programs Advanced Placement exam preparation; study abroad.

College Admission Counseling 62 students graduated in 2013; 44 went to college, including Brandeis University; Cornell University; Tulane University; University of Massachusetts Amherst; University of Rochester; Yale University. Other: 2 entered military service, 16 had other specific plans. Median SAT critical reading: 640, median SAT math: 645, median SAT writing: 660, median combined SAT: 1950, median composite ACT: 29.

Student Life Upper grades have specified standards of dress, student council, honor system. Discipline rests primarily with faculty. Attendance at religious services is required.

Tuition and Aid Day student tuition: $33,975. Tuition installment plan (FACTS Tuition Payment Plan). Need-based scholarship grants available. In 2013–14, 41% of upper-school students received aid. Total amount of financial aid awarded in 2013–14: $2,200,000.

Admissions Traditional secondary-level entrance grade is 9. For fall 2013, 115 students applied for upper-level admission, 112 were accepted, 64 enrolled. SSAT required. Deadline for receipt of application materials: January 31. Application fee required: $100. On-campus interview required.

Athletics Interscholastic: baseball (boys), basketball (b,g), cross-country running (b,g), lacrosse (b,g), soccer (b,g), softball (g), tennis (b,g), volleyball (g); intramural: basketball (b,g), tennis (b,g), volleyball (g); coed interscholastic: fitness, juggling, martial arts, ultimate Frisbee; coed intramural: fitness, golf, modern dance, table tennis, yoga. 26 coaches, 1 athletic trainer.

Computers Computers are regularly used in all classes. Computer network features include on-campus library services, Internet access, wireless campus network, Internet filtering or blocking technology, computer lab. Campus intranet, student e-mail accounts, and computer access in designated common areas are available to students. Students grades are available online. The school has a published electronic and media policy.

Contact Efraim Yudewitz, Director of Admissions. 781-642-6800. Fax: 781-642-6805. E-mail: eyudewitz@gannacademy.org. Website: www.gannacademy.org/

GARRISON FOREST SCHOOL

300 Garrison Forest Road
Owings Mills, Maryland 21117

Head of School: Mr. G. Peter O'Neill Jr.

General Information Girls' boarding and day (coeducational in lower grades) college-preparatory, arts, technology, Women in Science & Engineering (WISE), and The James Center at Garrison Forest School school. Boarding girls grades 8–12, day boys grades N–PK, day girls grades N–12. Founded: 1910. Setting: suburban. Nearest major city is Baltimore. Students are housed in single-sex dormitories. 110-acre campus. 18 buildings on campus. Approved or accredited by Association of Independent Maryland Schools, Middle States Association of Colleges and Schools, The Association of Boarding Schools, and Maryland Department of Education. Member of National Association of Independent Schools and Secondary School Admission Test Board. Endowment: $37 million. Total enrollment: 628. Upper school average class size: 14. Upper school faculty-student ratio: 1:8. There are 167 required school days per year for Upper School students. Upper School students typically attend 5 days per week. The average school day consists of 7 hours.

Upper School Student Profile Grade 9: 64 students (64 girls); Grade 10: 82 students (82 girls); Grade 11: 70 students (70 girls); Grade 12: 75 students (75 girls). 22% of students are boarding students. 85% are state residents. 11 states are represented in upper school student body. 14% are international students. International students from China, Germany, Mexico, and Republic of Korea.

Faculty School total: 116. In upper school: 6 men, 39 women; 32 have advanced degrees; 22 reside on campus.

Subjects Offered 3-dimensional art, 3-dimensional design, advanced chemistry, advanced math, algebra, American foreign policy, American government, American history, American history-AP, American literature, anatomy, ancient world history, animation, applied music, art, art history, art history-AP, arts and crafts, biology, calculus, calculus-AP, ceramics, chemistry, chemistry-AP, Chinese, Chinese studies, choral music, college counseling, college placement, college planning, computer science, computer skills, creative writing, dance, decision making skills, design, desktop publishing, digital applications, digital art, digital imaging, digital photography, drama, drawing, ecology, English, English composition, English literature, English-AP, environmental science-AP, environmental studies, equestrian sports, equine science, equitation, ESL, ethics, film studies, filmmaking, fine arts, French, French language-AP, French-AP, geometry, health and safety, health and wellness, history-AP, jewelry making, Latin, Latin-AP, leadership and service, life skills, mathematics, music, musical productions, painting, peace studies, peer counseling, philosophy, photography, physical education, physics, physics-AP, play production, portfolio art, pre-calculus, public policy, public policy issues and action, public service, public speaking, publications, science, science project, science research, sculpture, social justice, Spanish, Spanish language-AP, Spanish-AP, sports, stage design, statistics, student government, study skills, technological applications, technology, technology/design, theater, trigonometry, U.S. history-AP, values and decisions, voice ensemble, world history, writing, yearbook.

Graduation Requirements Arts and fine arts (art, music, dance, drama), decision making skills, English, foreign language, mathematics, physical education (includes health), science, social studies (includes history).

Special Academic Programs 12 Advanced Placement exams for which test preparation is offered; honors section; independent study; term-away projects; academic accommodation for the gifted, the musically talented, and the artistically talented; ESL (22 students enrolled).

College Admission Counseling 73 students graduated in 2013; all went to college, including Boston University; Columbia University; The Johns Hopkins University; University of Maryland, College Park; University of South Carolina; University of Virginia. 50% scored over 600 on SAT critical reading, 50% scored over 600 on SAT math, 50% scored over 600 on SAT writing, 50% scored over 26 on composite ACT.

Student Life Upper grades have uniform requirement, student council, honor system. Discipline rests equally with students and faculty.

Summer Programs Sports, art/fine arts programs offered; session focuses on extracurricular activities and young children; held on campus; accepts boys and girls; open to students from other schools. 400 students usually enrolled. 2014 schedule: June 16 to August 22. Application deadline: June 1.

Tuition and Aid Day student tuition: $26,110; 7-day tuition and room/board: $48,200. Tuition installment plan (FACTS Tuition Payment Plan). Merit scholarship grants, need-based scholarship grants, Merit-based Legacy Scholarship available. In 2013–14, 34% of upper-school students received aid; total upper-school merit-scholarship money awarded: $61,375. Total amount of financial aid awarded in 2013–14: $3,174,485.

Admissions Traditional secondary-level entrance grade is 9. For fall 2013, 162 students applied for upper-level admission, 81 were accepted, 35 enrolled. Admissions testing, ISEE, SSAT, TOEFL or WISC-R or WISC-III required. Deadline for receipt of application materials: December 13. Application fee required: $50. Interview required.

Athletics Interscholastic: badminton, basketball, cross-country running, equestrian sports, field hockey, golf, horseback riding, indoor soccer, indoor track, lacrosse, polo, soccer, softball, tennis, winter (indoor) track, winter soccer; intramural: aerobics, aerobics/dance, bowling, dance, fitness, horseback riding, modern dance, physical fitness, squash, strength & conditioning, swimming and diving, volleyball, yoga. 5 PE instructors, 12 coaches, 1 athletic trainer.

Computers Computers are regularly used in animation, art, college planning, design, desktop publishing, digital applications, English, ESL, foreign language, French, history, humanities, literary magazine, mathematics, newspaper, photography, publications, science, Spanish, study skills, technology, word processing, writing, yearbook classes. Computer network features include on-campus library services, Internet access, wireless campus network, Internet filtering or blocking technology, Moodle. Student e-mail accounts and computer access in designated common areas are available to students. Students grades are available online. The school has a published electronic and media policy.

Contact Mrs. Martha O'Connell, Interim Director of Admission and Senior College Counselor. 410-559-3111. Fax: 410-363-8441. E-mail: gfsinfo@gfs.org. Website: www.gfs.org

GASTON DAY SCHOOL

2001 Gaston Day School Road
Gastonia, North Carolina 28056

Head of School: Dr. Richard E. Rankin

General Information Coeducational day college-preparatory and arts school. Grades PS–12. Founded: 1967. Setting: suburban. Nearest major city is Charlotte. 60-acre campus. 4 buildings on campus. Approved or accredited by Southern Association of Colleges and Schools, Southern Association of Independent Schools, and North Carolina Department of Education. Member of National Association of Independent Schools. Endowment: $2.1 million. Total enrollment: 512. Upper school average class size: 12. Upper school faculty-student ratio: 1:7. There are 180 required school days per year for Upper School students. Upper School students typically attend 5 days per week. The average school day consists of 7 hours and 15 minutes.

Upper School Student Profile Grade 9: 46 students (18 boys, 28 girls); Grade 10: 37 students (15 boys, 22 girls); Grade 11: 41 students (20 boys, 21 girls); Grade 12: 34 students (19 boys, 15 girls).

Faculty School total: 53. In upper school: 7 men, 15 women; 14 have advanced degrees.

Subjects Offered Advanced chemistry, Advanced Placement courses, advanced studio art-AP, algebra, American history-AP, American literature, anatomy and physiology, art, band, biology, biology-AP, British literature, British literature (honors), calculus-AP, chemistry, chemistry-AP, choral music, chorus, creative writing, drama, English language and composition-AP, English language-AP, English literature and composition-AP, environmental science, environmental science-AP, film and literature, fine arts, French, general science, geometry, government/civics, honors algebra, honors English, honors geometry, honors U.S. history, honors world history, jazz band, journalism, learning lab, physics, pre-calculus, senior internship, Spanish, Spanish-AP, statistics-AP, student government, studio art-AP, study skills, U.S. government, U.S. history, U.S. history-AP, United States government-AP, visual arts, weight training, world literature, yearbook.

Graduation Requirements Arts and fine arts (art, music, dance, drama), electives, English, foreign language, mathematics, physical education (includes health), science, social studies (includes history), 25 hours of community service per year, seniors must complete a senior project.

Special Academic Programs Advanced Placement exam preparation; honors section; independent study; academic accommodation for the gifted; ESL (9 students enrolled).

College Admission Counseling 31 students graduated in 2013; all went to college, including Boston University; Pepperdine University; St. Lawrence University; The University of Alabama; The University of North Carolina at Chapel Hill; University of South Carolina. Mean SAT critical reading: 570, mean SAT math: 603, mean SAT writing: 598, mean combined SAT: 1771, mean composite ACT: 26.

Student Life Upper grades have specified standards of dress, student council, honor system. Discipline rests primarily with faculty.

Summer Programs Remediation, enrichment, advancement, sports, art/fine arts, computer instruction programs offered; session focuses on academic enrichment, advancement in sports and arts; held on campus; accepts boys and girls; open to students from other schools. 320 students usually enrolled. 2014 schedule: June to August.

Tuition and Aid Day student tuition: $14,390. Tuition installment plan (monthly payment plans, individually arranged payment plans). Merit scholarship grants, need-based scholarship grants available. In 2013–14, 55% of upper-school students received aid; total upper-school merit-scholarship money awarded: $147,914. Total amount of financial aid awarded in 2013–14: $199,200.

Admissions Traditional secondary-level entrance grade is 9. For fall 2013, 39 students applied for upper-level admission, 28 were accepted, 23 enrolled. ACT, ISEE, PSAT or SAT required. Deadline for receipt of application materials: none. Application fee required: $50. On-campus interview required.

Athletics Interscholastic: baseball (boys), basketball (b,g), cheering (g), cross-country running (b,g), golf (b), soccer (b,g), swimming and diving (b,g), tennis (b,g), track and field (b,g), volleyball (g); intramural: fitness (b,g). 1 PE instructor, 11 coaches, 1 athletic trainer.

Computers Computers are regularly used in art, English, foreign language, history, journalism, mathematics, newspaper, science, yearbook classes. Computer network features include on-campus library services, online commercial services, Internet access, wireless campus network, Internet filtering or blocking technology. Student e-mail accounts and computer access in designated common areas are available to students. Students grades are available online. The school has a published electronic and media policy.

Contact Mrs. Martha Jayne Rhyne, Director of Admission. 704-864-7744 Ext. 174. Fax: 704-865-3813. E-mail: mrhyne@gastonday.org. Website: www.gastonday.org

GATEWAY SCHOOL

Arlington, Texas
See Special Needs Schools section.

GEORGE SCHOOL

1690 Newtown Langhorne Road
PO Box 4460
Newtown, Pennsylvania 18940

Head of School: Nancy O. Starmer

General Information Coeducational boarding and day college-preparatory, arts, religious studies, bilingual studies, and technology school, affiliated with Society of Friends. Grades 9–12. Founded: 1893. Setting: suburban. Nearest major city is Philadelphia. Students are housed in single-sex dormitories. 265-acre campus. 19 buildings on campus. Approved or accredited by Friends Council on Education, International Baccalaureate Organization, Middle States Association of Colleges and Schools, The Association of Boarding Schools, The College Board, and Pennsylvania Department of Education. Member of National Association of Independent Schools and Secondary School Admission Test Board. Endowment: $134.6 million. Total enrollment: 545. Upper school average class size: 14. Upper school faculty-student ratio: 1:7. There are 165 required school days per year for Upper School students. Upper School students typically attend 5 days per week. The average school day consists of 6 hours.

Upper School Student Profile Grade 9: 129 students (72 boys, 57 girls); Grade 10: 137 students (60 boys, 77 girls); Grade 11: 146 students (66 boys, 80 girls); Grade 12: 133 students (64 boys, 69 girls). 51% of students are boarding students. 63% are state residents. 22 states are represented in upper school student body. 27% are international students. International students from China, Germany, Hong Kong, Republic of Korea, Taiwan, and Viet Nam; 39 other countries represented in student body. 15% of students are members of Society of Friends.

Faculty School total: 84. In upper school: 32 men, 44 women; 61 have advanced degrees; 55 reside on campus.

Subjects Offered African-American history, algebra, American history-AP, American literature, American literature-AP, art, Asian history, astronomy, athletics, Bible studies, biology, biology-AP, calculus, calculus-AP, ceramics, chemistry, chemistry-AP, Chinese, community service, composition, computer science, dance, drama, drawing, driver education, English, English literature, English literature and composition-AP, English literature-AP, English-AP, environmental science, ESL, fine arts, French, French language-AP, geometry, global studies, health, history-AP, horticulture, Latin, Latin American history, life science, literature, mathematics, Middle Eastern history, modern dance, modern European history, music theory, orchestra, painting, philosophy, photography, physical education, physics, pre-calculus, probability and statistics, religion, Russian history, science, science and technology, Spanish, Spanish language-AP, stagecraft, statistics-AP, theater, theory of knowledge, video film production, visual arts, vocal ensemble, woodworking, work camp program, world history, world literature.

Graduation Requirements Arts and fine arts (art, music, dance, drama), English, foreign language, geometry, mathematics, performing arts, religion (includes Bible studies and theology), science, social studies (includes history), 65 hours of community service.

Special Academic Programs International Baccalaureate program; Advanced Placement exam preparation; honors section; independent study; ESL.

College Admission Counseling 133 students graduated in 2013; 130 went to college, including Boston University; Drexel University; Guilford College; New York University; Skidmore College; University of Vermont. Other: 3 had other specific plans.

Student Life Upper grades have specified standards of dress, student council, honor system. Discipline rests equally with students and faculty. Attendance at religious services is required.

Summer Programs Enrichment, advancement, ESL programs offered; session focuses on academic and social preparation; held on campus; accepts boys and girls; not open to students from other schools. 80 students usually enrolled.

Tuition and Aid Day student tuition: $34,450; 7-day tuition and room/board: $51,250. Tuition installment plan (monthly payment plans, individually arranged payment plans). Merit scholarship grants, need-based scholarship grants available. In 2013–14, 50% of upper-school students received aid; total upper-school merit-scholarship money awarded: $300,250. Total amount of financial aid awarded in 2013–14: $8,364,060.

Admissions Traditional secondary-level entrance grade is 9. For fall 2013, 652 students applied for upper-level admission, 308 were accepted, 178 enrolled. SSAT or TOEFL or SLEP required. Deadline for receipt of application materials: February 1. Application fee required: $50. Interview required.

Athletics Interscholastic: baseball (boys), basketball (b,g), cross-country running (b,g), field hockey (g), football (b), hockey (g), lacrosse (b,g), soccer (b,g), softball (g), swimming and diving (b,g), tennis (b,g), track and field (b,g), volleyball (g), wrestling (b,g); coed interscholastic: cheering, equestrian sports, golf, horseback riding, indoor track, modern dance, winter (indoor) track; coed intramural: aerobics/dance, dance, horseback riding, strength & conditioning, yoga. 5 PE instructors, 5 coaches, 1 athletic trainer.

Computers Computers are regularly used in English, ESL, foreign language, history, mathematics, newspaper, photography, science, yearbook classes. Computer network features include on-campus library services, online commercial services, Internet access, wireless campus network, Internet filtering or blocking technology. Campus intranet and student e-mail accounts are available to students. Students grades are available online. The school has a published electronic and media policy.

Contact Jenna K. Davis, Interim Director of Admission and Financial Aid. 215-579-6547. Fax: 215-579-6549. E-mail: admission@georgeschool.org. Website: www.georgeschool.org

GEORGE STEVENS ACADEMY

23 Union Street
Blue Hill, Maine 04614

Head of School: Mr. Paul Perkinson

General Information Coeducational boarding and day college-preparatory and general academic school. Grades 9–12. Founded: 1803. Setting: small town. Nearest major city is Bangor. Students are housed in single-sex dormitories and host family homes. 20-acre campus. 6 buildings on campus. Approved or accredited by Independent Schools of Northern New England, New England Association of Schools and Colleges, The College Board, and Maine Department of Education. Member of Secondary School Admission Test Board. Endowment: $7 million. Total enrollment: 313. Upper school average class size: 15. Upper school faculty-student ratio: 1:10. There are 180 required school days per year for Upper School students. Upper School students typically attend 5 days per week. The average school day consists of 6 hours and 30 minutes.

Upper School Student Profile Grade 9: 78 students (35 boys, 43 girls); Grade 10: 84 students (42 boys, 42 girls); Grade 11: 69 students (46 boys, 23 girls); Grade 12: 82 students (42 boys, 40 girls). 8% of students are boarding students. 86% are state residents. 2 states are represented in upper school student body. 14% are international students. International students from Australia, China, France, Italy, Japan, and Republic of Korea.

Faculty School total: 34. In upper school: 17 men, 17 women; 18 have advanced degrees; 2 reside on campus.

Subjects Offered 20th century history, 3-dimensional design, advanced chemistry, advanced math, Advanced Placement courses, algebra, American literature, American literature-AP, art, art history, art-AP, arts and crafts, band, biology, British literature (honors), business mathematics, calculus-AP, carpentry, chamber groups, chemistry, computer applications, computer literacy, creative writing, critical thinking, desktop publishing, developmental language skills, drafting, drawing, driver education, earth science, electives, English, English-AP, environmental science, environmental science-AP, ESL, European history, fine arts, foreign language, forensics, French, general math, general science, geometry, German, health education, history, history-AP, honors algebra, honors English, honors geometry, honors U.S. history, human geography - AP, humanities, independent study, industrial arts, industrial technology, instrumental music, internship, jazz band, jazz ensemble, lab science, languages, Latin, literature, literature-AP, marine science, mathematics, mathematics-AP, mechanics, model United Nations, modern history, modern languages, modern problems, music, music theory, musical productions, mythology, personal fitness, photo shop, photography, physical education, physics, pre-algebra, pre-calculus, printmaking, psychology, reading/study skills, remedial study skills, science, senior project, shop, small engine repair, social issues, social sciences, Spanish, speech and debate, sports, statistics-AP, street law, student government, technology/design, TOEFL preparation, transportation technology, U.S. history, U.S. history-AP, Western civilization, wilderness education, woodworking, work-study, World-Wide-Web publishing, writing.

Graduation Requirements Arts and fine arts (art, music, dance, drama), electives, English, foreign language, history, mathematics, physical education (includes health), science, social sciences, U.S. history, senior debate.

Special Academic Programs Advanced Placement exam preparation; honors section; accelerated programs; independent study; term-away projects; study at local college for college credit; study abroad; academic accommodation for the gifted, the musically talented, and the artistically talented; remedial reading and/or remedial writing; remedial math; special instructional classes for deaf students, blind students; ESL (24 students enrolled).

College Admission Counseling 60 students graduated in 2012; 58 went to college, including Bowdoin College; Maine Maritime Academy; Simmons College; University of Maine; University of Southern Maine; University of Vermont. Other: 1 went to work, 1 entered military service. Mean SAT critical reading: 499, mean SAT math: 526, mean SAT writing: 508.

Student Life Upper grades have student council. Discipline rests primarily with faculty.

Tuition and Aid 7-day tuition and room/board: $37,400. Tuition installment plan (monthly payment plans, individually arranged payment plans). Need-based scholarship grants available. In 2012–13, 1% of upper-school students received aid.

Admissions Traditional secondary-level entrance grade is 9. International English Language Test, SSAT or TOEFL or SLEP required. Deadline for receipt of application materials: March 1. Application fee required: $75. Interview required.

Athletics Interscholastic: baseball (boys), basketball (b,g), cheering (b,g), cross-country running (b,g), golf (b,g), independent competitive sports (b,g), running (b,g), sailing (b,g), soccer (b,g), softball (g), swimming and diving (b,g), tennis (b,g), track and field (b,g), wrestling (b); coed intramural: backpacking, bocce, canoeing/kayaking, croquet, dance, dance team, fitness, fitness walking, flag football, floor hockey, Frisbee, hiking/backpacking, jogging, kayaking, modern dance, ocean paddling, outdoor activities, outdoor adventure, outdoor education, outdoor recreation, outdoor skills, paddle tennis, physical fitness, physical training, running, sailing, skateboarding, skiing (cross-country), skiing (downhill), snowboarding, snowshoeing, strength & conditioning, table tennis, ultimate Frisbee, volleyball, walking, weight lifting, weight training, wilderness, winter walking, yoga. 2 PE instructors, 26 coaches.

Computers Computers are regularly used in all academic, business skills, computer applications, creative writing, design, desktop publishing, drafting, English, foreign language, graphic design, photography, Web site design classes. Computer network features include on-campus library services, online commercial services, Internet access, wireless campus network, Internet filtering or blocking technology. Student e-mail accounts and computer access in designated common areas are available to students. Students grades are available online. The school has a published electronic and media policy.

Contact Mrs. Libby Chamberlain, Director of Admissions. 207-374-2808 Ext. 134. Fax: 207-374-2982. E-mail: l.chamberlain@georgestevens.org. Website: www.georgestevensacademy.org

GEORGETOWN DAY SCHOOL

4200 Davenport Street NW
Washington, District of Columbia 20016

Head of School: Russell Shaw

General Information Coeducational day college-preparatory, arts, and athletics school. Grades PK–12. Founded: 1945. Setting: urban. 6-acre campus. 1 building on campus. Approved or accredited by Association of Independent Maryland Schools, Middle States Association of Colleges and Schools, and District of Columbia Department of Education. Member of National Association of Independent Schools and Secondary School Admission Test Board. Endowment: $10.5 million. Total enrollment: 1,075. Upper school average class size: 15. Upper school faculty-student ratio: 1:7. There are 170 required school days per year for Upper School students. Upper School students typically attend 5 days per week. The average school day consists of 10 hours.

Upper School Student Profile Grade 9: 114 students (55 boys, 59 girls); Grade 10: 117 students (63 boys, 54 girls); Grade 11: 114 students (56 boys, 58 girls); Grade 12: 113 students (56 boys, 57 girls).

Faculty School total: 160. In upper school: 30 men, 40 women; 50 have advanced degrees.

Subjects Offered Algebra, American history, American literature, anthropology, art, art history, astronomy, biology, calculus, ceramics, chemistry, community service, computer science, creative writing, dance, drama, driver education, economics, English, environmental science-AP, European history, fine arts, French, geometry, government/civics, history, Latin, law, linear algebra, mathematics, music, photography, physical education, physics, psychology, science, social studies, Spanish, statistics-AP, theater, trigonometry, world history.

Graduation Requirements Arts and fine arts (art, music, dance, drama), English, foreign language, literature, mathematics, physical education (includes health), science, social studies (includes history). Community service is required.

Special Academic Programs 20 Advanced Placement exams for which test preparation is offered; honors section; independent study.

College Admission Counseling Colleges students went to include Brown University; Duke University; Harvard University; Stanford University; Wesleyan University; Yale University.

Student Life Upper grades have student council, honor system. Discipline rests primarily with faculty.

Summer Programs Enrichment programs offered; session focuses on based on interest; held on campus; accepts boys and girls; open to students from other schools. 120 students usually enrolled. 2014 schedule: June to August.

Tuition and Aid Day student tuition: $29,990–$34,325. Tuition installment plan (Insured Tuition Payment Plan, Academic Management Services Plan, monthly payment plans). Need-based scholarship grants available. In 2013–14, 20% of upper-school students received aid. Total amount of financial aid awarded in 2013–14: $1,000,000.

Admissions Traditional secondary-level entrance grade is 9. For fall 2013, 250 students applied for upper-level admission, 75 were accepted, 60 enrolled. ISEE or SSAT required. Deadline for receipt of application materials: January 10. Application fee required: $65. On-campus interview required.

Athletics Interscholastic: baseball (boys), basketball (b,g), crew (b,g), cross-country running (b,g), lacrosse (b,g); intramural: indoor soccer (b,g); coed interscholastic: golf, swimming and diving; coed intramural: flag football. 5 PE instructors, 6 coaches, 1 athletic trainer.

Computers Computers are regularly used in art, English, foreign language, history, mathematics, music, science classes. Computer network features include on-campus library services, online commercial services, Internet access, wireless campus network. Student e-mail accounts are available to students. The school has a published electronic and media policy.

Contact Vincent W. Rowe Jr., Director of Enrollment Management and Financial Aid. 202-274-3210. Fax: 202-274-3211. E-mail: vrowe@gds.org. Website: www.gds.org

GEORGETOWN PREPARATORY SCHOOL

10900 Rockville Pike
North Bethesda, Maryland 20852-3299

Head of School: Mr. Jeff Jones

General Information Boys' boarding and day college-preparatory, arts, religious studies, and technology school, affiliated with Roman Catholic Church. Grades 9–12. Founded: 1789. Setting: suburban. Nearest major city is Washington, DC. Students are housed in single-sex dormitories. 92-acre campus. 8 buildings on campus. Approved or accredited by Jesuit Secondary Education Association, Middle States Association of Colleges and Schools, National Catholic Education Association, The Association of Boarding Schools, and Maryland Department of Education. Member of National Association of Independent Schools and Secondary School Admission Test Board. Endowment: $20 million. Total enrollment: 490. Upper school average class size: 16. Upper school faculty-student ratio: 1:8. There are 150 required school days per year for Upper School students. Upper School students typically attend 5 days per week. The average school day consists of 6 hours and 30 minutes.

Upper School Student Profile Grade 9: 111 students (111 boys); Grade 10: 133 students (133 boys); Grade 11: 124 students (124 boys); Grade 12: 122 students (122 boys). 20% of students are boarding students. 60% are state residents. 18 states are represented in upper school student body. 30% are international students. International students from China, Mexico, Nigeria, Republic of Korea, Spain, and Taiwan; 24 other countries represented in student body. 70% of students are Roman Catholic.

Faculty School total: 60. In upper school: 40 men, 20 women; 55 have advanced degrees; 18 reside on campus.

Subjects Offered Algebra, American history, American literature, art, art history, Bible studies, biology, calculus, chemistry, computer programming, computer science, drama, driver education, economics, English, English literature, ESL, ethics, European history, fine arts, French, geometry, German, government/civics, history, journalism, Latin, mathematics, music, philosophy, physical education, physics, psychology, religion, science, social studies, Spanish, speech, stained glass, theater, theology, trigonometry, world history, world literature.

Graduation Requirements Arts and fine arts (art, music, dance, drama), classics, English, foreign language, mathematics, music theory, religion (includes Bible studies and theology), science, social studies (includes history), two years of Latin. Community service is required.

Special Academic Programs 24 Advanced Placement exams for which test preparation is offered; honors section; independent study; term-away projects; study abroad; academic accommodation for the gifted; ESL (14 students enrolled).

College Admission Counseling 111 students graduated in 2013; 110 went to college, including Boston College; Georgetown University; Stanford University; University of Notre Dame; University of Pennsylvania; University of Virginia. Other: 1 entered a postgraduate year. Mean SAT critical reading: 680, mean SAT math: 683, mean SAT writing: 637, mean combined SAT: 2000, mean composite ACT: 27.

Student Life Upper grades have specified standards of dress, student council. Discipline rests primarily with faculty. Attendance at religious services is required.

Summer Programs Remediation, enrichment, advancement, ESL, sports programs offered; session focuses on ESL; held on campus; accepts boys and girls; open to students from other schools. 75 students usually enrolled. 2014 schedule: June 28 to August 6. Application deadline: March 1.

Tuition and Aid Day student tuition: $29,625; 7-day tuition and room/board: $50,465. Tuition installment plan (FACTS Tuition Payment Plan). Need-based scholarship grants, middle-income loans available. In 2013–14, 25% of upper-school students received aid. Total amount of financial aid awarded in 2013–14: $2,000,000.

Admissions Traditional secondary-level entrance grade is 9. For fall 2013, 400 students applied for upper-level admission, 160 were accepted, 129 enrolled. SSAT required. Deadline for receipt of application materials: January 10. Application fee required: $100. Interview required.

Athletics Interscholastic: baseball, basketball, cross-country running, diving, fencing, football, golf, ice hockey, indoor soccer, indoor track & field, lacrosse, rugby, running, soccer, swimming and diving, tennis, track and field, winter (indoor) track, wrestling; intramural: basketball, canoeing/kayaking, fitness, flag football, floor hockey, Frisbee, hiking/backpacking, ice skating, indoor hockey, kayaking, life saving, martial arts, mountain biking, Nautilus, ocean paddling, paddle tennis, paint ball, physical fitness, physical training, power lifting, racquetball, rappelling, rock climbing, ropes courses, scuba diving, skiing (downhill), snowboarding, soccer, softball, strength & conditioning, table tennis, tennis, ultimate Frisbee, volleyball, weight training. 16 coaches, 3 athletic trainers.

Computers Computers are regularly used in art, classics, data processing, English, French, history, Latin, mathematics, music, religious studies, science, Spanish, writing classes. Computer network features include on-campus library services, online commercial services, Internet access, wireless campus network, Internet filtering or blocking technology. Campus intranet, student e-mail accounts, and computer access in designated common areas are available to students. Students grades are available online. The school has a published electronic and media policy.

Contact Mr. Brian J. Gilbert, Dean of Admissions. 301-214-1215. Fax: 301-493-6128. E-mail: admissions@gprep.org. Website: www.gprep.org

GEORGETOWN VISITATION PREPARATORY SCHOOL

1524 35th Street NW
Washington, District of Columbia 20007

Head of School: Daniel M. Kerns Jr.

General Information Girls' day college-preparatory school, affiliated with Roman Catholic Church. Grades 9–12. Founded: 1799. Setting: urban. 23-acre campus. 7 buildings on campus. Approved or accredited by Association of Independent Schools of Greater Washington, Middle States Association of Colleges and Schools, National Catholic Education Association, National Independent Private Schools Association, and District of Columbia Department of Education. Member of National Association of Independent Schools. Endowment: $16.7 million. Total enrollment: 490. Upper school average class size: 15. Upper school faculty-student ratio: 1:11. There are 181 required school days per year for Upper School students. Upper School students typically attend 5 days per week. The average school day consists of 5 hours and 30 minutes.

Upper School Student Profile Grade 9: 124 students (124 girls); Grade 10: 120 students (120 girls); Grade 11: 121 students (121 girls); Grade 12: 125 students (125 girls). 93% of students are Roman Catholic.

Faculty School total: 55. In upper school: 15 men, 40 women; 40 have advanced degrees.

Subjects Offered Advanced Placement courses, advanced studio art-AP, algebra, American history, American literature, anatomy, ancient world history, anthropology, art, art history, art history-AP, art-AP, Bible studies, biochemistry, bioethics, biology, biology-AP, calculus, calculus-AP, Catholic belief and practice, chemistry, chemistry-AP, chorus, comparative political systems-AP, computer science, conceptual physics, creative writing, dance, economics, electives, English, English language and composition-AP, English literature, English literature and composition-AP, English literature-AP, English/composition-AP, environmental science, environmental science-AP, ethics, European history, European history-AP, expository writing, fine arts, French, French-AP, geometry, government-AP, government/civics, health, health and wellness, history, Latin, madrigals, mathematics, music, neuroscience, personal development, physical education, physical fitness, physics, physics-AP, pre-calculus, psychology, psychology-AP, religion, science, social sciences, social studies, Spanish, Spanish-AP, speech, speech communications, studio art-AP, theology, trigonometry, U.S. government and politics-AP, U.S. history-AP, world history.

Graduation Requirements Arts and fine arts (art, music, dance, drama), English, foreign language, history, mathematics, physical education (includes health), religion (includes Bible studies and theology), science, social studies (includes history), speech, 80 hours of community service.

Special Academic Programs 18 Advanced Placement exams for which test preparation is offered; honors section; independent study; study at local college for college credit.

College Admission Counseling 121 students graduated in 2013; all went to college, including Boston University; College of Charleston; The College of William and Mary; University of Maryland, College Park; University of Virginia; Virginia Polytechnic Institute and State University. Mean SAT critical reading: 657, mean SAT math: 624, mean SAT writing: 675.

Student Life Upper grades have uniform requirement, student council, honor system. Discipline rests primarily with faculty. Attendance at religious services is required.

Summer Programs Remediation, enrichment, sports programs offered; held on campus; accepts girls; not open to students from other schools. 100 students usually enrolled. 2014 schedule: June to July. Application deadline: April.

Tuition and Aid Day student tuition: $25,500. Tuition installment plan (FACTS Tuition Payment Plan, individually arranged payment plans). Merit scholarship grants, need-based scholarship grants available. In 2013–14, 25% of upper-school students received aid; total upper-school merit-scholarship money awarded: $55,000. Total amount of financial aid awarded in 2013–14: $1,700,000.

Admissions Traditional secondary-level entrance grade is 9. High School Placement Test or High School Placement Test (closed version) from Scholastic Testing Service required. Deadline for receipt of application materials: December 6. Application fee required: $50. On-campus interview required.

Athletics Interscholastic: aerobics/dance, basketball, crew, cross-country running, dance, diving, field hockey, fitness, indoor track, lacrosse, soccer, softball, swimming and diving, tennis, track and field, volleyball, winter (indoor) track; intramural: cheering, flag football, strength & conditioning. 3 PE instructors, 23 coaches, 1 athletic trainer.

Computers Computers are regularly used in all academic, art, English, French, history, mathematics, religion, science, Spanish classes. Computer network features include on-campus library services, online commercial services, Internet access, wireless campus network, Internet filtering or blocking technology. Campus intranet and student e-mail accounts are available to students. Students grades are available online. The school has a published electronic and media policy.

Contact Janet Keller, Director of Admissions. 202-337-3350 Ext. 2241. Fax: 202-333-3522. E-mail: jkeller@visi.org. Website: www.visi.org

GEORGE WALTON ACADEMY

One Bulldog Drive
Monroe, Georgia 30655

Head of School: Mr. William M. Nicholson

General Information Coeducational day college-preparatory, arts, and technology school. Grades K4–12. Founded: 1969. Setting: small town. Nearest major city is Atlanta. 54-acre campus. 8 buildings on campus. Approved or accredited by Georgia Independent School Association, Southern Association of Colleges and Schools, and Georgia Department of Education. Total enrollment: 878. Upper school average class size: 17. Upper school faculty-student ratio: 1:12. There are 180 required school days per year for Upper School students. Upper School students typically attend 5 days per week. The average school day consists of 6 hours and 45 minutes.

Upper School Student Profile Grade 9: 75 students (45 boys, 30 girls); Grade 10: 71 students (36 boys, 35 girls); Grade 11: 92 students (44 boys, 48 girls); Grade 12: 78 students (41 boys, 37 girls).

Faculty School total: 83. In upper school: 15 men, 38 women; 20 have advanced degrees.

Subjects Offered Algebra, American history, American literature, anatomy, art, art history, Bible studies, biology, calculus, chemistry, creative writing, drama, economics, English, English literature, environmental science, European history, fine arts, geography, geometry, government/civics, grammar, health, history, journalism, Latin, mathematics, music, photography, physical education, physics, psychology, science, social sciences, social studies, sociology, Spanish, trigonometry, world history, world literature, writing.

Graduation Requirements Arts and fine arts (art, music, dance, drama), composition, English, foreign language, mathematics, physical education (includes health), science, social sciences, social studies (includes history), all students must be accepted to a college or university to graduate.

Special Academic Programs 11 Advanced Placement exams for which test preparation is offered; honors section; academic accommodation for the musically talented and the artistically talented.

College Admission Counseling 80 students graduated in 2012; all went to college, including Georgia College & State University; Georgia Institute of Technology; Georgia Southern University; Georgia State University; University of Georgia; University of North Georgia.

Student Life Upper grades have uniform requirement, student council, honor system. Discipline rests primarily with faculty.

Tuition and Aid Day student tuition: $8500. Tuition installment plan (monthly payment plans). Tuition reduction for siblings, need-based scholarship grants available. In 2012–13, 1% of upper-school students received aid.

Admissions Traditional secondary-level entrance grade is 9. ACT, CAT 5, CTBS, Stanford Achievement Test, any other standardized test, Otis-Lennon, Stanford Achievement Test, PSAT or SAT required. Deadline for receipt of application materials: none. Application fee required: $150. On-campus interview required.

Athletics Interscholastic: aquatics (boys, girls), baseball (b), basketball (b,g), cheering (g), cross-country running (b,g), dance squad (g), drill team (g), football (b), golf (b), physical fitness (b,g), soccer (b,g), softball (g), swimming and diving (b,g), tennis (b,g), track and field (b,g), volleyball (g), weight lifting (b), weight training (b,g), wrestling (b). 3 PE instructors, 8 coaches.

Computers Computers are regularly used in all academic classes. Computer network features include on-campus library services, online commercial services, Internet access, wireless campus network, Internet filtering or blocking technology. Computer access in designated common areas is available to students. Students grades are available online. The school has a published electronic and media policy.

Contact Ms. Chris Stancil, Director of Admissions. 770-207-5172 Ext. 234. Fax: 770-267-4023. E-mail: cstancil@gwa.com. Website: www.gwa.com

GERMANTOWN FRIENDS SCHOOL

31 West Coulter Street
Philadelphia, Pennsylvania 19144

Head of School: Dana O. Weeks

General Information Coeducational day college-preparatory, arts, and technology school, affiliated with Society of Friends. Grades K–12. Founded: 1845. Setting: urban. 21-acre campus. 21 buildings on campus. Approved or accredited by Friends Council on Education, Middle States Association of Colleges and Schools, National Independent Private Schools Association, and Pennsylvania Association of Independent Schools. Member of National Association of Independent Schools and Secondary School Admission Test Board. Endowment: $22 million. Total enrollment: 861. Upper school average class size: 18. Upper school faculty-student ratio: 1:9. There are 172 required school days per year for Upper School students. Upper School students typically attend 5 days per week. The average school day consists of 6 hours and 25 minutes.

Upper School Student Profile Grade 9: 119 students (43 boys, 76 girls); Grade 10: 120 students (45 boys, 75 girls); Grade 11: 94 students (38 boys, 56 girls); Grade 12: 86 students (38 boys, 48 girls). 6.3% of students are members of Society of Friends.

Faculty School total: 136. In upper school: 28 men, 30 women; 44 have advanced degrees.

Subjects Offered 3-dimensional art, advanced chemistry, advanced math, algebra, American history, ancient history, art, art history, biology, calculus, chemistry, choir, chorus, comparative cultures, computer applications, computer programming, creative writing, drama, dramatic arts, drawing, English, environmental education, environmental science, European history, French, geometry, Greek, health, human sexuality, independent study, instrumental music, jazz ensemble, Latin, Latin History, madrigals, mathematics, music, music theory, orchestra, painting, philosophy, photography, physical education, physics, pre-calculus, science, social studies, Spanish, sports, stagecraft, statistics, studio art, theater, trigonometry, vocal music.

Graduation Requirements English, foreign language, history, lab science, mathematics, music, physical education (includes health), month-long off-campus independent project.

Special Academic Programs Honors section; independent study; term-away projects; domestic exchange program (with The Network Program Schools, The Catlin Gabel School); study abroad; academic accommodation for the gifted, the musically talented, and the artistically talented; ESL (3 students enrolled).

College Admission Counseling 84 students graduated in 2013; all went to college, including Brown University; Columbia University; New York University; University of Colorado Boulder; University of Pennsylvania; Yale University. Mean SAT critical reading: 657, mean SAT math: 634, mean SAT writing: 629, mean combined SAT: 1985, mean composite ACT: 28.

Student Life Upper grades have student council. Discipline rests primarily with faculty. Attendance at religious services is required.

Summer Programs Enrichment, sports, art/fine arts, computer instruction programs offered; held both on and off campus; held at various locations around Philadelphia; accepts boys and girls; open to students from other schools. 2014 schedule: June 14 to August 31. Application deadline: June 1.

Tuition and Aid Day student tuition: $29,520. Tuition installment plan (FACTS Tuition Payment Plan). Need-based scholarship grants available. In 2013–14, 29% of upper-school students received aid. Total amount of financial aid awarded in 2013–14: $1,879,209.

Admissions Traditional secondary-level entrance grade is 9. For fall 2013, 111 students applied for upper-level admission, 69 were accepted, 33 enrolled. ISEE or SSAT required. Deadline for receipt of application materials: December 6. Application fee required: $40. On-campus interview required.

Athletics Interscholastic: baseball (boys), basketball (b,g), cross-country running (b,g), field hockey (g), indoor track & field (b,g), lacrosse (g), soccer (b,g), softball (g), squash (b,g), tennis (b,g), track and field (b,g), wrestling (b); intramural: flag football (b), rugby (b); coed intramural: physical training, strength & conditioning, weight training. 7 PE instructors, 37 coaches, 2 athletic trainers.

Computers Computers are regularly used in art, English, foreign language, history, mathematics, music, photography, publications, science classes. Computer network features include on-campus library services, online commercial services, Internet access, wireless campus network, Internet filtering or blocking technology. Campus intranet, student e-mail accounts, and computer access in designated common areas are available to students.

Contact Laura Sharpless Myran, Director, Enrollment and Financial Aid. 215-951-2346. Fax: 215-951-2370. E-mail: lauram@gfsnet.org. Website: www.germantownfriends.org

GILMAN SCHOOL

5407 Roland Avenue
Baltimore, Maryland 21210

Head of School: Mr. Henry P. A. Smyth

General Information Boys' day college-preparatory school. Grades K–12. Founded: 1897. Setting: suburban. 68-acre campus. 6 buildings on campus. Approved or accredited by Association of Independent Maryland Schools, Middle States Association of Colleges and Schools, and Maryland Department of Education. Member of National Association of Independent Schools and Secondary School Admission Test Board. Endowment: $110 million. Total enrollment: 1,033. Upper school average class size: 16. Upper school faculty-student ratio: 1:8. There are 172 required school days per year for Upper School students. Upper School students typically attend 5 days per week. The average school day consists of 9 hours.

Upper School Student Profile Grade 6: 83 students (83 boys); Grade 7: 87 students (87 boys); Grade 8: 95 students (95 boys); Grade 9: 115 students (115 boys); Grade 10: 113 students (113 boys); Grade 11: 117 students (117 boys); Grade 12: 116 students (116 boys).

Faculty School total: 147. In upper school: 59 men, 9 women; 57 have advanced degrees.

Subjects Offered Algebra, American history, American literature, anatomy, Arabic, architectural drawing, art, art history, biology, calculus, chemistry, Chinese, community service, computer math, computer programming, computer science, creative writing, drafting, drama, ecology, economics, English, English literature, environmental science, European history, expository writing, fine arts, French, geometry, German, government/civics, Greek, history, industrial arts, Latin, mathematics, mechanical drawing, music, photography, physical education, physics, physiology, religion, Russian, science, social studies, Spanish, speech, statistics, theater, trigonometry, writing.

Graduation Requirements Art history, athletics, English, foreign language, history, mathematics, music appreciation, religion (includes Bible studies and theology), science, senior project.

Special Academic Programs 30 Advanced Placement exams for which test preparation is offered; honors section; independent study; term-away projects; academic accommodation for the gifted, the musically talented, and the artistically talented.

College Admission Counseling 115 students graduated in 2013; 113 went to college, including Harvard University; Princeton University; The Johns Hopkins University; University of Maryland, College Park; University of Virginia. Other: 1 entered a postgraduate year, 1 had other specific plans. Mean SAT critical reading: 638, mean SAT math: 660, mean SAT writing: 637.

Student Life Upper grades have specified standards of dress, student council, honor system. Discipline rests equally with students and faculty.

Summer Programs Remediation, enrichment, advancement, sports, art/fine arts, rigorous outdoor training programs offered; session focuses on remediation and enrichment; held on campus; accepts boys and girls; open to students from other schools. 250 students usually enrolled. 2014 schedule: June 18 to July 26. Application deadline: June 18.

Tuition and Aid Day student tuition: $26,180. Tuition installment plan (Insured Tuition Payment Plan, FACTS Tuition Payment Plan, monthly payment plans). Need-based scholarship grants, need-based loans available. In 2013–14, 25% of upper-school students received aid. Total amount of financial aid awarded in 2013–14: $1,839,100.

Admissions Traditional secondary-level entrance grade is 9. For fall 2013, 170 students applied for upper-level admission, 58 were accepted, 31 enrolled. ISEE required. Deadline for receipt of application materials: December 20. Application fee required: $50. On-campus interview required.

Athletics Interscholastic: baseball, basketball, cross-country running, football, golf, ice hockey, indoor track, lacrosse, soccer, squash, swimming and diving, tennis, track and field, volleyball, water polo, winter (indoor) track, wrestling; intramural: basketball, bicycling, cross-country running, fitness, flag football, Frisbee, golf, physical fitness, rugby, table tennis, tennis, touch football, weight lifting. 3 PE instructors, 2 athletic trainers.

Computers Computers are regularly used in all academic, computer applications, design, digital applications classes. Computer network features include on-campus library services, Internet access, wireless campus network, Internet filtering or blocking technology. Campus intranet, student e-mail accounts, and computer access in designated common areas are available to students. Students grades are available online. The school has a published electronic and media policy.

Contact Danielle Moran, Admissions Assistant. 410-323-7169. Fax: 410-864-2825. E-mail: dmoran@gilman.edu. Website: www.gilman.edu

GILMOUR ACADEMY

34001 Cedar Road
Gates Mills, Ohio 44040-9356

Head of School: Br. Robert E. Lavelle, CSC

General Information Coeducational boarding and day and distance learning college-preparatory, arts, religious studies, and technology school, affiliated with Roman Catholic Church. Boarding grades 7–12, day grades PK–12. Distance learning grades 9–12. Founded: 1946. Setting: suburban. Nearest major city is Cleveland. Students are housed in coed dormitories and boys' wing and girls' wing dormitory. 144-acre campus. 15 buildings on campus. Approved or accredited by Independent Schools Association of the Central States, Midwest Association of Boarding Schools, National Catholic Education Association, North Central Association of Colleges and Schools, The Association of Boarding Schools, and Ohio Department of Education. Member of National Association of Independent Schools and Secondary School Admission Test Board. Endowment: $30 million. Total enrollment: 689. Upper school average class size: 14. Upper school faculty-student ratio: 1:9. Upper School students typically attend 5 days per week. The average school day consists of 7 hours and 20 minutes.

Upper School Student Profile Grade 9: 103 students (54 boys, 49 girls); Grade 10: 102 students (54 boys, 48 girls); Grade 11: 116 students (66 boys, 50 girls); Grade 12: 110 students (57 boys, 53 girls); Postgraduate: 1 student (1 boy). 13% of students are boarding students. 88% are state residents. 16 states are represented in upper school student body. 8% are international students. International students from Canada, China, and Republic of Korea; 1 other country represented in student body. 75% of students are Roman Catholic.

Faculty School total: 77. In upper school: 43 men, 34 women; 57 have advanced degrees; 4 reside on campus.

Subjects Offered Advanced Placement courses, advanced studio art-AP, algebra, American government, American history, American literature, art, band, Bible, biology, biology-AP, British literature, broadcast journalism, calculus, calculus-AP, ceramics, chemistry, chemistry-AP, chorus, community service, computer programming, computer science, computer science-AP, creative writing, drama, drawing, economics, English, English literature, English-AP, ensembles, ethics, European history, European history-AP, fine arts, French, French language-AP, French-AP, geometry, geometry with art applications, government, government-AP, government/civics, health, history, history of rock and roll, independent study, jazz ensemble, journalism, Latin, Latin-AP, law, leadership, mathematics, mathematics-AP, model United Nations, modern European history-AP, music, musical productions, oil painting, painting, photography, physical education, physical fitness, physics, physics-AP, pre-algebra, pre-calculus, religion, religious studies, SAT/ACT preparation, science, social studies, Spanish, Spanish language-AP, speech, speech and debate, statistics-AP, student government, student publications, studio art, studio art-AP, swimming, theater, trigonometry, U.S. history, U.S. history-AP, weight training, work-study, world history, writing, writing workshop, yearbook.

Graduation Requirements Arts and fine arts (art, music, dance, drama), English, foreign language, mathematics, physical education (includes health), religion (includes Bible studies and theology), science, social studies (includes history), speech, senior project. Community service is required.

Special Academic Programs Advanced Placement exam preparation; accelerated programs; independent study; study at local college for college credit; academic accommodation for the gifted, the musically talented, and the artistically talented.

College Admission Counseling 114 students graduated in 2012; 110 went to college, including Boston College; Case Western Reserve University; John Carroll University; Loyola University Chicago; Miami University; University of Dayton. Other: 4 had other specific plans. Mean SAT critical reading: 566, mean SAT math: 574, mean SAT writing: 564, mean combined SAT: 1704, mean composite ACT: 24.

Student Life Upper grades have specified standards of dress, student council, honor system. Discipline rests equally with students and faculty. Attendance at religious services is required.

Tuition and Aid Day student tuition: $10,160–$23,180; 7-day tuition and room/board: $38,895. Tuition installment plan (monthly payment plans, Tuition Management Systems). Tuition reduction for siblings, merit scholarship grants, need-based scholarship grants, need-based loans, paying campus jobs, endowed scholarships with criteria specified by donors available. In 2012–13, 50% of upper-school students received aid; total upper-school merit-scholarship money awarded: $95,000. Total amount of financial aid awarded in 2012–13: $3,500,000.

Admissions Traditional secondary-level entrance grade is 9. For fall 2012, 240 students applied for upper-level admission, 205 were accepted, 99 enrolled. ACT, ACT-Explore, ISEE, PSAT, SAT, SSAT or TOEFL required. Deadline for receipt of application materials: none. Application fee required: $35. Interview required.

Athletics Interscholastic: baseball (boys), basketball (b,g), cross-country running (b,g), football (b), gymnastics (g), hockey (b,g), ice hockey (b,g), lacrosse (b,g), running (b,g), soccer (b,g), softball (g), swimming and diving (b,g), tennis (b,g), track and field (b,g), volleyball (g), winter soccer (b,g); intramural: cheering (g), indoor soccer (b,g); coed interscholastic: figure skating, golf, indoor track, indoor track & field, winter (indoor) track; coed intramural: aerobics, alpine skiing, aquatics, basketball, bowling, broomball, figure skating, fitness, golf, ice skating, indoor track, paddle tennis, physical fitness, physical training, skiing (downhill), snowboarding, soccer, strength & conditioning, swimming and diving, tennis, volleyball, weight training, winter (indoor) track, winter soccer. 9 coaches, 3 athletic trainers.

Computers Computers are regularly used in all academic classes. Computer network features include on-campus library services, online commercial services, Internet access, wireless campus network, Internet filtering or blocking technology. Campus intranet, student e-mail accounts, and computer access in designated common areas are available to students. Students grades are available online. The school has a published electronic and media policy.

Contact Mr. Steve M. Scheidt, Director of Middle and Upper School Admissions. 440-473-8050. Fax: 440-473-8010. E-mail: admissions@gilmour.org. Website: www.gilmour.org

GIRARD COLLEGE

2101 South College Avenue
Box #121
Philadelphia, Pennsylvania 19121-4857
Head of School: Mr. Clarence D. Armbrister

General Information Coeducational boarding college-preparatory and general academic school. Grades 1–12. Founded: 1848. Setting: urban. Students are housed in single-sex dormitories. 43-acre campus. 10 buildings on campus. Approved or accredited by Middle States Association of Colleges and Schools, The Association of Boarding Schools, and Pennsylvania Department of Education. Member of National Association of Independent Schools. Endowment: $355 million. Total enrollment: 331. Upper school average class size: 22. Upper school faculty-student ratio: 1:16. There are 177 required school days per year for Upper School students. Upper School students typically attend 5 days per week. The average school day consists of 6 hours and 30 minutes.

Upper School Student Profile Grade 7: 31 students (12 boys, 19 girls); Grade 8: 35 students (15 boys, 20 girls); Grade 9: 23 students (13 boys, 10 girls); Grade 10: 36 students (13 boys, 23 girls); Grade 11: 37 students (19 boys, 18 girls); Grade 12: 39 students (16 boys, 23 girls). 100% of students are boarding students. 88% are state residents. 6 states are represented in upper school student body.

Faculty School total: 71. In upper school: 12 men, 9 women; 9 have advanced degrees; 1 resides on campus.

Subjects Offered Algebra, American history, American literature, anatomy, art, biology, calculus, chemistry, choir, college counseling, community service, computer literacy, earth science, English, English literature, European history, French, geometry, government/civics, health, honors algebra, honors English, honors geometry, honors U.S. history, instrumental music, jazz band, life management skills, mathematics, multicultural studies, music appreciation, physical education, physics, poetry, pre-calculus, SAT preparation, senior project, social studies, sociology, Spanish, video film production, world cultures.

Graduation Requirements College counseling, computer literacy, English, foreign language, mathematics, physical education (includes health), science, senior career experience, senior project, social sciences, social studies (includes history). Community service is required.

Special Academic Programs 1 Advanced Placement exam for which test preparation is offered; honors section; study at local college for college credit; remedial reading and/or remedial writing; remedial math.

College Admission Counseling 54 students graduated in 2013; 52 went to college, including Penn State University Park; Penn State University Park; Penn State University Park; Temple University; University of Pennsylvania; University of Pittsburgh. Other: 2 entered military service. Mean SAT critical reading: 473, mean SAT math: 463, mean SAT writing: 465, mean combined SAT: 1401, mean composite ACT: 26.

Student Life Upper grades have uniform requirement, student council. Discipline rests primarily with faculty.

Summer Programs Enrichment, advancement, sports, art/fine arts, computer instruction programs offered; session focuses on academic and recreation; held on campus; accepts boys and girls; open to students from other schools. 200 students usually enrolled. 2014 schedule: June 24 to August 2.

Tuition and Aid Full scholarships (if admission requirements met) available. In 2013–14, 100% of upper-school students received aid.

Admissions Admissions testing, math, reading, and mental ability tests and Otis-Lennon and 2 sections of ERB required. Deadline for receipt of application materials: none. No application fee required. On-campus interview required.

Athletics Interscholastic: baseball (boys), basketball (b,g), cross-country running (b,g), soccer (b,g), softball (g), tennis (g), track and field (b,g), winter (indoor) track (b,g), wrestling (b); intramural: bicycling (b), strength & conditioning (b,g), yoga (g); coed interscholastic: cheering; coed intramural: aerobics, aerobics/dance, aquatics, dance, fitness, flag football, indoor track & field, jogging, jump rope, life saving, martial arts, outdoor activities, outdoor adventure, physical fitness, running, swimming and diving, walking, weight training, winter walking. 1 PE instructor, 11 coaches.

Computers Computers are regularly used in college planning, English, foreign language, history, library, mathematics, newspaper, reading, research skills, SAT preparation, science, social studies, study skills, word processing, writing, yearbook classes. Computer network features include on-campus library services, online commercial services, Internet access, Internet filtering or blocking technology. Student e-mail accounts are available to students. The school has a published electronic and media policy.

Contact Aqila Clement, Admissions. 215-787-2621. Fax: 215-787-4402. E-mail: admissions@girardcollege.edu. Website: www.girardcollege.com

GIRLS PREPARATORY SCHOOL

205 Island Avenue
Chattanooga, Tennessee 37405
Head of School: Dr. Susan R. Groesbeck

General Information Girls' day college-preparatory, arts, and technology school. Grades 6–12. Founded: 1906. Setting: suburban. Nearest major city is Atlanta, GA. 55-

acre campus. 8 buildings on campus. Approved or accredited by Southern Association of Colleges and Schools and Southern Association of Independent Schools. Member of National Association of Independent Schools. Endowment: $25.3 million. Total enrollment: 584. Upper school average class size: 16. Upper school faculty-student ratio: 1:8. There are 180 required school days per year for Upper School students. Upper School students typically attend 5 days per week. The average school day consists of 7 hours and 10 minutes.

Upper School Student Profile Grade 9: 88 students (88 girls); Grade 10: 88 students (88 girls); Grade 11: 75 students (75 girls); Grade 12: 96 students (96 girls).

Faculty School total: 74. In upper school: 11 men, 34 women; 29 have advanced degrees.

Subjects Offered Advanced Placement courses, algebra, American history, American literature, art, art history, Basic programming, Bible studies, biology, calculus, chemistry, Chinese, choral music, computer science, dance, drama, engineering, English, English literature, environmental science, European history, fine arts, forensics, French, geometry, government/civics, graphic design, history, Latin, mathematics, modern civilization, music, physics, pottery, pre-calculus, public speaking, religion, science, Spanish, statistics, trigonometry, world history.

Graduation Requirements Arts and fine arts (art, music, dance, drama), electives, English, foreign language, history, mathematics, physical education (includes health), religion (includes Bible studies and theology), science.

Special Academic Programs 21 Advanced Placement exams for which test preparation is offered; honors section; independent study.

College Admission Counseling 89 students graduated in 2013; all went to college, including Auburn University; Samford University; Texas Christian University; The University of Tennessee; The University of Tennessee at Chattanooga; University of Georgia. Median SAT critical reading: 560, median SAT math: 580, median SAT writing: 570, median combined SAT: 1710, median composite ACT: 26. 36% scored over 600 on SAT critical reading, 36% scored over 600 on SAT math, 44% scored over 600 on SAT writing, 37% scored over 1800 on combined SAT, 58% scored over 26 on composite ACT.

Student Life Upper grades have uniform requirement, student council, honor system. Discipline rests primarily with faculty.

Summer Programs Remediation, enrichment, advancement, sports, art/fine arts, computer instruction programs offered; session focuses on summer fun and enrichment; held both on and off campus; held at Lupton Athletic fields and yacht club in Hixson, various locations throughout town, and Nantahala River Gorge; accepts boys and girls; open to students from other schools. 450 students usually enrolled. 2014 schedule: June 2 to July 18. Application deadline: June 1.

Tuition and Aid Day student tuition: $21,240. Tuition installment plan (Insured Tuition Payment Plan, FACTS Tuition Payment Plan, monthly payment plans, individually arranged payment plans, 60%/40% and 100% payment plans). Merit scholarship grants, need-based scholarship grants available. In 2013–14, 43% of upper-school students received aid; total upper-school merit-scholarship money awarded: $42,480. Total amount of financial aid awarded in 2013–14: $1,419,908.

Admissions Traditional secondary-level entrance grade is 9. For fall 2013, 40 students applied for upper-level admission, 28 were accepted, 15 enrolled. Admissions testing, mathematics proficiency exam and OLSAT, Stanford Achievement Test required. Deadline for receipt of application materials: none. Application fee required: $75. On-campus interview recommended.

Athletics Interscholastic: basketball, bowling, cheering, crew, cross-country running, diving, golf, lacrosse, rowing, soccer, softball, swimming and diving, tennis, track and field, volleyball; intramural: backpacking, bicycling, canoeing/kayaking, climbing, dance, dance squad, fitness, fitness walking, Frisbee, hiking/backpacking, jogging, kayaking, life saving, modern dance, mountain biking, outdoor activities, outdoor education, outdoor skills, paddle tennis, physical fitness, rafting, rock climbing, running, self defense, strength & conditioning, ultimate Frisbee, walking, weight training, wilderness, yoga; coed interscholastic: cheering. 6 PE instructors, 24 coaches, 1 athletic trainer.

Computers Computers are regularly used in all academic classes. Computer network features include on-campus library services, online commercial services, Internet access, wireless campus network, Internet filtering or blocking technology, network printing, scanning. Campus intranet and student e-mail accounts are available to students. Students grades are available online. The school has a published electronic and media policy.

Contact Debbie Bohner Young, Director of Admissions. 423-634-7647. Fax: 423-634-7643. E-mail: dyoung@gps.edu. Website: www.gps.edu

GLADES DAY SCHOOL

400 Gator Boulevard
Belle Glade, Florida 33430

Head of School: Mrs. Amie Pitts

General Information Coeducational day college-preparatory, general academic, vocational, and agriscience school. Grades PK–12. Founded: 1965. Setting: small town. Nearest major city is West Palm Beach. 21-acre campus. 4 buildings on campus. Approved or accredited by Florida Council of Independent Schools. Total enrollment: 307. Upper school average class size: 20. Upper school faculty-student ratio: 1:15. There are 180 required school days per year for Upper School students. Upper School

students typically attend 5 days per week. The average school day consists of 6 hours and 35 minutes.

Upper School Student Profile Grade 9: 34 students (21 boys, 13 girls); Grade 10: 24 students (17 boys, 7 girls); Grade 11: 30 students (24 boys, 6 girls); Grade 12: 35 students (21 boys, 14 girls).

Faculty School total: 20. In upper school: 8 men, 12 women; 3 have advanced degrees.

Subjects Offered ACT preparation, agriculture, algebra, American government, American history, American literature, anatomy, ancient history, art, Bible studies, biology, biology-AP, calculus, calculus-AP, chemistry, computer applications, computer skills, computer technologies, earth science, economics, English, English language and composition-AP, English literature, English literature and composition-AP, environmental science, European history, general math, geometry, government and politics-AP, grammar, health, health education, human geography - AP, journalism, keyboarding, literature and composition-AP, macroeconomics-AP, modern world history, music performance, physical education, pre-calculus, SAT/ACT preparation, Spanish, Spanish-AP, trigonometry, U.S. government and politics-AP, U.S. history, U.S. history-AP, weightlifting, world geography, world history, world history-AP, yearbook.

Graduation Requirements Algebra, American government, American literature, anatomy, ancient world history, arts and fine arts (art, music, dance, drama), biology, calculus, chemistry, computer applications, economics, English, English composition, English literature, geometry, health education, keyboarding, macroeconomics-AP, marine biology, modern world history, physical education (includes health), physical fitness, physical science, physics, pre-calculus, Spanish, U.S. history, world history.

Special Academic Programs 10 Advanced Placement exams for which test preparation is offered; honors section; independent study; study at local college for college credit; programs in general development for dyslexic students.

College Admission Counseling 32 students graduated in 2013; 30 went to college, including Florida Gulf Coast University; Florida State University; Palm Beach State College; Santa Fe College; University of Central Florida; University of Florida. Other: 2 went to work.

Student Life Upper grades have uniform requirement, student council, honor system. Discipline rests primarily with faculty.

Summer Programs Remediation programs offered; session focuses on remediation; held on campus; accepts boys and girls; not open to students from other schools. 7 students usually enrolled. 2014 schedule: June 7 to July 15. Application deadline: June 4.

Tuition and Aid Day student tuition: $6900–$8750. Tuition installment plan (FACTS Tuition Payment Plan, monthly payment plans, individually arranged payment plans). Tuition reduction for siblings, need-based scholarship grants available. In 2013–14, 10% of upper-school students received aid.

Admissions Traditional secondary-level entrance grade is 9. For fall 2013, 50 students applied for upper-level admission, 45 were accepted, 41 enrolled. Deadline for receipt of application materials: none. Application fee required: $400. On-campus interview required.

Athletics Interscholastic: baseball (boys), basketball (b,g), cheering (g), football (b), soccer (b,g), softball (g), track and field (b,g), volleyball (g); intramural: strength & conditioning (b,g), weight training (b,g). 2 PE instructors, 2 coaches.

Computers Computers are regularly used in English, journalism, science, Spanish, Web site design, word processing, yearbook classes. Computer network features include on-campus library services, Internet access, wireless campus network. Campus intranet and student e-mail accounts are available to students. Students grades are available online. The school has a published electronic and media policy.

Contact Mrs. Jamie Redish, High School Secretary. 561-996-6769 Ext. 10. Fax: 561-992-9274. E-mail: jredish@gladesdayschool.com. Website: www.gladesdayschool.com

GLENELG COUNTRY SCHOOL

12793 Folly Quarter Road
Ellicott City, Maryland 21042

Head of School: Mr. Gregory J. Ventre

General Information Coeducational day college-preparatory, arts, and technology school. Grades PK–12. Founded: 1954. Setting: suburban. Nearest major city is Baltimore. 87-acre campus. 1 building on campus. Approved or accredited by Association of Independent Maryland Schools, Middle States Association of Colleges and Schools, and Maryland Department of Education. Member of National Association of Independent Schools. Endowment: $900,000. Total enrollment: 768. Upper school average class size: 15. Upper school faculty-student ratio: 1:6. There are 175 required school days per year for Upper School students. Upper School students typically attend 5 days per week. The average school day consists of 7 hours.

Upper School Student Profile Grade 9: 61 students (31 boys, 30 girls); Grade 10: 70 students (35 boys, 35 girls); Grade 11: 69 students (39 boys, 30 girls); Grade 12: 81 students (41 boys, 40 girls).

Faculty School total: 131. In upper school: 26 men, 21 women; 37 have advanced degrees.

Subjects Offered Algebra, American history, American literature, art, art history, biology, biology-AP, calculus, calculus-AP, chemistry, chemistry-AP, Chinese, chorus, computer science, creative writing, drama, English, English literature, English-AP, European history, expository writing, French, French-AP, geometry, history, humanities, integrative seminar, Latin, Latin-AP, mathematics, photography, physical education, physical science, physics, physics-AP, pre-calculus, psychology, publications, science, social studies, Spanish, Spanish-AP, statistics, studio art, theater, trigonometry, world affairs.

Graduation Requirements Civics, English, foreign language, integrative seminar, mathematics, physical education (includes health), science, social studies (includes history), participation in Civic Leadership Program, 25 hours of community service per year.

Special Academic Programs 17 Advanced Placement exams for which test preparation is offered; honors section; independent study; academic accommodation for the gifted.

College Admission Counseling 66 students graduated in 2012; all went to college, including University of Maryland, College Park; University of South Carolina; Wake Forest University. Mean SAT critical reading: 600, mean SAT math: 620, mean SAT writing: 600, mean combined SAT: 1820. 51% scored over 600 on SAT critical reading, 53% scored over 600 on SAT math, 56% scored over 600 on SAT writing, 57% scored over 1800 on combined SAT.

Student Life Upper grades have uniform requirement, student council, honor system. Discipline rests equally with students and faculty.

Tuition and Aid Day student tuition: $24,170. Tuition installment plan (monthly payment plans, individually arranged payment plans, 2-payment plan). Merit scholarship grants, need-based scholarship grants available. In 2012–13, 40% of upper-school students received aid; total upper-school merit-scholarship money awarded: $150,000. Total amount of financial aid awarded in 2012–13: $1,850,000.

Admissions Traditional secondary-level entrance grade is 9. For fall 2012, 74 students applied for upper-level admission, 55 were accepted, 31 enrolled. ISEE or SSAT required. Deadline for receipt of application materials: January 15. Application fee required: $75. On-campus interview required.

Athletics Interscholastic: baseball (boys), basketball (b,g), cross-country running (b,g), field hockey (g), golf (b,g), ice hockey (b), indoor soccer (g), indoor track (b,g), lacrosse (b,g), soccer (b,g), tennis (b,g), volleyball (g), winter soccer (g), wrestling (b); coed interscholastic: golf, ice hockey, strength & conditioning; coed intramural: aerobics, aerobics/dance, dance, fitness, flag football, Frisbee, physical fitness, physical training, skiing (downhill), strength & conditioning, ultimate Frisbee, weight training, yoga. 5 PE instructors, 12 coaches, 1 athletic trainer.

Computers Computers are regularly used in all academic classes. Computer network features include on-campus library services, Internet access, wireless campus network. Campus intranet, student e-mail accounts, and computer access in designated common areas are available to students. Students grades are available online. The school has a published electronic and media policy.

Contact Mrs. Karen K. Wootton, Director of Admission and Financial Aid. 410-531-7346 Ext. 2203. Fax: 410-531-7363. E-mail: wootton@glenelg.org. Website: www.glenelg.org

THE GLENHOLME SCHOOL, DEVEREUX CONNECTICUT

Washington, Connecticut
See Special Needs Schools section.

GLENLYON NORFOLK SCHOOL

801 Bank Street
Victoria, British Columbia V8S 4A8, Canada

Head of School: Mr. Simon Bruce-Lockhart

General Information Coeducational day college-preparatory, arts, technology, and International Baccalaureate school. Grades JK–12. Founded: 1913. Setting: urban. 6-acre campus. 6 buildings on campus. Approved or accredited by International Baccalaureate Organization and British Columbia Department of Education. Affiliate member of National Association of Independent Schools. Language of instruction: English. Endowment: CAN$800,000. Total enrollment: 685. Upper school average class size: 18. Upper school faculty-student ratio: 1:8. There are 180 required school days per year for Upper School students. Upper School students typically attend 5 days per week. The average school day consists of 6 hours.

Upper School Student Profile Grade 9: 65 students (33 boys, 32 girls); Grade 10: 73 students (40 boys, 33 girls); Grade 11: 78 students (37 boys, 41 girls); Grade 12: 64 students (31 boys, 33 girls).

Faculty School total: 90. In upper school: 20 men, 21 women; 13 have advanced degrees.

Subjects Offered 20th century world history, art, band, biology, calculus, chemistry, choir, community service, comparative civilizations, concert band, creative writing, debate, directing, drama, English, English literature, European history, European literature, fine arts, French, geography, history, information technology, International Baccalaureate courses, jazz band, journalism, life skills, mathematics, music, newspaper, peer counseling, physical education, physics, public speaking, science, social studies, Spanish, stagecraft, theater arts, theory of knowledge, vocal jazz, world history, world literature, writing, yearbook.

Graduation Requirements Arts and fine arts (art, music, dance, drama), career planning, English, foreign language, information technology, mathematics, physical education (includes health), science, social studies (includes history). Community service is required.

Special Academic Programs International Baccalaureate program; honors section; term-away projects; ESL (10 students enrolled).

College Admission Counseling 56 students graduated in 2013; all went to college, including McGill University; The University of British Columbia; University of Calgary; University of Toronto; University of Victoria.

Student Life Upper grades have uniform requirement, student council, honor system. Discipline rests primarily with faculty.

Tuition and Aid Day student tuition: CAN$14,588–CAN$18,040. Guaranteed tuition plan. Tuition installment plan (monthly payment plans, individually arranged payment plans). Tuition reduction for siblings, bursaries, merit scholarship grants, tuition allowances for children of staff available. In 2013–14, 20% of upper-school students received aid; total upper-school merit-scholarship money awarded: CAN$23,050. Total amount of financial aid awarded in 2013–14: CAN$130,000.

Admissions Traditional secondary-level entrance grade is 9. SAT, SSAT or writing sample required. Deadline for receipt of application materials: none. Application fee required: CAN$200. Interview recommended.

Athletics Interscholastic: backpacking (boys, girls), badminton (b,g), basketball (b,g), canoeing/kayaking (b,g), climbing (b,g), crew (b,g), cross-country running (b,g), field hockey (g), fitness (b,g), kayaking (b,g), rock climbing (b,g), rowing (b,g), rugby (b), soccer (b,g), squash (b,g), swimming and diving (b,g), tennis (b,g), track and field (b,g), volleyball (g); intramural: badminton (b,g), ball hockey (b), basketball (b,g), floor hockey (b), outdoor education (b,g), outdoor recreation (b,g), outdoor skills (b,g), swimming and diving (b,g), track and field (b,g), ultimate Frisbee (b,g); coed interscholastic: backpacking, badminton, canoeing/kayaking, crew, cross-country running, fitness, golf, kayaking, sailing, tennis; coed intramural: badminton, basketball, outdoor education, outdoor recreation, outdoor skills, swimming and diving, track and field, ultimate Frisbee. 4 PE instructors, 12 coaches.

Computers Computers are regularly used in all classes. Computer network features include on-campus library services, Internet access, wireless campus network, Internet filtering or blocking technology. Campus intranet and student e-mail accounts are available to students. The school has a published electronic and media policy.

Contact Ms. Andrea Hughes, Admissions Associate. 250-370-6801. Fax: 250-370-6811. E-mail: admissions@mygns.ca. Website: www.mygns.ca

GONZAGA COLLEGE HIGH SCHOOL

19 Eye Street NW
Washington, District of Columbia 20001

Head of School: Mr. Thomas K. Every II

General Information Boys' day college-preparatory, arts, religious studies, and technology school, affiliated with Roman Catholic Church. Grades 9–12. Founded: 1821. Setting: urban. 1-acre campus. 9 buildings on campus. Approved or accredited by Association of Independent Schools of Greater Washington, Jesuit Secondary Education Association, Middle States Association of Colleges and Schools, and District of Columbia Department of Education. Member of National Association of Independent Schools. Endowment: $9.1 million. Total enrollment: 958. Upper school average class size: 26. Upper school faculty-student ratio: 1:15. There are 165 required school days per year for Upper School students. Upper School students typically attend 5 days per week. The average school day consists of 6 hours and 35 minutes.

Upper School Student Profile Grade 9: 241 students (241 boys); Grade 10: 243 students (243 boys); Grade 11: 234 students (234 boys); Grade 12: 240 students (240 boys). 85% of students are Roman Catholic.

Faculty School total: 63. In upper school: 48 men, 15 women; 57 have advanced degrees.

Subjects Offered Advanced Placement courses, African-American literature, algebra, American history, American literature, applied music, art, band, biology, broadcasting, calculus, calculus-AP, Catholic belief and practice, chemistry, chemistry-AP, Chinese, choir, choral music, Christian and Hebrew scripture, Christian ethics, Christian scripture, communications, community service, computer applications, computer math, computer programming, computer science, concert band, concert choir, creative writing, driver education, earth science, economics, economics-AP, English, English literature, English literature and composition-AP, English literature-AP, English-AP, environmental science-AP, ethics, ethics and responsibility, European history, European history-AP, expository writing, film appreciation, film studies, fine arts, French, French-AP, functions, geometry, government, government/civics, grammar, Greek, health, health education, history, honors algebra, honors English, honors geometry, human geography - AP, independent study, Irish literature, jazz ensemble, Latin, Latin-AP, mathematics, media communications, music, musicianship, philosophy, photography, physical education, physics, physics-AP, piano, poetry, political science, political systems, psychology, psychology-AP, religion, Russian history, Russian studies, science, social justice, social sciences, social studies, Spanish, Spanish-AP, statistics, statistics-AP, studio art-AP, symphonic band, theology, trigonometry, U.S. government and politics-AP, Web site design, world history, world literature.

Graduation Requirements Arts and fine arts (art, music, dance, drama), English, ethics, foreign language, mathematics, physical education (includes health), religion (includes Bible studies and theology), science, social justice, social sciences, social studies (includes history). Community service is required.

Special Academic Programs Advanced Placement exam preparation; honors section.

College Admission Counseling 235 students graduated in 2013; 234 went to college, including Penn State University Park; The Catholic University of America; University of Maryland, College Park; University of South Carolina; University of Virginia; Virginia Polytechnic Institute and State University. Other: 1 had other specific plans.

Student Life Upper grades have specified standards of dress, student council, honor system. Discipline rests primarily with faculty. Attendance at religious services is required.

Summer Programs Remediation, enrichment programs offered; session focuses on new student remediation, enrichment, and SAT preparation; held on campus; accepts boys and girls; open to students from other schools. 200 students usually enrolled. 2014 schedule: June to July. Application deadline: June 1.

Tuition and Aid Day student tuition: $19,275. Tuition installment plan (Insured Tuition Payment Plan, monthly payment plans). Merit scholarship grants, need-based scholarship grants available. In 2013–14, 33% of upper-school students received aid; total upper-school merit-scholarship money awarded: $100,000. Total amount of financial aid awarded in 2013–14: $2,400,000.

Admissions Traditional secondary-level entrance grade is 9. For fall 2013, 640 students applied for upper-level admission, 300 were accepted, 241 enrolled. High School Placement Test (closed version) from Scholastic Testing Service required. Deadline for receipt of application materials: December 10. Application fee required: $35.

Athletics Interscholastic: baseball, basketball, crew, cross-country running, diving, football, golf, ice hockey, indoor track & field, lacrosse, rugby, soccer, squash, swimming and diving, tennis, track and field, water polo, winter (indoor) track, wrestling; intramural: basketball, bowling, fencing, fishing, football, Frisbee, hiking/backpacking, martial arts, physical training, skiing (downhill), softball, strength & conditioning, table tennis, volleyball, weight lifting, whiffle ball. 2 PE instructors, 30 coaches, 2 athletic trainers.

Computers Computer network features include on-campus library services, Internet access. Student e-mail accounts are available to students. Students grades are available online. The school has a published electronic and media policy.

Contact Mr. Andrew C. Battaile, Dean of Admissions. 202-336-7101. Fax: 202-454-1188. E-mail: abattaile@gonzaga.org. Website: www.gonzaga.org

GOOD HOPE COUNTRY DAY SCHOOL

RR #1, Box 6199
Kingshill, Virgin Islands 00850-9807

Head of School: Mr. William D. Sinfield

General Information Coeducational day college-preparatory and technology school. Grades N–12. Founded: 1964. Setting: rural. Nearest major city is Christiansted, U.S. Virgin Islands. 25-acre campus. 6 buildings on campus. Approved or accredited by Middle States Association of Colleges and Schools and Virgin Islands Department of Education. Member of National Association of Independent Schools. Endowment: $574,000. Total enrollment: 440. Upper school average class size: 14. Upper school faculty-student ratio: 1:12. Upper School students typically attend 5 days per week. The average school day consists of 7 hours.

Upper School Student Profile Grade 9: 34 students (19 boys, 15 girls); Grade 10: 39 students (23 boys, 16 girls); Grade 11: 39 students (16 boys, 23 girls); Grade 12: 39 students (22 boys, 17 girls).

Faculty School total: 51. In upper school: 6 men, 17 women; 17 have advanced degrees.

Subjects Offered Algebra, American history, American literature, art, art history, arts, band, biology, calculus, ceramics, chemistry, chorus, community service, computer programming, computer science, creative writing, current events, dance, drama, earth science, ecology, economics, electronics, English, English literature, film, fine arts, French, geometry, government/civics, health, history, journalism, keyboarding, marine biology, mathematics, music, Native American studies, photography, physical education, physical science, physics, pre-calculus, psychology, public speaking, science, social studies, sociology, Spanish, statistics, swimming, theater, trigonometry, world history.

Graduation Requirements Arts and fine arts (art, music, dance, drama), computer science, English, foreign language, mathematics, physical education (includes health), science, social studies (includes history), swimming, typing. Community service is required.

Special Academic Programs Advanced Placement exam preparation.

College Admission Counseling 44 students graduated in 2013; all went to college, including Michigan Technological University; University of Pennsylvania; University of Pittsburgh; Vassar College. Median SAT critical reading: 520, median SAT math: 540, median composite ACT: 22. 35% scored over 600 on SAT critical reading, 25% scored over 600 on SAT math, 19% scored over 26 on composite ACT.

Student Life Upper grades have specified standards of dress, student council, honor system. Discipline rests primarily with faculty.

Tuition and Aid Day student tuition: $14,000. Tuition installment plan (monthly payment plans, individually arranged payment plans, semiannual and annual payment plans). Merit scholarship grants, need-based scholarship grants available. In 2013–14, 40% of upper-school students received aid; total upper-school merit-scholarship money awarded: $144,435. Total amount of financial aid awarded in 2013–14: $306,553.

Admissions Traditional secondary-level entrance grade is 9. For fall 2013, 25 students applied for upper-level admission, 10 were accepted, 10 enrolled. Essay and Test of Achievement and Proficiency required. Deadline for receipt of application materials: none. Application fee required: $150. On-campus interview required.

Athletics Interscholastic: baseball (boys), basketball (b,g), football (b), softball (g), tennis (b,g), volleyball (b,g); intramural: volleyball (b,g); coed interscholastic: aerobics, aquatics, basketball, cross-country running, sailing, soccer; coed intramural: basketball, soccer, ultimate Frisbee. 3 PE instructors, 4 coaches.

Computers Computers are regularly used in mathematics, music, science, yearbook classes. Computer network features include on-campus library services, online commercial services, Internet access. The school has a published electronic and media policy.

Contact Mrs. Alma V. Castro-Nieves, Registrar. 340-778-1974 Ext. 2108. Fax: 340-779-3331. E-mail: acastronieves@ghcds.org. Website: www.ghcds.org/

GOULD ACADEMY

PO Box 860
39 Church Street
Bethel, Maine 04217

Head of School: Matthew C. Ruby

General Information Coeducational boarding and day college-preparatory, arts, and technology school. Grades 9–PG. Founded: 1836. Setting: small town. Nearest major city is Portland. Students are housed in single-sex dormitories. 456-acre campus. 30 buildings on campus. Approved or accredited by Association of Independent Schools in New England, Independent Schools of Northern New England, New England Association of Schools and Colleges, The Association of Boarding Schools, and Maine Department of Education. Member of National Association of Independent Schools and Secondary School Admission Test Board. Endowment: $9.5 million. Total enrollment: 232. Upper school average class size: 12. Upper school faculty-student ratio: 1:6. There are 175 required school days per year for Upper School students. Upper School students typically attend 5 days per week. The average school day consists of 6 hours.

Upper School Student Profile Grade 9: 44 students (22 boys, 22 girls); Grade 10: 50 students (31 boys, 19 girls); Grade 11: 57 students (37 boys, 20 girls); Grade 12: 78 students (51 boys, 27 girls); Grade 13: 3 students (2 boys, 1 girl); Postgraduate: 4 students (4 boys). 71% of students are boarding students. 42% are state residents. 22 states are represented in upper school student body. 20% are international students. International students from China, Germany, Japan, Republic of Korea, Spain, and Taiwan; 2 other countries represented in student body.

Faculty School total: 44. In upper school: 23 men, 21 women; 25 have advanced degrees; 32 reside on campus.

Subjects Offered Acting, Advanced Placement courses, African-American literature, algebra, American foreign policy, American history, American literature, American literature-AP, analytic geometry, art, art history, athletic training, band, bioethics, DNA and culture, biology, biology-AP, British literature, British literature (honors), British literature-AP, calculus, calculus-AP, celestial navigation, ceramics, chemistry, chemistry-AP, chorus, Civil War, clayworking, college placement, computer information systems, computer music, computer programming, computer science, computers, conceptual physics, creative writing, debate, design, digital music, drama, drawing, earth science, Eastern religion and philosophy, ecology, economics, electives, electronic music, electronics, English, environmental science, environmental science-AP, ESL, European history, expository writing, foreign policy, French, geography, geometry, government and politics-AP, history, history-AP, honors algebra, honors English, honors world history, introduction to digital multitrack recording techniques, jazz band, jewelry making, Latin, learning strategies, literature by women, mathematics, music, music appreciation, music theory, musicianship, navigation, painting, philosophy, photography, physics, pottery, pre-calculus, printmaking, robotics, science, sculpture, Shakespeare, social studies, software design, Spanish, theater, U.S. government and politics-AP, video film production, women's literature, world history, writing.

Graduation Requirements English, foreign language, mathematics, physical education (includes health), science, social studies (includes history).

Special Academic Programs Advanced Placement exam preparation; honors section; independent study; academic accommodation for the gifted, the musically talented, and the artistically talented; ESL (25 students enrolled).

College Admission Counseling 59 students graduated in 2013; all went to college, including Bentley University; Lewis & Clark College; Rochester Institute of Technology; Saint Michael's College; University of Illinois at Urbana–Champaign; University of Vermont.

Student Life Upper grades have specified standards of dress, student council, honor system. Discipline rests equally with students and faculty.

Tuition and Aid Day student tuition: $30,300; 7-day tuition and room/board: $51,500. Tuition installment plan (Insured Tuition Payment Plan, individually arranged payment plans, full payment by August 15, 2/3 payment by August 12, 1/3 by December 1). Need-based scholarship grants, need-based loans available. In 2013–14, 38% of upper-school students received aid. Total amount of financial aid awarded in 2013–14: $1,355,000.

Admissions Traditional secondary-level entrance grade is 9. For fall 2013, 216 students applied for upper-level admission, 184 were accepted, 90 enrolled. SSAT or TOEFL or SLEP required. Deadline for receipt of application materials: February 1. Application fee required: $30. Interview required.

Athletics Interscholastic: alpine skiing (boys, girls), baseball (b), basketball (b,g), bicycling (b,g), cross-country running (b,g), field hockey (g), freestyle skiing (b,g); coed interscholastic: climbing, dance, dressage, equestrian sports, golf; coed intramural: golf. 11 coaches, 1 athletic trainer.

Computers Computers are regularly used in English, foreign language, history, mathematics, music, science, technology classes. Computer network features include on-campus library services, Internet access, wireless campus network. Student e-mail accounts are available to students. Students grades are available online. The school has a published electronic and media policy.

Contact Chris Hayward, Director of Admission. 207-824-7777. Fax: 207-824-2926. E-mail: haywardc@gouldacademy.org. Website: www.gouldacademy.org

THE GOVERNOR FRENCH ACADEMY

219 West Main Street
Belleville, Illinois 62220-1537

Head of School: Mr. Phillip E. Paeltz

General Information Coeducational boarding and day college-preparatory and bilingual studies school. Boarding grades 9–12, day grades K–12. Founded: 1983. Setting: urban. Nearest major city is St. Louis, MO. Students are housed in homes of local families. 3 buildings on campus. Approved or accredited by North Central Association of Colleges and Schools and Illinois Department of Education. Endowment: $100,000. Total enrollment: 157. Upper school average class size: 15. Upper school faculty-student ratio: 1:7. There are 176 required school days per year for Upper School students. Upper School students typically attend 5 days per week. The average school day consists of 7 hours and 15 minutes.

Upper School Student Profile Grade 9: 13 students (4 boys, 9 girls); Grade 10: 7 students (3 boys, 4 girls); Grade 11: 16 students (8 boys, 8 girls); Grade 12: 15 students (9 boys, 6 girls). 1% of students are boarding students. 99% are state residents. 1 state is represented in upper school student body. 1% are international students. International students from China and Republic of Korea.

Faculty School total: 12. In upper school: 3 men, 4 women; 4 have advanced degrees.

Subjects Offered Accounting, algebra, American history, American literature, anthropology, archaeology, biology, calculus, chemistry, creative writing, criminology, earth science, ecology, economics, engineering, English, English literature, environmental science, European history, expository writing, geography, geometry, government/civics, grammar, history, mathematics, physical education, physics, psychology, science, social sciences, social studies, statistics, theater arts, trigonometry, world history, world literature.

Graduation Requirements English, foreign language, history, mathematics, science, social sciences, vote of faculty.

Special Academic Programs 7 Advanced Placement exams for which test preparation is offered; accelerated programs; independent study; academic accommodation for the gifted and the artistically talented; programs in English for dyslexic students; ESL (4 students enrolled).

College Admission Counseling 13 students graduated in 2013; 12 went to college, including Saint Louis University; Southern Illinois University Edwardsville; Trinity College; University of Illinois at Urbana–Champaign; University of Kentucky; Washington University in St. Louis. Other: 1 went to work. Median composite ACT: 23. 20% scored over 26 on composite ACT.

Student Life Upper grades have uniform requirement, student council, honor system. Discipline rests primarily with faculty.

Summer Programs Remediation, enrichment, advancement programs offered; session focuses on academics; held on campus; accepts boys and girls; open to students from other schools. 25 students usually enrolled. 2014 schedule: June 16 to July 25. Application deadline: none.

Tuition and Aid Day student tuition: $6000; 7-day tuition and room/board: $22,200. Tuition installment plan (monthly payment plans). Tuition reduction for siblings available.

Admissions Traditional secondary-level entrance grade is 9. For fall 2013, 15 students applied for upper-level admission, 14 were accepted, 9 enrolled. School placement exam required. Deadline for receipt of application materials: none. No application fee required. Interview required.

Athletics Interscholastic: basketball (boys, girls), volleyball (b,g); coed interscholastic: cross-country running, soccer; coed intramural: independent competitive sports, softball.

Computers Computers are regularly used in computer applications, science, yearbook classes. Computer network features include Internet access, wireless campus network, Internet filtering or blocking technology. Computer access in designated common areas is available to students. The school has a published electronic and media policy.

Contact Ms. Carol S. Wilson, Director of Admissions. 618-233-7542. Fax: 618-233-0541. E-mail: admiss@governorfrench.com. Website: www.governorfrench.com

GRACE BAPTIST ACADEMY

7815 Shallowford Road
Chattanooga, Tennessee 37421

Head of School: Mr. Matthew Pollock

General Information Coeducational day college-preparatory and religious studies school, affiliated with Baptist Church. Grades K4–12. Founded: 1985. Setting: suburban. 2 buildings on campus. Approved or accredited by Association of Christian Schools International, Southern Association of Colleges and Schools, and Tennessee Department of Education. Total enrollment: 572. Upper school average class size: 18. Upper school faculty-student ratio: 1:12. Upper School students typically attend 5 days per week. The average school day consists of 7 hours.

Upper School Student Profile Grade 9: 41 students (23 boys, 18 girls); Grade 10: 45 students (18 boys, 27 girls); Grade 11: 49 students (20 boys, 29 girls); Grade 12: 41 students (19 boys, 22 girls). 75% of students are Baptist.

Faculty School total: 50. In upper school: 14 men, 20 women; 9 have advanced degrees.

Subjects Offered Advanced biology, advanced math, Advanced Placement courses, advanced studio art-AP, algebra, American government, American history, American literature, ancient world history, art, band, Bible, Bible studies, biology, biology-AP, calculus, calculus-AP, career/college preparation, chemistry, choir, Christian doctrine, Christian ethics, Christian testament, computer applications, consumer mathematics, drama performance, dramatic arts, economics, English, English composition, English literature, environmental studies, fitness, general math, general science, geometry, global studies, health, health and safety, honors English, honors world history, keyboarding, language arts, Life of Christ, mathematics, music, New Testament, painting, personal finance, physical education, physical fitness, physics, pre-algebra, pre-calculus, senior internship, senior project, Spanish, speech, state history, statistics-AP, studio art-AP, study skills, U.S. government and politics, U.S. history, U.S. history-AP, weight training, weightlifting, world geography, world religions, yearbook.

Graduation Requirements Algebra, Bible, biology, chemistry, economics, English, English literature, geometry, global studies, physical education (includes health), senior project, Spanish, speech, trigonometry, U.S. government, U.S. history, visual and performing arts, world geography.

Special Academic Programs 3 Advanced Placement exams for which test preparation is offered; honors section; study at local college for college credit.

College Admission Counseling 36 students graduated in 2013; 34 went to college, including Chattanooga State Community College; Tennessee Technological University; The University of Tennessee; The University of Tennessee at Chattanooga. Other: 1 went to work, 1 entered military service. Mean composite ACT: 24.

Student Life Upper grades have uniform requirement, student council, honor system. Discipline rests primarily with faculty. Attendance at religious services is required.

Summer Programs Remediation programs offered; session focuses on credit recovery; held on campus; accepts boys and girls; open to students from other schools. 45 students usually enrolled. 2014 schedule: June 17 to July 19. Application deadline: June 5.

Tuition and Aid Tuition installment plan (SMART Tuition Payment Plan, FACTS Tuition Payment Plan, monthly payment plans, individually arranged payment plans, bank draft). Tuition reduction for siblings, need-based scholarship grants available. In 2013–14, 5% of upper-school students received aid.

Admissions Traditional secondary-level entrance grade is 9. For fall 2013, 15 students applied for upper-level admission, 15 were accepted, 15 enrolled. Latest standardized score from previous school required. Deadline for receipt of application materials: none. Application fee required: $300. On-campus interview required.

Athletics Interscholastic: baseball (boys), basketball (b,g), cheering (g), cross-country running (b,g), football (b), soccer (b,g), softball (g), tennis (b,g), track and field (b,g), volleyball (g), weight training (b,g); intramural: physical training (b,g), strength & conditioning (b,g), weight lifting (b), weight training (b); coed interscholastic: archery, golf. 2 PE instructors, 5 coaches, 1 athletic trainer.

Computers Computers are regularly used in career education, career exploration, college planning, computer applications, keyboarding, mathematics, senior seminar, yearbook classes. Computer network features include on-campus library services, Internet access, wireless campus network, Internet filtering or blocking technology. Student e-mail accounts and computer access in designated common areas are available to students. Students grades are available online. The school has a published electronic and media policy.

Contact Mrs. Kristi Dolan, Admissions Director. 423-892-8222 Ext. 115. Fax: 423-892-1194. E-mail: kdolan@mygracechatt.org. Website: www.gracechatt.org

GRACE BRETHREN SCHOOL

1350 Cherry Avenue
Simi Valley, California 93065

Head of School: Mr. John Hynes

General Information Coeducational day college-preparatory, arts, vocational, religious studies, and bilingual studies school, affiliated with Brethren Church, Christian faith. Grades PS–12. Founded: 1979. Setting: suburban. Nearest major city is Los Angeles. 12-acre campus. 9 buildings on campus. Approved or accredited by Association of Christian Schools International, Western Association of Schools and Colleges, and California Department of Education. Total enrollment: 830. Upper school average class size: 22. Upper school faculty-student ratio: 1:11.

Upper School Student Profile 85% of students are Brethren, Christian.

Faculty School total: 36. In upper school: 18 men, 18 women; 15 have advanced degrees.

Subjects Offered Accounting, Advanced Placement courses, algebra, American literature, American literature-AP, anatomy and physiology, ancient world history, art, ASB Leadership, athletic training, band, baseball, basketball, Bible, Bible studies, biology, British literature, British literature-AP, career/college preparation, cheerleading, chemistry, choir, college counseling, computer graphics, computer music, computer tools, concert choir, critical thinking, critical writing, digital photography, drama, drama performance, environmental science, film studies, forensics, geometry, government and politics-AP, health, home economics, jazz ensemble, New Testament, photography, physical education, physics, physics-AP, pre-algebra, pre-calculus, set design, softball, Spanish, Spanish language-AP, speech, stage design, statistics, statistics-AP, technical theater, U.S. government and politics, U.S. government and politics-AP, U.S. history, U.S. history-AP, visual and performing arts, volleyball, world cultures, world geography, world history, yearbook.

Graduation Requirements Bible studies, electives, English, foreign language, mathematics, physical education (includes health), science, social studies (includes history), visual and performing arts.

Special Academic Programs Advanced Placement exam preparation; honors section; independent study; study at local college for college credit; remedial math.

College Admission Counseling 65 students graduated in 2013; 63 went to college, including California State University, Northridge; Moorpark College; The Master's College and Seminary; University of California, Los Angeles; Westmont College. Other: 2 entered a postgraduate year. Median combined SAT: 1480. 15% scored over 1800 on combined SAT.

Student Life Upper grades have uniform requirement, student council, honor system. Discipline rests primarily with faculty. Attendance at religious services is required.

Summer Programs Remediation, advancement programs offered; session focuses on remediation; held on campus; accepts boys and girls; open to students from other schools. 45 students usually enrolled.

Tuition and Aid Day student tuition: $9300. Guaranteed tuition plan. Tuition installment plan (monthly payment plans). Tuition reduction for siblings, need-based scholarship grants available. In 2013–14, 15% of upper-school students received aid.

Admissions Traditional secondary-level entrance grade is 9. For fall 2013, 71 students applied for upper-level admission, 68 were accepted, 64 enrolled. Math Placement Exam, Stanford Achievement Test and writing sample required. Deadline for receipt of application materials: none. Application fee required: $410. Interview required.

Athletics Interscholastic: aquatics (boys, girls), baseball (b), basketball (b,g), cheering (g), cross-country running (b,g), equestrian sports (b,g), flag football (b), football (b), golf (b,g), physical training (b,g), soccer (b,g), softball (g), strength & conditioning (b,g), swimming and diving (b,g), track and field (b,g), volleyball (g), weight training (b). 4 PE instructors, 16 coaches, 1 athletic trainer.

Computers Computers are regularly used in art, graphic arts, library, newspaper, photography, photojournalism, science, study skills, video film production, writing, yearbook classes. Computer network features include on-campus library services, Internet access, wireless campus network, Internet filtering or blocking technology. Computer access in designated common areas is available to students. Students grades are available online. The school has a published electronic and media policy.

Contact Mrs. Sheri Herr, Registrar. 805-522-4667 Ext. 2033. Fax: 805-522-5617. E-mail: sherr@gracebrethren.com. Website: www.gracebrethrenschools.com

GRACE CHRISTIAN SCHOOL

12407 Pintail Street
Anchorage, Alaska 99516

Head of School: Mr. Randy Karlberg

General Information Coeducational day college-preparatory, arts, religious studies, and technology school, affiliated with Christian faith. Grades K–12. Founded: 1980. Setting: urban. 7-acre campus. 1 building on campus. Approved or accredited by Association of Christian Schools International, Northwest Accreditation Commission, and Northwest Association of Schools and Colleges. Total enrollment: 617. Upper school average class size: 15. Upper school faculty-student ratio: 1:15. There are 180 required school days per year for Upper School students. Upper School students typically attend 5 days per week. The average school day consists of 6 hours and 50 minutes.

Upper School Student Profile Grade 7: 46 students (26 boys, 20 girls); Grade 8: 47 students (23 boys, 24 girls); Grade 9: 47 students (22 boys, 25 girls); Grade 10: 47 students (26 boys, 21 girls); Grade 11: 57 students (23 boys, 34 girls); Grade 12: 54 students (31 boys, 23 girls). 99% of students are Christian faith.

Faculty School total: 45. In upper school: 12 men, 16 women; 10 have advanced degrees.

Subjects Offered Algebra, American government, American history, art, Bible, biology, biology-AP, calculus-AP, chemistry, chemistry-AP, choir, computer skills, computer technologies, creative writing, drama, economics, English, English language and composition-AP, English literature and composition-AP, English literature-AP, English/composition-AP, film, fine arts, geometry, health, leadership and service, literature, media, music theory-AP, physical education, physical science, physics, psychology, publications, science, social studies, Spanish, speech, trigonometry, U.S. history, U.S. history-AP, weightlifting, world history, yearbook.

Graduation Requirements Algebra, American government, American literature, biology, British literature, consumer economics, electives, English composition, English literature, geometry, literary genres, literature, physical education (includes health), physical science, practical arts, U.S. history, world history, one year of Bible for every year attending, Old Testament survey in 9th grade, 10th Grade—New Testament survey, 11th Grade—Life and Times of Christ/Marriage and Family, 12th grade—Defending Your Faith/Understanding the Times.

Special Academic Programs Advanced Placement exam preparation.

College Admission Counseling 50 students graduated in 2013; 46 went to college, including Colorado State University; Corban University; The Master's College and Seminary; University of Alaska Anchorage; University of Alaska Fairbanks; Wheaton College. Other: 4 went to work. Mean SAT critical reading: 577, mean SAT math: 536, mean SAT writing: 544, mean combined SAT: 1657, mean composite ACT: 23.

Student Life Upper grades have specified standards of dress, student council, honor system. Discipline rests primarily with faculty. Attendance at religious services is required.

Summer Programs Enrichment programs offered; session focuses on science/forensics; held on campus; accepts boys and girls; open to students from other schools. 30 students usually enrolled. 2014 schedule: June 9 to June 13.

Tuition and Aid Day student tuition: $7750. Tuition installment plan (FACTS Tuition Payment Plan). Tuition reduction for siblings, need-based scholarship grants available. In 2013–14, 15% of upper-school students received aid. Total amount of financial aid awarded in 2013–14: $200,000.

Admissions Traditional secondary-level entrance grade is 9. For fall 2013, 36 students applied for upper-level admission, 34 were accepted, 34 enrolled. Math and English placement tests, school's own exam or Stanford Achievement Test required. Deadline for receipt of application materials: none. Application fee required: $50. Interview required.

Athletics Interscholastic: basketball (boys, girls), cheering (g), cross-country running (b,g), skiing (cross-country) (b,g), soccer (b,g), track and field (b,g), volleyball (g), wrestling (b). 2 PE instructors, 15 coaches, 1 athletic trainer.

Computers Computers are regularly used in career exploration, computer applications, media, publications, technology, video film production, yearbook classes. Computer network features include on-campus library services, online commercial services, Internet access, wireless campus network, Internet filtering or blocking technology. Students grades are available online.

Contact Mrs. Eva Hall, Admissions. 907-345-4814. Fax: 907-644-2260. E-mail: admissions@gracechristianalaska.org. Website: www.gracechristianalaska.org

THE GRAND RIVER ACADEMY

3042 College Street
Austinburg, Ohio 44010

Head of School: Tim Viands

General Information Boys' boarding college-preparatory, arts, technology, and ESL school; primarily serves underachievers, students with learning disabilities, and individuals with Attention Deficit Disorder. Grades 9–PG. Founded: 1831. Setting: small town. Nearest major city is Cleveland. Students are housed in single-sex dormitories. 200-acre campus. 11 buildings on campus. Approved or accredited by Independent Schools Association of the Central States, Midwest Association of Boarding Schools, North Central Association of Colleges and Schools, The Association of Boarding Schools, and Ohio Department of Education. Member of National Association of Independent Schools and Secondary School Admission Test Board. Endowment: $23 million. Total enrollment: 111. Upper school average class size: 7. Upper school faculty-student ratio: 1:6.

Upper School Student Profile Grade 9: 7 students (7 boys); Grade 10: 30 students (30 boys); Grade 11: 38 students (38 boys); Grade 12: 36 students (36 boys). 100% of students are boarding students. 30% are state residents. 18 states are represented in upper school student body. 16% are international students. International students from Brazil, Canada, China, Republic of Korea, Spain, and Thailand.

Faculty School total: 24. In upper school: 17 men, 7 women; 15 have advanced degrees; 21 reside on campus.

Subjects Offered 20th century American writers, 20th century history, 20th century world history, Advanced Placement courses, algebra, American history, American literature, art, biology, British literature (honors), calculus, calculus-AP, chemistry, civics, college writing, Coming of Age in the 20th Century, community service, comparative government and politics, computer science, creative writing, criminology, digital imaging, digital photography, economics, English, English as a foreign language, English literature, environmental science, ESL, ESL, European literature, fine arts, forensics, geography, government, government/civics, grammar, graphic design, health, history, integrated science, lab science, mathematics, music theory, photography, physical education, physics, physics-AP, pre-calculus, psychology, public speaking, science, social studies, Spanish, speech, TOEFL preparation, video and animation, video film production, Web site design, world civilizations, world history, world issues, world literature, yearbook.

Graduation Requirements Arts and fine arts (art, music, dance, drama), computer science, English, mathematics, physical education (includes health), science, social studies (includes history), acceptance at a college, passage of Ohio state-mandated proficiency tests. Community service is required.

Special Academic Programs 5 Advanced Placement exams for which test preparation is offered; honors section; independent study; study at local college for college credit; academic accommodation for the gifted; remedial reading and/or remedial writing; special instructional classes for students with Attention Deficit Disorder, students with Executive Functioning Disorder; ESL (18 students enrolled).

College Admission Counseling 33 students graduated in 2013; all went to college, including Baldwin Wallace University; Case Western Reserve University; Eastern Michigan University; John Carroll University; Penn State Erie, The Behrend College; Penn State University Park.

Student Life Upper grades have uniform requirement, student council, honor system. Discipline rests primarily with faculty.

Summer Programs Remediation, enrichment, advancement, ESL, sports, art/fine arts, computer instruction programs offered; session focuses on ESL, enrichment, and remediation; held on campus; accepts boys; open to students from other schools. 40 students usually enrolled. 2014 schedule: June 28 to August 8. Application deadline: June 22.

Tuition and Aid 5-day tuition and room/board: $37,000; 7-day tuition and room/board: $38,600. Need-based scholarship grants, prepGATE Loans available. In 2013–14, 10% of upper-school students received aid. Total amount of financial aid awarded in 2013–14: $205,000.

Admissions Traditional secondary-level entrance grade is 10. For fall 2013, 68 students applied for upper-level admission, 59 were accepted, 46 enrolled. Deadline for receipt of application materials: none. Application fee required: $35. On-campus interview required.

Athletics Interscholastic: baseball, basketball, cross-country running, golf, horseback riding, ice hockey, independent competitive sports, indoor soccer, soccer, swimming and diving, tennis, wrestling; intramural: backpacking, badminton, baseball, basketball, bicycling, billiards, bocce, bowling, canoeing/kayaking, equestrian sports, fishing, fitness, fitness walking, flag football, fly fishing, football, freestyle skiing, Frisbee, golf, hiking/backpacking, horseback riding, horseshoes, ice hockey, jogging, martial arts, mountain biking, Nautilus, outdoor activities, outdoor recreation, outdoor skills, paddle tennis, paint ball, physical fitness, physical training, power lifting, rafting, roller blading, roller skating, ropes courses, running, self defense, skateboarding, skiing (cross-country), skiing (downhill), snowboarding, soccer, softball, strength & conditioning, table tennis, tennis, touch football, ultimate Frisbee, volleyball, walking, weight lifting, weight training, whiffle ball, wrestling. 1 PE instructor, 10 coaches.

Computers Computers are regularly used in English, ESL, foreign language, history, mathematics, science classes. Computer resources include on-campus library services, online commercial services, Internet access, wireless campus network, Internet filtering or blocking technology, mobile learning lab, classrooms linked to T-1, SmartBoards technology. Campus intranet is available to students. Students grades are available online.

Contact Glenn Singer, Director of Admission. 440-275-2811 Ext. 225. Fax: 440-275-1825. E-mail: admissions@grandriver.org. Website: www.grandriver.org

THE GRAUER SCHOOL

1500 South El Camino Real
Encinitas, California 92024

Head of School: Dr. Stuart Robert Grauer

General Information Coeducational day college-preparatory, arts, and technology school. Grades 6–12. Founded: 1991. Setting: suburban. Nearest major city is San Diego. 5-acre campus. 6 buildings on campus. Approved or accredited by Western Association of Schools and Colleges and California Department of Education. Endowment: $150,000. Total enrollment: 161. Upper school average class size: 12. Upper school faculty-student ratio: 1:6. There are 178 required school days per year for Upper School students. Upper School students typically attend 5 days per week. The average school day consists of 6 hours and 30 minutes.

Upper School Student Profile Grade 6: 9 students (8 boys, 1 girl); Grade 7: 23 students (13 boys, 10 girls); Grade 8: 29 students (11 boys, 18 girls); Grade 9: 28 students (17 boys, 11 girls); Grade 10: 29 students (10 boys, 19 girls); Grade 11: 28 students (15 boys, 13 girls); Grade 12: 15 students (10 boys, 5 girls).

Faculty School total: 32. In upper school: 14 men, 16 women; 19 have advanced degrees.

Subjects Offered ACT preparation, advanced biology, advanced chemistry, advanced math, advanced TOEFL/grammar, algebra, alternative physical education, American government, American history, anatomy and physiology, ancient history, applied music, art, art appreciation, art history, ASB Leadership, athletic training, audio visual/media, backpacking, baseball, basketball, bell choir, biology, business mathematics, calculus, character education, chemistry, Chinese, choir, civics, classical music, college admission preparation, college planning, community service, computer applications, computer education, computer multimedia, computers, creative writing, culinary arts, drama, dramatic arts, earth and space science, economics, English literature, environmental education, ESL, ESL, experiential education, film studies, filmmaking, fitness, French, gardening, geography, geometry, global studies, health, high adventure outdoor program, honors algebra, honors English, honors geometry, honors U.S. history, honors world history, Japanese, keyboarding, leadership and service, marine science, multimedia, music, music appreciation, music performance, outdoor education, peace studies, personal fitness, photo shop, photography, physical education, physics, pre-algebra, pre-calculus, religion, religion and culture, robotics, SAT preparation, Spanish, speech and debate, studio art, study skills, surfing, tennis, theater arts, trigonometry, U.S. government, U.S. history, U.S. literature, world geography, world history, world religions.

Graduation Requirements Algebra, American history, art, biology, chemistry, college admission preparation, computer applications, computer skills, economics, English, experiential education, foreign language, French, geometry, life science, marine science, mathematics, non-Western literature, outdoor education, physical education (includes health), physical science, physics, science, senior project, social studies (includes history), studio art, U.S. government, U.S. history, U.S. literature, Western civilization, Western literature, wilderness education, world geography, world history, world literature, world religions, expeditionary learning in the field and 50 hours community service, all students graduate with distinction in a subject of their choice.

Special Academic Programs Advanced Placement exam preparation; honors section; independent study; study abroad; academic accommodation for the gifted, the musically talented, and the artistically talented; special instructional classes for deaf students; ESL (11 students enrolled).

College Admission Counseling 21 students graduated in 2013; all went to college, including High Point University; Lewis & Clark College; New York University; Pitzer College; The University of British Columbia; University of Southern California. Median SAT critical reading: 600, median SAT math: 560, median SAT writing: 600, median combined SAT: 1740, median composite ACT: 27.

Student Life Upper grades have specified standards of dress, student council, honor system. Discipline rests equally with students and faculty.

Summer Programs Remediation, enrichment, advancement, ESL, sports, art/fine arts, rigorous outdoor training, computer instruction programs offered; session focuses on academics and enrichment; held on campus; accepts boys and girls; open to students from other schools. 60 students usually enrolled.

Tuition and Aid Day student tuition: $22,000. Tuition installment plan (individually arranged payment plans, 3 payment plans). Tuition reduction for siblings, need-based scholarship grants available. In 2013–14, 14% of upper-school students received aid. Total amount of financial aid awarded in 2013–14: $156,977.

Admissions Traditional secondary-level entrance grade is 9. For fall 2013, 25 students applied for upper-level admission, 15 were accepted, 1 enrolled. Admissions testing, any standardized test and writing sample required. Deadline for receipt of application materials: February 28. Application fee required: $100. Interview required.

Athletics Interscholastic: tennis (boys, girls); intramural: basketball (b), football (b), soccer (b,g); triathlon (b,g), volleyball (b,g); coed interscholastic: aerobics/dance, archery, badminton, baseball, basketball, billiards, canoeing/kayaking, climbing, combined training, cooperative games, cross-country running, dance, fitness, fitness walking, flag football, Frisbee, hiking/backpacking, horseback riding, jogging, jump rope, kayaking, kickball, martial arts, modern dance, outdoor activities, outdoor adventure, outdoor education, outdoor recreation, outdoor skills, outdoors, physical fitness, physical training, rafting, rock climbing, roller skating, running, self defense, soccer, strength & conditioning, surfing, table tennis, tennis, track and field, volleyball, walking, wall climbing, weight training, yoga; coed intramural: cross-country running, dressage, equestrian sports, flag football, independent competitive sports, running, sailing, soccer, surfing, tennis, track and field, triathlon. 5 PE instructors, 5 coaches.

Computers Computers are regularly used in all classes. Computer network features include Internet access, wireless campus network, Internet filtering or blocking technology, online text books, online portfolios, all students required to have computers.. Campus intranet, student e-mail accounts, and computer access in designated common areas are available to students. Students grades are available online. The school has a published electronic and media policy.

Contact Ms. Elizabeth Braymen, Admissions Director. 760-274-2116. Fax: 760-944-6784. E-mail: admissions@grauerschool.com. Website: www.grauerschool.com

GREAT LAKES CHRISTIAN HIGH SCHOOL

4875 King Street
Beamsville, Ontario L0R 1B6, Canada

Head of School: Mr. Don Rose

General Information Coeducational boarding and day college-preparatory, general academic, arts, and religious studies school, affiliated with Church of Christ. Grades 9–12. Founded: 1952. 6 buildings on campus. Approved or accredited by Ontario Ministry of Education and Ontario Department of Education. Language of instruction: English. Endowment: CAN$500,000. Total enrollment: 94. Upper school average class size: 22.

Upper School Student Profile Grade 9: 18 students (10 boys, 8 girls); Grade 10: 22 students (10 boys, 12 girls); Grade 11: 25 students (11 boys, 14 girls); Grade 12: 33 students (19 boys, 14 girls). 60% of students are boarding students. 55% are province residents. 5 provinces are represented in upper school student body. 40% are international students. International students from China, Hong Kong, Republic of Korea, Taiwan, Thailand, and United States; 3 other countries represented in student body. 40% of students are members of Church of Christ.

Subjects Offered 20th century world history, accounting, algebra, arts appreciation, Bible, biology, calculus, career and personal planning, chemistry, computer science, computer technologies, dramatic arts, economics, English, English composition, English language and composition-AP, English literature, English-AP, ESL, family studies, finite math, French, geography, history, mathematics, mathematics-AP, media, music, music composition, physical education, physics, society, technology, world issues.

Graduation Requirements 20th century history, advanced math, art, Bible, business, Canadian geography, Canadian history, Canadian literature, career planning, civics, computer information systems, conceptual physics, critical thinking, current events, economics, English, English composition, English literature, French as a second language, geography, mathematics, physical education (includes health), science, society challenge and change, world geography, world history.

Special Academic Programs Independent study; ESL (18 students enrolled).

College Admission Counseling 26 students graduated in 2013; 17 went to college, including Carleton University; McMaster University; University of Ottawa; University of Toronto; Wilfrid Laurier University; York University. Other: 6 went to work, 1 entered military service.

Student Life Attendance at religious services is required.

Summer Programs Enrichment programs offered; session focuses on skill levels improvement; held on campus; accepts boys and girls; not open to students from other schools. 2014 schedule: June 25 to August 24. Application deadline: May 11.

Tuition and Aid Day student tuition: CAN$8800; 5-day tuition and room/board: CAN$13,400; 7-day tuition and room/board: CAN$15,200. Tuition installment plan (monthly payment plans, individually arranged payment plans). Tuition reduction for siblings, bursaries, merit scholarship grants, need-based scholarship grants, need-based loans, middle-income loans, paying campus jobs available. In 2013–14, 45% of upper-school students received aid; total upper-school merit-scholarship money awarded: CAN$8000. Total amount of financial aid awarded in 2013–14: CAN$150,000.

Admissions Traditional secondary-level entrance grade is 9. For fall 2013, 130 students applied for upper-level admission, 115 were accepted, 95 enrolled. CAT or SLEP required. Deadline for receipt of application materials: none. Application fee required: CAN$100. Interview recommended.

Athletics Interscholastic: badminton (boys, girls), basketball (b,g), cross-country running (b,g), golf (b), hockey (b,g), ice hockey (b,g), soccer (b,g), tennis (b,g), track and field (b,g), volleyball (b,g); intramural: aerobics (g), badminton (b,g), basketball (b,g), cooperative games (b,g), fitness (b,g), ice hockey (b,g), volleyball (b,g); coed interscholastic: badminton, indoor hockey, indoor soccer, netball, tennis; coed intramural: badminton, ball hockey, baseball, basketball, cooperative games, floor hockey, hockey, volleyball. 2 PE instructors, 2 coaches.

Computers Computers are regularly used in accounting, business, music, technology, typing classes. Computer network features include on-campus library services, Internet access, Internet filtering or blocking technology, grades are available online to parents. Campus intranet and computer access in designated common areas are available to students. Students grades are available online.

Contact Mrs. Sandy McBay, Admissions Liaison. 905-563-5374 Ext. 230. Fax: 905-563-0818. E-mail: study@glchs.on.ca. Website: www.glchs.on.ca

GREENHILL SCHOOL

4141 Spring Valley Road
Addison, Texas 75001

Head of School: Scott A. Griggs

General Information Coeducational day college-preparatory school. Grades PK–12. Founded: 1950. Setting: suburban. Nearest major city is Dallas. 78-acre campus. 8 buildings on campus. Approved or accredited by Independent Schools Association of the Southwest and Texas Department of Education. Member of National Association of Independent Schools and Secondary School Admission Test Board. Endowment: $30.3 million. Total enrollment: 1,276. Upper school average class size: 16. Upper school faculty-student ratio: 1:7. Upper School students typically attend 5 days per week. The average school day consists of 7 hours and 45 minutes.

Upper School Student Profile Grade 9: 121 students (61 boys, 60 girls); Grade 10: 119 students (59 boys, 60 girls); Grade 11: 118 students (57 boys, 61 girls); Grade 12: 118 students (62 boys, 56 girls).

Faculty School total: 171. In upper school: 34 men, 43 women; 52 have advanced degrees.

Subjects Offered Algebra, American history, American literature, art, art history, biology, calculus, ceramics, chemistry, Chinese, computer programming, computer science, creative writing, dance, drama, ecology, economics, English, English literature, European history, fine arts, French, geometry, government/civics, health, history, journalism, Latin, mathematics, music, philosophy, photography, physical education, physics, science, social studies, Spanish, speech, theater, trigonometry.

Graduation Requirements Arts and fine arts (art, music, dance, drama), classical language, computer studies, English, history, mathematics, modern languages, physical education (includes health), science. Community service is required.

Special Academic Programs Advanced Placement exam preparation; honors section; independent study; term-away projects.

College Admission Counseling 115 students graduated in 2013; 113 went to college, including Dartmouth College; New York University; The University of Texas at Austin; University of Pennsylvania; Vanderbilt University; Washington University in St. Louis. Other: 1 entered military service, 1 had other specific plans. Median SAT critical reading: 670, median SAT math: 680, median SAT writing: 680, median combined SAT: 2030, median composite ACT: 32. 79% scored over 600 on SAT critical reading, 79% scored over 600 on SAT math, 77% scored over 600 on SAT writing, 84% scored over 1800 on combined SAT, 89% scored over 26 on composite ACT.

Student Life Upper grades have specified standards of dress, student council, honor system. Discipline rests primarily with faculty.

Summer Programs Enrichment, sports, art/fine arts, computer instruction programs offered; session focuses on enrichment and sports; held on campus; accepts boys and girls; open to students from other schools. 1,300 students usually enrolled. 2014 schedule: June 2 to August 8. Application deadline: none.

Tuition and Aid Day student tuition: $24,850. Need-based scholarship grants available. In 2013–14, 20% of upper-school students received aid. Total amount of financial aid awarded in 2013–14: $1,755,310.

Admissions Traditional secondary-level entrance grade is 9. For fall 2013, 178 students applied for upper-level admission, 47 were accepted, 36 enrolled. ISEE required. Deadline for receipt of application materials: January 10. Application fee required: $175. Interview required.

Athletics Interscholastic: aquatics (boys, girls), baseball (b), basketball (b,g), cross-country running (b,g), field hockey (g), football (b), golf (b,g), lacrosse (b,g), running (b,g), soccer (b,g), softball (g), swimming and diving (b,g), tennis (b,g), track and field (b,g), volleyball (b,g), winter soccer (b,g); intramural: baseball (b), basketball (b,g), field hockey (g), fitness (b,g), football (b), lacrosse (b,g), physical fitness (b,g), running (b,g), soccer (b,g), softball (g), strength & conditioning (b,g), swimming and diving (b,g), tennis (b,g), track and field (b,g), volleyball (b,g), weight lifting (b,g), winter soccer (b,g); coed interscholastic: cheering; coed intramural: aquatics, ballet, cross-country running, dance, fitness, Frisbee, golf, physical fitness, running, soccer, strength & conditioning, swimming and diving, table tennis, tai chi, tennis, track and field, ultimate Frisbee, volleyball, weight lifting, weight training, winter soccer, yoga. 15 PE instructors, 4 athletic trainers.

Computers Computers are regularly used in computer applications, digital applications, independent study, programming, video film production, Web site design classes. Computer network features include on-campus library services, online commercial services, Internet access, wireless campus network, Internet filtering or blocking technology. Campus intranet, student e-mail accounts, and computer access in designated common areas are available to students. Students grades are available online. The school has a published electronic and media policy.

Contact Angela H. Woodson, Director of Admission. 972-628-5910. Fax: 972-404-8217. E-mail: admission@greenhill.org. Website: www.greenhill.org

GREENHILLS SCHOOL

850 Greenhills Drive
Ann Arbor, Michigan 48105

Head of School: Carl J. Pelofsky

General Information Coeducational day college-preparatory and arts school. Grades 6–12. Founded: 1968. Setting: suburban. Nearest major city is Detroit. 30-acre campus. 1 building on campus. Approved or accredited by Independent Schools Association of the Central States and Michigan Department of Education. Member of National Association of Independent Schools and Secondary School Admission Test Board. Endowment: $7 million. Total enrollment: 569. Upper school average class size: 16. Upper school faculty-student ratio: 1:8. There are 165 required school days per year for Upper School students. Upper School students typically attend 5 days per week. The average school day consists of 7 hours.

Upper School Student Profile Grade 9: 90 students (44 boys, 46 girls); Grade 10: 76 students (41 boys, 35 girls); Grade 11: 90 students (44 boys, 46 girls); Grade 12: 74 students (32 boys, 42 girls).

Faculty School total: 67. In upper school: 21 men, 30 women; 41 have advanced degrees.

Subjects Offered 3-dimensional art, advanced chemistry, Advanced Placement courses, African-American literature, algebra, American history, American literature, ancient history, art, astronomy, biology, calculus, calculus-AP, ceramics, chemistry, Chinese, Chinese studies, chorus, community service, creative writing, discrete mathematics, drama, drawing, economics, economics and history, English, English literature, ethics, European history, expository writing, fine arts, French, geometry, government, health, history, jazz, journalism, Latin, mathematics, music, orchestra, painting, photography, physical education, physical science, physics, science, social studies, Spanish, theater, trigonometry, world history, world literature, writing.

Graduation Requirements Arts and fine arts (art, music, dance, drama), English, foreign language, mathematics, physical education (includes health), science, social studies (includes history), senior project. Community service is required.

Special Academic Programs Advanced Placement exam preparation; honors section; independent study; programs in English, mathematics for dyslexic students; special instructional classes for blind students.

College Admission Counseling 90 students graduated in 2013; all went to college, including Brown University; Emory University; Michigan State University; Swarthmore College; The Johns Hopkins University; University of Michigan. Mean SAT critical reading: 654, mean SAT math: 660, mean SAT writing: 653, mean combined SAT: 1967, mean composite ACT: 29.

Student Life Upper grades have specified standards of dress, student council, honor system. Discipline rests equally with students and faculty.

Summer Programs Enrichment, sports, art/fine arts, rigorous outdoor training programs offered; session focuses on enrichment, academics, travel; held on campus; accepts boys and girls; open to students from other schools. 30 students usually enrolled. 2014 schedule: July 1 to July 30. Application deadline: none.

Tuition and Aid Day student tuition: $20,100. Tuition installment plan (FACTS Tuition Payment Plan, monthly payment plans). Need-based scholarship grants available. In 2013–14, 18% of upper-school students received aid. Total amount of financial aid awarded in 2013–14: $1,000,000.

Admissions Traditional secondary-level entrance grade is 9. For fall 2013, 85 students applied for upper-level admission, 52 were accepted, 36 enrolled. SSAT or TOEFL required. Deadline for receipt of application materials: none. Application fee required: $50. Interview required.

Athletics Interscholastic: baseball (boys), basketball (b,g), cross-country running (b,g), field hockey (g), golf (b,g), soccer (b,g), softball (g), tennis (b,g), track and field (b,g), volleyball (g); intramural: basketball (b,g), cross-country running (b,g), field hockey (g), soccer (b,g); coed interscholastic: equestrian sports, swimming and diving; coed intramural: hiking/backpacking, outdoor activities, outdoor education. 3 PE instructors, 36 coaches, 1 athletic trainer.

Computers Computers are regularly used in all academic classes. Computer network features include on-campus library services, online commercial services, Internet access, wireless campus network, Internet filtering or blocking technology. Campus intranet, student e-mail accounts, and computer access in designated common areas are available to students. Students grades are available online. The school has a published electronic and media policy.

Contact Betsy Ellsworth, Director of Admission and Financial Aid. 734-205-4061. Fax: 734-205-4056. E-mail: admission@greenhillsschool.org. Website: www.greenhillsschool.org

THE GREENWOOD SCHOOL

Putney, Vermont
See Junior Boarding Schools section.

GRIER SCHOOL

PO Box 308
Tyrone, Pennsylvania 16686-0308

Head of School: Mrs. Gina Borst

General Information Girls' boarding and day college-preparatory, arts, and business school. Boarding grades 7–PG, day grades 7–12. Founded: 1853. Setting: rural. Nearest major city is Pittsburgh. Students are housed in single-sex dormitories. 320-acre campus. 5 buildings on campus. Approved or accredited by Middle States Association of Colleges and Schools, Pennsylvania Association of Independent Schools, and The Association of Boarding Schools. Member of National Association of Independent Schools and Secondary School Admission Test Board. Endowment: $18 million. Total enrollment: 306. Upper school average class size: 10. Upper school faculty-student ratio: 1:7. There are 160 required school days per year for Upper School students. Upper School students typically attend 5 days per week. The average school day consists of 7 hours.

Upper School Student Profile Grade 9: 47 students (47 girls); Grade 10: 71 students (71 girls); Grade 11: 81 students (81 girls); Grade 12: 63 students (63 girls). 88% of students are boarding students. 18% are state residents. 30 states are represented in upper school student body. 50% are international students. International students from China, Germany, Mexico, Republic of Korea, Russian Federation, and Viet Nam; 6 other countries represented in student body.

Faculty School total: 62. In upper school: 18 men, 44 women; 36 have advanced degrees; 19 reside on campus.

Subjects Offered 3-dimensional art, acting, advanced biology, advanced chemistry, advanced studio art-AP, advanced TOEFL/grammar, algebra, American history, American history-AP, American literature, anatomy, art, art history, art history-AP, art-AP, ballet, ballet technique, batik, biology, biology-AP, British literature, British literature (honors), Broadway dance, calculus, calculus-AP, ceramics, chemistry, chemistry-AP, Chinese, choir, choral music, choreography, civics, community service, comparative religion, computer graphics, computer math, computer programming, computer-aided design, costumes and make-up, creative writing, criminology, current events, dance, desktop publishing, digital art, digital photography, directing, drama, drama performance, dramatic arts, drawing, earth science, ecology, economics, economics-AP, English, English as a foreign language, English literature, English literature and composition-AP, English literature-AP, environmental science, environmental science-AP, equine science, ESL, European history, European history-AP, fabric arts, fashion, fiber arts, filmmaking, finance, fine arts, French, French language-AP, French-AP, geography, geometry, government, government/civics, graphic arts, guitar, health, health and wellness, history, honors algebra, honors English, honors geometry, honors U.S. history, honors world history, human anatomy, human biology, instrumental music, international relations, jazz band, jazz dance, journalism, linguistics, macro/microeconomics-AP, macroeconomics-AP, marine biology, mathematics, microeconomics-AP, model United Nations, modern dance, music, music technology, music theater, music theory, music theory-AP, musical theater, musical theater dance, newspaper, oil painting, painting, personal finance, philosophy, photography, physical education, physics, physics-AP, physiology, piano, portfolio art, pre-algebra, pre-calculus, printmaking, probability and statistics, psychology, science, scuba diving, social studies, Spanish, Spanish language-AP, stagecraft, statistics-AP, studio art-AP, symphonic band, tap dance, theater, TOEFL preparation, trigonometry, typing, video film production, vocal ensemble, voice, weaving, women's studies, world history, world history-AP, world literature, writing, writing, writing workshop, yearbook.

Graduation Requirements Arts and fine arts (art, music, dance, drama), English, foreign language, mathematics, physical education (includes health), science, social sciences, social studies (includes history).

Special Academic Programs 19 Advanced Placement exams for which test preparation is offered; honors section; independent study; study abroad; academic accommodation for the gifted, the musically talented, and the artistically talented; remedial reading and/or remedial writing; remedial math; programs in English, general development for dyslexic students; special instructional classes for students with learning disabilities, Attention Deficit Disorder, and dyslexia; ESL (60 students enrolled).

College Admission Counseling 48 students graduated in 2013; all went to college, including Ithaca College; New York University; Penn State University Park; School of the Art Institute of Chicago; University of Illinois at Urbana–Champaign; University of Washington. Median SAT critical reading: 600, median SAT math: 640. 25% scored over 600 on SAT critical reading, 20% scored over 600 on SAT math.

Student Life Upper grades have specified standards of dress, student council, honor system. Discipline rests primarily with faculty.

Summer Programs Enrichment, ESL, sports, art/fine arts programs offered; session focuses on recreation and ESL; held on campus; accepts girls; open to students from other schools. 100 students usually enrolled. 2014 schedule: June 16 to September 7. Application deadline: none.

Tuition and Aid Day student tuition: $22,500; 7-day tuition and room/board: $47,800. Tuition installment plan (individually arranged payment plans). Tuition reduction for siblings, merit scholarship grants, need-based scholarship grants, need-based loans, paying campus jobs available. In 2013–14, 45% of upper-school students received aid; total upper-school merit-scholarship money awarded: $560,000. Total amount of financial aid awarded in 2013–14: $1,900,000.

Admissions Traditional secondary-level entrance grade is 9. For fall 2013, 275 students applied for upper-level admission, 170 were accepted, 127 enrolled. SSAT or WISC III required. Deadline for receipt of application materials: none. Application fee required: $50. Interview recommended.

Athletics Interscholastic: basketball, dance, equestrian sports, fencing, skiing (downhill), soccer, tennis, volleyball; intramural: aerobics, aerobics/dance, alpine skiing, aquatics, archery, badminton, ballet, basketball, bicycling, bowling, canoeing/kayaking, cheering, cross-country running, dance, equestrian sports, fencing, figure skating, fitness, fitness walking, fly fishing, golf, gymnastics, hiking/backpacking, horseback riding, jogging, jump rope, martial arts, modern dance, mountain biking, nordic skiing, outdoor recreation, paddle tennis, physical fitness, physical training, ropes courses, scuba diving, skiing (cross-country), skiing (downhill), snowboarding, soccer, swimming and diving, tennis, volleyball, walking, weight training, yoga. 3 PE instructors, 3 coaches, 3 athletic trainers.

Computers Computers are regularly used in creative writing, English, foreign language, graphic arts, mathematics, music technology, newspaper, science, yearbook classes. Computer network features include on-campus library services, online commercial services, Internet access, wireless campus network, Internet filtering or blocking technology. Campus intranet and student e-mail accounts are available to students. Students grades are available online. The school has a published electronic and media policy.

Contact Mr. Andrew M. Wilson, Headmaster/Director of Admissions. 814-684-3000 Ext. 106. Fax: 814-684-2177. E-mail: admissions@grier.org. Website: www.grier.org

See Display below, Close-Up on page 538, and Summer Program Close-Up on page 632.

GUAMANI PRIVATE SCHOOL

PO Box 3000
Guayama, Puerto Rico 00785

Head of School: Mr. Eduardo Delgado

General Information Coeducational day college-preparatory and bilingual studies school. Grades 1–12. Founded: 1914. Setting: urban. Nearest major city is Caguas. 1-acre campus. 1 building on campus. Approved or accredited by Middle States Association of Colleges and Schools, National Catholic Education Association, and Puerto Rico Department of Education. Total enrollment: 606. Upper school average class size: 20. Upper school faculty-student ratio: 1:13.

Faculty School total: 32. In upper school: 10 men, 10 women; 3 have advanced degrees.

Subjects Offered Advanced math, Advanced Placement courses, algebra, American government, American history, analysis and differential calculus, chemistry, civics, pre-algebra, pre-calculus, science project, science research, social sciences, social studies, sociology, Spanish, Spanish language-AP, U.S. literature, visual arts, world geography, world history.

Graduation Requirements Mathematics, science, social sciences, Spanish, acceptance into a college or university. Community service is required.

Special Academic Programs Advanced Placement exam preparation; honors section; independent study.

College Admission Counseling 23 students graduated in 2013; they went to Embry-Riddle Aeronautical University–Daytona; Syracuse University; University of Puerto Rico, Cayey University College; University of Puerto Rico, Mayagüez Campus; University of Puerto Rico, Río Piedras. Other: 23 entered a postgraduate year.

Student Life Upper grades have uniform requirement, student council, honor system. Discipline rests primarily with faculty.

Summer Programs Remediation, ESL programs offered; held on campus; accepts boys and girls; open to students from other schools. 30 students usually enrolled. 2014 schedule: June 1 to June 30. Application deadline: May 27.

Admissions Traditional secondary-level entrance grade is 9. For fall 2013, 30 students applied for upper-level admission, 21 were accepted, 20 enrolled. School's own test or Test of Achievement and Proficiency required. Deadline for receipt of application materials: none. Application fee required: $30. Interview required.

Athletics Interscholastic: aerobics/dance (girls), basketball (b,g), cheering (g), dance squad (g), volleyball (b,g); coed interscholastic: dance team. 3 PE instructors, 2 coaches.

Computers Computers are regularly used in aviation, English, mathematics, science, social sciences, Spanish, word processing classes. Computer resources include on-campus library services, Internet access, wireless campus network, Internet filtering or blocking technology. The school has a published electronic and media policy.

Contact Mrs. Digna Torres, Secretary. 787-864-6880. Fax: 787-866-4947. Website: www.guamani.com

GULLIVER PREPARATORY SCHOOL

6575 North Kendall Drive
Miami, Florida 33156

Head of School: John W. Krutulis

General Information Coeducational day college-preparatory, arts, technology, International Baccalaureate, architectural design, and pre-engineering, law and litigation, biomedical sciences school. Grades PK–12. Founded: 1926. Setting: suburban. 14-acre campus. 3 buildings on campus. Approved or accredited by CITA (Commission on International and Trans-Regional Accreditation), Southern Association of Colleges and Schools, Southern Association of Independent Schools, and Florida Department of Education. Member of Secondary School Admission Test Board. Total enrollment: 1,834. Upper school average class size: 14. Upper school faculty-student ratio: 1:8.

Faculty School total: 126. In upper school: 58 men, 68 women; 69 have advanced degrees.

Subjects Offered Algebra, American history, American literature, anatomy, architectural drawing, architecture, art, art history, biology, calculus, ceramics, chemistry, college admission preparation, college writing, computer animation, computer applications, computer processing, computer programming, computer programming-AP, computer science, computer science-AP, computer skills, computer studies, concert band, concert choir, creative writing, dance, desktop publishing, drafting, drama, economics, engineering, English, English literature, European history, fine arts, French, geometry, government/civics, history, Italian, keyboarding, Latin, marine biology, mathematics, mechanical drawing, music, newspaper, physical education, physics, psychology, science, social studies, Spanish, speech, statistics, theater, trigonometry, video, world history, world literature, yearbook, zoology.

Graduation Requirements Arts and fine arts (art, music, dance, drama), computer science, English, foreign language, mathematics, physical education (includes health), science, social studies (includes history). Community service is required.

GRIER school | grades 7-12
summer camps | ages 6-17

A boarding school for girls in grades 7-12 that features a diverse student body and a comprehensive college preparatory curriculum offering both academic rigor and learning support

admissions@grier.org | www.grier.org | 814.684.3000

Special Academic Programs International Baccalaureate program; Advanced Placement exam preparation; honors section; study at local college for college credit; academic accommodation for the gifted, the musically talented, and the artistically talented.

College Admission Counseling 180 students graduated in 2013; all went to college, including Boston University; Duke University; Florida International University; Florida State University; University of Florida; University of Miami. Mean SAT critical reading: 575, mean SAT math: 590, mean SAT writing: 578.

Student Life Upper grades have specified standards of dress, student council, honor system. Discipline rests primarily with faculty.

Summer Programs Remediation, enrichment, advancement, art/fine arts, rigorous outdoor training, computer instruction programs offered; session focuses on enrichment and reinforcement; held on campus; accepts boys and girls; not open to students from other schools. 175 students usually enrolled. 2014 schedule: June 7 to July 16. Application deadline: June 7.

Tuition and Aid Day student tuition: $12,760–$28,250. Tuition installment plan (monthly payment plans, school's own tuition recovery plan). Tuition reduction for siblings, need-based scholarship grants, application and matriculation fee waived for children of alumni available.

Admissions Traditional secondary-level entrance grade is 9. For fall 2013, 340 students applied for upper-level admission, 242 were accepted, 134 enrolled. School's own exam and SSAT required. Deadline for receipt of application materials: February 19. Application fee required: $100. Interview recommended.

Athletics Interscholastic: aerobics/Nautilus (girls); baseball (b); basketball (b,g); cross-country running (b,g); dance (g); dance squad (g); dance team (g); diving (b,g); football (b); golf (b,g); gymnastics (b,g); lacrosse (b); physical training (b,g); running (b,g); soccer (b,g); softball (g); swimming and diving (b,g); tennis (b,g); track and field (b,g); volleyball (g); water polo (b,g); intramural: boxing (b,g); weight training (b,g); coed interscholastic: aerobics, bowling, cheering, modern dance, yoga; coed intramural: aerobics/dance, aerobics/Nautilus, badminton, dance, dance squad, dance team, fitness, flag football, Frisbee, kickball, modern dance, netball, physical fitness, running, strength & conditioning, touch football, yoga. 6 PE instructors, 55 coaches, 2 athletic trainers.

Computers Computers are regularly used in architecture, art, college planning, drafting, English, graphic arts, graphic design, keyboarding, newspaper, programming, science, technology, word processing, yearbook classes. Computer network features include on-campus library services, online commercial services, Internet access, wireless campus network, Internet filtering or blocking technology, modified laptop program, SMART Boards and Audio enhancement systems. Students grades are available online. The school has a published electronic and media policy.

Contact Carol A. Bowen, Director of Admission. 305-666-7937 Ext. 1408. Fax: 305-665-3791. E-mail: bowc@gulliverschools.org. Website: www.gulliverschools.org

THE GUNNERY

99 Green Hill Road
Washington, Connecticut 06793

Head of School: Peter W. E. Becker

General Information Coeducational boarding and day college-preparatory, arts, and technology school. Boarding grades 9–PG, day grades 9–12. Founded: 1850. Setting: rural. Nearest major city is Hartford. Students are housed in single-sex dormitories. 220-acre campus. 27 buildings on campus. Approved or accredited by National Commission of Accreditation of Special Education Services, New England Association of Schools and Colleges, The Association of Boarding Schools, and Connecticut Department of Education. Member of National Association of Independent Schools and Secondary School Admission Test Board. Endowment: $21 million. Total enrollment: 298. Upper school average class size: 12. Upper school faculty-student ratio: 1:6. Upper School students typically attend 6 days per week.

Upper School Student Profile Grade 9: 49 students (29 boys, 20 girls); Grade 10: 67 students (44 boys, 23 girls); Grade 11: 90 students (60 boys, 30 girls); Grade 12: 95 students (74 boys, 21 girls); Postgraduate: 15 students (14 boys, 1 girl). 70% of students are boarding students. 50% are state residents. 26 states are represented in upper school student body. 20% are international students. International students from China, China, France, Germany, Japan, and Taiwan; 19 other countries represented in student body.

Faculty School total: 52. In upper school: 31 men, 21 women; 39 have advanced degrees; 46 reside on campus.

Subjects Offered Advanced chemistry, algebra, American history, American history-AP, American literature, anatomy, art, art history, biology, calculus, ceramics, chemistry, computer graphics, computer math, computer programming, computer science, creative writing, drama, drawing, earth science, economics, economics-AP, English, English language-AP, English literature, English literature-AP, environmental science, environmental studies, ESL, ethics, ethics and responsibility, European history, European history-AP, expository writing, fine arts, French, geometry, government/civics, grammar, health, history, history of rock and roll, honors algebra, honors English, honors geometry, human development, instruments, marine biology, mathematics, modern European history-AP, music, music composition, mythology, painting, photography, physical education, physical science, physics, physics-AP, physiology, political science, pottery, pre-calculus, psychology, public speaking,

science, social studies, sociology, Spanish, Spanish language-AP, Spanish literature-AP, speech, studio art, theater, trigonometry, U.S. history-AP, values and decisions, voice, world history, world literature, writing.

Graduation Requirements Arts and fine arts (art, music, dance, drama), English, ethics and responsibility, foreign language, history, human development, mathematics, physical education (includes health), public speaking, science, speech, Senior Capstone—30 hours of community service.

Special Academic Programs Advanced Placement exam preparation; honors section; independent study; term-away projects; study abroad; academic accommodation for the gifted, the musically talented, and the artistically talented; ESL (5 students enrolled).

College Admission Counseling 84 students graduated in 2013; 82 went to college, including Boston University; Hobart and William Smith Colleges; New York University; Northeastern University; United States Naval Academy; University of Wisconsin–Madison. Other: 2 had other specific plans.

Student Life Upper grades have specified standards of dress, student council, honor system. Discipline rests equally with students and faculty.

Tuition and Aid Day student tuition: $38,500; 7-day tuition and room/board: $51,200. Tuition installment plan (Insured Tuition Payment Plan, monthly payment plans). Merit scholarship grants, need-based scholarship grants, need-based loans available. In 2013–14, 49% of upper-school students received aid. Total amount of financial aid awarded in 2013–14: $3,800,000.

Admissions Traditional secondary-level entrance grade is 9. For fall 2013, 575 students applied for upper-level admission, 330 were accepted, 109 enrolled. ACT, PSAT or SAT or SSAT required. Deadline for receipt of application materials: January 31. Application fee required: $50. On-campus interview required.

Athletics Interscholastic: baseball (boys), basketball (b,g), crew (b,g), cross-country running (b,g), field hockey (g), football (b), ice hockey (b,g), lacrosse (b,g), skiing (downhill) (b,g), soccer (b,g), softball (g), strength & conditioning (b,g), tennis (b,g), wrestling (b); intramural: yoga (g); coed interscholastic: alpine skiing, Frisbee, golf; coed intramural: dance team, fitness, outdoor education, ultimate Frisbee. 2 coaches, 1 athletic trainer.

Computers Computers are regularly used in art, English, foreign language, history, mathematics, music, science classes. Computer network features include on-campus library services, Internet access, wireless campus network. Campus intranet and student e-mail accounts are available to students. Students grades are available online. The school has a published electronic and media policy.

Contact W. Jed Stuart, Director of Admissions. 860-868-7334. Fax: 860-868-1614. E-mail: admissions@gunnery.org. Website: www.gunnery.org

THE GUNSTON SCHOOL

911 Gunston Road
PO Box 200
Centreville, Maryland 21617

Head of School: Mr. John A. Lewis, IV

General Information Coeducational day college-preparatory, arts, and technology school. Grades 9–12. Founded: 1911. Setting: rural. Nearest major city is Annapolis. 32-acre campus. 4 buildings on campus. Approved or accredited by Association of Independent Maryland Schools, Middle States Association of Colleges and Schools, and Maryland Department of Education. Member of National Association of Independent Schools and Secondary School Admission Test Board. Endowment: $1 million. Total enrollment: 148. Upper school average class size: 10. Upper school faculty-student ratio: 1:6. There are 170 required school days per year for Upper School students. Upper School students typically attend 5 days per week. The average school day consists of 8 hours.

Upper School Student Profile Grade 9: 36 students (13 boys, 23 girls); Grade 10: 43 students (26 boys, 17 girls); Grade 11: 38 students (16 boys, 22 girls); Grade 12: 31 students (19 boys, 12 girls).

Faculty School total: 23. In upper school: 12 men, 11 women; 14 have advanced degrees.

Subjects Offered Advanced biology, advanced chemistry, advanced math, Advanced Placement courses, advanced studio art-AP, algebra, American government, American history, American literature, anatomy and physiology, ancient history, applied arts, art, art history, art history-AP, biology, biology-AP, British literature, British literature (honors), calculus, calculus-AP, calligraphy, ceramics, chemistry, chemistry-AP, Chesapeake Bay studies, Chinese literature, chorus, college counseling, college placement, college planning, community service, computer applications, computer science, digital photography, drama performance, economics, English, English as a foreign language, English literature, environmental science, environmental science-AP, ethical decision making, ethics, European history-AP, fine arts, fitness, freshman seminar, geometry, golf, government, government-AP, government/civics, health, health and wellness, history, history-AP, honors algebra, honors English, honors geometry, ideas, lab science, Latin, Latin-AP, mathematics, mathematics-AP, medieval history, Microsoft, music, music appreciation, music composition, music theory, painting, performing arts, photography, physics, physics-AP, play production, poetry, pottery, pre-calculus, pre-college orientation, printmaking, psychology, SAT preparation, SAT/ACT preparation, science, sculpture, senior internship, senior project, senior thesis, short story, silk screening, Spanish, Spanish-AP, sports, studio art, studio art-AP, swimming, tennis, trigonometry, U.S. government, U.S. government and politics-AP, U.S. history, U.S. history-AP, weight training, wellness, woodworking, world history, writing workshop.

Graduation Requirements Arts and fine arts (art, music, dance, drama), athletics, computer science, English, foreign language, history, mathematics, science, social sciences. Community service is required.

Special Academic Programs Advanced Placement exam preparation; honors section; independent study; term-away projects; study at local college for college credit; study abroad; academic accommodation for the gifted, the musically talented, and the artistically talented; ESL (27 students enrolled).

College Admission Counseling 35 students graduated in 2012; all went to college, including Dickinson College; Lehigh University; St. Mary's College of Maryland; University of Maryland, College Park; Virginia Polytechnic Institute and State University; Washington College. Mean SAT critical reading: 575, mean SAT math: 528, mean SAT writing: 546, mean combined SAT: 1649.

Student Life Upper grades have specified standards of dress, student council, honor system. Discipline rests primarily with faculty.

Tuition and Aid Day student tuition: $21,950. Tuition installment plan (monthly payment plans, individually arranged payment plans, Sallie Mae, Tuition Management Solutions). Merit scholarship grants, need-based scholarship grants available. In 2012–13, 50% of upper-school students received aid; total upper-school merit-scholarship money awarded: $10,000. Total amount of financial aid awarded in 2012–13: $860,000.

Admissions Traditional secondary-level entrance grade is 9. For fall 2012, 90 students applied for upper-level admission, 86 were accepted, 55 enrolled. ISEE or SSAT required. Deadline for receipt of application materials: February 1. Application fee required: $50. On-campus interview required.

Athletics Interscholastic: basketball (boys, girls), field hockey (g), lacrosse (b,g), soccer (b,g), tennis (b,g); intramural: independent competitive sports (b,g), tennis (b,g); coed interscholastic: crew, golf, sailing, tennis; coed intramural: badminton, equestrian sports, fitness, horseback riding, independent competitive sports, strength & conditioning, swimming and diving, tennis, weight training. 4 coaches.

Computers Computers are regularly used in English, foreign language, history, mathematics, science classes. Computer network features include on-campus library services, Internet access, wireless campus network, Internet filtering or blocking technology. Campus intranet, student e-mail accounts, and computer access in designated common areas are available to students.

Contact David Henry, Director of Admission and Financial Aid. 410-758-0620. Fax: 410-758-0628. E-mail: dhenry@gunston.org. Website: www.gunston.org

HAMPSHIRE COUNTRY SCHOOL

Rindge, New Hampshire
See Junior Boarding Schools section.

HAMPTON ROADS ACADEMY

739 Academy Lane
Newport News, Virginia 23602

Head of School: Mr. Peter Mertz

General Information Coeducational day college-preparatory school. Grades PK–12. Founded: 1959. Setting: suburban. 52-acre campus. 4 buildings on campus. Approved or accredited by Virginia Department of Education. Member of National Association of Independent Schools. Total enrollment: 588. Upper school average class size: 14. Upper school faculty-student ratio: 1:10. Upper School students typically attend 5 days per week. The average school day consists of 6 hours and 30 minutes.

Faculty School total: 70. In upper school: 13 men, 17 women; 19 have advanced degrees.

Subjects Offered African studies, algebra, American history, American literature, anatomy, art, biology, calculus, ceramics, chemistry, creative writing, drama, driver education, earth science, economics, English, English literature, European history, expository writing, fine arts, French, geography, geometry, government/civics, grammar, health, history, Latin, mathematics, music, photography, physical education, physics, physiology, science, social studies, Spanish, speech, statistics, theater, trigonometry, typing, world history, world literature, writing.

Graduation Requirements Arts and fine arts (art, music, dance, drama), English, foreign language, mathematics, physical education (includes health), science, social studies (includes history), community service. Community service is required.

Special Academic Programs 19 Advanced Placement exams for which test preparation is offered; honors section; independent study.

College Admission Counseling 74 students graduated in 2013; all went to college, including Hampden-Sydney College; James Madison University; The College of William and Mary; University of Virginia; Virginia Polytechnic Institute and State University. Median SAT critical reading: 600, median SAT math: 600, median SAT writing: 600, median combined SAT: 1800, median composite ACT: 22. 60% scored over 600 on SAT critical reading, 54% scored over 600 on SAT math, 56% scored over 600 on SAT writing, 57% scored over 1800 on combined SAT, 36% scored over 26 on composite ACT.

Student Life Upper grades have specified standards of dress, student council, honor system. Discipline rests primarily with faculty.

Summer Programs Enrichment, sports, art/fine arts, rigorous outdoor training, computer instruction programs offered; session focuses on K-8 students; held on campus; accepts boys and girls; open to students from other schools. 125 students usually enrolled. 2014 schedule: June 10 to July 30. Application deadline: none.

Tuition and Aid Day student tuition: $16,100. Tuition installment plan (SMART Tuition Payment Plan). Need-based scholarship grants available. In 2013–14, 18% of upper-school students received aid. Total amount of financial aid awarded in 2013–14: $900,000.

Admissions Traditional secondary-level entrance grade is 9. For fall 2013, 31 students applied for upper-level admission, 27 were accepted, 24 enrolled. ERB, school's own test and writing sample required. Deadline for receipt of application materials: none. Application fee required: $125. On-campus interview required.

Athletics Interscholastic: ball hockey (girls), baseball (b), basketball (b,g), cheering (g), cross-country running (b,g), equestrian sports (b,g), field hockey (g), football (b), golf (b,g), lacrosse (b), physical training (b,g), sailing (b,g), soccer (b,g), softball (g), swimming and diving (b,g), tennis (b,g), track and field (b,g), volleyball (g), weight training (b,g); intramural: hiking/backpacking (b,g), outdoor adventure (b,g), outdoor education (b,g), outdoor recreation (b,g), outdoor skills (b,g), outdoors (b,g), strength & conditioning (b,g); coed interscholastic: aquatics, cheering, equestrian sports; coed intramural: archery, equestrian sports, fitness, hiking/backpacking, outdoor adventure, outdoor education, outdoor recreation, outdoor skills, outdoors, physical fitness, physical training, ropes courses, strength & conditioning, ultimate Frisbee, weight training. 3 PE instructors, 44 coaches, 1 athletic trainer.

Computers Computers are regularly used in English, mathematics, music, science, writing, yearbook classes. Computer network features include on-campus library services, online commercial services, Internet access, wireless campus network, Internet filtering or blocking technology. Student e-mail accounts are available to students. Students grades are available online. The school has a published electronic and media policy.

Contact Rebecca Bresee, Director of Admission. 757-884-9148. Fax: 757-884-9137. E-mail: admissions@hra.org. Website: www.hra.org

HANALANI SCHOOLS

94-294 Anania Drive
Mililani, Hawaii 96789

Head of School: Mr. Mark Y. Sugimoto

General Information Coeducational day college-preparatory, arts, religious studies, bilingual studies, and technology school, affiliated with Christian faith. Grades PK–12. Founded: 1952. Setting: suburban. 6-acre campus. 6 buildings on campus. Approved or accredited by The Hawaii Council of Private Schools, Western Association of Schools and Colleges, and Hawaii Department of Education. Member of National Association of Independent Schools. Total enrollment: 700. Upper school average class size: 16. Upper school faculty-student ratio: 1:16. There are 175 required school days per year for Upper School students. Upper School students typically attend 5 days per week. The average school day consists of 7 hours and 5 minutes.

Upper School Student Profile Grade 7: 58 students (32 boys, 26 girls); Grade 8: 63 students (35 boys, 28 girls); Grade 9: 61 students (36 boys, 25 girls); Grade 10: 63 students (31 boys, 32 girls); Grade 11: 51 students (26 boys, 25 girls); Grade 12: 46 students (23 boys, 23 girls). 50% of students are Christian faith.

Faculty School total: 62. In upper school: 18 men, 14 women; 10 have advanced degrees.

Subjects Offered Advanced math, Advanced Placement courses, algebra, American government, American literature, art, band, basketball, Bible, Bible studies, biology, British literature, calculus, calculus-AP, cheerleading, chemistry, chemistry-AP, choir, chorus, Christian doctrine, Christian ethics, computer skills, concert band, consumer mathematics, drafting, drama, earth science, English composition, English literature, English-AP, ethics, geography, geometry, golf, grammar, handbells, intro to computers, Japanese, Japanese as Second Language, Japanese studies, journalism, keyboarding, language development, leadership, Life of Christ, life science, music, paleontology, physical education, physical science, physics, piano, pre-algebra, pre-calculus, robotics, SAT preparation, sign language, Spanish, speech, student government, student publications, study skills, theology, transition mathematics, trigonometry, U.S. history, U.S. history-AP, video, voice, volleyball, world history, writing, yearbook.

Graduation Requirements Arts and fine arts (art, music, dance, drama), Bible, Bible studies, electives, English, foreign language, guidance, mathematics, physical education (includes health), science, social studies (includes history), technology. Community service is required.

Special Academic Programs Advanced Placement exam preparation; honors section; independent study; remedial reading and/or remedial writing; remedial math.

College Admission Counseling 64 students graduated in 2013; 62 went to college, including Azusa Pacific University; Hawai'i Pacific University; Liberty University; University of Hawaii at Manoa. Other: 2 entered military service.

Student Life Upper grades have uniform requirement, student council, honor system. Discipline rests primarily with faculty. Attendance at religious services is required.

Summer Programs Remediation, enrichment, advancement, sports, art/fine arts, computer instruction programs offered; session focuses on enrichment and advancement; held both on and off campus; held at a variety of outdoor places; accepts boys and girls; open to students from other schools. 60 students usually enrolled. 2014 schedule: June 6 to July 15. Application deadline: May 15.

Tuition and Aid Day student tuition: $10,255. Tuition installment plan (SMART Tuition Payment Plan, monthly payment plans, lump sum payment, biannual payment). Tuition reduction for siblings, need-based scholarship grants, student referral credit available.

Admissions Traditional secondary-level entrance grade is 9. For fall 2013, 69 students applied for upper-level admission, 64 were accepted, 44 enrolled. Brigance Test of Basic Skills, SAT or SSAT required. Deadline for receipt of application materials: none. Application fee required: $50. Interview required.

Athletics Interscholastic: archery (boys), baseball (b), basketball (b,g), bowling (b,g), cheering (g), cross-country running (b,g), football (b), golf (b,g), outdoor education (b,g), soccer (b,g), track and field (b,g), volleyball (b,g), water polo (b); intramural: basketball (b,g), fitness (b,g), flag football (b,g), football (b,g), physical fitness (b,g), soccer (b,g), strength & conditioning (b,g), table tennis (b,g), track and field (b,g), volleyball (b,g), weight lifting (b,g), weight training (b,g); coed intramural: indoor soccer, jump rope, kickball, ropes courses, touch football. 3 PE instructors, 2 coaches, 1 athletic trainer.

Computers Computers are regularly used in all academic, journalism, newspaper, science, social sciences, yearbook classes. Computer network features include on-campus library services, online commercial services, Internet access, wireless campus network, Internet filtering or blocking technology, desktop publishing applications, Ebsco, Moodle. Campus intranet and student e-mail accounts are available to students. Students grades are available online. The school has a published electronic and media policy.

Contact Ms. Emily Engelsgjerd, Senior Admissions Associate. 808-625-0737 Ext. 456. Fax: 808-625-0691. E-mail: admissions@hanalani.org. Website: www.hanalani.org

HANK HANEY INTERNATIONAL JUNIOR GOLF ACADEMY

55 Hospital Center Common

Hilton Head Island, South Carolina 29926

Head of School: Tina Sprouse

General Information Coeducational boarding and day college-preparatory, arts, business, and bilingual studies school. Grades 5–PG. Founded: 1995. Setting: suburban. Nearest major city is Savannah, GA. Students are housed in single-sex cottages. 5-acre campus. 2 buildings on campus. Approved or accredited by South Carolina Department of Education. Candidate for accreditation by Southern Association of Colleges and Schools. Total enrollment: 140. Upper school average class size: 9. Upper school faculty-student ratio: 1:10. Upper School students typically attend 5 days per week. The average school day consists of 4 hours and 30 minutes.

Upper School Student Profile 95% of students are boarding students. 28 states are represented in upper school student body. 50% are international students. International students from Canada, Denmark, Japan, Mexico, Republic of Korea, and United Kingdom; 28 other countries represented in student body.

Faculty School total: 14. In upper school: 2 men, 12 women; 5 have advanced degrees.

Special Academic Programs Advanced Placement exam preparation; honors section; ESL.

Student Life Upper grades have specified standards of dress, student council, honor system. Discipline rests equally with students and faculty.

Summer Programs ESL, sports, art/fine arts programs offered; session focuses on golf; held on campus; accepts boys and girls; open to students from other schools. 350 students usually enrolled. 2014 schedule: June 6 to August 12. Application deadline: June 1.

Tuition and Aid Day student tuition: $38,900; 7-day tuition and room/board: $51,900. Guaranteed tuition plan. Tuition installment plan (individually arranged payment plans). Tuition reduction for siblings, Sallie Mae loans available.

Admissions Deadline for receipt of application materials: none. Application fee required: $50. Interview recommended.

Athletics Interscholastic: golf (boys, girls). 13 coaches.

Computers Computer resources include Internet access, wireless campus network. Computer access in designated common areas is available to students. Students grades are available online.

Contact Mary Noel Jordan, Admissions Administrator. 843-686-1500. Fax: 843-785-5116. E-mail: admissions@ijga.com. Website: www.ijga.com

HARGRAVE MILITARY ACADEMY

200 Military Drive

Chatham, Virginia 24531

Head of School: Brig. Gen. Don Broome, USA (Ret.)

General Information Boys' boarding and day college-preparatory, general academic, arts, religious studies, technology, academic postgraduate, leadership and ethics, and military school, affiliated with Baptist General Association of Virginia. Grades 7–PG. Founded: 1909. Setting: small town. Nearest major city is Danville. Students are housed in single-sex dormitories. 214-acre campus. 29 buildings on campus. Approved or accredited by Southern Association of Colleges and Schools, The Association of Boarding Schools, and Virginia Association of Independent Schools. Member of National Association of Independent Schools. Endowment: $3.5 million. Total enrollment: 310. Upper school average class size: 11. Upper school faculty-student ratio: 1:12. Upper School students typically attend 5 days per week.

Upper School Student Profile 24 states are represented in upper school student body. 20% of students are Baptist General Association of Virginia.

Faculty In upper school: 17 men, 13 women; 6 have advanced degrees; 8 reside on campus.

Subjects Offered Advanced biology, advanced chemistry, advanced math, Advanced Placement courses, algebra, American government, American history, American literature, art, astronomy, Bible studies, biology, calculus, chemistry, creative writing, debate, English, English literature, environmental science, ESL, functions, geometry, government/civics, health, history, journalism, leadership, leadership and service, leadership education training, Mandarin, mathematics, media production, physical education, physics, psychology, reading, religion, SAT/ACT preparation, science, social studies, sociology, Spanish, speech, study skills, TOEFL preparation, trigonometry.

Graduation Requirements English, foreign language, mathematics, physical education (includes health), religion (includes Bible studies and theology), science, social studies (includes history).

Special Academic Programs Advanced Placement exam preparation; honors section; independent study; study at local college for college credit; remedial reading and/or remedial writing; remedial math; programs in general development for dyslexic students; special instructional classes for students with Attention Deficit Disorder; ESL (7 students enrolled).

College Admission Counseling 50 students graduated in 2013; all went to college, including Hampden-Sydney College; The University of North Carolina at Charlotte; United States Military Academy; Virginia Military Institute; Virginia Polytechnic Institute and State University.

Student Life Upper grades have uniform requirement, student council, honor system. Discipline rests equally with students and faculty. Attendance at religious services is required.

Summer Programs Remediation, enrichment, advancement, ESL, sports, rigorous outdoor training, computer instruction programs offered; session focuses on academics/sports camps; held on campus; accepts boys; open to students from other schools. 140 students usually enrolled. 2014 schedule: June 30 to July 28. Application deadline: June 29.

Tuition and Aid Day student tuition: $12,900; 5-day tuition and room/board: $29,900. Guaranteed tuition plan. Tuition installment plan (monthly payment plans, individually arranged payment plans). Tuition reduction for siblings, merit scholarship grants, need-based scholarship grants, need-based loans, Sallie Mae loans available. In 2013–14, 35% of upper-school students received aid; total upper-school merit-scholarship money awarded: $52,000. Total amount of financial aid awarded in 2013–14: $525,000.

Admissions Traditional secondary-level entrance grade is 10. Math and English placement tests required. Deadline for receipt of application materials: none. Application fee required: $75. Interview recommended.

Athletics Interscholastic: aquatics, baseball, basketball, cross-country running, football, golf, independent competitive sports, lacrosse, marksmanship, riflery, soccer, swimming and diving, tennis, wrestling; intramural: aquatics, backpacking, billiards, canoeing/kayaking, climbing, cross-country running, drill team, fishing, fitness, fitness walking, hiking/backpacking, independent competitive sports, jogging, jump rope, kayaking, lacrosse, life saving, marksmanship, mountaineering, Nautilus, outdoor activities, outdoor adventure, outdoor recreation, paint ball, physical fitness, physical training, rappelling, riflery, rock climbing, ropes courses, running, scuba diving, skeet shooting, skiing (downhill), strength & conditioning, swimming and diving, table tennis, tennis, trap and skeet, walking, water polo, weight lifting, weight training. 1 PE instructor, 10 coaches, 1 athletic trainer.

Computers Computers are regularly used in all academic classes. Computer network features include on-campus library services, online commercial services, Internet access, wireless campus network, Internet filtering or blocking technology. Campus intranet, student e-mail accounts, and computer access in designated common areas are available to students. Students grades are available online. The school has a published electronic and media policy.

Contact Dr. Frank Martin, Chief of Staff/Director of Admissions. 434-432-2585. Fax: 434-432-3129. E-mail: admissions@hargrave.edu. Website: www.hargrave.edu

THE HARKER SCHOOL

500 Saratoga Avenue
San Jose, California 95129

Head of School: Christopher Nikoloff

General Information Coeducational day college-preparatory, arts, technology, and gifted students school. Grades K–12. Founded: 1893. Setting: urban. 16-acre campus. 7 buildings on campus. Approved or accredited by California Association of Independent Schools, Western Association of Schools and Colleges, and California Department of Education. Member of National Association of Independent Schools. Total enrollment: 1,819. Upper school average class size: 18. Upper school faculty-student ratio: 1:10. Upper School students typically attend 5 days per week.

Upper School Student Profile Grade 9: 190 students (88 boys, 102 girls); Grade 10: 187 students (99 boys, 88 girls); Grade 11: 175 students (99 boys, 76 girls); Grade 12: 175 students (85 boys, 90 girls).

Faculty School total: 187. In upper school: 40 men, 51 women; 80 have advanced degrees.

Subjects Offered 20th century American writers, acting, advanced math, algebra, American literature, anatomy and physiology, architecture, art history, art history-AP, Asian history, astronomy, baseball, basketball, biology, biology-AP, biotechnology, British literature, British literature (honors), calculus-AP, ceramics, cheerleading, chemistry, chemistry-AP, choreography, classical studies, college counseling, community service, computer science-AP, dance, dance performance, debate, discrete mathematics, drawing, ecology, economics, electronics, engineering, English literature and composition-AP, English literature-AP, environmental science-AP, ethics, European history-AP, evolution, expository writing, film and literature, fitness, forensics, French, French language-AP, French literature-AP, geometry, golf, graphic arts, great books, history of dance, Holocaust seminar, honors algebra, honors geometry, human geography - AP, Japanese, Japanese literature, jazz band, journalism, Latin, Latin-AP, linear algebra, literary magazine, macro/microeconomics-AP, macroeconomics-AP, Mandarin, medieval literature, mentorship program, music appreciation, music theory-AP, newspaper, orchestra, organic chemistry, painting, photography, physics, physics-AP, play production, poetry, political thought, pre-calculus, programming, psychology, psychology-AP, public policy, public speaking, research, robotics, scene study, sculpture, Shakespeare, softball, Spanish, Spanish language-AP, Spanish literature-AP, statistics, statistics-AP, stone carving, student government, studio art-AP, study skills, swimming, technical theater, tennis, theater arts, theater history, track and field, trigonometry, U.S. government and politics-AP, U.S. history, U.S. history-AP, video and animation, visual arts, vocal ensemble, volleyball, water polo, weight training, Western philosophy, world history, world history-AP, world religions, wrestling, yearbook, yoga.

Graduation Requirements Arts and fine arts (art, music, dance, drama), biology, chemistry, computer science, English, foreign language, mathematics, physical education (includes health), physics, public speaking, U.S. history, world history, 30 total hours of community service, one year arts survey theater, dance, music or visual arts).

Special Academic Programs Advanced Placement exam preparation; honors section; independent study; academic accommodation for the gifted.

College Admission Counseling 172 students graduated in 2012; all went to college, including Duke University; Santa Clara University; Stanford University; University of California, Berkeley; University of California, San Diego; University of Southern California. Mean SAT critical reading: 708, mean SAT math: 735, mean SAT writing: 731.

Student Life Upper grades have specified standards of dress, student council, honor system. Discipline rests primarily with faculty.

Tuition and Aid Day student tuition: $37,000. Need-based scholarship grants, need-based loans available. In 2012–13, 10% of upper-school students received aid.

Admissions Traditional secondary-level entrance grade is 9. ERB CTP IV, essay, ISEE or SSAT required. Deadline for receipt of application materials: January 17. Application fee required: $100. Interview required.

Athletics Interscholastic: baseball (boys), basketball (b,g), cross-country running (b,g), football (b), golf (b,g), lacrosse (g), soccer (b,g), softball (g), swimming and diving (b,g), tennis (b,g), track and field (b,g), volleyball (b,g), water polo (b,g); coed interscholastic: cheering, wrestling; coed intramural: aerobics/dance, dance, fencing, fitness, physical fitness, tennis, yoga. 4 PE instructors, 50 coaches, 1 athletic trainer.

Computers Computers are regularly used in all academic, college planning, graphic arts, newspaper, yearbook classes. Computer network features include on-campus library services, online commercial services, Internet access, wireless campus network, Internet filtering or blocking technology, ProQuest, Gale Group, InfoTrac, Facts On File. Campus intranet and student e-mail accounts are available to students. The school has a published electronic and media policy.

Contact Christianne Marra, Assistant to the Director of Admission. 408-249-2510. Fax: 408-984-2325. E-mail: ChristianneM@harker.org. Website: www.harker.org

THE HARLEY SCHOOL

1981 Clover Street
Rochester, New York 14618

Head of School: Mr. Ward J. Ghory

General Information Coeducational day college-preparatory and arts school. Grades N–12. Founded: 1917. Setting: suburban. 25-acre campus. 4 buildings on campus. Approved or accredited by National Independent Private Schools Association and New York State Association of Independent Schools. Member of National Association of Independent Schools. Endowment: $9.2 million. Total enrollment: 537. Upper school average class size: 8. Upper school faculty-student ratio: 1:8. There are 180 required school days per year for Upper School students. Upper School students typically attend 5 days per week. The average school day consists of 6 hours and 50 minutes.

Upper School Student Profile Grade 9: 48 students (18 boys, 30 girls); Grade 10: 48 students (20 boys, 28 girls); Grade 11: 46 students (22 boys, 24 girls); Grade 12: 44 students (23 boys, 21 girls).

Faculty School total: 90. In upper school: 14 men, 14 women; 28 have advanced degrees.

Subjects Offered 3-dimensional art, Advanced Placement courses, algebra, American history, anthropology, art, art history, art-AP, band, biology, calculus, calculus-AP, ceramics, chamber groups, chemistry, Chinese, choir, chorus, community service, comparative government and politics-AP, computer graphics, computer math, computer programming, computer science, creative writing, debate, desktop publishing, drama, drawing, driver education, economics-AP, English, English language and composition-AP, English literature, environmental science, ethics, European history, expository writing, film, fine arts, foreign language, French, gardening, geometry, graphic arts, Greek, health, jazz band, language-AP, Latin, mathematics, multimedia, music, music theory, orchestra, organic gardening, outdoor education, photography, physical education, physics, psychology, SAT preparation, science, Shakespeare, social studies, Spanish, speech, student government, study skills, theater, theater arts, theater production, U.S. history-AP, voice, world history, writing, yoga.

Graduation Requirements Arts and fine arts (art, music, dance, drama), computer science, English, foreign language, internship, mathematics, physical education (includes health), science, social studies (includes history), participation in team sports, community service. Community service is required.

Special Academic Programs 17 Advanced Placement exams for which test preparation is offered.

College Admission Counseling 32 students graduated in 2013; all went to college, including Brown University; New York University; Rochester Institute of Technology; State University of New York College at Geneseo; University of Pittsburgh; Vassar College. Mean SAT critical reading: 624, mean SAT math: 622, mean SAT writing: 615.

Student Life Upper grades have student council, honor system. Discipline rests primarily with faculty.

Summer Programs Remediation, enrichment, sports, art/fine arts, computer instruction programs offered; session focuses on day camp, outdoor skills, swimming, tennis, writing, college prep; held both on and off campus; held at field house, classrooms, grounds, field trips; accepts boys and girls; open to students from other schools. 150 students usually enrolled. 2014 schedule: June 9 to August 1. Application deadline: May.

Tuition and Aid Day student tuition: $18,500–$22,750. Tuition installment plan (Insured Tuition Payment Plan, monthly payment plans, 2-payment plan, prepaid discount plan). Tuition reduction for siblings, need-based scholarship grants available. In 2013–14, 33% of upper-school students received aid.

Admissions Traditional secondary-level entrance grade is 9. For fall 2013, 56 students applied for upper-level admission, 37 were accepted, 31 enrolled. Essay and Math Placement Exam required. Deadline for receipt of application materials: none. Application fee required: $50. On-campus interview required.

Athletics Interscholastic: baseball (boys), basketball (b,g), bowling (b,g), golf (b), skiing (downhill) (b,g), soccer (b,g), softball (b,g), swimming and diving (b,g), tennis (b,g), track and field (b,g), volleyball (b,g); coed interscholastic: cross-country running, outdoor education, running, yoga. 3 PE instructors, 11 coaches.

Computers Computers are regularly used in all academic, art classes. Computer network features include Internet access, wireless campus network. The school has a published electronic and media policy.

Contact Mrs. Ivone Foisy, Director of Admissions. 585-442-1770. Fax: 585-442-5758. E-mail: ifoisy@harleyschool.org. Website: www.harleyschool.org

THE HARPETH HALL SCHOOL

3801 Hobbs Road
PO Box 150207
Nashville, Tennessee 37215-0207

Head of School: Ann Teaff

General Information Girls' day college-preparatory, arts, and technology school. Grades 5–12. Founded: 1951. Setting: suburban. 41-acre campus. 7 buildings on campus. Approved or accredited by Southern Association of Colleges and Schools, Southern Association of Independent Schools, and Tennessee Association of

Independent Schools. Member of National Association of Independent Schools. Endowment: $33.4 million. Total enrollment: 671. Upper school average class size: 16. Upper school faculty-student ratio: 1:8. There are 185 required school days per year for Upper School students. Upper School students typically attend 5 days per week. The average school day consists of 8 hours.

Upper School Student Profile Grade 9: 108 students (108 girls); Grade 10: 105 students (105 girls); Grade 11: 95 students (95 girls); Grade 12: 88 students (88 girls).

Faculty School total: 89. In upper school: 13 men, 37 women; 40 have advanced degrees.

Subjects Offered Advanced Placement courses, algebra, American government, American history, American history-AP, American literature, art, art history, art history-AP, astronomy, athletics, audio visual/media, biology, biology-AP, botany, calculus, chamber groups, chemistry, chemistry-AP, Chinese, choir, choral music, college admission preparation, college counseling, comparative politics, computer math, computer programming, computer science, conceptual physics, contemporary issues, creative writing, dance, digital art, drama, ecology, English, English literature, environmental science, environmental studies, European history, European history-AP, expository writing, fine arts, French, French language-AP, French literature-AP, functions, geometry, government/civics, grammar, health, history, honors algebra, honors English, Latin, Latin-AP, life skills, Mandarin, mathematics, media arts, music, photography, physical education, physics, physics-AP, probability and statistics, psychology, science, social sciences, social studies, Spanish, Spanish language-AP, Spanish literature-AP, speech, statistics-AP, studio art-AP, theater, theater arts, trigonometry, video, world history, world history-AP, world literature, writing.

Graduation Requirements Arts and fine arts (art, music, dance, drama), electives, English, foreign language, mathematics, physical education (includes health), science, social sciences, participation in Winterim Program each year.

Special Academic Programs Advanced Placement exam preparation; honors section; independent study; term-away projects; study abroad; academic accommodation for the gifted, the musically talented, and the artistically talented.

College Admission Counseling 97 students graduated in 2013; all went to college, including Auburn University; Furman University; Texas Christian University; The University of Alabama; The University of North Carolina at Chapel Hill; University of Virginia. Mean SAT critical reading: 644, mean SAT math: 624, mean SAT writing: 646, mean combined SAT: 1914, mean composite ACT: 28.

Student Life Upper grades have uniform requirement, student council, honor system. Discipline rests primarily with faculty.

Summer Programs Enrichment, sports, art/fine arts, computer instruction programs offered; session focuses on enrichment classes and sports; held on campus; accepts girls; open to students from other schools. 750 students usually enrolled. 2014 schedule: May to August. Application deadline: none.

Tuition and Aid Day student tuition: $23,635. Tuition installment plan (monthly payment plans, individually arranged payment plans, Tuition Management Systems Plan). Need-based scholarship grants available. In 2013–14, 18% of upper-school students received aid. Total amount of financial aid awarded in 2013–14: $911,425.

Admissions Traditional secondary-level entrance grade is 9. For fall 2013, 71 students applied for upper-level admission, 35 were accepted, 27 enrolled. ISEE required. Deadline for receipt of application materials: January 1. Application fee required: $50. On-campus interview required.

Athletics Interscholastic: aquatics, basketball, bowling, crew, cross-country running, diving, golf, lacrosse, running, soccer, softball, swimming and diving, tennis, track and field, volleyball; intramural: aerobics/dance, cheering, climbing, cooperative games, dance, fitness, flag football, jogging, modern dance, outdoor activities, outdoor adventure, outdoor education, outdoor recreation, outdoor skills, physical training, rock climbing, self defense, strength & conditioning, ultimate Frisbee, walking, wall climbing, weight training, yoga. 3 PE instructors, 14 coaches, 1 athletic trainer.

Computers Computers are regularly used in all academic classes. Computer network features include on-campus library services, online commercial services, Internet access, wireless campus network, Internet filtering or blocking technology. Campus intranet and student e-mail accounts are available to students. The school has a published electronic and media policy.

Contact Sandy Binkley, Admission Coordinator. 615-346-0126. Fax: 615-297-0480. E-mail: binkley@harpethhall.org. Website: www.harpethhall.org

HARRELLS CHRISTIAN ACADEMY

360 Tomahawk Highway
PO Box 88
Harrells, North Carolina 28444

Head of School: Mr. Marcus P. Skipper

General Information Coeducational day college-preparatory school, affiliated with Christian faith. Grades K–12. Founded: 1969. Setting: rural. Nearest major city is Wilmington. 32-acre campus. 7 buildings on campus. Approved or accredited by Southern Association of Colleges and Schools, Southern Association of Independent Schools, and North Carolina Department of Education. Total enrollment: 412. Upper school average class size: 12. Upper school faculty-student ratio: 1:11. There are 176 required school days per year for Upper School students. Upper School students typically attend 5 days per week. The average school day consists of 5 hours and 36 minutes.

Upper School Student Profile Grade 9: 38 students (21 boys, 17 girls); Grade 10: 41 students (19 boys, 22 girls); Grade 11: 42 students (28 boys, 14 girls); Grade 12: 42 students (25 boys, 17 girls). 96% of students are Christian.

Faculty School total: 15. In upper school: 4 men, 11 women; 6 have advanced degrees.

Subjects Offered Algebra, animal science, art, art education, biology, biology-AP, calculus, ceramics, chemistry, chemistry-AP, computer art, earth science, English, English language and composition-AP, English literature, English literature and composition-AP, environmental science-AP, French, government/civics, history, journalism, mathematics, painting, photography, physical education, physical science, religion, social studies, Spanish, U.S. history-AP, weightlifting, world history-AP, yearbook.

Graduation Requirements Biology, computer applications, electives, English, environmental science, foreign language, mathematics, physical education (includes health), physical science, religious studies, social studies (includes history).

Special Academic Programs 5 Advanced Placement exams for which test preparation is offered; honors section; study at local college for college credit; programs in English, mathematics, general development for dyslexic students.

College Admission Counseling 32 students graduated in 2013; 31 went to college, including East Carolina University; North Carolina State University; The University of North Carolina at Chapel Hill; The University of North Carolina Wilmington. Other: 1 entered military service. Median SAT critical reading: 470, median SAT math: 470, median SAT writing: 460, median combined SAT: 1400, median composite ACT: 22. 17% scored over 600 on SAT critical reading, 17% scored over 600 on SAT math, 22% scored over 600 on SAT writing, 17% scored over 1800 on combined SAT, 1% scored over 26 on composite ACT.

Student Life Upper grades have specified standards of dress, honor system. Discipline rests primarily with faculty. Attendance at religious services is required.

Tuition and Aid Day student tuition: $8070. Tuition installment plan (monthly payment plans, individually arranged payment plans). Tuition reduction for siblings, need-based scholarship grants available. In 2013–14, 20% of upper-school students received aid. Total amount of financial aid awarded in 2013–14: $62,000.

Admissions Traditional secondary-level entrance grade is 9. For fall 2013, 15 students applied for upper-level admission, 14 were accepted, 14 enrolled. Admissions testing or Stanford Achievement Test required. Deadline for receipt of application materials: none. Application fee required: $35. On-campus interview required.

Athletics Interscholastic: baseball (boys), basketball (b,g), cheering (g), football (b), soccer (b,g), softball (g), tennis (g), volleyball (g); coed interscholastic: golf. 2 PE instructors, 1 coach.

Computers Computers are regularly used in art, English, journalism, yearbook classes. Computer resources include Internet access, wireless campus network, Internet filtering or blocking technology. Students grades are available online. The school has a published electronic and media policy.

Contact Mrs. Susan Frederick, Administrative Assistant. 910-532-4575 Ext. 221. Fax: 910-532-2958. E-mail: sfrederick@harrellsca.org. Website: www.harrellschristianacademy.com

THE HARRISBURG ACADEMY

10 Erford Road
Wormleysburg, Pennsylvania 17043

Head of School: Dr. James Newman

General Information Coeducational day college-preparatory and arts school. Grades PS–12. Founded: 1784. Setting: suburban. Nearest major city is Harrisburg. 23-acre campus. 1 building on campus. Approved or accredited by International Baccalaureate Organization, Middle States Association of Colleges and Schools, Pennsylvania Association of Independent Schools, and Pennsylvania Department of Education. Member of National Association of Independent Schools. Endowment: $5 million. Total enrollment: 400. Upper school average class size: 10. Upper school faculty-student ratio: 1:8. There are 172 required school days per year for Upper School students. Upper School students typically attend 5 days per week. The average school day consists of 7 hours.

Upper School Student Profile Grade 6: 28 students (14 boys, 14 girls); Grade 7: 28 students (18 boys, 10 girls); Grade 8: 20 students (10 boys, 10 girls); Grade 9: 20 students (10 boys, 10 girls); Grade 10: 22 students (12 boys, 10 girls); Grade 11: 25 students (15 boys, 10 girls); Grade 12: 23 students (10 boys, 13 girls).

Faculty School total: 55. In upper school: 8 men, 13 women; 9 have advanced degrees.

Subjects Offered Advanced Placement courses, algebra, American history, American literature, art, biology, calculus, ceramics, chemistry, computer science, creative writing, drama, economics, English, English literature, environmental science, European history, expository writing, fine arts, French, geography, geometry, grammar, health, history, International Baccalaureate courses, Latin, mathematics, music, philosophy, physical education, physics, science, social studies, Spanish, world history, world literature, writing.

Graduation Requirements Algebra, arts and fine arts (art, music, dance, drama), college planning, English, foreign language, geometry, physical education (includes health), public speaking, science, social studies (includes history). Community service is required.

Special Academic Programs International Baccalaureate program; Advanced Placement exam preparation; independent study.

College Admission Counseling 32 students graduated in 2012; all went to college, including American University; Dickinson College; Drexel University; Franklin & Marshall College; Penn State University Park; University of Pittsburgh. 50% scored over 600 on SAT critical reading, 50% scored over 600 on SAT math.

Student Life Upper grades have specified standards of dress, student council, honor system. Discipline rests primarily with faculty.

Tuition and Aid Day student tuition: $16,880. Tuition installment plan (Insured Tuition Payment Plan, monthly payment plans, individually arranged payment plans, need-based financial aid and merit scholarship programs). Tuition reduction for siblings, merit scholarship grants, need-based scholarship grants available. In 2012–13, 30% of upper-school students received aid; total upper-school merit-scholarship money awarded: $40,000. Total amount of financial aid awarded in 2012–13: $400,000.

Admissions Traditional secondary-level entrance grade is 9. For fall 2012, 14 students applied for upper-level admission, 10 were accepted, 8 enrolled. Admissions testing or TOEFL or SLEP required. Deadline for receipt of application materials: none. Application fee required: $75. Interview required.

Athletics Interscholastic: basketball (boys, girls), golf (b,g), lacrosse (b), soccer (b,g), swimming and diving (b,g), tennis (b,g); coed interscholastic: golf; coed intramural: cross-country running, skiing (downhill). 3 PE instructors, 18 coaches, 1 athletic trainer.

Computers Computers are regularly used in art, English, foreign language, graphic design, library, mathematics, music, science classes. Computer network features include on-campus library services, Internet access, wireless campus network, Internet filtering or blocking technology. Campus intranet and student e-mail accounts are available to students. Students grades are available online. The school has a published electronic and media policy.

Contact Mrs. Jessica Warren, Director of Admissions and Marketing. 717-763-7811 Ext. 313. Fax: 717-975-0894. E-mail: warren.j@harrisburgacademy.org. Website: www.harrisburgacademy.org

HARVARD-WESTLAKE SCHOOL

3700 Coldwater Canyon
Studio City, California 91604

Head of School: Richard B. Commons

General Information Coeducational day college-preparatory school, affiliated with Episcopal Church. Grades 7–12. Founded: 1989. Setting: urban. Nearest major city is Los Angeles. 26-acre campus. 12 buildings on campus. Approved or accredited by Western Association of Schools and Colleges. Member of National Association of Independent Schools. Endowment: $47.1 million. Total enrollment: 1,597. Upper school average class size: 16. Upper school faculty-student ratio: 1:8. Upper School students typically attend 5 days per week. The average school day consists of 6 hours and 35 minutes.

Upper School Student Profile Grade 9: 287 students (157 boys, 130 girls); Grade 10: 288 students (160 boys, 128 girls); Grade 11: 291 students (152 boys, 139 girls); Grade 12: 291 students (155 boys, 136 girls).

Faculty School total: 122. In upper school: 72 men, 50 women; 85 have advanced degrees.

Subjects Offered 3-dimensional art, advanced studio art-AP, algebra, American history, American literature, American literature-AP, anatomy, architecture, art, art history, art history-AP, Asian studies, astronomy, biology, biology-AP, calculus, calculus-AP, ceramics, chemistry, chemistry-AP, Chinese, choreography, chorus, classics, community service, comparative government and politics-AP, computer animation, computer programming, computer science, computer science-AP, creative writing, dance, drama, drawing, economics, economics-AP, electronics, English, English language and composition-AP, English literature, English literature-AP, environmental science, environmental science-AP, European history, expository writing, film, film studies, fine arts, French, French language-AP, French literature-AP, geography, geology, geometry, government and politics-AP, government/civics, grammar, health, human development, human geography - AP, Japanese, jazz, journalism, Latin, Latin-AP, logic, macro/microeconomics-AP, Mandarin, mathematics, music, music history, music theory-AP, oceanography, orchestra, painting, photography, physical education, physics, physics-AP, physiology, political science, pre-calculus, psychology, Russian, science, senior project, Shakespeare, social studies, Spanish, Spanish language-AP, Spanish literature-AP, statistics, statistics-AP, studio art-AP, technical theater, theater, trigonometry, U.S. government and politics-AP, U.S. history-AP, video, women's studies, world history, world history-AP, world literature, yearbook, zoology.

Graduation Requirements English, foreign language, history, human development, mathematics, performing arts, physical education (includes health), science, visual arts. Community service is required.

Special Academic Programs 30 Advanced Placement exams for which test preparation is offered; honors section; independent study; term-away projects; study abroad; academic accommodation for the gifted, the musically talented, and the artistically talented.

College Admission Counseling 285 students graduated in 2013; 284 went to college, including Cornell University; New York University; Stanford University; University of Michigan; University of Southern California; Washington University in St. Louis. Other: 1 had other specific plans. Mean SAT critical reading: 693, mean SAT math: 702, mean SAT writing: 718. 90% scored over 600 on SAT critical reading, 91% scored over 600 on SAT math.

Student Life Upper grades have specified standards of dress, student council, honor system. Discipline rests primarily with faculty.

Summer Programs Enrichment, sports, art/fine arts, rigorous outdoor training, computer instruction programs offered; session focuses on enrichment and sports; held on campus; accepts boys and girls; open to students from other schools. 500 students usually enrolled. 2014 schedule: June 9 to August 8. Application deadline: none.

Tuition and Aid Day student tuition: $32,300. Tuition installment plan (monthly payment plans, semi-annual payment plan, triennial payment plan). Need-based scholarship grants, short-term loans (payable by end of year in which loan is made) available. In 2013–14, 18% of upper-school students received aid. Total amount of financial aid awarded in 2013–14: $8,069,000.

Admissions Traditional secondary-level entrance grade is 9. For fall 2013, 540 students applied for upper-level admission, 130 were accepted, 93 enrolled. ISEE required. Deadline for receipt of application materials: January 17. Application fee required: $200. On-campus interview required.

Athletics Interscholastic: baseball (boys), basketball (b,g), cross-country running (b,g), field hockey (g), football (b), golf (b,g), gymnastics (g), lacrosse (b), soccer (b,g), softball (g), swimming and diving (b,g), tennis (b,g), track and field (b,g), volleyball (b,g), water polo (b,g), wrestling (b); coed interscholastic: diving, equestrian sports, fencing, martial arts; coed intramural: badminton. 6 PE instructors, 32 coaches, 3 athletic trainers.

Computers Computers are regularly used in art, English, foreign language, history, mathematics, music, science classes. Computer resources include on-campus library services, Internet access, wireless campus network, music composition and editing, foreign language lab, science lab. Campus intranet, student e-mail accounts, and computer access in designated common areas are available to students. Students grades are available online.

Contact Elizabeth Gregory, Director of Admission. 310-274-7281. Fax: 310-288-3212. E-mail: egregory@hw.com. Website: www.hw.com

THE HARVEY SCHOOL

260 Jay Street
Katonah, New York 10536

Head of School: Mr. Barry W. Fenstermacher

General Information Coeducational boarding and day and distance learning college-preparatory school. Boarding grades 9–12, day grades 6–12. Distance learning grades 6–12. Founded: 1916. Setting: suburban. Students are housed in single-sex dormitories. 125-acre campus. 14 buildings on campus. Approved or accredited by New York State Association of Independent Schools. Member of National Association of Independent Schools. Endowment: $2 million. Total enrollment: 334. Upper school average class size: 11. Upper school faculty-student ratio: 1:6. There are 165 required school days per year for Upper School students. Upper School students typically attend 5 days per week. The average school day consists of 8 hours and 50 minutes.

Upper School Student Profile Grade 9: 51 students (27 boys, 24 girls); Grade 10: 67 students (39 boys, 28 girls); Grade 11: 75 students (43 boys, 32 girls); Grade 12: 55 students (31 boys, 24 girls). 11% of students are boarding students. 75% are state residents. 3 states are represented in upper school student body.

Faculty School total: 56. In upper school: 27 men, 19 women; 34 have advanced degrees; 24 reside on campus.

Subjects Offered Algebra, American history, American literature, art, art history, biology, calculus, ceramics, chemistry, composition-AP, computer programming-AP, creative writing, drama, English, English literature, European history, expository writing, fine arts, French, general science, geology, geometry, government/civics, grammar, Greek, history, Japanese, Latin, mathematics, music, photography, physics, religion, science, social studies, Spanish, theater, trigonometry, world history, writing.

Graduation Requirements Arts and fine arts (art, music, dance, drama), computer literacy, English, foreign language, mathematics, science, social sciences, social studies (includes history).

Special Academic Programs 10 Advanced Placement exams for which test preparation is offered; honors section; independent study.

College Admission Counseling 63 students graduated in 2012; all went to college, including Barnard College; Bentley University; Cornell University; University of Connecticut; Villanova University.

Student Life Upper grades have specified standards of dress, student council. Discipline rests primarily with faculty.

Tuition and Aid Day student tuition: $31,250–$33,250; 5-day tuition and room/board: $40,250–$41,250. Tuition installment plan (FACTS Tuition Payment Plan, individually arranged payment plans). Need-based scholarship grants available. In 2012–13, 28% of upper-school students received aid. Total amount of financial aid awarded in 2012–13: $2,088,000.

Admissions Traditional secondary-level entrance grade is 9. For fall 2012, 134 students applied for upper-level admission, 94 were accepted, 59 enrolled. Deadline for receipt of application materials: none. Application fee required: $50. Interview required.

Athletics Interscholastic: baseball (boys), basketball (b,g), football (b), ice hockey (b), lacrosse (b,g), rugby (b), soccer (b,g), softball (g), volleyball (g); coed interscholastic: cross-country running, tennis, weight lifting; coed intramural: aerobics, dance, figure skating, fitness, fitness walking, Frisbee, golf, modern dance, strength & conditioning, tai chi, yoga. 1 athletic trainer.

Computers Computers are regularly used in English, foreign language, history, mathematics, science classes. Computer resources include on-campus library services, online commercial services, Internet access. The school has a published electronic and media policy.

Contact Mr. William Porter, Director of Admissions. 914-232-3161 Ext. 113. Fax: 914-232-6034. E-mail: wporter@harveyschool.org. Website: www.harveyschool.org

HAWAII BAPTIST ACADEMY

2429 Pali Highway
Honolulu, Hawaii 96817

Head of School: Richard Bento

General Information Coeducational day college-preparatory and Christian education school, affiliated with Southern Baptist Convention. Grades K–12. Founded: 1949. Setting: urban. 13-acre campus. 6 buildings on campus. Approved or accredited by Association of Christian Schools International and Western Association of Schools and Colleges. Member of National Association of Independent Schools and Secondary School Admission Test Board. Endowment: $4.7 million. Total enrollment: 1,106. Upper school average class size: 17. Upper school faculty-student ratio: 1:17. There are 176 required school days per year for Upper School students. Upper School students typically attend 5 days per week. The average school day consists of 6 hours.

Upper School Student Profile Grade 9: 124 students (58 boys, 66 girls); Grade 10: 110 students (46 boys, 64 girls); Grade 11: 116 students (52 boys, 64 girls); Grade 12: 119 students (63 boys, 56 girls). 12% of students are Southern Baptist Convention.

Faculty School total: 89. In upper school: 21 men, 24 women; 20 have advanced degrees.

Subjects Offered Advanced Placement courses, algebra, American history, American literature, ancient world history, art, Bible studies, biology, biology-AP, British literature, calculus-AP, chemistry, chemistry-AP, Chinese, Christian education, Christian ethics, Christian studies, communication skills, computer applications, concert band, digital photography, discrete mathematics, drafting, drama, drama performance, drawing, economics, English, English language and composition-AP, English literature, English literature-AP, environmental science, film, film history, fine arts, forensics, French, geometry, handbells, Japanese, journalism, mathematics, modern world history, music theory-AP, oceanography, physical education, physics, physics-AP, political science, pre-calculus, psychology, psychology-AP, religion, science, social studies, Spanish, speech, statistics, statistics-AP, trigonometry, U.S. history-AP, world history, world literature, writing.

Graduation Requirements Algebra, ancient history, arts and fine arts (art, music, dance, drama), Bible studies, biology, communication skills, computer applications, economics, English, foreign language, mathematics, physical education (includes health), political science, science, social studies (includes history), U.S. history, world history.

Special Academic Programs Advanced Placement exam preparation; independent study.

College Admission Counseling 113 students graduated in 2013; all went to college, including Chaminade University of Honolulu; Oregon State University; Seattle Pacific University; University of Hawaii at Manoa; University of Portland; Washington State University. Mean SAT critical reading: 551, mean SAT math: 599, mean SAT writing: 537, mean composite ACT: 25.

Student Life Upper grades have uniform requirement, student council. Discipline rests primarily with faculty. Attendance at religious services is required.

Summer Programs Remediation, enrichment, sports, art/fine arts, computer instruction programs offered; session focuses on academic/social preparation for entrance to regular school, instruction/remediation, and personal growth; held both on and off campus; held at various recreation sites; accepts boys and girls; open to students from other schools. 250 students usually enrolled. 2014 schedule: June 12 to July 8. Application deadline: April 15.

Tuition and Aid Day student tuition: $13,900. Guaranteed tuition plan. Tuition installment plan (Insured Tuition Payment Plan, monthly payment plans). Need-based scholarship grants available. In 2013–14, 20% of upper-school students received aid. Total amount of financial aid awarded in 2013–14: $367,247.

Admissions Traditional secondary-level entrance grade is 9. For fall 2013, 54 students applied for upper-level admission, 41 were accepted, 15 enrolled. Achievement tests and SSAT required. Deadline for receipt of application materials: January 31. Application fee required: $75. On-campus interview required.

Athletics Interscholastic: aquatics (boys, girls), baseball (b), basketball (b,g), bowling (b,g), canoeing/kayaking (b,g), cheering (g), cross-country running (b,g), diving (b,g), football (b), golf (b,g), judo (b,g), kayaking (b,g), riflery (b,g), soccer (b,g), softball (g), swimming and diving (b,g), tennis (b,g), track and field (b,g), volleyball (b,g), water polo (b,g), wrestling (b,g); coed interscholastic: canoeing/kayaking, cheering, golf, sailing. 3 PE instructors, 30 coaches, 2 athletic trainers.

Computers Computers are regularly used in college planning, digital applications, graphic design, journalism, keyboarding, media production, newspaper, video film production, word processing, yearbook classes. Computer network features include on-campus library services, online commercial services, Internet access, wireless campus network, Internet filtering or blocking technology, one-to-one iPads. Campus intranet, student e-mail accounts, and computer access in designated common areas are available to students. Students grades are available online. The school has a published electronic and media policy.

Contact Mrs. Katherine Lee, Director of Admissions. 808-595-7585. Fax: 808-564-0332. E-mail: klee@hba.net. Website: www.hba.net

HAWAI`I PREPARATORY ACADEMY

65-1692 Kohala Mountain Road
Kamuela, Hawaii 96743-8476

Head of School: Mr. Lindsay Barnes Jr.

General Information Coeducational boarding and day college-preparatory school. Boarding grades 9–PG, day grades K–12. Founded: 1949. Setting: small town. Nearest major city is Kona. Students are housed in single-sex by floor dormitories and single-sex dormitories. 220-acre campus. 22 buildings on campus. Approved or accredited by The Association of Boarding Schools and Western Association of Schools and Colleges. Member of National Association of Independent Schools and Secondary School Admission Test Board. Endowment: $16.4 million. Total enrollment: 620. Upper school average class size: 12. Upper school faculty-student ratio: 1:13. There are 163 required school days per year for Upper School students. Upper School students typically attend 5 days per week. The average school day consists of 8 hours.

Upper School Student Profile Grade 9: 75 students (37 boys, 38 girls); Grade 10: 99 students (44 boys, 55 girls); Grade 11: 115 students (51 boys, 64 girls); Grade 12: 107 students (61 boys, 46 girls); Postgraduate: 1 student (1 girl). 50% of students are boarding students. 50% are state residents. 14 states are represented in upper school student body. 20% are international students.

Faculty School total: 66. In upper school: 21 men, 20 women; 32 have advanced degrees; 22 reside on campus.

Subjects Offered 3-dimensional art, advanced computer applications, Advanced Placement courses, algebra, American literature, art history-AP, astronomy, band, biology, biology-AP, calculus, calculus-AP, ceramics, chemistry, chemistry-AP, choir, composition-AP, computer literacy, creative writing, digital photography, drama, drama performance, drawing, driver education, economics, English, environmental science, environmental science-AP, ESL, ethnic studies, film, fine arts, forensics, geology, geometry, Hawaiian history, Hawaiian language, honors world history, instrumental music, Japanese, literary genres, literature-AP, Mandarin, marine biology, marine science, math applications, mathematics, music theater, orchestra, photography, physical education, physical science, physics, physics-AP, pre-calculus, probability and statistics, psychology, psychology-AP, robotics, science research, Spanish, statistics-AP, strings, studio art, theater arts, theater production, trigonometry, U.S. history, U.S. history-AP, video film production, visual arts, vocal music, Web site design, world cultures, world history, world history-AP, world literature, yearbook.

Graduation Requirements Arts and fine arts (art, music, dance, drama), electives, English, mathematics, modern languages, science, social studies (includes history), sports, technology.

Special Academic Programs 14 Advanced Placement exams for which test preparation is offered; honors section; independent study; ESL (15 students enrolled).

College Admission Counseling 84 students graduated in 2013; all went to college, including Colorado State University; University of Hawaii at Manoa; University of Oregon; University of San Diego; University of Washington; Willamette University. Median SAT critical reading: 490, median SAT math: 520, median SAT writing: 480, median combined SAT: 1490. Mean composite ACT: 22. 12% scored over 600 on SAT critical reading, 37% scored over 600 on SAT math, 27% scored over 600 on SAT writing, 31% scored over 1800 on combined SAT, 17% scored over 26 on composite ACT.

Student Life Upper grades have specified standards of dress, student council, honor system. Discipline rests equally with students and faculty.

Summer Programs Enrichment, ESL programs offered; session focuses on academic enrichment; held on campus; accepts boys and girls; open to students from other schools. 100 students usually enrolled. 2014 schedule: June 23 to July 18. Application deadline: April 15.

Tuition and Aid Day student tuition: $22,300; 5-day tuition and room/board: $39,900; 7-day tuition and room/board: $44,100. Tuition installment plan (monthly payment plans, prepayment plan, 2-payment plan, 4-payment plan). Need-based scholarship grants, Hawaii residential boarding grants, Merit-based scholarship (75% demonstrated need to apply) available. In 2013–14, 36% of upper-school students received aid. Total amount of financial aid awarded in 2013–14: $1,500,000.

Admissions Traditional secondary-level entrance grade is 9. Any standardized test, ISEE or SSAT required. Deadline for receipt of application materials: February 1. Application fee required: $25. Interview required.

Athletics Interscholastic: baseball (boys), basketball (b,g), cross-country running (b,g), ocean paddling (b,g), soccer (b,g), softball (g), swimming and diving (b,g), tennis (b,g), track and field (b,g), volleyball (b,g), water polo (g), wrestling (b,g); intramural: baseball (b); coed interscholastic: diving, dressage, football, golf, horseback riding;

coed intramural: basketball, dance, dressage, golf, horseback riding, scuba diving, soccer, strength & conditioning, surfing, swimming and diving, tennis, ultimate Frisbee, volleyball, weight lifting, yoga. 1 athletic trainer.

Computers Computers are regularly used in computer applications, digital applications, science, video film production, yearbook classes. Computer network features include on-campus library services, online commercial services, Internet access, wireless campus network, Internet filtering or blocking technology. Campus intranet, student e-mail accounts, and computer access in designated common areas are available to students. Students grades are available online. The school has a published electronic and media policy.

Contact Mr. Joshua D. Clark, Director of Admission. 808-881-4074. Fax: 808-881-4003. E-mail: admissions@hpa.edu. Website: www.hpa.edu/

HAWKEN SCHOOL

12465 County Line Road
PO Box 8002
Gates Mills, Ohio 44040-8002

Head of School: D. Scott Looney

General Information Coeducational day college-preparatory, arts, business, STEMM (Science, Technology, Engineering, Math, Medicine), and Experiential and Service Learning school. Grades PS–12. Founded: 1915. Setting: suburban. Nearest major city is Cleveland. 325-acre campus. 5 buildings on campus. Approved or accredited by Ohio Association of Independent Schools and Ohio Department of Education. Member of National Association of Independent Schools. Endowment: $43.6 million. Total enrollment: 972. Upper school average class size: 15. Upper school faculty-student ratio: 1:9. There are 176 required school days per year for Upper School students. Upper School students typically attend 5 days per week. The average school day consists of 5 hours and 54 minutes.

Upper School Student Profile Grade 9: 119 students (61 boys, 58 girls); Grade 10: 101 students (53 boys, 48 girls); Grade 11: 109 students (57 boys, 52 girls); Grade 12: 95 students (51 boys, 44 girls).

Faculty School total: 143. In upper school: 29 men, 31 women; 43 have advanced degrees.

Subjects Offered 20th century world history, accounting, acting, advanced chemistry, advanced math, Advanced Placement courses, advanced studio art-AP, African-American literature, algebra, American Civil War, American history, American history-AP, American literature, animal science, art, art appreciation, art history, band, Bible as literature, biology, business, calculus, calculus-AP, ceramics, chemistry, chemistry-AP, Chinese, choir, choral music, chorus, Civil War, classical Greek literature, creative dance, creative writing, dance, dance performance, drama, drawing, ecology, economics, economics and history, engineering, English, English literature, English-AP, entrepreneurship, environmental science-AP, ethics, European history, experiential education, field ecology, film, film studies, fine arts, first aid, French, French studies, French-AP, geography, geometry, government/civics, graphic design, health, history, Holocaust and other genocides, humanities, improvisation, Latin, Latin-AP, mathematics, mathematics-AP, music, music theory, outdoor education, painting, performing arts, philosophy, photography, physical education, physics, physics-AP, physiology, poetry, probability and statistics, science, science research, sculpture, senior project, service learning/internship, social sciences, social studies, Spanish, Spanish literature-AP, speech, statistics-AP, strings, studio art-AP, swimming, theater, theater arts, theater design and production, theater production, trigonometry, U.S. history, U.S. history-AP, world history, world literature, World War I, World War II, writing.

Graduation Requirements Arts and fine arts (art, music, dance, drama), computer science, English, foreign language, history, mathematics, physical education (includes health), science. Community service is required.

Special Academic Programs 16 Advanced Placement exams for which test preparation is offered; honors section; accelerated programs; independent study; term-away projects; study abroad.

College Admission Counseling 113 students graduated in 2012; all went to college, including Brown University; Case Western Reserve University; Chicago State University; Southern Methodist University; The Ohio State University; Washington University in St. Louis. Median SAT critical reading: 630, median SAT math: 640, median SAT writing: 620, median combined SAT: 1910, median composite ACT: 28. 58% scored over 600 on SAT critical reading, 69% scored over 600 on SAT math, 61% scored over 600 on SAT writing, 64% scored over 1800 on combined SAT, 70% scored over 26 on composite ACT.

Student Life Upper grades have specified standards of dress, student council, honor system. Discipline rests equally with students and faculty.

Tuition and Aid Day student tuition: $23,115–$25,570. Tuition installment plan (Key Tuition Payment Plan, individually arranged payment plans, installment payment plan (60 percent by 8/15 and 40 percent by 1/15), AchieverLoans (Key Education Resources)). Merit scholarship grants, need-based scholarship grants, need-based loans available. In 2012–13, 37% of upper-school students received aid; total upper-school merit-scholarship money awarded: $162,000. Total amount of financial aid awarded in 2012–13: $5,102,962.

Admissions Traditional secondary-level entrance grade is 9. For fall 2012, 128 students applied for upper-level admission, 91 were accepted, 52 enrolled. ISEE

required. Deadline for receipt of application materials: December 19. Application fee required: $25. On-campus interview required.

Athletics Interscholastic: baseball (boys), basketball (b,g), cross-country running (b,g), diving (b,g), field hockey (g), football (b), golf (b,g), lacrosse (b,g), soccer (b,g), softball (g), swimming and diving (b,g), tennis (b,g), track and field (b,g), wrestling (b); intramural: basketball (b); coed intramural: dance, life saving, outdoor skills. 3 PE instructors, 33 coaches, 1 athletic trainer.

Computers Computers are regularly used in all classes. Computer network features include on-campus library services, Internet access, wireless campus network, Internet filtering or blocking technology. Campus intranet and student e-mail accounts are available to students. Students grades are available online. The school has a published electronic and media policy.

Contact Heather Willis Daly, Director of Admission and Financial Assistance. 440-423-2955. Fax: 440-423-2994. E-mail: hdaly@hawken.edu. Website: www.hawken.edu/

HAWTHORNE CHRISTIAN ACADEMY

2000 Route 208
Hawthorne, New Jersey 07506

Head of School: Mr. David Seidman

General Information Coeducational day college-preparatory, arts, religious studies, technology, music, and missions school, affiliated with Christian faith, Christian faith. Grades PS–12. Founded: 1981. Setting: suburban. Nearest major city is New York, NY. 22-acre campus. 4 buildings on campus. Approved or accredited by Association of Christian Schools International, Middle States Association of Colleges and Schools, and New Jersey Department of Education. Total enrollment: 496. Upper school average class size: 20. Upper school faculty-student ratio: 1:7. There are 180 required school days per year for Upper School students. Upper School students typically attend 5 days per week. The average school day consists of 6 hours and 40 minutes.

Upper School Student Profile Grade 9: 33 students (10 boys, 23 girls); Grade 10: 36 students (22 boys, 14 girls); Grade 11: 32 students (16 boys, 16 girls); Grade 12: 46 students (25 boys, 21 girls). 100% of students are Christian faith, Christian.

Faculty School total: 60. In upper school: 8 men, 14 women; 7 have advanced degrees.

Subjects Offered Accounting, advanced computer applications, Advanced Placement courses, algebra, anatomy and physiology, art and culture, band, Basic programming, bell choir, Bible, biology, biology-AP, business applications, calculus, calculus-AP, chemistry, choir, choral music, chorus, Christian ethics, composition, computer information systems, computer programming, computers, contemporary issues, creative writing, current events, drama, electives, English literature, English literature-AP, ensembles, foreign language, geometry, government, guidance, handbells, health, information technology, instrumental music, instruments, intro to computers, law, mathematics, music, music appreciation, music history, music theory, physical education, physical science, physics, politics, pre-calculus, psychology, Spanish, Spanish-AP, studio art, U.S. government, U.S. government and politics-AP, U.S. history-AP, video, visual arts, voice, Web site design, world history, yearbook.

Graduation Requirements Algebra, Bible, biology, chemistry, English literature, English literature-AP, geometry, intro to computers, mathematics, physical education (includes health), physical science, pre-calculus, Spanish, U.S. government, U.S. history, U.S. history-AP, world history, Christian service hours, Apologetics and Current Issues, specified number of Academic Elective Courses.

Special Academic Programs 5 Advanced Placement exams for which test preparation is offered.

College Admission Counseling 34 students graduated in 2013; 33 went to college, including Grove City College; Liberty University; New Jersey Institute of Technology; Palm Beach Atlantic University; Wheaton College. Other: 1 went to work. Mean SAT critical reading: 597, mean SAT math: 556, mean SAT writing: 590, mean combined SAT: 1153.

Student Life Upper grades have specified standards of dress, student council. Discipline rests primarily with faculty. Attendance at religious services is required.

Tuition and Aid Day student tuition: $11,070. Tuition installment plan (FACTS Tuition Payment Plan, monthly payment plans). Tuition reduction for siblings, merit scholarship grants, need-based scholarship grants, pastoral discounts, teacher/employee discounts available. In 2013–14, 29% of upper-school students received aid; total upper-school merit-scholarship money awarded: $23,000. Total amount of financial aid awarded in 2013–14: $74,440.

Admissions Traditional secondary-level entrance grade is 9. Admissions testing, Otis-Lennon School Ability Test or WRAT required. Deadline for receipt of application materials: none. Application fee required: $100. On-campus interview required.

Athletics Interscholastic: baseball (boys), basketball (b,g), soccer (b,g), softball (g), volleyball (g); coed interscholastic: bowling, cross-country running, track and field; coed intramural: strength & conditioning. 2 PE instructors.

Computers Computers are regularly used in computer applications, information technology, introduction to technology, lab/keyboard, library, technology, Web site design, yearbook classes. Computer network features include on-campus library services, Internet access, Internet filtering or blocking technology. Campus intranet is

available to students. Students grades are available online. The school has a published electronic and media policy.

Contact Mrs. Judith De Boer, Admissions Coordinator. 973-423-3331 Ext. 261. Fax: 973-238-1718. E-mail: jdeboer@hca.org. Website: www.hca.org/

HEAD-ROYCE SCHOOL

4315 Lincoln Avenue
Oakland, California 94602

Head of School: Robert Lake

General Information Coeducational day college-preparatory, arts, technology, and STEM, robotics, Global Online Academy school. Grades K–12. Founded: 1887. Setting: urban. 22-acre campus. 8 buildings on campus. Approved or accredited by Western Association of Schools and Colleges and California Department of Education. Member of National Association of Independent Schools. Endowment: $15 million. Total enrollment: 876. Upper school average class size: 16. Upper school faculty-student ratio: 1:9. There are 175 required school days per year for Upper School students. Upper School students typically attend 5 days per week. The average school day consists of 7 hours.

Upper School Student Profile Grade 9: 96 students (48 boys, 48 girls); Grade 10: 98 students (49 boys, 49 girls); Grade 11: 85 students (42 boys, 43 girls); Grade 12: 91 students (45 boys, 46 girls).

Faculty School total: 95. In upper school: 24 men, 19 women; 29 have advanced degrees.

Subjects Offered Algebra, American history, American literature, art, art history, astronomy, biology, calculus, ceramics, chemistry, Chinese, community service, computer programming, computer science, creative writing, debate, drama, ecology, English, English literature, European history, expository writing, fine arts, French, geometry, graphic arts, health, history, journalism, Latin, marine biology, mathematics, music, neurobiology, photography, physical education, physics, psychology, science, social studies, Spanish, theater, trigonometry, typing, video, world history, world literature, writing.

Graduation Requirements Art history, arts and fine arts (art, music, dance, drama), computer science, English, foreign language, mathematics, physical education (includes health), science, social studies (includes history), 40 hours of community service.

Special Academic Programs 24 Advanced Placement exams for which test preparation is offered; honors section; independent study; term-away projects; study at local college for college credit; study abroad; academic accommodation for the gifted, the musically talented, and the artistically talented.

College Admission Counseling 79 students graduated in 2013; all went to college, including Occidental College; Stanford University; University of California, Berkeley; University of California, Davis; University of California, Los Angeles; University of Southern California. Mean SAT critical reading: 691, mean SAT math: 689, mean SAT writing: 712.

Student Life Upper grades have specified standards of dress, student council, honor system. Discipline rests primarily with faculty.

Summer Programs Remediation, enrichment, advancement programs offered; session focuses on sports and enrichment; held on campus; accepts boys and girls; open to students from other schools. 800 students usually enrolled. 2014 schedule: June 16 to July 31. Application deadline: February.

Tuition and Aid Day student tuition: $33,525. Tuition installment plan (SMART Tuition Payment Plan, monthly payment plans). Need-based scholarship grants, paying campus jobs, tuition remission for children of faculty and staff available. In 2013–14, 30% of upper-school students received aid. Total amount of financial aid awarded in 2013–14: $2,296,400.

Admissions Traditional secondary-level entrance grade is 9. For fall 2013, 181 students applied for upper-level admission, 82 were accepted, 36 enrolled. ISEE or SSAT required. Deadline for receipt of application materials: January 16. Application fee required: $100. On-campus interview required.

Athletics Interscholastic: baseball (boys), basketball (b,g), cross-country running (b,g), dance squad (g), golf (b,g), lacrosse (b), modern dance (g), outdoor education (b,g), physical fitness (b,g), soccer (b,g), softball (g), strength & conditioning (b,g), swimming and diving (b,g), tennis (b,g), volleyball (b,g), weight lifting (b,g), weight training (b,g); coed interscholastic: cross-country running, golf, outdoor education, physical fitness, strength & conditioning, swimming and diving; coed intramural: bicycling, dance, ultimate Frisbee. 6 PE instructors, 39 coaches.

Computers Computers are regularly used in all academic, English, graphics, mathematics, science, yearbook classes. Computer network features include on-campus library services, online commercial services, Internet access, wireless campus network, laptop carts, Smartboards, iPad carts. Student e-mail accounts and computer access in designated common areas are available to students. Students grades are available online. The school has a published electronic and media policy.

Contact Mrs. Catherine Epstein, Director of Admissions and Financial Aid. 510-531-1300. Fax: 510-530-8329. E-mail: cepstein@headroyce.org. Website: www.headroyce.org

HEBREW ACADEMY

14401 Willow Lane
Huntington Beach, California 92647

Head of School: Dr. Megan Carlson

General Information Girls' boarding and coeducational day college-preparatory, general academic, religious studies, and technology school, affiliated with Jewish faith. Boarding girls grades 9–12, day boys grades N–8, day girls grades N–12. Founded: 1969. Setting: suburban. Students are housed in single-sex dormitories. 11-acre campus. 11 buildings on campus. Approved or accredited by Accrediting Commission for Schools and Western Association of Schools and Colleges. Total enrollment: 247. Upper school average class size: 10. Upper school faculty-student ratio: 1:4. There are 175 required school days per year for Upper School students. Upper School students typically attend 5 days per week. The average school day consists of 7 hours and 30 minutes.

Upper School Student Profile Grade 9: 15 students (15 girls); Grade 10: 6 students (6 girls); Grade 11: 11 students (11 girls); Grade 12: 4 students (4 girls). 10% of students are boarding students. 90% are state residents. 5 states are represented in upper school student body. 100% of students are Jewish.

Faculty School total: 41. In upper school: 6 men, 12 women; 2 have advanced degrees.

Subjects Offered Algebra, American history, American literature, art history, biology, earth science, economics, English, English literature, geography, government/civics, grammar, Hebrew, history, mathematics, physical education, physics, physiology, psychology, religion, science, social sciences, social studies, theology, world cultures, world history, writing.

Graduation Requirements Computer science, English, foreign language, mathematics, physical education (includes health), religion (includes Bible studies and theology), science, social sciences, social studies (includes history).

Special Academic Programs International Baccalaureate program; 5 Advanced Placement exams for which test preparation is offered; honors section; independent study; remedial reading and/or remedial writing; remedial math; programs in general development for dyslexic students.

Student Life Upper grades have uniform requirement, student council. Discipline rests primarily with faculty. Attendance at religious services is required.

Tuition and Aid Day student tuition: $13,000. Guaranteed tuition plan. Tuition installment plan (monthly payment plans, individually arranged payment plans). Tuition reduction for siblings, need-based scholarship grants available. In 2013–14, 30% of upper-school students received aid. Total amount of financial aid awarded in 2013–14: $30,000.

Admissions Traditional secondary-level entrance grade is 9. For fall 2013, 20 students applied for upper-level admission, 15 were accepted, 10 enrolled. Deadline for receipt of application materials: none. Application fee required: $100. On-campus interview required.

Athletics Interscholastic: aerobics/dance, aerobics/Nautilus, aquatics (b), archery (b), badminton, baseball (b), basketball (b), dance, jogging (b), physical fitness (b), soccer (b), softball (b), swimming and diving (b), volleyball. 1 PE instructor.

Computers Computers are regularly used in English, foreign language, science, technology classes. Computer network features include on-campus library services, online commercial services, Internet access, multimedia, including laser disks, digital cameras. Computer access in designated common areas is available to students. The school has a published electronic and media policy.

Contact Mrs. Alex Greenberg, Director of Admissions. 714-898-0051 Ext. 284. Fax: 714-898-0633. E-mail: agreenberg@hacds.org. Website: www.hebrewacademyhb.com

HEBREW ACADEMY OF THE FIVE TOWNS & ROCKAWAY

635 Central Avenue
Cedarhurst, New York 11516

Head of School: Ms. Naomi Lippman

General Information Coeducational day college-preparatory, arts, business, and religious studies school, affiliated with Jewish faith. Grades 9–12. Founded: 1978. Setting: suburban. Nearest major city is New York. 1 building on campus. Approved or accredited by Middle States Association of Colleges and Schools, The College Board, and New York Department of Education. Languages of instruction: English and Hebrew. Total enrollment: 388. Upper school average class size: 20. The average school day consists of 9 hours and 15 minutes.

Upper School Student Profile 100% of students are Jewish.

Faculty School total: 60.

Subjects Offered Advanced Placement courses, arts, English, fine arts, foreign language, Jewish studies, Judaic studies, mathematics, physical education, religion, science, social sciences, social studies.

Graduation Requirements Arts and fine arts (art, music, dance, drama), English, foreign language, Judaic studies, mathematics, physical education (includes health), religion (includes Bible studies and theology), science, social sciences, social studies (includes history), community service requirement.

Special Academic Programs 11 Advanced Placement exams for which test preparation is offered; honors section; independent study; study abroad; academic accommodation for the artistically talented.

College Admission Counseling 82 students graduated in 2013; all went to college, including Binghamton University, State University of New York; Columbia University; Cornell University; New York University; Queens College of the City University of New York; Yeshiva University. Median SAT critical reading: 590, median SAT math: 610, median SAT writing: 570. 48% scored over 600 on SAT critical reading, 56% scored over 600 on SAT math, 41% scored over 600 on SAT writing.

Student Life Upper grades have specified standards of dress, student council, honor system. Discipline rests primarily with faculty. Attendance at religious services is required.

Tuition and Aid Tuition installment plan (monthly payment plans, individually arranged payment plans). Need-based scholarship grants available.

Admissions Traditional secondary-level entrance grade is 9. Board of Jewish Education Entrance Exam required. Deadline for receipt of application materials: March 15. Application fee required. On-campus interview required.

Athletics Interscholastic: baseball (boys, girls), basketball (b,g), field hockey (b), softball (b,g), tennis (b,g), volleyball (g); coed intramural: skiing (downhill). 2 PE instructors, 8 coaches.

Computers Computers are regularly used in computer applications classes. Computer resources include on-campus library services, online commercial services, Internet access, Internet filtering or blocking technology. Student e-mail accounts are available to students. The school has a published electronic and media policy.

Contact Ms. Naomi Lippman, Principal, General Studies. 516-569-3807. Fax: 516-374-5761. Website: www.haftr.org

THE HEIGHTS SCHOOL

10400 Seven Locks Road
Potomac, Maryland 20854

Head of School: Mr. Alvaro J. de Vicente

General Information Boys' day college-preparatory and religious studies school, affiliated with Roman Catholic Church. Grades 3–12. Founded: 1969. Setting: suburban. Nearest major city is Washington, DC. 20-acre campus. 5 buildings on campus. Approved or accredited by Association of Independent Maryland Schools, Association of Independent Schools of Greater Washington, Middle States Association of Colleges and Schools, and Maryland Department of Education. Member of National Association of Independent Schools. Total enrollment: 460. Upper school average class size: 15. Upper school faculty-student ratio: 1:7. There are 173 required school days per year for Upper School students. Upper School students typically attend 5 days per week. The average school day consists of 6 hours and 45 minutes.

Upper School Student Profile Grade 6: 45 students (45 boys); Grade 7: 45 students (45 boys); Grade 8: 45 students (45 boys); Grade 9: 60 students (60 boys); Grade 10: 60 students (60 boys); Grade 11: 60 students (60 boys); Grade 12: 60 students (60 boys). 85% of students are Roman Catholic.

Faculty School total: 60. In upper school: 60 men; 37 have advanced degrees.

Subjects Offered Algebra, American history, American literature, American literature-AP, Ancient Greek, art history-AP, bioethics, biology, biology-AP, calculus, calculus-AP, chemistry, chemistry-AP, chorus, computer programming, computer science, drama, economics, economics-AP, English, English literature, ethics, European history, European history-AP, geology, geometry, government-AP, history, Latin, Latin-AP, macro/microeconomics-AP, macroeconomics-AP, mathematics, medieval history, music, philosophy, physical education, physics, physics-AP, post-calculus, religion, science, Spanish, Spanish language-AP, Spanish literature-AP, statistics-AP, studio art-AP, trigonometry, world literature, World War II, writing.

Graduation Requirements Athletics, electives, English, foreign language, history, mathematics, religion (includes Bible studies and theology), science.

Special Academic Programs Advanced Placement exam preparation; independent study; academic accommodation for the gifted.

College Admission Counseling 53 students graduated in 2013; 52 went to college, including The Catholic University of America; University of Maryland, College Park; University of Notre Dame; University of Virginia; Virginia Polytechnic Institute and State University. Other: 1 entered military service.

Student Life Upper grades have specified standards of dress, student council. Discipline rests primarily with faculty.

Summer Programs Remediation, enrichment, advancement, sports programs offered; session focuses on academic enrichment and outdoor adventure; held on campus; accepts boys; open to students from other schools. 100 students usually enrolled. 2014 schedule: June 23 to August 1. Application deadline: June.

Tuition and Aid Tuition installment plan (FACTS Tuition Payment Plan, monthly payment plans). Merit scholarship grants, need-based scholarship grants, need-based financial aid available. In 2013–14, 30% of upper-school students received aid; total upper-school merit-scholarship money awarded: $45,000. Total amount of financial aid awarded in 2013–14: $710,000.

Admissions Traditional secondary-level entrance grade is 9. For fall 2013, 69 students applied for upper-level admission, 25 were accepted, 15 enrolled. SSAT required. Deadline for receipt of application materials: January 25. Application fee required: $50. On-campus interview required.

Athletics Interscholastic: aquatics, baseball, basketball, cross-country running, diving, golf, lacrosse, rugby, soccer, squash, swimming and diving, tennis, track and field, wrestling; intramural: archery, basketball, cross-country running, rock climbing, skateboarding. 2 PE instructors, 1 athletic trainer.

Computers Computers are regularly used in computer applications, journalism, library skills, newspaper, programming, yearbook classes. Computer network features include on-campus library services, online commercial services, Internet access, wireless campus network, Internet filtering or blocking technology.

Contact Mrs. Dorothy Reilly, Coordinator of Admission. 301-765-2093. Fax: 301-365-4303. E-mail: dreilly@heights.edu. Website: www.heights.edu

HERITAGE CHRISTIAN ACADEMY

2003 McKnight Boulevard NE
Calgary, Alberta T2E 6L2, Canada

Head of School: Mr. Ryan Brennan

General Information Coeducational day college-preparatory, general academic, arts, religious studies, bilingual studies, and technology school, affiliated with Christian faith, Evangelical faith. Grades K–12. Founded: 1979. Setting: urban. 10-acre campus. 1 building on campus. Approved or accredited by Association of Christian Schools International, Association of Independent Schools and Colleges of Alberta, and Alberta Department of Education. Language of instruction: English. Total enrollment: 568. Upper school average class size: 27. Upper school faculty-student ratio: 1:9. There are 184 required school days per year for Upper School students. Upper School students typically attend 5 days per week. The average school day consists of 6 hours and 55 minutes.

Upper School Student Profile Grade 10: 51 students (21 boys, 30 girls); Grade 11: 40 students (25 boys, 15 girls); Grade 12: 30 students (13 boys, 17 girls). 100% of students are Christian, members of Evangelical faith.

Faculty School total: 34. In upper school: 6 men, 7 women; 2 have advanced degrees.

Subjects Offered Art, band, Bible, biology, career and personal planning, chemistry, choir, choral music, Christian education, computer applications, computer multimedia, creative writing, English, essential learning systems, French as a second language, health, language arts, mathematics, physical education, physics, psychology, religious studies, science, sewing, social studies, sports medicine, work experience.

Graduation Requirements Career and personal planning, English, mathematics, physical education (includes health), religious studies, science, social studies (includes history).

Special Academic Programs Independent study; remedial reading and/or remedial writing; remedial math; special instructional classes for deaf students, students with dyslexia addressed through IPPs and classroom accommodations.

College Admission Counseling 28 students graduated in 2012; 22 went to college, including Mount Royal University; The University of British Columbia; University of Alberta; University of Calgary; University of Lethbridge. Other: 5 went to work, 1 had other specific plans.

Student Life Upper grades have uniform requirement, student council, honor system. Discipline rests primarily with faculty. Attendance at religious services is required.

Tuition and Aid Day student tuition: CAN$3030. Tuition installment plan (monthly payment plans, individually arranged payment plans). Tuition reduction for siblings available.

Admissions Traditional secondary-level entrance grade is 10. For fall 2012, 6 students applied for upper-level admission, 6 were accepted, 6 enrolled. CTBS (or similar from their school) required. Deadline for receipt of application materials: none. Application fee required: CAN$100. Interview required.

Athletics Interscholastic: basketball (boys, girls), cross-country running (b,g), golf (b,g), track and field (b,g), volleyball (b,g), wrestling (b,g); coed interscholastic: floor hockey, track and field; coed intramural: basketball, climbing, floor hockey, indoor soccer, indoor track & field, outdoor activities, physical fitness, project adventure, soccer, touch football, track and field, volleyball, wall climbing. 1 PE instructor.

Computers Computers are regularly used in animation, Bible studies, career education, data processing, English, graphics, information technology, keyboarding, mathematics, multimedia, photography, science, social studies classes. Computer network features include Internet access, Internet filtering or blocking technology. Student e-mail accounts are available to students. The school has a published electronic and media policy.

Contact Office. 403-219-3201. Fax: 403-219-3210. E-mail: heritage_info@pallisersd.ab.ca. Website: www.hcacalgary.com

HERITAGE CHRISTIAN SCHOOL

9825 Woodley Avenue
North Hills, California 91343

Head of School: Mr. Lance Haliday

General Information Coeducational day college-preparatory, arts, religious studies, and technology school, affiliated with Christian faith. Grades 7–12. Founded: 1962. Setting: suburban. Nearest major city is Los Angeles. 11-acre campus. 5 buildings on campus. Approved or accredited by Association of Christian Schools

International and Western Association of Schools and Colleges. Total enrollment: 794. Upper school average class size: 30. Upper school faculty-student ratio: 1:22. There are 180 required school days per year for Upper School students. Upper School students typically attend 5 days per week. The average school day consists of 6 hours and 45 minutes.

Upper School Student Profile Grade 9: 137 students (69 boys, 68 girls); Grade 10: 156 students (72 boys, 84 girls); Grade 11: 179 students (100 boys, 79 girls); Grade 12: 171 students (81 boys, 90 girls).

Faculty School total: 40. In upper school: 12 men, 22 women; 26 have advanced degrees.

Subjects Offered 3-dimensional design, advanced computer applications, algebra, American history, American literature, analysis and differential calculus, anatomy and physiology, art, ASB Leadership, band, Bible studies, biology, biology-AP, calculus-AP, ceramics, chemistry, choir, choral music, Christian doctrine, Christian education, Christian ethics, computer applications, computer education, computer graphics, computer programming, computer science, computer skills, computer technologies, digital photography, drama, drama performance, earth science, economics, English, English literature, English-AP, expository writing, fine arts, French, French-AP, geography, geometry, government/civics, HTML design, intro to computers, jazz band, journalism, keyboarding, mathematics, music, photography, physical education, physics, physics-AP, practical arts, pre-calculus, psychology, psychology-AP, religion, science, social studies, Spanish, Spanish-AP, statistics, statistics-AP, studio art, theater arts, trigonometry, typing, U.S. history-AP, world history.

Graduation Requirements Arts and fine arts (art, music, dance, drama), English, foreign language, mathematics, physical education (includes health), practical arts, religion (includes Bible studies and theology), science, social studies (includes history).

Special Academic Programs Advanced Placement exam preparation; honors section; ESL (13 students enrolled).

College Admission Counseling 192 students graduated in 2013; 188 went to college, including California State University, Northridge; The Master's College and Seminary; University of California, Irvine; University of California, Los Angeles. Other: 2 went to work, 2 entered military service. Median SAT critical reading: 570, median SAT math: 565, median SAT writing: 550, median combined SAT: 1650, median composite ACT: 25.

Student Life Upper grades have uniform requirement, student council, honor system. Discipline rests primarily with faculty. Attendance at religious services is required.

Summer Programs Remediation, advancement, sports, computer instruction programs offered; session focuses on remediation and enrichment; held both on and off campus; held at Internet-based learning can be done from any computer; accepts boys and girls; open to students from other schools. 350 students usually enrolled. 2014 schedule: June 1 to July 30.

Tuition and Aid Day student tuition: $8778. Tuition installment plan (FACTS Tuition Payment Plan, monthly payment plans, 2-semester payment plan, annual payment plan). Need-based scholarship grants available. In 2013–14, 27% of upper-school students received aid. Total amount of financial aid awarded in 2013–14: $500,000.

Admissions Traditional secondary-level entrance grade is 9. For fall 2013, 130 students applied for upper-level admission, 124 were accepted, 110 enrolled. QUIC required. Deadline for receipt of application materials: August 1. Application fee required: $120. On-campus interview required.

Athletics Interscholastic: baseball (boys), basketball (b,g), cheering (g), cross-country running (b,g), football (b), golf (b), soccer (b,g), softball (g), tennis (g), track and field (b,g), volleyball (b,g). 2 PE instructors, 42 coaches.

Computers Computers are regularly used in animation, business applications, career technology, graphic design, graphics, introduction to technology, keyboarding, lab/keyboard, programming, technology, typing, Web site design, word processing classes. Computer network features include on-campus library services, Internet access, Internet filtering or blocking technology. The school has a published electronic and media policy.

Contact Mrs. Penny Lade, South Campus Registrar. 818-894-5742 Ext. 324. Fax: 818-892-5018. E-mail: plade@heritage-schools.org. Website: www.heritage-schools.org

HERITAGE CHRISTIAN SCHOOL

2850 Fourth Avenue
PO Box 400
Jordan, Ontario L0R 1S0, Canada

Head of School: Mr. A. Ben Harsevoort

General Information Coeducational day college-preparatory, general academic, arts, and religious studies school, affiliated with Reformed Church. Grades K–12. Founded: 1992. Setting: rural. Nearest major city is St. Catharines, Canada. 26-acre campus. 1 building on campus. Approved or accredited by Ontario Department of Education. Language of instruction: English. Total enrollment: 630. Upper school average class size: 50. Upper school faculty-student ratio: 1:15. There are 185 required school days per year for Upper School students. Upper School students typically attend 5 days per week. The average school day consists of 5 hours.

Upper School Student Profile Grade 9: 51 students (25 boys, 26 girls); Grade 10: 47 students (24 boys, 23 girls); Grade 11: 44 students (22 boys, 22 girls); Grade 12: 39 students (20 boys, 19 girls). 95% of students are Reformed.

Faculty School total: 35. In upper school: 11 men, 4 women; 4 have advanced degrees.

Subjects Offered 20th century American writers, 20th century physics, 20th century world history, advanced chemistry, advanced math, algebra, analysis and differential calculus, art, Bible, biology, bookkeeping, British literature, business mathematics, business studies, calculus, Canadian geography, Canadian history, Canadian law, Canadian literature, career education, chemistry, choral music, Christian and Hebrew scripture, Christian doctrine, Christian education, Christian ethics, Christian studies, Christian testament, Christianity, church history, civics, classical civilization, computer education, computer programming, computer skills, consumer mathematics, creative writing, culinary arts, drafting, English, English composition, English literature, entrepreneurship, environmental education, ethics, European civilization, European history, family studies, finite math, foods, foundations of civilization, French, French as a second language, general math, geography, geometry, grammar, health, history, honors algebra, honors English, honors geometry, honors world history, humanities, independent living, keyboarding, language and composition, language arts, law and the legal system, life science, literature, marketing, mathematics, media literacy, modern civilization, modern European history, modern Western civilization, music, music appreciation, novels, personal finance, physical education, physics, practicum, public speaking, religion and culture, religious education, religious studies, Shakespeare, society challenge and change, speech communications, technical drawing, vocal music, word processing, world civilizations, world literature, writing.

Graduation Requirements Ontario Secondary School Diploma requirements.

Special Academic Programs Remedial reading and/or remedial writing; remedial math.

College Admission Counseling 53 students graduated in 2013; 47 went to college, including Calvin College; Covenant College. Other: 6 went to work.

Student Life Upper grades have uniform requirement, student council. Discipline rests primarily with faculty. Attendance at religious services is required.

Tuition and Aid Day student tuition: CAN$12,500. Tuition installment plan (monthly payment plans).

Admissions Traditional secondary-level entrance grade is 9. Deadline for receipt of application materials: none. No application fee required. On-campus interview required.

Athletics Interscholastic: badminton (boys, girls), basketball (b,g), ice hockey (b), soccer (b,g), volleyball (b,g). 3 coaches.

Computers Computers are regularly used in accounting, business, economics, information technology, keyboarding, mathematics, newspaper, typing, yearbook classes. The school has a published electronic and media policy.

Contact Mrs. Mariam Sinke, Administrative Assistant. 905-562-7303 Ext. 221. Fax: 905-562-0020. E-mail: heritage@hcsjordan.ca. Website: www.hcsjordan.ca

THE HERITAGE SCHOOL

2093 Highway 29 North
Newnan, Georgia 30263

Head of School: J.P. Watson

General Information Coeducational day college-preparatory, arts, and technology school. Grades PK–12. Founded: 1970. Setting: suburban. Nearest major city is Atlanta. 62-acre campus. 13 buildings on campus. Approved or accredited by Georgia Independent School Association, Southern Association of Colleges and Schools, Southern Association of Independent Schools, and Georgia Department of Education. Member of National Association of Independent Schools. Endowment: $1.1 million. Total enrollment: 428. Upper school average class size: 14. Upper school faculty-student ratio: 1:8. There are 180 required school days per year for Upper School students. Upper School students typically attend 5 days per week. The average school day consists of 6 hours and 30 minutes.

Upper School Student Profile Grade 9: 44 students (16 boys, 28 girls); Grade 10: 39 students (22 boys, 17 girls); Grade 11: 51 students (26 boys, 25 girls); Grade 12: 36 students (24 boys, 12 girls).

Faculty School total: 53. In upper school: 6 men, 16 women; 8 have advanced degrees.

Subjects Offered Advanced studio art-AP, algebra, American government, American history, American history-AP, American literature, art, art history, art-AP, biology, biology-AP, calculus, calculus-AP, chemistry, chemistry-AP, college admission preparation, composition-AP, computer applications, digital photography, drama, economics, English, English language and composition-AP, English literature, English literature and composition-AP, environmental science, environmental science-AP, European history-AP, film appreciation, fitness, French, French language-AP, French-AP, gardening, geometry, government-AP, graphic arts, health, history, integrated science, language-AP, Latin, mathematics, music, music theory-AP, physical education, physical science, physics-AP, pre-calculus, psychology, psychology-AP, public speaking, Spanish, Spanish-AP, statistics-AP, strings, studio art-AP, U.S. history-AP, video film production, world history, world literature, writing workshop.

Graduation Requirements Arts and fine arts (art, music, dance, drama), computer science, electives, English, foreign language, mathematics, physical education (includes health), public speaking, science, social studies (includes history).

Special Academic Programs 16 Advanced Placement exams for which test preparation is offered; independent study.

College Admission Counseling 43 students graduated in 2013; all went to college, including Auburn University; Georgia Institute of Technology; Georgia Southern University; Kennesaw State University; University of Georgia; University of West Georgia. Mean SAT critical reading: 560, mean SAT math: 585, mean SAT writing: 550, mean combined SAT: 1695, mean composite ACT: 26.

Student Life Upper grades have specified standards of dress, student council, honor system. Discipline rests primarily with faculty.

Tuition and Aid Day student tuition: $7485–$14,180. Tuition installment plan (monthly payment plans). Tuition reduction for siblings, need-based scholarship grants available. In 2013–14, 30% of upper-school students received aid. Total amount of financial aid awarded in 2013–14: $367,651.

Admissions Traditional secondary-level entrance grade is 9. For fall 2013, 33 students applied for upper-level admission, 28 were accepted, 22 enrolled. Otis-Lennon School Ability Test required. Deadline for receipt of application materials: none. Application fee required: $50. On-campus interview required.

Athletics Interscholastic: aerobics/dance (girls), baseball (b), basketball (b,g), cheering (g), cross-country running (b,g), football (b), golf (b,g), soccer (b,g), softball (g), swimming and diving (b,g), tennis (b,g), track and field (b,g), volleyball (g), weight training (b,g); intramural: cheering (g), football (b); coed interscholastic: physical fitness; coed intramural: backpacking, basketball, canoeing/kayaking, climbing, equestrian sports, flag football, hiking/backpacking, horseback riding, kayaking, mountaineering, outdoor adventure, outdoor education, ropes courses, wilderness survival. 3 PE instructors, 1 athletic trainer.

Computers Computers are regularly used in college planning, creative writing, English, foreign language, publications, science, yearbook classes. Computer network features include on-campus library services, online commercial services, Internet access, wireless campus network, Internet filtering or blocking technology. Campus intranet, student e-mail accounts, and computer access in designated common areas are available to students. Students grades are available online. The school has a published electronic and media policy.

Contact Monica Haaland, Director of Admission and Marketing. 678-423-5393. Fax: 770-253-4850. E-mail: mhaaland@heritagehawks.org. Website: www.heritagehawks.org

THE HEWITT SCHOOL

45 East 75th Street
New York, New York 10021

Head of School: Ms. Joan Z. Lonergan

General Information Girls' day college-preparatory school. Grades K–12. Founded: 1920. Setting: urban. 1 building on campus. Approved or accredited by Middle States Association of Colleges and Schools, National Independent Private Schools Association, New York State Association of Independent Schools, and New York Department of Education. Member of National Association of Independent Schools and Secondary School Admission Test Board. Total enrollment: 520. Upper school average class size: 15. Upper school faculty-student ratio: 1:7. Upper School students typically attend 5 days per week. The average school day consists of 7 hours.

Upper School Student Profile Grade 9: 26 students (26 girls); Grade 10: 30 students (30 girls); Grade 11: 30 students (30 girls); Grade 12: 29 students (29 girls).

Faculty School total: 82. In upper school: 14 men, 16 women; 24 have advanced degrees.

Subjects Offered Algebra, American history, American literature, anatomy and physiology, art, biology, calculus, chemistry, computers, drama, earth science, English, English literature, European history, fine arts, French, genetics, geometry, history, Latin, mathematics, music, photography, physical education, physics, pre-calculus, science, Spanish, world history.

Graduation Requirements Creative arts, English, foreign language, history, mathematics, physical education (includes health), science, technology.

Special Academic Programs Advanced Placement exam preparation; honors section; independent study; term-away projects; study abroad.

College Admission Counseling 24 students graduated in 2012; all went to college, including Bard College; Barnard College; Bates College; Syracuse University; University of Michigan; University of Pennsylvania.

Student Life Upper grades have uniform requirement, student council. Discipline rests primarily with faculty.

Tuition and Aid Day student tuition: $38,550. Guaranteed tuition plan. Tuition installment plan (Insured Tuition Payment Plan, Key Tuition Payment Plan, monthly payment plans). Need-based scholarship grants available. In 2012–13, 22% of upper-school students received aid. Total amount of financial aid awarded in 2012–13: $1,394,709.

Admissions Traditional secondary-level entrance grade is 9. ERB and ISEE required. Deadline for receipt of application materials: December 1. Application fee required: $60. On-campus interview required.

Athletics Interscholastic: badminton, basketball, cross-country running, soccer, squash, swimming and diving, tennis, track and field, volleyball; intramural: badminton, basketball, crew, cross-country running, lacrosse, soccer, swimming and diving, tennis, track and field, volleyball. 4 PE instructors.

Computers Computers are regularly used in all academic, art, English, foreign language, history, humanities, mathematics, music, science classes. Computer network features include on-campus library services, online commercial services, Internet access, wireless campus network, Internet filtering or blocking technology. Campus intranet, student e-mail accounts, and computer access in designated common areas are available to students. The school has a published electronic and media policy.

Contact Ms. Jessica Acee, Director of Admissions, Middle and Upper School. 212-994-2623. Fax: 212-472-7531. E-mail: jacee@hewittschool.org. Website: hewittschool.org

HIGHLAND HALL WALDORF SCHOOL

17100 Superior Street
Northridge, California 91325

Head of School: Lynn Kern

General Information Coeducational day college-preparatory and arts school. Grades N–12. Founded: 1955. Setting: suburban. Nearest major city is Los Angeles. 11-acre campus. 4 buildings on campus. Approved or accredited by Association of Waldorf Schools of North America and Western Association of Schools and Colleges. Total enrollment: 241. Upper school average class size: 25. Upper school faculty-student ratio: 1:6. There are 175 required school days per year for Upper School students. Upper School students typically attend 5 days per week. The average school day consists of 7 hours and 10 minutes.

Upper School Student Profile Grade 9: 20 students (8 boys, 12 girls); Grade 10: 24 students (5 boys, 19 girls); Grade 11: 21 students (3 boys, 18 girls); Grade 12: 21 students (10 boys, 11 girls).

Faculty School total: 59. In upper school: 11 men, 15 women; 8 have advanced degrees.

Subjects Offered Algebra, American history, American literature, anatomy, ancient history, architecture, art, art history, astronomy, biology, bookbinding, botany, calculus, career/college preparation, cell biology, chemistry, choral music, chorus, clayworking, conflict resolution, CPR, creative writing, drama, drawing, earth science, economics, English, English literature, ethnic studies, European history, eurythmy, expository writing, geography, geology, geometry, German, government/civics, grammar, guidance, guitar, handbells, health, history, honors U.S. history, jazz ensemble, marine biology, mathematics, metalworking, music, music history, Native American history, orchestra, painting, physical education, physics, physiology, pre-algebra, pre-calculus, SAT preparation, sculpture, sewing, social studies, Spanish, speech, stone carving, theater, trigonometry, woodworking, world history, world literature, writing, yearbook, zoology.

Graduation Requirements 20th century history, 20th century world history, acting, algebra, American Civil War, anatomy, ancient history, ancient world history, architecture, art, art history, arts and crafts, arts and fine arts (art, music, dance, drama), atomic theory, bell choir, biology, bookbinding, botany, calculus, cell biology, chemistry, choral music, clayworking, college counseling, comparative religion, constitutional history of U.S., CPR, crafts, drama, drawing, earth science, economics, English, English composition, eurythmy, first aid, food and nutrition, foreign language, geography, geometry, German, government, health, history of architecture, history of music, human anatomy, human biology, human sexuality, inorganic chemistry, instrumental music, mathematics, music, music history, Native American history, novels, optics, orchestra, organic chemistry, physical education (includes health), physics, physiology, poetry, pre-calculus, probability, projective geometry, research skills, science, sculpture, sewing, Shakespeare, society and culture, Spanish, speech, student government, U.S. history, utopia, woodworking, world history, zoology. Community service is required.

Special Academic Programs Independent study; study abroad.

College Admission Counseling 22 students graduated in 2013; 20 went to college, including Berklee College of Music; Lewis & Clark College; Marlboro College; Middlebury College; Sarah Lawrence College; Vassar College. Other: 2 went to work. Mean SAT critical reading: 645, mean SAT math: 550, mean composite ACT: 27. 50% scored over 600 on SAT critical reading, 60% scored over 600 on SAT math, 50% scored over 26 on composite ACT.

Student Life Upper grades have specified standards of dress, student council. Discipline rests primarily with faculty.

Tuition and Aid Day student tuition: $22,175. Tuition installment plan (Insured Tuition Payment Plan, FACTS Tuition Payment Plan, monthly payment plans). Need-based scholarship grants available. In 2013–14, 19% of upper-school students received aid. Total amount of financial aid awarded in 2013–14: $204,600.

Admissions Traditional secondary-level entrance grade is 9. For fall 2013, 31 students applied for upper-level admission, 26 were accepted, 23 enrolled. Essay, math and English placement tests and writing sample required. Deadline for receipt of application materials: January 31. Application fee required: $100. On-campus interview required.

Athletics Interscholastic: baseball (boys), basketball (b,g), softball (g), volleyball (b,g); coed interscholastic: soccer; coed intramural: golf. 2 PE instructors, 2 coaches.

Computers Computers are regularly used in library skills, newspaper, yearbook classes. Computer network features include on-campus library services, Internet access, wireless campus network.

Contact Lynn van Schilfgaarde, Enrollment Director. 818-349-1394 Ext. 211. Fax: 818-349-2390. E-mail: lvs@highlandhall.org. Website: www.highlandhall.org

HIGH MOWING SCHOOL

222 Isaac Frye Highway
Wilton, New Hampshire 03086

Head of School: Rea Gill

General Information Coeducational boarding and day college-preparatory and arts school. Grades 9–12. Founded: 1942. Setting: rural. Nearest major city is Boston, MA. Students are housed in single-sex dormitories. 125-acre campus. 17 buildings on campus. Approved or accredited by Association of Independent Schools in New England, Association of Waldorf Schools of North America, Independent Schools of Northern New England, New England Association of Schools and Colleges, The Association of Boarding Schools, and New Hampshire Department of Education. Member of National Association of Independent Schools and Secondary School Admission Test Board. Endowment: $1 million. Total enrollment: 109. Upper school average class size: 10. Upper school faculty-student ratio: 1:5. There are 180 required school days per year for Upper School students. Upper School students typically attend 5 days per week. The average school day consists of 6 hours and 25 minutes.

Upper School Student Profile Grade 9: 26 students (7 boys, 19 girls); Grade 10: 16 students (7 boys, 9 girls); Grade 11: 32 students (17 boys, 15 girls); Grade 12: 35 students (18 boys, 17 girls). 56% of students are boarding students. 50% are state residents. 13 states are represented in upper school student body. 17% are international students. International students from China, Germany, Mexico, Spain, Switzerland, and Taiwan; 3 other countries represented in student body.

Faculty School total: 23. In upper school: 10 men, 13 women; 16 have advanced degrees; 15 reside on campus.

Subjects Offered Advanced chemistry, algebra, American history, American literature, anatomy, ancient history, ancient world history, art, art appreciation, art history, arts, batik, biochemistry, biology, botany, calculus, ceramics, chemistry, chorus, community service, computer programming, creative writing, digital art, drama, driver education, earth science, ecology, economics, English, English literature, environmental science, ESL, ethics, European history, eurythmy, expository writing, fiber arts, filmmaking, fine arts, French, geography, geology, geometry, government/civics, grammar, graphic arts, graphic design, health, health education, history, history of science, jazz band, mathematics, meteorology, music, mythology, nature study, optics, philosophy, photography, physical education, physics, physiology, probability and statistics, projective geometry, Russian literature, science, social sciences, social studies, Spanish, speech, studio art, theater, theory of knowledge, trigonometry, wilderness education, world history, world literature, writing, zoology.

Graduation Requirements Algebra, arts and fine arts (art, music, dance, drama), economics, English, foreign language, geometry, government, health, language arts, mathematics, performing arts, physical education (includes health), physics, science, social sciences, social studies (includes history), studio art, U.S. history. Community service is required.

Special Academic Programs Advanced Placement exam preparation; honors section; independent study; term-away projects; study abroad; academic accommodation for the musically talented and the artistically talented; remedial math; programs in mathematics for dyslexic students; ESL (14 students enrolled).

College Admission Counseling 26 students graduated in 2013; 23 went to college. Other: 3 had other specific plans. Mean SAT critical reading: 595, mean SAT math: 531, mean SAT writing: 568, mean combined SAT: 1694, mean composite ACT: 22.

Student Life Upper grades have specified standards of dress, student council. Discipline rests equally with students and faculty.

Tuition and Aid Day student tuition: $29,500; 7-day tuition and room/board: $47,000. Tuition installment plan (FACTS Tuition Payment Plan). Need-based scholarship grants available. In 2013–14, 45% of upper-school students received aid. Total amount of financial aid awarded in 2013–14: $600,000.

Admissions Traditional secondary-level entrance grade is 9. Deadline for receipt of application materials: February 15. Application fee required: $50. Interview required.

Athletics Interscholastic: baseball (boys), basketball (b,g), cross-country running (b,g), lacrosse (g), soccer (b,g); coed intramural: aerobics, alpine skiing, backpacking, bicycling, broomball, Circus, climbing, cross-country running, dance, fitness, fitness walking, Frisbee, hiking/backpacking, jogging, juggling, outdoor activities, outdoor education, outdoor recreation, outdoor skills, outdoors, physical fitness, physical training, rock climbing, running, skiing (cross-country), skiing (downhill), snowboarding, snowshoeing, tennis, ultimate Frisbee, volleyball, walking, wall climbing, wilderness, wilderness survival, wildernessways, yoga. 1 PE instructor, 8 coaches.

Computers Computers are regularly used in graphic arts, graphic design, mathematics, science, technology classes. Computer resources include on-campus library services, Internet access, wireless campus network. The school has a published electronic and media policy.

Contact Patricia Meissner, Director of Admissions. 603-654-2391 Ext. 109. Fax: 603-654-6588. E-mail: admissions@highmowing.org. Website: www.highmowing.org

HIGHROAD ACADEMY

46641 Chilliwack Central Road
Chilliwack, British Columbia V2P 1K3, Canada

Head of School: Mr. Stuart Morris

General Information Coeducational day college-preparatory and religious studies school, affiliated with Christian faith; primarily serves students with learning disabilities, individuals with Attention Deficit Disorder, individuals with emotional and behavioral problems, and dyslexic students. Grades K–12. Founded: 1978. Setting: small town. Nearest major city is Vancouver, Canada. 45-acre campus. 1 building on campus. Approved or accredited by British Columbia Department of Education. Language of instruction: English. Total enrollment: 390. Upper school average class size: 25. Upper school faculty-student ratio: 1:10. Upper School students typically attend 5 days per week. The average school day consists of 5 hours.

Upper School Student Profile Grade 6: 28 students (12 boys, 16 girls); Grade 7: 33 students (17 boys, 16 girls); Grade 8: 48 students (23 boys, 25 girls); Grade 9: 35 students (20 boys, 15 girls); Grade 10: 22 students (11 boys, 11 girls); Grade 11: 30 students (15 boys, 15 girls); Grade 12: 27 students (11 boys, 16 girls). 100% of students are Christian.

Faculty School total: 15. In upper school: 6 men, 5 women.

Graduation Requirements Bible.

Special Academic Programs Independent study; study at local college for college credit; ESL (23 students enrolled).

College Admission Counseling 27 students graduated in 2013; 8 went to college, including The University of British Columbia. Other: 6 went to work, 5 entered a postgraduate year, 6 had other specific plans.

Student Life Upper grades have uniform requirement, student council, honor system. Discipline rests primarily with faculty. Attendance at religious services is required.

Admissions Traditional secondary-level entrance grade is 10. Deadline for receipt of application materials: none. Application fee required: CAN$100. Interview required.

Athletics 1 PE instructor, 3 coaches.

Computers Computer network features include Internet access, wireless campus network, Internet filtering or blocking technology. Computer access in designated common areas is available to students. Students grades are available online.

Contact Mrs. Denise Kraubner, Office Manager. 604-792-4680. Fax: 604-792-2465. E-mail: dkraubner@highroadacademy.com. Website: www.highroadacademy.com

HILLSIDE SCHOOL

Marlborough, Massachusetts
See Junior Boarding Schools section.

THE HILL TOP PREPARATORY SCHOOL

Rosemont, Pennsylvania
See Special Needs Schools section.

HO'ALA SCHOOL

1067A California Avenue
Wahiawa, Hawaii 96786

Head of School: Linda Perry

General Information college-preparatory, arts, and Service Learning school. Founded: 1986. Setting: rural. Nearest major city is Honolulu. 1-acre campus. 1 building on campus. Approved or accredited by Western Association of Schools and Colleges and Hawaii Department of Education. Total enrollment: 73. Upper school average class size: 5. Upper school faculty-student ratio: 1:5. There are 182 required school days per year for Upper School students. Upper School students typically attend 5 days per week. The average school day consists of 5 hours and 30 minutes.

Upper School Student Profile Grade 6: 5 students (2 boys, 3 girls); Grade 7: 9 students (5 boys, 4 girls); Grade 8: 3 students (1 boy, 2 girls); Grade 9: 7 students (3 boys, 4 girls); Grade 10: 6 students (4 boys, 2 girls); Grade 12: 3 students (1 boy, 2 girls).

Faculty School total: 6. In upper school: 2 men, 4 women; 1 has an advanced degree.

Subjects Offered 1 1/2 elective credits, 20th century history, 20th century physics, 20th century world history, advanced biology, advanced chemistry, advanced computer applications, advanced math, Advanced Placement courses, advanced studio art-AP, algebra, alternative physical education, American Civil War, American government, American history, American history-AP, American literature, American literature-AP, analytic geometry, anthropology, art, art appreciation, art education, art history, art history-AP, athletics, basketball, biology, biology-AP, bowling, calculus, calculus-AP, character education, chemistry, chemistry-AP, civics, Civil War, civil war history, college admission preparation, college awareness, college counseling, college placement, college planning, college writing, community service, composition, composition-AP, computer applications, contemporary art, creative arts, creative dance, creative drama, creative thinking, creative writing, dance, drama, drama performance, drawing, drawing and design, English, English composition, English language and composition-AP, English language-AP, English literature and composition-AP, English literature-AP, English-AP, English/composition-AP, environmental science, environmental studies, fine arts, foreign language, general science, geometry, government/civics, government/civics-AP, grammar, guidance, Hawaiian history, health, health and safety, health and wellness, health education, history, home economics, honors algebra, honors English, honors geometry, honors U.S. history, honors world history, Internet, Internet research, lab science, language, language and composition, language-AP, life management skills, life skills, marine biology, marine science, mathematics-AP, mentorship program, modern dance, modern history, painting, personal and social education, physical education, physics, physics-AP, post-calculus, pre-algebra, pre-calculus, pre-college orientation, SAT/ACT preparation, science, scuba diving, senior career experience, senior project, service learning/internship, sewing, social sciences, social studies, Spanish, Spanish language-AP, Spanish-AP, student government, student teaching, studio art-AP, study skills, theater arts, volleyball, world geography, world governments, world history, world history-AP, writing, yearbook.

Special Academic Programs Advanced Placement exam preparation; honors section; academic accommodation for the gifted and the artistically talented; remedial reading and/or remedial writing; remedial math; programs in general development for dyslexic students.

College Admission Counseling 5 students graduated in 2013; all went to college.

Student Life Upper grades have uniform requirement, student council, honor system. Discipline rests primarily with faculty.

Tuition and Aid Day student tuition: $9800. Tuition installment plan (monthly payment plans, individually arranged payment plans). Tuition reduction for siblings, merit scholarship grants, need-based scholarship grants available. In 2013–14, 20% of upper-school students received aid. Total amount of financial aid awarded in 2013–14: $10,000.

Admissions Traditional secondary-level entrance grade is 9. For fall 2013, 2 students applied for upper-level admission. Admissions testing, High School Placement Test, school's own exam and writing sample required. Deadline for receipt of application materials: none. Application fee required: $50. Interview recommended.

Athletics Interscholastic: basketball (boys), cross-country running (b,g), swimming and diving (b,g), track and field (b,g); intramural: basketball (b). 5 PE instructors, 1 coach.

Computers Computers are regularly used in college planning, computer applications, English, health, history, keyboarding, lab/keyboard, mentorship program, science, Web site design, yearbook classes. Computer network features include wireless campus network. Students grades are available online.

Contact Mickie Hettema, Admissions Clerk. 808-621-1898. Fax: 808-622-3615. E-mail: Mickie@hoalaschool.org. Website: www.hoalaschool.org/

THE HOCKADAY SCHOOL

11600 Welch Road
Dallas, Texas 75229-2999

Head of School: Kim Wargo

General Information Girls' boarding and day and distance learning college-preparatory, arts, and technology school. Boarding grades 8–12, day grades PK–12. Distance learning grades 3–12. Founded: 1913. Setting: suburban. Students are housed in single-sex dormitories. 85-acre campus. 12 buildings on campus. Approved or accredited by Independent Schools Association of the Southwest and The Association of Boarding Schools. Member of National Association of Independent Schools and Secondary School Admission Test Board. Endowment: $121.5 million. Total enrollment: 1,086. Upper school average class size: 15. Upper school faculty-student ratio: 1:15. There are 160 required school days per year for Upper School students. Upper School students typically attend 5 days per week. The average school day consists of 6 hours and 40 minutes.

Upper School Student Profile Grade 9: 117 students (117 girls); Grade 10: 124 students (124 girls); Grade 11: 117 students (117 girls); Grade 12: 120 students (120 girls). 15% of students are boarding students. 86% are state residents. 10 states are represented in upper school student body. 11% are international students. International students from China, Jamaica, Mexico, Nigeria, Republic of Korea, and Taiwan; 7 other countries represented in student body.

Faculty School total: 128. In upper school: 18 men, 41 women; 47 have advanced degrees; 1 resides on campus.

Subjects Offered Acting, advanced math, advanced studio art-AP, algebra, American history, American history-AP, American literature, analytic geometry, anatomy, applied arts, applied music, art history, astronomy, athletics, audio visual/media, ballet, basketball, biology, biology-AP, body human, British literature, broadcast journalism, broadcasting, Broadway dance, calculus, calculus-AP, cell biology, ceramics, chemistry, chemistry-AP, college counseling, comparative religion, computer applications, computer science, computer science-AP, concert choir, consumer economics, CPR, creative writing, current events, dance, dance performance, debate, digital art, digital imaging, digital music, digital photography, directing, discrete mathematics, drawing and design, ecology, environmental systems, economics-AP, English, English literature, English literature and composition-AP, English-AP, environmental science, environmental science-AP, ESL, ESL, fencing, fine arts, finite math, first aid, French, French language-AP, French literature-AP, genetics, geometry,

guitar, health, health and wellness, honors English, humanities, information technology, interdisciplinary studies, journalism, Latin, Latin-AP, madrigals, Mandarin, microbiology, modern European history-AP, newspaper, non-Western literature, orchestra, philosophy, photography, physical education, physical fitness, physics, physics-AP, piano, pre-calculus, printmaking, probability and statistics, psychology, psychology-AP, self-defense, senior internship, set design, short story, Spanish, Spanish language-AP, Spanish literature-AP, stagecraft, studio art, studio art-AP, swimming, technology, tennis, track and field, U.S. government, U.S. history, U.S. history-AP, voice, volleyball, Web site design, wellness, world history, yearbook.

Graduation Requirements Algebra, American literature, art history, audio visual/media, biology-AP, chemistry, computer literacy, computer skills, English, English literature, geometry, history of music, information technology, languages, physical education (includes health), physics, senior project, U.S. government, U.S. history, world history, one semester of History of Art and Music, 60 hours of community service.

Special Academic Programs Advanced Placement exam preparation; honors section; independent study; term-away projects; study abroad; ESL (12 students enrolled).

College Admission Counseling 121 students graduated in 2012; all went to college, including Cornell University; Georgetown University; Harvard University; Northwestern University; Stanford University; Vanderbilt University.

Student Life Upper grades have uniform requirement, student council, honor system. Discipline rests primarily with faculty.

Tuition and Aid Day student tuition: $23,300–$23,925; 7-day tuition and room/board: $41,499–$46,258. Need-based scholarship grants, need-based financial aid available. In 2012–13, 22% of upper-school students received aid. Total amount of financial aid awarded in 2012–13: $1,851,800.

Admissions Traditional secondary-level entrance grade is 9. For fall 2012, 204 students applied for upper-level admission, 64 were accepted, 43 enrolled. Admissions testing required. Deadline for receipt of application materials: none. Application fee required: $175. Interview required.

Athletics Interscholastic: basketball, crew, cross-country running, fencing, field hockey, golf, independent competitive sports, jogging, lacrosse, rowing, running, soccer, softball, swimming and diving, tennis, track and field, volleyball, winter soccer; intramural: aerobics, aerobics/dance, aquatics, archery, ballet, basketball, cheering, cooperative games, dance, fitness, independent competitive sports, jogging, life saving, martial arts, modern dance, outdoor skills, physical fitness, physical training, project adventure, racquetball, ropes courses, running, self defense, strength & conditioning, swimming and diving, tennis, track and field, ultimate Frisbee, volleyball, weight lifting, weight training, yoga. 13 PE instructors, 9 coaches, 3 athletic trainers.

Computers Computers are regularly used in animation, art, computer applications, creative writing, dance, engineering, English, French, health, history, humanities, information technology, introduction to technology, journalism, Latin, mathematics, media, media production, media services, multimedia, music, newspaper, photography, photojournalism, psychology, publications, publishing, science, Spanish, technology, Web site design, yearbook classes. Computer network features include on-campus library services, online commercial services, Internet access, wireless campus network, Internet filtering or blocking technology. Campus intranet, student e-mail accounts, and computer access in designated common areas are available to students. Students grades are available online. The school has a published electronic and media policy.

Contact Jen Liggitt, Director of Admission. 214-363-6311. Fax: 214-265-1649. E-mail: admissions@mail.hockaday.org. Website: www.hockaday.org

See Display on next page and Close-Up on page 540.

HOLLAND HALL

5666 East 81st Street
Tulsa, Oklahoma 74137-2099

Head of School: Richard P. Hart

General Information Coeducational day college-preparatory, arts, religious studies, and technology school, affiliated with Episcopal Church. Grades PK–12. Founded: 1922. Setting: suburban. 162-acre campus. 5 buildings on campus. Approved or accredited by Independent Schools Association of the Southwest, National Association of Episcopal Schools, and Oklahoma Department of Education. Member of National Association of Independent Schools. Endowment: $68 million. Total enrollment: 995. Upper school average class size: 13. Upper school faculty-student ratio: 1:9. There are 172 required school days per year for Upper School students. Upper School students typically attend 5 days per week. The average school day consists of 6 hours and 52 minutes.

Upper School Student Profile Grade 6: 77 students (32 boys, 45 girls); Grade 7: 63 students (31 boys, 32 girls); Grade 8: 64 students (36 boys, 28 girls); Grade 9: 77 students (40 boys, 37 girls); Grade 10: 90 students (44 boys, 46 girls); Grade 11: 95 students (55 boys, 40 girls); Grade 12: 71 students (38 boys, 33 girls). 7% of students are members of Episcopal Church.

Faculty School total: 93. In upper school: 23 men, 19 women; 28 have advanced degrees.

Subjects Offered Algebra, American history, American studies, art, biology, calculus, calculus-AP, ceramics, chemistry, chemistry-AP, Chinese, computer programming, computer science, creative writing, dance, drama, driver education, ecology, economics, English, English literature, ethics, fine arts, French, geology, geometry, government/civics, history, Latin, mathematics, music, photography, physical education, physics, religion, science, social studies, Spanish, statistics-AP, theater, trigonometry, writing.

Graduation Requirements Arts and fine arts (art, music, dance, drama), English, foreign language, mathematics, physical education (includes health), religion (includes Bible studies and theology), science, social studies (includes history), senior intern program.

Special Academic Programs Advanced Placement exam preparation; honors section; independent study; study at local college for college credit; study abroad.

College Admission Counseling 74 students graduated in 2012; all went to college, including Oklahoma State University; Southern Methodist University; University of Oklahoma; University of Tulsa.

Student Life Upper grades have uniform requirement, student council, honor system. Discipline rests equally with students and faculty. Attendance at religious services is required.

Tuition and Aid Day student tuition: $17,300. Tuition installment plan (monthly payment plans, school's own payment plan). Merit scholarship grants, need-based scholarship grants available. In 2012–13, 28% of upper-school students received aid; total upper-school merit-scholarship money awarded: $154,900. Total amount of financial aid awarded in 2012–13: $928,525.

Admissions Traditional secondary-level entrance grade is 9. Admissions testing, Brigance Test of Basic Skills and ERB required. Deadline for receipt of application materials: none. Application fee required: $25. On-campus interview required.

Athletics Interscholastic: baseball (boys), basketball (b,g), cheering (g), cross-country running (b,g), field hockey (g), football (b), golf (b,g), modern dance (b,g), soccer (b,g), softball (b,g), tennis (b,g), track and field (b,g), volleyball (g); intramural: aerobics (b,g), dance (b,g), modern dance (b,g), soccer (b,g); coed interscholastic: cheering, crew, modern dance, physical training, strength & conditioning; coed intramural: fitness, modern dance, physical training, soccer, weight lifting. 39 coaches, 1 athletic trainer.

Computers Computers are regularly used in English, foreign language, history, mathematics, science classes. Computer network features include on-campus library services, online commercial services, Internet access, wireless campus network, Internet filtering or blocking technology. Student e-mail accounts and computer access in designated common areas are available to students. The school has a published electronic and media policy.

Contact Olivia Martin, Interim Director of Admission and Financial Aid. 918-481-1111 Ext. 740. Fax: 918-481-1145. E-mail: omartin@hollandhall.org. Website: www.hollandhall.org

HOLY CROSS HIGH SCHOOL

587 Oronoke Road
Waterbury, Connecticut 06708

Head of School: Mr. Timothy McDonald

General Information Coeducational day college-preparatory, arts, religious studies, and technology school, affiliated with Roman Catholic Church. Grades 9–12. Founded: 1968. Setting: suburban. 37-acre campus. 1 building on campus. Approved or accredited by National Catholic Education Association, New England Association of Schools and Colleges, and Connecticut Department of Education. Total enrollment: 630. Upper school average class size: 20. Upper school faculty-student ratio: 1:15. There are 160 required school days per year for Upper School students. Upper School students typically attend 5 days per week. The average school day consists of 6 hours.

Upper School Student Profile Grade 9: 129 students (60 boys, 69 girls); Grade 10: 156 students (83 boys, 73 girls); Grade 11: 165 students (86 boys, 79 girls); Grade 12: 177 students (97 boys, 80 girls). 85% of students are Roman Catholic.

Faculty School total: 60. In upper school: 28 men, 32 women; 37 have advanced degrees.

Subjects Offered Advanced biology, advanced math, Advanced Placement courses, advanced studio art-AP, algebra, American history, American history-AP, American literature, American literature-AP, American studies, anatomy, anatomy and physiology, art, art-AP, arts, band, Basic programming, biology, biology-AP, British literature, British literature-AP, business, business law, calculus, calculus-AP, campus ministry, Catholic belief and practice, chamber groups, chemistry, chemistry-AP, choir, computer applications, computer programming, computer science, concert band, concert choir, CPR, creative writing, drama, driver education, economics, economics and history, English, English literature, English-AP, environmental science, French, geometry, history, mathematics, music, physical education, physics, physiology, psychology, religion, science, social studies, Spanish, statistics, theater, theology, trigonometry, word processing, world history, world literature.

Graduation Requirements English, foreign language, mathematics, physical education (includes health), religion (includes Bible studies and theology), science, social studies (includes history).

Special Academic Programs Advanced Placement exam preparation; honors section; independent study; study at local college for college credit.

College Admission Counseling 196 students graduated in 2013; 187 went to college, including Central Connecticut State University; Naugatuck Valley Community College; Southern Connecticut State University; University of Connecticut; Western Connecticut State University. Other: 4 went to work, 2 entered military service, 3 entered a postgraduate year.

Student Life Upper grades have specified standards of dress, student council. Discipline rests primarily with faculty. Attendance at religious services is required.

Summer Programs Sports, art/fine arts programs offered; session focuses on basketball, volleyball, theatre; held on campus; accepts boys and girls; open to students from other schools.

Tuition and Aid Day student tuition: $11,650. Tuition installment plan (monthly payment plans, individually arranged payment plans, Tuition Management Systems (TMS)). Merit scholarship grants, need-based scholarship grants available. In 2013–14, 30% of upper-school students received aid; total upper-school merit-scholarship money awarded: $135,000. Total amount of financial aid awarded in 2013–14: $550,000.

Admissions Traditional secondary-level entrance grade is 9. For fall 2013, 365 students applied for upper-level admission, 321 were accepted, 130 enrolled. ETS HSPT (closed) required. Deadline for receipt of application materials: none. Application fee required: $25.

Athletics Interscholastic: baseball (boys), basketball (b,g), cheering (g), cross-country running (b,g), dance team (g), diving (b,g), football (b), golf (b,g), gymnastics (g), lacrosse (b,g), soccer (b,g), softball (g), swimming and diving (b,g), tennis (b,g), track and field (b,g), volleyball (g), winter (indoor) track (b,g), wrestling (b); intramural: basketball (b), skiing (downhill) (b,g), weight lifting (b); coed intramural: bowling, table tennis, ultimate Frisbee, yoga. 3 PE instructors, 22 coaches, 1 athletic trainer.

Computers Computers are regularly used in accounting, business, computer applications, creative writing, English, foreign language, French, history, mathematics, music technology, psychology, religious studies, science, social sciences, social studies, Spanish, technology, theology, Web site design, word processing, writing, writing, yearbook classes. Computer network features include on-campus library services, online commercial services, Internet access, wireless campus network. Campus intranet and computer access in designated common areas are available to students. Students grades are available online.

Contact Mrs. Jodie LaCava McGarrity, Director of Admissions. 203-757-9248. Fax: 203-757-3423. E-mail: jmcgarrity@holycrosshs-ct.com. Website: www.holycrosshs-ct.com

HOLY CROSS SCHOOL

5500 Paris Avenue
New Orleans, Louisiana 70122

Head of School: Mr. Charles DiGange

General Information Boys' day college-preparatory, arts, religious studies, and technology school, affiliated with Roman Catholic Church. Grades 5–12. Founded: 1849. Setting: suburban. 20-acre campus. 5 buildings on campus. Approved or accredited by National Catholic Education Association, Southern Association of Colleges and Schools, and Louisiana Department of Education. Total enrollment: 1,020. Upper school average class size: 21. Upper school faculty-student ratio: 1:13. There are 184 required school days per year for Upper School students. Upper School students typically attend 5 days per week. The average school day consists of 6 hours and 35 minutes.

Upper School Student Profile Grade 8: 156 students (156 boys); Grade 9: 166 students (166 boys); Grade 10: 154 students (154 boys); Grade 11: 138 students (138 boys); Grade 12: 115 students (115 boys). 80% of students are Roman Catholic.

Faculty School total: 66. In upper school: 35 men, 9 women; 22 have advanced degrees.

Graduation Requirements Community service requirement.

Special Academic Programs 11 Advanced Placement exams for which test preparation is offered; honors section; study at local college for college credit; academic accommodation for the gifted, the musically talented, and the artistically talented.

College Admission Counseling 112 students graduated in 2013; 111 went to college, including Louisiana State University and Agricultural and Mechanical College; Loyola University New Orleans; Spring Hill College; St. Edward's University; University of Louisiana at Lafayette; University of Southern Mississippi. Other: 1 entered military service.

Student Life Upper grades have uniform requirement, student council, honor system. Discipline rests primarily with faculty. Attendance at religious services is required.

Summer Programs Remediation, enrichment programs offered; session focuses on enrichment; held on campus; accepts boys; not open to students from other schools. 75 students usually enrolled. 2014 schedule: July 14 to July 28. Application deadline: May 31.

Tuition and Aid Day student tuition: $7277. Tuition installment plan (monthly payment plans). Tuition reduction for siblings, merit scholarship grants, need-based scholarship grants, paying campus jobs available. In 2013–14, 5% of upper-school students received aid; total upper-school merit-scholarship money awarded: $50,000.

Admissions Traditional secondary-level entrance grade is 8. For fall 2013, 350 students applied for upper-level admission, 235 were accepted, 210 enrolled. ACT-Explore or High School Placement Test required. Deadline for receipt of application materials: November 15. Application fee required: $20. Interview required.

Athletics Interscholastic: baseball, basketball, bowling, cheering, cross-country running, football, golf, indoor track, indoor track & field, power lifting, soccer, swimming and diving, tennis, wrestling; intramural: baseball, basketball, bicycling, fishing, flag football, football, Frisbee, lacrosse, martial arts, physical training, sailing, skateboarding, soccer, softball, strength & conditioning, ultimate Frisbee, volleyball, weight training. 10 PE instructors, 38 coaches, 2 athletic trainers.

Computers Computer network features include on-campus library services, online commercial services, Internet access, wireless campus network, Internet filtering or blocking technology. Student e-mail accounts and computer access in designated common areas are available to students. Students grades are available online. The school has a published electronic and media policy.

Contact Mr. Brian Kitchen, Director of Admissions. 504-942-3100. Fax: 504-284-3424. E-mail: bkitchen@holycrosstigers.com. Website: www.holycrosstigers.com

HOLY GHOST PREPARATORY SCHOOL

2429 Bristol Pike
Bensalem, Pennsylvania 19020

Head of School: Rev. Jeffrey T. Duaime, CSSP

General Information Boys' day college-preparatory, arts, and technology school, affiliated with Roman Catholic Church. Grades 9–12. Founded: 1897. Setting: suburban. Nearest major city is Philadelphia. 53-acre campus. 4 buildings on campus. Approved or accredited by Middle States Association of Colleges and Schools, National Catholic Education Association, and Pennsylvania Association of Independent Schools. Member of National Association of Independent Schools. Endowment: $2 million. Total enrollment: 480. Upper school average class size: 17. Upper school faculty-student ratio: 1:11. The average school day consists of 6 hours and 30 minutes.

Upper School Student Profile Grade 9: 106 students (106 boys); Grade 10: 124 students (124 boys); Grade 11: 127 students (127 boys); Grade 12: 123 students (123 boys). 94% of students are Roman Catholic.

Faculty School total: 50. In upper school: 32 men, 18 women; 34 have advanced degrees.

Subjects Offered 3-dimensional art, Advanced Placement courses, advanced studio art-AP, algebra, American government, American history, American history-AP, American literature, analysis, anatomy and physiology, art, Bible, biology, biology-AP, calculus, calculus-AP, campus ministry, career/college preparation, careers, ceremonies of life, chemistry, Chinese history, choral music, church history, college admission preparation, college counseling, communication arts, communication skills, computer programming-AP, computer science, computer science-AP, creative writing, drama performance, earth science, economics, English, English language and composition-AP, English literature, English literature and composition-AP, environmental science, European history, European history-AP, film, fine arts, French, French language-AP, geometry, government and politics-AP, government/civics, health, history, journalism, language-AP, Latin, Latin-AP, mathematics, modern European history-AP, music, music theory-AP, oral communications, physical education, physics, public speaking, religion, science, sexuality, social studies, Spanish, Spanish language-AP, Spanish-AP, speech, statistics, trigonometry, U.S. history-AP, United States government-AP, world cultures, world history, world history-AP, world literature, writing, yearbook.

Graduation Requirements Arts and fine arts (art, music, dance, drama), computer science, English, foreign language, mathematics, physical education (includes health), religion (includes Bible studies and theology), science, social studies (includes history), summer reading. Community service is required.

Special Academic Programs Advanced Placement exam preparation; honors section; independent study; study abroad.

College Admission Counseling 124 students graduated in 2012; all went to college, including Boston College; Duquesne University; Penn State University Park; Saint Joseph's University; University of Pennsylvania; Villanova University. Median SAT critical reading: 610, median SAT math: 640.

Student Life Upper grades have specified standards of dress, student council, honor system. Discipline rests primarily with faculty.

Tuition and Aid Day student tuition: $16,700. Tuition installment plan (monthly payment plans, quarterly and semi-annual payment plans). Merit scholarship grants, need-based scholarship grants, music scholarships, minority scholarships, art scholarships available. In 2012–13, 35% of upper-school students received aid; total upper-school merit-scholarship money awarded: $1,000,000. Total amount of financial aid awarded in 2012–13: $1,000,000.

Admissions Traditional secondary-level entrance grade is 9. For fall 2012, 398 students applied for upper-level admission, 158 were accepted, 106 enrolled. High School Placement Test (closed version) from Scholastic Testing Service required. Deadline for receipt of application materials: December 9. Application fee required: $60. On-campus interview required.

Athletics Interscholastic: baseball, basketball, bowling, cross-country running, golf, ice hockey, indoor track & field, lacrosse, soccer, Special Olympics, swimming and diving, tennis, track and field; intramural: basketball, fitness walking, flag football, football, Frisbee, soccer, street hockey, tennis, ultimate Frisbee. 10 coaches, 1 athletic trainer.

Computers Computers are regularly used in college planning, English, foreign language, mathematics, programming, publications, science, speech, yearbook classes. Computer network features include on-campus library services, online commercial services, Internet access, wireless campus network, Internet filtering or blocking technology. Student e-mail accounts are available to students.

Contact Mr. Ryan T. Abramson, Director of Admissions. 215-639-0811. Fax: 215-639-4225. E-mail: rabramson@holyghostprep.org. Website: www.holyghostprep.org

HOLY NAMES ACADEMY

728 21st Avenue East
Seattle, Washington 98112

Head of School: Elizabeth Swift

General Information Girls' day college-preparatory school, affiliated with Roman Catholic Church. Grades 9–12. Founded: 1880. Setting: urban. Approved or accredited by Northwest Accreditation Commission, Northwest Association of Independent Schools, and Washington Department of Education. Member of National Association of Independent Schools. Upper school average class size: 14.

Upper School Student Profile 74% of students are Roman Catholic.

Student Life Attendance at religious services is required.

Tuition and Aid Day student tuition: $12,396. Financial aid available to upper-school students. In 2013–14, 31% of upper-school students received aid.

Admissions Metropolitan Achievement Test required. Deadline for receipt of application materials: January 13. Application fee required: $30.

Contact 206-323-4272. Website: www.holynames-sea.org

HOLYOKE CATHOLIC HIGH SCHOOL

134 Springfield Street
Chicopee, Massachusetts 01013

Head of School: Mrs. Theresa J. Kitchell

General Information Coeducational day college-preparatory and arts school, affiliated with Roman Catholic Church. Grades 9–12. Founded: 1963. Setting: small town. Nearest major city is Springfield. 3 buildings on campus. Approved or accredited by New England Association of Schools and Colleges and Massachusetts Department of Education. Total enrollment: 298. Upper school average class size: 15. Upper school faculty-student ratio: 1:10. There are 180 required school days per year for Upper School students. Upper School students typically attend 5 days per week. The average school day consists of 6 hours.

Upper School Student Profile Grade 9: 71 students (32 boys, 39 girls); Grade 10: 78 students (32 boys, 46 girls); Grade 11: 66 students (29 boys, 37 girls); Grade 12: 83 students (34 boys, 49 girls). 90% of students are Roman Catholic.

Faculty School total: 31. In upper school: 13 men, 18 women; 21 have advanced degrees.

Subjects Offered Advanced biology, advanced math, algebra, American literature, American literature-AP, art, biology, calculus, calculus-AP, Catholic belief and practice, chemistry, English, English literature, environmental science, forensics, French, geometry, Latin, literature-AP, moral theology, multimedia design, performing arts, physics, pottery, pre-calculus, psychology, social sciences, Spanish, studio art, The 20th Century, U.S. history, U.S. history-AP, vocal ensemble, Web site design, world civilizations, world history, world religions, yearbook.

Graduation Requirements Electives, English, foreign language, mathematics, religion (includes Bible studies and theology), science, social studies (includes history), U.S. literature, community service hours at each grade level, English research paper at each level, Senior Internship Program.

Special Academic Programs 5 Advanced Placement exams for which test preparation is offered; honors section; independent study; study at local college for college credit; ESL (3 students enrolled).

College Admission Counseling 71 students graduated in 2012; all went to college, including Elms College; Fairfield University; Holyoke Community College; Western New England University; Westfield State University. Median composite ACT: 24. 1% scored over 26 on composite ACT.

Student Life Upper grades have uniform requirement, student council. Discipline rests primarily with faculty. Attendance at religious services is required.

Tuition and Aid Day student tuition: $7500. Tuition installment plan (FACTS Tuition Payment Plan). Merit scholarship grants, need-based scholarship grants available. In 2012–13, 30% of upper-school students received aid; total upper-school merit-scholarship money awarded: $1000. Total amount of financial aid awarded in 2012–13: $135,350.

Admissions Traditional secondary-level entrance grade is 9. For fall 2012, 113 students applied for upper-level admission, 107 were accepted, 73 enrolled. Scholastic Testing Service High School Placement Test required. Deadline for receipt of application materials: none. Application fee required: $100. Interview required.

Athletics Interscholastic: baseball (boys), basketball (b,g), cheering (g), cross-country running (b,g), football (b), indoor track & field (b,g), lacrosse (b,g), soccer (b,g), softball (g), winter (indoor) track (b,g); coed interscholastic: golf, hiking/backpacking, outdoor adventure, skiing (downhill), swimming and diving, tennis, unicycling; coed intramural: volleyball, weight training. 10 coaches.

Computers Computers are regularly used in multimedia classes. Computer network features include on-campus library services, Internet access, Internet filtering or blocking technology. Campus intranet and student e-mail accounts are available to students. Students grades are available online. The school has a published electronic and media policy.

Contact Mrs. Theresa Marie Zaborowski, Director of Admissions. 413-331-2480 Ext. 1132. Fax: 413-331-2708. E-mail: tzaborowski@holyokecatholichigh.org. Website: www.holyokecatholichigh.org

HOLY SAVIOR MENARD CATHOLIC HIGH SCHOOL

4603 Coliseum Boulevard
Alexandria, Louisiana 71303

Head of School: Mr. Joel Desselle

General Information Coeducational day college-preparatory and religious studies school, affiliated with Roman Catholic Church. Grades 7–12. Founded: 1930. Setting: suburban. 5-acre campus. 5 buildings on campus. Approved or accredited by National Catholic Education Association, Southern Association of Colleges and Schools, The College Board, and Louisiana Department of Education. Total enrollment: 494. Upper school average class size: 18. Upper school faculty-student ratio: 1:12. There are 178 required school days per year for Upper School students. Upper School students typically attend 5 days per week. The average school day consists of 7 hours and 15 minutes.

Upper School Student Profile Grade 9: 100 students (60 boys, 40 girls); Grade 10: 68 students (31 boys, 37 girls); Grade 11: 83 students (43 boys, 40 girls); Grade 12: 78 students (30 boys, 48 girls). 83% of students are Roman Catholic.

Faculty School total: 40. In upper school: 14 men, 26 women; 15 have advanced degrees.

Subjects Offered Advanced math, algebra, American history, anatomy and physiology, art, athletics, biology, biology-AP, British literature, British literature (honors), calculus-AP, campus ministry, Catholic belief and practice, cheerleading, chemistry, civics/free enterprise, computer applications, computer science, digital photography, English, English composition, English literature, English literature-AP, fine arts, French, general science, geometry, health, honors algebra, honors English, honors geometry, honors U.S. history, honors world history, journalism, language arts, law studies, moral reasoning, New Testament, newspaper, philosophy, physical education, physical science, physics, pre-algebra, pre-calculus, psychology, publications, reading/study skills, religion, sociology, Spanish, speech, world geography, world history, yearbook.

Graduation Requirements Algebra, American history, arts and fine arts (art, music, dance, drama), biology, chemistry, civics/free enterprise, computer applications, English, foreign language, geometry, physical science, religion (includes Bible studies and theology), world history, 27 credits required.

Special Academic Programs 4 Advanced Placement exams for which test preparation is offered; honors section; independent study; study at local college for college credit.

College Admission Counseling 63 students graduated in 2013; 62 went to college, including Louisiana State University and Agricultural and Mechanical College; Louisiana Tech University; Northwestern State University of Louisiana; Tulane University; University of Louisiana at Lafayette; University of New Orleans. Other: 1 went to work. Mean composite ACT: 23. 18% scored over 26 on composite ACT.

Student Life Upper grades have uniform requirement, student council, honor system. Discipline rests primarily with faculty. Attendance at religious services is required.

Tuition and Aid Day student tuition: $5900. Tuition installment plan (FACTS Tuition Payment Plan, monthly payment plans, individually arranged payment plans). Tuition reduction for siblings, merit scholarship grants, need-based scholarship grants available. In 2013–14, 12% of upper-school students received aid; total upper-school merit-scholarship money awarded: $5000. Total amount of financial aid awarded in 2013–14: $150,000.

Admissions Traditional secondary-level entrance grade is 9. For fall 2013, 20 students applied for upper-level admission, 20 were accepted, 20 enrolled. CTBS, Stanford Achievement Test, any other standardized test required. Deadline for receipt of application materials: March 15. Application fee required: $350. On-campus interview required.

Athletics Interscholastic: baseball (boys), basketball (b,g), cheering (g), cross-country running (b,g), danceline (g), football (b), golf (b,g), power lifting (b,g), running (b,g), soccer (b,g), softball (g), tennis (b,g), track and field (b,g); intramural: paddle tennis (b,g); coed interscholastic: swimming and diving; coed intramural: paddle tennis. 3 PE instructors, 3 coaches.

Computers Computers are regularly used in computer applications, English, journalism, mathematics, photography, publications, science, Web site design classes. Computer network features include on-campus library services, Internet access, wireless campus network, Internet filtering or blocking technology. Computer access in designated common areas is available to students. Students grades are available online.

Contact Mrs. Ashley Meadows, Guidance Secretary. 318-445-8233. Fax: 318-448-8170. E-mail: ameadows@holysaviormenard.com. Website: www.holysaviormenard.com

HOLY TRINITY DIOCESAN HIGH SCHOOL

98 Cherry Lane
Hicksville, New York 11801

Head of School: Mr. Gene Fennell

General Information Coeducational day college-preparatory school, affiliated with Roman Catholic Church. Grades 9–12. Founded: 1967. Setting: suburban. Nearest major city is New York. 1 building on campus. Approved or accredited by Middle States Association of Colleges and Schools, National Council for Private School Accreditation, New York State Board of Regents, The College Board, and New York

Department of Education. Total enrollment: 1,351. Upper school average class size: 32. Upper school faculty-student ratio: 1:17. There are 180 required school days per year for Upper School students. Upper School students typically attend 5 days per week.

Upper School Student Profile Grade 9: 323 students (150 boys, 173 girls); Grade 10: 349 students (180 boys, 169 girls); Grade 11: 356 students (167 boys, 189 girls); Grade 12: 323 students (165 boys, 158 girls). 90% of students are Roman Catholic.

Faculty School total: 82. In upper school: 29 men, 53 women; 77 have advanced degrees.

Subjects Offered Accounting, advanced math, Advanced Placement courses, American government, American history, American history-AP, American literature, American literature-AP, anatomy and physiology, architectural drawing, art, band, biology, biology-AP, British literature, British literature (honors), business law, calculus, calculus-AP, campus ministry, ceramics, chemistry, chemistry-AP, chorus, Christian scripture, Christian studies, Christian testament, comparative religion, composition, concert band, criminology, critical studies in film, dance, desktop publishing, earth science, economics, English, English composition, English language and composition-AP, English literature, English literature-AP, environmental science, film, food and nutrition, French, government and politics-AP, health, honors English, honors U.S. history, honors world history, intro to computers, jazz theory, keyboarding, literature and composition-AP, mathematics, music, performing arts, physical education, physics, physics-AP, pre-calculus, public speaking, religion, Spanish, Spanish language-AP, stagecraft, statistics, theater arts, theology, U.S. government and politics, U.S. government and politics-AP, U.S. history, U.S. history-AP, world wide web design.

Graduation Requirements Arts and fine arts (art, music, dance, drama), economics, English, foreign language, mathematics, physical education (includes health), religion (includes Bible studies and theology), science, U.S. government and politics.

Special Academic Programs Advanced Placement exam preparation; honors section; study at local college for college credit.

College Admission Counseling 326 students graduated in 2012; all went to college, including Adelphi University; Hofstra University; Nassau Community College; Stony Brook University, State University of New York. Mean SAT critical reading: 501, mean SAT math: 514, mean SAT writing: 503.

Student Life Upper grades have uniform requirement, student council. Discipline rests primarily with faculty.

Tuition and Aid Day student tuition: $8495. Tuition installment plan (monthly payment plans, individually arranged payment plans, 10-month tuition plan, 3-payment plan). Need-based scholarship grants available.

Admissions Traditional secondary-level entrance grade is 9. Catholic High School Entrance Examination required. Deadline for receipt of application materials: none. Application fee required. Interview recommended.

Athletics Interscholastic: badminton (girls), baseball (b), basketball (b,g), cheering (g), cross-country running (b,g), dance team (g), football (b), golf (b), gymnastics (g), indoor track (b,g), lacrosse (b,g), soccer (b,g), softball (g), swimming and diving (b,g), tennis (b,g), track and field (b,g), volleyball (b,g), weight lifting (b), weight training (b), winter (indoor) track (b,g), wrestling (b); intramural: physical training (b), weight training (b); coed interscholastic: bowling, fitness. 6 PE instructors, 1 athletic trainer.

Computers Computers are regularly used in college planning, computer applications, desktop publishing, drawing and design, economics, English, foreign language, graphic design, history, journalism, library, music technology, newspaper, occupational education, programming, research skills, SAT preparation, science, social studies, theater, Web site design, writing, yearbook classes. Computer network features include on-campus library services, Internet access, Internet filtering or blocking technology. Student e-mail accounts and computer access in designated common areas are available to students. Students grades are available online. The school has a published electronic and media policy.

Contact Admissions. 516-433-2900. Fax: 516-433-2827. E-mail: hths98@ holytrinityhs.echalk.com. Website: www.holytrinityhs.org

HOLY TRINITY SCHOOL

11300 Bayview Avenue
Richmond Hill, Ontario L4S 1L4, Canada

Head of School: Mr. Barry Hughes

General Information Coeducational day college-preparatory, arts, and business school, affiliated with Anglican Church of Canada. Grades JK–12. Founded: 1985. 37-acre campus. 1 building on campus. Approved or accredited by Canadian Association of Independent Schools, Conference of Independent Schools of Ontario, and Ontario Department of Education. Language of instruction: English. Endowment: CAN$6. Total enrollment: 750. Upper school average class size: 22. Upper school faculty-student ratio: 1:17. Upper School students typically attend 5 days per week. The average school day consists of 6 hours.

Upper School Student Profile Grade 9: 110 students (50 boys, 60 girls); Grade 10: 100 students (50 boys, 50 girls); Grade 11: 80 students (45 boys, 35 girls); Grade 12: 100 students (50 boys, 50 girls). 10% of students are members of Anglican Church of Canada.

Faculty In upper school: 30 men, 20 women; 25 have advanced degrees.

Special Academic Programs Advanced Placement exam preparation.

College Admission Counseling 88 students graduated in 2013; all went to college, including Queen's University at Kingston.

Student Life Upper grades have uniform requirement, student council, honor system. Discipline rests primarily with faculty. Attendance at religious services is required.

Summer Programs Enrichment, sports programs offered; held on campus; accepts boys and girls; open to students from other schools. 400 students usually enrolled. 2014 schedule: July 1 to August 7. Application deadline: April 30.

Tuition and Aid Day student tuition: CAN$22,200. Bursaries, need-based scholarship grants available. In 2013–14, 3% of upper-school students received aid. Total amount of financial aid awarded in 2013–14: 40,000 .

Admissions Traditional secondary-level entrance grade is 9. For fall 2013, 110 students applied for upper-level admission, 50 were accepted, 35 enrolled. SSAT required. Deadline for receipt of application materials: December 1. Application fee required: CAN$125. Interview required.

Athletics Interscholastic: field hockey (girls), hockey (b), ice hockey (b); coed interscholastic: baseball, cross-country running, Frisbee, indoor track & field, rugby, running, soccer, softball, tennis, track and field, ultimate Frisbee, volleyball. 4 PE instructors, 15 coaches, 1 athletic trainer.

Computers Computer network features include on-campus library services, Internet access, wireless campus network, Internet filtering or blocking technology. Campus intranet, student e-mail accounts, and computer access in designated common areas are available to students. Students grades are available online.

Contact Mrs. Mary-Lynn Seeley, Admission Assistant. 905-737-1114 Ext. 236. Fax: 905-737-5187. E-mail: mseeley@hts.on.ca. Website: www.hts.on.ca

HOPKINS SCHOOL

986 Forest Road
New Haven, Connecticut 06515

Head of School: Ms. Barbara M. Riley

General Information Coeducational day college-preparatory school. Grades 7–12. Founded: 1660. Setting: urban. Nearest major city is New York, NY. 108-acre campus. 10 buildings on campus. Approved or accredited by New England Association of Schools and Colleges and Connecticut Department of Education. Member of National Association of Independent Schools. Endowment: $68.6 million. Total enrollment: 711. Upper school average class size: 12. Upper school faculty-student ratio: 1:6. There are 170 required school days per year for Upper School students. Upper School students typically attend 5 days per week. The average school day consists of 7 hours and 30 minutes.

Upper School Student Profile Grade 9: 142 students (74 boys, 68 girls); Grade 10: 148 students (76 boys, 72 girls); Grade 11: 133 students (67 boys, 66 girls); Grade 12: 137 students (68 boys, 69 girls).

Faculty School total: 129. In upper school: 61 men, 68 women; 91 have advanced degrees.

Subjects Offered African-American history, algebra, American history, American literature, anatomy and physiology, ancient history, art, art history, art history-AP, Asian studies, biochemistry, biology, biology-AP, calculus, calculus-AP, ceramics, chemistry, chemistry-AP, Chinese, chorus, classical music, computer programming, creative writing, drama, earth science, economics, English, English literature, environmental science-AP, European history, European history-AP, expository writing, film, fine arts, forensics, French, French-AP, geometry, government/civics, Greek, history, Holocaust studies, HTML design, human geography - AP, human sexuality, Islamic history, Italian, jazz, Latin, Latin American history, Latin-AP, linear algebra, mathematics, military history, music, music theory, music theory-AP, philosophy, photography, physics, physics-AP, politics, probability and statistics, psychology, Spanish, Spanish-AP, statistics-AP, studio art, studio art-AP, theater, trigonometry, U.S. history-AP, urban studies, video, Web site design, woodworking, world literature, writing.

Graduation Requirements Arts and fine arts (art, music, dance, drama), English, foreign language, mathematics, physical education (includes health), science, social studies (includes history), swimming, grade 12 community service project.

Special Academic Programs Advanced Placement exam preparation; honors section; independent study; term-away projects; study abroad.

College Admission Counseling 133 students graduated in 2013; all went to college, including Barnard College; Brown University; Georgetown University; University of Chicago; University of Pennsylvania; Yale University. Mean SAT critical reading: 710, mean SAT math: 706, mean SAT writing: 718, mean combined SAT: 2134, mean composite ACT: 32.

Student Life Upper grades have specified standards of dress, student council, honor system. Discipline rests equally with students and faculty.

Summer Programs Remediation, enrichment, advancement, sports programs offered; session focuses on Grades 3 through 12 academics and some athletics; held on campus; accepts boys and girls; open to students from other schools. 180 students usually enrolled. 2014 schedule: June 30 to August 8. Application deadline: June 17.

Tuition and Aid Day student tuition: $35,500. Tuition installment plan (Academic Management Services Plan, Key Tuition Payment Plan). Need-based scholarship grants available. In 2013–14, 19% of upper-school students received aid. Total amount of financial aid awarded in 2013–14: $3,130,350.

Admissions Traditional secondary-level entrance grade is 9. For fall 2013, 304 students applied for upper-level admission, 117 were accepted, 71 enrolled. ISEE or SSAT required. Deadline for receipt of application materials: January 15. Application fee required: $75. On-campus interview required.

Athletics Interscholastic: aquatics (boys, girls), baseball (b), basketball (b,g), crew (b,g), cross-country running (b,g), diving (b,g), fencing (b,g), field hockey (g), football (b), golf (b,g), independent competitive sports (b,g), indoor track (b,g), lacrosse (b,g), soccer (b,g), softball (g), squash (b,g), swimming and diving (b,g), tennis (b,g), track and field (b,g), volleyball (g), water polo (b,g), wrestling (b); intramural: independent competitive sports (b,g); coed interscholastic: independent competitive sports, winter (indoor) track; coed intramural: aerobics, basketball, cooperative games, fencing, fitness, floor hockey, Frisbee, independent competitive sports, Nautilus, outdoor adventure, project adventure, ropes courses, running, soccer, squash, swimming and diving, tennis, volleyball, weight lifting, weight training, wilderness, yoga. 4 coaches, 3 athletic trainers.

Computers Computers are regularly used in art, English, foreign language, history, mathematics, science classes. Computer network features include on-campus library services, Internet access, wireless campus network, Internet filtering or blocking technology. Campus intranet and student e-mail accounts are available to students. The school has a published electronic and media policy.

Contact Ms. Gena Eggert, Administrative Assistant to Director of Admissions. 203-397-1001 Ext. 211. Fax: 203-389-2249. E-mail: admissions@hopkins.edu. Website: www.hopkins.edu

HOUGHTON ACADEMY

9790 Thayer Street
Houghton, New York 14744

Head of School: Mr. Scott Frazier

General Information Coeducational boarding and day college-preparatory, religious studies, and ELL school, affiliated with Wesleyan Church. Boarding grades 9–PG, day grades 6–PG. Founded: 1883. Setting: rural. Nearest major city is Buffalo. Students are housed in single-sex dormitories and staff homes. 25-acre campus. 6 buildings on campus. Approved or accredited by Association of Christian Schools International, Middle States Association of Colleges and Schools, The Association of Boarding Schools, and New York Department of Education. Member of National Association of Independent Schools. Endowment: $90,000. Total enrollment: 130. Upper school average class size: 16. Upper school faculty-student ratio: 1:8. There are 177 required school days per year for Upper School students. Upper School students typically attend 5 days per week. The average school day consists of 6 hours and 30 minutes.

Upper School Student Profile Grade 9: 13 students (8 boys, 5 girls); Grade 10: 23 students (12 boys, 11 girls); Grade 11: 40 students (24 boys, 16 girls); Grade 12: 31 students (12 boys, 19 girls). 51% of students are boarding students. 52% are state residents. 1 state is represented in upper school student body. 48% are international students. International students from China, Nigeria, Republic of Korea, Rwanda, Taiwan, and Viet Nam; 6 other countries represented in student body. 25% of students are members of Wesleyan Church.

Faculty School total: 18. In upper school: 8 men, 10 women; 10 have advanced degrees; 2 reside on campus.

Subjects Offered Algebra, American history, American literature, art, band, Bible, Bible studies, biology, business, business skills, calculus, chemistry, chorus, community service, computer science, creative writing, desktop publishing, driver education, earth science, economics, English, English literature, environmental science, ESL, ethics, fine arts, geography, geometry, government/civics, grammar, history, international relations, mathematics, music, photography, physical education, physics, science, social sciences, social studies, Spanish, speech, trigonometry, word processing, world history, writing.

Graduation Requirements Arts and fine arts (art, music, dance, drama), Bible, electives, English, mathematics, physical education (includes health), science, social studies (includes history).

Special Academic Programs 4 Advanced Placement exams for which test preparation is offered; honors section; independent study; study at local college for college credit; ESL.

College Admission Counseling 31 students graduated in 2013; 29 went to college, including George Mason University; Houghton College; Indiana University Bloomington; Rice University; State University of New York College at Geneseo; University of Massachusetts Boston. Other: 2 went to work.

Student Life Upper grades have uniform requirement, student council. Discipline rests primarily with faculty. Attendance at religious services is required.

Tuition and Aid Day student tuition: $5655; 7-day tuition and room/board: $28,210. Tuition installment plan (FACTS Tuition Payment Plan). Need-based scholarship grants available. In 2013–14, 25% of upper-school students received aid. Total amount of financial aid awarded in 2013–14: $95,000.

Admissions Traditional secondary-level entrance grade is 9. For fall 2013, 122 students applied for upper-level admission, 56 were accepted, 31 enrolled. PSAT or SAT for applicants to grade 11 and 12, SLEP, SSAT or TOEFL required. Deadline for receipt of application materials: February 14. Application fee required: $50. Interview required.

Athletics Interscholastic: basketball (boys, girls), cheering (g), soccer (b), volleyball (g); intramural: badminton (b,g), basketball (b,g), floor hockey (b,g), golf (b,g), indoor soccer (b,g), paddle tennis (b,g), racquetball (b,g), skiing (downhill) (b,g), soccer (b,g), table tennis (b,g), tennis (b,g), volleyball (b,g); coed interscholastic: golf; coed intramural: badminton, ball hockey, indoor soccer, paddle tennis, skiing (downhill), softball, table tennis. 2 PE instructors, 9 coaches, 1 athletic trainer.

Computers Computers are regularly used in accounting, Bible studies, college planning, English, graphic design, keyboarding, mathematics, multimedia, SAT preparation, science, word processing, yearbook classes. Computer network features include on-campus library services, Internet access, Internet filtering or blocking technology, electronic access to Houghton College Library holdings. Computer access in designated common areas is available to students. Students grades are available online. The school has a published electronic and media policy.

Contact Mrs. Sandy Merrill, Admission Coordinator. 585-567-8115. Fax: 585-567-8048. E-mail: admissions@houghtonacademy.org. Website: www.houghtonacademy.org

THE HOWARD SCHOOL

Atlanta, Georgia
See Special Needs Schools section.

THE HUDSON SCHOOL

601 Park Avenue
Hoboken, New Jersey 07030

Head of School: Mrs. Suellen F. Newman

General Information Coeducational day college-preparatory, arts, and music, theater, foreign languages school. Grades 5–12. Founded: 1978. Setting: urban. Nearest major city is New York, NY. 1 building on campus. Approved or accredited by Middle States Association of Colleges and Schools and New Jersey Department of Education. Member of National Association of Independent Schools. Endowment: $2 million. Total enrollment: 185. Upper school average class size: 18. Upper school faculty-student ratio: 1:4. There are 175 required school days per year for Upper School students. Upper School students typically attend 5 days per week. The average school day consists of 8 hours.

Upper School Student Profile Grade 9: 15 students (8 boys, 7 girls); Grade 10: 25 students (12 boys, 13 girls); Grade 11: 19 students (12 boys, 7 girls); Grade 12: 26 students (9 boys, 17 girls).

Faculty School total: 50. In upper school: 11 men, 16 women; 17 have advanced degrees.

Subjects Offered Advanced biology, advanced chemistry, advanced math, Advanced Placement courses, advanced studio art-AP, African drumming, algebra, American government, American history-AP, American literature, anatomy and physiology, Ancient Greek, art, art and culture, art history, art-AP, athletics, biology, biology-AP, British literature, calculus, calculus-AP, Caribbean history, chemistry, chemistry-AP, Chinese, chorus, computer graphics, computer science, computer science-AP, computers, conceptual physics, contemporary issues, creative writing, dance, electives, English, English literature, English literature-AP, English-AP, environmental education, environmental science, ethics, ethnic literature, film, French, French language-AP, gender issues, German, government-AP, guitar, health, history of music, HTML design, humanities, instrumental music, Japanese, jazz band, language arts, Latin, learning strategies, Mandarin, mathematics, media studies, microbiology, music, music history, music theory, mythology, neuroscience, performing arts, personal finance, personal money management, photo shop, photography, physical education, physics, physics-AP, poetry, post-calculus, pre-algebra, pre-calculus, psychology, psychology-AP, reading/study skills, robotics, Russian, science, science fiction, sculpture, senior project, senior seminar, skills for success, social justice, social sciences, Spanish, Spanish-AP, studio art, theater, trigonometry, U.S. history, U.S. history-AP, visual arts, voice, world civilizations, world cultures, world geography, world governments, world history, world literature, writing, yoga.

Graduation Requirements American history, art, art history, computer science, English, foreign language, Latin, mathematics, music history, personal finance, physical education (includes health), science, world history. Community service is required.

Special Academic Programs Advanced Placement exam preparation; honors section; accelerated programs; independent study; study at local college for college credit; study abroad; academic accommodation for the gifted, the musically talented, and the artistically talented; remedial reading and/or remedial writing; remedial math; ESL (6 students enrolled).

College Admission Counseling 22 students graduated in 2013; all went to college, including Barnard College; Columbia University; Macalester College; Rutgers, The State University of New Jersey, New Brunswick; Wellesley College. Median SAT critical reading: 620, median SAT math: 580, median SAT writing: 620, median combined SAT: 1770. 65% scored over 600 on SAT critical reading, 40% scored over 600 on SAT math, 65% scored over 600 on SAT writing, 45% scored over 1800 on combined SAT.

Student Life Upper grades have student council, honor system. Discipline rests primarily with faculty.

Summer Programs Art/fine arts programs offered; session focuses on theater; held on campus; accepts boys and girls; open to students from other schools. 20 students usually enrolled. 2014 schedule: July 1 to July 31. Application deadline: May 1.

Tuition and Aid Day student tuition: $17,130. Tuition installment plan (monthly payment plans, individually arranged payment plans, semiannual and annual payment plans, quarterly by special arrangement). Need-based scholarship grants available. In 2013–14, 45% of upper-school students received aid. Total amount of financial aid awarded in 2013–14: $363,025.

Admissions Traditional secondary-level entrance grade is 9. For fall 2013, 51 students applied for upper-level admission, 41 were accepted, 21 enrolled. ERB, ISEE or SSAT required. Deadline for receipt of application materials: December 15. Application fee required: $60. On-campus interview required.

Athletics Interscholastic: basketball (boys, girls), soccer (b,g), softball (g); intramural: modern dance (g); coed interscholastic: cheering, track and field; coed intramural: aerobics/dance, bowling, dance, fencing, Frisbee, outdoor education, physical fitness, ultimate Frisbee, yoga. 2 PE instructors, 4 coaches.

Computers Computers are regularly used in college planning, creative writing, desktop publishing, ESL, English, ethics, French, humanities, music, newspaper, philosophy, photography, photojournalism, programming, publications, Spanish, technology, theater, video film production, Web site design, word processing, writing, yearbook classes. Computer network features include Internet access, wireless campus network, Internet filtering or blocking technology. Campus intranet, student e-mail accounts, and computer access in designated common areas are available to students. Students grades are available online. The school has a published electronic and media policy.

Contact Mrs. Suellen F. Newman, Director. 201-659-8335 Ext. 107. Fax: 201-222-3669. E-mail: admissions@thehudsonschool.org. Website: www.thehudsonschool.org

HUMANEX ACADEMY

Englewood, Colorado
See Special Needs Schools section.

THE HUN SCHOOL OF PRINCETON

176 Edgerstoune Road
Princeton, New Jersey 08540

Head of School: Mr. Jonathan Brougham

General Information Coeducational boarding and day college-preparatory school. Boarding grades 9–PG, day grades 6–PG. Founded: 1914. Setting: suburban. Nearest major city is New York, NY. Students are housed in single-sex dormitories. 45-acre campus. 7 buildings on campus. Approved or accredited by Middle States Association of Colleges and Schools, The Association of Boarding Schools, and New Jersey Department of Education. Member of National Association of Independent Schools and Secondary School Admission Test Board. Endowment: $18 million. Total enrollment: 630. Upper school average class size: 13. Upper school faculty-student ratio: 1:8. Upper School students typically attend 5 days per week.

Upper School Student Profile Grade 9: 106 students (56 boys, 50 girls); Grade 10: 128 students (73 boys, 55 girls); Grade 11: 134 students (84 boys, 50 girls); Grade 12: 121 students (75 boys, 46 girls); Postgraduate: 13 students (12 boys, 1 girl). 35% of students are boarding students. 16 states are represented in upper school student body. 13% are international students. International students from China, Russian Federation, Saudi Arabia, Taiwan, United Kingdom, and Venezuela; 20 other countries represented in student body.

Faculty School total: 117. In upper school: 60 men, 57 women; 52 have advanced degrees; 29 reside on campus.

Subjects Offered 3-dimensional art, 3-dimensional design, advanced computer applications, Advanced Placement courses, advanced TOEFL/grammar, algebra, American government, American history, American history-AP, American literature, anatomy, architectural drawing, architecture, art, art history, art history-AP, astrophysics, biology, biology-AP, calculus, calculus-AP, ceramics, chemistry, chemistry-AP, chorus, community service, computer programming, computer science, drama, driver education, economics, engineering, English, English-AP, ESL, European history, fine arts, forensics, French, French-AP, geometry, government/civics, health, history, interdisciplinary studies, jazz band, Latin, Latin-AP, marine biology, mathematics, mechanical drawing, music, photography, physical education, physics, physics-AP, physiology, public speaking, science, social studies, Spanish, Spanish-AP, statistics-AP, television, theater, trigonometry, U.S. history-AP, video, video film production, world history.

Graduation Requirements Arts and fine arts (art, music, dance, drama), computer science, English, foreign language, health, history, mathematics, science, 10-20 hours of community service per year, summer reading, extracurricular activities.

Special Academic Programs Advanced Placement exam preparation; honors section; academic accommodation for the gifted; ESL (35 students enrolled).

College Admission Counseling 151 students graduated in 2013; all went to college, including Boston University; Lehigh University; Penn State University Park; Princeton University; Syracuse University. Median SAT critical reading: 590, median SAT math: 620, median SAT writing: 610, median composite ACT: 27.

Student Life Upper grades have specified standards of dress, student council, honor system. Discipline rests equally with students and faculty.

Summer Programs Remediation, enrichment, advancement, ESL, sports, art/fine arts, computer instruction programs offered; session focuses on make-up courses, enrichment, SAT and TOEFL preparation; held on campus; accepts boys and girls; open to students from other schools. 110 students usually enrolled. 2014 schedule: June 28 to July 23. Application deadline: none.

Tuition and Aid Day student tuition: $35,400; 7-day tuition and room/board: $51,500. Tuition installment plan (Academic Management Services Plan, FACTS Tuition Payment Plan, individually arranged payment plans). Merit scholarship grants, need-based scholarship grants, prepGATE loans available. In 2013–14, 30% of upper-school students received aid; total upper-school merit-scholarship money awarded: $50,000. Total amount of financial aid awarded in 2013–14: $4,000,000.

Admissions Traditional secondary-level entrance grade is 9. PSAT or SAT for applicants to grade 11 and 12, SSAT or TOEFL required. Deadline for receipt of application materials: January 31. Application fee required: $75. Interview required.

Athletics Interscholastic: baseball (boys), basketball (b,g), crew (b,g), cross-country running (b,g), fencing (b,g), field hockey (g), football (b), lacrosse (b,g), soccer (b,g), softball (g), tennis (b,g); intramural: dance squad (g), soccer (b,g), weight training (g); coed interscholastic: golf, ice hockey, swimming and diving, track and field; coed intramural: aerobics/dance, aerobics/Nautilus, ballet, basketball, cross-country running, dance, fitness, flag football, Frisbee, jogging, Nautilus, paint ball, physical fitness, running, skiing (downhill), strength & conditioning, touch football, ultimate Frisbee, volleyball, weight lifting. 3 coaches, 1 athletic trainer.

Computers Computers are regularly used in all academic classes. Computer network features include on-campus library services, online commercial services, Internet access, wireless campus network, Internet filtering or blocking technology. Campus intranet, student e-mail accounts, and computer access in designated common areas are available to students. Students grades are available online. The school has a published electronic and media policy.

Contact Mr. Steven C. Bristol, Director of Admissions. 609-921-7600. Fax: 609-279-9398. E-mail: admiss@hunschool.org. Website: www.hunschool.org

HUNTINGTON-SURREY SCHOOL

4804 Grover Avenue
Austin, Texas 78756

Head of School: Dr. Light Bailey German

General Information Coeducational day college-preparatory and writing school. Grades 9–12. Founded: 1973. Setting: urban. 1 building on campus. Approved or accredited by Southern Association of Colleges and Schools, The College Board, and Texas Department of Education. Total enrollment: 48. Upper school average class size: 8. Upper school faculty-student ratio: 1:4. There are 160 required school days per year for Upper School students. Upper School students typically attend 5 days per week. The average school day consists of 4 hours and 45 minutes.

Upper School Student Profile Grade 9: 7 students (5 boys, 2 girls); Grade 10: 16 students (6 boys, 10 girls); Grade 11: 16 students (10 boys, 6 girls); Grade 12: 9 students (5 boys, 4 girls).

Faculty School total: 20. In upper school: 5 men, 15 women; 10 have advanced degrees.

Subjects Offered Algebra, art, biology, calculus, chemistry, college planning, comparative religion, creative drama, discrete mathematics, drama, ecology, environmental systems, English, French, geometry, German, history, Latin, literature, math analysis, math review, mathematics, philosophy, physical science, physics, portfolio art, pre-algebra, pre-calculus, senior science survey, social studies, Spanish, student publications, study skills, theater arts, trigonometry, U.S. history, work-study, world history, writing, yearbook, yoga.

Graduation Requirements American literature, biology, British literature, economics, foreign language, mathematics, science, U.S. government, U.S. history, world history, world literature, writing, senior research project, school exit examinations: assertion with proof essay exam and mathematical competency exam, senior advisory course.

Special Academic Programs Accelerated programs; academic accommodation for the gifted.

College Admission Counseling 11 students graduated in 2013; 10 went to college, including Lewis & Clark College; Pacific University; St. Edward's University; Texas Tech University; The University of Texas at San Antonio; University of Massachusetts Amherst. Other: 1 went to work. Median SAT critical reading: 550, median SAT math: 520, median SAT writing: 470, median combined SAT: 1540.

Student Life Upper grades have student council, honor system. Discipline rests primarily with faculty.

Summer Programs Remediation, enrichment, advancement programs offered; session focuses on one-on-one teaching, or small classes; held on campus; accepts boys and girls; open to students from other schools. 12 students usually enrolled. 2014 schedule: June 9 to July 25. Application deadline: May 5.

Tuition and Aid Day student tuition: $1200. Tuition installment plan (monthly payment plans).

Admissions Traditional secondary-level entrance grade is 9. For fall 2013, 20 students applied for upper-level admission, 16 were accepted, 16 enrolled. Deadline for receipt of application materials: none. No application fee required. On-campus interview required.

Athletics Coed Intramural: yoga. 1 PE instructor.

Computers Computers are regularly used in study skills, writing classes. Computer resources include study hall computers and printers (available for student use). Computer access in designated common areas is available to students.

Contact Ms. Johni Walker-Little, Assistant Director. 512-478-4743. Fax: 512-457-0235. Website: www.huntingtonsurrey.com

HYDE PARK BAPTIST SCHOOL

3901 Speedway
Austin, Texas 78751

Head of School: Mr. Bob Liverman

General Information Coeducational day college-preparatory, arts, religious studies, and technology school, affiliated with Baptist Church. Grades PK–12. Founded: 1968. Setting: urban. 10-acre campus. 1 building on campus. Approved or accredited by Accreditation Commission of the Texas Association of Baptist Schools, Southern Association of Colleges and Schools, Texas Private School Accreditation Commission, and Texas Department of Education. Endowment: $236,500. Total enrollment: 599. Upper school average class size: 18. Upper school faculty-student ratio: 1:12. There are 175 required school days per year for Upper School students. Upper School students typically attend 5 days per week. The average school day consists of 7 hours and 20 minutes.

Upper School Student Profile Grade 9: 61 students (37 boys, 24 girls); Grade 10: 75 students (39 boys, 36 girls); Grade 11: 72 students (36 boys, 36 girls); Grade 12: 78 students (49 boys, 29 girls). 10% of students are Baptist.

Faculty School total: 30. In upper school: 8 men, 22 women; 7 have advanced degrees.

Subjects Offered Algebra, anatomy and physiology, art, athletics, Bible, Bible studies, biology, biology-AP, calculus, calculus-AP, cheerleading, chemistry, chemistry-AP, choir, choral music, Christian doctrine, Christian education, Christian ethics, Christian studies, college writing, communication skills, computer information systems, computer technologies, creative writing, digital photography, drama performance, earth science, economics, economics-AP, English, English language and composition-AP, English literature and composition-AP, English literature-AP, English-AP, environmental science, ESL, film and literature, French, geometry, government/civics, health, honors algebra, honors English, honors geometry, honors U.S. history, honors world history, internship, keyboarding, Latin, Latin-AP, macroeconomics-AP, marine biology, microeconomics-AP, musical productions, personal money management, physical education, physics, physics-AP, pre-algebra, pre-calculus, psychology, public speaking, SAT preparation, science, sign language, sociology, Spanish, Spanish-AP, speech, statistics-AP, study skills, theater, theater arts, U.S. government, U.S. government and politics-AP, U.S. history, U.S. history-AP, world geography, world history, writing, yearbook.

Graduation Requirements Arts and fine arts (art, music, dance, drama), Bible studies, computer science, electives, English, foreign language, mathematics, physical education (includes health), public speaking, science, social studies (includes history), 15 hours of community service per year.

Special Academic Programs Advanced Placement exam preparation; honors section; independent study; ESL (5 students enrolled).

College Admission Counseling 64 students graduated in 2013; all went to college, including Baylor University; Texas A&M University; Texas Christian University; Texas State University–San Marcos; The University of Texas at Austin. Mean SAT critical reading: 559, mean SAT math: 572, mean SAT writing: 565, mean combined SAT: 1696, mean composite ACT: 24. 36% scored over 600 on SAT critical reading, 41% scored over 600 on SAT math, 31% scored over 600 on SAT writing, 25% scored over 26 on composite ACT.

Student Life Upper grades have specified standards of dress, student council, honor system. Discipline rests primarily with faculty. Attendance at religious services is required.

Tuition and Aid Day student tuition: $13,800. Tuition installment plan (SMART Tuition Payment Plan, monthly payment plans). Tuition reduction for siblings, merit scholarship grants, need-based scholarship grants available. In 2013–14, 14% of upper-school students received aid; total upper-school merit-scholarship money awarded: $5000. Total amount of financial aid awarded in 2013–14: $145,250.

Admissions Traditional secondary-level entrance grade is 9. For fall 2013, 77 students applied for upper-level admission, 60 were accepted, 55 enrolled. ISEE required. Deadline for receipt of application materials: none. Application fee required: $150. On-campus interview required.

Athletics Interscholastic: baseball (boys), basketball (b,g), cheering (g), cross-country running (b,g), dance squad (g), dance team (g), drill team (g), football (b), golf (b,g), softball (g), strength & conditioning (b,g), tennis (b,g), track and field (b,g), volleyball (g). 1 PE instructor, 8 coaches, 1 athletic trainer.

Computers Computers are regularly used in business applications, computer applications, desktop publishing, keyboarding, multimedia, technology, Web site design, word processing, yearbook classes. Computer network features include on-campus library services, online commercial services, Internet access, wireless campus

network, Internet filtering or blocking technology. Students grades are available online. The school has a published electronic and media policy.

Contact Mrs. Lisa Thomas, Director of Admissions, High School. 512-465-8333. Fax: 512-827-2020. E-mail: lthomas@hp-schools.org. Website: www.hp-schools.org

HYMAN BRAND HEBREW ACADEMY OF GREATER KANSAS CITY

5801 West 115th Street
Overland Park, Kansas 66211

Head of School: Mr. Howard Haas

General Information Coeducational day college-preparatory, general academic, and religious studies school, affiliated with Jewish faith. Grades K–12. Founded: 1966. Setting: suburban. Nearest major city is Kansas City, MO. 32-acre campus. 1 building on campus. Approved or accredited by Independent Schools Association of the Central States. Languages of instruction: English and Hebrew. Endowment: $4.3 million. Total enrollment: 224. Upper school average class size: 11. Upper school faculty-student ratio: 1:5. There are 178 required school days per year for Upper School students. Upper School students typically attend 5 days per week. The average school day consists of 7 hours and 45 minutes.

Upper School Student Profile Grade 9: 4 students (1 boy, 3 girls); Grade 10: 11 students (5 boys, 6 girls); Grade 11: 9 students (4 boys, 5 girls); Grade 12: 15 students (8 boys, 7 girls). 100% of students are Jewish.

Faculty School total: 38. In upper school: 7 men, 10 women; 12 have advanced degrees.

Subjects Offered 3-dimensional design, algebra, American government, American history, American history-AP, American literature, anatomy and physiology, art, art history, Bible studies, biology, British literature, calculus-AP, chemistry, community service, computer applications, computer science, digital art, economics, English, English language and composition-AP, English literature, English literature and composition-AP, environmental science, ethics, European history, fine arts, geometry, health, Hebrew, Hebrew scripture, Holocaust seminar, Jewish studies, model United Nations, physical education, physics, statistics-AP, Talmud, trigonometry, U.S. government and politics-AP, world history, world literature, yearbook.

Graduation Requirements Arts and fine arts (art, music, dance, drama), English, foreign language, mathematics, physical education (includes health), religion (includes Bible studies and theology), science, social studies (includes history). Community service is required.

Special Academic Programs 6 Advanced Placement exams for which test preparation is offered; honors section; independent study; study at local college for college credit; academic accommodation for the gifted.

College Admission Counseling 10 students graduated in 2013; 9 went to college, including Georgetown University; Goucher College; Savannah College of Art and Design; School of the Art Institute of Chicago; The University of Kansas; University of Maryland, College Park. Other: 1 entered a postgraduate year. Mean composite ACT: 26. 50% scored over 26 on composite ACT.

Student Life Upper grades have specified standards of dress, student council. Discipline rests primarily with faculty. Attendance at religious services is required.

Tuition and Aid Day student tuition: $7250. Tuition installment plan (FACTS Tuition Payment Plan). Need-based scholarship grants available. In 2013–14, 26% of upper-school students received aid. Total amount of financial aid awarded in 2013–14: $41,800.

Admissions Traditional secondary-level entrance grade is 9. Writing sample required. Deadline for receipt of application materials: none. Application fee required: $50.

Athletics Interscholastic: basketball (boys, girls), soccer (b,g), tennis (b,g); coed interscholastic: cross-country running; coed intramural: tennis. 2 PE instructors, 6 coaches.

Computers Computers are regularly used in computer applications, desktop publishing, digital applications, economics, English, humanities, mathematics, newspaper, psychology, religious studies, science, social studies, writing, yearbook classes. Computer network features include on-campus library services, online commercial services, Internet access, wireless campus network. Student e-mail accounts and computer access in designated common areas are available to students. Students grades are available online. The school has a published electronic and media policy.

Contact Mrs. Tamara Lawson Schuster, Director of Admissions. 913-327-8135. Fax: 913-327-8180. E-mail: tschuster@hbha.edu. Website: www.hbha.edu

IC CATHOLIC PREP

217 Cottage Hill Avenue
Elmhurst, Illinois 60126

Head of School: Pamela M. Levar

General Information Coeducational day college-preparatory, arts, and religious studies school, affiliated with Roman Catholic Church. Grades 9–12. Founded: 1936. Setting: suburban. Nearest major city is Chicago. 3 buildings on campus. Approved or accredited by North Central Association of Colleges and Schools and Illinois

Department of Education. Member of National Association of Independent Schools. Total enrollment: 308. Upper school average class size: 18. Upper school faculty-student ratio: 1:9. There are 176 required school days per year for Upper School students. Upper School students typically attend 5 days per week. The average school day consists of 6 hours and 30 minutes.

Upper School Student Profile Grade 9: 75 students (40 boys, 35 girls); Grade 10: 85 students (49 boys, 36 girls); Grade 11: 73 students (30 boys, 43 girls); Grade 12: 75 students (45 boys, 30 girls). 91% of students are Roman Catholic.

Faculty School total: 28. In upper school: 8 men, 20 women; 14 have advanced degrees.

Subjects Offered 3-dimensional art, advanced chemistry, advanced math, algebra, American government, American history, anatomy and physiology, ancient world history, art, biology, biology-AP, British literature, business law, calculus, calculus-AP, campus ministry, career/college preparation, Catholic belief and practice, ceramics, chemistry, chemistry-AP, chorus, college counseling, computer applications, constitutional history of U.S., constitutional law, consumer education, current events, drawing, ecology, environmental systems, economics, English, English-AP, environmental science, fitness, foreign language, French, geometry, government/civics, health education, honors algebra, honors English, honors geometry, honors U.S. history, humanities, keyboarding, library, musical theater, newspaper, painting, physical education, physics, piano, pre-calculus, psychology, SAT/ACT preparation, sociology, Spanish, statistics, student government, trigonometry, U.S. government and politics-AP, U.S. history-AP, yearbook.

Graduation Requirements Algebra, American government, American literature, anatomy and physiology, art, biology, British literature, Catholic belief and practice, chemistry, computer applications, constitutional history of U.S., consumer education, English, foreign language, geometry, grammar, health, history, human biology, language and composition, mathematics, physical science, political science, pre-calculus, science, theology, trigonometry, U.S. history, world history, 40 hours of Christian service, attendance at retreat.

Special Academic Programs 5 Advanced Placement exams for which test preparation is offered; honors section; study at local college for college credit.

College Admission Counseling 77 students graduated in 2013; 74 went to college, including Eastern Illinois University; Illinois State University; Loyola University Chicago; University of Dayton; University of Illinois at Urbana–Champaign; University of Missouri. Other: 1 went to work, 2 had other specific plans.

Student Life Upper grades have uniform requirement, student council. Discipline rests primarily with faculty. Attendance at religious services is required.

Summer Programs Sports programs offered; session focuses on sports; held both on and off campus; held at Plunkett Field; accepts boys and girls; not open to students from other schools. 150 students usually enrolled. 2014 schedule: June 15 to July 28.

Tuition and Aid Day student tuition: $9800. Tuition installment plan (SMART Tuition Payment Plan). Tuition reduction for siblings, merit scholarship grants, need-based scholarship grants, merit scholarships (for placement test top scorers), externally funded scholarships (alumni, memorials), Catholic school teacher grants (1/3 reduction) available. In 2013–14, 59% of upper-school students received aid; total upper-school merit-scholarship money awarded: $15,000. Total amount of financial aid awarded in 2013–14: $175,000.

Admissions Traditional secondary-level entrance grade is 9. High School Placement Test (closed version) from Scholastic Testing Service required. Deadline for receipt of application materials: none. No application fee required.

Athletics Interscholastic: baseball (boys), basketball (b,g), bowling (b), cheering (g), cross-country running (b,g), dance team (g), football (b), lacrosse (b), pom squad (g), soccer (g), softball (g), strength & conditioning (b,g), tennis (g), track and field (b,g), volleyball (g), weight lifting (b), weight training (b,g), wrestling (b); intramural: ice hockey (b); coed interscholastic: fishing, golf. 2 PE instructors, 48 coaches, 2 athletic trainers.

Computers Computers are regularly used in accounting, business applications, business education, career exploration, college planning, computer applications, keyboarding, library, library skills, news writing, newspaper, publications, science, stock market, yearbook classes. Computer network features include on-campus library services, online commercial services, Internet access, wireless campus network, Internet filtering or blocking technology, Edline. Student e-mail accounts and computer access in designated common areas are available to students. Students grades are available online. The school has a published electronic and media policy.

Contact Mrs. Sarah Ford, Director of Admissions. 630-530-3484. Fax: 630-530-2290. E-mail: sford@iccatholicprep.org. Website: www.iccatholicprep.org

IDYLLWILD ARTS ACADEMY

52500 Temecula Road
PO Box 38
Idyllwild, California 92549

Head of School: Doug Ashcraft

General Information Coeducational boarding and day college-preparatory and arts school. Grades 9–PG. Founded: 1986. Setting: rural. Nearest major city is Los Angeles. Students are housed in single-sex dormitories. 205-acre campus. 44 buildings on campus. Approved or accredited by California Association of Independent Schools,

The Association of Boarding Schools, Western Association of Schools and Colleges, and California Department of Education. Member of National Association of Independent Schools and Secondary School Admission Test Board. Endowment: $3 million. Total enrollment: 295. Upper school average class size: 16. Upper school faculty-student ratio: 1:12. Upper School students typically attend 6 days per week.

Upper School Student Profile Grade 9: 39 students (16 boys, 23 girls); Grade 10: 61 students (28 boys, 33 girls); Grade 11: 77 students (37 boys, 40 girls); Grade 12: 83 students (41 boys, 42 girls); Postgraduate: 4 students (2 boys, 2 girls). 92% of students are boarding students. 38% are state residents. 35 states are represented in upper school student body. 44% are international students. International students from Australia, China, Japan, Mexico, Republic of Korea, and Taiwan; 16 other countries represented in student body.

Faculty School total: 65. In upper school: 24 men, 20 women; 30 have advanced degrees; 23 reside on campus.

Subjects Offered 3-dimensional art, 3-dimensional design, acting, advanced math, algebra, American government, American history, American literature, anatomy, art, art history, audio visual/media, audition methods, ballet, biology, Broadway dance, calculus, career/college preparation, ceramics, chemistry, choir, choral music, choreography, computer graphics, computer science, creative writing, critical studies in film, dance, digital art, directing, drama, drawing and design, economics, English, English literature, ensembles, environmental science, ESL, fiction, film and literature, film and new technologies, film appreciation, film history, film studies, filmmaking, fine arts, French, geography, geometry, government/civics, grammar, history, illustration, improvisation, jazz dance, jazz ensemble, jazz theory, mathematics, multimedia, music, music theater, music theory, musical productions, musical theater dance, orchestra, performing arts, photography, physical education, physics, play production, playwriting and directing, poetry, pottery, printmaking, science, social sciences, social studies, Spanish, tap dance, technical theater, technology/design, theater, video film production, vocal music, voice and diction, voice ensemble, world history, world literature, writing.

Graduation Requirements Art, arts and fine arts (art, music, dance, drama), English, foreign language, mathematics, performing arts, physical education (includes health), science, social sciences, social studies (includes history).

Special Academic Programs Advanced Placement exam preparation; honors section; ESL (45 students enrolled).

College Admission Counseling 68 students graduated in 2012; 66 went to college, including California Institute of the Arts; New York University; The Johns Hopkins University; The Juilliard School; University of California, Los Angeles; University of Rochester. Other: 2 went to work.

Student Life Upper grades have student council. Discipline rests equally with students and faculty.

Tuition and Aid Day student tuition: $36,000; 7-day tuition and room/board: $52,000. Tuition installment plan (Key Tuition Payment Plan, monthly payment plans, individually arranged payment plans, school's own payment plan). Need-based scholarship grants available. In 2012–13, 68% of upper-school students received aid. Total amount of financial aid awarded in 2012–13: $5,054,332.

Admissions Traditional secondary-level entrance grade is 10. For fall 2012, 400 students applied for upper-level admission, 400 were accepted, 295 enrolled. SLEP, SSAT or TOEFL required. Deadline for receipt of application materials: none. Application fee required: $50. Interview required.

Athletics Intramural: aerobics (boys, girls); coed intramural: aerobics, aerobics/dance, aerobics/Nautilus, ballet, basketball, bicycling, billiards, bowling, climbing, combined training, cooperative games, cross-country running, dance, fencing, fitness, Frisbee, hiking/backpacking, jogging, judo, martial arts, modern dance, mountain biking, outdoor activities, outdoor adventure, outdoor education, outdoor recreation, outdoors, physical fitness, physical training, rock climbing, soccer, swimming and diving, tennis, ultimate Frisbee, volleyball, walking, weight training, yoga. 1 PE instructor.

Computers Computers are regularly used in art, design, drafting, drawing and design, English, ESL, graphic design, media production, science classes. Computer resources include on-campus library services, Internet access, wireless campus network, Internet filtering or blocking technology. Computer access in designated common areas is available to students. Students grades are available online. The school has a published electronic and media policy.

Contact Mr. Marek Pramuka, Dean of Admission and Financial Aid. 951-659-2171 Ext. 2223. Fax: 951-659-3168. E-mail: admission@idyllwildarts.org. Website: www.idyllwildarts.org

IMMACULATA HIGH SCHOOL

600 Shawnee
Leavenworth, Kansas 66048

Head of School: Mrs. Helen C. Schwinn

General Information Coeducational day college-preparatory, arts, business, religious studies, and technology school, affiliated with Roman Catholic Church. Grades 9–12. Founded: 1924. Setting: suburban. Nearest major city is Kansas City. 2-acre campus. 1 building on campus. Approved or accredited by North Central Association of Colleges and Schools and Kansas Department of Education. Total enrollment: 122. Upper school average class size: 15. Upper school faculty-student ratio: 1:9. There are 171 required school days per year for Upper School students. Upper School students typically attend 5 days per week. The average school day consists of 7 hours and 30 minutes.

Upper School Student Profile Grade 9: 36 students (24 boys, 12 girls); Grade 10: 30 students (16 boys, 14 girls); Grade 11: 25 students (14 boys, 11 girls); Grade 12: 31 students (18 boys, 13 girls). 82% of students are Roman Catholic.

Faculty School total: 15. In upper school: 6 men, 9 women; 7 have advanced degrees.

Special Academic Programs Honors section; study at local college for college credit.

College Admission Counseling 26 students graduated in 2012; 24 went to college, including Johnson County Community College.

Student Life Upper grades have uniform requirement, student council. Discipline rests primarily with faculty. Attendance at religious services is required.

Admissions Traditional secondary-level entrance grade is 9. Achievement tests required. Deadline for receipt of application materials: none. No application fee required. Interview recommended.

Athletics Interscholastic: baseball (boys), basketball (b,g), cheering (g), dance team (g), football (b), golf (b), power lifting (b,g), soccer (b,g), softball (g), swimming and diving (b), tennis (b,g), track and field (b,g), volleyball (g), wrestling (b). 2 PE instructors, 4 coaches.

Computers Computers are regularly used in business education classes. Computer network features include Internet access, wireless campus network. Campus intranet is available to students. Students grades are available online.

Contact Paula Hyde, Academic Adviser. 913-682-3900. Fax: 913-682-9036. E-mail: phyde@archkckcs.org. Website: www.archkckcs.org/immaculata

IMMACULATA HIGH SCHOOL

240 Mountain Avenue
Somerville, New Jersey 08876

Head of School: Sr. Mary Smith

General Information Coeducational day college-preparatory and religious studies school, affiliated with Roman Catholic Church. Grades 9–12. Founded: 1962. Setting: suburban. 19-acre campus. 3 buildings on campus. Approved or accredited by Middle States Association of Colleges and Schools, National Catholic Education Association, New South Wales Department of School Education, and New Jersey Department of Education. Total enrollment: 690. Upper school average class size: 22. Upper school faculty-student ratio: 1:13. There are 180 required school days per year for Upper School students. Upper School students typically attend 5 days per week. The average school day consists of 6 hours and 30 minutes.

Upper School Student Profile Grade 9: 148 students (73 boys, 75 girls); Grade 10: 176 students (82 boys, 94 girls); Grade 11: 183 students (99 boys, 84 girls); Grade 12: 183 students (96 boys, 87 girls). 92% of students are Roman Catholic.

Faculty School total: 71. In upper school: 20 men, 51 women; 43 have advanced degrees.

Subjects Offered Accounting, advanced chemistry, advanced math, Advanced Placement courses, algebra, American history, American literature, anatomy, ancient world history, art, art history-AP, biology, British literature, business, calculus, calculus-AP, chemistry, chemistry-AP, creative writing, drama, drawing and design, driver education, Eastern world civilizations, ecology, English-AP, environmental science, environmental studies, European history-AP, film history, foreign language, French language-AP, geometry, global issues, global studies, graphic design, health, honors algebra, honors English, honors geometry, marching band, music theory, religious education, science, social studies, speech, trigonometry, U.S. history-AP.

Graduation Requirements Algebra, American literature, biology, British literature, chemistry, driver education, foreign language, geometry, health education, physical education (includes health), physics, theology, U.S. history.

Special Academic Programs Advanced Placement exam preparation; honors section; academic accommodation for the musically talented.

College Admission Counseling 191 students graduated in 2012; 187 went to college, including Loyola University Maryland; Penn State University Park; Rutgers, The State University of New Jersey, New Brunswick; Saint Joseph's University; Seton Hall University; The University of Scranton. Other: 2 entered military service, 2 had other specific plans. Mean SAT critical reading: 532, mean SAT math: 540, mean SAT writing: 554.

Student Life Upper grades have uniform requirement. Discipline rests primarily with faculty. Attendance at religious services is required.

Tuition and Aid Day student tuition: $10,400. Tuition installment plan (FACTS Tuition Payment Plan).

Admissions Traditional secondary-level entrance grade is 9. For fall 2012, 225 students applied for upper-level admission, 175 were accepted, 148 enrolled. High School Placement Test required. Deadline for receipt of application materials: December 31. Application fee required: $150. On-campus interview required.

Athletics Interscholastic: baseball (boys), basketball (b,g), cheering (g), cross-country running (b,g), football (b), lacrosse (b,g), soccer (b,g), softball (g), tennis (b,g); coed interscholastic: bowling, golf, swimming and diving. 4 PE instructors, 50 coaches, 1 athletic trainer.

Computers Computers are regularly used in graphic design, journalism, yearbook classes. Computer network features include on-campus library services, online commercial services, Internet access. Students grades are available online.

Contact Sr. Anne Brigid Gallagher, Assistant Principal/Academic Dean. 908-722-0200 Ext. 118. Fax: 908-218-7765. E-mail: sannebrigid@immaculatahighschool.org. Website: www.immaculatahighschool.org

IMMACULATA-LA SALLE HIGH SCHOOL

3601 South Miami Avenue
Miami, Florida 33133

Head of School: Sr. Kim Keraitis, FMA

General Information Coeducational day college-preparatory, arts, business, religious studies, and technology school, affiliated with Roman Catholic Church. Grades 9–12. Founded: 1958. Setting: urban. 13-acre campus. 7 buildings on campus. Approved or accredited by National Catholic Education Association, Southern Association of Colleges and Schools, The College Board, and Florida Department of Education. Endowment: $80,200. Total enrollment: 804. Upper school average class size: 24. Upper school faculty-student ratio: 1:15. There are 180 required school days per year for Upper School students. Upper School students typically attend 5 days per week. The average school day consists of 6 hours and 30 minutes.

Upper School Student Profile Grade 9: 190 students (75 boys, 115 girls); Grade 10: 187 students (77 boys, 110 girls); Grade 11: 215 students (79 boys, 136 girls); Grade 12: 212 students (80 boys, 132 girls). 95% of students are Roman Catholic.

Faculty School total: 65. In upper school: 30 men, 35 women; 24 have advanced degrees.

Subjects Offered 3-dimensional art, algebra, American government, American history, American history-AP, analytic geometry, anatomy, anatomy and physiology, art, band, Bible studies, biology, business technology, calculus, chemistry, chemistry-AP, Chinese, chorus, church history, comparative government and politics-AP, computer science, computer technology certification, creative writing, critical thinking, desktop publishing, digital photography, drama, driver education, economics, electronics, emerging technology, engineering, English, English language and composition-AP, English literature and composition-AP, environmental science-AP, ethics, European history-AP, filmmaking, finance, fine arts, first aid, French, French language-AP, geography, geometry, global studies, government and politics-AP, government/civics, graphic design, health, health and wellness, history, honors algebra, honors English, honors geometry, honors U.S. history, honors world history, keyboarding, marine biology, mathematics, music appreciation, physical education, physics, psychology, religion, science, social studies, sociology, Spanish, U.S. government, U.S. government and politics-AP, U.S. history, U.S. history-AP, weight training, world history, world religions, yearbook.

Graduation Requirements Arts and fine arts (art, music, dance, drama), business skills (includes word processing), English, foreign language, geometry, mathematics, physical education (includes health), religion (includes Bible studies and theology), science, social studies (includes history), 100 hours of community service.

Special Academic Programs Advanced Placement exam preparation; honors section; independent study; study at local college for college credit.

College Admission Counseling 186 students graduated in 2013; all went to college, including Barry University; Florida International University; Florida State University; Miami Dade College; University of Central Florida; University of Miami. Mean SAT critical reading: 500, mean SAT math: 506, mean SAT writing: 506, mean combined SAT: 1512, mean composite ACT: 21. 17% scored over 600 on SAT critical reading, 17% scored over 600 on SAT math, 16% scored over 600 on SAT writing, 15% scored over 1800 on combined SAT, 13% scored over 26 on composite ACT.

Student Life Upper grades have uniform requirement, student council, honor system. Discipline rests equally with students and faculty. Attendance at religious services is required.

Summer Programs Remediation, enrichment, advancement programs offered; session focuses on remediation and advancement; held on campus; accepts boys and girls; open to students from other schools. 150 students usually enrolled. 2014 schedule: June 16 to July 11. Application deadline: June 11.

Tuition and Aid Day student tuition: $11,000. Tuition installment plan (FACTS Tuition Payment Plan, monthly payment plans). Merit scholarship grants, paying campus jobs available. In 2013–14, 11% of upper-school students received aid; total upper-school merit-scholarship money awarded: $156,254. Total amount of financial aid awarded in 2013–14: $351,257.

Admissions Traditional secondary-level entrance grade is 9. For fall 2013, 406 students applied for upper-level admission, 314 were accepted, 245 enrolled. High School Placement Test (closed version) from Scholastic Testing Service required. Deadline for receipt of application materials: none. Application fee required: $50. On-campus interview required.

Athletics Interscholastic: baseball (boys), basketball (b,g), cheering (g), cross-country running (b,g), dance team (g), football (b), golf (b,g), lacrosse (b), soccer (b,g), softball (g), swimming and diving (b,g), tennis (b,g), track and field (b,g), volleyball (b,g), weight training (b,g), winter soccer (b,g); coed intramural: physical fitness. 3 PE instructors, 15 coaches, 1 athletic trainer.

Computers Computers are regularly used in business, business applications, economics, French, journalism, mathematics, programming, science, technology, word processing, yearbook classes. Computer network features include on-campus library services, Internet access, wireless campus network, Internet filtering or blocking technology. Campus intranet and student e-mail accounts are available to students. Students grades are available online. The school has a published electronic and media policy.

Contact Mrs. Jennifer Bonilla, Admissions Director. 305-854-2334 Ext. 130. Fax: 305-858-5971. E-mail: admissions@ilsroyals.com. Website: www.ilsroyals.com

IMMACULATE HEART HIGH SCHOOL AND MIDDLE SCHOOL

5515 Franklin Avenue
Los Angeles, California 90028-5999

Head of School: Ms. Virginia Hurst

General Information Girls' day college-preparatory school, affiliated with Roman Catholic Church. Grades 6–12. Founded: 1906. Setting: urban. 5-acre campus. 7 buildings on campus. Approved or accredited by Western Association of Schools and Colleges and California Department of Education. Upper school average class size: 18. Upper school faculty-student ratio: 1:15.

Faculty School total: 45. In upper school: 34 have advanced degrees.

Special Academic Programs Advanced Placement exam preparation; honors section; independent study.

Student Life Upper grades have uniform requirement, student council, honor system. Discipline rests primarily with faculty. Attendance at religious services is required.

Summer Programs Remediation, enrichment, sports, art/fine arts programs offered; held on campus; accepts boys and girls; open to students from other schools.

Tuition and Aid Tuition installment plan (The Tuition Plan). Merit scholarship grants, need-based scholarship grants available.

Admissions High School Placement Test or High School Placement Test (closed version) from Scholastic Testing Service required. Deadline for receipt of application materials: January 3. Application fee required: $75. On-campus interview required.

Computers Computer network features include Internet access, wireless campus network, Internet filtering or blocking technology. Campus intranet and student e-mail accounts are available to students. Students grades are available online.

Contact Ms. Jennie Lee, Director of Admissions. 323-461-3651 Ext. 240. Fax: 323-462-0610. E-mail: jlee@immaculateheart.org. Website: www.immaculateheart.org

INDEPENDENT SCHOOL

8317 East Douglas
Wichita, Kansas 67207

Head of School: Dr. Mary Dickerson

General Information Coeducational day college-preparatory, arts, and technology school. Grades PK–12. Founded: 1980. Setting: suburban. 22-acre campus. 2 buildings on campus. Approved or accredited by Independent Schools Association of the Central States. Total enrollment: 520. Upper school average class size: 15. Upper school faculty-student ratio: 1:9. There are 160 required school days per year for Upper School students. Upper School students typically attend 5 days per week. The average school day consists of 7 hours.

Upper School Student Profile Grade 9: 56 students (32 boys, 24 girls); Grade 10: 50 students (27 boys, 23 girls); Grade 11: 59 students (28 boys, 31 girls); Grade 12: 55 students (31 boys, 24 girls).

Faculty School total: 60. In upper school: 14 men, 11 women; 17 have advanced degrees.

Subjects Offered 3-dimensional art, advanced math, Advanced Placement courses, algebra, American government, American history, American history-AP, American literature, anatomy and physiology, art, biology, biology-AP, British literature, British literature (honors), calculus, calculus-AP, ceramics, chemistry, chemistry-AP, choir, computer applications, computer art, debate, economics, engineering, English literature-AP, film and new technologies, foreign language, forensics, geometry, health, health and wellness, Latin, music, music theory, music theory-AP, music-AP, newspaper, physics, physics-AP, psychology, psychology-AP, Spanish, Spanish-AP, statistics-AP, theater, theater arts, trigonometry, U.S. government and politics-AP, Web site design, weight training, yearbook.

Graduation Requirements Algebra, American government, American history, American literature, arts and fine arts (art, music, dance, drama), biology, British literature, chemistry, computer applications, computer literacy, English, foreign language, geography, geometry, humanities, physical education (includes health), world history, world literature, 50 hours of community service.

Special Academic Programs 14 Advanced Placement exams for which test preparation is offered; honors section; independent study; study at local college for college credit; academic accommodation for the gifted, the musically talented, and the artistically talented.

College Admission Counseling 54 students graduated in 2013; all went to college, including Kansas State University; Oklahoma State University; The University of Kansas; University of Tulsa. Mean SAT critical reading: 638, mean SAT math: 626, mean SAT writing: 589, mean combined SAT: 1853, mean composite ACT: 27.

Student Life Upper grades have specified standards of dress, student council, honor system. Discipline rests primarily with faculty.

Summer Programs Enrichment, advancement, sports, art/fine arts, computer instruction programs offered; held on campus; accepts boys and girls; open to students from other schools. 2014 schedule: May 20 to August 15.

Tuition and Aid Day student tuition: $10,800. Tuition installment plan (monthly payment plans, individually arranged payment plans). Need-based scholarship grants available. In 2013–14, 23% of upper-school students received aid.

Admissions Traditional secondary-level entrance grade is 9. For fall 2013, 49 students applied for upper-level admission, 45 were accepted, 41 enrolled. Admissions testing, non-standardized placement tests and Otis-Lennon Ability or Stanford Achievement Test required. Deadline for receipt of application materials: none. Application fee required: $40. Interview recommended.

Athletics Interscholastic: baseball (boys), basketball (b,g), cheering (g), cross-country running (b,g), dance team (g), football (b), golf (b,g), soccer (b,g), softball (g), strength & conditioning (b,g), swimming and diving (b,g), tennis (b,g), track and field (b,g), volleyball (g), weight training (b,g), wrestling (b); coed interscholastic: strength & conditioning, weight training. 2 PE instructors, 5 coaches, 1 athletic trainer.

Computers Computers are regularly used in art, college planning, economics, English, humanities, introduction to technology, library, literary magazine, mathematics, newspaper, photography, publications, Web site design, yearbook classes. Computer network features include on-campus library services, Internet access, wireless campus network, Internet filtering or blocking technology, homework online. Students grades are available online. The school has a published electronic and media policy.

Contact Ms. Danielle T. Dankey, Director of Admissions. 316-686-0152 Ext. 405. Fax: 316-686-3918. E-mail: danielle.dankey@theindependentschool.com. Website: www.theindependentschool.com

INDIAN CREEK SCHOOL

Lower, Middle Schools: 680 Evergreen Road and 1130 Anne Chambers Way
Upper School-1130 Anne Chambers Way
Crownsville, Maryland 21032

Head of School: Dr. Rick Branson

General Information college-preparatory school. Founded: 1973. Setting: small town. Nearest major city is Annapolis. 125-acre campus. 3 buildings on campus. Approved or accredited by Maryland Department of Education. Endowment: $35 million. Upper school average class size: 13. Upper School students typically attend 5 days per week. The average school day consists of 8 hours.

Special Academic Programs International Baccalaureate program; Advanced Placement exam preparation.

College Admission Counseling 49 students graduated in 2013; all went to college.

Student Life Upper grades have uniform requirement. Discipline rests equally with students and faculty.

Tuition and Aid Tuition installment plan (SMART Tuition Payment Plan). Merit scholarship grants, need-based scholarship grants available.

Admissions Traditional secondary-level entrance grade is 9. Application fee required: $50. Interview required.

Athletics Interscholastic: field hockey (girls), hockey (b), ice hockey (b); coed interscholastic: basketball, cross-country running, golf, horseback riding, lacrosse, sailing, soccer, tennis; coed intramural: aquatics, dance, equestrian sports, weight training. 15 coaches, 1 athletic trainer.

Computers Computer network features include on-campus library services, Internet access. Campus intranet and student e-mail accounts are available to students. The school has a published electronic and media policy.

Contact Ms. Tiffany McCormick, Director of Admission for Lower and Middle Schools. 410-923-3660. Fax: 410-923-0670. E-mail: tmccormick@indiancreekschool.org. Website: www.indiancreekschool.org

INSTITUTE OF NOTRE DAME

901 Aisquith Street
Baltimore, Maryland 21202-5499

Head of School: Dr. Mary L. Funke

General Information Girls' day college-preparatory, arts, business, religious studies, bilingual studies, and technology school, affiliated with Roman Catholic Church. Grades 9–12. Founded: 1847. Setting: urban. 2-acre campus. 1 building on campus. Approved or accredited by Association of Independent Maryland Schools, Middle States Association of Colleges and Schools, National Catholic Education Association, and Maryland Department of Education. Member of National Association of Independent Schools. Endowment: $5 million. Total enrollment: 367. Upper school average class size: 18. Upper school faculty-student ratio: 1:11. There are 180 required school days per year for Upper School students. Upper School students typically attend 5 days per week. The average school day consists of 6 hours and 20 minutes.

Upper School Student Profile Grade 9: 88 students (88 girls); Grade 10: 102 students (102 girls); Grade 11: 91 students (91 girls); Grade 12: 86 students (86 girls). 70% of students are Roman Catholic.

Faculty School total: 36. In upper school: 6 men, 30 women; 28 have advanced degrees.

Subjects Offered Accounting, algebra, American history, American literature, anatomy, art, Bible studies, biology, business, calculus, chemistry, Christianity, computer applications, computer math, computer programming, computer science, creative writing, criminal justice, dance, design, drama, drawing, driver education, earth science, engineering, English, English literature, environmental science, finance, fine arts, French, freshman seminar, geography, geology, geometry, government/civics, health, history, journalism, Latin, marine biology, mathematics, music, music history, physical education, physics, physiology, psychology, religion, science, social studies, sociology, Spanish, speech, theater, theology, trigonometry, women's studies, world history, world literature.

Graduation Requirements Arts and fine arts (art, music, dance, drama), business skills (includes word processing), computer science, English, foreign language, mathematics, physical education (includes health), religion (includes Bible studies and theology), science, social studies (includes history), 80 hours of community service.

Special Academic Programs 10 Advanced Placement exams for which test preparation is offered; honors section; accelerated programs; independent study; study at local college for college credit; academic accommodation for the gifted; remedial reading and/or remedial writing; remedial math.

College Admission Counseling Colleges students went to include Loyola University Maryland; Notre Dame of Maryland University; Stevenson University; Towson University; University of Maryland, Baltimore; University of Maryland, Baltimore County.

Student Life Upper grades have uniform requirement, student council, honor system. Discipline rests primarily with faculty. Attendance at religious services is required.

Summer Programs Remediation, enrichment, sports, art/fine arts, rigorous outdoor training, computer instruction programs offered; session focuses on community and incoming freshmen; held both on and off campus; held at Patterson Park, Herring Run Park, and Meadowood Regional Park; accepts girls; open to students from other schools. 150 students usually enrolled. 2014 schedule: June to July. Application deadline: none.

Tuition and Aid Day student tuition: $13,525. Tuition installment plan (monthly payment plans). Tuition reduction for siblings, merit scholarship grants, need-based scholarship grants, paying campus jobs, bank loans available. In 2013–14, 65% of upper-school students received aid; total upper-school merit-scholarship money awarded: $72,750. Total amount of financial aid awarded in 2013–14: $843,000.

Admissions Traditional secondary-level entrance grade is 9. For fall 2013, 220 students applied for upper-level admission, 195 were accepted, 88 enrolled. High School Placement Test required. Deadline for receipt of application materials: December 16. Application fee required: $30. On-campus interview required.

Athletics Interscholastic: aerobics/dance, badminton, basketball, cheering, crew, cross-country running, field hockey, golf, independent competitive sports, lacrosse, outdoor adventure, outdoors, physical training, pom squad, rowing, running, soccer, softball, strength & conditioning, swimming and diving, track and field, volleyball, winter (indoor) track, winter soccer; intramural: aerobics/dance, ballet, dance, dance squad, dance team, horseback riding, modern dance, outdoor adventure, self defense, weight training. 2 PE instructors, 27 coaches, 1 athletic trainer.

Computers Computers are regularly used in all academic classes. Computer network features include on-campus library services, online commercial services, Internet access, wireless campus network, Internet filtering or blocking technology. Campus intranet, student e-mail accounts, and computer access in designated common areas are available to students. Students grades are available online. The school has a published electronic and media policy.

Contact Ms. Helen Bruns, Director of Admissions. 410-522-7800 Ext. 220. Fax: 410-522-7810. E-mail: hbruns@indofmd.org. Website: www.indofmd.org

INSTITUT MONTE ROSA

57 Av. de Chillon
Montreux 1820, Switzerland

General Information Coeducational boarding and day college-preparatory, business, and bilingual studies school. Grades 7–12. Founded: 1874. Setting: small town. Students are housed in single-sex dormitories. 6-hectare campus. 2 buildings on campus. Approved or accredited by Swiss Federation of Private Schools. Languages of instruction: English and French. Upper school average class size: 8. Upper school faculty-student ratio: 1:5.

Special Academic Programs Advanced Placement exam preparation; ESL.

Student Life Upper grades have specified standards of dress, honor system. Discipline rests equally with students and faculty.

Summer Programs ESL, sports programs offered; session focuses on languages; held on campus; accepts boys and girls; open to students from other schools. 100 students usually enrolled.

Admissions Math and English placement tests required. Deadline for receipt of application materials: none. Application fee required: 800 Swiss francs. Interview recommended.

Athletics Coed Intramural: aerobics/dance, alpine skiing, aquatics, archery, badminton, basketball, bicycling, canoeing/kayaking, climbing, dance, equestrian sports, fitness, football, freestyle skiing, golf, gymnastics, handball, horseback riding, ice hockey, ice skating, indoor soccer, kayaking, modern dance, mountain biking, mountaineering, outdoor activities, outdoor education, outdoor recreation, paddling, physical fitness, physical training, rafting, skiing (cross-country), skiing (downhill), snowboarding, soccer, swimming and diving, tennis, water skiing.

Computers Computer resources include Internet access, wireless campus network, Internet filtering or blocking technology.

INTERLOCHEN ARTS ACADEMY

PO Box 199
4000 Highway M-137
Interlochen, Michigan 49643-0199

Head of School: Mr. Jeffrey S. Kimpton

General Information Coeducational boarding and day college-preparatory and arts school. Grades 9–PG. Founded: 1962. Setting: rural. Nearest major city is Traverse City. Students are housed in single-sex dormitories. 1,200-acre campus. 225 buildings on campus. Approved or accredited by North Central Association of Colleges and Schools and Michigan Department of Education. Member of National Association of Independent Schools and Secondary School Admission Test Board. Endowment: $61.7 million. Total enrollment: 471. Upper school average class size: 13. Upper school faculty-student ratio: 1:6. There are 151 required school days per year for Upper School students. Upper School students typically attend 5 days per week. The average school day consists of 6 hours and 40 minutes.

Upper School Student Profile Grade 9: 45 students (16 boys, 29 girls); Grade 10: 76 students (28 boys, 48 girls); Grade 11: 132 students (48 boys, 84 girls); Grade 12: 203 students (80 boys, 123 girls); Postgraduate: 15 students (9 boys, 6 girls). 95% of students are boarding students. 20% are state residents. 47 states are represented in upper school student body. 22% are international students. International students from Canada, China, Hong Kong, Mexico, Republic of Korea, and Taiwan; 21 other countries represented in student body.

Faculty School total: 82. In upper school: 43 men, 39 women; 74 have advanced degrees; 28 reside on campus.

Subjects Offered Algebra, American history, American literature, art, ballet, ballet technique, biology, British literature, calculus, ceramics, chamber groups, chemistry, chemistry-AP, choir, choral music, choreography, civil war history, computer math, computer science, contemporary art, creative writing, current events, dance, dance performance, drafting, drama, dramatic arts, earth science, ecology, English, English literature, environmental science, European history, expository writing, film, fine arts, French, geometry, government/civics, health, history, mathematics, music, philosophy, photography, physical education, physics, science, social studies, Spanish, speech, statistics, theater, trigonometry, world history, world literature, writing.

Graduation Requirements Arts and fine arts (art, music, dance, drama), English, mathematics, physical education (includes health), science, social studies (includes history).

Special Academic Programs Advanced Placement exam preparation; accelerated programs; independent study; term-away projects; academic accommodation for the gifted, the musically talented, and the artistically talented; ESL (41 students enrolled).

College Admission Counseling 217 students graduated in 2012; 206 went to college, including New York University; Oberlin College; University of Michigan; University of Rochester. Other: 5 entered a postgraduate year, 6 had other specific plans. Mean SAT critical reading: 586, mean SAT math: 558, mean SAT writing: 564, mean combined SAT: 1707, mean composite ACT: 25. 44% scored over 600 on SAT critical reading, 29% scored over 600 on SAT math, 33% scored over 600 on SAT writing, 32% scored over 1800 on combined SAT, 38% scored over 26 on composite ACT.

Student Life Upper grades have uniform requirement, student council, honor system. Discipline rests primarily with faculty.

Tuition and Aid Day student tuition: $30,580; 7-day tuition and room/board: $48,520. Tuition installment plan (monthly payment plans, individually arranged payment plans, Sallie Mae, Your Tuition Solution, PrepGate). Merit scholarship grants, need-based scholarship grants available. In 2012–13, 79% of upper-school students received aid; total upper-school merit-scholarship money awarded: $1,065,000. Total amount of financial aid awarded in 2012–13: $8,844,645.

Admissions Traditional secondary-level entrance grade is 11. For fall 2012, 1,083 students applied for upper-level admission, 582 were accepted, 471 enrolled. Achievement tests, any standardized test, audition, essay, placement test or SSAT required. Deadline for receipt of application materials: none. Application fee required: $60. Interview recommended.

Athletics 1 PE instructor.

Computers Computers are regularly used in graphic arts, mathematics, music, science, video film production classes. Computer network features include on-campus library services, online commercial services, Internet access, wireless campus network. Campus intranet and student e-mail accounts are available to students. The school has a published electronic and media policy.

Contact Jim Bekkering, Director of Admission and Financial Aid. 231-276-7472. Fax: 231-276-7464. E-mail: admission@interlochen.org. Website: www.interlochen.org

INTERMOUNTAIN CHRISTIAN SCHOOL

6515 South Lion Lane

Salt Lake City, Utah 84121

Head of School: Dean James Kerr

General Information Coeducational day college-preparatory, general academic, arts, business, and religious studies school, affiliated with Evangelical Free Church of America, Christian faith. Grades PK–12. Founded: 1982. Setting: suburban. 6-acre campus. 1 building on campus. Approved or accredited by Association of Christian Schools International, Northwest Accreditation Commission, Northwest Association of Schools and Colleges, and Utah Department of Education. Endowment: $79,000. Total enrollment: 285. Upper school average class size: 17. Upper school faculty-student ratio: 1:9. There are 180 required school days per year for Upper School students. Upper School students typically attend 5 days per week. The average school day consists of 7 hours.

Upper School Student Profile Grade 6: 21 students (8 boys, 13 girls); Grade 7: 22 students (9 boys, 13 girls); Grade 8: 18 students (13 boys, 5 girls); Grade 9: 21 students (10 boys, 11 girls); Grade 10: 10 students (5 boys, 5 girls); Grade 11: 10 students (5 boys, 5 girls); Grade 12: 14 students (8 boys, 6 girls). 97% of students are members of Evangelical Free Church of America, Christian.

Faculty School total: 33. In upper school: 7 men, 6 women; 9 have advanced degrees.

Subjects Offered Advanced Placement courses, algebra, American government, American history, American literature, American literature-AP, art, athletics, baseball, basketball, bell choir, Bible, biology, calculus, career education, ceramics, chemistry, choir, chorus, Christian doctrine, church history, community service, composition, computer science, computer skills, concert band, concert bell choir, concert choir, current events, debate, drama, drama performance, economics, economics and history, electives, English, English literature-AP, environmental science-AP, European history, European literature, family and consumer science, finance, fine arts, food science, geometry, government, handbells, health, history, independent study, instrumental music, jazz band, keyboarding, leadership and service, Life of Christ, mathematics, peer ministry, physical education, physics, pre-algebra, pre-calculus, science, senior seminar, sex education, social studies, Spanish, statistics, U.S. government, U.S. history, vocal ensemble, volleyball, world geography, world history.

Graduation Requirements Arts and fine arts (art, music, dance, drama), Bible, computer science, English, finance, foreign language, mathematics, physical education (includes health), science, social studies (includes history), class trips. Community service is required.

Special Academic Programs 3 Advanced Placement exams for which test preparation is offered; honors section; study at local college for college credit.

College Admission Counseling 15 students graduated in 2013; all went to college, including Clemson University; Grand Canyon University; Northwest Nazarene University; The University of Alabama; University of Utah. Mean SAT critical reading: 581, mean SAT math: 590, mean SAT writing: 543, mean combined SAT: 1714, mean composite ACT: 25. 33% scored over 600 on SAT critical reading, 44% scored over 600 on SAT math, 22% scored over 600 on SAT writing, 44% scored over 1800 on combined SAT, 38% scored over 26 on composite ACT.

Student Life Upper grades have specified standards of dress, student council, honor system. Discipline rests primarily with faculty. Attendance at religious services is required.

Tuition and Aid Day student tuition: $6470. Tuition installment plan (Insured Tuition Payment Plan, monthly payment plans, discounted up-front tuition payment). Tuition reduction for siblings, need-based scholarship grants available. In 2013–14, 19% of upper-school students received aid. Total amount of financial aid awarded in 2013–14: $24,904.

Admissions Traditional secondary-level entrance grade is 9. For fall 2013, 5 students applied for upper-level admission, 5 were accepted, 5 enrolled. School's own test required. Deadline for receipt of application materials: none. Application fee required: $90. On-campus interview required.

Athletics Interscholastic: baseball (boys), basketball (b,g), golf (b,g), soccer (b,g), volleyball (g). 2 PE instructors, 4 coaches.

Computers Computers are regularly used in art, computer applications, technology, writing classes. Computer network features include Internet access, wireless campus network, Internet filtering or blocking technology. Students grades are available online. The school has a published electronic and media policy.

Contact Eileen Rocco, Registrar. 801-942-8811. Fax: 801-942-8813. E-mail: rocco_e@slcics.org. Website: www.slcics.org

INTERNATIONAL HIGH SCHOOL

150 Oak Street

San Francisco, California 94102

Head of School: Ms. Ellen Deitsch Stern

General Information Coeducational day college-preparatory, arts, business, bilingual studies, technology, and Philosophy school. Grades PK–12. Founded: 1962. Setting: urban. 3-acre campus. 3 buildings on campus. Approved or accredited by Council of International Schools, French Ministry of Education, International Baccalaureate Organization, Western Association of Schools and Colleges, and California Department of Education. Member of National Association of Independent Schools, Secondary School Admission Test Board, and European Council of International Schools. Languages of instruction: English and French. Endowment: $5.1 million. Total enrollment: 1,046. Upper school average class size: 17. Upper school faculty-student ratio: 1:10. There are 165 required school days per year for Upper School students. Upper School students typically attend 5 days per week. The average school day consists of 7 hours.

Upper School Student Profile Grade 9: 89 students (43 boys, 46 girls); Grade 10: 79 students (38 boys, 41 girls); Grade 11: 88 students (36 boys, 52 girls); Grade 12: 81 students (35 boys, 46 girls).

Faculty School total: 139. In upper school: 33 men, 30 women; 35 have advanced degrees.

Subjects Offered Advanced chemistry, advanced math, algebra, American history, American literature, art, biology, calculus, chemistry, community service, current events, drama, earth science, economics, English, English literature, environmental science, ESL, European history, fine arts, French, geography, geometry, German, government/civics, history, International Baccalaureate courses, Mandarin, mathematics, music, philosophy, physical education, physics, science, social studies, Spanish, theater, theory of knowledge, trigonometry, world history, world literature, writing.

Graduation Requirements Arts and fine arts (art, music, dance, drama), English, foreign language, International Baccalaureate courses, mathematics, physical education (includes health), science, social studies (includes history), theory of knowledge, extended essay, 150 hours of CAS.

Special Academic Programs International Baccalaureate program; honors section; independent study; term-away projects; study abroad; academic accommodation for the gifted, the musically talented, and the artistically talented; ESL (12 students enrolled).

College Admission Counseling 73 students graduated in 2013; all went to college, including Boston University; McGill University; New York University; Oberlin College; University of California, Berkeley; University of California, Santa Cruz. Mean SAT critical reading: 614, mean SAT math: 615, mean SAT writing: 614.

Student Life Upper grades have student council. Discipline rests equally with students and faculty.

Summer Programs Remediation, enrichment, advancement programs offered; session focuses on enrichment; held on campus; accepts boys and girls; open to students from other schools. 15 students usually enrolled.

Tuition and Aid Day student tuition: $33,740. Tuition installment plan (FACTS Tuition Payment Plan). Need-based scholarship grants, French bourse available. In 2013–14, 25% of upper-school students received aid. Total amount of financial aid awarded in 2013–14: $748,000.

Admissions Traditional secondary-level entrance grade is 9. For fall 2013, 265 students applied for upper-level admission, 171 were accepted, 67 enrolled. Any standardized test, SSAT or writing sample required. Deadline for receipt of application materials: January 16. Application fee required: $100. Interview required.

Athletics Interscholastic: baseball (boys, girls), basketball (b,g), football (b), soccer (b,g), volleyball (b,g); intramural: ballet (b,g), baseball (b), basketball (b,g), floor hockey (b,g), soccer (b,g), softball (g), tennis (b,g), volleyball (b,g); coed interscholastic: badminton, cross-country running, swimming and diving, tennis, track and field; coed intramural: badminton, ballet, cross-country running, fencing, flagball, golf, handball, indoor hockey, outdoor activities, outdoor adventure, physical fitness, physical training, swimming and diving, water polo, weight training. 4 PE instructors, 8 coaches, 3 athletic trainers.

Computers Computers are regularly used in all academic classes. Computer network features include on-campus library services, online commercial services, Internet access, wireless campus network, iPad program for all high school students. Campus intranet, student e-mail accounts, and computer access in designated common areas are available to students. Students grades are available online. The school has a published electronic and media policy.

Contact Ms. Erin Cronin, Associate Director of Admission. 415-558-2093. Fax: 415-558-2085. E-mail: erinc@internationalsf.org. Website: www.internationalsf.org

INTERNATIONAL SCHOOL BANGKOK

39/7 Soi Nichada Thani, Samakee Road

Pakkret 11120, Thailand

Head of School: Dr. Andrew Davies

General Information Coeducational day college-preparatory, arts, and technology school. Grades PK–12. Founded: 1951. Setting: suburban. Nearest major city is Bangkok, Thailand. 37-acre campus. 2 buildings on campus. Approved or accredited by Ministry of Education (Thailand), Western Association of Schools and Colleges, and state department of education. Affiliate member of National Association of Independent Schools; member of European Council of International Schools. Language of instruction: English. Total enrollment: 1,896. Upper school average class size: 18. Upper school faculty-student ratio: 1:10. There are 183 required school days per year for Upper School students. Upper School students typically attend 5 days per week. The average school day consists of 6 hours.

Faculty School total: 229.

Subjects Offered 3-dimensional design, algebra, American history, American literature, art, art history, biology, business, business education, business studies, calculus, calculus-AP, ceramics, chemistry, choir, computer math, computer science, concert band, creative writing, dance, drama, drawing, drawing and design, Dutch, earth science, ecology, economics, economics and history, electives, English, English literature, environmental education, environmental science, environmental studies, ESL, European history, expository writing, fine arts, French, French studies, geography, geology, geometry, German, government/civics, health, history, humanities, industrial arts, Japanese, journalism, language arts, languages, mathematics, music, performing arts, philosophy, photography, physical education, physics, psychology, reading, robotics, science, social studies, sociology, Spanish, speech, statistics, Thai, theater, theory of knowledge, trigonometry, world history, world literature, writing.

Graduation Requirements Arts and fine arts (art, music, dance, drama), English, mathematics, physical education (includes health), science, social studies (includes history), community service hours, Senior Seminar, Global Citizenship Week, Thailand and Southeast Asia course. Community service is required.

Special Academic Programs International Baccalaureate program; Advanced Placement exam preparation; ESL.

College Admission Counseling 146 students graduated in 2013; all went to college, including Boston University; Northeastern University; Penn State University Park; The University of British Columbia; University of California, Los Angeles; University of Oregon.

Student Life Upper grades have uniform requirement, student council, honor system. Discipline rests primarily with faculty.

Summer Programs Remediation, enrichment, ESL, art/fine arts programs offered; held on campus; accepts boys and girls; open to students from other schools. 400 students usually enrolled. 2014 schedule: June to July. Application deadline: June 3.

Tuition and Aid Day student tuition: 803,000 Thai bahts. Tuition installment plan (individually arranged payment plans).

Admissions Math and English placement tests and school's own exam required. Deadline for receipt of application materials: none. Application fee required: 4500 Thai bahts. On-campus interview required.

Athletics Interscholastic: aquatics (boys, girls), badminton (b,g), basketball (b,g), cross-country running (b,g), dance (b,g), rugby (b,g), running (b,g), soccer (b,g), softball (b,g), swimming and diving (b,g), tennis (b,g), track and field (b,g), volleyball (b,g); intramural: aquatics (b,g), badminton (b,g), basketball (b,g), cross-country running (b,g), dance (b,g), fencing (b), rugby (b,g), running (b,g), swimming and diving (b,g), track and field (b,g), volleyball (b,g); coed interscholastic: dance team. 5 PE instructors.

Computers Computers are regularly used in all academic classes. Computer network features include on-campus library services, Internet access, wireless campus network, Internet filtering or blocking technology. Campus intranet, student e-mail accounts, and computer access in designated common areas are available to students. Students grades are available online. The school has a published electronic and media policy.

Contact Ms. Wendy Van Bramer, Admissions Director. 662-963-5800. Fax: 662-960-4103. E-mail: register@isb.ac.th. Website: www.isb.ac.th

INTERNATIONAL SCHOOL MANILA

University Parkway
Fort Bonifacio
1634 Taguig City, Philippines

Head of School: Supt. David Toze

General Information Coeducational day college-preparatory, arts, business, bilingual studies, and technology school. Grades PS–12. Founded: 1920. Setting: urban. Nearest major city is Manila, Philippines. 7-hectare campus. 1 building on campus. Approved or accredited by Western Association of Schools and Colleges. Affiliate member of National Association of Independent Schools; member of Secondary School Admission Test Board. Language of instruction: English. Endowment: $2 million. Total enrollment: 2,200. Upper school average class size: 16. Upper school faculty-student ratio: 1:9. There are 180 required school days per year for Upper School students. Upper School students typically attend 5 days per week. The average school day consists of 5 hours and 50 minutes.

Upper School Student Profile Grade 9: 196 students (98 boys, 98 girls); Grade 10: 195 students (96 boys, 99 girls); Grade 11: 193 students (92 boys, 101 girls); Grade 12: 196 students (100 boys, 96 girls).

Faculty School total: 220. In upper school: 42 men, 38 women; 60 have advanced degrees.

Subjects Offered Acting, anthropology, art, athletic training, band, Basic programming, biology, business, calculus-AP, chemistry, Chinese, choir, college

admission preparation, college awareness, college counseling, college placement, college planning, computer applications, computer graphics, computer literacy, computer multimedia, computer programming, computer science, creative writing, critical writing, dance, desktop publishing, digital photography, economics, economics and history, English, environmental science, ESL, film, filmmaking, foreign language, French, French as a second language, general science, geography, graphic design, health, health and wellness, health education, information technology, integrated mathematics, International Baccalaureate courses, international relations, Japanese, Japanese as Second Language, jazz band, leadership, math applications, math methods, mathematics, media studies, music, orchestra, parenting, peer counseling, personal fitness, Philippine culture, physical science, physics, political science, pre-calculus, programming, psychology, reading/study skills, remedial study skills, research, service learning/internship, sex education, Spanish, theater, theater arts, theory of knowledge, track and field, U.S. history, U.S. history-AP, video film production, visual and performing arts, visual arts, weight fitness, weight training, world history, world religions, writing.

Special Academic Programs International Baccalaureate program; Advanced Placement exam preparation; honors section; accelerated programs; independent study; academic accommodation for the gifted, the musically talented, and the artistically talented; remedial reading and/or remedial writing; remedial math; programs in English, mathematics, general development for dyslexic students; special instructional classes for deaf students; ESL (166 students enrolled).

College Admission Counseling 187 students graduated in 2013; all went to college, including New York University; Penn State University Park; Purdue University; The University of British Columbia; University of California, Berkeley; University of Southern California. Mean SAT critical reading: 581, mean SAT math: 649, mean SAT writing: 603, mean combined SAT: 1832, mean composite ACT: 26.

Student Life Upper grades have uniform requirement, student council, honor system. Discipline rests primarily with faculty.

Summer Programs ESL, sports programs offered; session focuses on academics for ESL; held on campus; accepts boys and girls; open to students from other schools. 80 students usually enrolled. 2014 schedule: June 10 to July 10. Application deadline: none.

Tuition and Aid Day student tuition: $24,000. Tuition installment plan (monthly payment plans, individually arranged payment plans, quarterly payment plan). Scholarships for low-income local students available.

Admissions Traditional secondary-level entrance grade is 9. For fall 2013, 273 students applied for upper-level admission, 76 were accepted, 76 enrolled. Iowa Tests of Basic Skills required. Deadline for receipt of application materials: none. Application fee required: $500. On-campus interview recommended.

Athletics Interscholastic: badminton (boys, girls), basketball (b,g), cheering (g), cross-country running (b,g), golf (b,g), gymnastics (b,g), martial arts (b,g), rugby (b,g), soccer (b,g), softball (b,g), swimming and diving (b,g), table tennis (b,g), tennis (b,g), track and field (b,g), volleyball (b,g), wall climbing (b,g); intramural: rugby (b,g), wall climbing (b,g), water polo (b,g); coed interscholastic: dance, wall climbing; coed intramural: volleyball, wall climbing. 5 PE instructors, 10 coaches.

Computers Computers are regularly used in art, English, foreign language, history, mathematics, music, science classes. Computer network features include on-campus library services, online commercial services, Internet access, wireless campus network, Internet filtering or blocking technology. Campus intranet, student e-mail accounts, and computer access in designated common areas are available to students. Students grades are available online. The school has a published electronic and media policy.

Contact Stephanie Hagedorn, Director of Admissions and Advancement. 63-2-840-8488. Fax: 63-2-840-8489. E-mail: admission@ismanila.org. Website: www.ismanila.org

INTERNATIONAL SCHOOL OF AMSTERDAM

Sportlaan 45
Amstelveen 1185 TB, Netherlands

Head of School: Dr. Ed Greene

General Information Coeducational day college-preparatory, arts, bilingual studies, and technology school. Grades PS–12. Founded: 1964. Setting: suburban. Nearest major city is Amsterdam, Netherlands. 1-acre campus. 2 buildings on campus. Approved or accredited by New England Association of Schools and Colleges. Member of European Council of International Schools. Language of instruction: English. Total enrollment: 1,008. Upper school average class size: 20. Upper school faculty-student ratio: 1:5. There are 177 required school days per year for Upper School students. Upper School students typically attend 5 days per week. The average school day consists of 7 hours.

Upper School Student Profile Grade 9: 67 students (39 boys, 28 girls); Grade 10: 62 students (32 boys, 30 girls); Grade 11: 64 students (28 boys, 36 girls); Grade 12: 53 students (26 boys, 27 girls).

Faculty School total: 180. In upper school: 29 men, 42 women; 28 have advanced degrees.

Subjects Offered Addiction, advanced math, algebra, American literature, art, biology, calculus, chemistry, community service, computer programming, computer science, drama, Dutch, economics, English, English literature, ESL, European history, food science, French, geography, geometry, German, history, Japanese, mathematics, music, photography, physical education, physics, science, social sciences, social studies, Spanish, technology, theater, theory of knowledge, trigonometry, world history, world literature.

Graduation Requirements Arts, computer science, English, foreign language, mathematics, physical education (includes health), science, social sciences, social studies (includes history). Community service is required.

Special Academic Programs International Baccalaureate program; independent study; academic accommodation for the gifted, the musically talented, and the artistically talented; remedial reading and/or remedial writing; remedial math; programs in English, mathematics, general development for dyslexic students; ESL (19 students enrolled).

College Admission Counseling 48 students graduated in 2012; 38 went to college, including Austin College; Brandeis University; Suffolk University; University of Arkansas. Other: 1 entered military service, 9 had other specific plans. Median SAT critical reading: 590, median SAT math: 630, median SAT writing: 600, median combined SAT: 1770. 45% scored over 600 on SAT critical reading, 55% scored over 600 on SAT math, 55% scored over 600 on SAT writing, 45% scored over 1800 on combined SAT.

Student Life Upper grades have specified standards of dress, student council, honor system. Discipline rests primarily with faculty.

Tuition and Aid Day student tuition: €21,375–€22,050. Tuition installment plan (monthly payment plans, individually arranged payment plans).

Admissions Traditional secondary-level entrance grade is 9. For fall 2012, 69 students applied for upper-level admission, 38 were accepted, 24 enrolled. Deadline for receipt of application materials: none. No application fee required. On-campus interview required.

Athletics Interscholastic: basketball (boys, girls), soccer (b,g), softball (b,g), swimming and diving (b,g), tennis (b,g), track and field (b,g), volleyball (g); coed intramural: aerobics, aerobics/dance, badminton, basketball, cricket, fitness, handball, hockey, netball, rugby, running, soccer, softball, tennis, track and field, volleyball. 7 PE instructors, 14 coaches, 14 athletic trainers.

Computers Computers are regularly used in art, drawing and design, English, foreign language, information technology, keyboarding, library, mathematics, music, science, yearbook classes. Computer network features include on-campus library services, online commercial services, Internet access, Internet filtering or blocking technology. Campus intranet and student e-mail accounts are available to students.

Contact Julia True, Director of Admissions. 31-20-347-1111. Fax: 31-20-347-1105. E-mail: admissions@isa.nl. Website: www.isa.nl

INTERNATIONAL SCHOOL OF INDIANA

4330 North Michigan Road
Indianapolis, Indiana 46208

Head of School: David Garner

General Information Coeducational day college-preparatory and bilingual studies school. Grades 5–12. Founded: 1994. Setting: urban. 63-acre campus. 4 buildings on campus. Approved or accredited by French Ministry of Education, Independent Schools Association of the Central States, International Baccalaureate Organization, and Indiana Department of Education. Member of National Association of Independent Schools and European Council of International Schools. Upper school average class size: 18. There are 180 required school days per year for Upper School students. Upper School students typically attend 5 days per week. The average school day consists of 7 hours and 35 minutes.

Subjects Offered International Baccalaureate courses.

Graduation Requirements International Baccalaureate courses.

Special Academic Programs International Baccalaureate program; study abroad; ESL (50 students enrolled).

College Admission Counseling 34 students graduated in 2013; all went to college, including Ball State University; Indiana University Bloomington; Purdue University. Mean SAT critical reading: 580, mean SAT math: 588, mean SAT writing: 590, mean combined SAT: 1758, mean composite ACT: 25.

Student Life Upper grades have specified standards of dress, student council, honor system. Discipline rests primarily with faculty.

Summer Programs Enrichment, ESL, sports, art/fine arts programs offered; session focuses on Languages and Sport Specific Camps-clinics; held on campus; accepts boys and girls; open to students from other schools. 70 students usually enrolled. 2014 schedule: June 10 to July 20. Application deadline: June 5.

Tuition and Aid Day student tuition: $16,608. Tuition installment plan (monthly payment plans). Merit scholarship grants, need-based scholarship grants available. In 2013–14, 24% of upper-school students received aid.

Admissions ISEE required. Deadline for receipt of application materials: none. Application fee required: $50. Interview required.

Athletics Interscholastic: basketball (boys, girls), crew (b,g), cross-country running (b,g), diving (g), golf (b,g), indoor track (b,g), indoor track & field (b,g), lacrosse (b,g), rowing (b,g), running (b,g), soccer (b,g), swimming and diving (b,g), tennis (b,g), track and field (b,g), volleyball (b,g), winter (indoor) track (b,g); intramural: badminton (b,g), fencing (b,g), fitness (b,g), flag football (b,g), floor hockey (b,g), Frisbee (b,g), gymnastics (b,g), indoor soccer (b,g), jogging (b,g), jump rope (b,g), kickball (b,g), modern dance (b,g), netball (b,g), outdoor activities (b,g), outdoor adventure (b,g), outdoor education (b,g), outdoor recreation (b,g), outdoor skills (b,g), outdoors (b,g), physical fitness (b,g), physical training (b,g), racquetball (b,g), rock climbing (b,g), roller blading (b,g), roller skating (b,g), ropes courses (b,g), rowing (b,g), rugby (b,g), running (b,g), sailing (b,g), self defense (b,g), skateboarding (b,g), skiing (cross-country) (b,g), skiing (downhill) (b,g), snowboarding (b,g), soccer (b,g), street hockey (b,g), strength & conditioning (b,g), synchronized swimming (g), table tennis (b,g), team handball (b,g), touch football (b,g), triathlon (b,g), ultimate Frisbee (b,g), walking (b,g), wall climbing (b,g), weight lifting (b,g), weight training (b,g), winter soccer (b,g), yoga (b,g); coed intramural: cricket. 4 PE instructors, 33 coaches, 1 athletic trainer.

Computers Computer network features include wireless campus network. Student e-mail accounts are available to students. The school has a published electronic and media policy.

Contact Kate Lock, Director of Admissions. 317-923-1951 Ext. 369. Fax: 317-923-1910. E-mail: klock@isind.org. Website: www.isind.org/

THE INTERNATIONAL SCHOOL OF LONDON

139 Gunnersbury Avenue
London W3 8LG, United Kingdom

Head of School: Mr. Huw Davies

General Information Coeducational day college-preparatory school. Grades K–12. Founded: 1972. Setting: urban. 2 buildings on campus. Member of European Council of International Schools. Language of instruction: English. Total enrollment: 340. Upper school average class size: 18. Upper school faculty-student ratio: 1:8. Upper School students typically attend 5 days per week.

Upper School Student Profile Grade 11: 30 students (15 boys, 15 girls); Grade 12: 30 students (15 boys, 15 girls).

Faculty School total: 67. In upper school: 15 men, 16 women; 21 have advanced degrees.

Subjects Offered Art, economics, English, French, geography, history, languages, mathematics, music, physical education, science, social sciences, Spanish, world affairs.

Graduation Requirements Foreign language, mathematics, science, social sciences. Community service is required.

Special Academic Programs International Baccalaureate program; ESL (47 students enrolled).

College Admission Counseling 22 students graduated in 2012; all went to college, including University of London; University of Oxford.

Student Life Upper grades have student council. Discipline rests primarily with faculty.

Tuition and Aid Day student tuition: £19,500.

Admissions For fall 2012, 36 students applied for upper-level admission, 30 were accepted, 30 enrolled. Deadline for receipt of application materials: July 30. Application fee required: £200. Interview recommended.

Athletics Interscholastic: basketball (boys, girls), soccer (b); intramural: badminton (b,g), softball (b,g), swimming and diving (b,g), table tennis (b,g), tennis (b,g); coed interscholastic: soccer; coed intramural: softball, swimming and diving, table tennis, tennis. 2 PE instructors, 2 coaches.

Computers Computers are regularly used in English, foreign language, mathematics, science classes. Computer network features include on-campus library services, Internet access, wireless campus network, Internet filtering or blocking technology. Student e-mail accounts are available to students. The school has a published electronic and media policy.

Contact Mr. Yoel Gordon, Director of Admissions. 20-8992-5823. Fax: 44-8993-7012. E-mail: ygordon@isllondon.org. Website: www.isllondon.org

IONA PREPARATORY SCHOOL

255 Wilmot Road
New Rochelle, New York 10804

Head of School: Br. Thomas Leto

General Information Boys' day college-preparatory, arts, religious studies, and technology school, affiliated with Roman Catholic Church. Grades 9–12. Founded: 1916. Setting: suburban. Nearest major city is New York. 27-acre campus. 3 buildings on campus. Approved or accredited by Christian Brothers Association, Middle States Association of Colleges and Schools, National Catholic Education Association, New York State Association of Independent Schools, and New York State Board of Regents. Member of National Association of Independent Schools. Endowment: $6 million. Total enrollment: 785. Upper school average class size: 23. Upper school faculty-student ratio: 1:13. There are 180 required school days per year for Upper School students. Upper School students typically attend 5 days per week. The average school day consists of 6 hours and 30 minutes.

Upper School Student Profile Grade 9: 213 students (213 boys); Grade 10: 195 students (195 boys); Grade 11: 188 students (188 boys); Grade 12: 189 students (189 boys). 87% of students are Roman Catholic.

Faculty School total: 67. In upper school: 47 men, 18 women; 65 have advanced degrees.

Subjects Offered Accounting, Advanced Placement courses, algebra, American history, American history-AP, American literature, anatomy, art, astronomy, biology, biology-AP, British literature, calculus, chemistry, chemistry-AP, communications, community service, composition-AP, computer programming, computer science, economics, English, English literature-AP, English/composition-AP, environmental science, European history, European history-AP, European literature, fine arts, French, French as a second language, geometry, government-AP, graphic design, health, health and safety, history, Italian, Latin, media, music, painting, physical education, physics, physiology, psychology, psychology-AP, religion, science, social sciences, social studies, Spanish, trigonometry, U.S. government and politics-AP, word processing, world literature, world religions.

Graduation Requirements Art, computer science, English, foreign language, mathematics, music, physical education (includes health), religion (includes Bible studies and theology), science, social studies (includes history), 100 hours of community service.

Special Academic Programs Advanced Placement exam preparation; honors section; study at local college for college credit; study abroad; academic accommodation for the gifted.

College Admission Counseling 180 students graduated in 2012; all went to college, including Boston College; Fairfield University; Fordham University; Iona College; Loyola University Maryland. Mean SAT critical reading: 610, mean SAT math: 620. 30% scored over 600 on SAT critical reading, 39% scored over 600 on SAT math.

Student Life Upper grades have specified standards of dress, student council, honor system. Discipline rests primarily with faculty. Attendance at religious services is required.

Tuition and Aid Day student tuition: $15,300. Tuition installment plan (monthly payment plans, individually arranged payment plans, 10-payment plan, semester payment plan). Merit scholarship grants, need-based scholarship grants available. In 2012–13, 31% of upper-school students received aid; total upper-school merit-scholarship money awarded: $190,000. Total amount of financial aid awarded in 2012–13: $325,000.

Admissions Traditional secondary-level entrance grade is 9. For fall 2012, 913 students applied for upper-level admission, 560 were accepted, 213 enrolled. Admissions testing, Catholic High School Entrance Examination, ISEE, SSAT, Test of Achievement and Proficiency or writing sample required. Deadline for receipt of application materials: none. No application fee required. Interview recommended.

Athletics Interscholastic: badminton, baseball, basketball, bowling, climbing, crew, cross-country running, diving, field hockey, flag football, football, golf, ice hockey, indoor track, indoor track & field, lacrosse, paint ball, physical fitness, rock climbing, running, soccer, swimming and diving, tennis, track and field, ultimate Frisbee, volleyball, weight lifting, weight training, winter (indoor) track, wrestling; intramural: baseball, basketball, climbing, fitness, flag football, floor hockey, Frisbee, physical fitness, physical training, rock climbing, soccer, strength & conditioning, tennis, volleyball, wall climbing, weight lifting. 3 PE instructors, 40 coaches, 1 athletic trainer.

Computers Computers are regularly used in all classes. Computer network features include on-campus library services, online commercial services, Internet access, wireless campus network, Internet filtering or blocking technology. Campus intranet and student e-mail accounts are available to students. The school has a published electronic and media policy.

Contact Mrs. Judy M. Musho, Director of Admissions. 914-632-0714 Ext. 215. Fax: 914-632-9760. E-mail: jmusho@ionaprep.org. Website: www.ionaprep.org

ISTANBUL INTERNATIONAL COMMUNITY SCHOOL

Buyukcekmece Karaagac Mahallesi 51. Sokak
Buyukcekmece
Istanbul 34500, Turkey

Head of School: Ms. Jane Thompson

General Information Coeducational day college-preparatory, general academic, and International Baccalaureate school. Grades 1–12. Founded: 1911. Setting: rural. 16-hectare campus. 4 buildings on campus. Approved or accredited by Council of International Schools, International Baccalaureate Organization, New England Association of Schools and Colleges, Northwest Association of Schools and Colleges, and The College Board. Affiliate member of National Association of Independent Schools; member of European Council of International Schools. Language of instruction: English. Endowment: $7 million. Total enrollment: 578. Upper school average class size: 20. Upper school faculty-student ratio: 1:9. There are 178 required school days per year for Upper School students. Upper School students typically attend 5 days per week. The average school day consists of 5 hours and 30 minutes.

Upper School Student Profile Grade 7: 45 students (26 boys, 19 girls); Grade 8: 55 students (35 boys, 20 girls); Grade 9: 44 students (23 boys, 21 girls); Grade 10: 37 students (23 boys, 14 girls); Grade 11: 55 students (27 boys, 28 girls); Grade 12: 32 students (20 boys, 12 girls).

Faculty School total: 76. In upper school: 21 men, 19 women; 24 have advanced degrees.

Graduation Requirements International Baccalaureate courses.

Special Academic Programs International Baccalaureate program; ESL.

College Admission Counseling 44 students graduated in 2013; 33 went to college, including Northeastern University; Skidmore College; Tufts University; Wheaton College. Mean SAT critical reading: 540, mean SAT math: 620, mean SAT writing: 660.

Student Life Upper grades have student council, honor system. Discipline rests primarily with faculty.

Tuition and Aid Day student tuition: $14,950–$29,900.

Admissions Comprehensive educational evaluation, English proficiency, school's own test or writing sample required. Application fee required: $1100. Interview required.

Athletics Interscholastic: basketball (boys, girls), equestrian sports (b,g), soccer (b,g), softball (b,g), volleyball (b,g); intramural: basketball (b,g), cross-country running (b,g), soccer (b,g), softball (b,g), volleyball (b,g); coed interscholastic: aquatics, badminton, ballet, cross-country running, horseback riding, table tennis, tennis; coed intramural: tennis. 6 PE instructors, 20 coaches.

Computers Computers are regularly used in all classes. Computer network features include on-campus library services, online commercial services, Internet access, wireless campus network, Internet filtering or blocking technology, 1 to 1 laptop program in grades 6-12 (student purchases/owns), 2 to 1 laptop program in grades 2-5, iPads for Preschool-Grade 1. Campus intranet and student e-mail accounts are available to students. Students grades are available online. The school has a published electronic and media policy.

Contact Mrs. Suzan Gurkan, Director of Admissions. 90-212-857-8264 Ext. 215. Fax: 90-212-857-8270. E-mail: admissions@iics.k12.tr. Website: www.iics.k12.tr

JACK M. BARRACK HEBREW ACADEMY

272 South Bryn Mawr Avenue
Bryn Mawr, Pennsylvania 19010

Head of School: Mrs. Sharon P. Levin

General Information Coeducational day college-preparatory, arts, religious studies, and bilingual studies school, affiliated with Jewish faith. Grades 6–12. Founded: 1946. Setting: suburban. Nearest major city is Philadelphia. 35-acre campus. 2 buildings on campus. Approved or accredited by Middle States Association of Colleges and Schools and Pennsylvania Department of Education. Member of National Association of Independent Schools. Languages of instruction: English and Hebrew. Endowment: $3.1 million. Total enrollment: 274. Upper school average class size: 16. Upper school faculty-student ratio: 1:15. There are 168 required school days per year for Upper School students. Upper School students typically attend 5 days per week. The average school day consists of 7 hours.

Upper School Student Profile Grade 9: 34 students (16 boys, 18 girls); Grade 10: 62 students (32 boys, 30 girls); Grade 11: 56 students (19 boys, 37 girls); Grade 12: 53 students (20 boys, 33 girls). 100% of students are Jewish.

Faculty School total: 53. In upper school: 17 men, 36 women; 40 have advanced degrees.

Subjects Offered Algebra, American history, American literature, art, astronomy, Bible studies, biology, calculus, chemistry, community service, computer math, computer programming, computer science, creative writing, earth science, English, English literature, environmental science, environmental science-AP, ethics, European history, French, geometry, government/civics, grammar, health, Hebrew, history, Jewish studies, Latin, mathematics, music, physical education, physics, public speaking, religion, science, social studies, Spanish, trigonometry, world history, writing.

Graduation Requirements English, foreign language, mathematics, physical education (includes health), religion (includes Bible studies and theology), science, social studies (includes history), senior community service project–150 hours in the senior year.

Special Academic Programs 8 Advanced Placement exams for which test preparation is offered; accelerated programs; independent study; term-away projects; study at local college for college credit; study abroad; academic accommodation for the gifted; remedial reading and/or remedial writing; remedial math; special instructional classes for deaf students.

College Admission Counseling 50 students graduated in 2012; all went to college, including Brandeis University; New York University; University of Maryland, College Park; University of Pennsylvania; University of Pittsburgh. Median SAT critical reading: 605, median SAT math: 642, median SAT writing: 605.

Student Life Upper grades have specified standards of dress, student council, honor system. Discipline rests primarily with faculty.

Tuition and Aid Day student tuition: $26,650. Tuition installment plan (Key Tuition Payment Plan, monthly payment plans, individually arranged payment plans). Tuition reduction for siblings, merit scholarship grants, need-based scholarship grants available. Total upper-school merit-scholarship money awarded for 2012–13: $151,200. Total amount of financial aid awarded in 2012–13: $1,483,690.

Admissions Traditional secondary-level entrance grade is 9. For fall 2012, 65 students applied for upper-level admission, 59 were accepted, 49 enrolled. ISEE required. Deadline for receipt of application materials: none. Application fee required: $75. On-campus interview required.

Athletics Interscholastic: baseball (boys), basketball (b,g), soccer (b,g), softball (g), tennis (b,g), track and field (g); intramural: basketball (b,g), field hockey (b,g), golf (b,g), lacrosse (g), running (b,g), soccer (b,g), squash (g), track and field (g), volleyball (b,g); coed interscholastic: cross-country running, soccer, swimming and diving. 2 PE instructors, 17 coaches.

Computers Computers are regularly used in foreign language, French, health, history, humanities, independent study, information technology, introduction to technology, journalism, keyboarding, Latin, library, literary magazine, mathematics, media production, multimedia, news writing, newspaper, photojournalism, programming, publications, remedial study skills, research skills, SAT preparation, science, social sciences, Spanish, study skills, technology, video film production, Web site design, word processing, writing, yearbook classes. Computer network features include on-campus library services, online commercial services, Internet access, wireless campus network, Internet filtering or blocking technology. Campus intranet, student e-mail accounts, and computer access in designated common areas are available to students. Students grades are available online. The school has a published electronic and media policy.

Contact Jennifer Groen, Director of Admission and Strategic Engagement. 610-922-2350. Fax: 610-922-2301. E-mail: jgroen@jbha.org. Website: www.jbha.org

JACKSON PREPARATORY SCHOOL

3100 Lakeland Drive
Jackson, Mississippi 39232

Head of School: Susan R. Lindsay

General Information Coeducational day college-preparatory school. Grades 6–12. Founded: 1970. Setting: urban. 74-acre campus. 6 buildings on campus. Approved or accredited by Mississippi Private School Association, Southern Association of Colleges and Schools, Southern Association of Independent Schools, and The College Board. Member of National Association of Independent Schools. Endowment: $993,373. Total enrollment: 800. Upper school average class size: 16. Upper school faculty-student ratio: 1:13. There are 176 required school days per year for Upper School students. Upper School students typically attend 5 days per week. The average school day consists of 6 hours and 45 minutes.

Upper School Student Profile Grade 10: 122 students (59 boys, 63 girls); Grade 11: 133 students (68 boys, 65 girls); Grade 12: 120 students (63 boys, 57 girls).

Faculty School total: 90. In upper school: 26 men, 49 women; 42 have advanced degrees.

Subjects Offered Accounting, advanced chemistry, Advanced Placement courses, algebra, American government, American history, American history-AP, American literature, art, Asian studies, Bible as literature, biology, biology-AP, British literature, calculus, calculus-AP, chemistry, chemistry-AP, choral music, civics, classical studies, computer science, creative writing, debate, discrete mathematics, drama, driver education, earth science, economics, English, English literature, English literature-AP, European history, film, fine arts, finite math, French, geography, geometry, government-AP, government/civics, grammar, Greek, Greek culture, history, honors algebra, honors English, honors geometry, journalism, Latin, Latin-AP, mathematics, music, physical education, physics, physics-AP, pre-algebra, pre-calculus, science, social studies, Spanish, trigonometry, U.S. government, U.S. government and politics-AP, U.S. history, U.S. history-AP, world history, world literature.

Graduation Requirements Arts and fine arts (art, music, dance, drama), computer applications, English, foreign language, mathematics, science, social studies (includes history).

Special Academic Programs Advanced Placement exam preparation; honors section; academic accommodation for the gifted, the musically talented, and the artistically talented; programs in English, mathematics, general development for dyslexic students.

College Admission Counseling 135 students graduated in 2012; all went to college, including Louisiana State University in Shreveport; Millsaps College; Mississippi College; Mississippi State University; The University of Alabama; University of Mississippi. Mean SAT critical reading: 617, mean SAT math: 621, mean SAT writing: 595, mean composite ACT: 25.

Student Life Upper grades have uniform requirement, student council, honor system. Discipline rests primarily with faculty.

Tuition and Aid Day student tuition: $12,543. Tuition installment plan (monthly payment plans). Need-based scholarship grants available. In 2012–13, 12% of upper-school students received aid. Total amount of financial aid awarded in 2012–13: $195,000.

Admissions Traditional secondary-level entrance grade is 10. For fall 2012, 16 students applied for upper-level admission, 11 were accepted, 10 enrolled. Non-standardized placement tests and OLSAT, Stanford Achievement Test required. Deadline for receipt of application materials: none. Application fee required: $40. Interview required.

Athletics Interscholastic: baseball (boys), basketball (b,g), cheering (g), cross-country running (b,g), dance team (g), football (b), Frisbee (b), soccer (b,g), softball (g), swimming and diving (b,g), tennis (b,g), track and field (b,g), ultimate Frisbee (b), volleyball (g); intramural: basketball (b,g), Frisbee (b), soccer (b,g), volleyball (b,g); coed interscholastic: cheering, golf. 4 coaches.

Computers Computers are regularly used in all classes. Computer network features include on-campus library services, online commercial services, Internet access, Electric Library, EBSCOhost, GaleNet, Grolier Online, NewsBank, online subscription services. The school has a published electronic and media policy.

Contact Lesley W. Morton, Director of Admission. 601-932-8106 Ext. 1. Fax: 601-936-4068. E-mail: lmorton@jacksonprep.net. Website: www.jacksonprep.net

JEAN AND SAMUEL FRANKEL JEWISH ACADEMY OF METROPOLITAN DETROIT

6600 West Maple Road
West Bloomfield, Michigan 48322

Head of School: Rabbi Eric Grossman

General Information Coeducational day college-preparatory, arts, business, and religious studies school, affiliated with Jewish faith. Grades 9–12. Founded: 2000. Setting: suburban. Nearest major city is West Bloomfield-Metro Detroit. 1 building on campus. Approved or accredited by Independent Schools Association of the Central States and Michigan Department of Education. Member of National Association of Independent Schools. Languages of instruction: English and Hebrew. Upper school average class size: 13. The average school day consists of 8 hours.

Upper School Student Profile Grade 9: 60 students (30 boys, 30 girls); Grade 10: 60 students (30 boys, 30 girls); Grade 11: 60 students (30 boys, 30 girls); Grade 12: 60 students (30 boys, 30 girls). 100% of students are Jewish.

Faculty In upper school: 30 have advanced degrees.

Special Academic Programs Advanced Placement exam preparation; honors section; study abroad; academic accommodation for the gifted; remedial reading and/or remedial writing; remedial math; special instructional classes for deaf students, blind students.

College Admission Counseling 56 went to college, including Michigan State University; University of Michigan–Dearborn.

Student Life Upper grades have specified standards of dress, student council, honor system. Discipline rests primarily with faculty. Attendance at religious services is required.

Tuition and Aid Day student tuition: $21,000. Tuition reduction for siblings, need-based scholarship grants available.

Admissions Traditional secondary-level entrance grade is 9. High School Placement Test required. Deadline for receipt of application materials: January 30. Application fee required: $100. Interview required.

Athletics 2 PE instructors, 8 coaches.

Computers Computer network features include on-campus library services, online commercial services, Internet access, wireless campus network, all students are given issued an iPad. Campus intranet and student e-mail accounts are available to students. Students grades are available online. The school has a published electronic and media policy.

Contact Lisa Gilan, Director of Admissions. 248-592-5263. Fax: 248-592-0022. E-mail: lgilan@frankelja.org. Website: www.frankelja.org/

JESUIT COLLEGE PREPARATORY SCHOOL

12345 Inwood Road
Dallas, Texas 75244

Head of School: Mr. Tom Garrison

General Information Boys' day college-preparatory school, affiliated with Roman Catholic Church (Jesuit order). Grades 9–12. Founded: 1942. Setting: suburban. 27-acre campus. 2 buildings on campus. Approved or accredited by Jesuit Secondary Education Association, National Catholic Education Association, Southern Association of Colleges and Schools, Texas Catholic Conference, and Texas Department of Education. Endowment: $25.6 million. Total enrollment: 1,095. Upper school average class size: 17. Upper school faculty-student ratio: 1:11. There are 190 required school days per year for Upper School students. Upper School students typically attend 5 days per week. The average school day consists of 6 hours.

Upper School Student Profile Grade 9: 282 students (282 boys); Grade 10: 290 students (290 boys); Grade 11: 266 students (266 boys); Grade 12: 257 students (257 boys). 81% of students are Roman Catholic Church (Jesuit order).

Faculty School total: 115. In upper school: 85 men, 30 women; 56 have advanced degrees.

Subjects Offered Advanced chemistry, advanced computer applications, advanced math, American literature-AP, American studies, art, art appreciation, art-AP, arts, band, Bible, biology, biology-AP, British literature, British literature-AP, calculus, calculus-AP, Catholic belief and practice, ceramics, chemistry, chemistry-AP, choir, Christian ethics, church history, civics, college counseling, community service, composition, composition-AP, computer applications, computer graphics, computer science, computer science-AP, contemporary issues, discrete mathematics, drama, drama performance, drama workshop, drawing, drawing and design, driver education, earth science, economics, economics-AP, English, English composition, English language and composition-AP, English language-AP, English literature, English literature and composition-AP, English literature-AP, English-AP, English/composition-AP, ethical decision making, European history, fine arts, French, French-AP, general science, geometry, government, government-AP, grammar, guitar, health, history, history-AP, honors algebra, honors English, honors geometry, honors U.S. history, honors world history, instrumental music, jazz band, journalism, Latin, literature and composition-

AP, marching band, mathematics, mathematics-AP, microcomputer technology applications, music, music appreciation, musical productions, orchestra, peace and justice, peer ministry, performing arts, physical education, physics, physics-AP, pottery, prayer/spirituality, pre-calculus, psychology, public speaking, publications, religion, scripture, social studies, Spanish, Spanish language-AP, Spanish literature-AP, Spanish-AP, speech, speech and debate, speech and oral interpretations, statistics, student government, student publications, studio art, studio art-AP, symphonic band, theater, theology, U.S. government, U.S. government and politics-AP, U.S. history, U.S. history-AP, U.S. literature, world history, world history-AP.

Graduation Requirements Arts and fine arts (art, music, dance, drama), computer science, English, foreign language, mathematics, physical education (includes health), science, social studies (includes history), theology. Community service is required.

Special Academic Programs 18 Advanced Placement exams for which test preparation is offered; honors section; independent study; study at local college for college credit.

College Admission Counseling 248 students graduated in 2013; 246 went to college, including Saint Louis University; Southern Methodist University; Texas A&M University; Texas Christian University; The University of Alabama; The University of Texas at Austin. Other: 2 had other specific plans. Mean SAT critical reading: 598, mean SAT math: 618, mean SAT writing: 595.

Student Life Upper grades have specified standards of dress, student council, honor system. Discipline rests primarily with faculty. Attendance at religious services is required.

Summer Programs Remediation, enrichment, advancement, sports, art/fine arts, computer instruction programs offered; session focuses on youth recreation; held on campus; accepts boys and girls; open to students from other schools. 800 students usually enrolled. 2014 schedule: June 15 to July 10. Application deadline: May 30.

Tuition and Aid Day student tuition: $15,200. Tuition installment plan (FACTS Tuition Payment Plan). Merit scholarship grants, need-based scholarship grants, paying campus jobs available. In 2013–14, 25% of upper-school students received aid; total upper-school merit-scholarship money awarded: $56,000. Total amount of financial aid awarded in 2013–14: $1,233,850.

Admissions Traditional secondary-level entrance grade is 9. For fall 2013, 513 students applied for upper-level admission, 326 were accepted, 282 enrolled. ISEE required. Deadline for receipt of application materials: January 7. Application fee required: $85. Interview required.

Athletics Interscholastic: baseball, basketball, bowling, crew, cross-country running, diving, fencing, football, golf, ice hockey, lacrosse, power lifting, rugby, soccer, swimming and diving, tennis, track and field, water polo, wrestling; intramural: basketball, bicycling, broomball, flagball, floor hockey, indoor soccer, ultimate Frisbee, volleyball; coed interscholastic: cheering, drill team. 6 PE instructors, 30 coaches, 2 athletic trainers.

Computers Computers are regularly used in college planning, desktop publishing, digital applications, engineering, English, foreign language, graphic design, graphics, humanities, introduction to technology, journalism, literary magazine, mathematics, media production, multimedia, newspaper, programming, publications, science, social studies, technology, video film production, Web site design, writing, yearbook classes. Computer network features include on-campus library services, online commercial services, Internet access, wireless campus network, Internet filtering or blocking technology. Campus intranet, student e-mail accounts, and computer access in designated common areas are available to students. Students grades are available online. The school has a published electronic and media policy.

Contact Mrs. Marueen Miramontes, Admissions Assistant. 972-387-8700 Ext. 453. Fax: 972-980-6707. E-mail: mmiramontes@jesuitcp.org. Website: www.jesuitcp.org

JESUIT HIGH SCHOOL OF TAMPA

4701 North Himes Avenue
Tampa, Florida 33614-6694

Head of School: Mr. Barry Neuburger

General Information Boys' day college-preparatory school, affiliated with Roman Catholic Church. Grades 9–12. Founded: 1899. Setting: urban. 40-acre campus. 9 buildings on campus. Approved or accredited by Jesuit Secondary Education Association, National Catholic Education Association, Southern Association of Colleges and Schools, and Florida Department of Education. Total enrollment: 758. Upper school average class size: 22. Upper school faculty-student ratio: 1:13. There are 175 required school days per year for Upper School students. Upper School students typically attend 5 days per week. The average school day consists of 7 hours and 23 minutes.

Upper School Student Profile Grade 9: 200 students (200 boys); Grade 10: 204 students (204 boys); Grade 11: 182 students (182 boys); Grade 12: 172 students (172 boys). 79% of students are Roman Catholic.

Faculty School total: 55. In upper school: 39 men, 16 women; 40 have advanced degrees.

Subjects Offered Algebra, American foreign policy, American government, American history, analytic geometry, anatomy, art, biology, calculus, calculus-AP, chemistry, chemistry-AP, chorus, computer science, economics, English, English language and composition-AP, English literature and composition-AP, environmental

science, ethics, European history, French, geometry, global studies, health, Latin, marine biology, math analysis, music, physical education, physics, physics-AP, physiology, pre-calculus, psychology, Spanish, Spanish language-AP, speech, statistics-AP, studio art-AP, theology, trigonometry, U.S. government and politics-AP, U.S. history-AP, world history, world history-AP, writing.

Graduation Requirements Arts and fine arts (art, music, dance, drama), English, foreign language, mathematics, physical education (includes health), science, social studies (includes history), theology, 150 hours of community service (additional 20 hours for National Honor Society members).

Special Academic Programs 14 Advanced Placement exams for which test preparation is offered; honors section.

College Admission Counseling 175 students graduated in 2013; all went to college, including Florida Gulf Coast University; Florida State University; University of Central Florida; University of Florida; University of South Florida. Mean SAT critical reading: 590, mean SAT math: 595, mean SAT writing: 589, mean combined SAT: 1776, mean composite ACT: 26.

Student Life Upper grades have specified standards of dress, student council. Discipline rests primarily with faculty. Attendance at religious services is required.

Summer Programs Remediation programs offered; session focuses on remediation; held on campus; accepts boys; not open to students from other schools. 50 students usually enrolled. 2014 schedule: June 18 to July 20.

Tuition and Aid Day student tuition: $13,400. Tuition installment plan (FACTS Tuition Payment Plan). Need-based scholarship grants available. In 2013–14, 24% of upper-school students received aid. Total amount of financial aid awarded in 2013–14: $1,342,290.

Admissions Traditional secondary-level entrance grade is 9. For fall 2013, 384 students applied for upper-level admission, 244 were accepted, 200 enrolled. High School Placement Test (closed version) from Scholastic Testing Service required. Deadline for receipt of application materials: January 12. Application fee required: $50.

Athletics Interscholastic: baseball, basketball, bowling, cross-country running, diving, football, golf, ice hockey, lacrosse, sailing, soccer, swimming and diving, tennis, track and field, wrestling; intramural: basketball, football, Frisbee, kickball, softball, ultimate Frisbee. 2 PE instructors, 1 athletic trainer.

Computers Computer network features include on-campus library services, online commercial services, Internet access, wireless campus network, Internet filtering or blocking technology. Campus intranet, student e-mail accounts, and computer access in designated common areas are available to students. Students grades are available online. The school has a published electronic and media policy.

Contact Mr. Steve Matesich, Director of Admissions. 813-877-5344 Ext. 509. Fax: 813-872-1853. E-mail: smatesich@jesuittampa.org. Website: www.jesuittampa.org

JOHN BURROUGHS SCHOOL

755 South Price Road
St. Louis, Missouri 63124

Head of School: Andy Abbott

General Information Coeducational day college-preparatory school. Grades 7–12. Founded: 1923. Setting: suburban. 47-acre campus. 7 buildings on campus. Approved or accredited by Independent Schools Association of the Central States. Member of National Association of Independent Schools and Secondary School Admission Test Board. Endowment: $42.8 million. Total enrollment: 600. Upper school average class size: 13. Upper school faculty-student ratio: 1:7. There are 163 required school days per year for Upper School students. Upper School students typically attend 5 days per week. The average school day consists of 8 hours.

Upper School Student Profile Grade 9: 104 students (51 boys, 53 girls); Grade 10: 102 students (51 boys, 51 girls); Grade 11: 99 students (49 boys, 50 girls); Grade 12: 104 students (53 boys, 51 girls).

Faculty School total: 111. In upper school: 45 men, 61 women; 83 have advanced degrees.

Subjects Offered Acting, Advanced Placement courses, African American history, algebra, American history, American literature, Ancient Greek, ancient world history, applied arts, architectural drawing, art, art history, art history-AP, astronomy, bioethics, biology, biology-AP, calculus, calculus-AP, ceramics, chemistry, chemistry-AP, Chinese, choral music, chorus, classical language, community service, comparative religion, computer math, computer science, computer skills, computer-aided design, creative writing, dance, debate, drama, earth science, ecology, engineering, English, English literature, environmental science, environmental systems, expository writing, fine arts, finite math, foreign language, French, French language-AP, gardening, geology, geometry, German, global issues, global studies, Greek, Greek culture, health, history, home economics, honors English, industrial arts, jazz, jazz band, keyboarding, lab science, Latin, Latin-AP, mathematics, mechanical drawing, meteorology, model United Nations, music, orchestra, organic chemistry, personal finance, photography, physical education, physics, poetry, pre-algebra, pre-calculus, probability and statistics, psychology, public speaking, reading/study skills, religion, Russian, science, social sciences, social studies, Spanish, Spanish-AP, speech and debate, statistics, trigonometry, vocal music, word processing, world civilizations, world history, world literature, world religions, writing.

Graduation Requirements Arts and fine arts (art, music, dance, drama), English, foreign language, history, mathematics, performing arts, physical education (includes health), practical arts, science, Senior May Project, Sophomore Diversity Seminar, Freshman Health.

Special Academic Programs 8 Advanced Placement exams for which test preparation is offered; honors section; independent study.

College Admission Counseling 99 students graduated in 2013; all went to college, including Boston University; Cornell University; Princeton University; Tufts University; Washington University in St. Louis; Yale University. Median SAT critical reading: 680, median SAT math: 690, median SAT writing: 670, median combined SAT: 2070, median composite ACT: 32. 81% scored over 600 on SAT critical reading, 92% scored over 600 on SAT math, 85% scored over 600 on SAT writing, 88% scored over 1800 on combined SAT, 97% scored over 26 on composite ACT.

Student Life Upper grades have student council, honor system. Discipline rests equally with students and faculty.

Tuition and Aid Day student tuition: $23,750. Tuition installment plan (monthly payment plans). Need-based scholarship grants, need-based loans available. In 2013–14, 21% of upper-school students received aid. Total amount of financial aid awarded in 2013–14: $2,051,000.

Admissions Traditional secondary-level entrance grade is 9. For fall 2013, 65 students applied for upper-level admission, 11 were accepted, 9 enrolled. SSAT required. Deadline for receipt of application materials: January 17. Application fee required: $40. On-campus interview required.

Athletics Interscholastic: baseball (boys), basketball (b,g), cheering (b,g), cross-country running (b,g), dance (g), dance squad (g), diving (b,g), field hockey (g), fitness (b,g), football (b), golf (b,g), ice hockey (b), independent competitive sports (b,g), lacrosse (b,g), modern dance (g), outdoor education (b,g), physical fitness (b,g), physical training (b,g), soccer (b,g), strength & conditioning (b,g), swimming and diving (b,g), tennis (b,g), track and field (b,g), volleyball (g), water polo (b), wrestling (b), yoga (b,g); coed interscholastic: cheering, dance, dance squad, ice hockey, modern dance, outdoor education, physical fitness, physical training, strength & conditioning, water polo, wrestling, yoga. 45 coaches, 1 athletic trainer.

Computers Computers are regularly used in all academic, animation, architecture, art, basic skills, cabinet making, college planning, current events, desktop publishing, drafting, drawing and design, industrial technology, keyboarding, lab/keyboard, library, library skills, media production, music, photography, photojournalism, remedial study skills, research skills, study skills, technical drawing, theater, video film production, Web site design, yearbook classes. Computer network features include on-campus library services, online commercial services, Internet access, wireless campus network, access to Google Apps, access to necessary curricular software, iPad/laptop check out from library. Campus intranet, student e-mail accounts, and computer access in designated common areas are available to students. The school has a published electronic and media policy.

Contact Caroline LaVigne, Director of Admissions and Tuition Aid. 314-993-4040. Fax: 314-567-2896. E-mail: clavigne@jburroughs.org. Website: www.jburroughs.org

JOHN HANCOCK ACADEMY

PO Drawer E
Sparta, Georgia 31087

Head of School: Mr. Steve James

General Information Coeducational day college-preparatory, general academic, arts, religious studies, and technology school, affiliated with Baptist Church, United Methodist Church. Grades K–12. Founded: 1966. Setting: rural. Nearest major city is Macon. 1 building on campus. Approved or accredited by Georgia Accrediting Commission, Georgia Independent School Association, and Georgia Department of Education. Languages of instruction: English and Spanish. Total enrollment: 122. Upper school average class size: 8. Upper school faculty-student ratio: 1:8. There are 180 required school days per year for Upper School students. Upper School students typically attend 5 days per week. The average school day consists of 8 hours.

Upper School Student Profile Grade 9: 11 students (7 boys, 4 girls); Grade 10: 13 students (6 boys, 7 girls); Grade 11: 11 students (7 boys, 4 girls); Grade 12: 9 students (4 boys, 5 girls). 80% of students are Baptist, United Methodist Church.

Faculty School total: 15. In upper school: 3 men, 5 women; 2 have advanced degrees.

Subjects Offered Advanced math, algebra, American government, American history, American literature, anatomy, art history, Bible, biology, botany, chemistry, computer applications, data processing, earth science, economics, English, English literature, environmental science, general math, geography, geometry, government, health, history, journalism, keyboarding, language arts, physical education, physical science, physics, pre-algebra, science, social studies, Spanish, state history, statistics, trigonometry, U.S. government, U.S. history, Web site design, weight training, world geography, world history, yearbook.

Special Academic Programs International Baccalaureate program; honors section; independent study.

College Admission Counseling 7 students graduated in 2012; 4 went to college, including University of Georgia; Valdosta State University. Other: 2 went to work, 1 had other specific plans.

Student Life Upper grades have specified standards of dress, student council, honor system. Discipline rests primarily with faculty.

Tuition and Aid Day student tuition: $4400. Tuition installment plan (monthly payment plans, individually arranged payment plans). Tuition reduction for siblings available.

Admissions Traditional secondary-level entrance grade is 9. ACT, any standardized test, OLSAT, Stanford Achievement Test, Otis-Lennon Ability or Stanford Achievement Test, PSAT or SAT required. Deadline for receipt of application materials: none. Application fee required: $100. Interview required.

Athletics Interscholastic: baseball (boys), basketball (b,g), cheering (g), football (b), golf (b,g), running (b,g), softball (g), tennis (b,g), track and field (b,g), volleyball (g), weight lifting (b,g); coed interscholastic: physical fitness. 1 PE instructor, 5 coaches.

Computers Computers are regularly used in keyboarding, Web site design, yearbook classes. Computer resources include Internet access.

Contact Mrs. Kaye Smith, Secretary. 706-444-6470. Fax: 706-444-6933. E-mail: johnhancockad@bellsouth.net. Website: www.johnhancockacademy.com/

JOHN T. MORGAN ACADEMY

2901 West Dallas Avenue
Selma, Alabama 36701

Head of School: Mrs. Martha McKnight

General Information Coeducational day college-preparatory school. Grades PK–12. Founded: 1965. Setting: small town. 26-acre campus. 5 buildings on campus. Approved or accredited by Southern Association of Colleges and Schools. Total enrollment: 500. Upper school average class size: 22. Upper school faculty-student ratio: 1:22. There are 178 required school days per year for Upper School students. Upper School students typically attend 5 days per week. The average school day consists of 6 hours.

Upper School Student Profile Grade 10: 48 students (26 boys, 22 girls); Grade 11: 31 students (18 boys, 13 girls); Grade 12: 43 students (24 boys, 19 girls).

Faculty School total: 36. In upper school: 6 men, 14 women; 6 have advanced degrees.

Subjects Offered World history.

Special Academic Programs Honors section.

College Admission Counseling 46 students graduated in 2013; all went to college, including Auburn University; The University of Alabama; Troy University. Median composite ACT: 22. 35% scored over 26 on composite ACT.

Student Life Upper grades have uniform requirement, student council, honor system. Discipline rests primarily with faculty.

Tuition and Aid Tuition installment plan (monthly payment plans).

Admissions Traditional secondary-level entrance grade is 10. For fall 2013, 8 students applied for upper-level admission, 8 were accepted, 8 enrolled. ACT or OLSAT/Stanford required. Deadline for receipt of application materials: none. Application fee required: $185. Interview required.

Athletics Interscholastic: baseball (boys), basketball (b,g), cheering (g), cross-country running (b,g), fitness (b,g), fitness walking (b,g), flag football (b), golf (b,g), physical fitness (b,g), running (b,g), scooter football (b), soccer (b,g), softball (g), strength & conditioning (b,g), tennis (b,g), track and field (b,g), volleyball (g), walking (b,g), weight lifting (b), weight training (b), whiffle ball (b,g), yoga (g); intramural: basketball (b,g), cooperative games (b,g), cross-country running (b,g), jogging (b,g), kickball (b,g), soccer (b,g), softball (g), tennis (b,g), touch football (b,g); coed interscholastic: golf, whiffle ball; coed intramural: cooperative games, jogging, jump rope, kickball. 2 PE instructors, 5 coaches.

Computers Computers are regularly used in computer applications classes. Computer network features include on-campus library services, Internet access, Internet filtering or blocking technology. Students grades are available online. The school has a published electronic and media policy.

Contact Mrs. Tina P. Cox, Secretary. 334-375-1044. Fax: 334-875-4465. E-mail: tcox@morganacademy.com. Website: www.morganacademy.com/

JOSEPHINUM ACADEMY

1501 North Oakley Boulevard
Chicago, Illinois 60622

Head of School: Mrs. Lourdes Weber

General Information Girls' day college-preparatory, arts, religious studies, and technology school, affiliated with Roman Catholic Church. Grades 9–12. Founded: 1890. Setting: urban. 2-acre campus. 1 building on campus. Approved or accredited by National Catholic Education Association, Network of Sacred Heart Schools, North Central Association of Colleges and Schools, and Illinois Department of Education. Endowment: $1.5 million. Total enrollment: 199. Upper school average class size: 20. Upper school faculty-student ratio: 1:10. There are 176 required school days per year for Upper School students. Upper School students typically attend 5 days per week. The average school day consists of 7 hours and 30 minutes.

Upper School Student Profile Grade 9: 48 students (48 girls); Grade 10: 58 students (58 girls); Grade 11: 54 students (54 girls); Grade 12: 39 students (39 girls). 50% of students are Roman Catholic.

Faculty School total: 24. In upper school: 6 men, 14 women; 16 have advanced degrees.

Subjects Offered ACT preparation, acting, advanced biology, advanced chemistry, Advanced Placement courses, algebra, American literature, applied arts, art, athletics, basketball, biology, biology-AP, business education, calculus-AP, campus ministry, Catholic belief and practice, chemistry, Christian studies, civics, college admission preparation, college awareness, college counseling, college placement, college planning, community garden, community service, computer education, constitutional history of U.S., consumer economics, consumer education, current events, drama, drama performance, electives, English, English literature-AP, English-AP, environmental science, fitness, foreign language, French, French as a second language, freshman seminar, geometry, global issues, global studies, health, health and wellness, history of the Americas, honors English, honors geometry, honors U.S. history, honors world history, Life of Christ, literature by women, modern history, moral theology, peer counseling, performing arts, physical education, physical science, physics, pre-calculus, religious studies, research seminar, senior project, senior thesis, Shakespeare, social justice, softball, Spanish, Spanish literature, Spanish-AP, speech, U.S. history, volleyball, water color painting, women's literature, women's studies, world history, world literature, world religions, world religions, writing, yearbook.

Graduation Requirements Algebra, arts and fine arts (art, music, dance, drama), biology, college admission preparation, computer science, consumer education, English, foreign language, health, mathematics, physical education (includes health), religion (includes Bible studies and theology), science, social sciences, social studies (includes history), technology, Senior Capstone Project, portfolio projects. Community service is required.

Special Academic Programs 6 Advanced Placement exams for which test preparation is offered; honors section; independent study; term-away projects; domestic exchange program (with Network of Sacred Heart Schools); study abroad; remedial reading and/or remedial writing; remedial math; ESL (5 students enrolled).

College Admission Counseling 38 students graduated in 2013; all went to college, including Carleton College; DePaul University; Grand Valley State University; Loyola University Chicago; University of Illinois at Chicago; University of Illinois at Urbana–Champaign.

Student Life Upper grades have uniform requirement, student council, honor system. Discipline rests primarily with faculty. Attendance at religious services is required.

Summer Programs Remediation, enrichment, sports, art/fine arts, computer instruction programs offered; session focuses on community service and educational advancement; held both on and off campus; held at Sacred Heart schools; accepts girls; open to students from other schools. 40 students usually enrolled.

Tuition and Aid Day student tuition: $4900. Tuition installment plan (SMART Tuition Payment Plan, monthly payment plans, individually arranged payment plans). Tuition reduction for siblings, merit scholarship grants, need-based scholarship grants available. In 2013–14, 89% of upper-school students received aid.

Admissions Traditional secondary-level entrance grade is 9. Catholic High School Entrance Examination required. Deadline for receipt of application materials: none. No application fee required. Interview recommended.

Athletics Interscholastic: basketball, soccer, softball, volleyball; intramural: fitness, football, track and field. 2 PE instructors, 5 coaches.

Computers Computers are regularly used in all academic classes. Computer network features include on-campus library services, online commercial services, Internet access, wireless campus network, Internet filtering or blocking technology, all students provided with iPads. Campus intranet, student e-mail accounts, and computer access in designated common areas are available to students. Students grades are available online. The school has a published electronic and media policy.

Contact Mrs. Alex Gonzalez, Director of Admissions. 773-276-1261 Ext. 234. Fax: 773-292-3963. E-mail: alex.gonzalez@josephinum.org. Website: www.josephinum.org

THE JOURNEYS SCHOOL OF TETON SCIENCE SCHOOL

700 Coyote Canyon Road
Jackson, Wyoming 83001

Head of School: Mr. Nate McClennen

General Information Coeducational day college-preparatory school. Grades K–12. Founded: 2001. Setting: rural. 800-acre campus. 1 building on campus. Approved or accredited by International Baccalaureate Organization, Northwest Association of Independent Schools, and Wyoming Department of Education. Member of National Association of Independent Schools. Endowment: $12 million. Total enrollment: 152. Upper school average class size: 10. Upper school faculty-student ratio: 1:7. There are 175 required school days per year for Upper School students. Upper School students typically attend 5 days per week. The average school day consists of 7 hours and 45 minutes.

Upper School Student Profile Grade 6: 13 students (10 boys, 3 girls); Grade 7: 16 students (6 boys, 10 girls); Grade 8: 12 students (5 boys, 7 girls); Grade 9: 8 students (1 boy, 7 girls); Grade 10: 12 students (7 boys, 5 girls); Grade 11: 13 students (6 boys, 7 girls); Grade 12: 9 students (9 girls).

Faculty In upper school: 8 men, 13 women; 13 have advanced degrees.

Subjects Offered International Baccalaureate courses.

Graduation Requirements International Baccalaureate courses.

Special Academic Programs International Baccalaureate program; independent study; academic accommodation for the gifted.

College Admission Counseling 8 students graduated in 2012; all went to college.

Student Life Upper grades have student council. Discipline rests equally with students and faculty.

Tuition and Aid Day student tuition: $18,900. Tuition installment plan (monthly payment plans, individually arranged payment plans). Need-based scholarship grants available. In 2012–13, 43% of upper-school students received aid. Total amount of financial aid awarded in 2012–13: $240,150.

Admissions Deadline for receipt of application materials: none. Application fee required: $50. Interview required.

Athletics Interscholastic: aerobics/dance (girls), alpine skiing (b,g), aquatics (g), baseball (b), basketball (b,g), cheering (g), cross-country running (b,g), dance (g), football (b), gymnastics (g), ice hockey (b,g), indoor track & field (g), martial arts (b,g), nordic skiing (b,g), soccer (b,g), swimming and diving (g), tennis (b,g), volleyball (g); intramural: dressage (g), equestrian sports (g), freestyle skiing (b,g), horseback riding (g), lacrosse (b,g), snowboarding (b,g); coed interscholastic: backpacking, skiing (cross-country), skiing (downhill), track and field; coed intramural: climbing, soccer, wall climbing. 1 PE instructor.

Computers Computer network features include Internet access, wireless campus network, Internet filtering or blocking technology. Campus intranet and student e-mail accounts are available to students. Students grades are available online.

Contact Tammie VanHolland, Director of Admissions. 307-734-3710. Fax: 307-733-3340. E-mail: tammie.vanholland@journeysschool.org. Website: www.tetonscience.org/index.cfm?id=journeys_home

THE JUDGE ROTENBERG EDUCATIONAL CENTER

Canton, Massachusetts
See Special Needs Schools section.

JUNIPERO SERRA HIGH SCHOOL

451 West 20th Avenue
San Mateo, California 94403-1385

Head of School: Lars Lund

General Information Boys' day college-preparatory, arts, business, religious studies, and technology school, affiliated with Roman Catholic Church. Grades 9–12. Founded: 1944. Setting: suburban. Nearest major city is San Francisco. 13-acre campus. 9 buildings on campus. Approved or accredited by Western Association of Schools and Colleges and Western Catholic Education Association. Endowment: $6.3 million. Total enrollment: 860. Upper school average class size: 26. Upper school faculty-student ratio: 1:27. There are 180 required school days per year for Upper School students. Upper School students typically attend 5 days per week. The average school day consists of 6 hours and 40 minutes.

Upper School Student Profile Grade 9: 226 students (226 boys); Grade 10: 228 students (228 boys); Grade 11: 216 students (216 boys); Grade 12: 190 students (190 boys). 68% of students are Roman Catholic.

Faculty School total: 76. In upper school: 59 men, 17 women; 37 have advanced degrees.

Subjects Offered Advanced biology, Advanced Placement courses, algebra, American history, American history-AP, American literature, analytic geometry, architectural drawing, architecture, art, art history-AP, athletic training, athletics, band, biology, biology-AP, business, calculus, calculus-AP, ceramics, chemistry, college admission preparation, college counseling, college planning, community service, comparative government and politics-AP, computer programming, computer science, creative writing, dance, drama, driver education, earth science, ecology, environmental systems, economics, electronics, English, English literature, English literature and composition-AP, English literature-AP, ethics, European history, fine arts, French, French language-AP, geography, geometry, German, government and politics-AP, government/civics, grammar, health, history, instrumental music, journalism, keyboarding, leadership and service, library skills, literature and composition-AP, Mandarin, mathematics, music, performing arts, photography, physical education, physics, pre-calculus, psychology, publications, religious studies, science, social sciences, social studies, Spanish, Spanish language-AP, Spanish-AP, speech, sports conditioning, statistics, student government, theater, trigonometry, U.S. government, U.S. government and politics-AP, U.S. history, U.S. history-AP, visual and performing arts, world history, writing.

Graduation Requirements All academic, arts and fine arts (art, music, dance, drama), computer science, English, foreign language, literature, mathematics, physical education (includes health), political systems, religion (includes Bible studies and theology), science, social sciences, social studies (includes history), 80 hours of community service. Community service is required.

Special Academic Programs 17 Advanced Placement exams for which test preparation is offered; honors section; study at local college for college credit.

College Admission Counseling 217 students graduated in 2013; all went to college, including California Polytechnic State University, San Luis Obispo; Saint Mary's College of California; Santa Clara University; The University of Arizona; University of California, Davis; University of Colorado Boulder.

Student Life Upper grades have specified standards of dress, student council, honor system. Discipline rests primarily with faculty. Attendance at religious services is required.

Summer Programs Remediation, enrichment, advancement, sports, art/fine arts, computer instruction programs offered; session focuses on enrichment and remediation; held on campus; accepts boys and girls; open to students from other schools. 480 students usually enrolled. 2014 schedule: June 16 to July 18. Application deadline: June 12.

Tuition and Aid Day student tuition: $17,975. Tuition installment plan (monthly payment plans, semester payment plan, annual payment plan, direct debit plan). Merit scholarship grants, need-based scholarship grants available. In 2013–14, 34% of upper-school students received aid; total upper-school merit-scholarship money awarded; $53,000. Total amount of financial aid awarded in 2013–14: $2,100,000.

Admissions Traditional secondary-level entrance grade is 9. For fall 2013, 425 students applied for upper-level admission, 315 were accepted, 226 enrolled. High School Placement Test required. Deadline for receipt of application materials: January 8. Application fee required: $75. On-campus interview required.

Athletics Interscholastic: baseball, basketball, crew, cross-country running, diving, football, golf, lacrosse, rowing, soccer, swimming and diving, tennis, track and field, volleyball, water polo, wrestling; intramural: basketball, bicycling, bowling, fishing, fitness, mountain biking, physical training, rock climbing, soccer, softball, strength & conditioning, surfing, touch football, weight lifting, weight training. 2 PE instructors, 48 coaches, 1 athletic trainer.

Computers Computers are regularly used in all academic classes. Computer network features include on-campus library services, Internet access, wireless campus network, Internet filtering or blocking technology. Campus intranet and student e-mail accounts are available to students. Students grades are available online. The school has a published electronic and media policy.

Contact Randy Vogel, Director of Admissions. 650-345-8242. Fax: 650-573-6638. E-mail: rvogel@serrahs.com. Website: www.serrahs.com

KALAMAZOO CHRISTIAN HIGH SCHOOL

2121 Stadium Drive
Kalamazoo, Michigan 49008-1692

Head of School: Mr. Bartel James Huizenga

General Information Coeducational day college-preparatory, general academic, arts, business, vocational, religious studies, bilingual studies, and technology school, affiliated with Christian Reformed Church, Reformed Church in America. Grades 9–12. Founded: 1877. Setting: urban. 3-acre campus. 1 building on campus. Approved or accredited by Christian Schools International, North Central Association of Colleges and Schools, and Michigan Department of Education. Endowment: $1 million. Total enrollment: 773. Upper school average class size: 22. Upper school faculty-student ratio: 1:12. There are 172 required school days per year for Upper School students. Upper School students typically attend 5 days per week. The average school day consists of 6 hours and 45 minutes.

Upper School Student Profile 45% of students are members of Christian Reformed Church, Reformed Church in America.

Faculty School total: 20. In upper school: 14 men, 6 women; 10 have advanced degrees.

Graduation Requirements 50 hours of community service.

Special Academic Programs Advanced Placement exam preparation; honors section; study at local college for college credit.

College Admission Counseling 67 students graduated in 2013; 65 went to college, including Calvin College; Grand Valley State University; Hope College; University of Michigan; Western Michigan University. Other: 1 entered military service, 1 had other specific plans. Median composite ACT: 23. 27% scored over 26 on composite ACT.

Student Life Upper grades have specified standards of dress, student council, honor system. Discipline rests primarily with faculty. Attendance at religious services is required.

Tuition and Aid Day student tuition: $8140. Tuition installment plan (FACTS Tuition Payment Plan, monthly payment plans, individually arranged payment plans). Tuition reduction for siblings, need-based scholarship grants available. In 2013–14, 50% of upper-school students received aid.

Admissions Traditional secondary-level entrance grade is 9. Deadline for receipt of application materials: none. Application fee required: $150. Interview required.

Athletics Interscholastic: baseball (boys), basketball (b,g), bowling (b,g), cheering (g), cross-country running (b,g), football (b), golf (b,g), hockey (b), physical fitness (b,g), soccer (b,g), softball (g), strength & conditioning (b,g), tennis (b,g), track and field (b,g), volleyball (g), weight lifting (b,g), weight training (b,g). 2 PE instructors, 32 coaches, 1 athletic trainer.

Computers Computers are regularly used in accounting, business, business applications, business skills, data processing, graphic arts, graphic design, keyboarding, lab/keyboard classes. Computer network features include on-campus library services,

online commercial services, Internet access. The school has a published electronic and media policy.

Contact Mr. Bartel James Huizenga, Principal. 269-381-2250 Ext. 220. Fax: 269-381-0319. E-mail: bhuizenga@kcsa.org. Website: www.kcsa.org

KANSAS CITY ACADEMY

7933 Main
Kansas City, Missouri 64114-2466

Head of School: Ms. Kathy Baldwin-Heitman

General Information Coeducational day college-preparatory and arts school. Grades 6–12. Founded: 1984. Setting: urban. 1-acre campus. 1 building on campus. Approved or accredited by North Central Association of Colleges and Schools. Total enrollment: 45. Upper school average class size: 10. Upper school faculty-student ratio: 1:6. There are 175 required school days per year for Upper School students. Upper School students typically attend 5 days per week. The average school day consists of 7 hours.

Upper School Student Profile Grade 9: 10 students (4 boys, 6 girls); Grade 10: 5 students (4 boys, 1 girl); Grade 11: 10 students (5 boys, 5 girls); Grade 12: 7 students (4 boys, 3 girls).

Faculty School total: 14. In upper school: 6 men, 8 women; 10 have advanced degrees.

Subjects Offered Acting, advanced biology, advanced math, algebra, American culture, American government, art, biology, British literature, career and personal planning, career/college preparation, ceramics, chemistry, composition, computer literacy, crafts, current events, digital photography, economics, English, ethical decision making, French, general science, geometry, health and wellness, integrated science, introduction to theater, journalism, language arts, literature, mathematics, Microsoft, music performance, personal finance, photography, physical fitness, physical science, pre-algebra, senior internship, social studies, Spanish, stage design, student government, technical theater, U.S. history, writing, yearbook.

Graduation Requirements Algebra, American government, arts and fine arts (art, music, dance, drama), biology, computer literacy, English, foreign language, geometry, health and wellness, interdisciplinary studies, personal finance, physical education (includes health), physical science, practical arts, U.S. history, world history.

Special Academic Programs Accelerated programs; independent study; special instructional classes for deaf students, blind students, students with Attention Deficit Disorder and dyslexia.

College Admission Counseling 8 students graduated in 2013; all went to college, including Johnson County Community College; University of Missouri. Median composite ACT: 21. 14% scored over 26 on composite ACT.

Student Life Upper grades have specified standards of dress, student council, honor system. Discipline rests equally with students and faculty.

Tuition and Aid Day student tuition: $11,975. Tuition installment plan (FACTS Tuition Payment Plan, monthly payment plans, individually arranged payment plans). Need-based scholarship grants available. In 2013–14, 55% of upper-school students received aid. Total amount of financial aid awarded in 2013–14: $121,000.

Admissions Traditional secondary-level entrance grade is 9. For fall 2013, 10 students applied for upper-level admission, 9 were accepted, 9 enrolled. Mathematics proficiency exam and writing sample required. Deadline for receipt of application materials: none. Application fee required: $70. On-campus interview required.

Athletics 1 PE instructor.

Computers Computers are regularly used in all academic classes. Computer network features include on-campus library services, Internet access, wireless campus network, Internet filtering or blocking technology. Students grades are available online. The school has a published electronic and media policy.

Contact Ms. Sheri Thomas, Director of Admissions and Records. 816-444-5225. Fax: 816-444-8354. E-mail: sthomas@kcacademy.org. Website: www.kcacademy.org

KENT DENVER SCHOOL

4000 East Quincy Avenue
Englewood, Colorado 80113

Head of School: Mr. Todd Horn

General Information Coeducational day college-preparatory and arts school. Grades 6–12. Founded: 1922. Setting: suburban. Nearest major city is Denver. 220-acre campus. 6 buildings on campus. Approved or accredited by Association of Colorado Independent Schools and Colorado Department of Education. Member of National Association of Independent Schools and Secondary School Admission Test Board. Endowment: $48 million. Total enrollment: 692. Upper school average class size: 15. Upper school faculty-student ratio: 1:7. There are 172 required school days per year for Upper School students. Upper School students typically attend 5 days per week. The average school day consists of 7 hours.

Upper School Student Profile Grade 9: 123 students (59 boys, 64 girls); Grade 10: 121 students (63 boys, 58 girls); Grade 11: 118 students (55 boys, 63 girls); Grade 12: 106 students (53 boys, 53 girls).

Faculty School total: 89. In upper school: 61 have advanced degrees.

Subjects Offered African-American literature, algebra, American history, American history-AP, American literature, ancient history, anthropology, art, art history, art history-AP, Asian studies, biology, calculus, calculus-AP, career education internship, ceramics, chemistry, choir, clayworking, college counseling, community service, computer math, computer programming, computer programming-AP, computer science, creative writing, drama, earth science, economics, English, English literature, English literature and composition-AP, environmental science, European history, European history-AP, fine arts, French, French language-AP, French literature-AP, French-AP, general science, genetics, geography, geology, geometry, government/civics, grammar, guitar, health and wellness, history, history-AP, human development, independent study, jazz band, Latin, Mandarin, mathematics, music, music performance, mythology, photography, physical education, physics, pre-calculus, science, social studies, Spanish, Spanish language-AP, Spanish literature-AP, statistics, studio art-AP, theater, Web site design, world history, world literature, writing.

Graduation Requirements Arts and fine arts (art, music, dance, drama), English, foreign language, history, internship, mathematics, participation in sports, science. Community service is required.

Special Academic Programs 18 Advanced Placement exams for which test preparation is offered; honors section; independent study; programs in general development for dyslexic students.

College Admission Counseling 105 students graduated in 2013; all went to college, including Dartmouth College; Duke University; Northwestern University; Princeton University; University of California, Berkeley; University of Southern California. Mean SAT critical reading: 628, mean SAT math: 639, mean SAT writing: 633, mean composite ACT: 28.

Student Life Upper grades have specified standards of dress, student council. Discipline rests equally with students and faculty.

Summer Programs Enrichment, sports, art/fine arts, computer instruction programs offered; session focuses on skill-building, arts, enrichment, athletics; held on campus; accepts boys and girls; open to students from other schools. 1,400 students usually enrolled. 2014 schedule: June 9 to July 25. Application deadline: none.

Tuition and Aid Day student tuition: $23,040. Tuition installment plan (Insured Tuition Payment Plan, Key Tuition Payment Plan, monthly payment plans). Need-based scholarship grants available. In 2013–14, 23% of upper-school students received aid. Total amount of financial aid awarded in 2013–14: $2,000,000.

Admissions Traditional secondary-level entrance grade is 9. For fall 2013, 161 students applied for upper-level admission, 75 were accepted, 49 enrolled. ISEE or SSAT required. Deadline for receipt of application materials: January 31. Application fee required: $60. Interview required.

Athletics Interscholastic: baseball (boys), basketball (b,g), cross-country running (b,g), diving (g), field hockey (g), football (b), golf (b,g), hockey (b), ice hockey (b), lacrosse (b,g), soccer (b,g), swimming and diving (g), tennis (b,g), track and field (b,g), volleyball (g); coed interscholastic: independent competitive sports, outdoor education, yoga; coed intramural: aerobics/Nautilus, bicycling, fitness, mountain biking, outdoor adventure, outdoor education, outdoor skills, physical fitness, physical training, strength & conditioning, weight lifting. 3 PE instructors, 17 coaches, 1 athletic trainer.

Computers Computers are regularly used in art, English, foreign language, history, mathematics, science classes. Computer network features include on-campus library services, online commercial services, Internet access, wireless campus network, Internet filtering or blocking technology. Student e-mail accounts and computer access in designated common areas are available to students. Students grades are available online. The school has a published electronic and media policy.

Contact Susan Green, Admission Office Manager. 303-770-7660 Ext. 237. Fax: 303-770-1398. E-mail: sgreen@kentdenver.org. Website: www.kentdenver.org

KENT PLACE SCHOOL

42 Norwood Avenue
Summit, New Jersey 07902-0308

Head of School: Mrs. Susan C. Bosland

General Information Coeducational day (boys' only in lower grades) college-preparatory school. Boys grades N–PK, girls grades N–12. Founded: 1894. Setting: suburban. Nearest major city is New York, NY. 25-acre campus. 6 buildings on campus. Approved or accredited by Middle States Association of Colleges and Schools and New Jersey Association of Independent Schools. Member of National Association of Independent Schools and Secondary School Admission Test Board. Endowment: $15 million. Total enrollment: 636. Upper school average class size: 16. Upper school faculty-student ratio: 1:7. There are 167 required school days per year for Upper School students. Upper School students typically attend 5 days per week. The average school day consists of 6 hours and 55 minutes.

Upper School Student Profile Grade 9: 69 students (69 girls); Grade 10: 78 students (78 girls); Grade 11: 67 students (67 girls); Grade 12: 63 students (63 girls).

Faculty School total: 119. In upper school: 7 men, 36 women; 35 have advanced degrees.

Subjects Offered Advanced Placement courses, algebra, American history, American history-AP, American literature, anatomy and physiology, art, art history-AP, biology, biology-AP, calculus, calculus-AP, ceramics, chemistry, chemistry-AP, computer literacy, computer programming-AP, computer science, creative writing, dance, drama, driver education, economics, English, English language-AP, English

literature, English literature-AP, environmental science, environmental science-AP, European history, expository writing, fine arts, French, French language-AP, French literature-AP, geometry, government/civics, grammar, health, history, independent study, Latin, Latin-AP, macroeconomics-AP, mathematics, modern European history-AP, music, music theory-AP, photography, physical education, physics, science, social studies, Spanish, Spanish language-AP, Spanish literature-AP, statistics, statistics-AP, theater, trigonometry, world history.

Graduation Requirements Arts and fine arts (art, music, dance, drama), English, foreign language, history, mathematics, physical education (includes health), science.

Special Academic Programs 22 Advanced Placement exams for which test preparation is offered; independent study.

College Admission Counseling 66 students graduated in 2013; all went to college, including Boston College; Colgate University; Cornell University; Princeton University; University of Pennsylvania; Yale University.

Student Life Upper grades have specified standards of dress, student council, honor system. Discipline rests equally with students and faculty.

Summer Programs Session focuses on traditional day camps and enrichment; held on campus; accepts boys and girls; open to students from other schools. 2014 schedule: June 11 to August 17.

Tuition and Aid Day student tuition: $32,788. Tuition installment plan (Insured Tuition Payment Plan, Key Tuition Payment Plan, monthly payment plans). Need-based scholarship grants available. In 2013–14, 20% of upper-school students received aid. Total amount of financial aid awarded in 2013–14: $1,299,061.

Admissions Traditional secondary-level entrance grade is 9. ISEE or SSAT required. Deadline for receipt of application materials: January 10. Application fee required: $70. On-campus interview required.

Athletics Interscholastic: basketball, cross-country running, field hockey, indoor track, lacrosse, soccer, softball, swimming and diving, tennis, track and field, volleyball, winter (indoor) track; intramural: dance, fencing, modern dance, physical fitness, squash. 4 PE instructors, 19 coaches, 1 athletic trainer.

Computers Computers are regularly used in all classes. Computer network features include on-campus library services, online commercial services, Internet access, wireless campus network, Internet filtering or blocking technology. Campus intranet, student e-mail accounts, and computer access in designated common areas are available to students. The school has a published electronic and media policy.

Contact Mrs. Julia Wall, Director of Admission and Financial Aid. 908-273-0900 Ext. 254. Fax: 908-273-9390. E-mail: admission@kentplace.org. Website: www.kentplace.org

KENT SCHOOL

PO Box 2006
Kent, Connecticut 06757

Head of School: Rev. Richardson W. Schell

General Information Coeducational boarding and day college-preparatory, arts, religious studies, technology, and pre-engineering school, affiliated with Episcopal Church. Grades 9–PG. Founded: 1906. Setting: small town. Nearest major city is Hartford. Students are housed in single-sex dormitories. 1,200-acre campus. 17 buildings on campus. Approved or accredited by Association of Independent Schools in New England, Connecticut Association of Independent Schools, National Association of Episcopal Schools, New England Association of Schools and Colleges, New York State Association of Independent Schools, The Association of Boarding Schools, and Connecticut Department of Education. Member of National Association of Independent Schools and Secondary School Admission Test Board. Endowment: $73.5 million. Total enrollment: 565. Upper school average class size: 12. Upper school faculty-student ratio: 1:7.

Upper School Student Profile Grade 9: 77 students (40 boys, 37 girls); Grade 10: 155 students (84 boys, 71 girls); Grade 11: 167 students (79 boys, 88 girls); Grade 12: 157 students (72 boys, 85 girls); Postgraduate: 15 students (1 boy, 14 girls). 90% of students are boarding students. 24% are state residents. 35 states are represented in upper school student body. 28% are international students. International students from Canada, China, Germany, Hong Kong, Republic of Korea, and Thailand; 40 other countries represented in student body.

Faculty School total: 73. In upper school: 43 men, 30 women; 55 have advanced degrees; 66 reside on campus.

Subjects Offered Advanced studio art-AP, African-American history, algebra, American history, American history-AP, American literature, architecture, art, art history-AP, Asian history, astronomy, Bible studies, biology, biology-AP, biotechnology, calculus, calculus-AP, ceramics, chemistry, chemistry-AP, Chinese, classical Greek literature, classical studies, composition-AP, computer math, computer programming, computer science, computer science-AP, digital imaging, drama, ecology, economics, English, English literature, English literature-AP, environmental science-AP, environmental studies, European history, European history-AP, expository writing, fine arts, French, French language-AP, French literature-AP, genetics, geology, geometry, German, German-AP, government and politics-AP, Greek, history, Latin, Latin American history, Latin-AP, law and the legal system, mathematics, meteorology, Middle Eastern history, modern European history-AP, music, music theory-AP, photography, physical education, physics, physics-AP, probability and statistics, psychology-AP, religion, science, sculpture, social studies, Spanish, Spanish language-AP, Spanish literature-AP, statistics-AP, theater, theology, trigonometry, U.S. government and politics-AP, world geography, world history, world literature.

Graduation Requirements Arts and fine arts (art, music, dance, drama), English, foreign language, history, mathematics, music, religion (includes Bible studies and theology), science, U.S. history.

Special Academic Programs 26 Advanced Placement exams for which test preparation is offered; honors section; independent study; academic accommodation for the gifted, the musically talented, and the artistically talented; ESL.

College Admission Counseling 171 students graduated in 2012; all went to college, including Boston University; Carnegie Mellon University; Colgate University; Cornell University; Princeton University; St. Lawrence University.

Student Life Upper grades have specified standards of dress, student council. Discipline rests equally with students and faculty. Attendance at religious services is required.

Tuition and Aid Day student tuition: $39,000; 7-day tuition and room/board: $49,500. Tuition installment plan (Key Tuition Payment Plan, monthly payment plans, individually arranged payment plans). Merit scholarship grants, need-based scholarship grants, need-based loans available. In 2012–13, 43% of upper-school students received aid. Total amount of financial aid awarded in 2012–13: $8,200,000.

Admissions Traditional secondary-level entrance grade is 9. For fall 2012, 1,200 students applied for upper-level admission, 450 were accepted, 190 enrolled. PSAT or SAT for applicants to grade 11 and 12, SSAT or TOEFL required. Deadline for receipt of application materials: January 15. Application fee required: $65. Interview required.

Athletics Interscholastic: baseball (boys), basketball (b,g), crew (b,g), cross-country running (b,g), diving (b,g), field hockey (g), football (b), golf (b,g), hockey (b,g), ice hockey (b,g), lacrosse (b,g), rowing (b,g), soccer (b,g), softball (g), squash (b,g), swimming and diving (b,g), tennis (b,g); intramural: basketball (b), crew (b,g), rowing (b,g); coed interscholastic: crew, dressage, equestrian sports, golf, horseback riding; coed intramural: aerobics/dance, aerobics/Nautilus, alpine skiing, ballet, bicycling, combined training, dance, dressage, equestrian sports, figure skating, fitness, hockey, horseback riding, ice skating, life saving, modern dance, mountain biking, physical fitness, physical training, ropes courses, sailing, skiing (downhill), snowboarding, soccer, squash, strength & conditioning, swimming and diving, tennis, ultimate Frisbee, weight training, yoga. 2 athletic trainers.

Computers Computers are regularly used in all academic, journalism, newspaper, yearbook classes. Computer network features include on-campus library services, online commercial services, Internet access, wireless campus network, students have online storage for schoolwork, Adobe Creative Suite, Autodesk, Mathcad, and Microsoft Office Software for all students. Campus intranet, student e-mail accounts, and computer access in designated common areas are available to students. The school has a published electronic and media policy.

Contact Ms. Kathryn F. Sullivan, Director of Admissions. 860-927-6111. Fax: 860-927-6109. E-mail: admissions@kent-school.edu. Website: www.kent-school.edu

KENTS HILL SCHOOL

PO Box 257
1614 Main Street, Route 17
Kents Hill, Maine 04349-0257

Head of School: Mr. Jeremy LaCasse

General Information Coeducational boarding and day college-preparatory, arts, technology, environmental studies, and ESL school, affiliated with Methodist Church. Grades 9–PG. Founded: 1824. Setting: rural. Nearest major city is Portland. Students are housed in single-sex dormitories. 400-acre campus. 24 buildings on campus. Approved or accredited by Association of Independent Schools in New England, Independent Schools of Northern New England, New England Association of Schools and Colleges, The Association of Boarding Schools, and Maine Department of Education. Member of National Association of Independent Schools and Secondary School Admission Test Board. Endowment: $4.9 million. Total enrollment: 250. Upper school average class size: 12. Upper school faculty-student ratio: 1:6. Upper School students typically attend 5 days per week. The average school day consists of 7 hours.

Upper School Student Profile Grade 9: 37 students (22 boys, 15 girls); Grade 10: 55 students (33 boys, 22 girls); Grade 11: 74 students (44 boys, 30 girls); Grade 12: 73 students (43 boys, 30 girls); Postgraduate: 10 students (8 boys, 2 girls). 75% of students are boarding students. 33% are state residents. 22 states are represented in upper school student body. 23% are international students. International students from Canada, China, Germany, Mexico, Republic of Korea, and Spain; 10 other countries represented in student body. 3% of students are Methodist.

Faculty School total: 46. In upper school: 26 men, 20 women; 22 have advanced degrees; 40 reside on campus.

Subjects Offered Acting, advanced math, Advanced Placement courses, advanced studio art-AP, African history, African-American literature, algebra, American history, American literature, art, art history, astronomy, biology, biotechnology, calculus, calculus-AP, ceramics, chemistry, college counseling, computer graphics, computer science-AP, computer-aided design, concert choir, creative writing, dance, drama, Eastern religion and philosophy, ecology, economics, English, English literature, environmental science, environmental science-AP, environmental studies, ESL, ethics,

ethics and responsibility, European history, filmmaking, fine arts, French, geology, geometry, government/civics, health, history, Holocaust, jazz ensemble, journalism, mathematics, music, photography, physics, psychology, religion, science, Shakespeare, Spanish, theater, U.S. history-AP, Western religions, woodworking, world history, writing.

Graduation Requirements English, environmental studies, foreign language, health, mathematics, science, social studies (includes history), visual and performing arts.

Special Academic Programs 11 Advanced Placement exams for which test preparation is offered; honors section; independent study; term-away projects; study abroad; academic accommodation for the gifted and the artistically talented; programs in general development for dyslexic students; special instructional classes for students with learning differences (through the Learning Skills Center); ESL (24 students enrolled).

College Admission Counseling 76 students graduated in 2012; 69 went to college. Other: 1 entered military service, 5 entered a postgraduate year, 1 had other specific plans.

Student Life Upper grades have specified standards of dress, student council, honor system. Discipline rests equally with students and faculty.

Tuition and Aid Day student tuition: $26,300; 7-day tuition and room/board: $48,300. Tuition installment plan (Insured Tuition Payment Plan, FACTS Tuition Payment Plan, monthly payment plans, individually arranged payment plans, 2-payment plan). Need-based scholarship grants available. In 2012–13, 41% of upper-school students received aid. Total amount of financial aid awarded in 2012–13: $2,200,000.

Admissions Traditional secondary-level entrance grade is 9. Deadline for receipt of application materials: February 1. Application fee required: $50. Interview required.

Athletics Interscholastic: baseball (boys), basketball (b,g), field hockey (g), football (b), ice hockey (b,g), lacrosse (b,g), soccer (b,g), softball (g), tennis (b,g); coed interscholastic: aerobics/dance, alpine skiing, bicycling, cross-country running, fencing, golf, horseback riding, independent competitive sports, mountain biking, skiing (downhill), snowboarding; coed intramural: alpine skiing, backpacking, canoeing/kayaking, dance, equestrian sports, fencing, figure skating, fitness, freestyle skiing, hiking/backpacking, horseback riding, ice skating, kayaking, mountain biking, nordic skiing, outdoor activities, outdoor recreation, physical training, skiing (cross-country), skiing (downhill), snowboarding, snowshoeing, strength & conditioning, tennis. 4 coaches, 1 athletic trainer.

Computers Computers are regularly used in all academic, college planning, desktop publishing, graphic design, media production, newspaper, photojournalism, publications, SAT preparation, video film production, Web site design, yearbook classes. Computer network features include on-campus library services, Internet access, wireless campus network, Internet filtering or blocking technology. Student e-mail accounts and computer access in designated common areas are available to students. Students grades are available online. The school has a published electronic and media policy.

Contact Mrs. Amy Smucker, Director of Admissions. 207-685-4914 Ext. 152. Fax: 207-685-9529. E-mail: asmucker@kentshill.org. Website: www.kentshill.org

KENTUCKY COUNTRY DAY SCHOOL

4100 Springdale Road
Louisville, Kentucky 40241

Head of School: Mr. Bradley E. Lyman

General Information Coeducational day college-preparatory, arts, technology, honors program, independent study, and advanced programs for academically exceptional students school. Grades JK–12. Founded: 1972. Setting: suburban. 85-acre campus. 3 buildings on campus. Approved or accredited by Independent Schools Association of the Central States. Member of National Association of Independent Schools. Endowment: $10.3 million. Total enrollment: 942. Upper school average class size: 16. Upper school faculty-student ratio: 1:7. There are 170 required school days per year for Upper School students. Upper School students typically attend 5 days per week. The average school day consists of 7 hours and 5 minutes.

Upper School Student Profile Grade 9: 78 students (34 boys, 44 girls); Grade 10: 63 students (30 boys, 33 girls); Grade 11: 66 students (30 boys, 36 girls); Grade 12: 80 students (38 boys, 42 girls).

Faculty School total: 125. In upper school: 22 men, 18 women; 32 have advanced degrees.

Subjects Offered Algebra, American history, American literature, art, biology, calculus, ceramics, chemistry, collage and assemblage, communications, computer math, computer programming, computer science, drama, economics, English, English literature, European history, fine arts, French, geology, geometry, government/civics, history, humanities, instrumental music, Latin, law, mathematics, multimedia, music, physical education, physics, play production, psychology, psychology-AP, science, sculpture, senior internship, senior project, social sciences, social studies, Spanish, Spanish language-AP, speech, stagecraft, statistics, studio art-AP, technical theater, theater, trigonometry, U.S. government and politics-AP, U.S. history-AP.

Graduation Requirements Arts and fine arts (art, music, dance, drama), communications, English, foreign language, mathematics, physical education (includes health), science, social studies (includes history).

Special Academic Programs 20 Advanced Placement exams for which test preparation is offered; honors section; independent study; term-away projects; study abroad; academic accommodation for the gifted, the musically talented, and the artistically talented.

College Admission Counseling 74 students graduated in 2012; all went to college, including Emory University; Indiana University Bloomington; Miami University; University of Kentucky; University of Louisville; University of Michigan. Median SAT critical reading: 570, median SAT math: 600, median SAT writing: 580, median combined SAT: 1750, median composite ACT: 26. 35% scored over 600 on SAT critical reading, 50% scored over 600 on SAT math, 35% scored over 600 on SAT writing, 40% scored over 1800 on combined SAT, 47% scored over 26 on composite ACT.

Student Life Upper grades have specified standards of dress, student council, honor system. Discipline rests equally with students and faculty.

Tuition and Aid Day student tuition: $17,800. Tuition installment plan (FACTS Tuition Payment Plan). Merit scholarship grants, need-based scholarship grants available. In 2012–13, 24% of upper-school students received aid; total upper-school merit-scholarship money awarded: $63,610. Total amount of financial aid awarded in 2012–13: $857,180.

Admissions Traditional secondary-level entrance grade is 9. For fall 2012, 40 students applied for upper-level admission, 30 were accepted, 21 enrolled. ERB Reading and Math required. Deadline for receipt of application materials: none. Application fee required: $50. On-campus interview required.

Athletics Interscholastic: baseball (boys), basketball (b,g), cross-country running (b,g), diving (b,g), field hockey (g), football (b), golf (b,g), lacrosse (b,g), soccer (b,g), softball (g), swimming and diving (b,g), tennis (b,g), track and field (b,g), volleyball (g), winter (indoor) track (b,g); coed interscholastic: weight training; coed intramural: bowling, project adventure, ropes courses, weight lifting. 7 PE instructors, 86 coaches, 1 athletic trainer.

Computers Computers are regularly used in all classes. Computer network features include on-campus library services, online commercial services, Internet access, wireless campus network, Internet filtering or blocking technology. Campus intranet and student e-mail accounts are available to students. Students grades are available online. The school has a published electronic and media policy.

Contact Mr. Jeff Holbrook, Director of Admissions. 502-814-4375. Fax: 502-814-4381. E-mail: admissions@kcd.org. Website: www.kcd.org

KESWICK CHRISTIAN SCHOOL

10101 54th Avenue North
St. Petersburg, Florida 33708

Head of School: Supt. Nick Stratis

General Information Coeducational day college-preparatory, arts, business, and religious studies school, affiliated with Bible Fellowship Church. Grades 1–12. Founded: 1953. Setting: rural. Nearest major city is Seminole. 10-acre campus. 3 buildings on campus. Approved or accredited by Florida Department of Education. Upper school average class size: 25. Upper school faculty-student ratio: 1:15. Upper School students typically attend 5 days per week. The average school day consists of 7 hours and 15 minutes.

Upper School Student Profile 50% of students are Bible Fellowship Church.

Faculty School total: 37. In upper school: 6 men, 15 women; 15 have advanced degrees.

Special Academic Programs International Baccalaureate program; Advanced Placement exam preparation; honors section; independent study.

College Admission Counseling 35 students graduated in 2012; 15 went to college. Other: 15 went to work, 1 entered military service, 2 entered a postgraduate year.

Student Life Upper grades have uniform requirement, student council, honor system. Discipline rests primarily with faculty. Attendance at religious services is required.

Tuition and Aid Day student tuition: $6700–$9900. Tuition installment plan (monthly payment plans, individually arranged payment plans). Tuition reduction for siblings, need-based scholarship grants available. In 2012–13, 50% of upper-school students received aid. Total amount of financial aid awarded in 2012–13: $25,000.

Admissions Traditional secondary-level entrance grade is 9. For fall 2012, 85 students applied for upper-level admission, 83 were accepted, 83 enrolled. Deadline for receipt of application materials: none. Application fee required: $225. Interview required.

Athletics Interscholastic: baseball (boys), basketball (b,g), cheering (g), cross-country running (b,g), flag football (b), football (b), golf (b), physical fitness (b), physical training (b), power lifting (b), soccer (b), volleyball (b), weight lifting (b), weight training (b), winter (indoor) track (b,g), winter soccer (b); coed interscholastic: cross-country running, running, swimming and diving, track and field, triathlon, winter (indoor) track. 4 PE instructors, 5 coaches, 1 athletic trainer.

Computers Computer network features include on-campus library services, wireless campus network, Internet filtering or blocking technology. Campus intranet and computer access in designated common areas are available to students. Students grades are available online.

Contact Sue Williams, Admissions Director. 727-393-9100 Ext. 416. Fax: 727-397-5378. E-mail: swilliams@keswickchristian.org. Website: keswickchristian.org/

THE KEW-FOREST SCHOOL

119-17 Union Turnpike
Forest Hills, New York 11375

Head of School: Mr. Mark P. Fish

General Information Coeducational day college-preparatory and arts school. Grades N–12. Founded: 1918. Setting: urban. Nearest major city is New York. 2-acre campus. 1 building on campus. Approved or accredited by Middle States Association of Colleges and Schools, New York Department of Education, and New York Department of Education. Member of National Association of Independent Schools and Secondary School Admission Test Board. Total enrollment: 238. Upper school average class size: 13. Upper school faculty-student ratio: 1:8. There are 181 required school days per year for Upper School students. Upper School students typically attend 5 days per week. The average school day consists of 6 hours and 35 minutes.

Upper School Student Profile Grade 6: 19 students (9 boys, 10 girls); Grade 7: 16 students (8 boys, 8 girls); Grade 8: 17 students (6 boys, 11 girls); Grade 9: 22 students (10 boys, 12 girls); Grade 10: 24 students (12 boys, 12 girls); Grade 11: 22 students (7 boys, 15 girls); Grade 12: 32 students (17 boys, 15 girls).

Faculty School total: 34. In upper school: 14 men, 7 women; 18 have advanced degrees.

Subjects Offered Algebra, American history, ancient history, art, biology, biology-AP, calculus, calculus-AP, chemistry, English, English composition, English language and composition-AP, English literature, French, French-AP, geometry, health, history, honors geometry, Latin, Latin-AP, marine biology, modern European history, philosophy, physical education, physics, physics-AP, pre-calculus, Spanish, Spanish-AP, trigonometry, U.S. government and politics.

Graduation Requirements Art, English, history, history of the Catholic Church, mathematics, modern languages, music appreciation, physical education (includes health), science, community service.

Special Academic Programs Advanced Placement exam preparation; honors section; independent study; academic accommodation for the gifted; ESL (20 students enrolled).

College Admission Counseling 21 students graduated in 2013; all went to college, including New York University; Vassar College. Median SAT critical reading: 520, median SAT math: 575, median SAT writing: 580. 25% scored over 600 on SAT critical reading, 40% scored over 600 on SAT math.

Student Life Upper grades have uniform requirement, student council, honor system. Discipline rests primarily with faculty.

Summer Programs Remediation, enrichment, advancement programs offered; session focuses on academic instruction; held on campus; accepts boys and girls; open to students from other schools. 50 students usually enrolled. 2014 schedule: July 1 to August 5.

Tuition and Aid Day student tuition: $32,775. Tuition installment plan (FACTS Tuition Payment Plan, Tuition Management Systems Plan). Need-based scholarship grants available. In 2013–14, 28% of upper-school students received aid. Total amount of financial aid awarded in 2013–14: $1,129,100.

Admissions Traditional secondary-level entrance grade is 9. ISEE or SSAT required. Deadline for receipt of application materials: none. Application fee required: $75. On-campus interview required.

Athletics Interscholastic: basketball (boys, girls), cross-country running (b,g), rowing (g), soccer (b,g), tennis (b,g), track and field (b,g), volleyball (g); intramural: basketball (b,g), soccer (b,g), tennis (b,g); coed interscholastic: archery, fencing, golf, sailing; coed intramural: badminton, cross-country running, fitness, physical fitness, rock climbing, running, strength & conditioning, volleyball. 2 PE instructors, 5 coaches.

Computers Computers are regularly used in all academic classes. Computer network features include on-campus library services, Internet access, wireless campus network, Internet filtering or blocking technology. Students grades are available online.

Contact Mr. Henry C. Horne, Director of Admission and Enrollment Management. 718-268-4667 Ext. 125. Fax: 718-268-9121. E-mail: hhorne@kewforest.org. Website: www.kewforest.org

THE KEY SCHOOL

534 Hillsmere Drive
Annapolis, Maryland 21403

Head of School: Marcella M. Yedid

General Information Coeducational day college-preparatory, arts, and outdoor education school. Grades PK–12. Founded: 1958. Setting: suburban. Nearest major city is Washington, DC. 15-acre campus. 10 buildings on campus. Approved or accredited by Association of Independent Maryland Schools and Maryland Department of Education. Member of National Association of Independent Schools. Endowment: $8.4 million. Total enrollment: 652. Upper school average class size: 14. Upper school faculty-student ratio: 1:7. There are 173 required school days per year for Upper School students. Upper School students typically attend 5 days per week.

Upper School Student Profile Grade 9: 53 students (26 boys, 27 girls); Grade 10: 47 students (19 boys, 28 girls); Grade 11: 43 students (17 boys, 26 girls); Grade 12: 53 students (28 boys, 25 girls).

Faculty School total: 112. In upper school: 19 men, 21 women; 26 have advanced degrees.

Subjects Offered Acting, algebra, American studies, ancient history, art, art history, biology, calculus, ceramics, chemistry, Chesapeake Bay studies, choir, computer science, conceptual physics, creative writing, dance, digital art, digital photography, drama, drama performance, drawing, economics, English, English literature, European history, fine arts, French, geometry, journalism, Latin, literature by women, music, photography, physical education, physics, physiology, playwriting, pre-calculus, printmaking, Russian literature, sculpture, Shakespeare, Spanish, Spanish literature, statistics, studio art, theater, theater production, trigonometry.

Graduation Requirements Arts and fine arts (art, music, dance, drama), English, foreign language, history, mathematics, performing arts, physical education (includes health), science.

Special Academic Programs Advanced Placement exam preparation; honors section; independent study; academic accommodation for the gifted.

College Admission Counseling 53 students graduated in 2013; 52 went to college, including Bard College; New York University; St. Mary's College of Maryland; University of Maryland, College Park; Yale University. Other: 1 had other specific plans.

Student Life Upper grades have student council. Discipline rests equally with students and faculty.

Summer Programs Remediation, enrichment, sports, art/fine arts, rigorous outdoor training programs offered; held both on and off campus; held at area pools, area parks, and other off-site locations; accepts boys and girls; open to students from other schools. 700 students usually enrolled. 2014 schedule: June 16 to August 15.

Tuition and Aid Day student tuition: $25,545. Tuition installment plan (FACTS Tuition Payment Plan, monthly payment plans). Tuition reduction for siblings, need-based scholarship grants available. In 2013–14, 23% of upper-school students received aid. Total amount of financial aid awarded in 2013–14: $439,397.

Admissions Traditional secondary-level entrance grade is 9. For fall 2013, 47 students applied for upper-level admission, 22 were accepted, 13 enrolled. ERB or ISEE required. Deadline for receipt of application materials: none. Application fee required: $45. Interview required.

Athletics Interscholastic: baseball (boys), basketball (b,g), field hockey (g), indoor soccer (g), lacrosse (b,g), soccer (b,g); intramural: field hockey (g), lacrosse (b,g); coed interscholastic: cross-country running, equestrian sports, golf, sailing, tennis; coed intramural: backpacking, basketball, canoeing/kayaking, climbing, cooperative games, dance, fitness, fitness walking, golf, hiking/backpacking, kayaking, kickball, modern dance, Newcombe ball, outdoor activities, project adventure, roller blading, running. 1 PE instructor, 44 coaches, 1 athletic trainer.

Computers Computers are regularly used in all academic classes. Computer network features include on-campus library services, online commercial services, Internet access, wireless campus network, online supplementary course materials. Campus intranet, student e-mail accounts, and computer access in designated common areas are available to students. The school has a published electronic and media policy.

Contact Jessie D. Dunleavy, Assistant Head of School for Enrollment Management. 410-263-9231. Fax: 410-280-5516. E-mail: jdunleavy@keyschool.org. Website: www.keyschool.org

KEYSTONE SCHOOL

119 East Craig Place
San Antonio, Texas 78212-3497

Head of School: Mr. Brian Yager

General Information Coeducational day college-preparatory and accelerated curriculum school. Grades PK–12. Founded: 1948. Setting: urban. 3-acre campus. 10 buildings on campus. Approved or accredited by Independent Schools Association of the Southwest and Texas Department of Education. Member of National Association of Independent Schools. Endowment: $327,000. Total enrollment: 431. Upper school average class size: 16. Upper school faculty-student ratio: 1:10. Upper School students typically attend 5 days per week. The average school day consists of 7 hours and 15 minutes.

Upper School Student Profile Grade 9: 34 students (14 boys, 20 girls); Grade 10: 34 students (22 boys, 12 girls); Grade 11: 36 students (16 boys, 20 girls); Grade 12: 24 students (15 boys, 9 girls).

Faculty School total: 49. In upper school: 11 men, 11 women; 14 have advanced degrees.

Subjects Offered Advanced Placement courses, algebra, American history, American history-AP, anatomy and physiology, biology, biology-AP, calculus-AP, chemistry, chemistry-AP, civics, community service, computer science-AP, creative writing, digital imaging, English, English language and composition-AP, English literature and composition-AP, English-AP, environmental science-AP, European history-AP, French, French language-AP, French-AP, geometry, health, history, history-AP, mathematics, performing arts, photojournalism, physical education, physics, physics-AP, political science, psychology, science, social studies, Spanish, Spanish literature-AP, Spanish-AP, statistics-AP, studio art, theater, theater arts, U.S. history-AP, world history.

Graduation Requirements Arts and fine arts (art, music, dance, drama), English, foreign language, mathematics, physical education (includes health), science, social studies (includes history), 4 Advanced Placement courses. Community service is required.

Special Academic Programs Advanced Placement exam preparation; honors section; academic accommodation for the gifted.

College Admission Counseling 32 students graduated in 2013; all went to college, including Barnard College; Harvard University; Texas A&M University; The University of Texas at Austin; Vanderbilt University; Yale University. Mean SAT critical reading: 679, mean SAT math: 652, mean SAT writing: 675, mean composite ACT: 31.

Student Life Upper grades have student council. Discipline rests primarily with faculty.

Summer Programs Sports programs offered; session focuses on sports camps; held on campus; accepts boys and girls; open to students from other schools. 60 students usually enrolled. 2014 schedule: June 2 to July 30. Application deadline: none.

Tuition and Aid Day student tuition: $16,290–$17,050. Tuition installment plan (monthly payment plans). Need-based scholarship grants available. In 2013–14, 15% of upper-school students received aid.

Admissions Traditional secondary-level entrance grade is 9. For fall 2013, 20 students applied for upper-level admission, 13 were accepted, 11 enrolled. ISEE, standardized test scores and writing sample required. Deadline for receipt of application materials: none. Application fee required: $50. On-campus interview required.

Athletics Interscholastic: basketball (boys, girls), golf (b,g), softball (g), tennis (b,g), volleyball (g); coed interscholastic: cross-country running, soccer; coed intramural: outdoor education. 3 PE instructors, 4 coaches.

Computers Computer network features include on-campus library services, online commercial services, Internet access, wireless campus network, Internet filtering or blocking technology, ProQuest Platinum. Computer access in designated common areas is available to students. Students grades are available online. The school has a published electronic and media policy.

Contact Mrs. Zina Wormley, Director of Admissions and Financial Aid. 210-735-4022. Fax: 210-734-5508. E-mail: zwormley@keystoneschool.org. Website: www.keystoneschool.org

KILDONAN SCHOOL

Amenia, New York
See Special Needs Schools section.

KIMBALL UNION ACADEMY

PO Box 188
Main Street
Meriden, New Hampshire 03770

Head of School: Mr. Michael J. Schafer

General Information Coeducational boarding and day college-preparatory, arts, and environmental science school. Grades 9–PG. Founded: 1813. Setting: small town. Nearest major city is Boston, MA. Students are housed in single-sex dormitories. 1,300-acre campus. 35 buildings on campus. Approved or accredited by Independent Schools of Northern New England, New England Association of Schools and Colleges, The Association of Boarding Schools, The College Board, and New Hampshire Department of Education. Member of National Association of Independent Schools and Secondary School Admission Test Board. Endowment: $23 million. Total enrollment: 338. Upper school average class size: 11. Upper school faculty-student ratio: 1:6. There are 159 required school days per year for Upper School students. Upper School students typically attend 6 days per week. The average school day consists of 5 hours and 8 minutes.

Upper School Student Profile Grade 9: 51 students (29 boys, 22 girls); Grade 10: 76 students (36 boys, 40 girls); Grade 11: 112 students (53 boys, 59 girls); Grade 12: 84 students (35 boys, 49 girls); Postgraduate: 8 students (8 boys). 66% of students are boarding students. 34% are state residents. 19 states are represented in upper school student body. 22% are international students. International students from Canada, China, Germany, Mexico, Republic of Korea, and Turkey; 16 other countries represented in student body.

Faculty School total: 48. In upper school: 32 men, 14 women; 26 have advanced degrees; 32 reside on campus.

Subjects Offered 3-dimensional design, acting, Advanced Placement courses, algebra, American history, American literature, anatomy, anthropology, architecture, art, art history, art history-AP, biology, biology-AP, calculus, calculus-AP, ceramics, chemistry, chemistry-AP, composition-AP, computer programming, creative writing, dance, digital photography, drama, driver education, English, English language and composition-AP, English literature, English literature and composition-AP, English-AP, environmental science, environmental science-AP, environmental studies, European history, fine arts, French, French language-AP, French literature-AP, geology, geometry, government/civics, grammar, health, history, history-AP, honors English, honors geometry, human geography - AP, independent study, international relations, jazz band, jazz ensemble, language-AP, Latin, Latin-AP, Mandarin, mathematical modeling, mathematics, modern European history-AP, modern world history, music, music history, music theory, music theory-AP, peer counseling, photo shop, photography, physics, physics-AP, physiology, playwriting, pottery, probability and statistics, programming, psychology, public speaking, science, social studies, Spanish, Spanish-

AP, stagecraft, statistics-AP, student publications, studio art, studio art-AP, theater, theater arts, theater design and production, trigonometry, U.S. government, U.S. history, U.S. history-AP, video film production, visual arts, woodworking, world history, world literature, writing.

Graduation Requirements Art, English, foreign language, history, mathematics, science.

Special Academic Programs 19 Advanced Placement exams for which test preparation is offered; honors section; independent study; term-away projects; study abroad.

College Admission Counseling 94 students graduated in 2013; 88 went to college, including Bates College; Boston University; Ithaca College; Norwich University; Providence College; St. Lawrence University. Other: 1 entered a postgraduate year, 5 had other specific plans.

Student Life Upper grades have specified standards of dress, student council, honor system. Discipline rests equally with students and faculty.

Summer Programs Enrichment, ESL, sports, art/fine arts programs offered; session focuses on environmental leadership (EE Just Institute) and ALPS (Accelerated Language Program) with Dartmouth College; held both on and off campus; held at Costa Rica; accepts boys and girls; open to students from other schools. 200 students usually enrolled. 2014 schedule: July 2 to July 30. Application deadline: April 15.

Tuition and Aid Day student tuition: $29,900; 7-day tuition and room/board: $49,500. Tuition installment plan (Insured Tuition Payment Plan, Academic Management Services Plan, Key Tuition Payment Plan, monthly payment plans). Merit scholarship grants, need-based scholarship grants, small merit scholarship program available. In 2013–14, 38% of upper-school students received aid. Total amount of financial aid awarded in 2013–14: $3,201,052.

Admissions Traditional secondary-level entrance grade is 9. For fall 2013, 474 students applied for upper-level admission, 332 were accepted, 127 enrolled. ACT, PSAT or SAT, SLEP, SSAT or TOEFL required. Deadline for receipt of application materials: February 1. Application fee required: $50. Interview required.

Athletics Interscholastic: alpine skiing (boys, girls), baseball (b), basketball (b,g), cross-country running (b,g), equestrian sports (b,g), field hockey (g), freestyle skiing (b,g), golf (b,g), hockey (b,g), horseback riding (b,g), ice hockey (b,g), lacrosse (b,g), nordic skiing (b,g), rugby (b), running (b,g), skiing (cross-country) (b,g), skiing (downhill) (b,g), snowboarding (b,g), soccer (b,g), softball (g), swimming and diving (b,g), tennis (b,g); coed interscholastic: bicycling, mountain biking; coed intramural: alpine skiing, backpacking, canoeing/kayaking, dance, equestrian sports, fitness, freestyle skiing, hiking/backpacking, modern dance, outdoor activities, physical fitness, rock climbing, squash, strength & conditioning, surfing, weight lifting, yoga. 1 coach, 2 athletic trainers.

Computers Computers are regularly used in architecture, computer applications, literary magazine, theater arts, woodworking classes. Computer network features include on-campus library services, Internet access, wireless campus network, Internet filtering or blocking technology, computer music studio/audio recording. Campus intranet, student e-mail accounts, and computer access in designated common areas are available to students. Students grades are available online. The school has a published electronic and media policy.

Contact Mr. Rich Ryerson, Director of Admissions. 603-469-2100. Fax: 603-469-2041. E-mail: admissions@kua.org. Website: www.kua.org

KING LOW HEYWOOD THOMAS

1450 Newfield Avenue
Stamford, Connecticut 06905

Head of School: Thomas B. Main

General Information Coeducational day college-preparatory and global studies, language distinctions, independent study school. Grades PK–12. Founded: 1865. Setting: suburban. Nearest major city is New York, NY. 40-acre campus. 3 buildings on campus. Approved or accredited by Connecticut Association of Independent Schools and New England Association of Schools and Colleges. Member of National Association of Independent Schools. Endowment: $19.1 million. Total enrollment: 692. Upper school average class size: 13. Upper school faculty-student ratio: 1:8. Upper School students typically attend 5 days per week. The average school day consists of 7 hours.

Upper School Student Profile Grade 9: 81 students (45 boys, 36 girls); Grade 10: 89 students (48 boys, 41 girls); Grade 11: 80 students (42 boys, 38 girls); Grade 12: 75 students (42 boys, 33 girls).

Faculty School total: 105. In upper school: 20 men, 27 women; 37 have advanced degrees.

Subjects Offered Acting, advanced chemistry, advanced computer applications, advanced math, Advanced Placement courses, algebra, American history, ancient history, ancient world history, ancient/medieval philosophy, anthropology, archaeology, art, biology, calculus, calculus-AP, chemistry, chemistry-AP, Chinese, choral music, college counseling, college planning, computer multimedia, computer programming, computer science-AP, digital photography, economics, economics-AP, English, English language and composition-AP, English literature, English literature-AP, environmental studies, ethics, European history, European history-AP, fine arts, forensics, French, French language-AP, general science, geometry, global studies, government, history, Holocaust, honors algebra, honors geometry, honors U.S. history, honors world history,

independent study, life skills, literature and composition-AP, macroeconomics-AP, mathematics, microeconomics-AP, model United Nations, modern European history-AP, modern languages, music theory-AP, musical productions, musical theater, oceanography, performing arts, philosophy, physics, physics-AP, play production, pre-calculus, psychology, public speaking, robotics, SAT preparation, SAT/ACT preparation, social studies, Spanish, Spanish language-AP, Spanish literature, Spanish literature-AP, statistics, statistics-AP, student government, student publications, studio art, theater arts, trigonometry, U.S. history-AP, U.S. literature, world history, world religions.

Graduation Requirements Arts and fine arts (art, music, dance, drama), English, ethics, foreign language, history, life skills, mathematics, science, sports, participation in one theater performance before graduation.

Special Academic Programs 17 Advanced Placement exams for which test preparation is offered; honors section; independent study; academic accommodation for the gifted, the musically talented, and the artistically talented.

College Admission Counseling 83 students graduated in 2013; 82 went to college, including Brown University; Bucknell University; Colgate University; Duke University; Elon University; Fairfield University. Other: 1 entered a postgraduate year. Median SAT critical reading: 565, median SAT math: 555, median SAT writing: 590, median combined SAT: 2400, median composite ACT: 26. 40% scored over 600 on SAT critical reading, 40% scored over 600 on SAT math, 49% scored over 600 on SAT writing, 41% scored over 1800 on combined SAT, 54% scored over 26 on composite ACT.

Student Life Upper grades have specified standards of dress, student council, honor system. Discipline rests primarily with faculty.

Summer Programs Remediation, enrichment, advancement, sports, art/fine arts programs offered; session focuses on academics (grades 6-12), enrichment (elementary school), and sports (grades 4-8) enrichment; held on campus; accepts boys and girls; open to students from other schools. 200 students usually enrolled. 2014 schedule: June 9 to August 1. Application deadline: June 1.

Tuition and Aid Day student tuition: $36,880. Tuition installment plan (Key Tuition Payment Plan). Need-based scholarship grants available. In 2013–14, 12% of upper-school students received aid. Total amount of financial aid awarded in 2013–14: $1,414,115.

Admissions Traditional secondary-level entrance grade is 9. For fall 2013, 193 students applied for upper-level admission, 67 were accepted, 35 enrolled. ISEE, school's own test or SSAT required. Deadline for receipt of application materials: January 1. Application fee required: $75. On-campus interview required.

Athletics Interscholastic: baseball (boys), basketball (b,g), cross-country running (b,g), field hockey (g), football (b), golf (b,g), ice hockey (b), independent competitive sports (b,g), lacrosse (b,g), soccer (b,g), softball (g), squash (b,g), tennis (b,g), volleyball (g); intramural: dance (g), physical training (b,g); coed interscholastic: independent competitive sports, squash; coed intramural: aerobics/dance, dance, fitness, physical training, strength & conditioning, weight lifting, weight training. 27 coaches, 2 athletic trainers.

Computers Computers are regularly used in college planning, economics, English, ethics, foreign language, French, history, mathematics, science, technology, writing, yearbook classes. Computer network features include on-campus library services, online commercial services, Internet access, wireless campus network, Internet filtering or blocking technology. Campus intranet, student e-mail accounts, and computer access in designated common areas are available to students. The school has a published electronic and media policy.

Contact Carrie Salvatore, Director of Admission and Financial Aid. 203-322-3496 Ext. 352. Fax: 203-505-6288. E-mail: csalvatore@klht.org. Website: www.klht.org

THE KING'S ACADEMY

202 Smothers Road
Seymour, Tennessee 37865

Head of School: Mr. Walter Grubb

General Information Coeducational boarding and day and distance learning college-preparatory and religious studies school, affiliated with Southern Baptist Convention. Boarding grades 7–12, day grades K4–12. Distance learning grades 9–12. Founded: 1880. Setting: suburban. Nearest major city is Knoxville. Students are housed in single-sex dormitories. 67-acre campus. 8 buildings on campus. Approved or accredited by Southern Association of Colleges and Schools and Tennessee Department of Education. Endowment: $3.1 million. Total enrollment: 471. Upper school average class size: 14. Upper school faculty-student ratio: 1:14. There are 180 required school days per year for Upper School students. Upper School students typically attend 5 days per week. The average school day consists of 7 hours.

Upper School Student Profile Grade 9: 45 students (25 boys, 20 girls); Grade 10: 40 students (21 boys, 19 girls); Grade 11: 47 students (27 boys, 20 girls); Grade 12: 37 students (23 boys, 14 girls). 24% of students are boarding students. 77% are state residents. 5 states are represented in upper school student body. 19% are international students. International students from China, Japan, Luxembourg, Nigeria, Rwanda, and Thailand; 4 other countries represented in student body. 80% of students are Southern Baptist Convention.

Faculty School total: 47. In upper school: 8 men, 13 women; 9 have advanced degrees; 9 reside on campus.

Subjects Offered Advanced Placement courses, algebra, American history, anatomy, art, Bible studies, biology, calculus, chemistry, Chinese, choir, drama, economics, English, English-AP, ESL, fine arts, geometry, government/civics, grammar, health, health and wellness, history, keyboarding, mathematics, music, orchestra, physical education, physics, physiology, religion, science, social studies, Spanish, world history.

Graduation Requirements Arts and fine arts (art, music, dance, drama), computer science, English, foreign language, mathematics, religion (includes Bible studies and theology), science, social studies (includes history), wellness.

Special Academic Programs Advanced Placement exam preparation; honors section; independent study; study at local college for college credit; ESL (18 students enrolled).

College Admission Counseling 37 students graduated in 2012; 34 went to college, including Boston College; Carson-Newman University; Georgia Institute of Technology; Penn State University Park; Purdue University; The University of Tennessee. Other: 3 went to work.

Student Life Upper grades have uniform requirement, student council. Discipline rests primarily with faculty. Attendance at religious services is required.

Tuition and Aid Day student tuition: $5500–$6600; 5-day tuition and room/board: $15,970–$20,680; 7-day tuition and room/board: $22,680–$27,390. Tuition installment plan (FACTS Tuition Payment Plan, monthly payment plans, individually arranged payment plans). Tuition reduction for siblings, need-based scholarship grants available. In 2012–13, 14% of upper-school students received aid. Total amount of financial aid awarded in 2012–13: $89,610.

Admissions Traditional secondary-level entrance grade is 9. For fall 2012, 34 students applied for upper-level admission, 33 were accepted, 22 enrolled. OLSAT, Stanford Achievement Test or TOEFL required. Deadline for receipt of application materials: none. Application fee required: $50. Interview recommended.

Athletics Interscholastic: baseball (boys), basketball (b,g), cheering (g), football (b), golf (b,g), soccer (b,g), tennis (b,g), volleyball (g), weight lifting (b,g), weight training (b,g); intramural: basketball (b,g), billiards (b,g), table tennis (b,g), tennis (b,g), volleyball (g), weight lifting (b,g), weight training (b,g); coed interscholastic: backpacking, bowling, cross-country running, rappelling, rock climbing, strength & conditioning, track and field; coed intramural: aerobics/Nautilus, canoeing/kayaking, cross-country running, fitness, outdoor education, physical fitness, physical training, rappelling, rock climbing, strength & conditioning, volleyball. 17 coaches, 1 athletic trainer.

Computers Computers are regularly used in business applications, computer applications, keyboarding, yearbook classes. Computer network features include Internet access. Students grades are available online.

Contact Mrs. Janice Mink, Director of Admissions. 865-573-8321. Fax: 865-573-8323. E-mail: jmink@thekingsacademy.net. Website: www.thekingsacademy.net

KINGS CHRISTIAN SCHOOL

900 East D Street
Lemoore, California 93245

Head of School: Mr. Steven W. Reynolds

General Information Coeducational day college-preparatory, general academic, arts, business, religious studies, and technology school, affiliated with Protestant-Evangelical faith. Grades PK–12. Founded: 1979. Setting: small town. Nearest major city is Fresno. 17-acre campus. 12 buildings on campus. Approved or accredited by Association of Christian Schools International and Western Association of Schools and Colleges. Total enrollment: 294. Upper school average class size: 20. Upper school faculty-student ratio: 1:11. There are 180 required school days per year for Upper School students. Upper School students typically attend 5 days per week. The average school day consists of 6 hours and 45 minutes.

Upper School Student Profile Grade 9: 16 students (10 boys, 6 girls); Grade 10: 21 students (13 boys, 8 girls); Grade 11: 27 students (16 boys, 11 girls); Grade 12: 24 students (13 boys, 11 girls). 70% of students are Protestant-Evangelical faith.

Faculty School total: 26. In upper school: 4 men, 7 women; 3 have advanced degrees.

Subjects Offered Accounting, advanced math, algebra, American government, art, auto mechanics, Bible studies, biology, business, business mathematics, calculus-AP, career education, cheerleading, chemistry, choir, chorus, Christian doctrine, Christian scripture, community service, computer applications, computer literacy, drama, drawing, driver education, economics, English, English composition, English literature-AP, ensembles, finance, fine arts, geography, geometry, health, home economics, HTML design, keyboarding, library skills, life skills, literature, mathematics, music, music theory, novels, painting, personal money management, physical education, physical science, physics, pre-algebra, religion, SAT preparation, science, Shakespeare, social sciences, social studies, Spanish, speech, U.S. history, weight training, word processing, yearbook.

Graduation Requirements Arts and fine arts (art, music, dance, drama), Bible studies, English, foreign language, mathematics, physical education (includes health), portfolio writing, science, social sciences, successfully pass Bible every year of attendance, proof of at least 9th grade proficiency (SAT Test).

Special Academic Programs 2 Advanced Placement exams for which test preparation is offered; honors section; accelerated programs; independent study; remedial reading and/or remedial writing; remedial math.

College Admission Counseling 26 students graduated in 2013; 22 went to college, including Azusa Pacific University; California State University, Fresno; The Master's College and Seminary; Vanguard University of Southern California; West Hills Community College. Other: 4 went to work. Median SAT critical reading: 520, median SAT math: 500, median SAT writing: 530, median combined SAT: 1550, median composite ACT: 20. 18% scored over 600 on SAT critical reading, 18% scored over 600 on SAT math, 18% scored over 600 on SAT writing, 45% scored over 1800 on combined SAT, 20% scored over 26 on composite ACT.

Student Life Upper grades have specified standards of dress, student council. Discipline rests primarily with faculty.

Tuition and Aid Day student tuition: $5999. Tuition installment plan (monthly payment plans). Tuition reduction for siblings, need-based scholarship grants, paying campus jobs available. In 2013–14, 19% of upper-school students received aid. Total amount of financial aid awarded in 2013–14: $61,750.

Admissions Traditional secondary-level entrance grade is 9. For fall 2013, 11 students applied for upper-level admission, 9 were accepted, 9 enrolled. PSAT or Terra Nova-CTB required. Deadline for receipt of application materials: none. Application fee required: $150.

Athletics Interscholastic: baseball (boys), basketball (b,g), football (b), softball (g), track and field (b,g), volleyball (g); intramural: physical fitness (b,g), physical training (b,g), power lifting (b), strength & conditioning (b,g), track and field (b,g), weight training (b,g); coed interscholastic: cheering, cross-country running, track and field; coed intramural: badminton, fitness, Frisbee, physical fitness, strength & conditioning, table tennis, track and field, volleyball. 5 PE instructors, 9 coaches, 2 athletic trainers.

Computers Computers are regularly used in Bible studies, college planning, English, introduction to technology, journalism, library skills, programming, SAT preparation, technical drawing, yearbook classes. Computer network features include on-campus library services, Internet access, wireless campus network, Internet filtering or blocking technology. Students grades are available online.

Contact Leslie Reynolds, Registrar. 559-924-8301 Ext. 107. Fax: 559-924-0607. E-mail: lreynolds@kcsnet.com. Website: www.kcsnet.com

KING'S-EDGEHILL SCHOOL

254 College Road
Windsor, Nova Scotia B0N 2T0, Canada

Head of School: Mr. Joseph Seagram

General Information Coeducational boarding and day college-preparatory school. Grades 6–12. Founded: 1788. Setting: small town. Nearest major city is Halifax, Canada. Students are housed in single-sex dormitories. 65-acre campus. 17 buildings on campus. Approved or accredited by California Association of Independent Schools and Nova Scotia Department of Education. Language of instruction: English. Total enrollment: 290. Upper school average class size: 15. Upper school faculty-student ratio: 1:10.

Upper School Student Profile Grade 10: 60 students (28 boys, 32 girls); Grade 11: 70 students (37 boys, 33 girls); Grade 12: 70 students (38 boys, 32 girls). 68% of students are boarding students. 55% are province residents. 13 provinces are represented in upper school student body. 30% are international students. International students from Germany, Hong Kong, Mexico, Republic of Korea, and Taiwan; 13 other countries represented in student body.

Faculty School total: 46. In upper school: 19 men, 23 women; 15 have advanced degrees; 22 reside on campus.

Subjects Offered Art, biology, calculus, chemistry, current events, drama, economics, English, French, geography, geology, history, mathematics, music, physics, political science, religion, science, social sciences, social studies, theater, theory of knowledge, world history.

Graduation Requirements English, foreign language, mathematics, science, social sciences, social studies (includes history).

Special Academic Programs International Baccalaureate program; honors section; term-away projects; study abroad; academic accommodation for the gifted; ESL (22 students enrolled).

College Admission Counseling 70 students graduated in 2013; all went to college, including Dalhousie University; McGill University; Queen's University at Kingston; The University of British Columbia; The University of Western Ontario; University of Toronto.

Student Life Upper grades have uniform requirement, student council, honor system. Discipline rests primarily with faculty. Attendance at religious services is required.

Tuition and Aid Day student tuition: CAN$16,100; 7-day tuition and room/board: CAN$37,700. Tuition installment plan (monthly payment plans, individually arranged payment plans). Bursaries, merit scholarship grants available. In 2013–14, 35% of upper-school students received aid. Total amount of financial aid awarded in 2013–14: CAN$900,000.

Admissions Traditional secondary-level entrance grade is 10. OLSAT and English Exam required. Deadline for receipt of application materials: none. Application fee required: CAN$100. Interview required.

Athletics Interscholastic: alpine skiing (boys, girls), aquatics (b,g), badminton (b,g), baseball (b,g), basketball (b,g), biathlon (b,g), bicycling (b,g), cross-country running (b,g), equestrian sports (b,g), fitness (b,g), Frisbee (b,g), golf (b,g), ice hockey (b,g), outdoor recreation (b,g), outdoor skills (b,g), physical fitness (b,g), rugby (b,g), skiing (cross-country) (b,g), skiing (downhill) (b,g), snowboarding (b,g), soccer (b,g), softball (b,g), table tennis (b,g), tennis (b,g), track and field (b,g), ultimate Frisbee (b,g), volleyball (b,g), weight lifting (b,g), wrestling (b,g); intramural: basketball (b,g), bicycling (b,g), cross-country running (b,g), golf (b,g), rugby (b,g), skiing (cross-country) (b,g), skiing (downhill) (b,g), snowboarding (b,g), soccer (b,g), softball (b,g), table tennis (b,g), tennis (b,g), track and field (b,g), weight lifting (b,g), yoga (b,g); coed interscholastic: alpine skiing, aquatics, bicycling, equestrian sports, fitness, Frisbee, outdoor recreation, outdoor skills, physical fitness, table tennis; coed intramural: bowling, curling, field hockey, table tennis, yoga. 2 PE instructors, 30 coaches.

Computers Computers are regularly used in computer applications, English, foreign language, mathematics, music, science classes. Computer network features include on-campus library services, online commercial services, Internet access, Internet filtering or blocking technology. Campus intranet, student e-mail accounts, and computer access in designated common areas are available to students.

Contact Mr. Chris B. Strickey, Director of Admission. 902-798-2278. Fax: 902-798-2105. E-mail: strickey@kes.ns.ca. Website: www.kes.ns.ca

KINGSWAY COLLEGE

1200 Leland Road
Oshawa, Ontario L1K 2H4, Canada

Head of School: Mr. Scott Bowes

General Information Coeducational boarding and day college-preparatory, general academic, arts, business, religious studies, bilingual studies, and technology school, affiliated with Seventh-day Adventists. Grades 9–12. Founded: 1903. Setting: small town. Nearest major city is Toronto, Canada. Students are housed in single-sex by floor dormitories. 100-acre campus. 9 buildings on campus. Approved or accredited by Ontario Ministry of Education and Ontario Department of Education. Language of instruction: English. Endowment: CAN$1.6 million. Total enrollment: 187. Upper school average class size: 13. Upper school faculty-student ratio: 1:12. There are 180 required school days per year for Upper School students. Upper School students typically attend 5 days per week. The average school day consists of 5 hours and 50 minutes.

Upper School Student Profile Grade 9: 31 students (18 boys, 13 girls); Grade 10: 52 students (28 boys, 24 girls); Grade 11: 46 students (26 boys, 20 girls); Grade 12: 58 students (26 boys, 32 girls). 56% of students are boarding students. 79% are province residents. 9 provinces are represented in upper school student body. 21% are international students. International students from Brazil, China, Kuwait, Republic of Korea, Ukraine, and United States; 2 other countries represented in student body. 80% of students are Seventh-day Adventists.

Faculty School total: 15. In upper school: 10 men, 5 women; 2 have advanced degrees; 2 reside on campus.

Subjects Offered Accounting, advanced chemistry, advanced computer applications, advanced math, algebra, American history, anthropology, band, biology, business studies, calculus, Canadian geography, Canadian history, Canadian law, career education, ceramics, chemistry, choir, civics, computer applications, computer information systems, computer programming, computer studies, concert band, English, English literature, ESL, French, healthful living, information processing, intro to computers, music, music performance, physical education, physics, psychology, religious education, science, sociology, study skills, U.S. history, visual arts, work-study, world civilizations, world religions.

Graduation Requirements Art, Canadian geography, Canadian history, careers, civics, English, French, mathematics, physical education (includes health), science, all students must take one religion course per year.

Special Academic Programs ESL (36 students enrolled).

College Admission Counseling 50 students graduated in 2013; 42 went to college, including Andrews University; McGill University; Southern Adventist University; University of Michigan; University of Toronto; Walla Walla University. Other: 1 had other specific plans.

Student Life Upper grades have specified standards of dress, student council. Discipline rests primarily with faculty.

Summer Programs ESL programs offered; session focuses on ESL; held both on and off campus; held at Toronto, Ontario and Niagara Falls, Ontario; accepts boys and girls; open to students from other schools. 60 students usually enrolled. 2014 schedule: August 5 to August 19. Application deadline: May 1.

Tuition and Aid Day student tuition: CAN$11,500; 7-day tuition and room/board: CAN$18,666. Tuition installment plan (monthly payment plans, individually arranged payment plans). Tuition reduction for siblings, merit scholarship grants, need-based scholarship grants, paying campus jobs available. In 2013–14, 45% of upper-school students received aid; total upper-school merit-scholarship money awarded: CAN$60,000. Total amount of financial aid awarded in 2013–14: CAN$200,000.

Admissions Traditional secondary-level entrance grade is 9. For fall 2013, 188 students applied for upper-level admission, 187 were accepted, 187 enrolled. Deadline for receipt of application materials: none. No application fee required. Interview recommended.

Athletics Interscholastic: basketball (boys, girls); intramural: basketball (b,g), flag football (b,g), floor hockey (b,g), ice hockey (b), indoor hockey (b,g), racquetball (b,g), soccer (b,g), softball (b,g), volleyball (b,g); coed interscholastic: backpacking; coed

intramural: badminton, canoeing/kayaking, gymnastics, hiking/backpacking, roller skating, skiing (downhill), snowboarding, volleyball. 1 PE instructor, 2 coaches.

Computers Computers are regularly used in accounting, business, career education, computer applications, data processing, English, ESL, history, programming, science, social sciences classes. Computer network features include Internet access, wireless campus network, Internet filtering or blocking technology. Student e-mail accounts and computer access in designated common areas are available to students. Students grades are available online. The school has a published electronic and media policy.

Contact Ms. Ashley Arriola, Communications Assistant. 905-433-1144 Ext. 211. Fax: 905-433-1156. E-mail: admissions@kingswaycollege.on.ca. Website: www.kingswaycollege.on.ca

KINGSWOOD-OXFORD SCHOOL

170 Kingswood Road
West Hartford, Connecticut 06119-1430

Head of School: Mr. Dennis Bisgaard

General Information Coeducational day college-preparatory school. Grades 6–12. Founded: 1909. Setting: suburban. Nearest major city is Hartford. 30-acre campus. 11 buildings on campus. Approved or accredited by New England Association of Schools and Colleges and Connecticut Department of Education. Member of National Association of Independent Schools and Secondary School Admission Test Board. Endowment: $25.7 million. Total enrollment: 511. Upper school average class size: 13. Upper school faculty-student ratio: 1:8. There are 160 required school days per year for Upper School students. Upper School students typically attend 5 days per week. The average school day consists of 7 hours.

Upper School Student Profile Grade 9: 85 students (36 boys, 49 girls); Grade 10: 99 students (57 boys, 42 girls); Grade 11: 88 students (44 boys, 44 girls); Grade 12: 93 students (45 boys, 48 girls).

Faculty School total: 53. In upper school: 27 men, 26 women; 33 have advanced degrees.

Subjects Offered Algebra, American history, American literature, art, art history-AP, band, biology, biology-AP, calculus, calculus-AP, chemistry, chemistry-AP, Chinese, Chinese studies, chorus, composition-AP, computer science, computer science-AP, concert band, concert choir, creative writing, digital music, digital photography, dramatic arts, drawing, economics, economics-AP, English, English language-AP, English literature, English literature-AP, environmental science, fine arts, forensics, French, French language-AP, geography, geometry, government/civics, jazz band, jazz ensemble, journalism, Latin, Latin-AP, marine biology, mathematics, media, music, orchestra, photography, physics, physics-AP, political science, public speaking, social studies, Spanish, Spanish language-AP, Spanish-AP, statistics, statistics-AP, theater, U.S. history-AP, visual arts, world history, world literature, writing.

Graduation Requirements Computer science, English, foreign language, mathematics, performing arts, science, social studies (includes history), technology, visual arts, participation on athletic teams, senior thesis in English, 30 hours of community service. Community service is required.

Special Academic Programs 17 Advanced Placement exams for which test preparation is offered; honors section; independent study; term-away projects; study at local college for college credit; study abroad.

College Admission Counseling 75 students graduated in 2013; all went to college, including Boston University; Bucknell University; Gettysburg College; Lehigh University; Union College; University of Connecticut. Median SAT critical reading: 615, median SAT math: 595, median SAT writing: 610, median combined SAT: 1820, median composite ACT: 27.

Student Life Upper grades have specified standards of dress, student council, honor system. Discipline rests equally with students and faculty.

Summer Programs Advancement, sports, art/fine arts programs offered; session focuses on academics, sports, and arts; held on campus; accepts boys and girls; open to students from other schools. 45 students usually enrolled.

Tuition and Aid Day student tuition: $34,500. Tuition installment plan (SMART Tuition Payment Plan). Merit scholarship grants, need-based scholarship grants available. In 2013–14, 35% of upper-school students received aid; total upper-school merit-scholarship money awarded: $276,500. Total amount of financial aid awarded in 2013–14: $2,300,000.

Admissions Traditional secondary-level entrance grade is 9. For fall 2013, 206 students applied for upper-level admission, 115 were accepted, 48 enrolled. SSAT required. Deadline for receipt of application materials: February 1. Application fee required: $55. On-campus interview required.

Athletics Interscholastic: baseball (boys), basketball (b,g), cross-country running (b,g), diving (b,g), field hockey (g), football (b), ice hockey (b,g), lacrosse (b,g), soccer (b,g), softball (g), squash (b,g), strength & conditioning (b,g), swimming and diving (b,g), tennis (b,g), track and field (b,g), volleyball (g); intramural: basketball (b,g), ice hockey (b), soccer (b,g), yoga (g); coed interscholastic: golf, skiing (downhill); coed intramural: strength & conditioning. 9 coaches, 2 athletic trainers.

Computers Computers are regularly used in English, foreign language, history, mathematics, music technology, photography, science classes. Computer resources include on-campus library services, Internet access, wireless campus network. Student e-mail accounts and computer access in designated common areas are available to students. Students grades are available online. The school has a published electronic and media policy.

Contact Mr. James E. ODonnell, Director of Enrollment Management. 860-727-5000. Fax: 860-236-3651. E-mail: odonnell.j@k-o.org. Website: www.kingswoodoxford.org

THE LAB SCHOOL OF WASHINGTON

Washington, District of Columbia
See Special Needs Schools section.

LA CHEIM SCHOOL

Antioch, California
See Special Needs Schools section.

LA JOLLA COUNTRY DAY SCHOOL

9490 Genesee Avenue
La Jolla, California 92037

Head of School: Mr. Christopher Schuck

General Information Coeducational day college-preparatory, arts, and technology school. Grades N–12. Founded: 1926. Setting: suburban. Nearest major city is San Diego. 24-acre campus. 8 buildings on campus. Approved or accredited by Western Association of Schools and Colleges and California Department of Education. Member of National Association of Independent Schools and Secondary School Admission Test Board. Endowment: $2.4 million. Total enrollment: 1,131. Upper school average class size: 16. Upper school faculty-student ratio: 1:16. There are 171 required school days per year for Upper School students. Upper School students typically attend 5 days per week. The average school day consists of 7 hours.

Upper School Student Profile Grade 9: 138 students (73 boys, 65 girls); Grade 10: 137 students (67 boys, 70 girls); Grade 11: 122 students (62 boys, 60 girls); Grade 12: 119 students (67 boys, 52 girls).

Faculty School total: 143. In upper school: 25 men, 26 women; 35 have advanced degrees.

Subjects Offered Advanced studio art-AP, algebra, Arabic, art, art history-AP, art-AP, ASB Leadership, astronomy, athletic training, band, baseball, basketball, biology, biology-AP, calculus, calculus-AP, ceramics, chemistry, chemistry-AP, choir, choral music, chorus, college counseling, community service, computer graphics, conceptual physics, concert band, creative writing, dance, dance performance, digital photography, drama, economics, economics-AP, English, English language-AP, English literature, English literature and composition-AP, English-AP, environmental science, European history, European history-AP, experiential education, Farsi, film studies, French, French language-AP, French literature-AP, French-AP, freshman seminar, geometry, golf, government, government and politics-AP, government-AP, history of drama, history-AP, honors algebra, honors geometry, independent study, instrumental music, journalism, linear algebra, madrigals, Mandarin, marine biology, modern European history-AP, music appreciation, music theory-AP, music-AP, neuroscience, performing arts, photography, physical education, physics, physics-AP, portfolio art, pre-calculus, programming, psychology, psychology-AP, Spanish, Spanish language-AP, Spanish literature-AP, Spanish-AP, speech, statistics-AP, strings, studio art, studio art-AP, technical theater, theater, theater arts, theater history, theater production, theory of knowledge, U.S. history-AP, world cultures, writing.

Graduation Requirements Arts and fine arts (art, music, dance, drama), English, foreign language, mathematics, performing arts, physical education (includes health), science, senior project, social sciences, speech, 40 hours of community service.

Special Academic Programs Advanced Placement exam preparation; honors section; study abroad.

College Admission Counseling 123 students graduated in 2013; 119 went to college, including Stanford University; University of Chicago; University of Southern California. Other: 4 had other specific plans. Mean SAT critical reading: 600, mean SAT math: 600, mean SAT writing: 622. 43% scored over 600 on SAT critical reading, 53% scored over 600 on SAT math.

Student Life Upper grades have specified standards of dress, student council. Discipline rests equally with students and faculty.

Summer Programs Remediation, enrichment, advancement, sports, art/fine arts, computer instruction programs offered; session focuses on academics, summer camp, sports camps; held on campus; accepts boys and girls; open to students from other schools. 300 students usually enrolled. 2014 schedule: June 22 to July 31. Application deadline: none.

Tuition and Aid Day student tuition: $28,650. Tuition installment plan (FACTS Tuition Payment Plan, monthly payment plans). Need-based scholarship grants available. In 2013–14, 28% of upper-school students received aid. Total amount of financial aid awarded in 2013–14: $2,748,943.

Admissions Traditional secondary-level entrance grade is 9. ERB (grade level), ISEE, TerraNova or writing sample required. Deadline for receipt of application materials: February 3. Application fee required: $125. On-campus interview required.

Athletics Interscholastic: aquatics (boys, girls), baseball (b), basketball (b,g), cross-country running (b,g), dance (b,g), fencing (b,g), football (b), golf (b,g), ice hockey (b), in-line hockey (b), independent competitive sports (b,g), lacrosse (b,g), roller hockey (b), soccer (b,g), softball (g), swimming and diving (b,g), tennis (b,g), track and field (b,g), volleyball (g), water polo (b,g); coed interscholastic: cheering, physical fitness, physical training, strength & conditioning, surfing, ultimate Frisbee, weight lifting, weight training; coed intramural: dance team, outdoor education, snowboarding. 7 PE instructors, 7 coaches, 1 athletic trainer.

Computers Computers are regularly used in art, English, French, history, mathematics, science, Spanish, technology classes. Computer network features include on-campus library services, online commercial services, Internet access, wireless campus network, Internet filtering or blocking technology, email connection from home. Student e-mail accounts are available to students. The school has a published electronic and media policy.

Contact Ms. Inez Odom, Director of Admission. 858-453-3440 Ext. 273. Fax: 858-453-8210. E-mail: Iodom@ljcds.org. Website: www.ljcds.org

LAKEFIELD COLLEGE SCHOOL

4391 County Road #29
Lakefield, Ontario K0L 2H0, Canada

Head of School: Mr. Struan Robertson

General Information Coeducational boarding and day and distance learning college-preparatory, arts, and athletics, music, outdoor education school, affiliated with Church of England (Anglican). Grades 9–12. Distance learning grades 9–12. Founded: 1879. Setting: small town. Nearest major city is Toronto, Canada. Students are housed in single-sex dormitories. 315-acre campus. 25 buildings on campus. Approved or accredited by Canadian Association of Independent Schools, Canadian Educational Standards Institute, The Association of Boarding Schools, and Ontario Department of Education. Affiliate member of National Association of Independent Schools; member of Secondary School Admission Test Board. Language of instruction: English. Endowment: CAN$22 million. Upper school average class size: 17. Upper school faculty-student ratio: 1:7. There are 195 required school days per year for Upper School students. Upper School students typically attend 6 days per week. The average school day consists of 5 hours.

Upper School Student Profile Grade 9: 62 students (31 boys, 31 girls); Grade 10: 81 students (41 boys, 40 girls); Grade 11: 120 students (57 boys, 63 girls); Grade 12: 103 students (57 boys, 46 girls). 68% of students are boarding students. 60% are province residents. 10 provinces are represented in upper school student body. 36% are international students. International students from Barbados, Bermuda, China, Democratic People's Republic of Korea, Germany, and Mexico; 23 other countries represented in student body.

Faculty School total: 53. In upper school: 27 men, 22 women; 12 have advanced degrees; 25 reside on campus.

Subjects Offered Algebra, art, art history, biology, calculus, chemistry, computer science, creative writing, drama, earth science, economics, English, English literature, environmental science, fine arts, French, geography, geometry, government/civics, health, history, kinesiology, mathematics, music, outdoor education, physical education, physics, science, social studies, sociology, Spanish, theater, trigonometry, vocal music, world history, world literature.

Graduation Requirements English, foreign language, mathematics, physical education (includes health), science, social studies (includes history).

Special Academic Programs 8 Advanced Placement exams for which test preparation is offered; term-away projects; study abroad.

College Admission Counseling 101 students graduated in 2013; 90 went to college, including McGill University; Ryerson University; The University of Western Ontario; Trent University; University of Ottawa; University of Toronto. Other: 11 had other specific plans.

Student Life Upper grades have uniform requirement, student council, honor system. Discipline rests equally with students and faculty.

Summer Programs Enrichment programs offered; session focuses on online courses; held off campus; held at via distance learning; accepts boys and girls; open to students from other schools. 100 students usually enrolled. 2014 schedule: June 22 to August 30.

Tuition and Aid Day student tuition: CAN$29,180; 7-day tuition and room/board: CAN$50,865. Tuition installment plan (Insured Tuition Payment Plan, monthly payment plans, individually arranged payment plans, 3-payment plans or custom payment plans if req'd). Bursaries, merit scholarship grants, need-based scholarship grants available. In 2013–14, 25% of upper-school students received aid; total upper-school merit-scholarship money awarded: CAN$22,000. Total amount of financial aid awarded in 2013–14: CAN$160,000.

Admissions Traditional secondary-level entrance grade is 9. For fall 2013, 218 students applied for upper-level admission, 190 were accepted, 135 enrolled. Otis-Lennon School Ability Test, SSAT or TOEFL or SLEP required. Deadline for receipt of application materials: none. Application fee required: CAN$100. Interview required.

Athletics Interscholastic: alpine skiing (boys, girls), baseball (b), basketball (g), crew (b,g), cross-country running (b,g), field hockey (g), hockey (b,g), ice hockey (b,g), nordic skiing (b,g), outdoor education (b,g), physical fitness (b,g), rock climbing (b,g), ropes courses (b,g), rowing (b,g), rugby (b,g), skiing (cross-country) (b,g), skiing (downhill) (b,g), snowboarding (b,g), soccer (b,g), softball (b), tennis (b), track and field (b,g), volleyball (g); intramural: aerobics/dance (g), basketball (b,g), cross-country running (b,g), fitness (b,g), running (b,g), skiing (cross-country) (b,g), tennis (b,g); coed interscholastic: alpine skiing, badminton, cross-country running, dressage, equestrian sports, Frisbee, hockey, horseback riding, ice hockey, nordic skiing, outdoor education, physical fitness, rock climbing, sailboarding, sailing, skiing (cross-country), skiing (downhill), snowboarding, tennis, track and field, ultimate Frisbee, wall climbing, windsurfing; coed intramural: basketball, canoeing/kayaking, climbing, cross-country running, dance, dance team, equestrian sports, fitness, ice hockey, kayaking, running, sailboarding, sailing, skiing (cross-country), skiing (downhill), softball, tennis, weight training, windsurfing, yoga.

Computers Computers are regularly used in all classes. Computer network features include on-campus library services, online commercial services, Internet access, wireless campus network, Internet filtering or blocking technology. Campus intranet, student e-mail accounts, and computer access in designated common areas are available to students. Students grades are available online. The school has a published electronic and media policy.

Contact Mrs. Barbara M. Rutherford, Assistant Director of Admissions. 705-652-3324 Ext. 345. Fax: 705-652-6320. E-mail: admissions@lcs.on.ca. Website: www.lcs.on.ca

LAKEHILL PREPARATORY SCHOOL

2720 Hillside Drive
Dallas, Texas 75214

Head of School: Roger L. Perry

General Information Coeducational day college-preparatory, arts, bilingual studies, and technology school. Grades K–12. Founded: 1971. Setting: urban. 23-acre campus. 4 buildings on campus. Approved or accredited by Independent Schools Association of the Southwest, Texas Private School Accreditation Commission, The College Board, and Texas Department of Education. Member of National Association of Independent Schools. Endowment: $300,000. Total enrollment: 400. Upper school average class size: 15. Upper school faculty-student ratio: 1:10. There are 175 required school days per year for Upper School students. Upper School students typically attend 5 days per week. The average school day consists of 7 hours and 30 minutes.

Upper School Student Profile Grade 9: 33 students (18 boys, 15 girls); Grade 10: 31 students (15 boys, 16 girls); Grade 11: 23 students (11 boys, 12 girls); Grade 12: 27 students (11 boys, 16 girls).

Faculty School total: 44. In upper school: 9 men, 13 women; 17 have advanced degrees.

Subjects Offered Advanced Placement courses, advanced studio art-AP, algebra, American history, American history-AP, American literature, art, art history, biology, calculus, calculus-AP, chemistry, college counseling, computer math, computer programming, computer programming-AP, computer science, digital photography, drama, earth science, economics, English, English language and composition-AP, English literature, environmental science-AP, European history, French, French language-AP, geography, geometry, government/civics, grammar, health, history, journalism, Latin, mathematics, music, music theater, physical education, physics, psychology, public speaking, publications, science, senior career experience, Shakespeare, social sciences, social studies, Spanish, Spanish language-AP, Spanish literature-AP, speech, statistics, theater, trigonometry, Western civilization, world history, world literature, writing.

Graduation Requirements Arts and fine arts (art, music, dance, drama), computer science, electives, English, foreign language, mathematics, science, social studies (includes history), Senior Internship Program.

Special Academic Programs 14 Advanced Placement exams for which test preparation is offered; honors section; independent study; study abroad.

College Admission Counseling 17 students graduated in 2013; all went to college, including Brown University; Rice University; The University of Kansas; The University of Texas at Austin; University of Oklahoma; University of Southern California. Median SAT critical reading: 623, median SAT math: 580, median SAT writing: 579, median combined SAT: 1782, median composite ACT: 24.

Student Life Upper grades have specified standards of dress, student council, honor system. Discipline rests primarily with faculty.

Summer Programs Enrichment, sports, art/fine arts, computer instruction programs offered; session focuses on enrichment; held on campus; accepts boys and girls; open to students from other schools. 200 students usually enrolled. 2014 schedule: June 9 to August 8. Application deadline: May 15.

Tuition and Aid Day student tuition: $18,500. Tuition installment plan (monthly payment plans). Tuition reduction for siblings, need-based scholarship grants available. In 2013–14, 18% of upper-school students received aid.

Admissions Traditional secondary-level entrance grade is 9. ERB CTP IV, ISEE or Stanford Achievement Test required. Deadline for receipt of application materials: January 17. Application fee required: $150. On-campus interview recommended.

Athletics Interscholastic: baseball (boys), basketball (b,g), cheering (g), cross-country running (b,g), football (b), golf (b,g), paddling (b,g), rock climbing (b,g), running (b,g), softball (g), swimming and diving (b,g), tennis (b,g), track and field (b,g), volleyball (g), weight training (b,g); coed interscholastic: soccer, swimming and diving, tennis; coed intramural: bowling. 3 PE instructors, 12 coaches, 1 athletic trainer.

Computers Computers are regularly used in art, college planning, creative writing, English, graphic design, journalism, mathematics, science, speech, Web site design, word processing, writing, yearbook classes. Computer network features include on-campus library services, online commercial services, Internet access, wireless campus network, Internet filtering or blocking technology. Student e-mail accounts and computer access in designated common areas are available to students. Students grades are available online. The school has a published electronic and media policy.

Contact Holly Walker, Director of Admission. 214-826-2931. Fax: 214-826-4623. E-mail: hwalker@lakehillprep.org. Website: www.lakehillprep.org

LAKE MARY PREPARATORY SCHOOL

650 Rantoul Lane
Lake Mary, Florida 32746

Head of School: Mr. Glenn Chapin

General Information Coeducational boarding and day and distance learning college-preparatory, arts, business, and technology school. Boarding grades 7–12, day grades PK–12. Distance learning grade X. Founded: 1999. Setting: suburban. Nearest major city is Orlando. Students are housed in single-sex dormitories. 48-acre campus. 1 building on campus. Approved or accredited by Florida Department of Education. Member of National Association of Independent Schools. Total enrollment: 640. Upper school average class size: 20. Upper school faculty-student ratio: 1:22. There are 180 required school days per year for Upper School students. Upper School students typically attend 5 days per week. The average school day consists of 7 hours and 30 minutes.

Upper School Student Profile Grade 6: 50 students (25 boys, 25 girls); Grade 7: 49 students (23 boys, 26 girls); Grade 8: 44 students (24 boys, 20 girls); Grade 9: 67 students (49 boys, 18 girls); Grade 10: 56 students (34 boys, 22 girls); Grade 11: 76 students (50 boys, 26 girls); Grade 12: 69 students (43 boys, 26 girls). 7% of students are boarding students. 93% are state residents. 2 states are represented in upper school student body. 7% are international students. International students from Brazil, China, Republic of Korea, Russian Federation, Turkey, and Viet Nam.

Faculty School total: 62. In upper school: 18 men, 21 women; 13 have advanced degrees; 8 reside on campus.

Subjects Offered 1968, 20th century American writers, 20th century ethnic conflicts, accounting, ACT preparation, addiction, ADL skills, advanced computer applications, advanced studio art-AP, advanced TOEFL/grammar, aerobics, aerospace education, aerospace science, aesthetics, African American history, African American studies, African dance, African drumming, African history, African literature, African studies, African-American history, African-American literature, African-American studies, agriculture, agroecology, Alabama history and geography, all , alternative physical education, American biography, American Civil War, American culture, American democracy, American foreign policy, American legal systems, American minority experience, American politics in film, American sign language, American studies, analysis, analysis and differential calculus, analysis of data, analytic geometry, anatomy and physiology, Ancient Greek, ancient history, ancient/medieval philosophy, animal behavior, animal husbandry, animal science, animation, anthropology, applied arts, applied music, applied skills, aquatics, Arabic, Arabic studies, archaeology, architecture, area studies, art and culture, art appreciation, art education, art history, art history-AP, art in New York, art-AP, arts, arts and crafts, arts appreciation, ASB Leadership, Asian history, Asian literature, Asian studies, astronomy, astrophysics, athletic training, atomic theory, audition methods, auto mechanics, automated accounting, aviation, backpacking, bacteriology, ballet technique, banking, basic imaging, basic language skills, Basic programming, basic skills, batik, bell choir, Bible, Bible as literature, Bible studies, biochemistry, bioethics, bioethics, DNA and culture, biotechnology, bivouac, Black history, boat building, boating, body human, Bolivian history, Bolivian social studies, bookbinding, bookkeeping, bookmaking, botany, bowling, brass choir, Brazilian history, Brazilian social studies, Brazilian studies, British history, British literature-AP, British National Curriculum, Broadway dance, Buddhism, business applications, business communications, business education, business law, business mathematics, business skills, business studies, business technology, cabinet making, California writers, calligraphy, campus ministry, Canadian geography, Canadian history, Canadian law, Canadian literature, Cantonese, career and personal planning, career and technology systems, career education, career education internship, career experience, career exploration, Career Passport, career planning, career technology, career/college preparation, careers, Caribbean history, carpentry, cartography, cartooning/animation, Catholic belief and practice, celestial navigation, ceramics, ceremonies of life, chamber groups, chaplaincy, Cherokee, Chesapeake Bay studies, Cheyenne history, Cheyenne language, child development, China/Japan history, Chinese, Chinese history, Chinese literature, Chinese studies, choir, choral music, Christian and Hebrew scripture, Christian doctrine, Christian education, Christian ethics, Christian scripture, Christian studies, Christian testament, Christianity, church history, circus acts, civics/free enterprise, civil rights, Civil War, civil war history, classical civilization, classical Greek literature, classical language, classical music, classical studies, classics, clinical chemistry, collage and assemblage, college admission preparation, college awareness, college placement, college planning, college writing, Colorado ecology, comedy, Coming of Age in the 20th Century, commercial art, communication arts, communication skills, communications, community garden, comparative civilizations, comparative cultures, comparative government and politics, comparative government and politics-AP, comparative political systems-AP, comparative politics, comparative religion, competitive science projects, composition, composition-AP, computer animation, computer applications, computer art, computer education, computer graphics, computer information systems, computer literacy, computer math, computer multimedia, computer music, computer processing, computer programming, computer programming-AP, computer resources, computer science, computer science-AP, computer skills, computer studies, computer technologies, computer technology certification, computer tools, computer-aided design, computers, conceptual physics, concert bell choir, concert choir, conservation, constitutional history of U.S., constitutional law, construction, consumer economics, consumer education, consumer law, consumer mathematics, contemporary art, contemporary history, contemporary issues, contemporary issues in science, contemporary math, contemporary problems, contemporary studies, contemporary technique, contemporary women writers, costumes and make-up, CPR, crafts, creation science, creative arts, creative dance, creative drama, creative thinking, creative writing, criminal justice, criminology, critical studies in film, critical thinking, critical writing, culinary arts, cultural arts, cultural criticism, cultural geography, current events, current history, dance performance, Danish, data analysis, data processing, death and loss, debate, decision making skills, democracy in America, design, desktop publishing, ESL, developmental language skills, developmental math, digital applications, digital imaging, digital music, directing, discrete mathematics, diversity studies, DNA, DNA research, DNA science lab, drafting, drama performance, drama workshop, dramatic arts, drawing, driver education, Dutch, early childhood, earth and space science, earth science, earth systems analysis, East Asian history, East European studies, Eastern religion and philosophy, Eastern world civilizations, Easterner in the West, ecology, ecology, environmental systems, education, Egyptian history, electronic imagery, electronic music, electronic publishing, electronic research, electronics, emergency medicine, emerging technology, engineering, English composition, English language and composition-AP, English language-AP, English literature, English literature and composition-AP, English-AP, English/composition-AP, ensembles, entomology, environmental education, environmental geography, environmental science, environmental science-AP, environmental studies, environmental systems, epic literature, equality and freedom, equestrian sports, equine management, equine science, equitation, essential learning systems, ethical decision making, ethics, ethics and responsibility, ethnic literature, ethnic studies, ethology, etymology, European civilization, European literature, eurythmics (guard), eurythmy, evolution, exercise science, existentialism, experiential education, experimental science, expository writing, expressive arts, fabric arts, family and consumer science, family living, family studies, Far Eastern history, Farsi, fashion, female experience in America, fencing, fiber arts, fiction, field ecology, Filipino, film and literature, film and new technologies, film appreciation, film history, film series, film studies, finance, finite math, Finnish, first aid, fitness, flight instruction, folk art, folk dance, folk music, food and nutrition, food science, foods, foreign policy, forensics, forest resources, forestry, foundations of civilization, four team activities, four units of summer reading, fractal geometry, French, French as a second language, French language-AP, French literature-AP, French studies, French-AP, freshman foundations, freshman seminar, functions, gardening, gender and religion, gender issues, general, general business, general math, general science, genetics, geography, geology, geometry with art applications, geopolitics, German, German literature, German-AP, gerontology, glassblowing, global issues, global science, global studies, golf, government, government and politics-AP, government/civics, government/civics-AP, grammar, graphic arts, graphics, great books, great issues, Greek, Greek culture, Greek drama, guidance, guitar, gymnastics, Haitian studies, handbells, Harlem Renaissance, Hausa, Hawaiian history, Hawaiian language, health, health and safety, health education, health enhancement, health immersion, health science, healthful living, Hebrew, Hebrew scripture, heritage of American Women, high adventure outdoor program, Hindi, Hispanic literature, histology, historical foundations for arts, historical research, historiography, history and culture of Portugal, history of architecture, history of China and Japan, history of computing, history of dance, history of drama, history of England, history of ideas, history of jazz, history of mathematics, history of music, history of religion, history of rock and roll, history of science, history of the Americas, history of the Catholic Church, history-AP, Holocaust, Holocaust and other genocides, Holocaust legacy, Holocaust seminar, Holocaust studies, holography, home economics, Homeric Greek, Honduran history, honors algebra, horticulture, HTML design, human anatomy, human biology, human development, human geography - AP, human issues, human movement and its application to health, human relations, human rights, human sexuality, humanities, hydrology, ideas, illustration, immunology, improvisation, independent living, independent study, Indian studies, Indonesian, Indonesian studies, industrial arts, industrial technology, information design technology, information processing, information technology, inorganic chemistry, inquiry into relationship, instrumental music, instruments, integrated arts, integrated mathematics, integrated physics, integrated science, integrated technology fundamentals, integrative seminar, interactive media, interdisciplinary studies, interior design, international affairs, International Baccalaureate courses, international foods, international relations, international studies, Internet, Internet research, internship, interpersonal skills, intro to computers, introduction to digital multitrack recording techniques, introduction to liberal studies, introduction to literature, introduction to technology, introduction to theater, Irish literature, Irish studies, Islamic history, Islamic studies, Israeli studies, issues of the 90's, Italian, Italian history, Japanese, Japanese and American values compared, Japanese as Second Language, Japanese history, Japanese literature, Japanese studies,

jazz, jazz dance, jazz ensemble, jazz theory, jewelry making, Jewish history, Jewish studies, John F. Kennedy, journalism, JROTC, JROTC or LEAD (Leadership Education and Development), Judaic studies, junior and senior seminars, justice seminar, Kentucky history, keyboarding, kinesiology, Korean, Korean culture, Korean literature, lab science, lab/keyboard, land and ranch management, land management, language, language and composition, language arts, language development, language enhancement and development, language of the theater, language structure, languages, Latin, Latin American history, Latin American literature, Latin American studies, Latin History, Latin-AP, law, law and the legal system, law studies, leadership, leadership and service, leadership education training, learning cognition, learning lab, learning strategies, leatherworking, lettering, library, library assistant, library research, library science, library skills, library studies, life issues, life management skills, Life of Christ, life saving, life science, life skills, limnology, linear algebra, linguistics, literacy, literary genres, literary magazine, literature, literature and composition-AP, literature by women, literature seminar, literature-AP, logarithms, logic, logic, rhetoric, and debate, macro/microeconomics-AP, macroeconomics-AP, madrigals, Malay, Malay culture, management information systems, Mandarin, marching band, marine ecology, marine science, marine studies, maritime history, marketing, martial arts, math applications, math methods, math review, mathematical modeling, mathematics, mathematics-AP, mechanical drawing, mechanics, mechanics of writing, media, media arts, media communications, media literacy, media production, media services, media studies, mediator, medieval history, medieval literature, medieval/Renaissance history, meditation, men's studies, mentorship program, metal fabrication technology, metalworking, meteorology, methods of research, Mexican history, Mexican literature, microbiology, microcomputer technology applications, microeconomics, microeconomics-AP, Microsoft, Middle East, Middle Eastern history, military history, military science, minority studies, model United Nations, modeling, modern Chinese history, modern civilization, modern dance, modern European history, modern European history-AP, modern history, modern languages, modern political theory, modern politics, modern problems, modern Western civilization, money management, Montana history, moral and social development, moral reasoning, moral theology, Moroccan studies, multicultural literature, multicultural studies, multimedia, multimedia design, museum science, music, music appreciation, music composition, music for dance, music history, music performance, music technology, music theater, music theory, music theory-AP, music-AP, musical productions, musical theater, musical theater dance, musicianship, mythology, nationalism and ethnic conflict, Native American arts and crafts, Native American history, Native American studies, natural history, natural resources management, nature study, nature writers, Navajo, naval science, navigation, neuroanatomy, neurobiology, neuroscience, New Testament, news writing, newspaper, NJROTC, non-Western literature, non-Western societies, North American literature, North Carolina history, Norwegian, novels, nuclear science, nutrition, occupational education, oceanography, official social customs, oil painting, opera, optics, oral communications, oral expression, orchestra, organ, organic biochemistry, organic chemistry, organic gardening, organizational studies, ornithology, outdoor education, Pacific art, Pacific Island studies, Pacific Northwest seminar, pack animal trips, painting, paleontology, parent/child development, parenting, participation in sports, peace and justice, peace education, peace studies, peer counseling, peer ministry, performing arts, permaculture, Persian, personal and social education, personal development, personal finance, personal fitness, personal growth, personal money management, Philippine culture, philosophy, philosophy of government, photo shop, photography, photojournalism, physical fitness, physical science, physiology, piano, piloting, play production, play/screen writing, playwriting, playwriting and directing, poetry, policy and value, Polish, political economy, political science, political systems, political thought, politics, Polynesian dance, portfolio art, portfolio writing, Portuguese, Portuguese literature, post-calculus, pottery, practical arts, practical living, practicum, pragmatics, prayer/spirituality, pre-calculus, pre-college orientation, pre-vocational education, printmaking, probability, probability and statistics, production, programming, projective geometry, psychology-AP, public policy, public policy issues and action, public service, public speaking, publications, publicity, publishing, Puerto Rican history, Quakerism and ethics, qualitative analysis, Rabbinic literature, radio broadcasting, reading, reading/study skills, reconstructive language, regional literature, relationships, religion, religion and culture, religious education, religious studies, remedial study skills, remedial/makeup course work, research, research and reference, research in consciousness, research seminar, research skills, rhetoric, rhetoric of war, rite of passage, robotics, Roman civilization, Roman culture, Roman historiography, Romantic period literature, ROTC, ROTC (for boys), Russia and contemporary Europe, Russian, Russian history, Russian literature, Russian studies, Sanskrit, SAT preparation, SAT/ACT preparation, scene study, science, science and technology, science fiction, science project, science research, scripture, scuba diving, sculpture, self-defense, senior career experience, senior composition, senior humanities, senior internship, senior project, senior science survey, senior seminar, senior thesis, Serbo-Croatian, service learning/internship, set design, sewing, sex education, sexuality, Shakespeare, Shakespearean histories, shop, short story, sign language, silk screening, single survival, Sinhalese, siSwati, skills for success, small engine repair, social doctrine, social education, social issues, social justice, social psychology, social sciences, social skills, social studies, society, society and culture, society challenge and change, society, politics and law, socioeconomic problems, sociology, softball, software design, sophomore skills, South African history, Southern literature, space and physical sciences, Spanish literature, Spanish literature-AP, Spanish-AP, speech, speech and oral interpretations, speech communications, speech origins of English, speech therapy, sports, sports conditioning, sports medicine, sports nutrition, sports performance development, sports psychology, sports science, sports team management, squash, stage and body movement, stage design, stained glass, standard curriculum, state government, state history, statistics, stock market, stone carving, strategies for success, street law, strings, student government, student publications, student teaching, studio art, studio art-AP, study skills, substance abuse, surfing, survival training, Swahili, Swedish, swimming, swimming competency, swimming test, Swiss culture, symphonic band, synchronized swimming, Talmud, Tamil, tap dance, taxonomy, technical arts, technical drawing, technical education, technical skills, technical studies, technical theater, technical writing, techniques of living and coping, technological applications, technology, technology/design, telecommunications, telecommunications and the Internet, television, tennis, Texas history, textiles, Thai, Thailand and Southeast Asia, The 20th Century, the comic tradition, the Presidency, the Sixties, the Web, theater, theater arts, theater design and production, theater history, theater production, theology, theology and the arts, theory of knowledge, therapeutic horseback riding, TOEFL preparation, Tok Pisin, topics in dramatic literature, track and field, traditional camping, training, transition mathematics, transportation technology, travel, trigonometry, tropical biology, tropical ecology, Turkish history, twentieth century ethnic conflicts, typing, U.S. and Virginia government, U.S. and Virginia government-AP, U.S. and Virginia history, U.S. constitutional history, U.S. government and politics, U.S. government and politics-AP, U.S. literature, U.S. Presidents, Ukolelc, Ukrainian, unified math, United Nations and international issues, urban design, urban studies, Urdu, utopia, values and decisions, Vedic science, veterinary science, video, video and animation, video communication, video film production, Vietnam, Vietnam history, Vietnam War, Virginia government, visual and performing arts, visual arts, visual literacy, visual reality, vocal ensemble, vocal jazz, vocal music, vocational arts, vocational skills, vocational-technical courses, voice, voice and diction, voice ensemble, volleyball, Washington State and Northwest History, water color painting, water polo, waterskiing, weaving, Web authoring, Web site design, weight fitness, weight reduction, weightlifting, welding, wellness, Western civilization, Western literature, Western philosophy, Western religions, white-water trips, wilderness education, wilderness experience, wind ensemble, wind instruments, windsurfing, women in literature, women in society, women in the classical world, women in world history, women spirituality and faith, women's health, women's literature, women's studies, wood lab, wood processing, woodworking, word processing, work camp program, work experience, work-study, world affairs, world arts, world civilizations, world cultures, world geography, world governments, world issues, world literature, world religions, world religions, world studies, World War I, World War II, world wide web design, World-Wide-Web publishing, wrestling, writing, writing, writing workshop, Yiddish, youth culture, Zen Buddhism, zoology.

Special Academic Programs Advanced Placement exam preparation; honors section; study abroad; ESL (52 students enrolled).

College Admission Counseling 72 students graduated in 2013; all went to college, including Florida State University; Penn State University Park; University of Central Florida; University of Florida; University of Miami; Wake Forest University. Median SAT critical reading: 510, median SAT math: 560, median SAT writing: 500, median combined SAT: 1560, median composite ACT: 24.

Student Life Upper grades have uniform requirement, student council, honor system. Discipline rests primarily with faculty.

Summer Programs Remediation, enrichment, ESL, art/fine arts, rigorous outdoor training, computer instruction programs offered; session focuses on enrichment activities; held on campus; accepts boys and girls; open to students from other schools. 450 students usually enrolled. 2014 schedule: June 7 to August 15. Application deadline: June 7.

Tuition and Aid Day student tuition: $13,575; 7-day tuition and room/board: $30,375. Tuition installment plan (monthly payment plans). Tuition reduction for siblings, merit scholarship grants, need-based scholarship grants available. In 2013–14, 10% of upper-school students received aid.

Admissions Traditional secondary-level entrance grade is 9. ISEE required. Deadline for receipt of application materials: none. Application fee required: $100. Interview required.

Athletics Interscholastic: aquatics (girls), baseball (b), basketball (b,g), bowling (b,g), cheering (g), cross-country running (b,g), dance (b,g), dance squad (b,g), dance team (b,g), diving (b,g), flag football (b,g), golf (b,g), lacrosse (b,g), soccer (b,g), softball (g), swimming and diving (b,g), tennis (b,g), track and field (b,g), volleyball (g), weight lifting (b,g), winter soccer (b,g). 4 PE instructors, 22 coaches, 1 athletic trainer.

Computers Computers are regularly used in all academic classes. Computer network features include on-campus library services, Internet access, wireless campus network, Internet filtering or blocking technology. Students grades are available online. The school has a published electronic and media policy.

Contact Cory Ostrowski, Director of Admissions. 407-805-0095 Ext. 105. Fax: 407-322-3872. E-mail: cory.ostrowski@lakemaryprep.com. Website: www.lakemaryprep.com/podium/default.aspx?t=134873

LANCASTER COUNTRY DAY SCHOOL

725 Hamilton Road
Lancaster, Pennsylvania 17603

Head of School: Mr. Steven D. Lisk

General Information Coeducational day college-preparatory school. Grades PS–12. Founded: 1908. Setting: suburban. Nearest major city is Philadelphia. 26-acre campus. 1 building on campus. Approved or accredited by Pennsylvania Department of Education. Member of National Association of Independent Schools. Endowment: $10 million. Total enrollment: 615. Upper school average class size: 12. Upper school faculty-student ratio: 1:6. There are 171 required school days per year for Upper School students. Upper School students typically attend 5 days per week. The average school day consists of 7 hours.

Upper School Student Profile Grade 9: 53 students (18 boys, 35 girls); Grade 10: 56 students (30 boys, 26 girls); Grade 11: 57 students (27 boys, 30 girls); Grade 12: 47 students (21 boys, 26 girls).

Faculty School total: 86. In upper school: 14 men, 25 women; 27 have advanced degrees.

Subjects Offered 20th century American writers, 20th century history, Advanced Placement courses, algebra, American history, American history-AP, American literature, American literature-AP, Asian studies, athletic training, Basic programming, bioethics, DNA and culture, biology, biology-AP, calculus, calculus-AP, ceramics, chamber groups, chemistry, chemistry-AP, China/Japan history, chorus, computer art, computer graphics, computer programming, computer programming-AP, computer science, computer science-AP, conceptual physics, contemporary history, contemporary issues, contemporary issues in science, creative writing, critical thinking, critical writing, dance, desktop publishing, digital imaging, drama, drawing, economics and history, English literature, English-AP, ensembles, environmental science, European civilization, European history, European literature, fine arts, French, French-AP, geometry, honors geometry, instrumental music, Latin, Mandarin, math applications, mathematics, model United Nations, music, music history, painting, photography, physical education, physics, pre-calculus, printmaking, programming, research seminar, senior project, service learning/internship, Spanish, Spanish-AP, sports medicine, statistics, statistics-AP, theater, trigonometry, U.S. history, U.S. history-AP, U.S. literature, United Nations and international issues, weight training, women in world history, world affairs, world civilizations, world history, world literature, writing, yearbook.

Graduation Requirements Arts, English, foreign language, history, Latin, mathematics, physical education (includes health), science.

Special Academic Programs 13 Advanced Placement exams for which test preparation is offered; accelerated programs; independent study; study at local college for college credit; academic accommodation for the gifted, the musically talented, and the artistically talented; programs in general development for dyslexic students; ESL (4 students enrolled).

College Admission Counseling 49 students graduated in 2013; all went to college, including American University; Bucknell University; Franklin & Marshall College; New York University; Penn State University Park; The George Washington University. Median SAT critical reading: 610, median SAT math: 620, median SAT writing: 600, median combined SAT: 1840, median composite ACT: 27. 51% scored over 600 on SAT critical reading, 59% scored over 600 on SAT math, 45% scored over 600 on SAT writing, 55% scored over 1800 on combined SAT, 51% scored over 26 on composite ACT.

Student Life Upper grades have specified standards of dress, student council, honor system. Discipline rests equally with students and faculty.

Tuition and Aid Day student tuition: $22,050. Tuition installment plan (monthly payment plans, 2-installment plan). Merit scholarship grants, need-based scholarship grants available. In 2013–14, 30% of upper-school students received aid; total upper-school merit-scholarship money awarded: $409,593. Total amount of financial aid awarded in 2013–14: $1,026,312.

Admissions Traditional secondary-level entrance grade is 9. For fall 2013, 89 students applied for upper-level admission, 40 were accepted, 24 enrolled. ERB CTP III required. Deadline for receipt of application materials: none. Application fee required: $75. Interview required.

Athletics Interscholastic: baseball (boys), basketball (b,g), cross-country running (b,g), dance (b,g), field hockey (g), football (b), lacrosse (b,g), modern dance (b,g), soccer (b,g), softball (g), tennis (b,g), volleyball (b,g), weight training (b,g), wrestling (b,g); coed interscholastic: bowling, golf, squash, swimming and diving, track and field, ultimate Frisbee. 4 PE instructors, 5 coaches, 1 athletic trainer.

Computers Computers are regularly used in all academic classes. Computer network features include on-campus library services, online commercial services, Internet access, wireless campus network, Internet filtering or blocking technology, Technology-rich environment with SmartBoards in every classroom, iPads for all students in grade 9-12 free of charge. Student e-mail accounts and computer access in designated common areas are available to students. Students grades are available online. The school has a published electronic and media policy.

Contact Jamie Beth Jamie Beth Schindler Schindler, Assistant Director of Admission. 717-392-2916 Ext. 228. Fax: 717-392-0425. E-mail: schindlerj@lancastercountryday.org. Website: www.lancastercountryday.org

LANCASTER MENNONITE HIGH SCHOOL

2176 Lincoln Highway East
Lancaster, Pennsylvania 17602

Head of School: Mr. Elvin Kennel

General Information Coeducational boarding and day college-preparatory, general academic, arts, vocational, religious studies, bilingual studies, and agriculture school, affiliated with Mennonite Church. Boarding grades 9–12, day grades 6–12. Founded: 1942. Setting: suburban. Nearest major city is Philadelphia. Students are housed in coed dormitories and single-sex by wings. 100-acre campus. 9 buildings on campus. Approved or accredited by Mennonite Education Agency, Mennonite Schools Council, Middle States Association of Colleges and Schools, and Pennsylvania Department of Education. Endowment: $12 million. Upper school average class size: 18. Upper school faculty-student ratio: 1:15. There are 182 required school days per year for Upper School students. Upper School students typically attend 5 days per week. The average school day consists of 6 hours and 30 minutes.

Upper School Student Profile Grade 9: 135 students (62 boys, 73 girls); Grade 10: 130 students (63 boys, 67 girls); Grade 11: 195 students (102 boys, 93 girls); Grade 12: 168 students (79 boys, 89 girls). 8% of students are boarding students. 89% are state residents. 4 states are represented in upper school student body. 11% are international students. International students from China, Ethiopia, Hong Kong, Republic of Korea, Spain, and Viet Nam; 13 other countries represented in student body. 30% of students are Mennonite.

Faculty School total: 77. In upper school: 38 men, 37 women; 50 have advanced degrees; 4 reside on campus.

Subjects Offered 1 1/2 elective credits, 3-dimensional art, 3-dimensional design, accounting, advanced biology, advanced chemistry, advanced math, Advanced Placement courses, agriculture, American government, American history, American history-AP, art appreciation, athletics, band, baseball, basketball, bell choir, Bible, Bible as literature, Bible studies, biology, biology-AP, bowling, business, business mathematics, calculus, calculus-AP, career experience, career exploration, career/college preparation, chemistry, chemistry-AP, Chinese, choir, chorus, Christian doctrine, Christian education, Christian scripture, Christian studies, church history, communications, community service, comparative government and politics, comparative government and politics-AP, concert band, concert choir, creative writing, culinary arts, drama, drawing, driver education, ecology, electives, English, English composition, English language and composition-AP, entrepreneurship, environmental science, ESL, European history, family and consumer science, family living, family studies, fashion, foods, foreign language, French, German, guitar, health education, history, human development, instrumental music, jazz band, language arts, Life of Christ, literary magazine, literature-AP, music, music appreciation, music composition, music performance, music theory, music-AP, musical productions, newspaper, orchestra, painting, parent/child development, participation in sports, performing arts, photography, physical education, physics, physics-AP, psychology, psychology-AP, public speaking, science, senior project, small engine repair, sociology, softball, Spanish, Spanish language-AP, statistics, statistics-AP, strings, student government, student publications, tennis, track and field, U.S. history, U.S. history-AP, U.S. literature, visual and performing arts, visual arts, voice, volleyball, weight training, welding, wind ensemble, wind instruments, woodworking, world history, world history-AP, writing.

Graduation Requirements A certain amount of credits are needed in various academic areas.

Special Academic Programs 13 Advanced Placement exams for which test preparation is offered; honors section; independent study; study at local college for college credit; academic accommodation for the musically talented; remedial reading and/or remedial writing; remedial math; special instructional classes for deaf students, blind students; ESL (40 students enrolled).

College Admission Counseling 147 students graduated in 2013; 96 went to college, including Eastern Mennonite University; Goshen College; Grove City College; Hesston College; Messiah College; Penn State University Park. Other: 26 went to work, 18 had other specific plans. Mean SAT critical reading: 552, mean SAT math: 545, mean SAT writing: 528, mean combined SAT: 1625.

Student Life Upper grades have specified standards of dress, student council. Discipline rests primarily with faculty. Attendance at religious services is required.

Summer Programs Enrichment, sports, art/fine arts programs offered; held on campus; accepts boys and girls; open to students from other schools. 200 students usually enrolled. 2014 schedule: June to August. Application deadline: none.

Tuition and Aid Day student tuition: $7500; 5-day tuition and room/board: $12,820; 7-day tuition and room/board: $15,990. Tuition installment plan (monthly payment plans). Tuition reduction for siblings, merit scholarship grants, need-based scholarship grants, paying campus jobs available. In 2013–14, 40% of upper-school students received aid; total upper-school merit-scholarship money awarded: $20,000. Total amount of financial aid awarded in 2013–14: $2,000,000.

Admissions Traditional secondary-level entrance grade is 9. For fall 2013, 112 students applied for upper-level admission, 112 were accepted, 112 enrolled. Deadline for receipt of application materials: none. Application fee required: $100. Interview recommended.

Athletics Interscholastic: ball hockey (girls), baseball (b), basketball (b,g), cross-country running (b,g), field hockey (g), football (b), golf (b), lacrosse (b), soccer (b,g), softball (g), tennis (b,g), track and field (b,g), volleyball (b,g); coed interscholastic: baseball, bowling. 4 PE instructors, 20 coaches, 1 athletic trainer.

Computers Computers are regularly used in all academic classes. Computer network features include on-campus library services, Internet access, wireless campus network, Internet filtering or blocking technology. Campus intranet and student e-mail accounts are available to students. Students grades are available online. The school has a published electronic and media policy.

Contact Christy L. Horst, Administrative Assistant for Admissions. 717-299-0436 Ext. 312. Fax: 717-299-0823. E-mail: horstcl@lancastermennonite.org. Website: www.lancastermennonite.org

LANDMARK CHRISTIAN ACADEMY

6502 Johnsontown Road
Louisville, Kentucky 40272

Head of School: Mr. Monte L. Ashworth

General Information Coeducational day college-preparatory and religious studies school, affiliated with Baptist Church. Grades K4–12. Founded: 1978. Setting: suburban. 5-acre campus. 1 building on campus. Approved or accredited by American Association of Christian Schools. Total enrollment: 140. Upper school average class size: 8. Upper school faculty-student ratio: 1:6. There are 177 required school days per year for Upper School students. Upper School students typically attend 5 days per week. The average school day consists of 6 hours and 50 minutes.

Upper School Student Profile Grade 9: 6 students (1 boy, 5 girls); Grade 10: 7 students (5 boys, 2 girls); Grade 11: 10 students (7 boys, 3 girls); Grade 12: 1 student (1 boy). 80% of students are Baptist.

Faculty School total: 16. In upper school: 5 men, 4 women; 2 have advanced degrees.

Subjects Offered Advanced math, algebra, American history, American literature, analytic geometry, ancient history, ancient world history, Bible, biology, business mathematics, chemistry, choir, computer technologies, consumer economics, consumer mathematics, economics, English composition, English literature, general science, geography, geometry, grammar, health, history, home economics, keyboarding, modern history, physical education, physics, pre-algebra, pre-calculus, speech, trigonometry, world geography, world history.

Graduation Requirements Bible, computers, English, foreign language, history, mathematics, science, social sciences.

College Admission Counseling 7 students graduated in 2013; 5 went to college, including University of Louisville. Other: 1 went to work, 1 had other specific plans. Mean composite ACT: 22.

Student Life Upper grades have uniform requirement. Discipline rests primarily with faculty.

Tuition and Aid Day student tuition: $3500. Tuition installment plan (FACTS Tuition Payment Plan). Tuition reduction for siblings available.

Admissions Traditional secondary-level entrance grade is 9. For fall 2013, 3 students applied for upper-level admission, 3 were accepted, 3 enrolled. Math and English placement tests required. Deadline for receipt of application materials: none. Application fee required: $275. On-campus interview required.

Athletics Interscholastic: basketball (boys), soccer (b), track and field (b,g), volleyball (g). 1 PE instructor, 3 coaches.

Computers Computers are regularly used in computer applications, keyboarding, Spanish classes. The school has a published electronic and media policy.

Contact Miss Gloria G. Ortegon, School Secretary. 502-933-3000. Fax: 502-933-5179. E-mail: LCAinfo@libcky.com. Website: www.lcaky.com/main.html

LANDMARK CHRISTIAN SCHOOL

50 SE Broad Street
Fairburn, Georgia 30213

Head of School: Mr. Mike Titus

General Information Coeducational day college-preparatory, arts, and religious studies school, affiliated with Christian faith, Protestant faith. Grades K4–12. Founded: 1989. Setting: suburban. Nearest major city is Atlanta. 62-acre campus. 4 buildings on campus. Approved or accredited by Southern Association of Colleges and Schools and Georgia Department of Education. Total enrollment: 862. Upper school average class size: 16. Upper school faculty-student ratio: 1:8. There are 179 required school days per year for Upper School students. Upper School students typically attend 5 days per week. The average school day consists of 7 hours and 15 minutes.

Upper School Student Profile Grade 9: 80 students (42 boys, 38 girls); Grade 10: 69 students (38 boys, 31 girls); Grade 11: 69 students (32 boys, 37 girls); Grade 12: 56 students (26 boys, 30 girls). 100% of students are Christian faith, Protestant.

Faculty School total: 74. In upper school: 13 men, 24 women; 17 have advanced degrees.

Subjects Offered Advanced biology, advanced chemistry, advanced math, Advanced Placement courses, advanced studio art-AP, algebra, American government, American literature-AP, anatomy and physiology, art, art-AP, athletic training, band, baseball, basketball, Bible, Bible studies, biology, biology-AP, British literature-AP, calculus, calculus-AP, chamber groups, cheerleading, chemistry, chemistry-AP, choral music, chorus, Christian studies, communications, composition, computer literacy, computer skills, computer technologies, computers, concert band, concert choir, drama, drama performance, economics, electives, English, English language and composition-AP, English literature, English literature-AP, English-AP, fine arts, foreign language, forensics, geometry, golf, government/civics-AP, health, health and wellness, history, history-AP, honors algebra, honors English, honors geometry, honors U.S. history, human anatomy, human biology, instrumental music, keyboarding, leadership education training, marine biology, music, music appreciation, music theater, physics, physics-AP, physiology, pre-calculus, social studies, Spanish, Spanish language-AP, Spanish-AP, speech, sports medicine, statistics, swimming, tennis, theater arts, U.S. history, U.S. history-AP, vocal ensemble, volleyball, weight training, writing, yearbook.

Special Academic Programs 9 Advanced Placement exams for which test preparation is offered; honors section; study at local college for college credit.

College Admission Counseling 52 students graduated in 2013; all went to college, including Georgia College & State University; Georgia Southern University; Mercer University; Samford University; University of Georgia. Median SAT critical reading: 540, median SAT math: 540, median SAT writing: 540, median combined SAT: 1620, median composite ACT: 24. 27% scored over 600 on SAT critical reading, 26% scored over 600 on SAT math, 26% scored over 600 on SAT writing, 25% scored over 1800 on combined SAT, 35% scored over 26 on composite ACT.

Student Life Upper grades have uniform requirement, student council, honor system. Discipline rests primarily with faculty. Attendance at religious services is required.

Summer Programs Computer instruction programs offered; held on campus; accepts boys and girls; not open to students from other schools. 20 students usually enrolled.

Tuition and Aid Day student tuition: $13,975. Tuition installment plan (monthly payment plans). Need-based scholarship grants available. In 2013–14, 20% of upper-school students received aid. Total amount of financial aid awarded in 2013–14: $250,000.

Admissions Traditional secondary-level entrance grade is 9. For fall 2013, 70 students applied for upper-level admission, 43 were accepted, 33 enrolled. School placement exam required. Deadline for receipt of application materials: February 14. Application fee required: $100. On-campus interview required.

Athletics Interscholastic: baseball (boys), basketball (b,g), cheering (g), cross-country running (b,g), football (b), golf (b,g), physical training (b,g), soccer (b,g), softball (g), strength & conditioning (b,g), swimming and diving (b,g), tennis (b,g), track and field (b,g), volleyball (g), weight lifting (b), wrestling (b). 5 PE instructors, 49 coaches, 2 athletic trainers.

Computers Computers are regularly used in all academic classes. Computer network features include on-campus library services, Internet access, Internet filtering or blocking technology, class assignments available online. Computer access in designated common areas is available to students. Students grades are available online.

Contact Mrs. Renee Chastain, Assistant to the Director of Admission. 770-692-6753. Fax: 770-969-6551. E-mail: admissions@landmark-cs.org. Website: www.landmarkchristianschool.org

LANDMARK SCHOOL

Prides Crossing, Massachusetts
See Special Needs Schools section.

LANDON SCHOOL

6101 Wilson Lane
Bethesda, Maryland 20817

Head of School: Mr. David M. Armstrong

General Information Boys' day college-preparatory, arts, and music school. Grades 3–12. Founded: 1929. Setting: suburban. Nearest major city is Washington, DC. 75-acre campus. 13 buildings on campus. Approved or accredited by Association of Independent Maryland Schools, Middle States Association of Colleges and Schools, and Maryland Department of Education. Member of National Association of Independent Schools. Endowment: $10.5 million. Total enrollment: 675. Upper school average class size: 15. Upper school faculty-student ratio: 1:6. There are 170 required school days per year for Upper School students. Upper School students typically attend 5 days per week. The average school day consists of 7 hours and 10 minutes.

Upper School Student Profile Grade 9: 81 students (81 boys); Grade 10: 83 students (83 boys); Grade 11: 88 students (88 boys); Grade 12: 78 students (78 boys).

Faculty School total: 108. In upper school: 43 men, 10 women; 35 have advanced degrees.

Subjects Offered Acting, algebra, American Civil War, American foreign policy, American history, American literature, American studies, art, art history-AP, biology, biology-AP, calculus, calculus-AP, ceramics, chemistry, chemistry-AP, Chinese, Chinese history, classics, computer science, computer science-AP, conceptual physics, constitutional law, creative writing, digital art, drama, drawing, earth science, economics-AP, engineering, English, English literature, environmental science-AP, environmental studies, ethics, European history, expository writing, fine arts, foreign policy, forensics, French, French language-AP, French literature-AP, French studies, freshman foundations, geography, geology, geometry, government/civics, grammar, handbells, health, history, humanities, international relations, jazz band, journalism,

justice seminar, Latin, mathematics, meteorology, Middle Eastern history, music, music history, music theory, music theory-AP, oceanography, painting, performing arts, photography, photojournalism, physical education, physics, physics-AP, pre-calculus, science, sculpture, senior project, Shakespeare, social studies, Spanish, Spanish language-AP, Spanish literature, statistics-AP, strings, technological applications, theater, trigonometry, typing, U.S. history, U.S. history-AP, world history, world literature, writing.

Graduation Requirements American Civil War, American government, arts and fine arts (art, music, dance, drama), biology, chemistry, English, ethics, foreign language, government, humanities, mathematics, music, physical education (includes health), pre-calculus, science, social studies (includes history), senior project, 2 year arts requirement.

Special Academic Programs Advanced Placement exam preparation; honors section; independent study; term-away projects; study abroad.

College Admission Counseling 78 students graduated in 2013; all went to college, including Bucknell University; Davidson College; Furman University; University of Colorado Boulder; University of Pennsylvania; University of Virginia. Mean SAT critical reading: 638, mean SAT math: 644, mean SAT writing: 653, mean combined SAT: 1935, mean composite ACT: 28.

Student Life Upper grades have specified standards of dress, student council, honor system. Discipline rests equally with students and faculty.

Summer Programs Remediation, enrichment, advancement, sports, art/fine arts programs offered; session focuses on enrichment, music, studio arts for Middle and Upper grades; advancement, remediation, and travel for Upper; held both on and off campus; held at locations in France, China and Spain; accepts boys and girls; open to students from other schools. 200 students usually enrolled. 2014 schedule: June 9. Application deadline: none.

Tuition and Aid Day student tuition: $33,565. Tuition installment plan (FACTS Tuition Payment Plan, monthly payment plans). Need-based scholarship grants, 50% tuition remission for faculty children available. In 2013–14, 25% of upper-school students received aid. Total amount of financial aid awarded in 2013–14: $1,535,509.

Admissions Traditional secondary-level entrance grade is 9. ISEE or SSAT required. Deadline for receipt of application materials: January 15. Application fee required: $75. On-campus interview required.

Athletics Interscholastic: baseball, basketball, cross-country running, diving, fencing, football, golf, ice hockey, lacrosse, riflery, rugby, soccer, squash, strength & conditioning, swimming and diving, tennis, track and field, ultimate Frisbee, water polo, winter (indoor) track, wrestling; intramural: basketball, Frisbee, physical fitness, softball, strength & conditioning, tennis, ultimate Frisbee, weight lifting. 13 coaches, 2 athletic trainers.

Computers Computers are regularly used in art, computer applications, photojournalism classes. Computer network features include on-campus library services, online commercial services, Internet access, wireless campus network, Internet filtering or blocking technology, password-accessed Web portals. Campus intranet, student e-mail accounts, and computer access in designated common areas are available to students. Students grades are available online. The school has a published electronic and media policy.

Contact Mr. George C. Mulligan, Director of Admissions. 301-320-1067. Fax: 301-320-1133. E-mail: george_mulligan@landon.net. Website: www.landon.net

LANSDALE CATHOLIC HIGH SCHOOL

700 Lansdale Avenue
Lansdale, Pennsylvania 19446-2995

Head of School: Mrs. Rita McGovern

General Information Coeducational day and distance learning college-preparatory, general academic, and religious studies school, affiliated with Roman Catholic Church. Grades 9–12. Distance learning grades 9–12. Founded: 1949. Setting: suburban. Nearest major city is Philadelphia. 33-acre campus. 1 building on campus. Approved or accredited by Middle States Association of Colleges and Schools, National Catholic Education Association, and Pennsylvania Department of Education. Total enrollment: 763. Upper school average class size: 30. Upper school faculty-student ratio: 1:21. There are 190 required school days per year for Upper School students. Upper School students typically attend 5 days per week. The average school day consists of 6 hours and 45 minutes.

Upper School Student Profile Grade 9: 177 students (85 boys, 92 girls); Grade 10: 193 students (98 boys, 95 girls); Grade 11: 213 students (121 boys, 92 girls); Grade 12: 180 students (101 boys, 79 girls). 99% of students are Roman Catholic.

Faculty School total: 37. In upper school: 17 men, 20 women; 18 have advanced degrees.

Subjects Offered Algebra, American government, American history, American history-AP, American literature, art, art history-AP, art-AP, band, biology-AP, business law, calculus, calculus-AP, career education, career planning, career/college preparation, Catholic belief and practice, chemistry, Chinese, choir, chorus, church history, college counseling, college placement, college planning, composition-AP, computer education, computer programming, drama, English language and composition-AP, English literature and composition-AP, English literature-AP, English/composition-AP, environmental science, European history, European history-AP, French, government-AP, health education, Italian, Latin, mathematics-AP, physical fitness, physical science, physics, pre-calculus, SAT/ACT preparation, Spanish, statistics, statistics-AP, student government, studio art, studio art-AP, The 20th Century, trigonometry, U.S. government and politics, U.S. government and politics-AP, U.S. history, U.S. history-AP, United States government-AP, Western civilization.

Graduation Requirements 30 hour service requirement by the middle of junior year.

Special Academic Programs 17 Advanced Placement exams for which test preparation is offered; honors section; study at local college for college credit.

College Admission Counseling 179 students graduated in 2013; 177 went to college, including Montgomery County Community College; Penn State University Park; Shippensburg University of Pennsylvania; Temple University; West Chester University of Pennsylvania. Other: 1 went to work, 1 entered military service.

Student Life Upper grades have uniform requirement, student council, honor system. Discipline rests primarily with faculty. Attendance at religious services is required.

Summer Programs Remediation, enrichment, advancement, sports, art/fine arts programs offered; held on campus; accepts boys and girls; open to students from other schools. 100 students usually enrolled. 2014 schedule: June to August.

Tuition and Aid Day student tuition: $6150. Tuition installment plan (monthly payment plans, individually arranged payment plans). Tuition reduction for siblings, merit scholarship grants, need-based scholarship grants, TAP Program available. In 2013–14, 20% of upper-school students received aid; total upper-school merit-scholarship money awarded: $57,900. Total amount of financial aid awarded in 2013–14: $106,000.

Admissions Traditional secondary-level entrance grade is 9. Deadline for receipt of application materials: none. Application fee required: $150. Interview recommended.

Athletics Interscholastic: baseball (boys), basketball (b,g), cheering (g), cross-country running (b,g), dance squad (b,g), field hockey (g), football (b), golf (b,g), ice hockey (b,g), lacrosse (b,g), rugby (b,g), soccer (b,g), softball (g), swimming and diving (b,g), tennis (b,g), track and field (b,g), volleyball (g), weight lifting (b), winter (indoor) track (b,g); intramural: flag football (b), ice hockey (b,g); coed interscholastic: bowling, diving, indoor track, indoor track & field; coed intramural: yoga. 1 PE instructor, 1 athletic trainer.

Computers Computers are regularly used in all classes. Computer network features include on-campus library services, online commercial services, Internet access, wireless campus network, Internet filtering or blocking technology. Computer access in designated common areas is available to students. Students grades are available online. The school has a published electronic and media policy.

Contact Mr. James Casey, President. 215-362-6160 Ext. 133. Fax: 215-362-5746. E-mail: jcasey@lansdalecatholic.com. Website: www.lansdalecatholic.com

LA SALLE HIGH SCHOOL

3880 East Sierra Madre Boulevard
Pasadena, California 91107-1996

Head of School: Br. Christopher Brady, FSC

General Information Coeducational day college-preparatory, arts, and religious studies school, affiliated with Roman Catholic Church. Grades 9–12. Founded: 1956. Setting: suburban. Nearest major city is Los Angeles. 10-acre campus. 3 buildings on campus. Approved or accredited by California Association of Independent Schools, Christian Brothers Association, Western Association of Schools and Colleges, Western Catholic Education Association, and California Department of Education. Total enrollment: 710. Upper school average class size: 26. Upper school faculty-student ratio: 1:11. There are 180 required school days per year for Upper School students. Upper School students typically attend 5 days per week. The average school day consists of 6 hours and 15 minutes.

Upper School Student Profile Grade 9: 171 students (107 boys, 64 girls); Grade 10: 181 students (95 boys, 86 girls); Grade 11: 179 students (90 boys, 89 girls); Grade 12: 179 students (93 boys, 86 girls). 66% of students are Roman Catholic.

Faculty School total: 69. In upper school: 43 men, 26 women; 44 have advanced degrees.

Subjects Offered 20th century history, acting, Advanced Placement courses, advanced studio art-AP, algebra, American Civil War, American government, American literature-AP, ancient world history, art, art-AP, ASB Leadership, band, biology-AP, business law, calculus, calculus-AP, campus ministry, Catholic belief and practice, chemistry-AP, chorus, Christian and Hebrew scripture, church history, civics, classical civilization, community service, comparative religion, composition, composition-AP, computer applications, computer education, computer graphics, computer literacy, computer programming, concert choir, constitutional history of U.S., creative writing, dance, dance performance, digital photography, drama, dramatic arts, drawing, ecology, environmental systems, economics, economics-AP, education, electives, English, English composition, English language-AP, English literature, English literature and composition-AP, English-AP, fiction, film, fine arts, foreign language, French, general math, general science, geometry, government, government/civics, government/civics-AP, health and safety, health education, Hispanic literature, history, history-AP, honors algebra, honors English, honors U.S. history, honors world history, integrated mathematics, introduction to theater, jazz, jazz band, jazz dance, jazz ensemble, journalism, keyboarding, lab science, lab/keyboard, law and the legal system, leadership, leadership and service, mathematics, mathematics-AP, microbiology, modern European history-AP, musical productions, newspaper, photo shop,

photography, physics, physics-AP, play production, pottery, pre-calculus, religion, religion and culture, religious studies, Roman civilization, science, social justice, Spanish, Spanish-AP, student government, studio art, studio art-AP, study skills, tap dance, technical theater, television, theater, theater arts, theater design and production, theater production, trigonometry, U.S. government, U.S. government and politics-AP, U.S. history, U.S. history-AP, U.S. literature, video communication, visual and performing arts, visual arts, wind instruments, world history, writing, yearbook.

Graduation Requirements Algebra, American literature, arts and fine arts (art, music, dance, drama), biology, campus ministry, chemistry, Christian and Hebrew scripture, Christian doctrine, church history, civics, computer literacy, economics, English, English composition, English literature, foreign language, geometry, integrated mathematics, physical education (includes health), physics, religious studies, U.S. history.

Special Academic Programs 15 Advanced Placement exams for which test preparation is offered; honors section.

College Admission Counseling 195 students graduated in 2012; all went to college, including Cornell University; Loyola Marymount University; Northern Arizona University; University of California, Berkeley; University of California, Santa Cruz; University of Southern California. Median SAT critical reading: 580, median SAT math: 590, median SAT writing: 590, median combined SAT: 1780, median composite ACT: 24. 42% scored over 600 on SAT critical reading, 47% scored over 600 on SAT math, 48% scored over 600 on SAT writing, 44% scored over 1800 on combined SAT, 38% scored over 26 on composite ACT.

Student Life Upper grades have uniform requirement, student council, honor system. Discipline rests primarily with faculty. Attendance at religious services is required.

Tuition and Aid Day student tuition: $13,920. Tuition installment plan (monthly payment plans, biannual). Merit scholarship grants, need-based scholarship grants available. In 2012–13, 40% of upper-school students received aid; total upper-school merit-scholarship money awarded: $80,000. Total amount of financial aid awarded in 2012–13: $1,450,000.

Admissions Traditional secondary-level entrance grade is 9. For fall 2012, 599 students applied for upper-level admission, 310 were accepted, 110 enrolled. STS required. Deadline for receipt of application materials: January 13. Application fee required: $80. Interview required.

Athletics Interscholastic: baseball (boys), basketball (b,g), cross-country running (b,g), dance team (g), equestrian sports (g), football (b), golf (b,g), soccer (b,g), softball (g), swimming and diving (b,g), tennis (b,g), track and field (b,g), volleyball (b,g), water polo (b,g); intramural: basketball (b,g), dance team (g), flag football (b); coed interscholastic: cheering, physical fitness, weight training; coed intramural: fitness, Frisbee, physical fitness, weight training. 2 PE instructors, 50 coaches, 2 athletic trainers.

Computers Computers are regularly used in all academic, computer applications, video film production classes. Computer resources include on-campus library services, online commercial services, Internet access. Students grades are available online. The school has a published electronic and media policy.

Contact Ms. Teresa Ring, Admissions Secretary. 626-351-8951. Fax: 626-696-4411. E-mail: tring@lasallehs.org. Website: www.lasallehs.org

LA SCUOLA D'ITALIA GUGLIELMO MARCONI

12 East 96th Street
New York, New York 10128

Head of School: Prof. Anna Fiore

General Information Coeducational day college-preparatory and bilingual studies school. Grades PK–12. Founded: 1977. Setting: urban. Nearest major city is Manhattan. 1 building on campus. Approved or accredited by New York Department of Education. Languages of instruction: English, French, and Italian. Total enrollment: 261. Upper school average class size: 10. There are 212 required school days per year for Upper School students. Upper School students typically attend 5 days per week.

Upper School Student Profile Grade 9: 12 students (5 boys, 7 girls); Grade 10: 13 students (7 boys, 6 girls); Grade 11: 11 students (4 boys, 7 girls); Grade 12: 8 students (3 boys, 5 girls).

Faculty School total: 48. In upper school: 6 men, 9 women; 15 have advanced degrees.

Special Academic Programs International Baccalaureate program; Advanced Placement exam preparation; honors section; study at local college for college credit; domestic exchange program; study abroad; remedial reading and/or remedial writing; remedial math; ESL (26 students enrolled).

College Admission Counseling 9 students graduated in 2013; all went to college.

Student Life Upper grades have uniform requirement, honor system. Discipline rests equally with students and faculty.

Tuition and Aid Day student tuition: $21,800. Tuition installment plan (The Tuition Plan). Tuition reduction for siblings, merit scholarship grants, need-based scholarship grants, need-based loans available.

Admissions Traditional secondary-level entrance grade is 9. For fall 2013, 17 students applied for upper-level admission, 17 were accepted, 16 enrolled. Application fee required: $100. Interview required.

Athletics Coed Interscholastic: artistic gym, basketball, fencing, soccer. 2 PE instructors, 2 coaches, 2 athletic trainers.

Computers Computer network features include on-campus library services, Internet access, Internet filtering or blocking technology. Computer access in designated common areas is available to students. The school has a published electronic and media policy.

Contact Mrs. Pia Pedicini, Deputy Head of School/Director of Admissions. 212-369-3290. Fax: 212-369-1164. E-mail: secretary@lascuoladitalia.org. Website: www.lascuoladitalia.org

THE LATIN SCHOOL OF CHICAGO

59 West North Boulevard
Chicago, Illinois 60610-1492

Head of School: Randall Dunn

General Information Coeducational day college-preparatory school. Grades JK–12. Founded: 1888. Setting: urban. 1-acre campus. 1 building on campus. Approved or accredited by Independent Schools Association of the Central States and Illinois Department of Education. Member of National Association of Independent Schools and Secondary School Admission Test Board. Endowment: $28.5 million. Total enrollment: 1,124. Upper school average class size: 15. Upper school faculty-student ratio: 1:8. There are 175 required school days per year for Upper School students. Upper School students typically attend 5 days per week. The average school day consists of 6 hours and 30 minutes.

Upper School Student Profile Grade 9: 115 students (56 boys, 59 girls); Grade 10: 115 students (52 boys, 63 girls); Grade 11: 106 students (45 boys, 61 girls); Grade 12: 108 students (46 boys, 62 girls).

Faculty School total: 160. In upper school: 33 men, 28 women; 49 have advanced degrees.

Subjects Offered Advanced Placement courses, advanced studio art-AP, African studies, African-American literature, algebra, American history, American history-AP, American literature, anatomy, animal behavior, art, art history, Asian studies, astronomy, biochemistry, biology, biology-AP, calculus, calculus-AP, chemistry, chemistry-AP, chorus, community service, composition, computer graphics, computer programming, computer science, creative writing, dance, drama, ecology, electives, electronics, English, English literature, environmental science, environmental science-AP, ethics, European civilization, European history, fine arts, French, French language-AP, French literature-AP, geography, geometry, history, history of ideas, honors U.S. history, human relations, human sexuality, humanities, independent study, instrumental music, Latin, Latin American history, Latin American literature, Latin-AP, literature by women, Mandarin, mathematical modeling, mathematics, mathematics-AP, Middle East, Middle Eastern history, music theory, photography, physical education, physics, physics-AP, physiology, poetry, probability and statistics, psychology, religion, science, social studies, Spanish, Spanish language-AP, Spanish literature, Spanish literature-AP, speech, stage design, statistics, studio art-AP, theater, trigonometry, women's literature, world history, world literature, writing.

Graduation Requirements Arts and fine arts (art, music, dance, drama), English, ethics, foreign language, human relations, human sexuality, mathematics, performing arts, physical education (includes health), science, social studies (includes history), technology, one-week non-credit course each year, service learning requirement. Community service is required.

Special Academic Programs Advanced Placement exam preparation; honors section; independent study; study abroad; academic accommodation for the gifted; remedial reading and/or remedial writing; remedial math; programs in general development for dyslexic students.

College Admission Counseling 106 students graduated in 2013; all went to college, including Miami University; Northwestern University; Tufts University; University of Chicago; University of Wisconsin–Madison; Yale University.

Student Life Upper grades have specified standards of dress, student council, honor system. Discipline rests equally with students and faculty.

Summer Programs Remediation, enrichment, advancement, sports, art/fine arts, rigorous outdoor training, computer instruction programs offered; session focuses on enrichment, remediation, sports, travel, and adventure; held both on and off campus; held at lakefront, city parks, wilderness experiences in the United States and abroad; accepts boys and girls; open to students from other schools. 180 students usually enrolled. 2014 schedule: June 9 to August 2. Application deadline: none.

Tuition and Aid Day student tuition: $29,985. Tuition installment plan (Insured Tuition Payment Plan, Key Tuition Payment Plan, FACTS Tuition Payment Plan, monthly payment plans, individually arranged payment plans). Need-based scholarship grants, need-based loans, middle-income loans, Key Education Achiever Loans available. In 2013–14, 20% of upper-school students received aid. Total amount of financial aid awarded in 2013–14: $2,300,000.

Admissions Traditional secondary-level entrance grade is 9. For fall 2013, 248 students applied for upper-level admission, 104 were accepted, 45 enrolled. ISEE

required. Deadline for receipt of application materials: February 1. Application fee required: $80. On-campus interview required.

Athletics Interscholastic: aquatics (boys, girls), badminton (g), baseball (b), basketball (b,g), cross-country running (b,g), field hockey (g), golf (b,g), ice hockey (b,g), soccer (b,g), softball (g), swimming and diving (b,g), tennis (b,g), track and field (b,g), volleyball (b,g), water polo (b,g); intramural: life saving (b,g); coed intramural: dance, kayaking, outdoor activities, outdoor adventure, outdoor education, outdoor recreation, physical fitness, physical training, skiing (downhill). 3 PE instructors, 20 coaches, 1 athletic trainer.

Computers Computers are regularly used in art, English, foreign language, mathematics, science classes. Computer network features include on-campus library services, online commercial services, Internet access, wireless campus network. Campus intranet, student e-mail accounts, and computer access in designated common areas are available to students. The school has a published electronic and media policy.

Contact Frankie Brown, Director of Enrollment Management. 312-582-6060. Fax: 312-582-6061. E-mail: fbrown@latinschool.org. Website: www.latinschool.org

LAURALTON HALL

200 High Street
Milford, Connecticut 06460

Head of School: Dr. Antoinette Iadarola

General Information Girls' day college-preparatory, arts, religious studies, and technology school, affiliated with Roman Catholic Church. Grades 9–12. Founded: 1905. Setting: suburban. Nearest major city is New Haven. 30-acre campus. 5 buildings on campus. Approved or accredited by Mercy Secondary Education Association, New England Association of Schools and Colleges, and Connecticut Department of Education. Member of National Association of Independent Schools. Total enrollment: 477. Upper school faculty-student ratio: 1:12. There are 165 required school days per year for Upper School students. Upper School students typically attend 5 days per week. The average school day consists of 6 hours and 15 minutes.

Upper School Student Profile Grade 9: 133 students (133 girls); Grade 10: 111 students (111 girls); Grade 11: 114 students (114 girls); Grade 12: 119 students (119 girls). 76% of students are Roman Catholic.

Faculty School total: 43. In upper school: 3 men, 40 women; 29 have advanced degrees.

Subjects Offered Algebra, American history, American literature, anatomy, art, biology, business, calculus, chemistry, Chinese, computer math, computer programming, English, English literature, environmental science, European history, fine arts, French, geometry, government/civics, health, history, journalism, Latin, mathematics, music, physical education, physics, physiology, religion, science, social studies, Spanish, trigonometry, world history, writing.

Graduation Requirements Arts and fine arts (art, music, dance, drama), English, foreign language, mathematics, physical education (includes health), religion (includes Bible studies and theology), science, social studies (includes history). Community service is required.

Special Academic Programs Honors section; study at local college for college credit.

College Admission Counseling 107 students graduated in 2013; all went to college, including Boston College; College of the Holy Cross; Fairfield University; Loyola University Maryland; Quinnipiac University; University of Connecticut. Mean SAT critical reading: 544, mean SAT math: 570, mean SAT writing: 563.

Student Life Upper grades have uniform requirement, student council, honor system. Discipline rests primarily with faculty. Attendance at religious services is required.

Tuition and Aid Day student tuition: $17,000. Tuition installment plan (FACTS Tuition Payment Plan, 1- and 2-payment plans). Tuition reduction for siblings, merit scholarship grants, need-based scholarship grants available. In 2013–14, 24% of upper-school students received aid; total upper-school merit-scholarship money awarded: $125,000. Total amount of financial aid awarded in 2013–14: $450,000.

Admissions Traditional secondary-level entrance grade is 9. High School Placement Test required. Deadline for receipt of application materials: none. Application fee required: $60.

Athletics Interscholastic: basketball, cheering, cross-country running, diving, field hockey, golf, gymnastics, ice hockey, indoor track, lacrosse, running, skiing (downhill), soccer, softball, swimming and diving, tennis, track and field, volleyball; intramural: basketball. 1 PE instructor, 27 coaches, 1 athletic trainer.

Computers Computers are regularly used in mathematics classes. Computer network features include on-campus library services, online commercial services, Internet access, wireless campus network, Internet filtering or blocking technology. Campus intranet, student e-mail accounts, and computer access in designated common areas are available to students. The school has a published electronic and media policy.

Contact Jessica Auscavitch, Marketing Coodinator. 203-878-3333. Fax: 203-876-9760. E-mail: jauscavitch@lauraltonhall.org. Website: www.lauraltonhall.org

See Display on next page and Close-Up on page 542.

THE LAUREATE ACADEMY

Winnipeg, Manitoba, Canada
See Special Needs Schools section.

LAUREL SPRINGS SCHOOL

302 West El Paseo Road
Ojai, California 93023

Head of School: Marilyn Mosley

General Information Distance learning only college-preparatory, arts, vocational, technology, and distance learning school. Distance learning grades K–12. Founded: 1991. Setting: small town. Nearest major city is Los Angeles. 1 building on campus. Approved or accredited by Western Association of Schools and Colleges and California Department of Education. Total enrollment: 1,529. Upper school average class size: 1. Upper school faculty-student ratio: 1:1. The average school day consists of 6 hours.

Upper School Student Profile Grade 9: 178 students (87 boys, 91 girls); Grade 10: 249 students (118 boys, 131 girls); Grade 11: 260 students (124 boys, 136 girls); Grade 12: 189 students (91 boys, 98 girls).

Faculty School total: 86. In upper school: 13 men, 51 women; 46 have advanced degrees.

Subjects Offered Algebra, American literature, art appreciation, art history, biology, biology-AP, British literature, British literature (honors), calculus, calculus-AP, career/college preparation, cartooning/animation, chemistry, chemistry-AP, college admission preparation, college counseling, driver education, earth science, economics, electives, English composition, English language and composition-AP, English literature and composition-AP, environmental education, environmental studies, French, French-AP, geometry, German, health, history of music, honors algebra, honors English, honors geometry, honors U.S. history, honors world history, Latin, macroeconomics-AP, Mandarin, microeconomics-AP, music history, mythology, photo shop, physical education, physics, physics-AP, pre-calculus, psychology, psychology-AP, SAT/ACT preparation, Shakespeare, sociology, Spanish, Spanish language-AP, statistics-AP, trigonometry, U.S. government, U.S. government and politics-AP, U.S. history, U.S. history-AP, world cultures, world history, world literature.

Graduation Requirements Arts and fine arts (art, music, dance, drama), electives, English, foreign language, mathematics, physical education (includes health), science, social studies (includes history).

Special Academic Programs Advanced Placement exam preparation; honors section; accelerated programs; independent study; term-away projects; academic accommodation for the gifted, the musically talented, and the artistically talented; remedial reading and/or remedial writing; remedial math; programs in English, mathematics, general development for dyslexic students; special instructional classes for students needing customized learning options.

College Admission Counseling 102 students graduated in 2012; 94 went to college, including Middle Tennessee State University; New York University; Purdue University; University of California, Los Angeles; University of California, Santa Barbara; University of Southern California. Other: 8 had other specific plans. Mean SAT critical reading: 562, mean SAT math: 519, mean SAT writing: 547, mean composite ACT: 23.

Student Life Upper grades have student council, honor system. Discipline rests equally with students and faculty.

Tuition and Aid Tuition installment plan (monthly payment plans, individually arranged payment plans). Tuition reduction for siblings, need-based scholarship grants available.

Admissions Traditional secondary-level entrance grade is 9. For fall 2012, 1,529 students applied for upper-level admission, 1,529 were accepted, 1,529 enrolled. Deadline for receipt of application materials: none. Application fee required: $250.

Computers Computers are regularly used in art, economics, English, foreign language, geography, health, history, independent study, information technology, language development, life skills, mathematics, psychology, SAT preparation, science, social studies, writing classes. Computer network features include on-campus library services, Internet access, 100 online courses. Students grades are available online.

Contact Admissions. 800-377-5890 Ext. 5502. Fax: 805-646-0186. Website: www.laurelsprings.com

LAWRENCE ACADEMY

26 Powderhouse Road
Groton, Massachusetts 01450

Head of School: Mr. Daniel Scheibe

General Information Coeducational boarding and day college-preparatory, interdisciplinary ninth grade curriculum, and student-centered learning school. Grades 9–12. Founded: 1793. Setting: small town. Nearest major city is Boston. Students are housed in single-sex dormitories. 115-acre campus. 31 buildings on campus. Approved or accredited by Association of Independent Schools in New England, New England Association of Schools and Colleges, The Association of Boarding Schools, and Massachusetts Department of Education. Member of National Association of Independent Schools and Secondary School Admission Test Board. Endowment: $18 million. Total enrollment: 399. Upper school average class size: 12. Upper school faculty-student ratio: 1:5. Upper School students typically attend 5 days per week. The average school day consists of 6 hours and 20 minutes.

Upper School Student Profile Grade 9: 79 students (40 boys, 39 girls); Grade 10: 111 students (61 boys, 50 girls); Grade 11: 108 students (59 boys, 49 girls); Grade 12: 101 students (51 boys, 50 girls). 50% of students are boarding students. 60% are state residents. 21 states are represented in upper school student body. 13% are international students. International students from China, Germany, Kazakhstan, Republic of Korea, Russian Federation, and Spain; 15 other countries represented in student body.

Faculty School total: 83. In upper school: 44 men, 39 women; 50 have advanced degrees; 39 reside on campus.

Subjects Offered Advanced Placement courses, African-American literature, algebra, American history, anatomy, art, astronomy, biology, botany, calculus, calculus-AP, ceramics, chemistry, composition, creative writing, criminal justice, dance, drawing, ecology, electives, electronics, English, English literature, entomology, environmental science-AP, ESL, European history, fine arts, finite math, fractal geometry, French, government/civics, history, independent study, John F. Kennedy, Latin, Latin American literature, limnology, marine science, mathematics, microbiology, music, music composition, music technology, music theory, music-AP, ornithology, painting, photography, physics, playwriting, pre-calculus, psychology, scene study, science, sculpture, Shakespeare, social psychology, Spanish, studio art, theater, tropical biology, U.S. government and politics-AP, writing.

Graduation Requirements Arts and fine arts (art, music, dance, drama), English, foreign language, history, mathematics, science, Winterim participation.

Special Academic Programs Advanced Placement exam preparation; honors section; independent study; term-away projects; study abroad; academic accommodation for the musically talented and the artistically talented; special instructional classes for deaf students, blind students; ESL (20 students enrolled).

College Admission Counseling 91 students graduated in 2013; all went to college, including Boston College; Boston University; Colby College; Skidmore College; University of New Hampshire; University of Vermont. Median SAT critical reading: 560, median SAT math: 580, median SAT writing: 570. 34% scored over 600 on SAT critical reading, 46% scored over 600 on SAT math, 40% scored over 600 on SAT writing, 37% scored over 1800 on combined SAT.

Student Life Upper grades have specified standards of dress, student council, honor system. Discipline rests primarily with faculty.

Tuition and Aid Day student tuition: $42,130; 7-day tuition and room/board: $54,750. Tuition installment plan (Key Tuition Payment Plan, monthly payment plans). Need-based scholarship grants, need-based loans, prepGATE loans available. In 2013–14, 29% of upper-school students received aid. Total amount of financial aid awarded in 2013–14: $3,450,000.

Admissions Traditional secondary-level entrance grade is 9. For fall 2013, 682 students applied for upper-level admission, 252 were accepted, 141 enrolled. PSAT or SAT, SSAT or TOEFL required. Deadline for receipt of application materials: February 1. Application fee required: $50. Interview required.

Athletics Interscholastic: baseball (boys), basketball (b,g), cross-country running (b,g), field hockey (g), football (b), golf (b,g), ice hockey (b,g), lacrosse (b,g), soccer (b,g), softball (g), tennis (b,g), track and field (b,g), volleyball (g), wrestling (b); intramural: tennis (b,g); coed interscholastic: alpine skiing, independent competitive sports, mountain biking, skiing (downhill), squash; coed intramural: dance, fitness, independent competitive sports, modern dance, outdoors, physical fitness, physical training, rappelling, skiing (downhill), snowboarding, strength & conditioning, volleyball, weight training, yoga. 5 coaches, 2 athletic trainers.

Computers Computers are regularly used in college planning, computer applications, ESL, library, media production, music, photography, SAT preparation, video film production, yearbook classes. Computer network features include on-campus library services, online commercial services, Internet access, wireless campus network, Internet filtering or blocking technology. Campus intranet, student e-mail accounts, and computer access in designated common areas are available to students. Students grades are available online. The school has a published electronic and media policy.

Contact Mr. Robert Olsen, Director of Admissions. 978-448-6535. Fax: 978-448-1519. E-mail: admiss@lacademy.edu. Website: www.lacademy.edu

LAWRENCE SCHOOL

Sagamore Hills, Ohio
See Special Needs Schools section.

THE LAWRENCEVILLE SCHOOL

PO Box 6008
2500 Main Street
Lawrenceville, New Jersey 08648
Head of School: Elizabeth A. Duffy

General Information Coeducational boarding and day college-preparatory, arts, religious studies, and technology school. Grades 9–PG. Founded: 1810. Setting: small town. Nearest major city is Philadelphia, PA. Students are housed in single-sex dormitories. 700-acre campus. 39 buildings on campus. Approved or accredited by Middle States Association of Colleges and Schools, New Jersey Association of Independent Schools, The Association of Boarding Schools, and New Jersey Department of Education. Member of National Association of Independent Schools and Secondary School Admission Test Board. Total enrollment: 819. Upper school average class size: 12. Upper school faculty-student ratio: 1:8. Upper School students typically attend 6 days per week. The average school day consists of 7 hours.

Upper School Student Profile 68% of students are boarding students. 45% are state residents. 32 states are represented in upper school student body. 15% are international students. International students from Canada, China, Hong Kong, Japan, Republic of Korea, and Saudi Arabia; 26 other countries represented in student body.

Faculty School total: 145. In upper school: 77 men, 68 women; all have advanced degrees.

Subjects Offered Acting, advanced chemistry, advanced computer applications, advanced studio art-AP, African-American literature, algebra, American Civil War, American foreign policy, American government, American history, American history-AP, American literature, American studies, architecture, art, art history, art history-AP, art-AP, arts, Asian history, astronomy, Basic programming, Bible, Bible studies, bioethics, bioethics, DNA and culture, biology, biology-AP, British literature, Buddhism, calculus, calculus-AP, Central and Eastern European history, ceramics, chamber groups, chemistry, chemistry-AP, China/Japan history, Chinese, Chinese studies, choir, chorus, Christian studies, Civil War, civil war history, classical Greek literature, classical language, comparative government and politics, conceptual physics, constitutional history of U.S., contemporary women writers, critical writing, dance, data analysis, design, digital applications, digital art, drama, dramatic arts, drawing, drawing and design, driver education, Eastern religion and philosophy, economics, electronic music, English, English literature, English literature-AP, English/composition-AP, environmental science, environmental studies, ethics, European history, European history-AP, European literature, evolution, field ecology, film and new technologies, film appreciation, filmmaking, foreign language, foreign policy, French, French language-AP, French literature-AP, French studies, French-AP, geometry, global science, Greek, health and wellness, Hebrew scripture, Hindi, historical foundations for arts, history of China and Japan, Holocaust, human biology, humanities, independent study, instruments, interdisciplinary studies, introduction to literature, introduction to theater, Irish literature, Irish studies, Islamic studies, Japanese, Japanese history, jazz, Jewish studies, John F. Kennedy, journalism, Latin, linear algebra, literature, medieval history, medieval literature, Middle East, Middle Eastern history, nature study, orchestra, organic chemistry, painting, participation in sports, personal development, philosophy, photography, physics, physics-AP, physiology, poetry, pre-algebra, pre-calculus, printmaking, probability and statistics, research seminar, robotics, science, set design, Shakespeare, short story, Southern literature, Spanish, Spanish language-AP, Spanish literature, studio art, the Presidency, the Sixties, theater, theater arts, U.S. constitutional history, U.S. government, U.S. government and politics, U.S. history, visual arts, water color painting, women in world history, world religions, world religions, writing.

Graduation Requirements Arts and fine arts (art, music, dance, drama), English, foreign language, interdisciplinary studies, mathematics, religion (includes Bible studies and theology), science, social sciences, social studies (includes history). Community service is required.

Special Academic Programs Honors section; independent study; term-away projects; study abroad.

College Admission Counseling 232 students graduated in 2012; 230 went to college, including Columbia College; New York University; Princeton University; University of Pennsylvania; Yale University. Other: 1 went to work, 1 entered a postgraduate year. Median SAT critical reading: 676, median SAT math: 697, median SAT writing: 687.

Student Life Upper grades have specified standards of dress, student council, honor system. Discipline rests equally with students and faculty.

Tuition and Aid Day student tuition: $38,050; 7-day tuition and room/board: $46,475. Tuition installment plan (one, two, and nine month installment plans are available). Need-based scholarship grants available. In 2012–13, 29% of upper-school students received aid. Total amount of financial aid awarded in 2012–13: $1,010,000.

Admissions Traditional secondary-level entrance grade is 9. For fall 2012, 1,929 students applied for upper-level admission, 244 enrolled. ISEE, PSAT and SAT for applicants to grade 11 and 12, SSAT or TOEFL or SLEP required. Deadline for receipt of application materials: January 31. Application fee required: $50. Interview required.

Athletics Interscholastic: baseball (boys), basketball (b,g), crew (b,g), cross-country running (b,g), fencing (b,g), field hockey (g), football (b), golf (b,g), hockey (b,g), ice hockey (b,g), indoor track (b,g), indoor track & field (b,g), lacrosse (b,g), rowing (b,g), soccer (b,g), softball (g), squash (b,g), swimming and diving (b,g), tennis (b,g), track and field (b,g), volleyball (b,g), water polo (b,g), winter (indoor) track (b,g); intramural: basketball (b,g), Frisbee (g), handball (b,g), team handball (b,g), ultimate Frisbee (g), weight lifting (b,g), weight training (b,g); coed interscholastic: wrestling; coed intramural: backpacking, bicycling, broomball, canoeing/kayaking, climbing, cricket, dance, fitness, hiking/backpacking, ice skating, kayaking, modern dance, Nautilus, outdoor activities, physical fitness, physical training, rock climbing, ropes courses, squash, strength & conditioning, wall climbing, yoga. 72 coaches, 4 athletic trainers.

Computers Computers are regularly used in art, English, mathematics, music, science, technology classes. Computer network features include on-campus library services, online commercial services, Internet access, wireless campus network, Internet filtering or blocking technology. Campus intranet, student e-mail accounts, and computer access in designated common areas are available to students. Students grades are available online. The school has a published electronic and media policy.

Contact Sally Fitzpatrick, Interim Dean of Admission. 800-735-2030. Fax: 609-895-2217. E-mail: sfitzpatrick@lawrenceville.org. Website: www.lawrenceville.org

See Display below and Close-Up on page 544.

LEE ACADEMY

26 Winn Road
Lee, Maine 04455

Head of School: Mr. W. Gus LeBlanc

General Information Coeducational boarding and day college-preparatory, arts, and vocational school. Boarding grades 9–PG, day grades 9–12. Founded: 1845. Setting: rural. Nearest major city is Bangor. Students are housed in single-sex dormitories. 400-acre campus. 15 buildings on campus. Approved or accredited by Independent Schools of Northern New England, New England Association of Schools and Colleges, and Maine Department of Education. Total enrollment: 260. Upper school average class size: 15. Upper school faculty-student ratio: 1:15. There are 175 required school days per year for Upper School students. Upper School students typically attend 5 days per week. The average school day consists of 7 hours and 30 minutes.

Upper School Student Profile Grade 9: 50 students (24 boys, 26 girls); Grade 10: 49 students (26 boys, 23 girls); Grade 11: 65 students (39 boys, 26 girls); Grade 12: 72 students (45 boys, 27 girls); Postgraduate: 15 students (15 boys). 43% of students are boarding students. 57% are state residents. 5 states are represented in upper school student body. 41% are international students. International students from Brazil, China, Democratic People's Republic of Korea, Germany, and Serbia and Montenegro; 11 other countries represented in student body.

Faculty School total: 28. In upper school: 15 men, 13 women; 9 have advanced degrees; 11 reside on campus.

Subjects Offered ACT preparation, advanced biology, advanced chemistry, advanced math, Advanced Placement courses, advanced studio art-AP, algebra, American government, American history-AP, anatomy and physiology, art, art-AP, athletics, audio visual/media, band, biology-AP, calculus, calculus-AP, chemistry, chemistry-AP, choir, choral music, chorus, civil rights, comparative government and politics-AP, composition, composition-AP, costumes and make-up, creative drama, developmental math, digital photography, drama, English, English as a foreign language, English language and composition-AP, English language-AP, English literature and composition-AP, English literature-AP, English-AP, English/composition-AP, environmental science-AP, ESL, ESL, foreign language, French, general math, geometry, government and politics-AP, government/civics, guitar, health, health and wellness, history, history-AP, honors English, honors geometry, honors U.S. history, industrial technology, integrated mathematics, introduction to theater, learning lab, literature and composition-AP, literature-AP, media arts, music, music appreciation, music performance, music theater, musical productions, musical theater, performing arts, photography, physical education, physical fitness, physics, physics-AP, piano, pre-college orientation, psychology-AP, SAT preparation, SAT/ACT preparation, Spanish, stage and body movement, stage design, stagecraft, statistics-AP, studio art-AP, theater, theater arts, theater design and production, theater production, TOEFL preparation, U.S. government and politics, U.S. government and politics-AP, U.S. history, U.S. history-AP, vocational skills, wellness, wind ensemble, wind instruments, world cultures, world history, yearbook.

Graduation Requirements Algebra, American history, arts, biology, civics, computer skills, English, foreign language, health and wellness, mathematics, physical education (includes health), science.

Special Academic Programs Advanced Placement exam preparation; honors section; independent study; study abroad; ESL (48 students enrolled).

College Admission Counseling 70 students graduated in 2013; they went to Arizona State University; Saint Joseph's College of Maine; St. Bonaventure University; University of Maine; University of Nevada, Las Vegas. Other: 1 entered military service, 2 entered a postgraduate year. Median SAT critical reading: 560, median SAT math: 622, median SAT writing: 570, median composite ACT: 26.

Student Life Upper grades have specified standards of dress, student council. Discipline rests primarily with faculty.

Summer Programs ESL programs offered; session focuses on ESL; held on campus; accepts boys and girls; open to students from other schools. 60 students usually enrolled. 2014 schedule: July to August. Application deadline: June.

Tuition and Aid Day student tuition: $9300; 7-day tuition and room/board: $35,400. Tuition installment plan (monthly payment plans, individually arranged payment plans). Need-based scholarship grants available.

Admissions Traditional secondary-level entrance grade is 9. TOEFL or SLEP or writing sample required. Deadline for receipt of application materials: none. No application fee required. Interview recommended.

Athletics Interscholastic: baseball (boys), basketball (b,g), cross-country running (b,g), nordic skiing (b,g), soccer (b,g), softball (g), tennis (b,g), track and field (b,g), wrestling (b); intramural: backpacking (b,g); coed interscholastic: alpine skiing, cheering, golf, running, skiing (downhill); coed intramural: aerobics, aerobics/dance, aerobics/Nautilus, archery, badminton, bicycling, billiards, bowling, canoeing/kayaking, climbing, cooperative games, cross-country running, fishing, fitness, fitness walking, freestyle skiing, Frisbee, golf, hiking/backpacking, horseback riding, in-line skating, indoor soccer, jogging, kayaking, kickball, mountain biking, Nautilus, outdoor activities, outdoor recreation, paint ball, physical fitness, physical training, rafting, running, skiing (downhill), snowboarding, ultimate Frisbee, walking, weight lifting, weight training. 1 PE instructor, 11 coaches, 1 athletic trainer.

Computers Computers are regularly used in architecture, drafting, English, ESL, independent study, library, literary magazine, SAT preparation, yearbook classes. Computer resources include on-campus library services, Internet access, wireless campus network, Internet filtering or blocking technology. Campus intranet, student e-mail accounts, and computer access in designated common areas are available to students. Students grades are available online. The school has a published electronic and media policy.

Contact Mrs. Deborah Jacobs, Director of Admission. 207-738-2252 Ext. 115. Fax: 207-738-3257. E-mail: admissions@leeacademy.org. Website: www.leeacademy.org

THE LEELANAU SCHOOL

Glen Arbor, Michigan
See Special Needs Schools section.

LEHIGH VALLEY CHRISTIAN HIGH SCHOOL

330 Howertown Road, Suite 101
Catasauqua, Pennsylvania 18032

Head of School: Mr. Robert J. Brennan Jr.

General Information Coeducational day college-preparatory, general academic, arts, business, religious studies, and technology school, affiliated with Protestant-Evangelical faith. Grades 9–12. Founded: 1988. Setting: urban. Nearest major city is Allentown. 2-acre campus. 1 building on campus. Approved or accredited by Association of Christian Schools International, Middle States Association of Colleges and Schools, and Pennsylvania Department of Education. Total enrollment: 122. Upper school average class size: 20. Upper school faculty-student ratio: 1:9. There are 180 required school days per year for Upper School students. Upper School students typically attend 5 days per week. The average school day consists of 6 hours and 45 minutes.

Upper School Student Profile Grade 9: 35 students (21 boys, 14 girls); Grade 10: 19 students (9 boys, 10 girls); Grade 11: 36 students (22 boys, 14 girls); Grade 12: 32 students (10 boys, 22 girls). 90% of students are Protestant-Evangelical faith.

Faculty School total: 13. In upper school: 7 men, 6 women; 9 have advanced degrees.

Subjects Offered Accounting, Advanced Placement courses, algebra, American history, ancient world history, art, Bible, biology, calculus-AP, chemistry, chorus, economics, English, English language and composition-AP, English literature and composition-AP, geometry, government, health, history, keyboarding, neuroscience, physical education, physical science, physics, pre-algebra, pre-calculus, Spanish, U.S. history, Western civilization.

Graduation Requirements Algebra, American history, American literature, art, Bible, Bible studies, biology, British literature, chemistry, choir, civics, computer applications, English, foreign language, geometry, mathematics, physical education (includes health), physical science, science, social sciences, Western civilization, general lifestyle not harmful to the testimony of the school as a Christian institution, minimum one year of full-time enrollment in LVCH or another Christian high school.

Special Academic Programs Advanced Placement exam preparation; honors section; accelerated programs; independent study; study at local college for college credit; academic accommodation for the gifted; programs in English, mathematics, general development for dyslexic students; special instructional classes for students needing learning support; ESL (2 students enrolled).

College Admission Counseling 28 students graduated in 2013; 26 went to college, including Cairn University; Eastern University; Lehigh University; Liberty University; Moravian College; Penn State University Park. Other: 2 went to work. Mean SAT critical reading: 531, mean SAT math: 539, mean SAT writing: 521, mean combined SAT: 1591.

Student Life Upper grades have uniform requirement, student council. Discipline rests primarily with faculty.

Summer Programs Remediation, advancement programs offered; session focuses on make-up courses; held both on and off campus; held at students' homes (for independent credit); accepts boys and girls; not open to students from other schools. 5 students usually enrolled. 2014 schedule: June 18 to August 11.

Tuition and Aid Day student tuition: $9408. Tuition installment plan (FACTS Tuition Payment Plan, individually arranged payment plans). Tuition reduction for siblings, need-based scholarship grants available. In 2013–14, 35% of upper-school students received aid. Total amount of financial aid awarded in 2013–14: $270,684.

Admissions Traditional secondary-level entrance grade is 9. For fall 2013, 36 students applied for upper-level admission, 36 were accepted, 35 enrolled. Achievement tests, Gates MacGinite Reading Tests or Wide Range Achievement Test required. Deadline for receipt of application materials: none. Application fee required: $200. On-campus interview required.

Athletics Interscholastic: baseball (boys), basketball (b,g), cheering (g), soccer (b,g), volleyball (g); coed interscholastic: cross-country running, track and field; coed intramural: fitness walking. 1 PE instructor.

Computers Computers are regularly used in graphic arts, keyboarding, library, multimedia, science, technology, writing, yearbook classes. Computer network features include on-campus library services, Internet access, Internet filtering or blocking technology. Students grades are available online. The school has a published electronic and media policy.

Contact Mrs. Kathy B VanDuzer, Director of Admissions. 610-403-1000 Ext. 15. Fax: 610-403-1004. E-mail: k.vanduzer@lvchs.org. Website: www.lvchs.org

LEHMAN HIGH SCHOOL

2400 Saint Mary Avenue
Sidney, Ohio 45365

Head of School: Mr. David Michael Barhorst

General Information Coeducational day and distance learning college-preparatory, arts, business, and religious studies school, affiliated with Roman Catholic Church. Grades 9–12. Distance learning grades 10–12. Founded: 1970. Setting: small town. Nearest major city is Dayton. 50-acre campus. 1 building on campus. Approved or accredited by North Central Association of Colleges and Schools, Ohio Catholic Schools Accreditation Association (OCSAA), and Ohio Department of Education. Endowment: $600,000. Total enrollment: 205. Upper school average class size: 15. Upper school faculty-student ratio: 1:15. There are 178 required school days per year for Upper School students. Upper School students typically attend 5 days per week. The average school day consists of 7 hours.

Upper School Student Profile Grade 9: 46 students (23 boys, 23 girls); Grade 10: 48 students (32 boys, 16 girls); Grade 11: 67 students (33 boys, 34 girls); Grade 12: 44 students (23 boys, 21 girls). 93% of students are Roman Catholic.

Faculty School total: 19. In upper school: 8 men, 11 women; 14 have advanced degrees.

Subjects Offered Accounting, algebra, American government, American literature, anatomy and physiology, art, art history, biology, biology-AP, British literature, British literature (honors), business, calculus, calculus-AP, ceramics, chemistry, chemistry-AP, choir, computer applications, concert band, drafting, earth science, English, English literature and composition-AP, environmental science, geography, geometry, government, health education, history of the Catholic Church, integrated science, intro to computers, Latin, moral theology, newspaper, painting, peace and justice, physical education, physics, pre-algebra, pre-calculus, psychology, sociology, Spanish, studio art, U.S. history, vocal music, weight fitness, world history, yearbook.

Graduation Requirements Biology, business, computer applications, electives, English composition, English literature, health education, mathematics, physical education (includes health), physical science, religion (includes Bible studies and theology), U.S. government, U.S. history, must attend a senior retreat.

Special Academic Programs Advanced Placement exam preparation; honors section; independent study; study at local college for college credit.

College Admission Counseling 47 students graduated in 2012; all went to college, including Miami University; Ohio University; The Ohio State University; University of Cincinnati; University of Dayton. Mean composite ACT: 24. 37% scored over 26 on composite ACT.

Student Life Upper grades have uniform requirement, student council, honor system. Discipline rests primarily with faculty. Attendance at religious services is required.

Tuition and Aid Day student tuition: $7150. Tuition installment plan (FACTS Tuition Payment Plan). Tuition reduction for siblings, need-based scholarship grants available. In 2012–13, 44% of upper-school students received aid. Total amount of financial aid awarded in 2012–13: $353,850.

Admissions Traditional secondary-level entrance grade is 9. For fall 2012, 5 students applied for upper-level admission, 5 were accepted, 5 enrolled. Achievement tests or any standardized test required. Deadline for receipt of application materials: none. Application fee required: $100. Interview recommended.

Athletics Interscholastic: baseball (boys), basketball (b,g), cheering (g), cross-country running (b,g), football (b), golf (b), soccer (b,g), softball (g), swimming and diving (b,g), tennis (b,g), track and field (b,g), volleyball (g), wrestling (b); intramural: strength & conditioning (b,g); coed intramural: indoor track. 1 PE instructor, 35 coaches, 1 athletic trainer.

Computers Computers are regularly used in accounting, computer applications, drafting, newspaper, science, yearbook classes. Computer resources include on-campus library services, Internet access, wireless campus network, Internet filtering or blocking technology. Students grades are available online. The school has a published electronic and media policy.

Contact Mrs. Denise Stauffer, Principal. 937-498-1161 Ext. 115. Fax: 937-492-9877. E-mail: d.stauffer@lehmancatholic.com. Website: www.lehmancatholic.com/

LEXINGTON CATHOLIC HIGH SCHOOL

2250 Clays Mill Road
Lexington, Kentucky 40503-1797

Head of School: Dr. Steven Angelucci

General Information Coeducational day college-preparatory and religious studies school, affiliated with Roman Catholic Church. Grades 9–12. Founded: 1823. Setting: urban. 7-acre campus. 3 buildings on campus. Approved or accredited by National Catholic Education Association, Southern Association of Colleges and Schools, and Kentucky Department of Education. Endowment: $500,000. Total enrollment: 810. Upper school average class size: 22. Upper school faculty-student ratio: 1:13. There are 177 required school days per year for Upper School students.

Upper School students typically attend 5 days per week. The average school day consists of 7 hours and 15 minutes.

Upper School Student Profile Grade 9: 202 students (111 boys, 91 girls); Grade 10: 212 students (98 boys, 114 girls); Grade 11: 209 students (103 boys, 106 girls); Grade 12: 187 students (99 boys, 88 girls). 77% of students are Roman Catholic.

Faculty School total: 64. In upper school: 33 men, 31 women; 48 have advanced degrees.

Subjects Offered Accounting, advanced chemistry, Advanced Placement courses, advanced studio art-AP, algebra, American government, American history, American history-AP, American literature, anatomy and physiology, art, astronomy, band, Bible as literature, biology, biology-AP, British literature, British literature (honors), calculus, calculus-AP, Catholic belief and practice, ceramics, chemistry, chemistry-AP, choral music, Christian and Hebrew scripture, church history, comparative religion, computer applications, computer programming, creative writing, drama, economics, English-AP, ethics, film, French, French-AP, geography, geology, geometry, government and politics-AP, health, history of the Catholic Church, honors English, honors geometry, honors U.S. history, honors world history, humanities, introduction to literature, Latin, Latin-AP, physical education, physics, psychology, religious studies, sociology, Spanish, Spanish language-AP, U.S. government, U.S. government and politics-AP, U.S. history, U.S. history-AP, world history, world literature.

Graduation Requirements American history, American literature, arts and fine arts (art, music, dance, drama), biology, British literature, Catholic belief and practice, chemistry, church history, computer applications, English, foreign language, mathematics, physical education (includes health), religion (includes Bible studies and theology), science, U.S. government, U.S. government and politics, U.S. history, world history.

Special Academic Programs 18 Advanced Placement exams for which test preparation is offered; honors section.

College Admission Counseling 191 students graduated in 2013; 187 went to college, including University of Kentucky. Other: 4 entered military service. Mean SAT critical reading: 572, mean SAT math: 574, mean SAT writing: 560, mean composite ACT: 25. 35% scored over 26 on composite ACT.

Student Life Upper grades have uniform requirement, student council, honor system. Discipline rests primarily with faculty. Attendance at religious services is required.

Summer Programs Computer instruction programs offered; session focuses on health, physical education, and computers; held on campus; accepts boys and girls; not open to students from other schools. 60 students usually enrolled. 2014 schedule: June to July.

Tuition and Aid Day student tuition: $8465. Tuition installment plan (monthly payment plans, individually arranged payment plans). Merit scholarship grants, need-based scholarship grants available. In 2013–14, 17% of upper-school students received aid; total upper-school merit-scholarship money awarded: $5000. Total amount of financial aid awarded in 2013–14: $495,000.

Admissions Traditional secondary-level entrance grade is 9. For fall 2013, 240 students applied for upper-level admission, 240 were accepted, 202 enrolled. Scholastic Testing Service High School Placement Test required. Deadline for receipt of application materials: none. Application fee required: $275.

Athletics Interscholastic: baseball (boys), basketball (b,g), cheering (g), cross-country running (b,g), dance team (g), diving (b,g), football (b), golf (b,g), soccer (b,g), softball (g), swimming and diving (b,g), tennis (b,g), track and field (b,g), volleyball (g); intramural: badminton (b,g), basketball (b,g), flag football (g), lacrosse (b), physical training (b,g); coed interscholastic: bowling, ultimate Frisbee; coed intramural: outdoor activities. 3 PE instructors, 2 athletic trainers.

Computers Computers are regularly used in all academic classes. Computer network features include on-campus library services, Internet access, wireless campus network, Internet filtering or blocking technology. Computer access in designated common areas is available to students. Students grades are available online. The school has a published electronic and media policy.

Contact Ms. MIndy Towles, Admissions Director. 859-277-7183 Ext. 231. Fax: 859-276-5086. E-mail: mtowles@lexingtoncatholic.com. Website: www.lexingtoncatholic.com

LICK-WILMERDING HIGH SCHOOL

755 Ocean Avenue
San Francisco, California 94112

Head of School: Eric Temple

General Information Coeducational day college-preparatory, arts, technology, and Technical Arts school. Grades 9–12. Founded: 1895. Setting: urban. 4-acre campus. 6 buildings on campus. Approved or accredited by Western Association of Schools and Colleges and California Department of Education. Member of National Association of Independent Schools and Secondary School Admission Test Board. Endowment: $43 million. Total enrollment: 460. Upper school average class size: 15. Upper school faculty-student ratio: 1:9. Upper School students typically attend 5 days per week. The average school day consists of 7 hours and 30 minutes.

Upper School Student Profile Grade 9: 118 students (66 boys, 52 girls); Grade 10: 120 students (60 boys, 60 girls); Grade 11: 111 students (52 boys, 59 girls); Grade 12: 112 students (53 boys, 59 girls).

Faculty School total: 63. In upper school: 26 men, 35 women; 55 have advanced degrees.

Subjects Offered Acting, adolescent issues, advanced chemistry, advanced math, African-American literature, algebra, American history, American literature, anatomy and physiology, architectural drawing, architecture, art, biology, calculus, chemistry, choral music, computer music, computer programming, computer science, creative writing, critical thinking, dance, digital imaging, drafting, drama, drama performance, drawing and design, electronics, English, English literature, ethical decision making, European history, film, fine arts, French, geometry, health and wellness, history, industrial arts, instrumental music, jazz band, jewelry making, journalism, junior and senior seminars, Mandarin, marine biology, mathematics, mechanical drawing, multimedia design, music, orchestra, outdoor education, peer counseling, photography, physical education, physics, playwriting and directing, politics, psychology, robotics, science, social studies, Spanish, Spanish literature, stage design, stagecraft, strategies for success, technical arts, technical skills, theater, theater design and production, trigonometry, U.S. history, urban design, video and animation, visual and performing arts, vocal ensemble, woodworking, word processing, world history, world literature, writing, yoga.

Graduation Requirements Arts and fine arts (art, music, dance, drama), English, foreign language, mathematics, physical education (includes health), science, social studies (includes history), technical arts, technology/design, junior project with technical arts.

Special Academic Programs Advanced Placement exam preparation; honors section; independent study.

College Admission Counseling 101 students graduated in 2013; all went to college, including Brown University; New York University; Stanford University; Tufts University; University of California, Berkeley; University of Southern California. Median SAT critical reading: 660, median SAT math: 680, median SAT writing: 700. 86% scored over 600 on SAT critical reading, 85% scored over 600 on SAT math, 89% scored over 600 on SAT writing.

Student Life Upper grades have student council. Discipline rests primarily with faculty.

Tuition and Aid Day student tuition: $39,395. Tuition installment plan (FACTS Tuition Payment Plan, 3- or 10-installment plans). Need-based scholarship grants available. In 2013–14, 38% of upper-school students received aid. Total amount of financial aid awarded in 2013–14: $4,300,000.

Admissions Traditional secondary-level entrance grade is 9. For fall 2013, 776 students applied for upper-level admission, 156 were accepted, 118 enrolled. ISEE or SSAT required. Deadline for receipt of application materials: January 16. Application fee required: $95. Interview required.

Athletics Interscholastic: baseball (boys), basketball (b,g), cross-country running (b,g), lacrosse (b,g), soccer (b,g), swimming and diving (b,g), tennis (b,g), track and field (b,g), volleyball (g); coed interscholastic: badminton, cross-country running, wrestling; coed intramural: dance, fitness, modern dance, physical fitness, rock climbing, ultimate Frisbee, yoga. 2 PE instructors, 25 coaches.

Computers Computers are regularly used in architecture, digital applications, drafting, history, journalism, library, literary magazine, mathematics, media, science, writing, yearbook classes. Computer network features include on-campus library services, online commercial services, Internet access, wireless campus network, Internet filtering or blocking technology. Campus intranet, student e-mail accounts, and computer access in designated common areas are available to students. Students grades are available online.

Contact Ms. Lisa Wu, Director of Admissions. 415-337-9990. Fax: 415-239-1230. E-mail: admissions@lwhs.org. Website: www.lwhs.org

LINCOLN ACADEMY

81 Academy Hill
Newcastle, Maine 04553

Head of School: Mr. John B. Pinkerton

General Information Coeducational day college-preparatory, general academic, arts, business, vocational, technology, advanced placement, and world languages school. Grades 9–12. Founded: 1801. Setting: small town. Nearest major city is Portland. 85-acre campus. 4 buildings on campus. Approved or accredited by New England Association of Schools and Colleges and Maine Department of Education. Endowment: $5.5 million. Total enrollment: 500. Upper school average class size: 18. Upper school faculty-student ratio: 1:13. There are 176 required school days per year for Upper School students. Upper School students typically attend 5 days per week. The average school day consists of 6 hours and 40 minutes.

Faculty School total: 43.

Subjects Offered 20th century history, 20th century world history, 3-dimensional art, 3-dimensional design, accounting, acting, advanced biology, advanced chemistry, advanced math, Advanced Placement courses, advanced studio art-AP, algebra, American history, American history-AP, American literature, American literature-AP, architectural drawing, art and culture, art-AP, athletics, audio visual/media, auto mechanics, band, basic language skills, biology, biology-AP, bookkeeping, business, business skills, calculus, calculus-AP, career/college preparation, chemistry, chemistry-AP, chorus, computer skills, conceptual physics, concert band, concert choir, desktop publishing, developmental language skills, developmental math, drafting, drama,

English composition, English language-AP, English literature-AP, English-AP, English/composition-AP, environmental science-AP, filmmaking, foreign language, French, French-AP, general math, geography, geometry, healthful living, history, history of rock and roll, honors algebra, honors English, honors geometry, honors U.S. history, honors world history, industrial arts, instrumental music, integrated physics, Italian, Japanese, jazz band, language arts, language development, marine science, mechanical drawing, music theory, music theory-AP, musical productions, performing arts, physical education, play production, play/screen writing, poetry, portfolio art, pre-algebra, pre-calculus, psychology, Russian, sculpture, social studies, Spanish, Spanish language-AP, studio art, technical drawing, technical education, U.S. history, U.S. history-AP, U.S. literature, visual and performing arts, work-study, world history, yearbook.

Graduation Requirements English, job shadow experiences, community service.

Special Academic Programs 12 Advanced Placement exams for which test preparation is offered; honors section; independent study.

College Admission Counseling 113 students graduated in 2012.

Student Life Upper grades have specified standards of dress, student council. Discipline rests primarily with faculty.

Tuition and Aid Day student tuition: $10,046.

Admissions Traditional secondary-level entrance grade is 9. CTBS or ERB required. Deadline for receipt of application materials: none. No application fee required. Interview recommended.

Athletics Interscholastic: baseball (boys), basketball (b,g), cheering (g), cross-country running (b,g), field hockey (g), golf (b), lacrosse (b,g), soccer (b,g), softball (g), swimming and diving (b,g), tennis (b,g), track and field (b,g), wrestling (g); coed interscholastic: indoor track, Special Olympics; coed intramural: dance team, outdoor activities.

Computers Computers are regularly used in all classes. Computer network features include on-campus library services, online commercial services, Internet access, wireless campus network. Campus intranet, student e-mail accounts, and computer access in designated common areas are available to students. Students grades are available online. The school has a published electronic and media policy.

Contact Sherry Stearns, Director of Admissions. 207-563-3596. Fax: 207-563-3599. E-mail: stearns@lincolnacademy.org. Website: www.lincolnacademy.org

LINCOLN SCHOOL

301 Butler Avenue
Providence, Rhode Island 02906-5556

Head of School: Julia Russell Eells

General Information Coeducational day (boys' only in lower grades) college-preparatory, arts, and technology school, affiliated with Society of Friends. Boys grades N–PK, girls grades N–12. Founded: 1884. Setting: urban. 46-acre campus. 5 buildings on campus. Approved or accredited by Association of Independent Schools in New England, Friends Council on Education, New England Association of Schools and Colleges, and Rhode Island Department of Education. Member of National Association of Independent Schools and Secondary School Admission Test Board. Endowment: $7 million. Total enrollment: 337. Upper school average class size: 13. Upper school faculty-student ratio: 1:4. Upper School students typically attend 5 days per week. The average school day consists of 7 hours and 13 minutes.

Upper School Student Profile Grade 9: 43 students (43 girls); Grade 10: 42 students (42 girls); Grade 11: 39 students (39 girls); Grade 12: 33 students (33 girls). 1% of students are members of Society of Friends.

Faculty School total: 75. In upper school: 11 men, 35 women; 24 have advanced degrees.

Subjects Offered Algebra, American history, American literature, anatomy, Arabic, art, biology, biology-AP, calculus, calculus-AP, ceramics, chemistry, chemistry-AP, college awareness, community service, computer science, creative writing, dance, English, English literature, environmental science, ethics, European history, European history-AP, French, French-AP, geometry, health, history, Latin, music, photography, physical education, physics, pre-calculus, Spanish, Spanish language-AP, statistics-AP, theater, trigonometry, U.S. history-AP, visual literacy, women's studies, world history, world literature.

Graduation Requirements Arts and fine arts (art, music, dance, drama), college planning, computer science, English, ethics, foreign language, mathematics, physical education (includes health), science, social studies (includes history), senior service trip. Community service is required.

Special Academic Programs Advanced Placement exam preparation; honors section; independent study; term-away projects; study at local college for college credit; study abroad; programs in general development for dyslexic students.

College Admission Counseling 48 students graduated in 2012; all went to college, including Boston University; Brown University; Hobart and William Smith Colleges; Worcester Polytechnic Institute. Median SAT critical reading: 590, median SAT math: 570, median SAT writing: 609.

Student Life Upper grades have uniform requirement, student council, honor system. Discipline rests equally with students and faculty.

Tuition and Aid Day student tuition: $28,650. Tuition installment plan (FACTS Tuition Payment Plan, Tuition Management Systems Plan). Merit scholarship grants, need-based scholarship grants available. In 2012–13, 40% of upper-school students received aid; total upper-school merit-scholarship money awarded: $15,000. Total amount of financial aid awarded in 2012–13: $2,000,000.

Admissions Traditional secondary-level entrance grade is 9. For fall 2012, 82 students applied for upper-level admission, 59 were accepted, 24 enrolled. ISEE or SSAT required. Deadline for receipt of application materials: February 15. Application fee required: $50. Interview required.

Athletics Interscholastic: basketball, crew, cross-country running, field hockey, lacrosse, soccer, squash, swimming and diving, tennis. 3 PE instructors, 17 coaches, 1 athletic trainer.

Computers Computers are regularly used in English, history, science classes. Computer network features include on-campus library services, Internet access, wireless campus network, Internet filtering or blocking technology. Student e-mail accounts and computer access in designated common areas are available to students. The school has a published electronic and media policy.

Contact Mrs. Diane Mota, Admission Office Administrative Assistant. 401-331-9696 Ext. 3157. Fax: 401-751-6670. E-mail: dmota@lincolnschool.org. Website: www.lincolnschool.org

LINDEN CHRISTIAN SCHOOL

877 Wilkes Avenue
Winnipeg, Manitoba R3P 1B8, Canada

Head of School: Mr. Robert Charach

General Information Coeducational day college-preparatory, arts, religious studies, and technology school, affiliated with Baptist Church. Grades 9–12. Founded: 1987. Setting: suburban. 1 building on campus. Approved or accredited by Association of Christian Schools International and Manitoba Department of Education. Language of instruction: English. Total enrollment: 876. Upper school average class size: 25. Upper school faculty-student ratio: 1:13.

Upper School Student Profile Grade 9: 77 students (32 boys, 45 girls); Grade 10: 67 students (33 boys, 34 girls); Grade 11: 50 students (19 boys, 31 girls); Grade 12: 69 students (33 boys, 36 girls).

Faculty School total: 61. In upper school: 14 men, 9 women.

Subjects Offered Choir, choral music, computer applications, computer information systems, computer science, computer studies, computer technologies, concert band, drama, dramatic arts, independent study, jazz band, jazz ensemble, leadership, leadership and service, music theater, religious studies, vocal jazz, voice ensemble.

Graduation Requirements Bible studies, English, mathematics, physical education (includes health), science, social studies (includes history).

Special Academic Programs Honors section; independent study.

College Admission Counseling 65 students graduated in 2012; 1 went to college, including Providence College; The University of Winnipeg; University of Manitoba; University of Toronto. Other: 53 entered a postgraduate year.

Student Life Upper grades have specified standards of dress, student council, honor system. Discipline rests primarily with faculty. Attendance at religious services is required.

Tuition and Aid Day student tuition: CAN$2940. Tuition installment plan (monthly payment plans). Tuition reduction for siblings, bursaries available. In 2012–13, 8% of upper-school students received aid.

Admissions Traditional secondary-level entrance grade is 9. PSAT required. Application fee required: CAN$25. Interview required.

Athletics Interscholastic: aerobics (boys, girls), badminton (b,g), baseball (b,g), basketball (b,g), bowling (b,g), broomball (b,g), climbing (b,g), cooperative games (b,g), cross-country running (b,g), curling (b,g), fitness (b,g), flag football (b,g), floor hockey (b,g), football (b,g), golf (b,g), ice hockey (b), life saving (b,g), physical fitness (b,g), soccer (b,g), track and field (b,g), volleyball (b,g); intramural: badminton (b,g), basketball (b,g), cross-country running (b,g), soccer (b,g), volleyball (b,g); coed interscholastic: aerobics, baseball, basketball, bowling, broomball, climbing, cooperative games, cross-country running, curling, fitness, football, golf, life saving, physical fitness, soccer, track and field, volleyball; coed intramural: basketball. 4 PE instructors.

Computers Computers are regularly used in all academic, art, Bible studies, career education, career exploration, Christian doctrine, college planning, creative writing, current events, data processing, desktop publishing, digital applications, drafting, drawing and design, ESL, geography, graphic arts, graphic design, health, history, independent study, information technology, lab/keyboard, learning cognition, library, library skills, life skills, literacy, mathematics, media, music, newspaper, photography, psychology, reading, religion, religious studies, research skills, science, social sciences, social studies, speech, study skills, technology, Web site design, word processing, writing, writing, yearbook classes. Computer network features include on-campus library services, Internet access, wireless campus network, Internet filtering or blocking technology. Student e-mail accounts are available to students. Students grades are available online. The school has a published electronic and media policy.

Contact Mrs. Colleen Job, Registrar. 204-989-6739. Fax: 204-487-7068. E-mail: colleenj@lindenchristian.org. Website: www.lindenchristian.org/

LINFIELD CHRISTIAN SCHOOL

31950 Pauba Road
Temecula, California 92592

Head of School: Karen Raftery

General Information Coeducational day college-preparatory, arts, religious studies, and technology school, affiliated with Christian faith. Grades JK–12. Founded: 1936. Setting: suburban. Nearest major city is San Diego. 105-acre campus. 6 buildings on campus. Approved or accredited by Association of Christian Schools International, Western Association of Schools and Colleges, and California Department of Education. Total enrollment: 757. Upper school average class size: 19. Upper school faculty-student ratio: 1:12. There are 171 required school days per year for Upper School students. Upper School students typically attend 5 days per week. The average school day consists of 5 hours and 55 minutes.

Upper School Student Profile Grade 6: 57 students (30 boys, 27 girls); Grade 7: 59 students (29 boys, 30 girls); Grade 8: 73 students (32 boys, 41 girls); Grade 9: 89 students (50 boys, 39 girls); Grade 10: 72 students (47 boys, 25 girls); Grade 11: 80 students (47 boys, 33 girls); Grade 12: 79 students (41 boys, 38 girls). 70% of students are Christian faith.

Faculty School total: 64. In upper school: 10 men, 15 women; 8 have advanced degrees.

Subjects Offered Advanced math, algebra, American sign language, anatomy and physiology, art, ASB Leadership, athletics, band, Bible, biology, calculus-AP, career/college preparation, chemistry, chemistry-AP, choir, computers, economics, English, English-AP, European history-AP, film, filmmaking, French, freshman foundations, general science, geometry, government, government-AP, health, physical education, physics, pre-calculus, public policy, senior seminar, service learning/internship, Spanish, Spanish-AP, speech and debate, sports medicine, studio art-AP, theater, U.S. history, U.S. history-AP, world history, world religions, yearbook.

Graduation Requirements Arts and fine arts (art, music, dance, drama), computer science, economics, English, foreign language, freshman foundations, government, mathematics, physical education (includes health), religion (includes Bible studies and theology), science, senior seminar, social sciences, social studies (includes history), speech and debate. Community service is required.

Special Academic Programs 12 Advanced Placement exams for which test preparation is offered; honors section.

College Admission Counseling 85 students graduated in 2013; 80 went to college, including California State University, San Marcos; Pepperdine University; San Diego State University; University of California, San Diego; University of Colorado Boulder. Other: 1 entered military service, 4 had other specific plans. Mean SAT critical reading: 508, mean SAT math: 551, mean SAT writing: 507, mean combined SAT: 1566.

Student Life Upper grades have uniform requirement, student council, honor system. Discipline rests primarily with faculty. Attendance at religious services is required.

Summer Programs Art/fine arts programs offered; held on campus; accepts boys and girls; open to students from other schools.

Tuition and Aid Day student tuition: $9780. Tuition installment plan (monthly payment plans). Need-based scholarship grants available. In 2013–14, 30% of upper-school students received aid.

Admissions Traditional secondary-level entrance grade is 9. TerraNova and writing sample required. Deadline for receipt of application materials: none. Application fee required: $75. On-campus interview required.

Athletics Interscholastic: baseball (boys), basketball (b,g), cheering (g), cross-country running (b,g), football (b), lacrosse (b), soccer (b,g), softball (g), tennis (b,g), track and field (b,g), volleyball (g); intramural: volleyball (g); coed interscholastic: equestrian sports, golf; coed intramural: cross-country running. 3 PE instructors, 16 coaches, 1 athletic trainer.

Computers Computers are regularly used in computer applications, keyboarding, science, senior seminar, yearbook classes. Computer network features include on-campus library services, Internet access, wireless campus network, Internet filtering or blocking technology. Campus intranet and computer access in designated common areas are available to students. Students grades are available online. The school has a published electronic and media policy.

Contact Mrs. Becky Swanson, Assistant Director of Admissions. 951-676-8111 Ext. 1402. Fax: 951-695-1291. E-mail: bswanson@linfield.com. Website: www.linfield.com

THE LINSLY SCHOOL

60 Knox Lane
Wheeling, West Virginia 26003-6489

Head of School: Mr. Chad Barnett

General Information Coeducational boarding and day college-preparatory, arts, technology, and science, mathematics, humanities, foreign language school. Boarding grades 7–12, day grades 5–12. Founded: 1814. Setting: suburban. Nearest major city is Pittsburgh, PA. Students are housed in single-sex dormitories. 60-acre campus. 19 buildings on campus. Approved or accredited by Independent Schools Association of the Central States, North Central Association of Colleges and Schools, The Association of Boarding Schools, and West Virginia Department of Education. Member of National Association of Independent Schools. Endowment: $16 million. Total enrollment: 443.

Upper school average class size: 15. Upper school faculty-student ratio: 1:10. There are 165 required school days per year for Upper School students. Upper School students typically attend 5 days per week. The average school day consists of 6 hours and 30 minutes.

Upper School Student Profile Grade 9: 79 students (42 boys, 37 girls); Grade 10: 72 students (34 boys, 38 girls); Grade 11: 83 students (53 boys, 30 girls); Grade 12: 64 students (32 boys, 32 girls). 27% of students are boarding students. 47% are state residents. 15 states are represented in upper school student body. 10% are international students. International students from Bahamas, China, Mexico, Republic of Korea, Saudi Arabia, and South Africa; 15 other countries represented in student body.

Faculty School total: 60. In upper school: 28 men, 15 women; 26 have advanced degrees; 24 reside on campus.

Subjects Offered Algebra, American history, American literature, art, art history, biology, biology-AP, calculus-AP, character education, chemistry, chemistry-AP, Chinese, chorus, college counseling, communications, computer programming, computer science, concert band, contemporary issues, creative writing, drama, earth science, economics, English, English language-AP, English literature, English literature-AP, environmental science, expository writing, fine arts, French, geometry, German, government/civics, health, history, human geography - AP, humanities, Latin, mathematics, model United Nations, multimedia design, music, newspaper, physical education, physics, physics-AP, psychology, psychology-AP, science, social studies, Spanish, speech, statistics, technology/design, theater, U.S. history-AP, world history, writing, yearbook, zoology.

Graduation Requirements Arts and fine arts (art, music, dance, drama), computer science, English, foreign language, mathematics, physical education (includes health), science, social studies (includes history), Senior Research Essay.

Special Academic Programs 12 Advanced Placement exams for which test preparation is offered; academic accommodation for the gifted.

College Admission Counseling 64 students graduated in 2013; all went to college, including Duquesne University; Marshall University; New York University; Ohio University; West Virginia University. Mean SAT critical reading: 580, mean SAT math: 580, mean SAT writing: 570, mean combined SAT: 1730, mean composite ACT: 26.

Student Life Upper grades have uniform requirement, student council, honor system. Discipline rests primarily with faculty.

Summer Programs Enrichment, advancement, computer instruction programs offered; held on campus; accepts boys and girls; open to students from other schools. 100 students usually enrolled. 2014 schedule: June 12 to July 12. Application deadline: June 12.

Tuition and Aid Day student tuition: $15,590; 5-day tuition and room/board: $32,170; 7-day tuition and room/board: $32,170. Need-based scholarship grants available. In 2013–14, 48% of upper-school students received aid. Total amount of financial aid awarded in 2013–14: $2,345,000.

Admissions Traditional secondary-level entrance grade is 9. Otis-Lennon, Stanford Achievement Test, SSAT or TOEFL or SLEP required. Deadline for receipt of application materials: none. No application fee required. Interview required.

Athletics Interscholastic: baseball (boys), basketball (b,g), cheering (g), cross-country running (b,g), diving (b,g), football (b), golf (b,g), ice hockey (b,g), lacrosse (b), soccer (b,g), softball (g), wrestling (b); intramural: flag football (b,g), floor hockey (b), football (b), hiking/backpacking (b,g), indoor soccer (b,g), indoor track (b,g), indoor track & field (b,g), life saving (b,g), mountain biking (b,g), outdoor activities (b,g), physical fitness (b,g), power lifting (b), rappelling (b,g), rock climbing (b,g), roller blading (b,g), ropes courses (b,g), running (b,g), street hockey (b); coed intramural: backpacking, badminton, bowling, canoeing/kayaking, climbing, combined training, cooperative games, cross-country running, fitness, Frisbee, ice skating, in-line skating, jogging, kayaking, kickball, life saving, mountain biking, Nautilus, physical fitness, physical training, rafting, rock climbing, ropes courses, running, scuba diving, soccer, softball. 4 PE instructors, 4 coaches, 1 athletic trainer.

Computers Computers are regularly used in economics, English, foreign language, humanities, journalism, mathematics, music, psychology, science classes. Computer network features include on-campus library services, online commercial services, Internet access, wireless campus network, Internet filtering or blocking technology. Student e-mail accounts are available to students. The school has a published electronic and media policy.

Contact Mr. Robert J. Zitzelsberger III, Director of Admissions. 304-233-1436. Fax: 304-234-4614. E-mail: admit@linsly.org. Website: www.linsly.org

See Display on next page and Close-Up on page 546.

LIPSCOMB ACADEMY

3901 Granny White Pike
Nashville, Tennessee 37204-3951

Head of School: Dr. Michael P. Hammond

General Information Coeducational day college-preparatory and religious studies school, affiliated with Church of Christ. Grades PK–12. Founded: 1891. Setting: suburban. 10-acre campus. 4 buildings on campus. Approved or accredited by National Christian School Association, Southern Association of Colleges and Schools, Southern Association of Independent Schools, and Tennessee Department of Education.

Endowment: $95,000. Total enrollment: 1,318. Upper school average class size: 18. Upper school faculty-student ratio: 1:15. Upper School students typically attend 5 days per week. The average school day consists of 7 hours and 15 minutes.

Upper School Student Profile Grade 9: 152 students (77 boys, 75 girls); Grade 10: 114 students (51 boys, 63 girls); Grade 11: 116 students (56 boys, 60 girls); Grade 12: 141 students (79 boys, 62 girls). 55% of students are members of Church of Christ.

Faculty School total: 37. In upper school: 16 men, 19 women; 25 have advanced degrees.

Subjects Offered Accounting, advanced computer applications, algebra, American government, American history, anatomy and physiology, art, band, biology, biology-AP, calculus-AP, chemistry, chemistry-AP, chorus, computer science, current history, drama, economics, English, French, geography, geometry, health, home economics, honors algebra, honors English, honors geometry, interior design, journalism, keyboarding, Latin, mathematics, modern history, painting, photography, physical education, physics, pre-algebra, psychology, religion, science, science research, social studies, Spanish, Spanish-AP, speech, statistics, trigonometry, visual arts, world history.

Graduation Requirements Economics, English, foreign language, mathematics, physical education (includes health), religion (includes Bible studies and theology), science, social studies (includes history), research paper, 60 hours of community service.

Special Academic Programs 4 Advanced Placement exams for which test preparation is offered; honors section; accelerated programs; study at local college for college credit; programs in general development for dyslexic students.

College Admission Counseling 132 students graduated in 2013; all went to college, including Belmont University; Harding University; Lipscomb University; Middle Tennessee State University; The University of Alabama; The University of Tennessee. Mean composite ACT: 25.

Student Life Upper grades have uniform requirement, student council. Discipline rests primarily with faculty. Attendance at religious services is required.

Summer Programs Remediation, enrichment, sports, art/fine arts programs offered; session focuses on mathematics and English remediation, Middle School Summer Academy; held on campus; accepts boys and girls; open to students from other schools. 100 students usually enrolled. 2014 schedule: June 1 to July 31. Application deadline: May 15.

Tuition and Aid Day student tuition: $10,990. Tuition installment plan (monthly payment plans, individually arranged payment plans). Tuition reduction for siblings, need-based scholarship grants available. In 2013–14, 8% of upper-school students received aid. Total amount of financial aid awarded in 2013–14: $183,000.

Admissions Traditional secondary-level entrance grade is 9. For fall 2013, 80 students applied for upper-level admission, 64 were accepted, 53 enrolled. Math and English placement tests or TOEFL required. Deadline for receipt of application materials: none. Application fee required: $100. Interview required.

Athletics Interscholastic: baseball (boys), basketball (b,g), bowling (b,g), cheering (g), cross-country running (b,g), football (b), golf (b,g), ice hockey (b,g), soccer (b,g), softball (g), tennis (b,g), track and field (b,g), volleyball (g), wrestling (b); intramural: basketball (b,g); coed intramural: basketball. 2 PE instructors, 16 coaches, 1 athletic trainer.

Computers Computer network features include on-campus library services, online commercial services, Internet access, wireless campus network, Internet filtering or blocking technology. Student e-mail accounts and computer access in designated common areas are available to students. Students grades are available online. The school has a published electronic and media policy.

Contact Mrs. Kim Schow, Administrative Assistant. 615-966-6409. Fax: 615-966-7639. E-mail: kim.schow@lipscomb.edu. Website: www.lipscombacademy.org

LITTLE KESWICK SCHOOL

Keswick, Virginia
See Special Needs Schools section.

LITTLE RED SCHOOL HOUSE AND ELISABETH IRWIN HIGH SCHOOL

272 Sixth Avenue
New York, New York 10014

Head of School: Philip Kassen

General Information Coeducational day college-preparatory, arts, and technology school. Grades N–12. Founded: 1921. Setting: urban. 2 buildings on campus. Approved or accredited by New York Department of Education. Member of National Association of Independent Schools. Total enrollment: 650. Upper school average class size: 15. Upper school faculty-student ratio: 1:7. There are 168 required school days per year for Upper School students. Upper School students typically attend 5 days per week. The average school day consists of 6 hours and 30 minutes.

Faculty School total: 100.

Subjects Offered 20th century American writers, 20th century physics, advanced biology, advanced chemistry, African-American literature, American culture, American history, American literature, art, art history, Asian history, astronomy, biology, calculus, chemistry, chorus, college counseling, college placement, community service, computer graphics, creative dance, dance, data analysis, drama, economics, environmental science, European history, film and literature, filmmaking, French, global studies, human rights, independent study, introduction to literature, introduction to technology, jazz band, journalism, Latin American literature, law, life issues, Mandarin, Middle

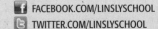

Eastern history, modern dance, modern European history, multimedia design, music, music technology, painting, photography, physical science, physics, playwriting, pre-calculus, printmaking, sculpture, senior internship, Shakespeare, Spanish, Spanish literature, studio art, theater, trigonometry, U.S. history, urban studies, world literature.

Graduation Requirements Arts and fine arts (art, music, dance, drama), English, foreign language, history, life issues, mathematics, physical education (includes health), science, senior project, technology, urban studies, 25 hours of community service per year.

Special Academic Programs Honors section; independent study; study at local college for college credit; study abroad.

College Admission Counseling 44 students graduated in 2013; all went to college, including Amherst College; Cornell University; Oberlin College; Vassar College.

Student Life Upper grades have student council, honor system. Discipline rests equally with students and faculty.

Tuition and Aid Day student tuition: $37,750. Tuition installment plan (Insured Tuition Payment Plan, SMART Tuition Payment Plan, monthly payment plans). Need-based scholarship grants available. In 2013–14, 25% of upper-school students received aid.

Admissions Traditional secondary-level entrance grade is 9. ISEE required. Deadline for receipt of application materials: December 1. Application fee required: $75. On-campus interview required.

Athletics Interscholastic: baseball (boys), basketball (b,g), soccer (b,g), softball (g), track and field (b,g), volleyball (g); coed interscholastic: cross-country running, golf, indoor track & field, judo, swimming and diving, tennis, winter (indoor) track; coed intramural: aerobics, aerobics/dance, dance, dance team, fitness, Frisbee, martial arts, modern dance, physical fitness, physical training, running, strength & conditioning, ultimate Frisbee, weight training, yoga. 5 PE instructors, 10 coaches, 1 athletic trainer.

Computers Computers are regularly used in all classes. Computer network features include on-campus library services, Internet access, wireless campus network, Internet filtering or blocking technology. Campus intranet, student e-mail accounts, and computer access in designated common areas are available to students. Students grades are available online. The school has a published electronic and media policy.

Contact Admissions Office. 212-477-5316. E-mail: admissions@lrei.org. Website: www.lrei.org

LODI ACADEMY
1230 South Central Avenue
Lodi, California 95242

Head of School: Mr. Harley Peterson

General Information Coeducational day college-preparatory, general academic, arts, and religious studies school, affiliated with Seventh-day Adventist Church. Boys grade 9, girls grade 12. Founded: 1908. Setting: small town. Nearest major city is Sacramento. 30-acre campus. 9 buildings on campus. Approved or accredited by Western Association of Schools and Colleges and California Department of Education. Endowment: $1.1 million. Total enrollment: 90. Upper school average class size: 23. Upper school faculty-student ratio: 1:9. There are 180 required school days per year for Upper School students. Upper School students typically attend 5 days per week. The average school day consists of 7 hours and 17 minutes.

Upper School Student Profile Grade 9: 30 students (14 boys, 16 girls); Grade 10: 14 students (8 boys, 6 girls); Grade 11: 23 students (14 boys, 9 girls); Grade 12: 23 students (10 boys, 13 girls). 80% of students are Seventh-day Adventists.

Faculty School total: 12. In upper school: 8 men, 4 women.

Subjects Offered Accounting, algebra, American history, American literature, art, auto mechanics, band, Bible, biology, chemistry, choir, chorus, computer applications, economics, English, English literature, English-AP, geography, geometry, government, health, life skills, music appreciation, physical education, physical science, physics, piano, pre-algebra, pre-calculus, Spanish, student publications, U.S. history, U.S. history-AP, world history, yearbook.

Graduation Requirements Algebra, American history, American literature, applied arts, arts and fine arts (art, music, dance, drama), Bible, biology, chemistry, computer applications, economics, English, English literature, geography, geometry, keyboarding, life skills, physical education (includes health), physical science, Spanish, U.S. government, U.S. history, work experience, world history, 100 hours of community service. Community service is required.

Special Academic Programs 2 Advanced Placement exams for which test preparation is offered.

College Admission Counseling 26 students graduated in 2013; 24 went to college, including La Sierra University; Pacific Union College; Walla Walla University. Other: 2 went to work.

Student Life Upper grades have specified standards of dress, student council. Discipline rests primarily with faculty. Attendance at religious services is required.

Tuition and Aid Day student tuition: $6350–$7950. Tuition installment plan (monthly payment plans, individually arranged payment plans). Tuition reduction for siblings, merit scholarship grants, need-based scholarship grants, paying campus jobs, low Income tuition available. In 2013–14, 40% of upper-school students received aid; total upper-school merit-scholarship money awarded: $7000. Total amount of financial aid awarded in 2013–14: $38,000.

Admissions Traditional secondary-level entrance grade is 9. For fall 2013, 35 students applied for upper-level admission, 32 were accepted, 30 enrolled. Achievement tests or Iowa Tests of Basic Skills required. Deadline for receipt of application materials: none. Application fee required: $300. Interview required.

Athletics Interscholastic: basketball (boys, girls), flag football (b,g), soccer (b,g), volleyball (g); intramural: basketball (b,g), flag football (b,g), volleyball (g); coed interscholastic: golf, softball. 1 PE instructor.

Computers Computers are regularly used in accounting, Bible studies, computer applications, English, mathematics classes. Computer network features include Internet access, wireless campus network, Internet filtering or blocking technology. Student e-mail accounts and computer access in designated common areas are available to students. Students grades are available online. The school has a published electronic and media policy.

Contact Mrs. Linda Mack, Registrar. 209-369-2781 Ext. 102. Fax: 209-368-6142. E-mail: lmack@lodiacademy.net. Website: www.lodiacademy.net

LONG ISLAND LUTHERAN MIDDLE AND HIGH SCHOOL
131 Brookville Road
Brookville, New York 11545-3399

Head of School: Dr. David Hahn

General Information Coeducational day college-preparatory, arts, business, religious studies, and technology school, affiliated with Lutheran Church. Grades 6–12. Founded: 1960. Setting: suburban. Nearest major city is New York. 32-acre campus. 6 buildings on campus. Approved or accredited by Evangelical Lutheran Church in America, Middle States Association of Colleges and Schools, US Department of State, and New York Department of Education. Member of National Association of Independent Schools. Endowment: $6.5 million. Total enrollment: 590. Upper school average class size: 18. Upper school faculty-student ratio: 1:9. There are 160 required school days per year for Upper School students. Upper School students typically attend 5 days per week. The average school day consists of 6 hours and 30 minutes.

Upper School Student Profile Grade 9: 118 students (57 boys, 61 girls); Grade 10: 98 students (46 boys, 52 girls); Grade 11: 94 students (49 boys, 45 girls); Grade 12: 103 students (52 boys, 51 girls). 25% of students are Lutheran.

Faculty School total: 58. In upper school: 21 men, 29 women; 47 have advanced degrees.

Subjects Offered Accounting, algebra, American history, American literature, anatomy, art, band, biology, biology-AP, business, business communications, business skills, calculus, calculus-AP, ceramics, choir, college planning, communication skills, computer programming, computer science, computer science-AP, creative writing, dance, decision making skills, driver education, earth science, economics-AP, English, English language-AP, English literature, English literature-AP, environmental science, ethics, European history, European history-AP, fine arts, French, French language-AP, freshman foundations, geography, geometry, government/civics, grammar, graphic arts, health, history, international relations, journalism, Mandarin, marketing, mathematics, multimedia, music, photography, physical education, physics, physics-AP, psychology, religion, social studies, Spanish, Spanish language-AP, technological applications, trigonometry, U.S. government and politics-AP, U.S. history-AP, video film production, word processing, world history, writing.

Graduation Requirements Arts and fine arts (art, music, dance, drama), business studies, English, foreign language, mathematics, physical education (includes health), religion (includes Bible studies and theology), science, social studies (includes history).

Special Academic Programs 14 Advanced Placement exams for which test preparation is offered; honors section; term-away projects; ESL (12 students enrolled).

College Admission Counseling 110 students graduated in 2013; all went to college, including Binghamton University, State University of New York; Fordham University; Hofstra University; New York University; Penn State University Park; Susquehanna University. Mean SAT critical reading: 572, mean SAT math: 564, mean SAT writing: 595, mean combined SAT: 1731, mean composite ACT: 24. 25% scored over 26 on composite ACT.

Student Life Upper grades have uniform requirement, student council, honor system. Discipline rests primarily with faculty. Attendance at religious services is required.

Summer Programs Sports, art/fine arts, computer instruction programs offered; session focuses on sports, recreation, and education; held both on and off campus; held at local satellite facilities; accepts boys and girls; open to students from other schools. 4,000 students usually enrolled. 2014 schedule: June 30 to August 22. Application deadline: January.

Tuition and Aid Day student tuition: $10,925–$12,945. Tuition installment plan (monthly payment plans, school's own payment plan). Tuition reduction for siblings, merit scholarship grants, need-based scholarship grants available. In 2013–14, 25% of upper-school students received aid; total upper-school merit-scholarship money awarded: $28,000. Total amount of financial aid awarded in 2013–14: $420,000.

Admissions Traditional secondary-level entrance grade is 9. For fall 2013, 138 students applied for upper-level admission, 86 were accepted, 56 enrolled. Cognitive Abilities Test, Math Placement Exam and writing sample required. Deadline for receipt of application materials: none. Application fee required: $100. On-campus interview required.

Athletics Interscholastic: baseball (boys, girls), basketball (b), cheering (g), dance team (g), football (b), lacrosse (b,g), roller hockey (b), soccer (b,g), softball (g), tennis (b,g), volleyball (g), wrestling (b); intramural: dance team (g), flag football (b), horseback riding (b,g); coed interscholastic: cross-country running, golf, running, track and field, winter (indoor) track; coed intramural: bowling, equestrian sports, physical training, skiing (downhill). 3 PE instructors, 30 coaches.

Computers Computers are regularly used in accounting, art, business, business skills, English, graphic design, history, journalism, library skills, mathematics, science classes. Computer network features include on-campus library services, Internet access, wireless campus network, Internet filtering or blocking technology, 1:1 Student iPad program required for all students. Student e-mail accounts and computer access in designated common areas are available to students. Students grades are available online. The school has a published electronic and media policy.

Contact Barbara Ward, Director of Admissions. 516-626-1700 Ext. 546. Fax: 516-622-7459. E-mail: barbara.ward@luhi.org. Website: www.luhi.org

LONG TRAIL SCHOOL

1045 Kirby Hollow Road
Dorset, Vermont 05251-9776

Head of School: Steven Dear

General Information Coeducational day college-preparatory and arts school. Grades 6–12. Founded: 1975. Setting: rural. Nearest major city is Rutland. Students are housed in private homes. 14-acre campus. 1 building on campus. Approved or accredited by International Baccalaureate Organization, New England Association of Schools and Colleges, and Vermont Department of Education. Member of National Association of Independent Schools. Endowment: $4.5 million. Total enrollment: 155. Upper school average class size: 10. Upper school faculty-student ratio: 1:8. There are 175 required school days per year for Upper School students. Upper School students typically attend 5 days per week. The average school day consists of 7 hours.

Upper School Student Profile Grade 9: 26 students (14 boys, 12 girls); Grade 10: 23 students (10 boys, 13 girls); Grade 11: 22 students (11 boys, 11 girls); Grade 12: 22 students (8 boys, 14 girls).

Faculty School total: 32. In upper school: 10 men, 22 women; 16 have advanced degrees.

Subjects Offered 20th century world history, acting, algebra, American literature, American literature-AP, art, band, biology, calculus, calculus-AP, chemistry, chorus, computer information systems, conceptual physics, concert band, drama, drawing, earth science, economics, English, English literature, English literature-AP, environmental science, environmental science-AP, French, geography, geometry, government/civics, history, mathematics, model United Nations, music, physical education, physical science, physics, political science, pre-algebra, pre-calculus, probability and statistics, psychology, psychology-AP, science, social studies, Spanish, statistics, statistics-AP, technical theater, theater, trigonometry, U.S. history, U.S. history-AP, world history, world literature, writing.

Graduation Requirements Arts and fine arts (art, music, dance, drama), computer science, English, foreign language, mathematics, physical education (includes health), science, social studies (includes history), brief graduation ceremony speech. Community service is required.

Special Academic Programs International Baccalaureate program; honors section; independent study; programs in English, mathematics, general development for dyslexic students; ESL (5 students enrolled).

College Admission Counseling 18 students graduated in 2013; 17 went to college, including Colgate University; Cornell University; Manhattanville College; Occidental College; Saint Michael's College; Temple University. Other: 1 entered military service. Mean SAT critical reading: 584, mean SAT math: 561, mean SAT writing: 554.

Student Life Upper grades have specified standards of dress, student council, honor system. Discipline rests equally with students and faculty.

Tuition and Aid Day student tuition: $16,950; 7-day tuition and room/board: $35,648. Tuition installment plan (monthly payment plans, individually arranged payment plans, Sallie Mae TuitionPay Plan). Merit scholarship grants, need-based scholarship grants available. In 2013–14, 25% of upper-school students received aid; total upper-school merit-scholarship money awarded: $9000. Total amount of financial aid awarded in 2013–14: $99,599.

Admissions Traditional secondary-level entrance grade is 9. For fall 2013, 20 students applied for upper-level admission, 13 were accepted, 9 enrolled. Admissions testing or essay required. Deadline for receipt of application materials: none. Application fee required: $75. On-campus interview required.

Athletics Interscholastic: baseball (boys), basketball (b,g), soccer (b,g), softball (g); coed interscholastic: alpine skiing, cross-country running, dance team, freestyle skiing, golf, rock climbing, skiing (downhill), snowboarding; coed intramural: aerobics/dance, alpine skiing, basketball, bicycling, dance, fitness walking, fly fishing, freestyle skiing, Frisbee, golf, ice skating, indoor soccer, mountain biking, nordic skiing, skiing (downhill), snowboarding, tennis, touch football, ultimate Frisbee, weight lifting. 1 PE instructor, 8 coaches.

Computers Computers are regularly used in art, English, foreign language, history, library, mathematics, music, science, technology, yearbook classes. Computer network features include on-campus library services, online commercial services, Internet access, wireless campus network, Internet filtering or blocking technology. Campus intranet is available to students. The school has a published electronic and media policy.

Contact Katie Redding, Director of Admissions. 802-867-5717 Ext. 106. Fax: 802-867-0147. E-mail: applylts@longtrailschool.org. Website: www.longtrailschool.org

LORETTO ACADEMY

1300 Hardaway Street
El Paso, Texas 79903

Head of School: Sr. Mary E. (Buffy) Boesen, SL

General Information Coeducational day (boys' only in lower grades) college-preparatory, arts, religious studies, and technology school, affiliated with Roman Catholic Church. Boys grades PK–5, girls grades PK–12. Founded: 1923. Setting: urban. 17-acre campus. 3 buildings on campus. Approved or accredited by Southern Association of Colleges and Schools and Texas Catholic Conference. Endowment: $4.1 million. Total enrollment: 636. Upper school average class size: 20. Upper school faculty-student ratio: 1:20. There are 180 required school days per year for Upper School students. Upper School students typically attend 5 days per week. The average school day consists of 7 hours.

Upper School Student Profile Grade 9: 98 students (98 girls); Grade 10: 89 students (89 girls); Grade 11: 92 students (92 girls); Grade 12: 86 students (86 girls). 90% of students are Roman Catholic.

Faculty School total: 52. In upper school: 7 men, 25 women; 15 have advanced degrees.

Subjects Offered Acting, advanced math, Advanced Placement courses, algebra, American government, American history, anatomy and physiology, art, art appreciation, art-AP, arts, arts and crafts, Bible, biology, business mathematics, calculus, calculus-AP, chemistry, choir, choral music, Christian and Hebrew scripture, college writing, computer applications, computer programming, computer science, English, environmental science, fine arts, French, geology, geometry, government, government-AP, health, honors algebra, honors English, honors geometry, Internet, journalism, keyboarding, life issues, literature, literature-AP, mathematics, modern dance, moral theology, music appreciation, photo shop, physical education, physics, religion, science, social studies, Spanish, Spanish language-AP, Spanish-AP, speech, speech and debate, student government, study skills, technical writing, theater production, world geography, world history, world religions, yearbook, zoology.

Graduation Requirements Algebra, American government, arts and fine arts (art, music, dance, drama), Bible studies, biology, Catholic belief and practice, chemistry, Christian and Hebrew scripture, Christian ethics, Christian studies, church history, computer programming, computer science, digital photography, economics, English, English composition, English literature, environmental science, foreign language, geography, government, health, human anatomy, journalism, lab/keyboard, life issues, mathematics, moral reasoning, physical education (includes health), physical science, physics, psychology, religion (includes Bible studies and theology), science, scripture, social justice, social studies (includes history), sociology, speech communications, technology, theology, world geography, service learning .5 credit, 4 credits of religion.

Special Academic Programs Advanced Placement exam preparation.

College Admission Counseling 76 students graduated in 2012; all went to college, including New Mexico State University; St. Edward's University; St. Mary's University; The University of Texas at El Paso; The University of Texas at San Antonio. Mean SAT critical reading: 508, mean SAT math: 481, mean SAT writing: 521. 14% scored over 600 on SAT critical reading, 8% scored over 600 on SAT math, 25% scored over 600 on SAT writing, 9% scored over 1800 on combined SAT, 5% scored over 26 on composite ACT.

Student Life Upper grades have uniform requirement, student council, honor system. Discipline rests primarily with faculty.

Tuition and Aid Day student tuition: $6700. Tuition installment plan (FACTS Tuition Payment Plan). Tuition reduction for siblings, need-based scholarship grants, paying campus jobs, need-based financial aid available. In 2012–13, 29% of upper-school students received aid. Total amount of financial aid awarded in 2012–13: $240,000.

Admissions Traditional secondary-level entrance grade is 9. For fall 2012, 72 students applied for upper-level admission, 60 were accepted, 55 enrolled. Educational Development Series or High School Placement Test required. Deadline for receipt of application materials: none. Application fee required: $10. On-campus interview required.

Athletics Interscholastic: aquatics, basketball, cross-country running, dance squad, dance team, golf, modern dance, soccer, softball, swimming and diving, tennis, track and field, volleyball. 2 PE instructors, 17 coaches.

Computers Computers are regularly used in all academic classes. Computer network features include on-campus library services, Internet access, Internet filtering or blocking technology. Computer access in designated common areas is available to students. Students grades are available online. The school has a published electronic and media policy.

Contact Mrs. Lily Miranda, Director of Admissions. 915-566-8400 Ext. 1109. Fax: 915-566-0636. E-mail: lmiranda@loretto.org. Website: www.loretto.org

LOS ANGELES LUTHERAN HIGH SCHOOL

Now Concordia Jr/Sr High

13570 Eldridge Avenue

Sylmar, California 91342

Head of School: Mr. Edward R. Amey

General Information Coeducational day and distance learning college-preparatory, arts, and religious studies school, affiliated with Lutheran Church–Missouri Synod, Lutheran Church. Grades K–12. Distance learning grades 10–12. Founded: 1953. Setting: suburban. Nearest major city is Los Angeles. 4-acre campus. 3 buildings on campus. Approved or accredited by National Lutheran School Accreditation, Western Association of Schools and Colleges, and California Department of Education. Endowment: $450,000. Total enrollment: 397. Upper school average class size: 22. Upper school faculty-student ratio: 1:10. There are 180 required school days per year for Upper School students. Upper School students typically attend 5 days per week. The average school day consists of 6 hours and 30 minutes.

Upper School Student Profile Grade 9: 20 students (9 boys, 11 girls); Grade 10: 29 students (13 boys, 16 girls); Grade 11: 48 students (29 boys, 19 girls); Grade 12: 49 students (24 boys, 25 girls). 30% of students are Lutheran Church–Missouri Synod, Lutheran.

Faculty School total: 22. In upper school: 11 men, 11 women; 7 have advanced degrees.

Subjects Offered 3-dimensional art, Advanced Placement courses, algebra, American literature, American sign language, anatomy and physiology, ancient history, band, bell choir, Bible, Bible studies, biology, biology-AP, British literature (honors), business applications, business law, business mathematics, calculus, career/college preparation, chemistry, choir, choral music, Christian doctrine, Christian scripture, classical music, composition, concert band, drawing, economics, English literature, English-AP, ESL, ethics, family studies, film appreciation, geography, geometry, German, government, jazz, jazz band, journalism, Life of Christ, math analysis, music theory, painting, physics, psychology, Spanish, U.S. history, world history, yearbook.

Graduation Requirements Advanced math, algebra, American government, American history, American literature, analytic geometry, ancient world history, biology, British literature, career education, chemistry, Christian doctrine, Christian testament, comparative religion, composition, economics, English composition, English literature, geometry, government, keyboarding, physical education (includes health), religious education, Spanish, U.S. government, U.S. history, world history.

Special Academic Programs 6 Advanced Placement exams for which test preparation is offered; honors section; study at local college for college credit; academic accommodation for the gifted, the musically talented, and the artistically talented; ESL (25 students enrolled).

College Admission Counseling 39 students graduated in 2012; 36 went to college, including California College of the Arts; California State University, Northridge; Concordia University. Other: 3 entered military service.

Student Life Upper grades have uniform requirement; student council. Discipline rests primarily with faculty. Attendance at religious services is required.

Tuition and Aid Day student tuition: $7200. Tuition installment plan (SMART Tuition Payment Plan, monthly payment plans). Merit scholarship grants, need-based scholarship grants available. In 2012–13, 30% of upper-school students received aid; total upper-school merit-scholarship money awarded: $16,000. Total amount of financial aid awarded in 2012–13: $100,000.

Admissions Traditional secondary-level entrance grade is 9. For fall 2012, 43 students applied for upper-level admission, 40 were accepted, 37 enrolled. Achievement/Aptitude/Writing or placement test required. Deadline for receipt of application materials: none. Application fee required: $300. Interview required.

Athletics Interscholastic: baseball (boys), basketball (b,g), cheering (g), drill team (g), flag football (b), football (b), soccer (b), volleyball (b,g); intramural: aerobics (b,g), fitness (b,g), jogging (b,g), physical fitness (b,g), physical training (b,g), strength & conditioning (b), tennis (b,g), track and field (b,g), ultimate Frisbee (b,g), walking (b,g), weight training (b,g); coed interscholastic: flag football, soccer; coed intramural: golf. 4 PE instructors, 8 coaches.

Computers Computers are regularly used in business, business applications, college planning, computer applications, desktop publishing, digital applications, keyboarding, lab/keyboard, media production, religion, science, yearbook classes. Computer network features include on-campus library services, online commercial services, Internet access, Internet filtering or blocking technology. Students grades are available online. The school has a published electronic and media policy.

Contact Ms. Barbara Winslow, Admissions Counselor. 818-362-5861. Fax: 818-367-0043. E-mail: barbara.winslow@concordiaschoolsla.org. Website: www.concordiahigh.org

LOUISVILLE COLLEGIATE SCHOOL

2427 Glenmary Avenue

Louisville, Kentucky 40204

Head of School: Junius Scott Prince

General Information Coeducational day college-preparatory, arts, and technology school. Grades JK–12. Founded: 1915. Setting: urban. 24-acre campus. 2 buildings on campus. Approved or accredited by Independent Schools Association of the Central States. Member of National Association of Independent Schools and Secondary School Admission Test Board. Endowment: $5.7 million. Total enrollment: 720. Upper school average class size: 15. Upper school faculty-student ratio: 1:8.

Faculty School total: 80. In upper school: 12 men, 10 women; 20 have advanced degrees.

Subjects Offered Algebra, American history, American literature, ancient history, art, art history, biology, calculus, chemistry, Chinese, chorus, community service, composition, computer science, creative writing, discrete mathematics, drama, economics, English, English literature, ensembles, environmental science, European history, fine arts, French, geometry, German, history, mathematics, media, music, music history, physical education, physics, physiology, pre-calculus, science, social studies, Spanish, statistics, studio art, theater, trigonometry, world history, world literature, writing.

Graduation Requirements Arts and fine arts (art, music, dance, drama), English, foreign language, mathematics, physical education (includes health), science, social studies (includes history), senior symposium in leadership and service, individual and class service projects, senior speech.

Special Academic Programs Advanced Placement exam preparation; honors section; independent study; term-away projects; study abroad.

College Admission Counseling 53 students graduated in 2012; all went to college, including Centre College; Miami University; Northwestern University; University of Louisville; Vanderbilt University; Wake Forest University. Median SAT critical reading: 605, median SAT math: 613, median SAT writing: 625, median composite ACT: 27.

Student Life Upper grades have uniform requirement, student council, honor system. Discipline rests equally with students and faculty.

Tuition and Aid Day student tuition: $20,600. Tuition installment plan (The Tuition Plan, monthly payment plans, individually arranged payment plans). Merit scholarship grants, need-based scholarship grants available. In 2012–13, 40% of upper-school students received aid.

Admissions Traditional secondary-level entrance grade is 9. School's own exam and SSAT required. Deadline for receipt of application materials: none. Application fee required: $50. Interview required.

Athletics Interscholastic: basketball (boys, girls), crew (g), cross-country running (b,g), field hockey (g), golf (b,g), indoor track (b,g), lacrosse (b,g), rowing (b,g), soccer (b,g), softball (g), strength & conditioning (b,g), swimming and diving (b,g), tennis (b,g), track and field (b,g), winter (indoor) track (b,g); intramural: basketball (b,g), soccer (b,g), tennis (b,g); coed interscholastic: soccer, strength & conditioning; coed intramural: soccer. 4 PE instructors, 60 coaches, 1 athletic trainer.

Computers Computers are regularly used in art, English, foreign language, history, mathematics, science classes. Computer network features include on-campus library services, online commercial services, Internet access, wireless campus network, Internet filtering or blocking technology. Student e-mail accounts and computer access in designated common areas are available to students. Students grades are available online. The school has a published electronic and media policy.

Contact Lynne Age, Admission Office Administrative Assistant. 502-479-0378. Fax: 502-454-0549. E-mail: lynne_age@loucol.com. Website: www.loucol.com

LOUISVILLE HIGH SCHOOL

22300 Mulholland Drive

Woodland Hills, California 91364

Head of School: Mrs. Kathleen Vercillo

General Information Girls' day college-preparatory, arts, religious studies, and technology school, affiliated with Roman Catholic Church. Grades 9–12. Founded: 1960. Setting: suburban. Nearest major city is Tarzana. 17-acre campus. 7 buildings on campus. Approved or accredited by National Catholic Education Association, Western Association of Schools and Colleges, Western Catholic Education Association, and California Department of Education. Total enrollment: 430. Upper school average class size: 25. Upper school faculty-student ratio: 1:25. There are 180 required school days per year for Upper School students. Upper School students typically attend 5 days per week. The average school day consists of 6 hours.

Upper School Student Profile Grade 9: 122 students (122 girls); Grade 10: 91 students (91 girls); Grade 11: 101 students (101 girls); Grade 12: 116 students (116 girls). 77% of students are Roman Catholic.

Faculty School total: 38. In upper school: 8 men, 30 women; 28 have advanced degrees.

Subjects Offered Advanced Placement courses, advanced studio art-AP, algebra, American history, American history-AP, American literature, American literature-AP, anatomy, art, Bible studies, biology, calculus, calculus-AP, campus ministry, ceramics, chemistry, computer science, creative writing, dance, drama, earth science, economics,

English, English literature, English literature-AP, European history, European history-AP, fine arts, French, geography, geometry, government/civics, government/civics-AP, grammar, health, history, journalism, law, mathematics, music, photography, physical education, physics, physics-AP, physiology, probability and statistics, psychology, religion, science, social sciences, social studies, Spanish, speech, theater, trigonometry, video film production, Web site design, world history, world literature.

Graduation Requirements Arts and fine arts (art, music, dance, drama), biology, chemistry, computer science, economics, English, foreign language, health, mathematics, performing arts, physical education (includes health), religion (includes Bible studies and theology), science, social sciences, social studies (includes history), U.S. government, U.S. history, visual arts, world history. Community service is required.

Special Academic Programs Advanced Placement exam preparation.

College Admission Counseling 112 students graduated in 2013; all went to college, including California State University, Northridge; Loyola Marymount University; University of California, Berkeley; University of California, Los Angeles; University of Portland; University of Southern California.

Student Life Upper grades have uniform requirement, student council, honor system. Discipline rests equally with students and faculty. Attendance at religious services is required.

Summer Programs Sports programs offered; session focuses on skill development; held both on and off campus; held at Los Angeles Pierce Community College and Balboa Park; accepts girls; open to students from other schools. 200 students usually enrolled. 2014 schedule: June 16 to August 8. Application deadline: May 23.

Tuition and Aid Day student tuition: $13,950. Tuition installment plan (FACTS Tuition Payment Plan). Merit scholarship grants, need-based scholarship grants available. In 2013–14, 40% of upper-school students received aid; total upper-school merit-scholarship money awarded: $86,500. Total amount of financial aid awarded in 2013–14: $682,000.

Admissions Traditional secondary-level entrance grade is 9. For fall 2013, 176 students applied for upper-level admission, 160 were accepted, 122 enrolled. High School Placement Test required. Deadline for receipt of application materials: February 1. Application fee required: $110. On-campus interview required.

Athletics Interscholastic: basketball, cross-country running, equestrian sports, field hockey, golf, lacrosse, soccer, softball, swimming and diving, tennis, track and field, volleyball, water polo; intramural: fitness walking, tennis, yoga. 2 PE instructors, 25 coaches, 1 athletic trainer.

Computers Computers are regularly used in all academic, college planning, computer applications, creative writing, economics, English, foreign language, French, graphic design, health, journalism, library, literary magazine, mathematics, media, media production, photography, religion, religious studies, science, social studies, Spanish, speech, technology, yearbook classes. Computer network features include on-campus library services, online commercial services, Internet access, wireless campus network, Internet filtering or blocking technology. Student e-mail accounts are available to students. Students grades are available online. The school has a published electronic and media policy.

Contact Mrs. Linda Klarin, Admissions Coordinator. 818-346-8812 Ext. 1000. Fax: 818-346-9483. E-mail: lklarin@louisvillehs.org. Website: www.louisvillehs.org

THE LOVETT SCHOOL

4075 Paces Ferry Road NW
Atlanta, Georgia 30327

Head of School: William S. Peebles

General Information Coeducational day college-preparatory school. Grades K–12. Founded: 1926. Setting: suburban. 100-acre campus. 8 buildings on campus. Approved or accredited by Southern Association of Colleges and Schools, Southern Association of Independent Schools, and Georgia Department of Education. Member of National Association of Independent Schools and Secondary School Admission Test Board. Endowment: $49.9 million. Total enrollment: 1,649. Upper school average class size: 13. Upper school faculty-student ratio: 1:8. There are 180 required school days per year for Upper School students. Upper School students typically attend 5 days per week. The average school day consists of 6 hours.

Upper School Student Profile Grade 9: 174 students (93 boys, 81 girls); Grade 10: 163 students (79 boys, 84 girls); Grade 11: 149 students (75 boys, 74 girls); Grade 12: 143 students (67 boys, 76 girls).

Faculty School total: 79. In upper school: 38 men, 41 women; 48 have advanced degrees.

Subjects Offered Advanced chemistry, advanced computer applications, advanced math, Advanced Placement courses, African American history, African history, African literature, African-American literature, algebra, American government, American history, American history-AP, American legal systems, American literature, ancient history, ancient world history, architecture, art, art history, Asian history, Asian studies, band, biology, botany, calculus, calculus-AP, career and personal planning, career/college preparation, ceramics, character education, chemistry, chorus, computer art, computer education, computer graphics, computer programming, computer science, creative writing, dance, debate, drama, driver education, earth science, ecology, economics, electronic music, English, English literature, English literature-AP, English-

AP, environmental science, ethics, European history, fiction, film history, fine arts, French, French language-AP, French literature-AP, French studies, French-AP, gender issues, genetics, geometry, German, history, human development, jazz dance, journalism, Latin, Latin-AP, leadership, marine biology, mathematics, medieval history, music theory, music theory-AP, newspaper, orchestra, painting, philosophy, photography, physical education, physics, portfolio art, pre-calculus, public speaking, religion, robotics, science, sculpture, social studies, Spanish, Spanish language-AP, Spanish literature-AP, speech, statistics, technical theater, theater, theater arts, trigonometry, U.S. government and politics-AP, video, Western civilization, Western philosophy, world cultures, world history, world literature, world religions, writing workshop, yearbook, zoology.

Graduation Requirements Algebra, American studies, arts and fine arts (art, music, dance, drama), biology, electives, English, foreign language, geometry, history, mathematics, physical education (includes health), religion (includes Bible studies and theology), science, Western civilization.

Special Academic Programs Advanced Placement exam preparation; honors section; independent study; term-away projects; study abroad; academic accommodation for the gifted, the musically talented, and the artistically talented.

College Admission Counseling 145 students graduated in 2013; all went to college, including Auburn University; Georgia Institute of Technology; The University of Alabama; The University of North Carolina at Chapel Hill; University of Georgia; University of Mississippi.

Student Life Upper grades have uniform requirement, student council, honor system. Discipline rests primarily with faculty. Attendance at religious services is required.

Summer Programs Remediation, enrichment, advancement programs offered; session focuses on academic course work; held on campus; accepts boys and girls; open to students from other schools. 130 students usually enrolled. 2014 schedule: June 3 to July 26. Application deadline: July 24.

Tuition and Aid Day student tuition: $20,000–$23,670. Tuition installment plan (individually arranged payment plans, 1/2 paid in July and 1/2 paid in November). Need-based scholarship grants available. In 2013–14, 14% of upper-school students received aid. Total amount of financial aid awarded in 2013–14: $1,230,000.

Admissions Traditional secondary-level entrance grade is 9. SSAT required. Deadline for receipt of application materials: February 1. Application fee required: $75. On-campus interview required.

Athletics Interscholastic: artistic gym (girls), baseball (b), basketball (b,g), cheering (g), cross-country running (b,g), dance (g), diving (b,g), football (b), golf (b,g), gymnastics (g), lacrosse (b,g), modern dance (g), soccer (b,g), softball (g), swimming and diving (b,g), tennis (b,g), track and field (b,g), volleyball (g), wrestling (b); intramural: aerobics/dance (g), dance (g), in-line hockey (b), modern dance (g), roller hockey (b); coed intramural: backpacking, bicycling, bowling, canoeing/kayaking, climbing, fitness, flag football, Frisbee, hiking/backpacking, kayaking, mountain biking, outdoor activities, physical fitness, physical training, rappelling, rock climbing, ropes courses, strength & conditioning, ultimate Frisbee, wall climbing, weight lifting, weight training, yoga. 3 PE instructors, 26 coaches, 2 athletic trainers.

Computers Computers are regularly used in all academic classes. Computer network features include on-campus library services, online commercial services, Internet access, wireless campus network, Internet filtering or blocking technology, central file storage. Student e-mail accounts and computer access in designated common areas are available to students. Students grades are available online.

Contact Ms. Debbie Lange, Director of Admission. 404-262-3032. Fax: 404-479-8463. E-mail: dlange@lovett.org. Website: www.lovett.org

THE LOWELL WHITEMAN SCHOOL

42605 County Road 36
Steamboat Springs, Colorado 80487

Head of School: Meg Morse

General Information Coeducational boarding and day college-preparatory school; primarily serves The Learning Center. Grades 9–12. Founded: 1957. Setting: rural. Nearest major city is Denver. Students are housed in single-sex dormitories. 192-acre campus. 10 buildings on campus. Approved or accredited by Association of Colorado Independent Schools, The Association of Boarding Schools, and Colorado Department of Education. Member of National Association of Independent Schools and Secondary School Admission Test Board. Endowment: $1 million. Total enrollment: 5,360. Upper school average class size: 8. Upper school faculty-student ratio: 1:7. There are 175 required school days per year for Upper School students. Upper School students typically attend 5 days per week. The average school day consists of 7 hours.

Upper School Student Profile Grade 9: 12 students (5 boys, 7 girls); Grade 10: 9 students (6 boys, 3 girls); Grade 11: 13 students (9 boys, 4 girls); Grade 12: 19 students (12 boys, 7 girls). 47% of students are boarding students. 65% are state residents. 24 states are represented in upper school student body. 6% are international students. International students from Canada, China, Germany, Mexico, United Arab Emirates, and United Kingdom.

Faculty School total: 20. In upper school: 8 men, 8 women; 7 have advanced degrees; 16 reside on campus.

Subjects Offered 20th century history, algebra, American history, American literature, American studies, anatomy, art, art history, biology, calculus, chemistry, computer math, computer programming, computer science, creative writing, drama, economics, English, English literature, expository writing, film, fine arts, French, geography, geology, geometry, government/civics, grammar, mathematics, physical education, physics, science, social sciences, social studies, Spanish, theater, trigonometry, typing, world history, writing.

Graduation Requirements Algebra, arts and fine arts (art, music, dance, drama), chemistry, computer science, English, foreign language, geography, geometry, mathematics, physical education (includes health), science, social sciences, social studies (includes history), Western civilization, foreign travel program, competitive ski/snowboarding program, outdoor program.

Special Academic Programs Advanced Placement exam preparation; honors section; independent study; study abroad; academic accommodation for the gifted.

College Admission Counseling 20 students graduated in 2013; 15 went to college, including Colorado State University; Middlebury College; Sierra College; The Colorado College; University of Colorado Boulder; University of Denver.

Student Life Upper grades have student council, honor system. Discipline rests equally with students and faculty.

Tuition and Aid Day student tuition: $17,700; 7-day tuition and room/board: $32,900. Tuition installment plan (individually arranged payment plans, school's own payment plan). Merit scholarship grants, need-based scholarship grants available. In 2013–14, 36% of upper-school students received aid; total upper-school merit-scholarship money awarded: $10,000. Total amount of financial aid awarded in 2013–14: $440,000.

Admissions Traditional secondary-level entrance grade is 9. For fall 2013, 25 students applied for upper-level admission, 23 were accepted, 18 enrolled. Deadline for receipt of application materials: none. Application fee required: $100. Interview required.

Athletics Interscholastic: alpine skiing (boys, girls), baseball (b), basketball (b,g), biathlon (b,g), cross-country running (b,g), dance team (g), freestyle skiing (b,g), golf (b,g), hockey (b,g), ice hockey (b,g), indoor hockey (b,g), mountain biking (b,g), mountaineering (b,g), nordic skiing (b,g), outdoor adventure (b,g), ski jumping (b,g), skiing (cross-country) (b,g), skiing (downhill) (b,g), snowboarding (b,g), soccer (b,g), tennis (b,g), wrestling (b); intramural: backpacking (b,g), basketball (b,g), bicycling (b,g), ice hockey (b,g), ice skating (b,g), independent competitive sports (b,g), indoor hockey (b,g), indoor soccer (b,g), jogging (b,g), lacrosse (g), mountain biking (b,g), mountaineering (b,g), outdoor adventure (b,g), rock climbing (b,g), skiing (cross-country) (b,g), skiing (downhill) (b,g), snowboarding (b,g), soccer (b,g); coed interscholastic: alpine skiing, biathlon, climbing, cross-country running, freestyle skiing, golf, ice hockey, indoor hockey, kayaking, mountain biking, mountaineering, nordic skiing, outdoor adventure, outdoor education, outdoor recreation, outdoor skills, rock climbing, ski jumping, skiing (cross-country), skiing (downhill), snowboarding, soccer, telemark skiing, wall climbing; coed intramural: aerobics, backpacking, badminton, bicycling, billiards, canoeing/kayaking, climbing, figure skating, fitness, flag football, Frisbee, golf, hiking/backpacking, horseback riding, ice hockey, ice skating, independent competitive sports, indoor hockey, indoor soccer, jogging, judo, juggling, kayaking, lacrosse, mountain biking, mountaineering, nordic skiing, outdoor adventure, outdoor education, outdoor recreation, outdoor skills, paint ball, physical fitness, physical training, rafting, rappelling, rock climbing, rugby, running, skateboarding, skiing (cross-country), skiing (downhill), snowboarding, snowshoeing, soccer, strength & conditioning, swimming and diving, table tennis, telemark skiing, tennis, volleyball, wall climbing, weight lifting, weight training, wilderness, wilderness survival, wildernessways, winter soccer, winter walking, yoga.

Computers Computers are regularly used in all academic classes. Computer network features include on-campus library services, online commercial services, Internet access, wireless campus network, Internet filtering or blocking technology. Campus intranet and student e-mail accounts are available to students. The school has a published electronic and media policy.

Contact Marta Miskolczy, Director of Admissions. 970-879-1350 Ext. 15. Fax: 970-879-0506. E-mail: marta@lws.edu. Website: www.lws.edu

LOYOLA-BLAKEFIELD

PO Box 6819
Baltimore, Maryland 21285-6819

Head of School: Mr. Anthony I. Day

General Information Boys' day college-preparatory, arts, and religious studies school, affiliated with Roman Catholic Church. Grades 6–12. Founded: 1852. Setting: suburban. 60-acre campus. 6 buildings on campus. Approved or accredited by Association of Independent Maryland Schools and Jesuit Secondary Education Association. Endowment: $22.5 million. Total enrollment: 983. Upper school average class size: 18. Upper school faculty-student ratio: 1:10. There are 175 required school days per year for Upper School students. Upper School students typically attend 5 days per week. The average school day consists of 7 hours.

Upper School Student Profile Grade 9: 184 students (184 boys); Grade 10: 192 students (192 boys); Grade 11: 186 students (186 boys); Grade 12: 182 students (182 boys). 78% of students are Roman Catholic.

Faculty School total: 98. In upper school: 50 men, 24 women; 55 have advanced degrees.

Subjects Offered Algebra, American government, American literature, American literature-AP, architecture, art, art history, band, biology, biology-AP, biotechnology,

British literature, British literature (honors), calculus, calculus-AP, chemistry, chemistry-AP, chorus, civil war history, composition, composition-AP, computer graphics, computer science, concert band, drawing, driver education, engineering, English, English language-AP, English literature-AP, European history-AP, film studies, fine arts, forensics, French, French language-AP, German, German-AP, government and politics-AP, Greek, history, history of music, honors algebra, honors English, honors geometry, honors world history, instrumental music, Italian, jazz ensemble, Latin, Latin-AP, marine science, mathematics, music history, oil painting, painting, photography, physical education, physics, physics-AP, poetry, pre-calculus, psychology, religion, science, Spanish, Spanish language-AP, statistics-AP, U.S. government and politics-AP, U.S. history, U.S. history-AP.

Graduation Requirements Arts and fine arts (art, music, dance, drama), computer science, English, foreign language, mathematics, physical education (includes health), religion (includes Bible studies and theology), science, social studies (includes history), 40 hours of Christian service.

Special Academic Programs 19 Advanced Placement exams for which test preparation is offered; honors section; academic accommodation for the gifted, the musically talented, and the artistically talented; programs in English, mathematics, general development for dyslexic students.

College Admission Counseling 181 students graduated in 2013; 180 went to college, including Loyola University Maryland; Mount St. Mary's University; University of Maryland, College Park; University of South Carolina; Virginia Polytechnic Institute and State University. Other: 1 had other specific plans. Median SAT critical reading: 580, median SAT math: 610, median SAT writing: 590, median combined SAT: 1790, median composite ACT: 26. 48% scored over 600 on SAT critical reading, 60% scored over 600 on SAT math, 47% scored over 600 on SAT writing, 49% scored over 1800 on combined SAT, 24% scored over 26 on composite ACT.

Student Life Upper grades have specified standards of dress, student council, honor system. Discipline rests primarily with faculty. Attendance at religious services is required.

Summer Programs Remediation, enrichment, advancement, sports, art/fine arts, computer instruction programs offered; held on campus; accepts boys and girls; open to students from other schools. 600 students usually enrolled. 2014 schedule: June 9 to August 1. Application deadline: none.

Tuition and Aid Day student tuition: $17,695. Tuition installment plan (Tuition Management Systems). Merit scholarship grants, need-based scholarship grants available. In 2013–14, 40% of upper-school students received aid; total upper-school merit-scholarship money awarded: $575,000. Total amount of financial aid awarded in 2013–14: $2,500,000.

Admissions Traditional secondary-level entrance grade is 9. For fall 2013, 321 students applied for upper-level admission, 277 were accepted, 112 enrolled. High School Placement Test or ISEE required. Deadline for receipt of application materials: December 15. No application fee required. On-campus interview required.

Athletics Interscholastic: baseball, basketball, cross-country running, diving, football, golf, ice hockey, indoor track & field, lacrosse, rugby, soccer, squash, swimming and diving, tennis, track and field, volleyball, water polo, winter (indoor) track, wrestling; intramural: basketball, flag football, indoor soccer, lacrosse, martial arts, rock climbing, tennis, ultimate Frisbee. 4 PE instructors, 30 coaches, 1 athletic trainer.

Computers Computers are regularly used in all classes. Computer network features include on-campus library services, online commercial services, Internet access, wireless campus network, Internet filtering or blocking technology. Campus intranet, student e-mail accounts, and computer access in designated common areas are available to students. Students grades are available online. The school has a published electronic and media policy.

Contact Ms. Paddy M. London, Admissions Assistant. 443-841-3680. Fax: 443-841-3105. E-mail: plondon@loyolablakefield.org. Website: www.loyolablakefield.org

LOYOLA SCHOOL

980 Park Avenue
New York, New York 10028-0020

Head of School: Mr. James F.X. Lyness

General Information Coeducational day college-preparatory school, affiliated with Roman Catholic Church (Jesuit order). Grades 9–12. Founded: 1900. Setting: urban. 2 buildings on campus. Approved or accredited by Jesuit Secondary Education Association, Middle States Association of Colleges and Schools, National Catholic Education Association, New York State Association of Independent Schools, and New York State Board of Regents. Member of National Association of Independent Schools and Secondary School Admission Test Board. Total enrollment: 202. Upper school average class size: 17. Upper school faculty-student ratio: 1:9. There are 180 required school days per year for Upper School students. Upper School students typically attend 5 days per week. The average school day consists of 6 hours and 20 minutes.

Upper School Student Profile Grade 9: 49 students (25 boys, 24 girls); Grade 10: 45 students (20 boys, 25 girls); Grade 11: 53 students (25 boys, 28 girls); Grade 12: 55 students (24 boys, 31 girls). 85% of students are Roman Catholic Church (Jesuit order).

Faculty School total: 30. In upper school: 16 men, 14 women; 28 have advanced degrees.

Subjects Offered Advanced Placement courses, algebra, American government, American history, American literature, art, art history, biology, calculus, chemistry, chorus, college counseling, community service, comparative religion, computer programming, computer science, creative writing, death and loss, discrete mathematics, drama, economics, English, English literature, ethics, European history, expository writing, film, film history, fine arts, French, geometry, grammar, health, history, instrumental music, journalism, language-AP, Latin, mathematics, music history, philosophy, photography, physical education, physics, political science, pre-calculus, religion, science, social studies, Spanish, speech, statistics-AP, student government, student publications, theater, theology, trigonometry, U.S. history-AP, world history, writing, yearbook.

Graduation Requirements Art history, computer literacy, English, foreign language, guidance, mathematics, music history, physical education (includes health), science, social studies (includes history), speech, theology, Christian service program hours each year.

Special Academic Programs Study abroad.

College Admission Counseling 55 students graduated in 2013; all went to college, including Cornell University; Fordham University; Georgetown University; New York University; The George Washington University. Median SAT critical reading: 620, median SAT math: 600, median SAT writing: 630.

Student Life Upper grades have specified standards of dress, student council, honor system. Discipline rests primarily with faculty. Attendance at religious services is required.

Tuition and Aid Day student tuition: $31,860. Tuition installment plan (SMART Tuition Payment Plan). Merit scholarship grants, need-based scholarship grants available. In 2013–14, 33% of upper-school students received aid; total upper-school merit-scholarship money awarded: $200,000. Total amount of financial aid awarded in 2013–14: $1,194,000.

Admissions Traditional secondary-level entrance grade is 9. High School Placement Test (closed version) from Scholastic Testing Service, ISEE or SSAT required. Deadline for receipt of application materials: November 16. Application fee required: $80. On-campus interview recommended.

Athletics Interscholastic: baseball (boys), basketball (b,g), cross-country running (b,g), soccer (b), softball (g), track and field (b,g), volleyball (g); intramural: basketball (b,g), dance (g); coed interscholastic: golf, physical fitness, soccer; coed intramural: Frisbee, hiking/backpacking, outdoor activities, outdoor adventure, physical fitness, physical training, track and field. 1 PE instructor, 9 coaches.

Computers Computers are regularly used in all academic classes. Computer network features include on-campus library services, online commercial services, Internet access, wireless campus network, Internet filtering or blocking technology. Campus intranet, student e-mail accounts, and computer access in designated common areas are available to students. The school has a published electronic and media policy.

Contact Mr. Gabriel Rotman, Associate Director of Admissions. 646-346-8131. Fax: 646-346-8175. E-mail: grotman@loyola-nyc.org. Website: www.loyola-nyc.org

LUSTRE CHRISTIAN HIGH SCHOOL

294 Lustre Rd.
Lustre, Montana 59225

Head of School: Wes Young

General Information Coeducational boarding and day college-preparatory, general academic, and religious studies school, affiliated with Mennonite Brethren Church, Christian faith. Grades 9–12. Founded: 1948. Setting: rural. Nearest major city is Glasgow. Students are housed in single-sex by floor dormitories. 20-acre campus. 1 building on campus. Approved or accredited by Association of Christian Schools International and Montana Department of Education. Endowment: $220,000. Total enrollment: 40. Upper school average class size: 7. Upper school faculty-student ratio: 1:4. There are 180 required school days per year for Upper School students. Upper School students typically attend 5 days per week. The average school day consists of 6 hours and 58 minutes.

Upper School Student Profile Grade 9: 16 students (7 boys, 9 girls); Grade 10: 6 students (3 boys, 3 girls); Grade 11: 11 students (8 boys, 3 girls); Grade 12: 7 students (1 boy, 6 girls). 63% of students are boarding students. 38% are state residents. 6 states are represented in upper school student body. 40% are international students. International students from China, Ethiopia, and Republic of Korea; 3 other countries represented in student body. 8% of students are members of Mennonite Brethren Church, Christian faith.

Faculty School total: 7. In upper school: 4 men, 3 women; 1 has an advanced degree; 5 reside on campus.

Subjects Offered Algebra, American literature, band, Bible studies, biology, British literature, chemistry, choir, Christian studies, computer science, computers, current events, English, fine arts, foreign language, geometry, health, journalism, mathematics, physical education, physical science, pre-calculus, religion, science, social sciences, social studies, U.S. government, U.S. history, world history.

Graduation Requirements Arts and fine arts (art, music, dance, drama), Bible, computer science, English, mathematics, physical education (includes health), science, social studies (includes history), senior chapel message (as part of senior Bible program).

College Admission Counseling 7 students graduated in 2013; all went to college, including Montana State University. Median composite ACT: 16.

Student Life Upper grades have specified standards of dress, student council. Discipline rests primarily with faculty. Attendance at religious services is required.

Tuition and Aid Day student tuition: $2850; 7-day tuition and room/board: $5050. Tuition installment plan (monthly payment plans, individually arranged payment plans). Need-based scholarship grants available. In 2013–14, 5% of upper-school students received aid.

Admissions Traditional secondary-level entrance grade is 9. For fall 2013, 16 students applied for upper-level admission, 13 were accepted, 10 enrolled. ITBS achievement test, PSAT, SLEP for foreign students or TOEFL or SLEP required. Deadline for receipt of application materials: none. No application fee required. Interview recommended.

Athletics Interscholastic: basketball (boys, girls), football (b), track and field (b,g), volleyball (g). 1 PE instructor, 1 coach.

Computers Computers are regularly used in Bible studies, English, history, journalism, mathematics, religious studies, science, yearbook classes. Computer network features include Internet access, wireless campus network.

Contact Wes Young, Principal. 406-392-5735. Fax: 406-392-5765. E-mail: wyoung@nemont.net. Website: www.lustrechristian.org

LUTHERAN HIGH SCHOOL NORTH

5401 Lucas Hunt Road
St. Louis, Missouri 63121

Head of School: Mr. Timothy Brackman

General Information Coeducational day college-preparatory, arts, business, religious studies, bilingual studies, and technology school, affiliated with Lutheran Church. Grades 9–12. Founded: 1946. Setting: urban. 47-acre campus. 1 building on campus. Approved or accredited by Lutheran School Accreditation Commission, National Lutheran School Accreditation, North Central Association of Colleges and Schools, and Missouri Department of Education. Endowment: $5.8 million. Total enrollment: 310. Upper school average class size: 20. Upper school faculty-student ratio: 1:10. There are 178 required school days per year for Upper School students. Upper School students typically attend 5 days per week. The average school day consists of 6 hours and 20 minutes.

Upper School Student Profile Grade 9: 74 students (38 boys, 36 girls); Grade 10: 88 students (50 boys, 38 girls); Grade 11: 81 students (36 boys, 45 girls); Grade 12: 67 students (35 boys, 32 girls). 47% of students are Lutheran.

Faculty School total: 30. In upper school: 17 men, 13 women; 26 have advanced degrees.

Subjects Offered Accounting, advanced chemistry, Advanced Placement courses, algebra, American history, American history-AP, American literature, anatomy, art, Bible studies, biology, business, business law, business skills, calculus, calculus-AP, ceramics, chemistry, child development, choir, Christian doctrine, Christian education, Christian ethics, Christian scripture, Christian studies, Christianity, church history, computer applications, computer multimedia, computer science, concert band, concert choir, data analysis, design, drawing, drawing and design, economics, English, English composition, English literature, English literature-AP, entrepreneurship, European history, family and consumer science, fashion, fine arts, finite math, food and nutrition, foods, French, geography, geometry, government, government/civics, health education, history, human anatomy, keyboarding, literature-AP, Mandarin, marketing, mathematics, media studies, multimedia design, music, organic chemistry, painting, physical education, physics, physiology, practical arts, pre-calculus, printmaking, probability and statistics, psychology, religion, research, science, social studies, society and culture, Spanish, speech, statistics, student publications, theology, U.S. government, U.S. history-AP, world geography, world history, world literature, world religions, writing.

Graduation Requirements American history, arts and fine arts (art, music, dance, drama), English, mathematics, physical education (includes health), practical arts, religion (includes Bible studies and theology), science, social studies (includes history), Saved to Serve (community service hours).

Special Academic Programs Advanced Placement exam preparation; honors section; independent study; study at local college for college credit.

College Admission Counseling 74 students graduated in 2013; all went to college, including Concordia University Chicago; Southeast Missouri State University; Truman State University; University of Central Missouri; University of Missouri. 50% scored over 26 on composite ACT.

Student Life Upper grades have uniform requirement, student council, honor system. Discipline rests primarily with faculty. Attendance at religious services is required.

Summer Programs Enrichment, sports programs offered; session focuses on fundamentals and enrichment; held on campus; accepts boys and girls; not open to students from other schools. 150 students usually enrolled. 2014 schedule: June 1 to July 31.

Tuition and Aid Day student tuition: $9875–$11,075. Tuition installment plan (FACTS Tuition Payment Plan, monthly payment plans, individually arranged payment plans, semester payment plan, full-year payment plan with discount). Tuition reduction for siblings, merit scholarship grants, need-based scholarship grants available. In 2013–

14, 66% of upper-school students received aid; total upper-school merit-scholarship money awarded: $22,000. Total amount of financial aid awarded in 2013–14: $750,000.

Admissions Traditional secondary-level entrance grade is 9. For fall 2013, 97 students applied for upper-level admission, 93 were accepted, 74 enrolled. ACT-Explore required. Deadline for receipt of application materials: none. Application fee required: $250. Interview recommended.

Athletics Interscholastic: baseball (boys), basketball (b,g), cheering (g), cross-country running (b,g), dance squad (g), football (b), golf (b), pom squad (g), soccer (b,g), softball (g), tennis (b,g), track and field (b,g), volleyball (g). 2 PE instructors.

Computers Computers are regularly used in art, business education, English, history, mathematics, science, social studies, yearbook classes. Computer network features include on-campus library services, Internet access, wireless campus network, Internet filtering or blocking technology, Internet college work program. Campus intranet and computer access in designated common areas are available to students. Students grades are available online. The school has a published electronic and media policy.

Contact Karen Kersten, Records Clerk. 314-389-3100 Ext. 406. Fax: 314-389-3103. E-mail: kkersten@lhsnstl.org. Website: www.lhsn.org

LUTHERAN HIGH SCHOOL NORTHWEST

1000 Bagley Avenue
Rochester Hills, Michigan 48309

Head of School: Mr. Paul Looker

General Information Coeducational day college-preparatory and religious studies school, affiliated with Lutheran Church–Missouri Synod. Grades 9–12. Founded: 1978. Setting: suburban. Nearest major city is Detroit. 30-acre campus. 1 building on campus. Approved or accredited by National Lutheran School Accreditation, North Central Association of Colleges and Schools, and Michigan Department of Education. Endowment: $1 million. Total enrollment: 289. Upper school average class size: 25. Upper school faculty-student ratio: 1:15. There are 185 required school days per year for Upper School students. Upper School students typically attend 5 days per week. The average school day consists of 7 hours and 20 minutes.

Upper School Student Profile Grade 9: 72 students (37 boys, 35 girls); Grade 10: 70 students (31 boys, 39 girls); Grade 11: 74 students (32 boys, 42 girls); Grade 12: 73 students (41 boys, 32 girls). 75% of students are Lutheran Church–Missouri Synod.

Faculty School total: 19. In upper school: 11 men, 8 women; 15 have advanced degrees.

Subjects Offered 20th century history, accounting, advanced chemistry, algebra, American history, American history-AP, art, audio visual/media, band, Basic programming, biology, biology-AP, bookkeeping, business, business applications, business mathematics, calculus, ceramics, chemistry, choral music, chorus, Christian doctrine, Christian scripture, computer education, computer science, conceptual physics, concert band, concert choir, desktop publishing, drawing, drawing and design, Eastern world civilizations, economics, English, English-AP, geography, geometry, German, government/civics, graphic arts, law, mathematics, music, painting, physical education, physical science, physics-AP, psychology, Spanish, statistics-AP, theology, trigonometry, U.S. government and politics-AP, world history.

Graduation Requirements Arts and fine arts (art, music, dance, drama), English, mathematics, physical education (includes health), religion (includes Bible studies and theology), science, social sciences, social studies (includes history). Community service is required.

Special Academic Programs 7 Advanced Placement exams for which test preparation is offered; honors section; independent study; study at local college for college credit.

College Admission Counseling 76 students graduated in 2013; 70 went to college, including Central Michigan University; Concordia University Chicago; Concordia University Wisconsin; Michigan State University; Oakland University; Western Michigan University. Other: 5 went to work, 1 entered military service. Median composite ACT: 24. 34% scored over 26 on composite ACT.

Student Life Upper grades have specified standards of dress, student council. Discipline rests primarily with faculty. Attendance at religious services is required.

Tuition and Aid Day student tuition: $7550. Tuition installment plan (monthly payment plans). Merit scholarship grants, need-based scholarship grants available. In 2013–14, 2% of upper-school students received aid; total upper-school merit-scholarship money awarded: $20,000. Total amount of financial aid awarded in 2013–14: $20,000.

Admissions Traditional secondary-level entrance grade is 9. High School Placement Test required. Deadline for receipt of application materials: none. Application fee required: $350. On-campus interview required.

Athletics Interscholastic: baseball (boys), basketball (b,g), cheering (g), cross-country running (b,g), dance team (g), football (b), golf (b,g), hockey (b), soccer (b,g), softball (g), track and field (b,g), volleyball (g), wrestling (b); intramural: indoor soccer (b,g); coed intramural: badminton, fitness, physical fitness, physical training, tennis, weight training.

Computers Computers are regularly used in journalism, keyboarding, mathematics, media, research skills, word processing, yearbook classes. Computer network features include Internet access, wireless campus network, Internet filtering or blocking technology. Students grades are available online. The school has a published electronic and media policy.

Contact Mr. Paul Looker, Principal. 248-852-6677. Fax: 248-852-2667. E-mail: plooker@lhsa.com. Website: www.lhnw.lhsa.com

LUTHERAN HIGH SCHOOL OF HAWAII

1404 University Avenue
Honolulu, Hawaii 96822-2494

Head of School: Daryl S. Utsumi

General Information Coeducational day college-preparatory school, affiliated with Lutheran Church–Missouri Synod. Grades 7–12. Founded: 1988. Setting: urban. 1-acre campus. 3 buildings on campus. Approved or accredited by Lutheran School Accreditation Commission, The Hawaii Council of Private Schools, Western Association of Schools and Colleges, and Hawaii Department of Education. Member of Secondary School Admission Test Board. Endowment: $43,000. Total enrollment: 55. Upper school average class size: 12. Upper school faculty-student ratio: 1:7. There are 178 required school days per year for Upper School students. Upper School students typically attend 5 days per week. The average school day consists of 7 hours and 15 minutes.

Upper School Student Profile Grade 7: 1 student (1 girl); Grade 8: 3 students (2 boys, 1 girl); Grade 9: 6 students (4 boys, 2 girls); Grade 10: 13 students (8 boys, 5 girls); Grade 11: 9 students (5 boys, 4 girls); Grade 12: 23 students (12 boys, 11 girls). 10% of students are Lutheran Church–Missouri Synod.

Faculty School total: 16. In upper school: 8 men, 8 women; 6 have advanced degrees.

Subjects Offered 20th century history, 3-dimensional art, advanced math, Advanced Placement courses, algebra, American government, American history, American literature, analytic geometry, art, art-AP, Bible studies, biology, British literature, calculus, calculus-AP, chemistry, choir, computer applications, computer programming, computer science, concert band, consumer economics, drama, earth science, economics, English, English literature, European history, expository writing, fine arts, food and nutrition, geometry, government/civics, grammar, health, history, home economics, Japanese, journalism, keyboarding, life skills, marine biology, mathematics, music, oceanography, photography, physical education, physics, psychology, religion, science, social sciences, social studies, Spanish, speech, theater, trigonometry, world history, world literature.

Graduation Requirements Arts and fine arts (art, music, dance, drama), computer science, English, health, mathematics, physical education (includes health), religion (includes Bible studies and theology), science, social studies (includes history).

Special Academic Programs Advanced Placement exam preparation; honors section; study at local college for college credit; academic accommodation for the musically talented and the artistically talented.

College Admission Counseling 23 students graduated in 2013; all went to college, including Kapiolani Community College; University of Hawaii at Manoa. Median composite ACT: 23. Mean SAT critical reading: 525, mean SAT math: 530, mean SAT writing: 525. 10% scored over 600 on SAT critical reading, 15% scored over 600 on SAT math.

Student Life Upper grades have uniform requirement, student council, honor system. Discipline rests primarily with faculty. Attendance at religious services is required.

Summer Programs Remediation, enrichment, advancement, sports, art/fine arts, computer instruction programs offered; held on campus; accepts boys and girls; open to students from other schools. 25 students usually enrolled. 2014 schedule: June 12 to July 20.

Tuition and Aid Day student tuition: $10,000–$11,490. Tuition installment plan (Insured Tuition Payment Plan). Tuition reduction for siblings, merit scholarship grants, need-based scholarship grants available. In 2013–14, 25% of upper-school students received aid; total upper-school merit-scholarship money awarded: $50,000. Total amount of financial aid awarded in 2013–14: $500,000.

Admissions Traditional secondary-level entrance grade is 9. For fall 2013, 25 students applied for upper-level admission, 20 were accepted, 15 enrolled. SSAT and TOEFL or SLEP required. Deadline for receipt of application materials: none. Application fee required: $30. Interview recommended.

Athletics Interscholastic: baseball (boys), basketball (b,g), bowling (b,g), canoeing/kayaking (b,g), cross-country running (b,g), diving (b,g), golf (b,g), judo (b,g), kayaking (b,g), paddling (b,g), soccer (b,g), softball (g), swimming and diving (b,g), tennis (b,g), track and field (b,g), volleyball (b,g), water polo (b,g), wrestling (b,g); coed interscholastic: cheering, football, gymnastics, sailing, strength & conditioning. 1 PE instructor, 5 coaches, 1 athletic trainer.

Computers Computers are regularly used in art, business applications, desktop publishing, English, history, journalism, library, mathematics, newspaper, photography, photojournalism, science, yearbook classes. Computer network features include on-campus library services, Internet access, wireless campus network, Internet filtering or blocking technology. Students grades are available online. The school has a published electronic and media policy.

Contact Lea Dominici, Admissions Officer. 808-949-5302. Fax: 808-947-3701. E-mail: office@lhshawaii.org. Website: www.lhshawaii.org

LUTHERAN HIGH SCHOOL OF INDIANAPOLIS

5555 South Arlington Avenue
Indianapolis, Indiana 46237-2366
Head of School: Mr. Michael Brandt

General Information Coeducational day college-preparatory, general academic, and religious studies school, affiliated with Lutheran Church–Missouri Synod. Grades 9–12. Founded: 1976. Setting: suburban. 14-acre campus. 1 building on campus. Approved or accredited by National Lutheran School Accreditation, North Central Association of Colleges and Schools, and Indiana Department of Education. Endowment: $600,000. Total enrollment: 216. Upper school average class size: 18. Upper school faculty-student ratio: 1:15. There are 180 required school days per year for Upper School students. Upper School students typically attend 5 days per week. The average school day consists of 7 hours and 15 minutes.

Upper School Student Profile Grade 9: 47 students (21 boys, 26 girls); Grade 10: 63 students (32 boys, 31 girls); Grade 11: 55 students (28 boys, 27 girls); Grade 12: 51 students (27 boys, 24 girls). 64% of students are Lutheran Church–Missouri Synod.

Faculty School total: 17. In upper school: 12 men, 5 women; 15 have advanced degrees.

Subjects Offered 3-dimensional art, Advanced Placement courses, advanced studio art-AP, algebra, American government, American history, American history-AP, American literature-AP, American sign language, anatomy, anatomy and physiology, art, art-AP, band, biology, biology-AP, calculus, calculus-AP, career experience, ceramics, chemistry, chemistry-AP, choir, chorus, Christian ethics, Christian scripture, Christian testament, computer information systems, computer programming, concert band, current events, desktop publishing, discrete mathematics, earth science, economics, English, English composition, English literature and composition-AP, English literature-AP, ethics, etymology, geography, geometry, German, health and wellness, honors algebra, humanities, integrated physics, math review, music theory, music theory-AP, New Testament, physical education, physical fitness, piano, pre-calculus, psychology, reading/study skills, sociology, Spanish, Spanish-AP, speech, statistics, studio art, U.S. government, U.S. history-AP, world history, world religions.

Graduation Requirements Arts and fine arts (art, music, dance, drama), biology, chemistry, Christian doctrine, Christian ethics, computer applications, economics, foreign language, geography, health and wellness, integrated physics, literature and composition-AP, New Testament, physical education (includes health), U.S. government, U.S. history, world religions.

Special Academic Programs 6 Advanced Placement exams for which test preparation is offered; honors section; independent study; study at local college for college credit; remedial reading and/or remedial writing; remedial math.

College Admission Counseling 74 students graduated in 2012; 72 went to college, including Ball State University; Indiana University Bloomington; Purdue University; Taylor University; University of Indianapolis. Other: 2 went to work. Mean SAT critical reading: 515, mean SAT math: 550, mean SAT writing: 502, mean combined SAT: 1567, mean composite ACT: 23.

Student Life Upper grades have uniform requirement, student council. Discipline rests primarily with faculty. Attendance at religious services is required.

Tuition and Aid Day student tuition: $9150. Tuition installment plan (monthly payment plans, In Full, by semester, or through 10 month payment plan). Tuition reduction for siblings, need-based scholarship grants, paying campus jobs, Simply Giving (Thrivent), church worker grants available. In 2012–13, 81% of upper-school students received aid. Total amount of financial aid awarded in 2012–13: $160,000.

Admissions Traditional secondary-level entrance grade is 9. For fall 2012, 64 students applied for upper-level admission, 61 were accepted, 61 enrolled. Math Placement Exam or SCAT required. Deadline for receipt of application materials: none. Application fee required: $200. On-campus interview required.

Athletics Interscholastic: baseball (boys), basketball (b,g), cross-country running (b,g), football (b), golf (b,g), soccer (b,g), softball (g), strength & conditioning (b,g), tennis (b,g), track and field (b,g), volleyball (b,g), weight lifting (b,g), weight training (b,g); intramural: basketball (b,g); coed interscholastic: cheering, physical fitness, weight training; coed intramural: bowling, fishing, football. 2 PE instructors, 22 coaches.

Computers Computers are regularly used in all academic classes. Computer network features include online commercial services, Internet access, wireless campus network, Internet filtering or blocking technology. Computer access in designated common areas is available to students. Students grades are available online. The school has a published electronic and media policy.

Contact Mrs. Tenille Bullock, Director of Admissions. 317-787-5474 Ext. 218. Fax: 317-787-2794. E-mail: admissions@lhsi.org. Website: www.lhsi.org

LUTHERAN HIGH SCHOOL OF SAN DIEGO

810 Buena Vista Way
Chula Vista, California 91910-6853
Head of School: Mr. Scott Dufresne

General Information Coeducational day and distance learning college-preparatory, arts, religious studies, and technology school, affiliated with Lutheran Church. Grades 9–12. Distance learning grades 9–12. Founded: 1975. Setting: urban. Nearest major city is San Diego. 9-acre campus. 6 buildings on campus. Approved or accredited by National Lutheran School Accreditation, Western Association of Schools and Colleges, and California Department of Education. Total enrollment: 88. Upper school average class size: 12. Upper school faculty-student ratio: 1:12. There are 180 required school days per year for Upper School students. Upper School students typically attend 5 days per week. The average school day consists of 6 hours and 30 minutes.

Upper School Student Profile Grade 9: 16 students (11 boys, 5 girls); Grade 10: 28 students (16 boys, 12 girls); Grade 11: 22 students (12 boys, 10 girls); Grade 12: 22 students (16 boys, 6 girls). 50% of students are Lutheran.

Faculty School total: 9. In upper school: 5 men, 4 women; 6 have advanced degrees.

Subjects Offered Accounting, acting, Advanced Placement courses, algebra, American government, American history, American literature, American literature-AP, analytic geometry, anatomy and physiology, applied arts, applied music, art, art appreciation, art history-AP, ASB Leadership, athletics, band, baseball, basketball, bell choir, Bible, biology, biology-AP, British literature, British literature-AP, calculus-AP, campus ministry, chemistry, choir, choral music, Christian education, Christian ethics, comparative religion, computer literacy, creative writing, drama, driver education, economics, English, English language and composition-AP, English language-AP, English literature and composition-AP, English literature-AP, English-AP, English/composition-AP, European history-AP, French, geometry, government, health education, history, music appreciation, physical education, physics, pre-calculus, softball, Spanish, Spanish language-AP, speech, student government, U.S. government and politics, yearbook.

Special Academic Programs Advanced Placement exam preparation.

College Admission Counseling 18 students graduated in 2012; 17 went to college, including Concordia University; Point Loma Nazarene University; San Diego State University; University of California, Irvine; University of California, Riverside. Other: 1 went to work. Mean SAT critical reading: 537, mean SAT math: 518, mean SAT writing: 540, mean combined SAT: 1595.

Student Life Upper grades have specified standards of dress, student council, honor system. Discipline rests primarily with faculty. Attendance at religious services is required.

Tuition and Aid Day student tuition: $8495. Tuition installment plan (monthly payment plans, individually arranged payment plans, Simply Giving—Thrivent Financial for Lutherans, Tuition Solution). Tuition reduction for siblings, merit scholarship grants, need-based scholarship grants available. In 2012–13, 31% of upper-school students received aid; total upper-school merit-scholarship money awarded: $8000. Total amount of financial aid awarded in 2012–13: $60,000.

Admissions Traditional secondary-level entrance grade is 9. Admissions testing required. Application fee required. Application fee required: $250. On-campus interview required.

Athletics Interscholastic: baseball (boys), basketball (b,g), cross-country running (b,g), football (b), softball (g), volleyball (b,g). 1 PE instructor, 10 coaches.

Computers Computer network features include on-campus library services, Internet access. Students grades are available online.

Contact Debbie Heien, Office Manager. 619-262-4444 Ext. 120. Fax: 619-872-0974. E-mail: debbie.heien@lhssd.org. Website: www.lutheranhighsandiego.org

LUTHER COLLEGE HIGH SCHOOL

1500 Royal Street
Regina, Saskatchewan S4T 5A5, Canada
Head of School: Dr. Mark Anderson

General Information Coeducational boarding and day college-preparatory, general academic, arts, International Baccalaureate, and ESL school, affiliated with Lutheran Church. Grades 9–12. Founded: 1913. Setting: urban. Nearest major city is Winnipeg, MB, Canada. Students are housed in single-sex dormitories. 27-acre campus. 5 buildings on campus. Approved or accredited by Saskatchewan Department of Education. Language of instruction: English. Endowment: CAN$600,000. Total enrollment: 430. Upper school average class size: 22. Upper school faculty-student ratio: 1:17. There are 190 required school days per year for Upper School students. Upper School students typically attend 5 days per week. The average school day consists of 7 hours.

Upper School Student Profile 14% of students are boarding students. 86% are province residents. 2 provinces are represented in upper school student body. 14% are international students. International students from China, Germany, Hong Kong, Republic of Korea, Taiwan, and Thailand; 6 other countries represented in student body. 22% of students are Lutheran.

Faculty School total: 36. In upper school: 19 men, 17 women; 5 have advanced degrees; 1 resides on campus.

Subjects Offered Band, biology, calculus, chemistry, choir, Christian ethics, computer science, drama, English, ESL, French, German, handbells, history, information processing, International Baccalaureate courses, Latin, mathematics, music, orchestra, physical fitness, physics, psychology, science, video film production.

Graduation Requirements Christian ethics, English, mathematics, science, social studies (includes history).

Special Academic Programs International Baccalaureate program; independent study; study abroad; academic accommodation for the gifted; ESL (15 students enrolled).

College Admission Counseling 91 students graduated in 2013; 75 went to college, including McGill University; University of Alberta; University of Calgary; University of Regina; University of Saskatchewan. Other: 16 went to work. 40% scored over 600 on SAT critical reading, 40% scored over 600 on SAT math, 40% scored over 600 on SAT writing, 20% scored over 1800 on combined SAT.

Student Life Upper grades have specified standards of dress. Discipline rests primarily with faculty. Attendance at religious services is required.

Summer Programs ESL programs offered; session focuses on ESL and cultural experience; held off campus; held at Luther College, University of Regina and Regina, Saskatchewan; accepts boys and girls; open to students from other schools. 7 students usually enrolled. 2014 schedule: July 28 to August 28.

Tuition and Aid Day student tuition: CAN$13,315; 7-day tuition and room/board: CAN$14,650–CAN$22,685. Tuition installment plan (monthly payment plans, individually arranged payment plans). Tuition reduction for siblings, bursaries, merit scholarship grants, need-based scholarship grants available. In 2013–14, 20% of upper-school students received aid; total upper-school merit-scholarship money awarded: CAN$30,000. Total amount of financial aid awarded in 2013–14: CAN$165,000.

Admissions Traditional secondary-level entrance grade is 9. For fall 2013, 184 students applied for upper-level admission, 174 were accepted, 164 enrolled. English entrance exam required. Deadline for receipt of application materials: March. Application fee required: CAN$400.

Athletics Interscholastic: badminton (boys, girls), baseball (b), basketball (b,g), bicycling (b,g), cheering (g), cross-country running (b,g), curling (b,g), football (b), golf (b,g), hockey (b,g), pom squad (g), rugby (b,g), soccer (b,g), softball (g), volleyball (g); intramural: basketball (b,g), floor hockey (b,g), soccer (b,g), volleyball (g); coed interscholastic: badminton, curling, pom squad, track and field; coed intramural: aerobics/dance, basketball, curling, floor hockey, football, outdoor education, table tennis, ultimate Frisbee. 2 PE instructors, 28 coaches, 2 athletic trainers.

Computers Computer network features include Internet access, wireless campus network, Internet filtering or blocking technology. Student e-mail accounts and computer access in designated common areas are available to students. Students grades are available online.

Contact Ms. Alanna Kalyniuk, Registrar. 306-791-9154. Fax: 306-359-6962. E-mail: lutherhs@luthercollege.edu. Website: www.luthercollege.edu

LUTHER NORTH COLLEGE PREP

5700 West Berteau Avenue
Chicago, Illinois 60634

Head of School: Mrs. Joy Mullaney

General Information Coeducational day and distance learning college-preparatory, general academic, arts, business, religious studies, and technology school, affiliated with Lutheran Church–Missouri Synod, Evangelical Lutheran Church in America; primarily serves students with learning disabilities and individuals with Attention Deficit Disorder. Grades 9–12. Distance learning grades 10–12. Founded: 1909. Setting: urban. 10-acre campus. 1 building on campus. Approved or accredited by Evangelical Lutheran Church in America, National Lutheran School Accreditation, North Central Association of Colleges and Schools, and Illinois Department of Education. Endowment: $200,000. Total enrollment: 180. Upper school average class size: 16. Upper school faculty-student ratio: 1:16. There are 179 required school days per year for Upper School students. Upper School students typically attend 5 days per week. The average school day consists of 7 hours.

Upper School Student Profile Grade 9: 45 students (25 boys, 20 girls); Grade 10: 40 students (20 boys, 20 girls); Grade 11: 54 students (29 boys, 25 girls); Grade 12: 41 students (21 boys, 20 girls). 47% of students are Lutheran Church–Missouri Synod, Evangelical Lutheran Church in America.

Faculty School total: 17. In upper school: 7 men, 10 women; 14 have advanced degrees.

Subjects Offered 20th century history, 3-dimensional art, accounting, ACT preparation, advanced computer applications, algebra, American legal systems, anatomy, art, astronomy, band, biology, business, calculus, ceramics, chemistry, chorus, composition, computer science, crafts, drawing, economics, English, English-AP, fine arts, geography, geometry, German, government-AP, government/civics, health, keyboarding, law, mathematics, music, painting, photography, physical education, physics, physiology, psychology, public speaking, reading, science, sewing, social sciences, social studies, Spanish, study skills, theology, trigonometry, U.S. history, word processing.

Graduation Requirements Arts and fine arts (art, music, dance, drama), English, foreign language, mathematics, physical education (includes health), religion (includes Bible studies and theology), science, social sciences, social studies (includes history), word processing, summative portfolio demonstration of faculty selected, extra and co-curricular participation annually.

Special Academic Programs Advanced Placement exam preparation; honors section; accelerated programs; independent study; study at local college for college credit; academic accommodation for the gifted, the musically talented, and the artistically talented; remedial reading and/or remedial writing; remedial math; programs in general development for dyslexic students; special instructional classes for students with learning differences.

College Admission Counseling 54 students graduated in 2012; 48 went to college, including Concordia University; DePaul University; Northeastern Illinois University; University of Illinois at Chicago; University of Illinois at Urbana–Champaign; Valparaiso University. Other: 2 went to work, 2 entered military service, 2 had other specific plans. Median composite ACT: 23. 20% scored over 26 on composite ACT.

Student Life Upper grades have specified standards of dress, student council, honor system. Discipline rests primarily with faculty. Attendance at religious services is required.

Tuition and Aid Day student tuition: $9400. Tuition installment plan (Insured Tuition Payment Plan, Academic Management Services Plan, SMART Tuition Payment Plan, monthly payment plans, individually arranged payment plans). Tuition reduction for siblings, merit scholarship grants, need-based scholarship grants, paying campus jobs available. In 2012–13, 70% of upper-school students received aid; total upper-school merit-scholarship money awarded: $30,000.

Admissions Traditional secondary-level entrance grade is 9. For fall 2012, 75 students applied for upper-level admission, 64 were accepted, 62 enrolled. Admissions testing and Stanford Achievement Test, Otis-Lennon School Ability Test required. Deadline for receipt of application materials: none. Application fee required: $175. On-campus interview recommended.

Athletics Interscholastic: baseball (boys), basketball (b,g), cross-country running (b,g), football (b), indoor track & field (b,g), softball (g), track and field (b,g), volleyball (g); coed interscholastic: indoor track; coed intramural: bowling. 2 PE instructors, 10 coaches, 1 athletic trainer.

Computers Computers are regularly used in all academic classes. Computer network features include on-campus library services, online commercial services, Internet access, wireless campus network, Internet filtering or blocking technology, workshops for students and parents in technology. Student e-mail accounts and computer access in designated common areas are available to students. Students grades are available online. The school has a published electronic and media policy.

Contact Mr. Wayne Wenzel, Assistant Principal. 773-286-3600. Fax: 773-286-0304. E-mail: wwenzel@luthernorth.org. Website: luthernorthcollegeprep.org/

LYCEE INTERNATIONAL DE LOS ANGELES

1105 W Riverside Drive
Burbank, California 91506

Head of School: Mrs. Anneli Harvey

General Information Coeducational day and distance learning college-preparatory, arts, bilingual studies, technology, Math and Sciences, and International Baccalaureate school. Grades PS–12. Distance learning grades 11–12. Founded: 1978. Setting: urban. Nearest major city is Los Angeles. 5-acre campus. 1 building on campus. Approved or accredited by French Ministry of Education, International Baccalaureate Organization, Western Association of Schools and Colleges, and California Department of Education. Languages of instruction: English and French. Total enrollment: 1,004. Upper school average class size: 13. Upper school faculty-student ratio: 1:9. There are 175 required school days per year for Upper School students. Upper School students typically attend 5 days per week. The average school day consists of 6 hours.

Upper School Student Profile Grade 9: 30 students (18 boys, 12 girls); Grade 10: 31 students (12 boys, 19 girls); Grade 11: 29 students (9 boys, 20 girls); Grade 12: 25 students (15 boys, 10 girls).

Faculty School total: 93. In upper school: 16 men, 16 women; 25 have advanced degrees.

Subjects Offered 20th century world history, advanced biology, advanced chemistry, advanced math, advanced studio art-AP, algebra, analysis and differential calculus, analytic geometry, art, biology, calculus, chemistry, civics, computer applications, economics, English, ESL, European history, film, fine arts, French, geography, geometry, health, history, honors English, industrial arts, integrated arts, integrated mathematics, integrated science, International Baccalaureate courses, lab science, Mandarin, mathematics, music, philosophy, physical education, physical science, physics, psychology, SAT preparation, science, science and technology, social studies, Spanish, technology/design, U.S. government, U.S. history, visual and performing arts, yearbook.

Graduation Requirements Advanced biology, algebra, arts and fine arts (art, music, dance, drama), biology, civics, computer science, English, French, geography, health, integrated mathematics, integrated science, mathematics, music, physical education (includes health), science, social studies (includes history), Spanish, U.S. government, U.S. history, 150 hours of CAS (creativity, action, service).

Special Academic Programs International Baccalaureate program; 3 Advanced Placement exams for which test preparation is offered; honors section; independent study; term-away projects; study abroad; ESL (15 students enrolled).

College Admission Counseling 18 students graduated in 2013; 17 went to college, including Bard College; Georgetown University; University of Pennsylvania. Other: 1 entered military service. Median SAT critical reading: 544, median SAT math: 600, median SAT writing: 570, median combined SAT: 1714, median composite ACT: 26. 12% scored over 600 on SAT math, 10% scored over 600 on SAT writing, 25% scored over 1800 on combined SAT, 40% scored over 26 on composite ACT.

Student Life Upper grades have specified standards of dress, student council, honor system. Discipline rests equally with students and faculty.

Tuition and Aid Day student tuition: $14,000–$16,300. Tuition installment plan (SMART Tuition Payment Plan). Tuition reduction for siblings, need-based scholarship grants available. In 2013–14, 24% of upper-school students received aid. Total amount of financial aid awarded in 2013–14: $563,569.

Admissions For fall 2013, 8 students applied for upper-level admission, 6 were accepted, 6 enrolled. Admissions testing, math and English placement tests and writing sample required. Deadline for receipt of application materials: none. Application fee required: $100. Interview required.

Athletics Interscholastic: basketball (boys, girls), volleyball (g); intramural: basketball (b,g), cross-country running (b,g), indoor soccer (b), skiing (downhill) (b,g), snowboarding (b,g), soccer (b), table tennis (b,g), volleyball (b,g); coed intramural: basketball, dance, horseback riding, running, swimming and diving, tennis. 2 PE instructors, 3 coaches.

Computers Computers are regularly used in art, computer applications, economics, English, ESL, foreign language, French, mathematics, science, technology classes. Computer network features include on-campus library services, Internet access, wireless campus network, Internet filtering or blocking technology, homework assignments available online, Smart Boards, iPads. Campus intranet, student e-mail accounts, and computer access in designated common areas are available to students. Students grades are available online. The school has a published electronic and media policy.

Contact Mme. Juliette Lange, Admissions Director. 626-695-5159. Fax: 818-994-2816. E-mail: juliette.lange@lilaschool.com. Website: www.lilaschool.com

LYNDON INSTITUTE

PO Box 127
College Road
Lyndon Center, Vermont 05850-0127

Head of School: Richard D. Hilton

General Information Coeducational boarding and day college-preparatory, general academic, arts, business, technology, and ESL school. Boarding grades 8–12, day grades 9–12. Founded: 1867. Setting: small town. Nearest major city is Burlington. Students are housed in single-sex dormitories. 150-acre campus. 27 buildings on campus. Approved or accredited by Independent Schools of Northern New England, New England Association of Schools and Colleges, The Association of Boarding Schools, and Vermont Department of Education. Endowment: $8 million. Upper school average class size: 16. Upper school faculty-student ratio: 1:10. There are 178 required school days per year for Upper School students. Upper School students typically attend 5 days per week. The average school day consists of 6 hours.

Upper School Student Profile Grade 9: 145 students (62 boys, 83 girls); Grade 10: 158 students (84 boys, 74 girls); Grade 11: 143 students (78 boys, 65 girls); Grade 12: 180 students (91 boys, 89 girls). 14% of students are boarding students. 91% are state residents. 2 states are represented in upper school student body. 9% are international students. International students from Afghanistan, China, Japan, Republic of Korea, Spain, and Taiwan; 1 other country represented in student body.

Faculty School total: 68. In upper school: 36 men, 32 women; 20 have advanced degrees; 3 reside on campus.

Subjects Offered 3-dimensional art, accounting, advanced chemistry, advanced math, algebra, American literature, ancient world history, animal science, art, auto mechanics, band, Basic programming, biology, bookmaking, business, business education, business mathematics, business technology, calculus, chemistry, chemistry-AP, chorus, college counseling, computer applications, computer graphics, computer information systems, computer science, computer skills, computer technologies, computer-aided design, concert band, consumer economics, creative writing, desktop publishing, drafting, drawing, driver education, economics, English, English language and composition-AP, English literature, entrepreneurship, environmental science, European history, family and consumer science, fashion, fine arts, French, general math, geography, geometry, graphic design, health, history, honors algebra, honors English, honors U.S. history, honors world history, industrial arts, information processing, information technology, instrumental music, jazz ensemble, keyboarding, Latin, literary magazine, mathematics, metalworking, music, music theory, philosophy, photography, physical education, physics, printmaking, science, social studies, Spanish, street law, studio art, studio art-AP, theater, theater arts, trigonometry, U.S. history, woodworking, word processing, world cultures, world history, writing.

Graduation Requirements Arts and fine arts (art, music, dance, drama), electives, English, health education, mathematics, physical education (includes health), science, social studies (includes history), U.S. history.

Special Academic Programs Advanced Placement exam preparation; honors section; independent study; study at local college for college credit; remedial reading and/or remedial writing; remedial math; ESL (50 students enrolled).

College Admission Counseling 148 students graduated in 2012; 117 went to college, including Purdue University; Saint Michael's College; University of Illinois at Urbana–Champaign; University of Vermont. Other: 19 went to work, 7 entered military service, 1 entered a postgraduate year, 4 had other specific plans.

Student Life Upper grades have specified standards of dress, student council. Discipline rests primarily with faculty.

Tuition and Aid Day student tuition: $14,004; 5-day tuition and room/board: $31,930; 7-day tuition and room/board: $44,700. Tuition installment plan (monthly payment plans, individually arranged payment plans). Need-based scholarship grants, prepGATE loans available. In 2012–13, 2% of upper-school students received aid.

Admissions Traditional secondary-level entrance grade is 9. International English Language Test, SSAT, ERB, PSAT, SAT, PLAN or ACT or TOEFL or SLEP required. Deadline for receipt of application materials: March 31. Application fee required: $50. Interview recommended.

Athletics Interscholastic: alpine skiing (boys, girls), baseball (b), basketball (b,g), cross-country running (b,g), field hockey (g), golf (b,g), ice hockey (b), nordic skiing (b,g), running (b,g), skiing (cross-country) (b,g), skiing (downhill) (b,g), soccer (b,g), softball (g), track and field (b,g), ultimate Frisbee (b,g); intramural: ballet (g), dance (b,g), volleyball (b,g); coed interscholastic: cheering, football, ice hockey, outdoor activities; coed intramural: aerobics/dance, bicycling, bowling, dance, dance team, equestrian sports, fitness walking, indoor soccer, indoor track, marksmanship, martial arts, modern dance, mountain biking, riflery, weight lifting. 2 PE instructors, 26 coaches, 2 athletic trainers.

Computers Computers are regularly used in architecture, business, business applications, business education, business skills, desktop publishing, drafting, engineering, graphic design, information technology, keyboarding, literary magazine, publishing, SAT preparation, science, technical drawing, technology, word processing, yearbook classes. Computer resources include on-campus library services, Internet access, Internet filtering or blocking technology, Big Chalk eLibrary, Vermont Online Library, NewsBank. Student e-mail accounts and computer access in designated common areas are available to students. The school has a published electronic and media policy.

Contact Mary B. Thomas, Assistant Head for Admissions. 802-626-5232. Fax: 802-626-6138. E-mail: mary.thomas@lyndoninstitute.org. Website: www.LyndonInstitute.org

THE MADEIRA SCHOOL

8328 Georgetown Pike
McLean, Virginia 22102-1200

Head of School: Ms. Pilar Cabeza de Vaca

General Information Girls' boarding and day college-preparatory school. Grades 9–12. Founded: 1906. Setting: suburban. Nearest major city is Washington, DC. Students are housed in single-sex dormitories. 376-acre campus. 34 buildings on campus. Approved or accredited by Association of Independent Schools of Greater Washington, The Association of Boarding Schools, and Virginia Department of Education. Member of National Association of Independent Schools and Secondary School Admission Test Board. Endowment: $56 million. Total enrollment: 310. Upper school average class size: 12. Upper school faculty-student ratio: 1:10. Upper School students typically attend 5 days per week.

Upper School Student Profile Grade 9: 76 students (76 girls); Grade 10: 70 students (70 girls); Grade 11: 86 students (86 girls); Grade 12: 78 students (78 girls). 52% of students are boarding students. 51% are state residents. 19 states are represented in upper school student body. 19% are international students. International students from Canada, China, France, Jamaica, Mexico, and Republic of Korea; 8 other countries represented in student body.

Faculty School total: 39. In upper school: 5 men, 29 women; 31 have advanced degrees; 14 reside on campus.

Subjects Offered Acting, advanced math, Advanced Placement courses, algebra, American literature, ancient history, Arabic, art history-AP, Asian literature, ballet, Basic programming, basketball, biology, biology-AP, British literature, calculus, calculus-AP, career/college preparation, ceramics, chamber groups, character education, chemistry, chemistry-AP, Chinese, chorus, college counseling, comparative religion, computer programming, conceptual physics, CPR, dance, digital photography, English, English composition, English language and composition-AP, English literature, English-AP, environmental science, equestrian sports, ESL, ethics, expository writing, Farsi, filmmaking, fine arts, forensics, French, French language-AP, geometry, global issues, grammar, graphic design, health, health and wellness, history, jazz dance, junior and senior seminars, Latin, Latin-AP, leadership education training, linear algebra, literature seminar, madrigals, mathematics, media literacy, Middle Eastern history, modern civilization, modern world history, music, musical productions, mythology, orchestra, performing arts, photography, physical education, physics, physics-AP, politics, pre-calculus, public speaking, science, science and technology, sex education, Spanish, Spanish language-AP, sports, statistics, statistics-AP, student government, student publications, studio art, study skills, swimming, theater, theater arts, trigonometry, U.S. government and politics-AP, U.S. history, U.S. history-AP, visual and performing arts, world civilizations, world history, world history-AP, world religions, writing, yearbook, yoga.

Graduation Requirements Arts and fine arts (art, music, dance, drama), English, foreign language, mathematics, physical education (includes health), science, social studies (includes history), co-curriculum program (off-campus internship program). Community service is required.

Special Academic Programs Advanced Placement exam preparation; independent study; ESL (10 students enrolled).

College Admission Counseling 71 students graduated in 2013; all went to college, including Kenyon College; Lehigh University; The College of William and Mary; The George Washington University; University of South Carolina; University of Virginia. Mean SAT critical reading: 649, mean SAT math: 639, mean SAT writing: 657.

Student Life Upper grades have specified standards of dress, student council, honor system. Discipline rests equally with students and faculty.

Summer Programs Enrichment, advancement, sports, art/fine arts programs offered; session focuses on field hockey, soccer, volleyball, tennis, basketball, lacrosse, softball, swimming for rising 6th-9th graders; held on campus; accepts boys and girls; open to students from other schools. 315 students usually enrolled. 2014 schedule: June 9 to August 8. Application deadline: none.

Tuition and Aid Day student tuition: $39,830; 7-day tuition and room/board: $52,710. Tuition installment plan (Insured Tuition Payment Plan, FACTS Tuition Payment Plan, monthly payment plans). Merit scholarship grants, need-based scholarship grants, need-based loans, middle-income loans available. In 2013–14, 28% of upper-school students received aid. Total amount of financial aid awarded in 2013–14: $2,776,071.

Admissions Traditional secondary-level entrance grade is 9. For fall 2013, 374 students applied for upper-level admission, 202 were accepted, 90 enrolled. ISEE, SSAT or TOEFL required. Deadline for receipt of application materials: January 31. Application fee required: $70. Interview required.

Athletics Interscholastic: aquatics, basketball, cross-country running, diving, equestrian sports, field hockey, horseback riding, lacrosse, soccer, softball, squash, swimming and diving, tennis, volleyball, winter soccer; intramural: dance, weight training, yoga. 5 PE instructors, 27 coaches, 1 athletic trainer.

Computers Computers are regularly used in art, English, foreign language, history, mathematics, science classes. Computer network features include on-campus library services, Internet access, wireless campus network, Internet filtering or blocking technology, campus interactive network. Campus intranet, student e-mail accounts, and computer access in designated common areas are available to students. Students grades are available online. The school has a published electronic and media policy.

Contact Ms. Ann Miller, Director of Admission and Financial Aid. 703-556-8273. Fax: 703-821-2845. E-mail: admission@madeira.org. Website: www.madeira.org

MADISON ACADEMY

325 Slaughter Road
Madison, Alabama 35758

Head of School: Dr. Robert F. Burton

General Information Coeducational day college-preparatory and religious studies school, affiliated with Church of Christ. Grades PS–12. Founded: 1955. Setting: suburban. Nearest major city is Huntsville. 160-acre campus. 5 buildings on campus. Approved or accredited by Southern Association of Colleges and Schools. Endowment: $1.5 million. Total enrollment: 900. Upper school average class size: 20. Upper school faculty-student ratio: 1:15. There are 180 required school days per year for Upper School students. Upper School students typically attend 5 days per week. The average school day consists of 6 hours.

Upper School Student Profile 35% of students are members of Church of Christ.

Faculty School total: 75. In upper school: 14 men, 20 women; 14 have advanced degrees.

Subjects Offered Accounting, advanced math, Alabama history and geography, algebra, American literature, anatomy, art, art history, arts, band, Bible studies, biology, calculus, calculus-AP, chemistry, choral music, chorus, Christian education, Christian ethics, Christian scripture, Christian studies, church history, community service, computer science, concert choir, consumer mathematics, creative writing, drama, earth science, economics, English, English literature, English/composition-AP, environmental science, European history, expository writing, French, general math, geography, geology, geometry, government/civics, health, human anatomy, journalism, keyboarding, music, photography, physical education, physical science, physics, physics-AP, physiology, pre-algebra, religion, Spanish, speech, studio art, trigonometry, U.S. government, U.S. government and politics, U.S. history, world geography, world history, world literature.

Graduation Requirements English, foreign language, mathematics, religion (includes Bible studies and theology), science, social sciences.

Special Academic Programs Honors section; accelerated programs; study at local college for college credit.

College Admission Counseling 70 students graduated in 2013; all went to college, including Abilene Christian University; Auburn University; Freed-Hardeman University; Lipscomb University; The University of Alabama. Mean composite ACT: 25.

Student Life Upper grades have uniform requirement, student council, honor system. Discipline rests primarily with faculty. Attendance at religious services is required.

Tuition and Aid Day student tuition: $7250. Tuition installment plan (monthly payment plans). Tuition reduction for siblings, need-based scholarship grants available. In 2013–14, 10% of upper-school students received aid. Total amount of financial aid awarded in 2013–14: $100,000.

Admissions Traditional secondary-level entrance grade is 9. For fall 2013, 100 students applied for upper-level admission, 50 were accepted, 41 enrolled. Stanford Achievement Test required. Deadline for receipt of application materials: none. Application fee required: $200. On-campus interview required.

Athletics Interscholastic: baseball (boys), basketball (b,g), cheering (g), football (b), golf (b,g), softball (g), swimming and diving (b,g), tennis (b,g), volleyball (g). 3 PE instructors, 36 coaches, 1 athletic trainer.

Computers Computers are regularly used in art, foreign language, science classes. Computer network features include on-campus library services, Internet access, wireless campus network, Internet filtering or blocking technology. Student e-mail accounts are available to students. The school has a published electronic and media policy.

Contact Dr. Michael Weimer, High School Principal. 256-469-6402. Fax: 256-649-6408. E-mail: mweimer@macademy.org. Website: www.macademy.org

MADISON COUNTRY DAY SCHOOL

5606 River Road
Waunakee, Wisconsin 53597

Head of School: Luke Felker

General Information Coeducational day college-preparatory and arts school. Grades PK–12. Founded: 1997. Setting: rural. Nearest major city is Madison. 75-acre campus. 1 building on campus. Approved or accredited by Independent Schools Association of the Central States and Wisconsin Department of Education. Member of National Association of Independent Schools. Total enrollment: 366. Upper school faculty-student ratio: 1:6. There are 173 required school days per year for Upper School students. Upper School students typically attend 5 days per week. The average school day consists of 7 hours and 30 minutes.

Upper School Student Profile Grade 9: 20 students (10 boys, 10 girls); Grade 10: 19 students (7 boys, 12 girls); Grade 11: 14 students (1 boy, 13 girls); Grade 12: 8 students (4 boys, 4 girls).

Faculty School total: 50. In upper school: 12 men, 38 women; 15 have advanced degrees.

Special Academic Programs International Baccalaureate program; study abroad.

Student Life Upper grades have specified standards of dress, student council. Discipline rests primarily with students.

Tuition and Aid Tuition installment plan (monthly payment plans, individually arranged payment plans). Tuition reduction for siblings, merit scholarship grants, need-based scholarship grants available. In 2013–14, 37% of upper-school students received aid.

Admissions Traditional secondary-level entrance grade is 9. ISEE required. Deadline for receipt of application materials: none. Application fee required.

Athletics Interscholastic: cross-country running (boys, girls), football (b), Frisbee (b,g), soccer (b,g), volleyball (g).

Computers Computer resources include on-campus library services, Internet access, wireless campus network. Students grades are available online. The school has a published electronic and media policy.

Contact Mrs. Dana Asmuth, Director of Marketing and Admissions. 608-850-6375. Fax: 608-850-6006. E-mail: dasmuth@madisoncountryday.org. Website: www.madisoncountryday.org

MAHARISHI SCHOOL OF THE AGE OF ENLIGHTENMENT

804 Dr. Robert Keith Wallace Drive
Fairfield, Iowa 52556-2200

Head of School: Dr. Richard Beall

General Information Coeducational boarding and day college-preparatory, arts, Science of Creative Intelligence: universal principles, and Transcendental Meditation: Research in Consciousness school. Boarding grades 9–12, day grades PS–12. Founded: 1972. Setting: small town. Nearest major city is Iowa City. Students are housed in host families. 10-acre campus. 5 buildings on campus. Approved or accredited by Independent Schools Association of the Central States and Iowa Department of Education. Member of National Association of Independent Schools. Total enrollment: 213. Upper school average class size: 15. Upper school faculty-student ratio: 1:12. There are 186 required school days per year for Upper School students. Upper School students typically attend 5 days per week. The average school day consists of 9 hours.

Upper School Student Profile Grade 9: 18 students (9 boys, 9 girls); Grade 10: 18 students (10 boys, 8 girls); Grade 11: 27 students (17 boys, 10 girls); Grade 12: 27 students (20 boys, 7 girls). 20% of students are boarding students. 80% are state residents. 6 states are represented in upper school student body. 20% are international students. International students from China, Germany, Mexico, Nepal, Netherlands, and South Africa; 20 other countries represented in student body.

Faculty School total: 54. In upper school: 11 men, 17 women; 12 have advanced degrees.

Subjects Offered Algebra, American government, American history, American literature, art, art history, basketball, British literature, business mathematics, chemistry, computer science, desktop publishing, digital photography, drama performance, driver education, economics, electives, environmental education, ESL, general math, integrated mathematics, photography, physical education, physiology, pre-calculus, Sanskrit, science project, senior thesis, Spanish, track and field, Vedic science, vocal music, volleyball, world history, world literature, writing, yoga.

Graduation Requirements Art history, computer science, economics, electives, English, foreign language, mathematics, physical education (includes health), science, senior thesis, social studies (includes history), writing, Science of Creative Intelligence course.

Special Academic Programs Honors section; academic accommodation for the gifted, the musically talented, and the artistically talented; remedial reading and/or remedial writing; remedial math; ESL (18 students enrolled).

College Admission Counseling 19 students graduated in 2013; all went to college, including Cornell College; Grinnell College; Maharishi University of Management; New York University; The University of Iowa; University of California, San Diego. Median SAT critical reading: 573, median SAT math: 605, median SAT writing: 610, median combined SAT: 1805, median composite ACT: 26. 58% scored over 600 on SAT critical reading, 42% scored over 600 on SAT math, 58% scored over 600 on SAT writing, 50% scored over 1800 on combined SAT, 43% scored over 26 on composite ACT.

Student Life Upper grades have uniform requirement, student council. Discipline rests primarily with faculty.

Summer Programs Enrichment, ESL, sports, art/fine arts programs offered; session focuses on interscholastic sports, arts; held both on and off campus; held at neighboring schools and universities; accepts boys and girls; not open to students from other schools. 40 students usually enrolled. 2014 schedule: June 15 to August 15. Application deadline: June 12.

Tuition and Aid Day student tuition: $13,900; 7-day tuition and room/board: $25,900–$42,000. Tuition installment plan (two semester payments). Tuition reduction for siblings, need-based scholarship grants available. In 2013–14, 85% of upper-school students received aid.

Admissions Traditional secondary-level entrance grade is 9. For fall 2013, 14 students applied for upper-level admission, 14 were accepted, 14 enrolled. International English Language Test or TOEFL or SLEP required. Deadline for receipt of application materials: none. No application fee required. Interview required.

Athletics Interscholastic: basketball (boys, girls), cheering (g), dance team (g), golf (b), indoor track & field (b,g), soccer (b), tennis (b,g), track and field (b,g), volleyball (g), winter (indoor) track (b,g); intramural: archery (b), badminton (b,g), ballet (g), baseball (b), basketball (b,g), canoeing/kayaking (b,g), dance (g), equestrian sports (g), fitness (b,g), fitness walking (g), handball (b,g), hiking/backpacking (b,g), jogging (b,g), life saving (b,g), modern dance (g), outdoor activities (b,g), outdoor recreation (b,g), physical fitness (b,g), physical training (b,g), running (b,g), strength & conditioning (b,g), table tennis (b,g), tennis (b,g), volleyball (g), wall climbing (b,g), winter (indoor) track (b,g), yoga (b,g). 3 PE instructors, 11 coaches.

Computers Computers are regularly used in business education, creative writing, desktop publishing, economics, English, ESL, geography, graphic design, history, independent study, library, library science, library skills, literacy, mathematics, multimedia, photography, programming, publications, science, senior seminar, social sciences, social studies, stock market, typing, video film production, writing classes. Computer network features include Internet access, Internet filtering or blocking technology, file and portfolio management. Campus intranet and computer access in designated common areas are available to students. Students grades are available online. The school has a published electronic and media policy.

Contact Ms. Springli Johnson, Director of International Admissions. 641-472-9400 Ext. 5538. Fax: 641-472-1211. E-mail: sjohnson@msae.edu. Website: www.maharishischooliowa.org

MAINE CENTRAL INSTITUTE

295 Main Street
Pittsfield, Maine 04967

Head of School: Christopher Hopkins

General Information Coeducational boarding and day college-preparatory, general academic, arts, vocational, bilingual studies, technology, humanities, and mathematics, the sciences school. Grades 9–PG. Founded: 1866. Setting: small town. Nearest major city is Portland. Students are housed in single-sex dormitories and honors dorm is coed. 23-acre campus. 19 buildings on campus. Approved or accredited by Independent Schools of Northern New England, New England Association of Schools and Colleges, The Association of Boarding Schools, and Maine Department of Education. Member of National Association of Independent Schools and Secondary School Admission Test Board. Endowment: $5 million. Total enrollment: 455. Upper school average class size: 16. Upper school faculty-student ratio: 1:14. There are 175 required school days per year for Upper School students. Upper School students typically attend 5 days per week. The average school day consists of 7 hours and 15 minutes.

Upper School Student Profile Grade 9: 94 students (48 boys, 46 girls); Grade 10: 103 students (61 boys, 42 girls); Grade 11: 123 students (61 boys, 62 girls); Grade

12: 133 students (75 boys, 58 girls). 71% are state residents. 11 states are represented in upper school student body. 85% are international students.

Faculty School total: 41. In upper school: 20 men, 21 women; 14 have advanced degrees; 25 reside on campus.

Subjects Offered Algebra, American history, American literature, anatomy, art, art-AP, Asian studies, astronomy, audio visual/media, ballet, biology, botany, calculus, calculus-AP, career exploration, chemistry, chemistry-AP, child development, civil rights, computer science, concert band, concert choir, contemporary issues, creative writing, drafting, drama, earth science, ecology, economics, electronic publishing, English, English literature, environmental science, ESL, ethics, fine arts, French, geology, geometry, government/civics, health, history, humanities, integrated science, jazz band, jazz dance, jazz ensemble, Latin, life management skills, literature-AP, mathematics, meteorology, music, music appreciation, music composition, music theory, personal finance, philosophy, photography, physical education, physics, physics-AP, piano, psychology, reading/study skills, SAT preparation, science, social sciences, social studies, sociology, Spanish, statistics, theater, trigonometry, video film production, Web site design, world history.

Graduation Requirements Arts and fine arts (art, music, dance, drama), computer skills, English, mathematics, physical education (includes health), science, senior project, social studies (includes history), Manson essay, Senior Project.

Special Academic Programs Advanced Placement exam preparation; honors section; study at local college for college credit; academic accommodation for the gifted and the musically talented; remedial reading and/or remedial writing; remedial math; programs in English, mathematics, general development for dyslexic students; ESL (50 students enrolled).

College Admission Counseling 112 students graduated in 2013; 90 went to college, including Husson University; Maine Maritime Academy; University of Maine; University of Maine at Farmington; University of Southern Maine. Other: 13 went to work, 3 entered military service, 6 had other specific plans. Median SAT critical reading: 428, median SAT math: 444, median SAT writing: 442, median combined SAT: 1314.

Student Life Upper grades have specified standards of dress, student council, honor system. Discipline rests primarily with faculty.

Summer Programs ESL, art/fine arts programs offered; session focuses on basic ESL, summer ballet; held on campus; accepts boys and girls; open to students from other schools. 35 students usually enrolled. 2014 schedule: July to August. Application deadline: none.

Tuition and Aid Day student tuition: $10,000; 7-day tuition and room/board: $42,000. Tuition installment plan (Key Tuition Payment Plan, SMART Tuition Payment Plan, monthly payment plans, school's own payment plan). Merit scholarship grants, need-based scholarship grants available. In 2013–14, 20% of upper-school students received aid; total upper-school merit-scholarship money awarded: $24,430. Total amount of financial aid awarded in 2013–14: $384,000.

Admissions Traditional secondary-level entrance grade is 9. For fall 2013, 385 students applied for upper-level admission, 352 were accepted, 140 enrolled. Deadline for receipt of application materials: none. Application fee required: $75. Interview recommended.

Athletics Interscholastic: baseball (boys), basketball (b,g), field hockey (g), football (b), riflery (b,g), soccer (b,g), softball (g); intramural: football (b); coed interscholastic: aerobics/dance, alpine skiing, ballet, cheering, cross-country running, dance, fencing, golf, modern dance, outdoor activities, outdoor adventure, physical training; coed intramural: alpine skiing, backpacking, basketball, billiards, canoeing/kayaking, climbing, cooperative games, fencing, fishing, flagball, floor hockey, handball, outdoor activities, rafting. 1 PE instructor, 30 coaches, 1 athletic trainer.

Computers Computer network features include on-campus library services, Internet access, wireless campus network, Internet filtering or blocking technology. Student e-mail accounts are available to students. Students grades are available online.

Contact Mr. Clint M. Williams, Dean of Admission. 207-487-2282 Ext. 128. Fax: 207-487-3512. E-mail: cwilliams@mci-school.org. Website: www.mci-school.org

See Display on next page and Close-Up on page 548.

MALVERN PREPARATORY SCHOOL

418 South Warren Avenue
Malvern, Pennsylvania 19355-2707

Head of School: Mr. Christian M. Talbot

General Information Boys' day college-preparatory school, affiliated with Roman Catholic Church. Grades 6–12. Founded: 1842. Setting: suburban. Nearest major city is Philadelphia. 104-acre campus. 18 buildings on campus. Approved or accredited by Middle States Association of Colleges and Schools, Pennsylvania Association of Independent Schools, and Pennsylvania Department of Education. Member of National Association of Independent Schools. Endowment: $5.2 million. Total enrollment: 595. Upper school average class size: 18. Upper school faculty-student ratio: 1:9. There are 180 required school days per year for Upper School students. Upper School students typically attend 5 days per week. The average school day consists of 7 hours.

Upper School Student Profile Grade 9: 112 students (112 boys); Grade 10: 110 students (110 boys); Grade 11: 109 students (109 boys); Grade 12: 103 students (103 boys). 85% of students are Roman Catholic.

Faculty School total: 74. In upper school: 54 men, 20 women; 49 have advanced degrees.

Subjects Offered Algebra, American history, American literature, art, Bible studies, biology, business, calculus, ceramics, chemistry, computer math, computer programming, computer science, concert band, creative writing, data analysis, drama, earth science, ecology, economics, English, English literature, environmental science, ethics, European history, expository writing, fine arts, French, geography, geometry, government/civics, grammar, health, history, jazz band, journalism, logic, mathematics, music, music performance, music theory, philosophy, photography, physical education, physics, printmaking, religion, science, sculpture, social sciences, social studies, sociology, Spanish, speech, sports medicine, studio art, theater, theology, trigonometry, world history, world literature, writing.

Graduation Requirements Arts and fine arts (art, music, dance, drama), computer science, English, foreign language, mathematics, physical education (includes health), religion (includes Bible studies and theology), science, senior career experience, social sciences, social studies (includes history). Community service is required.

Special Academic Programs Advanced Placement exam preparation; honors section; independent study.

College Admission Counseling 104 students graduated in 2012; all went to college, including Georgetown University; Penn State University Park; Saint Joseph's University; University of Pennsylvania; Villanova University.

Student Life Upper grades have specified standards of dress, student council. Discipline rests primarily with faculty.

Tuition and Aid Day student tuition: $24,450. Tuition installment plan (Insured Tuition Payment Plan, individually arranged payment plans, Bryn Mawr Trust Loan Program). Merit scholarship grants, need-based scholarship grants available. In 2012–13, 30% of upper-school students received aid; total upper-school merit-scholarship money awarded: $210,600. Total amount of financial aid awarded in 2012–13: $855,650.

Admissions Traditional secondary-level entrance grade is 9. Deadline for receipt of application materials: none. Application fee required: $25. On-campus interview required.

Athletics Interscholastic: aquatics, baseball, basketball, crew, cross-country running, diving, football, golf, ice hockey, lacrosse, soccer, squash, swimming and diving, tennis, track and field, water polo, winter (indoor) track. 4 PE instructors, 23 coaches, 1 athletic trainer.

Computers Computers are regularly used in all academic classes. Computer network features include on-campus library services, online commercial services, Internet access, Discovering Authors, Access PA Power Library, Electric Library, InfoTrac, SIRS Knowledge Source.

Contact William R. Gibson, Dean of Admissions. 484-595-1181. Fax: 484-595-1104. E-mail: wgibson@malvernprep.org. Website: www.malvernprep.org

MANHATTAN CHRISTIAN HIGH SCHOOL

8000 Churchill Road
Manhattan, Montana 59741

Head of School: Mr. Patrick J. De Jong

General Information Coeducational day and distance learning college-preparatory, general academic, arts, business, religious studies, and technology school, affiliated with Christian Reformed Church, Christian faith. Grades PK–12. Distance learning grades 9–12. Founded: 1907. Setting: rural. Nearest major city is Bozeman. 20-acre campus. 1 building on campus. Approved or accredited by Christian Schools International, Office for Standards in Education (OFSTED), The College Board, home study, and Montana Department of Education. Endowment: $5.5 million. Total enrollment: 266. Upper school average class size: 15. Upper school faculty-student ratio: 1:8. There are 175 required school days per year for Upper School students. Upper School students typically attend 5 days per week. The average school day consists of 6 hours and 19 minutes.

Upper School Student Profile Grade 6: 20 students (8 boys, 12 girls); Grade 7: 20 students (11 boys, 9 girls); Grade 8: 21 students (12 boys, 9 girls); Grade 9: 17 students (7 boys, 10 girls); Grade 10: 15 students (8 boys, 7 girls); Grade 11: 15 students (7 boys, 8 girls); Grade 12: 14 students (9 boys, 5 girls). 90% of students are members of Christian Reformed Church, Christian faith.

Faculty School total: 17. In upper school: 3 men, 5 women; 3 have advanced degrees.

Subjects Offered Art, Bible studies, business, community service, English, general science, mathematics, music, physical education, senior project, social studies, Spanish.

Graduation Requirements Arts and fine arts (art, music, dance, drama), business skills (includes word processing), English, mathematics, physical education (includes health), religion (includes Bible studies and theology), science, senior project, social studies (includes history), speech. Community service is required.

Special Academic Programs Advanced Placement exam preparation; honors section; independent study; term-away projects; study at local college for college credit; remedial reading and/or remedial writing; remedial math; programs in English, mathematics, general development for dyslexic students.

College Admission Counseling 20 students graduated in 2013; all went to college, including Azusa Pacific University; Dordt College; Montana State University; WyoTech Laramie. Mean composite ACT: 23.

Student Life Upper grades have specified standards of dress, student council, honor system. Discipline rests primarily with faculty. Attendance at religious services is required.

Tuition and Aid Day student tuition: $9200. Tuition installment plan (monthly payment plans, individually arranged payment plans). Tuition reduction for siblings, need-based scholarship grants available. In 2013–14, 95% of upper-school students received aid. Total amount of financial aid awarded in 2013–14: $297,100.

Admissions Traditional secondary-level entrance grade is 9. For fall 2013, 17 students applied for upper-level admission, 17 were accepted, 17 enrolled. Academic Profile Tests or any standardized test required. Deadline for receipt of application materials: none. Application fee required: $35. Interview required.

Athletics Interscholastic: baseball (boys), basketball (b,g), cheering (b,g), cross-country running (b,g), dance (g), football (b), golf (b,g), horseback riding (g), marksmanship (g), rodeo (g), track and field (b,g), volleyball (g). 1 PE instructor, 6 coaches, 2 athletic trainers.

Computers Computers are regularly used in business, English, science, senior seminar, social studies classes. Computer network features include on-campus library services, online commercial services, Internet access, wireless campus network, Internet filtering or blocking technology. Student e-mail accounts and computer access in designated common areas are available to students. Students grades are available online. The school has a published electronic and media policy.

Contact Mrs. Gloria Veltkamp, Admissions Director. 406-282-7261. Fax: 406-282-7701. E-mail: gveltkamp@manhattanchristian.org. Website: www.manhattanchristian.org

MAPLEBROOK SCHOOL

Amenia, New York
See Special Needs Schools section.

MARANATHA HIGH SCHOOL

169 South Saint John Avenue
Pasadena, California 91105

Head of School: Dr. David Gyertson

General Information Coeducational day college-preparatory, religious studies, and liberal arts school, affiliated with Christian faith. Grades 9–12. Founded: 1965. Setting: urban. 11-acre campus. 4 buildings on campus. Approved or accredited by Association of Christian Schools International, Western Association of Schools and Colleges, and California Department of Education. Endowment: $350,000. Total enrollment: 670. Upper school average class size: 24. Upper school faculty-student ratio: 1:14. There are 170 required school days per year for Upper School students. Upper School students typically attend 5 days per week. The average school day consists of 5 hours and 50 minutes.

Faculty School total: 50. In upper school: 21 men, 29 women; 35 have advanced degrees.

Subjects Offered Advanced math, algebra, American history, American history-AP, American literature, American sign language, anatomy and physiology, art, ASB Leadership, Bible, biology, biology-AP, calculus, calculus-AP, chemistry, chemistry-AP, choir, composition, conceptual physics, concert choir, drama performance, drawing, economics, English, English language-AP, English literature, English literature-AP, filmmaking, foreign language, French, geometry, government and politics-AP, government-AP, graphic design, honors algebra, honors English, honors U.S. history, jazz dance, learning lab, macroeconomics-AP, math analysis, modern world history, music theory, music theory-AP, musical theater, New Testament, orchestra, performing arts, photography, physical education, physical science, physics, physics-AP, psychology, psychology-AP, sociology, Spanish, Spanish language-AP, Spanish-AP, speech and debate, sports medicine, statistics-AP, studio art-AP, swimming, theater, theater arts, theology, theology and the arts, U.S. government, U.S. history-AP, weight training, world geography, world history, yearbook.

Graduation Requirements English, foreign language, history, life science, mathematics, performing arts, physical education (includes health), physical science, theology, visual arts, Theology must be taken every year student attends school. Community service is required.

Special Academic Programs 16 Advanced Placement exams for which test preparation is offered; honors section; study at local college for college credit; academic accommodation for the artistically talented; remedial reading and/or remedial writing; remedial math; special instructional classes for students with learning difficulties and Attention Deficit Disorder.

College Admission Counseling 165 students graduated in 2013; they went to Azusa Pacific University.

Student Life Upper grades have uniform requirement, student council, honor system. Discipline rests primarily with faculty. Attendance at religious services is required.

Summer Programs Remediation, enrichment, advancement, sports, art/fine arts programs offered; session focuses on science and math; held on campus; accepts boys and girls; open to students from other schools. 140 students usually enrolled. 2014 schedule: June 16 to July 27. Application deadline: February 3.

Tuition and Aid Day student tuition: $16,750. Tuition installment plan (SMART Tuition Payment Plan, monthly payment plans). Merit scholarship grants, need-based scholarship grants available. In 2013–14, 30% of upper-school students received aid.

Admissions Traditional secondary-level entrance grade is 9. ISEE required. Deadline for receipt of application materials: none. Application fee required: $75. Interview required.

Athletics Interscholastic: baseball (boys), basketball (b,g), cheering (g), cross-country running (b,g), diving (b,g), football (b), soccer (b,g), softball (g), swimming and diving (b,g), tennis (b,g), track and field (b,g), volleyball (b,g); coed interscholastic: dance team, equestrian sports, golf; coed intramural: hiking/backpacking, kayaking, outdoor activities, outdoor adventure, outdoor skills. 2 PE instructors, 27 coaches, 1 athletic trainer.

Computers Computers are regularly used in college planning, freshman foundations, graphic design, library, photography, research skills, yearbook classes. Computer network features include on-campus library services, online commercial services, Internet access, wireless campus network, Internet filtering or blocking technology, eLibrary, 1:1: iPad program. Campus intranet, student e-mail accounts, and computer access in designated common areas are available to students. Students grades are available online. The school has a published electronic and media policy.

Contact Mrs. Debbie Middlebrook, Admissions Administrative Assistant. 626-817-4021. Fax: 626-817-4040. E-mail: d_middlebrook@mhs-hs.org. Website: www.maranatha-hs.org

MARET SCHOOL

3000 Cathedral Avenue NW
Washington, District of Columbia 20008

Head of School: Marjo Talbott

General Information Coeducational day college-preparatory, arts, and technology school. Grades K–12. Founded: 1911. Setting: urban. 7-acre campus. 6 buildings on campus. Approved or accredited by Association of Independent Maryland Schools, Association of Independent Schools of Greater Washington, Middle States Association of Colleges and Schools, and District of Columbia Department of Education. Member of National Association of Independent Schools and Secondary School Admission Test Board. Endowment: $28.6 million. Total enrollment: 635. Upper school average class size: 18. Upper school faculty-student ratio: 1:6. Upper School students typically attend 5 days per week. The average school day consists of 7 hours.

Upper School Student Profile Grade 9: 78 students (37 boys, 41 girls); Grade 10: 72 students (37 boys, 35 girls); Grade 11: 76 students (37 boys, 39 girls); Grade 12: 79 students (41 boys, 38 girls).

Faculty School total: 108. In upper school: 40 men, 68 women; 78 have advanced degrees.

Subjects Offered 20th century history, 20th century world history, 3-dimensional art, acting, advanced biology, advanced chemistry, advanced computer applications, advanced math, advanced studio art-AP, African-American literature, algebra, American Civil War, American government, American history, American legal systems, American literature, Arabic, art, Asian history, Asian literature, Asian studies, biochemistry, bioethics, biology, biotechnology, Buddhism, calculus, calculus-AP, ceramics, chemistry, Chinese, choir, choral music, civil rights, classical civilization, classical language, classics, college admission preparation, college counseling, college planning, comedy, comparative religion, computer graphics, computer math, computer programming, computer science, concert choir, constitutional history of U.S., constitutional law, creative writing, critical thinking, critical writing, digital photography, drama, earth science, ecology, ecology, environmental systems, economics, English, English literature, environmental science, equality and freedom, ethics, European history, evolution, film history, fine arts, French, gender issues, geometry, global studies, government/civics, Hispanic literature, history, human development, human sexuality, humanities, Islamic history, Islamic studies, jazz band, jazz ensemble, Latin, madrigals, Mandarin, marine biology, marine ecology, mathematics, model United Nations, music, music theory, newspaper, organic chemistry, painting, photography, physical education, physics, pre-algebra, pre-calculus, psychology, science, science fiction, sculpture, senior project, service learning/internship, Shakespeare, Spanish, Spanish literature, statistics, technology, trigonometry, world history, world literature, writing.

Graduation Requirements Arts and fine arts (art, music, dance, drama), English, foreign language, history, mathematics, music, performing arts, physical education (includes health), science, 15 hours of community service in grades 9 and 10, additional 15 hours in grades 11 and 12.

Special Academic Programs 16 Advanced Placement exams for which test preparation is offered; honors section; independent study; study abroad; academic accommodation for the gifted, the musically talented, and the artistically talented; remedial reading and/or remedial writing; remedial math.

College Admission Counseling 84 students graduated in 2013; 83 went to college, including Columbia University; Harvard University; Oberlin College; Tulane University; Washington University in St. Louis; Wesleyan University. Other: 1 entered a postgraduate year.

Student Life Upper grades have student council. Discipline rests primarily with faculty.

Summer Programs Enrichment, advancement, sports, art/fine arts programs offered; session focuses on academics, athletics, and performing arts; held both on and off campus; held at Florida, France, India, Nicaragua, and Taiwan; accepts boys and girls; open to students from other schools. 450 students usually enrolled. 2014 schedule: June 17 to August 5. Application deadline: January 14.

Tuition and Aid Day student tuition: $33,810. Tuition installment plan (Tuition Management Systems (TMS)). Need-based scholarship grants available. In 2013–14, 24% of upper-school students received aid. Total amount of financial aid awarded in 2013–14: $1,660,000.

Admissions Traditional secondary-level entrance grade is 9. For fall 2013, 280 students applied for upper-level admission, 50 were accepted, 24 enrolled. Admissions testing, ISEE, PSAT, SSAT, Wechsler Intelligence Scale for Children, Wechsler Intelligence Scale for Children III or Woodcock-Johnson required. Deadline for receipt of application materials: January 6. Application fee required: $65. Interview required.

Athletics Interscholastic: baseball (boys), basketball (b,g), football (b), lacrosse (b,g), soccer (b,g), softball (g), tennis (b,g), volleyball (g), wrestling (b); intramural: ice hockey (b), squash (b,g); coed interscholastic: cross-country running, diving, golf, independent competitive sports, swimming and diving, track and field, ultimate Frisbee; coed intramural: flag football, indoor soccer, ultimate Frisbee, weight lifting, weight training, yoga. 6 PE instructors, 25 coaches, 1 athletic trainer.

Computers Computers are regularly used in graphic design, graphics, programming, publications, Web site design classes. Computer network features include on-campus library services, online commercial services, Internet access, wireless campus network, Internet filtering or blocking technology. Campus intranet and student e-mail accounts are available to students. Students grades are available online. The school has a published electronic and media policy.

Contact Annie M. Farquhar, Director of Admission and Financial Aid. 202-939-8814. Fax: 202-939-8845. E-mail: admissions@maret.org. Website: www.maret.org

MARIAN CATHOLIC HIGH SCHOOL

166 Marian Avenue

Tamaqua, Pennsylvania 18252-9789

Head of School: Sr. Bernard Agnes Smith, IHM

General Information Coeducational day college-preparatory, general academic, business, and technology school, affiliated with Roman Catholic Church. Grades 9–12. Founded: 1954. Setting: rural. Nearest major city is Hazleton. 1 building on campus. Approved or accredited by Middle States Association of Colleges and Schools, National Catholic Education Association, and Pennsylvania Department of Education. Total enrollment: 378. Upper school average class size: 23. Upper school faculty-student ratio: 1:11. The average school day consists of 6 hours and 14 minutes.

Upper School Student Profile Grade 9: 115 students (52 boys, 63 girls); Grade 10: 89 students (51 boys, 38 girls); Grade 11: 82 students (40 boys, 42 girls); Grade 12: 108 students (56 boys, 52 girls). 93% of students are Roman Catholic.

Faculty School total: 31. In upper school: 12 men, 19 women; 15 have advanced degrees.

Special Academic Programs Advanced Placement exam preparation; study at local college for college credit.

College Admission Counseling 62 went to college, including La Salle University; Penn State University Park. Other: 2 went to work, 1 entered a postgraduate year.

Student Life Upper grades have uniform requirement, student council, honor system. Discipline rests primarily with faculty. Attendance at religious services is required.

Summer Programs Sports programs offered; session focuses on sports camps; held on campus; accepts boys and girls; open to students from other schools. 60 students usually enrolled.

Tuition and Aid Day student tuition: $4350. Tuition installment plan (FACTS Tuition Payment Plan, monthly payment plans). Tuition reduction for siblings, merit scholarship grants, need-based scholarship grants available. In 2013–14, 45% of upper-school students received aid. Total amount of financial aid awarded in 2013–14: $102,000.

Admissions Traditional secondary-level entrance grade is 9. Deadline for receipt of application materials: none. Application fee required: $125. Interview recommended.

Athletics Interscholastic: baseball (boys), basketball (b,g), cheering (g), cross-country running (b,g), football (b), golf (b,g), softball (g), volleyball (g). 2 PE instructors, 20 coaches, 1 athletic trainer.

Computers Computer resources include on-campus library services, Internet access, Internet filtering or blocking technology. Student e-mail accounts are available to students. The school has a published electronic and media policy.

Contact Mrs. Teresa Sheer, Studies Director. 570-467-3335 Ext. 217. Fax: 570-467-0186. E-mail: tsheer@mariancatholichs.org. Website: www.mariancatholichs.org

MARIAN CENTRAL CATHOLIC HIGH SCHOOL

1001 McHenry Avenue

Woodstock, Illinois 60098

Head of School: Mr. Charles D. Rakers

General Information Coeducational day college-preparatory, arts, business, religious studies, bilingual studies, and technology school, affiliated with Roman Catholic Church. Grades 9–12. Founded: 1959. Setting: suburban. 42-acre campus. 1 building on campus. Approved or accredited by National Catholic Education Association, North Central Association of Colleges and Schools, and Illinois Department of Education. Endowment: $1.2 million. Total enrollment: 716. Upper school average class size: 23. Upper school faculty-student ratio: 1:17. There are 177 required school days per year for Upper School students. Upper School students typically attend 5 days per week. The average school day consists of 6 hours and 25 minutes.

Upper School Student Profile Grade 9: 201 students (100 boys, 101 girls); Grade 10: 167 students (100 boys, 67 girls); Grade 11: 186 students (100 boys, 86 girls); Grade 12: 162 students (79 boys, 83 girls). 89.3% of students are Roman Catholic.

Faculty School total: 46. In upper school: 21 men, 25 women; 34 have advanced degrees.

Subjects Offered Accounting, advanced biology, advanced chemistry, advanced math, Advanced Placement courses, algebra, American government, art, band, biology, biology-AP, business law, calculus, calculus-AP, chemistry, chemistry-AP, chorus, composition, computer applications, consumer economics, cultural geography, desktop publishing, engineering, English, English composition, English literature-AP, first aid, French, general science, geography, geometry, global issues, government, government and politics-AP, health, honors algebra, honors English, honors geometry, honors U.S. history, integrated science, marketing, photo shop, physical education, physical fitness, physical science, physics, pre-calculus, psychology, psychology-AP, publications, Spanish, speech, statistics-AP, theater, theology, U.S. history, U.S. history-AP, Web site design, world history, world history-AP.

Graduation Requirements Art, biology, consumer economics, electives, English, first aid, foreign language, government, mathematics, music, physical education (includes health), science, theology, U.S. history.

Special Academic Programs 9 Advanced Placement exams for which test preparation is offered; honors section; remedial reading and/or remedial writing; remedial math.

College Admission Counseling 158 students graduated in 2013; 150 went to college, including DePaul University; Loras College; Loyola University Chicago; Marquette University; Purdue University; University of Illinois at Urbana–Champaign. Other: 2 went to work, 1 entered military service, 2 entered a postgraduate year, 3 had other specific plans. Mean composite ACT: 25. 44% scored over 26 on composite ACT.

Student Life Upper grades have uniform requirement, student council. Discipline rests primarily with faculty. Attendance at religious services is required.

Summer Programs Enrichment, sports programs offered; session focuses on sports camps, study skills, Scholastic Bowl; held on campus; accepts boys and girls; open to students from other schools. 2014 schedule: June to August.

Tuition and Aid Day student tuition: $5920–$7930. Tuition installment plan (monthly payment plans, quarterly payment plan, semester payment plans, yearly payment plans). Tuition reduction for siblings, need-based scholarship grants, paying campus jobs available. In 2013–14, 21% of upper-school students received aid. Total amount of financial aid awarded in 2013–14: $301,400.

Admissions Traditional secondary-level entrance grade is 9. High School Placement Test (closed version) from Scholastic Testing Service required. Deadline for receipt of application materials: none. No application fee required.

Athletics Interscholastic: baseball (boys), basketball (b,g), cheering (g), cross-country running (b,g), dance team (g), football (b), golf (b,g), soccer (b,g), softball (g), tennis (b,g), track and field (b,g), volleyball (g), wrestling (b); coed interscholastic: fencing, fishing; coed intramural: floor hockey. 4 PE instructors, 52 coaches, 1 athletic trainer.

Computers Computers are regularly used in computer applications, desktop publishing, photography, publications, Web site design classes. Computer resources include on-campus library services, online commercial services, Internet access, Internet filtering or blocking technology. Students grades are available online. The school has a published electronic and media policy.

Contact Mrs. Barbara Villont, Director of Curriculum and Technology. 815-338-4220 Ext. 105. Fax: 815-338-4253. E-mail: bvillont@marian.com. Website: www.marian.com

MARIAN HIGH SCHOOL

1311 South Logan Street

Mishawaka, Indiana 46544

Head of School: Carl Loesch

General Information Coeducational day college-preparatory, arts, business, vocational, religious studies, bilingual studies, and technology school, affiliated with Roman Catholic Church. Grades 9–12. Founded: 1965. Setting: suburban. 135-acre campus. 1 building on campus. Approved or accredited by North Central Association of

Colleges and Schools, The College Board, and Indiana Department of Education. Total enrollment: 719. Upper school average class size: 27. Upper school faculty-student ratio: 1:24. There are 180 required school days per year for Upper School students. Upper School students typically attend 5 days per week. The average school day consists of 6 hours and 30 minutes.

Upper School Student Profile Grade 9: 199 students (89 boys, 110 girls); Grade 10: 182 students (102 boys, 80 girls); Grade 11: 172 students (86 boys, 86 girls); Grade 12: 166 students (82 boys, 84 girls). 83% of students are Roman Catholic.

Faculty School total: 48. In upper school: 18 men, 30 women; 22 have advanced degrees.

Subjects Offered 20th century history, 20th century physics, 20th century world history, 3-dimensional art, 3-dimensional design, accounting, acting, advanced chemistry, advanced computer applications, advanced math, algebra, alternative physical education, American government, American literature, analysis and differential calculus, analytic geometry, anatomy, ancient world history, art, art history, arts and crafts, arts appreciation, business law, calculus, Catholic belief and practice, chemistry, drama, drawing, drawing and design, economics, English composition, English literature-AP, environmental science, environmental studies, environmental systems, family and consumer science, family living, fashion, fine arts, food and nutrition, foods, French, French language-AP, general business, general math, geography, geometry, German, government and politics-AP, government-AP, government/civics, guidance, health, histology, honors world history, independent living, integrated science, keyboarding, Latin, Life of Christ, media, media arts, moral theology, music, music appreciation, nutrition, physics, physics-AP, pre-algebra, pre-calculus, psychology, religion, scripture, senior project, sewing, sociology, Spanish, Spanish language-AP, Spanish-AP, study skills, theology, U.S. government and politics-AP, U.S. history, U.S. history-AP, visual arts, vocal music, Western civilization.

Graduation Requirements Algebra, American government, American history, analytic geometry, arts and fine arts (art, music, dance, drama), biology, chemistry, computer information systems, computer skills, economics, English, English composition, English literature, French, keyboarding, languages, mathematics, science, scripture, writing, four years of theology.

Special Academic Programs Advanced Placement exam preparation; study at local college for college credit; remedial reading and/or remedial writing; remedial math.

College Admission Counseling 162 students graduated in 2012; 155 went to college, including Ball State University; DePaul University; Indiana University–Purdue University Fort Wayne; Indiana University Bloomington; Purdue University; University of Notre Dame. Other: 4 went to work, 1 entered military service, 2 had other specific plans. Mean SAT critical reading: 542, mean SAT math: 541, mean SAT writing: 537, mean composite ACT: 23.

Student Life Upper grades have specified standards of dress, student council, honor system. Discipline rests equally with students and faculty. Attendance at religious services is required.

Tuition and Aid Day student tuition: $5575–$6575. Tuition installment plan (The Tuition Plan, FACTS Tuition Payment Plan, individually arranged payment plans). Tuition reduction for siblings, need-based loans available. In 2012–13, 45% of upper-school students received aid. Total amount of financial aid awarded in 2012–13: $350,000.

Admissions Traditional secondary-level entrance grade is 9. For fall 2012, 210 students applied for upper-level admission, 210 were accepted, 199 enrolled. High School Placement Test, Math Placement Exam or placement test required. Deadline for receipt of application materials: September 9. Application fee required: $100. Interview required.

Athletics Interscholastic: aerobics/dance (girls), aquatics (b,g), baseball (b), basketball (b,g), cheering (b,g), Cosom hockey (b), cross-country running (b,g), dance team (g), diving (b,g), flag football (g), football (b), golf (b,g), gymnastics (g), hockey (b), ice hockey (b), indoor hockey (b), lacrosse (b,g), power lifting (b,g), rugby (b), soccer (b,g), softball (g), swimming and diving (b,g), tennis (b,g), track and field (b,g), volleyball (g), weight training (b,g), wrestling (b,g); intramural: basketball (b), flag football (g), pom squad (g); coed interscholastic: cheering, wrestling; coed intramural: alpine skiing, bowling. 2 PE instructors, 42 coaches, 1 athletic trainer.

Computers Computers are regularly used in business education, business skills, career education, commercial art, economics, foreign language, graphic arts, history, library, media arts, occupational education, publications, religion, yearbook classes. Computer network features include on-campus library services, online commercial services, Internet access, Internet filtering or blocking technology. Students grades are available online. The school has a published electronic and media policy.

Contact Mark B. Kirzeder, Assistant Principal of Academics. 574-259-5257 Ext. 318. Fax: 574-258-7668. E-mail: mkirzeder@marianhs.org. Website: www.marianhs.org/

MARIN ACADEMY

1600 Mission Avenue
San Rafael, California 94901-1859

Head of School: Travis Brownley

General Information Coeducational day college-preparatory, arts, technology, and outdoor education program school. Grades 9–12. Founded: 1971. Setting: suburban. Nearest major city is San Francisco. 10-acre campus. 11 buildings on

campus. Approved or accredited by California Association of Independent Schools, The College Board, and Western Association of Schools and Colleges. Member of National Association of Independent Schools and Secondary School Admission Test Board. Total enrollment: 406. Upper school average class size: 15. Upper school faculty-student ratio: 1:9. There are 180 required school days per year for Upper School students. Upper School students typically attend 5 days per week. The average school day consists of 6 hours and 45 minutes.

Upper School Student Profile Grade 9: 103 students (49 boys, 54 girls); Grade 10: 105 students (53 boys, 52 girls); Grade 11: 100 students (47 boys, 53 girls); Grade 12: 96 students (46 boys, 50 girls).

Faculty School total: 55. In upper school: 23 men, 32 women; 36 have advanced degrees.

Subjects Offered 20th century history, 20th century world history, 3-dimensional art, acting, adolescent issues, African history, algebra, American culture, American foreign policy, American government, American history, American literature, American minority experience, American studies, ancient world history, art, Asian history, Asian literature, biology, British literature (honors), calculus, ceramics, chemistry, college counseling, community service, creative writing, dance, digital imaging, digital photography, English, English literature, environmental science, European history, fine arts, French, geology, geometry, government/civics, health, history, honors U.S. history, human development, Islamic history, Islamic studies, Japanese, journalism, Mandarin, mathematics, music, oceanography, photography, physical education, physics, pre-calculus, science, social studies, Spanish, theater, trigonometry, world cultures, world history-AP.

Graduation Requirements Arts and fine arts (art, music, dance, drama), English, foreign language, health and wellness, health education, mathematics, physical education (includes health), science, social studies (includes history), annual one-week experiential education course. Community service is required.

Special Academic Programs 13 Advanced Placement exams for which test preparation is offered; honors section; independent study; term-away projects; study at local college for college credit; study abroad; academic accommodation for the gifted, the musically talented, and the artistically talented.

College Admission Counseling 102 students graduated in 2013; 100 went to college, including Middlebury College; Stanford University; Tufts University; University of Southern California; Washington University in St. Louis; Wesleyan University. Other: 2 had other specific plans. Median SAT critical reading: 670, median SAT math: 645, median SAT writing: 675, median combined SAT: 2000, median composite ACT: 28.

Student Life Upper grades have student council, honor system. Discipline rests primarily with faculty.

Summer Programs Art/fine arts programs offered; held on campus; accepts boys and girls; open to students from other schools. 40 students usually enrolled. 2014 schedule: June 15 to July 15. Application deadline: February 1.

Tuition and Aid Day student tuition: $37,430. Tuition installment plan (Tuition Management Systems (TMS)). Need-based scholarship grants available. In 2013–14, 21% of upper-school students received aid. Total amount of financial aid awarded in 2013–14: $2,500,000.

Admissions Traditional secondary-level entrance grade is 9. For fall 2013, 430 students applied for upper-level admission, 170 were accepted, 107 enrolled. SSAT required. Deadline for receipt of application materials: January 16. Application fee required: $100. On-campus interview required.

Athletics Interscholastic: aquatics (boys, girls), backpacking (b,g), baseball (b), basketball (b,g), bicycling (b,g), climbing (b,g), combined training (b,g), cross-country running (b,g), fencing (b,g), golf (b,g), independent competitive sports (b,g), lacrosse (b), mountain biking (b,g), soccer (b,g), swimming and diving (b,g), tennis (b,g), track and field (b,g), volleyball (g), water polo (b,g), wilderness (b,g); coed interscholastic: dance, golf; coed intramural: bicycling, climbing, fitness, flag football, Frisbee, hiking/backpacking, kayaking, martial arts, Nautilus, outdoor adventure, outdoor education, outdoor skills, physical fitness, rock climbing, scuba diving, ultimate Frisbee. 28 coaches, 1 athletic trainer.

Computers Computers are regularly used in art, English, foreign language, history, library skills, mathematics, music, photography, science, yearbook classes. Computer network features include on-campus library services, online commercial services, Internet access, wireless campus network, multimedia hardware and production applications. Student e-mail accounts and computer access in designated common areas are available to students.

Contact Dan Babior, Director of Admissions and Financial Aid. 415-453-4550 Ext. 216. Fax: 415-453-8905. E-mail: dbabior@ma.org. Website: www.ma.org

MARINE MILITARY ACADEMY

320 Iwo Jima Boulevard
Harlingen, Texas 78550

Head of School: Col. R Glenn Hill, USMC-Retd.

General Information Boys' boarding college-preparatory, general academic, and military school; primarily serves underachievers. Grades 8–PG. Founded: 1965. Setting: small town. Students are housed in single-sex dormitories. 142-acre campus. 43 buildings on campus. Approved or accredited by Military High School and College Association, Southern Association of Colleges and Schools, Southern Association of

Independent Schools, and Texas Department of Education. Endowment: $18 million. Total enrollment: 250. Upper school average class size: 13. Upper school faculty-student ratio: 1:13.

Upper School Student Profile Grade 8: 17 students (17 boys); Grade 9: 42 students (42 boys); Grade 10: 65 students (65 boys); Grade 11: 57 students (57 boys); Grade 12: 67 students (67 boys); Postgraduate: 3 students (3 boys). 100% of students are boarding students. 37% are state residents. 27 states are represented in upper school student body. 30% are international students. International students from China, Germany, Mexico, Panama, Russian Federation, and United Arab Emirates; 5 other countries represented in student body.

Faculty School total: 34. In upper school: 17 men, 17 women; 16 have advanced degrees; 24 reside on campus.

Subjects Offered Aerospace science, algebra, American history, band, biology, calculus, calculus-AP, chemistry, computer programming, computer science, economics, English, environmental science, geography, geometry, government/civics, history, journalism, JROTC, keyboarding, marine science, mathematics, military science, physics, physics-AP, political science, SAT preparation, science, social sciences, social studies, Spanish, Spanish-AP, speech, world history.

Graduation Requirements Business skills (includes word processing), computer science, English, foreign language, mathematics, military science, physical education (includes health), science, social sciences, social studies (includes history).

Special Academic Programs Advanced Placement exam preparation; honors section; study at local college for college credit; academic accommodation for the gifted; remedial reading and/or remedial writing; remedial math; ESL (60 students enrolled).

College Admission Counseling 54 students graduated in 2012; 53 went to college, including Texas A&M University; Texas Tech University; The Citadel, The Military College of South Carolina; United States Military Academy; United States Naval Academy; Virginia Military Institute. Other: 1 entered military service. 11.7% scored over 600 on SAT critical reading, 14% scored over 600 on SAT math.

Student Life Upper grades have uniform requirement, student council, honor system. Discipline rests equally with students and faculty. Attendance at religious services is required.

Tuition and Aid 7-day tuition and room/board: $33,000. Tuition installment plan (FACTS Tuition Payment Plan, monthly payment plans, individually arranged payment plans, Chief Financial Officer authorization required). Tuition reduction for siblings, merit scholarship grants, need-based scholarship grants, (Parent) Active Duty Military Discount, referral reward discount available. In 2012–13, 12% of upper-school students received aid. Total amount of financial aid awarded in 2012–13: $300,000.

Admissions For fall 2012, 195 students applied for upper-level admission, 172 were accepted, 142 enrolled. Deadline for receipt of application materials: none. Application fee required: $100.

Athletics Interscholastic: baseball, basketball, bicycling, boxing, cross-country running, diving, drill team, football, golf, JROTC drill, marksmanship, physical fitness, riflery, running, soccer, swimming and diving, tennis, track and field, winter soccer; intramural: baseball, basketball, boxing, climbing, fitness, flag football, football, judo, kickball, martial arts, outdoor activities, outdoor adventure, paint ball, physical fitness, physical training, power lifting, racquetball, rappelling, rock climbing, running, sailing, scuba diving, soccer, softball, swimming and diving, track and field, volleyball, wall climbing, weight lifting, weight training. 15 coaches, 1 athletic trainer.

Computers Computers are regularly used in English, foreign language, mathematics, science, yearbook classes. Computer network features include on-campus library services, online commercial services, Internet access, Internet filtering or blocking technology. Student e-mail accounts and computer access in designated common areas are available to students. Students grades are available online.

Contact Mrs. Jay Perez, Assistant Admissions Director. 956-423-6006 Ext. 251. Fax: 956-421-9273. E-mail: admissions@mma-tx.org. Website: www.mma-tx.org

See Display below and Close-Up on page 550.

MARION ACADEMY

1820 Prier Drive
Marion, Alabama 36756

Head of School: Mr. G. Travis Vaughn

General Information Coeducational day college-preparatory, general academic, arts, religious studies, bilingual studies, and technology school, affiliated with Christian faith. Grades K–12. Founded: 1987. Setting: small town. Nearest major city is Tuscaloosa. 5-acre campus. 1 building on campus. Approved or accredited by Southern Association of Colleges and Schools and Alabama Department of Education. Total enrollment: 96. Upper school average class size: 8. Upper school faculty-student ratio: 1:8. There are 180 required school days per year for Upper School students. Upper School students typically attend 5 days per week. The average school day consists of 6 hours and 30 minutes.

Upper School Student Profile Grade 7: 7 students (3 boys, 4 girls); Grade 8: 9 students (6 boys, 3 girls); Grade 9: 8 students (6 boys, 2 girls); Grade 10: 8 students (2 boys, 6 girls); Grade 11: 9 students (3 boys, 6 girls); Grade 12: 9 students (4 boys, 5 girls). 98% of students are Christian.

Faculty School total: 19. In upper school: 5 men, 5 women; 2 have advanced degrees.

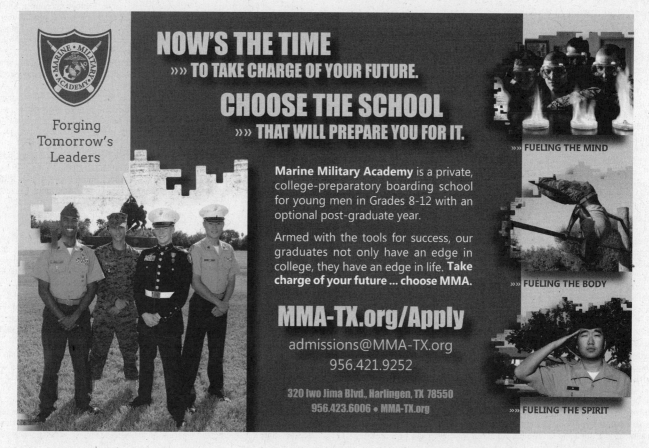

Subjects Offered 20th century history, 20th century world history, advanced computer applications, advanced math, Alabama history and geography, algebra, American government, anatomy and physiology, art, athletics, basic language skills, Bible studies, biology, cheerleading, college planning, creative writing, drama, earth science, economics, English language and composition-AP, English language-AP, English literature, English literature and composition-AP, foreign language, general math, geography, government, grammar, health education, history, honors algebra, honors English, human anatomy, Internet, language, language and composition, language arts, library, math applications, math methods, math review, mathematics, mathematics-AP, physical education, SAT/ACT preparation, speech, U.S. government, U.S. history.

Student Life Upper grades have specified standards of dress, student council, honor system. Discipline rests primarily with faculty.

Tuition and Aid Guaranteed tuition plan.

Admissions Traditional secondary-level entrance grade is 9. Deadline for receipt of application materials: none. Application fee required. Interview required.

Athletics Interscholastic: baseball (boys), basketball (b,g), cheering (g), cross-country running (b,g), football (b), softball (g), track and field (b,g), volleyball (g); coed interscholastic: track and field. 1 PE instructor, 2 coaches.

Computers Computers are regularly used in career education, library skills classes. Computer network features include Internet access. Student e-mail accounts are available to students.

Contact Mrs. Margaret S. Hallmon, Secretary. 334-683-8204. Fax: 334-683-4938. E-mail: marionacademy@hotmail.com. Website: www.marionacademy.org

MARIST SCHOOL

3790 Ashford-Dunwoody Road NE
Atlanta, Georgia 30319-1899

Head of School: Rev. Joel M. Konzen, SM

General Information Coeducational day college-preparatory, arts, business, religious studies, and technology school, affiliated with Roman Catholic Church. Grades 7–12. Founded: 1901. Setting: suburban. 77-acre campus. 18 buildings on campus. Approved or accredited by Southern Association of Colleges and Schools, Southern Association of Independent Schools, and Georgia Department of Education. Member of National Association of Independent Schools and Secondary School Admission Test Board. Endowment: $17.6 million. Total enrollment: 1,085. Upper school average class size: 18. Upper school faculty-student ratio: 1:12. There are 174 required school days per year for Upper School students. Upper School students typically attend 5 days per week. The average school day consists of 5 hours and 30 minutes.

Upper School Student Profile Grade 7: 145 students (76 boys, 69 girls); Grade 8: 150 students (74 boys, 76 girls); Grade 9: 206 students (98 boys, 108 girls); Grade 10: 190 students (98 boys, 92 girls); Grade 11: 194 students (97 boys, 97 girls); Grade 12: 200 students (94 boys, 106 girls). 74% of students are Roman Catholic.

Faculty School total: 100. In upper school: 52 men, 48 women; 78 have advanced degrees.

Subjects Offered Algebra, American history, American literature, ancient history, art, art history, biology, business skills, calculus, ceramics, chemistry, community service, computer programming, computer science, creative writing, dance, drama, driver education, economics, English, English literature, European history, fine arts, French, general science, geography, geology, geometry, German, government/civics, health, history, humanities, journalism, Latin, mathematics, music, peace and justice, philosophy, photography, physical education, physics, religion, science, social studies, Spanish, speech, statistics, studio art, theater, theology, world history, world literature, world religions, writing.

Graduation Requirements Arts and fine arts (art, music, dance, drama), business skills (includes word processing), computer science, English, foreign language, mathematics, physical education (includes health), religion (includes Bible studies and theology), science, social studies (includes history), community service requirements in all grades. Community service is required.

Special Academic Programs 21 Advanced Placement exams for which test preparation is offered; honors section; independent study.

College Admission Counseling 192 students graduated in 2013; 191 went to college, including Auburn University; Georgia Institute of Technology; The University of Alabama; University of Georgia; University of Mississippi; University of South Carolina. Other: 1 had other specific plans. 55% scored over 600 on SAT critical reading, 59% scored over 600 on SAT math, 54% scored over 600 on SAT writing, 60% scored over 1800 on combined SAT, 60% scored over 26 on composite ACT.

Student Life Upper grades have uniform requirement, student council, honor system. Discipline rests primarily with faculty. Attendance at religious services is required.

Summer Programs Enrichment, sports, art/fine arts programs offered; held on campus; accepts boys and girls; open to students from other schools.

Tuition and Aid Day student tuition: $16,725. Tuition installment plan (individually arranged payment plans, Tuition Management System). Need-based scholarship grants available. In 2013–14, 17% of upper-school students received aid. Total amount of financial aid awarded in 2013–14: $2,000,000.

Admissions Traditional secondary-level entrance grade is 9. For fall 2013, 270 students applied for upper-level admission, 107 were accepted, 64 enrolled. SSAT

required. Deadline for receipt of application materials: January 24. Application fee required: $75. On-campus interview required.

Athletics Interscholastic: baseball (boys), basketball (b,g), cheering (g), cross-country running (b,g), diving (b,g), football (b), golf (b,g), lacrosse (b,g), soccer (b,g), softball (g), swimming and diving (b,g), tennis (b,g), track and field (b,g), volleyball (g), wrestling (b); coed interscholastic: drill team; coed intramural: ultimate Frisbee. 6 PE instructors.

Computers Computers are regularly used in accounting, business applications, computer applications, drawing and design, English, foreign language, mathematics, music, science classes. Computer network features include on-campus library services, online commercial services, Internet access, wireless campus network, Internet filtering or blocking technology, one-to-one computing program, dedicated technical support website, on-site technology training. Student e-mail accounts and computer access in designated common areas are available to students. Students grades are available online. The school has a published electronic and media policy.

Contact Mr. Jim Byrne, Director of Admissions. 770-936-2214. Fax: 770-457-8402. E-mail: admissions@marist.com. Website: www.marist.com

MARMION ACADEMY

1000 Butterfield Road
Aurora, Illinois 60502

Head of School: Dr. James Quaid

General Information Boys' day college-preparatory, business, religious studies, Junior ROTC, and LEAD (Leadership Education and Development) school, affiliated with Roman Catholic Church. Grades 9–12. Founded: 1933. Setting: suburban. Nearest major city is Chicago. 325-acre campus. 5 buildings on campus. Approved or accredited by National Catholic Education Association, North Central Association of Colleges and Schools, and Illinois Department of Education. Member of Secondary School Admission Test Board. Endowment: $9 million. Total enrollment: 523. Upper school average class size: 27. Upper school faculty-student ratio: 1:11. The average school day consists of 7 hours and 25 minutes.

Upper School Student Profile Grade 9: 109 students (109 boys); Grade 10: 132 students (132 boys); Grade 11: 134 students (134 boys); Grade 12: 148 students (148 boys). 88% of students are Roman Catholic.

Faculty School total: 56. In upper school: 40 men, 16 women; 31 have advanced degrees.

Subjects Offered 1 1/2 elective credits, algebra, American history, American literature, anatomy, art, astronomy, band, biology, biology-AP, botany, calculus, calculus-AP, chemistry, chemistry-AP, community service, computer science, computer-aided design, creative writing, driver education, ecology, economics, English, English literature, English-AP, fine arts, French, French language-AP, general science, geometry, government/civics, history, history-AP, Italian, JROTC, Latin, Latin-AP, leadership, leadership education training, mathematics, mathematics-AP, meteorology, music, music theory-AP, philosophy, physical education, physics, physics-AP, physiology, psychology, religion, science, social sciences, social studies, sociology, Spanish, Spanish language-AP, statistics, statistics-AP, theology, trigonometry, Western civilization, zoology.

Graduation Requirements Arts and fine arts (art, music, dance, drama), English, foreign language, JROTC, leadership education training, mathematics, music appreciation, physical education (includes health), religion (includes Bible studies and theology), science, social sciences, social studies (includes history). Community service is required.

Special Academic Programs Advanced Placement exam preparation; honors section; independent study; academic accommodation for the gifted.

College Admission Counseling 120 students graduated in 2012; all went to college, including Marquette University; Purdue University; Saint Louis University; University of Dayton; University of Illinois. Mean composite ACT: 26.

Student Life Upper grades have uniform requirement, student council. Discipline rests primarily with faculty. Attendance at religious services is required.

Tuition and Aid Day student tuition: $10,100. Tuition installment plan (SMART Tuition Payment Plan, Tuition Management Systems). Merit scholarship grants, need-based scholarship grants, paying campus jobs available. In 2012–13, 30% of upper-school students received aid; total upper-school merit-scholarship money awarded: $155,000. Total amount of financial aid awarded in 2012–13: $342,800.

Admissions Traditional secondary-level entrance grade is 9. For fall 2012, 248 students applied for upper-level admission, 205 were accepted, 148 enrolled. High School Placement Test (closed version) from Scholastic Testing Service required. Deadline for receipt of application materials: none. Application fee required: $50. On-campus interview required.

Athletics Interscholastic: baseball, basketball, cross-country running, diving, football, golf, lacrosse, riflery, soccer, swimming and diving, tennis, track and field, wrestling; intramural: baseball, basketball, fencing, floor hockey, football, JROTC drill, outdoor activities, outdoors, soccer, swimming and diving, table tennis, tennis, volleyball, water polo, weight lifting. 2 PE instructors, 6 coaches, 1 athletic trainer.

Computers Computers are regularly used in design, science classes. Computer network features include on-campus library services, Internet access, wireless campus network, Internet filtering or blocking technology. Computer access in designated common areas is available to students. Students grades are available online. The school has a published electronic and media policy.

Contact William J. Dickson Jr., Director of Admissions. 630-897-6936. Fax: 630-897-7086. Website: www.marmion.org

MARSHALL SCHOOL

1215 Rice Lake Road

Duluth, Minnesota 55811

Head of School: Kevin Breen

General Information Coeducational day college-preparatory, arts, religious studies, and technology school. Grades 4–12. Founded: 1904. Setting: suburban. Nearest major city is Minneapolis. 40-acre campus. 1 building on campus. Approved or accredited by Independent Schools Association of the Central States. Member of National Association of Independent Schools. Endowment: $3.2 million. Total enrollment: 451. Upper school average class size: 18. Upper school faculty-student ratio: 1:11.

Faculty School total: 51. In upper school: 18 men, 13 women; 12 have advanced degrees.

Subjects Offered Algebra, American history, American literature, anatomy, art, biology, botany, calculus, calculus-AP, chemistry, community service, computer science, computer science-AP, creative writing, drama, earth science, English, English literature, English literature-AP, environmental science, European history, expository writing, fine arts; French, French-AP, geography, geometry, German, government/civics, health, history, law, mathematics, music, outdoor education, physical education, physics, poetry, religion, science, social studies, Spanish, Spanish-AP, speech, theater, theology, trigonometry, world history, world literature, writing.

Graduation Requirements Arts and fine arts (art, music, dance, drama), computer science, English, foreign language, mathematics, outdoor education, physical education (includes health), religion (includes Bible studies and theology), science, social studies (includes history). Community service is required.

Special Academic Programs 10 Advanced Placement exams for which test preparation is offered; honors section; independent study; study abroad; academic accommodation for the gifted; remedial reading and/or remedial writing; remedial math; programs in English, mathematics, general development for dyslexic students; special instructional classes for deaf students.

College Admission Counseling 87 students graduated in 2013; 85 went to college, including Saint John's University; University of Minnesota, Duluth; University of Minnesota, Twin Cities Campus; University of Wisconsin–Madison. Other: 2 had other specific plans: Median SAT critical reading: 630, median SAT math: 621, median composite ACT: 26.

Student Life Upper grades have student council, honor system. Discipline rests equally with students and faculty.

Summer Programs Remediation, enrichment, sports, art/fine arts, computer instruction programs offered; session focuses on enrichment and study skills; held both on and off campus; held at local parks; accepts boys and girls; open to students from other schools. 300 students usually enrolled. 2014 schedule: June 15 to August 18. Application deadline: none.

Tuition and Aid Day student tuition: $15,300. Tuition installment plan (Insured Tuition Payment Plan, Key Tuition Payment Plan, monthly payment plans). Need-based scholarship grants, paying campus jobs, AchieverLoans (Key Education Resources) available. In 2013–14, 39% of upper-school students received aid. Total amount of financial aid awarded in 2013–14: $1,400,000.

Admissions Traditional secondary-level entrance grade is 9. CTP or ERB required. Deadline for receipt of application materials: none. Application fee required: $75. On-campus interview required.

Athletics Interscholastic: baseball (boys), basketball (b,g), cheering (b,g), cross-country running (b,g), danceline (b,g), football (b), golf (b,g), ice hockey (b,g), nordic skiing (b,g), skiing (cross-country) (b,g), skiing (downhill) (b,g), soccer (b,g), softball (g), tennis (b,g), track and field (b,g), volleyball (g); coed interscholastic: alpine skiing, football; coed intramural: outdoor education. 4 PE instructors, 43 coaches, 1 athletic trainer.

Computers Computers are regularly used in English, foreign language, history, mathematics, science classes. Computer network features include on-campus library services, online commercial services, Internet access, wireless campus network, Internet filtering or blocking technology. Campus intranet and computer access in designated common areas are available to students. Students grades are available online. The school has a published electronic and media policy.

Contact Joe Wicklund, Director of Enrollment. 218-727-7266 Ext. 111. Fax: 218-727-1569. E-mail: joe.wicklund@marshallschool.org. Website: www.marshallschool.org

MARS HILL BIBLE SCHOOL

698 Cox Creek Parkway

Florence, Alabama 35630

Head of School: Mr. Dexter Rutherford

General Information Coeducational day college-preparatory, arts, and religious studies school, affiliated with Church of Christ. Grades K–12. Founded: 1947. Setting: suburban. Nearest major city is Huntsville. 80-acre campus.. 7 buildings on campus. Approved or accredited by National Christian School Association and Southern Association of Colleges and Schools. Endowment: $2.7 million. Total enrollment: 540. Upper school average class size: 22. Upper school faculty-student ratio: 1:14. There are 180 required school days per year for Upper School students. Upper School students typically attend 5 days per week. The average school day consists of 7 hours.

Upper School Student Profile Grade 9: 44 students (17 boys, 27 girls); Grade 10: 39 students (17 boys, 22 girls); Grade 11: 50 students (18 boys, 32 girls); Grade 12: 65 students (26 boys, 39 girls). 82% of students are members of Church of Christ.

Faculty School total: 42. In upper school: 11 men, 12 women; 14 have advanced degrees.

Subjects Offered ACT preparation, algebra, American government, American literature, American literature-AP, anatomy and physiology, ancient world history, band, Bible studies, biology, biology-AP, calculus, calculus-AP, chemistry, chorus, computer literacy, computer programming, computer science, concert band, concert choir, debate, drama, drama performance, driver education, ecology, economics, English, English composition, English literature, English literature and composition-AP, English literature-AP, ensembles, forensics, geometry, health, honors English, human anatomy, Internet research, jazz band, Life of Christ, marine biology, musical productions, physical education, physical science, physics, pre-algebra, pre-calculus, psychology, Spanish, speech, speech and debate, student government, student publications, U.S. history, U.S. history-AP, word processing, world geography, world history, yearbook.

Graduation Requirements Algebra, American government, American history, American literature, ancient world history, art, Bible, biology, British literature, chemistry, college writing, computer applications, computer literacy, economics, English composition, foreign language, geometry, health and wellness, introduction to literature, mathematics, physical education (includes health), physical science, science, social studies (includes history), speech communications. Community service is required.

Special Academic Programs 3 Advanced Placement exams for which test preparation is offered; honors section; independent study; study at local college for college credit; special instructional classes for students with learning disabilities, Attention Deficit Disorder, and dyslexia.

College Admission Counseling 64 students graduated in 2013; all went to college, including Auburn University; Freed-Hardeman University; Harding University; The University of Alabama; The University of Alabama at Birmingham; University of North Alabama. Median composite ACT: 25. 43% scored over 26 on composite ACT.

Student Life Upper grades have specified standards of dress, student council. Discipline rests primarily with faculty. Attendance at religious services is required.

Summer Programs Enrichment, sports, art/fine arts programs offered; session focuses on athletics, driver education, forensics, show choir, band; held on campus; accepts boys and girls; open to students from other schools. 180 students usually enrolled. 2014 schedule: June 1 to July 31. Application deadline: June 1.

Tuition and Aid Day student tuition: $6252. Tuition installment plan (FACTS Tuition Payment Plan, monthly payment plans). Tuition reduction for siblings, need-based scholarship grants available. In 2013–14, 20% of upper-school students received aid. Total amount of financial aid awarded in 2013–14: $150,000.

Admissions Traditional secondary-level entrance grade is 9. For fall 2013, 10 students applied for upper-level admission, 10 were accepted, 8 enrolled. Achievement tests, ACT-Explore, PSAT or Stanford Achievement Test required. Deadline for receipt of application materials: none. Application fee required: $100. Interview required.

Athletics Interscholastic: baseball (boys), basketball (b,g), cheering (g), cross-country running (b,g), football (b), golf (b,g), soccer (b,g), softball (g), tennis (b,g), track and field (b,g), volleyball (g); intramural: basketball (b,g). 3 PE instructors, 7 coaches.

Computers Computers are regularly used in all academic, Bible studies, English, history, remedial study skills, yearbook classes. Computer resources include on-campus library services, online commercial services, Internet access, wireless campus network, Internet filtering or blocking technology. Campus intranet and computer access in designated common areas are available to students. Students grades are available online. The school has a published electronic and media policy.

Contact Mrs. Jeannie Garrett, Director of Admissions. 256-767-1203 Ext. 2005. Fax: 256-767-6304. E-mail: jgarrett@mhbs.org. Website: www.mhbs.org

MARTIN LUTHER HIGH SCHOOL

60-02 Maspeth Avenue
Maspeth, New York 11378

Head of School: Mr. Randy Gast

General Information Coeducational day college-preparatory, arts, business, religious studies, and technology school, affiliated with Lutheran Church. Grades 6–12. Founded: 1960. Setting: urban. Nearest major city is New York. 1-acre campus. 1 building on campus. Approved or accredited by Middle States Association of Colleges and Schools and New York Department of Education. Total enrollment: 212. Upper school average class size: 22. Upper school faculty-student ratio: 1:12.

Upper School Student Profile Grade 9: 34 students (22 boys, 12 girls); Grade 10: 46 students (20 boys, 26 girls); Grade 11: 51 students (26 boys, 25 girls); Grade 12: 39 students (22 boys, 17 girls). 16% of students are Lutheran.

Faculty School total: 21. In upper school: 7 men, 11 women; 11 have advanced degrees.

Subjects Offered Algebra, American history, art, Bible studies, biology, business, business skills, calculus, calculus-AP, chemistry, chemistry-AP, computer programming, computer science, drama, driver education, earth science, economics, English, English literature, English literature-AP, environmental science-AP, ethics, European history, fine arts, French, geography, geometry, German, government/civics, grammar, health, history, journalism, marine biology, mathematics, music, philosophy, photography, physical education, physics, psychology, religion, science, social studies, Spanish, Spanish-AP, speech, theater, theology, trigonometry, U.S. history-AP, world history.

Graduation Requirements 1 1/2 elective credits, arts and fine arts (art, music, dance, drama), computer applications, English, foreign language, health, mathematics, physical education (includes health), religion (includes Bible studies and theology), science, social studies (includes history), service hours.

Special Academic Programs Advanced Placement exam preparation; honors section; independent study; study at local college for college credit; programs in general development for dyslexic students.

College Admission Counseling 53 students graduated in 2012; 51 went to college, including John Jay College of Criminal Justice of the City University of New York; Queens College of the City University of New York; St. Francis College; St. John's University; St. Joseph's College, New York. Other: 1 went to work, 1 entered military service. Mean SAT critical reading: 430, mean SAT math: 464.

Student Life Upper grades have uniform requirement, student council. Discipline rests primarily with faculty. Attendance at religious services is required.

Tuition and Aid Day student tuition: $8150. Tuition installment plan (monthly payment plans, Quarterly payment plan, one payment plan). Tuition reduction for siblings, merit scholarship grants, need-based scholarship grants available. In 2012–13, 50% of upper-school students received aid; total upper-school merit-scholarship money awarded: $40,800. Total amount of financial aid awarded in 2012–13: $1,955,670.

Admissions Traditional secondary-level entrance grade is 9. Iowa Test of Educational Development required. Deadline for receipt of application materials: none. Application fee required: $50. On-campus interview required.

Athletics Interscholastic: baseball (boys), basketball (b,g), cross-country running (b,g), fitness (b,g), soccer (b), softball (g), tennis (b,g), track and field (b,g), volleyball (g), wrestling (b,g); intramural: basketball (b,g), cross-country running (b,g), floor hockey (b,g), indoor hockey (b,g), soccer (b,g), weight lifting (b,g), wrestling (b); coed interscholastic: cross-country running, fitness, soccer; coed intramural: archery, badminton, cross-country running, fitness, handball, paddle tennis, racquetball, track and field, volleyball, wrestling. 2 PE instructors, 15 coaches.

Computers Computers are regularly used in business education, career education, Christian doctrine, computer applications, desktop publishing, history, keyboarding, newspaper, SAT preparation, Spanish, Web site design, yearbook classes. Computer resources include on-campus library services, Internet access. Student e-mail accounts are available to students. Students grades are available online.

Contact Ms. Patricia Dee, Admissions Administrator. 718-894-4000 Ext. 122. Fax: 718-894-1469. E-mail: pdee@martinluthernyc.org. Website: www.martinluthernyc.org

THE MARVELWOOD SCHOOL

476 Skiff Mountain Road
PO Box 3001
Kent, Connecticut 06757-3001

Head of School: Mr. Arthur Goodearl

General Information Coeducational boarding and day college-preparatory, arts, technology, field science, and community service, ESL school. Grades 9–12. Founded: 1957. Setting: rural. Nearest major city is Hartford. Students are housed in single-sex dormitories. 83-acre campus. 10 buildings on campus. Approved or accredited by New England Association of Schools and Colleges and Connecticut Department of Education. Member of National Association of Independent Schools and Secondary School Admission Test Board. Endowment: $1.6 million. Total enrollment: 165. Upper school average class size: 8. Upper school faculty-student ratio: 1:4. Upper School students typically attend 6 days per week. The average school day consists of 6 hours and 40 minutes.

Upper School Student Profile Grade 9: 20 students (12 boys, 8 girls); Grade 10: 40 students (25 boys, 15 girls); Grade 11: 55 students (37 boys, 18 girls); Grade 12: 37 students (21 boys, 16 girls). 94% of students are boarding students. 21% are state residents. 14 states are represented in upper school student body. 33% are international students. International students from China, Jamaica, Mexico, Republic of Korea, Spain, and United Kingdom; 7 other countries represented in student body.

Faculty School total: 48. In upper school: 19 men, 27 women; 24 have advanced degrees; 35 reside on campus.

Subjects Offered Algebra, American history, American literature, anatomy and physiology, art, art history, biology, calculus, ceramics, chemistry, chorus, college writing, community service, creative writing, drama, driver education, English, English literature, ESL, ethology, European history, film, fine arts, French, geography, geometry, history of China and Japan, Korean literature, limnology, mathematics, music, ornithology, photography, physics, pre-algebra, psychology, religion, SAT preparation, science, Shakespeare, social studies, Spanish, studio art, trigonometry, world cultures, world history, world literature.

Graduation Requirements Arts and fine arts (art, music, dance, drama), English, foreign language, mathematics, science, social studies (includes history), senior service project, daily participation in sports, weekly community service program.

Special Academic Programs Advanced Placement exam preparation; honors section; independent study; remedial reading and/or remedial writing; remedial math; programs in general development for dyslexic students; ESL (32 students enrolled).

College Admission Counseling 41 students graduated in 2012; all went to college, including Pace University; Suffolk University; Syracuse University; University of Hartford; Washington College. Median SAT critical reading: 458, median SAT math: 424, median SAT writing: 458.

Student Life Upper grades have specified standards of dress, student council, honor system. Discipline rests equally with students and faculty.

Tuition and Aid Day student tuition: $31,500; 7-day tuition and room/board: $48,200. Tuition installment plan (Insured Tuition Payment Plan, Academic Management Services Plan, SMART Tuition Payment Plan, individually arranged payment plans). Merit scholarship grants, need-based scholarship grants available. In 2012–13, 30% of upper-school students received aid; total upper-school merit-scholarship money awarded: $48,200. Total amount of financial aid awarded in 2012–13: $950,000.

Admissions Traditional secondary-level entrance grade is 9. For fall 2012, 257 students applied for upper-level admission, 168 were accepted, 58 enrolled. Deadline for receipt of application materials: none. Application fee required: $50. Interview required.

Athletics Interscholastic: baseball (boys), basketball (b,g), cross-country running (b,g), lacrosse (b), soccer (b,g), softball (g), tennis (b,g), volleyball (g), wrestling (b); intramural: lacrosse (g); coed interscholastic: alpine skiing, golf, outdoor activities, skiing (downhill); coed intramural: bicycling, canoeing/kayaking, climbing, dance, fishing, fly fishing, Frisbee, hiking/backpacking, horseback riding, kayaking, mountain biking, mountaineering, outdoor activities, physical training, rock climbing, ropes courses, skiing (downhill), snowboarding, strength & conditioning, weight training, wilderness, wildernessways, yoga. 1 coach, 1 athletic trainer.

Computers Computers are regularly used in computer applications, mathematics, newspaper, photography, science, writing classes. Computer network features include on-campus library services, Internet access, wireless campus network, Internet filtering or blocking technology. Campus intranet, student e-mail accounts, and computer access in designated common areas are available to students. The school has a published electronic and media policy.

Contact Mrs. Maureen Smith, Admissions Associate. 860-927-0047 Ext. 1005. Fax: 860-927-0021. E-mail: maureen.smith@marvelwood.org. Website: www.marvelwood.org

MARY INSTITUTE AND ST. LOUIS COUNTRY DAY SCHOOL (MICDS)

101 North Warson Road
St. Louis, Missouri 63124

Head of School: Lisa Lyle

General Information Coeducational day college-preparatory, arts, technology, Science, Engineer, and Math school. Grades JK–12. Founded: 1859. Setting: suburban. 100-acre campus. 9 buildings on campus. Approved or accredited by Independent Schools Association of the Central States and Missouri Department of Education. Member of National Association of Independent Schools and Secondary School Admission Test Board. Endowment: $91.1 million. Total enrollment: 1,247. Upper school average class size: 15. Upper school faculty-student ratio: 1:8. There are 170 required school days per year for Upper School students. Upper School students typically attend 5 days per week. The average school day consists of 7 hours and 15 minutes.

Upper School Student Profile Grade 9: 144 students (78 boys, 66 girls); Grade 10: 158 students (72 boys, 86 girls); Grade 11: 168 students (88 boys, 80 girls); Grade 12: 158 students (76 boys, 82 girls).

Faculty School total: 159. In upper school: 42 men, 34 women; 62 have advanced degrees.

Subjects Offered 20th century history, 20th century world history, 3-dimensional design, acting, algebra, analytic geometry, architecture, art history-AP, astronomy, astrophysics, audition methods, biology-AP, British literature, calculus, calculus-AP, ceramics, chamber groups, chemistry-AP, choir, Civil War, concert choir, constitutional law, creative writing, design, digital photography, discrete mathematics, drawing, economics, English, environmental science-AP, ethics, European history-AP, forensics, French, French-AP, German, German-AP, global issues, government-AP, health, Holocaust, independent study, integrated mathematics, internship, Italian, kinesiology, Latin, Latin-AP, linear algebra, macroeconomics-AP, Mandarin, marine biology, mathematical modeling, music theory-AP, neuroscience, painting, personal finance, personal growth, physics-AP, playwriting, programming, public speaking, robotics, sculpture, Shakespeare, short story, Spanish, Spanish-AP, stagecraft, statistics-AP, U.S. history, Web site design, world history, World War II.

Graduation Requirements Arts and fine arts (art, music, dance, drama), English, ethics, foreign language, health, mathematics, physical education (includes health), science, social studies (includes history). Community service is required.

Special Academic Programs Advanced Placement exam preparation; honors section; independent study; term-away projects; study abroad; academic accommodation for the gifted.

College Admission Counseling 147 students graduated in 2013; 146 went to college, including Purdue University; Southern Methodist University; The University of North Carolina at Chapel Hill; Tulane University; University of Miami; University of Missouri. Other: 1 entered military service. Median SAT critical reading: 630, median SAT math: 630, median SAT writing: 650, median combined SAT: 1895, median composite ACT: 29.

Student Life Upper grades have specified standards of dress, student council, honor system. Discipline rests equally with students and faculty.

Summer Programs Remediation, enrichment, advancement, sports, art/fine arts, rigorous outdoor training, computer instruction programs offered; session focuses on conditioning/training; held on campus; accepts boys and girls; open to students from other schools. 200 students usually enrolled. 2014 schedule: June 15 to July 24. Application deadline: January 14.

Tuition and Aid Day student tuition: $23,600. Tuition installment plan (FACTS Tuition Payment Plan, monthly plan through FACTS Management, Your Tuition Solution (Loan), credit card payment). Merit scholarship grants, need-based scholarship grants available. In 2013–14, 23% of upper-school students received aid; total upper-school merit-scholarship money awarded: $90,000. Total amount of financial aid awarded in 2013–14: $2,321,365.

Admissions Traditional secondary-level entrance grade is 9. For fall 2013, 120 students applied for upper-level admission, 53 were accepted, 43 enrolled. ISEE or SSAT required. Deadline for receipt of application materials: January 17. Application fee required: $40. Interview required.

Athletics Interscholastic: baseball (boys), cheering (g), crew (b,g), cross-country running (b,g), dance (b,g), diving (b,g), field hockey (g), football (b), golf (b,g), ice hockey (b), lacrosse (b,g), soccer (b,g), swimming and diving (b,g), tennis (b,g), track and field (b,g), volleyball (g), water polo (b), wrestling (b); intramural: fitness (b,g), independent competitive sports (b,g), jogging (b,g), modern dance (b,g), physical fitness (b,g), physical training (b,g), strength & conditioning (b,g), weight training (b,g); coed interscholastic: dance, water polo, wrestling; coed intramural: fitness, independent competitive sports, modern dance, physical fitness, physical training, strength & conditioning, ultimate Frisbee, weight training. 45 coaches.

Computers Computers are regularly used in art, English, foreign language, history, mathematics, music, science, vocational-technical courses classes. Computer network features include on-campus library services, online commercial services, Internet access, wireless campus network, Internet filtering or blocking technology, Intranet services and internet monitoring software. Student e-mail accounts and computer access in designated common areas are available to students. Students grades are available online. The school has a published electronic and media policy.

Contact Peggy B. Laramie, Director of Admission and Financial Aid. 314-995-7367. Fax: 314-872-3257. E-mail: plaramie@micds.org. Website: www.micds.org/home

THE MARY LOUIS ACADEMY

176-21 Wexford Terrace
Jamaica Estates, New York 11432-2926

Head of School: Sr. Kathleen M. McKinney CSJ, EdD

General Information Girls' day college-preparatory, arts, religious studies, and technology school, affiliated with Roman Catholic Church. Grades 9–12. Founded: 1936. Setting: suburban. Nearest major city is New York. 5-acre campus. 8 buildings on campus. Approved or accredited by Middle States Association of Colleges and Schools, National Catholic Education Association, New York Department of Education, New York State Board of Regents, and New York Department of Education. Total enrollment: 855. Upper school average class size: 25. Upper school faculty-student ratio: 1:13. There are 180 required school days per year for Upper School students. Upper School students typically attend 5 days per week. The average school day consists of 6 hours and 30 minutes.

Upper School Student Profile Grade 9: 191 students (191 girls); Grade 10: 208 students (208 girls); Grade 11: 207 students (207 girls); Grade 12: 249 students (249 girls). 74.5% of students are Roman Catholic.

Faculty School total: 75. In upper school: 16 men, 59 women; all have advanced degrees.

Subjects Offered 20th century American writers, 20th century history, 20th century physics, 20th century world history, 3-dimensional art, 3-dimensional design, advanced biology, advanced chemistry, advanced computer applications, advanced math, Advanced Placement courses, advanced studio art-AP, algebra, American Civil War, American culture, American democracy, American foreign policy, American government, American history, American history-AP, American literature, American literature-AP, anatomy, anatomy and physiology, ancient history, ancient world history, ancient/medieval philosophy, animation, anthropology, applied arts, applied music, art, art appreciation, art education, art history, art history-AP, art-AP, astronomy, athletics, Basic programming, Bible studies, biology, biology-AP, British history, British literature, business law, business skills, calculus, calculus-AP, career and personal planning, career exploration, career/college preparation, chemistry, chemistry-AP, Civil War, civil war history, college admission preparation, college planning, composition, computer animation, computer art, computer education, computer graphics, computer science, constitutional history of U.S., contemporary women writers, criminology, cultural geography, current events, current history, drawing, driver education, earth science, economics, engineering, English, English literature, ethics and responsibility, European history, European literature, family studies, female experience in America, fine arts, first aid, forensics, French, government/civics, health and wellness, health science, history, human development, Italian, Latin, law, leadership, leadership and service, literature, mathematics, microbiology, music, music theory, nutrition, painting, physical education, physics, political science, religion, robotics, SAT preparation, science, sculpture, social studies, Spanish, speech and debate, vocal music, women in society, women's health, world history, world literature.

Graduation Requirements Arts and fine arts (art, music, dance, drama), English, foreign language, mathematics, music, physical education (includes health), religion (includes Bible studies and theology), science, social studies (includes history), technology, community service project, Regents Diploma.

Special Academic Programs 17 Advanced Placement exams for which test preparation is offered; honors section; study at local college for college credit; academic accommodation for the gifted, the musically talented, and the artistically talented; programs in general development for dyslexic students.

College Admission Counseling 227 students graduated in 2013; all went to college, including Adelphi University; Binghamton University, State University of New York; Boston University; St. John's University; St. Joseph's College, New York; Syracuse University.

Student Life Upper grades have uniform requirement, student council. Discipline rests primarily with faculty. Attendance at religious services is required.

Summer Programs Remediation, enrichment, sports, art/fine arts programs offered; session focuses on Regents Competency Test preparation, Athletic Camps, Junior High student enrichment; held on campus; accepts girls; open to students from other schools. 100 students usually enrolled. 2014 schedule: July 1 to August 15. Application deadline: June 30.

Tuition and Aid Day student tuition: $7900. Tuition installment plan (monthly payment plans, quarterly payment plan, tuition in full (yearly)). Tuition reduction for siblings, merit scholarship grants, need-based scholarship grants available. In 2013–14, 26% of upper-school students received aid; total upper-school merit-scholarship money awarded: $411,326. Total amount of financial aid awarded in 2013–14: $528,811.

Admissions Traditional secondary-level entrance grade is 9. For fall 2013, 904 students applied for upper-level admission, 452 were accepted, 208 enrolled. Catholic High School Entrance Examination or school's own exam required. Deadline for receipt of application materials: February 1. Application fee required: $350. Interview recommended.

Athletics Interscholastic: aerobics, aerobics/dance, archery, badminton, basketball, billiards, bowling, cheering, cross-country running, dance, dance team, golf, gymnastics, indoor track, indoor track & field, lacrosse, running, self defense, soccer, softball, swimming and diving, tennis, track and field, volleyball, winter (indoor) track, yoga; intramural: basketball, billiards, fitness, self defense, soccer, yoga. 4 PE instructors, 32 coaches.

Computers Computers are regularly used in career exploration, college planning, English, foreign language, graphic design, history, library skills, literary magazine, mathematics, music, newspaper, science classes. Computer network features include on-campus library services, online commercial services, Internet access, wireless campus network, Internet filtering or blocking technology. Campus intranet and student e-mail accounts are available to students. Students grades are available online. The school has a published electronic and media policy.

Contact Sr. Lorraine O'Neill, CSJ, Administrative Secretary. 718-297-2120 Ext. 228. Fax: 718-739-0037. E-mail: loneill@tmla.org. Website: www.tmla.org

MARYMOUNT HIGH SCHOOL

10643 Sunset Boulevard
Los Angeles, California 90077

Head of School: Ms. Jacqueline Landry

General Information Girls' day college-preparatory, arts, religious studies, and technology school, affiliated with Roman Catholic Church. Grades 9–12. Founded: 1923. Setting: suburban. 5-acre campus. 6 buildings on campus. Approved or accredited by Western Association of Schools and Colleges, Western Catholic Education Association, and California Department of Education. Member of National Association of Independent Schools. Endowment: $5.7 million. Total enrollment: 374. Upper school average class size: 15. Upper school faculty-student ratio: 1:7. There are 170 required school days per year for Upper School students. Upper School students typically attend 5 days per week. The average school day consists of 6 hours and 15 minutes.

Upper School Student Profile Grade 9: 93 students (93 girls); Grade 10: 107 students (107 girls); Grade 11: 93 students (93 girls); Grade 12: 81 students (81 girls). 66% of students are Roman Catholic.

Faculty School total: 51. In upper school: 13 men, 38 women; 42 have advanced degrees.

Subjects Offered Acting, advanced studio art-AP, aerobics, African literature, algebra, American history, American legal systems, American literature, anatomy, art, art history, art-AP, biology, biology-AP, British literature, calculus, calculus-AP, ceramics, chemistry, choir, Christian testament, community service, computer literacy, computer science, contemporary issues, dance, death and loss, design, drama, drawing, ecology, economics, English, English literature, environmental science, environmental science-AP, ethics, fencing, film, fine arts, French, French-AP, gender and religion, geography, geometry, government/civics, Hebrew scripture, human development, Japanese literature, jazz ensemble, journalism, language and composition, literary magazine, literature, literature-AP, music, musical productions, oceanography, painting, peace studies, performing arts, photography, physical education, physics, physiology, pre-calculus, printmaking, psychology, religion, religious studies, robotics, science, self-defense, service learning/internship, social justice, social studies, softball, Spanish, Spanish language-AP, Spanish literature-AP, speech, swimming, theology, trigonometry, U.S. government and politics-AP, U.S. history, U.S. history-AP, vocal music, volleyball, women's studies, world religions, writing.

Graduation Requirements Arts and fine arts (art, music, dance, drama), English, foreign language, mathematics, performing arts, physical education (includes health), religion (includes Bible studies and theology), science, social studies (includes history).

Special Academic Programs 18 Advanced Placement exams for which test preparation is offered; honors section; independent study.

College Admission Counseling 92 students graduated in 2013; 91 went to college, including Boston College; Brown University; Santa Clara University; University of California, Berkeley; University of Colorado Boulder; Yale University. Other: 1 had other specific plans. Mean SAT critical reading: 629, mean SAT math: 620, mean SAT writing: 672, mean combined SAT: 1921, mean composite ACT: 27.

Student Life Upper grades have uniform requirement, student council, honor system. Discipline rests equally with students and faculty. Attendance at religious services is required.

Summer Programs Remediation, enrichment, advancement, sports, art/fine arts, computer instruction programs offered; session focuses on enrichment, advancement; held on campus; accepts girls; open to students from other schools. 100 students usually enrolled. 2014 schedule: June 23 to July 25. Application deadline: June 2.

Tuition and Aid Day student tuition: $28,900. Tuition installment plan (FACTS Tuition Payment Plan). Merit scholarship grants, need-based scholarship grants available. In 2013–14, 25% of upper-school students received aid; total upper-school merit-scholarship money awarded: $11,000. Total amount of financial aid awarded in 2013–14: $1,300,000.

Admissions Traditional secondary-level entrance grade is 9. For fall 2013, 173 students applied for upper-level admission, 156 were accepted, 93 enrolled. ISEE required. Deadline for receipt of application materials: January 13. Application fee required: $100. On-campus interview required.

Athletics Interscholastic: basketball, cross-country running, equestrian sports, golf, soccer, softball, swimming and diving, tennis, track and field, volleyball, water polo; intramural: aerobics, aerobics/dance, archery, crew, dance, fitness, physical fitness, self defense, strength & conditioning. 1 PE instructor, 31 coaches, 1 athletic trainer.

Computers Computers are regularly used in all academic classes. Computer network features include on-campus library services, online commercial services, Internet access, wireless campus network, Internet filtering or blocking technology, one-to-one student laptop program, access to UCLA Library, Loyola Marymount University Library, 14 independent high school libraries. Campus intranet, student e-mail accounts, and computer access in designated common areas are available to students. Students grades are available online. The school has a published electronic and media policy.

Contact Ms. Sarah Jallo, Director of Admission. 310-472-1205 Ext. 306. Fax: 310-440-4316. E-mail: sjallo@mhs-la.org. Website: www.mhs-la.org

MARYMOUNT INTERNATIONAL SCHOOL

Via di Villa Lauchli 180
Rome 00191, Italy

Head of School: Ms. Maria Castelluccio

General Information Coeducational day college-preparatory school, affiliated with Roman Catholic Church. Grades PK–12. Founded: 1946. Setting: suburban. 16-acre campus. 3 buildings on campus. Approved or accredited by New England Association of Schools and Colleges. Member of European Council of International Schools. Language of instruction: English. Total enrollment: 624. Upper school average class size: 18. Upper school faculty-student ratio: 1:15. There are 170 required school

days per year for Upper School students. Upper School students typically attend 5 days per week. The average school day consists of 6 hours and 45 minutes.

Upper School Student Profile Grade 9: 51 students (32 boys, 19 girls); Grade 10: 54 students (20 boys, 34 girls); Grade 11: 50 students (22 boys, 28 girls); Grade 12: 57 students (36 boys, 21 girls). 75% of students are Roman Catholic.

Faculty School total: 84. In upper school: 13 men, 34 women; 40 have advanced degrees.

Subjects Offered Algebra, American history, American literature, art, art history, art history-AP, biology, calculus, ceramics, chemistry, computer science, current events, drama, English, English literature, environmental science, ESL, European history, fine arts, French, geography, geometry, health, history, International Baccalaureate courses, international relations, Italian, Latin, mathematics, music, photography, physical education, physics, pre-calculus, psychology, religious education, science, social studies, Spanish, study skills, theater arts, theory of knowledge, trigonometry, world history.

Graduation Requirements Arts and fine arts (art, music, dance, drama), English, foreign language, mathematics, physical education (includes health), religion (includes Bible studies and theology), science, social studies (includes history).

Special Academic Programs International Baccalaureate program; ESL (30 students enrolled).

College Admission Counseling 51 students graduated in 2012; 49 went to college, including Boston University; New York University; Rensselaer Polytechnic Institute; The Johns Hopkins University; University of Southern California; University of Virginia. Other: 2 had other specific plans. Median SAT critical reading: 500, median SAT math: 500, median SAT writing: 520. 15% scored over 600 on SAT critical reading, 15% scored over 600 on SAT math, 15% scored over 600 on SAT writing.

Student Life Upper grades have specified standards of dress, student council, honor system. Discipline rests primarily with faculty. Attendance at religious services is required.

Tuition and Aid Day student tuition: €18,400.

Admissions Traditional secondary-level entrance grade is 9. For fall 2012, 52 students applied for upper-level admission, 38 were accepted, 24 enrolled. English proficiency or writing sample required. Deadline for receipt of application materials: none. Application fee required: €350. On-campus interview recommended.

Athletics Interscholastic: basketball (boys, girls), cheering (g), cross-country running (b,g), soccer (b,g); tennis (b,g), track and field (b,g), volleyball (b,g). 2 PE instructors, 9 coaches.

Computers Computers are regularly used in graphic arts classes. Computer network features include on-campus library services, Internet access, wireless campus network, Internet filtering or blocking technology, one to one laptop program in the middle school. Student e-mail accounts are available to students.

Contact Ms. Deborah Woods, Admissions Director. 39-063629101 Ext. 212. Fax: 39-0636301738. E-mail: admissions@marymountrome.org. Website: www.marymountrome.org

MARYMOUNT SCHOOL

1026 Fifth Avenue
New York, New York 10028

General Information Coeducational day (boys' only in lower grades) college-preparatory, arts, religious studies, and technology school, affiliated with Roman Catholic Church. Boys grades N–PK, girls grades N–12. Founded: 1926. Setting: urban. 3 buildings on campus. Approved or accredited by New York State Association of Independent Schools. Member of National Association of Independent Schools. Endowment: $800,000. Total enrollment: 608. Upper school average class size: 15. Upper school faculty-student ratio: 1:6. The average school day consists of 7 hours and 30 minutes.

See Display on next page and Close-Up on page 552.

THE MASTERS SCHOOL

49 Clinton Avenue
Dobbs Ferry, New York 10522

Head of School: Dr. Maureen Fonseca

General Information Coeducational boarding and day college-preparatory, arts, and technology school. Boarding grades 9–12, day grades 5–12. Founded: 1877. Setting: suburban. Nearest major city is New York. Students are housed in single-sex dormitories. 100-acre campus. 15 buildings on campus. Approved or accredited by Middle States Association of Colleges and Schools, The Association of Boarding Schools, and New York Department of Education. Member of National Association of Independent Schools and Secondary School Admission Test Board. Endowment: $30 million. Total enrollment: 650. Upper school average class size: 14. Upper school faculty-student ratio: 1:7. Upper School students typically attend 5 days per week. The average school day consists of 6 hours.

Upper School Student Profile Grade 9: 125 students (63 boys, 62 girls); Grade 10: 115 students (55 boys, 60 girls); Grade 11: 120 students (58 boys, 62 girls); Grade 12: 115 students (60 boys, 55 girls). 40% of students are boarding students. 50% are state residents. 20 states are represented in upper school student body. 18% are international students. International students from China, Germany, Republic of Korea,

Russian Federation, Switzerland, and Taiwan; 24 other countries represented in student body.

Faculty School total: 99. In upper school: 40 men, 50 women; 72 have advanced degrees; 60 reside on campus.

Subjects Offered Acting, algebra, American history, American literature, art history, biology, biology-AP, calculus, calculus-AP, ceramics, chemistry, chemistry-AP, computer math, computer programming, computer science, creative writing, dance, drama, driver education, earth science, electronics, English, English language-AP, English literature, English literature-AP, environmental science, ESL, ethics, European history, European history-AP, expository writing, fine arts, French, French language-AP, French literature-AP, geography, geometry, grammar, health, health and wellness, health education, jazz, jazz band, journalism, Latin, Latin-AP, mathematics, meteorology, music, music theory-AP, performing arts, photography, physical education, physics, physics-AP, pre-calculus, religion, science, senior thesis, social studies, Spanish, Spanish language-AP, Spanish literature-AP, speech, statistics, statistics-AP, studio art, studio art-AP, theater, trigonometry, U.S. history, U.S. history-AP, world history, world literature, world religions, writing, yearbook, yoga.

Graduation Requirements Arts and fine arts (art, music, dance, drama), computer science, English, foreign language, health, mathematics, physical education (includes health), public speaking, science, U.S. history, world history, world religions.

Special Academic Programs 19 Advanced Placement exams for which test preparation is offered; honors section; independent study; term-away projects; study at local college for college credit; study abroad; academic accommodation for the gifted, the musically talented, and the artistically talented; ESL (20 students enrolled).

College Admission Counseling 102 students graduated in 2013; all went to college, including Cornell University; Middlebury College; New York University; The Johns Hopkins University; University of Chicago; Williams College. Mean SAT critical reading: 660, mean SAT math: 640, mean SAT writing: 700, mean combined SAT: 2000. 61% scored over 600 on SAT critical reading, 57% scored over 600 on SAT math, 68% scored over 600 on SAT writing, 58% scored over 1800 on combined SAT.

Student Life Upper grades have specified standards of dress, student council, honor system. Discipline rests equally with students and faculty.

Tuition and Aid Day student tuition: $37,300; 7-day tuition and room/board: $52,430. Tuition installment plan (Insured Tuition Payment Plan, Key Tuition Payment Plan, monthly payment plans, individually arranged payment plans). Need-based scholarship grants available. In 2013–14, 25% of upper-school students received aid. Total amount of financial aid awarded in 2013–14: $5,000,000.

Admissions Traditional secondary-level entrance grade is 9. For fall 2013, 620 students applied for upper-level admission, 255 were accepted, 175 enrolled. ISEE, SSAT or TOEFL required. Deadline for receipt of application materials: February 1. Application fee required: $50. Interview required.

Athletics Interscholastic: baseball (boys), basketball (b,g), cross-country running (b,g), fencing (b,g), field hockey (g), lacrosse (b,g), soccer (b,g), softball (g), tennis (b,g), volleyball (g); coed interscholastic: dance, dance team, golf, indoor track, track and field; coed intramural: aerobics, aerobics/dance, aerobics/Nautilus, combined training, dance squad, dance team, fitness, Frisbee, martial arts, modern dance, outdoor activities, physical fitness, physical training, strength & conditioning, ultimate Frisbee, weight lifting, weight training, yoga. 2 PE instructors, 13 coaches, 1 athletic trainer.

Computers Computers are regularly used in computer applications, English, foreign language, graphic arts, graphic design, history, mathematics, newspaper, photography, programming, publications, science, senior seminar, study skills, video film production, Web site design, writing, yearbook classes. Computer network features include on-campus library services, online commercial services, Internet access, wireless campus network, Internet filtering or blocking technology. Student e-mail accounts and computer access in designated common areas are available to students. The school has a published electronic and media policy.

Contact Office of Admission. 914-479-6420. Fax: 914-693-7295. E-mail: admission@mastersny.org. Website: www.mastersny.org

MATIGNON HIGH SCHOOL

One Matignon Road
Cambridge, Massachusetts 02140

Head of School: Mr. Timothy M. Welsh

General Information Coeducational day college-preparatory, arts, business, religious studies, and technology school, affiliated with Roman Catholic Church. Grades 9–12. Founded: 1945. Setting: suburban. Nearest major city is Boston. 10-acre campus. 3 buildings on campus. Approved or accredited by Association of Independent Schools in New England, National Catholic Education Association, New England Association of Schools and Colleges, and Massachusetts Department of Education. Endowment: $253,000. Total enrollment: 458. Upper school average class size: 18. Upper school faculty-student ratio: 1:18. There are 180 required school days per year for Upper School students. Upper School students typically attend 5 days per week. The average school day consists of 7 hours.

Upper School Student Profile Grade 9: 105 students (43 boys, 62 girls); Grade 10: 127 students (50 boys, 77 girls); Grade 11: 108 students (43 boys, 65 girls); Grade 12: 118 students (48 boys, 70 girls). 75% of students are Roman Catholic.

Faculty School total: 34. In upper school: 12 men, 22 women; 23 have advanced degrees.

Subjects Offered 3-dimensional art, 3-dimensional design, accounting, adolescent issues, Advanced Placement courses, algebra, American history, American literature,

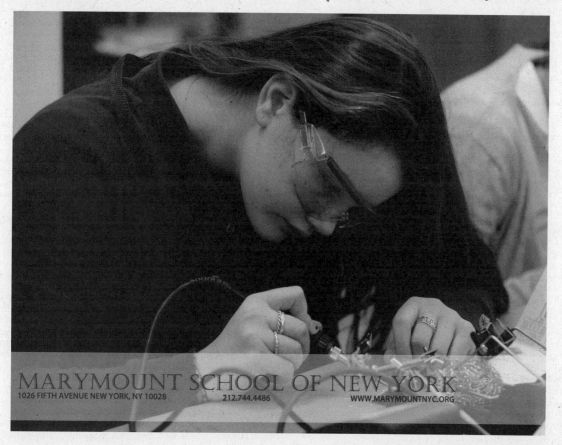

anatomy and physiology, art, art history, Bible studies, biology, calculus, chemistry, community service, computer science, drawing and design, economics, English, English literature, environmental science, fine arts, French, geometry, government/civics, grammar, health, history, Latin, law, mathematics, physical education, physics, psychology, religion, science, social sciences, social studies, Spanish, theology, trigonometry, world history, writing.

Graduation Requirements 20th century history, accounting, Advanced Placement courses, algebra, American history, anatomy and physiology, arts and fine arts (art, music, dance, drama), chemistry, computer science, English-AP, French, French-AP, geometry, health education, honors algebra, honors English, honors geometry, honors world history, Latin, law, physical education (includes health), psychology, religious studies, SAT preparation, senior internship, Spanish, Spanish-AP, U.S. history, U.S. history-AP, world cultures, world history, Christian service, 45 hours of community service (before junior year).

Special Academic Programs Advanced Placement exam preparation; honors section; independent study; study at local college for college credit; study abroad; ESL (25 students enrolled).

College Admission Counseling 114 students graduated in 2013; 110 went to college, including Boston University; Northeastern University; Stonehill College; Suffolk University; University of Massachusetts Amherst; University of Massachusetts Boston. Other: 2 went to work, 2 entered military service. Mean SAT critical reading: 500, mean SAT math: 559, mean SAT writing: 521, mean combined SAT: 1580. 21% scored over 600 on SAT critical reading, 23% scored over 600 on SAT math, 14% scored over 600 on SAT writing, 20% scored over 1800 on combined SAT.

Student Life Upper grades have uniform requirement, student council, honor system. Discipline rests primarily with faculty. Attendance at religious services is required.

Summer Programs Remediation, enrichment programs offered; session focuses on remediation/makeup and enrichment; held on campus; accepts boys and girls; open to students from other schools. 50 students usually enrolled. 2014 schedule: June 24 to July 19. Application deadline: none.

Tuition and Aid Day student tuition: $8900. Tuition installment plan (FACTS Tuition Payment Plan, monthly payment plans). Merit scholarship grants, need-based scholarship grants available. In 2013–14, 50% of upper-school students received aid; total upper-school merit-scholarship money awarded: $100,000. Total amount of financial aid awarded in 2013–14: $315,000.

Admissions Traditional secondary-level entrance grade is 9. For fall 2013, 410 students applied for upper-level admission, 362 were accepted, 108 enrolled. Catholic High School Entrance Examination, SSAT or TOEFL or SLEP required. Deadline for receipt of application materials: none. No application fee required. On-campus interview recommended.

Athletics Interscholastic: baseball (boys), basketball (b,g), cheering (g), cross-country running (b,g), football (b), ice hockey (b,g), lacrosse (b,g), soccer (b,g), softball (g), swimming and diving (b,g), tennis (b,g), track and field (b,g), volleyball (g); intramural: aerobics/dance (b,g), dance (b,g), dance squad (b,g), dance team (b,g), Frisbee (b,g), physical training (b,g), strength & conditioning (b,g), weight lifting (b,g), weight training (b,g); coed interscholastic: golf; coed intramural: table tennis, yoga. 1 PE instructor, 20 coaches, 1 athletic trainer.

Computers Computers are regularly used in all academic classes. Computer network features include on-campus library services, Internet access, wireless campus network, Internet filtering or blocking technology, all academic homework is provided online. Student e-mail accounts and computer access in designated common areas are available to students. Students grades are available online.

Contact Mr. Joseph A. DiSarcina, Principal. 617-876-1212 Ext. 14. Fax: 617-661-3905. E-mail: jdisarcina@matignon-hs.org. Website: www.matignon-hs.org

MAUI PREPARATORY ACADEMY

5095 Napilihau Street, #109B
PMB #186
Lahaina, Hawaii 96761

Head of School: Mr. George C. Baker

General Information Coeducational boarding and day and distance learning college-preparatory, arts, technology, and Project Based 21st Century Skills school. Grades PK–12. Distance learning grade X. Founded: 2005. Setting: small town. Students are housed in homestay. 20-acre campus. 7 buildings on campus. Approved or accredited by The Hawaii Council of Private Schools, Western Association of Schools and Colleges, and Hawaii Department of Education. Total enrollment: 200. Upper school average class size: 13. Upper school faculty-student ratio: 1:5. There are 178 required school days per year for Upper School students. Upper School students typically attend 5 days per week. The average school day consists of 5 hours and 45 minutes.

Upper School Student Profile Grade 9: 13 students (7 boys, 6 girls); Grade 10: 12 students (5 boys, 7 girls); Grade 11: 15 students (8 boys, 7 girls); Grade 12: 18 students (8 boys, 10 girls). 6% of students are boarding students. 4% are state residents. 2 states are represented in upper school student body. 2% are international students. International students from Canada and Japan.

Faculty School total: 21. In upper school: 8 men, 3 women; 9 have advanced degrees.

Subjects Offered Art, biology, calculus, chemistry, English, environmental science, foreign language, health, history, mathematics, physics, social studies, technology.

Graduation Requirements 1 1/2 elective credits, algebra, all academic, art, athletics, biology, chemistry, college planning, English, foreign language, geometry, science project, 25 hours of community service per year, two varsity teams per year.

Special Academic Programs Advanced Placement exam preparation; independent study; study at local college for college credit.

College Admission Counseling Colleges students went to include Chapman University; University of Miami; University of Oregon; University of San Diego; Utah State University. Mean SAT critical reading: 511, mean SAT math: 541, mean SAT writing: 525.

Student Life Upper grades have uniform requirement, student council, honor system. Discipline rests equally with students and faculty.

Tuition and Aid Day student tuition: $15,910; 7-day tuition and room/board: $27,000. Tuition installment plan (Insured Tuition Payment Plan, FACTS Tuition Payment Plan, monthly payment plans). Tuition reduction for siblings, merit scholarship grants, need-based scholarship grants available. In 2012–13, 40% of upper-school students received aid; total upper-school merit-scholarship money awarded: $123,697. Total amount of financial aid awarded in 2012–13: $465,785.

Admissions Traditional secondary-level entrance grade is 9. For fall 2012, 20 students applied for upper-level admission, 17 were accepted, 15 enrolled. CTP and ERB Mathematics required. Deadline for receipt of application materials: March 30. Application fee required: $100. Interview required.

Athletics Interscholastic: aquatics (boys, girls), canoeing/kayaking (b,g), cross-country running (b,g), golf (b), independent competitive sports (b,g), ocean paddling (b,g), surfing (b,g), swimming and diving (b,g), tennis (b,g), track and field (b,g), volleyball (g); intramural: basketball (b,g), surfing (b,g), windsurfing (b,g); coed interscholastic: ocean paddling; coed intramural: basketball, surfing, windsurfing. 1 PE instructor, 9 coaches.

Computers Computers are regularly used in all classes. Computer network features include on-campus library services, Internet access, wireless campus network. Campus intranet and student e-mail accounts are available to students. Students grades are available online. The school has a published electronic and media policy.

Contact Mrs. Cathi Minami, Admissions Coordinator. 808-665-9966. Fax: 808-665-1075. E-mail: cminami@mauiprep.org. Website: www.mauiprep.org

MAUR HILL-MOUNT ACADEMY

1000 Green Street
Atchison, Kansas 66002

Head of School: Mr. Phil Baniewicz

General Information Coeducational boarding and day college-preparatory, arts, religious studies, bilingual studies, and English as a Second language school, affiliated with Roman Catholic Church. Grades 9–12. Founded: 1863. Setting: small town. Nearest major city is Kansas City, MO. Students are housed in single-sex dormitories. 90-acre campus. 7 buildings on campus. Approved or accredited by National Catholic Education Association, North Central Association of Colleges and Schools, The Association of Boarding Schools, and Kansas Department of Education. Member of Secondary School Admission Test Board. Total enrollment: 195. Upper school average class size: 17. Upper school faculty-student ratio: 1:9. There are 182 required school days per year for Upper School students. Upper School students typically attend 5 days per week. The average school day consists of 6 hours and 30 minutes.

Upper School Student Profile Grade 9: 43 students (23 boys, 20 girls); Grade 10: 51 students (25 boys, 26 girls); Grade 11: 51 students (27 boys, 24 girls); Grade 12: 50 students (24 boys, 26 girls). 40% of students are boarding students. 50% are state residents. 14 states are represented in upper school student body. 30% are international students. International students from China, Mexico, Republic of Korea, Saudi Arabia, Spain, and Sweden; 9 other countries represented in student body. 65% of students are Roman Catholic.

Faculty School total: 21. In upper school: 13 men, 8 women; 11 have advanced degrees; 3 reside on campus.

Subjects Offered Algebra, American history, American literature, anatomy, art, Bible studies, biology, calculus, chemistry, computer science, drama, economics, English, English literature, ESL, fine arts, geography, geometry, government/civics, grammar, health, history, journalism, mathematics, music, photography, physical education, physics, physiology, psychology, religion, science, social sciences, social studies, sociology, Spanish, speech, theater, theology, trigonometry, typing, world history, world literature, writing.

Graduation Requirements Arts and fine arts (art, music, dance, drama), business skills (includes word processing), computer science, English, foreign language, mathematics, physical education (includes health), religion (includes Bible studies and theology), science, social sciences, social studies (includes history).

Special Academic Programs Advanced Placement exam preparation; honors section; study at local college for college credit; academic accommodation for the gifted; special instructional classes for students with Attention Deficit Disorder; ESL (15 students enrolled).

College Admission Counseling 45 students graduated in 2013; all went to college, including Benedictine College; Penn State University Park; Saint Louis University; The University of Kansas; The University of Texas at Austin.

Student Life Upper grades have uniform requirement, student council, honor system. Discipline rests primarily with faculty. Attendance at religious services is required.

Summer Programs ESL programs offered; session focuses on activities camp, ESL program; held on campus; accepts boys and girls; open to students from other schools. 17 students usually enrolled. 2014 schedule: July 5 to August 12. Application deadline: June 1.

Tuition and Aid 5-day tuition and room/board: $18,900; 7-day tuition and room/board: $20,500. Tuition installment plan (monthly payment plans, individually arranged payment plans, Sallie Mae). Tuition reduction for siblings, merit scholarship grants, need-based scholarship grants, need-based loans, paying campus jobs available. In 2013–14, 40% of upper-school students received aid. Total amount of financial aid awarded in 2013–14: $280,000.

Admissions Traditional secondary-level entrance grade is 10. For fall 2013, 138 students applied for upper-level admission, 95 were accepted, 74 enrolled. High School Placement Test required. Deadline for receipt of application materials: none. Application fee required: $50. Interview required.

Athletics Interscholastic: aquatics (girls), baseball (b), basketball (b,g), cheering (g), cross-country running (b,g), dance (g), dance squad (g), dance team (g), drill team (g), football (b), swimming and diving (b,g), tennis (b,g), track and field (b,g), volleyball (g); intramural: boxing (b), field hockey (b), fitness (b), flag football (b), floor hockey (b), football (b), running (b,g), skateboarding (b), skiing (downhill) (b,g), soccer (b,g), swimming and diving (b,g), touch football (b), track and field (b,g), weight lifting (b,g), weight training (b,g); coed interscholastic: bowling, golf, physical fitness, physical training, running, soccer, wrestling; coed intramural: baseball, basketball, Nautilus, physical fitness, physical training, roller blading, table tennis, tennis, volleyball, walking. 1 PE instructor, 10 coaches, 1 athletic trainer.

Computers Computer network features include on-campus library services, Internet access, wireless campus network, Internet filtering or blocking technology. Student e-mail accounts are available to students. Students grades are available online. The school has a published electronic and media policy.

Contact Mr. Deke Nolan, Admissions Director. 913-367-5482 Ext. 210. Fax: 913-367-5096. E-mail: admissions@mh-ma.com. Website: www.mh-ma.com

MCDONOGH SCHOOL

8600 McDonogh Road
Owings Mills, Maryland 21117-0380

Head of School: Charles W. Britton

General Information Coeducational boarding and day college-preparatory school. Boarding grades 9–12, day grades K–12. Founded: 1873. Setting: suburban. Nearest major city is Baltimore. Students are housed in single-sex dormitories. 800-acre campus. 46 buildings on campus. Approved or accredited by Association of Independent Maryland Schools. Member of National Association of Independent Schools. Endowment: $83 million. Total enrollment: 1,299. Upper school average class size: 15. Upper school faculty-student ratio: 1:9. There are 169 required school days per year for Upper School students. Upper School students typically attend 5 days per week. The average school day consists of 6 hours and 10 minutes.

Upper School Student Profile Grade 6: 104 students (54 boys, 50 girls); Grade 7: 107 students (58 boys, 49 girls); Grade 8: 114 students (61 boys, 53 girls); Grade 9: 149 students (82 boys, 67 girls); Grade 10: 147 students (76 boys, 71 girls); Grade 11: 146 students (79 boys, 67 girls); Grade 12: 143 students (76 boys, 67 girls). 5% of students are boarding students. 98% are state residents. 4 states are represented in upper school student body. 1% are international students.

Faculty School total: 177. In upper school: 37 men, 51 women; 60 have advanced degrees; 37 reside on campus.

Subjects Offered 20th century American writers, acting, Advanced Placement courses, African history, African literature, African-American studies, algebra, American history, American history-AP, American literature, American literature-AP, anatomy, art, art history, art-AP, Asian studies, band, biology, biology-AP, botany, calculus, calculus-AP, ceramics, chemistry, chemistry-AP, Chesapeake Bay studies, classical Greek literature, composition-AP, computer animation, computer graphics, computer music, computer programming, computer science, computer science-AP, concert band, concert choir, creative writing, dance, drama, drawing, ecology, economics, economics-AP, electives, engineering, English, English composition, English literature, English literature and composition-AP, English literature-AP, English-AP, English/composition-AP, environmental science, environmental science-AP, ethics, European history, film, film and literature, fine arts, fitness, foreign language, French, French language-AP, French literature-AP, French-AP, genetics, geology, geometry, German, German-AP, government and politics-AP, government-AP, government/civics, health and wellness, history, history-AP, honors algebra, honors English, honors geometry, honors U.S. history, honors world history, jazz band, jazz dance, journalism, language-AP, languages, Latin, Latin American literature, linguistics, literature and composition-AP, literature by women, marine biology, mathematics, Middle Eastern history, music, music theory, music theory-AP, oceanography, photography, physical education, physical fitness, physics, poetry, pre-calculus, psychology, religion, Russian history, science, senior project, set design, Shakespeare, short story, Spanish, Spanish language-AP, Spanish literature, Spanish literature-AP, Spanish-AP, speech, speech communications, statistics-AP, tap dance, theater, trigonometry, U.S. government and politics-AP, U.S. history, U.S. history-AP, video, visual arts, Web site design, woodworking, world history, world history-AP, world religions, world wide web design, writing workshop, yearbook.

Graduation Requirements Arts and fine arts (art, music, dance, drama), English, foreign language, mathematics, physical education (includes health), science, senior project, social studies (includes history). Community service is required.

Special Academic Programs Advanced Placement exam preparation; honors section; independent study; term-away projects.

College Admission Counseling 145 students graduated in 2013; all went to college. Mean SAT critical reading: 615, mean SAT math: 628, mean SAT writing: 606, mean combined SAT: 1850, mean composite ACT: 27.

Student Life Upper grades have uniform requirement, student council, honor system. Discipline rests primarily with faculty.

Summer Programs Enrichment, ESL, sports, art/fine arts, computer instruction programs offered; session focuses on recreation and sports camps; held both on and off campus; held at Gunpowder Falls State Park and Chesapeake Bay; accepts boys and girls; open to students from other schools. 1,700 students usually enrolled. 2014 schedule: June 17 to July 26. Application deadline: May 1.

Tuition and Aid Day student tuition: $26,100; 5-day tuition and room/board: $35,100. Tuition installment plan (Key Tuition Payment Plan, monthly payment plans, individually arranged payment plans). Need-based scholarship grants, need-based loans, middle-income loans available. In 2013–14, 28% of upper-school students received aid. Total amount of financial aid awarded in 2013–14: $3,247,700.

Admissions Traditional secondary-level entrance grade is 9. For fall 2013, 377 students applied for upper-level admission, 75 were accepted, 51 enrolled. ISEE required. Deadline for receipt of application materials: December 15. Application fee required: $55. On-campus interview required.

Athletics Interscholastic: aquatics (boys, girls), baseball (b), basketball (b,g), cross-country running (b,g), equestrian sports (b,g), field hockey (g), football (b), golf (b,g), indoor track & field (b,g), lacrosse (b,g), soccer (b,g), softball (g), swimming and diving (b,g), tennis (b,g), volleyball (g), water polo (b,g), winter (indoor) track (b,g), wrestling (b); coed interscholastic: cheering, equestrian sports, horseback riding, indoor track & field, squash, track and field; coed intramural: badminton, ballet, dance, fencing, fitness, squash, ultimate Frisbee. 14 PE instructors, 92 coaches, 2 athletic trainers.

Computers Computers are regularly used in all classes. Computer network features include on-campus library services, online commercial services, Internet access, wireless campus network, Internet filtering or blocking technology. Campus intranet, student e-mail accounts, and computer access in designated common areas are available to students. Students grades are available online. The school has a published electronic and media policy.

Contact Tim Fish, Director of Admissions. 410-581-4719. Fax: 410-998-3537. E-mail: tfish@mcdonogh.org. Website: www.mcdonogh.org

MCGILL-TOOLEN CATHOLIC HIGH SCHOOL

1501 Old Shell Road
Mobile, Alabama 36604-2291

Head of School: Mrs. Michelle T. Haas

General Information Coeducational day college-preparatory, arts, religious studies, and technology school, affiliated with Roman Catholic Church. Grades 9–12. Founded: 1896. Setting: urban. 18-acre campus. 5 buildings on campus. Approved or accredited by Southern Association of Colleges and Schools and Alabama Department of Education. Total enrollment: 1,170. Upper school average class size: 21. Upper school faculty-student ratio: 1:14. There are 180 required school days per year for Upper School students. Upper School students typically attend 5 days per week. The average school day consists of 6 hours and 40 minutes.

Upper School Student Profile Grade 9: 325 students (163 boys, 162 girls); Grade 10: 302 students (170 boys, 132 girls); Grade 11: 284 students (159 boys, 125 girls); Grade 12: 259 students (125 boys, 134 girls). 90.4% of students are Roman Catholic.

Faculty School total: 81. In upper school: 37 men, 43 women; 53 have advanced degrees.

Subjects Offered 3-dimensional art, 3-dimensional design, accounting, ACT preparation, advanced biology, advanced chemistry, advanced math, Advanced Placement courses, American government, American history, American history-AP, American literature, analytic geometry, anatomy and physiology, athletic training, band, baseball, basketball, Bible studies, biology, biology-AP, British literature, British literature (honors), calculus, calculus-AP, campus ministry, Catholic belief and practice, ceramics, cheerleading, chemistry, chemistry-AP, choir, choral music, chorus, church history, conceptual physics, concert choir, driver education, economics, English, English composition, English language and composition-AP, English-AP, French, geography, geometry, government, government and politics-AP, graphic design, health, health and wellness, history of the Catholic Church, honors algebra, honors English, honors geometry, honors U.S. history, honors world history, independent study, keyboarding, Latin, marine biology, modern European history-AP, modern world history, multimedia, music appreciation, painting, physical education, physical fitness, physics, physics-AP, pre-algebra, pre-calculus, psychology, reading, reading/study skills, softball, Spanish, Spanish language-AP, speech, studio art, studio art-AP, U.S. government, U.S. government and politics, U.S. government and politics-AP, U.S. history, U.S. history-AP, U.S. literature, video film production, vocal ensemble, volleyball, Web site design, weight fitness, weight training, world geography, world history, world history-AP, world literature, yearbook.

Graduation Requirements Electives, English, keyboarding, mathematics, physical education (includes health), religion (includes Bible studies and theology), science, social studies (includes history).

Special Academic Programs 14 Advanced Placement exams for which test preparation is offered; honors section; remedial reading and/or remedial writing; remedial math.

College Admission Counseling 294 students graduated in 2013; 279 went to college, including Auburn University; Louisiana State University and Agricultural and Mechanical College; Spring Hill College; The University of Alabama; University of South Alabama; University of Southern Mississippi. Other: 9 went to work, 6 entered military service. Median composite ACT: 24. 96% scored over 26 on composite ACT.

Student Life Upper grades have uniform requirement, student council. Discipline rests primarily with faculty. Attendance at religious services is required.

Summer Programs Remediation, enrichment programs offered; session focuses on math/reading/English transition to high school, remediation for religion courses; held on campus; accepts boys and girls; not open to students from other schools. 35 students usually enrolled. 2014 schedule: June 5 to June 27. Application deadline: May 29.

Tuition and Aid Day student tuition: $6500–$7800. Tuition installment plan (monthly payment plans, individually arranged payment plans). Tuition reduction for siblings, need-based scholarship grants available. In 2013–14, 26% of upper-school students received aid. Total amount of financial aid awarded in 2013–14: $958,000.

Admissions Traditional secondary-level entrance grade is 9. ACT-Explore required. Deadline for receipt of application materials: none. Application fee required: $100. On-campus interview recommended.

Athletics Interscholastic: baseball (boys), basketball (b,g), cheering (g), cross-country running (b,g), diving (b,g), football (b), golf (b,g), indoor track (g), soccer (b,g), softball (g), swimming and diving (b,g), tennis (b,g), track and field (b,g), volleyball (g). 4 PE instructors, 3 coaches, 1 athletic trainer.

Computers Computers are regularly used in current events, graphic design, keyboarding, reading, technology, video film production, Web site design, yearbook classes. Computer network features include on-campus library services, Internet access, wireless campus network, Internet filtering or blocking technology. Campus intranet, student e-mail accounts, and computer access in designated common areas are available to students. Students grades are available online. The school has a published electronic and media policy.

Contact Mr. Paul Knapstein, Director of Enrollment. 251-445-2934. Fax: 251-433-8356. E-mail: knapstp@mcgill-toolen.org. Website: www.mcgill-toolen.org/

MEADOWRIDGE SCHOOL

12224 240th Street
Maple Ridge, British Columbia V4R 1N1, Canada

Head of School: Mr. Hugh Burke

General Information Coeducational day college-preparatory, arts, technology, and International Baccalaureatte school. Grades JK–12. Founded: 1985. Setting: rural. Nearest major city is Vancouver, Canada. 27-acre campus. 1 building on campus. Approved or accredited by Canadian Association of Independent Schools, Council of International Schools, International Baccalaureate Organization, and British Columbia Department of Education. Language of instruction: English. Total enrollment: 540. Upper school average class size: 18. Upper school faculty-student ratio: 1:12. Upper School students typically attend 5 days per week. The average school day consists of 7 hours.

Faculty School total: 50. In upper school: 9 men, 15 women; 6 have advanced degrees.

Subjects Offered Accounting, art, biology, calculus, career and personal planning, chemistry, comparative civilizations, computer technologies, drama, English, English literature, fencing, French, geography, history, humanities, mathematics, photography, physical education, physics, science, Spanish, technology/design, theater, volleyball, weight training.

Graduation Requirements 3 provincially examinable courses, IB Diploma Programme.

Special Academic Programs International Baccalaureate program.

College Admission Counseling 36 students graduated in 2013; they went to McGill University; Queen's University at Kingston; Simon Fraser University; The University of British Columbia; University of Toronto; University of Victoria.

Student Life Upper grades have uniform requirement, student council, honor system. Discipline rests equally with students and faculty.

Tuition and Aid Day student tuition: CAN$17,000. Tuition installment plan (Insured Tuition Payment Plan, monthly payment plans). Tuition reduction for siblings, bursaries, merit scholarship grants available. Total upper-school merit-scholarship money awarded for 2013–14: CAN$22,000.

Admissions Traditional secondary-level entrance grade is 8. Admissions testing and writing sample required. Deadline for receipt of application materials: none. Application fee required: CAN$150. Interview required.

Athletics Interscholastic: aerobics/dance (boys, girls), badminton (b,g), basketball (b,g), physical fitness (b,g), rugby (b,g), soccer (b,g), volleyball (b,g); intramural:

aerobics/dance (b,g), basketball (b,g); coed interscholastic: aerobics/dance, cross-country running, flag football, outdoor activities, swimming and diving, track and field; coed intramural: aerobics/dance. 2 PE instructors.

Computers Computers are regularly used in art, English, history, humanities, industrial technology, library, library skills, mathematics, science, yearbook classes. Computer network features include on-campus library services, online commercial services, Internet access, wireless campus network, Internet filtering or blocking technology. Student e-mail accounts and computer access in designated common areas are available to students.

Contact Mrs. Tania Shepelska, Admissions. 604-467-4444. Fax: 604-467-4989. E-mail: tania.shepelska@meadowridge.bc.ca. Website: www.meadowridge.bc.ca

THE MEADOWS SCHOOL

8601 Scholar Lane
Las Vegas, Nevada 89128-7302

Head of School: Mr. Henry L. Chanin

General Information Coeducational day college-preparatory, arts, technology, and debate, foreign languages school. Grades PK–12. Founded: 1981. Setting: suburban. 42-acre campus. 11 buildings on campus. Approved or accredited by Northwest Accreditation Commission, Northwest Association of Independent Schools, Northwest Association of Schools and Colleges, and Nevada Department of Education. Member of National Association of Independent Schools and Secondary School Admission Test Board. Endowment: $14 million. Total enrollment: 895. Upper school average class size: 12. Upper school faculty-student ratio: 1:11. There are 181 required school days per year for Upper School students. Upper School students typically attend 5 days per week. The average school day consists of 7 hours.

Upper School Student Profile Grade 9: 75 students (29 boys, 46 girls); Grade 10: 63 students (27 boys, 36 girls); Grade 11: 66 students (29 boys, 37 girls); Grade 12: 69 students (27 boys, 42 girls).

Faculty School total: 87. In upper school: 18 men, 18 women; 25 have advanced degrees.

Subjects Offered 20th century American writers, 3-dimensional art, acting, advanced math, Advanced Placement courses, advanced studio art-AP, American literature, anatomy and physiology, anthropology, art, art history, art history-AP, athletics, band, banking, Basic programming, biology, biology-AP, British literature, British literature (honors), calculus, calculus-AP, ceramics, chemistry, chemistry-AP, choral music, chorus, composition, computer applications, computer graphics, computer literacy, computer programming, computer science, computer science-AP, concert choir, creative writing, dance, digital art, digital photography, drama, drama performance, drawing, drawing and design, economics, English, English composition, English language and composition-AP, English literature, English literature and composition-AP, European history, European history-AP, film studies, finance, fine arts, finite math, foreign language, forensics, French, French language-AP, genetics, geometry, government-AP, health, honors English, honors geometry, honors U.S. history, honors world history, human anatomy, instrumental music, integrated mathematics, international affairs, international relations, journalism, keyboarding, Latin, Latin-AP, literature and composition-AP, macro/microeconomics-AP, Mandarin, money management, music theater, music theory-AP, organic chemistry, painting, photography, physics, physics-AP, policy and value, pre-calculus, psychology-AP, Shakespeare, social justice, social sciences, Spanish, Spanish language-AP, Spanish literature, Spanish literature-AP, Spanish-AP, speech, speech and debate, speech and oral interpretations, sports medicine, statistics, statistics-AP, studio art, studio art-AP, technical theater, technology, theater production, trigonometry, U.S. government, U.S. government and politics-AP, U.S. history, U.S. history-AP, yearbook.

Graduation Requirements American literature, ancient world history, arts and fine arts (art, music, dance, drama), biology, English, English composition, English literature, European history, foreign language, geometry, mathematics, physical education (includes health), physics, pre-calculus, science, social studies (includes history), technical skills, U.S. government, U.S. history, seniors have a 24-hour per semester community service requirement, grades 9-11 have a 16-hour per semester community service requirement.

Special Academic Programs 24 Advanced Placement exams for which test preparation is offered; honors section; academic accommodation for the gifted, the musically talented, and the artistically talented.

College Admission Counseling 65 students graduated in 2013; all went to college, including Duke University; United States Military Academy; University of California, Los Angeles; University of California, San Diego; University of San Diego; University of Southern California. Median SAT critical reading: 660, median SAT math: 670, median SAT writing: 670, median combined SAT: 2000, median composite ACT: 30. 73% scored over 600 on SAT critical reading, 81% scored over 600 on SAT math, 84% scored over 600 on SAT writing, 84% scored over 1800 on combined SAT, 83% scored over 26 on composite ACT.

Student Life Upper grades have uniform requirement, student council, honor system. Discipline rests equally with students and faculty.

Summer Programs Enrichment, sports, art/fine arts programs offered; session focuses on enrichment; held on campus; accepts boys and girls; open to students from other schools. 50 students usually enrolled. 2014 schedule: June 9 to July 3. Application deadline: May 30.

Tuition and Aid Day student tuition: $21,660. Tuition installment plan (Insured Tuition Payment Plan, monthly payment plans, individually arranged payment plans, 2-payment plan, 70% by July 15 and 30% by February 15, 10 monthly payment plan using electronic withdrawal only). Need-based scholarship grants, need-based loans available. In 2013–14, 13% of upper-school students received aid. Total amount of financial aid awarded in 2013–14: $555,121.

Admissions Traditional secondary-level entrance grade is 9. ERB, ISEE, PSAT or SSAT required. Deadline for receipt of application materials: none. Application fee required: $100. On-campus interview required.

Athletics Interscholastic: baseball (boys), basketball (b,g), bowling (b,g), cheering (g), cross-country running (b,g), dance team (g), diving (b,g), football (b), softball (g), tennis (b,g), track and field (b,g), volleyball (g); coed interscholastic: golf, soccer. 1 PE instructor, 1 athletic trainer.

Computers Computers are regularly used in all academic, college planning, desktop publishing, English, foreign language, graphic design, history, independent study, introduction to technology, library, mathematics, music, news writing, photography, photojournalism, programming, publications, publishing, science, speech, technology, yearbook classes. Computer network features include on-campus library services, online commercial services, Internet access, wireless campus network, Internet filtering or blocking technology, SMART boards in all classrooms, 3 iPad carts, 8 Chromebooks carts, course syllabus and homework available online. Campus intranet, student e-mail accounts, and computer access in designated common areas are available to students. Students grades are available online. The school has a published electronic and media policy.

Contact 702-254-1610. Fax: 702-254-2452. Website: www.themeadowsschool.org

MEMORIAL HALL SCHOOL

5400 Mitchelldale, Ste,A-1
Houston, Texas 77092

Head of School: Rev. George C. Aurich

General Information Coeducational day college-preparatory, general academic, and bilingual studies school. Grades 6–12. Founded: 1966. Setting: urban. 1 building on campus. Approved or accredited by Southern Association of Colleges and Schools, Southern Association of Independent Schools, Texas Education Agency, and Texas Department of Education. Total enrollment: 75. Upper school average class size: 14. Upper school faculty-student ratio: 1:14. Upper School students typically attend 4 days per week. The average school day consists of 7 hours and 30 minutes.

Faculty School total: 11. In upper school: 4 men, 7 women; 3 have advanced degrees.

Subjects Offered Algebra, American history, art, biology, business mathematics, business skills, chemistry, computer science, economics, English, ESL, fine arts, geography, geometry, government/civics, health, history, journalism, mathematics, physical education, physics, psychology, science, social sciences, social studies, sociology, Spanish, trigonometry, world history.

Graduation Requirements Arts and crafts, arts and fine arts (art, music, dance, drama), business skills (includes word processing), computer science, English, foreign language, mathematics, physical education (includes health), science, social sciences, social studies (includes history), community service, foreign credit accepted upon completion.

Special Academic Programs Study at local college for college credit; remedial reading and/or remedial writing; remedial math; programs in English, mathematics, general development for dyslexic students; special instructional classes for students with learning disabilities, Attention Deficit Disorder, and dyslexia; ESL (60 students enrolled).

College Admission Counseling 24 students graduated in 2012; 22 went to college, including Baylor University; Sam Houston State University; St. Thomas University; Texas A&M University; The University of Texas at Austin; University of Houston. Other: 2 went to work.

Student Life Upper grades have uniform requirement, student council, honor system. Discipline rests equally with students and faculty.

Tuition and Aid Day student tuition: $12,200. Tuition installment plan (Insured Tuition Payment Plan, monthly payment plans, individually arranged payment plans). Tuition reduction for siblings available. In 2012–13, 5% of upper-school students received aid.

Admissions Traditional secondary-level entrance grade is 9. Stanford Achievement Test required. Deadline for receipt of application materials: none. Application fee required: $300. Interview required.

Athletics Interscholastic: aerobics (boys, girls), aerobics/dance (b,g), bowling (b,g), fitness (b,g), fitness walking (b,g), jump rope (b,g), yoga (b,g); intramural: cheering (g); coed interscholastic: bowling; coed intramural: dance, outdoor activities, physical fitness. 2 PE instructors.

Computers Computers are regularly used in all academic, basic skills, foreign language classes. Campus intranet is available to students.

Contact Ms. Kimberly Smith, Director. 713-688-5566. Fax: 713-956-9751. E-mail: memhallsch@aol.com. Website: www.memorialhall.org

MEMPHIS CATHOLIC HIGH SCHOOL AND MIDDLE SCHOOL

61 North Mclean Boulevard
Memphis, Tennessee 38104-2644

Head of School: Mr. Nicholas Green

General Information Coeducational day college-preparatory school, affiliated with Roman Catholic Church. Grades 7–12. Founded: 1954. Setting: urban. 4-acre campus. 1 building on campus. Approved or accredited by Southern Association of Colleges and Schools and Tennessee Department of Education. Upper school average class size: 20. Upper school faculty-student ratio: 1:15. There are 180 required school days per year for Upper School students. Upper School students typically attend 5 days per week. The average school day consists of 7 hours and 30 minutes.

Upper School Student Profile 30% of students are Roman Catholic.

Faculty School total: 15. In upper school: 7 men, 8 women; 12 have advanced degrees.

Student Life Upper grades have uniform requirement. Discipline rests equally with students and faculty. Attendance at religious services is required.

Admissions Traditional secondary-level entrance grade is 9. No application fee required.

Contact Mrs. Dell Russell, Admissions and Bookkeeper. 901-276-1221. Fax: 901-725-1447. E-mail: drussell@memphiscatholic.org. Website: www.memphiscatholic.org

MENAUL SCHOOL

301 Menaul Boulevard NE
Albuquerque, New Mexico 87107

Head of School: Mr. Lindsey R. Gilbert Jr.

General Information Coeducational boarding and day college-preparatory and college prep school, affiliated with Presbyterian Church. Boarding grades 9–12, day grades 6–12. Founded: 1896. Setting: urban. Students are housed in single-sex dormitories. 35-acre campus. 10 buildings on campus. Approved or accredited by Independent Schools Association of the Southwest, North Central Association of Colleges and Schools, The College Board, and New Mexico Department of Education. Endowment: $3.3 million. Total enrollment: 185. Upper school average class size: 12. Upper school faculty-student ratio: 1:9. There are 180 required school days per year for Upper School students. Upper School students typically attend 5 days per week. The average school day consists of 6 hours.

Upper School Student Profile 20% of students are boarding students. 80% are state residents. 3 states are represented in upper school student body. 20% are international students. International students from Belgium, China, Ukraine, and Viet Nam; 4 other countries represented in student body. 20% of students are Presbyterian.

Faculty School total: 25. In upper school: 13 men, 11 women; 16 have advanced degrees; 5 reside on campus.

Subjects Offered ACT preparation, Advanced Placement courses, algebra, American government, American history, American literature, art, arts and crafts, band, Bible studies, biology, calculus-AP, chemistry, clayworking, communications, computer graphics, computer programming, computer science, earth science, economics, English, English literature, English-AP, ethics, fine arts, geography, geometry, government/civics, history, Life of Christ, mathematics, music, Native American arts and crafts, physical education, physics, psychology, religion, science, social sciences, social studies, sociology, Spanish, theology, trigonometry, U.S. government and politics-AP, world history, world literature, writing, yearbook.

Graduation Requirements Arts and fine arts (art, music, dance, drama), communications, computer science, English, foreign language, mathematics, physical education (includes health), religion (includes Bible studies and theology), science, social sciences, social studies (includes history), 100 hours of community service.

Special Academic Programs Advanced Placement exam preparation; honors section; independent study; study at local college for college credit; academic accommodation for the gifted and the artistically talented; ESL (3 students enrolled).

College Admission Counseling 34 students graduated in 2012; all went to college, including New Mexico State University; University of New Mexico. 5% scored over 26 on composite ACT.

Student Life Upper grades have uniform requirement, student council, honor system. Discipline rests primarily with faculty. Attendance at religious services is required.

Tuition and Aid Day student tuition: $13,900; 5-day tuition and room/board: $29,000; 7-day tuition and room/board: $33,000. Tuition installment plan (FACTS Tuition Payment Plan). Need-based scholarship grants available. In 2012–13, 50% of upper-school students received aid. Total amount of financial aid awarded in 2012–13: $307,000.

Admissions Traditional secondary-level entrance grade is 9. Admissions testing, ERB, ISEE, SLEP for foreign students or SSAT required. Deadline for receipt of application materials: none. Application fee required: $35. Interview required.

Athletics Interscholastic: basketball (boys, girls), football (b), volleyball (g); intramural: lacrosse (b), soccer (b), touch football (b); coed interscholastic: golf, outdoor education, running, track and field; coed intramural: badminton, dance, modern dance. 2 PE instructors, 6 coaches, 1 athletic trainer.

Computers Computers are regularly used in art, college planning, English, graphics, history, mathematics, psychology, science, yearbook classes. Computer network features include on-campus library services, online commercial services, Internet access, wireless campus network, Internet filtering or blocking technology. Campus intranet and computer access in designated common areas are available to students. Students grades are available online. The school has a published electronic and media policy.

Contact Ericka Paul, Assistant to Admission. 505-341-7250. Fax: 505-344-2517. E-mail: epaul@menaulschool.com. Website: www.menaulschool.com

MENNONITE COLLEGIATE INSTITUTE

Box 250

Gretna, Manitoba R0G 0V0, Canada

Head of School: Mr. Darryl K. Loewen

General Information Coeducational boarding and day college-preparatory, general academic, arts, business, religious studies, and technology school, affiliated with Mennonite Church, Christian faith; primarily serves students with learning disabilities, individuals with Attention Deficit Disorder, individuals with emotional and behavioral problems, and dyslexic students. Boarding grades 9–12, day grades 7–12. Founded: 1889. Setting: small town. Nearest major city is Winnipeg, Canada. Students are housed in single-sex dormitories. 12-acre campus. 5 buildings on campus. Approved or accredited by The College Board and Manitoba Department of Education. Language of instruction: English. Endowment: CAN$500,000. Total enrollment: 140. Upper school average class size: 20. Upper school faculty-student ratio: 1:13. There are 196 required school days per year for Upper School students. Upper School students typically attend 5 days per week. The average school day consists of 7 hours and 10 minutes.

Upper School Student Profile Grade 9: 22 students (12 boys, 10 girls); Grade 10: 23 students (10 boys, 13 girls); Grade 11: 28 students (11 boys, 17 girls); Grade 12: 48 students (23 boys, 25 girls). 42% of students are boarding students. 95% are province residents. 3 provinces are represented in upper school student body. 3% are international students. International students from China, Congo, Democratic People's Republic of Korea, Hong Kong, Kenya, and Mexico; 1 other country represented in student body. 70% of students are Mennonite, Christian.

Faculty School total: 12. In upper school: 7 men, 5 women; 2 have advanced degrees; 2 reside on campus.

Subjects Offered Advanced TOEFL/grammar, agriculture, all academic, jazz ensemble, journalism, music.

Graduation Requirements English, geography, history, mathematics, physical education (includes health), compulsory religion courses at each grade level, compulsory religious history courses at one level.

Special Academic Programs 2 Advanced Placement exams for which test preparation is offered; independent study; academic accommodation for the musically talented; remedial reading and/or remedial writing; remedial math; programs in English, mathematics for dyslexic students; special instructional classes for blind students; ESL (8 students enrolled).

College Admission Counseling 36 students graduated in 2013; 24 went to college, including The University of Winnipeg; University of Manitoba. Other: 10 went to work, 2 had other specific plans.

Student Life Upper grades have uniform requirement, student council, honor system. Discipline rests primarily with faculty. Attendance at religious services is required.

Tuition and Aid Day student tuition: CAN$4800; 7-day tuition and room/board: CAN$18,200. Tuition installment plan (monthly payment plans, individually arranged payment plans). Tuition reduction for siblings, bursaries, merit scholarship grants, need-based scholarship grants, middle-income loans available. In 2013–14, 30% of upper-school students received aid; total upper-school merit-scholarship money awarded: CAN$9000. Total amount of financial aid awarded in 2013–14: CAN$40,000.

Admissions Traditional secondary-level entrance grade is 9. For fall 2013, 140 students applied for upper-level admission, 137 were accepted, 137 enrolled. Deadline for receipt of application materials: none. Application fee required: CAN$200. Interview recommended.

Athletics Interscholastic: badminton (boys, girls), baseball (b,g), basketball (b,g), cross-country running (b,g), curling (b,g), golf (b,g), soccer (b,g), track and field (b,g), volleyball (b,g); intramural: floor hockey (b,g), indoor soccer (b,g), paddle tennis (b,g), soccer (b,g), street hockey (b,g), table tennis (b,g); coed interscholastic: badminton, cross-country running, curling, golf, track and field; coed intramural: floor hockey, indoor soccer, paddle tennis, soccer, street hockey, table tennis. 3 PE instructors, 2 athletic trainers.

Computers Computers are regularly used in all academic classes. Computer network features include on-campus library services, Internet access, wireless campus network, Internet filtering or blocking technology. The school has a published electronic and media policy.

Contact Ms. Shanda Hochstettler, Admissions Counselor. 204-327-5891. Fax: 204-327-5872. E-mail: admissions@mciblues.net. Website: www.mciblues.net

MERCERSBURG ACADEMY

300 East Seminary Street

Mercersburg, Pennsylvania 17236

Head of School: Mr. Doug Hale

General Information Coeducational boarding and day college-preparatory school. Boarding grades 9–PG, day grades 9–11. Founded: 1893. Setting: small town. Nearest major city is Washington, DC. Students are housed in single-sex dormitories. 300-acre campus. 30 buildings on campus. Approved or accredited by Association of Independent Schools of Greater Washington, Middle States Association of Colleges and Schools, The Association of Boarding Schools, and Pennsylvania Department of Education. Member of National Association of Independent Schools and Secondary School Admission Test Board. Endowment: $193 million. Total enrollment: 430. Upper school average class size: 12. Upper school faculty-student ratio: 1:5. Upper School students typically attend 5 days per week. The average school day consists of 7 hours and 30 minutes.

Upper School Student Profile Grade 9: 82 students (43 boys, 39 girls); Grade 10: 107 students (49 boys, 58 girls); Grade 11: 113 students (65 boys, 48 girls); Grade 12: 110 students (63 boys, 47 girls); Postgraduate: 18 students (14 boys, 4 girls). 85% of students are boarding students. 30% are state residents. 33 states are represented in upper school student body. 18% are international students. International students from China, Germany, Republic of Korea, Saudi Arabia, Spain, and Thailand; 35 other countries represented in student body.

Faculty School total: 100. In upper school: 64 men, 33 women; 70 have advanced degrees; 45 reside on campus.

Subjects Offered 20th century American writers, 20th century world history, 3-dimensional art, acting, advanced chemistry, advanced computer applications, Advanced Placement courses, African American history, African dance, African drumming, algebra, American Civil War, American history, American history-AP, American literature, American literature-AP, art, art history, art history-AP, Asian history, astronomy, ballet, band, biology, biology-AP, botany, British literature-AP, Buddhism, calculus, calculus-AP, ceramics, chemistry, chemistry-AP, Chinese, choral music, chorus, comparative government and politics-AP, computer graphics, computer math, computer programming-AP, computer science, computer science-AP, concert band, creative writing, dance, digital art, drama, drawing, economics-AP, English, English literature, English literature and composition-AP, environmental science-AP, ethics, European history, European history-AP, film studies, fine arts, French, French language-AP, French literature-AP, genetics, geometry, German, German-AP, government and politics-AP, health, history, history of music, honors algebra, honors English, honors geometry, honors U.S. history, honors world history, humanities, Islamic studies, jazz band, journalism, Latin, Latin-AP, mathematics, modern European history-AP, music, music composition, music history, musical theater dance, orchestra, painting, personal fitness, physical education, physical science, physics, physics-AP, poetry, public speaking, religion, robotics, SAT preparation, science, sculpture, social studies, Spanish, Spanish language-AP, speech, stagecraft, statistics-AP, strings, studio art, theater, theater design and production, trigonometry, U.S. government and politics-AP, U.S. history-AP, United States government-AP, world history, world history-AP, world literature, yoga.

Graduation Requirements Arts and fine arts (art, music, dance, drama), English, foreign language, history, mathematics, physical education (includes health), religion (includes Bible studies and theology), science, participation in sports, performing arts, or other activities.

Special Academic Programs Advanced Placement exam preparation; honors section; independent study; term-away projects; study abroad; academic accommodation for the gifted, the musically talented, and the artistically talented.

College Admission Counseling 125 students graduated in 2013; all went to college, including Bryn Mawr College; Bucknell University; Georgetown University; Sewanee: The University of the South; United States Naval Academy; University of Pennsylvania.

Student Life Upper grades have specified standards of dress, student council, honor system. Discipline rests primarily with faculty.

Summer Programs Enrichment, ESL, sports, art/fine arts, rigorous outdoor training programs offered; session focuses on enrichment; held both on and off campus; held at various locations; accepts boys and girls; open to students from other schools. 2,300 students usually enrolled. 2014 schedule: June 10 to August 17. Application deadline: none.

Tuition and Aid Day student tuition: $36,580; 7-day tuition and room/board: $50,800. Tuition installment plan (Insured Tuition Payment Plan, Key Tuition Payment Plan, monthly payment plans). Merit scholarship grants, need-based scholarship grants, need-based loans available. In 2013–14, 48% of upper-school students received aid.

Admissions Traditional secondary-level entrance grade is 9. For fall 2013, 605 students applied for upper-level admission, 314 were accepted, 166 enrolled. ACT, ISEE, PSAT and SAT for applicants to grade 11 and 12, SAT, SSAT or TOEFL required. Deadline for receipt of application materials: January 31. Application fee required: $50. Interview required.

Athletics Interscholastic: baseball (boys), basketball (b,g), cross-country running (b,g), diving (b,g), field hockey (g), football (b), lacrosse (b,g), running (b,g), soccer (b,g), softball (g), squash (b,g), swimming and diving (b,g), tennis (b,g), track and field (b,g), volleyball (g), winter (indoor) track (b,g), wrestling (b); coed interscholastic: alpine skiing, golf; coed intramural: aerobics/dance, alpine skiing, backpacking, ballet, bicycling, canoeing/kayaking, climbing, dance, equestrian sports, fitness, freestyle skiing, Frisbee, golf, hiking/backpacking, horseback riding, kayaking, martial arts, modern dance, mountain biking, outdoor activities, outdoor adventure, outdoor education, outdoor recreation, outdoor skills, outdoors, paddling, physical fitness, physical training, rafting, rappelling, rock climbing, skiing (downhill), snowboarding, strength & conditioning, table tennis, ultimate Frisbee, wall climbing, weight lifting, weight training, wilderness survival, yoga. 4 PE instructors, 22 coaches, 2 athletic trainers.

Computers Computers are regularly used in art, English, foreign language, history, mathematics, music, science classes. Computer network features include on-campus library services, online commercial services, Internet access, wireless campus network. Student e-mail accounts and computer access in designated common areas are available to students. The school has a published electronic and media policy.

Contact Mr. Tommy W. Adams, Assistant Head of School for Enrollment. 717-328-6173. Fax: 717-328-6319. E-mail: admission@mercersburg.edu. Website: www.mercersburg.edu

MERCHISTON CASTLE SCHOOL

Colinton

Edinburgh EH13 0PU, United Kingdom

Head of School: Mr. Andrew R. Hunter

General Information Boys' boarding and day college-preparatory, arts, business, religious studies, bilingual studies, and technology school, affiliated with Christian faith. Ungraded, ages 8–18. Founded: 1833. Setting: small town. Students are housed in single-sex dormitories. 100-acre campus. 11 buildings on campus. Approved or accredited by Boarding Schools Association (UK) and Independent Schools Council (UK). Language of instruction: English. Upper school average class size: 9. Upper school faculty-student ratio: 1:9. The average school day consists of 9 hours.

Upper School Student Profile 70% of students are boarding students. 18% are international students. International students from China, France, Germany, Hong Kong, Russian Federation, and Spain; 15 other countries represented in student body. 50% of students are Christian faith.

Faculty School total: 64. In upper school: 38 men, 23 women; 37 have advanced degrees; 30 reside on campus.

Subjects Offered Algebra, art, biology, calculus, career education, chemistry, Chinese, computer science, creative writing, design, drama, Dutch, economics, electronics, English, English as a foreign language, English literature, European history, French, geography, geometry, German, government/civics, grammar, history, Italian, Japanese, Latin, Mandarin, mathematics, music, physical education, physics, political thought, politics, Portuguese, religion, Russian, science, social studies, Spanish, trigonometry, world history.

Graduation Requirements Any three A-level courses.

Special Academic Programs Independent study; term-away projects; study at local college for college credit; study abroad; academic accommodation for the gifted, the musically talented, and the artistically talented; remedial reading and/or remedial writing; remedial math; programs in English, mathematics, general development for dyslexic students; special instructional classes for deaf students, blind students; ESL (15 students enrolled).

College Admission Counseling 80 students graduated in 2013; 75 went to college. Other: 5 had other specific plans.

Student Life Upper grades have specified standards of dress, student council, honor system. Discipline rests equally with students and faculty.

Summer Programs ESL, sports programs offered; held on campus; accepts boys and girls; open to students from other schools. 40 students usually enrolled.

Tuition and Aid Day student tuition: £12,525–£20,190; 7-day tuition and room/board: £17,595–£27,465. Tuition reduction for siblings, bursaries available. In 2013–14, 20% of upper-school students received aid.

Admissions Traditional secondary-level entrance grade is 8. Traditional secondary-level entrance age is 13. Achievement/Aptitude/Writing, common entrance examinations and school's own exam required. Deadline for receipt of application materials: none. Application fee required: £100. Interview recommended.

Athletics Interscholastic: badminton (boys), ball hockey (b), basketball (b), boxing (b), cricket (b), cross-country running (b), curling (b), fencing (b), Fives (b), football (b), freestyle skiing (b), golf (b), hockey (b), indoor soccer (b), riflery (b), rugby (b), sailing (b), scuba diving (b), skiing (cross-country) (b), skiing (downhill) (b), soccer (b), squash (b), swimming and diving (b), table tennis (b), tennis (b), track and field (b), wall climbing (b); intramural: archery (b), badminton (b), ball hockey (b), basketball (b), bicycling (b), boxing (b), canoeing/kayaking (b), climbing (b), cricket (b), cross-country running (b), curling (b), diving (b), fencing (b), Fives (b), football (b), freestyle skiing (b), golf (b), gymnastics (b), hockey (b), indoor soccer (b), jogging (b), judo (b), life saving (b), marksmanship (b), martial arts (b), mountain biking (b), outdoor activities (b), outdoor education (b), outdoor skills (b), physical fitness (b), riflery (b), rock climbing (b), rugby (b), sailing (b), scuba diving (b), skiing (cross-country) (b), skiing (downhill) (b), soccer (b), squash (b), strength & conditioning (b), swimming and diving (b), table tennis (b), tennis (b), track and field (b), volleyball (b), wall climbing (b). 4 PE instructors, 2 coaches.

Computers Computers are regularly used in all academic, design, music classes. Computer network features include Internet access, wireless campus network, Internet

filtering or blocking technology. Campus intranet, student e-mail accounts, and computer access in designated common areas are available to students. The school has a published electronic and media policy.

Contact Mrs. Anne Rickard, Director of Admissions. 44-131-312-2201. Fax: 44-131-441 Ext. 6060. E-mail: admissions@merchiston.co.uk. Website: www.merchiston.co.uk

MERCY HIGH SCHOOL COLLEGE PREPARATORY

3250 19th Avenue

San Francisco, California 94132-2000

Head of School: Dr. Dorothy McCrea

General Information Girls' day college-preparatory, Women In Medicine, and Women in the Art school, affiliated with Roman Catholic Church. Grades 9–12. Founded: 1952. Setting: urban. Nearest major city is Daly City. 6-acre campus. 2 buildings on campus. Approved or accredited by Western Association of Schools and Colleges, Western Catholic Education Association, and California Department of Education. Endowment: $2 million. Total enrollment: 391. Upper school average class size: 25. Upper school faculty-student ratio: 1:14. There are 181 required school days per year for Upper School students. Upper School students typically attend 5 days per week. The average school day consists of 7 hours and 5 minutes.

Upper School Student Profile Grade 9: 97 students (97 girls); Grade 10: 87 students (87 girls); Grade 11: 102 students (102 girls); Grade 12: 105 students (105 girls). 60.9% of students are Roman Catholic.

Faculty School total: 27. In upper school: 4 men, 23 women; 21 have advanced degrees.

Subjects Offered 3-dimensional art, advanced studio art-AP, algebra, American history, American literature, art, biology, calculus, calculus-AP, ceramics, chemistry, chemistry-AP, chorus, creative writing, dance, dance performance, drama, English, English language-AP, English literature, English literature and composition-AP, environmental science, ethnic studies, expository writing, foreign language, French, geometry, government/civics, mathematics, physical education, physical science, physics, physics-AP, poetry, pre-calculus, religious studies, social justice, social studies, Spanish, speech, statistics, theater, trigonometry, U.S. history, United States government-AP, visual and performing arts, visual arts, world history, world literature.

Graduation Requirements Electives, English, languages, mathematics, physical science, religious studies, science, U.S. government, U.S. history, visual and performing arts, world history, 50 volunteer hours and a senior culminating project, Intersession. Community service is required.

Special Academic Programs Advanced Placement exam preparation; honors section; programs in English, mathematics, general development for dyslexic students; special instructional classes for McAuley Academic Program.

College Admission Counseling 108 students graduated in 2013; all went to college, including College of San Mateo; Dominican University; San Francisco State University; Sonoma State University; University of California, Davis; University of California, Los Angeles. Mean SAT critical reading: 500, mean SAT math: 499, mean SAT writing: 509, mean combined SAT: 1508, mean composite ACT: 26. 13% scored over 600 on SAT critical reading, 18% scored over 600 on SAT math, 15% scored over 600 on SAT writing, 15% scored over 1800 on combined SAT, 21% scored over 26 on composite ACT.

Student Life Upper grades have uniform requirement, student council, honor system. Discipline rests primarily with faculty. Attendance at religious services is required.

Summer Programs Enrichment, advancement programs offered; session focuses on pre-high program is enrichment only; secondary program is enrichment and remediation; held on campus; accepts boys and girls; open to students from other schools. 350 students usually enrolled. 2014 schedule: June 23 to July 18. Application deadline: June 19.

Tuition and Aid Day student tuition: $15,750. Tuition installment plan (individually arranged payment plans, TADS, 10 months payment (July-April), full pay and semiannual payment (July & December)). Merit scholarship grants, need-based scholarship grants available. In 2013–14, 40% of upper-school students received aid; total upper-school merit-scholarship money awarded: $30,000. Total amount of financial aid awarded in 2013–14: $1,200,000.

Admissions Traditional secondary-level entrance grade is 9. High School Placement Test required. Deadline for receipt of application materials: December 6. Application fee required: $80. On-campus interview required.

Athletics Interscholastic: basketball, cross-country running, dance, dance squad, self defense, soccer, softball, swimming and diving, tennis, track and field, volleyball. 2 PE instructors, 11 coaches.

Computers Computers are regularly used in all academic classes. Computer network features include on-campus library services, Internet access, wireless campus network, Internet filtering or blocking technology, RenWeb. Campus intranet, student e-mail accounts, and computer access in designated common areas are available to students. Students grades are available online. The school has a published electronic and media policy.

Contact Michelle Ferrari, Director of Community Outreach and Admissions. 415-584-5929. Fax: 415-334-9726. E-mail: mferrari@mercyhs.org. Website: www.mercyhs.org

MESA GRANDE SEVENTH-DAY ACADEMY

975 Fremont Street
Calimesa, California 92320
Head of School: Alfred J. Riddle

General Information Coeducational day college-preparatory, arts, religious studies, and technology school, affiliated with Seventh-day Adventists, Christian faith. Grades K–12. Founded: 1928. Setting: rural. Nearest major city is San Bernardino. 14-acre campus. 3 buildings on campus. Approved or accredited by Western Association of Schools and Colleges and California Department of Education. Endowment: $650,000. Total enrollment: 265. Upper school average class size: 30. Upper school faculty-student ratio: 1:10. There are 180 required school days per year for Upper School students. Upper School students typically attend 5 days per week. The average school day consists of 8 hours.

Upper School Student Profile Grade 9: 31 students (17 boys, 14 girls); Grade 10: 31 students (17 boys, 14 girls); Grade 11: 32 students (16 boys, 16 girls); Grade 12: 29 students (17 boys, 12 girls). 90% of students are Seventh-day Adventists, Christian.

Faculty School total: 23. In upper school: 6 men, 8 women; 8 have advanced degrees.

Subjects Offered Algebra, American literature, arts, ASB Leadership, auto mechanics, bell choir, biology, British literature, career education, chemistry, choral music, community service, composition, computer applications, computer-aided design, computers, concert choir, desktop publishing, drama, economics, economics and history, English, English composition, family living, fine arts, geometry, government/civics, graphic arts, handbells, health, instrumental music, keyboarding, lab science, marine biology, mathematics, music composition, music theory, physical education, physical science, physics, pre-calculus, relationships, religion, religious education, science, social sciences, social studies, Spanish, U.S. government, U.S. history, video film production, world history, world literature, yearbook.

Graduation Requirements Algebra, American government, applied skills, arts and fine arts (art, music, dance, drama), biology, British literature, career education, chemistry, computer education, computer technologies, economics, English, English composition, family living, industrial technology, keyboarding, mathematics, modern languages, physical education (includes health), physical fitness, physical science, physics, religious studies, science, social studies (includes history), Spanish, technical skills, work experience, community service.

Special Academic Programs ESL (8 students enrolled).

College Admission Counseling 30 students graduated in 2013; 25 went to college, including La Sierra University; Pacific Union College; Southern Adventist University; University of California, Irvine; University of California, Los Angeles; Walla Walla University. Other: 2 went to work, 1 entered military service, 1 had other specific plans.

Student Life Upper grades have uniform requirement, student council, honor system. Discipline rests primarily with faculty. Attendance at religious services is required.

Summer Programs Sports programs offered; held both on and off campus; held at Drayson Center, Loma Linda, CA; accepts boys and girls; open to students from other schools. 50 students usually enrolled. 2014 schedule: June 8 to August 3. Application deadline: May 5.

Tuition and Aid Day student tuition: $8000. Tuition installment plan (monthly payment plans, individually arranged payment plans). Need-based scholarship grants, need-based loans, middle-income loans available. In 2013–14, 25% of upper-school students received aid. Total amount of financial aid awarded in 2013–14: $35,000.

Admissions Traditional secondary-level entrance grade is 9. For fall 2013, 30 students applied for upper-level admission, 28 were accepted, 28 enrolled. Any standardized test, ITBS-TAP, Math Placement Exam or writing sample required. Deadline for receipt of application materials: none. Application fee required: $50. On-campus interview required.

Athletics Interscholastic: baseball (boys), basketball (b,g), flag football (b,g), softball (g), volleyball (b,g); coed interscholastic: cross-country running, golf, physical fitness, weight lifting. 2 PE instructors, 12 coaches, 2 athletic trainers.

Computers Computers are regularly used in art, design, graphic design, library skills, science, technical drawing, technology, typing, video film production, writing, yearbook classes. Computer network features include on-campus library services, online commercial services, Internet access, wireless campus network, Internet filtering or blocking technology. Student e-mail accounts and computer access in designated common areas are available to students. Students grades are available online. The school has a published electronic and media policy.

Contact Lois M. Myhre, Admissions Office. 909-795-1112 Ext. 257. Fax: 909-795-1653. E-mail: lois.myhre@mgak-12.org. Website: www.mesagrandeacademy.org

MIDDLESEX SCHOOL

1400 Lowell Road
Concord, Massachusetts 01742
Head of School: Kathleen C. Giles

General Information Coeducational boarding and day college-preparatory and arts school. Grades 9–12. Founded: 1901. Setting: suburban. Nearest major city is Boston. Students are housed in single-sex dormitories. 350-acre campus. 31 buildings on campus. Approved or accredited by New England Association of Schools and Colleges. Member of National Association of Independent Schools and Secondary School Admission Test Board. Endowment: $160 million. Total enrollment: 378. Upper school average class size: 12. Upper school faculty-student ratio: 1:6. There are 178 required school days per year for Upper School students. Upper School students typically attend 6 days per week. The average school day consists of 7 hours and 7 minutes.

Upper School Student Profile Grade 9: 81 students (36 boys, 45 girls); Grade 10: 100 students (47 boys, 53 girls); Grade 11: 100 students (55 boys, 45 girls); Grade 12: 97 students (52 boys, 45 girls). 67% of students are boarding students. 56% are state residents. 29 states are represented in upper school student body. 11% are international students. International students from Canada, China, Jamaica, Philippines, Republic of Korea, and Thailand; 13 other countries represented in student body.

Faculty School total: 62. In upper school: 36 men, 26 women; 44 have advanced degrees; 53 reside on campus.

Subjects Offered Acting, advanced biology, advanced chemistry, advanced computer applications, Advanced Placement courses, advanced studio art-AP, African American history, African history, African-American history, algebra, American literature, analytic geometry, art, art history, art history-AP, art-AP, Asian literature, astronomy, biology, biology-AP, British literature, calculus, calculus-AP, ceramics, chemistry, chemistry-AP, Chinese, classical Greek literature, computer programming, computer programming-AP, computer science, computer science-AP, creative writing, discrete mathematics, DNA, drama, economics, economics-AP, English, English literature, English literature and composition-AP, environmental science, environmental science-AP, ethics, European history, European history-AP, finite math, forensics, French, French language-AP, French literature-AP, geometry, Greek, history, history of jazz, Holocaust studies, independent study, jazz band, Latin, Latin American history, marine studies, mathematics, media, Middle East, Middle Eastern history, model United Nations, music, music theory, music theory-AP, philosophy, photography, physics, physics-AP, political science, religion, Shakespeare, Spanish, Spanish language-AP, Spanish literature-AP, statistics, statistics-AP, studio art-AP, theater, trigonometry, U.S. government and politics-AP, U.S. history, U.S. history-AP, video film production, Vietnam history, Vietnam War, vocal ensemble, women in world history, woodworking, world history, writing, writing workshop.

Graduation Requirements Algebra, analytic geometry, arts, English, English literature and composition-AP, European history, foreign language, geometry, science, trigonometry, U.S. history, completion of a wooden plaque.

Special Academic Programs 22 Advanced Placement exams for which test preparation is offered; honors section; independent study; academic accommodation for the gifted.

College Admission Counseling 101 students graduated in 2013; 100 went to college, including Amherst College; Boston College; Dartmouth College; Harvard University; Middlebury College; Trinity College. Other: 1 had other specific plans. Median SAT critical reading: 700, median SAT math: 690, median SAT writing: 700, median combined SAT: 2090, median composite ACT: 29. 89% scored over 600 on SAT critical reading, 89% scored over 600 on SAT math, 94% scored over 600 on SAT writing, 90% scored over 1800 on combined SAT, 88% scored over 26 on composite ACT.

Student Life Upper grades have specified standards of dress, student council, honor system. Discipline rests equally with students and faculty.

Tuition and Aid Day student tuition: $41,800; 7-day tuition and room/board: $52,300. Guaranteed tuition plan. Tuition installment plan (Insured Tuition Payment Plan, monthly payment plans, semiannual payment plan). Need-based scholarship grants, need-based loans available. In 2013–14, 28% of upper-school students received aid. Total amount of financial aid awarded in 2013–14: $4,300,000.

Admissions Traditional secondary-level entrance grade is 9. For fall 2013, 1,067 students applied for upper-level admission, 108 enrolled. ISEE, SSAT or TOEFL required. Deadline for receipt of application materials: January 15. Application fee required: $50. Interview recommended.

Athletics Interscholastic: alpine skiing (boys, girls), baseball (b), basketball (b,g), crew (b,g), cross-country running (b,g), field hockey (g), football (b), ice hockey (b,g), lacrosse (b,g), skiing (downhill) (b,g), soccer (b,g), softball (g), squash (b,g), tennis (b,g), volleyball (g), wrestling (b); coed interscholastic: golf, track and field; coed intramural: dance, fitness, physical training, squash, strength & conditioning, yoga. 1 PE instructor, 18 coaches, 2 athletic trainers.

Computers Computers are regularly used in all classes. Computer network features include on-campus library services, online commercial services, Internet access, wireless campus network, Internet filtering or blocking technology. Campus intranet, student e-mail accounts, and computer access in designated common areas are available to students. Students grades are available online. The school has a published electronic and media policy.

Contact Douglas C. Price, Director of Admissions. 978-371-6524. Fax: 978-402-1400. E-mail: admissions@mxschool.edu. Website: www.mxschool.edu

MIDDLE TENNESSEE CHRISTIAN SCHOOL

100 East MTCS Road
Murfreesboro, Tennessee 37129
Head of School: Dr. Phil Ellenburg

General Information Coeducational day college-preparatory, arts, religious studies, and technology school, affiliated with Church of Christ. Grades PK–12.

Founded: 1962. Setting: suburban. Nearest major city is Nashville. 37-acre campus. 3 buildings on campus. Approved or accredited by National Christian School Association, Southern Association of Colleges and Schools, Southern Association of Independent Schools, and Tennessee Department of Education. Member of National Association of Independent Schools. Total enrollment: 665. Upper school average class size: 18. Upper school faculty-student ratio: 1:18. There are 175 required school days per year for Upper School students. Upper School students typically attend 5 days per week. The average school day consists of 7 hours and 15 minutes.

Upper School Student Profile Grade 9: 47 students (29 boys, 18 girls); Grade 10: 47 students (26 boys, 21 girls); Grade 11: 45 students (24 boys, 21 girls); Grade 12: 50 students (28 boys, 22 girls). 52% of students are members of Church of Christ.

Faculty School total: 50. In upper school: 15 men, 15 women; 20 have advanced degrees.

Subjects Offered ACT preparation, advanced math, algebra, American history, American history-AP, American literature, anatomy, art, band, Bible, biology, biology-AP, calculus, chemistry, chorus, computer applications, computer technologies, driver education, economics, electives, English, French, geometry, integrated mathematics, keyboarding, physics, pre-algebra, pre-calculus, Spanish, speech, U.S. government, U.S. history, wellness, yearbook.

Graduation Requirements Algebra, arts, Bible, biology, chemistry, computer applications, economics, electives, English, French, geometry, keyboarding, physical science, pre-algebra, Spanish, speech, U.S. government, U.S. history, wellness, world history.

Special Academic Programs 3 Advanced Placement exams for which test preparation is offered; honors section; study at local college for college credit.

College Admission Counseling 56 students graduated in 2013; 55 went to college, including Freed-Hardeman University; Harding University; Lipscomb University; Middle Tennessee State University; Tennessee Technological University; The University of Tennessee at Chattanooga. Other: 1 entered military service. Median composite ACT: 24. 31% scored over 26 on composite ACT.

Student Life Upper grades have specified standards of dress, student council, honor system. Discipline rests primarily with faculty. Attendance at religious services is required.

Tuition and Aid Day student tuition: $7850. Tuition installment plan (monthly payment plans, individually arranged payment plans). Tuition reduction for siblings, need-based scholarship grants available.

Admissions Traditional secondary-level entrance grade is 9. For fall 2013, 39 students applied for upper-level admission, 36 were accepted, 30 enrolled. Achievement tests required. Deadline for receipt of application materials: none. Application fee required: $75. Interview required.

Athletics Interscholastic: baseball (boys), basketball (b,g), bowling (b,g), cheering (g), cross-country running (b,g), football (b), golf (b), skeet shooting (b,g), soccer (b,g), softball (g), tennis (b,g), trap and skeet (b,g), volleyball (g). 2 PE instructors.

Computers Computers are regularly used in engineering, keyboarding, mathematics, science, writing, yearbook classes. Computer network features include on-campus library services, Internet access, wireless campus network, Internet filtering or blocking technology. Student e-mail accounts and computer access in designated common areas are available to students. Students grades are available online. The school has a published electronic and media policy.

Contact Mrs. Jane Herring, Admissions and Public Relations. 615-893-0601. Fax: 615-895-8815. E-mail: janeherring@mtcscougars.org. Website: www.mtcscougars.org

MIDLAND SCHOOL

PO Box 8
5100 Figueroa Mountain Road
Los Olivos, California 93441

Head of School: Will Graham

General Information Coeducational boarding college-preparatory and environmental studies school. Grades 9–12. Founded: 1932. Setting: rural. Nearest major city is Santa Barbara. Students are housed in single-sex cabins. 2,860-acre campus. Approved or accredited by California Association of Independent Schools, The Association of Boarding Schools, and Western Association of Schools and Colleges. Member of National Association of Independent Schools and Secondary School Admission Test Board. Endowment: $14 million. Total enrollment: 77. Upper school average class size: 10. Upper school faculty-student ratio: 1:5. Upper School students typically attend 7 days per week. The average school day consists of 6 hours and 45 minutes.

Upper School Student Profile Grade 9: 20 students (9 boys, 11 girls); Grade 10: 21 students (14 boys, 7 girls); Grade 11: 22 students (11 boys, 11 girls); Grade 12: 14 students (6 boys, 8 girls). 100% of students are boarding students. 70% are state residents. 10 states are represented in upper school student body. 17% are international students. International students from China, India, Macao, and Republic of Korea.

Faculty School total: 23. In upper school: 14 men, 9 women; 9 have advanced degrees; 20 reside on campus.

Subjects Offered 3-dimensional art, advanced chemistry, advanced math, agroecology, algebra, American history, American literature, American studies, anthropology, backpacking, basketball, biology, ceramics, character education, chemistry, clayworking, community service, composition, creative writing, drama, economics, environmental education, environmental studies, equestrian sports, foreign language, gardening, geology, geometry, health education, human sexuality, hydrology, integrated science, land and ranch management, leadership, literature by women, metalworking, music, painting, physics, pre-calculus, senior project, senior seminar, senior thesis, Spanish, Spanish literature, statistics, U.S. history, volleyball, wilderness education, wilderness experience, world studies.

Graduation Requirements Arts and fine arts (art, music, dance, drama), English, foreign language, history, mathematics, science, senior thesis.

Special Academic Programs 9 Advanced Placement exams for which test preparation is offered; honors section; independent study.

College Admission Counseling 24 students graduated in 2013; all went to college, including Hampshire College; Hendrix College; Kenyon College; University of California, Berkeley; University of California, Santa Cruz; University of Southern California. Mean SAT critical reading: 571, mean SAT math: 567, mean SAT writing: 559, mean combined SAT: 1697, mean composite ACT: 25.

Student Life Upper grades have student council. Discipline rests equally with students and faculty.

Tuition and Aid 7-day tuition and room/board: $42,900. Tuition installment plan (monthly payment plans, Your Tuition Solution, Tuition Management Systems). Need-based scholarship grants available. In 2013–14, 50% of upper-school students received aid. Total amount of financial aid awarded in 2013–14: $1,000,000.

Admissions Traditional secondary-level entrance grade is 9. For fall 2013, 77 students applied for upper-level admission, 42 were accepted, 31 enrolled. ISEE, SSAT or TOEFL required. Deadline for receipt of application materials: February 15. Application fee required: $50. On-campus interview required.

Athletics Interscholastic: basketball (boys, girls), cross-country running (b,g), lacrosse (b,g), soccer (b,g), volleyball (g); intramural: table tennis (b,g); coed intramural: backpacking, equestrian sports, hiking/backpacking, horseback riding, outdoor adventure, outdoor skills, yoga.

Computers Computer network features include on-campus library services, online commercial services, Internet access, Internet filtering or blocking technology. Student e-mail accounts and computer access in designated common areas are available to students. The school has a published electronic and media policy.

Contact Amy E. Graham, Director of Admissions and Financial Aid. 805-688-5114 Ext. 114. Fax: 805-686-2470. E-mail: admissions@midland-school.org. Website: www.midland-school.org

MID-PACIFIC INSTITUTE

2445 Kaala Street
Honolulu, Hawaii 96822-2299

Head of School: Dr. Paul Turnbull, PhD

General Information Coeducational day college-preparatory, arts, bilingual studies, technology, and International Baccalaureate school; affiliated with United Church of Christ. Grades K–12. Founded: 1908. Setting: urban. 38-acre campus. 33 buildings on campus. Approved or accredited by International Baccalaureate Organization and Western Association of Schools and Colleges. Member of National Association of Independent Schools and Secondary School Admission Test Board. Total enrollment: 1,550. Upper school average class size: 20. Upper school faculty-student ratio: 1:20. Upper School students typically attend 5 days per week. The average school day consists of 6 hours and 15 minutes.

Faculty School total: 150. In upper school: 20 have advanced degrees.

Subjects Offered Algebra, American history, American literature, art, art history, astronomy, ballet, band, biology, business skills, calculus, career education, ceramics, chemistry, computer programming, computer science, creative writing, dance, debate, drama, drawing, economics, English, English literature, ESL, film, fine arts, first aid, French, general science, geography, geometry, Hawaiian history, health, history, instrumental music, Japanese, Latin, law, mathematics, oceanography, oral communications, painting, philosophy, photography, physical education, physics, printmaking, psychology, religion, science, sculpture, social sciences, social studies, Spanish, speech, swimming, swimming competency, technological applications, technology, theater, video, weight training, world history, world literature, writing.

Graduation Requirements Arts and fine arts (art, music, dance, drama), business skills (includes word processing), career education, computer science, English, foreign language, mathematics, oral communications, physical education (includes health), religion (includes Bible studies and theology), science, social sciences, social studies (includes history), speech, swimming competency.

Special Academic Programs International Baccalaureate program; Advanced Placement exam preparation; honors section; study at local college for college credit; academic accommodation for the gifted and the artistically talented; ESL (41 students enrolled).

College Admission Counseling 200 students graduated in 2013; all went to college, including Oregon State University; Seattle University; University of Hawaii at Manoa; University of Oregon; University of Southern California.

Student Life Upper grades have specified standards of dress, student council, honor system. Discipline rests primarily with faculty. Attendance at religious services is required.

Summer Programs Enrichment, advancement, ESL, art/fine arts, computer instruction programs offered; session focuses on physical fitness and skills; held on campus; accepts boys and girls; open to students from other schools. 1,200 students usually enrolled. 2014 schedule: June 5 to July 26. Application deadline: April 5.

Tuition and Aid Day student tuition: $19,050. Tuition installment plan (FACTS Tuition Payment Plan, monthly payment plans, semiannual payment plan). Merit scholarship grants, need-based scholarship grants, paying campus jobs, tuition reduction for children of employees available. In 2013–14, 17% of upper-school students received aid. Total amount of financial aid awarded in 2013–14: $2,900,000.

Admissions Traditional secondary-level entrance grade is 9. For fall 2013, 700 students applied for upper-level admission, 220 were accepted, 150 enrolled. SAT, SSAT and TOEFL required. Deadline for receipt of application materials: December 1. Application fee required: $125. Interview required.

Athletics Interscholastic: aquatics (boys, girls), baseball (b), basketball (b,g), bowling (b,g), canoeing/kayaking (b,g), cheering (g), cross-country running (b,g), football (b), golf (b,g), gymnastics (g), independent competitive sports (b,g), kayaking (b,g), ocean paddling (b,g), physical fitness (b,g), physical training (b,g), riflery (b,g), soccer (b,g), softball (g), strength & conditioning (b,g), surfing (b,g), swimming and diving (b,g), tennis (b,g), track and field (b,g), volleyball (b,g), water polo (b,g), wrestling (b,g); intramural: badminton (b,g), weight lifting (b,g), weight training (b,g); coed interscholastic: fitness, modern dance; coed intramural: badminton. 7 PE instructors, 40 coaches, 3 athletic trainers.

Computers Computers are regularly used in English, foreign language, mathematics, media arts, science classes. Computer network features include on-campus library services, online commercial services, Internet access, wireless campus network, Internet filtering or blocking technology, one-to-one iPad program. Campus intranet, student e-mail accounts, and computer access in designated common areas are available to students. Students grades are available online. The school has a published electronic and media policy.

Contact Ms. Heidi Bow, Admissions Assistant. 808-973-5005. Fax: 808-973-5099. E-mail: admissions@midpac.edu. Website: www.midpac.edu

MID-PENINSULA HIGH SCHOOL

1340 Willow Road
Menlo Park, California 94025-1516

Head of School: Douglas C. Thompson, PhD

General Information Coeducational day college-preparatory, general academic, and arts school; primarily serves underachievers, students with learning disabilities, individuals with Attention Deficit Disorder, individuals with emotional and behavioral problems, dyslexic students, and Asberger's Syndrome. Grades 9–12. Founded: 1979. Setting: suburban. Nearest major city is San Francisco. 2-acre campus. 1 building on campus. Approved or accredited by Western Association of Schools and Colleges and California Department of Education. Member of National Association of Independent Schools. Endowment: $2.4 million. Total enrollment: 117. Upper school average class size: 12. Upper school faculty-student ratio: 1:8. Upper School students typically attend 5 days per week. The average school day consists of 6 hours and 10 minutes.

Upper School Student Profile Grade 9: 25 students (11 boys, 14 girls); Grade 10: 30 students (17 boys, 13 girls); Grade 11: 34 students (22 boys, 12 girls); Grade 12: 27 students (19 boys, 8 girls).

Faculty School total: 18. In upper school: 6 men, 9 women; 5 have advanced degrees.

Subjects Offered Algebra, American sign language, art, biology, calculus, calculus-AP, chemistry, composition, contemporary issues, drama, driver education, English, geometry, government, human relations, mathematics, music performance, physical education, physics, SAT/ACT preparation, science, Spanish, sports, study skills, trigonometry, U.S. history, world studies.

Graduation Requirements American government, government, human relations, mathematics, physical education (includes health), science, social sciences, U.S. history. Community service is required.

Special Academic Programs Accelerated programs; independent study; remedial reading and/or remedial writing; remedial math.

College Admission Counseling Colleges students went to include California State University, Chico; California State University, East Bay; California State University, Monterey Bay; Pacific Lutheran University; University of San Francisco; Whittier College.

Student Life Discipline rests primarily with faculty.

Summer Programs Remediation, enrichment, art/fine arts programs offered; session focuses on academic support for current students; held on campus; accepts boys and girls; open to students from other schools. 104 students usually enrolled. 2014 schedule: June 23 to July 24. Application deadline: June 23.

Tuition and Aid Day student tuition: $29,740. Tuition installment plan (monthly payment plans, individually arranged payment plans, 2-payment plan). Need-based scholarship grants available. In 2013–14, 36% of upper-school students received aid.

Admissions Traditional secondary-level entrance grade is 9. Deadline for receipt of application materials: none. No application fee required. On-campus interview required.

Athletics Interscholastic: baseball (boys), basketball (b,g), softball (g), volleyball (b,g); coed interscholastic: cross-country running, soccer, track and field. 1 PE instructor, 4 coaches.

Computers Computers are regularly used in all academic, art, basic skills, college planning, desktop publishing, music, publications, SAT preparation, theater arts classes. Computer network features include Internet access, wireless campus network, Internet filtering or blocking technology. Campus intranet and computer access in designated common areas are available to students. The school has a published electronic and media policy.

Contact Ms. Andrea Henderson, Director of Admissions. 650-321-1991 Ext. 147. Fax: 650-321-9921. E-mail: andrea@mid-pen.com. Website: www.mid-pen.com

MILLBROOK SCHOOL

131 Millbrook School Road
Millbrook, New York 12545

Head of School: Mr. Drew Casertano

General Information Coeducational boarding and day college-preparatory, arts, environmental stewardship, and community service school. Grades 9–12. Founded: 1931. Setting: rural. Nearest major city is New York. Students are housed in single-sex dormitories. 800-acre campus. 40 buildings on campus. Approved or accredited by The Association of Boarding Schools and New York Department of Education. Member of National Association of Independent Schools and Secondary School Admission Test Board. Endowment: $27 million. Total enrollment: 283. Upper school average class size: 14. Upper school faculty-student ratio: 1:5. There are 179 required school days per year for Upper School students. Upper School students typically attend 6 days per week. The average school day consists of 7 hours.

Upper School Student Profile Grade 9: 50 students (25 boys, 25 girls); Grade 10: 71 students (42 boys, 29 girls); Grade 11: 79 students (37 boys, 42 girls); Grade 12: 78 students (45 boys, 33 girls); Postgraduate: 5 students (3 boys, 2 girls). 80% of students are boarding students. 40% are state residents. 24 states are represented in upper school student body. 15% are international students. International students from Canada, China, Ghana, Republic of Korea, Venezuela, and Viet Nam; 14 other countries represented in student body.

Faculty School total: 53. In upper school: 25 men, 28 women; 30 have advanced degrees; 45 reside on campus.

Subjects Offered Acting, advanced biology, advanced chemistry, advanced math, Advanced Placement courses, advanced studio art-AP, aesthetics, algebra, American history, American literature, ancient history, ancient world history, animal behavior, animal science, anthropology, art, art history, astronomy, biology, calculus, calculus-AP, ceramics, chemistry, choral music, constitutional law, creative writing, dance, dance performance, digital photography, drama, drama performance, drawing, ecology, English, English language-AP, English literature, English-AP, environmental science, European history, fine arts, forensics, French, French language-AP, French-AP, geometry, global studies, history, honors English, honors geometry, human biology, human development, independent study, instrumental music, jazz band, jazz ensemble, journalism, Mandarin, mathematics, medieval history, Middle Eastern history, music, music appreciation, music history, painting, philosophy, photography, physics, pre-calculus, psychology, science, senior project, social sciences, social studies, Spanish, Spanish-AP, studio art, study skills, theater, trigonometry, world history.

Graduation Requirements Biology, English, foreign language, history, mathematics, science, visual and performing arts.

Special Academic Programs 8 Advanced Placement exams for which test preparation is offered; honors section; independent study; term-away projects; study abroad.

College Admission Counseling 75 students graduated in 2013; 73 went to college, including Elon University; Hamilton College; New York University; Trinity College; Tulane University; Wesleyan University. Other: 2 had other specific plans. Mean SAT critical reading: 586, mean SAT math: 585, mean SAT writing: 589, mean combined SAT: 1760, mean composite ACT: 23.

Student Life Upper grades have specified standards of dress, student council. Discipline rests equally with students and faculty.

Tuition and Aid Day student tuition: $38,800; 7-day tuition and room/board: $51,375. Tuition installment plan (SMART Tuition Payment Plan). Need-based scholarship grants, need-based loans available. In 2013–14, 28% of upper-school students received aid. Total amount of financial aid awarded in 2013–14: $2,700,000.

Admissions Traditional secondary-level entrance grade is 9. For fall 2013, 560 students applied for upper-level admission, 270 were accepted, 106 enrolled. ISEE, PSAT or SAT for applicants to grade 11 and 12, SSAT, TOEFL or writing sample required. Deadline for receipt of application materials: January 15. Application fee required: $50. Interview required.

Athletics Interscholastic: baseball (boys), basketball (b,g), cross-country running (b,g), field hockey (g), ice hockey (b,g), lacrosse (b,g), soccer (b,g), softball (g), squash (b,g), tennis (b,g); coed interscholastic: golf; coed intramural: aerobics/dance, aerobics/Nautilus, alpine skiing, badminton, bicycling, dance, equestrian sports, fitness, hiking/backpacking, horseback riding, modern dance, outdoor education, physical training, running, skiing (downhill), snowboarding, strength & conditioning, weight training, yoga. 1 coach, 1 athletic trainer.

Computers Computers are regularly used in foreign language, French, history, journalism, mathematics, photography, science, study skills, video film production, yearbook classes. Computer network features include on-campus library services, online commercial services, Internet access, wireless campus network, Internet filtering or blocking technology. Campus intranet, student e-mail accounts, and computer access in designated common areas are available to students. Students grades are available online. The school has a published electronic and media policy.

Contact Mrs. Wendy Greenfield, Admission Office Assistant. 845-677-8261 Ext. 138. Fax: 845-677-1265. E-mail: admissions@millbrook.org. Website: www.millbrook.org

MILLER SCHOOL OF ALBEMARLE

1000 Samuel Miller Loop
Charlottesville, Virginia 22903-9328

Head of School: Mr. Patrick France

General Information Coeducational boarding and day college-preparatory and arts school. Grades 8–12. Founded: 1878. Setting: small town. Students are housed in single-sex dormitories. 1,600-acre campus. 6 buildings on campus. Approved or accredited by Missouri Independent School Association, The Association of Boarding Schools, Virginia Association of Independent Schools, and Virginia Department of Education. Member of National Association of Independent Schools and Secondary School Admission Test Board. Endowment: $15.4 million. Total enrollment: 173. Upper school average class size: 8. Upper school faculty-student ratio: 1:6. There are 180 required school days per year for Upper School students. Upper School students typically attend 5 days per week. The average school day consists of 5 hours and 10 minutes.

Upper School Student Profile Grade 8: 20 students (15 boys, 5 girls); Grade 9: 27 students (18 boys, 9 girls); Grade 10: 40 students (25 boys, 15 girls); Grade 11: 42 students (24 boys, 18 girls); Grade 12: 44 students (27 boys, 17 girls). 56% of students are boarding students. 60% are state residents. 13 states are represented in upper school student body. 24% are international students. International students from Brazil, China, Germany, Republic of Korea, Spain, and Viet Nam; 6 other countries represented in student body.

Faculty School total: 29. In upper school: 18 men, 11 women; 24 have advanced degrees; 23 reside on campus.

Subjects Offered Algebra, American government, American literature, ancient history, art, arts, baseball, basketball, biology, calculus, calculus-AP, carpentry, chemistry, civics, CPR, creative writing, drama performance, driver education, earth science, economics, economics and history, electives, English, English composition, English language and composition-AP, English language-AP, English literature, English literature and composition-AP, English literature-AP, English-AP, English/composition-AP, environmental science, environmental science-AP, environmental studies, environmental systems, ESL, European history, European history-AP, fine arts, fitness, foreign language, French, French language-AP, French literature-AP, French studies, French-AP, geography, geometry, government, government and politics-AP, government-AP, government/civics, history-AP, independent study, instrumental music, Latin, macroeconomics-AP, mathematics-AP, modern European history, modern European history-AP, music, music performance, musical productions, musical theater, participation in sports, photography, physical education, physical fitness, physical science, physics, poetry, pre-algebra, pre-calculus, reading/study skills, Spanish, Spanish language-AP, Spanish literature-AP, Spanish-AP, sports conditioning, statistics, student government, studio art, studio art-AP, study skills, tennis, trigonometry, U.S. government, U.S. government and politics-AP, U.S. history, U.S. history-AP, visual arts, volleyball, wood processing, woodworking, wrestling, yearbook.

Graduation Requirements Arts and fine arts (art, music, dance, drama), English, foreign language, mathematics, physical education (includes health), science, social studies (includes history). Community service is required.

Special Academic Programs 15 Advanced Placement exams for which test preparation is offered; honors section; accelerated programs; independent study; academic accommodation for the gifted, the musically talented, and the artistically talented; ESL (9 students enrolled).

College Admission Counseling 39 students graduated in 2012; 38 went to college, including James Madison University; Penn State University Park; The College of William and Mary; University of Virginia; Virginia Polytechnic Institute and State University; Washington and Lee University. Other: 1 went to work. Mean SAT critical reading: 510, mean SAT math: 559, mean SAT writing: 516. 40% scored over 600 on SAT critical reading, 40% scored over 600 on SAT math, 40% scored over 600 on SAT writing.

Student Life Upper grades have specified standards of dress, student council, honor system. Discipline rests equally with students and faculty.

Tuition and Aid Day student tuition: $19,000; 5-day tuition and room/board: $36,500; 7-day tuition and room/board: $39,400. Tuition installment plan (Insured Tuition Payment Plan, FACTS Tuition Payment Plan, individually arranged payment plans). Tuition reduction for siblings, need-based scholarship grants available. In 2012-13, 40% of upper-school students received aid. Total amount of financial aid awarded in 2012-13: $1,200,000.

Admissions Traditional secondary-level entrance grade is 9. For fall 2012, 210 students applied for upper-level admission, 102 were accepted, 60 enrolled. PSAT or SAT, SSAT, Stanford Achievement Test or TOEFL or SLEP required. Deadline for receipt of application materials: February 15. Application fee required: $50. Interview required.

Athletics Interscholastic: badminton (boys, girls), baseball (b), basketball (b,g), bicycling (b,g), cross-country running (b,g), lacrosse (b), mountain biking (b,g), outdoor activities (b,g), skiing (downhill) (b,g), snowboarding (b,g), soccer (b,g), tennis (b,g), volleyball (g), wrestling (b); intramural: bicycling (b,g); coed interscholastic: bicycling, equestrian sports, Frisbee, golf, horseback riding, mountain biking; coed intramural: aerobics/dance, basketball, bicycling, canoeing/kayaking, cross-country running, fishing, fitness, fitness walking, flag football, Frisbee, hiking/backpacking, indoor soccer, jogging, mountain biking, outdoor activities, paint ball, physical fitness, physical training, power lifting, running, skateboarding, soccer, softball, street hockey, strength & conditioning, swimming and diving, table tennis, tennis, touch football, ultimate Frisbee, volleyball, walking, weight lifting, weight training. 5 coaches, 1 athletic trainer.

Computers Computers are regularly used in English, foreign language, history, mathematics, science classes. Computer network features include on-campus library services, online commercial services, Internet access, wireless campus network, Internet filtering or blocking technology. Campus intranet and student e-mail accounts are available to students. Students grades are available online. The school has a published electronic and media policy.

Contact Ms. Dee Gregory, Assistant Director of Admissions. 434-823-4805 Ext. 248. Fax: 434-205-5007. E-mail: dgregory@millerschool.org. Website: www.millerschool.org

MILL SPRINGS ACADEMY

Alpharetta, Georgia
See Special Needs Schools section.

MILTON ACADEMY

170 Centre Street
Milton, Massachusetts 02186

General Information Coeducational boarding and day college-preparatory school. Boarding grades 9–12, day grades K–12. Founded: 1798. Setting: suburban. Nearest major city is Boston. Students are housed in single-sex dormitories. 125-acre campus. 25 buildings on campus. Approved or accredited by Association of Independent Schools in New England, New England Association of Schools and Colleges, The Association of Boarding Schools, and Massachusetts Department of Education. Member of National Association of Independent Schools and Secondary School Admission Test Board. Endowment: $167 million. Total enrollment: 980. Upper school average class size: 14. Upper school faculty-student ratio: 1:5. There are 162 required school days per year for Upper School students. Upper School students typically attend 5 days per week. The average school day consists of 7 hours.

See Display on next page and Close-Up on page 554.

MISS EDGAR'S AND MISS CRAMP'S SCHOOL

525 Mount Pleasant Avenue
Montreal, Quebec H3Y 3H6, Canada

Head of School: Ms. Katherine Nikidis

General Information Girls' day college-preparatory, arts, bilingual studies, and technology school. Grades K–11. Founded: 1909. Setting: urban. 4-acre campus. 1 building on campus. Approved or accredited by Canadian Association of Independent Schools, Quebec Association of Independent Schools, and Quebec Department of Education. Affiliate member of National Association of Independent Schools; member of Secondary School Admission Test Board. Languages of instruction: English and French. Total enrollment: 335. Upper school average class size: 19. Upper school faculty-student ratio: 1:9. There are 180 required school days per year for Upper School students. Upper School students typically attend 5 days per week. The average school day consists of 5 hours.

Upper School Student Profile Grade 9: 30 students (30 girls); Grade 10: 45 students (45 girls); Grade 11: 35 students (35 girls).

Faculty School total: 40. In upper school: 4 men, 14 women; 8 have advanced degrees.

Subjects Offered Art, art history, biology, calculus, career exploration, chemistry, computer science, creative writing, drama, ecology, economics, English, environmental science, European history, French, geography, history, mathematics, media, music, physical education, physics, science, social studies, Spanish, theater, women's studies, world history.

Graduation Requirements English, foreign language, mathematics, science, social studies (includes history).

Special Academic Programs 2 Advanced Placement exams for which test preparation is offered; honors section.

College Admission Counseling 36 students graduated in 2013; all went to college, including John Abbott College; Lower Canada College; Marianopolis College.

Student Life Upper grades have uniform requirement, student council, honor system. Discipline rests primarily with faculty.

Tuition and Aid Day student tuition: CAN$18,900. Tuition installment plan (individually arranged payment plans). Bursaries, merit scholarship grants available. In 2013–14, 18% of upper-school students received aid; total upper-school merit-scholarship money awarded: CAN$80,000. Total amount of financial aid awarded in 2013–14: CAN$135,000.

Admissions Traditional secondary-level entrance grade is 9. For fall 2013, 20 students applied for upper-level admission, 12 were accepted, 5 enrolled. CCAT, SSAT or writing sample required. Deadline for receipt of application materials: none. Application fee required: CAN$50. On-campus interview required.

Athletics Interscholastic: badminton, basketball, cross-country running, golf, hockey, ice hockey, running, soccer, swimming and diving, tennis, touch football, track and field, volleyball; intramural: badminton, baseball, basketball, crew, cross-country running, curling, dance, field hockey, gymnastics, ice hockey, outdoor adventure, outdoor education, outdoor skills, physical fitness, rugby, running, skiing (cross-country), soccer, softball, touch football, track and field, volleyball. 3 PE instructors, 11 coaches.

Computers Computers are regularly used in art, English, French, history, newspaper, writing, yearbook classes. Computer network features include on-campus library services, Internet access, wireless campus network, Internet filtering or blocking technology. Campus intranet, student e-mail accounts, and computer access in designated common areas are available to students. The school has a published electronic and media policy.

Contact Ms. Carla Bolsius, Admissions Coordinator. 514-935-6357 Ext. 254. Fax: 514-935-1099. E-mail: bolsiusc@ecs.qc.ca. Website: www.ecs.qc.ca

MISS HALL'S SCHOOL

492 Holmes Road
Pittsfield, Massachusetts 01201

Head of School: Dr. Mary Grant

General Information Girls' boarding and day college-preparatory, arts, technology, Community Service, and Leadership Development school. Grades 9–PG. Founded: 1898. Setting: suburban. Nearest major city is Albany, NY. Students are housed in single-sex dormitories. 80-acre campus. 9 buildings on campus. Approved or accredited by Association of Independent Schools in New England, New England Association of Schools and Colleges, The Association of Boarding Schools, The College Board, and Massachusetts Department of Education. Member of National Association of Independent Schools and Secondary School Admission Test Board. Endowment: $17.5 million. Total enrollment: 206. Upper school average class size: 11. Upper school faculty-student ratio: 1:6. There are 157 required school days per year for Upper School students. Upper School students typically attend 5 days per week. The average school day consists of 6 hours.

Upper School Student Profile Grade 9: 44 students (44 girls); Grade 10: 48 students (48 girls); Grade 11: 66 students (66 girls); Grade 12: 48 students (48 girls). 75% of students are boarding students. 34% are state residents. 21 states are represented in upper school student body. 34% are international students. International students from Canada, China, Japan, Republic of Korea, Taiwan, and Viet Nam; 16 other countries represented in student body.

Faculty School total: 36. In upper school: 8 men, 28 women; 25 have advanced degrees; 16 reside on campus.

Subjects Offered Advanced Placement courses, algebra, American government, American history, American literature, anatomy, art, art history, athletics, biology, business skills, calculus, career exploration, ceramics, chamber groups, character education, chemistry, Chinese, college counseling, community service, computer science, CPR, dance, drama, drawing, driver education, ecology, economics, English, English literature, English-AP, entrepreneurship, environmental science, ESL, ethics, ethics and responsibility, European history, European history-AP, expressive arts, field ecology, fine arts, forensics, French, gardening, geometry, government/civics, health, history, human sexuality, Latin, leadership and service, mathematics, media literacy, music, music history, painting, photography, physics, physiology, political science, psychology, robotics, science, senior internship, service learning/internship, social studies, sociology, Spanish, theater, trigonometry, world cultures, world history.

Graduation Requirements Arts, arts and fine arts (art, music, dance, drama), English, foreign language, history, mathematics, physical education (includes health), science. Community service is required.

Special Academic Programs Advanced Placement exam preparation; honors section; independent study; term-away projects; academic accommodation for the gifted, the musically talented, and the artistically talented; special instructional classes for students with mild learning disabilities and Attention Deficit Disorder; ESL (20 students enrolled).

College Admission Counseling 46 students graduated in 2013; all went to college.

Student Life Upper grades have specified standards of dress, student council, honor system. Discipline rests equally with students and faculty.

Tuition and Aid Day student tuition: $30,900; 7-day tuition and room/board: $49,850. Tuition installment plan (Insured Tuition Payment Plan, Academic Management Services Plan, Key Tuition Payment Plan, monthly payment plans, individually arranged payment plans). Merit scholarship grants, need-based scholarship grants available. In 2013–14, 50% of upper-school students received aid; total upper-school merit-scholarship money awarded: $275,000. Total amount of financial aid awarded in 2013–14: $3,000,000.

Milton Academy

Milton Academy cultivates in its students a passion for learning and a respect for others. Embracing diversity and the pursuit of excellence, we create a community in which individuals develop competence, confidence, and character.

Our active learning environment, in and out of the classroom, develops creative and critical thinkers who are unafraid to express their ideas and are prepared to seek meaningful lifetime success and to live by our motto, "Dare to be true."

For more information, please contact:
Milton Academy
170 Centre Street
Milton, MA 02186
www.milton.edu

Admissions Traditional secondary-level entrance grade is 9. For fall 2013, 244 students applied for upper-level admission, 126 were accepted, 74 enrolled. PSAT, SAT, SSAT or TOEFL required. Deadline for receipt of application materials: February 15. Application fee required: $50. Interview required.

Athletics Interscholastic: alpine skiing, basketball, cross-country running, field hockey, golf, lacrosse, skiing (downhill), soccer, softball, tennis, volleyball; intramural: aerobics, aerobics/dance, alpine skiing, dance, equestrian sports, fitness, fitness walking, golf, jogging, modern dance, outdoor activities, outdoor education, outdoor skills, physical fitness, rock climbing, ropes courses, running, skiing (cross-country), skiing (downhill), snowboarding, swimming and diving, tennis, walking, wall climbing, wilderness, yoga. 3 coaches, 1 athletic trainer.

Computers Computers are regularly used in computer applications, English, foreign language, history, mathematics, music, newspaper, photography, science, yearbook classes. Computer network features include on-campus library services, online commercial services, Internet access, wireless campus network, Internet filtering or blocking technology. Student e-mail accounts and computer access in designated common areas are available to students. The school has a published electronic and media policy.

Contact Ms. Julie Bradley, Director of Admission. 413-499-1300. Fax: 413-448-2994. E-mail: info@misshalls.org. Website: www.misshalls.org

MISSOURI MILITARY ACADEMY

204 Grand Avenue
Mexico, Missouri 65265

Head of School: Mr. Charles "Tony" A. McGeorge

General Information Boys' boarding and day college-preparatory, technology, ESL, military science, and military school, affiliated with Christian faith. Boarding grades 6–PG, day grades 6–12. Founded: 1889. Setting: small town. Nearest major city is St. Louis. Students are housed in single-sex dormitories. 288-acre campus. 19 buildings on campus. Approved or accredited by Independent Schools Association of the Central States and The Association of Boarding Schools. Member of National Association of Independent Schools and Secondary School Admission Test Board. Endowment: $39 million. Total enrollment: 210. Upper school average class size: 10. Upper school faculty-student ratio: 1:11. There are 175 required school days per year for Upper School students. Upper School students typically attend 5 days per week. The average school day consists of 5 hours and 50 minutes.

Upper School Student Profile Grade 9: 29 students (29 boys); Grade 10: 41 students (41 boys); Grade 11: 60 students (60 boys); Grade 12: 48 students (48 boys). 99% of students are boarding students. 20% are state residents. 30 states are represented in upper school student body. 40% are international students. International students from China, Mexico, Mongolia, Republic of Korea, Russian Federation, and Taiwan; 10 other countries represented in student body.

Faculty School total: 47. In upper school: 27 men, 8 women; 27 have advanced degrees; 5 reside on campus.

Subjects Offered Algebra, American literature, art, biology, broadcasting, business, business skills, calculus, chemistry, computer science, drama, economics, English, ESL, fine arts, French, geography, geometry, government/civics, history, honors algebra, honors English, honors U.S. history, humanities, instrumental music, Internet, jazz band, journalism, JROTC or LEAD (Leadership Education and Development), keyboarding, languages, Latin American studies, leadership, literary magazine, marching band, mathematics, military science, music, newspaper, physical education, physical science, physics, physics-AP, psychology, science, social studies, sociology, Spanish, speech, statistics, student government, student publications, swimming, theater, track and field, typing, U.S. government, U.S. history, vocal ensemble, vocal music, world history, wrestling, writing, yearbook.

Graduation Requirements Arts and fine arts (art, music, dance, drama), business skills (includes word processing), computer science, English, foreign language, JROTC, mathematics, physical education (includes health), science, social studies (includes history), 20 hours of community service per school year.

Special Academic Programs 9 Advanced Placement exams for which test preparation is offered; honors section; independent study; study at local college for college credit; academic accommodation for the gifted, the musically talented, and the artistically talented; remedial reading and/or remedial writing; remedial math; special instructional classes for students with Attention Deficit Disorder; ESL (33 students enrolled).

College Admission Counseling 52 students graduated in 2013; all went to college, including Texas A&M University; The University of Texas at Austin; University of California, Berkeley; University of Miami; University of Missouri; Washington University in St. Louis. Median SAT critical reading: 467, median SAT math: 547, median combined SAT: 1016, median composite ACT: 21.

Student Life Upper grades have uniform requirement, student council, honor system. Discipline rests equally with students and faculty. Attendance at religious services is required.

Summer Programs Remediation, enrichment, ESL, sports, rigorous outdoor training programs offered; session focuses on academics and leadership; held both on and off campus; held at water park in Jefferson City, MO and Courtois River for float/canoe trips; accepts boys and girls; open to students from other schools. 70

students usually enrolled. 2014 schedule: June 22 to July 18. Application deadline: June 15.

Tuition and Aid Day student tuition: $9100; 7-day tuition and room/board: $31,500. Guaranteed tuition plan. Tuition installment plan (individually arranged payment plans, school's own payment plan). Tuition reduction for siblings, merit scholarship grants, need-based scholarship grants, need-based loans available. In 2013–14, 30% of upper-school students received aid; total upper-school merit-scholarship money awarded: $25,000. Total amount of financial aid awarded in 2013–14: $875,000.

Admissions Traditional secondary-level entrance grade is 9. For fall 2013, 150 students applied for upper-level admission, 114 were accepted, 83 enrolled. SSAT or TOEFL or SLEP required. Deadline for receipt of application materials: none. Application fee required: $25. Interview required.

Athletics Interscholastic: aquatics, baseball, basketball, cross-country running, drill team, football, golf, JROTC drill, marksmanship, outdoor activities, riflery, soccer, swimming and diving, tennis, track and field, weight training, wrestling; intramural: aquatics, basketball, canoeing/kayaking, equestrian sports, fishing, fitness, fitness walking, flag football, horseback riding, indoor track, marksmanship, martial arts, outdoor activities, outdoor recreation, outdoor skills, paint ball, physical fitness, physical training, rappelling, riflery, roller blading, ropes courses, running, soccer, softball, strength & conditioning, swimming and diving, table tennis, tennis, touch football, track and field, volleyball, weight lifting, weight training, winter (indoor) track, wrestling. 12 coaches, 1 athletic trainer.

Computers Computers are regularly used in business, English, history, journalism, library, mathematics, newspaper, science, yearbook classes. Computer network features include on-campus library services, online commercial services, Internet access, wireless campus network, Internet filtering or blocking technology. Campus intranet, student e-mail accounts, and computer access in designated common areas are available to students. Students grades are available online. The school has a published electronic and media policy.

Contact Ms. Sandy Riutcel, Admissions Office Coordinator. 573-581-1776 Ext. 321. Fax: 573-581-0081. E-mail: sandy.riutcel@missourimilitaryacademy.com. Website: www.MissouriMilitaryAcademy.org

MISS PORTER'S SCHOOL

60 Main Street
Farmington, Connecticut 06032

Head of School: Dr. Katherine G. Windsor

General Information Girls' boarding and day college-preparatory and arts school. Grades 9–12. Founded: 1843. Setting: suburban. Nearest major city is Hartford. Students are housed in single-sex dormitories. 50-acre campus. 56 buildings on campus. Approved or accredited by New England Association of Schools and Colleges and Connecticut Department of Education. Member of National Association of Independent Schools and Secondary School Admission Test Board. Endowment: $93 million. Total enrollment: 311. Upper school average class size: 10. Upper school faculty-student ratio: 1:7. There are 170 required school days per year for Upper School students. Upper School students typically attend 5 days per week. The average school day consists of 7 hours.

Upper School Student Profile Grade 9: 68 students (68 girls); Grade 10: 74 students (74 girls); Grade 11: 89 students (89 girls); Grade 12: 80 students (80 girls). 66% of students are boarding students. 55% are state residents. 23 states are represented in upper school student body. 14% are international students. International students from China and Republic of Korea; 28 other countries represented in student body.

Faculty School total: 44. In upper school: 12 men, 32 women; 33 have advanced degrees; 34 reside on campus.

Subjects Offered Acting, advanced chemistry, advanced computer applications, advanced math, Advanced Placement courses, advanced studio art-AP, African history, algebra, American history, American literature, anatomy and physiology, aquatics, area studies, art history, art history-AP, arts, astronomy, athletics, ballet, biology, biology-AP, British literature, calculus, calculus-AP, career/college preparation, ceramics, chemistry, chemistry-AP, Chinese, Chinese history, classical language, college counseling, college planning, community service, computer applications, computer graphics, computer programming, computer science, creative writing, dance, dance performance, desktop publishing, drama, drama performance, economics, economics and history, engineering, English, English literature, environmental science, environmental science-AP, ethical decision making, ethics, European history, European history-AP, experiential education, expository writing, fitness, foreign language, forensics, French, French language-AP, French literature-AP, geometry, global issues, golf, graphic design, health and wellness, history, honors geometry, human rights, international relations, intro to computers, Japanese history, jazz, jewelry making, languages, Latin, Latin American literature, Latin-AP, leadership, mathematics, Middle Eastern history, model United Nations, modern dance, modern European history-AP, multicultural literature, music, music history, music performance, music theory, participation in sports, performing arts, personal finance, photography, physics, physics-AP, pre-calculus, printmaking, psychology, public speaking, science, Shakespeare, social studies, Spanish, Spanish language-AP, Spanish literature-AP, sports, squash, statistics, statistics-AP, student government, studio art, studio art-AP, swimming, swimming test, tennis, textiles, theater, trigonometry, U.S. history, U.S.

history-AP, video film production, visual arts, vocal music, Web site design, Western civilization, writing, yoga.

Graduation Requirements Arts and fine arts (art, music, dance, drama), athletics, computer science, English, experiential education, foreign language, leadership, mathematics, science, social studies (includes history), online course. Community service is required.

Special Academic Programs 26 Advanced Placement exams for which test preparation is offered; honors section; independent study; term-away projects; study abroad; ESL.

College Admission Counseling 77 students graduated in 2013; 75 went to college, including Carnegie Mellon University; Georgetown University; Middlebury College; New York University; The Johns Hopkins University; University of Chicago. Other: 2 had other specific plans. Mean SAT critical reading: 644, mean SAT math: 635, mean SAT writing: 660, mean combined SAT: 1939.

Student Life Upper grades have specified standards of dress, student council, honor system. Discipline rests equally with students and faculty.

Summer Programs Enrichment, advancement programs offered; session focuses on Model UN, leadership (for middle school girls); held on campus; accepts girls; open to students from other schools. 100 students usually enrolled. 2014 schedule: July 6 to July 19. Application deadline: none.

Tuition and Aid Day student tuition: $40,245; 7-day tuition and room/board: $50,455. Tuition installment plan (monthly payment plans, individually arranged payment plans). Merit scholarship grants, need-based scholarship grants available. In 2013–14, 38% of upper-school students received aid; total upper-school merit-scholarship money awarded: $50,000. Total amount of financial aid awarded in 2013–14: $3,100,000.

Admissions Traditional secondary-level entrance grade is 9. For fall 2013, 420 students applied for upper-level admission, 197 were accepted, 94 enrolled. ISEE, PSAT and SAT for applicants to grade 11 and 12, SSAT or TOEFL required. Deadline for receipt of application materials: January 15. Application fee required: $65. Interview required.

Athletics Interscholastic: alpine skiing, badminton, basketball, crew, cross-country running, dance, diving, equestrian sports, field hockey, Frisbee, golf, horseback riding, independent competitive sports, lacrosse, rowing, running, skiing (downhill), soccer, softball, squash, swimming and diving, tennis, track and field, ultimate Frisbee, volleyball; intramural: aerobics, aerobics/Nautilus, ballet, climbing, dance, equestrian sports, fitness, golf, horseback riding, jogging, life saving, martial arts, modern dance, outdoor adventure, outdoor recreation, physical fitness, physical training, rock climbing, running, self defense, skiing (downhill), snowboarding, squash, strength & conditioning, swimming and diving, tennis, wall climbing, weight training, yoga.

Computers Computers are regularly used in computer applications, desktop publishing, graphic design, graphics, introduction to technology, publications, Web site design classes. Computer network features include on-campus library services, online commercial services, Internet access, wireless campus network, Internet filtering or blocking technology, online courses. Campus intranet, student e-mail accounts, and computer access in designated common areas are available to students. Students grades are available online. The school has a published electronic and media policy.

Contact Liz Schmitt, Director of Admission. 860-409-3530. Fax: 860-409-3531. E-mail: liz_schmitt@missporters.org. Website: www.porters.org

MMI PREPARATORY SCHOOL

154 Centre Street
Freeland, Pennsylvania 18224

Head of School: Mr. Thomas G. Hood

General Information Coeducational day college-preparatory, arts, and technology school. Grades 6–12. Founded: 1879. Setting: small town. Nearest major city is Hazleton. 20-acre campus. 1 building on campus. Approved or accredited by Middle States Association of Colleges and Schools and Pennsylvania Department of Education. Member of National Association of Independent Schools. Endowment: $19 million. Total enrollment: 247. Upper school average class size: 16. Upper school faculty-student ratio: 1:11. There are 168 required school days per year for Upper School students. Upper School students typically attend 5 days per week. The average school day consists of 6 hours and 30 minutes.

Upper School Student Profile Grade 9: 42 students (25 boys, 17 girls); Grade 10: 35 students (22 boys, 13 girls); Grade 11: 44 students (24 boys, 20 girls); Grade 12: 36 students (18 boys, 18 girls).

Faculty School total: 27. In upper school: 10 men, 17 women; 19 have advanced degrees.

Subjects Offered 3-dimensional art, algebra, American history, American history-AP, American literature, anatomy, anthropology, art, art-AP, biology, biology-AP, calculus, chemistry, chemistry-AP, Chinese, computer programming, computer programming-AP, computer science, consumer education, creative writing, earth science, economics, English, English language and composition-AP, English literature, English literature and composition-AP, environmental science, European history, European history-AP, expository writing, fine arts, geography, geometry, German, government/civics, grammar, health, history, keyboarding, Latin, marine biology, mathematics, music, physical education, physics, physics-AP, physiology, psychology,

science, social studies, Spanish, speech, statistics, trigonometry, world history, world literature.

Graduation Requirements Analysis and differential calculus, arts and fine arts (art, music, dance, drama), college counseling, computer science, consumer education, economics, English, foreign language, mathematics, physical education (includes health), science, social studies (includes history), speech, independent research project presentation every spring, public speaking assembly project every year.

Special Academic Programs 10 Advanced Placement exams for which test preparation is offered; honors section; study at local college for college credit; academic accommodation for the gifted; special instructional classes for blind students.

College Admission Counseling 43 students graduated in 2013; 42 went to college, including Bucknell University; Drexel University; Lehigh University; Saint Joseph's University; The University of Scranton; University of Pennsylvania. Other: 1 entered military service. Mean SAT critical reading: 568, mean SAT math: 577, mean SAT writing: 574, mean combined SAT: 1719.

Student Life Upper grades have specified standards of dress, student council. Discipline rests primarily with faculty.

Tuition and Aid Day student tuition: $13,450. Tuition installment plan (monthly payment plans). Merit scholarship grants, need-based scholarship grants, paying campus jobs available. In 2013–14, 53% of upper-school students received aid; total upper-school merit-scholarship money awarded: $79,000. Total amount of financial aid awarded in 2013–14: $841,200.

Admissions Traditional secondary-level entrance grade is 9. For fall 2013, 36 students applied for upper-level admission, 30 were accepted, 17 enrolled. Cognitive Abilities Test and Iowa Tests of Basic Skills required. Deadline for receipt of application materials: none. Application fee required: $25. On-campus interview required.

Athletics Interscholastic: baseball (boys), basketball (b,g), cross-country running (b,g), soccer (b,g), softball (g), tennis (b,g), volleyball (g); intramural: bowling (b,g); coed interscholastic: golf; coed intramural: skiing (downhill), snowboarding. 2 PE instructors, 15 coaches, 1 athletic trainer.

Computers Computers are regularly used in all classes. Computer network features include on-campus library services, Internet access, wireless campus network, Internet filtering or blocking technology. Computer access in designated common areas is available to students. Students grades are available online. The school has a published electronic and media policy.

Contact Aprilaurie Whitley, Director of Admissions and Financial Aid. 570-636-1108 Ext. 136. Fax: 570-636-0742. E-mail: awhitley@mmiprep.org. Website: www.mmiprep.org

MODESTO CHRISTIAN SCHOOL

5901 Sisk Road
Modesto, California 95356

Head of School: Rev. Lance Lowell

General Information Coeducational day college-preparatory, arts, and religious studies school, affiliated with Assembly of God Church. Grades K–12. Founded: 1962. Setting: suburban. Nearest major city is Sacramento. 55-acre campus. 6 buildings on campus. Approved or accredited by Association of Christian Schools International, Western Association of Schools and Colleges, and California Department of Education. Total enrollment: 580. Upper school average class size: 20. Upper school faculty-student ratio: 1:10. There are 180 required school days per year for Upper School students. Upper School students typically attend 5 days per week. The average school day consists of 6 hours and 45 minutes.

Upper School Student Profile Grade 9: 65 students (41 boys, 24 girls); Grade 10: 66 students (41 boys, 25 girls); Grade 11: 71 students (37 boys, 34 girls); Grade 12: 78 students (43 boys, 35 girls). 10% of students are members of Assembly of God Church.

Faculty School total: 26. In upper school: 10 men, 16 women; 5 have advanced degrees.

Subjects Offered Advanced biology, algebra, American literature, American sign language, anatomy and physiology, arts, band, biology, biology-AP, calculus-AP, career education, chemistry, church history, consumer education, digital photography, drama, economics, English, English literature, environmental science, fine arts, French language-AP, general math, geometry, grammar, health, history, honors English, keyboarding, mathematics, physical education, physics, political science, pre-algebra, pre-calculus, religion, science, social sciences, social studies, Spanish, Spanish language-AP, speech, studio art-AP, study skills, U.S. government, U.S. history, U.S. history-AP, word processing, world history.

Graduation Requirements Arts and fine arts (art, music, dance, drama), computers, English, foreign language, health, mathematics, physical education (includes health), religion (includes Bible studies and theology), science, social studies (includes history), speech.

Special Academic Programs 7 Advanced Placement exams for which test preparation is offered; honors section; remedial reading and/or remedial writing; remedial math; programs in English, mathematics, general development for dyslexic students.

College Admission Counseling 68 students graduated in 2013; 66 went to college, including Azusa Pacific University; California Polytechnic State University,

San Luis Obispo; California State University, Stanislaus; Modesto Junior College. Other: 1 went to work, 1 entered military service. Median SAT critical reading: 524, median SAT math: 513, median SAT writing: 505, median combined SAT: 1037, median composite ACT: 24. 10% scored over 600 on SAT critical reading, 10% scored over 600 on SAT math, 6% scored over 600 on SAT writing, 14% scored over 1800 on combined SAT, 18% scored over 26 on composite ACT.

Student Life Upper grades have specified standards of dress, student council. Discipline rests primarily with faculty. Attendance at religious services is required.

Summer Programs Remediation, advancement programs offered; held on campus; accepts boys and girls; open to students from other schools. 2014 schedule: June 2 to July 8. Application deadline: May 25.

Tuition and Aid Day student tuition: $8270. Tuition installment plan (FACTS Tuition Payment Plan, monthly payment plans, individually arranged payment plans). Tuition reduction for siblings, merit scholarship grants, need-based scholarship grants, paying campus jobs available. In 2013–14, 20% of upper-school students received aid.

Admissions Traditional secondary-level entrance grade is 9. Admissions testing or Stanford Achievement Test required. Deadline for receipt of application materials: none. Application fee required: $275. On-campus interview required.

Athletics Interscholastic: baseball (boys), basketball (b,g), football (b), golf (b,g), soccer (b,g), softball (g), strength & conditioning (b,g), volleyball (g), wrestling (b); coed interscholastic: fitness, tennis, track and field, weight lifting. 2 PE instructors, 20 coaches.

Computers Computers are regularly used in career education, college planning, typing, yearbook classes. Computer resources include on-campus library services, wireless campus network, Internet filtering or blocking technology. Student e-mail accounts are available to students. Students grades are available online. The school has a published electronic and media policy.

Contact Mrs. Rachel Iversen, Admissions Office. 209-529-5510. Fax: 209-545-9930. E-mail: rachel.iversen@modestochristian.org. Website: www.modestochristian.org

MONSIGNOR DONOVAN HIGH SCHOOL

711 Hooper Avenue
Toms River, New Jersey 08753

Head of School: Edward Gere

General Information Coeducational day college-preparatory school, affiliated with Roman Catholic Church. Grades 9–12. Founded: 1962. Setting: suburban. 1 building on campus. Approved or accredited by Middle States Association of Colleges and Schools, National Catholic Education Association, and New Jersey Department of Education. Total enrollment: 726. Upper school average class size: 30. Upper school faculty-student ratio: 1:15.

Upper School Student Profile Grade 9: 161 students (77 boys, 84 girls); Grade 10: 182 students (79 boys, 103 girls); Grade 11: 181 students (88 boys, 93 girls); Grade 12: 202 students (95 boys, 107 girls). 85% of students are Roman Catholic.

Faculty School total: 61. In upper school: 28 men, 33 women.

Special Academic Programs Advanced Placement exam preparation; honors section; independent study; study at local college for college credit; academic accommodation for the gifted, the musically talented, and the artistically talented; remedial reading and/or remedial writing; remedial math.

College Admission Counseling 210 students graduated in 2012; 208 went to college. Other: 1 entered military service.

Student Life Upper grades have uniform requirement, student council, honor system. Discipline rests equally with students and faculty. Attendance at religious services is required.

Tuition and Aid Day student tuition: $10,875. Tuition installment plan (SMART Tuition Payment Plan, monthly payment plans). Merit scholarship grants, need-based scholarship grants, paying campus jobs available. In 2012–13, 20% of upper-school students received aid. Total amount of financial aid awarded in 2012–13: $400,000.

Admissions Traditional secondary-level entrance grade is 9. High School Placement Test (closed version) from Scholastic Testing Service or Scholastic Testing Service High School Placement Test required. Deadline for receipt of application materials: October 31. Application fee required: $50. On-campus interview recommended.

Athletics Interscholastic: baseball (boys), cheering (g), football (b), golf (b), ice hockey (b), lacrosse (g), softball (g), wrestling (b); coed interscholastic: basketball, bowling, cross-country running, dance, hiking/backpacking, sailing, skiing (cross-country), snowboarding, soccer, strength & conditioning, surfing, swimming and diving, tennis, weight lifting, weight training. 5 PE instructors, 22 coaches, 1 athletic trainer.

Computers Computers are regularly used in all academic classes. Computer network features include on-campus library services, Internet access, wireless campus network, Internet filtering or blocking technology. Student e-mail accounts are available to students. Students grades are available online.

Contact Mrs. Cynthia Saporito, Registrar. 732-349-8801 Ext. 2426. Fax: 732-505-8014. E-mail: csaporito@mondonhs.com. Website: www.mondonhs.com

MONTCLAIR KIMBERLEY ACADEMY

201 Valley Road
Montclair, New Jersey 07042

Head of School: Mr. Thomas W. Nammack

General Information Coeducational day college-preparatory, arts, and technology school. Grades PK–12. Founded: 1887. Setting: suburban. Nearest major city is New York, NY. 28-acre campus. 1 building on campus. Approved or accredited by Middle States Association of Colleges and Schools and National Lutheran School Accreditation. Member of National Association of Independent Schools and Secondary School Admission Test Board. Endowment: $12 million. Total enrollment: 1,031. Upper school average class size: 12. Upper school faculty-student ratio: 1:6. Upper School students typically attend 5 days per week. The average school day consists of 6 hours and 30 minutes.

Faculty School total: 73. In upper school: 40 men, 33 women; 64 have advanced degrees.

Subjects Offered Acting, advanced chemistry, advanced math, algebra, American history, American literature, architecture, art, astronomy, biology, biology-AP, British literature, calculus, calculus-AP, chemistry, chemistry-AP, Chinese, chorus, communications, concert band, creative writing, dance, digital photography, drama, driver education, ecology, economics, economics-AP, English, English literature, environmental science, ethics, European history, expository writing, fine arts, French, French language-AP, French literature-AP, geometry, government/civics, health, history, Latin, mathematics, music, photography, physical education, physics, physics-AP, post-calculus, Spanish, Spanish language-AP, Spanish literature-AP, statistics-AP, theater, trigonometry, world history, world literature, world wide web design, writing.

Graduation Requirements Art, arts and fine arts (art, music, dance, drama), English, foreign language, history, mathematics, music, physical education (includes health), science, swimming, citizenship. Community service is required.

Special Academic Programs Advanced Placement exam preparation; honors section; independent study; term-away projects; study abroad; academic accommodation for the gifted.

College Admission Counseling 105 students graduated in 2012; 104 went to college, including Georgetown University; Lafayette College; New York University; Penn State University Park; Princeton University; The George Washington University. Other: 1 entered a postgraduate year. Mean SAT critical reading: 630, mean SAT math: 647. 60% scored over 600 on SAT critical reading, 65% scored over 600 on SAT math.

Student Life Upper grades have specified standards of dress, student council, honor system. Discipline rests equally with students and faculty.

Tuition and Aid Day student tuition: $32,000. Tuition installment plan (Insured Tuition Payment Plan, monthly payment plans, individually arranged payment plans). Need-based scholarship grants available. In 2012–13, 15% of upper-school students received aid. Total amount of financial aid awarded in 2012–13: $1,281,308.

Admissions Traditional secondary-level entrance grade is 9. ISEE or SSAT required. Deadline for receipt of application materials: January 31. Application fee required: $50. On-campus interview required.

Athletics Interscholastic: baseball (boys), basketball (b,g), cheering (g), cross-country running (b,g), dance (b,g), dance team (b,g), fencing (b,g), field hockey (g), football (b), ice hockey (b), lacrosse (b,g), outdoor activities (b,g), physical fitness (b,g), soccer (b,g), softball (g), swimming and diving (b,g), tennis (b,g), track and field (b,g), volleyball (g), winter (indoor) track (b,g); coed interscholastic: golf. 5 PE instructors, 9 coaches, 2 athletic trainers.

Computers Computers are regularly used in all classes. Computer network features include on-campus library services, online commercial services, Internet access, wireless campus network, Internet filtering or blocking technology, 1:1 laptop school, community Intranet. Campus intranet and student e-mail accounts are available to students. The school has a published electronic and media policy.

Contact Sarah Rowland, Director of Admissions and Financial Aid. 973-509-7930. Fax: 973-509-4526. E-mail: srowland@mka.org. Website: www.mka.org

MONTGOMERY BELL ACADEMY

4001 Harding Road
Nashville, Tennessee 37205

Head of School: Bradford Gioia

General Information Boys' day college-preparatory and arts school. Grades 7–12. Founded: 1867. Setting: urban. 43-acre campus. 10 buildings on campus. Approved or accredited by Southern Association of Colleges and Schools, Southern Association of Independent Schools, and Tennessee Association of Independent Schools. Member of National Association of Independent Schools and Secondary School Admission Test Board. Endowment: $59.8 million. Total enrollment: 718. Upper school average class size: 13. Upper school faculty-student ratio: 1:7. There are 180 required school days per year for Upper School students. Upper School students typically attend 5 days per week. The average school day consists of 7 hours and 20 minutes.

Upper School Student Profile Grade 9: 131 students (131 boys); Grade 10: 130 students (130 boys); Grade 11: 121 students (121 boys); Grade 12: 113 students (113 boys).

Faculty School total: 98. In upper school: 76 men, 17 women; 63 have advanced degrees.

Subjects Offered Advanced Placement courses, algebra, American history, American history-AP, American literature, American literature-AP, art, art history, art history-AP, biology, biology-AP, calculus, calculus-AP, chemistry, chemistry-AP, Chinese, computer programming, computer science, computer science-AP, drama, earth science, economics, English, English literature, environmental science-AP, European history, European history-AP, fine arts, French, French language-AP, French literature-AP, French-AP, geography, geology, geometry, German, German-AP, government/civics, grammar, Greek, history, Latin, Latin-AP, mathematics, music, music history, music theory, music theory-AP, physical education, physics, physics-AP, science, social studies, Spanish, Spanish-AP, speech, statistics, statistics-AP, theater, trigonometry, U.S. government and politics-AP, U.S. history-AP, world history, world history-AP, writing.

Graduation Requirements Arts and fine arts (art, music, dance, drama), English, foreign language, mathematics, physical education (includes health), science, social studies (includes history).

Special Academic Programs Advanced Placement exam preparation; honors section; term-away projects; study abroad.

College Admission Counseling 124 students graduated in 2013; all went to college, including Auburn University at Montgomery; Furman University; The University of Tennessee; University of Mississippi; University of Virginia; Vanderbilt University. Mean SAT critical reading: 640, mean SAT math: 650, mean SAT writing: 620, mean combined SAT: 1910, mean composite ACT: 28.

Student Life Upper grades have specified standards of dress, student council, honor system. Discipline rests primarily with faculty.

Summer Programs Remediation, enrichment, sports, art/fine arts, rigorous outdoor training, computer instruction programs offered; session focuses on academics and athletics; held both on and off campus; held at Long Mountain, TN; accepts boys and girls; open to students from other schools. 2,400 students usually enrolled. 2014 schedule: June 1 to July 31.

Tuition and Aid Day student tuition: $22,280. Tuition installment plan (monthly payment plans, Dewar Tuition Refund Plan). Need-based scholarship grants available. In 2013–14, 23% of upper-school students received aid. Total amount of financial aid awarded in 2013–14: $1,300,000.

Admissions Traditional secondary-level entrance grade is 9. For fall 2013, 62 students applied for upper-level admission, 30 were accepted, 26 enrolled. ISEE required. Deadline for receipt of application materials: February 1. Application fee required: $50. Interview required.

Athletics Interscholastic: baseball, basketball, bowling, crew, cross-country running, diving, football, Frisbee, golf, hockey, ice hockey, lacrosse, riflery, rock climbing, rowing, soccer, swimming and diving, tennis, track and field, ultimate Frisbee, wrestling; intramural: backpacking, baseball, basketball, cheering, climbing, crew, cricket, fencing, flag football, fly fishing, football, Frisbee, hiking/backpacking, independent competitive sports, outdoor activities, paddle tennis, running, soccer, strength & conditioning, table tennis, track and field, weight training, wilderness, yoga. 2 PE instructors, 4 coaches, 2 athletic trainers.

Computers Computers are regularly used in all academic classes. Computer network features include on-campus library services, online commercial services, Internet access, wireless campus network, Internet filtering or blocking technology. Student e-mail accounts and computer access in designated common areas are available to students. Students grades are available online. The school has a published electronic and media policy.

Contact Mr. Greg Ferrell, Director, Admission and Financial Aid. 615-369-5311. Fax: 615-369-5316. E-mail: greg.ferrell@montgomerybell.edu. Website: www.montgomerybell.edu

MONT'KIARA INTERNATIONAL SCHOOL

22 Jalan Kiara
Mont Kiara
Kuala Lumpur 50480, Malaysia

Head of School: Brian Brumsickle

General Information Coeducational day college-preparatory school. Grades 1–12. Founded: 1994. Setting: suburban. 6-acre campus. 3 buildings on campus. Approved or accredited by Western Association of Schools and Colleges. Language of instruction: English. Total enrollment: 1,005. Upper school average class size: 20. Upper school faculty-student ratio: 1:10. There are 180 required school days per year for Upper School students. Upper School students typically attend 5 days per week. The average school day consists of 6 hours and 30 minutes.

Faculty School total: 135. In upper school: 35 men, 31 women; 28 have advanced degrees.

Subjects Offered Addiction.

Special Academic Programs International Baccalaureate program; ESL (112 students enrolled).

College Admission Counseling 58 students graduated in 2013; 45 went to college, including The University of British Columbia; University of Richmond. Other: 5 went to work, 5 entered military service, 3 had other specific plans. Mean SAT critical reading: 565, mean SAT math: 595, mean SAT writing: 532, mean combined SAT: 1692. 85% scored over 600 on SAT critical reading, 76% scored over 600 on SAT math, 91% scored over 600 on SAT writing, 84% scored over 1800 on combined SAT.

Student Life Upper grades have uniform requirement, student council. Discipline rests primarily with faculty.

Tuition and Aid Day student tuition: 98,839 Malaysian ringgits.

Admissions Traditional secondary-level entrance grade is 9. For fall 2013, 14 students applied for upper-level admission, 9 were accepted, 9 enrolled. Admissions testing, Math Placement Exam and Woodcock-Johnson Revised Achievement Test required. Deadline for receipt of application materials: none. Application fee required: 1000 Malaysian ringgits. On-campus interview required.

Athletics Interscholastic: baseball (boys, girls), basketball (b,g), martial arts (b,g), rugby (g), soccer (b,g), softball (b,g), swimming and diving (b,g), tennis (b,g), track and field (b,g), volleyball (b,g), wall climbing (b,g); coed interscholastic: aerobics/dance, aquatics, badminton, climbing, cooperative games, cross-country running, dance squad, swimming and diving, tennis, volleyball. 3 PE instructors, 2 coaches, 1 athletic trainer.

Computers Computers are regularly used in art classes. Computer network features include on-campus library services, online commercial services, Internet access, wireless campus network, Internet filtering or blocking technology. Student e-mail accounts and computer access in designated common areas are available to students. Students grades are available online. The school has a published electronic and media policy.

Contact Mohanaeswari Nadarajah, Executive Secretary, Admissions. 603-2093 8604. Fax: 603-2903 6045. E-mail: mohana@mkis.edu.my. Website: www.mkis.edu.my

MONTVERDE ACADEMY

17235 Seventh Street
Montverde, Florida 34756

Head of School: Mr. Kasey C. Kesselring

General Information Coeducational boarding and day college-preparatory and arts school. Boarding grades 7–PG, day grades PK–PG. Founded: 1912. Setting: small town. Nearest major city is Orlando. Students are housed in single-sex dormitories. 125-acre campus. 25 buildings on campus. Approved or accredited by Florida Council of Independent Schools, Southern Association of Colleges and Schools, Southern Association of Independent Schools, and The Association of Boarding Schools. Member of National Association of Independent Schools. Endowment: $8 million. Total enrollment: 1,010. Upper school average class size: 20. Upper school faculty-student ratio: 1:12. Upper School students typically attend 5 days per week.

Upper School Student Profile Grade 9: 91 students (51 boys, 40 girls); Grade 10: 138 students (77 boys, 61 girls); Grade 11: 163 students (104 boys, 59 girls); Grade 12: 166 students (102 boys, 64 girls). 65% of students are boarding students. 30% are state residents. 9 states are represented in upper school student body. 65% are international students. International students from China, Germany, Puerto Rico, Republic of Korea, Thailand, and Viet Nam; 34 other countries represented in student body.

Faculty School total: 57. In upper school: 14 men, 19 women; 20 have advanced degrees; 38 reside on campus.

Subjects Offered 20th century history, 3-dimensional art, accounting, acting, advanced computer applications, algebra, American history, American literature, anatomy, anatomy and physiology, ancient world history, art, art history, art history-AP, band, Basic programming, Bible studies, biochemistry, biology, biology-AP, broadcast journalism, business, business law, calculus, calculus-AP, ceramics, chemistry, chemistry-AP, Chinese, choral music, clayworking, comparative government and politics-AP, computer applications, computer graphics, computer programming, computer science, computer science-AP, concert band, concert choir, crafts, creative writing, digital applications, drama, economics, English, English language and composition-AP, English language-AP, English literature, English literature and composition-AP, English literature-AP, environmental science, ESL, European history, European history-AP, finance, fitness, genetics, geography, geometry, government, graphic design, health, history, honors algebra, honors English, honors geometry, honors U.S. history, human geography - AP, international affairs, introduction to theater, keyboarding, marine biology, marketing, mathematics, microeconomics-AP, modern world history, music appreciation, music theory-AP, personal finance, photo shop, photography, physical education, physics, physics-AP, physiology, piano, politics, pre-calculus, programming, psychology, psychology-AP, SAT/ACT preparation, science, Spanish, Spanish language-AP, statistics-AP, studio art, studio art-AP, study skills, symphonic band, technical theater, trigonometry, U.S. government and politics-AP, U.S. history, U.S. history-AP, Web site design, woodworking, world history, world history-AP, zoology.

Graduation Requirements Arts and fine arts (art, music, dance, drama), computer science, electives, English, foreign language, mathematics, physical education (includes health), science, social studies (includes history), international students are not required to take a foreign language if their native language is not English.

Special Academic Programs Advanced Placement exam preparation; honors section; ESL (106 students enrolled).

College Admission Counseling 171 students graduated in 2013; all went to college. Median SAT critical reading: 423, median SAT math: 542, median SAT writing: 442, median combined SAT: 1364, median composite ACT: 18.

Student Life Upper grades have uniform requirement, student council, honor system. Discipline rests equally with students and faculty.

Summer Programs Remediation, advancement, ESL programs offered; session focuses on academics; held on campus; accepts boys and girls; open to students from other schools. 50 students usually enrolled. 2014 schedule: June 21 to August 3. Application deadline: none.

Tuition and Aid Day student tuition: $11,812; 7-day tuition and room/board: $42,000. Tuition installment plan (monthly payment plans). Tuition reduction for siblings, need-based scholarship grants available. In 2013–14, 25% of upper-school students received aid. Total amount of financial aid awarded in 2013–14: $2,000,000.

Admissions Traditional secondary-level entrance grade is 9. ISEE or SSAT required. Deadline for receipt of application materials: none. Application fee required: $50. Interview recommended.

Athletics Interscholastic: baseball (boys), basketball (b,g), cheering (g), cross-country running (b,g), golf (b,g), soccer (b,g), tennis (b,g), track and field (b,g), volleyball (g), weight lifting (b,g); intramural: basketball (b,g), dance team (b,g), flag football (b), paddle tennis (b,g), soccer (b,g), softball (b,g), table tennis (b,g), tennis (b,g); coed interscholastic: equestrian sports, horseback riding, track and field, weight lifting; coed intramural: aerobics/dance, aquatics, basketball, bicycling, billiards, canoeing/kayaking, equestrian sports, fishing, fitness, fitness walking, Frisbee, horseback riding, jogging, juggling, kayaking, paddle tennis, physical fitness, physical training, running, soccer, strength & conditioning, ultimate Frisbee, walking, water skiing, yoga. 3 PE instructors, 16 coaches, 7 athletic trainers.

Computers Computers are regularly used in accounting, all academic, computer applications, digital applications, engineering, graphic design, information technology, language development, library skills, newspaper, programming, publications, SAT preparation, senior seminar, Web site design classes. Computer network features include on-campus library services, online commercial services, Internet access, wireless campus network, Internet filtering or blocking technology. Computer access in designated common areas is available to students. Students grades are available online. The school has a published electronic and media policy.

Contact Mr. Jon Hopman, Dean of Admission and Financial Aid. 407-469-2561 Ext. 4101. Fax: 407-469-3711. E-mail: jon.hopman@montverde.org. Website: www.montverde.org

MOORESTOWN FRIENDS SCHOOL

110 East Main Street
Moorestown, New Jersey 08057

Head of School: Mr. Laurence Van Meter

General Information Coeducational day college-preparatory, arts, religious studies, and technology school, affiliated with Society of Friends. Grades PS–12. Founded: 1785. Setting: suburban. Nearest major city is Philadelphia, PA. 48-acre campus. 9 buildings on campus. Approved or accredited by Friends Council on Education, Middle States Association of Colleges and Schools, and New Jersey Department of Education. Member of National Association of Independent Schools. Endowment: $8.3 million. Total enrollment: 722. Upper school average class size: 14. Upper school faculty-student ratio: 1:7. There are 170 required school days per year for Upper School students. Upper School students typically attend 5 days per week. The average school day consists of 7 hours and 5 minutes.

Upper School Student Profile Grade 9: 77 students (38 boys, 39 girls); Grade 10: 78 students (44 boys, 34 girls); Grade 11: 76 students (39 boys, 37 girls); Grade 12: 72 students (36 boys, 36 girls). 3% of students are members of Society of Friends.

Faculty School total: 100. In upper school: 18 men, 24 women; 28 have advanced degrees.

Subjects Offered Algebra, American history, American literature, art, art history, biology, calculus, ceramics, chemistry, Chinese, community service, computer programming, computer science, creative writing, drama, driver education, earth science, economics, English, English literature, environmental science, ethics, European history, expository writing, finance, fine arts, French, geometry, government/civics, grammar, health, history, mathematics, music, philosophy, photography, physical education, physics, psychology, religion, science, social studies, Spanish, theater, trigonometry, world history, writing.

Graduation Requirements Arts and fine arts (art, music, dance, drama), English, foreign language, history, mathematics, physical education (includes health), science, senior project, social studies (includes history). Community service is required.

Special Academic Programs Advanced Placement exam preparation; honors section; independent study; term-away projects; study abroad.

College Admission Counseling 71 students graduated in 2013; all went to college, including Boston University; Bucknell University; Cornell University; New York University; The Johns Hopkins University; University of Delaware. Mean SAT critical reading: 627, mean SAT math: 619, mean SAT writing: 631, mean combined SAT: 1877.

Student Life Upper grades have specified standards of dress, student council, honor system. Discipline rests primarily with faculty. Attendance at religious services is required.

Summer Programs Enrichment programs offered; held on campus; accepts boys and girls; open to students from other schools.

Tuition and Aid Day student tuition: $25,700. Tuition installment plan (Academic Management Services Plan, Tuition Refund Plan). Need-based scholarship grants, need-based loans, tuition reduction for children of faculty and staff available. In 2013–

14, 37% of upper-school students received aid. Total amount of financial aid awarded in 2013–14: $1,816,550.

Admissions Traditional secondary-level entrance grade is 9. For fall 2013, 77 students applied for upper-level admission, 35 were accepted, 29 enrolled. ERB CTP required. Deadline for receipt of application materials: none. Application fee required: $45. On-campus interview required.

Athletics Interscholastic: baseball (boys), basketball (b,g), crew (b,g), cross-country running (b,g), fencing (b,g), field hockey (g), independent competitive sports (b,g), lacrosse (b,g), physical training (b,g), soccer (b,g), swimming and diving (b,g), tennis (b,g); intramural: floor hockey (b), roller hockey (b), street hockey (b), weight training (b,g); coed interscholastic: golf; coed intramural: ultimate Frisbee. 5 PE instructors, 23 coaches, 1 athletic trainer.

Computers Computers are regularly used in English, foreign language, mathematics, media production, music, newspaper, photography, publications, religion, science, social studies, video film production, yearbook classes. Computer network features include on-campus library services, Internet access, wireless campus network, Internet filtering or blocking technology, campus portal. Campus intranet, student e-mail accounts, and computer access in designated common areas are available to students. Students grades are available online.

Contact Karin B. Miller, Director of Admission and Financial Aid. 856-235-2900 Ext. 227. Fax: 856-235-6684. E-mail: kmiller@mfriends.org. Website: www.mfriends.org

MOOSEHEART HIGH SCHOOL

255 James J. Davis Drive
Mooseheart, Illinois 60539

Head of School: Mr. Jeffrey Scott Szymczak

General Information Coeducational boarding and day college-preparatory, general academic, arts, business, vocational, religious studies, bilingual studies, technology, nursing, and cosmetology school, affiliated with Protestant faith, Roman Catholic Church; primarily serves underachievers. Grades K–12. Founded: 1913. Setting: small town. Nearest major city is Aurora. Students are housed in family homes. 1,000-acre campus. 40 buildings on campus. Approved or accredited by North Central Association of Colleges and Schools and Illinois Department of Education. Total enrollment: 212. Upper school average class size: 13. Upper school faculty-student ratio: 1:6. There are 176 required school days per year for Upper School students. Upper School students typically attend 5 days per week. The average school day consists of 6 hours and 45 minutes.

Upper School Student Profile Grade 6: 16 students (5 boys, 11 girls); Grade 7: 13 students (9 boys, 4 girls); Grade 8: 21 students (12 boys, 9 girls); Grade 9: 28 students (18 boys, 10 girls); Grade 10: 38 students (24 boys, 14 girls); Grade 11: 27 students (16 boys, 11 girls); Grade 12: 24 students (18 boys, 6 girls). 100% of students are boarding students. 65% are state residents. 22 states are represented in upper school student body. 6% are international students. International students from Canada, Ghana, and Sudan. 95% of students are Protestant, Roman Catholic.

Faculty School total: 45. In upper school: 9 men, 11 women; 6 have advanced degrees; 1 resides on campus.

Subjects Offered Algebra, American government, American history, auto mechanics, biology, business education, business law, career and personal planning, chemistry, child development, choral music, computer education, concert band, consumer education, ESL, geometry, government, health education, JROTC, language arts, mathematics, music technology, NJROTC, pre-algebra, religious education, vocational arts, world geography.

Special Academic Programs Independent study; remedial reading and/or remedial writing; remedial math; ESL (8 students enrolled).

College Admission Counseling 27 students graduated in 2013; 25 went to college, including Illinois State University; Illinois Wesleyan University; Northern Illinois University; Southern Illinois University Edwardsville; University of Illinois at Urbana–Champaign; Western Illinois University. Other: 1 went to work, 1 entered military service. Mean composite ACT: 16. 8% scored over 26 on composite ACT.

Student Life Upper grades have specified standards of dress, student council, honor system. Discipline rests primarily with faculty. Attendance at religious services is required.

Summer Programs Remediation, sports programs offered; session focuses on recreation; held on campus; accepts boys and girls; not open to students from other schools. 211 students usually enrolled. 2014 schedule: June 14 to August 13. Application deadline: none.

Admissions Traditional secondary-level entrance grade is 9. Mathematics proficiency exam required. Deadline for receipt of application materials: none. No application fee required. Interview recommended.

Athletics Interscholastic: basketball (boys, girls), cross-country running (b), drill team (b,g), football (b), indoor track & field (b,g), JROTC drill (b,g), track and field (b,g), volleyball (g), wrestling (b); intramural: aerobics (b), aerobics/dance (g), bowling (b,g); coed intramural: bowling. 2 PE instructors, 12 coaches, 1 athletic trainer.

Computers Computers are regularly used in word processing classes. Computer resources include on-campus library services, Internet access, wireless campus network, Internet filtering or blocking technology. Campus intranet and computer access in designated common areas are available to students. The school has a published electronic and media policy.

Contact Kyle Rife, Director of Admission. 630-906-3631 Ext. 3631. Fax: 630-906-3634 Ext. 3634. E-mail: krife@mooseheart.org. Website:

MORAVIAN ACADEMY

4313 Green Pond Road

Bethlehem, Pennsylvania 18020

Head of School: George N. King Jr.

General Information Coeducational day college-preparatory school, affiliated with Moravian Church. Grades PK–12. Founded: 1742. Setting: rural. Nearest major city is Philadelphia. 120-acre campus. 9 buildings on campus. Approved or accredited by Middle States Association of Colleges and Schools and Pennsylvania Department of Education. Member of National Association of Independent Schools and Secondary School Admission Test Board. Endowment: $16.8 million. Total enrollment: 750. Upper school average class size: 15. Upper school faculty-student ratio: 1:7. There are 173 required school days per year for Upper School students. Upper School students typically attend 5 days per week. The average school day consists of 7 hours and 15 minutes.

Upper School Student Profile Grade 9: 74 students (33 boys, 41 girls); Grade 10: 83 students (43 boys, 40 girls); Grade 11: 69 students (36 boys, 33 girls); Grade 12: 74 students (33 boys, 41 girls).

Faculty School total: 97. In upper school: 19 men, 24 women; 41 have advanced degrees.

Subjects Offered Acting, advanced biology, advanced chemistry, Advanced Placement courses, algebra, American history, American history-AP, American literature, anatomy, ancient history, ancient world history, art, bell choir, biology, biology-AP, botany, calculus, calculus-AP, ceramics, chemistry, chemistry-AP, Chinese, Chinese history, community service, drama, drawing, driver education, ecology, economics, English, English language-AP, English literature, English literature-AP, environmental science, environmental science-AP, ethics, European history, European history-AP, film, fine arts, French, French language-AP, geometry, government, health, history, honors geometry, Latin American history, mathematics, Middle East, music, painting, photography, physical education, physics, playwriting, poetry, probability and statistics, religion, science, short story, Spanish, Spanish language-AP, statistics, statistics-AP, theater, trigonometry, U.S. history-AP, woodworking, world history, world literature, zoology.

Graduation Requirements Arts and fine arts (art, music, dance, drama), English, foreign language, mathematics, physical education (includes health), religion (includes Bible studies and theology), science, social studies (includes history), service project.

Special Academic Programs 13 Advanced Placement exams for which test preparation is offered; honors section; independent study; study at local college for college credit.

College Admission Counseling 75 students graduated in 2013; all went to college, including Cornell University; Franklin & Marshall College; Lehigh University; Penn State University Park; Temple University; The George Washington University. Median SAT critical reading: 655, median SAT math: 630, median SAT writing: 645. 73% scored over 600 on SAT critical reading, 71% scored over 600 on SAT math, 74% scored over 600 on SAT writing.

Student Life Upper grades have specified standards of dress, student council. Discipline rests equally with students and faculty. Attendance at religious services is required.

Summer Programs Enrichment, sports, art/fine arts programs offered; session focuses on enrichment; held on campus; accepts boys and girls; open to students from other schools. 2014 schedule: June 8 to August 7.

Tuition and Aid Day student tuition: $25,130. Tuition installment plan (monthly payment plans). Need-based scholarship grants available. In 2013–14, 29% of upper-school students received aid. Total amount of financial aid awarded in 2013–14: $1,305,425.

Admissions Traditional secondary-level entrance grade is 9. For fall 2013, 59 students applied for upper-level admission, 41 were accepted, 27 enrolled. ERB and Otis-Lennon School Ability Test required. Deadline for receipt of application materials: none. Application fee required: $65. On-campus interview required.

Athletics Interscholastic: baseball (boys), basketball (b,g), field hockey (g), football (b), lacrosse (b,g), soccer (b,g), softball (g), tennis (b,g), track and field (b,g), volleyball (g), wrestling (b); coed interscholastic: cross-country running, golf, swimming and diving. 3 PE instructors, 15 coaches, 1 athletic trainer.

Computers Computers are regularly used in all academic, art, English, foreign language, history, mathematics, music, science classes. Computer resources include on-campus library services, Internet access, wireless campus network, 1:1 Program using MacBook Airs. Computer access in designated common areas is available to students. The school has a published electronic and media policy.

Contact Daniel Axford, Director of Upper School Admissions. 610-691-1600. Fax: 610-691-3354. E-mail: daxford@moravianacademy.org. Website: www.moravianacademy.org

See Display below and Close-Up on page 556.

MOREAU CATHOLIC HIGH SCHOOL

27170 Mission Boulevard
Hayward, California 94544

Head of School: Mr. Terry Lee

General Information Coeducational day college-preparatory, arts, business, religious studies, technology, and STEM school, affiliated with Roman Catholic Church. Grades 9–12. Founded: 1965. Setting: suburban. Nearest major city is San Francisco. 14-acre campus. 6 buildings on campus. Approved or accredited by National Catholic Education Association, Western Association of Schools and Colleges, Western Catholic Education Association, and California Department of Education. Total enrollment: 896. Upper school average class size: 24. Upper school faculty-student ratio: 1:18. There are 186 required school days per year for Upper School students. Upper School students typically attend 5 days per week. The average school day consists of 6 hours and 35 minutes.

Upper School Student Profile Grade 9: 256 students (138 boys, 118 girls); Grade 10: 242 students (107 boys, 135 girls); Grade 11: 196 students (105 boys, 91 girls); Grade 12: 202 students (103 boys, 99 girls). 72% of students are Roman Catholic.

Faculty School total: 69. In upper school: 30 men, 23 women; 27 have advanced degrees.

Subjects Offered Advanced Placement courses, aerobics, algebra, American Civil War, American history, American legal systems, American literature, anatomy, art, art history, ASB Leadership, astronomy, athletics, Bible as literature, biology, biology-AP, business, business law, business skills, calculus, calculus-AP, campus ministry, ceramics, cheerleading, chemistry, choral music, Christian ethics, Christian scripture, Christianity, church history, community service, computer education, computer math, computer programming, computer science, concert band, creative writing, drafting, drama, drama performance, driver education, earth science, economics, electronics, engineering, English, English literature, English/composition-AP, ethics, ethics and responsibility, European history, expository writing, fine arts, French, French-AP, geometry, government-AP, government/civics, grammar, health, health education, history, history of the Catholic Church, home economics, honors algebra, honors English, honors geometry, honors U.S. history, honors world history, human biology, instrumental music, jazz band, jazz ensemble, journalism, marching band, mathematics, mechanical drawing, media studies, moral and social development, moral theology, music, music appreciation, newspaper, physical education, physics, physics-AP, physiology, psychology, religion, science, sculpture, social sciences, social studies, Spanish, Spanish language-AP, speech, sports medicine, sports science, student government, student publications, symphonic band, the Sixties, theater, theology, trigonometry, typing, U.S. government, U.S. government and politics-AP, U.S. history, U.S. history-AP, weight training, world history, world literature, writing, yearbook.

Graduation Requirements Arts and fine arts (art, music, dance, drama), computer science, English, foreign language, mathematics, physical education (includes health), religion (includes Bible studies and theology), science, social sciences, social studies (includes history). Community service is required.

Special Academic Programs Advanced Placement exam preparation; honors section; special instructional classes for Saints and Scholars program for students with documented learning disabilities who require accommodations.

College Admission Counseling 229 students graduated in 2012; all went to college, including California State University; Saint Mary's College of California; Santa Clara University; Stanford University; University of California, Berkeley; University of San Francisco. Mean SAT critical reading: 527, mean SAT math: 546, mean SAT writing: 533, mean composite ACT: 24.

Student Life Upper grades have specified standards of dress, student council, honor system. Discipline rests primarily with faculty. Attendance at religious services is required.

Tuition and Aid Day student tuition: $15,096. Tuition installment plan (FACTS Tuition Payment Plan, monthly payment plans). Merit scholarship grants, need-based scholarship grants available. In 2012–13, 37% of upper-school students received aid. Total amount of financial aid awarded in 2012–13: $1,500,000.

Admissions Traditional secondary-level entrance grade is 9. Scholastic Testing Service High School Placement Test required. Deadline for receipt of application materials: January 4. Application fee required: $90. On-campus interview required.

Athletics Interscholastic: aquatics (boys, girls), badminton (b,g), baseball (b), basketball (b,g), cheering (g), cross-country running (b,g), dance squad (g), football (b), golf (b,g), soccer (b,g), softball (g), swimming and diving (b,g), tennis (b,g), track and field (b,g), volleyball (b,g), water polo (b,g); intramural: lacrosse (g); coed interscholastic: aerobics/dance, modern dance; coed intramural: equestrian sports, skiing (downhill), strength & conditioning. 5 PE instructors, 50 coaches, 1 athletic trainer.

Computers Computers are regularly used in career exploration, college planning, English, foreign language, history, journalism, keyboarding, mathematics, newspaper, religious studies, science, Spanish, technology, theology, writing, yearbook classes. Computer network features include on-campus library services, online commercial services, Internet access, wireless campus network, PowerSchool grade program, 1:1 student laptop program (every student at Moreau has a laptop), laptop included in tuition. Campus intranet, student e-mail accounts, and computer access in designated common areas are available to students. Students grades are available online. The school has a published electronic and media policy.

Contact Patricia Bevilacqua, Admissions Assistant. 510-881-4320. Fax: 510-582-8405. E-mail: admissions@moreaucatholic.org. Website: www.moreaucatholic.org

MORRISTOWN-BEARD SCHOOL

70 Whippany Road
Morristown, New Jersey 07960

Head of School: Mr. Peter Caldwell

General Information Coeducational day college-preparatory and arts school. Grades 6–12. Founded: 1891. Setting: suburban. Nearest major city is New York, NY. 22-acre campus. 11 buildings on campus. Approved or accredited by Middle States Association of Colleges and Schools, New Jersey Association of Independent Schools, and New Jersey Department of Education. Member of National Association of Independent Schools and Secondary School Admission Test Board. Endowment: $11 million. Total enrollment: 557. Upper school average class size: 12. Upper school faculty-student ratio: 1:7. There are 160 required school days per year for Upper School students. Upper School students typically attend 5 days per week. The average school day consists of 7 hours.

Upper School Student Profile Grade 9: 108 students (62 boys, 46 girls); Grade 10: 102 students (60 boys, 42 girls); Grade 11: 96 students (53 boys, 43 girls); Grade 12: 95 students (46 boys, 49 girls).

Faculty School total: 94. In upper school: 33 men, 37 women; 40 have advanced degrees.

Subjects Offered 20th century history, acting, advanced chemistry, advanced math, Advanced Placement courses, advanced studio art-AP, algebra, American history, American legal systems, American studies, anatomy and physiology, ancient world history, architecture, art, art history, astronomy, biology, biology-AP, calculus, calculus-AP, ceramics, chemistry, chemistry-AP, choir, chorus, community service, computer programming, computer science, computer skills, computer studies, constitutional law, creative writing, dance, digital art, drama, drawing, earth science, ecology, engineering, English, English-AP, fine arts, French, geometry, health, instrumental music, journalism, Latin, Middle Eastern history, mythology, nature writers, painting, photography, physical education, physical science, physics, physics-AP, public speaking, rite of passage, Spanish, Spanish-AP, speech, statistics, statistics-AP, studio art-AP, theater, trigonometry, U.S. history-AP, world history.

Graduation Requirements Arts and fine arts (art, music, dance, drama), English, foreign language, mathematics, physical education (includes health), science, service learning/internship, social studies (includes history). Community service is required.

Special Academic Programs 13 Advanced Placement exams for which test preparation is offered; honors section; independent study; term-away projects; study abroad.

College Admission Counseling 98 students graduated in 2012; 95 went to college, including American University; Boston College; Colgate University; New York University; University of Vermont; Wesleyan University. Other: 2 entered a postgraduate year, 1 had other specific plans. Mean SAT critical reading: 589, mean SAT math: 605, mean SAT writing: 613, mean composite ACT: 26.

Student Life Upper grades have specified standards of dress, student council, honor system. Discipline rests equally with students and faculty.

Tuition and Aid Day student tuition: $33,285. Tuition installment plan (Tuition Management Systems). Merit scholarship grants, need-based scholarship grants available. In 2012–13, 14% of upper-school students received aid; total upper-school merit-scholarship money awarded: $85,500. Total amount of financial aid awarded in 2012–13: $2,000,000.

Admissions Traditional secondary-level entrance grade is 9. For fall 2012, 377 students applied for upper-level admission, 225 were accepted, 127 enrolled. ISEE or SSAT required. Deadline for receipt of application materials: February 4. Application fee required: $60. On-campus interview required.

Athletics Interscholastic: baseball (boys), basketball (b,g), field hockey (g), football (b), ice hockey (b,g), lacrosse (b,g), skiing (downhill) (b,g), soccer (b,g), softball (g), swimming and diving (b,g), tennis (b,g), track and field (b,g), volleyball (g); coed interscholastic: alpine skiing, cross-country running, dance, golf, swimming and diving, track and field, yoga; coed intramural: dance, fitness, physical fitness, strength & conditioning. 4 PE instructors, 6 coaches, 1 athletic trainer.

Computers Computers are regularly used in architecture, art, English, foreign language, history, mathematics, music, science classes. Computer network features include on-campus library services, online commercial services, Internet access, wireless campus network, Internet filtering or blocking technology, Jstor, Jerseycat. Student e-mail accounts are available to students. Students grades are available online. The school has a published electronic and media policy.

Contact Mrs. Barbara Luperi, Admission Assistant. 973-539-3032. Fax: 973-539-1590. E-mail: bluperi@mbs.net. Website: www.mbs.net

MOTHER MCAULEY HIGH SCHOOL

3737 West 99th Street

Chicago, Illinois 60655-3133

Head of School: Mrs. Claudia Woodruff

General Information Girls' day college-preparatory, arts, religious studies, and technology school, affiliated with Roman Catholic Church. Grades 9–12. Founded: 1846. Setting: urban. 21-acre campus. 2 buildings on campus. Approved or accredited by Mercy Secondary Education Association, National Catholic Education Association, North Central Association of Colleges and Schools, The College Board, and Illinois Department of Education. Endowment: $2 million. Total enrollment: 1,215. Upper school average class size: 25. Upper school faculty-student ratio: 1:17. There are 180 required school days per year for Upper School students. Upper School students typically attend 5 days per week. The average school day consists of 6 hours and 30 minutes.

Upper School Student Profile Grade 9: 308 students (308 girls); Grade 10: 291 students (291 girls); Grade 11: 284 students (284 girls); Grade 12: 332 students (332 girls). 87% of students are Roman Catholic.

Faculty School total: 92. In upper school: 12 men, 80 women; 56 have advanced degrees.

Subjects Offered Anatomy and physiology, art history, art history-AP, calculus-AP, ceramics, chemistry-AP, English, English literature, English literature and composition-AP, European history-AP, first aid, French, French-AP, general science, geography, geometry, geometry with art applications, global issues, graphic design, history of the Catholic Church, honors algebra, honors English, honors geometry, honors U.S. history, honors world history, introduction to theater, journalism, Latin, Latin-AP, Life of Christ, marching band, media literacy, music appreciation, newspaper, orchestra, painting, photography, physical education, physics, play production, scripture, Spanish, Spanish-AP, speech, studio art, studio art-AP, theater, theology, U.S. history, U.S. history-AP, U.S. literature, Web site design, wind ensemble, world history, world history-AP, yearbook.

Graduation Requirements Art history, English, lab science, language, mathematics, music, physical education (includes health), social sciences, speech, technology, theology.

Special Academic Programs 16 Advanced Placement exams for which test preparation is offered; honors section; study at local college for college credit.

College Admission Counseling 331 students graduated in 2013; all went to college, including Eastern Illinois University; Illinois State University; Loyola University Chicago; University of Illinois at Chicago; University of Illinois at Urbana–Champaign. Mean composite ACT: 23.

Student Life Upper grades have uniform requirement, student council. Discipline rests primarily with faculty. Attendance at religious services is required.

Summer Programs Remediation, enrichment, advancement, sports, art/fine arts, computer instruction programs offered; session focuses on academics; held on campus; accepts girls; open to students from other schools. 200 students usually enrolled. 2014 schedule: June 16 to July 25. Application deadline: June 1.

Tuition and Aid Day student tuition: $9750. Tuition installment plan (monthly payment plans, individually arranged payment plans). Tuition reduction for siblings, merit scholarship grants, need-based scholarship grants, paying campus jobs available. In 2013–14, 40% of upper-school students received aid; total upper-school merit-scholarship money awarded: $30,000. Total amount of financial aid awarded in 2013–14: $1,000,000.

Admissions Traditional secondary-level entrance grade is 9. For fall 2013, 383 students applied for upper-level admission, 360 were accepted, 308 enrolled. High School Placement Test required. Deadline for receipt of application materials: June 1. Application fee required: $175.

Athletics Interscholastic: basketball, bowling, cross-country running, dance team, diving, golf, independent competitive sports, lacrosse, sailing, soccer, softball, swimming and diving, tennis, track and field, volleyball, water polo; intramural: aerobics, basketball, bowling, flag football, Frisbee, softball, touch football, ultimate Frisbee, volleyball. 3 PE instructors, 20 coaches, 1 athletic trainer.

Computers Computers are regularly used in accounting, art, basic skills, business education, drafting, drawing and design, English, foreign language, French, graphics, journalism, Latin, mathematics, music, newspaper, photography, science, social sciences, Spanish, theater, Web site design, writing, yearbook classes. Computer network features include on-campus library services, Internet access, wireless campus network, Internet filtering or blocking technology. Student e-mail accounts and computer access in designated common areas are available to students. Students grades are available online. The school has a published electronic and media policy.

Contact Mrs. Kathryn Klyczek, Director of Admissions and Financial Aid. 773-881-6534. Fax: 773-881-6515. E-mail: kklyczek@mothermcauley.org. Website: www.mothermcauley.org

MOUNT CARMEL SCHOOL

PO Box 500006

Saipan, Northern Mariana Islands 96950

Head of School: Mr. Galvin S. Deleon Guerrero

General Information Coeducational day college-preparatory, general academic, religious studies, and technology school, affiliated with Roman Catholic Church. Grades 1–12. Founded: 1952. Setting: rural. Nearest major city is Hagatna, Guam. 5-acre campus. 1 building on campus. Approved or accredited by Western Association of Schools and Colleges and Northern Mariana Islands Department of Education. Total enrollment: 378. Upper school average class size: 25. Upper school faculty-student ratio: 1:20. There are 180 required school days per year for Upper School students. Upper School students typically attend 5 days per week. The average school day consists of 6 hours and 5 minutes.

Upper School Student Profile Grade 9: 41 students (19 boys, 22 girls); Grade 10: 28 students (16 boys, 12 girls); Grade 11: 40 students (19 boys, 21 girls); Grade 12: 37 students (21 boys, 16 girls). 95% of students are Roman Catholic.

Faculty School total: 20. In upper school: 3 men, 6 women; 4 have advanced degrees.

Subjects Offered Advanced math, algebra, American government, American history, American history-AP, art, biology, British literature, calculus, calculus-AP, campus ministry, Catholic belief and practice, chemistry, Christian doctrine, Christian scripture, civics, composition, computer applications, computer science, drama, English, English literature, English literature-AP, foreign language, gardening, geometry, history of the Catholic Church, HTML design, independent study, Japanese, literature, media production, moral theology, physical education, physics, pre-calculus, Spanish, state history, theology, trigonometry, world history, world literature, world religions, yearbook.

Graduation Requirements Algebra, American history, art, biology, British literature, Catholic belief and practice, chemistry, Christian ethics, Christian scripture, church history, civics, composition, computer applications, English, English literature, foreign language, geometry, physical education (includes health), physics, theology, U.S. literature, world history.

Special Academic Programs 4 Advanced Placement exams for which test preparation is offered; independent study.

College Admission Counseling 45 students graduated in 2012; 25 went to college, including Northern Marianas College. Other: 3 went to work, 2 entered military service.

Student Life Upper grades have uniform requirement, student council, honor system. Discipline rests primarily with faculty. Attendance at religious services is required.

Tuition and Aid Day student tuition: $3530. Tuition installment plan (monthly payment plans). Tuition reduction for siblings, merit scholarship grants, need-based scholarship grants available. In 2012–13, 25% of upper-school students received aid; total upper-school merit-scholarship money awarded: $1000. Total amount of financial aid awarded in 2012–13: $30,000.

Admissions Traditional secondary-level entrance grade is 9. For fall 2012, 79 students applied for upper-level admission, 79 were accepted, 78 enrolled. Deadline for receipt of application materials: none. Application fee required: $50.

Athletics Interscholastic: aquatics (boys, girls), basketball (b,g), canoeing/kayaking (b,g), flag football (b), ocean paddling (b,g), softball (g), track and field (b,g), volleyball (b,g); intramural: badminton (b,g), basketball (b,g), flag football (b,g), floor hockey (b,g), soccer (b,g), volleyball (b,g); coed interscholastic: aquatics, ocean paddling, volleyball; coed intramural: badminton, soccer, volleyball. 1 PE instructor.

Computers Computers are regularly used in all academic, computer applications classes. Computer network features include on-campus library services, online commercial services, Internet access, wireless campus network, Internet filtering or blocking technology. Campus intranet is available to students. Students grades are available online. The school has a published electronic and media policy.

Contact Mr. Galvin S. Deleon Guerrero, President. 670-234-6184. Fax: 670-235-4751. E-mail: president.mcs@pticom.com. Website: www.mtcarmel-edu.net

MT. DE SALES ACADEMY

851 Orange Street

Macon, Georgia 31201

Head of School: Mr. David Held

General Information Coeducational day college-preparatory, arts, religious studies, and technology school, affiliated with Roman Catholic Church. Grades 6–12. Founded: 1876. Setting: urban. 72-acre campus. 10 buildings on campus. Approved or accredited by Georgia Independent School Association, Mercy Secondary Education Association, National Catholic Education Association, Southern Association of Colleges and Schools, Southern Association of Independent Schools, The College Board, and Georgia Department of Education. Member of National Association of Independent Schools. Endowment: $400,000. Total enrollment: 641. Upper school average class size: 19. Upper school faculty-student ratio: 1:9. There are 180 required school days per year for Upper School students. Upper School students typically attend 5 days per week. The average school day consists of 7 hours.

Upper School Student Profile Grade 6: 40 students (26 boys, 14 girls); Grade 7: 88 students (47 boys, 41 girls); Grade 8: 91 students (32 boys, 59 girls); Grade 9: 112 students (52 boys, 60 girls); Grade 10: 100 students (48 boys, 52 girls); Grade 11: 100

students (49 boys, 51 girls); Grade 12: 110 students (48 boys, 62 girls). 42% of students are Roman Catholic.

Faculty School total: 68. In upper school: 27 men, 20 women; 34 have advanced degrees.

Subjects Offered 20th century world history, advanced biology, advanced chemistry, advanced computer applications, advanced math, Advanced Placement courses, advanced studio art-AP, African American studies, algebra, American Civil War, American government, American history, American history-AP, American literature, American literature-AP, anatomy and physiology, art history-AP, astronomy, athletic training, band, biology, biology-AP, British literature, calculus, calculus-AP, chemistry, chemistry-AP, choral music, chorus, Christian education, Christian scripture, computer applications, computer multimedia, computer programming-AP, drawing and design, economics, English, English language and composition-AP, English literature and composition-AP, European history-AP, forensics, French, government, government and politics-AP, health, Holocaust studies, honors algebra, honors English, honors geometry, New Testament, physical education, physics-AP, portfolio art, pre-calculus, programming, psychology, psychology-AP, Spanish-AP, speech, statistics, statistics-AP, studio art, U.S. government, U.S. government and politics-AP, U.S. history, U.S. history-AP, visual arts, World War II, yearbook.

Graduation Requirements 1 1/2 elective credits, algebra, American government, American history, arts and fine arts (art, music, dance, drama), biology, chemistry, computer applications, economics, English, foreign language, government, health education, physical education (includes health), physics, religion (includes Bible studies and theology), theology, U.S. history, world history.

Special Academic Programs Honors section; study at local college for college credit.

College Admission Counseling 112 students graduated in 2013; they went to Georgia Institute of Technology; Georgia Southern University; Macon State College; University of Georgia. Mean SAT critical reading: 710, mean SAT math: 700, mean SAT writing: 720, mean combined SAT: 2130.

Student Life Upper grades have specified standards of dress, student council, honor system. Discipline rests primarily with faculty. Attendance at religious services is required.

Tuition and Aid Day student tuition: $11,000. Tuition installment plan (FACTS Tuition Payment Plan, monthly payment plans, individually arranged payment plans). Merit scholarship grants, need-based scholarship grants available. In 2013–14, 30% of upper-school students received aid; total upper-school merit-scholarship money awarded: $122,000. Total amount of financial aid awarded in 2013–14: $813,771.

Admissions Traditional secondary-level entrance grade is 9. For fall 2013, 92 students applied for upper-level admission, 68 were accepted, 46 enrolled. Naglieri Nonverbal School Ability Test required. Deadline for receipt of application materials: none. Application fee required: $50.

Athletics Interscholastic: baseball (boys), basketball (b,g), cheering (g), cross-country running (b,g), dance team (g), fitness (b,g), football (b), physical fitness (b,g), physical training (b,g), soccer (b,g), softball (g), strength & conditioning (b,g), swimming and diving (b,g), tennis (b,g), track and field (b,g), volleyball (g), weight training (b,g), wrestling (b); coed interscholastic: golf. 3 coaches.

Computers Computers are regularly used in all classes. Computer network features include on-campus library services, Internet access, wireless campus network, Internet filtering or blocking technology. Campus intranet, student e-mail accounts, and computer access in designated common areas are available to students. Students grades are available online. The school has a published electronic and media policy.

Contact Mrs. Linda Cardwell, Director of Admissions. 478-751-3244. Fax: 478-751-3241. E-mail: lcardwell@mountdesales.net. Website: www.mountdesales.net

MOUNT MERCY ACADEMY

88 Red Jacket Parkway
Buffalo, New York 14220

Head of School: Mrs. Margaret Staszak

General Information Girls' day college-preparatory, arts, and religious studies school, affiliated with Roman Catholic Church. Grades 9–12. Founded: 1904. Setting: urban. 2 buildings on campus. Approved or accredited by Middle States Association of Colleges and Schools and New York Department of Education. Total enrollment: 244. Upper school average class size: 20. Upper school faculty-student ratio: 1:20. There are 180 required school days per year for Upper School students. Upper School students typically attend 5 days per week. The average school day consists of 6 hours and 45 minutes.

Upper School Student Profile Grade 9: 67 students (67 girls); Grade 10: 53 students (53 girls); Grade 11: 74 students (74 girls); Grade 12: 50 students (50 girls). 97% of students are Roman Catholic.

Faculty School total: 32. In upper school: 6 men, 26 women.

Special Academic Programs Advanced Placement exam preparation; honors section; independent study.

College Admission Counseling 72 students graduated in 2012; all went to college.

Student Life Upper grades have uniform requirement, student council, honor system. Discipline rests equally with students and faculty. Attendance at religious services is required.

Tuition and Aid Day student tuition: $7800. Tuition installment plan (FACTS Tuition Payment Plan). Tuition reduction for siblings, merit scholarship grants, need-based scholarship grants, paying campus jobs available.

Admissions Traditional secondary-level entrance grade is 9. Admissions testing or High School Placement Test (closed version) from Scholastic Testing Service required. Deadline for receipt of application materials: none. Application fee required: $20. On-campus interview required.

Athletics Interscholastic: aquatics, basketball, bowling, cross-country running, golf, lacrosse, skiing (downhill), soccer, softball, swimming and diving, tennis, volleyball. 1 PE instructor, 13 coaches.

Computers Computers are regularly used in art, business, desktop publishing, keyboarding, study skills, yearbook classes. Computer network features include on-campus library services, Internet access, wireless campus network, Internet filtering or blocking technology. Campus intranet, student e-mail accounts, and computer access in designated common areas are available to students. Students grades are available online. The school has a published electronic and media policy.

Contact Mrs. Jeanne Burvid, Director of Admissions. 716-825-8796 Ext. 511. Fax: 716-825-0976. E-mail: jburvid@mtmercy.org. Website: www.mtmercy.org

MOUNT MICHAEL BENEDICTINE SCHOOL

22520 Mount Michael Road
Elkhorn, Nebraska 68022-3400

Head of School: Dr. David Peters

General Information Boys' boarding and day college-preparatory, arts, religious studies, and technology school, affiliated with Roman Catholic Church. Grades 9–12. Founded: 1970. Setting: suburban. Nearest major city is Omaha. Students are housed in single-sex dormitories and private homes. 440-acre campus. 1 building on campus. Approved or accredited by National Catholic Education Association, North Central Association of Colleges and Schools, The College Board, and Nebraska Department of Education. Endowment: $3.2 million. Total enrollment: 221. Upper school average class size: 15. Upper school faculty-student ratio: 1:8. There are 180 required school days per year for Upper School students. Upper School students typically attend 5 days per week. The average school day consists of 7 hours and 5 minutes.

Upper School Student Profile Grade 9: 56 students (56 boys); Grade 10: 64 students (64 boys); Grade 11: 58 students (58 boys); Grade 12: 58 students (58 boys). 68% of students are boarding students. 77% are state residents. 6 states are represented in upper school student body. 19% are international students. International students from China, Germany, Mexico, Republic of Korea, Rwanda, and Viet Nam; 2 other countries represented in student body. 81% of students are Roman Catholic.

Faculty School total: 31. In upper school: 21 men, 10 women; 23 have advanced degrees; 9 reside on campus.

Subjects Offered Accounting, Advanced Placement courses, algebra, American history, American history-AP, American literature, architectural drawing, art, band, Basic programming, basketball, bioethics, DNA and culture, biology, biology-AP, business, calculus-AP, ceramics, chemistry, chemistry-AP, chorus, Christian doctrine, Christian ethics, Christian scripture, Christianity, community service, composition-AP, computer programming, computer science, critical writing, drafting, drama, economics, English, English language-AP, English literature, English literature and composition-AP, European history, European history-AP, forensics, French, French language-AP, geography, geometry, government/civics, health education, Hebrew scripture, history of the Catholic Church, journalism, keyboarding, Latin, literature-AP, math applications, mathematics, music, philosophy, physical education, physics, physics-AP, psychology-AP, reading, robotics, science, social justice, social sciences, social studies, Spanish, Spanish-AP, speech, theater, theology, trigonometry, weight training, Western civilization, world religions, wrestling, writing, yearbook.

Graduation Requirements Advanced math, algebra, American government, American history, anatomy and physiology, biology, biology-AP, career/college preparation, chemistry, Christian studies, computer science, economics, economics and history, English, foreign language, geometry, government, mathematics, physical education (includes health), physics, pre-calculus, social studies (includes history), speech, Western civilization, world cultures, world religions, service hours requirement. Community service is required.

Special Academic Programs 11 Advanced Placement exams for which test preparation is offered; honors section; independent study; study at local college for college credit.

College Admission Counseling 57 students graduated in 2013; 37 went to college, including Benedictine College; Boston College; Creighton University; Saint John's University; Santa Clara University; University of Nebraska–Lincoln. Other: 2 entered military service. Median SAT critical reading: 630, median SAT math: 700, median SAT writing: 660, median combined SAT: 2000, median composite ACT: 28. 80% scored over 600 on SAT critical reading, 80% scored over 600 on SAT math, 100% scored over 600 on SAT writing, 80% scored over 1800 on combined SAT, 62% scored over 26 on composite ACT.

Student Life Upper grades have specified standards of dress, student council, honor system. Discipline rests primarily with faculty. Attendance at religious services is required.

Summer Programs Sports programs offered; session focuses on baseball; held on campus; accepts boys; open to students from other schools. 45 students usually enrolled. 2014 schedule: May 25 to August 10.

Tuition and Aid Day student tuition: $10,755–$11,075; 5-day tuition and room/board: $15,950–$16,270; 7-day tuition and room/board: $21,795–$22,115. Guaranteed tuition plan. Tuition installment plan (FACTS Tuition Payment Plan). Tuition reduction for siblings, bursaries, merit scholarship grants, need-based scholarship grants, need-based loans, paying campus jobs available. In 2013–14, 54% of upper-school students received aid; total upper-school merit-scholarship money awarded: $83,000. Total amount of financial aid awarded in 2013–14: $595,000.

Admissions Traditional secondary-level entrance grade is 9. For fall 2013, 114 students applied for upper-level admission, 74 were accepted, 56 enrolled. California Achievement Test, Explore, High School Placement Test, Iowa Tests of Basic Skills, SSAT, Stanford Achievement Test or TOEFL required. Deadline for receipt of application materials: July 1. Application fee required: $25. Interview required.

Athletics Interscholastic: baseball, basketball, bowling, cheering, cross-country running, diving, football, golf, soccer, swimming and diving, tennis, trap and skeet, wrestling; intramural: ball hockey, basketball, flag football, floor hockey, physical fitness, physical training, soccer, strength & conditioning, ultimate Frisbee, weight lifting, weight training. 1 PE instructor, 22 coaches, 2 athletic trainers.

Computers Computers are regularly used in architecture, career education, career exploration, career technology, college planning, drafting, economics, French, geography, history, journalism, keyboarding, library, mathematics, newspaper, science, Spanish, stock market, Web site design, yearbook classes. Computer network features include on-campus library services, online commercial services, Internet access, wireless campus network, Internet filtering or blocking technology. Campus intranet, student e-mail accounts, and computer access in designated common areas are available to students. Students grades are available online. The school has a published electronic and media policy.

Contact Mr. Eric Crawford, Director of Admissions. 402-253-0946. Fax: 402-289-4539. E-mail: ecrawford@mountmichael.org. Website: www.mountmichaelhs.com

MOUNT PARAN CHRISTIAN SCHOOL

1275 Stanley Road
Kennesaw, Georgia 30152

Head of School: Dr. David Tilley

General Information Coeducational day college-preparatory and religious studies school, affiliated with Christian faith. Grades K–12. Founded: 1976. Setting: suburban. Nearest major city is Marietta. 65-acre campus. 3 buildings on campus. Approved or accredited by Southern Association of Independent Schools. Total enrollment: 1,105. Upper school average class size: 17. There are 178 required school days per year for Upper School students. Upper School students typically attend 5 days per week. The average school day consists of 7 hours and 15 minutes.

Upper School Student Profile Grade 6: 96 students (50 boys, 46 girls); Grade 7: 114 students (58 boys, 56 girls); Grade 8: 114 students (58 boys, 56 girls); Grade 9: 108 students (56 boys, 52 girls); Grade 10: 123 students (55 boys, 68 girls); Grade 11: 98 students (52 boys, 46 girls); Grade 12: 77 students (26 boys, 51 girls). 100% of students are Christian faith.

Graduation Requirements Service hours.

Special Academic Programs 18 Advanced Placement exams for which test preparation is offered; honors section; study at local college for college credit; study abroad; academic accommodation for the gifted, the musically talented, and the artistically talented; remedial reading and/or remedial writing; remedial math; programs in English, general development for dyslexic students.

College Admission Counseling Colleges students went to include Auburn University; Georgia Institute of Technology; University of Georgia; Wheaton College.

Student Life Upper grades have uniform requirement. Discipline rests primarily with faculty. Attendance at religious services is required.

Tuition and Aid Day student tuition: $14,881. Tuition installment plan (monthly payment plans). Need-based scholarship grants available.

Admissions Any standardized test or Cognitive Abilities Test required. Deadline for receipt of application materials: none. Application fee required: $75. Interview required.

Athletics Interscholastic: baseball (boys), basketball (b,g), cheering (g), cross-country running (b,g), equestrian sports (g), football (b), golf (b,g), soccer (b,g), softball (g), strength & conditioning (b,g), tennis (b,g), track and field (b,g), volleyball (g), weight training (b), wrestling (b); coed interscholastic: aquatics, ballet, dance; coed intramural: fly fishing.

Computers Computers are regularly used in business, college planning, creative writing, current events, graphic design, keyboarding, library skills, research skills, yearbook classes. Computer network features include on-campus library services, online commercial services, Internet access, wireless campus network, Internet filtering or blocking technology. Campus intranet, student e-mail accounts, and computer access in designated common areas are available to students. Students grades are available online. The school has a published electronic and media policy.

Contact Mrs. Shaunda Brooks, Director of Admission. 770-578-0182 Ext. 2046. Fax: 770-977-9284. E-mail: sbrooks@mtparanschool.com. Website: www.mtparanschool.com

MOUNT SAINT CHARLES ACADEMY

800 Logee Street
Woonsocket, Rhode Island 02895-5599

Head of School: Mr. Herve E. Richer Jr.

General Information Coeducational day college-preparatory, arts, and religious studies school, affiliated with Roman Catholic Church. Grades 7–12. Founded: 1924. Setting: suburban. Nearest major city is Providence. 22-acre campus. 2 buildings on campus. Approved or accredited by New England Association of Schools and Colleges and Rhode Island Department of Education. Total enrollment: 699. Upper school average class size: 25. Upper school faculty-student ratio: 1:14. There are 180 required school days per year for Upper School students. The average school day consists of 6 hours and 15 minutes.

Upper School Student Profile Grade 7: 51 students (20 boys, 31 girls); Grade 8: 60 students (27 boys, 33 girls); Grade 9: 138 students (60 boys, 78 girls); Grade 10: 113 students (52 boys, 61 girls); Grade 11: 155 students (82 boys, 73 girls); Grade 12: 182 students (76 boys, 106 girls). 85% of students are Roman Catholic.

Faculty School total: 64. In upper school: 29 men, 34 women; 30 have advanced degrees.

Subjects Offered Advanced computer applications, algebra, American literature, architecture, art, art-AP, band, biology, biology-AP, British literature, calculus, calculus-AP, chemistry, chorus, computer science, creative writing, dance, drama, economics, English, English language and composition-AP, English literature, English literature and composition-AP, English literature-AP, environmental science, environmental science-AP, European history, European history-AP, fine arts, forensics, French, geography, geometry, government, government and politics-AP, government/civics, handbells, health education, history, history of the Catholic Church, honors U.S. history, honors world history, jazz band, mathematics, mathematics-AP, modern European history, music, music theory-AP, physical education, physics, physiology, psychology, psychology-AP, religion, science, social studies, Spanish, theater, trigonometry, U.S. history, U.S. history-AP, world history, world literature, writing, yearbook.

Graduation Requirements Arts and fine arts (art, music, dance, drama), computer science, English, foreign language, mathematics, physical education (includes health), religion (includes Bible studies and theology), science, social studies (includes history).

Special Academic Programs 14 Advanced Placement exams for which test preparation is offered; honors section.

College Admission Counseling 196 students graduated in 2013; 192 went to college. Other: 1 went to work, 2 entered military service, 1 entered a postgraduate year.

Student Life Upper grades have uniform requirement, student council. Discipline rests primarily with faculty. Attendance at religious services is required.

Summer Programs Sports, art/fine arts programs offered; session focuses on fine arts, soccer, hockey, basketball; held on campus; accepts boys and girls; open to students from other schools. 220 students usually enrolled. 2014 schedule: July 14 to July 25. Application deadline: none.

Tuition and Aid Day student tuition: $12,000. Tuition installment plan (FACTS Tuition Payment Plan, full payment discount plan). Need-based scholarship grants available. In 2013–14, 38% of upper-school students received aid. Total amount of financial aid awarded in 2013–14: $700,000.

Admissions Traditional secondary-level entrance grade is 7. For fall 2013, 250 students applied for upper-level admission, 200 were accepted, 130 enrolled. Diocesan Entrance Exam, ISEE, SAS, STS-HSPT, SSAT or STS required. Deadline for receipt of application materials: none. Application fee required: $25.

Athletics Interscholastic: baseball (boys), basketball (b,g), cross-country running (b,g), gymnastics (g), ice hockey (b,g), indoor track (b,g), lacrosse (b,g), sailing (b,g), soccer (b,g), softball (g), swimming and diving (b,g), tennis (b,g), track and field (b,g), volleyball (b,g), winter (indoor) track (b,g); intramural: aerobics/dance (g), basketball (b,g), dance (g); coed interscholastic: cheering, golf; coed intramural: billiards, bowling, dance team, flag football, indoor soccer, lacrosse, physical training, soccer, strength & conditioning, touch football. 4 PE instructors, 15 coaches, 1 athletic trainer.

Computers Computers are regularly used in accounting, architecture, art, computer applications, desktop publishing, graphic design, science, yearbook classes. Computer network features include on-campus library services, online commercial services, Internet access, Internet filtering or blocking technology, college/financial aid searches. Campus intranet, student e-mail accounts, and computer access in designated common areas are available to students. Students grades are available online. The school has a published electronic and media policy.

Contact Joseph J. O'Neill Jr., Registrar/Director of Admissions. 401-769-0310 Ext. 137. Fax: 401-762-2327. E-mail: admissions@mountsaintcharles.org. Website: www.mountsaintcharles.org

MT. SAINT DOMINIC ACADEMY

3 Ryerson Avenue
Caldwell, New Jersey 07006

Head of School: Sr. Frances Sullivan, OP

General Information Girls' day college-preparatory, arts, religious studies, and technology school, affiliated with Roman Catholic Church. Grades 9–12. Founded:

1892. Setting: suburban. Nearest major city is Newark. 70-acre campus. 3 buildings on campus. Approved or accredited by Middle States Association of Colleges and Schools, New Jersey Association of Independent Schools, and New Jersey Department of Education. Endowment: $1.5 million. Total enrollment: 315. Upper school average class size: 12. Upper school faculty-student ratio: 1:12. There are 180 required school days per year for Upper School students. Upper School students typically attend 5 days per week. The average school day consists of 6 hours.

Upper School Student Profile Grade 9: 98 students (98 girls); Grade 10: 65 students (65 girls); Grade 11: 86 students (86 girls); Grade 12: 66 students (66 girls). 88% of students are Roman Catholic.

Faculty School total: 39. In upper school: 5 men, 34 women; 16 have advanced degrees.

Subjects Offered Advanced math, advanced studio art-AP, algebra, American history-AP, American literature, American literature-AP, anatomy and physiology, art, Bible studies, biology, biology-AP, British literature, British literature (honors), calculus, calculus-AP, Catholic belief and practice, chemistry, choir, college counseling, college placement, college planning, communication skills, composition, composition-AP, computer applications, computer science, computer skills, computer technologies, concert choir, contemporary history, creative arts, creative writing, dance, debate, desktop publishing, digital photography, drama, drama workshop, drawing and design, driver education, ecology, environmental systems, English, English language and composition-AP, English literature, English literature and composition-AP, environmental science, forensics, French, geometry, health, history, Holocaust studies, literature, mathematics, music, photography, physical education, physics, pre-calculus, psychology, public speaking, religion, SAT preparation, science, Spanish, studio art-AP, U.S. history, U.S. history-AP, U.S. literature, word processing, world history, world literature, world wide web design.

Graduation Requirements 4 years of community service.

Special Academic Programs Advanced Placement exam preparation; honors section; independent study; academic accommodation for the gifted, the musically talented, and the artistically talented.

College Admission Counseling 99 students graduated in 2012; 96 went to college, including Loyola University Maryland; Montclair State University; Ramapo College of New Jersey; Rutgers, The State University of New Jersey, New Brunswick; Seton Hall University. Median SAT critical reading: 557, median SAT math: 541, median SAT writing: 573. 19% scored over 600 on SAT critical reading, 21% scored over 600 on SAT math, 18% scored over 600 on SAT writing.

Student Life Upper grades have uniform requirement, student council, honor system. Discipline rests primarily with faculty. Attendance at religious services is required.

Tuition and Aid Day student tuition: $14,150. Tuition installment plan (individually arranged payment plans, one payment in full, or otherwise monthly, quarterly, or semi-annually). Tuition reduction for siblings, merit scholarship grants, need-based scholarship grants available. In 2012–13, 16% of upper-school students received aid; total upper-school merit-scholarship money awarded: $95,000. Total amount of financial aid awarded in 2012–13: $192,000.

Admissions Traditional secondary-level entrance grade is 9. For fall 2012, 215 students applied for upper-level admission, 211 were accepted, 99 enrolled. Cooperative Entrance Exam (McGraw-Hill) required. Deadline for receipt of application materials: December 15. Application fee required: $40.

Athletics Interscholastic: aerobics/dance, aquatics, basketball, cross-country running, field hockey, indoor track, indoor track & field, lacrosse, soccer, softball, swimming and diving, tennis, track and field, volleyball; intramural: ballet, cheering, dance, dance squad, dance team, field hockey, modern dance. 1 PE instructor, 20 coaches, 1 athletic trainer.

Computers Computers are regularly used in English, foreign language, history, mathematics, music, science classes. Computer network features include on-campus library services, online commercial services, Internet access, wireless campus network, Internet filtering or blocking technology. Student e-mail accounts are available to students. Students grades are available online. The school has a published electronic and media policy.

Contact Pauline Condon, Director of Admission. 973-226-0660 Ext. 1114. Fax: 973-226-2135. E-mail: pcondon@msdacademy.org. Website: www.msdacademy.org

MOUNT SAINT JOSEPH ACADEMY

120 West Wissahickon Avenue
Flourtown, Pennsylvania 19031

Head of School: Sr. Kathleen Brabson, SSJ

General Information Girls' day college-preparatory school, affiliated with Roman Catholic Church. Grades 9–12. Founded: 1858. Setting: suburban. Nearest major city is Philadelphia. 78-acre campus. 1 building on campus. Approved or accredited by Middle States Association of Colleges and Schools, National Catholic Education Association, Pennsylvania Association of Independent Schools, and Pennsylvania Department of Education. Member of National Association of Independent Schools. Endowment: $4 million. Total enrollment: 550. Upper school average class size: 19. Upper school faculty-student ratio: 1:10. There are 180 required school days per year for Upper School students. Upper School students typically attend 5 days per week. The average school day consists of 6 hours and 45 minutes.

Upper School Student Profile Grade 9: 139 students (139 girls); Grade 10: 137 students (137 girls); Grade 11: 133 students (133 girls); Grade 12: 141 students (141 girls). 95% of students are Roman Catholic.

Faculty School total: 61. In upper school: 14 men, 47 women; 41 have advanced degrees.

Subjects Offered Accounting, algebra, American history, American history-AP, American literature, American studies, art, art history, astronomy, biochemistry, biology, calculus, calculus-AP, chemistry, chorus, communications, computer science, design, desktop publishing, drama, drawing, economics, English, English literature, English literature-AP, ethics, European history, film, fine arts, French, French-AP, geography, geometry, government/civics, health, history, human sexuality, instrumental music, journalism, keyboarding, Latin, literature, mathematics, music, music-AP, painting, physical education, physics, physics-AP, physiology, pre-calculus, psychology, religion, science, social studies, Spanish, Spanish-AP, speech, technology, theater, theology, trigonometry, word processing, world history, world literature, writing.

Graduation Requirements Arts and fine arts (art, music, dance, drama), computer science, English, foreign language, mathematics, physical education (includes health), religion (includes Bible studies and theology), science, social studies (includes history).

Special Academic Programs 13 Advanced Placement exams for which test preparation is offered; honors section; independent study; study at local college for college credit; academic accommodation for the gifted, the musically talented, and the artistically talented.

College Admission Counseling 142 students graduated in 2012; all went to college, including Drexel University; Fordham University; Penn State University Park; Temple University; University of Pennsylvania; University of Pittsburgh. Mean SAT critical reading: 632, mean SAT math: 610, mean SAT writing: 655, mean combined SAT: 1897. 60% scored over 600 on SAT critical reading, 57% scored over 600 on SAT math, 68% scored over 600 on SAT writing, 60% scored over 1800 on combined SAT.

Student Life Upper grades have uniform requirement, student council, honor system. Discipline rests primarily with faculty. Attendance at religious services is required.

Tuition and Aid Day student tuition: $13,800. Tuition installment plan (Higher Education Service, Inc., semester payment plan). Tuition reduction for siblings, merit scholarship grants, need-based scholarship grants available. In 2012–13, 20% of upper-school students received aid; total upper-school merit-scholarship money awarded: $398,900. Total amount of financial aid awarded in 2012–13: $699,113.

Admissions Traditional secondary-level entrance grade is 9. For fall 2012, 285 students applied for upper-level admission, 138 enrolled. High School Placement Test, SAS, STS-HSPT or school's own test required. Deadline for receipt of application materials: October 29. Application fee required: $75.

Athletics Interscholastic: basketball, crew, cross-country running, diving, field hockey, golf, indoor track, lacrosse, soccer, softball, swimming and diving, tennis, track and field, volleyball. 2 PE instructors, 24 coaches, 1 athletic trainer.

Computers Computers are regularly used in art, business studies, career exploration, college planning, commercial art, computer applications, desktop publishing, English, foreign language, graphic design, history, mathematics, music, science, theater arts, writing, writing, yearbook classes. Computer network features include on-campus library services, online commercial services, Internet access, wireless campus network, Internet filtering or blocking technology, video conferencing, SmartBoards. Campus intranet, student e-mail accounts, and computer access in designated common areas are available to students. Students grades are available online. The school has a published electronic and media policy.

Contact Ms. Carol Finney, Director of Admissions. 215-233-9133. Fax: 215-233-5887. E-mail: cfinney@msjacad.org. Website: www.msjacad.org

MOUNT VERNON PRESBYTERIAN SCHOOL

471 Mt. Vernon Highway NE
Atlanta, Georgia 30328

Head of School: Dr. Brett Jacobsen

General Information Coeducational day college-preparatory, arts, religious studies, technology, and Design Thinking school, affiliated with Presbyterian Church. Grades PK–12. Founded: 1972. Setting: suburban. 37-acre campus. 3 buildings on campus. Approved or accredited by Southern Association of Independent Schools and Georgia Department of Education. Member of National Association of Independent Schools and Secondary School Admission Test Board. Total enrollment: 891. Upper school average class size: 15. Upper school faculty-student ratio: 1:10. There are 175 required school days per year for Upper School students. Upper School students typically attend 5 days per week. The average school day consists of 7 hours.

Upper School Student Profile 15% of students are Presbyterian.

Faculty School total: 165. In upper school: 82 have advanced degrees.

Special Academic Programs ESL (4 students enrolled).

Student Life Upper grades have uniform requirement, student council, honor system. Discipline rests primarily with faculty. Attendance at religious services is required.

Summer Programs Remediation, enrichment, advancement, sports, art/fine arts programs offered; session focuses on enrichment; held on campus; accepts boys and girls; open to students from other schools. 100 students usually enrolled. 2014 schedule: May 25 to August 5. Application deadline: May.

Admissions ISEE, SSAT or Wechsler Intelligence Scale for Children required. Deadline for receipt of application materials: February 15. Application fee required: $100. Interview required.

Athletics Interscholastic: baseball (boys), basketball (b,g), cheering (g), football (b), softball (g), volleyball (g), wrestling (b); intramural: baseball (b), basketball (b,g), cheering (g), dance squad (g), dance team (g), flag football (b), football (b), softball (g); coed interscholastic: basketball, cross-country running, diving, golf, physical training, soccer, swimming and diving, tennis, track and field, weight training; coed intramural: basketball, golf, soccer, tennis, track and field, volleyball.

Contact Mrs. Kirsten Beard, Director of Admissions. 404-252-3448. Fax: 404-252-7154. E-mail: kbeard@mountvernonschool.org. Website: www.mountvernonschool.org/

MU HIGH SCHOOL

28 Heinkel
Columbia, Missouri 65211
Head of School: Dr. Kristi D. Smalley

General Information Coeducational day college-preparatory, general academic, and distance learning school. Grades 9–12. Founded: 1999. Setting: small town. Nearest major city is St. Louis. Approved or accredited by Missouri Independent School Association and North Central Association of Colleges and Schools.

Subjects Offered 1 1/2 elective credits, 20th century American writers, 20th century physics, 20th century world history, 3-dimensional art, accounting, advanced math, Advanced Placement courses, African-American literature, agriculture, Alabama history and geography, algebra, American biography, American Civil War, American culture, American democracy, American foreign policy, American government, American history, American history-AP, ancient world history, art, art appreciation, art history-AP, astronomy, basic language skills, Basic programming, biology, business applications, business skills, business studies, calculus, calculus-AP, career education, career exploration, career planning, career/college preparation, careers, character education, chemistry, child development, Chinese, civics, college planning, communication arts, comparative politics, comparative religion, computer applications, computer literacy, computer programming, computer science-AP, conservation, consumer economics, consumer education, consumer mathematics, contemporary history, contemporary issues, creative writing, decision making skills, economics, English, English literature and composition-AP, entrepreneurship, environmental science, European history-AP, European literature, family and consumer science, family living, family studies, female experience in America, fiction, film and literature, fitness, food and nutrition, French, general science, geography, geology, geometry, German, government, government and politics-AP, grammar, health and safety, health and wellness, history, independent study, integrated mathematics, interpersonal skills, Japanese, keyboarding, language, language arts, Latin, law and the legal system, literature, literature and composition-AP, literature by women, math applications, mathematics, media studies, medieval history, modern history, modern world history, music appreciation, mythology, newspaper, North American literature, novels, parent/child development, personal and social education, personal development, personal finance, personal fitness, personal money management, photography, poetry, political science, pre-algebra, pre-calculus, psychology, psychology-AP, reading/study skills, religious studies, science fiction, Shakespeare, short story, skills for success, social studies, sociology, Spanish, state history, statistics, study skills, trigonometry, U.S. constitutional history, U.S. government, U.S. government and politics, U.S. government and politics-AP, U.S. history, U.S. history-AP, U.S. literature, women's literature, world geography, world history, world religions, writing.

Graduation Requirements Missouri Department of Elementary and Secondary Education requirements.

Special Academic Programs Advanced Placement exam preparation; accelerated programs; independent study; study at local college for college credit; academic accommodation for the gifted, the musically talented, and the artistically talented; remedial reading and/or remedial writing.

College Admission Counseling 120 students graduated in 2013.

Summer Programs Remediation, enrichment, advancement programs offered; session focuses on online/distance education courses; held off campus; held at students can access coursework from anywhere that has Internet access; accepts boys and girls; open to students from other schools.

Admissions Deadline for receipt of application materials: none. Application fee required: $25.

Athletics 1 PE instructor.

Computers Computers are regularly used in accounting, art, business, business applications, business education, business skills, business studies, career education, career exploration, classics, college planning, computer applications, creative writing, current events, digital applications, economics, English, foreign language, French, French as a second language, geography, health, historical foundations for arts, history, humanities, independent study, information technology, journalism, keyboarding, language development, Latin, life skills, mathematics, media, music, news writing, occupational education, photography, programming, psychology, reading, religious studies, research skills, science, social sciences, social studies, Spanish, study skills, theater, theater arts, typing, writing, writing classes. Computer resources include on-campus library services, INET Library, Britannica Online School Edition, course

access. Computer access in designated common areas is available to students. Students grades are available online. The school has a published electronic and media policy.

Contact Alicia Bixby, Counselor. 573-882-7208. Fax: 573-884-9665. E-mail: bixbya@missouri.edu. Website: www.muhigh.missouri.edu/

MUNICH INTERNATIONAL SCHOOL

Schloss Buchhof
Starnberg D-82319, Germany
Head of School: Simon Taylor

General Information Coeducational day college-preparatory, arts, business, bilingual studies, and technology school. Grades PK–12. Founded: 1966. Setting: rural. Nearest major city is Munich, Germany. 26-acre campus. 5 buildings on campus. Approved or accredited by Council of International Schools, International Baccalaureate Organization, and New England Association of Schools and Colleges. Affiliate member of National Association of Independent Schools; member of Secondary School Admission Test Board and European Council of International Schools. Language of instruction: English. Total enrollment: 1,206. Upper school average class size: 21. Upper school faculty-student ratio: 1:6. There are 185 required school days per year for Upper School students. Upper School students typically attend 5 days per week. The average school day consists of 6 hours and 55 minutes.

Upper School Student Profile Grade 9: 115 students (55 boys, 60 girls); Grade 10: 106 students (52 boys, 54 girls); Grade 11: 106 students (59 boys, 47 girls); Grade 12: 97 students (45 boys, 52 girls).

Faculty School total: 162. In upper school: 26 men, 46 women; 34 have advanced degrees.

Subjects Offered Adolescent issues, algebra, art, biology, business, calculus, chemistry, computer science, computer-aided design, design, drama, Dutch, economics, English, English literature, ESL, European history, film studies, fine arts, French, geography, geometry, German, grammar, health, health education, history, home economics, Indonesian, information technology, instrumental music, integrated mathematics, International Baccalaureate courses, Japanese, journalism, lab/keyboard, library skills, math methods, mathematics, model United Nations, music, personal and social education, physical education, physics, SAT preparation, science, senior thesis, social sciences, social studies, Spanish, speech and debate, student government, Swedish, technology/design, theater, theory of knowledge, trigonometry, world history, world literature, writing, yearbook.

Graduation Requirements Arts and fine arts (art, music, dance, drama), English, foreign language, mathematics, philosophy, physical education (includes health), science, social sciences, social studies (includes history), theory of knowledge, extended essay, community service. Community service is required.

Special Academic Programs International Baccalaureate program; academic accommodation for the gifted; remedial math; ESL (12 students enrolled).

College Admission Counseling 94 students graduated in 2012; 68 went to college, including California Institute of Technology; Case Western Reserve University; New York University; Rensselaer Polytechnic Institute; Simon Fraser University; The University of British Columbia. Other: 1 went to work, 25 had other specific plans. Median SAT critical reading: 580, median SAT math: 610, median SAT writing: 620, median combined SAT: 1770, median composite ACT: 27. 34% scored over 600 on SAT critical reading, 60% scored over 600 on SAT math, 37% scored over 600 on SAT writing, 43% scored over 1800 on combined SAT, 69% scored over 26 on composite ACT.

Student Life Upper grades have specified standards of dress, student council, honor system. Discipline rests primarily with faculty.

Tuition and Aid Day student tuition: €17,850. Tuition installment plan (monthly payment plans, individually arranged payment plans, Tuition Fee Reduction Programme). Tuition reduction for siblings, need-based tuition remission for current students, need-based tution reduction available. In 2012–13, 1% of upper-school students received aid. Total amount of financial aid awarded in 2012–13: €27,250.

Admissions Traditional secondary-level entrance grade is 9. For fall 2012, 85 students applied for upper-level admission, 67 were accepted, 48 enrolled. English for Non-native Speakers, Math Placement Exam or Secondary Level English Proficiency required. Deadline for receipt of application materials: none. Application fee required: €100. On-campus interview recommended.

Athletics Interscholastic: alpine skiing (boys, girls), basketball (b,g), cross-country running (b,g), freestyle skiing (b,g), golf (b,g), rugby (b), skiing (downhill) (b,g), soccer (b,g), softball (g), swimming and diving (b,g), tennis (b,g), track and field (b,g), volleyball (b,g); intramural: badminton (b,g), ballet (b,g), basketball (b,g), canoeing/kayaking (b,g), climbing (b,g), cross-country running (b,g), dance (b,g), gymnastics (b,g), outdoor skills (b,g), soccer (b,g), strength & conditioning (b,g), swimming and diving (b,g), table tennis (b,g), tennis (b,g), track and field (b,g), volleyball (b,g), wall climbing (b,g); coed interscholastic: alpine skiing, cross-country running, golf, skiing (downhill), swimming and diving, tennis, track and field; coed intramural: ballet, canoeing/kayaking, climbing, dance, gymnastics, outdoor skills, swimming and diving, wall climbing. 5 PE instructors, 10 coaches.

Computers Computers are regularly used in all academic, current events, library skills, newspaper, research skills, yearbook classes. Computer network features include on-campus library services, Internet access, wireless campus network, Internet filtering or blocking technology. Campus intranet and student e-mail accounts are available to students. Students grades are available online. The school has a published electronic and media policy.

Contact Ms. Manuela Black, Director of Admissions. 49-8151-366 Ext. 120. Fax: 49-8151-366 Ext. 129. E-mail: admissions@mis-munich.de. Website: www.mis-munich.de

NATIONAL CATHEDRAL SCHOOL

3612 Woodley Road NW
Washington, District of Columbia 20016-5000

Head of School: Mrs. Kathleen O'Neill Jamieson

General Information Girls' day college-preparatory school, affiliated with Episcopal Church. Grades 4–12. Founded: 1900. Setting: urban. 59-acre campus. 7 buildings on campus. Approved or accredited by Association of Independent Maryland Schools, Association of Independent Schools of Greater Washington, Middle States Association of Colleges and Schools, National Association of Episcopal Schools, and District of Columbia Department of Education. Member of National Association of Independent Schools and Secondary School Admission Test Board. Endowment: $19 million. Total enrollment: 581. Upper school average class size: 14. Upper school faculty-student ratio: 1:7.

Upper School Student Profile Grade 9: 84 students (84 girls); Grade 10: 74 students (74 girls); Grade 11: 78 students (78 girls); Grade 12: 79 students (79 girls).

Faculty School total: 101. In upper school: 11 men, 34 women; 36 have advanced degrees.

Subjects Offered Advanced Placement courses, African American history, African-American literature, algebra, American history, American literature, art, art history, art history-AP, biology, calculus, ceramics, chemistry, Chinese, community service, computer programming, computer science, creative writing, dance, drama, earth science, economics, English, English literature, ethics, European history, expository writing, fine arts, French, geography, geometry, government/civics, Greek, history, Japanese, Latin, mathematics, music, photography, physical education, physics, political science, psychology, public speaking, religion, science, social studies, Spanish, statistics, theater, trigonometry, world history, writing.

Graduation Requirements Arts and fine arts (art, music, dance, drama), English, foreign language, mathematics, physical education (includes health), religion (includes Bible studies and theology), science, social studies (includes history). Community service is required.

Special Academic Programs 17 Advanced Placement exams for which test preparation is offered; honors section; independent study; term-away projects; study abroad; academic accommodation for the gifted.

College Admission Counseling 81 students graduated in 2013; all went to college, including Brown University; Dartmouth College; Princeton University; Stanford University; University of Pennsylvania; Yale University. Mean SAT critical reading: 718, mean SAT math: 698, mean SAT writing: 724.

Student Life Upper grades have specified standards of dress, student council, honor system. Discipline rests equally with students and faculty. Attendance at religious services is required.

Summer Programs Enrichment, sports, art/fine arts programs offered; held on campus; accepts boys and girls; open to students from other schools. 2014 schedule: June 11 to July 30. Application deadline: June 1.

Tuition and Aid Day student tuition: $36,255. Tuition installment plan (FACTS Tuition Payment Plan). Need-based scholarship grants available. In 2013–14, 17% of upper-school students received aid. Total amount of financial aid awarded in 2013–14: $917,760.

Admissions Traditional secondary-level entrance grade is 9. For fall 2013, 108 students applied for upper-level admission, 50 were accepted, 25 enrolled. ISEE, SSAT or Wechsler Intelligence Scale for Children required. Deadline for receipt of application materials: January 15. Application fee required: $75. Interview required.

Athletics Interscholastic: basketball, crew, dance team, field hockey, ice hockey, indoor soccer, indoor track, indoor track & field, lacrosse, Nautilus, rowing, soccer, softball, tennis, track and field, volleyball, winter (indoor) track; intramural: aerobics, aerobics/dance, aerobics/Nautilus, backpacking, ballet, canoeing/kayaking, climbing, dance, fitness, hiking/backpacking, independent competitive sports, kayaking, modern dance, mountain biking, outdoor adventure, physical fitness, rafting, rappelling, rock climbing, strength & conditioning, weight lifting, weight training, yoga; coed interscholastic: cross-country running, diving, swimming and diving. 11 PE instructors, 11 coaches, 1 athletic trainer.

Computers Computers are regularly used in art, English, foreign language, mathematics, multimedia, science classes. Computer network features include on-campus library services, online commercial services, Internet access, wireless campus network, Internet filtering or blocking technology. Student e-mail accounts and computer access in designated common areas are available to students. The school has a published electronic and media policy.

Contact Ms. Elizabeth Wilson, Admission Assistant. 202-537-6374. Fax: 202-537-2382. E-mail: ncs_admissions@cathedral.org. Website: www.ncs.cathedral.org

NAZARETH ACADEMY

1209 West Ogden Avenue
LaGrange Park, Illinois 60526

Head of School: Mrs. Deborah A. Tracy

General Information Coeducational day college-preparatory school, affiliated with Roman Catholic Church. Grades 9–12. Founded: 1900. Setting: suburban. Nearest major city is Chicago. 15-acre campus. 2 buildings on campus. Approved or accredited by North Central Association of Colleges and Schools, The College Board, and Illinois Department of Education. Total enrollment: 802. Upper school average class size: 24. Upper school faculty-student ratio: 1:18. There are 180 required school days per year for Upper School students. Upper School students typically attend 5 days per week. The average school day consists of 7 hours.

Upper School Student Profile Grade 9: 209 students (115 boys, 94 girls); Grade 10: 163 students (90 boys, 73 girls); Grade 11: 219 students (109 boys, 110 girls); Grade 12: 211 students (98 boys, 113 girls). 85% of students are Roman Catholic.

Faculty School total: 49. In upper school: 19 men, 30 women; 40 have advanced degrees.

Subjects Offered 3-dimensional design, acting, algebra, American government, American literature, art, biology, biology-AP, calculus-AP, chemistry, chemistry-AP, Chinese, computer programming, computer science-AP, concert band, concert choir, creative writing, drawing and design, economics, English, English language and composition-AP, English literature and composition-AP, environmental science, French, geometry, health, Italian, journalism, music theory, photography, physical education, physics, physics-AP, pre-calculus, psychology, religion, scripture, Spanish, speech, studio art, theater, trigonometry, U.S. history, U.S. history-AP, Western civilization, wind ensemble, world history, world literature, world religions.

Graduation Requirements Advanced math, algebra, American literature, arts and fine arts (art, music, dance, drama), biology, chemistry, church history, English, foreign language, geometry, physical education (includes health), physics, religion (includes Bible studies and theology), scripture, U.S. history, Western civilization, world literature, world religions, world studies, service hours, off-campus retreat for juniors.

Special Academic Programs 12 Advanced Placement exams for which test preparation is offered; honors section.

College Admission Counseling 201 students graduated in 2013; all went to college, including Loyola University Chicago; Marquette University; Northwestern University; University of Illinois at Chicago; University of Illinois at Urbana–Champaign; University of Notre Dame. Median composite ACT: 25. 34% scored over 26 on composite ACT.

Student Life Upper grades have uniform requirement, student council, honor system. Discipline rests primarily with faculty. Attendance at religious services is required.

Summer Programs Enrichment, sports, art/fine arts programs offered; session focuses on athletic camps; held on campus; accepts boys and girls; open to students from other schools.

Tuition and Aid Day student tuition: $11,250. Tuition installment plan (monthly payment plans). Tuition reduction for siblings, merit scholarship grants, need-based scholarship grants available. In 2013–14, 22% of upper-school students received aid; total upper-school merit-scholarship money awarded: $60,000. Total amount of financial aid awarded in 2013–14: $300,000.

Admissions Traditional secondary-level entrance grade is 9. For fall 2013, 350 students applied for upper-level admission, 222 enrolled. High School Placement Test required. Deadline for receipt of application materials: June 30. No application fee required. Interview recommended.

Athletics Interscholastic: baseball (boys), basketball (b,g), cheering (g), cross-country running (b,g), football (b), golf (b,g), lacrosse (b,g), pom squad (g), soccer (b,g), softball (g), tennis (b,g), track and field (b,g), volleyball (b,g), wrestling (b); intramural: weight training (b,g); coed interscholastic: hockey. 1 PE instructor, 1 coach, 1 athletic trainer.

Computers Computers are regularly used in all academic classes. Computer network features include on-campus library services, Internet access, wireless campus network, Internet filtering or blocking technology. Student e-mail accounts are available to students. Students grades are available online. The school has a published electronic and media policy.

Contact Mr. John Bonk, Recruitment Director. 708-387-8538. Fax: 708-354-0109. E-mail: jbonk@nazarethacademy.com. Website: www.nazarethacademy.com

NAZARETH ACADEMY HIGH SCHOOL FOR GIRLS

4001 Grant Avenue
Philadelphia, Pennsylvania 19114-2999

Head of School: Sr. Mary Joan Jacobs, EdD

General Information Girls' day college-preparatory, arts, business, religious studies, and technology school, affiliated with Roman Catholic Church. Grades 9–12. Founded: 1928. Setting: urban. 20-acre campus. 2 buildings on campus. Approved or accredited by Middle States Association of Colleges and Schools, National Catholic Education Association, and Pennsylvania Department of Education. Total enrollment: 378. Upper school average class size: 20. Upper school faculty-student ratio: 1:9. There are 180 required school days per year for Upper School students. Upper School students typically attend 5 days per week. The average school day consists of 6 hours.

Upper School Student Profile Grade 9: 95 students (95 girls); Grade 10: 90 students (90 girls); Grade 11: 87 students (87 girls); Grade 12: 106 students (106 girls). 95% of students are Roman Catholic.

Faculty School total: 46. In upper school: 12 men, 34 women; 29 have advanced degrees.

Subjects Offered Accounting, advanced biology, advanced computer applications, advanced math, Advanced Placement courses, algebra, American foreign policy, American government, American history, American history-AP, American literature, American literature-AP, analysis, analysis and differential calculus, analytic geometry, anatomy and physiology, art, art history, art history-AP, Bible studies, biology, British literature, British literature (honors), British literature-AP, business, business applications, business law, calculus, calculus-AP, career exploration, chemistry, choral music, church history, civics, college admission preparation, communication arts, comparative government and politics-AP, composition-AP, computer applications, computer math, computer programming, computer science, creative writing, dance, desktop publishing, desktop publishing, ESL, digital photography, driver education, earth science, economics, English, English language and composition-AP, English literature, English literature and composition-AP, English literature-AP, English/composition-AP, environmental science, environmental studies, European history, film studies, finance, food and nutrition, French, French as a second language, geography, geometry, government, government and politics-AP, government-AP, government/civics, grammar, health, history, history of mathematics, history of science, honors algebra, honors English, honors geometry, honors U.S. history, Irish literature, Italian, jazz band, journalism, Latin, law, law and the legal system, mathematics, microbiology, modern European history, music, music theory-AP, novels, physical education, physics, politics, pre-calculus, psychology, public speaking, religion, religious studies, research, research skills, science, sign language, social studies, sociology, Spanish, speech, statistics, statistics-AP, study skills, theater arts, theology, trigonometry, U.S. government and politics-AP, United States government-AP, world history, world literature, writing.

Graduation Requirements Arts and fine arts (art, music, dance, drama), English, mathematics, physical education (includes health), science, social studies (includes history), theology, 20 hours of service.

Special Academic Programs Advanced Placement exam preparation; honors section; study at local college for college credit; academic accommodation for the gifted, the musically talented, and the artistically talented.

College Admission Counseling 106 students graduated in 2013; all went to college, including Holy Family University; La Salle University; Penn State University Park; Saint Joseph's University; Temple University; The University of Scranton. Median SAT critical reading: 552, median SAT math: 518, median SAT writing: 542.

Student Life Upper grades have uniform requirement, student council, honor system. Discipline rests equally with students and faculty. Attendance at religious services is required.

Summer Programs Enrichment, advancement, sports, art/fine arts programs offered; session focuses on academics; held on campus; accepts girls; open to students from other schools. 250 students usually enrolled. 2014 schedule: June 24 to July 18. Application deadline: May 3.

Tuition and Aid Day student tuition: $8500. Tuition installment plan (FACTS Tuition Payment Plan). Tuition reduction for siblings, merit scholarship grants available. In 2013–14, 24% of upper-school students received aid; total upper-school merit-scholarship money awarded: $100,000.

Admissions Traditional secondary-level entrance grade is 9. For fall 2013, 376 students applied for upper-level admission, 250 were accepted, 95 enrolled. ETS HSPT (closed) required. Deadline for receipt of application materials: November 1. Application fee required: $250. On-campus interview required.

Athletics Interscholastic: basketball, cheering, cross-country running, dance, diving, field hockey, golf, indoor track & field, lacrosse, softball, swimming and diving, tennis, track and field, volleyball. 1 PE instructor, 18 coaches, 1 athletic trainer.

Computers Computers are regularly used in accounting, business applications, desktop publishing, ESL, English, library science, library skills, music, newspaper, programming, SAT preparation, science, word processing, yearbook classes. Computer resources include on-campus library services, Internet access, Internet filtering or blocking technology. Students grades are available online. The school has a published electronic and media policy.

Contact Mrs. Jacqui Makowski, Director of Admissions. 215-268-1026. Fax: 215-637-8523. E-mail: makowski@nazarethacademyhs.org. Website: www.nazarethacademyhs.org

NEBRASKA CHRISTIAN SCHOOLS

1847 Inskip Avenue
Central City, Nebraska 68826

Head of School: Mr. Josh Cumpston

General Information Coeducational boarding and day college-preparatory school, affiliated with Protestant-Evangelical faith. Boarding grades 7–12, day grades K–12. Founded: 1959. Setting: rural. Nearest major city is Lincoln. Students are housed in single-sex dormitories. 27-acre campus. 7 buildings on campus. Approved or accredited by Association of Christian Schools International and Nebraska Department of Education. Total enrollment: 204. Upper school average class size: 20. Upper school faculty-student ratio: 1:10. There are 155 required school days per year for Upper School students. Upper School students typically attend 4 days per week. The average school day consists of 8 hours.

Upper School Student Profile Grade 6: 10 students (4 boys, 6 girls); Grade 7: 16 students (10 boys, 6 girls); Grade 8: 16 students (11 boys, 5 girls); Grade 9: 27 students (10 boys, 17 girls); Grade 10: 23 students (10 boys, 13 girls); Grade 11: 35 students (20 boys, 15 girls); Grade 12: 33 students (16 boys, 17 girls). 33% of students are boarding students. 74% are state residents. 1 state is represented in upper school student body. 26% are international students. International students from China, Japan, Republic of Korea, Taiwan, Thailand, and Viet Nam. 90% of students are Protestant-Evangelical faith.

Faculty School total: 23. In upper school: 13 men, 7 women; 5 have advanced degrees; 5 reside on campus.

Subjects Offered Accounting, advanced math, algebra, American government, American history, American literature, anatomy and physiology, ancient world history, art, band, Bible, biology, business, business law, chemistry, choir, Christian doctrine, Christian ethics, Christian studies, composition, computer applications, computer programming, concert band, consumer mathematics, creation science, desktop publishing, economics, economics and history, English, English composition, ESL, family living, fitness, general math, geography, geometry, health and safety, history, keyboarding, lab science, language arts, Life of Christ, life science, literature, mathematics, music, music theory, physical education, physical fitness, physical science, physics, pre-calculus, SAT/ACT preparation, science, science project, social studies, Spanish, speech, trigonometry, U.S. government, vocal ensemble, vocal music, Web site design, word processing, world geography, world history, writing, yearbook.

Graduation Requirements Algebra, American government, American history, American literature, art, Bible, biology, chemistry, Christian doctrine, economics, English, family living, geometry, history, keyboarding, Life of Christ, music, physical education (includes health), physical science, world history.

Special Academic Programs Independent study; study at local college for college credit; ESL (16 students enrolled).

College Admission Counseling 36 students graduated in 2013; 34 went to college, including Hillsdale College; New York University; Palm Beach Atlantic University; Penn State University Park; University of Nebraska–Lincoln; Wheaton College. Other: 2 had other specific plans. Median composite ACT: 26. 30% scored over 26 on composite ACT.

Student Life Upper grades have specified standards of dress, student council, honor system. Discipline rests primarily with faculty. Attendance at religious services is required.

Tuition and Aid Day student tuition: $5000; 5-day tuition and room/board: $8000; 7-day tuition and room/board: $25,950. Guaranteed tuition plan. Tuition installment plan (FACTS Tuition Payment Plan, individually arranged payment plans). Tuition reduction for siblings, merit scholarship grants, need-based scholarship grants available. In 2013–14, 25% of upper-school students received aid; total upper-school merit-scholarship money awarded: $20,000. Total amount of financial aid awarded in 2013–14: $133,000.

Admissions Traditional secondary-level entrance grade is 9. For fall 2013, 27 students applied for upper-level admission, 24 were accepted, 18 enrolled. SLEP for foreign students or TOEFL or SLEP required. Deadline for receipt of application materials: none. Application fee required: $300. Interview recommended.

Athletics Interscholastic: basketball (boys, girls), cross-country running (b,g), football (b), track and field (b,g), volleyball (g), wrestling (b). 3 PE instructors, 7 coaches.

Computers Computers are regularly used in business applications, desktop publishing, Web site design, yearbook classes. Computer network features include Internet access, wireless campus network, Internet filtering or blocking technology. Students grades are available online.

Contact Mr. Larry Hoff, Director, International Programs. 308-946-3836. Fax: 308-946-3837. E-mail: lhoff@nebraskachristian.org. Website: www.nebraskachristian.org

NERINX HALL

530 East Lockwood Avenue
Webster Groves, Missouri 63119

Head of School: Mr. John Gabriel

General Information Girls' day college-preparatory and arts school, affiliated with Roman Catholic Church. Grades 9–12. Founded: 1924. Setting: suburban. Nearest major city is St. Louis. 12-acre campus. 4 buildings on campus. Approved or accredited by National Catholic Education Association, North Central Association of Colleges and Schools, and Missouri Department of Education. Endowment: $5 million. Total enrollment: 593. Upper school average class size: 20. Upper school faculty-student ratio: 1:10. There are 176 required school days per year for Upper School students. Upper School students typically attend 5 days per week. The average school day consists of 6 hours and 25 minutes.

Upper School Student Profile Grade 9: 120 students (120 girls); Grade 10: 159 students (159 girls); Grade 11: 151 students (151 girls); Grade 12: 163 students (163 girls). 89% of students are Roman Catholic.

Faculty School total: 54. In upper school: 12 men, 42 women; 48 have advanced degrees.

Subjects Offered Acting, advanced math, American government, American history, American literature, anatomy, anthropology, art, astronomy, athletics, biology, business, calculus, ceramics, chemistry, computer applications, computer graphics, conceptual physics, creative writing, death and loss, desktop publishing, drawing and design, Eastern world civilizations, economics, English composition, English literature, film appreciation, French, geology, German, graphics, health, history, Holocaust, honors algebra, honors English, honors geometry, honors U.S. history, instrumental music, jazz band, keyboarding, lab science, Latin, media, Middle East, model United Nations, multimedia, orchestra, painting, performing arts, personal finance, physics, pre-calculus, psychology, public speaking, religious education, Spanish, theology, Web site design, Western civilization.

Graduation Requirements Algebra, arts and fine arts (art, music, dance, drama), biology, chemistry, computer applications, foreign language, geometry, physical education (includes health), physical fitness, physics, theology, U.S. government and politics, U.S. history, U.S. literature, world history, writing. Community service is required.

Special Academic Programs 10 Advanced Placement exams for which test preparation is offered; honors section; study at local college for college credit.

College Admission Counseling 154 students graduated in 2013; 153 went to college, including Rockhurst University; Saint Louis University; Truman State University; University of Arkansas; University of Dayton; University of Missouri. Other: 1 entered military service. Mean composite ACT: 28.

Student Life Upper grades have uniform requirement, student council, honor system. Discipline rests primarily with faculty. Attendance at religious services is required.

Summer Programs Advancement programs offered; session focuses on advancement; held on campus; accepts girls; not open to students from other schools. 175 students usually enrolled.

Tuition and Aid Day student tuition: $11,900. Tuition installment plan (individually arranged payment plans). Tuition reduction for siblings, need-based scholarship grants, paying campus jobs available. In 2013–14, 27% of upper-school students received aid. Total amount of financial aid awarded in 2013–14: $695,529.

Admissions Traditional secondary-level entrance grade is 9. For fall 2013, 162 students applied for upper-level admission, 123 were accepted, 120 enrolled. Any standardized test or CTBS (or similar from their school) required. Deadline for receipt of application materials: December 2. Application fee required: $10. On-campus interview required.

Athletics Interscholastic: basketball, cross-country running, diving, field hockey, golf, lacrosse, racquetball, soccer, softball, swimming and diving, tennis, track and field, volleyball. 3 PE instructors, 25 coaches.

Computers Computers are regularly used in graphics, humanities, mathematics, science, speech, writing, writing classes. Computer network features include on-campus library services, Internet access, wireless campus network, Internet filtering or blocking technology. Student e-mail accounts are available to students. Students grades are available online. The school has a published electronic and media policy.

Contact Mrs. Mary Ann Gentry, Admissions. 314-968-1505 Ext. 151. Fax: 314-968-0604. E-mail: mgentry@nerinxhs.org. Website: www.nerinxhs.org

NEWARK ACADEMY

91 South Orange Avenue
Livingston, New Jersey 07039-4989

Head of School: M. Donald M. Austin

General Information Coeducational day college-preparatory, arts, technology, and International Baccalaureate school. Grades 6–12. Founded: 1774. Setting: suburban. Nearest major city is Morristown. 68-acre campus. 1 building on campus. Approved or accredited by Middle States Association of Colleges and Schools and New Jersey Department of Education. Member of National Association of Independent Schools and Secondary School Admission Test Board. Endowment: $25 million. Total enrollment: 582. Upper school average class size: 13. Upper school faculty-student ratio: 1:12. There are 165 required school days per year for Upper School students. Upper School students typically attend 5 days per week. The average school day consists of 6 hours.

Upper School Student Profile Grade 9: 106 students (57 boys, 49 girls); Grade 10: 105 students (55 boys, 50 girls); Grade 11: 93 students (49 boys, 44 girls); Grade 12: 101 students (48 boys, 53 girls).

Faculty School total: 78. In upper school: 39 men, 39 women; 66 have advanced degrees.

Subjects Offered Accounting, acting, advanced biology, advanced chemistry, advanced computer applications, advanced math, Advanced Placement courses, advanced studio art-AP, algebra, American history, American literature, anatomy, art, art history, arts, biology, botany, calculus, ceramics, chemistry, chorus, community service, computer programming, computer science, creative writing, drama, driver education, ecology, economics, English, English literature, European history, film studies, filmmaking, finance, fine arts, French, geometry, government/civics, grammar, health, history, history-AP, Holocaust studies, honors algebra, honors geometry, humanities, International Baccalaureate courses, jazz band, leadership, Mandarin,

mathematics, mechanical drawing, model United Nations, modern dance, money management, music, musical theater, newspaper, oil painting, participation in sports, peer counseling, philosophy, physical education, physical science, physics, play production, playwriting and directing, poetry, political science, pottery, pre-algebra, pre-calculus, probability and statistics, SAT/ACT preparation, science, Spanish, theater, theory of knowledge, trigonometry, world history, world literature, writing.

Graduation Requirements Arts and fine arts (art, music, dance, drama), computer science, English, foreign language, mathematics, physical education (includes health), science, social studies (includes history), 40-hour senior service project, community service.

Special Academic Programs International Baccalaureate program; 5 Advanced Placement exams for which test preparation is offered; honors section; accelerated programs; independent study; term-away projects; study abroad; academic accommodation for the gifted, the musically talented, and the artistically talented.

College Admission Counseling 104 students graduated in 2013; all went to college, including Cornell University; Georgetown University; Harvard University; New York University; The George Washington University; University of Pennsylvania. Median SAT critical reading: 688, median SAT math: 689, median SAT writing: 706, median combined SAT: 2083, median composite ACT: 30.

Student Life Upper grades have specified standards of dress, student council, honor system. Discipline rests primarily with faculty.

Summer Programs Remediation, enrichment, advancement, sports, art/fine arts, computer instruction programs offered; session focuses on enrichment and advancement; held on campus; accepts boys and girls; open to students from other schools. 1,250 students usually enrolled. 2014 schedule: June 27 to August 5. Application deadline: May 1.

Tuition and Aid Day student tuition: $33,300. Tuition installment plan (Insured Tuition Payment Plan, Key Tuition Payment Plan, monthly payment plans). Need-based scholarship grants available. In 2013–14, 19% of upper-school students received aid. Total amount of financial aid awarded in 2013–14: $1,776,490.

Admissions Traditional secondary-level entrance grade is 9. For fall 2013, 526 students applied for upper-level admission, 76 were accepted, 42 enrolled. ISEE or SSAT required. Deadline for receipt of application materials: December 9. Application fee required: $75. On-campus interview required.

Athletics Interscholastic: baseball (boys), basketball (b,g), cross-country running (b,g), fencing (b,g), field hockey (g), football (b), golf (b,g), lacrosse (b,g), running (b,g), skiing (downhill) (b,g), soccer (b,g), softball (g), swimming and diving (b,g), tennis (b,g), track and field (b,g), volleyball (g), wrestling (b); intramural: aerobics/dance (b,g), aerobics/Nautilus (b,g), baseball (b), basketball (b,g), bicycling (b,g), cross-country running (b,g), dance (b,g), dance team (b,g), field hockey (g), fitness (b,g), football (b), golf (b,g), hockey (b), ice hockey (b), lacrosse (b,g), modern dance (b,g), soccer (b,g), softball (g), swimming and diving (b,g), tennis (b,g), track and field (b,g), volleyball (g), weight lifting (b,g), wrestling (b), yoga (b,g); coed intramural: aerobics/dance, aerobics/Nautilus, bicycling, cricket, dance, dance team, fitness, modern dance, mountain biking, skiing (downhill), table tennis, ultimate Frisbee, weight lifting, yoga. 5 PE instructors, 10 coaches, 1 athletic trainer.

Computers Computers are regularly used in all academic classes. Computer network features include on-campus library services, online commercial services, Internet access, wireless campus network, Internet filtering or blocking technology. Campus intranet and student e-mail accounts are available to students. Students grades are available online. The school has a published electronic and media policy.

Contact Ms. Imaani F. Sanders, Admission Office Manager. 973-992-7000 Ext. 323. Fax: 973-488-0040. E-mail: Isanders@newarka.edu. Website: www.newarka.edu

NEW COVENANT ACADEMY

3304 South Cox Road
Springfield, Missouri 65807

Head of School: Mr. Matt Searson

General Information Coeducational day college-preparatory, arts, business, religious studies, technology, and science, math, foreign language, language arts school, affiliated with Christian faith. Grades JK–12. Founded: 1979. Setting: suburban. 27-acre campus. 1 building on campus. Approved or accredited by North Central Association of Colleges and Schools. Total enrollment: 397. There are 167 required school days per year for Upper School students. Upper School students typically attend 5 days per week. The average school day consists of 7 hours and 30 minutes.

Upper School Student Profile 99% of students are Christian.

Faculty School total: 30. In upper school: 5 men, 10 women.

Subjects Offered Advanced math, algebra, American government, American history, American literature, anatomy and physiology, ancient world history, art, athletics, Bible, biology, British literature, business, calculus, chemistry, Christianity, comparative government and politics, computer processing, computer technologies, computers, concert choir, economics, English, English composition, geology, geometry, health, history, independent study, Life of Christ, literature, mathematics, music appreciation, New Testament, oceanography, physical education, physics, pre-algebra, robotics, science, scripture, Spanish, trigonometry, world history, yearbook.

Special Academic Programs Study at local college for college credit.

College Admission Counseling 29 students graduated in 2013.

Student Life Upper grades have specified standards of dress, student council, honor system. Discipline rests primarily with faculty. Attendance at religious services is required.

Tuition and Aid Guaranteed tuition plan. Tuition installment plan (monthly payment plans, individually arranged payment plans). Need-based scholarship grants available.

Admissions Otis-Lennon School Ability Test, SLEP for foreign students or Stanford Achievement Test required. Deadline for receipt of application materials: none. Application fee required: $50. Interview required.

Athletics Interscholastic: basketball (boys, girls), cheering (g), golf (b), soccer (b,g), track and field (b,g), volleyball (g); intramural: basketball (b,g), soccer (b,g); coed interscholastic: golf. 1 PE instructor, 11 coaches.

Computers Computers are regularly used in computer applications, journalism, technology, word processing, yearbook classes. Computer network features include Internet access, Internet filtering or blocking technology. Student e-mail accounts and computer access in designated common areas are available to students. Students grades are available online.

Contact Mrs. Delana Reynolds, Admissions Officer. 417-887-9848 Ext. 6. Fax: 417-887-2419. E-mail: dreynolds@newcovenant.net. Website: www.newcovenant.net

NEWTON'S GROVE SCHOOL

1 City View Drive
Toronto, Ontario M9W 5A5, Canada

Head of School: Mrs. Gabrielle Bush

General Information Coeducational day college-preparatory, arts, business, technology, Science, and Math school. Grades JK–12. Founded: 1977. Setting: urban. 1 building on campus. Approved or accredited by Ontario Ministry of Education and Ontario Department of Education. Language of instruction: English. Total enrollment: 255. Upper school average class size: 18. Upper school faculty-student ratio: 1:18. There are 192 required school days per year for Upper School students. Upper School students typically attend 5 days per week. The average school day consists of 6 hours and 30 minutes.

Upper School Student Profile Grade 9: 29 students (21 boys, 8 girls); Grade 10: 34 students (20 boys, 14 girls); Grade 11: 29 students (16 boys, 13 girls); Grade 12: 28 students (14 boys, 14 girls).

Faculty School total: 35. In upper school: 9 men, 7 women; 2 have advanced degrees.

Subjects Offered Accounting, anthropology, biology, Canadian geography, Canadian history, Canadian law, chemistry, civics, communications, data processing, discrete mathematics, dramatic arts, English, film, French, functions, geometry, healthful living, information technology, learning strategies, mathematics, organizational studies, personal finance, philosophy, physics, psychology, reading, science, society challenge and change, sociology, visual arts, world history, writing.

Graduation Requirements English, Ontario Ministry of Education requirements.

Special Academic Programs ESL (15 students enrolled).

College Admission Counseling 34 students graduated in 2013; all went to college, including McMaster University; Ryerson University; University of Guelph; University of Ottawa; University of Toronto; York University.

Student Life Upper grades have uniform requirement, student council, honor system. Discipline rests primarily with faculty.

Summer Programs Remediation, enrichment, advancement, ESL, sports, art/fine arts, computer instruction programs offered; session focuses on academics; held on campus; accepts boys and girls; open to students from other schools. 100 students usually enrolled. 2014 schedule: July 7 to August 1. Application deadline: June 25.

Tuition and Aid Day student tuition: CAN$15,500. Tuition installment plan (individually arranged payment plans, MPS Payment Plan). Tuition reduction for siblings, early payment discount available.

Admissions Admissions testing required. Deadline for receipt of application materials: October 31. No application fee required. Interview required.

Athletics Interscholastic: baseball (boys, girls), basketball (b,g), flag football (b,g), football (b), indoor track & field (b,g), running (b,g), soccer (b,g), swimming and diving (b,g), track and field (b,g), volleyball (b,g); intramural: basketball (b,g), flag football (b,g), floor hockey (b,g), Frisbee (b,g), indoor hockey (b,g), physical fitness (b,g), rhythmic gymnastics (b,g), running (b,g), soccer (b,g), swimming and diving (b,g), touch football (b,g), track and field (b,g), ultimate Frisbee (b,g), volleyball (b,g), winter (indoor) track (b,g), winter soccer (b,g); coed interscholastic: aquatics, bowling, cross-country running, field hockey, flag football; coed intramural: badminton, baseball, basketball, bowling, cooperative games, cross-country running, flag football, table tennis, tennis. 2 PE instructors.

Computers Computers are regularly used in art, business education, computer applications, graphic arts, media arts, photography classes. Computer resources include Internet access, Internet filtering or blocking technology. Student e-mail accounts are available to students. The school has a published electronic and media policy.

Contact Mrs. Gabrielle Bush, Director. 416-745-1328. Fax: 416-745-4168. E-mail: gabriellebush@newtonsgroveschool.com. Website: www.newtonsgroveschool.com

NIAGARA CHRISTIAN COMMUNITY OF SCHOOLS

2619 Niagara Boulevard
Fort Erie, Ontario L2A 5M4, Canada

Head of School: Mr. Mark Thiessen

General Information Coeducational boarding and day college-preparatory, general academic, arts, business, vocational, religious studies, and technology school, affiliated with Brethren in Christ Church. Boarding grades 9–12, day grades 6–12. Founded: 1932. Setting: rural. Nearest major city is Niagara Falls, Canada. Students are housed in single-sex dormitories. 121-acre campus. 11 buildings on campus. Approved or accredited by Ontario Department of Education. Language of instruction: English. Total enrollment: 178. Upper school average class size: 17. Upper school faculty-student ratio: 1:16. There are 170 required school days per year for Upper School students. Upper School students typically attend 5 days per week. The average school day consists of 7 hours.

Upper School Student Profile Grade 9: 15 students (9 boys, 6 girls); Grade 10: 26 students (11 boys, 15 girls); Grade 11: 41 students (22 boys, 19 girls); Grade 12: 79 students (41 boys, 38 girls). 85% of students are boarding students. 15% are province residents. 4 provinces are represented in upper school student body. 85% are international students. International students from Hong Kong, Japan, Mexico, Nigeria, Republic of Korea, and Taiwan; 8 other countries represented in student body. 15% of students are Brethren in Christ Church.

Faculty School total: 22. In upper school: 8 men, 13 women; 2 have advanced degrees.

Subjects Offered Accounting, advanced chemistry, advanced computer applications, advanced math, advanced TOEFL/grammar, algebra, analysis and differential calculus, analysis of data, analytic geometry, anatomy, anthropology, art, art history, athletics, Bible, biology, business, business applications, business education, business mathematics, business technology, calculus, Canadian geography, Canadian history, Canadian literature, career education, chemistry, choir, civics, computer applications, computer programming, concert choir, data processing, discrete mathematics, early childhood, economics, English, English literature, ESL, exercise science, family studies, French as a second language, general math, geography, geometry, guidance, health education, history, information technology, instrumental music, integrated science, international affairs, leadership education training, Life of Christ, mathematics, media studies, modern world history, music, parenting, physical education, physics, politics, pre-calculus, science, Spanish, TOEFL preparation, world history, world issues, writing, writing.

Special Academic Programs Special instructional classes for students with learning disabilities; ESL (85 students enrolled).

College Admission Counseling 40 students graduated in 2013; 38 went to college, including Brock University; McMaster University; The University of Western Ontario; University of Toronto; University of Waterloo; Wilfrid Laurier University. Other: 2 went to work.

Student Life Upper grades have uniform requirement, student council, honor system. Discipline rests primarily with faculty. Attendance at religious services is required.

Summer Programs ESL programs offered; session focuses on ESL; held on campus; accepts boys and girls; not open to students from other schools. 70 students usually enrolled. 2014 schedule: July 5 to August 27. Application deadline: none.

Tuition and Aid Day student tuition: CAN$9050; 5-day tuition and room/board: CAN$29,895; 7-day tuition and room/board: CAN$38,840. Tuition installment plan (monthly payment plans, individually arranged payment plans, quarterly payment plan). Tuition reduction for siblings, bursaries, merit scholarship grants, need-based scholarship grants, paying campus jobs available. In 2013–14, 10% of upper-school students received aid; total upper-school merit-scholarship money awarded: CAN$50,000. Total amount of financial aid awarded in 2013–14: CAN$400,000.

Admissions Traditional secondary-level entrance grade is 9. For fall 2013, 50 students applied for upper-level admission, 50 were accepted, 50 enrolled. Admissions testing and English proficiency required. Deadline for receipt of application materials: none. Application fee required: CAN$100. Interview required.

Athletics Interscholastic: badminton (boys, girls), baseball (g), basketball (b,g), cross-country running (b,g), golf (b), soccer (b,g), track and field (b,g); coed interscholastic: badminton; coed intramural: aerobics, alpine skiing, aquatics, badminton, ball hockey, bowling, canoeing/kayaking, cross-country running, fitness, fitness walking, floor hockey, golf, ice skating, skiing (downhill), soccer. 1 PE instructor, 5 coaches.

Computers Computers are regularly used in accounting, all academic, business, data processing, economics, ESL, mathematics, science, yearbook classes. Computer network features include on-campus library services, Internet access, wireless campus network, Internet filtering or blocking technology. Campus intranet and computer access in designated common areas are available to students. Students grades are available online. The school has a published electronic and media policy.

Contact Mr. Rob Collier, Director of Residence and Student Life. 905-871-6980 Ext. 2244. Fax: 905-871-9260. E-mail: robcoll@niagaracc.com. Website: www.niagaracc.com

NOBLE ACADEMY

Greensboro, North Carolina

See Special Needs Schools section.

NOBLE AND GREENOUGH SCHOOL

10 Campus Drive

Dedham, Massachusetts 02026-4099

Head of School: Mr. Robert P. Henderson Jr.

General Information Coeducational boarding and day college-preparatory school. Boarding grades 9–12, day grades 7–12. Founded: 1866. Setting: suburban. Nearest major city is Boston. Students are housed in single-sex dormitories. 187-acre campus. 12 buildings on campus. Approved or accredited by Association of Independent Schools in New England, New England Association of Schools and Colleges, The College Board, and Massachusetts Department of Education. Member of National Association of Independent Schools and Secondary School Admission Test Board. Endowment: $104 million. Total enrollment: 613. Upper school average class size: 14. Upper school faculty-student ratio: 1:7. There are 162 required school days per year for Upper School students. Upper School students typically attend 5 days per week. The average school day consists of 7 hours and 5 minutes.

Upper School Student Profile Grade 9: 118 students (58 boys, 60 girls); Grade 10: 122 students (59 boys, 63 girls); Grade 11: 130 students (66 boys, 64 girls); Grade 12: 120 students (64 boys, 56 girls). 8% of students are boarding students. 99% are state residents. 3 states are represented in upper school student body.

Faculty School total: 125. In upper school: 65 men, 60 women; 34 reside on campus.

Subjects Offered 20th century history, Advanced Placement courses, African-American literature, algebra, American history, American literature, anatomy, ancient history, art, art history, astronomy, biology, calculus, ceramics, chemistry, community service, computer programming, computer science, concert band, creative writing, drama, drawing, earth science, ecology, economics, English, English literature, environmental science, ethics, European history, expository writing, fine arts, French, genetics, geography, geometry, government/civics, grammar, health, history, independent study, Japanese, journalism, Latin, Latin American history, marine biology, mathematics, music, painting, philosophy, photography, physics, physiology, printmaking, psychology, Roman civilization, science, senior internship, senior project, social studies, Spanish, speech, statistics, theater, trigonometry, Vietnam, world history, world literature, writing.

Graduation Requirements Arts and fine arts (art, music, dance, drama), computer science, English, foreign language, mathematics, performing arts, physical education (includes health), science, social studies (includes history), 80 hours of community service must be completed.

Special Academic Programs Advanced Placement exam preparation; honors section; independent study; term-away projects; study abroad; academic accommodation for the gifted, the musically talented, and the artistically talented.

College Admission Counseling 107 students graduated in 2013; all went to college, including Brown University; Colgate University; Cornell University; Harvard University; Middlebury College. 72% scored over 600 on SAT critical reading, 75% scored over 600 on SAT math, 80% scored over 600 on SAT writing.

Student Life Upper grades have specified standards of dress, student council, honor system. Discipline rests equally with students and faculty.

Tuition and Aid Day student tuition: $40,900; 5-day tuition and room/board: $46,700. Tuition installment plan (Tuition Management Systems). Need-based scholarship grants, need-based loans available. In 2013–14, 24% of upper-school students received aid. Total amount of financial aid awarded in 2013–14: $3,796,650.

Admissions Traditional secondary-level entrance grade is 9. For fall 2013, 582 students applied for upper-level admission, 134 were accepted, 76 enrolled. ISEE or SSAT required. Deadline for receipt of application materials: January 15. Application fee required: $60. On-campus interview required.

Athletics Interscholastic: baseball (boys), basketball (b,g), crew (b,g), cross-country running (b,g), field hockey (g), football (b); coed intramural: aerobics/dance, dance. 12 coaches, 2 athletic trainers.

Computers Computers are regularly used in English, foreign language, history, journalism, Latin, mathematics, music, science classes. Computer network features include on-campus library services, online commercial services, Internet access, Internet filtering or blocking technology, NoblesNet (first class email and bulletin board with electronic conferencing capability), wireless iBooks. Campus intranet, student e-mail accounts, and computer access in designated common areas are available to students. The school has a published electronic and media policy.

Contact Ms. Jennifer Hines, Dean of Enrollment Management. 781-320-7100. Fax: 781-320-1329. E-mail: admission@nobles.edu. Website: www.nobles.edu

THE NORA SCHOOL

955 Sligo Avenue

Silver Spring, Maryland 20910

Head of School: David E. Mullen

General Information Coeducational day college-preparatory, arts, and technology school. Grades 9–12. Founded: 1964. Setting: urban. Nearest major city is Washington, DC. 1-acre campus. 1 building on campus. Approved or accredited by Association of Independent Schools of Greater Washington, Middle States Association of Colleges and Schools, and Maryland Department of Education. Member of National Association of Independent Schools. Endowment: $250,000. Total enrollment: 60. Upper school average class size: 8. Upper school faculty-student ratio: 1:5. There are 175 required school days per year for Upper School students. Upper School students typically attend 5 days per week. The average school day consists of 5 hours and 35 minutes.

Upper School Student Profile Grade 9: 11 students (8 boys, 3 girls); Grade 10: 14 students (9 boys, 5 girls); Grade 11: 26 students (17 boys, 9 girls); Grade 12: 26 students (16 boys, 10 girls).

Faculty School total: 11. In upper school: 8 men, 3 women; all have advanced degrees.

Subjects Offered African-American literature, algebra, American literature, American studies, art, art history, astronomy, biology, British literature, calculus, ceramics, chemistry, college writing, community service, computer graphics, conceptual physics, conflict resolution, crafts, creative writing, economics, English composition, environmental science, expository writing, film and literature, forensics, geography, geometry, German, graphic design, illustration, integrated science, peace studies, peer counseling, photo shop, photography, physical education, physics, political science, pre-algebra, pre-calculus, psychology, sculpture, Shakespeare, social justice, Spanish, statistics, street law, studio art, trigonometry, U.S. history, wilderness education, women's literature, world history, world religions, writing.

Graduation Requirements Arts and fine arts (art, music, dance, drama), English, foreign language, lab science, mathematics, personal fitness, science, social studies (includes history), sports, U.S. history, wilderness education, writing, graduation portfolio. Community service is required.

Special Academic Programs Independent study; term-away projects; study at local college for college credit; academic accommodation for the gifted and the artistically talented; remedial reading and/or remedial writing; remedial math; programs in English, mathematics, general development for dyslexic students; special instructional classes for students with Attention Deficit Disorder and learning disabilities, students who have been unsuccessful in a traditional learning environment.

College Admission Counseling 19 students graduated in 2013; all went to college, including Bard College; Dickinson College; Goucher College; Guilford College; Loyola University Maryland; Mount Holyoke College.

Student Life Upper grades have student council. Discipline rests primarily with faculty.

Tuition and Aid Day student tuition: $25,800. Tuition installment plan (monthly payment plans). Need-based scholarship grants, Black Student Fund, Latino Student Fund, Washington Scholarship Fund available. In 2013–14, 24% of upper-school students received aid. Total amount of financial aid awarded in 2013–14: $167,000.

Admissions Traditional secondary-level entrance grade is 9. For fall 2013, 58 students applied for upper-level admission, 55 were accepted, 52 enrolled. Writing sample required. Deadline for receipt of application materials: none. Application fee required: $75. On-campus interview required.

Athletics Interscholastic: basketball (boys, girls); intramural: cheering (g); coed interscholastic: soccer, softball; coed intramural: alpine skiing, backpacking, bicycling, bowling, canoeing/kayaking, climbing, cooperative games, dance, Frisbee, hiking/backpacking, ice skating, kayaking, outdoor activities, outdoor adventure, rafting, rock climbing, ropes courses, running, skiing (downhill), table tennis, tennis, volleyball, wilderness. 2 coaches.

Computers Computers are regularly used in art, college planning, creative writing, design, drawing and design, English, graphic arts, graphic design, independent study, literary magazine, mathematics, photography, SAT preparation, writing, writing, yearbook classes. Computer network features include on-campus library services, online commercial services, Internet access, wireless campus network, Internet filtering or blocking technology. Students grades are available online. The school has a published electronic and media policy.

Contact Marcia D. Miller, Director of Admissions. 301-495-6672. Fax: 301-495-7829. E-mail: marcia@nora-school.org. Website: www.nora-school.org

NORFOLK ACADEMY

1585 Wesleyan Drive

Norfolk, Virginia 23502

Head of School: Mr. Dennis G. Manning

General Information Coeducational day college-preparatory school. Grades 1–12. Founded: 1728. Setting: suburban. 70-acre campus. 14 buildings on campus. Approved or accredited by Southern Association of Colleges and Schools, Southern Association of Independent Schools, The College Board, and Virginia Department of Education. Member of National Association of Independent Schools and Secondary

School Admission Test Board. Endowment: $40 million. Total enrollment: 1,248. Upper school average class size: 15. Upper school faculty-student ratio: 1:10. There are 175 required school days per year for Upper School students. Upper School students typically attend 5 days per week. The average school day consists of 7 hours.

Upper School Student Profile Grade 10: 122 students (66 boys, 56 girls); Grade 11: 135 students (63 boys, 72 girls); Grade 12: 122 students (67 boys, 55 girls).

Faculty School total: 124. In upper school: 39 men, 13 women; 32 have advanced degrees.

Subjects Offered Algebra, American history, American literature, art, art history, band, biology, calculus, chemistry, chorus, computer math, computer programming, computer science, dance, driver education, economics, English, English literature, environmental science, European history, film studies, fine arts, French, geography, geometry, German, government/civics, health, history, instrumental music, Italian, Latin, mathematics, music, music history, music theory, physical education, physics, science, social studies, Spanish, speech, statistics, studio art, theater arts, world history.

Graduation Requirements Arts and fine arts (art, music, dance, drama), English, foreign language, mathematics, physical education (includes health), science, social studies (includes history), 8-minute senior speech, seminar program. Community service is required.

Special Academic Programs Advanced Placement exam preparation; independent study; study abroad; academic accommodation for the gifted, the musically talented, and the artistically talented.

College Admission Counseling 117 students graduated in 2013; all went to college, including Hampden-Sydney College; James Madison University; The College of William and Mary; University of Virginia; Virginia Polytechnic Institute and State University. Mean SAT critical reading: 628, mean SAT math: 648, mean SAT writing: 622.

Student Life Upper grades have specified standards of dress, student council, honor system. Discipline rests equally with students and faculty.

Summer Programs Enrichment, advancement, sports, art/fine arts programs offered; session focuses on academics, arts, athletics, day camp for children; held both on and off campus; held at surfing camp located at beach and Business internships; accepts boys and girls; open to students from other schools. 500 students usually enrolled. 2014 schedule: June 17 to July 26.

Tuition and Aid Day student tuition: $21,500. Tuition installment plan (Key Tuition Payment Plan, monthly payment plans). Need-based scholarship grants available. In 2013–14, 20% of upper-school students received aid.

Admissions Traditional secondary-level entrance grade is 10. For fall 2013, 30 students applied for upper-level admission, 9 were accepted, 8 enrolled. ERB Achievement Test, ERB CTP IV, essay, Individual IQ, Otis-Lennon School Ability Test or SSAT required. Deadline for receipt of application materials: February 1. Application fee required: $50. On-campus interview required.

Athletics Interscholastic: baseball (boys), basketball (b,g), cheering (g), crew (b,g), cross-country running (b,g), dance (b,g), diving (b,g), field hockey (g), football (b), golf (b,g), indoor track (b,g), lacrosse (b,g), sailing (b,g), soccer (b,g), softball (g), swimming and diving (b,g), tennis (b,g), track and field (b,g), volleyball (g), winter (indoor) track (b,g), wrestling (b); intramural: dance (g), dance team (g). 2 PE instructors, 3 athletic trainers.

Computers Computers are regularly used in all academic classes. Computer network features include on-campus library services, online commercial services, Internet access, wireless campus network, Internet filtering or blocking technology, online library resources, video production, curriculum-based software, desktop publishing, campus-wide media distribution system. Campus intranet, student e-mail accounts, and computer access in designated common areas are available to students. Students grades are available online. The school has a published electronic and media policy.

Contact Mr. James H. Lasley Jr., Director of Admissions. 757-455-5582 Ext. 5337. Fax: 757-455-3199. E-mail: jlasley@norfolkacademy.org. Website: www.norfolkacademy.org

NORMAN HOWARD SCHOOL

Rochester, New York
See Special Needs Schools section.

THE NORTH BROWARD PREPARATORY UPPER SCHOOL

7600 Lyons Road
Coconut Creek, Florida 33073

Head of School: Elise R. Ecoff, EdD

General Information Coeducational boarding and day college-preparatory, arts, and technology school. Boarding grades 8–12, day grades PK–12. Founded: 1957. Setting: suburban. Students are housed in single-sex dormitories. 75-acre campus. 10 buildings on campus. Approved or accredited by Florida Council of Independent Schools and Southern Association of Colleges and Schools. Total enrollment: 1,375. Upper school average class size: 18. Upper school faculty-student ratio: 1:18. There are 177 required school days per year for Upper School students. Upper School students

typically attend 5 days per week. The average school day consists of 6 hours and 20 minutes.

Upper School Student Profile Grade 6: 92 students (56 boys, 36 girls); Grade 7: 119 students (74 boys, 45 girls); Grade 8: 108 students (66 boys, 42 girls); Grade 9: 131 students (63 boys, 68 girls); Grade 10: 166 students (85 boys, 81 girls); Grade 11: 230 students (150 boys, 80 girls); Grade 12: 169 students (93 boys, 76 girls). 30% of students are boarding students. 85% are state residents. 3 states are represented in upper school student body. 30% are international students. International students from Brazil, China, Germany, Italy, Republic of Korea, and Russian Federation; 6 other countries represented in student body.

Faculty School total: 104. In upper school: 39 men, 65 women; 45 have advanced degrees; 7 reside on campus.

Subjects Offered Algebra, American history-AP, analysis and differential calculus, analytic geometry, ancient world history, art, art history, audio visual/media, Basic programming, biology, biology-AP, British literature, broadcast journalism, business, calculus, calculus-AP, chemistry, chemistry-AP, choir, choral music, college counseling, computer applications, computer graphics, computer programming, computer programming-AP, computers, concert band, concert choir, contemporary women writers, drama workshop, dramatic arts, ecology, environmental systems, economics, English, English composition, English literature, English literature and composition-AP, environmental science, environmental science-AP, ESL, European history, European history-AP, forensics, French, French language-AP, French literature-AP, geometry, guitar, honors algebra, honors English, honors geometry, honors U.S. history, honors world history, jazz band, jazz dance, jazz ensemble, keyboarding, Latin, model United Nations, modern European history, modern European history-AP, music, music appreciation, performing arts, physical education, physical fitness, physics-AP, psychology-AP, robotics, SAT preparation, Shakespeare, skills for success, sociology, Spanish, Spanish language-AP, Spanish literature, Spanish literature-AP, U.S. government, U.S. government and politics-AP, U.S. history, U.S. literature, wind ensemble, wind instruments, women in literature, world history-AP.

Graduation Requirements Algebra, American history, American literature, biology, calculus, chemistry, computer applications, electives, English, European history, foreign language, geometry, performing arts, physical education (includes health), physics, U.S. government, U.S. literature, world cultures. Community service is required.

Special Academic Programs International Baccalaureate program; Advanced Placement exam preparation; honors section; independent study; study at local college for college credit; academic accommodation for the gifted, the musically talented, and the artistically talented; remedial reading and/or remedial writing; remedial math; programs in English, mathematics, general development for dyslexic students; ESL (80 students enrolled).

College Admission Counseling 180 students graduated in 2013; all went to college, including Boston University; Duke University; Florida State University; University of Florida; University of Miami; University of Pennsylvania. Mean SAT critical reading: 517, mean SAT math: 571, mean SAT writing: 524. 27% scored over 600 on SAT critical reading, 29% scored over 600 on SAT math, 25% scored over 600 on SAT writing, 23% scored over 1800 on combined SAT, 26% scored over 26 on composite ACT.

Student Life Upper grades have uniform requirement, student council, honor system. Discipline rests equally with students and faculty.

Summer Programs Remediation, enrichment, advancement, sports, art/fine arts, computer instruction programs offered; session focuses on enrichment; held on campus; accepts boys and girls; open to students from other schools. 750 students usually enrolled. 2014 schedule: June 9 to August 1.

Tuition and Aid Day student tuition: $19,910–$23,610. Tuition installment plan (monthly payment plans). Tuition reduction for siblings, merit scholarship grants, need-based scholarship grants available. In 2013–14, 22% of upper-school students received aid; total upper-school merit-scholarship money awarded: $1,300,000. Total amount of financial aid awarded in 2013–14: $2,400,000.

Admissions Traditional secondary-level entrance grade is 9. For fall 2013, 160 students applied for upper-level admission, 121 were accepted, 70 enrolled. SSAT required. Deadline for receipt of application materials: none. Application fee required: $150. Interview required.

Athletics Interscholastic: aquatics (boys, girls), baseball (b), basketball (b,g), bowling (g), cross-country running (b,g), dance (g), dance squad (g), dance team (g), flag football (g), football (b), golf (b,g), ice hockey (b), lacrosse (b,g), physical fitness (b,g), rugby (b), soccer (b,g), softball (g), swimming and diving (b,g), tennis (b,g), track and field (b,g), volleyball (g), water polo (b,g), winter soccer (b,g); coed interscholastic: aquatics, bowling, cheering, cross-country running, dressage, fencing, golf, physical fitness; coed intramural: basketball, flag football, scuba diving, strength & conditioning. 4 PE instructors, 18 coaches, 1 athletic trainer.

Computers Computers are regularly used in all academic classes. Computer network features include on-campus library services, online commercial services, Internet access, wireless campus network, Internet filtering or blocking technology. Campus intranet, student e-mail accounts, and computer access in designated common areas are available to students. Students grades are available online. The school has a published electronic and media policy.

Contact Jackie Fagan, Director of Admissions. 954-247-0011 Ext. 303. Fax: 954-247-0012. E-mail: faganj@nbps.org. Website: www.nbps.org

NORTH CENTRAL TEXAS ACADEMY

3846 North Highway 144
Granbury, Texas 76048

Head of School: Mrs. Jennifer Smith

General Information Coeducational boarding and day and distance learning college-preparatory, arts, and agriculture/FFA school, affiliated with Christian faith. Grades PK–12. Distance learning grade X. Founded: 1975. Setting: rural. Nearest major city is Dallas. Students are housed in single-sex residences. 500-acre campus. 1 building on campus. Approved or accredited by Association of Christian Schools International, Southern Association of Colleges and Schools, and The Association of Boarding Schools. Member of National Association of Independent Schools. Total enrollment: 194. Upper school average class size: 8. Upper school faculty-student ratio: 1:7. There are 170 required school days per year for Upper School students. Upper School students typically attend 5 days per week. The average school day consists of 6 hours and 30 minutes.

Upper School Student Profile 70% of students are boarding students. 70% are state residents. 8 states are represented in upper school student body. 10% are international students. International students from China, Congo, Hong Kong, Nigeria, Taiwan, and Viet Nam; 3 other countries represented in student body. 65% of students are Christian.

Faculty School total: 33. In upper school: 4 men, 22 women; 9 have advanced degrees; 10 reside on campus.

Subjects Offered 1 1/2 elective credits, advanced math, Advanced Placement courses, agriculture, algebra, all academic, American history, American literature, animal husbandry, animal science, applied music, art, athletics, basketball, Bible, biology, calculus, cheerleading, chemistry, choir, classical music, computer education, computer literacy, computer skills, concert choir, desktop publishing, drawing, driver education, economics, economics-AP, electives, English, English literature, English-AP, fine arts, gardening, general math, general science, geometry, golf, government, government-AP, guitar, health, history, horticulture, instruments, journalism, language arts, library, life science, mathematics, mathematics-AP, music, music appreciation, music performance, music theory, newspaper, physical education, physics, pottery, pre-algebra, pre-calculus, science, scripture, social studies, Spanish, speech, sports, tennis, track and field, trigonometry, U.S. government, U.S. history, vocal ensemble, volleyball, weight training, woodworking, world history, yearbook.

Special Academic Programs Honors section; independent study; study at local college for college credit; academic accommodation for the gifted, the musically talented, and the artistically talented; ESL (14 students enrolled).

College Admission Counseling 15 students graduated in 2013; 14 went to college, including Southwestern University; Texas A&M University; Texas Christian University; Texas State University–San Marcos; Texas Wesleyan University; United States Air Force Academy. Other: 1 entered military service.

Student Life Upper grades have uniform requirement, student council, honor system. Discipline rests primarily with faculty. Attendance at religious services is required.

Summer Programs Remediation, enrichment, ESL, sports, art/fine arts programs offered; session focuses on enrichment; held on campus; accepts boys and girls; not open to students from other schools. 160 students usually enrolled. 2014 schedule: June 4 to July 13.

Tuition and Aid Day student tuition: $5000–$9600; 7-day tuition and room/board: $12,000–$36,000. Tuition installment plan (monthly payment plans, individually arranged payment plans). Tuition reduction for siblings, need-based scholarship grants available. In 2013–14, 88% of upper-school students received aid.

Admissions Traditional secondary-level entrance grade is 10. Achievement tests, English for Non-native Speakers, Stanford Achievement Test or writing sample required. Deadline for receipt of application materials: none. Application fee required: $60. Interview required.

Athletics Interscholastic: baseball (boys), basketball (b,g), cheering (g), cross-country running (b,g), football (b), golf (b,g), horseback riding (b,g), outdoor education (b,g), physical fitness (b,g), running (b,g), soccer (g), softball (g), strength & conditioning (b,g), tennis (b,g), track and field (b,g), volleyball (g), weight training (b,g). 2 PE instructors, 4 coaches.

Computers Computers are regularly used in computer applications, creative writing, desktop publishing, English, journalism, library, newspaper, yearbook classes. Computer resources include on-campus library services, Internet access, wireless campus network, Internet filtering or blocking technology. Computer access in designated common areas is available to students. Students grades are available online.

Contact Mr. Todd L. Shipman, President/Chief Financial Officer. 254-897-4822. Fax: 254-897-7650. E-mail: todd@happyhillfarm.org. Website: www.NorthCentralTexasAcademy.org

NORTHFIELD MOUNT HERMON SCHOOL

One Lamplighter Way
Mount Hermon, Massachusetts 01354

Head of School: Peter B. Fayroian

General Information Coeducational boarding and day college-preparatory, College Model Academic Planning, and more than 150 courses school. Grades 9–PG. Founded: 1879. Setting: rural. Nearest major city is Hartford, CT. Students are housed in single-sex by floor dormitories and single-sex dormitories. 1,565-acre campus. 35 buildings on campus. Approved or accredited by Association of Independent Schools in New England, New England Association of Schools and Colleges, and Massachusetts Department of Education. Member of National Association of Independent Schools and Secondary School Admission Test Board. Endowment: $120 million. Total enrollment: 650. Upper school average class size: 12. Upper school faculty-student ratio: 1:6. There are 160 required school days per year for Upper School students. Upper School students typically attend 5 days per week. The average school day consists of 8 hours.

Upper School Student Profile Grade 9: 101 students (51 boys, 50 girls); Grade 10: 178 students (88 boys, 90 girls); Grade 11: 191 students (94 boys, 97 girls); Grade 12: 152 students (76 boys, 76 girls); Postgraduate: 31 students (25 boys, 6 girls). 82% of students are boarding students. 31% are state residents. 31 states are represented in upper school student body. 25% are international students. International students from China, Hong Kong, Mexico, Republic of Korea, Russian Federation, and Thailand; 47 other countries represented in student body.

Faculty School total: 99. In upper school: 53 men, 42 women; 68 have advanced degrees; all reside on campus.

Subjects Offered 3-dimensional art, acting, Advanced Placement courses, aerobics, algebra, American history, American history-AP, American literature, American literature-AP, analytic geometry, anatomy, anatomy and physiology, ancient history, applied music, Arabic, art, art-AP, arts, astronomy, athletics, ballet, band, baseball, Basic programming, basketball, Bible, bioethics, biology, biology-AP, botany, broadcasting, calculus, calculus-AP, campus ministry, cell biology, ceramics, chamber groups, chemistry, chemistry-AP, Chinese, Chinese literature, choir, choral music, choreography, chorus, Christian doctrine, Christianity, Civil War, collage and assemblage, college admission preparation, college counseling, community service, computers, concert band, concert choir, creative writing, dance, dance performance, debate, digital imaging, digital music, digital photography, drama, drama performance, drama workshop, dramatic arts, drawing, driver education, earth science, economics, economics-AP, electives, English, English composition, English language-AP, English literature and composition-AP, English-AP, English/composition-AP, ensembles, environmental science, environmental science-AP, environmental studies, epic literature, equality and freedom, ESL, ethics, European history, European history-AP, European literature, expository writing, fiction, film, film and literature, film history, film studies, fine arts, fitness, foreign language, French, French language-AP, French-AP, functions, general science, genetics, geology, geometry, global issues, global studies, golf, government, graphic design, great books, guitar, Harlem Renaissance, health, health and wellness, health education, history, history of jazz, history of music, history of religion, history-AP, honors algebra, honors English, honors geometry, honors U.S. history, honors world history, human anatomy, humanities, independent study, instrumental music, instruments, introduction to literature, introduction to theater, jazz, jazz band, jewelry making, journalism, language-AP, languages, Latin, Latin-AP, life science, linear algebra, literary magazine, literature, literature seminar, literature-AP, macro/microeconomics-AP, Mandarin, martial arts, mathematics, mathematics-AP, mechanics of writing, media arts, meditation, microeconomics, model United Nations, modern dance, modern European history, modern European history-AP, modern history, modern Western civilization, modern world history, music, music history, music performance, music theater, music theory, music theory-AP, musical productions, musical theater, musicianship, New Testament, news writing, newspaper, non-Western literature, non-Western societies, North American literature, novels, oral communications, oral expression, orchestra, outdoor education, painting, performing arts, philosophy, photography, physical education, physical fitness, physical science, physics, physics-AP, physiology, piano, play production, poetry, political science, portfolio art, pottery, pre-calculus, printmaking, programming, psychology-AP, public speaking, publications, radio broadcasting, religion, religion and culture, religious studies, research skills, robotics, Russian studies, SAT preparation, SAT/ACT preparation, science, science research, scripture, sculpture, Shakespeare, short story, social studies, society, politics and law, Spanish, Spanish language-AP, Spanish literature, Spanish-AP, speech, speech and debate, stage design, stagecraft, statistics, statistics-AP, strings, student government, student publications, studio art, studio art-AP, study skills, swimming, tennis, The 20th Century, theater, theater arts, theater design and production, theater production, topics in dramatic literature, track and field, travel, trigonometry, Turkish history, U.S. history, U.S. history-AP, U.S. literature, United States government-AP, video, video film production, visual and performing arts, visual arts, vocal ensemble, vocal music, voice ensemble, volleyball, Western religions, wilderness experience, wind ensemble, work experience, work-study, world cultures, world governments, world history, world issues, world literature, world religions, world religions, world studies, wrestling, writing, writing, writing workshop, yearbook, yoga.

Graduation Requirements Arts and fine arts (art, music, dance, drama), English, foreign language, mathematics, physical education (includes health), religion (includes Bible studies and theology), science, social studies (includes history), participation in work program.

Special Academic Programs Advanced Placement exam preparation; honors section; independent study; term-away projects; study abroad; academic accommodation for the gifted, the musically talented, and the artistically talented; ESL (32 students enrolled).

College Admission Counseling 193 students graduated in 2013; 189 went to college, including Brown University; Colby College; Cornell University; New York University; Skidmore College; University of Massachusetts Amherst. Other: 4 had other specific plans. Mean SAT critical reading: 598, mean SAT math: 604, mean SAT writing: 653, mean combined SAT: 1855, mean composite ACT: 24.

Student Life Upper grades have student council, honor system. Discipline rests primarily with faculty.

Summer Programs Remediation, enrichment, ESL, art/fine arts programs offered; session focuses on intense academic preparation; held on campus; accepts boys and girls; open to students from other schools. 2014 schedule: June to August.

Tuition and Aid Day student tuition: $35,700; 7-day tuition and room/board: $52,200. Tuition installment plan (Tuition Pay 10-Month). Need-based scholarship grants, need-based loans, Sallie Mae K–12 Family Education Loans, Your Solution Education available. In 2013–14, 30% of upper-school students received aid. Total amount of financial aid awarded in 2013–14: $6,300,000.

Admissions Traditional secondary-level entrance grade is 9. For fall 2013, 1,500 students applied for upper-level admission, 475 were accepted, 240 enrolled. ACT, ISEE, PSAT, SAT, SSAT or TOEFL required. Deadline for receipt of application materials: February 1. Application fee required: $50. Interview recommended.

Athletics Interscholastic: alpine skiing (boys, girls), baseball (b), basketball (b,g), crew (b,g), cross-country running (b,g), field hockey (g), football (b), Frisbee (b,g), hockey (b,g), ice hockey (b,g), lacrosse (b,g), nordic skiing (b,g), skiing (cross-country) (b,g), skiing (downhill) (b,g), soccer (b,g), softball (g), swimming and diving (b,g), tennis (b,g), track and field (b,g), ultimate Frisbee (b,g), volleyball (b,g), wrestling (b); coed interscholastic: dance, dance team, golf, modern dance; coed intramural: aerobics, aerobics/dance, alpine skiing, aquatics, backpacking, badminton, ballet, basketball, bicycling, canoeing/kayaking, climbing, dance, dance team, fencing, fitness, Frisbee, hiking/backpacking, kayaking, lacrosse, martial arts, modern dance, nordic skiing, outdoor activities, outdoor education, physical fitness, physical training, rock climbing, running, sailing, skiing (cross-country), skiing (downhill), soccer, softball, strength & conditioning, ultimate Frisbee, volleyball, weight training, wilderness, yoga.

Computers Computers are regularly used in all academic classes. Computer network features include on-campus library services, online commercial services, Internet access, wireless campus network, Internet filtering or blocking technology. Campus intranet, student e-mail accounts, and computer access in designated common areas are available to students. Students grades are available online. The school has a published electronic and media policy.

Contact Office of Admission. 413-498-3227. Fax: 413-498-3152. E-mail: admission@nmhschool.org. Website: www.nmhschool.org

NORTH SHORE COUNTRY DAY SCHOOL

310 Green Bay Road
Winnetka, Illinois 60093-4094

Head of School: Mr. Tom Doar III

General Information Coeducational day college-preparatory, arts, technology, global, and service learning school. Grades PK–12. Founded: 1919. Setting: suburban. Nearest major city is Chicago. 16-acre campus. 6 buildings on campus. Approved or accredited by Independent Schools Association of the Central States and Illinois Department of Education. Member of National Association of Independent Schools and Secondary School Admission Test Board. Endowment: $20 million. Total enrollment: 510. Upper school average class size: 14. Upper school faculty-student ratio: 1:8. Upper School students typically attend 5 days per week. The average school day consists of 6 hours and 30 minutes.

Upper School Student Profile Grade 9: 51 students (23 boys, 28 girls); Grade 10: 51 students (28 boys, 23 girls); Grade 11: 51 students (27 boys, 24 girls); Grade 12: 47 students (24 boys, 23 girls).

Faculty School total: 80. In upper school: 27 men, 35 women; 42 have advanced degrees.

Subjects Offered Algebra, American history, American literature, anatomy and physiology, art, Asian studies, biology, biology-AP, calculus, calculus-AP, ceramics, chemistry, chemistry-AP, creative writing, drama, earth science, ecology, economics, English, English literature, English-AP, European history, expository writing, fine arts, French, French-AP, geography, geometry, government/civics, grammar, journalism, Mandarin, mathematics, music, photography, physical education, physics, physics-AP, printmaking, science, social studies, Spanish, Spanish-AP, speech, statistics, statistics-AP, technology, theater, trigonometry, U.S. history-AP, world history, world literature, writing.

Graduation Requirements Arts and fine arts (art, music, dance, drama), English, foreign language, mathematics, physical education (includes health), physical fitness, science, service learning/internship, social studies (includes history), technology, one stage performance in four years, completion of senior service project in May, completion of one-week community service project in four years.

Special Academic Programs Advanced Placement exam preparation; independent study; term-away projects; study at local college for college credit; study abroad.

College Admission Counseling 52 students graduated in 2013; all went to college, including Southern Methodist University; University of Illinois at Urbana–Champaign.

Student Life Upper grades have specified standards of dress, student council, honor system. Discipline rests primarily with faculty.

Tuition and Aid Day student tuition: $24,800–$25,800. Tuition installment plan (Insured Tuition Payment Plan, Key Tuition Payment Plan, monthly payment plans, individually arranged payment plans, trimester payment plan). Merit scholarship grants, need-based scholarship grants, need-based loans, middle-income loans available. In 2013–14, 16% of upper-school students received aid. Total amount of financial aid awarded in 2013–14: $1,500,000.

Admissions Traditional secondary-level entrance grade is 9. ERB and writing sample required. Deadline for receipt of application materials: January 31. Application fee required: $75. On-campus interview required.

Athletics Interscholastic: baseball (boys), basketball (b,g), cross-country running (b,g), field hockey (g), football (b), golf (b,g), indoor track & field (b,g), soccer (b,g), tennis (b,g), track and field (b,g), volleyball (g); intramural: physical training (b,g), weight lifting (b,g); coed intramural: dance, sailing. 4 PE instructors, 24 coaches, 1 athletic trainer.

Computers Computers are regularly used in all academic classes. Computer network features include on-campus library services, online commercial services, Internet access, wireless campus network, Internet filtering or blocking technology. Campus intranet and student e-mail accounts are available to students. The school has a published electronic and media policy.

Contact Ms. Julie Schmidt, Admissions Liaison. 847-881-8800. Fax: 847-446-0675. E-mail: jschmidt@nscds.org. Website: www.nscds.org

NORTH TORONTO CHRISTIAN SCHOOL

255 Yorkland Boulevard
Toronto, Ontario M2J 1S3, Canada

Head of School: Mr. Allen Schenk

General Information Coeducational day college-preparatory and religious studies school, affiliated with Protestant-Evangelical faith. Grades JK–12. Founded: 1981. Setting: urban. 6-acre campus. 1 building on campus. Approved or accredited by Association of Christian Schools International and Ontario Department of Education. Language of instruction: English. Total enrollment: 438. Upper school average class size: 25. Upper school faculty-student ratio: 1:15. There are 184 required school days per year for Upper School students. Upper School students typically attend 5 days per week. The average school day consists of 6 hours.

Faculty School total: 31. In upper school: 11 men, 12 women; 8 have advanced degrees.

Subjects Offered Accounting, biology, business, calculus, Canadian geography, Canadian law, career exploration, chemistry, civics, computer applications, discrete mathematics, English, French, functions, geography, geometry, healthful living, information technology, instrumental music, marketing, physics, visual arts, world history, world issues, world religions.

Graduation Requirements 40 hours of community service, Successful completion of the Ontario Secondary School Literacy Test.

Special Academic Programs Independent study; ESL (21 students enrolled).

College Admission Counseling 62 students graduated in 2013; 61 went to college, including Brock University; McMaster University; Queen's University at Kingston; The University of Western Ontario; University of Toronto; York University. Other: 1 had other specific plans.

Student Life Upper grades have uniform requirement. Discipline rests primarily with faculty. Attendance at religious services is required.

Tuition and Aid Day student tuition: CAN$7536. Tuition installment plan (monthly payment plans, individually arranged payment plans). Tuition reduction for siblings, bursaries available.

Admissions Traditional secondary-level entrance grade is 9. Deadline for receipt of application materials: none. Application fee required: CAN$150. On-campus interview required.

Athletics Interscholastic: rugby (girls); coed interscholastic: aquatics, badminton, ball hockey, basketball, cross-country running, golf, soccer, softball, squash, swimming and diving, table tennis, tennis, track and field, volleyball, wrestling; coed intramural: alpine skiing, canoeing/kayaking, diving, fitness, floor hockey, judo, kayaking, outdoor education, outdoor skills, street hockey, water polo. 6 PE instructors.

Computers Computers are regularly used in business applications, information technology, introduction to technology, keyboarding, mathematics, programming, science, typing, word processing classes. Computer network features include Internet access, wireless campus network. The school has a published electronic and media policy.

Contact Mr. Gordon Cooke, Administrator. 416-491-7667. Fax: 416-491-3806. E-mail: gcooke@ntcs.on.ca. Website: www.ntcs.on.ca

NORTHWEST ACADEMY

1130 Southwest Main Street
Portland, Oregon 97205

Head of School: Mary Vinton Folberg

General Information Coeducational day college-preparatory, arts, and bilingual studies school. Grades 6–12. Founded: 1996. Setting: urban. 4 buildings on campus. Approved or accredited by Northwest Accreditation Commission, Northwest

Association of Independent Schools, and Oregon Department of Education. Member of National Association of Independent Schools. Total enrollment: 182. Upper school average class size: 15. Upper school faculty-student ratio: 1:4. Upper School students typically attend 5 days per week. The average school day consists of 7 hours and 30 minutes.

Upper School Student Profile Grade 9: 31 students (12 boys, 19 girls); Grade 10: 19 students (7 boys, 12 girls); Grade 11: 15 students (6 boys, 9 girls); Grade 12: 15 students (5 boys, 10 girls).

Faculty School total: 41. In upper school: 17 men, 22 women; 18 have advanced degrees.

Subjects Offered 20th century history, acting, algebra, anatomy and physiology, animation, art history, ballet, biology, calculus, career/college preparation, chemistry, comparative government and politics, comparative politics, comparative religion, computer animation, computer literacy, computer music, creative writing, critical thinking, dance performance, desktop publishing, digital art, drama workshop, drawing, earth and space science, ecology, environmental systems, English literature, European civilization, film studies, French, geometry, history of music, human anatomy, humanities, illustration, independent study, internship, introduction to digital multitrack recording techniques, jazz band, jazz dance, jazz ensemble, journalism, keyboarding, media arts, medieval/Renaissance history, multimedia design, music composition, music history, music performance, musical theater, painting, photo shop, physics, play/screen writing, political systems, pre-calculus, printmaking, senior thesis, Shakespeare, social sciences, Spanish, student publications, tap dance, theater, trigonometry, U.S. government and politics, U.S. history, video film production, visual arts, vocal ensemble, vocal jazz, world cultures, world history, world wide web design, writing, yoga.

Graduation Requirements 4 years of English/humanities, senior thesis seminar, 3 years of both math and science, 2 years of foreign language, 7 units of credit of arts electives, community service, computer literacy, physical education.

Special Academic Programs Accelerated programs; independent study; study at local college for college credit; academic accommodation for the gifted, the musically talented, and the artistically talented.

College Admission Counseling 14 students graduated in 2013; 13 went to college, including California College of the Arts; Goucher College; Oregon State University; Savannah College of Art and Design; Whitman College. Other: 1 went to work. Median SAT critical reading: 590, median SAT math: 520, median SAT writing: 570, median combined SAT: 1640. 46% scored over 600 on SAT critical reading, 16% scored over 600 on SAT math, 31% scored over 600 on SAT writing, 30% scored over 1800 on combined SAT.

Student Life Upper grades have student council, honor system. Discipline rests primarily with faculty.

Tuition and Aid Day student tuition: $18,500. Tuition installment plan (FACTS Tuition Payment Plan). Need-based scholarship grants available. In 2013–14, 22% of upper-school students received aid. Total amount of financial aid awarded in 2013–14: $457,300.

Admissions Traditional secondary-level entrance grade is 9. For fall 2013, 26 students applied for upper-level admission, 20 were accepted, 12 enrolled. Admissions testing, placement test and writing sample required. Deadline for receipt of application materials: January 31. Application fee required: $100. Interview required.

Athletics Coed Intramural: aerobics, aerobics/dance, artistic gym, ballet, basketball, cooperative games, dance, modern dance, tai chi, yoga.

Computers Computers are regularly used in all academic, yearbook classes. Computer network features include Internet access, wireless campus network, film and audio editing, sound design, animation, Flash. Campus intranet and computer access in designated common areas are available to students. The school has a published electronic and media policy.

Contact Lainie Keslin Ettinger, Director of Admissions and Marketing. 503-223-3367 Ext. 104. Fax: 503-402-1043. E-mail: lettinger@nwacademy.org. Website: www.nwacademy.org

NORTHWEST CATHOLIC HIGH SCHOOL

29 Wampanoag Drive
West Hartford, Connecticut 06117

Head of School: Mr. David Eustis

General Information Coeducational day college-preparatory school, affiliated with Roman Catholic Church. Grades 9–12. Founded: 1961. Setting: suburban. Nearest major city is Hartford. 1 building on campus. Approved or accredited by New England Association of Schools and Colleges and Connecticut Department of Education. Total enrollment: 601. Upper school average class size: 18. Upper school faculty-student ratio: 1:12. There are 180 required school days per year for Upper School students. Upper School students typically attend 5 days per week. The average school day consists of 6 hours and 18 minutes.

Upper School Student Profile Grade 9: 169 students (78 boys, 91 girls); Grade 10: 152 students (74 boys, 78 girls); Grade 11: 143 students (78 boys, 65 girls); Grade 12: 137 students (61 boys, 76 girls). 77% of students are Roman Catholic.

Faculty School total: 47. In upper school: 20 men, 27 women; 33 have advanced degrees.

Subjects Offered Biology-AP, calculus-AP, chemistry-AP, computer science-AP, English language and composition-AP, English literature and composition-AP, French language-AP, Latin-AP, music theory-AP, physics-AP, Spanish-AP, statistics-AP, studio art-AP, U.S. government and politics-AP, U.S. history-AP.

Graduation Requirements Arts and fine arts (art, music, dance, drama), English, foreign language, health education, mathematics, physical education (includes health), religion (includes Bible studies and theology), science, social studies (includes history), 25 hours of community service.

Special Academic Programs 15 Advanced Placement exams for which test preparation is offered; honors section; study at local college for college credit.

College Admission Counseling 169 students graduated in 2013; 168 went to college, including Bates College; Boston College; College of the Holy Cross; Providence College; Quinnipiac University; University of Connecticut. Other: 1 entered military service. Mean SAT critical reading: 555, mean SAT math: 560, mean SAT writing: 560.

Student Life Upper grades have uniform requirement, student council, honor system. Discipline rests primarily with faculty. Attendance at religious services is required.

Summer Programs Sports programs offered; session focuses on grades 3-8; held both on and off campus; held at Northwest Catholic High facilities and St.Thomas Seminary fields; accepts boys and girls; open to students from other schools. 100 students usually enrolled. 2014 schedule: June to August. Application deadline: May 31.

Tuition and Aid Day student tuition: $13,600. Tuition installment plan (monthly payment plans). Tuition reduction for siblings, merit scholarship grants, need-based scholarship grants available. Total amount of financial aid awarded in 2013–14: $1,300,000.

Admissions Traditional secondary-level entrance grade is 9. High School Placement Test required. Deadline for receipt of application materials: March 1. Application fee required: $25.

Athletics Interscholastic: baseball (boys), basketball (b,g), cheering (g), cross-country running (b,g), field hockey (g), golf (b,g), ice hockey (b), indoor track & field (b,g), lacrosse (b,g), soccer (b,g), softball (g), tennis (b,g), track and field (b,g), volleyball (g), winter (indoor) track (b,g); intramural: basketball (b,g); coed interscholastic: diving, football, swimming and diving; coed intramural: canoeing/kayaking, climbing, dance team, fitness, flag football, hiking/backpacking, indoor soccer, outdoor adventure, rappelling, rock climbing, scuba diving, skiing (downhill), snowboarding, snowshoeing, strength & conditioning, ultimate Frisbee, weight training, whiffle ball. 1 PE instructor, 1 athletic trainer.

Computers Computers are regularly used in all academic classes. Computer network features include on-campus library services, Internet access, wireless campus network, Internet filtering or blocking technology. Student e-mail accounts and computer access in designated common areas are available to students. Students grades are available online. The school has a published electronic and media policy.

Contact Mrs. Nancy Scully Bannon, Director of Admissions. 860-236-4221 Ext. 124. Fax: 860-570-0080. E-mail: nbannon@nwcath.org. Website: www.northwestcatholic.org

THE NORTHWEST SCHOOL

1415 Summit Avenue
Seattle, Washington 98122

Head of School: Mike McGill

General Information Coeducational boarding and day college-preparatory, arts, and ESL school. Boarding grades 9–12, day grades 6–12. Founded: 1978. Setting: urban. Students are housed in coed dormitories. 1-acre campus. 4 buildings on campus. Approved or accredited by Northwest Accreditation Commission, Northwest Association of Independent Schools, and Washington Department of Education. Member of National Association of Independent Schools. Endowment: $1.6 million. Total enrollment: 478. Upper school average class size: 16. Upper school faculty-student ratio: 1:9. There are 168 required school days per year for Upper School students. Upper School students typically attend 5 days per week. The average school day consists of 7 hours and 20 minutes.

Upper School Student Profile Grade 9: 77 students (38 boys, 39 girls); Grade 10: 101 students (54 boys, 47 girls); Grade 11: 80 students (41 boys, 39 girls); Grade 12: 81 students (43 boys, 38 girls). 14% of students are boarding students. 80% are state residents. 2 states are represented in upper school student body. 20% are international students. International students from China, Japan, Republic of Korea, Taiwan, Thailand, and Viet Nam; 2 other countries represented in student body.

Faculty School total: 75. In upper school: 23 men, 36 women; 40 have advanced degrees.

Subjects Offered Advanced chemistry, algebra, astronomy, biology, calculus, ceramics, chemistry, Chinese, chorus, computer skills, contemporary problems, dance, drama, drawing, earth science, English, ESL, evolution, fiber arts, film, fine arts, French, geometry, health, history, humanities, illustration, improvisation, jazz dance, jazz ensemble, journalism, life science, literature, math analysis, mathematics, mentorship program, musical theater, orchestra, outdoor education, painting, performing arts, philosophy, photography, physical education, physical science, physics, play production, pre-algebra, pre-calculus, printmaking, Spanish, statistics, strings, textiles, theater, trigonometry, U.S. government and politics, U.S. history, visual arts, Washington State and Northwest History, water color painting, wilderness education, world history, writing.

Graduation Requirements English, foreign language, history, humanities, mathematics, physical education (includes health), science, senior project, social studies (includes history), visual and performing arts, participation in environmental maintenance program.

Special Academic Programs ESL (50 students enrolled).

College Admission Counseling 87 students graduated in 2012; 86 went to college, including Brown University; Haverford College; Rhode Island School of Design; The University of British Columbia; University of California, Los Angeles; University of Washington. Other: 1 had other specific plans.

Student Life Upper grades have honor system. Discipline rests primarily with faculty.

Tuition and Aid Day student tuition: $29,930; 7-day tuition and room/board: $43,655. Tuition installment plan (school's own payment plan). Need-based scholarship grants available. In 2012–13, 16% of upper-school students received aid. Total amount of financial aid awarded in 2012–13: $1,142,451.

Admissions Traditional secondary-level entrance grade is 9. For fall 2012, 252 students applied for upper-level admission, 159 were accepted, 64 enrolled. ISEE, SSAT or TOEFL required. Deadline for receipt of application materials: January 12. Application fee required: $70. Interview required.

Athletics Interscholastic: basketball (boys, girls), cross-country running (b,g), soccer (b,g), track and field (b,g), ultimate Frisbee (b,g), volleyball (g); coed intramural: fitness, hiking/backpacking, outdoor education, physical fitness, rock climbing, ropes courses, skiing (cross-country), skiing (downhill). 2 PE instructors, 30 coaches.

Computers Computers are regularly used in art, English, ESL, foreign language, graphic design, health, history, humanities, journalism, library, mathematics, music, science, social studies, theater, video film production, writing, yearbook classes. Computer network features include on-campus library services, Internet access, wireless campus network, ProQuest, ABC-Cleo, JSTOR, eLibrary, CultureGrams, World Conflicts and Online Encyclopedias. Computer access in designated common areas is available to students. Students grades are available online. The school has a published electronic and media policy.

Contact Douglas Leek, Director of Admissions and Enrollment Management. 206-682-7309. Fax: 206-467-7353. E-mail: douglas.leek@northwestschool.org. Website: www.northwestschool.org

NORTHWOOD SCHOOL

PO Box 1070
92 Northwood Road
Lake Placid, New York 12946

Head of School: Edward M. Good

General Information Coeducational boarding and day college-preparatory and arts school. Grades 9–PG. Founded: 1905. Setting: small town. Nearest major city is Albany. Students are housed in single-sex dormitories. 80-acre campus. 8 buildings on campus. Approved or accredited by New York State Association of Independent Schools and The Association of Boarding Schools. Member of National Association of Independent Schools and Secondary School Admission Test Board. Endowment: $8 million. Total enrollment: 182. Upper school average class size: 9. Upper school faculty-student ratio: 1:6. There are 180 required school days per year for Upper School students. Upper School students typically attend 5 days per week. The average school day consists of 7 hours.

Upper School Student Profile Grade 9: 17 students (8 boys, 9 girls); Grade 10: 48 students (30 boys, 18 girls); Grade 11: 58 students (38 boys, 20 girls); Grade 12: 59 students (38 boys, 21 girls). 79% of students are boarding students. 39% are state residents. 19 states are represented in upper school student body. 36% are international students. International students from Canada, China, Finland, Mexico, Republic of Korea, and Spain; 6 other countries represented in student body.

Faculty School total: 33. In upper school: 22 men, 8 women; 15 have advanced degrees; 17 reside on campus.

Subjects Offered Algebra, American history, American literature, art, biology, calculus, ceramics, chemistry, computer science, drama, earth science, English, English literature, ensembles, environmental science, expository writing, fiber arts, French, geography, geology, geometry, government/civics, great issues, health, history, journalism, mathematics, music, photography, physical education, physics, psychology, SAT preparation, science, social studies, sociology, Spanish, theater, trigonometry, world history.

Graduation Requirements Arts and fine arts (art, music, dance, drama), English, foreign language, mathematics, physical education (includes health), science, social studies (includes history).

Special Academic Programs 5 Advanced Placement exams for which test preparation is offered; honors section; independent study; remedial reading and/or remedial writing; ESL (25 students enrolled).

College Admission Counseling 69 students graduated in 2012; 60 went to college, including Clarkson University; New York University; Penn State University Park; Skidmore College; St. Lawrence University; Syracuse University. Other: 3 entered a postgraduate year, 6 had other specific plans. Median SAT critical reading: 520, median SAT math: 500, median SAT writing: 510.

Student Life Upper grades have specified standards of dress, student council, honor system. Discipline rests primarily with faculty.

Tuition and Aid Day student tuition: $25,450; 7-day tuition and room/board: $44,425. Tuition installment plan (The Tuition Plan). Need-based scholarship grants available. In 2012–13, 56% of upper-school students received aid.

Admissions Traditional secondary-level entrance grade is 11. For fall 2012, 255 students applied for upper-level admission, 163 were accepted, 99 enrolled. Any standardized test or TOEFL or SLEP required. Deadline for receipt of application materials: none. Application fee required: $50. Interview required.

Athletics Interscholastic: crew (boys, girls), hockey (b,g), ice hockey (b,g), ice skating (b,g), lacrosse (b,g), nordic skiing (b,g), ski jumping (b,g), skiing (downhill) (b,g), soccer (b,g), telemark skiing (b,g), tennis (b,g); intramural: hockey (b,g), ice hockey (b,g), ice skating (b,g), skiing (downhill) (b,g), snowboarding (b,g); coed interscholastic: alpine skiing, figure skating, fitness, freestyle skiing, golf, nordic skiing, skiing (cross-country), snowboarding, telemark skiing; coed intramural: alpine skiing, backpacking, bicycling, canoeing/kayaking, climbing, combined training, cross-country running, figure skating, fishing, fitness, fly fishing, freestyle skiing, golf, hiking/backpacking, jogging, kayaking, luge, mountain biking, mountaineering, nordic skiing, outdoor adventure, physical training, rafting, rappelling, rock climbing, ropes courses, rowing, running, skiing (cross-country), skiing (downhill), snowboarding, street hockey, strength & conditioning, tennis, walking, wall climbing, weight training, wilderness, wilderness survival, wildernessways, winter walking. 1 coach, 1 athletic trainer.

Computers Computers are regularly used in English, foreign language, history, mathematics, science classes. Computer network features include on-campus library services, online commercial services, Internet access, wireless campus network, Internet filtering or blocking technology. Students grades are available online. The school has a published electronic and media policy.

Contact Elenor Mandigo, Admissions Assistant. 518-523-3382 Ext. 204. Fax: 518-523-3405. E-mail: younge@northwoodschool.com. Website: www.northwoodschool.com

NORTH YARMOUTH ACADEMY

148 Main Street
Yarmouth, Maine 04096

Head of School: Brad Choyt

General Information Coeducational day college-preparatory, arts, and technology school. Grades 5–12. Founded: 1814. Setting: suburban. Nearest major city is Portland. 25-acre campus. 14 buildings on campus. Approved or accredited by Association of Independent Schools in New England, Independent Schools of Northern New England, New England Association of Schools and Colleges, and Maine Department of Education. Member of National Association of Independent Schools and Secondary School Admission Test Board. Endowment: $3 million. Total enrollment: 280. Upper school average class size: 15. Upper school faculty-student ratio: 1:8. There are 277 required school days per year for Upper School students. Upper School students typically attend 5 days per week. The average school day consists of 5 hours and 45 minutes.

Upper School Student Profile Grade 9: 50 students (25 boys, 25 girls); Grade 10: 55 students (31 boys, 24 girls); Grade 11: 47 students (22 boys, 25 girls); Grade 12: 48 students (26 boys, 22 girls).

Faculty School total: 42. In upper school: 16 men, 26 women; 26 have advanced degrees.

Subjects Offered Algebra, American government, American history, American history-AP, ancient world history, art, art history-AP, art-AP, biology-AP, calculus-AP, chemistry, chorus, classical language, college counseling, composition-AP, computer graphics, contemporary issues, drama, drawing and design, earth science, English, English composition, English literature, English literature and composition-AP, English-AP, environmental science-AP, European history, European history-AP, experiential education, fine arts, French, French-AP, genetics, geometry, history, instrumental music, jazz, language-AP, Latin, Latin-AP, mathematics, model United Nations, modern European history, modern European history-AP, music, music theory-AP, music-AP, painting, photography, physical education, physical science, physics, physics-AP, pottery, pre-algebra, pre-calculus, psychology, science, senior project, social issues, social studies, society challenge and change, Spanish, Spanish-AP, statistics, statistics-AP, student publications, studio art, studio art-AP, technology, theater, trigonometry, U.S. government and politics-AP, U.S. history, U.S. history-AP, visual and performing arts, vocal music, world history.

Graduation Requirements Arts and fine arts (art, music, dance, drama), English, foreign language, history, mathematics, science, senior project, speech, two-week volunteer senior service project, senior speech, participation in athletics or performing arts program each season (3).

Special Academic Programs Advanced Placement exam preparation; honors section; study abroad; ESL (6 students enrolled).

College Admission Counseling 52 students graduated in 2012; 50 went to college, including Case Western Reserve University; Colby College; Kalamazoo College; Mount Holyoke College; Tufts University. Other: 2 had other specific plans. Median SAT critical reading: 600, median SAT math: 600. 50% scored over 600 on SAT critical reading, 50% scored over 600 on SAT math.

Student Life Upper grades have specified standards of dress, student council, honor system. Discipline rests equally with students and faculty.

Tuition and Aid Day student tuition: $25,400. Tuition installment plan (Insured Tuition Payment Plan, monthly payment plans). Need-based scholarship grants available. In 2012–13, 45% of upper-school students received aid. Total amount of financial aid awarded in 2012–13: $904,000.

Admissions Traditional secondary-level entrance grade is 9. For fall 2012, 57 students applied for upper-level admission, 45 were accepted, 29 enrolled. School placement exam, SSAT or writing sample required. Deadline for receipt of application materials: February 1. Application fee required: $45. On-campus interview required.

Athletics Interscholastic: baseball (boys), basketball (b,g), crew (b,g), cross-country running (b,g), fencing (b), field hockey (g), golf (b,g), ice hockey (b,g), indoor track (b,g), indoor track & field (b,g), lacrosse (b,g), nordic skiing (b,g), sailing (b,g), skiing (cross-country) (b,g), soccer (b,g), softball (g), swimming and diving (b,g), tennis (b,g), track and field (b,g). 1 PE instructor, 17 coaches, 1 athletic trainer.

Computers Computers are regularly used in English, foreign language, graphic design, history, mathematics, science, technology classes. Computer network features include on-campus library services, Internet access. Campus intranet, student e-mail accounts, and computer access in designated common areas are available to students. The school has a published electronic and media policy.

Contact Laurie D. Hyndman, Director of Admission and Financial Aid. 207-846-2376 Ext. 407. Fax: 207-846-2382. E-mail: admission@nya.org. Website: www.nya.org

THE NORWICH FREE ACADEMY

305 Broadway
Norwich, Connecticut 06360

Head of School: Mr. David J. Klein

General Information Coeducational day college-preparatory, general academic, arts, business, vocational, bilingual studies, and technology school. Grades 9–12. Founded: 1856. Setting: suburban. 15-acre campus. 11 buildings on campus. Approved or accredited by New England Association of Schools and Colleges and Connecticut Department of Education. Member of National Association of Independent Schools. Total enrollment: 2,300. Upper school average class size: 24. Upper school faculty-student ratio: 1:22. There are 181 required school days per year for Upper School students. Upper School students typically attend 5 days per week. The average school day consists of 7 hours.

Faculty School total: 171. In upper school: 66 men, 105 women.

Subjects Offered 3-dimensional art, 3-dimensional design, accounting, advanced biology, advanced chemistry, advanced computer applications, advanced math, Advanced Placement courses, advanced studio art-AP, algebra, American history, American history-AP, American literature, anatomy and physiology, Arabic, architectural drawing, art, art history-AP, audio visual/media, band, biology, biology-AP, biotechnology, British literature, British literature-AP, business technology, calculus-AP, chemistry, chemistry-AP, Chinese, choir, chorus, civics, composition-AP, computer science-AP, dance, digital photography, discrete mathematics, drafting, drama, drawing, drawing and design, early childhood, economics, economics-AP, English language and composition-AP, English literature and composition-AP, environmental science-AP, European history-AP, exercise science, family and consumer science, finance, foods, forensics, French, French language-AP, geometry, Greek, health, jazz band, jazz dance, journalism, kinesiology, Latin, Latin-AP, marching band, marine biology, marketing, mathematical modeling, metalworking, music theory-AP, oceanography, personal finance, photo shop, photography, physical education, physics, physics-AP, piano, political science, politics, pre-calculus, printmaking, psychology, psychology-AP, public speaking, Spanish language-AP, speech communications, sports science, television, U.S. history, U.S. history-AP, visual arts, vocal ensemble, woodworking, zoology.

Special Academic Programs 20 Advanced Placement exams for which test preparation is offered; honors section; study at local college for college credit; remedial reading and/or remedial writing; remedial math; special instructional classes for students with learning disabilities, Attention Deficit Disorder, emotional and behavioral problems, and dyslexia; ESL (90 students enrolled).

College Admission Counseling 569 students graduated in 2013; 444 went to college. Other: 30 went to work, 10 entered military service, 33 entered a postgraduate year, 16 had other specific plans. Mean SAT critical reading: 513, mean SAT math: 512, mean SAT writing: 508, mean composite ACT: 24.

Student Life Upper grades have specified standards of dress, student council, honor system. Discipline rests primarily with faculty.

Summer Programs Remediation, enrichment, ESL, sports programs offered; held on campus; accepts boys and girls; not open to students from other schools. 250 students usually enrolled. 2014 schedule: July 1 to July 29. Application deadline: June 1.

Tuition and Aid Day student tuition: $11,720.

Admissions Traditional secondary-level entrance grade is 9. Deadline for receipt of application materials: none. No application fee required. Interview required.

Athletics Interscholastic: baseball (boys), basketball (b,g), cheering (b,g), cross-country running (b,g), fencing (b,g), field hockey (g), football (b), golf (b,g), gymnastics (g), hockey (b), ice hockey (b), indoor track (b,g), indoor track & field (b,g),

lacrosse (b,g), running (b,g), soccer (b,g), softball (g), Special Olympics (b,g), swimming and diving (b,g), tennis (b,g), track and field (b,g), volleyball (b,g), winter (indoor) track (b,g), wrestling (b); intramural: skiing (downhill) (b,g), snowboarding (b); coed interscholastic: drill team; coed intramural: dance, dance team, physical fitness, physical training, power lifting, skateboarding, snowboarding, strength & conditioning, weight lifting, weight training. 4 PE instructors, 25 coaches, 5 athletic trainers.

Computers Computer network features include on-campus library services, Internet access, wireless campus network, Internet filtering or blocking technology. Student e-mail accounts are available to students. The school has a published electronic and media policy.

Contact Mr. John Iovino, Director of Student Affairs. 860-425-5510. Fax: 860-889-7124. E-mail: iovinoj@nfaschool.org. Website: www.nfaschool.org

NOTRE DAME ACADEMY

2851 Overland Avenue
Los Angeles, California 90064

Head of School: Ms. Lilliam Paetzold

General Information Girls' day college-preparatory, arts, religious studies, technology, and athletics school, affiliated with Roman Catholic Church. Grades 9–12. Founded: 1949. Setting: urban. 1 building on campus. Approved or accredited by Western Association of Schools and Colleges, Western Catholic Education Association, and California Department of Education. Total enrollment: 380. Upper school average class size: 23. Upper school faculty-student ratio: 1:12.

Upper School Student Profile 86% of students are Roman Catholic.

Faculty School total: 35. In upper school: 11 men, 24 women; 21 have advanced degrees.

Subjects Offered Advanced studio art-AP, algebra, American history, art, art history-AP, athletic training, biology, biology-AP, calculus, calculus-AP, campus ministry, chemistry, chemistry-AP, choir, Christian and Hebrew scripture, community service, computer science, dance, design, digital photography, drama, drama performance, economics, English, English language and composition-AP, English literature and composition-AP, environmental science-AP, European history-AP, French, French-AP, geometry, government and politics-AP, government/civics, health, history, honors geometry, Japanese, law, leadership, photography, physical education, physics, pre-calculus, psychology, psychology-AP, religion, Spanish, Spanish language-AP, speech and oral interpretations, statistics, trigonometry, U.S. government and politics-AP, U.S. history-AP, world civilizations, world history-AP.

Graduation Requirements Arts and fine arts (art, music, dance, drama), computer science, English, foreign language, mathematics, physical education (includes health), religion (includes Bible studies and theology), science, social studies (includes history), speech. Community service is required.

Special Academic Programs 16 Advanced Placement exams for which test preparation is offered; honors section.

College Admission Counseling 75 students graduated in 2013; 74 went to college, including Arizona State University; Loyola Marymount University; University of California, Berkeley; University of California, Davis; University of California, Los Angeles; University of Southern California. Other: 1 entered military service. Median SAT critical reading: 580, median SAT math: 540, median SAT writing: 570. Mean combined SAT: 1683, mean composite ACT: 25.

Student Life Upper grades have uniform requirement, student council, honor system. Discipline rests primarily with faculty. Attendance at religious services is required.

Summer Programs Remediation, enrichment, advancement, sports, art/fine arts, computer instruction programs offered; session focuses on academic advancement, required prerequisites, enrichment; held both on and off campus; held at various athletic facilities; accepts boys and girls; open to students from other schools. 300 students usually enrolled. 2014 schedule: June 9 to July 18. Application deadline: May.

Tuition and Aid Day student tuition: $11,900. Tuition installment plan (FACTS Tuition Payment Plan, monthly payment plans). Merit scholarship grants, need-based scholarship grants, paying campus jobs available. In 2013–14, 30% of upper-school students received aid.

Admissions Traditional secondary-level entrance grade is 9. High School Placement Test (closed version) from Scholastic Testing Service required. Deadline for receipt of application materials: January 10. Application fee required: $75. On-campus interview required.

Athletics Interscholastic: basketball, cross-country running, dance, equestrian sports, soccer, softball, swimming and diving, tennis, track and field, volleyball. 1 PE instructor, 18 coaches, 1 athletic trainer.

Computers Computers are regularly used in all academic, computer applications, design, journalism, photography, yearbook classes. Computer network features include on-campus library services, online commercial services, Internet access, wireless campus network, Internet filtering or blocking technology, 1-to-1 iPad program. Student e-mail accounts and computer access in designated common areas are available to students. Students grades are available online. The school has a published electronic and media policy.

Contact Ms. Brigid Williams, Director of Admissions. 310-839-5289 Ext. 218. Fax: 310-839-7957. E-mail: bwilliams@ndala.com. Website: www.ndala.com

NOTRE DAME ACADEMY

1073 Main Street
Hingham, Massachusetts 02043

Head of School: Sr. Barbara A. Barry, SND

General Information Girls' day college-preparatory, arts, business, religious studies, and technology school, affiliated with Roman Catholic Church. Grades 7–12. Founded: 1853. Setting: suburban. Nearest major city is Boston. 68-acre campus. 1 building on campus. Approved or accredited by Association of Independent Schools in New England, National Catholic Education Association, New England Association of Schools and Colleges, and Massachusetts Department of Education. Endowment: $4.9 million. Total enrollment: 568. Upper school average class size: 20. Upper school faculty-student ratio: 1:11. There are 180 required school days per year for Upper School students. Upper School students typically attend 5 days per week. The average school day consists of 6 hours and 30 minutes.

Upper School Student Profile 94% of students are Roman Catholic.

Faculty School total: 54. In upper school: 10 men, 44 women; 50 have advanced degrees.

Subjects Offered Acting, advanced chemistry, Advanced Placement courses, advanced studio art-AP, algebra, American history, American history-AP, American literature, anatomy, anatomy and physiology, art, art history, Bible studies, bioethics, biology, biology-AP, business, business skills, calculus, calculus-AP, campus ministry, Catholic belief and practice, ceramics, chemistry, community service, computer science, driver education, economics, English, English literature, ethics, European history, fine arts, French, geometry, government/civics, history, Latin, mathematics, music, photography, physical education, physics, physiology, psychology, religion, science, social sciences, social studies, Spanish, trigonometry, U.S. government and politics-AP, world history, world literature.

Graduation Requirements Art, computer applications, English, foreign language, guidance, mathematics, music, physical education (includes health), religion (includes Bible studies and theology), science, social studies (includes history).

Special Academic Programs 17 Advanced Placement exams for which test preparation is offered; honors section; independent study; ESL (7 students enrolled).

College Admission Counseling 144 students graduated in 2013; all went to college, including Holy Cross College; Loyola University Maryland; Northeastern University; Providence College; Saint Anselm College; University of Massachusetts Amherst.

Student Life Upper grades have uniform requirement, student council, honor system. Discipline rests primarily with faculty. Attendance at religious services is required.

Tuition and Aid Day student tuition: $1765. Tuition installment plan (FACTS Tuition Payment Plan). Merit scholarship grants, need-based scholarship grants available. In 2013–14, 33% of upper-school students received aid; total upper-school merit-scholarship money awarded: $200,000. Total amount of financial aid awarded in 2013–14: $600,000.

Admissions Traditional secondary-level entrance grade is 9. For fall 2013, 350 students applied for upper-level admission, 275 were accepted, 146 enrolled. Diocesan Entrance Exam required. Deadline for receipt of application materials: December 1. Application fee required: $30.

Athletics Interscholastic: alpine skiing, basketball, cheering, cross-country running, dance team, diving, field hockey, golf, gymnastics, ice hockey, indoor track & field, lacrosse, sailing, skiing (downhill), soccer, softball, strength & conditioning, swimming and diving, tennis, track and field, volleyball, weight training, winter (indoor) track; intramural: crew, dance team. 1 PE instructor, 26 coaches, 1 athletic trainer.

Computers Computers are regularly used in art, college planning, English, foreign language, history, mathematics, music, religion, science classes. Computer network features include on-campus library services, Internet access, wireless campus network, Internet filtering or blocking technology. Campus intranet, student e-mail accounts, and computer access in designated common areas are available to students. Students grades are available online. The school has a published electronic and media policy.

Contact Mrs. Patricia Spatola, Director of Admissions. 781-749-5930 Ext. 235. Fax: 781-749-8366. E-mail: pspatola@ndahingham.com. Website: www.ndahingham.com

NOTRE DAME COLLEGE PREP

7655 West Dempster Street
Niles, Illinois 60714-2098

Head of School: Mr. Daniel Tully

General Information Boys' day college-preparatory, arts, business, religious studies, and technology school, affiliated with Roman Catholic Church. Grades 9–12. Founded: 1955. Setting: suburban. Nearest major city is Chicago. 28-acre campus. 1 building on campus. Approved or accredited by National Catholic Education Association, North Central Association of Colleges and Schools, and Illinois Department of Education. Endowment: $1.2 million. Total enrollment: 834. Upper school average class size: 17. Upper school faculty-student ratio: 1:17. There are 175 required school days per year for Upper School students. Upper School students typically attend 5 days per week. The average school day consists of 6 hours and 50 minutes.

Upper School Student Profile Grade 9: 239 students (239 boys); Grade 10: 216 students (216 boys); Grade 11: 192 students (192 boys); Grade 12: 187 students (187 boys). 87% of students are Roman Catholic.

Faculty School total: 62. In upper school: 33 men, 29 women; 43 have advanced degrees.

Subjects Offered 3-dimensional art, accounting, advanced biology, advanced chemistry, advanced math, algebra, American literature, art, art history, art history-AP, band, Bible as literature, Bible studies, bioethics, biology, biology-AP, British literature, British literature (honors), calculus, calculus-AP, Catholic belief and practice, chemistry, chemistry-AP, choir, comedy, computer literacy, computer programming, concert band, concert choir, contemporary history, creative writing, debate, drama, dramatic arts, economics, English, English-AP, environmental science, ESL, ethics, European history-AP, film appreciation, fine arts, geography, geometry, government-AP, health, history, honors algebra, honors English, honors geometry, honors world history, Italian, jazz, jazz band, journalism, Latin, Latin-AP, leadership, life skills, mathematics, music, music appreciation, music theory, philosophy, physical education, physics, physics-AP, pre-algebra, pre-calculus, psychology, reading/study skills, religion, science, social studies, sociology, Spanish, Spanish-AP, speech, statistics, studio art-AP, theology, trigonometry, U.S. history, U.S. history-AP, Web site design, weight training, weightlifting, Western civilization, world history-AP, world literature, world religions.

Graduation Requirements Algebra, American literature, arts and fine arts (art, music, dance, drama), biology, British literature, computer literacy, constitutional law, English, foreign language, geometry, health, mathematics, physical education (includes health), religion (includes Bible studies and theology), science, social studies (includes history), U.S. history, Western civilization, world literature, writing, four years of religious retreats and community services.

Special Academic Programs 12 Advanced Placement exams for which test preparation is offered; honors section; study at local college for college credit; academic accommodation for the gifted; remedial reading and/or remedial writing; remedial math; special instructional classes for remedial English, math, religion, science and social studies; ESL (5 students enrolled).

College Admission Counseling 171 students graduated in 2013; 164 went to college, including Illinois State University; Loras College; Loyola University Chicago; The University of Iowa; University of Illinois at Chicago; University of Illinois at Urbana–Champaign. Other: 2 went to work, 3 entered military service, 2 had other specific plans. Mean composite ACT: 24. 32% scored over 26 on composite ACT.

Student Life Upper grades have specified standards of dress, student council, honor system. Discipline rests primarily with faculty. Attendance at religious services is required.

Summer Programs Remediation, enrichment, sports, art/fine arts, computer instruction programs offered; session focuses on remediation/make up; held on campus; accepts boys and girls; open to students from other schools. 200 students usually enrolled. 2014 schedule: June 3 to August 1.

Tuition and Aid Day student tuition: $9950. Tuition installment plan (FACTS Tuition Payment Plan). Tuition reduction for siblings, merit scholarship grants, need-based scholarship grants, paying campus jobs available. In 2013–14, 43% of upper-school students received aid; total upper-school merit-scholarship money awarded: $94,000.

Admissions Traditional secondary-level entrance grade is 9. For fall 2013, 260 students applied for upper-level admission, 252 were accepted, 243 enrolled. High School Placement Test or TOEFL or SLEP required. Deadline for receipt of application materials: June 1. Application fee required: $25. Interview recommended.

Athletics Interscholastic: baseball, basketball, bowling, cross-country running, diving, football, golf, ice hockey, lacrosse, soccer, swimming and diving, tennis, track and field, volleyball, wrestling; intramural: baseball, basketball, boxing, combined training, flag football, floor hockey, football, outdoor adventure, paddle tennis, physical fitness, softball, table tennis, ultimate Frisbee, volleyball, weight lifting, weight training, wrestling. 4 PE instructors, 25 coaches, 1 athletic trainer.

Computers Computers are regularly used in accounting, art, computer applications, English, ESL, geography, health, history, science, Web site design classes. Computer network features include on-campus library services, Internet access, wireless campus network, Internet filtering or blocking technology, college search and scholarships. Student e-mail accounts are available to students. Students grades are available online. The school has a published electronic and media policy.

Contact Mrs. LaVerne Bontempo, Assistant Director of Enrollment. 847-779-8615. Fax: 847-965-2975. E-mail: lbontempo@nddons.org. Website: www.nddons.org

NOTRE DAME HIGH SCHOOL

596 South Second Street
San Jose, California 95112

Head of School: Mrs. Mary Elizabeth Riley

General Information Girls' day college-preparatory, arts, religious studies, and technology school, affiliated with Roman Catholic Church. Grades 9–12. Founded: 1851. Setting: urban. 2-acre campus. 4 buildings on campus. Approved or accredited by Western Association of Schools and Colleges, Western Catholic Education Association, and California Department of Education. Endowment: $1 million. Total enrollment: 628. Upper school average class size: 22. Upper school faculty-student ratio: 1:16.

There are 202 required school days per year for Upper School students. Upper School students typically attend 5 days per week. The average school day consists of 6 hours and 55 minutes.

Upper School Student Profile Grade 9: 170 students (170 girls); Grade 10: 158 students (158 girls); Grade 11: 161 students (161 girls); Grade 12: 139 students (139 girls). 56% of students are Roman Catholic.

Faculty School total: 43. In upper school: 6 men, 37 women; 33 have advanced degrees.

Subjects Offered Advanced biology, advanced chemistry, Advanced Placement courses, algebra, art, ASB Leadership, athletics, band, Basic programming, biology, biology-AP, calculus, calculus-AP, campus ministry, ceramics, chemistry, chorus, Christian and Hebrew scripture, college admission preparation, computer programming, computer science, creative writing, dance, decision making skills, digital photography, drama, drama performance, economics, English, English language and composition-AP, English literature, English literature and composition-AP, environmental science-AP, film and literature, fine arts, French, French language-AP, French literature-AP, geography, geometry, global studies, government/civics, healthful living, honors algebra, honors English, honors geometry, honors U.S. history, honors world history, journalism, library research, library skills, mathematics, modern world history, moral and social development, musical theater, painting, peer counseling, peer ministry, philosophy, photography, physical education, physical fitness, physics, post-calculus, pre-calculus, psychology, psychology-AP, public speaking, religion, research skills, robotics, science, service learning/internship, social justice, social psychology, social studies, Spanish, Spanish language-AP, Spanish literature-AP, speech and debate, statistics, study skills, theater, trigonometry, U.S. government, U.S. government and politics-AP, U.S. history, U.S. history-AP, video film production, Web site design, women in society, world history, world history-AP, world religions, yearbook.

Graduation Requirements Arts and fine arts (art, music, dance, drama), English, foreign language, mathematics, physical education (includes health), religion (includes Bible studies and theology), science, social studies (includes history), community service learning program.

Special Academic Programs 10 Advanced Placement exams for which test preparation is offered; honors section; independent study; study at local college for college credit.

College Admission Counseling 155 students graduated in 2013; all went to college, including California Polytechnic State University, San Luis Obispo; Santa Clara University; Seattle University; Sonoma State University; University of San Francisco; University of Southern California. Median SAT critical reading: 569, median SAT math: 572, median SAT writing: 590. 40% scored over 600 on SAT critical reading, 41% scored over 600 on SAT math, 47% scored over 600 on SAT writing.

Student Life Upper grades have uniform requirement, student council, honor system. Discipline rests primarily with faculty. Attendance at religious services is required.

Summer Programs Enrichment, advancement programs offered; session focuses on enrichment; held on campus; accepts boys and girls; open to students from other schools. 125 students usually enrolled. 2014 schedule: June to July.

Tuition and Aid Day student tuition: $15,600. Tuition installment plan (FACTS Tuition Payment Plan, annual payment plan, 2-payment plan). Merit scholarship grants, need-based scholarship grants, individual sponsored grants available. In 2013–14, 22% of upper-school students received aid; total upper-school merit-scholarship money awarded: $13,000. Total amount of financial aid awarded in 2013–14: $767,000.

Admissions Traditional secondary-level entrance grade is 9. For fall 2013, 388 students applied for upper-level admission, 273 were accepted, 170 enrolled. High School Placement Test required. Deadline for receipt of application materials: January 15. Application fee required: $70.

Athletics Interscholastic: aquatics (girls), basketball (g), cross-country running (g), golf (g), lacrosse (g), soccer (g), softball (g), swimming and diving (g), tennis (g), track and field (g), volleyball (g); intramural: badminton (g), basketball (g), volleyball (g). 2 PE instructors, 25 coaches, 2 athletic trainers.

Computers Computers are regularly used in all academic, English, foreign language, history, mathematics, science classes. Computer network features include on-campus library services, online commercial services, Internet access, wireless campus network, Internet filtering or blocking technology. Student e-mail accounts are available to students. Students grades are available online. The school has a published electronic and media policy.

Contact Ms. Susana Garcia, Director of Enrollment Management. 408-294-1113 Ext. 2159. Fax: 408-293-9779. E-mail: sgarcia@ndsj.org. Website: www.ndsj.org

NOTRE DAME HIGH SCHOOL

601 Lawrence Road
Lawrenceville, New Jersey 08648

Heads of School: Mr. Barry Edward Breen and Ms. Mary Liz Ivins

General Information Coeducational day college-preparatory school, affiliated with Roman Catholic Church. Grades 9–12. Founded: 1957. Setting: suburban. Nearest major city is Trenton. 100-acre campus. 1 building on campus. Approved or accredited by Middle States Association of Colleges and Schools, National Catholic Education Association, and New Jersey Department of Education. Total enrollment: 1,299. Upper school average class size: 23. Upper school faculty-student ratio: 1:13. There are 180 required school days per year for Upper School students. Upper School students typically attend 5 days per week. The average school day consists of 6 hours and 30 minutes.

Upper School Student Profile Grade 9: 347 students (171 boys, 176 girls); Grade 10: 333 students (168 boys, 165 girls); Grade 11: 312 students (157 boys, 155 girls); Grade 12: 307 students (161 boys, 146 girls). 82% of students are Roman Catholic.

Faculty School total: 96. In upper school: 36 men, 60 women; 42 have advanced degrees.

Subjects Offered 20th century history, 3-dimensional art, 3-dimensional design, accounting, acting, advanced chemistry, advanced computer applications, advanced math, Advanced Placement courses, algebra, American government, American history, American history-AP, American literature, ancient world history, applied music, art, art and culture, art-AP, athletics, Basic programming, Bible studies, biology, biology-AP, British literature, business, business applications, business studies, calculus, calculus-AP, campus ministry, Catholic belief and practice, ceramics, chemistry, chemistry-AP, choir, chorus, Christian doctrine, community service, comparative religion, computer applications, computer science, concert band, concert choir, constitutional law, contemporary issues, creative writing, dance, dance performance, discrete mathematics, drama, driver education, ecology, environmental systems, economics, economics-AP, English, English composition, English language and composition-AP, English literature and composition-AP, English literature-AP, environmental science-AP, etymology, European history-AP, film appreciation, film studies, filmmaking, first aid, French, French-AP, geometry, German, German literature, government-AP, health education, honors algebra, honors English, honors world history, independent study, Italian, Japanese, jazz band, journalism, kinesiology, language-AP, Latin, law, leadership service, leadership education training, literature and composition-AP, literature-AP, macro/microeconomics-AP, madrigals, math review, media literacy, newspaper, orchestra, painting, peer counseling, peer ministry, personal finance, philosophy, photography, physical education, physics, physics-AP, piano, portfolio art, pottery, pre-algebra, pre-calculus, probability and statistics, psychology, psychology-AP, public speaking, reading/study skills, religion, religion and culture, robotics, Russian, SAT preparation, scripture, senior internship, senior project, service learning/internship, sociology, Spanish, Spanish literature, Spanish-AP, speech and debate, sports medicine, statistics-AP, studio art-AP, U.S. government, U.S. government and politics-AP, U.S. literature, women spirituality and faith, world history, world literature, writing.

Graduation Requirements Biology, English, foreign language, integrated technology fundamentals, lab science, mathematics, physical education (includes health), religion (includes Bible studies and theology), U.S. history, world history, service-learning. Community service is required.

Special Academic Programs 15 Advanced Placement exams for which test preparation is offered; honors section; independent study; study at local college for college credit; remedial reading and/or remedial writing; remedial math.

College Admission Counseling 285 students graduated in 2012; 282 went to college, including Loyola University Maryland; Rutgers, The State University of New Jersey, New Brunswick; Saint Joseph's University; Seton Hall University; The College of New Jersey; University of Delaware. Other: 1 went to work, 2 entered military service. Mean SAT critical reading: 554, mean SAT math: 557, mean SAT writing: 555, mean combined SAT: 1666. 30% scored over 600 on SAT critical reading, 34% scored over 600 on SAT math, 28% scored over 600 on SAT writing, 26% scored over 1800 on combined SAT.

Student Life Upper grades have uniform requirement, student council, honor system. Discipline rests primarily with faculty. Attendance at religious services is required.

Tuition and Aid Day student tuition: $10,920. Tuition installment plan (Tuition Management Systems Plan). Tuition reduction for siblings, need-based scholarship grants available. In 2012–13, 10% of upper-school students received aid. Total amount of financial aid awarded in 2012–13: $375,000.

Admissions Traditional secondary-level entrance grade is 9. For fall 2012, 550 students applied for upper-level admission, 425 were accepted, 347 enrolled. Scholastic Testing Service High School Placement Test required. Deadline for receipt of application materials: November 30. Application fee required: $50. On-campus interview required.

Athletics Interscholastic: baseball (boys), basketball (b,g), cheering (g), cross-country running (b,g), dance (g), field hockey (g), football (b), golf (b,g), ice hockey (b), indoor track (b,g), lacrosse (b,g), soccer (b,g), softball (g), swimming and diving (b,g), tennis (b,g), track and field (b,g), winter (indoor) track (b,g), wrestling (b); intramural: touch football (g), volleyball (b,g); coed interscholastic: cheering, dance, diving, fitness, strength & conditioning; coed intramural: Frisbee, outdoor activities, outdoor recreation, physical fitness, ultimate Frisbee, volleyball, weight lifting, weight training. 9 PE instructors, 65 coaches, 1 athletic trainer.

Computers Computers are regularly used in all academic classes. Computer network features include on-campus library services, online commercial services, Internet access, wireless campus network, Internet filtering or blocking technology. Campus intranet and computer access in designated common areas are available to students. Students grades are available online. The school has a published electronic and media policy.

Contact Ms. Peggy Miller, Director of Enrollment Management. 609-882-7900 Ext. 139. Fax: 609-882-6599. E-mail: miller@ndnj.org. Website: www.ndnj.org

NOTRE DAME HIGH SCHOOL

2701 Vermont Avenue
Chattanooga, Tennessee 37404

Head of School: Mr. Perry L. Storey

General Information Coeducational day college-preparatory, arts, religious studies, technology, and Microsoft IT Academy Certification school, affiliated with Roman Catholic Church. Grades 9–12. Founded: 1876. Setting: urban. 22-acre campus. 3 buildings on campus. Approved or accredited by Southern Association of Colleges and Schools and Tennessee Department of Education. Endowment: $750,000. Total enrollment: 407. Upper school average class size: 18. Upper school faculty-student ratio: 1:10. There are 180 required school days per year for Upper School students. Upper School students typically attend 5 days per week. The average school day consists of 5 hours and 50 minutes.

Upper School Student Profile Grade 9: 115 students (57 boys, 58 girls); Grade 10: 82 students (42 boys, 40 girls); Grade 11: 107 students (49 boys, 58 girls); Grade 12: 103 students (54 boys, 49 girls). 77% of students are Roman Catholic.

Faculty School total: 40. In upper school: 16 men, 24 women; 27 have advanced degrees.

Subjects Offered 3-dimensional art, ACT preparation, Advanced Placement courses, algebra, American history-AP, American literature, anatomy, anatomy and physiology, art-AP, band, biology, biology-AP, British literature, calculus, Catholic belief and practice, chemistry, choir, civics, conceptual physics, creative dance, criminal justice, drama, economics, electives, English composition, English literature, English-AP, environmental science-AP, European history-AP, foreign language, French, geometry, German, government, government/civics, health and wellness, history-AP, honors algebra, honors English, honors geometry, honors U.S. history, honors world history, Latin, physics, religion, Spanish, U.S. government and politics-AP, weight training, wellness, world geography, world history, world history-AP, writing, yoga.

Special Academic Programs Advanced Placement exam preparation; honors section; independent study; study at local college for college credit.

College Admission Counseling 126 students graduated in 2012; 125 went to college, including Auburn University; Middle Tennessee State University; The University of Tennessee; The University of Tennessee at Chattanooga; University of Georgia. Other: 1 had other specific plans.

Student Life Upper grades have uniform requirement, student council, honor system. Discipline rests primarily with faculty. Attendance at religious services is required.

Tuition and Aid Day student tuition: $9150–$11,754. Tuition installment plan (Insured Tuition Payment Plan, FACTS Tuition Payment Plan, monthly payment plans, individually arranged payment plans). Tuition reduction for siblings, need-based scholarship grants available. In 2012–13, 30% of upper-school students received aid. Total amount of financial aid awarded in 2012–13: $378,271.

Admissions Traditional secondary-level entrance grade is 9. ACT-Explore required. Deadline for receipt of application materials: none. Application fee required: $100. On-campus interview required.

Athletics Interscholastic: aerobics/dance (girls), baseball (b), basketball (b,g), bowling (b,g), cross-country running (b,g), dance (g), dance squad (g), dance team (g), diving (b,g), football (b), golf (b,g), modern dance (g), physical training (b,g), running (b,g), soccer (b,g), softball (g), swimming and diving (b,g), tennis (b,g), track and field (b,g), volleyball (g), weight training (b,g), wrestling (b); intramural: aerobics/dance (g), cheering (g), indoor soccer (b), indoor track (b,g), lacrosse (b,g); coed interscholastic: cheering, yoga; coed intramural: backpacking, canoeing/kayaking, climbing, crew, hiking/backpacking, kayaking, mountaineering, outdoors, rafting, rappelling, rock climbing, rowing, skiing (downhill), snowboarding, wall climbing. 4 PE instructors, 30 coaches, 2 athletic trainers.

Computers Computers are regularly used in information technology classes. Computer network features include on-campus library services, Internet access, wireless campus network, Internet filtering or blocking technology, language software labs, Microsoft IT Academy Training. Student e-mail accounts and computer access in designated common areas are available to students. Students grades are available online. The school has a published electronic and media policy.

Contact Ms. Jenny Rittgers, Admissions Director. 423-624-4618 Ext. 1004. Fax: 423-624-4621. E-mail: admissions@myndhs.com. Website: www.myndhs.com

NOTRE DAME JUNIOR/SENIOR HIGH SCHOOL

60 Spangenburg Avenue
East Stroudsburg, Pennsylvania 18301-2799

Head of School: Mr. Jeffrey Neill Lyons

General Information Coeducational day college-preparatory, arts, and religious studies school, affiliated with Roman Catholic Church. Grades 7–12. Founded: 1967. Setting: suburban. 40-acre campus. 4 buildings on campus. Approved or accredited by Middle States Association of Colleges and Schools, National Catholic Education Association, and Pennsylvania Department of Education. Total enrollment: 270. Upper school average class size: 25. Upper school faculty-student ratio: 1:15. There are 180 required school days per year for Upper School students. Upper School students typically attend 5 days per week. The average school day consists of 6 hours and 30 minutes.

Upper School Student Profile Grade 7: 43 students (19 boys, 24 girls); Grade 8: 33 students (12 boys, 21 girls); Grade 9: 35 students (13 boys, 22 girls); Grade 10: 67 students (33 boys, 34 girls); Grade 11: 47 students (22 boys, 25 girls); Grade 12: 45 students (23 boys, 22 girls). 88% of students are Roman Catholic.

Faculty School total: 25. In upper school: 8 men, 16 women; 12 have advanced degrees.

Graduation Requirements Lab/keyboard, mathematics, moral theology, physical education (includes health), physical science, religion (includes Bible studies and theology), senior project, U.S. history, U.S. literature, word processing, world cultures, world religions.

Special Academic Programs Advanced Placement exam preparation; honors section; study at local college for college credit.

College Admission Counseling 58 students graduated in 2013; 56 went to college, including Marywood University; Mount St. Mary's University; Penn State University Park; Saint Joseph's University; Temple University; The University of Scranton. Other: 2 went to work. Median SAT critical reading: 500, median SAT math: 460, median SAT writing: 500, median combined SAT: 1460. 10% scored over 600 on SAT critical reading, 15% scored over 600 on SAT math, 10% scored over 600 on SAT writing, 25% scored over 1800 on combined SAT.

Student Life Upper grades have uniform requirement, student council. Discipline rests primarily with faculty. Attendance at religious services is required.

Tuition and Aid Tuition installment plan (FACTS Tuition Payment Plan). Tuition reduction for siblings, need-based scholarship grants available. In 2013–14, 30% of upper-school students received aid.

Admissions Traditional secondary-level entrance grade is 7. Achievement tests or TerraNova required. Deadline for receipt of application materials: May 1. No application fee required. Interview required.

Athletics Interscholastic: baseball (boys), basketball (b,g), cheering (g), field hockey (g), soccer (b,g), softball (g), swimming and diving (b,g), tennis (b,g), winter soccer (b,g); coed interscholastic: golf, soccer; coed intramural: cross-country running, indoor soccer, jogging, strength & conditioning. 2 PE instructors, 15 coaches, 1 athletic trainer.

Computers Computer network features include on-campus library services, Internet access, Internet filtering or blocking technology. The school has a published electronic and media policy.

Contact Mr. Jeffrey Neill Lyons, Principal. 570-421-0466. Fax: 570-476-0629. E-mail: principal@ndhigh.org. Website: www.ndhigh.org

OAK GROVE SCHOOL

220 West Lomita Avenue
Ojai, California 93023

Head of School: Meredy Benson Rice

General Information Coeducational boarding and day college-preparatory and arts school. Boarding grades 9–12, day grades PK–12. Founded: 1975. Setting: small town. Nearest major city is Los Angeles. Students are housed in coed dormitories. 150-acre campus. 6 buildings on campus. Approved or accredited by The Association of Boarding Schools, Western Association of Schools and Colleges, and California Department of Education. Member of National Association of Independent Schools and Secondary School Admission Test Board. Endowment: $1.2 million. Total enrollment: 209. Upper school average class size: 15. Upper school faculty-student ratio: 1:7. There are 170 required school days per year for Upper School students. Upper School students typically attend 5 days per week. The average school day consists of 8 hours and 30 minutes.

Upper School Student Profile 35% of students are boarding students. 83% are state residents. 2 states are represented in upper school student body. 23% are international students. International students from Brazil, China, India, Japan, Republic of Korea, and Viet Nam.

Faculty School total: 35. In upper school: 6 men, 5 women; 5 have advanced degrees; 2 reside on campus.

Subjects Offered Algebra, American history, American literature, anatomy, art, art history, biology, calculus, ceramics, chemistry, communications, community service, comparative religion, computer science, drama, earth science, economics, English, English literature, ethics, film and new technologies, fine arts, gardening, geography, geometry, global studies, history, horticulture, human development, inquiry into relationship, mathematics, music, permaculture, photography, physical education, physics, relationships, religion and culture, science, social studies, Spanish, studio art, theater, world cultures, world history, world literature.

Graduation Requirements Algebra, American history, arts and fine arts (art, music, dance, drama), backpacking, biology, chemistry, college admission preparation, comparative religion, economics and history, English, ethics and responsibility, foreign language, geometry, mathematics, science, social studies (includes history), Spanish, world religions, participation in camping and travel programs and sports, one year of visual and performing arts. Community service is required.

Special Academic Programs 3 Advanced Placement exams for which test preparation is offered; honors section; ESL (4 students enrolled).

College Admission Counseling 12 students graduated in 2013; 11 went to college, including California Institute of the Arts; New York University; Pace University; The Colorado College; University of California, Berkeley. Other: 1 had other specific plans. Mean SAT critical reading: 627, mean SAT math: 580, mean SAT writing: 617. 57% scored over 600 on SAT critical reading, 28% scored over 600 on SAT math, 42% scored over 600 on SAT writing.

Student Life Upper grades have student council, honor system. Discipline rests equally with students and faculty.

Summer Programs ESL programs offered; held on campus; accepts boys and girls; open to students from other schools. 15 students usually enrolled. 2014 schedule: July to August. Application deadline: June.

Tuition and Aid Day student tuition: $16,000; 7-day tuition and room/board: $36,200. Tuition installment plan (FACTS Tuition Payment Plan, annual and semiannual payment plans). Need-based scholarship grants, African-American scholarships available. In 2013–14, 40% of upper-school students received aid. Total amount of financial aid awarded in 2013–14: $60,000.

Admissions Traditional secondary-level entrance grade is 9. For fall 2013, 31 students applied for upper-level admission, 22 were accepted, 8 enrolled. SSAT or TOEFL or SLEP required. Deadline for receipt of application materials: none. Application fee required: $50. Interview required.

Athletics Interscholastic: soccer (boys, girls), volleyball (b,g); intramural: equestrian sports (g), soccer (b,g), volleyball (b,g); coed intramural: backpacking, fitness, hiking/backpacking, outdoor activities, outdoor education, outdoor skills, physical fitness, ropes courses, skiing (downhill), table tennis, tennis, wilderness. 1 PE instructor, 3 coaches.

Computers Computers are regularly used in art, ESL, graphic arts, history, independent study, library, mathematics, multimedia, photography, SAT preparation, science, technology, typing, writing, yearbook classes. Computer network features include on-campus library services, online commercial services, Internet access, wireless campus network, Internet filtering or blocking technology. Computer access in designated common areas is available to students.

Contact Joy Maguire-Parsons, Director of Admissions. 805-646-8236 Ext. 109. Fax: 805-646-6509. E-mail: enroll@oakgroveschool.org. Website: www.oakgroveschool.org

THE OAKLAND SCHOOL

362 McKee Place
Pittsburgh, Pennsylvania 15213

Head of School: Mr. Jack C. King

General Information Coeducational day college-preparatory and arts school. Grades 8–12. Founded: 1982. Setting: urban. 1 building on campus. Approved or accredited by Pennsylvania Department of Education. Candidate for accreditation by Middle States Association of Colleges and Schools. Total enrollment: 40. Upper school average class size: 6. Upper school faculty-student ratio: 1:6. There are 180 required school days per year for Upper School students. Upper School students typically attend 5 days per week. The average school day consists of 5 hours and 30 minutes.

Upper School Student Profile Grade 8: 2 students (1 boy, 1 girl); Grade 9: 7 students (3 boys, 4 girls); Grade 10: 10 students (5 boys, 5 girls); Grade 11: 10 students (5 boys, 5 girls); Grade 12: 11 students (6 boys, 5 girls).

Faculty School total: 10. In upper school: 3 men, 7 women; 5 have advanced degrees.

Subjects Offered Advanced math, algebra, American history, American literature, art, art history, biology, business skills, calculus, chemistry, computer math, computer science, creative writing, drama, earth science, ecology, economics, English, English literature, environmental science, ESL, expository writing, fine arts, French, geography, geometry, German, government/civics, history, mathematics, physical education, physics, pre-calculus, psychology, SAT/ACT preparation, science, social studies, Spanish, speech, trigonometry, world history, world literature, writing.

Graduation Requirements Arts and fine arts (art, music, dance, drama), computer literacy, English, mathematics, physical education (includes health), science, social studies (includes history), community service.

Special Academic Programs Honors section; accelerated programs; independent study; study at local college for college credit; academic accommodation for the gifted and the artistically talented; remedial reading and/or remedial writing; remedial math; ESL (2 students enrolled).

College Admission Counseling 11 students graduated in 2013; 10 went to college, including Ohio University; Penn State University Park; Rochester Institute of Technology; University of Pittsburgh. Other: 1 had other specific plans. Mean SAT critical reading: 530, mean SAT math: 512, mean SAT writing: 550.

Student Life Upper grades have student council. Discipline rests primarily with faculty.

Tuition and Aid Day student tuition: $10,000. Tuition installment plan (monthly payment plans, individually arranged payment plans, quarterly payment plan, semiannual payment plan). Tuition reduction for siblings, merit scholarship grants, need-based scholarship grants available. In 2013–14, 20% of upper-school students received aid. Total amount of financial aid awarded in 2013–14: $26,000.

Admissions Traditional secondary-level entrance grade is 10. For fall 2013, 24 students applied for upper-level admission, 20 were accepted, 14 enrolled. WRAT required. Deadline for receipt of application materials: none. Application fee required: $100. On-campus interview required.

Athletics Intramural: aerobics/dance (girls), dance (g); coed intramural: baseball, basketball, bicycling, billiards, bowling, cooperative games, cross-country running, fitness, fitness walking, flag football, Frisbee, golf, hiking/backpacking, ice skating, jogging, jump rope, kickball, martial arts, racquetball, running, skateboarding, skiing

(cross-country), skiing (downhill), snowboarding, softball, swimming and diving, tai chi, tennis, volleyball, walking. 1 PE instructor.

Computers Computers are regularly used in all academic classes. Computer network features include Internet access, wireless campus network. Student e-mail accounts and computer access in designated common areas are available to students. Students grades are available online.

Contact Admissions Desk. 412-621-7878. Fax: 412-621-7881. E-mail: oschool@stargate.net. Website: www.theoaklandschool.org

OAKLAND SCHOOL

Keswick, Virginia
See Special Needs Schools section.

THE OAKRIDGE SCHOOL

5900 West Pioneer Parkway
Arlington, Texas 76013-2899

Head of School: Mr. Jonathan Kellam

General Information Coeducational day college-preparatory, arts, and technology school. Grades PS–12. Founded: 1979. Setting: suburban. 90-acre campus. 12 buildings on campus. Approved or accredited by Independent Schools Association of the Southwest and Texas Department of Education. Member of National Association of Independent Schools. Endowment: $672,406. Total enrollment: 858. Upper school average class size: 16. Upper school faculty-student ratio: 1:11. There are 171 required school days per year for Upper School students. Upper School students typically attend 5 days per week. The average school day consists of 7 hours.

Upper School Student Profile Grade 9: 82 students (41 boys, 41 girls); Grade 10: 75 students (38 boys, 37 girls); Grade 11: 83 students (36 boys, 47 girls); Grade 12: 74 students (42 boys, 32 girls).

Faculty School total: 82. In upper school: 12 men, 14 women; 26 have advanced degrees.

Subjects Offered 3-dimensional art, acting, Advanced Placement courses, advanced studio art-AP, algebra, American history, American history-AP, American literature, anatomy, ancient world history, anthropology, archaeology, art, art history-AP, athletics, biology, British literature, calculus, calculus-AP, chemistry, chemistry-AP, Chinese, choir, choral music, college admission preparation, college counseling, college writing, community service, comparative religion, composition-AP, computer art, computer graphics, computer literacy, computer multimedia, computer science-AP, concert choir, creative writing, current events, desktop publishing, digital applications, digital art, digital imaging, digital photography, discrete mathematics, drama, drama performance, drama workshop, dramatic arts, drawing, drawing and design, economics, economics and history, English, English language and composition-AP, English literature and composition-AP, environmental science-AP, European civilization, European history-AP, expository writing, film and literature, fine arts, fractal geometry, French, French language-AP, French-AP, geometry, golf, government, government and politics-AP, government-AP, government/civics, graphic arts, graphic design, graphics, honors algebra, honors English, honors geometry, honors world history, human biology, independent study, language and composition, language arts, literature and composition-AP, modern European history-AP, modern world history, music theory, music theory-AP, musical productions, physics, physics-AP, play production, poetry, portfolio art, portfolio writing, pre-algebra, pre-calculus, probability and statistics, programming, public service, public speaking, reading/study skills, SAT preparation, SAT/ACT preparation, Spanish, Spanish-AP, strings, theater, track and field, U.S. government, U.S. government and politics, U.S. government and politics-AP, U.S. history, U.S. history-AP, United States government-AP, video, video communication, video film production, visual and performing arts, voice, voice ensemble, Web site design, weightlifting, world history.

Graduation Requirements Arts and fine arts (art, music, dance, drama), English, foreign language, mathematics, physical education (includes health), science, social studies (includes history), participation in six seasons of athletics, 60 hours of community service. Community service is required.

Special Academic Programs 21 Advanced Placement exams for which test preparation is offered; honors section; independent study; study at local college for college credit; study abroad; academic accommodation for the gifted, the musically talented, and the artistically talented.

College Admission Counseling 78 students graduated in 2012; all went to college, including Austin College; Oklahoma State University; Texas A&M University; Texas Christian University; The University of Texas at Austin; University of Arkansas. Mean SAT critical reading: 600, mean SAT math: 619, mean SAT writing: 595, mean combined SAT: 1814, mean composite ACT: 27.

Student Life Upper grades have uniform requirement, student council, honor system. Discipline rests primarily with faculty.

Tuition and Aid Day student tuition: $18,300. Tuition installment plan (FACTS Tuition Payment Plan, early discount option). Need-based scholarship grants available. In 2012–13, 22% of upper-school students received aid. Total amount of financial aid awarded in 2012–13: $523,375.

Admissions Traditional secondary-level entrance grade is 9. For fall 2012, 49 students applied for upper-level admission, 38 were accepted, 31 enrolled. ERB Reading and Math, ISEE or Otis-Lennon School Ability Test required. Deadline for receipt of application materials: March 1. Application fee required: $75. Interview required.

Athletics Interscholastic; baseball (boys), basketball (b,g), cheering (g), cross-country running (b,g), field hockey (g), football (b), golf (b,g), physical fitness (b,g), physical training (b,g), power lifting (b), soccer (b,g), softball (g), strength & conditioning (b,g), swimming and diving (b,g), tennis (b,g), track and field (b,g), volleyball (g), weight lifting (b), wrestling (b); intramural: fitness (b,g), physical fitness (b,g), physical training (b,g), strength & conditioning (b,g), weight lifting (b), weight training (b); coed intramural: outdoor activities, outdoor education. 7 PE instructors, 10 coaches, 2 athletic trainers.

Computers Computers are regularly used in art, English, foreign language, history, mathematics, programming, science, stock market, technology, video film production, Web site design, writing, yearbook classes. Computer network features include on-campus library services, online commercial services, Internet access, wireless campus network, Internet filtering or blocking technology. Campus intranet, student e-mail accounts, and computer access in designated common areas are available to students. Students grades are available online. The school has a published electronic and media policy.

Contact Dr. Jerry A. Davis Jr., Director of Admissions. 817-451-4994 Ext. 2708. Fax: 817-457-6681. E-mail: jadavis@theoakridgeschool.org. Website: www.theoakridgeschool.org

OAKWOOD FRIENDS SCHOOL

22 Spackenkill Road
Poughkeepsie, New York 12603

Head of School: Peter F. Baily

General Information Coeducational boarding and day college-preparatory and arts school, affiliated with Society of Friends. Boarding grades 9–12, day grades 6–12. Founded: 1796. Setting: suburban. Nearest major city is New York. Students are housed in single-sex dormitories. 63-acre campus. 22 buildings on campus. Approved or accredited by Friends Council on Education, New York State Association of Independent Schools, New York State Board of Regents, The Association of Boarding Schools, and New York Department of Education. Member of National Association of Independent Schools and Secondary School Admission Test Board. Endowment: $3 million. Total enrollment: 125. Upper school average class size: 11. Upper school faculty-student ratio: 1:4. There are 167 required school days per year for Upper School students. Upper School students typically attend 5 days per week. The average school day consists of 5 hours.

Upper School Student Profile Grade 9: 23 students (15 boys, 8 girls); Grade 10: 24 students (9 boys, 15 girls); Grade 11: 32 students (17 boys, 15 girls); Grade 12: 26 students (17 boys, 9 girls). 50% of students are boarding students. 74% are state residents. 8 states are represented in upper school student body. 33% are international students. International students from Canada, China, Ghana, Republic of Korea, Rwanda, and Spain; 2 other countries represented in student body. 1% of students are members of Society of Friends.

Faculty School total: 33. In upper school: 15 men, 14 women; 23 have advanced degrees; 24 reside on campus.

Subjects Offered Acting, algebra, American history, American literature, American sign language, anthropology, art, art history, biology, calculus, ceramics, chemistry, community service, computer applications, conceptual physics, critical thinking, directing, drama, drawing, ecology, English, English literature, ensembles, environmental science, ESL, European history, existentialism, expository writing, fashion, fine arts, French, geometry, health, history, interdisciplinary studies, introduction to theater, mathematics, media arts, music, music theater, painting, photography, physical education, physics, playwriting and directing, pre-calculus, psychology, public speaking, Quakerism and ethics, robotics, science, sculpture, social studies, Spanish, statistics-AP, theater, world history, writing.

Graduation Requirements Advanced math, algebra, American history, arts and fine arts (art, music, dance, drama), biology, chemistry, computer literacy, conceptual physics, English, foreign language, geometry, health, interdisciplinary studies, physical education (includes health), Quakerism and ethics, U.S. history, world history, senior orientation trip in September, senior evaluation trip in June, community service. Community service is required.

Special Academic Programs 8 Advanced Placement exams for which test preparation is offered; independent study; special instructional classes for students with mild learning differences; ESL (44 students enrolled).

College Admission Counseling 35 students graduated in 2012; all went to college, including American University; Goucher College; Hobart and William Smith Colleges; Rensselaer Polytechnic Institute; Skidmore College; The George Washington University. Median SAT critical reading: 530, median SAT math: 500, median SAT writing: 530. 15% scored over 600 on SAT critical reading, 38% scored over 600 on SAT math, 27% scored over 600 on SAT writing.

Student Life Upper grades have specified standards of dress, student council, honor system. Discipline rests equally with students and faculty. Attendance at religious services is required.

Tuition and Aid Day student tuition: $24,220; 5-day tuition and room/board: $36,598; 7-day tuition and room/board: $41,980. Tuition installment plan (FACTS Tuition Payment Plan, monthly payment plans). Tuition reduction for siblings, need-based scholarship grants available. In 2012–13, 39% of upper-school students received aid. Total amount of financial aid awarded in 2012–13: $808,000.

Admissions Traditional secondary-level entrance grade is 9. For fall 2012, 110 students applied for upper-level admission, 75 were accepted, 40 enrolled. TOEFL or writing sample required. Deadline for receipt of application materials: none. Application fee required: $40. Interview required.

Athletics Interscholastic: baseball (boys), basketball (b,g), cross-country running (b,g), Frisbee (b,g), independent competitive sports (b,g), running (b,g), soccer (b,g), softball (g), tennis (b,g), volleyball (g); coed interscholastic: swimming and diving, ultimate Frisbee; coed intramural: badminton, basketball, bowling, cooperative games, cross-country running, dance team, fitness, fitness walking, indoor soccer, jogging, kickball, martial arts, outdoor activities, physical training, ropes courses, running, strength & conditioning, table tennis, tai chi, ultimate Frisbee, volleyball, walking, weight lifting, whiffle ball, yoga.

Computers Computers are regularly used in computer applications, English, foreign language, history, science, writing classes. Computer network features include on-campus library services, online commercial services, Internet access, wireless campus network, Internet filtering or blocking technology. Computer access in designated common areas is available to students. Students grades are available online. The school has a published electronic and media policy.

Contact Barbara Lonczak, Director of Admissions. 845-462-4200 Ext. 215. Fax: 845-462-4251. E-mail: blonczak@oakwoodfriends.org. Website: www.oakwoodfriends.org

OJAI VALLEY SCHOOL

723 El Paseo Road
Ojai, California 93023

Head of School: Mr. Michael J. Hall-Mounsey

General Information Coeducational boarding and day college-preparatory, arts, and technology school; primarily serves students with learning disabilities, individuals with Attention Deficit Disorder, and dyslexic students. Boarding grades 3–12, day grades PK–12. Founded: 1911. Setting: rural. Nearest major city is Los Angeles. Students are housed in single-sex dormitories. 200-acre campus. 13 buildings on campus. Approved or accredited by California Association of Independent Schools, The Association of Boarding Schools, Western Association of Schools and Colleges, and California Department of Education. Member of National Association of Independent Schools and Secondary School Admission Test Board. Endowment: $1 million. Total enrollment: 288. Upper school average class size: 12. Upper school faculty-student ratio: 1:6.

Upper School Student Profile Grade 9: 24 students (15 boys, 9 girls); Grade 10: 31 students (12 boys, 19 girls); Grade 11: 24 students (14 boys, 10 girls); Grade 12: 30 students (19 boys, 11 girls). 72% of students are boarding students. 46% are state residents. 7 states are represented in upper school student body. 44% are international students. International students from China, Japan, Mexico, Republic of Korea, Taiwan, and Thailand; 3 other countries represented in student body.

Faculty School total: 54. In upper school: 11 men, 12 women; 10 have advanced degrees; 10 reside on campus.

Subjects Offered 20th century history, algebra, American history, American literature, art, art history, biology, biology-AP, calculus-AP, chemistry, chemistry-AP, community service, computer science, conceptual physics, creative writing, drama, ecology, economics, English, English literature, English-AP, environmental science, equestrian sports, ESL, fine arts, geography, geometry, government/civics, grammar, history, honors English, humanities, independent study, mathematics, music, music theory-AP, photography, physical education, physics, psychology, science, social studies, Spanish, Spanish-AP, speech, statistics, studio art, studio art-AP, theater, trigonometry, wilderness education, world history, writing.

Graduation Requirements Arts and fine arts (art, music, dance, drama), economics, English, foreign language, government, mathematics, science, social studies (includes history).

Special Academic Programs 11 Advanced Placement exams for which test preparation is offered; honors section; accelerated programs; independent study; study abroad; academic accommodation for the gifted and the artistically talented; remedial reading and/or remedial writing; remedial math; ESL (12 students enrolled).

College Admission Counseling 23 students graduated in 2012; all went to college, including Boston University; New York University; The Johns Hopkins University; University of California, Riverside; University of California, Santa Barbara. Median SAT critical reading: 540, median SAT math: 625, median SAT writing: 585, median combined SAT: 1750. 25% scored over 600 on SAT math.

Student Life Upper grades have specified standards of dress, student council, honor system. Discipline rests equally with students and faculty.

Tuition and Aid Day student tuition: $19,500; 7-day tuition and room/board: $47,950. Tuition installment plan (individually arranged payment plans). Need-based scholarship grants, need-based loans available. In 2012–13, 15% of upper-school students received aid. Total amount of financial aid awarded in 2012–13: $347,360.

Admissions Traditional secondary-level entrance grade is 9. For fall 2012, 150 students applied for upper-level admission, 65 were accepted, 32 enrolled. Any standardized test, SSAT or TOEFL required. Deadline for receipt of application materials: none. Application fee required: $50. Interview required.

Athletics Interscholastic: baseball (boys), basketball (b,g), cross-country running (b,g), dressage (b,g), football (b), lacrosse (b,g), soccer (b,g), volleyball (b,g); coed interscholastic: equestrian sports, golf, track and field; coed intramural: backpacking, basketball, bicycling, climbing, cross-country running, equestrian sports, fencing, fitness, fitness walking, golf, hiking/backpacking, horseback riding, kayaking, martial arts, mountain biking, outdoor education, physical fitness, rappelling, rock climbing, ropes courses, surfing, swimming and diving, weight training, yoga. 2 PE instructors, 2 coaches, 2 athletic trainers.

Computers Computers are regularly used in economics, English, ESL, geography, history, humanities, journalism, mathematics, music, photography, SAT preparation, science, social sciences, yearbook classes. Computer resources include on-campus library services, online commercial services, Internet access, wireless campus network, Internet filtering or blocking technology. The school has a published electronic and media policy.

Contact Ms. Tracy Wilson, Director of Admission. 805-646-1423. Fax: 805-646-0362. E-mail: admission@ovs.org. Website: www.ovs.org

OLDENBURG ACADEMY

1 Twister Circle
Oldenburg, Indiana 47036

Head of School: Ms. Diane H Laake

General Information Coeducational day college-preparatory, arts, and religious studies school, affiliated with Roman Catholic Church. Grades 9–12. Founded: 1852. Setting: small town. Nearest major city is Cincinnati, OH. 23-acre campus. 3 buildings on campus. Approved or accredited by North Central Association of Colleges and Schools and Indiana Department of Education. Total enrollment: 198. Upper school average class size: 15. Upper school faculty-student ratio: 1:12. There are 180 required school days per year for Upper School students. The average school day consists of 7 hours.

Upper School Student Profile Grade 9: 61 students (28 boys, 33 girls); Grade 10: 52 students (25 boys, 27 girls); Grade 11: 51 students (22 boys, 29 girls); Grade 12: 34 students (10 boys, 24 girls). 80% of students are Roman Catholic.

Faculty School total: 17. In upper school: 8 men, 9 women; 13 have advanced degrees.

Graduation Requirements 40 hours of community service.

Special Academic Programs Advanced Placement exam preparation; honors section; ESL (8 students enrolled).

College Admission Counseling Colleges students went to include Butler University; Indiana University Bloomington; Purdue University.

Student Life Upper grades have uniform requirement, student council, honor system. Discipline rests primarily with faculty. Attendance at religious services is required.

Tuition and Aid Day student tuition: $7200. Tuition installment plan (FACTS Tuition Payment Plan). Tuition reduction for siblings, merit scholarship grants, need-based scholarship grants available. In 2013–14, 35% of upper-school students received aid; total upper-school merit-scholarship money awarded: $25,000. Total amount of financial aid awarded in 2013–14: $65,000.

Admissions Traditional secondary-level entrance grade is 9. High School Placement Test (closed version) from Scholastic Testing Service required. Deadline for receipt of application materials: none. Application fee required: $350. Interview recommended.

Athletics Interscholastic: baseball (boys), basketball (b,g), cheering (g), cross-country running (b,g), dance (b), dance team (g), football (b), physical fitness (b,g), soccer (b,g), softball (g), swimming and diving (b,g), tennis (b,g), track and field (b,g), volleyball (g), wrestling (b). 1 PE instructor, 9 coaches, 1 athletic trainer.

Computers Computer network features include on-campus library services, Internet access, wireless campus network, Internet filtering or blocking technology, one-to-one student iPad program. Campus intranet, student e-mail accounts, and computer access in designated common areas are available to students. Students grades are available online. The school has a published electronic and media policy.

Contact Mrs. Bettina Rose, Principal. 812-934-4440 Ext. 223. Fax: 812-934-4838. E-mail: brose@oldenburgacademy.org. Website: www.oldenburgacademy.org/

THE O'NEAL SCHOOL

3300 Airport Road
PO Box 290
Southern Pines, North Carolina 28388-0290

Head of School: Mr. Alan Barr

General Information Coeducational day college-preparatory school. Grades PK–12. Founded: 1971. Setting: small town. Nearest major city is Raleigh. 40-acre campus. 3 buildings on campus. Approved or accredited by Southern Association of Colleges and Schools, Southern Association of Independent Schools, and North Carolina Department of Education. Endowment: $1.6 million. Total enrollment: 415. Upper school average class size: 15. Upper school faculty-student ratio: 1:12. There are 170 required school days per year for Upper School students. Upper School students

typically attend 5 days per week. The average school day consists of 6 hours and 15 minutes.

Upper School Student Profile Grade 9: 47 students (19 boys, 28 girls); Grade 10: 37 students (13 boys, 24 girls); Grade 11: 39 students (20 boys, 19 girls); Grade 12: 35 students (18 boys, 17 girls).

Faculty School total: 54. In upper school: 9 men, 7 women; 8 have advanced degrees.

Subjects Offered Algebra, American history, American literature, art, art history, art history-AP, biology, biology-AP, calculus-AP, chemistry, community service, computer science, drama, economics, English, English language-AP, English literature, English literature-AP, environmental science, environmental science-AP, European history, European history-AP, expository writing, film, filmmaking, fine arts, French, geometry, government-AP, mathematics, photography, physical education, physics-AP, political science, pottery, pre-calculus, public speaking, science, social studies, Spanish, statistics-AP, U.S. history-AP, world history, world literature, yearbook.

Graduation Requirements Arts and fine arts (art, music, dance, drama), English, foreign language, mathematics, physical education (includes health), science, social studies (includes history), 36 hours of community service.

Special Academic Programs 13 Advanced Placement exams for which test preparation is offered; independent study; study at local college for college credit.

College Admission Counseling 41 students graduated in 2013; 40 went to college, including Appalachian State University; East Carolina University; North Carolina State University; The University of North Carolina at Chapel Hill; The University of North Carolina at Charlotte; Western Carolina University. Other: 1 entered a postgraduate year. Median SAT critical reading: 540, median SAT math: 530, median SAT writing: 510, median combined SAT: 1580. 29% scored over 600 on SAT critical reading, 30% scored over 600 on SAT math, 19% scored over 600 on SAT writing, 19% scored over 1800 on combined SAT.

Student Life Upper grades have specified standards of dress, student council, honor system. Discipline rests primarily with faculty.

Tuition and Aid Day student tuition: $15,950. Tuition installment plan (Insured Tuition Payment Plan, monthly payment plans, individually arranged payment plans). Merit scholarship grants, need-based scholarship grants available. In 2013–14, 34% of upper-school students received aid; total upper-school merit-scholarship money awarded: $47,850. Total amount of financial aid awarded in 2013–14: $465,050.

Admissions Traditional secondary-level entrance grade is 9. For fall 2013, 26 students applied for upper-level admission, 23 were accepted, 17 enrolled. Admissions testing, essay, OLSAT, Stanford Achievement Test, PSAT and SAT for applicants to grade 11 and 12, WRAT or writing sample required. Deadline for receipt of application materials: none. Application fee required: $100. On-campus interview required.

Athletics Interscholastic: baseball (boys), basketball (b,g), cheering (g), cross-country running (b,g), soccer (b,g), swimming and diving (b,g), tennis (b,g), track and field (b,g), volleyball (g); coed interscholastic: golf. 2 PE instructors, 2 coaches.

Computers Computers are regularly used in all academic classes. Computer network features include on-campus library services, Internet access, wireless campus network, Internet filtering or blocking technology, EBSCO, World Book Online. Student e-mail accounts and computer access in designated common areas are available to students. The school has a published electronic and media policy.

Contact Mrs. Alice Droppers, Director of Admissions and Financial Aid. 910-692-6920 Ext. 103. Fax: 910-692-6930. E-mail: adroppers@onealschool.org. Website: www.onealschool.org

ONEIDA BAPTIST INSTITUTE

11 Mulberry Street
Oneida, Kentucky 40972

Head of School: Mr. Larry Allen Gritton Jr.

General Information Coeducational boarding and day college-preparatory, general academic, arts, vocational, religious studies, bilingual studies, and agriculture school, affiliated with Southern Baptist Convention. Grades 6–12. Founded: 1899. Setting: rural. Nearest major city is Lexington. Students are housed in single-sex dormitories. 200-acre campus. 15 buildings on campus. Approved or accredited by The Kentucky Non-Public School Commission, The National Non-Public School Commission, and Kentucky Department of Education. Endowment: $15 million. Total enrollment: 275. Upper school average class size: 11. Upper school faculty-student ratio: 1:11. There are 174 required school days per year for Upper School students. Upper School students typically attend 5 days per week. The average school day consists of 6 hours.

Upper School Student Profile Grade 9: 42 students (23 boys, 19 girls); Grade 10: 65 students (36 boys, 29 girls); Grade 11: 50 students (27 boys, 23 girls); Grade 12: 53 students (30 boys, 23 girls). 80% of students are boarding students. 50% are state residents. 26 states are represented in upper school student body. 20% are international students. International students from China, Ethiopia, Nigeria, Republic of Korea, Thailand, and United Republic of Tanzania; 12 other countries represented in student body. 25% of students are Southern Baptist Convention.

Faculty School total: 50. In upper school: 18 men, 18 women; 10 have advanced degrees; 42 reside on campus.

Subjects Offered Agriculture, algebra, band, Bible, biology, biology-AP, calculus-AP, chemistry, child development, choir, commercial art, computers, cultural geography, drama, earth and space science, English, English-AP, ESL, geography, geometry, government, government-AP, guitar, health, language arts, life skills, literature, mathematics, physical education, physical science, piano, pre-calculus, social sciences, Spanish, stagecraft, U.S. history, U.S. history-AP, vocal ensemble, weight training, world history.

Graduation Requirements Arts and fine arts (art, music, dance, drama), Bible, computer literacy, English, foreign language, mathematics, physical education (includes health), science, social studies (includes history), field placement.

Special Academic Programs 6 Advanced Placement exams for which test preparation is offered; independent study; remedial reading and/or remedial writing; remedial math; ESL (14 students enrolled).

College Admission Counseling 46 students graduated in 2013; 43 went to college, including Berea College; Eastern Kentucky University; Lindsey Wilson College; University of Kentucky; University of the Cumberlands; Western Kentucky University. Other: 3 went to work.

Student Life Upper grades have specified standards of dress. Discipline rests primarily with faculty. Attendance at religious services is required.

Summer Programs Remediation, enrichment, advancement programs offered; session focuses on remediation and make-up courses; held on campus; accepts boys and girls; open to students from other schools. 125 students usually enrolled. 2014 schedule: June 2 to July 11. Application deadline: none.

Tuition and Aid 7-day tuition and room/board: $5750–$12,500. Tuition installment plan (monthly payment plans). Need-based scholarship grants available. In 2013–14, 100% of upper-school students received aid.

Admissions Traditional secondary-level entrance grade is 9. Deadline for receipt of application materials: none. Application fee required: $35. On-campus interview required.

Athletics Interscholastic: baseball (boys), basketball (b,g), cheering (g), cross-country running (b,g), softball (g), swimming and diving (b,g), tennis (b,g), track and field (b,g), volleyball (g); coed interscholastic: soccer. 2 PE instructors.

Computers Computers are regularly used in commercial art classes. Computer resources include Internet access, Internet filtering or blocking technology. The school has a published electronic and media policy.

Contact Admissions. 606-847-4111 Ext. 233. Fax: 606-847-4496. E-mail: admissions@oneidaschool.org. Website: www.oneidaschool.org

OREGON EPISCOPAL SCHOOL

6300 Southwest Nicol Road
Portland, Oregon 97223-7566

Head of School: Mrs. Mo Copeland

General Information Coeducational boarding and day college-preparatory, arts, religious studies, technology, and science school, affiliated with Episcopal Church. Boarding grades 9–12, day grades PK–12. Founded: 1869. Setting: suburban. Students are housed in single-sex dormitories. 59-acre campus. 9 buildings on campus. Approved or accredited by National Association of Episcopal Schools, Northwest Accreditation Commission, Northwest Association of Independent Schools, Northwest Association of Schools and Colleges, and Oregon Department of Education. Member of National Association of Independent Schools and Secondary School Admission Test Board. Endowment: $20.9 million. Total enrollment: 858. Upper school average class size: 15. Upper school faculty-student ratio: 1:7. There are 175 required school days per year for Upper School students. Upper School students typically attend 5 days per week. The average school day consists of 7 hours.

Upper School Student Profile Grade 9: 73 students (39 boys, 34 girls); Grade 10: 84 students (47 boys, 37 girls); Grade 11: 79 students (38 boys, 41 girls); Grade 12: 80 students (44 boys, 36 girls). 18% of students are boarding students. 83% are state residents. 3 states are represented in upper school student body. 12% are international students. International students from Canada, China, Republic of Korea, Taiwan, Thailand, and Viet Nam; 1 other country represented in student body. 11% of students are members of Episcopal Church.

Faculty School total: 121. In upper school: 19 men, 28 women; 36 have advanced degrees; 12 reside on campus.

Subjects Offered Advanced chemistry, advanced math, Advanced Placement courses, algebra, American history, American literature, American studies, anatomy, anatomy and physiology, Arabic studies, art, Asian history, astronomy, athletic training, Basic programming, biology, Buddhism, calculus, calculus-AP, ceramics, chemistry, Chinese, chorus, Christian studies, Christianity, college counseling, college planning, college writing, community service, computer graphics, computer science, computer science-AP, constitutional law, creative writing, dance, debate, discrete mathematics, drama, drawing, driver education, East Asian history, ecology, electronics, engineering, English, English literature, environmental science, ESL, ESL, European history, fencing, film, film and literature, filmmaking, fine arts, finite math, foreign language, foreign policy, French, French language-AP, French-AP, freshman seminar, functions, gardening, geology, geometry, graphic arts, graphic design, graphics, health, health and wellness, history, history of China and Japan, history of ideas, history of rock and roll, history-AP, human anatomy, human relations, human sexuality, humanities, independent study, international affairs, international relations, jazz band, jazz dance, jazz ensemble, journalism, literature, marine biology, marine ecology, mathematics, mathematics-AP, microbiology, model United Nations, modern Chinese history, music, music history, music technology, musical productions, musical theater, newspaper,

painting, personal finance, personal fitness, philosophy, photography, photojournalism, physical education, physical fitness, physics, playwriting and directing, poetry, pre-algebra, pre-calculus, psychology, psychology-AP, religion, religion and culture, research, science, science project, science research, service learning/internship, sex education, sexuality, Shakespeare, social studies, Spanish, Spanish language-AP, Spanish literature, Spanish-AP, speech, stagecraft, statistics, statistics-AP, tennis, theater, theater design and production, theology, track and field, trigonometry, U.S. history, U.S. history-AP, urban studies, video and animation, video film production, visual arts, vocal ensemble, vocal music, weight training, weightlifting, wellness, wilderness education, wilderness experience, world history, world literature, world religions, world religions, world wide web design, yearbook, yoga, zoology.

Graduation Requirements Arts and fine arts (art, music, dance, drama), electives, English, foreign language, health education, humanities, mathematics, philosophy, physical education (includes health), religion (includes Bible studies and theology), science, service learning/internship, U.S. history, Winterim, College Decisions (for juniors).

Special Academic Programs Advanced Placement exam preparation; honors section; independent study; term-away projects; study abroad; academic accommodation for the gifted; ESL (9 students enrolled).

College Admission Counseling 67 students graduated in 2013; all went to college, including New York University; Oregon State University; Santa Clara University; Stanford University; University of Southern California; University of Washington. Median SAT critical reading: 620, median SAT math: 690, median SAT writing: 650, median combined SAT: 1980, median composite ACT: 29. 60% scored over 600 on SAT critical reading, 78% scored over 600 on SAT math, 65% scored over 600 on SAT writing, 74% scored over 1800 on combined SAT, 66% scored over 26 on composite ACT.

Student Life Upper grades have specified standards of dress, student council. Discipline rests equally with students and faculty. Attendance at religious services is required.

Summer Programs Remediation, enrichment, advancement, sports, art/fine arts, computer instruction programs offered; session focuses on a variety of academic, sports, and artistic enrichment programs; held both on and off campus; held at local/regional trips are offered through summer programs for experiential education and science and research: marine ecology trip on Oregon Coast, backpacking on Mt. Hood, etc.; accepts boys and girls; open to students from other schools. 2,200 students usually enrolled. 2014 schedule: June 17 to August 23.

Tuition and Aid Day student tuition: $26,544; 7-day tuition and room/board: $50,709. Tuition installment plan (Insured Tuition Payment Plan, monthly payment plans). Need-based scholarship grants available. In 2013–14, 17% of upper-school students received aid. Total amount of financial aid awarded in 2013–14: $801,155.

Admissions Traditional secondary-level entrance grade is 9. For fall 2013, 162 students applied for upper-level admission, 41 were accepted, 25 enrolled. SSAT or TOEFL required. Deadline for receipt of application materials: January 22. Application fee required: $75. Interview required.

Athletics Interscholastic: alpine skiing (boys, girls), basketball (b,g), cross-country running (b,g), fencing (b,g), golf (b,g), lacrosse (b,g), skiing (downhill) (b,g), soccer (b,g), tennis (b,g), track and field (b,g), volleyball (g); intramural: backpacking (b,g), hiking/backpacking (b,g), outdoor activities (b,g), snowboarding (b,g), yoga (b,g); coed intramural: outdoor education, physical fitness, physical training, rock climbing, ropes courses. 2 PE instructors, 47 coaches, 1 athletic trainer.

Computers Computers are regularly used in art, English, foreign language, history, humanities, independent study, mathematics, music, philosophy, religion, science, social sciences, technology classes. Computer network features include on-campus library services, online commercial services, Internet access, wireless campus network, Internet filtering or blocking technology, one-to-one laptop program. Campus intranet, student e-mail accounts, and computer access in designated common areas are available to students. Students grades are available online. The school has a published electronic and media policy.

Contact Ms. Marcy Morris, Admissions Associate. 503-768-3115. Fax: 503-768-3140. E-mail: admit@oes.edu. Website: www.oes.edu

ORINDA ACADEMY

19 Altarinda Road
Orinda, California 94563-2602

Head of School: Ron Graydon

General Information Coeducational day college-preparatory, general academic, and arts school. Grades 7–12. Founded: 1982. Setting: suburban. Nearest major city is Walnut Creek. 1-acre campus. 2 buildings on campus. Approved or accredited by East Bay Independent Schools Association, The College Board, and Western Association of Schools and Colleges. Total enrollment: 90. Upper school average class size: 10. Upper school faculty-student ratio: 1:9. There are 180 required school days per year for Upper School students. Upper School students typically attend 5 days per week. The average school day consists of 6 hours and 30 minutes.

Upper School Student Profile Grade 9: 18 students (13 boys, 5 girls); Grade 10: 20 students (11 boys, 9 girls); Grade 11: 18 students (12 boys, 6 girls); Grade 12: 25 students (10 boys, 15 girls).

Faculty School total: 19. In upper school: 8 men, 11 women; 9 have advanced degrees.

Subjects Offered Algebra, American history, American literature, American sign language, art, basketball, biology, calculus, chemistry, community service, computer graphics, computer multimedia, computer music, contemporary issues, creative writing, dance, drama, earth science, economics, English, English literature, English literature and composition-AP, ensembles, environmental science, ESL, European history, film history, fine arts, French, geography, geometry, government/civics, health, history, history of music, introduction to theater, journalism, mathematics, music, music performance, musical productions, performing arts, physical education, physics, science, social studies, Spanish, Spanish language-AP, theater, trigonometry, visual arts, yearbook.

Graduation Requirements Algebra, biology, civics, composition, economics, English, foreign language, geometry, physical education (includes health), science, trigonometry, U.S. history, visual and performing arts. Community service is required.

Special Academic Programs 2 Advanced Placement exams for which test preparation is offered; honors section; accelerated programs; academic accommodation for the gifted; ESL (2 students enrolled).

College Admission Counseling 16 students graduated in 2013; 14 went to college, including American University; Lewis & Clark College; Saint Mary's College of California; Scripps College; Seattle University; Willamette University. Other: 1 went to work, 1 entered military service. Mean SAT critical reading: 533, mean SAT math: 504, mean SAT writing: 534, mean combined SAT: 1571. 20% scored over 600 on SAT critical reading, 13% scored over 600 on SAT math, 27% scored over 600 on SAT writing, 7% scored over 1800 on combined SAT.

Student Life Upper grades have specified standards of dress, student council, honor system. Discipline rests primarily with faculty.

Summer Programs Remediation, enrichment, advancement programs offered; session focuses on academics; held on campus; accepts boys and girls; open to students from other schools. 50 students usually enrolled. 2014 schedule: June 23 to August 8. Application deadline: none.

Tuition and Aid Day student tuition: $31,975. Tuition installment plan (FACTS Tuition Payment Plan). Tuition reduction for siblings, need-based scholarship grants available. In 2013–14, 25% of upper-school students received aid. Total amount of financial aid awarded in 2013–14: $400,000.

Admissions Traditional secondary-level entrance grade is 9. For fall 2013, 70 students applied for upper-level admission, 46 were accepted, 26 enrolled. ISEE, SSAT or Star-9 required. Deadline for receipt of application materials: January 16. Application fee required: $75. On-campus interview required.

Athletics Interscholastic: baseball (boys), basketball (b,g); coed interscholastic: soccer; coed intramural: soccer, softball. 1 PE instructor, 1 coach.

Computers Computers are regularly used in English, French, media arts, social sciences, Spanish, writing, yearbook classes. Computer network features include Internet access, Internet filtering or blocking technology. Student e-mail accounts and computer access in designated common areas are available to students. The school has a published electronic and media policy.

Contact Laurel Evans, Director of Admissions. 925-254-7553 Ext. 305. Fax: 925-254-4768. E-mail: laurel@orindaacademy.org. Website: www.orindaacademy.org

THE ORME SCHOOL

HC 63, Box 3040
Mayer, Arizona 86333

Head of School: Dr. Mike Gemma

General Information Coeducational boarding and day college-preparatory, arts, bilingual studies, ESL program, and horsemanship school. Grades 8–PG. Founded: 1929. Setting: rural. Nearest major city is Phoenix. Students are housed in single-sex dormitories. 360-acre campus. 30 buildings on campus. Approved or accredited by North Central Association of Colleges and Schools, The Association of Boarding Schools, and Arizona Department of Education. Member of National Association of Independent Schools and Secondary School Admission Test Board. Endowment: $1 million. Upper school average class size: 12. Upper school faculty-student ratio: 1:6. There are 179 required school days per year for Upper School students. Upper School students typically attend 5 days per week. The average school day consists of 7 hours.

Upper School Student Profile Grade 8: 9 students (5 boys, 4 girls); Grade 9: 22 students (12 boys, 10 girls); Grade 10: 27 students (16 boys, 11 girls); Grade 11: 26 students (14 boys, 12 girls); Grade 12: 23 students (14 boys, 9 girls); Postgraduate: 2 students (1 boy, 1 girl). 95% of students are boarding students. 60% are state residents. 15 states are represented in upper school student body. 33% are international students. International students from China, Colombia, Germany, Norway, Russian Federation, and Turkey; 5 other countries represented in student body.

Faculty School total: 25. In upper school: 10 men, 12 women; 15 have advanced degrees; 20 reside on campus.

Subjects Offered Advanced Placement courses, advanced TOEFL/grammar, algebra, American history, American history-AP, American literature, American literature-AP, ancient world history, art, art history, astronomy, band, biology, British literature (honors), calculus, calculus-AP, ceramics, chemistry, choir, college admission preparation, college counseling, community service, computer programming, computer science, creative writing, drama, drama performance, ecology, English, English

language and composition-AP, English literature, English literature and composition-AP, European history, European history-AP, fine arts, French, geography, geology, geometry, government, grammar, history, history of music, honors English, honors U.S. history, humanities, Latin, mathematics, music, performing arts, photography, physics, physics-AP, psychology, science, social sciences, social studies, Spanish, statistics-AP, student government, theater, trigonometry, U.S. history, U.S. history-AP, weightlifting, world cultures, world history, world literature, writing.

Graduation Requirements Advanced Placement courses, arts and fine arts (art, music, dance, drama), computer science, English, equine science, ESL, foreign language, humanities, mathematics, science, social sciences, social studies (includes history), students must participate in annual outdoor programs such as Fall outing and Caravan. Community service is required.

Special Academic Programs Advanced Placement exam preparation; independent study; ESL (20 students enrolled).

College Admission Counseling 33 students graduated in 2013; 22 went to college, including Arizona State University; Boston University; Columbia University; Cornell University; Dartmouth College; Northern Arizona University. Other: 1 went to work. Mean SAT critical reading: 500, mean SAT math: 533, mean SAT writing: 495, mean combined SAT: 1528, mean composite ACT: 21. 19% scored over 600 on SAT critical reading, 12% scored over 1800 on combined SAT, 9% scored over 26 on composite ACT.

Student Life Upper grades have specified standards of dress, student council, honor system. Discipline rests equally with students and faculty.

Summer Programs Remediation, advancement, ESL programs offered; session focuses on advancement; held on campus; accepts boys and girls; open to students from other schools. 12 students usually enrolled. 2014 schedule: June 27 to July 25. Application deadline: none.

Tuition and Aid Day student tuition: $20,650; 5-day tuition and room/board: $36,000; 7-day tuition and room/board: $41,400. Tuition installment plan (individually arranged payment plans). Need-based scholarship grants available. In 2013–14, 40% of upper-school students received aid. Total amount of financial aid awarded in 2013–14: $1,200,000.

Admissions Traditional secondary-level entrance grade is 9. For fall 2013, 91 students applied for upper-level admission, 66 were accepted, 33 enrolled. PSAT and SAT for applicants to grade 11 and 12, SSAT, standardized test scores, TOEFL or SLEP and writing sample required. Deadline for receipt of application materials: February 15. Application fee required: $50. Interview required.

Athletics Interscholastic: baseball (boys), basketball (b,g), cross-country running (b,g), equestrian sports (b,g), football (b), pom squad (g), rodeo (b,g), softball (g), tennis (b,g), track and field (b,g), volleyball (g); intramural: aerobics/dance (g), climbing (b,g), fitness (b,g), physical training (b,g), rappelling (b,g), rock climbing (b,g), rodeo (b,g), strength & conditioning (b,g), tennis (b,g), wall climbing (b,g), weight lifting (b,g), weight training (b,g), wilderness (b,g), wilderness survival (b,g), wrestling (b); coed interscholastic: equestrian sports, horseback riding, rodeo; coed intramural: backpacking, climbing, fitness, fitness walking, hiking/backpacking, horseback riding, mountain biking, mountaineering, outdoor activities, outdoor adventure, outdoor recreation, outdoor skills, outdoors, physical training, power lifting, rappelling, rock climbing, rodeo, skiing (downhill), snowboarding, soccer, strength & conditioning, walking, wall climbing, weight lifting, weight training, wilderness, wilderness survival.

Computers Computers are regularly used in all academic classes. Computer network features include on-campus library services, Internet access, wireless campus network, Internet filtering or blocking technology. Campus intranet and computer access in designated common areas are available to students. Students grades are available online. The school has a published electronic and media policy.

Contact Ms. Margaret 'Meg' Casey, Director of Admission and Financial Aid. 928-632-7601. Fax: 928-632-7605. E-mail: mcasey@ormeschool.org. Website: www.ormeschool.org

OUR LADY OF MERCY ACADEMY

1001 Main Road
Newfield, New Jersey 08344

Head of School: Sr. Grace Marie Scandale

General Information Girls' day college-preparatory, arts, religious studies, bilingual studies, and technology school, affiliated with Roman Catholic Church. Grades 9–12. Founded: 1962. Setting: rural. Nearest major city is Vineland. 58-acre campus. 2 buildings on campus. Approved or accredited by British Accreditation Council, Middle States Association of Colleges and Schools, and National Catholic Education Association. Endowment: $255,000. Total enrollment: 150. Upper school average class size: 20. Upper school faculty-student ratio: 1:11. There are 180 required school days per year for Upper School students. Upper School students typically attend 5 days per week. The average school day consists of 6 hours and 30 minutes.

Upper School Student Profile Grade 9: 27 students (27 girls); Grade 10: 38 students (38 girls); Grade 11: 29 students (29 girls); Grade 12: 44 students (44 girls); Postgraduate: 138 students (138 girls). 90% of students are Roman Catholic.

Faculty School total: 22. In upper school: 22 women; 10 have advanced degrees.

Subjects Offered Algebra, American history, American literature, art, biology, botany, British literature (honors), career and personal planning, Catholic belief and practice, chemistry, choral music, chorus, Christian ethics, Christian scripture, Christian testament, Christianity, college counseling, computer technologies, CPR, current events, death and loss, driver education, economics, electronic publishing, English literature, first aid, food and nutrition, French, graphic design, honors algebra, honors geometry, Middle Eastern history, physics, pre-calculus, probability and statistics, psychology, publications, religion, social justice, sociology, technology, Western civilization.

Graduation Requirements Algebra, biology, chemistry, English, geometry, physical education (includes health), religion (includes Bible studies and theology), religious studies, technology, U.S. history, Western civilization.

Special Academic Programs Honors section; study at local college for college credit.

College Admission Counseling 33 students graduated in 2013; all went to college, including La Salle University; Rutgers, The State University of New Jersey, New Brunswick; Saint Joseph's University; Seton Hall University; The University of Scranton; University of Pennsylvania.

Student Life Upper grades have uniform requirement, student council, honor system. Discipline rests primarily with faculty. Attendance at religious services is required.

Tuition and Aid Day student tuition: $10,544. Tuition installment plan (SMART Tuition Payment Plan, monthly payment plans, individually arranged payment plans). Tuition reduction for siblings, merit scholarship grants, need-based scholarship grants, paying campus jobs available. In 2013–14, 15% of upper-school students received aid; total upper-school merit-scholarship money awarded: $34,500. Total amount of financial aid awarded in 2013–14: $35,000.

Admissions Traditional secondary-level entrance grade is 9. For fall 2013, 35 students applied for upper-level admission, 26 were accepted, 26 enrolled. High School Placement Test (closed version) from Scholastic Testing Service required. Deadline for receipt of application materials: none. Application fee required: $200.

Athletics Interscholastic: basketball, cheering, crew, lacrosse, soccer, softball, strength & conditioning, swimming and diving, tennis, track and field, volleyball; intramural: badminton, basketball, flag football, golf, gymnastics, physical fitness, soccer, softball, synchronized swimming, volleyball. 2 PE instructors, 12 coaches.

Computers Computers are regularly used in all academic, career exploration, college planning, creative writing, graphic design, graphics, library, library skills, photography, publications, research skills, technology, typing, Web site design, word processing, yearbook classes. Computer network features include on-campus library services, Internet access, wireless campus network, Internet filtering or blocking technology. Computer access in designated common areas is available to students. Students grades are available online. The school has a published electronic and media policy.

Contact Sr. Grace Marie Scandale, Principal. 856-697-2008. Fax: 856-697-2887. E-mail: srgrace@olmanj.org. Website: www.olmanj.org

OUR LADY OF MOUNT CARMEL HIGH SCHOOL

1706 Old Eastern Avenue
Baltimore, Maryland 21221-2203

Head of School: Mr. Christopher Ashby

General Information Coeducational day college-preparatory, arts, religious studies, and technology school, affiliated with Roman Catholic Church. Grades PK–12. Founded: 1959. Setting: suburban. 1 building on campus. Approved or accredited by Middle States Association of Colleges and Schools and Maryland Department of Education. Upper school average class size: 16. Upper school faculty-student ratio: 1:16. There are 182 required school days per year for Upper School students. Upper School students typically attend 5 days per week. The average school day consists of 6 hours and 30 minutes.

Faculty School total: 82.

Special Academic Programs Advanced Placement exam preparation; honors section; study at local college for college credit.

Student Life Upper grades have uniform requirement, student council, honor system. Discipline rests primarily with faculty. Attendance at religious services is required.

Summer Programs Enrichment, sports programs offered; held on campus; accepts boys and girls; open to students from other schools.

Tuition and Aid Tuition installment plan (FACTS Tuition Payment Plan). Tuition reduction for siblings, merit scholarship grants, need-based scholarship grants, paying campus jobs available.

Admissions High School Placement Test (closed version) from Scholastic Testing Service required. Deadline for receipt of application materials: none. No application fee required. Interview required.

Athletics Interscholastic: baseball (boys), basketball (b,g), football (b), soccer (b,g), volleyball (g), wrestling (b); coed interscholastic: aerobics, aerobics/dance, ballet, cheering, dance, golf. 2 PE instructors, 8 coaches, 1 athletic trainer.

Computers Computer network features include on-campus library services, Internet access. The school has a published electronic and media policy.

Contact Mrs. Laura Cummins, Admissions. 410-238-1163. Fax: 410-686-2361. E-mail: lcummins@olmcmd.org. Website: www.olmcmd.org

OUT-OF-DOOR-ACADEMY

5950 Deer Drive
Sarasota, Florida 34240

Head of School: Mr. David Mahler

General Information Coeducational day college-preparatory school. Grades PK–12. Founded: 1924. Setting: suburban. Nearest major city is Tampa. 85-acre campus. 9 buildings on campus. Approved or accredited by Florida Council of Independent Schools and National Independent Private Schools Association. Member of National Association of Independent Schools. Endowment: $10 million. Total enrollment: 680. Upper school average class size: 16. Upper school faculty-student ratio: 1:7. There are 172 required school days per year for Upper School students. Upper School students typically attend 5 days per week. The average school day consists of 7 hours.

Upper School Student Profile Grade 9: 76 students (44 boys, 32 girls); Grade 10: 53 students (27 boys, 26 girls); Grade 11: 64 students (26 boys, 38 girls); Grade 12: 54 students (27 boys, 27 girls).

Faculty School total: 88. In upper school: 13 men, 23 women; 20 have advanced degrees.

Subjects Offered Advanced Placement courses, advanced studio art-AP, algebra, American history-AP, art history, biology, biology-AP, British literature, calculus, calculus-AP, chemistry, chemistry-AP, college counseling, computers, drama, drama performance, dramatic arts, English, English composition, English language and composition-AP, English literature, English literature and composition-AP, English-AP, European history-AP, expository writing, French, French language-AP, geometry, graphic design, health and wellness, history-AP, honors algebra, honors geometry, Latin, Latin-AP, literature, literature and composition-AP, music, newspaper, photography, portfolio art, robotics, Spanish, Spanish language-AP, studio art, studio art-AP, U.S. government, U.S. history, U.S. history-AP, women's studies, world cultures, world literature, world studies, yearbook, zoology.

Graduation Requirements Arts and fine arts (art, music, dance, drama), electives, English, foreign language, health, history, mathematics, performing arts, personal fitness, science. Community service is required.

Special Academic Programs 21 Advanced Placement exams for which test preparation is offered; honors section; independent study.

College Admission Counseling 52 students graduated in 2013; all went to college, including Duke University; Florida State University; New York University; Rollins College; Stanford University; University of Florida. Mean SAT critical reading: 611, mean SAT math: 611, mean SAT writing: 612, mean combined SAT: 1222.

Student Life Upper grades have specified standards of dress, student council, honor system. Discipline rests equally with students and faculty.

Summer Programs Enrichment, sports, art/fine arts programs offered; held on campus; accepts boys and girls; open to students from other schools. 150 students usually enrolled. 2014 schedule: June 4 to August 10. Application deadline: May.

Tuition and Aid Day student tuition: $19,700. Tuition installment plan (FACTS Tuition Payment Plan). Need-based scholarship grants, faculty/staff tuition remission available. In 2013–14, 30% of upper-school students received aid. Total amount of financial aid awarded in 2013–14: $869,850.

Admissions Traditional secondary-level entrance grade is 9. For fall 2013, 76 students applied for upper-level admission, 42 were accepted, 32 enrolled. ERB or SSAT required. Deadline for receipt of application materials: March 1. Application fee required: $100. Interview required.

Athletics Interscholastic: baseball (boys), basketball (b,g), cheering (g), cross-country running (b,g), football (b), golf (b,g), independent competitive sports (b,g), lacrosse (b,g), soccer (b,g), softball (g), swimming and diving (b,g), tennis (b,g), track and field (b,g), volleyball (g); intramural: fitness (b,g); coed interscholastic: sailing; coed intramural: physical fitness, physical training, strength & conditioning, weight training. 4 PE instructors, 35 coaches, 1 athletic trainer.

Computers Computers are regularly used in all academic, computer applications, English, foreign language, French, graphic design, history, Latin, mathematics, newspaper, science, senior seminar, social studies, Spanish, yearbook classes. Computer network features include on-campus library services, online commercial services, Internet access, wireless campus network, Internet filtering or blocking technology, digital video production. Campus intranet, student e-mail accounts, and computer access in designated common areas are available to students. Students grades are available online. The school has a published electronic and media policy.

Contact Mr. Michael Salmon, Director of Middle and Upper School Admissions. 941-554-5955. Fax: 941-907-1251. E-mail: msalmon@oda.edu. Website: www.oda.edu

THE OVERLAKE SCHOOL

20301 Northeast 108th Street
Redmond, Washington 98053

Head of School: Matthew P. Horvat

General Information Coeducational day college-preparatory school. Grades 5–12. Founded: 1967. Setting: rural. Nearest major city is Seattle. 75-acre campus. 22 buildings on campus. Approved or accredited by Northwest Accreditation Commission, Northwest Association of Independent Schools, The College Board, and Washington Department of Education. Member of National Association of Independent Schools. Endowment: $15 million. Total enrollment: 534. Upper school average class size: 14.

Upper school faculty-student ratio: 1:9. There are 173 required school days per year for Upper School students. Upper School students typically attend 5 days per week. The average school day consists of 6 hours.

Upper School Student Profile Grade 9: 80 students (43 boys, 37 girls); Grade 10: 79 students (38 boys, 41 girls); Grade 11: 74 students (37 boys, 37 girls); Grade 12: 71 students (34 boys, 37 girls).

Faculty School total: 62. In upper school: 21 men, 27 women; 30 have advanced degrees.

Subjects Offered 3-dimensional art, 3-dimensional design, acting, advanced chemistry, Advanced Placement courses, aerobics, African studies, algebra, American history, American literature, anatomy and physiology, art, art history-AP, arts, athletic training, athletics, backpacking, band, Basic programming, bioethics, biology-AP, calculus, calculus-AP, career/college preparation, ceramics, chamber groups, chemistry, chemistry-AP, Chinese, choir, chorus, college admission preparation, community service, computer graphics, computer programming, computer science-AP, concert band, concert choir, constitutional history of U.S., constitutional law, creative arts, drama, drama performance, drawing, English, English literature, English literature and composition-AP, English literature-AP, fine arts, fitness, foreign language, forensics, French, French language-AP, geometry, global issues, graphic design, health, Holocaust and other genocides, honors algebra, honors U.S. history, industrial arts, instrumental music, integrated science, Japanese, jazz, jazz band, jazz ensemble, lab science, Latin, Latin-AP, life skills, literature, mathematics, metalworking, Middle East, modern history, music, music theater, musical productions, orchestra, outdoor education, painting, participation in sports, performing arts, personal fitness, photography, physical education, physics-AP, pre-calculus, programming, psychology, science, senior project, Spanish, Spanish language-AP, Spanish literature-AP, sports conditioning, sports medicine, stage design, stagecraft, statistics-AP, studio art, theater, theater arts, traditional camping, U.S. history, video film production, vocal music, woodworking, world history, world literature, yearbook.

Graduation Requirements Arts and fine arts (art, music, dance, drama), English, foreign language, history, lab science, mathematics, outdoor education, physical education (includes health), senior project, annual Project Week, 2 co-curricular activities. Community service is required.

Special Academic Programs 14 Advanced Placement exams for which test preparation is offered; honors section; independent study.

College Admission Counseling 66 students graduated in 2013; all went to college, including Gonzaga University; Santa Clara University; Scripps College; University of Southern California; University of Washington. Median SAT critical reading: 665, median SAT math: 695, median SAT writing: 675, median composite ACT: 30. 82% scored over 600 on SAT critical reading, 91% scored over 600 on SAT math, 87% scored over 600 on SAT writing.

Student Life Upper grades have student council. Discipline rests equally with students and faculty.

Summer Programs Sports programs offered; session focuses on skill-building sports camps; held both on and off campus; held at sports programs are on campus; outdoor program trips are in the mountains, etc.; accepts boys and girls; not open to students from other schools. 75 students usually enrolled. 2014 schedule: June 9 to August 15. Application deadline: June 9.

Tuition and Aid Day student tuition: $28,065. Tuition installment plan (10-payment schedule). Need-based scholarship grants, 50% tuition remission for faculty and staff, Malone Scholarship, Gibson Scholarship available. In 2013–14, 18% of upper-school students received aid. Total amount of financial aid awarded in 2013–14: $675,904.

Admissions Traditional secondary-level entrance grade is 9. For fall 2013, 72 students applied for upper-level admission, 31 were accepted, 21 enrolled. ISEE or SSAT required. Deadline for receipt of application materials: January 14. Application fee required: $50. Interview required.

Athletics Interscholastic: baseball (boys), basketball (b,g), cross-country running (b,g), golf (b,g), lacrosse (b,g), soccer (b,g), tennis (b,g), ultimate Frisbee (b,g), volleyball (g); intramural: basketball (b,g), physical fitness (b,g), strength & conditioning (b,g), weight lifting (b,g), weight training (b,g); coed interscholastic: squash, tennis; coed intramural: backpacking, canoeing/kayaking, climbing, fitness, hiking/backpacking, kayaking, mountain biking, mountaineering, outdoor activities, outdoor education, outdoor skills, physical fitness, physical training, rafting, rappelling, rock climbing, ropes courses, skiing (downhill), snowshoeing, table tennis, wall climbing, wilderness, yoga. 4 PE instructors, 45 coaches, 2 athletic trainers.

Computers Computers are regularly used in all classes. Computer network features include on-campus library services, online commercial services, Internet access, wireless campus network. Campus intranet and computer access in designated common areas are available to students. Students grades are available online. The school has a published electronic and media policy.

Contact Lori Maughan, Director of Admission and Financial Aid. 425-868-1000. Fax: 425-868-5771. E-mail: lmaughan@overlake.org. Website: www.overlake.org

THE OXFORD ACADEMY

1393 Boston Post Road
Westbrook, Connecticut 06498-0685

Head of School: Philip B. Cocchiola

General Information Boys' boarding college-preparatory, general academic, arts, bilingual studies, and ESL school. Grades 9–PG. Founded: 1906. Setting: small town. Nearest major city is New Haven. Students are housed in single-sex dormitories. 13-acre campus. 8 buildings on campus. Approved or accredited by Connecticut Association of Independent Schools, New England Association of Schools and Colleges, The Association of Boarding Schools, and Connecticut Department of Education. Member of National Association of Independent Schools and Secondary School Admission Test Board. Endowment: $250,000. Total enrollment: 38. Upper school average class size: 1. Upper school faculty-student ratio: 1:1.

Upper School Student Profile Grade 9: 4 students (4 boys); Grade 10: 5 students (5 boys); Grade 11: 10 students (10 boys); Grade 12: 17 students (17 boys). 100% of students are boarding students. 35% are state residents. 8 states are represented in upper school student body. 33% are international students. International students from Bahamas, Bermuda, France, Mexico, Republic of Korea, and Saudi Arabia.

Faculty School total: 22. In upper school: 15 men, 7 women; 10 have advanced degrees; 12 reside on campus.

Subjects Offered Algebra, American history, American literature, anatomy, astronomy, biology, botany, calculus, chemistry, creative writing, earth science, ecology, economics, English, English literature, environmental science, ESL, European history, expository writing, French, geography, geology, geometry, German, government/civics, grammar, history, Latin, marine biology, mathematics, oceanography, paleontology, philosophy, physical education, physics, physiology, psychology, science, social studies, sociology, Spanish, study skills, trigonometry, world history, world literature, writing, zoology.

Graduation Requirements English, foreign language, mathematics, science, social studies (includes history). Community service is required.

Special Academic Programs Advanced Placement exam preparation; honors section; accelerated programs; independent study; academic accommodation for the gifted; remedial reading and/or remedial writing; remedial math; special instructional classes for students with mild ADD and learning differences; ESL (6 students enrolled).

College Admission Counseling 17 students graduated in 2012; all went to college, including Bucknell University; Georgia Southern University; Lynn University; Rhode Island School of Design; Suffolk University; Wheaton College. 20% scored over 600 on SAT critical reading, 20% scored over 600 on SAT math, 20% scored over 600 on SAT writing.

Student Life Upper grades have specified standards of dress, student council, honor system. Discipline rests equally with students and faculty.

Tuition and Aid 7-day tuition and room/board: $54,900. Tuition installment plan (monthly payment plans, individually arranged payment plans). Tuition reduction for siblings, need-based scholarship grants available. In 2012–13, 1% of upper-school students received aid.

Admissions For fall 2012, 22 students applied for upper-level admission, 19 were accepted, 13 enrolled. SLEP for foreign students, Stanford Achievement Test, Otis-Lennon School Ability Test, TOEFL, WISC or WAIS or Woodcock-Johnson required. Deadline for receipt of application materials: none. Application fee required: $65. Interview recommended.

Athletics Interscholastic: basketball, soccer, tennis; intramural: basketball, flag football, Frisbee, golf, hiking/backpacking, paint ball, physical fitness, power lifting, roller blading, running, sailing, skateboarding, strength & conditioning, table tennis, tennis, ultimate Frisbee, walking, weight lifting, weight training. 6 coaches.

Computers Computers are regularly used in mathematics classes. Computer network features include Internet access. Student e-mail accounts are available to students. The school has a published electronic and media policy.

Contact Mrs. Patricia Davis, Director of Admissions. 860-399-6247 Ext. 100. Fax: 860-399-6805. E-mail: admissions@oxfordacademy.net. Website: www.oxfordacademy.net

PACIFIC ACADEMY

679 Encinitas Boulevard
Suite 205
Encinitas, California 92024

Head of School: Dr. Erika Sanchez

General Information Coeducational day college-preparatory and arts school; primarily serves students with learning disabilities, individuals with Attention Deficit Disorder, and dyslexic students. Grades 7–12. Founded: 1997. Setting: small town. Nearest major city is San Diego. 1 building on campus. Approved or accredited by Western Association of Schools and Colleges and California Department of Education. Languages of instruction: English and Spanish. Total enrollment: 21. Upper school average class size: 6. Upper school faculty-student ratio: 1:5.

Faculty School total: 5. In upper school: 3 men, 2 women; 4 have advanced degrees.

Subjects Offered Algebra, American government, American literature, American studies, art history, biology, business mathematics, chemistry, computer applications, earth science, economics, English, ethnic studies, general math, geography, geometry, history, language arts, life science, literature, physical science, physics, pre-algebra, pre-calculus, Spanish, U.S. history, world history, world literature.

Graduation Requirements Arts and fine arts (art, music, dance, drama), computer studies, English, foreign language, mathematics, physical education (includes health), practical arts, science, social studies (includes history), community service hours in 11th and 12th grade.

Special Academic Programs Advanced Placement exam preparation; honors section; accelerated programs; academic accommodation for the gifted.

College Admission Counseling 5 students graduated in 2012.

Student Life Upper grades have honor system. Discipline rests primarily with faculty.

Tuition and Aid Day student tuition: $13,600–$15,000. Tuition installment plan (monthly payment plans). Tuition reduction for siblings available. In 2012–13, 5% of upper-school students received aid.

Admissions Traditional secondary-level entrance grade is 10. California Achievement Test required. Deadline for receipt of application materials: none. Application fee required: $50. On-campus interview required.

Athletics 1 PE instructor.

Computers Computers are regularly used in all academic, yearbook classes. Computer network features include online commercial services, Internet access, wireless campus network.

Contact Ms. Annie Chang, Director of Admissions. 760-634-1188. Fax: 760-436-5718. E-mail: achang@pacificacademy.org. Website: www.pacificacademy.org

PACIFIC CREST COMMUNITY SCHOOL

116 Northeast 29th Street
Portland, Oregon 97232

Head of School: Becky Lukens

General Information Coeducational day college-preparatory and arts school. Grades 6–12. Founded: 1993. Setting: urban. 1 building on campus. Approved or accredited by Northwest Accreditation Commission, Northwest Association of Schools and Colleges, and Oregon Department of Education. Total enrollment: 85. Upper school average class size: 10. Upper school faculty-student ratio: 1:9. There are 180 required school days per year for Upper School students. Upper School students typically attend 5 days per week. The average school day consists of 6 hours.

Faculty School total: 14. In upper school: 6 men, 8 women; 11 have advanced degrees.

Subjects Offered Acting, advanced math, African drumming, algebra, American government, American history, American literature, animal behavior, anthropology, art history, Asian history, bioethics, botany, calculus, cell biology, chemistry, civil war history, comparative religion, computer applications, creative writing, cultural criticism, current events, drama, drawing, ecology, economics, English literature, entomology, ethics, European history, filmmaking, foreign language, geometry, government, health, history of mathematics, HTML design, Japanese studies, linear algebra, literature by women, logic, marine biology, medieval history, Pacific Island studies, personal finance, philosophy, physical education, physics, play/screen writing, pre-algebra, pre-calculus, printmaking, probability and statistics, psychology, public speaking, SAT preparation, science fiction, senior seminar, service learning/internship, set design, Shakespeare, short story, sociology, Spanish, stage design, theater arts, U.S. government, U.S. history, visual literacy, Web site design, women's literature, writing.

Graduation Requirements Senior seminar/dissertation.

Special Academic Programs Independent study; study at local college for college credit; academic accommodation for the gifted.

College Admission Counseling 16 students graduated in 2013; 13 went to college. Other: 3 had other specific plans.

Student Life Discipline rests equally with students and faculty.

Tuition and Aid Day student tuition: $12,000. Tuition installment plan (monthly payment plans). Need-based scholarship grants available. In 2013–14, 15% of upper-school students received aid. Total amount of financial aid awarded in 2013–14: $60,000.

Admissions Traditional secondary-level entrance grade is 9. For fall 2013, 22 students applied for upper-level admission, 19 were accepted, 19 enrolled. Deadline for receipt of application materials: March 1. Application fee required: $100. Interview required.

Athletics Coed Intramural: artistic gym, basketball, bicycling, bowling, canoeing/kayaking, hiking/backpacking, outdoor adventure, outdoor education, outdoor skills, rock climbing, running, skiing (cross-country). 2 PE instructors.

Computers Computer network features include Internet access, wireless campus network. Student e-mail accounts are available to students.

Contact Jenny Osborne, Co-Director. 503-234-2826. Fax: 503-234-3186. E-mail: Jenny@pcrest.org. Website: www.pcrest.org

PADUA FRANCISCAN HIGH SCHOOL

6740 State Road
Parma, Ohio 44134-4598

Head of School: Mr. David Stec

General Information Coeducational day college-preparatory, arts, business, religious studies, and technology school, affiliated with Roman Catholic Church. Grades 9–12. Founded: 1961. Setting: suburban. Nearest major city is Cleveland. 40-acre campus. 1 building on campus. Approved or accredited by North Central Association of Colleges and Schools, Ohio Catholic Schools Accreditation Association (OCSAA), and Ohio Department of Education. Endowment: $1.5 million. Total enrollment: 755. Upper school average class size: 25. Upper school faculty-student ratio: 1:19. There are 179 required school days per year for Upper School students. Upper School students typically attend 5 days per week. The average school day consists of 6 hours and 30 minutes.

Upper School Student Profile Grade 9: 173 students (84 boys, 89 girls); Grade 10: 176 students (87 boys, 89 girls); Grade 11: 229 students (131 boys, 98 girls); Grade 12: 177 students (96 boys, 81 girls). 90% of students are Roman Catholic.

Faculty School total: 56. In upper school: 23 men, 33 women; 30 have advanced degrees.

Subjects Offered Accounting, algebra, American government, art appreciation, biology-AP, business, calculus-AP, chemistry, child development, Christian ethics, church history, computers, concert band, concert choir, consumer economics, current events, design, drawing, earth science, economics, English, English language-AP, ensembles, fitness, food and nutrition, French, French-AP, geography, geometry, German, German-AP, honors algebra, honors English, honors geometry, honors U.S. history, integrated science, interior design, Italian, Latin, Latin-AP, marching band, marketing, math analysis, music appreciation, music theory, orchestra, painting, photography, physics, pre-calculus, programming, psychology, social issues, social justice, sociology, Spanish, Spanish-AP, stagecraft, symphonic band, theater, trigonometry, U.S. history, U.S. history-AP, world cultures, world history.

Graduation Requirements Arts and fine arts (art, music, dance, drama), computer science, English, foreign language, lab science, mathematics, physical education (includes health), social studies (includes history), theology, four years of service projects.

Special Academic Programs Advanced Placement exam preparation; honors section; accelerated programs; study at local college for college credit; study abroad; remedial reading and/or remedial writing; remedial math; programs in English, mathematics for dyslexic students; special instructional classes for students with learning disabilities.

College Admission Counseling 207 students graduated in 2013; 203 went to college, including Cleveland State University; John Carroll University; Kent State University; The Ohio State University; The University of Akron; The University of Toledo. Other: 3 went to work, 1 entered military service. Median SAT critical reading: 548, median SAT math: 551, median SAT writing: 541, median combined SAT: 1640, median composite ACT: 23. 23% scored over 600 on SAT critical reading, 32% scored over 600 on SAT math, 22% scored over 600 on SAT writing, 34% scored over 26 on composite ACT.

Student Life Upper grades have specified standards of dress, student council, honor system. Discipline rests primarily with faculty. Attendance at religious services is required.

Summer Programs Enrichment, sports, art/fine arts, computer instruction programs offered; session focuses on introducing students to school, programs, coaches, and other students; PE for credit; held on campus; accepts boys and girls; open to students from other schools. 175 students usually enrolled. 2014 schedule: June 16 to June 20. Application deadline: May 16.

Tuition and Aid Day student tuition: $9625. Tuition installment plan (monthly payment plans, individually arranged payment plans). Tuition reduction for siblings, merit scholarship grants, need-based scholarship grants, paying campus jobs available. In 2013–14, 45% of upper-school students received aid; total upper-school merit-scholarship money awarded: $400,750. Total amount of financial aid awarded in 2013–14: $452,650.

Admissions Traditional secondary-level entrance grade is 9. For fall 2013, 214 students applied for upper-level admission, 178 were accepted, 173 enrolled. High School Placement Test or STS required. Deadline for receipt of application materials: January 31. Application fee required: $50.

Athletics Interscholastic: aquatics (boys, girls), baseball (b), basketball (b,g), bowling (b,g), cheering (g), combined training (b,g), cross-country running (b,g), dance team (g), diving (b,g), football (b), golf (b,g), ice hockey (b), lacrosse (b), physical fitness (b,g), soccer (b,g), softball (g), strength & conditioning (b,g), swimming and diving (b,g), tennis (g), track and field (b,g), volleyball (g), wrestling (b); intramural: basketball (b), flag football (b), football (b), freestyle skiing (b,g), golf (g), gymnastics (g), power lifting (b), touch football (b), weight lifting (b), weight training (b,g), winter soccer (b), yoga (b); coed interscholastic: figure skating, fitness; coed intramural: alpine skiing, backpacking, canoeing/kayaking, fishing, hiking/backpacking, skiing (downhill), snowboarding, wilderness, wilderness survival, wildernessways. 3 PE instructors, 30 coaches, 5 athletic trainers.

Computers Computers are regularly used in all academic classes. Computer network features include on-campus library services, online commercial services, Internet access, wireless campus network. Computer access in designated common areas is

available to students. Students grades are available online. The school has a published electronic and media policy.

Contact Mrs. Rachel DeGirolamo, Admissions Coordinator. 440-845-2444 Ext. 112. Fax: 440-845-5710. E-mail: rdegirolamo@paduafranciscan.com. Website: www.paduafranciscan.com

THE PAIDEIA SCHOOL

1509 Ponce de Leon Avenue
Atlanta, Georgia 30307

Head of School: Paul F. Bianchi

General Information Coeducational day college-preparatory, arts, and technology school. Grades PK–12. Founded: 1971. Setting: urban. 28-acre campus. 13 buildings on campus. Approved or accredited by Georgia Independent School Association, Southern Association of Colleges and Schools, Southern Association of Independent Schools, and Georgia Department of Education. Member of National Association of Independent Schools. Endowment: $13.2 million. Total enrollment: 987. Upper school average class size: 13. Upper school faculty-student ratio: 1:10. There are 178 required school days per year for Upper School students. Upper School students typically attend 5 days per week. The average school day consists of 6 hours and 45 minutes.

Upper School Student Profile Grade 9: 111 students (50 boys, 61 girls); Grade 10: 105 students (52 boys, 53 girls); Grade 11: 101 students (55 boys, 46 girls); Grade 12: 103 students (49 boys, 54 girls).

Faculty School total: 141. In upper school: 34 men, 31 women; 55 have advanced degrees.

Subjects Offered 20th century history, acting, African drumming, African-American history, African-American literature, algebra, American culture, American government, American history, American literature, anatomy, anatomy and physiology, art, art history, Asian history, Asian studies, athletic training, auto mechanics, bioethics, biology, biology-AP, calculus, ceramics, chemistry, chemistry-AP, chorus, community service, comparative religion, computer programming, creative writing, drama, drawing, ecology, environmental systems, economics, English, English literature, environmental science, ethics, European history-AP, expository writing, filmmaking, fine arts, forensics, French, French studies, gardening, geography, geology, geometry, government/civics, health, health and wellness, history, humanities, jazz band, jewelry making, journalism, literature, mathematics, medieval history, music theory-AP, Native American studies, orchestra, photography, physical education, physics, physics-AP, play production, playwriting and directing, poetry, pre-calculus, psychology, psychology-AP, Shakespeare, social studies, Spanish, Spanish literature, speech, stage design, statistics, statistics-AP, studio art, theater, theater arts, trigonometry, U.S. history, Web site design, weight training, women's health, women's studies, world civilizations, world history, world literature, writing, yearbook.

Graduation Requirements Arts and fine arts (art, music, dance, drama), English, foreign language, mathematics, physical education (includes health), science, social studies (includes history), 60 hours of community service with local, non-profit agency(ies). Community service is required.

Special Academic Programs 11 Advanced Placement exams for which test preparation is offered; honors section; independent study.

College Admission Counseling 103 students graduated in 2013; 101 went to college, including Emory University; Georgia Institute of Technology; Georgia State University; Oberlin College; Tulane University; University of Georgia. Other: 1 went to work, 1 had other specific plans.

Student Life Upper grades have student council, honor system. Discipline rests equally with students and faculty.

Tuition and Aid Day student tuition: $20,835. Tuition installment plan (bank-arranged tuition loan program). Need-based scholarship grants, need-based tuition assistance available. In 2013–14, 19% of upper-school students received aid. Total amount of financial aid awarded in 2013–14: $1,255,760.

Admissions Traditional secondary-level entrance grade is 9. Deadline for receipt of application materials: January 27. Application fee required: $75. On-campus interview required.

Athletics Interscholastic: baseball (boys), basketball (b,g), cross-country running (b,g), diving (b,g), soccer (b,g), softball (g), swimming and diving (b,g), tennis (b,g), track and field (b,g), ultimate Frisbee (b,g), volleyball (g); coed interscholastic: golf; coed intramural: basketball, bicycling, bowling, fitness, flag football, hiking/backpacking, outdoor education, soccer, softball, strength & conditioning, tai chi, ultimate Frisbee, volleyball, weight lifting, weight training, yoga. 2 PE instructors, 2 athletic trainers.

Computers Computers are regularly used in science classes. Computer network features include on-campus library services, online commercial services, Internet access, wireless campus network, Internet filtering or blocking technology, technology assistant program, computer borrowing program for students, technology courses. Campus intranet, student e-mail accounts, and computer access in designated common areas are available to students. The school has a published electronic and media policy.

Contact Admissions Office. 404-270-2312. Fax: 404-270-2312. E-mail: admissions@paideiaschool.org. Website: www.paideiaschool.org

PALMA SCHOOL

919 Iverson Street
Salinas, California 93901

Head of School: Br. Patrick D. Dunne, CFC

General Information Boys' day college-preparatory and religious studies school, affiliated with Roman Catholic Church. Grades 7–12. Founded: 1951. Setting: suburban. Nearest major city is San Jose. 25-acre campus. 16 buildings on campus. Approved or accredited by Western Association of Schools and Colleges, Western Catholic Education Association, and California Department of Education. Endowment: $250,000. Total enrollment: 534. Upper school average class size: 25. Upper school faculty-student ratio: 1:15. Upper School students typically attend 5 days per week.

Upper School Student Profile Grade 9: 101 students (101 boys); Grade 10: 102 students (102 boys); Grade 11: 102 students (102 boys); Grade 12: 97 students (97 boys). 69% of students are Roman Catholic.

Faculty School total: 31. In upper school: 26 men, 5 women; 19 have advanced degrees.

Subjects Offered Algebra, American history, American literature, anatomy, art, art history, band, biology, business, calculus, calculus-AP, chemistry, Chinese, Christian and Hebrew scripture, church history, civics, community service, computer applications, computer art, computer math, computer multimedia, computer programming, computer programming-AP, computer science, computer-aided design, creative writing, debate, digital art, driver education, earth science, economics, English, English language and composition-AP, English literature, English literature-AP, ethics, European history, European history-AP, expository writing, film, film studies, fine arts, French, geography, geometry, government/civics, grammar, health, health education, history, honors algebra, honors geometry, Japanese, jazz ensemble, journalism, Latin, mathematics, music, participation in sports, physical education, physical science, physics, pre-calculus, psychology, religion, Russian, Russian literature, science, social studies, Spanish, Spanish language-AP, speech, statistics-AP, student government, theology, trigonometry, typing, U.S. government and politics-AP, U.S. history-AP, video film production, world history, world literature, world religions, writing.

Graduation Requirements Advanced biology, arts and fine arts (art, music, dance, drama), English, foreign language, mathematics, physical education (includes health), religion (includes Bible studies and theology), science, social studies (includes history), religious retreat (8th, 9th, 10th grades), 60 hours of community service, must take the ACT College Entrance Exam.

Special Academic Programs Advanced Placement exam preparation; honors section; study at local college for college credit.

College Admission Counseling 109 students graduated in 2013; 107 went to college, including California Polytechnic State University, San Luis Obispo; California State University, Fresno; California State University, Monterey Bay; Saint Mary's College of California; Santa Clara University; University of California, Davis. Other: 2 went to work.

Student Life Upper grades have specified standards of dress, student council, honor system. Discipline rests primarily with faculty. Attendance at religious services is required.

Summer Programs Remediation, enrichment, advancement, sports, art/fine arts programs offered; session focuses on remediation, advancement, and enrichment; held on campus; accepts boys and girls; open to students from other schools. 150 students usually enrolled. 2014 schedule: June 15 to July 25. Application deadline: May 1.

Tuition and Aid Day student tuition: $9900. Tuition installment plan (Insured Tuition Payment Plan, monthly payment plans, 2-payment plan). Merit scholarship grants, need-based scholarship grants available. In 2013–14, 15% of upper-school students received aid. Total amount of financial aid awarded in 2013–14: $229,000.

Admissions Traditional secondary-level entrance grade is 9. For fall 2013, 65 students applied for upper-level admission, 45 were accepted, 40 enrolled. ETS high school placement exam and ETS HSPT (closed) required. Deadline for receipt of application materials: none. Application fee required: $75. On-campus interview required.

Athletics Interscholastic: baseball, basketball, cross-country running, diving, field hockey, football, golf, mountain biking, soccer, swimming and diving, tennis, track and field, volleyball, water polo, winter soccer, wrestling; intramural: basketball, indoor soccer, physical training, skiing (downhill), snowboarding, ultimate Frisbee, weight training. 5 PE instructors, 15 coaches, 1 athletic trainer.

Computers Computers are regularly used in art, economics, English, foreign language, history, mathematics, multimedia, music, newspaper, photography, science, social sciences, video film production, writing, yearbook classes. Computer network features include on-campus library services, online commercial services, Internet access, wireless campus network, Internet filtering or blocking technology. Student e-mail accounts and computer access in designated common areas are available to students. Students grades are available online. The school has a published electronic and media policy.

Contact Mrs. Lisa Laycock, Director of Admissions. 831-422-6391. Fax: 831-422-5065. E-mail: laycock@palmahschool.org. Website: www.palmaschool.org

PALMER TRINITY SCHOOL

7900 Southwest 176th Street
Palmetto Bay, Florida 33157
Head of School: Sean Murphy

General Information Coeducational day college-preparatory, arts, religious studies, technology, and ESL school, affiliated with Episcopal Church. Grades 6–12. Founded: 1972. Setting: suburban. Nearest major city is Miami. 55-acre campus. 10 buildings on campus. Approved or accredited by Florida Council of Independent Schools, National Association of Episcopal Schools, Southern Association of Colleges and Schools, Southern Association of Independent Schools, and Florida Department of Education. Member of National Association of Independent Schools and Secondary School Admission Test Board. Endowment: $5 million. Total enrollment: 660. Upper school average class size: 13. Upper school faculty-student ratio: 1:50. There are 175 required school days per year for Upper School students. Upper School students typically attend 5 days per week. The average school day consists of 6 hours.

Upper School Student Profile Grade 9: 100 students (48 boys, 52 girls); Grade 10: 93 students (45 boys, 48 girls); Grade 11: 105 students (42 boys, 63 girls); Grade 12: 83 students (40 boys, 43 girls). 10% of students are members of Episcopal Church.

Faculty School total: 89. In upper school: 22 men, 33 women; 55 have advanced degrees.

Subjects Offered Algebra, American government, American studies, art, art-AP, Basic programming, biology, biology-AP, British literature, calculus, calculus-AP, ceramics, chemistry, chemistry-AP, choir, computer science, concert band, creative writing, dance, drama, earth science, ecology, economics, English, English language and composition-AP, English literature, English literature and composition-AP, environmental studies, ESL, European history, European history-AP, film, fine arts, forensics, French, French language-AP, geometry, global studies, guitar, health and wellness, history, honors algebra, honors English, honors geometry, honors U.S. history, honors world history, journalism, keyboarding, literature, macroeconomics-AP, marine biology, mathematics, model United Nations, multimedia, music, newspaper, physical education, physical science, physics, physics-AP, pre-algebra, pre-calculus, psychology, religion, religion and culture, science, sculpture, Spanish, Spanish language-AP, Spanish literature-AP, theater, U.S. history, U.S. history-AP, United States government-AP, world history, world literature, yearbook.

Graduation Requirements 1 1/2 elective credits, arts and fine arts (art, music, dance, drama), computer programming, English, foreign language, history, humanities, mathematics, physical education (includes health), religious studies, science, minimum 20 hours of community service per year.

Special Academic Programs 21 Advanced Placement exams for which test preparation is offered; honors section; accelerated programs; independent study; term-away projects; study at local college for college credit; study abroad; academic accommodation for the gifted, the musically talented, and the artistically talented; ESL (27 students enrolled).

College Admission Counseling 85 students graduated in 2012; all went to college, including Boston College; Florida State University; Texas Christian University; The George Washington University; University of Florida; University of Miami. Mean SAT critical reading: 616, mean SAT math: 618, mean SAT writing: 628, mean combined SAT: 1872, mean composite ACT: 27.

Student Life Upper grades have uniform requirement, student council, honor system. Discipline rests equally with students and faculty.

Tuition and Aid Day student tuition: $26,000. Tuition installment plan (Insured Tuition Payment Plan, monthly payment plans). Need-based scholarship grants available. In 2012–13, 17% of upper-school students received aid. Total amount of financial aid awarded in 2012–13: $940,300.

Admissions Traditional secondary-level entrance grade is 9. For fall 2012, 119 students applied for upper-level admission, 64 were accepted, 39 enrolled. ACT, ISEE, PSAT and SAT for applicants to grade 11 and 12, SLEP for foreign students or SSAT required. Deadline for receipt of application materials: February 1. Application fee required: $115. On-campus interview required.

Athletics Interscholastic: baseball (boys), basketball (b,g), cheering (g), cross-country running (b,g), dance (g), football (b), golf (b,g), lacrosse (b,g), soccer (b,g), softball (g), strength & conditioning (b), tennis (b,g), track and field (b,g), volleyball (g), wrestling (b); intramural: basketball (b,g), dance team (g), floor hockey (b), hockey (b), in-line hockey (b), in-line skating (b), rugby (b), volleyball (g), weight training (b,g); coed intramural: climbing, ice hockey, outdoor education, physical training, rock climbing, strength & conditioning, weight training. 3 PE instructors, 20 coaches, 1 athletic trainer.

Computers Computers are regularly used in all academic, art, college planning, design, desktop publishing, graphic arts, library skills classes. Computer network features include on-campus library services, online commercial services, Internet access, wireless campus network, Internet filtering or blocking technology, laptop program in all academic areas. Student e-mail accounts are available to students. Students grades are available online. The school has a published electronic and media policy.

Contact Danny Reynolds, Director of Admission, College Counseling, and Financial Aid. 305-969-4204. Fax: 305-251-0607. E-mail: dreynolds@palmertrinity.org. Website: www.palmertrinity.org

PALO ALTO PREPARATORY SCHOOL

2462 Wyandotte Street
Mountain View, California 94043
Head of School: Christopher Morley Keck

General Information Coeducational day and distance learning college-preparatory school. Grades 8–12. Distance learning grades 9–12. Founded: 1986. Setting: suburban. Nearest major city is Palo Alto. 1 building on campus. Approved or accredited by Western Association of Schools and Colleges and California Department of Education. Total enrollment: 65. Upper school average class size: 8. Upper school faculty-student ratio: 1:8. There are 180 required school days per year for Upper School students. Upper School students typically attend 5 days per week. The average school day consists of 6 hours.

Upper School Student Profile Grade 8: 2 students (2 boys); Grade 9: 16 students (11 boys, 5 girls); Grade 10: 22 students (16 boys, 6 girls); Grade 11: 19 students (11 boys, 8 girls); Grade 12: 19 students (12 boys, 7 girls).

Faculty School total: 11. In upper school: 7 men, 4 women; 5 have advanced degrees.

Subjects Offered 3-dimensional design.

Graduation Requirements Senior Project.

Special Academic Programs International Baccalaureate program; 3 Advanced Placement exams for which test preparation is offered; accelerated programs; independent study; study at local college for college credit; study abroad; programs in English, mathematics for dyslexic students.

College Admission Counseling 15 students graduated in 2013; 13 went to college, including California Polytechnic State University, San Luis Obispo; California State University, Dominguez Hills. Other: 1 had other specific plans.

Student Life Upper grades have specified standards of dress, student council, honor system. Discipline rests primarily with faculty.

Summer Programs Remediation, rigorous outdoor training programs offered; session focuses on outdoor excursions and classes for makeup or to get ahead; held on campus; accepts boys and girls; open to students from other schools. 40 students usually enrolled. 2014 schedule: July 1 to August 9. Application deadline: May 15.

Tuition and Aid Day student tuition: $25,000. Tuition installment plan (SMART Tuition Payment Plan). Need-based scholarship grants available.

Admissions Traditional secondary-level entrance grade is 8. Deadline for receipt of application materials: none. No application fee required. On-campus interview required.

Computers Computer network features include Internet access, wireless campus network, Internet filtering or blocking technology. Campus intranet and student e-mail accounts are available to students. Students grades are available online. The school has a published electronic and media policy.

Contact Lisa Ohearn-Keck, Dean of Students. 650-493-7071 Ext. 102. Fax: 650-493-7073. E-mail: lisa@paloaltoprep.com. Website: www.paloaltoprep.com

PARADISE ADVENTIST ACADEMY

5699 Academy Drive
PO Box 2169
Paradise, California 95969
Head of School: Mr. Lance Taggart

General Information Coeducational day college-preparatory school, affiliated with Seventh-day Adventists. Grades K–12. Founded: 1908. Setting: small town. Nearest major city is Sacramento. 12-acre campus. 6 buildings on campus. Approved or accredited by Western Association of Schools and Colleges and California Department of Education. Endowment: $200,000. Total enrollment: 180. Upper school average class size: 20. Upper school faculty-student ratio: 1:8. There are 180 required school days per year for Upper School students. Upper School students typically attend 5 days per week. The average school day consists of 8 hours and 5 minutes.

Upper School Student Profile Grade 9: 18 students (6 boys, 12 girls); Grade 10: 17 students (12 boys, 5 girls); Grade 11: 25 students (12 boys, 13 girls); Grade 12: 16 students (9 boys, 7 girls). 80% of students are Seventh-day Adventists.

Faculty School total: 20. In upper school: 7 men, 3 women; 6 have advanced degrees.

Subjects Offered Advanced biology, advanced computer applications, advanced math, algebra, American government, American history, auto mechanics, band, basketball, Bible, biology, career education, carpentry, chemistry, choir, computer applications, computers, drama, earth science, English, geometry, health, keyboarding, military history, physical education, physical science, physics, pre-algebra, pre-calculus, Spanish, speech, U.S. government, U.S. history, volleyball, weightlifting, woodworking, world history, yearbook.

Graduation Requirements Advanced computer applications, algebra, American government, American history, arts and fine arts (art, music, dance, drama), Bible, biology, career and personal planning, career education, chemistry, computer literacy, electives, English, keyboarding, languages, life skills, physical education (includes health), physics, Spanish, world history, 100 hours of community service, 20 credits of fine arts, 100 hours of work experience.

Special Academic Programs Accelerated programs; independent study; remedial math.

College Admission Counseling 26 students graduated in 2013; 25 went to college, including Concordia University; New York University; Pacific Union College; Southern Adventist University; Walla Walla University. Other: 1 entered military service. Median SAT critical reading: 570, median SAT math: 550, median SAT writing: 530, median combined SAT: 1650, median composite ACT: 22. 23% scored over 600 on SAT critical reading, 36% scored over 600 on SAT math, 17% scored over 600 on SAT writing, 23% scored over 1800 on combined SAT, 25% scored over 26 on composite ACT.

Student Life Upper grades have specified standards of dress, student council. Discipline rests primarily with faculty. Attendance at religious services is required.

Summer Programs Sports programs offered; session focuses on basketball; held on campus; accepts boys and girls; open to students from other schools. 30 students usually enrolled. 2014 schedule: June 9 to June 13. Application deadline: June 9.

Tuition and Aid Day student tuition: $8700. Tuition installment plan (monthly payment plans, individually arranged payment plans, By year-$50 off, 10 or 12 month plan, Automatic Bank withdrawal). Tuition reduction for siblings, merit scholarship grants, need-based scholarship grants, paying campus jobs available. In 2013–14, 25% of upper-school students received aid; total upper-school merit-scholarship money awarded: $800. Total amount of financial aid awarded in 2013–14: $50,000.

Admissions Traditional secondary-level entrance grade is 9. For fall 2013, 10 students applied for upper-level admission, 10 were accepted, 10 enrolled. Any standardized test required. Deadline for receipt of application materials: August 17. Application fee required: $50. Interview required.

Athletics Interscholastic: basketball (boys, girls), cheering (g), football (b,g), soccer (b), volleyball (g). 1 PE instructor, 2 coaches.

Computers Computers are regularly used in all academic classes. Computer network features include on-campus library services, Internet access, wireless campus network, Internet filtering or blocking technology. Campus intranet, student e-mail accounts, and computer access in designated common areas are available to students. Students grades are available online. The school has a published electronic and media policy.

Contact Mrs. Brenda Muth, Registrar. 530-877-6540 Ext. 3010. Fax: 530-877-0870. E-mail: bmuth@mypaa.net. Website: www.mypaa.net

PARISH EPISCOPAL SCHOOL

4101 Sigma Road
Dallas, Texas 75244

Head of School: Mr. Dave Monaco

General Information Coeducational day college-preparatory and arts school, affiliated with Episcopal Church. Grades PK–12. Founded: 1972. Setting: suburban. 50-acre campus. 1 building on campus. Approved or accredited by Independent Schools Association of the Southwest, Southwest Association of Episcopal Schools, and Texas Department of Education. Member of National Association of Independent Schools. Endowment: $23 million. Total enrollment: 1,100. Upper school average class size: 18. The average school day consists of 7 hours and 45 minutes.

Upper School Student Profile 25% of students are members of Episcopal Church.

Special Academic Programs Honors section.

College Admission Counseling 96 students graduated in 2013.

Student Life Upper grades have uniform requirement, student council, honor system. Discipline rests primarily with faculty. Attendance at religious services is required.

Summer Programs Enrichment, advancement, sports, art/fine arts, computer instruction programs offered; held on campus; accepts boys and girls; open to students from other schools. 2014 schedule: June 1 to August 3. Application deadline: none.

Tuition and Aid Day student tuition: $22,000. Guaranteed tuition plan. Tuition installment plan (Insured Tuition Payment Plan, FACTS Tuition Payment Plan). Need-based scholarship grants available.

Admissions Traditional secondary-level entrance grade is 9. ISEE required. Deadline for receipt of application materials: January 17. Application fee required: $150. Interview required.

Athletics Interscholastic: baseball (boys), basketball (b,g), cheering (g), dance (b,g), dance squad (b,g), drill team (g), field hockey (g), football (b), golf (b,g), lacrosse (b,g), soccer (b,g), softball (g), strength & conditioning (b,g), swimming and diving (b,g), track and field (b,g), volleyball (g), weight training (b,g), winter soccer (b,g); intramural: aerobics/dance (g), dance (g); coed interscholastic: cross-country running, golf, tennis; coed intramural: physical fitness, strength & conditioning, weight training.

Computers Computer resources include on-campus library services, Internet access, Internet filtering or blocking technology. Campus intranet, student e-mail accounts, and computer access in designated common areas are available to students. Students grades are available online. The school has a published electronic and media policy.

Contact Ms. Gina Wallace, Admission Coordinator. 972-239-8011. Fax: 972-991-1237. E-mail: gwallace@parishepiscopal.org. Website: www.parishepiscopal.org

THE PARK SCHOOL OF BALTIMORE

2425 Old Court Road
Baltimore, Maryland 21208

Head of School: Mr. Daniel Paradis

General Information Coeducational day college-preparatory school. Grades PK–12. Founded: 1912. Setting: suburban. 100-acre campus. 4 buildings on campus.

Approved or accredited by Association of Independent Maryland Schools and Maryland Department of Education. Member of National Association of Independent Schools. Endowment: $30.2 million. Total enrollment: 833. Upper school average class size: 15. Upper school faculty-student ratio: 1:7. There are 170 required school days per year for Upper School students. Upper School students typically attend 5 days per week. The average school day consists of 7 hours.

Upper School Student Profile Grade 9: 86 students (43 boys, 43 girls); Grade 10: 74 students (38 boys, 36 girls); Grade 11: 94 students (51 boys, 43 girls); Grade 12: 77 students (33 boys, 44 girls).

Faculty School total: 119. In upper school: 25 men, 23 women; 39 have advanced degrees.

Subjects Offered 20th century world history, 3-dimensional art, acting, advanced chemistry, advanced math, African studies, anatomy, animal behavior, architectural drawing, art history, astronomy, audio visual/media, biochemistry, bioethics, DNA and culture, biology, British literature, calculus, ceramics, chemistry, Chinese, Chinese history, Chinese literature, choir, choral music, computer animation, computer programming, criminal justice, criminology, debate, design, digital art, digital music, digital photography, discrete mathematics, drama workshop, drawing, ecology, economics, English, English composition, English literature, environmental science, equality and freedom, etymology, European history, film studies, filmmaking, French, French studies, functions, Greek drama, health education, human sexuality, illustration, independent study, Islamic studies, jazz ensemble, jewelry making, keyboarding, madrigals, mathematics, Middle East, modern languages, multicultural studies, music composition, music performance, musical theater, organic chemistry, painting, photography, physical education, physics, playwriting and directing, poetry, publications, sculpture, senior project, set design, Shakespeare, social justice, Spanish, Spanish literature, statistics, studio art, theater, theater arts, U.S. history, visual and performing arts, vocal ensemble, Web site design, women in literature, woodworking, world religions, World War II, World-Wide-Web publishing, writing workshop.

Graduation Requirements Arts and fine arts (art, music, dance, drama), English, history, mathematics, modern languages, physical education (includes health), science.

Special Academic Programs Advanced Placement exam preparation; independent study; term-away projects; study abroad; academic accommodation for the gifted, the musically talented, and the artistically talented.

College Admission Counseling 81 students graduated in 2013; 80 went to college, including Brown University; Franklin & Marshall College; New York University; The Johns Hopkins University; University of Maryland, College Park; Vassar College. Other: 1 had other specific plans.

Student Life Upper grades have student council. Discipline rests equally with students and faculty.

Summer Programs Held on campus; accepts boys and girls; open to students from other schools. 2014 schedule: June 23 to August 1.

Tuition and Aid Day student tuition: $26,390. Tuition installment plan (The Tuition Plan, Insured Tuition Payment Plan, FACTS Tuition Payment Plan, monthly payment plans). Need-based scholarship grants available. In 2013–14, 22% of upper-school students received aid. Total amount of financial aid awarded in 2013–14: $1,270,175.

Admissions Traditional secondary-level entrance grade is 9. For fall 2013, 108 students applied for upper-level admission, 63 were accepted, 24 enrolled. ISEE required. Deadline for receipt of application materials: January 1. Application fee required: $50. Interview required.

Athletics Interscholastic: baseball (boys), basketball (b,g), cross-country running (b,g), field hockey (g), indoor soccer (g), lacrosse (b,g), soccer (b,g), softball (g), squash (b,g), tennis (b,g), winter soccer (g); coed intramural: climbing, Frisbee, strength & conditioning, ultimate Frisbee, wall climbing, yoga. 3 PE instructors, 19 coaches, 1 athletic trainer.

Computers Computers are regularly used in art, computer applications, creative writing, desktop publishing, English, foreign language, French, graphic design, history, journalism, library skills, mathematics, media production, music, music technology, news writing, newspaper, photojournalism, programming, publications, science, Spanish, theater, theater arts, video film production, woodworking, writing, writing, yearbook classes. Computer network features include on-campus library services, online commercial services, Internet access, wireless campus network, Internet filtering or blocking technology, access to course materials and assignments through faculty Web pages and wikis, discounted software purchase plan. Campus intranet, student e-mail accounts, and computer access in designated common areas are available to students. Students grades are available online. The school has a published electronic and media policy.

Contact Rachel Hockett, Administrative Assistant. 410-339-4130. Fax: 410-339-4127. E-mail: admission@parkschool.net. Website: www.parkschool.net

THE PARK SCHOOL OF BUFFALO

4625 Harlem Road
Snyder, New York 14226

Head of School: Christopher J. Lauricella

General Information Coeducational boarding and day college-preparatory and arts school. Boarding grades 9–12, day grades PK–12. Founded: 1912. Setting:

suburban. Nearest major city is Buffalo. Students are housed in host families. 34-acre campus. 13 buildings on campus. Approved or accredited by National Independent Private Schools Association, New York Department of Education, and New York Department of Education. Member of National Association of Independent Schools. Endowment: $1.6 million. Total enrollment: 290. Upper school average class size: 16. Upper school faculty-student ratio: 1:8. There are 167 required school days per year for Upper School students. Upper School students typically attend 5 days per week. The average school day consists of 7 hours.

Upper School Student Profile Grade 9: 34 students (13 boys, 21 girls); Grade 10: 36 students (15 boys, 21 girls); Grade 11: 32 students (16 boys, 16 girls); Grade 12: 31 students (23 boys, 8 girls). 18% of students are boarding students. 82% are state residents. 18% are international students. International students from Canada, China, Panama, and Republic of Korea.

Faculty School total: 39. In upper school: 13 men, 12 women; 20 have advanced degrees.

Subjects Offered Advanced studio art-AP, algebra, American history, American history-AP, American literature, American literature-AP, art, band, biology, biology-AP, calculus, calculus-AP, ceramics, chemistry, chorus, college admission preparation, college counseling, community service, computer applications, computer programming, critical thinking, drama, drawing, economics, English, environmental science, fine arts, forensics, French, French language-AP, freshman seminar, geometry, government/civics, health, junior and senior seminars, marine biology, media, media production, metalworking, music, orchestra, organic chemistry, photography, physical education, physics, senior project, senior seminar, senior thesis, sophomore skills, Spanish, Spanish-AP, studio art-AP, trigonometry, U.S. government and politics-AP, woodworking, world history, yearbook.

Graduation Requirements Arts and fine arts (art, music, dance, drama), computer science, English, foreign language, mathematics, physical education (includes health), science, senior project, senior thesis, social sciences, social studies (includes history). Community service is required.

Special Academic Programs Advanced Placement exam preparation; honors section; accelerated programs; independent study; study at local college for college credit; study abroad; academic accommodation for the gifted; ESL (27 students enrolled).

College Admission Counseling 26 students graduated in 2013; 24 went to college, including Carleton College; City College of the City University of New York; Skidmore College; State University of New York College at Geneseo; The George Washington University; Trinity College. Other: 1 entered military service, 1 had other specific plans. Median SAT critical reading: 590, median SAT math: 580, median SAT writing: 580, median combined SAT: 1750, median composite ACT: 25. 37% scored over 600 on SAT critical reading, 44% scored over 600 on SAT math, 32% scored over 600 on SAT writing, 32% scored over 1800 on combined SAT, 43% scored over 26 on composite ACT.

Student Life Upper grades have specified standards of dress, student council, honor system. Discipline rests equally with students and faculty.

Summer Programs Remediation, enrichment, advancement, ESL, sports, art/fine arts programs offered; session focuses on recreational day camp, basketball camps, soccer camp, ESL, summer scholars; held on campus; accepts boys and girls; open to students from other schools. 585 students usually enrolled. 2014 schedule: July 7 to August 29. Application deadline: January 6.

Tuition and Aid Day student tuition: $19,000–$19,975; 5-day tuition and room/board: $28,000; 7-day tuition and room/board: $32,000. Tuition installment plan (Insured Tuition Payment Plan, FACTS Tuition Payment Plan). Tuition reduction for siblings, merit scholarship grants, need-based scholarship grants available. In 2013–14, 40% of upper-school students received aid; total upper-school merit-scholarship money awarded: $160,837. Total amount of financial aid awarded in 2013–14: $518,154.

Admissions Traditional secondary-level entrance grade is 9. For fall 2013, 50 students applied for upper-level admission, 38 were accepted, 28 enrolled. ERB Reading and Math, Otis-Lennon School Ability Test or TOEFL required. Deadline for receipt of application materials: none. Application fee required: $50. Interview required.

Athletics Interscholastic: basketball (boys, girls), bowling (b,g), golf (b), lacrosse (b), soccer (b,g), tennis (b,g); coed interscholastic: soccer; coed intramural: bicycling, cooperative games, cross-country running, fitness, flag football, floor hockey, Frisbee, hiking/backpacking, indoor soccer, outdoor activities, outdoor adventure, outdoor education, outdoor recreation, outdoor skills, outdoors, physical fitness, running, skiing (downhill), snowboarding, snowshoeing, soccer, strength & conditioning, weight lifting, weight training, winter walking, yoga. 2 PE instructors, 14 coaches.

Computers Computers are regularly used in creative writing, current events, data processing, English, graphic arts, independent study, mathematics, media, media arts, media services, newspaper, photography, science, word processing, yearbook classes. Computer network features include on-campus library services, online commercial services, Internet access, wireless campus network, Internet filtering or blocking technology. Campus intranet, student e-mail accounts, and computer access in designated common areas are available to students. Students grades are available online. The school has a published electronic and media policy.

Contact Marnie Cerrato, Director of Enrollment Management. 716-839-1242 Ext. 107. Fax: 716-408-9511. E-mail: mcerrato@theparkschool.org. Website: www.theparkschool.org

PARKVIEW ADVENTIST ACADEMY

5505 College Avenue
Lacombe, Alberta T4L 2E7, Canada

Head of School: Ms. Angie Bishop

General Information Coeducational boarding and day college-preparatory, general academic, arts, vocational, religious studies, and technology school, affiliated with Seventh-day Adventist Church. Grades 10–12. Founded: 1907. Setting: small town. Nearest major city is Edmonton, Canada. Students are housed in single-sex by floor dormitories. Approved or accredited by National Council for Private School Accreditation and Alberta Department of Education. Language of instruction: English. Upper school average class size: 20. Upper school faculty-student ratio: 1:10. There are 188 required school days per year for Upper School students. Upper School students typically attend 5 days per week. The average school day consists of 5 hours and 50 minutes.

Upper School Student Profile Grade 10: 30 students (15 boys, 15 girls); Grade 11: 32 students (17 boys, 15 girls); Grade 12: 45 students (24 boys, 21 girls). 40% of students are boarding students. 70% are province residents. 4 provinces are represented in upper school student body. 1% are international students. International students from Rwanda; 3 other countries represented in student body. 80% of students are Seventh-day Adventists.

Faculty School total: 9. In upper school: 3 men, 6 women; 2 have advanced degrees; 1 resides on campus.

Subjects Offered Advanced math, art, arts, band, biology, career and technology systems, chemistry, choir, choral music, English, fine arts, foods, French, home economics, industrial arts, instrumental music, language arts, mathematics, mechanics, metalworking, music, photography, physical education, physics, religion, religious studies, science, social sciences, social studies, welding, woodworking.

Graduation Requirements Computer processing, keyboarding, physical education (includes health), word processing.

Special Academic Programs ESL.

College Admission Counseling 36 went to college. Other: 3 went to work.

Student Life Upper grades have specified standards of dress, student council, honor system. Discipline rests primarily with faculty. Attendance at religious services is required.

Tuition and Aid Day student tuition: CAN$5657; 7-day tuition and room/board: CAN$11,724. Tuition installment plan (monthly payment plans, individually arranged payment plans). Tuition reduction for siblings, merit scholarship grants available.

Admissions Traditional secondary-level entrance grade is 10. Deadline for receipt of application materials: none. Application fee required: CAN$20. Interview required.

Athletics Interscholastic: aquatics (boys), basketball (b,g), hockey (b), soccer (b), volleyball (b,g); intramural: basketball (b,g), football (b), softball (g); coed interscholastic: baseball, basketball, soccer; coed intramural: baseball, basketball. 1 PE instructor, 3 coaches.

Computers Computer network features include on-campus library services, Internet access, wireless campus network, Internet filtering or blocking technology. Student e-mail accounts are available to students. Students grades are available online. The school has a published electronic and media policy.

Contact Mr. Rodney Jamieson, Vice Principal. 403-782-3381 Ext. 4111. Fax: 866-931-2652. E-mail: rjamieso@paa.ca. Website: www.paa.ca/

THE PATHWAY SCHOOL

Norristown, Pennsylvania
See Special Needs Schools section.

PATTEN ACADEMY OF CHRISTIAN EDUCATION

2433 Coolidge Avenue
Oakland, California 94601

Head of School: Dr. Sharon Anderson

General Information Coeducational day college-preparatory, arts, religious studies, and bilingual studies school, affiliated with Christian faith. Grades K–12. Founded: 1944. Setting: urban. Nearest major city is San Francisco. 3 buildings on campus. Approved or accredited by Western Association of Schools and Colleges and California Department of Education. Total enrollment: 117. Upper school average class size: 11. Upper school faculty-student ratio: 1:6. There are 185 required school days per year for Upper School students. Upper School students typically attend 5 days per week. The average school day consists of 6 hours and 45 minutes.

Upper School Student Profile Grade 9: 12 students (7 boys, 5 girls); Grade 10: 11 students (6 boys, 5 girls); Grade 11: 12 students (6 boys, 6 girls); Grade 12: 9 students (4 boys, 5 girls). 11% of students are Christian faith.

Faculty School total: 14. In upper school: 5 men, 2 women; 6 have advanced degrees.

Subjects Offered Algebra, American literature, art, arts, band, Bible studies, biology, chemistry, choir, community service, computer science, economics, English, English literature, fine arts, geometry, health, instrumental music, introduction to literature, language arts, life skills, mathematics, music, physical education, physical science, physics, piano, pre-calculus, religion, science, social studies, Spanish, strings,

U.S. government, U.S. history, vocal music, world geography, world history, world literature, writing.

Graduation Requirements Arts and fine arts (art, music, dance, drama), environmental science, foreign language, mathematics, science, social studies (includes history). Community service is required.

College Admission Counseling 12 students graduated in 2012; 11 went to college, including California State University, East Bay; Morehouse College; Patten University; Saint Mary's College of California; University of California, Berkeley. Other: 1 went to work.

Student Life Upper grades have uniform requirement, student council, honor system. Discipline rests primarily with faculty. Attendance at religious services is required.

Tuition and Aid Day student tuition: $5999. Tuition installment plan (monthly payment plans). Tuition reduction for siblings, need-based scholarship grants available. In 2012–13, 27% of upper-school students received aid. Total amount of financial aid awarded in 2012–13: $23,797.

Admissions Traditional secondary-level entrance grade is 9. For fall 2012, 10 students applied for upper-level admission, 9 were accepted, 9 enrolled. Deadline for receipt of application materials: none. Application fee required: $50. On-campus interview required.

Athletics Interscholastic: basketball (boys, girls), volleyball (b,g). 1 PE instructor.

Computers Computer network features include Internet access.

Contact Mrs. Sharon Moncher, Coordinator. 510-533-3121. Fax: 510-535-9381. Website: www.pattenacademy.org

PEDDIE SCHOOL

201 South Main Street
Hightstown, New Jersey 08520

Head of School: John F. Green

General Information Coeducational boarding and day college-preparatory, arts, and technology school. Grades 9–PG. Founded: 1864. Setting: small town. Nearest major city is Princeton. Students are housed in single-sex dormitories. 230-acre campus. 53 buildings on campus. Approved or accredited by Middle States Association of Colleges and Schools, The Association of Boarding Schools, and New Jersey Department of Education. Member of National Association of Independent Schools and Secondary School Admission Test Board. Endowment: $278 million. Total enrollment: 550. Upper school average class size: 12. Upper school faculty-student ratio: 1:6. Upper School students typically attend 6 days per week. The average school day consists of 7 hours.

Upper School Student Profile Grade 9: 114 students (61 boys, 53 girls); Grade 10: 133 students (71 boys, 62 girls); Grade 11: 144 students (73 boys, 71 girls); Grade 12: 141 students (70 boys, 71 girls); Postgraduate: 16 students (13 boys, 3 girls). 63% of students are boarding students. 24 states are represented in upper school student body. 13% are international students. International students from China, Hong Kong, Japan, Republic of Korea, Thailand, and United Kingdom; 34 other countries represented in student body.

Faculty School total: 84. In upper school: 48 men, 36 women; 58 have advanced degrees; 72 reside on campus.

Subjects Offered Acting, African studies, algebra, American history, American literature, American studies, anatomy, architecture, art, art history, art history-AP, Asian studies, astronomy, Bible studies, biology, biology-AP, calculus, calculus-AP, chemistry, Chinese, comedy, comparative religion, computer programming, computer science, creative writing, debate, digital imaging, DNA, DNA science lab, drama, earth science, ecology, economics, English, English literature, environmental science, environmental science-AP, European history, European history-AP, expository writing, film history, fine arts, forensics, French, French language-AP, French literature-AP, geometry, global issues, global science, government/civics, health, history, information technology, Latin, Latin-AP, mathematics, Middle East, music, music theory-AP, neuroscience, philosophy, photography, physical education, physics, physics-AP, psychology, psychology-AP, robotics, science, Shakespeare, social studies, Spanish, Spanish language-AP, Spanish literature-AP, speech, statistics, statistics-AP, studio art-AP, theater, trigonometry, U.S. history, U.S. history-AP, video film production, world history, world literature, World War I, World War II, writing.

Graduation Requirements Arts and fine arts (art, music, dance, drama), computer science, English, foreign language, history, mathematics, physical education (includes health), science. Community service is required.

Special Academic Programs Advanced Placement exam preparation; honors section; independent study; term-away projects; study abroad.

College Admission Counseling 140 students graduated in 2012; all went to college, including Carnegie Mellon University; Cornell University; Princeton University; The George Washington University; The Johns Hopkins University; University of Pennsylvania.

Student Life Upper grades have specified standards of dress, student council. Discipline rests primarily with faculty.

Tuition and Aid Day student tuition: $39,000; 7-day tuition and room/board: $47,500. Tuition installment plan (Academic Management Services Plan, monthly payment plans, individually arranged payment plans). Merit scholarship grants, need-based scholarship grants, need-based loans available. In 2012–13, 40% of upper-school

students received aid; total upper-school merit-scholarship money awarded: $70,000. Total amount of financial aid awarded in 2012–13: $5,000,000.

Admissions Traditional secondary-level entrance grade is 9. For fall 2012, 1,561 students applied for upper-level admission, 310 were accepted, 171 enrolled. ISEE or SSAT required. Deadline for receipt of application materials: January 15. Application fee required: $50. Interview required.

Athletics Interscholastic: baseball (boys), basketball (b,g), crew (b,g), cross-country running (b,g), diving (b,g), field hockey (g), fitness (b,g), football (b), golf (b,g), indoor track & field (b,g), lacrosse (b,g), soccer (b,g), softball (g), strength & conditioning (b,g), swimming and diving (b,g), tennis (b,g), track and field (b,g), winter (indoor) track (b,g), wrestling (b), yoga (b,g); intramural: weight lifting (b,g), weight training (b,g); coed intramural: bicycling, bowling, dance, physical fitness, physical training, softball. 9 coaches, 3 athletic trainers.

Computers Computers are regularly used in English, foreign language, history, mathematics, science classes. Computer network features include on-campus library services, online commercial services, Internet access, wireless campus network, Internet filtering or blocking technology, NewsBank, Britannica, GaleNet, Electric Library. Student e-mail accounts are available to students. Students grades are available online. The school has a published electronic and media policy.

Contact Raymond H. Cabot, Director of Admission. 609-944-7501. Fax: 609-944-7901. E-mail: admission@peddie.org. Website: www.peddie.org

THE PENNINGTON SCHOOL

112 West Delaware Avenue
Pennington, New Jersey 08534-1601

Head of School: Mrs. Stephanie (Penny) G. Townsend

General Information Coeducational boarding and day college-preparatory and arts school, affiliated with Methodist Church. Boarding grades 8–12, day grades 6–12. Founded: 1838. Setting: small town. Nearest major city is Philadelphia, PA. Students are housed in single-sex by floor dormitories and single-sex dormitories. 54-acre campus. 17 buildings on campus. Approved or accredited by Middle States Association of Colleges and Schools, National Independent Private Schools Association, The Association of Boarding Schools, The College Board, University Senate of United Methodist Church, and New Jersey Department of Education. Member of National Association of Independent Schools and Secondary School Admission Test Board. Endowment: $25 million. Total enrollment: 487. Upper school average class size: 13. Upper school faculty-student ratio: 1:8. There are 180 required school days per year for Upper School students. Upper School students typically attend 5 days per week. The average school day consists of 7 hours.

Upper School Student Profile Grade 9: 96 students (51 boys, 45 girls); Grade 10: 103 students (62 boys, 41 girls); Grade 11: 95 students (61 boys, 34 girls); Grade 12: 112 students (62 boys, 50 girls). 25% of students are boarding students. 61% are state residents. 5 states are represented in upper school student body. 11% are international students. International students from Australia, China, Germany, Republic of Korea, Spain, and Taiwan. 5% of students are Methodist.

Faculty School total: 87. In upper school: 31 men, 38 women; 55 have advanced degrees; 50 reside on campus.

Subjects Offered Advanced studio art-AP, advanced TOEFL/grammar, African-American history, algebra, American history, American literature, anatomy, anatomy and physiology, art, bioethics, DNA and culture, biology, British literature-AP, calculus-AP, cheerleading, chemistry, chemistry-AP, Chinese, chorus, computer applications, computer skills, drama, economics, English, English literature, English literature-AP, English-AP, environmental science, ESL, fine arts, forensics, French, French language-AP, genetics, geometry, German, government and politics-AP, Greek, Greek culture, health, history-AP, honors algebra, honors English, honors geometry, honors U.S. history, jazz ensemble, Latin, macroeconomics-AP, music, music history, music theory, organic chemistry, photography, physics, physics-AP, pottery, pre-calculus, psychology, public speaking, religion, robotics, senior internship, Spanish, Spanish literature, Spanish-AP, stage design, stagecraft, technical theater, U.S. government and politics-AP, Web site design, weight training, world history, world history-AP.

Graduation Requirements Algebra, American history, arts and fine arts (art, music, dance, drama), athletics, biology, chemistry, computer education, English, foreign language, geometry, health education, public speaking, religion (includes Bible studies and theology), religion and culture, world history.

Special Academic Programs 18 Advanced Placement exams for which test preparation is offered; honors section; independent study; term-away projects; study at local college for college credit; study abroad; academic accommodation for the gifted; programs in English for dyslexic students; ESL (41 students enrolled).

College Admission Counseling 94 students graduated in 2013; all went to college, including Boston University; Drexel University; Fordham University; New York University; Princeton University; Syracuse University. Mean combined SAT: 1695, mean composite ACT: 25.

Student Life Upper grades have specified standards of dress, student council, honor system. Discipline rests equally with students and faculty. Attendance at religious services is required.

Tuition and Aid Day student tuition: $32,170; 7-day tuition and room/board: $47,770. Tuition installment plan (monthly payment plans). Need-based scholarship grants available. In 2013–14, 28% of upper-school students received aid. Total amount of financial aid awarded in 2013–14: $3,000,000.

Admissions Traditional secondary-level entrance grade is 9. For fall 2013, 463 students applied for upper-level admission, 213 were accepted, 78 enrolled. SSAT or TOEFL required. Deadline for receipt of application materials: February 1. Application fee required: $50. Interview required.

Athletics Interscholastic: baseball (boys), basketball (b,g), cheering (g), field hockey (g), football (b), ice hockey (b), softball (g); intramural: aquatics (b,g), bowling (b,g); coed interscholastic: cross-country running, golf, indoor track, lacrosse, soccer, swimming and diving, tennis, track and field, water polo, weight training, winter (indoor) track; coed intramural: dance team, fitness, physical training, strength & conditioning, weight training. 3 coaches, 2 athletic trainers.

Computers Computers are regularly used in art, college planning, computer applications, creative writing, desktop publishing, graphic design, library, literary magazine, mathematics, music, newspaper, research skills, science, video film production, yearbook classes. Computer network features include on-campus library services, online commercial services, Internet access, wireless campus network, Internet filtering or blocking technology. Campus intranet, student e-mail accounts, and computer access in designated common areas are available to students. Students grades are available online. The school has a published electronic and media policy.

Contact Ms. Grace Megaffin, Admission Officer. 609-737-6128. Fax: 609-730-1405. E-mail: gmegaffin@pennington.org. Website: www.pennington.org

See Display below and Close-Up on page 558.

PENSACOLA CATHOLIC HIGH SCHOOL

3043 West Scott Street
Pensacola, Florida 32505

Head of School: Sr. Kierstin Martin

General Information Coeducational day college-preparatory and technology school, affiliated with Roman Catholic Church. Grades 9–12. Founded: 1941. Setting: urban. 25-acre campus. 5 buildings on campus. Approved or accredited by Southern Association of Colleges and Schools. Total enrollment: 611. Upper school average class size: 25. Upper school faculty-student ratio: 1:18. There are 180 required school days per year for Upper School students. Upper School students typically attend 5 days per week. The average school day consists of 7 hours.

Upper School Student Profile Grade 9: 144 students (89 boys, 55 girls); Grade 10: 160 students (98 boys, 62 girls); Grade 11: 161 students (96 boys, 65 girls); Grade 12: 146 students (83 boys, 63 girls). 70% of students are Roman Catholic.

Faculty School total: 50. In upper school: 15 men, 35 women; 15 have advanced degrees.

Subjects Offered Advanced math, Advanced Placement courses, algebra, American government, American history, American history-AP, American literature, analysis and differential calculus, analytic geometry, anatomy and physiology, art, art appreciation, arts and crafts, athletics, band, baseball, basketball, Bible, Bible studies, biology, botany, British literature, broadcast journalism, business law, calculus, calculus-AP, campus ministry, Catholic belief and practice, chemistry, Christian ethics, Christian scripture, Christian studies, Christian testament, church history, civics, college counseling, comparative religion, composition, composition-AP, computer applications, computer graphics, consumer mathematics, CPR, creative arts, criminal justice, desktop publishing, digital photography, drawing, earth science, economics, electives, English, English composition, English language and composition-AP, English literature, English literature and composition-AP, environmental science, fabric arts, film appreciation, film history, filmmaking, foreign language, French, general science, genetics, geography, geometry, government, government-AP, grammar, graphic arts, guidance, health education, history, history of the Catholic Church, honors algebra, honors English, honors geometry, honors U.S. history, honors world history, human sexuality, journalism, keyboarding, lab science, library, library assistant, Life of Christ, literature and composition-AP, marine biology, music appreciation, music history, physical education, physical science, physics, pottery, pre-algebra, pre-calculus, probability and statistics, reading, religion, sex education, social studies, Spanish, student government, student publications, telecommunications and the Internet, television, the Web, trigonometry, U.S. government, U.S. government and politics-AP, U.S. history, U.S. literature, vocal music, weight training, Western civilization, world geography, world history, world religions.

Graduation Requirements American government, American history, American literature, art appreciation, biology, economics, government, music appreciation, sociology, U.S. history, Western civilization, world geography.

Special Academic Programs Advanced Placement exam preparation; honors section; independent study; study at local college for college credit; academic accommodation for the gifted; remedial reading and/or remedial writing; remedial math; programs in English, mathematics, general development for dyslexic students; special instructional classes for deaf students, blind students.

College Admission Counseling 132 students graduated in 2013; 130 went to college, including Florida State University; Mississippi State University; Pensacola State College; The University of Alabama; University of Florida. Other: 2 entered military service. Mean SAT critical reading: 525, mean SAT math: 520, mean SAT writing: 533, mean combined SAT: 1578, mean composite ACT: 24.

Student Life Upper grades have specified standards of dress, student council. Discipline rests primarily with faculty. Attendance at religious services is required.

Summer Programs Remediation, enrichment programs offered; session focuses on religion courses, enrichment, and study skills; held on campus; accepts boys and girls; not open to students from other schools.

success...

Consider The Pennington School if you can think for yourself, like to be creative and have fun, and believe that the arts, athletics, and service are just as important as academic excellence.

We are an extraordinary, diverse, and empowering community.

Talk with us.

609 737 6128 | admiss@pennington.org | www.pennington.org

Find it
@THE
PENNINGTON
SCHOOL

Grades 6–12
coed, day and boarding

Tuition and Aid Tuition installment plan (individually arranged payment plans). Tuition reduction for siblings, need-based scholarship grants available.

Admissions Traditional secondary-level entrance grade is 9. ETS high school placement exam required. Deadline for receipt of application materials: none. Application fee required: $125. On-campus interview required.

Athletics Interscholastic: baseball (boys), basketball (b,g), cheering (b,g), golf (b,g), physical training (b), soccer (b,g), softball (g), swimming and diving (b,g), wrestling (b).

Computers Computers are regularly used in Bible studies, computer applications, creative writing, desktop publishing, foreign language, French, geography, graphic design, history, independent study, keyboarding, mathematics, publications, reading, religion, science, social studies, Spanish, stock market, study skills, video film production, Web site design, word processing, yearbook classes. Computer network features include on-campus library services, online commercial services, Internet access, wireless campus network, Internet filtering or blocking technology. Student e-mail accounts and computer access in designated common areas are available to students. Students grades are available online. The school has a published electronic and media policy.

Contact Mary Kyte, Senior Guidance Counselor. 850-436-6400 Ext. 120. Fax: 850-436-6405. E-mail: mkyte@pensacolachs.org. Website: www.pensacolachs.org

PEOPLES CHRISTIAN ACADEMY

245 Renfrew Drive
Markham, Ontario L3R 6G3, Canada

Head of School: Mr. Reg Andrews

General Information Coeducational day college-preparatory and religious studies school, affiliated with Christian faith. Grades JK–12. Founded: 1971. Setting: urban. Nearest major city is Toronto, Canada. 5-acre campus. 1 building on campus. Approved or accredited by Association of Christian Schools International, Christian Schools International, Ontario Ministry of Education, and Ontario Department of Education. Language of instruction: English. Endowment: CAN$15,000. Total enrollment: 339. Upper school average class size: 20. Upper school faculty-student ratio: 1:10. There are 176 required school days per year for Upper School students. Upper School students typically attend 5 days per week. The average school day consists of 7 hours.

Upper School Student Profile Grade 9: 22 students (13 boys, 9 girls); Grade 10: 29 students (12 boys, 17 girls); Grade 11: 27 students (16 boys, 11 girls); Grade 12: 32 students (15 boys, 17 girls). 85% of students are Christian.

Faculty School total: 36. In upper school: 9 men, 13 women; 4 have advanced degrees.

Subjects Offered Accounting, Bible, biology, calculus, Canadian geography, Canadian history, Canadian law, careers, chemistry, civics, discrete mathematics, dramatic arts, economics, English, exercise science, family studies, French, functions, geography, geometry, health education, healthful living, ideas, information technology, instrumental music, journalism, keyboarding, literature, mathematics, media arts, organizational studies, philosophy, physical education, physics, psychology, science, sociology, visual arts, vocal music, world history, world religions, writing.

Graduation Requirements Arts, Canadian geography, Canadian history, careers, civics, English, French as a second language, mathematics, physical education (includes health), science, must complete Bible course curriculum for all grades.

College Admission Counseling 42 students graduated in 2012; 40 went to college, including McMaster University; The University of Western Ontario; University of Guelph; University of Toronto; Wilfrid Laurier University; York University. Other: 2 had other specific plans.

Student Life Upper grades have uniform requirement, student council, honor system. Discipline rests primarily with faculty. Attendance at religious services is required.

Tuition and Aid Day student tuition: CAN$9630. Tuition installment plan (monthly payment plans). Tuition reduction for siblings, bursaries, need-based scholarship grants, alumni scholarships, prepayment tuition reduction available. In 2012–13, 2% of upper-school students received aid. Total amount of financial aid awarded in 2012–13: CAN$30,000.

Admissions Traditional secondary-level entrance grade is 9. For fall 2012, 15 students applied for upper-level admission, 10 were accepted, 10 enrolled. CTBS (or similar from their school) required. Deadline for receipt of application materials: none. Application fee required: CAN$150. Interview required.

Athletics Interscholastic: badminton (boys, girls), baseball (b,g), basketball (b,g), cross-country running (b,g), Frisbee (b,g), running (b,g), track and field (b,g), volleyball (b,g); intramural: badminton (b,g), basketball (b,g), cross-country running (b,g), floor hockey (b,g), running (b,g); coed interscholastic: badminton, baseball, basketball, cross-country running, Frisbee, running, swimming and diving, track and field; coed intramural: badminton, basketball, cross-country running, floor hockey, running, volleyball. 2 PE instructors.

Computers Computers are regularly used in business studies, drawing and design, graphics, information technology, introduction to technology, journalism, mathematics, yearbook classes. Computer network features include Internet access, Internet filtering or blocking technology. The school has a published electronic and media policy.

Contact School Office. 416-733-2010 Ext. 204. Fax: 416-733-2011. E-mail: admissions@pca.ca. Website: www.pca.ca

THE PHELPS SCHOOL

583 Sugartown Road
Malvern, Pennsylvania 19355

Head of School: Mr. Daniel E. Knopp

General Information Boys' boarding and day college-preparatory, Academic Support Program (ASP), and ESL program school. Grades 7–PG. Founded: 1946. Setting: suburban. Nearest major city is Philadelphia. Students are housed in single-sex dormitories. 75-acre campus. 18 buildings on campus. Approved or accredited by Academy of Orton-Gillingham Practitioners and Educators, Middle States Association of Colleges and Schools, The Association of Boarding Schools, and Pennsylvania Department of Education. Member of National Association of Independent Schools and Secondary School Admission Test Board. Total enrollment: 110. Upper school average class size: 8. Upper school faculty-student ratio: 1:4. There are 160 required school days per year for Upper School students. The average school day consists of 7 hours and 5 minutes.

Upper School Student Profile Grade 7: 3 students (3 boys); Grade 8: 5 students (5 boys); Grade 9: 18 students (18 boys); Grade 10: 23 students (23 boys); Grade 11: 25 students (25 boys); Grade 12: 32 students (32 boys); Postgraduate: 4 students (4 boys). 75% of students are boarding students. 32% are state residents. 10 states are represented in upper school student body. 40% are international students. International students from China, Ghana, Republic of Korea, Saudi Arabia, Spain, and Taiwan; 8 other countries represented in student body.

Faculty School total: 22. In upper school: 15 men, 6 women; 9 have advanced degrees; 18 reside on campus.

Subjects Offered Algebra, American history, art, biology, calculus, calculus-AP, chemistry, college admission preparation, earth science, English, environmental science, ESL, fitness, general math, geometry, government, health, learning strategies, mathematics, participation in sports, photography, physical education, physical science, physics, pre-algebra, pre-calculus, psychology, reading, reading/study skills, remedial study skills, SAT preparation, Spanish, study skills, weight training, world history, yearbook.

Graduation Requirements English, mathematics, physical education (includes health), science, social studies (includes history). Community service is required.

Special Academic Programs Advanced Placement exam preparation; independent study; academic accommodation for the gifted; remedial reading and/or remedial writing; remedial math; programs in English, mathematics, general development for dyslexic students; ESL (31 students enrolled).

College Admission Counseling 35 students graduated in 2013; 33 went to college, including Drexel University; Immaculata University; Michigan State University; The University of Alabama at Birmingham; The University of Arizona; Villanova University. Other: 1 went to work, 1 entered military service.

Student Life Upper grades have uniform requirement, student council. Discipline rests primarily with faculty.

Summer Programs Sports programs offered; session focuses on sports; held on campus; accepts boys and girls; open to students from other schools. 20 students usually enrolled. 2014 schedule: June 10 to August 15.

Tuition and Aid Day student tuition: $23,850; 7-day tuition and room/board: $42,950. Tuition installment plan (FACTS Tuition Payment Plan). Merit scholarship grants, need-based scholarship grants available. In 2013–14, 37% of upper-school students received aid. Total amount of financial aid awarded in 2013–14: $850,000.

Admissions Traditional secondary-level entrance grade is 7. Deadline for receipt of application materials: none. Application fee required: $50. Interview required.

Athletics Interscholastic: baseball, basketball, cross-country running, golf, lacrosse, soccer, street hockey, tennis; intramural: bowling, climbing, fitness, horseback riding, in-line skating, independent competitive sports, indoor soccer, martial arts, physical fitness, roller blading, roller hockey, strength & conditioning, weight lifting, weight training, winter soccer, wrestling. 1 PE instructor, 16 coaches, 1 athletic trainer.

Computers Computers are regularly used in all classes. Computer network features include Internet access, wireless campus network, Internet filtering or blocking technology, all students are provided a laptop with the option to buy. Campus intranet, student e-mail accounts, and computer access in designated common areas are available to students. Students grades are available online. The school has a published electronic and media policy.

Contact Mrs. Lisa Ballard, Admissions Associate. 610-644-1754. Fax: 610-644-6679. E-mail: admis@thephelpsschool.org. Website: www.thephelpsschool.org

PHILADELPHIA-MONTGOMERY CHRISTIAN ACADEMY

35 Hillcrest Avenue
Erdenheim, Pennsylvania 19038

Head of School: Mr. Donald B. Beebe

General Information Coeducational day college-preparatory, arts, and religious studies school, affiliated with Christian faith. Grades K–12. Founded: 1943. Setting: suburban. Nearest major city is Philadelphia. 1-acre campus. 1 building on campus. Approved or accredited by Christian Schools International and Middle States Association of Colleges and Schools. Endowment: $150,205. Total enrollment: 309.

Upper school average class size: 18. Upper school faculty-student ratio: 1:10. There are 178 required school days per year for Upper School students. Upper School students typically attend 5 days per week. The average school day consists of 6 hours and 50 minutes.

Upper School Student Profile Grade 9: 32 students (13 boys, 19 girls); Grade 10: 41 students (20 boys, 21 girls); Grade 11: 30 students (17 boys, 13 girls); Grade 12: 37 students (19 boys, 18 girls). 99% of students are Christian.

Faculty School total: 33. In upper school: 10 men, 8 women; 8 have advanced degrees.

Subjects Offered Algebra, American history, American literature, art, art history, biology, calculus, ceramics, chemistry, creative writing, drama, English, English literature, ethics, European history, fine arts, geography, geometry, German, government/civics, grammar, health, history, mathematics, music, physical education, physics, religion, science, social studies, sociology, Spanish, theater, trigonometry, typing, world history, writing.

Graduation Requirements Arts and fine arts (art, music, dance, drama), Bible, English, languages, mathematics, physical education (includes health), science, social studies (includes history).

Special Academic Programs 4 Advanced Placement exams for which test preparation is offered; honors section; academic accommodation for the gifted, the musically talented, and the artistically talented; ESL (10 students enrolled).

College Admission Counseling 17 students graduated in 2013; all went to college, including Eastern Michigan University; Liberty University; Penn State University Park; Temple University; West Chester University of Pennsylvania. Mean SAT critical reading: 568, mean SAT math: 551, mean SAT writing: 557, mean combined SAT: 1676.

Student Life Upper grades have uniform requirement, student council. Discipline rests primarily with faculty. Attendance at religious services is required.

Summer Programs ESL programs offered; session focuses on Intensive English and cultural immersion; held on campus; accepts boys and girls; not open to students from other schools. 6 students usually enrolled. 2014 schedule: August 18 to August 29.

Tuition and Aid Day student tuition: $12,799. Tuition installment plan (FACTS Tuition Payment Plan). Tuition reduction for siblings, need-based scholarship grants available. In 2013–14, 55% of upper-school students received aid. Total amount of financial aid awarded in 2013–14: $500,000.

Admissions Traditional secondary-level entrance grade is 9. For fall 2013, 23 students applied for upper-level admission, 21 were accepted, 17 enrolled. Brigance Test of Basic Skills or Iowa Tests of Basic Skills required. Deadline for receipt of application materials: none. Application fee required: $100. Interview required.

Athletics Interscholastic: baseball (boys), basketball (b,g), soccer (b,g), softball (g), tennis (g), track and field (b,g), wrestling (b); coed interscholastic: cross-country running. 2 PE instructors, 6 coaches.

Computers Computers are regularly used in art, English, mathematics, yearbook classes. Computer resources include on-campus library services, Internet access, Internet filtering or blocking technology, online college search. Students grades are available online. The school has a published electronic and media policy.

Contact Phil VanVeldhuizen, Admissions and Marketing Manager. 215-233-0782 Ext. 408. Fax: 215-233-0829. E-mail: admissions@phil-mont.com. Website: www.phil-mont.com

PHILLIPS ACADEMY (ANDOVER)

180 Main Street
Andover, Massachusetts 01810-4161

Head of School: John G. Palfrey Jr.

General Information Coeducational boarding and day college-preparatory school. Grades 9–PG. Founded: 1778. Setting: suburban. Nearest major city is Boston. Students are housed in single-sex dormitories and 9th graders housed separately from other students. 500-acre campus. 160 buildings on campus. Approved or accredited by New England Association of Schools and Colleges and The Association of Boarding Schools. Member of National Association of Independent Schools and Secondary School Admission Test Board. Endowment: $785 million. Total enrollment: 1,143. Upper school average class size: 13. Upper school faculty-student ratio: 1:5. There are 157 required school days per year for Upper School students. Upper School students typically attend 5 days per week. The average school day consists of 8 hours.

Upper School Student Profile Grade 9: 214 students (106 boys, 108 girls); Grade 10: 293 students (151 boys, 142 girls); Grade 11: 308 students (160 boys, 148 girls); Grade 12: 328 students (166 boys, 162 girls); Postgraduate: 28 students (20 boys, 8 girls). 75% of students are boarding students. 41% are state residents. 47 states are represented in upper school student body. 8% are international students. International students from Canada, China, Hong Kong, Republic of Korea, Thailand, and United Kingdom; 35 other countries represented in student body.

Faculty School total: 219. In upper school: 105 men, 114 women; 171 have advanced degrees; 190 reside on campus.

Subjects Offered Algebra, American history, American literature, ancient history, animal behavior, animation, Arabic studies, architecture, art, art history, astronomy, band, Bible studies, biology, calculus, ceramics, chamber groups, chemistry, Chinese, chorus, computer graphics, computer programming, computer science, creative writing, dance, drama, drawing, driver education, ecology, economics, English, English literature, environmental science, ethics, European history, expository writing, film, fine arts, French, geology, geometry, German, government/civics, grammar, Greek, health, history, international relations, Japanese, jazz, Latin, Latin American studies, life issues, literature, mathematics, Middle Eastern history, music, mythology, oceanography, painting, philosophy, photography, physical education, physics, physiology, printmaking, psychology, religion, Russian, Russian studies, science, sculpture, social sciences, social studies, sociology, Spanish, speech, swimming, theater, trigonometry, video, world history, writing.

Graduation Requirements Arts and fine arts (art, music, dance, drama), English, foreign language, history, life issues, mathematics, philosophy, physical education (includes health), religion (includes Bible studies and theology), science, social sciences, swimming test.

Special Academic Programs Advanced Placement exam preparation; honors section; independent study; term-away projects; study abroad; academic accommodation for the gifted, the musically talented, and the artistically talented; programs in English, mathematics, general development for dyslexic students; special instructional classes for deaf students, blind students.

College Admission Counseling 313 students graduated in 2012; 306 went to college, including Columbia University; Cornell University; Stanford University; University of Pennsylvania; Wesleyan University; Yale University. Other: 7 had other specific plans. Mean SAT critical reading: 678, mean SAT math: 684, mean SAT writing: 675.

Student Life Upper grades have student council, honor system. Discipline rests primarily with faculty.

Tuition and Aid Day student tuition: $34,500; 7-day tuition and room/board: $44,500. Tuition installment plan (individually arranged payment plans, The Andover Plan). Need-based scholarship grants, middle-income loans, Andover is a true need-blind school that admits students without regard to a family's financial situation available. In 2012–13, 46% of upper-school students received aid. Total amount of financial aid awarded in 2012–13: $18,157,000.

Admissions For fall 2012, 3,154 students applied for upper-level admission, 444 were accepted, 371 enrolled. ISEE or SSAT required. Deadline for receipt of application materials: February 1. Application fee required: $40. Interview required.

Athletics Interscholastic: baseball (boys), basketball (b,g), bicycling (b,g), crew (b,g), cross-country running (b,g), diving (b,g), field hockey (g), football (b), golf (b,g), ice hockey (b,g), indoor track & field (b,g), lacrosse (b,g), nordic skiing (b,g), skiing (cross-country) (b,g), soccer (b,g), softball (g), squash (b,g), swimming and diving (b,g), tennis (b,g), track and field (b,g), volleyball (b,g), water polo (b,g), winter (indoor) track (b,g), wrestling (b); intramural: aerobics/dance (b,g), backpacking (b,g), basketball (b,g), crew (b,g), martial arts (b,g), physical fitness (b,g), physical training (b,g); coed interscholastic: bicycling, Frisbee, golf, ultimate Frisbee, wrestling; coed intramural: badminton, ballet, canoeing/kayaking, cheering, cross-country running, dance, fencing, fitness, fitness walking, hiking/backpacking, martial arts, modern dance, outdoor adventure, outdoor education, physical fitness, physical training, rappelling, rock climbing, ropes courses, soccer, softball, strength & conditioning, tennis, wall climbing. 7 PE instructors, 25 coaches, 3 athletic trainers.

Computers Computers are regularly used in animation, architecture, art, classics, computer applications, digital applications, English, foreign language, history, mathematics, music, photography, psychology, religious studies, science, theater, video film production classes. Computer network features include on-campus library services, online commercial services, Internet access, wireless campus network. Campus intranet and student e-mail accounts are available to students. The school has a published electronic and media policy.

Contact Jim Ventre, Interim Dean of Admission and Director of Financial Aid. 978-749-4050. Fax: 978-749-4068. E-mail: admissions@andover.edu. Website: www.andover.edu

PHILLIPS EXETER ACADEMY

20 Main Street
Exeter, New Hampshire 03833-2460

Head of School: Mr. Thomas E. Hassan

General Information Coeducational boarding and day college-preparatory school. Grades 9–PG. Founded: 1781. Setting: small town. Nearest major city is Boston, MA. Students are housed in single-sex dormitories. 670-acre campus. 130 buildings on campus. Approved or accredited by Association of Independent Schools in New England, New England Association of Schools and Colleges, and The Association of Boarding Schools. Member of National Association of Independent Schools and Secondary School Admission Test Board. Upper school average class size: 12. Upper school faculty-student ratio: 1:5.

Upper School Student Profile 80% of students are boarding students. 45 states are represented in upper school student body. 10% are international students.

Faculty School total: 258.

Subjects Offered Algebra, American history, American literature, anatomy, anthropology, Arabic, archaeology, architecture, art, art history, astronomy, biology, botany, calculus, ceramics, chemistry, Chinese, classics, computer programming, computer science, creative writing, dance, discrete mathematics, drama, driver education, ecology, economics, electronics, English, English literature, environmental science, ethics, European history, evolution, existentialism, expository writing, film, fine arts, French, genetics, geology, geometry, German, Greek, health, history, Italian, Japanese, Latin, linear algebra, logic, marine biology, mathematics, music, music composition, ornithology, philosophy, photography, physical education, physics, physiology, psychology, religion, Russian, science, sculpture, Spanish, statistics, theater, trigonometry, world literature, writing, Zen Buddhism.

Graduation Requirements American history, art, biology, computer science, English, foreign language, mathematics, physical education (includes health), physical science, religion (includes Bible studies and theology), science.

Special Academic Programs Advanced Placement exam preparation; honors section; independent study; term-away projects; study abroad; academic accommodation for the gifted, the musically talented, and the artistically talented.

College Admission Counseling Colleges students went to include Harvard University; New York University; Stanford University; The George Washington University; The Johns Hopkins University; University of Pennsylvania.

Student Life Upper grades have specified standards of dress, student council, honor system. Discipline rests primarily with faculty.

Summer Programs Enrichment programs offered; session focuses on academic enrichment; held on campus; accepts boys and girls; open to students from other schools. Application deadline: none.

Tuition and Aid Day student tuition: $35,750; 7-day tuition and room/board: $46,030. Tuition installment plan (Academic Management Services Plan, Tuition Management Systems Plan). Need-based scholarship grants available.

Admissions Traditional secondary-level entrance grade is 9. PSAT or SAT, SSAT or TOEFL required. Deadline for receipt of application materials: January 15. Application fee required: $50. Interview required.

Athletics Interscholastic: baseball (boys), basketball (b,g), crew (b,g), cross-country running (b,g), field hockey (g), football (b), golf (b,g), ice hockey (b,g), lacrosse (b,g), soccer (b,g), softball (g), squash (b,g), swimming and diving (b,g), tennis (b,g), track and field (b,g), volleyball (g), water polo (b,g), wrestling (b); coed interscholastic: bicycling, winter (indoor) track.

Computers Computers are regularly used in computer applications, foreign language, mathematics, science classes. Computer network features include on-campus library services, Internet access, Internet filtering or blocking technology. Campus intranet and student e-mail accounts are available to students.

Contact Director of Admissions. 603-777-3437. Fax: 603-777-4399. E-mail: admit@exeter.edu. Web site: www.exeter.edu.

See Summer Program Close-Up on page 634.

PHOENIX CHRISTIAN UNIFIED SCHOOLS

1751 West Indian School Road
Phoenix, Arizona 85015

Head of School: Dr. Phil Adams

General Information Coeducational day college-preparatory, general academic, religious studies, and AP/Honors school, affiliated with Christian faith. Grades PS–12. Founded: 1949. Setting: urban. 12-acre campus. 10 buildings on campus. Approved or accredited by Association of Christian Schools International, North Central Association of Colleges and Schools, and Arizona Department of Education. Total enrollment: 424. Upper school average class size: 20. Upper school faculty-student ratio: 1:20. There are 178 required school days per year for Upper School students. Upper School students typically attend 5 days per week. The average school day consists of 6 hours and 40 minutes.

Upper School Student Profile Grade 6: 19 students (10 boys, 9 girls); Grade 7: 18 students (7 boys, 11 girls); Grade 8: 31 students (12 boys, 19 girls); Grade 9: 49 students (27 boys, 22 girls); Grade 10: 63 students (27 boys, 36 girls); Grade 11: 50 students (25 boys, 25 girls); Grade 12: 69 students (37 boys, 32 girls).

Faculty School total: 23. In upper school: 11 men, 9 women; 19 have advanced degrees.

Subjects Offered Advanced computer applications, algebra, American literature, American literature-AP, anatomy, art, arts, band, Bible, biology, biology-AP, calculus, calculus-AP, career and personal planning, chemistry, choir, choral music, computer applications, computers, creative writing, culinary arts, drama, drama performance, drawing, economics, English, English literature, English literature-AP, English-AP, geometry, government, government-AP, home economics, instrumental music, integrated science, internship, intro to computers, language-AP, library, literature, literature-AP, marching band, photography, physical education, physics, pre-algebra, pre-calculus, psychology, religious education, sociology, Spanish, Spanish language-AP, statistics, student government, study skills, U.S. government, U.S. history, U.S. history-AP, Web site design, world history, yearbook.

Graduation Requirements Advanced math, Advanced Placement courses, algebra, American literature, arts and fine arts (art, music, dance, drama), biology, British literature, chemistry, computer education, economics, English, English composition, English literature, foreign language, geometry, government, integrated science, pre-calculus, religious studies, study skills, U.S. history, world history, world literature.

Special Academic Programs Advanced Placement exam preparation; honors section; independent study; study at local college for college credit; ESL (3 students enrolled).

College Admission Counseling 47 students graduated in 2013; 45 went to college, including Arizona Christian University; Arizona State University; Grand Canyon University; Northern Arizona University; The University of Arizona. Other: 1 entered military service, 1 had other specific plans. Mean SAT critical reading: 544, mean SAT math: 544, mean SAT writing: 532, mean composite ACT: 23.

Student Life Upper grades have uniform requirement, student council. Discipline rests primarily with faculty.

Summer Programs Remediation, advancement, sports programs offered; session focuses on advance education, redemption, refine skills; held on campus; accepts boys and girls; open to students from other schools. 40 students usually enrolled. 2014 schedule: June 1 to July 15. Application deadline: May 15.

Tuition and Aid Day student tuition: $8411. Tuition installment plan (FACTS Tuition Payment Plan, monthly payment plans, individually arranged payment plans). Tuition reduction for siblings, merit scholarship grants, need-based scholarship grants available.

Admissions Traditional secondary-level entrance grade is 9. Achievement tests, any standardized test or placement test required. Deadline for receipt of application materials: none. Application fee required: $50. Interview required.

Athletics Interscholastic: baseball (boys), basketball (b,g), cheering (g), football (b), softball (g), volleyball (g), wrestling (b); intramural: football (g), volleyball (b); coed interscholastic: cross-country running, diving, golf, soccer, swimming and diving, tennis, track and field, weight lifting, weight training. 1 PE instructor, 7 coaches, 1 athletic trainer.

Computers Computers are regularly used in career exploration, college planning, computer applications, keyboarding, library, media services, Web site design, yearbook classes. Computer resources include on-campus library services, Internet access, wireless campus network, Internet filtering or blocking technology. Campus intranet and computer access in designated common areas are available to students. Students grades are available online. The school has a published electronic and media policy.

Contact Mrs. Gretchen Janes, Admissions Coordinator. 602-265-4707 Ext. 270. Fax: 602-277-7170. E-mail: gjanes@phoenixchristian.org. Website: www.phoenixchristian.org

PHOENIX COUNTRY DAY SCHOOL

3901 East Stanford Drive
Paradise Valley, Arizona 85253

Head of School: Mr. Andrew Rodin

General Information Coeducational day college-preparatory, arts, performing and studio arts, extensive athletics, and community service, global citizenship, and travel school. Grades PK–12. Founded: 1961. Setting: suburban. Nearest major city is Phoenix. 40-acre campus. 8 buildings on campus. Approved or accredited by Independent Schools Association of the Southwest and National Independent Private Schools Association. Member of National Association of Independent Schools. Endowment: $15 million. Total enrollment: 724. Upper school average class size: 15. Upper school faculty-student ratio: 1:8. There are 173 required school days per year for Upper School students. Upper School students typically attend 5 days per week. The average school day consists of 5 hours.

Upper School Student Profile Grade 9: 70 students (33 boys, 37 girls); Grade 10: 64 students (29 boys, 35 girls); Grade 11: 57 students (20 boys, 37 girls); Grade 12: 62 students (25 boys, 37 girls).

Faculty School total: 90. In upper school: 17 men, 13 women; 23 have advanced degrees.

Subjects Offered Acting, advanced biology, advanced chemistry, advanced math, Advanced Placement courses, African-American literature, algebra, American government, American history, American history-AP, American literature, anatomy, anatomy and physiology, anthropology, art, art history, art history-AP, astronomy, band, baseball, basketball, biology, biology-AP, British literature, calculus, calculus-AP, ceramics, chemistry, chemistry-AP, Chinese, Chinese studies, choir, chorus, computer programming, computer science, creative writing, digital photography, directing, discrete mathematics, drawing, ecology, English, English composition, English literature, environmental science, environmental science-AP, ethics, European history, evolution, fine arts, French, French-AP, geography, geology, geometry, government/civics, history, Holocaust studies, jazz band, journalism, Latin, Latin American literature, Latin-AP, literature, Mandarin, marine biology, mathematics, music, oceanography, orchestra, painting, photography, physical education, physics, physics-AP, physiology, pre-calculus, probability and statistics, psychology, scene study, science, Shakespeare, social sciences, social studies, Spanish, Spanish-AP, speech, statistics, statistics-AP, theater, theater arts, trigonometry, world history, world literature, world religions.

Graduation Requirements Advanced biology, American history, American literature, ancient world history, arts and fine arts (art, music, dance, drama), biology, chemistry, English, foreign language, mathematics, physical education (includes health), physics, science, U.S. history, Western civilization, world history, 40 hours of community service.

Special Academic Programs 15 Advanced Placement exams for which test preparation is offered; honors section; independent study; study abroad.

College Admission Counseling 58 students graduated in 2012; all went to college, including Arizona State University; Harvard University; Massachusetts

Institute of Technology; New York University; Southern Methodist University; University of Southern California. Median SAT critical reading: 670, median SAT math: 680, median SAT writing: 690, median combined SAT: 2010, median composite ACT: 29. 77% scored over 600 on SAT critical reading, 86% scored over 600 on SAT math, 86% scored over 600 on SAT writing, 86% scored over 1800 on combined SAT, 78% scored over 26 on composite ACT.

Student Life Upper grades have specified standards of dress, student council, honor system. Discipline rests primarily with faculty.

Tuition and Aid Day student tuition: $22,100. Tuition installment plan (Insured Tuition Payment Plan, monthly payment plans, individually arranged payment plans, 10 months, quarterly, semiannual, and yearly payment plans). Need-based scholarship grants available. In 2012–13, 21% of upper-school students received aid. Total amount of financial aid awarded in 2012–13: $1,016,600.

Admissions Traditional secondary-level entrance grade is 9. For fall 2012, 82 students applied for upper-level admission, 45 were accepted, 31 enrolled. Achievement/Aptitude/Writing, ERB CTP IV, Math Placement Exam, Otis-Lennon IQ and writing sample required. Deadline for receipt of application materials: March 1. Application fee required: $100. Interview required.

Athletics Interscholastic: baseball (boys), basketball (b,g), cheering (g), diving (b,g), flag football (b), golf (b,g), lacrosse (b,g), soccer (b,g), softball (g), winter soccer (g); intramural: archery (b,g), badminton (b,g), basketball (b,g), lacrosse (b,g), outdoor education (b,g), outdoor recreation (b,g), physical fitness (b,g), softball (g), strength & conditioning (b,g), yoga (b,g); coed interscholastic: cheering, diving, swimming and diving, tennis, volleyball; coed intramural: basketball, cross-country running, flag football, golf, hiking/backpacking, running, soccer, swimming and diving, tennis, volleyball, weight lifting, winter soccer. 5 PE instructors, 23 coaches, 1 athletic trainer.

Computers Computers are regularly used in art, college planning, creative writing, data processing, desktop publishing, economics, engineering, English, foreign language, French, history, humanities, independent study, information technology, keyboarding, library, library skills, literary magazine, mathematics, news writing, newspaper, photography, programming, publications, research skills, science, social sciences, social studies, Spanish, stock market, Web site design, writing, yearbook classes. Computer network features include on-campus library services, online commercial services, Internet access, wireless campus network, Internet filtering or blocking technology. Campus intranet, student e-mail accounts, and computer access in designated common areas are available to students. Students grades are available online. The school has a published electronic and media policy.

Contact Sandy Orrick, Admissions Assistant. 602-955-8200 Ext. 2255. Fax: 602-381-4554. E-mail: sandy.orrick@pcds.org. Website: www.pcds.org

PICKENS ACADEMY

225 Ray Bass Road
Carrollton, Alabama 35447
Head of School: Mr. Brach White

General Information Coeducational day college-preparatory, general academic, and technology school. Grades K4–12. Founded: 1970. Setting: rural. Nearest major city is Tuscaloosa. 3 buildings on campus. Approved or accredited by Distance Education and Training Council, Southern Association of Colleges and Schools, and Alabama Department of Education. Total enrollment: 265. Upper school average class size: 25. Upper school faculty-student ratio: 1:20. There are 180 required school days per year for Upper School students. Upper School students typically attend 5 days per week. The average school day consists of 7 hours.

Upper School Student Profile Grade 7: 25 students (11 boys, 14 girls); Grade 8: 28 students (11 boys, 17 girls); Grade 9: 15 students (7 boys, 8 girls); Grade 10: 26 students (13 boys, 13 girls); Grade 11: 19 students (7 boys, 12 girls); Grade 12: 34 students (15 boys, 19 girls).

Faculty School total: 21. In upper school: 5 men, 16 women; 8 have advanced degrees.

Subjects Offered 20th century history, 20th century world history, advanced chemistry, advanced computer applications, advanced math, Alabama history and geography, algebra, American democracy, American government, American history, American literature, anatomy and physiology, ancient history, ancient world history, applied music, art, band, baseball, basketball, biology, British literature, business mathematics, calculus, career/college preparation, cheerleading, chemistry, civics, college admission preparation, composition, computer literacy, consumer economics, CPR, creative writing, desktop publishing, economics, English composition, English literature, environmental science, family and consumer science, French, geography, government, grammar, health education, history, keyboarding, land management, leadership education training, library assistant, Microsoft, music, music appreciation, physical education, physical science, physics, research skills, science, student government, trigonometry, U.S. government and politics, Web site design, weight training, weightlifting.

Graduation Requirements 20th century world history, advanced math, American government, American history, anatomy and physiology, calculus, economics, English, English composition, English literature, physics, research skills, trigonometry.

Special Academic Programs Study at local college for college credit.

College Admission Counseling 24 students graduated in 2012; 17 went to college, including Auburn University; Mississippi State University; The University of Alabama. Other: 1 went to work, 1 entered military service. Median composite ACT: 21. 8% scored over 26 on composite ACT.

Student Life Upper grades have specified standards of dress, student council. Discipline rests primarily with faculty.

Tuition and Aid Day student tuition: $3000. Guaranteed tuition plan. Tuition installment plan (Insured Tuition Payment Plan, monthly payment plans).

Admissions Traditional secondary-level entrance grade is 9. PSAT or Stanford Achievement Test, Otis-Lennon School Ability Test required. Deadline for receipt of application materials: none. No application fee required. On-campus interview required.

Athletics Interscholastic: baseball (boys), basketball (b,g), cheering (g), cross-country running (b,g), danceline (g), football (b), golf (b,g), softball (g), volleyball (g), weight lifting (b,g); coed interscholastic: tennis, track and field. 1 PE instructor, 2 coaches.

Computers Computers are regularly used in all academic classes. Computer network features include on-campus library services, Internet access, Internet filtering or blocking technology. Student e-mail accounts are available to students. Students grades are available online. The school has a published electronic and media policy.

Contact Admissions. 205-367-8144. Fax: 205-367-8145. Website: www.pickensacademy.com

PICKERING COLLEGE

16945 Bayview Avenue
Newmarket, Ontario L3Y 4X2, Canada
Head of School: Mr. Peter C. Sturrup

General Information Coeducational boarding and day college-preparatory, arts, technology, film studies and radio station, and leadership school. Boarding grades 7–12, day grades JK–12. Founded: 1842. Setting: suburban. Nearest major city is Toronto, Canada. Students are housed in single-sex dormitories. 42-acre campus. 6 buildings on campus. Approved or accredited by Canadian Association of Independent Schools, Canadian Educational Standards Institute, National Independent Private Schools Association, Ontario Ministry of Education, The Association of Boarding Schools, and Ontario Department of Education. Affiliate member of National Association of Independent Schools; member of Secondary School Admission Test Board. Language of instruction: English. Total enrollment: 373. Upper school average class size: 18. Upper school faculty-student ratio: 1:9. There are 164 required school days per year for Upper School students. Upper School students typically attend 5 days per week. The average school day consists of 8 hours.

Upper School Student Profile Grade 9: 42 students (26 boys, 16 girls); Grade 10: 54 students (32 boys, 22 girls); Grade 11: 57 students (31 boys, 26 girls); Grade 12: 65 students (32 boys, 33 girls). 35% of students are boarding students. 60% are province residents. 40% are international students. International students from Barbados, China, Germany, Japan, Mexico, and Russian Federation; 18 other countries represented in student body.

Faculty School total: 42. In upper school: 17 men, 12 women; 7 have advanced degrees; 15 reside on campus.

Subjects Offered Algebra, art, art history, biology, business, business skills, business studies, calculus, Canadian geography, Canadian history, careers, chemistry, community service, computer applications, computer multimedia, computer programming, computer science, concert band, creative writing, drama, dramatic arts, economics, English, English composition, English literature, entrepreneurship, environmental science, ESL, experiential education, family studies, filmmaking, fine arts, finite math, French, geography, geometry, government/civics, guitar, health, health education, history, instrumental music, jazz band, law, leadership, literature, mathematics, media studies, music, physical education, physics, politics, science, social sciences, social studies, theater, video film production, visual arts, vocal music, world history.

Graduation Requirements English, 60 hours of community service completed over 4 years before graduation.

Special Academic Programs Independent study; ESL (25 students enrolled).

College Admission Counseling 69 students graduated in 2012; 67 went to college, including Dalhousie University; McGill University; Queen's University at Kingston; The University of Western Ontario; University of Toronto; University of Waterloo. Other: 1 entered military service, 1 had other specific plans.

Student Life Upper grades have uniform requirement, student council, honor system. Discipline rests equally with students and faculty.

Tuition and Aid Day student tuition: CAN$19,130–CAN$23,000; 7-day tuition and room/board: CAN$47,700–CAN$49,930. Tuition installment plan (Insured Tuition Payment Plan, monthly payment plans). Tuition reduction for siblings, bursaries, merit scholarship grants, need-based scholarship grants available. In 2012–13, 4% of upper-school students received aid; total upper-school merit-scholarship money awarded: CAN$13,000. Total amount of financial aid awarded in 2012–13: CAN$100,000.

Admissions Traditional secondary-level entrance grade is 9. For fall 2012, 109 students applied for upper-level admission, 52 enrolled. CAT, International English Language Test, SLEP for foreign students, SSAT or TOEFL required. Deadline for receipt of application materials: none. Application fee required: CAN$200. Interview required.

Athletics Interscholastic: badminton (boys, girls), basketball (b,g), cross-country running (b,g), figure skating (b,g), hockey (b), horseback riding (b,g), ice hockey (b), ice skating (b,g), rugby (b,g), skiing (downhill) (b,g), snowboarding (b,g), soccer (b,g), softball (b,g), swimming and diving (b,g), tennis (b,g), track and field (b,g), volleyball (b,g); intramural: badminton (b,g), ball hockey (b,g), combined training (b,g), figure skating (b,g), floor hockey (b,g), hockey (b,g), horseback riding (b,g), ice skating (b,g), outdoor activities (b,g), outdoor adventure (b,g), outdoor recreation (b,g), paddle tennis (b,g), physical training (b,g), running (b,g), skiing (downhill) (b,g), soccer (b,g), strength & conditioning (b,g), swimming and diving (b,g), tennis (b,g), track and field (b,g), volleyball (b,g); coed interscholastic: alpine skiing, aquatics, badminton, cross-country running, equestrian sports, figure skating, hockey, horseback riding, ice hockey, ice skating, mountain biking, skiing (downhill), snowboarding, soccer, swimming and diving, tennis, track and field; coed intramural: aerobics/dance, badminton, ball hockey, basketball, bowling, broomball, canoeing/kayaking, cooperative games, cross-country running, dance squad, equestrian sports, figure skating, fitness, floor hockey, Frisbee, golf, hockey, horseback riding, ice skating, indoor soccer, mountain biking, nordic skiing, outdoor adventure, outdoor education, paint ball, rock climbing, skiing (downhill), soccer, strength & conditioning, swimming and diving, table tennis, tennis, touch football, track and field, volleyball, wilderness survival, yoga. 3 PE instructors, 2 coaches, 1 athletic trainer.

Computers Computers are regularly used in all classes. Computer network features include on-campus library services, Internet access, wireless campus network, Internet filtering or blocking technology. Student e-mail accounts are available to students. Students grades are available online. The school has a published electronic and media policy.

Contact Mrs. Susan Hundert, Admission Associate, Day and North American Boarding. 905-895-1700 Ext. 259. Fax: 905-895-1306. E-mail: admission@pickeringcollege.on.ca. Website: www.pickeringcollege.on.ca

PIEDMONT ACADEMY

PO Box 231
126 Highway 212 West
Monticello, Georgia 31064

Head of School: Mr. Tony Tanner

General Information Coeducational day college-preparatory, arts, business, vocational, religious studies, bilingual studies, technology, and joint enrollment with Georgia Military College school, affiliated with Protestant faith. Grades 1–12. Founded: 1970. Setting: rural. Nearest major city is Atlanta. 22-acre campus. 8 buildings on campus. Approved or accredited by Georgia Accrediting Commission, Georgia Independent School Association, and Southern Association of Independent Schools. Total enrollment: 277. Upper school average class size: 15. Upper school faculty-student ratio: 1:13. There are 180 required school days per year for Upper School students. Upper School students typically attend 5 days per week. The average school day consists of 7 hours.

Upper School Student Profile Grade 9: 23 students (14 boys, 9 girls); Grade 10: 26 students (14 boys, 12 girls); Grade 11: 33 students (22 boys, 11 girls); Grade 12: 27 students (14 boys, 13 girls). 98% of students are Protestant.

Faculty School total: 31. In upper school: 6 men, 15 women; 15 have advanced degrees.

Subjects Offered Advanced chemistry, advanced computer applications, advanced math, algebra, American government, American history, American history-AP, anatomy and physiology, band, biology, business law, calculus, calculus-AP, chemistry, chemistry-AP, civics, computer science, computer science-AP, computers, concert band, concert choir, consumer economics, consumer law, economics, English, English-AP, geometry, government and politics-AP, government-AP, government/civics, grammar, health education, honors algebra, honors English, honors geometry, Internet, intro to computers, keyboarding, language arts, leadership and service, literature, mathematics, performing arts, personal finance, physical fitness, physical science, physics, pre-calculus, science, sociology, Spanish, student government, wind instruments, world history, yearbook.

Graduation Requirements Algebra, American government, American literature, biology, calculus, chemistry, civics, English composition, English literature, geometry, government, grammar, history, keyboarding, mathematics, physical education (includes health), physical science, science, Spanish.

Special Academic Programs Study at local college for college credit.

College Admission Counseling 24 students graduated in 2013; all went to college, including Georgia Institute of Technology; Georgia Perimeter College; University of Georgia; University of North Georgia.

Student Life Upper grades have uniform requirement, student council, honor system. Discipline rests primarily with faculty.

Tuition and Aid Day student tuition: $4480–$6360. Guaranteed tuition plan. Tuition installment plan (monthly payment plans, individually arranged payment plans, APOGEE School Choice Scholarship, Financial Assistance (Grant)). Tuition reduction for siblings, need-based scholarship grants available. In 2013–14, 8% of upper-school students received aid. Total amount of financial aid awarded in 2013–14: $25,000.

Admissions Traditional secondary-level entrance grade is 9. For fall 2013, 48 students applied for upper-level admission, 48 were accepted, 45 enrolled. Cognitive

Abilities Test, OLSAT, Stanford Achievement Test or WAIS, WICS required. Deadline for receipt of application materials: none. Application fee required: $75. Interview required.

Athletics Interscholastic: baseball (boys), basketball (b,g), cheering (b,g), fitness (b,g), flag football (b,g), football (b), golf (b,g), power lifting (b,g); coed interscholastic: cross-country running, skeet shooting; coed intramural: cross-country running, flag football. 6 PE instructors, 10 coaches.

Computers Computers are regularly used in all academic classes. Computer network features include on-campus library services, online commercial services, Internet access, wireless campus network, Internet filtering or blocking technology. Campus intranet is available to students. Students grades are available online. The school has a published electronic and media policy.

Contact Judy M. Nelson, Director of Admissions/Public and Alumni Relations. 706-468-8818 Ext. 304. Fax: 706-468-2409. E-mail: judy_nelson@piedmontacademy.com. Website: www.piedmontacademy.com

PINECREST ACADEMY

955 Peachtree Parkway
Cumming, Georgia 30041

Head of School: Fr. Robert Presutti, LC, PhD

General Information Coeducational day college-preparatory, arts, religious studies, and technology school, affiliated with Roman Catholic Church. Grades PK–12. Founded: 1993. Setting: suburban. Nearest major city is Atlanta. 70-acre campus. 4 buildings on campus. Approved or accredited by Georgia Independent School Association, National Catholic Education Association, Southern Association of Colleges and Schools, The College Board, and Georgia Department of Education. Member of Secondary School Admission Test Board. Total enrollment: 790. Upper school average class size: 18. Upper school faculty-student ratio: 1:9. There are 180 required school days per year for Upper School students. Upper School students typically attend 5 days per week. The average school day consists of 7 hours and 30 minutes.

Upper School Student Profile Grade 9: 83 students (47 boys, 36 girls); Grade 10: 72 students (37 boys, 35 girls); Grade 11: 66 students (28 boys, 38 girls); Grade 12: 54 students (28 boys, 26 girls). 82% of students are Roman Catholic.

Faculty School total: 29. In upper school: 14 men, 15 women; 9 have advanced degrees.

Subjects Offered Advanced chemistry, advanced math, Advanced Placement courses, advanced studio art-AP, algebra, American history, American history-AP, American literature, anatomy and physiology, art, art history-AP, art-AP, arts, band, biology, biology-AP, British literature, British literature AP, business communications, calculus, calculus-AP, chemistry, chemistry-AP, chorus, Christian ethics, church history, classical language, composition, composition-AP, computer science-AP, concert band, creative writing, debate, digital imaging, drama, dramatic arts, drawing, drawing and design, economics, electives, engineering, English, English as a foreign language, English composition, English language and composition-AP, English language-AP, English literature, English literature and composition-AP, English literature-AP, English-AP, English/composition-AP, environmental science, ESL, ESL, European history-AP, French, general science, geometry, German, government and politics-AP, health education, history of the Catholic Church, history-AP, honors algebra, honors English, honors geometry, honors U.S. history, honors world history, instrumental music, instruments, journalism, language, language and composition, language arts, language-AP, languages, Latin, Latin-AP, law, Life of Christ, literature and composition-AP, macroeconomics-AP, microeconomics-AP, modern Western civilization, music, music theory, music theory-AP, oceanography, painting, personal fitness, philosophy, physical education, physics, play production, pre-algebra, pre-calculus, psychology, psychology-AP, public speaking, SAT preparation, SAT/ACT preparation, science, science and technology, scripture, sculpture, Spanish, Spanish language-AP, Spanish literature, Spanish literature-AP, Spanish-AP, speech and debate, statistics, statistics-AP, studio art, studio art-AP, symphonic band, technology, theater arts, theology, U.S. government and politics, U.S. government and politics-AP, U.S. history, U.S. history-AP, Web site design, weight fitness, weight training, weightlifting, world history, world history-AP, world literature, world wide web design, yearbook.

Special Academic Programs 22 Advanced Placement exams for which test preparation is offered; honors section; independent study; ESL (14 students enrolled).

College Admission Counseling 51 students graduated in 2013; all went to college, including Furman University; Georgia College & State University; Georgia Institute of Technology; University of Georgia; University of North Georgia; University of South Carolina. Mean SAT critical reading: 590, mean SAT math: 591, mean SAT writing: 590, mean combined SAT: 1771, mean composite ACT: 25. 34% scored over 600 on SAT critical reading, 51% scored over 600 on SAT math, 40% scored over 600 on SAT writing, 38% scored over 1800 on combined SAT, 49% scored over 26 on composite ACT.

Student Life Upper grades have uniform requirement, student council, honor system. Discipline rests primarily with faculty. Attendance at religious services is required.

Summer Programs Advancement programs offered; session focuses on math programs; held on campus; accepts boys and girls; not open to students from other schools. 8 students usually enrolled.

Tuition and Aid Day student tuition: $14,500. Tuition installment plan (monthly payment plans). Tuition reduction for siblings, need-based scholarship grants available.

Admissions Traditional secondary-level entrance grade is 9. For fall 2013, 42 students applied for upper-level admission, 41 were accepted, 38 enrolled. Admissions testing, Individual IQ, Achievement and behavior rating scale, PSAT or SAT for applicants to grade 11 and 12, psychoeducational evaluation, school's own exam, SSAT or TOEFL required. Deadline for receipt of application materials: none. Application fee required: $150. Interview required.

Athletics Interscholastic: baseball (boys), basketball (b,g), cheering (g), cross-country running (b,g), football (b), golf (b), lacrosse (b,g), soccer (b,g), softball (g), swimming and diving (b,g), tennis (b,g), track and field (b,g), volleyball (g), weight training (b,g); intramural: baseball (b), basketball (b,g), cheering (g), cross-country running (b,g), football (b), lacrosse (b,g), soccer (b,g), swimming and diving (b,g), tennis (b,g), track and field (b,g), volleyball (g); coed intramural: fencing. 1 PE instructor, 13 coaches.

Computers Computers are regularly used in all classes. Computer network features include on-campus library services, online commercial services, Internet access, wireless campus network, Internet filtering or blocking technology, homework is available online. Campus intranet, student e-mail accounts, and computer access in designated common areas are available to students. Students grades are available online.

Contact Ms. Melissa McWaters, Admissions Assistant. 770-888-4477 Ext. 245. Fax: 770-888-0404. E-mail: mmcwaters@pinecrestacademy.org. Website: www.pinecrestacademy.org/

PINE CREST SCHOOL

1501 Northeast 62nd Street
Fort Lauderdale, Florida 33334-5116

Head of School: Dr. Dana Markham

General Information Coeducational day college-preparatory school. Grades PK–12. Founded: 1934. Setting: urban. 49-acre campus. 22 buildings on campus. Approved or accredited by Florida Council of Independent Schools, Southern Association of Colleges and Schools, and Southern Association of Independent Schools. Member of National Association of Independent Schools and Secondary School Admission Test Board. Endowment: $36.2 million. Total enrollment: 1,755. Upper school average class size: 17. Upper school faculty-student ratio: 1:14. The average school day consists of 6 hours and 30 minutes.

Upper School Student Profile Grade 9: 214 students (98 boys, 116 girls); Grade 10: 200 students (107 boys, 93 girls); Grade 11: 185 students (97 boys, 88 girls); Grade 12: 207 students (101 boys, 106 girls).

Faculty School total: 219. In upper school: 42 men, 59 women; 61 have advanced degrees.

Subjects Offered Algebra, American history, art, art history, ballet, band, biology, calculus, ceramics, chemistry, Chinese, chorus, comparative government and politics-AP, computer graphics, computer programming, computer science, dance, drama, economics, English, environmental science, ethics, European history, fine arts, forensics, French, geometry, German, government/civics, history, mathematics, music, orchestra, photography, physical education, physics, psychology, Spanish, speech, statistics.

Graduation Requirements Arts and fine arts (art, music, dance, drama), English, ethics, foreign language, humanities, mathematics, physical education (includes health), science, social studies (includes history), speech.

Special Academic Programs Advanced Placement exam preparation; honors section; ESL (12 students enrolled).

College Admission Counseling 206 students graduated in 2012; 205 went to college, including Cornell University; The George Washington University; The Johns Hopkins University; University of Florida; University of Miami; University of Pennsylvania. Other: 1 entered a postgraduate year. Median SAT critical reading: 640, median SAT math: 650, median SAT writing: 650, median combined SAT: 1950, median composite ACT: 29. 70% scored over 600 on SAT critical reading, 77% scored over 600 on SAT math, 69% scored over 600 on SAT writing, 76% scored over 1800 on combined SAT, 80% scored over 26 on composite ACT.

Student Life Upper grades have uniform requirement, student council, honor system. Discipline rests primarily with faculty.

Tuition and Aid Day student tuition: $24,440. Tuition installment plan (The Tuition Refund Plan). Need-based scholarship grants available. In 2012–13, 18% of upper-school students received aid. Total amount of financial aid awarded in 2012–13: $1,888,380.

Admissions Traditional secondary-level entrance grade is 9. For fall 2012, 187 students applied for upper-level admission, 114 were accepted, 76 enrolled. SSAT required. Deadline for receipt of application materials: none. Application fee required: $100. Interview required.

Athletics Interscholastic: aquatics (boys, girls), baseball (b), basketball (b,g), crew (b,g), cross-country running (b,g), diving (b,g), football (b), golf (b,g), lacrosse (b,g), physical fitness (b,g), soccer (b,g), softball (g), strength & conditioning (b,g), swimming and diving (b,g), tennis (b,g), track and field (b,g), volleyball (b,g), weight lifting (b,g); intramural: aquatics (b,g), swimming and diving (b,g); coed

interscholastic: ballet, cheering; coed intramural: ballet, physical training, strength & conditioning. 8 PE instructors, 1 athletic trainer.

Computers Computer network features include on-campus library services, online commercial services, Internet access, wireless campus network, Internet filtering or blocking technology, laptop program (grades 6-12), SmartBoards in classrooms. Campus intranet and student e-mail accounts are available to students. Students grades are available online. The school has a published electronic and media policy.

Contact Mrs. Elena Del Alamo, Director of Admission and Financial Aid. 954-492-4103. Fax: 954-492-4188. E-mail: pcadmit@pinecrest.edu. Website: www.pinecrest.edu

PINEHURST SCHOOL

St. Catharines, Ontario, Canada
See Special Needs Schools section.

PINEWOOD - THE INTERNATIONAL SCHOOL OF THESSALONIKI, GREECE

PO Box 60606
Thermi
Thessaloniki 57001, Greece

Head of School: Dr. Roxanne Giampapa

General Information Coeducational boarding and day college-preparatory, arts, and bilingual studies school. Boarding grades 7–12, day grades PK–12. Founded: 1950. Setting: suburban. Students are housed in coed dormitories. 4-acre campus. 2 buildings on campus. Approved or accredited by International Baccalaureate Organization, Middle States Association of Colleges and Schools, The College Board, US Department of State, and state department of education. Member of European Council of International Schools. Language of instruction: English. Total enrollment: 205. Upper school average class size: 10. Upper school faculty-student ratio: 1:5. There are 174 required school days per year for Upper School students. The average school day consists of 6 hours and 30 minutes.

Upper School Student Profile Grade 9: 15 students (9 boys, 6 girls); Grade 10: 10 students (5 boys, 5 girls); Grade 11: 25 students (12 boys, 13 girls); Grade 12: 25 students (14 boys, 11 girls). 10% of students are boarding students. 80% are international students. International students from Bulgaria, China, Italy, Spain, and United States; 20 other countries represented in student body.

Faculty School total: 35. In upper school: 7 men, 14 women; 14 have advanced degrees.

Subjects Offered Algebra, art, biology, chemistry, computer applications, computer science, computers, economics, electives, English, English literature, ESL, European history, French, general science, geography, geometry, Greek, Greek culture, history, honors English, honors U.S. history, library, literature, math methods, mathematics, modern European history, music, physical education, physical science, physics, pre-algebra, psychology, science, social sciences, social studies, U.S. history, world cultures, world geography, world history, world literature, yearbook.

Graduation Requirements Electives, English, European history, foreign language, mathematics, physical education (includes health), science, social studies (includes history), world history.

Special Academic Programs International Baccalaureate program; honors section; accelerated programs; independent study; study at local college for college credit; ESL (30 students enrolled).

College Admission Counseling 8 students graduated in 2012; 7 went to college, including Bard College. Other: 1 had other specific plans.

Student Life Upper grades have specified standards of dress, student council, honor system. Discipline rests primarily with faculty.

Tuition and Aid Day student tuition: €10,812; 7-day tuition and room/board: €22,500. Tuition installment plan (monthly payment plans, individually arranged payment plans, 3-payment plan). Merit scholarship grants, need-based scholarship grants available. In 2012–13, 5% of upper-school students received aid.

Admissions Traditional secondary-level entrance grade is 10. English entrance exam or English language required. Deadline for receipt of application materials: none. No application fee required. Interview required.

Athletics Interscholastic: aerobics/dance (girls), basketball (b,g), dance (g), fitness (b,g), football (b), soccer (b,g), volleyball (b,g); intramural: basketball (b,g), cheering (g), flag football (b,g), floor hockey (b,g), football (b,g), soccer (b,g), table tennis (b,g), tennis (b,g), volleyball (b,g); coed interscholastic: gymnastics, indoor soccer, juggling; coed intramural: baseball, gymnastics, juggling, softball, table tennis. 2 PE instructors, 3 coaches, 2 athletic trainers.

Computers Computers are regularly used in English, science, word processing, yearbook classes. Computer network features include on-campus library services, Internet access, wireless campus network. Student e-mail accounts are available to students. Students grades are available online. The school has a published electronic and media policy.

Contact Mrs. Youli Andrianopoulou, Executive Assistant to the Director/Head of Admissions. 30-2310-301221 Ext. 13. Fax: 30-2310-323196. E-mail: admissions@pinewood.gr. Website: www.pinewood.gr

THE PINGREE SCHOOL

537 Highland Street

South Hamilton, Massachusetts 01982

Head of School: Dr. Timothy M. Johnson

General Information Coeducational day college-preparatory school. Grades 9–12. Founded: 1961. Setting: suburban. Nearest major city is Boston. 100-acre campus. 2 buildings on campus. Approved or accredited by Association of Independent Schools in New England, National Independent Private Schools Association, and New England Association of Schools and Colleges. Member of National Association of Independent Schools and Secondary School Admission Test Board. Endowment: $9.3 million. Total enrollment: 330. Upper school average class size: 15. Upper school faculty-student ratio: 1:7. There are 162 required school days per year for Upper School students. Upper School students typically attend 5 days per week. The average school day consists of 8 hours.

Upper School Student Profile Grade 9: 85 students (34 boys, 51 girls); Grade 10: 86 students (43 boys, 43 girls); Grade 11: 78 students (38 boys, 40 girls); Grade 12: 81 students (31 boys, 50 girls).

Faculty School total: 58. In upper school: 23 men, 35 women; 45 have advanced degrees.

Subjects Offered Algebra, American history, American literature, American studies, art, art history, astronomy, biology, calculus, ceramics, chemistry, computer programming, computer science, creative writing, dance, drama, driver education, earth science, ecology, economics, engineering, English, English literature, European history, fine arts, French, geometry, history, Latin, mathematics, music, oceanography, philosophy, photography, physics, psychology, Russian literature, science, social studies, Spanish, theater, trigonometry, writing.

Graduation Requirements Arts and fine arts (art, music, dance, drama), English, foreign language, mathematics, science, social studies (includes history), senior projects.

Special Academic Programs Advanced Placement exam preparation; honors section; independent study; term-away projects.

College Admission Counseling 84 students graduated in 2013; 82 went to college, including Boston University; Colby College; Providence College; The Colorado College; University of Denver; University of Michigan. Other: 1 entered a postgraduate year, 1 had other specific plans. Median SAT critical reading: 590, median SAT math: 610, median SAT writing: 600, median combined SAT: 1800, median composite ACT: 26. 45% scored over 600 on SAT critical reading, 57% scored over 600 on SAT math, 51% scored over 600 on SAT writing, 51% scored over 1800 on combined SAT, 50% scored over 26 on composite ACT.

Student Life Upper grades have specified standards of dress, student council, honor system. Discipline rests equally with students and faculty.

Tuition and Aid Day student tuition: $37,500. Tuition installment plan (Academic Management Services Plan). Merit scholarship grants, need-based scholarship grants, need-based loans available. In 2013–14, 30% of upper-school students received aid; total upper-school merit-scholarship money awarded: $144,000. Total amount of financial aid awarded in 2013–14: $2,500,000.

Admissions Traditional secondary-level entrance grade is 9. For fall 2013, 400 students applied for upper-level admission, 200 were accepted, 100 enrolled. ISEE or SSAT required. Deadline for receipt of application materials: January 15. Application fee required: $50. On-campus interview required.

Athletics Interscholastic: baseball (boys), basketball (b,g), cross-country running (b,g), field hockey (g), football (b), golf (b,g), ice hockey (b,g), lacrosse (b,g), running (b,g), soccer (b,g), softball (g), swimming and diving (b,g), tennis (b,g), volleyball (g); coed interscholastic: Frisbee, sailing, ultimate Frisbee; coed intramural: dance, fitness, golf, hiking/backpacking, modern dance, mountaineering, outdoor adventure, outdoor education, outdoor skills, physical fitness, physical training, skiing (downhill), strength & conditioning, weight lifting, weight training, wilderness. 24 coaches, 2 athletic trainers.

Computers Computers are regularly used in college planning, computer applications, desktop publishing, digital applications, drawing and design, English, foreign language, graphic arts, graphic design, independent study, information technology, mathematics, programming, publications, science, technology, Web site design, word processing, writing, yearbook classes. Computer network features include on-campus library services, online commercial services, Internet access, wireless campus network, Internet filtering or blocking technology. Campus intranet, student e-mail accounts, and computer access in designated common areas are available to students. Students grades are available online. The school has a published electronic and media policy.

Contact Mrs. Jody MacWhinnie, Admission Office Coordinator. 978-468-4415 Ext. 262. Fax: 978-468-3758. E-mail: jmacwhinnie@pingree.org. Website: www.pingree.org

THE PINGRY SCHOOL

Martinsville Road

131 Martinsville Road

Basking Ridge, New Jersey 07920

Head of School: Mr. Nathaniel Conard

General Information Coeducational day college-preparatory and arts school. Grades K–12. Founded: 1861. Setting: suburban. Nearest major city is New York, NY. 240-acre campus. 1 building on campus. Approved or accredited by Middle States Association of Colleges and Schools and New Jersey Department of Education. Member of National Association of Independent Schools. Endowment: $80 million. Total enrollment: 1,084. Upper school average class size: 14. Upper school faculty-student ratio: 1:8. There are 168 required school days per year for Upper School students. Upper School students typically attend 5 days per week. The average school day consists of 6 hours and 15 minutes.

Upper School Student Profile Grade 9: 146 students (80 boys, 66 girls); Grade 10: 134 students (67 boys, 67 girls); Grade 11: 144 students (71 boys, 73 girls); Grade 12: 132 students (63 boys, 69 girls).

Faculty School total: 120. In upper school: 47 men, 37 women; 61 have advanced degrees.

Subjects Offered Algebra, American literature, analysis, analysis and differential calculus, anatomy, architecture, art, art history-AP, biology, biology-AP, brass choir, calculus, chemistry, chemistry-AP, Chinese, clayworking, comparative cultures, computer science-AP, creative writing, drafting, drama, driver education, English, ethics, European literature, filmmaking, French, French-AP, geometry, German, German-AP, Greek drama, health, jazz band, jewelry making, Latin, literature by women, macro/microeconomics-AP, macroeconomics-AP, modern European history, music theory, mythology, orchestra, painting, peer counseling, photography, physics, physics-AP, physiology, psychology, psychology-AP, sculpture, Shakespeare, Spanish, Spanish-AP, studio art-AP, trigonometry, U.S. government and politics-AP, U.S. history-AP, wind ensemble, world literature, yearbook.

Graduation Requirements Arts and fine arts (art, music, dance, drama), English, foreign language, mathematics, physical education (includes health), science, social studies (includes history). Community service is required.

Special Academic Programs 20 Advanced Placement exams for which test preparation is offered; honors section; independent study; term-away projects; study abroad; academic accommodation for the gifted.

College Admission Counseling 131 students graduated in 2013; 128 went to college, including Boston College; Cornell University; Georgetown University; Hamilton College; Princeton University; University of Pennsylvania. Other: 3 had other specific plans. Mean SAT critical reading: 686, mean SAT math: 693, mean SAT writing: 698, mean composite ACT: 30.

Student Life Upper grades have specified standards of dress, student council, honor system. Discipline rests equally with students and faculty.

Summer Programs Enrichment, sports programs offered; session focuses on enrichment, writing, and study skills; held on campus; accepts boys and girls; open to students from other schools. 30 students usually enrolled. 2014 schedule: June 27 to August 8.

Tuition and Aid Day student tuition: $29,509–$34,714. Tuition installment plan (monthly payment plans, individually arranged payment plans, My Tuition Solutions). Need-based scholarship grants available. In 2013–14, 15% of upper-school students received aid. Total amount of financial aid awarded in 2013–14: $4,657,269.

Admissions Traditional secondary-level entrance grade is 9. For fall 2013, 298 students applied for upper-level admission, 97 were accepted, 69 enrolled. ERB, ISEE, SSAT or Wechsler Intelligence Scale for Children required. Deadline for receipt of application materials: January 5. Application fee required: $90. On-campus interview required.

Athletics Interscholastic: alpine skiing (boys, girls), baseball (b), basketball (b,g), cross-country running (b,g), fencing (b,g), field hockey (g), football (b), golf (b,g), ice hockey (b,g), lacrosse (b,g), skiing (downhill) (b,g), soccer (b,g), softball (g), squash (b,g), swimming and diving (b,g), tennis (b,g), track and field (b,g), wrestling (b); intramural: fitness (b,g), yoga (b,g); coed interscholastic: dance, physical fitness, physical training, water polo. 3 PE instructors, 15 coaches, 1 athletic trainer.

Computers Computers are regularly used in all academic classes. Computer network features include on-campus library services, online commercial services, Internet access, wireless campus network, Internet filtering or blocking technology. Campus intranet, student e-mail accounts, and computer access in designated common areas are available to students. The school has a published electronic and media policy.

Contact Mrs. Samantha Schifano, Admission Coordinator and Counselor. 908-647-5555 Ext. 1228. Fax: 908-647-4395. E-mail: sschifano@pingry.org. Website: www.pingry.org

PIONEER VALLEY CHRISTIAN SCHOOL

965 Plumtree Road
Springfield, Massachusetts 01119

Head of School: Mr. Timothy L. Duff

General Information Coeducational day college-preparatory, religious studies, bilingual studies, and technology school, affiliated with Protestant faith, Evangelical faith. Grades PS–12. Founded: 1972. Setting: suburban. 25-acre campus. 1 building on campus. Approved or accredited by Association of Christian Schools International, New England Association of Schools and Colleges, and Massachusetts Department of Education. Total enrollment: 270. Upper school average class size: 20. Upper school faculty-student ratio: 1:4. There are 181 required school days per year for Upper School students. Upper School students typically attend 5 days per week. The average school day consists of 6 hours and 40 minutes.

Upper School Student Profile Grade 9: 21 students (10 boys, 11 girls); Grade 10: 23 students (14 boys, 9 girls); Grade 11: 18 students (10 boys, 8 girls); Grade 12: 9 students (4 boys, 5 girls). 95% of students are Protestant, members of Evangelical faith.

Faculty School total: 31. In upper school: 6 men, 10 women; 9 have advanced degrees.

Subjects Offered Advanced math, algebra, American literature, American literature-AP, anatomy, art, athletics, baseball, basketball, bell choir, Bible studies, biology, British literature, British literature-AP, calculus-AP, chemistry, choir, choral music, Christian education, drama, economics, English, English-AP, French, geometry, government, history, instrumental music, music, physical education, physical science, physics, pre-algebra, sociology, softball, Spanish, speech, sports, technology, tennis, U.S. history, volleyball, weight training, Western civilization, world history, yearbook.

Graduation Requirements Algebra, American literature, arts and fine arts (art, music, dance, drama), Bible, biology, British literature, economics, English, foreign language, government, physical education (includes health), physical science, sociology, speech, U.S. history, Christian/community service hours.

Special Academic Programs Advanced Placement exam preparation; honors section; remedial reading and/or remedial writing; remedial math; programs in English, mathematics, general development for dyslexic students; special instructional classes for students with learning disabilities, Attention Deficit Disorder, and dyslexia.

College Admission Counseling 20 students graduated in 2013; all went to college, including American International College; Gordon College; Taylor University; Western New England University. Median SAT critical reading: 480, median SAT math: 490, median SAT writing: 510.

Student Life Upper grades have uniform requirement, honor system. Discipline rests primarily with faculty. Attendance at religious services is required.

Tuition and Aid Day student tuition: $10,700. Tuition installment plan (monthly payment plans, Electronic Funds Transfer, weekly, biweekly, monthly). Need-based scholarship grants, need-based financial aid and scholarship available. In 2013–14, 38% of upper-school students received aid. Total amount of financial aid awarded in 2013–14: $80,300.

Admissions Traditional secondary-level entrance grade is 9. For fall 2013, 72 students applied for upper-level admission, 53 were accepted, 52 enrolled. Admissions testing required. Deadline for receipt of application materials: none. Application fee required: $100. Interview required.

Athletics Interscholastic: baseball (boys), basketball (b,g), softball (g), tennis (b,g), volleyball (g); intramural: soccer (b,g); coed interscholastic: soccer, weight training; coed intramural: combined training, physical training, soccer, strength & conditioning. 2 PE instructors, 16 coaches.

Computers Computers are regularly used in all academic classes. Computer network features include Internet access, Internet filtering or blocking technology, homework assignments available online.

Contact Mr. Pat Sterlacci, Director of Admissions. 413-782-8031. Fax: 413-782-8033. E-mail: psterlacci@pvcs.org. Website: www.pvcs.org

POPE JOHN XXIII REGIONAL HIGH SCHOOL

28 Andover Road
Sparta, New Jersey 07871

Head of School: Mr. Brian Vohden

General Information Coeducational day college-preparatory, arts, business, religious studies, and technology school, affiliated with Roman Catholic Church. Grades 8–12. Founded: 1956. Setting: suburban. Nearest major city is New York, NY. 15-acre campus. 1 building on campus. Approved or accredited by New Jersey Department of Education. Total enrollment: 943. Upper school average class size: 20. Upper school faculty-student ratio: 1:13. There are 180 required school days per year for Upper School students. Upper School students typically attend 5 days per week. The average school day consists of 5 hours and 42 minutes.

Upper School Student Profile Grade 8: 139 students (80 boys, 59 girls); Grade 9: 196 students (104 boys, 92 girls); Grade 10: 198 students (89 boys, 109 girls); Grade 11: 210 students (116 boys, 94 girls); Grade 12: 201 students (90 boys, 111 girls). 80% of students are Roman Catholic.

Faculty School total: 78. In upper school: 36 men, 42 women; 35 have advanced degrees.

Subjects Offered Advanced chemistry, advanced computer applications, advanced math, Advanced Placement courses, algebra, American literature, American studies, anatomy and physiology, art, biology, biology-AP, British literature, business, business law, calculus, calculus-AP, chemistry, chemistry-AP, choral music, computer literacy, computer science, computer science-AP, conceptual physics, concert choir, earth science, economics, English, English language-AP, English literature, English literature and composition-AP, environmental science, environmental science-AP, European history-AP, fine arts, French, French-AP, geometry, German, global issues, government and politics-AP, graphic arts, health and safety, history-AP, honors algebra, honors English, honors geometry, honors U.S. history, honors world history, human geography - AP, Italian, Japanese, jazz band, journalism, lab science, Latin, macroeconomics-AP, microeconomics-AP, modern politics, music theory, physical education, physics, physics-AP, pre-calculus, psychology, psychology-AP, public speaking, reading/study skills, robotics, Spanish, Spanish language-AP, statistics, statistics-AP, theater arts, theology, U.S. government, U.S. government and politics-AP, U.S. history, U.S. history-AP, world cultures, world history-AP, zoology.

Graduation Requirements Arts and fine arts (art, music, dance, drama), English, foreign language, health and safety, mathematics, science, social studies (includes history), theology, 60 hours of community service (15 hours per year).

Special Academic Programs Advanced Placement exam preparation; honors section; ESL (15 students enrolled).

College Admission Counseling 219 students graduated in 2013; 216 went to college, including Drexel University; Moravian College; Northeastern University; Rutgers, The State University of New Jersey, New Brunswick; Saint Joseph's University; The Catholic University of America. Other: 3 had other specific plans. Mean SAT critical reading: 527, mean SAT math: 558, mean SAT writing: 535, mean combined SAT: 1620.

Student Life Upper grades have uniform requirement, student council. Discipline rests primarily with faculty. Attendance at religious services is required.

Summer Programs Remediation, enrichment, sports programs offered; session focuses on sports; held on campus; accepts boys and girls; open to students from other schools. 200 students usually enrolled.

Tuition and Aid Day student tuition: $14,000. Guaranteed tuition plan. Tuition installment plan (SMART Tuition Payment Plan). Need-based scholarship grants available.

Admissions Traditional secondary-level entrance grade is 9. CTB/McGraw-Hill/Macmillan Co-op Test, Math Placement Exam, placement test and writing sample required. Deadline for receipt of application materials: none. No application fee required. Interview required.

Athletics Interscholastic: baseball (boys), basketball (b,g), cheering (g), cross-country running (b,g), field hockey (g), football (b), ice hockey (b), indoor track & field (b,g), lacrosse (b,g), running (b,g), skiing (downhill) (b,g), softball (g), swimming and diving (b,g), tennis (b,g), track and field (b,g), volleyball (b,g), winter (indoor) track (b,g), wrestling (b); coed interscholastic: golf.

Computers Computers are regularly used in graphic arts, programming classes. Computer network features include Internet access, wireless campus network, Internet filtering or blocking technology, Naviance Succeed. Computer access in designated common areas is available to students. Students grades are available online. The school has a published electronic and media policy.

Contact Mrs. Anne Kaiser, Administrative Assistant for Admissions. 973-729-6125 Ext. 255. Fax: 973-729-4536. E-mail: annekaiser@popejohn.org. Website: www.popejohn.org

PORTER-GAUD SCHOOL

300 Albemarle Road
Charleston, South Carolina 29407

Head of School: Mr. David DuBose Egleston Jr.

General Information Coeducational day college-preparatory, arts, religious studies, and technology school, affiliated with Christian faith, Episcopal Church. Grades 1–12. Founded: 1867. Setting: suburban. 80-acre campus. 7 buildings on campus. Approved or accredited by National Association of Episcopal Schools, National Independent Private Schools Association, Southern Association of Colleges and Schools, Southern Association of Independent Schools, and South Carolina Department of Education. Member of National Association of Independent Schools and Secondary School Admission Test Board. Endowment: $12 million. Total enrollment: 886. Upper school average class size: 12. Upper school faculty-student ratio: 1:12. There are 175 required school days per year for Upper School students. Upper School students typically attend 5 days per week. The average school day consists of 7 hours and 15 minutes.

Upper School Student Profile Grade 9: 97 students (63 boys, 34 girls); Grade 10: 88 students (57 boys, 31 girls); Grade 11: 85 students (50 boys, 35 girls); Grade 12: 89 students (58 boys, 31 girls); Postgraduate: 359 students (228 boys, 131 girls). 80% of students are Christian, members of Episcopal Church.

Faculty School total: 98. In upper school: 15 men, 25 women; 30 have advanced degrees.

Subjects Offered Advanced Placement courses, algebra, American history, American literature, art, art history, art-AP, biology, calculus, calculus-AP, chemistry, computer programming, computer science, drama, economics, English, English literature, ethics, European history, expository writing, fine arts, French, geometry, government/civics, health, Latin, Latin-AP, music, music appreciation, music theory-AP, physical education, physics, pre-calculus, Spanish, Spanish language-AP, world history, world literature.

Graduation Requirements Algebra, American literature, art education, arts and fine arts (art, music, dance, drama), biology, chemistry, computer science, English, English composition, English literature, European history, foreign language, geometry, health, physical education (includes health), physics, pre-calculus, religion (includes Bible studies and theology), trigonometry, U.S. history, world history.

Special Academic Programs 19 Advanced Placement exams for which test preparation is offered; honors section; independent study.

College Admission Counseling 80 students graduated in 2013; all went to college, including Clemson University; Georgetown University; Sewanee: The University of the South; University of South Carolina; University of Virginia. Mean SAT critical reading: 624, mean SAT math: 616, mean SAT writing: 628, mean combined SAT: 1868, mean composite ACT: 28.

Student Life Upper grades have uniform requirement, student council, honor system. Discipline rests equally with students and faculty. Attendance at religious services is required.

Summer Programs Remediation, enrichment programs offered; session focuses on remedial; held on campus; accepts boys and girls; open to students from other schools. 15 students usually enrolled. 2014 schedule: June to August. Application deadline: June.

Tuition and Aid Day student tuition: $19,950. Tuition installment plan (FACTS Tuition Payment Plan, monthly payment plans, individually arranged payment plans, 60/40 payment plan). Need-based scholarship grants available. In 2013–14, 20% of upper-school students received aid. Total amount of financial aid awarded in 2013–14: $467,620.

Admissions Traditional secondary-level entrance grade is 9. For fall 2013, 60 students applied for upper-level admission, 53 were accepted, 29 enrolled. ISEE or SSAT required. Deadline for receipt of application materials: January 30. Application fee required: $75. Interview recommended.

Athletics Interscholastic: baseball (boys), basketball (b,g), cheering (g), fencing (b), football (b), hockey (b), ice hockey (b), lacrosse (b), physical training (b,g), soccer (b,g), softball (b,g), squash (b), strength & conditioning (b,g), swimming and diving (b,g), tennis (b,g), track and field (b,g), volleyball (g), weight lifting (b,g), weight training (b,g), wrestling (b); intramural: basketball (b,g), Frisbee (b,g), lacrosse (b); coed interscholastic: cross-country running, golf, Nautilus, sailing; coed intramural: Frisbee, ultimate Frisbee. 4 PE instructors, 26 coaches, 1 athletic trainer.

Computers Computers are regularly used in all classes. Computer network features include on-campus library services, Internet access, wireless campus network, Internet filtering or blocking technology, 4-year Computer Science degree with college credit earned. Campus intranet, student e-mail accounts, and computer access in designated common areas are available to students. Students grades are available online. The school has a published electronic and media policy.

Contact Mrs. Eleanor W. Hurtes, Director of Admissions. 843-402-4775. Fax: 843-556-7404. E-mail: eleanor.hurtes@portergaud.edu. Website: www.portergaud.edu

PORTSMOUTH ABBEY SCHOOL

285 Cory's Lane
Portsmouth, Rhode Island 02871

Head of School: Dr. James De Vecchi

General Information Coeducational boarding and day college-preparatory, arts, religious studies, and music, classics, humanities school, affiliated with Roman Catholic Church. Grades 9–12. Founded: 1926. Setting: small town. Nearest major city is Providence. Students are housed in single-sex dormitories. 550-acre campus. 36 buildings on campus. Approved or accredited by Association of Independent Schools in New England, National Independent Private Schools Association, New England Association of Schools and Colleges, and The Association of Boarding Schools. Member of National Association of Independent Schools and Secondary School Admission Test Board. Endowment: $30 million. Total enrollment: 357. Upper school average class size: 13. Upper school faculty-student ratio: 1:7. There are 180 required school days per year for Upper School students. Upper School students typically attend 6 days per week. The average school day consists of 7 hours.

Upper School Student Profile Grade 9: 77 students (42 boys, 35 girls); Grade 10: 111 students (64 boys, 47 girls); Grade 11: 76 students (42 boys, 34 girls); Grade 12: 93 students (44 boys, 49 girls). 70% of students are boarding students. 35% are state residents. 22 states are represented in upper school student body. 19% are international students. International students from China, Dominican Republic, Guatemala, Republic of Korea, Spain, and Trinidad and Tobago; 10 other countries represented in student body. 60% of students are Roman Catholic.

Faculty School total: 52. In upper school: 35 men, 17 women; 41 have advanced degrees; 34 reside on campus.

Subjects Offered Algebra, American literature, art, art history, art history-AP, art-AP, biology, biology-AP, calculus, calculus-AP, chemistry, chemistry-AP, Chinese, Christian doctrine, Christian ethics, computer programming-AP, computer science, computer science-AP, creative writing, drama, drama workshop, economics, English, English language and composition-AP, English literature, English literature and

composition-AP, fine arts, French, French language-AP, French literature-AP, geometry, government/civics, Greek, health, history, history-AP, humanities, international relations, Latin, Latin-AP, Mandarin, marine biology, mathematics, mathematics-AP, modern European history-AP, music, music composition, music theory, music theory-AP, philosophy, photography, physics, physics-AP, physiology, political science, religion, science, social sciences, Spanish, Spanish language-AP, Spanish literature-AP, statistics-AP, studio art-AP, theater, theology, trigonometry, U.S. history, U.S. history-AP, world history, writing workshop.

Graduation Requirements Arts and fine arts (art, music, dance, drama), English, foreign language, history, Latin, mathematics, religion (includes Bible studies and theology), science, humanities.

Special Academic Programs 19 Advanced Placement exams for which test preparation is offered; honors section; independent study; academic accommodation for the gifted.

College Admission Counseling 105 students graduated in 2012; all went to college, including Boston College; Brown University; Georgetown University; New York University; Northeastern University; The George Washington University.

Student Life Upper grades have specified standards of dress, student council, honor system. Discipline rests primarily with faculty. Attendance at religious services is required.

Tuition and Aid Day student tuition: $33,025; 7-day tuition and room/board: $48,850. Tuition installment plan (monthly payment plans, individually arranged payment plans, Tuition Management Systems Plan). Merit scholarship grants, need-based scholarship grants available. In 2012–13, 37% of upper-school students received aid; total upper-school merit-scholarship money awarded: $300,000. Total amount of financial aid awarded in 2012–13: $3,600,000.

Admissions Traditional secondary-level entrance grade is 9. For fall 2012, 512 students applied for upper-level admission, 246 were accepted, 117 enrolled. PSAT or SAT for applicants to grade 11 and 12, SSAT and TOEFL required. Deadline for receipt of application materials: January 31. Application fee required: $50. Interview required.

Athletics Interscholastic: baseball (boys), basketball (b,g), cross-country running (b,g), field hockey (g), football (b), golf (b,g), ice hockey (b,g), lacrosse (b,g), soccer (b,g), softball (g), squash (b,g), swimming and diving (b,g), tennis (b,g), track and field (b,g), wrestling (g); coed interscholastic: cross-country running, sailing, swimming and diving, track and field; coed intramural: ballet, dance, equestrian sports, fitness, horseback riding, modern dance, strength & conditioning, weight training. 1 athletic trainer.

Computers Computer network features include on-campus library services, Internet access, wireless campus network. Campus intranet and student e-mail accounts are available to students. Students grades are available online.

Contact Mrs. Ann Motta, Admissions Coordinator. 401-643-1248. Fax: 401-643-1355. E-mail: admissions@portsmouthabbey.org. Website: www.portsmouthabbey.org

PORTSMOUTH CHRISTIAN ACADEMY

20 Seaborne Drive
Dover, New Hampshire 03820

Head of School: Mr. Dennis Runey

General Information Coeducational day college-preparatory, arts, religious studies, technology, science/mathematics/fine arts, and communication school, affiliated with Christian faith. Grades K–12. Founded: 1979. Setting: rural. Nearest major city is Portsmouth. 50-acre campus. 2 buildings on campus. Approved or accredited by Association of Christian Schools International, New England Association of Schools and Colleges, and New Hampshire Department of Education. Total enrollment: 617. Upper school average class size: 17. Upper school faculty-student ratio: 1:13. There are 172 required school days per year for Upper School students. Upper School students typically attend 5 days per week. The average school day consists of 7 hours and 5 minutes.

Upper School Student Profile Grade 9: 46 students (21 boys, 25 girls); Grade 10: 51 students (25 boys, 26 girls); Grade 11: 36 students (21 boys, 15 girls); Grade 12: 48 students (15 boys, 33 girls). 70% of students are Christian faith.

Faculty School total: 71. In upper school: 12 men, 13 women; 14 have advanced degrees.

Subjects Offered 20th century American writers, 20th century history, 3-dimensional art, 3-dimensional design, ACT preparation, advanced chemistry, advanced computer applications, advanced math, Advanced Placement courses, advanced studio art-AP, African drumming, algebra, alternative physical education, American history, American literature, American literature-AP, analysis and differential calculus, anatomy and physiology, applied music, art, art appreciation, art education, art history, art history-AP, arts appreciation, astronomy, athletic training, athletics, band, baseball, basketball, Bible, Bible studies, biochemistry, biology, British literature, British literature (honors), calculus, calculus-AP, chemistry, chemistry-AP, choir, choral music, chorus, Christian doctrine, Christian education, Christian ethics, Christian scripture, Christian studies, Christian testament, Christianity, church history, civics, college admission preparation, college awareness, college counseling, college placement, college planning, college writing, comparative religion, composition, composition-AP, computer applications, computer education, computer graphics, computer processing, computer resources, computer skills, computer-aided design, contemporary issues, current history, debate, digital art, digital photography, drama,

drama performance, drama workshop, drawing, drawing and design, driver education, economics, economics and history, English, English as a foreign language, English composition, English language and composition-AP, English literature and composition-AP, English literature-AP, English-AP, environmental science, European history, film and literature, foreign language, French, French language-AP, French studies, geometry, government, government/civics, guitar, health, health and wellness, honors algebra, honors English, honors geometry, honors world history, human anatomy, instrumental music, integrated physics, jazz band, lab science, law studies, learning lab, literature, literature and composition-AP, literature-AP, logic, rhetoric, and debate, marine science, math review, mathematics, microbiology, modern European history, modern history, music, music appreciation, musical productions, musical theater, New Testament, novels, performing arts, photography, physics, physics-AP, physiology, political economy, pre-calculus, religion and culture, rhetoric, SAT preparation, SAT/ACT preparation, Shakespeare, Spanish, Spanish language-AP, Spanish-AP, student government, symphonic band, theater arts, theology, U.S. history, U.S. history-AP, U.S. literature, world history, World War II, writing, writing workshop, yearbook.

Graduation Requirements 20th century history, algebra, arts and fine arts (art, music, dance, drama), biology, chemistry, comparative cultures, composition, computer skills, foreign language, geometry, physical education (includes health), physical science, U.S. history, writing, one Bible course for each year of Upper School attendance, service hours.

Special Academic Programs Advanced Placement exam preparation; honors section; accelerated programs; independent study; study at local college for college credit; academic accommodation for the gifted and the musically talented; special instructional classes for students with Attention Deficit Disorder and dyslexia; ESL (22 students enrolled).

College Admission Counseling 34 students graduated in 2013; 33 went to college, including Pepperdine University; Rochester Institute of Technology; Seattle Pacific University; Texas A&M University; University of Massachusetts Amherst; University of New Hampshire. Other: 1 had other specific plans. Mean SAT critical reading: 562, mean SAT math: 536, mean SAT writing: 551.

Student Life Upper grades have specified standards of dress, student council, honor system. Discipline rests primarily with faculty.

Summer Programs Remediation, enrichment, ESL, sports programs offered; session focuses on soccer, basketball, and volleyball; held on campus; accepts boys and girls; open to students from other schools. 75 students usually enrolled. 2014 schedule: July 1 to August 25. Application deadline: June 1.

Tuition and Aid Day student tuition: $10,420. Tuition installment plan (monthly payment plans, FAST Tuition Payment Plan). Tuition reduction for siblings, need-based scholarship grants, Tuition Assistance available. In 2013–14, 36% of upper-school students received aid. Total amount of financial aid awarded in 2013–14: $180,000.

Admissions Traditional secondary-level entrance grade is 9. Achievement tests, PSAT or SAT, PSAT or SAT for applicants to grade 11 and 12, PSAT, SAT, or ACT for applicants to grade 11 and 12, SAT, standardized test scores, Stanford Achievement Test, Test of Achievement and Proficiency, TOEFL, TOEFL or SLEP or writing sample required. Deadline for receipt of application materials: none. Application fee required: $100. Interview required.

Athletics Interscholastic: baseball (boys), basketball (b,g), cross-country running (b,g), indoor track & field (b,g), soccer (b,g), softball (g), tennis (b,g), track and field (b,g), volleyball (g), winter (indoor) track (b,g); intramural: golf (b,g), skiing (cross-country) (b,g), skiing (downhill) (b,g), snowboarding (b,g), tennis (b,g); coed interscholastic: alpine skiing, cross-country running, fitness, indoor track & field, winter (indoor) track; coed intramural: skiing (cross-country), skiing (downhill), snowboarding, tennis. 1 PE instructor, 14 coaches.

Computers Computers are regularly used in art, Bible studies, career education, Christian doctrine, classics, college planning, desktop publishing, economics, English, foreign language, graphic design, history, humanities, independent study, library, library skills, mathematics, media arts, photography, religion, religious studies, SAT preparation, science, social studies, writing, yearbook classes. Computer network features include on-campus library services, online commercial services, Internet access, Internet filtering or blocking technology. Computer access in designated common areas is available to students. Students grades are available online. The school has a published electronic and media policy.

Contact Mrs. Wendy Moran, Director of Admissions. 603-742-3617 Ext. 116. Fax: 603-750-0490. E-mail: wmoran@pcaschool.org. Website: www.pcaschool.org

THE POTOMAC SCHOOL

1301 Potomac School Road
McLean, Virginia 22101

Head of School: John Kowalik

General Information Coeducational day college-preparatory and liberal arts, arts, athletics, and character education school. Grades K–12. Founded: 1904. Setting: suburban. Nearest major city is Washington, DC. 90-acre campus. Approved or accredited by Association of Independent Schools of Greater Washington and Virginia Association of Independent Schools. Member of National Association of Independent Schools and Secondary School Admission Test Board. Endowment: $31 million. Total

enrollment: 1,024. Upper school average class size: 14. Upper school faculty-student ratio: 1:6.

Upper School Student Profile Grade 9: 105 students (51 boys, 54 girls); Grade 10: 104 students (50 boys, 54 girls); Grade 11: 117 students (57 boys, 60 girls); Grade 12: 97 students (44 boys, 53 girls).

Faculty School total: 160. In upper school: 32 men, 34 women.

Subjects Offered 20th century American writers, 20th century world history, 3-dimensional art, 3-dimensional design, acting, advanced computer applications, advanced math, Advanced Placement courses, advanced studio art-AP, African-American literature, African-American studies, algebra, American literature, anatomy and physiology, ancient world history, art, art history, band, bell choir, Bible as literature, bioethics, biology, biology-AP, British literature, calculus, calculus-AP, ceramics, chamber groups, character education, chemistry, chemistry-AP, Chinese history, choral music, community service, comparative religion, computer programming, computer programming-AP, computer science, conceptual physics, concert band, creative writing, debate, directing, drama, drama performance, drawing and design, economics and history, engineering, English, English literature, environmental science, European history, expository writing, fine arts, French, French language-AP, French literature-AP, functions, geometry, global studies, government/civics, handbells, Harlem Renaissance, history of music, independent study, jazz band, Latin, Latin American history, Latin-AP, leadership, literary magazine, madrigals, mathematics, Middle Eastern history, model United Nations, modern European history, music, music composition, music theory-AP, newspaper, painting, performing arts, photography, physical education, physics, physics-AP, portfolio art, pre-calculus, robotics, science, science and technology, sculpture, senior project, Shakespeare, short story, Spanish, Spanish language-AP, Spanish literature-AP, stagecraft, statistics-AP, strings, student government, studio art-AP, theater arts, trigonometry, U.S. government and politics, U.S. history-AP, vocal music, yearbook.

Graduation Requirements Arts and fine arts (art, music, dance, drama), English, foreign language, history, mathematics, physical education (includes health), science, senior project, month-long senior project.

Special Academic Programs Advanced Placement exam preparation; honors section; independent study.

College Admission Counseling 100 students graduated in 2013; 99 went to college, including Duke University; Georgetown University; Northwestern University; Southern Methodist University; University of Virginia; Washington University in St. Louis. Median SAT critical reading: 670, median SAT math: 680, median SAT writing: 690.

Student Life Upper grades have specified standards of dress, student council, honor system. Discipline rests equally with students and faculty.

Summer Programs Enrichment, advancement, sports, art/fine arts programs offered; session focuses on academics and enrichment; held on campus; accepts boys and girls; open to students from other schools. 2014 schedule: June 16 to August 15. Application deadline: none.

Tuition and Aid Day student tuition: $34,660. Tuition installment plan (Insured Tuition Payment Plan, FACTS Tuition Payment Plan, monthly payment plans). Need-based scholarship grants available. In 2013–14, 18% of upper-school students received aid.

Admissions Traditional secondary-level entrance grade is 9. ISEE or SSAT required. Deadline for receipt of application materials: January 10. Application fee required: $65. On-campus interview required.

Athletics Interscholastic: baseball (boys), basketball (b,g), cross-country running (b,g), field hockey (g), football (b), lacrosse (b,g), soccer (b,g), softball (g), squash (b,g), tennis (b,g), track and field (b,g), wrestling (b); intramural: independent competitive sports (b,g), weight lifting (b,g); coed interscholastic: golf, ice hockey, swimming and diving, winter (indoor) track; coed intramural: canoeing/kayaking, dance, fitness, hiking/backpacking, ice hockey, outdoor education, physical fitness, physical training, sailing, strength & conditioning, weight training, yoga. 5 PE instructors, 60 coaches, 2 athletic trainers.

Computers Computers are regularly used in all academic, computer applications, drawing and design, independent study, literary magazine, newspaper, photography, programming, yearbook classes. Computer network features include on-campus library services, online commercial services, Internet access, wireless campus network, Internet filtering or blocking technology, eBooks. Campus intranet and student e-mail accounts are available to students. Students grades are available online. The school has a published electronic and media policy.

Contact Vickie Pierce, Admission Services Coordinator. 703-749-6313. Fax: 703-356-1764. Website: www.potomacschool.org

POUGHKEEPSIE DAY SCHOOL

260 Boardman Road
Poughkeepsie, New York 12603

Head of School: Josie Holford

General Information Coeducational day college-preparatory and arts school. Grades PK–12. Founded: 1934. Setting: suburban. Nearest major city is New York. 35-acre campus. 2 buildings on campus. Approved or accredited by New York Department of Education. Member of National Association of Independent Schools. Endowment: $4.1 million. Total enrollment: 280. Upper school average class size: 12. Upper school faculty-student ratio: 1:7. There are 165 required school days per year for Upper School students. Upper School students typically attend 5 days per week. The average school day consists of 7 hours.

Upper School Student Profile Grade 9: 19 students (8 boys, 11 girls); Grade 10: 32 students (14 boys, 18 girls); Grade 11: 39 students (19 boys, 20 girls); Grade 12: 25 students (14 boys, 11 girls).

Faculty School total: 52. In upper school: 5 men, 12 women; 13 have advanced degrees.

Subjects Offered 3-dimensional art, acting, advanced math, Advanced Placement courses, African drumming, algebra, American literature, American literature-AP, analysis and differential calculus, analytic geometry, anatomy, anatomy and physiology, ancient history, ancient world history, art history, arts, Basic programming, bioethics, biology, calculus, calculus-AP, chamber groups, chemistry, collage and assemblage, college admission preparation, college planning, community service, computer programming, computer science, computer-aided design, conflict resolution, contemporary art, creative arts, creative drama, creative writing, decision making skills, desktop publishing, digital art, digital photography, discrete mathematics, drama, drama performance, drawing, ecology, economics, English, English literature, English literature-AP, English-AP, ensembles, European civilization, European history, fiction, filmmaking, fine arts, French, French language-AP, French-AP, geology, geometry, guitar, history, Holocaust and other genocides, Holocaust studies, independent study, instrumental music, integrated arts, interdisciplinary studies, Islamic studies, jazz band, jazz ensemble, lab science, leadership, life saving, life skills, linear algebra, literary magazine, literature, literature-AP, mathematics, modern European history, multicultural literature, multicultural studies, music, music appreciation, music composition, music performance, music theory, music theory-AP, musical productions, oil painting, painting, peer counseling, performing arts, photography, physical education, physical science, physics, physiology, play production, playwriting and directing, pre-calculus, printmaking, probability and statistics, religion and culture, SAT preparation, science, senior internship, service learning/internship, social issues, social studies, Spanish, Spanish language-AP, Spanish-AP, stained glass, statistics, strings, studio art, theater arts, theater production, trigonometry, U.S. history, video film production, visual arts, voice ensemble, Web site design, Western civilization, wind ensemble, writing workshop, yearbook, zoology.

Graduation Requirements Algebra, arts, biology, chemistry, classical Greek literature, college planning, electives, English, English literature, foreign language, geometry, interdisciplinary studies, life skills, mathematics, music, performing arts, physical education (includes health), physics, physiology, pre-calculus, SAT preparation, senior internship, senior thesis, trigonometry, visual arts, four-week off-campus senior internship. Community service is required.

Special Academic Programs Advanced Placement exam preparation; honors section; independent study; term-away projects; study at local college for college credit; academic accommodation for the gifted, the musically talented, and the artistically talented; ESL (19 students enrolled).

College Admission Counseling 23 students graduated in 2013; 21 went to college, including Barnard College; Clark University; Hampshire College; New York University; Smith College; Stanford University. Mean SAT critical reading: 660, mean SAT math: 600, mean SAT writing: 640, mean combined SAT: 1900. 79% scored over 600 on SAT critical reading, 53% scored over 600 on SAT math, 63% scored over 600 on SAT writing, 74% scored over 1800 on combined SAT.

Student Life Upper grades have student council, honor system. Discipline rests primarily with faculty.

Summer Programs Art/fine arts programs offered; session focuses on visual and performing arts; held on campus; accepts boys and girls; open to students from other schools. 45 students usually enrolled. 2014 schedule: June 14 to August 7. Application deadline: May 15.

Tuition and Aid Day student tuition: $23,200. Tuition installment plan (FACTS Tuition Payment Plan, The Tuition Refund Plan). Need-based scholarship grants, tuition reduction for children of full-time faculty and staff available. In 2013–14, 44% of upper-school students received aid. Total amount of financial aid awarded in 2013–14: $551,160.

Admissions Traditional secondary-level entrance grade is 9. For fall 2013, 52 students applied for upper-level admission, 27 were accepted, 12 enrolled. School's own exam required. Deadline for receipt of application materials: January 15. Application fee required: $50. On-campus interview required.

Athletics Interscholastic: baseball (boys), basketball (b,g), cross-country running (b,g), soccer (b,g), softball (g); intramural: basketball (b,g), softball (g); coed interscholastic: cross-country running, Frisbee, soccer, ultimate Frisbee; coed intramural: alpine skiing, basketball, bicycling, cooperative games, cross-country running, dance, figure skating, fitness, fitness walking, Frisbee, hiking/backpacking, ice skating, jogging, life saving, outdoor education, outdoor skills, skiing (downhill), snowboarding, soccer, swimming and diving, tennis, ultimate Frisbee, volleyball, walking, yoga. 2 PE instructors, 5 coaches.

Computers Computers are regularly used in all academic, college planning, desktop publishing, journalism, library skills, literary magazine, media, music, newspaper, photography, photojournalism, programming, SAT preparation, video film production,

Web site design, yearbook classes. Computer network features include on-campus library services, online commercial services, Internet access, wireless campus network, EBSCOhost, Maps101, Web Feet Guides, Gale databases, ProQuest, unitedstreaming, Britannica Online, World Book Online, Grolier Online. Campus intranet, student e-mail accounts, and computer access in designated common areas are available to students. The school has a published electronic and media policy.

Contact Tammy Reilly, Assistant Director of Enrollment and International Student Coordinator. 845-462-7600 Ext. 201. Fax: 845-462-7602. E-mail: treilly@poughkeepsieday.org. Website: www.poughkeepsieday.org/

POWERS CATHOLIC HIGH SCHOOL

1505 West Court Street
Flint, Michigan 48503

Head of School: Mrs. Sally Bartos

General Information Coeducational day college-preparatory, arts, business, religious studies, and technology school, affiliated with Roman Catholic Church. Grades 9–12. Founded: 1970. Setting: urban. 80-acre campus. 1 building on campus. Approved or accredited by National Catholic Education Association, North Central Association of Colleges and Schools, and Michigan Department of Education. Endowment: $3 million. Total enrollment: 545. Upper school average class size: 25. Upper school faculty-student ratio: 1:18. There are 188 required school days per year for Upper School students. Upper School students typically attend 5 days per week. The average school day consists of 6 hours and 51 minutes.

Upper School Student Profile Grade 9: 133 students (68 boys, 65 girls); Grade 10: 126 students (67 boys, 59 girls); Grade 11: 163 students (80 boys, 83 girls); Grade 12: 123 students (64 boys, 59 girls). 75% of students are Roman Catholic.

Faculty School total: 31. In upper school: 12 men, 19 women; 24 have advanced degrees.

Subjects Offered Art, art-AP, biology, biology-AP, calculus-AP, ceramics, chemistry, choir, computer skills, concert band, drafting, economics, English, English literature and composition-AP, European history-AP, French, geometry, government, government-AP, health, honors algebra, honors English, honors geometry, integrated science, interdisciplinary studies, macroeconomics-AP, marching band, math analysis, math applications, mechanical drawing, physics, pre-algebra, pre-calculus, psychology, psychology-AP, public speaking, religion, social justice, Spanish, state history, studio art-AP, theology, trigonometry, U.S. history, wind ensemble, world geography, world history, world religions, yearbook.

Graduation Requirements American history, English, government, health, mathematics, science, theology, world history, 40 hours of community service (5 hours for each semester in attendance at Powers).

Special Academic Programs 7 Advanced Placement exams for which test preparation is offered; honors section; remedial reading and/or remedial writing; remedial math.

College Admission Counseling 122 students graduated in 2013; 119 went to college, including Central Michigan University; Grand Valley State University; Michigan State University; Saginaw Valley State University; University of Michigan; University of Michigan–Dearborn. Other: 1 entered military service, 2 had other specific plans. Mean composite ACT: 23.

Student Life Upper grades have uniform requirement, student council. Discipline rests primarily with faculty. Attendance at religious services is required.

Tuition and Aid Day student tuition: $8200. Tuition installment plan (SMART Tuition Payment Plan). Tuition reduction for siblings, need-based scholarship grants available. In 2013–14, 50% of upper-school students received aid. Total amount of financial aid awarded in 2013–14: $450,300.

Admissions Traditional secondary-level entrance grade is 9. ACT-Explore required. Deadline for receipt of application materials: none. Application fee required: $100. Interview required.

Athletics Interscholastic: alpine skiing (boys, girls), baseball (b), basketball (b,g), bowling (b,g), cross-country running (b,g), dance squad (g), dance team (g), diving (b,g), football (b), golf (b,g), ice hockey (b), lacrosse (b,g), skiing (downhill) (b,g), soccer (b,g), softball (g), swimming and diving (b,g), tennis (b,g), track and field (b,g), volleyball (g), wrestling (b); coed interscholastic: cheering, equestrian sports, indoor track, power lifting, skeet shooting, strength & conditioning, weight lifting; coed intramural: ultimate Frisbee, weight training. 2 PE instructors.

Computers Computers are regularly used in accounting, business applications, drafting, graphic design, keyboarding, yearbook classes. Computer network features include on-campus library services, Internet access, wireless campus network, Internet filtering or blocking technology. Computer access in designated common areas is available to students. Students grades are available online. The school has a published electronic and media policy.

Contact Mr. Brian Sheeran, Assistant Principal/Athletic Director. 810-591-4741. Fax: 810-591-1794. E-mail: bsheeran@powerscatholic.org. Website: www.powerscatholic.org/

PRESBYTERIAN PAN AMERICAN SCHOOL

PO Box 1578
223 North FM Road 772
Kingsville, Texas 78364-1578

Head of School: Dr. Doug Dalglish

General Information Coeducational boarding and day and distance learning college-preparatory school, affiliated with Presbyterian Church (U.S.A.). Grades 9–12. Distance learning grades 9–12. Founded: 1912. Setting: rural. Nearest major city is Corpus Christi. Students are housed in single-sex dormitories. 670-acre campus. 22 buildings on campus. Approved or accredited by Southern Association of Colleges and Schools, Texas Private School Accreditation Commission, and Texas Department of Education. Endowment: $5.3 million. Total enrollment: 160. Upper school average class size: 20. Upper school faculty-student ratio: 1:10. There are 180 required school days per year for Upper School students. Upper School students typically attend 5 days per week. The average school day consists of 8 hours.

Upper School Student Profile Grade 9: 32 students (12 boys, 20 girls); Grade 10: 46 students (20 boys, 26 girls); Grade 11: 30 students (16 boys, 14 girls); Grade 12: 51 students (22 boys, 29 girls). 100% of students are boarding students. 6% are state residents. 1 state is represented in upper school student body. 94% are international students. International students from China, Costa Rica, Mexico, Republic of Korea, and Rwanda. 40% of students are Presbyterian Church (U.S.A.).

Faculty School total: 17. In upper school: 6 men, 11 women; 5 have advanced degrees; 3 reside on campus.

Subjects Offered Algebra, American history, American literature, animal science, art, arts, Bible studies, biology, calculus, career exploration, chemistry, choir, communications, computer science, debate, economics, English, English literature, ESL, geography, geometry, government/civics, health, horticulture, journalism, literary genres, mathematical modeling, physical education, physics, pre-calculus, religion, Spanish, theater arts, U.S. history, world history, world literature, yearbook.

Graduation Requirements Arts and fine arts (art, music, dance, drama), career exploration, economics, English, foreign language, mathematics, religion (includes Bible studies and theology), science, social sciences, social studies (includes history), TOEFL score of 550, or SAT Reading of 550.

Special Academic Programs Study at local college for college credit; ESL (45 students enrolled).

College Admission Counseling 51 students graduated in 2013; 50 went to college, including Schreiner University; Texas A&M University; Texas A&M University–Kingsville; The University of Texas at Austin; The University of Texas at San Antonio; University of Houston. Median SAT critical reading: 410, median SAT math: 450, median SAT writing: 420. 4% scored over 600 on SAT critical reading, 5% scored over 600 on SAT math.

Student Life Upper grades have uniform requirement, student council, honor system. Discipline rests primarily with faculty. Attendance at religious services is required.

Tuition and Aid Day student tuition: $8500; 7-day tuition and room/board: $15,000. Guaranteed tuition plan. Tuition installment plan (monthly payment plans, individually arranged payment plans, quarterly payment plan, semester payment plan). Tuition reduction for siblings, merit scholarship grants, need-based scholarship grants, need-based financial aid, discounts tied to enrollment referred by current student families available. In 2013–14, 91% of upper-school students received aid. Total amount of financial aid awarded in 2013–14: $1,161,400.

Admissions Traditional secondary-level entrance grade is 9. For fall 2013, 95 students applied for upper-level admission, 70 were accepted, 55 enrolled. TOEFL required. Deadline for receipt of application materials: none. Application fee required: $75. Interview recommended.

Athletics Interscholastic: baseball (boys), basketball (b,g), cheering (b,g), cross-country running (b,g), soccer (b,g), track and field (b,g), volleyball (g); intramural: billiards (b), jogging (b,g), life saving (b,g), paddle tennis (b,g), physical fitness (b,g), strength & conditioning (b,g), table tennis (b,g), tennis (b,g), volleyball (b), walking (b,g), winter walking (b,g); coed intramural: aquatics, fitness walking, jogging, life saving, paddle tennis, strength & conditioning, table tennis, volleyball, walking, winter walking. 1 PE instructor, 2 coaches, 1 athletic trainer.

Computers Computers are regularly used in all academic, English, ESL, mathematics, publications, yearbook classes. Computer resources include on-campus library services, Internet access, Internet filtering or blocking technology. Campus intranet, student e-mail accounts, and computer access in designated common areas are available to students. Students grades are available online. The school has a published electronic and media policy.

Contact Joe L. Garcia, Director of Admissions. 361-592-4307 Ext. 1004. Fax: 361-592-6126. E-mail: jlgarcia@ppas.org. Website: www.ppas.org

See Display below and Close-Up on page 560.

PRESTON HIGH SCHOOL

2780 Schurz Avenue
Bronx, New York 10465

Head of School: Mrs. Jane Grendell

General Information Girls' day college-preparatory, arts, religious studies, and technology school, affiliated with Roman Catholic Church. Grades 9–12. Founded: 1947. Setting: urban. Nearest major city is New York. 5-acre campus. 2 buildings on campus. Approved or accredited by Middle States Association of Colleges and Schools and New York Department of Education. Total enrollment: 600. Upper school average class size: 25. Upper school faculty-student ratio: 1:25. There are 180 required school

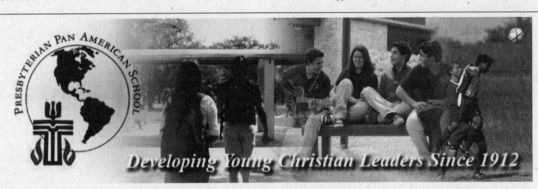

days per year for Upper School students. Upper School students typically attend 5 days per week. The average school day consists of 5 hours and 20 minutes.

Upper School Student Profile Grade 9: 165 students (165 girls); Grade 10: 137 students (137 girls); Grade 11: 134 students (134 girls); Grade 12: 131 students (131 girls). 83% of students are Roman Catholic.

Faculty School total: 50. In upper school: 15 men, 35 women; 37 have advanced degrees.

Subjects Offered Advanced computer applications, advanced math, Advanced Placement courses, algebra, American history, American history-AP, anatomy and physiology, art, biology, biology-AP, British literature, British literature (honors), calculus-AP, Catholic belief and practice, chemistry, chorus, communication skills, computer education, computer graphics, computer programming, creative writing, earth science, economics and history, English, English literature and composition-AP, film history, foreign language, geometry, global studies, government-AP, graphic design, health, honors algebra, honors English, honors geometry, honors U.S. history, honors world history, Italian, Latin, law, media studies, moral theology, music, peer counseling, philosophy, physical education, physics, play/screen writing, religious studies, service learning/internship, Spanish, Spanish language-AP, Spanish literature-AP, U.S. government and politics-AP, women in world history, world literature.

Graduation Requirements All academic.

Special Academic Programs Advanced Placement exam preparation; honors section; independent study; study at local college for college credit.

College Admission Counseling 168 students graduated in 2013; 167 went to college, including Binghamton University, State University of New York; Fordham University; Iona College; Manhattan College; New York University; University at Albany, State University of New York. Other: 1 entered military service. Mean SAT critical reading: 512, mean SAT math: 506, mean SAT writing: 517, mean combined SAT: 1535.

Student Life Upper grades have uniform requirement, student council, honor system. Discipline rests equally with students and faculty. Attendance at religious services is required.

Summer Programs Remediation, enrichment programs offered; session focuses on enrichment for incoming freshmen; held on campus; accepts girls; not open to students from other schools. 30 students usually enrolled. 2014 schedule: July 1 to July 31.

Tuition and Aid Day student tuition: $8515. Tuition installment plan (SMART Tuition Payment Plan, monthly payment plans). Tuition reduction for siblings, merit scholarship grants, need-based scholarship grants available. In 2013–14, 14% of upper-school students received aid; total upper-school merit-scholarship money awarded: $421,315. Total amount of financial aid awarded in 2013–14: $808,360.

Admissions Traditional secondary-level entrance grade is 9. For fall 2013, 586 students applied for upper-level admission, 444 were accepted, 165 enrolled. Math, reading, and mental ability tests, school placement exam and writing sample required. Deadline for receipt of application materials: December 6. No application fee required. Interview recommended.

Athletics Interscholastic: basketball, cheering, fitness, soccer, softball, volleyball; intramural: yoga. 2 PE instructors, 9 coaches.

Computers Computers are regularly used in graphic design, video film production, Web site design classes. Computer network features include on-campus library services, Internet access, Internet filtering or blocking technology. The school has a published electronic and media policy.

Contact Mrs. Cristina Fragale, Director of Admissions. 718-863-9134 Ext. 132. Fax: 718-863-6125. E-mail: cfragale@prestonhs.org. Website: www.prestonhs.org

PRESTONWOOD CHRISTIAN ACADEMY

6801 West Park Boulevard
Plano, Texas 75093

Head of School: Dr. Larry Taylor

General Information Coeducational day and distance learning college-preparatory and Bible courses school, affiliated with Southern Baptist Convention. Grades PK–12. Distance learning grades 6–12. Founded: 1997. Setting: suburban. Nearest major city is Dallas. 44-acre campus. 2 buildings on campus. Approved or accredited by Southern Association of Colleges and Schools and Texas Department of Education. Total enrollment: 1,472. Upper school average class size: 18. Upper school faculty-student ratio: 1:11. There are 172 required school days per year for Upper School students. Upper School students typically attend 5 days per week. The average school day consists of 7 hours and 35 minutes.

Upper School Student Profile Grade 9: 130 students (75 boys, 55 girls); Grade 10: 125 students (55 boys, 70 girls); Grade 11: 122 students (60 boys, 62 girls); Grade 12: 114 students (63 boys, 51 girls). 66% of students are Southern Baptist Convention.

Faculty School total: 115. In upper school: 17 men, 23 women; 20 have advanced degrees.

Subjects Offered 20th century history, 20th century physics, advanced chemistry, advanced math, Advanced Placement courses, algebra, American history-AP, American literature, anatomy and physiology, art, art-AP, band, Bible, biology, biology-AP, British literature, calculus-AP, ceramics, chemistry, choir, Christian doctrine, computer applications, conceptual physics, debate, drama, drawing, economics, ethics, fine arts, fitness, geometry, government, government-AP, health, honors algebra, honors English,

honors geometry, honors U.S. history, honors world history, internship, language-AP, leadership education training, learning lab, literature-AP, logic, multimedia, multimedia design, newspaper, painting, performing arts, personal fitness, philosophy, photo shop, physical fitness, physics, physics-AP, pre-calculus, printmaking, sculpture, service learning/internship, Spanish, Spanish-AP, speech, statistics, strings, student government, studio art, U.S. government and politics-AP, U.S. history, Web site design, Western literature, world history, world religions, yearbook.

Graduation Requirements 1 1/2 elective credits, algebra, arts and fine arts (art, music, dance, drama), Bible, biology, British literature, chemistry, Christian doctrine, computer applications, economics, English, English literature, ethics, foreign language, geometry, government, mathematics, philosophy, physical education (includes health), physics, speech, U.S. history, Western literature, world history, mission trip.

Special Academic Programs Advanced Placement exam preparation; honors section; academic accommodation for the gifted.

College Admission Counseling 124 students graduated in 2012; all went to college, including Baylor University; Oklahoma State University; Southern Methodist University; Texas A&M University; The University of Texas at Austin; University of Oklahoma. Median SAT critical reading: 560, median SAT math: 550, median SAT writing: 550, median combined SAT: 1540, median composite ACT: 24. 37% scored over 600 on SAT critical reading, 35% scored over 600 on SAT math, 31% scored over 600 on SAT writing, 47% scored over 1800 on combined SAT, 38% scored over 26 on composite ACT.

Student Life Upper grades have uniform requirement, student council, honor system. Discipline rests primarily with faculty.

Tuition and Aid Day student tuition: $16,297–$16,779. Tuition installment plan (FACTS Tuition Payment Plan, monthly payment plans, individually arranged payment plans). Tuition reduction for siblings, need-based scholarship grants available. In 2012–13, 21% of upper-school students received aid. Total amount of financial aid awarded in 2012–13: $734,381.

Admissions Traditional secondary-level entrance grade is 9. For fall 2012, 109 students applied for upper-level admission, 65 were accepted, 54 enrolled. ISEE or Stanford Achievement Test required. Deadline for receipt of application materials: none. Application fee required: $100. Interview required.

Athletics Interscholastic: baseball (boys), basketball (b,g), cheering (g), cross-country running (b,g), drill team (g), football (b), golf (b,g), soccer (b,g), softball (g), swimming and diving (b,g), tennis (b,g), track and field (b,g), volleyball (g). 42 coaches.

Computers Computers are regularly used in all academic, technology classes. Computer network features include on-campus library services, Internet access, wireless campus network, Internet filtering or blocking technology. Student e-mail accounts are available to students. Students grades are available online. The school has a published electronic and media policy.

Contact Mrs. Marsha Backof, Admissions Assistant. 972-930-4010. Fax: 972-930-4008. E-mail: mbackof@prestonwoodchristian.org. Website: www.prestonwoodchristian.org

PROCTOR ACADEMY

PO Box 500
204 Main Street
Andover, New Hampshire 03216

Head of School: Mr. Michael Henriques

General Information Coeducational boarding and day college-preparatory, arts, technology, environmental studies, and experiential learning programs school. Grades 9–12. Founded: 1848. Setting: small town. Nearest major city is Concord. Students are housed in single-sex dormitories. 3,000-acre campus. 46 buildings on campus. Approved or accredited by Association for Experiential Education, Association of Independent Schools in New England, Independent Schools of Northern New England, New England Association of Schools and Colleges, The Association of Boarding Schools, and New Hampshire Department of Education. Member of National Association of Independent Schools and Secondary School Admission Test Board. Endowment: $25 million. Total enrollment: 360. Upper school average class size: 12. Upper school faculty-student ratio: 1:5. There are 170 required school days per year for Upper School students. Upper School students typically attend 6 days per week. The average school day consists of 5 hours and 35 minutes.

Upper School Student Profile Grade 9: 63 students (36 boys, 27 girls); Grade 10: 92 students (55 boys, 37 girls); Grade 11: 105 students (61 boys, 44 girls); Grade 12: 91 students (52 boys, 39 girls); Postgraduate: 9 students (7 boys, 2 girls). 77% of students are boarding students. 31% are state residents. 30 states are represented in upper school student body. 7% are international students. International students from China, Hong Kong, Mexico, Republic of Korea, Spain, and Viet Nam; 9 other countries represented in student body.

Faculty School total: 85. In upper school: 39 men, 46 women; 66 have advanced degrees; 35 reside on campus.

Subjects Offered Algebra, American history, American literature, art, art history, biology, boat building, calculus, ceramics, chemistry, computer math, computer programming, creative writing, drama, economics, English, English literature, environmental science, European history, fine arts, finite math, forestry, French, genetics, geometry, health, history, industrial arts, mathematics, Middle Eastern history, music, music history, music technology, Native American history, performing arts, photography, physical education, physics, piano, play/screen writing, poetry, political thought, probability and statistics, psychology, public speaking, publications, science, senior project, social sciences, Spanish, sports medicine, studio art, study skills, the Web, theater, theater history, U.S. government and politics-AP, U.S. history-AP, Vietnam history, voice, voice ensemble, wilderness experience, woodworking, world literature, writing, writing workshop.

Graduation Requirements Arts and fine arts (art, music, dance, drama), English, foreign language, mathematics, science, social sciences.

Special Academic Programs 14 Advanced Placement exams for which test preparation is offered; honors section; independent study; term-away projects; study at local college for college credit; study abroad; academic accommodation for the gifted; programs in general development for dyslexic students.

College Admission Counseling 98 students graduated in 2013; they went to Connecticut College; Elon University; Endicott College; St. Lawrence University; University of Denver; University of New Hampshire. Other: 6 had other specific plans. Mean SAT critical reading: 555, mean SAT math: 560, mean SAT writing: 545, mean combined SAT: 1660, mean composite ACT: 23. 20% scored over 600 on SAT critical reading, 24% scored over 600 on SAT math, 22% scored over 600 on SAT writing, 24% scored over 26 on composite ACT.

Student Life Upper grades have student council, honor system. Discipline rests equally with students and faculty.

Tuition and Aid Day student tuition: $31,400; 7-day tuition and room/board: $51,700. Tuition installment plan (Academic Management Services Plan, monthly payment plans). Need-based scholarship grants available. In 2013–14, 28% of upper-school students received aid. Total amount of financial aid awarded in 2013–14: $3,200,000.

Admissions Traditional secondary-level entrance grade is 9. For fall 2013, 482 students applied for upper-level admission, 270 were accepted, 125 enrolled. ISEE, PSAT or SAT for applicants to grade 11 and 12, SSAT, TOEFL or SLEP, WISC/Woodcock-Johnson or writing sample required. Deadline for receipt of application materials: February 1. Application fee required: $50. Interview required.

Athletics Interscholastic: alpine skiing (boys, girls), archery (b,g), baseball (b), basketball (b,g), bicycling (b,g), canoeing/kayaking (b,g), cross-country running (b,g), field hockey (g), football (b), hockey (b,g), ice hockey (b,g), lacrosse (b,g), nordic skiing (b,g), skiing (downhill) (b,g), snowboarding (b,g), soccer (b,g), softball (g), tennis (b,g); intramural: alpine skiing (b,g), snowboarding (b,g); coed interscholastic: dance, freestyle skiing, golf, horseback riding, kayaking, ski jumping, skiing (cross-country); coed intramural: aerobics/dance, aerobics/Nautilus, backpacking, ballet, broomball, canoeing/kayaking, climbing, combined training, dance, equestrian sports, fencing, fitness, Frisbee, hiking/backpacking, horseback riding, kayaking, martial arts, modern dance, mountain biking, mountaineering, outdoor activities, outdoor adventure, outdoor education, outdoor recreation, outdoor skills, outdoors, paint ball, rock climbing, running, skiing (downhill), snowshoeing, strength & conditioning, ultimate Frisbee, wall climbing, weight lifting, weight training, wilderness, yoga. 5 coaches, 2 athletic trainers.

Computers Computers are regularly used in all academic classes. Computer network features include on-campus library services, online commercial services, Internet access, wireless campus network, Internet filtering or blocking technology. Campus intranet and student e-mail accounts are available to students. Students grades are available online. The school has a published electronic and media policy.

Contact Charlie Durell, Admissions Coordinator. 603-735-6312. Fax: 603-735-6284. E-mail: charlie_durell@proctornet.com. Website: www.proctoracademy.org

PROFESSIONAL CHILDREN'S SCHOOL

132 West 60th Street
New York, New York 10023

Head of School: Dr. James Dawson

General Information Coeducational day college-preparatory school. Grades 6–12. Founded: 1914. Setting: urban. 1 building on campus. Approved or accredited by New York State Association of Independent Schools. Member of National Association of Independent Schools. Endowment: $2.7 million. Total enrollment: 195. Upper school average class size: 10. Upper school faculty-student ratio: 1:8. There are 163 required school days per year for Upper School students. Upper School students typically attend 5 days per week. The average school day consists of 7 hours.

Upper School Student Profile Grade 9: 23 students (8 boys, 15 girls); Grade 10: 36 students (12 boys, 24 girls); Grade 11: 46 students (14 boys, 32 girls); Grade 12: 55 students (35 boys, 20 girls).

Faculty School total: 28. In upper school: 12 men, 14 women; 26 have advanced degrees.

Subjects Offered Advanced math, algebra, American government, American history, biology, calculus, chemistry, chorus, computer education, constitutional history of U.S., constitutional law, creative writing, drama, English, English literature, environmental science, ESL, foreign language, French, general math, geometry, health education, introduction to literature, keyboarding, library research, library skills, physical education, physics, pre-algebra, pre-calculus, Spanish, studio art, U.S. government, U.S. history.

Graduation Requirements Art, English, foreign language, health, history, mathematics, science.

Special Academic Programs ESL (25 students enrolled).

College Admission Counseling 55 students graduated in 2013; 46 went to college, including American Academy of Dramatic Arts–New York; New York University; Pace University; The Juilliard School. Other: 5 went to work, 4 had other specific plans.

Student Life Upper grades have student council, honor system. Discipline rests primarily with faculty.

Tuition and Aid Day student tuition: $35,200. Tuition installment plan (Tuition Management Systems). Need-based scholarship grants available. In 2013–14, 30% of upper-school students received aid. Total amount of financial aid awarded in 2013–14: $862,000.

Admissions Traditional secondary-level entrance grade is 9. For fall 2013, 86 students applied for upper-level admission, 80 were accepted, 53 enrolled. ERB, ISEE, SSAT or Stanford Achievement Test required. Deadline for receipt of application materials: none. Application fee required: $75. On-campus interview recommended.

Athletics 1 PE instructor.

Computers Computers are regularly used in all academic classes. Computer network features include on-campus library services, Internet access, wireless campus network, Internet filtering or blocking technology. Student e-mail accounts and computer access in designated common areas are available to students. The school has a published electronic and media policy.

Contact Ms. Shari Honig, Director of Admissions. 212-582-3116 Ext. 112. Fax: 212-307-6542. E-mail: admissions@pcs-nyc.org. Website: www.pcs-nyc.org

THE PROUT SCHOOL

4640 Tower Hill Road
Wakefield, Rhode Island 02879

Head of School: Mr. David Carradini

General Information Coeducational day college-preparatory, arts, religious studies, and technology school, affiliated with Roman Catholic Church. Grades 9–12. Founded: 1966. Setting: small town. Nearest major city is Providence. 25-acre campus. 1 building on campus. Approved or accredited by International Baccalaureate Organization, New England Association of Schools and Colleges, Rhode Island State Certified Resource Progam, and Rhode Island Department of Education. Total enrollment: 640. Upper school average class size: 23. Upper school faculty-student ratio: 1:18. There are 182 required school days per year for Upper School students. Upper School students typically attend 5 days per week. The average school day consists of 6 hours and 30 minutes.

Upper School Student Profile 75% of students are Roman Catholic.

Faculty School total: 53. In upper school: 25 men, 28 women; 40 have advanced degrees.

Subjects Offered Acting, American literature, anatomy and physiology, art education, art history, athletic training, ballet, ballet technique, band, biology, calculus, chemistry, Chinese, choir, chorus, Christian doctrine, Christian education, Christian ethics, Christian scripture, Christian studies, Christianity, church history, clayworking, college planning, college writing, community service, comparative religion, computer applications, computer art, computer education, computer graphics, computer multimedia, computer programming, computer science, computer skills, computer studies, contemporary history, contemporary issues, costumes and make-up, CPR, creative dance, creative drama, creative thinking, critical studies in film, critical writing, dance performance, drama performance, drama workshop, dramatic arts, drawing, drawing and design, earth science, economics, economics and history, English, English composition, English literature, environmental science, environmental studies, first aid, fitness, food and nutrition, foreign language, French, general science, government, graphic arts, graphic design, health, health and wellness, history, history of the Catholic Church, honors English, honors U.S. history, honors world history, human anatomy, instruments, introduction to theater, Italian, jazz band, keyboarding, lab science, language, language and composition, law and the legal system, life science, marine science, mathematics, modern history, music performance, music theater, musical theater, musical theater dance, oceanography, personal fitness, physical fitness, physics, play production, portfolio art, pre-calculus, public service, religion, religion and culture, religious education, religious studies, scene study, science, science research, scripture, set design, Spanish, sports nutrition, stage and body movement, stage design, theater, theater arts, theater design and production, theater history, visual and performing arts, yearbook.

Graduation Requirements Computers, English, foreign language, health education, history, lab science, mathematics, oceanography, physical education (includes health), religion (includes Bible studies and theology), science.

Special Academic Programs International Baccalaureate program; Advanced Placement exam preparation; honors section.

College Admission Counseling 158 students graduated in 2012; 152 went to college, including Johnson & Wales University; Providence College; Salve Regina University; University of New Hampshire; University of Rhode Island. Other: 1 went to work, 2 entered military service, 3 entered a postgraduate year.

Student Life Upper grades have uniform requirement, student council, honor system. Discipline rests primarily with faculty. Attendance at religious services is required.

Tuition and Aid Day student tuition: $10,750. Tuition installment plan (FACTS Tuition Payment Plan). Tuition reduction for siblings, need-based scholarship grants available. In 2012–13, 28% of upper-school students received aid. Total amount of financial aid awarded in 2012–13: $225,000.

Admissions Traditional secondary-level entrance grade is 9. For fall 2012, 310 students applied for upper-level admission, 228 were accepted, 167 enrolled. Admissions testing and essay required. Deadline for receipt of application materials: December 22. Application fee required: $25.

Athletics Interscholastic: baseball (boys), basketball (b,g), cheering (g), cross-country running (b,g), gymnastics (g), lacrosse (b,g), soccer (b,g), softball (g), swimming and diving (b,g), tennis (b,g), track and field (b,g), volleyball (g); intramural: dance (g), outdoor recreation (b,g); coed interscholastic: aquatics, golf, ice hockey; coed intramural: aerobics, aerobics/dance, ballet, bicycling, fitness, outdoor recreation, sailing, strength & conditioning, table tennis, weight lifting, weight training. 3 PE instructors, 14 coaches.

Computers Computers are regularly used in all academic classes. Computer resources include on-campus library services, Internet access, Internet filtering or blocking technology. Computer access in designated common areas is available to students. The school has a published electronic and media policy.

Contact Ms. Kristen Need, Director of Admissions. 401-789-9262 Ext. 515. Fax: 401-782-2262. E-mail: kneed@theproutschool.org. Website: www.theproutschool.org

PROVIDENCE ACADEMY

15100 Schmidt Lake Road
Plymouth, Minnesota 55446

Head of School: Dr. Todd Flanders

General Information Coeducational day college-preparatory, arts, and religious studies school, affiliated with Roman Catholic Church. Grades PK–12. Founded: 2001. Setting: suburban. Nearest major city is Minneapolis. 42-acre campus. 1 building on campus. Approved or accredited by Independent Schools Association of the Central States and Minnesota Department of Education. Member of National Association of Independent Schools. Total enrollment: 867. Upper school average class size: 20. Upper school faculty-student ratio: 1:11. There are 172 required school days per year for Upper School students. Upper School students typically attend 5 days per week. The average school day consists of 6 hours and 45 minutes.

Upper School Student Profile Grade 9: 82 students (40 boys, 42 girls); Grade 10: 100 students (44 boys, 56 girls); Grade 11: 78 students (39 boys, 39 girls); Grade 12: 77 students (38 boys, 39 girls). 67% of students are Roman Catholic.

Faculty School total: 70. In upper school: 54 have advanced degrees.

Subjects Offered Advanced biology, advanced chemistry.

Special Academic Programs 14 Advanced Placement exams for which test preparation is offered; honors section; study at local college for college credit; study abroad.

College Admission Counseling 62 students graduated in 2013; all went to college, including Creighton University; Iowa State University of Science and Technology; Southern Methodist University; University of Minnesota, Twin Cities Campus; University of Notre Dame; University of St. Thomas. Median SAT critical reading: 620, median SAT math: 605, median SAT writing: 630, median combined SAT: 1885, median composite ACT: 28. 66% scored over 600 on SAT critical reading, 61% scored over 600 on SAT math, 66% scored over 600 on SAT writing, 66% scored over 1800 on combined SAT, 55% scored over 26 on composite ACT.

Student Life Upper grades have uniform requirement, student council, honor system. Discipline rests primarily with faculty. Attendance at religious services is required.

Summer Programs Enrichment, sports, art/fine arts programs offered; session focuses on Enrichment; held on campus; accepts boys and girls; open to students from other schools. 17 students usually enrolled. 2014 schedule: June 10 to August 6. Application deadline: May 1.

Tuition and Aid Tuition installment plan (individually arranged payment plans). Merit scholarship grants, need-based scholarship grants available. In 2013–14, 31% of upper-school students received aid; total upper-school merit-scholarship money awarded: $60,000. Total amount of financial aid awarded in 2013–14: $941,948.

Admissions Traditional secondary-level entrance grade is 9. For fall 2013, 44 students applied for upper-level admission, 44 were accepted, 33 enrolled. ISEE required. Deadline for receipt of application materials: January 18. Application fee required: $25. Interview required.

Athletics Interscholastic: baseball (boys), basketball (b,g), cross-country running (b,g), football (b), golf (b,g), hockey (b,g), lacrosse (b), soccer (b,g), softball (g), swimming and diving (b,g), tennis (b,g), track and field (b,g), volleyball (g); coed intramural: sailing, skiing (cross-country), skiing (downhill). 4 PE instructors, 80 coaches, 1 athletic trainer.

Computers Computer resources include on-campus library services, Internet access, wireless campus network, Internet filtering or blocking technology. Campus intranet, student e-mail accounts, and computer access in designated common areas are available to students. Students grades are available online. The school has a published electronic and media policy.

Contact Mrs. Susan Truax, Admissions Assistant. 763-258-2502. Fax: 763-258-2503. E-mail: susan.truax@providenceacademy.org. Website: www.providenceacademy.org/

PROVIDENCE CATHOLIC SCHOOL, THE COLLEGE PREPARATORY SCHOOL FOR GIRLS GRADES 6-12

1215 North St. Mary's
San Antonio, Texas 78215-1787

Head of School: Ms. Alicia Garcia

General Information Girls' day college-preparatory, arts, and religious studies school, affiliated with Roman Catholic Church. Grades 6–12. Founded: 1951. Setting: urban. 3-acre campus. 4 buildings on campus. Approved or accredited by Southern Association of Colleges and Schools, Southern Association of Independent Schools, Texas Catholic Conference, and Texas Education Agency. Total enrollment: 315. Upper school average class size: 22. Upper school faculty-student ratio: 1:11. There are 186 required school days per year for Upper School students. Upper School students typically attend 5 days per week. The average school day consists of 7 hours.

Upper School Student Profile Grade 9: 63 students (63 girls); Grade 10: 47 students (47 girls); Grade 11: 45 students (45 girls); Grade 12: 38 students (38 girls). 80% of students are Roman Catholic.

Faculty School total: 30. In upper school: 6 men, 19 women; 18 have advanced degrees.

Subjects Offered Acting, advanced biology, advanced chemistry, advanced math, Advanced Placement courses, aerobics, algebra, American history, American history-AP, American literature, American literature-AP, anatomy, ancient world history, art, athletics, audio visual/media, band, biology, biology-AP, British literature, British literature-AP, broadcast journalism, broadcasting, calculus-AP, career education internship, Catholic belief and practice, cheerleading, chemistry, choir, choral music, church history, composition-AP, computer information systems, concert band, concert choir, conflict resolution, creative writing, dance, dance performance, desktop publishing, drama, drama performance, drama workshop, economics, English, English language and composition-AP, English language-AP, English literature, English literature and composition-AP, English literature-AP, English-AP, film, fitness, foreign language, French, geography, government, government and politics-AP, history, history-AP, human anatomy, jazz band, journalism, JROTC, JROTC or LEAD (Leadership Education and Development), Latin, law, leadership, literature and composition-AP, music theory, newspaper, peer ministry, personal fitness, photography, photojournalism, physical education, physical fitness, physical science, physics, play production, psychology, social justice, sociology, softball, Spanish, Spanish language-AP, Spanish-AP, speech, sports, statistics-AP, student government, student publications, swimming, swimming competency, tennis, Texas history, the Web, theater, theater arts, theater design and production, theater production, theology, track and field, U.S. government and politics, U.S. government and politics-AP, U.S. history, U.S. history-AP, volleyball, Web site design, world geography, world history, yearbook.

Graduation Requirements All academic, 100 hours of community service completed by grade 12, senior retreat participation.

Special Academic Programs International Baccalaureate program; 13 Advanced Placement exams for which test preparation is offered; honors section; independent study; study at local college for college credit.

College Admission Counseling 48 students graduated in 2013; all went to college, including St. Mary's University; Texas A&M University; The University of Texas at Austin; The University of Texas at San Antonio; University of the Incarnate Word.

Student Life Upper grades have uniform requirement, student council, honor system. Discipline rests primarily with faculty. Attendance at religious services is required.

Summer Programs Remediation, enrichment, advancement, sports, art/fine arts, computer instruction programs offered; session focuses on getting ahead (improvement); held on campus; accepts girls; open to students from other schools. 100 students usually enrolled. 2014 schedule: June 6 to July 14. Application deadline: May 25.

Tuition and Aid Day student tuition: $7392. Tuition installment plan (FACTS Tuition Payment Plan, Middle School Tuition $4,202). Tuition reduction for siblings, merit scholarship grants, need-based scholarship grants available. In 2013–14, 20% of upper-school students received aid; total upper-school merit-scholarship money awarded: $70,210. Total amount of financial aid awarded in 2013–14: $200,000.

Admissions Traditional secondary-level entrance grade is 9. High School Placement Test or QUIC required. Deadline for receipt of application materials: none. No application fee required. On-campus interview recommended.

Athletics Interscholastic: aerobics, aerobics/dance, basketball, bowling, cheering, cross-country running, dance, dance team, JROTC drill, physical fitness, physical training, running, soccer, softball, tennis, track and field, volleyball, weight training, winter soccer; coed interscholastic: aquatics. 1 PE instructor, 7 coaches, 1 athletic trainer.

Computers Computers are regularly used in desktop publishing, journalism, newspaper, Web site design, yearbook classes. Computer network features include on-campus library services, online commercial services, Internet access, Internet filtering or blocking technology, online classrooms. Campus intranet and student e-mail accounts are available to students. Students grades are available online. The school has a published electronic and media policy.

Contact Mrs. Stephanie Takas-Mercer, Admissions Director. 210-224-6651 Ext. 210. Fax: 210-224-9242. E-mail: stakas-mercer@providencehs.net. Website: www.providencehs.net

PROVIDENCE COUNTRY DAY SCHOOL

660 Waterman Avenue

East Providence, Rhode Island 02914-1724

Head of School: Mr. Vince Watchorn

General Information Coeducational day college-preparatory and arts school. Grades 6–12. Founded: 1923. Setting: suburban. Nearest major city is Providence. 18-acre campus. 6 buildings on campus. Approved or accredited by Association of Independent Schools in New England, New England Association of Schools and Colleges, The College Board, and Rhode Island Department of Education. Member of National Association of Independent Schools and Secondary School Admission Test Board. Endowment: $1.6 million. Total enrollment: 200. Upper school average class size: 12. Upper school faculty-student ratio: 1:7. There are 166 required school days per year for Upper School students. Upper School students typically attend 5 days per week. The average school day consists of 6 hours and 50 minutes.

Upper School Student Profile Grade 9: 34 students (21 boys, 13 girls); Grade 10: 42 students (26 boys, 16 girls); Grade 11: 41 students (24 boys, 17 girls); Grade 12: 48 students (32 boys, 16 girls).

Faculty School total: 40. In upper school: 14 men, 16 women; 19 have advanced degrees.

Subjects Offered Advanced Placement courses, algebra, American government, American history, American history-AP, American literature, ancient history, art, art history-AP, Asian studies, Bible as literature, bioethics, biology, biology-AP, British literature, calculus, calculus-AP, ceramics, chemistry, choir, computer graphics, conceptual physics, creative writing, drama, earth science, electives, English, English literature, English literature-AP, environmental science, European civilization, European history, European history-AP, expository writing, fine arts, foreign language, forensics, French, geography, geometry, government/civics, graphic design, health, history, independent study, jazz ensemble, journalism, Latin, mathematics, media production, modern European history, music, performing arts, photography, physical education, physics, pottery, pre-algebra, pre-calculus, public speaking, science, senior internship, social studies, Spanish, Spanish language-AP, studio art, theater, trigonometry, U.S. government and politics-AP, visual arts, world history, writing.

Graduation Requirements Arts and fine arts (art, music, dance, drama), English, foreign language, history, mathematics, physical education (includes health), science, senior independent project, community service hours.

Special Academic Programs 9 Advanced Placement exams for which test preparation is offered; honors section; independent study; term-away projects; academic accommodation for the gifted, the musically talented, and the artistically talented.

College Admission Counseling 48 students graduated in 2013; all went to college, including Bates College; Connecticut College; Rensselaer Polytechnic Institute; Skidmore College; The College of William and Mary; University of Rhode Island. Mean SAT critical reading: 568, mean SAT math: 580, mean SAT writing: 572, mean combined SAT: 1721, mean composite ACT: 23.

Student Life Upper grades have specified standards of dress, student council, honor system. Discipline rests primarily with faculty.

Summer Programs Sports, art/fine arts programs offered; held on campus; accepts boys and girls; not open to students from other schools.

Tuition and Aid Day student tuition: $29,400–$29,900. Tuition installment plan (FACTS Tuition Payment Plan, monthly payment plans). Merit scholarship grants, need-based scholarship grants available. In 2013–14, 41% of upper-school students received aid. Total amount of financial aid awarded in 2013–14: $1,500,000.

Admissions Traditional secondary-level entrance grade is 9. For fall 2013, 127 students applied for upper-level admission, 116 were accepted, 47 enrolled. ISEE or SSAT required. Deadline for receipt of application materials: February 1. Application fee required: $55. On-campus interview required.

Athletics Interscholastic: baseball (boys), basketball (b,g), cross-country running (b,g), football (b), golf (b,g), ice hockey (b), indoor track & field (b,g), lacrosse (b,g), sailing (b,g), soccer (b,g), swimming and diving (b,g), tennis (b,g), track and field (b,g), winter (indoor) track (b,g), wrestling (b); coed interscholastic: physical fitness, yoga; coed intramural: strength & conditioning, weight training. 2 PE instructors, 8 coaches, 1 athletic trainer.

Computers Computers are regularly used in art, English, foreign language, history, mathematics, music, science classes. Computer network features include on-campus library services, online commercial services, Internet access, Internet filtering or blocking technology. Campus intranet, student e-mail accounts, and computer access in designated common areas are available to students. The school has a published electronic and media policy.

Contact Ms. Ashley E. Randlett, Director of Admissions and Financial Aid. 401-438-5170 Ext. 102. Fax: 401-435-4514. E-mail: randlett@providencecountryday.org. Website: www.providencecountryday.org

PROVIDENCE DAY SCHOOL

5800 Sardis Road

Charlotte, North Carolina 28270

Head of School: Dr. Glyn Cowlishaw

General Information Coeducational day college-preparatory and global studies diploma program school. Grades PK–12. Founded: 1971. Setting: suburban. 44-acre campus. 18 buildings on campus. Approved or accredited by Southern Association of Colleges and Schools, Southern Association of Independent Schools, and North Carolina Department of Education. Member of National Association of Independent Schools. Endowment: $4 million. Total enrollment: 1,580. Upper school average class size: 18. Upper school faculty-student ratio: 1:9. There are 176 required school days per year for Upper School students. Upper School students typically attend 5 days per week. The average school day consists of 7 hours and 10 minutes.

Upper School Student Profile Grade 9: 143 students (71 boys, 72 girls); Grade 10: 143 students (73 boys, 70 girls); Grade 11: 142 students (70 boys, 72 girls); Grade 12: 142 students (71 boys, 71 girls).

Faculty School total: 148. In upper school: 46 men, 34 women; 56 have advanced degrees.

Subjects Offered 3-dimensional design, accounting, African-American history, algebra, American history, American literature, art, art history-AP, Asian history, band, biology, biology-AP, calculus-AP, chemistry, chemistry-AP, chorus, Civil War, composition, computer graphics, computer programming, computer science, computer science-AP, drama, economics, English, English literature, English-AP, environmental science, environmental science-AP, fine arts, French, French-AP, geometry, German, German-AP, government-AP, government/civics, health, history, history-AP, instrumental music, international relations, journalism, Judaic studies, keyboarding, Latin, Latin-AP, literature, Mandarin, mathematics, music-AP, photography, physical education, physical science, physics, physics-AP, political science, pre-calculus, psychology, science, set design, social studies, Spanish, Spanish-AP, sports medicine, statistics-AP, theater, word processing, world history, writing, yearbook.

Graduation Requirements Arts and fine arts (art, music, dance, drama), computer science, English, foreign language, mathematics, physical education (includes health), science, social studies (includes history), Global Studies Diploma.

Special Academic Programs 24 Advanced Placement exams for which test preparation is offered; honors section; accelerated programs; domestic exchange program; study abroad; academic accommodation for the gifted, the musically talented, and the artistically talented.

College Admission Counseling 135 students graduated in 2013; all went to college, including Appalachian State University; Duke University; North Carolina State University; The University of North Carolina at Chapel Hill; Vanderbilt University; Wake Forest University. Median SAT critical reading: 650, median SAT math: 660, median SAT writing: 650, median combined SAT: 1960, median composite ACT: 28. 73% scored over 600 on SAT critical reading, 80% scored over 600 on SAT math, 71% scored over 600 on SAT writing, 73% scored over 1800 on combined SAT.

Student Life Upper grades have specified standards of dress, student council, honor system. Discipline rests equally with students and faculty.

Summer Programs Remediation, enrichment, advancement, sports, art/fine arts, computer instruction programs offered; session focuses on academics, enrichment; held both on and off campus; held at various parks, recreation centers, museums; accepts boys and girls; open to students from other schools. 2,500 students usually enrolled. 2014 schedule: June 7 to August 6. Application deadline: none.

Tuition and Aid Day student tuition: $22,080. Tuition installment plan (Academic Management Services Plan, SMART Tuition Payment Plan, monthly payment plans). Need-based scholarship grants available. In 2013–14, 14% of upper-school students received aid. Total amount of financial aid awarded in 2013–14: $1,056,585.

Admissions Traditional secondary-level entrance grade is 9. For fall 2013, 113 students applied for upper-level admission, 65 were accepted, 39 enrolled. Cognitive Abilities Test, ERB CTP IV, ISEE, SSAT, ERB, PSAT, SAT, PLAN or ACT or Woodcock-Johnson Educational Evaluation, WISC III required. Deadline for receipt of application materials: January 15. Application fee required: $90. On-campus interview required.

Athletics Interscholastic: aerobics/dance (girls), aquatics (b,g), baseball (b), basketball (b,g), cheering (g), cross-country running (b,g), dance squad (g), field hockey (g), football (b), golf (b,g), lacrosse (b,g), soccer (b,g), softball (g), swimming and diving (b,g), tennis (b,g), track and field (b,g), volleyball (g), wrestling (b); intramural: indoor hockey (b,g), indoor soccer (b,g), Newcombe ball (b,g), physical fitness (b,g), pillo polo (b,g), soccer (b,g), softball (b,g), strength & conditioning (b,g), volleyball (b,g); coed intramural: indoor hockey, indoor soccer, Newcombe ball, physical fitness, pillo polo, soccer, softball, strength & conditioning, tennis, volleyball. 4 PE instructors, 36 coaches, 2 athletic trainers.

Computers Computers are regularly used in English, mathematics, science, technology, word processing classes. Computer network features include on-campus library services, online commercial services, Internet access, wireless campus network, Internet filtering or blocking technology, wireless iBook lab available for individual student check-out, iPads. Student e-mail accounts and computer access in designated common areas are available to students. Students grades are available online. The school has a published electronic and media policy.

Contact Mrs. Carissa Goddard, Admissions Assistant. 704-887-7040. Fax: 704-887-7520 Ext. 7041. E-mail: carissa.goddard@providenceday.org. Website: www.providenceday.org

PROVIDENCE HIGH SCHOOL

511 South Buena Vista Street
Burbank, California 91505-4865

Head of School: Mr. Joe Sciuto

General Information Coeducational day college-preparatory, arts, religious studies, and technology school, affiliated with Roman Catholic Church. Grades 9–12. Founded: 1955. Setting: urban. Nearest major city is Los Angeles. 4-acre campus. 7 buildings on campus. Approved or accredited by National Catholic Education Association, The College Board, Western Association of Schools and Colleges, Western Catholic Education Association, and California Department of Education. Endowment: $1.6 million. Total enrollment: 419. Upper school average class size: 20. Upper school faculty-student ratio: 1:9. There are 182 required school days per year for Upper School students. Upper School students typically attend 5 days per week. The average school day consists of 6 hours.

Upper School Student Profile Grade 9: 107 students (43 boys, 64 girls); Grade 10: 115 students (56 boys, 59 girls); Grade 11: 119 students (52 boys, 67 girls); Grade 12: 78 students (38 boys, 40 girls). 71% of students are Roman Catholic.

Faculty School total: 48. In upper school: 22 men, 26 women; 29 have advanced degrees.

Subjects Offered 3-dimensional art, accounting, advanced computer applications, Advanced Placement courses, advanced studio art-AP, algebra, American history, American history-AP, American literature, American literature-AP, Basic programming, Bible studies, biology, biology-AP, business mathematics, calculus, calculus-AP, Catholic belief and practice, ceramics, chemistry, chemistry-AP, choral music, chorus, Christian and Hebrew scripture, community service, computer animation, computer art, computer programming, computer science, computer science-AP, criminal justice, digital photography, drama, economics, economics-AP, English, English literature, English literature and composition-AP, environmental science, environmental science-AP, ethics, film, fine arts, French, geometry, graphic arts, history, instruments, journalism, language-AP, Latin, law, leadership, Mandarin, mathematics, media studies, music, photography, physical education, physics, physics-AP, pre-calculus, psychology, psychology-AP, public speaking, religion, robotics, science, social studies, Spanish, Spanish-AP, theater, trigonometry, U.S. government, U.S. government and politics-AP, U.S. history-AP, United States government-AP, video, video and animation, video film production, visual and performing arts, volleyball, world history, world religions, world religions, writing, yearbook, yoga.

Graduation Requirements Advanced math, American government, American history, American literature, art, biology, British literature, chemistry, comparative religion, computer science, economics, electives, English, ethics, foreign language, mathematics, physical education (includes health), religion (includes Bible studies and theology), science, social studies (includes history), world history, world literature, completion of Christian Service hours.

Special Academic Programs 15 Advanced Placement exams for which test preparation is offered; honors section; academic accommodation for the musically talented and the artistically talented.

College Admission Counseling 87 students graduated in 2013; 86 went to college, including California State University, Northridge; Mount St. Mary's College; Pasadena City College; University of California, Riverside; University of San Francisco. Other: 1 entered military service. Mean SAT critical reading: 533, mean SAT math: 535, mean SAT writing: 520.

Student Life Upper grades have uniform requirement, student council. Discipline rests equally with students and faculty. Attendance at religious services is required.

Summer Programs Remediation, enrichment, advancement, sports, art/fine arts, computer instruction programs offered; session focuses on enrichment, remediation, and extracurricular activities; held on campus; accepts boys and girls; open to students from other schools. 250 students usually enrolled. 2014 schedule: June 16 to July 11. Application deadline: May 30.

Tuition and Aid Day student tuition: $13,750. Tuition installment plan (The Tuition Plan, 1-payment plan: payment in full due July 1st, 2-payment plan-60% due July 1st, 40% due January 1st, 10-payment plan: monthly beginning July 1, ending April 1). Merit scholarship grants, need-based scholarship grants, PSJMC Employee Discount available. In 2013–14, 47% of upper-school students received aid; total upper-school merit-scholarship money awarded: $169,000. Total amount of financial aid awarded in 2013–14: $459,500.

Admissions Traditional secondary-level entrance grade is 9. For fall 2013, 245 students applied for upper-level admission, 225 were accepted, 107 enrolled. Admissions testing or High School Placement Test required. Deadline for receipt of application materials: January 11. Application fee required: $75. On-campus interview required.

Athletics Interscholastic: baseball (boys), basketball (b,g), combined training (b), cross-country running (b,g), fitness (b,g), golf (b), physical fitness (b,g), soccer (b,g), softball (g), strength & conditioning (b,g), volleyball (b,g), weight training (b); coed interscholastic: cheering, cross-country running, dance team, track and field, yoga; coed intramural: kickball, volleyball. 4 PE instructors, 25 coaches.

Computers Computers are regularly used in accounting, animation, computer applications, desktop publishing, digital applications, information technology, journalism, library, literary magazine, media, media production, newspaper, photography, programming, publications, video film production, Web site design, word processing, writing, yearbook classes. Computer network features include on-campus library services, online commercial services, Internet access, wireless campus network, Microsoft Office Suite XP Professional, extranet portal. Student e-mail accounts are available to students. Students grades are available online. The school has a published electronic and media policy.

Contact Mrs. Judy Umeck, Director of Admissions. 818-846-8141 Ext. 14501. Fax: 818-843-8421. E-mail: judy.umeck@providencehigh.org. Website: www.providencehigh.org

PUNAHOU SCHOOL

1601 Punahou Street
Honolulu, Hawaii 96822

Head of School: Dr. James K. Scott

General Information Coeducational day and distance learning college-preparatory, arts, and technology school. Grades K–12. Distance learning grades 9–12. Founded: 1841. Setting: urban. 76-acre campus. 21 buildings on campus. Approved or accredited by Western Association of Schools and Colleges. Member of National Association of Independent Schools and Secondary School Admission Test Board. Endowment: $194.3 million. Total enrollment: 3,771. Upper school average class size: 21. Upper school faculty-student ratio: 1:10. There are 174 required school days per year for Upper School students. Upper School students typically attend 5 days per week. The average school day consists of 7 hours.

Upper School Student Profile Grade 9: 448 students (219 boys, 229 girls); Grade 10: 439 students (215 boys, 224 girls); Grade 11: 415 students (200 boys, 215 girls); Grade 12: 436 students (207 boys, 229 girls).

Faculty School total: 336. In upper school: 73 men, 99 women; 124 have advanced degrees.

Subjects Offered Acting, advanced biology, advanced chemistry, Advanced Placement courses, algebra, American literature, American studies, anatomy and physiology, anthropology, art, Asian history, astronomy, ballet, Bible as literature, bioethics, biology, biology-AP, biotechnology, British literature, calculus, calculus-AP, career/college preparation, ceramics, character education, chemistry, chemistry-AP, child development, Chinese, choir, choral music, chorus, clayworking, college admission preparation, college counseling, college planning, college writing, community garden, composition, computer science, computer science-AP, concert band, contemporary issues, CPR, creative writing, dance, digital art, drama performance, drawing, driver education, economics, English, English composition, environmental science, environmental science-AP, European history, European history-AP, film and literature, French, French language-AP, geometry, glassblowing, government and politics-AP, guitar, Hawaiian history, Hawaiian language, humanities, independent study, Japanese, jewelry making, journalism, JROTC or LEAD (Leadership Education and Development), law, Mandarin, marching band, marine biology, mechanical drawing, medieval history, money management, music theory, musical theater, oceanography, painting, peer counseling, photography, physical education, physics, physics-AP, pre-calculus, psychology, psychology-AP, religion, robotics, SAT preparation, sculpture, Shakespeare, social studies, Spanish, Spanish-AP, statistics-AP, studio art, studio art-AP, symphonic band, technical theater, theater design and production, U.S. government and politics-AP, U.S. history, U.S. history-AP, video, video film production, Western literature, wind ensemble, world civilizations, world literature, writing, yoga.

Graduation Requirements Electives, English, foreign language, mathematics, physical education (includes health), science, social studies (includes history), visual and performing arts, seniors are required to take a CapSeeds course that combines economics and community service, one course with the Spiritual, Ethical, Community Responsibility (SECR) designation.

Special Academic Programs 17 Advanced Placement exams for which test preparation is offered; honors section; independent study; study abroad.

College Admission Counseling 422 students graduated in 2013; 417 went to college, including Loyola Marymount University; Santa Clara University; Seattle University; University of Hawaii at Manoa; University of Southern California. Other: 2 entered military service, 3 had other specific plans. Median SAT critical reading: 610, median SAT math: 670, median SAT writing: 620, median combined SAT: 1910. 51% scored over 600 on SAT critical reading, 75% scored over 600 on SAT math, 59% scored over 600 on SAT writing, 68% scored over 1800 on combined SAT.

Student Life Upper grades have specified standards of dress, student council, honor system. Discipline rests primarily with faculty. Attendance at religious services is required.

Summer Programs Enrichment, advancement, sports, art/fine arts programs offered; session focuses on enrichment and graduation credit; held both on and off campus; held at Japan, Costa Rica, China; accepts boys and girls; not open to students from other schools. 3,925 students usually enrolled. 2014 schedule: June 16 to July 18. Application deadline: April 11.

Tuition and Aid Day student tuition: $19,800. Tuition installment plan (Insured Tuition Payment Plan, monthly payment plans, semester payment plan; annual payment plan). Merit scholarship grants, need-based scholarship grants available. In 2013–14, 15% of upper-school students received aid. Total amount of financial aid awarded in 2013–14: $2,687,980.

Admissions Traditional secondary-level entrance grade is 9. For fall 2013, 392 students applied for upper-level admission, 132 were accepted, 97 enrolled. SAT or SSAT required. Deadline for receipt of application materials: November 1. Application fee required: $125. Interview required.

Athletics Interscholastic: baseball (boys), basketball (b,g), bowling (b,g), canoeing/kayaking (b,g), cheering (g), cross-country running (b,g), football (b), golf (b,g), judo (b,g), kayaking (b,g), paddling (b,g), riflery (b,g), sailing (b,g), soccer (b,g), softball (g), swimming and diving (b,g), tennis (b,g), track and field (b,g), volleyball (b,g), water polo (b,g), wrestling (b,g); coed interscholastic: canoeing/kayaking, paddling. 4 PE instructors, 266 coaches, 4 athletic trainers.

Computers Computers are regularly used in all academic classes. Computer network features include on-campus library services, online commercial services, Internet access, wireless campus network, Internet filtering or blocking technology. Campus intranet, student e-mail accounts, and computer access in designated common areas are available to students. The school has a published electronic and media policy.

Contact Mrs. Betsy S. Hata, Director of Admission and Financial Aid. 808-944-5714. Fax: 808-943-3602. E-mail: admission@punahou.edu. Website: www.punahou.edu

PUSCH RIDGE CHRISTIAN ACADEMY

9500 North Oracle Road
Tucson, Arizona 85704

Head of School: Mr. Jason A Clapero

General Information Coeducational day college-preparatory, arts, and religious studies school, affiliated with Presbyterian Church in America. Grades 6–12. Founded: 2000. Setting: suburban. Nearest major city is Oro Valley. 48-acre campus. 2 buildings on campus. Approved or accredited by Association of Christian Schools International and Arizona Department of Education. Endowment: $40,000. Upper school average class size: 22. Upper school faculty-student ratio: 1:16. There are 176 required school days per year for Upper School students. Upper School students typically attend 5 days per week. The average school day consists of 6 hours and 30 minutes.

Upper School Student Profile Grade 9: 81 students (38 boys, 43 girls); Grade 10: 79 students (41 boys, 38 girls); Grade 11: 73 students (48 boys, 25 girls); Grade 12: 78 students (31 boys, 47 girls). 15% of students are Presbyterian Church in America.

Faculty School total: 29. In upper school: 13 men, 16 women; 13 have advanced degrees.

Subjects Offered 3-dimensional art, acting, advanced biology, advanced chemistry, advanced math, Advanced Placement courses, algebra, American Civil War, American government, American history, American history-AP, American literature, American literature-AP, analytic geometry, anatomy, art, ASB Leadership, athletics, band, Bible, biology, chemistry, chemistry-AP, choir, choral music, chorus, college admission preparation, college counseling, college placement, college planning, computer-aided design, concert band, concert choir, creative writing, drama performance, drawing and design, economics, economics-AP, electives, English, English composition, English language and composition-AP, English language-AP, English literature, English literature and composition-AP, English literature-AP, English-AP, English/composition-AP, environmental science, geometry, government, government-AP, graphic arts, honors algebra, honors English, honors geometry, introduction to theater, Latin, leadership, New Testament, physics, SAT preparation, Spanish, Spanish language-AP, statistics, U.S. government, U.S. history, U.S. history-AP, Web site design, world geography, world history.

Graduation Requirements Algebra, American government, American history, American literature, Bible, biology, electives, English, geography, geometry, U.S. government, U.S. history, world history.

Special Academic Programs Advanced Placement exam preparation; honors section; study at local college for college credit.

College Admission Counseling 57 students graduated in 2013; 55 went to college. 46% scored over 600 on SAT critical reading, 38% scored over 600 on SAT math, 43% scored over 600 on SAT writing, 41% scored over 1800 on combined SAT.

Student Life Upper grades have specified standards of dress, student council, honor system. Discipline rests primarily with faculty. Attendance at religious services is required.

Tuition and Aid Day student tuition: $8437. Tuition installment plan (monthly payment plans). Tuition reduction for siblings, need-based scholarship grants available. In 2013–14, 85% of upper-school students received aid. Total amount of financial aid awarded in 2013–14: $2,000,000.

Admissions Traditional secondary-level entrance grade is 9. For fall 2013, 40 students applied for upper-level admission, 33 were accepted, 32 enrolled. Admissions testing, Gates MacGinite Reading Tests and school's own exam required. Deadline for receipt of application materials: none. Application fee required: $100. Interview required.

Athletics Interscholastic: baseball (boys), basketball (b,g), cheering (g), flagball (b), soccer (b,g), softball (g), swimming and diving (b,g), tennis (b,g), track and field (b,g), volleyball (g); coed interscholastic: cross-country running, golf. 1 PE instructor, 38 coaches, 1 athletic trainer.

Computers Computers are regularly used in college planning, graphic arts, photography, SAT preparation, science, wilderness education classes. Computer network features include Internet access, Internet filtering or blocking technology. Campus intranet is available to students. The school has a published electronic and media policy.

Contact Mrs. Paula Donley, Director of Admissions. 520-797-0107 Ext. 502. Fax: 520-797-0598. E-mail: paula.donley@prca-tucson.org. Website: www.prca-cca.com/

QUEEN MARGARET'S SCHOOL

660 Brownsey Avenue
Duncan, British Columbia V9L 1C2, Canada

Head of School: Mrs. Wilma Jamieson

General Information Girls' boarding and coeducational day college-preparatory, arts, technology, Equestrian Studies, and STEM school, affiliated with Anglican Church of Canada. Boarding girls grades 6–12, day boys grades PS–8, day girls grades PS–12. Founded: 1921. Setting: small town. Nearest major city is Victoria, Canada. Students are housed in single-sex dormitories. 27-acre campus. 9 buildings on campus. Approved or accredited by Canadian Association of Independent Schools, Canadian Educational Standards Institute, The Association of Boarding Schools, and British Columbia Department of Education. Affiliate member of National Association of Independent Schools; member of Secondary School Admission Test Board and Canadian Association of Independent Schools. Language of instruction: English. Endowment: CAN$500,000. Total enrollment: 317. Upper school average class size: 16. Upper school faculty-student ratio: 1:8. There are 168 required school days per year for Upper School students. Upper School students typically attend 5 days per week. The average school day consists of 7 hours.

Upper School Student Profile Grade 9: 25 students (25 girls); Grade 10: 38 students (38 girls); Grade 11: 34 students (34 girls); Grade 12: 31 students (31 girls). 59% of students are boarding students. 47% are province residents. 7 provinces are represented in upper school student body. 51% are international students. International students from China, Hong Kong, Japan, Mexico, Spain, and United States; 15 other countries represented in student body.

Faculty School total: 45. In upper school: 5 men, 17 women; 9 have advanced degrees; 4 reside on campus.

Subjects Offered Acting, advanced math, advanced studio art-AP, all academic, animal science, applied skills, art, band, biology, business education, business skills, calculus, calculus-AP, Canadian history, career and personal planning, career exploration, chemistry, chorus, college planning, communications, computer science, creative writing, drama, engineering, English, English language-AP, English literature, equestrian sports, equine management, equine science, equitation, ESL, finance, fine arts, food and nutrition, French, geography, grammar, health, history, home economics, information technology, instrumental music, international relations, international studies, Japanese, jazz ensemble, journalism, leadership, leadership and service, mathematics, media, media arts, music, outdoor education, photography, physical education, physics, science, social studies, society, politics and law, speech, sports, sports psychology, textiles, theater, visual arts, world history, writing, yearbook.

Graduation Requirements Arts and fine arts (art, music, dance, drama), career and personal planning, English, language arts, mathematics, physical education (includes health), science, social studies (includes history). Community service is required.

Special Academic Programs Advanced Placement exam preparation; independent study; study at local college for college credit; academic accommodation for the gifted, the musically talented, and the artistically talented; ESL (40 students enrolled).

College Admission Counseling 29 students graduated in 2013; 27 went to college, including Carleton University; Queen's University at Kingston; University of Alberta; University of Calgary; University of Toronto; University of Victoria. Other: 2 went to work.

Student Life Upper grades have uniform requirement, student council, honor system. Discipline rests primarily with faculty. Attendance at religious services is required.

Summer Programs Enrichment, ESL, sports programs offered; session focuses on ESL group camps, equestrian riding, and pre-vet camp; held on-campus; accepts boys and girls; open to students from other schools. 25 students usually enrolled. 2014 schedule: July 6 to August 29. Application deadline: May 15.

Tuition and Aid Day student tuition: CAN$10,850–CAN$13,000; 5-day tuition and room/board: CAN$31,950; 7-day tuition and room/board: CAN$38,325–CAN$52,790. Tuition installment plan (Insured Tuition Payment Plan, monthly payment plans, individually arranged payment plans). Tuition reduction for siblings, bursaries, merit scholarship grants, need-based scholarship grants, tuition reduction for children of staff available. In 2013–14, 35% of upper-school students received aid; total upper-school merit-scholarship money awarded: CAN$50,000. Total amount of financial aid awarded in 2013–14: CAN$150,000.

Admissions Traditional secondary-level entrance grade is 9. Deadline for receipt of application materials: none. Application fee required: CAN$200. Interview required.

Athletics Interscholastic: aquatics, badminton, basketball (b), canoeing/kayaking, cross-country running (b), dressage, equestrian sports (b), field hockey, horseback riding (b), soccer (b), swimming and diving (b), track and field (b), volleyball (b); intramural: aerobics, aerobics/dance, golf (b), modern dance, rafting, rappelling, rugby (b), running (b), sailing, scuba diving, sea rescue, snowshoeing, surfing, track and field (b), ultimate Frisbee, volleyball (b), wrestling (b), yoga (b); coed intramural: alpine skiing, aquatics, archery, badminton, ball hockey, baseball, basketball, cooperative games, cross-country running, dance, dressage, equestrian sports, field hockey, figure skating, fitness, flag football, floor hockey, freestyle skiing, Frisbee, gymnastics, hiking/backpacking, hockey, horseback riding, ice skating, kayaking, ocean paddling, outdoor activities, outdoor adventure, outdoor education, outdoor recreation, outdoor skills, outdoors, paddling, physical fitness, physical training, rugby, skiing (downhill), snowboarding, soccer, softball, street hockey, strength & conditioning, swimming and diving, tennis, weight training. 2 PE instructors, 3 coaches, 2 athletic trainers.

Computers Computers are regularly used in all academic, art, career education, career exploration, college planning, creative writing, English, ESL, French, information technology, introduction to technology, journalism, mathematics, media arts, media production, science, social sciences, technology classes. Computer network features include on-campus library services, Internet access, wireless campus network, Internet filtering or blocking technology. Campus intranet and student e-mail accounts are available to students. The school has a published electronic and media policy.

Contact Admissions Coordinator. 250-746-4185. Fax: 250-746-4187. E-mail: admissions@qms.bc.ca. Website: www.qms.bc.ca

QUINTE CHRISTIAN HIGH SCHOOL

138 Wallbridge-Loyalist Road
RR 2
Belleville, Ontario K8N 4Z2, Canada

Head of School: Mr. Johan Cooke

General Information Coeducational day college-preparatory, general academic, arts, business, vocational, religious studies, bilingual studies, and technology school, affiliated with Christian faith, Protestant faith. Grades 9–12. Founded: 1977. Setting: suburban. Nearest major city is Toronto, Canada. 25-acre campus. 1 building on campus. Approved or accredited by Christian Schools International, Ontario Ministry of Education, and Ontario Department of Education. Language of instruction: English. Total enrollment: 161. Upper school average class size: 15. Upper school faculty-student ratio: 1:15. There are 176 required school days per year for Upper School students. Upper School students typically attend 5 days per week. The average school day consists of 6 hours and 10 minutes.

Upper School Student Profile Grade 9: 36 students (22 boys, 14 girls); Grade 10: 35 students (16 boys, 19 girls); Grade 11: 37 students (13 boys, 24 girls); Grade 12: 45 students (25 boys, 20 girls). 90% of students are Christian, Protestant.

Faculty School total: 16. In upper school: 9 men, 7 women; 2 have advanced degrees.

Subjects Offered Accounting, art, Bible, biology, calculus, careers, chemistry, Christian education, civics, computers, drama, English, English literature, ESL, French, geography, history, law, leadership education training, mathematics, mathematics-AP, media, music, peer counseling, physical education, physics, religious education, science, shop, society challenge and change, technical education, transportation technology, world issues, world religions.

Graduation Requirements Accounting, applied arts, careers, Christian education, civics, computers, English, French, geography, mathematics, physical education (includes health), religious education, science, social studies (includes history), world religions, Ontario Christian School diploma requirements.

Special Academic Programs Special instructional classes for students with learning disabilities.

College Admission Counseling 39 students graduated in 2012; 20 went to college, including Calvin College; Dordt College; Queen's University at Kingston; Redeemer University College; University of Guelph; University of Waterloo. 100% scored over 26 on composite ACT.

Student Life Upper grades have specified standards of dress, student council, honor system. Discipline rests primarily with faculty. Attendance at religious services is required.

Tuition and Aid Day student tuition: CAN$12,200. Tuition installment plan (monthly payment plans, individually arranged payment plans). Tuition reduction for siblings, need-based scholarship grants available. In 2012–13, 18% of upper-school students received aid.

Admissions Traditional secondary-level entrance grade is 9. Deadline for receipt of application materials: March 31. Application fee required: CAN$250. Interview required.

Athletics Interscholastic: badminton (boys, girls), basketball (b,g), cross-country running (b,g), track and field (b,g), volleyball (b,g); coed interscholastic: badminton; coed intramural: badminton, basketball, fitness walking, indoor soccer, physical training, volleyball. 3 PE instructors.

Computers Computers are regularly used in all classes. Computer network features include on-campus library services, Internet access, wireless campus network, Internet filtering or blocking technology. Campus intranet, student e-mail accounts, and computer access in designated common areas are available to students. The school has a published electronic and media policy.

Contact Mrs. Hermien Hogewoning, Administrative Assistant. 613-968-7870. Fax: 613-968-7970. E-mail: admin@qchs.ca. Website: www.qchs.ca

RABUN GAP-NACOOCHEE SCHOOL

339 Nacoochee Drive
Rabun Gap, Georgia 30568

Head of School: Dr. Anthony Sgro

General Information Coeducational boarding and day college-preparatory, arts, ESL, and performing arts school, affiliated with Presbyterian Church. Boarding grades 7–12, day grades 5–12. Founded: 1903. Setting: rural. Nearest major city is Atlanta. Students are housed in single-sex dormitories. 1,400-acre campus. 14 buildings on campus. Approved or accredited by North Carolina Association of Independent Schools, Southern Association of Colleges and Schools, Southern Association of Independent Schools, The Association of Boarding Schools, and Georgia Department of Education. Member of National Association of Independent Schools and Secondary School Admission Test Board. Endowment: $50 million. Total enrollment: 404. Upper school average class size: 16. Upper school faculty-student ratio: 1:10. There are 172 required school days per year for Upper School students. Upper School students typically attend 5 days per week. The average school day consists of 6 hours and 15 minutes.

Upper School Student Profile Grade 9: 68 students (34 boys, 34 girls); Grade 10: 89 students (49 boys, 40 girls); Grade 11: 83 students (45 boys, 38 girls); Grade 12: 66 students (41 boys, 25 girls). 53% of students are boarding students. 65% are state residents. 11 states are represented in upper school student body. 25% are international students. International students from Bahamas, China, Germany, Mexico, Republic of Korea, and Taiwan; 17 other countries represented in student body. 10% of students are Presbyterian.

Faculty School total: 54. In upper school: 19 men, 21 women; 26 have advanced degrees; 49 reside on campus.

Subjects Offered Advanced Placement courses, algebra, American literature, anatomy, ancient world history, art, art history, art history-AP, band, Bible studies, biology, biology-AP, botany, calculus-AP, chemistry, chemistry-AP, chorus, computer-aided design, creative writing, economics, English language-AP, English literature-AP, environmental science, environmental science-AP, ESL, European history-AP, French, French-AP, geography, geometry, government, government-AP, health, health education, history-AP, honors algebra, honors English, honors U.S. history, honors world history, industrial arts, journalism, life science, mathematics, modern European history-AP, modern world history, music, orchestra, physical education, physical science, physics, physics-AP, pre-algebra, pre-calculus, probability and statistics, psychology, science, Spanish, Spanish language-AP, Spanish-AP, studio art-AP, theater, U.S. government and politics-AP, U.S. history, U.S. history-AP, wind ensemble, world geography, world history, world literature, yearbook.

Graduation Requirements Algebra, ancient world history, arts and fine arts (art, music, dance, drama), biology, chemistry, English, foreign language, geometry, mathematics, modern world history, physical education (includes health), physics, religion (includes Bible studies and theology), science, social studies (includes history), U.S. history, participation in Intersession/G.A.P. Week, science symposium, Project Eagle.

Special Academic Programs Advanced Placement exam preparation; honors section; independent study; study abroad; ESL (16 students enrolled).

College Admission Counseling 69 students graduated in 2013; all went to college, including Emory University; Georgia Institute of Technology; The University of North Carolina at Chapel Hill; University of Georgia; Wofford College.

Student Life Upper grades have uniform requirement, student council, honor system. Discipline rests equally with students and faculty. Attendance at religious services is required.

Summer Programs Remediation, advancement, sports programs offered; session focuses on fall sports team preparation, math remedial and enrichment programs; held both on and off campus; held at online; accepts boys and girls; not open to students from other schools. 130 students usually enrolled. 2014 schedule: July 30 to August 22.

Tuition and Aid Day student tuition: $17,330; 7-day tuition and room/board: $42,890. Tuition installment plan (monthly payment plans, semester payment plan). Merit scholarship grants, need-based scholarship grants, tuition remission for children of faculty and staff available. In 2013–14, 73% of upper-school students received aid; total upper-school merit-scholarship money awarded: $300,000. Total amount of financial aid awarded in 2013–14: $5,000,000.

Admissions Traditional secondary-level entrance grade is 9. For fall 2013, 365 students applied for upper-level admission, 196 were accepted, 81 enrolled. ISEE, SSAT or TOEFL required. Deadline for receipt of application materials: February 7. Application fee required: $85. Interview required.

Athletics Interscholastic: baseball (boys), basketball (b,g), cross-country running (b,g), football (b), soccer (b,g), softball (g), swimming and diving (b,g), tennis (b,g), volleyball (g), wrestling (b); intramural: soccer (b,g), swimming and diving (b,g), tennis (b,g); coed interscholastic: Circus, dance team, golf, tennis; coed intramural: aerobics/dance, ballet, basketball, bicycling, canoeing/kayaking, Circus, climbing, combined training, dance, dance team, fitness, fitness walking, hiking/backpacking, kayaking, modern dance, mountain biking, Nautilus, outdoor activities, physical training, rafting, rock climbing, strength & conditioning, swimming and diving, tennis, triathlon, ultimate Frisbee, wall climbing, weight lifting, yoga. 1 PE instructor, 22 coaches, 1 athletic trainer.

Computers Computers are regularly used in English, library skills, literary magazine, technical drawing, theater arts, writing, yearbook classes. Computer network features include on-campus library services, online commercial services, Internet access, wireless campus network, Internet filtering or blocking technology, application and re-enrollment online services. Campus intranet, student e-mail accounts, and computer access in designated common areas are available to students. The school has a published electronic and media policy.

Contact Mrs. Kathy Watts, Admission Assistant. 706-746-7720. Fax: 706-746-7797. E-mail: kwatts@rabungap.org. Website: www.rabungap.org

RAMONA CONVENT SECONDARY SCHOOL

1701 West Ramona Road

Alhambra, California 91803-3080

Head of School: Ms. Tina Bonacci

General Information Girls' day college-preparatory, arts, business, religious studies, bilingual studies, and technology school, affiliated with Roman Catholic Church. Grades 7–12. Founded: 1889. Setting: suburban. Nearest major city is Los Angeles. 19-acre campus. 10 buildings on campus. Approved or accredited by Western Association of Schools and Colleges, Western Catholic Education Association, and California Department of Education. Endowment: $2 million. Total enrollment: 272. Upper school average class size: 22. Upper school faculty-student ratio: 1:9. There are 180 required school days per year for Upper School students. Upper School students typically attend 5 days per week. The average school day consists of 6 hours and 30 minutes.

Upper School Student Profile Grade 9: 60 students (60 girls); Grade 10: 53 students (53 girls); Grade 11: 69 students (69 girls); Grade 12: 76 students (76 girls). 88% of students are Roman Catholic.

Faculty School total: 30. In upper school: 6 men, 24 women; all have advanced degrees.

Subjects Offered Advanced Placement courses, advanced studio art-AP, algebra, American history, American literature, art history, Bible studies, biology, biology-AP, calculus, calculus-AP, ceramics, chemistry, chemistry-AP, computer programming, computer science, dance, drama, economics, English, English literature, environmental science, European history, European history-AP, fine arts, French, French-AP, geography, geometry, government/civics, grammar, graphic arts, health, history, honors English, honors geometry, mathematics, music, photography, physical education, physics, pre-calculus, religion, science, social sciences, social studies, Spanish, Spanish language-AP, Spanish literature-AP, speech, theater, theology, trigonometry, U.S. government and politics-AP, visual arts, word processing, world history, world literature.

Graduation Requirements Arts and fine arts (art, music, dance, drama), business skills (includes word processing), computer science, English, foreign language, mathematics, physical education (includes health), religion (includes Bible studies and theology), science, social studies (includes history), speech, passing grade in the Ramona Arithmetic Proficiency Test.

Special Academic Programs Advanced Placement exam preparation; honors section; independent study; study abroad; academic accommodation for the gifted, the musically talented, and the artistically talented.

College Admission Counseling 89 students graduated in 2012; all went to college, including California State University, Los Angeles; Loyola Marymount University; Mount St. Mary's College; Pitzer College; University of California, Irvine; University of California, Los Angeles. Mean SAT critical reading: 532, mean SAT math: 511, mean SAT writing: 536.

Student Life Upper grades have uniform requirement, student council, honor system. Discipline rests primarily with faculty. Attendance at religious services is required.

Tuition and Aid Day student tuition: $12,000. Tuition installment plan (monthly payment plans, quarterly and semester payment plans). Merit scholarship grants, need-based scholarship grants, paying campus jobs available. In 2012–13, 33% of upper-school students received aid; total upper-school merit-scholarship money awarded: $18,000. Total amount of financial aid awarded in 2012–13: $350,000.

Admissions Traditional secondary-level entrance grade is 9. For fall 2012, 190 students applied for upper-level admission, 150 were accepted, 78 enrolled. High School Placement Test required. Deadline for receipt of application materials: January 24. Application fee required: $75. On-campus interview required.

Athletics Interscholastic: basketball, cross-country running, soccer, softball, swimming and diving, tennis, track and field, volleyball. 1 PE instructor, 9 coaches.

Computers Computers are regularly used in all academic classes. Computer network features include on-campus library services, Internet access, wireless campus network, Internet filtering or blocking technology. Student e-mail accounts and computer access in designated common areas are available to students. Students grades are available online. The school has a published electronic and media policy.

Contact Mrs. Veronica Fernandez, Associate Director of Enrollment and Public Relations. 626-282-4151 Ext. 168. Fax: 626-281-0797. E-mail: vfernandez@ramonaconvent.org. Website: www.ramonaconvent.org

RANDOLPH-MACON ACADEMY

200 Academy Drive

Front Royal, Virginia 22630

Head of School: Maj. Gen. Maurice Forsyth

General Information Coeducational boarding and day college-preparatory, religious studies, technology, Air Force Junior ROTC, ESL, and military school, affiliated with Methodist Church. Grades 6–PG. Founded: 1892. Setting: small town. Nearest major city is Washington, DC. Students are housed in single-sex dormitories. 135-acre campus. 9 buildings on campus. Approved or accredited by Southern Association of Colleges and Schools, The Association of Boarding Schools, University Senate of United Methodist Church, and Virginia Department of Education. Member of National Association of Independent Schools. Endowment: $5 million. Total enrollment: 330. Upper school average class size: 13. Upper school faculty-student ratio: 1:14. There are 180 required school days per year for Upper School students. Upper School students typically attend 5 days per week. The average school day consists of 7 hours.

Upper School Student Profile Grade 9: 51 students (37 boys, 14 girls); Grade 10: 69 students (45 boys, 24 girls); Grade 11: 62 students (38 boys, 24 girls); Grade 12: 76 students (49 boys, 27 girls); Postgraduate: 6 students (5 boys, 1 girl). 81% of students are boarding students. 45% are state residents. 25 states are represented in upper school student body. 25% are international students. International students from Angola, China, Democratic People's Republic of Korea, Nigeria, Saudi Arabia, and Viet Nam; 11 other countries represented in student body. 14% of students are Methodist.

Faculty School total: 34. In upper school: 24 men, 10 women; 22 have advanced degrees; 18 reside on campus.

Subjects Offered Advanced math, aerospace science, algebra, American government, American history, American history-AP, American literature, American literature-AP, anatomy, anatomy and physiology, art, art history, art history-AP, Asian history, aviation, band, Bible studies, biology, biology-AP, British literature, calculus, calculus-AP, career education, chemistry, chorus, college counseling, comparative religion, composition-AP, computer applications, computer literacy, conceptual physics, concert band, concert choir, critical thinking, desktop publishing, discrete mathematics, drama, English, English composition, English literature, English literature and composition-AP, English-AP, epic literature, ESL, European history-AP, flight instruction, geometry, German, German-AP, government/civics, handbells, history, honors algebra, honors English, honors geometry, honors U.S. history, independent study, journalism, JROTC, keyboarding, life management skills, mathematics, music, music appreciation, New Testament, personal finance, personal fitness, photography, physical education, physics, physics-AP, physiology, pre-algebra, pre-calculus, psychology, religion, SAT preparation, science, senior seminar, Shakespeare, social studies, Spanish, Spanish literature-AP, speech and debate, statistics-AP, studio art, theater arts, trigonometry, U.S. government, U.S. history, world history, yearbook.

Graduation Requirements Aerospace science, arts and fine arts (art, music, dance, drama), computer science, English, foreign language, mathematics, physical education (includes health), religion (includes Bible studies and theology), science, social studies (includes history), Air Force Junior ROTC for each year student is enrolled.

Special Academic Programs Advanced Placement exam preparation; honors section; independent study; study at local college for college credit; study abroad; academic accommodation for the gifted; ESL (18 students enrolled).

College Admission Counseling 82 students graduated in 2013; all went to college, including George Mason University; Howard University; Michigan State University; The College of William and Mary; Virginia Military Institute; Virginia Polytechnic Institute and State University. Median SAT critical reading: 522, median SAT math: 560, median SAT writing: 511, median combined SAT: 1590, median composite ACT: 22.

Student Life Upper grades have uniform requirement, student council, honor system. Discipline rests equally with students and faculty. Attendance at religious services is required.

Summer Programs Remediation, enrichment, advancement, ESL, art/fine arts, computer instruction programs offered; session focuses on remediation, new courses, ESL, flight, college counseling; held on campus; accepts boys and girls; open to students from other schools. 180 students usually enrolled. 2014 schedule: June 29 to July 25. Application deadline: June 20.

Tuition and Aid Day student tuition: $16,762; 7-day tuition and room/board: $33,399. Tuition installment plan (monthly payment plans, 2-payment plan). Tuition reduction for siblings, merit scholarship grants, need-based scholarship grants, paying campus jobs, Methodist Church scholarships available. In 2013–14, 36% of upper-school students received aid; total upper-school merit-scholarship money awarded: $70,000. Total amount of financial aid awarded in 2013–14: $304,242.

Admissions Traditional secondary-level entrance grade is 9. For fall 2013, 207 students applied for upper-level admission, 149 were accepted, 112 enrolled. Any standardized test or SSAT required. Deadline for receipt of application materials: none. Application fee required: $75. Interview required.

Athletics Interscholastic: baseball (boys), basketball (b,g), cross-country running (b,g), football (b), lacrosse (b), soccer (b,g), softball (g), swimming and diving (b,g), tennis (b,g), track and field (b,g), volleyball (b,g), wrestling (b); intramural: basketball (b,g), horseback riding (g), independent competitive sports (b,g), soccer (b,g), softball (g), strength & conditioning (b,g), swimming and diving (b,g), tennis (b,g), track and field (b,g), volleyball (b,g); coed interscholastic: cheering, drill team, golf, JROTC drill; coed intramural: golf, horseback riding, indoor soccer, jogging, JROTC drill, outdoor activities, outdoor recreation, physical fitness, soccer, strength & conditioning, swimming and diving, table tennis, volleyball, weight lifting, weight training. 2 PE instructors, 1 athletic trainer.

Computers Computers are regularly used in aerospace science, aviation, English, ESL, foreign language, independent study, mathematics, science, yearbook classes. Computer network features include on-campus library services, online commercial services, Internet access, Internet filtering or blocking technology. Campus intranet and student e-mail accounts are available to students. Students grades are available online. The school has a published electronic and media policy.

Contact Mrs. Lauren Mattingly, Communications Coordinator. 540-636-5484. Fax: 540-636-5419. E-mail: lmattingly@rma.edu. Website: www.rma.edu

RANDOLPH SCHOOL

1005 Drake Avenue SE
Huntsville, Alabama 35802

Head of School: Dr. Byron C. Hulsey

General Information Coeducational day college-preparatory and arts school. Grades K–12. Founded: 1959. Setting: suburban. 67-acre campus. 3 buildings on campus. Approved or accredited by Southern Association of Colleges and Schools, Southern Association of Independent Schools, and The College Board. Member of National Association of Independent Schools. Endowment: $11 million. Total enrollment: 1,001. Upper school average class size: 13. Upper school faculty-student ratio: 1:10. The average school day consists of 7 hours.

Faculty School total: 106. In upper school: 16 men, 25 women; 21 have advanced degrees.

Subjects Offered 3-dimensional art, acting, algebra, American history, American history-AP, American literature, anatomy, art, art-AP, band, biology, biology-AP, calculus, calculus-AP, ceramics, chemistry, chemistry-AP, comparative government and politics-AP, computer math, concert choir, creative writing, drama, drama workshop, economics, English, English literature, English-AP, environmental science, European history, European history-AP, film appreciation, filmmaking, fine arts, French, French-AP, geometry, history, journalism, Latin, marine biology, mathematics, music, music theory-AP, physical education, physics, physics-AP, physiology, psychology, science, social studies, Southern literature, Spanish, Spanish-AP, speech, stage design, stagecraft, student publications, studio art-AP, theater, trigonometry, U.S. government and politics-AP, U.S. history-AP, world history, world history-AP, world literature, writing, yearbook.

Graduation Requirements Algebra, arts and fine arts (art, music, dance, drama), biology, chemistry, English, foreign language, geometry, health, literature, mathematics, science, social studies (includes history), U.S. history, world history.

Special Academic Programs 12 Advanced Placement exams for which test preparation is offered; honors section; independent study; study at local college for college credit.

College Admission Counseling 80 students graduated in 2012; all went to college, including Auburn University; Birmingham-Southern College; Sewanee: The University of the South; The University of Alabama; The University of Alabama at Birmingham; Vanderbilt University. Mean SAT critical reading: 632, mean SAT math: 637, mean SAT writing: 634, mean combined SAT: 1903, mean composite ACT: 28. 53% scored over 600 on SAT critical reading, 57% scored over 600 on SAT math, 55% scored over 600 on SAT writing, 55% scored over 1800 on combined SAT, 66% scored over 26 on composite ACT.

Student Life Upper grades have specified standards of dress, student council, honor system. Discipline rests primarily with faculty.

Tuition and Aid Day student tuition: $12,460–$16,615. Tuition installment plan (Insured Tuition Payment Plan, 2- and 10-month payment plans). Need-based scholarship grants, middle-income loans available. In 2012–13, 9% of upper-school students received aid. Total amount of financial aid awarded in 2012–13: $258,240.

Admissions Traditional secondary-level entrance grade is 9. For fall 2012, 42 students applied for upper-level admission, 27 were accepted, 22 enrolled. ISEE or writing sample required. Deadline for receipt of application materials: none. Application fee required: $75. On-campus interview required.

Athletics Interscholastic: baseball (boys), basketball (b,g), cheering (g), cross-country running (b,g), diving (b,g), football (b), golf (b,g), indoor track & field (b,g), physical fitness (b,g), physical training (b,g), soccer (b,g), softball (g), swimming and diving (b,g), tennis (b,g), track and field (b,g), volleyball (g), winter (indoor) track (b,g); coed interscholastic: diving. 2 PE instructors, 19 coaches, 2 athletic trainers.

Computers Computers are regularly used in all academic classes. Computer network features include on-campus library services, online commercial services, Internet access, wireless campus network, Internet filtering or blocking technology, laptops. Campus intranet, student e-mail accounts, and computer access in designated common areas are available to students. Students grades are available online. The school has a published electronic and media policy.

Contact Glynn Below, Director of Admissions. 256-799-6104. Fax: 256-881-1784. E-mail: gbelow@randolphschool.net. Website: www.randolphschool.net

RANNEY SCHOOL

235 Hope Road
Tinton Falls, New Jersey 07724

Head of School: Dr. John W. Griffith

General Information Coeducational day college-preparatory school. Grades N–12. Founded: 1960. Setting: suburban. Nearest major city is New York, NY. 60-acre campus. 3 buildings on campus. Approved or accredited by Middle States Association of Colleges and Schools and New Jersey Department of Education. Member of National Association of Independent Schools and Secondary School Admission Test Board. Total enrollment: 820. Upper school average class size: 13. Upper school faculty-student ratio: 1:9. There are 170 required school days per year for Upper School students. Upper School students typically attend 5 days per week. The average school day consists of 7 hours.

Upper School Student Profile Grade 9: 87 students (51 boys, 36 girls); Grade 10: 78 students (30 boys, 48 girls); Grade 11: 80 students (27 boys, 53 girls); Grade 12: 59 students (30 boys, 29 girls).

Faculty School total: 94. In upper school: 20 have advanced degrees.

Subjects Offered ACT preparation, Advanced Placement courses, algebra, American history, American literature, anatomy and physiology, art, art history, art history-AP, astronomy, biology, biology-AP, British literature (honors), calculus, calculus-AP, ceramics, chemistry, chemistry-AP, computer programming, computer science, computer science-AP, ecology, environmental systems, economics, economics-AP, English, English language-AP, English literature, English literature-AP, environmental science, environmental science-AP, ethics, European history, European history-AP, fine arts, French, French-AP, geometry, government, government and politics-AP, grammar, health, history, honors English, honors geometry, journalism, macro/microeconomics-AP, macroeconomics-AP, Mandarin, marine biology, mathematics, music, music history, music theory-AP, music-AP, physical education, physics, physics-AP, SAT preparation, science, senior internship, senior thesis, Spanish, Spanish language-AP, strings, studio art, studio art-AP, theater arts, world history, world history-AP, world literature, writing.

Graduation Requirements Arts and fine arts (art, music, dance, drama), English, foreign language, history, mathematics, physical education (includes health), science.

Special Academic Programs 19 Advanced Placement exams for which test preparation is offered; honors section; independent study.

College Admission Counseling 50 students graduated in 2013; all went to college, including Boston College; Georgetown University; New York University; Rutgers, The State University of New Jersey, New Brunswick; The George Washington University; Tulane University. Mean SAT critical reading: 626, mean SAT math: 621, mean SAT writing: 638, mean combined SAT: 1884.

Student Life Upper grades have specified standards of dress, student council, honor system. Discipline rests equally with students and faculty.

Summer Programs Enrichment, sports, art/fine arts, computer instruction programs offered; session focuses on academic, enrichment, and Gifted and Talented; held on campus; accepts boys and girls; open to students from other schools. 200 students usually enrolled. 2014 schedule: June 30 to August 22. Application deadline: none.

Tuition and Aid Day student tuition: $25,500–$26,500. Tuition installment plan (Tuiton Management Systems (TMS)). Tuition reduction for siblings, need-based scholarship grants, Tuition discount beginning with the 3rd child, Reduced tuition for children of employees available. In 2013–14, 6% of upper-school students received aid. Total amount of financial aid awarded in 2013–14: $362,000.

Admissions Traditional secondary-level entrance grade is 9. For fall 2013, 80 students applied for upper-level admission, 44 were accepted, 32 enrolled. ERB required. Deadline for receipt of application materials: none. Application fee required: $75. On-campus interview required.

Athletics Interscholastic: baseball (boys), basketball (b,g), cheering (g), field hockey (g), indoor track (b,g), lacrosse (b,g), soccer (b,g), softball (g), tennis (b,g); coed interscholastic: aquatics, crew, cross-country running, golf, swimming and diving, track and field; coed intramural: aquatics, climbing, crew, dance team, fencing, fishing, fitness, indoor track, ropes courses, running, squash, strength & conditioning, weight training. 7 PE instructors, 27 coaches, 1 athletic trainer.

Computers Computers are regularly used in all academic classes. Computer network features include on-campus library services, Internet access, wireless campus network, Internet filtering or blocking technology, 1:1 laptop program in grades 6-12. Campus intranet, student e-mail accounts, and computer access in designated common areas are available to students. Students grades are available online. The school has a published electronic and media policy.

Contact Mr. Lee S. Bostic, Director of Admission and Financial Aid. 732-542-4777 Ext. 1107. Fax: 732-460-1078. E-mail: lbostic@ranneyschool.org. Website: www.ranneyschool.org

See Display on next page and Close-Up on page 562.

RANSOM EVERGLADES SCHOOL

3575 Main Highway
Miami, Florida 33133

Head of School: Mrs. Ellen Y. Moceri

General Information Coeducational day college-preparatory school. Grades 6–12. Founded: 1903. Setting: urban. 11-acre campus. 19 buildings on campus. Approved or accredited by Southern Association of Colleges and Schools, Southern Association of Independent Schools, and Florida Department of Education. Member of National Association of Independent Schools and Secondary School Admission Test Board. Endowment: $25.6 million. Total enrollment: 1,064. Upper school average class size: 14. Upper school faculty-student ratio: 1:10. There are 175 required school days per year for Upper School students. Upper School students typically attend 5 days per week. The average school day consists of 5 hours and 40 minutes.

Upper School Student Profile Grade 9: 156 students (84 boys, 72 girls); Grade 10: 146 students (74 boys, 72 girls); Grade 11: 153 students (73 boys, 80 girls); Grade 12: 153 students (79 boys, 74 girls).

Faculty School total: 99. In upper school: 30 men, 24 women; 44 have advanced degrees.

Subjects Offered Advanced Placement courses, algebra, American history, American history-AP, American literature, anatomy and physiology, art, art history, art history-AP, Asian studies, astronomy, band, biology, calculus, calculus-AP, ceramics, chemistry, chemistry-AP, Chinese, choir, chorus, college counseling, comparative government and politics-AP, computer math, computer programming, computer science, computer science-AP, computer-aided design, concert band, creative writing, dance, dance performance, debate, digital photography, drama, earth science, ecology, economics, economics-AP, engineering, English, English literature, English literature and composition-AP, English-AP, environmental science, environmental science-AP, environmental studies, ethical decision making, ethics, ethics and responsibility, European history, European history-AP, experiential education, fine arts, French, French language-AP, French-AP, geography, geology, geometry, government and politics-AP, government/civics, grammar, graphic design, guitar, health, health and wellness, history, history-AP, human anatomy, interdisciplinary studies, jazz ensemble, journalism, macro/microeconomics-AP, macroeconomics-AP, Mandarin, marine biology, mathematics, mathematics-AP, music, music theory, music theory-AP, music-AP, mythology, philosophy, photography, physical education, physics, physics-AP, probability and statistics, psychology, psychology-AP, robotics, science, sculpture, social studies, sociology, Spanish, Spanish language-AP, Spanish literature-AP, speech, speech and debate, statistics, statistics-AP, theater, theory of knowledge, trigonometry, U.S. government and politics-AP, U.S. history, U.S. history-AP, world history, world history-AP, world literature, writing, yearbook.

Graduation Requirements Arts and fine arts (art, music, dance, drama), computer science, English, foreign language, mathematics, physical education (includes health), science, social studies (includes history).

Special Academic Programs 22 Advanced Placement exams for which test preparation is offered; honors section.

College Admission Counseling 151 students graduated in 2013; all went to college, including New York University; Stanford University; The Johns Hopkins University; University of Chicago; University of Miami; University of Pennsylvania. Median SAT critical reading: 660, median SAT math: 690, median SAT writing: 670, median combined SAT: 2020, median composite ACT: 30. 74% scored over 600 on SAT critical reading, 84% scored over 600 on SAT math, 85% scored over 600 on SAT writing, 84% scored over 1800 on combined SAT, 88% scored over 26 on composite ACT.

Student Life Upper grades have specified standards of dress, student council, honor system. Discipline rests primarily with faculty.

Summer Programs Enrichment, advancement, computer instruction programs offered; session focuses on enrichment to reinforce basic skills and advancement for credit; held on campus; accepts boys and girls; open to students from other schools. 90 students usually enrolled. 2014 schedule: June 9 to July 18. Application deadline: June 6.

Tuition and Aid Day student tuition: $29,450. Tuition installment plan (monthly payment plans, 60%/40% payment plan). Need-based scholarship grants available. In 2013–14, 16% of upper-school students received aid. Total amount of financial aid awarded in 2013–14: $2,309,780.

Admissions Traditional secondary-level entrance grade is 9. For fall 2013, 100 students applied for upper-level admission, 11 were accepted, 6 enrolled. SSAT required. Deadline for receipt of application materials: December 1. Application fee required: $100. On-campus interview required.

Athletics Interscholastic: baseball (boys), basketball (b,g), canoeing/kayaking (b,g), cheering (g), crew (b,g), cross-country running (b,g), dance (g), dance team (g), football (b), golf (b,g), kayaking (b,g), lacrosse (b,g), physical training (b,g), sailing (b,g), soccer (b,g), softball (g), swimming and diving (b,g), tennis (b,g), track and field (b,g), volleyball (b,g), water polo (b,g), wrestling (b); coed interscholastic: crew, kayaking, sailing. 4 PE instructors, 80 coaches, 2 athletic trainers.

Computers Computers are regularly used in all classes. Computer network features include on-campus library services, online commercial services, Internet access, wireless campus network, Internet filtering or blocking technology. Student e-mail accounts and computer access in designated common areas are available to students. Students grades are available online. The school has a published electronic and media policy.

Contact Amy Sayfie Zichella, Director of Admission. 305-250-6875. Fax: 305-854-1846. E-mail: asayfie@ransomeverglades.org. Website: www.ransomeverglades.org

RAVENSCROFT SCHOOL

7409 Falls of the Neuse Road
Raleigh, North Carolina 27615

Head of School: Mrs. Doreen C. Kelly

General Information Coeducational day college-preparatory, arts, and technology school. Grades PK–12. Founded: 1862. Setting: suburban. 127-acre campus. 13 buildings on campus. Approved or accredited by Southern Association of Colleges and Schools, Southern Association of Independent Schools, and North Carolina Department of Education. Member of National Association of Independent Schools. Endowment: $15 million. Total enrollment: 1,210. Upper school average class size: 13. Upper school faculty-student ratio: 1:8. There are 179 required school days per year for Upper School students. Upper School students typically attend 5 days per week. The average school day consists of 7 hours and 10 minutes.

Faculty School total: 156. In upper school: 25 men, 30 women; 42 have advanced degrees.

Subjects Offered Advanced Placement courses, algebra, American history, American literature, anatomy, art, art history, astronomy, biology, biotechnology, calculus, chemistry, computer programming, computer science, discrete mathematics, drama, economics, engineering, English, English literature, environmental science, environmental science-AP, European history, expository writing, fine arts, French, geometry, government/civics, Greek, health, history, journalism, Latin, mathematics, music, photography, physical education, physics, psychology, science, social sciences, social studies, Spanish, speech, sports medicine, stagecraft, statistics-AP, theater, world history, writing.

Graduation Requirements Arts and fine arts (art, music, dance, drama), composition, English, foreign language, mathematics, physical education (includes health), science, social sciences, social studies (includes history). Community service is required.

Special Academic Programs 24 Advanced Placement exams for which test preparation is offered; honors section; independent study; term-away projects; study at local college for college credit; study abroad; academic accommodation for the gifted, the musically talented, and the artistically talented.

College Admission Counseling 115 students graduated in 2012; 114 went to college, including Appalachian State University; Davidson College; East Carolina University; North Carolina State University; The University of North Carolina at Chapel Hill; Virginia Polytechnic Institute and State University. Other: 1 entered a postgraduate year. Median SAT critical reading: 640, median SAT math: 660, median SAT writing: 640, median combined SAT: 1950, median composite ACT: 27. 61% scored over 600 on SAT critical reading, 71% scored over 600 on SAT math, 62% scored over 600 on SAT writing, 68% scored over 1800 on combined SAT, 55% scored over 26 on composite ACT.

Student Life Upper grades have specified standards of dress, student council, honor system. Discipline rests equally with students and faculty.

Tuition and Aid Day student tuition: $19,550. Tuition installment plan (individually arranged payment plans). Merit scholarship grants, need-based scholarship grants, need-based loans available. In 2012–13, 7% of upper-school students received aid.

Admissions Traditional secondary-level entrance grade is 9. ERB and SSAT required. Deadline for receipt of application materials: none. Application fee required: $70. On-campus interview required.

Athletics Interscholastic: baseball (boys), basketball (b,g), cheering (g), cross-country running (b,g), dance squad (g); field hockey (g), fitness (b,g), football (b), golf (b,g), lacrosse (b,g), physical training (b,g), soccer (b,g), softball (g), strength & conditioning (b,g), swimming and diving (b,g), tennis (b,g), track and field (b,g), volleyball (g), weight training (b,g), wrestling (b); intramural: baseball (b), basketball (b,g), cheering (g), dance team (g), football (b,g), lacrosse (b), soccer (b,g), softball (g), strength & conditioning (b,g), swimming and diving (b,g), tennis (b,g), track and field (b,g), volleyball (g), wrestling (b); coed interscholastic: life saving. 10 PE instructors, 68 coaches, 2 athletic trainers.

Computers Computers are regularly used in economics, English, foreign language, history, mathematics, science, social studies, writing classes. Computer network features include on-campus library services, online commercial services, Internet access, wireless campus network, Internet filtering or blocking technology. Campus intranet, student e-mail accounts, and computer access in designated common areas are available to students. Students grades are available online. The school has a published electronic and media policy.

Contact Mrs. Pamela J. Jamison, Director of Admissions. 919-847-0900 Ext. 2226. Fax: 919-846-2371. E-mail: admissions@ravenscroft.org. Website: www.ravenscroft.org

REALMS OF INQUIRY

120 W. Vine Street
Murray, Utah 84107

Head of School: Mr. Ross Jones

General Information Coeducational day college-preparatory, general academic, arts, bilingual studies, and outdoor education school; primarily serves gifted students. Grades 6–12. Founded: 1972. Setting: urban. Nearest major city is Salt Lake City. 1-

acre campus. 1 building on campus. Approved or accredited by Northwest Accreditation Commission and Northwest Association of Independent Schools. Total enrollment: 14. Upper school average class size: 7. Upper school faculty-student ratio: 1:7. There are 180 required school days per year for Upper School students. Upper School students typically attend 5 days per week. The average school day consists of 6 hours and 15 minutes.

Upper School Student Profile Grade 7: 2 students (1 boy, 1 girl); Grade 8: 2 students (2 boys); Grade 9: 1 student (1 boy); Grade 10: 3 students (3 boys); Grade 11: 3 students (1 boy, 2 girls); Grade 12: 3 students (1 boy, 2 girls).

Faculty School total: 5. In upper school: 2 men, 1 woman; 1 has an advanced degree.

Subjects Offered Algebra, art, band, biology, calculus, chemistry, computer literacy, drama, earth science, English, geometry, history, life skills, outdoor education, photography, physical education, physics, pre-calculus, Spanish, writing.

Graduation Requirements Arts and fine arts (art, music, dance, drama), computer science, English, foreign language, mathematics, outdoor education, physical education (includes health), science, social sciences, social studies (includes history), 30 volunteer service hours per year.

Special Academic Programs Accelerated programs; independent study; study at local college for college credit; study abroad; academic accommodation for the gifted, the musically talented, and the artistically talented; programs in English, mathematics, general development for dyslexic students.

College Admission Counseling 5 students graduated in 2013; 4 went to college, including Beloit College; University of Utah; Westminster College. Other: 1 had other specific plans. Median SAT critical reading: 690, median SAT math: 640, median SAT writing: 670, median combined SAT: 2000, median composite ACT: 28. 100% scored over 600 on SAT critical reading, 100% scored over 600 on SAT math, 100% scored over 600 on SAT writing, 100% scored over 1800 on combined SAT, 100% scored over 26 on composite ACT.

Student Life Upper grades have student council, honor system. Discipline rests equally with students and faculty.

Summer Programs Rigorous outdoor training programs offered; session focuses on climbing, rafting, wilderness skills; held both on and off campus; held at various locations; accepts boys and girls; open to students from other schools. 10 students usually enrolled.

Tuition and Aid Day student tuition: $12,900. Tuition installment plan (monthly payment plans, individually arranged payment plans). Tuition reduction for siblings, need-based scholarship grants available. In 2013–14, 30% of upper-school students received aid. Total amount of financial aid awarded in 2013–14: $40,000.

Admissions Admissions testing, WISC-III and Woodcock-Johnson, WISC/Woodcock-Johnson or Woodcock-Johnson required. Deadline for receipt of application materials: none. Application fee required: $25. Interview required.

Athletics Coed Interscholastic: backpacking, bicycling, canoeing/kayaking, climbing, combined training, cooperative games, cross-country running, dance, fencing, fishing, fitness, flag football, Frisbee, gymnastics, hiking/backpacking, independent competitive sports, jogging, kayaking, life saving, martial arts, modern dance, mountain biking, mountaineering, nordic skiing, outdoor activities, outdoor adventure, outdoor education, outdoor recreation, outdoor skills, outdoors, paddling, physical fitness, physical training, project adventure, rafting, rappelling, rock climbing, running, skateboarding, ski jumping, skiing (cross-country), skiing (downhill), snowboarding, snowshoeing, soccer, strength & conditioning, swimming and diving, table tennis, telemark skiing, touch football, ultimate Frisbee, unicycling, volleyball, walking, wall climbing, weight lifting, weight training, wilderness, wilderness survival, wildernessways, winter walking, yoga.

Computers Computers are regularly used in all academic, career exploration, college planning, commercial art, computer applications, creative writing, current events, design, desktop publishing, digital applications, drafting, drawing and design, engineering, English, foreign language, graphic design, graphics, history, independent study, mathematics, media, media arts, media production, media services, music, photography, photojournalism, publishing, research skills, SAT preparation, science, social sciences, social studies classes. Computer network features include on-campus library services, Internet access, wireless campus network. Computer access in designated common areas is available to students. Students grades are available online. The school has a published electronic and media policy.

Contact Karri Van Tongeren, Front Desk. 801-467-5911. Fax: 801-590-7701. E-mail: frontdesk@realmsofinquiry.org. Website: www.realmsofinquiry.org

THE RECTORY SCHOOL

Pomfret, Connecticut
See Junior Boarding Schools section.

REDEEMER CHRISTIAN HIGH SCHOOL

82 Colonnade Road North
Ottawa, Ontario K2E 7L2, Canada

Head of School: Mr. Chuck Schoenmaker

General Information Coeducational day college-preparatory, general academic, and religious studies school, affiliated with Christian faith. Grades 9–12. Founded:

1975. Setting: urban. 2-acre campus. 1 building on campus. Approved or accredited by Christian Schools International and Ontario Department of Education. Language of instruction: English. Total enrollment: 167. Upper school average class size: 20. Upper school faculty-student ratio: 1:9. There are 186 required school days per year for Upper School students. Upper School students typically attend 5 days per week. The average school day consists of 6 hours and 20 minutes.

Upper School Student Profile Grade 9: 52 students (26 boys, 26 girls); Grade 10: 38 students (19 boys, 19 girls); Grade 11: 44 students (22 boys, 22 girls); Grade 12: 33 students (19 boys, 14 girls). 95% of students are Christian faith.

Faculty School total: 18. In upper school: 10 men, 8 women; 5 have advanced degrees.

Graduation Requirements Graduating students must have proof they have completed a minimum of 60 volunteer hours in the community.

Student Life Upper grades have uniform requirement, student council, honor system. Discipline rests primarily with faculty. Attendance at religious services is required.

Admissions Deadline for receipt of application materials: none. Application fee required: CAN$250. Interview required.

Contact Mrs. Mary Joustra, Office Administrator. 613-723-9262 Ext. 21. Fax: 613-723-9321. E-mail: info@rchs.on.ca. Website: www.rchs.on.ca/

REDWOOD CHRISTIAN SCHOOLS

4200 James Avenue
Castro Valley, California 94546
Head of School: Mr. Bruce D. Johnson

General Information Coeducational day college-preparatory and religious studies school, affiliated with Christian faith. Grades K–12. Founded: 1970. Setting: urban. Nearest major city is Oakland. 10-acre campus. 11 buildings on campus. Approved or accredited by Association of Christian Schools International, Western Association of Schools and Colleges, and California Department of Education. Total enrollment: 692. Upper school average class size: 20. Upper school faculty-student ratio: 1:10. There are 175 required school days per year for Upper School students. Upper School students typically attend 5 days per week. The average school day consists of 6 hours and 50 minutes.

Upper School Student Profile Grade 9: 73 students (40 boys, 33 girls); Grade 10: 71 students (33 boys, 38 girls); Grade 11: 79 students (46 boys, 33 girls); Grade 12: 70 students (44 boys, 26 girls). 50% of students are Christian.

Faculty School total: 27. In upper school: 16 men, 11 women; 9 have advanced degrees.

Subjects Offered Advanced math, Advanced Placement courses, algebra, art, athletics, band, baseball, basketball, Bible studies, biology, calculus-AP, chemistry, choir, civics, computer literacy, concert band, creative writing, drama, drama performance, economics, English, English language and composition-AP, English literature and composition-AP, ensembles, European history-AP, fitness, geometry, honors English, keyboarding, macro/microeconomics-AP, physical education, physical science, physics, softball, Spanish, speech, track and field, trigonometry, U.S. government, U.S. history, vocal music, woodworking, world history, world history-AP, yearbook.

Graduation Requirements Arts and fine arts (art, music, dance, drama), Bible, computer literacy, electives, English, foreign language, mathematics, physical education (includes health), science, speech, world history.

Special Academic Programs Advanced Placement exam preparation; honors section; study at local college for college credit; remedial reading and/or remedial writing; remedial math; programs in English, mathematics, general development for dyslexic students; ESL (30 students enrolled).

College Admission Counseling 56 students graduated in 2013; 54 went to college, including Azusa Pacific University; Michigan State University; Santa Monica College; University of California, Davis; University of California, Los Angeles; University of Oregon. Other: 2 went to work. Mean SAT critical reading: 499, mean SAT math: 558, mean SAT writing: 504, mean combined SAT: 1555. 11% scored over 600 on SAT critical reading, 40% scored over 600 on SAT math, 28% scored over 600 on SAT writing, 21% scored over 1800 on combined SAT.

Student Life Upper grades have specified standards of dress, student council, honor system. Discipline rests primarily with faculty.

Tuition and Aid Day student tuition: $9291–$22,400. Tuition installment plan (FACTS Tuition Payment Plan, monthly payment plans, individually arranged payment plans). Tuition reduction for siblings, merit scholarship grants, need-based scholarship grants, paying campus jobs available. In 2013–14, 30% of upper-school students received aid. Total amount of financial aid awarded in 2013–14: $400,000.

Admissions Traditional secondary-level entrance grade is 9. For fall 2013, 74 students applied for upper-level admission, 69 were accepted, 54 enrolled. Stanford Achievement Test required. Deadline for receipt of application materials: none. Application fee required: $175. On-campus interview required.

Athletics Interscholastic: baseball (boys), basketball (b,g), cross-country running (b,g), soccer (b,g), softball (g), tennis (b,g), track and field (b,g), volleyball (b,g). 2 PE instructors, 1 coach.

Computers Computers are regularly used in computer applications, keyboarding, yearbook classes. Computer network features include on-campus library services, Internet access, wireless campus network, 1:1 iPad Initiative for grades 9-12. Campus

intranet and student e-mail accounts are available to students. Students grades are available online. The school has a published electronic and media policy.

Contact Mrs. Deborah Wright, Administrative Assistant. 510-889-7526. Fax: 510-881-0127. E-mail: deborahwright@rcs.edu. Website: www.rcs.edu

REGINA JUNIOR-SENIOR HIGH SCHOOL

2150 Rochester Avenue
Iowa City, Iowa 52245
Head of School: Glenn Plummer

General Information college-preparatory school, affiliated with Roman Catholic Church. Approved or accredited by National Catholic Education Association and Iowa Department of Education. Total enrollment: 902. Upper school average class size: 17. There are 180 required school days per year for Upper School students. Upper School students typically attend 5 days per week.

Upper School Student Profile 85% of students are Roman Catholic.

Special Academic Programs Advanced Placement exam preparation.

College Admission Counseling 64 students graduated in 2013; 63 went to college, including Iowa State University of Science and Technology; The University of Iowa; University of Northern Iowa. Other: 1 entered military service.

Student Life Upper grades have specified standards of dress, student council. Attendance at religious services is required.

Summer Programs Sports programs offered; session focuses on strength and conditioning; held on campus; accepts boys and girls; open to students from other schools. 2014 schedule: June to August.

Tuition and Aid Tuition installment plan (SMART Tuition Payment Plan). Tuition reduction for siblings, need-based scholarship grants available.

Admissions Deadline for receipt of application materials: none. Application fee required: $100. Interview required.

Athletics Interscholastic: baseball (boys), basketball (b,g), bowling (b,g), cross-country running (b,g), football (b), golf (b,g), soccer (b,g), track and field (b,g), volleyball (g), wrestling (b); coed interscholastic: dance team, strength & conditioning, weight training. 1 PE instructor, 1 athletic trainer.

Computers Student e-mail accounts are available to students.

Contact 319-338-5436. Fax: 319-337-4109. Website: www.icregina.com/jr__sr_high/

REGIS HIGH SCHOOL

55 East 84th Street
New York, New York 10028-0884
Head of School: Dr. Gary J. Tocchet

General Information Boys' day college-preparatory school, affiliated with Roman Catholic Church. Grades 9–12. Founded: 1914. Setting: urban. 3-acre campus. 1 building on campus. Approved or accredited by Jesuit Secondary Education Association, Middle States Association of Colleges and Schools, and New York Department of Education. Total enrollment: 530. Upper school average class size: 15. Upper school faculty-student ratio: 1:15. There are 180 required school days per year for Upper School students. Upper School students typically attend 5 days per week. The average school day consists of 6 hours and 50 minutes.

Upper School Student Profile Grade 9: 137 students (137 boys); Grade 10: 134 students (134 boys); Grade 11: 128 students (128 boys); Grade 12: 131 students (131 boys). 100% of students are Roman Catholic.

Faculty School total: 62. In upper school: 42 men, 20 women; 52 have advanced degrees.

Subjects Offered Algebra, American history, American literature, art, art history, band, biology, calculus, chemistry, Chinese, computer programming, computer science, creative writing, drama, driver education, economics, English, English literature, ethics, European history, expository writing, film, French, geometry, German, health, history, Latin, mathematics, music, physical education, physics, psychology, social studies, Spanish, speech, statistics, theater, theology, trigonometry, writing.

Graduation Requirements Art, computer literacy, English, foreign language, history, mathematics, music, physical education (includes health), science, theology, Christian service program.

Special Academic Programs 14 Advanced Placement exams for which test preparation is offered; independent study; study abroad.

College Admission Counseling 131 students graduated in 2013; all went to college, including College of the Holy Cross; Fordham University; Georgetown University; Polytechnic Institute of New York University; University of Notre Dame; University of Virginia. Mean SAT critical reading: 713, mean SAT math: 713, mean SAT writing: 719, mean combined SAT: 2145.

Student Life Upper grades have specified standards of dress, student council. Discipline rests primarily with faculty. Attendance at religious services is required.

Tuition and Aid Tuition-free school available.

Admissions Traditional secondary-level entrance grade is 9. For fall 2013, 707 students applied for upper-level admission, 144 were accepted, 137 enrolled. Admissions testing required. Deadline for receipt of application materials: October 19. Application fee required: $50. On-campus interview required.

Athletics Interscholastic: baseball, basketball, cross-country running, fencing, floor hockey, indoor track & field, volleyball; intramural: baseball, basketball, cross-country running, floor hockey, indoor soccer. 2 PE instructors, 10 coaches.

Computers Computers are regularly used in all academic classes. Computer network features include on-campus library services, Internet access, wireless campus network, Internet filtering or blocking technology. Campus intranet, student e-mail accounts, and computer access in designated common areas are available to students.

Contact Mr. Eric P. DiMichele, Director of Admissions. 212-288-1100 Ext. 2057. Fax: 212-794-1221. E-mail: edimiche@regis.org. Website: www.regis.org

REGIS JESUIT HIGH SCHOOL, GIRLS DIVISION

6300 South Lewiston Way
Aurora, Colorado 80016

Head of School: Ms. Gretchen M. Kessler

General Information Coeducational day college-preparatory, arts, and religious studies school, affiliated with Roman Catholic Church (Jesuit order). Grades 9–12. Founded: 2003. Setting: suburban. 64-acre campus. 2 buildings on campus. Approved or accredited by American Association of Christian Schools and Colorado Department of Education. Total enrollment: 1,700. Upper school average class size: 20. Upper school faculty-student ratio: 1:8. Upper School students typically attend 5 days per week. The average school day consists of 6 hours and 45 minutes.

Upper School Student Profile Grade 9: 460 students (270 boys, 190 girls); Grade 10: 420 students (240 boys, 180 girls); Grade 11: 420 students (240 boys, 180 girls); Grade 12: 400 students (225 boys, 175 girls). 65% of students are Roman Catholic Church (Jesuit order).

Faculty School total: 175. In upper school: 24 men, 57 women.

Special Academic Programs International Baccalaureate program; Advanced Placement exam preparation; academic accommodation for the gifted, the musically talented, and the artistically talented; remedial reading and/or remedial writing; remedial math; special instructional classes for deaf students, blind students.

College Admission Counseling Colleges students went to include Adams State University.

Student Life Upper grades have specified standards of dress, student council, honor system. Discipline rests primarily with faculty. Attendance at religious services is required.

Tuition and Aid Financial aid available to upper-school students. In 2012–13, 35% of upper-school students received aid.

Admissions Traditional secondary-level entrance grade is 9. For fall 2012, 900 students applied for upper-level admission, 500 were accepted, 460 enrolled. Deadline for receipt of application materials: December 12. Application fee required.

Athletics Interscholastic: aerobics/dance (girls), aquatics (b,g), baseball (b,g), basketball (b,g), cheering (g), cross-country running (b,g), dance (g), dance team (g), field hockey (g), fitness (b,g), football (b), golf (b,g), ice hockey (b), modern dance (g), physical fitness (b,g), power lifting (b), rhythmic gymnastics (g), rugby (b), running (b,g), soccer (b,g), swimming and diving (b,g), tennis (b,g), track and field (b,g), volleyball (b,g), wrestling (b); intramural: basketball (b,g), flag football (b), football (b), golf (b,g), soccer (b,g), whiffle ball (b). 10 PE instructors, 30 coaches, 3 athletic trainers.

Computers Computer network features include on-campus library services, Internet access, wireless campus network, Internet filtering or blocking technology. Campus intranet, student e-mail accounts, and computer access in designated common areas are available to students. Students grades are available online. The school has a published electronic and media policy.

Contact Ms. Patricia Long, Director of Admissions. 303-269-8164. Fax: 303-221-4776. E-mail: plong@regisjesuit.com. Website: www.regisjesuit.com

REJOICE CHRISTIAN SCHOOLS

12200 East 86th Street North
Owasso, Oklahoma 74055

Head of School: Dr. Craig D. Shaw

General Information Coeducational day college-preparatory school, affiliated with Free Will Baptist Church. Grades P3–12. Founded: 1992. Setting: suburban. Nearest major city is Tulsa. 1 building on campus. Approved or accredited by Association of Christian Schools International and Oklahoma Department of Education. Total enrollment: 713. Upper school average class size: 12. Upper school faculty-student ratio: 1:12.

Upper School Student Profile Grade 6: 36 students (14 boys, 22 girls); Grade 7: 40 students (17 boys, 23 girls); Grade 8: 37 students (20 boys, 17 girls); Grade 9: 35 students (14 boys, 21 girls); Grade 10: 17 students (8 boys, 9 girls); Grade 11: 17 students (10 boys, 7 girls); Grade 12: 15 students (9 boys, 6 girls). 30% of students are Free Will Baptist Church.

Faculty School total: 22. In upper school: 5 men, 17 women; 8 have advanced degrees.

Subjects Offered Advanced biology, advanced chemistry, Advanced Placement courses, algebra, American democracy, American government, American history,

American history-AP, anatomy, anatomy and physiology, art, art appreciation, art education, art history, athletic training, athletics, band, basketball, Bible, Bible studies, biology, biology-AP, business, business education, calculus, calculus-AP, cheerleading, chemistry, chemistry-AP, choir, chorus, Christian education, civics, computer skills, electives, English, English language-AP, English literature and composition-AP, English literature-AP, English-AP, English/composition-AP, fitness, general business, general math, geography, geometry, golf, government, government and politics-AP, government-AP, government/civics, government/civics-AP, history, honors algebra, honors English, honors geometry, honors U.S. history, honors world history, journalism, language, language arts, library, mathematics, mathematics-AP, media, music, novels, physical education, physical fitness, physical science, pre-algebra, pre-calculus, Spanish, Spanish language-AP, speech, speech and debate, sports, sports conditioning, state history, technology, track and field, trigonometry, U.S. government, U.S. government and politics-AP, U.S. history, U.S. history-AP, weight training, world history, world history-AP, yearbook.

Special Academic Programs Honors section; study at local college for college credit.

Student Life Upper grades have student council, honor system. Discipline rests primarily with faculty.

Tuition and Aid Tuition installment plan (SMART Tuition Payment Plan, monthly payment plans). Need-based scholarship grants available.

Admissions Gates MacGinite Reading Tests, Gates MacGinite Reading/Key Math or Stanford Achievement Test required. Deadline for receipt of application materials: none. Application fee required: $160. Interview required.

Athletics Interscholastic: basketball (boys, girls), cheering (g), cross-country running (b,g), fitness (b,g), flag football (b,g), football (b), golf (b,g), jogging (b,g), outdoor activities (b,g), outdoor recreation (b,g), physical fitness (b,g), physical training (b,g), ropes courses (b,g), running (b,g), strength & conditioning (b,g), track and field (b,g), volleyball (g), weight lifting (b), weight training (b,g). 2 PE instructors, 15 coaches, 2 athletic trainers.

Computers Computers are regularly used in English, journalism, library, media, newspaper, yearbook classes. Computer network features include on-campus library services, Internet access, wireless campus network, Internet filtering or blocking technology. Campus intranet is available to students. Students grades are available online. The school has a published electronic and media policy.

Contact Mrs. Julie Long, High School Registrar. 918-516-0050. Fax: 918-516-0299. E-mail: jlong@rejoiceschool.com. Website: www.rejoiceschool.com

RIDLEY COLLEGE

2 Ridley Road
St. Catharines, Ontario L2R7C3, Canada

Head of School: Mr. Edward Kidd

General Information Coeducational boarding and day college-preparatory, arts, business, and technology school, affiliated with Church of England (Anglican). Boarding grades 5–PG, day grades JK–PG. Founded: 1889. Setting: suburban. Nearest major city is Buffalo, NY. Students are housed in single-sex dormitories. 100-acre campus. 13 buildings on campus. Approved or accredited by Canadian Association of Independent Schools, Canadian Educational Standards Institute, Conference of Independent Schools of Ontario, Headmasters' Conference, International Baccalaureate Organization, National Independent Private Schools Association, Ontario Ministry of Education, The Association of Boarding Schools, and Ontario Department of Education. Affiliate member of National Association of Independent Schools; member of Secondary School Admission Test Board. Language of instruction: English. Endowment: CAN$23 million. Total enrollment: 651. Upper school average class size: 17. Upper school faculty-student ratio: 1:7. There are 232 required school days per year for Upper School students. Upper School students typically attend 6 days per week. The average school day consists of 6 hours.

Upper School Student Profile Grade 9: 72 students (43 boys, 29 girls); Grade 10: 111 students (68 boys, 43 girls); Grade 11: 146 students (89 boys, 57 girls); Grade 12: 136 students (68 boys, 68 girls); Postgraduate: 5 students (3 boys, 2 girls). 64% of students are boarding students. 63% are province residents. 25 provinces are represented in upper school student body. 32% are international students. International students from China, Germany, Hong Kong, Mexico, Russian Federation, and United States; 30 other countries represented in student body. 20% of students are members of Church of England (Anglican).

Faculty School total: 77. In upper school: 37 men, 40 women; 26 have advanced degrees; 40 reside on campus.

Subjects Offered Accounting, algebra, American history, anthropology, art, art history, biology, business mathematics, business skills, calculus, Canadian history, Canadian law, chemistry, computer programming, computer science, creative writing, drafting, drama, dramatic arts, driver education, economics, English, English literature, ESL, finance, fine arts, French, geography, German, International Baccalaureate courses, kinesiology, Latin, Mandarin, mathematics, music, physical education, physics, science, social sciences, social studies, Spanish, sports science, theater, world history, world religions, writing.

Graduation Requirements Arts and fine arts (art, music, dance, drama), business skills (includes word processing), English, foreign language, mathematics, physical education (includes health), science, social sciences, social studies (includes history).

Special Academic Programs International Baccalaureate program; honors section; independent study; study abroad; academic accommodation for the musically talented and the artistically talented; ESL (20 students enrolled).

College Admission Counseling 126 students graduated in 2013; 116 went to college, including Brock University; Queen's University at Kingston; The University of Western Ontario; University of Guelph; University of Toronto; University of Waterloo. Other: 4 entered a postgraduate year, 6 had other specific plans.

Student Life Upper grades have uniform requirement, student council, honor system. Discipline rests primarily with faculty. Attendance at religious services is required.

Tuition and Aid Day student tuition: CAN$28,458; 5-day tuition and room/board: CAN$40,035; 7-day tuition and room/board: CAN$50,388. Tuition installment plan (monthly payment plans, individually arranged payment plans). Bursaries, merit scholarship grants, need-based scholarship grants, need-based loans available. In 2013–14, 38% of upper-school students received aid; total upper-school merit-scholarship money awarded: CAN$300,000. Total amount of financial aid awarded in 2013–14: CAN$3,000,000.

Admissions Traditional secondary-level entrance grade is 9. For fall 2013, 452 students applied for upper-level admission, 334 were accepted, 210 enrolled. Deadline for receipt of application materials: none. Application fee required: CAN$150. Interview required.

Athletics Interscholastic: aerobics/dance (girls), artistic gym (g), baseball (b,g), basketball (b,g), crew (b,g), cross-country running (b,g), dance (g), dance squad (g), dance team (g), field hockey (g), fitness walking (g), gymnastics (g), hockey (b,g), ice hockey (b,g), rowing (b,g), rugby (b,g), running (b,g), soccer (b,g), softball (b,g), squash (b,g), swimming and diving (b,g), tennis (b,g), track and field (b,g), volleyball (g); intramural: aerobics (g), aerobics/dance (g), ball hockey (b), ballet (g), Cosom hockey (g), hockey (b,g), ice hockey (b,g), running (b,g); coed interscholastic: golf, tennis; coed intramural: alpine skiing, aquatics, backpacking, badminton, baseball, basketball, bicycling, bowling, canoeing/kayaking, climbing, cooperative games, curling, drill team, equestrian sports, fencing, fitness, Frisbee, golf, hiking/backpacking, horseback riding, ice skating, jogging, life saving, martial arts, modern dance, outdoor activities, outdoor education, outdoor recreation, outdoor skills, physical fitness, physical training, power lifting, racquetball, rock climbing, ropes courses, sailing, scuba diving, self defense, skiing (cross-country), skiing (downhill), snowboarding, snowshoeing, soccer, softball, squash, strength & conditioning, swimming and diving, table tennis, tennis, track and field, triathlon, ultimate Frisbee, volleyball, walking, wall climbing, weight lifting, weight training, wilderness survival, yoga. 8 coaches, 3 athletic trainers.

Computers Computers are regularly used in all academic classes. Computer network features include on-campus library services, online commercial services, Internet access, wireless campus network, Internet filtering or blocking technology. Student e-mail accounts and computer access in designated common areas are available to students. Students grades are available online. The school has a published electronic and media policy.

Contact Mrs. Stephanie Park, Admissions Administrative Assistant. 905-684-1889 Ext. 2207. Fax: 905-684-8875. E-mail: admissions@ridleycollege.com. Website: www.ridleycollege.com

RIVERDALE COUNTRY SCHOOL

5250 Fieldston Road
Bronx, New York 10471-2999

Head of School: Dominic A.A. Randolph

General Information Coeducational day college-preparatory school. Grades PK–12. Founded: 1907. Setting: suburban. Nearest major city is New York. 27-acre campus. 9 buildings on campus. Approved or accredited by New York Department of Education. Member of National Association of Independent Schools and Secondary School Admission Test Board. Endowment: $58.2 million. Total enrollment: 1,125. Upper school average class size: 16. Upper school faculty-student ratio: 1:8. Upper School students typically attend 5 days per week.

Faculty School total: 185.

Subjects Offered Algebra, American literature, anatomy, art, art history, biology, calculus, ceramics, chemistry, community service, computer math, computer programming, computer science, creative writing, drama, driver education, earth science, ecology, economics, English, English literature, environmental science, European history, expository writing, fine arts, French, geology, geometry, government/civics, grammar, health, history, history of science, introduction to liberal studies, Japanese, journalism, Latin, Mandarin, marine biology, mathematics, music, oceanography, philosophy, photography, physical education, physics, psychology, science, social studies, Spanish, speech, statistics, theater, theory of knowledge, trigonometry, world history, writing.

Graduation Requirements American studies, arts and fine arts (art, music, dance, drama), computer science, English, foreign language, mathematics, physical education (includes health), science, social studies (includes history), integrated liberal studies. Community service is required.

Special Academic Programs Honors section; independent study; term-away projects; study abroad; academic accommodation for the gifted, the musically talented, and the artistically talented.

College Admission Counseling 122 students graduated in 2013; all went to college, including Cornell University; Dartmouth College; Duke University; Harvard University; Stanford University; Yale University.

Student Life Upper grades have student council, honor system. Discipline rests equally with students and faculty.

Summer Programs Enrichment programs offered; session focuses on science research; held on campus; accepts boys and girls; not open to students from other schools.

Tuition and Aid Day student tuition: $43,600. Tuition installment plan (monthly payment plans). Need-based scholarship grants available. In 2013–14, 20% of upper-school students received aid.

Admissions Traditional secondary-level entrance grade is 9. ISEE or SSAT required. Deadline for receipt of application materials: November 15. Application fee required: $60. On-campus interview required.

Athletics Interscholastic: baseball (boys), basketball (b,g), crew (b,g), field hockey (g), football (b), gymnastics (g), lacrosse (b,g), soccer (b,g), softball (g), tennis (b,g), volleyball (g), wrestling (b); intramural: baseball (b), basketball (b,g), field hockey (g), football (b), gymnastics (g), lacrosse (b,g), soccer (b,g), softball (g), tennis (b,g), volleyball (g), wrestling (b); coed interscholastic: cross-country running, fencing, golf, squash, swimming and diving, track and field, ultimate Frisbee; coed intramural: cross-country running, dance, fencing, fitness, physical fitness, squash, swimming and diving, tennis, track and field, ultimate Frisbee, yoga. 7 PE instructors, 31 coaches, 1 athletic trainer.

Computers Computers are regularly used in art, English, foreign language, history, mathematics, music, science classes. Computer network features include on-campus library services, online commercial services, Internet access, wireless campus network, Internet filtering or blocking technology, off-campus email, off-campus library services. Student e-mail accounts and computer access in designated common areas are available to students. The school has a published electronic and media policy.

Contact Jenna Rogers King, Director of Middle and Upper School Admission. 718-519-2715. Fax: 718-519-2793. E-mail: jrking@riverdale.edu. Website: www.riverdale.edu

RIVER OAKS BAPTIST SCHOOL

2300 Willowick
Houston, Texas 77027

Head of School: Mrs. Leanne Reynolds

General Information Coeducational day college-preparatory and Character education school, affiliated with Christian faith. Grades PK–8. Founded: 1955. Setting: urban. Approved or accredited by Accreditation Commission of the Texas Association of Baptist Schools, Independent Schools Association of the Southwest, and Texas Department of Education. Member of National Association of Independent Schools. Endowment: $30 million. Total enrollment: 732. There are 187 required school days per year for Upper School students.

Upper School Student Profile Grade 6: 80 students (40 boys, 40 girls); Grade 7: 80 students (40 boys, 40 girls); Grade 8: 80 students (40 boys, 40 girls). 95% of students are Christian.

Faculty School total: 91.

Student Life Upper grades have uniform requirement, honor system. Discipline rests primarily with faculty. Attendance at religious services is required.

Tuition and Aid Tuition installment plan (Insured Tuition Payment Plan, monthly payment plans). Need-based scholarship grants available.

Admissions Individual IQ, ISEE and OLSAT, Stanford Achievement Test required. Deadline for receipt of application materials: none. Application fee required: $100. On-campus interview required.

Computers Computer network features include on-campus library services, wireless campus network, Internet filtering or blocking technology. Campus intranet and student e-mail accounts are available to students. Students grades are available online. The school has a published electronic and media policy.

Contact Mrs. Kristin Poe, Director of Admission. 713-623-6938. Fax: 713-623-0650. E-mail: kpoe@robs.org. Website: www.robs.org

RIVERSIDE MILITARY ACADEMY

2001 Riverside Drive
Gainesville, Georgia 30501

Head of School: Dr. James H. Benson, Col., USMC-Retd.

General Information Boys' boarding and day college-preparatory, arts, technology, JROTC (grades 9-12), and military school, affiliated with Christian faith. Grades 7–12. Founded: 1907. Setting: suburban. Nearest major city is Atlanta. Students are housed in single-sex dormitories. 206-acre campus. 9 buildings on campus. Approved or accredited by Southern Association of Colleges and Schools, Southern Association of Independent Schools, and Georgia Department of Education. Member of National Association of Independent Schools. Endowment: $52 million. Total enrollment: 423. Upper school average class size: 14. Upper school faculty-student ratio: 1:14. There are 180 required school days per year for Upper School students. Upper School students typically attend 5 days per week. The average school day consists of 5 hours and 45 minutes.

Upper School Student Profile Grade 9: 74 students (74 boys); Grade 10: 69 students (69 boys); Grade 11: 97 students (97 boys); Grade 12: 98 students (98 boys). 95% of students are boarding students. 56% are state residents. 30 states are represented in upper school student body. 29% are international students. International students from China, Colombia, Dominican Republic, Kazakhstan, Mexico, and Republic of Korea; 16 other countries represented in student body. 80% of students are Christian faith.

Faculty School total: 45. In upper school: 35 men, 10 women; 30 have advanced degrees; 20 reside on campus.

Subjects Offered Algebra, American literature, art, art appreciation, band, biology, biology-AP, calculus, calculus-AP, ceramics, chemistry, chemistry-AP, chorus, computer applications, computer education, computer programming, computer science, computer skills, computer studies, computer technologies, desktop publishing, drama, drawing, earth science, economics, English, English composition, English literature, English/composition-AP, ESL, ethics, European history, fine arts, geography, geometry, German, government/civics, grammar, health, history-AP, honors English, honors geometry, honors U.S. history, honors world history, JROTC, keyboarding, Latin, leadership, mathematics, military science, modern world history, music, music technology, music theory, painting, physical education, physics, physics-AP, pre-algebra, pre-calculus, science, social studies, Spanish, statistics, swimming, theater, U.S. government, U.S. government and politics-AP, U.S. history, U.S. history-AP, U.S. literature, visual arts, weight training, world geography, world history, world history-AP, world literature, yearbook.

Graduation Requirements Arts and fine arts (art, music, dance, drama), computer science, electives, English, foreign language, JROTC, lab science, mathematics, military science, physical education (includes health), science, social studies (includes history).

Special Academic Programs 8 Advanced Placement exams for which test preparation is offered; honors section; independent study; special instructional classes for Attention Deficit Hyperactivity Disorder, Attention Deficit Disorder; ESL (24 students enrolled).

College Admission Counseling 83 students graduated in 2012; 64 went to college, including The Citadel, The Military College of South Carolina; The University of Alabama; University of California, Los Angeles; University of Florida; University of Georgia. Other: 2 went to work, 3 entered military service. Median SAT critical reading: 484, median SAT math: 511, median SAT writing: 462, median combined SAT: 1458, median composite ACT: 20.

Student Life Upper grades have uniform requirement, student council, honor system. Discipline rests equally with students and faculty. Attendance at religious services is required.

Tuition and Aid Day student tuition: $17,150; 7-day tuition and room/board: $28,600. Tuition installment plan (Key Tuition Payment Plan, FACTS Tuition Payment Plan, monthly payment plans). Need-based scholarship grants available. In 2012–13, 10% of upper-school students received aid.

Admissions Traditional secondary-level entrance grade is 10. Any standardized test required. Deadline for receipt of application materials: none. Application fee required: $100. Interview required.

Athletics Interscholastic: aquatics, baseball, basketball, crew, cross-country running, drill team, football, golf, JROTC drill, lacrosse, marksmanship, outdoor adventure, outdoor skills, paint ball, riflery, ropes courses, soccer, strength & conditioning, swimming and diving, tennis, track and field, weight lifting, weight training, wrestling; intramural: aquatics, backpacking, baseball, basketball, billiards, canoeing/kayaking, cheering, climbing, combined training, crew, cross-country running, fencing, fishing, fitness, flag football, football, hiking/backpacking, indoor soccer, indoor track, indoor track & field, jogging, JROTC drill, kayaking, marksmanship, mountaineering, outdoor activities, paddle tennis, physical fitness, physical training, rafting, rappelling, riflery, rock climbing, ropes courses, running, skateboarding, soccer, softball, swimming and diving, table tennis, tennis, volleyball, wall climbing, water polo, water volleyball, weight lifting, wilderness. 5 PE instructors, 20 coaches, 1 athletic trainer.

Computers Computers are regularly used in college planning, desktop publishing, English, ESL, foreign language, library, mathematics, multimedia, music, SAT preparation, science, Spanish, technology, theater, yearbook classes. Computer network features include on-campus library services, Internet access, wireless campus network, Internet filtering or blocking technology. Campus intranet, student e-mail accounts, and computer access in designated common areas are available to students. Students grades are available online. The school has a published electronic and media policy.

Contact Admissions Office. 800-462-2338. Fax: 678-291-3364. E-mail: apply@riversidemilitary.com. Website: www.riversidemilitary.com

THE RIVERS SCHOOL
333 Winter Street
Weston, Massachusetts 02493-1040
Head of School: Thomas P. Olverson

General Information Coeducational day college-preparatory and arts school. Grades 6–12. Founded: 1915. Setting: suburban. Nearest major city is Boston. 53-acre campus. 8 buildings on campus. Approved or accredited by Association of Independent Schools in New England and New England Association of Schools and Colleges. Member of National Association of Independent Schools and Secondary School Admission Test Board. Endowment: $18.5 million. Total enrollment: 479. Upper school average class size: 12. Upper school faculty-student ratio: 1:6. Upper School students typically attend 5 days per week. The average school day consists of 7 hours and 15 minutes.

Upper School Student Profile Grade 9: 93 students (43 boys, 50 girls); Grade 10: 90 students (50 boys, 40 girls); Grade 11: 93 students (56 boys, 37 girls); Grade 12: 83 students (42 boys, 41 girls).

Faculty School total: 86. In upper school: 43 men, 43 women; 56 have advanced degrees.

Subjects Offered Advanced Placement courses, algebra, American history, American literature, art, art history, art history-AP, astronomy, biochemistry, biology, biology-AP, calculus, calculus-AP, ceramics, chamber groups, chemistry, chemistry-AP, chorus, civil rights, Civil War, computer graphics, computer science, computer science-AP, creative writing, drama, earth science, economics-AP, English, English language and composition-AP, English literature, English literature and composition-AP, environmental science-AP, European history, expository writing, film studies, filmmaking, fine arts, French, French-AP, geography, geometry, history, Holocaust, jazz band, journalism, kinesiology, Latin, Latin-AP, Mandarin, mathematics, modern European history-AP, music, photography, physics, physics-AP, playwriting, science, Spanish, Spanish-AP, statistics-AP, the Presidency, theater, theater arts, trigonometry, U.S. history-AP, world history, world literature.

Graduation Requirements Algebra, athletics, English, foreign language, geometry, history, mathematics, modern European history, science, U.S. history, visual and performing arts, participation in athletics. Community service is required.

Special Academic Programs Advanced Placement exam preparation; honors section; independent study; study at local college for college credit.

College Admission Counseling 84 students graduated in 2013; all went to college, including Babson College; Brown University; Bucknell University; Colby College; Colgate University; Lehigh University. Median SAT critical reading: 650, median SAT math: 690, median SAT writing: 680, median combined SAT: 2000. 82% scored over 600 on SAT critical reading, 75% scored over 600 on SAT math, 76% scored over 600 on SAT writing, 82% scored over 1800 on combined SAT.

Student Life Upper grades have specified standards of dress, student council, honor system. Discipline rests primarily with faculty.

Tuition and Aid Day student tuition: $40,200. Tuition installment plan (Academic Management Services Plan, Key Tuition Payment Plan, monthly payment plans). Need-based scholarship grants available. In 2013–14, 30% of upper-school students received aid. Total amount of financial aid awarded in 2013–14: $3,065,050.

Admissions Traditional secondary-level entrance grade is 9. ISEE or SSAT required. Deadline for receipt of application materials: February 1. Application fee required: $40. On-campus interview required.

Athletics Interscholastic: alpine skiing (boys, girls), baseball (b), basketball (b,g), cross-country running (b,g), field hockey (g), football (b), ice hockey (b,g), lacrosse (b,g), skiing (downhill) (b,g), soccer (b,g), softball (g), strength & conditioning (b,g), tennis (b,g); intramural: basketball (b,g), tennis (g); coed interscholastic: fitness, physical training, track and field, weight lifting, weight training; coed intramural: strength & conditioning. 4 coaches, 2 athletic trainers.

Computers Computers are regularly used in art, English, foreign language, history, humanities, language development, mathematics, newspaper, publications, science, writing, yearbook classes. Computer network features include on-campus library services, online commercial services, Internet access, wireless campus network, Internet filtering or blocking technology, language lab. Campus intranet, student e-mail accounts, and computer access in designated common areas are available to students. Students grades are available online. The school has a published electronic and media policy.

Contact Gillian Lloyd, Director of Admissions. 781-235-9300. Fax: 781-239-3614. E-mail: g.lloyd@rivers.org. Website: www.rivers.org

RIVERSTONE INTERNATIONAL SCHOOL
5521 Warm Springs Avenue
Boise, Idaho 83716
Head of School: Mr. Bob Carignan

General Information Coeducational day college-preparatory school. Grades PS–12. Founded: 1997. Setting: suburban. 14-acre campus. 3 buildings on campus. Approved or accredited by Council of International Schools, International Baccalaureate Organization, Northwest Association of Independent Schools, Northwest Association of Schools and Colleges, and Idaho Department of Education. Member of National Association of Independent Schools. Total enrollment: 314. Upper school average class size: 12. Upper school faculty-student ratio: 1:6. There are 169 required school days per year for Upper School students. Upper School students typically attend 5 days per week. The average school day consists of 6 hours and 45 minutes.

Upper School Student Profile Grade 9: 20 students (12 boys, 8 girls); Grade 10: 28 students (15 boys, 13 girls); Grade 11: 24 students (12 boys, 12 girls); Grade 12: 22 students (11 boys, 11 girls).

Faculty School total: 59. In upper school: 8 men, 14 women; 12 have advanced degrees.

Subjects Offered International Baccalaureate courses.

Graduation Requirements Art, English, foreign language, history, mathematics, science.

Special Academic Programs International Baccalaureate program; independent study; study abroad; ESL (15 students enrolled).

College Admission Counseling 23 students graduated in 2013; all went to college, including Bowdoin College; Columbia University; Harvard University; Middlebury College; Montana State University; The College of Idaho. Mean SAT critical reading: 621, mean SAT math: 616, mean SAT writing: 627, mean combined SAT: 1864.

Student Life Upper grades have specified standards of dress, student council, honor system. Discipline rests equally with students and faculty.

Summer Programs Enrichment, ESL, sports, art/fine arts, rigorous outdoor training programs offered; session focuses on camps, ESL, and outdoor education; held both on and off campus; held at Boise River, Boise Foothills, and Sawtooth and White Cloud Mountains; accepts boys and girls; open to students from other schools. 100 students usually enrolled. 2014 schedule: June 11 to August 16. Application deadline: June 1.

Tuition and Aid Day student tuition: $14,550. Tuition installment plan (monthly payment plans). Need-based scholarship grants available. In 2013–14, 20% of upper-school students received aid.

Admissions Traditional secondary-level entrance grade is 9. For fall 2013, 43 students applied for upper-level admission, 30 were accepted, 18 enrolled. Deadline for receipt of application materials: none. Application fee required: $75. Interview required.

Athletics Interscholastic: basketball (boys, girls), volleyball (g); coed interscholastic: alpine skiing, nordic skiing, skiing (cross-country), skiing (downhill), snowboarding, soccer; coed intramural: backpacking, canoeing/kayaking, climbing, flag football, hiking/backpacking, ice skating, kayaking, lacrosse, nordic skiing, outdoor activities, outdoor adventure, outdoor education, outdoor recreation, outdoor skills, outdoors, physical fitness, rafting, rock climbing, ropes courses, skiing (cross-country), skiing (downhill), snowboarding, snowshoeing, tennis, wilderness. 1 PE instructor, 3 coaches.

Computers Computers are regularly used in art, college planning, English, ESL, foreign language, French, history, lab/keyboard, music, research skills, Spanish, writing, yearbook classes. Computer network features include online commercial services, Internet access, wireless campus network. Student e-mail accounts are available to students. Students grades are available online. The school has a published electronic and media policy.

Contact Ms. Rachel Pusch, Director of Admissions and Institutional Advancement. 208-424-5000 Ext. 2104. Fax: 208-424-0033. E-mail: rpusch@riverstoneschool.org. Website: www.riverstoneschool.org

ROCKHURST HIGH SCHOOL

9301 State Line Road
Kansas City, Missouri 64114-3299

Head of School: Rev. Terrence Baum

General Information Boys' day college-preparatory, arts, business, religious studies, and technology school, affiliated with Roman Catholic Church. Grades 9–12. Founded: 1910. Setting: suburban. 36-acre campus. 3 buildings on campus. Approved or accredited by Jesuit Secondary Education Association, North Central Association of Colleges and Schools, and Missouri Department of Education. Member of National Association of Independent Schools. Endowment: $12 million. Upper school average class size: 23. Upper school faculty-student ratio: 1:12. There are 167 required school days per year for Upper School students. Upper School students typically attend 5 days per week. The average school day consists of 7 hours.

Upper School Student Profile Grade 9: 267 students (267 boys); Grade 10: 284 students (284 boys); Grade 11: 286 students (286 boys); Grade 12: 263 students (263 boys). 80% of students are Roman Catholic.

Faculty School total: 98. In upper school: 82 men, 15 women; 61 have advanced degrees.

Subjects Offered Algebra, American history, American literature, anatomy, art, Bible studies, biology, business, business skills, calculus, ceramics, chemistry, computer math, computer programming, computer science, creative writing, drama, economics, English, English literature, European history, fine arts, forensics, French, geography, geometry, government/civics, Greek, history, journalism, Latin, mathematics, music, photography, physical education, physics, physiology, religion, science, social studies, Spanish, speech, theater, theology, trigonometry, vocal music, word processing.

Graduation Requirements Arts and fine arts (art, music, dance, drama), computer science, English, foreign language, mathematics, physical education (includes

health), religion (includes Bible studies and theology), science, social studies (includes history), technological applications, attendance at retreats, community service hours.

Special Academic Programs Advanced Placement exam preparation; honors section; study at local college for college credit; special instructional classes for students with Attention Deficit Disorder.

College Admission Counseling 242 students graduated in 2013; all went to college, including Kansas State University; Rockhurst University; The University of Kansas; University of Arkansas; University of Central Missouri; University of Missouri-Columbia. Mean SAT critical reading: 629, mean SAT math: 650, mean SAT writing: 636, mean combined SAT: 1915, mean composite ACT: 27.

Student Life Upper grades have specified standards of dress, student council. Discipline rests primarily with faculty. Attendance at religious services is required.

Summer Programs Remediation, enrichment, sports, art/fine arts, computer instruction programs offered; session focuses on transition to high school and enrichment; held on campus; accepts boys and girls; open to students from other schools. 350 students usually enrolled. 2014 schedule: June 2 to July 3. Application deadline: none.

Tuition and Aid Day student tuition: $11,550. Tuition installment plan (monthly payment plans, individually arranged payment plans). Merit scholarship grants, need-based scholarship grants, paying campus jobs available. In 2013–14, 35% of upper-school students received aid; total upper-school merit-scholarship money awarded: $20,250. Total amount of financial aid awarded in 2013–14: $1,800,000.

Admissions Traditional secondary-level entrance grade is 9. For fall 2013, 360 students applied for upper-level admission, 340 were accepted, 267 enrolled. High School Placement Test and STS required. Deadline for receipt of application materials: December 15. Application fee required: $15.

Athletics Interscholastic: baseball, basketball, cheering, cross-country running, diving, football, golf, ice hockey, lacrosse, soccer, swimming and diving, tennis, track and field, ultimate Frisbee, wrestling; intramural: basketball, fencing, flag football, football, mountain biking, rugby, soccer, softball, volleyball, weight lifting, weight training. 2 PE instructors, 17 coaches, 1 athletic trainer.

Computers Computers are regularly used in mathematics, science, technology classes. Computer network features include on-campus library services, online commercial services, Internet access. Campus intranet and student e-mail accounts are available to students. Students grades are available online. The school has a published electronic and media policy.

Contact Jack Reichmeier, Director of Admission and Financial Aid. 816-363-2036 Ext. 558. Fax: 816-363-3764. E-mail: jreichme@rockhursths.edu. Website: www.rockhursths.edu

ROCKWAY MENNONITE COLLEGIATE

110 Doon Road
Kitchener, Ontario N2G 3C8, Canada

Head of School: Mr. Dennis Wikerd

General Information Coeducational boarding and day college-preparatory, arts, religious studies, and technology school, affiliated with Mennonite Church USA. Grades 7–12. Founded: 1945. Setting: suburban. Nearest major city is Toronto, Canada. Students are housed in host family homes. 14-acre campus. 7 buildings on campus. Approved or accredited by Mennonite Schools Council and Ontario Department of Education. Language of instruction: English. Endowment: CAN$450,000. Total enrollment: 285. Upper school average class size: 19. Upper school faculty-student ratio: 1:10. There are 194 required school days per year for Upper School students. Upper School students typically attend 5 days per week. The average school day consists of 5 hours and 55 minutes.

Upper School Student Profile 1% of students are boarding students. 85% are province residents. 1 province is represented in upper school student body. 15% are international students. International students from China, Democratic People's Republic of Korea, Germany, Hong Kong, Japan, and Taiwan; 2 other countries represented in student body. 38% of students are Mennonite Church USA.

Faculty School total: 45. In upper school: 20 men, 20 women; 8 have advanced degrees.

Subjects Offered Algebra, auto mechanics, Bible, biology, calculus, Canadian history, career education, chemistry, choral music, civics, computer science, computer studies, construction, dramatic arts, English, entrepreneurship, ESL, family studies, finite math, food and nutrition, French, functions, geography, geometry, German, guidance, health, healthful living, history, information technology, instrumental music, integrated technology fundamentals, Mandarin, mathematics, music, orchestra, parenting, personal finance, philosophy, physical education, physics, religious studies, science, strings, technology/design, transportation technology, visual arts, vocal music, wind instruments, world history, world religions.

Graduation Requirements Ontario Ministry of Education requirements, 2 credits in a language other than English, religious studies courses through grade 10.

Special Academic Programs Independent study; academic accommodation for the gifted; ESL (34 students enrolled).

College Admission Counseling 68 students graduated in 2012; 58 went to college, including Carleton University; The University of Western Ontario; University of Guelph; University of Toronto; University of Waterloo; Wilfrid Laurier University. Other: 8 went to work, 2 had other specific plans.

Student Life Upper grades have specified standards of dress, student council. Discipline rests primarily with faculty. Attendance at religious services is required.

Tuition and Aid Day student tuition: CAN$12,360; 7-day tuition and room/board: CAN$20,860. Tuition installment plan (monthly payment plans, individually arranged payment plans). Tuition reduction for siblings, bursaries, need-based scholarship grants, paying campus jobs available. In 2012–13, 25% of upper-school students received aid. Total amount of financial aid awarded in 2012–13: CAN$170,000.

Admissions Traditional secondary-level entrance grade is 9. For fall 2012, 60 students applied for upper-level admission, 56 were accepted, 55 enrolled. Deadline for receipt of application materials: none. Application fee required: CAN$100.

Athletics Interscholastic: badminton (boys, girls), baseball (b,g), basketball (b,g), cross-country running (b,g), soccer (b), softball (b,g), track and field (b,g), volleyball (b,g), wrestling (b,g); intramural: ball hockey (b,g), baseball (b,g), basketball (b,g), cooperative games (b,g), dance (b,g), field hockey (b,g), flag football (b,g), flagball (b,g), floor hockey (b,g), football (b,g), indoor soccer (b,g), nordic skiing (b,g), outdoor education (b,g), physical training (b,g), power lifting (b,g), rock climbing (b,g), rugby (b,g), skiing (downhill) (b,g), soccer (b,g), strength & conditioning (b,g), volleyball (b,g); coed interscholastic: soccer; coed intramural: baseball, canoeing/kayaking, cooperative games, outdoor education, roller skating, skiing (downhill), street hockey, table tennis, track and field. 4 PE instructors.

Computers Computers are regularly used in Bible studies, business, career technology, college planning, construction, drafting, English, geography, library, mathematics, religious studies, science, typing, Web site design classes. Computer resources include on-campus library services, Internet access, Internet filtering or blocking technology.

Contact Mr. Tom Bileski, Director of Community Relations. 519-342-0007 Ext. 3029. Fax: 519-743-5935. E-mail: admin@rockway.ca. Website: www.rockway.ca

ROLAND PARK COUNTRY SCHOOL

5204 Roland Avenue
Baltimore, Maryland 21210

Head of School: Mrs. Jean Waller Brune

General Information Coeducational day (boys only in lower grades) and distance learning college-preparatory and arts school. Boys grade PS, girls grades PS–12. Distance learning grades 9–12. Founded: 1901. Setting: suburban. 21-acre campus. 1 building on campus. Approved or accredited by Association of Independent Maryland Schools. Member of National Association of Independent Schools and Secondary School Admission Test Board. Endowment: $54.1 million. Total enrollment: 676. Upper school average class size: 14. Upper school faculty-student ratio: 1:7. There are 176 required school days per year for Upper School students. Upper School students typically attend 5 days per week. The average school day consists of 7 hours and 45 minutes.

Upper School Student Profile Grade 9: 83 students (83 girls); Grade 10: 84 students (84 girls); Grade 11: 80 students (80 girls); Grade 12: 69 students (69 girls).

Faculty School total: 97. In upper school: 6 men, 41 women; 36 have advanced degrees.

Subjects Offered 3-dimensional art, advanced biology, advanced chemistry, advanced math, Advanced Placement courses, advanced studio art-AP, algebra, American history-AP, American literature, American literature-AP, anatomy, ancient world history, Arabic, archaeology, art, art history, art history-AP, astronomy, biology, biology-AP, calculus, calculus-AP, ceramics, chemistry, chemistry-AP, Chesapeake Bay studies, Chinese, community service, computer programming, computer science, creative writing, dance, drama, ecology, economics, engineering, English, English language-AP, English literature, English literature-AP, English-AP, environmental science, environmental studies, European civilization, European history, European history-AP, French, French language-AP, French literature-AP, geometry, German, government/civics, Greek, health, integrated mathematics, Latin, music, philosophy, photography, physical education, physics, physiology, religion, Russian, science, social studies, Spanish, speech, statistics, theater, trigonometry, world history.

Graduation Requirements Adolescent issues, arts and fine arts (art, music, dance, drama), biology, chemistry, English, foreign language, history, mathematics, physical education (includes health), physics, public speaking, science. Community service is required.

Special Academic Programs Advanced Placement exam preparation; honors section; independent study; term-away projects; study abroad.

College Admission Counseling 79 students graduated in 2013; all went to college, including New York University; Skidmore College; The George Washington University; University of Pennsylvania; University of Virginia; Washington and Lee University. Mean SAT critical reading: 581, mean SAT math: 587, mean SAT writing: 604, mean combined SAT: 1772, mean composite ACT: 25.

Student Life Upper grades have uniform requirement, student council, honor system. Discipline rests equally with students and faculty.

Summer Programs Remediation, enrichment, advancement, sports, art/fine arts programs offered; session focuses on summer camp, arts, some academics; held both on and off campus; held at off-site pool and venues for outdoor education programs and various sites around Baltimore for art projects; accepts boys and girls; open to students from other schools. 600 students usually enrolled. 2014 schedule: June 16 to August 22. Application deadline: none.

Tuition and Aid Day student tuition: $24,995. Tuition installment plan (FACTS Tuition Payment Plan, individually arranged payment plans). Need-based scholarship grants, paying campus jobs available. In 2013–14, 31% of upper-school students received aid. Total amount of financial aid awarded in 2013–14: $1,346,750.

Admissions Traditional secondary-level entrance grade is 9. For fall 2013, 119 students applied for upper-level admission, 78 were accepted, 32 enrolled. ERB CTP IV or ISEE required. Deadline for receipt of application materials: December 20. Application fee required: $60. Interview required.

Athletics Interscholastic: badminton, basketball, crew, cross-country running, field hockey, golf, independent competitive sports, indoor soccer, indoor track, lacrosse, soccer, softball, squash, swimming and diving, tennis, volleyball, winter (indoor) track, winter soccer; intramural: dance, fitness, modern dance, outdoor education, physical fitness, rock climbing, strength & conditioning. 7 PE instructors, 1 athletic trainer.

Computers Computers are regularly used in all classes. Computer network features include on-campus library services, online commercial services, Internet access, wireless campus network, Internet filtering or blocking technology, online database. Campus intranet, student e-mail accounts, and computer access in designated common areas are available to students. Students grades are available online. The school has a published electronic and media policy.

Contact Peggy Wolf, Director of Admissions. 410-323-5500. Fax: 410-323-2164. E-mail: admissions@rpcs.org. Website: www.rpcs.org

ROLLING HILLS PREPARATORY SCHOOL

One Rolling Hills Prep Way
San Pedro, California 90732

Head of School: Peter McCormack

General Information Coeducational day college-preparatory, arts, and technology school. Grades 6–12. Founded: 1981. Setting: suburban. Nearest major city is Los Angeles. 21-acre campus. 20 buildings on campus. Approved or accredited by Western Association of Schools and Colleges and California Department of Education. Member of National Association of Independent Schools. Endowment: $100,000. Total enrollment: 225. Upper school average class size: 16. Upper school faculty-student ratio: 1:9. There are 180 required school days per year for Upper School students. Upper School students typically attend 5 days per week. The average school day consists of 6 hours.

Upper School Student Profile Grade 9: 30 students (15 boys, 15 girls); Grade 10: 32 students (16 boys, 16 girls); Grade 11: 31 students (16 boys, 15 girls); Grade 12: 37 students (21 boys, 16 girls).

Faculty School total: 36. In upper school: 7 men, 21 women; 13 have advanced degrees.

Subjects Offered Algebra, American history, American literature, American sign language, anatomy, art, biology, calculus, ceramics, chemistry, Chinese, computer science, creative writing, drama, economics, English, English literature, European history, fine arts, French, geography, geometry, government/civics, history, mathematics, music, photography, physical education, physics, pre-calculus, robotics, science, social studies, Spanish, speech, statistics, theater, trigonometry, world history.

Graduation Requirements Arts and fine arts (art, music, dance, drama), English, foreign language, mathematics, outdoor education, physical education (includes health), science, social studies (includes history), two-week senior internship, senior speech.

Special Academic Programs 10 Advanced Placement exams for which test preparation is offered; honors section; independent study; academic accommodation for the gifted; programs in general development for dyslexic students; ESL (16 students enrolled).

College Admission Counseling 45 students graduated in 2013; 43 went to college, including Berklee College of Music; Carnegie Mellon University; Lewis & Clark College; University of California, Berkeley; University of California, Los Angeles; University of Southern California. Other: 2 had other specific plans. Mean SAT critical reading: 620, mean SAT math: 600, mean SAT writing: 610. 45% scored over 600 on SAT critical reading, 40% scored over 600 on SAT math, 45% scored over 600 on SAT writing.

Student Life Upper grades have specified standards of dress, student council, honor system. Discipline rests primarily with faculty.

Summer Programs Enrichment, art/fine arts programs offered; session focuses on algebra and photography; held on campus; accepts boys and girls; open to students from other schools. 30 students usually enrolled. 2014 schedule: June 26 to August 28. Application deadline: June 1.

Tuition and Aid Day student tuition: $25,650. Tuition installment plan (Insured Tuition Payment Plan, Key Tuition Payment Plan, monthly payment plans). Merit scholarship grants, need-based scholarship grants available. In 2013–14, 35% of upper-school students received aid. Total amount of financial aid awarded in 2013–14: $660,000.

Admissions Traditional secondary-level entrance grade is 9. For fall 2013, 22 students applied for upper-level admission, 15 were accepted, 10 enrolled. ISEE or TOEFL required. Deadline for receipt of application materials: none. Application fee required: $125. Interview required.

Athletics Interscholastic: baseball (boys), basketball (b,g), cheering (g), football (b), soccer (b,g), softball (g), track and field (g), volleyball (b,g); intramural: cheering (g), dance (g); coed interscholastic: cross-country running, golf, roller hockey, running, track and field; coed intramural: backpacking, climbing, fitness, hiking/backpacking, outdoor education, physical fitness, rock climbing, ropes courses. 4 PE instructors, 10 coaches, 1 athletic trainer.

Computers Computers are regularly used in English, foreign language, history, mathematics, photography, science classes. Computer network features include on-campus library services, Internet access, wireless campus network. The school has a published electronic and media policy.

Contact Ryan Tillson, Director of Admission. 310-791-1101 Ext. 148. Fax: 310-373-4931. E-mail: rtillson@rollinghillsprep.org. Website: www.rollinghillsprep.org

ROSSEAU LAKE COLLEGE

1967 Bright Street
Rosseau, Ontario P0C 1J0, Canada

Head of School: Mr. Lance Postma

General Information Coeducational boarding and day college-preparatory, arts, business, and technology school. Grades 7–12. Founded: 1967. Setting: rural. Nearest major city is Toronto, Canada. Students are housed in single-sex dormitories. 53-acre campus. 13 buildings on campus. Approved or accredited by Canadian Association of Independent Schools, Canadian Educational Standards Institute, Ontario Ministry of Education, The Association of Boarding Schools, and Ontario Department of Education. Languages of instruction: English and French. Endowment: CAN$100,000. Total enrollment: 84. Upper school average class size: 15. Upper school faculty-student ratio: 1:6. There are 176 required school days per year for Upper School students. Upper School students typically attend 5 days per week. The average school day consists of 7 hours and 30 minutes.

Upper School Student Profile Grade 7: 4 students (2 boys, 2 girls); Grade 8: 6 students (6 boys); Grade 9: 17 students (12 boys, 5 girls); Grade 10: 22 students (17 boys, 5 girls); Grade 11: 18 students (10 boys, 8 girls); Grade 12: 17 students (10 boys, 7 girls). 62% of students are boarding students. 54% are province residents. 2 provinces are represented in upper school student body. 46% are international students. International students from Brazil, China, Germany, Japan, Mexico, and Spain; 4 other countries represented in student body.

Faculty School total: 19. In upper school: 8 men, 11 women; 3 have advanced degrees; 11 reside on campus.

Subjects Offered Accounting, algebra, art, art history, biology, business, calculus, Canadian law, career and personal planning, chemistry, civics, computer programming, computer science, data analysis, economics, English, entrepreneurship, ESL, European history, experiential education, fine arts, French, geography, geometry, health, history, information technology, marketing, mathematics, music, outdoor education, physical education, physics, political science, science, social sciences, trigonometry, visual arts, world governments, writing.

Graduation Requirements Arts and fine arts (art, music, dance, drama), business skills (includes word processing), career planning, civics, computer science, English, foreign language, mathematics, physical education (includes health), science, social studies (includes history).

Special Academic Programs Accelerated programs; independent study; term-away projects; study abroad; academic accommodation for the gifted; remedial reading and/or remedial writing; remedial math; ESL (18 students enrolled).

College Admission Counseling 15 students graduated in 2013; all went to college, including McMaster University; Queen's University at Kingston; The University of Western Ontario; University of Guelph; University of Toronto; York University.

Student Life Upper grades have uniform requirement, student council, honor system. Discipline rests equally with students and faculty.

Summer Programs Remediation, enrichment, advancement programs offered; session focuses on academics; held on campus; accepts boys and girls; open to students from other schools. 10 students usually enrolled. 2014 schedule: July 1 to July 30. Application deadline: June 15.

Tuition and Aid Day student tuition: CAN$17,700; 7-day tuition and room/board: CAN$40,500. Tuition installment plan (monthly payment plans, individually arranged payment plans). Merit scholarship grants, need-based scholarship grants available. In 2013–14, 10% of upper-school students received aid; total upper-school merit-scholarship money awarded: CAN$40,000. Total amount of financial aid awarded in 2013–14: CAN$160,000.

Admissions Traditional secondary-level entrance grade is 9. For fall 2013, 35 students applied for upper-level admission, 27 were accepted, 26 enrolled. Admissions testing and English Composition Test for ESL students required. Deadline for receipt of application materials: none. Application fee required: CAN$150. Interview required.

Athletics Interscholastic: baseball (boys), basketball (b,g), cross-country running (b,g), field hockey (g), hockey (b), ice hockey (b), mountain biking (b,g), nordic skiing (b,g), rugby (b), running (b,g), skiing (cross-country) (b,g), snowboarding (b,g), soccer (b,g), softball (b), swimming and diving (b,g), tennis (b,g), track and field (b,g), volleyball (b,g); intramural: alpine skiing (b,g), baseball (b), basketball (b,g), cross-country running (b,g), field hockey (g), hockey (b,g), ice hockey (b,g), rugby (b), running (b,g), skiing (cross-country) (b,g), snowboarding (b,g); coed interscholastic: bicycling, canoeing/kayaking, climbing, golf, kayaking, mountain biking, nordic skiing, running, skiing (cross-country), skiing (downhill), snowboarding, softball, track and

field; coed intramural: aerobics, aerobics/dance, aquatics, backpacking, ball hockey, baseball, basketball, bicycling, bowling, broomball, canoeing/kayaking, climbing, combined training, cooperative games, Cosom hockey, cross-country running, equestrian sports, fishing, fitness, fitness walking, flag football, floor hockey, fly fishing, freestyle skiing, Frisbee, golf, hiking/backpacking, horseback riding, ice skating, indoor hockey, indoor soccer, jogging, kayaking, life saving, mountain biking, mountaineering, nordic skiing, outdoor activities, paddle tennis, paddling, physical fitness, physical training, rappelling, rock climbing, ropes courses, sailboarding, sailing, scuba diving, skateboarding, skiing (cross-country), skiing (downhill), snowboarding, snowshoeing, soccer, softball, squash, street hockey, strength & conditioning, swimming and diving, table tennis, tennis, track and field, triathlon, ultimate Frisbee, volleyball, walking, wall climbing, water skiing, weight lifting, weight training, wilderness, wilderness survival, wildernessways, windsurfing, winter walking, yoga. 2 PE instructors, 2 coaches.

Computers Computers are regularly used in geography, graphic arts, information technology classes. Computer network features include on-campus library services, Internet access, wireless campus network, Internet filtering or blocking technology. Campus intranet, student e-mail accounts, and computer access in designated common areas are available to students. The school has a published electronic and media policy.

Contact Ms. Lynda Marshall, Director of Admissions. 705-732-4351 Ext. 12. Fax: 705-732-6319. E-mail: lynda.marshall@rlc.on.ca. Website: www.rosseaulakecollege.com

ROSS SCHOOL

18 Goodfriend Drive
East Hampton, New York 11937

Head of School: Ms. Patricia Lein

General Information Coeducational boarding and day college-preparatory, Globally-focused, integrated curriculum, and ESOL curriculum school. Boarding grades 7–12, day grades N–12. Founded: 1991. Setting: small town. Nearest major city is New York City. Students are housed in single-sex dormitories. 100-acre campus. 7 buildings on campus. Approved or accredited by Middle States Association of Colleges and Schools, The Association of Boarding Schools, and New York Department of Education. Member of National Association of Independent Schools and Secondary School Admission Test Board. Total enrollment: 521. Upper school average class size: 15. Upper school faculty-student ratio: 1:7. There are 175 required school days per year for Upper School students. Upper School students typically attend 5 days per week. The average school day consists of 8 hours.

Upper School Student Profile 66% of students are boarding students. 6 states are represented in upper school student body. 60% are international students. International students from Brazil, China, Germany, Republic of Korea, Russian Federation, and Taiwan; 19 other countries represented in student body.

Faculty School total: 94. In upper school: 21 men, 33 women; 41 have advanced degrees; 19 reside on campus.

Subjects Offered 20th century world history, 3-dimensional design, acting, advanced biology, advanced chemistry, advanced computer applications, advanced math, African drumming, algebra, American history, art history, athletics, audio visual/media, biology, calculus, chemistry, Chinese, chorus, college counseling, computer multimedia, concert band, contemporary issues, creative writing, current events, dance, digital imaging, drawing, electives, English, English literature, entrepreneurship, ESL, filmmaking, French, geometry, global issues, health, health and wellness, history, independent study, integrated arts, interdisciplinary studies, jazz band, literature by women, marine biology, mathematics, media arts, media production, media studies, model United Nations, music, musical productions, performing arts, philosophy, photography, physics, pre-algebra, pre-calculus, probability and statistics, psychology, religion, SAT preparation, science, science and technology, senior internship, senior project, Spanish, studio art, technological applications, theater arts, United Nations and international issues, visual arts, Web site design, wood lab, world history.

Graduation Requirements 60 hours of community service.

Special Academic Programs 9 Advanced Placement exams for which test preparation is offered; honors section; independent study; term-away projects; ESL (158 students enrolled).

College Admission Counseling 68 students graduated in 2013; all went to college, including Bard College; Boston University; Cornell University; New York University; Parsons The New School for Design; Stanford University. Median SAT critical reading: 520, median SAT math: 560, median SAT writing: 510.

Student Life Upper grades have uniform requirement, student council, honor system. Discipline rests primarily with faculty.

Summer Programs ESL, sports, art/fine arts programs offered; session focuses on ESOL, cultural history curriculum, test prep, and wellness activities; held on campus; accepts boys and girls; open to students from other schools. 60 students usually enrolled. 2014 schedule: June 23 to August 1. Application deadline: none.

Tuition and Aid Day student tuition: $36,200; 7-day tuition and room/board: $54,200. Tuition installment plan (monthly payment plans). Tuition reduction for siblings, need-based scholarship grants available. In 2013–14, 35% of upper-school students received aid.

Admissions Traditional secondary-level entrance grade is 9. Any standardized test required. Deadline for receipt of application materials: none. Application fee required: $100. Interview required.

Athletics Interscholastic: baseball (boys), basketball (b,g), cross-country running (b,g), golf (b,g), soccer (b,g), softball (g), tennis (b,g), track and field (b,g), volleyball (g); coed interscholastic: cheering, rowing, sailing; coed intramural: archery, dance, kayaking, modern dance, mountain biking, sailing, strength & conditioning, surfing, tai chi, yoga. 6 PE instructors, 8 coaches, 1 athletic trainer.

Computers Computers are regularly used in all classes. Computer network features include on-campus library services, online commercial services, Internet access, wireless campus network, Internet filtering or blocking technology. Campus intranet and student e-mail accounts are available to students. Students grades are available online. The school has a published electronic and media policy.

Contact Ms. Kristin Eberstadt, Director of Admissions. 631-907-5205. Fax: 631-907-5563. E-mail: keberstadt@ross.org. Website: www.ross.org

ROTHESAY NETHERWOOD SCHOOL

40 College Hill Road
Rothesay, New Brunswick E2E 5H1, Canada

Head of School: Mr. Paul G. Kitchen

General Information Coeducational boarding and day college-preparatory, arts, and technology school, affiliated with Anglican Church of Canada. Grades 6–12. Founded: 1877. Setting: small town. Nearest major city is Saint John, Canada. Students are housed in single-sex dormitories. 260-acre campus. 26 buildings on campus. Approved or accredited by Canadian Association of Independent Schools, Conference of Independent Schools of Ontario, International Baccalaureate Organization, The Association of Boarding Schools, and New Brunswick Department of Education. Affiliate member of National Association of Independent Schools. Languages of instruction: English and French. Endowment: CAN$3.5 million. Total enrollment: 265. Upper school average class size: 16. Upper school faculty-student ratio: 1:8. There are 176 required school days per year for Upper School students. Upper School students typically attend 5 days per week. The average school day consists of 7 hours and 45 minutes.

Upper School Student Profile Grade 9: 41 students (21 boys, 20 girls); Grade 10: 52 students (28 boys, 24 girls); Grade 11: 47 students (20 boys, 27 girls); Grade 12: 64 students (39 boys, 25 girls). 58% of students are boarding students. 66% are province residents. 9 provinces are represented in upper school student body. 17% are international students. International students from Bermuda, China, Dominica, Germany, Mexico, and Republic of Korea; 8 other countries represented in student body. 30% of students are members of Anglican Church of Canada.

Faculty School total: 42. In upper school: 15 men, 15 women; 6 have advanced degrees; 35 reside on campus.

Subjects Offered 3-dimensional design, advanced chemistry, art, art history, biology, Canadian history, chemistry, computer programming, computer science, CPR, digital art, drama, driver education, English, English literature, ESL, European history, fine arts, French, geography, geometry, health, history, information technology, International Baccalaureate courses, leadership, math applications, mathematics, music, outdoor education, physical education, physics, science, social studies, Spanish, theater arts, world history, writing.

Graduation Requirements Arts and fine arts (art, music, dance, drama), computer science, English, foreign language, mathematics, physical education (includes health), science, social sciences, social studies (includes history), IB Theory of Knowledge, IB designation CAS hours (creativity, action, service), Extended Essay, Outward Bound adventure.

Special Academic Programs International Baccalaureate program; honors section; independent study; term-away projects; study at local college for college credit; academic accommodation for the gifted, the musically talented, and the artistically talented; ESL (10 students enrolled).

College Admission Counseling 59 students graduated in 2012; all went to college, including Acadia University; Dalhousie University; Mount Allison University; Queen's University at Kingston; St. Francis Xavier University; University of Toronto.

Student Life Upper grades have uniform requirement, student council, honor system. Discipline rests primarily with faculty. Attendance at religious services is required.

Tuition and Aid Day student tuition: CAN$19,850; 7-day tuition and room/board: CAN$32,840. Tuition installment plan (monthly payment plans, individually arranged payment plans). Tuition reduction for siblings, bursaries, merit scholarship grants, need-based scholarship grants available. In 2012–13, 32% of upper-school students received aid.

Admissions Traditional secondary-level entrance grade is 9. For fall 2012, 91 students applied for upper-level admission, 82 were accepted, 63 enrolled. Deadline for receipt of application materials: none. Application fee required: CAN$100. Interview required.

Athletics Interscholastic: basketball (boys, girls), crew (b,g), cross-country running (b,g), field hockey (g), ice hockey (b,g), rowing (b,g), rugby (b,g), running (b,g), soccer (b,g), squash (b,g), tennis (b,g), track and field (b,g), volleyball (b,g); intramural: crew (b,g), cross-country running (b,g), golf (b,g), ice hockey (b,g), indoor soccer (b), squash (b,g), tennis (b,g), track and field (b,g), yoga (g); coed interscholastic: badminton, crew, cross-country running, ice hockey, rowing, tennis, track and field; coed intramural:

aerobics, aerobics/dance, backpacking, badminton, bicycling, billiards, broomball, canoeing/kayaking, climbing, cooperative games, crew, cross-country running, fitness, fitness walking, floor hockey, golf, hiking/backpacking, ice hockey, ice skating, indoor soccer, jogging, kayaking, outdoor activities, outdoor education, physical fitness, physical training, rock climbing, running, skiing (cross-country), skiing (downhill), snowboarding, snowshoeing, squash, street hockey, strength & conditioning, tennis, track and field, ultimate Frisbee, volleyball, walking, wall climbing, weight training. 3 PE instructors.

Computers Computers are regularly used in all classes. Computer network features include on-campus library services, Internet access, wireless campus network, Internet filtering or blocking technology, Web site for each academic course, informative, interactive online community for parents, teachers, and students. Campus intranet and student e-mail accounts are available to students. Students grades are available online. The school has a published electronic and media policy.

Contact Mrs. Elizabeth Kitchen, Associate Director of Admission. 506-848-0866. Fax: 506-848-0851. E-mail: Elizabeth.Kitchen@rns.cc. Website: www.rns.cc

ROWLAND HALL

843 South Lincoln Street
Salt Lake City, Utah 84102

Head of School: Mr. Alan C. Sparrow

General Information Coeducational day college-preparatory school. Grades PK–12. Founded: 1867. Setting: urban. 4-acre campus. 1 building on campus. Approved or accredited by National Association of Episcopal Schools, Northwest Accreditation Commission, Northwest Association of Independent Schools, Northwest Association of Schools and Colleges, The College Board, and Utah Department of Education. Member of National Association of Independent Schools. Endowment: $7.2 million. Total enrollment: 927. Upper school average class size: 16. Upper school faculty-student ratio: 1:7. There are 170 required school days per year for Upper School students. Upper School students typically attend 5 days per week. The average school day consists of 6 hours.

Upper School Student Profile Grade 9: 89 students (44 boys, 45 girls); Grade 10: 78 students (30 boys, 48 girls); Grade 11: 64 students (25 boys, 39 girls); Grade 12: 69 students (39 boys, 30 girls).

Faculty School total: 43. In upper school: 21 men, 22 women; 32 have advanced degrees.

Subjects Offered Adolescent issues, algebra, biology, biology-AP, calculus, calculus-AP, ceramics, chemistry, chemistry-AP, Chinese, chorus, computer graphics, creative writing, dance, debate, drama, English, English language and composition-AP, English literature and composition-AP, environmental science, ethics, European history-AP, French, French language-AP, French literature-AP, geometry, graphic arts, graphic design, history, human development, jazz band, Latin, Latin-AP, math applications, modern European history-AP, music theory, newspaper, orchestra, photography, physical education, physics, physics-AP, political science, pre-calculus, psychology-AP, Spanish, Spanish-AP, statistics-AP, studio art, studio art-AP, theater, trigonometry, U.S. history, U.S. history-AP, weight training, Western civilization, world cultures, world religions, yearbook.

Graduation Requirements American history, arts and fine arts (art, music, dance, drama), biology, chemistry, English, ethics, foreign language, health education, mathematics, physical education (includes health), physics, science, social studies (includes history), world religions.

Special Academic Programs 17 Advanced Placement exams for which test preparation is offered; honors section; independent study.

College Admission Counseling 85 students graduated in 2013; 82 went to college, including Arizona State University; University of Oregon; University of Oregon; University of Southern California; University of Utah; Wellesley College. Other: 3 entered a postgraduate year. Median SAT critical reading: 620, median SAT math: 640, median SAT writing: 620, median combined SAT: 1870, median composite ACT: 29. 53% scored over 600 on SAT critical reading, 63% scored over 600 on SAT math, 53% scored over 600 on SAT writing, 58% scored over 1800 on combined SAT, 65% scored over 26 on composite ACT.

Student Life Upper grades have specified standards of dress, student council, honor system. Discipline rests equally with students and faculty.

Summer Programs Enrichment, advancement, sports, art/fine arts, computer instruction programs offered; session focuses on advancement and elective courses; held on campus; accepts boys and girls; open to students from other schools. 40 students usually enrolled. 2014 schedule: June 17 to August 9. Application deadline: none.

Tuition and Aid Day student tuition: $18,170. Tuition installment plan (monthly payment plans, individually arranged payment plans, 2-installment plan). Merit scholarship grants, need-based scholarship grants, Ethnic/Racial Diversity scholarship grants, Malone Family Foundation Academically Talented/need-based scholarships available. In 2013–14, 23% of upper-school students received aid; total upper-school merit-scholarship money awarded: $53,500. Total amount of financial aid awarded in 2013–14: $591,190.

Admissions Traditional secondary-level entrance grade is 9. For fall 2013, 78 students applied for upper-level admission, 48 were accepted, 34 enrolled. ACT-Explore, ERB CTP IV, ISEE, PSAT, TOEFL or writing sample required. Deadline for receipt of application materials: March 1. Application fee required: $60. Interview required.

Athletics Interscholastic: alpine skiing (boys, girls), baseball (b), basketball (b,g), golf (b,g), skiing (downhill) (b,g), soccer (b,g), softball (g), swimming and diving (b,g), tennis (b,g), volleyball (g); intramural: skiing (downhill) (b,g); coed interscholastic: alpine skiing, cross-country running, dance, modern dance, skiing (downhill), track and field; coed intramural: climbing, deck hockey, hiking/backpacking, mountain biking, outdoor activities, outdoor education, physical fitness, physical training, rock climbing, ropes courses, skiing (cross-country), skiing (downhill), snowboarding, strength & conditioning, swimming and diving, telemark skiing, weight training, yoga. 6 PE instructors, 22 coaches, 1 athletic trainer.

Computers Computers are regularly used in desktop publishing, graphic design, yearbook classes. Computer network features include on-campus library services, Internet access, wireless campus network, Internet filtering or blocking technology, all students have their own laptop computer. Campus intranet, student e-mail accounts, and computer access in designated common areas are available to students. Students grades are available online. The school has a published electronic and media policy.

Contact Kathryn B. Gundersen, Director of Admission. 801-924-2950. Fax: 801-363-5521. E-mail: kathygundersen@rowlandhall.org. Website: www.rowlandhall.org

THE ROXBURY LATIN SCHOOL

101 St. Theresa Avenue
West Roxbury, Massachusetts 02132

Head of School: Mr. Kerry Paul Brennan

General Information Boys' day college-preparatory school. Grades 7–12. Founded: 1645. Setting: urban. Nearest major city is Boston. 117-acre campus. 10 buildings on campus. Approved or accredited by Association of Independent Schools in New England, Headmasters' Conference, and New England Association of Schools and Colleges. Member of National Association of Independent Schools and Secondary School Admission Test Board. Endowment: $105 million. Total enrollment: 299. Upper school average class size: 13. Upper school faculty-student ratio: 1:7. There are 176 required school days per year for Upper School students. Upper School students typically attend 5 days per week. The average school day consists of 6 hours and 30 minutes.

Upper School Student Profile Grade 7: 43 students (43 boys); Grade 8: 42 students (42 boys); Grade 9: 53 students (53 boys); Grade 10: 52 students (52 boys); Grade 11: 56 students (56 boys); Grade 12: 53 students (53 boys).

Faculty School total: 40. In upper school: 35 men, 5 women; 31 have advanced degrees.

Subjects Offered Advanced biology, advanced chemistry, advanced math, algebra, American Civil War, American government, American history, American literature, American studies, analysis, analytic geometry, Ancient Greek, ancient history, ancient world history, applied arts, art, art history, arts, biology, calculus, calculus-AP, chemistry, classical Greek literature, classical language, college counseling, college placement, computer science, computer science-AP, creative writing, design, drama, earth science, English, English literature, environmental science, European history, expository writing, fine arts, French, French language-AP, geometry, global studies, government/civics, grammar, history, Indian studies, Latin, Latin-AP, life science, macro/microeconomics-AP, mathematics, Middle East, model United Nations, music, music theory-AP, personal development, photography, physical education, physical science, physics, pre-algebra, science, senior project, Spanish, Spanish language-AP, Spanish-AP, statistics-AP, studio art, theater, trigonometry, U.S. history, visual arts, water color painting, Western civilization, world history, writing.

Graduation Requirements Arts, English, foreign language, history, Latin, mathematics, science, U.S. history, Western civilization, independent senior project.

Special Academic Programs 11 Advanced Placement exams for which test preparation is offered; honors section; independent study; academic accommodation for the gifted, the musically talented, and the artistically talented.

College Admission Counseling 51 students graduated in 2013; all went to college, including Boston College; Columbia University; Dartmouth College; Davidson College; Harvard University; Yale University. Median SAT critical reading: 740, median SAT math: 770, median SAT writing: 770, median combined SAT: 2240. 96% scored over 600 on SAT critical reading, 98% scored over 600 on SAT math, 98% scored over 600 on SAT writing, 98% scored over 1800 on combined SAT.

Student Life Upper grades have specified standards of dress, student council, honor system. Discipline rests equally with students and faculty.

Summer Programs Enrichment, sports, computer instruction programs offered; held on campus; accepts boys and girls; open to students from other schools. 75 students usually enrolled. 2014 schedule: June 12 to July 31. Application deadline: none.

Tuition and Aid Day student tuition: $26,100. Tuition installment plan (Insured Tuition Payment Plan, Key Tuition Payment Plan, 2-payment plan). Need-based scholarship grants available. In 2013–14, 37% of upper-school students received aid. Total amount of financial aid awarded in 2013–14: $2,087,325.

Admissions Traditional secondary-level entrance grade is 7. For fall 2013, 494 students applied for upper-level admission, 65 were accepted, 55 enrolled. ISEE or SSAT required. Deadline for receipt of application materials: January 6. No application fee required. On-campus interview required.

Athletics Interscholastic: baseball, basketball, cross-country running, football, ice hockey, lacrosse, soccer, tennis, track and field, wrestling. 7 coaches, 1 athletic trainer.

Computers Computers are regularly used in all academic, desktop publishing, literary magazine, newspaper, yearbook classes. Computer network features include on-campus library services, online commercial services, Internet access, wireless campus network, Internet filtering or blocking technology. Campus intranet, student e-mail accounts, and computer access in designated common areas are available to students. The school has a published electronic and media policy.

Contact Ms. Lindsay Schuyler, Assistant Director of Admission. 617-325-4920. Fax: 617-325-3585. E-mail: admission@roxburylatin.org. Website: www.roxburylatin.org

ROYAL CANADIAN COLLEGE

8610 Ash Street
Vancouver, British Columbia V6P 3M2, Canada

Head of School: Mr. Howard H. Jiang

General Information Coeducational day college-preparatory and general academic school. Grades 8–12. Founded: 1989. Setting: suburban. 1-acre campus. 2 buildings on campus. Approved or accredited by British Columbia Department of Education. Language of instruction: English. Total enrollment: 110. Upper school average class size: 20. Upper school faculty-student ratio: 1:20. There are 197 required school days per year for Upper School students. Upper School students typically attend 5 days per week. The average school day consists of 5 hours and 30 minutes.

Upper School Student Profile Grade 10: 19 students (12 boys, 7 girls); Grade 11: 18 students (12 boys, 6 girls); Grade 12: 73 students (36 boys, 37 girls).

Faculty School total: 6. In upper school: 5 men, 1 woman; 1 has an advanced degree.

Subjects Offered Accounting, applied skills, biology, calculus, Canadian history, career planning, chemistry, communications, computer science, computer science-AP, drama, economics, English, ESL, fine arts, general science, geography, history, information technology, Mandarin, mathematics, physical education, physics, pre-calculus, social sciences, world history, writing.

Graduation Requirements Applied skills, arts and fine arts (art, music, dance, drama), career and personal planning, language arts, mathematics, science, social studies (includes history).

Special Academic Programs ESL (10 students enrolled).

College Admission Counseling 48 students graduated in 2013; 45 went to college, including McGill University; Simon Fraser University; The University of British Columbia; University of Toronto; University of Victoria. Other: 3 had other specific plans.

Student Life Upper grades have student council, honor system. Discipline rests primarily with faculty.

Summer Programs ESL programs offered; session focuses on learning survival English conversational skills, and Canadian cultural experience; held on campus; accepts boys and girls; open to students from other schools. 30 students usually enrolled. 2014 schedule: July 2 to August 22. Application deadline: May 31.

Tuition and Aid Day student tuition: CAN$13,500. Merit scholarship grants available. In 2013–14, 4% of upper-school students received aid; total upper-school merit-scholarship money awarded: CAN$10,000. Total amount of financial aid awarded in 2013–14: CAN$18,000.

Admissions Traditional secondary-level entrance grade is 11. For fall 2013, 7 students applied for upper-level admission, 5 were accepted, 5 enrolled. English language required. Deadline for receipt of application materials: none. Application fee required: CAN$200. Interview recommended.

Athletics Intramural: badminton (boys, girls), baseball (b,g), basketball (b,g), soccer (b,g), table tennis (b,g), ultimate Frisbee (b,g), volleyball (b,g); coed intramural: badminton, baseball, soccer, table tennis, ultimate Frisbee, volleyball. 1 PE instructor.

Computers Computers are regularly used in accounting, career exploration, English, information technology, programming, science, social studies classes. Computer network features include Internet access, wireless campus network, Internet filtering or blocking technology. Computer access in designated common areas is available to students.

Contact Ms. Alice Syn, Admissions Manager. 604-738-2221. Fax: 604-738-2282. E-mail: alice.syn@royalcanadiancollege.com. Website: www.royalcanadiancollege.com

ROYCEMORE SCHOOL

1200 Davis Street
Evanston, Illinois 60201

Head of School: Mr. Joseph A. Becker

General Information Coeducational day college-preparatory and arts school. Grades PK–12. Founded: 1915. Setting: suburban. Nearest major city is Chicago. 2.4-acre campus. 1 building on campus. Approved or accredited by Independent Schools Association of the Central States and Illinois Department of Education. Member of National Association of Independent Schools. Endowment: $11,000. Total enrollment: 292. Upper school average class size: 9. Upper school faculty-student ratio: 1:5. There are 172 required school days per year for Upper School students. Upper School students typically attend 5 days per week. The average school day consists of 7 hours.

Upper School Student Profile Grade 9: 21 students (9 boys, 12 girls); Grade 10: 27 students (14 boys, 13 girls); Grade 11: 20 students (12 boys, 8 girls); Grade 12: 28 students (13 boys, 15 girls).

Faculty School total: 40. In upper school: 5 men, 15 women; 14 have advanced degrees.

Subjects Offered African-American literature, algebra, American literature, art, biology, biology-AP, calculus-AP, chemistry, choir, comedy, composition, drawing, English language and composition-AP, English literature, environmental science, European history-AP, French, French-AP, geometry, government/civics, human development, independent study, international relations, introduction to theater, literature-AP, microeconomics, modern European history, music composition, music history, music theory, music theory-AP, mythology, painting, physical education, physics, physics-AP, pottery, public speaking, sculpture, society, politics and law, sociology, Spanish, Spanish-AP, studio art-AP, trigonometry, U.S. history, U.S. history-AP, world history, world literature, world religions, yearbook.

Graduation Requirements Arts and fine arts (art, music, dance, drama), English, foreign language, mathematics, physical education (includes health), science, social studies (includes history), participation in a 3-week January short-term project each year.

Special Academic Programs 10 Advanced Placement exams for which test preparation is offered; accelerated programs; independent study; study at local college for college credit.

College Admission Counseling 32 students graduated in 2012; all went to college, including DePaul University; Indiana University Bloomington; Knox College; University of Illinois at Urbana–Champaign; University of Wisconsin–Madison. Median SAT critical reading: 630, median SAT math: 630, median SAT writing: 560, median combined SAT: 1760, median composite ACT: 26. 55% scored over 600 on SAT critical reading, 55% scored over 600 on SAT math, 38% scored over 600 on SAT writing, 52% scored over 1800 on combined SAT, 48% scored over 26 on composite ACT.

Student Life Upper grades have specified standards of dress, student council, honor system. Discipline rests primarily with faculty.

Tuition and Aid Day student tuition: $24,425. Tuition installment plan (individually arranged payment plans, semi-annual payment plan, 9-month payment plan). Merit scholarship grants, need-based scholarship grants, discounts for children of Northwestern University and NorthShore University HealthSystem employees available. In 2012–13, 47% of upper-school students received aid; total upper-school merit-scholarship money awarded: $66,150. Total amount of financial aid awarded in 2012–13: $699,821.

Admissions Traditional secondary-level entrance grade is 9. Any standardized test or writing sample required. Deadline for receipt of application materials: none. Application fee required: $75. Interview required.

Athletics Interscholastic: basketball (boys, girls), volleyball (g); intramural: softball (b), strength & conditioning (b), volleyball (b); coed interscholastic: soccer; coed intramural: gymnastics, table tennis. 3 PE instructors, 2 coaches.

Computers Computers are regularly used in all academic classes. Computer network features include on-campus library services, Internet access, wireless campus network. The school has a published electronic and media policy.

Contact Ms. Amanda Avery, Director of Admissions. 847-866-6055. Fax: 847-866-6545. E-mail: aavery@roycemoreschool.org. Website: www.roycemoreschool.org

RUMSEY HALL SCHOOL

Washington Depot, Connecticut
See Junior Boarding Schools section.

RUNDLE COLLEGE

4411 Manitoba Road SE
Calgary, Alberta T2G 4B9, Canada

Head of School: Mr. David Hauk

General Information Coeducational day college-preparatory, arts, business, bilingual studies, and technology school. Grades PK–12. Founded: 1985. Setting: suburban. 20-acre campus. 1 building on campus. Approved or accredited by Canadian Association of Independent Schools and Alberta Department of Education. Member of Secondary School Admission Test Board. Language of instruction: English. Total enrollment: 811. Upper school average class size: 14. Upper school faculty-student ratio: 1:14. There are 187 required school days per year for Upper School students. Upper School students typically attend 5 days per week. The average school day consists of 6 hours.

Upper School Student Profile Grade 10: 84 students (37 boys, 47 girls); Grade 11: 94 students (46 boys, 48 girls); Grade 12: 78 students (41 boys, 37 girls).

Faculty School total: 45. In upper school: 14 men, 31 women; 15 have advanced degrees.

Subjects Offered Accounting, art, band, biology, calculus, chemistry, computer science, drama, English, French, general science, mathematics, physical education, physics, science, social studies, Spanish, theater.

Graduation Requirements Career and personal planning, English, mathematics, physical education (includes health), science, social sciences.

Special Academic Programs Honors section; study abroad.

College Admission Counseling 81 students graduated in 2012; 79 went to college, including Queen's University at Kingston; St. Francis Xavier University; The University of British Columbia; University of Alberta; University of Calgary; University of Victoria. Other: 1 went to work, 1 had other specific plans.

Student Life Upper grades have uniform requirement, student council, honor system. Discipline rests primarily with faculty.

Tuition and Aid Day student tuition: CAN$12,000. Tuition installment plan (monthly payment plans). Bursaries, merit scholarship grants available. In 2012–13, 1% of upper-school students received aid; total upper-school merit-scholarship money awarded: CAN$24,000. Total amount of financial aid awarded in 2012–13: CAN$90,000.

Admissions Traditional secondary-level entrance grade is 10. For fall 2012, 50 students applied for upper-level admission, 25 were accepted, 20 enrolled. Achievement tests and SSAT or WISC III required. Deadline for receipt of application materials: none. Application fee required: CAN$100. On-campus interview required.

Athletics Interscholastic: badminton (boys, girls), basketball (b,g), cross-country running (b,g), curling (b,g), dance squad (b,g), flag football (b,g), floor hockey (b,g), football (b), golf (b,g), rugby (b,g), soccer (b,g), track and field (b,g), volleyball (b,g), wrestling (b,g); intramural: aerobics (g), badminton (b,g), dance (g), football (b); coed interscholastic: badminton, softball; coed intramural: badminton, baseball, basketball, cross-country running, flag football, football, lacrosse, outdoor recreation, skiing (downhill), soccer, table tennis, track and field, volleyball, weight lifting, wrestling. 4 PE instructors.

Computers Computers are regularly used in technology classes. Computer network features include Internet access, wireless campus network; Web page hosting, multimedia productions, streaming video student news. Student e-mail accounts and computer access in designated common areas are available to students. Students grades are available online. The school has a published electronic and media policy.

Contact Ms. Nicola Spencer, Director of Admissions. 403-291-3866 Ext. 106. Fax: 403-291-5458. E-mail: spencer@rundle.ab.ca. Website: www.rundle.ab.ca

RYE COUNTRY DAY SCHOOL

Cedar Street
Rye, New York 10580-2034

General Information Coeducational day college-preparatory, arts, and technology school. Grades PK–12. Founded: 1869. Setting: suburban. Nearest major city is New York. 30-acre campus. 8 buildings on campus. Approved or accredited by New York Department of Education. Member of National Association of Independent Schools and Secondary School Admission Test Board. Endowment: $29 million. Total enrollment: 886. Upper school average class size: 13. Upper school faculty-student ratio: 1:7. There are 165 required school days per year for Upper School students. Upper School students typically attend 5 days per week. The average school day consists of 6 hours and 50 minutes.

See Display on next page and Close-Up on page 564.

SACRAMENTO ADVENTIST ACADEMY

5601 Winding Way
Carmichael, California 95608-1298

Head of School: John Soule

General Information Coeducational day college-preparatory, general academic, arts, business, vocational, religious studies, bilingual studies, and technology school, affiliated with Seventh-day Adventist Church. Grades K–12. Founded: 1957. Setting: suburban. Nearest major city is Sacramento. 36-acre campus. 5 buildings on campus. Approved or accredited by Board of Regents, General Conference of Seventh-day Adventists, National Council for Private School Accreditation, Western Association of Schools and Colleges, and California Department of Education. Total enrollment: 222. Upper school average class size: 29. Upper school faculty-student ratio: 1:12. There are 180 required school days per year for Upper School students. Upper School students typically attend 5 days per week. The average school day consists of 7 hours and 15 minutes.

Upper School Student Profile 96% of students are Seventh-day Adventists.

Faculty School total: 25. In upper school: 8 men, 4 women; 4 have advanced degrees.

Subjects Offered Accounting, advanced math, Advanced Placement courses, algebra, art, band, Bible, biology, biology-AP, business technology, calculus-AP, chemistry, choir, computer applications, computer education, conceptual physics, concert band, consumer mathematics, driver education, economics, English, English composition, English language and composition-AP, geometry, graphic design, handbells, health, health education, keyboarding, life skills, microcomputer technology applications, photography, physical education, physics, public speaking, religion, softball, Spanish, Spanish-AP, speech, technical skills, U.S. government, U.S. history, word processing, world history, world history-AP, World War I.

Graduation Requirements Arts and fine arts (art, music, dance, drama), biology, computer applications, economics, English, keyboarding, life skills, mathematics,

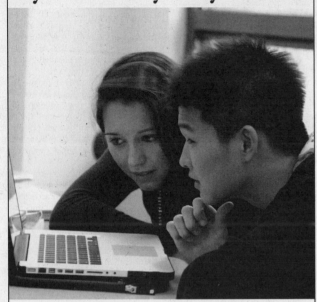
physical education (includes health), religion (includes Bible studies and theology), science, U.S. government, U.S. history, 100 hours of documented work experience, 25 hours of documented community service per year of attendance.

Special Academic Programs 2 Advanced Placement exams for which test preparation is offered; honors section; accelerated programs; study at local college for college credit; remedial math.

College Admission Counseling 27 students graduated in 2012; 24 went to college, including American River College; La Sierra University; Pacific Union College; Sierra College; Walla Walla University. Other: 2 went to work, 1 entered military service. Mean SAT critical reading: 559, mean SAT math: 566, mean composite ACT: 23. 22% scored over 600 on SAT critical reading, 44% scored over 600 on SAT math, 45% scored over 26 on composite ACT.

Student Life Upper grades have specified standards of dress, student council. Discipline rests primarily with faculty.

Tuition and Aid Day student tuition: $5470–$9740. Tuition installment plan (monthly payment plans, individually arranged payment plans). Tuition reduction for siblings, paying campus jobs, academy day scholarships available. In 2012–13, 5% of upper-school students received aid. Total amount of financial aid awarded in 2012–13: $10,000.

Admissions Traditional secondary-level entrance grade is 9. Deadline for receipt of application materials: none. Application fee required: $25. Interview required.

Athletics Interscholastic: baseball (girls), basketball (b,g), flag football (b,g), golf (b), softball (b,g), volleyball (g). 1 PE instructor, 1 coach.

Computers Computers are regularly used in accounting, business applications, English, history, keyboarding, religion, word processing classes. Computer network features include on-campus library services, online commercial services, Internet access.

Contact Mrs. Sheri Miller, Registrar/Guidance Counselor. 916-481-2300 Ext. 102. Fax: 916-481-7426. E-mail: smiller@sacaa.org. Website: www.sacaa.org

SACRAMENTO COUNTRY DAY SCHOOL

2636 Latham Drive
Sacramento, California 95864-7198

Head of School: Stephen T. Repsher

General Information Coeducational day college-preparatory, arts, and technology school. Grades PK–12. Founded: 1964. Setting: suburban. 12-acre campus. 8 buildings on campus. Approved or accredited by California Association of Independent Schools and Western Association of Schools and Colleges. Member of National Association of Independent Schools. Endowment: $2 million. Total enrollment: 481. Upper school average class size: 12. Upper school faculty-student ratio: 1:9. There are 175 required school days per year for Upper School students. Upper School students typically attend 5 days per week. The average school day consists of 6 hours and 25 minutes.

Upper School Student Profile Grade 9: 27 students (15 boys, 12 girls); Grade 10: 33 students (15 boys, 18 girls); Grade 11: 31 students (15 boys, 16 girls); Grade 12: 24 students (13 boys, 11 girls).

Faculty School total: 65. In upper school: 18 men, 10 women; 19 have advanced degrees.

Subjects Offered Acting, algebra, American history, American literature, ancient history, ancient/medieval philosophy, art, art history, art history-AP, art-AP, band, biology, biology-AP, British literature, calculus, calculus-AP, ceramics, chamber groups, chemistry, chemistry-AP, community service, computer skills, computer technologies, concert band, creative writing, digital imaging, digital music, drama, drama performance, drawing, earth science, economics, English, English literature, European history, fine arts, French, French-AP, geography, geometry, government/civics, grammar, history, international relations, jazz band, journalism, language and composition, Latin, Latin-AP, mathematics, microeconomics, newspaper, nutrition, orchestra, physical education, physics, physics-AP, physiology, pre-calculus, public speaking, science, social studies, Spanish, Spanish-AP, speech, studio art, studio art-AP, technology/design, theater, trigonometry, U.S. history, U.S. history-AP, world history, world literature, writing.

Graduation Requirements Arts and fine arts (art, music, dance, drama), computer science, electives, English, foreign language, history, interdisciplinary studies, mathematics, physical education (includes health), science, Senior Seminors. Community service is required.

Special Academic Programs Advanced Placement exam preparation; independent study; study at local college for college credit.

College Admission Counseling 41 students graduated in 2013; all went to college, including California College of the Arts; Chapman University; Occidental College; University of California, Berkeley; University of California, Los Angeles; University of California, San Diego. Median SAT critical reading: 605, median SAT math: 611, median SAT writing: 621, median combined SAT: 1836. 100% scored over 600 on SAT critical reading, 100% scored over 600 on SAT math, 100% scored over 600 on SAT writing, 100% scored over 1800 on combined SAT.

Student Life Upper grades have specified standards of dress, student council, honor system. Discipline rests primarily with faculty.

Tuition and Aid Day student tuition: $16,970–$21,700. Tuition installment plan (Insured Tuition Payment Plan, monthly payment plans, individually arranged payment plans). Need-based scholarship grants available. In 2013–14, 28% of upper-school students received aid. Total amount of financial aid awarded in 2013–14: $429,050.

Admissions Traditional secondary-level entrance grade is 9. For fall 2013, 37 students applied for upper-level admission, 19 were accepted, 13 enrolled. ERB, Otis-Lennon Mental Ability Test and writing sample required. Deadline for receipt of application materials: none. Application fee required: $50. Interview required.

Athletics Interscholastic: baseball (boys), basketball (b,g), flag football (b), lacrosse (b), soccer (b,g), softball (g), swimming and diving (b,g), track and field (b,g), volleyball (b,g); coed interscholastic: cross-country running, golf, skiing (downhill), snowboarding, tennis, wrestling. 3 PE instructors, 14 coaches.

Computers Computers are regularly used in all academic classes. Computer network features include on-campus library services, online commercial services, Internet access, wireless campus network, Internet filtering or blocking technology. Campus intranet and student e-mail accounts are available to students. The school has a published electronic and media policy.

Contact Lonna Bloedau, Director of Admission. 916-481-8811. Fax: 916-481-6016. E-mail: lbloedau@saccds.org. Website: www.saccds.org

SACRED HEART/GRIFFIN HIGH SCHOOL

1200 West Washington
Springfield, Illinois 62702-4794

Head of School: Sr. Margaret Joanne Grueter, OP

General Information Coeducational day college-preparatory school, affiliated with Roman Catholic Church. Grades 9–12. Founded: 1895. Setting: urban. 13-acre campus. 2 buildings on campus. Approved or accredited by National Catholic Education Association, North Central Association of Colleges and Schools, and Illinois Department of Education. Endowment: $8.7 million. Total enrollment: 781. Upper school average class size: 24. Upper school faculty-student ratio: 1:24. There are 176 required school days per year for Upper School students. Upper School students typically attend 5 days per week. The average school day consists of 7 hours.

Upper School Student Profile Grade 9: 207 students (91 boys, 116 girls); Grade 10: 192 students (101 boys, 91 girls); Grade 11: 217 students (122 boys, 95 girls); Grade 12: 165 students (84 boys, 81 girls). 88% of students are Roman Catholic.

Faculty School total: 52. In upper school: 24 men, 28 women; 26 have advanced degrees.

Subjects Offered Advanced biology.

Graduation Requirements 80 hours of service to community or approved organizations.

Special Academic Programs 9 Advanced Placement exams for which test preparation is offered; honors section; academic accommodation for the gifted, the musically talented, and the artistically talented.

College Admission Counseling 191 students graduated in 2012; 187 went to college. Other: 2 entered military service, 2 had other specific plans. Median composite ACT: 24.

Student Life Upper grades have uniform requirement, student council, honor system. Discipline rests primarily with faculty. Attendance at religious services is required.

Tuition and Aid Day student tuition: $7275. Tuition installment plan (FACTS Tuition Payment Plan, individually arranged payment plans). Tuition reduction for siblings, merit scholarship grants, need-based scholarship grants available. In 2012–13, 30% of upper-school students received aid; total upper-school merit-scholarship money awarded: $12,900. Total amount of financial aid awarded in 2012–13: $443,093.

Admissions Traditional secondary-level entrance grade is 9. For fall 2012, 207 students applied for upper-level admission, 207 were accepted, 207 enrolled. Explore required. Deadline for receipt of application materials: none. Application fee required: $225. Interview recommended.

Athletics Interscholastic: aquatics (boys, girls), baseball (b), basketball (b,g), cheering (g), cross-country running (b,g), diving (b,g), football (b), golf (b,g), hockey (b), pom squad (g), soccer (b,g), softball (g), tennis (b,g), track and field (b,g), volleyball (g). 1 PE instructor, 3 coaches, 1 athletic trainer.

Computers Computers are regularly used in all academic classes. Computer network features include on-campus library services, Internet access, wireless campus network, Internet filtering or blocking technology. Students grades are available online. The school has a published electronic and media policy.

Contact Erica Cusumano, Marketing/Alumni Coordinator. 217-787-9732. Fax: 217-726-9791. E-mail: Cusumano@shg.org. Website: www.shg.org

SACRED HEART SCHOOL OF HALIFAX

5820 Spring Garden Road
Halifax, Nova Scotia B3H 1X8, Canada

Head of School: Sr. Anne Wachter

General Information Coeducational day college-preparatory and religious studies school, affiliated with Roman Catholic Church. Grades K–12. Founded: 1849. Setting: urban. 1 building on campus. Approved or accredited by Canadian Association of Independent Schools, Network of Sacred Heart Schools, and Nova Scotia Department of Education. Language of instruction: English. Total enrollment: 461.

Upper school average class size: 18. Upper school faculty-student ratio: 1:10. There are 175 required school days per year for Upper School students. Upper School students typically attend 5 days per week. The average school day consists of 7 hours.

Upper School Student Profile Grade 7: 40 students (18 boys, 22 girls); Grade 8: 51 students (10 boys, 41 girls); Grade 9: 56 students (23 boys, 33 girls); Grade 10: 48 students (23 boys, 25 girls); Grade 11: 36 students (12 boys, 24 girls); Grade 12: 36 students (8 boys, 28 girls). 60% of students are Roman Catholic.

Faculty School total: 65. In upper school: 7 men, 28 women; 22 have advanced degrees.

Subjects Offered 20th century history, 20th century world history, algebra, art, Bible studies, biology, calculus, Canadian history, chemistry, creative writing, earth science, economics, English, English literature, environmental science, European history, expository writing, French, geography, geometry, government/civics, grammar, health, history, mathematics, music, physical education, physics, religion, science, social studies, sociology, Spanish, theater, trigonometry, world history, writing.

Graduation Requirements Arts and fine arts (art, music, dance, drama), English, foreign language, history, mathematics, physical education (includes health), religion (includes Bible studies and theology), science. Community service is required.

Special Academic Programs 8 Advanced Placement exams for which test preparation is offered; honors section; domestic exchange program (with Network of Sacred Heart Schools); study abroad; ESL (19 students enrolled).

College Admission Counseling 35 students graduated in 2013; 32 went to college, including Acadia University; Carleton University; Dalhousie University; Mount Allison University; Saint Mary's University; St. Francis Xavier University. Other: 1 had other specific plans.

Student Life Upper grades have uniform requirement, student council, honor system. Discipline rests primarily with faculty. Attendance at religious services is required.

Summer Programs Remediation, enrichment programs offered; session focuses on French remediation, debate; held on campus; accepts boys and girls; open to students from other schools. 50 students usually enrolled. Application deadline: none.

Tuition and Aid Day student tuition: CAN$12,977. Tuition installment plan (monthly payment plans, individually arranged payment plans). Tuition reduction for siblings, bursaries, merit scholarship grants, need-based scholarship grants available. In 2013–14, 12% of upper-school students received aid; total upper-school merit-scholarship money awarded: CAN$106,000. Total amount of financial aid awarded in 2013–14: CAN$138,000.

Admissions Traditional secondary-level entrance grade is 7. Otis-Lennon School Ability Test and school's own test required. Deadline for receipt of application materials: none. Application fee required: CAN$100. On-campus interview required.

Athletics Interscholastic: aquatics (girls), badminton (b,g), basketball (b,g), cross-country running (b,g), field hockey (g), ice hockey (b), soccer (b,g), swimming and diving (b,g), tennis (g), volleyball (g); intramural: alpine skiing (b,g), badminton (b,g), basketball (b,g), cross-country running (b,g), curling (g), fitness walking (g), jogging (b,g), running (b,g), skiing (downhill) (b,g), soccer (b,g), swimming and diving (b), tennis (g), track and field (g), volleyball (g). 3 PE instructors.

Computers Computer network features include on-campus library services, Internet access, wireless campus network, Internet filtering or blocking technology. Campus intranet and student e-mail accounts are available to students. The school has a published electronic and media policy.

Contact Ms. Pauline Scott, Principal, Sacred Heart High School. 902-422-4459 Ext. 209. Fax: 902-423-7691. E-mail: pscott@shsh.ca. Website: www.sacredheartschool.ns.ca

SADDLEBACK VALLEY CHRISTIAN SCHOOL

26333 Oso Road
San Juan Capistrano, California 92675

Head of School: Mr. Edward Carney

General Information Coeducational day college-preparatory, general academic, arts, religious studies, and technology school, affiliated with Christian faith. Grades PK–12. Founded: 1997. Setting: suburban. Nearest major city is Irvine/Anaheim. 69-acre campus. 6 buildings on campus. Approved or accredited by Association of Christian Schools International, Western Association of Schools and Colleges, and California Department of Education. Total enrollment: 911. Upper school average class size: 24. Upper school faculty-student ratio: 1:15. There are 180 required school days per year for Upper School students. Upper School students typically attend 5 days per week. The average school day consists of 6 hours and 35 minutes.

Upper School Student Profile Grade 9: 89 students (49 boys, 40 girls); Grade 10: 108 students (49 boys, 59 girls); Grade 11: 103 students (55 boys, 48 girls); Grade 12: 76 students (36 boys, 40 girls). 75% of students are Christian faith.

Faculty School total: 75. In upper school: 12 men, 22 women; 10 have advanced degrees.

Subjects Offered 1 1/2 elective credits, algebra, American history, American history-AP, American literature, American sign language, anatomy and physiology, applied arts, art, art history-AP, ASB Leadership, athletic training, Bible, Bible as literature, biology, biology-AP, British literature, business mathematics, calculus-AP, chemistry, computers, concert choir, debate, drama, English language and composition-AP, English literature and composition-AP, environmental science, ESL, geography, geometry, government and politics-AP, history, honors English, music, musical theater, oceanography, psychology-AP, public speaking, religious studies, science, senior project, Spanish, Spanish language-AP, speech and debate, sports, statistics-AP, studio art-AP, trigonometry, U.S. government and politics, U.S. government and politics-AP, U.S. history, U.S. history-AP, visual and performing arts, world history, world literature, world religions, yearbook.

Graduation Requirements Algebra, American history, American literature, anatomy and physiology, art, Bible, biology, British literature, earth science, English, English literature, foreign language, geometry, history, life science, physical education (includes health), physical science, science, senior project, Spanish, speech, trigonometry, U.S. history, visual arts, world history, Senior Project required for seniors to graduate.

Special Academic Programs 11 Advanced Placement exams for which test preparation is offered; honors section; independent study; study at local college for college credit; study abroad; remedial reading and/or remedial writing; remedial math; programs in English, mathematics, general development for dyslexic students; special instructional classes for students with learning disabilities; ESL (24 students enrolled).

College Admission Counseling 64 students graduated in 2012; 50 went to college, including Biola University; California Polytechnic State University, San Luis Obispo; Point Loma Nazarene University; University of California, Los Angeles; University of California, San Diego. Other: 10 went to work, 4 had other specific plans. Median SAT critical reading: 540, median SAT math: 540, median SAT writing: 540, median combined SAT: 1620, median composite ACT: 22. 32% scored over 600 on SAT critical reading, 21% scored over 600 on SAT math, 32% scored over 600 on SAT writing, 26% scored over 1800 on combined SAT, 27% scored over 26 on composite ACT.

Student Life Upper grades have uniform requirement, student council, honor system. Discipline rests primarily with faculty. Attendance at religious services is required.

Tuition and Aid Day student tuition: $8600. Tuition installment plan (monthly payment plans). Tuition reduction for siblings, need-based scholarship grants available. In 2012–13, 25% of upper-school students received aid. Total amount of financial aid awarded in 2012–13: $175,000.

Admissions Traditional secondary-level entrance grade is 9. For fall 2012, 70 students applied for upper-level admission, 65 were accepted, 60 enrolled. Placement test required. Deadline for receipt of application materials: none. Application fee required: $200. Interview required.

Athletics Interscholastic: baseball (boys), basketball (b,g), cheering (g), cross-country running (b,g), football (b), golf (b,g), soccer (b,g), softball (g), swimming and diving (b,g), tennis (g), track and field (b,g), volleyball (b,g); intramural: equestrian sports (g); coed interscholastic: dance team. 5 PE instructors, 15 coaches, 4 athletic trainers.

Computers Computers are regularly used in computer applications classes. Computer network features include Internet access, Internet filtering or blocking technology. Student e-mail accounts are available to students. Students grades are available online. The school has a published electronic and media policy.

Contact Mrs. Denise Karlsen, Registrar. 949-443-4050 Ext. 1201. Fax: 949-443-3941. E-mail: denisek@svcschools.org. Website: www.svcschools.org

SADDLEBROOK PREPARATORY SCHOOL

5700 Saddlebrook Way
Wesley Chapel, Florida 33543

Head of School: Mr. Larry W. Robison

General Information Coeducational boarding and day college-preparatory school. Boarding grades 6–12, day grades 3–12. Founded: 1993. Setting: suburban. Nearest major city is Tampa. Students are housed in single-sex dormitories. 50-acre campus. 8 buildings on campus. Approved or accredited by Southern Association of Colleges and Schools and Florida Department of Education. Total enrollment: 80. Upper school average class size: 8. Upper school faculty-student ratio: 1:8. There are 175 required school days per year for Upper School students. Upper School students typically attend 5 days per week. The average school day consists of 7 hours and 15 minutes.

Upper School Student Profile Grade 9: 14 students (12 boys, 2 girls); Grade 10: 18 students (13 boys, 5 girls); Grade 11: 13 students (10 boys, 3 girls); Grade 12: 18 students (13 boys, 5 girls); Postgraduate: 3 students (3 boys). 55% of students are boarding students. 20% are state residents. 12 states are represented in upper school student body. 69% are international students. International students from Brazil, China, India, Mexico, Russian Federation, and Turkey; 19 other countries represented in student body.

Faculty School total: 12. In upper school: 1 man, 6 women; 6 have advanced degrees.

Subjects Offered Algebra, American government, American history, biology, calculus, chemistry, economics, English, French, geometry, marine biology, physical science, physics, pre-algebra, pre-calculus, probability and statistics, SAT preparation, Spanish, world geography, world history.

Graduation Requirements Algebra, American government, American history, biology, chemistry, economics, English, geometry, mathematics, physical education (includes health), physical science, science, social studies (includes history), world history.

Special Academic Programs Honors section; ESL (18 students enrolled).

College Admission Counseling 16 students graduated in 2013; all went to college, including College of Charleston; Francis Marion University; Northwestern University; The Johns Hopkins University; The University of Tampa; University of Richmond.

Student Life Upper grades have uniform requirement, student council, honor system. Discipline rests primarily with faculty.

Summer Programs Remediation, enrichment, advancement, ESL, sports, art/fine arts programs offered; session focuses on academics; held on campus; accepts boys and girls; open to students from other schools. 8 students usually enrolled. 2014 schedule: June 4 to August 2. Application deadline: May 25.

Tuition and Aid Day student tuition: $16,885; 7-day tuition and room/board: $32,885. Tuition installment plan (individually arranged payment plans). Tuition reduction for siblings available.

Admissions Traditional secondary-level entrance grade is 12. For fall 2013, 60 students applied for upper-level admission, 51 were accepted, 46 enrolled. Deadline for receipt of application materials: none. Application fee required: $50. Interview recommended.

Athletics Interscholastic: golf (boys). 28 coaches, 3 athletic trainers.

Computers Computers are regularly used in English, foreign language, history, mathematics, science classes. Computer network features include on-campus library services, online commercial services, Internet access, wireless campus network, Internet filtering or blocking technology, RenWeb. Student e-mail accounts and computer access in designated common areas are available to students. Students grades are available online. The school has a published electronic and media policy.

Contact Ms. Donna Claggett, Administrative Manager. 813-907-4525. Fax: 813-991-4713. E-mail: dclaggett@saddlebrook.com. Website: www.saddlebrookprep.com

SAGE HILL SCHOOL

20402 Newport Coast Drive
Newport Coast, California 92657-0300

Head of School: Mr. Gordon McNeill

General Information Coeducational day college-preparatory and arts school. Grades 9–12. Founded: 2000. Setting: suburban. Nearest major city is Newport Beach. 30-acre campus. 6 buildings on campus. Approved or accredited by Western Association of Schools and Colleges and California Department of Education. Member of National Association of Independent Schools. Endowment: $12.2 million. Total enrollment: 479. Upper school average class size: 15. Upper school faculty-student ratio: 1:10. There are 165 required school days per year for Upper School students. Upper School students typically attend 5 days per week. The average school day consists of 6 hours and 20 minutes.

Upper School Student Profile Grade 9: 129 students (62 boys, 67 girls); Grade 10: 126 students (64 boys, 62 girls); Grade 11: 117 students (57 boys, 60 girls); Grade 12: 107 students (51 boys, 56 girls).

Faculty School total: 46. In upper school: 22 men, 24 women; 24 have advanced degrees.

Subjects Offered Advanced biology, advanced chemistry, advanced math, Advanced Placement courses, algebra, American history, American history-AP, art, art history-AP, athletics, biology, biology-AP, British literature, calculus, calculus-AP, ceramics, chemistry, chemistry-AP, Chinese, choral music, computer science-AP, dance, dance performance, digital art, economics-AP, English, English literature and composition-AP, English-AP, environmental science-AP, French, geometry, honors algebra, honors English, honors geometry, human anatomy, instrumental music, international relations, Latin, marine science, modern dance, modern world history, music, music theory-AP, physical science, physics-AP, pre-calculus, psychology, psychology-AP, Spanish, Spanish-AP, statistics-AP, studio art-AP, theater, theater design and production, U.S. history, U.S. history-AP, United States government-AP, wind ensemble.

Graduation Requirements Arts, English, history, languages, mathematics, physical education (includes health), science.

Special Academic Programs 19 Advanced Placement exams for which test preparation is offered; honors section; independent study; academic accommodation for the gifted, the musically talented, and the artistically talented.

College Admission Counseling 118 students graduated in 2013; all went to college, including Cornell University; New York University; Southern Methodist University; University of California, Berkeley; University of Pennsylvania. Mean SAT critical reading: 638, mean SAT math: 646, mean SAT writing: 658, mean combined SAT: 1942, mean composite ACT: 29.

Student Life Upper grades have specified standards of dress, student council, honor system. Discipline rests equally with students and faculty.

Summer Programs Remediation, enrichment, advancement, sports, art/fine arts programs offered; session focuses on academics; held on campus; accepts boys and girls; open to students from other schools. 400 students usually enrolled. 2014 schedule: June to July.

Tuition and Aid Day student tuition: $31,770. Tuition installment plan (SMART Tuition Payment Plan, monthly payment plans). Need-based scholarship grants available. In 2013–14, 14% of upper-school students received aid. Total amount of financial aid awarded in 2013–14: $1,862,760.

Admissions Traditional secondary-level entrance grade is 9. For fall 2013, 296 students applied for upper-level admission, 207 were accepted, 139 enrolled. ISEE required. Deadline for receipt of application materials: February 15. Application fee required: $100. On-campus interview required.

Athletics Interscholastic: baseball (boys), basketball (b,g), cross-country running (b,g), diving (b,g), football (b), golf (b,g), lacrosse (b,g), soccer (b,g), swimming and diving (b,g), tennis (b,g), track and field (b,g), volleyball (b,g), water polo (b). 3 PE instructors, 45 coaches, 1 athletic trainer.

Computers Computers are regularly used in computer applications, digital applications, video film production classes. Computer network features include on-campus library services, online commercial services, Internet access, wireless campus network, Internet filtering or blocking technology. Student e-mail accounts and computer access in designated common areas are available to students. Students grades are available online. The school has a published electronic and media policy.

Contact Ms. Elaine Mijalis-Kahn, Director of Admission and Financial Aid. 949-219-1337. Fax: 949-219-1399. E-mail: mijaliskahne@sagehillschool.org. Website: www.sagehillschool.org

SAGE RIDGE SCHOOL

2515 Crossbow Court
Reno, Nevada 89511

General Information Coeducational day college-preparatory, arts, and technology school. Grades 5–12. Founded: 1997. Setting: suburban. 44-acre campus. 2 buildings on campus. Approved or accredited by Northwest Association of Independent Schools and Nevada Department of Education. Member of National Association of Independent Schools. Total enrollment: 215. Upper school average class size: 14. Upper school faculty-student ratio: 1:6. There are 180 required school days per year for Upper School students. Upper School students typically attend 5 days per week. The average school day consists of 7 hours and 10 minutes.

Upper School Student Profile Grade 9: 31 students (18 boys, 13 girls); Grade 10: 18 students (9 boys, 9 girls); Grade 11: 20 students (11 boys, 9 girls); Grade 12: 16 students (6 boys, 10 girls).

Faculty School total: 32. In upper school: 8 men, 8 women; 9 have advanced degrees.

Subjects Offered Advanced chemistry, algebra, American history-AP, American literature, American literature-AP, analytic geometry, anatomy and physiology, ancient world history, art history, biology, biology-AP, British literature, British literature-AP, calculus, calculus-AP, ceramics, chemistry, choir, classical language, college counseling, conceptual physics, creative writing, debate, drama performance, electives, English language and composition-AP, English language-AP, English literature and composition-AP, English literature-AP, European history, European literature, foreign language, geometry, honors algebra, honors English, lab science, language-AP, Latin, Latin-AP, medieval history, modern European history, music history, music performance, music theory, outdoor education, philosophy, physical education, physical fitness, physics, playwriting and directing, poetry, pre-algebra, pre-calculus, probability and statistics, public speaking, senior internship, senior seminar, senior thesis, Spanish, Spanish language-AP, Spanish literature, Spanish literature-AP, Spanish-AP, statistics, studio art, studio art-AP, theater, theater arts, theater history, theory of knowledge, trigonometry, U.S. government and politics-AP, U.S. history, U.S. history-AP, Western literature, world history.

Graduation Requirements 20th century world history, algebra, American history, American literature, analytic geometry, ancient world history, art history, biology, British literature, chemistry, conceptual physics, English composition, European history, foreign language, history of music, modern European history, music, outdoor education, participation in sports, pre-calculus, public speaking, science, senior internship, senior thesis, speech, theater history, trigonometry, U.S. history, 15 hours of community service per year, senior thesis and senior internship, two mini-semester seminars per year.

Special Academic Programs 16 Advanced Placement exams for which test preparation is offered; honors section; independent study.

College Admission Counseling 20 students graduated in 2012; all went to college, including Dartmouth College; Duke University; Pepperdine University. Mean SAT critical reading: 612, mean SAT math: 660, mean SAT writing: 636, mean combined SAT: 1907, mean composite ACT: 27.

Student Life Upper grades have uniform requirement, student council, honor system. Discipline rests equally with students and faculty.

Tuition and Aid Day student tuition: $18,300. Tuition installment plan (Insured Tuition Payment Plan). Need-based scholarship grants available. In 2012–13, 13% of upper-school students received aid. Total amount of financial aid awarded in 2012–13: $179,225.

Admissions Traditional secondary-level entrance grade is 9. ERB required. Deadline for receipt of application materials: none. Application fee required: $50. Interview required.

Athletics Interscholastic: alpine skiing (boys, girls), basketball (b,g), cross-country running (b,g), golf (b), skiing (downhill) (b,g), track and field (b,g), volleyball (g), wrestling (b,g); intramural: alpine skiing (b,g), basketball (b,g), cross-country running (b,g), golf (b,g), skiing (downhill) (b,g), swimming and diving (b,g), track and field (b,g), volleyball (g); coed intramural: bicycling, Frisbee, lacrosse, outdoor education, ropes courses, soccer. 2 PE instructors, 13 coaches.

Computers Computers are regularly used in art, classics, college planning, current events, English, foreign language, history, humanities, independent study, Latin, literary magazine, mathematics, newspaper, publications, SAT preparation, science, senior seminar, social sciences, social studies, Spanish, speech, word processing, writing, yearbook classes. Computer network features include on-campus library services, online commercial services, Internet access, wireless campus network, Internet filtering or blocking technology. Student e-mail accounts are available to students. Students grades are available online. The school has a published electronic and media policy.

Contact Mrs. Laurice Antoun-Becker, Director of Admission. 775-852-6222 Ext. 509. Fax: 775-852-6228. E-mail: LBecker@sageridge.org. Website: www.sageridge.org

ST. AGNES ACADEMY

9000 Bellaire Boulevard
Houston, Texas 77036

Head of School: Sr. Jane Meyer

General Information Girls' day college-preparatory, arts, business, religious studies, and technology school, affiliated with Roman Catholic Church. Grades 9–12. Founded: 1906. Setting: urban. 33-acre campus. 3 buildings on campus. Approved or accredited by Southern Association of Colleges and Schools, Texas Catholic Conference, and Texas Department of Education. Endowment: $9 million. Total enrollment: 899. Upper school average class size: 19. Upper school faculty-student ratio: 1:12. There are 180 required school days per year for Upper School students. Upper School students typically attend 5 days per week. The average school day consists of 6 hours and 50 minutes.

Upper School Student Profile Grade 9: 232 students (232 girls); Grade 10: 236 students (236 girls); Grade 11: 226 students (226 girls); Grade 12: 205 students (205 girls). 76% of students are Roman Catholic.

Faculty School total: 87. In upper school: 21 men, 66 women; 55 have advanced degrees.

Subjects Offered Accounting, acting, algebra, American history, American literature, art, art history, biology, business law, business skills, calculus, chemistry, community service, computer programming, computer science, creative writing, dance, digital photography, drama, economics, English, English literature, European history, fine arts, French, geology, geometry, government/civics, health, history, integrated physics, journalism, keyboarding, Latin, marine biology, mathematics, music, philosophy, photography, physical education, physics, physiology, psychology, religion, science, social sciences, social studies, Spanish, speech, theater, theology, trigonometry, video film production, world history, world literature.

Graduation Requirements Advanced Placement courses, arts and fine arts (art, music, dance, drama), computer science, electives, English, foreign language, mathematics, physical education (includes health), religion (includes Bible studies and theology), science, social sciences, social studies (includes history), speech, 100 hours of community service.

Special Academic Programs Advanced Placement exam preparation; honors section; independent study.

College Admission Counseling 207 students graduated in 2013; all went to college, including Louisiana State University and Agricultural and Mechanical College; St. Edward's University; Texas A&M University; The University of Texas at Austin; The University of Texas at San Antonio. Mean SAT critical reading: 620, mean SAT math: 620, mean composite ACT: 26. 56% scored over 600 on SAT critical reading, 58% scored over 600 on SAT math, 50% scored over 26 on composite ACT.

Student Life Upper grades have uniform requirement, student council, honor system. Discipline rests primarily with faculty. Attendance at religious services is required.

Summer Programs Remediation, art/fine arts, computer instruction programs offered; session focuses on remediation and elective credit; held on campus; accepts girls; not open to students from other schools. 100 students usually enrolled. 2014 schedule: June to June.

Tuition and Aid Day student tuition: $15,450. Tuition installment plan (plans arranged through local bank). Merit scholarship grants, need-based scholarship grants available. In 2013–14, 30% of upper-school students received aid; total upper-school merit-scholarship money awarded: $24,000. Total amount of financial aid awarded in 2013–14: $983,000.

Admissions Traditional secondary-level entrance grade is 9. For fall 2013, 552 students applied for upper-level admission, 321 were accepted, 232 enrolled. High School Placement Test or ISEE required. Deadline for receipt of application materials: January 15. Application fee required: $75.

Athletics Interscholastic: aquatics, basketball, cheering, cross-country running, dance team, diving, field hockey, golf, lacrosse, soccer, softball, swimming and diving, tennis, track and field, volleyball, water polo, winter soccer; intramural: badminton, floor hockey, volleyball, yoga. 5 PE instructors, 8 coaches, 1 athletic trainer.

Computers Computers are regularly used in all classes. Computer network features include on-campus library services, online commercial services, Internet access, wireless campus network, Internet filtering or blocking technology. Campus intranet and student e-mail accounts are available to students. Students grades are available online. The school has a published electronic and media policy.

Contact Maddy Echols, Admissions Coordinator. 713-219-5400. Fax: 713-219-5499. E-mail: maddy.echols@st-agnes.org. Website: www.st-agnes.org

ST. ALBANS SCHOOL

Mount Saint Alban
Washington, District of Columbia 20016

Head of School: Mr. Vance Wilson

General Information Boys' boarding and day college-preparatory school, affiliated with Episcopal Church. Boarding grades 9–12, day grades 4–12. Founded: 1909. Setting: urban. Students are housed in single-sex dormitories. 54-acre campus. 7 buildings on campus. Approved or accredited by Association of Independent Maryland Schools, Association of Independent Schools of Greater Washington, The Association of Boarding Schools, Western Catholic Education Association, and District of Columbia Department of Education. Member of National Association of Independent Schools and Secondary School Admission Test Board. Endowment: $51.3 million. Total enrollment: 593. Upper school average class size: 13. Upper school faculty-student ratio: 1:7. There are 170 required school days per year for Upper School students. Upper School students typically attend 5 days per week. The average school day consists of 9 hours and 30 minutes.

Upper School Student Profile Grade 9: 84 students (84 boys); Grade 10: 82 students (82 boys); Grade 11: 80 students (80 boys); Grade 12: 77 students (77 boys). 9% of students are boarding students. 47% are state residents. 5 states are represented in upper school student body. 2% are international students. International students from Bulgaria, China, and United Kingdom. 20% of students are members of Episcopal Church.

Faculty School total: 80. In upper school: 49 men, 21 women; 45 have advanced degrees; 6 reside on campus.

Subjects Offered Advanced Placement courses, algebra, American history, American literature, Ancient Greek, art, art history, art history-AP, Bible studies, biology, biotechnology, calculus, ceramics, chemistry, Chinese, community service, computer math, computer programming, computer science, creative writing, dance, directing, drama, earth science, economics, engineering, English, English literature, ethics, European history, expository writing, filmmaking, fine arts, French, geography, geology, geometry, government/civics, Greek, history, Japanese, Latin, marine biology, mathematics, music, photography, physical education, physics, religion, science, sculpture, social studies, Spanish, speech, stagecraft, theater, zoology.

Graduation Requirements American history, ancient history, arts and fine arts (art, music, dance, drama), English, ethics, foreign language, mathematics, physical education (includes health), science, participation in athletic program, participation in community service. Community service is required.

Special Academic Programs Advanced Placement exam preparation; honors section; independent study; term-away projects; study abroad.

College Admission Counseling 79 students graduated in 2013; all went to college, including Dartmouth College; Georgetown University; Harvard University; University of Pennsylvania; Wake Forest University; Yale University.

Student Life Upper grades have specified standards of dress, student council, honor system. Discipline rests equally with students and faculty. Attendance at religious services is required.

Summer Programs Remediation, enrichment, advancement, ESL, sports, art/fine arts, rigorous outdoor training, computer instruction programs offered; session focuses on academics, day camp, and sports camps; held on campus; accepts boys and girls; open to students from other schools. 1,500 students usually enrolled. 2014 schedule: June 10 to August 23. Application deadline: none.

Tuition and Aid Day student tuition: $38,082; 7-day tuition and room/board: $53,870. Tuition installment plan (Insured Tuition Payment Plan, monthly payment plans, individually arranged payment plans). Need-based scholarship grants, need-based loans available. In 2013–14, 27% of upper-school students received aid. Total amount of financial aid awarded in 2013–14: $2,541,164.

Admissions Traditional secondary-level entrance grade is 9. For fall 2013, 149 students applied for upper-level admission, 57 were accepted, 32 enrolled. ISEE or SSAT required. Deadline for receipt of application materials: January 10. Application fee required: $80. Interview required.

Athletics Interscholastic: aquatics, baseball, basketball, canoeing/kayaking, climbing, crew, cross-country running, diving, football, golf, ice hockey, independent competitive sports, indoor soccer, indoor track, indoor track & field, kayaking, lacrosse, rappelling, rock climbing, soccer, swimming and diving, tennis, track and field, wall climbing, weight training, winter (indoor) track, winter soccer, wrestling; intramural: aquatics, basketball, combined training, dance, fitness, indoor soccer, outdoor activities, physical training, tennis, track and field, weight lifting, yoga. 5 coaches, 2 athletic trainers.

Computers Computers are regularly used in all academic, mathematics, programming, science classes. Computer network features include on-campus library services, online commercial services, Internet access, wireless campus network. Campus intranet and student e-mail accounts are available to students. The school has a published electronic and media policy.

Contact Mrs. Melissa Larocque, Admissions and Financial Aid Coordinator. 202-537-6440. Fax: 202-537-2225. E-mail: mlarocque@cathedral.org. Website: www.stalbansschool.org/

SAINT ALBERT JUNIOR-SENIOR HIGH SCHOOL

400 Gleason Avenue
Council Bluffs, Iowa 51503

Head of School: Mr. David M. Schweitzer

General Information college-preparatory school, affiliated with Roman Catholic Church. Founded: 1963. Setting: suburban. 5-acre campus. 1 building on campus. Approved or accredited by North Central Association of Colleges and Schools and Iowa Department of Education. Endowment: $1 million. Total enrollment: 740. Upper school average class size: 20. Upper school faculty-student ratio: 1:10. There are 190 required school days per year for Upper School students. Upper School students typically attend 5 days per week. The average school day consists of 7 hours.

Upper School Student Profile Grade 7: 51 students (31 boys, 20 girls); Grade 8: 72 students (35 boys, 37 girls); Grade 9: 45 students (18 boys, 27 girls); Grade 10: 55 students (24 boys, 31 girls); Grade 11: 57 students (34 boys, 23 girls); Grade 12: 50 students (30 boys, 20 girls). 98% are state residents. 2 states are represented in upper school student body. 1% are international students. 85% of students are Roman Catholic.

Faculty School total: 33. In upper school: 13 men, 20 women; 18 have advanced degrees.

Subjects Offered U.S. history.

Graduation Requirements World religions.

Special Academic Programs 9 Advanced Placement exams for which test preparation is offered; honors section; study at local college for college credit; academic accommodation for the gifted; remedial reading and/or remedial writing; remedial math; special instructional classes for deaf students.

College Admission Counseling 43 students graduated in 2013; all went to college, including Iowa State University of Science and Technology; The University of Iowa; University of Nebraska–Lincoln; University of Nebraska at Omaha; University of Northern Iowa. Median composite ACT: 24. 60% scored over 26 on composite ACT.

Student Life Upper grades have uniform requirement, student council. Discipline rests primarily with faculty. Attendance at religious services is required.

Summer Programs Remediation programs offered; held on campus; accepts boys and girls; not open to students from other schools. 10 students usually enrolled. 2014 schedule: June 1 to June 30.

Tuition and Aid Day student tuition: $7200. Tuition installment plan (monthly payment plans, individually arranged payment plans). Tuition reduction for siblings, merit scholarship grants, need-based scholarship grants, paying campus jobs available. In 2013–14, 30% of upper-school students received aid; total upper-school merit-scholarship money awarded: $15,000. Total amount of financial aid awarded in 2013–14: $380,000.

Admissions Traditional secondary-level entrance grade is 9. For fall 2013, 15 students applied for upper-level admission, 12 were accepted, 10 enrolled. Deadline for receipt of application materials: none. No application fee required. Interview recommended.

Athletics Interscholastic: baseball (boys), basketball (b,g), bowling (b,g), cheering (g), cross-country running (b,g), dance (g), dance squad (g), dance team (g), football (b), golf (b,g), soccer (b,g), softball (g), swimming and diving (b,g), tennis (b,g), track and field (b,g), wrestling (b). 3 PE instructors, 53 coaches, 1 athletic trainer.

Computers Computers are regularly used in all classes. Computer network features include Internet access, wireless campus network, Internet filtering or blocking technology. Campus intranet and student e-mail accounts are available to students. Students grades are available online. The school has a published electronic and media policy.

Contact Ms. Abby Jares, Admissions Coordinator. 712-328-2316. Fax: 712-328-0228. E-mail: jaresa@saintalbertschools.org. Website: www.saintalbertschools.org/

ST. ANDREW'S COLLEGE

15800 Yonge Street
Aurora, Ontario L4G 3H7, Canada

Head of School: Mr. Kevin R. McHenry

General Information Boys' boarding and day college-preparatory, arts, business, and technology school. Grades 5–12. Founded: 1899. Setting: small town. Nearest major city is Toronto, Canada. Students are housed in single-sex dormitories. 110-acre campus. 24 buildings on campus. Approved or accredited by Canadian Association of Independent Schools, Canadian Educational Standards Institute, Conference of Independent Schools of Ontario, Ontario Ministry of Education, The Association of Boarding Schools, and Ontario Department of Education. Affiliate member of National Association of Independent Schools; member of Secondary School Admission Test Board. Language of instruction: English. Endowment: CAN$25 million. Total enrollment: 613. Upper school average class size: 17. Upper school faculty-student ratio: 1:8. There are 158 required school days per year for Upper School students. Upper School students typically attend 5 days per week. The average school day consists of 5 hours and 20 minutes.

Upper School Student Profile Grade 9: 109 students (109 boys); Grade 10: 108 students (108 boys); Grade 11: 128 students (128 boys); Grade 12: 101 students (101 boys). 50% of students are boarding students. 71% are province residents. 7 provinces are represented in upper school student body. 27% are international students.

International students from China, Hong Kong, Mexico, Republic of Korea, Russian Federation, and United States; 34 other countries represented in student body.

Faculty School total: 72. In upper school: 47 men, 7 women; 16 have advanced degrees; 24 reside on campus.

Subjects Offered Accounting, Advanced Placement courses, algebra, American history, art, biology, business, calculus, chemistry, communications, community service, computer science, creative writing, drama, economics, English, English literature, environmental science, fine arts, French, geography, geometry, health, history, mathematics, music, physical education, physics, physiology, science, social sciences, social studies, sociology, Spanish, statistics, world history, world religions.

Graduation Requirements Arts, arts and fine arts (art, music, dance, drama), business, careers, civics, computer science, drama, English, foreign language, French, geography, health education, history, mathematics, physical education (includes health), science, science and technology, social sciences. Community service is required.

Special Academic Programs 10 Advanced Placement exams for which test preparation is offered; honors section; accelerated programs; independent study; term-away projects; study abroad; ESL (60 students enrolled).

College Admission Counseling 133 students graduated in 2013; 128 went to college, including Queen's University at Kingston; The University of British Columbia; The University of Western Ontario; University of Guelph; University of Toronto; Wilfrid Laurier University. Other: 5 had other specific plans.

Student Life Upper grades have uniform requirement, student council, honor system. Discipline rests equally with students and faculty. Attendance at religious services is required.

Summer Programs Remediation, advancement, ESL, sports, art/fine arts programs offered; session focuses on Scottish music (piping and drumming), sports/arts camps, leadership camps, academics; held on campus; accepts boys and girls; open to students from other schools. 1,200 students usually enrolled. 2014 schedule: June 19 to August 15. Application deadline: none.

Tuition and Aid Day student tuition: CAN$30,280; 5-day tuition and room/board: CAN$48,725; 7-day tuition and room/board: CAN$48,725. Tuition installment plan (monthly payment plans, one-time payment, three installments plan, Plastiq). Bursaries, merit scholarship grants, need-based scholarship grants available. In 2013–14, 26% of upper-school students received aid; total upper-school merit-scholarship money awarded: CAN$363,000. Total amount of financial aid awarded in 2013–14: CAN$1,877,530.

Admissions Traditional secondary-level entrance grade is 9. For fall 2013, 162 students applied for upper-level admission, 108 were accepted, 88 enrolled. CAT, SSAT or TOEFL or SLEP required. Deadline for receipt of application materials: none. Application fee required: CAN$150. Interview required.

Athletics Interscholastic: alpine skiing, aquatics, badminton, baseball, basketball, biathlon, cricket, cross-country running, curling, fencing, football, golf, ice hockey, indoor track, indoor track & field, lacrosse, marksmanship, nordic skiing, rugby, running, skiing (cross-country), skiing (downhill), soccer, softball, squash, swimming and diving, table tennis, tennis, track and field, triathlon, volleyball, winter (indoor) track; intramural: aquatics, archery, backpacking, badminton, baseball, basketball, canoeing/kayaking, climbing, cooperative games, cross-country running, curling, fencing, fitness, floor hockey, football, golf, hiking/backpacking, ice hockey, ice skating, jogging, lacrosse, marksmanship, mountain biking, nordic skiing, outdoor activities, outdoor education, outdoor recreation, outdoor skills, physical fitness, riflery, rock climbing, ropes courses, running, scuba diving, self defense, skiing (cross-country), skiing (downhill), soccer, softball, squash, strength & conditioning, swimming and diving, table tennis, tennis, touch football, track and field, triathlon, ultimate Frisbee, volleyball, wall climbing, water polo, weight lifting, weight training, wilderness survival, yoga. 5 athletic trainers.

Computers Computers are regularly used in all academic classes. Computer network features include on-campus library services, online commercial services, Internet access, wireless campus network, Internet filtering or blocking technology. The school has a published electronic and media policy.

Contact Mrs. Wendy Coates, Admission Associate. 905-727-3178 Ext. 303. Fax: 905-727-9032. E-mail: admission@sac.on.ca. Website: www.sac.on.ca

ST. ANDREW'S EPISCOPAL SCHOOL

8804 Postoak Road
Potomac, Maryland 20854

Head of School: Mr. Robert Kosasky

General Information Coeducational day college-preparatory school, affiliated with Episcopal Church. Grades PS–12. Founded: 1978. Setting: suburban. Nearest major city is Washington, DC. 19-acre campus. 5 buildings on campus. Approved or accredited by Association of Independent Maryland Schools, Association of Independent Schools of Greater Washington, Middle States Association of Colleges and Schools, and National Association of Episcopal Schools. Member of National Association of Independent Schools and Secondary School Admission Test Board. Endowment: $6 million. Total enrollment: 506. Upper school average class size: 14. Upper school faculty-student ratio: 1:7. There are 172 required days per year for Upper School students. Upper School students typically attend 5 days per week. The average school day consists of 6 hours and 40 minutes.

Upper School Student Profile Grade 6: 22 students (11 boys, 11 girls); Grade 7: 37 students (16 boys, 21 girls); Grade 8: 47 students (25 boys, 22 girls); Grade 9: 75 students (38 boys, 37 girls); Grade 10: 60 students (38 boys, 22 girls); Grade 11: 65 students (29 boys, 36 girls); Grade 12: 60 students (36 boys, 24 girls). 21% of students are members of Episcopal Church.

Faculty School total: 66. In upper school: 18 men, 22 women; 27 have advanced degrees.

Subjects Offered 20th century history, 3-dimensional art, 3-dimensional design, acting, Advanced Placement courses, advanced studio art-AP, algebra, American history, American literature, art, art history, art history-AP, art-AP, athletics, band, Bible, biology, biology-AP, British literature, calculus, calculus-AP, ceramics, chemistry, chorus, civics, college counseling, composition-AP, computer animation, computer art, computer graphics, computer science, creative writing, dance, digital photography, drama, dramatic arts, earth science, English, English literature, English literature and composition-AP, English-AP, ethics, European history, fine arts, French, French language-AP, French literature-AP, geography, geometry, global studies, government/civics, guitar, health, history, instrumental music, jazz band, journalism, Latin, Latin American studies, Latin-AP, mathematics, modern European history, music, musical theater, newspaper, orchestra, organic biochemistry, painting, photography, physical education, physical science, physics, physics-AP, pre-algebra, pre-calculus, public speaking, religion, robotics, science, service learning/internship, Spanish, Spanish language-AP, Spanish literature-AP, Spanish-AP, sports, stage design, statistics, student publications, studio art, studio art-AP, theater, theater design and production, theology, trigonometry, U.S. history, U.S. history-AP, video, visual and performing arts, vocal music, world cultures, world history, world religions, writing, yearbook.

Graduation Requirements English, foreign language, history, mathematics, performing arts, physical education (includes health), religion (includes Bible studies and theology), science, senior thesis, visual arts. Community service is required.

Special Academic Programs Advanced Placement exam preparation; independent study; special instructional classes for deaf students; ESL (4 students enrolled).

College Admission Counseling 72 students graduated in 2013; all went to college, including American University; Duke University; Franklin & Marshall College; University of Delaware; University of Maryland, College Park; Wake Forest University.

Student Life Upper grades have specified standards of dress, student council, honor system. Discipline rests primarily with faculty. Attendance at religious services is required.

Summer Programs Enrichment, advancement, sports, art/fine arts programs offered; session focuses on advancement and enrichment; held on campus; accepts boys and girls; open to students from other schools. 400 students usually enrolled. 2014 schedule: June 17 to August 2. Application deadline: none.

Tuition and Aid Day student tuition: $36,000. Tuition installment plan (FACTS Tuition Payment Plan, monthly payment plans). Need-based scholarship grants, Achiever Loans (Key Education Resources) available. In 2013–14, 22% of upper-school students received aid. Total amount of financial aid awarded in 2013–14: $2,193,800.

Admissions Traditional secondary-level entrance grade is 9. Comprehensive educational evaluation, ISEE or SSAT required. Deadline for receipt of application materials: January 15. Application fee required: $50. On-campus interview required.

Athletics Interscholastic: baseball (boys), basketball (b,g), cross-country running (b,g), lacrosse (b,g), soccer (b,g), softball (g), tennis (b,g), volleyball (g); coed interscholastic: equestrian sports, golf, track and field, wrestling; coed intramural: dance, fitness, physical fitness, weight training, winter (indoor) track. 12 coaches, 1 athletic trainer.

Computers Computers are regularly used in English, foreign language, graphic arts, history, journalism, mathematics, music, science classes. Computer network features include on-campus library services, online commercial services, Internet access, wireless campus network, Internet filtering or blocking technology. Campus intranet and student e-mail accounts are available to students. Students grades are available online. The school has a published electronic and media policy.

Contact Mrs. Aileen Moodie, Associate Director of Admission and Admission Office Coordinator. 301-983-5200 Ext. 236. Fax: 301-983-4620. E-mail: admission@saes.org. Website: www.saes.org

ST. ANDREW'S REGIONAL HIGH SCHOOL

880 Mckenzie Avenue
Victoria, British Columbia V8X 3G5, Canada

Head of School: Mr. Andrew Keleher

General Information Coeducational day college-preparatory, general academic, and religious studies school, affiliated with Roman Catholic Church. Grades 8–12. Founded: 1983. Setting: urban. 2-acre campus. 1 building on campus. Approved or accredited by British Columbia Department of Education. Language of instruction: English. Upper school average class size: 24. Upper school faculty-student ratio: 1:14. There are 178 required school days per year for Upper School students. Upper School students typically attend 5 days per week. The average school day consists of 5 hours.

Upper School Student Profile 65% of students are Roman Catholic.

Faculty School total: 30. In upper school: 14 men, 14 women; 11 have advanced degrees.

Subjects Offered Religious education, yoga.

Graduation Requirements Religious studies.

Special Academic Programs Honors section.

College Admission Counseling 103 students graduated in 2013. Other: 10 went to work, 90 entered a postgraduate year, 3 had other specific plans.

Student Life Upper grades have uniform requirement, student council, honor system. Discipline rests primarily with faculty. Attendance at religious services is required.

Tuition and Aid Tuition reduction for siblings, bursaries available.

Admissions Deadline for receipt of application materials: February 28. Application fee required: CAN$50. Interview required.

Athletics Interscholastic: badminton (boys, girls), basketball (b,g), bicycling (b,g), cross-country running (b,g); intramural: basketball (b,g); coed interscholastic: aquatics; coed intramural: dance team, floor hockey, indoor soccer.

Computers Computers are regularly used in business education, career education, computer applications, digital applications, photography classes. Computer resources include on-campus library services, Internet access, Internet filtering or blocking technology. The school has a published electronic and media policy.

Contact Diane Chimich, Vice Principal. 250-479-1414. Fax: 250-479-5356. E-mail: dchimich@cisdv.bc.ca. Website: www.standrewshigh.ca/

ST. ANDREW'S SCHOOL

63 Federal Road
Barrington, Rhode Island 02806

Head of School: Mr. John D. Martin

General Information Coeducational boarding and day college-preparatory and arts school. Boarding grades 9–12, day grades 6–12. Founded: 1893. Setting: suburban. Nearest major city is Providence. Students are housed in single-sex dormitories. 100-acre campus. 33 buildings on campus. Approved or accredited by Massachusetts Department of Education, National Association of Episcopal Schools, New England Association of Schools and Colleges, Rhode Island State Certified Resource Progam, The Association of Boarding Schools, and Rhode Island Department of Education. Member of National Association of Independent Schools and Secondary School Admission Test Board. Endowment: $16.4 million. Total enrollment: 205. Upper school average class size: 12. Upper school faculty-student ratio: 1:5. There are 150 required school days per year for Upper School students. Upper School students typically attend 5 days per week. The average school day consists of 8 hours.

Upper School Student Profile Grade 9: 34 students (23 boys, 11 girls); Grade 10: 40 students (22 boys, 18 girls); Grade 11: 47 students (31 boys, 16 girls); Grade 12: 51 students (32 boys, 19 girls); Postgraduate: 3 students (3 boys). 31% of students are boarding students. 59% are state residents. 8 states are represented in upper school student body. 18% are international students. International students from China, India, Republic of Korea, South Africa, Taiwan, and United Kingdom; 2 other countries represented in student body.

Faculty School total: 42. In upper school: 14 men, 24 women; 25 have advanced degrees; 21 reside on campus.

Subjects Offered Advanced biology, Advanced Placement courses, algebra, American history, ancient history, art, astronomy, biology, calculus, calculus-AP, ceramics, chemistry, chorus, college counseling, computer applications, creative writing, digital applications, digital photography, drawing, English, environmental science, ESL, European history, French, geometry, human anatomy, humanities, jewelry making, lab science, music history, music theory, music theory-AP, oceanography, oral communications, physical education, physics, pre-calculus, printmaking, probability and statistics, remedial study skills, Spanish, stagecraft, statistics-AP, studio art, study skills, technical theater, theater, TOEFL preparation, trigonometry, water color painting, yearbook.

Graduation Requirements Arts and fine arts (art, music, dance, drama), English, mathematics, physical education (includes health), science, social studies (includes history), community service.

Special Academic Programs Advanced Placement exam preparation; honors section; independent study; remedial reading and/or remedial writing; programs in English for dyslexic students; special instructional classes for deaf students, blind students, students with mild language-based learning disabilities, students with attention/organizational issues (ADHD); ESL (24 students enrolled).

College Admission Counseling 47 students graduated in 2013; 44 went to college, including Bard College; Brandeis University; Emory University; Fordham University; Gettysburg College; Worcester Polytechnic Institute. Other: 3 went to work. Median SAT critical reading: 480, median SAT math: 520, median SAT writing: 490, median combined SAT: 1540, median composite ACT: 20. 10% scored over 600 on SAT critical reading, 21% scored over 600 on SAT math, 10% scored over 600 on SAT writing, 10% scored over 1800 on combined SAT.

Student Life Upper grades have specified standards of dress, student council. Discipline rests primarily with faculty.

Summer Programs Remediation, enrichment, advancement, ESL, sports, art/fine arts, rigorous outdoor training, computer instruction programs offered; session focuses on skills development; held on campus; accepts boys and girls; open to students from

other schools. 800 students usually enrolled. 2014 schedule: June 23 to August 15. Application deadline: none.

Tuition and Aid Day student tuition: $32,800; 7-day tuition and room/board: $49,500. Tuition installment plan (Key Tuition Payment Plan). Need-based scholarship grants, need-based loans available. In 2013–14, 47% of upper-school students received aid. Total amount of financial aid awarded in 2013–14: $2,117,710.

Admissions Traditional secondary-level entrance grade is 9. For fall 2013, 291 students applied for upper-level admission, 137 were accepted, 52 enrolled. Any standardized test required. Deadline for receipt of application materials: January 15. Application fee required: $50. Interview required.

Athletics Interscholastic: basketball (boys, girls), cross-country running (b,g), golf (b), lacrosse (b,g), soccer (b,g), tennis (b,g); coed interscholastic: soccer; coed intramural: badminton, ball hockey, basketball, bicycling, billiards, bocce, cooperative games, croquet, dance, fitness, fitness walking, flag football, floor hockey, Frisbee, horseshoes, jogging, physical fitness, project adventure, ropes courses, running, soccer, strength & conditioning, tennis, touch football, ultimate Frisbee, walking, weight lifting, weight training, yoga. 1 PE instructor, 20 coaches, 1 athletic trainer.

Computers Computers are regularly used in all academic, computer applications, library skills, multimedia, photography, SAT preparation, yearbook classes. Computer network features include on-campus library services, Internet access, wireless campus network, Internet filtering or blocking technology, NetClassroom is available for parents and students. Campus intranet, student e-mail accounts, and computer access in designated common areas are available to students. Students grades are available online. The school has a published electronic and media policy.

Contact Kristel Dunphy, Assistant Director to Admissions. 401-246-1230 Ext. 3053. Fax: 401-246-0510. E-mail: kdunphy@standrews-ri.org. Website: www.standrews-ri.org

See Display on next page and Close-Up on page 566.

ST. ANDREW'S–SEWANEE SCHOOL

290 Quintard Road
Sewanee, Tennessee 37375-3000

Head of School: Rev. John T. Thomas

General Information Coeducational boarding and day college-preparatory, arts, and science school, affiliated with Episcopal Church. Boarding grades 9–12, day grades 6–12. Founded: 1868. Setting: small town. Nearest major city is Chattanooga. Students are housed in single-sex dormitories. 550-acre campus. 19 buildings on campus. Approved or accredited by National Association of Episcopal Schools, Southern Association of Colleges and Schools, Southern Association of Independent Schools, The Association of Boarding Schools, and Tennessee Department of Education. Member of National Association of Independent Schools and Secondary School Admission Test Board. Endowment: $11 million. Total enrollment: 248. Upper school average class size: 13. Upper school faculty-student ratio: 1:4. There are 168 required school days per year for Upper School students. Upper School students typically attend 5 days per week. The average school day consists of 4 hours and 30 minutes.

Upper School Student Profile Grade 9: 38 students (17 boys, 21 girls); Grade 10: 44 students (31 boys, 13 girls); Grade 11: 59 students (16 boys, 43 girls); Grade 12: 45 students (27 boys, 18 girls). 44% of students are boarding students. 72% are state residents. 14 states are represented in upper school student body. 16% are international students. International students from China, Costa Rica, Denmark, Germany, Republic of Korea, and Taiwan; 10 other countries represented in student body. 33% of students are members of Episcopal Church.

Faculty School total: 39. In upper school: 13 men, 23 women; 24 have advanced degrees; 26 reside on campus.

Subjects Offered 20th century history, acting, adolescent issues, advanced biology, advanced chemistry, advanced TOEFL/grammar, aerobics, African history, African-American literature, algebra, American history, American literature, American studies, art, Asian history, band, biology, British literature, British literature (honors), calculus, chamber groups, chemistry, Chinese, choir, college counseling, community service, comparative religion, creative writing, drama, dramatic arts, ecology, English, English literature, environmental systems, ESL, European literature, filmmaking, fine arts, general science, geometry, history, humanities, Latin, Latin American literature, leadership, literature, mathematics, minority studies, music, philosophy, physical education, physics, poetry, pottery, pre-algebra, psychology, religion, religious studies, science, social studies, Southern literature, Spanish, statistics, theater, trigonometry, world history, yearbook.

Graduation Requirements Arts and fine arts (art, music, dance, drama), English, foreign language, mathematics, physical education (includes health), religion (includes Bible studies and theology), science, social studies (includes history), senior lecture series, creedal statement. Community service is required.

Special Academic Programs Advanced Placement exam preparation; independent study; term-away projects; study at local college for college credit; study abroad; academic accommodation for the gifted, the musically talented, and the artistically talented; remedial reading and/or remedial writing; remedial math; ESL (16 students enrolled).

College Admission Counseling 46 students graduated in 2012; 42 went to college, including Northeastern University; Sewanee: The University of the South. Other: 4 went to work.

Student Life Upper grades have specified standards of dress, student council, honor system. Discipline rests equally with students and faculty. Attendance at religious services is required.

Tuition and Aid Day student tuition: $16,500; 7-day tuition and room/board: $40,000. Tuition installment plan (monthly payment plans). Merit scholarship grants, need-based scholarship grants available. In 2012–13, 48% of upper-school students received aid; total upper-school merit-scholarship money awarded: $148,000. Total amount of financial aid awarded in 2012–13: $1,365,590.

Admissions Traditional secondary-level entrance grade is 9. For fall 2012, 118 students applied for upper-level admission, 68 were accepted, 48 enrolled. SLEP, TOEFL or writing sample required. Deadline for receipt of application materials: none. Application fee required: $50. Interview required.

Athletics Interscholastic: baseball (boys), basketball (b,g), cross-country running (b,g), football (b), soccer (b,g), softball (g), swimming and diving (b,g), tennis (b,g), track and field (b,g), volleyball (g), wrestling (b,g); intramural: ballet (g); coed interscholastic: bicycling, cross-country running, golf, mountain biking, ultimate Frisbee; coed intramural: aerobics, aerobics/dance, backpacking, bicycling, billiards, canoeing/kayaking, climbing, combined training, dance, dance team, fishing, fitness, fly fishing, hiking/backpacking, independent competitive sports, kayaking, modern dance, mountain biking, mountaineering, outdoor activities, outdoor adventure, outdoor education, outdoor recreation, outdoor skills, outdoors, paint ball, physical fitness, physical training, rafting, rappelling, rock climbing, ropes courses, running, soccer, strength & conditioning, table tennis, tennis, touch football, triathlon, walking, wall climbing, weight training, wilderness, wilderness survival, yoga. 8 coaches.

Computers Computers are regularly used in all academic, art, college planning, creative writing, design, desktop publishing, digital applications, English, foreign language, graphic arts, graphic design, history, humanities, introduction to technology, Latin, literary magazine, mathematics, religion, SAT preparation, science, Spanish, yearbook classes. Computer network features include on-campus library services, online commercial services, Internet access, wireless campus network, Internet filtering or blocking technology, access to University of the South technology facilities. Student e-mail accounts and computer access in designated common areas are available to students. Students grades are available online.

Contact Ms. Anne Chenoweth, Director of Admission and Financial Aid. 931-598-5651 Ext. 2117. Fax: 931-914-1222. E-mail: admission@sasweb.org. Website: www.sasweb.org

ST. ANNE'S–BELFIELD SCHOOL

2132 Ivy Road
Charlottesville, Virginia 22903

Head of School: Mr. David S. Lourie

General Information Coeducational boarding and day college-preparatory, arts, religious studies, and ESL school, affiliated with Christian faith. Boarding grades 9–12, day grades PK–12. Founded: 1910. Setting: small town. Nearest major city is Washington, DC. Students are housed in coed dormitories. 49-acre campus. 6 buildings on campus. Approved or accredited by The Association of Boarding Schools and Virginia Association of Independent Schools. Member of National Association of Independent Schools and Secondary School Admission Test Board. Endowment: $25 million. Total enrollment: 869. Upper school average class size: 12. Upper school faculty-student ratio: 1:8. There are 180 required school days per year for Upper School students. Upper School students typically attend 5 days per week. The average school day consists of 7 hours and 30 minutes.

Upper School Student Profile Grade 9: 94 students (49 boys, 45 girls); Grade 10: 86 students (42 boys, 44 girls); Grade 11: 78 students (34 boys, 44 girls); Grade 12: 88 students (49 boys, 39 girls). 18% of students are boarding students. 87% are state residents. 7 states are represented in upper school student body. 9% are international students. International students from Azerbaijan, China, Ethiopia, Republic of Korea, Saint Kitts and Nevis, and South Africa; 22 other countries represented in student body.

Faculty School total: 111. In upper school: 16 men, 25 women; 35 have advanced degrees; 7 reside on campus.

Subjects Offered 1968, algebra, art, biology, biology-AP, calculus-AP, ceramics, chemistry, chemistry-AP, choir, conceptual physics, drama, economics, English, environmental science-AP, ESL, French, French language-AP, geometry, honors algebra, honors geometry, humanities, Latin, Latin-AP, modern European history-AP, modern world history, music theory, music theory-AP, orchestra, photography, physics, physics-AP, pre-calculus, religion, sculpture, Spanish, Spanish language-AP, statistics, statistics-AP, theology, trigonometry, U.S. history, U.S. history-AP, video, world history, writing workshop.

Graduation Requirements Art, English, foreign language, history, mathematics, physical education (includes health), religion (includes Bible studies and theology), science. Community service is required.

Special Academic Programs 14 Advanced Placement exams for which test preparation is offered; honors section; independent study; study at local college for college credit; ESL (12 students enrolled).

College Admission Counseling Colleges students went to include James Madison University; Lynchburg College; The College of William and Mary; University of Mary Washington; University of Virginia; Virginia Commonwealth University.

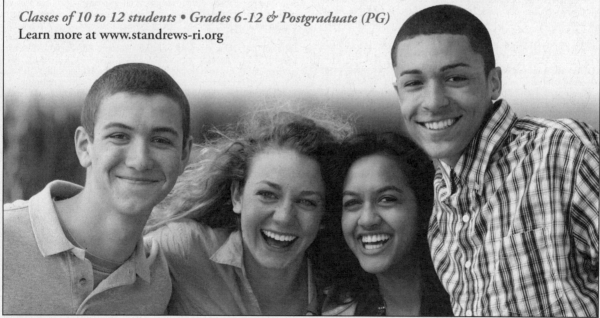

Other: 1 had other specific plans. Median SAT critical reading: 630, median SAT math: 620. Mean SAT writing: 622. 59% scored over 600 on SAT critical reading, 57% scored over 600 on SAT math, 68% scored over 600 on SAT writing, 72% scored over 1800 on combined SAT.

Student Life Upper grades have uniform requirement, student council, honor system. Discipline rests primarily with faculty. Attendance at religious services is required.

Tuition and Aid Day student tuition: $22,000; 5-day tuition and room/board: $36,200; 7-day tuition and room/board: $46,000. Tuition installment plan (Insured Tuition Payment Plan, FACTS Tuition Payment Plan, monthly payment plans). Need-based scholarship grants, need-based financial aid available. In 2012–13, 38% of upper-school students received aid. Total amount of financial aid awarded in 2012–13: $4,500,000.

Admissions Traditional secondary-level entrance grade is 9. For fall 2012, 104 students applied for upper-level admission, 60 were accepted, 45 enrolled. ERB verbal, ERB math, SSAT, TOEFL or writing sample required. Deadline for receipt of application materials: February 15. Application fee required: $30. Interview required.

Athletics Interscholastic: baseball (boys), basketball (b,g), cross-country running (b,g), field hockey (g), football (b), golf (b,g), lacrosse (b,g), soccer (b,g), softball (g), squash (b,g), swimming and diving (b,g), tennis (b,g), track and field (b,g), volleyball (g), wrestling (b); coed interscholastic: cross-country running, golf, squash, swimming and diving, track and field; coed intramural: aerobics, aerobics/dance, alpine skiing, dance, fitness, physical fitness, yoga. 6 PE instructors, 8 coaches, 2 athletic trainers.

Computers Computers are regularly used in all academic classes. Computer network features include on-campus library services, online commercial services, Internet access, wireless campus network. Student e-mail accounts and computer access in designated common areas are available to students. Students grades are available online. The school has a published electronic and media policy.

Contact Mrs. Kai'li Millner, Assistant Director of Admission for Grades 5-12. 434-296-5106. Fax: 434-979-1486. E-mail: kmillner@stab.org. Website: www.stab.org

ST. ANTHONY CATHOLIC HIGH SCHOOL

3200 McCullough Avenue
San Antonio, Texas 78212-3099

Head of School: Mr. Rene Escobedo

General Information Coeducational boarding and day and distance learning college-preparatory, arts, religious studies, technology, AP Dual Credit, and college course credit school, affiliated with Roman Catholic Church. Grades 9–12. Distance learning grades 9–12. Founded: 1903. Setting: urban. Students are housed in single-sex by floor dormitories. 14-acre campus. 5 buildings on campus. Approved or accredited by National Catholic Education Association, Southern Association of Colleges and Schools, Texas Catholic Conference, The College Board, and Texas Department of Education. Total enrollment: 391. Upper school average class size: 19. Upper school faculty-student ratio: 1:12. There are 180 required school days per year for Upper School students. Upper School students typically attend 5 days per week. The average school day consists of 7 hours.

Upper School Student Profile Grade 9: 96 students (59 boys, 37 girls); Grade 10: 93 students (50 boys, 43 girls); Grade 11: 108 students (65 boys, 43 girls); Grade 12: 94 students (55 boys, 39 girls). 4% of students are boarding students. 89% are state residents. 1 state is represented in upper school student body. 11% are international students. International students from China, Japan, Mexico, Republic of Korea, Spain, and Viet Nam; 1 other country represented in student body. 85% of students are Roman Catholic.

Faculty School total: 35. In upper school: 19 men, 16 women; 19 have advanced degrees.

Subjects Offered Advanced biology, advanced chemistry, advanced math, Advanced Placement courses, algebra, anatomy and physiology, art, athletics, band, Bible studies, biology, calculus, Catholic belief and practice, chemistry, choir, computer graphics, computer literacy, dance, drama, economics, English, English language and composition-AP, English literature, English literature and composition-AP, environmental science, ESL, film appreciation, geology, geometry, government, graphic arts, graphic design, health, history, history of the Catholic Church, honors algebra, Japanese, jazz band, keyboarding, Latin, mathematical modeling, media literacy, moral theology, photography, photojournalism, physical education, physics, pre-calculus, psychology, sexuality, sociology, Spanish, Spanish-AP, speech, theater, theater arts, theology, trigonometry, U.S. government, U.S. history, U.S. history-AP, world history, world history-AP, world religions, writing, yearbook.

Graduation Requirements Arts and fine arts (art, music, dance, drama), computer applications, economics, English, foreign language, government, health, mathematics, physical education (includes health), religion (includes Bible studies and theology), science, speech, U.S. history, world history.

Special Academic Programs Advanced Placement exam preparation; honors section; independent study; study at local college for college credit; study abroad; academic accommodation for the gifted; ESL (34 students enrolled).

College Admission Counseling 109 students graduated in 2012; all went to college, including San Antonio College; St. Mary's University; Texas A&M University; The University of Texas at San Antonio; University of the Incarnate Word. 8.3% scored over 600 on SAT critical reading, 15.6% scored over 600 on SAT math, 5.5% scored

over 600 on SAT writing, 5.5% scored over 1800 on combined SAT, 4.6% scored over 26 on composite ACT.

Student Life Upper grades have uniform requirement, student council, honor system. Discipline rests primarily with faculty. Attendance at religious services is required.

Tuition and Aid Day student tuition: $8575; 7-day tuition and room/board: $19,000. Tuition installment plan (monthly payment plans). Tuition reduction for siblings, merit scholarship grants, need-based scholarship grants available. In 2012–13, 37% of upper-school students received aid; total upper-school merit-scholarship money awarded: $50,000. Total amount of financial aid awarded in 2012–13: $175,000.

Admissions Traditional secondary-level entrance grade is 9. For fall 2012, 422 students applied for upper-level admission, 402 were accepted, 391 enrolled. High School Placement Test required. Deadline for receipt of application materials: none. No application fee required. Interview required.

Athletics Interscholastic: baseball (boys), basketball (b,g), cross-country running (b,g), dance team (g), football (b), lacrosse (b), soccer (b,g), softball (g), swimming and diving (b,g), tennis (b,g), track and field (b,g), volleyball (g); coed interscholastic: cheering, golf. 2 PE instructors, 32 coaches, 1 athletic trainer.

Computers Computers are regularly used in all academic classes. Computer network features include on-campus library services, Internet access, wireless campus network, Internet filtering or blocking technology. Student e-mail accounts are available to students. Students grades are available online. The school has a published electronic and media policy.

Contact Mr. Alejandro Calderon, Director of Enrollment. 210-832-5632. Fax: 210-832-5633. E-mail: sachs@uiwtx.edu. Website: www.sachs.org

SAINT ANTHONY HIGH SCHOOL

620 Olive Avenue
Long Beach, California 90802

Head of School: Mr. Mike Schabert

General Information Coeducational day college-preparatory, arts, business, religious studies, technology, Marine Science Academy, and Theatre Arts Program school, affiliated with Roman Catholic Church. Grades 9–12. Founded: 1920. Setting: urban. 15-acre campus. 5 buildings on campus. Approved or accredited by National Catholic Education Association, Western Association of Schools and Colleges, Western Catholic Education Association, and California Department of Education. Total enrollment: 480. Upper school average class size: 25. Upper school faculty-student ratio: 1:19. There are 180 required school days per year for Upper School students. Upper School students typically attend 5 days per week. The average school day consists of 7 hours and 15 minutes.

Upper School Student Profile 80% of students are Roman Catholic.

Faculty School total: 25. In upper school: 13 men, 12 women; 23 have advanced degrees.

Subjects Offered ACT preparation, acting, Advanced Placement courses, algebra, American history, American history-AP, American literature-AP, anatomy and physiology, art, ASB Leadership, athletics, band, Bible studies, biology, biology-AP, British literature, calculus, calculus-AP, campus ministry, career and personal planning, career/college preparation, Catholic belief and practice, ceramics, cheerleading, chemistry, chemistry-AP, choir, Christian doctrine, Christian ethics, Christian scripture, Christian studies, Christian testament, Christianity, church history, civics, college admission preparation, college awareness, college counseling, college planning, college writing, comparative religion, computer resources, computer technologies, constitutional history of U.S., drama, economics, economics-AP, English, English language and composition-AP, English language-AP, English literature, English literature and composition-AP, English literature-AP, English-AP, environmental science, environmental science-AP, ethics, fine arts, geometry, government, government-AP, government/civics, health, health education, history, honors English, honors geometry, honors U.S. history, honors world history, integrated technology fundamentals, jazz band, leadership, leadership and service, Life of Christ, literature and composition-AP, macroeconomics-AP, marching band, marine biology, marine science, mathematics, mathematics-AP, music, music appreciation, musical productions, New Testament, peace and justice, physical education, physics, physics-AP, play production, prayer/spirituality, pre-algebra, pre-calculus, religion, religious education, religious studies, SAT/ACT preparation, science, social justice, social sciences, social studies, Spanish, Spanish language-AP, Spanish-AP, student government, theater, U.S. government, U.S. government and politics, U.S. government and politics-AP, U.S. history, U.S. history-AP, world history, world history-AP, world religions, yearbook.

Graduation Requirements Arts and fine arts (art, music, dance, drama), English, foreign language, mathematics, physical education (includes health), religion (includes Bible studies and theology), science, social sciences, social studies (includes history), Christian service hours. Community service is required.

Special Academic Programs Advanced Placement exam preparation; honors section; academic accommodation for the gifted and the artistically talented; remedial reading and/or remedial writing; remedial math.

College Admission Counseling 59 students graduated in 2012; 58 went to college, including California State University, Dominguez Hills; California State University, Long Beach; Loyola Marymount University; University of California, Irvine; University of California, Los Angeles; University of California, San Diego.

Other: 1 entered military service. Mean SAT critical reading: 471, mean SAT math: 445, mean SAT writing: 451, mean combined SAT: 1367. 7% scored over 600 on SAT critical reading, 5% scored over 600 on SAT math, 4% scored over 600 on SAT writing, 4% scored over 1800 on combined SAT.

Student Life Upper grades have uniform requirement, student council, honor system. Discipline rests primarily with faculty. Attendance at religious services is required.

Tuition and Aid Day student tuition: $6400. Tuition installment plan (SMART Tuition Payment Plan, monthly payment plans, individually arranged payment plans). Tuition reduction for siblings, merit scholarship grants, need-based scholarship grants, Catholic Education Foundation (CEF) assistance available. In 2012–13, 55% of upper-school students received aid.

Admissions Traditional secondary-level entrance grade is 9. For fall 2012, 250 students applied for upper-level admission, 130 enrolled. High School Placement Test required. Deadline for receipt of application materials: none. Application fee required: $50. On-campus interview required.

Athletics Interscholastic: baseball (boys), basketball (b,g), cheering (g), cross-country running (b,g), dance squad (g), diving (b,g), football (b), independent competitive sports (b,g), running (b,g), soccer (b,g), softball (g), strength & conditioning (b,g), track and field (b,g), volleyball (b,g), weight training (b,g); coed interscholastic: aquatics, cheering; coed intramural: fitness, golf, physical fitness, roller blading, roller hockey, running, tennis. 31 coaches, 1 athletic trainer.

Computers Computers are regularly used in aerospace science, all academic, aviation, basic skills, Bible studies, business, career education, Christian doctrine, college planning, creative writing, current events, design, drawing and design, economics, English, foreign language, graphic arts, graphic design, graphics, historical foundations for arts, history, journalism, keyboarding, library, mathematics, media, media arts, media production, media services, mentorship program, multimedia, news writing, newspaper, photojournalism, publications, publishing, religion, religious studies, remedial study skills, research skills, SAT preparation, science, technology, theater arts, word processing, writing, writing, yearbook classes. Computer network features include online commercial services, Internet access, wireless campus network, Internet filtering or blocking technology, fiber optic, multimedia laboratory, iPad for every student. Campus intranet, student e-mail accounts, and computer access in designated common areas are available to students. Students grades are available online. The school has a published electronic and media policy.

Contact Ms. Lori Tribble, Registrar. 562-435-4496 Ext. 1200. Fax: 562-437-3055. E-mail: lori.tribble@longbeachsaints.org. Website: www.longbeachsaints.org

SAINT ANTHONY HIGH SCHOOL

304 East Roadway Avenue
Effingham, Illinois 62401

Head of School: Mr. Greg Fearday

General Information Coeducational day college-preparatory, arts, business, religious studies, bilingual studies, and technology school, affiliated with Roman Catholic Church. Grades 9–12. Setting: small town. Nearest major city is St. Louis, MO. 1 building on campus. Approved or accredited by Illinois Department of Education. Total enrollment: 190. Upper school average class size: 20. Upper school faculty-student ratio: 1:10. There are 176 required school days per year for Upper School students. Upper School students typically attend 5 days per week. The average school day consists of 5 hours and 42 minutes.

Upper School Student Profile Grade 9: 40 students (20 boys, 20 girls); Grade 10: 41 students (16 boys, 25 girls); Grade 11: 49 students (27 boys, 22 girls); Grade 12: 40 students (24 boys, 16 girls). 97% of students are Roman Catholic.

Faculty School total: 21. In upper school: 6 men, 15 women; 8 have advanced degrees.

Subjects Offered Accounting, advanced math, algebra, American government, anatomy, art appreciation, band, biology, British literature, calculus-AP, career exploration, Catholic belief and practice, ceramics, chemistry, chorus, communications, composition, computer applications, conceptual physics, concert band, consumer education, criminal justice, current events, drawing, earth science, English literature, English-AP, environmental science, finite math, forensics, general math, geography, geometry, health, microbiology, music appreciation, physical education, physical science, physics, pre-algebra, psychology, publications, Spanish, statistics-AP, U.S. history, world history, world wide web design.

Graduation Requirements American government, arts and fine arts (art, music, dance, drama), computer science, consumer education, English, mathematics, physical education (includes health), religion (includes Bible studies and theology), science, social sciences, speech, U.S. history, world history.

Special Academic Programs International Baccalaureate program; 3 Advanced Placement exams for which test preparation is offered; independent study; study at local college for college credit; remedial math; special instructional classes for deaf students.

College Admission Counseling 52 students graduated in 2013; 51 went to college, including Eastern Illinois University; Southern Illinois University Edwardsville; University of Illinois at Urbana–Champaign. Other: 1 entered military service. Median composite ACT: 24.

Student Life Upper grades have specified standards of dress, student council. Discipline rests primarily with faculty. Attendance at religious services is required.

Tuition and Aid Tuition installment plan (monthly payment plans). Need-based scholarship grants available.

Admissions Traditional secondary-level entrance grade is 9. Deadline for receipt of application materials: none. No application fee required.

Athletics Interscholastic: baseball (boys), basketball (b,g), bowling (b,g), cheering (g), dance team (g), golf (b,g), soccer (b,g), softball (g), tennis (b,g), track and field (b,g), volleyball (g), wrestling (b); coed interscholastic: cross-country running. 2 PE instructors, 19 coaches.

Computers Computers are regularly used in drafting, publications, yearbook classes. Computer network features include on-campus library services, Internet access, Internet filtering or blocking technology. Student e-mail accounts are available to students. Students grades are available online. The school has a published electronic and media policy.

Contact Mr. Greg Fearday, Principal. 217-342-6969. Fax: 217-342-6997. E-mail: gfearday@stanthony.com. Website: www.stanthony.com

ST. ANTHONY'S JUNIOR-SENIOR HIGH SCHOOL

1618 Lower Main Street
Wailuku, Hawaii 96793

Head of School: Mrs. Patricia Rickard

General Information Coeducational day college-preparatory, general academic, arts, religious studies, technology, and college courses offered for dual credit school, affiliated with Roman Catholic Church. Grades 7–12. Founded: 1848. Setting: small town. 15-acre campus. 13 buildings on campus. Approved or accredited by National Catholic Education Association, Western Association of Schools and Colleges, and Hawaii Department of Education. Member of National Association of Independent Schools. Endowment: $216,177. Total enrollment: 155. Upper school average class size: 22. Upper school faculty-student ratio: 1:10. There are 180 required school days per year for Upper School students. Upper School students typically attend 5 days per week. The average school day consists of 6 hours and 45 minutes.

Upper School Student Profile Grade 9: 34 students (14 boys, 20 girls); Grade 10: 18 students (10 boys, 8 girls); Grade 11: 32 students (18 boys, 14 girls); Grade 12: 22 students (10 boys, 12 girls). 65% of students are Roman Catholic.

Faculty School total: 20. In upper school: 8 men, 12 women; 10 have advanced degrees.

Subjects Offered Advanced math, American government, American history, American literature, anatomy and physiology, applied arts, art, athletic training, athletics, baseball, basic skills, basketball, Bible, Bible as literature, Bible studies, biology, bowling, British literature, business, calculus-AP, campus ministry, chemistry, college counseling, college planning, computer education, computer graphics, computer literacy, computer skills, computer technologies, computer technology certification, computer tools, computers, drawing, drawing and design, electives, English, English language and composition-AP, English literature, English literature and composition-AP, environmental science, environmental science-AP, foreign language, health, keyboarding, mathematics, music, physical education, pre-algebra, pre-calculus, religion, religious studies, SAT preparation, SAT/ACT preparation, science, social studies, sports medicine, standard curriculum, technology, U.S. history-AP, world geography, writing, writing, yearbook.

Graduation Requirements Art, English, languages, mathematics, physical education (includes health), religion (includes Bible studies and theology), science, social studies (includes history), technology.

Special Academic Programs 6 Advanced Placement exams for which test preparation is offered; honors section; study at local college for college credit.

College Admission Counseling 24 students graduated in 2012; all went to college, including University of Hawaii at Manoa; University of Notre Dame; University of Portland; Western Washington University. Median SAT critical reading: 518, median SAT math: 526, median SAT writing: 495, median combined SAT: 1539, median composite ACT: 22. 33% scored over 600 on SAT critical reading, 33% scored over 600 on SAT math, 33% scored over 600 on SAT writing, 33% scored over 1800 on combined SAT.

Student Life Upper grades have uniform requirement, student council. Discipline rests primarily with faculty. Attendance at religious services is required.

Tuition and Aid Day student tuition: $7500–$10,300. Tuition installment plan (FACTS Tuition Payment Plan). Tuition reduction for siblings, merit scholarship grants, need-based scholarship grants, alumni discount, new student referral discount available. In 2012–13, 50% of upper-school students received aid; total upper-school merit-scholarship money awarded: $4000. Total amount of financial aid awarded in 2012–13: $207,000.

Admissions Traditional secondary-level entrance grade is 9. For fall 2012, 27 students applied for upper-level admission, 27 were accepted, 20 enrolled. Achievement tests, Educational Development Series or standardized test scores required. Deadline for receipt of application materials: none. Application fee required: $300. Interview required.

Athletics Interscholastic: aquatics (boys, girls), baseball (b), basketball (b), bowling (b,g), canoeing/kayaking (b,g), cross-country running (b,g), drill team (b,g), football (b), golf (b,g), judo (b,g), ocean paddling (b,g), paddling (b,g), racquetball (b,g), riflery (b,g), running (b,g), soccer (b,g), softball (g), strength & conditioning (b,g), surfing (b,g), swimming and diving (b,g), tennis (b,g), track and field (b,g), volleyball (g), weight lifting (b,g), weight training (b,g), wrestling (b,g); intramural: basketball (b,g), flag football (b,g); coed interscholastic: cheering, flag football, paddling, racquetball; coed intramural: flag football. 2 PE instructors, 36 coaches, 1 athletic trainer.

Computers Computers are regularly used in college planning, computer applications, digital applications, graphic design, independent study, photography, technology, Web site design, yearbook classes. Computer network features include on-campus library services, Internet access, Internet filtering or blocking technology. Student e-mail accounts and computer access in designated common areas are available to students. Students grades are available online. The school has a published electronic and media policy.

Contact Mrs. Cindy Martin, Guidance/College Counselor. 808-244-4190 Ext. 224. Fax: 808-242-8081. E-mail: cmartin@sasmaui.org. Website: www.sasmaui.org

ST. AUGUSTINE HIGH SCHOOL

3266 Nutmeg Street
San Diego, California 92104-5199

Head of School: James Walter Horne

General Information Boys' day college-preparatory and religious studies school, affiliated with Roman Catholic Church. Grades 9–12. Founded: 1922. Setting: urban. 7-acre campus. 10 buildings on campus. Approved or accredited by National Catholic Education Association, Western Association of Schools and Colleges, and Western Catholic Education Association. Endowment: $1 million. Total enrollment: 700. Upper school average class size: 25. Upper school faculty-student ratio: 1:25. There are 180 required school days per year for Upper School students. Upper School students typically attend 5 days per week. The average school day consists of 5 hours and 50 minutes.

Upper School Student Profile Grade 9: 190 students (190 boys); Grade 10: 180 students (180 boys); Grade 11: 170 students (170 boys); Grade 12: 160 students (160 boys). 94% of students are Roman Catholic.

Faculty School total: 50. In upper school: 38 men, 10 women; 37 have advanced degrees.

Subjects Offered Algebra, American history, American literature, anatomy, art, art history, arts, Bible studies, biology, calculus, chemistry, computer science, driver education, economics, economics-AP, English, English literature, English-AP, ethics, fine arts, French, geometry, government/civics, grammar, health, history, Latin, Latin-AP, mathematics, music, philosophy, physical education, physics, physiology, psychology, religion, science, social studies, Spanish, speech, theology, trigonometry, world history, world literature, writing.

Graduation Requirements Arts and fine arts (art, music, dance, drama), English, foreign language, mathematics, physical education (includes health), religion (includes Bible studies and theology), science, social studies (includes history), speech, 100 hours of Christian service over four years.

Special Academic Programs Advanced Placement exam preparation; honors section; study abroad; academic accommodation for the gifted; remedial reading and/or remedial writing; remedial math; programs in English, mathematics, general development for dyslexic students; special instructional classes for blind students.

College Admission Counseling 169 students graduated in 2013; all went to college, including Gonzaga University; San Diego State University; University of California, Los Angeles; University of California, San Diego; University of Notre Dame; University of San Diego. 45% scored over 600 on SAT critical reading, 45% scored over 600 on SAT math, 45% scored over 600 on SAT writing, 55% scored over 26 on composite ACT.

Student Life Upper grades have specified standards of dress, student council, honor system. Discipline rests primarily with faculty. Attendance at religious services is required.

Summer Programs Remediation, enrichment, advancement, sports, rigorous outdoor training programs offered; session focuses on preparing students for fall semester; held on campus; accepts boys and girls; open to students from other schools. 150 students usually enrolled. 2014 schedule: June 20 to July 29. Application deadline: none.

Tuition and Aid Day student tuition: $15,000. Tuition installment plan (SMART Tuition Payment Plan, monthly payment plans, quarterly and annual payment plans). Merit scholarship grants, need-based scholarship grants, paying campus jobs available. In 2013–14, 50% of upper-school students received aid.

Admissions Traditional secondary-level entrance grade is 9. For fall 2013, 340 students applied for upper-level admission, 220 were accepted, 190 enrolled. ACT-Explore required. Deadline for receipt of application materials: January 25. Application fee required: $50. Interview required.

Athletics Interscholastic: baseball, basketball, cross-country running, diving, football, golf, in-line hockey, lacrosse, roller hockey, rugby, running, soccer, surfing, swimming and diving, tennis, track and field, volleyball, winter soccer, wrestling; intramural: basketball, bicycling, crew, fishing, fitness, flag football, Frisbee, kickball, mountain biking, ocean paddling, outdoor activities, outdoor adventure, outdoor education, outdoor recreation, physical fitness, physical training, racquetball, scuba diving, speedball, street hockey, strength & conditioning, table tennis, ultimate Frisbee, volleyball, weight lifting, weight training, yoga. 5 PE instructors, 26 coaches, 1 athletic trainer.

Computers Computers are regularly used in foreign language, mathematics, science, Web site design, writing classes. Computer resources include on-campus library services, online commercial services, Internet access, wireless campus network, Internet filtering or blocking technology, online databases, remote access. Campus intranet, student e-mail accounts, and computer access in designated common areas are available to students. Students grades are available online. The school has a published electronic and media policy.

Contact Jeannie Oliwa, Registrar. 619-282-2184 Ext. 5512. Fax: 619-282-1203. E-mail: joliwa@sahs.org. Website: www.sahs.org

SAINT AUGUSTINE PREPARATORY SCHOOL

611 Cedar Avenue
PO Box 279
Richland, New Jersey 08350

Head of School: Rev. Donald F. Reilly, OSA

General Information Boys' day college-preparatory and religious studies school, affiliated with Roman Catholic Church. Grades 9–12. Founded: 1959. Setting: rural. Nearest major city is Vineland. 120-acre campus. 4 buildings on campus. Approved or accredited by Middle States Association of Colleges and Schools, National Catholic Education Association, and New Jersey Department of Education. Endowment: $250,000. Total enrollment: 680. Upper school average class size: 17. Upper school faculty-student ratio: 1:12. There are 180 required school days per year for Upper School students. Upper School students typically attend 5 days per week. The average school day consists of 6 hours and 8 minutes.

Upper School Student Profile Grade 9: 163 students (163 boys); Grade 10: 183 students (183 boys); Grade 11: 178 students (178 boys); Grade 12: 156 students (156 boys). 78% of students are Roman Catholic.

Faculty School total: 61. In upper school: 47 men, 14 women; 31 have advanced degrees.

Subjects Offered 20th century history, accounting, advanced chemistry, Advanced Placement courses, advanced studio art-AP, algebra, American Civil War, American history-AP, American literature, anatomy and physiology, ancient world history, Arabic, Arabic studies, art, band, Bible, biology, biology-AP, British literature, British literature (honors), calculus, calculus-AP, Catholic belief and practice, chemistry, chemistry-AP, choir, Christian and Hebrew scripture, Christian doctrine, Christian ethics, church history, classical language, college counseling, college planning, community service, comparative religion, computer applications, computer programming, computer science, computer science-AP, computer-aided design, concert choir, culinary arts, current events, drama, drama performance, driver education, economics, engineering, English, English composition, English literature, English literature-AP, environmental education, ethics and responsibility, European history, European history-AP, finance, French, geometry, German, grammar, guitar, history, history-AP, Holocaust, Holocaust and other genocides, honors algebra, honors English, honors geometry, honors U.S. history, independent study, jazz band, jazz ensemble, lab science, language-AP, Latin, marine biology, mathematics-AP, model United Nations, moral theology, music history, music theory-AP, peer ministry, philosophy, photojournalism, physical education, physics, physics-AP, political science, pre-calculus, psychology, psychology-AP, public speaking, religion, religious studies, SAT preparation, scripture, service learning/internship, social skills, sociology, Spanish, Spanish language-AP, Spanish literature-AP, Spanish-AP, studio art, theater, travel, U.S. history-AP, vocal music, Web site design, world cultures, world religions, writing.

Graduation Requirements Electives, English, foreign language, lab science, mathematics, religion (includes Bible studies and theology), science, service learning/internship, U.S. history, world cultures, social service project (approximately 100 hours), retreat experiences, third semester experiences (travel; hands-on learning.

Special Academic Programs 18 Advanced Placement exams for which test preparation is offered; honors section; independent study; study at local college for college credit; study abroad; programs in general development for dyslexic students.

College Admission Counseling 173 students graduated in 2013; 170 went to college, including Drexel University; La Salle University; Rowan University; Saint Joseph's University; University of Delaware; Villanova University. Other: 3 had other specific plans. Mean SAT critical reading: 551, mean SAT math: 583, mean SAT writing: 557, mean combined SAT: 1691, mean composite ACT: 24. 32% scored over 600 on SAT critical reading, 43% scored over 600 on SAT math, 31% scored over 600 on SAT writing, 31% scored over 1800 on combined SAT, 31% scored over 26 on composite ACT.

Student Life Upper grades have uniform requirement, student council, honor system. Discipline rests primarily with faculty. Attendance at religious services is required.

Summer Programs Enrichment, advancement, sports, art/fine arts, rigorous outdoor training programs offered; session focuses on academic enrichment, community relations, sports camps; held both on and off campus; held at crew camp on nearby lake; accepts boys and girls; open to students from other schools. 656 students usually enrolled. 2014 schedule: July 7 to August 8. Application deadline: June 13.

Tuition and Aid Day student tuition: $15,600. Tuition installment plan (FACTS Tuition Payment Plan, individually arranged payment plans, credit card payment). Merit scholarship grants, need-based scholarship grants available. In 2013–14, 38% of upper-school students received aid; total upper-school merit-scholarship money awarded: $206,500. Total amount of financial aid awarded in 2013–14: $1,100,000.

Admissions Traditional secondary-level entrance grade is 9. For fall 2013, 270 students applied for upper-level admission, 217 were accepted, 163 enrolled. School's own exam required. Deadline for receipt of application materials: January 31. Application fee required: $75. On-campus interview recommended.

Athletics Interscholastic: baseball, basketball, bowling, crew, cross-country running, fencing, football, golf, ice hockey, indoor track, lacrosse, rowing, rugby, sailing, soccer, squash, swimming and diving, tennis, track and field, volleyball, winter (indoor) track, wrestling; intramural: basketball, physical training, ultimate Frisbee, weight training. 2 PE instructors, 11 coaches, 1 athletic trainer.

Computers Computers are regularly used in all academic, art, career education, computer applications, design, photojournalism, SAT preparation classes. Computer network features include on-campus library services, online commercial services, Internet access, wireless campus network, Internet filtering or blocking technology, syllabus, current grades, and assignments available online for all courses. Student e-mail accounts and computer access in designated common areas are available to students. Students grades are available online. The school has a published electronic and media policy.

Contact Mr. Stephen Cappuccio, Dean of Enrollment Management. 856-697-2600 Ext. 112. Fax: 856-697-8389. E-mail: mr.cappuccio@hermits.com. Website: www.hermits.com

ST. BENEDICT AT AUBURNDALE

8250 Varnavas Drive
Cordova, Tennessee 38016

Head of School: Mrs. Sondra Morris

General Information Coeducational day college-preparatory, arts, business, religious studies, bilingual studies, and technology school, affiliated with Roman Catholic Church. Grades 9–12. Founded: 1966. Setting: suburban. Nearest major city is Memphis. 40-acre campus. 1 building on campus. Approved or accredited by National Catholic Education Association, Southern Association of Colleges and Schools, and Tennessee Department of Education. Endowment: $200,000. Total enrollment: 945. Upper school average class size: 26. Upper school faculty-student ratio: 1:16. There are 186 required school days per year for Upper School students. Upper School students typically attend 5 days per week. The average school day consists of 7 hours and 15 minutes.

Upper School Student Profile Grade 9: 230 students (110 boys, 120 girls); Grade 10: 252 students (122 boys, 130 girls); Grade 11: 240 students (110 boys, 130 girls); Grade 12: 223 students (100 boys, 123 girls). 85% of students are Roman Catholic.

Faculty School total: 65. In upper school: 15 men, 50 women; 40 have advanced degrees.

Subjects Offered Accounting, acting, algebra, American government, American history, American history-AP, American literature-AP, anatomy and physiology, applied music, art, art appreciation, art education, art history, art-AP, astronomy, band, biology, calculus, calculus-AP, Catholic belief and practice, chemistry, choir, choral music, choreography, chorus, church history, cinematography, clayworking, comparative religion, composition-AP, computer graphics, computer multimedia, computers, creative writing, dance, digital art, digital photography, drama, drama performance, drawing, driver education, ecology, economics, economics-AP, English, English language-AP, English literature-AP, English-AP, English/composition-AP, etymology, European history, film, filmmaking, fine arts, first aid, fitness, forensics, French, French-AP, general business, geometry, German, government, government-AP, graphic arts, graphic design, health and wellness, health education, history, history of the Catholic Church, history-AP, honors algebra, honors English, honors geometry, honors U.S. history, human anatomy, human biology, instrumental music, internship, jazz band, jazz dance, journalism, keyboarding, lab/keyboard, Latin, literature-AP, macroeconomics-AP, marketing, modern history, music appreciation, music history, music theory, newspaper, performing arts, personal finance, photography, physical education, physical science, physics, play production, pre-algebra, pre-calculus, psychology, religion, set design, sociology, Spanish, Spanish-AP, speech, sports conditioning, stage design, statistics-AP, student publications, U.S. government and politics-AP, U.S. history-AP, world geography, world history, yearbook.

Graduation Requirements Arts and fine arts (art, music, dance, drama), economics, English, foreign language, government, mathematics, physical education (includes health), religion (includes Bible studies and theology), science, social studies (includes history), technology, theology.

Special Academic Programs 10 Advanced Placement exams for which test preparation is offered; study at local college for college credit; academic accommodation for the gifted, the musically talented, and the artistically talented; remedial reading and/or remedial writing; remedial math; programs in English, mathematics, general development for dyslexic students; special instructional classes for students with diagnosed learning disabilities and Attention Deficit Disorder.

College Admission Counseling 243 students graduated in 2013; all went to college, including Christian Brothers University; Middle Tennessee State University; Mississippi State University; The University of Alabama; The University of Tennessee; University of Memphis. Mean SAT critical reading: 570, mean SAT math: 560, mean composite ACT: 24. 38% scored over 600 on SAT critical reading, 37% scored over 600 on SAT math, 30% scored over 26 on composite ACT.

Student Life Upper grades have uniform requirement, student council, honor system. Discipline rests primarily with faculty. Attendance at religious services is required.

Summer Programs Remediation, enrichment programs offered; session focuses on enrichment for math and language; held on campus; accepts boys and girls; not open to students from other schools. 30 students usually enrolled. 2014 schedule: July 5 to July 29. Application deadline: none.

Tuition and Aid Day student tuition: $8600. Tuition installment plan (FACTS Tuition Payment Plan, monthly payment plans, individually arranged payment plans). Merit scholarship grants, need-based scholarship grants available. In 2013–14, 4% of upper-school students received aid; total upper-school merit-scholarship money awarded: $30,000. Total amount of financial aid awarded in 2013–14: $35,000.

Admissions Traditional secondary-level entrance grade is 9. For fall 2013, 270 students applied for upper-level admission, 270 were accepted, 260 enrolled. High School Placement Test required. Deadline for receipt of application materials: none. Application fee required: $75. Interview required.

Athletics Interscholastic: baseball (boys), basketball (b,g), bowling (b,g), cheering (g), cross-country running (b,g), dance (g), dance squad (g), dance team (g), football (b), Frisbee (b,g), golf (b,g), lacrosse (b,g), pom squad (g), soccer (b,g), softball (g), strength & conditioning (b), swimming and diving (b,g), tennis (b,g), track and field (b,g), volleyball (g), weight lifting (b), weight training (b), wrestling (b); coed interscholastic: water polo; coed intramural: Frisbee. 4 PE instructors, 17 coaches, 1 athletic trainer.

Computers Computers are regularly used in all academic, art, business, commercial art, current events, dance, design, desktop publishing, economics, French, graphic arts, graphic design, health, history, journalism, lab/keyboard, Latin, mathematics, music, newspaper, photography, psychology, publications, religion, science, social sciences, social studies, Spanish, speech, study skills, technology, theater, theater arts, theology, Web site design, writing, yearbook classes. Computer network features include on-campus library services, Internet access, wireless campus network, Internet filtering or blocking technology. Campus intranet and student e-mail accounts are available to students. Students grades are available online. The school has a published electronic and media policy.

Contact Mrs. Terri Heath, Director of Admissions. 901-260-2873. Fax: 901-260-2850. E-mail: heatht@sbaeagles.org. Website: www.sbaeagles.org

ST. BERNARD HIGH SCHOOL

1593 Norwich-New London Turnpike
Uncasville, Connecticut 06382

Head of School: Mr. Thomas J. Doherty III

General Information Coeducational day college-preparatory school, affiliated with Roman Catholic Church. Grades 6–12. Founded: 1956. Setting: suburban. Nearest major city is Hartford. 113-acre campus. 2 buildings on campus. Approved or accredited by New England Association of Schools and Colleges and Connecticut Department of Education. Member of National Association of Independent Schools. Endowment: $1 million. Total enrollment: 369. Upper school average class size: 20. Upper school faculty-student ratio: 1:12. There are 177 required school days per year for Upper School students. Upper School students typically attend 5 days per week. The average school day consists of 6 hours.

Upper School Student Profile Grade 9: 57 students (30 boys, 27 girls); Grade 10: 72 students (26 boys, 46 girls); Grade 11: 60 students (34 boys, 26 girls); Grade 12: 72 students (36 boys, 36 girls). 60% of students are Roman Catholic.

Faculty School total: 33. In upper school: 19 men, 12 women; 26 have advanced degrees.

Subjects Offered 3-dimensional art, accounting, acting, algebra, anatomy and physiology, athletic training, biology, biology-AP, calculus, calculus-AP, chemistry, chemistry-AP, Christian doctrine, Christian ethics, Christian scripture, church history, conceptual physics, concert band, concert choir, creative writing, design, drawing and design, economics, English, English literature and composition-AP, environmental science, European history-AP, fine arts, forensics, French, French-AP, geometry, global issues, health, honors algebra, honors English, honors geometry, honors U.S. history, honors world history, integrated science, intro to computers, modern world history, moral theology, music, music theory, music theory-AP, Native American studies, nutrition, organic chemistry, painting, peace and justice, peer counseling, peer ministry, performing arts, personal finance, personal fitness, philosophy, photography, physical education, physics, pottery, pre-algebra, pre-calculus, printmaking, psychology-AP, public speaking, religious studies, scripture, sociology, Spanish, Spanish-AP, sports conditioning, sports nutrition, statistics, street law, strings, studio art, technology, theater arts, U.S. history, U.S. history-AP, world history.

Graduation Requirements Art, biology, chemistry, English, health education, history, intro to computers, mathematics, physical education (includes health), theology, U.S. history, world history, all students are required to complete 100 hours of community service prior to high school graduation.

Special Academic Programs Honors section; study at local college for college credit.

College Admission Counseling 74 students graduated in 2012; 72 went to college, including Keene State College; Providence College; Roger Williams University; Saint Michael's College; University of Connecticut; Worcester Polytechnic

Institute. Other: 2 entered military service. Mean SAT critical reading: 546, mean SAT math: 518, mean SAT writing: 533.

Student Life Upper grades have uniform requirement, student council, honor system. Discipline rests primarily with faculty. Attendance at religious services is required.

Tuition and Aid Day student tuition: $11,400. Tuition installment plan (SMART Tuition Payment Plan, FACTS Tuition Payment Plan, monthly payment plans, individually arranged payment plans). Tuition reduction for siblings, merit scholarship grants, need-based scholarship grants available. In 2012–13, 32% of upper-school students received aid; total upper-school merit-scholarship money awarded: $166,050. Total amount of financial aid awarded in 2012–13: $354,257.

Admissions Traditional secondary-level entrance grade is 9. For fall 2012, 136 students applied for upper-level admission, 120 were accepted, 110 enrolled. High School Placement Test (closed version) from Scholastic Testing Service and Scholastic Testing Service required. Deadline for receipt of application materials: January 15. No application fee required. On-campus interview recommended.

Athletics Interscholastic: baseball (boys), basketball (b,g), cheering (g), cross-country running (b,g), diving (b,g), fencing (b,g), football (b), golf (b,g), ice hockey (b), indoor track & field (b,g), lacrosse (b,g), physical fitness (b,g), soccer (b,g), softball (g), swimming and diving (b,g), tennis (b,g), track and field (b,g), wrestling (b,g); coed interscholastic: cheering, cross-country running, fencing, golf, physical fitness, soccer, swimming and diving, wrestling; coed intramural: skiing (cross-country), skiing (downhill), snowboarding, strength & conditioning, volleyball, weight training. 2 PE instructors, 50 coaches, 1 athletic trainer.

Computers Computers are regularly used in computer applications, design classes. Computer resources include on-campus library services, Internet access, wireless campus network, Internet filtering or blocking technology. Campus intranet, student e-mail accounts, and computer access in designated common areas are available to students. Students grades are available online. The school has a published electronic and media policy.

Contact Mrs. Cathy Brown, Director of Admissions (gr. 6-8) and International Programs. 860-848-1271 Ext. 108. Fax: 860-848-1274. E-mail: Admissions@Saint-Bernard.com. Website: www.saint-bernard.com

ST. BERNARD'S CATHOLIC SCHOOL

222 Dollison Street
Eureka, California 95501

Head of School: Mr. David Sharp

General Information Coeducational boarding and day college-preparatory and religious studies school, affiliated with Roman Catholic Church. Boarding grades 9–12, day grades PK–12. Founded: 1912. Setting: small town. Nearest major city is San Francisco. 5-acre campus. 4 buildings on campus. Approved or accredited by National Catholic Education Association, Western Association of Schools and Colleges, Western Catholic Education Association, and California Department of Education. Endowment: $63,000. Total enrollment: 300. Upper school average class size: 20. Upper school faculty-student ratio: 1:12. There are 162 required school days per year for Upper School students. Upper School students typically attend 5 days per week. The average school day consists of 6 hours.

Upper School Student Profile 25% of students are boarding students. 75% are state residents. 25% are international students. International students from China, Republic of Korea, and Viet Nam. 35% of students are Roman Catholic.

Faculty School total: 20. In upper school: 9 men, 11 women; 5 have advanced degrees.

Subjects Offered Arts, community service, English, fine arts, mathematics, physical education, religion, science, social studies.

Graduation Requirements Arts and fine arts (art, music, dance, drama), English, foreign language, mathematics, physical education (includes health), science, social studies (includes history), theology, follow the University of California requirements (250 units). Community service is required.

Special Academic Programs Advanced Placement exam preparation; honors section; remedial reading and/or remedial writing; remedial math; special instructional classes for students with learning disabilities.

College Admission Counseling 44 students graduated in 2012; 43 went to college, including College of the Redwoods; Humboldt State University; Pacific University; Sonoma State University; University of California, San Diego; University of San Francisco. Other: 1 entered military service.

Student Life Upper grades have specified standards of dress, student council. Discipline rests equally with students and faculty. Attendance at religious services is required.

Tuition and Aid Day student tuition: $6300. Tuition installment plan (monthly payment plans, individually arranged payment plans, 3% reduction if paid in full by July 10). Tuition reduction for siblings, merit scholarship grants, need-based scholarship grants, paying campus jobs available. In 2012–13, 47% of upper-school students received aid; total upper-school merit-scholarship money awarded: $2500. Total amount of financial aid awarded in 2012–13: $55,000.

Admissions Traditional secondary-level entrance grade is 9. Admissions testing required. Deadline for receipt of application materials: none. Application fee required: $40. Interview required.

Athletics Interscholastic: baseball (boys), basketball (b,g), football (b), golf (b,g), soccer (b,g), softball (g), tennis (b,g), volleyball (g), wrestling (b); intramural: cheering (g); coed interscholastic: track and field. 1 PE instructor, 15 coaches, 1 athletic trainer.

Computers Computers are regularly used in graphic design, journalism, yearbook classes. Computer network features include on-campus library services, Internet access, wireless campus network, Internet filtering or blocking technology. Students grades are available online. The school has a published electronic and media policy.

Contact Mrs. Shirley Sobol, Domestic Admissions. 707-443-2735 Ext. 115. Fax: 707-443-4723. E-mail: sobol@saintbernards.us. Website: www.saintbernards.us/

ST. BRENDAN HIGH SCHOOL

2950 Southwest 87th Avenue
Miami, Florida 33165-3295

Head of School: Mr. Jose Rodelgo-Bueno

General Information Coeducational day college-preparatory, general academic, arts, business, religious studies, bilingual studies, and technology school, affiliated with Roman Catholic Church. Grades 9–12. Founded: 1975. Setting: urban. 34-acre campus. 3 buildings on campus. Approved or accredited by Southern Association of Colleges and Schools and Florida Department of Education. Total enrollment: 1,118. Upper school average class size: 28. Upper school faculty-student ratio: 1:15. There are 180 required school days per year for Upper School students. Upper School students typically attend 5 days per week. The average school day consists of 7 hours and 45 minutes.

Upper School Student Profile 98% of students are Roman Catholic.

Faculty School total: 76. In upper school: 22 men, 54 women; 34 have advanced degrees.

Graduation Requirements Algebra, students must complete 100 community service hours in their four years of high school.

Special Academic Programs 10 Advanced Placement exams for which test preparation is offered; honors section; study at local college for college credit; academic accommodation for the gifted; remedial reading and/or remedial writing; remedial math.

College Admission Counseling 315 students graduated in 2012; 310 went to college, including Florida International University; Florida State University; Miami Dade College; University of Central Florida; University of Florida; University of Miami. Other: 5 had other specific plans. Median SAT critical reading: 480, median SAT math: 460, median SAT writing: 470, median combined SAT: 1410, median composite ACT: 20. 10% scored over 26 on composite ACT.

Student Life Upper grades have uniform requirement, student council, honor system. Discipline rests primarily with faculty. Attendance at religious services is required.

Tuition and Aid Tuition installment plan (FACTS Tuition Payment Plan, monthly payment plans). Need-based scholarship grants, paying campus jobs available. In 2012–13, 23% of upper-school students received aid. Total amount of financial aid awarded in 2012–13: $266,000.

Admissions Traditional secondary-level entrance grade is 9. Catholic High School Entrance Examination or placement test required. Deadline for receipt of application materials: January 22. Application fee required: $50.

Athletics Interscholastic: baseball (boys), basketball (b,g), cheering (g), cross-country running (b,g), dance team (g), soccer (b,g), softball (g), swimming and diving (b,g), tennis (b,g), track and field (b,g), volleyball (b,g). 2 PE instructors, 17 coaches, 1 athletic trainer.

Computers Computers are regularly used in business, computer applications, graphic design, mathematics, media arts, media production, newspaper, programming, reading, remedial study skills, research skills, science, speech, Web site design, word processing, yearbook classes. Computer network features include on-campus library services, Internet access, wireless campus network, Internet filtering or blocking technology, 1:1 iPad program. Computer access in designated common areas is available to students. Students grades are available online. The school has a published electronic and media policy.

Contact Melissa Ferrer, Director of Admissions. 305-223-5181 Ext. 578. Fax: 305-220-7434. E-mail: mferrer@stbhs.org. Website: www.stbhs.org

ST. CATHERINE'S ACADEMY

Anaheim, California
See Junior Boarding Schools section.

ST. CROIX SCHOOLS

1200 Oakdale Avenue
West St. Paul, Minnesota 55118

Head of School: Dr. Gene Pfeifer

General Information Coeducational boarding and day college-preparatory, general academic, arts, business, vocational, religious studies, bilingual studies, technology, and ESL school, affiliated with Wisconsin Evangelical Lutheran Synod, Christian faith. Grades 6–12. Founded: 1958. Setting: suburban. Nearest major city is St. Paul. Students are housed in single-sex dormitories. 30-acre campus. 3 buildings on campus. Approved or accredited by Minnesota Department of Education. Endowment: $1.6 million. Total enrollment: 500. Upper school average class size: 21. Upper school faculty-student ratio: 1:15. There are 176 required school days per year for Upper School students. Upper School students typically attend 5 days per week. The average school day consists of 5 hours and 30 minutes.

Upper School Student Profile Grade 9: 110 students (52 boys, 58 girls); Grade 10: 110 students (57 boys, 53 girls); Grade 11: 110 students (56 boys, 54 girls); Grade 12: 110 students (53 boys, 57 girls). 30% of students are boarding students. 74% are state residents. 7 states are represented in upper school student body. 22% are international students. International students from China, Japan, Republic of Korea, Taiwan, Thailand, and Viet Nam; 11 other countries represented in student body. 62% of students are Wisconsin Evangelical Lutheran Synod, Christian.

Faculty School total: 35. In upper school: 24 men, 11 women; 21 have advanced degrees; 4 reside on campus.

Subjects Offered Accounting, advanced biology, advanced chemistry, advanced math, Advanced Placement courses, algebra, American history, American literature, applied skills, art, band, Bible studies, biology, biology-AP, business skills, calculus, chemistry, choir, chorus, computer programming, computer science, drama, economics, engineering, English, English literature, environmental science, general science, geography, geology, geometry, German, home economics, keyboarding, Latin, literature, Mandarin, mathematics, music, physical education, physics, pre-algebra, reading, religion, science, social sciences, social studies, Spanish, speech, trigonometry, world history, writing.

Graduation Requirements Algebra, arts and fine arts (art, music, dance, drama), biology, chemistry, English, English composition, English literature, foreign language, geometry, government, grammar, literature, physical education (includes health), physics, religion (includes Bible studies and theology), science, social studies (includes history), speech, world geography.

Special Academic Programs 12 Advanced Placement exams for which test preparation is offered; honors section; independent study; academic accommodation for the gifted, the musically talented, and the artistically talented; remedial reading and/or remedial writing; remedial math; programs in English for dyslexic students; special instructional classes for students with learning disabilities; ESL (30 students enrolled).

College Admission Counseling 115 students graduated in 2013; 111 went to college, including Bethany Lutheran College; Cornell College; Martin Luther College; Minnesota State University Mankato; University of Minnesota, Twin Cities Campus; University of Wisconsin–Madison. Other: 1 went to work, 3 entered military service. Mean composite ACT: 25.

Student Life Upper grades have specified standards of dress, student council, honor system. Discipline rests equally with students and faculty.

Summer Programs ESL, sports programs offered; session focuses on ESL and activities, and a variety of sports camps; held on campus; accepts boys and girls; open to students from other schools. 80 students usually enrolled. 2014 schedule: July 15 to August 2. Application deadline: May 15.

Tuition and Aid 7-day tuition and room/board: $26,800. Tuition installment plan (SMART Tuition Payment Plan). Merit scholarship grants, need-based scholarship grants available. In 2013–14, 40% of upper-school students received aid; total upper-school merit-scholarship money awarded: $25,000. Total amount of financial aid awarded in 2013–14: $600,000.

Admissions Traditional secondary-level entrance grade is 9. For fall 2013, 163 students applied for upper-level admission, 124 were accepted, 100 enrolled. Secondary Level English Proficiency or writing sample required. Deadline for receipt of application materials: none. Application fee required: $100. Interview recommended.

Athletics Interscholastic: baseball (boys), basketball (b,g), bowling (b,g), cheering (g), cross-country running (b,g), dance team (g), football (b), golf (b,g), hockey (b,g), ice hockey (b,g), soccer (b,g), softball (g), swimming and diving (b,g), tennis (b,g), track and field (b,g), volleyball (g), wrestling (b); intramural: badminton (b,g), basketball (b,g); coed intramural: alpine skiing, ball hockey, basketball, bowling, cheering, cross-country running, dance team, flag football, floor hockey, Frisbee, jogging, juggling, kickball, physical fitness, physical training, power lifting, skiing (downhill), snowboarding, softball, strength & conditioning, swimming and diving, table tennis, tennis, touch football, track and field, ultimate Frisbee, volleyball, weight lifting, weight training, whiffle ball. 3 PE instructors, 3 coaches, 2 athletic trainers.

Computers Computers are regularly used in accounting, computer applications, desktop publishing, economics, graphic design, keyboarding, media production, writing, yearbook classes. Computer network features include on-campus library services, online commercial services, Internet access, wireless campus network, Internet filtering or blocking technology. Computer access in designated common areas is available to students. Students grades are available online. The school has a published electronic and media policy.

Contact Dr. Jeff Lemke, Admissions Director. 651-455-1521. Fax: 651-451-3968. E-mail: international@stcroixlutheran.org. Website: www.stcroixlutheran.org

SAINT DOMINIC ACADEMY

Bishop Joseph OSB Boulevard
121 Gracelawn Road
Auburn, Maine 04210

Head of School: Mr. Donald Fournier

General Information Coeducational day and distance learning college-preparatory, arts, business, and religious studies school, affiliated with Roman Catholic Church. Grades PK–12. Distance learning grades 11–12. Founded: 1941. Setting: suburban. 70-acre campus. 1 building on campus. Approved or accredited by Maine Department of Education. Total enrollment: 571. Upper school average class size: 18. Upper school faculty-student ratio: 1:12. There are 175 required school days per year for Upper School students. Upper School students typically attend 5 days per week. The average school day consists of 6 hours and 15 minutes.

Upper School Student Profile 70% of students are Roman Catholic.

Faculty School total: 25. In upper school: 10 men, 15 women.

Special Academic Programs International Baccalaureate program; Advanced Placement exam preparation; honors section; independent study.

College Admission Counseling 53 students graduated in 2013; 52 went to college. Other: 1 entered military service. Median SAT critical reading: 542, median SAT math: 534, median SAT writing: 524, median combined SAT: 1600.

Student Life Upper grades have specified standards of dress, student council, honor system. Discipline rests primarily with faculty. Attendance at religious services is required.

Summer Programs Enrichment, sports, art/fine arts programs offered; session focuses on recreation/theater/math and science; held both on and off campus; held at various venues; accepts boys and girls; open to students from other schools.

Tuition and Aid Day student tuition: $11,414. Tuition installment plan (FACTS Tuition Payment Plan). Merit scholarship grants, need-based scholarship grants available. In 2013–14, 40% of upper-school students received aid.

Admissions Traditional secondary-level entrance grade is 9. Scholastic Testing Service High School Placement Test required. Deadline for receipt of application materials: none. Application fee required: $50. Interview required.

Athletics Interscholastic: baseball (boys), basketball (b,g), field hockey (g), ice hockey (b,g), indoor track & field (b,g), soccer (b,g), softball (b,g), swimming and diving (b); coed interscholastic: alpine skiing, aquatics, cheering, cross-country running, dance team, golf, nordic skiing. 1 PE instructor, 30 coaches, 1 athletic trainer.

Computers Computer network features include on-campus library services, online commercial services, Internet access, wireless campus network, Internet filtering or blocking technology. Campus intranet, student e-mail accounts, and computer access in designated common areas are available to students. Students grades are available online. The school has a published electronic and media policy.

Contact Mr. James Boulet, Director of Admissions. 207-782-6911 Ext. 2110. Fax: 207-795-6439. E-mail: james.boulet@portlanddiocese.org. Website: www.stdomsmaine.org

SAINT EDWARD'S SCHOOL

1895 Saint Edward's Drive
Vero Beach, Florida 32963

Head of School: Mr. Michael J. Mersky

General Information Coeducational day college-preparatory, technology, and advanced placement school, affiliated with Episcopal Church. Grades PK–12. Founded: 1965. Setting: suburban. Nearest major city is West Palm Beach. 26-acre campus. 12 buildings on campus. Approved or accredited by Florida Council of Independent Schools, National Association of Episcopal Schools, Southern Association of Colleges and Schools, and The College Board. Member of National Association of Independent Schools and Secondary School Admission Test Board. Endowment: $6 million. Total enrollment: 500. Upper school average class size: 12. Upper school faculty-student ratio: 1:8. There are 176 required school days per year for Upper School students. Upper School students typically attend 5 days per week. The average school day consists of 6 hours and 30 minutes.

Upper School Student Profile Grade 9: 50 students (30 boys, 20 girls); Grade 10: 51 students (30 boys, 21 girls); Grade 11: 66 students (36 boys, 30 girls); Grade 12: 58 students (26 boys, 32 girls).

Faculty School total: 60. In upper school: 14 men, 14 women; 18 have advanced degrees.

Subjects Offered Advanced Placement courses, algebra, American history, American literature, anatomy and physiology, art, band, biology, biology-AP, calculus, calculus-AP, chemistry, chemistry-AP, Chinese, choir, choral music, chorus, Christian ethics, computer science-AP, concert band, concert choir, contemporary issues, contemporary studies, drama, economics, economics-AP, electronic music, English, English as a foreign language, English language and composition-AP, English literature and composition-AP, ethics, fine arts, geometry, global studies, government, government-AP, graphic design, health and wellness, honors algebra, honors English, honors geometry, human geography - AP, instrumental music, Internet research, Mandarin, marine biology, mathematics, model United Nations, modern European history-AP, music, music theory-AP, neuroscience, performing arts, physical education, physical fitness, physics, physics-AP, pre-calculus, psychology, religion, science, senior internship, senior project, social sciences, social studies, sociology, Spanish, Spanish language-AP, sports medicine, statistics-AP, theater arts, U.S. government and politics-AP, U.S. history-AP, world history, world history-AP.

Graduation Requirements Arts and fine arts (art, music, dance, drama), English, foreign language, mathematics, physical education (includes health), religion (includes Bible studies and theology), science, social sciences, social studies (includes history), 25 hours of community service each year of high school.

Special Academic Programs Advanced Placement exam preparation; honors section; independent study; study at local college for college credit; study abroad; academic accommodation for the gifted, the musically talented, and the artistically talented; ESL (25 students enrolled).

College Admission Counseling 42 students graduated in 2013; all went to college, including Franklin & Marshall College; The Catholic University of America; University of Colorado Boulder; University of Florida; University of South Carolina; University of South Florida. Mean SAT critical reading: 581, mean SAT math: 584, mean SAT writing: 570, mean combined SAT: 1735, mean composite ACT: 25.

Student Life Upper grades have specified standards of dress, student council, honor system. Discipline rests primarily with faculty. Attendance at religious services is required.

Summer Programs Remediation, enrichment, sports, art/fine arts, computer instruction programs offered; session focuses on enrichment, water activities, sports, study skills; held both on and off campus; held at Waterfront Indian River Lagoon; accepts boys and girls; open to students from other schools. 870 students usually enrolled. 2014 schedule: June 9 to August 15. Application deadline: none.

Tuition and Aid Day student tuition: $6000–$24,900. Tuition installment plan (FACTS Tuition Payment Plan, 1-, 2-, and 10-payment plans). Need-based scholarship grants available. In 2013–14, 27% of upper-school students received aid. Total amount of financial aid awarded in 2013–14: $1,750,000.

Admissions Traditional secondary-level entrance grade is 9. For fall 2013, 61 students applied for upper-level admission, 55 were accepted, 37 enrolled. ACT, PSAT, SAT or SSAT required. Deadline for receipt of application materials: February 15. Application fee required: $50. Interview recommended.

Athletics Interscholastic: baseball (boys), basketball (b,g), cheering (g), crew (b,g), cross-country running (b,g), football (b), golf (b,g), independent competitive sports (b,g), lacrosse (b,g), soccer (b,g), swimming and diving (b,g), tennis (b,g), volleyball (g), weight lifting (b,g); intramural: baseball (b), basketball (b,g), cheering (g), cross-country running (b,g), flagball (b), football (b), golf (b,g), lacrosse (b,g), physical fitness (b,g), sailing (b,g), soccer (b,g), tennis (b,g), volleyball (g); coed interscholastic: aquatics, swimming and diving; coed intramural: aquatics, outdoor education, physical fitness, soccer, softball. 4 PE instructors, 14 coaches, 1 athletic trainer.

Computers Computers are regularly used in all academic classes. Computer network features include on-campus library services, online commercial services, Internet access, wireless campus network, Internet filtering or blocking technology, issuance of tablet technology to all students in grades 6-12, electronic submission of homework, class assignments and homework available online. Campus intranet and student e-mail accounts are available to students. Students grades are available online. The school has a published electronic and media policy.

Contact Ms. Peggy Anderson, Director of Admission. 772-492-2364. Fax: 772-231-2427. E-mail: panderson@steds.org. Website: www.steds.org

SAINT ELIZABETH HIGH SCHOOL

1530 34th Avenue
Oakland, California 94601

Head of School: Mr. Martin Procaccio

General Information Coeducational day college-preparatory, arts, and religious studies school, affiliated with Roman Catholic Church. Grades 9–12. Founded: 1921. Setting: urban. Nearest major city is Berkeley. 2-acre campus. 1 building on campus. Approved or accredited by National Catholic Education Association, Western Association of Schools and Colleges, and California Department of Education. Endowment: $100,000. Total enrollment: 143. Upper school average class size: 16. Upper school faculty-student ratio: 1:15. There are 180 required school days per year for Upper School students. Upper School students typically attend 5 days per week. The average school day consists of 6 hours and 48 minutes.

Upper School Student Profile Grade 9: 50 students (31 boys, 19 girls); Grade 10: 30 students (16 boys, 14 girls); Grade 11: 27 students (14 boys, 13 girls); Grade 12: 36 students (19 boys, 17 girls). 80% of students are Roman Catholic.

Faculty School total: 17. In upper school: 5 men, 10 women; 8 have advanced degrees.

Subjects Offered Advanced math, algebra, American literature, American literature-AP, anatomy and physiology, art and culture, biology, business mathematics, calculus-AP, Catholic belief and practice, chemistry, Christian and Hebrew scripture, Christian testament, civics, composition, computer applications, computer graphics, computer literacy, creative writing, drawing and design, economics, economics and history, English, English literature and composition-AP, geometry, journalism, learning strategies, moral and social development, physical education, physical science, physics, pre-algebra, pre-calculus, psychology, social justice, Spanish, Spanish language-AP, Spanish literature-AP, speech, speech communications, trigonometry, U.S. history, world cultures, world geography, world history, world religions.

Graduation Requirements Arts and fine arts (art, music, dance, drama), electives, English, foreign language, mathematics, physical education (includes health), religious studies, science, social sciences, 100 hours of community service.

Special Academic Programs 3 Advanced Placement exams for which test preparation is offered; honors section; remedial reading and/or remedial writing; remedial math; programs in English, mathematics for dyslexic students; special instructional classes for students with learning disabilities, Attention Deficit Disorder, dyslexia, and emotional and behavioral problems.

College Admission Counseling 42 students graduated in 2013; all went to college, including California State University, East Bay; San Francisco State University; San Jose State University; University of California, Berkeley; University of California, Davis.

Student Life Upper grades have specified standards of dress, honor system. Discipline rests primarily with faculty. Attendance at religious services is required.

Summer Programs Remediation programs offered; session focuses on academics; held on campus; accepts boys and girls; not open to students from other schools. 25 students usually enrolled. 2014 schedule: June 17 to July 16. Application deadline: June 1.

Tuition and Aid Day student tuition: $11,200. Tuition installment plan (SMART Tuition Payment Plan). Tuition reduction for siblings, merit scholarship grants, need-based scholarship grants available. In 2013–14, 90% of upper-school students received aid; total upper-school merit-scholarship money awarded: $67,000. Total amount of financial aid awarded in 2013–14: $990,000.

Admissions Traditional secondary-level entrance grade is 9. For fall 2013, 88 students applied for upper-level admission, 70 were accepted, 50 enrolled. High School Placement Test required. Deadline for receipt of application materials: none. Application fee required: $75. Interview required.

Athletics Interscholastic: baseball (boys), basketball (b,g), cross-country running (b,g), soccer (b,g), softball (g), track and field (b,g), volleyball (b,g). 1 PE instructor, 9 coaches.

Computers Computer network features include on-campus library services, Internet access, wireless campus network, Internet filtering or blocking technology. Students grades are available online. The school has a published electronic and media policy.

Contact Lisseth Aguilar, Executive Assistant. 510-532-8947. Fax: 510-532-9754. E-mail: laguilar@stliz-hs.org. Website: www.stliz-hs.org

ST. FRANCIS DE SALES HIGH SCHOOL

2323 West Bancroft Street
Toledo, Ohio 43607

Head of School: Mr. Eric J. Smola

General Information Boys' day college-preparatory, religious studies, AP courses, and community service school, affiliated with Roman Catholic Church. Grades 9–12. Founded: 1955. Setting: urban. Nearest major city is Cleveland. 25-acre campus. 1 building on campus. Approved or accredited by Ohio Catholic Schools Accreditation Association (OCSAA) and Ohio Department of Education. Endowment: $9 million. Total enrollment: 612. Upper school average class size: 24. Upper school faculty-student ratio: 1:14. There are 180 required school days per year for Upper School students. Upper School students typically attend 5 days per week. The average school day consists of 6 hours and 30 minutes.

Upper School Student Profile Grade 9: 167 students (167 boys); Grade 10: 139 students (139 boys); Grade 11: 154 students (154 boys); Grade 12: 152 students (152 boys). 73% of students are Roman Catholic.

Faculty School total: 54. In upper school: 41 men, 13 women; 33 have advanced degrees.

Subjects Offered Advanced Placement courses, advanced studio art-AP, algebra, American history, American history-AP, American literature, American literature-AP, anatomy, animation, art, biology, biology-AP, British literature, calculus, calculus-AP, ceramics, chemistry, chemistry-AP, Chinese, chorus, church history, community service, computer science, computer-aided design, creative writing, criminal justice, drawing, economics, English literature, English-AP, environmental science, expository writing, French, French-AP, geometry, government/civics, grammar, graphic design, health, journalism, Latin, Latin-AP, macroeconomics-AP, math analysis, mathematics, microeconomics-AP, military history, music, mythology, New Testament, physical education, physical science, physics, physics-AP, pre-calculus, psychology, psychology-AP, public speaking, science, social justice, social studies, sociology, Spanish, Spanish-AP, statistics, theology, trigonometry, U.S. government, U.S. government and politics-AP, U.S. history-AP, Web site design, world geography, world history, yearbook.

Graduation Requirements Art, computer science, English, foreign language, mathematics, physical education (includes health), religion (includes Bible studies and theology), science, social studies (includes history), participation in religious retreats four of 4 years. Community service is required.

Special Academic Programs Advanced Placement exam preparation; honors section; study at local college for college credit; ESL (6 students enrolled).

College Admission Counseling 124 students graduated in 2013; 123 went to college, including Baldwin Wallace University; Bowling Green State University; Miami University; The Ohio State University; The University of Toledo; University of

Dayton. Other: 1 had other specific plans. Mean SAT critical reading: 551, mean SAT math: 560, mean SAT writing: 513, mean composite ACT: 24.

Student Life Upper grades have specified standards of dress, student council. Discipline rests primarily with faculty. Attendance at religious services is required.

Summer Programs Enrichment programs offered; session focuses on mathematics, English; held on campus; accepts boys; not open to students from other schools. 100 students usually enrolled. 2014 schedule: June 9 to June 27. Application deadline: June 1.

Tuition and Aid Day student tuition: $10,300. Tuition installment plan (monthly payment plans, quarterly payment plan). Tuition reduction for siblings, merit scholarship grants, need-based scholarship grants, paying campus jobs available. In 2013–14, 70% of upper-school students received aid; total upper-school merit-scholarship money awarded: $394,450. Total amount of financial aid awarded in 2013–14: $1,665,000.

Admissions Traditional secondary-level entrance grade is 9. For fall 2013, 219 students applied for upper-level admission, 185 were accepted, 167 enrolled. STS required. Deadline for receipt of application materials: none. No application fee required. On-campus interview required.

Athletics Interscholastic: baseball, basketball, bowling, crew, cross-country running, diving, football, golf, ice hockey, lacrosse, soccer, swimming and diving, tennis, track and field, water polo, winter (indoor) track, wrestling; intramural: basketball, football. 4 PE instructors, 49 coaches, 2 athletic trainers.

Computers Computers are regularly used in animation, art, desktop publishing, English, mathematics, science, Web site design classes. Computer network features include Internet access, Internet filtering or blocking technology. Student e-mail accounts and computer access in designated common areas are available to students. Students grades are available online. The school has a published electronic and media policy.

Contact Mrs. Jacqueline VanDemark, Administrative Assistant. 419-531-1618. Fax: 419-531-9740. E-mail: jvandemark@sfstoledo.org. Website: www.sfstoledo.org

SAINT FRANCIS GIRLS HIGH SCHOOL

5900 Elvas Avenue
Sacramento, California 95819

Head of School: Mrs. Margo Brown

General Information Girls' day college-preparatory, arts, and religious studies school, affiliated with Roman Catholic Church. Grades 9–12. Founded: 1940. Setting: urban. 11-acre campus. 11 buildings on campus. Approved or accredited by Western Association of Schools and Colleges, Western Catholic Education Association, and California Department of Education. Total enrollment: 1,078. Upper school average class size: 26. Upper school faculty-student ratio: 1:15. There are 180 required school days per year for Upper School students. Upper School students typically attend 5 days per week. The average school day consists of 7 hours.

Upper School Student Profile Grade 9: 262 students (262 girls); Grade 10: 270 students (270 girls); Grade 11: 261 students (261 girls); Grade 12: 285 students (285 girls). 72.6% of students are Roman Catholic.

Faculty School total: 68. In upper school: 18 men, 50 women; 62 have advanced degrees.

Subjects Offered Acting, advanced biology, advanced chemistry, advanced computer applications, advanced math, Advanced Placement courses, advanced studio art-AP, algebra, American government, American history, American history-AP, American literature, anatomy and physiology, art, art history-AP, biology, biology-AP, biotechnology, calculus, calculus-AP, chemistry, chemistry-AP, choir, Christian ethics, church history, civics, computer graphics, computer science-AP, dance, drawing, economics, English literature and composition-AP, equality and freedom, ethics, film and literature, fitness, French, French literature-AP, French-AP, geography, geometry, health, Hebrew scripture, integrated science, Italian, jazz, Latin, model United Nations, orchestra, painting, philosophy, physics, prayer/spirituality, pre-calculus, robotics, sculpture, Spanish, Spanish language-AP, Spanish literature-AP, speech, statistics, studio art-AP, U.S. government and politics-AP, U.S. history, U.S. history-AP, world history, world religions, yearbook, yoga.

Special Academic Programs 13 Advanced Placement exams for which test preparation is offered; honors section.

College Admission Counseling 258 students graduated in 2013; 255 went to college, including California Polytechnic State University, San Luis Obispo; California State University, Sacramento; Texas Christian University; The University of Arizona; University of California, Davis; University of Nevada, Reno. Other: 3 had other specific plans. Mean SAT critical reading: 574, mean SAT math: 552, mean SAT writing: 593, mean composite ACT: 25.

Student Life Upper grades have uniform requirement, student council, honor system. Discipline rests primarily with faculty. Attendance at religious services is required.

Summer Programs Enrichment, advancement, sports, art/fine arts programs offered; held on campus; accepts boys and girls; open to students from other schools. 750 students usually enrolled. 2014 schedule: June 16 to July 25. Application deadline: none.

Tuition and Aid Day student tuition: $12,200. Tuition installment plan (monthly payment plans, Semi-Annual, Annual). Need-based scholarship grants available. In 2013–14, 26% of upper-school students received aid. Total amount of financial aid awarded in 2013–14: $1,200,000.

Admissions Traditional secondary-level entrance grade is 9. CTBS (or similar from their school) required. Deadline for receipt of application materials: January 24. No application fee required. Interview required.

Athletics Interscholastic: aerobics, basketball, cheering, cross-country running, diving, golf, lacrosse, physical training, soccer, softball, swimming and diving, tennis, track and field, volleyball, water polo. 4 PE instructors, 45 coaches, 2 athletic trainers.

Computers Computer resources include on-campus library services, Internet access, wireless campus network, Internet filtering or blocking technology. Student e-mail accounts and computer access in designated common areas are available to students. Students grades are available online. The school has a published electronic and media policy.

Contact Mrs. Lisa Wilkins, Director of Admissions. 916-452-3461 Ext. 195. Fax: 916-452-6046. E-mail: lwilkins@stfrancishs.org. Website: www.stfrancishs.org

SAINT FRANCIS HIGH SCHOOL

200 Foothill Boulevard
La Canada Flintridge, California 91011

Head of School: Mr. Thomas G. Moran

General Information Boys' day college-preparatory and religious studies school, affiliated with Roman Catholic Church. Grades 9–12. Founded: 1946. Setting: suburban. Nearest major city is Los Angeles. 19-acre campus. 5 buildings on campus. Approved or accredited by Western Association of Schools and Colleges and Western Catholic Education Association. Total enrollment: 678. Upper school average class size: 28. Upper school faculty-student ratio: 1:15. There are 182 required school days per year for Upper School students. Upper School students typically attend 5 days per week. The average school day consists of 6 hours.

Upper School Student Profile Grade 9: 173 students (173 boys); Grade 10: 177 students (177 boys); Grade 11: 164 students (164 boys); Grade 12: 164 students (164 boys). 67% of students are Roman Catholic.

Faculty School total: 48. In upper school: 38 men, 10 women; 20 have advanced degrees.

Subjects Offered Advanced Placement courses, computer skills, English, fine arts, foreign language, history, mathematics, physical education, religion, science, social sciences, technology.

Graduation Requirements Arts and fine arts (art, music, dance, drama), English, foreign language, mathematics, physical education (includes health), religion (includes Bible studies and theology), science, social sciences, technology, Christian service hours, retreat each year of attendance. Community service is required.

Special Academic Programs Advanced Placement exam preparation; honors section.

College Admission Counseling 141 students graduated in 2013; 137 went to college, including California State University, Northridge; California State University Channel Islands; Santa Clara University; Texas Christian University. Other: 4 had other specific plans. Mean SAT critical reading: 561, mean SAT math: 557, mean SAT writing: 538, mean composite ACT: 23.

Student Life Upper grades have specified standards of dress, student council. Discipline rests primarily with faculty. Attendance at religious services is required.

Summer Programs Remediation, enrichment, sports programs offered; session focuses on remediation and enrichment; held on campus; accepts boys and girls; open to students from other schools. 400 students usually enrolled. 2014 schedule: June 23 to July 25. Application deadline: June 16.

Tuition and Aid Day student tuition: $13,300. Tuition installment plan (FACTS Tuition Payment Plan, monthly payment plans). Merit scholarship grants, need-based scholarship grants available. In 2013–14, 20% of upper-school students received aid; total upper-school merit-scholarship money awarded: $55,000. Total amount of financial aid awarded in 2013–14: $700,000.

Admissions Traditional secondary-level entrance grade is 9. For fall 2013, 400 students applied for upper-level admission, 210 were accepted, 173 enrolled. High School Placement Test required. Deadline for receipt of application materials: January 25. Application fee required: $75. On-campus interview required.

Athletics Interscholastic: baseball, basketball, cross-country running, football, golf, lacrosse, soccer, tennis, track and field, volleyball. 3 PE instructors, 14 coaches, 1 athletic trainer.

Computers Computers are regularly used in all academic, yearbook classes. Computer network features include on-campus library services, Internet access, wireless campus network, Internet filtering or blocking technology. Students grades are available online. The school has a published electronic and media policy.

Contact Mrs. Stephanie Martinez, Registrar. 818-790-0325 Ext. 502. Fax: 818-790-5542. E-mail: martinezs@sfhs.net. Website: www.sfhs.net

SAINT FRANCIS HIGH SCHOOL

1885 Miramonte Avenue
Mountain View, California 94040
Head of School: Mr. Kevin Makley

General Information Coeducational day college-preparatory, arts, religious studies, and technology school, affiliated with Roman Catholic Church, Roman Catholic Church. Grades 9–12. Founded: 1954. Setting: suburban. Nearest major city is San Jose. 25-acre campus. 10 buildings on campus. Approved or accredited by Western Association of Schools and Colleges and California Department of Education. Total enrollment: 1,753. Upper school average class size: 29. Upper school faculty-student ratio: 1:29. There are 180 required school days per year for Upper School students. Upper School students typically attend 5 days per week. The average school day consists of 6 hours and 30 minutes.

Upper School Student Profile Grade 9: 458 students (229 boys, 229 girls); Grade 10: 451 students (234 boys, 217 girls); Grade 11: 409 students (216 boys, 193 girls); Grade 12: 435 students (212 boys, 223 girls). 70% of students are Roman Catholic, Roman Catholic.

Faculty School total: 103. In upper school: 56 men, 47 women; 63 have advanced degrees.

Subjects Offered 20th century American writers, 3-dimensional design, accounting, algebra, American literature, analytic geometry, anatomy and physiology, Arabic studies, band, biology, biology-AP, British literature, British literature (honors), business, calculus-AP, chemistry, chemistry-AP, Christianity, computer graphics, computer literacy, computer programming, computer science, computer science-AP, concert band, concert choir, contemporary issues, contemporary problems, creative writing, design, drama, drawing, economics, electronic music, English, English literature-AP, film and literature, French, French-AP, geography, geometry, German, German-AP, global science, graphics, health science, human biology, information technology, Irish literature, jazz band, jazz ensemble, journalism, music, oil painting, philosophy, physical education, physical science, pre-calculus, printmaking, psychology, religious studies, science fiction, short story, social justice, Spanish, Spanish-AP, speech, speech communications, statistics, symphonic band, technical drawing, technology, trigonometry, typing, U.S. government, U.S. government and politics-AP, U.S. history, U.S. history-AP, water color painting, word processing, world history, world religions.

Graduation Requirements Computer literacy, English, foreign language, human biology, mathematics, physical education (includes health), religious studies, science, social studies (includes history).

Special Academic Programs Advanced Placement exam preparation; honors section; study at local college for college credit.

College Admission Counseling 412 students graduated in 2013; all went to college, including Loyola Marymount University; Stanford University; University of California, Berkeley; University of California, Los Angeles; University of Southern California. Mean SAT critical reading: 711, mean SAT math: 743, mean SAT writing: 742.

Student Life Upper grades have specified standards of dress, student council. Discipline rests primarily with faculty. Attendance at religious services is required.

Summer Programs Remediation, enrichment, advancement, sports, art/fine arts, computer instruction programs offered; session focuses on academics and enrichment; held on campus; accepts boys and girls; open to students from other schools. 1,000 students usually enrolled. 2014 schedule: June 15 to July 30. Application deadline: June 10.

Tuition and Aid Day student tuition: $15,500. Tuition installment plan (monthly payment plans, individually arranged payment plans). Need-based scholarship grants, paying campus jobs available. In 2013–14, 18% of upper-school students received aid. Total amount of financial aid awarded in 2013–14: $2,100,000.

Admissions Traditional secondary-level entrance grade is 9. For fall 2013, 1,300 students applied for upper-level admission, 650 were accepted, 458 enrolled. High School Placement Test required. Deadline for receipt of application materials: December 13. Application fee required: $65. On-campus interview required.

Athletics Interscholastic: aquatics (boys, girls), baseball (b,g), basketball (b,g), cheering (g), cross-country running (b,g), dance squad (g), diving (b,g), drill team (b,g), field hockey (g), football (b), golf (b,g), gymnastics (g), lacrosse (b,g), soccer (b,g), softball (g), strength & conditioning (b,g), swimming and diving (b,g), track and field (b,g), volleyball (b,g), water polo (b,g), wrestling (b); intramural: cooperative games (b,g), crew (g), flag football (b,g), indoor soccer (b,g), physical fitness (b,g), rugby (b,g), soccer (b,g), strength & conditioning (b,g), swimming and diving (b,g), table tennis (b,g), volleyball (b,g), whiffle ball (b,g); coed interscholastic: cheering; coed intramural: basketball, cooperative games, flag football, indoor soccer, soccer, volleyball, whiffle ball. 6 PE instructors, 51 coaches, 1 athletic trainer.

Computers Computers are regularly used in creative writing, current events, digital applications, graphic arts, graphic design, photography, publications classes. Computer network features include on-campus library services, Internet access, wireless campus network, Internet filtering or blocking technology. Campus intranet, student e-mail accounts, and computer access in designated common areas are available to students. Students grades are available online.

Contact Mr. Simon Raines, Director of Admissions. 650-968-1213 Ext. 213. Fax: 650-968-1706. E-mail: simonraines@sfhs.com. Website: www.sfhs.com

ST. FRANCIS HIGH SCHOOL

233 West Broadway
Louisville, Kentucky 40202
Head of School: Ms. Alexandra Schreiber Thurstone

General Information Coeducational day college-preparatory and arts school. Grades 9–12. Founded: 1976. Setting: urban. 2-acre campus. 1 building on campus. Approved or accredited by Independent Schools Association of the Central States and Kentucky Department of Education. Member of National Association of Independent Schools. Endowment: $1 million. Total enrollment: 150. Upper school average class size: 12. Upper school faculty-student ratio: 1:9. There are 174 required school days per year for Upper School students. Upper School students typically attend 5 days per week. The average school day consists of 7 hours.

Upper School Student Profile Grade 9: 38 students (17 boys, 21 girls); Grade 10: 44 students (18 boys, 26 girls); Grade 11: 33 students (14 boys, 19 girls); Grade 12: 35 students (20 boys, 15 girls).

Faculty School total: 20. In upper school: 12 men, 8 women; 15 have advanced degrees.

Subjects Offered African studies, algebra, American history, ancient history, ancient world history, art, biology, biology-AP, business, calculus, calculus-AP, chemistry, chemistry-AP, Chinese, Chinese history, civil rights, community service, creative writing, drama, drawing, English, English literature, English literature-AP, environmental science, environmental science-AP, European history, European history-AP, film studies, filmmaking, fine arts, finite math, French, French language-AP, French literature-AP, French-AP, gender and religion, gender issues, geometry, health, history-AP, journalism, law, medieval history, modern civilization, photography, physical education, physics, physics-AP, playwriting, pre-calculus, senior project, Spanish, Spanish language-AP, Spanish literature-AP, Spanish-AP, statistics, statistics-AP, The 20th Century, U.S. history-AP, video film production, world history, writing, zoology.

Graduation Requirements Arts and fine arts (art, music, dance, drama), English, foreign language, history, mathematics, physical education (includes health), science, senior project (year-long research project on a topic of student's choice). Community service is required.

Special Academic Programs Advanced Placement exam preparation; independent study; study abroad; academic accommodation for the gifted and the artistically talented.

College Admission Counseling 35 students graduated in 2013; all went to college.

Student Life Upper grades have student council. Discipline rests equally with students and faculty.

Summer Programs Remediation, enrichment, advancement, sports programs offered; session focuses on enrichment; held on campus; accepts boys and girls; open to students from other schools. 40 students usually enrolled. 2014 schedule: June 1 to August 13. Application deadline: April 1.

Tuition and Aid Day student tuition: $19,950. Tuition installment plan (Insured Tuition Payment Plan, FACTS Tuition Payment Plan, monthly payment plans). Merit scholarship grants, need-based scholarship grants, tuition remission for children of faculty and staff available. In 2013–14, 52% of upper-school students received aid.

Admissions Traditional secondary-level entrance grade is 9. For fall 2013, 47 students applied for upper-level admission, 42 were accepted, 39 enrolled. Deadline for receipt of application materials: January 15. Application fee required: $50. On-campus interview required.

Athletics Interscholastic: basketball (boys, girls), bicycling (b,g), bowling (g), field hockey (g), fitness (b,g), lacrosse (b), running (b,g), tennis (b,g), track and field (b,g), volleyball (g); intramural: indoor hockey (g), indoor soccer (b); coed interscholastic: indoor track & field, soccer; coed intramural: dance team, fitness, physical fitness, physical training, power lifting, racquetball, rowing, ultimate Frisbee, wall climbing, wallyball, weight lifting, weight training, yoga. 1 PE instructor, 12 coaches.

Computers Computers are regularly used in English, French, history, mathematics, science, Spanish classes. Computer network features include Internet access, wireless campus network, word processing, publishing, and Web page programs. Student e-mail accounts and computer access in designated common areas are available to students. The school has a published electronic and media policy.

Contact Ms. Lucy Wathen, Director of Admissions. 502-736-1009. Fax: 502-736-1049. E-mail: lwathen@stfrancisschool.org. Website: www.stfrancisschool.org

ST. GEORGE'S INDEPENDENT SCHOOL

1880 Wolf River Road
Collierville, Tennessee 38017
Head of School: Mr. William W. Taylor

General Information Coeducational day college-preparatory school, affiliated with Christian faith. Grades PK–12. Founded: 1959. Setting: suburban. Nearest major city is Memphis. 250-acre campus. 5 buildings on campus. Approved or accredited by Southern Association of Colleges and Schools and Southern Association of Independent Schools. Member of National Association of Independent Schools. Endowment: $3.4 million. Total enrollment: 1,213. Upper school average class size: 19. Upper school faculty-student ratio: 1:7. There are 175 required school days per year for

Upper School students. Upper School students typically attend 5 days per week. The average school day consists of 7 hours and 18 minutes.

Subjects Offered Algebra, American literature, astronomy, band, biology, biology-AP, calculus, calculus-AP, chemistry, chemistry-AP, chorus, computer programming, drawing, English, English language and composition-AP, English literature and composition-AP, environmental science, ethics, European history-AP, European literature, film, French, French language-AP, geometry, global studies, government and politics-AP, government/civics, honors algebra, honors geometry, human anatomy, independent study, journalism, Latin, Latin-AP, painting, philosophy, photography, physics, physics-AP, pottery, pre-calculus, printmaking, psychology, psychology-AP, religion, short story, social justice, Southern literature, Spanish, Spanish language-AP, statistics-AP, theater, trigonometry, U.S. history, U.S. history-AP, visual arts, wellness, world history, world history-AP.

Graduation Requirements Art, electives, English, history, independent study, language, mathematics, religion (includes Bible studies and theology), science, wellness, senior independent study, senior Global Challenge.

Special Academic Programs Advanced Placement exam preparation; honors section; independent study.

College Admission Counseling Mean SAT critical reading: 619, mean SAT math: 598, mean SAT writing: 608, mean combined SAT: 1825, mean composite ACT: 28.

Student Life Upper grades have specified standards of dress, student council, honor system. Discipline rests equally with students and faculty. Attendance at religious services is required.

Summer Programs Remediation, enrichment, advancement, sports, art/fine arts, computer instruction programs offered; session focuses on enrichment; held on campus; accepts boys and girls; open to students from other schools. 2014 schedule: June to August. Application deadline: June.

Tuition and Aid Day student tuition: $17,171. Tuition installment plan (individually arranged payment plans, One payment per year, two payments per year, and four payments per year.). Need-based scholarship grants available. In 2013–14, 14% of upper-school students received aid. Total amount of financial aid awarded in 2013–14: $389,652.

Admissions Traditional secondary-level entrance grade is 9. Admissions testing or ISEE required. Deadline for receipt of application materials: none. Application fee required: $50. Interview required.

Athletics Interscholastic: baseball (boys), basketball (b,g), cheering (g), cross-country running (b,g), football (b), golf (b,g), lacrosse (b,g), pom squad (g), soccer (b,g), softball (g), tennis (b,g), track and field (b,g), volleyball (g), wrestling (b); coed interscholastic: swimming and diving; coed intramural: equestrian sports.

Computers Computers are regularly used in all classes. Computer network features include on-campus library services, Internet access, wireless campus network, Internet filtering or blocking technology. Campus intranet, student e-mail accounts, and computer access in designated common areas are available to students. Students grades are available online. The school has a published electronic and media policy.

Contact Mrs. Jennifer Taylor, Director of Admission. 901-457-2000. Fax: 901-457-2111. E-mail: jtaylor@sgis.org. Website: www.sgis.org

ST. GEORGE'S SCHOOL

372 Purgatory Road
Middletown, Rhode Island 02842-5984

Head of School: Eric F. Peterson

General Information Coeducational boarding and day college-preparatory, arts, religious studies, technology, and marine sciences school, affiliated with Episcopal Church. Grades 9–12. Founded: 1896. Setting: suburban. Nearest major city is Providence. Students are housed in single-sex dormitories. 125-acre campus. 47 buildings on campus. Approved or accredited by Association of Independent Schools in New England, National Association of Episcopal Schools, New England Association of Schools and Colleges, The Association of Boarding Schools, and Rhode Island Department of Education. Member of National Association of Independent Schools and Secondary School Admission Test Board. Endowment: $120 million. Total enrollment: 365. Upper school average class size: 11. Upper school faculty-student ratio: 1:6. Upper School students typically attend 6 days per week. The average school day consists of 6 hours and 50 minutes.

Upper School Student Profile Grade 9: 76 students (38 boys, 38 girls); Grade 10: 104 students (50 boys, 54 girls); Grade 11: 89 students (43 boys, 46 girls); Grade 12: 90 students (43 boys, 47 girls). 85% of students are boarding students. 20% are state residents. 31 states are represented in upper school student body. 15% are international students. International students from Canada, China, Germany, and Republic of Korea; 18 other countries represented in student body.

Faculty School total: 70. In upper school: 32 men, 37 women; 55 have advanced degrees; 60 reside on campus.

Subjects Offered 3-dimensional art, 3-dimensional design, acting, advanced biology, advanced chemistry, advanced computer applications, advanced math, Advanced Placement courses, advanced studio art-AP, African American history, African American studies, algebra, American history, American history-AP, American literature, American literature-AP, American studies, analytic geometry, architectural drawing, architecture, art, art history, art-AP, Asian studies, Bible, Bible as literature,

Bible studies, biology, biology-AP, calculus, calculus-AP, ceramics, chemistry, chemistry-AP, Chinese, computer graphics, computer math, computer programming, computer science, computer science-AP, creative writing, dance, DNA, drama, dramatic arts, drawing, ecology, economics, economics-AP, English, English language and composition-AP, English literature, English literature-AP, environmental science, environmental science-AP, ethics, European history, European history-AP, expository writing, fine arts, French, French language-AP, geometry, global studies, government/civics, grammar, health, history, journalism, Latin, Latin-AP, law, logic, macro/microeconomics-AP, Mandarin, marine biology, mathematics, microbiology, music, music theory-AP, navigation, oceanography, philosophy, photography, physics, physics-AP, psychology, public speaking, religion, robotics, science, sculpture, social studies, Spanish, Spanish language-AP, Spanish literature-AP, statistics, studio art-AP, theater, theology, trigonometry, U.S. government and politics-AP, veterinary science, world history, world history-AP, world literature, writing.

Graduation Requirements Arts and fine arts (art, music, dance, drama), computer science, English, foreign language, mathematics, physical education (includes health), religion (includes Bible studies and theology), science, social studies (includes history).

Special Academic Programs Advanced Placement exam preparation; honors section; independent study; term-away projects; study abroad; academic accommodation for the gifted, the musically talented, and the artistically talented.

College Admission Counseling 90 students graduated in 2013; 89 went to college, including Babson College; Boston College; Georgetown University; Middlebury College; The George Washington University; Wake Forest University. Other: 1 entered a postgraduate year. Mean SAT critical reading: 630, mean SAT math: 655, mean SAT writing: 630, mean combined SAT: 1915.

Student Life Upper grades have specified standards of dress, student council, honor system. Discipline rests primarily with faculty. Attendance at religious services is required.

Tuition and Aid Day student tuition: $35,700; 7-day tuition and room/board: $52,000. Tuition installment plan (Insured Tuition Payment Plan, monthly payment plans, individually arranged payment plans). Need-based scholarship grants, need-based loans, middle-income loans available. In 2013–14, 30% of upper-school students received aid. Total amount of financial aid awarded in 2013–14: $3,700,000.

Admissions Traditional secondary-level entrance grade is 9. For fall 2013, 756 students applied for upper-level admission, 211 were accepted, 119 enrolled. ISEE, PSAT, SSAT or TOEFL required. Deadline for receipt of application materials: February 1. Application fee required: $50. Interview recommended.

Athletics Interscholastic: baseball (boys), basketball (b,g), cross-country running (b,g), field hockey (g), football (b), hockey (b,g), ice hockey (b,g), lacrosse (b,g), sailing (b,g), soccer (b,g), softball (g), squash (b,g), swimming and diving (b,g), tennis (b,g), track and field (b,g); coed interscholastic: dance, golf, sailing; coed intramural: aerobics/dance, dance, modern dance, mountain biking, Nautilus, soccer, softball, squash, strength & conditioning. 3 coaches, 3 athletic trainers.

Computers Computers are regularly used in art, English, foreign language, history, mathematics, music, religion, science, theater classes. Computer network features include on-campus library services, online commercial services, Internet access, wireless campus network, Internet filtering or blocking technology, scanners, digital cameras, and access to printers. Campus intranet, student e-mail accounts, and computer access in designated common areas are available to students. Students grades are available online. The school has a published electronic and media policy.

Contact Ryan P. Mulhern, Director of Admission. 401-842-6600. Fax: 401-842-6696. E-mail: admission@stgeorges.edu. Website: www.stgeorges.edu

ST. GEORGE'S SCHOOL

4175 West 29th Avenue
Vancouver, British Columbia V6S 1V1, Canada

Head of School: Dr. Tom Matthews

General Information Boys' boarding and day college-preparatory, arts, business, bilingual studies, and technology school. Boarding grades 8–12, day grades 1–12. Founded: 1930. Setting: urban. Students are housed in single-sex dormitories. 27-acre campus. 2 buildings on campus. Approved or accredited by Canadian Association of Independent Schools, Northwest Association of Independent Schools, The Association of Boarding Schools, and British Columbia Department of Education. Affiliate member of National Association of Independent Schools; member of Secondary School Admission Test Board. Language of instruction: English. Total enrollment: 1,157. Upper school average class size: 19. Upper school faculty-student ratio: 1:8. There are 157 required school days per year for Upper School students. Upper School students typically attend 5 days per week. The average school day consists of 6 hours.

Upper School Student Profile Grade 8: 144 students (144 boys); Grade 9: 152 students (152 boys); Grade 10: 162 students (162 boys); Grade 11: 162 students (162 boys); Grade 12: 161 students (161 boys). 18% of students are boarding students. 91% are province residents. 9 provinces are represented in upper school student body. 9% are international students. International students from China, Germany, Hong Kong, Mexico, Taiwan, and United States; 13 other countries represented in student body.

Faculty School total: 130. In upper school: 62 men, 31 women; 55 have advanced degrees; 14 reside on campus.

Subjects Offered Advanced chemistry, advanced computer applications, advanced math, algebra, analysis and differential calculus, applied arts, applied music, applied skills, architecture, art, art history, art history-AP, biology, biology-AP, business, business skills, calculus, calculus-AP, Canadian geography, Canadian history, Canadian literature, career and personal planning, ceramics, chemistry, chemistry-AP, comparative government and politics-AP, computer graphics, computer programming, computer programming-AP, computer science, computer science-AP, creative writing, critical thinking, debate, drama, drama performance, dramatic arts, earth science, economics, economics-AP, English, English literature, English literature-AP, environmental science, European history, expository writing, film, fine arts, French, French-AP, geography, geology, geometry, German, German-AP, government/civics, grammar, history, industrial arts, introduction to theater, Japanese, journalism, Latin, Latin-AP, law, library, Mandarin, mathematics, mathematics-AP, music, music-AP, performing arts, photography, physical education, physical fitness, physics, physics-AP, psychology, psychology-AP, science, social studies, society, politics and law, Spanish, Spanish-AP, speech and debate, studio art, studio art-AP, technical theater, theater, trigonometry, typing, U.S. history-AP, United States government-AP, Western civilization, world history, world literature, writing.

Graduation Requirements Arts and fine arts (art, music, dance, drama), business skills (includes word processing), English, foreign language, mathematics, physical education (includes health), science, social studies (includes history).

Special Academic Programs Advanced Placement exam preparation; honors section; remedial reading and/or remedial writing.

College Admission Counseling 162 students graduated in 2013; 157 went to college, including McGill University; Queen's University at Kingston; The University of British Columbia; The University of Western Ontario; University of Toronto. Other: 5 had other specific plans.

Student Life Upper grades have uniform requirement, student council, honor system. Discipline rests primarily with faculty.

Summer Programs Advancement, ESL, sports, art/fine arts, computer instruction programs offered; session focuses on recreation and enrichment; held both on and off campus; held at other schools in area (outdoor education); accepts boys and girls; open to students from other schools. 1,000 students usually enrolled. 2014 schedule: July 2 to August 15. Application deadline: none.

Tuition and Aid Day student tuition: CAN$18,140–CAN$29,880; 7-day tuition and room/board: CAN$42,000–CAN$53,500. Tuition installment plan (monthly payment plans, individually arranged payment plans, term payment plan, one-time payment plan). Tuition reduction for siblings, bursaries, merit scholarship grants, need-based scholarship grants available. In 2013–14, 7% of upper-school students received aid. Total amount of financial aid awarded in 2013–14: CAN$800,000.

Admissions Traditional secondary-level entrance grade is 8. For fall 2013, 225 students applied for upper-level admission, 92 were accepted, 51 enrolled. School's own exam and SSAT required. Deadline for receipt of application materials: December 2. Application fee required: CAN$250. Interview required.

Athletics Interscholastic: badminton, basketball, cricket, cross-country running, field hockey, golf, ice hockey, rowing, rugby, soccer, swimming and diving, tennis, track and field, triathlon, volleyball, water polo; intramural: badminton, ball hockey, basketball, bicycling, canoeing/kayaking, cross-country running, flag football, floor hockey, ice hockey, martial arts, outdoor education, outdoor recreation, physical fitness, rugby, running, sailing, skiing (downhill), soccer, softball, squash, swimming and diving, table tennis, tennis, track and field, ultimate Frisbee, volleyball, water polo, weight lifting. 10 PE instructors, 3 coaches, 2 athletic trainers.

Computers Computers are regularly used in desktop publishing, history, information technology, mathematics, media, publications, science, technology classes. Computer network features include on-campus library services, online commercial services, Internet access, wireless campus network, Internet filtering or blocking technology. Campus intranet, student e-mail accounts, and computer access in designated common areas are available to students. Students grades are available online. The school has a published electronic and media policy.

Contact Mr. Gordon C. Allan, Director of Admissions. 604-221-3881. Fax: 604-221-3893. E-mail: gallan@stgeorges.bc.ca. Website: www.stgeorges.bc.ca

ST. GEORGE'S SCHOOL OF MONTREAL

3100 The Boulevard
Montreal, Quebec H3Y 1R9, Canada

Head of School: Mr. James A. Officer

General Information Coeducational day college-preparatory, arts, bilingual studies, technology, Sports études, and Performing Arts études school. Grades K–11. Founded: 1930. Setting: urban. 2-acre campus. 1 building on campus. Approved or accredited by Canadian Association of Independent Schools, Quebec Association of Independent Schools, and Quebec Department of Education. Affiliate member of National Association of Independent Schools. Languages of instruction: English and French. Total enrollment: 426. Upper school average class size: 19. Upper school faculty-student ratio: 1:15. There are 180 required school days per year for Upper School students. Upper School students typically attend 5 days per week. The average school day consists of 6 hours and 45 minutes.

Upper School Student Profile Grade 7: 50 students (25 boys, 25 girls); Grade 8: 45 students (28 boys, 17 girls); Grade 9: 47 students (36 boys, 11 girls); Grade 10: 58 students (31 boys, 27 girls); Grade 11: 36 students (17 boys, 19 girls).

Faculty School total: 33. In upper school: 14 men, 19 women; 16 have advanced degrees.

Subjects Offered Advanced math, advanced studio art-AP, algebra, ancient history, art, art appreciation, art history, biology, calculus, calculus-AP, Canadian history, chemistry, college counseling, communication skills, community service, competitive science projects, computer animation, computer art, computer multimedia, concert band, concert choir, contemporary issues, creative thinking, creative writing, critical thinking, dance, debate, desktop publishing, digital art, drama, drama performance, earth science, English, English literature and composition-AP, English-AP, environmental education, environmental science, ESL, ethics, experimental science, expository writing, filmmaking, fine arts, fitness, food and nutrition, French as a second language, French studies, French-AP, general math, general science, geography, government/civics, health education, independent study, instrumental music, integrated science, interdisciplinary studies, Internet research, jazz band, jazz ensemble, leadership, leadership education training, library research, marine biology, mathematics, media arts, media literacy, mentorship program, model United Nations, music, music appreciation, musical productions, musical theater dance, oral communications, outdoor education, performing arts, photography, physical education, physical fitness, physics, play production, play/screen writing, portfolio art, pre-calculus, psychology, psychology-AP, research skills, robotics, science and technology, science project, set design, sex education, social studies, Spanish, sports science, student publications, studio art-AP, swimming, tennis, track and field, writing, yoga.

Graduation Requirements Art, electives, English, ethics, French as a second language, mathematics, physical education (includes health), science, social studies (includes history), community learning.

Special Academic Programs 7 Advanced Placement exams for which test preparation is offered; honors section; independent study; academic accommodation for the gifted, the musically talented, and the artistically talented; remedial reading and/or remedial writing; remedial math; ESL (7 students enrolled).

College Admission Counseling 36 students graduated in 2013; all went to college.

Student Life Upper grades have specified standards of dress, student council. Discipline rests primarily with faculty.

Tuition and Aid Guaranteed tuition plan. Tuition installment plan (4 Payments (1, 2 or 4 Payments)). Tuition reduction for siblings, need-based scholarship grants available.

Admissions Traditional secondary-level entrance grade is 7. For fall 2013, 132 students applied for upper-level admission, 70 were accepted, 49 enrolled. Academic Profile Tests or placement test required. Deadline for receipt of application materials: January 25. Application fee required: CAN$50. Interview required.

Athletics Interscholastic: badminton (boys, girls), basketball (b,g), cross-country running (b,g), flag football (g), football (b), golf (b,g), rugby (b), running (b,g), soccer (b,g), swimming and diving (b,g), tennis (b,g), track and field (b,g); intramural: badminton (b,g); coed interscholastic: aquatics, independent competitive sports, jogging; coed intramural: aerobics, aquatics, ball hockey, baseball, basketball, bicycling, canoeing/kayaking, climbing, cooperative games, Cosom hockey, cross-country running, curling, dance, fencing, fitness, fitness walking, floor hockey, ice hockey, indoor soccer, jogging, martial arts, outdoor recreation, physical fitness, scuba diving, self defense, skiing (cross-country), soccer, squash, track and field, volleyball, wall climbing, yoga. 2 PE instructors, 8 coaches.

Computers Computers are regularly used in all classes. Computer network features include on-campus library services, Internet access, wireless campus network, Internet filtering or blocking technology. Campus intranet and student e-mail accounts are available to students. The school has a published electronic and media policy.

Contact Ms. Kathay Carson, Director of Admissions. 514-904-0542. Fax: 514-933-3621. E-mail: kathay.carson@stgeorges.qc.ca. Website: www.stgeorges.qc.ca

SAINT GERTRUDE HIGH SCHOOL

3215 Stuart Avenue
Richmond, Virginia 23221

Head of School: Mrs. Susan Walker

General Information Girls' day college-preparatory and religious studies school, affiliated with Roman Catholic Church. Grades 9–12. Founded: 1922. Setting: urban. 1 building on campus. Approved or accredited by National Independent Private Schools Association, Southern Association of Colleges and Schools, and Virginia Department of Education. Member of National Association of Independent Schools. Total enrollment: 266. Upper school average class size: 15. Upper school faculty-student ratio: 1:9. There are 180 required school days per year for Upper School students. The average school day consists of 7 hours.

Upper School Student Profile Grade 9: 62 students (62 girls); Grade 10: 83 students (83 girls); Grade 11: 55 students (55 girls); Grade 12: 66 students (66 girls). 67% of students are Roman Catholic.

Faculty School total: 30. In upper school: 3 men, 27 women; 26 have advanced degrees.

Subjects Offered Advanced Placement courses, algebra, American history, American history-AP, American literature, American literature-AP, anatomy, art, bell choir, Bible studies, biology, calculus, calculus-AP, ceramics, chemistry, chemistry-AP, chorus, church history, community service, computer science, drama, drawing, driver education, English, English language and composition-AP, English language-AP, English literature, English literature and composition-AP, environmental science, European history, expository writing, fine arts, French, geometry, government and politics-AP, government/civics, grammar, history, honors algebra, honors English, honors world history, humanities, keyboarding, Latin, mathematics, media, music, painting, physical education, physics, physics-AP, pre-calculus, probability and statistics, psychology, religion, science, social sciences, social studies, sociology, Spanish, Spanish literature, studio art-AP, theater, theology, trigonometry, U.S. government and politics-AP, world history, world literature, writing, yearbook.

Graduation Requirements Arts and fine arts (art, music, dance, drama), computer science, English, keyboarding, mathematics, physical education (includes health), religion (includes Bible studies and theology), science, social sciences, social studies (includes history), 4 years Theology. Community service is required.

Special Academic Programs Advanced Placement exam preparation; honors section.

College Admission Counseling 66 students graduated in 2013; all went to college, including James Madison University; The College of William and Mary; University of Virginia; Virginia Commonwealth University; Virginia Polytechnic Institute and State University.

Student Life Upper grades have uniform requirement, student council, honor system. Discipline rests equally with students and faculty. Attendance at religious services is required.

Tuition and Aid Day student tuition: $14,600. Tuition installment plan (FACTS Tuition Payment Plan, monthly payment plans). Merit scholarship grants, need-based scholarship grants available. In 2013–14, 24% of upper-school students received aid.

Admissions Traditional secondary-level entrance grade is 9. Admissions testing, latest standardized score from previous school and Otis-Lennon School Ability Test required. Deadline for receipt of application materials: January 31. Application fee required: $50. On-campus interview required.

Athletics Interscholastic: basketball, cross-country running, field hockey, golf, indoor track, lacrosse, soccer, softball, swimming and diving, tennis, track and field, volleyball; coed interscholastic; swimming and diving, track and field. 1 PE instructor, 14 coaches, 1 athletic trainer.

Computers Computers are regularly used in all academic classes. Computer network features include on-campus library services, Internet access, wireless campus network, Internet filtering or blocking technology. Campus intranet, student e-mail accounts, and computer access in designated common areas are available to students. Students grades are available online. The school has a published electronic and media policy.

Contact Maureen Williams, Director of Admission and Marketing. 804-358-9885 Ext. 341. Fax: 804-353-8929. E-mail: mwilliams@saintgertrude.org. Website: www.saintgertrude.org

ST. GREGORY COLLEGE PREPARATORY SCHOOL

3231 North Craycroft Road
Tucson, Arizona 85712

Head of School: Mr. A. Richard Belding

General Information Coeducational day college-preparatory and arts school. Grades 6–12. Founded: 1980. Setting: suburban. 40-acre campus. 9 buildings on campus. Approved or accredited by Independent Schools Association of the Southwest, The College Board, and Arizona Department of Education. Member of National Association of Independent Schools and Secondary School Admission Test Board. Total enrollment: 299. Upper school average class size: 16. Upper school faculty-student ratio: 1:9. Upper School students typically attend 5 days per week. The average school day consists of 7 hours and 30 minutes.

Upper School Student Profile Grade 9: 41 students (19 boys, 22 girls); Grade 10: 42 students (21 boys, 21 girls); Grade 11: 54 students (31 boys, 23 girls); Grade 12: 52 students (27 boys, 25 girls).

Faculty School total: 34. In upper school: 11 men, 12 women; 17 have advanced degrees.

Subjects Offered Advanced studio art-AP, algebra, American history, American literature, anatomy and physiology, ancient world history, art, art history, band, biology, biology-AP, calculus, ceramics, chemistry, chemistry-AP, choir, chorus, college counseling, college placement, community service, comparative government and politics-AP, computer programming, creative writing, drama, earth science, ecology, economics, English, English literature, English-AP, ethics, European history, European history-AP, expository writing, fine arts, finite math, French, French language-AP, French-AP, geography, geology, geometry, government and politics-AP, government/civics, government/civics-AP, grammar, history, history of drama, history of music, humanities, independent study, jazz band, journalism, Latin, Latin-AP, literature, marine biology, mathematics, music, music theory, music theory-AP, newspaper, photography, physical education, physical science, physics, pre-calculus, religion, SAT preparation, science, social studies, Spanish, Spanish language-AP, Spanish-AP, speech, stage design, stagecraft, studio art-AP, theater, trigonometry, U.S. government and politics-AP, U.S. history-AP, world history, writing.

Graduation Requirements Arts and fine arts (art, music, dance, drama), English, foreign language, history, humanities, mathematics, science, senior internships. Community service is required.

Special Academic Programs Advanced Placement exam preparation; honors section; accelerated programs; independent study; term-away projects; study at local college for college credit; academic accommodation for the gifted, the musically talented, and the artistically talented.

College Admission Counseling 29 students graduated in 2012; 28 went to college, including Brown University; Princeton University; Smith College; Stanford University; The University of Arizona. Other: 1 went to work. Mean SAT critical reading: 573, mean SAT math: 590, mean composite ACT: 26.

Student Life Upper grades have specified standards of dress, student council, honor system. Discipline rests primarily with faculty.

Tuition and Aid Day student tuition: $14,950–$15,950. Tuition installment plan (monthly payment plans, 2- and 10-payment plans). Need-based scholarship grants available. In 2012–13, 42% of upper-school students received aid. Total amount of financial aid awarded in 2012–13: $1,200,000.

Admissions Traditional secondary-level entrance grade is 9. ERB CTP IV and writing sample required. Deadline for receipt of application materials: February. Application fee required: $45. Interview recommended.

Athletics Interscholastic: baseball (boys), basketball (b,g), golf (b,g), soccer (b,g), softball (g), swimming and diving (b,g), tennis (b,g), volleyball (b,g); intramural: touch football (b); coed interscholastic: cross-country running, hiking/backpacking, outdoor education, ropes courses, strength & conditioning; coed intramural: basketball, cooperative games, cross-country running, dance, flag football, football, hiking/backpacking, outdoor education, outdoor recreation, outdoor skills, physical training, ropes courses, strength & conditioning, volleyball, weight training, yoga. 3 PE instructors, 12 coaches, 1 athletic trainer.

Computers Computers are regularly used in English, foreign language, history, journalism, mathematics, newspaper, photography, science classes. Computer network features include on-campus library services, online commercial services, Internet access, wireless campus network, Internet filtering or blocking technology. Campus intranet, student e-mail accounts, and computer access in designated common areas are available to students. Students grades are available online. The school has a published electronic and media policy.

Contact Director of Admissions. 520-327-6395 Ext. 209. Fax: 520-327-8276. E-mail: admissions@stgregoryschool.org. Website: www.stgregoryschool.org

SAINT JOAN ANTIDA HIGH SCHOOL

1341 North Cass Street
Milwaukee, Wisconsin 53202

Head of School: Mr. Paul Gessner

General Information Girls' day college-preparatory, arts, business, religious studies, technology, and engineering school, affiliated with Roman Catholic Church. Grades 9–12. Founded: 1954. Setting: urban. 2 buildings on campus. Approved or accredited by North Central Association of Colleges and Schools and Wisconsin Department of Education. Total enrollment: 250. Upper school average class size: 25. Upper school faculty-student ratio: 1:14. Upper School students typically attend 5 days per week.

Upper School Student Profile Grade 9: 83 students (83 girls); Grade 10: 66 students (66 girls); Grade 11: 46 students (46 girls); Grade 12: 52 students (52 girls). 50% of students are Roman Catholic.

Faculty School total: 25. In upper school: 7 men, 18 women; 9 have advanced degrees.

Subjects Offered 3-dimensional art, advanced chemistry, advanced math, Advanced Placement courses, algebra, American history-AP, American literature, American literature-AP, anatomy, art, bell choir, biology, biotechnology, British literature, business, calculus, campus ministry, career planning, career/college preparation, Catholic belief and practice, ceramics, chemistry, chemistry-AP, choir, Christian and Hebrew scripture, church history, clayworking, college admission preparation, college counseling, composition, composition-AP, concert choir, keyboarding, leadership and service.

Graduation Requirements Advanced Placement courses, algebra, American history, chemistry, Christian studies, church history, composition, electives, English composition, English literature, English literature, history of the Americas, history of the Catholic Church, physics, religion (includes Bible studies and theology), science, speech.

Special Academic Programs Advanced Placement exam preparation; honors section; study at local college for college credit; remedial reading and/or remedial writing; remedial math.

College Admission Counseling 52 students graduated in 2012; 50 went to college, including University of Wisconsin–Milwaukee. Other: 2 went to work.

Student Life Upper grades have uniform requirement, student council, honor system. Discipline rests primarily with faculty. Attendance at religious services is required.

Tuition and Aid Day student tuition: $6500. Tuition installment plan (SMART Tuition Payment Plan). Merit scholarship grants, need-based scholarship grants available. In 2012–13, 98% of upper-school students received aid.

Admissions Traditional secondary-level entrance grade is 9. For fall 2012, 150 students applied for upper-level admission, 120 were accepted, 118 enrolled. Explore required. Deadline for receipt of application materials: December 31. No application fee required. On-campus interview recommended.

Athletics Interscholastic: basketball, cheering, cross-country running, drill team, soccer, tennis, volleyball. 1 PE instructor.

Computers Computers are regularly used in business, engineering, keyboarding classes. Computer network features include on-campus library services, Internet access, wireless campus network, Internet filtering or blocking technology. The school has a published electronic and media policy.

Contact Ms. Marcela O. Garcia, Director of Admissions. 414-274-4709. Fax: 414-272-3135. E-mail: mgarcia@saintjoanantida.org. Website: www.saintjoanantida.org/

ST. JOHN'S PREPARATORY SCHOOL

72 Spring Street
Danvers, Massachusetts 01923

Head of School: Dr. Edward P. Hardiman

General Information Boys' day college-preparatory, arts, religious studies, and technology school, affiliated with Roman Catholic Church. Grades 9–12. Founded: 1907. Setting: suburban. Nearest major city is Boston. 175-acre campus. 9 buildings on campus. Approved or accredited by National Catholic Education Association and New England Association of Schools and Colleges. Member of National Association of Independent Schools. Endowment: $1.2 million. Total enrollment: 1,200. Upper school average class size: 18. Upper school faculty-student ratio: 1:11. There are 161 required school days per year for Upper School students. Upper School students typically attend 5 days per week. The average school day consists of 6 hours and 9 minutes.

Upper School Student Profile Grade 9: 300 students (300 boys); Grade 10: 300 students (300 boys); Grade 11: 300 students (300 boys); Grade 12: 300 students (300 boys). 70% of students are Roman Catholic.

Faculty School total: 108. In upper school: 67 men, 41 women; 86 have advanced degrees.

Subjects Offered Accounting, acting, aerospace science, African American history, algebra, American history, American history-AP, American literature, anatomy and physiology, art, biology, biology-AP, business, calculus, calculus-AP, ceramics, chemistry, chemistry-AP, Chinese, chorus, computer programming, computer science, computer science-AP, desktop publishing, drama, driver education, economics, economics-AP, English, English literature, English-AP, environmental science, environmental studies, ethics, European history, European history-AP, geometry, German, German-AP, government/civics, Holocaust, human geography - AP, jazz ensemble, Latin, Latin-AP, law studies, mathematics, music, neuroscience, physical education, physics, physics-AP, religion, robotics, science, sculpture, social studies, society, politics and law, Spanish, Spanish-AP, statistics, statistics-AP, studio art, technology, trigonometry, U.S. government and politics-AP, U.S. history-AP, video, world history, world religions.

Graduation Requirements Arts and fine arts (art, music, dance, drama), English, foreign language, mathematics, physical education (includes health), religion (includes Bible studies and theology), science, social studies (includes history).

Special Academic Programs Advanced Placement exam preparation; honors section; independent study; study abroad; academic accommodation for the gifted, the musically talented, and the artistically talented.

College Admission Counseling 300 students graduated in 2013; 292 went to college, including Boston College; Northeastern University; Providence College; University of Connecticut; University of Massachusetts Amherst; University of New Hampshire. Other: 1 went to work, 6 entered a postgraduate year, 1 had other specific plans.

Student Life Upper grades have specified standards of dress, student council. Discipline rests primarily with faculty. Attendance at religious services is required.

Summer Programs Enrichment, advancement, sports, art/fine arts, computer instruction programs offered; session focuses on academic enrichment, study skills, arts, and fitness; held on campus; accepts boys and girls; open to students from other schools.

Tuition and Aid Day student tuition: $19,950. Tuition installment plan (SMART Tuition Payment Plan). Merit scholarship grants, need-based scholarship grants available. In 2013–14, 31% of upper-school students received aid. Total amount of financial aid awarded in 2013–14: $2,900,000.

Admissions Traditional secondary-level entrance grade is 9. SSAT or STS, Diocese Test required. Deadline for receipt of application materials: December 20. Application fee required: $50.

Athletics Interscholastic: alpine skiing, baseball, basketball, cross-country running, fencing, football, Frisbee, golf, hockey, ice hockey, indoor track, lacrosse, rugby, sailing, skiing (downhill), soccer, swimming and diving, tennis, track and field, ultimate Frisbee, volleyball, water polo, winter (indoor) track, wrestling; intramural: baseball, basketball, bicycling, bocce, bowling, boxing, climbing, combined training, cooperative games, crew, flag football, floor hockey, Frisbee, golf, ice hockey, martial arts, mountain biking, Nautilus, physical fitness, rowing, sailing, skiing (downhill), snowboarding, strength & conditioning, surfing, table tennis, tennis, touch football, ultimate Frisbee, volleyball, weight lifting, weight training, whiffle ball. 2 PE instructors, 57 coaches, 2 athletic trainers.

Computers Computers are regularly used in all academic, career exploration, college planning, research skills classes. Computer network features include on-campus

library services, Internet access, wireless campus network, Internet filtering or blocking technology, student access to 300 computer workstations. Student e-mail accounts are available to students. Students grades are available online. The school has a published electronic and media policy.

Contact Ms. Maureen Ward, Administrative Assistant. 978-624-1301. Fax: 978-624-1315. E-mail: mward@stjohnsprep.org. Website: www.stjohnsprep.org

SAINT JOHN'S PREPARATORY SCHOOL

Box 4000
2280 Watertower Road
Collegeville, Minnesota 56321

Head of School: Fr. Jonathan Licari, OSB

General Information Coeducational boarding and day college-preparatory, arts, religious studies, bilingual studies, and Theatre school, affiliated with Roman Catholic Church. Boarding grades 9–PG, day grades 6–PG. Founded: 1857. Setting: rural. Nearest major city is Minneapolis/St. Paul. Students are housed in single-sex dormitories. 2,700-acre campus. 23 buildings on campus. Approved or accredited by Independent Schools Association of the Central States, International Baccalaureate Organization, Midwest Association of Boarding Schools, The Association of Boarding Schools, and Minnesota Department of Education. Member of National Association of Independent Schools. Endowment: $9 million. Total enrollment: 295. Upper school average class size: 16. Upper school faculty-student ratio: 1:10. There are 172 required school days per year for Upper School students. Upper School students typically attend 5 days per week. The average school day consists of 5 hours and 35 minutes.

Upper School Student Profile Grade 9: 40 students (19 boys, 21 girls); Grade 10: 51 students (23 boys, 28 girls); Grade 11: 72 students (42 boys, 30 girls); Grade 12: 56 students (22 boys, 34 girls). 37% of students are boarding students. 63% are state residents. 4 states are represented in upper school student body. 25% are international students. International students from Austria, Chile, China, Mexico, Republic of Korea, and Taiwan; 18 other countries represented in student body. 50% of students are Roman Catholic.

Faculty School total: 34. In upper school: 18 men, 16 women; 24 have advanced degrees; 2 reside on campus.

Subjects Offered 3-dimensional design, advanced chemistry, Advanced Placement courses, algebra, American history, American literature, art, art history, band, Bible studies, biology, biology-AP, British literature, calculus, ceramics, chemistry, Chinese, choir, civics, conceptual physics, creative writing, current events, drawing, earth science, economics, English, English literature, English-AP, environmental science-AP, ESL, European history, fine arts, geometry, German, government/civics, health, history, International Baccalaureate courses, mathematics, music, orchestra, photography, physical education, physics, pre-calculus, religion, science, social studies, Spanish, speech, statistics, theology, trigonometry, world history, world literature, writing.

Graduation Requirements American literature, British literature, English, theology and the arts, world literature.

Special Academic Programs International Baccalaureate program; Advanced Placement exam preparation; honors section; independent study; term-away projects; study at local college for college credit; study abroad; ESL (23 students enrolled).

College Admission Counseling 51 students graduated in 2013; all went to college, including Carleton College; College of Saint Benedict; St. John's University; University of Minnesota, Twin Cities Campus. Mean SAT critical reading: 713, mean SAT math: 685, mean SAT writing: 672, mean combined SAT: 2070, mean composite ACT: 27.

Student Life Upper grades have specified standards of dress, student council, honor system. Discipline rests primarily with faculty. Attendance at religious services is required.

Summer Programs Enrichment, advancement, art/fine arts programs offered; session focuses on fun camp experiences; held on campus; accepts boys and girls; open to students from other schools. 1,000 students usually enrolled. 2014 schedule: June 16 to August 8. Application deadline: June 1.

Tuition and Aid Day student tuition: $14,995; 5-day tuition and room/board: $30,352; 7-day tuition and room/board: $33,870. Tuition installment plan (monthly payment plans, individually arranged payment plans, semester payment plan). Merit scholarship grants, need-based scholarship grants, paying campus jobs available. In 2013–14, 46% of upper-school students received aid; total upper-school merit-scholarship money awarded: $30,000. Total amount of financial aid awarded in 2013–14: $750,000.

Admissions Traditional secondary-level entrance grade is 9. For fall 2013, 144 students applied for upper-level admission, 77 were accepted, 48 enrolled. International English Language Test, SSAT or TOEFL required. Deadline for receipt of application materials: none. Application fee required: $25. Interview required.

Athletics Interscholastic: alpine skiing (boys, girls), aquatics (g), baseball (b), basketball (b,g), cross-country running (b,g), diving (g), football (b), gymnastics (g), ice hockey (b,g), indoor track & field (b,g), nordic skiing (b,g), soccer (b,g), softball (g), swimming and diving (b,g), tennis (b,g), track and field (b,g); intramural: aerobics (g), aerobics/dance (g), dance (g), figure skating (g), golf (b,g), ice skating (g); coed intramural: bicycling, canoeing/kayaking, cross-country running, fitness, fitness walking, flag football, floor hockey, Frisbee, indoor soccer, mountain biking, nordic skiing, physical fitness, physical training, racquetball, rock climbing, roller blading, skiing (cross-country), skiing (downhill), soccer, strength & conditioning, swimming and diving, ultimate Frisbee, volleyball, walking, wall climbing, wallyball, weight lifting, weight training, winter (indoor) track, winter soccer, winter walking, yoga. 1 PE instructor, 21 coaches.

Computers Computers are regularly used in all academic, English, science classes. Computer network features include on-campus library services, Internet access, wireless campus network, Internet filtering or blocking technology. Student e-mail accounts and computer access in designated common areas are available to students. Students grades are available online. The school has a published electronic and media policy.

Contact Jennine Klosterman, Director of Admissions. 320-363-3321. Fax: 320-363-3322. E-mail: jklosterman@sjprep.net. Website: www.sjprep.net

ST. JOHN'S-RAVENSCOURT SCHOOL

400 South Drive
Winnipeg, Manitoba R3T 3K5, Canada

Head of School: Dr. Stephen Johnson

General Information Coeducational boarding and day college-preparatory school. Boarding grades 8–12, day grades K–12. Founded: 1820. Setting: suburban. Students are housed in single-sex dormitories. 23-acre campus. 6 buildings on campus. Approved or accredited by Canadian Association of Independent Schools, Canadian Educational Standards Institute, The Association of Boarding Schools, and Manitoba Department of Education. Language of instruction: English. Endowment: CAN$8.3 million. Total enrollment: 822. Upper school average class size: 20. Upper school faculty-student ratio: 1:9. There are 172 required school days per year for Upper School students.

Upper School Student Profile Grade 9: 96 students (49 boys, 47 girls); Grade 10: 88 students (53 boys, 35 girls); Grade 11: 100 students (60 boys, 40 girls); Grade 12: 89 students (47 boys, 42 girls). 4% of students are boarding students. 96% are province residents. 5 provinces are represented in upper school student body. 2% are international students. International students from China, Democratic People's Republic of Korea, Germany, Hong Kong, Taiwan, and United States; 2 other countries represented in student body.

Faculty School total: 78. In upper school: 25 men, 23 women; 13 have advanced degrees; 4 reside on campus.

Subjects Offered Advanced Placement courses, algebra, American history, animation, art, biology, biology-AP, calculus, calculus-AP, Canadian geography, Canadian history, chemistry, chemistry-AP, computer science, debate, drama, driver education, economics, English, English literature, European history, European history-AP, French, French-AP, geography, geometry, history, information technology, law, linear algebra, mathematics, music, physical education, physics, physics-AP, pre-calculus, psychology, psychology-AP, science, social studies, Spanish, theater, visual arts, Web site design, world issues.

Graduation Requirements Canadian geography, Canadian history, computer science, English, French, geography, history, mathematics, physical education (includes health), pre-calculus, science, social sciences.

Special Academic Programs Advanced Placement exam preparation; honors section; independent study; study at local college for college credit; ESL (27 students enrolled).

College Admission Counseling 99 students graduated in 2012; 98 went to college, including McGill University; Queen's University at Kingston; The University of British Columbia; The University of Western Ontario; University of Manitoba; University of Toronto.

Student Life Upper grades have uniform requirement, student council, honor system. Discipline rests equally with students and faculty.

Tuition and Aid Day student tuition: CAN$18,650; 7-day tuition and room/board: CAN$34,790–CAN$45,400. Tuition installment plan (monthly payment plans, individually arranged payment plans). Bursaries, merit scholarship grants available. In 2012–13, 21% of upper-school students received aid; total upper-school merit-scholarship money awarded: CAN$95,000. Total amount of financial aid awarded in 2012–13: CAN$262,250.

Admissions Traditional secondary-level entrance grade is 9. For fall 2012, 72 students applied for upper-level admission, 47 were accepted, 39 enrolled. Otis-Lennon School Ability Test, school's own exam or TOEFL or SLEP required. Deadline for receipt of application materials: none. Application fee required: CAN$125. Interview recommended.

Athletics Interscholastic: aerobics (boys, girls), badminton (b,g), basketball (b,g), cross-country running (b,g), Frisbee (b,g), golf (b), hockey (b,g), ice hockey (b,g), indoor track (b,g), indoor track & field (b,g), lacrosse (b,g); intramural: badminton (b,g), basketball (b,g), cross-country running (b,g), dance (b,g), hockey (b,g); coed interscholastic: badminton, Frisbee, physical fitness; coed intramural: badminton, flag football, floor hockey. 6 PE instructors.

Computers Computers are regularly used in business skills, career exploration, college planning, creative writing, English, history, library skills, newspaper, science, social studies, yearbook classes. Computer network features include on-campus library services, Internet access, wireless campus network, Internet filtering or blocking technology, EBSCO. Campus intranet and student e-mail accounts are available to students. The school has a published electronic and media policy.

Contact Mr. Paul Prieur, Director of Admissions and Marketing. 204-477-2400. Fax: 204-477-2429. E-mail: admissions@sjr.mb.ca. Website: www.sjr.mb.ca

ST. JOSEPH ACADEMY

155 State Road 207
St. Augustine, Florida 32084

Head of School: Mr. Thomas McGlinn

General Information Coeducational day college-preparatory, arts, religious studies, and technology school, affiliated with Roman Catholic Church. Grades 9–12. Founded: 1866. Setting: suburban. 33-acre campus. 13 buildings on campus. Approved or accredited by Southern Association of Colleges and Schools and Florida Department of Education. Total enrollment: 260. Upper school average class size: 14. Upper school faculty-student ratio: 1:11. There are 182 required school days per year for Upper School students. Upper School students typically attend 5 days per week. The average school day consists of 6 hours and 40 minutes.

Upper School Student Profile Grade 9: 61 students (31 boys, 30 girls); Grade 10: 63 students (31 boys, 32 girls); Grade 11: 61 students (28 boys, 33 girls); Grade 12: 75 students (36 boys, 39 girls). 84% of students are Roman Catholic.

Faculty School total: 22. In upper school: 12 men, 10 women; 10 have advanced degrees.

Subjects Offered Advanced computer applications, advanced math, Advanced Placement courses, advanced studio art-AP, algebra, American government, American history, American sign language, anatomy and physiology, ancient world history, applied arts, art, art history, Bible studies, biology, calculus-AP, career education, career exploration, career planning, Catholic belief and practice, chemistry, Christianity, church history, clayworking, college counseling, college placement, college planning, community service, computer applications, computer education, computer skills, costumes and make-up, creative drama, drama, drama performance, drama workshop, drawing, English, English composition, English language-AP, environmental science, government, history of the Catholic Church, honors algebra, honors English, honors geometry, honors U.S. history, honors world history, integrated mathematics, Internet research, life management skills, marine biology, Microsoft, moral theology, peer ministry, personal fitness, physical education, physics, play production, portfolio art, pottery, pre-calculus, psychology, religious education, Shakespeare, Spanish, Spanish language-AP, Spanish literature-AP, theology, U.S. history, weight training.

Graduation Requirements Advanced Placement courses, career/college preparation, Catholic belief and practice, college writing, computer literacy, dramatic arts, economics, English, environmental science, foreign language, government, mathematics, physical education (includes health), religion (includes Bible studies and theology), social studies (includes history), theology.

Special Academic Programs Advanced Placement exam preparation; honors section; study at local college for college credit; academic accommodation for the gifted and the artistically talented; special instructional classes for students with Attention Deficit Disorder.

College Admission Counseling 58 students graduated in 2013; all went to college, including Florida Atlantic University; Florida State University; Florida State University; University of Central Florida; University of Florida; University of North Florida.

Student Life Upper grades have uniform requirement, student council, honor system. Discipline rests primarily with faculty. Attendance at religious services is required.

Summer Programs Sports, computer instruction programs offered; session focuses on football conditioning, weight training, basketball clinics and tournaments; held on campus; accepts boys and girls; not open to students from other schools. 86 students usually enrolled. 2014 schedule: June 1 to July 31.

Tuition and Aid Day student tuition: $8125–$10,250. Tuition installment plan (FACTS Tuition Payment Plan). Tuition reduction for siblings, need-based scholarship grants available. In 2013–14, 43% of upper-school students received aid. Total amount of financial aid awarded in 2013–14: $120,000.

Admissions Traditional secondary-level entrance grade is 9. For fall 2013, 103 students applied for upper-level admission, 98 were accepted, 93 enrolled. ACT-Explore, Iowa Tests of Basic Skills, Iowa Tests of Basic Skills-Grades 7-8, Archdiocese HSEPT-Grade 9, PSAT or SAT required. Deadline for receipt of application materials: none. Application fee required: $600. Interview recommended.

Athletics Interscholastic: baseball (boys), basketball (b,g), cheering (g), cross-country running (b,g), football (b), golf (b,g), physical fitness (b,g), physical training (b,g), soccer (b,g), softball (g), swimming and diving (b,g), tennis (b,g), track and field (b,g), volleyball (g), weight training (b), winter soccer (b,g); intramural: lacrosse (b,g). 2 PE instructors, 3 coaches, 1 athletic trainer.

Computers Computers are regularly used in all academic, animation, computer applications, media classes. Computer network features include on-campus library services, Internet access, wireless campus network, Internet filtering or blocking technology. Student e-mail accounts and computer access in designated common areas are available to students. Students grades are available online. The school has a published electronic and media policy.

Contact Mr. Patrick M. Keane, Director of Admissions. 904-824-0431 Ext. 305. Fax: 904-824-4412. E-mail: admissions@sjaweb.org. Website: www.sjaweb.org

SAINT JOSEPH ACADEMY HIGH SCHOOL

3470 Rocky River Drive
Cleveland, Ohio 44111

Head of School: Dr. Jim Cantwell

General Information Girls' day college-preparatory, technology, pre-engineering, and Mandarin school, affiliated with Roman Catholic Church. Grades 9–12. Founded: 1890. Setting: urban. 44-acre campus. 2 buildings on campus. Approved or accredited by North Central Association of Colleges and Schools, Ohio Catholic Schools Accreditation Association (OCSAA), and Ohio Department of Education. Endowment: $3.5 million. Upper school average class size: 23. Upper school faculty-student ratio: 1:12. The average school day consists of 7 hours.

Upper School Student Profile Grade 9: 180 students (180 girls); Grade 10: 175 students (175 girls); Grade 11: 148 students (148 girls); Grade 12: 162 students (162 girls). 90% of students are Roman Catholic.

Faculty School total: 63. In upper school: 15 men, 48 women; 38 have advanced degrees.

Subjects Offered ACT preparation, advanced biology, advanced chemistry, Advanced Placement courses, advanced studio art-AP, algebra, art, biology-AP, calculus, calculus-AP, chemistry-AP, Chinese, creative writing, English language-AP, European history-AP, film studies, filmmaking, French-AP, geometry, government and politics-AP, graphic design, Greek, honors U.S. history, honors world history, Latin, Latin-AP, model United Nations, physics-AP, psychology-AP, Spanish, Spanish-AP, speech and debate, statistics-AP, studio art-AP, U.S. history-AP, world history-AP.

Graduation Requirements 4 credits of Theology, 4 credits of Mathematics.

Special Academic Programs 13 Advanced Placement exams for which test preparation is offered; honors section; independent study; study abroad.

College Admission Counseling 163 students graduated in 2012; 161 went to college, including Cleveland State University; John Carroll University; Kent State University; Miami University; Ohio University; University of Dayton. Other: 2 went to work. Mean SAT critical reading: 557, mean SAT math: 531, mean SAT writing: 554, mean combined SAT: 1642, mean composite ACT: 24.

Student Life Upper grades have uniform requirement, student council, honor system. Discipline rests primarily with faculty. Attendance at religious services is required.

Tuition and Aid Day student tuition: $10,600. Tuition installment plan (monthly payment plans). Tuition reduction for siblings, merit scholarship grants, need-based scholarship grants, need-based loans, paying campus jobs available. In 2012–13, 65% of upper-school students received aid; total upper-school merit-scholarship money awarded: $130,000. Total amount of financial aid awarded in 2012–13: $900,000.

Admissions Traditional secondary-level entrance grade is 9. For fall 2012, 245 students applied for upper-level admission, 195 were accepted, 181 enrolled. ACT-Explore required. Deadline for receipt of application materials: none. No application fee required. Interview required.

Athletics Interscholastic: basketball, cheering, crew, cross-country running, diving, golf, rugby, soccer, softball, swimming and diving, tennis, track and field, volleyball; intramural: alpine skiing, dance team, physical fitness, strength & conditioning. 2 PE instructors, 14 coaches, 1 athletic trainer.

Computers Computer network features include on-campus library services, Internet access, wireless campus network, Internet filtering or blocking technology. Student e-mail accounts and computer access in designated common areas are available to students. Students grades are available online. The school has a published electronic and media policy.

Contact Ms. Diane Marie Kanney, Director of Admissions. 216-251-4868 Ext. 220. Fax: 216-251-5809. E-mail: admissions@sja1890.org. Website: www.sja1890.org

ST. JOSEPH HIGH SCHOOL

2320 Huntington Turnpike
Trumbull, Connecticut 06611

Head of School: Pres. William J. Fitzgerald, PhD

General Information Coeducational day college-preparatory, arts, business, religious studies, and technology school, affiliated with Roman Catholic Church. Grades 9–12. Founded: 1962. Setting: suburban. Nearest major city is Bridgeport. 25-acre campus. 2 buildings on campus. Approved or accredited by New England Association of Schools and Colleges and Connecticut Department of Education. Total enrollment: 830. Upper school average class size: 24. Upper school faculty-student ratio: 1:20. Upper School students typically attend 5 days per week. The average school day consists of 6 hours.

Upper School Student Profile 85% of students are Roman Catholic.

Faculty School total: 64. In upper school: 25 men, 39 women; 50 have advanced degrees.

Subjects Offered Accounting, Advanced Placement courses, algebra, American history, American literature, art, art history, band, biology, business skills, calculus, chemistry, chorus, community service, computer applications, current events, design, drawing, earth science, ecology, economics, English, English literature, European history, finance, fine arts, French, geography, geometry, government/civics, health, history, international relations, Italian, journalism, law, mathematics, music, painting, philosophy, physical education, physics, poetry, pre-calculus, psychology, religion,

science, sculpture, Shakespeare, social studies, sociology, Spanish, statistics, study skills, theology, trigonometry, word processing.

Graduation Requirements Arts and fine arts (art, music, dance, drama), English, foreign language, mathematics, physical education (includes health), religion (includes Bible studies and theology), science, social studies (includes history). Community service is required.

Special Academic Programs 7 Advanced Placement exams for which test preparation is offered; honors section; study at local college for college credit; academic accommodation for the gifted; special instructional classes for students with learning disabilities and Attention Deficit Disorder; ESL (14 students enrolled).

College Admission Counseling 182 students graduated in 2013; 175 went to college, including Boston College; Boston University; Fairfield University; Providence College; Southern Connecticut State University; University of Connecticut. Other: 1 entered military service, 1 entered a postgraduate year. Mean SAT critical reading: 535, mean SAT math: 516, mean SAT writing: 540, mean combined SAT: 1597, mean composite ACT: 21.

Student Life Upper grades have uniform requirement, student council. Discipline rests primarily with faculty. Attendance at religious services is required.

Summer Programs Sports programs offered; session focuses on soccer and basketball; held on campus. 2014 schedule: July 1 to August 30.

Tuition and Aid Day student tuition: $9775. Tuition installment plan (monthly payment plans, one lump sum payment with discount by June 1 or two payments by semester, payment plan through People's Bank). Tuition reduction for siblings, merit scholarship grants, need-based scholarship grants available. In 2013–14, 34% of upper-school students received aid; total upper-school merit-scholarship money awarded: $148,000. Total amount of financial aid awarded in 2013–14: $235,000.

Admissions Admissions testing, High School Placement Test and STS - Educational Development Series required. Deadline for receipt of application materials: December 1. Application fee required: $50.

Athletics Interscholastic: baseball (boys), basketball (b,g), cheering (g), cross-country running (b,g), diving (g), football (b), hockey (b,g), ice hockey (b,g), indoor track & field (b,g), lacrosse (b,g), softball (g), swimming and diving (g), tennis (b,g), track and field (b,g), volleyball (b,g); coed interscholastic: bowling, golf. 2 PE instructors, 65 coaches, 2 athletic trainers.

Computers Computer network features include on-campus library services, online commercial services, Internet access, wireless campus network, Internet filtering or blocking technology. Campus intranet and student e-mail accounts are available to students. Students grades are available online. The school has a published electronic and media policy.

Contact Peggy Kuhar Marino '71, Director of Admission. 203-378-9378 Ext. 308. Fax: 203-378-7306. E-mail: pmarino@sjcadets.org. Website: www.sjcadets.org

SAINT JOSEPH HIGH SCHOOL

10900 West Cermak Road
Westchester, Illinois 60154-4299

Head of School: Mr. Ronald Hoover

General Information Coeducational day college-preparatory, arts, business, vocational, religious studies, bilingual studies, and technology school, affiliated with Roman Catholic Church. Grades 9–12. Founded: 1960. Setting: suburban. Nearest major city is Chicago. 21-acre campus. 2 buildings on campus. Approved or accredited by Christian Brothers Association, North Central Association of Colleges and Schools, and Illinois Department of Education. Total enrollment: 476. Upper school average class size: 25. Upper school faculty-student ratio: 1:16. There are 176 required school days per year for Upper School students. Upper School students typically attend 5 days per week. The average school day consists of 6 hours and 30 minutes.

Upper School Student Profile Grade 9: 122 students (72 boys, 50 girls); Grade 10: 109 students (66 boys, 43 girls); Grade 11: 125 students (65 boys, 60 girls); Grade 12: 120 students (62 boys, 58 girls). 39% of students are Roman Catholic.

Faculty School total: 32. In upper school: 17 men, 13 women; 15 have advanced degrees.

Subjects Offered Accounting, ACT preparation, acting, algebra, American history, anatomy and physiology, art, band, biology, business law, calculus, calculus-AP, chemistry, Christian ethics, computer applications, computer programming, computer-aided design, creative writing, current events, digital photography, economics, English, English-AP, film studies, fine arts, geometry, graphic arts, health, human biology, Italian, journalism, moral and social development, music appreciation, peace and justice, peer ministry, photography, physical education, physics, pre-algebra, pre-calculus, reading, reading/study skills, sociology, Spanish, Spanish-AP, speech, sports conditioning, studio art, theater production, U.S. history, video and animation, video film production, Web site design, world cultures, world religions.

Graduation Requirements Arts and fine arts (art, music, dance, drama), economics, English, foreign language, health, mathematics, physical education (includes health), religion (includes Bible studies and theology), science, social studies (includes history), each student must complete 40 community service hours.

Special Academic Programs 4 Advanced Placement exams for which test preparation is offered; honors section; independent study; study at local college for college credit; remedial reading and/or remedial writing; remedial math; special instructional classes for deaf students, blind students.

College Admission Counseling 146 students graduated in 2013; 136 went to college, including Illinois State University; Saint Mary's University of Minnesota; Saint Xavier University; Triton College; University of Illinois at Urbana–Champaign; Western Illinois University. Other: 10 went to work. Median composite ACT: 20. 11% scored over 26 on composite ACT.

Student Life Upper grades have uniform requirement, student council, honor system. Discipline rests primarily with faculty. Attendance at religious services is required.

Summer Programs Remediation, sports programs offered; session focuses on remediation/make-up; held on campus; accepts boys and girls; open to students from other schools. 200 students usually enrolled. 2014 schedule: June 16 to July 28. Application deadline: June 2.

Tuition and Aid Day student tuition: $9100. Tuition installment plan (monthly payment plans, individually arranged payment plans, based on parents income special arrangements are made with income tax return). Tuition reduction for siblings, merit scholarship grants, need-based scholarship grants, paying campus jobs available. In 2013–14, 65% of upper-school students received aid; total upper-school merit-scholarship money awarded: $110,000. Total amount of financial aid awarded in 2013–14: $1,000,000.

Admissions Traditional secondary-level entrance grade is 9. For fall 2013, 261 students applied for upper-level admission, 261 were accepted, 122 enrolled. High School Placement Test (closed version) from Scholastic Testing Service required. Deadline for receipt of application materials: none. Application fee required: $300. On-campus interview required.

Athletics Interscholastic: aerobics/dance (girls), baseball (b), basketball (b,g), bowling (b,g), cheering (g), cross-country running (b,g), dance team (g), football (b), golf (b,g), hockey (g), indoor soccer (b,g), indoor track (b,g), soccer (b,g), softball (g), strength & conditioning (b,g), tennis (b,g), track and field (b,g), volleyball (b,g), wrestling (b); coed intramural: yoga. 3 PE instructors, 30 coaches, 1 athletic trainer.

Computers Computers are regularly used in business applications, current events, economics, English, graphic arts, graphic design, health, history, journalism, mathematics, music, newspaper, photography, reading, religion, science, social studies, Spanish, speech, technology, theater arts, video film production, writing, yearbook classes. Computer network features include Internet access, wireless campus network, Internet filtering or blocking technology, 10th, 11th, and 12th have a laptop computer with wireless access to the Internet, anywhere on campus, 9th graders take part in a digital citizenship course in which they learn about the computers. Campus intranet and student e-mail accounts are available to students. Students grades are available online. The school has a published electronic and media policy.

Contact Mrs. Tricia McGleam, Admissions Director. 708-562-4433 Ext. 117. Fax: 708-562-4459. E-mail: tmcgleam@stjoeshs.org. Website: www.stjoeshs.org/pages/StJosephHS

SAINT JOSEPH HIGH SCHOOL

145 Plainfield Avenue
Metuchen, New Jersey 08840

Head of School: Mr. John A. Anderson '70

General Information Boys' day college-preparatory, arts, religious studies, and technology school, affiliated with Roman Catholic Church. Grades 9–12. Founded: 1961. Setting: suburban. Nearest major city is New York, NY. 68-acre campus. 8 buildings on campus. Approved or accredited by Middle States Association of Colleges and Schools, National Catholic Education Association, and New Jersey Department of Education. Endowment: $2 million. Total enrollment: 760. Upper school average class size: 24. Upper school faculty-student ratio: 1:16. There are 170 required school days per year for Upper School students. Upper School students typically attend 5 days per week. The average school day consists of 6 hours and 12 minutes.

Upper School Student Profile Grade 9: 181 students (181 boys); Grade 10: 200 students (200 boys); Grade 11: 210 students (210 boys); Grade 12: 170 students (170 boys). 75% of students are Roman Catholic.

Faculty School total: 68. In upper school: 44 men, 24 women; 44 have advanced degrees.

Subjects Offered Accounting, acting, Advanced Placement courses, algebra, American Civil War, American government, American history, American literature, art, arts, astronomy, biology, biology-AP, calculus, calculus-AP, campus ministry, career education, Catholic belief and practice, chemistry, chemistry-AP, Christian ethics, Christian scripture, Christian studies, Christianity, church history, computer animation, computer applications, computer programming, computer science, computer science-AP, desktop publishing, discrete mathematics, driver education, English, English literature, English-AP, European history, European history-AP, French, French as a second language, French-AP, geometry, German, German literature, guitar, health, history, lab science, Latin, mathematics, mathematics-AP, meteorology, music, personal finance, photo shop, photography, physical education, physics, physics-AP, pre-calculus, public speaking, religion, social studies, Spanish, Spanish-AP, technical drawing, theology, U.S. government and politics-AP, U.S. history-AP, Web site design, world literature, world religions, writing.

Graduation Requirements Arts and fine arts (art, music, dance, drama), career education, computer science, English, foreign language, lab science, mathematics, physical education (includes health), religion (includes Bible studies and theology), science, social studies (includes history). Community service is required.

Special Academic Programs 33 Advanced Placement exams for which test preparation is offered; honors section; independent study; study at local college for college credit; academic accommodation for the gifted.

College Admission Counseling 184 students graduated in 2012; all went to college, including Penn State University Park; Rutgers, The State University of New Jersey, Rutgers College; Saint Joseph's University; Seton Hall University; The College of New Jersey; University of Notre Dame. Mean SAT critical reading: 551, mean SAT math: 587, mean SAT writing: 551.

Student Life Upper grades have specified standards of dress, student council, honor system. Discipline rests primarily with faculty. Attendance at religious services is required.

Tuition and Aid Tuition installment plan (FACTS Tuition Payment Plan, monthly payment plans, individually arranged payment plans). Merit scholarship grants, need-based scholarship grants available. In 2012–13, 10% of upper-school students received aid; total upper-school merit-scholarship money awarded: $150,000. Total amount of financial aid awarded in 2012–13: $250,000.

Admissions Traditional secondary-level entrance grade is 9. For fall 2012, 400 students applied for upper-level admission, 280 were accepted, 225 enrolled. High School Placement Test required. Deadline for receipt of application materials: none. No application fee required. On-campus interview recommended.

Athletics Interscholastic: baseball, basketball, bowling, cross-country running, football, golf, ice hockey, indoor track & field, lacrosse, soccer, swimming and diving, tennis, track and field, volleyball, winter (indoor) track; intramural: crew, flag football, Frisbee, skiing (downhill), snowboarding, strength & conditioning, ultimate Frisbee, volleyball, weight lifting, weight training. 3 PE instructors, 41 coaches, 1 athletic trainer.

Computers Computers are regularly used in animation, computer applications, desktop publishing, desktop publishing, ESL, drawing and design, graphic design, graphics, journalism, lab/keyboard, mathematics, news writing, newspaper, photography, publications, publishing, science, technical drawing, technology, Web site design, word processing, yearbook classes. Computer network features include on-campus library services, online commercial services, Internet access, Internet filtering or blocking technology. Students grades are available online. The school has a published electronic and media policy.

Contact Mr. Marc Moreau, Director of Admissions. 732-549-7600 Ext. 221. Fax: 732-549-0282. E-mail: admissions@stjoes.org. Website: www.stjoes.org

ST. JOSEPH'S ACADEMY

3015 Broussard Street
Baton Rouge, Louisiana 70808

Head of School: Mrs. Linda Fryoux Harvison

General Information Girls' day college-preparatory, arts, religious studies, and technology school, affiliated with Roman Catholic Church. Grades 9–12. Founded: 1868. Setting: urban. 14-acre campus. 8 buildings on campus. Approved or accredited by National Catholic Education Association, Southern Association of Colleges and Schools, Southern Association of Independent Schools, and Louisiana Department of Education. Endowment: $2.2 million. Total enrollment: 1,048. Upper school average class size: 24. Upper school faculty-student ratio: 1:15. There are 177 required school days per year for Upper School students. Upper School students typically attend 5 days per week. The average school day consists of 7 hours and 20 minutes.

Upper School Student Profile Grade 9: 285 students (285 girls); Grade 10: 272 students (272 girls); Grade 11: 246 students (246 girls); Grade 12: 245 students (245 girls). 95% of students are Roman Catholic.

Faculty School total: 71. In upper school: 9 men, 61 women; 31 have advanced degrees.

Subjects Offered Accounting, acting, advanced biology, advanced chemistry, advanced computer applications, advanced math, Advanced Placement courses, algebra, American history, American history-AP, American literature, American literature-AP, analysis, analysis and differential calculus, art, art appreciation, band, Basic programming, biology, biology-AP, business law, calculus-AP, campus ministry, Catholic belief and practice, chemistry, child development, choir, choral music, chorus, Christian and Hebrew scripture, church history, civics, civics/free enterprise, computer applications, computer information systems, computer multimedia, computer programming, computer technologies, computer technology certification, CPR, critical studies in film, dance, desktop publishing, drama, drama performance, economics, English, English literature-AP, English-AP, environmental science, European history-AP, family and consumer science, film and literature, fine arts, foreign language, French, French as a second language, geometry, grammar, health, health and safety, health education, Hebrew scripture, honors algebra, honors English, honors geometry, human sexuality, independent study, information technology, Latin, marching band, media arts, media production, music, novels, physical education, physical fitness, physics, poetry, pre-calculus, public speaking, religion, research, Shakespeare, social justice, Spanish, speech, speech communications, technology, the Web, transition mathematics, U.S. history, U.S. history-AP, U.S. literature, visual arts, vocal ensemble, vocal music, Web authoring, Web site design, world history-AP.

Graduation Requirements Advanced math, algebra, American history, arts and fine arts (art, music, dance, drama), biology, chemistry, civics, computer applications, English, foreign language, geometry, physical education (includes health), physical science, physics, religion (includes Bible studies and theology), world history, service hours.

Special Academic Programs Advanced Placement exam preparation; honors section; independent study; study at local college for college credit.

College Admission Counseling 249 students graduated in 2013; all went to college, including Auburn University; Louisiana State University and Agricultural and Mechanical College; Louisiana Tech University; Loyola University New Orleans; The University of Alabama; University of Louisiana at Lafayette. 49% scored over 26 on composite ACT.

Student Life Upper grades have uniform requirement, student council, honor system. Discipline rests primarily with faculty. Attendance at religious services is required.

Summer Programs Computer instruction programs offered; session focuses on computer orientation for incoming 9th grade students; held on campus; accepts girls; not open to students from other schools. 285 students usually enrolled. 2014 schedule: June 2 to June 13. Application deadline: November 22.

Tuition and Aid Day student tuition: $9799. Tuition installment plan (monthly debit plan). Need-based scholarship grants available. In 2013–14, 9% of upper-school students received aid. Total amount of financial aid awarded in 2013–14: $411,306.

Admissions Traditional secondary-level entrance grade is 9. ACT-Explore required. Deadline for receipt of application materials: November 22. Application fee required: $50. On-campus interview required.

Athletics Interscholastic: ballet, basketball, bowling, cheering, cross-country running, dance squad, golf, gymnastics, indoor track, modern dance, physical fitness, physical training, rodeo, running, soccer, softball, strength & conditioning, swimming and diving, tennis, track and field, triathlon, volleyball, weight training, winter (indoor) track, winter soccer; coed intramural: volleyball. 6 PE instructors, 7 coaches, 1 athletic trainer.

Computers Computers are regularly used in all classes. Computer network features include on-campus library services, online commercial services, Internet access, wireless campus network, Internet filtering or blocking technology, administrative software/grading/scheduling. Student e-mail accounts are available to students. Students grades are available online. The school has a published electronic and media policy.

Contact Mrs. Sheri Gillio, Assistant Principal. 225-388-2243. Fax: 225-344-5714. E-mail: gillios@sjabr.org. Website: www.sjabr.org

ST. JOSEPH'S CATHOLIC SCHOOL

100 St. Joseph's Drive
Greenville, South Carolina 29607

Head of School: Mr. Keith F. Kiser

General Information Coeducational day college-preparatory school, affiliated with Roman Catholic Church. Grades 6–12. Founded: 1993. Setting: suburban. 36-acre campus. 3 buildings on campus. Approved or accredited by South Carolina Department of Education. Total enrollment: 669. Upper school average class size: 19. Upper school faculty-student ratio: 1:13. There are 175 required school days per year for Upper School students. Upper School students typically attend 5 days per week. The average school day consists of 7 hours and 10 minutes.

Upper School Student Profile Grade 9: 101 students (47 boys, 54 girls); Grade 10: 107 students (56 boys, 51 girls); Grade 11: 94 students (50 boys, 44 girls); Grade 12: 103 students (50 boys, 53 girls). 73% of students are Roman Catholic.

Faculty School total: 57. In upper school: 22 men, 31 women; 4 have advanced degrees.

Subjects Offered Advanced Placement courses, algebra, American history, American literature, ancient world history, art, arts appreciation, bell choir, bioethics, biology, biology-AP, calculus, calculus-AP, chemistry, chemistry-AP, choral music, chorus, Christian doctrine, Christian ethics, church history, composition, computer applications, computer graphics, creative writing, dance, directing, drama workshop, dramatic arts, drawing, economics, economics-AP, English language and composition-AP, English literature and composition-AP, ensembles, environmental science, European history, European history-AP, European literature, exercise science, film, film studies, fine arts, forensics, French, geometry, government, government-AP, honors algebra, honors English, honors geometry, honors U.S. history, human anatomy, human movement and its application to health, instrumental music, keyboarding, Latin, literary magazine, literature, media, medieval/Renaissance history, moral theology, newspaper, personal finance, physical education, physics, physics-AP, pre-algebra, pre-calculus, psychology, science fiction, Shakespeare, Spanish, Spanish language-AP, Spanish-AP, speech, sports conditioning, statistics-AP, strings, theater arts, theater production, U.S. history, U.S. history-AP, yearbook.

Graduation Requirements 65 hours of community service.

Special Academic Programs Advanced Placement exam preparation; honors section.

College Admission Counseling 77 students graduated in 2013; all went to college, including Clemson University; College of Charleston; Furman University; University of South Carolina. Mean SAT critical reading: 601, mean SAT math: 587, mean SAT writing: 583, mean combined SAT: 1771, mean composite ACT: 26.

Student Life Upper grades have uniform requirement, student council, honor system. Discipline rests primarily with faculty. Attendance at religious services is required.

Summer Programs Sports, art/fine arts programs offered; held on campus; accepts boys and girls; open to students from other schools. 2014 schedule: June to August.

Tuition and Aid Day student tuition: $10,335. Tuition installment plan (monthly payment plans, yearly payment plan, semiannual payment plan). Tuition reduction for siblings, merit scholarship grants, need-based scholarship grants, tuition reduction for staff available. In 2013–14, 33% of upper-school students received aid; total upper-school merit-scholarship money awarded: $41,340. Total amount of financial aid awarded in 2013–14: $454,986.

Admissions Traditional secondary-level entrance grade is 9. For fall 2013, 82 students applied for upper-level admission, 60 were accepted, 41 enrolled. Scholastic Testing Service High School Placement Test (open version) required. Deadline for receipt of application materials: none. Application fee required: $125. On-campus interview required.

Athletics Interscholastic: baseball (boys), basketball (b,g), cheering (g), cross-country running (b,g), football (b), golf (b), lacrosse (b,g), soccer (b,g), softball (g), swimming and diving (b,g), tennis (b,g), track and field (b,g), volleyball (g), wrestling (b); intramural: basketball (b,g), flag football (b), Frisbee (b,g), soccer (b,g), volleyball (g); coed interscholastic: golf; coed intramural: dance, weight training.

Computers Computers are regularly used in computer applications, graphic design, keyboarding, programming, yearbook classes. Computer network features include Internet access.

Contact Mrs. Barbara L. McGrath, Director of Admissions. 864-234-9009 Ext. 104. Fax: 864-234-5516. E-mail: bmcgrath@sjcatholicschool.org. Website: www.sjcatholicschool.org

ST. JOSEPH'S PREPARATORY SCHOOL

1733 Girard Avenue
Philadelphia, Pennsylvania 19130

Head of School: Rev. George W. Bur, SJ

General Information Boys' day college-preparatory, arts, and religious studies school, affiliated with Roman Catholic Church. Grades 9–12. Founded: 1851. Setting: urban. 7-acre campus. 3 buildings on campus. Approved or accredited by Jesuit Secondary Education Association, Middle States Association of Colleges and Schools, National Catholic Education Association, and Pennsylvania Department of Education. Member of National Association of Independent Schools. Endowment: $9 million. Total enrollment: 968. Upper school average class size: 22. Upper school faculty-student ratio: 1:16. There are 156 required school days per year for Upper School students. Upper School students typically attend 5 days per week. The average school day consists of 6 hours.

Upper School Student Profile Grade 9: 248 students (248 boys); Grade 10: 225 students (225 boys); Grade 11: 244 students (244 boys); Grade 12: 251 students (251 boys). 95% of students are Roman Catholic.

Faculty School total: 75. In upper school: 60 men, 15 women; 65 have advanced degrees.

Subjects Offered Algebra, American history, American literature, anatomy, archaeology, art, biology, business, calculus, chemistry, classics, computer math, computer programming, computer science, earth science, economics, English, English literature, environmental science, ethics, European history, fine arts, French, geometry, German, government/civics, Greek, history, Latin, Mandarin, marine biology, mathematics, photography, physical education, physics, physiology, religion, science, social sciences, social studies, Spanish, speech, trigonometry, world history, world literature.

Graduation Requirements Arts and fine arts (art, music, dance, drama), classics, computer science, English, foreign language, mathematics, physical education (includes health), religion (includes Bible studies and theology), science, social sciences, social studies (includes history), Christian service hours in junior and senior year.

Special Academic Programs International Baccalaureate program; 15 Advanced Placement exams for which test preparation is offered; honors section; independent study; study at local college for college credit; study abroad; academic accommodation for the gifted, the musically talented, and the artistically talented.

College Admission Counseling 241 students graduated in 2013; 239 went to college, including Fordham University; Penn State University Park; Saint Joseph's University; Temple University; University of Pennsylvania; University of Pittsburgh. Other: 2 had other specific plans. Mean SAT critical reading: 621, mean SAT math: 619, mean SAT writing: 609, mean combined SAT: 1849. 55% scored over 600 on SAT critical reading, 55% scored over 600 on SAT math, 55% scored over 600 on SAT writing, 55% scored over 1800 on combined SAT.

Student Life Upper grades have specified standards of dress, student council. Discipline rests primarily with faculty. Attendance at religious services is required.

Summer Programs Remediation, enrichment, sports, art/fine arts, computer instruction programs offered; session focuses on pre-8th grade enrichment; held on campus; accepts boys and girls; open to students from other schools. 500 students usually enrolled. 2014 schedule: June 26 to July 26. Application deadline: none.

Tuition and Aid Day student tuition: $19,900. Tuition installment plan (monthly payment plans). Tuition reduction for siblings, merit scholarship grants, need-based scholarship grants, need-based loans, middle-income loans, paying campus jobs available. In 2013–14, 36% of upper-school students received aid; total upper-school merit-scholarship money awarded: $500,000. Total amount of financial aid awarded in 2013–14: $3,250,000.

Admissions Traditional secondary-level entrance grade is 9. For fall 2013, 650 students applied for upper-level admission, 320 were accepted, 248 enrolled. 3-R Achievement Test, High School Placement Test or High School Placement Test (closed version) from Scholastic Testing Service required. Deadline for receipt of application materials: November 15. Application fee required: $50. On-campus interview recommended.

Athletics Interscholastic: baseball, basketball, bowling, crew, cross-country running, diving, football, Frisbee, golf, ice hockey, indoor track & field, lacrosse, rowing, rugby, running, soccer, squash, swimming and diving, tennis, track and field, ultimate Frisbee, volleyball, winter (indoor) track, wrestling; intramural: basketball, flag football, handball, martial arts, paint ball, physical fitness, table tennis, team handball, volleyball, water polo. 35 coaches, 1 athletic trainer.

Computers Computers are regularly used in English, mathematics, science classes. Computer network features include on-campus library services, online commercial services, Internet access, wireless campus network, Internet filtering or blocking technology. Student e-mail accounts and computer access in designated common areas are available to students. Students grades are available online. The school has a published electronic and media policy.

Contact Jason M. Zazyczny, Director of Admission. 215-978-1958. Fax: 215-978-1920. E-mail: jzazyczny@sjprep.org. Website: www.sjprep.org

ST. JUDE'S SCHOOL

888 Trillium Drive
Kitchener, Ontario N2R 1K4, Canada

Head of School: Mr. Frederick T. Gore

General Information Coeducational day college-preparatory, arts, and bright learning disabled school; primarily serves underachievers, students with learning disabilities, individuals with Attention Deficit Disorder, and dyslexic students. Grades 1–12. Founded: 1982. Setting: small town. Nearest major city is Toronto, Canada. 10-acre campus. 1 building on campus. Approved or accredited by Ontario Ministry of Education and Ontario Department of Education. Language of instruction: English. Total enrollment: 30. Upper school average class size: 6. Upper school faculty-student ratio: 1:6. There are 200 required school days per year for Upper School students. Upper School students typically attend 5 days per week. The average school day consists of 7 hours.

Upper School Student Profile Grade 10: 2 students (2 boys); Grade 11: 1 student (1 boy).

Faculty School total: 6. In upper school: 3 men, 3 women; 3 have advanced degrees.

Subjects Offered 20th century history, 20th century physics, 20th century world history, accounting, acting, adolescent issues, advanced chemistry, advanced math, algebra, analytic geometry, ancient history, ancient world history, ancient/medieval philosophy, anthropology, applied arts, art, art appreciation, art education, art history, basic skills, biology, bookkeeping, business education, business law, business mathematics, business studies, calculus, Canadian history, Canadian law, Canadian literature, career and personal planning, career education, chemistry, civics, college counseling, communication skills, computer literacy, computer science, computer skills, computer studies, discrete mathematics, dramatic arts, drawing and design, earth and space science, ecology, ecology, environmental systems, economics, economics and history, English, English literature, environmental studies, ESL, family studies, fencing, finite math, general science, geography, health, health education, history, honors algebra, honors English, honors geometry, independent study, intro to computers, keyboarding, law, law studies, marketing, media studies, modern Western civilization, modern world history, philosophy, physical education, physical fitness, remedial study skills, remedial/makeup course work, science, science and technology, society, politics and law, sociology, Spanish, study skills, visual arts, Western philosophy, world issues.

Graduation Requirements Ontario requirements.

Special Academic Programs Remedial reading and/or remedial writing; remedial math; programs in English, mathematics, general development for dyslexic students; special instructional classes for students with learning disabilities, Attention Deficit Disorder, and dyslexia; ESL (2 students enrolled).

College Admission Counseling 5 students graduated in 2012; all went to college, including University of Waterloo; Wilfrid Laurier University.

Student Life Upper grades have uniform requirement, student council, honor system. Discipline rests primarily with faculty.

Tuition and Aid Day student tuition: CAN$16,900. Tuition installment plan (monthly payment plans, individually arranged payment plans).

Admissions For fall 2012, 5 students applied for upper-level admission, 5 were accepted, 5 enrolled. Academic Profile Tests, achievement tests, Woodcock Reading Mastery Key Math and Woodcock-Johnson Educational Evaluation, WISC III required. Deadline for receipt of application materials: none. No application fee required. Interview required.

Athletics Interscholastic: synchronized swimming (girls); coed interscholastic: basketball, bowling, cross-country running, fencing, golf; coed intramural: badminton, ball hockey, baseball, basketball, bowling, cross-country running, curling, fencing, fitness, floor hockey, golf, martial arts. 2 PE instructors.

Computers Computers are regularly used in all classes. Computer network features include Internet access, Internet filtering or blocking technology.

Contact Frederick T. Gore, Director of Education. 519-888-0807. Fax: 519-888-0316. E-mail: director@stjudes.com. Website: www.stjudes.com

SAINT LAWRENCE ACADEMY

2000 Lawrence Court
Santa Clara, California 95051

Head of School: Mr. Phil Dolan

General Information Coeducational day college-preparatory, arts, business, religious studies, and technology school, affiliated with Roman Catholic Church. Grades 9–12. Founded: 1975. Setting: urban. Nearest major city is San Jose. 9-acre campus. 3 buildings on campus. Approved or accredited by National Catholic Education Association, Western Association of Schools and Colleges, and California Department of Education. Total enrollment: 250. Upper school average class size: 21. Upper school faculty-student ratio: 1:15. There are 169 required school days per year for Upper School students. Upper School students typically attend 5 days per week. The average school day consists of 6 hours and 35 minutes.

Upper School Student Profile 65% of students are Roman Catholic.

Faculty School total: 27. In upper school: 12 men, 15 women; 17 have advanced degrees.

Subjects Offered Accounting, algebra, American history, American history-AP, American literature, American sign language, art, biology, biology-AP, career exploration, chemistry, computer programming, computer science, consumer economics, drama, earth science, economics, English, English literature, ethics, French, geometry, government/civics, health, keyboarding, mathematics, music, physical education, physical science, physics, religion, science, social studies, Spanish, Spanish-AP, technology, theater, trigonometry, word processing, world history, world literature, yearbook.

Graduation Requirements Arts and fine arts (art, music, dance, drama), computer science, English, foreign language, mathematics, physical education (includes health), religion (includes Bible studies and theology), science, social sciences. Community service is required.

Special Academic Programs Study at local college for college credit.

College Admission Counseling 55 students graduated in 2013; 54 went to college, including De Anza College; San Francisco State University; San Jose State University; Santa Clara University; University of California, Irvine; West Valley College. Other: 1 went to work. Mean SAT critical reading: 526, mean SAT math: 545. 13% scored over 600 on SAT critical reading, 20% scored over 600 on SAT math.

Student Life Upper grades have uniform requirement, student council, honor system. Discipline rests primarily with faculty. Attendance at religious services is required.

Tuition and Aid Day student tuition: $15,000. Tuition installment plan (monthly payment plans). Merit scholarship grants, need-based scholarship grants, diocesan scholarship for Catholic students available.

Admissions Traditional secondary-level entrance grade is 9. Catholic High School Entrance Examination required. Deadline for receipt of application materials: January 15. Application fee required: $75. Interview required.

Athletics Interscholastic: baseball (boys), basketball (b,g), cross-country running (b,g), golf (b), roller hockey (b), soccer (b), tennis (b,g), track and field (b,g), volleyball (g); coed interscholastic: golf, roller hockey, soccer; coed intramural: aerobics/dance, bowling, dance. 3 coaches, 1 athletic trainer.

Computers Computers are regularly used in all academic, science classes. Computer network features include Internet access, wireless campus network, Internet filtering or blocking technology. Campus intranet and student e-mail accounts are available to students. Students grades are available online. The school has a published electronic and media policy.

Contact Mrs. Mary Dixon, Admissions Director. 408-296-6391. Fax: 408-296-3794. E-mail: mdixon@saintlawrence.org. Website: www.saintlawrenceacademy.com

ST. LAWRENCE SEMINARY HIGH SCHOOL

301 Church Street
Mount Calvary, Wisconsin 53057

Head of School: Fr. John Holly, OFMCAP

General Information Boys' boarding college-preparatory and religious studies school, affiliated with Roman Catholic Church. Grades 9–12. Founded: 1860. Setting: rural. Nearest major city is Milwaukee. Students are housed in single-sex dormitories. 150-acre campus. 11 buildings on campus. Approved or accredited by National Catholic Education Association, North Central Association of Colleges and Schools, and Wisconsin Department of Education. Total enrollment: 195. Upper school average class size: 17. Upper school faculty-student ratio: 1:9. There are 167 required school days per year for Upper School students. Upper School students typically attend 5 days per week. The average school day consists of 7 hours and 25 minutes.

Upper School Student Profile Grade 9: 57 students (57 boys); Grade 10: 50 students (50 boys); Grade 11: 55 students (55 boys); Grade 12: 33 students (33 boys); Postgraduate: 195 students (195 boys). 100% of students are boarding students. 30% are state residents. 18 states are represented in upper school student body. 12% are international students. International students from Ghana, India, Philippines, Republic of Korea, Saudi Arabia, and Viet Nam; 4 other countries represented in student body. 100% of students are Roman Catholic.

Faculty School total: 25. In upper school: 19 men, 6 women; 12 have advanced degrees; 6 reside on campus.

Subjects Offered Accounting, algebra, American history, American literature, art, biology, business, business law, calculus, chemistry, classical studies, computer science, English, English literature, fine arts, geometry, German, government/civics, health, health and wellness, humanities, industrial arts, lab/keyboard, Latin, literary genres, mathematics, mechanical drawing, music, physical education, physics, psychology, religion, science, socioeconomic problems, Spanish, theology, trigonometry, world history, world literature.

Graduation Requirements Arts and fine arts (art, music, dance, drama), business skills (includes word processing), computer science, English, foreign language, health education, humanities, mathematics, physical education (includes health), religion (includes Bible studies and theology), science, social studies (includes history), study skills, ministry hours.

Special Academic Programs Study at local college for college credit.

College Admission Counseling 37 students graduated in 2013; all went to college, including Marquette University; Saint Xavier University; University of Chicago; University of Dallas; University of Minnesota, Duluth; University of Wisconsin–Madison. Median SAT critical reading: 550, median SAT math: 600, median SAT writing: 540, median combined SAT: 1630; median composite ACT: 23. 10% scored over 600 on SAT critical reading, 50% scored over 600 on SAT math, 20% scored over 600 on SAT writing, 30% scored over 1800 on combined SAT, 23% scored over 26 on composite ACT.

Student Life Upper grades have specified standards of dress, student council, honor system. Discipline rests primarily with faculty. Attendance at religious services is required.

Tuition and Aid 7-day tuition and room/board: $10,800. Tuition installment plan (SMART Tuition Payment Plan, monthly payment plans, individually arranged payment plans). Need-based scholarship grants available. In 2013–14, 73% of upper-school students received aid. Total amount of financial aid awarded in 2013–14: $778,110.

Admissions Traditional secondary-level entrance grade is 9. For fall 2013, 81 students applied for upper-level admission, 79 were accepted, 74 enrolled. 3-R Achievement Test and any standardized test required. Deadline for receipt of application materials: none. Application fee required: $300. Interview recommended.

Athletics Interscholastic: baseball, basketball, cross-country running, soccer, tennis, track and field, wrestling; intramural: basketball, bicycling, billiards, bowling, floor hockey, Frisbee, handball, kickball, outdoor activities, outdoor recreation, physical fitness, physical training, racquetball, skiing (downhill), softball, table tennis, tennis, volleyball, wallyball, weight lifting, winter soccer. 3 PE instructors, 8 coaches, 1 athletic trainer.

Computers Computers are regularly used in accounting, business education, classics, creative writing, drafting, economics, English, keyboarding, mathematics, psychology, science, typing, writing, yearbook classes. Computer network features include on-campus library services, Internet access, Internet filtering or blocking technology. Campus intranet, student e-mail accounts, and computer access in designated common areas are available to students. The school has a published electronic and media policy.

Contact Mrs. Deann Sippel, Administrative Assistant to Admissions. 920-753-7570. Fax: 920-753-7507. E-mail: dsippel@stlawrence.edu. Website: www.stlawrence.edu

SAINT LUCY'S PRIORY HIGH SCHOOL

655 West Sierra Madre Avenue
Glendora, California 91741-1997

Head of School: Sr. Monica Collins, OSB

General Information Girls' day college-preparatory, arts, religious studies, and technology school, affiliated with Roman Catholic Church. Grades 9–12. Founded: 1962. Setting: suburban. Nearest major city is Pasadena. 14-acre campus. 4 buildings on campus. Approved or accredited by Western Association of Schools and Colleges and California Department of Education. Endowment: $2 million. Total enrollment: 647. Upper school average class size: 17. Upper school faculty-student ratio: 1:17. There are 182 required school days per year for Upper School students. Upper School students typically attend 5 days per week. The average school day consists of 6 hours and 45 minutes.

Upper School Student Profile Grade 9: 166 students (166 girls); Grade 10: 151 students (151 girls); Grade 11: 152 students (152 girls); Grade 12: 178 students (178 girls). 80% of students are Roman Catholic.

Faculty School total: 41. In upper school: 9 men, 32 women; 15 have advanced degrees.

Subjects Offered Adolescent issues, advanced math, algebra, art, art appreciation, ASB Leadership, athletics, Bible studies, biology, biology-AP, calculus, calculus-AP, calligraphy, chemistry, child development, Christian ethics, Christian scripture, church history, commercial art, computer art, creative dance, creative writing, dance, drama,

drawing, early childhood, economics, English, English language and composition-AP, English literature, English literature-AP, ethics, European history-AP, film studies, French, geometry, health, health education, Hebrew scripture, journalism, kinesiology, library assistant, literary magazine, mechanical drawing, media arts, meditation, modern European history-AP, moral and social development, moral theology, musical productions, painting, physical education, physical science, physics, physiology, psychology, religion, sculpture, sewing, Spanish, Spanish-AP, studio art, theater production, trigonometry, U.S. government, U.S. government and politics-AP, U.S. history, U.S. history-AP, voice, world history, yearbook.

Graduation Requirements Arts and fine arts (art, music, dance, drama), English, foreign language, mathematics, physical education (includes health), religion (includes Bible studies and theology), science, social sciences, social studies (includes history).

Special Academic Programs Advanced Placement exam preparation; honors section.

College Admission Counseling 171 students graduated in 2012; all went to college, including Azusa Pacific University; California State Polytechnic University, Pomona; Loyola Marymount University; Mount St. Mary's College; University of California, Irvine; University of California, Riverside. Mean SAT critical reading: 540, mean SAT math: 521, mean SAT writing: 548, mean composite ACT: 23. 40% scored over 600 on SAT critical reading, 20% scored over 600 on SAT math, 35% scored over 600 on SAT writing, 46% scored over 26 on composite ACT.

Student Life Upper grades have uniform requirement, student council. Discipline rests equally with students and faculty. Attendance at religious services is required.

Tuition and Aid Day student tuition: $7800. Tuition installment plan (SMART Tuition Payment Plan, monthly payment plans, individually arranged payment plans, quarterly payment plan). Tuition reduction for siblings, merit scholarship grants, need-based scholarship grants available. In 2012–13, 5% of upper-school students received aid; total upper-school merit-scholarship money awarded: $3500. Total amount of financial aid awarded in 2012–13: $90,000.

Admissions Traditional secondary-level entrance grade is 9. STS required. Deadline for receipt of application materials: January 21. Application fee required: $75. On-campus interview required.

Athletics Interscholastic: basketball, cheering, cross-country running, drill team, soccer, softball, swimming and diving, tennis, track and field, volleyball, water polo; intramural: badminton, basketball, cheering, dance, dance squad, dance team, jogging, physical fitness, soccer, softball, yoga. 2 PE instructors, 36 coaches, 1 athletic trainer.

Computers Computers are regularly used in art, drawing and design, English, graphic arts, history, journalism, library science, literary magazine, mathematics, media production, music, psychology, science, yearbook classes. Computer resources include Internet access, wireless campus network, Internet filtering or blocking technology. Campus intranet and computer access in designated common areas are available to students. Students grades are available online.

Contact Mrs. Irma Esparza, Secretary. 626-335-3322. Fax: 626-335-4373. Website: www.stlucys.com

ST. MARK'S SCHOOL OF TEXAS

10600 Preston Road
Dallas, Texas 75230-4000

Head of School: Mr. Arnold E. Holtberg

General Information Boys' day college-preparatory, arts, technology, and advanced placement school. Grades 1–12. Founded: 1906. Setting: urban. 40-acre campus. 13 buildings on campus. Approved or accredited by Independent Schools Association of the Southwest. Member of National Association of Independent Schools and Secondary School Admission Test Board. Endowment: $120 million. Total enrollment: 851. Upper school average class size: 14. Upper school faculty-student ratio: 1:8. There are 172 required school days per year for Upper School students. Upper School students typically attend 5 days per week. The average school day consists of 7 hours and 55 minutes.

Upper School Student Profile Grade 9: 96 students (96 boys); Grade 10: 90 students (90 boys); Grade 11: 92 students (92 boys); Grade 12: 86 students (86 boys).

Subjects Offered 3-dimensional art, acting, algebra, American history-AP, ancient world history, art, art history, astronomy, Basic programming, biology, biology-AP, calculus, calculus-AP, ceramics, chemistry, chemistry-AP, Chinese, choir, civil rights, community service, computer programming, computer science, computer science-AP, conceptual physics, concert band, creative drama, creative writing, debate, digital art, digital photography, directing, DNA science lab, drama, drama workshop, economics, economics-AP, English, English literature and composition-AP, English literature-AP, environmental science-AP, European history, European history-AP, film studies, fine arts, gender issues, geology, geometry, history, honors English, honors geometry, humanities, independent study, Japanese, journalism, Latin, Latin-AP, macroeconomics-AP, marine ecology, mathematics, microeconomics-AP, modern European history-AP, modern world history, music, oceanography, photography, physical education, physics, physics-AP, piano, science, science fiction, sculpture, senior project, Spanish, Spanish language-AP, Spanish literature-AP, statistics-AP, strings, theater, trigonometry, U.S. history, video film production, Web site design, woodworking, world history, world religions.

Graduation Requirements Arts and fine arts (art, music, dance, drama), English, foreign language, mathematics, physical education (includes health), science, social studies (includes history), senior exhibition. Community service is required.

Special Academic Programs Advanced Placement exam preparation; honors section; independent study; term-away projects; study abroad; academic accommodation for the gifted.

College Admission Counseling 92 students graduated in 2013; all went to college, including Dartmouth College; New York University; Southern Methodist University; The University of Texas at Austin; University of Southern California; Vanderbilt University. Mean SAT critical reading: 689, mean SAT math: 715, mean SAT writing: 686, mean combined SAT: 2090, mean composite ACT: 32.

Student Life Upper grades have uniform requirement, student council, honor system. Discipline rests primarily with faculty. Attendance at religious services is required.

Tuition and Aid Day student tuition: $25,258–$26,914. Tuition installment plan (Insured Tuition Payment Plan, individually arranged payment plans, financial aid student monthly payment plan). Need-based scholarship grants, tuition remission for sons of faculty and staff, need-based middle-income financial aid available. In 2013–14, 15% of upper-school students received aid. Total amount of financial aid awarded in 2013–14: $1,013,991.

Admissions Traditional secondary-level entrance grade is 9. For fall 2013, 109 students applied for upper-level admission, 21 were accepted, 19 enrolled. ISEE required. Deadline for receipt of application materials: January 6. Application fee required: $175. Interview required.

Athletics Interscholastic: backpacking, baseball, basketball, cheering, climbing, crew, cross-country running, diving, fencing, football, golf, hiking/backpacking, hockey, ice hockey, lacrosse, outdoor education, outdoor skills, physical fitness, physical training, soccer, strength & conditioning, swimming and diving, tennis, track and field, volleyball, wall climbing, water polo, weight training, wilderness, winter soccer, wrestling; intramural: basketball, bicycling, cooperative games, cross-country running, fitness, flag football, floor hockey, jump rope, kickball, lacrosse, physical fitness, physical training, soccer, softball, swimming and diving, table tennis, team handball, tennis, track and field, volleyball, water polo, weight training, winter soccer, wrestling. 11 PE instructors, 69 coaches, 2 athletic trainers.

Computers Computers are regularly used in English, foreign language, humanities, mathematics, science classes. Computer network features include on-campus library services, online commercial services, Internet access, wireless campus network, Internet filtering or blocking technology. Student e-mail accounts and computer access in designated common areas are available to students. Students grades are available online. The school has a published electronic and media policy.

Contact Mr. David P. Baker, Director of Admission and Financial Aid. 214-346-8171. Fax: 214-346-8701. E-mail: admission@smtexas.org. Website: www.smtexas.org

ST. MARTIN'S EPISCOPAL SCHOOL

225 Green Acres Road
Metairie, Louisiana 70003

Head of School: Merry Sorrells

General Information Coeducational day college-preparatory school, affiliated with Episcopal Church. Grades PK–12. Founded: 1947. Setting: suburban. Nearest major city is New Orleans. 18-acre campus. 13 buildings on campus. Approved or accredited by Independent Schools Association of the Southwest, National Association of Episcopal Schools, Southern Association of Colleges and Schools, Southwest Association of Episcopal Schools, The College Board, and Louisiana Department of Education. Member of National Association of Independent Schools. Endowment: $8.1 million. Total enrollment: 483. Upper school average class size: 17. Upper school faculty-student ratio: 1:6. There are 180 required school days per year for Upper School students. Upper School students typically attend 5 days per week. The average school day consists of 5 hours and 10 minutes.

Upper School Student Profile Grade 9: 37 students (28 boys, 9 girls); Grade 10: 47 students (27 boys, 20 girls); Grade 11: 60 students (32 boys, 28 girls); Grade 12: 61 students (31 boys, 30 girls). 10% of students are members of Episcopal Church.

Faculty School total: 88. In upper school: 14 men, 20 women; 17 have advanced degrees.

Subjects Offered Advanced chemistry, advanced math, Advanced Placement courses, advanced studio art-AP, algebra, American history, American history-AP, American literature, American literature-AP, art, art history, band, baseball, basketball, bell choir, Bible studies, biology, biology-AP, calculus, calculus-AP, career education internship, career/college preparation, ceramics, cheerleading, chemistry, chemistry-AP, Chinese studies, chorus, civics, college counseling, community garden, community service, computer literacy, creative writing, digital photography, drama, earth science, economics, economics and history, English, English language and composition-AP, English literature, English literature and composition-AP, English literature-AP, environmental science, ethics, European history-AP, film studies, fine arts, French, French-AP, geography, geology, geometry, grammar, history-AP, honors algebra, honors English, honors geometry, humanities, internship, journalism, lab science, Latin, Latin-AP, leadership and service, life management skills, life skills, literary magazine, Mandarin, mathematics, model United Nations, music, music appreciation, music-AP, musical productions, newspaper, philosophy, physical education, physics, pre-algebra, publications, religion, SAT preparation, science, scripture, senior internship, social

studies, softball, Spanish, Spanish-AP, speech, statistics-AP, student government, studio art, studio art-AP, swimming, tennis, theater, theater design and production, theology, track and field, trigonometry, U.S. history-AP, volleyball, world history, world literature, world religions, writing.

Graduation Requirements Arts and fine arts (art, music, dance, drama), electives, English, foreign language, life skills, mathematics, physical education (includes health), religion (includes Bible studies and theology), science, senior internship, social studies (includes history), senior intern program, 50 hours of community service.

Special Academic Programs 12 Advanced Placement exams for which test preparation is offered; honors section; independent study.

College Admission Counseling 58 students graduated in 2013; all went to college, including Louisiana State University and Agricultural and Mechanical College; Loyola University New Orleans; Rhodes College; Spring Hill College; The University of Alabama; University of Mississippi. Median SAT critical reading: 570, median SAT math: 570, median SAT writing: 590, median combined SAT: 1730, median composite ACT: 27. 40% scored over 600 on SAT critical reading, 35% scored over 600 on SAT math, 40% scored over 600 on SAT writing, 44% scored over 1800 on combined SAT, 40% scored over 26 on composite ACT.

Student Life Upper grades have specified standards of dress, student council, honor system. Discipline rests primarily with faculty. Attendance at religious services is required.

Summer Programs Remediation, enrichment, advancement, sports, art/fine arts, computer instruction programs offered; session focuses on academics, athletics, creative arts, and enrichment; held on campus; accepts boys and girls; open to students from other schools. 267 students usually enrolled. 2014 schedule: June 1 to August 7. Application deadline: May 15.

Tuition and Aid Day student tuition: $18,800. Tuition installment plan (local bank-arranged plan). Merit scholarship grants, need-based scholarship grants available. In 2013–14, 35% of upper-school students received aid; total upper-school merit-scholarship money awarded: $238,250. Total amount of financial aid awarded in 2013–14: $583,060.

Admissions Traditional secondary-level entrance grade is 9. For fall 2013, 26 students applied for upper-level admission, 24 were accepted, 12 enrolled. Admissions testing, CTP, ISEE, math and English placement tests, WISC III or other aptitude measures; standardized achievement test or writing sample required. Deadline for receipt of application materials: none. Application fee required: $50. On-campus interview required.

Athletics Interscholastic: baseball (boys), basketball (b,g), cross-country running (b,g), flag football (b), football (b), golf (b,g), soccer (b,g), softball (g), swimming and diving (b,g), tennis (b,g), track and field (b,g), volleyball (g); intramural: basketball (b,g), cheering (b,g), cross-country running (b,g), golf (b,g), ropes courses (b,g), soccer (b,g), swimming and diving (b,g), tennis (b,g), track and field (b,g), volleyball (g); coed intramural: lacrosse, project adventure. 6 PE instructors, 6 coaches, 1 athletic trainer.

Computers Computers are regularly used in all academic classes. Computer network features include on-campus library services, online commercial services, Internet access, wireless campus network, Internet filtering or blocking technology, VPN for teachers, staff, and students. Campus intranet, student e-mail accounts, and computer access in designated common areas are available to students. Students grades are available online. The school has a published electronic and media policy.

Contact Mrs. Danielle Calamia, Admission Assistant. 504-736-9917. Fax: 504-736-8802. E-mail: danielle.calamia@stmsaints.com. Website: www.stmsaints.com

ST. MARY'S EPISCOPAL SCHOOL

60 Perkins Extended
Memphis, Tennessee 38117-3199

Head of School: Mr. Albert L. Throckmorton

General Information Girls' day college-preparatory, arts, religious studies, technology, and Global issues, Science school, affiliated with Episcopal Church. Grades PK–12. Founded: 1847. Setting: urban. 25-acre campus. 8 buildings on campus. Approved or accredited by National Association of Episcopal Schools, Southern Association of Colleges and Schools, Southern Association of Independent Schools, The College Board, and Tennessee Department of Education. Member of National Association of Independent Schools. Endowment: $19 million. Total enrollment: 849. Upper school average class size: 13. Upper school faculty-student ratio: 1:13. There are 175 required school days per year for Upper School students. Upper School students typically attend 5 days per week. The average school day consists of 6 hours and 15 minutes.

Upper School Student Profile Grade 9: 67 students (67 girls); Grade 10: 64 students (64 girls); Grade 11: 56 students (56 girls); Grade 12: 59 students (59 girls). 15% of students are members of Episcopal Church.

Faculty School total: 113. In upper school: 9 men, 29 women; 30 have advanced degrees.

Subjects Offered Algebra, anatomy and physiology, art history, art history-AP, biology, biology-AP, calculus, calculus-AP, chamber groups, chemistry, chemistry-AP, choir, comparative religion, economics, English, English language and composition-AP, English literature and composition-AP, ethics, French, French-AP, geography, geometry, global issues, guitar, health, humanities, instrumental music, Latin, Latin-AP,

Mandarin, microbiology, music theory-AP, performing arts, physical education, physics, physics-AP, pre-calculus, psychology, religion, robotics, Spanish, Spanish-AP, speech, studio art, studio art-AP, technology, theater, U.S. government, U.S. history, U.S. history-AP, wind ensemble, world history, world history-AP.

Graduation Requirements 1 1/2 elective credits, algebra, arts and fine arts (art, music, dance, drama), biology, calculus, chemistry, computer skills, economics, English, English language-AP, English literature-AP, foreign language, geometry, physical education (includes health), physics, pre-calculus, religion (includes Bible studies and theology), social studies (includes history), U.S. history, world history.

Special Academic Programs 16 Advanced Placement exams for which test preparation is offered; honors section; independent study; academic accommodation for the gifted, the musically talented, and the artistically talented.

College Admission Counseling 64 students graduated in 2013; all went to college, including Sewanee: The University of the South; Texas Christian University; The University of Alabama; The University of Tennessee; University of Arkansas; University of Mississippi. Median SAT critical reading: 630, median SAT math: 620, median SAT writing: 660, median combined SAT: 1870, median composite ACT: 30. 67% scored over 600 on SAT critical reading, 56% scored over 600 on SAT math, 81% scored over 600 on SAT writing, 67% scored over 1800 on combined SAT, 86% scored over 26 on composite ACT.

Student Life Upper grades have specified standards of dress, student council, honor system. Discipline rests equally with students and faculty. Attendance at religious services is required.

Summer Programs Enrichment, sports, art/fine arts programs offered; session focuses on summer enrichment, reading; held both on and off campus; held at predominantly held on the school campus. Swimming component at a neighborhood pool; accepts boys and girls; open to students from other schools. 500 students usually enrolled. 2014 schedule: May 28 to August 10. Application deadline: none.

Tuition and Aid Day student tuition: $18,100. Tuition installment plan (monthly payment plans, credit card payment). Need-based scholarship grants, discounts for children of faculty, staff, and clergy available. In 2013–14, 19% of upper-school students received aid. Total amount of financial aid awarded in 2013–14: $352,800.

Admissions Traditional secondary-level entrance grade is 9. For fall 2013, 23 students applied for upper-level admission, 21 were accepted, 11 enrolled. ISEE and writing sample required. Deadline for receipt of application materials: none. Application fee required: $75. On-campus interview required.

Athletics Interscholastic: basketball, bowling, cross-country running, dance team, golf, lacrosse, soccer, softball, swimming and diving, tennis, track and field, volleyball. 1 PE instructor, 7 coaches, 1 athletic trainer.

Computers Computers are regularly used in all academic, career exploration, college planning, creative writing, library, literary magazine, music, newspaper, research skills, SAT preparation, speech, theater arts, yearbook classes. Computer network features include on-campus library services, Internet access, wireless campus network, Internet filtering or blocking technology, online database services for research available at school and at home. Campus intranet, student e-mail accounts, and computer access in designated common areas are available to students. Students grades are available online. The school has a published electronic and media policy.

Contact Ms. Nicole Hernandez, Director of Admission and Financial Aid. 901-537-1405. Fax: 901-685-1098. E-mail: nhernandez@stmarysschool.org. Website: www.stmarysschool.org

SAINT MARY'S HALL

9401 Starcrest Drive
San Antonio, Texas 78217

Head of School: Mr. Bob Windham

General Information Coeducational day college-preparatory and arts school. Grades PK–12. Founded: 1879. Setting: suburban. 60-acre campus. 15 buildings on campus. Approved or accredited by Independent Schools Association of the Southwest. Member of National Association of Independent Schools and Secondary School Admission Test Board. Endowment: $31.7 million. Total enrollment: 1,008. Upper school average class size: 15. Upper school faculty-student ratio: 1:6. There are 173 required school days per year for Upper School students. Upper School students typically attend 5 days per week. The average school day consists of 7 hours and 15 minutes.

Upper School Student Profile Grade 9: 101 students (45 boys, 56 girls); Grade 10: 101 students (50 boys, 51 girls); Grade 11: 93 students (52 boys, 41 girls); Grade 12: 102 students (44 boys, 58 girls).

Faculty School total: 102. In upper school: 29 men, 20 women; 37 have advanced degrees.

Subjects Offered 3-dimensional art, Advanced Placement courses, algebra, American history-AP, American literature, anatomy and physiology, art, art history, art history-AP, art-AP, athletic training, ballet, baseball, basketball, biology, biology-AP, British literature, calculus, calculus-AP, cell biology, ceramics, chemistry, chemistry-AP, choir, college counseling, composition, computer science, computer science-AP, concert choir, creative writing, dance, digital photography, directing, drama, drawing, drawing and design, economics, economics-AP, English language and composition-AP, English literature and composition-AP, environmental science-AP, European history, European history-AP, fitness, French, French language-AP, genetics, geology,

geometry, golf, government/civics, great books, guitar, health, human geography - AP, jazz band, Latin, Latin-AP, literary magazine, marine biology, model United Nations, music theory, painting, photography, physical education, physics, physics-AP, piano, pre-calculus, religious studies, science research, sculpture, set design, softball, Spanish, Spanish language-AP, Spanish literature-AP, speech, statistics-AP, swimming, technical theater, tennis, track and field, U.S. history, voice, volleyball, Web site design, world geography, world history, world literature, world religions, yearbook, zoology.

Graduation Requirements Arts and fine arts (art, music, dance, drama), athletics, electives, English, foreign language, mathematics, physical education (includes health), science, social studies (includes history), 40 hours of community service.

Special Academic Programs 25 Advanced Placement exams for which test preparation is offered; honors section; independent study; study abroad.

College Admission Counseling 94 students graduated in 2013; all went to college, including Harvard University; Southern Methodist University; The University of Texas at Austin; Trinity University; University of Southern California; Vanderbilt University. Median SAT critical reading: 610, median SAT math: 623, median SAT writing: 615.

Student Life Upper grades have uniform requirement, student council, honor system. Discipline rests primarily with faculty. Attendance at religious services is required.

Summer Programs Enrichment, sports, art/fine arts, computer instruction programs offered; held on campus; accepts boys and girls; open to students from other schools. 837 students usually enrolled. 2014 schedule: June 1 to August 5. Application deadline: May 13.

Tuition and Aid Day student tuition: $20,435. Tuition installment plan (monthly payment plans, individually arranged payment plans, full-year payment plan, 2-payment plan, monthly payment plan). Merit scholarship grants, need-based scholarship grants available. In 2013–14, 22% of upper-school students received aid; total upper-school merit-scholarship money awarded: $538,960. Total amount of financial aid awarded in 2013–14: $621,990.

Admissions Traditional secondary-level entrance grade is 9. For fall 2013, 133 students applied for upper-level admission, 79 were accepted, 47 enrolled. ISEE required. Deadline for receipt of application materials: November 14. Application fee required: $50. Interview required.

Athletics Interscholastic: ballet (boys, girls), baseball (b), basketball (b,g), cheering (g), dance (b,g), field hockey (g), fitness (b,g), football (b), golf (b,g), independent competitive sports (b,g), lacrosse (b), soccer (b,g), softball (g), volleyball (b,g); coed interscholastic: cross-country running, physical fitness, physical training, strength & conditioning, tennis, track and field, weight training. 14 coaches, 2 athletic trainers.

Computers Computers are regularly used in media arts classes. Computer network features include on-campus library services, Internet access, wireless campus network, Internet filtering or blocking technology, SmartBoards. Student e-mail accounts are available to students. Students grades are available online. The school has a published electronic and media policy.

Contact Mrs. Julie Hellmund, Director of Admission. 210-483-9234. Fax: 210-655-5211. E-mail: jhellmund@smhall.org. Website: www.smhall.org

SAINT MARY'S HIGH SCHOOL

2525 North Third Street
Phoenix, Arizona 85004

Head of School: Mrs. Suzanne M. Fessler

General Information Coeducational day college-preparatory, general academic, arts, and religious studies school, affiliated with Roman Catholic Church. Grades 9–12. Founded: 1917. Setting: urban. 6-acre campus. 5 buildings on campus. Approved or accredited by North Central Association of Colleges and Schools, Western Catholic Education Association, and Arizona Department of Education. Endowment: $1 million. Total enrollment: 503. Upper school average class size: 25. Upper school faculty-student ratio: 1:15. There are 180 required school days per year for Upper School students. Upper School students typically attend 5 days per week. The average school day consists of 6 hours and 45 minutes.

Upper School Student Profile Grade 9: 158 students (80 boys, 78 girls); Grade 10: 124 students (62 boys, 62 girls); Grade 11: 115 students (60 boys, 55 girls); Grade 12: 106 students (42 boys, 64 girls). 85% of students are Roman Catholic.

Faculty School total: 32. In upper school: 12 men, 20 women; 18 have advanced degrees.

Subjects Offered Advanced Placement courses, algebra, American government, American history, American history-AP, American literature, art, band, biology, British literature, British literature (honors), calculus-AP, Catholic belief and practice, chemistry, Christian and Hebrew scripture, composition, dance, drama, economics, electives, English, English composition, English language and composition-AP, English literature, English literature and composition-AP, fine arts, foreign language, French, geometry, health, history, history of the Catholic Church, honors algebra, honors English, honors geometry, honors U.S. history, Latin, Life of Christ, physical education, physical science, physics, prayer/spirituality, pre-calculus, religious education, social studies, Spanish, Spanish language-AP, standard curriculum, state government, state history, theology, trigonometry, U.S. government and politics-AP, world geography, world history, world religions, yearbook.

Graduation Requirements Advanced math, algebra, American government, American history, American literature, anatomy and physiology, arts and fine arts (art, music, dance, drama), biology, British literature, Catholic belief and practice, chemistry, Christian and Hebrew scripture, composition, economics, electives, English, foreign language, geometry, health education, history of the Catholic Church, language and composition, physical education (includes health), physics, pre-calculus, theology, trigonometry, world history, world literature, 90 hours of Christian community service, 4 credtis of Catholic Theology courses.

Special Academic Programs 5 Advanced Placement exams for which test preparation is offered; honors section; study at local college for college credit; remedial reading and/or remedial writing; remedial math.

College Admission Counseling 123 students graduated in 2013; 120 went to college, including Arizona State University; Grand Canyon University; Northern Arizona University; The University of Arizona. Other: 2 went to work, 1 entered military service.

Student Life Upper grades have uniform requirement, student council. Discipline rests primarily with faculty. Attendance at religious services is required.

Summer Programs Remediation, enrichment, advancement, sports, art/fine arts programs offered; session focuses on high school preparation for incoming freshmen and advancement for upper classmen; held on campus; accepts boys and girls; open to students from other schools. 200 students usually enrolled. 2014 schedule: June 3 to July 11. Application deadline: May 9.

Tuition and Aid Day student tuition: $12,600. Tuition installment plan (monthly payment plans, individually arranged payment plans, quarterly and semester payment plans). Need-based scholarship grants, paying campus jobs available. In 2013–14, 80% of upper-school students received aid. Total amount of financial aid awarded in 2013–14: $2,200,000.

Admissions Traditional secondary-level entrance grade is 9. For fall 2013, 180 students applied for upper-level admission, 170 were accepted, 160 enrolled. High School Placement Test required. Deadline for receipt of application materials: none. Application fee required: $300. On-campus interview required.

Athletics Interscholastic: baseball (boys), basketball (b,g), cheering (g), football (b), golf (b,g), physical fitness (b,g), soccer (b,g), softball (g), strength & conditioning (b,g), tennis (b,g), volleyball (b,g), weight training (b,g), winter soccer (b,g); intramural: dance (g); coed interscholastic: cross-country running, physical fitness, strength & conditioning, swimming and diving, track and field, weight training. 3 PE instructors, 20 coaches, 1 athletic trainer.

Computers Computers are regularly used in digital applications, graphics, yearbook classes. Computer resources include on-campus library services, online commercial services, Internet access, wireless campus network, Internet filtering or blocking technology. Student e-mail accounts are available to students. Students grades are available online. The school has a published electronic and media policy.

Contact Mrs. Sarah Yerden, Director of Admissions. 602-251-2515. Fax: 602-251-2595. E-mail: syerden@smknights.org. Website: www.smknights.org

SAINT MARY'S HIGH SCHOOL

113 Duke of Gloucester Street
Annapolis, Maryland 21401

Head of School: Mr. Richard Bayhan

General Information Coeducational day college-preparatory, arts, religious studies, bilingual studies, and technology school, affiliated with Roman Catholic Church. Grades 9–12. Founded: 1946. Setting: small town. 5-acre campus. 3 buildings on campus. Approved or accredited by Southern Association of Independent Schools and Maryland Department of Education. Total enrollment: 500. Upper school average class size: 22. Upper school faculty-student ratio: 1:15. Upper School students typically attend 5 days per week. The average school day consists of 6 hours and 25 minutes.

Upper School Student Profile 80% of students are Roman Catholic.

Faculty School total: 32. In upper school: 17 men, 15 women.

Subjects Offered Accounting, algebra, American government, American literature, art, art history, art history-AP, biology, biology-AP, British literature, calculus-AP, Catholic belief and practice, chemistry, chemistry-AP, Christian scripture, Christianity, cinematography, computer applications, creative writing, current events, drama, economics, environmental science, European history-AP, fiction, forensics, French, geography, geometry, health, integrated mathematics, interdisciplinary studies, Irish literature, Latin, literature and composition-AP, math analysis, mathematics, mechanical drawing, microbiology, musical theater, peace and justice, physical education, physical science, physics, physics-AP, pre-calculus, psychology, public speaking, relationships, religion, religion and culture, senior project, Shakespeare, social justice, sociology, Spanish, sports conditioning, studio art, trigonometry, U.S. government and politics-AP, U.S. history, U.S. history-AP, weight training, world arts, world history, world literature, writing, zoology.

Graduation Requirements Arts and fine arts (art, music, dance, drama), computers, English, foreign language, mathematics, physical education (includes health), religion (includes Bible studies and theology), science, social studies (includes history).

Special Academic Programs Advanced Placement exam preparation; honors section; study at local college for college credit; study abroad; academic accommodation for the gifted.

College Admission Counseling 110 students graduated in 2013; all went to college.

Student Life Upper grades have uniform requirement, student council, honor system. Discipline rests primarily with faculty. Attendance at religious services is required.

Tuition and Aid Day student tuition: $13,660. Tuition installment plan (monthly payment plans). Merit scholarship grants, need-based scholarship grants available. In 2013–14, 25% of upper-school students received aid; total upper-school merit-scholarship money awarded: $30,000. Total amount of financial aid awarded in 2013–14: $250,000.

Admissions Traditional secondary-level entrance grade is 9. For fall 2013, 285 students applied for upper-level admission, 138 enrolled. High School Placement Test required. Deadline for receipt of application materials: January 6. Application fee required: $75.

Athletics Interscholastic: baseball (boys), basketball (b,g), cross-country running (b,g), dance team (g), field hockey (g), football (b), golf (b,g), lacrosse (b,g), soccer (b,g), swimming and diving (b,g), tennis (b,g), track and field (b,g), volleyball (g), wrestling (b); intramural: crew (g); coed interscholastic: weight training; coed intramural: dance team, fishing, Frisbee, sailing, yoga. 2 PE instructors, 56 coaches, 1 athletic trainer.

Computers Computers are regularly used in all classes. Computer network features include on-campus library services, online commercial services, Internet access, wireless campus network. Student e-mail accounts are available to students. Students grades are available online. The school has a published electronic and media policy.

Contact Mrs. Chrissie Chomo, Director of Admissions. 410-990-4236. Fax: 410-269-7843. E-mail: cchomo@stmarysannapolis.org. Website: www.stmarysannapolis.org

ST. MARY'S PREPARATORY SCHOOL

3535 Indian Trail
Orchard Lake, Michigan 48324

Head of School: James Glowacki

General Information Boys' boarding and day college-preparatory school, affiliated with Roman Catholic Church. Grades 9–12. Founded: 1885. Setting: suburban. Nearest major city is Detroit. Students are housed in single-sex dormitories. 80-acre campus. 12 buildings on campus. Approved or accredited by Michigan Association of Non-Public Schools and Michigan Department of Education. Total enrollment: 480. Upper school average class size: 18. Upper school faculty-student ratio: 1:10. There are 185 required school days per year for Upper School students. Upper School students typically attend 5 days per week. The average school day consists of 7 hours.

Upper School Student Profile Grade 9: 147 students (147 boys); Grade 10: 130 students (130 boys); Grade 11: 122 students (122 boys); Grade 12: 94 students (94 boys). 15% of students are boarding students. 80% are state residents. 5 states are represented in upper school student body. 15% are international students. International students from Brazil, China, Poland, Republic of Korea, Russian Federation, and Taiwan. 80% of students are Roman Catholic.

Faculty School total: 58. In upper school: 43 men, 15 women; 16 have advanced degrees; 6 reside on campus.

Subjects Offered Algebra, American history, American literature, art, band, Bible studies, biology, business, business skills, calculus, chemistry, Chinese, computer programming, computer science, creative writing, drafting, driver education, earth science, ecology, economics, English, English literature, expository writing, fine arts, French, geometry, government/civics, grammar, health, history, journalism, law, mathematics, music technology, mythology, physical education, physics, Polish, psychology, religion, robotics, science, social sciences, social studies, Spanish, speech, theology, trigonometry, world history, writing.

Graduation Requirements Arts and fine arts (art, music, dance, drama), business skills (includes word processing), computer science, English, foreign language, mathematics, physical education (includes health), religion (includes Bible studies and theology), science, social sciences, social studies (includes history).

Special Academic Programs Advanced Placement exam preparation; honors section; study at local college for college credit; academic accommodation for the musically talented and the artistically talented; programs in general development for dyslexic students; special instructional classes for students with learning disabilities, Attention Deficit Disorder, and dyslexia; ESL (60 students enrolled).

College Admission Counseling 125 students graduated in 2012; 119 went to college, including Michigan State University; Oakland University; University of Detroit Mercy; University of Michigan; Wayne State University; Western Michigan University. Other: 1 entered a postgraduate year, 5 had other specific plans. Median SAT critical reading: 503, median SAT math: 600, median SAT writing: 510, median combined SAT: 1613, median composite ACT: 25. 5% scored over 600 on SAT critical reading, 15% scored over 600 on SAT math, 40% scored over 26 on composite ACT.

Student Life Upper grades have specified standards of dress, student council, honor system. Discipline rests primarily with faculty. Attendance at religious services is required.

Tuition and Aid Day student tuition: $9800; 5-day tuition and room/board: $20,000; 7-day tuition and room/board: $22,000. Tuition installment plan (FACTS Tuition Payment Plan, individually arranged payment plans). Tuition reduction for siblings, merit scholarship grants, need-based scholarship grants available. In 2012–13, 80% of upper-school students received aid.

Admissions Traditional secondary-level entrance grade is 9. For fall 2012, 300 students applied for upper-level admission, 200 were accepted, 150 enrolled. STS and TOEFL required. Deadline for receipt of application materials: none. Application fee required: $35. Interview recommended.

Athletics Interscholastic: alpine skiing, baseball, basketball, crew, cross-country running, football, freestyle skiing, golf, hockey, ice hockey, indoor track, indoor track & field, jogging, lacrosse, rowing, skiing (downhill), soccer, track and field, wrestling; intramural: aerobics/Nautilus, aquatics, basketball, bicycling, billiards, bowling, broomball, fitness, Frisbee, golf, hockey, ice hockey, ice skating, indoor hockey, indoor soccer, indoor track, jogging, lacrosse, mountain biking, Nautilus, physical fitness, physical training, rowing, running, skeet shooting, skiing (downhill), snowboarding, soccer, strength & conditioning, swimming and diving, table tennis, tennis, weight lifting, weight training, whiffle ball. 2 PE instructors, 25 coaches, 3 athletic trainers.

Computers Computers are regularly used in desktop publishing, drafting, engineering, yearbook classes. Computer network features include on-campus library services, Internet access, Internet filtering or blocking technology. Campus intranet and student e-mail accounts are available to students. Students grades are available online.

Contact Candace Knight, Dean of Admissions. 248-683-0514. Fax: 248-683-1740. E-mail: cknight@stmarysprep.com. Website: www.stmarysprep.com/

SAINT MARY'S SCHOOL

900 Hillsborough Street
Raleigh, North Carolina 27603-1689

Head of School: Dr. Monica M. Gillespie

General Information Girls' boarding and day college-preparatory, arts, religious studies, bilingual studies, and technology school, affiliated with Episcopal Church. Grades 9–12. Founded: 1842. Setting: urban. Students are housed in single-sex dormitories. 23-acre campus. 26 buildings on campus. Approved or accredited by National Association of Episcopal Schools, North Carolina Association of Independent Schools, Southern Association of Colleges and Schools, Southern Association of Independent Schools, and The Association of Boarding Schools. Member of National Association of Independent Schools and Secondary School Admission Test Board. Total enrollment: 237. Upper school average class size: 12. Upper school faculty-student ratio: 1:8. Upper School students typically attend 5 days per week. The average school day consists of 7 hours.

Upper School Student Profile Grade 9: 49 students (49 girls); Grade 10: 67 students (67 girls); Grade 11: 63 students (63 girls); Grade 12: 58 students (58 girls). 48% of students are boarding students. 78% are state residents. 12 states are represented in upper school student body. 11% are international students. International students from China, Republic of Korea, Russian Federation, Spain, United Kingdom, and Viet Nam; 1 other country represented in student body. 20% of students are members of Episcopal Church.

Faculty School total: 40. In upper school: 10 men, 30 women; 30 have advanced degrees; 36 reside on campus.

Subjects Offered 3-dimensional art, acting, advanced chemistry, advanced math, Advanced Placement courses, algebra, American government, American history, American history-AP, American literature, anatomy, art, astronomy, athletics, ballet, biology, biology-AP, calculus, calculus-AP, ceramics, chemistry, chemistry-AP, choir, choral music, computer science, dance, drama, drama performance, drawing, drawing and design, earth science, ecology, English, English literature, English literature-AP, European history, French, French language-AP, geometry, government, government-AP, government/civics, honors English, honors geometry, honors U.S. history, honors world history, Latin, Latin-AP, mathematics, philosophy, physical education, physics, physics-AP, piano, psychology-AP, religion, senior project, Spanish, Spanish language-AP, speech, U.S. government and politics-AP, U.S. history, U.S. history-AP, Western civilization, world literature, yearbook, yoga.

Graduation Requirements Algebra, arts and fine arts (art, music, dance, drama), biology, electives, English, foreign language, geometry, government, physical education (includes health), physical science, religion (includes Bible studies and theology), social sciences, U.S. history, Western civilization.

Special Academic Programs Advanced Placement exam preparation; honors section; independent study; study at local college for college credit; study abroad; academic accommodation for the gifted, the musically talented, and the artistically talented.

College Admission Counseling 71 students graduated in 2012; all went to college, including Clemson University; Elon University; North Carolina State University; The University of North Carolina at Chapel Hill; University of Georgia; University of South Carolina.

Student Life Upper grades have specified standards of dress, student council, honor system. Discipline rests equally with students and faculty. Attendance at religious services is required.

Tuition and Aid Day student tuition: $19,100; 7-day tuition and room/board: $40,800. Tuition installment plan (FACTS Tuition Payment Plan, monthly payment plans). Merit scholarship grants, need-based scholarship grants available.

Admissions Traditional secondary-level entrance grade is 9. For fall 2012, 183 students applied for upper-level admission, 127 were accepted, 81 enrolled. SSAT and

TOEFL required. Deadline for receipt of application materials: none. Application fee required: $100. Interview required.

Athletics Interscholastic: basketball, cross-country running, field hockey, golf, lacrosse, soccer, softball, swimming and diving, tennis, track and field, volleyball; intramural: ballet, dance, dance team, modern dance. 2 PE instructors, 32 coaches, 1 athletic trainer.

Computers Computers are regularly used in dance, English, foreign language, history, introduction to technology, mathematics, newspaper, publications, science, senior seminar, writing, yearbook classes. Computer network features include on-campus library services, online commercial services, Internet access, wireless campus network, Internet filtering or blocking technology. Student e-mail accounts are available to students. Students grades are available online. The school has a published electronic and media policy.

Contact Mrs. Elizabeth Lynnes, Manager of Admission Systems and Data. 919-424-4003. Fax: 919-424-4122. E-mail: admission@sms.edu. Website: www.sms.edu

ST. MARY'S SCHOOL

816 Black Oak Drive
Medford, Oregon 97504-8504

Head of School: Mr. Frank Phillips

General Information Coeducational boarding and day college-preparatory, arts, religious studies, and ESL school, affiliated with Roman Catholic Church. Boarding grades 9–12, day grades 6–12. Founded: 1865. Setting: small town. Nearest major city is Eugene. Students are housed in single-sex dormitories. 23-acre campus. 9 buildings on campus. Approved or accredited by National Catholic Education Association, Northwest Association of Independent Schools, Northwest Association of Schools and Colleges, and Oregon Department of Education. Member of National Association of Independent Schools. Total enrollment: 461. Upper school average class size: 18. Upper school faculty-student ratio: 1:11. There are 180 required school days per year for Upper School students. Upper School students typically attend 5 days per week. The average school day consists of 7 hours and 15 minutes.

Upper School Student Profile Grade 9: 74 students (37 boys, 37 girls); Grade 10: 85 students (49 boys, 36 girls); Grade 11: 81 students (29 boys, 52 girls); Grade 12: 72 students (35 boys, 37 girls). 15% of students are boarding students. 85% are state residents. 2 states are represented in upper school student body. 15% are international students. International students from China, Republic of Korea, Rwanda, and Thailand; 4 other countries represented in student body. 35% of students are Roman Catholic.

Faculty School total: 48. In upper school: 22 men, 26 women; 21 have advanced degrees; 2 reside on campus.

Subjects Offered Advanced Placement courses, advanced TOEFL/grammar, algebra, American history, American history-AP, American literature, ancient history, art, art history-AP, biology, biology-AP, calculus-AP, chamber groups, chemistry, chemistry-AP, chorus, community service, computer programming-AP, computer science, creative writing, drama, earth science, economics-AP, English, English-AP, environmental science-AP, ESL, ethics, European history, European history-AP, expository writing, fine arts, general science, geometry, German, government/civics, government/civics-AP, grammar, health, history, human geography - AP, instrumental music, jazz band, Latin, Latin-AP, mathematics, music theory-AP, physical education, physics, physics-AP, religion, science, social sciences, social studies, Spanish, Spanish-AP, speech, studio art-AP, trigonometry, world history, world literature, writing.

Graduation Requirements Arts and fine arts (art, music, dance, drama), electives, English, foreign language, mathematics, physical education (includes health), religion (includes Bible studies and theology), science, social sciences, social studies (includes history), 28 credits required for graduation, 100 hours of community service (25 each year in Upper School).

Special Academic Programs 20 Advanced Placement exams for which test preparation is offered; independent study; study at local college for college credit; academic accommodation for the gifted, the musically talented, and the artistically talented; ESL (35 students enrolled).

College Admission Counseling 79 students graduated in 2013; 78 went to college, including Oregon State University; Portland State University; Santa Clara University; University of Oregon; University of Portland; University of San Diego. Other: 1 had other specific plans. Mean SAT critical reading: 568, mean SAT math: 568, mean SAT writing: 564, mean combined SAT: 1700, mean composite ACT: 25.

Student Life Upper grades have specified standards of dress, student council, honor system. Discipline rests equally with students and faculty. Attendance at religious services is required.

Summer Programs Enrichment, advancement, sports programs offered; session focuses on enrichment and SAT prep; held both on and off campus; held at Various Camp Locations; accepts boys and girls; open to students from other schools. 75 students usually enrolled. 2014 schedule: July 1 to August 27. Application deadline: none.

Tuition and Aid Day student tuition: $12,900. Tuition installment plan (monthly payment plans, annual payment plan). Need-based scholarship grants available. In 2013–14, 47% of upper-school students received aid. Total amount of financial aid awarded in 2013–14: $850,000.

Admissions Traditional secondary-level entrance grade is 9. Deadline for receipt of application materials: February 15. Application fee required: $50. Interview required.

Athletics Interscholastic: baseball (boys), basketball (b,g), combined training (b,g), cross-country running (b,g), football (b), golf (b,g), independent competitive sports (b,g), soccer (b,g), softball (g), tennis (b,g), track and field (b,g), volleyball (g); intramural: alpine skiing (b,g), canoeing/kayaking (b,g), equestrian sports (b,g), flag football (g), hiking/backpacking (b,g); coed interscholastic: martial arts; coed intramural: backpacking, bicycling, fencing, fitness, floor hockey, kayaking, outdoor activities, outdoor adventure, rafting, skiing (downhill), strength & conditioning, tennis, weight lifting. 2 PE instructors.

Computers Computers are regularly used in English, history, mathematics, science, speech classes. Computer network features include on-campus library services, online commercial services, Internet access, wireless campus network, Internet filtering or blocking technology, access to homework, daily bulletins, and teachers via email, Wifi. Campus intranet and computer access in designated common areas are available to students. Students grades are available online. The school has a published electronic and media policy.

Contact Ms. Rebecca Naumes, Director of Admissions. 541-773-7877. Fax: 541-772-8973. E-mail: admissions@smschool.us. Website: www.smschool.us

SAINT MAUR INTERNATIONAL SCHOOL

83 Yamate-cho, Naka-ku
Yokohama 231-8654, Japan

Head of School: Mrs. Catherine Osias Endo

General Information Coeducational day college-preparatory, general academic, arts, religious studies, technology, and science school, affiliated with Roman Catholic Church. Grades PK–12. Founded: 1872. Setting: urban. 1-hectare campus. 7 buildings on campus. Approved or accredited by Council of International Schools, East Asia Regional Council of Schools, International Baccalaureate Organization, Ministry of Education, Japan, and New England Association of Schools and Colleges. Language of instruction: English. Total enrollment: 436. Upper school average class size: 15. Upper school faculty-student ratio: 1:4. There are 175 required school days per year for Upper School students. Upper School students typically attend 5 days per week. The average school day consists of 5 hours and 30 minutes.

Upper School Student Profile Grade 9: 37 students (15 boys, 22 girls); Grade 10: 39 students (16 boys, 23 girls); Grade 11: 34 students (15 boys, 19 girls); Grade 12: 18 students (9 boys, 9 girls). 25% of students are Roman Catholic.

Faculty School total: 60. In upper school: 19 men, 15 women; 11 have advanced degrees.

Subjects Offered Art, biology, calculus-AP, chemistry, computer science, drama, drama performance, economics, economics-AP, English, fine arts, French, geography, information technology, Japanese, Japanese history, mathematics, music, music performance, physical education, physics, psychology, religious studies, robotics, science, social studies, Spanish, theory of knowledge, TOEFL preparation, visual arts, world history.

Graduation Requirements Arts and fine arts (art, music, dance, drama), English, foreign language, mathematics, physical education (includes health), religion (includes Bible studies and theology), science, social studies (includes history).

Special Academic Programs International Baccalaureate program; 10 Advanced Placement exams for which test preparation is offered; independent study; academic accommodation for the gifted, the musically talented, and the artistically talented; ESL.

College Admission Counseling 26 students graduated in 2013; 25 went to college, including McGill University; The University of British Columbia; University of California, Berkeley; University of Toronto. Other: 1 had other specific plans. Median combined SAT: 1860. Mean SAT critical reading: 538, mean SAT math: 663, mean SAT writing: 575. 43% scored over 600 on SAT critical reading, 70% scored over 600 on SAT math, 43% scored over 600 on SAT writing, 52% scored over 1800 on combined SAT.

Student Life Upper grades have uniform requirement, student council. Discipline rests primarily with faculty. Attendance at religious services is required.

Summer Programs Enrichment, advancement, ESL, sports, art/fine arts, computer instruction programs offered; session focuses on TOEFL and SAT preparation; held both on and off campus; held at various off-campus locations; accepts boys and girls; open to students from other schools. 130 students usually enrolled. 2014 schedule: June 16 to July 11. Application deadline: May 15.

Tuition and Aid Day student tuition: ¥2,145,000.

Admissions For fall 2013, 98 students applied for upper-level admission, 95 were accepted, 90 enrolled. School's own test required. Deadline for receipt of application materials: none. Application fee required: ¥20,000. On-campus interview required.

Athletics Interscholastic: baseball (boys), basketball (b,g), cross-country running (b,g), soccer (b,g), volleyball (g); intramural: soccer (b); coed interscholastic: table tennis. 2 PE instructors.

Computers Computers are regularly used in art, computer applications, economics, English, foreign language, French, geography, independent study, information technology, mathematics, media, music, psychology, SAT preparation, science, social studies, Spanish, technology classes. Computer network features include on-campus library services, Internet access, wireless campus network, Internet filtering or blocking technology. Campus intranet, student e-mail accounts, and computer access in designated common areas are available to students. Students grades are available online. The school has a published electronic and media policy.

Contact Mr. Richard B. Rucci, Director of Admissions. 81-(0) 45-641-5751. Fax: 81-(0) 45-641-6688. E-mail: rrucci@stmaur.ac.jp. Website: www.stmaur.ac.jp

ST. MICHAEL'S COLLEGE SCHOOL

1515 Bathurst Street
Toronto, Ontario M5P 3H4, Canada

Head of School: Mr. Terrance Sheridan

General Information Boys' day college-preparatory and religious studies school, affiliated with Roman Catholic Church. Grades 7–12. Founded: 1852. Setting: urban. 10-acre campus. 2 buildings on campus. Approved or accredited by Ontario Ministry of Education and Ontario Department of Education. Member of Secondary School Admission Test Board. Language of instruction: English. Total enrollment: 1,067. Upper school average class size: 24. Upper school faculty-student ratio: 1:16. There are 184 required school days per year for Upper School students. Upper School students typically attend 5 days per week. The average school day consists of 6 hours and 19 minutes.

Upper School Student Profile Grade 9: 221 students (221 boys); Grade 10: 220 students (220 boys); Grade 11: 214 students (214 boys); Grade 12: 215 students (215 boys). 90% of students are Roman Catholic.

Faculty School total: 74. In upper school: 64 men, 10 women; 20 have advanced degrees.

Subjects Offered Advanced Placement courses, all academic, American history, anatomy and physiology, ancient history, art, biology, calculus, calculus-AP, Canadian geography, Canadian history, Canadian law, Canadian literature, career and personal planning, career education, chemistry, civics, computer multimedia, economics, English, English composition, English literature, finite math, French, functions, geography, history, history-AP, Italian, Latin, leadership, mathematics, media arts, modern Western civilization, outdoor education, physical education, religion, science, Spanish, theology, world religions.

Graduation Requirements 20 hours of community service, 20 hours of Christian service must be completed over the 4 years of high school.

Special Academic Programs Advanced Placement exam preparation.

College Admission Counseling 217 students graduated in 2013; all went to college, including Queen's University at Kingston; Ryerson University; The University of Western Ontario; University of Guelph; University of Toronto; York University.

Student Life Upper grades have uniform requirement, student council, honor system. Discipline rests primarily with faculty. Attendance at religious services is required.

Tuition and Aid Day student tuition: CAN$17,000. Tuition installment plan (monthly payment plans, individually arranged payment plans, all up front-$300 discount, three monthly installments (March, June, August)-$100 discount). Bursaries, merit scholarship grants, need-based scholarship grants available. In 2013–14, 15% of upper-school students received aid; total upper-school merit-scholarship money awarded: CAN$105,000. Total amount of financial aid awarded in 2013–14: CAN$1,800,000.

Admissions Traditional secondary-level entrance grade is 9. For fall 2013, 296 students applied for upper-level admission, 199 were accepted, 144 enrolled. SSAT required. Deadline for receipt of application materials: none. Application fee required: CAN$125.

Athletics Interscholastic: alpine skiing, aquatics, archery, badminton, baseball, basketball, cross-country running, football, golf, ice hockey, indoor track & field, lacrosse, mountain biking, nordic skiing, rugby, skiing (cross-country), skiing (downhill), snowboarding, soccer, softball, swimming and diving, tennis, track and field, volleyball; intramural: archery, badminton, ball hockey, basketball, fishing, fitness, flag football, ice hockey, indoor soccer, outdoor education, power lifting, soccer, tennis, touch football.

Computers Computers are regularly used in all academic, media arts classes. Computer network features include on-campus library services, Internet access, wireless campus network, Internet filtering or blocking technology. Student e-mail accounts and computer access in designated common areas are available to students. The school has a published electronic and media policy.

Contact Ms. Marilyn Furgiuele, Admissions Assistant. 416-653-3180 Ext. 438. Fax: 416-653-7704. E-mail: furgiuele@smcsmail.com. Website: www.stmichaelscollegeschool.com

ST. MICHAEL'S PREPARATORY SCHOOL OF THE NORBERTINE FATHERS

19292 El Toro Road
Silverado, California 92676-9710

Head of School: Rev. Victor J. Szczurek, OPRAEM

General Information Boys' boarding college-preparatory and religious studies school, affiliated with Roman Catholic Church. Grades 9–12. Founded: 1961. Setting: suburban. Nearest major city is Los Angeles. Students are housed in single-sex dormitories. 35-acre campus. 4 buildings on campus. Approved or accredited by

National Catholic Education Association, Western Association of Schools and Colleges, and California Department of Education. Total enrollment: 67. Upper school average class size: 12. Upper school faculty-student ratio: 1:3. There are 180 required school days per year for Upper School students. Upper School students typically attend 5 days per week. The average school day consists of 7 hours.

Upper School Student Profile 100% of students are boarding students. 90% are state residents. 4% are international students. International students from China, Hong Kong, Spain, and Viet Nam; 1 other country represented in student body. 95% of students are Roman Catholic.

Faculty School total: 20. In upper school: 18 men, 2 women; 18 have advanced degrees; 13 reside on campus.

Subjects Offered Algebra, American history, American history-AP, American literature, ancient history, art history, Bible studies, biology, calculus-AP, chemistry, chorus, economics, economics-AP, English, English literature, ethics, fine arts, geography, geometry, government-AP, government/civics, Greek, health, history, Latin, Latin-AP, mathematics, philosophy, physical education, physical science, physics, pre-calculus, religion, science, social studies, Spanish, Spanish-AP, theology, trigonometry, world literature.

Graduation Requirements Arts and fine arts (art, music, dance, drama), English, foreign language, mathematics, physical education (includes health), religion (includes Bible studies and theology), science, social studies (includes history), Senior Matura.

Special Academic Programs Advanced Placement exam preparation; honors section; independent study; ESL (1 student enrolled).

College Admission Counseling 11 students graduated in 2013; all went to college, including California State Polytechnic University, Pomona; California State University, Fullerton; California State University, Long Beach; Thomas Aquinas College; University of California, Davis; University of Notre Dame. Mean SAT critical reading: 514, mean SAT math: 530.

Student Life Upper grades have uniform requirement, student council, honor system. Discipline rests equally with students and faculty. Attendance at religious services is required.

Tuition and Aid 5-day tuition and room/board: $21,700. Tuition installment plan (FACTS Tuition Payment Plan, monthly payment plans, individually arranged payment plans). Need-based scholarship grants available. Total amount of financial aid awarded in 2013–14: $500,000.

Admissions High School Placement Test required. Deadline for receipt of application materials: none. Application fee required: $100. Interview required.

Athletics Interscholastic: baseball, basketball, cross-country running, football, soccer; intramural: field hockey, outdoor activities, swimming and diving, table tennis, volleyball, weight lifting. 1 PE instructor, 2 coaches.

Computers Computers are regularly used in English, mathematics, science classes. Computer resources include on-campus library services, Internet access, Internet filtering or blocking technology. Computer access in designated common areas is available to students. Students grades are available online.

Contact Mrs. Pamela M. Christian, School Secretary. 949-858-0222 Ext. 237. Fax: 949-858-7365. E-mail: admissions@stmichaelsprep.org. Website: www.stmichaelsprep.org

SAINT PATRICK HIGH SCHOOL

5900 West Belmont Avenue
Chicago, Illinois 60634

Head of School: Br. Konrad Diebold

General Information Boys' day college-preparatory, arts, and religious studies school, affiliated with Roman Catholic Church. Grades 9–12. Founded: 1861. Setting: urban. 1 building on campus. Approved or accredited by Christian Brothers Association, National Catholic Education Association, North Central Association of Colleges and Schools, and Illinois Department of Education. Endowment: $6.8 million. Total enrollment: 710. Upper school average class size: 22. Upper school faculty-student ratio: 1:17. There are 178 required school days per year for Upper School students. Upper School students typically attend 5 days per week. The average school day consists of 6 hours and 40 minutes.

Upper School Student Profile Grade 9: 154 students (154 boys); Grade 10: 204 students (204 boys); Grade 11: 183 students (183 boys); Grade 12: 169 students (169 boys). 75% of students are Roman Catholic.

Faculty School total: 59. In upper school: 43 men, 16 women; 39 have advanced degrees.

Subjects Offered Accounting, algebra, American history, American literature, anatomy, art, art history, biology, broadcasting, business, business skills, calculus, chemistry, Chinese, chorus, computer graphics, computer science, creative writing, drama, driver education, ecology, economics, English, English literature, ESL, ethics, European history, fine arts, French, geography, geometry, government/civics, grammar, health, history, journalism, keyboarding, mathematics, music, physical education, physics, psychology, religion, science, social sciences, social studies, sociology, Spanish, speech, theater, trigonometry, word processing, world history, writing.

Graduation Requirements Arts and fine arts (art, music, dance, drama), business skills (includes word processing), computer science, English, mathematics, physical education (includes health), religion (includes Bible studies and theology),

science, service learning/internship, social sciences, social studies (includes history), participation in a retreat program. Community service is required.

Special Academic Programs Advanced Placement exam preparation; honors section; study at local college for college credit; remedial reading and/or remedial writing; remedial math.

College Admission Counseling 195 students graduated in 2012; 183 went to college, including DePaul University; Lewis University; Northeastern Illinois University; Northern Illinois University; University of Illinois at Chicago; University of Illinois at Urbana–Champaign. Other: 2 went to work, 3 entered military service, 7 had other specific plans. Mean composite ACT: 21. 28% scored over 26 on composite ACT.

Student Life Upper grades have specified standards of dress, student council, honor system. Discipline rests primarily with faculty. Attendance at religious services is required.

Tuition and Aid Day student tuition: $9400. Tuition installment plan (monthly payment plans, quarterly payment plan). Merit scholarship grants, need-based scholarship grants, legacy (sons and grandsons of alumni) available. In 2012–13, 50% of upper-school students received aid. Total amount of financial aid awarded in 2012–13: $1,025,000.

Admissions Traditional secondary-level entrance grade is 9. For fall 2012, 212 students applied for upper-level admission, 210 were accepted, 154 enrolled. ACT-Explore or any standardized test required. Deadline for receipt of application materials: none. No application fee required. On-campus interview required.

Athletics Interscholastic: baseball, basketball, bowling, cross-country running, diving, fishing, football, golf, hockey, soccer, swimming and diving, tennis, track and field, volleyball, water polo, wrestling; intramural: basketball, football, volleyball. 4 PE instructors, 19 coaches, 1 athletic trainer.

Computers Computers are regularly used in business, English, foreign language, geography, graphic arts, graphic design, graphics, history, information technology, introduction to technology, library skills, mathematics, media arts, media production, media services, newspaper, photojournalism, religion, remedial study skills, research skills, science, typing, word processing, yearbook classes. Computer network features include on-campus library services, online commercial services, Internet access, wireless campus network, Internet filtering or blocking technology. Student e-mail accounts are available to students. Students grades are available online. The school has a published electronic and media policy.

Contact Christopher Perez, Director of Curriculum. 773-282-8844 Ext. 228. Fax: 773-282-2361. E-mail: cperez@stpatrick.org. Website: www.stpatrick.org

SAINT PATRICK - SAINT VINCENT HIGH SCHOOL

1500 Benicia Road
Vallejo, California 94591

Head of School: Ms. Mary Ellen Ryan

General Information Coeducational day college-preparatory, arts, business, religious studies, and technology school, affiliated with Roman Catholic Church. Grades 9–12. Founded: 1870. Setting: suburban. 31-acre campus. 8 buildings on campus. Approved or accredited by Western Association of Schools and Colleges, Western Catholic Education Association, and California Department of Education. Total enrollment: 502. Upper school average class size: 30. Upper school faculty-student ratio: 1:30. There are 180 required school days per year for Upper School students. Upper School students typically attend 5 days per week. The average school day consists of 6 hours and 15 minutes.

Upper School Student Profile Grade 9: 117 students (46 boys, 71 girls); Grade 10: 129 students (63 boys, 66 girls); Grade 11: 119 students (72 boys, 47 girls); Grade 12: 137 students (64 boys, 73 girls). 80% of students are Roman Catholic.

Faculty School total: 43. In upper school: 19 men, 21 women; 24 have advanced degrees.

Subjects Offered Algebra, art, biology, calculus-AP, campus ministry, Catholic belief and practice, chemistry, chemistry-AP, choir, civics, college counseling, college planning, computer multimedia, computer science-AP, concert bell choir, concert choir, economics, English, English-AP, environmental science, environmental studies, ethnic studies, film appreciation, French, French language-AP, geometry, health, history-AP, honors English, human biology, keyboarding, leadership, organic chemistry, physical education, physics, psychology, religion, science, Spanish, Spanish language-AP, statistics, statistics-AP, studio art-AP, theater arts, U.S. history, vocal jazz, world history, world history-AP.

Graduation Requirements English, foreign language, mathematics, physical education (includes health), religion (includes Bible studies and theology), science, social studies (includes history), Christian service.

Special Academic Programs 8 Advanced Placement exams for which test preparation is offered; honors section; academic accommodation for the gifted; remedial math.

College Admission Counseling 140 students graduated in 2012; 137 went to college, including California State University, Sacramento; San Jose State University; Sonoma State University; University of California, Davis; University of California, Los Angeles; University of California, San Diego. Other: 3 entered military service.

Student Life Upper grades have specified standards of dress, student council, honor system. Discipline rests primarily with faculty. Attendance at religious services is required.

Tuition and Aid Day student tuition: $11,650. Tuition installment plan (FACTS Tuition Payment Plan). Tuition reduction for siblings, need-based scholarship grants available. In 2012–13, 30% of upper-school students received aid. Total amount of financial aid awarded in 2012–13: $680,000.

Admissions Traditional secondary-level entrance grade is 9. For fall 2012, 179 students applied for upper-level admission, 165 were accepted, 131 enrolled. High School Placement Test required. Deadline for receipt of application materials: none. Application fee required: $50. Interview required.

Athletics Interscholastic: baseball (boys), basketball (b,g), cross-country running (b,g), golf (b,g), soccer (b,g), softball (g), swimming and diving (b,g), tennis (b,g), track and field (b,g), volleyball (b,g), water polo (b,g), wrestling (b,g); coed interscholastic: cheering, football, yoga. 3 PE instructors, 67 coaches, 1 athletic trainer.

Computers Computers are regularly used in business applications, business education, business studies, career education, career exploration, college planning, computer applications, desktop publishing, drawing and design, economics, English, foreign language, graphic arts, graphic design, history, library, library skills, mathematics, psychology, religious studies, science, social studies, Spanish, theater arts, theology, Web site design, word processing, yearbook classes. Computer network features include on-campus library services, Internet access, wireless campus network, Internet filtering or blocking technology. Student e-mail accounts are available to students. Students grades are available online. The school has a published electronic and media policy.

Contact Mrs. Sheila Williams, Director of Admissions. 707-644-4425 Ext. 448. Fax: 707-644-4770. E-mail: s.williams@spsv.org. Website: spsv.org

ST. PATRICK'S REGIONAL SECONDARY

115 East 11th Avenue
Vancouver, British Columbia V5T 2C1, Canada

Head of School: Mr. Ralph J Gabriele

General Information Coeducational day college-preparatory, general academic, arts, business, religious studies, and technology school, affiliated with Roman Catholic Church. Grades 8–12. Founded: 1923. Setting: urban. 2 buildings on campus. Approved or accredited by British Columbia Department of Education. Language of instruction: English. Total enrollment: 500. Upper school average class size: 25. The average school day consists of 6 hours.

Upper School Student Profile Grade 8: 99 students (38 boys, 61 girls); Grade 9: 101 students (35 boys, 66 girls); Grade 10: 104 students (33 boys, 71 girls); Grade 11: 101 students (36 boys, 65 girls); Grade 12: 101 students (38 boys, 63 girls). 97% of students are Roman Catholic.

Faculty School total: 35. In upper school: 15 men, 15 women; 8 have advanced degrees.

Special Academic Programs Advanced Placement exam preparation; ESL (15 students enrolled).

College Admission Counseling 100 students graduated in 2013; all went to college, including University of Alaska Fairbanks.

Student Life Upper grades have uniform requirement. Attendance at religious services is required.

Tuition and Aid Tuition installment plan (monthly payment plans).

Admissions Application fee required: CAN$100. Interview required.

Athletics Interscholastic: basketball (boys, girls), soccer (b,g), track and field (b,g), volleyball (g), wrestling (b,g); coed intramural: badminton. 5 PE instructors, 5 coaches.

Contact Mr. Ralph J Gabriele, Principal. 604-874-6422. Fax: 604-874-5176. E-mail: administration@stpats.bc.ca. Website: www.stpats.bc.ca

ST. PAUL ACADEMY AND SUMMIT SCHOOL

1712 Randolph Avenue
St. Paul, Minnesota 55105

Head of School: Bryn S. Roberts

General Information Coeducational day college-preparatory school. Grades K–12. Founded: 1900. Setting: urban. 32-acre campus. 4 buildings on campus. Approved or accredited by Independent Schools Association of the Central States and Minnesota Department of Education. Member of National Association of Independent Schools. Endowment: $31 million. Total enrollment: 901. Upper school average class size: 14. Upper school faculty-student ratio: 1:7. Upper School students typically attend 5 days per week.

Upper School Student Profile Grade 9: 113 students (60 boys, 53 girls); Grade 10: 96 students (41 boys, 55 girls); Grade 11: 89 students (41 boys, 48 girls); Grade 12: 92 students (45 boys, 47 girls).

Faculty School total: 101. In upper school: 15 men, 25 women; 32 have advanced degrees.

Subjects Offered Algebra, American literature, art, biology, calculus, ceramics, chemistry, Chinese, creative writing, current events, debate, drama, earth science, economics, English, English literature, European history, expository writing, fine arts, French, geometry, German, journalism, law and the legal system, marine biology, mathematics, multicultural studies, music, music theory, newspaper, photography, physical education, physics, psychology, science, senior project, Shakespeare, social psychology, social studies, sociology, space and physical sciences, Spanish, trigonometry, world history, world literature, world religions, yearbook.

Graduation Requirements Arts and fine arts (art, music, dance, drama), English, foreign language, mathematics, physical education (includes health), science, social studies (includes history), month-long senior project, senior speech.

Special Academic Programs Honors section; independent study; term-away projects; study abroad.

College Admission Counseling 88 students graduated in 2013; 84 went to college, including Brown University; Princeton University; St. Olaf College; University of Minnesota, Twin Cities Campus; University of St. Thomas; University of Wisconsin–Madison. Other: 1 entered military service, 3 had other specific plans. Mean SAT critical reading: 638, mean SAT math: 638, mean SAT writing: 634, mean combined SAT: 1911, mean composite ACT: 30. 70% scored over 600 on SAT critical reading, 67% scored over 600 on SAT math, 60% scored over 600 on SAT writing, 63% scored over 1800 on combined SAT, 82% scored over 26 on composite ACT.

Student Life Upper grades have specified standards of dress, student council. Discipline rests equally with students and faculty.

Summer Programs Enrichment programs offered; held on campus; accepts boys and girls; open to students from other schools.

Tuition and Aid Day student tuition: $25,560. Tuition installment plan (Insured Tuition Payment Plan, monthly payment plans). Need-based scholarship grants available. In 2013–14, 29% of upper-school students received aid. Total amount of financial aid awarded in 2013–14: $1,810,480.

Admissions Traditional secondary-level entrance grade is 9. For fall 2013, 75 students applied for upper-level admission, 49 were accepted, 37 enrolled. SSAT, ERB, PSAT, SAT, PLAN or ACT or writing sample required. Deadline for receipt of application materials: February 1. Application fee required: $75. Interview required.

Athletics Interscholastic: alpine skiing (boys, girls), baseball (b), basketball (b,g), cross-country running (b,g), dance (g), dance team (g), diving (b,g), fencing (b,g), football (b), golf (b,g), ice hockey (b,g), skiing (cross-country) (b,g), skiing (downhill) (b,g), soccer (b,g), softball (g), swimming and diving (b,g), tennis (b,g); intramural: outdoor adventure (b,g); coed interscholastic: lacrosse, strength & conditioning, track and field; coed intramural: hiking/backpacking, physical fitness, snowboarding, table tennis. 1 PE instructor, 85 coaches, 1 athletic trainer.

Computers Computers are regularly used in all academic classes. Computer network features include on-campus library services, online commercial services, Internet access, wireless campus network, Internet filtering or blocking technology, laptop program (beginning in grade 7). Student e-mail accounts and computer access in designated common areas are available to students. The school has a published electronic and media policy.

Contact Mrs. Heather Cameron Ploen, Director of Admission and Financial Aid. 651-698-2451. Fax: 651-698-6787. E-mail: hploen@spa.edu. Website: www.spa.edu

ST. PAUL PREPARATORY SCHOOL

380 Jackson Street
Suite 100
Saint Paul, Minnesota 55101

Head of School: Dr. Charles Briscoe

General Information Coeducational day college-preparatory, general academic, arts, business, bilingual studies, technology, and Liberal arts school. Grades 9–12. Founded: 2003. Setting: urban. Nearest major city is St. Paul. 2-acre campus. 2 buildings on campus. Approved or accredited by National Association of Episcopal Schools, North Central Association of Colleges and Schools, and Minnesota Department of Education. Total enrollment: 203. Upper school average class size: 11. Upper school faculty-student ratio: 1:12. There are 160 required school days per year for Upper School students. Upper School students typically attend 5 days per week. The average school day consists of 5 hours and 45 minutes.

Upper School Student Profile Grade 9: 8 students (4 boys, 4 girls); Grade 10: 24 students (13 boys, 11 girls); Grade 11: 57 students (31 boys, 26 girls); Grade 12: 115 students (66 boys, 49 girls).

Faculty School total: 21. In upper school: 4 men, 16 women; 10 have advanced degrees.

Subjects Offered Advanced Placement courses, algebra, American government, American history, American literature, Arabic, art, art history, aviation, biology, British literature, calculus, chemistry, chemistry-AP, Chinese, Chinese studies, choir, college admission preparation, composition, computer science, computer science-AP, creative writing, drama, drawing, earth science, economics, English as a foreign language, English composition, English literature and composition-AP, ESL, European history-AP, fitness, French, geography, geometry, German, German literature, guitar, health, internship, intro to computers, introduction to literature, literature, modern European history, music, music theory-AP, musical theater, painting, physical education, physical fitness, physical science, physics, pre-calculus, psychology, robotics, SAT preparation, sociology, Spanish, Spanish literature, speech, statistics-AP, theater, trigonometry, U.S. history, U.S. history-AP, United States government-AP, Web authoring, world civilizations, world cultures, world history, world history-AP, world literature, writing, writing, writing, writing workshop, yearbook.

Special Academic Programs 11 Advanced Placement exams for which test preparation is offered; honors section; accelerated programs; independent study; study at local college for college credit; study abroad; academic accommodation for the gifted, the musically talented, and the artistically talented; remedial reading and/or remedial writing; remedial math; ESL (122 students enrolled).

College Admission Counseling 80 students graduated in 2013; 72 went to college, including Gustavus Adolphus College; Hamline University; University of St. Thomas. Mean composite ACT: 21.

Student Life Upper grades have specified standards of dress, student council, honor system. Discipline rests equally with students and faculty.

Summer Programs Enrichment, advancement, ESL programs offered; session focuses on language and culture; held both on and off campus; held at Various international countries; accepts boys and girls; open to students from other schools. 30 students usually enrolled. 2014 schedule: July 8 to August 3. Application deadline: May.

Tuition and Aid Day student tuition: $9000. Tuition installment plan (monthly payment plans). Tuition reduction for siblings, merit scholarship grants, need-based scholarship grants, paying campus jobs available. In 2013–14, 50% of upper-school students received aid; total upper-school merit-scholarship money awarded: $476,250. Total amount of financial aid awarded in 2013–14: $764,650.

Admissions Traditional secondary-level entrance grade is 11. For fall 2013, 203 students applied for upper-level admission, 203 were accepted, 203 enrolled. Iowa Tests of Basic Skills, Stanford Achievement Test or TOEFL or SLEP required. Deadline for receipt of application materials: none. No application fee required. Interview required.

Athletics Interscholastic: basketball (boys, girls), soccer (b,g). 1 PE instructor, 2 coaches.

Computers Computers are regularly used in aviation, college planning, computer applications, creative writing, English, ESL, foreign language, information technology, mathematics, SAT preparation, science, social sciences, Web site design, writing, yearbook classes. Computer network features include Internet access, wireless campus network, Internet filtering or blocking technology, PowerSchool Database Host. Campus intranet and computer access in designated common areas are available to students. Students grades are available online. The school has a published electronic and media policy.

Contact Jennifer Bratulich, Director of Admissions. 651-288-4610. Fax: 651-288-4616. E-mail: jbratulich@stpaulprep.org. Website: www.stpaulprep.org

ST. PAUL'S EPISCOPAL SCHOOL

161 Dogwood Lane
Mobile, Alabama 36608

Head of School: Mr. F. Martin Lester Jr.

General Information Coeducational day college-preparatory, arts, technology, and honors, Advanced Placement school, affiliated with Episcopal Church. Grades PK–12. Founded: 1947. Setting: suburban. 32-acre campus. 10 buildings on campus. Approved or accredited by National Association of Episcopal Schools, Southern Association of Colleges and Schools, Southern Association of Independent Schools, and Alabama Department of Education. Member of National Association of Independent Schools and Secondary School Admission Test Board. Endowment: $1.6 million. Total enrollment: 1,222. Upper school average class size: 20. Upper school faculty-student ratio: 1:12. There are 177 required school days per year for Upper School students. Upper School students typically attend 5 days per week. The average school day consists of 6 hours and 10 minutes.

Upper School Student Profile Grade 9: 102 students (56 boys, 46 girls); Grade 10: 98 students (52 boys, 46 girls); Grade 11: 89 students (40 boys, 49 girls); Grade 12: 92 students (48 boys, 44 girls).

Faculty School total: 143. In upper school: 21 men, 35 women; 48 have advanced degrees.

Subjects Offered Advanced biology, advanced chemistry, advanced math, Advanced Placement courses, advanced studio art-AP, algebra, American history, American literature, anatomy and physiology, art, arts, band, biology, biology-AP, calculus, calculus-AP, chemistry, chemistry-AP, choir, choral music, civics, composition, computer science, concert choir, digital photography, drama, driver education, economics, economics-AP, English, English literature, English-AP, environmental science, environmental science-AP, European history, European history-AP, fine arts, foreign language, French, French-AP, geometry, government-AP, government/civics, grammar, history, history-AP, honors algebra, honors English, honors geometry, human anatomy, instrumental music, journalism, Latin, marching band, marine biology, mathematics, music, oil painting, painting, photography, physical education, physics, physics-AP, pre-algebra, pre-calculus, public service, Spanish, speech, theater, theater arts, trigonometry, U.S. history-AP, weight training, world history, yearbook.

Graduation Requirements Arts and fine arts (art, music, dance, drama), electives, English, foreign language, history, mathematics, science, 4 years of English, mathematics, social studies, and science, 2 year minimum foreign language, 60 hours of community service. Community service is required.

Special Academic Programs Advanced Placement exam preparation; honors section; study at local college for college credit; remedial reading and/or remedial

writing; remedial math; special instructional classes for students with diagnosed learning disabilities.

College Admission Counseling 130 students graduated in 2012; all went to college, including Auburn University; Birmingham-Southern College; The University of Alabama; University of Mississippi; University of South Alabama; Vanderbilt University.

Student Life Upper grades have uniform requirement, student council, honor system. Discipline rests primarily with faculty. Attendance at religious services is required.

Tuition and Aid Tuition installment plan (Insured Tuition Payment Plan, monthly payment plans, individually arranged payment plans, semiannual payment plan). Need-based scholarship grants available.

Admissions Traditional secondary-level entrance grade is 9. ERB CTP IV or Otis-Lennon and 2 sections of ERB required. Deadline for receipt of application materials: none. Application fee required. Interview required.

Athletics Interscholastic: baseball (boys), basketball (b,g), cheering (g), cross-country running (b,g), diving (b,g), football (b), golf (b,g), indoor track & field (b,g), soccer (b,g), softball (g), strength & conditioning (b,g), swimming and diving (b,g), tennis (b,g), track and field (b,g), volleyball (g), weight training (b), winter (indoor) track (b,g); intramural: basketball (b,g), soccer (b,g), volleyball (g), weight training (b); coed interscholastic: fencing. 6 PE instructors, 13 coaches, 4 athletic trainers.

Computers Computers are regularly used in economics, English, foreign language, history, independent study, journalism, keyboarding, mathematics, newspaper, publications, science, Spanish, writing, yearbook classes. Computer network features include on-campus library services, online commercial services, Internet access, wireless campus network, Internet filtering or blocking technology. Campus intranet, student e-mail accounts, and computer access in designated common areas are available to students. Students grades are available online. The school has a published electronic and media policy.

Contact Ms. Julie L. Taylor, Admissions Director. 251-461-2129. Fax: 251-342-1844. E-mail: jtaylor@stpaulsmobile.net. Website: www.stpaulsmobile.net

ST. PAUL'S HIGH SCHOOL

2200 Grant Avenue
Winnipeg, Manitoba R3P 0P8, Canada

Head of School: Fr. Len Altilia, SJ

General Information Boys' day college-preparatory, arts, religious studies, and technology school, affiliated with Roman Catholic Church. Grades 9–12. Founded: 1926. Setting: suburban. 18-acre campus. 6 buildings on campus. Approved or accredited by Jesuit Secondary Education Association and Manitoba Department of Education. Language of instruction: English. Endowment: CAN$7.5 million. Total enrollment: 596. Upper school average class size: 26. Upper school faculty-student ratio: 1:14. There are 196 required school days per year for Upper School students. Upper School students typically attend 5 days per week. The average school day consists of 5 hours and 50 minutes.

Upper School Student Profile Grade 9: 149 students (149 boys); Grade 10: 153 students (153 boys); Grade 11: 150 students (150 boys); Grade 12: 144 students (144 boys). 68% of students are Roman Catholic.

Faculty School total: 43. In upper school: 33 men, 10 women; 16 have advanced degrees.

Subjects Offered Algebra, American history, art, biology, calculus, chemistry, classics, computer science, current events, economics, English, ethics, French, geography, geometry, history, law, mathematics, media, multimedia, multimedia design, music, Native American studies, physical education, physics, political science, psychology, religion, science, social studies, speech, theology, world wide web design.

Graduation Requirements English, mathematics, physical education (includes health), religion (includes Bible studies and theology), science, social studies (includes history), completion of Christian service program.

Special Academic Programs Advanced Placement exam preparation; honors section; remedial math.

College Admission Counseling 138 students graduated in 2013; 131 went to college, including McGill University; Queen's University at Kingston; The University of British Columbia; The University of Winnipeg; University of Manitoba; University of Toronto. Other: 2 went to work, 5 had other specific plans.

Student Life Upper grades have specified standards of dress, student council, honor system. Discipline rests primarily with faculty. Attendance at religious services is required.

Summer Programs Sports programs offered; session focuses on sport skills and relationship building; held on campus; accepts boys; open to students from other schools. 80 students usually enrolled. 2014 schedule: August 20 to September 2.

Tuition and Aid Day student tuition: CAN$8050. Tuition installment plan (Insured Tuition Payment Plan, monthly payment plans, individually arranged payment plans). Bursaries, need-based loans available. In 2013–14, 14% of upper-school students received aid. Total amount of financial aid awarded in 2013–14: CAN$340,000.

Admissions Traditional secondary-level entrance grade is 9. For fall 2013, 295 students applied for upper-level admission, 168 were accepted, 157 enrolled. Achievement tests and STS required. Deadline for receipt of application materials: February 1. Application fee required: CAN$100. On-campus interview required.

Athletics Interscholastic: badminton, basketball, cross-country running, curling, football, golf, ice hockey, indoor track, indoor track & field, rugby, soccer, track and field, volleyball, wrestling; intramural: badminton, basketball, curling, fitness, flag football, golf, physical fitness, physical training, skiing (downhill), strength & conditioning, table tennis, volleyball, weight training. 4 PE instructors, 1 athletic trainer.

Computers Computers are regularly used in French, French as a second language, geography, mathematics, multimedia, religious studies, science, Web site design classes. Computer network features include on-campus library services, online commercial services, Internet access, wireless campus network, Internet filtering or blocking technology. Campus intranet, student e-mail accounts, and computer access in designated common areas are available to students. Students grades are available online. The school has a published electronic and media policy.

Contact Mr. Tom Lussier, Principal. 204-831-2300. Fax: 204-831-2340. E-mail: tlussier@stpauls.mb.ca. Website: www.stpauls.mb.ca

ST. PIUS X CATHOLIC HIGH SCHOOL

2674 Johnson Road NE
Atlanta, Georgia 30345

Head of School: Mr. Steve Spellman

General Information Coeducational day college-preparatory school, affiliated with Roman Catholic Church. Grades 9–12. Founded: 1958. Setting: suburban. 33-acre campus. 8 buildings on campus. Approved or accredited by National Catholic Education Association, Southern Association of Colleges and Schools, The College Board, and Georgia Department of Education. Member of Secondary School Admission Test Board. Total enrollment: 1,100. Upper school average class size: 21. Upper school faculty-student ratio: 1:12. There are 180 required school days per year for Upper School students. The average school day consists of 7 hours.

Upper School Student Profile Grade 9: 275 students (140 boys, 135 girls); Grade 10: 285 students (140 boys, 145 girls); Grade 11: 260 students (130 boys, 130 girls); Grade 12: 260 students (130 boys, 130 girls). 84% of students are Roman Catholic.

Faculty School total: 97. In upper school: 49 men, 45 women; 67 have advanced degrees.

Subjects Offered Accounting, algebra, American history, American literature, anatomy, art, band, biology, business, business law, calculus, ceramics, chemistry, chorus, computer programming, computer science, creative writing, current events, dance, drama, driver education, economics, English, English literature, European history, expository writing, forensics, French, geography, geometry, German, government/civics, health, history, instrumental music, journalism, Latin, mathematics, music, physical education, physical science, physics, physiology, psychology, religion, science, social studies, sociology, Spanish, speech, statistics, theater, trigonometry, world history, world literature.

Graduation Requirements American history, computer science, English, foreign language, mathematics, physical education (includes health), religion (includes Bible studies and theology), science, social studies (includes history), Works of Mercy.

Special Academic Programs 20 Advanced Placement exams for which test preparation is offered; honors section; special instructional classes for students with learning disabilities and Attention Deficit Disorder.

College Admission Counseling 250 students graduated in 2013; 248 went to college, including Emory University; Georgia Institute of Technology; Georgia State University; University of Georgia; University of Notre Dame. Other: 1 entered military service. 60% scored over 600 on SAT critical reading, 60% scored over 600 on SAT math, 50% scored over 26 on composite ACT.

Student Life Upper grades have uniform requirement, student council, honor system. Discipline rests equally with students and faculty. Attendance at religious services is required.

Summer Programs Enrichment, sports, art/fine arts programs offered; held on campus; accepts boys and girls; open to students from other schools. 500 students usually enrolled. 2014 schedule: June 3 to July 30.

Tuition and Aid Day student tuition: $11,800. Tuition installment plan (FACTS Tuition Payment Plan, monthly payment plans). Tuition reduction for siblings, need-based scholarship grants available. In 2013–14, 18% of upper-school students received aid. Total amount of financial aid awarded in 2013–14: $400,000.

Admissions Traditional secondary-level entrance grade is 9. For fall 2013, 547 students applied for upper-level admission, 300 were accepted, 275 enrolled. SSAT required. Deadline for receipt of application materials: February 1. Application fee required: $100.

Athletics Interscholastic: baseball (boys), basketball (b,g), cheering (b,g), cross-country running (b,g), dance (b), dance squad (g), dance team (g), diving (b,g), drill team (g), football (b), golf (b,g), lacrosse (b,g), soccer (b,g), softball (g), strength & conditioning (b,g), swimming and diving (b,g), tennis (b,g), track and field (b,g), volleyball (g), water polo (b,g), weight training (b,g), wrestling (b); coed interscholastic: sailing, water polo. 4 PE instructors, 35 coaches, 1 athletic trainer.

Computers Computer network features include on-campus library services, online commercial services, Internet access, wireless campus network, Internet filtering or blocking technology. Campus intranet, student e-mail accounts, and computer access in

designated common areas are available to students. Students grades are available online. The school has a published electronic and media policy.

Contact Terry Sides, Coordinator of Admissions. 404-636-0323 Ext. 291. Fax: 404-636-2118. E-mail: tsides@spx.org. Website: www.spx.org

ST. PIUS X HIGH SCHOOL

811 West Donovan Street
Houston, Texas 77091-5699

Head of School: Sr. Donna M. Pollard, OP

General Information Coeducational day college-preparatory, arts, business, religious studies, and technology school, affiliated with Roman Catholic Church. Grades 9–12. Founded: 1956. Setting: urban. 26-acre campus. 1 building on campus. Approved or accredited by Southern Association of Colleges and Schools, Texas Catholic Conference, The College Board, and Texas Department of Education. Endowment: $3.5 million. Total enrollment: 670. Upper school average class size: 20. Upper school faculty-student ratio: 1:12. There are 180 required school days per year for Upper School students. Upper School students typically attend 5 days per week. The average school day consists of 7 hours.

Upper School Student Profile Grade 9: 159 students (93 boys, 66 girls); Grade 10: 168 students (93 boys, 75 girls); Grade 11: 167 students (85 boys, 82 girls); Grade 12: 155 students (82 boys, 73 girls). 71% of students are Roman Catholic.

Faculty School total: 57. In upper school: 21 men, 36 women; 41 have advanced degrees.

Subjects Offered Advanced chemistry, advanced computer applications, advanced math, Advanced Placement courses, advanced studio art-AP, algebra, American history-AP, American literature, American literature-AP, art, band, biology, biology-AP, business law, calculus, calculus-AP, campus ministry, Catholic belief and practice, chemistry, choir, chorus, Christian ethics, church history, college counseling, communications, community service, computer applications, computer multimedia, computer programming, computer science-AP, cultural geography, dance, death and loss, desktop publishing, earth and space science, economics, English language-AP, English literature-AP, environmental science, film history, fine arts, foreign language, French, geography, geometry, graphic design, health, health education, history of the Catholic Church, honors geometry, honors world history, introduction to theater, jewelry making, language arts, Latin, Latin-AP, library assistant, marching band, modern world history, moral and social development, moral theology, musical productions, painting, personal finance, philosophy, photography, physical education, physics, psychology, reading/study skills, SAT/ACT preparation, Shakespeare, social justice, sociology, Spanish, Spanish language-AP, Spanish-AP, speech, speech communications, stagecraft, student government, student publications, technical theater, theology, U.S. government, U.S. government and politics-AP, U.S. history, U.S. history-AP, Web site design, world history, world religions, yearbook.

Graduation Requirements Advanced math, algebra, American government, American history, ancient world history, art, biology, chemistry, communications, economics, electives, English, geometry, government, health, integrated physics, physical education (includes health), physics, theology, 2 years of foreign language or reading development, Christian Service Learning (100 hours of community service), 4 years of theology.

Special Academic Programs 10 Advanced Placement exams for which test preparation is offered; honors section; study at local college for college credit; remedial reading and/or remedial writing; remedial math; programs in English, mathematics, general development for dyslexic students.

College Admission Counseling 175 students graduated in 2013; 170 went to college, including Stephen F. Austin State University; Texas A&M University; Texas State University–San Marcos; Texas Tech University; The University of Texas at San Antonio; University of Houston. Mean SAT critical reading: 517, mean SAT math: 505, mean SAT writing: 492, mean combined SAT: 1517, mean composite ACT: 23. 12% scored over 600 on SAT critical reading, 12% scored over 600 on SAT math, 13% scored over 600 on SAT writing, 11% scored over 1800 on combined SAT, 19% scored over 26 on composite ACT.

Student Life Upper grades have uniform requirement, student council, honor system. Discipline rests primarily with faculty. Attendance at religious services is required.

Summer Programs Enrichment, sports, art/fine arts, computer instruction programs offered; held on campus; accepts boys and girls; not open to students from other schools. 100 students usually enrolled. 2014 schedule: June 6 to July 30. Application deadline: May 1.

Tuition and Aid Day student tuition: $11,700. Tuition installment plan (monthly payment plans, individually arranged payment plans). Tuition reduction for siblings, merit scholarship grants, need-based scholarship grants available. In 2013–14, 26% of upper-school students received aid; total upper-school merit-scholarship money awarded: $53,500. Total amount of financial aid awarded in 2013–14: $711,000.

Admissions Traditional secondary-level entrance grade is 9. For fall 2013, 375 students applied for upper-level admission, 275 were accepted, 199 enrolled. Catholic High School Entrance Examination required. Deadline for receipt of application materials: January 15. Application fee required: $50. Interview required.

Athletics Interscholastic: baseball (boys), basketball (b,g), cheering (g), cross-country running (b,g), dance squad (g), dance team (b,g), drill team (g), football (b), golf (b,g), rugby (b,g), soccer (b,g), softball (g), swimming and diving (b,g), tennis (b,g), track and field (b,g), volleyball (g), wrestling (b). 1 PE instructor, 1 athletic trainer.

Computers Computers are regularly used in art, career exploration, career technology, desktop publishing, drawing and design, graphic design, journalism, mathematics, multimedia, news writing, newspaper, publications, technology, video film production, yearbook classes. Computer network features include on-campus library services, Internet access, wireless campus network, Internet filtering or blocking technology, faculty Web pages for courses. Student e-mail accounts and computer access in designated common areas are available to students. Students grades are available online. The school has a published electronic and media policy.

Contact Ms. Susie Kramer, Admissions Director. 713-579-7507. Fax: 713-692-5725. E-mail: kramers@stpiusx.org. Website: www.stpiusx.org

ST. STANISLAUS COLLEGE

304 South Beach Boulevard
Bay St. Louis, Mississippi 39520

Head of School: Br. Francis David, SC

General Information Boys' boarding and day college-preparatory, business, religious studies, technology, and ESL school, affiliated with Roman Catholic Church. Grades 7–12. Founded: 1854. Setting: small town. Nearest major city is New Orleans, LA. Students are housed in single-sex dormitories. 30-acre campus. 8 buildings on campus. Approved or accredited by National Catholic Education Association, Southern Association of Colleges and Schools, Southern Association of Independent Schools, and Mississippi Department of Education. Member of National Association of Independent Schools. Endowment: $5 million. Total enrollment: 352. Upper school average class size: 22. Upper school faculty-student ratio: 1:12. There are 180 required school days per year for Upper School students. Upper School students typically attend 5 days per week. The average school day consists of 6 hours and 23 minutes.

Upper School Student Profile Grade 9: 65 students (65 boys); Grade 10: 64 students (64 boys); Grade 11: 66 students (66 boys); Grade 12: 55 students (55 boys). 25% of students are boarding students. 90% are state residents. 6 states are represented in upper school student body. 1% are international students. International students from Angola, China, Mexico, Republic of Korea, Taiwan, and Thailand. 80% of students are Roman Catholic.

Faculty School total: 34. In upper school: 28 men, 6 women; 21 have advanced degrees; 8 reside on campus.

Subjects Offered Accounting, ACT preparation, advanced biology, advanced chemistry, advanced computer applications, advanced math, Advanced Placement courses, algebra, American history, American history-AP, American literature, anatomy, art, astronomy, biology, biology-AP, business, business education, business law, calculus, calculus-AP, campus ministry, ceramics, chemistry, chemistry-AP, computer programming, computer science, computer science-AP, creative writing, desktop publishing, drama, economics, economics and history, English, English language and composition-AP, English literature, English literature and composition-AP, environmental science, ESL, finance, French, French as a second language, genetics, geography, geology, geometry, government, government/civics, grammar, guidance, health, health education, history, journalism, law, marine biology, marine science, mathematics, music, music performance, physical education, physics, physics-AP, pre-calculus, psychology, psychology-AP, religion, science, scuba diving, short story, social sciences, social studies, sociology, Spanish, speech, swimming, symphonic band, theater, theater arts, theology, track and field, trigonometry, typing, U.S. history-AP, world history, world literature.

Graduation Requirements Arts and fine arts (art, music, dance, drama), computer science, English, foreign language, mathematics, physical education (includes health), religion (includes Bible studies and theology), science, social sciences, social studies (includes history), service hours are required.

Special Academic Programs 8 Advanced Placement exams for which test preparation is offered; honors section; study at local college for college credit; remedial reading and/or remedial writing; remedial math; ESL (10 students enrolled).

College Admission Counseling 59 students graduated in 2013; all went to college, including Louisiana State University and Agricultural and Mechanical College; Mississippi State University; University of Mississippi; University of New Orleans; University of South Alabama; University of Southern Mississippi. Median SAT critical reading: 520, median SAT math: 620, median SAT writing: 570, median composite ACT: 21. 40% scored over 600 on SAT critical reading, 50% scored over 600 on SAT math, 35% scored over 600 on SAT writing, 22% scored over 1800 on combined SAT, 17% scored over 26 on composite ACT.

Student Life Upper grades have uniform requirement, student council, honor system. Discipline rests primarily with faculty. Attendance at religious services is required.

Summer Programs ESL programs offered; session focuses on water sports summer camp and ESL, cultural summer camp; held both on and off campus; held at Mississippi, Louisiana, and Florida; accepts boys and girls; open to students from other schools. 180 students usually enrolled. 2014 schedule: June 15 to July 13. Application deadline: none.

Tuition and Aid Day student tuition: $6090; 7-day tuition and room/board: $23,257. Tuition installment plan (monthly payment plans, individually arranged payment plans). Need-based scholarship grants, paying campus jobs available.

Admissions Traditional secondary-level entrance grade is 9. For fall 2013, 100 students applied for upper-level admission, 90 were accepted, 80 enrolled. Deadline for receipt of application materials: none. Application fee required: $100. Interview required.

Athletics Interscholastic: baseball, basketball, cross-country running, football, golf, power lifting, soccer, track and field; intramural: baseball, basketball, billiards, cheering, fishing, flag football, floor hockey, football, hiking/backpacking, jogging, outdoor activities, outdoor adventure, outdoor education, outdoor recreation, outdoor skills, outdoors, physical fitness, physical training, power lifting, scuba diving, swimming and diving, table tennis, tennis, touch football, volleyball, water polo, water skiing, weight lifting, weight training; coed interscholastic: sailing, swimming and diving, tennis. 5 PE instructors, 16 coaches, 1 athletic trainer.

Computers Computers are regularly used in accounting, English, mathematics, religion, SAT preparation, science, Spanish classes. Computer network features include on-campus library services, online commercial services, Internet access, wireless campus network, Internet filtering or blocking technology. Campus intranet and computer access in designated common areas are available to students. Students grades are available online.

Contact Mr. Richard Gleber, Assistant Director of Admissions. 228-467-9057 Ext. 249. Fax: 228-466-2972. E-mail: richard@ststan.com. Website: www.ststan.com

ST. STEPHEN'S & ST. AGNES SCHOOL

1000 St. Stephen's Road
Alexandria, Virginia 22304

Head of School: Mrs. Joan G. Ogilvy Holden

General Information Coeducational day college-preparatory, arts, religious studies, and technology school, affiliated with Episcopal Church. Grades JK–12. Founded: 1924. Setting: suburban. Nearest major city is Washington, DC. 58-acre campus. 5 buildings on campus. Approved or accredited by Association of Independent Schools of Greater Washington, National Association of Episcopal Schools, and Virginia Association of Independent Schools. Member of National Association of Independent Schools and Secondary School Admission Test Board. Endowment: $23.6 million. Total enrollment: 1,144. Upper school average class size: 14. Upper school faculty-student ratio: 1:9. There are 170 required school days per year for Upper School students. Upper School students typically attend 5 days per week. The average school day consists of 7 hours and 10 minutes.

Upper School Student Profile Grade 9: 115 students (59 boys, 56 girls); Grade 10: 115 students (57 boys, 58 girls); Grade 11: 107 students (50 boys, 57 girls); Grade 12: 119 students (70 boys, 49 girls). 22% of students are members of Episcopal Church.

Faculty School total: 142. In upper school: 24 men, 29 women; 41 have advanced degrees.

Subjects Offered 1 1/2 elective credits, Advanced Placement courses, algebra, American history, American literature, art, art history, art history-AP, bioethics, biology, biology-AP, calculus, calculus-AP, ceramics, chemistry, chemistry-AP, Christian education, Christian ethics, Christian scripture, Christian testament, comparative government and politics-AP, concert choir, directing, drama, drawing, economics, English, English-AP, ensembles, environmental science-AP, ethics, European history, European history-AP, forensics, French, French language-AP, geometry, government/civics-AP, history, honors English, honors geometry, honors U.S. history, honors world history, instrumental music, jazz ensemble, Latin, Latin-AP, macro/microeconomics-AP, Mandarin, mathematics, medieval history, medieval/Renaissance history, microeconomics-AP, music, music theory-AP, newspaper, painting, physical education, physics, physics-AP, playwriting and directing, pre-calculus, psychology-AP, religion, robotics, sculpture, senior project, Spanish, Spanish language-AP, Spanish literature-AP, sports, sports medicine, statistics-AP, studio art, studio art-AP, technical theater, theater, theater arts, trigonometry, U.S. history-AP, world history, writing, yearbook, yoga.

Graduation Requirements Arts and fine arts (art, music, dance, drama), English, family studies, foreign language, history, mathematics, physical education (includes health), religion (includes Bible studies and theology), science, technological applications, senior year independent off-campus project, 40 hours of community service.

Special Academic Programs 22 Advanced Placement exams for which test preparation is offered; honors section; independent study; term-away projects; study abroad; academic accommodation for the gifted, the musically talented, and the artistically talented.

College Admission Counseling 111 students graduated in 2013; all went to college, including The College of William and Mary; University of Michigan; University of Pennsylvania; University of Virginia; Washington and Lee University; Yale University. Mean SAT critical reading: 597, mean SAT math: 608, mean SAT writing: 602, mean combined SAT: 1807.

Student Life Upper grades have specified standards of dress, student council, honor system. Discipline rests equally with students and faculty. Attendance at religious services is required.

Summer Programs Enrichment, advancement, sports, art/fine arts, computer instruction programs offered; session focuses on enrichment; held both on and off campus; held at Chesapeake Bay, DC, VA and MD area, auxiliary camps held on our campus—Johns Hopkins University, Center for Talented Youth, and ASM Summer

Tennis Camp, Terrence Austin's Football Camp, USA Chess Camp and Animation Creation; accepts boys and girls; open to students from other schools. 1,750 students usually enrolled. 2014 schedule: June 16 to August 15. Application deadline: April 15.

Tuition and Aid Day student tuition: $32,074. Tuition installment plan (FACTS Tuition Payment Plan). Need-based scholarship grants available. In 2013–14, 27% of upper-school students received aid. Total amount of financial aid awarded in 2013–14: $2,327,954.

Admissions Traditional secondary-level entrance grade is 9. ISEE or SSAT required. Deadline for receipt of application materials: January 15. Application fee required: $70. Interview required.

Athletics Interscholastic: baseball (boys), basketball (b,g), field hockey (g), football (b), ice hockey (b), lacrosse (b,g), soccer (b,g), softball (g), swimming and diving (b,g), tennis (b,g), track and field (b,g), volleyball (g), winter soccer (g), wrestling (b); intramural: dance team (g), independent competitive sports (b,g); coed interscholastic: cross-country running, diving, golf, winter (indoor) track; coed intramural: basketball, fitness, independent competitive sports, jogging, physical fitness, physical training, strength & conditioning, weight lifting, weight training, yoga. 6 PE instructors, 14 coaches, 2 athletic trainers.

Computers Computers are regularly used in all academic classes. Computer network features include on-campus library services, online commercial services, Internet access, wireless campus network, Internet filtering or blocking technology, computer labs for foreign language, math, technology, library, newspaper, physics, and chemistry, homework assignments posted online, mobile wireless laptop cart, iPads, computers available in study hall and library. Campus intranet, student e-mail accounts, and computer access in designated common areas are available to students. Students grades are available online. The school has a published electronic and media policy.

Contact Mr. Jon Kunz, Director of Admission, Grades 6-12. 703-212-2706. Fax: 703-212-2788. E-mail: jkunz@sssas.org. Website: www.sssas.org

SAINT STEPHEN'S EPISCOPAL SCHOOL

315 41st Street West
Bradenton, Florida 34209

Head of School: Janet S. Pullen

General Information Coeducational day college-preparatory, arts, religious studies, and marine science school, affiliated with Episcopal Church. Grades PK–12. Founded: 1970. Setting: small town. Nearest major city is Tampa. 35-acre campus. 3 buildings on campus. Approved or accredited by Florida Council of Independent Schools, National Association of Episcopal Schools, Southern Association of Colleges and Schools, and Southern Association of Independent Schools. Member of National Association of Independent Schools. Endowment: $1.2 million. Total enrollment: 654. Upper school average class size: 11. Upper school faculty-student ratio: 1:11. There are 177 required school days per year for Upper School students. Upper School students typically attend 5 days per week. The average school day consists of 7 hours.

Upper School Student Profile Grade 9: 62 students (32 boys, 30 girls); Grade 10: 54 students (26 boys, 28 girls); Grade 11: 73 students (38 boys, 35 girls); Grade 12: 70 students (34 boys, 36 girls); Postgraduate: 2 students (2 boys). 15% of students are members of Episcopal Church.

Faculty School total: 90. In upper school: 13 men, 18 women; 21 have advanced degrees.

Subjects Offered 3-dimensional art, Advanced Placement courses, advanced studio art-AP, algebra, American government, American history, American history-AP, American literature, art, art history, art history-AP, art-AP, astronomy, band, biology, biology-AP, British literature, broadcast journalism, calculus, calculus-AP, ceramics, chemistry, chemistry-AP, choir, chorus, community service, comparative religion, composition, composition-AP, computer programming, computer programming-AP, computer science, computer science-AP, conceptual physics, debate, digital art, digital photography, discrete mathematics, drama, economics, English, English language and composition-AP, English language-AP, English literature, English literature and composition-AP, English literature-AP, English-AP, environmental science-AP, European history, European history-AP, French, French language-AP, geometry, graphic design, humanities, international relations, journalism, Latin, Latin-AP, marine biology, marine science, music, newspaper, organic chemistry, painting, photography, physical education, physics, physics-AP, portfolio art, pre-calculus, probability and statistics, psychology, public speaking, science research, Spanish, Spanish language-AP, speech and debate, studio art, studio art-AP, trigonometry, U.S. history, U.S. history-AP, weight training, Western civilization, world history, world history-AP.

Graduation Requirements Arts and fine arts (art, music, dance, drama), electives, English, foreign language, mathematics, physical education (includes health), science, social studies (includes history), senior speech. Community service is required.

Special Academic Programs 17 Advanced Placement exams for which test preparation is offered; honors section.

College Admission Counseling 52 students graduated in 2012; all went to college, including Florida State University; University of Central Florida; University of Florida; University of Miami; University of South Florida. Mean SAT critical reading: 570, mean SAT math: 614, mean SAT writing: 579, mean composite ACT: 25. 39% scored over 600 on SAT critical reading, 56% scored over 600 on SAT math, 36% scored over 600 on SAT writing, 38% scored over 26 on composite ACT.

Student Life Upper grades have specified standards of dress, student council, honor system. Discipline rests primarily with faculty. Attendance at religious services is required.

Tuition and Aid Day student tuition: $18,550. Tuition installment plan (monthly payment plans). Need-based scholarship grants available. In 2012–13, 6% of upper-school students received aid. Total amount of financial aid awarded in 2012–13: $9250.

Admissions Traditional secondary-level entrance grade is 9. For fall 2012, 37 students applied for upper-level admission, 34 were accepted, 34 enrolled. School's own exam required. Deadline for receipt of application materials: none. Application fee required: $100. Interview recommended.

Athletics Interscholastic: aerobics/dance (girls), aquatics (b,g), baseball (b), basketball (b,g), cheering (g), cross-country running (b,g), dance (g), dance team (g), diving (b,g), football (b), golf (b,g), independent competitive sports (b,g), lacrosse (b), soccer (b,g), softball (g), swimming and diving (b,g), tennis (b,g), track and field (b,g), volleyball (g), winter soccer (b,g), wrestling (b); intramural: aerobics/dance (g), ballet (g), basketball (b,g), cheering (g), cross-country running (b,g), dance (g), fitness (b,g), horseback riding (b,g), jogging (b,g), lacrosse (b,g), physical fitness (b,g), physical training (b,g), running (b,g), sailing (b,g), soccer (b,g), softball (b,g), strength & conditioning (b,g), tennis (b,g), track and field (b,g), volleyball (b,g), weight training (b,g), wrestling (b); coed intramural: kayaking, yoga. 8 PE instructors, 14 coaches, 1 athletic trainer.

Computers Computers are regularly used in art, computer applications, foreign language, journalism, library, mathematics, media, science, social sciences, word processing, writing, yearbook classes. Computer network features include on-campus library services, online commercial services, Internet access, wireless campus network, Internet filtering or blocking technology, Microsoft Office. Computer access in designated common areas is available to students. Students grades are available online. The school has a published electronic and media policy.

Contact Linda G. Lutz, Director of Admissions. 941-746-2121 Ext. 1568. Fax: 941-345-1237. E-mail: llutz@saintstephens.org. Website: www.saintstephens.org

ST. STEPHEN'S EPISCOPAL SCHOOL

6500 St. Stephen's Drive
Austin, Texas 78746

Head of School: Mr. Robert Kirkpatrick

General Information Coeducational boarding and day college-preparatory and theater school, affiliated with Episcopal Church. Boarding grades 8–12, day grades 6–12. Founded: 1950. Setting: suburban. Students are housed in single-sex dormitories. 370-acre campus. 45 buildings on campus. Approved or accredited by Independent Schools Association of the Southwest, National Association of Episcopal Schools, The Association of Boarding Schools, and Texas Department of Education. Member of National Association of Independent Schools and Secondary School Admission Test Board. Endowment: $320,000. Total enrollment: 689. Upper school average class size: 17. Upper school faculty-student ratio: 1:8. There are 165 required school days per year for Upper School students. Upper School students typically attend 5 days per week. The average school day consists of 7 hours and 35 minutes.

Upper School Student Profile Grade 9: 119 students (62 boys, 57 girls); Grade 10: 132 students (70 boys, 62 girls); Grade 11: 126 students (66 boys, 60 girls); Grade 12: 110 students (53 boys, 57 girls). 35% of students are boarding students. 80% are state residents. 7 states are represented in upper school student body. 20% are international students. International students from Bahamas, China, Hong Kong, Mexico, Saudi Arabia, and Taiwan; 15 other countries represented in student body. 18% of students are members of Episcopal Church.

Faculty School total: 98. In upper school: 40 men, 35 women; 45 have advanced degrees; 36 reside on campus.

Subjects Offered 3-dimensional design, acting, algebra, American history, American history-AP, anthropology, art, art history, astrophysics, ballet, band, biology, calculus, ceramics, chamber groups, chemistry, Chinese, choreography, classics, computer applications, computer math, computer science, computer studies, creative writing, directing, drama, English, English literature, environmental science, European history, fine arts, French, geology, geometry, government/civics, graphic design, history, jazz band, Latin, mathematics, music, musical theater, photography, physical education, physics, physics-AP, play/screen writing, pre-calculus, psychology, public policy issues and action, public speaking, religion, science, social studies, Spanish, theater arts, theology, video, world history, world literature.

Graduation Requirements Arts and fine arts (art, music, dance, drama), electives, English, foreign language, mathematics, physical education (includes health), religion (includes Bible studies and theology), science, social studies (includes history), community service requirement in middle and upper schools.

Special Academic Programs Advanced Placement exam preparation; honors section; independent study; study abroad; ESL (23 students enrolled).

College Admission Counseling 107 students graduated in 2013; all went to college, including Southern Methodist University; The Colorado College; The University of Texas at Austin; University of California, Berkeley. Mean SAT critical reading: 625, mean SAT math: 662, mean SAT writing: 640, mean combined SAT: 1967, mean composite ACT: 28.

Student Life Upper grades have specified standards of dress, student council. Discipline rests equally with students and faculty. Attendance at religious services is required.

Summer Programs Sports, art/fine arts programs offered; session focuses on soccer, tennis, travel abroad, foreign language/culture, fine arts, community service; held both on and off campus; held at locations in Europe, El Salvador, Nicaragua, Costa Rica, American wilderness areas; accepts boys and girls; open to students from other schools. 120 students usually enrolled. 2014 schedule: June 1 to July 31. Application deadline: none.

Tuition and Aid Day student tuition: $23,160; 7-day tuition and room/board: $46,780. Tuition installment plan (individually arranged payment plans). Merit scholarship grants, need-based scholarship grants available. In 2013–14, 16% of upper-school students received aid; total upper-school merit-scholarship money awarded: $30,000. Total amount of financial aid awarded in 2013–14: $2,800,000.

Admissions Traditional secondary-level entrance grade is 9. For fall 2013, 331 students applied for upper-level admission, 135 were accepted, 92 enrolled. ISEE or SSAT required. Deadline for receipt of application materials: January 25. Application fee required: $100. Interview required.

Athletics Interscholastic: baseball (boys), basketball (b,g), cheering (b,g), crew (b,g), cross-country running (b,g), field hockey (g), football (b), golf (b,g), lacrosse (b,g), running (b,g), soccer (b,g), softball (g), swimming and diving (b,g), tennis (b,g), track and field (b,g), volleyball (g), winter soccer (b,g); intramural: bicycling (b,g), climbing (b,g), combined training (b,g), dance (b,g), fitness (b,g), hiking/backpacking (b,g), independent competitive sports (b,g), indoor hockey (b,g), modern dance (b,g), mountain biking (b,g), mountaineering (b,g), outdoor adventure (b,g), outdoor education (b,g), physical fitness (b,g), physical training (b,g), rappelling (b,g), rock climbing (b,g), ropes courses (b,g), strength & conditioning (b,g), surfing (b,g), wall climbing (b,g), weight training (b,g). 2 PE instructors, 9 coaches, 3 athletic trainers.

Computers Computer network features include on-campus library services, online commercial services, Internet access, wireless campus network, Internet filtering or blocking technology, online schedules, syllabi, homework, examples, and links to information sources. Campus intranet, student e-mail accounts, and computer access in designated common areas are available to students. Students grades are available online. The school has a published electronic and media policy.

Contact Lawrence Sampleton, Director of Admission. 512-327-1213 Ext. 210. Fax: 512-327-6771. E-mail: admission@sstx.org. Website: www.sstx.org

ST. STEPHEN'S SCHOOL, ROME

Via Aventina 3
Rome 00153, Italy

Head of School: Ms. Lesley Jane Murphy

General Information Coeducational boarding and day college-preparatory, arts, and bilingual studies school. Grades 9–PG. Founded: 1964. Setting: urban. Students are housed in single-sex by floor dormitories. 2-acre campus. 2 buildings on campus. Approved or accredited by International Baccalaureate Organization, New England Association of Schools and Colleges, and US Department of State. Affiliate member of National Association of Independent Schools; member of European Council of International Schools. Language of instruction: English. Endowment: $3.5 million. Total enrollment: 278. Upper school average class size: 13. Upper school faculty-student ratio: 1:7. There are 175 required school days per year for Upper School students. Upper School students typically attend 5 days per week. The average school day consists of 7 hours.

Upper School Student Profile Grade 9: 63 students (32 boys, 31 girls); Grade 10: 56 students (27 boys, 29 girls); Grade 11: 83 students (37 boys, 46 girls); Grade 12: 75 students (39 boys, 36 girls); Postgraduate: 1 student (1 boy). 14% of students are boarding students. 64% are international students. International students from China, Germany, Russian Federation, Sri Lanka, United Kingdom, and United States; 29 other countries represented in student body.

Faculty School total: 46. In upper school: 12 men, 34 women; 38 have advanced degrees; 8 reside on campus.

Subjects Offered 20th century history, algebra, American literature, art, art history, biology, calculus, chemistry, chorus, classical studies, creative writing, dance, drama, economics, English, English literature, environmental systems, European history, French, geometry, health, instrumental music, Islamic studies, Italian, Latin, music theory, photography, physical education, physics, pre-calculus, Roman civilization, sculpture, Spanish, theory of knowledge, trigonometry, U.S. history, world literature.

Graduation Requirements Arts and fine arts (art, music, dance, drama), English, foreign language, mathematics, physical education (includes health), science, social studies (includes history), senior essay, computer proficiency examination, service.

Special Academic Programs International Baccalaureate program; 8 Advanced Placement exams for which test preparation is offered; domestic exchange program (with Buckingham Browne & Nichols School, Choate Rosemary Hall); ESL (4 students enrolled).

College Admission Counseling 62 students graduated in 2013; 55 went to college, including Boston University; Duke University; Georgetown University; Stanford University; Wellesley College; Worcester Polytechnic Institute. Other: 1

entered a postgraduate year, 6 had other specific plans. Mean SAT critical reading: 611, mean SAT math: 628, mean SAT writing: 627, mean combined SAT: 1866.

Student Life Upper grades have student council. Discipline rests equally with students and faculty.

Summer Programs Enrichment, art/fine arts programs offered; session focuses on liberal arts/pre-college; held both on and off campus; held at off-campus sites include museum visits and visits to various historical sites within the city; accepts boys and girls; open to students from other schools. 50 students usually enrolled. 2014 schedule: July 1 to August 4. Application deadline: June 19.

Tuition and Aid Day student tuition: €22,750–€23,250; 7-day tuition and room/board: €34,000–€34,500. Tuition installment plan (individually arranged payment plans). Tuition reduction for siblings, merit scholarship grants, need-based scholarship grants available. In 2013–14, 5% of upper-school students received aid; total upper-school merit-scholarship money awarded: €30,000. Total amount of financial aid awarded in 2013–14: €405,150.

Admissions Traditional secondary-level entrance grade is 9. For fall 2013, 165 students applied for upper-level admission, 117 were accepted, 110 enrolled. School's own exam required. Deadline for receipt of application materials: February 7. Application fee required: €150. Interview required.

Athletics Interscholastic: basketball (boys, girls), soccer (b,g), volleyball (b,g); intramural: basketball (b,g), soccer (b,g), volleyball (b,g); coed interscholastic: track and field; coed intramural: dance, self defense, track and field, yoga. 1 PE instructor, 6 coaches.

Computers Computers are regularly used in English, foreign language, mathematics, photography, science, social studies classes. Computer network features include on-campus library services, Internet access, wireless campus network, Internet filtering or blocking technology, In house technical assistance. Campus intranet, student e-mail accounts, and computer access in designated common areas are available to students. Students grades are available online. The school has a published electronic and media policy.

Contact Ms. Alex Perniciaro, Admissions Coordinator. 39-06-575-0605. Fax: 39-06-574-1941. E-mail: admissions@ststephens-rome.com. Website: www.sssrome.it

SAINT TERESA'S ACADEMY

5600 Main Street
Kansas City, Missouri 64113

Head of School: Mrs. Nan Tiehen Bone

General Information Girls' day college-preparatory school, affiliated with Roman Catholic Church. Grades 9–12. Founded: 1866. Setting: urban. 20-acre campus. 4 buildings on campus. Approved or accredited by National Catholic Education Association, North Central Association of Colleges and Schools, and Missouri Department of Education. Endowment: $150,000. Total enrollment: 607. Upper school average class size: 21. Upper school faculty-student ratio: 1:12. There are 174 required school days per year for Upper School students. Upper School students typically attend 5 days per week. The average school day consists of 6 hours and 40 minutes.

Upper School Student Profile Grade 9: 168 students (168 girls); Grade 10: 158 students (158 girls); Grade 11: 145 students (145 girls); Grade 12: 135 students (135 girls). 87% of students are Roman Catholic.

Faculty School total: 48. In upper school: 8 men, 40 women; 33 have advanced degrees.

Subjects Offered Advanced chemistry, advanced math, algebra, American government, American history, American history-AP, American literature, American literature-AP, analysis, anatomy and physiology, art, athletics, basketball, biology, biology-AP, botany, British literature, calculus, career/college preparation, chamber groups, chemistry, chemistry-AP, choir, chorus, computer graphics, computer programming, current events, dance, directing, drama, drawing, ecology, English, English language and composition-AP, English language-AP, English literature, European history-AP, fiber arts, fitness, foreign language, forensics, French, French language-AP, French-AP, freshman seminar, geometry, golf, graphic design, health, independent study, journalism, keyboarding, language arts, Latin, Latin History, music-AP, newspaper, painting, physical education, physics, piano, playwriting, portfolio art, pre-calculus, probability and statistics, psychology, psychology-AP, Shakespeare, social issues, social studies, sociology, softball, Spanish, Spanish language-AP, Spanish literature-AP, Spanish-AP, speech, speech and debate, speech communications, sports conditioning, sports performance development, stagecraft, swimming, technical theater, tennis, theater, theology and the arts, track and field, trigonometry, U.S. government, U.S. government and politics, U.S. government and politics-AP, U.S. history, U.S. history-AP, volleyball, Western civilization, women in literature, women spirituality and faith, world geography, world religions, world religions, writing, writing, yearbook.

Graduation Requirements Arts and fine arts (art, music, dance, drama), computer science, electives, English, foreign language, mathematics, physical education (includes health), science, social studies (includes history), theology. Community service is required.

Special Academic Programs 10 Advanced Placement exams for which test preparation is offered; honors section; study at local college for college credit.

College Admission Counseling 133 students graduated in 2013; all went to college, including Kansas State University; Saint Louis University; The University of Kansas; University of Arkansas; University of Missouri. Mean SAT critical reading:

600, mean SAT math: 580, mean SAT writing: 610, mean combined SAT: 1780, mean composite ACT: 26.

Student Life Upper grades have uniform requirement, student council. Discipline rests primarily with faculty. Attendance at religious services is required.

Summer Programs Enrichment, sports, art/fine arts, computer instruction programs offered; session focuses on fine arts, sports, credit bearing courses, and enrichment summer school programs; held on campus; accepts girls; open to students from other schools. 145 students usually enrolled. 2014 schedule: June 3 to July 15. Application deadline: May 1.

Tuition and Aid Day student tuition: $10,650. Tuition installment plan (SMART Tuition Payment Plan). Tuition reduction for siblings, merit scholarship grants, need-based scholarship grants available. In 2013–14, 25% of upper-school students received aid; total upper-school merit-scholarship money awarded: $125,000. Total amount of financial aid awarded in 2013–14: $150,000.

Admissions Traditional secondary-level entrance grade is 9. For fall 2013, 181 students applied for upper-level admission, 175 were accepted, 162 enrolled. Placement test required. Deadline for receipt of application materials: February 28. No application fee required.

Athletics Interscholastic: aerobics/dance, basketball, cross-country running, diving, drill team, golf, lacrosse, soccer, softball, swimming and diving, tennis, track and field, volleyball; intramural: aerobics/dance, badminton, fitness, fitness walking, jogging, physical fitness, physical training, running, strength & conditioning, table tennis, volleyball, walking, weight lifting, weight training. 1 PE instructor, 25 coaches, 1 athletic trainer.

Computers Computers are regularly used in business education, creative writing, graphics, journalism, library, newspaper, photography, research skills, science, writing, yearbook classes. Computer network features include on-campus library services, Internet access, wireless campus network, Internet filtering or blocking technology. Campus intranet is available to students. Students grades are available online. The school has a published electronic and media policy.

Contact Mrs. Roseann Hudnall, Admissions Director. 816-501-0011 Ext. 135. Fax: 816-523-0232. E-mail: rhudnall@stteresasacademy.org. Website: www.stteresasacademy.org

SAINT THOMAS ACADEMY

949 Mendota Heights Road
Mendota Heights, Minnesota 55120

Head of School: Thomas B. Mich, PhD

General Information Boys' day college-preparatory and military school, affiliated with Roman Catholic Church. Grades 7–12. Founded: 1885. Setting: suburban. Nearest major city is St. Paul. 72-acre campus. 4 buildings on campus. Approved or accredited by Independent Schools Association of the Central States. Member of National Association of Independent Schools. Endowment: $16.3 million. Total enrollment: 671. Upper school average class size: 18. Upper school faculty-student ratio: 1:10. There are 172 required school days per year for Upper School students. Upper School students typically attend 5 days per week. The average school day consists of 6 hours and 40 minutes.

Upper School Student Profile Grade 9: 126 students (126 boys); Grade 10: 148 students (148 boys); Grade 11: 129 students (129 boys); Grade 12: 143 students (143 boys). 80% of students are Roman Catholic.

Faculty School total: 59. In upper school: 37 men, 17 women; 48 have advanced degrees.

Subjects Offered Advanced biology, advanced computer applications, advanced math, Advanced Placement courses, algebra, American democracy, American government, American history, American history-AP, American literature, American literature-AP, American studies, art, art and culture, art appreciation, art history, band, biology, biology-AP, calculus, campus ministry, chemistry, Chinese, computer science, creative writing, earth science, economics, English, English literature, environmental studies, fine arts, French, geometry, government/civics, health, history, JROTC, Latin, mathematics, military science, music, physical education, physics, psychology, religion, science, social studies, Spanish, trigonometry, world history, world literature, writing.

Graduation Requirements Arts and fine arts (art, music, dance, drama), biology, chemistry, English, foreign language, health education, JROTC or LEAD (Leadership Education and Development), mathematics, physical education (includes health), science, social studies (includes history), theology, U.S. history, world history, 100 hours of community service in 12th grade.

Special Academic Programs 11 Advanced Placement exams for which test preparation is offered; honors section; independent study; study at local college for college credit.

College Admission Counseling 120 students graduated in 2012; 118 went to college, including Boston College; Iowa State University of Science and Technology; University of Minnesota, Twin Cities Campus; University of Notre Dame; University of St. Thomas; University of Wisconsin–Madison. Other: 2 had other specific plans. Mean SAT critical reading: 611, mean SAT math: 626, mean SAT writing: 586, mean composite ACT: 26.

Student Life Upper grades have uniform requirement, student council, honor system. Discipline rests primarily with faculty. Attendance at religious services is required.

Tuition and Aid Day student tuition: $17,950. Tuition installment plan (SMART Tuition Payment Plan, monthly payment plans, individually arranged payment plans, quarterly payment plan). Merit scholarship grants, need-based scholarship grants available. In 2012–13, 40% of upper-school students received aid; total upper-school merit-scholarship money awarded: $115,000. Total amount of financial aid awarded in 2012–13: $2,500,000.

Admissions Traditional secondary-level entrance grade is 9. For fall 2012, 125 students applied for upper-level admission, 112 were accepted, 82 enrolled. Cognitive Abilities Test required. Deadline for receipt of application materials: none. No application fee required. On-campus interview recommended.

Athletics Interscholastic: alpine skiing, baseball, basketball, cross-country running, drill team, fitness, football, golf, hockey, ice hockey, JROTC drill, lacrosse, marksmanship, nordic skiing, outdoor skills, physical fitness, riflery, skiing (cross-country), skiing (downhill), soccer, swimming and diving, tennis, track and field, wrestling; intramural: basketball, bowling, football, hockey, physical training, strength & conditioning, table tennis, weight lifting, weight training. 3 PE instructors, 1 athletic trainer.

Computers Computers are regularly used in all academic, art, foreign language, music classes. Computer network features include on-campus library services, online commercial services, Internet access, wireless campus network, Internet filtering or blocking technology. Student e-mail accounts are available to students. Students grades are available online. The school has a published electronic and media policy.

Contact Peggy Mansur, Admissions Assistant. 651-683-1515. Fax: 651-683-1576. E-mail: pmansur@cadets.com. Website: www.cadets.com

ST. THOMAS AQUINAS HIGH SCHOOL

2801 Southwest 12th Street
Fort Lauderdale, Florida 33312-2999

Head of School: Mrs. Tina Jones

General Information Coeducational day college-preparatory, arts, religious studies, technology, Campus Ministry, and college preparatory school, affiliated with Roman Catholic Church. Grades 9–12. Founded: 1936. Setting: suburban. 24-acre campus. 23 buildings on campus. Approved or accredited by National Catholic Education Association, Southern Association of Colleges and Schools, and Florida Department of Education. Total enrollment: 2,194. Upper school average class size: 25. Upper school faculty-student ratio: 1:18. There are 180 required school days per year for Upper School students. Upper School students typically attend 5 days per week. The average school day consists of 6 hours and 30 minutes.

Upper School Student Profile Grade 9: 549 students (253 boys, 296 girls); Grade 10: 566 students (296 boys, 270 girls); Grade 11: 544 students (278 boys, 266 girls); Grade 12: 535 students (261 boys, 274 girls). 96% of students are Roman Catholic.

Faculty School total: 127. In upper school: 56 men, 71 women; 73 have advanced degrees.

Subjects Offered 20th century history, 20th century world history, 3-dimensional art, acting, advanced chemistry, advanced computer applications, advanced math, Advanced Placement courses, advanced studio art-AP, aerobics, algebra, American government, American history, American history-AP, American literature, anatomy and physiology, art, art appreciation, art history-AP, athletics, biology, biology-AP, British literature, British literature (honors), British literature-AP, broadcast journalism, calculus, calculus-AP, chemistry, chemistry-AP, Chinese, choir, choral music, chorus, Christianity, church history, comparative government and politics-AP, comparative political systems-AP, composition-AP, computer art, computer graphics, computer programming-AP, computer science-AP, debate, desktop publishing, digital art, digital imaging, directing, drama, drama performance, drawing, economics-AP, electives, English, English language and composition-AP, English literature, English literature and composition-AP, English literature-AP, English-AP, English/composition-AP, environmental science, environmental science-AP, European history, European history-AP, film and literature, film and new technologies, fitness, food science, forensics, French, French language-AP, French literature-AP, French-AP, general science, geometry, government, government and politics-AP, government-AP, government/civics-AP, grammar, graphic arts, graphic design, health, health and safety, health and wellness, health education, health enhancement, health science, healthful living, Hispanic literature, history, history of drama, history-AP, Holocaust, honors algebra, honors English, honors geometry, honors U.S. history, honors world history, human anatomy, human geography - AP, jazz, jazz band, journalism, keyboarding, lab science, language, language and composition, language arts, language-AP, Latin, Latin-AP, leadership, leadership and service, leadership education training, Life of Christ, literature, literature and composition-AP, literature-AP, macro/microeconomics-AP, macroeconomics-AP, marine biology, marine studies, mathematics-AP, media, microeconomics, microeconomics-AP, model United Nations, modern European history, modern European history-AP, news writing, newspaper, nutrition, oral expression, orchestra, peace and justice, peace education, peace studies, performing arts, photography, photojournalism, physical education, physical fitness, physics, physics-AP, play production, playwriting and directing, poetry, political systems, pottery, pre-algebra, pre-calculus, probability and statistics, psychology, psychology-AP, public speaking, reading, SAT preparation, SAT/ACT preparation, Spanish, Spanish language-AP, Spanish literature, Spanish literature-AP, Spanish-AP, speech, speech and debate, speech and oral interpretations, speech communications, sports team management, stage design, stagecraft, statistics, statistics-AP, student government, student publications, studio art, technical theater, television, trigonometry, U.S. government and·politics-AP, U.S. history, U.S. history-AP, United States government-AP, world history, world history-AP.

Graduation Requirements Arts and fine arts (art, music, dance, drama), computer science, electives, English, foreign language, health, mathematics, personal fitness, science, social sciences, theology.

Special Academic Programs Advanced Placement exam preparation; honors section; study at local college for college credit; remedial reading and/or remedial writing; remedial math.

College Admission Counseling 553 students graduated in 2013; 547 went to college, including Florida Atlantic University; Florida State University; University of Central Florida; University of Florida; University of Miami; University of North Florida. Other: 1 entered military service, 5 had other specific plans. Mean SAT critical reading: 556, mean SAT math: 557, mean SAT writing: 563, mean composite ACT: 24.

Student Life Upper grades have uniform requirement, student council, honor system. Discipline rests primarily with faculty. Attendance at religious services is required.

Summer Programs Remediation, enrichment, advancement, art/fine arts, computer instruction programs offered; session focuses on enrichment; held on campus; accepts boys and girls; open to students from other schools. 1,000 students usually enrolled. 2014 schedule: June 10 to June 26. Application deadline: June 10.

Tuition and Aid Tuition installment plan (monthly payment plans, TADS). Need-based scholarship grants available.

Admissions Traditional secondary-level entrance grade is 9. For fall 2013, 700 students applied for upper-level admission, 598 were accepted, 549 enrolled. High School Placement Test required. Deadline for receipt of application materials: March 31. Application fee required: $50. Interview required.

Athletics Interscholastic: baseball (boys), basketball (b,g), bowling (b,g), cheering (g), cross-country running (b,g), dance (b,g), dance squad (g), diving (b,g), drill team (g), football (b), golf (b,g), lacrosse (b,g), physical fitness (b,g), running (b,g), sailing (b,g), soccer (b,g), softball (g), swimming and diving (b,g), tennis (b,g), track and field (b,g), volleyball (b,g), water polo (b,g), wrestling (b); intramural: dance team (g), danceline (g), drill team (g); coed interscholastic: ballet, bowling, hockey, ice hockey, indoor hockey, physical training; coed intramural: physical training, running. 2 PE instructors, 39 coaches, 1 athletic trainer.

Computers Computers are regularly used in all academic, data processing, desktop publishing, graphic arts, graphic design, graphics, journalism, keyboarding, lab/keyboard, media, media arts, media production, media services, news writing, newspaper, programming, publications, publishing, technology, video film production, Web site design, word processing classes. Computer network features include on-campus library services, online commercial services, Internet access, wireless campus network, Internet filtering or blocking technology. Campus intranet, student e-mail accounts, and computer access in designated common areas are available to students. Students grades are available online. The school has a published electronic and media policy.

Contact Admissions Office. 954-581-2127 Ext. 8623. Fax: 954-327-2193. E-mail: mary.facella@aquinas-sta.org. Website: www.aquinas-sta.org

SAINT THOMAS AQUINAS HIGH SCHOOL

11411 Pflumm Road
Overland Park, Kansas 66215-4816

Head of School: Dr. William P. Ford

General Information Coeducational day college-preparatory, religious studies, and technology school, affiliated with Roman Catholic Church. Grades 9–12. Founded: 1988. Setting: suburban. Nearest major city is Kansas City, MO. 44-acre campus. 2 buildings on campus. Approved or accredited by National Catholic Education Association, North Central Association of Colleges and Schools, and Kansas Department of Education. Total enrollment: 937. Upper school average class size: 24. Upper school faculty-student ratio: 1:15. There are 180 required school days per year for Upper School students. Upper School students typically attend 5 days per week. The average school day consists of 7 hours.

Upper School Student Profile Grade 9: 224 students (112 boys, 112 girls); Grade 10: 223 students (111 boys, 112 girls); Grade 11: 240 students (122 boys, 118 girls); Grade 12: 219 students (110 boys, 109 girls). 97% of students are Roman Catholic.

Faculty School total: 66. In upper school: 30 men, 36 women; 64 have advanced degrees.

Graduation Requirements Arts and fine arts (art, music, dance, drama), computer technologies, electives, English, Latin, mathematics, modern languages, physical education (includes health), science, social studies (includes history), speech, theology, service (one fourth credit each of 4 years).

Special Academic Programs Advanced Placement exam preparation; honors section; study at local college for college credit; academic accommodation for the gifted; remedial reading and/or remedial writing; remedial math.

College Admission Counseling 246 students graduated in 2013; 245 went to college, including Benedictine College; Johnson County Community College; Kansas State University; Saint Louis University; The University of Kansas; University of Notre Dame. Other: 1 entered military service. Mean SAT critical reading: 619, mean SAT math: 638, mean SAT writing: 603, mean composite ACT: 25.

Student Life Upper grades have uniform requirement, student council. Discipline rests primarily with faculty. Attendance at religious services is required.

Summer Programs Remediation, advancement, sports, computer instruction programs offered; session focuses on sports camps and selected academic coursework; held on campus; accepts boys and girls; open to students from other schools.

Tuition and Aid Day student tuition: $8100–$9100. Tuition installment plan (SMART Tuition Payment Plan). Need-based scholarship grants available.

Admissions Traditional secondary-level entrance grade is 9. ACT-Explore required. Deadline for receipt of application materials: none. Application fee required: $175. Interview required.

Athletics Interscholastic: baseball (boys), basketball (b,g), bowling (b,g), cross-country running (b,g), dance team (g), diving (b,g), football (b), golf (b,g), soccer (b,g), softball (g), swimming and diving (b,g), tennis (b,g), track and field (b,g), volleyball (g), wrestling (b); intramural: field hockey (g), lacrosse (b); coed interscholastic: cheering; coed intramural: table tennis, ultimate Frisbee. 3 PE instructors, 1 athletic trainer.

Computers Computers are regularly used in all academic, computer applications, desktop publishing, programming, video film production, Web site design classes. Computer network features include on-campus library services, Internet access, wireless campus network, computer labs and laptop carts. Student e-mail accounts are available to students. Students grades are available online. The school has a published electronic and media policy.

Contact Mrs. Diane Pyle, Director of Admissions. 913-319-2423. Fax: 913-345-2319. E-mail: dpyle@stasaints.net. Website: www.stasaints.net

ST. THOMAS AQUINAS HIGH SCHOOL

197 Dover Point Road
Dover, New Hampshire 03820

Head of School: Mr. Kevin Collins

General Information Coeducational day college-preparatory and religious studies school, affiliated with Roman Catholic Church. Grades 9–12. Founded: 1960. Setting: small town. Nearest major city is Boston, MA. 11-acre campus. 2 buildings on campus. Approved or accredited by New England Association of Schools and Colleges and New Hampshire Department of Education. Total enrollment: 585. Upper school average class size: 18. Upper school faculty-student ratio: 1:14. There are 186 required school days per year for Upper School students. Upper School students typically attend 5 days per week. The average school day consists of 6 hours and 25 minutes.

Faculty School total: 51. In upper school: 27 men, 24 women; 25 have advanced degrees.

Subjects Offered Algebra, anatomy and physiology, biology, biology-AP, calculus, calculus-AP, chemistry, chorus, Christian ethics, civics, concert band, contemporary studies, drawing, economics, English, environmental science-AP, finite math, French, geography, geometry, honors algebra, honors English, honors geometry, humanities, international relations, introduction to technology, Latin, marine biology, math applications, media arts, music appreciation, music theory, painting, physics, prayer/spirituality, pre-calculus, psychology, science, scripture, sculpture, social justice, sociology, Spanish, statistics-AP, studio art, theology, trigonometry, U.S. government and politics-AP, U.S. history, U.S. history-AP, wellness, Western civilization, world religions.

Graduation Requirements Arts and fine arts (art, music, dance, drama), Christian ethics, electives, English, foreign language, freshman seminar, mathematics, prayer/spirituality, science, scripture, social justice, social studies (includes history), theology, world religions, 40 hour community service requirement.

Special Academic Programs Advanced Placement exam preparation; honors section; independent study.

College Admission Counseling 157 students graduated in 2013; 152 went to college, including Keene State College; Merrimack College; Saint Michael's College; Suffolk University; University of New Hampshire; University of Vermont. Other: 3 entered a postgraduate year, 2 had other specific plans. Mean SAT critical reading: 565, mean SAT math: 561, mean SAT writing: 561, mean composite ACT: 24.

Student Life Upper grades have specified standards of dress, student council. Discipline rests primarily with faculty. Attendance at religious services is required.

Summer Programs Enrichment, advancement programs offered; held on campus; accepts boys and girls; not open to students from other schools.

Tuition and Aid Day student tuition: $11,350. Tuition installment plan (annual, semiannual, and 10-month payment plans). Need-based scholarship grants available. In 2013–14, 25% of upper-school students received aid.

Admissions Traditional secondary-level entrance grade is 9. Scholastic Testing Service High School Placement Test required. Deadline for receipt of application materials: December 20. Application fee required: $40.

Athletics Interscholastic: baseball (boys), basketball (b,g), cross-country·running (b,g), field hockey (g), football (b), golf (b,g), ice hockey (b,g), lacrosse (b,g), skiing (downhill) (b,g), soccer (b,g), softball (g), swimming and diving (b,g), tennis (b,g), track and field (b,g), volleyball (g), winter (indoor) track (b,g), wrestling (b); intramural: dance team (g). 51 coaches, 1 athletic trainer.

Computers Computers are regularly used in introduction to technology, media arts classes. Computer network features include on-campus library services, Internet access, wireless campus network. Student e-mail accounts and computer access in designated common areas are available to students. Students grades are available online.

Contact Mr. Keith Adams, Director of Admissions. 603-742-3206. Fax: 603-749-7822. E-mail: kadams@stalux.org. Website: www.stalux.org

ST. THOMAS HIGH SCHOOL

4500 Memorial Drive
Houston, Texas 77007-7332

Head of School: Rev. Patrick Fulton, CSB

General Information Boys' day college-preparatory and religious studies school, affiliated with Roman Catholic Church. Grades 9–12. Founded: 1900. Setting: urban. 37-acre campus. 6 buildings on campus. Approved or accredited by Southern Association of Colleges and Schools, Texas Catholic Conference, Texas Education Agency, and Texas Department of Education. Member of National Association of Independent Schools. Endowment: $12 million. Total enrollment: 752. Upper school average class size: 18. Upper school faculty-student ratio: 1:14. There are 185 required school days per year for Upper School students. Upper School students typically attend 5 days per week. The average school day consists of 7 hours and 20 minutes.

Upper School Student Profile Grade 9: 230 students (230 boys); Grade 10: 175 students (175 boys); Grade 11: 179 students (179 boys); Grade 12: 173 students (173 boys). 72% of students are Roman Catholic.

Faculty School total: 54. In upper school: 33 men, 21 women; 28 have advanced degrees.

Subjects Offered Algebra, American government, American history, American history-AP, American literature, anatomy and physiology, ancient history, art, arts, Basic programming, Bible studies, bioethics, biology, biology-AP, British literature, calculus, calculus-AP, ceramics, chemistry, chemistry-AP, civics/free enterprise, classical civilization, college counseling, comparative government and politics-AP, computer applications, computer information systems, computer programming, computer studies, creative writing, critical thinking, critical writing, decision making skills, desktop publishing, digital photography, drama, drawing, ecology, environmental systems, economics, economics-AP, English, English language-AP, English literature, English literature-AP, environmental education, environmental science, ethics, European history, fine arts, forensics, French, geography, geology, geometry, government and politics-AP, government/civics, grammar, guidance, health, health education, history of the Catholic Church, Holocaust studies, instrumental music, jazz band, journalism, Latin, marine biology, mathematics, military history, oceanography, oral communications, orchestra, painting, photography, physical education, physics, physics-AP, pre-calculus, programming, public speaking, publications, religion, social studies, Spanish, Spanish language-AP, speech, student government, student publications, theater, theology, trigonometry, U.S. government and politics-AP, world history, world literature.

Graduation Requirements Arts and fine arts (art, music, dance, drama), computer applications, English, foreign language, mathematics, physical education (includes health), religion (includes Bible studies and theology), science, social studies (includes history).

Special Academic Programs 10 Advanced Placement exams for which test preparation is offered; honors section.

College Admission Counseling 171 students graduated in 2012; all went to college, including Louisiana State University and Agricultural and Mechanical College; Texas A&M University; Texas Tech University; The University of Texas at Austin; The University of Texas at San Antonio; University of Houston. Mean composite ACT: 26.

Student Life Upper grades have specified standards of dress, student council, honor system. Discipline rests primarily with faculty. Attendance at religious services is required.

Tuition and Aid Day student tuition: $13,250. Tuition installment plan (monthly payment plans). Merit scholarship grants, need-based scholarship grants, middle-income loans available. In 2012–13, 34% of upper-school students received aid; total upper-school merit-scholarship money awarded: $200,000. Total amount of financial aid awarded in 2012–13: $1,300,000.

Admissions Traditional secondary-level entrance grade is 9. For fall 2012, 587 students applied for upper-level admission, 315 were accepted, 232 enrolled. High School Placement Test required. Deadline for receipt of application materials: January 15. Application fee required: $75.

Athletics Interscholastic: baseball, basketball, cross-country running, football, golf, lacrosse, rugby, soccer, swimming and diving, tennis, track and field, wrestling; intramural: basketball, bowling, flag football, Frisbee, roller hockey, table tennis, weight lifting. 2 PE instructors, 2 coaches, 1 athletic trainer.

Computers Computers are regularly used in data processing, desktop publishing, multimedia, newspaper, photography, programming, publications, Web site design, word processing classes. Computer network features include on-campus library services, Internet access, wireless campus network, Internet filtering or blocking technology. Campus intranet, student e-mail accounts, and computer access in designated common areas are available to students. Students grades are available online. The school has a published electronic and media policy.

Contact Ms. Christine Westman, Assistant Principal. 713-864-6348. Fax: 713-864-5750. E-mail: chris.westman@sths.org. Website: www.sths.org

SAINT THOMAS MORE CATHOLIC HIGH SCHOOL

450 East Farrel Road
Lafayette, Louisiana 70508

Head of School: Mr. Richard Lavergne

General Information Coeducational day college-preparatory, arts, business, religious studies, bilingual studies, and technology school, affiliated with Roman Catholic Church. Grades 9–12. Founded: 1982. Setting: suburban. Nearest major city is Baton Rouge. 45-acre campus. 1 building on campus. Approved or accredited by Southern Association of Colleges and Schools and Louisiana Department of Education. Endowment: $2.5 million. Total enrollment: 1,085. Upper school average class size: 25. Upper school faculty-student ratio: 1:25. There are 180 required school days per year for Upper School students. Upper School students typically attend 5 days per week. The average school day consists of 7 hours.

Upper School Student Profile Grade 9: 274 students (144 boys, 130 girls); Grade 10: 288 students (142 boys, 146 girls); Grade 11: 265 students (124 boys, 141 girls); Grade 12: 258 students (119 boys, 139 girls). 89% of students are Roman Catholic.

Faculty School total: 90. In upper school: 27 men, 47 women; 23 have advanced degrees.

Subjects Offered ACT preparation, advanced chemistry, advanced math, Advanced Placement courses, advanced studio art-AP, algebra, American history, anatomy and physiology, applied music, art, athletics, band, biology, business, calculus-AP, campus ministry, chemistry, chemistry-AP, civics/free enterprise, computer science, computer skills, creative writing, debate, desktop publishing, drama, economics and history, English, English language and composition-AP, English literature and composition-AP, environmental science, European history-AP, film studies, fitness, French, geography, geometry, health, honors algebra, honors English, honors U.S. history, honors world history, independent study, kinesiology, mathematics, newspaper, photography, physical education, physical science, physics, play production, pre-calculus, psychology, public speaking, religion, Spanish, speech, speech and debate, studio art-AP, study skills, theology, trigonometry, U.S. history-AP, Web site design, weight training, world history, yearbook.

Graduation Requirements Arts and fine arts (art, music, dance, drama), business applications, English, French, keyboarding, mathematics, physical education (includes health), religion (includes Bible studies and theology), science, social studies (includes history), Spanish, world history.

Special Academic Programs 10 Advanced Placement exams for which test preparation is offered; honors section; independent study; study at local college for college credit; academic accommodation for the gifted; remedial reading and/or remedial writing; remedial math.

College Admission Counseling 250 students graduated in 2013; 244 went to college, including Louisiana State University and Agricultural and Mechanical College; Spring Hill College; Texas Christian University; University of Louisiana at Lafayette; University of Mississippi. Other: 2 went to work, 1 entered military service, 3 had other specific plans. Median composite ACT: 24.

Student Life Upper grades have uniform requirement, student council, honor system. Discipline rests primarily with faculty. Attendance at religious services is required.

Tuition and Aid Day student tuition: $6070–$6270. Tuition installment plan (monthly payment plans, individually arranged payment plans). Merit scholarship grants, need-based scholarship grants, paying campus jobs available. In 2013–14, 5% of upper-school students received aid; total upper-school merit-scholarship money awarded: $98,000. Total amount of financial aid awarded in 2013–14: $100,000.

Admissions Traditional secondary-level entrance grade is 9. Achievement tests, ACT-Explore, any standardized test, Explore, latest standardized score from previous school and standardized test scores required. Deadline for receipt of application materials: none. No application fee required.

Athletics Interscholastic: aquatics (boys, girls), baseball (b), basketball (b,g), bowling (b,g), cheering (g), cross-country running (b,g), dance squad (g), dance team (g), floor hockey (b), football (b), golf (b,g), indoor track (b,g), indoor track & field (b,g), physical training (b,g), soccer (b,g), softball (g), strength & conditioning (b,g), tennis (b,g), track and field (b,g), volleyball (g), weight lifting (b,g), weight training (b,g), wrestling (b); intramural: flag football (b,g), indoor hockey (b), lacrosse (b); coed interscholastic: Special Olympics. 4 PE instructors, 4 coaches.

Computers Computers are regularly used in all academic, library classes. Computer network features include on-campus library services, online commercial services, Internet access, wireless campus network, Internet filtering or blocking technology, computer access in the library before and after school and during lunch. Campus intranet, student e-mail accounts, and computer access in designated common areas are available to students. Students grades are available online. The school has a published electronic and media policy.

Contact Ms. Natalie D. Broussard '00, Assistant Director of Admissions. 337-988-7779. Fax: 337-988-2911. E-mail: natalie.broussard@stmcougars.net. Website: www.stmcougars.net

ST. TIMOTHY'S SCHOOL

8400 Greenspring Avenue

Stevenson, Maryland 21153

Head of School: Randy S. Stevens

General Information Girls' boarding and day college-preparatory, arts, and IB (International Baccalaureate diploma program) school, affiliated with Episcopal Church. Grades 9–12. Founded: 1882. Setting: suburban. Nearest major city is Baltimore. Students are housed in single-sex dormitories. 145-acre campus. 23 buildings on campus. Approved or accredited by Association of Independent Maryland Schools, International Baccalaureate Organization, Middle States Association of Colleges and Schools, National Association of Episcopal Schools, The Association of Boarding Schools, and Maryland Department of Education. Member of National Association of Independent Schools and Secondary School Admission Test Board. Endowment: $10 million. Total enrollment: 165. Upper school average class size: 10. Upper school faculty-student ratio: 1:6. There are 175 required school days per year for Upper School students. Upper School students typically attend 5 days per week. The average school day consists of 7 hours.

Upper School Student Profile Grade 9: 42 students (42 girls); Grade 10: 48 students (48 girls); Grade 11: 41 students (41 girls); Grade 12: 34 students (34 girls). 67% of students are boarding students. 40% are state residents. 18 states are represented in upper school student body. 31% are international students. International students from China, Germany, Ghana, Japan, Nigeria, and Republic of Korea; 15 other countries represented in student body.

Faculty School total: 26. In upper school: 7 men, 16 women; 17 have advanced degrees; 16 reside on campus.

Subjects Offered Algebra, American literature, art, art history, bell choir, biology, British literature, calculus, chemistry, Chinese, choir, college counseling, comparative politics, creative writing, dance, drama, drama performance, drama workshop, English, English composition, English literature, ESL, ethics, European history, fine arts, foreign language, French, geometry, history, integrated mathematics, International Baccalaureate courses, Latin, Mandarin, mathematics, modern dance, music, photography, physics, piano, religion, SAT preparation, science, Spanish, U.S. history, world history, world literature, writing.

Graduation Requirements Arts and fine arts (art, music, dance, drama), English, foreign language, history, mathematics, physical education (includes health), religion (includes Bible studies and theology), science, Theory of Knowledge course, extended essay, Community, Action, and Service (CAS). Community service is required.

Special Academic Programs International Baccalaureate program; independent study; ESL (23 students enrolled).

College Admission Counseling 35 students graduated in 2013; all went to college, including Barnard College; Columbia University; University of Maryland, College Park; University of Michigan; University of Virginia; Wake Forest University.

Student Life Upper grades have uniform requirement, student council, honor system. Discipline rests equally with students and faculty. Attendance at religious services is required.

Summer Programs Enrichment, ESL programs offered; session focuses on global immersion/intensive language and college prep; held on campus; accepts boys and girls; open to students from other schools.

Tuition and Aid Day student tuition: $28,000; 7-day tuition and room/board: $49,100. Tuition installment plan (FACTS Tuition Payment Plan). Merit scholarship grants, need-based scholarship grants, need-based loans available. In 2013–14, 52% of upper-school students received aid; total upper-school merit-scholarship money awarded: $100,000. Total amount of financial aid awarded in 2013–14: $2,500,000.

Admissions Traditional secondary-level entrance grade is 9. For fall 2013, 206 students applied for upper-level admission, 123 were accepted, 72 enrolled. ISEE, SLEP for foreign students, SSAT or TOEFL required. Deadline for receipt of application materials: February 1. Application fee required: $50. Interview required.

Athletics Interscholastic: badminton, basketball, dressage, equestrian sports, field hockey, golf, horseback riding, ice hockey, indoor soccer, lacrosse, soccer, softball, squash, swimming and diving, tennis, volleyball; intramural: ballet, dance, dance squad, equestrian sports, horseback riding, modern dance, outdoor adventure, weight training, yoga. 3 coaches, 1 athletic trainer.

Computers Computers are regularly used in art, college planning, English, mathematics, publications, SAT preparation, science, yearbook classes. Computer network features include on-campus library services, online commercial services, Internet access, wireless campus network, Internet filtering or blocking technology. Student e-mail accounts are available to students. The school has a published electronic and media policy.

Contact Anne Mickle, Director of Admissions. 410-486-7401. Fax: 410-486-1167. E-mail: amickle@stt.org. Website: www.stt.org

SAINT URSULA ACADEMY

4025 Indian Road

Toledo, Ohio 43606

Head of School: Mrs. Mary Werner

General Information Girls' day college-preparatory, arts, business, religious studies, bilingual studies, technology, and College Preparatory school, affiliated with Roman Catholic Church. Grades 6–12. Founded: 1854. Setting: suburban. 16-acre campus. 1 building on campus. Approved or accredited by North Central Association of Colleges and Schools, Ohio Catholic Schools Accreditation Association (OCSAA), and Ohio Department of Education. Total enrollment: 549. Upper school average class size: 16. Upper school faculty-student ratio: 1:12. There are 180 required school days per year for Upper School students. Upper School students typically attend 5 days per week. The average school day consists of 7 hours and 20 minutes.

Upper School Student Profile Grade 6: 20 students (20 girls); Grade 7: 30 students (30 girls); Grade 8: 20 students (20 girls); Grade 9: 125 students (125 girls); Grade 10: 141 students (141 girls); Grade 11: 120 students (120 girls); Grade 12: 121 students (121 girls). 75% of students are Roman Catholic.

Faculty School total: 51. In upper school: 9 men, 41 women; 32 have advanced degrees.

Subjects Offered 3-dimensional art, accounting, Advanced Placement courses, advanced studio art-AP, algebra, American government, American history, American history-AP, American literature, anatomy, anatomy and physiology, art, art-AP, ballet, biology, British literature, British literature-AP, business law, calculus-AP, career exploration, Catholic belief and practice, ceramics, chemistry, chemistry-AP, choral music, choreography, chorus, church history, comparative government and politics-AP, comparative religion, composition-AP, computer applications, computer graphics, concert choir, dance, digital photography, drama, drawing, economics, electives, engineering, English language and composition-AP, English literature and composition-AP, fashion, female experience in America, film history, foreign language, French language-AP, geometry, government, government and politics-AP, graphic arts, health, history of the Catholic Church, honors algebra, honors English, honors geometry, honors world history, human geography - AP, instrumental music, Latin, Latin-AP, literature, literature and composition-AP, Mandarin, marketing, mathematics-AP, microeconomics, music, music theory-AP, New Testament, orchestra, painting, personal finance, photography, physical education, physics, physiology, pre-calculus, printmaking, probability and statistics, psychology, psychology-AP, religion and culture, religious education, sculpture, single survival, social psychology, Spanish, Spanish language-AP, speech, statistics, statistics-AP, student publications, studio art-AP, symphonic band, theology, trigonometry, U.S. government and politics, U.S. government and politics-AP, U.S. history, U.S. history-AP, U.S. literature, United States government-AP, vocal music, women's health, women's studies, yearbook.

Graduation Requirements Arts and fine arts (art, music, dance, drama), computers, English, foreign language, mathematics, physical education (includes health), science, social studies (includes history), theology, community service, Career Exploration Experience.

Special Academic Programs 15 Advanced Placement exams for which test preparation is offered; honors section; study at local college for college credit.

College Admission Counseling 125 students graduated in 2013; 123 went to college, including Miami University; The Ohio State University; The University of Toledo; University of Dayton; University of Michigan. Other: 1 went to work, 1 entered military service. Mean SAT critical reading: 570, mean SAT math: 554, mean SAT writing: 577, mean composite ACT: 25. 40% scored over 600 on SAT critical reading, 25% scored over 600 on SAT math, 58% scored over 600 on SAT writing, 37% scored over 26 on composite ACT.

Student Life Upper grades have uniform requirement, student council, honor system. Discipline rests primarily with faculty. Attendance at religious services is required.

Summer Programs Enrichment, advancement, sports, art/fine arts, computer instruction programs offered; session focuses on athletics and academics; held both on and off campus; held at golf course; accepts girls; open to students from other schools. 300 students usually enrolled. 2014 schedule: June 6 to July 29. Application deadline: June 1.

Tuition and Aid Tuition installment plan (SMART Tuition Payment Plan). Tuition reduction for siblings, merit scholarship grants, need-based scholarship grants, paying campus jobs available. In 2013–14, 68% of upper-school students received aid. Total amount of financial aid awarded in 2013–14: $1,299,000.

Admissions Traditional secondary-level entrance grade is 9. For fall 2013, 160 students applied for upper-level admission, 151 were accepted, 121 enrolled. High School Placement Test or placement test required. Deadline for receipt of application materials: none. Application fee required.

Athletics Interscholastic: aerobics/dance, ballet, basketball, bowling, broomball, cheering, crew, cross-country running, dance team, diving, equestrian sports, fencing, golf, gymnastics, horseback riding, independent competitive sports, lacrosse, modern dance, physical fitness, physical training, rowing, soccer, softball, swimming and diving, tennis, track and field, volleyball, water polo, weight training; intramural: badminton, cooperative games, volleyball. 1 PE instructor, 32 coaches, 1 athletic trainer.

Computers Computers are regularly used in accounting, computer applications, graphic arts, newspaper, Web site design, yearbook classes. Computer network features include on-campus library services, Internet access, wireless campus network, Internet filtering or blocking technology. Campus intranet, student e-mail accounts, and computer access in designated common areas are available to students. Students grades are available online. The school has a published electronic and media policy.

Contact Mrs. Nichole Flores, Principal. 419-329-2279. Fax: 419-531-4575. E-mail: nflores@toledosua.org. Website: www.toledosua.org

SAINT VIATOR HIGH SCHOOL

1213 East Oakton Street
Arlington Heights, Illinois 60004

Head of School: Rev. Corey Brost, CSV

General Information Coeducational day college-preparatory, arts, religious studies, bilingual studies, and technology school, affiliated with Roman Catholic Church. Grades 9–12. Founded: 1961. Setting: suburban. Nearest major city is Chicago. 1 building on campus. Approved or accredited by North Central Association of Colleges and Schools and Illinois Department of Education. Upper school average class size: 25. Upper school faculty-student ratio: 1:13. There are 190 required school days per year for Upper School students. Upper School students typically attend 5 days per week. The average school day consists of 6 hours and 35 minutes.

Faculty School total: 77. In upper school: 30 men, 47 women; 50 have advanced degrees.

Graduation Requirements 25 hours of Christian Service each year (100 total hours).

College Admission Counseling 246 students graduated in 2013; all went to college, including DePaul University; Indiana University Bloomington; Loyola University Chicago; The University of Iowa; University of Dayton; University of Illinois at Urbana–Champaign. Mean composite ACT: 26.

Student Life Upper grades have uniform requirement, student council, honor system. Discipline rests primarily with faculty. Attendance at religious services is required.

Summer Programs Enrichment, advancement, sports, art/fine arts, computer instruction programs offered; held on campus; accepts boys and girls; not open to students from other schools. 2014 schedule: June 10 to July 26.

Tuition and Aid Day student tuition: $11,850. Tuition installment plan (monthly payment plans). Need-based scholarship grants available. In 2013–14, 28% of upper-school students received aid. Total amount of financial aid awarded in 2013–14: $1,300,000.

Admissions Traditional secondary-level entrance grade is 9. ETS high school placement exam required. Application fee required: $400.

Athletics Interscholastic: baseball (boys), basketball (b,g), cheering (g), cross-country running (b,g), football (b), golf (b,g), ice hockey (b), lacrosse (b,g), pom squad (g), soccer (b,g), softball (g), swimming and diving (b,g), tennis (b,g), track and field (b,g), volleyball (b,g), water polo (b,g), wrestling (b); coed intramural: outdoor adventure. 3 PE instructors, 101 coaches, 2 athletic trainers.

Computers Computer network features include Internet access, wireless campus network, Internet filtering or blocking technology, faculty Web pages. Students grades are available online. The school has a published electronic and media policy.

Contact Mrs. Eileen Manno, Principal. 847-392-4050 Ext. 229. Fax: 847-392-4101. E-mail: emanno@saintviator.com. Website: www.saintviator.com

ST. XAVIER CATHOLIC SCHOOL

200 North Washington
Junction City, Kansas 66441

General Information college-preparatory and general academic school. Approved or accredited by Kansas Department of Education. Upper school average class size: 12.

Student Life Attendance at religious services is required.

Admissions Application fee required. On-campus interview required.

Athletics Interscholastic: basketball (boys, girls), cross-country running (b), volleyball (g); coed interscholastic: cheering, track and field.

Contact 785-238-2841. Fax: 785-238-5021. Website: www.saintxrams.org

SALEM ACADEMY

500 Salem Avenue
Winston-Salem, North Carolina 27101-0578

Head of School: Mr. Karl Sjolund

General Information Girls' boarding and day college-preparatory and arts school, affiliated with Moravian Church. Grades 9–12. Founded: 1772. Setting: urban. Students are housed in single-sex dormitories. 60-acre campus. 4 buildings on campus. Approved or accredited by Southern Association of Colleges and Schools, The Association of Boarding Schools, and North Carolina Department of Education. Member of National Association of Independent Schools and Secondary School Admission Test Board. Endowment: $7 million. Total enrollment: 160. Upper school average class size: 10. Upper school faculty-student ratio: 1:7. There are 172 required school days per year for Upper School students. Upper School students typically attend 5 days per week. The average school day consists of 7 hours and 30 minutes.

Upper School Student Profile Grade 9: 31 students (31 girls); Grade 10: 39 students (39 girls); Grade 11: 44 students (44 girls); Grade 12: 38 students (38 girls). 60% of students are boarding students. 30% are state residents. 11 states are represented in upper school student body. 33% are international students. International students from China, Germany, and Republic of Korea; 3 other countries represented in student body. 4% of students are Moravian.

Faculty School total: 24. In upper school: 2 men, 22 women; 13 have advanced degrees; 3 reside on campus.

Subjects Offered Algebra, American history, art, biology, calculus, chemistry, dance, drama, economics, English, European history, fine arts, French, geometry, government/civics, Latin, mathematics, music, physical education, physics, pre-calculus, psychology, religion, science, social sciences, social studies, Spanish, theater, trigonometry, world history.

Graduation Requirements Arts and fine arts (art, music, dance, drama), English, foreign language, mathematics, physical education (includes health), religion (includes Bible studies and theology), science, social sciences, social studies (includes history), completion of January term.

Special Academic Programs 8 Advanced Placement exams for which test preparation is offered; honors section; term-away projects; study at local college for college credit; study abroad; programs in general development for dyslexic students; ESL (8 students enrolled).

College Admission Counseling 40 students graduated in 2013; all went to college, including New York University; Penn State University Park; The University of North Carolina at Chapel Hill; The University of North Carolina at Greensboro. Mean SAT critical reading: 575, mean SAT math: 631, mean SAT writing: 598, mean combined SAT: 1876.

Student Life Upper grades have specified standards of dress, student council, honor system. Discipline rests equally with students and faculty.

Tuition and Aid Day student tuition: $19,940; 7-day tuition and room/board: $40,490. Tuition installment plan (Key Tuition Payment Plan, monthly payment plans). Merit scholarship grants, need-based scholarship grants available. In 2013–14, 45% of upper-school students received aid; total upper-school merit-scholarship money awarded: $123,100. Total amount of financial aid awarded in 2013–14: $1,033,794.

Admissions Traditional secondary-level entrance grade is 9. For fall 2013, 160 students applied for upper-level admission, 85 were accepted, 65 enrolled. ACT, PSAT, SAT, SSAT or TOEFL required. Deadline for receipt of application materials: none. Application fee required: $50. Interview required.

Athletics Interscholastic: basketball, cross-country running, fencing, field hockey, golf, soccer, softball, swimming and diving, tennis, track and field, volleyball; intramural: aerobics/dance, archery, badminton, dance, fitness, flag football, floor hockey, golf, horseback riding, indoor hockey, indoor soccer, self defense. 2 PE instructors, 15 coaches, 1 athletic trainer.

Computers Computers are regularly used in all academic classes. Computer network features include on-campus library services, online commercial services, Internet access, wireless campus network. Student e-mail accounts and computer access in designated common areas are available to students. Students grades are available online.

Contact C. Lucia Higgins, Director of Admissions. 336-721-2643. Fax: 336-917-5340. E-mail: academy@salem.edu. Website: www.salemacademy.com

SALEM ACADEMY

942 Lancaster Drive NE
Salem, Oregon 97301

Head of School: Stan Baker

General Information Coeducational day college-preparatory, general academic, arts, vocational, religious studies, bilingual studies, and technology school, affiliated with Protestant Church. Grades K–12. Founded: 1945. Setting: suburban. 34-acre campus. 6 buildings on campus. Approved or accredited by Association of Christian Schools International, Northwest Accreditation Commission, and Oregon Department of Education. Total enrollment: 631. Upper school average class size: 20. Upper school faculty-student ratio: 1:9. Upper School students typically attend 5 days per week. The average school day consists of 7 hours and 15 minutes.

Upper School Student Profile 90% of students are Protestant.

Faculty School total: 48. In upper school: 12 men, 15 women; 5 have advanced degrees.

Subjects Offered Advanced chemistry, Advanced Placement courses, algebra, American history, American literature, anatomy and physiology, art, athletics, auto mechanics, baseball, Bible, Bible studies, biology, business, calculus, ceramics, cheerleading, chemistry, choir, college counseling, college writing, computer programming, computer science, drama, drama performance, economics, English, English literature, English literature and composition-AP, English literature-AP, ESL, foods, geography, geometry, government/civics, grammar, health, history, history-AP, home economics, honors English, industrial arts, Japanese, jazz ensemble, mathematics, music, physical education, physical science, physics, psychology, religion, SAT preparation, science, shop, social sciences, social studies, softball, Spanish, speech, track and field, typing, U.S. history-AP, vocal music, volleyball, weight training, woodworking, world history, world literature, writing.

Graduation Requirements English, foreign language, mathematics, physical education (includes health), religion (includes Bible studies and theology), science, social sciences, social studies (includes history), one credit in biblical studies for each year attended, 40 hours of community service (high school).

Special Academic Programs 7 Advanced Placement exams for which test preparation is offered; honors section; independent study; study at local college for college credit; academic accommodation for the musically talented and the artistically talented; ESL (23 students enrolled).

College Admission Counseling 59 students graduated in 2013; 48 went to college, including Chemeketa Community College; Corban University; George Fox University; Oregon State University; University of Oregon; Washington State University. Other: 11 went to work. Mean SAT critical reading: 531, mean SAT math: 549, mean SAT writing: 524, mean combined SAT: 1605.

Student Life Upper grades have specified standards of dress, student council, honor system. Discipline rests primarily with faculty.

Tuition and Aid Tuition installment plan (monthly payment plans). Tuition reduction for siblings, need-based scholarship grants available. In 2013–14, 25% of upper-school students received aid.

Admissions Traditional secondary-level entrance grade is 9. Math Placement Exam, Reading for Understanding, school's own exam and writing sample required. Deadline for receipt of application materials: none. Application fee required: $50. On-campus interview required.

Athletics Interscholastic: baseball (boys), basketball (b,g), cheering (g), cross-country running (b,g), football (b), golf (b,g), softball (g), track and field (b,g), volleyball (g); coed interscholastic: equestrian sports, swimming and diving; coed intramural: racquetball. 2 PE instructors, 36 coaches.

Computers Computers are regularly used in computer applications, design, digital applications, media, media production, multimedia, music technology, photography, photojournalism, video film production, yearbook classes. Computer network features include on-campus library services, Internet access, wireless campus network, Internet filtering or blocking technology. Students grades are available online. The school has a published electronic and media policy.

Contact Mr. Shannon deVries, Dean of Students. 503-378-1211. Fax: 503-375-3265. E-mail: sdevries@salemacademy.org. Website: www.salemacademy.org

SALESIAN HIGH SCHOOL

2851 Salesian Avenue
Richmond, California 94804

Head of School: Mr. Timothy J. Chambers

General Information Coeducational day college-preparatory, arts, religious studies, and technology school, affiliated with Roman Catholic Church. Grades 9–12. Founded: 1960. Setting: urban. Nearest major city is San Francisco. 21-acre campus. 3 buildings on campus. Approved or accredited by National Catholic Education Association, Western Association of Schools and Colleges, Western Catholic Education Association, and California Department of Education. Endowment: $200,000. Total enrollment: 473. Upper school average class size: 18. Upper school faculty-student ratio: 1:18. There are 177 required school days per year for Upper School students. Upper School students typically attend 5 days per week. The average school day consists of 6 hours and 50 minutes.

Upper School Student Profile Grade 9: 107 students (55 boys, 52 girls); Grade 10: 130 students (68 boys, 62 girls); Grade 11: 106 students (57 boys, 49 girls); Grade 12: 130 students (58 boys, 72 girls). 65% of students are Roman Catholic.

Faculty School total: 36. In upper school: 17 men, 15 women; 25 have advanced degrees.

Subjects Offered Advanced math, advanced studio art-AP, algebra, American history-AP, American literature, American literature-AP, anatomy, ancient world history, art, art history, art history-AP, biology, calculus, calculus-AP, Catholic belief and practice, Christian scripture, Christianity, classical language, computer literacy, drama, dramatic arts, economics, English, English composition, English language and composition-AP, English literature, English literature-AP, English-AP, environmental science, French, French language-AP, French-AP, geometry, government, government/civics, health and wellness, history of the Catholic Church, history-AP, honors U.S. history, mathematics, mathematics-AP, performing arts, physical education, physics, pre-algebra, pre-calculus, psychology, religion, SAT preparation, science, Spanish, Spanish language-AP, Spanish-AP, U.S. government, U.S. history, visual and performing arts, world history, world religions.

Graduation Requirements Arts and fine arts (art, music, dance, drama), English, foreign language, mathematics, physical education (includes health), religion (includes Bible studies and theology), science, social sciences, theology, Christian service projects.

Special Academic Programs 11 Advanced Placement exams for which test preparation is offered; honors section; remedial reading and/or remedial writing; remedial math.

College Admission Counseling 144 students graduated in 2012; 142 went to college, including San Francisco State University; University of California, Berkeley; University of California, Davis; University of California, Santa Cruz. Other: 2 entered military service.

Student Life Upper grades have uniform requirement, student council. Discipline rests primarily with faculty. Attendance at religious services is required.

Tuition and Aid Day student tuition: $13,250. Tuition installment plan (SMART Tuition Payment Plan). Merit scholarship grants, need-based scholarship grants available. In 2012–13, 45% of upper-school students received aid; total upper-school merit-scholarship money awarded: $50,000. Total amount of financial aid awarded in 2012–13: $1,400,000.

Admissions Traditional secondary-level entrance grade is 9. For fall 2012, 270 students applied for upper-level admission, 150 were accepted, 107 enrolled. High School Placement Test and High School Placement Test (closed version) from Scholastic Testing Service required. Deadline for receipt of application materials: none. Application fee required: $850. On-campus interview required.

Athletics Interscholastic: baseball (boys), basketball (b,g), cheering (g), cross-country running (b,g), football (b), physical training (b), soccer (b,g), softball (g), swimming and diving (b,g), volleyball (b,g), weight training (b), winter soccer (b,g); intramural: basketball (b,g), floor hockey (b,g), football (b), weight training (b); coed interscholastic: cross-country running, golf, track and field. 1 PE instructor, 25 coaches.

Computers Computers are regularly used in all academic, computer applications, history, library, stock market, yearbook classes. Computer network features include on-campus library services, Internet access, wireless campus network, Internet filtering or blocking technology. Student e-mail accounts and computer access in designated common areas are available to students. Students grades are available online. The school has a published electronic and media policy.

Contact Mrs. Connie Decuir, Director of Admissions. 510-234-4433 Ext. 1128. Fax: 510-236-4636. E-mail: cdecuir@salesian.com. Website: www.salesian.com

SALESIANUM SCHOOL

1801 North Broom Street
Wilmington, Delaware 19802-3891

Head of School: Rev. J. Christian Beretta, OSFS

General Information Boys' day college-preparatory school, affiliated with Roman Catholic Church. Grades 9–12. Founded: 1903. Setting: suburban. 22-acre campus. 1 building on campus. Approved or accredited by Middle States Association of Colleges and Schools and Delaware Department of Education. Total enrollment: 970. Upper school average class size: 20. Upper school faculty-student ratio: 1:12.

Upper School Student Profile Grade 9: 258 students (258 boys); Grade 10: 245 students (245 boys); Grade 11: 235 students (235 boys); Grade 12: 232 students (232 boys). 87% of students are Roman Catholic.

Faculty School total: 92. In upper school: 67 men, 25 women; 53 have advanced degrees.

Subjects Offered Algebra, American history, American history-AP, American literature, anatomy, architecture, art, art-AP, band, biology, biology-AP, business, business law, calculus, calculus-AP, career/college preparation, chemistry, chemistry-AP, chorus, community service, computer applications, computer programming, computer science, computer science-AP, drafting, driver education, ecology, economics, English, English literature, English-AP, ensembles, environmental science-AP, European history-AP, fine arts, foreign policy, French, French-AP, geometry, German-AP, government/civics, health, journalism, Latin, law, literature, marketing, mathematics, physical education, physics, physics-AP, pre-calculus, psychology, psychology-AP, religion, science, social sciences, social studies, Spanish, Spanish-AP, statistics, statistics-AP, television, trigonometry, U.S. government and politics-AP, video, Western literature, world affairs, world history, world literature.

Graduation Requirements Arts and fine arts (art, music, dance, drama), college planning, computer science, driver education, electives, English, foreign language, mathematics, physical education (includes health), religion (includes Bible studies and theology), science, social sciences, social studies (includes history). Community service is required.

Special Academic Programs Advanced Placement exam preparation; honors section; independent study; study at local college for college credit; domestic exchange program (with Ursuline Academy, Padua Academy); academic accommodation for the gifted; remedial reading and/or remedial writing; remedial math.

College Admission Counseling 261 students graduated in 2012; 258 went to college, including Penn State University Park; Saint Joseph's University; University of Delaware; Villanova University; Virginia Polytechnic Institute and State University. Other: 2 went to work, 1 entered military service. Mean SAT critical reading: 574, mean SAT math: 589, mean SAT writing: 558, mean combined SAT: 1721. 32% scored over 600 on SAT critical reading, 41% scored over 600 on SAT math, 27% scored over 600 on SAT writing.

Student Life Upper grades have specified standards of dress, student council. Discipline rests primarily with faculty. Attendance at religious services is required.

Tuition and Aid Day student tuition: $12,600. Tuition installment plan (Insured Tuition Payment Plan, monthly payment plans, semester payment plan, annual payment plan, monthly payment plan). Merit scholarship grants, need-based scholarship grants, paying campus jobs available. In 2012–13, 23% of upper-school students received aid; total upper-school merit-scholarship money awarded: $315,000. Total amount of financial aid awarded in 2012–13: $650,000.

Admissions Traditional secondary-level entrance grade is 9. Scholastic Testing Service High School Placement Test required. Deadline for receipt of application materials: November 30. Application fee required: $65.

Athletics Interscholastic: baseball, basketball, cross-country running, diving, football, golf, ice hockey, lacrosse, soccer, swimming and diving, tennis, track and field, volleyball, wrestling; intramural: basketball, bowling, flag football, Frisbee, lacrosse, roller hockey, rowing, skateboarding, tennis, ultimate Frisbee, weight lifting. 4 PE instructors, 58 coaches, 1 athletic trainer.

Computers Computers are regularly used in architecture, college planning, drafting, English, foreign language, mathematics, science, social studies, yearbook classes. Computer network features include on-campus library services, online commercial services, Internet access, wireless campus network, Internet filtering or blocking technology. Campus intranet and computer access in designated common areas are available to students. Students grades are available online.

Contact Mrs. Barbara Palena, Administrative Assistant to the Admissions Office. 302-654-2495 Ext. 148. Fax: 302-654-7767. E-mail: bpalena@salesianum.org. Website: www.salesianum.org

SALPOINTE CATHOLIC HIGH SCHOOL

1545 East Copper Street
Tucson, Arizona 85719-3199

Head of School: Mrs. Kay Sullivan

General Information Coeducational day college-preparatory, religious studies, Humanities, and STEM school, affiliated with Roman Catholic Church. Grades 9–12. Founded: 1950. Setting: urban. 40-acre campus. 10 buildings on campus. Approved or accredited by National Catholic Education Association, North Central Association of Colleges and Schools, Western Catholic Education Association, and Arizona Department of Education. Endowment: $3.9 million. Total enrollment: 1,041. Upper school average class size: 24. Upper school faculty-student ratio: 1:15. There are 180 required school days per year for Upper School students. Upper School students typically attend 5 days per week. The average school day consists of 6 hours and 50 minutes.

Upper School Student Profile Grade 9: 251 students (133 boys, 118 girls); Grade 10: 267 students (135 boys, 132 girls); Grade 11: 255 students (135 boys, 120 girls); Grade 12: 268 students (142 boys, 126 girls). 77% of students are Roman Catholic.

Faculty School total: 83. In upper school: 27 men, 49 women; 66 have advanced degrees.

Subjects Offered 3-dimensional art, 3-dimensional design, accounting, acting, advanced biology, advanced chemistry, advanced math, Advanced Placement courses, advanced studio art-AP, aerobics, algebra, American culture, American government, American history, American history-AP, American literature, American literature-AP, American studies, analysis and differential calculus, animation, art, art appreciation, art history, art history-AP, art-AP, arts, athletic training, athletics, band, Bible studies, biology, biology-AP, bookkeeping, British literature, British literature (honors), business, calculus, calculus-AP, career and personal planning, career and technology systems, career planning, career technology, career/college preparation, Catholic belief and practice, ceramics, chemistry, chemistry-AP, choir, choral music, classics, comparative religion, composition, computer animation, computer art, computer programming, computer science, computer skills, computer-aided design, computers, concert band, concert choir, constitutional history of U.S., consumer economics, creative writing, dance, desktop publishing, digital art, digital photography, discrete mathematics, drama, drama performance, drawing and design, earth science, economics, electives, electronic publishing, engineering, English, English literature, English literature and composition-AP, English literature-AP, environmental science, environmental science-AP, European history, film and literature, finance, fitness, French, French language-AP, French literature-AP, French-AP, general business, general math, geography, geometry, government, government and politics-AP, government/civics, history, Holocaust, honors algebra, honors English, honors geometry, honors U.S. history, humanities, instrumental music, jazz, jazz band, jazz ensemble, journalism, language arts, Latin, Latin-AP, law, leadership, leadership and service, learning lab, Life of Christ, literary magazine, macroeconomics-AP, marching band, marketing, music history, music theory, newspaper, non-Western literature, orchestra, painting, performing arts, personal fitness, philosophy, photo shop, photography, photojournalism, physical fitness, physics, physics-AP, play production, politics, pottery, pre-algebra, pre-calculus, probability and statistics, programming, psychology, rhetoric, SAT/ACT preparation, scripture, sculpture, Shakespeare, social justice, softball, space and physical sciences, Spanish, Spanish language-AP, Spanish literature, Spanish literature-AP, Spanish-AP, sports conditioning, sports medicine, statistics, statistics-AP, student government, student publications, studio art, studio art-AP, symphonic band, theater, theology, trigonometry, U.S. government and politics, U.S. history-AP, United States government-AP, visual and performing arts, visual arts, vocal music, voice ensemble, water color painting, weight fitness, weight training, weightlifting, world history, world history-AP, world literature, world religions, world studies, writing, writing workshop, yearbook.

Graduation Requirements Arts and fine arts (art, music, dance, drama), career and technology systems, English, exercise science, mathematics, modern languages, science, social studies (includes history), theology, Theology.

Special Academic Programs 18 Advanced Placement exams for which test preparation is offered; honors section; study at local college for college credit; remedial reading and/or remedial writing; remedial math; programs in English, mathematics, general development for dyslexic students.

College Admission Counseling 282 students graduated in 2013; 280 went to college, including Arizona State University; Northern Arizona University; Pima Community College; Texas Christian University; The University of Arizona; University of San Diego. Other: 1 went to work, 1 entered military service. Median SAT critical reading: 550, median SAT math: 540, median SAT writing: 520, median combined SAT: 1630, median composite ACT: 25. 30% scored over 600 on SAT critical reading, 29% scored over 600 on SAT math, 23% scored over 600 on SAT writing, 25% scored over 1800 on combined SAT, 35% scored over 26 on composite ACT.

Student Life Upper grades have specified standards of dress, student council, honor system. Discipline rests primarily with faculty. Attendance at religious services is required.

Summer Programs Remediation, enrichment, advancement, sports, computer instruction programs offered; session focuses on advancement, remediation, sports camps; held on campus; accepts boys and girls; open to students from other schools. 1,100 students usually enrolled. 2014 schedule: May 28 to July 31. Application deadline: May 25.

Tuition and Aid Day student tuition: $8200. Tuition installment plan (monthly payment plans, individually arranged payment plans). Merit scholarship grants, need-based scholarship grants, USS Education Loan Program available. In 2013–14, 47% of upper-school students received aid; total upper-school merit-scholarship money awarded: $52,000. Total amount of financial aid awarded in 2013–14: $1,678,295.

Admissions Traditional secondary-level entrance grade is 9. For fall 2013, 355 students applied for upper-level admission, 344 were accepted, 268 enrolled. High School Placement Test or TOEFL required. Deadline for receipt of application materials: none. Application fee required: $60. On-campus interview required.

Athletics Interscholastic: aerobics/dance (girls), baseball (b), basketball (b,g), cheering (g), cross-country running (b,g), dance team (g), diving (b,g), football (b), golf (b,g), independent competitive sports (b,g), lacrosse (b), physical fitness (b,g), physical training (b,g), soccer (b,g), softball (g), strength & conditioning (b,g), swimming and diving (b,g), tennis (b,g), track and field (b,g), volleyball (b,g), weight lifting (b,g), wrestling (b); intramural: aerobics (g); coed interscholastic: strength & conditioning. 3 PE instructors, 110 coaches, 2 athletic trainers.

Computers Computers are regularly used in all academic classes. Computer network features include on-campus library services, Internet access, wireless campus network, Internet filtering or blocking technology. Campus intranet, student e-mail accounts, and computer access in designated common areas are available to students. Students grades are available online. The school has a published electronic and media policy.

Contact Mrs. Meg Gossmann, Admissions Coordinator. 520-547-4460. Fax: 520-327-8477. E-mail: mgossmann@salpointe.org. Website: www.salpointe.org

SANDIA PREPARATORY SCHOOL

532 Osuna Road NE
Albuquerque, New Mexico 87113

Head of School: B. Stephen Albert

General Information Coeducational day college-preparatory and arts school. Grades 6–12. Founded: 1966. Setting: suburban. 30-acre campus. 13 buildings on campus. Approved or accredited by Independent Schools Association of the Southwest and New Mexico Department of Education. Member of National Association of Independent Schools. Endowment: $506 million. Total enrollment: 612. Upper school average class size: 15. Upper school faculty-student ratio: 1:7. There are 180 required school days per year for Upper School students. Upper School students typically attend 5 days per week. The average school day consists of 7 hours and 30 minutes.

Upper School Student Profile Grade 9: 92 students (51 boys, 41 girls); Grade 10: 84 students (49 boys, 35 girls); Grade 11: 89 students (45 boys, 44 girls); Grade 12: 83 students (40 boys, 43 girls).

Faculty School total: 80. In upper school: 37 men, 25 women; 47 have advanced degrees.

Subjects Offered 20th century American writers, 3-dimensional art, adolescent issues, advanced biology, advanced chemistry, advanced computer applications, advanced math, algebra, American history, American literature, American politics in film, anatomy and physiology, ancient world history, art, astronomy, band, biology, calculus, ceramics, chemistry, chorus, computer programming, computer science, creative writing, digital photography, drawing, earth science, ecology, environmental systems, economics, English, English literature, environmental science, film, film history, filmmaking, fine arts, foreign language, French, French as a second language, geology, geometry, global issues, grammar, guitar, healthful living, history, jazz band, journalism, language arts, library skills, life science, mathematics, media communications, modern world history, music, newspaper, orchestra, outdoor education, painting, performing arts, personal development, philosophy, photography, physical education, physics, pottery, pre-algebra, pre-calculus, science, Shakespearean histories, social studies, Spanish, state history, statistics, technical theater, technology, theater, trigonometry, women in world history, world history, world literature, World War I, World War II, yearbook.

Graduation Requirements Arts and fine arts (art, music, dance, drama), electives, English, foreign language, mathematics, physical education (includes health), science, social studies (includes history), completion of a one-month volunteer Senior Experience in a professional, academic, or volunteer area of interest during May of senior year.

Special Academic Programs Independent study; study at local college for college credit; study abroad; academic accommodation for the gifted, the musically talented, and the artistically talented.

College Admission Counseling 91 students graduated in 2013; all went to college, including Carnegie Mellon University; Duke University; Knox College; Lake Forest Academy; Trinity University; University of New Mexico. Median SAT critical reading: 660, median SAT math: 610, median composite ACT: 27. 65% scored over 600 on SAT critical reading, 59% scored over 600 on SAT math, 60% scored over 26 on composite ACT.

Student Life Upper grades have specified standards of dress, student council. Discipline rests primarily with faculty.

Summer Programs Enrichment, sports, art/fine arts, computer instruction programs offered; session focuses on summer enrichment; held on campus; accepts boys and girls; open to students from other schools. 350 students usually enrolled. 2014 schedule: June 2 to July 11. Application deadline: May 1.

Tuition and Aid Day student tuition: $19,420. Tuition installment plan (FACTS Tuition Payment Plan, monthly payment plans). Need-based scholarship grants available. In 2013–14, 20% of upper-school students received aid. Total amount of financial aid awarded in 2013–14: $950,000.

Admissions Traditional secondary-level entrance grade is 9. For fall 2013, 54 students applied for upper-level admission, 24 were accepted, 19 enrolled. Admissions testing required. Deadline for receipt of application materials: February 8. Application fee required: $55. On-campus interview required.

Athletics Interscholastic: baseball (boys), basketball (b,g), cross-country running (b,g), dance squad (g), golf (b,g), soccer (b,g), softball (g), swimming and diving (b,g), table tennis (b), tennis (b,g), track and field (b,g), volleyball (g); intramural: basketball (b,g), self defense (g); coed interscholastic: aquatics, bowling, dance, kickball; coed intramural: backpacking, bocce, canoeing/kayaking, climbing, Frisbee, hiking/backpacking, kayaking, lacrosse, modern dance, nordic skiing, ocean paddling, outdoor adventure, outdoor education, outdoor skills, rock climbing, yoga. 5 PE instructors, 40 coaches, 1 athletic trainer.

Computers Computers are regularly used in art, college planning, graphic arts, history, information technology, journalism, library skills, literacy, mathematics, multimedia, newspaper, photography, publications, science, study skills, technology, typing, word processing, yearbook classes. Computer network features include on-campus library services, online commercial services, Internet access, Internet filtering or blocking technology, individual student accounts, productivity software. Student e-mail accounts are available to students. Students grades are available online. The school has a published electronic and media policy.

Contact Laura Fitzpatrick, Director of Admission. 505-338-3000. Fax: 505-338-3099. E-mail: lfitzpatrick@sandiaprep.org. Website: www.sandiaprep.org

SAN DIEGO JEWISH ACADEMY

11860 Carmel Creek Road
San Diego, California 92130

Head of School: Chaim Heller

General Information Coeducational day college-preparatory, arts, and religious studies school, affiliated with Jewish faith. Grades K–12. Founded: 1979. Setting: suburban. 56-acre campus. 3 buildings on campus. Approved or accredited by National Independent Private Schools Association, Western Association of Schools and Colleges, and California Department of Education. Languages of instruction: English and Hebrew. Endowment: $2.5 million. Total enrollment: 485. Upper school average class size: 20. Upper school faculty-student ratio: 1:18. Upper School students typically attend 5 days per week. The average school day consists of 7 hours and 15 minutes.

Upper School Student Profile Grade 6: 39 students (14 boys, 25 girls); Grade 7: 55 students (27 boys, 28 girls); Grade 8: 39 students (14 boys, 25 girls); Grade 9: 46 students (24 boys, 22 girls); Grade 10: 46 students (28 boys, 18 girls); Grade 11: 51 students (24 boys, 27 girls); Grade 12: 38 students (16 boys, 22 girls). 99% of students are Jewish.

Faculty School total: 35. In upper school: 12 men, 19 women; 17 have advanced degrees.

Subjects Offered 20th century history, 20th century world history, advanced biology, advanced chemistry, Advanced Placement courses, algebra, American government, American history, American history-AP, American literature, American literature-AP, analytic geometry, art, art history-AP, athletics, baseball, basketball, Bible, Bible studies, biology, biology-AP, British history, British literature, British literature (honors), calculus-AP, chemistry, college admission preparation, college counseling, community service, competitive science projects, composition-AP, conceptual physics, creative drama, digital photography, dramatic arts, economics, economics and history, electives, English, English composition, English language and composition-AP, English language-AP, English literature, English literature and composition-AP, English literature-AP, English/composition-AP, European history, European history-AP, European literature, fitness, foreign language, golf, government,

government/civics, guitar, Hebrew, Hebrew scripture, history, Holocaust, Holocaust studies, honors algebra, honors English, honors geometry, honors world history, humanities, independent study, instrumental music, instruments, Jewish history, Jewish studies, Judaic studies, languages, literature and composition-AP, literature-AP, music, musical theater dance, photography, physical education, physics, physics-AP, prayer/spirituality, pre-algebra, pre-calculus, pre-college orientation, psychology, Rabbinic literature, religious education, religious studies, social sciences, Spanish, standard curriculum, statistics-AP, student government, theater, trigonometry, U.S. government, U.S. history, U.S. history-AP, U.S. literature, video film production, visual arts, volleyball, weight fitness, weightlifting, world history, world literature, yearbook.

Special Academic Programs 19 Advanced Placement exams for which test preparation is offered; honors section; independent study.

College Admission Counseling Colleges students went to include Chapman University; San Diego State University; The George Washington University; The University of Arizona; University of Redlands. Other: 1 had other specific plans. Mean SAT critical reading: 592, mean SAT math: 593, mean SAT writing: 606, mean composite ACT: 26.

Student Life Upper grades have specified standards of dress, student council, honor system. Discipline rests primarily with faculty. Attendance at religious services is required.

Summer Programs Sports, rigorous outdoor training programs offered; session focuses on complete athletic development; held on campus; accepts boys and girls; open to students from other schools. 50 students usually enrolled. 2014 schedule: June 14 to August 20. Application deadline: June 1.

Tuition and Aid Day student tuition: $21,995–$22,395. Tuition installment plan (FACTS Tuition Payment Plan, monthly payment plans). Tuition reduction for siblings, merit scholarship grants, need-based scholarship grants available. In 2013–14, 20% of upper-school students received aid; total upper-school merit-scholarship money awarded: $50,000. Total amount of financial aid awarded in 2013–14: $553,000.

Admissions Traditional secondary-level entrance grade is 9. For fall 2013, 50 students applied for upper-level admission, 40 were accepted, 40 enrolled. Deadline for receipt of application materials: none. Application fee required: $100. On-campus interview required.

Athletics Interscholastic: aquatics (boys, girls), baseball (b), basketball (b,g), cross-country running (b,g), football (b), golf (b), independent competitive sports (b,g), soccer (b,g), softball (g), swimming and diving (b,g), tennis (b,g), volleyball (g), winter soccer (b,g); coed interscholastic: flag football, track and field; coed intramural: aerobics/dance, baseball, basketball, dance, fencing, fitness, flag football, football, martial arts, physical fitness, physical training, self defense, soccer, softball, strength & conditioning, tennis, track and field, volleyball, weight lifting, weight training, winter soccer. 4 PE instructors, 50 coaches, 2 athletic trainers.

Computers Computers are regularly used in college planning, economics, English, foreign language, graphic design, history, humanities, mathematics, newspaper, photography, psychology, religious studies, science, social studies, video film production, writing, yearbook classes. Computer network features include on-campus library services, online commercial services, Internet access, Internet filtering or blocking technology. Student e-mail accounts are available to students. Students grades are available online.

Contact Leslie Cohen Kastner, Admissions Director. 858-704-3716. Fax: 858-704-3850. E-mail: lkastner@sdja.com. Website: www.sdja.com

SAN DOMENICO SCHOOL

1500 Butterfield Road
San Anselmo, California 94960

Head of School: Ms. Cecily Stock

General Information Girls' boarding and coeducational day college-preparatory, arts, religious studies, music, and theater arts, dance school, affiliated with Roman Catholic Church. Boarding girls grades 9–12, day boys grades PK–8, day girls grades PK–12. Founded: 1850. Setting: suburban. Nearest major city is San Francisco. Students are housed in single-sex dormitories. 515-acre campus. 4 buildings on campus. Approved or accredited by California Association of Independent Schools, Western Association of Schools and Colleges, and Western Catholic Education Association. Member of National Association of Independent Schools. Endowment: $9 million. Total enrollment: 598. Upper school average class size: 12. Upper school faculty-student ratio: 1:5. There are 180 required school days per year for Upper School students. Upper School students typically attend 5 days per week. The average school day consists of 7 hours.

Upper School Student Profile Grade 9: 51 students (51 girls); Grade 10: 42 students (42 girls); Grade 11: 47 students (47 girls); Grade 12: 30 students (30 girls). 56% of students are boarding students. 59% are state residents. 2 states are represented in upper school student body. 41% are international students. International students from China, Hong Kong, Japan, Mexico, Republic of Korea, and Taiwan. 25% of students are Roman Catholic.

Faculty School total: 35. In upper school: 7 men, 28 women; 17 have advanced degrees; 7 reside on campus.

Subjects Offered Acting, advanced studio art-AP, algebra, American history, American literature, art, art history, biology, biology-AP, calculus, calculus-AP, ceramics, chemistry, chemistry-AP, community service, drama, English, English language and composition-AP, English literature, English literature-AP, environmental science, environmental science-AP, ESL, ethics, European history, expository writing, fine arts, geometry, government/civics, grammar, history, Mandarin, mathematics, modern world history, music, music composition, music theater, music theory, music theory-AP, musical productions, musicianship, photography, physical education, physics, physics-AP, psychology-AP, religion, science, social studies, sociology, Spanish, Spanish language-AP, statistics-AP, studio art-AP, theater, theology, trigonometry, U.S. history-AP, world history, world literature.

Graduation Requirements Arts and fine arts (art, music, dance, drama), English, foreign language, health, mathematics, physical education (includes health), religion (includes Bible studies and theology), science, social studies (includes history). Community service is required.

Special Academic Programs Advanced Placement exam preparation; honors section; independent study; academic accommodation for the musically talented; ESL (18 students enrolled).

College Admission Counseling 37 students graduated in 2013; all went to college, including California Polytechnic State University, San Luis Obispo; Drexel University; New York University; University of California, Berkeley; University of California, San Diego; University of San Diego. Mean SAT critical reading: 584, mean SAT math: 606, mean SAT writing: 592, mean combined SAT: 1782, mean composite ACT: 29.

Student Life Upper grades have specified standards of dress, student council, honor system. Discipline rests primarily with faculty.

Tuition and Aid Day student tuition: $34,700; 5-day tuition and room/board: $51,000; 7-day tuition and room/board: $51,006. Tuition installment plan (Insured Tuition Payment Plan, monthly payment plans). Need-based scholarship grants available. In 2013–14, 46% of upper-school students received aid. Total amount of financial aid awarded in 2013–14: $2,000,000.

Admissions Traditional secondary-level entrance grade is 9. For fall 2013, 174 students applied for upper-level admission, 113 were accepted, 62 enrolled. High School Placement Test, ISEE or SSAT required. Deadline for receipt of application materials: January 16. Application fee required: $100. Interview required.

Athletics Interscholastic: badminton, basketball, cross-country running, equestrian sports, horseback riding, soccer, swimming and diving, tennis, volleyball; intramural: dance, golf, modern dance. 1 PE instructor, 5 coaches.

Computers Computers are regularly used in English, mathematics, science, social studies, yearbook classes. Computer network features include on-campus library services, online commercial services, Internet access, wireless campus network, Internet filtering or blocking technology. Student e-mail accounts are available to students. Students grades are available online. The school has a published electronic and media policy.

Contact Ms. Jennifer Durante, Interim Director, High School Admissions. 415-258-1905. Fax: 415-258-1906. E-mail: admissions@sandomenico.org. Website: www.sandomenico.org/

SANDY SPRING FRIENDS SCHOOL

16923 Norwood Road
Sandy Spring, Maryland 20860

Head of School: Thomas R. Gibian

General Information Coeducational boarding and day college-preparatory, arts, and ESL school, affiliated with Society of Friends. Boarding grades 9–12, day grades PK–12. Founded: 1961. Setting: suburban. Nearest major city is Washington, DC. Students are housed in single-sex by floor dormitories. 140-acre campus. 15 buildings on campus. Approved or accredited by Association of Independent Maryland Schools, Association of Independent Schools of Greater Washington, Friends Council on Education, The Association of Boarding Schools, and Maryland Department of Education. Member of National Association of Independent Schools and Secondary School Admission Test Board. Endowment: $1.1 million. Total enrollment: 572. Upper school average class size: 14. Upper school faculty-student ratio: 1:8. There are 171 required school days per year for Upper School students. Upper School students typically attend 5 days per week. The average school day consists of 7 hours and 30 minutes.

Upper School Student Profile Grade 9: 57 students (19 boys, 38 girls); Grade 10: 59 students (30 boys, 29 girls); Grade 11: 75 students (33 boys, 42 girls); Grade 12: 72 students (47 boys, 25 girls). 31% of students are boarding students. 71% are state residents. 6 states are represented in upper school student body. 24% are international students. International students from China, Jamaica, Rwanda, Thailand, Turkey, and Viet Nam; 2 other countries represented in student body. 11% of students are members of Society of Friends.

Faculty School total: 68. In upper school: 12 men, 20 women; 22 have advanced degrees; 6 reside on campus.

Subjects Offered Algebra, American history, American literature, art, biology, British literature-AP, calculus, calculus-AP, ceramics, chemistry, chemistry-AP, choral music, creative writing, cultural geography, dance, dance performance, desktop publishing, drama, drawing, English, English as a foreign language, English literature and composition-AP, English literature-AP, environmental science-AP, ESL, ESL, French, French language-AP, geology, geometry, grammar, history, mathematics, music, music theory-AP, Native American history, painting, photography, physical

education, physics, poetry, Quakerism and ethics, Russian literature, science, Spanish, Spanish language-AP, statistics-AP, trigonometry, U.S. history-AP, weaving, Western civilization, world literature.

Graduation Requirements Art, English, foreign language, history, mathematics, physical education (includes health), religion (includes Bible studies and theology), science. Community service is required.

Special Academic Programs 15 Advanced Placement exams for which test preparation is offered; honors section; independent study; academic accommodation for the gifted, the musically talented, and the artistically talented; ESL (25 students enrolled).

College Admission Counseling 72 students graduated in 2013; 70 went to college, including McDaniel College; Penn State University Park; Purdue University; St. Mary's College of Maryland; Syracuse University; Washington College. Other: 1 entered a postgraduate year, 1 had other specific plans. Median SAT critical reading: 580, median SAT math: 590, median SAT writing: 580, median combined SAT: 1750, median composite ACT: 24. 23% scored over 600 on SAT critical reading, 20% scored over 600 on SAT math, 19% scored over 600 on SAT writing, 23% scored over 1800 on combined SAT, 4% scored over 26 on composite ACT.

Student Life Upper grades have specified standards of dress, student council, honor system. Discipline rests equally with students and faculty. Attendance at religious services is required.

Summer Programs Enrichment, ESL, sports, art/fine arts programs offered; session focuses on recreational and enrichment; held on campus; accepts boys and girls; open to students from other schools. 1,200 students usually enrolled. 2014 schedule: June 21 to August 21. Application deadline: May 1.

Tuition and Aid Day student tuition: $29,200; 5-day tuition and room/board: $43,000; 7-day tuition and room/board: $53,800. Tuition installment plan (FACTS Tuition Payment Plan). Need-based scholarship grants available. In 2013–14, 31% of upper-school students received aid. Total amount of financial aid awarded in 2013–14: $3,035,000.

Admissions Traditional secondary-level entrance grade is 9. For fall 2013, 198 students applied for upper-level admission, 106 were accepted, 57 enrolled. PSAT, SSAT or TOEFL or SLEP required. Deadline for receipt of application materials: January 15. Application fee required: $75. Interview required.

Athletics Interscholastic: baseball (boys), basketball (b,g), cross-country running (b,g), ice hockey (b), lacrosse (b,g), soccer (b,g), softball (g), tennis (b,g), volleyball (g); coed interscholastic: cooperative games, golf, kickball, modern dance, running, track and field; coed intramural: basketball, cooperative games, dance, Frisbee, hiking/backpacking, jogging, outdoor activities, outdoor adventure, outdoor education, outdoor recreation, outdoor skills, outdoors, physical fitness, physical training, rappelling, rock climbing, ropes courses, running, skiing (downhill), snowboarding, strength & conditioning, table tennis, track and field, ultimate Frisbee, walking, wall climbing, weight lifting, weight training, wilderness, wilderness survival, wrestling, yoga. 5 PE instructors, 3 coaches, 1 athletic trainer.

Computers Computers are regularly used in all academic classes. Computer network features include on-campus library services, Internet access, wireless campus network. Student e-mail accounts and computer access in designated common areas are available to students. Students grades are available online.

Contact Yasmin McGinnis, Director of Enrollment Management. 301-774-7455 Ext. 182. Fax: 301-924-1115. E-mail: yasmin.mcginnis@ssfs.org. Website: www.ssfs.org

SAN MARCOS BAPTIST ACADEMY

2801 Ranch Road Twelve
San Marcos, Texas 78666-9406

Head of School: Dr. John H. Garrison

General Information Coeducational boarding and day college-preparatory, arts, business, religious studies, technology, learning skills, and ESL school, affiliated with Baptist General Conference. Grades 7–12. Founded: 1907. Setting: small town. Nearest major city is Austin. Students are housed in single-sex dormitories. 220-acre campus. 9 buildings on campus. Approved or accredited by Accreditation Commission of the Texas Association of Baptist Schools, Southern Association of Colleges and Schools, and Texas Department of Education. Member of National Association of Independent Schools. Endowment: $5.8 million. Total enrollment: 286. Upper school average class size: 12. Upper school faculty-student ratio: 1:7. There are 180 required school days per year for Upper School students. Upper School students typically attend 5 days per week. The average school day consists of 7 hours and 40 minutes.

Upper School Student Profile Grade 9: 39 students (28 boys, 11 girls); Grade 10: 65 students (47 boys, 18 girls); Grade 11: 71 students (42 boys, 29 girls); Grade 12: 62 students (37 boys, 25 girls). 56% of students are boarding students. 62% are state residents. 5 states are represented in upper school student body. 35% are international students. International students from China, Japan, Mexico, Nigeria, Republic of Korea, and Viet Nam; 9 other countries represented in student body. 14% of students are Baptist General Conference.

Faculty School total: 39. In upper school: 18 men, 21 women; 23 have advanced degrees; 4 reside on campus.

Subjects Offered Advanced math, Advanced Placement courses, algebra, American government, American history, American literature, analysis and differential calculus, analytic geometry, anatomy and physiology, ancient world history, applied arts, applied music, art, athletic training, athletics, band, baseball, Basic programming, basketball, Bible, Bible studies, biology, biology-AP, British literature, British literature (honors), British literature-AP, business applications, calculus, calculus-AP, career/college preparation, character education, cheerleading, chemistry, choir, Christian scripture, Christian testament, Christianity, civics, civics/free enterprise, clayworking, college admission preparation, college counseling, college planning, communication skills, community service, comparative religion, computer applications, computer information systems, computer programming, computer science, computers, concert band, concert choir, contemporary art, critical thinking, desktop publishing, digital photography, drama, drama performance, drama workshop, dramatic arts, drawing, driver education, earth and space science, earth science, economics, economics and history, English, English as a foreign language, English composition, English literature, English literature and composition-AP, English literature-AP, English-AP, ESL, family and consumer science, fine arts, foreign language, French, geography, geometry, golf, government/civics, grammar, guidance, health, health education, history, history of the Americas, honors algebra, honors geometry, honors U.S. history, honors world history, HTML design, human anatomy, human biology, instrumental music, instruments, intro to computers, introduction to theater, jazz band, journalism, JROTC, JROTC or LEAD (Leadership Education and Development), keyboarding, language and composition, language arts, leadership, leadership and service, leadership education training, learning strategies, library, library skills, library studies, Life of Christ, life skills, literature, literature and composition-AP, literature-AP, logic, mathematical modeling, mathematics, mathematics-AP, military science, music, music appreciation, music performance, music theory, musical productions, musical theater, musicianship, New Testament, news writing, newspaper, novels, painting, participation in sports, personal and social education, personal fitness, personal growth, photography, photojournalism, physical education, physical fitness, physical science, physics, piano, play production, pottery, prayer/spirituality, pre-calculus, psychology, public speaking, reading, reading/study skills, religion, religious education, remedial study skills, research skills, SAT preparation, SAT/ACT preparation, science, social skills, social studies, society and culture, sociology, softball, Spanish, speech, speech and debate, speech communications, sports, sports conditioning, sports performance development, sports team management, state government, state history, stock market, student government, student publications, study skills, swimming, tennis, Texas history, theater, theater arts, theater production, theology, TOEFL preparation, track and field, U.S. government, U.S. government and politics, U.S. history, U.S. literature, visual arts, vocal ensemble, vocal jazz, vocal music, voice, voice and diction, voice ensemble, volleyball, Web site design, weight training, weightlifting, Western civilization, world civilizations, world cultures, world geography, world history, world issues, world literature, world religions, world religions, world studies, world wide web design, yearbook.

Graduation Requirements Arts and fine arts (art, music, dance, drama), computer science, economics, electives, English, foreign language, JROTC or LEAD (Leadership Education and Development), mathematics, physical education (includes health), religion (includes Bible studies and theology), science, social studies (includes history), speech.

Special Academic Programs 7 Advanced Placement exams for which test preparation is offered; honors section; accelerated programs; independent study; study at local college for college credit; academic accommodation for the gifted, the musically talented, and the artistically talented; remedial reading and/or remedial writing; remedial math; programs in English, mathematics, general development for dyslexic students; special instructional classes for deaf students, students with Section 504 learning disabilities, Attention Deficit Disorder, and dyslexia; ESL (30 students enrolled).

College Admission Counseling 61 students graduated in 2013; 58 went to college, including Michigan State University; Texas State University–San Marcos; Texas Tech University; The University of Texas at Austin; University of Illinois at Urbana–Champaign; University of Notre Dame. Other: 1 entered military service, 2 had other specific plans. Median combined SAT: 450, median composite ACT: 19. Mean SAT critical reading: 459, mean SAT math: 525, mean SAT writing: 460. 16.4% scored over 600 on SAT critical reading, 32.8% scored over 600 on SAT math, 14.9% scored over 600 on SAT writing, 14.9% scored over 1800 on combined SAT, 7% scored over 26 on composite ACT.

Student Life Upper grades have uniform requirement, student council, honor system. Discipline rests primarily with faculty. Attendance at religious services is required.

Tuition and Aid Day student tuition: $9260; 7-day tuition and room/board: $29,650. Guaranteed tuition plan. Tuition installment plan (monthly payment plans, individually arranged payment plans). Need-based scholarship grants available. In 2013–14, 85% of upper-school students received aid. Total amount of financial aid awarded in 2013–14: $439,180.

Admissions Traditional secondary-level entrance grade is 9. For fall 2013, 130 students applied for upper-level admission, 109 were accepted, 85 enrolled. Deadline for receipt of application materials: none. Application fee required: $100. Interview required.

Athletics Interscholastic: baseball (boys), basketball (b,g), cross-country running (b,g), football (b), golf (b,g), JROTC drill (b,g), power lifting (b,g), softball (g), swimming and diving (b,g), tennis (b,g), track and field (b,g), volleyball (g), weight lifting (b,g); coed interscholastic: equestrian sports, flag football, marksmanship, soccer, winter soccer; coed intramural: cheering, Frisbee, horseback riding, ropes

courses, table tennis, weight lifting, weight training. 3 PE instructors, 20 coaches, 1 athletic trainer.

Computers Computers are regularly used in all classes. Computer network features include on-campus library services, online commercial services, Internet access, wireless campus network, Internet filtering or blocking technology, 1:1 computer device program for high school students. Student e-mail accounts and computer access in designated common areas are available to students. Students grades are available online. The school has a published electronic and media policy.

Contact Mrs. Shelley L Henry, Director of Admissions and Communications. 800-428-5120. Fax: 512-753-8031. E-mail: admissions@smba.org. Website: www.smabears.org

SANTA CATALINA SCHOOL

1500 Mark Thomas Drive
Monterey, California 93940-5291

Head of School: Sr. Claire Barone

General Information Girls' boarding and day college-preparatory, liberal arts, and marine biology school, affiliated with Roman Catholic Church. Grades 9–12. Founded: 1950. Setting: small town. Nearest major city is San Francisco. Students are housed in single-sex dormitories. 36-acre campus. 21 buildings on campus. Approved or accredited by National Catholic Education Association, The Association of Boarding Schools, The College Board, Western Association of Schools and Colleges, and California Department of Education. Member of National Association of Independent Schools and Secondary School Admission Test Board. Endowment: $24 million. Total enrollment: 259. Upper school average class size: 12. Upper school faculty-student ratio: 1:8. There are 172 required school days per year for Upper School students. Upper School students typically attend 5 days per week. The average school day consists of 5 hours and 25 minutes.

Upper School Student Profile Grade 9: 62 students (62 girls); Grade 10: 61 students (61 girls); Grade 11: 55 students (55 girls); Grade 12: 80 students (80 girls). 45% of students are boarding students. 77% are state residents. 11 states are represented in upper school student body. 17% are international students. International students from Canada, China, Democratic People's Republic of Korea, Hong Kong, Mexico, and Singapore; 9 other countries represented in student body. 49% of students are Roman Catholic.

Faculty School total: 35. In upper school: 17 men, 18 women; 27 have advanced degrees; 13 reside on campus.

Subjects Offered Algebra, American literature, art, art history-AP, ballet, biology, biology-AP, calculus, calculus-AP, ceramics, chemistry, chemistry-AP, Chinese, choir, college counseling, conceptual physics, dance, digital art, drama, drama performance, English, English language-AP, English literature, English literature-AP, ensembles, environmental science-AP, European history, fine arts, French, French language-AP, geometry, health, honors algebra, honors English, honors geometry, jazz dance, Latin, Latin-AP, Mandarin, marine science, media arts, music, music performance, peace and justice, philosophy, photography, physical education, physics, physics-AP, pre-calculus, Spanish, Spanish language-AP, Spanish literature-AP, studio art, studio art-AP, theater, theology, trigonometry, U.S. history, U.S. history-AP, women spirituality and faith, world history, world history-AP, world issues, world literature, world religions.

Graduation Requirements Arts, English, foreign language, history, lab science, mathematics, physical education (includes health), religious studies.

Special Academic Programs 16 Advanced Placement exams for which test preparation is offered; honors section; academic accommodation for the gifted, the musically talented, and the artistically talented.

College Admission Counseling 59 students graduated in 2013; all went to college, including Boston University; Duke University; New York University; University of California, Davis; University of California, Santa Barbara; University of Southern California. Mean SAT critical reading: 607, mean SAT math: 611, mean SAT writing: 616.

Student Life Upper grades have uniform requirement, student council. Discipline rests equally with students and faculty. Attendance at religious services is required.

Summer Programs Enrichment, sports, art/fine arts programs offered; session focuses on recreation and enrichment fun; held on campus; accepts girls; open to students from other schools. 215 students usually enrolled. 2014 schedule: June 22 to July 26. Application deadline: none.

Tuition and Aid Day student tuition: $30,800; 7-day tuition and room/board: $47,400. Tuition installment plan (monthly payment plans, Tuition Management Systems). Merit scholarship grants, need-based scholarship grants available. In 2013–14, 40% of upper-school students received aid. Total amount of financial aid awarded in 2013–14: $2,100,000.

Admissions Traditional secondary-level entrance grade is 9. For fall 2013, 206 students applied for upper-level admission, 111 were accepted, 71 enrolled. ISEE, SSAT or TOEFL required. Deadline for receipt of application materials: February 1. Application fee required: $75. Interview required.

Athletics Interscholastic: basketball, cross-country running, diving, equestrian sports, field hockey, golf, lacrosse, soccer, softball, swimming and diving, tennis, track and field, volleyball, water polo; intramural: ballet, canoeing/kayaking, dance, fencing, fitness, horseback riding, kayaking, modern dance, outdoor activities, physical fitness, rafting, rock climbing, self defense, strength & conditioning, surfing, weight training, yoga. 1 PE instructor, 26 coaches.

Computers Computers are regularly used in English, foreign language, mathematics, media arts, science, yearbook classes. Computer network features include on-campus library services, Internet access, wireless campus network, Internet filtering or blocking technology, iPad initiative for freshman and sophomore classes. Campus intranet, student e-mail accounts, and computer access in designated common areas are available to students. The school has a published electronic and media policy.

Contact Mrs. Jamie Buffington Browne '85, Director of Admission. 831-655-9356. Fax: 831-655-7535. E-mail: jamie.brown@santacatalina.org. Website: www.santacatalina.org

SANTA FE PREPARATORY SCHOOL

1101 Camino de la Cruz Blanca
Santa Fe, New Mexico 87505

Head of School: Mr. James W. Leonard

General Information Coeducational day college-preparatory, arts, and community service school. Grades 7–12. Founded: 1961. Setting: suburban. 13-acre campus. 4 buildings on campus. Approved or accredited by Independent Schools Association of the Southwest and New Mexico Department of Education. Member of National Association of Independent Schools. Endowment: $4.3 million. Total enrollment: 303. Upper school average class size: 13. Upper school faculty-student ratio: 1:16. There are 171 required school days per year for Upper School students. Upper School students typically attend 5 days per week. The average school day consists of 6 hours and 23 minutes.

Upper School Student Profile Grade 9: 49 students (30 boys, 19 girls); Grade 10: 74 students (31 boys, 43 girls); Grade 11: 39 students (24 boys, 15 girls); Grade 12: 42 students (16 boys, 26 girls).

Faculty School total: 48. In upper school: 19 men, 20 women; 27 have advanced degrees.

Subjects Offered Acting, advanced chemistry, advanced computer applications, advanced math, algebra, American Civil War, American culture, American democracy, American government, American history, American history-AP, American literature, analytic geometry, art, art appreciation, art history, art history-AP, arts, athletics, basketball, biology, calculus, calculus-AP, ceramics, chemistry, chemistry-AP, chorus, clayworking, college counseling, community service, computer applications, computer graphics, computer literacy, computer programming, computer science, conceptual physics, creative writing, drama, drama performance, dramatic arts, driver education, earth science, English, English literature, European history, fine arts, French, geography, geometry, health, history, humanities, journalism, keyboarding, Latin, mathematics, music, photography, physical education, physics, psychology, science, social studies, Spanish, theater, trigonometry, world history, world literature, writing.

Graduation Requirements Arts and fine arts (art, music, dance, drama), computer science, English, foreign language, history, humanities, mathematics, music appreciation, physical education (includes health), science, social studies (includes history), senior seminar program. Community service is required.

Special Academic Programs 5 Advanced Placement exams for which test preparation is offered; honors section; independent study; study at local college for college credit; study abroad.

College Admission Counseling 52 students graduated in 2012; all went to college, including Middlebury College; University of Denver; University of New Mexico; University of Redlands; Whitman College; Williams College. Median SAT critical reading: 620, median SAT math: 610, median SAT writing: 600, median combined SAT: 1850, median composite ACT: 28. 61% scored over 600 on SAT critical reading, 61% scored over 600 on SAT math, 54% scored over 600 on SAT writing, 61% scored over 1800 on combined SAT, 58% scored over 26 on composite ACT.

Student Life Upper grades have specified standards of dress, student council. Discipline rests equally with students and faculty.

Tuition and Aid Day student tuition: $18,906. Tuition installment plan (individually arranged payment plans, Tuition Management Systems Plan). Need-based scholarship grants, tuition remission for faculty available. In 2012–13, 30% of upper-school students received aid.

Admissions Traditional secondary-level entrance grade is 9. For fall 2012, 22 students applied for upper-level admission, 22 were accepted, 22 enrolled. Mathematics proficiency exam required. Deadline for receipt of application materials: none. Application fee required: $55. On-campus interview required.

Athletics Interscholastic: baseball (boys), basketball (b,g), cross-country running (b,g), diving (b,g), lacrosse (b,g), soccer (b,g), softball (g), swimming and diving (b,g), tennis (b,g), track and field (b,g), volleyball (g); intramural: basketball (b,g), cross-country running (b,g), football (b,g), soccer (b,g), tennis (b,g), track and field (b,g), volleyball (g); coed interscholastic: aerobics/dance, dance team; coed intramural: basketball, bowling, skiing (downhill), swimming and diving. 1 PE instructor, 16 coaches, 1 athletic trainer.

Computers Computers are regularly used in current events, English, French, freshman foundations, geography, graphic arts, history, humanities, journalism, library, literary magazine, mathematics, newspaper, photography, photojournalism, science, social sciences, writing, yearbook classes. Computer network features include on-campus library services, Internet access, wireless campus network, Internet filtering or

blocking technology. Campus intranet, student e-mail accounts, and computer access in designated common areas are available to students. The school has a published electronic and media policy.

Contact Michael Multari, Director of Admissions. 505-982-1829 Ext. 1212. Fax: 505-982-2897. E-mail: mmultari@sfprep.org. Website: www.santafeprep.org

SBEC (SOUTHERN BAPTIST EDUCATIONAL CENTER)

7400 Getwell Road
Southaven, Mississippi 38672

Head of School: Mr. David H. Manley

General Information Coeducational day college-preparatory, arts, religious studies, and technology school, affiliated with Christian faith, Baptist Church. Grades PK–12. Founded: 1972. Setting: suburban. Nearest major city is Memphis, TN. 61-acre campus. 2 buildings on campus. Approved or accredited by Southern Association of Independent Schools. Total enrollment: 1,077. Upper school average class size: 21. Upper school faculty-student ratio: 1:13. There are 177 required school days per year for Upper School students. Upper School students typically attend 5 days per week. The average school day consists of 7 hours and 5 minutes.

Upper School Student Profile Grade 7: 79 students (41 boys, 38 girls); Grade 8: 69 students (39 boys, 30 girls); Grade 9: 84 students (42 boys, 42 girls); Grade 10: 74 students (35 boys, 39 girls); Grade 11: 81 students (38 boys, 43 girls); Grade 12: 87 students (40 boys, 47 girls). 90% of students are Christian, Baptist.

Faculty School total: 99. In upper school: 11 men, 30 women; 16 have advanced degrees.

Subjects Offered Advanced math, algebra, American government, American history, anatomy and physiology, art, arts, band, Bible, Bible studies, biology, calculus-AP, chemistry, computer programming, computer science, drafting, drama, driver education, economics, English, English-AP, French, geometry, home economics, journalism, keyboarding, Latin, physical education, physics, pre-algebra, psychology, sociology, Spanish, U.S. government and politics-AP, vocal music, world history, yearbook.

Graduation Requirements 20th century world history, advanced math, algebra, American history, anatomy and physiology, Bible, chemistry, Christian studies, computer programming, economics, English, French, geometry, independent living, Latin, physical education (includes health), physics, psychology, Spanish, U.S. government and politics-AP, world history, world history-AP.

Special Academic Programs Advanced Placement exam preparation; honors section; academic accommodation for the gifted; remedial reading and/or remedial writing; remedial math; programs in English, mathematics, general development for dyslexic students.

College Admission Counseling 85 students graduated in 2012; 83 went to college, including Mississippi College; Mississippi State University; Samford University; University of Memphis; University of Mississippi. Other: 1 went to work, 1 had other specific plans. Mean composite ACT: 31. 35% scored over 26 on composite ACT.

Student Life Upper grades have specified standards of dress, student council. Discipline rests primarily with faculty. Attendance at religious services is required.

Tuition and Aid Day student tuition: $4756–$5300. Tuition installment plan (monthly payment arrangements with local bank). Tuition reduction for siblings, need-based scholarship grants available. In 2012–13, 13% of upper-school students received aid. Total amount of financial aid awarded in 2012–13: $67,675.

Admissions Traditional secondary-level entrance grade is 8. For fall 2012, 40 students applied for upper-level admission, 38 were accepted, 36 enrolled. Admissions testing required. Deadline for receipt of application materials: none. Application fee required: $225. On-campus interview required.

Athletics Interscholastic: baseball (boys), basketball (b,g), cheering (g), cross-country running (b,g), drill team (g), football (b), golf (b,g), soccer (b,g), softball (g), strength & conditioning (b,g), swimming and diving (b,g), tennis (b,g), track and field (b,g), volleyball (g); intramural: soccer (b,g); coed intramural: soccer. 2 PE instructors, 1 coach, 1 athletic trainer.

Computers Computers are regularly used in all classes. Computer network features include on-campus library services, Internet access, wireless campus network. Students grades are available online.

Contact Mrs. Sheila Sheron, Director of Admission. 662-349-5127. Fax: 662-349-4962. E-mail: ssheron@sbectrojans.com. Website:

SCATTERGOOD FRIENDS SCHOOL

1951 Delta Avenue
West Branch, Iowa 52358-8507

Head of School: Ms. Christine Ashley

General Information Coeducational boarding and day college-preparatory and arts school, affiliated with Society of Friends. Boarding grades 9–PG, day grades 9–12. Founded: 1890. Setting: rural. Nearest major city is Iowa City. Students are housed in single-sex dormitories. 120-acre campus. 15 buildings on campus. Approved or accredited by Friends Council on Education, Independent Schools Association of the Central States, Midwest Association of Boarding Schools, and The Association of Boarding Schools. Endowment: $4.4 million. Total enrollment: 40. Upper school average class size: 10. Upper school faculty-student ratio: 1:2. There are 180 required school days per year for Upper School students. Upper School students typically attend 5 days per week. The average school day consists of 7 hours.

Upper School Student Profile Grade 9: 5 students (2 boys, 3 girls); Grade 10: 8 students (4 boys, 4 girls); Grade 11: 12 students (7 boys, 5 girls); Grade 12: 15 students (5 boys, 10 girls). 98% of students are boarding students. 38% are state residents. 9 states are represented in upper school student body. 30% are international students. International students from Bolivia, China, Ethiopia, Mexico, Rwanda, and Spain; 6 other countries represented in student body. 14% of students are members of Society of Friends.

Faculty School total: 20. In upper school: 11 men, 7 women; 14 have advanced degrees; all reside on campus.

Subjects Offered Advanced TOEFL/grammar, agriculture, algebra, alternative physical education, American government, American history, art, biology, calculus, career/college preparation, ceramics, chemistry, college admission preparation, community service, creative writing, critical thinking, dance performance, digital art, drama, drama performance, drawing and design, ecology, environmental systems, environmental science, ESL, ethics, expository writing, fencing, fine arts, gardening, geometry, government/civics, history, independent study, Internet research, library research, martial arts, mathematics, organic gardening, physics, portfolio writing, pottery, Quakerism and ethics, religion, research seminar, SAT/ACT preparation, science, senior seminar, social studies, Spanish, studio art, U.S. history, wilderness education, woodworking, writing workshop, yearbook, yoga.

Graduation Requirements Algebra, American literature, biology, chemistry, English, foreign language, geometry, government, health and wellness, history, humanities, junior and senior seminars, physical education (includes health), physics, portfolio writing, Quakerism and ethics, religious studies, SAT/ACT preparation, U.S. government, U.S. history, world literature, 30 hours of community service per year in attendance, 20-page senior research paper with a thesis defense presentation, Acceptance at 4-year college or university.

Special Academic Programs Honors section; accelerated programs; independent study; term-away projects; study abroad; ESL (11 students enrolled).

College Admission Counseling 12 students graduated in 2013; 11 went to college, including Earlham College; Iowa State University of Science and Technology; Kansas State University; The University of Iowa. Other: 1 went to work. Median SAT critical reading: 620, median SAT math: 530, median SAT writing: 570, median combined SAT: 1720. 71% scored over 600 on SAT critical reading, 29% scored over 600 on SAT math, 43% scored over 600 on SAT writing, 43% scored over 1800 on combined SAT.

Student Life Upper grades have specified standards of dress, student council. Discipline rests equally with students and faculty. Attendance at religious services is required.

Tuition and Aid Day student tuition: $16,950; 5-day tuition and room/board: $27,600; 7-day tuition and room/board: $27,600. Tuition installment plan (Academic Management Services Plan, monthly payment plans, individually arranged payment plans). Merit scholarship grants, need-based scholarship grants, Scholarships for Quaker students available. In 2013–14, 75% of upper-school students received aid; total upper-school merit-scholarship money awarded: $1000. Total amount of financial aid awarded in 2013–14: $500,000.

Admissions Traditional secondary-level entrance grade is 9. Deadline for receipt of application materials: none. Application fee required: $65. Interview required.

Athletics Coed Interscholastic: basketball, fencing, soccer; coed intramural: archery, backpacking, ball hockey, bicycling, canoeing/kayaking, combined training, cooperative games, dance, fitness, hiking/backpacking, jogging, juggling, martial arts, modern dance, physical fitness, running, strength & conditioning, ultimate Frisbee, yoga.

Computers Computers are regularly used in all classes. Computer network features include online commercial services, Internet access, wireless campus network, Internet filtering or blocking technology, Laptops and campus-wide wifi for each student. Campus intranet, student e-mail accounts, and computer access in designated common areas are available to students. Students grades are available online. The school has a published electronic and media policy.

Contact Ms. Alicia Streeter, Director of Admissions. 319-643-7628. Fax: 319-643-3735. E-mail: admissions@scattergood.org. Website: www.scattergood.org

SCHOLAR'S HALL PREPARATORY SCHOOL

888 Trillium Drive
Kitchener, Ontario N2R 1K4, Canada

Head of School: Mr. Frederick T. Gore

General Information Coeducational day college-preparatory, general academic, arts, and business school. Grades JK–12. Founded: 1997. Setting: small town. Nearest major city is Toronto, Canada. 10-acre campus. 1 building on campus. Approved or accredited by Ontario Department of Education. Language of instruction: English. Total enrollment: 105. Upper school average class size: 10. Upper school faculty-student ratio: 1:10. There are 200 required school days per year for Upper School students.

Upper School students typically attend 5 days per week. The average school day consists of 7 hours.

Upper School Student Profile Grade 6: 10 students (5 boys, 5 girls); Grade 7: 10 students (5 boys, 5 girls); Grade 8: 10 students (5 boys, 5 girls); Grade 9: 10 students (5 boys, 5 girls); Grade 10: 10 students (5 boys, 5 girls); Grade 11: 10 students (5 boys, 5 girls); Grade 12: 10 students (5 boys, 5 girls).

Faculty School total: 10. In upper school: 5 men, 5 women; 5 have advanced degrees.

Special Academic Programs ESL (20 students enrolled).

College Admission Counseling 10 students graduated in 2012; 2 went to college, including The University of Western Ontario; University of Waterloo; Wilfrid Laurier University. Other: 8 entered a postgraduate year.

Student Life Upper grades have uniform requirement, student council, honor system. Discipline rests primarily with faculty.

Tuition and Aid Day student tuition: CAN$10,900. Guaranteed tuition plan. Tuition installment plan (The The Tuition Plan, monthly payment plans, individually arranged payment plans). Tuition reduction for siblings, bursaries available. In 2012–13, 10% of upper-school students received aid. Total amount of financial aid awarded in 2012–13: CAN$20,000.

Admissions Traditional secondary-level entrance grade is 9. For fall 2012, 20 students applied for upper-level admission, 15 were accepted, 15 enrolled. Woodcock-Johnson Educational Evaluation, WISC III required. Deadline for receipt of application materials: June 1. No application fee required. Interview required.

Athletics Coed Interscholastic: badminton, ball hockey, baseball, basketball, cross-country running, fencing, fitness, fitness walking, flag football, floor hockey, Frisbee, golf, independent competitive sports, martial arts, outdoor activities, outdoor education, physical fitness, self defense, soccer, softball, table tennis, volleyball; coed intramural: badminton, ball hockey, baseball, basketball, bowling, cross-country running, fencing, fitness, fitness walking, flag football, floor hockey, Frisbee, golf, martial arts, outdoor activities, outdoor education, physical fitness, self defense, soccer, softball, table tennis, volleyball. 2 PE instructors.

Computers Computers are regularly used in all classes. Computer network features include Internet access, wireless campus network, Internet filtering or blocking technology. Campus intranet is available to students. The school has a published electronic and media policy.

Contact 519-888-6620. Fax: 519-884-0316. Website: www.scholarshall.com

SCOTTSDALE CHRISTIAN ACADEMY

14400 North Tatum Boulevard
Phoenix, Arizona 85032

Head of School: Mr. Sean Greene

General Information Coeducational day college-preparatory and religious studies school, affiliated with Christian faith. Grades PK–12. Founded: 1968. Setting: suburban. 14-acre campus. 6 buildings on campus. Approved or accredited by Association of Christian Schools International and North Central Association of Colleges and Schools. Total enrollment: 851. Upper school average class size: 22. Upper school faculty-student ratio: 1:15. There are 180 required school days per year for Upper School students. Upper School students typically attend 5 days per week. The average school day consists of 7 hours.

Upper School Student Profile 99% of students are Christian.

Faculty School total: 61. In upper school: 10 men, 8 women; 4 have advanced degrees.

Subjects Offered Advanced Placement courses, algebra, American history, American history-AP, American literature, anatomy, art, Bible studies, biology, calculus, chemistry, creative writing, drama, economics, English, English-AP, fine arts, French, geography, geometry, government/civics, graphic design, guitar, history, honors geometry, honors U.S. history, mathematics, music, physical education, physical science, physics, physics-AP, religion, science, social studies, Spanish, speech, trigonometry, world history.

Graduation Requirements American government, American history, ancient world history, arts and fine arts (art, music, dance, drama), Bible, biology, chemistry, Christian ethics, economics, English, foreign language, government, mathematics, physical education (includes health), religion (includes Bible studies and theology), science, social sciences, social studies (includes history), speech, U.S. history, world history.

Special Academic Programs Advanced Placement exam preparation; honors section; independent study; study at local college for college credit.

College Admission Counseling 69 students graduated in 2013; 67 went to college, including Arizona Christian University; Arizona State University; Baylor University; Biola University; Grand Canyon University; The University of Arizona.

Student Life Upper grades have specified standards of dress, student council. Discipline rests primarily with faculty. Attendance at religious services is required.

Summer Programs Sports, art/fine arts programs offered; session focuses on camps; held on campus; accepts boys and girls; open to students from other schools. 300 students usually enrolled. 2014 schedule: June to June.

Tuition and Aid Day student tuition: $10,000. Tuition installment plan (Academic Management Services Plan). Tuition reduction for siblings, need-based scholarship grants available.

Admissions Traditional secondary-level entrance grade is 9. Deadline for receipt of application materials: none. Application fee required: $100. On-campus interview required.

Athletics Interscholastic: baseball (boys), basketball (b,g), cheering (g), cross-country running (b,g), football (b), golf (b,g), soccer (b,g), softball (g), swimming and diving (b,g), tennis (b,g), track and field (b,g), volleyball (b,g), winter soccer (b); intramural: weight lifting (b); coed intramural: martial arts. 3 PE instructors, 50 coaches, 1 athletic trainer.

Computers Computers are regularly used in computer applications, graphic design, Latin, photography, video film production, yearbook classes. Computer network features include on-campus library services, Internet access, wireless campus network, Internet filtering or blocking technology, EXPAN. Campus intranet and student e-mail accounts are available to students. Students grades are available online. The school has a published electronic and media policy.

Contact Joan Rockwell, Admissions. 602-992-5100 Ext. 1095. Fax: 602-992-0575. E-mail: jrockwell@scamail.org. Website: www.scarizona.org

SCOTUS CENTRAL CATHOLIC HIGH SCHOOL

1554 18th Avenue
Columbus, Nebraska 68601-5132

Head of School: Mr. Wayne Morfeld

General Information Coeducational day college-preparatory, arts, business, religious studies, and technology school, affiliated with Roman Catholic Church. Grades 7–12. Founded: 1884. Setting: small town. Nearest major city is Omaha. 1-acre campus. 1 building on campus. Approved or accredited by National Catholic Education Association, North Central Association of Colleges and Schools, and Nebraska Department of Education. Endowment: $7.6 million. Total enrollment: 396. Upper school average class size: 20. Upper school faculty-student ratio: 1:14. There are 174 required school days per year for Upper School students. Upper School students typically attend 5 days per week. The average school day consists of 6 hours and 40 minutes.

Upper School Student Profile Grade 9: 68 students (36 boys, 32 girls); Grade 10: 71 students (41 boys, 30 girls); Grade 11: 52 students (25 boys, 27 girls); Grade 12: 66 students (29 boys, 37 girls). 95% of students are Roman Catholic.

Faculty School total: 28. In upper school: 11 men, 17 women; 9 have advanced degrees.

Subjects Offered Accounting, advanced math, Advanced Placement courses, algebra, American history, art, astronomy, band, Bible studies, biology, bookkeeping, calculus, calculus-AP, campus ministry, career and personal planning, career exploration, career/college preparation, Catholic belief and practice, character education, chemistry, child development, choir, choral music, chorus, community service, computer applications, computer multimedia, computer technologies, concert band, concert choir, consumer economics, consumer mathematics, contemporary problems, CPR, current events, digital applications, drama, earth science, economics, English, fabric arts, family and consumer science, fitness, food and nutrition, geography, government, guidance, health and safety, history, human development, instrumental music, jazz band, jazz ensemble, journalism, keyboarding, life management skills, life skills, marching band, modern world history, personal fitness, physical education, physical science, physics, physiology, psychology, reading/study skills, sociology, Spanish, speech, speech and debate, student publications, textiles, theater, U.S. history, vocal ensemble, weight training, world history, yearbook.

Graduation Requirements Algebra, American government, American history, biology, chemistry, computer applications, electives, English, geometry, mathematics, modern history, physical education (includes health), religion (includes Bible studies and theology), Spanish, speech, U.S. history, world history, 80 hours of Living the Faith community/church/school service.

Special Academic Programs Advanced Placement exam preparation; study at local college for college credit.

College Admission Counseling 66 students graduated in 2013; 64 went to college, including Rockhurst University; The University of South Dakota; University of Nebraska–Lincoln; University of Nebraska at Kearney; University of Nebraska at Omaha; University of Notre Dame. Other: 2 entered military service. Median composite ACT: 23. 21% scored over 26 on composite ACT.

Student Life Upper grades have uniform requirement, student council, honor system. Discipline rests equally with students and faculty. Attendance at religious services is required.

Tuition and Aid Day student tuition: $2475–$2575. Tuition installment plan (monthly payment plans). Need-based scholarship grants, paying campus jobs available. In 2013–14, 29% of upper-school students received aid. Total amount of financial aid awarded in 2013–14: $110,000.

Admissions Traditional secondary-level entrance grade is 9. Deadline for receipt of application materials: none. No application fee required. Interview recommended.

Athletics Interscholastic: baseball (boys), basketball (b,g), cheering (g), cross-country running (b,g), football (b), golf (b,g), soccer (b,g), softball (g), swimming and diving (b,g), tennis (b,g), track and field (b,g), volleyball (g), wrestling (b). 3 PE instructors, 15 coaches, 2 athletic trainers.

Computers Computers are regularly used in business, computer applications, journalism, keyboarding, newspaper, publications, technology, Web site design, word processing, yearbook classes. Computer network features include on-campus library services, Internet access, wireless campus network, Internet filtering or blocking technology. Campus intranet, student e-mail accounts, and computer access in designated common areas are available to students. Students grades are available online. The school has a published electronic and media policy.

Contact Mrs. Pamela K. Weir, 7-12 Guidance Counselor. 402-564-7165 Ext. 121. Fax: 402-564-6004. E-mail: pweir@scotuscc.org. Website: www.scotuscc.org

SEABURY HALL

480 Olinda Road
Makawao, Hawaii 96768-9399

Head of School: Mr. Joseph J. Schmidt

General Information Coeducational day college-preparatory, arts, and technology school, affiliated with Episcopal Church. Grades 6–12. Founded: 1964. Setting: rural. Nearest major city is Kahului. 73-acre campus. 8 buildings on campus. Approved or accredited by Western Association of Schools and Colleges. Member of National Association of Independent Schools and Secondary School Admission Test Board. Endowment: $27 million. Total enrollment: 443. Upper school average class size: 16. Upper school faculty-student ratio: 1:11. There are 175 required school days per year for Upper School students. Upper School students typically attend 5 days per week. The average school day consists of 7 hours and 30 minutes.

Upper School Student Profile Grade 9: 82 students (32 boys, 50 girls); Grade 10: 82 students (29 boys, 53 girls); Grade 11: 70 students (28 boys, 42 girls); Grade 12: 77 students (34 boys, 43 girls). 5% of students are members of Episcopal Church.

Faculty School total: 56. In upper school: 23 men, 15 women; 23 have advanced degrees.

Subjects Offered Acting, algebra, American history, American history-AP, American literature, American literature-AP, art, band, biology, biology-AP, calculus-AP, ceramics, chemistry, chorus, college counseling, college placement, college planning, community service, comparative religion, computer programming, dance, drawing, economics, engineering, English, English literature, ethics, European history-AP, expository writing, fine arts, geometry, global studies, government, Hawaiian history, Hawaiian language, history, Japanese, keyboarding, mathematics, mythology, painting, philosophy, physical education, physical science, physics, physics-AP, political science, pre-algebra, pre-calculus, religion, SAT preparation, science, set design, social studies, Spanish, Spanish-AP, speech, studio art-AP, yearbook.

Graduation Requirements Arts and fine arts (art, music, dance, drama), English, foreign language, mathematics, physical education (includes health), religion (includes Bible studies and theology), science, social studies (includes history), speech. Community service is required.

Special Academic Programs 13 Advanced Placement exams for which test preparation is offered; honors section; independent study; academic accommodation for the gifted.

College Admission Counseling 72 students graduated in 2012; 71 went to college, including California Polytechnic State University, San Luis Obispo; Chapman University; Colorado State University; University of Colorado Boulder; University of Hawaii at Manoa; University of San Francisco. Other: 1 entered military service. Mean SAT critical reading: 550, mean SAT math: 570, mean SAT writing: 565, mean combined SAT: 1685, mean composite ACT: 25.

Student Life Upper grades have specified standards of dress, student council, honor system. Discipline rests primarily with faculty.

Tuition and Aid Day student tuition: $17,330. Tuition installment plan (FACTS Tuition Payment Plan). Need-based scholarship grants available. In 2012–13, 36% of upper-school students received aid. Total amount of financial aid awarded in 2012–13: $956,860.

Admissions Traditional secondary-level entrance grade is 9. For fall 2012, 173 students applied for upper-level admission, 136 were accepted, 102 enrolled. ERB CTP III, ISEE or SSAT required. Deadline for receipt of application materials: February 16. Application fee required: $65. Interview required.

Athletics Interscholastic: basketball (boys, girls), cross-country running (b,g), dance (g), golf (b,g), paddling (b,g), physical fitness (b,g), soccer (b,g), swimming and diving (b,g), tennis (b,g), track and field (b,g), volleyball (b,g); intramural: basketball (b,g), dance (g), fitness (b,g), strength & conditioning (b,g); coed interscholastic: baseball, dance, paddling, physical fitness; coed intramural: ballet, baseball, cross-country running, dance, fitness, track and field, volleyball. 4 PE instructors, 12 coaches, 1 athletic trainer.

Computers Computers are regularly used in art, economics, English, foreign language, history, journalism, mathematics, newspaper, science, speech, yearbook classes. Computer network features include on-campus library services, online commercial services, Internet access, wireless campus network, Internet filtering or blocking technology. Campus intranet, student e-mail accounts, and computer access in designated common areas are available to students. Students grades are available online. The school has a published electronic and media policy.

Contact Elaine V. Nelson, Director of Admissions. 808-572-0807. Fax: 808-572-2042. E-mail: enelson@seaburyhall.org. Website: www.seaburyhall.org

SEATTLE ACADEMY OF ARTS AND SCIENCES

1201 East Union Street
Seattle, Washington 98122

Head of School: Joe Puggelli

General Information Coeducational day college-preparatory, arts, and technology school. Grades 6–12. Founded: 1983. Setting: urban. 3-acre campus. 5 buildings on campus. Approved or accredited by Northwest Accreditation Commission, Northwest Association of Independent Schools, Northwest Association of Schools and Colleges, and Washington Department of Education. Member of National Association of Independent Schools. Endowment: $12.2 million. Total enrollment: 720. Upper school average class size: 18. Upper school faculty-student ratio: 1:9. There are 170 required school days per year for Upper School students. Upper School students typically attend 5 days per week. The average school day consists of 6 hours and 45 minutes.

Upper School Student Profile Grade 9: 126 students (66 boys, 60 girls); Grade 10: 106 students (52 boys, 54 girls); Grade 11: 106 students (53 boys, 53 girls); Grade 12: 103 students (50 boys, 53 girls).

Faculty School total: 115. In upper school: 53 men, 62 women; 76 have advanced degrees.

Subjects Offered 20th century world history, acting, advanced chemistry, algebra, American history, American literature, Asian studies, biology, biotechnology, calculus, chemistry, choir, civics, community service, dance, debate, drawing, economics, English, environmental systems, French, geometry, health, history, humanities, independent study, instrumental music, lab science, literature, Mandarin, marine science, math analysis, musical productions, painting, physical education, physics, printmaking, robotics, sculpture, Spanish, speech, stagecraft, statistics, visual arts, vocal music, world literature, yearbook.

Graduation Requirements Arts and fine arts (art, music, dance, drama), English, foreign language, history, mathematics, physical education (includes health), science, social studies (includes history). Community service is required.

Special Academic Programs Honors section; independent study; term-away projects; study abroad; academic accommodation for the gifted, the musically talented, and the artistically talented; remedial reading and/or remedial writing; remedial math; programs in English, mathematics, general development for dyslexic students.

College Admission Counseling 102 students graduated in 2013; 101 went to college, including California Polytechnic State University, San Luis Obispo; New York University; Northwestern University; Tulane University; University of Washington; Western Washington University. Other: 1 had other specific plans. Mean SAT critical reading: 621, mean SAT math: 595, mean SAT writing: 611, mean combined SAT: 1828, mean composite ACT: 27.

Student Life Upper grades have student council, honor system. Discipline rests equally with students and faculty.

Summer Programs Enrichment, sports, art/fine arts programs offered; held both on and off campus; held at outdoor trips to various national and international locations; accepts boys and girls; open to students from other schools. 100 students usually enrolled. 2014 schedule: June 16 to August 15.

Tuition and Aid Day student tuition: $28,380. Tuition installment plan (Academic Management Services Plan, monthly payment plans). Need-based scholarship grants available. In 2013–14, 20% of upper-school students received aid.

Admissions Traditional secondary-level entrance grade is 9. ISEE required. Deadline for receipt of application materials: January 14. Application fee required: $100. Interview required.

Athletics Interscholastic: basketball (boys, girls), cross-country running (b,g), Frisbee (b,g), golf (b,g), soccer (b,g), tennis (b,g), track and field (b,g), ultimate Frisbee (b,g), volleyball (g); coed interscholastic: dance, dance squad, dance team; coed intramural: alpine skiing, bowling, climbing, in-line skating, outdoor activities, paint ball, roller blading, roller skating, skateboarding, skiing (cross-country), skiing (downhill), snowboarding, squash, weight training. 5 PE instructors, 30 coaches, 2 athletic trainers.

Computers Computers are regularly used in all academic, computer applications, English, foreign language, graphic design, history, mathematics, newspaper, science, speech, study skills, theater arts, video film production, Web site design, yearbook classes. Computer network features include on-campus library services, online commercial services, Internet access, wireless campus network, Internet filtering or blocking technology. Student e-mail accounts are available to students. Students grades are available online. The school has a published electronic and media policy.

Contact Jim Rupp, Admission Director. 206-324-7227. Fax: 206-323-6618. E-mail: jrupp@seattleacademy.org. Website: www.seattleacademy.org

SEISEN INTERNATIONAL SCHOOL

12-15 Yoga 1-chome, Setagaya-ku
Tokyo 158-0097, Japan

Head of School: Sr. Margaret Scott

General Information Coeducational day (boys' only in lower grades) college-preparatory school, affiliated with Roman Catholic Church. Boys grade K, girls grades K–12. Founded: 1962. Setting: urban. 1-hectare campus. 3 buildings on campus. Approved or accredited by Council of International Schools, Department of Defense Dependents Schools, International Baccalaureate Organization, Ministry of Education, Japan, National Catholic Education Association, and New England Association of Schools and Colleges. Member of Secondary School Admission Test Board. Language of instruction: English. Total enrollment: 634. Upper school average class size: 20. Upper school faculty-student ratio: 1:6. There are 172 required school days per year for Upper School students. Upper School students typically attend 5 days per week. The average school day consists of 6 hours.

Upper School Student Profile Grade 9: 57 students (57 girls); Grade 10: 59 students (59 girls); Grade 11: 46 students (46 girls); Grade 12: 36 students (36 girls). 20% of students are Roman Catholic.

Faculty School total: 87. In upper school: 15 men, 34 women; 30 have advanced degrees.

Subjects Offered 3-dimensional art, advanced math, art, bell choir, biology, business, career planning, chemistry, Chinese, choir, college planning, computer graphics, computers, Danish, drama, English, environmental studies, ESL, French, geography, geometry, health education, history, honors algebra, honors geometry, information technology, International Baccalaureate courses, Japanese, journalism, Korean, library, math methods, mathematics, model United Nations, music, music composition, music performance, painting, performing arts, personal and social education, physical education, physics, pottery, psychology, religion, science, social sciences, social studies, Spanish, speech, theory of knowledge, trigonometry, visual arts, world history, yearbook.

Graduation Requirements Electives, English, foreign language, mathematics, physical education (includes health), religion (includes Bible studies and theology), science, social studies (includes history).

Special Academic Programs International Baccalaureate program; honors section; independent study; remedial reading and/or remedial writing; remedial math; ESL (11 students enrolled).

College Admission Counseling 32 students graduated in 2013; 30 went to college, including Carnegie Mellon University; New York University; The George Washington University; The University of British Columbia; University of California, San Diego; Waseda University. Other: 2 had other specific plans. Median SAT critical reading: 570, median SAT math: 640, median SAT writing: 600, median combined SAT: 1790. 40% scored over 600 on SAT critical reading, 64% scored over 600 on SAT math, 56% scored over 600 on SAT writing, 48% scored over 1800 on combined SAT.

Student Life Upper grades have uniform requirement, student council, honor system. Discipline rests primarily with faculty.

Summer Programs Remediation, ESL programs offered; session focuses on high school remedial work only; held on campus; accepts girls; not open to students from other schools. 8 students usually enrolled. 2014 schedule: June 9 to June 27. Application deadline: May 1.

Tuition and Aid Day student tuition: ¥1,940,000. Tuition installment plan (monthly payment plans, individually arranged payment plans). Tuition reduction for siblings, need-based scholarship grants available. In 2013–14, 2% of upper-school students received aid. Total amount of financial aid awarded in 2013–14: ¥1,170,000.

Admissions Traditional secondary-level entrance grade is 9. For fall 2013, 17 students applied for upper-level admission, 11 were accepted, 10 enrolled. Admissions testing, mathematics proficiency exam, Reading for Understanding or writing sample required. Deadline for receipt of application materials: none. Application fee required: ¥20,000. On-campus interview required.

Athletics Interscholastic: basketball, cross-country running, running, soccer, swimming and diving, tennis, track and field, volleyball; intramural: badminton, outdoor activities, running, soccer, table tennis, tennis, winter soccer. 3 PE instructors.

Computers Computers are regularly used in art, business studies, career education, college planning, English, foreign language, graphic design, history, information technology, journalism, mathematics, music, psychology, science, study skills, writing, yearbook classes. Computer network features include on-campus library services, online commercial services, Internet access, wireless campus network, Internet filtering or blocking technology. Campus intranet, student e-mail accounts, and computer access in designated common areas are available to students.

Contact Sr. Margaret Scott, School Head. 81-3-3704-2661. Fax: 81-3-3701-1033. E-mail: sisinfo@seisen.com. Website: www.seisen.com

SETON CATHOLIC HIGH SCHOOL

1150 North Dobson Road
Chandler, Arizona 85224

Head of School: Patricia L. Collins

General Information Coeducational day college-preparatory, arts, religious studies, technology, and dual enrollment with Seton Hill Univ. in specific classes school, affiliated with Roman Catholic Church. Grades 9–12. Founded: 1954. Setting: suburban. Nearest major city is Phoenix. 30-acre campus. 11 buildings on campus. Approved or accredited by North Central Association of Colleges and Schools, Western Catholic Education Association, and Arizona Department of Education. Endowment: $342,000. Total enrollment: 580. Upper school average class size: 21. Upper school faculty-student ratio: 1:12. There are 182 required school days per year for Upper School students. Upper School students typically attend 5 days per week. The average school day consists of 6 hours and 55 minutes.

Upper School Student Profile Grade 9: 159 students (84 boys, 75 girls); Grade 10: 155 students (79 boys, 76 girls); Grade 11: 127 students (62 boys, 65 girls); Grade 12: 138 students (70 boys, 68 girls). 96% of students are Roman Catholic.

Faculty School total: 45. In upper school: 21 men, 24 women; 29 have advanced degrees.

Subjects Offered Aerobics, algebra, American government, American history, anatomy, art, athletic training, Basic programming, biology, biology-AP, calculus, chemistry, chemistry-AP, choir, Christian and Hebrew scripture, Christian scripture, church history, computer applications, dance, drama, drawing, economics, English, English-AP, European history-AP, fitness, foreign language, French, geometry, government, guitar, health, honors English, honors geometry, honors U.S. history, keyboarding, Latin, Latin-AP, personal fitness, photography, physics, pre-calculus, psychology, reading/study skills, religion, scripture, social justice, Spanish, Spanish-AP, study skills, television, theology, U.S. government, U.S. history, video film production, weight training, world history, world religions, yearbook.

Graduation Requirements Arts and fine arts (art, music, dance, drama), computer applications, computer literacy, English, foreign language, mathematics, physical education (includes health), religion (includes Bible studies and theology), science, social studies (includes history), study skills.

Special Academic Programs 11 Advanced Placement exams for which test preparation is offered; honors section.

College Admission Counseling 127 students graduated in 2013; 126 went to college, including Arizona State University; Northern Arizona University; The University of Arizona. Other: 1 had other specific plans. Mean SAT critical reading: 565, mean SAT math: 578, mean SAT writing: 543, mean composite ACT: 25. 26% scored over 600 on SAT critical reading, 31% scored over 600 on SAT math, 20% scored over 600 on SAT writing.

Student Life Upper grades have uniform requirement, student council, honor system. Discipline rests primarily with faculty. Attendance at religious services is required.

Summer Programs Enrichment, advancement, sports, art/fine arts programs offered; session focuses on academic support for incoming students, athletic camps, theatre camp; held on campus; accepts boys and girls; open to students from other schools. 60 students usually enrolled. 2014 schedule: June 1 to June 30. Application deadline: May 30.

Tuition and Aid Day student tuition: $13,030. Tuition installment plan (FACTS Tuition Payment Plan, monthly payment plans). Merit scholarship grants, need-based scholarship grants, Catholic Tuition Organization of Diocese of Phoenix available. In 2013–14, 50% of upper-school students received aid; total upper-school merit-scholarship money awarded: $44,000. Total amount of financial aid awarded in 2013–14: $705,000.

Admissions Traditional secondary-level entrance grade is 9. For fall 2013, 249 students applied for upper-level admission, 185 were accepted, 164 enrolled. Catholic High School Entrance Examination or Scholastic Testing Service High School Placement Test required. Deadline for receipt of application materials: January 31. Application fee required: $75. Interview required.

Athletics Interscholastic: baseball (boys), basketball (b,g), cheering (g), cross-country running (b,g), dance squad (g), danceline (g), diving (b,g), football (b), golf (b,g), soccer (b,g), softball (g), swimming and diving (b,g), tennis (b,g), track and field (b,g), volleyball (b,g), wrestling (b); coed interscholastic: aerobics/dance, dance, dance team, football, physical fitness, strength & conditioning, weight training. 2 PE instructors, 70 coaches, 1 athletic trainer.

Computers Computers are regularly used in all academic, religious studies, yearbook classes. Computer network features include on-campus library services, Internet access, wireless campus network, Internet filtering or blocking technology, Turnitin. Campus intranet and student e-mail accounts are available to students. Students grades are available online. The school has a published electronic and media policy.

Contact Mr. Chris Moore, Director of Admission. 480-963-1900 Ext. 2008. Fax: 480-963-1974. E-mail: cmoore@setoncatholic.org. Website: www.setoncatholic.org

THE SEVEN HILLS SCHOOL

5400 Red Bank Road
Cincinnati, Ohio 45227

Head of School: Mr. Christopher P. Garten

General Information Coeducational day college-preparatory, arts, and technology school. Grades PK–12. Founded: 1974. Setting: suburban. 35-acre campus. 16 buildings on campus. Approved or accredited by Ohio Department of Education. Member of National Association of Independent Schools and Secondary School Admission Test Board. Endowment: $19.2 million. Total enrollment: 1,028. Upper school average class size: 15. Upper school faculty-student ratio: 1:9. There are 178 required school days per year for Upper School students. Upper School students typically attend 5 days per week. The average school day consists of 7 hours and 5 minutes.

Upper School Student Profile Grade 9: 86 students (47 boys, 39 girls); Grade 10: 85 students (40 boys, 45 girls); Grade 11: 81 students (49 boys, 32 girls); Grade 12: 63 students (31 boys, 32 girls).

Faculty School total: 128. In upper school: 20 men, 25 women; 40 have advanced degrees.

Subjects Offered Acting, advanced computer applications, Advanced Placement courses, algebra, American history, American literature, ancient history, art, art history, biology, British literature, calculus, ceramics, chemistry, computer programming, computer science, economics, English, European history, fine arts, French, geometry, journalism, Latin, linear algebra, Mandarin, medieval/Renaissance history, modern political theory, music, physical education, physics, pre-calculus, psychology, Spanish, speech, theater, world history, world literature, writing.

Graduation Requirements Algebra, arts and fine arts (art, music, dance, drama), biology, chemistry, computer science, English, foreign language, geometry, performing arts, physical education (includes health), physics, U.S. history, U.S. literature, completion of a personal challenge project, successfully pass writing competency exam, 30 hours of community service.

Special Academic Programs 16 Advanced Placement exams for which test preparation is offered; honors section; independent study; term-away projects; study abroad; academic accommodation for the gifted.

College Admission Counseling 83 students graduated in 2013; 81 went to college, including Duke University; Massachusetts Institute of Technology; Miami University; Northwestern University; Tufts University; Washington University in St. Louis. Median SAT critical reading: 661, median SAT math: 663, median SAT writing: 666, median composite ACT: 29. 74% scored over 600 on SAT critical reading, 87% scored over 600 on SAT math, 84% scored over 600 on SAT writing.

Student Life Upper grades have specified standards of dress, student council. Discipline rests primarily with faculty.

Summer Programs Enrichment programs offered; session focuses on SAT review, sports clinics, and acting workshop; held on campus; accepts boys and girls; open to students from other schools. 400 students usually enrolled. 2014 schedule: June 16 to August 8. Application deadline: none.

Tuition and Aid Day student tuition: $21,022–$21,565. Tuition installment plan (monthly payment plans, individually arranged payment plans). Merit scholarship grants, need-based scholarship grants available. In 2013–14, 17% of upper-school students received aid; total upper-school merit-scholarship money awarded: $157,900. Total amount of financial aid awarded in 2013–14: $530,000.

Admissions Traditional secondary-level entrance grade is 9. For fall 2013, 55 students applied for upper-level admission, 42 were accepted, 26 enrolled. ISEE required. Deadline for receipt of application materials: November 26. Application fee required: $50. On-campus interview required.

Athletics Interscholastic: baseball (boys), basketball (b,g), cheering (g), cross-country running (b,g), golf (b), gymnastics (g), lacrosse (b,g), soccer (b,g), softball (g), swimming and diving (b,g), tennis (b,g), volleyball (g); coed interscholastic: track and field. 3 PE instructors, 9 coaches.

Computers Computers are regularly used in foreign language, mathematics, science classes. Computer network features include on-campus library services, online commercial services, Internet access, wireless campus network, Internet filtering or blocking technology. Computer access in designated common areas is available to students. Students grades are available online. The school has a published electronic and media policy.

Contact Mrs. Janet S. Hill, Director of Admission and Financial Aid. 513-728-2405. Fax: 513-728-2409. E-mail: janet.hill@7hills.org. Website: www.7hills.org

SEVERN SCHOOL

201 Water Street
Severna Park, Maryland 21146

Head of School: Douglas H. Lagarde

General Information Coeducational day college-preparatory, arts, and technology school. Grades 6–12. Founded: 1914. Setting: suburban. Nearest major city is Annapolis. 19-acre campus. 8 buildings on campus. Approved or accredited by Association of Independent Maryland Schools, Middle States Association of Colleges and Schools, and Maryland Department of Education. Member of National Association of Independent Schools and Secondary School Admission Test Board. Endowment: $6 million. Total enrollment: 582. Upper school average class size: 15. Upper school faculty-student ratio: 1:8. There are 175 required school days per year for Upper School students. Upper School students typically attend 5 days per week. The average school day consists of 6 hours and 35 minutes.

Upper School Student Profile Grade 9: 99 students (43 boys, 56 girls); Grade 10: 105 students (47 boys, 58 girls); Grade 11: 94 students (51 boys, 43 girls); Grade 12: 89 students (48 boys, 41 girls).

Faculty School total: 81. In upper school: 27 men, 30 women; 38 have advanced degrees.

Subjects Offered Algebra, American history, American literature, art, biology, calculus, ceramics, chemistry, community service, computer programming, computer science, CPR, creative writing, dance, desktop publishing, digital art, digital imaging, digital photography, discrete mathematics, drama, drama performance, dramatic arts, drawing, drawing and design, earth science, ecology, economics, economics-AP, English, English literature, environmental science, environmental systems, European civilization, European history, European history-AP, expository writing, fine arts, forensics, French, French language-AP, French literature-AP, geometry, government/civics, grammar, graphic arts, health, history, journalism, Latin, marine biology, mathematics, multimedia, music, photography, physical education, physics, psychology, science, social studies, Spanish, speech, theater, trigonometry, world history, world literature, writing.

Graduation Requirements Arts and fine arts (art, music, dance, drama), computer science, CPR, English, foreign language, mathematics, physical education (includes health), science, social studies (includes history). Community service is required.

Special Academic Programs Advanced Placement exam preparation; honors section; independent study; study abroad; academic accommodation for the gifted, the musically talented, and the artistically talented.

College Admission Counseling 100 students graduated in 2012; all went to college, including Boston University; Elon University; The George Washington University; The Johns Hopkins University; The University of Alabama; University of Maryland, College Park. Median SAT critical reading: 600, median SAT math: 630, median SAT writing: 620, median combined SAT: 1860, median composite ACT: 26. 47% scored over 600 on SAT critical reading, 56% scored over 600 on SAT math, 55% scored over 600 on SAT writing, 58% scored over 1800 on combined SAT, 47% scored over 26 on composite ACT.

Student Life Upper grades have uniform requirement, student council, honor system. Discipline rests primarily with faculty.

Tuition and Aid Day student tuition: $22,150. Tuition installment plan (Academic Management Services Plan). Need-based scholarship grants available. In 2012–13, 24% of upper-school students received aid. Total amount of financial aid awarded in 2012–13: $1,115,305.

Admissions Traditional secondary-level entrance grade is 9. For fall 2012, 105 students applied for upper-level admission, 55 were accepted, 44 enrolled. ISEE required. Deadline for receipt of application materials: January 20. Application fee required: $55. On-campus interview required.

Athletics Interscholastic: baseball (boys), basketball (b,g), combined training (b,g), dance team (g), field hockey (g), football (b), lacrosse (b,g), soccer (b,g), tennis (b,g), wrestling (b); coed interscholastic: cross-country running, dance, diving, fitness, golf, outdoor education, physical fitness, sailing, strength & conditioning, swimming and diving, track and field, weight training; coed intramural: aerobics/dance, ice hockey, outdoor adventure, paint ball, table tennis. 4 PE instructors, 56 coaches, 2 athletic trainers.

Computers Computers are regularly used in all academic classes. Computer network features include on-campus library services, online commercial services, Internet access, Internet filtering or blocking technology. Campus intranet, student e-mail accounts, and computer access in designated common areas are available to students. Students grades are available online. The school has a published electronic and media policy.

Contact Ellen Murray, Associate Director of Admissions. 410-647-7701 Ext. 2266. Fax: 410-544-9451. E-mail: e.murray@severnschool.com. Website: www.severnschool.com

SEWICKLEY ACADEMY

315 Academy Avenue
Sewickley, Pennsylvania 15143

Head of School: Mr. Kolia J. O'Connor

General Information Coeducational day college-preparatory, arts, and technology school. Grades PK–12. Founded: 1838. Setting: suburban. Nearest major city is Pittsburgh. 30-acre campus. 10 buildings on campus. Approved or accredited by Pennsylvania Department of Education. Member of National Association of Independent Schools and Secondary School Admission Test Board. Endowment: $31 million. Total enrollment: 708. Upper school average class size: 15. Upper school faculty-student ratio: 1:7. There are 167 required school days per year for Upper School students. Upper School students typically attend 5 days per week. The average school day consists of 7 hours.

Upper School Student Profile Grade 9: 72 students (41 boys, 31 girls); Grade 10: 67 students (34 boys, 33 girls); Grade 11: 71 students (34 boys, 37 girls); Grade 12: 79 students (44 boys, 35 girls).

Faculty School total: 106. In upper school: 28 men, 28 women; 32 have advanced degrees.

Subjects Offered Advanced chemistry, advanced studio art-AP, African studies, algebra, American history, American history-AP, American literature, American literature-AP, art, art-AP, astronomy, band, biology, biology-AP, calculus, calculus-AP, ceramics, chemistry, chemistry-AP, choral music, chorus, clayworking, computer applications, computer art, computer programming, computer science, computer science-AP, concert band, concert choir, contemporary issues, creative writing, dance, dance performance, digital art, drama, drama performance, drama workshop, drawing, driver education, economics, English, English literature, environmental science, ethics, European history, European history-AP, expository writing, fine arts, French, French language-AP, French literature-AP, geometry, German, German-AP, government/civics, health, health education, history, Italian, keyboarding, Mandarin, music, musical theater, performing arts, photography, physical education, physics, physics-AP, pre-calculus, psychology, psychology-AP, senior project, Spanish, Spanish literature, Spanish-AP, speech and debate, statistics, statistics-AP, studio art, theater, trigonometry, U.S. history-AP, U.S. literature, Vietnam War, world history, world literature, writing.

Graduation Requirements Arts and fine arts (art, music, dance, drama), English, foreign language, health education, mathematics, physical education (includes health), science, social studies (includes history), U.S. history, world cultures, world studies. Community service is required.

Special Academic Programs Advanced Placement exam preparation; honors section; independent study; term-away projects; study at local college for college credit; study abroad.

College Admission Counseling 62 students graduated in 2013; all went to college, including Boston University; Bucknell University; Colgate University; Dartmouth College; Emory University; Princeton University.

Student Life Upper grades have specified standards of dress, student council, honor system. Discipline rests equally with students and faculty.

Summer Programs Enrichment, advancement, sports, art/fine arts programs offered; session focuses on academics, athletics, and musical theater; held on campus; accepts boys and girls; open to students from other schools. 150 students usually enrolled. 2014 schedule: June 11 to August 10. Application deadline: none.

Tuition and Aid Day student tuition: $23,935. Tuition installment plan (monthly payment plans). Need-based scholarship grants available. In 2013–14, 20% of upper-school students received aid. Total amount of financial aid awarded in 2013–14: $600,000.

Admissions Traditional secondary-level entrance grade is 9. ISEE or SSAT required. Deadline for receipt of application materials: February 7. Application fee required: $50. Interview required.

Athletics Interscholastic: baseball (boys), basketball (b,g), cross-country running (b,g), golf (b,g), ice hockey (b), lacrosse (b,g), physical fitness (b,g), soccer (b,g), softball (g), tennis (b,g); coed interscholastic: bowling, diving, field hockey, physical fitness, swimming and diving, track and field. 5 PE instructors, 5 coaches, 1 athletic trainer.

Computers Computers are regularly used in all academic classes. Computer network features include on-campus library services, online commercial services, Internet access, wireless campus network, Internet filtering or blocking technology. Campus intranet, student e-mail accounts, and computer access in designated common areas are available to students. The school has a published electronic and media policy.

Contact Ms. Wendy Berns, Admission Assistant. 412-741-2235. Fax: 412-741-1411. E-mail: wberns@sewickley.org. Website: www.sewickley.org

SHADY SIDE ACADEMY

423 Fox Chapel Road
Pittsburgh, Pennsylvania 15238

Head of School: Mr. Thomas Cangiano

General Information Coeducational boarding and day college-preparatory school. Boarding grades 9–12, day grades PK–12. Founded: 1883. Setting: suburban. Students are housed in single-sex dormitories. 130-acre campus. 26 buildings on campus. Approved or accredited by Middle States Association of Colleges and Schools, The Association of Boarding Schools, and Pennsylvania Department of Education. Member of National Association of Independent Schools. Endowment: $50.3 million. Total enrollment: 935. Upper school average class size: 13. Upper school faculty-student ratio: 1:8. There are 172 required school days per year for Upper School students. Upper School students typically attend 5 days per week.

Upper School Student Profile Grade 9: 115 students (68 boys, 47 girls); Grade 10: 131 students (73 boys, 58 girls); Grade 11: 119 students (61 boys, 58 girls); Grade 12: 127 students (62 boys, 65 girls). 10% of students are boarding students. 97% are state residents. 7 states are represented in upper school student body.

Faculty School total: 121. In upper school: 34 men, 28 women; 39 have advanced degrees; 22 reside on campus.

Subjects Offered 3-dimensional art, advanced biology, advanced chemistry, advanced computer applications, advanced math, Advanced Placement courses, algebra, American history, American literature, architectural drawing, architecture, art, art history, band, biology, calculus, calculus-AP, ceramics, chemistry, Chinese, Chinese history, choir, college counseling, computer graphics, computer math, computer programming, computer science, computer science-AP, concert band, creative writing, drama, economics, English, English literature, environmental science, ethics, European history, expository writing, film and literature, fine arts, fractal geometry, French, French-AP, gender issues, geography, geometry, German, German-AP, health, history, introduction to theater, jazz ensemble, Latin, linear algebra, logic, mathematics, music, music technology, musical theater, philosophy, photography, physical education, physics, pre-calculus, probability and statistics, religion and culture, science, senior project, social studies, Spanish, Spanish-AP, speech, statistics, studio art, technical theater, theater arts, trigonometry, world history, world literature, writing.

Graduation Requirements Art, athletics, computer science, English, foreign language, history, mathematics, physical education (includes health), science, participation in five seasons of athletics.

Special Academic Programs 6 Advanced Placement exams for which test preparation is offered; honors section; accelerated programs; independent study; term-away projects; study at local college for college credit; study abroad; academic accommodation for the gifted, the musically talented, and the artistically talented.

College Admission Counseling 118 students graduated in 2013; 116 went to college, including Furman University; Lehigh University; New York University; Penn

State University Park; The George Washington University; University of Pittsburgh. Other: 1 entered a postgraduate year, 1 had other specific plans. Median SAT critical reading: 620, median SAT math: 650, median SAT writing: 640, median combined SAT: 1910, median composite ACT: 30. 63% scored over 600 on SAT critical reading, 72% scored over 600 on SAT math, 64% scored over 600 on SAT writing, 69% scored over 1800 on combined SAT, 53% scored over 26 on composite ACT.

Student Life Upper grades have specified standards of dress, student council. Discipline rests primarily with faculty.

Summer Programs Remediation, enrichment, advancement, sports, art/fine arts, computer instruction programs offered; session focuses on academic and non-academic enrichment; held on campus; accepts boys and girls; open to students from other schools. 1,200 students usually enrolled. 2014 schedule: June 9 to August 15. Application deadline: none.

Tuition and Aid Day student tuition: $27,875; 5-day tuition and room/board: $38,925. Tuition installment plan (monthly payment plans, Tuition Refund Plan available through Dewar's). Tuition reduction for siblings, merit scholarship grants, need-based scholarship grants, merit-based scholarships are for boarding students, FAME awards (Fund for the Advancement of Minorities Through Education), partial tuition remission for children of full-time employees available. In 2013–14, 22% of upper-school students received aid; total upper-school merit-scholarship money awarded: $50,000. Total amount of financial aid awarded in 2013–14: $2,012,350.

Admissions Traditional secondary-level entrance grade is 9. For fall 2013, 123 students applied for upper-level admission, 96 were accepted, 60 enrolled. ISEE, SSAT or TOEFL required. Deadline for receipt of application materials: February 4. Application fee required: $50. On-campus interview required.

Athletics Interscholastic: baseball (boys), basketball (b,g), cheering (g), crew (g), cross-country running (b,g), field hockey (g), football (b), golf (b,g), ice hockey (b,g), lacrosse (b,g), soccer (b,g), softball (g), squash (b,g), swimming and diving (b,g), tennis (b,g), track and field (b,g), wrestling (b); intramural: volleyball (g); coed interscholastic: ultimate Frisbee; coed intramural: aerobics/dance, badminton, bowling, cricket, fitness, ultimate Frisbee, weight lifting. 1 PE instructor, 47 coaches, 2 athletic trainers.

Computers Computers are regularly used in all classes. Computer network features include on-campus library services, online commercial services, Internet access, wireless campus network, Internet filtering or blocking technology, report cards are available online four times a year. Student e-mail accounts and computer access in designated common areas are available to students. The school has a published electronic and media policy.

Contact Ms. Katherine H. Mihm, Director of Enrollment Management and Marketing. 412-968-3179. Fax: 412-968-3213. E-mail: kmihm@shadysideacademy.org. Website: www.shadysideacademy.org

SHANLEY HIGH SCHOOL

5600 25th Street South
Fargo, North Dakota 58104

Head of School: Mr. Edward M. Mitchell

General Information Coeducational day college-preparatory and religious studies school, affiliated with Roman Catholic Church. Grades 9–12. Founded: 1882. Setting: suburban. 1 building on campus. Approved or accredited by North Dakota Department of Education. Total enrollment: 313. Upper school average class size: 20. Upper school faculty-student ratio: 1:18. There are 175 required school days per year for Upper School students. Upper School students typically attend 5 days per week. The average school day consists of 6 hours and 30 minutes.

Upper School Student Profile Grade 9: 81 students (45 boys, 36 girls); Grade 10: 80 students (35 boys, 45 girls); Grade 11: 77 students (46 boys, 31 girls); Grade 12: 75 students (36 boys, 39 girls). 80% of students are Roman Catholic.

Faculty School total: 24. In upper school: 10 men, 14 women; 12 have advanced degrees.

Subjects Offered Accounting, advanced chemistry, advanced math, Advanced Placement courses, algebra, American history, anatomy and physiology, art, band, biology, British literature-AP, business applications, business law, calculus-AP, ceramics, chemistry, chemistry-AP, choir, computer applications, conservation, ecology, economics, English, English literature-AP, general math, geography, global issues, health, journalism, Latin, leadership, modern European history-AP, physical education, physics, pre-algebra, pre-calculus, psychology-AP, religion, science, social studies, U.S. government, U.S. history, world history.

Special Academic Programs 5 Advanced Placement exams for which test preparation is offered; independent study.

College Admission Counseling 82 students graduated in 2013; 81 went to college, including Concordia College; North Dakota State University; University of Mary; University of North Dakota. Other: 1 entered military service. Median composite ACT: 24.

Student Life Upper grades have specified standards of dress, student council, honor system. Discipline rests primarily with faculty. Attendance at religious services is required.

Tuition and Aid Tuition installment plan (FACTS Tuition Payment Plan, monthly payment plans). Tuition reduction for siblings, merit scholarship grants, need-based scholarship grants available. In 2013–14, 54% of upper-school students received aid.

Admissions Traditional secondary-level entrance grade is 9. For fall 2013, 29 students applied for upper-level admission, 29 were accepted, 29 enrolled. Application fee required: $50. Interview required.

Athletics Interscholastic: aquatics (boys, girls), baseball (b), basketball (b,g), cheering (g), cross-country running (b,g), diving (b,g), football (b), golf (b,g), hockey (b), track and field (b,g), volleyball (g).

Computers Computers are regularly used in all academic classes. Computer resources include on-campus library services, Internet access, wireless campus network, Internet filtering or blocking technology. Campus intranet and student e-mail accounts are available to students. Students grades are available online.

Contact Ms. Lori K Hager, Director of Admissions, Marketing and Rercruitment. 701-893-3271. Fax: 701-893-3277. E-mail: lori.hager@jp2schools.org. Website: www.jp2schools.org

THE SHARON ACADEMY

Post Office Box 207
Sharon, Vermont 05065

Head of School: Michael B. Livingston

General Information Coeducational day college-preparatory school. Grades 7–12. Founded: 1996. Setting: rural. 80-acre campus. 1 building on campus. Approved or accredited by Independent Schools of Northern New England and Vermont Department of Education. Candidate for accreditation by New England Association of Schools and Colleges. Member of National Association of Independent Schools. Total enrollment: 165. Upper school average class size: 16. Upper school faculty-student ratio: 1:16. There are 175 required school days per year for Upper School students. Upper School students typically attend 5 days per week. The average school day consists of 7 hours.

Upper School Student Profile Grade 9: 33 students (16 boys, 17 girls); Grade 10: 34 students (15 boys, 19 girls); Grade 11: 31 students (16 boys, 15 girls); Grade 12: 30 students (12 boys, 18 girls).

Graduation Requirements Junior and Senior Exhibitions, community service.

Special Academic Programs Independent study; term-away projects; study abroad.

College Admission Counseling 32 students graduated in 2013; all went to college.

Student Life Upper grades have student council, honor system. Discipline rests equally with students and faculty.

Admissions Traditional secondary-level entrance grade is 9. Deadline for receipt of application materials: none. No application fee required. On-campus interview required.

Computers Computer network features include on-campus library services, Internet access, wireless campus network, Internet filtering or blocking technology. Campus intranet, student e-mail accounts, and computer access in designated common areas are available to students. Students grades are available online. The school has a published electronic and media policy.

Contact Amber Wylie, Associate Director of Communications and Admissions. 802-763-2500 Ext. 120. Fax: 802-763-2502. E-mail: awylie@sharonacademy.net. Website: www.SharonAcademy.org

SHATTUCK-ST. MARY'S SCHOOL

1000 Shumway Avenue
PO Box 218
Faribault, Minnesota 55021

Head of School: Kathy Layendecker

General Information Coeducational boarding and day college-preparatory, arts, and BioScience, STEM Education school, affiliated with Episcopal Church. Grades 6–PG. Founded: 1858. Setting: small town. Nearest major city is Minneapolis/St. Paul. Students are housed in single-sex dormitories. 250-acre campus. 10 buildings on campus. Approved or accredited by Independent Schools Association of the Central States, Midwest Association of Boarding Schools, National Association of Episcopal Schools, The Association of Boarding Schools, and Minnesota Department of Education. Member of National Association of Independent Schools and Secondary School Admission Test Board. Total enrollment: 443. Upper school average class size: 11. Upper school faculty-student ratio: 1:9. There are 167 required school days per year for Upper School students. Upper School students typically attend 5 days per week. The average school day consists of 7 hours.

Upper School Student Profile Grade 6: 7 students (4 boys, 3 girls); Grade 7: 11 students (7 boys, 4 girls); Grade 8: 23 students (13 boys, 10 girls); Grade 9: 63 students (35 boys, 28 girls); Grade 10: 91 students (61 boys, 30 girls); Grade 11: 128 students (78 boys, 50 girls); Grade 12: 114 students (66 boys, 48 girls); Postgraduate: 7 students (2 boys, 5 girls). 75% of students are boarding students. 25% are state residents. 44 states are represented in upper school student body. 32% are international students. International students from Canada, China, Mexico, Republic of Korea, Russian Federation, and Taiwan; 25 other countries represented in student body.

Faculty School total: 80. In upper school: 25 men, 30 women; 42 have advanced degrees; 60 reside on campus.

Subjects Offered 20th century world history, Advanced Placement courses, advanced studio art-AP, advanced TOEFL/grammar, algebra, American Civil War, American history, American history-AP, American literature, American sign language, anatomy and physiology, art, art history, astronomy, ballet, band, Bible studies, bioethics, biology, British literature, calculus, calculus-AP, ceramics, chamber groups, chemistry, chemistry-AP, choir, choral music, community service, composition, dance, digital photography, drama, drawing, economics, English, English language and composition-AP, English literature, English literature and composition-AP, environmental science-AP, ESL, ethics, European civilization, European history, European history-AP, expository writing, field ecology, film studies, fine arts, French, French language-AP, geography, geometry, government/civics, grammar, Greek, high adventure outdoor program, history, human anatomy, Latin, Latin American history, Mandarin, mathematics, microbiology, Middle Eastern history, music, Native American history, oil painting, orchestra, painting, physics, physics-AP, piano, pottery, pre-algebra, pre-calculus, psychology, psychology-AP, public speaking, religion, robotics, Roman civilization, science, social studies, South African history, Spanish, Spanish-AP, speech, statistics, statistics-AP, theater, trigonometry, U.S. history-AP, world geography, world history, world history-AP, writing.

Graduation Requirements Arts and fine arts (art, music, dance, drama), English, foreign language, mathematics, religion (includes Bible studies and theology), science, social studies (includes history), 20 hours of community service per year.

Special Academic Programs 17 Advanced Placement exams for which test preparation is offered; honors section; independent study; academic accommodation for the gifted, the musically talented, and the artistically talented; remedial reading and/or remedial writing; remedial math; programs in English, mathematics, general development for dyslexic students; ESL (67 students enrolled).

College Admission Counseling 106 students graduated in 2013; 101 went to college, including Butler University; Cornell University; University of Illinois at Urbana–Champaign; University of Minnesota, Twin Cities Campus; University of Rochester; University of Wisconsin–Madison. Other: 3 entered a postgraduate year, 2 had other specific plans.

Student Life Upper grades have uniform requirement, student council. Discipline rests primarily with faculty. Attendance at religious services is required.

Summer Programs ESL, sports, art/fine arts programs offered; session focuses on challenging, diversified instruction in the arts and athletics; ESL summer program; held on campus; accepts boys and girls; open to students from other schools.

Tuition and Aid Day student tuition: $28,100; 7-day tuition and room/board: $42,175. Tuition installment plan (Insured Tuition Payment Plan, monthly payment plans). Merit scholarship grants, need-based scholarship grants, Performing arts scholarship, Headmasters scholarship available. In 2013–14, 44% of upper-school students received aid. Total amount of financial aid awarded in 2013–14: $3,900,000.

Admissions Traditional secondary-level entrance grade is 10. For fall 2013, 1,012 students applied for upper-level admission, 312 were accepted, 184 enrolled. SSAT or TOEFL required. Deadline for receipt of application materials: none. Application fee required: $75. Interview required.

Athletics Interscholastic: baseball (boys), basketball (b,g), fencing (b,g), golf (b,g), ice hockey (b,g), indoor hockey (b,g), indoor soccer (b,g), lacrosse (b,g), soccer (b,g), tennis (b,g), volleyball (g); intramural: drill team (b,g), weight training (b,g); coed interscholastic: figure skating, soccer; coed intramural: basketball, dance, dance team, Frisbee, ice skating, jogging, modern dance, outdoor activities, outdoor recreation, ropes courses, strength & conditioning, table tennis, ultimate Frisbee, yoga. 29 coaches, 3 athletic trainers.

Computers Computers are regularly used in animation, college planning, creative writing, English, ESL, foreign language, history, independent study, mathematics, photography, SAT preparation, science, senior seminar, speech, writing, writing, yearbook classes. Computer network features include on-campus library services, Internet access, wireless campus network, Internet filtering or blocking technology. Campus intranet, student e-mail accounts, and computer access in designated common areas are available to students. Students grades are available online. The school has a published electronic and media policy.

Contact Mr. Jesse W. Fortney, Director of Admissions. 800-421-2724. Fax: 507-333-1661. E-mail: admissions@s-sm.org. Website: www.s-sm.org

SHAWE MEMORIAL JUNIOR/SENIOR HIGH SCHOOL

201 West State Street
Madison, Indiana 47250-2899

Head of School: Mr. Steven J. Hesse

General Information Coeducational day college-preparatory and religious studies school, affiliated with Roman Catholic Church. Grades 7–12. Founded: 1954. Setting: small town. 30-acre campus. 1 building on campus. Approved or accredited by North Central Association of Colleges and Schools and Indiana Department of Education. Total enrollment: 342. Upper school average class size: 12. Upper school faculty-student ratio: 1:9. There are 180 required school days per year for Upper School students. Upper School students typically attend 5 days per week. The average school day consists of 7 hours.

Upper School Student Profile Grade 9: 25 students (12 boys, 13 girls); Grade 10: 23 students (11 boys, 12 girls); Grade 11: 41 students (22 boys, 19 girls); Grade 12: 19 students (11 boys, 8 girls). 70% of students are Roman Catholic.

Faculty School total: 19. In upper school: 3 men, 16 women; 10 have advanced degrees.

Subjects Offered Advanced Placement courses.

Special Academic Programs International Baccalaureate program; 6 Advanced Placement exams for which test preparation is offered; honors section; independent study; study at local college for college credit; academic accommodation for the gifted; remedial reading and/or remedial writing; special instructional classes for deaf students, some special needs students can be accommodated on an individual basis.

College Admission Counseling 39 students graduated in 2013; 37 went to college, including Ball State University; Bellarmine University; Indiana University Bloomington; Purdue University; University of Cincinnati. Other: 2 went to work. Mean SAT critical reading: 534, mean SAT math: 516, mean SAT writing: 515, mean combined SAT: 1565. 24% scored over 600 on SAT critical reading, 19% scored over 600 on SAT math, 27% scored over 600 on SAT writing.

Student Life Upper grades have specified standards of dress, student council. Discipline rests primarily with faculty. Attendance at religious services is required.

Tuition and Aid Day student tuition: $5915. Tuition installment plan (The Tuition Plan, FACTS Tuition Payment Plan, individually arranged payment plans, multiple options). Tuition reduction for siblings, need-based scholarship grants available. In 2013–14, 35% of upper-school students received aid. Total amount of financial aid awarded in 2013–14: $161,537.

Admissions Traditional secondary-level entrance grade is 9. For fall 2013, 23 students applied for upper-level admission, 19 were accepted, 19 enrolled. Deadline for receipt of application materials: none. Application fee required: $150. Interview required.

Athletics Interscholastic: archery (boys), baseball (b), basketball (b,g), cheering (g), cross-country running (b,g), fencing (b), golf (b,g), soccer (b,g), softball (g), tennis (b,g), track and field (b,g), volleyball (g). 2 PE instructors, 10 coaches, 1 athletic trainer.

Computers Computer network features include on-campus library services, Internet access, wireless campus network, Internet filtering or blocking technology. Campus intranet is available to students. Students grades are available online.

Contact Mr. Philip J. Kahn, President. 812-273-5835 Ext. 245. Fax: 812-273-8975. E-mail: poppresident@popeace.org. Website: www.popeaceschools.org/

SHAWNIGAN LAKE SCHOOL

1975 Renfrew Road
Shawnigan Lake, British Columbia V0R 2W1, Canada

Head of School: Mr. David Robertson

General Information Coeducational boarding and day college-preparatory, arts, athletics, leadership, citizenship, and entrepreneurship, and language studies school. Grades 8–12. Founded: 1916. Setting: rural. Nearest major city is Victoria, Canada. Students are housed in single-sex dormitories. 300-acre campus. 50 buildings on campus. Approved or accredited by British Columbia Independent Schools Association, Canadian Association of Independent Schools, The Association of Boarding Schools, Western Boarding Schools Association, and British Columbia Department of Education. Affiliate member of National Association of Independent Schools; member of Secondary School Admission Test Board. Languages of instruction: English and French. Endowment: CAN$9 million. Total enrollment: 457. Upper school average class size: 15. Upper school faculty-student ratio: 1:8. Upper School students typically attend 6 days per week.

Upper School Student Profile Grade 8: 34 students (19 boys, 15 girls); Grade 9: 61 students (41 boys, 20 girls); Grade 10: 121 students (69 boys, 52 girls); Grade 11: 125 students (75 boys, 50 girls); Grade 12: 116 students (69 boys, 47 girls). 90% of students are boarding students. 60% are province residents. 17 provinces are represented in upper school student body. 20% are international students. International students from China, Democratic People's Republic of Korea, Germany, Hong Kong, Mexico, and United States; 19 other countries represented in student body.

Faculty School total: 69. In upper school: 41 men, 28 women; 23 have advanced degrees; 44 reside on campus.

Subjects Offered Advanced Placement courses, advanced studio art-AP, algebra, architectural drawing, art, art history, art history-AP, biology, biology-AP, business skills, calculus, calculus-AP, career and personal planning, chemistry, chemistry-AP, choir, comparative civilizations, computer science, computer science-AP, creative writing, earth science, economics, English, English language and composition-AP, English literature, English literature and composition-AP, English-AP, entrepreneurship, environmental science, European history-AP, fine arts, French, French language-AP, French literature-AP, French-AP, geography, geometry, health, history, human geography - AP, industrial arts, information technology, law, mathematics, media studies, music, philosophy, physical education, physics, physics-AP, science, social studies, Spanish, sports science, study skills, theater, trigonometry, U.S. history-AP, woodworking, writing.

Graduation Requirements Arts and fine arts (art, music, dance, drama), career and personal planning, English, mathematics, physical education (includes health), science, social studies (includes history), graduation requirements are mandated by the BC Provincial Government and include English 12 plus 4 additional grade 12 courses, and 30 hours of work experience, refer to the curriculum courses to see the subject offerings.

Special Academic Programs Advanced Placement exam preparation; honors section; academic accommodation for the gifted; remedial reading and/or remedial writing; remedial math; ESL (10 students enrolled).

College Admission Counseling 117 students graduated in 2013; 113 went to college, including McGill University; Queen's University at Kingston; The University of British Columbia; The University of Western Ontario; University of Toronto; University of Victoria. Other: 2 went to work, 2 had other specific plans.

Student Life Upper grades have uniform requirement, student council, honor system. Discipline rests equally with students and faculty. Attendance at religious services is required.

Summer Programs Sports programs offered; session focuses on rugby; held on campus; accepts boys and girls; open to students from other schools.

Tuition and Aid Day student tuition: CAN$22,200; 7-day tuition and room/board: CAN$41,300–CAN$54,700. Tuition reduction for siblings, merit scholarship grants available. In 2013–14, 25% of upper-school students received aid; total upper-school merit-scholarship money awarded: CAN$300,000. Total amount of financial aid awarded in 2013–14: CAN$1,000,000.

Admissions Traditional secondary-level entrance grade is 8. For fall 2013, 302 students applied for upper-level admission, 182 were accepted, 168 enrolled. English entrance exam and Math Placement Exam required. Deadline for receipt of application materials: none. Application fee required: CAN$200. Interview required.

Athletics Interscholastic: basketball (boys, girls), crew (b,g), cross-country running (b,g), field hockey (g), golf (b,g), hockey (b), ice hockey (b), rowing (b,g), rugby (b,g), soccer (b,g), squash (b,g), tennis (b,g), volleyball (g); intramural: ballet (g), basketball (b,g), crew (b,g), field hockey (g), golf (b,g), rowing (b,g), rugby (b,g), soccer (b,g), squash (b,g), strength & conditioning (b,g), tennis (b,g), volleyball (g), weight training (b,g), winter soccer (g); coed interscholastic: hockey, ice hockey; coed intramural: aerobics, aerobics/dance, alpine skiing, aquatics, backpacking, badminton, canoeing/kayaking, climbing, cross-country running, dance, fitness, golf, hiking/backpacking, jogging, kayaking, modern dance, nordic skiing, ocean paddling, outdoor activities, outdoor adventure, outdoor education, outdoor recreation, outdoor skills, outdoors, physical fitness, physical training, rock climbing, running, skiing (cross-country), skiing (downhill), snowboarding, snowshoeing, swimming and diving, track and field, triathlon, wilderness survival, yoga. 3 PE instructors, 11 coaches, 1 athletic trainer.

Computers Computers are regularly used in animation, architecture, art, business, college planning, computer applications, design, drafting, drawing and design, foreign language, graphic arts, history, information technology, library, mathematics, photography, research skills, science, social studies, video film production, yearbook classes. Computer network features include on-campus library services, online commercial services, Internet access, wireless campus network, Internet filtering or blocking technology. Campus intranet and student e-mail accounts are available to students. Students grades are available online. The school has a published electronic and media policy.

Contact Ms. Margot Allen, Associate Director of Admissions. 250-743-6207. Fax: 250-743-6280. E-mail: admissions@shawnigan.ca. Website: www.shawnigan.ca

SHELTON SCHOOL AND EVALUATION CENTER
Dallas, Texas
See Special Needs Schools section.

THE SHIPLEY SCHOOL
814 Yarrow Street
Bryn Mawr, Pennsylvania 19010-3525
Head of School: Dr. Steven S. Piltch

General Information Coeducational day college-preparatory school. Grades PK–12. Founded: 1894. Setting: suburban. Nearest major city is Philadelphia. 36-acre campus. 4 buildings on campus. Approved or accredited by Middle States Association of Colleges and Schools and Pennsylvania Association of Independent Schools. Member of National Association of Independent Schools and Secondary School Admission Test Board. Endowment: $33.2 million. Total enrollment: 823. Upper school average class size: 12. Upper school faculty-student ratio: 1:7. There are 173 required school days per year for Upper School students. Upper School students typically attend 5 days per week. The average school day consists of 7 hours and 30 minutes.

Upper School Student Profile Grade 9: 84 students (39 boys, 45 girls); Grade 10: 89 students (43 boys, 46 girls); Grade 11: 105 students (55 boys, 50 girls); Grade 12: 74 students (40 boys, 34 girls).

Faculty School total: 139. In upper school: 30 men, 37 women; 48 have advanced degrees.

Subjects Offered Advanced studio art-AP, algebra, American history, American literature, ancient world history, art, art history, athletic training, athletics, band, bioethics, biology, calculus, chamber groups, chemistry, chorus, classical language, college admission preparation, college counseling, conceptual physics, concert bell choir, CPR, drama, drama performance, dramatic arts, ecology, environmental systems, economics, economics and history, English, English literature, European history, film studies, fine arts, forensics, French, geometry, global issues, global studies, grammar, health, health and wellness, health education, Homeric Greek, honors English, honors geometry, honors U.S. history, honors world history, independent study, introduction to theater, jazz band, Latin, leadership, library skills, Mandarin, mathematics, medieval history, Middle East, model United Nations, music, music theory, musical productions, orchestra, performing arts, philosophy, photography, physical education, physical fitness, physics, pre-calculus, research skills, science, senior project, senior seminar, service learning/internship, Shakespeare, Spanish, speech and debate, statistics, student publications, studio art-AP, theater, theater arts, urban studies, wind ensemble, world history, world literature.

Graduation Requirements English, foreign language, interdisciplinary studies, mathematics, performing arts, physical education (includes health), research skills, science, senior project, senior seminar, social studies (includes history), studio art, 40 hours of community service/service learning.

Special Academic Programs 1 Advanced Placement exam for which test preparation is offered; honors section; accelerated programs; independent study; term-away projects; study abroad; academic accommodation for the gifted.

College Admission Counseling 84 students graduated in 2013; all went to college, including Harvard University; New York University; Syracuse University; The George Washington University; University of Pennsylvania; University of Pittsburgh. Mean SAT critical reading: 631, mean SAT math: 641, mean SAT writing: 646, mean combined SAT: 1903, mean composite ACT: 27.

Student Life Upper grades have specified standards of dress, student council, honor system. Discipline rests equally with students and faculty.

Tuition and Aid Day student tuition: $32,625. Tuition installment plan (monthly payment plans). Need-based scholarship grants available. In 2013–14, 31% of upper-school students received aid. Total amount of financial aid awarded in 2013–14: $2,504,090.

Admissions Traditional secondary-level entrance grade is 9. For fall 2013, 321 students applied for upper-level admission, 216 were accepted, 128 enrolled. ISEE, SSAT or Wechsler Intelligence Scale for Children required. Deadline for receipt of application materials: January 17. Application fee required: $50. On-campus interview required.

Athletics Interscholastic: baseball (boys), basketball (b,g), crew (b,g), cross-country running (b,g), field hockey (g), independent competitive sports (b,g), lacrosse (b,g), rowing (b,g), soccer (b,g), softball (g), squash (b,g), tennis (b,g), volleyball (g), weight training (b,g); intramural: aerobics (b,g), aerobics/Nautilus (b,g), dance (g), modern dance (g), Nautilus (b,g); coed interscholastic: diving, golf, independent competitive sports, swimming and diving, weight training; coed intramural: fitness, Nautilus, physical fitness, yoga. 10 PE instructors, 57 coaches, 2 athletic trainers.

Computers Computers are regularly used in all classes. Computer network features include on-campus library services, online commercial services, Internet access, wireless campus network, Internet filtering or blocking technology, all progress, midterm, and final reports are online, 3D printer. Campus intranet, student e-mail accounts, and computer access in designated common areas are available to students. Students grades are available online. The school has a published electronic and media policy.

Contact Mrs. Zoe Marshall, Assistant to the Director of Admissions. 610-525-4300 Ext. 4118. Fax: 610-525-5082. E-mail: zmarshall@shipleyschool.org. Website: www.shipleyschool.org

SHOORE CENTRE FOR LEARNING
Toronto, Ontario, Canada
See Special Needs Schools section.

SHORELINE CHRISTIAN
2400 Northeast 147th Street
Shoreline, Washington 98155
Head of School: Mr. Timothy E. Visser

General Information Coeducational day college-preparatory, general academic, and religious studies school, affiliated with Christian faith. Grades PS–12. Founded: 1952. Setting: suburban. Nearest major city is Seattle. 7-acre campus. 3 buildings on campus. Approved or accredited by Christian Schools International, Northwest Accreditation Commission, Northwest Association of Schools and Colleges, and Washington Department of Education. Total enrollment: 212. Upper school average class size: 16. Upper school faculty-student ratio: 1:7. There are 180 required school days per year for Upper School students. Upper School students typically attend 5 days per week. The average school day consists of 6 hours and 30 minutes.

Upper School Student Profile Grade 6: 12 students (7 boys, 5 girls); Grade 7: 13 students (6 boys, 7 girls); Grade 8: 9 students (5 boys, 4 girls); Grade 9: 11 students (5 boys, 6 girls); Grade 10: 17 students (10 boys, 7 girls); Grade 11: 16 students (9 boys, 7 girls); Grade 12: 18 students (12 boys, 6 girls). 100% of students are Christian faith.

Faculty School total: 27. In upper school: 5 men, 9 women; 6 have advanced degrees.

Subjects Offered 20th century history, advanced math, Advanced Placement courses, algebra, American history, American literature, art, band, Bible, biology,

British literature, calculus, calculus-AP, chemistry, choir, Christian doctrine, college writing, composition, computer applications, consumer education, current events, current history, drama, drawing, English, English composition, English literature, fine arts, geography, geometry, global studies, government, health, human anatomy, jazz band, keyboarding, language arts, life science, life skills, literature, mathematics, mathematics-AP, music appreciation, physical education, physical science, physics, pre-calculus, psychology, sculpture, sociology, Spanish, speech, study skills, U.S. history, Washington State and Northwest History, weight training, Western civilization, world literature, world religions, yearbook.

Graduation Requirements American government, American literature, Bible, British literature, composition, electives, English, global issues, keyboarding, mathematics, occupational education, physical education (includes health), portfolio art, portfolio writing, science, social sciences, speech, U.S. history, Washington State and Northwest History, Western civilization, world literature.

Special Academic Programs Honors section; independent study; study at local college for college credit; remedial reading and/or remedial writing; programs in English for dyslexic students.

College Admission Counseling 25 students graduated in 2013; 23 went to college, including Edmonds Community College; Seattle Pacific University; University of Washington; Washington State University; Western Washington University; Whitworth University. Other: 1 went to work, 1 had other specific plans. Median SAT critical reading: 521, median SAT math: 512, median SAT writing: 528, median combined SAT: 1561, median composite ACT: 26. 32% scored over 600 on SAT critical reading, 28% scored over 600 on SAT math, 33% scored over 600 on SAT writing, 31% scored over 1800 on combined SAT, 67% scored over 26 on composite ACT.

Student Life Upper grades have specified standards of dress, student council, honor system. Discipline rests primarily with faculty. Attendance at religious services is required.

Tuition and Aid Day student tuition: $10,200–$11,675. Tuition installment plan (monthly payment plans, individually arranged payment plans, prepaid cash tuition discount, quarterly or semi-annual payment plans). Tuition reduction for siblings, need-based scholarship grants, discount for qualifying Pastor families, discount for staff available. In 2013–14, 29% of upper-school students received aid. Total amount of financial aid awarded in 2013–14: $170,000.

Admissions Traditional secondary-level entrance grade is 9. For fall 2013, 6 students applied for upper-level admission, 5 were accepted, 5 enrolled. Deadline for receipt of application materials: none. Application fee required: $100. Interview required.

Athletics Interscholastic: basketball (boys, girls), soccer (b), volleyball (g); coed interscholastic: golf, soccer, track and field. 1 PE instructor, 17 coaches.

Computers Computers are regularly used in all academic, art, computer applications, library, music, occupational education, research skills, yearbook classes. Computer network features include on-campus library services, Internet access, wireless campus network, Internet filtering or blocking technology. Campus intranet, student e-mail accounts, and computer access in designated common areas are available to students. Students grades are available online. The school has a published electronic and media policy.

Contact Mrs. Laurie Dykstra, Director of Development. 206-364-7777 Ext. 308. Fax: 206-364-0349. E-mail: ldykstra@shorelinechristian.org. Website: www.shorelinechristian.org

SIGNET CHRISTIAN SCHOOL

95 Jonesville Crescent
North York, Ontario M4A 1H2, Canada

Head of School: Mr. Trent Mansell

General Information Coeducational day college-preparatory, business, and Science school, affiliated with Christian faith. Grades JK–12. Founded: 1975. Setting: urban. Nearest major city is Toronto, Canada. 1-acre campus. 1 building on campus. Approved or accredited by Association of Christian Schools International and Ontario Department of Education. Language of instruction: English. Total enrollment: 37. Upper school average class size: 6. Upper school faculty-student ratio: 1:5. There are 178 required school days per year for Upper School students. Upper School students typically attend 5 days per week. The average school day consists of 6 hours and 30 minutes.

Upper School Student Profile Grade 10: 2 students (1 boy, 1 girl); Grade 11: 5 students (3 boys, 2 girls); Grade 12: 9 students (6 boys, 3 girls). 80% of students are Christian.

Faculty School total: 11. In upper school: 2 men, 3 women; 1 has an advanced degree.

Subjects Offered Biology, business studies, calculus, Canadian geography, Canadian history, career education, chemistry, civics, English, ESL, French as a second language, math analysis, math applications, physics, science, visual arts.

Graduation Requirements English, Ontario Ministry of Education requirements.

Special Academic Programs Independent study; ESL (3 students enrolled).

Student Life Upper grades have uniform requirement, student council. Discipline rests primarily with faculty. Attendance at religious services is required.

Tuition and Aid Day student tuition: CAN$7000. Tuition installment plan (individually arranged payment plans). Tuition reduction for siblings available.

Admissions SLEP required. Deadline for receipt of application materials: none. No application fee required.

Athletics Coed Intramural: basketball, bowling, cross-country running, ice skating, skiing (downhill), snowboarding, soccer, table tennis, track and field.

Computers Computers are regularly used in English, mathematics, technology classes. Computer network features include Internet access.

Contact Admissions. 416-750-7515. Fax: 416-750-7720. E-mail: scs@titan.tcn.net. Website: www.signetschool.ca

SMITH SCHOOL

New York, New York
See Special Needs Schools section.

SOLOMON COLLEGE

Suite 228, 10621 100th Avenue
Edmonton, Alberta T5J 0B3, Canada

Head of School: Ms. Ping Ping Lee

General Information Coeducational day and distance learning college-preparatory, general academic, vocational, bilingual studies, and ESL school. Grades 10–12. Distance learning grades 10–12. Founded: 1994. Setting: urban. 1 building on campus. Approved or accredited by Association of Independent Schools and Colleges of Alberta and Alberta Department of Education. Language of instruction: English. Total enrollment: 25. Upper school average class size: 10. Upper school faculty-student ratio: 1:10. There are 225 required school days per year for Upper School students. Upper School students typically attend 5 days per week. The average school day consists of 4 hours and 30 minutes.

Upper School Student Profile Grade 11: 3 students (3 boys); Grade 12: 10 students (5 boys, 5 girls).

Faculty School total: 5. In upper school: 2 men, 3 women; 2 have advanced degrees.

Subjects Offered Biology, calculus, career and personal planning, chemistry, Chinese, computer information systems, computer skills, computer technologies, English literature, ESL, keyboarding, mathematics, physics, social studies.

Special Academic Programs ESL (80 students enrolled).

College Admission Counseling 10 students graduated in 2012; 8 went to college, including University of Alberta; University of Calgary; University of Lethbridge.

Student Life Discipline rests equally with students and faculty.

Tuition and Aid Day student tuition: CAN$5800.

Admissions Traditional secondary-level entrance grade is 10. For fall 2012, 13 students applied for upper-level admission, 13 were accepted, 13 enrolled. Placement test required. Deadline for receipt of application materials: August 31. Application fee required: CAN$200.

Computers Computer network features include Internet access, wireless campus network, Internet filtering or blocking technology. Campus intranet is available to students.

Contact Mr. Sunny Ip, Registrar. 780-431-1516. Fax: 780-431-1644. E-mail: sunnyi@solomoncollege.ca. Website: www.solomoncollege.ca/index_home.htm

SONOMA ACADEMY

2500 Farmers Lane
Santa Rosa, California 95404

Head of School: Janet Durgin

General Information Coeducational day college-preparatory and Environmental Leadership & Global Citizenship concentrations school. Grades 9–12. Founded: 1999. Setting: suburban. Nearest major city is San Francisco. 34-acre campus. 3 buildings on campus. Approved or accredited by Western Association of Schools and Colleges and California Department of Education. Member of National Association of Independent Schools. Total enrollment: 268. Upper school average class size: 15. Upper school faculty-student ratio: 1:12. Upper School students typically attend 5 days per week. The average school day consists of 6 hours and 30 minutes.

Upper School Student Profile Grade 9: 68 students (33 boys, 35 girls); Grade 10: 60 students (31 boys, 29 girls); Grade 11: 71 students (37 boys, 34 girls); Grade 12: 69 students (27 boys, 42 girls).

Faculty School total: 26. In upper school: 12 men, 14 women; 17 have advanced degrees.

Subjects Offered Algebra, anatomy and physiology, arts, British literature, calculus, calculus-AP, chemistry, chemistry-AP, choir, computer programming, constitutional law, creative writing, digital photography, economics, engineering, English language and composition-AP, English literature and composition-AP, environmental studies, expository writing, French, genetics, geometry, historiography, literature, Mandarin, music history, oceanography, philosophy, physics, physics-AP, Shakespeare, Spanish, Spanish language-AP, studio art, theater.

Special Academic Programs 7 Advanced Placement exams for which test preparation is offered; honors section; independent study; study abroad.

College Admission Counseling 48 students graduated in 2013; all went to college, including Amherst College; Reed College; Tulane University. Mean SAT critical reading: 607, mean SAT math: 595, mean SAT writing: 595, mean combined SAT: 1797.

Student Life Upper grades have student council. Discipline rests equally with students and faculty.

Tuition and Aid Day student tuition: $36,140. Tuition installment plan (Insured Tuition Payment Plan, monthly payment plans). Need-based scholarship grants, STEM Scholarships available. In 2013–14, 50% of upper-school students received aid. Total amount of financial aid awarded in 2013–14: $2,600,000.

Admissions Traditional secondary-level entrance grade is 9. SSAT required. Deadline for receipt of application materials: January 9. Application fee required: $90. Interview required.

Athletics Interscholastic: baseball (boys), basketball (b,g), cross-country running (b,g), equestrian sports (b,g), lacrosse (b,g), soccer (b,g), track and field (b,g), volleyball (g); coed intramural: aerobics/dance, combined training, dance, fencing, fitness, flag football, Frisbee, kickball, martial arts, outdoor education, physical fitness, physical training, power lifting, rock climbing, softball, strength & conditioning, tai chi, ultimate Frisbee, weight training, yoga.

Computers Computers are regularly used in all classes. Computer network features include on-campus library services, online commercial services, Internet access, wireless campus network, Internet filtering or blocking technology, one-to-one laptop program, digital technology center, broadcast studio. Campus intranet and student e-mail accounts are available to students. Students grades are available online. The school has a published electronic and media policy.

Contact Sandy Stack, Director of Enrollment and Marketing. 707-545-1770. Fax: 707-636-2474. E-mail: sandy.stack@sonomaacademy.org. Website: www.sonomaacademy.org/

SOUNDVIEW PREPARATORY SCHOOL

370 Underhill Avenue
Yorktown Heights, New York 10598

Head of School: W. Glyn Hearn

General Information Coeducational day college-preparatory, arts, and technology school. Grades 6–PG. Founded: 1989. Setting: suburban. Nearest major city is New York. 13-acre campus. 7 buildings on campus. Approved or accredited by New York Department of Education. Member of National Association of Independent Schools. Total enrollment: 68. Upper school average class size: 7. Upper school faculty-student ratio: 1:5. There are 164 required school days per year for Upper School students. Upper School students typically attend 5 days per week. The average school day consists of 6 hours and 47 minutes.

Upper School Student Profile Grade 9: 14 students (8 boys, 6 girls); Grade 10: 17 students (9 boys, 8 girls); Grade 11: 13 students (5 boys, 8 girls); Grade 12: 12 students (4 boys, 8 girls).

Faculty School total: 15. In upper school: 3 men, 11 women; 10 have advanced degrees.

Subjects Offered Advanced Placement courses, advanced studio art-AP, algebra, American history, American literature, anatomy and physiology, art, art-AP, biology, calculus, chemistry, computer science, computer science-AP, earth science, English, English literature, English-AP, European history-AP, French, geometry, health, Italian, Latin, mathematics, music, physical education, physics, psychology-AP, science, social studies, Spanish, study skills, U.S. history-AP, world history.

Graduation Requirements Art, electives, English, foreign language, health, history, mathematics, physical education (includes health), science.

Special Academic Programs 6 Advanced Placement exams for which test preparation is offered; honors section; accelerated programs; independent study; academic accommodation for the gifted, the musically talented, and the artistically talented; special instructional classes for students needing wheelchair accessibility.

College Admission Counseling 16 students graduated in 2013; 15 went to college, including Boston University; Clark University; Sarah Lawrence College; Skidmore College; University of Vermont; Wheaton College. Other: 1 had other specific plans. Mean SAT critical reading: 600, mean SAT math: 590, mean SAT writing: 560, mean composite ACT: 28.

Student Life Discipline rests primarily with faculty.

Tuition and Aid Day student tuition: $34,300–$35,500. Need-based scholarship grants available. In 2013–14, 20% of upper-school students received aid. Total amount of financial aid awarded in 2013–14: $420,000.

Admissions Traditional secondary-level entrance grade is 9. For fall 2013, 30 students applied for upper-level admission, 21 were accepted, 17 enrolled. ERB (CTP-Verbal, Quantitative) or ERB Mathematics required. Deadline for receipt of application materials: none. Application fee required: $50. On-campus interview required.

Athletics Coed Interscholastic: basketball, soccer, ultimate Frisbee; coed intramural: skiing (downhill). 1 PE instructor, 1 coach.

Computers Computers are regularly used in all academic classes. Computer network features include Internet access, wireless campus network, Internet filtering or blocking technology. Campus intranet and student e-mail accounts are available to students. The school has a published electronic and media policy.

Contact Mary E. Ivanyi, Assistant Head. 914-962-2780. Fax: 914-302-2769. E-mail: mivanyi@soundviewprep.org. Website: www.soundviewprep.org

See Display on next page and Close-Up on page 568.

SOUTHFIELD CHRISTIAN HIGH SCHOOL

28650 Lahser Road
Southfield, Michigan 48034-2099

Head of School: Mrs. Sue Hoffenbacher

General Information Coeducational day and distance learning college-preparatory, arts, religious studies, and technology school, affiliated with Christian faith, Evangelical faith. Grades PK–12. Distance learning grades 9–12. Founded: 1970. Setting: suburban. Nearest major city is Detroit. 28-acre campus. 1 building on campus. Approved or accredited by Association of Christian Schools International, Independent Schools Association of the Central States, North Central Association of Colleges and Schools, and Michigan Department of Education. Endowment: $1.5 million. Total enrollment: 577. Upper school average class size: 22. Upper school faculty-student ratio: 1:20. There are 176 required school days per year for Upper School students. Upper School students typically attend 5 days per week. The average school day consists of 7 hours.

Upper School Student Profile Grade 9: 56 students (19 boys, 37 girls); Grade 10: 46 students (27 boys, 19 girls); Grade 11: 48 students (27 boys, 21 girls); Grade 12: 59 students (25 boys, 34 girls). 100% of students are Christian faith, members of Evangelical faith.

Faculty School total: 28. In upper school: 14 men, 14 women; 13 have advanced degrees.

Subjects Offered Accounting, Advanced Placement courses, algebra, American government, American history, American history-AP, American literature, American literature-AP, ancient world history, art, band, Bible, biology, biology-AP, British literature, calculus-AP, chemistry, chemistry-AP, choir, chorus, communication arts, composition-AP, computer applications, computer programming, conceptual physics, creative writing, drawing and design, economics, English language-AP, English literature and composition-AP, film and literature, French, geography, geometry, government, graphic design, health, instrumental music, Life of Christ, literature and composition-AP, Middle Eastern history, New Testament, organic chemistry, photography, physical education, physics-AP, pre-calculus, probability and statistics, Russian history, senior project, Spanish, speech and debate, U.S. history, vocal music, Web site design, world studies, yearbook.

Special Academic Programs Advanced Placement exam preparation; honors section; independent study.

College Admission Counseling 41 students graduated in 2013; all went to college, including Grand Valley State University; Hope College; Michigan State University; Oakland University; University of Michigan; Wheaton College. Median SAT critical reading: 460, median SAT math: 430, median SAT writing: 480, median composite ACT: 24. 25% scored over 26 on composite ACT.

Student Life Upper grades have uniform requirement, student council. Discipline rests primarily with faculty. Attendance at religious services is required.

Summer Programs Rigorous outdoor training programs offered; session focuses on physical education; held on campus; accepts boys and girls; not open to students from other schools. 10 students usually enrolled. 2014 schedule: June 16 to June 27. Application deadline: May 1.

Tuition and Aid Day student tuition: $8930. Tuition installment plan (FACTS Tuition Payment Plan). Tuition reduction for siblings, need-based scholarship grants available. In 2013–14, 10% of upper-school students received aid.

Admissions Traditional secondary-level entrance grade is 9. For fall 2013, 65 students applied for upper-level admission, 25 were accepted, 16 enrolled. Any standardized test required. Deadline for receipt of application materials: none. No application fee required. On-campus interview required.

Athletics Interscholastic: baseball (boys), basketball (b,g), cheering (g), cross-country running (b,g), football (b), soccer (b,g), softball (g), track and field (b,g), volleyball (g); coed interscholastic: golf; coed intramural: skiing (downhill), weight lifting. 1 PE instructor, 1 athletic trainer.

Computers Computers are regularly used in art, commercial art, computer applications, creative writing, drawing and design, graphic arts, graphic design, independent study, media production, programming, publishing, Web site design, writing, yearbook classes. Computer network features include on-campus library services, Internet access, wireless campus network, Internet filtering or blocking technology. Student e-mail accounts are available to students. Students grades are available online. The school has a published electronic and media policy.

Contact Mrs. Alisa Ruffin, High School Principal. 248-357-3660 Ext. 278. Fax: 248-357-5271. E-mail: aruffin@southfieldchristian.org. Website: www.southfieldchristian.org

SOUTHWEST CHRISTIAN SCHOOL, INC.

7001 Benbrook Lake Drive
Fort Worth, Texas 76132

Head of School: Dr. Penny Armstrong

General Information Coeducational day college-preparatory, arts, religious studies, and technology school, affiliated with Christian faith. Grades PK–12. Founded: 1969. Setting: suburban. 39-acre campus. 3 buildings on campus. Approved or accredited by Southern Association of Colleges and Schools and Texas Department of Education. Member of National Association of Independent Schools. Total enrollment: 861. Upper school average class size: 16. Upper school faculty-student ratio: 1:11. There are 176 required school days per year for Upper School students. Upper School students typically attend 5 days per week. The average school day consists of 7 hours.

Upper School Student Profile Grade 7: 76 students (35 boys, 41 girls); Grade 8: 67 students (28 boys, 39 girls); Grade 9: 65 students (21 boys, 44 girls); Grade 10: 85 students (39 boys, 46 girls); Grade 11: 79 students (43 boys, 36 girls); Grade 12: 68 students (33 boys, 35 girls).

Faculty School total: 130. In upper school: 13 men, 35 women; 34 have advanced degrees.

Subjects Offered 1 1/2 elective credits, advanced math, algebra, American government, American literature, American literature-AP, anatomy and physiology, art, Bible studies, biology, biology-AP, British literature, British literature-AP, calculus, calculus-AP, chemistry, chemistry-AP, choir, drama, English, English literature-AP, English-AP, foreign language, French, geometry, government, history, honors algebra, honors English, honors geometry, honors U.S. history, honors world history, journalism, keyboarding, lab science, leadership, literature and composition-AP, physics, physics-AP, pre-algebra, pre-calculus, psychology, SAT preparation, Spanish, speech, technology, U.S. history, U.S. history-AP, Web site design.

Graduation Requirements 4 years of Bible courses.

Special Academic Programs Advanced Placement exam preparation; honors section; accelerated programs; study at local college for college credit; study abroad; academic accommodation for the gifted.

College Admission Counseling 77 students graduated in 2012; 74 went to college. Other: 3 entered military service.

Student Life Upper grades have uniform requirement, student council, honor system. Discipline rests primarily with faculty. Attendance at religious services is required.

Tuition and Aid Day student tuition: $10,275–$13,700. Tuition installment plan (FACTS Tuition Payment Plan). Need-based scholarship grants available. In 2012–13, 20% of upper-school students received aid. Total amount of financial aid awarded in 2012–13: $455,000.

Admissions Traditional secondary-level entrance grade is 9. For fall 2012, 106 students applied for upper-level admission, 99 were accepted, 62 enrolled. Stanford 9 required. Deadline for receipt of application materials: none. No application fee required. Interview required.

Athletics Interscholastic: aerobics/dance (girls), baseball (b), basketball (b,g), cheering (g), cross-country running (b,g), dance team (g), equestrian sports (b,g), football (b), golf (b,g), soccer (b,g), softball (g), track and field (b,g), volleyball (g), wrestling (b); intramural: physical training (b,g); coed interscholastic: aquatics, equestrian sports, paint ball, rodeo; coed intramural: aquatics, fitness, strength & conditioning, weight training. 2 PE instructors, 12 coaches, 1 athletic trainer.

Computers Computers are regularly used in all academic classes. Computer network features include on-campus library services, online commercial services, Internet access, wireless campus network, Internet filtering or blocking technology, computer carts for classroom use. Student e-mail accounts and computer access in designated common areas are available to students. Students grades are available online. The school has a published electronic and media policy.

Contact Mr. Travis Crow, Dean of Student Services. 817-294-9596 Ext. 207. Fax: 817-294-9603. E-mail: tcrow@southwestchristian.org. Website: www.southwestchristian.org

SOUTHWESTERN ACADEMY

Beaver Creek Ranch Campus
Rimrock, Arizona 86335

Head of School: Mr. Kenneth Veronda

General Information Coeducational boarding and day college-preparatory, general academic, and arts school. Grades 9–PG. Founded: 1963. Setting: rural. Nearest major city is Sedona. Students are housed in single-sex dormitories. 185-acre campus. 24 buildings on campus. Approved or accredited by The Association of Boarding Schools and Arizona Department of Education. Member of Secondary School Admission Test Board. Endowment: $10 million. Total enrollment: 17. Upper school average class size: 6. Upper school faculty-student ratio: 1:3. There are 184 required school days per year for Upper School students. Upper School students typically attend 5 days per week. The average school day consists of 8 hours.

Upper School Student Profile Grade 9: 3 students (2 boys, 1 girl); Grade 10: 4 students (2 boys, 2 girls); Grade 11: 6 students (3 boys, 3 girls); Grade 12: 4 students (2 boys, 2 girls). 100% of students are boarding students. 3% are state residents. 2 states are represented in upper school student body. 70% are international students. International students from China, Indonesia, Mexico, Saudi Arabia, and Serbia and Montenegro.

Faculty School total: 9. In upper school: 8 men, 1 woman; 4 have advanced degrees; 6 reside on campus.

Subjects Offered Advanced math, Advanced Placement courses, algebra, American history, American literature, American literature-AP, art, art appreciation, art history, astronomy, biology, biology-AP, British literature, calculus, chemistry, earth science, ecology, economics, English, English composition, environmental education, environmental science, environmental studies, ESL, fashion, fine arts, general math, geometry, health, integrated science, Latin, math review, mathematics, music, music appreciation, outdoor education, physics, pre-algebra, Spanish, studio art, U.S. government, world cultures, yearbook.

Graduation Requirements Algebra, American government, American history, American literature, British literature, computer literacy, economics, electives, English, foreign language, geometry, lab science, mathematics, physical education (includes health), visual and performing arts, world cultures. Community service is required.

Special Academic Programs Study at local college for college credit; ESL (10 students enrolled).

College Admission Counseling 8 students graduated in 2013; all went to college, including Arizona State University; Drexel University; The University of Arizona; University of Nevada, Las Vegas. Median SAT critical reading: 550, median SAT math: 700, median SAT writing: 550, median combined SAT: 1800.

Student Life Upper grades have specified standards of dress, student council, honor system. Discipline rests primarily with faculty.

Summer Programs Remediation, enrichment, advancement, ESL, art/fine arts, rigorous outdoor training programs offered; session focuses on academics and outdoor/environmental education; held on campus; accepts boys and girls; open to students from other schools. 30 students usually enrolled. 2014 schedule: June 23 to August 15. Application deadline: none.

Tuition and Aid Day student tuition: $16,550; 7-day tuition and room/board: $33,750. Tuition installment plan (monthly payment plans, individually arranged payment plans). Need-based scholarship grants available. In 2013–14, 40% of upper-school students received aid. Total amount of financial aid awarded in 2013–14: $600,000.

Admissions Traditional secondary-level entrance grade is 9. For fall 2013, 49 students applied for upper-level admission, 28 were accepted, 17 enrolled. English language, English proficiency, ESL, High School Placement Test, International English Language Test, international math and English tests, SLEP, SLEP for foreign students, TOEFL or writing sample required. Deadline for receipt of application materials: none. Application fee required: $100. Interview required.

Athletics Interscholastic: basketball (boys, girls), volleyball (g); coed interscholastic: golf, soccer; coed intramural: alpine skiing, aquatics, archery, backpacking, badminton, ballet, baseball, basketball, bicycling, billiards, canoeing/kayaking, climbing, croquet, cross-country running, equestrian sports, fishing, fitness, fitness walking, flag football, Frisbee, golf, hiking/backpacking, horseback riding, horseshoes, ice skating, mountain biking, outdoor activities, outdoor adventure, outdoor education, outdoor recreation, outdoor skills, outdoors, paint ball, physical fitness, rafting, rock climbing, ropes courses, running, skiing (cross-country), skiing (downhill), snowboarding, soccer, softball, swimming and diving, table tennis, tennis, touch football, track and field, volleyball, walking, weight lifting, weight training, wilderness. 1 PE instructor, 2 coaches.

Computers Computers are regularly used in all academic, animation, architecture, art, basic skills, career education, career exploration, classics, college planning, commercial art, computer applications, creative writing, current events, data processing, design, digital applications, drafting, drawing and design, economics, English, ESL, ethics, foreign language, geography, graphic arts, graphic design, graphics, health, historical foundations for arts, history, humanities, independent study, information technology, journalism, keyboarding, lab/keyboard, language development, learning cognition, library, life skills, literacy, literary magazine, mathematics, media, media arts, media production, media services, mentorship program, multimedia, music, music technology, news writing, newspaper, occupational education, philosophy, photography, photojournalism, programming, psychology, publications, publishing, reading, research skills, SAT preparation, science, senior seminar, social sciences, social studies, Spanish, speech, stock market, study skills, technical drawing, technology, theater, theater arts, typing, video film production, vocational-technical courses, Web site design, wilderness education, word processing, writing, writing, yearbook classes. Computer network features include on-campus library services, Internet access, wireless campus network, Internet filtering or blocking technology. Student e-mail accounts and computer access in designated common areas are available to students.

Contact Mr. Joseph M. Blake, Director of Admissions and Outreach. 626-799-5010 Ext. 203. Fax: 626-799-0407. E-mail: jblake@southwesternacademy.edu. Website: www.southwesternacademy.edu

See Display below, Close-Up on page 570, and Summer Program Close-Up on page 636.

SOUTHWESTERN ACADEMY

2800 Monterey Road
San Marino, California 91108

Head of School: Mr. Kenneth R. Veronda

General Information Coeducational boarding and day college-preparatory, general academic, arts, and ESL school. Grades 6–PG. Founded: 1924. Setting: suburban. Nearest major city is Los Angeles. Students are housed in single-sex dormitories. 8-acre campus. 9 buildings on campus. Approved or accredited by The Association of Boarding Schools, Western Association of Schools and Colleges, and

SOUTHWESTERN ACADEMY
BEAVER CREEK RANCH CAMPUS
Beaver Creek, Arizona

Set on 180 acres, outside the city of Sedona in northern Arizona, you'll find a school like no other!

FOR MORE INFORMATION:
admissions@southwesternacademy.edu
http://www.southwesternacademy.edu

California Department of Education. Member of Secondary School Admission Test Board. Endowment: $15 million. Upper school average class size: 12. Upper school faculty-student ratio: 1:6. There are 184 required school days per year for Upper School students. Upper School students typically attend 5 days per week. The average school day consists of 8 hours.

Upper School Student Profile Grade 9: 20 students (16 boys, 4 girls); Grade 10: 34 students (20 boys, 14 girls); Grade 11: 37 students (23 boys, 14 girls); Grade 12: 32 students (20 boys, 12 girls); Postgraduate: 1 student (1 girl). 75% of students are boarding students. 29% are state residents. 7 states are represented in upper school student body. 55% are international students. International students from China, Germany, Japan, Russian Federation, Taiwan, and Viet Nam; 19 other countries represented in student body.

Faculty School total: 27. In upper school: 12 men, 11 women; 15 have advanced degrees; 10 reside on campus.

Subjects Offered Algebra, American history, American literature, animation, art, art history, audio visual/media, biology, calculus, calculus-AP, chemistry, college counseling, creative writing, drama, earth science, economics, English, English literature, ESL, European history, expository writing, fashion, fine arts, geography, geology, geometry, government/civics, grammar, health, history, journalism, mathematics, music, photography, physical education, physics, psychology, science, social sciences, social studies, Spanish, speech, world cultures, world history, world literature, writing.

Graduation Requirements Algebra, American government, American history, American literature, biology, British literature, computer literacy, economics, electives, English, foreign language, geometry, lab science, mathematics, physical education (includes health), visual and performing arts, world cultures, 100 hours of community service. Community service is required.

Special Academic Programs Advanced Placement exam preparation; honors section; independent study; study at local college for college credit; academic accommodation for the musically talented and the artistically talented; ESL (39 students enrolled).

College Admission Counseling 36 students graduated in 2013; 34 went to college, including Drexel University; Marymount College, Palos Verdes, California; Pepperdine University; Syracuse University; University of California, Los Angeles; University of Virginia. Other: 1 entered military service, 1 had other specific plans.

Student Life Upper grades have specified standards of dress, student council, honor system. Discipline rests primarily with faculty.

Summer Programs Remediation, enrichment, advancement, ESL, art/fine arts, computer instruction programs offered; session focuses on academics; held on campus; accepts boys and girls; open to students from other schools. 60 students usually enrolled. 2014 schedule: June 14 to September 11. Application deadline: none.

Tuition and Aid Day student tuition: $16,550; 7-day tuition and room/board: $33,750. Tuition installment plan (monthly payment plans, individually arranged payment plans). Need-based scholarship grants available. In 2013–14, 20% of upper-school students received aid. Total amount of financial aid awarded in 2013–14: $600,000.

Admissions Traditional secondary-level entrance grade is 9. For fall 2013, 192 students applied for upper-level admission, 88 were accepted, 59 enrolled. TOEFL or SLEP or writing sample required. Deadline for receipt of application materials: none. Application fee required: $100. Interview required.

Athletics Interscholastic: baseball (boys), basketball (b,g), track and field (b,g), volleyball (b,g); intramural: baseball (b), basketball (b,g), track and field (b,g), volleyball (b,g); coed interscholastic: baseball, bowling, climbing, cross-country running, fishing, fitness, fitness walking, flag football, horseback riding, soccer, tennis; coed intramural: archery, backpacking, baseball, bicycling, bowling, climbing, cross-country running, fishing, fitness, fitness walking, golf, hiking/backpacking, horseback riding, jogging, mountain biking, outdoor activities, outdoor adventure, outdoor education, outdoor recreation, outdoor skills, outdoors, paddle tennis, physical fitness, physical training, skiing (downhill), snowboarding, soccer, table tennis, tennis, weight training. 2 PE instructors, 4 coaches, 1 athletic trainer.

Computers Computers are regularly used in all academic, animation, art, career exploration, classics, college planning, computer applications, creative writing, current events, design, desktop publishing, digital applications, economics, English, ESL, foreign language, geography, graphic arts, graphic design, graphics, historical foundations for arts, history, humanities, independent study, journalism, language development, library, life skills, literary magazine, mathematics, media, media arts, media production, media services, mentorship program, multimedia, music, music technology, news writing, photography, photojournalism, publications, publishing, reading, SAT preparation, science, senior seminar, social sciences, social studies, Spanish, speech, study skills, technology, theater, theater arts, typing, video film production, word processing, writing, writing, yearbook classes. Computer network features include on-campus library services, online commercial services, Internet access, wireless campus network, Internet filtering or blocking technology. Student e-mail accounts and computer access in designated common areas are available to students. The school has a published electronic and media policy.

Contact Mr. Joseph M. Blake, Director of Admissions and Outreach. 626-799-5010 Ext. 1203. Fax: 626-799-0407. E-mail: jblake@southwesternacademy.edu. Website: www.SouthwesternAcademy.edu

See Display below, Close-Up on page 572, and Summer Program Close-Up on page 638.

SPARTANBURG DAY SCHOOL

1701 Skylyn Drive
Spartanburg, South Carolina 29307

Head of School: Mrs. Rachel S. Deems

General Information Coeducational day college-preparatory and arts school. Grades PK–12. Founded: 1957. Setting: suburban. Nearest major city is Greenville. 52-acre campus. 10 buildings on campus. Approved or accredited by Southern Association of Colleges and Schools and Southern Association of Independent Schools. Member of National Association of Independent Schools. Endowment: $4.1 million. Total enrollment: 449. Upper school average class size: 12. Upper school faculty-student ratio: 1:9. There are 175 required school days per year for Upper School students. Upper School students typically attend 5 days per week. The average school day consists of 8 hours and 45 minutes.

Upper School Student Profile Grade 9: 40 students (18 boys, 22 girls); Grade 10: 35 students (16 boys, 19 girls); Grade 11: 36 students (16 boys, 20 girls); Grade 12: 34 students (20 boys, 14 girls).

Faculty School total: 55. In upper school: 8 men, 14 women; 19 have advanced degrees.

Subjects Offered Advanced chemistry, advanced math, Advanced Placement courses, algebra, American government, American history, American history-AP, American literature, applied music, art, art history-AP, arts appreciation, band, biology, biology-AP, calculus, calculus-AP, career/college preparation, character education, chemistry, chemistry-AP, chorus, college counseling, college placement, college writing, community service, computer education, concert band, creative drama, creative writing, critical thinking, critical writing, cultural arts, debate, drama performance, drawing, drawing and design, earth science, English, English composition, English literature, English literature-AP, European history, fine arts, French, French language-AP, geometry, government/civics, history, jazz band, keyboarding, Latin, Latin-AP, mathematics, modern European history-AP, music, music theory, philosophy, physics, physics-AP, science, Spanish, Spanish language-AP, speech, statistics, statistics-AP, studio art-AP, trigonometry, U.S. government and politics-AP, world history.

Graduation Requirements Algebra, arts and fine arts (art, music, dance, drama), biology, chemistry, English, foreign language, geometry, history, physics, Ancient or European history, one additional lab science, participation in one sport per year.

Special Academic Programs 19 Advanced Placement exams for which test preparation is offered; honors section; study at local college for college credit; academic accommodation for the gifted and the artistically talented; programs in English, mathematics, general development for dyslexic students; ESL (3 students enrolled).

College Admission Counseling 27 students graduated in 2012; all went to college, including College of Charleston; University of Virginia; Washington and Lee University; Wofford College. Mean SAT critical reading: 595, mean SAT math: 602, mean SAT writing: 584.

Student Life Upper grades have specified standards of dress, student council, honor system. Discipline rests primarily with faculty.

Tuition and Aid Day student tuition: $14,425. Tuition installment plan (monthly payment plans, tuition insurance). Merit scholarship grants, need-based scholarship grants, tuition reduction for children of faculty and staff, tuition reduction for children of benefit-receiving employees of Wofford College, Converse College, UCSUpstate available. In 2012–13, 24% of upper-school students received aid.

Admissions Traditional secondary-level entrance grade is 9. ERB, Kaufman Test of Educational Achievement, Metropolitan Test, ITBS, Otis-Lennon School Ability Test, Stanford Achievement Test or writing sample required. Deadline for receipt of application materials: none. Application fee required: $50. On-campus interview recommended.

Athletics Interscholastic: baseball (boys), basketball (b,g), cheering (g), soccer (b,g), swimming and diving (b,g), tennis (b,g), volleyball (g); coed interscholastic: aquatics, cooperative games, cross-country running, fitness, golf, martial arts, physical fitness, physical training, track and field, weight training. 4 PE instructors, 8 coaches, 1 athletic trainer.

Computers Computers are regularly used in art, English, French, history, Latin, mathematics, philosophy, science, Spanish classes. Computer network features include on-campus library services, Internet access, wireless campus network, Internet filtering or blocking technology, multimedia presentation stations. Student e-mail accounts are available to students. The school has a published electronic and media policy.

Contact Mr. Shawn Wilson, Director of Admissions. 864-582-7539 Ext. 2906. Fax: 864-582-7530. E-mail: shawn.wilson@sdsgriffin.org. Website: www.spartanburgdayschool.org

THE SPENCE SCHOOL

22 East 91st Street
New York, New York 10128-0657

Head of School: Ellanor (Bodie) N. Brizendine

General Information Girls' day college-preparatory, arts, and technology school. Grades K–12. Founded: 1892. Setting: urban. 2 buildings on campus. Approved or accredited by New York State Association of Independent Schools. Member of National Association of Independent Schools and Secondary School Admission Test Board. Total enrollment: 725. Upper school average class size: 14. Upper school faculty-student ratio: 1:7. There are 164 required school days per year for Upper School students. Upper School students typically attend 5 days per week. The average school day consists of 7 hours.

Upper School Student Profile Grade 9: 61 students (61 girls); Grade 10: 55 students (55 girls); Grade 11: 61 students (61 girls); Grade 12: 57 students (57 girls).

Faculty School total: 128. In upper school: 21 men, 50 women; 59 have advanced degrees.

Subjects Offered 20th century American writers, 20th century history, 20th century world history, 3-dimensional design, acting, addiction, advanced chemistry, advanced math, aerobics, African history, African literature, African-American literature, algebra, alternative physical education, American culture, American history, American literature, art, art and culture, art history, art-AP, Asian history, Asian literature, bioethics, bioethics, DNA and culture, biology, calculus, ceramics, chemistry, Chinese, Chinese history, Chinese literature, civil rights, college admission preparation, composition, computer programming, computer science, constitutional law, CPR, critical writing, dance, dance performance, design, digital imaging, digital photography, discrete mathematics, drama, drama performance, dramatic arts, drawing, earth science, economics, English, environmental science, equality and freedom, European history, exercise science, female experience in America, fiber arts, film studies, first aid, fitness, foreign language, French, geometry, global studies, health, health and wellness, history, instrumental music, Israeli studies, Japanese history, Japanese literature, Latin, Latin American history, Latin American literature, Latin American studies, linear algebra, literature, mathematics, media literacy, Middle East, modern European history, multimedia, music, music composition, music theory, non-Western literature, novels, painting, performing arts, photo shop, photography, physical education, physics, poetry, pre-algebra, printmaking, psychology, robotics, science, science research, sculpture, self-defense, Shakespeare, South African history, Spanish, Spanish literature, speech, statistics, technology, theater production, U.S. history, video film production, visual and performing arts, women's studies, world history, world religions, world studies, yoga.

Graduation Requirements Advanced math, algebra, American literature, art, biology, chemistry, computer science, dance, English, European history, foreign language, geometry, global studies, health, history, languages, music, non-Western societies, performing arts, physical education (includes health), physics, science, Shakespeare, speech, technology, U.S. history, visual and performing arts, visual arts, world religions, world studies.

Special Academic Programs 1 Advanced Placement exam for which test preparation is offered; independent study; term-away projects; study abroad.

College Admission Counseling 59 students graduated in 2013; all went to college, including Bowdoin College; Middlebury College; Northwestern University; Princeton University; University of Pennsylvania; Yale University. Median SAT critical reading: 710, median SAT math: 690, median SAT writing: 720, median combined SAT: 2150, median composite ACT: 32. 90% scored over 600 on SAT critical reading, 94% scored over 600 on SAT math, 94% scored over 600 on SAT writing, 93% scored over 1800 on combined SAT, 96% scored over 26 on composite ACT.

Student Life Upper grades have uniform requirement, student council. Discipline rests primarily with faculty.

Tuition and Aid Day student tuition: $40,975. Tuition installment plan (Academic Management Services Plan). Need-based scholarship grants, prepGATE loans, Academic Management Services private loans available. In 2013–14, 26% of upper-school students received aid. Total amount of financial aid awarded in 2013–14: $1,911,707.

Admissions Traditional secondary-level entrance grade is 9. ISEE or SSAT required. Deadline for receipt of application materials: December 1. Application fee required: $65. On-campus interview required.

Athletics Interscholastic: badminton, basketball, cross-country running, field hockey, lacrosse, soccer, softball, squash, swimming and diving, tennis, track and field, volleyball; intramural: fencing. 8 PE instructors, 29 coaches, 2 athletic trainers.

Computers Computers are regularly used in art, computer applications, creative writing, design, economics, foreign language, history, independent study, journalism, mathematics, science, technology classes. Computer network features include on-campus library services, online commercial services, Internet access, wireless campus network, iPads for every 9th grader to keep throughout Upper School, all classrooms equipped with SMART Boards. Campus intranet, student e-mail accounts, and computer access in designated common areas are available to students. The school has a published electronic and media policy.

Contact Susan Parker, Director of Admissions. 212-710-8140. Fax: 212-289-6025. E-mail: sparker@spenceschool.org. Website: www.spenceschool.org

SPRING CREEK ACADEMY

6000 Custer Road
Building 5
Plano, Texas 75023

General Information Coeducational boarding and day and distance learning college-preparatory school. Grades K–12. Distance learning grade X. Founded: 1997. Setting: suburban. Nearest major city is Dallas. 3 buildings on campus. Approved or accredited by Southern Association of Colleges and Schools, Texas Education Agency, Texas Private School Accreditation Commission, and Texas Department of Education. Upper school average class size: 6. Upper school faculty-student ratio: 1:6. There are

180 required school days per year for Upper School students. Upper School students typically attend 5 days per week. The average school day consists of 2 hours and 30 minutes.

Faculty School total: 22. In upper school: 4 men, 18 women; 12 have advanced degrees.

Special Academic Programs Advanced Placement exam preparation; honors section.

College Admission Counseling 14 students graduated in 2012; all went to college.

Student Life Upper grades have specified standards of dress, student council, honor system. Discipline rests primarily with faculty.

Admissions Iowa Tests of Basic Skills required. Deadline for receipt of application materials: none. Application fee required: $300. On-campus interview required.

Computers Computer network features include Internet access, wireless campus network, Internet filtering or blocking technology. Computer access in designated common areas is available to students. Students grades are available online. The school has a published electronic and media policy.

Contact 972-517-6730. Fax: 972-517-8750. Website: springcreekacademy.com/

SPRINGSIDE CHESTNUT HILL ACADEMY

500 West Willow Grove Avenue
Philadelphia, Pennsylvania 19118
Head of School: Dr. Priscilla Sands

General Information Coeducational day college-preparatory, arts, technology, science, and math school. Grades PK–12. Founded: 1861. Setting: suburban. 62-acre campus. 4 buildings on campus. Approved or accredited by Pennsylvania Department of Education. Member of National Association of Independent Schools and Secondary School Admission Test Board. Endowment: $37.5 million. Total enrollment: 1,102. Upper school average class size: 16. Upper school faculty-student ratio: 1:7. There are 175 required school days per year for Upper School students. Upper School students typically attend 5 days per week. The average school day consists of 7 hours and 30 minutes.

Upper School Student Profile Grade 9: 120 students (55 boys, 65 girls); Grade 10: 115 students (46 boys, 69 girls); Grade 11: 120 students (63 boys, 57 girls); Grade 12: 117 students (62 boys, 55 girls).

Faculty School total: 141. In upper school: 32 men, 40 women; 53 have advanced degrees.

Subjects Offered Advanced math, Advanced Placement courses, African studies, algebra, American history, art, art history, biology, biology-AP, calculus, calculus-AP, ceramics, chamber groups, chemistry, Chinese, choral music, college counseling, community service, comparative government and politics-AP, computer animation, computer programming, computer science, dance, dance performance, drama, drawing and design, East Asian history, English, English literature, English-AP, environmental science, European history, European history-AP, fine arts, forensics, French, French language-AP, geometry, handbells, health, history-AP, independent study, jazz ensemble, Latin, mathematics, music, oceanography, orchestra, peer counseling, photography, physical education, physics, physics-AP, physiology, printmaking, robotics, science, senior project, social studies, Spanish, Spanish-AP, statistics, statistics-AP, theater, trigonometry, U.S. government and politics-AP, U.S. history, weight reduction, woodworking, world history, world history-AP, writing, writing workshop, yearbook.

Graduation Requirements Arts, English, foreign language, health, history, mathematics, music, physical education (includes health), science, senior project, sports, senior speech, Center for Entrepreneurial Leadership seminars.

Special Academic Programs 9 Advanced Placement exams for which test preparation is offered; honors section; independent study.

College Admission Counseling 106 students graduated in 2013; all went to college, including Elon University; Ithaca College; Northeastern University; Penn State University Park; University of Pennsylvania; Ursinus College. Mean SAT critical reading: 625, mean SAT math: 620, mean SAT writing: 650, mean composite ACT: 28.

Student Life Upper grades have uniform requirement, student council, honor system. Discipline rests equally with students and faculty.

Summer Programs Remediation, enrichment, sports, art/fine arts, computer instruction programs offered; session focuses on to offer a variety of interesting opportunities for kids of all ages and interests; held on campus; accepts boys and girls; open to students from other schools. 250 students usually enrolled. 2014 schedule: June 9 to August 15.

Tuition and Aid Day student tuition: $30,390. Tuition installment plan (monthly payment plans, Higher Education Service, Inc). Merit scholarship grants, need-based scholarship grants available. In 2013–14, 40% of upper-school students received aid. Total amount of financial aid awarded in 2013–14: $3,379,780.

Admissions Traditional secondary-level entrance grade is 9. For fall 2013, 206 students applied for upper-level admission, 119 were accepted, 67 enrolled. ISEE or SSAT required. Deadline for receipt of application materials: January 15. Application fee required: $50. On-campus interview required.

Athletics Interscholastic: basketball (boys, girls), crew (b,g), cross-country running (b,g), field hockey (g), golf (b,g), ice hockey (b), independent competitive sports (g), lacrosse (b,g), rowing (b,g), soccer (b,g), softball (g), squash (b,g), swimming and diving (b,g), tennis (b,g), track and field (b,g), volleyball (g), winter (indoor) track (b,g), wrestling (b). 6 PE instructors, 58 coaches, 2 athletic trainers.

Computers Computers are regularly used in all classes. Computer network features include on-campus library services, online commercial services, Internet access, wireless campus network, Internet filtering or blocking technology, SCH is a 1:1 school in grades 3-12, and 1:2 in PK-2, many faculty are 1+1 with iPads and Laptops. Campus intranet, student e-mail accounts, and computer access in designated common areas are available to students. Students grades are available online. The school has a published electronic and media policy.

Contact Ms. Murielle Telemaque, Admissions Office Manager. 215-247-7007. Fax: 215-242-4055. E-mail: mtelemaque@sch.org. Website: www.sch.org

SQUAW VALLEY ACADEMY

235 Squaw Valley Road
Olympic Valley, California 96146
Head of School: Mr. Donald Rees

General Information Coeducational boarding and day college-preparatory and arts school. Grades 9–12. Founded: 1978. Setting: rural. Nearest major city is Reno, NV. Students are housed in single-sex by floor dormitories and single-sex dormitories. 3-acre campus. 4 buildings on campus. Approved or accredited by National Independent Private Schools Association, Western Association of Schools and Colleges, and California Department of Education. Member of National Association of Independent Schools and Secondary School Admission Test Board. Total enrollment: 100. Upper school average class size: 8. Upper school faculty-student ratio: 1:8. Upper School students typically attend 5 days per week. The average school day consists of 8 hours.

Upper School Student Profile 100% of students are boarding students. 75% are international students. International students from Bangladesh, China, Japan, Kyrgyzstan, Republic of Korea, and Russian Federation; 8 other countries represented in student body.

Faculty School total: 12. In upper school: 9 men, 3 women; 6 have advanced degrees; 4 reside on campus.

Subjects Offered Addiction, advanced biology, advanced chemistry, advanced math, Advanced Placement courses, advanced TOEFL/grammar, algebra, American democracy, American government, American history, American history-AP, American literature, American literature-AP, anatomy, applied arts, applied music, art, art education, art history, backpacking, band, biology, biology-AP, calculus, calculus-AP, ceramics, chemistry, civics, college admission preparation, college counseling, college placement, college planning, college writing, computer science, computers, creative writing, drama, English, English literature, environmental science, expository writing, fine arts, French, geography, geometry, government/civics, grammar, health, history, history-AP, instruments, Internet, Internet research, jazz, language-AP, linear algebra, literature-AP, martial arts, mathematics, mathematics-AP, music, music appreciation, music history, music performance, music theory, novels, outdoor education, photography, physical education, physics, physics-AP, pre-calculus, psychology, publications, research and reference, SAT preparation, SAT/ACT preparation, science, social sciences, social studies, Spanish, Spanish-AP, student government, student publications, studio art, surfing, swimming, TOEFL preparation, travel, trigonometry, typing, video, visual and performing arts, weight fitness, world history, world history-AP, writing, yearbook, yoga.

Graduation Requirements Arts and fine arts (art, music, dance, drama), college admission preparation, English, foreign language, mathematics, physical education (includes health), science, social sciences, participation in skiing and snowboarding, seniors must gain acceptance into a minimum of one (1) college or university.

Special Academic Programs 15 Advanced Placement exams for which test preparation is offered; honors section; accelerated programs; independent study; study at local college for college credit; academic accommodation for the gifted, the musically talented, and the artistically talented; programs in English, mathematics for dyslexic students; special instructional classes for students with ADD and dyslexia; ESL (15 students enrolled).

College Admission Counseling 17 students graduated in 2013; all went to college, including Michigan State University; Penn State University Park; The Johns Hopkins University; University of California, Davis; University of Colorado Boulder; University of Oregon. Median combined SAT: 1650. 20% scored over 600 on SAT critical reading, 40% scored over 600 on SAT math, 20% scored over 600 on SAT writing, 20% scored over 1800 on combined SAT.

Student Life Upper grades have uniform requirement, student council, honor system. Discipline rests primarily with faculty.

Summer Programs Remediation, enrichment, advancement, ESL, sports, art/fine arts programs offered; session focuses on academics and mountain sports; held both on and off campus; held at Lake Tahoe; accepts boys and girls; open to students from other schools. 25 students usually enrolled. 2014 schedule: June 30 to August 10. Application deadline: none.

Tuition and Aid 7-day tuition and room/board: $48,789. Tuition installment plan (individually arranged payment plans). Tuition reduction for siblings, merit scholarship grants, need-based scholarship grants available. In 2013–14, 10% of upper-school students received aid; total upper-school merit-scholarship money awarded: $175,000. Total amount of financial aid awarded in 2013–14: $175,000.

Admissions Traditional secondary-level entrance grade is 10. For fall 2013, 120 students applied for upper-level admission, 110 were accepted, 100 enrolled. Math Placement Exam and writing sample required. Deadline for receipt of application materials: none. Application fee required: $100. Interview required.

Athletics Interscholastic: alpine skiing (boys, girls), freestyle skiing (b,g), skiing (downhill) (b,g), snowboarding (b,g); intramural: aerobics (b,g), aerobics/Nautilus (b,g), alpine skiing (b,g), aquatics (b,g), backpacking (b,g), badminton (b,g), basketball (b,g), bicycling (b,g), billiards (b,g), blading (b,g), bowling (b,g), canoeing/kayaking (b,g), climbing (b,g), combined training (b,g), croquet (b,g), cross-country running (b,g), field hockey (b,g), fishing (b,g), fitness (b,g), fitness walking (b,g), flag football (b,g), fly fishing (b,g), freestyle skiing (b,g), Frisbee (b,g), golf (b,g), hiking/backpacking (b,g), horseback riding (b,g), ice skating (b,g), jogging (b,g), kayaking (b,g), mountain biking (b,g), mountaineering (b,g), nordic skiing (b,g), outdoor activities (b,g), outdoor adventure (b,g), outdoor education (b,g), outdoor recreation (b,g), outdoor skills (b,g), outdoors (b,g), paddling (b,g), paint ball (b,g), physical fitness (b,g), physical training (b,g), rafting (b,g), rock climbing (b,g), ropes courses (b,g), running (b,g), self defense (b,g), skateboarding (b,g), skiing (cross-country) (b,g), skiing (downhill) (b,g), snowboarding (b,g), snowshoeing (b,g), strength & conditioning (b,g), swimming and diving (b,g), table tennis (b,g), telemark skiing (b,g), tennis (b,g), ultimate Frisbee (b,g), volleyball (b,g), walking (b,g), wall climbing (b,g), weight lifting (b,g), weight training (b,g), yoga (b,g); coed interscholastic: alpine skiing, freestyle skiing, skiing (downhill), snowboarding, soccer; coed intramural: aerobics, aerobics/Nautilus, alpine skiing, aquatics, backpacking, badminton, baseball, basketball, bicycling, billiards, blading, bowling, canoeing/kayaking, climbing, combined training, croquet, cross-country running, field hockey, fishing, fitness, fitness walking, flag football, fly fishing, freestyle skiing, Frisbee, golf, hiking/backpacking, horseback riding, ice skating, jogging, kayaking, mountain biking, mountaineering, nordic skiing, outdoor activities, outdoor adventure, outdoor education, outdoor recreation, outdoor skills, outdoors, paddling, paint ball, physical fitness, physical training, rafting, rock climbing, ropes courses, running, self defense, skateboarding, skiing (cross-country), skiing (downhill), snowboarding, snowshoeing, soccer, softball, strength & conditioning, swimming and diving, table tennis, telemark skiing, tennis, ultimate Frisbee, volleyball, walking, wall climbing, weight lifting, weight training, yoga.

Computers Computers are regularly used in all academic classes. Computer network features include on-campus library services, online commercial services, Internet access, wireless campus network, Internet filtering or blocking technology. Computer access in designated common areas is available to students.

Contact Adrienne Forbes, M.Ed., Admissions Director. 530-583-9393 Ext. 105. Fax: 530-581-1111. E-mail: enroll@sva.org. Website: www.sva.org

STEPHEN T. BADIN HIGH SCHOOL

571 New London Road
Hamilton, Ohio 45013

Head of School: Mr. Brian Pendergest

General Information Coeducational day college-preparatory, general academic, arts, business, vocational, religious studies, and technology school, affiliated with Roman Catholic Church. Grades 9–12. Founded: 1966. Setting: urban. Nearest major city is Cincinnati. 22-acre campus. 2 buildings on campus. Approved or accredited by National Catholic Education Association, North Central Association of Colleges and Schools, Ohio Catholic Schools Accreditation Association (OCSAA), and Ohio Department of Education. Endowment: $120,000. Total enrollment: 509. Upper school average class size: 24. Upper school faculty-student ratio: 1:19. There are 182 required school days per year for Upper School students. Upper School students typically attend 5 days per week. The average school day consists of 6 hours and 55 minutes.

Upper School Student Profile Grade 9: 158 students (83 boys, 75 girls); Grade 10: 126 students (68 boys, 58 girls); Grade 11: 125 students (65 boys, 60 girls); Grade 12: 100 students (60 boys, 40 girls). 90% of students are Roman Catholic.

Faculty School total: 35. In upper school: 19 men, 15 women; 23 have advanced degrees.

Subjects Offered Accounting, algebra, American history, American literature, art, band, biology, British literature, calculus, calculus-AP, chemistry, chorus, computer programming, computer resources, consumer economics, consumer mathematics, economics, English, English literature, English-AP, French, geometry, government-AP, government/civics, history, integrated science, intro to computers, journalism, Latin, marketing, mathematics, music, music theory, physical education, physical science, physics, physiology, pre-calculus, publications, religion, science, social studies, Spanish, Web site design, Western literature, world history.

Graduation Requirements Computer science, English, mathematics, physical education (includes health), religion (includes Bible studies and theology), science, social studies (includes history), 15 hours of community service per year for seniors.

Special Academic Programs 8 Advanced Placement exams for which test preparation is offered; honors section; study at local college for college credit; study abroad; remedial reading and/or remedial writing; remedial math.

College Admission Counseling 124 students graduated in 2012; 120 went to college, including College of Mount St. Joseph; Miami University; Ohio University; The Ohio State University; University of Cincinnati; Xavier University. Other: 2 went to work, 2 entered military service. Median SAT critical reading: 526, median SAT

math: 521, median SAT writing: 529, median combined SAT: 1574, median composite ACT: 23. 21% scored over 600 on SAT critical reading, 11% scored over 600 on SAT math, 16% scored over 600 on SAT writing, 20% scored over 1800 on combined SAT, 25% scored over 26 on composite ACT.

Student Life Upper grades have uniform requirement, student council. Discipline rests primarily with faculty. Attendance at religious services is required.

Tuition and Aid Day student tuition: $7800. Tuition installment plan (monthly payment plans, individually arranged payment plans, quarterly payment plan). Merit scholarship grants, need-based scholarship grants, paying campus jobs available. In 2012–13, 36% of upper-school students received aid; total upper-school merit-scholarship money awarded: $23,000. Total amount of financial aid awarded in 2012–13: $300,000.

Admissions Traditional secondary-level entrance grade is 9. Deadline for receipt of application materials: none. No application fee required. On-campus interview recommended.

Athletics Interscholastic: aquatics (boys, girls), baseball (b), basketball (b,g), bowling (b,g), cheering (g), diving (b,g), football (b), golf (b,g), gymnastics (g), hockey (b), ice hockey (b), rowing (b), soccer (b,g), softball (g), swimming and diving (b,g), tennis (g), volleyball (b,g); coed interscholastic: fishing. 2 PE instructors, 35 coaches, 1 athletic trainer.

Computers Computers are regularly used in mathematics, music, science, Web site design classes. Computer network features include on-campus library services, Internet access, wireless campus network, Internet filtering or blocking technology, scanners, travelling laptops, digital cameras. Campus intranet, student e-mail accounts, and computer access in designated common areas are available to students. Students grades are available online. The school has a published electronic and media policy.

Contact Mrs. Angie Gray, Director of Recruitment. 513-863-3993 Ext. 145. Fax: 513-785-2844. E-mail: agray@mail.badinhs.org. Website: www.badinhs.org/index.asp

STEVENSON SCHOOL

3152 Forest Lake Road
Pebble Beach, California 93953

Head of School: Mr. Joseph E. Wandke

General Information Coeducational boarding and day college-preparatory, arts, and technology school. Boarding grades 9–12, day grades PK–12. Founded: 1952. Setting: suburban. Nearest major city is San Francisco. Students are housed in single-sex by floor dormitories, coed dormitories, and single-sex dormitories. 65-acre campus. 24 buildings on campus. Approved or accredited by The Association of Boarding Schools, Western Association of Schools and Colleges, and California Department of Education. Member of National Association of Independent Schools and Secondary School Admission Test Board. Endowment: $25 million. Total enrollment: 747. Upper school average class size: 14. Upper school faculty-student ratio: 1:10. Upper School students typically attend 5 days per week. The average school day consists of 6 hours and 30 minutes.

Upper School Student Profile Grade 9: 109 students (61 boys, 48 girls); Grade 10: 139 students (74 boys, 65 girls); Grade 11: 143 students (68 boys, 75 girls); Grade 12: 129 students (62 boys, 67 girls). 58% of students are boarding students. 47% are state residents. 19 states are represented in upper school student body. 23% are international students. International students from China, Hong Kong, Republic of Korea, Russian Federation, Taiwan, and Viet Nam; 24 other countries represented in student body.

Faculty School total: 71. In upper school: 47 men, 24 women; 46 have advanced degrees; 36 reside on campus.

Subjects Offered 3-dimensional art, advanced chemistry, Advanced Placement courses, algebra, American history, American literature, American literature-AP, architecture, art, art history, art-AP, biology, biology-AP, broadcasting, calculus, calculus-AP, ceramics, chemistry, chemistry-AP, Chinese, computer programming, computer science, concert band, creative writing, dance, dance performance, drama, drama performance, drama workshop, dramatic arts, drawing, drawing and design, driver education, economics, economics-AP, English, English literature, English-AP, environmental science, environmental science-AP, ethics, European civilization, European history, expository writing, fine arts, French, French-AP, geometry, government/civics, grammar, history of ideas, history-AP, honors algebra, honors English, honors geometry, honors U.S. history, Japanese, jazz, jazz band, jazz ensemble, jazz theory, journalism, Latin, Latin-AP, macroeconomics-AP, marine biology, mathematics, mathematics-AP, microbiology, music, musical productions, musical theater, ornithology, photography, physical education, physics, physics-AP, portfolio art, pre-calculus, psychology, science, social studies, Spanish, Spanish-AP, speech, stage design, stagecraft, studio art-AP, tap dance, theater, trigonometry, U.S. history-AP, visual and performing arts, visual arts, vocal ensemble, wilderness education, wilderness experience, wind ensemble, world cultures, world history, world literature, world studies, writing, yearbook.

Graduation Requirements Arts and fine arts (art, music, dance, drama), English, foreign language, mathematics, physical education (includes health), science, social studies (includes history).

Special Academic Programs 22 Advanced Placement exams for which test preparation is offered; honors section; independent study; term-away projects; study abroad.

College Admission Counseling 127 students graduated in 2013; all went to college, including New York University; University of California, Berkeley; University of California, Los Angeles; University of Colorado Boulder; University of Southern California; University of Washington. Mean SAT critical reading: 630, mean SAT math: 652, mean SAT writing: 624, mean combined SAT: 1946, mean composite ACT: 28.

Student Life Upper grades have specified standards of dress, student council, honor system. Discipline rests equally with students and faculty.

Summer Programs Enrichment, sports, art/fine arts programs offered; held on campus; accepts boys and girls; open to students from other schools. 140 students usually enrolled. 2014 schedule: June 23 to August 22. Application deadline: none.

Tuition and Aid Day student tuition: $33,200; 7-day tuition and room/board: $54,600. Tuition installment plan (Insured Tuition Payment Plan). Need-based scholarship grants available. In 2013–14, 24% of upper-school students received aid. Total amount of financial aid awarded in 2013–14: $3,100,000.

Admissions Traditional secondary-level entrance grade is 9. For fall 2013, 436 students applied for upper-level admission, 213 were accepted, 111 enrolled. SSAT required. Deadline for receipt of application materials: February 1. Application fee required: $75. Interview required.

Athletics Interscholastic: baseball (boys), basketball (b,g), cross-country running (b,g), diving (b,g), field hockey (g), football (b), golf (b,g), lacrosse (b,g), sailing (b,g), soccer (b,g), softball (g), swimming and diving (b,g), tennis (b,g), track and field (b,g), volleyball (g), water polo (b,g); intramural: dance (b,g), golf (b,g), horseback riding (b,g), kayaking (b,g), modern dance (b,g), mountaineering (b,g), outdoor education (b,g), outdoors (b,g), power lifting (b,g), rock climbing (b,g), strength & conditioning (b,g), table tennis (b,g), weight lifting (b,g), wilderness (b,g), yoga (b,g); coed interscholastic: sailing; coed intramural: basketball, bicycling, climbing, dance, equestrian sports, fencing, horseback riding, kayaking, modern dance, mountaineering, outdoor education, outdoors, rock climbing, sailing, softball, strength & conditioning, table tennis, weight lifting, wilderness, yoga. 30 coaches.

Computers Computers are regularly used in all classes. Computer network features include on-campus library services, online commercial services, Internet access, wireless campus network, Internet filtering or blocking technology. Campus intranet and student e-mail accounts are available to students. Students grades are available online. The school has a published electronic and media policy.

Contact Ms. Susan Rymzo, Director of Admission. 831-625-8309. Fax: 831-625-5208. E-mail: info@stevensonschool.org. Website: www.stevensonschool.org

THE STORM KING SCHOOL

314 Mountain Road
Cornwall-on-Hudson, New York 12520-1899

Head of School: Mr. Paul Domingue

General Information Coeducational boarding and day college-preparatory and arts school. Grades 8–12. Founded: 1867. Setting: small town. Nearest major city is New York. Students are housed in single-sex dormitories. 55-acre campus. 24 buildings on campus. Approved or accredited by Middle States Association of Colleges and Schools, The Association of Boarding Schools, and New York Department of Education. Member of National Association of Independent Schools and Secondary School Admission Test Board. Endowment: $1 million. Total enrollment: 139. Upper school average class size: 12. Upper school faculty-student ratio: 1:6. There are 166 required school days per year for Upper School students. Upper School students typically attend 5 days per week. The average school day consists of 8 hours.

Upper School Student Profile Grade 8: 7 students (5 boys, 2 girls); Grade 9: 21 students (10 boys, 11 girls); Grade 10: 28 students (19 boys, 9 girls); Grade 11: 41 students (23 boys, 18 girls); Grade 12: 42 students (16 boys, 26 girls). 85% of students are boarding students. 32% are state residents. 6 states are represented in upper school student body. 47% are international students. International students from China, Italy, Republic of Korea, Russian Federation, Taiwan, and Viet Nam; 13 other countries represented in student body.

Faculty School total: 36. In upper school: 21 men, 15 women; 23 have advanced degrees; 16 reside on campus.

Subjects Offered Acting, Advanced Placement courses, advanced studio art-AP, advanced TOEFL/grammar, algebra, American history, American literature, American sign language, art, art history-AP, art-AP, astronomy, athletics, biology, biology-AP, calculus, calculus-AP, chemistry, Chinese, choir, choral music, college counseling, college planning, community service, computer graphics, computer programming-AP, computer science-AP, creative writing, dance, dance performance, digital art, drama, drawing, earth science, economics, economics-AP, English, English literature, English literature-AP, English-AP, environmental science, ESL, ESL, fine arts, foreign language, geometry, government/civics, guitar, health, health education, high adventure outdoor program, history, humanities, literacy, literature, macro/microeconomics-AP, macroeconomics-AP, Mandarin, mathematics, music, music composition, musical productions, outdoor education, painting, performing arts, photography, physical education, physics, physics-AP, piano, pre-calculus, psychology, psychology-AP, SAT preparation, science, Spanish, stage design, stagecraft, statistics-AP, student government, studio art-AP, theater, theater design and production, U.S. history, world history, world literature, writing, yearbook.

Graduation Requirements English, foreign language, Internet, mathematics, performing arts, public speaking, science, social studies (includes history), visual arts,

at least two community service, outdoor adventure, and cultural experiences per year. Community service is required.

Special Academic Programs 10 Advanced Placement exams for which test preparation is offered; honors section; academic accommodation for the gifted, the musically talented, and the artistically talented; remedial reading and/or remedial writing; programs in English, mathematics, general development for dyslexic students; ESL (50 students enrolled).

College Admission Counseling 42 students graduated in 2013; all went to college, including Drexel University; Pace University; Penn State University Park; Rensselaer Polytechnic Institute; University of Connecticut; University of Rochester. Median SAT critical reading: 530, median SAT math: 620, median SAT writing: 500, median combined SAT: 1580, median composite ACT: 19. 15% scored over 600 on SAT critical reading, 57% scored over 600 on SAT math, 15% scored over 600 on SAT writing, 18% scored over 1800 on combined SAT, 22% scored over 26 on composite ACT.

Student Life Upper grades have specified standards of dress, student council, honor system. Discipline rests primarily with faculty.

Tuition and Aid Day student tuition: $24,970; 7-day tuition and room/board: $46,750. Tuition installment plan (individually arranged payment plans). Tuition reduction for siblings, merit scholarship grants, need-based scholarship grants available. In 2013–14, 26% of upper-school students received aid; total upper-school merit-scholarship money awarded: $32,500. Total amount of financial aid awarded in 2013–14: $405,575.

Admissions Traditional secondary-level entrance grade is 9. For fall 2013, 254 students applied for upper-level admission, 96 were accepted, 51 enrolled. Admissions testing, SSAT or TOEFL or SLEP required. Deadline for receipt of application materials: none. Application fee required: $85. Interview required.

Athletics Interscholastic: basketball (boys, girls), bicycling (b,g), lacrosse (b,g), soccer (b,g), softball (g), volleyball (g), wrestling (b); coed interscholastic: crew, cross-country running, fencing, golf, jogging, rowing, running, sailing, skiing (downhill), snowboarding, tennis; coed intramural: aerobics/dance, alpine skiing, backpacking, ballet, bicycling, bocce, bowling, canoeing/kayaking, climbing, dance, fitness, fitness walking, freestyle skiing, golf, hiking/backpacking, ice skating, jogging, kayaking, modern dance, mountain biking, mountaineering, Nautilus, outdoor activities, outdoor adventure, outdoor education, outdoor recreation, outdoor skills, outdoors, paddle tennis, paddling, physical fitness, physical training, power lifting, rafting, rappelling, rock climbing, ropes courses, skiing (cross-country), skiing (downhill), snowboarding, snowshoeing, strength & conditioning, table tennis, tennis, touch football, track and field, walking, wall climbing, weight lifting, weight training, wilderness, winter walking, yoga. 3 coaches, 1 athletic trainer.

Computers Computers are regularly used in all academic, art, college planning, computer applications, drawing and design, economics, English, ESL, foreign language, graphic design, history, mathematics, music technology, photography, psychology, video film production, yearbook classes. Computer network features include on-campus library services, online commercial services, Internet access, wireless campus network, Internet filtering or blocking technology, parent/student/teacher communication portal. Campus intranet, student e-mail accounts, and computer access in designated common areas are available to students. Students grades are available online. The school has a published electronic and media policy.

Contact Mr. Marek Pramuka, Director of Admissions and Marketing. 845-458-7542. Fax: 845-534-4128. E-mail: mpramuka@sks.org. Website: www.sks.org

STRATFORD ACADEMY

6010 Peake Road
Macon, Georgia 31220-3903

Head of School: Dr. Robert E. Veto

General Information Coeducational day college-preparatory, arts, and technology school. Grades 1–12. Founded: 1960. Setting: suburban. Nearest major city is Atlanta. 70-acre campus. 4 buildings on campus. Approved or accredited by Georgia Independent School Association, Southern Association of Colleges and Schools, Southern Association of Independent Schools, and Georgia Department of Education. Member of National Association of Independent Schools. Endowment: $1 million. Total enrollment: 962. Upper school average class size: 17. Upper school faculty-student ratio: 1:13. There are 180 required school days per year for Upper School students. Upper School students typically attend 5 days per week. The average school day consists of 6 hours.

Faculty School total: 89. In upper school: 24 men, 23 women; 25 have advanced degrees.

Subjects Offered Advanced Placement courses, algebra, American history, American literature, anatomy, art, art history, art-AP, athletics, baseball, basketball, biology, biology-AP, calculus, calculus-AP, chemistry, chemistry-AP, community service, comparative government and politics-AP, computer programming, computer science, creative writing, drama, drama performance, driver education, earth science, economics, English, English literature, English literature-AP, English-AP, European history, European history-AP, expository writing, French, French-AP, geography, geometry, government/civics, grammar, history, history-AP, humanities, journalism, keyboarding, Latin, Latin-AP, madrigals, mathematics, mathematics-AP, music, physical education, physical science, physics, pre-calculus, science, social sciences, social studies, sociology, Spanish, Spanish-AP, speech, speech and debate, theater, trigonometry, U.S. government and politics-AP, water color painting, world history, world literature, writing.

Graduation Requirements English, foreign language, math applications, mathematics, science, senior seminar, social sciences, social studies (includes history), community service. Community service is required.

Special Academic Programs Advanced Placement exam preparation; independent study; special instructional classes for students with learning disabilities, Attention Deficit Disorder, and dyslexia.

College Admission Counseling 73 students graduated in 2012; all went to college, including Auburn University; Davidson College; Georgia Institute of Technology; Georgia Southern University; Harvard University; University of Georgia.

Student Life Upper grades have uniform requirement, student council, honor system. Discipline rests primarily with faculty.

Tuition and Aid Day student tuition: $12,995. Tuition installment plan (Insured Tuition Payment Plan, monthly payment plans, individually arranged payment plans). Merit scholarship grants, need-based scholarship grants available. Total upper-school merit-scholarship money awarded for 2012–13: $12,995.

Admissions Traditional secondary-level entrance grade is 9. ERB required. Deadline for receipt of application materials: none. Application fee required: $50. On-campus interview required.

Athletics Interscholastic: aerobics (girls), aquatics (b,g), baseball (b), basketball (b,g), cheering (g), cross-country running (b,g), dance team (g), drill team (g), fitness (b,g), football (b), horseback riding (b,g), physical training (b,g), soccer (b,g), softball (g), tennis (b,g), track and field (b,g), volleyball (g), wrestling (b), yoga (g); coed interscholastic: badminton, golf. 9 PE instructors, 6 coaches, 2 athletic trainers.

Computers Computers are regularly used in art, creative writing, English, French, graphics, information technology, Spanish classes. Computer network features include on-campus library services, Internet access, wireless campus network. Computer access in designated common areas is available to students. The school has a published electronic and media policy.

Contact Mrs. Lori Palmer, Associate Director of Admissions. 478-477-8073 Ext. 298. Fax: 478-477-0299. E-mail: lori.palmer@stratford.org. Website: www.stratford.org

STRATHCONA-TWEEDSMUIR SCHOOL

RR 2
Okotoks, Alberta T1S 1A2, Canada

Head of School: Mr. William Jones

General Information Coeducational day college-preparatory, arts, and technology school. Grades 1–12. Founded: 1905. Setting: rural. Nearest major city is Calgary, Canada. 200-acre campus. 1 building on campus. Approved or accredited by Canadian Association of Independent Schools, Canadian Educational Standards Institute, International Baccalaureate Organization, and Alberta Department of Education. Affiliate member of National Association of Independent Schools; member of Secondary School Admission Test Board. Language of instruction: English. Endowment: CAN$5 million. Total enrollment: 667. Upper school average class size: 20. Upper school faculty-student ratio: 1:9. There are 174 required school days per year for Upper School students. Upper School students typically attend 5 days per week. The average school day consists of 6 hours and 40 minutes.

Upper School Student Profile Grade 6: 44 students (27 boys, 17 girls); Grade 7: 65 students (26 boys, 39 girls); Grade 8: 68 students (33 boys, 35 girls); Grade 9: 74 students (44 boys, 30 girls); Grade 10: 85 students (46 boys, 39 girls); Grade 11: 79 students (44 boys, 35 girls); Grade 12: 79 students (41 boys, 38 girls).

Faculty School total: 80. In upper school: 24 men, 27 women; 15 have advanced degrees.

Subjects Offered Art, band, biology, calculus, chemistry, computer science, drama, English, fine arts, French, Latin, mathematics, music, outdoor education, physical education, physics, science, social sciences, social studies, Spanish, theater.

Graduation Requirements Arts and fine arts (art, music, dance, drama), business skills (includes word processing), English, foreign language, mathematics, physical education (includes health), science, social sciences, social studies (includes history).

Special Academic Programs International Baccalaureate program; term-away projects.

College Admission Counseling 75 students graduated in 2012; all went to college, including Acadia University; Queen's University at Kingston; The University of British Columbia; The University of Western Ontario; University of Calgary; University of Victoria.

Student Life Upper grades have uniform requirement, student council, honor system. Discipline rests primarily with faculty.

Tuition and Aid Day student tuition: CAN$15,760–CAN$18,090. Tuition installment plan (monthly payment plans). Bursaries, merit scholarship grants, need-based scholarship grants available. In 2012–13, 10% of upper-school students received aid; total upper-school merit-scholarship money awarded: CAN$100,000. Total amount of financial aid awarded in 2012–13: CAN$137,913.

Admissions Traditional secondary-level entrance grade is 10. CTBS, OLSAT, Differential Aptitude Test, Henmon-Nelson or SSAT required. Deadline for receipt of application materials: none. Application fee required: CAN$100. Interview required.

Athletics Interscholastic: badminton (boys, girls), basketball (b,g), canoeing/kayaking (b,g), cross-country running (b,g), fencing (b,g), field hockey (g), golf (b,g), hiking/backpacking (b,g), jump rope (b,g), nordic skiing (b,g), outdoor activities (b,g), outdoor education (b,g), rugby (b), soccer (g), telemark skiing (b,g), track and field (b,g), triathlon (b,g), volleyball (b,g), wall climbing (b,g); coed interscholastic: alpine skiing, backpacking, badminton, bicycling, canoeing/kayaking, climbing, cross-country running, hiking/backpacking, jump rope, mountain biking, mountaineering, nordic skiing, outdoor activities, outdoor education; coed intramural: basketball, volleyball. 10 PE instructors, 38 coaches, 2 athletic trainers.

Computers Computers are regularly used in all classes. Computer network features include on-campus library services, online commercial services, Internet access, wireless campus network, Internet filtering or blocking technology. Campus intranet and student e-mail accounts are available to students. Students grades are available online. The school has a published electronic and media policy.

Contact Ms. Lydia J Hawkins, Director of Enrollment. 403-938-8303. Fax: 403-938-4492. E-mail: hawkinl@sts.ab.ca. Website: www.sts.ab.ca

STRATTON MOUNTAIN SCHOOL

World Cup Circle
Stratton Mountain, Vermont 05155

Head of School: Christopher G. Kaltsas

General Information Coeducational boarding and day college-preparatory, arts, bilingual studies, and technology school. Grades 7–PG. Founded: 1972. Setting: rural. Nearest major city is Albany, NY. Students are housed in single-sex by floor dormitories. 12-acre campus. 7 buildings on campus. Approved or accredited by New England Association of Schools and Colleges and Vermont Department of Education. Member of National Association of Independent Schools. Endowment: $2.4 million. Total enrollment: 124. Upper school average class size: 10. Upper school faculty-student ratio: 1:6. There are 170 required school days per year for Upper School students. Upper School students typically attend 5 days per week. The average school day consists of 5 hours.

Upper School Student Profile Grade 9: 23 students (11 boys, 12 girls); Grade 10: 26 students (17 boys, 9 girls); Grade 11: 18 students (9 boys, 9 girls); Grade 12: 24 students (11 boys, 13 girls); Postgraduate: 10 students (5 boys, 5 girls). 54% of students are boarding students. 46% are state residents. 22 states are represented in upper school student body. 5% are international students. International students from Australia, Italy, Japan, New Zealand, and Switzerland.

Faculty School total: 21. In upper school: 7 men, 10 women; 8 have advanced degrees; 8 reside on campus.

Subjects Offered Algebra, American history, American literature, art, biology, calculus, chemistry, computer science, English, English literature, environmental science, French, geography, geometry, grammar, health, history, journalism, mathematics, nutrition, physical education, physics, science, social studies, Spanish, world history.

Graduation Requirements Arts and fine arts (art, music, dance, drama), computer education, English, foreign language, health education, mathematics, science, social studies (includes history), superior competence in winter sports (skiing/snowboarding). Community service is required.

Special Academic Programs Independent study; ESL (3 students enrolled).

College Admission Counseling 21 students graduated in 2012; 14 went to college, including Dartmouth College; Middlebury College; St. Lawrence University; University of Colorado Boulder; University of New Hampshire; University of Vermont. Other: 7 entered a postgraduate year. Mean SAT critical reading: 580, mean SAT math: 570, mean SAT writing: 600, mean combined SAT: 1750. 32% scored over 600 on SAT critical reading, 21% scored over 600 on SAT math, 47% scored over 600 on SAT writing, 42% scored over 1800 on combined SAT.

Student Life Upper grades have specified standards of dress, student council, honor system. Discipline rests primarily with faculty.

Tuition and Aid Day student tuition: $32,500; 7-day tuition and room/board: $44,500. Tuition installment plan (choice of one or two tuition installments plus advance deposit). Need-based scholarship grants, need-based loans available. In 2012–13, 48% of upper-school students received aid. Total amount of financial aid awarded in 2012–13: $800,000.

Admissions Traditional secondary-level entrance grade is 9. For fall 2012, 50 students applied for upper-level admission, 30 were accepted, 22 enrolled. Mathematics proficiency exam required. Deadline for receipt of application materials: March 15. Application fee required: $100. On-campus interview required.

Athletics Interscholastic: alpine skiing (boys, girls), bicycling (b,g), cross-country running (b,g), freestyle skiing (b,g), golf (b,g), lacrosse (b,g), mountain biking (b,g), nordic skiing (b,g), skiing (cross-country) (b,g), skiing (downhill) (b,g), snowboarding (b,g), soccer (b,g), tennis (b,g); intramural: strength & conditioning (b,g), tennis (b,g), yoga (b,g); coed intramural: skateboarding, tennis, yoga. 24 coaches, 1 athletic trainer.

Computers Computers are regularly used in computer applications, graphic design, mathematics, media production, research skills, science, Web site design, yearbook classes. Computer network features include on-campus library services, online commercial services, Internet access, Internet filtering or blocking technology. Student e-mail accounts are available to students. The school has a published electronic and media policy.

Contact Mrs. Kate Nolan Joyce, Director of Admissions. 802-856-1124. Fax: 802-297-0020. E-mail: knolan@gosms.org. Website: www.gosms.org

STUART HALL

235 West Frederick Street
PO Box 210
Staunton, Virginia 24401

Head of School: Mr. Mark H. Eastham

General Information Girls' boarding and coeducational day college-preparatory and arts school, affiliated with Episcopal Church. Boarding girls grades 8–12, day boys grades PK–12, day girls grades PK–12. Founded: 1844. Setting: small town. Nearest major city is Richmond. Students are housed in single-sex dormitories. 8-acre campus. 6 buildings on campus. Approved or accredited by National Association of Episcopal Schools, Virginia Association of Independent Schools, and Virginia Department of Education. Member of National Association of Independent Schools and Secondary School Admission Test Board. Endowment: $1 million. Total enrollment: 300. Upper school average class size: 10. Upper school faculty-student ratio: 1:12. There are 172 required school days per year for Upper School students. Upper School students typically attend 5 days per week. The average school day consists of 6 hours and 20 minutes.

Upper School Student Profile Grade 9: 22 students (7 boys, 15 girls); Grade 10: 32 students (4 boys, 28 girls); Grade 11: 36 students (4 boys, 32 girls); Grade 12: 34 students (6 boys, 28 girls). 48% of students are boarding students. 82% are state residents. 3 states are represented in upper school student body. 17% are international students. International students from China, Republic of Korea, and Rwanda; 3 other countries represented in student body. 25% of students are members of Episcopal Church.

Faculty School total: 40. In upper school: 12 men, 12 women; 16 have advanced degrees; 4 reside on campus.

Subjects Offered Algebra, American literature, ancient world history, applied arts, applied music, art appreciation, art history, biology, biology-AP, British literature, calculus-AP, career education, career/college preparation, ceramics, chamber groups, chemistry, chemistry-AP, choir, choral music, chorus, civics, college counseling, composition, creative writing, drama, drama performance, dramatic arts, English, English composition, English language and composition-AP, English literature-AP, English-AP, environmental science, environmental science-AP, ESL, fine arts, French, French language-AP, geometry, grammar, guitar, health education, history of drama, history of music, history-AP, honors algebra, honors English, honors geometry, honors world history, instrumental music, lab science, language and composition, learning lab, mathematics, modern world history, music, music composition, music history, music performance, music theater, music theory, philosophy, photography, physical education, physical fitness, physics, piano, playwriting and directing, portfolio art, pre-algebra, pre-calculus, probability and statistics, religion, SAT preparation, science, social studies, Spanish, Spanish language-AP, Spanish-AP, stage and body movement, stage design, strings, student government, student publications, study skills, theater, theater arts, theater history, theater production, trigonometry, U.S. government, U.S. government and politics-AP, U.S. history, U.S. history-AP, visual and performing arts, visual arts, vocal ensemble, vocal music, voice, voice ensemble, world geography, world history, world history-AP, world literature, yearbook.

Graduation Requirements Arts and fine arts (art, music, dance, drama), English, foreign language, mathematics, philosophy, physical education (includes health), religion (includes Bible studies and theology), SAT preparation, science, social studies (includes history).

Special Academic Programs Advanced Placement exam preparation; honors section; study at local college for college credit; academic accommodation for the gifted, the musically talented, and the artistically talented; ESL (30 students enrolled).

College Admission Counseling 31 students graduated in 2012; 26 went to college, including Brandeis University; New England Conservatory of Music; Roanoke College; University of Virginia; Virginia Military Institute; Virginia Polytechnic Institute and State University. Mean SAT critical reading: 577, mean SAT math: 567, mean SAT writing: 561.

Student Life Upper grades have specified standards of dress, student council, honor system. Discipline rests equally with students and faculty.

Tuition and Aid Day student tuition: $13,400; 5-day tuition and room/board: $28,000; 7-day tuition and room/board: $41,500. Tuition installment plan (Insured Tuition Payment Plan, monthly payment plans, individually arranged payment plans). Need-based scholarship grants available. In 2012–13, 33% of upper-school students received aid. Total amount of financial aid awarded in 2012–13: $850,000.

Admissions Traditional secondary-level entrance grade is 10. For fall 2012, 10 students applied for upper-level admission, 6 were accepted, 6 enrolled. TOEFL or SLEP required. Deadline for receipt of application materials: February 1. Application fee required: $45. Interview required.

Athletics Interscholastic: basketball (boys, girls), cheering (g), golf (b,g), horseback riding (b,g), jogging (b,g), lacrosse (b,g), soccer (b,g), track and field (b,g), volleyball (g); intramural: cheering (g), skiing (downhill) (b,g), snowboarding (b,g); coed interscholastic: cross-country running, lacrosse, running, soccer; coed intramural: golf. 1 PE instructor, 1 coach.

Computers Computers are regularly used in all classes. Computer network features include on-campus library services, Internet access, wireless campus network, Internet filtering or blocking technology. Student e-mail accounts and computer access in designated common areas are available to students. The school has a published electronic and media policy.

Contact Mrs. Mia Kivlighan, Director, Day Enrollment. 888-306-8926. Fax: 540-886-2275. E-mail: mkivlighan@stuart-hall.org. Website: www.stuart-hall.org

THE STUDY

3233 The Boulevard
Westmount, Quebec H3Y 1S4, Canada

Head of School: Nancy Sweer

General Information Girls' day college-preparatory, arts, bilingual studies, technology, and science school. Grades K–11. Founded: 1915. Setting: urban. Nearest major city is Montreal, Canada. 2 buildings on campus. Approved or accredited by Canadian Association of Independent Schools, Quebec Association of Independent Schools, and Quebec Department of Education. Affiliate member of National Association of Independent Schools. Languages of instruction: English and French. Endowment: CAN$5 million. Total enrollment: 316. Upper school average class size: 18. Upper school faculty-student ratio: 1:8. There are 180 required school days per year for Upper School students. Upper School students typically attend 5 days per week.

Upper School Student Profile Grade 7: 29 students (29 girls); Grade 8: 35 students (35 girls); Grade 9: 14 students (14 girls); Grade 10: 17 students (17 girls); Grade 11: 27 students (27 girls).

Faculty School total: 80. In upper school: 1 man, 28 women; 8 have advanced degrees.

Subjects Offered Algebra, art, art history, arts appreciation, biology, chemistry, computer science, ecology, economics, English, entrepreneurship, environmental science, ethics, European history, French, gender issues, geography, geometry, history, Mandarin, mathematics, music, philosophy, physical education, physics, religion and culture, science, social studies, Spanish, stagecraft, technology, theater, world history.

Graduation Requirements English, ethics, foreign language, French, mathematics, physical education (includes health), science, social studies (includes history), technology. Community service is required.

Special Academic Programs Advanced Placement exam preparation.

College Admission Counseling 24 students graduated in 2013; 21 went to college.

Student Life Upper grades have uniform requirement, student council, honor system. Discipline rests primarily with faculty.

Tuition and Aid Day student tuition: CAN$17,285. Tuition installment plan (monthly payment plans, individually arranged payment plans, 2-payment plan). Bursaries, merit scholarship grants, need-based scholarship grants available. In 2013–14, 18% of upper-school students received aid. Total amount of financial aid awarded in 2013–14: CAN$405,857.

Admissions Traditional secondary-level entrance grade is 7. CAT or SSAT required. Deadline for receipt of application materials: none. Application fee required: CAN$200. On-campus interview required.

Athletics Interscholastic: alpine skiing, badminton, basketball, crew, cross-country running, flag football, golf, hockey, ice hockey, rowing, running, skiing (cross-country), soccer, tennis, touch football, track and field, volleyball; intramural: aerobics, aerobics/dance, aerobics/Nautilus, badminton, ballet, basketball, bicycling, cooperative games, dance, fitness, ice hockey, jump rope, martial arts, outdoor activities, soccer, squash, touch football, track and field, ultimate Frisbee, volleyball. 3 PE instructors, 8 coaches.

Computers Computers are regularly used in art, English, history, mathematics, science classes. Computer network features include on-campus library services, Internet access, wireless campus network, Internet filtering or blocking technology. Campus intranet, student e-mail accounts, and computer access in designated common areas are available to students. The school has a published electronic and media policy.

Contact Antonia Zannis, Deputy Head of School. 514-935-9352. Fax: 514-935-1721. E-mail: admissions@thestudy.qc.ca. Website: www.thestudy.qc.ca

SUBIACO ACADEMY

405 North Subiaco Avenue
Subiaco, Arkansas 72865

Head of School: Mr. Matthew C. Stengel

General Information Boys' boarding and day college-preparatory, arts, religious studies, bilingual studies, technology, and art and performing art school, affiliated with Roman Catholic Church. Grades 7–12. Founded: 1887. Setting: rural. Nearest major city is Little Rock. Students are housed in single-sex dormitories. 100-acre campus. 10 buildings on campus. Approved or accredited by Headmasters' Conference, Independent Schools Association of the Central States, National Catholic Education Association, North Central Association of Colleges and Schools, The Association of Boarding Schools, and Arkansas Department of Education. Arkansas Non-Public Schools Accrediting Association. Member of National Association of Independent Schools. Endowment: $3.5 million. Total enrollment: 182. Upper school average class size: 18. Upper school faculty-student ratio: 1:9. There are 179 required school days per year for Upper School students. Upper School students typically attend 5 days per week. The average school day consists of 6 hours and 25 minutes.

Upper School Student Profile Grade 7: 10 students (10 boys); Grade 8: 18 students (18 boys); Grade 9: 34 students (34 boys); Grade 10: 41 students (41 boys); Grade 11: 45 students (45 boys); Grade 12: 34 students (34 boys). 60% of students are boarding students. 57% are state residents. 18 states are represented in upper school student body. 17% are international students. International students from China, Japan, Mexico, Nigeria, Republic of Korea, and Viet Nam; 1 other country represented in student body. 65% of students are Roman Catholic.

Faculty School total: 31. In upper school: 21 men, 10 women; 18 have advanced degrees; 9 reside on campus.

Subjects Offered Algebra, American history, American history-AP, art, art-AP, band, biology, biology-AP, broadcasting, calculus, calculus-AP, chemistry, chemistry-AP, choral music, chorus, Christian doctrine, Christian education, Christian scripture, Christian studies, Christian testament, church history, communications, computer art, computer science, drama, drama workshop, driver education, earth and space science, earth science, economics, English, English literature, English literature and composition-AP, English-AP, finance, fine arts, geography, geometry, government/civics, jazz ensemble, journalism, Latin, mathematics-AP, music, physical education, physics, piano, psychology, religion, sociology, Spanish, speech, statistics-AP, Western civilization, world history.

Graduation Requirements Arts and fine arts (art, music, dance, drama), computer science, English, foreign language, mathematics, physical education (includes health), religion (includes Bible studies and theology), science, social studies (includes history), Western civilization. Community service is required.

Special Academic Programs 8 Advanced Placement exams for which test preparation is offered; honors section; academic accommodation for the gifted, the musically talented, and the artistically talented; ESL (11 students enrolled).

College Admission Counseling 40 students graduated in 2013; 39 went to college, including Hendrix College; Penn State University Park; Rhodes College; Texas Christian University; University of Arkansas; University of Dallas. Other: 1 entered military service.

Student Life Upper grades have uniform requirement, student council. Discipline rests primarily with faculty. Attendance at religious services is required.

Summer Programs Remediation programs offered; held on campus; accepts boys; not open to students from other schools.

Tuition and Aid Day student tuition: $6800; 5-day tuition and room/board: $20,600; 7-day tuition and room/board: $23,000. Tuition installment plan (monthly payment plans, individually arranged payment plans). Need-based scholarship grants available. In 2013–14, 35% of upper-school students received aid. Total amount of financial aid awarded in 2013–14: $449,540.

Admissions Traditional secondary-level entrance grade is 9. For fall 2013, 71 students applied for upper-level admission, 57 were accepted, 45 enrolled. International English Language Test, Junior TOEFL, or TOEFL required. Deadline for receipt of application materials: none. Application fee required: $50. Interview required.

Athletics Interscholastic: baseball, basketball, cross-country running, football, golf, soccer, tennis, track and field; intramural: archery, backpacking, baseball, basketball, bicycling, billiards, blading, bowling, canoeing/kayaking, cheering, climbing, cross-country running, diving, fishing, fitness, fly fishing, football, Frisbee, golf, handball, hiking/backpacking, horseshoes, in-line skating, indoor soccer, jogging, kayaking, marksmanship, outdoor activities, physical fitness, physical training, power lifting, riflery, rock climbing, roller blading, running, skateboarding, skeet shooting, skiing (downhill), soccer, softball, strength & conditioning, tennis, walking, wall climbing, weight lifting. 1 PE instructor, 12 coaches.

Computers Computers are regularly used in art, Christian doctrine, commercial art, creative writing, desktop publishing, digital applications, drawing and design, economics, English, geography, graphic arts, history, journalism, keyboarding, literary magazine, mathematics, news writing, newspaper, photography, photojournalism, publications, religion, religious studies, SAT preparation, science, Spanish, stock market, video film production, word processing, writing, yearbook classes. Computer network features include on-campus library services, Internet access, wireless campus network, Internet filtering or blocking technology. Computer access in designated common areas is available to students. Students grades are available online. The school has a published electronic and media policy.

Contact Ms. Evelyn Bauer, Assistant Director of Admissions. 800-364-7824. Fax: 479-934-1033. E-mail: ebauer@subi.org. Website: www.subi.org

THE SUDBURY VALLEY SCHOOL

2 Winch Street
Framingham, Massachusetts 01701

Head of School: Samuel McGuire

General Information Coeducational day college-preparatory and general academic school. Grades PS–12. Founded: 1968. Setting: suburban. Nearest major city is Boston. 10-acre campus. 2 buildings on campus. Approved or accredited by Massachusetts Department of Education. Total enrollment: 160. Upper school faculty-student ratio: 1:16. There are 180 required school days per year for Upper School students. Upper School students typically attend 5 days per week. The average school day consists of 6 hours.

Faculty School total: 8. In upper school: 5 men, 3 women; 3 have advanced degrees.

Subjects Offered Algebra, American history, American literature, anatomy, anthropology, archaeology, art, art history, Bible studies, biology, botany, business, calculus, ceramics, chemistry, computer programming, computer science, creative writing, dance, drama, economics, English, English literature, ethics, European history, expository writing, French, geography, geometry, German, government/civics, grammar, Hebrew, history, history of ideas, history of science, home economics, Latin, mathematics, music, philosophy, photography, physical education, physics, physiology, psychology, religion, social studies, Spanish, speech, theater, trigonometry, typing, world history, world literature, writing.

Graduation Requirements Students must justify the proposition that they have developed the problem solving skill, the adaptability, and the abilities needed to function, independently in the world.

Special Academic Programs Independent study.

College Admission Counseling 6 students graduated in 2013; 4 went to college. Other: 2 went to work.

Student Life Upper grades have student council, honor system. Discipline rests equally with students and faculty.

Tuition and Aid Day student tuition: $8200. Tuition reduction for siblings available.

Admissions Deadline for receipt of application materials: none. Application fee required: $50. On-campus interview required.

Computers Computer network features include on-campus library services, Internet access. Student e-mail accounts are available to students. The school has a published electronic and media policy.

Contact Hanna Greenberg, Admissions Clerk. 508-877-3030. Fax: 508-788-0674. E-mail: office@sudval.org. Website: www.sudval.org

SUMMERFIELD WALDORF SCHOOL

655 Willowside Road
Santa Rosa, California 95401

Head of School: Mr. Bob Flagg

General Information Coeducational day college-preparatory, arts, and Waldorf Curriculum school. Grades K–12. Founded: 1974. Setting: rural. 38-acre campus. 8 buildings on campus. Approved or accredited by Association of Waldorf Schools of North America, Western Association of Schools and Colleges, and California Department of Education. Total enrollment: 409. Upper school average class size: 28. Upper school faculty-student ratio: 1:7. Upper School students typically attend 5 days per week. The average school day consists of 7 hours.

Faculty School total: 23. In upper school: 11 men, 12 women; all have advanced degrees.

Subjects Offered Advanced chemistry, arts, history, humanities, literature, mathematics, music, science.

Graduation Requirements All , Senior Thesis Project.

Special Academic Programs Honors section; study abroad.

College Admission Counseling 22 students graduated in 2013; 21 went to college, including Bennington College; Cornell University; Oberlin College; Sonoma State University; University of California, Davis; University of Redlands. Other: 1 went to work.

Student Life Upper grades have specified standards of dress, student council, honor system. Discipline rests primarily with faculty.

Tuition and Aid Day student tuition: $17,000. Tuition installment plan (FACTS Tuition Payment Plan, monthly payment plans). Tuition reduction for siblings, need-based scholarship grants available. In 2013–14, 40% of upper-school students received aid.

Admissions Traditional secondary-level entrance grade is 9. For fall 2013, 56 students applied for upper-level admission, 38 were accepted, 34 enrolled. Deadline for receipt of application materials: January 16. Application fee required: $75. On-campus interview required.

Athletics Interscholastic: basketball (boys, girls), soccer (b,g), volleyball (b,g); coed interscholastic: tennis. 5 PE instructors, 5 coaches.

Computers The school has a published electronic and media policy.

Contact Ms. Sallie Miller, Admissions Director. 707-575-7194 Ext. 102. Fax: 707-575-3217. E-mail: sallie@summerfieldwaldof.org. Website: www.summerfieldwaldorf.org

THE SUMMIT COUNTRY DAY SCHOOL

2161 Grandin Road
Cincinnati, Ohio 45208-3300

Head of School: Mr. Rich Wilson

General Information Coeducational day college-preparatory school, affiliated with Roman Catholic Church. Grades PK–12. Founded: 1890. Setting: suburban. 24-acre campus. 2 buildings on campus. Approved or accredited by Independent Schools

Association of the Central States, The College Board, and Ohio Department of Education. Member of National Association of Independent Schools. Endowment: $20 million. Total enrollment: 1,020. Upper school average class size: 16. Upper school faculty-student ratio: 1:9. There are 187 required school days per year for Upper School students. Upper School students typically attend 5 days per week. The average school day consists of 6 hours and 30 minutes.

Upper School Student Profile Grade 9: 87 students (47 boys, 40 girls); Grade 10: 87 students (32 boys, 55 girls); Grade 11: 96 students (51 boys, 45 girls); Grade 12: 99 students (47 boys, 52 girls). 60% of students are Roman Catholic.

Faculty School total: 136. In upper school: 14 men, 23 women; 31 have advanced degrees.

Subjects Offered Advanced Placement courses, algebra, American history, American history-AP, American literature, anatomy and physiology, archaeology, art, biology, biology-AP, business law, calculus, calculus-AP, ceramics, chemistry, chemistry-AP, chorus, college admission preparation, college placement, community service, computer applications, computer science, computer science-AP, concert choir, critical studies in film, drama, economics, English, English literature, English-AP, environmental science, European history, European history-AP, fine arts, French, French-AP, geometry, government-AP, government/civics, grammar, graphic design, health, history, history of science, history-AP, Holocaust studies, language-AP, Latin, Latin-AP, leadership, leadership and service, leadership education training, literary magazine, mathematics, music, music theory-AP, music-AP, philosophy, physical education, physics, physics-AP, pre-calculus, psychology, psychology-AP, public speaking, religion, religious studies, science, senior career experience, service learning/internship, social studies, Spanish, Spanish language-AP, Spanish-AP, speech, speech communications, statistics-AP, student government, studio art, studio art-AP, study skills, theater, trigonometry, U.S. government and politics-AP, world history, world history-AP, world literature, world religions, writing.

Graduation Requirements Arts and fine arts (art, music, dance, drama), computer applications, computer science, English, foreign language, mathematics, physical education (includes health), religion (includes Bible studies and theology), science, social sciences, social studies (includes history), speech communications, junior year leadership course (one semester), junior year speech course, 40 hours of community service, senior search (2-week field experience in career of interest area).

Special Academic Programs 19 Advanced Placement exams for which test preparation is offered; honors section; independent study; study abroad; academic accommodation for the gifted and the artistically talented.

College Admission Counseling 97 students graduated in 2013; all went to college, including Denison University; Indiana University Bloomington; Loyola University Chicago; Purdue University; The Ohio State University; University of Cincinnati. Median SAT critical reading: 631, median SAT math: 609, median composite ACT: 28.

Student Life Upper grades have uniform requirement, student council, honor system. Discipline rests equally with students and faculty. Attendance at religious services is required.

Summer Programs Enrichment, advancement, sports, art/fine arts, computer instruction programs offered; session focuses on enrichment, academic advancement; held both on and off campus; held at 16-acre athletic sports complex; accepts boys and girls; open to students from other schools. 2014 schedule: June 7 to August 15. Application deadline: none.

Tuition and Aid Day student tuition: $19,250–$19,750. Tuition installment plan (Insured Tuition Payment Plan, monthly payment plans, individually arranged payment plans). Merit scholarship grants, need-based scholarship grants available. In 2013–14, 50% of upper-school students received aid.

Admissions Traditional secondary-level entrance grade is 9. For fall 2013, 285 students applied for upper-level admission, 173 were accepted, 50 enrolled. High School Placement Test or ISEE required. Deadline for receipt of application materials: December 13. Application fee required: $50. On-campus interview required.

Athletics Interscholastic: baseball (boys, girls), basketball (b,g), bowling (b,g), cheering (g), cross-country running (b,g), diving (b,g), field hockey (g), football (b), golf (b,g), lacrosse (b), soccer (b,g), softball (g), swimming and diving (b,g), tennis (b,g), track and field (b,g), volleyball (g), wrestling (b); intramural: dance team (g); coed interscholastic: weight lifting. 52 coaches, 1 athletic trainer.

Computers Computers are regularly used in all classes. Computer network features include on-campus library services, online commercial services, Internet access, wireless campus network, Internet filtering or blocking technology, mobile laptop computer lab, School wude PORTAL/Grades, Sketchpad, 8 full-text databases including Big Chalk, World Book, Children's Lit, SIRS, Biography Resource Center, Wilson Web, INFOhio, JSTOR. Campus intranet, student e-mail accounts, and computer access in designated common areas are available to students. Students grades are available online. The school has a published electronic and media policy.

Contact Mrs. Kelley Schiess, Director of Admission. 513-871-4700 Ext. 207. Fax: 513-533-5350. E-mail: schiess_k@summitcds.org. Website: www.summitcds.org

SUMMIT PREPARATORY SCHOOL

Kalispell, Montana
See Special Needs Schools section.

SUNSHINE BIBLE ACADEMY

400 Sunshine Drive
Miller, South Dakota 57362-6821

Head of School: Jason Watson

General Information Coeducational boarding and day college-preparatory, general academic, arts, business, vocational, religious studies, bilingual studies, and technology school, affiliated with Christian faith. Boarding grades 8–12, day grades K–12. Founded: 1951. Setting: rural. Nearest major city is Pierre. Students are housed in single-sex dormitories. 160-acre campus. 20 buildings on campus. Approved or accredited by Association of Christian Schools International and South Dakota Department of Education. Total enrollment: 94. Upper school average class size: 20. Upper school faculty-student ratio: 1:9. There are 180 required school days per year for Upper School students. Upper School students typically attend 5 days per week. The average school day consists of 6 hours and 40 minutes.

Upper School Student Profile Grade 9: 13 students (4 boys, 9 girls); Grade 10: 15 students (10 boys, 5 girls); Grade 11: 16 students (9 boys, 7 girls); Grade 12: 21 students (9 boys, 12 girls). 91% of students are boarding students. 70% are state residents. 7 states are represented in upper school student body. 15% are international students. International students from Ethiopia, Japan, and Republic of Korea. 100% of students are Christian faith.

Faculty School total: 16. In upper school: 8 men, 3 women; 4 have advanced degrees; 13 reside on campus.

Subjects Offered Accounting, advanced math, algebra, American history, American literature, band, bell choir, Bible, Bible studies, biology, chemistry, choir, Christian doctrine, Christian ethics, computer science, creative writing, drama, drama performance, economics, English, English literature, ethics, fine arts, geography, geometry, government/civics, grammar, health, history, HTML design, journalism, mathematics, music, music appreciation, music composition, music history, music performance, newspaper, physical education, physics, science, social sciences, social studies, Spanish, speech, speech and oral interpretations, trigonometry, typing, U.S. government, U.S. history, vocal music, world geography, world history, writing, yearbook.

Graduation Requirements Arts and fine arts (art, music, dance, drama), Bible, computer science, English, mathematics, science, social sciences, social studies (includes history).

Special Academic Programs Independent study; study at local college for college credit; academic accommodation for the musically talented; remedial math.

College Admission Counseling 21 students graduated in 2013; 18 went to college, including Dordt College; North Dakota State University; South Dakota State University; The George Washington University; University of Maryland, Baltimore County; University of Massachusetts Amherst. Other: 3 went to work. Median composite ACT: 23. 8% scored over 26 on composite ACT.

Student Life Upper grades have specified standards of dress, student council, honor system. Discipline rests primarily with faculty. Attendance at religious services is required.

Tuition and Aid Day student tuition: $5565; 7-day tuition and room/board: $7950. Tuition installment plan (monthly payment plans). Tuition reduction for siblings, need-based scholarship grants available. In 2013–14, 20% of upper-school students received aid. Total amount of financial aid awarded in 2013–14: $38,520.

Admissions Traditional secondary-level entrance grade is 9. For fall 2013, 22 students applied for upper-level admission, 22 were accepted, 20 enrolled. Deadline for receipt of application materials: none. Application fee required: $50. On-campus interview required.

Athletics Interscholastic: basketball (boys, girls), cheering (g), cross-country running (b,g), football (b), track and field (b,g), volleyball (g), wrestling (b); intramural: physical fitness (b,g), physical training (b,g), strength & conditioning (b,g), weight lifting (b,g), weight training (b,g). 1 PE instructor, 6 coaches.

Computers Computers are regularly used in art, journalism, newspaper, publications, publishing, research skills, speech, typing, Web site design, writing, yearbook classes. Computer resources include on-campus library services, Internet access, wireless campus network, Internet filtering or blocking technology. Student e-mail accounts are available to students.

Contact Mr. Andrew Boersma, Dean of Students. 605-853-3071 Ext. 14. Fax: 605-853-3072. E-mail: andrew.boersma@k12.sd.us. Website: www.sunshinebible.org

THE TAFT SCHOOL

110 Woodbury Road
Watertown, Connecticut 06795

Head of School: Mr. William R. MacMullen

General Information Coeducational boarding and day college-preparatory, arts, and humanities school. Grades 9–PG. Founded: 1890. Setting: small town. Nearest major city is Waterbury. Students are housed in single-sex dormitories. 224-acre campus. 20 buildings on campus. Approved or accredited by New England Association of Schools and Colleges, The Association of Boarding Schools, The College Board, and Connecticut Department of Education. Member of National Association of Independent Schools and Secondary School Admission Test Board. Endowment: $208 million. Total enrollment: 579. Upper school average class size: 12. Upper school faculty-student ratio: 1:5. Upper School students typically attend 6 days per week. The average school day consists of 7 hours.

Upper School Student Profile Grade 9: 106 students (50 boys, 56 girls); Grade 10: 148 students (74 boys, 74 girls); Grade 11: 161 students (79 boys, 82 girls); Grade 12: 161 students (85 boys, 76 girls); Postgraduate: 12 students (9 boys, 3 girls). 82% of students are boarding students. 37% are state residents. 37 states are represented in upper school student body. 16% are international students. International students from Bermuda, Canada, China, Hong Kong, Republic of Korea, and Viet Nam; 27 other countries represented in student body.

Faculty School total: 124. In upper school: 61 men, 63 women; 92 have advanced degrees; 118 reside on campus.

Subjects Offered Acting, adolescent issues, advanced biology, advanced chemistry, advanced computer applications, advanced math, Advanced Placement courses, advanced studio art-AP, African-American literature, algebra, American history, American history-AP, American literature, anatomy, anatomy and physiology, animal behavior, architectural drawing, architecture, art, art history, art history-AP, astronomy, biology, biology-AP, calculus, calculus-AP, ceramics, chamber groups, character education, chemistry, chemistry-AP, Chinese, computer math, computer programming, computer science, computer science-AP, concert choir, creative writing, dance, design, digital imaging, drama, drawing, ecology, economics, economics-AP, English, English literature, English literature-AP, environmental science, environmental science-AP, ethics, European history, European history-AP, expository writing, film studies, fine arts, forensics, French, French language-AP, geography, geology, geometry, government-AP, government/civics, grammar, Greek, history, history of rock and roll, history of science, honors algebra, honors English, honors geometry, human rights, humanities, Islamic studies, Japanese, jazz band, Latin, Mandarin, marine biology, mathematics, music, music theory-AP, philosophy, photography, physical education, physics, physics-AP, physiology, pre-calculus, psychology, religion, science, senior project, senior thesis, service learning/internship, sex education, South African history, Spanish, Spanish literature-AP, Spanish-AP, speech, statistics, statistics-AP, studio art-AP, theater, theology, trigonometry, U.S. government and politics-AP, U.S. history-AP, video film production, world history, world literature, writing, zoology.

Graduation Requirements American history, arts and fine arts (art, music, dance, drama), English, foreign language, mathematics, science, social studies (includes history), three semesters of arts.

Special Academic Programs 29 Advanced Placement exams for which test preparation is offered; honors section; independent study; term-away projects; study abroad; academic accommodation for the gifted, the musically talented, and the artistically talented.

College Admission Counseling 165 students graduated in 2013; 161 went to college, including Cornell University; Georgetown University; Hamilton College; Trinity College; University of Southern California; Wesleyan University. Other: 4 entered a postgraduate year. Mean SAT critical reading: 630, mean SAT math: 650, mean SAT writing: 648, mean combined SAT: 1928. 67% scored over 600 on SAT critical reading, 75% scored over 600 on SAT math, 69% scored over 600 on SAT writing, 72% scored over 1800 on combined SAT.

Student Life Upper grades have specified standards of dress, student council, honor system. Discipline rests equally with students and faculty.

Summer Programs Enrichment, ESL, sports, art/fine arts programs offered; session focuses on academic enrichment; held on campus; accepts boys and girls; open to students from other schools. 150 students usually enrolled. 2014 schedule: June 25 to July 30. Application deadline: none.

Tuition and Aid Day student tuition: $37,300; 7-day tuition and room/board: $50,300. Tuition installment plan (SMART Tuition Payment Plan). Need-based scholarship grants, need-based loans available. In 2013–14, 37% of upper-school students received aid. Total amount of financial aid awarded in 2013–14: $7,300,000.

Admissions Traditional secondary-level entrance grade is 9. For fall 2013, 1,600 students applied for upper-level admission, 323 were accepted, 184 enrolled. SSAT required. Deadline for receipt of application materials: January 15. Application fee required: $50. Interview required.

Athletics Interscholastic: alpine skiing (boys, girls), baseball (b), basketball (b,g), crew (b,g), cross-country running (b,g), field hockey (g), football (b), golf (b,g), hockey (b,g), ice hockey (b,g), lacrosse (b,g), rowing (b,g), soccer (b,g), softball (g), squash (b,g), tennis (b,g), track and field (b,g), ultimate Frisbee (b,g), volleyball (g), wrestling (b); coed interscholastic: dressage, equestrian sports, horseback riding; coed intramural: aerobics, aerobics/dance, ballet, basketball, climbing, cross-country running, dance, dressage, equestrian sports, figure skating, fitness, fitness walking, Frisbee, hockey, horseback riding, ice hockey, ice skating, jogging, martial arts, modern dance, outdoor activities, physical fitness, rock climbing, rowing, running, soccer, squash, strength & conditioning, tennis, track and field, ultimate Frisbee, walking, wall climbing, weight lifting, weight training, yoga. 1 coach, 3 athletic trainers.

Computers Computers are regularly used in art, English, foreign language, geography, history, mathematics, music, science classes. Computer network features

include on-campus library services, online commercial services, Internet access, wireless campus network, Internet filtering or blocking technology. Campus intranet, student e-mail accounts, and computer access in designated common areas are available to students. The school has a published electronic and media policy.

Contact Mr. Peter A. Frew, Director of Admissions. 860-945-7700. Fax: 860-945-7808. E-mail: admissions@taftschool.org. Website: www.taftschool.org

TAIPEI AMERICAN SCHOOL

800 Chung Shan North Road, Section 6
Taipei 11152, Taiwan

Head of School: Dr. Sharon Hennessy

General Information Coeducational day college-preparatory, arts, technology, and fine and performing arts, STEM, robotics school. Grades PK–12. Founded: 1949. Setting: urban. 15-acre campus. 5 buildings on campus. Approved or accredited by International Baccalaureate Organization, US Department of State, and Western Association of Schools and Colleges. Affiliate member of National Association of Independent Schools; member of European Council of International Schools. Language of instruction: English. Endowment: 499 million Taiwan dollars. Total enrollment: 2,235. Upper school average class size: 17. Upper school faculty-student ratio: 1:9. There are 180 required school days per year for Upper School students. Upper School students typically attend 5 days per week. The average school day consists of 6 hours and 40 minutes.

Upper School Student Profile Grade 9: 215 students (120 boys, 95 girls); Grade 10: 225 students (107 boys, 118 girls); Grade 11: 216 students (97 boys, 119 girls); Grade 12: 228 students (116 boys, 112 girls).

Faculty School total: 249. In upper school: 53 men, 50 women; 85 have advanced degrees.

Subjects Offered Advanced math, Advanced Placement courses, advanced studio art-AP, algebra, American literature, art history, Asian studies, biology, business, calculus, ceramics, chemistry, chemistry-AP, Chinese, choir, computer science, computer science-AP, contemporary history, current history, dance, debate, digital photography, drawing, earth science, English, English language-AP, English literature-AP, environmental science-AP, European history-AP, expository writing, fitness, forensics, French, French-AP, geography, geometry, health, International Baccalaureate courses, Japanese, jazz ensemble, journalism, Latin, linear algebra, macro/microeconomics-AP, macroeconomics-AP, Mandarin, microeconomics-AP, music theory-AP, orchestra, physical education, physics, physics-AP, pre-algebra, pre-calculus, psychology, research seminar, rhetoric, robotics, Spanish, Spanish-AP, speech and debate, statistics-AP, theater, theory of knowledge, trigonometry, U.S. history, U.S. history-AP, video film production, visual arts, wind ensemble, world cultures, world history, world literature, yearbook.

Graduation Requirements English, mathematics, modern languages, performing arts, physical education (includes health), public speaking, science, social studies (includes history).

Special Academic Programs International Baccalaureate program; 26 Advanced Placement exams for which test preparation is offered; honors section; ESL.

College Admission Counseling 217 students graduated in 2012; 214 went to college, including New York University; University of California, Berkeley; University of California, Los Angeles; University of California, San Diego; University of Pennsylvania; University of Southern California. Other: 2 entered military service, 1 had other specific plans. Mean SAT critical reading: 614, mean SAT math: 684, mean SAT writing: 631, mean combined SAT: 1929.

Student Life Upper grades have specified standards of dress, student council, honor system. Discipline rests primarily with faculty.

Tuition and Aid Day student tuition: 563,855 Taiwan dollars. Tuition installment plan (individually arranged payment plans).

Admissions Traditional secondary-level entrance grade is 9. For fall 2012, 117 students applied for upper-level admission, 68 were accepted, 54 enrolled. California Achievement Test, English for Non-native Speakers, ERB CTP IV, Iowa Tests of Basic Skills, ISEE, latest standardized score from previous school, PSAT, SAT, SSAT or Stanford Achievement Test required. Deadline for receipt of application materials: none. Application fee required: 10,000 Taiwan dollars.

Athletics Interscholastic: badminton (boys, girls), basketball (b,g), cross-country running (b,g), dance (b,g), golf (b,g), rugby (b,g), soccer (b,g), softball (b,g), swimming and diving (b,g), tennis (b,g), track and field (b,g), volleyball (b,g); intramural: swimming and diving (b,g). 6 PE instructors, 1 athletic trainer.

Computers Computers are regularly used in all academic classes. Computer network features include on-campus library services, online commercial services, Internet access, wireless campus network, Internet filtering or blocking technology. Campus intranet, student e-mail accounts, and computer access in designated common areas are available to students. Students grades are available online. The school has a published electronic and media policy.

Contact Dr. Winnie Tang, Admissions Officer. 886-2-2873-9900 Ext. 328. Fax: 886-2-2873-1641. E-mail: admissions@tas.edu.tw. Website: www.tas.edu.tw

TAMPA PREPARATORY SCHOOL

727 West Cass Street
Tampa, Florida 33606

Head of School: Mr. Kevin M. Plummer

General Information Coeducational day college-preparatory, arts, bilingual studies, and technology school. Grades 6–12. Founded: 1974. Setting: urban. 12-acre campus. 4 buildings on campus. Approved or accredited by Southern Association of Colleges and Schools and Florida Department of Education. Member of National Association of Independent Schools and Secondary School Admission Test Board. Total enrollment: 576. Upper school average class size: 18. Upper school faculty-student ratio: 1:10. There are 180 required school days per year for Upper School students. Upper School students typically attend 5 days per week. The average school day consists of 7 hours and 10 minutes.

Upper School Student Profile Grade 6: 44 students (25 boys, 19 girls); Grade 7: 62 students (29 boys, 33 girls); Grade 8: 67 students (33 boys, 34 girls); Grade 9: 98 students (61 boys, 37 girls); Grade 10: 102 students (53 boys, 49 girls); Grade 11: 118 students (51 boys, 67 girls); Grade 12: 102 students (44 boys, 58 girls).

Faculty School total: 71. In upper school: 31 men, 40 women; 31 have advanced degrees.

Subjects Offered Advanced biology, advanced chemistry, Advanced Placement courses, athletic training, college counseling, creative writing, digital photography, engineering, global studies, leadership education training, marine biology, model United Nations, musical theater, personal fitness, photography, play/screen writing, public speaking, religion and culture, senior internship, senior project, sports medicine, statistics, technical theater, theater, theater arts, video film production, world history.

Graduation Requirements Algebra, arts and fine arts (art, music, dance, drama), English, foreign language, geometry, history, physical education (includes health), pre-calculus, science.

Special Academic Programs 21 Advanced Placement exams for which test preparation is offered; honors section; independent study; study abroad; academic accommodation for the gifted, the musically talented, and the artistically talented.

College Admission Counseling 98 students graduated in 2013; all went to college, including Emory University; Florida State University; Southern Methodist University; University of Central Florida; University of Florida; University of Pennsylvania.

Student Life Upper grades have specified standards of dress, student council, honor system. Discipline rests equally with students and faculty.

Summer Programs Remediation, enrichment, advancement, computer instruction programs offered; session focuses on grades 8-12 summer camp, acclerated academics, enrichment classes; held on campus; accepts boys and girls; open to students from other schools. 400 students usually enrolled. 2014 schedule: June 8 to July 31. Application deadline: none.

Tuition and Aid Day student tuition: $17,050. Guaranteed tuition plan. Tuition installment plan (FACTS Tuition Payment Plan, individually arranged payment plans). Merit scholarship grants, need-based scholarship grants available. In 2013–14, 16% of upper-school students received aid; total upper-school merit-scholarship money awarded: $90,500. Total amount of financial aid awarded in 2013–14: $650,000.

Admissions Traditional secondary-level entrance grade is 9. For fall 2013, 212 students applied for upper-level admission, 180 were accepted, 139 enrolled. ISEE, PSAT or SAT for applicants to grade 11 and 12, SSAT, TOEFL or writing sample required. Deadline for receipt of application materials: February 15. Application fee required: $75. On-campus interview recommended.

Athletics Interscholastic: baseball (boys), basketball (b,g), crew (b,g), cross-country running (b,g), dance team (g), diving (b,g), golf (b,g), lacrosse (b), rowing (b,g), running (b,g), soccer (b,g), softball (g), swimming and diving (b,g), tennis (b,g), track and field (b,g), volleyball (b,g), wrestling (b); intramural: dance team (g), physical fitness (b,g), racquetball (b,g); coed interscholastic: aquatics, bowling; coed intramural: badminton, dance, fitness, flag football, modern dance, physical training, sailing, scuba diving, strength & conditioning, table tennis, weight training. 4 PE instructors, 57 coaches, 2 athletic trainers.

Computers Computers are regularly used in all academic, creative writing, economics, graphic design, journalism, mathematics, science, yearbook classes. Computer network features include on-campus library services, online commercial services, Internet access, wireless campus network, Internet filtering or blocking technology. Campus intranet, student e-mail accounts, and computer access in designated common areas are available. Students grades are available online. The school has a published electronic and media policy.

Contact Mrs. Linda Y. Quinn, Admissions Assistant. 813-251-8481 Ext. 4011. Fax: 813-254-2106. E-mail: lquinn@tampaprep.org. Website: www.tampaprep.org

TANDEM FRIENDS SCHOOL

279 Tandem Lane
Charlottesville, Virginia 22902

Head of School: Andy Jones-Wilkins

General Information Coeducational day college-preparatory and arts school, affiliated with Society of Friends. Grades 5–12. Founded: 1970. Setting: small town. Nearest major city is Richmond. 23-acre campus. 7 buildings on campus. Approved or accredited by Friends Council on Education and Virginia Association of Independent Schools. Member of National Association of Independent Schools. Endowment: $3.3 million. Total enrollment: 207. Upper school average class size: 12. Upper school faculty-student ratio: 1:6. There are 180 required school days per year for Upper School students. Upper School students typically attend 5 days per week. The average school day consists of 7 hours.

Upper School Student Profile Grade 9: 30 students (13 boys, 17 girls); Grade 10: 21 students (12 boys, 9 girls); Grade 11: 27 students (9 boys, 18 girls); Grade 12: 31 students (13 boys, 18 girls). 3% of students are members of Society of Friends.

Faculty School total: 36. In upper school: 7 men, 10 women; 10 have advanced degrees.

Subjects Offered Algebra, American literature, anatomy, art, bioethics, biology, biology-AP, calculus, calculus-AP, ceramics, chemistry, chemistry-AP, college counseling, computer applications, creative writing, cultural geography, discrete mathematics, drama, economics, economics and history, English, English-AP, environmental science-AP, expository writing, fine arts, French, French-AP, geometry, health and wellness, jazz ensemble, Latin, Latin-AP, marine biology, media studies, modern world history, music, musical productions, performing arts, photo shop, photography, physics, Quakerism and ethics, senior project, Spanish, Spanish-AP, statistics, statistics-AP, student government, student publications, studio art, theater, trigonometry, U.S. government, U.S. history, U.S. history-AP, weaving, world history, world literature, writing, yearbook.

Graduation Requirements Arts and fine arts (art, music, dance, drama), computer science, English, foreign language, government/civics, history, mathematics, science, senior year independent experiential learning project. Community service is required.

Special Academic Programs Advanced Placement exam preparation; independent study; academic accommodation for the gifted; remedial reading and/or remedial writing; remedial math.

College Admission Counseling 36 students graduated in 2012; 32 went to college, including Bates College; James Madison University; The College of William and Mary; University of North Carolina at Asheville; University of Virginia; Virginia Polytechnic Institute and State University. Other: 4 had other specific plans. Median SAT critical reading: 642, median SAT math: 599, median SAT writing: 620, median combined SAT: 1241, median composite ACT: 26.

Student Life Upper grades have student council, honor system. Discipline rests equally with students and faculty. Attendance at religious services is required.

Tuition and Aid Day student tuition: $17,900. Tuition installment plan (Insured Tuition Payment Plan, monthly payment plans, individually arranged payment plans). Need-based scholarship grants, tuition remission for children of full-time faculty available. In 2012–13, 34% of upper-school students received aid. Total amount of financial aid awarded in 2012–13: $379,110.

Admissions Traditional secondary-level entrance grade is 9. For fall 2012, 76 students applied for upper-level admission, 71 were accepted, 59 enrolled. Woodcock-Johnson required. Deadline for receipt of application materials: none. Application fee required: $50. Interview required.

Athletics Interscholastic: basketball (boys, girls), field hockey (g), lacrosse (b,g), soccer (b,g), tennis (b,g), volleyball (g); coed interscholastic: cross-country running, fencing, golf, mountain biking, track and field; coed intramural: fencing. 2 PE instructors, 24 coaches.

Computers Computers are regularly used in all academic classes. Computer network features include on-campus library services, online commercial services, Internet access, wireless campus network, Internet filtering or blocking technology, virtual classroom, iPad program for grades 5, 6, and 9. Student e-mail accounts and computer access in designated common areas are available to students. Students grades are available online. The school has a published electronic and media policy.

Contact Louise DeCamp Cole, Director of Admissions. 434-951-9314. Fax: 434-296-1886. E-mail: lcole@tandemfs.org. Website: www.tandemfs.org

TAPPLY BINET COLLEGE

245 Garner Road West
Ancaster, Ontario L9G 3K9, Canada

Head of School: Ms. Sue Davidson

General Information Coeducational day college-preparatory and general academic school. Grades 7–12. Founded: 1997. Setting: small town. Nearest major city is Hamilton, Canada. 1-acre campus. 1 building on campus. Approved or accredited by Ontario Ministry of Education and Ontario Department of Education. Language of instruction: English. Total enrollment: 17. Upper school average class size: 6. Upper school faculty-student ratio: 1:3.

Upper School Student Profile Grade 9: 2 students (1 boy, 1 girl); Grade 10: 3 students (2 boys, 1 girl); Grade 11: 2 students (1 boy, 1 girl); Grade 12: 10 students (7 boys, 3 girls).

Faculty School total: 6. In upper school: 1 man, 3 women; 3 have advanced degrees.

College Admission Counseling 4 students graduated in 2012; they went to Brock University; Trent University; Wilfrid Laurier University.

Student Life Upper grades have uniform requirement, student council, honor system. Discipline rests primarily with faculty.

Admissions Battery of testing done through outside agency required. Deadline for receipt of application materials: none. No application fee required.

Athletics Coed Interscholastic: aerobics/Nautilus. 1 PE instructor.

Contact Ms. Sue Davidson, Principal. 905-648-2737. Fax: 905-648-8762. E-mail: tapplybinetcollege@cogeco.net. Website: www.tapplybinetcollege.com

TASIS THE AMERICAN SCHOOL IN ENGLAND

Coldharbour Lane

Thorpe, Surrey TW20 8TE, United Kingdom

General Information Coeducational boarding and day college-preparatory and arts school. Boarding grades 9–13, day grades N–13. Founded: 1976. Setting: rural. Nearest major city is London, United Kingdom. Students are housed in single-sex dormitories. 46-acre campus. 26 buildings on campus. Approved or accredited by Council of International Schools, International Baccalaureate Organization, New England Association of Schools and Colleges, Office for Standards in Education (OFSTED), The Association of Boarding Schools, and state department of education. Affiliate member of National Association of Independent Schools; member of Secondary School Admission Test Board and European Council of International Schools. Language of instruction: English. Total enrollment: 750. Upper school average class size: 15. Upper school faculty-student ratio: 1:8. There are 171 required school days per year for Upper School students. Upper School students typically attend 5 days per week. The average school day consists of 6 hours.

See Display below and Close-Up on page 574.

TASIS, THE AMERICAN SCHOOL IN SWITZERLAND

Via Collina d'Oro

Montagnola-Lugano CH-6926, Switzerland

General Information Coeducational boarding and day college-preparatory, arts, and sports school. Boarding grades 7–PG, day grades 1–PG. Founded: 1956. Setting: small town. Nearest major city is Lugano, Switzerland. Students are housed in single-sex dormitories. 9-acre campus. 19 buildings on campus. Approved or accredited by New England Association of Schools and Colleges and Swiss Federation of Private Schools. Affiliate member of National Association of Independent Schools; member of Secondary School Admission Test Board. Language of instruction: English. Total

enrollment: 642. Upper school average class size: 14. Upper school faculty-student ratio: 1:5. Upper School students typically attend 5 days per week.

See Display on next page, Close-Up on page 576, and Summer Program Close-Up on page 640.

TELLURIDE MOUNTAIN SCHOOL

200 San Miguel River Drive

Telluride, Colorado 81435

Head of School: Mr. Joseph Stefani

General Information Coeducational day college-preparatory, arts, technology, and music, visual and dramatic arts school. Grades PK–12. Founded: 1999. Setting: small town. Nearest major city is Denver. 1 building on campus. Approved or accredited by Association of Colorado Independent Schools and Colorado Department of Education. Member of National Association of Independent Schools. Total enrollment: 88. Upper school average class size: 4. Upper school faculty-student ratio: 1:5. There are 165 required school days per year for Upper School students. Upper School students typically attend 5 days per week. The average school day consists of 6 hours and 30 minutes.

Upper School Student Profile Grade 6: 6 students (2 boys, 4 girls); Grade 7: 7 students (5 boys, 2 girls); Grade 8: 8 students (7 boys, 1 girl); Grade 9: 5 students (3 boys, 2 girls); Grade 10: 6 students (3 boys, 3 girls); Grade 11: 3 students (1 boy, 2 girls).

Faculty School total: 15. In upper school: 4 men, 4 women; 4 have advanced degrees.

Subjects Offered Algebra, alternative physical education, American Civil War, American history, American literature, ancient world history, applied music, art, backpacking, biology, calculus, character education, chemistry, civil rights, college admission preparation, college counseling, college planning, community service, computer education, computer literacy, computer multimedia, computer music, CPR, creative writing, critical thinking, critical writing, digital music, drama, dramatic arts, English composition, English literature, environmental education, European history, film studies, geography, geology, geometry, grammar, guitar, history, history of rock and roll, instrumental music, Internet research, keyboarding, Latin American literature, leadership, leadership and service, music, music performance, music technology, outdoor education, painting, portfolio writing, pre-algebra, pre-calculus, public speaking, reading/study skills, Spanish, Spanish literature, studio art, trigonometry, video film production, visual arts, white-water trips, wilderness education, world history.

Graduation Requirements Algebra, biology, chemistry, college admission preparation, college counseling, dramatic arts, English, English composition, English

TASIS

THE AMERICAN SCHOOL IN ENGLAND

Scan this QR code with your smartphone to find out more about TASIS England.

Coeducational • Day (3-18 yrs) • Boarding (14-18 yrs)
American High School Diploma • AP Classes • IB Diploma
Excellent university placement in the US, UK & worldwide
Welcoming international community • Near London

Coldharbour Lane, Thorpe, Surrey TW20 8TE
Tel: +44 1932 582316
ukadmissions@tasisengland.org

www.tasisengland.org

US Office:
Tel: 703 299 8150
usadmissions@tasis.com

literature, geometry, grammar, history, music, physics, pre-calculus, Spanish, trigonometry, U.S. history, visual arts, wilderness education, world history.

Special Academic Programs Independent study; study abroad.

College Admission Counseling 4 students graduated in 2013; 3 went to college, including Bennington College; Eckerd College; Whitman College. Other: 1 had other specific plans.

Student Life Upper grades have specified standards of dress. Discipline rests primarily with faculty.

Tuition and Aid Day student tuition: $23,150. Tuition installment plan (monthly payment plans, individually arranged payment plans). Merit scholarship grants, need-based scholarship grants available. In 2013–14, 45% of upper-school students received aid. Total amount of financial aid awarded in 2013–14: $181,243.

Admissions Traditional secondary-level entrance grade is 9. For fall 2013, 3 students applied for upper-level admission, 3 were accepted, 3 enrolled. Deadline for receipt of application materials: none. Application fee required: $50. Interview required.

Athletics Interscholastic: alpine skiing (boys, girls), freestyle skiing (b,g), skiing (cross-country) (b,g), skiing (downhill) (b,g), snowboarding (b,g); coed interscholastic: backpacking, canoeing/kayaking, climbing, cooperative games, hiking/backpacking, ice skating, kayaking, mountaineering, nordic skiing, outdoor activities, outdoor adventure, outdoor education, outdoor recreation, outdoor skills, outdoors, rafting, rappelling, rock climbing, telemark skiing, wilderness, wilderness survival, yoga; coed intramural: alpine skiing. 1 PE instructor, 5 coaches.

Computers Computers are regularly used in all classes. Computer network features include Internet access, wireless campus network. Campus intranet, student e-mail accounts, and computer access in designated common areas are available to students. The school has a published electronic and media policy.

Contact Mrs. Jamie Intemann, Program Coordinator. 970-728-1969. Fax: 970-369-4412. E-mail: jintemann@telluridemtnschool.org. Website: www.telluridemtnschool.org/

TEMPLE GRANDIN SCHOOL

Boulder, Colorado
See Special Needs Schools section.

THE TENNEY SCHOOL

2055 South Gessner
Houston, Texas 77063

Head of School: Mr. Michael E. Tenney

General Information Coeducational day college-preparatory and general academic school; primarily serves individuals with Attention Deficit Disorder. Grades 6–12. Founded: 1973. Setting: suburban. 1-acre campus. 1 building on campus. Approved or accredited by Southern Association of Colleges and Schools and Texas Department of Education. Total enrollment: 57. Upper school average class size: 1. Upper school faculty-student ratio: 1:2. There are 170 required school days per year for Upper School students. Upper School students typically attend 5 days per week. The average school day consists of 5 hours.

Upper School Student Profile Grade 6: 6 students (4 boys, 2 girls); Grade 7: 5 students (3 boys, 2 girls); Grade 8: 9 students (3 boys, 6 girls); Grade 9: 6 students (3 boys, 3 girls); Grade 10: 13 students (7 boys, 6 girls); Grade 11: 11 students (7 boys, 4 girls); Grade 12: 7 students (4 boys, 3 girls).

Faculty School total: 27. In upper school: 3 men, 24 women; 14 have advanced degrees.

Subjects Offered Accounting, algebra, American history, American literature, biology, British literature, business law, calculus, chemistry, computer programming, computer studies, creative writing, economics, English, fine arts, geometry, government, health, independent study, journalism, keyboarding, mathematics, microcomputer technology applications, physical education, physical science, physics, pre-calculus, psychology, science, social studies, sociology, Spanish, studio art, study skills, world geography, world history, world literature, yearbook.

Graduation Requirements American government, American history.

Special Academic Programs Advanced Placement exam preparation; honors section; academic accommodation for the gifted, the musically talented, and the artistically talented; remedial reading and/or remedial writing; remedial math; special instructional classes for deaf students; ESL (10 students enrolled).

College Admission Counseling 16 students graduated in 2013; all went to college, including Houston Baptist University; St. Thomas University; Texas A&M University; The University of Texas at Austin; University of Houston.

Student Life Upper grades have specified standards of dress. Discipline rests primarily with faculty.

Summer Programs Remediation, enrichment, advancement programs offered; session focuses on academic course work; held on campus; accepts boys and girls; open to students from other schools. 45 students usually enrolled. 2014 schedule: June 6 to June 28. Application deadline: June 1.

Tuition and Aid Day student tuition: $23,000.

Admissions Traditional secondary-level entrance grade is 9. For fall 2013, 40 students applied for upper-level admission, 18 were accepted, 17 enrolled. Naglieri Nonverbal School Ability Test or Scholastic Achievement Test required. Deadline for receipt of application materials: none. No application fee required. On-campus interview required.

Athletics 1 PE instructor.

Computers Computers are regularly used in computer applications, creative writing, desktop publishing, English, foreign language, journalism, keyboarding, speech, word processing, yearbook classes. Computer network features include on-campus library services, Internet access, wireless campus network, Internet filtering or blocking technology. Campus intranet and computer access in designated common areas are available to students. Students grades are available online.

Contact Mr. Michael E. Tenney, Director. 713-783-6990. Fax: 713-783-0786. E-mail: mtenney@tenneyschool.com. Website: www.tenneyschool.com

TEURLINGS CATHOLIC HIGH SCHOOL

139 Teurlings Drive
Lafayette, Louisiana 70501-3832

Head of School: Mr. Michael Harrison Boyer

General Information Coeducational day and distance learning college-preparatory and religious studies school, affiliated with Roman Catholic Church. Grades 9–12. Distance learning grades 10–12. Founded: 1955. Setting: urban. Nearest major city is Baton Rouge. 25-acre campus. 13 buildings on campus. Approved or accredited by National Catholic Education Association, Southern Association of Colleges and Schools, and Louisiana Department of Education. Endowment: $140,000. Total enrollment: 681. Upper school average class size: 21. Upper school faculty-student ratio: 1:21. There are 179 required school days per year for Upper School students. Upper School students typically attend 5 days per week. The average school day consists of 6 hours and 50 minutes.

Upper School Student Profile Grade 9: 207 students (100 boys, 107 girls); Grade 10: 165 students (88 boys, 77 girls); Grade 11: 172 students (89 boys, 83 girls); Grade 12: 137 students (64 boys, 73 girls). 94% of students are Roman Catholic.

Faculty School total: 44. In upper school: 16 men, 25 women; 13 have advanced degrees.

Subjects Offered Accounting, acting, advanced chemistry, advanced computer applications, advanced math, algebra, American history, American literature, anatomy and physiology, art, biology, business applications, calculus, campus ministry, chemistry, civics/free enterprise, computer science, drama, English, environmental science, fine arts, French, geography, geometry, health, honors algebra, honors English, honors geometry, honors U.S. history, honors world history, interpersonal skills, physical education, physical science, physics, public speaking, publications, Spanish, speech, sports medicine, theology, world history.

Graduation Requirements Advanced math, algebra, American history, American literature, biology, chemistry, civics, civics/free enterprise, electives, English, geometry, literature, physical education (includes health), physical science, theology, world geography, world history.

Special Academic Programs Honors section; study at local college for college credit.

College Admission Counseling 166 students graduated in 2013; 158 went to college, including Centenary College of Louisiana; Louisiana State University and Agricultural and Mechanical College; Louisiana State University at Eunice; Northwestern State University of Louisiana; Tulane University; University of Louisiana at Lafayette. Other: 2 went to work, 3 entered military service, 3 had other specific plans. Median composite ACT: 22. 11% scored over 26 on composite ACT.

Student Life Upper grades have uniform requirement, student council. Discipline rests equally with students and faculty. Attendance at religious services is required.

Tuition and Aid Day student tuition: $5400. Tuition installment plan (monthly payment plans). Need-based scholarship grants, paying campus jobs available. In 2013–14, 20% of upper-school students received aid. Total amount of financial aid awarded in 2013–14: $84,000.

Admissions Traditional secondary-level entrance grade is 9. For fall 2013, 202 students applied for upper-level admission, 181 were accepted, 151 enrolled. ACT, ACT-Explore, Explore, PSAT or Stanford Achievement Test required. Deadline for receipt of application materials: January 27. No application fee required.

Athletics Interscholastic: baseball (boys), basketball (b,g), bowling (b,g), cheering (b,g), cross-country running (b,g), dance team (g), football (b), golf (b,g), gymnastics (b,g), indoor track & field (b,g), soccer (b,g), softball (g), strength & conditioning (b,g), swimming and diving (b,g), tennis (b,g), track and field (b,g), volleyball (g), winter (indoor) track (b,g), wrestling (b); intramural: cheering (g); coed interscholastic: riflery, skeet shooting, trap and skeet. 3 coaches.

Computers Computers are regularly used in business applications, English, French, geography, history, mathematics, publications, science, Spanish, theater classes. Computer network features include on-campus library services, Internet access, wireless campus network, Internet filtering or blocking technology. Student e-mail accounts and computer access in designated common areas are available to students. Students grades are available online. The school has a published electronic and media policy.

Contact Mrs. Kathy Dodson, Administrative Secretary. 337-235-5711 Ext. 101. Fax: 337-234-8057. E-mail: kdodson@tchs.net. Website: www.tchs.net

THE THACHER SCHOOL

5025 Thacher Road
Ojai, California 93023

Head of School: Mr. Michael K. Mulligan

General Information Coeducational boarding and day college-preparatory, arts, and technology school. Grades 9–12. Founded: 1889. Setting: small town. Nearest major city is Santa Barbara. Students are housed in single-sex dormitories. 450-acre campus. 89 buildings on campus. Approved or accredited by The Association of Boarding Schools, Western Association of Schools and Colleges, and California Department of Education. Member of National Association of Independent Schools and Secondary School Admission Test Board. Endowment: $116.9 million. Total enrollment: 252. Upper school average class size: 11. Upper school faculty-student ratio: 1:6. Upper School students typically attend 5 days per week. The average school day consists of 7 hours.

Upper School Student Profile Grade 9: 63 students (33 boys, 30 girls); Grade 10: 63 students (31 boys, 32 girls); Grade 11: 63 students (32 boys, 31 girls); Grade 12: 63 students (29 boys, 34 girls). 90% of students are boarding students. 53% are state residents. 24 states are represented in upper school student body. 12% are international students. International students from Australia, China, Hong Kong, Japan, Republic of Korea, and Saudi Arabia; 5 other countries represented in student body.

Faculty School total: 45. In upper school: 24 men, 21 women; 31 have advanced degrees; all reside on campus.

Subjects Offered 3-dimensional art, ACT preparation, acting, advanced chemistry, advanced math, Advanced Placement courses, advanced studio art-AP, algebra, American history, American history-AP, American literature, art, art history, art history-AP, astronomy, biology, biology-AP, calculus, calculus-AP, ceramics, chemistry, chemistry-AP, Chinese, computer math, computer science, computer science-AP, conceptual physics, creative writing, dance, drama, ecology, economics, economics and history, electronic music, English, English literature, English literature-AP, English/composition-AP, environmental science, environmental science-AP, European history, European history-AP, film, fine arts, French, French language-AP, French literature-AP, geography, geometry, health, history, journalism, Latin, logic, marine biology, mathematics, music, music theory-AP, philosophy, photography, physical education, physics, physics-AP, psychology, religion, science, social studies, Spanish, Spanish language-AP, Spanish literature-AP, statistics, studio art-AP, theater, trigonometry, U.S. history-AP, world history, world literature, writing.

Graduation Requirements Arts and fine arts (art, music, dance, drama), English, foreign language, mathematics, physical education (includes health), science, social studies (includes history), senior exhibition program (students choose an academic topic of interest and study it for one year, culminating in a school-wide presentation).

Special Academic Programs 17 Advanced Placement exams for which test preparation is offered; honors section; independent study; study abroad; academic accommodation for the gifted, the musically talented, and the artistically talented.

College Admission Counseling 69 students graduated in 2013; all went to college, including Colby College; Columbia College; Cornell University; Middlebury College; Stanford University. Median SAT critical reading: 720, median SAT math: 720, median SAT writing: 730, median combined SAT: 2160.

Student Life Upper grades have specified standards of dress, student council, honor system. Discipline rests equally with students and faculty.

Tuition and Aid Day student tuition: $33,470; 7-day tuition and room/board: $50,550. Tuition installment plan (monthly payment plans). Need-based scholarship grants available. In 2013–14, 27% of upper-school students received aid. Total amount of financial aid awarded in 2013–14: $2,351,000.

Admissions Traditional secondary-level entrance grade is 9. For fall 2013, 625 students applied for upper-level admission, 89 were accepted, 69 enrolled. ACT-Explore, ISEE, PSAT or SSAT required. Deadline for receipt of application materials: January 15. Application fee required: $75. Interview required.

Athletics Interscholastic: baseball (boys), basketball (b,g), cross-country running (b,g), dance (b,g), football (b), lacrosse (b,g), soccer (b,g), tennis (b,g), track and field (b,g), volleyball (g); intramural: aerobics (b,g), backpacking (b,g), ballet (b,g), bicycling (b,g), canoeing/kayaking (b,g), climbing (b,g), dance (b,g), dance squad (b,g), horseback riding (b,g), outdoor activities (b,g), weight training (b,g), wilderness (b,g), wilderness survival (b,g), yoga (b,g); coed interscholastic: dance, equestrian sports; coed intramural: aerobics, backpacking, ballet, bicycling, bowling, canoeing/kayaking, climbing, dance, equestrian sports, fencing, Frisbee, golf, handball, hiking/backpacking, horseback riding, kayaking, modern dance, mountain biking, outdoor activities, paddle tennis, pistol, polo, Polocrosse, riflery, rock climbing, rodeo, skiing (downhill), surfing, trap and skeet, ultimate Frisbee, wall climbing, weight lifting, yoga. 18 coaches, 1 athletic trainer.

Computers Computers are regularly used in English, foreign language, history, mathematics, science classes. Computer network features include on-campus library services, online commercial services, Internet access, wireless campus network, Internet filtering or blocking technology. Campus intranet, student e-mail accounts, and computer access in designated common areas are available to students. Students grades are available online. The school has a published electronic and media policy.

Contact Mr. William P. McMahon, Director of Admission. 805-640-3210. Fax: 805-640-9377. E-mail: admission@thacher.org. Website: www.thacher.org

THINK GLOBAL SCHOOL

One Embarcadero Center
Suite 500
San Francisco, California 94111

Head of School: Mr. Alun Cooper

General Information Coeducational boarding college-preparatory and IB curriculum school. Grades 9–12. Founded: 2009. Setting: suburban. Students are housed in coed facilities in host city. Approved or accredited by International Baccalaureate Organization and Western Association of Schools and Colleges. Endowment: $10 million. Total enrollment: 36. Upper school average class size: 12. Upper school faculty-student ratio: 1:3. There are 193 required school days per year for Upper School students. Upper School students typically attend 5 days per week. The average school day consists of 6 hours and 45 minutes.

Upper School Student Profile Grade 9: 6 students (2 boys, 4 girls); Grade 10: 12 students (5 boys, 7 girls); Grade 11: 18 students (8 boys, 10 girls). 100% of students are boarding students. 9 states are represented in upper school student body. 75% are international students. International students from Bhutan, Singapore, Sweden, Thailand, and United Kingdom; 14 other countries represented in student body.

Faculty School total: 14. In upper school: 7 men, 7 women; 10 have advanced degrees; 13 reside on campus.

Subjects Offered All academic.

Special Academic Programs International Baccalaureate program; study abroad.

Student Life Upper grades have specified standards of dress, student council, honor system. Discipline rests equally with students and faculty.

Tuition and Aid 7-day tuition and room/board: $79,000. Tuition installment plan (monthly payment plans, individually arranged payment plans). Need-based scholarship grants available.

Admissions Traditional secondary-level entrance grade is 9. For fall 2012, 135 students applied for upper-level admission, 14 were accepted, 13 enrolled. Admissions testing or English proficiency required. Deadline for receipt of application materials: none. No application fee required. Interview required.

Computers Computers are regularly used in all classes. Computer network features include Internet access, wireless campus network, Internet filtering or blocking technology, all students are provided with laptops, iPads, and phones. Campus intranet and student e-mail accounts are available to students. Students grades are available online. The school has a published electronic and media policy.

Contact Mrs. Lily Just, Director of Admissions. 202-580-8405. E-mail: ljust@thinkglobalschool.org. Website: www.thinkglobalschool.org

THOMAS JEFFERSON SCHOOL

4100 South Lindbergh Boulevard
St. Louis, Missouri 63127

Head of School: Dr. Elizabeth L. Holekamp

General Information Coeducational boarding and day college-preparatory and classical liberal-arts education school. Grades 7–PG. Founded: 1946. Setting: suburban. Students are housed in single-sex dormitories. 20-acre campus. 12 buildings on campus. Approved or accredited by Independent Schools Association of the Central States, Midwest Association of Boarding Schools, and The Association of Boarding Schools. Member of National Association of Independent Schools and Secondary School Admission Test Board. Endowment: $1.5 million. Total enrollment: 91. Upper school average class size: 14. Upper school faculty-student ratio: 1:6. There are 130 required school days per year for Upper School students. Upper School students typically attend 5 days per week. The average school day consists of 8 hours and 30 minutes.

Upper School Student Profile Grade 9: 16 students (10 boys, 6 girls); Grade 10: 17 students (10 boys, 7 girls); Grade 11: 17 students (11 boys, 6 girls); Grade 12: 18 students (10 boys, 8 girls). 57% of students are boarding students. 43% are state residents. 10 states are represented in upper school student body. 30% are international students. International students from Canada, China, Japan, Poland, Republic of Korea, and Taiwan; 3 other countries represented in student body.

Faculty School total: 19. In upper school: 5 men, 8 women; 10 have advanced degrees; 5 reside on campus.

Subjects Offered Advanced Placement courses, algebra, American history-AP, ancient history, ancient world history, art, art history, biology, biology-AP, calculus, calculus-AP, ceramics, chemistry, chemistry-AP, dance, earth science, English, English language-AP, English literature-AP, ESL, fine arts, French, geography, geometry, government and politics-AP, government/civics, Greek, history, Homeric Greek, Italian,

Latin, life science, mathematics, music, physical science, physics, physics-AP, science, social studies, trigonometry, U.S. history-AP, world history, world history-AP.

Graduation Requirements Arts and fine arts (art, music, dance, drama), English, foreign language, mathematics, science, social studies (includes history). Community service is required.

Special Academic Programs 10 Advanced Placement exams for which test preparation is offered; honors section; academic accommodation for the gifted; ESL (10 students enrolled).

College Admission Counseling 14 students graduated in 2012; all went to college, including Cornell University; Haverford College; Mount Holyoke College; Stanford University; University of Chicago; University of Illinois at Urbana–Champaign. Median SAT critical reading: 700, median SAT math: 660, median SAT writing: 690, median combined SAT: 2050.

Student Life Upper grades have specified standards of dress, student council, honor system. Discipline rests equally with students and faculty.

Tuition and Aid Day student tuition: $22,750; 5-day tuition and room/board: $37,750; 7-day tuition and room/board: $39,500. Tuition installment plan (monthly payment plans, individually arranged payment plans, Sallie Mae TuitionPay). Merit scholarship grants, need-based scholarship grants, paying campus jobs available. In 2012–13, 35% of upper-school students received aid; total upper-school merit-scholarship money awarded: $10,000. Total amount of financial aid awarded in 2012–13: $640,000.

Admissions Traditional secondary-level entrance grade is 9. For fall 2012, 47 students applied for upper-level admission, 14 were accepted, 11 enrolled. SSAT or TOEFL required. Deadline for receipt of application materials: February 15. Application fee required: $40. Interview required.

Athletics Interscholastic: basketball (boys, girls), soccer (b,g), volleyball (b,g); intramural: basketball (b,g), soccer (b,g), volleyball (b,g); coed interscholastic: soccer; coed intramural: dance, fitness, physical fitness, tennis, weight training, yoga.

Computers Computers are regularly used in foreign language, mathematics, science, yearbook classes. Computer network features include online commercial services, Internet access, wireless campus network, Internet filtering or blocking technology. Campus intranet, student e-mail accounts, and computer access in designated common areas are available to students. The school has a published electronic and media policy.

Contact Mrs. Barbara Fraser, Director of Admissions. 314-843-4151 Ext. 2341. Fax: 314-843-3527. E-mail: admissions@tjs.org. Website: www.tjs.org

See Display on next page and Close-Up on page 578.

THORNTON ACADEMY

438 Main Street
Saco, Maine 04072

Head of School: Mr. Rene Menard

General Information Coeducational boarding and day college-preparatory, general academic, arts, and technology school. Boarding grades 8–12, day grades 6–12. Founded: 1811. Setting: small town. Nearest major city is Boston, MA. Students are housed in single-sex dormitories and homestay. 80-acre campus. 10 buildings on campus. Approved or accredited by Independent Schools of Northern New England, New England Association of Schools and Colleges, and Maine Department of Education. Member of National Association of Independent Schools. Endowment: $8 million. Total enrollment: 1,503. Upper school average class size: 22. Upper school faculty-student ratio: 1:14. Upper School students typically attend 5 days per week. The average school day consists of 7 hours.

Upper School Student Profile Grade 7: 65 students (35 boys, 30 girls); Grade 8: 65 students (30 boys, 35 girls); Grade 9: 287 students (145 boys, 142 girls); Grade 10: 284 students (136 boys, 148 girls); Grade 11: 274 students (147 boys, 127 girls); Grade 12: 234 students (113 boys, 121 girls). 10% of students are boarding students. 3 states are represented in upper school student body. 90% are international students. International students from China, Kazakhstan, Spain, Thailand, Turkey, and Viet Nam; 20 other countries represented in student body.

Faculty School total: 89. In upper school: 42 men, 46 women; 44 have advanced degrees; 12 reside on campus.

Subjects Offered Accounting, Advanced Placement courses, algebra, American history, art, band, biology, business mathematics, calculus, chemistry, chorus, computer programming, computer science, dance, desktop publishing, drafting, drama, economics, English, environmental science, European history, family studies, film, fine arts, four team activities, French, geography, geometry, German, health, instrumental music, journalism, keyboarding, Latin, marketing, mathematics, music, music theory, nutrition, painting, photography, physical education, physical fitness, physics, political science, pottery, psychology, science, sculpture, social studies, sociology, Spanish, statistics, studio art, theater, trigonometry, word processing.

Graduation Requirements Arts and fine arts (art, music, dance, drama), business skills (includes word processing), computer science, English, foreign language, mathematics, physical education (includes health), science, social studies (includes history).

Special Academic Programs Advanced Placement exam preparation; honors section; accelerated programs; independent study; term-away projects; academic accommodation for the gifted, the musically talented, and the artistically talented;

remedial reading and/or remedial writing; remedial math; programs in English, mathematics, general development for dyslexic students.

College Admission Counseling 188 students graduated in 2013; 128 went to college, including Saint Joseph's College; Southern Maine Community College; University of Maine; University of Maine at Farmington; University of New Hampshire; University of Southern Maine. Other: 55 went to work, 5 entered military service. Median SAT critical reading: 500, median SAT math: 490, median composite ACT: 28. 6% scored over 600 on SAT critical reading, 15% scored over 600 on SAT math, 100% scored over 26 on composite ACT.

Student Life Upper grades have student council, honor system. Discipline rests primarily with faculty.

Summer Programs Remediation, enrichment, ESL, sports, art/fine arts, computer instruction programs offered; held on campus; accepts boys and girls; open to students from other schools. 50 students usually enrolled. Application deadline: none.

Tuition and Aid Day student tuition: $12,500; 7-day tuition and room/board: $42,000. Tuition installment plan (monthly payment plans). Merit scholarship grants, need-based scholarship grants available. In 2013–14, 5% of upper-school students received aid.

Admissions Traditional secondary-level entrance grade is 9. TOEFL required. Deadline for receipt of application materials: none. No application fee required. Interview required.

Athletics Interscholastic: baseball (boys), basketball (b,g), cheering (g), cross-country running (b,g), field hockey (g), football (b), ice hockey (b), lacrosse (b,g), soccer (b,g), softball (g), tennis (b,g), track and field (b,g), volleyball (g); intramural: lacrosse (b); coed interscholastic: golf, running, swimming and diving; coed intramural: aerobics/dance, bicycling, dance, freestyle skiing, modern dance, mountain biking, outdoor activities, paint ball, physical fitness, rafting, skiing (cross-country), skiing (downhill), snowboarding. 3 PE instructors, 1 athletic trainer.

Computers Computers are regularly used in art, English, foreign language, mathematics, science, social studies classes. Computer network features include on-campus library services, online commercial services, Internet access, wireless campus network, Internet filtering or blocking technology, student laptops. Student e-mail accounts and computer access in designated common areas are available to students. Students grades are available online. The school has a published electronic and media policy.

Contact Ms. Pat Olinger, Admissions Manager, PDSO. 207-282-3361 Ext. 4458. Fax: 207-282-3508. E-mail: pat.olinger@thorntonacademy.org. Website: www.thorntonacademy.org

TIDEWATER ACADEMY

217 Church Street
Post Office Box 1000
Wakefield, Virginia 23888

Head of School: Mr. Rodney L. Taylor

General Information Coeducational day college-preparatory, arts, and technology school. Grades PK–12. Founded: 1964. Setting: rural. Nearest major city is Richmond. 10-acre campus. 4 buildings on campus. Approved or accredited by Virginia Association of Independent Schools. Total enrollment: 153. Upper school average class size: 15. Upper school faculty-student ratio: 1:15. There are 180 required school days per year for Upper School students. Upper School students typically attend 5 days per week. The average school day consists of 6 hours and 50 minutes.

Upper School Student Profile Grade 8: 14 students (6 boys, 8 girls); Grade 9: 11 students (8 boys, 3 girls); Grade 10: 14 students (6 boys, 8 girls); Grade 11: 12 students (4 boys, 8 girls); Grade 12: 11 students (7 boys, 4 girls).

Faculty School total: 25. In upper school: 4 men, 9 women; 2 have advanced degrees.

Subjects Offered Algebra, American history, American literature, art, arts, biology, calculus, chemistry, computer applications, creative writing, driver education, earth science, English, English literature, English-AP, fine arts, geography, geometry, government/civics, grammar, health, history, journalism, life skills, mathematics, music, physical education, science, social sciences, social studies, Spanish, world history, world literature, writing.

Graduation Requirements Arts and fine arts (art, music, dance, drama), business skills (includes word processing), computer science, English, foreign language, mathematics, physical education (includes health), science, social sciences, social studies (includes history).

Special Academic Programs 6 Advanced Placement exams for which test preparation is offered; honors section; independent study.

College Admission Counseling 23 students graduated in 2012; 18 went to college, including James Madison University; Lynchburg College; Radford University; Randolph-Macon College. Other: 4 went to work, 1 entered military service. Median SAT critical reading: 516, median SAT math: 501. 5% scored over 600 on SAT critical reading.

Student Life Upper grades have specified standards of dress, student council, honor system. Discipline rests primarily with faculty.

Tuition and Aid Day student tuition: $6575. Tuition installment plan (FACTS Tuition Payment Plan, monthly payment plans, individually arranged payment plans). Need-based scholarship grants available. In 2012–13, 40% of upper-school students received aid. Total amount of financial aid awarded in 2012–13: $125,000.

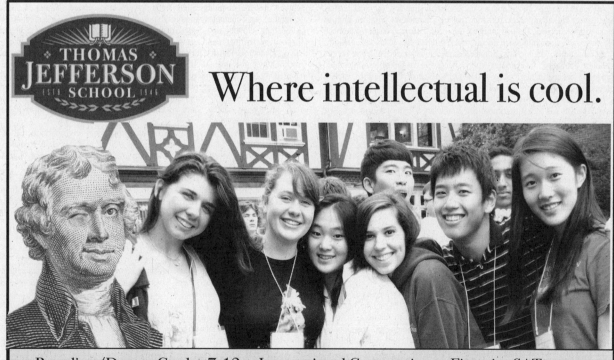

THOMAS JEFFERSON SCHOOL ESTD 1946

Where intellectual is cool.

Boarding/Day ❖ Grades 7-12 ❖ International Community ❖ First-tier SAT scores
TJS.org ❖ admissions@tjs.org ❖ 4100 S. Lindbergh Blvd., St. Louis, MO

Admissions Traditional secondary-level entrance grade is 10. For fall 2012, 9 students applied for upper-level admission, 6 were accepted, 6 enrolled. Any standardized test required. Deadline for receipt of application materials: none. Application fee required: $25. On-campus interview required.

Athletics Interscholastic: baseball (boys), basketball (b,g), cheering (g), football (b), softball (g), tennis (b,g), volleyball (g). 2 PE instructors, 2 coaches.

Computers Computers are regularly used in yearbook classes. Computer network features include on-campus library services, Internet access, wireless campus network. Campus intranet is available to students.

Contact Robyn Croft, Admissions Counselor. 757-899-5401. Fax: 757-899-2521. E-mail: r_croft@tidewateracademy-pvt-va.us. Website: www.tawarriors.org

TILTON SCHOOL

30 School Street
Tilton, New Hampshire 03276
Head of School: Peter Saliba

General Information Coeducational boarding and day college-preparatory school; primarily serves students with learning disabilities, individuals with Attention Deficit Disorder, and dyslexic students. Grades 9–PG. Founded: 1845. Setting: small town. Nearest major city is Concord. Students are housed in single-sex by floor dormitories and single-sex dormitories. 150-acre campus. 30 buildings on campus. Approved or accredited by Association of Independent Schools in New England, Independent Schools of Northern New England, New England Association of Schools and Colleges, The Association of Boarding Schools, and New Hampshire Department of Education. Member of National Association of Independent Schools and Secondary School Admission Test Board. Endowment: $1.6 million. Total enrollment: 222. Upper school average class size: 12. Upper school faculty-student ratio: 1:5. There are 187 required school days per year for Upper School students. Upper School students typically attend 6 days per week. The average school day consists of 7 hours.

Upper School Student Profile Grade 9: 31 students (19 boys, 12 girls); Grade 10: 50 students (34 boys, 16 girls); Grade 11: 57 students (37 boys, 20 girls); Grade 12: 63 students (41 boys, 22 girls); Postgraduate: 21 students (17 boys, 4 girls). 75% of students are boarding students. 35% are state residents. 17 states are represented in upper school student body. 27% are international students. International students from Canada, China, Italy, Republic of Korea, Spain, and Taiwan; 2 other countries represented in student body.

Faculty School total: 40. In upper school: 27 men, 13 women; 19 have advanced degrees; 38 reside on campus.

Subjects Offered Advanced chemistry, advanced math, advanced studio art-AP, advertising design, algebra, American history, American literature, anatomy and physiology, art, biology, biology-AP, calculus, calculus-AP, ceramics, chemistry, chemistry-AP, clayworking, college counseling, computer graphics, criminal justice, criminology, dance, digital art, drama, drawing, ecology, economics, English, English language and composition-AP, English literature-AP, ESL, European history, European history-AP, forensics, French, French literature-AP, French-AP, functions, geology, geometry, global studies, graphic arts, graphic design, guitar, honors algebra, honors English, honors geometry, independent study, integrated mathematics, integrated science, Japanese, leadership, marine ecology, music, music appreciation, music theory, musical productions, painting, photography, physics, physics-AP, politics, pre-calculus, psychology, psychology-AP, Russian, SAT preparation, sociology, Spanish, Spanish literature-AP, Spanish-AP, statistics, studio art, studio art-AP, theater, trigonometry, wilderness education, world cultures, world literature, world religions, yearbook.

Graduation Requirements American history, arts and fine arts (art, music, dance, drama), English, foreign language, history, lab science, mathematics, science, annual participation in Plus/5 (including activities in art and culture, athletics, community service, leadership, and outdoor experience).

Special Academic Programs 11 Advanced Placement exams for which test preparation is offered; honors section; independent study; ESL (22 students enrolled).

College Admission Counseling 96 students graduated in 2013; 91 went to college, including Endicott College; Hobart and William Smith Colleges; Northeastern University; Saint Michael's College; St. Lawrence University; University of New Hampshire. Other: 1 went to work, 1 entered military service, 3 had other specific plans. Mean SAT critical reading: 515, mean SAT math: 557, mean SAT writing: 527, mean combined SAT: 1599.

Student Life Upper grades have specified standards of dress, student council, honor system. Discipline rests primarily with faculty.

Summer Programs Enrichment, advancement, ESL, sports, art/fine arts, computer instruction programs offered; held both on and off campus; held at Mountain Bike Park few miles away; accepts boys and girls; open to students from other schools.

Tuition and Aid Day student tuition: $28,650; 7-day tuition and room/board: $49,750. Tuition installment plan (FACTS Tuition Payment Plan, individually arranged payment plans). Merit scholarship grants, need-based scholarship grants, need-based loans available. In 2013–14, 50% of upper-school students received aid; total upper-school merit-scholarship money awarded: $422,300. Total amount of financial aid awarded in 2013–14: $2,338,710.

Admissions Traditional secondary-level entrance grade is 9. For fall 2013, 507 students applied for upper-level admission, 307 were accepted, 101 enrolled. ACT, PSAT, PSAT or SAT for applicants to grade 11 and 12, SAT, SLEP, SSAT, SSAT, ERB,

PSAT, SAT, PLAN or ACT, TOEFL, TOEFL or SLEP, WAIS, WICS or writing sample required. Deadline for receipt of application materials: February 1. Application fee required: $50. Interview required.

Athletics Interscholastic: baseball (boys), basketball (b,g), field hockey (g), football (b), ice hockey (b,g), lacrosse (b,g), soccer (b,g), softball (g), tennis (b,g); coed interscholastic: alpine skiing, cross-country running, golf, mountain biking, skiing (downhill), snowboarding, weight lifting, weight training, wrestling; coed intramural: canoeing/kayaking, hiking/backpacking, outdoor activities, outdoor education, outdoor skills, rock climbing, squash, strength & conditioning, wall climbing, weight training, wilderness survival. 1 athletic trainer.

Computers Computers are regularly used in English, foreign language, graphic arts, history, mathematics, newspaper, science, yearbook classes. Computer network features include on-campus library services, online commercial services, Internet access, wireless campus network, Internet filtering or blocking technology, USB ports, Smart Media Readers. Campus intranet, student e-mail accounts, and computer access in designated common areas are available to students. Students grades are available online. The school has a published electronic and media policy.

Contact Sharon Trudel, Admissions Assistant. 603-286-1733. Fax: 603-286-1705. E-mail: admissions@tiltonschool.org. Website: www.tiltonschool.org

TIMOTHY CHRISTIAN HIGH SCHOOL

1061 South Prospect Avenue
Elmhurst, Illinois 60126
Head of School: Mr. Bradford Mitchell

General Information Coeducational day college-preparatory, general academic, arts, business, vocational, religious studies, and technology school, affiliated with Christian faith. Grades K–12. Founded: 1911. Setting: suburban. Nearest major city is Chicago. 26-acre campus. 1 building on campus. Approved or accredited by Christian Schools International, North Central Association of Colleges and Schools, and Illinois Department of Education. Total enrollment: 1,030. Upper school average class size: 13. Upper school faculty-student ratio: 1:13. There are 176 required school days per year for Upper School students. Upper School students typically attend 5 days per week. The average school day consists of 6 hours and 45 minutes.

Upper School Student Profile Grade 9: 73 students (45 boys, 28 girls); Grade 10: 102 students (50 boys, 52 girls); Grade 11: 86 students (49 boys, 37 girls); Grade 12: 94 students (36 boys, 58 girls). 99% of students are Christian.

Faculty School total: 30. In upper school: 17 men, 13 women; 24 have advanced degrees.

Subjects Offered Advanced math, algebra, American literature, anatomy and physiology, art, band, Bible, biology, British literature, business studies, calculus-AP, ceramics, chemistry, child development, choir, Christian doctrine, Christian ethics, church history, communication skills, community service, computer applications, computer art, computer graphics, computer-aided design, concert choir, desktop publishing, drawing and design, economics, electives, English, English literature-AP, expository writing, food and nutrition, geometry, health, home economics, honors algebra, honors geometry, human anatomy, independent living, industrial arts, industrial technology, instrumental music, interior design, jazz ensemble, music, music appreciation, music theory, New Testament, oral communications, orchestra, parent/child development, photography, physical education, physics, physics-AP, pre-calculus, psychology, sewing, Spanish, trigonometry, U.S. government, U.S. history, U.S. history-AP, United States government-AP, Western civilization, world cultures, world literature.

Graduation Requirements Computer processing, English, mathematics, music, physical education (includes health), religious studies, science, social studies (includes history), senior service retreat at end of 12th grade, service requirement in grades 9-11 (10 hours per year).

Special Academic Programs 6 Advanced Placement exams for which test preparation is offered; honors section; remedial reading and/or remedial writing.

College Admission Counseling 99 students graduated in 2013; 97 went to college, including Calvin College; Dordt College; Hope College; Trinity Christian College. Other: 1 went to work, 1 had other specific plans.

Student Life Upper grades have specified standards of dress, student council, honor system. Discipline rests primarily with faculty. Attendance at religious services is required.

Summer Programs Sports, art/fine arts programs offered; session focuses on athletics; held on campus; accepts boys and girls; open to students from other schools. 136 students usually enrolled.

Tuition and Aid Day student tuition: $8930–$18,000. Tuition installment plan (FACTS Tuition Payment Plan, FACTS is required unless paying the total tuition at once). Need-based scholarship grants, some need-based financial assistance available through school foundation available. In 2013–14, 13% of upper-school students received aid.

Admissions Traditional secondary-level entrance grade is 9. Scholastic Testing Service, Scholastic Testing Service High School Placement Test, school's own exam or TOEFL or SLEP required. Deadline for receipt of application materials: none. Application fee required: $50. On-campus interview required.

Athletics Interscholastic: baseball (boys), basketball (b,g), cross-country running (b,g), pom squad (g), soccer (b,g), softball (g), tennis (b,g), track and field (b,g), volleyball (g); intramural: basketball (b), flag football (b); coed interscholastic: cheering, golf; coed intramural: volleyball. 2 PE instructors, 1 athletic trainer.

Computers Computers are regularly used in art, computer applications, English, graphic design, industrial technology, keyboarding, science, writing classes. Computer network features include on-campus library services, Internet access, wireless campus network, Internet filtering or blocking technology. Student e-mail accounts are available to students. Students grades are available online. The school has a published electronic and media policy.

Contact Mr. Rudi Gesch, Marketing Director. 630-782-4043. Fax: 630-833-9238. E-mail: gesch@timothychristian.com. Website: www.timothychristian.com

TMI - THE EPISCOPAL SCHOOL OF TEXAS

20955 West Tejas Trail
San Antonio, Texas 78257

Head of School: Dr. John W. Cooper

General Information Coeducational boarding and day college-preparatory, arts, religious studies, technology, and military school, affiliated with Episcopal Church, Christian faith. Boarding grades 8–12, day grades 6–12. Founded: 1893. Setting: suburban. Students are housed in single-sex dormitories. 80-acre campus. 17 buildings on campus. Approved or accredited by Independent Schools Association of the Southwest, National Association of Episcopal Schools, Southwest Association of Episcopal Schools, The Association of Boarding Schools, and Texas Department of Education. Member of National Association of Independent Schools. Total enrollment: 470. Upper school average class size: 16. Upper school faculty-student ratio: 1:10. There are 168 required school days per year for Upper School students. Upper School students typically attend 5 days per week. The average school day consists of 6 hours and 10 minutes.

Upper School Student Profile Grade 6: 36 students (17 boys, 19 girls); Grade 7: 45 students (25 boys, 20 girls); Grade 8: 49 students (30 boys, 19 girls); Grade 9: 98 students (55 boys, 43 girls); Grade 10: 82 students (48 boys, 34 girls); Grade 11: 85 students (43 boys, 42 girls); Grade 12: 76 students (44 boys, 32 girls). 15% of students are boarding students. 96% are state residents. 2 states are represented in upper school student body. 3% are international students. International students from China, El Salvador, Mexico, and Nigeria. 86% of students are members of Episcopal Church, Christian.

Faculty School total: 55. In upper school: 29 men, 21 women; 35 have advanced degrees; 13 reside on campus.

Subjects Offered 20th century history, acting, Advanced Placement courses, advanced studio art-AP, algebra, American Civil War, American history, American literature, anatomy and physiology, astronomy, athletics, biology, British literature, calculus, ceramics, chemistry, choir, computer programming, conceptual physics, earth science, economics, English, English literature, environmental science, fine arts, geometry, government, Greek, history, JROTC, Latin, meteorology, military history, philosophy, photography, physics, playwriting, religion, Spanish, statistics, studio art, theater arts, theater design and production, world history, writing.

Graduation Requirements Arts and fine arts (art, music, dance, drama), electives, English, foreign language, history, mathematics, philosophy, physical education (includes health), religion (includes Bible studies and theology), science, senior chapel talk, community service requirement.

Special Academic Programs Advanced Placement exam preparation; honors section; independent study; ESL (27 students enrolled).

College Admission Counseling 72 students graduated in 2013; all went to college, including Baylor University; Southern Methodist University; Southwestern University; Texas A&M University; Texas Christian University; United States Military Academy. Median SAT critical reading: 600, median SAT math: 590, median SAT writing: 610, median combined SAT: 1800.

Student Life Upper grades have uniform requirement, student council, honor system. Discipline rests equally with students and faculty. Attendance at religious services is required.

Summer Programs Enrichment, advancement, sports programs offered; session focuses on academics and enrichment; held on campus; accepts boys and girls; open to students from other schools. 100 students usually enrolled. 2014 schedule: June to July. Application deadline: May.

Tuition and Aid Day student tuition: $20,905; 5-day tuition and room/board: $37,860; 7-day tuition and room/board: $41,520. Tuition installment plan (FACTS Tuition Payment Plan). Merit scholarship grants, need-based scholarship grants, tuition remission for children of faculty available. In 2013–14, 25% of upper-school students received aid; total upper-school merit-scholarship money awarded: $55,000. Total amount of financial aid awarded in 2013–14: $555,500.

Admissions Traditional secondary-level entrance grade is 9. For fall 2013, 130 students applied for upper-level admission, 105 were accepted, 70 enrolled. ERB, ISEE, PSAT or SAT, SSAT and TOEFL required. Deadline for receipt of application materials: none. Application fee required: $75. Interview required.

Athletics Interscholastic: baseball (boys), basketball (b,g), cheering (g), cross-country running (b,g), dance (g), fitness (b,g), football (b), golf (b,g), independent competitive sports (b,g), lacrosse (b,g), soccer (b,g), softball (g), strength & conditioning (b,g), swimming and diving (b,g), tennis (b,g), track and field (b,g), volleyball (g), weight training (b,g); coed interscholastic: JROTC drill, marksmanship,

physical fitness, physical training, riflery, strength & conditioning. 10 coaches, 1 athletic trainer.

Computers Computers are regularly used in journalism, language development, literary magazine, newspaper, programming, science, yearbook classes. Computer network features include on-campus library services, online commercial services, Internet access, Internet filtering or blocking technology. Campus intranet, student e-mail accounts, and computer access in designated common areas are available to students. Students grades are available online. The school has a published electronic and media policy.

Contact Mr. Aaron Hawkins, Director of Admissions. 210-564-6152. Fax: 210-698-0715. E-mail: a.hawkins@tmi-sa.org. Website: www.tmi-sa.org

TOWER HILL SCHOOL

2813 West 17th Street
Wilmington, Delaware 19806

Head of School: Dr. Christopher D. Wheeler

General Information Coeducational day college-preparatory, arts, and technology school. Grades PS–12. Founded: 1919. Setting: suburban. Nearest major city is Philadelphia, PA. 45-acre campus. 4 buildings on campus. Approved or accredited by Middle States Association of Colleges and Schools and Delaware Department of Education. Member of National Association of Independent Schools and Secondary School Admission Test Board. Endowment: $31 million. Total enrollment: 747. Upper school average class size: 14. Upper school faculty-student ratio: 1:6. There are 162 required school days per year for Upper School students. Upper School students typically attend 5 days per week. The average school day consists of 7 hours.

Upper School Student Profile Grade 9: 68 students (35 boys, 33 girls); Grade 10: 63 students (36 boys, 27 girls); Grade 11: 64 students (31 boys, 33 girls); Grade 12: 57 students (33 boys, 24 girls).

Faculty School total: 113. In upper school: 23 men, 23 women; 32 have advanced degrees.

Subjects Offered Acting, advanced biology, advanced chemistry, advanced computer applications, advanced math, advanced studio art-AP, algebra, American literature, art, art history, band, biology, British literature, calculus, calculus-AP, chemistry, China/Japan history, chorus, civil rights, classical Greek literature, community service, computer science, creative writing, current events, DNA, drama, drawing, driver education, engineering, English, English literature, European history, film, fine arts, French, geometry, health and wellness, historical research, history, human anatomy, jazz band, Latin, Latin American literature, mathematics, music, music theory, organic chemistry, painting, photography, physical science, physics, poetry, politics, pre-calculus, psychology, SAT preparation, science, Shakespeare, Spanish, Spanish literature, strings, theater, theater design and production, U.S. constitutional history, U.S. history, U.S. history-AP, Vietnam War, woodworking, world history, writing, writing.

Graduation Requirements Arts and fine arts (art, music, dance, drama), athletics, English, foreign language, mathematics, science, social studies (includes history). Community service is required.

Special Academic Programs Advanced Placement exam preparation; honors section; independent study; academic accommodation for the gifted, the musically talented, and the artistically talented.

College Admission Counseling 54 students graduated in 2013; all went to college, including Colgate University; New York University; The George Washington University; University of Delaware; Virginia Polytechnic Institute and State University; Wake Forest University. Mean SAT critical reading: 601, mean SAT math: 646, mean SAT writing: 635, mean composite ACT: 28. 69% scored over 600 on SAT critical reading, 73% scored over 600 on SAT math, 69% scored over 600 on SAT writing, 64% scored over 26 on composite ACT.

Student Life Upper grades have specified standards of dress, student council, honor system. Discipline rests equally with students and faculty.

Summer Programs Enrichment, sports programs offered; session focuses on sports camps and science enrichments; held on campus; accepts boys and girls; open to students from other schools. 60 students usually enrolled. 2014 schedule: June 9 to August 8. Application deadline: May 1.

Tuition and Aid Day student tuition: $25,850–$26,425. Tuition installment plan (The Tuition Plan, monthly payment plans, individually arranged payment plans, 60/40). Merit scholarship grants, need-based scholarship grants available. In 2013–14, 21% of upper-school students received aid; total upper-school merit-scholarship money awarded: $134,000. Total amount of financial aid awarded in 2013–14: $1,091,005.

Admissions Traditional secondary-level entrance grade is 9. For fall 2013, 77 students applied for upper-level admission, 49 were accepted, 20 enrolled. ISEE, PSAT or SAT for applicants to grade 11 and 12, SSAT or writing sample required. Deadline for receipt of application materials: January 2. Application fee required: $40. On-campus interview required.

Athletics Interscholastic: baseball (boys), basketball (b,g), cross-country running (b,g), field hockey (g), football (b), indoor track (b,g), lacrosse (b,g), soccer (b,g), swimming and diving (b,g), tennis (b,g), track and field (b,g), volleyball (g), winter (indoor) track (b,g), wrestling (b); intramural: fitness (g), physical fitness (g), self defense (g), yoga (g); coed interscholastic: golf; coed intramural: aerobics/Nautilus, physical training, strength & conditioning, weight lifting. 24 coaches, 2 athletic trainers.

Computers Computers are regularly used in all academic classes. Computer network features include on-campus library services, Internet access, wireless campus network, Internet filtering or blocking technology. Student e-mail accounts and computer access in designated common areas are available to students. Students grades are available online. The school has a published electronic and media policy.

Contact Mr. William R. Ushler, Associate Director of Admission. 302-657-8350. Fax: 302-657-8377. E-mail: wushler@towerhill.org. Website: www.towerhill.org

TRAFALGAR CASTLE SCHOOL

401 Reynolds Street

Whitby, Ontario L1N 3W9, Canada

Head of School: Mr. Adam de Pencier

General Information Girls' boarding and day college-preparatory, arts, business, bilingual studies, and technology school. Boarding grades 7–12, day grades 5–12. Founded: 1874. Setting: small town. Nearest major city is Toronto, Canada. Students are housed in single-sex dormitories. 28-acre campus. 2 buildings on campus. Approved or accredited by Canadian Association of Independent Schools, Canadian Educational Standards Institute, Conference of Independent Schools of Ontario, Ontario Ministry of Education, The Association of Boarding Schools, and Ontario Department of Education. Affiliate member of National Association of Independent Schools. Language of instruction: English. Endowment: CAN$153,000. Total enrollment: 191. Upper school average class size: 15. Upper school faculty-student ratio: 1:9. There are 170 required school days per year for Upper School students. Upper School students typically attend 5 days per week. The average school day consists of 7 hours and 30 minutes.

Upper School Student Profile Grade 9: 26 students (26 girls); Grade 10: 36 students (36 girls); Grade 11: 36 students (36 girls); Grade 12: 36 students (36 girls). 38% of students are boarding students. 75% are province residents. 2 provinces are represented in upper school student body. 25% are international students. International students from Bahamas, Barbados, China, Democratic People's Republic of Korea, Mexico, and Republic of Korea; 1 other country represented in student body.

Faculty School total: 27. In upper school: 7 men, 20 women; 9 have advanced degrees; 5 reside on campus.

Subjects Offered Algebra, art, art history, biology, business skills, calculus, chemistry, computer math, computer science, creative writing, drama, earth science, economics, English, English literature, environmental science, ESL, European history, fine arts, French, geography, geometry, grammar, Latin, law, mathematics, music, photography, physical education, physics, science, social studies, world history, world literature, writing.

Graduation Requirements Arts and fine arts (art, music, dance, drama), business skills (includes word processing), computer science, English, foreign language, mathematics, physical education (includes health), science, social studies (includes history).

Special Academic Programs Advanced Placement exam preparation; honors section; independent study; term-away projects; domestic exchange program; special instructional classes for students with slight learning disabilities; ESL (20 students enrolled).

College Admission Counseling 34 students graduated in 2013; all went to college, including Dalhousie University; McGill University; Queen's University at Kingston; The University of British Columbia; The University of Western Ontario; University of Toronto.

Student Life Upper grades have uniform requirement, student council. Discipline rests primarily with faculty.

Tuition and Aid Day student tuition: CAN$21,115–CAN$23,390; 5-day tuition and room/board: CAN$41,475; 7-day tuition and room/board: CAN$44,940. Tuition installment plan (monthly payment plans, individually arranged payment plans, early payment discounts). Tuition reduction for siblings, bursaries, merit scholarship grants, need-based scholarship grants available. In 2013–14, 3% of upper-school students received aid; total upper-school merit-scholarship money awarded: CAN$16,000. Total amount of financial aid awarded in 2013–14: CAN$43,000.

Admissions Traditional secondary-level entrance grade is 9. For fall 2013, 75 students applied for upper-level admission, 70 were accepted, 64 enrolled. Cognitive Abilities Test required. Deadline for receipt of application materials: none. Application fee required: CAN$2500. Interview required.

Athletics Interscholastic: badminton, baseball, basketball, cross-country running, field hockey, gymnastics, ice hockey, independent competitive sports, soccer, softball, swimming and diving, synchronized swimming, tennis, track and field, volleyball; intramural: badminton, baseball, basketball, cross-country running, dance team, field hockey, fitness, fitness walking, gymnastics, ice hockey, outdoor activities, outdoor adventure, outdoor education, physical fitness, ropes courses, rowing, running, skiing (cross-country), skiing (downhill), snowboarding, soccer, softball, swimming and diving, synchronized swimming, tennis, track and field, volleyball, yoga. 3 PE instructors.

Computers Computers are regularly used in all academic classes. Computer network features include on-campus library services, Internet access, wireless campus network,

Internet filtering or blocking technology. Campus intranet and student e-mail accounts are available to students. Students grades are available online. The school has a published electronic and media policy.

Contact Mr. Sharon Magor, Acting Admissions Director. 905-668-3358 Ext. 247. Fax: 905-668-4136. E-mail: magor.sharon@trafalgarcastle.ca. Website: www.trafalgarcastle.ca

TREVOR DAY SCHOOL

1 West 88th Street

New York, New York 10024

Head of School: Pamela J. Clarke

General Information Coeducational day college-preparatory, arts, and technology school. Grades N–12. Founded: 1930. Setting: urban. 1 building on campus. Approved or accredited by New York Department of Education. Member of National Association of Independent Schools and Secondary School Admission Test Board. Endowment: $16 million. Total enrollment: 800. Upper school average class size: 15. Upper school faculty-student ratio: 1:6.

Upper School Student Profile Grade 6: 66 students (38 boys, 28 girls); Grade 7: 61 students (28 boys, 33 girls); Grade 8: 65 students (35 boys, 30 girls); Grade 9: 66 students (32 boys, 34 girls); Grade 10: 62 students (33 boys, 29 girls); Grade 11: 57 students (23 boys, 34 girls); Grade 12: 63 students (30 boys, 33 girls).

Faculty School total: 145. In upper school: 37 men, 38 women; 55 have advanced degrees.

Subjects Offered Advanced chemistry, advanced computer applications, advanced math, African-American literature, algebra, American history, American literature, ancient world history, animation, architectural drawing, art, art history, Asian literature, Basic programming, biology, British literature, calculus, calculus-AP, ceramics, chemistry, choreography, chorus, college counseling, community service, computer programming, computer science, computer studies, concert band, creative writing, dance, discrete mathematics, drama, drama performance, drawing, economics, English, English literature, environmental science, equality and freedom, ethics, European history, expository writing, film and literature, filmmaking, fine arts, foreign language, forensics, French, French language-AP, genetics, geometry, grammar, Harlem Renaissance, health, Hispanic literature, history, honors English, independent study, intro to computers, Italian, jazz ensemble, literary magazine, madrigals, mathematics, model United Nations, music, musical productions, newspaper, peer counseling, performing arts, photography, photojournalism, physical education, physics, play production, playwriting, poetry, pottery, pre-calculus, Russian literature, science, senior internship, Shakespeare, Shakespearean histories, social studies, Spanish, Spanish language-AP, stained glass, statistics, statistics-AP, student government, studio art, technical theater, theater, U.S. history-AP, video, Web site design, wilderness education, world history, world literature, writing, yearbook.

Graduation Requirements Arts and fine arts (art, music, dance, drama), computer science, English, ethics, foreign language, mathematics, physical education (includes health), science, social studies (includes history), 80 hours of community service.

Special Academic Programs Advanced Placement exam preparation; honors section; independent study; term-away projects; study at local college for college credit; study abroad.

College Admission Counseling 58 students graduated in 2013; all went to college, including Brown University; New York University; Oberlin College; University of Michigan; University of Pennsylvania; Vassar College.

Student Life Upper grades have student council. Discipline rests equally with students and faculty.

Tuition and Aid Day student tuition: $27,250–$39,625. Tuition installment plan (FACTS Tuition Payment Plan, plan A: balance (85%) due August 15, plan B: 45% due July 24 - balance due December 30, plan C: 9-monthly installments). Need-based scholarship grants available. In 2013–14, 20% of upper-school students received aid. Total amount of financial aid awarded in 2013–14: $4,700,000.

Admissions Traditional secondary-level entrance grade is 9. ERB, ISEE or SSAT required. Deadline for receipt of application materials: January 1. Application fee required: $50. On-campus interview required.

Athletics Interscholastic: baseball (boys), basketball (b,g), soccer (b,g), softball (g), tennis (b,g), volleyball (g), wrestling (b); coed interscholastic: cross-country running, dance, fitness walking, modern dance, outdoor education, project adventure, track and field. 4 PE instructors, 12 coaches.

Computers Computers are regularly used in art, English, foreign language, history, mathematics, music, science classes. Computer network features include on-campus library services, online commercial services, Internet access, wireless campus network, Internet filtering or blocking technology, personal portals with homework and schedules for each student. Campus intranet and student e-mail accounts are available to students. The school has a published electronic and media policy.

Contact Kristin Harman, Director of Admissions. 212-426-3389. Fax: 646-672-5579. E-mail: kharman@trevor.org. Website: www.trevor.org

TRI-CITY CHRISTIAN ACADEMY

2211 W Germann Road
Chandler, Arizona 85286

Head of School: Pastor Thad E. Todd

General Information Coeducational day college-preparatory, religious studies, and music school, affiliated with Baptist Church. Grades K4–12. Founded: 1971. Setting: suburban. Nearest major city is Phoenix. 9-acre campus. 1 building on campus. Approved or accredited by Association of Christian Schools International and North Central Association of Colleges and Schools. Total enrollment: 304. Upper school average class size: 23. Upper school faculty-student ratio: 1:16. There are 169 required school days per year for Upper School students. Upper School students typically attend 5 days per week. The average school day consists of 7 hours and 5 minutes.

Upper School Student Profile Grade 9: 30 students (13 boys, 17 girls); Grade 10: 17 students (10 boys, 7 girls); Grade 11: 23 students (12 boys, 11 girls); Grade 12: 22 students (11 boys, 11 girls). 40% of students are Baptist.

Faculty School total: 19. In upper school: 6 men, 4 women; 2 have advanced degrees.

Subjects Offered 20th century history, 20th century world history, algebra, American government, American history, American literature, applied music, athletic training, athletics, band, basic language skills, basketball, bell choir, Bible, Bible studies, biology, brass choir, business mathematics, calculus, career and personal planning, career/college preparation, cheerleading, chemistry, choir, choral music, chorus, Christian doctrine, Christian education, Christian ethics, Christian scripture, civics, computer applications, computer studies, computers, concert choir, debate, drama, drama performance, dramatic arts, English, English composition, English literature, ESL, foreign language, geometry, government, journalism, keyboarding, library skills, public speaking, Spanish, strings, U.S. history, voice and diction, volleyball, wind instruments, world history, yearbook.

Special Academic Programs Independent study; study at local college for college credit; ESL (10 students enrolled).

College Admission Counseling 15 students graduated in 2013; 13 went to college, including Arizona State University; Bob Jones University; Northern Arizona University. Other: 2 went to work.

Student Life Upper grades have uniform requirement, student council, honor system. Discipline rests primarily with faculty.

Tuition and Aid Day student tuition: $5125. Tuition installment plan (monthly payment plans). Tuition reduction for siblings, tuition tax scholarships available. In 2013–14, 30% of upper-school students received aid. Total amount of financial aid awarded in 2013–14: $25,000.

Admissions Traditional secondary-level entrance grade is 9. For fall 2013, 13 students applied for upper-level admission, 13 were accepted, 12 enrolled. Deadline for receipt of application materials: none. Application fee required: $225. On-campus interview required.

Athletics Interscholastic: basketball (boys), golf (b), soccer (b,g), volleyball (g); coed interscholastic: soccer. 2 PE instructors.

Computers Computers are regularly used in ESL, foreign language, journalism classes. Computer resources include Internet access. Students grades are available online.

Contact 480-245-7902. Fax: 480-245-7908. Website: www.tcawarriors.org

TRI-CITY CHRISTIAN SCHOOLS

1737 West Vista Way
Vista, California 92083

Head of School: Mr. Clark Gilbert

General Information Coeducational day college-preparatory, general academic, arts, vocational, religious studies, bilingual studies, and technology school, affiliated with Christian faith. Grades PK–12. Founded: 1971. Setting: suburban. Nearest major city is San Diego. 4-acre campus. 4 buildings on campus. Approved or accredited by Association of Christian Schools International and Western Association of Schools and Colleges. Endowment: $100,000. Total enrollment: 571. Upper school average class size: 22. Upper school faculty-student ratio: 1:12. There are 180 required school days per year for Upper School students. Upper School students typically attend 5 days per week. The average school day consists of 7 hours and 25 minutes.

Upper School Student Profile Grade 9: 47 students (24 boys, 23 girls); Grade 10: 52 students (23 boys, 29 girls); Grade 11: 50 students (22 boys, 28 girls); Grade 12: 71 students (28 boys, 43 girls). 25% of students are Christian faith.

Faculty School total: 25. In upper school: 9 men, 16 women; 12 have advanced degrees.

Subjects Offered Algebra, American literature, American sign language, art, Bible studies, biology, biology-AP, British literature (honors), business mathematics, calculus, calculus-AP, chemistry, civics, computer science, drama, economics, English, English language-AP, English literature, English literature-AP, environmental science, European history, geometry, government/civics, guitar, health education, history, honors English, honors U.S. history, honors world history, journalism, library skills, mathematics, philosophy, physical education, physical science, physiology, religion, science, social studies, Spanish, speech, trigonometry, U.S. history, U.S. history-AP, world history, world literature.

Graduation Requirements Arts and fine arts (art, music, dance, drama), computer studies, English, foreign language, mathematics, physical education (includes health), religion (includes Bible studies and theology), science, social studies (includes history), speech, student portfolio. Community service is required.

Special Academic Programs International Baccalaureate program; Advanced Placement exam preparation; honors section; independent study.

College Admission Counseling 77 students graduated in 2012; all went to college, including Azusa Pacific University; California State University, San Marcos; MiraCosta College; Palomar College; Point Loma Nazarene University; Vanguard University of Southern California. Mean SAT critical reading: 546, mean SAT math: 532, mean SAT writing: 544.

Student Life Upper grades have uniform requirement, student council. Discipline rests primarily with faculty. Attendance at religious services is required.

Tuition and Aid Day student tuition: $7100–$9100. Tuition installment plan (monthly payment plans, individually arranged payment plans). Tuition reduction for siblings, need-based scholarship grants, paying campus jobs, church affiliation grants available. In 2012–13, 5% of upper-school students received aid. Total amount of financial aid awarded in 2012–13: $50,000.

Admissions Traditional secondary-level entrance grade is 9. Any standardized test, English entrance exam and Math Placement Exam required. Deadline for receipt of application materials: none. Application fee required: $425. On-campus interview required.

Athletics Interscholastic: aerobics/dance (girls), baseball (b), basketball (b,g), cheering (g), cross-country running (b,g), flag football (b), football (b), golf (b), soccer (b,g), softball (g), tennis (b,g), touch football (b), track and field (b,g), volleyball (b,g), weight training (b,g); intramural: dance (g), physical fitness (b,g); coed interscholastic: equestrian sports, golf, horseback riding, lacrosse, martial arts, snowboarding. 2 PE instructors, 20 coaches, 1 athletic trainer.

Computers Computers are regularly used in animation, business applications, career exploration, computer applications, media production, news writing, science, video film production classes. Computer network features include on-campus library services, Internet access, Internet filtering or blocking technology. Campus intranet and student e-mail accounts are available to students. Students grades are available online. The school has a published electronic and media policy.

Contact Mrs. Terri Montano, Registrar. 760-806-8247 Ext. 200. Fax: 760-906-9002. E-mail: Terri.Montano@tccs.org. Website: www.tccs.org

TRINITY CHRISTIAN ACADEMY

10 Windy City Road
Jackson, Tennessee 38305

Head of School: Mr. Jon Holley

General Information Coeducational day college-preparatory school. Grades PS–12. Founded: 1986. Setting: small town. Nearest major city is Memphis. 30-acre campus. 1 building on campus. Approved or accredited by Association of Christian Schools International, Southern Association of Colleges and Schools, and Tennessee Department of Education. Total enrollment: 772. Upper school average class size: 22. Upper school faculty-student ratio: 1:7. There are 176 required school days per year for Upper School students. Upper School students typically attend 5 days per week. The average school day consists of 5 hours and 35 minutes.

Faculty School total: 65. In upper school: 11 men, 10 women; 12 have advanced degrees.

Subjects Offered Algebra, art, Bible studies, biology, biology-AP, British literature, British literature (honors), calculus-AP, chemistry, choir, computers, drama, economics, English, etymology, fine arts, forensics, geography, geometry, government, personal finance, photography, physical fitness, physical science, physics, physics-AP, pre-calculus, U.S. history, U.S. history-AP, wellness, world history, yearbook.

Graduation Requirements Arts and fine arts (art, music, dance, drama), Bible, computers, English, foreign language, history, mathematics, science, speech, wellness, 80 hours of community service and participation in the Footprints program.

Special Academic Programs Honors section; study at local college for college credit.

College Admission Counseling 60 students graduated in 2013; 58 went to college, including Middle Tennessee State University; The University of Tennessee; The University of Tennessee at Chattanooga; The University of Tennessee at Martin; Union University. Other: 1 went to work, 1 entered military service. Median composite ACT: 24.

Student Life Upper grades have uniform requirement, student council, honor system. Discipline rests primarily with faculty. Attendance at religious services is required.

Tuition and Aid Day student tuition: $8000. Guaranteed tuition plan. Tuition installment plan (FACTS Tuition Payment Plan, monthly payment plans). Need-based scholarship grants available.

Admissions Traditional secondary-level entrance grade is 9. For fall 2013, 48 students applied for upper-level admission, 48 were accepted, 48 enrolled. SAT required. Deadline for receipt of application materials: none. Application fee required: $200. On-campus interview required.

Athletics Interscholastic: baseball (girls), basketball (b,g), cheering (b), cross-country running (b,g), football (g), golf (b,g), in-line hockey (b), soccer (b,g), softball (g), tennis (b,g), track and field (b,g), trap and skeet (b), volleyball (b). 2 PE instructors.

Computers Computers are regularly used in computer applications, keyboarding classes. Computer resources include Internet access, Internet filtering or blocking technology. Students grades are available online.

Contact Mrs. Kathleen George, Admissions Director. 731-668-8500 Ext. 107. Fax: 731-668-3232. E-mail: kgeorge@tcalions.com. Website: www.tcalions.com

TRINITY COLLEGE SCHOOL

55 Deblaquire Street North
Port Hope, Ontario L1A 4K7, Canada

Head of School: Mr. Stuart K.C. Grainger

General Information Coeducational boarding and day college-preparatory and Liberal Arts school, affiliated with Church of England (Anglican). Boarding grades 9–12, day grades 5–12. Founded: 1865. Setting: small town. Nearest major city is Toronto, Canada. Students are housed in single-sex dormitories. 100-acre campus. 15 buildings on campus. Approved or accredited by Canadian Association of Independent Schools, Conference of Independent Schools of Ontario, The Association of Boarding Schools, and Ontario Department of Education. Affiliate member of National Association of Independent Schools; member of Secondary School Admission Test Board. Language of instruction: English. Endowment: CAN$25 million. Total enrollment: 554. Upper school average class size: 16. Upper school faculty-student ratio: 1:8. There are 165 required school days per year for Upper School students. Upper School students typically attend 5 days per week. The average school day consists of 6 hours.

Upper School Student Profile Grade 9: 81 students (48 boys, 33 girls); Grade 10: 94 students (54 boys, 40 girls); Grade 11: 138 students (82 boys, 56 girls); Grade 12: 135 students (66 boys, 69 girls). 60% of students are boarding students. 61% are province residents. 8 provinces are represented in upper school student body. 33% are international students. International students from Bermuda, China, Germany, Mexico, Nigeria, and Saudi Arabia; 25 other countries represented in student body. 30% of students are members of Church of England (Anglican).

Faculty School total: 86. In upper school: 37 men, 29 women; 17 have advanced degrees; 11 reside on campus.

Subjects Offered Algebra, American history, art, art history-AP, astronomy, biology, biology-AP, calculus, calculus-AP, Canadian geography, Canadian history, Canadian law, career education, career/college preparation, chemistry, chemistry-AP, civics, classical civilization, community service, comparative government and politics-AP, computer programming, computer science, computer science-AP, creative writing, dramatic arts, earth science, economics, English, English language-AP, English literature, English literature-AP, environmental science, environmental science-AP, environmental studies, ESL, fine arts, finite math, French, French-AP, general science, geography, geometry, German, guidance, health education, history, human geography - AP, independent study, Latin, law, mathematics, microeconomics-AP, music, music theory-AP, outdoor education, philosophy, physical education, physics, physics-AP, political science, politics, society challenge and change, Spanish, statistics-AP, studio art-AP, world history, world history-AP.

Graduation Requirements Arts, Canadian geography, Canadian history, civics, English, French, guidance, mathematics, physical education (includes health), science, social sciences, technology, minimum 40 hours of community service, provincial literacy test completion.

Special Academic Programs Advanced Placement exam preparation; independent study; term-away projects; study abroad; ESL (20 students enrolled).

College Admission Counseling 139 students graduated in 2013; 126 went to college, including Dalhousie University; Queen's University at Kingston; The University of Western Ontario; University of Guelph; University of Toronto; University of Waterloo. Other: 2 went to work, 11 had other specific plans.

Student Life Upper grades have uniform requirement, student council, honor system. Discipline rests primarily with faculty. Attendance at religious services is required.

Summer Programs Enrichment, advancement, ESL programs offered; session focuses on advancement through cultural enrichment; held both on and off campus; held at England; accepts boys and girls; not open to students from other schools. 30 students usually enrolled. 2014 schedule: July 3 to August 30. Application deadline: May 1.

Tuition and Aid Day student tuition: CAN$21,750–CAN$29,950; 7-day tuition and room/board: CAN$49,450–CAN$52,950. Tuition installment plan (monthly payment plans, quarterly payment plan (domestic students only), three payment option (international students)). Bursaries, need-based scholarship grants available. In 2013–14, 27% of upper-school students received aid. Total amount of financial aid awarded in 2013–14: CAN$1,750,000.

Admissions Traditional secondary-level entrance grade is 9. For fall 2013, 198 students applied for upper-level admission, 198 were accepted, 134 enrolled. Otis-Lennon Ability or Stanford Achievement Test, SSAT or TOEFL required. Deadline for receipt of application materials: none. Application fee required: CAN$150. Interview required.

Athletics Interscholastic: baseball (boys), basketball (b,g), cricket (b), field hockey (g), football (b), hockey (g), ice hockey (b,g), rugby (b,g), soccer (b,g), squash (b,g), tennis (b,g), volleyball (g); coed interscholastic: badminton, cross-country running, golf, nordic skiing, outdoor education, rowing, swimming and diving, track and field; coed intramural: aerobics, aerobics/dance, badminton, basketball, cooperative games, cricket, cross-country running, dance, equestrian sports, fitness, fitness walking, golf,

ice hockey, ice skating, skiing (downhill), snowboarding, soccer, softball, squash, strength & conditioning, swimming and diving, table tennis, tennis, ultimate Frisbee, weight lifting, weight training, yoga. 4 PE instructors, 5 coaches, 2 athletic trainers.

Computers Computers are regularly used in all academic classes. Computer network features include on-campus library services, Internet access, wireless campus network, Internet filtering or blocking technology. Campus intranet and student e-mail accounts are available to students. The school has a published electronic and media policy.

Contact Ms. Kathryn A. LaBranche, Director of Admissions. 905-885-3209. Fax: 905-885-7444. E-mail: admissions@tcs.on.ca. Website: www.tcs.on.ca

TRINITY HIGH SCHOOL

4011 Shelbyville Road
Louisville, Kentucky 40207-9427

Head of School: Robert J. Mullen, EdD

General Information Boys' day college-preparatory, arts, business, religious studies, and technology school, affiliated with Roman Catholic Church. Grades 9–12. Founded: 1953. Setting: suburban. 110-acre campus. 11 buildings on campus. Approved or accredited by National Catholic Education Association, Southern Association of Colleges and Schools, Southern Association of Independent Schools, and Kentucky Department of Education. Member of National Association of Independent Schools. Endowment: $16 million. Total enrollment: 1,320. Upper school average class size: 20. Upper school faculty-student ratio: 1:12. There are 175 required school days per year for Upper School students. Upper School students typically attend 5 days per week. The average school day consists of 7 hours.

Upper School Student Profile Grade 9: 349 students (349 boys); Grade 10: 324 students (324 boys); Grade 11: 318 students (318 boys); Grade 12: 329 students (329 boys). 84% of students are Roman Catholic.

Faculty School total: 120. In upper school: 88 men, 30 women; 110 have advanced degrees.

Subjects Offered 20th century history, 3-dimensional art, accounting, acting, adolescent issues, advanced chemistry, advanced computer applications, advanced math, Advanced Placement courses, advanced studio art-AP, algebra, American Civil War, American democracy, American foreign policy, American government, American history, American history-AP, American literature, American literature-AP, analysis and differential calculus, analysis of data, anatomy and physiology, ancient history, ancient world history, applied arts, applied music, art, art and culture, art appreciation, art education, art history, art-AP, arts, arts appreciation, athletic training, athletics, band, banking, Basic programming, Bible as literature, biology, biology-AP, broadcasting, business, business education, business law, business mathematics, business studies, business technology, calculus, calculus-AP, campus ministry, career exploration, career planning, career/college preparation, cell biology, character education, cheerleading, chemistry, chemistry-AP, choir, choral music, chorus, Christian doctrine, Christian ethics, Christian scripture, church history, cinematography, civics, Civil War, classical civilization, classical Greek literature, classical music, college admission preparation, college awareness, college counseling, college placement, college planning, communication arts, communication skills, community service, comparative cultures, comparative government and politics, composition-AP, computer animation, computer applications, computer art, computer education, computer graphics, computer information systems, computer literacy, computer math, computer multimedia, computer music, computer processing, computer programming, computer science, computer skills, computer studies, computer technologies, computer technology certification, computer tools, computers, concert band, concert choir, conflict resolution, constitutional law, contemporary art, CPR, creative writing, critical studies in film, critical thinking, critical writing, data analysis, data processing, death and loss, decision making skills, developmental math, digital photography, DNA research, drama, drama performance, drawing, drawing and design, earth and space science, earth science, ecology, economics, economics and history, economics-AP, English, English language and composition-AP, English literature, English-AP, environmental studies, European civilization, European history, evolution, family living, fencing, film, film studies, finite math, first aid, forensics, French, general science, geography, geometry, German, health, health science, Hebrew scripture, Holocaust studies, HTML design, humanities, independent study, information technology, instrumental music, integrated mathematics, interdisciplinary studies, Internet, jazz band, journalism, keyboarding, language arts, leadership and service, literature, literature-AP, martial arts, mathematics, modern civilization, moral and social development, multimedia design, music performance, musical theater, New Testament, news writing, newspaper, oil painting, painting, peace and justice, philosophy, photography, photojournalism, physical education, physical fitness, physical science, physics, physics-AP, post-calculus, pottery, pre-algebra, pre-calculus, probability and statistics, programming, psychology, public speaking, religion, religious studies, Roman civilization, Romantic period literature, Russian history, SAT/ACT preparation, science, sculpture, senior seminar, social justice, social psychology, social sciences, social studies, sociology, software design, space and physical sciences, Spanish, Spanish literature, Spanish-AP, speech and debate, sports medicine, sports nutrition, stage design, stained glass, statistics, student government, student publications, technology, trigonometry, U.S. government and politics-AP, U.S. history-AP, video film production, Web site design, weight training, Western civilization, work-study, world civilizations, world history, world history-AP, yearbook.

Graduation Requirements Communication arts, English, foreign language, humanities, lab science, mathematics, physical education (includes health), religion (includes Bible studies and theology), science, social studies (includes history), several elective offerings, must have taken the ACT. Community service is required.

Special Academic Programs Advanced Placement exam preparation; honors section; independent study; study at local college for college credit; study abroad; academic accommodation for the gifted, the musically talented, and the artistically talented; remedial reading and/or remedial writing; remedial math; programs in English, mathematics, general development for dyslexic students; special instructional classes for deaf students, blind students.

College Admission Counseling 315 students graduated in 2013; 310 went to college, including Bellarmine University; Eastern Kentucky University; Indiana University Bloomington; University of Dayton; University of Kentucky; University of Louisville. Other: 3 went to work, 2 entered military service. Mean combined SAT: 1854, mean composite ACT: 24.

Student Life Upper grades have specified standards of dress, student council, honor system. Discipline rests primarily with faculty. Attendance at religious services is required.

Summer Programs Remediation, enrichment, advancement, sports, art/fine arts, computer instruction programs offered; session focuses on academic advancement and enrichment/sports camps; held on campus; accepts boys; not open to students from other schools. 1,000 students usually enrolled. 2014 schedule: June 1 to August 3. Application deadline: May 15.

Tuition and Aid Day student tuition: $11,775. Guaranteed tuition plan. Tuition installment plan (monthly payment plans, individually arranged payment plans, Tuition Management Systems). Merit scholarship grants, need-based scholarship grants, paying campus jobs available. In 2013–14, 40% of upper-school students received aid; total upper-school merit-scholarship money awarded: $120,000. Total amount of financial aid awarded in 2013–14: $2,500,000.

Admissions Traditional secondary-level entrance grade is 9. High School Placement Test required. Deadline for receipt of application materials: none. Application fee required: $75. Interview required.

Athletics Interscholastic: archery, baseball, basketball, bicycling, bowling, cheering, crew, cross-country running, diving, fishing, football, golf, hockey, ice hockey, lacrosse, power lifting, rugby, soccer, swimming and diving, tennis, track and field, volleyball, weight lifting, wrestling; intramural: alpine skiing, basketball, bocce, climbing, cricket, fencing, fishing, flag football, freestyle skiing, Frisbee, golf, hiking/backpacking, indoor soccer, judo, kickball, life saving, martial arts, mountain biking, outdoor adventure, paddle tennis, rock climbing, rowing, skiing (downhill), snowboarding, soccer, softball, strength & conditioning, table tennis, ultimate Frisbee, volleyball, water polo, weight lifting, weight training; coed intramural: bowling. 5 PE instructors, 30 coaches, 3 athletic trainers.

Computers Computers are regularly used in all classes. Computer network features include on-campus library services, online commercial services, Internet access, wireless campus network, Internet filtering or blocking technology, free use of Office 365, cloud-based document storage. Campus intranet, student e-mail accounts, and computer access in designated common areas are available to students. Students grades are available online. The school has a published electronic and media policy.

Contact Mr. Joseph M. Porter Jr., Vice President for Advancement. 502-736-2119. Fax: 502-899-2052. E-mail: porter@thsrock.net. Website: www.trinityrocks.com

TRINITY HIGH SCHOOL

581 Bridge Street
Manchester, New Hampshire 03104

Head of School: Mr. Denis Mailloux

General Information Coeducational day college-preparatory, arts, religious studies, and technology school, affiliated with Roman Catholic Church. Grades 9–12. Founded: 1886. Setting: urban. Nearest major city is Boston, MA. 5-acre campus. 2 buildings on campus. Approved or accredited by National Catholic Education Association, New England Association of Schools and Colleges, and New Hampshire Department of Education. Total enrollment: 442. Upper school average class size: 15. Upper school faculty-student ratio: 1:12. There are 180 required school days per year for Upper School students. Upper School students typically attend 5 days per week. The average school day consists of 6 hours and 40 minutes.

Upper School Student Profile Grade 9: 108 students (57 boys, 51 girls); Grade 10: 117 students (69 boys, 48 girls); Grade 11: 105 students (58 boys, 47 girls); Grade 12: 112 students (56 boys, 56 girls). 80% of students are Roman Catholic.

Faculty School total: 37. In upper school: 18 men, 17 women; 21 have advanced degrees.

Subjects Offered 3-dimensional art, advanced biology, advanced math, Advanced Placement courses, algebra, American government, American history, American history-AP, American literature, analysis, anatomy and physiology, art, Bible studies, biology, calculus, calculus-AP, chemistry, computer science, driver education, English, English literature, English-AP, ethics, French, geometry, grammar, health, history, human development, journalism, Latin, mathematics, physical education, physics, psychology, psychology-AP, religion, science, social studies, sociology, Spanish, theology, trigonometry, U.S. history-AP, world history, world literature.

Special Academic Programs 5 Advanced Placement exams for which test preparation is offered; honors section; study at local college for college credit.

College Admission Counseling 100 students graduated in 2013; 97 went to college, including Boston University; Keene State College; Northeastern University; Saint Anselm College; Stonehill College; University of New Hampshire. Other: 1 went to work, 1 entered military service, 1 entered a postgraduate year.

Student Life Upper grades have specified standards of dress, student council, honor system. Discipline rests primarily with faculty. Attendance at religious services is required.

Tuition and Aid Day student tuition: $8940. Tuition installment plan (FACTS Tuition Payment Plan). Need-based scholarship grants available. In 2013–14, 10% of upper-school students received aid.

Admissions Traditional secondary-level entrance grade is 9. STS required. Deadline for receipt of application materials: none. Application fee required: $50. Interview recommended.

Athletics Interscholastic: baseball (boys), basketball (b,g), cheering (g), cross-country running (b,g), football (b), gymnastics (g), hockey (b), ice hockey (b), indoor track & field (b,g), lacrosse (b), skiing (cross-country) (b,g), skiing (downhill) (b,g), soccer (b,g), softball (g), swimming and diving (b,g), tennis (b,g), volleyball (g), winter (indoor) track (b,g), wrestling (b); coed interscholastic: alpine skiing, golf, track and field; coed intramural: gymnastics. 1 PE instructor, 25 coaches, 1 athletic trainer.

Computers Computers are regularly used in all academic, English, journalism, science, social sciences, yearbook classes. Computer network features include Internet access, wireless campus network. Campus intranet and student e-mail accounts are available to students. Students grades are available online.

Contact Mr. Patrick Smith, Dean of Students and Director of Admissions. 603-668-2910 Ext. 18. Fax: 603-668-2913. E-mail: psmith@trinity-hs.org. Website: www.trinity-hs.org

TRINITY HIGH SCHOOL

12425 Granger Road
Garfield Heights, Ohio 44125

Head of School: Mrs. Linda Bacho

General Information Coeducational day college-preparatory, arts, business, religious studies, technology, technical, and medical school, affiliated with Roman Catholic Church. Grades 9–12. Founded: 1926. Setting: suburban. Nearest major city is Cleveland. 26-acre campus. 3 buildings on campus. Approved or accredited by National Catholic Education Association, North Central Association of Colleges and Schools, Ohio Catholic Schools Accreditation Association (OCSAA), and Ohio Department of Education. Total enrollment: 352. Upper school average class size: 17. Upper school faculty-student ratio: 1:12. There are 199 required school days per year for Upper School students. Upper School students typically attend 5 days per week. The average school day consists of 7 hours.

Upper School Student Profile Grade 9: 93 students (46 boys, 47 girls); Grade 10: 107 students (41 boys, 66 girls); Grade 11: 66 students (19 boys, 47 girls); Grade 12: 86 students (43 boys, 43 girls). 89% of students are Roman Catholic.

Faculty School total: 34. In upper school: 12 men, 18 women; 15 have advanced degrees.

Subjects Offered 3-dimensional art, accounting, advanced biology, advanced chemistry, advanced computer applications, advanced math, Advanced Placement courses, advanced studio art-AP, algebra, American government, American history, American history-AP, American literature, analysis and differential calculus, anatomy and physiology, animation, art, athletics, automated accounting, band, Bible, Bible studies, biology, bookkeeping, British literature, British literature (honors), business applications, business skills, business technology, calculus-AP, campus ministry, career and personal planning, career education, career education internship, career experience, career exploration, career planning, career/college preparation, Catholic belief and practice, ceramics, chemistry, choir, Christian and Hebrew scripture, Christian doctrine, Christian ethics, Christian scripture, Christian testament, church history, college admission preparation, college awareness, college counseling, college placement, college planning, college writing, communication skills, community service, comparative religion, competitive science projects, computer animation, computer applications, computer art, computer education, computer graphics, computer information systems, computer multimedia, computer technologies, computer technology certification, computer-aided design, concert band, concert choir, consumer economics, creative writing, critical thinking, critical writing, culinary arts, digital applications, drama performance, drawing and design, earth science, economics and history, electives, English, English literature and composition-AP, environmental science, ethics, European history, food and nutrition, foods, foreign language, four units of summer reading, geometry, global studies, government-AP, graphic arts, graphic design, graphics, guidance, health education, honors algebra, honors English, honors geometry, human anatomy, human biology, instrumental music, integrated mathematics, Internet research, internship, lab science, library, life issues, Life of Christ, marching band, marine biology, Microsoft, moral theology, musical theater, neuroscience, oral communications, participation in sports, peace and justice, peer ministry, personal finance, photo shop, physical education, physics, play production, portfolio art, prayer/spirituality, pre-algebra, pre-calculus, psychology, public speaking, SAT/ACT preparation, speech, sports, studio art-AP, study skills, symphonic band, theology, U.S.

government and politics-AP, video, video and animation, vocal ensemble, Web site design, wind ensemble, word processing, world history, yearbook.

Graduation Requirements Arts and fine arts (art, music, dance, drama), electives, English, government, human relations, mathematics, physical education (includes health), science, social studies (includes history), theology, Western civilization, service hours, internship.

Special Academic Programs Advanced Placement exam preparation; honors section; independent study; academic accommodation for the gifted and the artistically talented; remedial math; programs in English, mathematics, general development for dyslexic students.

College Admission Counseling 78 students graduated in 2013; 74 went to college, including John Carroll University; Kent State University; Miami University; Ohio University; The Ohio State University; University of Dayton. Other: 2 went to work, 1 entered military service, 1 had other specific plans. Median SAT critical reading: 485, median SAT math: 450, median SAT writing: 450, median combined SAT: 1385, median composite ACT: 21. 27% scored over 600 on SAT critical reading, 18% scored over 600 on SAT math, 18% scored over 600 on SAT writing, 10% scored over 1800 on combined SAT, 11% scored over 26 on composite ACT.

Student Life Upper grades have uniform requirement, student council. Discipline rests primarily with faculty. Attendance at religious services is required.

Summer Programs Enrichment, advancement, sports, art/fine arts programs offered; session focuses on recruitment; held both on and off campus; held at other schools; accepts boys and girls; open to students from other schools. 125 students usually enrolled. 2014 schedule: June to August. Application deadline: May.

Tuition and Aid Day student tuition: $9900. Guaranteed tuition plan. Tuition installment plan (individually arranged payment plans, private bank loans). Tuition reduction for siblings, need-based scholarship grants, middle-income loans, private bank loans available. In 2013–14, 25% of upper-school students received aid. Total amount of financial aid awarded in 2013–14: $138,000.

Admissions Traditional secondary-level entrance grade is 9. For fall 2013, 121 students applied for upper-level admission, 100 were accepted, 93 enrolled. Scholastic Testing Service High School Placement Test required. Deadline for receipt of application materials: none. Application fee required: $20. On-campus interview required.

Athletics Interscholastic: baseball (boys), basketball (b,g), cheering (g), cross-country running (b,g), danceline (g), football (b), soccer (b,g), softball (g), track and field (b,g), volleyball (g), wrestling (b); intramural: danceline (g); coed interscholastic: golf, indoor track & field; coed intramural: skiing (downhill), snowboarding. 1 PE instructor, 34 coaches, 1 athletic trainer.

Computers Computers are regularly used in all academic classes. Computer network features include on-campus library services, online commercial services, Internet access, wireless campus network, Internet filtering or blocking technology, Citrix, network printing, personal storage on network, weekly email grade reports, electronic newsletters, remote access, school Web site, online homework tracking system. Computer access in designated common areas is available to students. Students grades are available online. The school has a published electronic and media policy.

Contact Sr. Dian Majsterek, Administrative Assistant, Admissions and Marketing. 216-581-1061. Fax: 216-581-9348. E-mail: SisterDian@ths.org. Website: www.ths.org

TRINITY-PAWLING SCHOOL

700 Route 22
Pawling, New York 12564

Head of School: Mr. Archibald A. Smith III

General Information Boys' boarding and day college-preparatory, arts, religious studies, technology, and ESL school, affiliated with Episcopal Church. Boarding grades 9–PG, day grades 7–PG. Founded: 1907. Setting: small town. Nearest major city is New York. Students are housed in single-sex dormitories. 140-acre campus. 31 buildings on campus. Approved or accredited by New York State Association of Independent Schools, New York State Board of Regents, and The Association of Boarding Schools. Member of National Association of Independent Schools and Secondary School Admission Test Board. Endowment: $35 million. Total enrollment: 283. Upper school average class size: 12. Upper school faculty-student ratio: 1:8. There are 186 required school days per year for Upper School students. Upper School students typically attend 6 days per week. The average school day consists of 6 hours and 30 minutes.

Upper School Student Profile Grade 9: 38 students (38 boys); Grade 10: 54 students (54 boys); Grade 11: 83 students (83 boys); Grade 12: 69 students (69 boys); Postgraduate: 16 students (16 boys). 80% of students are boarding students. 20% are state residents. 19 states are represented in upper school student body. 25% are international students. International students from Brazil, Canada, China, Republic of Korea, Saudi Arabia, and Viet Nam; 14 other countries represented in student body. 20% of students are members of Episcopal Church.

Faculty School total: 53. In upper school: 36 men, 15 women; 40 have advanced degrees; 50 reside on campus.

Subjects Offered Advanced Placement courses, advanced studio art-AP, algebra, American government, American history, American legal systems, American literature, American studies, anatomy, anatomy and physiology, architectural drawing, art, art history, art history-AP, Asian history, Asian studies, astronomy, Bible, biology, biology-AP, calculus, calculus-AP, ceramics, chemistry, chemistry-AP, choir, chorus, Christian

ethics, civil rights, composition-AP, computer applications, computer information systems, computer math, computer music, computer programming, computer science, computer science-AP, computer technologies, constitutional history of U.S., data analysis, drafting, drama, drama performance, earth science, East Asian history, ecology, economics, economics-AP, English, English language-AP, English literature, English literature-AP, English-AP, English/composition-AP, environmental science, environmental science-AP, environmental studies, ESL, ethics, European history, European history-AP, fine arts, French, French language-AP, French studies, geology, geometry, government, government and politics-AP, government/civics, grammar, health science, history, honors algebra, honors English, honors geometry, honors U.S. history, honors world history, human anatomy, keyboarding, Latin, Latin American literature, Latin-AP, law and the legal system, literature, literature and composition-AP, Mandarin, mathematics, mechanical drawing, model United Nations, music, philosophy, photography, physical education, physics, physics-AP, physiology, political science, pre-calculus, probability and statistics, psychology, public speaking, reading/study skills, religion, religious education, religious studies, SAT preparation, science, Shakespeare, social justice, social sciences, social studies, Spanish, Spanish language-AP, Spanish literature-AP, statistics-AP, studio art, studio art-AP, study skills, theater, theology, trigonometry, U.S. government and politics, U.S. history, U.S. history-AP, Vietnam War, word processing, world history, writing, yearbook.

Graduation Requirements Arts and fine arts (art, music, dance, drama), English, foreign language, mathematics, physical education (includes health), religion (includes Bible studies and theology), science, social studies (includes history).

Special Academic Programs 17 Advanced Placement exams for which test preparation is offered; honors section; remedial reading and/or remedial writing; programs in English for dyslexic students; ESL (25 students enrolled).

College Admission Counseling 85 students graduated in 2013; all went to college, including Boston University; Hobart and William Smith Colleges; Purdue University; Trinity College; Tulane University; University of Vermont. Mean SAT critical reading: 580, mean SAT math: 570.

Student Life Upper grades have specified standards of dress, student council, honor system. Discipline rests equally with students and faculty. Attendance at religious services is required.

Tuition and Aid Day student tuition: $36,250; 7-day tuition and room/board: $51,000. Tuition installment plan (Academic Management Services Plan, individually arranged payment plans, payment plans arranged directly with the school business office). Need-based scholarship grants, need-based loans available. In 2013–14, 35% of upper-school students received aid. Total amount of financial aid awarded in 2013–14: $3,300,000.

Admissions Traditional secondary-level entrance grade is 9. For fall 2013, 412 students applied for upper-level admission, 301 were accepted, 101 enrolled. PSAT or SAT, SSAT, TOEFL, Wechsler Intelligence Scale for Children III or WISC-R required. Deadline for receipt of application materials: February 1. Application fee required: $50. On-campus interview required.

Athletics Interscholastic: alpine skiing, baseball, basketball, cross-country running, football, golf, hockey, ice hockey, lacrosse, ropes courses, skiing (downhill), soccer, squash, strength & conditioning, tennis, track and field, weight lifting, weight training, wrestling; intramural: alpine skiing, basketball, bicycling, climbing, fishing, fitness, floor hockey, fly fishing, Frisbee, golf, hiking/backpacking, ice skating, mountain biking, outdoor education, outdoor recreation, physical training, polo, rock climbing, running, skiing (downhill), snowboarding, soccer, softball, squash, strength & conditioning, tennis, trap and skeet, ultimate Frisbee, wall climbing, weight lifting. 30 coaches, 2 athletic trainers.

Computers Computers are regularly used in English, history, mathematics, remedial study skills, science classes. Computer network features include on-campus library services, online commercial services, Internet access, wireless campus network, Internet filtering or blocking technology. Campus intranet, student e-mail accounts, and computer access in designated common areas are available to students. Students grades are available online. The school has a published electronic and media policy.

Contact Mrs. Denise Palmer, Admission Office Manager. 845-855-4825. Fax: 845-855-4827. E-mail: denisepalmer@trinitypawling.org. Website: www.trinitypawling.org

See Display on next page and Close-Up on page 580.

TRINITY PREPARATORY SCHOOL

5700 Trinity Prep Lane
Winter Park, Florida 32792

Head of School: Craig S. Maughan

General Information Coeducational day college-preparatory, arts, technology, and Stanford Online video conferencing courses school, affiliated with Episcopal Church. Grades 6–12. Founded: 1966. Setting: suburban. Nearest major city is Orlando. 100-acre campus. 12 buildings on campus. Approved or accredited by Florida Department of Education. Member of National Association of Independent Schools and Secondary School Admission Test Board. Endowment: $9.2 million. Total enrollment: 865. Upper school average class size: 17. Upper school faculty-student ratio: 1:10. There are 175 required school days per year for Upper School students. Upper School students typically attend 5 days per week. The average school day consists of 5 hours and 45 minutes.

Upper School Student Profile Grade 9: 130 students (74 boys, 56 girls); Grade 10: 127 students (72 boys, 55 girls); Grade 11: 134 students (70 boys, 64 girls); Grade 12: 129 students (62 boys, 67 girls). 7% of students are members of Episcopal Church.

Faculty School total: 85. In upper school: 28 men, 39 women; 46 have advanced degrees.

Subjects Offered 20th century American writers, 20th century world history, 3-dimensional art, advanced math, Advanced Placement courses, advanced studio art-AP, algebra, American history, American literature, anatomy, animal science, art, athletic training, audio visual/media, band, Basic programming, Bible, biology, biology-AP, calculus, calculus-AP, character education, chemistry, chemistry-AP, chorus, civics, Civil War, comparative religion, computer graphics, computer multimedia, computer processing, computer programming, computer programming-AP, concert band, concert choir, creative writing, critical studies in film, digital photography, drama, drawing, economics, economics-AP, English, English language and composition-AP, English literature, English literature and composition-AP, environmental science, environmental science-AP, ethics, European history, European history-AP, filmmaking, fine arts, forensics, French, French language-AP, French literature-AP, geography, geometry, government and politics-AP, health, honors algebra, honors English, honors geometry, journalism, Latin, Latin-AP, life management skills, mathematics, music, music theory-AP, newspaper, painting, physical education, physics, physics-AP, portfolio art, pottery, pre-algebra, pre-calculus, probability and statistics, psychology, psychology-AP, science, sculpture, social studies, Spanish, Spanish language-AP, Spanish literature-AP, speech, strings, studio art-AP, theater, trigonometry, U.S. government and politics-AP, U.S. history-AP, weight training, world history, world wide web design, writing, yearbook.

Graduation Requirements 1 1/2 elective credits, arts and fine arts (art, music, dance, drama), computer science, electives, English, foreign language, life management skills, mathematics, physical education (includes health), science, social sciences, 1/2 additional social studies credit.

Special Academic Programs 25 Advanced Placement exams for which test preparation is offered; honors section; independent study; study at local college for college credit; study abroad; academic accommodation for the gifted, the musically talented, and the artistically talented.

College Admission Counseling 120 students graduated in 2013; all went to college, including Florida State University; New York University; Rollins College; University of Central Florida; University of Florida; University of Miami.

Student Life Upper grades have specified standards of dress, student council, honor system. Discipline rests primarily with faculty. Attendance at religious services is required.

Summer Programs Remediation, enrichment, advancement, sports, art/fine arts, computer instruction programs offered; session focuses on enrichment; held on campus; accepts boys and girls; open to students from other schools. 300 students usually enrolled. 2014 schedule: June 14 to August 8. Application deadline: none.

Tuition and Aid Day student tuition: $17,950. Tuition installment plan (Insured Tuition Payment Plan, monthly payment plans, semiannual and annual payment plans). Need-based scholarship grants available. In 2013–14, 25% of upper-school students received aid. Total amount of financial aid awarded in 2013–14: $1,972,600.

Admissions Traditional secondary-level entrance grade is 9. For fall 2013, 65 students applied for upper-level admission, 39 were accepted, 29 enrolled. CTP, ISEE, PSAT, SAT or SSAT required. Deadline for receipt of application materials: February 8. Application fee required: $75. Interview required.

Athletics Interscholastic: baseball (boys), basketball (b,g), bowling (b,g), cheering (g), cross-country running (b,g), diving (b,g), fitness (b,g), football (b), golf (b,g), lacrosse (b,g), physical fitness (b,g), soccer (b,g), softball (g), strength & conditioning (b,g), swimming and diving (b,g), tennis (b,g), track and field (b,g), volleyball (g), weight lifting (b,g), weight training (b,g); intramural: ropes courses (b,g), strength & conditioning (b,g). 5 PE instructors, 48 coaches, 1 athletic trainer.

Computers Computers are regularly used in all classes. Computer network features include on-campus library services, online commercial services, Internet access, wireless campus network, Internet filtering or blocking technology. Student e-mail accounts and computer access in designated common areas are available to students. Students grades are available online. The school has a published electronic and media policy.

Contact Sherryn M. Hay, Director of Admission. 321-282-2523. Fax: 407-671-6935. E-mail: hays@trinityprep.org. Website: www.trinityprep.org

TRINITY SCHOOL OF TEXAS

215 Teague Street
Longview, Texas 75601

Head of School: Mr. Gary L. Whitwell

General Information Coeducational day college-preparatory, arts, religious studies, and technology school, affiliated with Episcopal Church. Grades PK–12. Founded: 1957. Setting: small town. Nearest major city is Dallas. 14-acre campus. 4 buildings on campus. Approved or accredited by National Association of Episcopal Schools, Southern Association of Colleges and Schools, Southwest Association of Episcopal Schools, and Texas Department of Education. Endowment: $315,000. Total enrollment: 275. Upper school average class size: 12. Upper school faculty-student ratio: 1:8. There are 174 required school days per year for Upper School students. Upper School students typically attend 5 days per week. The average school day consists of 6 hours and 20 minutes.

Upper School Student Profile Grade 9: 15 students (9 boys, 6 girls); Grade 10: 15 students (6 boys, 9 girls); Grade 11: 11 students (7 boys, 4 girls); Grade 12: 12 students (4 boys, 8 girls). 11% of students are members of Episcopal Church.

Faculty School total: 38. In upper school: 3 men, 13 women; 3 have advanced degrees.

Subjects Offered Advanced studio art-AP, algebra, American history, art, astronomy, athletics, biology, biology-AP, calculus, calculus-AP, Central and Eastern European history, character education, chemistry, chemistry-AP, choral music, college admission preparation, college writing, community service, computer applications, computer literacy, conflict resolution, creative writing, desktop publishing, digital photography, drama performance, earth science, economics, English-AP, environmental studies, European history-AP, geography, geometry, government, government/civics, grammar, health, junior and senior seminars, keyboarding, language and composition, language arts, leadership and service, library, life science, literature and composition-AP, mathematics, modern European history, modern Western civilization, modern world history, music, music performance, mythology, newspaper, participation in sports, personal finance, photography, photojournalism, physical education, physical fitness, physical science, physics, pre-algebra, pre-calculus, probability and statistics, psychology, psychology-AP, religious studies, research seminar, research skills, SAT preparation, SAT/ACT preparation, sociology, Spanish, Spanish language-AP, sports, statistics, student publications, studio art, Texas history, U.S. government, U.S. history, world geography, world history, world religions, yearbook.

Graduation Requirements Arts and fine arts (art, music, dance, drama), computers, English, government/civics, languages, mathematics, physical education (includes health), science, social sciences, speech, theology.

Special Academic Programs Advanced Placement exam preparation; accelerated programs; independent study; term-away projects; study at local college for college credit; study abroad; academic accommodation for the gifted, the musically talented, and the artistically talented; programs in English, mathematics for dyslexic students.

College Admission Counseling 12 students graduated in 2013; all went to college, including Louisiana State University and Agricultural and Mechanical College; Texas A&M University; The University of Texas at Austin. Median SAT critical reading: 530, median SAT math: 620, median SAT writing: 535, median combined SAT: 1690, median composite ACT: 23. 18% scored over 600 on SAT critical reading, 23% scored over 600 on SAT math, 13% scored over 600 on SAT writing, 42% scored over 26 on composite ACT.

Student Life Upper grades have specified standards of dress, student council, honor system. Discipline rests primarily with faculty. Attendance at religious services is required.

Summer Programs Remediation, enrichment, advancement programs offered; session focuses on broad, age-appropriate opportunities for child development; held both on and off campus; held at a wide variety of excursions related to weekly themes; accepts boys and girls; open to students from other schools. 47 students usually enrolled. 2014 schedule: May 31 to July 29. Application deadline: April 15.

Tuition and Aid Day student tuition: $8250–$8500. Tuition installment plan (FACTS Tuition Payment Plan, monthly payment plans, individually arranged payment plans, semester payment plan). Merit scholarship grants, need-based scholarship grants available. In 2013–14, 22% of upper-school students received aid; total upper-school merit-scholarship money awarded: $650,000.

Admissions Traditional secondary-level entrance grade is 9. For fall 2013, 12 students applied for upper-level admission, 12 were accepted, 12 enrolled. Otis-Lennon, Stanford Achievement Test, PSAT or SAT for applicants to grade 11 and 12, Woodcock-Johnson Revised Achievement Test and writing sample required. Deadline for receipt of application materials: none. Application fee required: $850. On-campus interview required.

Athletics Interscholastic: baseball (boys), basketball (b,g), cheering (g), football (b), golf (b,g), physical fitness (b), power lifting (b), tennis (b,g), track and field (b,g), volleyball (g); intramural: football (b), physical fitness (b,g), tennis (b,g), volleyball (g); coed interscholastic: soccer; coed intramural: soccer, track and field, weight training. 2 PE instructors, 4 coaches.

Computers Computers are regularly used in college planning, computer applications, creative writing, English, geography, history, journalism, keyboarding, library, mathematics, newspaper, photography, photojournalism, psychology, publications, publishing, research skills, SAT preparation, science, senior seminar, Spanish, technology, writing, yearbook classes. Computer network features include on-campus library services, online commercial services, Internet access, Internet filtering or blocking technology. The school has a published electronic and media policy.

Contact Mrs. Cissy Abernathy, Director of Admission. 903-753-0612 Ext. 236. Fax: 903-753-4812. E-mail: cabernathy@trinityschooloftexas.com. Website: www.trinityschooloftexas.com

TRINITY VALLEY SCHOOL

7500 Dutch Branch Road
Fort Worth, Texas 76132

Head of School: Dr. Gary Krahn

General Information Coeducational day college-preparatory school. Grades K–12. Founded: 1959. Setting: urban. 75-acre campus. 7 buildings on campus. Approved or accredited by Independent Schools Association of the Southwest and Texas Department of Education. Member of National Association of Independent Schools. Endowment: $38 million. Total enrollment: 970. Upper school average class size: 16. Upper school faculty-student ratio: 1:5. There are 170 required school days per year for Upper School students. Upper School students typically attend 5 days per week. The average school day consists of 7 hours and 45 minutes.

Upper School Student Profile Grade 9: 88 students (45 boys, 43 girls); Grade 10: 89 students (49 boys, 40 girls); Grade 11: 83 students (39 boys, 44 girls); Grade 12: 88 students (39 boys, 49 girls).

Faculty School total: 110. In upper school: 27 men, 36 women; 44 have advanced degrees.

Subjects Offered Algebra, American culture, American history, American history-AP, ancient history, ancient world history, art, Asian history, biology, biology-AP, British history, calculus, calculus-AP, ceramics, chemistry, chemistry-AP, Chinese, choir, computer graphics, computer science, computer science-AP, constitutional law, creative writing, debate, digital imaging, economics, economics-AP, English, English language-AP, English literature-AP, environmental science, French, French-AP, geometry, government/civics, humanities, journalism, Latin, Latin-AP, leadership, modern European history, photography, physical education, physics, physics-AP, psychology-AP, Spanish, Spanish-AP, statistics, statistics-AP, technical theater, theater arts, U.S. government, U.S. government and politics-AP, video film production, writing workshop, yearbook.

Graduation Requirements Algebra, American government, American history, arts and fine arts (art, music, dance, drama), biology, chemistry, economics, English, foreign language, geometry, physical education (includes health), physics, pre-calculus, Western civilization, students must complete 60 hours of community service in the U.S.. Community service is required.

Special Academic Programs 22 Advanced Placement exams for which test preparation is offered; honors section; academic accommodation for the gifted, the musically talented, and the artistically talented.

College Admission Counseling 73 students graduated in 2013; 72 went to college, including Southern Methodist University; Texas A&M University; Texas Christian University; The University of Alabama; The University of Texas at Austin; University of Oklahoma. Other: 1 had other specific plans. Mean combined SAT: 1922, mean composite ACT: 28.

Student Life Upper grades have uniform requirement, student council, honor system. Discipline rests equally with students and faculty.

Summer Programs Enrichment, advancement, sports, art/fine arts, rigorous outdoor training, computer instruction programs offered; session focuses on enrichment; held both on and off campus; held at New Mexico and Colorado (backpacking); accepts boys and girls; open to students from other schools. 200 students usually enrolled. 2014 schedule: June 4 to July 27. Application deadline: May 15.

Tuition and Aid Day student tuition: $19,200. Tuition installment plan (monthly payment plans). Need-based scholarship grants available. In 2013–14, 16% of upper-school students received aid. Total amount of financial aid awarded in 2013–14: $764,080.

Admissions Traditional secondary-level entrance grade is 9. For fall 2013, 43 students applied for upper-level admission, 23 were accepted, 17 enrolled. ISEE required. Deadline for receipt of application materials: March 7. Application fee required: $75. Interview required.

Athletics Interscholastic: baseball (boys), basketball (b,g), cross-country running (b,g), field hockey (g), football (b), golf (b,g), lacrosse (b), soccer (b,g), softball (g), tennis (b,g), track and field (b,g), volleyball (b,g). 5 PE instructors, 6 coaches, 2 athletic trainers.

Computers Computers are regularly used in all academic classes. Computer network features include on-campus library services, online commercial services, Internet access, wireless campus network, Internet filtering or blocking technology. Campus intranet, student e-mail accounts, and computer access in designated common areas are available to students. Students grades are available online. The school has a published electronic and media policy.

Contact Judith Kinser, Director of Admissions and Financial Aid. 817-321-0116. Fax: 817-321-0105. E-mail: kinserj@trinityvalleyschool.org. Website: www.trinityvalleyschool.org

TURNING WINDS ACADEMIC INSTITUTE

Bonners Ferry, Idaho
See Special Needs Schools section.

TYLER STREET CHRISTIAN ACADEMY

915 West 9th Street
Dallas, Texas 75208

Head of School: Dr. Karen J. Egger

General Information Coeducational day college-preparatory, general academic, arts, religious studies, and technology school, affiliated with Christian faith. Grades P3–12. Founded: 1972. Setting: urban. 5-acre campus. 2 buildings on campus. Approved or accredited by Association of Christian Schools International, Southern Association of

Colleges and Schools, Texas Private School Accreditation Commission, and Texas Department of Education. Endowment: $120,000. Total enrollment: 198. Upper school average class size: 10. Upper school faculty-student ratio: 1:13. There are 176 required school days per year for Upper School students. Upper School students typically attend 5 days per week. The average school day consists of 7 hours and 40 minutes.

Upper School Student Profile Grade 9: 32 students (14 boys, 18 girls); Grade 10: 12 students (8 boys, 4 girls); Grade 11: 10 students (4 boys, 6 girls); Grade 12: 12 students (7 boys, 5 girls). 75% of students are Christian faith.

Faculty School total: 31. In upper school: 6 men, 8 women; 5 have advanced degrees.

Subjects Offered Advanced Placement courses, algebra, American government, American history, art, art appreciation, art history, arts and crafts, athletic training, ballet, band, bell choir, Bible studies, biology, British literature, British literature (honors), calculus, calculus-AP, cheerleading, chemistry, choir, choral music, Christian education, college admission preparation, college counseling, college planning, community service, composition, computer applications, computer literacy, computer skills, computer technologies, computer-aided design, concert band, concert bell choir, CPR, critical writing, economics, English literature, family living, freshman seminar, geography, geometry, government, grammar, guidance, health, history, Holocaust studies, honors algebra, honors English, honors geometry, human anatomy, human biology, integrated physics, keyboarding, lab science, lab/keyboard, leadership, leadership and service, literature, mathematics-AP, musical productions, physical education, physical science, physics, physiology, pre-calculus, religion, robotics, science, social studies, Spanish, speech communications, student government, track and field, U.S. government, U.S. history, U.S. literature, volleyball, weight training, world geography, world history, world literature, yearbook.

Graduation Requirements Algebra, American government, arts and fine arts (art, music, dance, drama), Bible, biology, calculus, chemistry, computer science, economics, English, geometry, physical education (includes health), physical science, physics, Spanish, speech communications, U.S. history, world geography, world history.

Special Academic Programs International Baccalaureate program; 1 Advanced Placement exam for which test preparation is offered; honors section; independent study; study at local college for college credit.

College Admission Counseling 12 students graduated in 2013; all went to college, including Baylor University; Rice University; Texas A&M University; Texas Tech University; The University of Texas at Arlington; University of North Texas. Mean SAT critical reading: 564, mean SAT math: 506, mean composite ACT: 25. 43% scored over 600 on SAT critical reading, 15% scored over 600 on SAT math, 28% scored over 600 on SAT writing, 15% scored over 1800 on combined SAT, 9% scored over 26 on composite ACT.

Student Life Upper grades have uniform requirement, student council, honor system. Discipline rests primarily with faculty. Attendance at religious services is required.

Summer Programs Session focuses on grades PK-6th summer camp; held on campus; accepts boys and girls; open to students from other schools. 25 students usually enrolled. 2014 schedule: June 4 to August 7. Application deadline: April 27.

Tuition and Aid Day student tuition: $7200. Tuition installment plan (FACTS Tuition Payment Plan). Merit scholarship grants, need-based scholarship grants available. In 2013–14, 66% of upper-school students received aid; total upper-school merit-scholarship money awarded: $2500. Total amount of financial aid awarded in 2013–14: $92,200.

Admissions Traditional secondary-level entrance grade is 9. For fall 2013, 51 students applied for upper-level admission, 49 were accepted, 34 enrolled. Admissions testing, English entrance exam, mathematics proficiency exam and writing sample required. Deadline for receipt of application materials: none. Application fee required: $50. On-campus interview required.

Athletics Interscholastic: ballet (boys, girls), basketball (b,g), cheering (g), dance squad (b,g), football (b), independent competitive sports (b,g), life saving (b,g), martial arts (b,g), modern dance (g), physical training (b,g), strength & conditioning (b,g), track and field (b,g), volleyball (g), weight lifting (b,g), weight training (b,g); coed interscholastic: cooperative games, life saving, physical training. 1 PE instructor, 4 coaches, 1 athletic trainer.

Computers Computers are regularly used in business applications, career exploration, computer applications, data processing, desktop publishing, graphic arts, information technology, introduction to technology, keyboarding, lab/keyboard, library, library skills, literacy, photojournalism, reading, technology, word processing, yearbook classes. Computer network features include on-campus library services, Internet access, Internet filtering or blocking technology, on-campus library services for Accelerated Reader Program. Computer access in designated common areas is available to students. Students grades are available online. The school has a published electronic and media policy.

Contact Mrs. Lynsey Corley, Registrar. 214-941-9717 Ext. 200. Fax: 214-941-0324. E-mail: lynseycorley@tsca.org. Website: www.tsca.org

UNITED MENNONITE EDUCATIONAL INSTITUTE
614 Mersea Road 6, RR 5
Leamington, Ontario N8H 3V8, Canada

Head of School: Mrs. Sonya A. Bedal

General Information Coeducational day college-preparatory, arts, and religious studies school, affiliated with Mennonite Church USA. Grades 9–12. Founded: 1945. Setting: rural. Nearest major city is Windsor, Canada. 12-acre campus. 3 buildings on campus. Approved or accredited by Mennonite Schools Council and Ontario Department of Education. Language of instruction: English. Total enrollment: 48. Upper school average class size: 12. Upper school faculty-student ratio: 1:15. The average school day consists of 6 hours.

Upper School Student Profile Grade 9: 16 students (7 boys, 9 girls); Grade 10: 8 students (6 boys, 2 girls); Grade 11: 9 students (3 boys, 6 girls); Grade 12: 15 students (8 boys, 7 girls). 65% of students are Mennonite Church USA.

Faculty School total: 10. In upper school: 4 men, 6 women; 1 has an advanced degree.

Subjects Offered 20th century physics, advanced chemistry, advanced math, algebra, American history, ancient world history, art, Bible, biology, business studies, career exploration, chemistry, choir, choral music, Christian ethics, church history, civics, communication arts, computer applications, computer studies, computer technologies, English, environmental geography, family studies, film and new technologies, foreign language, French as a second language, German, instrumental music, introduction to theater, mathematics, orchestra, parenting, religious studies, society challenge and change, theater arts.

Graduation Requirements Arts, Canadian geography, Canadian history, careers, civics, English, French, mathematics, physical education (includes health), science.

College Admission Counseling 12 students graduated in 2013; 10 went to college. Other: 1 went to work, 1 had other specific plans.

Student Life Upper grades have specified standards of dress, student council. Discipline rests equally with students and faculty. Attendance at religious services is required.

Tuition and Aid Day student tuition: CAN$6530. Tuition installment plan (monthly payment plans). Tuition reduction for siblings, bursaries, need-based scholarship grants, need-based loans available. In 2013–14, 17% of upper-school students received aid. Total amount of financial aid awarded in 2013–14: CAN$20,000.

Admissions Traditional secondary-level entrance grade is 9. For fall 2013, 20 students applied for upper-level admission, 20 were accepted, 20 enrolled. Deadline for receipt of application materials: none. No application fee required.

Athletics Interscholastic: badminton (boys, girls), baseball (b,g), basketball (b,g), cross-country running (b,g), floor hockey (b,g), golf (b,g), soccer (b), softball (g), volleyball (b,g); intramural: badminton (b,g), baseball (b,g), basketball (b,g), bicycling (b), fitness (b,g), football (b), indoor hockey (b,g), indoor soccer (b,g), outdoor activities (b,g), soccer (b,g), volleyball (b,g); coed intramural: ultimate Frisbee, weight lifting, yoga. 1 PE instructor, 4 coaches.

Computers Computers are regularly used in all classes. Computer network features include on-campus library services, Internet access, wireless campus network, Internet filtering or blocking technology. The school has a published electronic and media policy.

Contact Mrs. Sonya A. Bedal, Principal. 519-326 7448. Fax: 519-326 0278. E-mail: umeiadm@gmail.com. Website: www.umei.ca

UNIVERSITY LIGGETT SCHOOL
1045 Cook Road
Grosse Pointe Woods, Michigan 48236

Head of School: Dr. Joseph P. Healey

General Information Coeducational day college-preparatory, arts, and technology school. Grades PK–12. Founded: 1878. Setting: suburban. Nearest major city is Detroit. 50-acre campus. 4 buildings on campus. Approved or accredited by Independent Schools Association of the Central States. Member of National Association of Independent Schools. Total enrollment: 616. Upper school average class size: 14. Upper school faculty-student ratio: 1:8. There are 170 required school days per year for Upper School students. The average school day consists of 7 hours.

Upper School Student Profile Grade 9: 73 students (36 boys, 37 girls); Grade 10: 75 students (36 boys, 39 girls); Grade 11: 65 students (34 boys, 31 girls); Grade 12: 68 students (34 boys, 34 girls).

Faculty School total: 94. In upper school: 23 men, 16 women; 27 have advanced degrees.

Subjects Offered Algebra, American history, American literature, art, art history, biology, calculus, ceramics, chemistry, creative writing, drama, engineering, English, English literature, environmental science-AP, European history, fine arts, French, geology, geometry, government/civics, Greek, health and wellness, history of jazz, instrumental music, Latin, mathematics, media arts, modern languages, photography, physical education, physical fitness, physics, physiology, psychology, SAT preparation, science, social studies, Spanish, technology, theater, Vietnam, world history.

Graduation Requirements Algebra, arts and fine arts (art, music, dance, drama), biology, chemistry, computer science, English, foreign language, geometry, government, mathematics, physical education (includes health), science, U.S. history, world history, Advanced Research Project. Community service is required.

Special Academic Programs Honors section; independent study; term-away projects; study abroad; academic accommodation for the gifted, the musically talented, and the artistically talented; special instructional classes for deaf students.

College Admission Counseling 77 students graduated in 2013; all went to college, including Boston College; Kalamazoo College; Michigan State University; University of Michigan; Western Michigan University; Williams College. Mean SAT critical reading: 610, mean SAT math: 590, mean SAT writing: 590, mean composite ACT: 27. 54% scored over 600 on SAT critical reading, 43% scored over 600 on SAT math, 54% scored over 600 on SAT writing.

Student Life Upper grades have specified standards of dress, student council, honor system. Discipline rests primarily with faculty.

Summer Programs Remediation, enrichment, sports programs offered; session focuses on SAT preparation; held on campus; accepts boys and girls; open to students from other schools. 400 students usually enrolled. 2014 schedule: June 22 to August 12. Application deadline: none.

Tuition and Aid Day student tuition: $17,880–$22,480. Tuition installment plan (Insured Tuition Payment Plan, monthly payment plans, individually arranged payment plans, 2- and 4-payment plans). Tuition reduction for siblings, merit scholarship grants, need-based scholarship grants, scholarships for children of alumni available. In 2013–14, 35% of upper-school students received aid; total upper-school merit-scholarship money awarded: $250,000. Total amount of financial aid awarded in 2013–14: $2,600,000.

Admissions Traditional secondary-level entrance grade is 9. For fall 2013, 285 students applied for upper-level admission, 72 were accepted, 44 enrolled. ERB CTP III or SSAT required. Deadline for receipt of application materials: none. Application fee required: $50. Interview required.

Athletics Interscholastic: baseball (boys), basketball (b,g), field hockey (g), football (b), golf (b), ice hockey (b,g), lacrosse (b,g), soccer (b,g), softball (g), tennis (b,g), volleyball (g); coed interscholastic: physical training, swimming and diving; coed intramural: aerobics/dance, ultimate Frisbee, weight lifting. 4 PE instructors, 15 coaches, 1 athletic trainer.

Computers Computers are regularly used in all academic classes. Computer network features include on-campus library services, online commercial services, Internet access, wireless campus network, Internet filtering or blocking technology. Campus intranet, student e-mail accounts, and computer access in designated common areas are available to students. Students grades are available online. The school has a published electronic and media policy.

Contact Ms. Anne Sheppard, Assistant Head of Enrollment, Director of Admissions and Financial Aid. 313-884-4444 Ext. 405. Fax: 313-884-1775. E-mail: asheppard@uls.org. Website: www.uls.org

UNIVERSITY OF CHICAGO LABORATORY SCHOOLS

1362 East 59th Street
Chicago, Illinois 60637

Head of School: Dr. David W. Magill

General Information Coeducational day college-preparatory school. Grades N–12. Founded: 1896. Setting: urban. 15-acre campus. 3 buildings on campus. Approved or accredited by Independent Schools Association of the Central States, North Central Association of Colleges and Schools, and Illinois Department of Education. Member of National Association of Independent Schools. Endowment: $17.8 million. Total enrollment: 1,888. Upper school average class size: 16. Upper school faculty-student ratio: 1:10. There are 170 required school days per year for Upper School students. Upper School students typically attend 5 days per week. The average school day consists of 7 hours and 5 minutes.

Upper School Student Profile Grade 9: 134 students (62 boys, 72 girls); Grade 10: 135 students (66 boys, 69 girls); Grade 11: 121 students (59 boys, 62 girls); Grade 12: 125 students (56 boys, 69 girls).

Faculty School total: 233. In upper school: 30 men, 40 women; 59 have advanced degrees.

Subjects Offered Acting, advanced biology, advanced chemistry, African-American history, algebra, American history, art, art history, biology, calculus, calculus-AP, chemistry, Chinese, community service, computer science, computer science-AP, CPR, creative writing, discrete mathematics, drama, drawing, driver education, English, English literature, European history, expository writing, fine arts, French, French-AP, geometry, German, German-AP, government/civics, history, Holocaust, jazz band, journalism, Latin, Mandarin, mathematics, modern European history, music, music theory-AP, newspaper, orchestra, painting, photography, photojournalism, physical education, physics, play production, post-calculus, science, sculpture, social studies, Spanish, Spanish language-AP, Spanish-AP, statistics, statistics-AP, studio art, theater, trigonometry, U.S. history, Web site design, Western civilization, world history, writing, yearbook.

Graduation Requirements Arts and fine arts (art, music, dance, drama), computer science, English, foreign language, mathematics, music, physical education (includes health), science, social studies (includes history). Community service is required.

Special Academic Programs 8 Advanced Placement exams for which test preparation is offered; accelerated programs; independent study; study at local college for college credit.

College Admission Counseling 127 students graduated in 2013; 116 went to college, including Brown University; DePaul University; New York University; Stanford University; University of Chicago; University of Illinois at Urbana–Champaign. Other: 1 had other specific plans. Median SAT critical reading: 661, median SAT math: 695, median SAT writing: 664, median combined SAT: 2020, median composite ACT: 30.

Student Life Upper grades have student council. Discipline rests primarily with faculty.

Summer Programs Enrichment, advancement, sports programs offered; session focuses on advancement of placement in courses; held on campus; accepts boys and girls; open to students from other schools. 125 students usually enrolled. 2014 schedule: June 23 to August 1. Application deadline: May 15.

Tuition and Aid Day student tuition: $28,290. Tuition installment plan (monthly payment plans, quarterly payment plan). Need-based scholarship grants available. In 2013–14, 16% of upper-school students received aid. Total amount of financial aid awarded in 2013–14: $1,182,716.

Admissions Traditional secondary-level entrance grade is 9. For fall 2013, 157 students applied for upper-level admission, 52 were accepted, 26 enrolled. ISEE required. Deadline for receipt of application materials: November 30. Application fee required: $80. On-campus interview required.

Athletics Interscholastic: baseball (boys), basketball (b,g), cross-country running (b,g), indoor track & field (b,g), soccer (b,g), swimming and diving (b,g), tennis (b,g), track and field (b,g), volleyball (g), winter (indoor) track (b,g); intramural: dance squad (g), weight training (b,g); coed interscholastic: cross-country running, fencing, golf; coed intramural: life saving. 12 PE instructors, 31 coaches, 1 athletic trainer.

Computers Computers are regularly used in mathematics, music, newspaper, science, yearbook classes. Computer network features include on-campus library services, Internet access, wireless campus network. Student e-mail accounts and computer access in designated common areas are available to students. Students grades are available online. The school has a published electronic and media policy.

Contact Irene Reed, Executive Director of Admissions and Financial Aid. 773-702-9451. Fax: 773-702-7455. E-mail: ireed@ucls.uchicago.edu. Website: www.ucls.uchicago.edu/

See Close-Up on page 582.

UNIVERSITY OF DETROIT JESUIT HIGH SCHOOL AND ACADEMY

8400 South Cambridge Avenue
Detroit, Michigan 48221

Head of School: Mr. Anthony Trudel

General Information Boys' day college-preparatory, arts, religious studies, and technology school, affiliated with Roman Catholic Church (Jesuit order). Grades 7–12. Founded: 1877. Setting: urban. 12-acre campus. 1 building on campus. Approved or accredited by Jesuit Secondary Education Association, Michigan Association of Non-Public Schools, North Central Association of Colleges and Schools, and Michigan Department of Education. Endowment: $15 million. Total enrollment: 873. Upper school average class size: 22. Upper school faculty-student ratio: 1:14. There are 183 required school days per year for Upper School students. Upper School students typically attend 5 days per week. The average school day consists of 6 hours and 45 minutes.

Upper School Student Profile Grade 9: 212 students (212 boys); Grade 10: 190 students (190 boys); Grade 11: 190 students (190 boys); Grade 12: 160 students (160 boys). 72% of students are Roman Catholic Church (Jesuit order).

Faculty School total: 61. In upper school: 41 men, 20 women; 40 have advanced degrees.

Subjects Offered Acting, African-American history, algebra, American history, American history-AP, American literature, anatomy, art, Bible studies, biochemistry, biology, biology-AP, calculus, calculus-AP, ceramics, chemistry, chemistry-AP, Chinese, Christian and Hebrew scripture, Christian doctrine, Christian education, Christian ethics, Christian studies, Christian testament, church history, comparative religion, computer applications, computer programming, computer-aided design, drawing, earth science, economics, English, English literature, English literature-AP, English-AP, environmental science, ethics, European history, expository writing, French, geography, geometry, government-AP, government/civics, history, history of the Catholic Church, history-AP, Latin, Latin-AP, Mandarin, mathematics, music, physical education, physical science, physics, physics-AP, psychology, public speaking, religion, science, social studies, sociology, Spanish, Spanish-AP, speech, theology, trigonometry, U.S. government and politics-AP, U.S. history, U.S. history-AP, world history, world literature, writing.

Graduation Requirements Arts and fine arts (art, music, dance, drama), business skills (includes word processing), English, foreign language, mathematics, physical education (includes health), public speaking, religion (includes Bible studies and theology), science, social studies (includes history), senior community service program.

Special Academic Programs 14 Advanced Placement exams for which test preparation is offered; honors section; independent study; study at local college for college credit.

College Admission Counseling 156 students graduated in 2012; 155 went to college, including Michigan State University; University of Dayton; University of Michigan; University of Michigan–Dearborn; University of Notre Dame; Wayne State University. Other: 1 had other specific plans. Mean SAT critical reading: 593, mean SAT math: 603, mean SAT writing: 611.

Student Life Upper grades have specified standards of dress, student council, honor system. Discipline rests primarily with faculty. Attendance at religious services is required.

Tuition and Aid Day student tuition: $10,980. Tuition installment plan (FACTS Tuition Payment Plan). Merit scholarship grants, need-based scholarship grants available. In 2012–13, 34% of upper-school students received aid; total upper-school merit-scholarship money awarded: $250,000. Total amount of financial aid awarded in 2012–13: $1,610,000.

Admissions Traditional secondary-level entrance grade is 9. For fall 2012, 500 students applied for upper-level admission, 360 were accepted, 212 enrolled. Scholastic Testing Service High School Placement Test or STS - Educational Development Series required. Deadline for receipt of application materials: none. No application fee required. On-campus interview recommended.

Athletics Interscholastic: baseball, basketball, bowling, cross-country running, diving, football, golf, ice hockey, lacrosse, skiing (downhill), soccer, swimming and diving, tennis, track and field, wrestling; intramural: basketball, bowling, flag football, football, Frisbee, soccer, ultimate Frisbee. 2 PE instructors, 15 coaches, 2 athletic trainers.

Computers Computers are regularly used in all academic, art, history, mathematics, science, speech classes. Computer network features include on-campus library services, online commercial services, Internet access, wireless campus network, Internet filtering or blocking technology. Student e-mail accounts are available to students. Students grades are available online. The school has a published electronic and media policy.

Contact Mr. Atif Lodhi, Director of Admissions. 313-862-5400 Ext. 2380. Fax: 313-862-3299. E-mail: atif.lodhi@uofdjesuit.org. Website: www.uofdjesuit.org/

UNIVERSITY PREP

8000 25th Avenue NE
Seattle, Washington 98115

Head of School: Erica L. Hamlin

General Information Coeducational day college-preparatory, arts, bilingual studies, technology, and global education school; primarily serves students with learning disabilities, individuals with Attention Deficit Disorder, and dyslexic students. Grades 6–12. Founded: 1976. Setting: urban. 6-acre campus. 5 buildings on campus. Approved or accredited by Northwest Accreditation Commission, Northwest Association of Independent Schools, and Washington Department of Education. Member of National Association of Independent Schools. Endowment: $6 million. Total enrollment: 511. Upper school average class size: 17. Upper school faculty-student ratio: 1:9. There are 169 required school days per year for Upper School students. Upper School students typically attend 5 days per week. The average school day consists of 6 hours and 50 minutes.

Upper School Student Profile Grade 9: 80 students (40 boys, 40 girls); Grade 10: 77 students (41 boys, 36 girls); Grade 11: 78 students (40 boys, 38 girls); Grade 12: 67 students (32 boys, 35 girls).

Faculty School total: 59. In upper school: 20 men, 23 women; 30 have advanced degrees.

Subjects Offered 3-dimensional art, advanced chemistry, advanced math, African-American studies, algebra, American government, American history, American literature, applied arts, applied music, art, art and culture, art history, Asian literature, Asian studies, astronomy, athletics, audio visual/media, band, biology, British literature, calculus, career and personal planning, career planning, career/college preparation, chemistry, Chinese, Chinese studies, choir, chorus, civil rights, classical civilization, college counseling, college placement, college planning, community service, comparative government and politics, comparative religion, composition, computer art, computer literacy, computer science, conceptual physics, creative dance, creative drama, creative writing, critical thinking, critical writing, dance, decision making skills, democracy in America, design, digital art, digital photography, diversity studies, drafting, drama, drama performance, dramatic arts, drawing, ecology, economics, electives, English, English composition, English literature, ensembles, environmental education, environmental science, environmental studies, ethnic studies, European history, expository writing, film studies, fine arts, fitness, foreign language, French, freshman seminar, geography, geometry, global studies, golf, government, government/civics, graphic design, health, history, history of religion, independent study, information technology, introduction to technology, Japanese, Japanese history, Japanese studies, jazz ensemble, journalism, languages, Latin American studies, library, life skills, literary magazine, mathematics, media, medieval/Renaissance history, minority studies, multicultural studies, music, music performance, music theory, orchestra, Pacific Northwest seminar, painting, performing arts, personal fitness, philosophy, photography, physical education, physical fitness, physics, play production, play/screen writing, poetry, political science, politics, psychology, public policy,

publishing, research, Russian studies, science, senior thesis, social justice, Spanish, stagecraft, statistics, student publications, theater, theater arts, theater design and production, trigonometry, vocal ensemble, weight training, weightlifting, wilderness education, wilderness experience, women in society, world literature, yearbook.

Graduation Requirements American history, arts and fine arts (art, music, dance, drama), biology, chemistry, English, foreign language, life skills, mathematics, Pacific Northwest seminar, physical education (includes health), physics, science, senior thesis, social studies (includes history). Community service is required.

Special Academic Programs Independent study; term-away projects; domestic exchange program; study abroad; programs in English, mathematics, general development for dyslexic students; special instructional classes for college-bound students with high intellectual potential who have diagnosed specific learning disability.

College Admission Counseling 68 students graduated in 2012; all went to college, including Chapman University; Dartmouth College; Occidental College; Santa Clara University; University of Pennsylvania; University of Washington. Median SAT critical reading: 620, median SAT math: 610, median SAT writing: 620, median combined SAT: 1855, median composite ACT: 28. 60% scored over 600 on SAT critical reading, 52% scored over 600 on SAT math, 60% scored over 600 on SAT writing, 57% scored over 1800 on combined SAT, 64% scored over 26 on composite ACT.

Student Life Upper grades have student council, honor system. Discipline rests equally with students and faculty.

Tuition and Aid Day student tuition: $28,080. Tuition installment plan (Insured Tuition Payment Plan, Key Tuition Payment Plan, monthly payment plans, individually arranged payment plans, Dewar Tuition Refund Plan). Need-based scholarship grants available. In 2012–13, 21% of upper-school students received aid. Total amount of financial aid awarded in 2012–13: $1,392,423.

Admissions Traditional secondary-level entrance grade is 9. For fall 2012, 206 students applied for upper-level admission, 43 were accepted, 23 enrolled. ISEE required. Deadline for receipt of application materials: January 15. Application fee required: $75. On-campus interview required.

Athletics Interscholastic: baseball (boys), basketball (b,g), cross-country running (b,g), flag football (b), Frisbee (b,g), soccer (b,g), softball (g), tennis (b,g), track and field (b,g), volleyball (g); intramural: golf (b,g), ultimate Frisbee (b,g); coed interscholastic: ultimate Frisbee; coed intramural: aerobics, aerobics/dance, backpacking, climbing, dance, fitness, hiking/backpacking, modern dance, outdoor activities, outdoor adventure, outdoor education, outdoor skills, outdoors, rock climbing, skiing (downhill), snowboarding, strength & conditioning, ultimate Frisbee, wall climbing, weight training, wilderness, yoga. 5 PE instructors, 65 coaches, 1 athletic trainer.

Computers Computers are regularly used in all academic, art, creative writing, English, foreign language, geography, history, information technology, journalism, library, mathematics, media, music, photography, publications, publishing, research skills, science, technology, writing, writing, yearbook classes. Computer network features include on-campus library services, online commercial services, Internet access, wireless campus network, Internet filtering or blocking technology, RYOD - Required your on device. Campus intranet, student e-mail accounts, and computer access in designated common areas are available to students. Students grades are available online. The school has a published electronic and media policy.

Contact Melaine Taylor, Associate Director of Admission. 206-523-6407. Fax: 206-525-5320. E-mail: admissionoffice@universityprep.org. Website: www.universityprep.org

UNIVERSITY SCHOOL OF JACKSON

232/240 McClellan Road
Jackson, Tennessee 38305

Head of School: Stuart Hirstein

General Information Coeducational day college-preparatory, arts, and technology school. Grades PK–12. Founded: 1970. Setting: suburban. 130-acre campus. 4 buildings on campus. Approved or accredited by Southern Association of Colleges and Schools and Tennessee Department of Education. Member of National Association of Independent Schools. Endowment: $85,000. Total enrollment: 1,150. Upper school average class size: 20. Upper school faculty-student ratio: 1:13. There are 180 required school days per year for Upper School students. Upper School students typically attend 5 days per week. The average school day consists of 7 hours and 10 minutes.

Upper School Student Profile Grade 9: 94 students (48 boys, 46 girls); Grade 10: 80 students (38 boys, 42 girls); Grade 11: 74 students (33 boys, 41 girls); Grade 12: 67 students (32 boys, 35 girls).

Faculty School total: 94. In upper school: 15 men, 20 women; 30 have advanced degrees.

Subjects Offered 3-dimensional art, 3-dimensional design, accounting, acting, advanced biology, advanced chemistry, advanced math, Advanced Placement courses, advanced studio art-AP, algebra, American history, American literature, anatomy, anatomy and physiology, art, band, biology, biology-AP, broadcast journalism, calculus, calculus-AP, character education, chemistry, chemistry-AP, chorus, computer applications, computer programming, computer science, creative writing, current events, dramatic arts, ecology, economics, economics and history, English, English language-AP, English literature and composition-AP, English literature-AP, environmental science, environmental science-AP, European history, fine arts, French, geography, geology, geometry, government, government/civics, honors algebra, honors English, honors geometry, humanities, keyboarding, macroeconomics-AP, mathematics, music theory, music theory-AP, music-AP, performing arts, photography, physical education, physical science, physics, pre-calculus, psychology, science, social studies, Spanish, Spanish language-AP, studio art-AP, trigonometry, U.S. history, U.S. history-AP, vocal ensemble, world history, world religions, yearbook.

Graduation Requirements Arts and fine arts (art, music, dance, drama), computer science, English, foreign language, mathematics, science, social studies (includes history), 50 hours of community service.

Special Academic Programs 11 Advanced Placement exams for which test preparation is offered; honors section; academic accommodation for the gifted, the musically talented, and the artistically talented; ESL (10 students enrolled).

College Admission Counseling 88 students graduated in 2013; all went to college, including Mississippi State University; Rhodes College; Tennessee Technological University; The University of Tennessee; Union University; University of Arkansas. Median SAT critical reading: 501, median SAT math: 539, median SAT writing: 542, median combined SAT: 1582, median composite ACT: 26. 20% scored over 600 on SAT critical reading, 20% scored over 600 on SAT math, 20% scored over 600 on SAT writing, 20% scored over 1800 on combined SAT, 45% scored over 26 on composite ACT.

Student Life Upper grades have uniform requirement, student council, honor system. Discipline rests equally with students and faculty.

Summer Programs Remediation, enrichment, sports, art/fine arts, computer instruction programs offered; session focuses on enrichment and remediation; held on campus; accepts boys and girls; open to students from other schools. 500 students usually enrolled. 2014 schedule: June 1 to July 31. Application deadline: none.

Tuition and Aid Day student tuition: $6400–$8470. Tuition installment plan (FACTS Tuition Payment Plan, monthly payment plans, quarterly payment plan). Tuition reduction for siblings, need-based scholarship grants, need-based financial aid available. In 2013–14, 3% of upper-school students received aid. Total amount of financial aid awarded in 2013–14: $150,000.

Admissions Traditional secondary-level entrance grade is 9. For fall 2013, 21 students applied for upper-level admission, 16 were accepted, 15 enrolled. Math Placement Exam, Otis-Lennon School Ability Test and writing sample required. Deadline for receipt of application materials: none. Application fee required: $50. On-campus interview required.

Athletics Interscholastic: baseball (boys), basketball (b,g), cheering (g), cross-country running (b,g), football (b), golf (b,g), physical fitness (b,g), soccer (b,g), softball (g), tennis (b,g), track and field (b,g), volleyball (g), weight lifting (b,g), weight training (b,g); intramural: bowling (b,g), in-line hockey (b); coed intramural: bowling. 2 coaches.

Computers Computers are regularly used in art, English, foreign language, history, journalism, keyboarding, music, science, technology, theater arts, word processing, writing, yearbook classes. Computer network features include on-campus library services, online commercial services, Internet access, wireless campus network, Internet filtering or blocking technology. Campus intranet and computer access in designated common areas are available to students. Students grades are available online. The school has a published electronic and media policy.

Contact Kay Shearin, Director of Admissions. 731-660-1692. Fax: 731-668-6910. E-mail: kshearin@usjbruins.org. Website: www.usjbruins.org

UNIVERSITY SCHOOL OF MILWAUKEE

2100 West Fairy Chasm Road
Milwaukee, Wisconsin 53217

Head of School: Laura J. Fuller

General Information Coeducational day college-preparatory, arts, and technology school. Grades PK–12. Founded: 1851. Setting: suburban. 131-acre campus. 2 buildings on campus. Approved or accredited by Independent Schools Association of the Central States and Wisconsin Department of Education. Member of National Association of Independent Schools and Secondary School Admission Test Board. Endowment: $47 million. Total enrollment: 1,120. Upper school average class size: 15. Upper school faculty-student ratio: 1:9. There are 178 required school days per year for Upper School students. Upper School students typically attend 5 days per week. The average school day consists of 6 hours and 45 minutes.

Upper School Student Profile Grade 9: 91 students (43 boys, 48 girls); Grade 10: 101 students (61 boys, 40 girls); Grade 11: 88 students (43 boys, 45 girls); Grade 12: 96 students (48 boys, 48 girls).

Faculty School total: 121. In upper school: 24 men, 30 women; 35 have advanced degrees.

Subjects Offered Algebra, American history, American literature, art, art history, band, biology, calculus, chemistry, computer programming, computer science, concert choir, discrete mathematics, drama, drawing, economics, English, English literature, European history, expository writing, French, geometry, health, Latin, mathematics, music, orchestra, painting, photography, physical education, physics, printmaking, psychology, SAT/ACT preparation, sculpture, Spanish, statistics, theater, U.S. history, world history, world literature.

Graduation Requirements Arts and fine arts (art, music, dance, drama), English, foreign language, history, mathematics, physical education (includes health), science, 40 hours of community service.

Special Academic Programs Advanced Placement exam preparation; honors section; independent study; study at local college for college credit.

College Admission Counseling 76 students graduated in 2013; all went to college, including Elon University; High Point University; Marquette University; Miami University; Saint Louis University; University of Wisconsin–Madison. Mean SAT critical reading: 653, mean SAT math: 638, mean SAT writing: 642, mean combined SAT: 1934, mean composite ACT: 29. 71% scored over 600 on SAT critical reading, 71% scored over 600 on SAT math, 68% scored over 600 on SAT writing, 71% scored over 1800 on combined SAT, 80% scored over 26 on composite ACT.

Student Life Upper grades have specified standards of dress, student council, honor system. Discipline rests equally with students and faculty.

Summer Programs Enrichment, sports, art/fine arts, computer instruction programs offered; session focuses on reading, writing, math, science, sports, visual arts, music, drama, and computer enrichment/instruction; held on campus; accepts boys and girls; open to students from other schools. 1,400 students usually enrolled. 2014 schedule: June 10 to August 16. Application deadline: none.

Tuition and Aid Day student tuition: $21,907. Tuition installment plan (SMART Tuition Payment Plan). Merit scholarship grants, need-based scholarship grants available. In 2013–14, 26% of upper-school students received aid; total upper-school merit-scholarship money awarded: $188,167. Total amount of financial aid awarded in 2013–14: $1,025,310.

Admissions Traditional secondary-level entrance grade is 9. For fall 2013, 66 students applied for upper-level admission, 39 were accepted, 26 enrolled. ERB Achievement Test required. Deadline for receipt of application materials: January 3. Application fee required: $50. Interview required.

Athletics Interscholastic: baseball (boys), basketball (b,g), cross-country running (b,g), dance team (g), diving (b,g), field hockey (g), football (b), golf (b), ice hockey (b,g), lacrosse (b), skiing (downhill) (b,g), soccer (b,g), swimming and diving (b,g), tennis (b,g), track and field (b,g), volleyball (g). 2 PE instructors, 46 coaches, 2 athletic trainers.

Computers Computers are regularly used in college planning, creative writing, English, foreign language, history, journalism, mathematics, science, yearbook classes. Computer network features include on-campus library services, online commercial services, Internet access, wireless campus network, Internet filtering or blocking technology. Student e-mail accounts are available to students. Students grades are available online. The school has a published electronic and media policy.

Contact Kathleen Friedman, Director of Admissions. 414-540-3321. Fax: 414-352-8076. E-mail: kfriedman@usmk12.org. Website: www.usmk12.org

UNIVERSITY SCHOOL OF NOVA SOUTHEASTERN UNIVERSITY

3375 SW 75 Avenue
Lower School Building
Fort Lauderdale, Florida 33314

Head of School: Dr. Jerome S. Chermak

General Information Coeducational day college-preparatory, arts, and technology school. Grades PK–12. Founded: 1970. Setting: suburban. 300-acre campus. 4 buildings on campus. Approved or accredited by Association of Independent Schools of Florida, Southern Association of Colleges and Schools, and Florida Department of Education. Member of National Association of Independent Schools. Endowment: $750,000. Total enrollment: 1,845. Upper school average class size: 20. Upper school faculty-student ratio: 1:18. There are 180 required school days per year for Upper School students. Upper School students typically attend 5 days per week. The average school day consists of 6 hours.

Upper School Student Profile Grade 9: 167 students (84 boys, 83 girls); Grade 10: 188 students (100 boys, 88 girls); Grade 11: 180 students (99 boys, 81 girls); Grade 12: 179 students (89 boys, 90 girls).

Faculty School total: 181. In upper school: 26 men, 35 women; 43 have advanced degrees.

Subjects Offered Advanced Placement courses, advanced studio art-AP, algebra, American government, American history, American literature, anatomy, art, band, biology, calculus, ceramics, chemistry, chorus, community service, computer programming, computer science, creative writing, debate, directing, drawing and design, economics, English, English literature, environmental science, expository writing, fine arts, forensics, French, geometry, grammar, guitar, journalism, keyboarding, media production, music, music appreciation, music theory, orchestra, performing arts, personal fitness, physical education, physics, portfolio art, pre-calculus, psychology, public speaking, Spanish, speech, theater, trigonometry, video film production, world geography, world history, world literature, writing.

Graduation Requirements Art, computer science, electives, English, expository writing, foreign language, health education, journalism, mathematics, music, personal fitness, physical education (includes health), public speaking, science, social studies (includes history), speech and debate. Community service is required.

Special Academic Programs Advanced Placement exam preparation; honors section; accelerated programs; independent study; term-away projects; study at local college for college credit; academic accommodation for the gifted, the musically talented, and the artistically talented; remedial reading and/or remedial writing; ESL (5 students enrolled).

College Admission Counseling 166 students graduated in 2013; all went to college, including Boston University; Florida State University; University of Central Florida; University of Florida; University of Miami; University of Pennsylvania.

Student Life Upper grades have uniform requirement, student council. Discipline rests primarily with faculty.

Summer Programs Remediation, enrichment, advancement, sports, art/fine arts programs offered; session focuses on sports, arts, and academics; held on campus; accepts boys and girls; open to students from other schools. 400 students usually enrolled. 2014 schedule: June 4 to August 11. Application deadline: none.

Tuition and Aid Day student tuition: $20,500. Tuition installment plan (Tuition management Systems). Tuition reduction for siblings, need-based scholarship grants available. In 2013–14, 15% of upper-school students received aid. Total amount of financial aid awarded in 2013–14: $1,500,000.

Admissions Traditional secondary-level entrance grade is 9. For fall 2013, 175 students applied for upper-level admission, 116 were accepted, 75 enrolled. SSAT required. Deadline for receipt of application materials: none. Application fee required: $100. Interview required.

Athletics Interscholastic: baseball (boys), basketball (b,g), cheering (g), crew (b,g), cross-country running (b,g), dance team (g), diving (b,g), football (b,g), golf (b,g), ice hockey (b), lacrosse (b,g), soccer (b,g), softball (g), swimming and diving (b,g), tennis (b,g), track and field (b,g), volleyball (b,g), wrestling (b); coed interscholastic: cross-country running, dance. 3 PE instructors, 43 coaches, 1 athletic trainer.

Computers Computer network features include on-campus library services, online commercial services, Internet access, wireless campus network, Internet filtering or blocking technology. Student e-mail accounts and computer access in designated common areas are available to students. Students grades are available online. The school has a published electronic and media policy.

Contact Ms. Allison Musso, Coordinator of Admissions. 954-262-4405. Fax: 954-262-3691. E-mail: amusso@nova.edu. Website: www.uschool.nova.edu

UPPER CANADA COLLEGE

200 Lonsdale Road
Toronto, Ontario M4V 1W6, Canada

Head of School: Dr. James Power

General Information Boys' boarding and day college-preparatory, arts, bilingual studies, technology, and International Baccalaureate school. Boarding grades 8–12, day grades K–12. Founded: 1829. Setting: urban. Students are housed in single-sex dormitories. 16-hectare campus. 4 buildings on campus. Approved or accredited by Canadian Association of Independent Schools, Conference of Independent Schools of Ontario, International Baccalaureate Organization, Ontario Ministry of Education, The Association of Boarding Schools, and Ontario Department of Education. Affiliate member of National Association of Independent Schools; member of Secondary School Admission Test Board. Language of instruction: English. Total enrollment: 1,190. Upper school average class size: 20. Upper school faculty-student ratio: 1:8. There are 210 required school days per year for Upper School students. Upper School students typically attend 5 days per week. The average school day consists of 6 hours and 30 minutes.

Upper School Student Profile Grade 6: 80 students (80 boys); Grade 7: 120 students (120 boys); Grade 8: 125 students (125 boys); Grade 9: 145 students (145 boys); Grade 10: 159 students (159 boys); Grade 11: 165 students (165 boys); Grade 12: 165 students (165 boys). 15% of students are boarding students. 90% are province residents. 3 provinces are represented in upper school student body. 45% are international students. International students from Bangladesh, China, Hong Kong, Russian Federation, and United States; 21 other countries represented in student body.

Faculty School total: 138. In upper school: 57 men, 28 women; 17 reside on campus.

Subjects Offered 3-dimensional design, advanced biology, advanced chemistry, advanced math, algebra, all academic, American history, art, athletics, biology, calculus, career and personal planning, chemistry, Chinese, civics, community service, computer multimedia, computer programming, computer science, creative arts, creative writing, digital art, drama, economics, English, English literature, environmental science, equality and freedom, European history, expository writing, film, film studies, fine arts, French, functions, geography, geometry, German, health, history, instrumental music, International Baccalaureate courses, Latin, mathematics, music, physical education, physics, science, social sciences, social studies, Spanish, theater, theater arts, theory of knowledge, trigonometry, visual arts, world history, writing.

Graduation Requirements English, foreign language, mathematics, science, social sciences. Community service is required.

Special Academic Programs International Baccalaureate program; honors section; term-away projects; study abroad.

College Admission Counseling 165 students graduated in 2013; 157 went to college, including Georgetown University; McGill University; Queen's University at Kingston; The University of Western Ontario; University of Toronto; University of Waterloo. Other: 3 had other specific plans.

Student Life Upper grades have specified standards of dress, student council. Discipline rests equally with students and faculty.

Summer Programs Enrichment, advancement, art/fine arts, computer instruction programs offered; session focuses on enrichment and credit courses; held on campus; accepts boys and girls; open to students from other schools. 300 students usually enrolled. 2014 schedule: June 15 to August 30. Application deadline: none.

Tuition and Aid Day student tuition: CAN$32,150; 7-day tuition and room/board: CAN$52,010–CAN$58,510. Tuition installment plan (twice annual payment plan or full-payment discount plan). Bursaries, merit scholarship grants, need-based scholarship grants, need-based financial assistance available. In 2013–14, 15% of upper-school students received aid; total upper-school merit-scholarship money awarded: CAN$50,000. Total amount of financial aid awarded in 2013–14: CAN$3,700,000.

Admissions Traditional secondary-level entrance grade is 9. SSAT or SSAT, ERB, PSAT, SAT, PLAN or ACT required. Deadline for receipt of application materials: none. Application fee required: CAN$200. Interview required.

Athletics Interscholastic: aquatics, badminton, baseball, basketball, crew, cricket, cross-country running, dance, football, golf, hockey, ice hockey, lacrosse, rowing, rugby, running, soccer, softball, squash, swimming and diving, tennis, track and field, volleyball; intramural: alpine skiing, backpacking, ball hockey, basketball, bicycling, canoeing/kayaking, climbing, combined training, cooperative games, fencing, field hockey, floor hockey, hiking/backpacking, hockey, ice hockey, in-line hockey, indoor hockey, indoor soccer, kayaking, martial arts, mountain biking, outdoor activities, outdoor adventure, outdoor education, outdoor recreation, outdoor skills, physical training, power lifting, rock climbing, ropes courses, self defense, skiing (downhill), snowboarding, soccer, softball, street hockey, strength & conditioning, tai chi, volleyball, weight training, wilderness, winter soccer.

Computers Computers are regularly used in business education, computer applications, digital applications, graphic arts, graphic design, graphics, media arts, technology classes. Computer network features include on-campus library services, online commercial services, Internet access, wireless campus network, Internet filtering or blocking technology, laptop school; laptop use across all subjects. Campus intranet, student e-mail accounts, and computer access in designated common areas are available to students. The school has a published electronic and media policy.

Contact Tricia Rankin, Associate Director of Admission. 416-488-1125 Ext. 2221. Fax: 416-484-8618. E-mail: trankin@ucc.on.ca. Website: www.ucc.on.ca

THE URSULINE ACADEMY OF DALLAS

4900 Walnut Hill Lane
Dallas, Texas 75229

Head of School: Mrs. Birgitt Lopez

General Information Girls' day college-preparatory, arts, religious studies, and technology school, affiliated with Roman Catholic Church. Grades 9–12. Founded: 1874. Setting: urban. 26-acre campus. 5 buildings on campus. Approved or accredited by Independent Schools Association of the Southwest, National Catholic Education Association, Texas Catholic Conference, The College Board, and Texas Department of Education. Total enrollment: 800. Upper school average class size: 18. Upper school faculty-student ratio: 1:10.

Upper School Student Profile Grade 9: 200 students (200 girls); Grade 10: 200 students (200 girls); Grade 11: 200 students (200 girls); Grade 12: 200 students (200 girls). 85% of students are Roman Catholic.

Faculty School total: 92. In upper school: 17 men, 75 women; 71 have advanced degrees.

Subjects Offered 20th century history, Advanced Placement courses, algebra, anatomy, anatomy and physiology, Arabic, band, biology, calculus, ceramics, chemistry, Chinese, choir, Christian and Hebrew scripture, community service, comparative government and politics, comparative religion, computer programming, computer science, concert choir, creative writing, current events, dance, design, digital imaging, digital photography, discrete mathematics, drama, drawing, economics, English literature, environmental science, ethics, European history, fitness, French, geography, geology, geometry, government, government/civics, graphic design, health and wellness, journalism, Mandarin, newspaper, oceanography, orchestra, painting, peer ministry, photography, physical education, physics, pre-calculus, printmaking, psychology, social justice, Spanish, speech, statistics, theater, theology, U.S. history, U.S. literature, Web authoring, Western civilization, world history, world literature, yearbook.

Graduation Requirements Arts and fine arts (art, music, dance, drama), computer science, English, foreign language, mathematics, physical education (includes health), religion (includes Bible studies and theology), science, social studies (includes history), speech. Community service is required.

Special Academic Programs Advanced Placement exam preparation; honors section; independent study.

College Admission Counseling 191 students graduated in 2013; all went to college. Mean SAT critical reading: 619, mean SAT math: 619, mean SAT writing: 639, mean combined SAT: 1877, mean composite ACT: 28.

Student Life Upper grades have uniform requirement, student council, honor system. Discipline rests equally with students and faculty. Attendance at religious services is required.

Summer Programs Remediation, advancement, art/fine arts, computer instruction programs offered; session focuses on remediation and advancement; held on campus;

accepts girls; not open to students from other schools. 200 students usually enrolled. 2014 schedule: June 5 to July 2. Application deadline: April 16.

Tuition and Aid Day student tuition: $17,400. Tuition installment plan (individually arranged payment plans, annual, semi-annual, and monthly (by bank draft) payment plans). Merit scholarship grants, need-based scholarship grants available. In 2013–14, 23% of upper-school students received aid; total upper-school merit-scholarship money awarded: $68,000. Total amount of financial aid awarded in 2013–14: $898,100.

Admissions Traditional secondary-level entrance grade is 9. For fall 2013, 400 students applied for upper-level admission, 210 enrolled. ISEE required. Deadline for receipt of application materials: January 10. Application fee required: $60. Interview required.

Athletics Interscholastic: basketball, cheering, crew, cross-country running, diving, drill team, golf, lacrosse, soccer, softball, swimming and diving, tennis, track and field, volleyball; intramural: crew, drill team. 3 PE instructors, 15 coaches, 1 athletic trainer.

Computers Computers are regularly used in all classes. Computer network features include on-campus library services, online commercial services, Internet access, wireless campus network. Campus intranet and student e-mail accounts are available to students. Students grades are available online.

Contact Mrs. Jill Tilden, Admissions Assistant. 469-232-1804. Fax: 469-232-1836. E-mail: jtilden@ursulinedallas.org. Website: www.ursulinedallas.org

VALLE CATHOLIC HIGH SCHOOL

40 North Fourth Street
Ste. Genevieve, Missouri 63670

Head of School: Dr. Mark Gilligan

General Information Coeducational day college-preparatory, arts, business, vocational, religious studies, and technology school, affiliated with Roman Catholic Church. Grades 9–12. Founded: 1837. Setting: small town. Nearest major city is St. Louis. 3-acre campus. 4 buildings on campus. Approved or accredited by North Central Association of Colleges and Schools and Missouri Department of Education. Endowment: $2 million. Total enrollment: 152. Upper school average class size: 15. Upper school faculty-student ratio: 1:9. There are 171 required school days per year for Upper School students. Upper School students typically attend 5 days per week. The average school day consists of 6 hours and 30 minutes.

Upper School Student Profile Grade 9: 42 students (20 boys, 22 girls); Grade 10: 29 students (20 boys, 9 girls); Grade 11: 42 students (20 boys, 22 girls); Grade 12: 39 students (16 boys, 23 girls). 98% of students are Roman Catholic.

Faculty School total: 14. In upper school: 5 men, 9 women; 8 have advanced degrees.

Subjects Offered Accounting, advanced chemistry, advanced computer applications, advanced math, algebra, American democracy, American history, American literature, analysis and differential calculus, anatomy and physiology, architectural drawing, art, art history, band, biology, British literature, business, business applications, business law, business studies, calculus, calculus-AP, Catholic belief and practice, chemistry-AP, Christian and Hebrew scripture, Christian scripture, church history, civics, civics/free enterprise, classics, communications, comparative religion, composition, computer applications, computer multimedia, computer science, computer skills, concert band, consumer economics, consumer law, drafting, drama, drama performance, drawing, economics, economics and history, English, entrepreneurship, environmental science, foreign language, geography, geometry, history of the Catholic Church, honors algebra, honors English, honors U.S. history, human anatomy, marching band, math analysis, mathematics, media communications, moral theology, novels, orchestra, painting, peace and justice, physical education, physics, practical arts, psychology, religion, science, social studies, sociology, Spanish, technical drawing, U.S. government, values and decisions, visual arts, Western civilization, yearbook.

Graduation Requirements Advanced math, algebra, American history, American literature, biology, Catholic belief and practice, chemistry, Christian and Hebrew scripture, civics, English, English composition, ethical decision making, foreign language, geometry, government/civics, history of the Catholic Church, mathematics, physical education (includes health), practical arts, religion (includes Bible studies and theology), science, senior composition, social justice, social studies (includes history), Spanish, 80 hours of community service.

Special Academic Programs Honors section; study at local college for college credit; academic accommodation for the gifted, the musically talented, and the artistically talented; remedial reading and/or remedial writing; remedial math.

College Admission Counseling 23 students graduated in 2013; all went to college, including Fontbonne University; Missouri State University; Saint Louis University; Southeast Missouri State University; Truman State University; University of Missouri. Mean SAT critical reading: 720, mean SAT math: 780, mean composite ACT: 24. 100% scored over 600 on SAT critical reading, 100% scored over 600 on SAT math, 26% scored over 26 on composite ACT.

Student Life Upper grades have uniform requirement, student council, honor system. Discipline rests primarily with faculty. Attendance at religious services is required.

Summer Programs Remediation, enrichment, advancement programs offered; session focuses on advancement and remediation/make-up; held on campus; accepts boys and girls; not open to students from other schools. 2 students usually enrolled. 2014 schedule: June 3 to July 31.

Tuition and Aid Day student tuition: $3800. Tuition installment plan (The Tuition Plan, monthly payment plans, individually arranged payment plans, tuition assistance through the St. Louis Archdiocese and Scholarships available through the School). Tuition reduction for siblings, merit scholarship grants, need-based scholarship grants, tuition relief funds available from St. Louis Archdiocese available. In 2013–14, 25% of upper-school students received aid; total upper-school merit-scholarship money awarded: $10,000. Total amount of financial aid awarded in 2013–14: $165,000.

Admissions Traditional secondary-level entrance grade is 9. For fall 2013, 43 students applied for upper-level admission, 43 were accepted, 42 enrolled. Any standardized test, school placement exam and writing sample required. Deadline for receipt of application materials: none. Application fee required: $25. Interview recommended.

Athletics Interscholastic: baseball (boys), basketball (b,g), dance team (g), drill team (g), football (b), track and field (b,g), volleyball (g), weight training (b); coed interscholastic: cheering, cross-country running, golf, physical training, strength & conditioning, weight lifting. 1 PE instructor.

Computers Computers are regularly used in accounting, business, career exploration, college planning, English, geography, history, humanities, journalism, mathematics, psychology, science, Spanish, writing, yearbook classes. Computer network features include Internet access, wireless campus network, Internet filtering or blocking technology. Student e-mail accounts and computer access in designated common areas are available to students. Students grades are available online. The school has a published electronic and media policy.

Contact Mrs. Dawn C. Basler, Registrar. 573-883-7496 Ext. 242. Fax: 573-883-9142. E-mail: baslerd@valleschools.org. Website: www.valleschools.org

VALLEY CHRISTIAN HIGH SCHOOL

100 Skyway Drive
San Jose, California 95111

Head of School: Dr. Clifford Daugherty

General Information Coeducational day and distance learning college-preparatory, arts, religious studies, technology, Conservatory of the Arts, and Applied Math, Science and Engineering Institute school, affiliated with Christian faith. Grades K–12. Distance learning grades 8–12. Founded: 1960. Setting: suburban. 53-acre campus. 6 buildings on campus. Approved or accredited by Association of Christian Schools International, Western Association of Schools and Colleges, and California Department of Education. Total enrollment: 2,475. Upper school average class size: 28. Upper school faculty-student ratio: 1:17. There are 174 required school days per year for Upper School students. Upper School students typically attend 5 days per week. The average school day consists of 6 hours and 45 minutes.

Upper School Student Profile Grade 9: 380 students (198 boys, 182 girls); Grade 10: 340 students (172 boys, 168 girls); Grade 11: 380 students (195 boys, 185 girls); Grade 12: 336 students (176 boys, 160 girls). 85% of students are Christian.

Faculty School total: 146. In upper school: 40 men, 51 women; 26 have advanced degrees.

Subjects Offered 20th century American writers, acting, advanced chemistry, advanced computer applications, advanced math, Advanced Placement courses, advanced studio art-AP, aerospace education, algebra, American history, American literature, American sign language, anatomy and physiology, ancient world history, applied music, art, audio visual/media, Basic programming, Bible, Bible studies, biology, biology-AP, biotechnology, British literature-AP, broadcasting, calculus-AP, career and personal planning, career planning, cheerleading, chemistry, chemistry-AP, Chinese, choir, choral music, choreography, Christian doctrine, Christian ethics, Christian scripture, Christian studies, college admission preparation, college counseling, college planning, comparative political systems-AP, composition-AP, computer art, computer literacy, computer music, computer programming, computer science-AP, computer-aided design, concert choir, consumer mathematics, critical studies in film, dance, dance performance, digital art, drama, drama performance, dramatic arts, electronics, engineering, English, English language and composition-AP, English literature-AP, environmental science-AP, European history-AP, film appreciation, film studies, filmmaking, finite math, foreign language, French, French studies, geometry, global studies, government, grammar, guitar, health education, health science, history, history of music, honors English, honors U.S. history, honors world history, HTML design, instrumental music, introduction to theater, Japanese, Japanese as Second Language, jazz band, jazz dance, jazz ensemble, journalism, keyboarding, Latin, leadership, leadership and service, literature and composition-AP, macro/microeconomics-AP, Mandarin, marching band, marine biology, mathematics, mathematics-AP, Microsoft, music theater, music theory-AP, musical productions, musical theater, photo shop, photojournalism, physical science, physics, physics-AP, play/screen writing, pre-algebra, pre-calculus, radio broadcasting, SAT preparation, sign language, Spanish, Spanish-AP, stage design, statistics, statistics-AP, student government, studio art-AP, symphonic band, tap dance, technical theater, telecommunications, theater arts, theater production, trigonometry, U.S. government, U.S. government and politics-AP, U.S. history, U.S. history-AP, video film production, vocal ensemble, weight training, wind ensemble, world history, yearbook.

Graduation Requirements Arts and fine arts (art, music, dance, drama), Bible studies, biology, Christian and Hebrew scripture, Christian doctrine, Christian studies, computers, economics, economics and history, English, English composition, English literature, foreign language, global studies, health and wellness, mathematics, physical education (includes health), physical science, science, technology, U.S. government, U.S. history, world geography, world history.

Special Academic Programs 22 Advanced Placement exams for which test preparation is offered; honors section; academic accommodation for the musically talented and the artistically talented; programs in English, mathematics, general development for dyslexic students.

College Admission Counseling 326 students graduated in 2013; 324 went to college, including Azusa Pacific University; California Polytechnic State University, San Luis Obispo; California State University, Chico; San Jose State University; University of California, Berkeley; University of California, Davis. Other: 1 entered military service. Median SAT critical reading: 540, median SAT math: 530, median SAT writing: 590, median combined SAT: 1660. 35% scored over 600 on SAT critical reading, 38% scored over 600 on SAT math, 32% scored over 600 on SAT writing, 31% scored over 1800 on combined SAT.

Student Life Upper grades have specified standards of dress, student council, honor system. Discipline rests primarily with faculty.

Summer Programs Remediation, enrichment, advancement, sports, art/fine arts, computer instruction programs offered; session focuses on advancement, remediation, and enrichment; held on campus; accepts boys and girls; open to students from other schools. 500 students usually enrolled. 2014 schedule: June 21 to July 30. Application deadline: none.

Tuition and Aid Day student tuition: $16,176. Tuition installment plan (FACTS Tuition Payment Plan). Need-based scholarship grants available. In 2013–14, 20% of upper-school students received aid. Total amount of financial aid awarded in 2013–14: $1,300,000.

Admissions Traditional secondary-level entrance grade is 9. For fall 2013, 448 students applied for upper-level admission, 353 were accepted, 245 enrolled. Admissions testing, essay, Iowa Subtests, mathematics proficiency exam, school's own test or TOEFL required. Deadline for receipt of application materials: none. Application fee required: $70. Interview required.

Athletics Interscholastic: aquatics (boys, girls), baseball (b), basketball (b,g), cheering (b,g), cross-country running (b,g), dance squad (b,g), dance team (b), diving (b,g), football (b), golf (b,g), ice hockey (b,g), soccer (b,g), softball (g), swimming and diving (b,g), tennis (b,g), track and field (b,g), volleyball (b,g), water polo (b,g), weight training (b,g), wrestling (b); intramural: weight training (b,g). 3 PE instructors, 23 coaches, 2 athletic trainers.

Computers Computers are regularly used in aerospace science, Bible studies, college planning, computer applications, digital applications, engineering, foreign language, graphic arts, graphic design, journalism, keyboarding, lab/keyboard, library, mathematics, media arts, music, music technology, news writing, newspaper, photography, photojournalism, research skills, science, technology, typing, video film production, Web site design, word processing, writing, yearbook classes. Computer network features include on-campus library services, Internet access, wireless campus network, Internet filtering or blocking technology, ten online classes, through two online learning labs. Campus intranet, student e-mail accounts, and computer access in designated common areas are available to students. Students grades are available online. The school has a published electronic and media policy.

Contact Alana James, High School Admissions Coordinator. 408-513-2512. Fax: 408-513-2517. E-mail: ajames@vcs.net. Website: www.vcs.net

VALLEY FORGE MILITARY ACADEMY & COLLEGE

1001 Eagle Road
Wayne, Pennsylvania 19087-3695

Head of School: Col. James J. Doyle, USMC-Retd.

General Information Boys' boarding and day college-preparatory, arts, business, religious studies, bilingual studies, technology, music, and military school. Boarding grades 7–PG, day grades 7–12. Founded: 1928. Setting: suburban. Nearest major city is Philadelphia. Students are housed in single-sex dormitories. 100-acre campus. 83 buildings on campus. Approved or accredited by Middle States Association of Colleges and Schools, The Association of Boarding Schools, and Pennsylvania Department of Education. Member of National Association of Independent Schools and Secondary School Admission Test Board. Endowment: $12 million. Total enrollment: 248. Upper school average class size: 12. Upper school faculty-student ratio: 1:11. There are 175 required school days per year for Upper School students. Upper School students typically attend 5 days per week. The average school day consists of 5 hours and 50 minutes.

Upper School Student Profile Grade 9: 34 students (34 boys); Grade 10: 37 students (37 boys); Grade 11: 74 students (74 boys); Grade 12: 59 students (59 boys); Postgraduate: 23 students (23 boys). 100% of students are boarding students. 30% are state residents. 35 states are represented in upper school student body. 15% are international students. International students from China, Egypt, Mexico, Republic of Korea, Russian Federation, and Saudi Arabia; 29 other countries represented in student body.

Faculty School total: 30. In upper school: 16 men, 12 women; 18 have advanced degrees; 14 reside on campus.

Subjects Offered ACT preparation, algebra, American government, American history-AP, anatomy and physiology, ancient world history, applied music, art, biology,

calculus, chemistry, Chinese, computer programming, creative writing, driver education, earth science, English, English literature and composition-AP, ESL, ESL, European history, French, French studies, geometry, government/civics, health, health education, honors geometry, honors U.S. history, instrumental music, Latin, mathematics, modern world history, music, music theory, physical education, physics, physics-AP, pre-algebra, Russian, social sciences, sociology, Spanish, speech, statistics-AP, TOEFL preparation, U.S. government, U.S. history, U.S. history-AP, world history, world religions, world religions.

Special Academic Programs Advanced Placement exam preparation; honors section; independent study; study at local college for college credit; study abroad; academic accommodation for the musically talented and the artistically talented; remedial reading and/or remedial writing; remedial math; ESL (24 students enrolled).

College Admission Counseling 73 students graduated in 2012; 65 went to college, including Drexel University; George Mason University; Penn State University Park; United States Military Academy; United States Naval Academy; University of Chicago. Other: 3 went to work, 1 entered a postgraduate year, 4 had other specific plans. Median SAT critical reading: 500, median SAT math: 530, median SAT writing: 450, median combined SAT: 1440. 28% scored over 600 on SAT critical reading, 38% scored over 600 on SAT math, 16% scored over 600 on SAT writing, 16% scored over 1800 on combined SAT.

Student Life Upper grades have uniform requirement, student council, honor system. Discipline rests equally with students and faculty. Attendance at religious services is required.

Tuition and Aid Day student tuition: $21,250; 5-day tuition and room/board: $34,000; 7-day tuition and room/board: $32,500. Tuition installment plan (monthly payment plans, individually arranged payment plans, HES). Tuition reduction for siblings, merit scholarship grants, need-based scholarship grants available. In 2012–13, 73% of upper-school students received aid; total upper-school merit-scholarship money awarded: $2,230,907. Total amount of financial aid awarded in 2012–13: $2,230,907.

Admissions Traditional secondary-level entrance grade is 11. For fall 2012, 339 students applied for upper-level admission, 204 were accepted, 105 enrolled. TOEFL or SLEP required. Deadline for receipt of application materials: none. Application fee required: $100. Interview required.

Athletics Interscholastic: baseball, basketball, climbing, cross-country running, dressage, drill team, equestrian sports, fitness, football, golf, horseback riding, indoor track, judo, lacrosse, marksmanship, outdoor activities, outdoor recreation, physical fitness, physical training, soccer, swimming and diving, weight lifting, weight training, wrestling; intramural: boxing, fencing, hockey, indoor hockey, indoor soccer, life saving, martial arts, paint ball, physical training, rugby, scuba diving, soccer, street hockey, ultimate Frisbee. 3 PE instructors, 12 coaches, 2 athletic trainers.

Computers Computers are regularly used in all classes. Computer network features include on-campus library services, Internet access, wireless campus network, Internet filtering or blocking technology, Blackboard. Campus intranet, student e-mail accounts, and computer access in designated common areas are available to students. Students grades are available online. The school has a published electronic and media policy.

Contact Col. John Ford, Academy Headmaster and Interim Director of Enrollment. 610-989-1490. Fax: 610-340-2194. E-mail: admissions@vfmac.edu. Website: www.vfmac.edu

VALLEY LUTHERAN HIGH SCHOOL

5199 North 7th Avenue
Phoenix, Arizona 85013-2043

Head of School: Mr. Robert Koehne

General Information Coeducational day college-preparatory, arts, religious studies, and technology school, affiliated with Lutheran Church–Missouri Synod. Grades 9–12. Founded: 1981. Setting: urban. 10-acre campus. 4 buildings on campus. Approved or accredited by National Lutheran School Accreditation, North Central Association of Colleges and Schools, and Arizona Department of Education. Total enrollment: 184. Upper school average class size: 15. Upper school faculty-student ratio: 1:10. There are 180 required school days per year for Upper School students. Upper School students typically attend 5 days per week. The average school day consists of 6 hours and 45 minutes.

Upper School Student Profile Grade 9: 37 students (20 boys, 17 girls); Grade 10: 45 students (23 boys, 22 girls); Grade 11: 60 students (38 boys, 22 girls); Grade 12: 42 students (23 boys, 19 girls). 56% of students are Lutheran Church–Missouri Synod.

Faculty School total: 18. In upper school: 10 men, 8 women; 7 have advanced degrees.

Subjects Offered Advanced Placement courses, advanced studio art-AP, algebra, American government, American history, American history-AP, American literature, American politics in film, anatomy and physiology, art, athletics, band, Bible, biology, British literature, British literature (honors), calculus, calculus-AP, career and personal planning, chemistry, choir, choral music, chorus, Christian doctrine, Christian education, Christian ethics, computer skills, concert band, consumer mathematics, creative writing, current history, economics, English, English literature and composition-AP, environmental science, film history, foreign language, freshman seminar, geography, government, government-AP, honors algebra, honors geometry, human biology, intro to computers, music, music appreciation, New Testament, oral communications, physical education, physical fitness, physics, portfolio art, pre-algebra, pre-calculus, psychology, religion, SAT preparation, SAT/ACT preparation, Spanish, speech, speech communications, trigonometry, U.S. government, U.S. history-AP, United States government-AP, weightlifting, world geography, world history, world literature, World-Wide-Web publishing, yearbook.

Special Academic Programs 4 Advanced Placement exams for which test preparation is offered; honors section; term-away projects; academic accommodation for the gifted; remedial math; special instructional classes for deaf students.

College Admission Counseling 63 students graduated in 2012; 50 went to college, including Arizona State University; Azusa Pacific University; Concordia University; Grand Canyon University; Northern Arizona University; The University of Arizona. Other: 3 went to work, 8 entered military service, 1 entered a postgraduate year, 1 had other specific plans. Median SAT critical reading: 550, median SAT math: 560, median SAT writing: 500, median combined SAT: 1610, median composite ACT: 24.

Student Life Upper grades have specified standards of dress, student council, honor system. Discipline rests primarily with faculty. Attendance at religious services is required.

Tuition and Aid Day student tuition: $8500. Tuition installment plan (monthly payment plans, individually arranged payment plans, Vanco Services online payments). Merit scholarship grants, need-based scholarship grants, association grants, Christian worker discounts available. In 2012–13, 30% of upper-school students received aid. Total amount of financial aid awarded in 2012–13: $166,770.

Admissions Traditional secondary-level entrance grade is 9. For fall 2012, 68 students applied for upper-level admission, 68 were accepted, 64 enrolled. High School Placement Test and school's own test required. Deadline for receipt of application materials: none. Application fee required: $50. On-campus interview required.

Athletics Interscholastic: baseball (boys), basketball (b,g), cheering (g), cross-country running (b,g), football (b), pom squad (g), soccer (b,g), softball (g), track and field (b,g), volleyball (g), wrestling (b); coed interscholastic: golf, running, strength & conditioning, tennis, weight training. 13 coaches.

Computers Computers are regularly used in computer applications, desktop publishing, photography, Web site design, word processing, yearbook classes. Computer network features include Internet access, Internet filtering or blocking technology. Students grades are available online. The school has a published electronic and media policy.

Contact Mr. Robert Koehne, Principal. 602-230-1600 Ext. 120. Fax: 602-230-1602. E-mail: rkoehne@vlhs.org. Website: www.vlhs.org/

THE VALLEY SCHOOL

5255 S. Linden Rd.
Swartz Creek, Michigan 48473

Head of School: Kaye C. Panchula

General Information Coeducational day college-preparatory and arts school. Grades PK–12. Founded: 1970. Setting: urban. Nearest major city is Flint. 5-acre campus. 1 building on campus. Candidate for accreditation by Independent Schools Association of the Central States. Total enrollment: 58. Upper school average class size: 15. Upper school faculty-student ratio: 1:8. There are 180 required school days per year for Upper School students. Upper School students typically attend 5 days per week. The average school day consists of 5 hours and 30 minutes.

Upper School Student Profile Grade 9: 3 students (2 boys, 1 girl); Grade 10: 6 students (3 boys, 3 girls); Grade 11: 1 student (1 girl); Grade 12: 4 students (4 boys).

Faculty School total: 13. In upper school: 4 men, 3 women; 4 have advanced degrees.

Subjects Offered Algebra, American history, American literature, anatomy, art, art history, biology, chemistry, current events, earth science, English, English literature, European history, expository writing, fine arts, geometry, government/civics, grammar, history, mathematics, music, physical education, physics, probability and statistics, SAT/ACT preparation, science, social sciences, Spanish, trigonometry, world cultures, world history, world literature, writing.

Graduation Requirements Arts and fine arts (art, music, dance, drama), biology, college counseling, English, foreign language, mathematics, science, social sciences, social studies (includes history), senior project off campus.

Special Academic Programs Study at local college for college credit; academic accommodation for the gifted and the artistically talented.

College Admission Counseling 5 students graduated in 2013; all went to college, including Central Michigan University; University of Michigan. Median composite ACT: 24.

Student Life Upper grades have student council. Discipline rests equally with students and faculty.

Tuition and Aid Day student tuition: $9899. Tuition installment plan (FACTS Tuition Payment Plan). Tuition reduction for siblings, merit scholarship grants, need-based scholarship grants available. In 2013–14, 83% of upper-school students received aid; total upper-school merit-scholarship money awarded: $28,199. Total amount of financial aid awarded in 2013–14: $51,376.

Admissions Traditional secondary-level entrance grade is 9. For fall 2013, 8 students applied for upper-level admission, 7 were accepted, 7 enrolled. School's own exam required. Deadline for receipt of application materials: none. No application fee required. On-campus interview required.

Athletics Interscholastic: basketball (boys, girls), golf (b), outdoor skills (b,g), outdoors (b,g), physical fitness (b,g), soccer (b,g), tennis (g), volleyball (g). 2 PE instructors, 3 coaches.

Computers Computers are regularly used in art, English, mathematics, science, social sciences, stock market, study skills, writing classes. Computer resources include Internet access, wireless campus network. Computer access in designated common areas is available to students.

Contact Ms. Minka Owens, Director of Admissions. 810-767-4004. Fax: 810-655-0853. E-mail: email@valleyschool.org. Website: www.valleyschool.org

VALLEY VIEW SCHOOL

North Brookfield, Massachusetts
See Special Needs Schools section.

VANDEBILT CATHOLIC HIGH SCHOOL

209 South Hollywood Road
Houma, Louisiana 70360

Head of School: Mr. David T. Keife

General Information Coeducational day college-preparatory, arts, business, religious studies, and technology school, affiliated with Roman Catholic Church. Grades 8–12. Founded: 1965. Setting: suburban. Nearest major city is New Orleans. 29-acre campus. 8 buildings on campus. Approved or accredited by Southern Association of Colleges and Schools and Louisiana Department of Education. Endowment: $620,000. Total enrollment: 921. Upper school average class size: 25. Upper school faculty-student ratio: 1:25.

Upper School Student Profile Grade 8: 186 students (93 boys, 93 girls); Grade 9: 185 students (93 boys, 92 girls); Grade 10: 201 students (94 boys, 107 girls); Grade 11: 165 students (78 boys, 87 girls); Grade 12: 179 students (81 boys, 98 girls). 85% of students are Roman Catholic.

Faculty School total: 63. In upper school: 25 men, 38 women; 20 have advanced degrees.

Subjects Offered 20th century world history, 3-dimensional art, accounting, advanced chemistry, advanced math, algebra, American history, art, band, biology, bookkeeping, business education, calculus, chemistry, choir, civics, computer applications, computer science, driver education, earth science, English, English literature, French, general business, geography, history of music, honors algebra, honors English, honors geometry, honors U.S. history, keyboarding, Latin, leadership, mathematics, media, music appreciation, physical education, physical science, physics, pre-algebra, reading, reading/study skills, religion, Spanish, speech, world history.

Graduation Requirements Algebra, American history, athletics, biology, chemistry, civics, civics/free enterprise, computer applications, English, geometry, physical education (includes health), religion (includes Bible studies and theology), science, social studies (includes history).

Special Academic Programs Programs in English, mathematics for dyslexic students; special instructional classes for students with Attention Deficit Disorder and dyslexia.

College Admission Counseling 166 students graduated in 2013; 165 went to college, including Louisiana State University and Agricultural and Mechanical College; Louisiana Tech University; Loyola University New Orleans; Nicholls State University; Tulane University; University of Louisiana at Lafayette. Other: 1 went to work. Mean composite ACT: 23. 40% scored over 26 on composite ACT.

Student Life Upper grades have uniform requirement, student council. Discipline rests primarily with faculty. Attendance at religious services is required.

Tuition and Aid Day student tuition: $6770. Tuition installment plan (monthly payment plans). Merit scholarship grants, need-based scholarship grants, middle-income loans available. In 2013–14, 8% of upper-school students received aid; total upper-school merit-scholarship money awarded: $25,000. Total amount of financial aid awarded in 2013–14: $125,000.

Admissions Traditional secondary-level entrance grade is 8. For fall 2013, 895 students applied for upper-level admission, 894 were accepted, 894 enrolled. Deadline for receipt of application materials: none. No application fee required. On-campus interview required.

Athletics Interscholastic: baseball (boys), basketball (b,g), bowling (b,g), cheering (g), cross-country running (b,g), dance team (g), football (b), golf (b), gymnastics (b,g), indoor track & field (b,g), power lifting (b), soccer (b,g), softball (g), swimming and diving (b,g), tennis (b,g), track and field (b,g), volleyball (g), weight training (b,g). 5 PE instructors, 15 coaches.

Computers Computers are regularly used in accounting, aerospace science, all academic, animation, architecture, art, aviation, basic skills, Bible studies, business, business applications, business education, business skills, business studies, cabinet making, career education, career exploration, career technology, Christian doctrine, classics, college planning, commercial art, computer applications, construction, creative writing, current events, dance, data processing, design, desktop publishing, desktop publishing, ESL, digital applications, drafting, drawing and design, economics, engineering, English, ESL, ethics, foreign language, French, French as a second language, freshman foundations, geography, graphic design, graphics, health, historical foundations for arts, history, human geography - AP, humanities, independent study, industrial technology, information technology, introduction to technology, journalism, JROTC, lab/keyboard, language development, Latin, learning cognition, library, library science, library skills, life skills, literacy, literary magazine, mathematics, media, media arts, media production, media services, mentorship program, multimedia, music, music technology, news writing, newspaper, NJROTC, occupational education, philosophy, photography, photojournalism, programming, psychology, publications, publishing, reading, religion, religious studies, remedial study skills, research skills, SAT preparation, science, senior seminar, social sciences, social studies, Spanish, speech, stock market, study skills, technical drawing, technology, theater, theater arts, theology, typing, video film production, vocational-technical courses, Web site design, wilderness education, woodworking, word processing, writing, writing classes. Computer network features include on-campus library services, Internet access, Internet filtering or blocking technology. Computer access in designated common areas is available to students. Students grades are available online. The school has a published electronic and media policy.

Contact Mr. Quinn Moreaux, Assistant Principal. 985-876-2551. Fax: 985-868-9774. E-mail: qmoreaux@htdiocese.org. Website: www.vandebiltcatholic.org

THE VANGUARD SCHOOL

Lake Wales, Florida
See Special Needs Schools section.

VENTA PREPARATORY SCHOOL

2013 Old Carp Road
Ottawa, Ontario K0A 1L0, Canada
Head of School: Ms. Marilyn Mansfield
General Information Coeducational boarding and day college-preparatory, arts, and music school. Boarding grades 1–10, day grades JK–10. Founded: 1981. Setting: small town. Students are housed in single-sex by floor dormitories. 50-acre campus. 8 buildings on campus. Approved or accredited by Ontario Ministry of Education and Ontario Department of Education. Member of Secondary School Admission Test Board. Language of instruction: English. Total enrollment: 74. Upper school average class size: 12. Upper school faculty-student ratio: 1:6. There are 175 required school days per year for Upper School students. Upper School students typically attend 5 days per week. The average school day consists of 8 hours and 30 minutes.
Upper School Student Profile Grade 8: 7 students (5 boys, 2 girls); Grade 9: 8 students (3 boys, 5 girls); Grade 10: 8 students (7 boys, 1 girl). 40% of students are boarding students. 90% are province residents. 2 provinces are represented in upper school student body. International students from Bermuda, China, Hong Kong, Mexico, and United States.
Faculty School total: 18. In upper school: 7 men, 11 women; 4 have advanced degrees; 6 reside on campus.
Special Academic Programs Independent study; academic accommodation for the gifted; remedial reading and/or remedial writing; remedial math; programs in English, mathematics, general development for dyslexic students.
Student Life Upper grades have uniform requirement, honor system. Discipline rests primarily with faculty.
Tuition and Aid Day student tuition: CAN$17,070–CAN$18,585; 5-day tuition and room/board: CAN$30,965–CAN$33,895; 7-day tuition and room/board: CAN$34,465–CAN$37,395. Tuition installment plan (monthly payment plans, individually arranged payment plans). Tuition reduction for siblings available.
Admissions Traditional secondary-level entrance grade is 8. For fall 2013, 5 students applied for upper-level admission, 3 were accepted, 3 enrolled. Psychoeducational evaluation, Wechsler Individual Achievement Test and Wechsler Intelligence Scale for Children III required. Deadline for receipt of application materials: none. Application fee required: CAN$150. On-campus interview required.
Athletics Coed Interscholastic: basketball, rugby, soccer; coed intramural: ball hockey, baseball, basketball, canoeing/kayaking, fitness, football, ice hockey, jogging, outdoor recreation, running, soccer, track and field, ultimate Frisbee. 4 PE instructors.
Computers Computers are regularly used in current events, geography, keyboarding, mathematics, research skills, science classes. Computer network features include Internet access, wireless campus network, Internet filtering or blocking technology. The school has a published electronic and media policy.
Contact Ms. Tanya Kaye, Manager, Marketing and Admissions. 613-839-2175 Ext. 240. Fax: 613-839-1956. E-mail: info@ventaprep.com. Website: www.ventapreparatoryschool.com

VIANNEY HIGH SCHOOL

1311 South Kirkwood Road
St. Louis, Missouri 63122
Head of School: Dr. Timothy Dilg
General Information Boys' day college-preparatory, arts, business, religious studies, and technology school, affiliated with Roman Catholic Church. Grades 9–12. Founded: 1960. Setting: suburban. 37-acre campus. 6 buildings on campus. Approved or accredited by National Catholic Education Association, North Central Association of Colleges and Schools, and The College Board. Total enrollment: 640. Upper school average class size: 22. Upper school faculty-student ratio: 1:13. There are 165 required school days per year for Upper School students. Upper School students typically attend 5 days per week. The average school day consists of 6 hours and 5 minutes.
Upper School Student Profile Grade 9: 163 students (163 boys); Grade 10: 165 students (165 boys); Grade 11: 172 students (172 boys); Grade 12: 140 students (140 boys). 98% of students are Roman Catholic.
Faculty School total: 50. In upper school: 40 men, 8 women; 37 have advanced degrees.
Subjects Offered Accounting, advanced chemistry, Advanced Placement courses, algebra, American government, American history, American literature, analysis, analytic geometry, architectural drawing, art, art education, art history, arts appreciation, athletic training, band, British literature (honors), business law, business mathematics, calculus, calculus-AP, Catholic belief and practice, chemistry, Christian and Hebrew scripture, Christian ethics, Christian studies, college writing, communication skills, composition, computer applications, computer programming, computer skills, constitutional history of U.S., consumer education, current events, drama, economics, English composition, English literature, European history, expository writing, foreign language, fractal geometry, French, geometry, German, German literature, government, health and wellness, honors algebra, honors English, honors geometry, honors U.S. history, journalism, keyboarding, leadership, mythology, probability and statistics, publications, research skills, scripture, sex education, Shakespeare, Spanish, Spanish literature, sports conditioning, stage design, stagecraft, technical drawing, technology, technology/design, the Web, theater arts, theater design and production, theater history, trigonometry, U.S. government, U.S. history, U.S. literature, Web site design, weight training, world civilizations, world history, writing.
Graduation Requirements American history, American literature, arts and fine arts (art, music, dance, drama), biology, English, English composition, food science, foods, foreign language, government/civics, grammar, history, keyboarding, mathematics, physical education (includes health), physical fitness, religious studies, science, social issues, 100 hours of community service, forensic science.
Special Academic Programs 5 Advanced Placement exams for which test preparation is offered; honors section; study at local college for college credit; special instructional classes for students with learning disabilities, Attention Deficit Disorder, dyslexia, emotional and behavioral problems.
College Admission Counseling 147 students graduated in 2012; 146 went to college, including Missouri State University; Saint Louis University; Southeast Missouri State University; St. Louis Community College at Meramec; University of Missouri. Other: 1 entered military service. Median composite ACT: 24. 25% scored over 26 on composite ACT.
Student Life Upper grades have specified standards of dress, student council, honor system. Discipline rests primarily with faculty. Attendance at religious services is required.
Tuition and Aid Day student tuition: $12,000. Tuition installment plan (The Tuition Plan, FACTS Tuition Payment Plan, monthly payment plans, individually arranged payment plans). Tuition reduction for siblings, merit scholarship grants, need-based scholarship grants, paying campus jobs available. In 2012–13, 27% of upper-school students received aid; total upper-school merit-scholarship money awarded: $135,127. Total amount of financial aid awarded in 2012–13: $316,127.
Admissions Traditional secondary-level entrance grade is 9. For fall 2012, 172 students applied for upper-level admission, 167 were accepted, 163 enrolled. Explore required. Deadline for receipt of application materials: none. No application fee required. On-campus interview required.
Athletics Interscholastic: aquatics, baseball, basketball, cross-country running, diving, football, golf, ice hockey, lacrosse, racquetball, roller hockey, soccer, swimming and diving, tennis, track and field, volleyball, wrestling; intramural: bowling, flag football, paint ball, Special Olympics, touch football. 3 PE instructors, 40 coaches, 1 athletic trainer.
Computers Computers are regularly used in all academic, architecture, computer applications, creative writing, drafting, journalism, yearbook classes. Computer network features include on-campus library services, online commercial services, Internet access, wireless campus network, Internet filtering or blocking technology. Campus intranet, student e-mail accounts, and computer access in designated common areas are available to students. Students grades are available online. The school has a published electronic and media policy.
Contact Mr. Tom Mulvihill, Director of Admissions. 314-965-4853 Ext. 142. Fax: 314-965-1950. E-mail: tmulvihill@vianney.com. Website: www.vianney.com

VICKSBURG CATHOLIC SCHOOL

1900 Grove Street
Vicksburg, Mississippi 39183
Head of School: Mrs. Michele Connelly
General Information Coeducational day college-preparatory and religious studies school, affiliated with Roman Catholic Church. Grades PK–12. Founded: 1860. Setting: urban. Nearest major city is Jackson. 8-acre campus. 2 buildings on campus. Approved or accredited by National Catholic Education Association, Southern Association of Colleges and Schools, and Mississippi Department of Education.

Endowment: $350,000. Total enrollment: 577. Upper school average class size: 16. Upper school faculty-student ratio: 1:11. There are 180 required school days per year for Upper School students. Upper School students typically attend 5 days per week. The average school day consists of 5 hours and 50 minutes.

Upper School Student Profile Grade 7: 56 students (26 boys, 30 girls); Grade 8: 44 students (22 boys, 22 girls); Grade 9: 45 students (25 boys, 20 girls); Grade 10: 43 students (25 boys, 18 girls); Grade 11: 44 students (20 boys, 24 girls); Grade 12: 38 students (24 boys, 14 girls). 50% of students are Roman Catholic.

Faculty School total: 51. In upper school: 10 men, 14 women; 5 have advanced degrees.

Subjects Offered Accounting, ACT preparation, algebra, American government, American history, American history-AP, anatomy, anatomy and physiology, art, band, biology, biology-AP, calculus-AP, chemistry, chemistry-AP, choir, computer applications, desktop publishing, drama, earth science, economics, English, English language and composition-AP, environmental science, foreign language, geography, geology, geometry, government and politics-AP, health, honors algebra, honors English, honors geometry, humanities, keyboarding, learning lab, music, personal finance, physical education, physics, physics-AP, pre-algebra, pre-calculus, psychology, public speaking, sociology, Spanish, state history, theology, trigonometry, U.S. government, U.S. government and politics-AP, U.S. history, world history, yearbook.

Graduation Requirements Algebra, American government, American history, biology, computer skills, economics, English, geography, geometry, government, health, history, lab science, law, physical education (includes health), Spanish, theology, U.S. government, U.S. history, world history, Mississippi state requirements.

Special Academic Programs 7 Advanced Placement exams for which test preparation is offered; honors section; study at local college for college credit; special instructional classes for students with learning disabilities, Attention Deficit Disorder, dyslexia, emotional and behavioral problems.

College Admission Counseling 36 students graduated in 2013; 34 went to college, including Delta State University; Hinds Community College; Louisiana State University and Agricultural and Mechanical College; Mississippi State University; University of Mississippi; University of Southern Mississippi. Other: 2 entered military service. Median composite ACT: 20. 17% scored over 26 on composite ACT.

Student Life Upper grades have uniform requirement, student council, honor system. Discipline rests primarily with faculty. Attendance at religious services is required.

Tuition and Aid Day student tuition: $6200. Tuition installment plan (FACTS Tuition Payment Plan). Tuition reduction for siblings, need-based scholarship grants available. In 2013–14, 14% of upper-school students received aid. Total amount of financial aid awarded in 2013–14: $75,000.

Admissions Traditional secondary-level entrance grade is 7. For fall 2013, 16 students applied for upper-level admission, 16 were accepted, 16 enrolled. Admissions testing required. Deadline for receipt of application materials: none. Application fee required: $75. Interview required.

Athletics Interscholastic: baseball (boys), basketball (b,g), cheering (g), cross-country running (b,g), dance squad (g), football (b), golf (b,g), power lifting (b), soccer (b,g), softball (g), swimming and diving (b,g), tennis (b,g), track and field (b,g); coed interscholastic: swimming and diving, tennis. 2 PE instructors, 4 coaches.

Computers Computers are regularly used in accounting, computer applications, desktop publishing, keyboarding classes. Computer network features include on-campus library services, online commercial services, Internet access, Internet filtering or blocking technology. Students grades are available online. The school has a published electronic and media policy.

Contact Mrs. Patricia Rabalais, Registrar. 601-636-2256 Ext. 16. Fax: 601-631-0430. E-mail: patricia.rabalais@vicksburgcatholic.org. Website: www.vicksburgcatholic.org

VICTOR VALLEY CHRISTIAN SCHOOL

15260 Nisqualli Road
Victorville, California 92395

Head of School: Pastor John Martin

General Information Coeducational day college-preparatory, arts, religious studies, and bilingual studies school, affiliated with Assemblies of God. Grades K–12. Founded: 1972. Setting: suburban. Nearest major city is Los Angeles. 8-acre campus. 5 buildings on campus. Approved or accredited by Association of Christian Schools International and Western Association of Schools and Colleges. Languages of instruction: English and Spanish. Total enrollment: 300. Upper school average class size: 20. Upper school faculty-student ratio: 1:15. There are 179 required school days per year for Upper School students. Upper School students typically attend 5 days per week. The average school day consists of 7 hours and 15 minutes.

Upper School Student Profile 15% of students are Assemblies of God.

Faculty School total: 17. In upper school: 4 men, 7 women; 3 have advanced degrees.

Subjects Offered Algebra, American history, art, arts, Bible studies, biology, biology-AP, calculus-AP, chemistry, chorus, Christian education, computer literacy, computer science, drama, English, English as a foreign language, English language and composition-AP, English literature-AP, fine arts, geometry, government, health, mathematics, physical education, physics, pre-calculus, psychology-AP, religion, science, social sciences, social studies, Spanish, U.S. history, U.S. history-AP, word processing, world history, world history-AP, yearbook.

Graduation Requirements Arts and fine arts (art, music, dance, drama), English, foreign language, government, health, mathematics, religion (includes Bible studies and theology), science, social sciences, community service.

Special Academic Programs 5 Advanced Placement exams for which test preparation is offered; honors section; accelerated programs; independent study; study at local college for college credit; academic accommodation for the gifted; special instructional classes for students with learning disabilities; ESL (18 students enrolled).

College Admission Counseling 30 students graduated in 2013; all went to college, including California State University, Fullerton; California State University, San Bernardino; The University of Arizona; University of California, Irvine. Mean SAT critical reading: 480, mean SAT math: 470, mean SAT writing: 475, mean composite ACT: 22. 10% scored over 600 on SAT math.

Student Life Upper grades have uniform requirement, student council. Discipline rests primarily with faculty.

Summer Programs Remediation, enrichment programs offered; held on campus; accepts boys and girls; open to students from other schools. 8 students usually enrolled. 2014 schedule: June to August. Application deadline: June.

Tuition and Aid Tuition installment plan (FACTS Tuition Payment Plan, monthly payment plans, individually arranged payment plans). Tuition reduction for siblings, need-based scholarship grants available. In 2013–14, 10% of upper-school students received aid.

Admissions Traditional secondary-level entrance grade is 9. For fall 2013, 19 students applied for upper-level admission, 18 were accepted, 18 enrolled. Deadline for receipt of application materials: none. No application fee required. Interview required.

Athletics Interscholastic: baseball (boys), basketball (b,g), cheering (g), cross-country running (b,g), football (b), softball (g), track and field (b,g), volleyball (g); coed interscholastic: golf, soccer. 2 PE instructors, 7 coaches, 1 athletic trainer.

Computers Computers are regularly used in desktop publishing, graphic arts, journalism, yearbook classes. Computer resources include on-campus library services, Internet access, wireless campus network, Internet filtering or blocking technology. Campus intranet is available to students. Students grades are available online.

Contact Mrs. Deb Clarkson, Principal. 760-241-8827. Fax: 760-243-0654. E-mail: dclarkson@vfassembly.org. Website: www.vvcs.org

VIEWPOINT SCHOOL

23620 Mulholland Highway
Calabasas, California 91302

Head of School: Dr. Robert J. Dworkoski

General Information Coeducational day college-preparatory and arts school. Grades K–12. Founded: 1961. Setting: suburban. Nearest major city is Los Angeles. 25-acre campus. 5 buildings on campus. Approved or accredited by Western Association of Schools and Colleges and California Department of Education. Member of National Association of Independent Schools. Endowment: $11 million. Total enrollment: 1,212. Upper school average class size: 18. Upper school faculty-student ratio: 1:10. There are 180 required school days per year for Upper School students. Upper School students typically attend 5 days per week. The average school day consists of 7 hours.

Upper School Student Profile Grade 9: 147 students (69 boys, 78 girls); Grade 10: 124 students (64 boys, 60 girls); Grade 11: 113 students (58 boys, 55 girls); Grade 12: 121 students (69 boys, 52 girls).

Faculty School total: 164. In upper school: 36 men, 45 women; 75 have advanced degrees.

Subjects Offered Adolescent issues, advanced chemistry, advanced computer applications, advanced studio art-AP, African literature, algebra, American history, American history-AP, American literature, ancient history, ancient world history, animation, art, art appreciation, art history, art history-AP, Asian history, Asian studies, ballet, Basic programming, basic skills, Bible as literature, biology, biology-AP, British literature, business skills, calculus, calculus-AP, California writers, ceramics, character education, chemistry, chemistry-AP, Chinese, Chinese studies, choir, choreography, chorus, clayworking, college admission preparation, community service, comparative government and politics, comparative government and politics-AP, comparative politics, computer animation, computer programming, computer science, computer science-AP, concert band, contemporary women writers, creative writing, critical studies in film, dance, debate, decision making skills, diversity studies, drama, drama performance, dramatic arts, drawing and design, earth science, economics, English, English language-AP, English literature, English literature-AP, ensembles, environmental education, environmental science, environmental science-AP, European history, European history-AP, film, film appreciation, filmmaking, fine arts, French, French language-AP, French literature-AP, geometry, global science, government/civics, history, history-AP, Holocaust and other genocides, honors algebra, honors English, honors geometry, human development, humanities, instrumental music, international relations, jazz, jazz band, jazz dance, jazz ensemble, journalism, keyboarding, Latin, Latin American history, Latin History, Latin-AP, library skills, literary magazine, literature by women, mathematics, medieval history, multicultural literature, music, music composition, music history, music theory-AP, newspaper, oceanography, outdoor education, performing arts, photography, physical education, physics, physics-AP, physiology, poetry, probability and statistics, psychology, psychology-AP, public speaking, robotics, science, sculpture, senior project, Shakespeare, short story, social studies, sociology, Spanish, Spanish language-AP,

Spanish literature-AP, speech and debate, student publications, studio art-AP, study skills, swimming, theater, trigonometry, U.S. government and politics-AP, video, vocal jazz, women's literature, word processing, world history, yearbook.

Graduation Requirements Arts and fine arts (art, music, dance, drama), computer science, English, foreign language, global studies, mathematics, physical education (includes health), science, social studies (includes history). Community service is required.

Special Academic Programs 29 Advanced Placement exams for which test preparation is offered; honors section; independent study; study abroad.

College Admission Counseling 109 students graduated in 2013; all went to college, including Stanford University; University of California, Berkeley; University of California, Los Angeles; University of California, San Diego; University of Southern California. Mean SAT critical reading: 642, mean SAT math: 652, mean SAT writing: 660, mean composite ACT: 26.

Student Life Upper grades have specified standards of dress, student council, honor system. Discipline rests primarily with faculty.

Summer Programs Remediation, enrichment, advancement, sports, art/fine arts, computer instruction programs offered; session focuses on academics, arts, sports, and recreation; held on campus; accepts boys and girls; open to students from other schools. 315 students usually enrolled. 2014 schedule: June 16 to August 20. Application deadline: none.

Tuition and Aid Day student tuition: $32,750. Tuition installment plan (monthly payment plans). Need-based scholarship grants available. In 2013–14, 25% of upper-school students received aid. Total amount of financial aid awarded in 2013–14: $2,645,439.

Admissions Traditional secondary-level entrance grade is 9. For fall 2013, 165 students applied for upper-level admission, 102 were accepted, 62 enrolled. ISEE or SSAT required. Deadline for receipt of application materials: December 15. Application fee required: $125. Interview required.

Athletics Interscholastic: aerobics/dance (boys, girls), ballet (b,g), baseball (b), basketball (b,g), cooperative games (b,g), football (b), lacrosse (b), soccer (b,g), softball (g), volleyball (b,g); intramural: backpacking (b,g), ball hockey (b,g), ballet (b,g), baseball (b), basketball (b,g), soccer (b,g), softball (g), volleyball (b,g); coed interscholastic: cross-country running, dance, dance squad, dressage, equestrian sports, fencing, flag football, golf, modern dance, swimming and diving, tennis; coed intramural: cheering, cross-country running, dance, dance squad, dance team, fencing, football, golf, hiking/backpacking, modern dance, outdoor education, outdoor recreation, outdoor skills, physical fitness, physical training, strength & conditioning, swimming and diving, weight training. 15 PE instructors, 15 coaches, 1 athletic trainer.

Computers Computers are regularly used in animation, basic skills, college planning, English, foreign language, history, keyboarding, library skills, mathematics, multimedia, music, newspaper, publications, science, video film production, Web site design, word processing, yearbook classes. Computer network features include on-campus library services, online commercial services, Internet access, wireless campus network, Internet filtering or blocking technology. Campus intranet and student e-mail accounts are available to students. The school has a published electronic and media policy.

Contact Mr. Patrick LaBo, Admission and Financial Aid Coordinator. 818-591-6560. Fax: 818-591-0834. E-mail: admission@viewpoint.org. Website: www.viewpoint.org

VILLA ANGELA-ST. JOSEPH HIGH SCHOOL

18491 Lakeshore Boulevard
Cleveland, Ohio 44119-1212

Head of School: Mr. David Csank

General Information Coeducational day college-preparatory, general academic, arts, business, vocational, religious studies, bilingual studies, and technology school, affiliated with Roman Catholic Church. Grades 9–12. Founded: 1990. Setting: urban. 5-acre campus. 2 buildings on campus. Approved or accredited by North Central Association of Colleges and Schools and Ohio Department of Education. Endowment: $3 million. Total enrollment: 375. Upper school average class size: 20. Upper school faculty-student ratio: 1:12. There are 179 required school days per year for Upper School students. Upper School students typically attend 5 days per week. The average school day consists of 7 hours and 8 minutes.

Upper School Student Profile 50% of students are Roman Catholic.

Faculty School total: 61. In upper school: 28 men, 19 women; 27 have advanced degrees.

Subjects Offered 20th century American writers, 20th century history, 20th century physics, 20th century world history, 3-dimensional art, 3-dimensional design, accounting, ACT preparation, advanced chemistry, advanced computer applications, advanced math, Advanced Placement courses, African American history, African-American history, algebra, alternative physical education, American Civil War, American culture, American democracy, American government, American history, American history-AP, American literature, analysis, analytic geometry, anatomy, anatomy and physiology, applied skills, architectural drawing, art, art and culture, art appreciation, art education, art history, arts, arts and crafts, arts appreciation, audio visual/media, auto mechanics, band, basic skills, Bible, Bible studies, biology, biology-AP, British literature, British literature (honors), business, business skills, business studies, calculus, calculus-AP, campus ministry, career and personal planning, career

education, career education internship, career experience, career exploration, career planning, career/college preparation, carpentry, cartooning/animation, Catholic belief and practice, chemistry, chemistry-AP, child development, choir, choral music, chorus, Christian doctrine, Christian education, Christian ethics, Christian scripture, Christian studies, Christian testament, Christianity, church history, civics, Civil War, civil war history, college admission preparation, college placement, community service, composition, computer education, computer information systems, computer literacy, computer multimedia, computer programming, computer resources, computer science, computer skills, computer studies, computer technologies, computer technology certification, computer tools, computer-aided design, computers, conceptual physics, concert band, creative arts, creative writing, critical thinking, critical writing, culinary arts, current events, current history, debate, design, desktop publishing, diversity studies, drawing, drawing and design, early childhood, engineering, English, English composition, English language and composition-AP, English language-AP, English literature, English literature and composition-AP, English literature-AP, English-AP, English/composition-AP, environmental education, environmental geography, environmental science, environmental studies, epic literature, ethnic literature, ethnic studies, European civilization, European history, expressive arts, family and consumer science, family living, family studies, fiction, fine arts, food and nutrition, foods, foreign language, French, freshman foundations, functions, gender and religion, general, general business, general math, general science, geography, geometry, global issues, global science, government, government-AP, government/civics, health, health education, health science, history, history of religion, history of the Catholic Church, history-AP, honors algebra, honors English, honors geometry, honors U.S. history, honors world history, human development, human relations, human sexuality, independent living, industrial arts, industrial technology, instrumental music, instruments, interactive media, Internet, Internet research, intro to computers, introduction to literature, introduction to technology, keyboarding, lab science, lab/keyboard, language and composition, language arts, languages, Latin, life management skills, life science, life skills, literary genres, literary magazine, literature, literature and composition-AP, literature-AP, logarithms, logic, rhetoric, and debate, math analysis, math applications, math methods, math review, mathematical modeling, mathematics, mathematics-AP, mechanics of writing, Microsoft, minority studies, modern civilization, modern European history, modern history, modern politics, modern Western civilization, modern world history, moral and social development, multicultural studies, multimedia design, music, music performance, music theater, musical productions, musical theater, newspaper, nutrition, painting, parent/child development, peer ministry, performing arts, personal and social education, physical education, physical science, physics, physics-AP, prayer/spirituality, pre-algebra, pre-calculus, programming, publications, reading, reading/study skills, relationships, religion, religion and culture, religious education, religious studies, research skills, Romantic period literature, SAT preparation, SAT/ACT preparation, science, science and technology, scripture, sculpture, sewing, sex education, shop, skills for success, social education, social issues, social justice, social sciences, social studies, society, politics and law, space and physical sciences, Spanish, Spanish literature, speech and debate, student government, student publications, studio art, study skills, technology, technology/design, the Web, theology, theology and the arts, trigonometry, typing, U.S. government, U.S. government and politics, U.S. government and politics-AP, U.S. history, U.S. literature, U.S. Presidents, United Nations and international issues, United States government-AP, Vietnam, Vietnam history, Vietnam War, visual and performing arts, visual arts, vocal ensemble, vocal music, vocational skills, vocational-technical courses, Web authoring, Web site design, Western civilization, Western literature, wood lab, woodworking, word processing, world civilizations, world cultures, world geography, world governments, world history, world issues, world literature, world religions, world religions, world studies, World War I, World War II, world wide web design, writing, writing, writing workshop, yearbook.

Graduation Requirements Students are required to complete a total of 50 hours of service work to be eligible for graduation.

Special Academic Programs Advanced Placement exam preparation; honors section; study at local college for college credit; remedial reading and/or remedial writing; remedial math.

College Admission Counseling 55 students graduated in 2013; all went to college, including Bowling Green State University; John Carroll University; Kent State University; Ohio University; The Ohio State University; University of Dayton.

Student Life Upper grades have uniform requirement, student council, honor system. Discipline rests primarily with faculty. Attendance at religious services is required.

Summer Programs Remediation, sports, art/fine arts programs offered; session focuses on athletic and summer camps; held on campus; accepts boys and girls; open to students from other schools. 70 students usually enrolled. 2014 schedule: June to August. Application deadline: June.

Tuition and Aid Day student tuition: $8250. Tuition installment plan (monthly payment plans). Merit scholarship grants, need-based scholarship grants available. In 2013–14, 70% of upper-school students received aid.

Admissions Traditional secondary-level entrance grade is 9. Deadline for receipt of application materials: none. No application fee required. On-campus interview required.

Athletics Interscholastic: baseball (boys), basketball (b,g), cheering (g), cross-country running (b,g), dance team (g), football (b), golf (b,g), hockey (b), ice hockey (b), indoor track (b,g), indoor track & field (b,g), soccer (b,g), softball (g), track and field (b,g), volleyball (g), wrestling (g); intramural: basketball (b,g), flag football (g);

coed interscholastic: bowling; coed intramural: flag football, Frisbee, touch football, ultimate Frisbee, volleyball. 1 PE instructor, 60 coaches, 2 athletic trainers.

Computers Computers are regularly used in architecture, business, career education, career exploration, college planning, creative writing, data processing, design, desktop publishing, drafting, drawing and design, English, industrial technology, information technology, introduction to technology, keyboarding, lab/keyboard, literary magazine, newspaper, publications, publishing, research skills, science, technical drawing, technology, typing, vocational-technical courses, Web site design, word processing, writing, writing, yearbook classes. Computer network features include on-campus library services, online commercial services, Internet access, wireless campus network, Internet filtering or blocking technology, Schoology (online learning information system). Campus intranet, student e-mail accounts, and computer access in designated common areas are available to students. Students grades are available online. The school has a published electronic and media policy.

Contact Mrs. Terri Richards, Director of Admissions. 216-481-8414 Ext. 254. Fax: 216-486-1035. E-mail: trichards@vasj.com. Website: www.vasj.com

VILLA DUCHESNE AND OAK HILL SCHOOL

801 South Spoede Road
St. Louis, Missouri 63131

Head of School: Sr. Lucie Nordmann, RSCJ

General Information Coeducational day college-preparatory, arts, religious studies, and technology school, affiliated with Roman Catholic Church. Boys grades JK–6, girls grades JK–12. Founded: 1929. Setting: suburban. 60-acre campus. 2 buildings on campus. Approved or accredited by Independent Schools Association of the Central States, National Catholic Education Association, Network of Sacred Heart Schools, North Central Association of Colleges and Schools, and Missouri Department of Education. Member of National Association of Independent Schools. Total enrollment: 640. Upper school average class size: 15. Upper school faculty-student ratio: 1:9. There are 180 required school days per year for Upper School students. Upper School students typically attend 5 days per week. The average school day consists of 7 hours.

Upper School Student Profile 88% of students are Roman Catholic.

Faculty School total: 89. In upper school: 13 men, 44 women; 40 have advanced degrees.

Subjects Offered American government, American literature, American literature-AP, anatomy and physiology, art, biology, biology-AP, British literature, calculus, calculus-AP, campus ministry, ceramics, chemistry, chorus, civics, computers, creative writing, discrete mathematics, drawing, economics, English, European history, European history-AP, Far Eastern history, French, geography, geometry, health, integrated physics, math analysis, Middle East, music, newspaper, painting, personal development, physical education, physics, pre-algebra, pre-calculus, printmaking, psychology, public speaking, religion, scripture, sculpture, social justice, Spanish, studio art, studio art-AP, theater arts, U.S. history, U.S. history-AP, Western civilization, women's studies, world literature, yearbook.

Graduation Requirements All academic, students must perform community service to graduate.

Special Academic Programs International Baccalaureate program; 11 Advanced Placement exams for which test preparation is offered; honors section; independent study; term-away projects; study at local college for college credit; domestic exchange program (with Network of Sacred Heart Schools); study abroad; remedial reading and/or remedial writing; remedial math.

College Admission Counseling 97 students graduated in 2012; all went to college, including Marquette University; Saint Louis University; Texas Christian University; University of Missouri. Mean combined SAT: 1827, mean composite ACT: 28.

Student Life Upper grades have uniform requirement, student council, honor system. Discipline rests primarily with faculty. Attendance at religious services is required.

Tuition and Aid Day student tuition: $17,980. Tuition installment plan (monthly payment plans, individually arranged payment plans, 8-month plan, trimester plan, or full-payment plan). Tuition reduction for siblings, need-based scholarship grants available. In 2012–13, 31% of upper-school students received aid. Total amount of financial aid awarded in 2012–13: $1,148,249.

Admissions Traditional secondary-level entrance grade is 9. SSAT required. Deadline for receipt of application materials: November 21. Application fee required: $40. On-campus interview required.

Athletics Interscholastic: basketball (girls), cross-country running (g), diving (g), field hockey (g), golf (g), lacrosse (g), racquetball (g), soccer (g), softball (g), swimming and diving (g), tennis (g), track and field (g), volleyball (g). 7 PE instructors, 34 coaches, 1 athletic trainer.

Computers Computers are regularly used in all academic classes. Computer network features include on-campus library services, online commercial services, Internet access, wireless campus network, Internet filtering or blocking technology, students in grades 7 to 12 have personal HP tablet PCs. Campus intranet, student e-mail accounts, and computer access in designated common areas are available to students. Students grades are available online. The school has a published electronic and media policy.

Contact Mrs. Elaine Brooks, Admissions Assistant. 314-810-3566. Fax: 314-432-0199. E-mail: ebrooks@vdoh.org. Website: www.vdoh.org

VILLA JOSEPH MARIE HIGH SCHOOL

1180 Holland Road
Holland, Pennsylvania 18966

Head of School: Mrs. Mary T. Michel

General Information Girls' day college-preparatory, arts, religious studies, and drama school, affiliated with Roman Catholic Church. Grades 9–12. Founded: 1932. Setting: suburban. Nearest major city is Philadelphia. 55-acre campus. 3 buildings on campus. Approved or accredited by Middle States Association of Colleges and Schools and Pennsylvania Department of Education. Member of National Association of Independent Schools. Total enrollment: 363. Upper school average class size: 15. Upper school faculty-student ratio: 1:9. There are 169 required school days per year for Upper School students. Upper School students typically attend 5 days per week. The average school day consists of 6 hours and 45 minutes.

Upper School Student Profile Grade 9: 91 students (91 girls); Grade 10: 97 students (97 girls); Grade 11: 87 students (87 girls); Grade 12: 88 students (88 girls). 98% of students are Roman Catholic.

Faculty School total: 44. In upper school: 9 men, 35 women; 27 have advanced degrees.

Subjects Offered Algebra, American government, American history, American history-AP, anatomy and physiology, ancient history, art, art appreciation, biology, biology-AP, business mathematics, calculus-AP, chemistry, chemistry-AP, chorus, conceptual physics, dance, drama, earth science, English, English literature-AP, environmental science, environmental science-AP, European history-AP, film and literature, forensics, French, geometry, graphic design, health, Italian, Latin, music, physical education, physics, physics-AP, pre-calculus, psychology, psychology-AP, sociology, Spanish, speech, studio art, theology, trigonometry, world history, writing.

Graduation Requirements Arts and fine arts (art, music, dance, drama), English, foreign language, mathematics, physical education (includes health), religion (includes Bible studies and theology), science, social sciences, social studies (includes history), service hours requirement.

Special Academic Programs 10 Advanced Placement exams for which test preparation is offered; honors section; independent study; study at local college for college credit; academic accommodation for the gifted.

College Admission Counseling 84 students graduated in 2013; all went to college, including Penn State University Park; Saint Joseph's University; The University of Scranton; University of Pittsburgh; Villanova University; West Chester University of Pennsylvania. Mean SAT critical reading: 571, mean SAT math: 584, mean SAT writing: 604.

Student Life Upper grades have uniform requirement, student council, honor system. Discipline rests primarily with faculty. Attendance at religious services is required.

Summer Programs Enrichment, advancement, sports, art/fine arts programs offered; session focuses on enrichment; held on campus; accepts girls; open to students from other schools. 150 students usually enrolled. 2014 schedule: July to July.

Tuition and Aid Day student tuition: $12,150. Tuition installment plan (monthly payment plans, individually arranged payment plans). Tuition reduction for siblings, merit scholarship grants, need-based scholarship grants available. In 2013–14, 6% of upper-school students received aid; total upper-school merit-scholarship money awarded: $160,000.

Admissions Traditional secondary-level entrance grade is 9. For fall 2013, 200 students applied for upper-level admission, 130 were accepted, 91 enrolled. High School Placement Test required. Deadline for receipt of application materials: November 16. Application fee required: $65. On-campus interview required.

Athletics Interscholastic: basketball, bowling, cheering, cross-country running, field hockey, golf, indoor track, lacrosse, soccer, softball, swimming and diving, tennis, track and field, volleyball, winter (indoor) track. 1 PE instructor, 17 coaches, 1 athletic trainer.

Computers Computers are regularly used in art, college planning, creative writing, English, foreign language, health, history, library, literary magazine, mathematics, religion, science, yearbook classes. Computer network features include on-campus library services, online commercial services, Internet access, wireless campus network, Internet filtering or blocking technology. Computer access in designated common areas is available to students. Students grades are available online. The school has a published electronic and media policy.

Contact Mrs. Laura Lasky, Director of Admissions. 215-357-8810 Ext. 193. Fax: 215-357-9410. E-mail: llasky@vjmhs.org. Website: www.vjmhs.org

VILLA MADONNA ACADEMY

2500 Amsterdam Road
Covington, Kentucky 41017

Head of School: Mrs. Pamela McQueen

General Information Coeducational day college-preparatory school, affiliated with Roman Catholic Church. Grades 7–12. Founded: 1904. Setting: suburban. Nearest major city is Cincinnati, OH. 234-acre campus. 3 buildings on campus. Approved or accredited by Commission on Secondary and Middle Schools, Southern Association of Colleges and Schools, and Kentucky Department of Education. Total enrollment: 426. Upper school average class size: 11. Upper school faculty-student ratio: 1:8. There are 177 required school days per year for Upper School students. Upper School students typically attend 5 days per week. The average school day consists of 6 hours and 30 minutes.

Upper School Student Profile Grade 7: 27 students (10 boys, 17 girls); Grade 8: 38 students (20 boys, 18 girls); Grade 9: 23 students (12 boys, 11 girls); Grade 10: 39 students (10 boys, 29 girls); Grade 11: 34 students (11 boys, 23 girls); Grade 12: 36 students (9 boys, 27 girls). 70% of students are Roman Catholic.

Faculty School total: 26. In upper school: 9 men, 17 women; 18 have advanced degrees.

Subjects Offered Accounting, advanced biology, advanced chemistry, Advanced Placement courses, advanced studio art-AP, algebra, American history, American history-AP, art, art history, biology, calculus, calculus-AP, campus ministry, chemistry, chorus, computer programming-AP, computer science, desktop publishing, drama, English, English-AP, European history, French, French-AP, geometry, government/civics, health, honors English, Latin, Latin-AP, macro/microeconomics-AP, media production, music, music theory-AP, physical education, physics, physics-AP, pre-calculus, psychology-AP, religion, Spanish, Spanish-AP, speech, speech communications, world cultures.

College Admission Counseling 56 went to college, including University of Cincinnati; University of Louisville.

Student Life Upper grades have uniform requirement, student council, honor system. Discipline rests primarily with faculty. Attendance at religious services is required.

Tuition and Aid Tuition installment plan (FACTS Tuition Payment Plan). Tuition reduction for siblings, merit scholarship grants, need-based scholarship grants available.

Admissions Traditional secondary-level entrance grade is 9. Diocesan Entrance Exam required. Deadline for receipt of application materials: none. No application fee required. On-campus interview recommended.

Athletics Interscholastic: baseball (boys), basketball (b,g), cross-country running (b,g), golf (b,g), soccer (b,g), softball (g), swimming and diving (b,g), tennis (b,g), track and field (b,g), volleyball (g).

Computers Computers are regularly used in all classes. Computer network features include on-campus library services, Internet access, wireless campus network, Internet filtering or blocking technology. Student e-mail accounts are available to students. Students grades are available online. The school has a published electronic and media policy.

Contact Mrs. Janet Baugh, Admissions Director. 859-331-6333 Ext. 139. Fax: 859-331-8615. E-mail: admissions@villamadonna.net. Website: www.villamadonna.net/

VILLA VICTORIA ACADEMY

376 West Upper Ferry Road
Ewing, New Jersey 08628

Head of School: Sr. Lillian Harrington, MPF

General Information Girls' day college-preparatory, arts, religious studies, and technology school, affiliated with Roman Catholic Church. Grades PK–12. Founded: 1933. Setting: suburban. Nearest major city is Trenton. 44-acre campus. 7 buildings on campus. Approved or accredited by Middle States Association of Colleges and Schools, National Catholic Education Association, and New Jersey Department of Education. Member of National Association of Independent Schools. Total enrollment: 168. Upper school average class size: 12. Upper school faculty-student ratio: 1:8. There are 180 required school days per year for Upper School students. Upper School students typically attend 5 days per week. The average school day consists of 6 hours and 20 minutes.

Upper School Student Profile Grade 9: 14 students (14 girls); Grade 10: 15 students (15 girls); Grade 11: 14 students (14 girls); Grade 12: 12 students (12 girls). 65% of students are Roman Catholic.

Faculty School total: 35. In upper school: 5 men, 16 women; 13 have advanced degrees.

Subjects Offered Algebra, American literature, art, art history, art-AP, arts, arts appreciation, athletics, Bible studies, biology, calculus, calculus-AP, campus ministry, career and personal planning, career exploration, career planning, career/college preparation, Catholic belief and practice, ceramics, character education, chemistry, chemistry-AP, Chinese studies, choir, choral music, chorus, Christian education, Christian ethics, Christianity, church history, clayworking, college admission preparation, college awareness, college counseling, college placement, college planning, college writing, communication skills, community service, computer science, concert band, concert choir, creative thinking, creative writing, critical thinking, critical writing, cultural arts, current events, drama, drawing, drawing and design, earth science, English, English composition, English language and composition-AP, English literature, English literature-AP, English-AP, ethics and responsibility, European history, fiction, fine arts, French, French language-AP, French studies, French-AP, gender and religion, general business, general math, general science, geography, geometry, global issues, government, government and politics-AP, government-AP, government/civics, government/civics-AP, grammar, health, health and safety, health and wellness, health education, history, history of music, history of religion, history of the Americas, history of the Catholic Church, history-AP, honors algebra, honors English, honors geometry, honors U.S. history, honors world history, humanities, independent study, interdisciplinary studies, Internet, Internet research, interpersonal skills, language and composition, Latin, leadership, leadership and service, library research, library skills, life management skills, Life of Christ, linguistics, literary

magazine, literature, literature-AP, math analysis, math applications, math methods, math review, mathematics, mathematics-AP, mechanics of writing, modern history, modern languages, modern world history, money management, moral and social development, moral reasoning, moral theology, multimedia, music, music appreciation, music history, music performance, music theater, music theory, musical productions, musical theater, musical theater dance, oil painting, painting, participation in sports, peer ministry, performing arts, personal development, personal finance, personal fitness, personal money management, photography, physical education, physics, physics-AP, play production, poetry, portfolio art, pottery, prayer/spirituality, pre-algebra, pre-calculus, public service, public speaking, qualitative analysis, reading/study skills, religion, religion and culture, religious education, research, research skills, rhetoric, SAT preparation, SAT/ACT preparation, science, science and technology, sculpture, senior humanities, senior project, senior seminar, set design, Shakespeare, skills for success, social skills, social studies, society and culture, Spanish, Spanish language-AP, Spanish-AP, sports, sports conditioning, stage design, stagecraft, strategies for success, student government, student publications, theater, theater design and production, trigonometry, U.S. history, United States government-AP, values and decisions, visual and performing arts, visual arts, vocal ensemble, world civilizations, world cultures, world history, world issues, world literature, world religions, writing.

Graduation Requirements American literature, art history, arts and fine arts (art, music, dance, drama), biology, British literature, chemistry, computer science, English, foreign language, mathematics, physical education (includes health), physics, religion (includes Bible studies and theology), SAT/ACT preparation, science, social studies (includes history), world cultures, world literature, interdisciplinary humanities. Community service is required.

Special Academic Programs Advanced Placement exam preparation; honors section; independent study; academic accommodation for the gifted, the musically talented, and the artistically talented.

College Admission Counseling 17 students graduated in 2013; all went to college, including Boston University; Fordham University; New York University; The George Washington University; University of Pennsylvania; Villanova University. Median combined SAT: 1814.

Student Life Upper grades have uniform requirement, student council, honor system. Discipline rests primarily with faculty. Attendance at religious services is required.

Tuition and Aid Day student tuition: $12,000. Tuition installment plan (FACTS Tuition Payment Plan, individually arranged payment plans, 2-payment plan). Tuition reduction for siblings, merit scholarship grants, need-based scholarship grants available. In 2013–14, 30% of upper-school students received aid; total upper-school merit-scholarship money awarded: $50,000.

Admissions Traditional secondary-level entrance grade is 9. High School Placement Test (closed version) from Scholastic Testing Service or school placement exam required. Deadline for receipt of application materials: December 13. Application fee required: $50. On-campus interview required.

Athletics Interscholastic: basketball, cross-country running, soccer, softball, tennis, track and field; intramural: dance, outdoor activities, outdoor education, walking. 1 PE instructor, 4 coaches.

Computers Computers are regularly used in art, English, foreign language, history, mathematics, music, SAT preparation, science, theater classes. Computer network features include on-campus library services, Internet access, wireless campus network, Internet filtering or blocking technology, each student in 9-11 grade have their own NetBook for use in school and home. Computer access in designated common areas is available to students. Students grades are available online. The school has a published electronic and media policy.

Contact Ms. Lori Hoffman, Director of Admissions. 609-882-1700 Ext. 19. Fax: 609-882-8421. E-mail: lhoffman@villavictoria.org. Website: www.villavictoria.org

VILLA WALSH ACADEMY

455 Western Avenue
Morristown, New Jersey 07960

Head of School: Sr. Patricia Pompa

General Information Girls' day college-preparatory, arts, religious studies, and technology school, affiliated with Roman Catholic Church. Grades 7–12. Founded: 1967. Setting: suburban. Nearest major city is New York, NY. 130-acre campus. 4 buildings on campus. Approved or accredited by Middle States Association of Colleges and Schools, National Catholic Education Association, New Jersey Department of Education, and New Jersey Department of Education. Endowment: $6 million. Total enrollment: 252. Upper school average class size: 12. Upper school faculty-student ratio: 1:8. There are 176 required school days per year for Upper School students. Upper School students typically attend 5 days per week. The average school day consists of 6 hours and 30 minutes.

Upper School Student Profile Grade 9: 57 students (57 girls); Grade 10: 54 students (54 girls); Grade 11: 55 students (55 girls); Grade 12: 56 students (56 girls). 90% of students are Roman Catholic.

Faculty School total: 35. In upper school: 3 men, 32 women; 20 have advanced degrees.

Subjects Offered Advanced Placement courses, algebra, American history, American literature, anatomy and physiology, art, Bible as literature, biology, biology-AP, British literature, British literature (honors), calculus, calculus-AP, career/college preparation, chemistry, chemistry-AP, choral music, chorus, church history, college admission preparation, computer applications, computer graphics, computer literacy, computer processing, computer programming, computer science, computer skills, CPR, creative writing, desktop publishing, driver education, economics, English, English language and composition-AP, English literature, ethics, European civilization, European history-AP, family living, finite math, first aid, French, French language-AP, French-AP, geometry, health education, honors English, honors geometry, honors U.S. history, Italian, keyboarding, life science, mathematics, modern European history, moral theology, philosophy, physical education, physics, physics-AP, pre-algebra, pre-calculus, psychology, psychology-AP, religion, Spanish, Spanish-AP, statistics-AP, studio art, theology, U.S. government and politics, U.S. history, U.S. history-AP, voice ensemble, Web site design, world history, world literature.

Graduation Requirements Arts and fine arts (art, music, dance, drama), English, foreign language, mathematics, physical education (includes health), science, social studies (includes history), theology.

Special Academic Programs 14 Advanced Placement exams for which test preparation is offered; honors section; independent study; academic accommodation for the gifted, the musically talented, and the artistically talented.

College Admission Counseling 57 students graduated in 2013; all went to college, including Boston College; College of the Holy Cross; Georgetown University; Loyola University Maryland; University of Notre Dame; Villanova University. Mean SAT critical reading: 640, mean SAT math: 620, mean SAT writing: 670, mean combined SAT: 1930.

Student Life Upper grades have uniform requirement, student council, honor system. Discipline rests primarily with faculty. Attendance at religious services is required.

Tuition and Aid Day student tuition: $17,500. Tuition installment plan (Insured Tuition Payment Plan, Key Tuition Payment Plan, individually arranged payment plans). Merit scholarship grants, need-based scholarship grants available. In 2013–14, 11% of upper-school students received aid; total upper-school merit-scholarship money awarded: $10,000. Total amount of financial aid awarded in 2013–14: $110,000.

Admissions Traditional secondary-level entrance grade is 9. For fall 2013, 150 students applied for upper-level admission, 70 were accepted, 60 enrolled. Math, reading, and mental ability tests and writing sample required. Deadline for receipt of application materials: none. Application fee required: $50. On-campus interview required.

Athletics Interscholastic: basketball, cross-country running, indoor track, lacrosse, soccer, softball, swimming and diving, tennis, track and field, volleyball, winter (indoor) track. 1 PE instructor, 32 coaches, 1 athletic trainer.

Computers Computers are regularly used in college planning, desktop publishing, independent study, keyboarding, library science, mathematics, newspaper, programming, SAT preparation, science, technology, Web site design, word processing, yearbook classes. Computer network features include on-campus library services, Internet access, wireless campus network, Internet filtering or blocking technology. Campus intranet is available to students. The school has a published electronic and media policy.

Contact Sr. Doris Lavinthal, Director. 973-538-3680 Ext. 175. Fax: 973-538-6733. E-mail: lavinthald@aol.com. Website: www.villawalsh.org

VISITATION ACADEMY

3020 North Ballas Road
St. Louis, Missouri 63131

Head of School: Mrs. Rosalie Henry

General Information Coeducational day (boys' only in lower grades) college-preparatory, arts, and technology school, affiliated with Roman Catholic Church. Boys grade PK, girls grades PK–12. Founded: 1833. Setting: suburban. 30-acre campus. 1 building on campus. Approved or accredited by Independent Schools Association of the Central States, National Catholic Education Association, North Central Association of Colleges and Schools, and Missouri Department of Education. Member of National Association of Independent Schools. Endowment: $7 million. Total enrollment: 642. Upper school average class size: 16. Upper school faculty-student ratio: 1:9. There are 176 required school days per year for Upper School students. Upper School students typically attend 5 days per week. The average school day consists of 7 hours.

Upper School Student Profile Grade 7: 44 students (44 girls); Grade 8: 66 students (66 girls); Grade 9: 88 students (88 girls); Grade 10: 89 students (89 girls); Grade 11: 98 students (98 girls); Grade 12: 93 students (93 girls). 84% of students are Roman Catholic.

Faculty School total: 53. In upper school: 8 men, 45 women; 45 have advanced degrees.

Subjects Offered Adolescent issues, advanced biology, advanced chemistry, advanced math, Advanced Placement courses, algebra, American history, American history-AP, American literature, American literature-AP, anatomy, anatomy and physiology, art, art appreciation, art history, bell choir, Bible studies, biology, biology-AP, calculus, calculus-AP, ceramics, character education, chemistry, chemistry-AP, choral music, chorus, Christian studies, Christian testament, church history, civics, classical language, computer art, computer math, computer programming, computer science, concert choir, creative writing, drama, earth science, economics, economics and history, engineering, English, English literature, English literature-AP, environmental science, European history, European history-AP, expository writing, fine

arts, French, French-AP, genetics, geography, geometry, government/civics, grammar, health, history, independent study, journalism, keyboarding, Latin, mathematics, music, New Testament, photo shop, photography, physical education, physical science, physics, pre-calculus, psychology, robotics, science, social studies, Spanish, speech, statistics-AP, theater, theology, trigonometry, U.S. history-AP, world geography, world literature.

Graduation Requirements Arts and fine arts (art, music, dance, drama), computers, electives, English, foreign language, mathematics, physical education (includes health), science, service learning/internship, social studies (includes history), theology, 120 hours of community service.

Special Academic Programs 12 Advanced Placement exams for which test preparation is offered; honors section; independent study; study at local college for college credit; special instructional classes for students with mild learning differences.

College Admission Counseling 62 students graduated in 2013; all went to college, including Creighton University; Rockhurst University; Saint Louis University; University of Dayton; University of Missouri; Washington University in St. Louis. Median SAT critical reading: 620, median SAT math: 610, median SAT writing: 600, median combined SAT: 1830, median composite ACT: 29.

Student Life Upper grades have uniform requirement, student council. Discipline rests primarily with faculty. Attendance at religious services is required.

Summer Programs Sports programs offered; session focuses on athletics—basketball, soccer, volleyball, cheerleading; held on campus; accepts girls; open to students from other schools. 200 students usually enrolled.

Tuition and Aid Day student tuition: $17,305. Tuition installment plan (FACTS Tuition Payment Plan). Need-based scholarship grants available. In 2013–14, 10% of upper-school students received aid.

Admissions Traditional secondary-level entrance grade is 7. For fall 2013, 134 students applied for upper-level admission, 112 were accepted, 75 enrolled. SSAT required. Deadline for receipt of application materials: January 17. Application fee required: $75. On-campus interview required.

Athletics Interscholastic: basketball, cheering, cross-country running, dance, diving, field hockey, golf, lacrosse, racquetball, soccer, softball, swimming and diving, tennis, track and field, volleyball; intramural: cheering, dance. 4 PE instructors, 17 coaches, 1 athletic trainer.

Computers Computers are regularly used in all academic, art, English, foreign language, history, mathematics, science, theology classes. Computer network features include on-campus library services, Internet access, wireless campus network, Internet filtering or blocking technology. Campus intranet and student e-mail accounts are available to students. Students grades are available online. The school has a published electronic and media policy.

Contact Mrs. Ashley Giljum, Director of Admission. 314-625-9102. Fax: 314-432-7210. E-mail: agiljum@visitationacademy.org. Website: www.visitationacademy.org

WAKEFIELD SCHOOL

4439 Old Tavern Road
PO Box 107
The Plains, Virginia 20198

Head of School: Mr. Ed Costello

General Information Coeducational day college-preparatory and arts school. Grades PS–12. Founded: 1972. Setting: rural. Nearest major city is Washington, DC. 65-acre campus. 6 buildings on campus. Approved or accredited by Virginia Department of Education. Member of National Association of Independent Schools. Total enrollment: 397. Upper school average class size: 10. Upper school faculty-student ratio: 1:11. There are 180 required school days per year for Upper School students. Upper School students typically attend 5 days per week. The average school day consists of 7 hours.

Upper School Student Profile Grade 9: 48 students (22 boys, 26 girls); Grade 10: 43 students (17 boys, 26 girls); Grade 11: 28 students (14 boys, 14 girls); Grade 12: 33 students (11 boys, 22 girls).

Faculty School total: 45. In upper school: 16 men, 14 women; 24 have advanced degrees.

Subjects Offered Acting, Advanced Placement courses, algebra, American government, American history-AP, American literature, art, art history, bell choir, biology, biology-AP, British history, British literature, British literature-AP, calculus, calculus-AP, chemistry, chemistry-AP, chorus, classical language, composition, computer applications, computer programming, conservation, drama, dramatic arts, earth science, Eastern world civilizations, ecology, English language and composition-AP, English literature and composition-AP, environmental science, environmental science-AP, European history-AP, French, French language-AP, geometry, geopolitics, government and politics-AP, government/civics, Latin, Latin-AP, model United Nations, music, music composition, music history, music theory, music theory-AP, physical fitness, physics, physics-AP, political science, psychology, publications, senior thesis, Spanish, Spanish language-AP, statistics, statistics-AP, studio art, studio art-AP, U.S. history, world civilizations, world literature.

Graduation Requirements Advanced math, algebra, American history, American literature, arts, British literature, composition, computer literacy, English, foreign language, geometry, government/civics, grammar, lab science, language, literature, physical education (includes health), pre-calculus, world civilizations, 2 interdisciplinary compositions, 2 thesis and portfolio projects, including senior thesis.

Special Academic Programs 14 Advanced Placement exams for which test preparation is offered; honors section; independent study; programs in general development for dyslexic students.

College Admission Counseling 33 students graduated in 2013; all went to college, including Elon University; George Mason University; Rhode Island School of Design; University of Mary Washington; University of Virginia. Mean SAT critical reading: 622, mean SAT math: 597, mean SAT writing: 601, mean combined SAT: 1820.

Student Life Upper grades have uniform requirement, student council, honor system. Discipline rests equally with students and faculty.

Summer Programs Remediation, enrichment, advancement, sports, art/fine arts, computer instruction programs offered; session focuses on academics, athletics, fine arts, fun; held both on and off campus; held at various locations; accepts boys and girls; open to students from other schools. 200 students usually enrolled. 2014 schedule: June 15 to July 25.

Tuition and Aid Day student tuition: $3080–$23,950. Tuition installment plan (FACTS Tuition Payment Plan, monthly payment plans, The Tuition Refund Plan). Need-based scholarship grants available. In 2013–14, 25% of upper-school students received aid. Total amount of financial aid awarded in 2013–14: $1,500,000.

Admissions Traditional secondary-level entrance grade is 9. Admissions testing or SSAT required. Deadline for receipt of application materials: none. Application fee required: $60. Interview required.

Athletics Interscholastic: basketball (boys, girls), field hockey (g), lacrosse (b,g), soccer (b,g), squash (b), strength & conditioning (b,g), tennis (b,g), volleyball (g); intramural: field hockey (g), fitness (b,g), lacrosse (b,g), outdoor activities (b,g), soccer (b,g), squash (b), strength & conditioning (b,g), tennis (b,g), volleyball (g), weight training (b,g); coed interscholastic: aquatics, cross-country running, equestrian sports, fitness, golf, physical fitness, squash, swimming and diving; coed intramural: aquatics, cross-country running, squash, swimming and diving. 2 PE instructors, 5 coaches, 1 athletic trainer.

Computers Computers are regularly used in all academic, publications, yearbook classes. Computer network features include on-campus library services, online commercial services, Internet access, wireless campus network, Internet filtering or blocking technology, new Science and Technology building opened in January 2007, student center login/password protected portal for students on new Web site. Campus intranet, student e-mail accounts, and computer access in designated common areas are available to students. Students grades are available online. The school has a published electronic and media policy.

Contact Office of Admissions. 540-253-7600. Fax: 540-253-5492. E-mail: admissions@wakefieldschool.org. Website: www.wakefieldschool.org

WALDORF HIGH SCHOOL OF MASSACHUSETTS BAY

160 Lexington Street
Belmont, Massachusetts 02478

Head of School: Mara D. White

General Information Coeducational day college-preparatory and arts school. Grades 9–12. Founded: 1996. Setting: suburban. Nearest major city is Boston. 1 building on campus. Approved or accredited by Association of Independent Schools in New England, Association of Waldorf Schools of North America, New England Association of Schools and Colleges, and Massachusetts Department of Education. Total enrollment: 55. Upper school average class size: 14. Upper school faculty-student ratio: 1:7. There are 165 required school days per year for Upper School students. Upper School students typically attend 5 days per week. The average school day consists of 6 hours and 30 minutes.

Upper School Student Profile Grade 9: 10 students (4 boys, 6 girls); Grade 10: 17 students (5 boys, 12 girls); Grade 11: 19 students (7 boys, 12 girls); Grade 12: 9 students (6 boys, 3 girls).

Faculty School total: 12. In upper school: 4 men, 4 women; 3 have advanced degrees.

Subjects Offered Algebra, American history, American literature, American studies, analysis and differential calculus, anatomy and physiology, ancient history, ancient world history, art, art history, astronomy, athletics, Bible as literature, biology, bookbinding, botany, calculus, chemistry, chorus, classical Greek literature, college admission preparation, college counseling, college placement, community service, computer applications, computer programming, creative writing, current events, digital art, drama, drama performance, earth science, electives, English, English literature, epic literature, European history, expository writing, fine arts, fitness, geography, geometry, global studies, grammar, health education, jazz ensemble, mathematics, medieval/Renaissance history, model United Nations, modern history, music, Native American history, painting, photography, physical education, physics, play production, poetry, projective geometry, Russian literature, SAT preparation, senior internship, senior seminar, Spanish, theory of knowledge, trigonometry, U.S. government, woodworking, world history, world literature, writing, yearbook, zoology.

Graduation Requirements Algebra, arts and fine arts (art, music, dance, drama), chemistry, English, English literature, foreign language, geometry, global studies,

mathematics, music, performing arts, physical education (includes health), physics, practical arts, science, social studies (includes history). Community service is required.

Special Academic Programs Honors section; independent study; term-away projects; study abroad.

College Admission Counseling 16 students graduated in 2013; 12 went to college, including Connecticut College; Guilford College; Northeastern University; Occidental College; Smith College; University of Massachusetts Amherst. Other: 4 went to work.

Student Life Upper grades have specified standards of dress, student council. Discipline rests primarily with faculty.

Tuition and Aid Day student tuition: $25,800. Tuition installment plan (monthly payment plans, individually arranged payment plans). Tuition reduction for siblings, merit scholarship grants, need-based scholarship grants available. In 2013–14, 40% of upper-school students received aid; total upper-school merit-scholarship money awarded: $2000. Total amount of financial aid awarded in 2013–14: $357,455.

Admissions Traditional secondary-level entrance grade is 9. For fall 2013, 38 students applied for upper-level admission, 28 were accepted, 18 enrolled. Essay, grade equivalent tests or math and English placement tests required. Deadline for receipt of application materials: none. Application fee required: $50. Interview required.

Athletics Interscholastic: basketball (boys, girls), soccer (b,g); coed interscholastic: ultimate Frisbee. 2 coaches.

Computers Computers are regularly used in college planning, creative writing, current events, independent study, mathematics, photography, research skills, SAT preparation, Spanish, yearbook classes. Computer network features include Internet access, Internet filtering or blocking technology. Computer access in designated common areas is available to students. The school has a published electronic and media policy.

Contact Susan Morris, Enrollment Coordinator. 617-489-6600 Ext. 11. Fax: 617-489-6619. E-mail: s.morris@waldorfhighschool.org. Website: www.waldorfhighschool.org

THE WALDORF SCHOOL OF GARDEN CITY

225 Cambridge Avenue
Garden City, New York 11530

Head of School: Ms. Sabine Kully

General Information Coeducational day college-preparatory, arts, and liberal arts school. Grades N–12. Founded: 1947. Setting: suburban. Nearest major city is New York. 10-acre campus. 1 building on campus. Approved or accredited by Association of Waldorf Schools of North America, Middle States Association of Colleges and Schools, and New York Department of Education. Member of National Association of Independent Schools and Secondary School Admission Test Board. Endowment: $4 million. Total enrollment: 350. Upper school average class size: 25. Upper school faculty-student ratio: 1:5. There are 170 required school days per year for Upper School students. Upper School students typically attend 5 days per week. The average school day consists of 7 hours and 10 minutes.

Upper School Student Profile Grade 6: 21 students (11 boys, 10 girls); Grade 7: 23 students (7 boys, 16 girls); Grade 8: 23 students (10 boys, 13 girls); Grade 9: 29 students (14 boys, 15 girls); Grade 10: 25 students (13 boys, 12 girls); Grade 11: 24 students (11 boys, 13 girls); Grade 12: 27 students (14 boys, 13 girls).

Faculty School total: 50. In upper school: 9 men, 12 women; 14 have advanced degrees.

Subjects Offered Algebra, American history, American literature, anatomy, art, art history, biology, botany, calculus, cartography, chemistry, computer science, creative writing, dance, drama, earth science, economics, English, English literature, European history, expository writing, fine arts, French, geography, geology, geometry, German, government/civics, grammar, health, history, mathematics, model United Nations, music, physical education, physics, physiology, science, sculpture, social studies, speech, trigonometry, woodworking, world history, world literature, writing, zoology.

Graduation Requirements Applied arts, arts and fine arts (art, music, dance, drama), English, French, German, history of architecture, history of drama, history of music, history of science, literature, medieval history, medieval/Renaissance history, music, organic chemistry, physical education (includes health), science, social studies (includes history).

Special Academic Programs Independent study; study at local college for college credit; study abroad; academic accommodation for the musically talented and the artistically talented.

College Admission Counseling Colleges students went to include American University; Boston College; Dartmouth College; Fordham University; Rochester Institute of Technology; Wellesley College. 35% scored over 600 on SAT critical reading, 40% scored over 600 on SAT math, 14% scored over 600 on SAT writing, 45% scored over 26 on composite ACT.

Student Life Upper grades have specified standards of dress, student council, honor system. Discipline rests equally with students and faculty.

Summer Programs Enrichment programs offered; session focuses on music, drama, field trips, tennis, painting, crafts, puppetry, swimming, athletics; held both on and off campus; held at Camp Glen Brook (programs in summer and winter); accepts boys and girls; open to students from other schools. 80 students usually enrolled. 2014 schedule: June 25 to August 3. Application deadline: none.

Tuition and Aid Day student tuition: $22,300. Tuition installment plan (FACTS Tuition Payment Plan). Merit scholarship grants, need-based scholarship grants available. In 2013–14, 35% of upper-school students received aid; total upper-school merit-scholarship money awarded: $30,000. Total amount of financial aid awarded in 2013–14: $180,000.

Admissions SSAT required. Deadline for receipt of application materials: none. Application fee required: $75. On-campus interview required.

Athletics Interscholastic: baseball (boys, girls), basketball (b,g), cross-country running (b,g), independent competitive sports (b,g), physical fitness (b,g), soccer (b,g), softball (g), volleyball (g); intramural: artistic gym (b,g), cooperative games (b,g), dance (b,g), fitness (b,g), volleyball (b,g); coed interscholastic: outdoor education, ropes courses, soccer; coed intramural: artistic gym, dance, fitness, volleyball. 2 PE instructors, 6 coaches.

Computers Computers are regularly used in research skills, science, yearbook classes. Computer network features include on-campus library services, online commercial services, Internet access, wireless campus network, Internet filtering or blocking technology. Campus intranet, student e-mail accounts, and computer access in designated common areas are available to students. The school has a published electronic and media policy.

Contact Mrs. Carol Proctor, Admissions Assistant. 516-742-3434 Ext. 129. Fax: 516-742-3457. E-mail: proctorc@waldorfgarden.org. Website: www.waldorfgarden.org

THE WALDORF SCHOOL OF SARATOGA SPRINGS

122 Regent Street
Saratoga Springs, New York 12866
Head of School: Ms. Katherine Scharff

General Information Coeducational day college-preparatory, general academic, and arts school. Grades PK–12. Founded: 1981. Setting: suburban. 5-acre campus. 1 building on campus. Approved or accredited by Association of Waldorf Schools of North America and New York Department of Education. Total enrollment: 241. Upper school average class size: 13. Upper school faculty-student ratio: 1:13. There are 170 required school days per year for Upper School students. Upper School students typically attend 5 days per week. The average school day consists of 7 hours and 20 minutes.

Upper School Student Profile Grade 9: 9 students (4 boys, 5 girls); Grade 10: 10 students (4 boys, 6 girls); Grade 11: 17 students (10 boys, 7 girls); Grade 12: 12 students (6 boys, 6 girls).

Faculty School total: 30. In upper school: 6 men, 11 women; 9 have advanced degrees.

Subjects Offered All academic.

Graduation Requirements Art, chemistry, earth science, English, eurythmy, foreign language, history, life science, mathematics, music, physical education (includes health), physics, juniors must complete an internship program, seniors must complete a senior project.

Special Academic Programs Independent study; study abroad; remedial reading and/or remedial writing; remedial math.

College Admission Counseling 8 students graduated in 2013; 7 went to college, including Bard College; Bowdoin College; Pratt Institute; Rensselaer Polytechnic Institute; Skidmore College; University of Massachusetts Amherst. Other: 1 went to work.

Student Life Upper grades have specified standards of dress, honor system. Discipline rests primarily with faculty.

Tuition and Aid Day student tuition: $15,195. Tuition installment plan (monthly payment plans). Tuition reduction for siblings, need-based scholarship grants, Tuition Assistance Program available. In 2013–14, 30% of upper-school students received aid.

Admissions Traditional secondary-level entrance grade is 9. For fall 2013, 11 students applied for upper-level admission, 11 were accepted, 9 enrolled. Non-standardized placement tests required. Deadline for receipt of application materials: none. No application fee required. Interview required.

Athletics Interscholastic: cross-country running (boys, girls), rowing (b,g); coed intramural: archery, climbing, golf, hiking/backpacking, outdoor activities, outdoor adventure, outdoor education, outdoor recreation, outdoor skills, rock climbing, tennis, walking, yoga. 1 PE instructor.

Computers Computers are regularly used in computer applications, graphic design, yearbook classes. Students grades are available online. The school has a published electronic and media policy.

Contact Mrs. Debra Nicastro, Admissions Coordinator. 518-587-2224. Fax: 518-581-1466. E-mail: admissions@waldorfsaratoga.org. Website: www.waldorfsaratoga.org/

WALNUT HILL SCHOOL FOR THE ARTS

12 Highland Street
Natick, Massachusetts 01760-2199
Head of School: Mr. Antonio Viva

General Information Coeducational boarding and day college-preparatory and arts school. Grades 9–PG. Founded: 1893. Setting: suburban. Nearest major city is Boston. Students are housed in single-sex dormitories. 30-acre campus. 19 buildings on campus. Approved or accredited by New England Association of Schools and Colleges and Massachusetts Department of Education. Member of National Association of Independent Schools and Secondary School Admission Test Board. Endowment: $12 million. Total enrollment: 298. Upper school average class size: 14. Upper school faculty-student ratio: 1:6.

Upper School Student Profile Grade 9: 43 students (15 boys, 28 girls); Grade 10: 71 students (19 boys, 52 girls); Grade 11: 86 students (27 boys, 59 girls); Grade 12: 98 students (36 boys, 62 girls). 80% of students are boarding students. 31% are state residents. 32 states are represented in upper school student body. 32% are international students. International students from Canada, China, Republic of Korea, Taiwan, Thailand, and United Kingdom; 6 other countries represented in student body.

Faculty School total: 51. In upper school: 24 men, 27 women; 47 have advanced degrees; 20 reside on campus.

Subjects Offered 20th century world history, 3-dimensional art, acting, advanced chemistry, advanced math, algebra, American history, American literature, art history, arts, ballet, ballet technique, biology, calculus, ceramics, chemistry, choral music, choreography, chorus, classical music, college counseling, community service, creative writing, dance, directing, drama, drawing, English, English literature, environmental science, ESL, fine arts, French, geometry, health, history, history of dance, jazz dance, mathematics, modern dance, music history, music theory, musical theater, musical theater dance, opera, orchestra, painting, photography, physics, piano, poetry, pre-calculus, research seminar, science, sculpture, set design, Shakespeare, social studies, Spanish, stage design, technical theater, theater, theater design and production, theater production, U.S. history, visual and performing arts, visual arts, vocal music, voice, voice ensemble, world history, writing.

Graduation Requirements Arts, English, foreign language, mathematics, science, social studies (includes history), U.S. history, completion of arts portfolio, body of writing, or participation in performing arts ensembles and/or solo recital.

Special Academic Programs Advanced Placement exam preparation; honors section; independent study; academic accommodation for the gifted, the musically talented, and the artistically talented; ESL (35 students enrolled).

College Admission Counseling 96 students graduated in 2012; 90 went to college, including New England Conservatory of Music; New York University; Peabody Conservatory of The Johns Hopkins University; Pratt Institute; School of the Art Institute of Chicago; The Juilliard School. Other: 6 had other specific plans. Median SAT critical reading: 590, median SAT math: 580, median SAT writing: 580, median composite ACT: 26.

Student Life Upper grades have student council. Discipline rests equally with students and faculty.

Tuition and Aid Day student tuition: $35,000; 7-day tuition and room/board: $45,900. Tuition installment plan (Insured Tuition Payment Plan, Academic Management Services Plan, monthly payment plans). Need-based scholarship grants available. In 2012–13, 50% of upper-school students received aid. Total amount of financial aid awarded in 2012–13: $2,900,000.

Admissions Traditional secondary-level entrance grade is 10. For fall 2012, 407 students applied for upper-level admission, 178 were accepted, 119 enrolled. Any standardized test, audition, TOEFL or SLEP or writing sample required. Deadline for receipt of application materials: February 1. Application fee required: $65. Interview recommended.

Athletics Intramural: self defense (girls); coed intramural: aerobics, aerobics/dance, ballet, dance, fitness, modern dance, outdoor activities, physical fitness, physical training, self defense, yoga. 3 athletic trainers.

Computers Computer network features include on-campus library services, Internet access, wireless campus network, Internet filtering or blocking technology. Campus intranet, student e-mail accounts, and computer access in designated common areas are available to students. The school has a published electronic and media policy.

Contact Mike Bucco Sr., Acting Director of Admission. 508-650-5020. Fax: 508-655-3726. E-mail: admissions@walnuthillarts.org. Website: why.walnuthillarts.org/

WALSINGHAM ACADEMY

1100 Jamestown Road
PO Box 8702
Williamsburg, Virginia 23187-8702
Head of School: Sr. Mary Jeanne Oesterle, RSM

General Information Coeducational day college-preparatory, arts, religious studies, and technology school, affiliated with Roman Catholic Church. Grades PK–12. Founded: 1947. Setting: small town. Nearest major city is Richmond. 30-acre campus. 2 buildings on campus. Approved or accredited by National Catholic Education Association and Southern Association of Colleges and Schools. Endowment: $3 million. Total enrollment: 533. Upper school average class size: 16. Upper school faculty-student ratio: 1:7. There are 182 required school days per year for Upper School students. Upper School students typically attend 5 days per week. The average school day consists of 6 hours and 30 minutes.

Upper School Student Profile Grade 8: 47 students (21 boys, 26 girls); Grade 9: 41 students (23 boys, 18 girls); Grade 10: 35 students (18 boys, 17 girls); Grade 11: 53 students (32 boys, 21 girls); Grade 12: 43 students (19 boys, 24 girls). 47% of students are Roman Catholic.

Faculty School total: 30. In upper school: 9 men, 21 women; 25 have advanced degrees.

Subjects Offered 3-dimensional art, advanced math, Advanced Placement courses, advanced studio art-AP, algebra, American history, American history-AP, American literature, American literature-AP, ancient world history, art, band, Bible, Bible studies, biology, biology-AP, British literature-AP, calculus, calculus-AP, Catholic belief and practice, chemistry, chemistry-AP, choral music, Christian ethics, Christian scripture, church history, driver education, earth science, economics, English, English language and composition-AP, English literature, English literature and composition-AP, English literature-AP, environmental science, environmental science-AP, fine arts, French, French-AP, geography, geometry, government/civics, health, history, honors English, independent study, Latin, Latin-AP, marine science, mathematics, medieval/Renaissance history, modern world history, music, music theory-AP, newspaper, physical education, physics, physics-AP, pre-calculus, psychology, public speaking, religion, science, social justice, social studies, Spanish, Spanish-AP, statistics, statistics-AP, studio art-AP, theology, trigonometry, U.S. government and politics-AP, U.S. history-AP, world history, yearbook.

Graduation Requirements Arts and fine arts (art, music, dance, drama), English, foreign language, mathematics, physical education (includes health), religion (includes Bible studies and theology), science, social studies (includes history), 20 hours of community service each year.

Special Academic Programs 16 Advanced Placement exams for which test preparation is offered; honors section; independent study.

College Admission Counseling 62 students graduated in 2012; all went to college, including James Madison University; The Catholic University of America; University of Georgia; University of Virginia; Virginia Polytechnic Institute and State University; Wake Forest University. Mean SAT critical reading: 570, mean SAT math: 589, mean SAT writing: 574.

Student Life Upper grades have uniform requirement, student council, honor system. Discipline rests primarily with faculty. Attendance at religious services is required.

Tuition and Aid Day student tuition: $12,534. Tuition installment plan (FACTS Tuition Payment Plan). Tuition reduction for siblings, need-based scholarship grants available. Total amount of financial aid awarded in 2012–13: $190,000.

Admissions Traditional secondary-level entrance grade is 8. For fall 2012, 21 students applied for upper-level admission, 20 were accepted, 20 enrolled. Kuhlmann-Anderson Level G (for grades 7-9) or Level H (for grades 10-12), TerraNova or TOEFL or SLEP required. Deadline for receipt of application materials: none. Application fee required: $100. On-campus interview required.

Athletics Interscholastic: baseball (boys), basketball (b,g), cross-country running (b,g), field hockey (g), golf (b,g), lacrosse (b,g), soccer (b,g), swimming and diving (b,g), tennis (b,g), track and field (b,g), volleyball (g); coed interscholastic: sailing. 2 PE instructors, 32 coaches, 1 athletic trainer.

Computers Computers are regularly used in all classes. Computer network features include on-campus library services, Internet access, wireless campus network, Internet filtering or blocking technology. Students grades are available online. The school has a published electronic and media policy.

Contact Mrs. Anita Magliola, Director of Admissions. 757-229-6026. E-mail: amagliola@walsingham.org. Website: www.walsingham.org

WALTHER CHRISTIAN ACADEMY

900 Chicago Avenue
Melrose Park, Illinois 60160

Head of School: Mr. James Craven

General Information college-preparatory school, affiliated with Lutheran Church–Missouri Synod. Founded: 1954. Setting: suburban. Nearest major city is Chicago. Approved or accredited by Illinois Department of Education. Language of instruction: Spanish. Upper school average class size: 16. Upper school faculty-student ratio: 1:12.

Upper School Student Profile 90% are state residents. 10% are international students. 35% of students are Lutheran Church–Missouri Synod.

Special Academic Programs Advanced Placement exam preparation; honors section; independent study; study at local college for college credit; academic accommodation for the gifted, the musically talented, and the artistically talented; remedial reading and/or remedial writing; remedial math; special instructional classes for deaf students, blind students.

College Admission Counseling 93 students graduated in 2013; all went to college.

Student Life Upper grades have specified standards of dress, student council, honor system. Discipline rests primarily with faculty. Attendance at religious services is required.

Summer Programs Remediation, enrichment, advancement programs offered; held on campus; open to students from other schools.

Tuition and Aid Tuition installment plan (monthly payment plans, individually arranged payment plans, FAST). Tuition reduction for siblings, merit scholarship grants, need-based scholarship grants, need-based loans, middle-income loans, paying campus jobs available.

Admissions Deadline for receipt of application materials: none. Application fee required: $20.

Athletics Interscholastic: baseball (boys), basketball (b,g), cheering (g), cross-country running (b,g), dance team (g), football (b), golf (b,g), pom squad (g), softball (g), tennis (b,g), track and field (b,g), wrestling (b); coed intramural: floor hockey.

Computers Computer network features include on-campus library services, online commercial services, Internet access, wireless campus network, Internet filtering or blocking technology. Campus intranet and computer access in designated common areas are available to students. Students grades are available online. The school has a published electronic and media policy.

Contact 708-344-0404. Fax: 708-344-0525. Website: www.walther.com

WASATCH ACADEMY

120 South 100 West
Mt. Pleasant, Utah 84647

Head of School: Mr. Joseph Loftin

General Information Coeducational boarding and day college-preparatory, arts, bilingual studies, technology, and debate school. Grades 7–PG. Founded: 1875. Setting: small town. Nearest major city is Provo. Students are housed in single-sex dormitories. 40-acre campus. 31 buildings on campus. Approved or accredited by Northwest Association of Independent Schools, Northwest Association of Schools and Colleges, The Association of Boarding Schools, and Utah Department of Education. Member of National Association of Independent Schools. Endowment: $2 million. Total enrollment: 304. Upper school average class size: 12. Upper school faculty-student ratio: 1:10.

Upper School Student Profile Grade 9: 27 students (16 boys, 11 girls); Grade 10: 73 students (43 boys, 30 girls); Grade 11: 96 students (59 boys, 37 girls); Grade 12: 93 students (62 boys, 31 girls); Postgraduate: 1 student (1 boy). 78% of students are boarding students. 26% are state residents. 25 states are represented in upper school student body. 53% are international students. International students from Brazil, China, Russian Federation, Spain, Taiwan, and Viet Nam; 26 other countries represented in student body.

Faculty School total: 53. In upper school: 25 men, 26 women; 19 have advanced degrees; 48 reside on campus.

Subjects Offered 3-dimensional art, 3-dimensional design, acting, advanced computer applications, Advanced Placement courses, advanced studio art-AP, advanced TOEFL/grammar, algebra, American Civil War, American history, American history-AP, American literature-AP, anatomy, animation, art, athletic training, audio visual/media, ballet, biology, biology-AP, broadcast journalism, business mathematics, calculus-AP, ceramics, chemistry, chemistry-AP, Chinese, choir, cinematography, Civil War, college counseling, college placement, comedy, community garden, community service, dance, design, drama, drawing, drawing and design, driver education, earth science, electronic music, emerging technology, English, English language and composition-AP, English literature and composition-AP, English-AP, ensembles, environmental science-AP, equestrian sports, equine science, ESL, ESL, European history, European history-AP, film, filmmaking, fine arts, forensics, French, geography, geology, global issues, golf, guitar, honors algebra, honors English, honors U.S. history, jazz ensemble, jewelry making, Latin, learning strategies, martial arts, math applications, music, music theory, outdoor education, painting, performing arts, philosophy, photography, physical education, physical science, physics, physics-AP, piano, play production, pottery, pre-calculus, reading, SAT/ACT preparation, Spanish, Spanish-AP, speech and debate, stained glass, statistics-AP, student government, studio art-AP, study skills, theater, theater arts, theater design and production, TOEFL preparation, U.S. government, U.S. history, U.S. history-AP, United Nations and international issues, Vietnam War, weightlifting, Western civilization, woodworking, world religions, yearbook, yoga.

Graduation Requirements Arts and fine arts (art, music, dance, drama), computer literacy, English, foreign language, mathematics, physical education (includes health), science, social sciences, social studies (includes history), U.S. history, outdoor, cultural, community service, and recreational requirements.

Special Academic Programs 16 Advanced Placement exams for which test preparation is offered; honors section; accelerated programs; independent study; study at local college for college credit; programs in English, mathematics, general development for dyslexic students; ESL (29 students enrolled).

College Admission Counseling 87 students graduated in 2013; 85 went to college, including Boston University; Michigan State University; Parsons The New School for Design; Penn State University Park; Smith College; University of Utah. Other: 1 entered a postgraduate year, 1 had other specific plans. Median SAT critical reading: 500, median SAT math: 480, median composite ACT: 22. Mean SAT writing: 564, mean combined SAT: 1892. 13% scored over 600 on SAT critical reading, 9% scored over 600 on SAT math, 27% scored over 26 on composite ACT.

Student Life Upper grades have specified standards of dress, student council, honor system. Discipline rests primarily with faculty.

Summer Programs Remediation, enrichment, advancement, ESL programs offered; held on campus; accepts boys and girls; open to students from other schools. 50 students usually enrolled. 2014 schedule: June 23 to August 3. Application deadline: none.

Tuition and Aid Day student tuition: $25,850; 5-day tuition and room/board: $44,200; 7-day tuition and room/board: $47,200. Tuition installment plan (Key Tuition Payment Plan, monthly payment plans, individually arranged payment plans). Merit scholarship grants, need-based scholarship grants, need-based loans available. In 2013–14, 38% of upper-school students received aid; total upper-school merit-scholarship money awarded: $126,000. Total amount of financial aid awarded in 2013–14: $2,650,000.

Admissions Traditional secondary-level entrance grade is 9. For fall 2013, 188 students applied for upper-level admission, 153 were accepted, 111 enrolled. Deadline for receipt of application materials: none. Application fee required: $100. Interview required.

Athletics Interscholastic: alpine skiing (boys, girls), baseball (b), basketball (b,g), climbing (b,g), cross-country running (b,g), dance (b,g), dressage (b,g), equestrian sports (b,g), golf (b,g), horseback riding (b,g), outdoor activities (b,g), outdoor education (b,g), paint ball (b,g), physical training (b,g), rodeo (b,g), running (b,g), skiing (cross-country) (b,g), skiing (downhill) (b,g), snowboarding (b,g), snowshoeing (b,g), soccer (b,g), tennis (b,g), track and field (b,g), volleyball (g), weight training (b,g); intramural: alpine skiing (b,g), dance (g), skiing (downhill) (b,g), soccer (b,g), table tennis (b,g); coed interscholastic: aerobics/dance, backpacking, ballet, bicycling, canoeing/kayaking, cheering, climbing, combined training, cross-country running, dance, dressage, equestrian sports, fishing, golf, hiking/backpacking, horseback riding, kayaking, martial arts, modern dance, mountain biking, nordic skiing, outdoor activities, paint ball, physical training, rock climbing, rodeo, running, ski jumping, skiing (cross-country), skiing (downhill), snowboarding, snowshoeing, swimming and diving, table tennis, telemark skiing, tennis, track and field, weight training, yoga; coed intramural: aerobics/dance, aquatics, backpacking, badminton, ballet, bicycling, billiards, blading, bowling, canoeing/kayaking, climbing, combined training, cooperative games, dance team, equestrian sports, fishing, fitness, flag football, freestyle skiing, Frisbee, golf, hiking/backpacking, horseback riding, horseshoes, jogging, lacrosse, modern dance, mountain biking, nordic skiing, outdoor activities, paint ball, physical training, power lifting, rafting, rappelling, rock climbing, running, skateboarding, skiing (downhill), snowshoeing, swimming and diving, table tennis, telemark skiing, ultimate Frisbee, volleyball, weight lifting, weight training, yoga. 2 coaches, 1 athletic trainer.

Computers Computers are regularly used in all academic classes. Computer network features include on-campus library services, online commercial services, Internet access, wireless campus network, Internet filtering or blocking technology. Campus intranet and student e-mail accounts are available to students. Students grades are available online.

Contact Mrs. Kimberly Stephens, Director of Admissions. 435-462-1443. Fax: 435-462-1450. E-mail: kimberly.stephens@wasatchacademy.org. Website: www.wasatchacademy.org

WASHINGTON INTERNATIONAL SCHOOL

3100 Macomb Street NW
Washington, District of Columbia 20008

Head of School: Clayton W. Lewis

General Information Coeducational day college-preparatory, bilingual studies, and International Baccalaureate school. Grades PK–12. Founded: 1966. Setting: urban. 6-acre campus. 8 buildings on campus. Approved or accredited by International Baccalaureate Organization, Middle States Association of Colleges and Schools, and District of Columbia Department of Education. Member of National Association of Independent Schools, Secondary School Admission Test Board, and European Council of International Schools. Languages of instruction: English, French, and Spanish. Endowment: $4 million. Total enrollment: 899. Upper school average class size: 12. Upper school faculty-student ratio: 1:7. There are 175 required school days per year for Upper School students. Upper School students typically attend 5 days per week. The average school day consists of 5 hours and 25 minutes.

Upper School Student Profile Grade 9: 66 students (36 boys, 30 girls); Grade 10: 69 students (34 boys, 35 girls); Grade 11: 66 students (26 boys, 40 girls); Grade 12: 69 students (34 boys, 35 girls).

Faculty School total: 105. In upper school: 16 men, 20 women; 24 have advanced degrees.

Subjects Offered Advanced chemistry, advanced math, art, arts, biology, calculus, chemistry, chorus, community service, comparative government and politics, contemporary history, drama, Dutch, economics, English, English literature, environmental science, fine arts, French, geography, history, information technology, integrated mathematics, International Baccalaureate courses, literature seminar, music, musical productions, physical education, physics, science, social sciences, Spanish, theater, theory of knowledge, world history.

Graduation Requirements Algebra, arts, arts and fine arts (art, music, dance, drama), biology, calculus, chemistry, economics, English, environmental science, foreign language, geography, geometry, physical education (includes health), physics, trigonometry, world history, world literature, IB program. Community service is required.

Special Academic Programs International Baccalaureate program.

College Admission Counseling 61 students graduated in 2013; all went to college, including McGill University; New York University; The Johns Hopkins University; University of California, Berkeley; University of California, San Diego; Vassar College. Mean SAT critical reading: 648, mean SAT math: 635, mean SAT writing: 657.

Student Life Upper grades have specified standards of dress, student council, honor system. Discipline rests primarily with faculty.

Summer Programs ESL programs offered; held on campus; accepts boys and girls; open to students from other schools. 2014 schedule: June 24 to August 9. Application deadline: June 24.

Tuition and Aid Day student tuition: $33,260. Tuition installment plan (monthly payment plans, 2-payment plan). Need-based scholarship grants available.

Admissions Traditional secondary-level entrance grade is 9. School's own exam required. Deadline for receipt of application materials: January 10. Application fee required: $50. Interview required.

Athletics Interscholastic: baseball (boys), basketball (b,g), soccer (b,g), softball (g), tennis (b,g), track and field (b,g), volleyball (b,g); coed interscholastic: cross-country running, golf; coed intramural: swimming and diving. 3 PE instructors, 1 athletic trainer.

Computers Computers are regularly used in all classes. Computer network features include on-campus library services, online commercial services, Internet access, wireless campus network, Internet filtering or blocking technology. Campus intranet and student e-mail accounts are available to students. The school has a published electronic and media policy.

Contact Ms. Mary Hastings Moore, Associate Director of Admissions. 202-243-1815. Fax: 202-243-1807. E-mail: moore@wis.edu. Website: www.wis.edu

THE WATERFORD SCHOOL

1480 East 9400 South
Sandy, Utah 84093

Head of School: Mrs. Nancy M. Heuston

General Information Coeducational day college-preparatory, arts, technology, and visual arts, music, photography, dance, and theater school. Grades PK–12. Founded: 1981. Setting: suburban. Nearest major city is Salt Lake City. 40-acre campus. 10 buildings on campus. Approved or accredited by Northwest Accreditation Commission, Northwest Association of Independent Schools, Northwest Association of Schools and Colleges, and Utah Department of Education. Member of National Association of Independent Schools. Endowment: $2 million. Total enrollment: 875. Upper school average class size: 16. Upper school faculty-student ratio: 1:4. There are 169 required school days per year for Upper School students. Upper School students typically attend 5 days per week. The average school day consists of 6 hours.

Upper School Student Profile Grade 9: 77 students (45 boys, 32 girls); Grade 10: 65 students (33 boys, 32 girls); Grade 11: 60 students (24 boys, 36 girls); Grade 12: 56 students (27 boys, 29 girls).

Faculty School total: 68. In upper school: 37 men, 31 women; 51 have advanced degrees.

Subjects Offered 20th century history, 3-dimensional design, acting, advanced math, Advanced Placement courses, aerobics, algebra, American history, American history-AP, American literature, art, Asian history, basketball, biology, biology-AP, British literature, calculus, calculus-AP, ceramics, chemistry, chemistry-AP, chorus, computer applications, computer art, computer graphics, computer programming, computer science, computer science-AP, creative writing, debate, drama, drama performance, drama workshop, drawing, ecology, economics, English-AP, European history, European history-AP, French, French-AP, genetics, geology, geometry, German, German-AP, Japanese, jazz ensemble, Latin, Latin American literature, music history, music performance, music theater, outdoor education, painting, philosophy, photography, physical education, physics, physics-AP, pre-calculus, probability and statistics, psychology, sculpture, Spanish, Spanish-AP, statistics-AP, strings, studio art-AP, trigonometry, voice ensemble, volleyball, weight training, wind ensemble, world literature, writing workshop, yearbook, zoology.

Graduation Requirements 20th century world history, algebra, American history, American literature, biology, British literature, calculus, chemistry, computer science, English, European history, foreign language, geometry, music performance, physics, pre-calculus, trigonometry, visual arts, world history, writing workshop, six terms of physical education or participation on athletic teams.

Special Academic Programs 15 Advanced Placement exams for which test preparation is offered; honors section; independent study; term-away projects; academic accommodation for the gifted, the musically talented, and the artistically talented.

College Admission Counseling 55 students graduated in 2013; all went to college. Mean SAT critical reading: 633, mean SAT math: 633, mean SAT writing: 628, mean combined SAT: 1890, mean composite ACT: 28.

Student Life Upper grades have uniform requirement, student council, honor system. Discipline rests equally with students and faculty.

Summer Programs Enrichment, advancement, sports, art/fine arts, rigorous outdoor training programs offered; session focuses on enrichment and advancement; held both on and off campus; held at various locations in Utah and abroad; accepts boys and girls; not open to students from other schools. 100 students usually enrolled. 2014 schedule: June 10 to August 15. Application deadline: March 15.

Tuition and Aid Day student tuition: $19,875. Tuition installment plan (Insured Tuition Payment Plan, monthly payment plans). Tuition reduction for siblings, need-based scholarship grants available. In 2013–14, 10% of upper-school students received aid. Total amount of financial aid awarded in 2013–14: $1,700,000.

Admissions Traditional secondary-level entrance grade is 9. For fall 2013, 56 students applied for upper-level admission, 32 were accepted, 27 enrolled. ERB CTP IV, school's own test or TOEFL required. Deadline for receipt of application materials: none. Application fee required: $35. On-campus interview required.

Athletics Interscholastic: basketball (boys, girls), crew (b,g), cross-country running (b,g), golf (b,g), lacrosse (b,g), soccer (b,g), tennis (b,g), volleyball (g); coed interscholastic: alpine skiing, aquatics, ballet, dance, Frisbee, racquetball, skiing (downhill), ultimate Frisbee; coed intramural: aerobics, backpacking, climbing, crew, hiking/backpacking, nordic skiing, outdoor activities, outdoor adventure, outdoor education, outdoor recreation, outdoor skills, outdoors, rock climbing, skiing (cross-country), skiing (downhill), snowshoeing, strength & conditioning, weight training, yoga. 6 PE instructors, 15 coaches.

Computers Computers are regularly used in animation, college planning, graphic design, library, literary magazine, newspaper, photography, publications, yearbook classes. Computer network features include on-campus library services, online commercial services, Internet access, wireless campus network, Internet filtering or blocking technology. Campus intranet, student e-mail accounts, and computer access in designated common areas are available to students. Students grades are available online. The school has a published electronic and media policy.

Contact Mr. Todd Winters, Director of Admissions. 801-816-2213. Fax: 801-572-1787. E-mail: toddwinters@waterfordschool.org. Website: www.waterfordschool.org

WATKINSON SCHOOL

180 Bloomfield Avenue
Hartford, Connecticut 06105

Head of School: Mr. John W. Bracker

General Information Coeducational day college-preparatory, arts, technology, and athletics, global systems school. Grades 6–PG. Founded: 1881. Setting: suburban. 40-acre campus. 5 buildings on campus. Approved or accredited by Association of Independent Schools in New England, New England Association of Schools and Colleges, and Connecticut Department of Education. Member of National Association of Independent Schools and Secondary School Admission Test Board. Endowment: $4.4 million. Total enrollment: 266. Upper school average class size: 12. Upper school faculty-student ratio: 1:6. There are 165 required school days per year for Upper School students. Upper School students typically attend 5 days per week. The average school day consists of 7 hours and 30 minutes.

Upper School Student Profile Grade 9: 39 students (18 boys, 21 girls); Grade 10: 43 students (21 boys, 22 girls); Grade 11: 57 students (32 boys, 25 girls); Grade 12: 46 students (23 boys, 23 girls); Postgraduate: 7 students (5 boys, 2 girls).

Faculty School total: 47. In upper school: 13 men, 24 women; 21 have advanced degrees.

Subjects Offered African history, algebra, American history, American literature, American sign language, anatomy, ancient world history, art, Asian history, biology, calculus, ceramics, chemistry, creative writing, dance, drama, drawing, earth science, English, English literature, environmental science, European history, expository writing, fine arts, forensics, French, geography, geometry, health, history, internship, mathematics, modern European history, painting, photography, physics, pottery, science, social studies, Spanish, theater, U.S. history, world history, world literature, writing.

Graduation Requirements Arts and fine arts (art, music, dance, drama), English, foreign language, health and wellness, mathematics, science, social studies (includes history), technology.

Special Academic Programs Independent study; study at local college for college credit; academic accommodation for the gifted, the musically talented, and the artistically talented; programs in English, mathematics, general development for dyslexic students; special instructional classes for deaf students.

College Admission Counseling 32 students graduated in 2013; 30 went to college, including Clark University; Hofstra University; University of Vermont. Other: 2 had other specific plans. Median SAT critical reading: 600, median SAT math: 560, median SAT writing: 550, median combined SAT: 1690, median composite ACT: 26. 34% scored over 600 on SAT critical reading, 24% scored over 600 on SAT math, 27% scored over 600 on SAT writing, 29% scored over 1800 on combined SAT, 35% scored over 26 on composite ACT.

Student Life Upper grades have specified standards of dress, student council. Discipline rests equally with students and faculty.

Summer Programs Remediation, enrichment programs offered; session focuses on academics; held on campus; accepts boys and girls; open to students from other schools. 8 students usually enrolled. 2014 schedule: June 30 to August 1. Application deadline: none.

Tuition and Aid Day student tuition: $35,200. Tuition installment plan (Insured Tuition Payment Plan, SMART Tuition Payment Plan). Need-based scholarship grants available. In 2013–14, 42% of upper-school students received aid. Total amount of financial aid awarded in 2013–14: $1,689,180.

Admissions Traditional secondary-level entrance grade is 9. For fall 2013, 164 students applied for upper-level admission, 101 were accepted, 67 enrolled. ISEE or SSAT required. Deadline for receipt of application materials: February 1. Application fee required: $50. On-campus interview required.

Athletics Interscholastic: baseball (boys), basketball (b,g), crew (b,g), cross-country running (b,g), lacrosse (b,g), soccer (b,g), softball (g), tennis (b,g), volleyball (g); coed interscholastic: crew, cross-country running, tennis, ultimate Frisbee; coed intramural: alpine skiing, ballet, Circus, climbing, combined training, dance, fencing, fitness, juggling, martial arts, outdoor activities, outdoor adventure, physical fitness, physical training, skiing (downhill), snowboarding, street hockey, strength & conditioning, tennis, ultimate Frisbee, volleyball, weight lifting, yoga. 4 coaches.

Computers Computers are regularly used in computer applications, desktop publishing classes. Computer network features include on-campus library services, online commercial services, Internet access, wireless campus network, Internet filtering or blocking technology. Campus intranet, student e-mail accounts, and computer access in designated common areas are available to students. Students grades are available online. The school has a published electronic and media policy.

Contact Mrs. Cathy Batson, Admissions Office Assistant. 860-236-5618 Ext. 136. Fax: 860-233-8295. E-mail: cathy_batson@watkinson.org. Website: www.watkinson.org

WAYNFLETE SCHOOL

360 Spring Street
Portland, Maine 04102

Head of School: Geoffrey Wagg

General Information Coeducational day college-preparatory school. Grades PK–12. Founded: 1898. Setting: urban. Nearest major city is Boston, MA. 37-acre campus. 10 buildings on campus. Approved or accredited by Association of Independent Schools in New England, Independent Schools of Northern New England, New England Association of Schools and Colleges, The College Board, and Maine Department of Education. Member of National Association of Independent Schools. Endowment: $21.5 million. Total enrollment: 575. Upper school average class size: 13. Upper school faculty-student ratio: 1:12. There are 172 required school days per year for Upper School students. Upper School students typically attend 5 days per week. The average school day consists of 7 hours and 15 minutes.

Upper School Student Profile Grade 9: 70 students (28 boys, 42 girls); Grade 10: 59 students (30 boys, 29 girls); Grade 11: 70 students (33 boys, 37 girls); Grade 12: 62 students (26 boys, 36 girls).

Faculty School total: 75. In upper school: 19 men, 23 women; 30 have advanced degrees.

Subjects Offered 20th century American writers, 3-dimensional art, 3-dimensional design, advanced biology, African literature, algebra, American history, American literature, ancient/medieval philosophy, art history, astrophysics, bioethics, biology, British literature (honors), Buddhism, calculus, ceramics, chemistry, composition, constitutional history of U.S., creative writing, drama, drama workshop, English, English composition, English literature, environmental science, equality and freedom, European history, expository writing, French, geometry, government/civics, health, Latin, Mandarin, marine biology, Mexican history, Middle Eastern history, modern European history, music, physical education, physics, pre-calculus, printmaking, psychology, Russian history, Spanish, statistics, studio art, trigonometry, U.S. constitutional history, Vietnam, world history, world literature.

Graduation Requirements Arts, biology, English, foreign language, geometry, history, mathematics, performing arts, science, sports, U.S. history. Seniors may design a month-long Senior Project, which allows them to pursue academic interests, potential careers, fine arts, or community service. Community service is required.

Special Academic Programs Independent study; term-away projects; study abroad.

College Admission Counseling 63 students graduated in 2013; 62 went to college, including Hamilton College; Kenyon College; Tufts University; Wheaton College. Other: 1 had other specific plans. Median SAT critical reading: 630, median SAT math: 610, median SAT writing: 630, median combined SAT: 1870. 57% scored over 600 on SAT critical reading, 60% scored over 600 on SAT math, 60% scored over 600 on SAT writing, 59% scored over 1800 on combined SAT.

Student Life Upper grades have student council. Discipline rests primarily with faculty.

Summer Programs Enrichment, sports, art/fine arts programs offered; session focuses on sports, gymnastics, martial arts, robotics, fine/performing arts, digital media, sustainable ocean studies; held both on and off campus; held at Fore River Fields, Portland, ME and Pensobscot Bay, Darling Marine Center, Mt. Desert Island; accepts boys and girls; open to students from other schools. 750 students usually enrolled. 2014 schedule: June 16 to July 25. Application deadline: none.

Tuition and Aid Day student tuition: $26,235. Tuition installment plan (Insured Tuition Payment Plan, monthly payment plans). Need-based scholarship grants available. In 2013–14, 31% of upper-school students received aid. Total amount of financial aid awarded in 2013–14: $1,509,056.

Admissions Traditional secondary-level entrance grade is 9. For fall 2013, 62 students applied for upper-level admission, 37 were accepted, 26 enrolled. Writing sample required. Deadline for receipt of application materials: February 10. Application fee required: $40. Interview required.

Athletics Interscholastic: baseball (boys), basketball (b,g), cross-country running (b,g), field hockey (g), golf (b,g), hockey (g), lacrosse (b,g), skiing (cross-country) (b,g), soccer (b,g), tennis (b,g); coed interscholastic: crew, nordic skiing, rowing, sailing, swimming and diving, track and field; coed intramural: dance, fitness walking, modern dance, physical fitness, sailing, swimming and diving, tennis, weight lifting, weight training, yoga. 4 PE instructors, 20 coaches, 1 athletic trainer.

Computers Computers are regularly used in all academic classes. Computer network features include on-campus library services, online commercial services, Internet access, wireless campus network, Internet filtering or blocking technology, Google doc accounts; academic data bases, including JSTOR, MARVEL, Infotrac, Noodle Tools, and URSUS. Student e-mail accounts and computer access in designated common areas are available to students. The school has a published electronic and media policy.

Contact Admission Office. 207-774-5721 Ext. 1224. Fax: 207-772-4782. E-mail: admissionoffice@waynflete.org. Website: www.waynflete.org

WEBB SCHOOL OF KNOXVILLE

9800 Webb School Drive
Knoxville, Tennessee 37923-3399

Head of School: Mr. Scott L. Hutchinson

General Information Coeducational day college-preparatory, arts, religious studies, and technology school. Grades K–12. Founded: 1955. Setting: urban. Nearest major city is Chattanooga. 114-acre campus. 8 buildings on campus. Approved or accredited by Southern Association of Colleges and Schools, Southern Association of Independent Schools, and Tennessee Department of Education. Member of National Association of Independent Schools and Secondary School Admission Test Board. Endowment: $325 million. Total enrollment: 1,034. Upper school average class size: 16. Upper school faculty-student ratio: 1:10. There are 174 required school days per year for Upper School students. Upper School students typically attend 5 days per week. The average school day consists of 8 hours and 5 minutes.

Upper School Student Profile Grade 9: 118 students (52 boys, 66 girls); Grade 10: 104 students (53 boys, 51 girls); Grade 11: 134 students (75 boys, 59 girls); Grade 12: 115 students (58 boys, 57 girls).

Faculty School total: 98. In upper school: 17 men, 28 women; 40 have advanced degrees.

Subjects Offered 3-dimensional design, algebra, American sign language, anatomy and physiology, art history-AP, biology, biology-AP, calculus, calculus-AP, ceramics, chamber groups, chemistry, chemistry-AP, computer science-AP, concert choir, digital imaging, drama, drawing, economics, engineering, English, English language and composition-AP, English literature and composition-AP, English-AP, environmental science-AP, forensics, French, French-AP, geometry, government and politics-AP, history of rock and roll, honors algebra, honors English, honors geometry, honors world history, journalism, Latin, Latin-AP, macroeconomics-AP, Mandarin, modern European history-AP, modern world history, music theory-AP, painting, photography, physics, physics-AP, pre-calculus, probability and statistics, psychology-AP, robotics, Spanish, Spanish-AP, stage design, statistics-AP, strings, studio art-AP, trigonometry, U.S. history, U.S. history-AP, wind ensemble, world history, world history-AP, world religions, yearbook.

Graduation Requirements Algebra, American history, arts and fine arts (art, music, dance, drama), biology, chemistry, English, foreign language, geometry, history, mathematics, physical education (includes health), public service, science, world history, world religions, public speaking (two chapel talks), 25 hours of community service per year.

Special Academic Programs 28 Advanced Placement exams for which test preparation is offered; honors section; independent study; study abroad; remedial reading and/or remedial writing; remedial math.

College Admission Counseling 104 students graduated in 2013; all went to college, including Belmont University; The University of Alabama; The University of Tennessee; University of Georgia; Washington University in St. Louis. Mean SAT critical reading: 625, mean SAT math: 613, mean SAT writing: 615, mean composite ACT: 28. 62% scored over 600 on SAT critical reading, 54% scored over 600 on SAT math, 51% scored over 600 on SAT writing, 76% scored over 26 on composite ACT.

Student Life Upper grades have uniform requirement, student council, honor system. Discipline rests equally with students and faculty.

Summer Programs Remediation, enrichment, advancement, sports, art/fine arts programs offered; session focuses on academic and sports-oriented fun; held on campus; accepts boys and girls; open to students from other schools. 1,200 students usually enrolled. 2014 schedule: June 2 to August 1. Application deadline: June 2.

Tuition and Aid Day student tuition: $17,170. Tuition installment plan (monthly payment plans, individually arranged payment plans, Tuition Payments can also be paid in two installments-last calendar day in July and November). Need-based scholarship grants available. In 2013–14, 14% of upper-school students received aid. Total amount of financial aid awarded in 2013–14: $722,480.

Admissions Traditional secondary-level entrance grade is 9. For fall 2013, 61 students applied for upper-level admission, 57 were accepted, 47 enrolled. ISEE required. Deadline for receipt of application materials: January 31. Application fee required: $75. On-campus interview required.

Athletics Interscholastic: baseball (boys), basketball (b,g), bowling (b,g), cheering (g), climbing (b,g), cross-country running (b,g), dance squad (g), field hockey (g), football (b), golf (b,g), lacrosse (b), soccer (b,g), softball (g), swimming and diving

(b,g), tennis (b,g), track and field (b,g), volleyball (g), wrestling (b); coed interscholastic: sailing. 27 coaches, 1 athletic trainer.

Computers Computers are regularly used in all classes. Computer network features include on-campus library services, Internet access, wireless campus network, Internet filtering or blocking technology, all students in grades 4-12 own/lease iPads for school. Student e-mail accounts are available to students. Students grades are available online. The school has a published electronic and media policy.

Contact Mrs. Christy Widener, Admissions Administrative Assistant. 865-291-3830. Fax: 865-291-1532. E-mail: christy_widener@webbschool.org. Website: www.webbschool.org

THE WEBB SCHOOLS

1175 West Baseline Road
Claremont, California 91711

Head of School: Mr. Taylor Stockdale

General Information Coeducational boarding and day college-preparatory school. Grades 9–12. Founded: 1922. Setting: suburban. Nearest major city is Los Angeles. Students are housed in single-sex dormitories. 70-acre campus. Approved or accredited by The Association of Boarding Schools, Western Association of Schools and Colleges, Western Catholic Education Association, and California Department of Education. Member of National Association of Independent Schools and Secondary School Admission Test Board. Endowment: $30.2 million. Upper school average class size: 15. Upper school faculty-student ratio: 1:8.

Upper School Student Profile Grade 9: 91 students (46 boys, 45 girls); Grade 10: 103 students (55 boys, 48 girls); Grade 11: 104 students (50 boys, 54 girls); Grade 12: 107 students (52 boys, 55 girls). 60% of students are boarding students. 70% are state residents. 14 states are represented in upper school student body. 22% are international students. International students from China, Hong Kong, Republic of Korea, Russian Federation, Saudi Arabia, and Taiwan; 9 other countries represented in student body.

Faculty School total: 55. In upper school: 29 men, 26 women; 45 have advanced degrees; 39 reside on campus.

Subjects Offered Algebra, American history, American history-AP, American literature, ancient world history, art, astronomy, biology, biology-AP, calculus, calculus-AP, chamber groups, chemistry, chemistry-AP, Chinese, chorus, computer programming, economics, engineering, English, English language and composition-AP, English literature and composition-AP, environmental science, environmental science-AP, French, French language-AP, health and wellness, history, integrated mathematics, journalism, linear algebra, literature, marine biology, media arts, modern world history, music theory, oceanography, orchestra, paleontology, physics, physics-AP, pre-calculus, psychology, sculpture, Spanish, Spanish language-AP, Spanish literature-AP, statistics, statistics-AP, theater, U.S. history-AP, world history-AP, writing.

Graduation Requirements Arts and fine arts (art, music, dance, drama), English, foreign language, health, history, mathematics, physical education (includes health), science.

Special Academic Programs 15 Advanced Placement exams for which test preparation is offered; honors section; academic accommodation for the gifted.

College Admission Counseling 94 students graduated in 2013; all went to college, including Columbia University; Georgetown University; Scripps College; University of Chicago; University of Southern California; Washington University in St. Louis. Mean combined SAT: 2000.

Student Life Upper grades have specified standards of dress, student council, honor system. Discipline rests equally with students and faculty.

Summer Programs Enrichment, advancement, sports, art/fine arts, computer instruction programs offered; session focuses on academic enrichment; held on campus; accepts boys and girls; open to students from other schools. 450 students usually enrolled. 2014 schedule: June to July.

Tuition and Aid Day student tuition: $36,635; 7-day tuition and room/board: $51,515. Tuition installment plan (Insured Tuition Payment Plan, monthly payment plans). Need-based scholarship grants available. In 2013–14, 33% of upper-school students received aid. Total amount of financial aid awarded in 2013–14: $3,600,000.

Admissions Traditional secondary-level entrance grade is 9. For fall 2013, 445 students applied for upper-level admission, 171 were accepted, 109 enrolled. ISEE, SSAT or TOEFL required. Deadline for receipt of application materials: January 15. Application fee required: $75. On-campus interview required.

Athletics Interscholastic: baseball (boys), basketball (b,g), cross-country running (b,g), football (b), golf (b,g), soccer (b,g), softball (g), swimming and diving (b,g), tennis (b,g), track and field (b,g), volleyball (b,g), water polo (b,g), wrestling (b); coed interscholastic: badminton; coed intramural: dance, fitness, outdoor activities, triathlon, yoga. 30 coaches, 1 athletic trainer.

Computers Computers are regularly used in all academic classes. Computer network features include on-campus library services, online commercial services, Internet access, wireless campus network, Internet filtering or blocking technology. Campus intranet and student e-mail accounts are available to students. Students grades are available online. The school has a published electronic and media policy.

Contact Mr. Leo Marshall, Director of Admission and Financial Aid. 909-482-5214. Fax: 909-445-8269. E-mail: admission@webb.org. Website: www.webb.org/admission

WELLSPRING FOUNDATION

Bethlehem, Connecticut
See Special Needs Schools section.

WELLSPRINGS FRIENDS SCHOOL

3590 West 18th Avenue
Eugene, Oregon 97402

Head of School: Dennis Hoerner

General Information Coeducational day college-preparatory and general academic school, affiliated with Society of Friends; primarily serves underachievers. Grades 9–12. Founded: 1994. Setting: small town. Nearest major city is Portland. 4-acre campus. 2 buildings on campus. Approved or accredited by Northwest Accreditation Commission, Northwest Association of Schools and Colleges, and Oregon Department of Education. Member of National Association of Independent Schools. Endowment: $8,000. Total enrollment: 45. Upper school average class size: 10. Upper school faculty-student ratio: 1:8. There are 175 required school days per year for Upper School students. Upper School students typically attend 5 days per week. The average school day consists of 6 hours.

Upper School Student Profile Grade 9: 4 students (2 boys, 2 girls); Grade 10: 5 students (3 boys, 2 girls); Grade 11: 7 students (2 boys, 5 girls); Grade 12: 12 students (5 boys, 7 girls); Grade 13: 2 students (1 boy, 1 girl).

Faculty School total: 6. In upper school: 3 men, 2 women; 3 have advanced degrees.

Subjects Offered 20th century world history, advanced math, algebra, creative writing, English, film, finance, fine arts, geometry, German, government, human sexuality, life science, personal finance, physical education, physical science, poetry, pre-algebra, reading, Spanish, U.S. history.

Graduation Requirements English, foreign language, mathematics, science, social studies (includes history), Community Building. Community service is required.

Special Academic Programs Independent study; remedial reading and/or remedial writing; remedial math.

College Admission Counseling 17 students graduated in 2013; 9 went to college, including Lane Community College; University of Oregon. Other: 5 went to work, 3 had other specific plans.

Student Life Upper grades have student council. Discipline rests equally with students and faculty.

Tuition and Aid Day student tuition: $7000. Tuition installment plan (monthly payment plans, individually arranged payment plans). Need-based scholarship grants available.

Admissions Traditional secondary-level entrance grade is 9. For fall 2013, 12 students applied for upper-level admission, 12 were accepted, 10 enrolled. Deadline for receipt of application materials: none. No application fee required. Interview required.

Athletics Coed Intramural: basketball, bocce, football, Frisbee, hiking/backpacking, physical fitness, skateboarding. 1 PE instructor.

Computers Computers are regularly used in career education, career exploration, music, writing, yearbook classes. Computer network features include Internet access, wireless campus network.

Contact Office Manager. 541-686-1223. Fax: 541-687-1493. E-mail: info@wellspringsfriends.org. Website: www.wellspringsfriends.org

WESLEYAN ACADEMY

PO Box 1489
Guaynabo, Puerto Rico 00970-1489

Head of School: Rev. Fernando Vazquez

General Information Coeducational day college-preparatory school, affiliated with Wesleyan Church. Grades PK–12. Founded: 1955. Setting: urban. Nearest major city is San Juan. 6-acre campus. 1 building on campus. Approved or accredited by Association of Christian Schools International, Middle States Association of Colleges and Schools, and Puerto Rico Department of Education. Total enrollment: 959. Upper school average class size: 25. Upper school faculty-student ratio: 1:23. There are 180 required school days per year for Upper School students. Upper School students typically attend 6 days per week. The average school day consists of 6 hours and 15 minutes.

Upper School Student Profile Grade 9: 68 students (35 boys, 33 girls); Grade 10: 57 students (32 boys, 25 girls); Grade 11: 52 students (27 boys, 25 girls); Grade 12: 52 students (27 boys, 25 girls). 50% of students are members of Wesleyan Church.

Faculty School total: 72. In upper school: 8 men, 18 women; 5 have advanced degrees.

Subjects Offered Accounting, advanced math, algebra, American history, anatomy and physiology, art, athletics, Bible, biology, calculus, career and personal planning, career planning, chemistry, choir, Christian education, college planning, computer skills, critical writing, dance, drama, earth science, English, English literature, French, general math, general science, geography, geometry, global studies, golf, guidance, guitar, handbells, health, history, Internet, intro to computers, keyboarding, lab science, library, mathematics, music, music appreciation, personal development, piano, poetry, pre-algebra, pre-calculus, pre-college orientation, Puerto Rican history, science, social

sciences, Spanish, swimming, trigonometry, U.S. government, volleyball, world affairs, world history, yearbook.

Graduation Requirements American government, American history, Bible, computer science, electives, English, foreign language, health, history, lab science, mathematics, physical education (includes health), science, service learning/internship, social sciences, social studies (includes history), Spanish, 84 accumulative hours of community service during high school years.

Special Academic Programs Advanced Placement exam preparation; honors section; independent study.

College Admission Counseling 40 students graduated in 2013; all went to college, including Boston University; Florida International University; Lynn University; Stetson University; Syracuse University; Virginia Polytechnic Institute and State University. Mean SAT critical reading: 526, mean SAT math: 498, mean SAT writing: 527, mean combined SAT: 1551. 18% scored over 600 on SAT critical reading, 14% scored over 600 on SAT math, 22% scored over 600 on SAT writing, 14% scored over 1800 on combined SAT.

Student Life Upper grades have uniform requirement, student council, honor system. Discipline rests primarily with faculty.

Summer Programs Remediation, enrichment, advancement programs offered; session focuses on remediation and enrichment classes; held on campus; accepts boys and girls; open to students from other schools. 100 students usually enrolled. 2014 schedule: June 2 to June 27. Application deadline: May 30.

Tuition and Aid Day student tuition: $6700. Guaranteed tuition plan. Tuition installment plan (monthly payment plans, full-payment discount plan, semester payment plan). Need-based scholarship grants, need-based financial aid available. In 2013–14, 2% of upper-school students received aid. Total amount of financial aid awarded in 2013–14: $1000.

Admissions Traditional secondary-level entrance grade is 9. For fall 2013, 165 students applied for upper-level admission, 150 were accepted, 143 enrolled. Academic Profile Tests, admissions testing, mathematics proficiency exam and Metropolitan Achievement Test required. Deadline for receipt of application materials: none. Application fee required: $100. On-campus interview required.

Athletics Interscholastic: basketball (boys, girls), golf (b,g), indoor soccer (b,g), soccer (b,g), swimming and diving (b,g), tennis (b,g), track and field (b,g), volleyball (b,g); intramural: basketball (b,g), indoor soccer (b,g), soccer (b,g), track and field (b,g), volleyball (b,g); coed interscholastic: tennis. 3 PE instructors, 3 coaches.

Computers Computers are regularly used in all academic classes. Computer network features include on-campus library services, Internet access, wireless campus network, Internet filtering or blocking technology. Student e-mail accounts and computer access in designated common areas are available to students. Students grades are available online. The school has a published electronic and media policy.

Contact Mrs. Mae Ling Cardona, Admissions Clerk. 787-720-8959 Ext. 1235. Fax: 787-790-0730. E-mail: mcardona@wesleyanacademy.org. Website: www.wesleyanacademy.org

WESTBURY CHRISTIAN SCHOOL

10420 Hillcroft
Houston, Texas 77096

Head of School: Mr. Greg J. Glenn

General Information Coeducational day college-preparatory, arts, business, religious studies, and technology school, affiliated with Church of Christ. Grades PK–12. Founded: 1975. Setting: urban. 13-acre campus. 1 building on campus. Approved or accredited by National Christian School Association, Southern Association of Colleges and Schools, Texas Private School Accreditation Commission, The College Board, and Texas Department of Education. Endowment: $300,000. Total enrollment: 480. Upper school average class size: 22. Upper school faculty-student ratio: 1:10. There are 180 required school days per year for Upper School students. Upper School students typically attend 5 days per week. The average school day consists of 7 hours and 45 minutes.

Upper School Student Profile Grade 9: 42 students (19 boys, 23 girls); Grade 10: 34 students (3 boys, 31 girls); Grade 11: 69 students (38 boys, 31 girls); Grade 12: 53 students (30 boys, 23 girls). 18% of students are members of Church of Christ.

Faculty School total: 52. In upper school: 19 men, 15 women; 13 have advanced degrees.

Subjects Offered Accounting, algebra, anatomy and physiology, art, athletics, band, basketball, Bible, biology, biology-AP, business, calculus-AP, cheerleading, chemistry, chemistry-AP, community service, computer applications, debate, drama, economics, English, English language and composition-AP, English literature and composition-AP, geography, geometry, government, government-AP, health, human geography - AP, journalism, macro/microeconomics-AP, photography, physical education, physical science, physics, pre-calculus, psychology-AP, robotics, Spanish, speech, statistics-AP, studio art-AP, U.S. history, U.S. history-AP, vocal music, weight training, world history, world history-AP.

Graduation Requirements Arts and fine arts (art, music, dance, drama), Bible, electives, English, foreign language, geometry, mathematics, physical education (includes health), science, social studies (includes history), speech, continuous participation in student activities programs, community service each semester.

Special Academic Programs 15 Advanced Placement exams for which test preparation is offered; independent study.

College Admission Counseling 57 students graduated in 2013; all went to college, including Harding University; Houston Baptist University; Texas A&M University; Texas Tech University; The University of Texas at Austin; University of Houston. Mean SAT critical reading: 496, mean SAT math: 545, mean SAT writing: 495, mean combined SAT: 1536, mean composite ACT: 23. 9% scored over 600 on SAT critical reading, 25% scored over 600 on SAT math, 17% scored over 600 on SAT writing, 48% scored over 1800 on combined SAT, 36% scored over 26 on composite ACT.

Student Life Upper grades have uniform requirement, student council, honor system. Discipline rests primarily with faculty.

Summer Programs Enrichment, sports, art/fine arts programs offered; session focuses on week-long basketball, football, and volleyball instruction camps; held both on and off campus; held at Wildcat athletic complex, 10402 Fondren, Houston; accepts boys and girls; open to students from other schools. 200 students usually enrolled. 2014 schedule: June 3 to July 26. Application deadline: none.

Tuition and Aid Day student tuition: $12,120. Tuition installment plan (FACTS Tuition Payment Plan). Merit scholarship grants, need-based scholarship grants available. In 2013–14, 16% of upper-school students received aid; total upper-school merit-scholarship money awarded: $20,000. Total amount of financial aid awarded in 2013–14: $182,294.

Admissions Traditional secondary-level entrance grade is 9. For fall 2013, 95 students applied for upper-level admission, 68 were accepted, 55 enrolled. ISEE, Otis-Lennon School Ability Test and SLEP for foreign students required. Deadline for receipt of application materials: none. Application fee required: $75. Interview required.

Athletics Interscholastic: baseball (boys), basketball (b,g), cheering (g), cross-country running (b,g), football (b), golf (b,g), soccer (b,g), softball (g), strength & conditioning (b,g), swimming and diving (b,g), tennis (b,g), track and field (b,g), volleyball (g). 1 PE instructor, 7 coaches, 1 athletic trainer.

Computers Computers are regularly used in all academic classes. Computer network features include on-campus library services, online commercial services, Internet access, wireless campus network, Internet filtering or blocking technology. Campus intranet and student e-mail accounts are available to students. Students grades are available online. The school has a published electronic and media policy.

Contact Mrs. Phylis Frye, Director of Admissions. 713-551-8100 Ext. 1018. Fax: 713-551-8117. E-mail: admissions@westburychristian.org. Website: www.westburychristian.org

WEST CATHOLIC HIGH SCHOOL

1801 Bristol Avenue NW
Grand Rapids, Michigan 49504

Head of School: Mrs. Cynthia Kneibel

General Information Coeducational day college-preparatory and religious studies school, affiliated with Roman Catholic Church. Grades 9–12. Founded: 1962. Setting: urban. 20-acre campus. 1 building on campus. Approved or accredited by National Catholic Education Association, North Central Association of Colleges and Schools, and Michigan Department of Education. Endowment: $1 million. Total enrollment: 437. Upper school average class size: 30. Upper school faculty-student ratio: 1:30. There are 181 required school days per year for Upper School students. Upper School students typically attend 5 days per week. The average school day consists of 6 hours.

Upper School Student Profile Grade 9: 87 students (43 boys, 44 girls); Grade 10: 117 students (60 boys, 57 girls); Grade 11: 112 students (69 boys, 43 girls); Grade 12: 121 students (60 boys, 61 girls). 95% of students are Roman Catholic.

Faculty School total: 26. In upper school: 13 men, 13 women; 20 have advanced degrees.

Subjects Offered 20th century world history, acting, advanced chemistry, advanced computer applications, advanced math, American government, American literature, anatomy, art, band, Basic programming, biology, biology-AP, calculus, calculus-AP, career planning, chemistry, choir, Christian doctrine, composition, composition-AP, computer applications, computer programming, concert band, desktop publishing, drama, drawing, earth science, economics, economics-AP, English, English language and composition-AP, English literature, English literature and composition-AP, English literature-AP, environmental science, family living, French, general math, geometry, government, government and politics-AP, government-AP, government/civics, history, history of the Catholic Church, honors algebra, honors English, honors geometry, honors world history, human anatomy, intro to computers, jazz band, journalism, marching band, physics, pre-algebra, pre-calculus, psychology, sexuality, social justice, sociology, Spanish, U.S. government and politics-AP, U.S. history, Web site design, world history, yearbook.

Graduation Requirements Economics, electives, English composition, foreign language, government, health, mathematics, religion (includes Bible studies and theology), science, social studies (includes history), U.S. history, visual arts.

Special Academic Programs Advanced Placement exam preparation; honors section; independent study; remedial reading and/or remedial writing.

College Admission Counseling 121 students graduated in 2012; 117 went to college, including Central Michigan University; Grand Valley State University; Loyola University Chicago; Saint Mary's College; University of Dayton. Other: 1 went to work, 3 entered military service. 45% scored over 600 on SAT critical reading, 67% scored over 600 on SAT math, 45% scored over 600 on SAT writing, 45% scored over 1800 on combined SAT, 31% scored over 26 on composite ACT.

Student Life Upper grades have uniform requirement, student council, honor system. Discipline rests primarily with faculty. Attendance at religious services is required.

Tuition and Aid Day student tuition: $8170. Tuition installment plan (FACTS Tuition Payment Plan, individually arranged payment plans). Need-based scholarship grants available. In 2012–13, 25% of upper-school students received aid.

Admissions Traditional secondary-level entrance grade is 9. For fall 2012, 10 students applied for upper-level admission, 10 were accepted, 10 enrolled. Essay, High School Placement Test and Math Placement Exam required. Deadline for receipt of application materials: February 1. Application fee required: $150.

Athletics Interscholastic: baseball (boys), basketball (b,g), bowling (b,g), cheering (g), cross-country running (b,g), diving (b,g), football (b), golf (b,g), gymnastics (g), hockey (b), ice hockey (b), pom squad (g), skiing (downhill) (b,g), soccer (b,g), softball (g), swimming and diving (b,g), tennis (b,g), track and field (b,g), volleyball (g), weight lifting (b), weight training (b), wrestling (b); intramural: basketball (b,g). 1 PE instructor, 66 coaches, 2 athletic trainers.

Computers Computers are regularly used in all academic classes. Computer network features include Internet access, wireless campus network, Internet filtering or blocking technology. Student e-mail accounts and computer access in designated common areas are available to students. Students grades are available online. The school has a published electronic and media policy.

Contact Mrs. Lauri Ford, Guidance Secretary. 616-233-5909. Fax: 616-453-4320. E-mail: lauriford@grcss.org. Website: www.grwestcatholic.org

WESTCHESTER COUNTRY DAY SCHOOL

2045 North Old Greensboro Road
High Point, North Carolina 27265

Head of School: Mr. Cobb Atkinson

General Information Coeducational day and distance learning college-preparatory, arts, bilingual studies, and technology school. Grades PK–12. Distance learning grades 6–12. Founded: 1967. Setting: rural. 53-acre campus. 6 buildings on campus. Approved or accredited by Southern Association of Colleges and Schools, Southern Association of Independent Schools, and North Carolina Department of Education. Member of National Association of Independent Schools. Endowment: $2.5 million. Total enrollment: 355. Upper school average class size: 16. Upper school faculty-student ratio: 1:6. There are 176 required school days per year for Upper School students. Upper School students typically attend 5 days per week. The average school day consists of 5 hours and 40 minutes.

Upper School Student Profile Grade 9: 31 students (13 boys, 18 girls); Grade 10: 32 students (21 boys, 11 girls); Grade 11: 24 students (13 boys, 11 girls); Grade 12: 39 students (25 boys, 14 girls).

Faculty School total: 56. In upper school: 9 men, 16 women; 15 have advanced degrees.

Subjects Offered Advanced chemistry, Advanced Placement courses, advanced studio art-AP, algebra, American history, American literature, American literature-AP, art, art history-AP, art-AP, athletics, biology, biology-AP, British literature, calculus, calculus-AP, chamber groups, character education, chemistry, chemistry-AP, choral music, chorus, college admission preparation, college counseling, college placement, college planning, college writing, computer science, creative writing, dance, debate, earth science, economics, English, English language-AP, English literature, English literature-AP, environmental science, European history, European history-AP, exercise science, film and literature, fine arts, French, geography, geometry, global studies, government/civics, grammar, health, health education, history, Mandarin, mathematics, music, music theory-AP, physical education, physics, probability and statistics, science, social studies, Spanish, Spanish language-AP, statistics-AP, theater, U.S. history-AP, voice ensemble, Web site design, world history, world literature, writing.

Graduation Requirements Arts and fine arts (art, music, dance, drama), civics, English, foreign language, mathematics, physical education (includes health), science, social studies (includes history), community service project, senior speech.

Special Academic Programs 15 Advanced Placement exams for which test preparation is offered; honors section; independent study.

College Admission Counseling 43 students graduated in 2013; all went to college, including Appalachian State University; Clemson University; East Carolina University; North Carolina State University; The University of North Carolina at Chapel Hill; The University of North Carolina Wilmington. Median combined SAT: 1170. Mean SAT critical reading: 571, mean SAT math: 566, mean SAT writing: 555.

Student Life Upper grades have specified standards of dress, student council, honor system. Discipline rests primarily with faculty.

Summer Programs Enrichment, sports, art/fine arts, computer instruction programs offered; session focuses on academics, sports, hobby-related; held on campus; accepts boys and girls; open to students from other schools. 267 students usually enrolled. 2014 schedule: May 31 to August 12. Application deadline: none.

Tuition and Aid Day student tuition: $5000–$15,720. Guaranteed tuition plan. Tuition installment plan (FACTS Tuition Payment Plan, monthly payment plans). Tuition reduction for siblings, merit scholarship grants, need-based scholarship grants available. In 2013–14, 31% of upper-school students received aid; total upper-school merit-scholarship money awarded: $68,000. Total amount of financial aid awarded in 2013–14: $450,000.

Admissions Traditional secondary-level entrance grade is 9. Brigance Test of Basic Skills, ERB CTP IV, grade equivalent tests, Metropolitan Achievement Test, Wide Range Achievement Test or Woodcock-Johnson Revised Achievement Test required. Deadline for receipt of application materials: none. Application fee required: $75. Interview recommended.

Athletics Interscholastic: baseball (boys), basketball (b,g), cheering (g), dance (g), dance team (g), soccer (b,g), softball (g), tennis (b,g), volleyball (g); coed interscholastic: aquatics, cross-country running, golf, physical fitness, swimming and diving, track and field. 2 PE instructors, 15 coaches, 1 athletic trainer.

Computers Computers are regularly used in English, foreign language, history, library science, mathematics, science, Web site design, yearbook classes. Computer network features include on-campus library services, Internet access, wireless campus network, Internet filtering or blocking technology. Campus intranet, student e-mail accounts, and computer access in designated common areas are available to students. Students grades are available online. The school has a published electronic and media policy.

Contact Mrs. Kerie Beth Scott, Director of Admissions. 336-822-4005. Fax: 336-869-6685. E-mail: keriebeth.scott@westchestercds.org. Website: www.westchestercds.org

WEST ISLAND COLLEGE

7410 Blackfoot Trail SE
Calgary, Alberta T2H IM5, Canada

Head of School: Ms. Carol Grant-Watt

General Information Coeducational day college-preparatory, arts, business, bilingual studies, technology, and advanced placement school. Grades 7–12. Founded: 1982. Setting: urban. 18-acre campus. 2 buildings on campus. Approved or accredited by Canadian Association of Independent Schools and Alberta Department of Education. Languages of instruction: English, French, and Spanish. Total enrollment: 451. Upper school average class size: 18. Upper school faculty-student ratio: 1:17. There are 182 required school days per year for Upper School students. Upper School students typically attend 5 days per week. The average school day consists of 6 hours and 13 minutes.

Upper School Student Profile Grade 10: 75 students (36 boys, 39 girls); Grade 11: 95 students (45 boys, 50 girls); Grade 12: 68 students (33 boys, 35 girls).

Faculty School total: 45. In upper school: 20 men, 21 women; 15 have advanced degrees.

Subjects Offered Advanced Placement courses, anthropology, art, arts, biology, business, chemistry, choral music, communications, debate, drama, English, European history, experiential education, French, French studies, health, information processing, information technology, leadership, literature, mathematics, modern languages, music, outdoor education, philosophy, physical education, physics, political thought, politics, psychology, public speaking, science, social sciences, social studies, sociology, Spanish, standard curriculum, study skills, world geography, world history, world religions.

Graduation Requirements Alberta Education requirements.

Special Academic Programs 10 Advanced Placement exams for which test preparation is offered; honors section; independent study; study abroad; academic accommodation for the gifted.

College Admission Counseling 71 students graduated in 2012; 69 went to college, including McGill University; Queen's University at Kingston; The University of British Columbia; University of Alberta; University of Calgary; University of Victoria. Other: 2 had other specific plans.

Student Life Upper grades have uniform requirement, student council, honor system. Discipline rests equally with students and faculty.

Tuition and Aid Day student tuition: CAN$12,800. Tuition installment plan (monthly payment plans).

Admissions Traditional secondary-level entrance grade is 10. For fall 2012, 24 students applied for upper-level admission, 23 were accepted, 19 enrolled. 3-R Achievement Test, CCAT, CTBS, OLSAT, Gates MacGinite Reading Tests and Otis-Lennon IQ Test required. Deadline for receipt of application materials: none. Application fee required: CAN$100. Interview required.

Athletics Interscholastic: basketball (boys, girls), field hockey (g), rugby (b), track and field (b,g), volleyball (b,g); intramural: aquatics (b,g), basketball (b,g), floor hockey (b,g), track and field (b,g), volleyball (b,g); coed interscholastic: badminton, climbing, cross-country running, soccer; coed intramural: alpine skiing, backpacking, badminton, bicycling, bowling, canoeing/kayaking, climbing, cross-country running, curling, dance, fitness, golf, hiking/backpacking, kayaking, mountaineering, nordic skiing, outdoor activities, outdoor education, physical fitness, physical training, rock climbing, sailing, skiing (cross-country), skiing (downhill), snowboarding, soccer, wilderness survival, wildernessways. 4 PE instructors, 10 coaches, 2 athletic trainers.

Computers Computers are regularly used in business, career education, career exploration, career technology, economics, English, French, independent study, mathematics, media arts, media production, multimedia, science, social studies, technology, word processing classes. Computer network features include on-campus library services, online commercial services, Internet access, wireless campus network, Internet filtering or blocking technology. Campus intranet, student e-mail accounts, and computer access in designated common areas are available to students. Students grades are available online. The school has a published electronic and media policy.

Contact Ms. Nicole Bernard, Director of Admissions. 403-444-0023. Fax: 403-444-2820. E-mail: admissions@westislandcollege.ab.ca. Website: www.westislandcollege.ab.ca

WESTMINSTER CHRISTIAN ACADEMY

186 Westminster Drive
Opelousas, Louisiana 70570

Head of School: Mrs. Merida Brooks

General Information Coeducational day college-preparatory, arts, religious studies, bilingual studies, and technology school, affiliated with Protestant-Evangelical faith, Christian faith. Grades PK–12. Founded: 1978. Setting: rural. Nearest major city is Lafayette. 30-acre campus. 6 buildings on campus. Approved or accredited by Association of Christian Schools International and Louisiana Department of Education. Endowment: $300,000. Total enrollment: 1,143. Upper school average class size: 23. Upper school faculty-student ratio: 1:13. There are 175 required school days per year for Upper School students. Upper School students typically attend 5 days per week. The average school day consists of 7 hours.

Upper School Student Profile Grade 9: 70 students (37 boys, 33 girls); Grade 10: 67 students.(38 boys, 29 girls); Grade 11: 63 students (31 boys, 32 girls); Grade 12: 47 students (26 boys, 21 girls). 95% of students are Protestant-Evangelical faith, Christian faith.

Faculty School total: 66. In upper school: 15 men, 15 women; 5 have advanced degrees.

Subjects Offered Advanced math, algebra, American history, art, biology, calculus, calculus-AP, ceramics, chemistry, chemistry-AP, civics, concert choir, creative writing, drama, economics, English, English-AP, fine arts, French, geometry, guitar, history-AP, Latin, music, physics, religion, Spanish, world history, yearbook.

Graduation Requirements Arts and fine arts (art, music, dance, drama), computer literacy, English, foreign language, mathematics, physical education (includes health), religion (includes Bible studies and theology), science, social studies (includes history).

Special Academic Programs 6 Advanced Placement exams for which test preparation is offered; honors section; accelerated programs; study at local college for college credit; special instructional classes for students with mild learning disabilities and Attention Deficit Disorder.

College Admission Counseling 51 students graduated in 2013; 48 went to college, including Baylor University; Louisiana State University and Agricultural and Mechanical College; Louisiana State University at Eunice; Louisiana Tech University; University of Louisiana at Lafayette. Other: 1 went to work, 1 entered a postgraduate year, 1 had other specific plans. Mean SAT math: 581, mean SAT writing: 680, mean composite ACT: 26.

Student Life Upper grades have uniform requirement, student council. Discipline rests primarily with faculty. Attendance at religious services is required.

Summer Programs Enrichment, sports, art/fine arts programs offered; session focuses on training for football; held on campus; accepts boys; not open to students from other schools. 150 students usually enrolled. 2014 schedule: June 1 to July 31. Application deadline: May 15.

Tuition and Aid Day student tuition: $5935. Tuition installment plan (monthly payment plans, individually arranged payment plans, annual and biannual payment plans). Need-based scholarship grants, pastor discounts available. In 2013–14, 10% of upper-school students received aid. Total amount of financial aid awarded in 2013–14: $70,000.

Admissions Traditional secondary-level entrance grade is 9. For fall 2013, 24 students applied for upper-level admission, 21 were accepted, 17 enrolled. School's own exam and Terra Nova-CTB required. Deadline for receipt of application materials: none. Application fee required: $150. On-campus interview required.

Athletics Interscholastic: baseball (boys), basketball (b,g), cheering (g), cross-country running (b,g), football (b), soccer (b,g), softball (g), swimming and diving (b,g), track and field (b,g), volleyball (g); coed interscholastic: golf, hiking/backpacking, soccer, wilderness survival. 3 PE instructors, 2 coaches, 1 athletic trainer.

Computers Computers are regularly used in computer applications classes. Computer network features include on-campus library services, Internet access, wireless campus network, Internet filtering or blocking technology, one-to-one iPad program for grades 9-12. Student e-mail accounts and computer access in designated common areas are available to students. Students grades are available online. The school has a published electronic and media policy.

Contact Mrs. Michelle Nezat, Director of Institutional Advancement. 337-948-4623 Ext. 123. Fax: 337-948-4090. E-mail: mnezat@wcala.org. Website: www.wcala.org

WESTMINSTER CHRISTIAN SCHOOL

6855 Southwest 152nd Street
Palmetto Bay, Florida 33157

Head of School: Mr. Peter Cabrera

General Information Coeducational day and distance learning college-preparatory, arts, and religious studies school, affiliated with Christian faith. Grades PK–12. Distance learning grades 9–12. Founded: 1961. Setting: suburban. Nearest major city is Miami. 26-acre campus. 9 buildings on campus. Approved or accredited by Christian Schools of Florida, Southern Association of Colleges and Schools, and Florida Department of Education. Endowment: $2.2 million. Total enrollment: 1,068. Upper school average class size: 17. Upper school faculty-student ratio: 1:15. There are 173 required school days per year for Upper School students. Upper School students typically attend 5 days per week. The average school day consists of 7 hours.

Upper School Student Profile Grade 9: 128 students (50 boys, 78 girls); Grade 10: 121 students (61 boys, 60 girls); Grade 11: 120 students (72 boys, 48 girls); Grade 12: 105 students (42 boys, 63 girls). 100% of students are Christian.

Faculty School total: 104. In upper school: 23 men, 24 women; 35 have advanced degrees.

Subjects Offered Advanced Placement courses, algebra, American history, American literature, anatomy, art, Bible studies, biology, biology-AP, business law, business skills, calculus, ceramics, chemistry, chemistry-AP, community service, computer programming, computer science, creative writing, drama, economics, English, English literature, fine arts, French, French-AP, general science, geometry, government-AP, government/civics, grammar, health, history, macroeconomics-AP, marine biology, mathematics, music, musical theater, organic chemistry, photography, physical education, physics, physiology, psychology, religion, SAT preparation, science, scripture, sculpture, social studies, sociology, softball, Spanish, Spanish language-AP, Spanish-AP, speech, sports, statistics-AP, strings, study skills, swimming, theater, track and field, trigonometry, typing, U.S. government, U.S. government and politics-AP, U.S. history, U.S. history-AP, vocal ensemble, volleyball, weightlifting, wind ensemble, world history, world literature, wrestling, writing, yearbook.

Graduation Requirements Arts and fine arts (art, music, dance, drama), Bible, computer science, electives, English, foreign language, health science, lab science, mathematics, physical education (includes health), science, social studies (includes history), speech. Community service is required.

Special Academic Programs 16 Advanced Placement exams for which test preparation is offered; honors section; accelerated programs; independent study; academic accommodation for the gifted, the musically talented, and the artistically talented; programs in English, mathematics for dyslexic students.

College Admission Counseling 116 students graduated in 2013; all went to college, including Florida International University; Florida State University; University of Central Florida; University of Florida; University of Miami. Mean SAT critical reading: 552, mean SAT math: 539, mean SAT writing: 559, mean combined SAT: 1651, mean composite ACT: 24. 15% scored over 600 on SAT critical reading, 10% scored over 600 on SAT math, 10% scored over 600 on SAT writing, 10% scored over 1800 on combined SAT, 15% scored over 26 on composite ACT.

Student Life Upper grades have uniform requirement, student council, honor system. Discipline rests primarily with faculty. Attendance at religious services is required.

Summer Programs Remediation, advancement, computer instruction programs offered; session focuses on academics and athletics; held on campus; accepts boys and girls; open to students from other schools. 50 students usually enrolled. 2014 schedule: June 7 to July 30.

Tuition and Aid Day student tuition: $17,200. Tuition installment plan (monthly payment plans, individually arranged payment plans, semiannual and annual payment plans). Need-based scholarship grants available. In 2013–14, 15% of upper-school students received aid. Total amount of financial aid awarded in 2013–14: $750,000.

Admissions Traditional secondary-level entrance grade is 9. For fall 2013, 140 students applied for upper-level admission, 70 were accepted, 52 enrolled. Iowa Tests of Basic Skills and writing sample required. Deadline for receipt of application materials: February 1. Application fee required: $125. On-campus interview required.

Athletics Interscholastic: baseball (boys), basketball (b,g), cheering (g), cross-country running (b,g), football (b), golf (b,g), soccer (b,g), softball (g), swimming and diving (b,g), tennis (b,g), track and field (b,g), volleyball (b,g), wrestling (b). 8 PE instructors, 75 coaches, 2 athletic trainers.

Computers Computers are regularly used in accounting, art, Bible studies, business applications, career exploration, college planning, computer applications, creative writing, economics, English, foreign language, keyboarding, mathematics, music, photography, programming, science, word processing, writing, writing, yearbook classes. Computer network features include on-campus library services, online commercial services, Internet access, wireless campus network, Internet filtering or blocking technology. Campus intranet and student e-mail accounts are available to students. Students grades are available online. The school has a published electronic and media policy.

Contact Mrs. Lisa North, Director of Admission. 305-233-2030 Ext. 1246. Fax: 305-253-9623. E-mail: lnorth@wcsmiami.org. Website: www.wcsmiami.org

WESTMINSTER SCHOOL

995 Hopmeadow Street
Simsbury, Connecticut 06070

Head of School: Mr. William V.N. Philip

General Information Coeducational boarding and day college-preparatory, arts, and technology school. Grades 9–PG. Founded: 1888. Setting: suburban. Nearest major city is Hartford. Students are housed in single-sex dormitories. 230-acre campus. 39 buildings on campus. Approved or accredited by New England Association of Schools and Colleges, The Association of Boarding Schools, and Connecticut Department of Education. Member of National Association of Independent Schools and Secondary School Admission Test Board. Endowment: $85 million. Total enrollment: 390. Upper school average class size: 12. Upper school faculty-student ratio: 1:6. There are 183 required school days per year for Upper School students. Upper School students typically attend 6 days per week. The average school day consists of 6 hours and 30 minutes.

Upper School Student Profile Grade 9: 68 students (38 boys, 30 girls); Grade 10: 109 students (56 boys, 53 girls); Grade 11: 105 students (53 boys, 52 girls); Grade 12: 97 students (51 boys, 46 girls); Postgraduate: 12 students (8 boys, 4 girls). 67% of students are boarding students. 49% are state residents. 24 states are represented in upper school student body. 12% are international students. International students from Bermuda, Canada, China, Hong Kong, Republic of Korea, and Taiwan; 13 other countries represented in student body.

Faculty School total: 58. In upper school: 33 men, 25 women; 51 have advanced degrees; 53 reside on campus.

Subjects Offered Acting, advanced chemistry, advanced computer applications, advanced math, Advanced Placement courses, advanced studio art-AP, African American history, algebra, American history, American history-AP, American literature, American literature-AP, anatomy and physiology, Ancient Greek, architecture, art, art history, art history-AP, art-AP, Asian history, astronomy, athletics, band, biology, biology-AP, calculus, calculus-AP, character education, chemistry, chemistry-AP, Chinese, choir, choral music, comparative government and politics-AP, computer programming, computer science-AP, creative writing, dance, discrete mathematics, drama, drama workshop, drawing, drawing and design, driver education, ecology, economics, economics-AP, English, English literature, English-AP, English/composition-AP, environmental science-AP, ethics, ethics and responsibility, European history, European history-AP, female experience in America, fine arts, French, French language-AP, French literature-AP, geology, geometry, graphic design, health, history, honors algebra, honors English, honors geometry, illustration, Latin, Latin-AP, literature and composition-AP, macro/microeconomics-AP, mathematics, mathematics-AP, mechanical drawing, modern European history-AP, music, music appreciation, music composition, music theory-AP, musical theater, Native American history, painting, philosophy, photography, physics, physics-AP, pre-calculus, probability and statistics, psychology-AP, SAT preparation, SAT/ACT preparation, science, set design, social studies, Spanish, Spanish language-AP, Spanish literature, Spanish literature-AP, stagecraft, statistics, statistics-AP, studio art-AP, theater, trigonometry, U.S. history-AP, world history, writing.

Graduation Requirements Arts, English, foreign language, history, mathematics, science.

Special Academic Programs 23 Advanced Placement exams for which test preparation is offered; honors section; independent study; term-away projects; study abroad.

College Admission Counseling 104 students graduated in 2013; all went to college, including Boston College; Bucknell University; Trinity College; Union College; University of Richmond. Median SAT critical reading: 617, median SAT math: 623, median SAT writing: 632, median combined SAT: 1871.

Student Life Upper grades have specified standards of dress, student council. Discipline rests primarily with faculty.

Summer Programs Enrichment, sports programs offered; session focuses on soccer, lacrosse, science; held on campus; accepts boys and girls; open to students from other schools. 400 students usually enrolled. 2014 schedule: July 9 to August 3.

Tuition and Aid Day student tuition: $39,000; 7-day tuition and room/board: $52,000. Tuition installment plan (Academic Management Services Plan). Need-based scholarship grants available. In 2013–14, 33% of upper-school students received aid. Total amount of financial aid awarded in 2013–14: $4,459,000.

Admissions Traditional secondary-level entrance grade is 9. For fall 2013, 1,087 students applied for upper-level admission, 272 were accepted, 125 enrolled. PSAT and SAT for applicants to grade 11 and 12, SSAT or TOEFL required. Deadline for receipt of application materials: January 15. Application fee required: $75. On-campus interview required.

Athletics Interscholastic: baseball (boys), basketball (b,g), cross-country running (b,g), diving (b,g), field hockey (g), football (b), golf (b,g), hockey (b,g), ice hockey (b,g), lacrosse (b,g), soccer (b,g), softball (g), squash (b,g), swimming and diving (b,g), tennis (b,g), track and field (b,g); intramural: strength & conditioning (b,g); coed interscholastic: dance, martial arts, modern dance; coed intramural: aerobics/dance, ballet, bowling, canoeing/kayaking, dance, fly fishing, freestyle skiing, ice skating, modern dance, mountain biking, outdoor activities, rugby, skiing (cross-country), skiing (downhill), table tennis, unicycling. 2 athletic trainers.

Computers Computers are regularly used in English, foreign language, history, mathematics, science classes. Computer network features include on-campus library services, online commercial services, Internet access, wireless campus network, Internet filtering or blocking technology. Campus intranet, student e-mail accounts, and computer access in designated common areas are available to students. The school has a published electronic and media policy.

Contact Mrs. Rhonda Smith, Admissions Assistant. 860-408-3060. Fax: 860-408-3042. E-mail: admit@westminster-school.org. Website: www.westminster-school.org

THE WESTMINSTER SCHOOL AT OAK MOUNTAIN

5080 Cahaba Valley Trace
Birmingham, Alabama 35252

Head of School: Robbie Hinton

General Information college-preparatory, general academic, arts, and religious studies school. Approved or accredited by Alabama Department of Education. Total enrollment: 508. Upper School students typically attend 5 days per week.

Upper School Student Profile 100% are state residents.

Student Life Upper grades have uniform requirement.

Tuition and Aid Tuition reduction for siblings available.

Admissions Application fee required: $300. Interview required.

Athletics Interscholastic: basketball (boys, girls), cross-country running (b,g), indoor track & field (b,g), soccer (b,g), tennis (b,g), track and field (b,g).

Computers Computer network features include wireless campus network. Students grades are available online. The school has a published electronic and media policy.

Contact 205-995-9694. Website: www.westminsterknights.org/

WESTOVER SCHOOL

1237 Whittemore Road
Middlebury, Connecticut 06762

Head of School: Mrs. Ann S. Pollina

General Information Girls' boarding and day college-preparatory, arts, technology, and mathematics and science school. Grades 9–12. Founded: 1909. Setting: small town. Nearest major city is New York, NY. Students are housed in single-sex dormitories. 145-acre campus. 11 buildings on campus. Approved or accredited by Association of Independent Schools in New England, New England Association of Schools and Colleges, The Association of Boarding Schools, and Connecticut Department of Education. Member of National Association of Independent Schools and Secondary School Admission Test Board. Endowment: $46 million. Total enrollment: 204. Upper school average class size: 12. Upper School faculty-student ratio: 1:7. There are 183 required school days per year for Upper School students. Upper School students typically attend 6 days per week. The average school day consists of 6 hours.

Upper School Student Profile Grade 9: 37 students (37 girls); Grade 10: 61 students (61 girls); Grade 11: 52 students (52 girls); Grade 12: 54 students (54 girls). 62% of students are boarding students. 53% are state residents. 16 states are represented in upper school student body. 19% are international students. International students from China, Japan, Mexico, Republic of Korea, Russian Federation, and Rwanda; 11 other countries represented in student body.

Faculty School total: 39. In upper school: 8 men, 31 women; 35 have advanced degrees; 20 reside on campus.

Subjects Offered Advanced chemistry, Advanced Placement courses, African-American studies, algebra, American history, American history-AP, American literature, art, art history, art-AP, astronomy, ballet technique, bell choir, biology, biology-AP, calculus, calculus-AP, ceramics, chemistry, clayworking, community service, computer literacy, computer science, computer science-AP, creative writing, dance, drama, drawing, English, English language and composition-AP, English literature, environmental science, ESL, etymology, European history, European history-AP, filmmaking, fine arts, French, French-AP, geography, geometry, grammar, health and wellness, journalism, Latin, mathematics, model United Nations, music, music theory-AP, musical productions, painting, performing arts, photo shop, photography, physics, physics-AP, poetry, politics, portfolio art, pre-calculus, religion, robotics, science, sculpture, Shakespeare, short story, social studies, Spanish, Spanish-AP, speech, studio art-AP, theater, trigonometry, wilderness education, women's studies, world history, writing.

Graduation Requirements Art, athletics, English, foreign language, general science, mathematics, science, summer reading. Community service is required.

Special Academic Programs 15 Advanced Placement exams for which test preparation is offered; honors section; independent study; term-away projects; study abroad; academic accommodation for the gifted, the musically talented, and the artistically talented; special instructional classes for deaf students; ESL (5 students enrolled).

College Admission Counseling 43 students graduated in 2013; all went to college, including Stanford University. Median composite ACT: 27. Mean SAT critical reading: 597, mean SAT math: 594, mean SAT writing: 621. 61% scored over 600 on SAT critical reading, 59% scored over 600 on SAT math, 64% scored over 600 on SAT writing, 54% scored over 1800 on combined SAT, 56% scored over 26 on composite ACT.

Student Life Upper grades have specified standards of dress, student council, honor system. Discipline rests equally with students and faculty.

Tuition and Aid Day student tuition: $35,300; 7-day tuition and room/board: $49,100. Tuition installment plan (The Tuition Plan, Insured Tuition Payment Plan, FACTS Tuition Payment Plan, monthly payment plans). Need-based scholarship grants, need-based loans, middle-income loans available. In 2013–14, 50% of upper-school students received aid.

Admissions Traditional secondary-level entrance grade is 9. For fall 2013, 232 students applied for upper-level admission, 105 were accepted, 61 enrolled. ISEE, SSAT or TOEFL required. Deadline for receipt of application materials: January 15. Application fee required: $50. On-campus interview required.

Athletics Interscholastic: basketball, cross-country running, field hockey, golf, independent competitive sports, lacrosse, outdoor activities, soccer, softball, squash, swimming and diving, tennis, volleyball; intramural: aerobics, aerobics/dance, alpine skiing, backpacking, ballet, canoeing/kayaking, climbing, dance, fitness, fitness walking, Frisbee, hiking/backpacking, jogging, kayaking, modern dance, outdoor activities, outdoor education, outdoor skills, outdoors, paddle tennis, physical fitness, physical training, rappelling, rock climbing, running, self defense, skiing (downhill), snowboarding, strength & conditioning, tennis, ultimate Frisbee, walking, wall climbing, weight lifting, weight training, wilderness, yoga. 2 PE instructors, 10 coaches, 1 athletic trainer.

Computers Computers are regularly used in all academic classes. Computer network features include on-campus library services, online commercial services, Internet access, wireless campus network, Internet filtering or blocking technology. Campus intranet, student e-mail accounts, and computer access in designated common areas are available to students. Students grades are available online. The school has a published electronic and media policy.

Contact Mrs. Laura Volovski, Director of Admission. 203-577-4521. Fax: 203-577-4588. E-mail: admission@westoverschool.org. Website: www.westoverschool.org

WESTRIDGE SCHOOL

324 Madeline Drive
Pasadena, California 91105-3399

Head of School: Ms. Elizabeth J. McGregor

General Information Girls' day college-preparatory, arts, and technology school. Grades 4–12. Founded: 1913. Setting: suburban. Nearest major city is Los Angeles. 9-acre campus. 11 buildings on campus. Approved or accredited by National Independent Private Schools Association, The College Board, Western Association of Schools and Colleges, and California Department of Education. Member of National Association of Independent Schools. Endowment: $16.5 million. Total enrollment: 482. Upper school average class size: 10. Upper school faculty-student ratio: 1:6. Upper School students typically attend 5 days per week. The average school day consists of 6 hours and 30 minutes.

Upper School Student Profile Grade 9: 82 students (82 girls); Grade 10: 48 students (48 girls); Grade 11: 62 students (62 girls); Grade 12: 72 students (72 girls).

Faculty School total: 58. In upper school: 13 men, 25 women; 27 have advanced degrees.

Subjects Offered Acting, Advanced Placement courses, algebra, American history, American literature, art, art history, biology, calculus, cell biology, ceramics, chemistry, Chinese, chorus, classical language, college counseling, computer applications, computer graphics, computer science, creative writing, dance, directing, drama, earth science, English, English literature, environmental science, European history, fine arts, French, geometry, government/civics, history, Latin, life science, Mandarin, mathematics, modern languages, music, orchestra, photography, physical education, physical science, physics, physiology, pre-calculus, science, Spanish, Spanish literature, statistics, studio art, theater, trigonometry, video, visual and performing arts, visual arts, world history, world literature.

Graduation Requirements Art, college counseling, cultural arts, English, foreign language, history, mathematics, music, physical education (includes health), science, senior project, statistics. Community service is required.

Special Academic Programs Advanced Placement exam preparation; honors section; independent study.

College Admission Counseling 67 students graduated in 2013; 66 went to college, including Emerson College; Stanford University; University of California, Berkeley; University of Pennsylvania; University of Southern California; Vassar College. Other: 1 had other specific plans. Median SAT critical reading: 630, median SAT math: 630, median SAT writing: 660, median combined SAT: 1930, median composite ACT: 27.

Student Life Upper grades have uniform requirement, student council. Discipline rests primarily with faculty.

Tuition and Aid Day student tuition: $31,300. Tuition installment plan (monthly payment plans, full payment, two payment plan, 10-month tuition payment). Need-based scholarship grants available. In 2013–14, 38% of upper-school students received aid. Total amount of financial aid awarded in 2013–14: $1,742,800.

Admissions Traditional secondary-level entrance grade is 9. For fall 2013, 86 students applied for upper-level admission, 53 were accepted, 21 enrolled. ISEE or writing sample required. Deadline for receipt of application materials: January 24. Application fee required: $85. On-campus interview required.

Athletics Interscholastic: aerobics/dance, basketball, cross-country running, dance, diving, fencing, golf, lacrosse, martial arts, modern dance, physical fitness, soccer, softball, swimming and diving, tennis, track and field, volleyball, water polo, yoga. 26 coaches.

Computers Computers are regularly used in art, English, foreign language, history, library skills, mathematics, science, yearbook classes. Computer network features include on-campus library services, online commercial services, Internet access, wireless campus network, Internet filtering or blocking technology, course Web sites, remote access to email and files, school Internet portal/Web site. Student e-mail accounts are available to students. The school has a published electronic and media policy.

Contact Ms. Helen V. Hopper, Director of Admissions. 626-799-1153 Ext. 213. Fax: 626-799-7068. E-mail: hhopper@westridge.org. Website: www.westridge.org

WEST SOUND ACADEMY

16571 Creative Drive NE
Poulsbo, Washington 98370

Head of School: Joe Kennedy

General Information Coeducational boarding and day college-preparatory, arts, and International Baccalaureate school. Boarding grades 8–12, day grades 6–12. Founded: 1998. Setting: rural. Nearest major city is Seattle. Students are housed in dormitories. 20-acre campus. 4 buildings on campus. Approved or accredited by International Baccalaureate Organization, Northwest Accreditation Commission, Northwest Association of Independent Schools, and Washington Department of Education. Total enrollment: 95. Upper school average class size: 11. Upper school faculty-student ratio: 1:7. There are 178 required school days per year for Upper School students. Upper School students typically attend 5 days per week. The average school day consists of 6 hours and 15 minutes.

Upper School Student Profile Grade 9: 12 students (6 boys, 6 girls); Grade 10: 11 students (9 boys, 2 girls); Grade 11: 22 students (7 boys, 15 girls); Grade 12: 16 students (7 boys, 9 girls). 18% of students are boarding students. 66% are state residents. 1 state is represented in upper school student body. 34% are international students. International students from China, Ghana, Republic of Korea, Slovakia, Tunisia, and Turkey; 2 other countries represented in student body.

Faculty School total: 19. In upper school: 6 men, 8 women; 9 have advanced degrees.

Subjects Offered Advanced biology, advanced math, advanced TOEFL/grammar, algebra, American history, American literature, analytic geometry, ancient world history, art, art history, Basic programming, biology, calculus, calculus-AP, ceramics, chemistry, civics, college admission preparation, college awareness, college counseling, college planning, community service, computer skills, contemporary issues, creative writing, dance, drama, drawing, earth science, electives, English, ESL, film studies, filmmaking, fitness, four units of summer reading, French, geometry, global issues, guitar, history, improvisation, independent study, International Baccalaureate courses, journalism, linear algebra, literary magazine, logarithms, marine biology, music, music performance, non-Western literature, non-Western societies, outdoor education, painting, performing arts, photography, physics, poetry, portfolio art, portfolio writing, SAT preparation, senior thesis, set design, Spanish, speech, sports, student government, studio art, technology, theory of knowledge, U.S. history, visual arts, Washington State and Northwest History, Western civilization, Western literature, white-water trips, wilderness experience, world cultures, world history, world literature, yearbook.

Graduation Requirements Biology, chemistry, English, foreign language, history, International Baccalaureate courses, mathematics, physics, senior thesis, service learning/internship, theory of knowledge, visual arts, West Sound Academy has a 4-1-4 academic calendar; students are required to complete a Jan-Term, courses are 3-week-long short courses of intense study in a variety of subjects outside the usual curriculum, fall and spring trips to varied locations teach leadership, environmental ethics, and technical skills.

Special Academic Programs International Baccalaureate program; Advanced Placement exam preparation; independent study; term-away projects; academic accommodation for the gifted, the musically talented, and the artistically talented; ESL (20 students enrolled).

College Admission Counseling 8 students graduated in 2013; 7 went to college, including Indiana University Bloomington; Lewis & Clark College; University of Virginia; University of Washington; Western Washington University; Whitman College. Other: 1 entered a postgraduate year. Median SAT critical reading: 570, median SAT math: 580, median SAT writing: 580, median combined SAT: 1790. 43% scored over 600 on SAT critical reading, 43% scored over 600 on SAT math, 29% scored over 600 on SAT writing, 38% scored over 1800 on combined SAT.

Student Life Upper grades have specified standards of dress, student council, honor system. Discipline rests primarily with faculty.

Summer Programs Enrichment programs offered; session focuses on math enrichment for Algebra II, Geometry, IB Math Studies; held on campus; accepts boys and girls; open to students from other schools. 10 students usually enrolled. 2014 schedule: August 11 to August 22. Application deadline: August 1.

Tuition and Aid Day student tuition: $15,805; 7-day tuition and room/board: $41,460. Tuition installment plan (Insured Tuition Payment Plan, monthly payment plans). Merit scholarship grants, need-based scholarship grants available. In 2013–14,

36% of upper-school students received aid; total upper-school merit-scholarship money awarded: $101,450. Total amount of financial aid awarded in 2013–14: $251,931.

Admissions Traditional secondary-level entrance grade is 9. For fall 2013, 40 students applied for upper-level admission, 33 were accepted, 20 enrolled. International English Language Test or TOEFL required, Deadline for receipt of application materials: none. Application fee required: $60. Interview required.

Athletics Interscholastic: basketball (boys), lacrosse (g), sailing (b), soccer (b,g), swimming and diving (b), volleyball (g); coed intramural: climbing, hiking/backpacking, kayaking, outdoor activities, outdoor education, outdoor recreation, rafting, rappelling, rock climbing.

Computers Computers are regularly used in all classes. Computer network features include on-campus library services, Internet access, wireless campus network, Internet filtering or blocking technology. Student e-mail accounts are available to students. Students grades are available online. The school has a published electronic and media policy.

Contact Lisa Gsellman, Director of Admissions. 360-598-5954. Fax: 360-598-5494. E-mail: lgsellman@westsoundacademy.org. Website: www.westsoundacademy.org/

WESTTOWN SCHOOL

975 Westtown Road
West Chester, Pennsylvania 19382-5700

Head of School: John W. Baird

General Information Coeducational boarding and day college-preparatory, arts, and religious studies school, affiliated with Society of Friends. Boarding grades 9–12, day grades PK–10. Founded: 1799. Setting: suburban. Nearest major city is Philadelphia. Students are housed in single-sex by floor dormitories and single-sex dormitories. 600-acre campus. 38 buildings on campus. Approved or accredited by Friends Council on Education, Middle States Association of Colleges and Schools, and Pennsylvania Department of Education. Member of National Association of Independent Schools and Secondary School Admission Test Board. Endowment: $70 million. Total enrollment: 632. Upper school average class size: 15. Upper school faculty-student ratio: 1:8. Upper School students typically attend 5 days per week. The average school day consists of 9 hours and 20 minutes.

Upper School Student Profile Grade 9: 80 students (35 boys, 45 girls); Grade 10: 103 students (44 boys, 59 girls); Grade 11: 76 students (42 boys, 34 girls); Grade 12: 122 students (54 boys, 68 girls). 76% of students are boarding students. 58% are state residents. 17 states are represented in upper school student body. 18% are international students. International students from China, Germany, Republic of Korea, Thailand, Turkey, and Viet Nam; 14 other countries represented in student body. 15% of students are members of Society of Friends.

Faculty School total: 112. In upper school: 32 men, 34 women; 52 have advanced degrees; 62 reside on campus.

Subjects Offered 3-dimensional art, ACT preparation, advanced biology, advanced chemistry, advanced math, algebra, American culture, American foreign policy, American history, American literature, Ancient Greek, ancient history, art, Asian history, astronomy, astrophysics, ballet, band, baseball, basketball, Bible, Bible studies, biology, botany, British literature, calculus, Chinese, choir, choral music, chorus, Christian and Hebrew scripture, classical language, classical studies, comparative religion, computer applications, concert band, concert choir, crafts, creative dance, creative writing, dance, dance performance, digital art, drama, drama performance, drama workshop, drawing, drawing and design, earth science, Eastern religion and philosophy, ecology, ecology, environmental systems, electives, engineering, English, English as a foreign language, English composition, English literature, environmental science, environmental studies, environmental systems, ESL, European history, film and literature, folk art, foreign language, foreign policy, fractal geometry, French, functions, geometry, German, graphic design, Greek, Holocaust and other genocides, honors algebra, honors geometry, honors U.S. history, honors world history, Japanese, jazz, jazz band, jazz dance, jazz ensemble, lab science, language, Latin, Latin American history, leadership, library research, linear algebra, literature, literature seminar, Mandarin, mathematics, model United Nations, modern dance, music, music composition, music performance, music theater, musical theater, mythology, nature writers, non-Western literature, peace and justice, physics, piano, play production, playwriting and directing, pre-algebra, pre-calculus, Quakerism and ethics, religion, robotics, SAT preparation, science, senior project, senior seminar, Shakespeare, Spanish, Spanish literature, stage design, statistics, student government, student publications, studio art, swimming, tennis, theater, theater design and production, theater history, theater production, trigonometry, U.S. history, U.S. literature, visual and performing arts, visual arts, vocal ensemble, vocal music, water color painting, weight fitness, Western civilization, Western literature, Western religions, woodworking, world history, world literature, world religions, wrestling, writing, writing workshop, yearbook.

Graduation Requirements Arts and fine arts (art, music, dance, drama), English, foreign language, health education, history, mathematics, physical education (includes health), religion (includes Bible studies and theology), religious studies, science, senior project, service learning/internship, social sciences.

Special Academic Programs Advanced Placement exam preparation; honors section; independent study; study abroad; academic accommodation for the gifted, the musically talented, and the artistically talented; remedial math; ESL (18 students enrolled).

College Admission Counseling 79 students graduated in 2013; all went to college, including Franklin & Marshall College; Guilford College; New York University; Northwestern University; Pomona College; Smith College.

Student Life Upper grades have specified standards of dress, student council, honor system. Discipline rests equally with students and faculty. Attendance at religious services is required.

Tuition and Aid Day student tuition: $30,200; 7-day tuition and room/board: $48,140. Tuition installment plan (Key Tuition Payment Plan, monthly payment plans). Merit scholarship grants, need-based scholarship grants available.

Admissions Traditional secondary-level entrance grade is 9. For fall 2013, 333 students applied for upper-level admission, 163 were accepted, 86 enrolled. SSAT or TOEFL required. Deadline for receipt of application materials: none. Application fee required: $50. Interview required.

Athletics Interscholastic: baseball (boys), basketball (b,g), cross-country running (b,g), field hockey (g), independent competitive sports (b,g), lacrosse (b,g), soccer (b,g), softball (g), swimming and diving (b,g), tennis (b,g), track and field (b,g), volleyball (g); coed interscholastic: dance, dance team, golf, independent competitive sports, indoor track, indoor track & field; coed intramural: aquatics, ballet, basketball, canoeing/kayaking, combined training, dance, fitness, hiking/backpacking, indoor soccer, life saving, modern dance, outdoor activities, outdoor education, outdoor recreation, physical fitness, physical training, ropes courses, running, strength & conditioning, weight training, yoga. 18 coaches, 2 athletic trainers.

Computers Computers are regularly used in all academic, art, career exploration, college planning, current events, desktop publishing, digital applications, introduction to technology, library, library skills, literary magazine, publications, research skills, theater classes. Computer network features include on-campus library services, online commercial services, Internet access, wireless campus network, Internet filtering or blocking technology. Campus intranet, student e-mail accounts, and computer access in designated common areas are available to students. Students grades are available online. The school has a published electronic and media policy.

Contact Nathan Bohn, Director of Admission. 610-399-7900. Fax: 610-399-7909. E-mail: admissions@westtown.edu. Website: www.westtown.edu

WESTVIEW SCHOOL

Los Angeles, California
See Special Needs Schools section.

WHEATON ACADEMY

900 Prince Crossing Road
West Chicago, Illinois 60185

Head of School: Dr. Gene Frost

General Information Coeducational day college-preparatory and religious studies school, affiliated with Christian faith. Grades 9–12. Founded: 1853. Setting: suburban. Nearest major city is Chicago. 43-acre campus. 8 buildings on campus. Approved or accredited by Association of Christian Schools International, North Central Association of Colleges and Schools, and Illinois Department of Education. Total enrollment: 640. Upper school average class size: 21. Upper school faculty-student ratio: 1:15. There are 175 required school days per year for Upper School students. Upper School students typically attend 5 days per week. The average school day consists of 6 hours and 30 minutes.

Upper School Student Profile Grade 9: 169 students (82 boys, 87 girls); Grade 10: 158 students (77 boys, 81 girls); Grade 11: 165 students (82 boys, 83 girls); Grade 12: 168 students (82 boys, 86 girls). 98% of students are Christian faith.

Faculty School total: 51. In upper school: 29 men, 22 women; 33 have advanced degrees.

Subjects Offered ACT preparation, algebra, art, arts and crafts, band, Bible, Bible studies, biology, biology-AP, British literature, business, business applications, calculus, calculus-AP, ceramics, chemistry, chemistry-AP, child development, choir, Christian doctrine, Christian education, classics, comparative government and politics-AP, computer art, computer education, computer graphics, computer multimedia, computer processing, computer programming-AP, computer science, concert choir, consumer economics, creative writing, debate, desktop publishing, drama, drama workshop, drawing, driver education, earth science, economics, engineering, English, English language and composition-AP, English literature, English literature and composition-AP, environmental science, environmental science-AP, European history, European history-AP, family living, fiber arts, fine arts, foods, French, French language-AP, freshman seminar, geology, geometry, government/civics, graphic design, Greek, health, health and wellness, history, honors English, honors geometry, honors U.S. history, industrial arts, internship, journalism, keyboarding, leadership, literature, mathematics, multimedia design, music, music theory-AP, novels, orchestra, personal growth, physical education, physics, physics-AP, portfolio art, pre-algebra, psychology, publications, science, social sciences, social studies, sociology, Spanish, Spanish language-AP, speech, statistics, statistics-AP, student publications, theater, theology,

trigonometry, U.S. government, U.S. government and politics-AP, U.S. history, U.S. history-AP, U.S. literature, world history, world history-AP, world literature, writing.

Graduation Requirements Arts and fine arts (art, music, dance, drama), English, mathematics, physical education (includes health), religion (includes Bible studies and theology), science, social sciences, social studies (includes history), Winterim (2-week period during January allowing students to take two classes beyond the typical curriculum).

Special Academic Programs 17 Advanced Placement exams for which test preparation is offered; honors section; independent study; term-away projects; study at local college for college credit; academic accommodation for the gifted, the musically talented, and the artistically talented; remedial reading and/or remedial writing; remedial math; special instructional classes for students with learning disabilities; ESL (50 students enrolled).

College Admission Counseling 167 students graduated in 2013; 163 went to college, including Calvin College; Hope College; Lipscomb University; Taylor University; University of Illinois at Urbana–Champaign; Wheaton College. Other: 1 went to work, 3 had other specific plans. Median composite ACT: 25. 45% scored over 26 on composite ACT.

Student Life Upper grades have specified standards of dress, student council, honor system. Discipline rests primarily with faculty. Attendance at religious services is required.

Summer Programs Enrichment, advancement, sports, art/fine arts, computer instruction programs offered; held on campus; accepts boys and girls; open to students from other schools. 75 students usually enrolled. 2014 schedule: June 9 to June 27.

Tuition and Aid Day student tuition: $14,000. Tuition installment plan (monthly payment plans, semester payment plan). Tuition reduction for siblings, merit scholarship grants, need-based scholarship grants, paying campus jobs available. In 2013–14, 35% of upper-school students received aid; total upper-school merit-scholarship money awarded: $15,000. Total amount of financial aid awarded in 2013–14: $600,000.

Admissions Traditional secondary-level entrance grade is 9. ACT-Explore and placement test required. Deadline for receipt of application materials: February 15. Application fee required: $50. On-campus interview required.

Athletics Interscholastic: baseball (boys), basketball (b,g), cheering (g), cross-country running (b,g), dance team (g), football (b), golf (b,g), ice hockey (b), lacrosse (b), pom squad (g), soccer (b,g), softball (g), tennis (b,g), track and field (b,g), volleyball (b,g); intramural: aerobics (g), flagball (g), ice hockey (b), wilderness survival (b); coed interscholastic: modern dance, physical training, running; coed intramural: climbing, floor hockey, hiking/backpacking, outdoor education, outdoor skills, power lifting, project adventure, riflery, rock climbing, skiing (cross-country), strength & conditioning, wall climbing, weight lifting, weight training. 2 PE instructors, 6 coaches, 1 athletic trainer.

Computers Computers are regularly used in Bible studies, graphic design, independent study, mathematics, multimedia, writing, yearbook classes. Computer network features include on-campus library services, online commercial services, Internet access, wireless campus network, Internet filtering or blocking technology. Student e-mail accounts are available to students. Students grades are available online. The school has a published electronic and media policy.

Contact Mr. Ryan Hall, Admissions Counselor. 630-562-7500 Ext. 7501. Fax: 630-231-1469. E-mail: rhall@wheatonacademy.org. Website: www.wheatonacademy.org

THE WHEELER SCHOOL

216 Hope Street
Providence, Rhode Island 02906

Head of School: Mr. Dan Miller, PhD

General Information Coeducational day college-preparatory, arts, Community Action Program (service-based learning), and AERIE Program (individual academic enrichment grades 9-12) school. Grades N–12. Founded: 1889. Setting: urban. 5-acre campus. 8 buildings on campus. Approved or accredited by Association of Independent Schools in New England, New England Association of Schools and Colleges, and Rhode Island Department of Education. Member of National Association of Independent Schools. Endowment: $21.3 million. Total enrollment: 817. Upper school average class size: 15. Upper school faculty-student ratio: 1:7. There are 165 required school days per year for Upper School students. Upper School students typically attend 5 days per week. The average school day consists of 6 hours and 25 minutes.

Upper School Student Profile Grade 9: 91 students (53 boys, 38 girls); Grade 10: 95 students (52 boys, 43 girls); Grade 11: 83 students (40 boys, 43 girls); Grade 12: 81 students (41 boys, 40 girls).

Faculty School total: 124. In upper school: 23 men, 30 women; 36 have advanced degrees.

Subjects Offered 20th century American writers, 20th century world history, acting, Advanced Placement courses, advanced studio art-AP, algebra, American history, anatomy, art, art history, biology, biology-AP, biotechnology, Black history, broadcasting, business skills, calculus, calculus-AP, ceramics, chemistry, Chinese, Chinese studies, choral music, civil rights, computer programming, computer science, contemporary issues, dance, drama, drawing, economics, engineering, English, English literature, English-AP, environmental science, environmental science-AP, European history, film studies, fine arts, forensics, French, geometry, guitar, Japanese, jazz ensemble, kinesiology, Latin, Latin American history, Latin American studies, mathematics, Middle Eastern history, music, nutrition, photography, physical education, physics, physiology, pre-calculus, printmaking, psychology, research, science, sculpture, social studies, Spanish, statistics, theater, trigonometry, Web site design, Western civilization.

Graduation Requirements Arts and fine arts (art, music, dance, drama), English, foreign language, history, mathematics, performing arts, physical education (includes health), science, community service, Unity and Diversity Curriculum.

Special Academic Programs 18 Advanced Placement exams for which test preparation is offered; honors section; independent study; term-away projects; study at local college for college credit; study abroad; academic accommodation for the gifted; programs in general development for dyslexic students.

College Admission Counseling 81 students graduated in 2013; all went to college, including Brown University; Dickinson College; Georgetown University; Northeastern University; Stanford University; Yale University. Mean SAT critical reading: 625, mean SAT math: 637, mean SAT writing: 651, mean combined SAT: 1913, mean composite ACT: 28.

Student Life Upper grades have specified standards of dress, student council. Discipline rests equally with students and faculty.

Summer Programs Enrichment, sports, art/fine arts programs offered; session focuses on Jazz Camp, Basketball Camp, Kayaking/Voyager Camps, Sports Academy; held on campus; accepts boys and girls; open to students from other schools. 175 students usually enrolled. 2014 schedule: June 16 to August 8. Application deadline: none.

Tuition and Aid Day student tuition: $30,115–$38,715. Tuition installment plan (Key Tuition Payment Plan, monthly payment plans). Need-based scholarship grants available. In 2013–14, 23% of upper-school students received aid. Total amount of financial aid awarded in 2013–14: $1,601,835.

Admissions Traditional secondary-level entrance grade is 9. For fall 2013, 154 students applied for upper-level admission, 56 were accepted, 29 enrolled. ISEE or SSAT required. Deadline for receipt of application materials: January 31. Application fee required: $60. On-campus interview required.

Athletics Interscholastic: baseball (boys), basketball (b,g), cross-country running (b,g), field hockey (g), football (b), ice hockey (b,g), lacrosse (b,g), soccer (b,g), softball (g), swimming and diving (b,g), tennis (b,g), track and field (b,g), winter (indoor) track (b,g); coed interscholastic: golf, squash. 6 PE instructors, 35 coaches, 1 athletic trainer.

Computers Computers are regularly used in all classes. Computer network features include on-campus library services, online commercial services, Internet access, wireless campus network. Campus intranet and student e-mail accounts are available to students. The school has a published electronic and media policy.

Contact Mrs. Jeanette Epstein, Director of Admission. 401-421-8100. Fax: 401-751-7674. E-mail: jeanetteepstein@wheelerschool.org. Website: www.wheelerschool.org

WHITEFIELD ACADEMY

1 Whitefield Drive SE
Mableton, Georgia 30126

Head of School: Dr. John H. Lindsell

General Information Coeducational day college-preparatory, arts, religious studies, technology, and life and career planning school, affiliated with Christian faith. Grades PK–12. Founded: 1996. Setting: suburban. Nearest major city is Atlanta. 75-acre campus. 5 buildings on campus. Approved or accredited by Southern Association of Colleges and Schools and Southern Association of Independent Schools. Member of Secondary School Admission Test Board. Total enrollment: 649. Upper school average class size: 18. Upper school faculty-student ratio: 1:18. The average school day consists of 6 hours and 45 minutes.

Upper School Student Profile Grade 9: 48 students (27 boys, 21 girls); Grade 10: 58 students (30 boys, 28 girls); Grade 11: 48 students (24 boys, 24 girls); Grade 12: 62 students (32 boys, 30 girls). 100% of students are Christian faith.

Faculty School total: 122. In upper school: 12 men, 11 women; 13 have advanced degrees.

Graduation Requirements Algebra, American history, American literature, arts and fine arts (art, music, dance, drama), biology, British literature, chemistry, Christian studies, English, foreign language, geometry, health education, modern European history, physical fitness, physics, pre-calculus, public speaking, Western civilization, Life and Career Planning program; Community Service Hour Requirements. Community service is required.

Special Academic Programs Advanced Placement exam preparation; honors section; independent study; special instructional classes for deaf students, blind students.

College Admission Counseling 68 students graduated in 2012; all went to college, including Auburn University; Furman University; Georgia Institute of Technology; The University of Alabama; University of Georgia.

Student Life Upper grades have uniform requirement, student council, honor system. Discipline rests primarily with faculty. Attendance at religious services is required.

Tuition and Aid Day student tuition: $19,410. Tuition installment plan (FACTS Tuition Payment Plan). Need-based financial assistance (through SSS application),

AchieverLoans, and PrepGATE loans available. In 2012–13, 18% of upper-school students received aid. Total amount of financial aid awarded in 2012–13: $800,000.

Admissions Traditional secondary-level entrance grade is 9. SSAT required. Deadline for receipt of application materials: February 15. Application fee required: $65. Interview required.

Athletics Interscholastic: baseball (boys), basketball (b,g), cheering (g), cross-country running (b,g), diving (b,g), football (b), golf (b,g), lacrosse (b), physical fitness (b,g), physical training (b,g), soccer (b,g), softball (g), strength & conditioning (b,g), swimming and diving (b,g), tennis (b,g), track and field (b,g), volleyball (g), weight lifting (b,g), weight training (b,g), wrestling (b); coed interscholastic: cross-country running, diving, golf, physical fitness, physical training, strength & conditioning, swimming and diving, tennis, track and field, weight lifting, weight training. 2 PE instructors, 5 coaches, 2 athletic trainers.

Computers Computer network features include on-campus library services, online commercial services, Internet access, wireless campus network, Internet filtering or blocking technology. Students grades are available online. The school has a published electronic and media policy.

Contact Mrs. Linda J. Simpson, Admission Director. 678-305-3027. Fax: 678-305-3010. E-mail: lsimpson@whitefieldacademy.com. Website: www.whitefieldacademy.com

WHITEFIELD ACADEMY

7711 Fegenbush Lane
Louisville, Kentucky 40228

Head of School: Mr. Gary W. Mounce

General Information Coeducational day college-preparatory, arts, religious studies, and technology school, affiliated with Baptist Church. Grades PS–12. Founded: 1976. Setting: suburban. 30-acre campus. 2 buildings on campus. Approved or accredited by Association of Christian Schools International, CITA (Commission on International and Trans-Regional Accreditation), Christian Schools International, Council of Accreditation and School Improvement, Southern Association of Colleges and Schools, and Kentucky Department of Education. Total enrollment: 778. Upper school average class size: 20. Upper school faculty-student ratio: 1:20. There are 178 required school days per year for Upper School students. Upper School students typically attend 5 days per week. The average school day consists of 6 hours and 25 minutes.

Upper School Student Profile Grade 9: 42 students (21 boys, 21 girls); Grade 10: 54 students (29 boys, 25 girls); Grade 11: 49 students (27 boys, 22 girls); Grade 12: 42 students (17 boys, 25 girls). 35% of students are Baptist.

Faculty School total: 68. In upper school: 8 men, 7 women; 9 have advanced degrees.

Subjects Offered Adolescent issues, advanced math, algebra, anatomy, art, arts, band, Bible studies, biology, calculus, calculus-AP, chemistry, choir, choral music, chorus, Christian education, Christian studies, college placement, college planning, college writing, communication skills, composition, computer applications, computer education, computers, current events, drama, drama performance, economics, English, English composition, English literature, English literature-AP, foreign language, geometry, history, honors English, library, mathematics, music, political science, pre-calculus, reading, SAT/ACT preparation, science, science project, sex education, social sciences, Spanish, speech and debate, student government, student publications, U.S. history, U.S. history-AP.

Graduation Requirements Arts and fine arts (art, music, dance, drama), Bible, electives, English, foreign language, health, mathematics, physical education (includes health), science, social studies (includes history), Religious Studies.

Special Academic Programs 6 Advanced Placement exams for which test preparation is offered; honors section; independent study; study at local college for college credit; academic accommodation for the gifted.

College Admission Counseling 47 students graduated in 2013; 43 went to college, including Bellarmine University; Eastern Kentucky University; Jefferson Community and Technical College; University of Kentucky; University of Louisville; Western Kentucky University. Other: 2 went to work, 2 had other specific plans. Median composite ACT: 26. 43% scored over 26 on composite ACT.

Student Life Upper grades have uniform requirement, student council, honor system. Discipline rests primarily with faculty. Attendance at religious services is required.

Summer Programs Enrichment, sports, art/fine arts programs offered; session focuses on academic enrichment; held on campus; accepts boys and girls; open to students from other schools. 60 students usually enrolled.

Tuition and Aid Day student tuition: $6700. Tuition installment plan (FACTS Tuition Payment Plan, annual payment in full plan). Tuition reduction for siblings, need-based scholarship grants available. In 2013–14, 13% of upper-school students received aid. Total amount of financial aid awarded in 2013–14: $42,175.

Admissions Traditional secondary-level entrance grade is 9. For fall 2013, 27 students applied for upper-level admission, 21 were accepted, 21 enrolled. Stanford Achievement Test required. Deadline for receipt of application materials: none. Application fee required: $350. On-campus interview required.

Athletics Interscholastic: aquatics (boys, girls), baseball (b), basketball (b,g), cheering (b,g), cross-country running (b,g), golf (b,g), soccer (b,g), softball (g), swimming and diving (b,g), tennis (b,g), track and field (b,g), volleyball (g); intramural:

aerobics (g), fitness (b,g), outdoor activities (b,g), physical fitness (b,g), volleyball (g), weight lifting (b,g). 2 PE instructors.

Computers Computers are regularly used in all academic, college planning, library, newspaper, SAT preparation, theater arts, yearbook classes. Computer network features include on-campus library services, Internet access, wireless campus network, Internet filtering or blocking technology. Computer access in designated common areas is available to students. Students grades are available online. The school has a published electronic and media policy.

Contact Mrs. Diane Fow, Director of Admissions. 502-231-6261. Fax: 502-239-3144. E-mail: dfow@whitefield.org. Website: www.whitefield.org/

THE WHITE MOUNTAIN SCHOOL

371 West Farm Road
Bethlehem, New Hampshire 03574

Head of School: Tim Breen, PhD

General Information Coeducational boarding and day college-preparatory, arts, and sustainability studies school, affiliated with Episcopal Church. Grades 9–PG. Founded: 1886. Setting: rural. Nearest major city is Concord. Students are housed in single-sex dormitories. 250-acre campus. 13 buildings on campus. Approved or accredited by Association for Experiential Education, National Association of Episcopal Schools, New England Association of Schools and Colleges, The Association of Boarding Schools, and New Hampshire Department of Education. Member of National Association of Independent Schools and Secondary School Admission Test Board. Endowment: $1.5 million. Total enrollment: 112. Upper school average class size: 9. Upper school faculty-student ratio: 1:5. Upper School students typically attend 6 days per week. The average school day consists of 5 hours and 45 minutes.

Upper School Student Profile Grade 9: 24 students (12 boys, 12 girls); Grade 10: 20 students (9 boys, 11 girls); Grade 11: 42 students (20 boys, 22 girls); Grade 12: 26 students (12 boys, 14 girls). 85% of students are boarding students. 25% are state residents. 22 states are represented in upper school student body. 30% are international students. International students from China, Ethiopia, Kenya, Republic of Korea, Ukraine, and Zambia; 5 other countries represented in student body. 5% of students are members of Episcopal Church.

Faculty School total: 28. In upper school: 15 men, 13 women; 15 have advanced degrees; 24 reside on campus.

Subjects Offered Algebra, American literature, American studies, anatomy and physiology, biology, Buddhism, calculus, Caribbean history, ceramics, chemistry, college counseling, community garden, community service, creative writing, drawing and design, earth science, economics, English, environmental education, environmental science, environmental studies, ESL, ethics, French, geometry, health, history of jazz, human development, independent study, jazz theory, learning strategies, literature, Middle Eastern history, music history, painting, philosophy, photography, physics, pre-calculus, printmaking, senior project, social justice, Spanish, studio art, theater arts, theater production, U.S. history, world history, writing.

Graduation Requirements Algebra, American history, arts and fine arts (art, music, dance, drama), English, geometry, health, literature, non-Western societies, physical science, theology, Western civilization, writing, field courses, sustainability studies, community service. Community service is required.

Special Academic Programs 6 Advanced Placement exams for which test preparation is offered; honors section; independent study; term-away projects; academic accommodation for the gifted, the musically talented, and the artistically talented; programs in English, mathematics, general development for dyslexic students; special instructional classes for students with dysgraphia and other learning differences; ESL (19 students enrolled).

College Admission Counseling 27 students graduated in 2013; all went to college, including Fort Lewis College; St. Lawrence University; The College of Wooster; University of Vermont; Warren Wilson College; Western State Colorado University. 10% scored over 600 on SAT critical reading, 24% scored over 600 on SAT math.

Student Life Upper grades have specified standards of dress, student council, honor system. Discipline rests primarily with faculty.

Summer Programs Sports programs offered; session focuses on whitewater kayaking, rock climbing, and hiking; held both on and off campus; held at local rivers and open water and White Mountain National Forest; accepts boys and girls; open to students from other schools. 40 students usually enrolled. 2014 schedule: June 15 to July 30.

Tuition and Aid Day student tuition: $23,600; 7-day tuition and room/board: $49,200. Tuition installment plan (Insured Tuition Payment Plan, Academic Management Services Plan, 2-payment plan). Merit scholarship grants, need-based scholarship grants available. In 2013–14, 47% of upper-school students received aid. Total amount of financial aid awarded in 2013–14: $1,412,000.

Admissions For fall 2013, 126 students applied for upper-level admission, 65 were accepted, 39 enrolled. SSAT, ERB, PSAT, SAT, PLAN or ACT, TOEFL or SLEP, WISC III or other aptitude measures; standardized achievement test or writing sample required. Deadline for receipt of application materials: January 31. Application fee required: $60. Interview required.

Athletics Interscholastic: basketball (boys, girls), lacrosse (b,g), soccer (b,g); intramural: dance (g); coed interscholastic: climbing, cross-country running, freestyle skiing, mountain biking, rock climbing, snowboarding; coed intramural: aerobics/Nautilus, alpine skiing, backpacking, bicycling, canoeing/kayaking, climbing, combined training, fitness, freestyle skiing, Frisbee, hiking/backpacking, kayaking, martial arts, mountain biking, mountaineering, Nautilus, nordic skiing, outdoor activities, outdoor adventure, outdoor education, outdoor recreation, outdoor skills, outdoors, paddling, physical fitness, physical training, rappelling, rock climbing, running, skiing (cross-country), skiing (downhill), snowboarding, snowshoeing, strength & conditioning, telemark skiing, ultimate Frisbee, wall climbing, wilderness, wilderness survival, yoga. 1 athletic trainer.

Computers Computers are regularly used in college planning, foreign language, library skills, mathematics, media arts, science, yearbook classes. Computer network features include on-campus library services, online commercial services, Internet access, wireless campus network, Internet filtering or blocking technology. Student e-mail accounts and computer access in designated common areas are available to students. The school has a published electronic and media policy.

Contact Cindy Silver, Admission Office Manager. 603-444-2928 Ext. 26. Fax: 603-444-5568. E-mail: cindy.silver@whitemountain.org. Website: www.whitemountain.org

WHITFIELD SCHOOL

175 South Mason Road
St. Louis, Missouri 63141

Head of School: Mr. John Delautre

General Information Coeducational day college-preparatory school. Grades 6–12. Founded: 1952. Setting: suburban. 25-acre campus. 3 buildings on campus. Approved or accredited by Independent Schools Association of the Central States. Member of National Association of Independent Schools. Endowment: $7.4 million. Total enrollment: 379. Upper school average class size: 12. Upper school faculty-student ratio: 1:8.

Upper School Student Profile Grade 6: 24 students (13 boys, 11 girls); Grade 7: 51 students (26 boys, 25 girls); Grade 8: 57 students (30 boys, 27 girls); Grade 9: 63 students (24 boys, 39 girls); Grade 10: 65 students (28 boys, 37 girls); Grade 11: 59 students (28 boys, 31 girls); Grade 12: 60 students (31 boys, 29 girls).

Faculty School total: 60. In upper school: 23 men, 27 women; 30 have advanced degrees.

Subjects Offered Advanced chemistry, algebra, American history, American literature, art, biochemistry, biology, calculus, calculus-AP, ceramics, chemistry, chemistry-AP, choir, college counseling, college placement, college planning, community service, concert band, earth science, English, European history, fine arts, French, French-AP, geometry, health, history, junior and senior seminars, Latin, mathematics, modern world history, music, painting, photography, physical education, physics, pre-algebra, pre-calculus, science, senior internship, social studies, sophomore skills, Spanish, Spanish-AP, symphonic band, theater, trigonometry, visual and performing arts, Western civilization, world cultures, world history, world literature.

Graduation Requirements Arts and fine arts (art, music, dance, drama), English, foreign language, mathematics, physical education (includes health), science, social studies (includes history), sophomore, junior, and senior seminars.

Special Academic Programs Advanced Placement exam preparation; honors section; independent study; academic accommodation for the gifted, the musically talented, and the artistically talented.

College Admission Counseling 56 students graduated in 2013; all went to college, including Miami University; Saint Louis University; Southern Methodist University; Syracuse University; University of Missouri; Vanderbilt University. Mean SAT critical reading: 680, mean SAT math: 640, mean SAT writing: 640, mean composite ACT: 27.

Student Life Upper grades have specified standards of dress, student council, honor system. Discipline rests primarily with faculty.

Summer Programs Enrichment, sports, art/fine arts, computer instruction programs offered; session focuses on athletics, arts, technology and summer fun programs; held on campus; accepts boys and girls; open to students from other schools. 250 students usually enrolled. 2014 schedule: June 16 to August 1. Application deadline: none.

Tuition and Aid Day student tuition: $23,350. Tuition installment plan (Key Tuition Payment Plan, monthly payment plans, 1-, 2-, and 10-payment plans). Need-based scholarship grants available. In 2013–14, 26% of upper-school students received aid. Total amount of financial aid awarded in 2013–14: $1,350,000.

Admissions Traditional secondary-level entrance grade is 7. SSAT required. Deadline for receipt of application materials: January 17. Application fee required: $75. On-campus interview required.

Athletics Interscholastic: baseball (boys), basketball (b,g), cheering (g), cross-country running (b,g), dance team (g), field hockey (g), golf (b), ice hockey (b), lacrosse (b,g), soccer (b,g), tennis (b), track and field (b,g), volleyball (g), wrestling (b); intramural: baseball (b), basketball (b,g), cheering (g), cross-country running (b,g), dance team (g), field hockey (g), soccer (b,g), volleyball (g), wrestling (b); coed interscholastic: dance team, golf, ice hockey, tennis; coed intramural: ice hockey. 4 PE instructors, 9 coaches, 1 athletic trainer.

Computers Computers are regularly used in all classes. Computer network features include on-campus library services, online commercial services, Internet access, wireless campus network, off-campus library and database searches, Tablet PC program running Microsoft Windows. Campus intranet and student e-mail accounts are available to students. The school has a published electronic and media policy.

Contact Lou Sabino, Director of Admission. 314-415-1256. Fax: 314-434-6193. E-mail: lou.sabino@whitfieldschool.org. Website: www.whitfieldschool.org

WHITINSVILLE CHRISTIAN SCHOOL

279 Linwood Avenue
Whitinsville, Massachusetts 01588

General Information Coeducational day college-preparatory school, affiliated with Christian Reformed Church. Grades K–12. Founded: 1928. Setting: small town. Nearest major city is Worcester. 40-acre campus. 1 building on campus. Approved or accredited by Massachusetts Department of Education. Total enrollment: 499. Upper school average class size: 13. Upper school faculty-student ratio: 1:8. There are 180 required school days per year for Upper School students. The average school day consists of 6 hours and 15 minutes.

Upper School Student Profile Grade 9: 32 students (20 boys, 12 girls); Grade 10: 39 students (20 boys, 19 girls); Grade 11: 60 students (33 boys, 27 girls); Grade 12: 49 students (25 boys, 24 girls). 35% of students are members of Christian Reformed Church.

Faculty In upper school: 16 have advanced degrees.

Special Academic Programs 5 Advanced Placement exams for which test preparation is offered; honors section; ESL (14 students enrolled).

College Admission Counseling 49 students graduated in 2013; all went to college, including Gordon College; Palm Beach Atlantic University; University of Massachusetts Amherst; University of Massachusetts Dartmouth.

Student Life Upper grades have specified standards of dress, student council. Discipline rests primarily with faculty. Attendance at religious services is required.

Admissions Deadline for receipt of application materials: none. Application fee required: $75. Interview required.

Athletics Interscholastic: baseball (boys), basketball (b,g), cross-country running (b,g), golf (b), indoor track & field (b,g), soccer (b,g), softball (g), tennis (b,g), track and field (b,g), volleyball (g). 2 PE instructors.

Computers Computer resources include Internet access, wireless campus network, Internet filtering or blocking technology. Students grades are available online. The school has a published electronic and media policy.

Contact 508-234-8211. Fax: 508-234-0624. Website: www.whitinsvillechristian.org/

WILBRAHAM & MONSON ACADEMY

423 Main Street
Wilbraham, Massachusetts 01095

Head of School: Mr. Rodney LaBrecque

General Information Coeducational boarding and day college-preparatory, arts, business, and technology school. Boarding grades 9–PG, day grades 6–PG. Founded: 1804. Setting: small town. Nearest major city is Springfield. Students are housed in single-sex by floor dormitories and single-sex dormitories. 300-acre campus. 24 buildings on campus. Approved or accredited by Association of Independent Schools in New England, New England Association of Schools and Colleges, and The Association of Boarding Schools. Member of National Association of Independent Schools and Secondary School Admission Test Board. Endowment: $5 million. Total enrollment: 431. Upper school average class size: 12. Upper school faculty-student ratio: 1:6. Upper School students typically attend 5 days per week.

Upper School Student Profile Grade 6: 21 students (12 boys, 9 girls); Grade 7: 23 students (15 boys, 8 girls); Grade 8: 30 students (20 boys, 10 girls); Grade 9: 59 students (33 boys, 26 girls); Grade 10: 81 students (51 boys, 30 girls); Grade 11: 120 students (69 boys, 51 girls); Grade 12: 86 students (52 boys, 34 girls); Postgraduate: 12 students (11 boys, 1 girl). 53% of students are boarding students. 73% are state residents. 12 states are represented in upper school student body. 30% are international students. International students from Bermuda, China, Italy, Japan, Republic of Korea, and Russian Federation; 25 other countries represented in student body.

Faculty School total: 61. In upper school: 34 men, 27 women; 41 have advanced degrees; 26 reside on campus.

Subjects Offered Advanced Placement courses, algebra, American history, American literature, art, art history, biology, biology-AP, bookmaking, calculus, calculus-AP, ceramics, chemistry, chemistry-AP, college admission preparation, computer programming, computer science, computer-aided design, conceptual physics, creative writing, critical studies in film, decision making skills, desktop publishing, drama, driver education, economics, economics-AP, English, English literature, English-AP, entrepreneurship, environmental science, environmental science-AP, ESL, ethical decision making, European history, European history-AP, finance, fine arts, French, French-AP, geometry, global studies, honors algebra, honors geometry, honors U.S. history, honors world history, humanities, instrumental music, instruments, Internet research, Irish literature, Latin, Latin-AP, leadership, Mandarin, mathematics, modern European history, modern European history-AP, music-AP, painting, performing arts, personal finance, photography, physical education, physics, play/screen writing, poetry, pre-algebra, pre-calculus, pre-college orientation, probability and statistics, public speaking, research and reference, SAT preparation, science, sculpture, Shakespeare, short story, social studies, sociology, Spanish, Spanish-

AP, statistics-AP, studio art, studio art-AP, the Web, theater, U.S. history, U.S. history-AP, Vietnam War, visual arts, vocal ensemble, Web site design, world history, world literature, writing, writing workshop.

Graduation Requirements Algebra, American history, arts and fine arts (art, music, dance, drama), English, foreign language, geometry, lab science, physical education (includes health).

Special Academic Programs Advanced Placement exam preparation; honors section; independent study; academic accommodation for the musically talented and the artistically talented; ESL (8 students enrolled).

College Admission Counseling 91 students graduated in 2013; all went to college, including Boston University; Bryant University; Connecticut College; Princeton University; Smith College; University of Massachusetts Amherst. Mean SAT critical reading: 531, mean SAT math: 621, mean SAT writing: 561, mean combined SAT: 1713.

Student Life Upper grades have specified standards of dress, student council, honor system. Discipline rests equally with students and faculty.

Summer Programs Enrichment, ESL programs offered; session focuses on intensive English studies, entrepreneurial studies; held on campus; accepts boys and girls; open to students from other schools. 50 students usually enrolled. 2014 schedule: June 17 to July 7. Application deadline: March 1.

Tuition and Aid Day student tuition: $34,600; 7-day tuition and room/board: $50,985. Tuition installment plan (The Tuition Plan, Academic Management Services Plan, monthly payment plans, Tuition Management Systems Plan, Key Bank). Tuition reduction for siblings, need-based scholarship grants, need-based loans available. In 2013–14, 37% of upper-school students received aid.

Admissions Traditional secondary-level entrance grade is 9. For fall 2013, 649 students applied for upper-level admission, 315 were accepted, 146 enrolled. Deadline for receipt of application materials: February 1. Application fee required: $75. Interview required.

Athletics Interscholastic: baseball (boys), basketball (b,g), cross-country running (b,g), field hockey (g), football (b), independent competitive sports (b,g), lacrosse (b,g), soccer (b,g), softball (g), swimming and diving (b,g), tennis (b,g), track and field (b,g), volleyball (g), wrestling (b); intramural: basketball (b,g); coed interscholastic: alpine skiing, dance, golf, independent competitive sports, modern dance, riflery, skiing (downhill), water polo, winter (indoor) track; coed intramural: aerobics, aerobics/dance, aerobics/Nautilus, backpacking, canoeing/kayaking, climbing, fitness, hiking/backpacking, jogging, kayaking, life saving, outdoor adventure, physical fitness, physical training, rock climbing, running, snowboarding, strength & conditioning, tai chi, tennis, weight lifting, weight training, yoga. 1 PE instructor, 11 coaches, 1 athletic trainer.

Computers Computers are regularly used in architecture, art, college planning, drawing and design, English, graphic design, library skills, literary magazine, mathematics, music, newspaper, research skills, science, Web site design, yearbook classes. Computer network features include on-campus library services, online commercial services, Internet access, wireless campus network, Internet filtering or blocking technology. Campus intranet and student e-mail accounts are available to students. Students grades are available online. The school has a published electronic and media policy.

Contact Ms. Loretta J. Fograshy, Administrative Assistant, Admission. 413-596-6811 Ext. 107. Fax: 413-599-1749. E-mail: lfograshy@wma.us. Website: www.wma.us

WILLIAM PENN CHARTER SCHOOL

3000 West School House Lane
Philadelphia, Pennsylvania 19144

Head of School: Darryl J. Ford

General Information Coeducational day college-preparatory school, affiliated with Society of Friends. Grades PK–12. Founded: 1689. Setting: urban. 44-acre campus. 8 buildings on campus. Approved or accredited by Middle States Association of Colleges and Schools and Pennsylvania Association of Independent Schools. Member of National Association of Independent Schools and Secondary School Admission Test Board. Endowment: $63 million. Total enrollment: 966. Upper school average class size: 16. Upper school faculty-student ratio: 1:9. There are 181 required school days per year for Upper School students. Upper School students typically attend 5 days per week. The average school day consists of 6 hours.

Upper School Student Profile Grade 6: 55 students (29 boys, 26 girls); Grade 7: 73 students (39 boys, 34 girls); Grade 8: 81 students (46 boys, 35 girls); Grade 9: 120 students (60 boys, 60 girls); Grade 10: 113 students (66 boys, 47 girls); Grade 11: 115 students (57 boys, 58 girls); Grade 12: 110 students (75 boys, 35 girls). 3% of students are members of Society of Friends.

Faculty School total: 134. In upper school: 36 men, 37 women; 57 have advanced degrees.

Subjects Offered Algebra, American history, American literature, architectural drawing, art, art history-AP, Asian studies, band, Bible studies, bioethics, biology, biology-AP, botany, British literature, calculus, calculus-AP, calligraphy, ceramics, chemistry, chemistry-AP, choral music, chorus, college counseling, computer math, computer programming, computer science, creative writing, design, drama, drawing, earth science, Eastern religion and philosophy, ecology, economics, electronic music, English, English literature, environmental science, environmental science-AP, ethics,

European history, European history-AP, film, filmmaking, fine arts, French, French-AP, genetics, geology, geometry, government and politics-AP, health, Hebrew scripture, history, history of rock and roll, history of science, human anatomy, independent study, Irish literature, jazz band, junior and senior seminars, Latin, learning cognition, learning strategies, marine biology, mathematics, Middle East, model United Nations, modern European history-AP, music, music performance, oceanography, organic chemistry, painting, peace and justice, photography, physical education, physics, physics-AP, pottery, pre-calculus, public speaking, Quakerism and ethics, religion, science, sculpture, senior project, service learning/internship, Shakespeare, social studies, Spanish, Spanish-AP, speech, statistics-AP, symphonic band, theater, theater arts, theater design and production, theater production, trigonometry, U.S. history-AP, United States government-AP, video, visual and performing arts, world history, world literature, world religions, writing.

Graduation Requirements Computer science, English, foreign language, mathematics, music, physical education (includes health), religious studies, science, social studies (includes history), theater, visual arts.

Special Academic Programs 14 Advanced Placement exams for which test preparation is offered; honors section; independent study; study at local college for college credit; academic accommodation for the gifted, the musically talented, and the artistically talented.

College Admission Counseling 116 students graduated in 2013; all went to college, including Boston College; Lehigh University; The George Washington University; University of Pennsylvania; University of Vermont; University of Virginia.

Student Life Upper grades have specified standards of dress, student council, honor system. Discipline rests equally with students and faculty. Attendance at religious services is required.

Summer Programs Enrichment, advancement, sports, art/fine arts programs offered; held on campus; accepts boys and girls; open to students from other schools. 37 students usually enrolled. 2014 schedule: June 16 to August 1. Application deadline: June 16.

Tuition and Aid Day student tuition: $30,400. Tuition installment plan (Academic Management Services Plan, monthly payment plans, individually arranged payment plans, Sallie Mae TuitionPay). Need-based scholarship grants available. In 2013–14, 38% of upper-school students received aid. Total amount of financial aid awarded in 2013–14: $2,321,390.

Admissions Traditional secondary-level entrance grade is 9. For fall 2013, 247 students applied for upper-level admission, 68 were accepted, 43 enrolled. ISEE or SSAT required. Deadline for receipt of application materials: January 10. Application fee required: $30. On-campus interview required.

Athletics Interscholastic: aquatics (boys, girls), baseball (b), basketball (b,g), crew (b,g), cross-country running (b,g), diving (b,g), field hockey (g), football (b), golf (b,g), lacrosse (b,g), soccer (b,g), softball (g), squash (b,g), swimming and diving (b,g), tennis (b,g), track and field (b,g), water polo (b,g), wrestling (b); intramural: basketball (b,g); coed intramural: ultimate Frisbee. 10 PE instructors, 46 coaches, 2 athletic trainers.

Computers Computers are regularly used in all classes. Computer network features include on-campus library services, online commercial services, Internet access, wireless campus network, Internet filtering or blocking technology, 1:1 laptop program. Campus intranet, student e-mail accounts, and computer access in designated common areas are available to students. The school has a published electronic and media policy.

Contact Beth Johnson, Director of Middle and Upper School Admissions. 215-844-3460 Ext. 104. Fax: 215-843-3939. E-mail: bjohnson@penncharter.com. Website: www.penncharter.com

THE WILLIAMS SCHOOL

182 Mohegan Avenue
New London, Connecticut 06320-4110
Head of School: Mr. Mark Fader

General Information Coeducational day college-preparatory and arts school. Grades 7–12. Founded: 1891. Setting: urban. 25-acre campus. 2 buildings on campus. Approved or accredited by Connecticut Association of Independent Schools, New England Association of Schools and Colleges, and Connecticut Department of Education. Member of National Association of Independent Schools and Secondary School Admission Test Board. Endowment: $4 million. Total enrollment: 238. Upper school average class size: 13. Upper school faculty-student ratio: 1:9. There are 165 required school days per year for Upper School students. Upper School students typically attend 5 days per week. The average school day consists of 6 hours and 48 minutes.

Upper School Student Profile Grade 9: 43 students (16 boys, 27 girls); Grade 10: 40 students (21 boys, 19 girls); Grade 11: 50 students (24 boys, 26 girls); Grade 12: 54 students (23 boys, 31 girls).

Faculty School total: 36. In upper school: 18 men, 18 women; 26 have advanced degrees.

Subjects Offered Algebra, American history, art, band, biology, biology-AP, calculus, calculus-AP, chemistry, chemistry-AP, chorus, dance, digital art, drama, economics, English, English literature, English-AP, environmental science, European history, expository writing, fine arts, French, French-AP, geography, geometry, Greek, history, jazz, Latin-AP, mathematics, modern European history, music, music composition, music history, music theory, music theory-AP, physical education,

physics, physics-AP, pre-calculus, science, social studies, Spanish, Spanish-AP, theater, trigonometry, world history, world literature.

Graduation Requirements Arts and fine arts (art, music, dance, drama), classical language, English, foreign language, mathematics, physical education (includes health), science, senior project, social studies (includes history), at least one year of Latin, four years of math in Upper School or through precalculus.

Special Academic Programs 10 Advanced Placement exams for which test preparation is offered; honors section; independent study; study at local college for college credit; study abroad; academic accommodation for the gifted, the musically talented, and the artistically talented.

College Admission Counseling 67 students graduated in 2012; all went to college, including Boston University; Connecticut College; Goucher College; New York University; Tufts University; University of Connecticut. Mean SAT critical reading: 614, mean SAT math: 584, mean SAT writing: 590, mean combined SAT: 1788, mean composite ACT: 26. 67% scored over 600 on SAT critical reading, 45% scored over 600 on SAT math, 46% scored over 600 on SAT writing.

Student Life Upper grades have specified standards of dress, student council. Discipline rests primarily with faculty.

Tuition and Aid Day student tuition: $26,600. Tuition installment plan (Insured Tuition Payment Plan, FACTS Tuition Payment Plan, monthly payment plans, individually arranged payment plans). Need-based scholarship grants available. In 2012–13, 40% of upper-school students received aid. Total amount of financial aid awarded in 2012–13: $1,270,680.

Admissions Traditional secondary-level entrance grade is 9. For fall 2012, 68 students applied for upper-level admission, 61 were accepted, 30 enrolled. SSAT required. Deadline for receipt of application materials: February 1. Application fee required: $50. On-campus interview required.

Athletics Interscholastic: baseball (boys), basketball (b,g), field hockey (g), lacrosse (b,g), soccer (b,g), tennis (b,g); intramural: dance (b,g), dance team (b,g), fencing (b,g), fitness (b,g), yoga (b); coed interscholastic: cross-country running, sailing, squash, swimming and diving; coed intramural: dance, dance team, fencing, fitness, golf, modern dance, weight training. 2 PE instructors, 19 coaches, 1 athletic trainer.

Computers Computers are regularly used in creative writing, English, French, graphic design, history, Latin, mathematics, music, photography, SAT preparation, science, social studies, Spanish, study skills, theater, writing, yearbook classes. Computer network features include on-campus library services, online commercial services, Internet access, wireless campus network, Internet filtering or blocking technology. Campus intranet, student e-mail accounts, and computer access in designated common areas are available to students. The school has a published electronic and media policy.

Contact Cristan Harris, Director of Admission. 860-439-2789. Fax: 860-439-2796. E-mail: charris@williamsschool.org. Website: www.williamsschool.org

THE WILLISTON NORTHAMPTON SCHOOL

19 Payson Avenue
Easthampton, Massachusetts 01027
Head of School: Mr. Robert W. Hill III

General Information Coeducational boarding and day college-preparatory school. Boarding grades 9–PG, day grades 7–12. Founded: 1841. Setting: small town. Nearest major city is Northampton. Students are housed in single-sex dormitories. 125-acre campus. 57 buildings on campus. Approved or accredited by Association of Independent Schools in New England, New England Association of Schools and Colleges, and The Association of Boarding Schools. Member of National Association of Independent Schools and Secondary School Admission Test Board. Endowment: $40 million. Total enrollment: 544. Upper school average class size: 13. Upper school faculty-student ratio: 1:6. There are 160 required school days per year for Upper School students. Upper School students typically attend 5 days per week. The average school day consists of 8 hours and 30 minutes.

Upper School Student Profile Grade 9: 78 students (42 boys, 36 girls); Grade 10: 107 students (47 boys, 60 girls); Grade 11: 134 students (71 boys, 63 girls); Grade 12: 134 students (74 boys, 60 girls); Postgraduate: 16 students (11 boys, 5 girls). 65% of students are boarding students. 40% are state residents. 28 states are represented in upper school student body. 19% are international students. International students from Bermuda, Canada, China, Hong Kong, Republic of Korea, and Taiwan; 27 other countries represented in student body.

Faculty School total: 75. In upper school: 37 men, 38 women; 49 have advanced degrees; 50 reside on campus.

Subjects Offered African-American history, algebra, American history, American literature, anatomy and physiology, animal behavior, art, art history, astronomy, biology, biology-AP, calculus, calculus-AP, chemistry, chemistry-AP, China/Japan history, Chinese, choral music, choreography, Christian and Hebrew scripture, comparative government and politics-AP, comparative politics, computer math, computer programming, computer science, computer science-AP, constitutional law, creative writing, dance, discrete mathematics, drama, economics, economics and history, economics-AP, English, English language-AP, English literature, English literature-AP, environmental science, ESL, ethics, European history, expository writing, fine arts, French, French language-AP, French literature-AP, French-AP, genetics, geometry, global studies, government/civics, health, history, history of jazz, honors algebra, honors English, honors geometry, Islamic studies, Latin, Latin American history, Latin-AP, mathematics, music, music theory, organic biochemistry, organic chemistry, philosophy, photography, photojournalism, physics, physics-AP, play production, playwriting, poetry, psychology, psychology-AP, religion, religion and culture, Russian history, science, sculpture, social studies, Spanish, Spanish language-AP, Spanish literature-AP, statistics-AP, theater, theology, trigonometry, U.S. history-AP, world history, world literature, writing workshop.

Graduation Requirements Arts and fine arts (art, music, dance, drama), English, foreign language, history, mathematics, science, participation in Afternoon Program.

Special Academic Programs 18 Advanced Placement exams for which test preparation is offered; honors section; independent study; term-away projects; study abroad; academic accommodation for the gifted, the musically talented, and the artistically talented; special instructional classes for deaf students; ESL (12 students enrolled).

College Admission Counseling 113 students graduated in 2013; 108 went to college, including Babson College; Carleton College; Hobart and William Smith Colleges; New York University; Union College; University of Pennsylvania. Other: 1 entered military service, 4 had other specific plans. Mean SAT critical reading: 574, mean SAT math: 609, mean SAT writing: 591, mean combined SAT: 1773, mean composite ACT: 25.

Student Life Upper grades have specified standards of dress, student council, honor system. Discipline rests equally with students and faculty.

Tuition and Aid Day student tuition: $34,800; 7-day tuition and room/board: $50,900. Tuition installment plan (Insured Tuition Payment Plan, monthly payment plans, individually arranged payment plans, Tuition Management Systems). Merit scholarship grants, need-based scholarship grants available. In 2013–14, 42% of upper-school students received aid; total upper-school merit-scholarship money awarded: $139,000. Total amount of financial aid awarded in 2013–14: $6,169,500.

Admissions Traditional secondary-level entrance grade is 9. For fall 2013, 824 students applied for upper-level admission, 275 were accepted, 130 enrolled. ACT, ISEE, PSAT or SAT for applicants to grade 11 and 12, SSAT or TOEFL required. Deadline for receipt of application materials: January 15. Application fee required: $50. Interview required.

Athletics Interscholastic: alpine skiing (boys, girls), baseball (b), basketball (b,g), crew (b,g), cross-country running (b,g), field hockey (g), football (b), golf (b,g), ice hockey (b,g), lacrosse (b,g), soccer (b,g), softball (g), squash (b,g), strength & conditioning (b,g), swimming and diving (b,g), tennis (b,g), track and field (b,g), volleyball (g), water polo (b,g), wrestling (b); intramural: self defense (g); coed interscholastic: dance, diving, physical training, ultimate Frisbee; coed intramural: aerobics, aerobics/dance, dance, dance team, equestrian sports, fitness, horseback riding, judo, martial arts, modern dance, mountain biking, snowboarding, weight lifting, weight training, yoga. 1 PE instructor, 5 coaches, 2 athletic trainers.

Computers Computers are regularly used in college planning, geography, graphic design, history, library, mathematics, newspaper, photography, photojournalism, programming, science, yearbook classes. Computer network features include on-campus library services, online commercial services, Internet access, wireless campus network, Internet filtering or blocking technology. Campus intranet, student e-mail accounts, and computer access in designated common areas are available to students. Students grades are available online. The school has a published electronic and media policy.

Contact Mr. Derek Cunha, Associate Director of Admission. 413-529-3241. Fax: 413-527-9494. E-mail: dcunha@williston.com. Website: www.williston.com

See Display below and Close-Up on page 584.

THE WILLOWS ACADEMY

1015 Rose Avenue
Des Plaines, Illinois 60016

Head of School: Mrs. Jeanne Petros

General Information Girls' day college-preparatory, arts, religious studies, technology, and College Preparatory school, affiliated with Roman Catholic Church. Grades 6–12. Founded: 1974. Setting: suburban. Nearest major city is Chicago. 4-acre campus. 1 building on campus. Approved or accredited by Illinois Department of Education. Total enrollment: 230. Upper school average class size: 18. Upper school faculty-student ratio: 1:10. Upper School students typically attend 5 days per week. The average school day consists of 6 hours and 30 minutes.

Upper School Student Profile Grade 6: 23 students (23 girls); Grade 7: 29 students (29 girls); Grade 8: 25 students (25 girls); Grade 9: 42 students (42 girls); Grade 10: 37 students (37 girls); Grade 11: 30 students (30 girls); Grade 12: 42 students (42 girls). 85% of students are Roman Catholic.

Faculty School total: 35. In upper school: 27 women; 15 have advanced degrees.

Subjects Offered Algebra, American history, American literature, art, biology, calculus, chemistry, choir, choral music, computer graphics, computer programming, computer science, economics, English, English literature, ethics, European history, fine arts, four units of summer reading, French, geography, geometry, government/civics, grammar, health, history, instrumental music, Latin, mathematics, music, music history, music theory, musical productions, philosophy, physical education, physics, pre-calculus, science, social studies, Spanish, statistics, theology, visual arts, vocal music, world history, world literature, writing.

Graduation Requirements Arts and fine arts (art, music, dance, drama), English, foreign language, four units of summer reading, mathematics, physical education (includes health), religion (includes Bible studies and theology), science, social studies (includes history), 40 hours of service work per year.

Special Academic Programs Advanced Placement exam preparation; honors section.

College Admission Counseling 35 students graduated in 2012; all went to college, including Marquette University; Northwestern University; Purdue University; University of Dallas; University of Illinois at Urbana–Champaign; University of Notre Dame. Mean SAT critical reading: 695, mean SAT math: 658, mean SAT writing: 672, mean composite ACT: 26.

Student Life Upper grades have uniform requirement, student council, honor system. Discipline rests primarily with faculty.

Tuition and Aid Day student tuition: $14,000. Tuition installment plan (Insured Tuition Payment Plan, monthly payment plans, quarterly, semiannual, and annual payment plans). Tuition reduction for siblings, need-based scholarship grants available. In 2012–13, 30% of upper-school students received aid.

Admissions Traditional secondary-level entrance grade is 9. For fall 2012, 80 students applied for upper-level admission, 80 were accepted, 66 enrolled. Any standardized test, ISEE or school's own exam required. Deadline for receipt of application materials: none. Application fee required: $50. On-campus interview required.

Athletics Interscholastic: basketball, cross-country running, dance team, soccer, softball, swimming and diving, volleyball; intramural: strength & conditioning. 1 PE instructor, 8 coaches.

Computers Computers are regularly used in graphic design, history, mathematics, music, music technology, science classes. Computer network features include Internet access, Internet filtering or blocking technology. Computer access in designated common areas is available to students. Students grades are available online.

Contact Stephanie Sheffield, Director of Admissions. 847-824-6900. Fax: 847-824-7089. E-mail: sheffield@willowsacademy.org. Website: www.willowsacademy.org

WILMINGTON CHRISTIAN SCHOOL

825 Loveville Road
Hockessin, Delaware 19707

Head of School: Mr. William F. Stevens Jr.

General Information Coeducational day college-preparatory, arts, religious studies, and technology school, affiliated with Protestant faith. Grades PK–12. Founded: 1946. Setting: suburban. Nearest major city is Wilmington. 15-acre campus. 1 building on campus. Approved or accredited by Association of Christian Schools International, Middle States Association of Colleges and Schools, and Delaware Department of Education. Endowment: $400,000. Total enrollment: 517. Upper school average class size: 25. Upper school faculty-student ratio: 1:15. There are 177 required school days per year for Upper School students. Upper School students typically attend 5 days per week. The average school day consists of 6 hours and 40 minutes.

Upper School Student Profile Grade 9: 45 students (23 boys, 22 girls); Grade 10: 60 students (29 boys, 31 girls); Grade 11: 69 students (34 boys, 35 girls); Grade 12: 58 students (30 boys, 28 girls). 90% of students are Protestant.

Faculty School total: 52. In upper school: 11 men, 20 women; 13 have advanced degrees.

Subjects Offered Accounting, advanced math, algebra, American history, American history-AP, American minority experience, anatomy and physiology, art, band, biology, calculus, calculus-AP, chemistry, chorus, Christian doctrine, Christian ethics, church history, civics, computer applications, consumer mathematics, creative writing, democracy in America, driver education, ecology, economics, English, geometry, German, health, honors algebra, honors English, honors geometry, information processing, journalism, lab science, library assistant, marine biology, modern history, music theory, novels, physical education, physical science, physics, pre-calculus, Spanish, speech, study skills, trigonometry, world civilizations, world religions, yearbook.

Graduation Requirements Bible studies, English, foreign language, health education, mathematics, physical education (includes health), science, social studies (includes history), 40 hours of community service.

Special Academic Programs Advanced Placement exam preparation; honors section; study at local college for college credit; remedial reading and/or remedial writing; remedial math; ESL (9 students enrolled).

College Admission Counseling 52 students graduated in 2013; all went to college, including Drexel University; Eastern University; Gordon College; Liberty University; Messiah College; University of Delaware.

Student Life Upper grades have uniform requirement, student council, honor system. Discipline rests primarily with faculty. Attendance at religious services is required.

Summer Programs Remediation, advancement programs offered; session focuses on to attract more students to the school; held on campus; accepts boys and girls; open to students from other schools. 12 students usually enrolled. 2014 schedule: June 15 to August 5.

Tuition and Aid Day student tuition: $12,290. Tuition installment plan (STEP Plan (monthly deduction from a checking account)). Tuition reduction for siblings, need-based scholarship grants available. In 2013–14, 47% of upper-school students received aid. Total amount of financial aid awarded in 2013–14: $292,720.

Admissions Traditional secondary-level entrance grade is 9. For fall 2013, 68 students applied for upper-level admission, 35 were accepted, 32 enrolled. Stanford Achievement Test required. Deadline for receipt of application materials: August 1. Application fee required: $125. On-campus interview required.

Athletics Interscholastic: baseball (boys), basketball (b,g), cheering (g), field hockey (g), lacrosse (b), soccer (b,g), softball (g), volleyball (g), wrestling (b); coed interscholastic: cross-country running, golf, running. 2 PE instructors, 16 coaches, 1 athletic trainer.

Computers Computers are regularly used in accounting, business education, data processing, information technology, newspaper, yearbook classes. Computer network features include on-campus library services, Internet access. The school has a published electronic and media policy.

Contact Mrs. Carol Allston-Stiles, Admissions/Assistant to the Head of School. 302-239-2121 Ext. 3205. Fax: 302-239-2778. E-mail: admissions@WilmingtonChristian.org. Website: www.wilmingtonchristian.org

WILMINGTON FRIENDS SCHOOL

101 School Road
Wilmington, Delaware 19803

Head of School: Bryan K. Garman

General Information Coeducational day college-preparatory school, affiliated with Society of Friends. Grades PS–12. Founded: 1748. Setting: suburban. Nearest major city is Philadelphia, PA. 57-acre campus. 4 buildings on campus. Approved or accredited by Friends Council on Education, International Baccalaureate Organization, Middle States Association of Colleges and Schools, and Delaware Department of Education. Member of National Association of Independent Schools. Endowment: $22 million. Total enrollment: 765. Upper school average class size: 15. Upper school faculty-student ratio: 1:10. There are 169 required school days per year for Upper School students. Upper School students typically attend 5 days per week. The average school day consists of 7 hours.

Upper School Student Profile Grade 9: 69 students (33 boys, 36 girls); Grade 10: 72 students (36 boys, 36 girls); Grade 11: 58 students (29 boys, 29 girls); Grade 12: 70 students (37 boys, 33 girls). 5% of students are members of Society of Friends.

Faculty School total: 92. In upper school: 13 men, 13 women; 26 have advanced degrees.

Subjects Offered 3-dimensional art, advanced chemistry, art, biology, calculus, chemistry, community service, computer art, driver education, English, environmental science, European history, French, history, human development, improvisation, independent study, integrated mathematics, jazz ensemble, journalism, Mandarin, mathematics, music, music theory, peace and justice, physical education, physics, pre-calculus, programming, Quakerism and ethics, religion, science, social sciences, Spanish, studio art, theater, theater arts, theory of knowledge, U.S. history, Web site design, wellness, wind ensemble, world history.

Graduation Requirements Computer science, English, foreign language, human development, mathematics, participation in sports, performing arts, religion (includes Bible studies and theology), science, service learning/internship, social sciences, visual arts, wellness, 50 hours of community service (single organization) before senior year, Global Peace and Justice course, Visual and Performing Arts courses,, Human Dynamics and Development course.

Special Academic Programs International Baccalaureate program; 2 Advanced Placement exams for which test preparation is offered; honors section; independent study; term-away projects; study abroad; academic accommodation for the gifted, the musically talented, and the artistically talented.

College Admission Counseling 69 students graduated in 2013; 66 went to college, including Bates College; Penn State University Park; University of Delaware; University of Miami; University of South Carolina; Wake Forest University. Other: 2 had other specific plans. Mean SAT critical reading: 607, mean SAT math: 628, mean SAT writing: 611, mean combined SAT: 1846, mean composite ACT: 27.

Student Life Upper grades have specified standards of dress, student council. Discipline rests primarily with faculty. Attendance at religious services is required.

Tuition and Aid Day student tuition: $22,425. Tuition installment plan (Tuition Management Systems (purchased Key Tuition Plan)). Need-based scholarship grants available. In 2013–14, 31% of upper-school students received aid. Total amount of financial aid awarded in 2013–14: $1,088,338.

Admissions Traditional secondary-level entrance grade is 9. For fall 2013, 78 students applied for upper-level admission, 33 were accepted, 20 enrolled. CTP, ERB and ISEE required. Deadline for receipt of application materials: none. Application fee required: $50. Interview required.

Athletics Interscholastic: baseball (boys), basketball (b,g), cross-country running (b,g), field hockey (g), football (b), lacrosse (b,g), soccer (b,g), swimming and diving (b,g), tennis (b,g), track and field (b,g), volleyball (g), wrestling (b); intramural: strength & conditioning (b,g); coed interscholastic: winter (indoor) track; coed intramural: aerobics. 3 PE instructors, 43 coaches, 1 athletic trainer.

Computers Computers are regularly used in art, English, French, library skills, literary magazine, mathematics, music, newspaper, science, social studies, Spanish, yearbook classes. Computer network features include on-campus library services, online commercial services, Internet access, wireless campus network, Internet filtering or blocking technology, 1:1 laptop program, Google Docs account, off campus library services, online access to attendance, personalized Web site login for data driven Web site, open wireless network for personal devices, document storage, backup, and security. Campus intranet and computer access in designated common areas are available to students. Students grades are available online. The school has a published electronic and media policy.

Contact Ms. Kathleen Hopkins, Director of Admissions and Financial Aid. 302-576-2930. Fax: 302-576-2939. E-mail: khopkins@wilmingtonfriends.org. Website: www.wilmingtonfriends.org/

WILSON HALL

520 Wilson Hall Road
Sumter, South Carolina 29150

Head of School: Mr. Frederick B. Moulton Sr.

General Information Coeducational day college-preparatory, arts, and technology school. Grades PS–12. Founded: 1966. Setting: small town. Nearest major city is Columbia. 17-acre campus. 6 buildings on campus. Approved or accredited by Southern Association of Colleges and Schools, Southern Association of Independent Schools, and South Carolina Department of Education. Endowment: $280,000. Total enrollment: 778. Upper school average class size: 18. Upper school faculty-student ratio: 1:13. There are 180 required school days per year for Upper School students. Upper School students typically attend 5 days per week. The average school day consists of 6 hours and 20 minutes.

Upper School Student Profile Grade 9: 65 students (32 boys, 33 girls); Grade 10: 64 students (32 boys, 32 girls); Grade 11: 59 students (28 boys, 31 girls); Grade 12: 54 students (32 boys, 22 girls).

Faculty School total: 84. In upper school: 15 men, 28 women; 22 have advanced degrees.

Subjects Offered 3-dimensional design, algebra, anatomy, biology-AP, calculus-AP, chemistry-AP, computer applications, computer programming, computer programming-AP, drawing, economics, English, English language-AP, English literature-AP, environmental science, European history-AP, French, French language-AP, government, government-AP, journalism, Latin, Latin-AP, Middle Eastern history, multimedia, music theory-AP, philosophy, physical education, physical science, physics-AP, pottery, sculpture, Spanish, Spanish language-AP, studio art-AP, trigonometry, U.S. history-AP, world history.

Graduation Requirements Arts and fine arts (art, music, dance, drama), computer science, English, foreign language, mathematics, physical education (includes health), science, social studies (includes history), acceptance into four-year college or university, 20 hours community service.

Special Academic Programs 16 Advanced Placement exams for which test preparation is offered; honors section.

College Admission Counseling 67 students graduated in 2013; all went to college, including Clemson University; College of Charleston; Duke University; Furman University; The Citadel, The Military College of South Carolina; University of South Carolina. Mean SAT critical reading: 568, mean SAT math: 588, mean SAT writing: 554, mean combined SAT: 1711, mean composite ACT: 24.

Student Life Upper grades have specified standards of dress, honor system. Discipline rests primarily with faculty.

Summer Programs Enrichment, sports, art/fine arts, computer instruction programs offered; session focuses on enrichment; held on campus; accepts boys and girls; not open to students from other schools. 100 students usually enrolled. 2014 schedule: June 1 to July 15. Application deadline: May 20.

Tuition and Aid Day student tuition: $5175–$6195. Tuition installment plan (monthly payment plans). Need-based scholarship grants available. In 2013–14, 6% of upper-school students received aid. Total amount of financial aid awarded in 2013–14: $135,000.

Admissions Traditional secondary-level entrance grade is 9. For fall 2013, 140 students applied for upper-level admission, 101 were accepted, 101 enrolled. ACT, CTBS, OLSAT, Iowa Tests of Basic Skills, PSAT and SAT for applicants to grade 11 and 12, school's own test or Stanford Achievement Test, Otis-Lennon School Ability Test required. Deadline for receipt of application materials: none. Application fee required: $150. Interview recommended.

Athletics Interscholastic: baseball (boys), basketball (b,g), bowling (b,g), cheering (g), cross-country running (b,g), equestrian sports (g), fishing (b), football (b), golf (b,g), marksmanship (b), Nautilus (b,g), riflery (b), running (b,g), skeet shooting (b), softball (g), strength & conditioning (b,g), swimming and diving (b,g), tennis (b,g), track and field (b,g), trap and skeet (b), volleyball (g), wrestling (b); intramural: table tennis (b), weight lifting (b,g), weight training (b,g); coed interscholastic: climbing, outdoor adventure, outdoor education, paint ball, riflery, skeet shooting, soccer; coed intramural: archery, outdoor adventure, rafting, rock climbing, ropes courses, table tennis. 5 PE instructors, 12 coaches.

Computers Computers are regularly used in computer applications, English, journalism, literary magazine, technology, yearbook classes. Computer network features include on-campus library services, online commercial services, Internet access, wireless campus network, Internet filtering or blocking technology. Students grades are available online. The school has a published electronic and media policy.

Contact Mr. Sean Hoskins, Director of Admissions and Public Relations. 803-469-3475 Ext. 107. Fax: 803-469-3477. E-mail: sean_hoskins@hotmail.com. Website: www.wilsonhall.org

WINDELLS ACADEMY

PO Box 6
Brightwood, Oregon 97011

Head of School: Mike Hanley

General Information Coeducational boarding college-preparatory, general academic, and skateboarding, freestyle skiing, and snowboarding school. Grades 9–12. Founded: 2009. Setting: rural. Nearest major city is Portland. Students are housed in single-sex dormitories. 53-acre campus. 16 buildings on campus. Approved or accredited by Northwest Accreditation Commission and Oregon Department of Education. Upper school average class size: 25. Upper school faculty-student ratio: 1:7. There are 208 required school days per year for Upper School students. Upper School students typically attend 7 days per week. The average school day consists of 4 hours.

Upper School Student Profile Grade 9: 2 students (2 boys); Grade 10: 7 students (7 boys); Grade 11: 4 students (4 boys); Grade 12: 12 students (9 boys, 3 girls). 100% of students are boarding students. 4% are state residents. 17 states are represented in upper school student body. 32% are international students. International students from Australia, Canada, Chile, France, Switzerland, and Thailand.

Faculty School total: 6. In upper school: 1 man, 2 women; 3 have advanced degrees.

Subjects Offered Accounting, ACT preparation, advanced biology, advanced chemistry, advanced math, Advanced Placement courses, algebra, American government, American history, American legal systems, American literature, art history, arts appreciation, biology, biology-AP, business law, business skills, calculus, calculus-AP, career planning, chemistry, chemistry-AP, Chinese, civics, computer literacy, computer science, computer science-AP, consumer mathematics, contemporary issues, creative writing, digital imaging, digital photography, driver education, earth and space science, earth science, economics, economics and history, economics-AP, English, English as a foreign language, English language-AP, English literature, English literature-AP, English-AP, environmental science, environmental science-AP, European history, European history-AP, fine arts, French, French language-AP, French studies, French-AP, geography, geometry, German, German-AP, grammar, health, health and wellness, integrated mathematics, Japanese, journalism, Latin, life science, life skills, Mandarin, marketing, personal finance, physical education, physical fitness, physical science, physics, physics-AP, pre-algebra, pre-calculus, programming, psychology, psychology-AP, skills for success, sociology, Spanish, statistics, statistics-AP, trigonometry, U.S. government, U.S. government and politics, U.S. government and politics-AP, U.S. history, U.S. history-AP, video, video film production, world history, world history-AP, world literature.

Graduation Requirements Our students receive a diploma through the Keystone online school.

College Admission Counseling 5 students graduated in 2012; 2 went to college, including University of Utah. Other: 1 went to work, 2 had other specific plans.

Student Life Discipline rests primarily with faculty.

Tuition and Aid 7-day tuition and room/board: $35,000–$40,000. Guaranteed tuition plan. Tuition installment plan (monthly payment plans, individually arranged payment plans). Merit scholarship grants, need-based scholarship grants, academic scholarships, athletic scholarships, and partial media scholarships available. In 2012–13, 20% of upper-school students received aid.

Admissions Traditional secondary-level entrance grade is 10. For fall 2012, 27 students applied for upper-level admission, 25 were accepted, 25 enrolled. Deadline for receipt of application materials: none. No application fee required. On-campus interview required.

Athletics Intramural: skateboarding (boys, girls), ski jumping (b,g), snowboarding (b,g); coed intramural: skateboarding, ski jumping, snowboarding. 4 coaches.

Computers Computers are regularly used in all classes. Computer resources include Internet access, wireless campus network. Computer access in designated common areas is available to students. Students grades are available online.

Contact Ally Ryoppy, Academy Director. 503-622-8751. Fax: 503-622-4582. E-mail: ally@windellsacademy.com. Website: windellsacademy.com/

WINDERMERE PREPARATORY SCHOOL

6189 Winter Garden-Vineland Road
Windermere, Florida 34786

Head of School: Thomas L. Marcy, EdD

General Information Boys' boarding and coeducational day college-preparatory, arts, and technology school. Boarding boys grades 9–12, day boys grades PK–12, day girls grades PK–12. Founded: 2000. Setting: suburban. Nearest major city is Orlando. Students are housed in single-sex dormitories. 48-acre campus. 3 buildings on campus. Approved or accredited by Association of Independent Schools of Florida, International Baccalaureate Organization, National Independent Private Schools Association, Southern Association of Colleges and Schools, Southern Association of Independent Schools, and Florida Department of Education. Total enrollment: 1,193. Upper school average class size: 17. Upper school faculty-student ratio: 1:11. There are 180 required school days per year for Upper School students. Upper School students typically attend 5 days per week. The average school day consists of 7 hours and 15 minutes.

Upper School Student Profile Grade 6: 85 students (40 boys, 45 girls); Grade 7: 97 students (54 boys, 43 girls); Grade 8: 87 students (44 boys, 43 girls); Grade 9: 85 students (37 boys, 48 girls); Grade 10: 116 students (56 boys, 60 girls); Grade 11: 128 students (58 boys, 70 girls); Grade 12: 103 students (50 boys, 53 girls). 10% of students are boarding students. 91% are state residents. 10% are international students. International students from Austria, Canada, China, Germany, Switzerland, and Turkey; 8 other countries represented in student body.

Faculty School total: 103. In upper school: 14 men, 21 women; 30 have advanced degrees; 3 reside on campus.

Subjects Offered 20th century history, 3-dimensional art, acting, algebra, American government, American history, American literature, art, biology, business, calculus, ceramics, chemistry, choir, chorus, creative writing, dance, dance performance, drama, drama performance, economics, electives, English, English composition, English literature, environmental science, ethics, film, forensics, French, geometry, graphic design, honors algebra, honors English, honors U.S. history, honors world history, International Baccalaureate courses, Latin, music, music theory, personal fitness, physical education, physics, pre-calculus, psychology, Spanish, speech and debate, theory of knowledge, world history, world literature, yearbook.

Graduation Requirements Arts and fine arts (art, music, dance, drama), electives, English, foreign language, history, mathematics, performing arts, physical fitness, science, 6 additional elective credits. Community service is required.

Special Academic Programs International Baccalaureate program; 2 Advanced Placement exams for which test preparation is offered; honors section; independent study; academic accommodation for the musically talented and the artistically talented; ESL (22 students enrolled).

College Admission Counseling 91 students graduated in 2013; 86 went to college, including Florida State University; Penn State University Park; Rollins College; University of Central Florida; University of Florida. Other: 5 had other specific plans. Mean SAT critical reading: 509, mean SAT math: 579, mean SAT writing: 573, mean combined SAT: 1601, mean composite ACT: 25. 23.6% scored over 600 on SAT critical reading, 47.2% scored over 600 on SAT math, 22.2% scored over 600 on SAT writing, 20.8% scored over 1800 on combined SAT, 48.9% scored over 26 on composite ACT.

Student Life Upper grades have uniform requirement, student council, honor system. Discipline rests primarily with faculty.

Summer Programs Enrichment, sports, art/fine arts, computer instruction programs offered; session focuses on enrichment, academics, and athletics; held on campus; accepts boys and girls; open to students from other schools. 200 students usually enrolled. 2014 schedule: June to August. Application deadline: May.

Tuition and Aid Day student tuition: $16,975; 7-day tuition and room/board: $47,775. Tuition installment plan (monthly payment plans). Merit scholarship grants, need-based scholarship grants available. In 2013–14, 8% of upper-school students received aid; total upper-school merit-scholarship money awarded: $72,000. Total amount of financial aid awarded in 2013–14: $411,445.

Admissions Traditional secondary-level entrance grade is 9. For fall 2013, 200 students applied for upper-level admission, 150 were accepted, 134 enrolled. Stanford Achievement Test required. Deadline for receipt of application materials: none. Application fee required: $100. Interview recommended.

Athletics Interscholastic: ballet (girls), baseball (b), basketball (b,g), cheering (g), dance (g), dance team (g), golf (b,g), lacrosse (b,g), modern dance (g), physical fitness (b,g), physical training (b,g), soccer (b,g), softball (g), strength & conditioning (b,g), swimming and diving (b,g), tennis (b,g), track and field (b,g), volleyball (g), weight training (g); coed interscholastic: crew, cross-country running, dance, track and field; coed intramural: flag football, golf. 8 PE instructors, 47 coaches, 1 athletic trainer.

Computers Computers are regularly used in all academic classes. Computer network features include on-campus library services, Internet access, wireless campus network, Internet filtering or blocking technology. Student e-mail accounts are available to students. Students grades are available online. The school has a published electronic and media policy.

Contact Mrs. Carol Riggs, Director of Admissions. 407-905-7737 Ext. 3228. Fax: 407-905-7710. E-mail: carol.riggs@windermereprep.com. Website: www.windermereprep.com

THE WINDSOR SCHOOL

37-02 Main St. / 3rd Floor
Flushing, New York 11354

Head of School: Mr. James Seery

General Information Coeducational day college-preparatory and arts school. Grades 6–PG. Founded: 1969. Setting: urban. Nearest major city is New York. 1 building on campus. Approved or accredited by Middle States Association of Colleges and Schools, New York Department of Education, New York State Board of Regents, The College Board, US Department of State, and New York Department of Education. Total enrollment: 180. Upper school average class size: 14. Upper school faculty-student ratio: 1:14. There are 185 required school days per year for Upper School students. Upper School students typically attend 5 days per week. The average school day consists of 6 hours and 5 minutes.

Upper School Student Profile Grade 8: 10 students (4 boys, 6 girls); Grade 9: 12 students (4 boys, 8 girls); Grade 10: 45 students (27 boys, 18 girls); Grade 11: 60 students (35 boys, 25 girls); Grade 12: 65 students (34 boys, 31 girls).

Faculty School total: 14. In upper school: 5 men, 9 women; all have advanced degrees.

Subjects Offered Advanced Placement courses, algebra, American history, American literature, art, basic skills, biology, business, business applications, calculus, chemistry, computer science, computer skills, creative writing, economics, English, English literature, environmental science, ESL, European history, fine arts, French, geometry, government/civics, grammar, health, marketing, mathematics, music, physical education, physics, pre-calculus, psychology, science, social sciences, social studies, Spanish, trigonometry, world affairs, world history.

Graduation Requirements Arts and fine arts (art, music, dance, drama), English, foreign language, health education, mathematics, physical education (includes health), science, social studies (includes history).

Special Academic Programs Advanced Placement exam preparation; honors section; accelerated programs; independent study; academic accommodation for the gifted, the musically talented, and the artistically talented; remedial reading and/or remedial writing; remedial math; ESL (27 students enrolled).

College Admission Counseling 68 students graduated in 2013; all went to college, including Binghamton University, State University of New York; Michigan State University; Penn State University Park; Queens College of the City University of New York; St. John's University. Median SAT critical reading: 440, median SAT math: 550, median SAT writing: 460. 10% scored over 600 on SAT critical reading, 35% scored over 600 on SAT math, 10% scored over 600 on SAT writing.

Student Life Upper grades have specified standards of dress. Discipline rests primarily with faculty.

Summer Programs Remediation, enrichment, advancement, ESL programs offered; session focuses on advancement, enrichment, remediation; held on campus; accepts boys and girls; open to students from other schools. 450 students usually enrolled. 2014 schedule: July 1 to August 18. Application deadline: June 30.

Tuition and Aid Day student tuition: $23,800. Tuition installment plan (individually arranged payment plans). Tuition reduction for siblings available. In 2013–14, 5% of upper-school students received aid. Total amount of financial aid awarded in 2013–14: $20,000.

Admissions Traditional secondary-level entrance grade is 10. For fall 2013, 80 students applied for upper-level admission, 76 were accepted, 73 enrolled. Achievement tests and school's own exam required. Deadline for receipt of application materials: none. No application fee required. On-campus interview recommended.

Athletics Interscholastic: basketball (boys, girls), soccer (b,g), track and field (b,g); intramural: basketball (b,g), cooperative games (b,g), fitness (b,g), jump rope (g), physical fitness (b,g), soccer (b,g), table tennis (b,g), tennis (b,g), volleyball (b,g), yoga (b,g); coed interscholastic: basketball, soccer, track and field; coed intramural: basketball, fitness, jump rope, physical fitness, soccer, table tennis, tennis, volleyball, yoga. 2 PE instructors, 2 coaches.

Computers Computers are regularly used in art, mathematics, research skills, yearbook classes. Computer network features include Internet access, Internet filtering or blocking technology. Campus intranet and computer access in designated common areas are available to students. The school has a published electronic and media policy.

Contact Ms. Emily Yu, Director of Admissions. 718-359-8300. Fax: 718-359-1876. E-mail: admin@thewindsorschool.com. Website: www.windsorschool.com

WINSTON PREPARATORY SCHOOL

New York, New York
See Special Needs Schools section.

THE WINSTON SCHOOL

Dallas, Texas
See Special Needs Schools section.

THE WINSTON SCHOOL SAN ANTONIO

San Antonio, Texas
See Special Needs Schools section.

THE WOODHALL SCHOOL

PO Box 550
58 Harrison Lane
Bethlehem, Connecticut 06751

Head of School: Matthew C. Woodhall

General Information Boys' boarding and day college-preparatory and arts school; primarily serves students with above-average intellectual ability who have had difficulties in traditional school environments. Grades 9–PG. Founded: 1983. Setting: rural. Nearest major city is Waterbury. Students are housed in single-sex dormitories.

38-acre campus. 5 buildings on campus. Approved or accredited by Association of Independent Schools in New England, New England Association of Schools and Colleges, and Connecticut Department of Education. Member of National Association of Independent Schools. Endowment: $450,000. Total enrollment: 43. Upper school average class size: 4. Upper school faculty-student ratio: 1:4. There are 184 required school days per year for Upper School students. Upper School students typically attend 6 days per week. The average school day consists of 6 hours.

Upper School Student Profile Grade 9: 5 students (5 boys); Grade 10: 13 students (13 boys); Grade 11: 15 students (15 boys); Grade 12: 10 students (10 boys). 97% of students are boarding students. 16% are state residents. 20 states are represented in upper school student body. 6% are international students. International students from Canada and United Kingdom; 1 other country represented in student body.

Faculty School total: 16. In upper school: 13 men, 3 women; 13 have advanced degrees; 13 reside on campus.

Subjects Offered Algebra, American history, anatomy, art, biology, calculus, chemistry, comparative government and politics, drama, English, environmental science, geometry, Greek, language and composition, Latin, physics, pre-calculus, Spanish, world civilizations.

Graduation Requirements Arts and fine arts (art, music, dance, drama), communication skills, English, foreign language, mathematics, physical education (includes health), science, social studies (includes history).

Special Academic Programs Advanced Placement exam preparation; independent study; special instructional classes for students with Attention Deficit Disorder and non-verbal learning disabilities; ESL.

College Admission Counseling 12 students graduated in 2013; 10 went to college, including Adelphi University; Goucher College; Guilford College; Manhattanville College; Quinnipiac University; University of the Ozarks. Other: 2 entered a postgraduate year. Median SAT critical reading: 560, median SAT math: 615, median SAT writing: 565, median combined SAT: 1695, median composite ACT: 26. 50% scored over 600 on SAT critical reading, 60% scored over 600 on SAT math, 30% scored over 600 on SAT writing, 40% scored over 1800 on combined SAT, 60% scored over 26 on composite ACT.

Student Life Upper grades have specified standards of dress, student council, honor system. Discipline rests primarily with faculty.

Tuition and Aid Day student tuition: $45,810; 7-day tuition and room/board: $59,500. Tuition installment plan (individually arranged payment plans).

Admissions Traditional secondary-level entrance grade is 10. For fall 2013, 47 students applied for upper-level admission, 33 were accepted, 20 enrolled. Deadline for receipt of application materials: none. Application fee required: $100. On-campus interview required.

Athletics Interscholastic: basketball, cross-country running, lacrosse, soccer, wrestling; intramural: alpine skiing, basketball, canoeing/kayaking, cross-country running, fishing, fitness, fitness walking, hiking/backpacking, jogging, lacrosse, outdoor activities, outdoor education, outdoor recreation, physical fitness, physical training, rafting, running, skiing (cross-country), soccer, strength & conditioning, volleyball, walking, wall climbing, weight lifting, winter walking, wrestling. 1 athletic trainer.

Computers Computers are regularly used in art, English, foreign language, history, mathematics, science, social sciences classes. Computer resources include Internet access. The school has a published electronic and media policy.

Contact Matthew C. Woodhall, Head of School. 203-266-7788. Fax: 203-266-5896. E-mail: mwoodhall@woodhallschool.org. Website: www.woodhallschool.org

WOODLYNDE SCHOOL

445 Upper Gulph Road
Strafford, Pennsylvania 19087

Head of School: Christopher M. Fulco, EdD

General Information Coeducational day college-preparatory, arts, and technology school; primarily serves students with learning disabilities, individuals with Attention Deficit Disorder, dyslexic students, Executive Function Disorder, and Auditory Processing Disorder. Grades K–12. Founded: 1976. Setting: suburban. Nearest major city is Philadelphia. 8-acre campus. 2 buildings on campus. Approved or accredited by Pennsylvania Department of Education. Member of National Association of Independent Schools. Endowment: $559,699. Total enrollment: 262. Upper school average class size: 10. Upper school faculty-student ratio: 1:5. There are 168 required school days per year for Upper School students. Upper School students typically attend 5 days per week. The average school day consists of 6 hours and 55 minutes.

Upper School Student Profile Grade 9: 23 students (13 boys, 10 girls); Grade 10: 22 students (12 boys, 10 girls); Grade 11: 22 students (12 boys, 10 girls); Grade 12: 26 students (14 boys, 12 girls).

Faculty School total: 62. In upper school: 15 men, 18 women; 8 have advanced degrees.

Subjects Offered Algebra, American history, American literature, art, art-AP, arts, biology, chemistry, creative writing, earth science, English, English literature, English-AP, European history, fine arts, French, geometry, government/civics, health, history, journalism, mathematics, music, photography, physical education, physics, political science, psychology, science, social studies, Spanish, studio art, world history, world literature, writing.

Graduation Requirements Arts and fine arts (art, music, dance, drama), English, foreign language, internship, mathematics, physical education (includes health), science, social studies (includes history), community service, senior project, senior speech.

Special Academic Programs Advanced Placement exam preparation; honors section; study at local college for college credit; remedial reading and/or remedial writing; remedial math; programs in English, general development for dyslexic students.

College Admission Counseling 24 students graduated in 2013; 23 went to college, including Albright College; Cabrini College; Emerson College; Lynn University; Oberlin College; Sarah Lawrence College. Other: 1 had other specific plans.

Student Life Upper grades have uniform requirement, student council. Discipline rests primarily with faculty.

Summer Programs Remediation, enrichment, advancement, sports, art/fine arts programs offered; session focuses on mathematics and reading enrichment; held both on and off campus; held at Camp Nock-A-Mixon; accepts boys and girls; not open to students from other schools. 75 students usually enrolled. 2014 schedule: June 20 to July 22. Application deadline: May 30.

Tuition and Aid Day student tuition: $32,150. Tuition installment plan (FACTS Tuition Payment Plan, monthly payment plans). Need-based scholarship grants available. In 2013–14, 35% of upper-school students received aid. Total amount of financial aid awarded in 2013–14: $525,475.

Admissions Traditional secondary-level entrance grade is 9. For fall 2013, 19 students applied for upper-level admission, 10 were accepted, 6 enrolled. Individual IQ required. Deadline for receipt of application materials: none. Application fee required: $100. On-campus interview required.

Athletics Interscholastic: basketball (boys, girls), lacrosse (b,g), softball (g), tennis (b,g), volleyball (g); coed interscholastic: cross-country running, golf, soccer; coed intramural: aerobics/dance, dance, yoga. 2 PE instructors, 12 coaches, 1 athletic trainer.

Computers Computers are regularly used in all academic, art, college planning, creative writing, drawing and design, English, foreign language, French, graphic arts, graphic design, health, history, journalism, Latin, learning cognition, mathematics, music, newspaper, photography, psychology, publications, science, social studies, Spanish, study skills, technology, word processing, writing, writing, yearbook classes. Computer network features include on-campus library services, Internet access, wireless campus network, Internet filtering or blocking technology. Campus intranet and student e-mail accounts are available to students. Students grades are available online. The school has a published electronic and media policy.

Contact Dorinda Shank, Director of Admissions. 610-687-9660 Ext. 624. Fax: 610-687-4752. E-mail: shankd@woodlynde.org. Website: www.woodlynde.org

WOODWARD ACADEMY

1662 Rugby Avenue
College Park, Georgia 30337

Head of School: Mr. Stuart Gulley, PhD

General Information Coeducational day college-preparatory and arts school. Grades PK–12. Founded: 1900. Setting: suburban. Nearest major city is Atlanta. 112-acre campus. 50 buildings on campus. Approved or accredited by Georgia Independent School Association, Southern Association of Colleges and Schools, and Georgia Department of Education. Member of National Association of Independent Schools and Secondary School Admission Test Board. Endowment: $122 million. Total enrollment: 2,738. Upper school average class size: 17.

Faculty School total: 363. In upper school: 56 men, 81 women.

Subjects Offered 20th century world history, 3-dimensional art, 3-dimensional design, acting, Advanced Placement courses, algebra, American government, American history, American history-AP, anatomy and physiology, art, astronomy, audio visual/media, band, biology, biology-AP, calculus, calculus-AP, ceramics, chemistry, chemistry-AP, choir, choral music, chorus, comparative religion, computer education, computer programming, computer programming-AP, computer science, computer science-AP, concert band, contemporary history, contemporary issues, creative writing, dance, debate, digital music, drama, drama performance, drawing, drawing and design, earth science, ecology, economics, economics and history, economics-AP, English, English language and composition-AP, English literature, English literature and composition-AP, English-AP, environmental science, environmental science-AP, European history, European history-AP, fine arts, French, French language-AP, French-AP, geography, geometry, government and politics-AP, government/civics, grammar, health, history, history-AP, honors English, honors geometry, honors U.S. history, honors world history, independent study, Japanese, jewelry making, journalism, Latin, literature and composition-AP, marching band, marine ecology, mathematics, meteorology, microeconomics-AP, Middle East, modern European history-AP, multicultural literature, music, oceanography, performing arts, personal fitness, photography, physical education, physics, physics-AP, pre-calculus, probability and statistics, science, social studies, Spanish, Spanish language-AP, Spanish-AP, speech communications, statistics, statistics-AP, television, the Sixties, theater, trigonometry, U.S. government and politics, U.S. government and politics-AP, U.S. history, U.S. history-AP, video, voice ensemble, world history, world literature, world religions, yearbook.

Graduation Requirements Arts and fine arts (art, music, dance, drama), computer science, English, foreign language, mathematics, physical education (includes health), religion (includes Bible studies and theology), science, social studies (includes history).

Special Academic Programs 20 Advanced Placement exams for which test preparation is offered; honors section; independent study.

College Admission Counseling 257 students graduated in 2013; all went to college, including Auburn University; Georgia Institute of Technology; Georgia Southern University; The University of Alabama; University of Georgia.

Student Life Upper grades have uniform requirement, student council, honor system. Discipline rests primarily with faculty.

Summer Programs Enrichment, advancement, sports, art/fine arts, computer instruction programs offered; held on campus; accepts boys and girls; open to students from other schools. 2,300 students usually enrolled.

Tuition and Aid Day student tuition: $23,950. Tuition installment plan (SMART Tuition Payment Plan, Your Tuition Solution—Springstone Financial, Sallie Mae). Need-based scholarship grants available. In 2013–14, 10% of upper-school students received aid.

Admissions Traditional secondary-level entrance grade is 9. SSAT required. Deadline for receipt of application materials: February 28. Application fee required: $75. On-campus interview required.

Athletics Interscholastic: baseball (boys), basketball (b,g), cheering (g), cross-country running (b,g), diving (b,g), football (b), golf (b,g), lacrosse (b,g), soccer (b,g), softball (g), swimming and diving (b,g), tennis (b,g), track and field (b,g), volleyball (g); intramural: basketball (b,g), cheering (g), football (b), soccer (b,g), softball (g), swimming and diving (b,g), tennis (b,g), track and field (b,g), volleyball (g); coed interscholastic: Frisbee, power lifting, ultimate Frisbee, weight lifting; coed intramural: fencing, horseback riding. 4 PE instructors, 34 coaches, 1 athletic trainer.

Computers Computers are regularly used in creative writing, English, foreign language, graphic design, journalism, literary magazine, mathematics, media production, newspaper, science, yearbook classes. Computer network features include on-campus library services, online commercial services, Internet access, wireless campus network. Student e-mail accounts are available to students. Students grades are available online.

Contact Russell L. Slider, Vice President/Dean of Admissions. 404-765-4001. Fax: 404-765-4009. E-mail: rusty.slider@woodward.edu. Website: www.woodward.edu

THE WOODWARD SCHOOL

1102 Hancock Street
Quincy, Massachusetts 02169

Head of School: Carol Andrews, JD

General Information Girls' day college-preparatory, arts, and technology school. Grades 6–12. Founded: 1869. Setting: urban. Nearest major city is Boston. 2-acre campus. 2 buildings on campus. Approved or accredited by Association of Independent Schools in New England, New England Association of Schools and Colleges, and Massachusetts Department of Education. Member of Secondary School Admission Test Board. Total enrollment: 125. Upper school average class size: 12. Upper school faculty-student ratio: 1:8. There are 165 required school days per year for Upper School students. Upper School students typically attend 5 days per week. The average school day consists of 6 hours and 35 minutes.

Upper School Student Profile Grade 9: 19 students (19 girls); Grade 10: 20 students (20 girls); Grade 11: 20 students (20 girls); Grade 12: 22 students (22 girls).

Faculty School total: 20. In upper school: 3 men, 17 women; 14 have advanced degrees.

Subjects Offered Advanced computer applications, algebra, American history, American literature, anatomy, art, arts, biology, calculus, calculus-AP, chemistry, chorus, classical studies, classics, community service, computer graphics, computer math, computer science, computer skills, constitutional law, drama, ecology, English, English language and composition-AP, environmental science, filmmaking, fine arts, French, health and wellness, health science, language arts, Latin, Latin-AP, law and the legal system, literature, literature and composition-AP, mathematics, media studies, music, music appreciation, physics, physics-AP, physiology, political science, portfolio art, pre-algebra, psychology, rhetoric, SAT preparation, science, senior project, social sciences, social studies, sociology, Spanish, study skills, theater arts, U.S. government, U.S. history, Web authoring, Web site design, world history, world literature, World War II, writing.

Graduation Requirements Arts and fine arts (art, music, dance, drama), computer science, English, foreign language, mathematics, science, senior project, social studies (includes history). Community service is required.

Special Academic Programs 6 Advanced Placement exams for which test preparation is offered; honors section; independent study; ESL (11 students enrolled).

College Admission Counseling 22 students graduated in 2013; all went to college, including Boston College; Boston University; Northeastern University; University of Massachusetts Amherst; University of Massachusetts Boston.

Student Life Upper grades have specified standards of dress, student council, honor system. Discipline rests primarily with faculty.

Tuition and Aid Day student tuition: $13,100. Tuition installment plan (monthly payment plans, individually arranged payment plans, Tuition Management Systems).

Tuition reduction for siblings, merit scholarship grants, need-based scholarship grants, prepGATE K-12 education loan available. In 2013–14, 42% of upper-school students received aid; total upper-school merit-scholarship money awarded: $38,500. Total amount of financial aid awarded in 2013–14: $200,298.

Admissions Traditional secondary-level entrance grade is 9. For fall 2013, 37 students applied for upper-level admission, 22 were accepted, 15 enrolled. ERB, ISEE, school's own exam, SSAT or writing sample required. Deadline for receipt of application materials: none. Application fee required: $50. Interview required.

Athletics Interscholastic: basketball, soccer, softball; intramural: running. 2 PE instructors, 6 coaches, 1 athletic trainer.

Computers Computers are regularly used in all classes. Computer network features include on-campus library services, Internet access, wireless campus network, Internet filtering or blocking technology. Computer access in designated common areas is available to students. The school has a published electronic and media policy.

Contact Sarah Jacobs, Director of Admissions. 617-773-5610. Fax: 617-770-1551. E-mail: sjacobs@thewoodwardschool.org. Website: www.thewoodwardschool.org

WORCESTER ACADEMY

81 Providence Street
Worcester, Massachusetts 01604

Head of School: Ronald Cino

General Information Coeducational boarding and day college-preparatory, arts, technology, and ESL school. Boarding grades 9–PG, day grades 6–12. Founded: 1834. Setting: urban. Nearest major city is Boston. Students are housed in single-sex dormitories. 60-acre campus. 14 buildings on campus. Approved or accredited by Association of Independent Schools in New England, New England Association of Schools and Colleges, and The Association of Boarding Schools. Member of National Association of Independent Schools and Secondary School Admission Test Board. Endowment: $22 million. Total enrollment: 625. Upper school average class size: 13. Upper school faculty-student ratio: 1:8. There are 160 required school days per year for Upper School students. Upper School students typically attend 5 days per week. The average school day consists of 6 hours and 45 minutes.

Upper School Student Profile Grade 6: 31 students (16 boys, 15 girls); Grade 7: 39 students (20 boys, 19 girls); Grade 8: 45 students (21 boys, 24 girls); Grade 9: 80 students (40 boys, 40 girls); Grade 10: 128 students (74 boys, 54 girls); Grade 11: 156 students (75 boys, 81 girls); Grade 12: 128 students (61 boys, 67 girls); Postgraduate: 18 students (18 boys). 33% of students are boarding students. 72% are state residents. 15 states are represented in upper school student body. 20% are international students. International students from China, Hong Kong, Japan, Republic of Korea, Taiwan, and Viet Nam; 26 other countries represented in student body.

Faculty School total: 73. In upper school: 41 men, 32 women; 61 have advanced degrees; 27 reside on campus.

Subjects Offered Acting, advanced studio art-AP, algebra, American history, American history-AP, American literature, American studies, anatomy, Ancient Greek, architecture, art, art-AP, band, biology, biology-AP, British literature, calculus, calculus-AP, ceramics, chemistry, chemistry-AP, Chinese, choral music, chorus, computer programming, computer science-AP, contemporary issues, creative writing, directing, economics, English, English language-AP, English literature, English literature-AP, English-AP, environmental science, environmental studies, ESL, ESL, ethics, European history, European history-AP, French, geography, geometry, government-AP, health, history, Holocaust studies, honors English, honors world history, human anatomy, journalism, Latin, mathematics, music, music theory, physical education, physics, post-calculus, pre-algebra, pre-calculus, sculpture, Spanish, statistics, studio art-AP, U.S. government and politics-AP, U.S. history-AP, world history, world history-AP, world religions, World War II.

Graduation Requirements Algebra, American literature, arts and fine arts (art, music, dance, drama), biology, chemistry, English, foreign language, geometry, health and wellness, mathematics, physical education (includes health), social sciences, U.S. history, world literature, writing, senior projects, community service.

Special Academic Programs 16 Advanced Placement exams for which test preparation is offered; honors section; independent study; ESL (8 students enrolled).

College Admission Counseling 137 students graduated in 2013; all went to college, including Boston College; Bowdoin College; College of the Holy Cross; Emory University; University of Illinois at Urbana–Champaign; Worcester Polytechnic Institute. Mean SAT critical reading: 600, mean SAT math: 650, mean composite ACT: 26. 45% scored over 600 on SAT critical reading, 50% scored over 600 on SAT math, 50% scored over 26 on composite ACT.

Student Life Upper grades have specified standards of dress, student council, honor system. Discipline rests equally with students and faculty.

Summer Programs ESL programs offered; session focuses on English preparation, TOEFL and SAT preparation; held on campus; accepts boys and girls; open to students from other schools. 20 students usually enrolled. 2014 schedule: August 7 to August 28.

Tuition and Aid Day student tuition: $30,360; 5-day tuition and room/board: $44,190; 7-day tuition and room/board: $53,460. Tuition installment plan (Academic Management Services Plan, FACTS Tuition Payment Plan). Need-based scholarship grants, paying campus jobs available. In 2013–14, 36% of upper-school students received aid. Total amount of financial aid awarded in 2013–14: $4,400,000.

Admissions Traditional secondary-level entrance grade is 9. For fall 2013, 704 students applied for upper-level admission, 332 were accepted, 172 enrolled. ACT, ISEE, PSAT or SAT for applicants to grade 11 and 12, SSAT or TOEFL required. Deadline for receipt of application materials: January 15. Application fee required: $60. Interview required.

Athletics Interscholastic: baseball (boys), basketball (b,g), cross-country running (b,g), field hockey (g), football (b), ice hockey (b,g), lacrosse (b,g), skiing (downhill) (b,g), soccer (b,g), softball (g), tennis (b,g), track and field (b,g), volleyball (b), wrestling (b); coed interscholastic: crew, golf, swimming and diving; coed intramural: aerobics/dance, dance team, paddle tennis. 3 PE instructors, 10 coaches, 3 athletic trainers.

Computers Computers are regularly used in all academic, art, college planning, library, media arts, music, theater arts, video film production, yearbook classes. Computer network features include on-campus library services, online commercial services, Internet access, wireless campus network, Internet filtering or blocking technology. Campus intranet, student e-mail accounts, and computer access in designated common areas are available to students. Students grades are available online. The school has a published electronic and media policy.

Contact Roberta Osorio, Director of Admission and Financial Aid. 508-754-5302 Ext. 199. Fax: 508-752-2382. E-mail: roberta.osorio@worcesteracademy.org. Website: www.worcesteracademy.org

WORCESTER PREPARATORY SCHOOL

508 South Main Street
PO Box 1006
Berlin, Maryland 21811

Head of School: Dr. Barry W. Tull

General Information Coeducational day college-preparatory, arts, and technology school. Grades PK–12. Founded: 1970. Setting: small town. Nearest major city is Ocean City. 45-acre campus. 7 buildings on campus. Approved or accredited by Association of Independent Maryland Schools, Middle States Association of Colleges and Schools, and Maryland Department of Education. Member of National Association of Independent Schools. Total enrollment: 525. Upper school average class size: 14. Upper school faculty-student ratio: 1:9. There are 173 required school days per year for Upper School students. Upper School students typically attend 5 days per week. The average school day consists of 6 hours and 30 minutes.

Upper School Student Profile Grade 6: 42 students (18 boys, 24 girls); Grade 7: 45 students (28 boys, 17 girls); Grade 8: 37 students (13 boys, 24 girls); Grade 9: 52 students (27 boys, 25 girls); Grade 10: 48 students (24 boys, 24 girls); Grade 11: 48 students (20 boys, 28 girls); Grade 12: 53 students (25 boys, 28 girls).

Faculty School total: 62. In upper school: 13 men, 21 women; 29 have advanced degrees.

Subjects Offered Advanced Placement courses, algebra, American history, American literature, art, art history, biology, biology-AP, calculus, calculus-AP, chemistry, chemistry-AP, computer programming, computer programming-AP, computer science, creative writing, dance, dance performance, drama, earth science, economics, English, English literature, English literature and composition-AP, English-AP, European history, fine arts, French, geography, geometry, government/civics, Latin, literature and composition-AP, literature-AP, mathematics, military history, music, music theory, physical education, physics, physics-AP, psychology, SAT preparation, science, social sciences, social studies, Spanish, speech, statistics, technological applications, technology/design, theater, typing, U.S. history-AP, vocal music, world history, world history-AP, world literature, writing.

Graduation Requirements Art appreciation, arts and fine arts (art, music, dance, drama), computer science, English, foreign language, mathematics, music appreciation, physical education (includes health), science, social sciences.

Special Academic Programs 8 Advanced Placement exams for which test preparation is offered; honors section; independent study; academic accommodation for the gifted.

College Admission Counseling 44 students graduated in 2013; all went to college, including Brown University; Cornell University; Georgetown University; New York University; The College of William and Mary; University of Delaware.

Student Life Upper grades have uniform requirement, student council, honor system. Discipline rests primarily with faculty.

Tuition and Aid Day student tuition: $12,310. Tuition installment plan (Key Tuition Payment Plan, monthly payment plans, individually arranged payment plans). Need-based scholarship grants available. In 2013–14, 1% of upper-school students received aid.

Admissions Traditional secondary-level entrance grade is 9. For fall 2013, 23 students applied for upper-level admission, 19 were accepted, 18 enrolled. Achievement/Aptitude/Writing and writing sample required. Deadline for receipt of application materials: none. Application fee required: $50. On-campus interview required.

Athletics Interscholastic: basketball (boys, girls), field hockey (g), lacrosse (b,g), soccer (b,g), tennis (b,g), volleyball (g), weight training (b,g), winter soccer (b,g); intramural: basketball (b,g), dance (b,g), dance squad (b,g), flag football (b,g), soccer (b,g); coed interscholastic: cheering, golf, tennis; coed intramural: dance, dance squad. 3 PE instructors, 12 coaches, 1 athletic trainer.

Computers Computers are regularly used in all classes. Computer network features include on-campus library services, online commercial services, Internet access, wireless campus network, Internet filtering or blocking technology. Campus intranet, student e-mail accounts, and computer access in designated common areas are available to students. The school has a published electronic and media policy.

Contact Tara F. Becker, Director of Admissions. 410-641-3575 Ext. 107. Fax: 410-641-3586. E-mail: tbecker@worcesterprep.org. Website: www.worcesterprep.org

WYOMING SEMINARY

201 North Sprague Avenue
Kingston, Pennsylvania 18704-3593

Head of School: Dr. Kip P. Nygren

General Information Coeducational boarding and day college-preparatory school, affiliated with United Methodist Church. Grades 9–PG. Founded: 1844. Setting: suburban. Nearest major city is Wilkes-Barre. Students are housed in single-sex dormitories. 22-acre campus. 12 buildings on campus. Approved or accredited by Middle States Association of Colleges and Schools, Pennsylvania Association of Independent Schools, The Association of Boarding Schools, The College Board, University Senate of United Methodist Church, and Pennsylvania Department of Education. Member of National Association of Independent Schools and Secondary School Admission Test Board. Endowment: $50 million. Total enrollment: 756. Upper school average class size: 14. Upper school faculty-student ratio: 1:8. There are 170 required school days per year for Upper School students. Upper School students typically attend 5 days per week. The average school day consists of 7 hours.

Upper School Student Profile Grade 9: 80 students (40 boys, 40 girls); Grade 10: 103 students (47 boys, 56 girls); Grade 11: 121 students (67 boys, 54 girls); Grade 12: 100 students (47 boys, 53 girls); Postgraduate: 15 students (11 boys, 4 girls). 41% of students are boarding students. 66% are state residents. 17 states are represented in upper school student body. 25% are international students. International students from Canada, China, Germany, Republic of Korea, Taiwan, and Viet Nam; 10 other countries represented in student body. 10% of students are United Methodist Church.

Faculty School total: 57. In upper school: 31 men, 26 women; 42 have advanced degrees; 37 reside on campus.

Subjects Offered 20th century world history, 3-dimensional design, algebra, alternative physical education, American Civil War, American history, American literature, analysis and differential calculus, analytic geometry, anatomy and physiology, ancient world history, art, art appreciation, art history, art history-AP, Bible studies, biology, biology-AP, botany, British literature, calculus, calculus-AP, ceramics, chemistry, chemistry-AP, choral music, college admission preparation, college counseling, computer programming, computer science, conceptual physics, creative writing, critical writing, discrete mathematics, drama, drawing and design, ecology, English, English literature, environmental science, environmental science-AP, ESL, European history, European history-AP, expository writing, fine arts, French, French-AP, geometry, health education, history, history of music, independent study, Judaic studies, Latin, Latin-AP, mathematics, music, music theory, music theory-AP, philosophy, photography, physics, poetry, pre-calculus, printmaking, psychology, psychology-AP, public speaking, religion, Russian, science, science research, Shakespeare, social studies, sociology, Spanish, Spanish-AP, statistics, statistics-AP, studio art-AP, theater, trigonometry, U.S. government and politics-AP, U.S. history-AP, women in literature, world civilizations, world cultures, world history, world literature, world religions, World War II, zoology.

Graduation Requirements Art history, Bible as literature, biology, computer science, English, foreign language, health education, mathematics, music history, physical education (includes health), public speaking, science, social studies (includes history), U.S. history, world civilizations, 40 hours of community service, extracurricular participation.

Special Academic Programs 21 Advanced Placement exams for which test preparation is offered; honors section; independent study; term-away projects; study at local college for college credit; study abroad; ESL (47 students enrolled).

College Admission Counseling 100 students graduated in 2012; 98 went to college, including Boston University; Bucknell University; Drexel University; New York University; Penn State University Park. Other: 1 went to work, 1 entered a postgraduate year. Mean SAT critical reading: 572, mean SAT math: 633, mean SAT writing: 582, mean combined SAT: 1787.

Student Life Upper grades have specified standards of dress, student council, honor system. Discipline rests equally with students and faculty. Attendance at religious services is required.

Tuition and Aid Day student tuition: $21,850; 7-day tuition and room/board: $43,200. Tuition installment plan (FACTS Tuition Payment Plan, monthly payment plans). Merit scholarship grants, need-based scholarship grants, need-based loans, prepGATE loans available. In 2012–13, 50% of upper-school students received aid; total upper-school merit-scholarship money awarded: $400,000. Total amount of financial aid awarded in 2012–13: $6,000,000.

Admissions Traditional secondary-level entrance grade is 9. For fall 2012, 356 students applied for upper-level admission, 199 were accepted, 106 enrolled. ACT, PSAT or SAT for applicants to grade 11 and 12, SSAT or TOEFL or SLEP required. Deadline for receipt of application materials: none. Application fee required: $75. Interview required.

Athletics Interscholastic: baseball (boys), basketball (b,g), cross-country running (b,g), diving (b,g), field hockey (g), ice hockey (b,g), lacrosse (b,g), soccer (b,g), softball (g), swimming and diving (b,g), tennis (b,g), wrestling (b); coed interscholastic: golf, strength & conditioning; coed intramural: ballet, combined training, dance, fitness, martial arts, modern dance, outdoor activities, outdoor recreation, physical training, wall climbing. 2 PE instructors, 6 coaches, 1 athletic trainer.

Computers Computers are regularly used in art, English, foreign language, history, mathematics, music, science classes. Computer network features include on-campus library services, online commercial services, Internet access, wireless campus network, Internet filtering or blocking technology. Campus intranet, student e-mail accounts, and computer access in designated common areas are available to students. Students grades are available online. The school has a published electronic and media policy.

Contact Mr. Eric Turner, Director of Enrollment Management. 570-270-2160. Fax: 570-270-2191. E-mail: admission@wyomingseminary.org. Website: www.wyomingseminary.org

XAVERIAN HIGH SCHOOL

7100 Shore Road
Brooklyn, New York 11209

Head of School: Mr. Robert Alesi

General Information Boys' day college-preparatory, arts, business, religious studies, and technology school, affiliated with Roman Catholic Church. Grades 9–12. Founded: 1957. Setting: urban. 1 building on campus. Approved or accredited by Middle States Association of Colleges and Schools, New York Department of Education, New York State Board of Regents, and New York Department of Education. Total enrollment: 1,088. Upper school average class size: 27. Upper school faculty-student ratio: 1:26. There are 180 required school days per year for Upper School students. Upper School students typically attend 5 days per week. The average school day consists of 6 hours.

Special Academic Programs Advanced Placement exam preparation; honors section; study at local college for college credit; academic accommodation for the gifted and the musically talented; remedial reading and/or remedial writing; remedial math; programs in English, mathematics, general development for dyslexic students.

College Admission Counseling 270 students graduated in 2012.

Student Life Upper grades have uniform requirement. Attendance at religious services is required.

Tuition and Aid Day student tuition: $11,600. Tuition installment plan (SMART Tuition Payment Plan). Merit scholarship grants, need-based scholarship grants, need-based loans available. In 2012–13, 30% of upper-school students received aid.

Admissions For fall 2012, 800 students applied for upper-level admission. New York Archdiocesan Cooperative Entrance Examination required. Deadline for receipt of application materials: December 1. No application fee required.

Athletics Interscholastic: aquatics, baseball, basketball, billiards, bowling, cross-country running, diving, fitness, football, golf, handball, ice hockey, indoor track, indoor track & field, jogging, lacrosse, physical fitness, physical training, power lifting, running, soccer, strength & conditioning, swimming and diving, team handball, tennis, track and field, volleyball, weight lifting, weight training, winter (indoor) track, wrestling; intramural: Frisbee, independent competitive sports, Nautilus, ultimate Frisbee.

Computers Computers are regularly used in all classes. Computer network features include on-campus library services, online commercial services, Internet access, wireless campus network, Internet filtering or blocking technology, students are issued iPad 2s when they enter the school. Campus intranet and student e-mail accounts are available to students. Students grades are available online. The school has a published electronic and media policy.

Contact Deacon Kevin McCormack, Principal. 718-836-7100. Fax: 718-836-7114. E-mail: kmccormack@xaverian.org. Website: www.xaverian.org

XAVIER COLLEGE PREPARATORY

4710 North Fifth Street
Phoenix, Arizona 85012

Head of School: Sr. Joan Fitzgerald, BVM

General Information Girls' day college-preparatory, arts, religious studies, technology, great books, Advanced Placement, dual college enrollment,, and STEM education school, affiliated with Roman Catholic Church. Grades 9–12. Founded: 1943. Setting: urban. 20-acre campus. 10 buildings on campus. Approved or accredited by National Catholic Education Association, North Central Association of Colleges and Schools, Western Catholic Education Association, and Arizona Department of Education. Endowment: $2 million. Total enrollment: 1,173. Upper school average class size: 24. Upper school faculty-student ratio: 1:22. There are 180 required school days per year for Upper School students. Upper School students typically attend 5 days per week. The average school day consists of 5 hours.

Upper School Student Profile Grade 9: 303 students (303 girls); Grade 10: 310 students (310 girls); Grade 11: 292 students (292 girls); Grade 12: 268 students (268 girls). 75% of students are Roman Catholic.

Faculty School total: 95. In upper school: 20 men, 75 women; 70 have advanced degrees.

Subjects Offered Accounting, advanced biology, advanced chemistry, advanced computer applications, Advanced Placement courses, advanced studio art-AP, algebra, American government, American history, American history-AP, American literature, analysis and differential calculus, anatomy and physiology, architecture, art, art history, astronomy, athletic training, audition methods, band, bell choir, biology, biology-AP, calculus, calculus-AP, ceramics, cheerleading, chemistry, chemistry-AP, child development, Chinese, choir, church history, community service, computer programming-AP, computer science, computer studies, concert choir, contemporary issues, culinary arts, dance, dance performance, digital photography, drama, economics, English, English language and composition-AP, English literature-AP, environmental science-AP, ethics, European history-AP, family and consumer science, film studies, fine arts, French, French language-AP, geography, geometry, graphic design, great books, guitar, jazz band, Latin, Latin-AP, music, music theory-AP, musical theater, New Testament, newspaper, philosophy, physical education, physics, physics-AP, pre-calculus, psychology, sociology, Spanish, Spanish language-AP, Spanish literature-AP, sports medicine, stagecraft, statistics-AP, student government, theology, trigonometry, U.S. government and politics-AP, visual arts, weight training, weightlifting, world history-AP, world literature.

Graduation Requirements American literature, arts and fine arts (art, music, dance, drama), computer science, English, foreign language, mathematics, physical education (includes health), religion (includes Bible studies and theology), science, social studies (includes history), Arizona history and free enterprise independent study, summer reading program, 50 hours of community service.

Special Academic Programs 22 Advanced Placement exams for which test preparation is offered; honors section; independent study; study at local college for college credit; study abroad; academic accommodation for the gifted and the artistically talented.

College Admission Counseling 301 students graduated in 2013; 298 went to college, including Arizona State University; Northern Arizona University; The University of Arizona; University of California, Los Angeles; University of Notre Dame; University of San Diego. Other: 3 had other specific plans. Median composite ACT: 26. Mean SAT critical reading: 575, mean SAT math: 561, mean SAT writing: 579.

Student Life Upper grades have uniform requirement, student council, honor system. Discipline rests primarily with faculty. Attendance at religious services is required.

Summer Programs Enrichment, advancement, sports, art/fine arts, computer instruction programs offered; session focuses on academic advancement; held on campus; accepts girls; not open to students from other schools. 700 students usually enrolled. 2014 schedule: May 27 to June 27. Application deadline: April 1.

Tuition and Aid Day student tuition: $12,564–$16,227. Tuition installment plan (monthly payment plans, semester payment plan). Need-based scholarship grants, reduced tuition rate for Catholic families registered in Catholic parishes of the Diocese of Phoenix available. In 2013–14, 40% of upper-school students received aid. Total amount of financial aid awarded in 2013–14: $1,500,000.

Admissions Traditional secondary-level entrance grade is 9. For fall 2013, 510 students applied for upper-level admission, 375 were accepted, 340 enrolled. High School Placement Test required. Deadline for receipt of application materials: January 30. Application fee required: $50.

Athletics Interscholastic: aerobics/dance, badminton, basketball, cheering, crew, cross-country running, dance squad, dance team, danceline, diving, fitness, golf, lacrosse, pom squad, rowing, soccer, softball, strength & conditioning, swimming and diving, tennis, track and field, volleyball, winter soccer; intramural: archery, crew, dance, floor hockey, modern dance, tennis, weight training; coed interscholastic: ice hockey; coed intramural: flag football, tennis, volleyball. 4 PE instructors, 21 coaches, 2 athletic trainers.

Computers Computers are regularly used in all classes. Computer network features include on-campus library services, online commercial services, Internet access, wireless campus network, Internet filtering or blocking technology, Blackboard Learning Systems, Blackbaud NetClassroom. Student e-mail accounts and computer access in designated common areas are available to students. Students grades are available online. The school has a published electronic and media policy.

Contact Mrs. Paula Petrowski, Director of Admissions. 602-277-3772 Ext. 3104. Fax: 602-240-3175. E-mail: ppetrowski@xcp.org. Website: www.xcp.org

YESHIVA HIGH SCHOOL

7135 North Carpenter Road
Skokie, Illinois 60077

Head of School: Rabbi Moshe Wender

General Information Boys' boarding and day college-preparatory, religious studies, and technology school, affiliated with Jewish faith. Grades 9–12. Founded: 1922. Setting: suburban. Nearest major city is Chicago. Students are housed in single-sex dormitories. 11-acre campus. 2 buildings on campus. Approved or accredited by North Central Association of Colleges and Schools and Illinois Department of Education. Language of instruction: Hebrew. Total enrollment: 145. Upper school average class size: 1. Upper school faculty-student ratio: 1:13. There are 197 required school days per year for Upper School students. Upper School students typically attend 5 days per week.

Upper School Student Profile Grade 9: 35 students (35 boys); Grade 10: 39 students (39 boys); Grade 11: 35 students (35 boys); Grade 12: 36 students (36 boys). 33% of students are boarding students. 68% are state residents. 13 states are represented in upper school student body. International students from Canada and Mexico. 100% of students are Jewish.

Faculty School total: 34. In upper school: 15 have advanced degrees; 1 resides on campus.

Subjects Offered Bible, computers, economics, English, Hebrew, Jewish history, mathematics, physical education, science, social studies, Talmud.

Special Academic Programs 7 Advanced Placement exams for which test preparation is offered; honors section; independent study; academic accommodation for the gifted; remedial reading and/or remedial writing; remedial math.

College Admission Counseling 25 students graduated in 2013; all went to college, including Loyola University Chicago; Northwestern University; University of Illinois at Chicago; Yeshiva University. Mean SAT critical reading: 600, mean SAT math: 610, mean composite ACT: 27.

Student Life Upper grades have specified standards of dress, student council. Discipline rests primarily with faculty. Attendance at religious services is required.

Tuition and Aid 7-day tuition and room/board: $15,315. Tuition installment plan (monthly payment plans, individually arranged payment plans). Need-based loans available. In 2013–14, 60% of upper-school students received aid.

Admissions Traditional secondary-level entrance grade is 9. For fall 2013, 55 students applied for upper-level admission, 39 were accepted, 24 enrolled. ACT-Explore, admissions testing or any standardized test required. Deadline for receipt of application materials: none. Application fee required. On-campus interview required.

Athletics Interscholastic: basketball, physical training; intramural: aerobics, basketball, fitness, flag football, football, martial arts, soccer, softball. 1 PE instructor, 4 coaches.

Computers Computers are regularly used in stock market classes. Computer network features include on-campus library services, Internet access.

Contact Rabbi Joshua Zisook, Director of Admissions. 847-982-2500. Fax: 847-677-6381. E-mail: zisook@htc.edu. Website: www.htc.edu/fasman-yeshiva-high-school.html

YORK CATHOLIC HIGH SCHOOL

601 East Springettsbury Avenue
York, Pennsylvania 17403

Head of School: Mrs. Adrienne K. Seufert

General Information Coeducational day college-preparatory and general academic school, affiliated with Roman Catholic Church. Grades 7–12. Founded: 1927. Setting: suburban. 19-acre campus. 1 building on campus. Approved or accredited by Middle States Association of Colleges and Schools, National Catholic Education Association, and Pennsylvania Department of Education. Total enrollment: 636. Upper school average class size: 21. Upper school faculty-student ratio: 1:16. There are 180 required school days per year for Upper School students. Upper School students typically attend 5 days per week. The average school day consists of 6 hours and 15 minutes.

Upper School Student Profile Grade 9: 99 students (40 boys, 59 girls); Grade 10: 106 students (49 boys, 57 girls); Grade 11: 136 students (60 boys, 76 girls); Grade 12: 99 students (52 boys, 47 girls). 89% of students are Roman Catholic.

Faculty School total: 46. In upper school: 16 men, 30 women.

Special Academic Programs Advanced Placement exam preparation; honors section; study at local college for college credit.

College Admission Counseling 110 students graduated in 2012; 104 went to college. Other: 6 entered military service. Median SAT critical reading: 547, median SAT math: 533, median SAT writing: 546, median combined SAT: 1626.

Student Life Upper grades have uniform requirement, student council, honor system. Discipline rests primarily with faculty. Attendance at religious services is required.

Tuition and Aid Day student tuition: $4800. Tuition installment plan (SMART Tuition Payment Plan). Tuition reduction for siblings, need-based scholarship grants available. In 2012–13, 28% of upper-school students received aid. Total amount of financial aid awarded in 2012–13: $250,000.

Admissions Traditional secondary-level entrance grade is 9. Deadline for receipt of application materials: none. No application fee required. Interview required.

Athletics Interscholastic: baseball (boys), basketball (b,g), cheering (g), cross-country running (b,g), football (b), golf (b,g), lacrosse (b,g), running (b,g), soccer (b,g), softball (g), tennis (b,g), track and field (b,g), volleyball (g), wrestling (b); intramural: strength & conditioning (b); coed intramural: bowling, ice hockey, skiing (downhill), table tennis.

Computers Computer resources include on-campus library services, Internet access, Internet filtering or blocking technology. Campus intranet is available to students. Students grades are available online. The school has a published electronic and media policy.

Contact Ms. Heather Hoffman, Director of Admissions. 717-846-8871 Ext. 20. Fax: 717-843-4588. E-mail: hhoffman@yorkcatholic.org. Website: www.yorkcatholic.org

YORK PREPARATORY SCHOOL

40 West 68th Street
New York, New York 10023-6092

Head of School: Ronald P. Stewart

General Information Coeducational day college-preparatory, arts, technology, music (practical and theory), and drama school. Grades 6–12. Founded: 1969. Setting: urban. 1 building on campus. Approved or accredited by Middle States Association of Colleges and Schools, National Independent Private Schools Association, and New York Department of Education. Member of National Association of Independent Schools. Total enrollment: 358. Upper school average class size: 15. Upper school faculty-student ratio: 1:6. There are 158 required school days per year for Upper School students. Upper School students typically attend 5 days per week. The average school day consists of 6 hours and 30 minutes.

Upper School Student Profile Grade 9: 73 students (44 boys, 29 girls); Grade 10: 64 students (35 boys, 29 girls); Grade 11: 61 students (36 boys, 25 girls); Grade 12: 64 students (40 boys, 24 girls).

Faculty School total: 64. In upper school: 24 men, 40 women; 48 have advanced degrees.

Subjects Offered 20th century history, 20th century world history, 3-dimensional art, advanced chemistry, advanced computer applications, Advanced Placement courses, advanced studio art-AP, algebra, American history, American history-AP, American literature, anatomy, animation, anthropology, art, art appreciation, astronomy, biology, calculus, calculus-AP, ceramics, chemistry, chemistry-AP, comparative religion, computer math, computer programming, computer science, computer skills, concert band, creative writing, current events, drama, drama performance, driver education, earth science, economics, English, English literature, English-AP, environmental science, ethics, European history, expository writing, filmmaking, fine arts, French, genetics, geography, geology, geometry, government/civics, grammar, health education, Holocaust studies, law, literary magazine, mathematics, music, music history, philosophy, photography, physical education, physics, physiology, political science, politics, pre-calculus, psychology, reading/study skills, research skills, SAT preparation, science, science project, social studies, Spanish, statistics, theater, trigonometry, typing, world history, world literature, writing, zoology.

Graduation Requirements Arts and fine arts (art, music, dance, drama), English, foreign language, mathematics, physical education (includes health), science, social studies (includes history). Community service is required.

Special Academic Programs Advanced Placement exam preparation; honors section; independent study; study at local college for college credit; academic accommodation for the gifted, the musically talented, and the artistically talented; programs in English, mathematics, general development for dyslexic students; special instructional classes for students with mild learning issues (extra tutoring program).

College Admission Counseling 51 students graduated in 2012; all went to college, including American University; Boston University; Harvard University; Massachusetts Institute of Technology; Syracuse University; The Johns Hopkins University.

Student Life Upper grades have specified standards of dress, student council, honor system. Discipline rests primarily with faculty.

Tuition and Aid Day student tuition: $40,700–$41,300. Tuition installment plan (Insured Tuition Payment Plan, monthly payment plans, individually arranged payment plans). Tuition reduction for siblings, merit scholarship grants, need-based scholarship grants available. In 2012–13, 20% of upper-school students received aid. Total amount of financial aid awarded in 2012–13: $1,000,000.

Admissions Traditional secondary-level entrance grade is 9. ISEE or SSAT required. Deadline for receipt of application materials: January 15. Application fee required: $50. On-campus interview required.

Athletics Interscholastic: baseball (boys), basketball (b,g), cross-country running (b,g), soccer (b,g), softball (b,g), volleyball (b,g); intramural: cheering (g), volleyball (b,g); coed interscholastic: basketball, cross-country running, golf, tennis, track and field; coed intramural: aerobics, aerobics/Nautilus, aquatics, basketball, bicycling, combined training, cross-country running, dance, fitness, Frisbee, golf, indoor track, physical fitness, physical training, skiing (downhill), soccer, softball, swimming and diving, ultimate Frisbee, weight training, yoga. 6 PE instructors, 6 coaches, 2 athletic trainers.

Computers Computers are regularly used in all academic classes. Computer network features include on-campus library services, online commercial services, Internet access, wireless campus network, Internet filtering or blocking technology. Computer access in designated common areas is available to students. Students grades are available online. The school has a published electronic and media policy.

Contact Ms. Cathy Minaudo, Director of Admissions. 212-362-0400 Ext. 106. Fax: 212-362-7424. E-mail: cminaudo@yorkprep.org. Website: www.yorkprep.org

See Display on next page and Close-Up on page 586.

YORK SCHOOL

9501 York Road
Monterey, California 93940

Head of School: Chuck Harmon

General Information Coeducational day college-preparatory, arts, bilingual studies, and technology school, affiliated with Episcopal Church. Grades 8–12. Founded: 1959. Setting: suburban. Nearest major city is San Jose. 126-acre campus. 6 buildings on campus. Approved or accredited by California Association of Independent Schools, National Association of Episcopal Schools, Western Association of Schools and Colleges, and California Department of Education. Member of National Association of Independent Schools. Endowment: $5.8 million. Total enrollment: 225. Upper school average class size: 14. Upper school faculty-student ratio: 1:8. Upper School students typically attend 5 days per week. The average school day consists of 7 hours.

Upper School Student Profile Grade 8: 18 students (7 boys, 11 girls); Grade 9: 62 students (34 boys, 28 girls); Grade 10: 56 students (28 boys, 28 girls); Grade 11: 43 students (17 boys, 26 girls); Grade 12: 50 students (27 boys, 23 girls).

Faculty School total: 32. In upper school: 16 men, 16 women; 24 have advanced degrees.

Subjects Offered Advanced studio art-AP, algebra, American history-AP, anatomy, ancient history, art, art history, Asian history, band, biology, biology-AP, calculus, calculus-AP, chemistry, chemistry-AP, choir, community service, computer science, creative writing, digital art, drama, English, English-AP, environmental science, film, fine arts, French, French language-AP, geometry, Greek, jazz, Latin, Latin-AP, marine biology, mathematics, music, music theory-AP, orchestra, painting, philosophy, photography, physical education, physical science, physics, physics-AP, physiology, pre-calculus, psychology-AP, science, social studies, Spanish, Spanish language-AP, statistics, studio art, U.S. history, U.S. history-AP, world history, yearbook.

Graduation Requirements Arts and fine arts (art, music, dance, drama), computer science, English, foreign language, mathematics, physical education (includes health), science, social studies (includes history), ensemble participation. Community service is required.

Special Academic Programs Advanced Placement exam preparation; honors section.

College Admission Counseling 49 students graduated in 2012; 46 went to college, including Boston University; Princeton University; University of California, Santa Barbara; Whittier College. Other: 3 had other specific plans. Mean SAT critical reading: 670, mean SAT math: 657, mean SAT writing: 665, mean combined SAT: 1992, mean composite ACT: 28.

Student Life Upper grades have specified standards of dress, student council, honor system. Discipline rests primarily with faculty.

Tuition and Aid Day student tuition: $27,600. Tuition installment plan (individually arranged payment plans, 2 Payments, 10 Payments). Need-based scholarship grants available. In 2012–13, 46% of upper-school students received aid. Total amount of financial aid awarded in 2012–13: $1,463,100.

Admissions Traditional secondary-level entrance grade is 9. For fall 2012, 133 students applied for upper-level admission. Admissions testing required. Deadline for receipt of application materials: February 1. Application fee required: $75. Interview required.

Athletics Interscholastic: basketball (boys, girls), cross-country running (b,g), diving (b,g), field hockey (g), golf (b,g), soccer (b,g), softball (g), swimming and diving (b,g), tennis (b,g), volleyball (g); coed interscholastic: dance, lacrosse; coed intramural: badminton, basketball, fitness walking, independent competitive sports, jogging, soccer, ultimate Frisbee, volleyball, walking, weight training, yoga. 18 coaches.

Computers Computers are regularly used in computer applications, technology, yearbook classes. Computer network features include on-campus library services, Internet access, wireless campus network. The school has a published electronic and media policy.

Contact Rachel Gaudoin, Admission Associate. 831-372-7338 Ext. 116. Fax: 831-372-8055. E-mail: rachel@york.org Website: www.york.org

THE YORK SCHOOL

1320 Yonge Street
Toronto, Ontario M4T 1X2, Canada

Head of School: Mr. Conor Jones

General Information Coeducational day college-preparatory and International Baccalaureate school. Grades JK–12. Founded: 1965. Setting: urban. 1-acre campus. 1 building on campus. Approved or accredited by Canadian Association of Independent Schools, Canadian Educational Standards Institute, Conference of Independent Schools of Ontario, International Baccalaureate Organization, and Ontario Department of Education. Member of Secondary School Admission Test Board. Language of instruction: English. Total enrollment: 600. Upper school average class size: 18. Upper school faculty-student ratio: 1:16. Upper School students typically attend 5 days per week. The average school day consists of 7 hours.

Faculty School total: 80. In upper school: 12 men, 20 women.

Subjects Offered 20th century history, American history, biology, calculus, Canadian geography, Canadian history, Canadian law, careers, chemistry, civics, discrete mathematics, dramatic arts, economics, English, environmental systems, French, functions, geography, geometry, global issues, healthful living, instrumental music, Mandarin, physical education, physics, social sciences, society challenge and change, Spanish, theater arts, theory of knowledge, visual arts, vocal music, world history, world religions.

Graduation Requirements International Baccalaureate diploma exams.

Special Academic Programs International Baccalaureate program; honors section; independent study; study abroad; academic accommodation for the gifted, the musically talented, and the artistically talented.

College Admission Counseling 54 students graduated in 2013; all went to college, including McGill University; McMaster University; Queen's University at Kingston; The University of Western Ontario; University of Toronto; University of Waterloo.

Student Life Upper grades have uniform requirement, student council, honor system. Discipline rests primarily with faculty.

Tuition and Aid Day student tuition: CAN$27,000. Tuition installment plan (monthly payment plans, individually arranged payment plans). Merit scholarship grants, need-based scholarship grants available. In 2013–14, 5% of upper-school students received aid.

Admissions Traditional secondary-level entrance grade is 9. For fall 2013, 100 students applied for upper-level admission, 81 were accepted, 34 enrolled. School's own exam required. Deadline for receipt of application materials: December 6. Application fee required: CAN$200. Interview recommended.

Athletics Interscholastic: aerobics/dance (boys, girls), aerobics/Nautilus (b,g), alpine skiing (b,g), badminton (b,g), baseball (b,g), basketball (b,g), cooperative games (b,g), cross-country running (b,g), fitness (b,g), floor hockey (b,g), outdoor activities (b,g), outdoor education (b,g), running (b,g), soccer (b,g), softball (b,g), strength & conditioning (b,g), track and field (b,g); intramural: aerobics/Nautilus (b,g), badminton (b,g), baseball (b,g), basketball (b,g), outdoor education (b,g), volleyball (b,g); coed interscholastic: badminton, cooperative games, cross-country running, floor hockey, ice skating, outdoor activities, outdoor education, running, strength & conditioning, track and field, ultimate Frisbee; coed intramural: backpacking, badminton, curling, Frisbee, hiking/backpacking, outdoor adventure, outdoor education, outdoor skills, track and field, ultimate Frisbee. 4 PE instructors.

Computers Computers are regularly used in all academic classes. Computer network features include on-campus library services, Internet access, wireless campus network, Internet filtering or blocking technology. Campus intranet, student e-mail accounts, and computer access in designated common areas are available to students. Students grades are available online. The school has a published electronic and media policy.

Contact Ms. Julia Gordon, Admission Assistant. 416-646-5275. Fax: 416-926-9592. E-mail: jgordon@yorkschool.com. Website: www.yorkschool.com

ZURICH INTERNATIONAL SCHOOL

Steinacherstrasse 140
Wdenswil 8820, Switzerland

Head of School: Jeff Paulson

General Information Coeducational day college-preparatory, technology, and International Baccalaureate Diploma and Advanced Placement school. Grades PS–13. Founded: 1963. Setting: suburban. Nearest major city is Zurich, Switzerland. 6-acre campus. 1 building on campus. Approved or accredited by International Baccalaureate Organization, New England Association of Schools and Colleges, and Swiss Federation of Private Schools. Member of European Council of International Schools. Language of instruction: English. Total enrollment: 1,493. Upper school average class size: 16. Upper school faculty-student ratio: 1:7. There are 175 required school days per year for Upper School students. Upper School students typically attend 5 days per week. The average school day consists of 7 hours.

Upper School Student Profile Grade 9: 111 students (61 boys, 50 girls); Grade 10: 110 students (50 boys, 60 girls); Grade 11: 122 students (70 boys, 52 girls); Grade 12: 117 students (49 boys, 68 girls).

Faculty School total: 230. In upper school: 31 men, 35 women; 46 have advanced degrees.

Subjects Offered Acting, Advanced Placement courses, art history, art history-AP, art-AP, biology, biology-AP, calculus, calculus-AP, chemistry-AP, computer programming-AP, concert band, concert choir, digital photography, drama, drama performance, economics, economics-AP, English, English language and composition-AP, English literature, English literature and composition-AP, ESL, European history-AP, fine arts, French, French language-AP, German, German-AP, health, history, history-AP, International Baccalaureate courses, journalism, macro/microeconomics-AP, macroeconomics-AP, mathematics, microeconomics-AP, music, philosophy, photography, physical education, physics-AP, pre-calculus, psychology-AP, public speaking, robotics, science, social studies, Spanish language-AP, statistics-AP, studio art, studio art-AP, theater, U.S. history-AP, visual arts, world history, world history-AP, writing.

Graduation Requirements Arts and fine arts (art, music, dance, drama), English, foreign language, mathematics, physical education (includes health), science, social studies (includes history), completion of a yearly service project. Community service is required.

Special Academic Programs International Baccalaureate program; 22 Advanced Placement exams for which test preparation is offered; honors section; independent study; remedial reading and/or remedial writing; remedial math; ESL (9 students enrolled).

College Admission Counseling 121 students graduated in 2012; 110 went to college, including Northeastern University; Northwestern University; Princeton University; University of California, Los Angeles; University of Chicago; University of Virginia. Other: 2 went to work, 3 entered military service, 6 had other specific plans. Median SAT critical reading: 570, median SAT math: 560, median SAT writing: 570, median combined SAT: 1700. 46% scored over 600 on SAT critical reading, 39% scored over 600 on SAT math, 42% scored over 600 on SAT writing.

Student Life Upper grades have specified standards of dress, student council. Discipline rests primarily with faculty.

Tuition and Aid Day student tuition: 33,900 Swiss francs. Tuition installment plan (monthly payment plans). Need-based scholarship grants available. In 2012–13, 3% of upper-school students received aid. Total amount of financial aid awarded in 2012–13: 67,700 Swiss francs.

Admissions Traditional secondary-level entrance grade is 9. For fall 2012, 141 students applied for upper-level admission, 58 were accepted, 58 enrolled. English for Non-native Speakers or math and English placement tests required. Deadline for receipt of application materials: none. Application fee required: 500 Swiss francs.

Athletics Interscholastic: basketball (boys, girls), rugby (b), soccer (b,g), softball (g), tennis (b,g), volleyball (b,g); intramural: indoor soccer (b,g); coed interscholastic: alpine skiing, cross-country running, golf, skiing (cross-country), skiing (downhill), swimming and diving, track and field, ultimate Frisbee; coed intramural: aerobics/dance, badminton, basketball, canoeing/kayaking, climbing, dance, fitness, Frisbee, juggling, kayaking, outdoor activities, rock climbing, sailing, swimming and diving, wall climbing, yoga. 5 PE instructors, 15 coaches.

Computers Computers are regularly used in all classes. Computer network features include on-campus library services, online commercial services, Internet access, wireless campus network, one to one Tablet Program, Moodle, VHS, MAC lab, iPad pilot in upper school. Campus intranet, student e-mail accounts, and computer access in designated common areas are available to students. Students grades are available online. The school has a published electronic and media policy.

Contact Dale Braunschweig, Head Admissions. 41-58 750 2531. Fax: 41-58 750 2501. E-mail: dbraunschweig@zis.ch. Website: www.zis.ch

Traditional Day and Boarding School Close-Ups

AMERICAN HERITAGE SCHOOL

Plantation and Delray Beach, Florida

Type: Coeducational, day, independent, nonsectarian
Grades: PK-3–grade 12
Enrollment: 2,400, Plantation campus; 1,098, Boca/Delray campus
Head of School: William Laurie, President and Founder

THE SCHOOL

American Heritage School's mission is to graduate students who are prepared in mind, body, and spirit to meet the requirements of the colleges of their choice. To this end, the School strives to offer a challenging college preparatory curriculum, opportunities for leadership, and superior programs in the arts and athletics. American Heritage is committed to providing a safe and nurturing environment for learning so that children of average to gifted intelligence may achieve their full potential to be intelligent, creative, and contributing members of society. Students receive a well-rounded education that provides opportunities for leadership and character building and extensive opportunities for growth in the arts, athletics, and new technology.

ACADEMIC PROGRAM

The curriculum for the preprimary child is developmental and age appropriate at each level. Daily language, speech, and auditory development activities help children to listen, understand, speak, and learn effectively. The program seeks to maximize the academic potential of each child, while fostering a positive self-image and providing the skills necessary for the next level of education.

The Lower School is committed to developing a student's basic skills, helping the student master content areas, and maintaining the student's enthusiasm for learning. Students learn the fundamentals of reading, process writing, mathematics, and English through a logical progressive sequence, and they learn social studies, handwriting, spelling, science, and health, with an emphasis on the development of good study skills. In math and reading, students are grouped according to ability. Enrichment classes in computer education, art, media center, music, Spanish, Chinese, physical education, and investigative science lab are offered. Field trips, special projects and events, and assemblies supplement the work introduced in class.

Math, reading, grammar, literature, social studies, and science are the core subjects of the junior high curriculum, where critical-thinking skills become increasingly important. Writing skills are emphasized, helping students become literate and articulate thinkers and writers. Enrichment courses are an important part of the junior high curriculum, with courses rotated on a nine-week basis. Honors classes are available in all core subject areas.

At the high school level, emphasis is placed on college preparation and on higher-level thinking skills. Students are challenged by required research and speech and writing assignments in all subject areas. An extensive variety of classes in all areas of the fine arts is available. A selection of electives—from marine biology to Advanced Placement Chinese to stagecraft—rounds out the students' schedules, allowing them to explore other interests and talents. In addition to traditional lecture and discussion, teachers supplement the text curriculum with activities, projects, and field trips that make subjects more relevant and meaningful to the students.

Honors and Advanced Placement (AP) courses are available to qualified students. Students may gain college credit as a benefit of the successful completion of AP courses, which include American government, American history, biology, calculus, chemistry, economics, English language, English literature, environmental studies, European history, French, music theory, physics, psychology, Spanish, and world history.

American Heritage School offers unique premedical, prelaw, and pre-engineering programs to qualified high school students. The programs challenge those ninth- through twelfth-grade students who have an interest in these fields of study and encourage students to consider these areas as potential career choices. The many course offerings are most often taught by working professionals in each area. In addition to course work for both programs, there are required internships that match students with professionals in their area of study.

In 2013, the school had 34 National Merit Scholarship Finalists and was the top-ranked private school at the National Mu Alpha Theta (mathematics honor society) annual conference.

Through the international program, in addition to an international student's regular academic classes, one to two hours of English language instruction is provided daily. Living with an American family produces more opportunity for language development and practice.

FACULTY AND ADVISERS

The students at American Heritage are served by 211 teachers, counselors, and administrators at the Plantation location, and 124 teachers, counselors, and administrators at the Delray campus. Sixty-two percent hold master's or doctoral degrees. Teachers actively seek out both school-year and summer workshops to attend, and they return with creative ideas for their teaching. Faculty turnover is minimal. The faculty is also committed to the Heritage philosophy of developing good character and self-esteem as well as the reinforcement of traditional values in students. Teachers maintain close communication with parents regarding their child's progress, with frequent written progress reports, phone calls, and scheduled conference days. The school provides a web-based service on which students and parents can access information ranging from general school, club, and sports topics to specific content for individual classes. Classes are small, with a 17:1 student-teacher ratio.

COLLEGE ADMISSION COUNSELING

At American Heritage, the goal is to send seniors to colleges that match their goals and expectations for college life. There are 10 full-time guidance counselors in the high school, including a Director of College Planning and an International Counselor.

The college placement process begins in seventh grade with academic advising about curriculum and course selection and continues through high school with college-preparation advising. The counselors keep abreast of current admissions trends through attendance at national and local conferences and frequent contact with college admissions representatives.

The preparation for college intensifies as students in grades 9 through 12 follow a program designed to help them score well on the SATs. The program includes SAT prep mini-exercises in their English and math classes. In tenth grade and above, students may take an intensive daily SAT prep class taught on campus during the regular school day.

At this level, academic counseling gives consideration to graduation requirements and course selection, study skills and time management, leadership and club involvement, and referral to mentoring or professional tutoring, if needed. College advising is offered in the classroom on topics such as standardized test taking, the college application process, resume and essay writing,

and searching for colleges and majors. The School reviews all college applications sent, writes letters of recommendation, finds scholarships for students, prepares students for college interviews, invites college admission representatives to campus, hosts a college fair, and proctors AP exams.

Virtually all graduates continue their educations and are admitted to the nation's finest colleges and universities. In recent years, graduates have been admitted to such schools as Boston College, Colgate, Columbia, Cornell, Duke, Harvard, Georgetown, MIT, NYU, Pepperdine, Princeton, Rutgers, Tufts, Wake Forest, West Point, Yale, and the Universities of Connecticut, Maryland, Pennsylvania, and Southern California.

STUDENT BODY AND CONDUCT

In the Lower School, the PK-3 classes enroll about 16 students; PK-4, 17; Kindergarten, 18; grades 1 and 2, 21; grades 3 and 4, 22; and grades 5 and 6, 23. In preschool through grade six, each class has a teacher and a full-time assistant. Grades 7 through 12 in the Upper School average 17 students.

The Plantation campus has 2,400 students, with 733 in the Lower School and 1,667 in the Upper School. The Boca/Delray student population totals 1,098 with 258 students in the Lower School and 840 in the Upper School. The School's day population is culturally diverse, with students representing forty-three countries from around the world.

ACADEMIC FACILITIES

The Plantation campus includes a fully equipped science lab, fifteen state-of-the-art computer rooms, and a $25-million Center for the Arts that houses a state-of-the-art 800-seat theater, a black-box theater, spacious art studios, a graphic design lab, choral and band rooms, and individual practice rooms. There are two new library/media centers, one that services the Lower School and another that meets all the technological requirements of students in the Upper School. Heritage has an excellent physical education center that includes an Olympic-sized swimming and diving facility, a gymnasium, six tennis courts, a track, four modern locker rooms, a weight-training room, and acres of well-maintained athletic fields.

The American Heritage Boca/Delray campus provides seven state-of-the-art iMac computer labs, fully equipped science labs, art studios, a college guidance computer lab, a library/media center and research lab, a new $8 million elementary/junior high classroom building, a $20 million center for the arts, an Olympic-sized swimming pool with eight racing lanes, a 2,600-square-foot teaching pool, a 25,000-square-foot gymnasium/auditorium, six lighted tennis courts, a football and soccer field, fully equipped weight training room, locker rooms, two well-equipped playgrounds, acres of well-maintained baseball and softball fields, practice fields for soccer and football, and beautifully landscaped grounds and courtyards.

ATHLETICS

The athletic program is an important part of the sense of community that has developed at Heritage. Parents, teachers, administrators, and students develop a special kind of camaraderie while cheering on the Patriot and Stallion teams. Awards evenings are held for athletes and parents at the conclusion of each season. Heritage offers a complete competitive sports program. A "no-cut" policy allows every student who wants to participate an opportunity to play on the Patriot team of his or her choice. Coaches provide high-quality instruction in all sports. Sportsmanship, teamwork, recognition of effort, and thorough training and preparation are the goals toward which the School works every day. Each year, a number of student-athletes receive financial help for their college education based on their athletic ability and their performance. More importantly, however, for those who do not have the ability—or maybe the desire—to participate at the collegiate level, athletic opportunities offer a very enjoyable and memorable experience, with accomplishments and relationships that last a lifetime. American Heritage competes as a member of the Florida High School Activities Association, and the athletics programs are consistently ranked in the top ten in the state of Florida.

EXTRACURRICULAR OPPORTUNITIES

The extensive activities offered at Heritage serve several purposes. Primarily, they assist in the growth and development of students, but they also provide opportunities for leadership and excellence, which are increasingly required for college admission. Among the activities and clubs offered to high school students are the National Honor Society; Student Council; Spanish/French Honor Society; Premed, Prelaw, and Pre-engineering Clubs; the Modern Language Club; Mu Alpha Theta (math club); SADD; the computer club; yearbook; the student newspaper; thespians; marching band; orchestra; jazz band; and chorus. Lower School students can take after-school classes in art, dance, instrumental music, karate, cooking, computers, and other areas of interest. Students may also participate in Student Council, Junior Thespians, or advanced math competitions.

American Heritage School provides an outstanding fine arts program to students in PK-3 through grade 12. The Center for the Arts is a beautiful, specially designed facility that enhances the arts program. Students participating in art, music, and drama programs have won awards at local, state, and national levels of competition in recent years. This recognition includes the Florida State Thespians Critics Choice awards, Florida Vocal Association (superior ratings for choir, solo, and ensemble), Florida Orchestra Association (superior ratings for solo and ensemble/guitar and strings), American Choral Directors Award, and National Scholastic Art Competition (gold and silver medals).

Many students participate in enrichment and leadership programs offered in Broward County, including the National Conference for Community and Justice, Leadership Broward, Boys and Girls Clubs, Silver Knights, and the Institute for Math and Computer Science. Nationally, students have participated in Hugh O'Brian Youth Foundation, Freedoms Foundation, Presidential Classroom, and Global Young Leaders Conference. In addition, American Heritage School is home to the Center for the Arts Scholarship Foundation, a nonprofit fund-raising organization that awards scholarships to talented students in the arts.

SUMMER PROGRAMS

American Heritage has provided summer fun for young campers since 1981. Summer camp provides activities that help build confidence and self-esteem. Campers enjoy the challenges and rewards of teamwork as they work and play. Through the numerous activities that are offered, campers continue to develop the socialization skills begun in school. Campers enjoy good relationships with the high school and college counselors, who serve as role models for them. American Heritage Day Camp sessions are available for students 13 years old and under.

For students who have failed a credit course in high school or have been required by their current school to attend summer school in order to pass to the next grade level, summer school is a necessity. However, many others can benefit from American Heritage's summer academic program, including preschoolers who need readiness skills to succeed in kindergarten or first grade; elementary and junior high students who need practice and development of basic skills in math, reading, and language arts; any students who perform one or two years below grade level; students for whom English is a second language; high school students who want to advance themselves academically by earning extra credits during the summer; and high school students who will soon take the SAT or ACT tests for college admission. More information can be obtained by contacting the American Heritage School.

COSTS AND FINANCIAL AID

In 2013–14, tuition and fees total between $19,013 for preschoolers and $23,930 for twelfth-grade students. An international program is available at additional cost for the academic school year—August through May—and includes tuition, housing, three meals a day, books, uniforms, and 2 hours a day of English language.

American Heritage offers financial aid to parents who qualify.

ADMISSIONS INFORMATION

Enrollment at American Heritage School is limited to students who are above average to gifted in intelligence and who are working at or above grade level. Math, reading, vocabulary, and IQ tests are administered and are used to determine if the student has the background and basic skills necessary to be successful. The results of these entrance exams are discussed with the parents at a conference following the testing. I-20 visas are granted to international students who are accepted. Details are available from the Director of Admissions. Students are admitted without regard to race, creed, or national origin.

For acceptance into American Heritage's international program, families must supply complete academic records from the age of 12, translated into English; two teacher letters of recommendation, translated into English; copies of the student's passport; and a completed American Heritage School application form. The American Heritage Admissions Committee reviews the student's records and determines suitable placement. Full tuition for the school year is due upon acceptance. After tuition has been received, the School issues an I-20 form, which must be taken to the U.S. Embassy in the student's country to obtain a student visa.

APPLICATION TIMETABLE

First-semester classes begin in late August. For information regarding specific deadlines, students should contact American Heritage School's Plantation campus.

ADMISSIONS CORRESPONDENCE

Attn: Admissions

American Heritage School
12200 West Broward Boulevard
Plantation, Florida 33325
United States
Phone: 954-472-0022
E-mail: admissions@ahschool.com
Website: http://www.ahschool.com

American Heritage School Boca/Delray
6200 Linton Boulevard
Delray Beach, Florida 33484
United States
Phone: 561-495-7272
E-mail: admissions.bd@ahschool.com
Website: http://www.ahschool.com

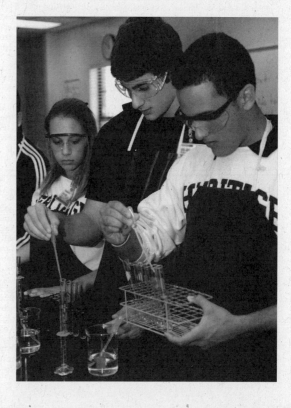

THE ATHENIAN SCHOOL

Danville, California

THE ATHENIAN SCHOOL

Type: Coeducational day and boarding college-preparatory school
Grades: 6–12: Middle School, day only, 6–8; Upper School, boarding and day, 9–12
Enrollment: School total: 475; Upper School: 316
Head of School: Eric Niles, Head

THE SCHOOL

Founded in 1965 by Dyke Brown, a graduate of Yale Law School and Vice President of the Ford Foundation, Athenian has as its goal the development of each student for a life of purpose and personal fulfillment as a citizen of the world. An Athenian education equips graduates with a deep understanding of themselves, extraordinary skills for achievement, and the compassion to make a positive difference in the world.

With distinctive programs, Athenian powerfully prepares students for outstanding colleges by engaging them in their education. Meaningful hands-on classes and programs make learning exciting and motivating. Classes average 15 to 16 students, so teachers know each student and involve them in intellectually challenging discussions and activities. Athenian's diverse student body comes from throughout the East Bay and more than ten countries. The international programs broaden students' perspectives, with opportunities across the globe for exchanges, service projects, interim trips, and conferences. Students build important skills in activities such as an electric car project, a championship robotics team, athletics, and art, music, chorus, and theater. All students participate in community service each year and, in grade 11, complete the Athenian Wilderness Experience. Few schools offer an experience as academically and personally enriching as Athenian's.

Nearly 100 percent of Athenian graduates are admitted to an outstanding array of four-year colleges and universities. Athenian helps students find the colleges that fit them best. Most importantly, Athenian inspires students to become lifelong learners and confident, successful adults.

Athenian's beautiful 75-acre campus of rolling hills is located 32 miles east of San Francisco at the base of Mt. Diablo. Athenian students access the cultural and educational resources of the San Francisco Bay Area via Athenian's shuttles, buses, and nearby BART stations (the Bay Area rapid transit system). Students also enjoy activities on the nearby Pacific Coast and the majestic Sierra mountains.

A nonprofit institution, Athenian is governed by a 25-member Board of Trustees. The School's operating budget is $15 million for 2013–14. The endowment is $9 million.

The Athenian School is fully accredited by the Western Association of Schools and Colleges. It is a member of the National Association of Independent Schools, the California Association of Independent Schools, A Better Chance, Western Boarding Schools, the College Board, the National Association for College Admission Counseling, and the Round Square Conference of International Schools.

ACADEMIC PROGRAM

Athenian's exciting broad curriculum develops analytical thinking and communication skills in all disciplines, offering a wide variety of enriching courses in English, history, math, science, fine arts, foreign language, and physical education. The ninth-grade humanities program studies major world cultures through literature, history, and art courses. The sophomore humanities program focuses on American studies in history and literature. Juniors and seniors choose enriching and varied seminars in history and literature, including honors and AP preparation. Athenian's mathematics program features statistics and AP statistics courses in addition to two yearlong consecutive AP calculus courses.

Science features first-year and second-year courses in physics, chemistry, and biology in addition to environmental science, geology, applied science, and the art of science and making. Modern languages offer courses with honors and/or AP options in French, Mandarin Chinese, and Spanish. Fine and performing arts feature courses in drawing, painting, sculpture, pottery, stained glass, photography, dance, musical performance, drama, theater tech, and several arts and society courses. Many honors or Advanced Placement and/or honors options are offered.

The academic year is divided into two semesters. The daily schedule includes six academic periods ranging from 50 to 85 minutes each. Each course meets four times a week.

Courses required for graduation are as follows: English, 4 years; laboratory science, 3 years; mathematics, 3 years; history, 3 years (including freshman humanities, American studies, and three 1-semester elective history seminars in the junior or senior year); 3 years of a foreign language; and 2.5 years of fine arts. Most students exceed these requirements. Students also fulfill graduation requirements in community service each year and must participate in the Athenian Wilderness Experience in grade 11.

Some of the electives offered are studio arts, drama workshops, instrumental ensembles, and additional courses in academic subjects. Required seminars (chosen by students) for English and history may include Shakespeare, science fiction, Russian fiction, Latin American fiction, African American studies, creative writing, or women writers. Science offers inspiring applied science, geology, and environmental science courses and extracurricular programs in building an electric car and robotics. Mathematics courses go beyond two Advanced Placement calculus courses to offer statistics and AP statistics yearlong courses.

Class size varies from 8 to 20, and the average class has 15 students. The overall student-teacher ratio is 10:1. Study for boarding students is supervised by faculty members assigned to dormitories during the evenings.

Athenian offers intermediate and advanced English learning courses to students for whom English is not the first language. ESL students take part in the in the regular curriculum for subjects other than English and history. Field trips help familiarize international students with northern California and U.S. culture.

Opportunities for independent study are provided for selected students by the academic departments. Athenian students have access to unmatched international experiences. Student exchanges can be arranged either domestically or internationally. The Athenian School is a founding member of a notable consortium of international schools, The Round Square, which offers students academic exchanges, international community service opportunities, and participation in an annual international student conference. Class field trips in the San Francisco Bay Area are frequent. Students may also participate in off-campus internships oriented toward community service and career exploration. Qualified seniors may take advantage of an accelerated high school program arrangement at the University of California at Berkeley.

A distinctive element of the curriculum is the Athenian Wilderness Experience, required of all students in their junior year. AWE enhances self-confidence, communication skills, and perseverance in addition to fostering an appreciation of the environment.

FACULTY AND ADVISERS

There are 55 full-time and 15 part-time faculty members, 42 of whom hold advanced degrees. Twenty-five faculty members live on-campus with their families.

Eric Niles, Head since 2009, has graduated from the University of Pennsylvania, Wharton School of Economics, and UCLA Law School. Prior to his career in education, he served as counsel to a member of the House of Representatives. Beginning in 1995 he taught and served as Dean of Students at Midland School and then Emma Willard School, where he became Assistant Head in 2005. In 2009 the Athenian Board of Trustees and community selected Mr. Niles as Athenian's Head of School.

The Athenian School maintains an excellent faculty by seeking the most talented people in their respective fields, by encouraging teachers to continue their education, and by providing financial support for professional growth. Enthusiasm for teaching and teaching skills for this age group are qualities also sought in faculty members.

Faculty members perform dormitory supervision, take charge of activities several weekends a year, organize community service activities, and lead adventurous trips and activities during Interim period each spring. Each faculty member also acts as an adviser for 8 to 10 students.

COLLEGE ADMISSION COUNSELING

Two college counselors provide expert advice to students choosing colleges. College counseling starts in the junior year and includes sessions with each student and with parents, as well as preparation for the PSAT and SAT. Trips to campuses throughout the country are available. The Athenian School is visited by numerous college representatives each year.

The following is a representative list of the institutions to which graduates have been admitted: Amherst, Brown, Columbia, Cornell, Dartmouth, Duke, Evergreen State, Georgetown, Johns Hopkins, MIT, NYU, Occidental, Pomona, Princeton, Reed, Stanford, USC, Yale, and the Universities of California (all campuses), Chicago, and Pennsylvania.

STUDENT BODY AND CONDUCT

In 2013–14, there were 72 freshmen (33 boys and 39 girls), 82 sophomores (42 boys and 40 girls), 81 juniors (37 boys and 44 girls), and 76 seniors (41 boys and 35 girls). Of these 311 students, 41 (21 boys and 20 girls) were boarders and 270 (132 boys and 138 girls) were day students.

Eighty-nine percent of the students are from California, and 11 percent are international students from more than ten different countries. Forty-seven percent are members of ethnic minority groups.

Living as a community requires cooperation, social responsibility, and a sense of having a real influence on the quality of life and the decision-making process. A strong feeling of community promotes a good rapport between students and faculty members, and faculty members help students behave with respect toward themselves, others, and the school community.

The rules encourage high ethical standards and the ability to live with others harmoniously. The use of tobacco, alcohol, and illegal drugs is prohibited. Cheating and dishonesty of all kinds are also major rule violations. Infractions of these rules often result either in referral by the Dean of Students to the Student Discipline Committee or expulsion. Town Meeting is the student government of the School and provides a forum for the discussion of community issues and standards.

ACADEMIC FACILITIES

Academic facilities include classrooms; a science building with four labs; a library holding 16,000 print volumes, forty-three periodical subscriptions, and six electronic subscriptions; a Center for the Arts with gallery, black box theater, drawing and painting, sculpture and pottery, and a dance studio; a new music and multipurpose building, which houses large choral and instrumental rooms, an ensemble room, and two smaller practice rooms; several computer labs; and the improved and renamed Maker's Studio, a significant facility for applied science and robotics.

BOARDING AND GENERAL FACILITIES

There are three dormitories and sixteen faculty homes. A number of faculty members reside in apartments or town houses on campus.

Returning students in grades 11 and 12 generally choose single rooms. The Director of the Boarding Program and dormitory parents match the new and younger students with roommates for the double rooms. Ninth graders receive support and guidance from carefully selected seniors through this all-important transition. Supervision of each dorm at the School is the responsibility of a faculty dorm head, assisted by older students who act as proctors.

Students most often arrange to spend the two-week winter and spring vacations with nearby relatives or friends, if they do not travel back to their homes. If needed, the School assists international students in finding suitable homestays during shorter vacation periods. Some trips are also provided during vacations.

The Dyke Brown Main Hall contains the kitchen, dining area, and administrative offices. The Boarding Center provides a gathering place for resident students.

The School nurse visits the dorms each day and advises what action should be taken for any students reported ill. She is available for emergencies as well as drop-in visits during scheduled hours. The School counselor is also available as a resource if needed.

ATHLETICS

Physical education, interscholastic sport, or dance is required of all students.

Athenian teams compete with other schools in the North Bay Conference of the California Interscholastic Federation. The School fields interscholastic teams in thirteen sports. These are badminton, baseball (for boys), basketball, cross-country, golf, soccer, softball (for girls), swimming, tennis, track and field, volleyball, and wrestling.

There are also junior varsity teams in most of these sports. Athenian's teams have won league championships in a number of sports in recent years. Athenian also has sailing and equestrian teams. Its cross-country program ranks sixth in the state of California.

Noncompetitive activities include rock-climbing, hiking, skiing, bicycling, weight training, conditioning, and jazz dance.

Campus facilities include two gyms, nearby tennis courts, a 25-meter pool, a soccer field, and baseball and softball diamonds.

EXTRACURRICULAR OPPORTUNITIES

The School plans occasional trips to museums, plays, the opera, concerts, art exhibits, and lectures in the Bay Area. There are also skiing trips to the Sierra Nevada and excursions to spots on the coast.

On-campus activities include the School newspaper, debate, Interweave, yearbook, and Multicultural Alliance, among many others.

Community service is required of all students. Service projects include cross-country skiing with the visually handicapped, running the scholarship auction, helping at soup kitchens in San Francisco, working with disadvantaged children or the elderly, and working on environmental projects.

DAILY LIFE

A typical day begins with breakfast between 7:30 and 8. Day students arrive in time for classes, which begin at 8:10. A hot lunch prepared at the School is served at noon. Classes end at 2:40 and are followed by sports and performing arts. Dinner is at 6. Clubs, activities, School meetings, and study occupy a portion of each day.

Faculty-supervised evening study hours are from 7:30 to 9:30, when the dormitories are kept quiet. All boarding students are in their dorms by 10:30 p.m., Sunday through Thursday, and by midnight on Friday and Saturday.

WEEKEND LIFE

Weekend activities are arranged by faculty members on duty. They may include hikes on Mt. Diablo, visits to San Francisco and Berkeley, trips to the coast or the Sierra, and an attendance of the Oregon Shakespeare Festival. Boarding students may spend weekends off campus with permission from the Dean of Students and their parents.

Day students are encouraged to participate in all activities available to boarding students and to spend the night on campus from time to time. An outdoor education program is available throughout the year.

COSTS AND FINANCIAL AID

Tuition for 2013–14 is $33,516 for day students and $53,650 for boarding students. Additional expenditures are estimated at $1,000. They include such expenses as books and athletic uniforms. Tuition insurance and a tuition payment plan are available.

Financial aid is based on need; eligibility is determined by the School and Student Service for Financial Aid. For 2013–14, scholarship aid of over $2.1 million was awarded to 90 students.

ADMISSIONS INFORMATION

Admission seeks talent, fit, and diversity in the student body. Athenian seeks students who will prosper in an informal, caring environment, want a rigorous academic course of studies, support Athenian's mission, and will contribute to the on-campus community. Admission is selective and based upon the applicant's intellectual ability, academic achievement, character, motivation, creativity, talents, and interests. The School seeks a student body that includes a diversity of geographical, economic, cultural, and ethnic backgrounds.

Each applicant must submit an application, including transcripts and recommendations, have a personal interview, and take an entrance examination, the ISEE, or the SSAT. ESL candidates must take the TOEFL, IELTS, or SLEP.

Priority is given to ninth graders and then to tenth graders. Admission is granted to a smaller number of eleventh graders and occasionally to a twelfth grader.

APPLICATION TIMETABLE

Initial inquiries should be made in the fall of the year preceding anticipated entrance. The School catalog and application forms are available from the Admission Office upon request. Campus visits and interviews may be arranged at any time during the academic year on weekdays between 8:30 and 3. The application deadline is January 15, and notification of admission is given no later than March 19. After this date, applications may still be received and reviewed until all places are filled.

ADMISSIONS CORRESPONDENCE

Christopher Beeson, Director of Admission
The Athenian School
2100 Mt. Diablo Scenic Boulevard
Danville, California 94506
United States
Phone: 925-362-7223
Fax: 925-362-7228
E-mail: admission@athenian.org
Website: http://www.athenian.org

BERKELEY PREPARATORY SCHOOL

Tampa, Florida

Type: Coeducational independent college-preparatory day school
Grades: PK–12: Lower Division, prekindergarten–5; Middle Division, 6–8; Upper Division, 9–12
Enrollment: School total: 1,300; Lower Division: 400; Middle Division: 325; Upper Division: 575
Head of School: Joseph W. Seivold, Headmaster

THE SCHOOL

The Latin words *Disciplina, Diligentia,* and *Integritas* in Berkeley's motto describe the school's mission to nurture students' intellectual, emotional, spiritual and physical development so they can achieve their highest human potential. Episcopal in heritage, Berkeley was founded in 1960 and opened for grades 7–12 the following year. Kindergarten through grade 6 was added in 1967, and prekindergarten began in 1988. Berkeley's purpose is to enable its students to achieve academic excellence in preparation for higher education and to instill in students a strong sense of morality, ethics, and social responsibility.

Berkeley is located on an 80-acre campus in Tampa, Florida, a location that attracts students from Hillsborough, Pinellas, Pasco, Polk, and Hernando Counties and throughout the greater Tampa Bay area. Private bus transportation is available.

Berkeley is incorporated as a nonprofit institution and is governed by a 27-member Board of Trustees that includes alumni, parents of current students, and parents of alumni. The presidents of the Alumni Association and Parents' Club are also members of the Board.

ACADEMIC PROGRAM

The school year runs from the end of August to the first week of June and includes Thanksgiving, Christmas, and spring vacations. The curriculum naturally varies within each division.

In the Lower Division, the program seeks to provide appropriate, challenging learning experiences in a safe environment that reflects the academic, social, moral, and ethical values the school espouses in its philosophy. Curricular emphasis is on core subjects of reading and mathematics. An interdisciplinary approach is used in world language and social studies, and manipulatives are used extensively in the science and mathematics programs. Each student also receives instruction in library skills and integration of technology and learning.

Academic requirements in the Middle Division, where classes average 16 to 20 students, are English, English expression, mathematics, global studies, world language, science, technology, physical education, art, drama, and music. All students in grades 6 and 7 take Latin and their choice of French, Spanish, or Chinese. Continuing grade 8 students have the option of Latin, French, Spanish, or Chinese. Classes meet five days a week on a rotating schedule. Extra help is available from teachers, and grades are sent to parents four times a year.

The Upper Division program, with an average class size of 15 to 20 students, requires students to take four or five credit courses a year, in addition to fine arts and physical education requirements. To graduate, a student must complete 23 credits, including 4 in English, 4 in mathematics, and 3 in history, science, and foreign language. Students must also complete one year of personal fitness/health and an additional year of physical education, two years of fine arts, and two electives. In addition, Berkeley students are required to take a semester of religious studies each year and complete 76 hours of community service. More than twenty Advanced Placement courses are offered. The Upper Division program is designed to provide students with the atmosphere and advantages of a small liberal arts college. Students are offered a choice of more than forty student activities and clubs, and they may be selected to join several nationally recognized academic honor groups, including the Cum Laude Society and National Honor Society.

FACULTY AND ADVISERS

There are more than 250 full-time faculty members and administrators. They hold baccalaureate, more than 100 graduate, and several doctoral degrees. Headmaster Seivold graduated Phi Beta Kappa from the University of North Carolina at Chapel Hill with a degree in history. He holds a master's degree in education administration from St. Mary's University of Minnesota. He came to Berkeley from The Blake School in Minnesota.

In addition to teaching responsibilities, faculty members are involved in Berkeley's co-curricular programs as coaches and student activity advisers. In the Upper Division, 3 teach part-time and serve as academic grade advisers for students in grades 9 and 10, and 3 full-time college counselors assist students in grades 11 and 12 with academic advising and the college process. Berkeley faculty members receive support for professional development opportunities and several faculty members have been recognized as some of the top teachers among their peers nationally.

COLLEGE ADMISSION COUNSELING

Traditionally, Berkeley's entire graduating class goes on to attend college. Although Berkeley does not rank its students, more than 125 colleges visit the School each year to recruit its graduates. The average SAT score for the class of 2013 was 1245 (1870). Berkeley's college counseling department works to assist students and their families

in selecting colleges that best suit their academic, financial, and social needs.

Recent graduates are attending Boston College, Brown, Cornell, Dartmouth, Duke, Emory, Georgetown, Harvard, Northwestern, Notre Dame, NYU, Princeton, Stanford, Vanderbilt, Villanova, Yale, and the Universities of Florida, Miami, Michigan, North Carolina, Pennsylvania, and Virginia. Scholarship offers totaling more than $9 million were made to the class of 2013.

STUDENT BODY AND CONDUCT

In all divisions, Berkeley students are expected to maintain high standards. Mature conduct and use of manners are expected, and an honor code outlines students' responsibilities. In exchange, students are entrusted with certain privileges, such as direct access to the administration and the opportunity to initiate School-sponsored clubs. Students wear uniforms to class.

CAMPUS FACILITIES

The 80-acre campus is located in Town 'n' Country, a suburb of Tampa. The campus consists of classrooms; a fine arts wing; a science wing; two libraries; technology labs; general convocation rooms; physical education fields; a 19,000-square-foot student center; the 425-seat Berkeley Café; a prekindergarten wing; and administrative offices for the Lower, Middle, and Upper Divisions.

The fine arts program is enhanced by the Lykes Center for the Arts, a 634-seat performing arts center, which also includes a gallery for visual arts displays, a flex studio for dance and small drama productions, dressing rooms, and an orchestra pit.

ATHLETICS

Varsity sports for boys include baseball, basketball, crew, cross-country, diving, football, golf, lacrosse, soccer, hockey, swimming, tennis, track, and wrestling. Girls compete in basketball, crew, cross-country, diving, golf, lacrosse, soccer, softball, swimming, tennis, track, and volleyball. Berkeley has been recognized as the Florida High School Athletic Association's overall 4A state academic champion for three consecutive years and has several individual and team champions.

Berkeley's athletic facilities include the new 53,000 square-foot Straz Family Field House; two gymnasiums; a junior Olympic swimming pool; a wrestling/gymnastics room; a weight room; a rock-climbing wall; a varsity level soccer field; a tennis complex; a high- and low-ropes course; a baseball and softball complex; a state-of-the-art track, a stadium; and practice fields for football, soccer, and lacrosse. Seasonal sports award banquets and a homecoming football game are scheduled annually.

EXTRACURRICULAR OPPORTUNITIES

In addition to its broad-based commitment to student organizations and clubs and its community service requirements, Berkeley offers its students a vast array of possibilities beyond the classrooms. Student artwork is accepted each year into the prestigious Scarfone Gallery Art Show, and several students receive gold key awards each year from the Alliance for Young Artists and Writers. An after-school Lower Division chess club attracts close to 100 students from kindergarten through grade 5. Middle and Upper Division students, as well as many faculty members, participate in several international experiences, visiting countries such as England, New Zealand, the Dominican Republic, Ghana, Australia, China, France, Italy, Switzerland, and Spain.

DAILY LIFE

Students in prekindergarten through grade 5 attend classes from 8 to 3:10. Middle and Upper Division students also begin at 8 and end at 3:20. Teachers are available to assist students and offer extra help during activity periods, which are scheduled into each class day. Supervised study halls are also scheduled for some students.

SUMMER PROGRAMS

A six-week summer academic program for prekindergarten through grade 12 students is offered. More information is available online at www.berkeleyprep.org/summer.

COSTS AND FINANCIAL AID

The tuition schedule for 2013–14 is as follows: $16,860 for prekindergarten and kindergarten, $17,260 for grades 1–5, $19,140 for grades 6–8, and $20,550 for grades 9–12. Tuition is payable in eight installments and must be paid in full by January 1. Tuition payments do not cover costs of uniforms, laptops, supplies, transportation, special event admission fees, or other expenses incurred in the ordinary course of student activities at Berkeley.

Berkeley makes all admission decisions without regard to financial status. Families who have reviewed their financial situation and feel that help may be needed in paying tuition should apply for aid. Financial aid awards are available at any grade level to students who demonstrate need. In determining need, the guidelines of the School and Student Service for Financial Aid (SSS) are used. Each award is individualized based upon the financial assessment of each applicant. It is important to note that Berkeley may not be able to accommodate all financial aid applications in a given year.

Berkeley is also fortunate to have a number of scholarships available to students. In addition to demonstrated financial need, specific criteria such as academic achievement and leadership potential are also components of a separate scholarship application process. Receiving a scholarship is a great honor; therefore, the process is both competitive and selective. A selection committee will review the completed applications and announce the scholarship recipients in early March.

ADMISSIONS INFORMATION

In considering applicants, Berkeley evaluates a student's talent, academic skills, personal interests, motivation to learn, and desire to attend. Special consideration is given to qualified applicants who are children of faculty members or alumni or who have siblings currently attending Berkeley.

Lower Division candidates visit age-appropriate classrooms and are evaluated through grade level assessments. Middle and Upper Division candidates are required to take the Secondary School Admissions Test (SSAT) and generally register for a November, December, or January test date. In addition to the SSAT, all applicants schedule an appointment with the Admissions Office for Otis-Lennon testing and a writing sample. Entering juniors and seniors may submit PSAT, SAT, PLAN, or ACT scores in place of sitting for the SSAT.

The admission process is selective and is based on information gathered from the application form, interviews, the candidate's record, admission tests, and teacher recommendations.

Berkeley admits students of any race, color, sex, religion, and national or ethnic origin and does not discriminate on the basis of any category protected by law in the administration of its educational policies; admission policies; and scholarship, financial aid, athletic, and other school-administered programs.

APPLICATION TIMETABLE

Applications should be submitted by the fall one year prior to the student's entrance into Berkeley. The Lower and Upper Division Admissions Committees begin evaluation of applicants in mid-February and decisions are made in March. The Middle Division Admissions Committee begins evaluation of completed files in mid-January with notification on a rolling basis from the end of January until vacancies are filled. All applications after the initial selection process are considered on a space-available basis.

Berkeley welcomes inquiries from families throughout the year. However, because of the competitive nature of the admission process, families are encouraged to visit the campus as early as possible to become familiar with the School, its programs, and its admission procedure.

ADMISSIONS CORRESPONDENCE

Janie McIlvaine
Director of Admissions
Berkeley Preparatory School
4811 Kelly Road
Tampa, Florida 33615
United States
Phone: 813-885-1673
Fax: 813-886-6933
E-mail: mcilvjan@berkeleyprep.org
Website: www.berkeleyprep.org/admissions

BERKSHIRE SCHOOL

Sheffield, Massachusetts

Type: Coeducational boarding and day college-preparatory school
Grades: 9–12 (Forms III–VI), postgraduate year
Enrollment: 391
Interim Head of School: Pieter Mulder

THE SCHOOL

Berkshire School is a coed, college preparatory boarding and day school that prepares 391 ninth through twelfth graders and postgraduates for a global future. Pioneering programs—such as Advanced Math/Science Research, Advanced Humanities Research, and Sustainability and Resource Management—coexist with advanced sections and AP offerings in all disciplines. With a range of artistic and athletic offerings; a new, state-of-the-art math and science center; a 117,000-square-foot athletic facility; an 8-acre solar field providing 38 percent of the School's energy needs; and national recognition for its efforts in environmental conservation, Berkshire School is an extraordinary setting in which students are encouraged to embrace the school motto: *Pro Vita Non Pro Schola Discimus,* "Learning—not just for school, but for life."

In 1907, Mr. and Mrs. Seaver B. Buck, graduates of Harvard and Smith respectively, rented the building of Glenny Farm at the foot of Mt. Everett and founded Berkshire School. For thirty-five years, the Bucks devoted themselves to educating young men to the values of academic excellence, physical vigor, and high personal standards. In 1969, this commitment to excellence was extended to include girls.

Situated at the base of Mt. Everett, the second-highest mountain in Massachusetts, Berkshire's campus spans 400 acres. It is a 75-minute drive to both Albany International Airport and Hartford's Bradley International Airport and just over 2 hours from Boston and New York City.

Berkshire School is incorporated as a not-for-profit institution, governed by a 30-member self-perpetuating Board of Trustees. The School has a $112-million endowment. Annual operating expenses exceed $21 million. Annual Giving in 2012–13 exceeded $2.5 million. The Berkshire Chapter of the Cum Laude Society was established in 1942.

Berkshire School is accredited by the New England Association of Schools and Colleges and holds memberships in the Independent School Association of Massachusetts, the National Association of Independent Schools, the College Entrance Examination Board, the National Association for College Admission Counseling, the Secondary School Admission Test Board, and the Association of Boarding Schools.

ACADEMIC PROGRAM

Berkshire's academic program is firmly rooted in a college-preparatory curriculum that features advanced and AP courses across all disciplines. In addition, unique opportunities to excel in math/science research, student-directed independent study, and electives in science, history, and fine arts allow students to pursue advanced study at Berkshire. As creative and agile problem solvers, strong critical thinkers, persuasive communicators, and active global citizens, Berkshire's students are equipped with the skills required to excel in the twenty-first century. The School's balance between academic rigor and possibility allows students to flourish as independent learners, community members, and professionals.

Believing that the best preparation for college is the acquisition of knowledge from a variety of disciplines, Berkshire requires the

following credits: 4 years of English; 3 years each of mathematics, a foreign language, and history; 2 years of science; and 1 year of the visual or performing arts. All departments provide for accelerated sections, and students are placed at a level commensurate with their skills and talent. Many students take one or more of the sixteen Advanced Placement courses offered.

Most students carry five courses. The average number of students in a class is 12, and the student-teacher ratio is 5:1. The academic year is divided into two semesters, each culminating with an assessment period. Students receive grades, teacher comments, and adviser letters twice each semester. Berkshire uses a traditional letter-grading system of A–F (D is passing).

In 2007, Berkshire introduced its Advanced Math/Science Research course in which students use the strong foundation of knowledge acquired in the regular Berkshire curriculum as a springboard for beyond-the-curriculum projects in areas of cutting-edge research and other fields. Students intern with a professional scientist to conduct research in facilities located in the nearby Hartford, Connecticut and Albany, New York areas. Students work closely with their mentor in the field of their choice for 4 to 8 hours a week. The course culminates with a critical review paper and a research paper, both in scientific format.

FACULTY AND ADVISERS

The Berkshire teaching faculty numbers 65, and 88 including nonteaching faculty. Forty-four teachers hold a master's degree and 8 hold doctorates. Faculty members contribute to both the academic and personal development of each student. The small size of the Berkshire community permits faculty members to become involved in students' lives outside, as well as inside, the classroom. Each student is paired with a faculty adviser who provides guidance, monitors academic progress, and serves as a liaison with the student's family. Berkshire also retains the services of 4 pediatricians, a nurse practitioner, 4 registered nurses, and 2 certified athletic trainers.

Pieter M. Mulder was named Berkshire's interim head of school in the spring of 2013. He holds a bachelor's degree in American studies from Williams College with minors in architecture and environmental science, and a master's degree in mathematics with a concentration in creative writing from Wesleyan University. Mr. Mulder is in his ninth year at Berkshire. He lives on campus with his wife, Lucia, and their two children.

COLLEGE ADMISSION COUNSELING

College counseling at Berkshire . is the responsibility of 5 professionals who assist students and their parents in the search for an appropriate college or university. The formal process begins in the Fifth Form, with individual conferences with the college counselors, and the opportunity to meet with some of the approximately 100 college admissions representatives who visit the campus. In February, Fifth Formers and their parents attend a two-day seminar on the college admission process. Admission strategies are discussed and specific institutions are identified for each student's consideration. During the summer, students are encouraged to visit

colleges and write the first draft of their college application essay. The application process is generally completed by winter vacation in the Sixth Form year.

Members of the classes of 2011–2013 enrolled at a variety of four-year colleges or universities, including Amherst, Bard, Bates, Berkeley, Boston College, Boston University, Bowdoin, Brown, Bucknell, Caltech, Carnegie Mellon, Colby, Colgate, Colorado College, Columbia, Cornell, Dartmouth, Denison, Dickinson, Elon, Emory, Franklin & Marshall, Hamilton, Harvard, Johns Hopkins, Kenyon, Lehigh, Middlebury, MIT, NYU, Northeastern, Northwestern, Princeton, SMU, St. Lawrence, Syracuse, Union, USC, Vanderbilt, Villanova, West Point, Whitman, Williams, Yale, and the Universities of Connecticut, Massachusetts, Michigan, Pennsylvania, Vermont, and Wisconsin.

STUDENT BODY AND CONDUCT

In the 2013–14 academic year, there are 353 boarders and 38 day students. The student body is drawn from thirty-two states and twenty-eight countries.

Students contribute directly to the life of the school community through involvement in the Student Government, the Prefect Program, dormitory life, and various clubs and activities. Participation gives students a positive growth experience in keeping with the School's motto, *Pro Vita Non Pro Schola Discimus,* "Learning—not just for school, but for life." The rules at Berkshire are simple and straightforward and are consistent with the values and ideals of the School. They are designed to help students live orderly lives within an environment of mutual trust and respect.

ACADEMIC FACILITIES

Berkshire Hall, the primary academic facility built in 1930 and the centerpiece of the campus, reopened in the fall of 2008 after a full renovation. It now features larger classrooms with state-of-the-art technology, new administrative offices, a two-story atrium, and a Great Room for student study and special functions. A new music center opened in the fall of 2010, featuring two specially designed classrooms to meet the needs of the instrumental, choral, and chamber music programs. The center has five practice rooms, plenty of spacious storage cabinets for instruments, a recording studio, and storage and office space for the music program. A new dance studio also opened in the fall of 2010 as part of the existing gymnasium. In 2009, the School opened its Center for Writing and Critical Thinking, which is home to a nightly writing tutoring program. The center also hosts faculty forums and guest speakers.

In the fall of 2011, Allen Theater reopened after a complete renovation. The Allen renovation also included new academic spaces for the Kenefick Center for Learning, new classrooms for the theater and film department and the SAT tutoring program, and a new studio for WBSL, the School's own radio station.

In October 2012, Berkshire inaugurated the state-of-the-art Bellas/Dixon Math and Science Center. This new, 48,000-square-foot building provides students and teachers with facilities that will allow them to pursue academic excellence and innovation at the highest level while adhering to the School's commitment to sustainability. The 2013 school year saw the opening of the School's new fine arts center, which includes a new gallery, department offices, and new classrooms for studio and digital art and ceramics.

The Geier Library contains approximately 43,000 volumes in open stacks, an extensive reference collection in both print and electronic format, numerous periodicals, and a fine audiovisual collection. The library has wireless Internet access, as well as twenty computers with Internet access and an online card catalog for student use. ProQuest Direct, the Expanded Academic Index ASAP, the *New York Times* full text (1994 to present), and the current ninety days' full text of 150 Northeastern newspapers, including the *Wall Street Journal* online, keep the library fully up-to-date on breaking information. In addition, in 2011 the Library acquired access to JSTOR, an online database of more than 1,000 academic journals, containing literally millions of peer-reviewed articles, images, reviews, and primary sources.

At the Dixon Observatory, computer-synchronized telescopes make it possible to view and photograph objects in the solar system and beyond. Given the combination of equipment, software, and location, Berkshire's observatory is among the best in New England.

BOARDING AND GENERAL FACILITIES

Berkshire has ten residential houses, including two girls' dormitories that were completed in the fall of 2002. Three faculty families generally reside in each house along with a prefect—Sixth Formers whose primary responsibility is to assist dorm parents with daily routines, such as study hall and room inspection. Dorm rooms all have Internet access and private phone lines. There is a common room in each house, where students may relax or study. Benson Commons, the school center, features a dining hall, a post office, the School bookstore, the Music Center, the Student Life Office, and recreational spaces. In 2011 an 8-acre solar field was built on campus and it now provides up to 38 percent of the School's electricity needs.

ATHLETICS

Berkshire enjoys a proud tradition of athletic excellence. The School provides competition in twenty-seven interscholastic sports, including baseball, basketball, crew, cross-country running, field hockey, football, golf, ice hockey, lacrosse, mountain biking, skiing, soccer, softball, squash, tennis, track and field, and volleyball. Students may also participate in the Ritt Kellogg Mountain Program, a program that utilizes Berkshire's natural environment and its proximity to the Appalachian Trail to present athletic challenges, teach leadership, and foster environmental responsibility.

In January 2009, the 117,000-square-foot Jackman L. Stewart Athletic Center opened. The facility offers two ice rinks (one Olympic-size), fourteen locker rooms, seating for 800 spectators, a 34-machine fitness center and athletic training rooms. It can also be used for indoor tennis and can accommodate all-school functions. A second athletic center features full-size courts for basketball and volleyball, four international squash courts, a climbing wall, and a dance studio. Other facilities include the new Thomas H. Young Field for baseball,

softball fields, an all-weather track, a lighted football field, and two synthetic-turf fields. A twelve-court tennis facility was completed in the fall of 2010.

EXTRACURRICULAR OPPORTUNITIES

Berkshire offers students a variety of opportunities to express their talents and passions. Students publish a newspaper, a yearbook, and a literary magazine that features student writing, art, and photography. The Ritt Kellogg Mountain Program offers backcountry skills, boatbuilding, fly fishing, hiking, kayaking, rock climbing, and winter mountaineering.

There are a number of active clubs, including the Drama Club, the International Club, the Investment Club, the Maple Syrup Program, the Philanthropy Society, and a Student Activities Committee.

Berkshire's student-run FM radio station, WBSL, operates with a power of 250 watts and is capable of reaching 10,000 listeners. Berkshire is one of the few secondary schools to hold membership in the Intercollegiate Broadcasting System and the only one affiliated with both the Associated Press wire service and its radio service.

Berkshire students pursue the arts in the classroom and in extracurricular activities. The theater program offers two plays in the fall and spring as well as a winter musical. There are three choral groups: Ursa Major, an all-school chorus; Ursa Minor, a girls' a cappella group; and Greensleeves, an all-male chorus. There are two music groups: a jazz band and a chamber music ensemble. Students can also take private voice and instrumental lessons. Each season the Berkshire community looks forward to various performances, such as dance and music recitals, a jazz café, and poetry readings. Visual arts include painting, drawing, sculpture, digital art, photography, and ceramics. Students display their work in galleries in the Student Center and in Berkshire Hall.

DAILY LIFE

The first of the six class periods in a school day begins at 8 a.m., and the final class concludes at 2:45 p.m., except on Wednesday and Saturday, when the last class ends by 11:35 a.m. Berkshire follows a rotating schedule in which classes meet at different times each day.

Athletics, outdoor experiences, and art activities occupy the afternoon. Clubs often meet after dinner, before the 2-hour supervised study period that begins at 8 p.m.

WEEKEND LIFE

Weekend activities are planned by a Director of Student Activities and include first-run movies, dances with live bands, and other dances hosted by DJs. There are trips to local amusement parks and theaters as well as shopping trips to Hartford and Albany. In addition, students and faculty members journey to New York and Boston to visit museums, attend theater and music productions, or take in professional sports events.

COSTS AND FINANCIAL AID

For the 2013–14 academic year, tuition is $52,150 for boarding students and $42,150 for

day students. For most students, $100 a month is sufficient personal spending money. Ten percent of the tuition is paid upon enrollment, 50 percent is payable on July 1, and 40 percent is payable on November 30. Various tuition payment plans are available.

Financial aid is awarded on the basis of need to about 30 percent of the student body. The total financial aid spent in 2013–14 was $4.4 million. The School and Student Service (SSS) Parents Financial Statement and a 1040 form are required.

ADMISSIONS INFORMATION

Berkshire adheres to the principle that in diversity there is strength and therefore, actively seeks students from a broad range of geographic, ethnic, religious, and socioeconomic backgrounds. Admission is most common in the Third and Fourth Forms, and the School enrolls a small number of Fifth Formers and postgraduates each year.

In order to assess the student's academic record, potential, character, and contributions to his or her school, Berkshire requires a personal interview, a transcript, test scores, and recommendations from English and mathematics teachers, along with the actual application. Candidates should have their Secondary School Admission Test (SSAT) scores forwarded to Berkshire School (school code 1612). International students are required to have their Test of English as a Foreign Language (TOEFL) scores forwarded in addition to their SSAT (school code 3252).

APPLICATION TIMETABLE

Interested families are encouraged to visit the campus in the fall or winter preceding the September in which admission is desired. Visits are arranged according to the academic schedule, Monday, Tuesday, Thursday, and Friday, from 8 a.m. to 2 p.m. and Wednesday and Saturday from 8 to 10:45 a.m. January 15 is the deadline for submitting applications; late applications are accepted as long as space is anticipated. Berkshire adheres to the standard notification date of March 10 and the families' reply date of April 10. Depending on availability, late applications are processed on a rolling basis. Applications to Berkshire School can be submitted using Gateway to Prep Schools and SSAT.

ADMISSIONS CORRESPONDENCE

Andrew Bogardus, Director of Admission
Berkshire School
245 North Undermountain Road
Sheffield, Massachusetts 01257
United States
Phone: 413-229-1003
Fax: 413-229-1016
E-mail: admission@berkshireschool.org
Website: http://www.berkshireschool.org

THE BOLLES SCHOOL

Jacksonville, Florida

THE
BOLLES™
SCHOOL
ALL THINGS POSSIBLE

Type: Coeducational boarding (7–12) and day (PK–12) college-preparatory school
Grades: PK–12: Lower Schools, PK–5; Middle School, 6–8; Upper School, 9–12
Enrollment: School total: 1,648; Lower Schools, 462; Middle School, 405; Upper School, 781
Head of School: Bradley R. Johnson, President and Head of School

THE SCHOOL

Bolles offers a comprehensive college-preparatory program. Bolles prepares students for the future by offering them an education that challenges and guides them in the belief that all things are possible. Moral development is encouraged by an emphasis on respect for self and others, volunteerism, and personal responsibility.

Bolles has served as the educational inspiration for three generations, with a strong and unshakable commitment to providing the finest preparatory education possible for each student. Located in Jacksonville, Florida, Bolles was founded in 1933 as an all-boys military school on the San Jose Campus. In 1962, the School dropped its military status; in 1971, it began admitting girls.

In 1981, the Lower School Whitehurst Campus for grades K–5 was begun. A separate campus for middle school students in grades 6–8 was achieved in 1991 with the acquisition of Bartram School, an independent girls' school operating since 1934 and now known as the Bolles Middle School Bartram Campus. In 1998, the Bolles Lower School Ponte Vedra Beach Campus opened its doors to serve students in pre-kindergarten through grade 5.

Today, with nearly 1,700 students on four campuses, Bolles is recognized as one of the finest college-preparatory institutions in the nation. All of its students are college-bound. Bolles students consistently place in the top 10 percent of Advanced Placement scores from throughout the country. The School prepares students for the future by providing them with a variety of activities and a myriad of challenges that promote growth and development in four primary areas: academics, arts, activities, and athletics. Students learn to make decisions and budget time by balancing homework, sports, extracurricular, family, and community service responsibilities.

Students from all walks of life, cultures, religions, and races learn together at Bolles, a microcosm of the world that they will inherit. The School's excellent academic and athletic offerings attracted students from twenty-three countries and eleven states to participate in the resident program for the 2012–13 school year. This blend of cultures and interests sets Bolles apart from other independent college-preparatory institutions in the Southeast and fosters a level of mutual respect that is crucial in learning how to meet global challenges.

The School's locations are in suburban neighborhoods. The Upper School San Jose Campus and the Lower School Whitehurst Campus occupy 52 acres on the St. Johns River. Five miles to the northeast, the Middle School Bartram Campus is set on 23 acres. The Bolles Lower School Ponte Vedra Beach Campus is located on 12 acres in Ponte Vedra Beach, east of Jacksonville.

Jacksonville, a major metropolitan area in northeast Florida, is home to the Jaguars National Football League team and many cultural associations, such as the Jacksonville Symphony, the Florida Ballet, several professional theater companies, three major museums, the Jacksonville Zoo, and several professional sports teams. Downtown Jacksonville is located approximately 35 minutes from the Jacksonville Beach area, which includes Ponte Vedra Beach, and about an hour from St. Augustine, the oldest city in the United States.

A not-for-profit institution, Bolles is governed by a self-perpetuating board of 32 trustees. The School also works with a 37-member Board of Visitors and an Alumni Board that represents more than 8,300 living graduates.

The School's operating budget is more than $30 million. The annual giving goal for 2012–13 was $1.35 million, which included more than $900,000 in unrestricted funds. The School's endowment is more than $11.6 million.

The School is accredited by the Southern Association of Colleges and Schools and the Florida Council of Independent Schools and holds membership in the National Association of Independent Schools, the Council for Spiritual and Ethical Education, the Secondary School Admission Test Board, and the Southeastern Association of Boarding Schools.

ACADEMIC PROGRAM

The Middle School curriculum includes English, government, world cultures, world geography, U.S. history, mathematics through algebra, and science, and world languages. Students may select from a varied fine and performing arts program and may choose among band, chorus, drama, dance, graphics, drawing and painting, ceramics and sculpture, and computer elective. Each student has an adviser, and a full-time, on-campus guidance counselor assists with decision-making skills, peer relations, and alcohol- and drug-abuse awareness.

Upper School students must earn 22 credits for graduation, with a college-certifying grade of at least C-. Specific requirements are 4 years of English; 2 of a single foreign language; 3 of social studies, including U.S. and world history; 3 of mathematics through algebra II; 3 of science, including biology and chemistry; 2 of physical education; 1 of fine arts; ½ year of life management skills; and 3½ years of additional electives. The average class size is 15 students.

Among the full-year courses are English, French, Latin, Spanish, Japanese, Chinese, world and U.S. history, algebra, geometry, pre-calculus, physical science, biology, chemistry, marine science, environmental science, band, introduction to dance, intermediate dance, upper-level dance, AP drawing, AP portfolio 2-D, AP portfolio 3-D, advanced acting, portfolio development honors, men's chorus, women's chorus, concert choir, and symphonic band. There are honors sections in English, geometry, algebra, biology, chemistry, physics, neurobiology, languages, and social studies. Courses designed to prepare students for Advanced Placement examinations are available in English, U.S. and European history, American and comparative government, languages (French, Latin, Spanish, and Chinese), calculus, computer science, statistics, biology, chemistry, physics, computer science, statistics, portfolio art, and art history. A postgraduate program is available to students seeking an additional year of academics prior to entering college.

Students choose from such semester electives as composition, Latin American history, Middle Eastern history, art history, humanities, economics, human anatomy, neuroscience, psychology, mythology, foundations of studio art, drawing and painting, ceramics and sculpture, creative writing, acting, directing, production, public speaking, computer or multimedia applications, robotics, statistics, algebra III, and trigonometry.

The school offers an English as a second language curriculum to students in grades 7–12 for those students whose level of proficiency indicates this need.

Opportunities for off-campus projects sponsored directly by the School include the Outdoor Academy and French, Spanish, Japanese, and Chinese exchange programs as well as a study-abroad experience to Spain.

Grades, with narrative reports from faculty advisers, are sent to parents twice each quarter.

FACULTY AND ADVISERS

Bradley R. Johnson was appointed President and Head of School in 2013. A 1979 graduate of The Bolles School, Johnson received a B.A. in economics and B.A. in psychology cum laude from Duke University and graduated with honors from the University of Florida College of Law. Johnson is board-certified in civil trial law by the Florida Bar and has practiced with some of Jacksonville's most venerable firms during his 26-year legal carer, most recently as a partner in the firm Taylor, Day, Grimm, Boyd, & Johnson. A longtime member of the Bolles community as both a volunteer and parent of triplets, Johnson demonstrates the School's motto "Pursing excellence through courage, integrity, and compassion" with his unwavering commitment to the School.

Bolles has 147 full-time faculty members; there are 68 professional staff members who hold master's degrees and 11 who hold doctorates.

Each student in the Middle and Upper Schools is assigned to a faculty member, whose primary responsibility is to serve as an adviser. A minimal class load makes the adviser readily accessible to both students and parents. The School maintains an Office of Student Counseling to assist students in addressing issues that fall outside the traditional categories of academic advising.

COLLEGE ADMISSION COUNSELING

The aim of the college counseling program is to help students and their families to find college options and ultimately to find the most appropriate college choice. At the start of the second semester of the junior year, a daylong meeting is held to begin the more structured aspect of the process, and each student is assigned a college-placement adviser. An evening parent meeting provides additional information. The Williams Guidance Center offers a full range of up-to-date college reference materials, which include catalogs, videotapes, and computer search programs. In addition, approximately 100 college representatives visit the campus each year to meet with students, counselors, and parents.

In each of the past five years, 98 percent of graduates have attended four-year colleges and universities. A small number of students defer admission, and a small percentage attend two-year schools.

The middle 50 percent of scores for the last three graduating classes on the SAT Reasoning Test are 1080–1320 on a 1600 scale. The middle 50 percent of ACT scores are 23–29. Teachers in English and mathematics classes work with students in preparation for college admission testing.

STUDENT BODY AND CONDUCT

The Upper School numbers 787 students, with between 190 and 200 students in each grade. There are 91 boarding students.

There is an Honor Code and a Values Statement, and the Honor Council of Upper School students administers the Code and serves as the judiciary court for infractions against the Code. The Student Council is very active and serves as a proactive body for legislation of student privileges, organizes activities, and offers advice to the Upper School administration.

ACADEMIC FACILITIES

On the Upper School San Jose Campus, Bolles Hall houses classrooms, boys' dormitory rooms, a dining room and kitchen, offices, and three meeting rooms. Other academic buildings are Clifford G. Schultz Hall, with seventeen classrooms; the Michael Marco Science Center, which houses three science labs; the Joan W. and Martin E. Stein Computer Laboratory; the Hirsig Life Science Center; Ulmer Hall, which includes fifteen classrooms, a language lab, and two science labs; and a marine science classroom along the St. Johns River. In 2012 the traffic flow and parking areas were completely restructured and paved, and iron security gates were added to the entrance.

The Swisher Library houses the Meadow Multimedia Center, with a large-screen television, two satellite dishes, and computer labs. Other facilities include the McGehee Auditorium, which seats more than 600, and the Cindy and Jay Stein Fine Arts Center, which contains the Independent Life Music Building, the Lucy B. Gooding Art Gallery, and the Lynch Theater.

Middle School academic facilities include Murchison-Lane Hall for classrooms and administrative offices, the Art Barn, a marine science classroom along Pottsburg Creek, girls' dormitory rooms, the Pratt Library, and the Betsy Lovett Arts Center, which opened in 2007.

The Lower School Whitehurst Campus houses each grade separately in homelike classrooms set around a natural playground. The Lower School Ponte Vedra Beach Campus is a modern campus that includes an administration/classroom facility as well as the McLauchlan-Evans Building, housing classrooms, and the River Branch Building, which is the location of both the Ullmann Family Art Room and the Loeb-Lovett Family Music Room. In 2012 an area below the main building was completely renovated and is now a cafetorium with a large open space. This building also houses a new campus store.

BOARDING AND GENERAL FACILITIES

All boarding students are housed in rooms that accommodate 2 students. Boys and girls reside on separate campuses. Students are assigned roommates based upon age and interests.

Upper School athletic facilities include Collins Stadium at the Donovan Baseball Field, Hodges Field, the Bent Tennis Complex, the Baker-Gate Petroleum Company Track Facility, and Skinner-Barco Stadium. The Davis Sports Complex includes the Huston Student Center, basketball and volleyball courts, the 25-yard Lobrano and 50-meter Uible swimming pools, the Cassidy Aquatic Fitness Center, and the Garces Diving Facility. The Agnes Cain Gymnasium features

a wrestling room and athletic offices. The newly constructed Peyton Boathouse and Rice Family Crew Complex, and the Bent Student Center are proud additions to the San Jose Campus.

Among the Middle School athletic facilities are a football and soccer field, the Conroy Athletic Center, and Meninak Field, which includes Collins Baseball Stadium.

ATHLETICS

Bolles is a member of the Florida High School Athletic Association. Boys' teams compete in baseball, basketball, crew, cross-country, football, golf, lacrosse, soccer, swimming, tennis, track, wrestling, and weightlifting. Girls' teams compete in basketball, cheerleading, crew, cross-country, golf, soccer, softball, swimming, tennis, track, and volleyball. Middle School boys' teams compete in baseball, basketball, crew, football, lacrosse, soccer, swimming, track, and wrestling. Middle School girls' teams compete in basketball, cheerleading, crew, soccer, softball, swimming, track, and volleyball.

EXTRACURRICULAR OPPORTUNITIES

Extracurricular activities offered include Student Government; National Honor Society; language honor societies; Amnesty International; Interact, a service club; a mentor program; three student after-school tutoring programs; Student Advocate Council, which promotes community spirit among the students; an array of other community service opportunities; language clubs; special interest clubs; Community Service Leadership Council; Sophomore Leadership Council; class-sponsored activities; *Turris* (yearbook); *The Bugle* (newspaper); and *Perspective* (literary magazine).

DAILY LIFE

The daily schedule for the Upper School, which lasts from 8 a.m. until 3:45 p.m., includes seven 45-minute periods and "Zero Hour," a 30-minute period reserved for individual conferences and extra help. Boarders have evening study in their rooms, with faculty members available for extra help, and supervised study halls are provided for students needing more structured assistance.

WEEKEND LIFE

Resident students are strongly encouraged to take advantage of the excellent recreational facilities at Bolles. On weekends, the waterfront is open for resident students, weather permitting. In addition, regular off-campus trips are organized, as are, from time to time, special trips.

COSTS AND FINANCIAL AID

Upper School tuition costs for the 2013–14 school year are as follows: tuition, room, and meals for boarding students (grades 7–12) totals $43,300, and tuition for day students (grades 9–12) totals $21,200. Additional fees include $500–$750 for books, $30–$35 per gym uniform set, $375 for driver education, a one-time $500 facilities fee, and $45–$65 for the yearbook. Essential services fees for boarding students include $315 for the School clinic, $100 for emergency escrow, and an allowance of $40 per week ($1,440 per school year) for students in grades 7–8, $45 per week ($1,620 per school year) for students in grades 9–11, and $50 per week ($1,800 per school year) for students in grade 12. Lunches and snacks are available for purchase by day students.

The School awarded over $3.5 million in financial aid for the 2012–13 academic year.

ADMISSIONS INFORMATION

The School seeks students who demonstrate the ability to meet the requirements of a rigorous college-preparatory curriculum. In addition, special talents and strengths that allow the applicant to achieve distinction within the applicant pool are desired. The ISEE or its equivalent is required of all applicants, as are a personal interview, teacher recommendations, and transcripts. There is a $45 application fee for day students and a $75 application fee for international students.

APPLICATION TIMETABLE

The Admission Office accepts applications beginning in the fall, with an initial deadline of January 10. Applications received after that date are considered on a rolling basis as space becomes available. Upon acceptance, the applicant must respond with a deposit of 10 percent of the total tuition and pay the facilities fee within two weeks.

ADMISSIONS CORRESPONDENCE

The Bolles School
7400 San Jose Boulevard
Jacksonville, Florida 32217
United States
Phone: 904-256-5030
Fax: 904-739-9929
Website: http://www.Bolles.org

CAMPBELL HALL (EPISCOPAL)

North Hollywood, California

Campbell Hall
EPISCOPAL

Type: Coeducational day college-preparatory school
Grades: K–12: Lower School, K–6; Middle School, 7–8; Upper School, 9–12
Enrollment: School total: 1,100; Upper School: 544
Head of School: The Reverend Canon Julian Bull, Headmaster

THE SCHOOL

"Campbell Hall is a community of inquiry committed to academic excellence and to the nurturing of decent, loving, and responsible human beings." So says the mission statement for this independent, K–12, coeducational, nonprofit day school.

Campbell Hall is both progressive and traditional, with one of the most innovative schedules in the independent school world and a dynamic, research-based educational program. Affiliated with the Episcopal Church and its 500-year history of academic excellence, Campbell Hall is also one of the most religiously and racially diverse schools in Southern California. Believing both discipline and balance to be crucial in healthy, productive lives, the program provides a vast range of possibilities for intellectual, creative, and athletic pursuits.

Located in the San Fernando Valley, Campbell Hall has a 15-acre campus with lush landscaping and the atmosphere of an oasis in the midst of the city. In addition to classroom spaces, the campus comprises athletic fields, six science labs, playgrounds, four art studios, two gymnasiums, a theater, three dance studios, music practice rooms, nine computer labs, amphitheaters, and other outdoor teaching spaces. The Arts and Education Center, which opened for the 2012–13 school year, houses new classrooms, music and art rooms, a video production studio and lab, a recording studio, a photography and digital arts center, and an art gallery.

Campbell Hall was founded in 1944 by the Reverend Alexander K. Campbell as a school dedicated not only to the finest in academic education but also to the discovery of the values of a religious heritage. Campbell Hall enrolls students in kindergarten through the twelfth grade.

The basic structure and operation of the school and the formulation of educational and other school policies are guided by a 24-member Board of Directors. The board is composed of community leaders, alumni, and parents of Campbell Hall students. The Headmaster has traditionally served as a liaison between the board and the various segments of the school community.

The school's advancement programs include annual and capital campaigns.

Campbell Hall is accredited by the Western Association of Schools and Colleges and the California Association of Independent Schools. The school is also accredited by the Episcopal Diocesan Commission on Schools. It holds memberships in the National Association of Independent Schools, National Association of Episcopal Schools, Episcopal Diocesan Commission on Schools, Educational Records Bureau, National Association of College Admission Counselors, Council for Advancement and Support of Education, College Board, Council for Religion in Independent Schools, and Cum Laude Society.

ACADEMIC PROGRAM

Students at the high school must complete 7½ units in the humanities, including 4 units of the English component, 3 units of the history component, and ½ unit of senior seminar. Other requirements for graduation include 3 units of mathematics, 3 of a world language, 3 of a laboratory science, 2 years of physical education, 1 year of a visual or performing art, ½ year of art history, ½ year of music history, and ½ year of human development. In addition to the graduation requirements, students must complete additional units chosen from electives, such as music theory, creative writing, economics, ethics, physiology, poetry, computer programming, philosophy, psychology, and visual and performing arts. Students must also complete 20 hours of approved community service each year.

A number of special academic options attract qualified students. Twenty-one Advanced Placement courses and eighteen honors courses are offered and include calculus (AB and BC), probability and statistics, English, Chinese, French, Japanese, Spanish, European history, U.S. history, government/politics, human geography, biology, chemistry, physics, music theory, art history, psychology, economics, and computer science. In addition, qualified seniors may take college-level courses through the Talented High School Student Program of the California State University at Northridge, through local community colleges, through the UCLA High School Scholars' Program, and through approved online course providers.

Classes range in size from 8 or fewer students in advanced courses to 19 in some of the required courses. An online pilot program is available to students who wish to petition for specific courses in which they are particularly interested that are not part of the curriculum.

The school's grading system uses percentages: 100–90 is an A; 89–80 is a B; 79–70 is a C; 69–60 is a D, and no credit is given for a grade of 59 or below. Report cards, which are issued electronically each semester and trimester, include letter grades, as well as evaluations of work habits and cooperation.

At the end of each year, students who earn all A's in all classes are eligible for the Headmaster's List; students who earn a 3.6 academic average qualify for the Honor Roll primarily on the basis of grade point average. Academically outstanding juniors and seniors are eligible for membership in the Cum Laude Society.

FACULTY AND ADVISERS

There are 151 teaching faculty members; 58 hold master's degrees and 5 have doctorates. The school has a strong professional growth and development program, funded in part by the school's charitable giving program. Faculty members are encouraged to attend seminars and conferences in their fields. In addition to giving academic and social guidance to individual students, faculty advisers work closely with class officers to ensure unity and success in various class projects and social activities.

The Reverend Canon Julian Bull was appointed Headmaster in 2003. He is a graduate of Dartmouth (B.A., 1982), Boston College (M.A., 1988), and received his M.Div. from Virginia Theological Seminary in 2007.

Mr. Bull was formerly Head of School at Trinity Episcopal in New Orleans, Louisiana.

COLLEGE ADMISSION COUNSELING

The college counseling office provides students with support and guidance to facilitate their postsecondary educational plans. College counselors work with individual students on a personalized basis to find the best option that is consistent with each student's interests, values, abilities, and educational goals. Students are encouraged to seek opportunities that will best allow them to continue their intellectual and personal development.

In October, all sophomores and juniors take the PSAT. Throughout their high school years, students receive extensive college counseling through group workshops and in-depth individual conferences with the college counseling staff members. Throughout the school year, the college counseling office offers a number of programs to help students and parents understand the college admissions process. These programs often include meeting college admission representatives. In recent years, speakers from Brown, California Institute of the Arts, Columbia, Duke, NYU, Northwestern, Pitzer College, Sarah Lawrence, Stanford, UCLA, and USC have participated in these programs. One hundred percent of Campbell Hall graduates are accepted to four-year colleges or universities. They are drawn to a broad range of schools, and in recent years have enrolled at Berklee College of Music, Berkeley, Brown, Carnegie Mellon, Claremont McKenna, Columbia, Cornell, Duke, Emory, Georgetown, Grinnell College, Julliard, Middlebury, NYU, Northwestern, Pomona, Rhode Island School of Design, Rice, Scripps, UCLA, USC, Spelman, Stanford, Swarthmore, Tufts, the U.S. Air Force Academy, Vassar, Washington (St. Louis), Wesleyan, Whitman, Yale, and the Universities of Chicago, Michigan, and Pennsylvania.

STUDENT BODY AND CONDUCT

Of the 544 boys and girls in the Upper School (grades 9–12), 135 are in the ninth grade, 151 in the tenth, 126 in the eleventh, and 132 in the twelfth. Most students live in the suburban areas of Los Angeles.

Because Campbell Hall is concerned with the formation of character traits and values that reflect a sense of responsibility as well as a concern for the needs of others, misconduct is subject to disciplinary action. Violation of school rules and regulations may result in suspension or expulsion.

ACADEMIC FACILITIES

Campus academic facilities include classroom complexes, seven science labs, four computer labs, the Fine Arts Building, the Arts and Education Center, and a theater. A 22,000-square-foot library and academic center serves as the hub for the school's state-of-the-art technological resources which include campus-wide high-speed wireless Internet access and hundreds of laptops, tablets, and desktops deployed throughout the campus. Carefully researched iPad pilot programs and online education and digital media projects ensure that the school continues to teach for the twenty-first century; its philosophy blends technological sophistication with a strong sense of community and opportunity in this world center for the arts, sciences, and communications. All faculty members have school-supplied iPads and laptops and significant professional development resources available to them. The school library subscribes to a number of online databases.

The new 111,000-square-foot Arts and Education Center includes three two-story connected buildings, a multilevel subterranean parking garage, twenty-four state-of-the-art classrooms, an art gallery, a television studio, a video production lab, a photography lab and darkroom, a recording studio, a faculty resource center, outdoor learning spaces, terraces, and gardens, with extensive use of multimedia throughout. Designed by Gensler, an architectural firm renowned for its expertise in education design and innovative sustainability practices, the project is LEED certified.

ATHLETICS

There are two basic components to the athletics program. First, physical education courses provide basic and advanced instruction for sports that are in season; and second, Campbell Hall is a member of the California Interscholastic Federation (Gold Coast Athletic Association) and field teams in baseball, basketball, cheerleading, cross-country, tackle football, equestrian, golf, soccer, softball, tennis, track and field, and volleyball.

The school has two well-equipped gymnasiums, a baseball diamond, an artificial turf football and soccer field, a softball field, and five outdoor basketball/volleyball courts.

EXTRACURRICULAR OPPORTUNITIES

An active student government with elected officers represents each division of the student body. Among the student-planned events are dances; homecoming; the Winter Formal; and the Halloween, Christmas, and Valentine's Day celebrations. The year's social schedule culminates in a spring prom, planned by the student activities committee to honor the senior class.

There are also many curricular field trips and about sixty special interest groups, such as the Speech and Debate Team, Highlanders, the Cultural Awareness Club, the Spirit Club, Thespians, the Creative Writing Club, Amnesty International, Junior Statesmen of America, GSA, the Community Service Committee, and the High School Academic Honor Board.

DAILY LIFE

Monday through Thursday, there are four 75-minute blocks that meet between 8:50 a.m. and 3:40 p.m. Four days per week, 40 minutes are devoted to chapel (every Monday and Thursday), advisee group meetings, or clubs. On Wednesdays, the secondary school begins at 9:30 a.m. to allow for student/faculty conferences. There is a daily 45-minute lunch break. Interspersed among the academic courses are electives that provide enrichment in the fine arts (painting, drawing, ceramics, sculpture, and photography), the performing arts (chorus, instrumental music, drama, stagecraft, and dance), sports (physical education and team sports), robotics, computer programming, etc. Yearbook, newspaper, and journalism are also available as curricular classes.

SUMMER PROGRAMS

The school offers a full complement of summer programs for students in kindergarten through grade 12, including academic courses, a creative arts academy, and sports camps. Additional information may be obtained by contacting the Summer Programs Director.

COSTS AND FINANCIAL AID

Tuition for 2013–14, including fees, ranges from $26,980 to $33,100. Tuition payments may be made annually, biannually or in ten monthly installments. Students may either bring their own lunches to school or purchase them at the student store or from a school-sponsored caterer at the school at lunchtime. Uniforms are worn Monday through Thursday, with free dress on Fridays. There are four bus routes.

Financial aid is available and is awarded on the basis of family need. Continuing students have priority for renewal. In 2012–13, 24 percent of Middle and Upper School students received financial aid.

ADMISSIONS INFORMATION

The school seeks students who are able to benefit from a rigorous college-preparatory curriculum and who will contribute to extracurricular as well as other community activities. Campbell Hall admits students of any race, color, national or ethnic origin to all the rights, privileges, programs, and activities generally accorded or made available to the students at the school. It does not discriminate on the basis of race, color, national or ethnic origin, or any other legally protected status in administration of its educational policies, admissions policies, scholarship programs and athletic and other school-administered programs. Campbell Hall is a diverse school community. Students of color make up 33 percent of the student body, and diverse faiths and family structures are also represented.

An entrance examination is required, as are recommendations from 2 teachers and a school administrator, a transcript from the school in which the applicant is currently enrolled, and an interview.

APPLICATION TIMETABLE

The Admissions Office is open from 8 a.m. to 4 p.m., Monday through Friday, to answer inquiries and to arrange interviews and campus visits. Applicants for the 2014–15 school year should file an application, accompanied by a $135 fee, by December 18, 2013. Applicants take the Independent School Entrance Examination.

The school makes most decisions concerning new admissions by March. Parents are expected to reply to an offer of acceptance within two weeks and to pay a deposit, which is credited toward the first semester's tuition.

ADMISSIONS CORRESPONDENCE

Alice Fleming, Director of Admissions
George White, Associate Director
Campbell Hall
4533 Laurel Canyon Boulevard
North Hollywood, California 91617
United States
Phone: 818-980-7280
Website: http://www.campbellhall.org

CANTERBURY SCHOOL

Ft. Myers, Florida

CANTERBURY SCHOOL
Education • Character • Leadership • Service

Type: Coeducational, day, college-preparatory
Grades: Prekindergarten–12: Lower School, Pre-K–3; Intermediate School, 4–6; Middle School, 7–8; Upper School, 9–12
Enrollment: 600; Upper School, 220
Head of School: Anthony J. Paulus

THE SCHOOL

Founded in 1964, the Canterbury School sits on 32 acres located on College Parkway between U.S. 41 and McGregor Boulevard. The School is dedicated to academic excellence within a caring and supportive community, preparing students of ability, promise, and diverse backgrounds for selective colleges. Canterbury's motto, "Education, character, leadership, service," defines the focus of the School's program and underscores all that its students do in and out of the classroom.

There are four divisions—Lower (grades prekindergarten–3), Intermediate (grades 4–6), Middle (grades 7–8), and Upper (grades 9–12). At all levels, the academic program emphasizes individual growth, skill development, a high caliber of instruction, collaboration, and high standards. Canterbury provides all students with an opportunity to challenge themselves and take risks in an atmosphere of mutual respect and partnership among students, parents, and teachers. Canterbury's integrated, innovative curriculum emphasizes group and individual study of the liberal arts, in addition to experiential learning and community service opportunities.

The Canterbury School is accredited by the Southern Association of Independent Schools (SAIS), Southern Association of Colleges and Schools/Council on Accreditation and School Improvement (SACS/CASI), Florida Council of Independent Schools (FCIS), the College Board, and the Florida Kindergarten Council (FKC).

ACADEMIC PROGRAM

All students pursue a demanding schedule of college-preparatory classes for four years in the Upper School, earning a minimum of 25 credits to graduate. Students play an active role in their course of study, and juniors and seniors may pursue advanced work in areas of significant interest or expertise. Although Honors and Advanced Placement courses, as well as independent studies, give students extra challenges, even the standard-level courses thoroughly prepare students for college work. Offering a rigorous and rewarding liberal arts curriculum, the Upper School program is rich in math, science, modern and classical languages, music, visual arts, social sciences, foreign language, and drama, with a special emphasis on writing, research, and the discourse of ideas. Study strategies, self-discipline, academic responsibility, and fluency in technology are underscored in each content area. Students learn academic honesty, competitive fair play, and good citizenship through a respected honor code. Students master key skills that will serve them well in their college careers as they actively participate in intellectual inquiry, analysis, and evaluation.

Middle School students take one course in each of the major disciplines every year—English, mathematics, science, social studies, and foreign language—and classes in the arts and in physical education/health, as well as other electives.

Canterbury's Intermediate School offers instruction in a math, science, and technology triad, as well as the Writing Across the Curriculum initiative, which links critical thinking and written expression in every curriculum area. Lower School celebrates childhood in an age-appropriate, developmental learning environment for students in prekindergarten through third grade; a balance between hard work and fun creates an environment where children are encouraged to take risks and assume personal responsibility for their learning as they embark upon their learning journey.

FACULTY AND ADVISERS

There are 80 faculty members, 38 of whom teach in the Upper School. Canterbury's talented and dedicated faculty seeks to inspire young minds through a rigorous and rewarding curriculum. Passionate about ideas and mentoring, instructors understand how students learn most effectively. Teaching is more than facts, figures, and formulas—it's a way of life. Canterbury's teachers personalize their approach to meet individual student needs. Small class sizes allow one-on-one time for personal attention, challenging and supporting students as they stretch their minds and their opportunities.

COLLEGE ADMISSION COUNSELING

College preparation is a primary focus of Canterbury's curriculum, so students receive the highly personalized direction and encouragement they need to choose the undergraduate institution with the right fit. An experienced college counselor guides juniors and seniors, as well as their families, through the process—helping them gain a comprehensive understanding of college acceptance practices. The result? An ongoing tradition of a 100 percent college-acceptance rate among Canterbury graduates. Recent graduates have been accepted to such distinguished institutions as Carnegie Mellon, Dartmouth, Georgetown, Harvard, Princeton, and Yale.

STUDENT BODY AND CONDUCT

Six hundred students are enrolled in grades prekindergarten–12. They come from diverse backgrounds, but the majority live in Fort Myers, Cape Coral, Sanibel, and the surrounding area.

ACADEMIC FACILITIES

The Canterbury School Libraries offer instruction, materials, and technology to promote the skills of information literacy and fluency, the love of reading, and the joy of intellectual discovery. By providing resources for both academic and recreational reading needs, the libraries help students develop research competencies for college and facilitate lifelong learning. The libraries also provide space for individual reflection and creation, as well as a forum for the sharing of ideas within the Canterbury community. The Ellenberg Library (grades 6–12) has established several special collections, in addition to the familiar biography, fiction, nonfiction, periodical, reference, and story collections. The Hilliard Library serves students from pre-K through fifth grade and their teachers. The library collection, of both print and nonprint resources, includes books, videotapes, magazines, Internet access, professional resources, and online subscription databases.

The Lower and Intermediate schools have dedicated art and music classrooms, science laboratories, computer labs and classrooms. They share a library. The Middle and Upper schools share a library, a language listening lab, and music and art classrooms, but they have separate science laboratories, computer labs, classrooms, and commons areas. The entire school shares the dining hall, a gymnasium and a sports center, an outdoor marine biology touch tank and classroom, and the Performing Arts Center.

ATHLETICS

At Canterbury, the life of the mind is complemented by a strong athletic program. Canterbury School fields teams in soccer, basketball, baseball, football, volleyball, swimming, tennis, golf, cross-country, track and field, and lacrosse. Students are encouraged to become involved with athletics; around 85 percent of all Middle and Upper School students participate in interscholastic sports. Canterbury School is a member of the Florida High School Athletic Association (FHSAA) and is accredited by the Southern Association of Schools and Colleges (SACS). The Middle School belongs to the Suncoast Middle School League.

EXTRACURRICULAR OPPORTUNITIES

Clubs and organizations play key roles in student life. Students can choose from more than twenty active clubs on campus, including yearbook, newspaper, chess, mock trial, and Model UN, which meet regularly throughout the year. Students can also participate in a variety of local, state, national, and international scholastic competitions.

DAILY LIFE

Students spend their days in class, followed by after-school activities ranging from community service, student government, and athletics to clubs and study groups.

SUMMER PROGRAMS

Summer academic programs are available to students of all ages. Students can brush up their math, writing, or Spanish skills or take SAT-prep courses. Canterbury provides a recommended summer reading list for prekindergarten to fifth grade students so that they can begin, continue, and support the process of developing comprehension and analytical skills. Students in grades 6–12 receive a required summer reading list to support their academic course selection for the following year.

COSTS AND FINANCIAL AID

Upper School students pay $19,155 plus fees per academic year. Tuition is $14,395 for prekindergarten and kindergarten, $16,600 for grades 1–3, $17,915 for grades 4–6, and $18,545 for Middle School. Fees are additional. In 2013–14, Canterbury provided more than $1.5 million in financial assistance to 25 percent of the student body, with awards ranging from 20 percent to 95 percent of tuition.

Tuition payments include both a nonrefundable deposit and the remaining tuition balance. The nonrefundable 20 percent deposit is due upon enrollment and must accompany the student's enrollment contract. On July 1, another 30 percent of tuition is due, and the remaining 50 percent is due October 1. With this plan, tuition refund insurance is optional. Payment plan options are presented in the addendum to the enrollment contract.

ADMISSIONS INFORMATION

As a college-preparatory school with high academic standards, Canterbury seeks students of demonstrated abilities with potential for intellectual growth. Boys and girls entering prekindergarten through grade eleven are invited to apply, beginning the fall prior to the school year they wish to attend. Applications can be submitted online or by mail and must include the $100 application fee.

Applicants are first evaluated by testing, using the ERB, CTP 4 Test, or the SSAT in grades 4–11. Next, candidates' files are forwarded to the Admission Committee, which assesses each application based on the student's past academic achievement, performance on the admission test, a written essay, personal recommendations, and an interview with the division head and director of admission.

APPLICATION TIMETABLE

Open houses are scheduled October through March; attendees must reserve a space by contacting the admission office. Applications are accepted continually.

ADMISSIONS CORRESPONDENCE

Julie Peters, Director of Admissions
Canterbury School
8141 College Parkway
Fort Myers, Florida 33919
United States
Phone: 239-415-8945
Fax: 239-481-8339
E-mail: jpeters@canterburyfortmyers.org
Website:
http://www.canterburyfortmyers.org/

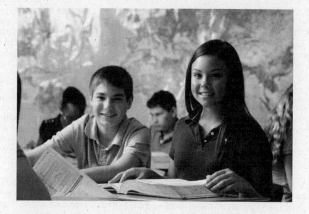

THE CASCADILLA SCHOOL

Ithaca, New York

 Cascadilla School

Type: Coeducational boarding and day college-preparatory school
Grades: 9–12, postgraduate year
Enrollment: 60
Head of School: Patricia A. Kendall, Headmistress

THE SCHOOL

The Cascadilla School was founded in 1870 as a preparatory school for Cornell University. In 1939, it was reorganized as a nonprofit corporation under a Board of Trustees and granted an absolute charter by the Board of Regents of the State of New York.

The philosophy of education at Cascadilla is to provide a flexible, accelerated program within which each individual can achieve his or her goals in preparation for a successful college career. This learning experience emphasizes the steady development of an adult viewpoint and a mature approach to life.

The School is located in the heart of the Finger Lakes region in Ithaca, a city of 50,000 people, 20,000 of whom are college and university students. This scenic college town provides many cultural activities as well as athletics events. The School is located on the edge of the Cornell University campus, and students are encouraged to take advantage of the community's outstanding offerings, which include restaurants, shops, theater, and recreational facilities. There is direct air and bus service from New York City and other major U.S. cities.

The Cascadilla School is run by a 5-member Board of Trustees that is drawn from the business and professional community. Patricia A. Kendall is currently President of the Board and also Headmistress.

The School is privately endowed and nondenominational and has assets of approximately $1.2 million. Tuition charges provide more than 90 percent of its funding, and gifts from alumni and friends make up the remainder.

The Cascadilla School is registered with the New York State Board of Regents.

ACADEMIC PROGRAM

The Cascadilla School offers a complete high school curriculum. The School's goal is to prepare students for college in an accelerated program. Full-unit high school courses are taught by the semester; the typical student completes between 7 and 8 units per year.

Twenty-three units are required for graduation, including 5 in English, 4 in social sciences, 3 in math, 3 in science, 1 in a language other than English, 1 in art and/or music, 2 in physical education, ½ in health, and 3½ in electives. All courses are taught on the New York State Regents level. In addition to taking Advanced Placement courses, seniors may enroll in actual college course work at Cornell, Ithaca College, or Tompkins Cortland Community College.

Extra help and supervised study are available in the afternoon until 5 p.m. The library and the laboratories are open until then. No evening study hall is required unless a student's academic performance falls below acceptable standards.

All class grouping is heterogeneous. Class size averages 8 students, and the student-teacher ratio is 6:1.

The Cascadilla School uses a numerical grading system that runs from 0 to 100, with 70 the minimum passing grade and 75 the start of college-recommending grades. Reports, with individual comments, are sent home monthly; more frequent reports are developed in special situations. Certain reading and writing skills are required for entrance into English III. A three-level skills program is used for students who do not meet these requirements. All students are assisted in their process of application to American universities and colleges.

FACULTY AND ADVISERS

The Cascadilla School has 9 full-time and 6 part-time teachers. All have bachelor's degrees, and 14 have master's degrees. The small size and personal nature of the School make every teacher an adviser. An attempt is made to make time in the school day for personal contact outside of regularly scheduled classes.

There is very little turnover in the full-time staff. The part-time staff is drawn from the Cornell and Ithaca college communities and changes as courses demand.

The Headmistress' academic background includes a B.S. degree from Syracuse University, an M.S. degree from Nazareth College, and an administrative degree in education from the State University of New York at Cortland. Mrs. Kendall brings nearly forty years of experience in education to Cascadilla School.

COLLEGE ADMISSION COUNSELING

Planning for college begins almost as soon as a student enters Cascadilla. The School has entered a partnership with Kaplan Educational Centers, through which Cascadilla students are provided preparation for the SAT exams on campus. Kaplan tailors its SAT preparation program to meet the needs of Cascadilla students. A section of the library is devoted to college catalogs and career information. College visits are encouraged, and the School provides transportation for them. Involvement with the Cornell University community provides valuable stimulation for most Cascadilla students.

SAT scores for 2012–13 ranged from 1560 to 2280. Approximately one third of the graduating seniors also took the ACT.

The School averages between 17 and 20 graduates per year. Ninety-eight percent go on to further their education, and about 98 percent attend four-year colleges. Recent graduates are attending Columbia, Cornell, Hamilton, Northwestern, NYU, various SUNY colleges and universities, and the Universities of Colorado, Georgia, Illinois, Michigan, and Wisconsin.

STUDENT BODY AND CONDUCT

The Cascadilla School attracts students from a wide geographic area. Since 2008, students have come from the U.S. and eight other countries. The School has room for 25–30 boarders; day students make up the rest of the School population. Seventy percent of the students are juniors, seniors, and postgraduates; Cascadilla is interested primarily in students who are planning to be at the School for two to three years. The accelerated program works best when the students have the emotional maturity to establish goals and work toward them.

ACADEMIC FACILITIES

The classroom building was opened in 1890. It contains eight classrooms, a science laboratory, a language laboratory, a computer room, and a library of nearly 9,000 volumes.

Students who are interested in music or the visual arts may use the programs and facilities of Cornell University or Ithaca College.

BOARDING AND GENERAL FACILITIES

The two dormitories are designed to bring together the elements of a family environment, college life, and apartment living. Single and double rooms are available, each with its own refrigerator; each dormitory has a snack kitchen and a TV lounge. Supervision is provided by dorm parents. The School tries to create a living environment that reinforces its academic programs.

The Cascadilla School has no formal dining facilities of its own; therefore, most students use the dorm facilities for breakfast and take the fourteen-meal option of the Cornell University Meal Plan for lunch and dinner, although a twenty-one-meal option is available. This daily exposure to the university helps them to become familiar with its programs and facilities.

ATHLETICS

Cascadilla's physical education program offers bowling, cross-country skiing, rowing, and sailboarding. Students are also encouraged to join the YMCA, which includes the weight room and aerobics, swimming, and racquetball facilities. The Cascadilla School's Gryphons soccer team also provides an interscholastic athletic program throughout the academic year.

EXTRACURRICULAR OPPORTUNITIES

Most extracurricular opportunities are available through the university and the community. The area is rich in cultural events that range from lectures and plays to musical performances of all types.

DAILY LIFE

Most students have 6 hours of academic course work between 9 a.m. and 4 p.m. All students and faculty members share a common lunch period. The afternoon program varies from day to day and may include physical education; special courses, such as SAT preparation through Kaplan, photography, and drawing; and opportunities to get extra help or tutoring. Many students also work on the School's news magazine and yearbook. After dinner, evenings typically involve study, recreation, and a movie or TV.

WEEKEND LIFE

The School sponsors movies and occasional parties. There may also be ski trips that include transportation, instruction, and rental of equipment. In addition, as is true of extracurricular activities during the week, students may take advantage of the wide range of opportunities at Cornell and other local schools and colleges.

COSTS AND FINANCIAL AID

Tuition, a double room, and board fees for the 2013–14 school year are $39,000. Additional charges are made for single rooms and for unusually heavy course loads.

The Cascadilla School is interested in attracting good students from all cultures and socioeconomic groups. Last year, 40 percent of the School's students received some type of financial aid or scholarship. There are also several opportunities for part-time work at the School.

ADMISSIONS INFORMATION

The Cascadilla School is looking for students who are ready to put their high school program together and prepare for college. The SSAT is not required. The School, however, seeks students with academic potential, if not achievement.

An admission interview is required for all U.S. applicants, and a $50 application fee is required of all U.S. applicants. An application fee is also required of international applicants.

The Cascadilla School admits students of any race, color, and national or ethnic origin to all the rights, privileges, programs, and activities generally accorded or made available to students at the School. It does not discriminate on the basis of race, color, or national and ethnic origin in administration of its educational policies, admissions policies, and scholarship, athletic, and other School-administered programs.

APPLICATION TIMETABLE

The Cascadilla School has a rolling admission process; however, the recommended application deadlines are January 15, June 30, and September 1, depending on the term in which a student wishes to begin. A $5,000 deposit is required upon acceptance. It is strongly suggested that applications be submitted by June 1 for September entrance, as the amount of dormitory space is extremely limited.

ADMISSIONS CORRESPONDENCE

Patricia A. Kendall, Headmistress
The Cascadilla School
116 Summit Street
Ithaca, New York 14850
United States
Phone: 607-272-3110
Fax: 607-272-0747
E-mail: admissions@cascadillaschool.org
Website: http://www.cascadillaschool.org/

CHARLOTTE LATIN SCHOOL

Charlotte, North Carolina

CHARLOTTE
LATIN
SCHOOL

Type: Independent, college-preparatory, nonsectarian, coeducational day school
Grades: Transitional kindergarten–Grade 12
Enrollment: 1,402
Head of School: Arch N. McIntosh, Jr., Headmaster

THE SCHOOL

Founded in 1970, Charlotte Latin School (CLS) is located on a 122-acre campus in southeast Charlotte, North Carolina. The school community, which includes students, parents, alumni, and faculty and staff members, embraces a shared mission, core values, and a commitment to academic excellence. Latin is a school that is traditional by design yet innovative in implementation. The School's emphasis is for its students to maintain balance in their lives, which is enhanced by a curriculum built upon a foundation of academic rigor, the arts, and athletics. Students are presented with many growth-promoting opportunities to explore and develop their interests, including a variety of co-curricular options and a TK–12 community service program that fosters a lifelong commitment to service through age-appropriate activities. Students also are encouraged to explore their world and are supported in this endeavor through active international sister schools and study-abroad programs.

Charlotte Latin remains true to its founding parents' original vision as a place where a stimulating learning environment is united with a vibrant family life. Named for America's early Latin schools, in which colonial children pursued classical studies under the careful tutelage of their teachers, Charlotte Latin similarly fosters a close relationship between its faculty and students. With their teachers' guidance, students of all ages study and serve the community that surrounds them and the world that beckons them, in preparation to care for and succeed in the global community they will inherit as adults. Their parents, too, are partners with the School in their education and are frequently seen on campus attending special events, cheering on a Hawks athletic team, sharing lunch with their children in Founders' Hall, or serving on the Board of Trustees, Parents' Council, or one of the many volunteer committees that make Charlotte Latin a special place. Alumni, too, often return to campus to visit former teachers, and in some cases, to visit their own children at Latin. More than 3,500 alumni are members of the active CLS Alumni Association.

Charlotte Latin School is accredited by and is a member of the National, Southern, and North Carolina Associations of Independent Schools. The most recent reaccreditation by SAIS-SACS (the Southern Association of Independent Schools and Southern Association of Colleges and Schools) was in 2011. The School is also accredited by the North Carolina Department of Public Instruction. Latin is the youngest school in the United States to receive a Cum Laude chapter, and it has been named a Blue Ribbon School of Excellence three times by the U.S. Department of Education.

ACADEMIC PROGRAM

Charlotte Latin is organized into three divisions: the Lower School includes transitional kindergarten through fifth grade; the Middle School encompasses the sixth through eighth grades; and the Upper School comprises the ninth through twelfth grades.

The academic program prepares students to succeed in college and beyond by instilling a lifelong love of learning. Charlotte Latin School's curriculum is designed so that each successive grade adds to the students' mastery of skills and continued maturation. Through the leadership of the Division Heads and Curriculum Coordinator, the curriculum is constantly reviewed and refined to ensure that best practices are adopted to create a strong academic foundation.

The class of 2013's SAT scores reflect this academic strength. The middle 50 percent of scores are 560–690 for critical reading, 600–710 for mathematics, and 600–720 for writing. The class's middle 50 percent ACT composite score is 25–31.

While Latin has high expectations for its students, the School provides a nurturing environment and individual support, including a learning resources coordinator and guidance counselor for each division.

FACULTY AND ADVISORS

At Latin's core is a dedicated faculty composed of more than 160 experienced educators. The School's low student-teacher ratios and considerable professional development resources demonstrate that Latin values its teachers and celebrates learning. Active Middle School and Upper School advisory programs foster strong ties between faculty members and students, which enable these adults to serve as positive role models for maturing adolescents.

COLLEGE ADMISSION COUNSELING

As a college preparatory school, Charlotte Latin provides a College Center that guides students and their families through every step of the college admission process. The College Center is staffed by three full-time college counselors and a full-time registrar who work actively with both students and their families throughout the Upper School years. The support is individualized and proactive, and is designed to empower the student to take ownership of the process. The success of Latin's approach to college admissions is evidenced annually; 100 percent of the School's graduates are accepted to prestigious colleges and universities across the United States and beyond.

STUDENT BODY AND CONDUCT

The Charlotte Latin community is guided by the CLS Honor Code. A plaque bearing the inscription "Honor above all" is posted in every classroom as a constant reminder of the importance of this creed in the life of Charlotte Latin School. Adherence to the Honor Pledge is a condition of enrollment in the Upper School. Students may participate with administrators and faculty members as representatives of the Upper School Honor Council after demonstrating successive levels of leadership and personally modeling honorable conduct.

ACADEMIC FACILITIES

Latin's campus features distinct areas and buildings for each of the three divisions as well as shared facilities, such as the 17,630-square-foot Media Center and 13,275-square-foot Founders' Hall dining facility. Connected by covered walkways, each area of campus is appropriate for the developmental stage of the students while also enhancing a sense of school unity. The Horne Performing Arts Center, which opened in 2011, provides state-of-the-art instructional and performance spaces for the vocal and instrumental music programs. The theater program benefits from the performing arts center's 740-seat Thies Auditorium and Anne's Black Box Theater.

Wired and wireless computer connectivity is available in every building via a campuswide fiber-optic network and a dedicated 300MB line for high-speed data transmission. Computer labs and mobile laptop labs are utilized by students at all grade levels. Internet access via the academic network is filtered by the School to ensure that students view only appropriate online content.

The Hawks Quest low ropes challenge course opened in 2013 to enhance students' experiential and outdoor learning opportunities.

ATHLETICS

Interscholastic athletics have a long and rich tradition at Charlotte Latin School. Throughout its more than forty-year history, students have proven they can compete on the playing field as well as in the classroom. Along with the many conference and state titles earned over the years, the School has always placed a premium on the values instilled and the life lessons learned from athletic competition.

Latin sponsors more than sixty-five athletic teams in seventeen men's and women's sports, and more than 90 percent of students in grades 7–12 participate in at least one sport.

Athletic facilities include three gymnasiums, an all-weather track surrounding the 1,450-seat Patten Stadium; six tennis courts; seven playing fields; an Olympic-quality natatorium; a cross-country course; and the Beck Student Activities Center, which includes an arena, fitness facility, indoor track, and dedicated wrestling room.

The Charlotte Latin Hawks won the Wells Fargo/Wachovia Cup for overall excellence in high school athletics every year from 2005 through 2011. A commitment to athletic excellence is not only reflected in the many championship banners collected over the years but also through Latin's adherence to high standards of personal conduct and good sportsmanship on the part of student athletes, coaches, and fans.

EXTRACURRICULAR OPPORTUNITIES

Charlotte Latin offers a balanced program that provides creative outlets for students' intellectual and physical energies. Beginning in the fourth grade, a broad selection of clubs and organizations is available to encourage students to pursue their interests and explore new opportunities. Leadership development is a key component of participation, with students accepting increasing responsibility

for managing organizations such as the Student Council, Service Program, and the Mosaic Club, which fosters inclusiveness and promotes awareness of diversity issues.

SUMMER PROGRAMS

The goal of Charlotte Latin Summer Programs is to provide an environment that promotes a joy for learning, where campers can develop cognitively, socially, emotionally, and physically through growth-promoting experiences. A professional and caring staff sustains a safe, structured, and innovative environment that sparks children's excitement about exploring new possibilities. Camps are primarily designed for boys and girls in Lower School and Middle School. Fees vary depending on the camp(s) selected. For more information, call 704-846-7277.

COSTS AND FINANCIAL AID

Tuition for the 2013–2014 school year is as follows: transitional kindergarten and kindergarten, $16,100; grades 1–5, $18,700; and grades 6–12, $20,250.

Charlotte Latin has need-based financial aid funds available for qualified families. Application for financial aid is made during the admissions application process. Charlotte Latin is a Malone Scholar School, and other scholarships are available to students based upon specific qualifying criteria.

ADMISSIONS INFORMATION

Charlotte Latin School's admission policies were established to fulfill the School's

philosophy: to initiate in its students a love of and a respect for learning, to help them develop self-discipline, and to encourage creativity. The School seeks to attract a variety of students who demonstrate motivation and the ability to respond to the total School program. Charlotte Latin welcomes students who indicate a willingness to participate and a desire to do their best. The School believes that students with a breadth of talents and interests will contribute to the creation of a dynamic learning environment. Charlotte Latin School does not discriminate on the basis of sex, race, color, religion, sexual orientation, or national origin in the administration of its educational programs, admissions policies, financial aid policies, employment practices, or other School-administered programs.

APPLICATION TIMETABLE

Additional information about Charlotte Latin School's admissions process and key dates is available online at www.charlottelatin.org/admissions.

ADMISSIONS CORRESPONDENCE

Charlotte Latin School
9502 Providence Road
Charlotte, North Carolina 28277
United States
Phone: 704-846-1100
E-mail: inquiries@charlottelatin.org
Website: http://www.charlottelatin.org

CONVENT OF THE SACRED HEART
Greenwich, Connecticut

Type: Independent, Catholic day school for girls in kindergarten through twelfth grade, with coed preschool and kindergarten
Grades: P–12: Barat Center for Early Childhood Education, P–PreK; Lower School, K–4; Middle School, 5–8; Upper School, 9–12
Enrollment: School total: 737; Upper School: 295
Head of School: Pamela Juan Hayes, Head of School

THE SCHOOL

Convent of the Sacred Heart is situated on a beautiful 118-acre wooded campus in Greenwich, Connecticut. Greenwich is a suburban town located about 30 miles from New York City and 40 minutes from New Haven. An independent Catholic school for girls in preschool through grade 12 with a coed preschool and prekindergarten, Sacred Heart was first established in New York City in 1848 and moved to Greenwich in 1945. Convent of the Sacred Heart is one of twenty-two Sacred Heart schools in the United States and part of an international network of schools that includes more than 200 schools in twenty-eight countries around the world.

A Sacred Heart education provides a strong academic foundation appropriate to each student's individual talents and abilities within an environment that fosters the development of her spiritual life and a strong sense of personal values. True to its international heritage, the school welcomes students and faculty members of diverse backgrounds and faiths, so that each student will grow in her understanding of different cultures and peoples. Graduates are prepared to become leaders with broad intellectual and spiritual horizons.

Convent of the Sacred Heart is a nonprofit institution governed by a 22-member Board of Trustees, which is responsible to the Society of the Sacred Heart for the implementation of the society's educational philosophy. Parents, religious, alumnae, and educators serve on the board. Sacred Heart benefits from the active involvement and strong support of its parent and alumnae organizations.

The school is accredited by the New England Association of Schools and Colleges and approved by the Connecticut State Board of Education. It is a member of the National Association of Independent Schools, the Connecticut Association of Independent Schools, the Cum Laude Society, the College Board, the National Association of College Admissions Counselors, the National Coalition of Girls' Schools, and the Network of Sacred Heart Schools in the United States.

ACADEMIC PROGRAM

Sacred Heart is committed to the development of each student's intellectual, physical, spiritual, and emotional well-being. The academic program in the Upper School provides a rigorous educational foundation that enables students to become independent and creative thinkers. Students are active participants in the learning process, expanding their experience through exploration, inquiry, and discovery. Students analyze, critique, evaluate, and make important connections with the concepts they learn.

Sacred Heart's academic program is comprehensive, rigorous, and flexible. Serious study is emphasized, and the development of essential academic skills necessary for success in college and life is encouraged. College-preparatory, honors, and advanced-placement courses are offered throughout the core curriculum, which includes mathematics, science, English, history and social sciences, world languages, theology, and the arts. A student is afforded opportunities for exploration of her own talents and interests through special projects, study abroad, summer programs, and independent study. Emphasizing the connection between the disciplines is critical to learning at Sacred Heart. Faculty collaboration helps students in discovering and understanding the relevance of all subject areas and the importance of their learning in relationship to society and their daily lives.

A student's schedule for the three-term academic year is planned individually. The student plans her course of study with the support of her teachers and her Academic Dean. Course levels are chosen according to academic readiness, ability, and talent in an academic area. Each student typically takes between 6 and 8 credits per school year in a combination of required courses and electives.

Graduation requirements are based on the expectations of highly selective colleges and universities; all of Sacred Heart's graduates choose to attend college. To receive a diploma, students must complete a minimum of 25 credits, although the majority of students complete more than this minimum number. The requirements include 4 credits of English, 4 credits in theology, 3 credits in history, 3 credits in mathematics, 3 credits in a world language, 3 credits in science, and 2 elective credits, at least 1 of which must be in the arts. Students must also complete 2 years of physical education and a 2-year health education requirement.

All academic disciplines employ the computer as a tool for writing, research, analysis, and presentation, including the use of multimedia presentations, spreadsheets and databases for organization and analysis, and desktop publishing. The program also addresses the possibilities and responsibilities associated with the use of technology in today's society. All students in grades 6–12 use laptop computers in the classroom and anywhere else they study or work. iPads are available from preschool through Middle School. Netbooks are used in fifth grade.

FACULTY AND ADVISERS

High expectations and positive role models are important to the success of girls and young women. A student-faculty ratio of 7:1 and an average class size of approximately 13 students ensure the teachers know every student. Assured of the faculty's support, students are motivated to take risks through which confidence and self-discipline develop. Individual teaching styles are complemented by a common commitment to the goals and criteria of a Sacred Heart education.

Convent of the Sacred Heart has 125 faculty members, with 50 full-time and 1 part-time members teaching in the Upper School. They also serve as academic advisers to small groups of about 10 advisees, and many serve as club moderators and coaches as well. Students meet with their advisers regularly during a special advisory period. Each day begins with an all-school assembly and students and faculty members attend an Upper School chapel service once per cycle.

Teachers regularly participate in workshops, summer study, curriculum development, travel, and research. Approximately 77 percent of the faculty members hold advanced degrees, including 8 who have doctoral degrees. The full-time faculty has an average of fifteen years of teaching experience.

COLLEGE ADMISSION COUNSELING

The College Guidance Department at Sacred Heart believes in the importance of an individualized college process and works hard to find the best match possible for each student. An informational parent meeting in the sophomore year helps to set this tone. The Directors of College Guidance also review PSAT scores, and help their student advisees plan schedules for appropriate SAT Subject Tests.

In junior year, students and parents meet with the Directors of College Guidance to identify goals and discuss expectations about college plans. The college search process is explained at an evening winter program, which features college representatives and the college counselors. Juniors also attend guidance classes that explore issues surrounding the college selection process, including identifying prospective colleges, the campus visit and interview, the college essay, and financial aid and scholarships. Students have access to a variety of college search resources, including guidebooks, Internet search engines, and an internal software program. Students are also encouraged to take advantage of opportunities to meet with the many college representatives who visit Sacred Heart in the fall.

During the senior year, each student and her parents examine the more specific details of the application process: deadlines, the submission of standardized test scores, the college essay, resumes, and financial aid. In the school's 165-year history, Sacred Heart graduates have attended many of the nation's finest colleges and universities. Recent graduates are currently attending schools such as Boston College, Brown, Cornell, Georgetown, Harvard, Holy Cross, Johns Hopkins, Notre Dame, Stanford, Yale, and the University of Virginia.

STUDENT BODY AND CONDUCT

There are 737 students enrolled in preschool through grade 12, with 295 students enrolled in the Upper School. Students join the high school from more than sixty-seven different communities, coming from public, private, and parochial schools in Connecticut and New York State. The student body includes a diversity of ethnic, socioeconomic, and religious backgrounds that allows for a dynamic community with a wide range of interests, talents, and passions.

School policies and practices foster the acceptance of responsibility, self-discipline, respect for the self and others, and caring for the school and wider community. The student government, student/faculty disciplinary board, and the administration work together to establish and enforce policies and minimal rules that govern the school community.

ACADEMIC FACILITIES

Overlooking Long Island Sound, the campus consists of modern classrooms, science laboratories, an observatory, playgrounds, synthetic-turf fields, a media center, a theater, a chapel, a broadcast journalism studio, a gymnasium, a fitness room, a swimming pool, and a dance studio.

The media center holds a collection of 30,000 books, 1,000 e-books, online databases and encyclopedias, and DVDs and videos in a fully wireless environment. The library recently purchased a Backbone Media table for small-group collaboration.

A 29,000-square-foot science center has state-of-the-art science laboratories for all three divisions, including the Upper School's Science Research Program, in addition to space for the Upper School art studio, special space for drama and music, classrooms, and offices. On campus, there is a free-standing state-of-the-art observatory, which offers students interested in astronomy the opportunity for viewings of the night sky through a computerized, 16-inch telescope with 800x magnification. In addition, outside the observatory there is a pad with ten 8-inch telescopes.

The broadcast journalism studio consists of control, editing, and recording rooms. Students learn how to operate camera, audio, lighting, and editing equipment to tell their stories. This state-of-the-art space provides students with the opportunity to practice media literacy in a meaningful, hands-on fashion.

Students studying art, environmental science, and ecology make frequent use of the school's acres of woods, trails, fields, and a working vegetable garden. The campus is further enlivened by traditions and events unique to Convent of the Sacred Heart.

ATHLETICS

The energy of the Sacred Heart community extends beyond the walls of the school buildings. The indoor competition swimming pool, tennis courts, and the synthetic and grass playing fields outside are showcases for girls accepting challenges, testing limits, and cooperating with teammates. Sacred Heart provides a full schedule of varsity, junior varsity, and thirds sports, including basketball, crew, cross-country, field hockey, golf, lacrosse, soccer, softball, squash, swimming and diving, tennis, and volleyball. The teams are supported with the very best facilities and equipment, including two synthetic-turf fields. Convent of the Sacred Heart is a member of the twelve-school Fairchester League and the New England Preparatory School Athletic Council (NEPSAC). A certified athletic trainer services both the Middle and Upper School student-athletes.

The physical education program is designed to develop skills for a healthy and active life. Opportunities are provided for competition, excellence, and fun in a variety of activities for all students.

EXTRACURRICULAR OPPORTUNITIES

A wide range of clubs, committees, and activities provide opportunities for students to contribute to the school community, pursue their interests, and develop leadership and team skills. Students produce major theatrical productions, govern the student body through extensive collaboration with student-elected representatives, and produce award-winning publications, which include a school newspaper and a literary and art magazine in English and another in a variety of world languages. Sacred Heart students participate in local, regional, and national competitions with their peers from other schools through programs such as forensics/speech and debate, science research, broadcast journalism, and Model United Nations. These programs are designed to promote self-expression, intellectual challenge, and individual leadership opportunities.

Music, dramatic readings, and gallery art shows are an important part of the Upper School experience. Diverse curricular offerings in visual arts, theater, and music provide opportunities for interdisciplinary study, and core academic classes often collaborate on thematic projects with the arts departments.

Recognizing that one's own creative development emerges from exposure to the creativity of others, Sacred Heart emphasizes a balance between performance and appreciation. Guest artists, performers, and lecturers regularly visit the school. Proximity to New York City creates opportunities to investigate unlimited cultural resources, while student exhibitions and performances showcase the talents cultivated in the school's classes and studios.

The Community Service Program is also an integral part of the Upper School experience at Sacred Heart. Using age-appropriate tools, students study a wide range of issues, including racism, poverty, housing, and education. Analysis of social injustices helps the students recognize that they can use their talents to be agents of change in the world. The Community Service Program explores domestic and global issues and includes guest speakers, individual yearly projects, service trips, and retreats. While service is required for Upper School students, most exceed the graduation requirement of 100 hours with extra volunteer work. The Barat Foundation is a student-run philanthropic organization that awards grants to community nonprofits and teaches financial literacy to students.

The Sacred Heart Exchange Program allows students to experience different cultures in the United States and around the world. Upper School students may complete an academic exchange of two to ten weeks at another Sacred Heart school. Convent of the Sacred Heart also welcomes exchange students to its campus. Recently, Sacred Heart students have studied in England, France, Spain, Taiwan, Australia, Chile, Mexico, and Nova Scotia. Upon graduating, students are given an international Sacred Heart Passport listing the Sacred Heart schools throughout the world where they are always welcome.

DAILY LIFE

The first academic period begins at 8:25 a.m. The school day includes six academic periods with time built in for advisory periods, assembly periods, and activities and club meetings. The day concludes at 3:25 p.m. Sports and a variety of activities occur after school. Students may buy or bring their lunch. A hot lunch is provided for a yearly fee.

SUMMER PROGRAMS

Convent of the Sacred Heart offers a summer enrichment program for its students and siblings in June. In August, the School hosts a study skills development program for incoming Middle School students.

In addition, as part of its mission Sacred Heart hosts an annual Summer Outreach Program for 250 boys and girls in grades 2 through 9 from low-income families. The five-week academic program is augmented with extracurricular activities, including team sports, swimming lessons, and hands-on experience with a vegetable garden. Many Sacred Heart students volunteer to help with this program.

COSTS AND FINANCIAL AID

An education at Sacred Heart is an investment that provides many important and valuable opportunities. Tuition for 2013–14 was $35,900 for grades 9–12. The Financial Aid Committee is committed to helping families find ways to make an education at Convent of the Sacred Heart affordable. The Financial Aid Committee works with families to determine personalized need-based assistance and financial planning. Applying for financial aid has no bearing on admission to Convent of the Sacred Heart.

ADMISSIONS INFORMATION

Sacred Heart admits students without regard to race, religion, nationality, or ethnic origin. Applicants are considered on the basis of their school records, teacher recommendations, admission test scores, class visit, and personal interview. Entrance exams are administered at the school in November and January and at other local independent schools throughout the fall.

Families are encouraged to attend the Open House for kindergarten through grade 12 in November or Thursday morning Tour Day programs (October, November, December, and January). Sacred Heart also hosts an evening Upper School Open House in October for students interested in grades 9–12. Open house dates for the preschool and prekindergarten, The Barat Center for Early Childhood Education, are in November and January. Specific dates for these events will be available on the School's website at http://www.cshgreenwich.org. Individual tours and interviews are also available.

APPLICATION TIMETABLE

All application materials and visits must be completed by February 1. Decision letters are mailed by March 1. Applications for financial aid with supporting documentation are due by February 15.

ADMISSIONS CORRESPONDENCE

Catherine Cullinane, Director of Admission and
    Financial Aid
Convent of the Sacred Heart
1177 King Street
Greenwich, Connecticut 06831
United States
Phone: 203-532-3534
Fax: 203-532-3301
E-mail: admission@cshct.org
Website: http://www.cshgreenwich.org

DEERFIELD ACADEMY
Deerfield, Massachusetts

DEERFIELD ACADEMY

Type: Coeducational boarding and day college-preparatory school
Grades: 9–12, postgraduate year
Enrollment: 630
Head of School: Dr. Margarita O'Byrne Curtis

THE SCHOOL

Since its founding in 1797, Deerfield Academy has provided a unique and challenging opportunity for young people. Deerfield Academy is a vibrant learning community nurturing high standards of scholarship, citizenship, and personal responsibility. Through a demanding liberal arts curriculum, extensive cocurricular program, and supportive residential environment, Deerfield encourages each student to develop an inquisitive and creative mind, sound body, strong moral character, and commitment to service. The setting of the campus, which is rich in tradition and beauty, inspires reflection, study and play, the cultivation of friendships, and the growth of a defining community spirit.

The school's 280-acre campus is located in the center of Historic Deerfield, a restored Colonial village in western Massachusetts, 90 miles from Boston and 55 miles from Hartford. Only 20 minutes south is the five-college area that includes Amherst, Smith, Mount Holyoke, and Hampshire Colleges and the University of Massachusetts, providing rich cultural and intellectual resources.

A 30-member Board of Trustees is the Academy's governing body. The endowment is valued at approximately $422 million. In 2012–13, operating expenses totaled $50.7 million, capital gifts amounted to $18.7 million, and Annual Giving was $5.5 million, with 40 percent of the 9,811 alumni participating.

Deerfield is accredited by the New England Association of Schools and Colleges. It is a member of the National Association of Independent Schools, the Independent School Association of Massachusetts, and the Secondary School Admission Test Board.

ACADEMIC PROGRAM

Deerfield's curriculum is designed to enable its students to assume active and intelligent roles in the world community. Courses and teaching methods are aimed at developing logical and imaginative thinking, systematic approaches to problem solving, clear and correct expression in writing and speech, and the confidence to pursue creatively one's interests and talents. Students take five courses per trimester. Their schedules are planned individually in consultation with advisers and the Academic Dean.

Graduation requirements include English, 4 years; mathematics, 3 years; foreign language, 3 years of a language (Arabic, Chinese, French, Greek, Latin, or Spanish); history, 2 years (including 1 year of U.S. history); laboratory science, 2 years; fine arts, two terms; and philosophy and religious studies, one term. All sophomores take a one-term course in health issues. In addition, all new students take a required course in library skills. Honors and Advanced Placement (AP) courses are offered in nineteen subject areas. Last year, 320 students sat for 709 AP exams. Ninety-one percent of the tests received qualifying scores of 3 or better. Independent study is offered in all departments.

During the spring term, seniors may engage in off-campus alternate-studies projects, ranging from working in a local hospital to serving as an intern for a member of Congress. Juniors may spend half of their year at the Maine Coast Semester, which combines regular classes with studies of environmental issues;

at the Mountain School in Vermont; or at a boarding school in South Africa, Botswana, or Kenya. Sophomores and juniors may spend a semester at the Island School on Eleuthera in the Bahamas. The Swiss Semester in Zermatt is a program that gives sophomores an opportunity to study geology, European history, and foreign language at the foot of the Matterhorn. Deerfield participates in the School Year Abroad program in China, France, Italy, Japan, Spain, and Vietnam, which is available for juniors and seniors. Students may also choose from many exchange programs, including programs in Australia, Hong Kong, Jordan, and New Zealand. Summer opportunities are available in China, the Dominican Republic, France, Greece, Italy, Spain, and Uruguay.

The average class size is 12. The overall faculty-student ratio is 1:6. Placement in AP courses, honors sections, and accelerated courses is based upon preparedness, ability, and interest. All students have study hours Sunday through Thursday evenings.

The school year is divided into three 11-week terms. Grades are sent at the end of each term and at midterm. In the fall and spring, the student's academic adviser prepares a formal written report, commenting extensively on the student's academic performance, attitude, work habits, dormitory life, and participation in athletics and cocurricular activities and as a citizen of the school.

Grading is based on a numerical scale of 0 to 100; 60 is passing. The honor roll is made up of students with minimum averages of 90, and the high honor roll recognizes students with averages of 93 and above. Students in academic difficulty are reviewed by the Academic Standing Committee at the end of each term. Teachers are available during evenings, weekends, and free periods to assist students individually. Students can also get help from the Study Skills Coordinator.

FACULTY AND ADVISERS

The high quality of Deerfield's faculty is the school's greatest endowment.

The faculty consists of 119 members (55 women and 64 men); 73 percent hold advanced degrees. Ninety percent reside on campus or live in the village of Deerfield. All faculty members act as advisers to students, coach sports, head tables in the dining hall, and serve on various committees. Teachers receive summer grants and time away from the Academy for advanced study, travel, and exchange teaching.

Dr. Margarita O'Byrne Curtis was appointed Head of School in July 2006. She earned her B.A. from Tulane, her B.S. from Mankato State, and a Ph.D. in Romance languages and literature from Harvard.

COLLEGE ADMISSION COUNSELING

College advising is coordinated by 4 college advisers. Beginning in their junior year, all students attend small-group discussions that help them make informed decisions about college. In mid-winter, every junior is assigned to an individual college adviser, who further develops, with parental consultation, a list of prospective colleges. In the fall of the senior year, college advisers assist students in narrowing their college choices and in making the most effective presentation of their strengths. During the fall, representatives of

approximately 160 colleges visit the Academy for presentations and interviews.

Normally, sophomores and juniors take the PSAT in October. Juniors take the SAT in January; SAT Subject Tests in December, May, and June; and Advanced Placement (AP) tests in May. Seniors, whenever advisable, take the SAT in the fall and additional AP tests later in the year. The average SAT scores for the class of 2013 was 656 critical reading, 666 math, and 662 writing.

Of the 204 graduates in 2013, 196 are attending college, 8 students deferred admission to college for a year. Colleges attended by 5 or more students are: Cornell, Dartmouth, Duke, Georgetown, Harvard, Pennsylvania, Princeton, Stanford, Virginia, Williams, and Yale.

STUDENT BODY AND CONDUCT

In fall 2012, Deerfield enrolled 633 students: 309 girls and 324 boys. There were 95 boarders and 17 day students in the ninth grade, 125 boarders and 26 day students in the tenth grade, 148 boarders and 18 day students in the eleventh grade, and 188 boarders and 16 day students in the twelfth grade (including 20 postgraduates). Recognizing that diversity enriches the school, the Academy seeks to foster an appreciation of difference. To that end, international students made up 16 percent of the student body, and those from minority groups made up 30 percent. Deerfield students came from thirty-nine states and thirty-three countries.

In all communities, a healthy tension exists between the need for individuality and the need for common values and standards. A community's shared values define the place, giving it a distinct sense of itself. In all facets of school life, Deerfield strives to teach that honesty, tolerance, compassion, and responsibility are essential to the well-being of the individual, the school, and society. Deerfield Academy is a residential community in which students learn to conduct themselves according to high standards of citizenship. Expectations for students are clear, and the response to misbehavior is timely and as supportive as possible of the students involved.

ACADEMIC FACILITIES

Deerfield's campus has eighty-one buildings. The Frank L. Boyden Library has a collection of more than 85,000 books, periodicals, and films. Most of the library's collection is accessible via a fully integrated online catalog. The Koch Center, a new, state-of-the-art 80,000-square-foot center for science, mathematics, and technology, includes a new planetarium; thirty classroom and laboratory spaces, including dedicated spaces for independent research; a 225-seat auditorium; the Star Terrace; and a central atrium.

The Memorial Building contains the main auditorium, Hilson Gallery, Russell Gallery, art studios, a black-box theater, a dance facility, and music recital and practice rooms.

BOARDING AND GENERAL FACILITIES

There are eighteen dormitories. Faculty members live in apartments attached to each dorm corridor and maintain a close, supportive relationship with students. Two senior proctors also live on the freshman and sophomore corridors. Eighty-five percent of the boarding students have single rooms.

The fifteen-bed health center, Dewey House, is staffed full-time by a physician and registered nurses.

ATHLETICS

Participation in sports—at the student's level of ability—is the athletic program's central focus. The Academy fields interscholastic teams in baseball, basketball, crew, cross-country, cycling, diving, field hockey, football, golf, ice hockey, lacrosse, skiing, soccer, softball, squash, swimming, tennis, track, volleyball, water polo, and wrestling. Supervised recreational activities include aerobics, cycling, dance, skiing, squash, strength training, tennis, and an outdoor skills program.

Deerfield's gymnasium complex contains three basketball courts; a wrestling arena; an indoor hockey rink; a new 5,500-square-foot fitness center with state-of-the-art cardiovascular and weight lifting equipment, trainer's room, and locker rooms; the Dewey Squash Center, a 16,000-square-foot facility housing ten international squash courts and tournament seating; and the largest preparatory school natatorium in New England, which includes an indoor, eight-lane, 25-yard pool with a separate diving well. Ninety acres of playing fields include three football fields, twelve soccer/lacrosse fields, three field hockey fields, eighteen tennis courts, a major-league-quality baseball field, a softball field, paddle tennis courts, a new boathouse and crew facility, and a new eight-lane track. Two synthetic turf fields were added in the summer of 2008.

EXTRACURRICULAR OPPORTUNITIES

Deerfield students and faculty members are extraordinarily productive in the performing and visual arts. Musical groups include wind ensemble, chamber music, string orchestra, jazz ensemble, Deerfield Choral Society, madrigal singers, a cappella groups, and the Academy Chorus. Many opportunities exist for acting as well. In addition to the three major theater productions each year, plays and scenes are also performed by advanced acting classes. Students who are interested in dance may explore modern, jazz, and ballet, with the opportunity to perform all three terms.

Cocurricular organizations include Peer Counselors, the Diversity Task Force, Amnesty International, and debate, photography, and political clubs. Outing groups offer opportunities to ski, rock climb, and bike on weekends. Publications include an award-winning campus newspaper, the yearbook, and literary publications.

Students provide service as tutors, dormitory proctors, tour guides, and waiters in the dining hall. Students serve responsibly on various standing and ad hoc administrative committees and play an especially important role on the disciplinary committee. Students are also involved in various community service projects. The Community Service program encourages Deerfield students and faculty members to broaden their perspectives by sharing with and learning from people of different ages, abilities, cultures, and economic backgrounds.

Ongoing projects include mentoring at nearby schools, volunteering in shelters and day-care centers, tutoring, organic farming and on-campus recycling, visiting nursing homes, and sponsoring Red Cross blood drives. Some students also serve as Big Brothers or Big Sisters to local youth. In addition, each sophomore also participates in Deerfield Perspectives, an on-campus service program.

DAILY LIFE

Students normally take five courses each term, and each course meets four times per week. The length of a class period ranges from 45 to 70 minutes. Classes begin at 8:30 and end at 3:05, except on Wednesday, when classes end at 12:45 and are followed by interscholastic athletics and cocurricular activities. Classes do not meet on Saturdays. One morning a week, students and faculty members gather together for a school meeting, and students and faculty members attend seven family-style meals per week. All sports and drama activities take place after classes. Clubs and cocurricular groups meet between dinner and study hours or on weekends.

Students study in their dormitory rooms between 7:45 and 9:45 p.m., Sunday through Thursday. They may also study in the library, perform laboratory experiments, or seek help from a faculty member or the student tutoring service. During the school week, the curfew for freshmen and sophomores is 7:45; for juniors and seniors, it is 9:45.

WEEKEND LIFE

In addition to athletic events on Saturday afternoon, there are films, theatrical productions, and musical performances. Social activities, sponsored by the Student Activities Committee and chaperoned by faculty members, include coffeehouses, talent shows, concerts, and dances. Deerfield's rural setting and extensive athletic facilities are ideal for recreational hiking, rock climbing, skiing, swimming, ice skating, and other activities.

The Academy Events Committee plans and sponsors events throughout the school year. The Robert Crow Lecture Series brings to the Academy leaders in politics, government, education, science, and journalism. Students attend concerts and film series. Art exhibitions and numerous dramatic productions provide recognition for promising young artists, photographers, and actors. Students also have access to cultural programs in the five-college area.

Freshmen may take two weekends off campus in the fall term and three each in the winter and spring terms; sophomores may take two weekends in fall, three in winter, and an unlimited number in spring; juniors and seniors in good standing may take unlimited weekends. On weekends, the curfew for freshmen and sophomores is at 10:30 p.m. on Friday and 11 on Saturday. For juniors and seniors, Friday curfew is at 11; Saturday curfew is at 11:30.

COSTS AND FINANCIAL AID

For 2012–13 school year, the cost for boarding students was $47,500; for day students, it was $34,050. Additional fees included $2,045 for books, infirmary, and technology. Tuition is payable in two installments, on August 1 and December 1. A $2,500 deposit (credited to the August tuition bill) is due within four weeks of the student's acceptance by Deerfield.

Deerfield awards financial aid to 35 percent of its students. Financial aid totaled more than $7 million for the 2012–13 academic year; grants, based on demonstrated need and procedures established by the School and Student Service for Financial Aid, range from $2,500 to full tuition.

ADMISSIONS INFORMATION

Deerfield maintains rigorous academic standards and seeks a diverse student body—geographic, socioeconomic, and racial. Selection is based upon academic ability and performance, character and maturity, and promise as a positive community citizen. The Admission Committee closely examines candidates' teacher and school recommendations and personal essays.

The SSAT or ISEE is required of applicants for grades 9 and 10 and should be taken during an applicant's current academic year. The SSAT, ISEE, or PSAT is required for eleventh-grade applicants, and the PSAT, SAT or ACT is required for twelfth-grade and postgraduate candidates. The TOEFL may be taken in place of the aforementioned tests by students for whom English is not their first language.

Deerfield Academy does not discriminate on the basis of race, color, creed, handicap, sexual orientation, or national or ethnic origin in its admission policies or financial aid program.

APPLICATION TIMETABLE

Applicants normally visit the Academy in the year prior to the proposed date of entrance. Campus tours and interviews are conducted from 8:30 to 2:20 on Monday, Tuesday, Thursday, and Friday; from 8:15 to noon on Wednesday; and at 9, 10, and 11 on Saturday. Weekdays are preferable, since there are no Saturday classes. The completed application—including teacher recommendations, the school transcript, and essays—should be submitted no later than the January 15 deadline. Applicants receive notification of the admission decision on March 10. The candidate reply date is April 10. Specific dates can be found on the Academy's website at http://deerfield.edu/apply/how-to-apply.

ADMISSIONS CORRESPONDENCE

Pam Safford
Dean of Admission and Financial Aid
Deerfield Academy
Deerfield, Massachusetts 01342
United States
Phone: 413-774-1400
E-mail: admission@deerfield.edu
Website: http://www.deerfield.edu

DELBARTON SCHOOL

Morristown, New Jersey

Type: Boys' day college-preparatory school
Grades: 7–12: Middle School, 7–8; Upper School, 9–12
Enrollment: School total: 558; Upper School: 491
Head of School: Br. Paul Diveny, O.S.B., Headmaster

THE SCHOOL

Delbarton School was established in 1939 by the Benedictine monks of Saint Mary's Abbey as an independent boarding and day school. Now a day school, Delbarton is located on a 200-acre woodland campus 3 miles west of historic Morristown and 30 miles west of New York City. Adjacent to the campus is Jockey Hollow, a national historic park.

Delbarton School seeks to enroll boys of good character who have demonstrated scholastic achievement and the capacity for further growth. The faculty strives to support each boy's efforts toward intellectual development and to reinforce his commitment to help build a community of responsible individuals. The faculty encourages each boy to become an independent seeker of information, not a passive recipient, and to assume responsibility for gaining both knowledge and judgment that will strengthen his contribution to the life of the School and his later contribution to society. While the School offers much, it also seeks boys who are willing to give much and who are eager to understand as well as to be understood.

The School is governed by the 9-member Board of Trustees of the Order of Saint Benedict of New Jersey, located at Saint Mary's Abbey in Morristown. Delbarton's 2013–14 annual operating expenses totaled $20.5 million. It has an endowment of $30 million. This includes annual fund-raising support from 38 percent of the alumni.

Delbarton School is accredited by the Middle States Association of Colleges and Schools and approved by the Department of Education of the State of New Jersey. It is a member of the National Association of Independent Schools, the New Jersey Association of Independent Schools, the Council for Advancement and Support of Education, the National Catholic Educational Association, and the New Jersey State Interscholastic Athletic Association.

ACADEMIC PROGRAM

The academic program in the Upper School is college preparatory. The course of study offers preparation in all major academic subjects and a number of electives. The studies are intended to help a boy shape a thought and a sentence, speak clearly about ideas and effectively about feelings, and suspend judgment until all the facts are known. Course work, on the whole, is intensive and involves about 20 hours of outside preparation each week. The curriculum contains both a core of required subjects that are fundamental to a liberal education and various elective courses that are designed to meet the individual interests of the boys. Instruction is given in all areas that are necessary for gaining admission to liberal arts or technical institutions of higher learning.

The school year is divided into three academic terms. In each term, every boy must take five major courses, physical education, and religious studies. The specific departmental requirements in grades 9 through 12 are English (4 years), mathematics (4 years), foreign language (3 years), science (3 years), history (3 years), religious studies (2 terms in each of 4 years), physical education and health (4 years), fine arts (1 major course, 1 term of art, and 1 term of music), and computer technology (2 terms). For qualified boys in the junior and senior years, all departments offer Advanced Placement courses, and it is also possible in certain instances to pursue work through independent study or to study at neighboring colleges.

The grading system uses A to F (failing) designations with pluses and minuses. Advisory reports are sent to parents in the middle of each term as well as at the end of the three terms. Parents are also contacted when a student has received an academic warning or is placed on probation. The average class size is 15, and the student-teacher ratio is about 7:1, which fosters close student-faculty relations.

FACULTY AND ADVISERS

In 2013–14 the faculty consisted of 6 Benedictine monks and 76 lay teachers. Sixty-two are full-time members, with 58 holding advanced degrees.

Br. Paul Diveny, O.S.B., became Headmaster in July 2007. Br. Paul received his B.A. from the Catholic University of America in 1975; his diploma in Monastic Studies from the Pontificio Ateneo Sant'Anselmo in Rome, Italy in 1982; and his M.A. in German from Middlebury College in 1987. He has served the School previously as a teacher of Latin, German, ancient history, and religious studies, and as Assistant Headmaster.

The teaching tradition of the School has called upon faculty members to serve as coaches, counselors, or administrators. A genuine interest in the development of people leads the faculty to be involved in many student activities. Every boy is assigned to a guidance counselor, who advises in the selection of courses that meet School and college requirements as well as personal interests. Individual conferences are regularly arranged to discuss academic and personal development. The counselor also contacts the boy's parents when it seems advisable.

COLLEGE ADMISSION COUNSELING

Preparation for college begins when a boy enters Delbarton. The PSAT is given to everyone in the tenth and eleventh grades. Guidance for admission to college is directed by the senior class counselor. This process generally begins in the fall of the junior year, when the junior class counselor meets

with each boy to help clarify his goals and interests. Many college admissions officers visit the School annually for conferences. Every effort is made to direct each boy toward an institution that will challenge his abilities and satisfy his interests.

The mean SAT critical reading and math score for the class of 2013 was 1350. More than 25 percent of the young men in the classes of 2010, 2011, 2012, and 2013 have been named National Merit Scholars, Semifinalists, or Commended Students. In addition, 85 percent of the members of the class of 2013 were enrolled in at least one AP course.

All of the graduates of the classes of 2010, 2011, 2012, and 2013 went on to college, with 4 or more attending such schools as Boston College, Columbia, Cornell, Dartmouth, Duke, Georgetown, Harvard, Holy Cross, Johns Hopkins, Middlebury, Notre Dame, Princeton, Villanova, Williams, Yale, and the Universities of Pennsylvania and Virginia.

STUDENT BODY AND CONDUCT

The 2013–14 Upper School student body consisted of 127 ninth graders, 117 tenth graders, 117 eleventh graders, and 130 twelfth graders. The Middle School has 34 seventh and 33 eighth graders. All of the students are from New Jersey, particularly the counties of Morris, Essex, Somerset, Union, Bergen, Hunterdon, Passaic, and Sussex.

Regulations, academic and social, are relatively few. The School eschews the manipulative, the coercive, the negative, or the merely punitive approach to discipline. The basic understanding underlying the School's regulations is that each boy, entering with others in a common educational enterprise, shares responsibility with his fellow students and with faculty members for developing and maintaining standards that contribute to the welfare of the entire School community. Moreover, shared responsibility is essential to the growth of the community; at the same time, much of an individual boy's growth, the increase in his capacity for self-renewal, his sense of belonging, and his sense of identity spring from his eagerness and willingness to contribute to the life of the School. Each class has a moderator, who is available for advice and assistance. The moderator works closely with the boys, assisting them in their progress.

ACADEMIC FACILITIES

The physical facilities include two classroom buildings, a fine arts center, a science pavilion, a greenhouse, the church, and the dining hall. Academic facilities include thirty-seven classrooms, six science laboratories, art and music studios, and a library of more than 20,000 volumes. The five computer laboratories consist of 250 workstations in a networked system. The school recently adopted a one-to-one laptop program for the students and provides several charging stations throughout the campus. Three computer laboratories and dedicated classroom computers also provide over 100 workstations in a networked system. Some individual academic departments offer personal computers for advanced study in their discipline as well.

ATHLETICS

Sports at the School are an integral part of student life. The School holds the traditional belief that much can be learned about cooperation, competition, and character through participating in sports. Almost 85 percent of the boys participate on one or more interscholastic athletics teams. Varsity sports offered in the fall term are football, soccer, and cross-country; in the winter term, basketball, wrestling, track, hockey, squash, bowling, and swimming (in an off-campus pool); and in the spring, baseball, track, lacrosse, tennis, and golf. In most of these sports, there are junior varsity, freshman, and Middle School teams. Some intramural sports are available, depending upon interest, every year.

The facilities consist of two gymnasiums, eight athletics fields, six tennis courts, and an outdoor pool for swimming during warm weather. Students who join the golf team are able to play at nearby golf clubs.

EXTRACURRICULAR OPPORTUNITIES

The School provides opportunities for individual development outside the classroom as well as within. The faculty encourages the boys to express their intellectual, cultural, social, and recreational interests through a variety of activities and events. For example, fine arts at Delbarton are available both within and outside the curriculum. Studio hours accommodate boys after school, and students visit galleries and museums. In the music department, vocal and instrumental instruction is available. Performing ensembles include an orchestra, band, and chorus and smaller vocal and instrumental ensembles. Under the aegis of the Abbey Players, drama productions are staged three times a year, involving boys in a wide variety of experiences.

Other activities include Deaneries (student support groups promoting School unity and spirit), the *Courier* (the School newspaper), the *Archway* (the yearbook), *Schola Cantorum* (a vocal ensemble), the Abbey Orchestra, and the Model UN, Mock Trial, Speech and Debate, Junior Statesmen, Art, History, Chess, Cycling, Stock Exchange, and Future Business Leaders clubs. In addition, faculty moderators of the Ski Club

regularly organize and chaperone trips during School vacations.

To expose students to other cultures and to enhance their understanding of the world, faculty members have organized trips to Europe, Africa, and Latin America. The Campus Ministry office is active in sponsoring several outreach programs that lead boys to an awareness of the needs of others and the means to answer calls for help. The outreach programs include community soup kitchens, Big Brothers of America, Adopt-a-Grandparent, Basketball Clinic for exceptional children, and a program in which volunteers travel to Appalachia during break to contribute various services to the poor of that area.

Students' imagination and initiative are also given opportunities for expression through Student Council committees and assemblies. The students are also offered School-sponsored trips to cultural and recreational events at area colleges and in nearby cities.

DAILY LIFE

Classes begin at 8:15 a.m. and end at 2:34 p.m. The average number of classes per day for each student is six. Two classes are an hour long, while the remainder are 40 minutes each. The School operates on a six-day cycle, and each class meets five days per cycle. Physical education classes are held during the school day. After classes, students are involved in athletics and the arts. Clubs and organizations also meet after school, while many meet at night.

COSTS AND FINANCIAL AID

Charges at Delbarton for the 2013–14 academic year are $32,200. These are comprehensive fees that include a daily hot lunch as well as library and athletics fees. The only other major expenses are the bookstore bill and transportation, the cost of which varies. Optional expenses may arise for such items as the yearbook, music lessons, or trips.

Because of the School's endowment and generous alumni and parent support, a financial aid program enables many boys to attend the School. All awards are based on financial need, as determined by the criteria set by the School and Student Service for Financial Aid. No academic or athletics scholarships are awarded. Financial aid is granted to boys in grades 7 through 12. This year, the School was able to grant $1.7 million to students.

ADMISSIONS INFORMATION

Delbarton School selects students whose academic achievement and personal promise indicate that they are likely to become

positive members of the community. The object of the admissions procedure is for the School and prospective student to learn as much as possible about each other. Admission is based on the candidate's overall qualifications, without regard to race, color, religion, or national or ethnic origin.

The typical applicant takes one of the three entrance tests administered by the School in October, November, and December. Candidates are considered on the basis of their transcript, recommendations, test results, and personal interview in addition to the formal application. In 2013–14, 381 students were tested for entrance in grades 7 and 9; of these, 148 were accepted. One hundred percent of the students who were accepted for the seventh grade were enrolled; 82 percent of those accepted for the ninth grade were enrolled. Delbarton does not admit postgraduate students or students who are entering the twelfth grade.

APPLICATION TIMETABLE

The School welcomes inquiries at any time during the year. Students who apply are invited to spend a day at Delbarton attending classes with a School host. Interested applicants should arrange this day visit through the Admissions Office. Tours of the campus are generally given in conjunction with interviews, from 9 a.m. to noon on Saturdays in the fall, or by special arrangement. The formal application for admission must be accompanied by a nonrefundable fee of $65. Application fee waivers are available upon request.

It is advisable to initiate the admissions process in the early fall. Acceptance notifications for applicants to grades 7 and 9 are made by the end of January. Applicants to all remaining grades, as well as students placed in a wait pool, are given acceptance notification as late as June. Parents are expected to reply to acceptances two to three weeks after notification. A refundable deposit is also required. Application for financial aid should be made as early as possible; the committee hopes to notify financial aid applicants by the middle of March.

ADMISSIONS CORRESPONDENCE

Dr. David Donovan
Dean of Admissions
Delbarton School
Morristown, New Jersey 07960
United States
Phone: 973-538-3231 Ext. 3019
Fax: 973-538-8836
E-mail: admissions@delbarton.org
Website: http://www.delbarton.org/
    admissions

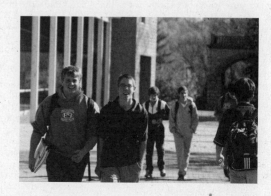

THE DERRYFIELD SCHOOL

Manchester, New Hampshire

Type: Coeducational, college-preparatory day school
Grades: Grades 6–12
Enrollment: Total: 387; Middle School: 116; Upper School: 271
Head of School: Mary Halpin Carter, Ph.D., Head of School

THE SCHOOL

The Derryfield School, an independent, coeducational, college-preparatory day school, was founded by local citizens in 1964 to provide an outstanding secondary education for students who want to live at home.

Derryfield inspires bright, motivated young people to be their best, and provides them with the skills and experiences needed to be valued, dynamic, confident, and purposeful members of any community.

The School is governed by a 20-member Board of Trustees and, in addition to tuition, is supported financially through annual giving and an endowment fund of more than $4.4 million.

Derryfield is accredited by the New England Association of Schools and Colleges and is a member of the National Association of Independent Schools (NAIS), the Association of Independent Schools of New England (AISNE), and the Independent Schools Association of Northern New England (ISANNE).

ACADEMIC PROGRAM

Derryfield's challenging academic program combines a seriousness of purpose with a sense of spirit. A core college-preparatory curriculum is enhanced by more than seventy elective classes and independent learning opportunities.

Students entering Derryfield in the Middle School participate in a curriculum that provides a firm background in skills and basic discipline areas in preparation for Upper School courses. All students in grades 6, 7, and 8 take English, mathematics, science, history, and a foreign language. In addition, all Middle School students participate in drama, music, wellness, physical education, and art.

Students entering the Upper School (grades 9–12) plan their course of study in the context of graduation requirements, college plans, and interests. A total of 18 academic credits is required with the following departmental distribution: 4 credits in English, 2 credits in history, 3 credits in mathematics, 3 credits in a world language, 2-1/3 credits in science, 1 credit in fine arts, and participation in either the alternative sports program or a team sport two seasons per year. Each student carries a minimum of five courses each term. The academic year consists of three terms.

The Independent Senior Project is an option for seniors during the final six weeks of the spring term. The project allows students to explore their interests and to gain practical experience outside of the classroom.

FACULTY AND ADVISERS

The Derryfield faculty consists of 46 members (25 men and 21 women). Master's degrees are held by 28 members and Ph.D.'s are held by 4 members. Twenty-four faculty members have taught at Derryfield for ten or more years, and annual faculty turnover is low. The student-faculty ratio is 8:1.

Faculty members are hired on the basis of a high level of expertise in their academic areas as well as enthusiasm to contribute to the overall success of their students and the School. In addition to their classroom obligations, faculty members advise approximately 8 students, coach Derryfield's athletic and academic teams, advise student activities, and make themselves available to counsel students in other areas of student life.

COLLEGE ADMISSION COUNSELING

A dedicated college counselor begins working with students in February of their junior year. College counseling is an active process that includes group seminars and individual meetings with students and their families. More than 90 college representatives visit Derryfield each year.

The average SAT scores for the class of 2013 were 607 in critical reading, 613 in math, and 616 in the writing section. Fifty-six students graduated in 2013, with 100 percent of the class going to college. A sampling of the colleges and universities currently attended by 2 or more Derryfield graduates includes American, Barnard, Bates, Boston College, Colby, Cornell, Dartmouth, Elon, George Washington, Holy Cross, Johns Hopkins, Middlebury, NYU, Northeastern, Providence, Quinnipiac, RIT, St. Lawrence, Syracuse, Tufts, and the Universities of Colorado–Boulder, Michigan, Vermont, and Virginia.

STUDENT BODY AND CONDUCT

Of the 387 students enrolled at The Derryfield School, 116 students attend the Middle School program and 271 students attend the Upper School program. Students come from fifty local communities.

Violations of School rules are handled by the Discipline Committee, which consists of elected students and faculty members who evaluate discipline issues and make recommendations to the Head of School.

ACADEMIC FACILITIES

Derryfield's academic facilities include classroom buildings with five fully equipped science laboratories, a STEM classroom, a technology center with workstations and laptops, a 95-seat multimedia lyceum, a 17,000-volume library with a large subscription database, two art studios, an art gallery, and a 400-seat performing arts center. Outdoor classroom facilities include several miles of cross-country trails, high and low ropes courses, and many acres of woods. A turf field, a full-sized gymnasium, weight-training area, and trainer's room are also valuable learning sites for courses in physical education and health and wellness. In addition, the School opened the new 8,000-square-foot Gateway Building in 2011, which houses administrative offices, the Breakthrough Manchester Program, and two additional teaching spaces.

ATHLETICS

"A sound mind in a healthy body" defined the Greek ideal and is the concept at the core of Derryfield's physical education, health and wellness, and athletics philosophy.

All Middle Schoolers (grades 6–8) take physical education and health and wellness. Seventh and eighth graders also have competitive athletic requirements. Offerings include alpine skiing, baseball, basketball, cross-country running, field hockey, lacrosse, Nordic skiing, soccer, softball, and tennis.

In the Upper School (grades 9–12), two levels of competitive sports teams (junior varsity and varsity), as well as some alternative physical activities (e.g., yoga, dance, weight training) are offered. Upper School athletics include alpine skiing, baseball, basketball, crew, cross-country running, equestrian, field hockey, golf, lacrosse, Nordic skiing, soccer, softball, swimming, and tennis. The School also honors areas of physical interest that it does not offer on site; students may request that an independent physical activity be a replacement for one of the two required seasons.

Derryfield is a member of the New Hampshire Interscholastic Athletic Association, participating in Divisions I, II, III, and IV, according to sport. Derryfield currently has the most athletic offerings of any Division IV school in New Hampshire and has garnered more than thirty-three state championships in the last ten years.

EXTRACURRICULAR OPPORTUNITIES

Derryfield's commitment to the arts is evident. High school students perform two large-scale drama productions each year, while seventh and eighth graders take part in their own musical. Each sixth grade drama class produces its own junior musical. Instrumental ensembles that include classical, jazz, and orchestral instruments are active in both the Middle and Upper School. There are vocal groups in both schools, and Upper School students may audition for a select chorus. All musicians participate in two concerts per year and frequently in talent shows and assemblies. Students are encouraged to audition for the New Hampshire All-State Chorus and Band. Visual art students regularly submit materials to the New Hampshire Student Artist Awards and the Boston Globe Scholastic Art Awards, and help organize displays of their own work in Derryfield's art gallery openings.

In each of the two schools, Middle and Upper, students participate in more than a dozen student-organized clubs. Choices include School Council, Conservation Club, Art Club, Gay/Straight Alliance, Empower Women Club, Robotics Club, Social Media Ambassadors, and Chinese Culture Club, among others. Derryfield also offers competitive clubs, including Math Team, Debate Team, Mock Trial, Granite State Challenge, and Model United Nations. Student publications include newspapers, literary magazines, academic journals, and a yearbook.

Field trips, organized through classes or clubs, include regular visits to New York City, Boston, and Manchester museums, theaters, courtrooms, and outdoor areas of interest. Each year, different faculty members lead groups of students on cultural or service-learning outings. Upper School trips for the 2013–14 school year include a science-oriented trip to the Amazon in Peru, a Habitat for Humanity work project in North Carolina, and a trip to England that will focus on the literature and history of the country. Middle School opportunities include Washington, D.C. and Costa Rica. In the summer of 2013, Derryfield experienced its first exchange with a girls' school in South Africa; this year, there are exchanges at the same girls' school in Durban, as well as at a boys' school in Cape Town.

In its dedication to local and global communities, Derryfield's Key Club actively partners with the National Honor Society and more than a dozen organizations, including the New Hampshire Food Bank, the American Cancer Society, New Horizons Soup Kitchen, Boys and Girls Club, and local immigrant relocation programs.

Breakthrough Manchester, a year-round, tuition-free academic program, is also an important part of The Derryfield School. Breakthrough offers motivated students from Manchester's public elementary schools the opportunity to learn from outstanding high school and college students. Several Derryfield faculty members work as mentor teachers, while a large number of Derryfield students teach for Breakthrough.

Traditional Derryfield events and celebrations include Founders' Day, Winter Carnival, Grandparents' Day, Head's Holiday, Country Fair, Moose Revue talent show, and the Prom.

DAILY LIFE

Because Derryfield students come from approximately fifty different surrounding towns, the School itself becomes a hub for learning, playing, serving, and socializing.

A full Derryfield School day begins at 7:55 a.m. and ends between 2:45 and 3:20 p.m. Departure times vary, depending on grade, a student's level of involvement in extracurricular activities or desire to obtain extra help from a teacher, use the library, or attend study hall.

Homeroom gatherings occur two mornings per week, and advisories meet three times per week. The Tuesday and Friday class schedules allow time for an activities period, during which clubs meet. A 30-minute all-school assembly takes place each Monday morning. The class schedule is a seven-period, seven-"day," rotating schedule.

SUMMER PROGRAMS

Derryfield offers several summer camps, including lacrosse, soccer, and a very popular theater camp. There are also a number of academic options, featuring robotics, academic skills, SAT preparation, creative writing, and writing for the college process.

COSTS AND FINANCIAL AID

Tuition and fees for 2013–14 are $28,535. In addition to the need-based Financial Aid Program and the Merit Scholarship Program, which offer direct grants, the School offers installment payment options.

The Financial Aid Program is designed to make a Derryfield education accessible to qualified students who could not otherwise afford the cost of attending. On average, Derryfield provides financial assistance to 25 percent of the student body, with awards that vary from 5 to 95 percent of tuition. Derryfield awards nearly $1.5 million in financial aid grants annually.

The Merit Scholarship Program is designed to recognize students who demonstrate qualities that will add meaning and vitality to Derryfield's core values or are distinguished by a commitment to purposeful involvement in both the local and global community. Awards of up to $15,000 are made annually.

The Malone Scholars Program was established in 2012 with a $2 million award from the Malone Foundation in recognition of the School's academic program. The Foundation's goal is to improve access to quality education for gifted students who lack the financial resources to develop their talents. Currently, the school has three Malone Scholars, and anticipates that additional Scholars will be added for the 2014–15 school year.

ADMISSIONS INFORMATION

The Admission Committee considers applications from students entering grades 6 through 12. Although the largest number of students enters in grades 6, 7, 8, and 9, spaces are often available in other grades as well.

Applicants are required to complete an on-campus interview and a written application. The SSAT is required for all applications to grades 6 through 9. Applicants to grade 10, 11, and 12 have the option to submit their PSAT or SAT scores.

APPLICATION TIMETABLE

The priority deadline for applications is January 31. Tours and interviews are offered through the Admission Office. There is a $50 preliminary application fee for applicants.

Notification of acceptance is mailed on March 10, and families are expected to reply by April 10.

ADMISSIONS CORRESPONDENCE

Admission Office
The Derryfield School
2108 River Road
Manchester, New Hampshire 03104-1396
United States
Phone: 603-669-4524
Fax: 603-641-9521
E-mail: admission@derryfield.org
Website: http://www.derryfield.org

GRIER SCHOOL
Tyrone, Pennsylvania

Type: Girls' boarding and day college-preparatory school
Grades: 7–PG: Middle School, 7–8; Upper School: 9–12, postgraduate year
Enrollment: School total: 304
Heads of School: Douglas A. Grier, Director; Andrew Wilson, Headmaster; Gina Borst, Head of School

THE SCHOOL

Grier School was founded in 1853 as the Mountain Female Seminary and was reincorporated in 1857 under the direction of Dr. Lemuel Grier. The School has been successfully operated under the management of four generations of the Grier family. In 1957, the School was reincorporated as a nonprofit foundation administered by an alumnae Board of Trustees. Grier is located on a 300-acre campus in the country, 3 miles from Tyrone, Pennsylvania, and halfway between State College (where Penn State University is located) and Altoona.

The School is committed to a highly supportive philosophy aimed at developing each girl's full potential as an individual. Competitive sports are offered but do not overshadow the many intramural, life-sports, and creative arts opportunities available to each girl. Grier does not seek an elitist or high-pressure label and is proud of its family-like environment. "Friendliness" is the word most often used by visitors to describe the atmosphere.

The current endowment stands at approximately $18 million, supplemented by $520,000 raised through the most recent Annual and Capital Giving program.

Grier School is accredited by the Middle States Association of Colleges and Schools. It has memberships in the National Association of Independent Schools, the Pennsylvania Association of Independent Schools, and the Secondary School Admission Test Board.

ACADEMIC PROGRAM

Grier offers a multi-track academic program. The Elite Scholars Program is well suited for high-achieving students interested in honors and AP courses. AP courses are offered in all subject areas as twenty class offerings. While all classes are college preparatory in nature, the Learning Skills and Student Support programs ensure that all students receive the support they need to empower themselves as learners. Every attempt is made to pace the curriculum to the needs of individual students, and crossover is encouraged between the academic tracks according to the abilities of the students.

Learning Skills, a course taught by 3 specialists, is available for students who require additional academic structure and provides opportunities for tutoring and the development of strong study habits. This program serves the needs of approximately 50 students at Grier. A comprehensive English as a second language program is offered to international students. Girls who test below 100 on the TOEFL Internet-based test are required to attend an intensive summer session.

Students are encouraged to take at least one elective in the arts each year. The variety of course offerings is designed to provide students with the opportunity to pursue areas of interest and to develop and enhance their individual talents. Strong programs are offered in studio art, ceramics, jewelry making, photography, weaving, costume design, dance, music, and drama. Art faculty members help students assemble portfolios in preparation for higher education.

FACULTY AND ADVISERS

The full-time faculty consists of 43 women and 10 men, more than half of whom have received advanced degrees.

Douglas A. Grier, Director of the School for the past thirty years, is a graduate of Princeton and has an M.A. and a Ph.D. from the University of Michigan. Andrew Wilson and Gina Borst are co-heads of the School. Headmaster Andrew Wilson has a B.A. from Middlebury College and has worked at Grier for twenty-eight years. Head of School Gina Borst has a B.S. and an M.Ed. from Penn State University. She has worked at Grier for twenty-one years.

Many faculty members live on campus, and 25 housemothers supervise the dormitories. Faculty members are available for extra academic help on a daily basis. Faculty members also serve as advisers to students and participate in various clubs and sports activities.

COLLEGE ADMISSION COUNSELING

The School has a full-time college counselor who works with students in their junior and senior years. College counseling begins in the winter term of the junior year with class discussions about colleges, admissions requirements, and application procedures. The college counselor then discusses specific colleges with each student individually and helps the student develop a preliminary list of colleges to investigate and visit over the summer, thus refining the list. In the fall of the senior year, the counselor reviews each student's list again and encourages the student to apply to at least six colleges. Applications are usually sent by Thanksgiving (or before Christmas break at the latest).

Graduates of the class of 2013 were accepted at various colleges and universities, including Boston College, Boston University, College of William and Mary, UCLA, Fashion Institute of Technology, Lehigh, Parsons, Elon, Skidmore, and the Universities of Illinois and Wisconsin.

STUDENT BODY AND CONDUCT

Students come from thirty states and sixteen other countries.

Students are expected to follow the rules as defined in the student handbook. A Discipline Committee composed of students, faculty members, and administrators handles all infractions. Grier believes that good citizenship should be encouraged through incentive, and girls earn merits for good conduct, honors grades, and academic effort.

The student government consists of a Student Council with representatives from each class. The council serves as a forum for student concerns and helps plan the weekend programs.

ACADEMIC FACILITIES

Trustees Building is a modern classroom facility that was completely remodeled in summer 2002. It houses classrooms, two science labs, a supervised study room, and studios for ceramics, batik, and photo printmaking. Adjoining buildings house computer studios, language classrooms, and the Landon Library, which houses 16,000 volumes. The Fine Arts Center, housing extensive facilities for music and art classes, opened in January 2002. The Science Center opened in August 2003. Grier's Performing Arts Center, containing practice and performance space for dance and drama, opened in June 2006. Three new classrooms and four music practice rooms were added to the academic facilities when a new dormitory was completed in September 2012.

BOARDING AND GENERAL FACILITIES

The living quarters consist of seven dormitory areas and five cottages. The dorms and cottages provide a modern private bath for every two rooms. Two girls share a room, and each combination of two rooms and bath is called a suite. All students must leave the campus for Thanksgiving, Christmas, and spring break, though the School does sponsor trips during Thanksgiving and spring break.

Multiple student lounges with TVs and games are available, and a School-operated snack bar is located in a remodeled eighteenth-century log cabin.

The Health Center is located on the campus and is staffed at all times for emergencies or any medical concern that may arise.

ATHLETICS

Students of all ability levels are encouraged to participate in either the interscholastic sports program, which includes riding, dance, basketball, soccer, volleyball, and tennis, or the life-sports program of riding, dance, swimming, tennis, fencing, archery, badminton, yoga, body sculpting, scuba diving, and skiing/snowboarding. Grier has an excellent horseback riding program with 3 full-time instructors and 1 part-time instructor. Four stables accommodate 35 School horses and up to 15 privately owned horses. Two indoor and two outdoor rings are located on the campus within an easy walking distance of the dorm. Grier's Western indoor ring was completed in September of 2012.

The School's gymnasium is well suited for basketball and volleyball. Grier's state-of-the-art fitness center opened in September 2006. Five tennis courts and ample playing fields round out the School's physical education facilities.

EXTRACURRICULAR OPPORTUNITIES

Student groups active on campus include Grier Dance; Grier Equestrians; the Athletic Association; drama, cooking, baking, outing, ecology, modern languages, and Grier Giving Back clubs; and the yearbook and School newspaper. In addition, students participate in "Green and Gold" intramural sports, which often include soccer, volleyball, basketball, softball, and horseback riding.

Creative arts play an important part in school life, and girls can participate in several activities for enjoyment and credit, including drama, photography, art, instrumental music, voice, and dance.

Nearby Penn State University provides many cultural, social, and educational opportunities. A wide variety of field trips are offered each year, ranging from rock concerts to ski weekends to trips to Washington, D.C.,

Pittsburgh, and New York City. A regular schedule of visiting artists and a movie series complete the social activities.

DAILY LIFE

Classes begin at 8 and run until 2:37, Monday through Friday; sports activities are scheduled during the next 3 hours. A 40-minute period is set aside daily for student-teacher conferences, and an all-school meeting is held daily. Students have a 105-minute supervised study period in the dormitories Sunday through Thursday nights.

WEEKEND LIFE

Because most of Grier's students are boarders, a comprehensive program of weekend activities is planned. Approximately eight dances are planned annually, usually for Saturday evenings. The Outing Club uses the nearby facilities of Raystown Lake for camping and hiking, and canoeing and white-water rafting on the Youghiogheny River are also popular. Tussey Mountain Ski Resort, near Penn State University, is 40 minutes away.

COSTS AND FINANCIAL AID

Tuition, room, and board for the 2013–14 school year was $47,800. Books cost approximately $400 per year. Off-campus entertainment is optional, with additional costs charged based on individual participation. A deposit of $4,000 is due with the Enrollment Contract. Parents may elect to pay the entire tuition by July 1 or pay 80 percent in July and the balance in December.

Financial aid is based primarily on need. To apply, parents must submit the Parents' Financial Statement to the School

and Student Service for Financial Aid in Princeton, New Jersey. In 2012–13, 35 percent of the student body received a total of $2.0 million in financial aid.

ADMISSIONS INFORMATION

Grier seeks college-bound students of average to above-average ability who possess interest in sports and the arts as well as a desire to work in a challenging yet supportive academic atmosphere. Applicants are accepted in grades 7 through 12 (and occasionally for a postgraduate year) on the basis of previous record, recommendations, and an interview. Grier School admits students of any race, nationality, religion, or ethnic background.

Approximately 50 percent of all applicants are accepted for admission.

APPLICATION TIMETABLE

Grier has rolling admissions, and the Selection Committee meets on a regular basis to consider students whose files are complete. Candidates are asked to file an application and transcript release form with a $50 application fee, submit two teacher's recommendations, and have a personal interview on campus. The Admissions Office is open for interviews and tours during both the academic year and the summer.

ADMISSIONS CORRESPONDENCE

Andrew Wilson, Director of Admissions
Grier School
Tyrone, Pennsylvania 16686
United States
Phone: 814-684-3000
Fax: 814-684-2177
E-mail: admissions@grier.org
Website: http://www.grier.org

THE HOCKADAY SCHOOL

Dallas, Texas

Type: Girls' day college-preparatory (prekindergarten–grade 12) and boarding (grades 8–12) school
Grades: Prekindergarten–12: Lower School, Prekindergarten–4; Middle School, 5–8; Upper School, 9–12 (Forms I–IV)
Enrollment: School total: 1,087
Head of School: Kim Wargo, Eugene McDermott Headmistress

THE SCHOOL

The Hockaday School, founded a century ago in 1913, provides a nationally recognized college-preparatory education for bright girls of strong potential who will assume positions of responsibility and leadership in a rapidly changing world. Ela Hockaday dedicated herself to giving each girl a foundation for living based on scholarship, character, courtesy, and athletics—the traditional Four Cornerstones that remain the dominant influence in the School's educational philosophy today.

Hockaday's campus encompasses 88 acres of open fields and wooded creeks in residential north Dallas. The School's contemporary architectural setting features an academic quadrangle built to provide views of exterior gardens and landscaped terraces.

A Board of Trustees is the governing body. The School's endowment is more than $132 million, and the operating income is supplemented by Annual Fund giving of more than $2 million. The Alumnae Association, with more than 11,000 graduates and former students, contributes significantly to the ongoing programs of the School.

The Hockaday School is accredited by the Independent Schools Association of the Southwest. It holds membership in the National Association of Boarding Schools, the Heads Network, the College Board, the National Association for College Admission Counseling, the Educational Records Bureau, the National Coalition of Girls' Schools, the Online School for Girls, and the Secondary School Admission Test Board.

ACADEMIC PROGRAM

Students are exposed to a rigorous academic curriculum that offers core educational subjects as well as unique offerings in technology, the arts, and leadership and personal development. Graduation requirements (in years) include English, 4; mathematics, 3; history, 2.5; foreign language, 2; laboratory science, 3; fine arts, 1.5; physical education and health, 4; and academic electives from any department. Hockaday offers 121 courses, including many honors courses. Advanced Placement courses are offered in eighteen subjects, including English, modern European history, U.S. history, AB and BC calculus, statistics, physics, chemistry, biology, studio art, Latin, French, Mandarin Chinese, Spanish, computer science, and economics. For some selected courses, Hockaday has an option allowing girls to take classes via the Online School for Girls. Private lessons in cello, flute, guitar, piano, violin, and voice are also available.

An English for Speakers of Other Languages (ESOL) program is offered to students at the intermediate and advanced levels. Intensive language training in academic writing, critical reading, listening, and speaking skills is the focus of the program. Students may continue at Hockaday after the first year, following acceptance into the regular academic program. International students with intermediate or advanced English proficiency may study at Hockaday. Along with these special classes, students may study math, science, fine arts, and other courses in the mainstream curriculum. First-year ESOL students travel to the Texas Hill Country and Washington, D.C.

Class sizes average 15 students, with an overall student-teacher ratio of 10:1.

The grading system in grades 7–12 uses A to F designations with pluses and minuses. Reports are sent to parents at the end of each quarter period. High achievement in the Upper School is recognized by inclusion on the Headmistress's List and by initiation into a number of honor societies, including the Cum Laude Society.

Each student receives careful counseling throughout her Hockaday career. Academic counseling begins even in the admissions process and continues under the supervision of the division offices, which coordinates the faculty adviser system and general counseling program. Each student has an interested, concerned faculty adviser to assist her with academic or personal matters on a daily basis.

FACULTY AND ADVISERS

The Hockaday faculty comprises accomplished individuals, most of whom have advanced degrees, with 10 holding doctoral degrees.

Hockaday's teachers are chosen for their depth of knowledge in their fields of specialization, personal integrity, and the ability to facilitate the progress of individual students. Many are successful writers, lecturers, artists, musicians, photographers, or composers. Summer study grants are awarded to faculty members to encourage both research and professional development.

Ms. Kim Wargo, Eugene McDermott Headmistress, holds a bachelor's degree in journalism from Louisiana State University, where she graduated summa cum laude with minors in history and English. She earned a master's degree in history from Tulane University.

COLLEGE ADMISSION COUNSELING

The college counselors work directly with Upper School students in their college planning. Each student participates with her parents in conferences with the counselor concerning applications and final selection.

In 2013, the middle 50 percent SAT scores ranged from 640 to 760 in critical reading, 640 to 760 in math, and 670 to 780 in writing. The class of 2013 had 23 National Merit Finalists, 24 National Merit Semifinalists, 29 National Merit Commended Students, 1 National Achievement Finalist, 1 National Achievement Semifinalist, 1 National Achievement Outstanding Participant, 3 National Hispanic Scholars, and 1 National Hispanic Honorable Mention Finalist. Hockaday alumnae include Hesburgh-Yusko Scholars (Notre Dame), Jefferson-Echols Scholars (Virginia), Marshall Scholars, Morehead-Cain Scholars (UNC-CH), a Rhodes Scholar, and Truman Scholars. They have received the Michael C. Rockefeller Memorial Fellowship at Harvard and have been named to the Gates Millennium Scholars Program. Traditionally, 100 percent of Hockaday graduates attend four-year colleges or universities. The 116 members of the class of 2013 were admitted to 173 institutions, including Bowdoin, Carnegie Mellon, Claremont McKenna, Duke, George Washington, Harvard, Middlebury, Northwestern, Princeton, SMU, Stanford, Vanderbilt, Wake Forest, Washington University in St. Louis, Yale, and the Universities of Chicago and Texas at Austin, among others.

STUDENT BODY AND CONDUCT

The student body is composed of 1,087 girls (74 of whom board) from eight states and thirteen countries besides the United States. Thirty-eight percent of the girls are members of minority groups.

The Upper School Student Council and the Honor Council exert strong, active, and responsible leadership in student affairs. In addition to planning activities, allocating funds, and serving as a forum for student concerns, these councils promote and exemplify the School's written Honor Code.

Students are expected to abide by the guidelines set forth in the Upper School manual. Disciplinary measures rest primarily with the Head of the Upper School and the Headmistress.

ACADEMIC FACILITIES

The campus includes twelve buildings. The Liza Lee Academic Research Center is 52,000-square-feet and hosts two expansive libraries, several computer labs, debate team space, a state-of-the-art communications hub, a versatile hall that doubles as a lecture facility and audiovisual theater, a blue room, and an editing suite. In the academic area are classrooms; laboratories for languages, computers, and reading; and a study center. The campus is fully wireless, and all classrooms are equipped with SmartBoard technology for use in conjunction with students' laptops, required for every girl in grades 6–12. The Fine Arts facilities include a 600-seat auditorium, instrumental and voice studios, practice rooms, a painting studio, ceramics facilities with outdoor kilns, a photography laboratory, printmaking facilities, and an electronic music studio. The new Centennial Center, which will house an interdisciplinary arts and sciences program, is under construction (Phase I) and will include a lecture hall, study lounges, classrooms, modern laboratories, a green roof outdoor learning facility, planetarium, and engineering lab. The Wellness Center includes the 5,000-square-foot Hill Family Fitness Center, an 1,800-square-foot aerobics room with state-of-the-art aerobic and resistance equipment, and athletic training facilities fully equipped for the treatment of sports-related injuries.

BOARDING AND GENERAL FACILITIES

Accommodations for boarding students are newly renovated, comfortable dormitories with study areas and lounges. Girls of similar grades are normally housed on the same hall, each with its own lounge, kitchen, large-screen plasma television, DVR, and laundry room. The dormitories are wireless and all laptops are equipped with Skype. An additional common lounge has also been updated with a large-screen television, kitchen, and fireplace, which overlooks an outdoor swimming pool and tennis courts. Rooms are shared by two students, and each hall contains a small suite for the dorm mom in charge. The dormitories are closed for Thanksgiving, Christmas, and spring vacations.

The School's Health Center is located on the ground floor of the dormitory area, with a registered nurse on duty at all times and the School doctor on call. Campus security is maintained 24 hours a day.

The Wellness Center features an aerobics center, a fitness testing area, a trainer's facility, and the Hill Fitness Center, a 5,000-square-foot facility offering aerobic, resistance, and circuit training equipment.

ATHLETICS

Athletic facilities include two gymnasiums housing basketball courts (convertible to volleyball and indoor tennis courts), two racquetball courts, a swimming pool, and a dance studio. On the grounds are six athletic fields, a softball complex, an all-weather track, a tennis center with ten courts and seating for 90 people. Interscholastic sports include basketball, crew, cross-country, fencing, field hockey, golf, lacrosse, soccer, softball, swimming and diving, tennis, track, and volleyball.

EXTRACURRICULAR OPPORTUNITIES

The Hockaday educational experience includes far more than just the classroom. There is a vast range of extracurricular opportunities for students to take part in: more than seventy student clubs, community service projects that impact the world beyond the campus, international and domestic class bonding trips that build lifelong friendships, world-renowned speakers who expand students' perspectives, talent showcases at the Coffeehouse, and more.

To encourage student creativity, the Upper School sponsors a literary and journalistic magazine, a newspaper, and the Hockaday yearbook. These publications are edited by students with the guidance of faculty advisers. The literary magazine, *Vibrato*, won a gold medal with one all-Columbian honor from the Columbia Scholastic Press Association (CSPA). *Vibrato* has won top distinctions in ten of the last eleven years. Hockaday's student newspaper, *The Fourcast*, was awarded a gold medal with three all-Columbian honors, the highest score possible. NSPA rated the magazine first class with two marks of distinction. The yearbook, *Cornerstones*, was featured in a full-page treatment in the 2010 edition of Taylor Publishing's *Yearbook*. All three of Hockaday's scholastic press publications were featured in the NSPA's *Best of the High School Press*.

Service to the School and its surrounding community is an important part of a girl's life at Hockaday. Each Upper School student is required to contribute a minimum of 15 volunteer hours per year in service to the wider community.

DAILY LIFE

Upper School classes begin at 8:30 a.m. and end at 4:00 p.m. Monday through Friday. The daily schedule provides time for academic help sessions and club meetings.

Varsity sports meet after the close of the regular school day. Boarding students have a 2-hour required study time, Sunday through Thursday nights.

WEEKEND LIFE

Off-campus activities each weekend enable resident students to take advantage of the many cultural and recreational resources in the Dallas–Fort Worth area. Faculty members are frequently involved in boarding activities, as are families of the Hockaday Parents' Association, who sponsor girls who are new to Hockaday and include them in family activities. Each resident student is matched with a local Dallas family through the Host Family Program. The host families offer local support for the girls and encourage their participation in social activities outside of school.

SUMMER PROGRAMS

A six-week coed academic summer session is offered for day and boarding students. Students may attend three- or six-week sessions beginning in June and July. Summer boarding is available. Programs in language immersion, math and science enrichment, computers, sports, SAT preparation, study skills, English, creative writing, and arts/theater are offered. The academic courses focus on enrichment opportunities. English as a second language, an international program lasting three weeks, begins in July. Information on the summer session is available in late spring. Applications are accepted until all spaces are filled, although students are encouraged to apply early to ensure their preferred course selection.

COSTS AND FINANCIAL AID

In 2013–14, tuition for Upper School day students averages $26,000. For resident students, costs are approximately $47,000 for tuition, room, and board. Additional expenses for both day and resident students include, among others, those for books and uniforms. A deposit of $1,000 for day students or $2,500 for boarding students is due with the signed enrollment contract, and the balance of tuition and fees is due by June 1, prior to entrance in August. Partial payment for room and board for resident students is also made at this time. The room and board balance for resident students is payable by December 1 following entrance in August.

The Hockaday Financial Aid Program offers assistance based on financial need. Parents of all applicants for financial aid must provide financial information as required by the Financial Aid Committee. Over $3 million was awarded to students in 2012–13. Details of the programs are available from the Admission Office.

ADMISSIONS INFORMATION

Applicants to Hockaday's Upper School are considered on the basis of their previous academic records, results of aptitude and achievement testing, teacher and head of school evaluations, and, in most cases, a personal interview. Because the School requires a student to attend the School for at least two years to be eligible for graduation, new students are not normally admitted to the senior class. In order to qualify for admission and have a successful experience at Hockaday, girls need to possess strong potential and a desire to learn.

APPLICATION TIMETABLE

Initial inquiries are welcome at any time, and applications are received continuously. There is a nonrefundable application fee for both day-student and boarding-student applications. Entrance tests are scheduled in December, January, and February and periodically throughout the spring and summer. Campus tours are available at convenient times during the year. Notification of the admission decision is made approximately six weeks after testing. Parents are expected to reply to an offer of admission within two weeks.

ADMISSIONS CORRESPONDENCE

Jen Liggitt, Assistant Head for Admission and
 Enrollment Management
The Hockaday School
11600 Welch Road
Dallas, Texas 75229-2999
United States
Phone: 214-363-6311
Fax: 214-265-1649
E-mail: admissions@mail.hockaday.org
Web site: http://www.hockaday.org

LAURALTON HALL, THE ACADEMY OF OUR LADY OF MERCY

Milford, Connecticut

Type: Girls college-preparatory day school
Grades: 9–12
Enrollment: 460+
Head of School: Antoinette Iadarola, Ph.D., President

THE ACADEMY

Lauralton Hall, the Academy of Our Lady of Mercy, is a Catholic college-preparatory high school, founded in 1905 by the Sisters of Mercy. The first Catholic college-prep school for young women in Connecticut, it is over 100 years old—a major milestone for any school and even more significant for a Catholic girls' school. A member of the National Coalition of Girls' Schools, Lauralton Hall is accredited by the New England Association of Schools and Colleges and the Connecticut Department of Education. The Lauralton day-school experience prepares girls to become competent, confident, and compassionate women, aligning with the school's mission of "Empowering women for life." Lauralton students are giving of themselves, especially to those in need, and are challenged to succeed academically.

Lauralton Hall is one of a select group of Catholic girls' schools that has remained true to its original mission, which is to foster a community atmosphere enriched by the Mercy tradition and to educate young women to pursue knowledge, recognize truth, and respond to the needs of others. This empowers young women to excel in any endeavor, to find their own voices, and to be bearers of mercy for others. Since Lauralton believes character formation is as essential as academic achievement, the core values of a Mercy education play an integral role in a Lauralton Hall education: compassion and service, educational excellence, concern for women and women's issues, global vision and responsibility, spiritual growth and development, and collaboration.

Centrally located in historic downtown Milford and within walking distance of a train station, Lauralton attracts more than 460 students from over 35 towns. Students come by train, car, or bus, seeking the same rigorous preparation for college as the more than 6,000 alumnae who have passed through Lauralton's halls for over 100 years. The student body is composed of young women from diverse socioeconomic, religious, and ethnic backgrounds.

ACADEMIC PROGRAM

The well-rounded Lauralton Hall curriculum fully prepares students for college study, with demanding honors and advanced placement classes offered in all academic disciplines. As an added dimension, the formation of character is valued as highly as intellectual achievement. In keeping with the tradition of the Sisters of Mercy, students are constantly challenged to think of others and to reach out to those in need. They are expected to become Renaissance women for the twenty-first century—articulate and poised, confident and compassionate, gracious in their strength, at home in their own times, respectful of the past, and fully prepared to embrace the future.

Lauralton strives to develop clear, independent thinkers who appreciate knowledge and the learning process. The school offers a solid and well-balanced college-preparatory curriculum, which emphasizes a mastery of analytical and critical thinking skills, problem solving, and the ability to communicate ideas effectively. Challenging and demanding college-preparatory, honors, and advanced placement courses are offered. Courses are also available through the UConn Early College Experience (ECE), a concurrent enrollment program that allows motivated high school students to take UConn courses at their high schools for both high school and college credit. Every course taken through the UConn ECE is equivalent to the same course at the University of Connecticut. Established in 1955, the UConn ECE is the nation's longest running concurrent enrollment program and is nationally accredited by the National Alliance of Concurrent Enrollment Partnerships (NACEP).

Lauralton Hall offers advanced placement (AP) courses in calculus, chemistry, English language and composition, English literature and composition, environmental science, European history, French, Latin, music theory, physics, Spanish, and United States history. UConn ECE courses are offered in biology, elementary discrete mathematics, English literature and composition, European history, finite mathematics, French, fundamentals of music theory, Spanish IV, and U.S. history.

In order to graduate, a minimum of 25 credits must be earned, which must include six major subject areas (English, world languages, history, mathematics, science, and religion), a fine arts course, physical education, and 75 hours of community service.

FACULTY AND ADVISERS

There are 43 faculty members, 7 administrators, 4 guidance counselors, and 2 library media specialists. About 81 percent of the faculty members hold advanced degrees. The school is privileged to have the presence of a Sister of Mercy on the school campus and 2 sisters active on the Board of Trustees.

COLLEGE ADMISSION COUNSELING

Individual conferences and group sessions are an integral, ongoing part of each student's guidance experience during her four years at Lauralton Hall. The counselors guide students in making appropriate college choices and help students with the application process.

In recent years, Lauralton Hall graduates have attended top-tier institutions such as Boston College, Brown, Carnegie Mellon, College of the Holy Cross, Columbia, Dartmouth, Duke, Georgetown, Harvard, Rensselaer Polytechnic Institute, the United States Military Academy, the United States Naval Academy, the University of Pennsylvania, Vanderbilt, and Vassar, to name a few.

STUDENT BODY AND CONDUCT

More than 460 young women from 35 Connecticut towns attend Lauralton Hall. The students are from diverse socioeconomic, religious, and ethnic backgrounds; about 77 percent are Catholic, and 16 percent are members of minority groups. Students are expected to abide by the codes of conduct found in the school's Student/Parent Handbook of Standards and Expectations.

ACADEMIC FACILITIES

The beautiful 30-acre campus surrounds a Victorian Gothic mansion built in 1864. The mansion and its property were purchased by the Sisters of Mercy in 1905 for use as a school. The administrative building, known as Mercy Hall, and the St. Joseph school building were added to provide classrooms, offices, an auditorium, a library/media center, and the school chapel. The school also has a music building, an athletic center, five new state-of-the-art science labs, and recently renovated art rooms.

ATHLETICS

At Lauralton Hall, students have the opportunity to participate in many different interscholastic athletics and are required to take physical education classes. "We've got the spirit!" summarizes what student athletes at Lauralton Hall experience: the joy of competition, pride in school and personal accomplishments, and the ability to win or lose with heads held high. Lauralton Hall athletes are expected to play fair, enjoy honest competition, and demonstrate sportsmanship, dedication, and compassion for one another, opponents, officials, and spectators. The school is a member of the Connecticut Interscholastic Athletic Conference (CIAC) and the South West Conference (SWC). There are fifteen varsity sports: basketball, cheerleading, cross-country, field hockey, golf, gymnastics, ice hockey, lacrosse, skiing, soccer, softball, swimming and diving, tennis, track and field, and volleyball.

The campus has its own playing fields and an athletic center, which houses a basketball court as well as a fully equipped fitness center.

EXTRACURRICULAR OPPORTUNITIES

In preparing its young women to become visionary leaders and active members of their communities, Lauralton encourages each student to become involved in at least one extracurricular activity. Clubs, organizations, and activities bring new experiences, new challenges, and new friends. With more than thirty clubs and organizations to choose from, there is something to fit the interest of every young woman. Extracurricular activities include culture trips, student council, national and language honor societies, a fall musical, a spring play, Christmas and spring concerts, art club, youth and government, environmental club, percussion ensemble, Shakespeare club, humanities, classic film, dance club, Key club, debate club, world language clubs, student literary publications, yearbook, and school mixers/dances. New groups and activities are added yearly, based on student interest.

CAMPUS MINISTRY

Lauralton students are sisters in faith. They help the less fortunate and are stewards of the earth. They have retreats, liturgies, and prayer services.

The Office of Campus Ministry annually sponsors special collections to benefit those less fortunate. Lauralton's students generously embrace these initiatives. The four-year service program builds compassion and links the school to the global community through national and international mission trips.

The Lauralton Hall Women of Mercy award was created in 2004 to recognize young women, chosen by their peers, who exemplify the qualities of mercy established by Catherine McAuley: compassion, kindness, honesty, integrity, and care for the least of God's people.

DAILY LIFE

Classes begin at 8 a.m. with homeroom and end at 2:20 p.m., Monday through Friday. Sports and activities are offered after school.

SUMMER PROGRAMS

Lauralton Hall offers summer sports and enrichment programs for girls and boys. A qualified adult staff guides children through a week of learning and fun in a safe environment. Open to students ages 6 and up, these high-quality, educational, fun programs offer participants an opportunity to experience community and engage in diverse activities on the beautiful Lauralton Hall campus at various times and dates from the end of June through August.

Enrichment programs include a variety of offerings in art, sports, science, writing, cooking, and more. Recent sessions have included STEM Gems, video making, baking, all levels of cooking, Art Adventure, Fun Adventures, creative writing, CSI, physics, soccer, basketball, baseball, field hockey, lacrosse, softball, and cheerleading.

COSTS AND FINANCIAL AID

Tuition for 2013–14 is $17,000, plus the cost of books and uniform. There is also a $150 athletics fee per sport per athlete. Financial aid and scholarships are available. About 24 percent of students receive financial aid.

ADMISSIONS INFORMATION

Interested parents and prospective students, including transfer students, may request information by contacting Mrs. Kathleen O. Shine, Director of Enrollment Management at kshine@lauraltonhall.org or 203-878-3333. Information can also be accessed on the school website, www.lauraltonhall.org. Prospective students are also welcome to spend a day at the school.

APPLICATION TIMETABLE

Inquiries are welcome anytime. Applications should be submitted online by November 15, but they are accepted later, space permitting. The application fee is $60.

ADMISSIONS CORRESPONDENCE

Admissions Office
Lauralton Hall
200 High Street
Milford, Connecticut 06460
United States
Phone: 203-878-3333
Fax: 203-876-9760
E-mail: admission@lauraltonhall.org
Website: http://www.lauraltonhall.org

THE LAWRENCEVILLE SCHOOL

Lawrenceville, New Jersey

Type: Coeducational boarding and day college-preparatory school
Grades: 9–PG (Second–Fifth Forms): Lower School, Second Form; Circle/Crescent Level, Third–Fourth Forms; Fifth Form
Enrollment: 816
Head of School: Elizabeth A. Duffy, Head Master

THE SCHOOL

The Lawrenceville School was founded in 1810 by Isaac Van Arsdale Brown as the Maidenhead Academy. Throughout the 1900s, Lawrenceville continued to develop as a leader in academic innovation, including early adoption of Advanced Placement (AP) courses and the introduction of nationally and internationally known guest speakers designed to broaden the intellectual horizons of young Lawrentians. Among the most-lasting changes was the introduction in 1936 of the Harkness method of education, which sought to bring the benefits of the House system to the classroom by providing an intimate environment for intellectual discourse.

Discussion of coeducation began in earnest in the 1970s, and after a lengthy, but thoughtful analysis of what it would mean both pedagogically and practically to the school, the Board elected to accept female students in 1985. The first girls arrived on campus in 1987 and brought a new vitality to the campus community. As the twentieth century drew to a close, the School embraced the ever-increasing diversity of its students in gender, geography, faith, race, and socioeconomic status, focusing on the need for a Lawrentian education to include broad exposure to all facets of the global community and an appreciation for and understanding of multiculturalism.

For more than 200 years, Lawrenceville graduates have gone on to success in their chosen fields, prepared by their education for the changing world around them. As the School enters its third century of educating students, it welcomes new students to join the legacy of Lawrenceville and discover what it means to be a Lawrentian in the twenty-first century.

The Lawrenceville School is located on 700 acres in the historic village of Lawrenceville, New Jersey.

The mission of the School is to inspire and educate promising young people from diverse backgrounds for responsible leadership, personal fulfillment, and enthusiastic participation in the world. Through its unique House system, collaborative Harkness approach to teaching and learning, close mentoring relationships, and extensive co-curricular opportunities, Lawrenceville helps students to develop high standards of character and scholarship; a passion for learning; an appreciation for diversity; a global perspective; and strong commitments to personal, community, and environmental responsibility.

Lawrenceville is accredited by the Middle States Association of Colleges and Schools and is a member of the Secondary School Admission Test Board, the National Association of Independent Schools, the New Jersey Association of Independent Schools, and the Council for Religion in Independent Schools.

ACADEMIC PROGRAM

The School's graduation requirements are designed to ensure students receive a strong foundation in all disciplines during their first two years that can be built upon in the upper forms. The requirements meet NCAA standards and are aligned with standard requirements for college admissions.

The requirements for entering Second Formers are: arts, 3 terms; English, 9 terms; history, 6 terms; humanities–English, 3 terms; humanities–cultural studies, 3 terms; interdisciplinary, 2 terms (at the advanced level); language through unit 9 (foundational level–through unit 6)*; mathematics through advanced algebra or precalculus (foundational level–through math 3)*; religion and philosophy, 2 terms; and science, 9 terms (foundational level–6 terms)*. Students are also required to give at least 40 hours of community service before they graduate. (*Students may opt to finish their course work in one of these disciplines at the foundational level with approval.)

Individual participation is encouraged in small classroom sections that average 12 students. Classes are grouped randomly and are taught around a large oval table called the Harkness table. Evening study periods, held in the Houses, are supervised by the Housemaster, the Assistant Housemaster, or an Associate Housemaster.

Students may also apply for independent study, off-campus projects, or the Lawrenceville international programs. Recent destinations include China, the Dominican Republic, Mexico, Japan, France, Peru, Nicaragua, Ghana, the Galapagos, Great Britain, South Africa, and Tanzania. Other opportunities include language immersion trips, where students reside with host families. Driver's education is also available.

Lawrenceville uses a letter grading system (A–F) in which D– is passing and B+ qualifies for honors.

The school year is divided into three 10-week terms. Full reports are sent home at the end of each term, with interim reports at midterm. The full reports include comments and grades from each of a student's teachers indicating his or her accomplishments, efforts, and attitudes. Less formal progress reports are also written by teachers throughout the term as needed. Students in academic difficulty are placed on academic review, which entails close supervision and additional communication with parents.

FACULTY AND ADVISERS

There are 104 full-time, four part-time faculty members, and six teaching fellows, all of whom hold numerous degrees: 11 doctorates; 88 master's degrees; and 15 bachelor's degrees. Most faculty members reside on the campus, and many serve as residential Housemasters, coaches, and club advisers. All are active in advising and counseling students.

Elizabeth A. Duffy was appointed the twelfth Head Master of the Lawrenceville School in 2003. Ms. Duffy graduated magna cum laude from Princeton University in 1988 with an A.B. in molecular biology. In 1993, she received an M.B.A. from the Graduate School of Business at Stanford University and an A.M. in administration and policy analysis from the School of Education there. She has spent her entire career working with educators at all levels.

COLLEGE ADMISSION COUNSELING

The College Counseling Office supports, informs, and encourages students and their families as they navigate the exciting, complex, and ever-changing process of college admissions. The counselors educate students and families about the nuances of admissions, advise students about college options that best suit their individual needs, and support and encourage students as they complete the application process.

Lawrenceville's college counselors offer students decades of professional experience as college counselors and college admissions officers. The counseling staff provides valuable and timely advice to families as the process unfolds and helps students present their abilities, talents, and experiences to colleges in the most appropriate manner. The 5 counselors carry a small average case load of 45 students, which allows for personal attention and sustained involvement in all aspects of the residential school community. Over the course of their Lawrenceville careers, families and students receive information through form-specific newsletters, classwide meetings, and Parent Weekend programming. They also have access to Naviance, an online college admission management tool. All of these resources help ensure that students and their families are well prepared to embrace the college counseling process when students are

officially assigned to individual counselors in the middle of their Fourth Form year.

Median SAT scores are: 689 critical reading, 703 math, and 703 writing. Between 2011 and 2013, the twenty colleges most attended by Lawrenceville students were: Princeton, Duke, Georgetown, NYU, University of Virginia, Dartmouth, Brown, Cornell, University of Pennsylvania, Stanford, University of Chicago, Trinity College (Connecticut), Columbia, Colgate, George Washington, Johns Hopkins, University of St. Andrews (Scotland), Yale, Davidson, and Harvard.

STUDENT BODY AND CONDUCT

For 2013–14, there are 816 students: boarding 555, day 261, male 419, and female 397. Students are from 34 states and 38 countries.

Lawrenceville expects its students to achieve good records and develop self-control, systematic study habits, and a clear sense of responsibility. The School has a high regard for energy, initiative, a positive attitude, and active cooperation. Students accepting this premise have no trouble following the basic regulations.

The student body elects 5 governing officers from among students in the Fifth Form, and each House elects its own Student Council.

ACADEMIC FACILITIES

Lawrenceville's first rate, state-of-the art academic facilities, which include Fathers' Building, the Kirby Arts Center, Gruss Center of Visual Arts, the F. M. Kirby Science Center, the Juliet Lyell Staunton Clark Music Center, Bunn Library, and the Noyes History Center, offer a unique opportunity for all students. Each building houses an entire academic discipline, so students are immersed within a particular subject from the minute they enter the building until the minute they leave.

Lawrenceville supports excellent teaching with outstanding educational and campus resources. The Bicentennial Campaign, completed in 2010 in honor of the School's 200th anniversary, demonstrated the intense willingness of alumni, parents, and friends to provide the absolute best facilities and support for students and faculty. This most ambitious campaign raised $218.5 million, exceeding the $200 million goal, for student financial aid, faculty support, academic programs, and student life. Among the campaign's successes were the new Al Rashid Health and Wellness Center, a state-of-the-art facility for both treatment and prevention; Carter House, a fifth girls' residential house; and lighted turf fields of the Getz Sports Complex.

BOARDING AND GENERAL FACILITIES

Lawrenceville's most distinguishing feature is its House system. In each of the twenty Houses, the Housemaster maintains close contact with the residents. House athletics teams compete on an intramural level, and House identity is maintained through separate dining rooms in the Irwin Dining Center for the underformers. This distinctive system provides a small social environment in which each student's contribution is important and measurable.

Services in the Edith Memorial Chapel are nondenominational. The Al Rashid Health and Wellness Center offers inpatient and outpatient medical care, including psychological counseling services, and a consulting staff who offer gynecological care, orthopedic/sports medicine, and nutrition. Certified athletic trainers provide rehabilitation services for injuries. The Center's health professionals seek to educate and encourage students to develop the knowledge and skills needed to sustain a lifetime of healthy function.

ATHLETICS

Lawrenceville regards athletics as yet another educational opportunity for students and a valuable complement to the School's rigorous academic expectations. The importance of commitment; satisfaction of teamwork; hard lessons of failure; courage to surmount pain, fatigue, and frustration for a common goal; the virtue of physical conditioning; imperatives of sportsmanship; and the sheer joy of healthy competition are values Lawrenceville's athletic program is uniquely suited to teach. In addition, the School's proud interscholastic tradition and comprehensive intramural program, along with instruction in lifetime sports, ensure that each student experiences the challenge and reward of athletic competition.

The School takes pride in its first-class outdoor sports facilities: two FieldTurf artificial playing surfaces with lights for field hockey, lacrosse, and soccer; and eighteen other multipurpose natural grass athletic fields, including five intramural fields and two softball and two baseball diamonds. There are also twelve tennis courts, a nine-hole golf course, and a quarter-mile all-weather track. The crew program enjoys the use of a bay and other facilities at the Mercer Lake Rowing Association boathouse.

The Edward J. Lavino Field House is one of the finest in any independent school. The main arena has a Mondo surface with three combination basketball-volleyball-tennis courts; a four-lane 200-meter banked indoor track, with an eight-lane straightaway; and long jump, shot put, pole vault, and high jump areas. Along each side of the arena are two gymnasiums, a six-lane competition swimming pool, a wrestling room, a performance center, and an athletic training wellness room. A modern, enclosed ice hockey rink is attached to the Lavino Field House, and there are ten Anderson international squash courts. Nearby, a separate building houses the state-of-the-art, 4,500-square-foot Al Rashid Strength and Conditioning Center that is supervised by 2 certified coaches.

Students must participate in an approved form of athletic activity each term. Rehabilitation of athletic injuries and fitness testing are an important part of the athletic program and are available to students by Lawrenceville's 2 certified athletic trainers.

The School's outdoor, experientially based programs and initiatives educate students in responsible leadership, community membership, and character development and provide interactions in the outdoor environment, enhancing both academic and nonacademic skills development. Lawrentians have traveled the globe through outdoor program courses, scaling glaciers in Patagonia, trekking through the desert in South Africa, and sea kayaking among icebergs in Newfoundland. Athletic credit is given to participants.

Lawrenceville's ropes course offers students the opportunity to accept a challenge and work toward conquering it as a group. The course, created and built by an outdoor experiential education expert, is designed to help students listen to each other, trust each other, and work toward a common goal.

EXTRACURRICULAR OPPORTUNITIES

Lawrenceville provides a numerous opportunities for students to explore outside the classroom. There are more than eighty clubs and organizations specializing in interests such as writing, acting, debate, music, art, history, religion, science, photography, woodworking, and scuba diving.

Through the required Community Service Program, students serve as tutors, elementary school study center supervisors, and group activity counselors. The School sponsors organized educational and cultural trips to New York City and Washington, D.C.

Exhibits occur throughout the year. Several lecture programs bring speakers and artists to the campus. Annual events include Parents' Weekend in the fall, Parents' Winter Gathering, and Alumni Weekend in the spring.

DAILY LIFE

Lawrenceville students have their schedules packed full of classes, study hours, athletic practice, rehearsals, and time for friends, special events, eating, and sleeping. Students learn to manage their time, meet their commitments, and enjoy their friendships.

Classes begin at 8 a.m. on most days, and the dining center opens at 7 a.m. for breakfast. Each class meets four times a week for 55-minute sessions. Science and advanced classes have an additional 55-minute period each week for labs, extended discussions, test practice, writing workshops, etc. There also are three 40-minute periods each week for student-teacher consultations. Students are highly encouraged to take advantage of consultation periods.

The entire School eats lunch at the same time, and each House dines together. This tradition is yet another example of how the House system defines the Lawrenceville experience. On Mondays, students take lunch with their academic advisers. Each advisee group shares a table, and time is spent discussing both individual and group concerns; if needed, students can schedule a private meeting with their adviser.

The entire School assembles once a week for an all-School community meeting. These gatherings feature readings, reflections, and announcements. School meeting agendas include outside speakers, special guests, musical presentations, and opportunities to examine student issues.

Classes end at 3:05 p.m., but then there is more to do—sports or community service. On Wednesdays, classes end at 12:20 p.m., and students have the option of studying, rehearsing, practicing sports, working on publications, or fulfilling their community service requirement. Saturday classes end at 11:30 a.m..

Dinner is served from 5:30 to 7 p.m. All Forms eat in the Irwin Dining Center, except for the Fifth Form, which takes meals in the Abbott Dining Room in the Upper House. After dinner, there is time for clubs, activities, homework, and socializing. Check-in is at 8 p.m. for Lower School, 8:30 p.m. for Crescent and Circle Houses, and 9 p.m. for the Fifth Form, Sunday–Friday. Permission to leave the House after check-in to go to the library, rehearsals, club meetings, or to meet a teacher for consultation is granted after check-in time, but students must check back in with the Housemaster on duty by 10 p.m. (11 p.m. on Saturday).

WEEKEND LIFE

On weekends, at least one House sponsors an all-School social event, which may include carnivals, concerts, formal dinners, and dances. Faculty members are on hand to take trips to local shopping areas and movie theaters. Reach Out to the Arts is a faculty-led club that takes weekly trips to cultural events in New York. Day students are encouraged to attend all-campus activities.

COSTS AND FINANCIAL AID

The annual charges for 2013–14 are $53,320 for boarding students and $44,100 for day students.

Through the generosity of alumni, friends, and foundations, approximately $10.7 million in funds are available to provide financial assistance to qualified students. Currently, 29 percent of the student body receives assistance. Awards are made on the basis of character, ability, past performance, and future promise. Amounts are based solely on need and are determined by procedures established by the School and Student Service for Financial Aid.

ADMISSIONS INFORMATION

All students who enter must be able to meet the academic standards. Lawrenceville also looks for students who possess the potential to become vitally interested members of the student body—students who make individual contributions.

Selection is based on all-around qualifications without regard to race, creed, or national origin. Character, seriousness of purpose, and future promise as well as past performance, the recommendation of a headmaster or principal, and SSAT results are all taken into consideration by the Admission Committee.

For fall 2013, there were 2,072 formal applications for grades 9–12, of which 246 enrolled. Thirty-four percent were from public schools, 44 percent from private schools, 17 percent from international schools, and five percent from church-related schools.

Required for admission is the formal application, which includes a written essay, a transcript of the applicant's school record, a letter of recommendation from the head of the current school, three reference letters, SSAT or ISEE and/or TOEFL scores, and an on-campus interview.

APPLICATION TIMETABLE

Campus interviews are conducted during the week from 9 a.m. to 2 p.m. Monday, Tuesday, Thursday, and Friday. Applicants can also interview on Wednesdays from 9 to 10:30 and on Saturdays from 8:30 to 10:30. Interviews are not conducted on Saturdays during the summer months.

The application deadline is January 15 for boarding and day students, at which time all application materials must be submitted and interviews completed. The notification date is March 10, and parents reply by April 10.

ADMISSIONS CORRESPONDENCE

Dean of Admission
The Lawrenceville School
2500 Main Street
P.O. Box 6008
Lawrenceville, New Jersey 08648
United States
Phone: 609-895-2030
800-735-2030 (toll-free outside New Jersey)
Fax: 609-895-2217
E-mail: admission@lawrenceville.org
Website: http://www.lawrenceville.org

THE LINSLY SCHOOL
Wheeling, West Virginia

The Linsly School
FORWARD AND NO RETREAT
1814   2014
Celebrating 200 Years

Type: Independent, coeducational, college-preparatory boarding and day school
Grades: 5–12
Enrollment: 440 students; 100 boarding students
Head of School: Chad Barnett

THE SCHOOL

Founded in 1814, and celebrating its bicentennial anniversary this academic year, the Linsly School is a private, coeducational, independent day and boarding school for students in grades 5 through 12. Located in Wheeling, West Virginia, the School offers a college-preparatory curriculum that combines the traditional values of hard work, respect, honor, honesty, and self-discipline within a challenging academic program designed to unlock the potential of each student.

The family-like atmosphere at Linsly helps students grow and develop under the guidance of faculty members who know them by name and care about their future. Learning is not limited to the classroom—it happens over lunch, dinner, evening study hall, and at any time—learning at Linsly never ends.

Linsly is a place where lifelong friendships between students and faculty are formed. Students wear uniforms, not to encourage conformity, but to ensure that they are known for their unique ideas and abilities. Linsly is a school where long-forgotten traditional values live on in everyday curriculum.

With 100 percent college placement, Linsly's record as an excellent college-preparatory academy speaks for itself. But the School also teaches that there is more to education than test scores and college acceptance letters. Every day, students learn by living many of life's most important principles: responsibility, commitment, time management, sportsmanship, maturity, and even disappointment. The School's no-quit policy teaches students to finish what they start and to follow through with their commitments.

The education a student earns at Linsly is both deep and lasting because life's lessons continually emerge. The experience fosters lifelong learning to prepare students for college and life.

ACADEMIC PROGRAM

At Linsly, academic excellence has always been developed through a traditional curriculum enhanced with contemporary courses. While some schools claim to go back to basics, Linsly is proud to have never left them.

The academic program is rigorous and challenging to every student. Advanced-level courses are available in both the high school and the middle school curriculum, ensuring that even the most gifted students will be intellectually challenged.

Class grades are computed on a numerical basis. All grades below 70 percent are considered failing. Certain grades are indicated by letter grade (92 and up, A; 83–91, B; 74–82, C; 70–73, D). Report cards are mailed home four times a year at the end of every grading period. Students receive a separate report for each subject. A student having attained an average of 92 percent has earned second honors. A student having received an average of 95 percent has earned first honors. In addition, deficiency reports and/or progress reports are mailed to parents at the midpoint of each grading period. Lower School students receive letter grades in computer and physical education/health twice a

year, at the end of each semester. Lower School students receive letter grades in fine arts courses every grading period.

A full program of college preparatory subjects is offered at Linsly. All students must carry a five-course per semester class load (excluding physical education). Full credit courses meet five times weekly for the entire year. However, there are certain half-credit courses which meet three times weekly for a year, or every day for a semester. Twenty credits are required for graduation and must include the following minimums: 4 credits of English, 4 credits of mathematics, 3 credits of social studies, 3 credits of the same world language, 3 credits of science (2 laboratory sciences), physical education, 1 full credit of fine arts including art appreciation and music appreciation, ½ credit of computer science, and the Senior Research Essay.

FACULTY AND ADVISERS

Linsly teachers share a common calling. They are not individuals who see education as an 8-to-3 job. They are not individuals who see themselves as specialists in a very narrow area, uninterested in broadening the education of their students. Linsly teachers are interested in the complete development of their students. They are diverse in their talents, varied in their interests, and committed to a model of education that places the relationship with their students at the heart of the teaching experience.

Many of Linsly's faculty members live on campus, making them readily accessible for extra help and counsel. As advisers, the faculty members build strong and lasting relationships with their students. This strong sense of community is felt in all aspects of school life at Linsly. The School is extremely proud of its accomplished and respected faculty and administrative team.

Linsly's Advisory Program provides guidance from the faculty members in both academic and personal matters and allows a small group of students and a faculty mentor to get to know one another personally outside of the academic environment. Students meet daily for the first 10 minutes of the academic day with other advisees. While this is an ideal time for group discussions, students may call upon their faculty adviser for help or advice whenever needed. The average advisory group consists of 10 students. New students are assigned advisers, and returning students choose their adviser at the end of every year. The adviser becomes the student's close personal contact with the School, and advisers are available to offer assistance in all areas of a student's life.

COLLEGE ADMISSION COUNSELING

Linsly's college counseling office seeks to find the best college or university to match each individual student's needs and interests. The School's director of college counseling conducts a thorough program of testing and interviews with both students and parents throughout each high school student's Linsly career. College counseling begins in the sophomore year when students sit for their first PSAT and SAT tests. Taking these exams early allows students

to become familiar with their test-taking abilities and provides instructors with the data necessary to help meet the academic needs of a particular individual or body of students. This individual attention and concern helps students gain an understanding of their academic and personal priorities when selecting institutions of higher learning.

A multiyear, comprehensive SAT-preparation program begins in the sophomore year and concludes prior to the student's first senior SAT. In addition to regular administration of the PSAT, SAT, and SAT Subject Tests, each student goes through a thorough interview process including the Strong Interest Inventory to help them discover academic and career interests. This individual attention and concern helps students gain an understanding of their academic and personal priorities when selecting institutions of higher learning.

STUDENT BODY AND CONDUCT

There are approximately 440 students enrolled at the Linsly School during the academic year. Students in grades 5 through 8 are considered members of Linsly's Lower School. The Upper School is comprised of students in grades 9 through 12.

Daily life at Linsly is based on principles of mutual respect and cooperation. Students are encouraged to accept responsibility, express themselves openly, and develop a strong sense of self-awareness and self-confidence. Boys and girls adhere to a dress code designed to distinguish themselves by their accomplishments rather than by their appearance.

ACADEMIC FACILITIES

Linsly's scenic 65-acre campus offers an ideal setting for a safe and vibrant learning community. Tucked behind Wheeling's historic National Road, and bordered by Wheeling Creek, the Linsly campus functions as an extensive classroom. The School's location makes it an attractive educational option for families throughout West Virginia, Pennsylvania, Ohio, and beyond.

With nearly twenty faculty residences situated throughout campus, Linsly's neighborhood feeling provides all students an encouraging and attentive place to grow and learn.

Linsly's Banes Hall serves as the School's primary academic building. The 80,000-square-foot structure, which houses twenty-seven classrooms, modern science laboratories, upgraded computer centers, a technology-rich library, music room, swimming pool, and cafeteria, is being expanded as part of the School's 200th Anniversary Campaign. The expansion to Banes Hall will include a new twenty-first century library, a high-tech classroom with stadium-style seating, an alumni dining hall, and a new academic wing. The Williams Visual Arts Center provides top-quality studio, classroom, and gallery space, while the Hess Center offers equipment for students interested in woodworking. The Dlesk Conference Center is a unique place for meetings or searching the Linsly history archives housed there.

BOARDING AND GENERAL FACILITIES

Any student living outside the day student area (as defined by the School) must live in a Linsly dormitory. Weiss Hall, Merriman Hall, Yost Hall, and the Dicke Dorm are operated for those students who reside outside the Wheeling area and who have a strong desire to participate in the Linsly education program.

The layout of each of the dormitories is different. Within each dormitory there are faculty members assigned a specific section or wing. The Dormitory Master for that section is responsible for prescribing specific rules and the conduct of the residents. Students are not permitted in other dormitories or in other wings without consent.

The Linsly campus is located approximately 1 hour from the Pittsburgh International Airport. If necessary, the School can help parents arrange transportation to and from the airport for boarding students.

ATHLETICS

At Linsly, athletics are an important part of a well-rounded education; they not only contribute to physical well-being, but they also teach valuable lessons. Through athletics, students learn that hard work, perseverance, sportsmanship, and teamwork count at least as much as winning.

Every Linsly student is encouraged to participate in athletics. Lower School students can play on interscholastic teams, and all participate in a spring intramural sports program. The Upper School athletic program includes more than twenty interscholastic teams, which compete in both the Ohio Valley Athletic Conference (OVAC) and the Interstate Prep School League. Even students who are not athletically inclined can choose an appropriate sport and work with a coach to gain satisfaction of meeting the sport's physical and mental challenges.

EXTRACURRICULAR OPPORTUNITIES

Linsly provides a wide range of extracurricular options considered essential to the overall educational process. The Student Life program gives each student the opportunity to express his or her individuality through participation in activities that meet a variety of needs and interests.

Throughout the year, the School sponsors dances, fun activities, and on-campus events that highlight the talents of the diverse student body. A weekly all-school meeting is held to recognize accomplishments both in and outside of school.

Linsly offers a variety of special interest and community service clubs and organizations to give students the opportunity to participate in

areas where they have interests and abilities. Participation helps each student develop a sense of responsibility for their community that is important to the individual and the school. Once a student begins a commitment, they must finish the commitment. The clubs and organizations meet regularly during specified times during the school day or after school. Some of the extracurricular activities offered include animal shelter club, Lower School band, yearbook, newspaper, chorus, Upper and Lower School drama, stage band, forensics, French club, German club, Fellowship of Christian Athletes, Key Club, Shakespeare club, Spanish club, Upper School math club, chess club, Lower School newspaper, classical club, puzzlemaniacs, history club, Model United Nations, environmental club, outdoor adventure club, multicultural club, technology club, Scrabble club, and Students Against Destructive Decisions.

DAILY LIFE

The school day begins at 8 a.m. when students meet in adviser groups for 10 minutes. Fifty-minute academic periods begin at 8:10. At 9:50 there is a half-hour flexible period to allow School clubs and class meetings to take place. The five remaining 50-minute periods are broken up by a half-hour lunch period. The Lower School eats at noon, and the Upper School eats at 12:50.

COSTS AND FINANCIAL AID

Tuition for the 2013–14 academic year is $15,590 for day students and $32,170 for boarding students. The cost of books, uniforms, and supplies is approximately $1,000.

The Linsly School seeks to attract and maintain a highly capable and diverse student body. To help meet that commitment the School offers financial aid to qualified students on the basis of the demonstrated financial need of the family and the availability of funds. Families should not be discouraged from applying because of limited financial resources. For the 2013–14 academic year, approximately 40 percent of Linsly students received awards totaling $1.8 million.

The Linsly School now proudly ranks among fifty other independent schools across the United States to have been awarded the prestigious Malone Scholars Grant, a $2 million endowment designed to support the School's scholarship program.

The Linsly School does not offer merit scholarships; the financial aid program is need-based. It is the School's expectation that families receiving financial assistance embrace the value of a Linsly education and make it a priority in their financial planning.

Financial aid decisions are made independent of admission decisions. Once students who have applied for financial aid

are accepted in the admission process, they are referred to the Financial Aid Committee, which reviews the family's financial information, calculates their demonstrated need, and determines their financial aid awards.

Questions or concerns about financial aid or the financial aid application process should be directed to R. J. Zitzelsberger, Linsly's Director of Admissions and Financial Aid.

ADMISSIONS INFORMATION

Families interested in learning more about Linsly can request information by calling the Admissions Office at 304-233-1436 or e-mailing admit@linsly.org. In addition, families can submit an inquiry form via the Linsly School's Web site at www.linsly.org/admissions.

There are three main steps to Linsly's admissions process. The first is to schedule a visit by contacting the Admissions Office, Monday–Friday, 8 a.m. to 4 p.m. Weekend visits are also available. A campus visit will last approximately 2 hours and will include a tour of campus, an interview with the admissions director, and the completion of the School's admissions test. Interested students may also attend a Campus Visit Day.

The second step is to complete and submit an application and supporting materials (two essays, teacher recommendations, standardized test scores, and a parent survey). Finally, if the applicant family plans to apply for financial aid, they need to notify the admissions office; the application information will be forwarded to them.

Once an application for admission is completed, the admissions committee meets to discuss each applicant. When a decision is made, the admissions office will notify the applicant of the decision.

APPLICATION TIMETABLE

An application for admissions and all supporting documents should be submitted to the admissions office by mid-December (decision by mid-January) or mid-February (decision by mid-March). Specific deadline dates for each year are available on the School's Web site. The deadline for International Student applications is usually the end of January.

ADMISSIONS CORRESPONDENCE

R. J. Zitzelsberger III
Director of Admissions
Linsly School
60 Knox Lane
Wheeling, West Virginia 26003
United States
Phone: 304-233-1436
E-mail: admit@linsly.org
Web site: http://www.linsly.org/admissions

MAINE CENTRAL INSTITUTE
Pittsfield, Maine

Type: Coeducational traditional boarding and day college-preparatory and comprehensive curriculum
Grades: 9–12, postgraduate year
Enrollment: 433
Head of School: Christopher Hopkins

THE SCHOOL

Founded in 1866 by Free Will Baptists, Maine Central Institute (MCI) retains the inventive spirit and philosophy of its founders but no longer has a formal affiliation with the church. During the school's pioneer years, MCI served as a feeder school to Bates College in nearby Lewiston, Maine. Although adhering to upstanding and traditional educational values, MCI is progressive and broadminded, pledging to provide a comprehensive college-preparatory education to a multicultural student body diverse in talents, abilities, and interests.

MCI regards each student as an individual with individual needs and aspirations. In keeping with its belief in individuality, MCI strives to foster an overall environment of mutual respect, cooperation, and tolerance among all of its members and with the surrounding community. In a safe and caring atmosphere, students are encouraged to develop a moral and social consciousness, self-esteem, and social responsibility and to become globally aware, lifelong learners.

The rural town of Pittsfield (population 4,500) is nestled in between the Atlantic Ocean and the mountains of western Maine. The region of central Maine provides prime opportunities for hiking, skiing, biking, fishing, skating, and snowmobiling. The campus is within walking distance of local eateries, recreational parks, shopping, hiking trails, and a movie theater.

Maine Central Institute is accredited by the New England Association of Schools and Colleges and approved by the State of Maine Department of Education. MCI is also a member of the College Board and the National Association of Independent Schools.

ACADEMIC PROGRAM

MCI offers a rigorous comprehensive curriculum to accommodate various learning styles and academic abilities. MCI fosters the intellectual curiosities of its student body by offering accelerated and advanced placement courses in all core subject areas.

For grades 9–12, 20 credits are required for graduation. Students must successfully complete units in English (4), mathematics (4), social studies (3, including U.S. history), science (4), physical education (1), fine arts (1), computer science (½), and health (½). Students are required to take the equivalent of at least 6 units each semester. MCI also offers a postgraduate academic year with college prep and advanced placement courses.

MCI's math and science programs exceed national standards and utilize state-of-the-art technology and academic facilities.

Students in MCI's well-known humanities program understand the culture of an era through a study of its history, literature, and art. The school has an award-winning music program.

The world language program includes four levels of French and Spanish. In 2009, MCI added a Chinese Mandarin program to the world languages, which is taught by a teacher from China. In addition to the traditional offerings, students may take courses in psychology, guitar, business, sociology, public speaking, computer-assisted drawing, vocational subjects, and piano.

MCI offers a structured ESL program for the international student who is planning for a university education. Students receive individual testing before placement at one of four levels of ESL. The extensive ESL program includes American history for international students and carefully structured math classes that focus on the development of math language skills. MCI also offers a two-week summer program for ESL which is required for all new international students.

FACULTY AND ADVISERS

The 2013–14 faculty consists of 44 full-time members. More than a quarter of the faculty and staff members reside on campus, while the rest live in nearby towns such as Newport, Waterville, and Bangor.

Faculty members are selected on the basis of three main criteria. They must possess a strong subject-matter background, the ability to relate to students, and an educational philosophy consistent with that of the institution and its mission. Faculty members are also expected to become actively involved in coaching, supervising dormitories, advising, counseling, and student affairs.

COLLEGE ADMISSION COUNSELING

A guidance team of 5 professionals is available for students. Counselors are responsible primarily for helping students with post-secondary placement and academic program planning. Approximately 75 college admissions representatives visit MCI's campus annually. Career counseling is also an integral part of the counseling department. Financial aid workshops for seniors, postgraduates, and their parents are offered. Preparation for the SAT and ACT is offered within the math and English curricula. Supplemental SAT preparation is offered outside of the school day.

MCI has a strong history of placing students in post-secondary schools. Schools attended by recent graduates include Bates, Boston College, Boston University, Brown, Colby, Cornell, Emerson, Emory, George Mason, Hofstra, Husson, Maine Maritime Academy, Michigan State, Muhlenberg, Northeastern, NYU, Penn State, Simmons, Syracuse, Tufts, and the Universities of Connecticut, California, Maine, New England, New Hampshire, North Carolina–Chapel Hill, Rhode Island, and Washington.

STUDENT BODY AND CONDUCT

The 2013–14 enrollment of 433 includes day and boarding students. Students come to MCI from six states and ten countries.

Students at MCI are expected to be good citizens and are held responsible for their behavior. The rules that provide the structure for the school community are written in the student handbook. Disciplinary issues are the responsibility of the administration, the faculty, and the residence hall staff.

ACADEMIC FACILITIES

There are seventeen buildings housed on the 23-acre campus. Visitors are greeted upon entrance with the stoic simplicity of the campus with its brick-front buildings and the historic bell tower of Founder's Hall.

The Math and Science Center is a 23,000-square-foot recent addition to MCI, including fifteen instructional spaces, a computer classroom, and a nearby greenhouse. MCI adopted a one-to-one computer program in 2013, providing every student with an iPad for use at school and at home. Students can access Wi-Fi throughout campus and the dormitories. The school also has 100 additional computers are available for student use. Students have access to both the Powell Memorial Library and the Pittsfield Public Library.

BOARDING AND GENERAL FACILITIES

Boarding students reside in single-sex residence halls on campus, supervised by resident faculty and staff members. There is also an option for the highest-achieving residential students to live in the Honors Dormitory. Each residence hall has its own recreation room and laundry facilities. The Trustee Memorial Student Center was recently added to the MCI campus. It is home to the dining hall, student lounge, and garden sitting area, including a performance stage, food court, garden benches, and game room.

Weymouth Hall houses the ESL Center, the Wellness Center, the school bookstore, and an additional student lounge.

MCI offers a unique Host Family Program. Participating students are paired with a family from the community that makes the student a part of its family for the school year. Students may spend time with their host family on weekends, after school, and during vacations.

ATHLETICS

MCI believes that athletics are an important part of the education process, a dynamic lesson in teamwork, and a hallmark of personal dedication. The school offers a comprehensive athletic program for student-athletes of varying levels of ability by offering JV, varsity, and club-level sports.

There are eighteen sports teams for boys and girls, including baseball, basketball, cheering, field hockey, football, golf, lacrosse, rifle, skiing, soccer, softball, tennis, track, and wrestling.

Wright Gymnasium and Parks Gymnasium are multiple-use athletic facilities, and each contains a weight room and locker facilities. Located on the main campus are a football field, a practice field, a ¼-mile track, and a rifle range. By fall of 2014, three additional fields are slated to be available on campus for team practice and games. Manson Park has fields for soccer, field hockey, baseball, and softball as well as three tennis courts. The school has the use of a local golf course and ski areas for competitive teams and recreation.

EXTRACURRICULAR OPPORTUNITIES

MCI students may choose from among more than thirty campus organizations, which represent some of the following interests: drama production; world languages and travel to places such as Costa Rica, Spain, France, Italy, and Russia; chess; robotics; Kindness Krew; Outdoor adventure team, which includes hiking, biking, canoeing, and other activities; weight lifting; Key Club, which is the school's community service organization; computer science; and public speaking. Students may participate in Student Council; MCI's strong, award-winning music program includes concert band, concert choir, chamber choir, vocal jazz ensemble, instrumental jazz ensemble, jazz combo, percussion ensemble, and pep band; and the Math Team which competes locally and statewide.

Bossov Ballet Theatre offers MCI students a unique opportunity to study classical ballet as part of the academic curriculum. Ballet classes are taught by Natalya Nikolaevna Getman, a former dancer with the Moscow Ballet. The program allows students to earn full academic credit for ballet training. Students who complete the program are uniquely positioned either to matriculate to an outstanding college or join a professional ballet company.

DAILY LIFE

The school day begins at 7:45 a.m. and ends at 2:45 p.m., with a 40-minute lunch break.

Classes run from Monday through Friday, with dinner served from 5 to 6:30 p.m. Sunday through Thursday, there is a mandatory supervised study hall from 7 to 8:30 p.m. for all boarding students. Honors Study is available to high-achieving students.

WEEKEND LIFE

Supervised weekend activities include trips to Canada, Boston, the nearby capital of Augusta, the city of Portland, historic ports, lighthouses and coastal towns along the Atlantic shoreline, and cultural and athletic events both on and off campus. Activities such as whale watching, white-water rafting, and skiing at Sugarloaf Resort are also offered. With parental permission, students are allowed to go home on weekends or visit the home of their host family.

COSTS AND FINANCIAL AID

The 2013–14 tuition, room, and board are $42,000 for boarding students, and tuition is $10,000 for private day students. The cost for ESL support is $3,000 for the first class and $2,000 for each additional class. The nonrefundable deposit of $5,000 is due within two weeks of an offer of admission. A variety of payment plans are available.

Financial aid is awarded on a need basis, determined by information shown on the Parents' Confidential Statement and any additional financial information that is requested.

ADMISSIONS INFORMATION

MCI's Admissions Committee screens all applicants to determine their compatibility with MCI's philosophy that students should assume a mature responsibility for their own education. No entrance tests are required, but an on-campus or online video conference interview with each student and his or her parents is strongly recommended. School transcripts and results of standardized tests are used to determine academic ability and appropriate academic placement in classes in accordance with the student's individual needs, abilities, and interests.

Maine Central Institute does not discriminate on the basis of race, sex, age, sexual preference, disability, religion, or national or ethnic origin in the administration of its educational and admission policies, financial aid programs, and athletic or other school-administered programs and activities.

APPLICATION TIMETABLE

Inquiries and applications are welcome at any time; however, applying by June 1 is recommended. Visits may be scheduled at any time during the year but are most effective when school is in session. Tours and interviews can be arranged by calling the Admissions Office, which is open Monday through Friday from 8 a.m. to 4:30 p.m. A nonrefundable application fee of $75 is required.

ADMISSIONS CORRESPONDENCE

Clint M. Williams, Dean of Admission
Maine Central Institute
295 Main Street
Pittsfield, Maine 04967
United States
Phone: 207-487-2282
Fax: 207-487-3512
E-mail: cwilliams@mci-school.org
Website: http://www.mci-school.org
Skype: mciadmission

MARINE MILITARY ACADEMY

Harlingen, Texas

Type: All-boys, college-preparatory, military boarding school
Grades: 8–12 with an optional postgraduate year
Enrollment: 250
Head of School: Col. R. Glenn Hill, USMC (Ret.)

THE SCHOOL

Marine Military Academy (MMA) is a private, college-preparatory, boarding school for young men in grades 8–12 with an optional postgraduate year. Located in sunny South Texas, MMA is the only private secondary school based on the traditions, values, and ideals of the U.S. Marine Corps. Since 1965, MMA has been home to adolescent sons from all over the world. MMA takes young men and fuels their minds, bodies, and spirits.

MMA's purpose is to inspire positive academic, physical, and moral growth in every cadet. To achieve this, MMA provides a structured, distraction-free setting that allows cadets to focus on their educational and personal development. At the center of this environment are eight principles that govern each cadet's actions: leadership, character, confidence, courage, responsibility, self-discipline, loyalty, and respect.

Throughout this journey, cadets learn to take ownership of their lives and develop the critical tools they need to succeed not only in college, but in life. MMA's proven education model makes it among the world's top private military schools for adolescent males.

In the early 1960s, Capt. William A. Gary, an Arizona rancher and retired U.S. Marine Corps Reservist, wanted to send his son to a school that embraced the ideology of the Marine Corps. He believed that the Marine Corps' concepts of leadership, discipline, responsibility, and moral values could be successfully applied to a college-preparatory education. Captain Gary could not find such a school, so in 1963 he and a group of retired Marines set out on a mission to start one.

Captain Gary and his team discovered a former Air Force navigation school in Harlingen, Texas, a city located in the southernmost part of the state. The Marines envisioned the 142-acre campus as an all-boys, military boarding school and began building the educational laboratory that would develop today's young men into tomorrow's leaders.

In September 1965, Marine Military Academy opened its doors to 58 cadets; six would comprise the first graduating class of 1966. Today, MMA is home to hundreds of young men from across the globe and the alma mater to thousands of alumni.

ACADEMIC PROGRAM

To prepare cadets for the rigor of college course work and help them earn college credit, MMA offers and promotes dual enrollment and Advanced Placement (AP) courses. MMA's academic program is accredited by the Southern Association of

Colleges and Schools. One hundred percent of MMA graduates are accepted into colleges or universities.

In addition to its core classes, MMA offers two popular elective classes: aerospace/flight training and marine science/sailing.

When school is out, MMA holds a four-week summer camp for boys who wish to engage in numerous outdoor activities and challenges designed to build their strength, confidence, concentration, and self-discipline. MMA also offers a concurrent ESL Summer Camp for students who wish to learn English.

FACULTY AND ADVISERS

With a student-teacher ratio of 12:1, MMA provides small class sizes so cadets receive more personalized instruction. The daily afternoon tutorial period allows cadets to seek extra assistance from their teachers on subjects they find challenging. The grade point average (GPA) for new cadets increases by an average of 1.71.

COLLEGE ADMISSION COUNSELING

The College Placement Officer at MMA assists all cadets with their college or service academy selection and the application process. The College Placement Officer is located in the College Placement Office, a library that houses hundreds of resources, such as college catalogs, study guides for college admission tests, financial aid and scholarship information, and other print and online data.

MMA's distinguished Marine Corps Junior ROTC program makes it a Naval Honor School. As a Naval Honor School, MMA has the privilege of nominating cadets each year for placement in the U.S. service academies.

STUDENT BODY AND CONDUCT

Approximately 250 cadets attend MMA. As an international boarding school, MMA cadets represent at least 12 different countries. No matter where they hail from, all cadets form a bond of brotherhood and become part of the "Leatherneck" family.

Marine Military Academy's mission is to develop disciplined, morally strong, college-ready young men who are prepared for responsible leadership. MMA provides sound academic preparation so cadets may enter the university or service academy of their choice. In addition, MMA is globally recognized as a premier private school for adolescent men on course to achieve their post-secondary education and career goals.

MMA is guided by the three Marine Corps values: honor, courage, and commitment.

Cadets are held to the highest ethical and moral standards. Respect for others is essential. Cadets will face their fears and overcome them. They will do what is right no matter the consequences. Cadets strive for excellence and never give up. Duty to others is fundamental.

ACADEMIC FACILITIES

MMA is located on a 142-acre, gated campus in Harlingen, Texas, and offers an impressive array of facilities for academics, athletics, and ceremonies. The Tom T. East Center is home to the mathematics and science departments and the synergistic lab, which allows cadets to explore a wide variety of physical phenomena in a hands-on manner including light, sound, flight, and bridge design. Coleman Hall houses the English department, SAT Prep computer lab, and College Placement Office. The social sciences and foreign language departments are located in Belle Blaschke Hall. With over 18,000 books and hundreds of print and online resources, the Harold James Memorial Library reinforces MMA's strong educational program and is the nucleus for academic activities.

The Col Philip J. Yeckel Memorial Auditorium seats 1,070 people and is used for concerts, theater productions, and special events. Throughout the school year, MMA hosts a number of battalion-size parades that are open to the public on its Parade Ground.

MMA is also proud to serve as the home of the Iwo Jima Monument. On February 23, 1945, news photographer Joe Rosenthal captured five Marines and one Navy Corpsman erecting an American flag atop Mount Suribachi. At the time the photo was released, sculptor Dr. Felix W. de Weldon was on duty with the U.S. Navy. After World War II ended, de Weldon felt that the inspiring event should be depicted on a massive scale in our nation's capital. Over a nine-and-a-half-year period, he created a statue that would be cast in bronze and erected in Arlington, Virginia. It would be known as the U.S. Marine Corps War Memorial.

In 1981, de Weldon gifted the original working model of the Iwo Jima Memorial to MMA. The statue, which came in numerous parts, arrived at MMA on October 10, 1981. Just six months later, on April 16, 1982, MMA held the dedication ceremony for this distinguished American icon.

There were several important reasons why MMA was selected by de Weldon as the monument's home. The main street of the campus was appropriately named Iwo Jima Boulevard by its founders in

1965. The fairly constant temperature and humidity in Harlingen, Texas, are ideal for the preservation of the plaster figures. The Marine depicted at the base of the flagpole was a South Texas native, Cpl. Harlon H. Block of Weslaco, Texas; his gravesite is directly behind the Iwo Jima Monument. In addition, MMA is the only place outside of the nation's capital where proper honors are rendered with battalion-size, dress-blue parades.

Since 1982, the Jima Monument has been an inspiration to MMA cadets and visitors from all over the world. All MMA parades are held in front of this magnificent sculpture and an American flag flies above it 24 hours a day.

ATHLETICS AND EXTRACURRICULAR OPPORTUNITIES

All MMA cadets are required to participate in at least one sport or activity. MMA offers 15 sports and three activities for cadets to join. The campus boasts four athletic fields, three tennis courts, three gyms, a swimming pool, a marksmanship center, and the 40-acre Leadership Enhancement and Development (LEAD) Complex.

The sports and activities MMA currently offers include band, boxing, baseball, basketball, cross-country, cycling, drill team and color guard, football, golf, jujitsu, rifle team, rock climbing, soccer, swimming, track and field, tennis, weightlifting, and wrestling.

DAILY LIFE

Cadets reside in barracks with a live-in drill instructor. There are approximately 50 cadets in each barrack; two cadets share a room equipped with a bathroom. Each barrack has two community rooms, a

computer study room with filtered Internet access and a television room. Cadets eat three times a day in the Mess Hall.

A typical day for the cadets includes the following:

6 a.m.—Reveille
6:10 a.m.—Physical training
6:40 a.m.—Breakfast
7:30 a.m.—Clean up and prepare for school
8:35 a.m.—Morning colors
8:50 a.m.—Morning classes
12:10 p.m.—Pass in review/formation and lunch
1:15 p.m.—Afternoon classes
2:55 p.m.—Tutoring
3:35 p.m.—Activities
6 p.m.—Dinner
7 p.m.—Study period
9:15 p.m.—Free time
10 p.m.—Lights out

Cadets earn liberty on the weekends and may leave the MMA campus for leisure, such as spending a day at the local movie theater or mall. The young men often use their liberty to perform community service. MMA cadets contribute approximately 3,000 hours a year to the local community.

COSTS AND FINANCIAL AID

Tuition and fees for the school year are $33,000, and the uniform fee is $1,400. The application fee is $100 and a security deposit of $1,800 is required. Payment plan information is available by contacting the Admissions Office at 956-421-9252 or admissions@MMA-TX.org.

Financial assistance is available in the form of scholarships. Scholarships are never full, only partial. Prospective students can contact MMA's chief financial officer at 956-421-9240 for more scholarship information.

ADMISSIONS INFORMATION

Applications for the school year are accepted all year, but students enter at the beginning of the fall or spring semester. Acceptance to MMA is based on a number of factors: prior academic history and curriculum, discipline history, health history, and, very importantly, potential. Because of the nature of the academic setting, the committee looks for young men who have the potential to adapt to MMA's program.

A guided tour is highly recommended as it gives the applicant and his family a sense of daily life at MMA. Ideally located, MMA is just a five-minute walk from Valley International Airport, the region's largest airport, and a 40-minute drive from South Padre Island. To schedule a tour, contact Admissions at 956-421-9252 or admissions@MMA-TX.org.

Marine Military Academy does not discriminate on the basis of race, religion, color, or national or ethnic origin in the administration of its educational policies, admission policies, scholarship or loan programs, or athletic and other academy-administered programs.

ADMISSIONS CORRESPONDENCE

Marine Military Academy
Admissions Office
320 Iwo Jima Boulevard
Harlingen, Texas 78550
United States
Phone: 956-421-9252
Fax: 956-421-9273
E-mail: admissions@MMA-TX.org
Website: MMA-TX.org

MARYMOUNT SCHOOL OF NEW YORK
New York, New York

Type: Girls' independent college-preparatory Catholic day school
Grades: N–XII: Lower School, Nursery–III; Lower Middle School, IV–V; Upper Middle School, VI–VIII, Upper School, IX–XII
Enrollment: School total: 704; Upper School: 213
Head of School: Concepcion R. Alvar

THE SCHOOL

Marymount School of New York is an independent Catholic day school that educates girls in a tradition of academic excellence and moral values. The School promotes in each student a respect for her own unique abilities and provides a foundation for exploring and acting on questions of integrity and ethical decision-making. Founded by Mother Marie Joseph Butler in 1926 as part of a worldwide network of schools directed by the Religious of the Sacred Heart of Mary, Marymount remains faithful to its mission "to educate young women who question, risk, and grow; young women who care, serve, and lead; young women prepared to challenge, shape, and change the world." Committed to its Catholic heritage, the School welcomes and values the religious diversity of its student body and seeks to give all students a deeper understanding of the role of the spiritual in life. The School also has an active social service program and integrates social justice and human rights into the curriculum.

Marymount occupies three adjoining landmark Beaux Arts mansions, located on Fifth Avenue's historic Museum Mile, a fourth mansion on East 82nd Street, and a recently renovated 42,000-square-foot facility on East 97th Street. The Metropolitan Museum of Art and Central Park, both located directly across the street from the Fifth Avenue Campus, provide resources that are integral to the School's academic and extracurricular programs. Several studio art classes meet in the Museum's Carroll Classroom. As part of the Class IX humanities curriculum and in advanced art history courses, Upper School students have classes in the Museum weekly. Central Park is used for science and fitness classes as well as extracurricular activities. Other city sites, such as the United Nations, the Tenement Museum, Ellis Island, the New York Zoological Society, the American Museum of Natural History, the Rose Planetarium, MoMA, the Guggenheim, and El Museo Del Barrio are also frequent extensions of the classroom for Marymount students.

Since 1969, the School has been independently incorporated under the direction of a 30-member Board of Trustees made up of parents, alumnae, educators, and members of the founding order. The School benefits from a strong Parents' Association; an active Alumnae Association; the involvement of parents, alumnae, and student volunteers; and a successful Annual Giving Program.

Marymount is accredited by the New York State Association of Independent Schools (NYSAIS). The School holds membership in the National Association of Independent Schools (NAIS), NYSAIS, the Independent Schools Admissions Association of Greater New York (ISAAGNY), the National Catholic Education Association, the National Coalition of Girls' Schools (NCGS), and the Educational Records Bureau (ERB).

ACADEMIC PROGRAM

The study of classic disciplines at Marymount is dynamic and innovative. The rigorous college-preparatory curriculum emphasizes critical thinking, collaboration, communication, and creativity. Students are encouraged to question and explore topics in depth, to take intellectual risks, and to work independently and collaboratively to find alternative approaches to problems. With its focus on the education of young women, Marymount allows each student to find her own voice. Students develop the skills necessary to succeed in competitive colleges and in life beyond the classroom: self-confidence, leadership ability, a risk-taking spirit, and joy in learning.

A commitment to the study of science, technology, engineering, and mathematics (STEM) is reflected in Marymount's curriculum, which fully integrates information and communication technologies into all subject areas. Students have access to desktop and laptop computers, iPads, and other mobile computing devices throughout the School. Students in Classes K through V use iPads for individual and collaborative exploration, creation, and communication. Students in Classes VI through XII and staff members each have a school-supplied MacBook, school email, and Google account and use digital media to carry out research, create presentations, publish work, communicate, and demonstrate ideas and concepts. Students learn a wide variety of authoring tools as well as programming languages to create and publish digital media. Using an array of interactive media, students extend discussions and collaborations beyond the classroom. Using online tools and video-conferencing, students collaborate on projects with other Marymount Schools and with students and researchers around the globe.

Marymount's position at the forefront of educational technology relies on more than the investment in laptops, iPads, interactive displays, software, and networks. To maintain its cutting-edge program—which has been recognized for excellence by NAIS, NCGS, and Apple Inc.—the School offers technology workshops throughout the school year for the faculty and other NAIS-school faculty members.

High school graduation requirements include satisfactory completion of 4 years of English, 3 years of history, 3 years of math, 3 years of laboratory science, 3 years of a world language, 4 years of religious studies, 4 years of physical education, 3 semesters of visual/performing arts, 1 year of computer science, and 6 semesters of health/guidance. These requirements provide a broad, solid base of knowledge while sharpening problem-solving and research skills and promoting critical and creative thinking. Upper School students are formally evaluated four times a year, using an A–F grading scale. The evaluation process includes written reports and biannual parent/student/teacher conferences.

The School offers honors and Advanced Placement courses as well as electives and studio courses, such as AP art history, economics, classical Greek, music history, introduction to acting, two AP studio art courses, African studies, critical thinking in the arts, Middle Eastern studies, history of modern China, physical computing, and engineering. In senior English, students choose from seminars that cover topics from Shakespeare's history plays to contemporary American drama to the literature of African-American and Asian-American women writers. Most students elect to take a fourth year of math; advanced offerings include AP calculus AB, AP calculus BC, AP statistics, and calculus. Fourth-year science courses include AP biology, AP chemistry, AP physics C, advanced physics, molecular biology, and atmospheric science. The science program connects with and utilizes the research of numerous institutions, including the New York Academy of Sciences and Princeton University, as well as participating in the STEM Internship Program, the STEM Research Program, and the GAINS Network. Class XII students may elect to take AP psychology or other advanced courses through Marymount's affiliate membership in Online School for Girls.

While a leader in science and technological education, Marymount is also committed to the study of humanities. All Class IX students take part in the Integrated Humanities program, an interdisciplinary curriculum that focuses on history, literature, and art history in the study of ancient civilizations. Classes are held at the Metropolitan Museum of Art at least once a week. The program includes a performance-based World Civilizations Festival and collaborative research projects in history and art history. As a culminating project, seniors submit an interdisciplinary writing portfolio of selected work from their last three years of high school.

The visual and performing arts offerings include studio art, media arts, AP 2-D design, AP drawing, ensemble music, choral music, chamber choir, and introduction to acting. The after-school chorus, Marymount Singers, performs regularly at masses and concerts, and the Marymount Players stage two productions annually.

The religious studies program includes comparative religions, Hebrew scriptures, the New Testament, social justice, and ethics. With a focus on moral and ethical decision-making, students analyze systemic social issues and immerse themselves in the community through numerous service projects, as well as the Marymount Philanthropy and Community Transformation (M-PACT) program. The Catholic-Jewish Initiative provides students with a deeper understanding of the Judeo-Christian tradition and includes Holocaust studies and a trip to the National Holocaust Museum in Washington, D.C.

During the summer after junior year, each student participates in an off-campus internship to gain exposure to a career of interest. Students have interned at hospitals, research laboratories, law firms, financial organizations, theaters, schools, nonprofit organizations, and corporations. They also attend a career day, with visiting alumnae as guest speakers. A financial literacy program prepares graduates for the financial challenges of college and life.

As members of a worldwide network of schools, students may opt to spend the second semester of their sophomore year at a Marymount International School in London or Rome. There is also the opportunity for a summer exchange to an RSHM school in Brazil. Annual concert and study tours and service trips extend the curriculum. Recent study tours have included exploring scientists and poets in England and Scotland, mathematics and culture of ancient Greece, the ecology of the Galapagos Islands, the theater and literature of Shakespeare's London and Stratford-upon-Avon, and the music, language, and culture of Italy, France, and Spain. Recent service trips have brought students to work with disabled orphans in Jamaica, rebuild homes in New Orleans, and promote justice for trafficked women in New York City. The Marymount Singers enjoy an annual concert tour every spring and have performed domestically and abroad.

Housed in a newly renovated facility on East 97th Street, the Upper Middle School encourages, supports, and challenges early adolescent students as they continue to develop independence, leadership, and achievement. Experiential, inquiry-based learning offers students opportunities to question their thinking, shape their understanding, and explore varied points of view as they become critical thinkers and innovative problem-solvers. Studio courses allow students to tinker, explore, and practice creative expression. Students in the Upper Mid are expected to be both independent and collaborative, curious and compassionate, bold and reflective.

The Lower Middle School curriculum welcomes the diverse interests of young adolescents and is structured to channel their energy and natural love of learning. The integrated core curriculum gradually increases in the degree of departmentalization at each grade level, and challenging learning activities and flexible groupings in main subject areas ensure that the students achieve their full potential. Speech classes prepare the girls for dramatic presentations reflective of their social studies and literature curriculum, and Class V students visit the Metropolitan Museum of Art for studio art and social studies classes. Uptown Broadway, an extracurricular option, allows the students to participate in a full-scale musical production.

The Lower School provides child-centered, creative learning within a challenging, structured environment. The curriculum focuses on the acquisition of foundational skills, often through an interdisciplinary approach. Programs engage students in the exciting process of learning about themselves, their surroundings, and the larger world. Introductory lessons in Spanish complement the social studies curriculum. A hands-on science program, an emphasis on technology integration, a study of robotics, a popular School chorus, and an extensive after-school program are some highlights of the Lower School.

FACULTY AND ADVISORS

There are 103 full-time and 16 part-time faculty members, allowing for a 6:1 student-teacher ratio. Eighty-three percent of the faculty members hold master's degrees, and 11 percent hold doctoral degrees. In Nursery through Class II, each class has a head teacher and at least one assistant teacher. In Classes III through V, each class has three homeroom teachers. In Classes VI–XII, each student has a homeroom teacher and an advisor, usually one of her teachers, who follows her academic progress and provides guidance and support. Learning resource specialists, school nurses, an athletic trainer, artists-in-residence, and school psychologists work with students throughout the School.

Concepcion R. Alvar was appointed Headmistress in 2004 after serving thirteen years as the Director of Admissions and three years as a head teacher. She also served as the Director and Supervisor of Marymount Summer for sixteen years. Mrs. Alvar holds a B.S. from Maryknoll College (Philippines) and an M.A. from Columbia University, Teachers College.

COLLEGE ADMISSION COUNSELING

Under the guidance of the Director of College Counseling, Marymount's formal college counseling program begins during the junior year. Two College Nights are held for Class XI students and parents. Individual counseling throughout the semester directs each student to those colleges that best match her achievements and interests. Students participate in weekly guidance classes to learn about general requirements for college admission, the application process, and standardized tests. During the fall of their senior year, students continue the weekly sessions, focusing on essay writing, admissions interviews, and financial aid applications.

Graduates from recent classes are attending the following colleges and universities: Amherst, Barnard, Boston College, Boston University, Bowdoin, Brown, Columbia, Cooper Union, Connecticut, Cornell, Dartmouth, Davidson, Duke, Fairfield, Fordham, George Washington, Georgetown, Harvard, Holy Cross, Kenyon, Middlebury, NYU, Oberlin, Princeton, Skidmore, Smith, Stanford, Trinity, Tufts, Vanderbilt, Villanova, Wake Forest, Wellesley, Wesleyan, Wheaton, Williams, Yale, and the Universities of Notre Dame, Pennsylvania, St. Andrew's (Scotland), and Virginia.

STUDENT BODY AND CONDUCT

Marymount's enrollment is 704 students in Nursery through Class XII, with 213 girls in the Upper School. Most students reside in the five boroughs of New York City; however, Upper School students also commute from Long Island, New Jersey, and Westchester County. Students wear uniforms, except on special days; participate in

athletic and extracurricular activities; and attend weekly chapel services, all-school masses, and annual class retreats.

Marymount encourages students to be active participants in their education and in the life of the School community. Students seek out leadership and volunteer opportunities, serving as advocates for one another through peer mentoring, retreat teams, and the Big Sister/Little Sister program. Student government and campus ministry provide social and service opportunities that enable students to broaden their perspectives, develop as leaders, sharpen public-speaking skills, and form lasting friendships. Teachers and administrators encourage each student to respect herself and others and to be responsible members of the community.

ACADEMIC FACILITIES

The Beaux Arts mansions on Fifth Avenue provide rooms for Lower and Upper School classes, and include four science laboratories, two art studios, a math center, a Fab Lab, a gymnasium, an auditorium, a courtyard play area, a chapel, and a library complex. The East 82nd Street facility is the home of the Lower Middle School. Students in the Lower Mid, Upper Mid, and Upper Schools also attend classes at the East 97th Street campus. This renovated facility is the home of the Upper Middle School and includes a gymnasium, cafeteria, and three floors of classrooms. The fourth floor of the 97th Street Campus features several science classrooms and laboratories as well as a media-production lab, and a Fab Lab where students can design, engineer, and fabricate an array of objects and solutions using 3-D printers, laser cutters, and other fabrication tools. The additional campus also offers classrooms for humanities classes, space for visual and performing arts, and a fitness room. All classrooms feature interactive boards and multimedia displays.

ATHLETICS

The athletics program promotes good health, physical fitness, coordination, skill development, confidence, and a spirit of competition and collaboration through its physical education classes, the electives program for Classes X–XII, and individual and team sports.

Marymount provides a full schedule for varsity and junior varsity sports, as well as teams at the V/VI and VII/VIII class levels. Participants in Classes V/VI stay two days per week for an after-school sports program; students in Classes VII/VIII commit to three afternoons per week. The junior varsity and varsity teams compete within the Athletic Association of Independent Schools League (AAIS) in badminton, basketball, cross-country, fencing, field hockey, lacrosse, soccer, softball, swimming, tennis, track and field, and volleyball.

In addition to its gymnasiums, Marymount uses the facilities of nearby Catholic schools, the Harlem Armory, Riverbank State Park, and Roberto Clemente State Park. Central Park, Randall's Island, and Van Cortlandt Park are sites for field sports. Tennisport, Riverbank State Park, and Flushing Meadows are competitive sites for the tennis and swim teams. Additional facilities are used throughout New York City.

EXTRACURRICULAR OPPORTUNITIES

A wide range of clubs and activities complement the academic program, promote student initiative, and provide opportunities to contribute to the School community and develop communication, cooperation, and leadership skills. Student-led clubs include Amnesty International, book club, digital photography, science and the environment club, film club, finance club, forensics team, Mathletes, philosophy club, set design/tech crew, student government, and women in action. Campus Ministry, CAMBIAS (Cultural Awareness Club), Marymount Singers, Marymount Players, Mock Trial, Model UN, and National Honor Society offer additional opportunities for student service, leadership, and performance. Student publications include a yearbook (Marifia), a newspaper (Joritan), and an award-winning literary/arts journal (Muse). A wide range of weekly clubs in the Lower and Upper Middle Schools includes Student Council; Italian, Latin, and French clubs; altar servers; handbells; environmental science; art; drama; handwork; and the literary magazine, Chez Nous.

Each year, the Upper School presents two dramatic productions, including a musical; organizes either a Harambee Celebration during Black History Month or a Bias Awareness Day; sponsors an Art Festival; and participates in numerous community service projects, local and national competitions, and conferences with other schools.

The School brings people of stature and high achievement to address students, including Nobel Peace Prize winner Leymah Gbowee, former poet laureate Billy Collins, athlete Tegla Laroupe, author Jhumpa Lahiri, bioethicist Ronald Green, nanotechnologist Dr. Susan Arney, African American painter Philomena Williamson, feminist Gloria Steinem, Sr. Helen Prejean, author of *Dead Man Walking*, and Sheryl WuDunn, coauthor of *Half the Sky*. The Maggie Murray Fund supports a series of writing-related events to enrich the students' literary experiences and has given students the opportunity to attend conversations with such celebrated writers as Toni Morrison and Chinua Achebe.

Students have the opportunity to interact with boys from neighboring schools through dramatic productions, community service projects, walkathons, dances, and other student-run social activities.

DAILY LIFE

Upper School classes are held from 8 a.m. to 2:50 p.m. Class periods are 45, 60, or 75 minutes in length and typically meet four days in an eight-day cycle. After classes have ended, most students remain for sports, extracurricular activities, and/or independent study.

COSTS AND FINANCIAL AID

The tuition for the 2013–14 academic year ranges from $24,425 for Nursery to $41,865 for Class XII. In February, parents are required to make a deposit of $5,000, which is credited toward the November tuition. The Key Education Resources Payment Plan is available.

Roughly $3 million in financial aid was awarded in 2012–13 to students after establishing need through School and Student Services. Twenty-two percent of Marymount students receive need-based financial aid.

ADMISSIONS INFORMATION

As a college-preparatory school, Marymount aims to enroll young women of academic promise and sound character who seek a challenging educational environment and opportunities for learning outside the classroom. Educational Records Bureau tests, school records, and interviews are used in selecting students.

The School admits students of any race, color, and national or ethnic origin to all the rights, privileges, programs, and activities generally accorded or made available to students at the School and does not discriminate on these bases in the administration of its educational policies, admissions policies, scholarship or loan programs, athletic programs, or other School programs.

APPLICATION TIMETABLE

Interested students are encouraged to contact the Admissions Office as early as possible in the fall for admission the following year. The application deadline is November 30, but may be changed at the discretion of the Director of Admissions. Notification of admissions decisions is sent during February, according to the dates established by the Independent School Admissions Association of Greater New York.

ADMISSIONS CORRESPONDENCE

Lillian Issa
Deputy Head/Director of Admissions
Marymount School of New York
1026 Fifth Avenue
New York, New York 10028
United States
Phone: 212-744-4486
Fax: 212-744-0163 (general)
212-744-0716 (admissions)
E-mail: admissions@marymountnyc.org
Website: http://marymountnyc.org

MILTON ACADEMY

Milton, Massachusetts

Type: Coeducational boarding and day college-preparatory school
Grades: K–12: (Lower School: K–8; Upper School: 9–12)
Enrollment: School total: 980; Upper School: 680
Head of School: Todd Bland

THE SCHOOL

The Academy received its charter in 1798 under the Massachusetts land-grant policy. It bequeathed to the school a responsibility to "open the way for all the people to a higher order of education than the common schools can supply." Milton's motto, "Dare to be true," not only states a core value, it describes Milton's culture. Milton fosters intellectual inquiry and encourages initiative and the open exchange of ideas. Teaching and learning at Milton are active processes that recognize the intelligence, talents, and potential of each member of the Academy.

For more than 200 years, Milton has developed confident, independent thinkers in an intimate, friendly setting where students and faculty members understand that the life of the mind is the pulse of the school. A gifted and dedicated faculty motivates a diverse student body, providing students with the structure to learn and the support to take risks. The faculty's teaching expertise and passion for scholarship generates extraordinary growth in students who learn to expect the most of themselves. The Milton community connects purposefully with world issues. Students graduate with a clear sense of themselves, their world, and how to contribute.

From Milton Academy's suburban 125-acre campus, 8 miles south of Boston in the town of Milton (population 26,000), students and faculty members access the vast cultural resources of Boston and Cambridge. Minutes from campus is the Blue Hills Reservation, 6,000 wooded acres of hiking trails and ski slopes.

Milton Academy is a nonprofit organization with a self-perpetuating Board of Trustees. Its endowment is $212 million (as of June 2013).

Milton Academy is accredited by the New England Association of Schools and Colleges and holds memberships in the National Association of Independent Schools, the Cum Laude Society, and the Association of Independent Schools in New England.

ACADEMIC PROGRAM

Milton students and faculty members are motivated participants in the world of ideas, concepts, and values. Milton's curriculum provides rigorous preparation for college and includes more than 182 courses in nine academic departments. For students entering Milton in the ninth grade, a minimum of 18 credits are required for graduation. This includes 4 years of English, 2 years of history (including U.S. and modern world history), 2 years of science, 1 year of an arts course, and successful completion of algebra II, geometry, and a level III foreign language course. Noncredit requirements include current events/public speaking, physical education, a ninth-grade arts course (music/drama/visual arts), and a four-year affective education curriculum that includes health, values, social awareness, and senior transitions.

Electives are offered in all academic areas. Examples of electives include computer programming, comparative government, performing literature, Spanish film and social change, advanced architecture, philosophy and literature, choreography, film and video production, psychology, engineering, nuclear physics, issues in environmental science, creative writing, music theory, observational astronomy, and marine biology. Students may petition to take independent study courses, and Advanced Placement courses leading to college credit are offered in most subject areas.

In January, seniors submit a proposal for a five-week spring independent project, on or off campus. Senior projects give students the opportunity to pursue in-depth interests stemming from their work at Milton.

The typical class size is 14 students, and the overall student-teacher ratio is 5:1. Nightly 2-hour study periods in the houses are supervised for boarding students.

Faculty members are available for individual help throughout the day and in the houses at night. Students seeking assistance with assignments or help with specific skills, organization, and/or time management visit the Academic Skills Center, which is staffed throughout the day.

The school year, which is divided into two semesters, runs from early September to early June with an examination period at the end of January. Students typically take five courses per semester. Students earn letter grades from E (failure) through A+, and comments prepared by each student's teachers and adviser are sent to parents three times a year in November, February, and June.

All academic buildings and residential houses are part of a campuswide computer network. MiltONline, the Academy's e-mail and conferencing system, allows students to join conference discussions for many classes and extracurricular activities, communicate with faculty members and friends, and submit assignments. Students have access to the Milton Intranet as well as the Internet.

Class II students (eleventh graders) may apply to spend either the fall or spring semester at the Mountain School Program of Milton Academy (an interdisciplinary academic program set on a working 300-acre farm in Vermont); at CITYterm at the Master's School in Dobbs Ferry, New York; or at the Maine Coast Semester at Chewonki. Through School Year Abroad, Milton provides opportunities in Spain, France, Italy, and China. Milton also offers six- to eight-week exchange programs with schools in Spain, France, and China.

FACULTY AND ADVISERS

The deep commitment of a learned and experienced group of teachers is Milton's greatest treasure. Teaching in Classes IV–I (grades 9–12) are 133 full-time faculty members, 78 percent of whom hold advanced degrees (Ph.D. and master's degrees). Eighty-five percent of faculty members live on campus.

In addition to teaching, faculty members also serve as house parents and coaches, as well as advisers to student clubs, organizations, publications, and activities. Each faculty member is an adviser to a group of 6 to 8 students and supports the students' emotional, social, and academic well-being at Milton.

COLLEGE ADMISSION COUNSELING

Four college counselors work one-on-one with students, beginning in their Class II (eleventh grade) year, in a highly personal and effective approach toward the college admissions process.

For the graduating classes of 2011, 2012, and 2013 the top college enrollments were Harvard (28), Tufts (18), Cornell (17), Boston College (16), Colby College (16), NYU (16), University of Chicago (15), Brown (14), and Wesleyan University (14).

STUDENT BODY AND CONDUCT

Of the 680 students in the Upper School, 50 percent are boys and 50 percent are girls; 50 percent are boarding students and 50 percent are day students. Forty percent of Milton's enrolled students are students of color. Eleven percent of the Upper School students are international, coming from twenty-four countries across the globe. Thirty percent of Milton students receive financial aid, and the average grants account for 75 percent of tuition.

All Upper School students from Classes IV–I (grades 9–12) participate in the Self-Governing Association, led by 2 elected student representatives, 1 senior girl and 1 senior boy. Elected class representatives serve with faculty members on the Discipline Committee, which recommends to the Head of School appropriate responses when infractions of major school rules occur. Rules at Milton Academy foster the cohesion and morale of the community and enhance education by upholding standards of conduct developed by generations of students and faculty members.

ACADEMIC FACILITIES

Among the prominent buildings on the Milton campus are three primarily academic buildings: Warren Hall (English), Wigglesworth Hall (history), and Ware Hall (math and foreign languages); the Kellner Performing Arts Center, with a 350-seat teaching theater, a studio theater, dressing rooms, scene shop, practice rooms, orchestral rehearsal room, dance studio, and speech/debate room; the Athletic and Convocation Center, with a hockey rink, a fitness center, three basketball courts, and an indoor track; the Williams Squash Courts; the Ayer Observatory; and Apthorp Chapel. The Pritzker Science Center, which opened in 2010, integrates classroom areas with laboratory tables and equipment to create an environment that allows students to work collaboratively and move seamlessly between discussion and hands-on lab work. The Art and Media Center is home to numerous visual art studios and public display spaces, including the Nesto Gallery and the Greely auditorium.

Cox Library contains more than 46,000 volumes, more than 150 periodicals with back issues on microfilm, and a newspaper collection dating back to 1704. It also provides CD-ROM sources, Internet access and online search capabilities. Within Cox Library is one of several computer laboratories.

BOARDING AND GENERAL FACILITIES

Milton Academy students live in one of eight single-sex houses ranging in size from 31 to 48 students; four for boys and four for girls. Single rooms house one third of the students, while the other two thirds of the students reside in double rooms. Milton houses include all four classes as well as faculty members' families. Students spend all their Milton years in one house, experiencing a family-at-school context for developing close relationships with valued adults, learning about responsibility to the community, taking leadership roles with peers, and sharing social and cultural traditions. All rooms are networked, and school computers are available for student use in the house common rooms.

The Health and Counseling Center and the Academic Skills Center, as well as house parents in each residential house, class deans, and the office of the school chaplain, are available to meet students' needs.

ATHLETICS

Milton believes that teamwork, sportsmanship, and the pursuit of excellence are important values and that regular vigorous exercise is a foundation of good health. Milton offers a comprehensive athletic program that includes physical education classes and a range of intramural and interscholastic sports geared to the needs and interests of every student.

The school's offerings in interscholastic sports are Alpine skiing, baseball, basketball, cross-country, field hockey, football, golf, ice hockey, lacrosse, sailing, soccer, softball, squash, swimming and diving, tennis, track, volleyball, and wrestling.

Intramural offerings include the outdoor program, Pilates, soccer, squash, strength and conditioning, tennis, Ultimate (Frisbee), and yoga.

Sports facilities include four athletic buildings, an ice hockey rink and fitness center, two indoor climbing walls, twelve playing fields, seventeen tennis courts, seven international squash courts, an all-weather track, a cross-country course, and a ropes course.

EXTRACURRICULAR OPPORTUNITIES

The breadth of extracurricular opportunities means that every student finds a niche—a comfortable place to develop new skills, take on leadership, show commitment, make friends, and have fun. Clubs and organizations include cultural groups such as the Asian Society, Latino Association, Onyx, and Common Ground (an umbrella organization for the various groups); the Arts Board; the Outdoor Club; the Chinese, French, and Spanish clubs; the debate, math, and speech teams; and Students for Gender Equality. There are eleven student publications, among them *The Asian, La Voz, MAGUS/MABUS, Mille Tonnes, Milton Measure, Milton Paper,* and the yearbook. Music programs include the chamber singers, the gospel choir, the glee club, the orchestra, improvisational jazz combos, and five a cappella groups. The performing arts are an important part of the extracurricular offerings at Milton. Main stage theater productions, studio theater productions, play readings, and speech and debate team are a few of the available opportunities. Milton stages twelve major theater productions each year, including a Class IV (ninth grade) play, student directed one-act plays, a dance concert, and a biennial musical. Service opportunities include the audiovisual crew, community service, Lorax (environmental group), Orange and Blue Key (admission tour guides and leaders), and the Public Issues Board.

DAILY LIFE

The academic day runs from 8 a.m. to 2:55 p.m., except on Wednesday, when classes end at 1:15 p.m. There are no classes on Saturday or Sunday. Cafeteria-style lunch is served from 11 a.m. to 1:30 p.m., and students eat during a free period within that time. The students' activities period is from 3 to 3:30 p.m. Athletics and extracurricular activities take place from 3:30 to 5:30 p.m. Family-style dinner is at 6 p.m., and the evening study period runs from 7:30 to 9:30 p.m. Lights-out time depends on the grade level of each student.

WEEKEND LIFE

Interscholastic games are held on Wednesday, Friday, and Saturday afternoons. Social activities on Friday and Saturday evenings are planned by the Student Activities Association. Day students join boarders every weekend for events such as dances with live or recorded music, classic and new films, concerts, plays, drama readings, dormitory open houses, and trips to professional sports events, arts events, or local museums.

Prior to leaving campus, students must check their plans with house parents, who must approve their whereabouts and any overnight plans.

SUMMER PROGRAMS

Milton Academy does not run its own summer programs on campus. Professional development opportunities are made available to faculty members, including the Cultural Diversity Institute and the Boarding Staff Conference for teachers from across the country. In addition, Milton hosts many outside programs, including sports camps and academic enrichment programs.

COSTS AND FINANCIAL AID

For the 2013–14 academic year, tuition is $49,400 for boarding students and $40,550 for day students.

Milton seeks to enroll the most qualified applicants regardless of their financial circumstances. To that end, more than $8.6 million in financial aid will be provided to students in the 2014–15 school year. All financial aid at Milton is awarded on the basis of need. In addition to the program of direct grants, the school offers installment payment options and two low-interest loan programs.

ADMISSIONS INFORMATION

Milton Academy seeks students who are able, energetic, intellectually curious, and have strong values and a willingness to grow. Applicants must submit the Secondary School Admission Test (SSAT) scores (students applying for eleventh grade may submit PSAT or SAT scores if applicable). All applicants must also submit a school transcript, teacher recommendations, parental statement, and two essays. An interview, on or off campus, is also required.

APPLICATION TIMETABLE

The deadline for applying is January 15. Notification letters are sent out March 10; the reply date is April 10. There is a $50 application fee for U.S. applicants and a $100 fee for international applicants.

ADMISSIONS CORRESPONDENCE

Paul Rebuck, Dean of Admission
Milton Academy
170 Centre Street
Milton, Massachusetts 02186
United States
Phone: 617-898-2227
Fax: 617-898-1701
E-mail: admissions@milton.edu
Website: http://www.milton.edu

MORAVIAN ACADEMY

Bethlehem, Pennsylvania

Type: Day college-preparatory school
Grades: PK–12: Lower School, Prekindergarten–5; Middle School, 6–8; Upper School, 9–12
Enrollment: School total: 748 ; Upper School: 300
Head of School: George N. King Jr., Headmaster

THE SCHOOL

Moravian Academy (MA) traces its origin back to 1742 and the Moravians who settled Bethlehem. Guided by the wisdom of John Amos Comenius, Moravian bishop and renowned educator, the Moravian Church established schools in every community in which it settled. Moravian Academy became incorporated in 1971 when Moravian Seminary for Girls and Moravian Preparatory School were merged. The school has two campuses: the Lower–Middle School campus in the historic downtown area of Bethlehem and the Upper School campus on a 120-acre estate 6 miles to the east.

For more than 270 years, Moravian Academy has encouraged sound innovations to meet contemporary challenges while recognizing the permanence of basic human values. The school seeks to promote young people's full development in mind, body, and spirit by fostering a love for learning, respect for others, joy in participation and service, and skill in decision-making. Preparation for college occurs in an atmosphere characterized by an appreciation for the individual.

Moravian Academy is governed by a Board of Trustees. Six members are representatives of the Moravian Church. As of June 30, 2013, the net asset value of the Academy is $38.6 million, of which $16.8 million is endowment. In 2012–13, Annual Giving was $424,064, and operating expenses were $15.4 million.

Moravian Academy is accredited by the Middle States Association of Colleges and Schools and the Pennsylvania Association of Independent Schools. The school is a member of the National Association of Independent Schools, the Association of Delaware Valley Independent Schools, the College Board, the Council for Spiritual and Ethical Education, the School and Student Service for Financial Aid, and the Secondary School Admission Test Board.

Moravian Academy does not discriminate on the basis of race, nationality, sex, sexual orientation, religious affiliation, or ethnic origin in the administration of its educational and admission policies, financial aid awards, and athletic or other school-administered programs. Applicants who are disabled (or applicants' family members who are disabled) and require any type of accommodation during the application process, or at any other time, are encouraged to identify themselves and indicate what type of accommodation is needed.

ACADEMIC PROGRAM

Students are required to carry five major courses per year. Minimum graduation requirements include English, 4 credits; mathematics, 3 credits; lab sciences, 3 credits; global language, 3 credits; social studies, 3 credits; fine arts, 2 credits; and physical education and health. All students must successfully complete a semester course in world religions or ethics. Community service is an integral part of the curriculum. Electives are offered in all areas, including fine and performing arts, sciences, English, math, history, and global languages. Moravian Academy offers Advanced Placement courses, numerous honors courses, and the opportunity to pursue an honors independent study project under the mentorship of a faculty member. The Academy also participates in a high school scholars program that enables a small number of highly qualified students to take college courses at no cost. The overall student-faculty ratio is about 9:1, with classes ranging from 10 to 18 students.

Grades in most courses are A–F; D is a passing grade. However, a C- is required to advance to the next level in math and global languages. Reports are sent to parents on a monthly basis, and parent-conference opportunities are scheduled in the fall semester. Faculty and staff members are available for additional conferences whenever necessary. Examinations are held at the end of each seventeen-week semester in all major subjects. In the senior year, final examinations are given in May to allow seniors time for a two-week Post Term Experience before graduation.

FACULTY AND ADVISORS

The Upper School has 35 full-time and 8 part-time faculty members. Ninety-five percent of the full-time Upper School faculty members have advanced degrees. Several faculty members have degrees in counseling in addition to other subjects, and the entire faculty shares in counseling through the Faculty-Student Advisor Program.

George N. King Jr. was appointed Headmaster in 2007. He previously served as the Head of the Wooster School in Danbury, Connecticut. Mr. King received his B.A. from Murray State University and his M.A. from the New England Conservatory of Music.

COLLEGE ADMISSION COUNSELING

The Director of College Counseling begins group work in college guidance in the tenth grade. Tenth graders take a practice PSAT and repeat it the following year. Sophomore Seminar encourages students to familiarize themselves with the college application process; the focus is on understanding academic options and participation in school and community life. College Night is held annually for juniors and their parents.

Junior Seminar meets weekly in small groups for college counseling during the second semester and includes an individual family conference in the spring. They take the PSAT, SAT, and Subject Tests. Some students also elect to take the ACT in their junior or senior year. Senior Seminar meets weekly in small groups during the first semester for additional guidance and seniors are led through the college application process. They take the SAT and Subject Tests again, if necessary. In recent years, approximately 85 to 90 percent of the senior class takes at least one Advanced Placement exam and earns a score of 3 or higher.

Average SAT scores of 2013 graduates were 637 critical reading, 656 math, and 650 writing. Graduates of 2013 are attending Boston University, Brown, Bryn Mawr, Bucknell, Carleton, Clarkson, College of William and Mary, Cornell, Davidson, Drexel, Earlham, Elizabethtown, Elon, Emory, Fordham, Franklin and Marshall, George Washington, Hamilton, Harvard, Haverford, Hobart and William Smith, Lafayette, Lehigh, Muhlenberg, Northeastern, Penn State, RIT, Roger Williams, Rollins, Rose-Hulman, Saint Joseph's (Pennsylvania), School of Visual Arts, Siena, Smith, SMU, Susquehanna, Temple, Ursinus, Villanova, Washington and Lee, Wellesley, Williams, and the Universities of Miami, Michigan, Pittsburgh, Richmond, Rochester, Vermont, and Virginia. Some students participate in travel abroad or gap year programs before attending college.

STUDENT BODY AND CONDUCT

The Upper School has 300 students. The school understands the value of diversity in the educational setting. In all divisions, students and faculty members from a variety of ethnic, cultural, religious, and socioeconomic backgrounds carry on this commitment. Through classroom activities, nondenominational chapel services discussing many faiths, and active engagement with each other, students at Moravian Academy are encouraged to appreciate one another's individuality.

Students enjoy the small classes and the opportunity for participation in sports and other activities. Students are expected to wear clothing that is neat and appropriate for school. Denim is not permitted during the school day, and a school uniform is required for members of performing groups. Students participate actively in a Student Council. Serious matters of discipline come before a faculty-student discipline committee.

ACADEMIC FACILITIES

Snyder House, Walter Hall, Couch Fine Arts Center, and the Heath Science

Complex hold the classrooms, studios, and laboratories (environmental science, physics, and biology). The Academy's arts program is enhanced by the courses offered in the Van S. Merle-Smith Woodworking Studio. All of the library's resources are integrated with the instructional program to intensify and individualize the educational experience. Technology plays an important role in enhancing learning and students get hands-on experience with the latest equipment in classrooms and labs. The 1:1 program gives all students their own MacBook Air computer; use of the computer is integrated into the curriculum and is an integral part of the learning program. SmartBoards and Smart TVs are used in all divisions to enhance the learning process. The Couch Fine Arts Center houses the studio arts department. A 350-seat auditorium enhances the music and theater programs. Students can also use the resources and facilities of the seven colleges and universities in the area.

ATHLETICS

A strong athletics program meets the guidelines of the school's philosophy that a person must be nurtured in body, as well as in mind and spirit, and that respect for others and participation are important goals. A new 40,000-square-foot athletic and wellness center is under construction and scheduled for completion by December 2013. In addition, eight athletics fields, and six tennis courts provide the school with facilities for varsity and junior varsity teams in boys' and girls' lacrosse and baseball; girls' field hockey; boys' and girls' basketball, cross-country, soccer, swimming, and tennis; coeducational golf; and a girls' varsity softball team. Students also have the opportunity to participate in girls' volleyball, football, track, and wrestling in co-operative programs with a local school. A gymnasium that includes a weight room complements the physical education facilities in Walter Hall. An outdoor recreational pool is available for special student functions as well as the Academy's summer day camp program for younger children.

All students take part in team sports. In any given athletic season, more than one third of the Upper School student body participates in after-school athletics at the Academy.

EXTRACURRICULAR OPPORTUNITIES

Moravian Academy's activity program provides opportunities for varied interests and talents. Included are service projects, outdoor education, International Club, *Legacy* (yearbook), *Green Ponderer* (literary magazine), Model Congress, Model UN, PJAS, Scholastic Scrimmage, and a variety of activities that change in response to student interests. A fine arts series combines music, art, drama, and dance. In addition, the Academy's outdoor education program offers a variety of off-campus experiences in hiking, rock climbing, and white water rafting/kayaking. The annual Country Fair gives students an opportunity to work with the Parents' Association to create a family fun day for the school and Lehigh Valley community. Rooted in Moravian tradition, a strong appreciation of music has continued. There are several student musical groups, including chorale, MA Chamber Singers, Coda Red (an a cappella group), handbell choirs, and instrumental ensembles. Highlights of the year include the Christmas Vespers Service and the spring concert.

DAILY LIFE

A typical school day begins at 8 a.m., and classes run until 3:15 p.m. on Monday, Tuesday, Wednesday, and Friday. On Thursday, classes conclude at 2:55. The average length of class periods is about 40 minutes. Students usually take five major classes daily along with courses in the fine and performing arts, physical education, and health/driver's education.

A weekly nondenominational chapel service is held on Thursday mornings. On Monday, Tuesday, Wednesday, and Friday, there is a period for class meetings, all-school meetings, advisory meetings, or activity periods.

COSTS AND FINANCIAL AID

Tuition for 2013–14 is $25,130. There is an additional dining fee for students. An initial deposit of $1,000 is required upon acceptance, and the remainder of the fee is to be paid in two installments, unless other arrangements are made. An additional fee for tuition insurance is recommended for all new students.

Financial aid is available. Moravian Academy uses the services of the School and Student Service for Financial Aid by NAIS. Aid is awarded on the basis of demonstrated financial need. Aid is received by approximately 29 percent of Upper School students.

ADMISSIONS INFORMATION

Students are admitted in grades 9–11. Each applicant is carefully considered. Students who demonstrate an ability and willingness to handle a rigorous academic program as well as such qualities as intellectual curiosity, responsibility, creativity, and enthusiasm for school and community life, are encouraged to apply. Scores on tests administered by the school are also used in the admission process. In addition, school records, recommendations, and a personal interview are required. Admissions are usually completed by May, but there are sometimes openings available after that time.

APPLICATION TIMETABLE

Inquiries are welcome at any time. The Admission Office makes arrangements for tours and classroom visits during the school week. If necessary, other arrangements for tours can be made. The application fee is $65. Test dates are scheduled on specified Saturday mornings from January through March. Notifications are sent after February 15, and families are asked to respond within two weeks.

ADMISSIONS CORRESPONDENCE

Daniel J. Axford
Director of Admissions, Upper School
Moravian Academy
4313 Green Pond Road
Bethlehem, Pennsylvania 18020
United States
Phone: 610-691-1600
Website: http://www.moravianacademy.org

THE PENNINGTON SCHOOL

Pennington, New Jersey

Type: Coeducational day and boarding college-preparatory school
Grades: 6–12: Middle School, 6–8; Upper School, 9–12
Enrollment: School total: 487; Middle School, 81; Upper School: 406
Head of School: Stephanie G. Townsend, Head of School

THE SCHOOL

The Pennington School is an independent coeducational school for students in grades 6 through 12, with both day and boarding programs. The curriculum is college preparatory, with an emphasis on fostering the development of the whole student through academics, athletics, community service, and the creative and performing arts. There are also specialized programs within the curriculum for international students and for students with learning differences. Founded in 1838, The Pennington School values both tradition and innovation, applying to a rapidly-changing world the values gleaned from centuries of learning, along with the most up-to-date knowledge. The School's faculty members focus not only on what they can teach the students but also on what the varied perspectives of the extraordinarily diverse student body can impart to the overall educational experience.

The 54-acre campus is strategically located in a suburban setting just 60 miles from New York City, 40 miles from Philadelphia, and within 8 miles of Princeton. This location makes it convenient for cultural and educational field trips.

The governing body is a 36-member Board of Trustees. Pennington's endowment currently stands at $31 million.

The Pennington School is accredited by the Middle States Association of Colleges and Schools and approved by the New Jersey Association of Independent Schools. It is a member of the National Association of Independent Schools, the New Jersey Association of Independent Schools, and the Secondary School Admission Test Board. The Pennington School is affiliated with the University Senate and the Board of Higher Education and Ministry of the United Methodist Church.

ACADEMIC PROGRAM

The Pennington School's objectives are to offer a rigorous, challenging, and broad academic program that best prepares its students for life as college students.

Middle School students concentrate on five major subject areas: mathematics, English, social studies, science, and foreign language. All students rotate through a series of exploratory courses during the year, including art/drama, music, health, technology, public speaking, and ethics.

Students in the Upper School usually take six classes per day. The minimum number of credits necessary for graduation is 20. Requirements include the following: English, 4; mathematics, 3; history, 3; science, 3; foreign language, 2; religion, 1; art, 1; health, 1; technology, ½; and public speaking, ¼. Honors and Advanced Placement courses are offered in all disciplines.

The student-teacher ratio is 8:1, and the average class size is 13, with a maximum of 18 students in any one class. A two-hour evening study period for boarders is supervised. The School library is open a half-hour before the school day begins until the conclusion of study hall on school nights and for limited hours on weekends.

The School uses the semester system, but, with midterm evaluations, there are four marking periods. Parent-teacher or parent-adviser-student conferences are held twice a year. Individual conferences are arranged as required.

Official grades are issued at the conclusion of each semester. The Pennington School uses a letter grading system in which D (60) is a passing grade but C– (70) is the minimum grade for a course to count toward graduation requirements.

The Pennington School has two programs that offer learning support: the Center for Learning, a unique program designed for bright, academically talented students with language-based learning differences, and an English as a second language (ESL) program.

FACULTY AND ADVISERS

The faculty consists of 100 men and women, about half of whom live on campus. Seventy percent of the faculty members hold advanced degrees. Faculty members serve as advisers for 6 to 8 students, and oversee all aspects of each student's life at the School. Trained counselors are available to all students for specific needs. Teachers also serve as hall parents, providing the basis for yet another kind of close relationship.

Stephanie (Penny) Townsend, appointed Head of School in 2006, earned her bachelor's degree from the University of Connecticut and her master's degree from Middlebury College. Before coming to The Pennington School, she taught Spanish at Northfield Mount Hermon School in Massachusetts and at the Taft School in Connecticut. Most recently, Townsend served as the Dean of Faculty at the Taft School.

COLLEGE ADMISSION COUNSELING

College guidance is the responsibility of trained counselors who coordinate all aspects of the college planning and placement process, including the taking of PSAT, ACT Plan, SAT, ACT, SAT II, TOEFL, and Advanced Placement tests. Representatives from almost 200 colleges visit The Pennington School each year to meet with students. Juniors and seniors meet individually with their college counselors and attend college admission panels. Juniors attend special college programs, including two spring on-campus college fairs, and take a college admission seminar.

The School's recent graduates attend such colleges and universities as American, Boston College, Boston University, Brown, Bucknell, Columbia, Emory, Georgetown, Harvey Mudd, Hofstra, Lafayette, Lehigh, NYU, Parsons, Princeton, Rutgers, Syracuse, Trinity (Hartford), Villanova, Williams, the University of Pennsylvania, and the University of St. Andrews (Scotland).

STUDENT BODY AND CONDUCT

Of The Pennington School's 487 students, 81 are in the Middle School and 406 are in the Upper School; 385 are day students, and 102 are boarding students. Current students represent seven states and come from a number of countries, including Australia, the Bahamas, China, Germany, South Korea, Spain, Taiwan, and the West Indies. Twenty-six percent of the students belong to minority groups.

There is a student government, elected by the student body. Students are expected to follow the School Honor Code and the rules defined in the *Student/Parent Handbook*. Violations may be dealt with by the Behavior Review Board, which is made up of students and faculty members.

During class hours, Upper School boys must wear collared shirts, slacks, and dress shoes; on certain days, shirts and ties are required. Upper School girls must wear slacks or skirts with collared shirts or blouses. Middle School boys wear polo shirts and slacks; girls wear polo shirts with slacks or skirts or polo dresses. Monday night formal dinners and certain programs call for jackets and ties for boys and dresses or skirts and blouses for girls. The dress code permits jeans, T-shirts, and sneakers to be worn by students after class hours, on weekends, and on dress-down days but not during class time.

ACADEMIC FACILITIES

The centers of academic activities are Stainton Hall, a classroom/administration building; the Campus Center, containing art and music classrooms and studios, a theater, foreign language classrooms, and the Student Center; Meckler Library, which contains the academic book collection, online databases, and the technology classrooms; and Old Main, which houses classrooms and five residence halls. A new building to house humanities classes is in the planning stages and is slated to be completed by September 2015.

BOARDING AND GENERAL FACILITIES

In addition to Old Main, which contains five residence halls, there are also two dormitories containing another five residence halls: Becher Hall, a one-story residence with ten student rooms and two faculty apartments, and Buck Hall, containing four halls with double rooms and private bathrooms. There are eight faculty apartments in this building. The School has an attractive dining facility and a health center, with 2 registered nurses in residence. Boarding facilities close for the Thanksgiving, Christmas, and spring holidays, so all students must leave the campus during those vacation periods. The Pennington School also has numerous athletic facilities, as described below.

ATHLETICS

The Pennington School believes that the lessons learned through athletic involvement are valuable ones. Thus, every student is expected to participate in a team or individual sport that fits his or her own ability level. Although The Pennington School's athletic teams are very successful and frequently win state championships, the emphasis is on participation, collective effort, sportsmanship, and personal growth. All students must participate in at least one sport per year. Boarders must take three terms of activities. When boarding students are not involved in a sport, they must be involved in other extracurricular activities.

The sports available for boys and girls in grades 9 to 12 are basketball, cheerleading, cross-country, golf, lacrosse, soccer, swimming, tennis, track and field, and water polo. In addition, field hockey and softball are available for girls, and baseball, football, and ice hockey are offered for boys.

In addition to a gymnasium/swimming pool complex, The Pennington School has five tennis courts, 30 acres of playing fields, an all-weather-surface track, and a lighted artificial turf field lined for lacrosse, soccer, and football. The School also offers weight training with a facility housing the SOURCE Institute for Human Performance.

EXTRACURRICULAR OPPORTUNITIES

Life at The Pennington School is more than classrooms, laboratories, and the library, essential as these are. Opportunities exist for participation in a wide range of extracurricular activities.

Apart from the athletics program, there are many clubs and organizations that students may join. These include three drama productions a year, the Pennington Singers, Mock Trial, Peer Leadership, National Honor Society, Photography Club, International Thespian Society, Model United Nations, Pennington Sports News, Campus Guides, United People of Many Colors, jazz ensemble, chamber ensemble, Junior Proctors, foreign language clubs, and staffs of the yearbook, newspaper, and literary magazine, which contains creative writing and artistic work of students. All students are encouraged to do community service during the year. Students do volunteer work for hospitals and charitable organizations in Pennington, Princeton, and Trenton and travel globally on service-related trips during School vacations.

A student activities program provides for social events such as dances, ski trips, movies, theater presentations, and visits to area places of interest.

Life at The Pennington School also includes a weekly chapel service. Chapel services are a peaceful time for reflection and thought about life and love, friendship and community, right and wrong—themes that are important in every religion and in every country. The School's students come from many faiths and traditions, including Christianity, Hinduism, Islam, Judaism, Quakerism, and Buddhism.

DAILY LIFE

The class day begins at 8:00 a.m. and concludes at 3:00 p.m. There is an activities period on Fridays, a biweekly community meeting on Mondays, and special programs on many Wednesdays. There are two lunch periods. An extra-help conference period follows the class day. Sports practice takes place from 3:30 to 5:30, and dinner follows at 5:30 for boarding students. A monitored study period for boarders from 7:30 to 9:30 completes the day. Lights are out at 10:30 p.m. on weekdays.

WEEKEND LIFE

Day students and boarders are encouraged to participate in weekend activities coordinated by residential faculty. These include functions on campus as well as trips off campus to attend plays, museums, festivals, and professional sports contests. The library, swimming pool, and gymnasium are open on weekends. Transportation is also provided to shopping centers, where students may shop, eat, or see a movie.

COSTS AND FINANCIAL AID

The 2013–14 charges are $32,170 for Upper School students and $31,250 for Middle School students, with a $15,600 supplement for boarding. There are supplemental charges for Center for Learning and ESL classes as well. Additional costs are a campus store deposit and an activity fee. There are special fees for private music lessons and tutoring, if desired.

Financial aid is based on demonstrated need. Parents applying for aid must submit the required paperwork and forms through TADS. Financial aid is granted on an annual basis. Thirty percent of the students received financial aid for the 2013–14 school year.

ADMISSIONS INFORMATION

The Pennington School seeks students who have strong academic ability, as demonstrated on their school transcript and the SSAT, good character, and a record of good citizenship. Approximately 40 percent of the applicants are accepted for admission.

The School does not discriminate on the basis of race, color, religion, gender, or national or ethnic origin in the administration of its admission or educational policies or the financial aid, athletic, or other School-administered programs.

APPLICATION TIMETABLE

Students should begin the application process for The Pennington School early in the fall. The School uses a March 10 notification date and an April 10 reply date; late applications are considered only if space is available. Students must have their application and all supplemental materials submitted and the interview completed by February 1. The Admission Office is open throughout the year for interviews and tours of the campus from 8:00 to 4:00, Monday through Friday, by appointment.

ADMISSIONS CORRESPONDENCE

Stephen D. Milich
Director of Admission and Financial Aid
The Pennington School
Pennington, New Jersey 08534
United States
Phone: 609-737-6128
Fax: 609-730-1405
E-mail: admiss@pennington.org
Website: http://www.pennington.org

PRESBYTERIAN PAN AMERICAN SCHOOL

Kingsville, Texas

Type: Coeducational college-preparatory boarding school and day school
Grades: 9–12 plus a fifth/bridge year
Enrollment: 170
Head of School: Dr. Robert L. (Doug) Dalglish

THE SCHOOL

Presbyterian Pan American School (Pan Am) was founded in 1911 on land from the world-renowned King Ranch. Pan Am has distinguished itself over the past century with its commitment to preparing international students, along with racial and ethnic minorities, for a university-level education. Although students come from many countries around the world including the United States, English is used in all classrooms. English as a Second Language (ESL) is the foundation of an international student's first year, with faculty and classes assigned based on language proficiency testing administered during the first week on campus.

Pan Am seeks student applicants who demonstrate an ease in communicating with others, who are open to experiencing the wider world, and who are eager to discover and explore the possibilities the global community holds for them.

Enrollment at Pan Am ranges from 150 to 175, typically with an even ratio of boys and girls. In recent years, students have come to Pan Am from South Korea, Mexico, China, Japan, Rwanda, Ecuador, Peru, Bolivia, Hong Kong, Taiwan, Guatemala, Colombia, Costa Rica, Spain, Equatorial Guinea, and the United States.

As a mission school of the Presbyterian Church (U.S.A.), Pan Am offers generous financial aid. The majority of students come from Christian families (Protestant or Roman Catholic); however, the admissions process is impartial to both religion and economic situation. Students attend chapel services and take elective courses in Bible. During the junior and senior years, students participate in seminars that require critical thinking about selected topics in ethics, economic justice, and human rights, particularly informed by the teachings and ideals of the Protestant Reformation. However, the school does not attempt to proselytize and teaches a wholesome respect for the reality and diversity of God's creation.

Pan Am is located on a 670-acre working cattle ranch in Kingsville, Texas, which is less than an hour's drive from the Corpus Christi International Airport and about an hour and a half north of the U.S. border with Mexico.

The school is accredited by the Southern Association of Colleges and Schools (SACS) and is a member of the Texas Association of Non-Public Schools (TANS). The Texas Education Agency (TEA) sets graduation requirements.

ACADEMIC PROGRAM

Classroom instruction, along with a student's social formation, is designed to equip the student for success in college and eventually in a satisfying career. A student who fully utilizes Pan American School's many resources should be able to achieve a minimum average grade of 85 in college. Each student is mentored to attain a score of 550 on the standardized Test of English as a Foreign Language (TOEFL).

In addition to traditional high school subjects, Pan Am offers instruction in speech, journalism, economics, fine arts, computers, horticulture and agriculture, health and hygiene, physical education, and religious studies. Practical experience in robotics is offered periodically. For those students eager for the experience, the school offers a supervised 4-H program where participants raise their own animal that will eventually be sold at the annual livestock show and auction. No previous ranch experience is required.

Classes average about 20 students each. The student-faculty ratio is 10:1.

Senior students who score well on a college placement exam have the option of taking college-level classes for dual credit at Coastal Bend College. Typically, up to one third of the senior class will graduate with college credits in math, English, government, or economics.

Pan Am also offers a fifth "bridge" year for international students who are academically strong but whose English language proficiency might place them at a competitive disadvantage in a U.S. college classroom. The emphasis of the bridge year is to strengthen a student's English reading comprehension, speaking, writing, and listening skills.

FACULTY AND ADVISERS

The professional staff includes classroom teachers; resource specialists; specialists in art, music, and physical education; a school principal (or dean); academic and psychological counselors; a computer network engineer; and a library and media specialist. Many are graduates of Texas A&M University–Kingsville and/or are working toward advanced degrees.

Several staff members, including the president and spiritual life director, live on campus. Parents are invited to visit, phone, or e-mail faculty members. Each student's family receives an online password to access their child's grades, along with comments and observations from teachers and counselors.

COLLEGE ADMISSION COUNSELING

Academic counselors advise each student regarding options for college. Each senior is required to apply to a minimum of three colleges or universities, which may be in the United States, the student's home country, or elsewhere in the world. Many choose to study in Texas before returning home.

Presbyterian Pan American School is proud of its nearly 100 percent college acceptance rate among senior class students. In recent years, Pan Am's graduates have been accepted by such fine institutions as Baylor, Dordt, Schreiner, Tecnológico de Monterrey, Texas A&M, Trinity (San Antonio), Universidad Autónoma de Nuevo León, Universidad Iberoamericana, Universidad Nacional Autónoma de México, University of Houston, The University of Texas at Austin, and other locations in The University of Texas and Texas A&M University systems.

ACADEMIC FACILITIES

The Pan Am campus includes four classroom buildings offering science labs, an art studio, choir room, and computer lab and a library with a media center. The campus is served by multiple T-1 high-speed Internet lines and also provides wireless access. Also, all students have a school e-mail address.

BOARDING AND GENERAL FACILITIES

In addition to the academic facilities, there are a number of other buildings on the 50-acre campus. A kitchen and a dining hall serve three meals daily to the student body and staff. The Morris Chapel is the center of worship and spiritual life. Boys and girls live in their respective dormitory complexes, each with lounge facilities and a resident adult staff of dorm parents and assistants. A gymnasium contains basketball and volleyball courts. In addition, there are administrative offices, a teachers' lounge, offices, and a student union building.

ATHLETICS

Presbyterian Pan American School points proudly to a string of Texas state championships in boys' soccer. In addition, the school offers girls' soccer, boys' and girls' basketball, girls' volleyball, cheerleading, girls' and boys' track, and boys' baseball. There is also an outdoor basketball court, a tennis court, a soccer field and track, and a swimming pool. Student lifeguards are Red Cross–trained and certified. The boys' and girls' dorm complexes include fitness facilities and boys' and girls' common areas.

EXTRACURRICULAR OPPORTUNITIES

Pan Am firmly believes that social and personal formation is as vital as academic information in preparing young people to take their places in the world. While athletics offer the most obvious extracurricular outlets, the school provides additional activities as well. A professionally led choir affords training and vocal coaching. Choir members have the opportunity to compete at the annual Texas Association of Private and Parochial Schools (TAAPS) All-State Choir competition. The Morris Chapel Choir visits around the state and serves as a powerful outreach for the school. The 4-H Club presents opportunities to participate in raising lambs on the school's extensive ranch. Quilting and photography students also participate and compete in 4-H competitions. Student Council, Drama Club, Yearbook, and National Honor Society further develop leadership and organizational ability. The chapel's praise band offers students the opportunity to perform in an organized musical group. Student-led committees abound, ranging from worship to waste recycling. There are frequent class fund-raising projects and opportunities to contribute to the student-produced newspaper.

DAILY LIFE

Students clean their rooms each morning in preparation for inspection. Breakfast is at 7:15 a.m. on weekdays and later on weekends. The first class of the day begins at 7:45. The work program, choir, and athletic activities are held after classes dismiss in the afternoon. Computer lab is held on alternate evenings for boys and girls. Free time for informal athletics, board games, jogging, and other recreation is available following dinner. There is a required chapel worship service twice a week and on Sunday, with students working alongside the Director of Spiritual Life to plan and lead the worship. Students typically have several hours of homework to complete before lights-out at 10:30 p.m.

Since the school's founding in 1911, the student work program has been an integral component of the weekday routine. Each student is required to perform 6 hours per week of supervised on-campus work, which may include cleaning the library or public areas of the dorms, assisting in the kitchen, sanitizing tables in the dining hall, maintenance of facilities, collecting trash, gardening, or other routine tasks.

Weekends at Pan Am are as important as weekdays and begin when the last class ends on Friday. There is no work program on Fridays, and evening activities in the Student Union Building (SUB) may include movies and dances, cards and chess, and pool and ping-pong. Saturdays and Sundays are also times when students may be driven into Kingsville or the malls in Corpus Christi for supervised excursions to shop and hang out together. Seasonal weekend activities include occasional barbecues over native mesquite cut from the ranch, outings to NCAA Division II athletic events, or gatherings at the swimming pool. Many students enjoy the tree-covered campus as a pleasant place to come together to play the guitar, sing, and be with friends. Students are required to attend worship services on Sunday mornings. Students who live within driving distance of the campus can sign out of the dorm with parental permission and spend an occasional weekend at home, often inviting friends and roommates to go with them.

COSTS AND FINANCIAL AID

Tuition and fees in 2013–14 were $15,000 for boarding students and $8,500 for day students. The costs include room, board, tuition, and fees for such college entrance exams and other academic tests as the PSAT, SAT, and TOEFL.

The school offers a tuition installment plan and accepts online payments via credit card. As a mission school of the Presbyterian Church (U.S.A.), Pan Am remains committed to being financially accessible to families with modest financial resources. Most years, about 85 percent of the student body receives some degree of need-based financial aid. Nearly $1,100,000 in need-based financial aid was awarded for the 2012–13 school year.

ADMISSIONS INFORMATION

Presbyterian Pan American School admits students into grades 9 through 12. The school also offers a post–high school year of intensive English language studies for international students preparing to apply to a U.S. college. Interested parents and prospective students may find further information online at www.ppas.org. Admission packets are available on the website or by contacting the Office of Admissions. Scheduled visits to the campus are recommended. For families living far from the United States, the Director of Admissions can conduct a webcam interview over the Internet.

Once an international student has been admitted, the school will issue a U.S. Department of Homeland Security Form I-20, the application for an F-1 Student Visa. Once Form I-20 has been completed and received by Pan Am, students must make an appointment with the U.S. Embassy or a consular office in their home country, where they will be interviewed regarding their reasons for wishing to study in the United States as well as their future plans back home.

APPLICATION TIMETABLE

Inquiries are welcome at any time. The school begins receiving applications in January of each year. Admissions decisions will not be made until the applicant's file is complete. Applications should be received by June 30 of each year. Late applications may be considered if space is available. The application fee is $75, payable either in cash or online.

ADMISSIONS CORRESPONDENCE

Mr. Joe L. Garcia, Director of Admissions
Presbyterian Pan American School
Post Office Box 1578
223 North FM Road 772
Kingsville, Texas 78364
United States
Phone: 361-592-4307
Fax: 361-592-6126
E-mail: jlgarcia@ppas.org
Website: www.ppas.org

RANNEY SCHOOL

Tinton Falls, New Jersey

Type: Coeducational college-preparatory day school
Grades: BG (3 years old)–grade 12: Lower School, BG–Grade 5; Middle School, Grades 6–8; Upper School, Grades 9–12
Enrollment: School total: 820
Head of School: Dr. John W. Griffith

THE SCHOOL

Ranney School was founded in 1960 by Russell G. Ranney for the purpose of fostering high academic achievement. A former Associate Director of the New York University Reading Institute, Mr. Ranney was a firm believer in the three R's. An 18-member Board of Trustees, plus the Head of School, supervises the School's operation on its campus of more than 60 acres in a residential neighborhood located approximately 45 miles south of New York City.

Ranney School is dedicated to engaging its students in an exemplary, well-rounded education, one that promotes the development of every child's intellectual, personal, creative, and moral promise. By serving a diverse community that values a rigorous, wide-ranging program of study, Ranney students are inspired to reach their full potential. Guided by dedicated and compassionate professionals, the Ranney experience is distinguished by the heartfelt bond between student and teacher—the hallowed principle celebrating the unique nature of every child. In an environment with contemporary learning resources, students learn the value of contributing to their local and global communities through leadership and service. The School's motto, "knowledge, vision, honor," is as much an inspiration as it is a social imperative, one that informs the thinking and actions the School's students. Awakening students' intellectual potential and encouraging them to communicate with confidence in their own unique voice remains fundamental to the Ranney experience. The ultimate success of Ranney students is the result of a simple yet powerful mission-promise, that every child is known and valued.

The Board of Trustees is the School's governing body. During 2012–13, annual giving totaled $701,000; annual operating expenses average $21 million.

Ranney School alumni number approximately 1,760. The Office of Development and Alumni Relations oversees alumni activities.

Ranney School is accredited by the Middle States Association of Colleges and Schools. The School maintains active membership in the National Association of Independent Schools (NAIS), the New Jersey Association of Independent Schools (NJAIS), the Council for Advancement and Support of Education (CASE), the Educational Records Bureau (ERB), and the National Association for College Admission Counseling (NACAC).

ACADEMIC PROGRAM

The Lower School (beginners [age 3] through grade 5) curriculum is designed to stimulate a child's natural love of learning and to inspire each child to reach his or her best potential. Goals are set forth in a program consistent with the stages of child development and innovative curriculum and instruction. The primary goal of the Lower School is to maximize the growth of each individual. The curriculum remains rooted in the development of language arts. Course time is allotted to vocabulary building, spelling, grammar usage, reading, and the development of creative writing skills. Strong programs in mathematics, science, social studies, and computer education complement these courses. Students are also introduced to studies in the fine arts, performing arts, music, and world languages. Aquatics and physical education complete the course of study. Teaching strategies include differentiated instruction, cooperative

learning, and interdisciplinary activities and instruction.

The Ranney Middle School provides academic challenge in a community-like setting, where students are able to feel supported and comfortable in their surroundings. The developmentally appropriate curriculum is rigorous and skills based, allowing students to develop both self-knowledge and knowledge of the world, while developing personal values and preparing for the challenges of higher education. The comprehensive English and mathematics programs initiated in the lower grades are continued in the Middle School, and learning is further enhanced through engaging programs in history, lab-based science classes and full-time world language study, including Mandarin Chinese. Students are also exposed to computer technology, visual art, drama and music through the yearly academic electives program. Beginning in the sixth grade, students are taught study skills and organizational strategies, which include the use of their laptop computer, provided through Ranney's grades 6–12 one-to-one laptop computer plan. The rich and demanding academic schedule is made approachable for all students through the advisory program, ensuring that all students have the necessary guidance and support as they navigate their way through the Middle School years.

The Upper School (grades 9 through 12) graduation requirements include a minimum of 21 academic credits, plus 4 units in health and physical education. All students are expected to take 5 full credits of course work each year. Specific requirements include English (4 credits), world language (3 credits), history (3 credits, 2 of which must be American history), mathematics (3 credits), science (3 credits with lab, including biology and chemistry), art (1/2 credit), music (1/2 credit), and physical education (4 credits). In addition to required courses, a number of full-year electives are available to sophomores, juniors, and seniors. The Upper School curriculum also offers many honors and college-level Advanced Placement (AP) courses. Eighteen AP courses are available to students who are capable of accelerated study. All Upper School students receive a laptop computer in addition to the digital media center on campus. A full-year capstone project is available to seniors.

Ranney utilizes a numeric grading system with a 100-point scale. The school year consists of two semesters and four marking periods, with grades and written evaluations being sent home at the end of the first and third marking periods. Report cards with grades only are sent at the end of each semester. Midterm exams are given in January and final exams in June.

FACULTY AND ADVISERS

There are 92 full-time faculty members, plus 4 part-time instructors. Approximately 50 percent of the faculty holds graduate degrees; seven have doctorates. Each Middle and Upper School faculty member serves as an adviser to an average of 6 to 8 students. Ranney School also employs 2 full-time registered nurses who support students on campus and during off-campus field trips and retreats as well. The nurses work closely with the athletic trainer who provides an additional layer of support for on-campus athletic practices and games. Ranney faculty members are accomplished and recognized professionals whose contributions to the growth and status of their calling often extend outside the School community.

Dr. John W. Griffith was appointed Headmaster in July 2013. Dr. Griffith holds a bachelor's degree in English from Middlebury College, an M.A. in educational leadership from Columbia University, and a Ph.D. and M.Phil. in English (modern British literature) from Oxford University.

COLLEGE ADMISSION COUNSELING

The College Guidance Office is one of the distinguishing features of Ranney School. The Upper School students' first interaction with the College Guidance Office begins in ninth grade, where all student course schedules pass through the college guidance office for review. Staff members then work closely with students, parents, and advisers throughout the Upper School years to ensure that each student follows an appropriate academic course, with clear and achievable goals. Beginning in tenth grade, students take the PSAT and the PLAN test and are guided by their college counselor to focus on either the ACT or SAT exam.

During junior year, Ranney's college counselors meet one-on-one with students and parents to discuss all the variables in the college selection process and help focus each student's priorities, goals, and aspirations. Students enter the admission process well-prepared and well-informed, benefiting from individualized counseling designed to ensure success. Ranney's success is evident: 100 percent of graduates go on to attend four-year schools, 75 percent are admitted to their first- or second-choice college, and Ranney students regularly earn more than $2.55 million in scholarships.

All seniors receive direction from the College Guidance Office in writing college essays, interviewing skills, and preparing their final applications.

The mean SAT scores for 2013 graduates were 620 critical reading, 630 writing, and 630 math.

The senior class of 2013 achieved 100 percent college acceptance and matriculated at schools such as Boston College, Georgetown, George Washington, NYU, Rutgers, Tulane, and the University of Miami.

STUDENT BODY AND CONDUCT

The 2013–14 student body consists of 820 students, as follows: 156 boys and 163 girls in the Lower School, 104 boys and 94 girls in the Middle School, and 138 boys and 166 girls in the Upper School.

Ranney's families represent many countries, including China, India, Japan, and Russia. The School sponsors an International Week of Celebration each year in all three divisions.

A Judicial Board handles routine disciplinary issues in the Upper School. The board consists of 2 faculty members and 2 students and is chaired by the Dean of Students. Recommendations are given to the Principal and the Headmaster for review and decision.

ACADEMIC FACILITIES

The Lower School is comprised of three buildings and has its own computer lab, two science labs, a library, and The Commons, the Lower School cafeteria. Ranney is a completely wireless campus with over 100 laptops and 40 iPads available in the Lower School. In addition, each classroom is equipped with two computers and Smart Board technology. The Middle School and Upper School are housed in Ranney's modern and high-tech academic complex. The facility offers thirty-three classrooms; state-of-the-art biology, chemistry, physics, and robotics laboratories; a world language laboratory; a college guidance center; a modern library with digital media center; student assembly areas and access to laptops to complement the 1:1 laptop program in grades 6–12, and a unique Distance Learning Center. The entire building offers wireless Internet access. In addition, the Middle and Upper Schools have their own dining hall. All divisions on campus experience physical education and aquatics instruction in the Gerhard Pavilion for Athletics and the Walling Aquatics Center. Performing arts programs and division assemblies are conducted in Panther Hall.

ATHLETICS

Ranney School encourages students to participate in sports and views athletics as an important part of the educational program. All students are eligible to participate regardless of ability. Ranney School offers twenty-five varsity-level sport teams, as well as a coed squash club. Ranney School also offers fourteen interscholastic teams on the middle school level, along with four club sports, including winter track, fencing, crew, and golf. Ranney competes against other accredited public and private schools in the area and maintains active membership in the Shore Conference of High Schools, the New Jersey Independent School Athletic Association, and the New Jersey State Interscholastic Athletic Association. Interscholastic competition begins in the sixth grade. The School has two gymnasiums; a newly renovated 25-meter indoor swimming pool; five new tennis courts; a baseball and softball field; and brand-new athletic facilities, including a synthetic turf field and all-weather track. In addition, there is a new fitness center. Ranney also employs an athletic trainer with MA ATC/L certification.

EXTRACURRICULAR OPPORTUNITIES

Ranney Plus is a robust, all-inclusive, after-school program that enriches opportunities for students of all ages at the School. Across the divisions, Ranney Plus plays an important role for students. It provides opportunities for students to explore activities that encompass global perspectives in the areas of performing arts, technology, science, math, and athletics, and also allows them to receive teacher-supported assistance with homework, study skills, or preparation for a specific subject assessment or project. Each division offers an array of selections for students to explore after school, such as clubs, specialized student activities, and athletic teams and interscholastic sports. Ranney Plus also provides complimentary after-care programs for students in the Lower and Middle Schools.

In addition to Ranney Plus, the Lower School offers a variety of extracurricular and after-school activities for students in grades kindergarten through 5, and periodically offers parent programs. Student programs include computers, art instruction, creative writing, chorus, band, cooking, swimming, soccer, golf, fencing, lacrosse, baseball, and others.

On Saturday mornings throughout the school year, Ranney families gather on campus for Panther Cubs, a parent-driven athletic enrichment program, open to Ranney students in kindergarten through fifth grade. This program allows boys and girls to learn the basics of soccer, basketball, swimming, baseball, tennis, and/ or lacrosse in a fun and structured setting that focuses on teamwork and good sportsmanship, laying the groundwork for participation in the Middle and Upper School Panther athletic programs.

Both schools have a student council, world language, science, technology, and arts-related programs. Performing arts opportunities include band, chorus, orchestra, and both divisions offer state-recognized forensics programs. Students in grades 7–12 are eligible to join the Middle or Upper School Science Olympiad teams, which travel to a variety of locations for local and state-level competition.

The Upper School has an active chapter of the National Honor Society, seven academic honor societies, and a Cum Laude Society chapter. Students can also participate in Mock Trial, math, chess, and academic bowl teams. Chorus and drama clubs offer students an opportunity to perform for friends, parents, and peers. Publications include *Horizons* (the School's award-winning yearbook), *The Torch* (the Ranney School newspaper, named a silver medalist by the Columbia Scholastic Press Association), *The Beacon* (college guidance magazine), and *RSVP* (Ranney School Verse and Prose, named a gold medalist by the Columbia Scholastic Press Association), which showcases the talents of Ranney's young artists and authors.

Throughout the year, the Ranney School Fine Arts Department and Thespian Troupe present art exhibitions, music recitals, and two major drama productions. Traditional events include Spirit Day/Homecoming, International Week, Halloween Parade, Grandparents' Thanksgiving Feast, and Parents' Day Tea. Field trips, both international and local, offer cultural exposure outside the Ranney campus for students in the middle and upper divisions. International student travel takes place each year, with students immersed in the culture of countries such as England, France, Italy, Costa Rica, and Spain.

DAILY LIFE

The typical school day consists of seven 45-minute academic periods, two 40-minute periods, and one 60-minute period, with a 10-minute break between second and third periods, plus two lunch periods. Most periods meet every five out of six days. Assemblies are held throughout the year. Each week, grades 6–12 meet with their advisers for approximately 20 minutes during an adviser period. School begins at 8:25 a.m. and ends at 3:25 p.m. The cafeteria serves hot and cold lunches. Bus transportation is available to most students.

SUMMER PROGRAMS

Students in kindergarten–grade 12 can enroll in two to eight weeks of talent development and academic study courses for enrichment, preview, review, and/or credit in several academic subject areas. Several courses are taught by Ranney School faculty members. In addition, four- and five-year-olds can enroll in one-week Interactive Preschool Adventure programs designed to specifically meet their emerging cognitive, psychomotor, and social/emotional needs. Ranney Summer Programs also provide an eight-, six-, or four-week summer day camp program available for boys and girls ages 3 through 13 and a Counselor-in-Training program is available for 14-year-olds. Ranney Day Camp is fully accredited by the American Camping Association.

COSTS AND FINANCIAL AID

Tuition for 2013–14 ranges from $10,550 to $26,500. Extras include books (Lower School: $150–$550; Middle School: $400–$650; Upper School: $600–$900), transportation ($4,500–$5,000), and the academic technology fee (grades 6–12) $435. Parents of students in grades pre-K through 12 are required to purchase a $1,000 bond, which is redeemed when the child either graduates or leaves Ranney School.

Ranney School is committed to awarding financial aid to those students who demonstrate a financial need. Families who feel that a need for assistance exists are encouraged to apply. The Financial Aid Committee of the Board of Trustees bases financial aid decisions on the formula provided by the School and Student Service for Financial Aid (SSS) in Princeton, New Jersey. The Financial Aid Committee diligently reviews each application in order to distribute available funds equitably. All applications are held in strict confidence. Each student applying for aid must be in good standing in all aspects of student life. Parents must complete the SSS financial aid form annually and should send it to Princeton as early as possible. Inquiries should be directed to the Director of Admission and Financial Aid.

Parents can arrange to pay the tuition over a ten-month period through Tuition Management Services. An enrollment deposit must be paid directly to the School upon registration.

ADMISSION INFORMATION

The first step in applying to Ranney School is to complete the information request form, or call 732-542-4777 to receive an admission packet with application. Once the application and non-refundable $75 application fee has been returned, the student will be contacted to schedule a test date (or play date for Beginners through Kindergarten) and a campus visit. Please see the Admission Process links on Ranney School's Admission webpage for additional information specific to Early Childhood, Lower School, Middle School or Upper School admission.

APPLICATION TIMETABLE

Ranney School does not stipulate a formal application deadline for Lower and Middle Schools, but it is strongly recommended that parents contact the Admission Office during the fall to enroll for the next academic year. All interested applicants for Upper School must complete the admission process by January 15. All applications received after January 15 will receive a rolling decision after February 1 based on space availability.

ADMISSION CORRESPONDENCE

Lee S. Bostic
Director of Admission and Financial Aid
Ranney School
235 Hope Road
Tinton Falls, New Jersey 07724
United States
Phone: 732-542-4777 Ext. 1107
Fax: 732-460-1078
E-mail: lbostic@ranneyschool.org
Website: http://www.ranneyschool.org

RYE COUNTRY DAY SCHOOL
Rye, New York

Type: Coeducational day college-preparatory school
Grades: P–12: Lower School, Prekindergarten–4; Middle School, 5–8; Upper School, 9–12
Enrollment: School total: 893; Upper School: 398
Head of School: Scott A. Nelson, Headmaster

THE SCHOOL

Founded in 1869, Rye Country Day School (RCDS) is entering its 144th year. Reflecting and reaffirming the School's purposes, the RCDS mission statement states, "Rye Country Day School is a coeducational, college-preparatory school dedicated to providing students from Pre-Kindergarten through Grade Twelve with an excellent education using both traditional and innovative approaches. In a nurturing and supportive environment, we offer a challenging program that stimulates individuals to achieve their maximum potential through academic, athletic, creative, and social endeavors. We are actively committed to diversity. We expect and promote moral responsibility, and strive to develop strength of character within a respectful school community. Our goal is to foster a lifelong passion for learning, understanding, and service in an ever-changing world."

Rye Country Day School acts consciously and deliberately in order to create and sustain an inclusive community. According to the School's diversity mission statement, "At Rye Country Day, we believe that diversity is the existence of human variety. As such, each one of us is diverse in multiple ways and in a variety of contexts. We recognize diversity as including, but not limited to, differences in ability/disability, age, ethnicity, family structures, gender, geographic origin, life experiences, physical appearance, race, religion, sexual orientation, and socioeconomic status. As educators, we are committed to creating and sustaining a school community that is diverse and inclusive, one in which all members can participate fully and maximize their potential. We believe that only an inclusive school community can be equitable and just. We are proactive about teaching our students the importance of diversity and inclusion in an increasingly interconnected, multicultural, and ever-changing world. As we prepare our students for leadership in the world beyond Rye Country Day, we are responsible for teaching them how to communicate with and be respectful of others—beginning with those in our school community and extending to those who live beyond our nation's borders. Every global citizen should be able to thrive in a diverse and interconnected society. Our commitment to inclusion enriches our community with diverse ideas and perspectives. Students grow and flourish in this type of environment, where they can safely explore their individual identity while developing and exercising strength of character, healthy self-esteem, and confidence. Through our commitment to diversity and inclusion, we strive to be good role models for the individuals in our care so that their present and future actions and choices may positively impact the world."

The 26-acre campus is located in Rye at the junction of routes I-95 and I-287, one block from the train station. The School's location, 25 miles from Manhattan, provides easy access to both New York City and to a suburban setting with ample playing fields and open spaces. Through frequent field trips, internships, and community service projects, the School takes considerable advantage of the cultural opportunities in the New York metropolitan area.

A nonprofit, nonsectarian institution, Rye Country Day is governed by a 26-member Board of Trustees that includes parents and alumni. The annual operating budget is $28.2 million, and the physical plant assets have a book value in excess of $53.1 million. Annual gifts from parents, alumni, and friends amount to more than $3.4 million. The endowment of the School is valued at more than $37.6 million.

Rye Country Day School is accredited by the Middle States Association of Colleges and Schools and the New York State Association of Independent Schools and is chartered and registered by the New York State Board of Regents. It is a member of the National Association of Independent Schools, the

New York State Association of Independent Schools, the Educational Records Bureau, the College Board, and the National Association for College Admission Counseling.

ACADEMIC PROGRAM

Leading to the college-preparatory program of the Upper School, the program in the Middle School (grades 5–8) emphasizes the development of skills and the acquisition of information needed for success at the secondary school level by exposing students to a wide range of opportunities. The academic program is fully departmentalized. Spanish or French is offered to all students in grades 2–5. Starting in grade 6 students may choose Latin or Mandarin Chinese or continue with Spanish or French. The math, foreign language, and writing programs lead directly into the Upper School curriculum. Programs in art, music (vocal and instrumental), computer use, and dramatics are offered in all grades. Students in kindergarten through grade 6 are scheduled for sports for 45 to 75 minutes daily, and a full interscholastic sports program is available to both boys and girls in grades 7 and 8, and in the Upper School.

Sixteen courses are required for Upper School graduation, including 4 years of English, 3 years of mathematics, 3 years of one foreign language, 2 years of science, and 2 years of history. Students entering the School by grade 9 must complete ½ unit in art and music survey, and ½ unit in the arts. Seniors must successfully complete an off-campus Senior Term community service program in June. Students are expected to carry five academic courses per year.

Full-year courses in English include English 9, 10, and 11; major American writers; English and American literature; and creative and expository writing. Required mathematics courses are algebra I, algebra II, trigonometry, and geometry. Regular course work extends through calculus BC, and tutorials are available for more advanced students. Yearlong courses in science are environmental science, biology, chemistry, and physics. Science courses are laboratory based. The computer science department offers beginning and advanced programming, software applications courses, desktop publishing, and independent study opportunities.

The modern language department offers five years of Mandarin Chinese, French, and Spanish, and the classics department teaches five years of Latin. History courses include world civilizations, U.S. history, government, and modern European history. Semester electives in the humanities include philosophy, psychology, government, and economics.

In the arts, full-year courses in studio art, art history, and music theory are available. Participation in the Concert Choir and Wind Ensemble earns students full academic credit. Semester courses in drawing, printmaking, sculpture, graphic design, ceramics, and photography are available. The drama department offers electives in technique, history, oral presentation, technical theater, and dance.

Advanced Placement courses leading to the AP examinations are offered in biology, environmental science, chemistry, physics, psychology, economics, statistics, calculus, English, U.S. government, U.S. and modern European history, Mandarin Chinese, French, Spanish, Latin, music theory, photography, studio art, history of art, and computer science. Honors sections are scheduled in tenth- and eleventh-grade English, math, physics, biology, and chemistry, and in foreign languages at all levels. Independent study is available in grades 11 and 12 in all disciplines.

The student-teacher ratio is 8:1, and the average class size in the Upper School is 12. Extra help is provided for students as needed.

The year is divided into two semesters. Examinations are given in March. Grades are scaled from A to F and are given four times a year. Written comments accompany grades at the end of each quarter.

Academic classes travel to New York City and other areas to supplement classroom work. Although not a graduation requirement, all students are involved in community service programs. Class projects, club-based programs, and individual service experiences involve work with Charity: Water, City Harvest, Haiti Lumiere de Demain, Village Health Works, Big Brother-Big Sister, Doctors Without Borders, St. Jude Children's Research Hospital, and numerous local community partners.

Students in grades 7–12 are required to have laptop computers. The campus supports wireless Internet connection and provides appropriate filters for student and faculty educational use. A technology department supports and updates the network and assists students with software and hardware issues. Students receiving financial aid awards receive new laptop computers from the school which are replaced every three years.

FACULTY AND ADVISERS

The Upper School faculty consists of 65 full-time teachers—35 men and 30 women, the large majority of whom hold at least one advanced degree. The average length of service is eight years, and annual faculty turnover averages fewer than 6 teachers.

Scott A. Nelson became Headmaster in 1993. He holds a B.A. from Brown University and an M.A. from Fordham University. Prior to his appointment at Rye, he served as Upper School Director both at the Marlborough School in Los Angeles and at the Hackley School in Tarrytown, New York. Mr. Nelson and his family reside on campus.

Nearly all faculty members in the Middle and Upper Schools serve as advisers for 5 to 12 students each. In addition to helping students select courses, faculty advisers monitor the students' progress in all areas of school life and provide ongoing support. The advisers also meet with students' parents at various times throughout the year.

Rye Country Day seeks faculty members who are effective teachers in their field and who, by virtue of their sincere interest in the students' overall well-being, will further the broad goals of the School's philosophy. The School supports the continuing education of its faculty through grants and summer sabbaticals totaling more than $409,000 a year.

COLLEGE ADMISSION COUNSELING

The college selection process is supervised by a full-time Director of College Counseling and 2 Associate Directors, and support is provided by an administrative assistant. Advising is done in groups and on an individual basis, with the staff meeting with both students and their families. More than 100 college representatives visit the campus each year.

The 85 graduates of the class of 2013 enrolled in forty-nine colleges and universities, including Barnard, Boston College, Brown, Colby, Colgate, Columbia, Dartmouth, Duke, University of Edinburgh, Emory, Georgetown, Georgia Tech, Harvard, Michigan, Middlebury, NYU, Northwestern, Notre Dame, Oberlin Conservatory of Music, University of Pennsylvania, Swarthmore, Trinity College, Tufts, Vanderbilt, University of Virginia, Wellesley, Wesleyan, and Williams.

STUDENT BODY AND CONDUCT

The Upper School enrollment for 2013–14 totaled 398: 214 boys and 184 girls. There were 97 students in grade 9, 101 in grade 10, 103 in grade 11, and 97 in grade 12. Members of minority groups represented 36 percent of the student body in grades 5–12. Students came from roughly forty different school districts in Westchester and Fairfield counties as well as New York City. Students holding citizenship in twenty countries were enrolled.

While School regulations are few, the School consciously and directly emphasizes a cooperative, responsible, and healthy community life. The Student Council plays a major role in administering School organizations and activities. Minor disciplinary problems are handled by the Division Principal or Grade Level Dean; more serious matters in the Upper School may be brought before the Disciplinary Committee. There is student representation on the Academic Affairs and other major committees.

ACADEMIC FACILITIES

Academic facilities at Rye Country Day School include the Main Building (1927) and Main Building Addition (2002), with separate areas for kindergarten through grade 4, grades 5 and 6, and grades 7 and 8. The Lower and Middle School divisions have separate art, computer, and science facilities.

The Upper School is housed in the Pinkham Building (1964), which was completely renovated in 2010. The new 14,000-square-foot addition includes a 140-seat auditorium, a college counseling center, faculty offices, classrooms, and three science labs.

There are two libraries on campus—the Lower School Library (2002) and the Klingenstein Library (1984), which serves the Middle and Upper School divisions. The Klingenstein Library contains more than 25,000 volumes with fully automated circulation and collection management technology. Resources include significant periodical and reference materials that are available via direct online services and the Internet, CD-ROM, and substantial videotape collection.

The school has invested in technology infrastructure and classroom SmartBoards in all three divisions. Laptop computers, which are required for all students in grades 7 through 12, are used extensively throughout the curriculum. Access to the RCDS network and Internet is via a campuswide wireless network. In total, there are over 650 networked computers on campus.

The performing arts programs are housed in the Dunn Performing Arts Center (1990), which includes a 400-seat theater-auditorium and classroom spaces for vocal music, instrumental music, and a dance studio. There also are five music practice rooms which adjunct faculty use for private music lessons.

ATHLETICS

Rye Country Day's athletic program offers seventy-two interscholastic teams for students in grades 7 through 12. Varsity competition includes boys' and girls' teams in soccer, cross-country, basketball, ice hockey, fencing, squash, tennis, golf, track and field, sailing, and lacrosse, as well as football, field hockey, wrestling, baseball, and softball. Approximately 70 percent of the students participate in at least one team sport.

The physical education department offers classes throughout the year in fitness center training, yoga, boot camp, kickboxing, Zumba, tennis, squash, dance, running, and skating.

Athletic facilities include the LaGrange Field House (1972) with its indoor ice rink/tennis courts; a multipurpose gymnasium which serves as the home for the wrestling and fencing programs; the Scott A. Nelson Athletic Center (2000), which houses a two-court gymnasium, four squash courts, four locker rooms, and an athletic training facility; a multipurpose room; and a state-of-the-art fitness center. Between 2007 and 2009, the School installed four artificial turf fields, making it the premier outdoor athletic facility in the area.

EXTRACURRICULAR OPPORTUNITIES

More than fifty extracurricular activities are available. Students can choose vocal music (Concert Choir, Madrigal Singers, and solfeggio classes)

and instrumental music (Wind Ensemble, Concert Band, and Jazz Band). Many of these offerings have curricular status. The performance groups give local concerts and occasionally travel to perform at schools and universities here and abroad. In addition, professional instructors offer private instrumental and voice lessons during and after the school day. The drama department presents major productions three times a year. Recent productions have included *The Laramie Project, South Pacific, Dark of the Moon, The Mystery of Edwin Drood, Macbeth, The Pajama Game, The Arabian Nights, Anything Goes, Alice in Wonderland, Urinetown, Museum, Bye Bye Birdie, The Comedy of Errors, The Boys from Syracuse, Working, The Miracle Worker,* and *Guys and Dolls.*

Student publications include a yearbook, newspaper, literary magazine, graphic arts and photography magazines, and a public affairs journal, each of which is composed using student publications desktop publishing facilities. The School's website (http://www.ryecountryday.org) is an ever-changing location for student- and staff-provided information on and perspectives of the School. Students participate in Model Congress programs on campus and at other schools and colleges.

The School's new focus on public purpose goes beyond community service by challenging community members to use rich and varied methods to identify, examine, and research social inequities and plan a partnership-based course of action that is responsive to community needs. Using an interdisciplinary service-learning approach, the School encourages students to question their assumptions, integrate community and global themes into their academic work, and realize their potential to empower others and themselves as empathic, interconnected citizens. Rye Country Day is committed to leveraging its human and educational resources to co-create sustainable solutions to real-world problems. The School's public purpose mission statement reads: "Since 1869, Rye Country Day School's motto, 'Not for self, but for service,' has been integral to the culture of the School. The Rye Country Day School philosophy states, 'A superior education embraces the concept that to educate is to do more than to teach.' Through service learning, we will provide transformative educational opportunities that prepare our students to be responsible citizens with an ethic of service and empathy for our shared human experience. We believe that meaningful and mutually beneficial partnerships emanate from a curriculum enhanced by community engagement. Rye Country Day School's sustained commitment to making a positive impact on the community and contributing to the common good defines our public purpose."

DAILY LIFE

Beginning each day at 8:05, the Upper School utilizes a six-day schedule cycle. Most courses meet five of the six days, with one or two longer, 70-minute periods per cycle. The day includes an activity/meeting period and two lunch periods as well as seven class periods. Class periods end at 2:50, and team sport practices and games begin at 3:30. Breakfast and lunch may be purchased in the school dining room; seniors may have lunch off campus. Study halls are required for grade 9.

SUMMER PROGRAMS

The Rye Country Day Summer School enrolls approximately 100 students—rising students to grades 6 to postgraduate—in remedial, enrichment, and advanced-standing courses. Some courses prepare students for the New York State Regents exams that may be taken at the local public schools. The program is six weeks long and runs on a five-period schedule from 8 a.m. to noon, Monday through Friday. Tuition averages $1,300 per course. A brochure is available after April 1 from the Director of the Summer School or on the School's website.

In addition to the Summer School, Rye conducts a summer program, the ACTION Program, an academic enrichment program at Rye for highly motivated public school students who will be entering grades 7, 8, and 9. The ACTION Program seeks to expand the academic and intellectual horizons of very capable and responsible students from local communities who may not have the resources available to provide such summer programs. The program promotes confidence and strength of character while helping students grow academically and develop as leaders.

The ACTION Program runs for four weeks in July. Its philosophy emphasizes learning for the sake of learning. All students take project-based courses in math, science, history, leadership, Presidential election coverage, creative writing, drama, and yoga/kickboxing. Once a week, the curriculum is reinforced with experiential learning opportunities outside the classroom. Field trips include seeing a Broadway musical, participating in a high ropes adventures program, and sailing aboard a schooner in the Long Island Sound.

COSTS AND FINANCIAL AID

Tuition for grade 9 for 2013–14 is $34,600. Additional charges are made for textbooks, lunches, sports, field trips, and private music lessons, as appropriate.

Tuition aid is available on a need basis. For the 2013–14 academic year, 141 students received a total of more than $4.2 million in aid. All aid applications are processed through the School and Student Service for Financial Aid.

ADMISSIONS INFORMATION

Students are accepted in all grades. In 2013–14, 24 new students enrolled in the ninth grade, 9 in the tenth grade, and 2 in the eleventh grade. Academic readiness is a prerequisite; a diversity of skills and interests, as well as general academic aptitude, is eagerly sought. The School seeks and enrolls students of all backgrounds; a diverse student body is an important part of the School's educational environment.

Required in the admissions process are the results of the Educational Records Bureau's Independent School Entrance Examination (ISEE) or the Secondary School Admission Test (SSAT); the student's school record; and school and faculty recommendations. A visit to the campus and an interview are also required.

APPLICATION TIMETABLE

Inquiries are welcome throughout the year. Interviews and tours of the campus begin in late September. To be considered in initial admissions decisions, applicants must fully complete the Application by December 15. All other parts of the Application Folder (transcripts, testing, recommendation forms, interview, etc.) are due by January 15. Candidates whose Application Folders are complete by that date are notified by approximately February 15. Applications received after December 15 are evaluated on a rolling basis. All application materials are available online (www.ryecountryday.org/admissions).

ADMISSIONS CORRESPONDENCE

Matthew J. M. Suzuki, Director of Admissions
Rye Country Day School
Cedar Street
Rye, New York 10580-2034
United States
Phone: 914-925-4513
Fax: 914-921-2147
E-mail: matt_suzuki@ryecountryday.org
Website: http://www.ryecountryday.org

ST. ANDREW'S SCHOOL

Barrington, Rhode Island

St. Andrew's School
Rhode Island

Type: Coeducational, boarding and day college-preparatory school
Grades: 6–12 and postgraduate (PG): Middle School, 6–8; Upper School and Boarding, 9–12 and postgraduate (PG)
Enrollment: School total: 215; Upper School: 181
Head of School: John D. Martin

THE SCHOOL

St. Andrew's School is a coeducational boarding and day school for students in grades 6–12 and postgraduate (PG), with the boarding program starting in the ninth grade. The School is located on a 100-acre campus in Barrington (population approximately 16,000), a suburban community 10 miles southeast of Providence on Narragansett Bay. The campus contains open space and woodlands. Its proximity to Providence and Newport, as well as Boston, offers a wide variety of cultural opportunities for students.

St. Andrew's School was founded in 1893 by Rev. William Merrick Chapin as a school for homeless boys. From these simple beginnings through its years as a working farm school to its present role as a coeducational boarding and day college preparatory school, St. Andrew's steadfastly maintains the same sense of purpose and concern for the individual. The curriculum is designed to prepare students for college, with emphasis on helping them to develop stronger academic skills, study habits, and self-esteem.

Every St. Andrew's teacher is trained to teach using a multisensory approach for the different ways students may learn. St. Andrew's students find that when they get to college, they are well prepared to handle the course work because they have a true understanding of how they learn and an awareness of the tools they need to achieve their best.

St. Andrew's School is a nonsectarian, nonprofit corporation. A Board of Trustees governs the School; this 21-member board meets five times a year. The School's physical plant is valued at approximately $45 million. The School's endowment is currently valued at more than $15.2 million.

St. Andrew's is accredited by the New England Association of Schools and Colleges. It is a member of the National Association of Independent Schools, the Association of Independent Schools in New England, the Association of Boarding Schools, and the Independent Schools Association of Rhode Island.

ACADEMIC PROGRAM

St. Andrew's School believes that every student can find success in the classroom. With a 5:1 student-teacher ratio, the average class size at St. Andrew's is 7–10 students with a class maximum of 12. Small classes, along with twice-daily adviser meetings, help to ensure that no student is overlooked. The homelike community, nurturing environment, and hands-on approach to learning and teaching help maintain close student-teacher relationships.

To graduate from the Upper School, a student must complete 26 credits: 24 academic credits and 2 credits in physical education. Students are expected to take course work in English, math, science, social studies, and physical education each year. Preparation in a foreign language is also highly recommended. Students may only have one study hall in their schedule. Seniors must pass the equivalent of five full-credit courses in order to graduate.

Specific minimum requirements for Upper School students are 4 credits in English, 3 credits in social studies (including 1 in U.S. history), 3 credits in mathematics, 3 credits in science (including 2 in a lab science), 2 credits in physical education, 1 credit in art, and 10 elective credits. An English as a Second Language (ESL) Program is provided for international students. The School's computer network, which is available to all students, provides Internet access from all classrooms, dorm rooms, and offices.

The School's Learning Services program, for students who have been identified with language-based learning differences or attentional challenges, is taught by learning support teachers. All students enrolled in a program receive instruction and support to enable academic success in the School's college-preparatory course of study. An Individual Education Plan is designed and updated annually with input from the student, family, and each teacher. This plan identifies both the skills and support to be provided throughout the year to guide learning success. Individualized programs are available to support the advancement of reading, writing, speech and language, and study skills (e.g., materials management, test preparation, focus and homework strategies, time management, organization, and planning).

The school year runs on a semester basis. Students are evaluated frequently by their teachers so that each student's progress is monitored closely throughout the year. Each advisee meets twice a day with his or her adviser to discuss issues pertaining to the student's academic progress and his or her involvement in the School community. Advisers communicate with families every three weeks by phone or e-mail.

FACULTY AND ADVISERS

The faculty numbers 42, with 14 men and 28 women. Twenty-one reside with their families on campus and nine of them serve as dorm parents. All full-time faculty members serve as advisers. John D. Martin was appointed Head of School on July 1, 1996, and has an extensive background in independent schools, including teaching and administrative positions at Sewickley Academy, Peddie School, and Tabor Academy. He holds a Master of Divinity degree from Yale University, a Master of Education degree from American International College, and a Bachelor of Arts degree from Tufts University.

COLLEGE ADMISSION COUNSELING

All of St. Andrew's graduates enter four-year colleges, two-year colleges, postgraduate programs, or technical schools upon graduation each year. Goal setting, short- and long-term planning, and informal discussions about careers and postsecondary plans are ongoing between students and advisers from the moment a student enters the Upper School. Formal college counseling begins in the eleventh grade. The college counselor works with students and their parents to assist in determining the best steps for each student. The advisers and other

faculty members assist the college counselor in assessing each student's options. PSATs are administered in the fall and students take the test in the sophomore and junior years. SATs should be taken during the junior and senior years. College representatives visit the campus throughout the year to meet with interested students.

St. Andrew's graduates have matriculated to colleges and universities such as Boston University, Brandeis, Brown, Dartmouth, Emmanuel, Emory, Fairfield, Indiana, Michigan State, Mount Holyoke, Parsons, Penn State, Pratt, Providence, Ringling College of Art and Design, Rhode Island College, Roger Williams, Sacred Heart, Salve Regina, Seton Hall, Suffolk, Syracuse, Tulane, and the Universities of California, Hawaii, Illinois, Massachusetts, Rhode Island, Vermont, and Washington.

STUDENT BODY AND CONDUCT

The School enrolls both boarding and day students. Approximately one third of the Upper School population boards. Approximately 21 percent of the School's population is enrolled in the Middle School, and less than 35 percent of the School's population participates in the Resource/Focus Programs.

Over the years, St. Andrew's School has attracted boarding students from all corners of the United States and other countries, including Canada, China, France, Germany, Greece, Haiti, India, Israel, Jamaica, Japan, Montenegro, Senegal, South Africa, South Korea, Taiwan, and Turkey.

Each student is required to read the *Parent and Student Handbook,* which defines expectations for students within the community. Difficulties, if they arise, are handled according to degree; minor issues are handled by teachers and dorm parents, while major offenses are handled by the Director of Student Life in conjunction with a joint student-faculty disciplinary committee. Faculty advisers play a major role in working with students to help them understand the expectations of them as members of the community.

ACADEMIC FACILITIES

Stone Academic Center (1988) houses fifteen classrooms, a renovated resource wing with five classrooms for instruction, a computer lab, academic offices, and a faculty workroom. It is also the site of the Rooke Library, which features study carrels, meeting rooms, and computer workstations. Hardy Hall (1898) was renovated in 2008 and houses the Middle School (6–8). The classrooms are designed for interactive learning in groups of 5 to 12 students. The George M. Sage Gymnasium (2001) and the Karl P. Jones Gymnasium (1965) each house a full-size gymnasium and locker room facilities. The Annie Lee Steele Adams Memorial Student Service Center (1997) houses the Health Center, classrooms, and additional office space. The David A. Brown '52 Science Center houses four science labs, two regular classrooms, and the office of the Director of College Counseling. The Norman E. and Dorothy R. McCulloch Center for the Arts (2004) houses a 287-seat theater, two visual art classrooms, a ceramics lab, a music classroom, music practice rooms, a black-box/theater classroom, a computer graphics lab, storage, and theater scene shop.

BOARDING AND GENERAL FACILITIES

Upper School girls live in the newly renovated and expanded Margot's House (formerly Cady House, 1969). Upper School boys live in Bill's House (1970), Coleman House (circa 1795), and Perry Hall (1927). Students are assigned to single or double rooms. Each dormitory is supervised by faculty dorm parents, who are aided by the Director of Residential Life and the Director of Student Life. Each dorm has a common room, laundry facilities, access to a kitchen area, and ample storage space. Gardiner Hall (1926) has seating for 175 and the Head Master's Dining Room. McVickar Hall (1913) houses the Admissions office, the Head Master's office, the Development and Communications department, and reception area. Peck Hall (circa 1895) contains the Business office. Clark Hall (1899) houses the Student Center, offering students space for entertainment and relaxation. The second floor provides faculty housing.

Coleman House and the Rectory, the Head Master's house, are late-eighteenth-century buildings that were acquired by the School from two local estates. Both buildings are said to have been stops for travelers on the Underground Railroad. The Rectory has a hidden back staircase and room.

ATHLETICS

Upper School students participate in athletics at the completion of each class day. St. Andrew's fields varsity teams in boys' and girls' basketball, cross-country, golf, lacrosse, soccer, and tennis. Intramural sports programs are also offered and include fitness training, weight training, yoga, biking, lawn games, and Project Adventure Ropes Course. St. Andrew's also offers a state-of-the-art health and fitness center that comprises separate cardio and weight-training facilities.

EXTRACURRICULAR OPPORTUNITIES

The School's proximity to Providence, Newport, and Boston provides a myriad of cultural and recreational activities. Students may take advantage of museums, movies, concerts, plays, rock climbing, skating, bowling, skiing, and professional and collegiate sporting events. Among the on-campus extracurricular activities are theater, photography, and yearbook. The St. Andrew's Parent Association (SAPA) organizes a wide variety of social activities for students throughout the year, from dances to laser tag to paintball to barbecues.

DAILY LIFE

Boarding students generally rise at about 7:00 a.m. and are responsible for making their beds, cleaning their rooms, and performing other assorted dorm chores. Breakfast is served at 7:30 and is a favorite gathering time for day and boarding students alike. Students assemble for Morning Meeting at 8:00 and then meet in their advising groups. Classes begin at 8:30. Adviser meetings are held again at the end of the day. Activities and athletics begin at 3:00 p.m. and run until approximately 4:00. Students may leave the campus between athletics and dinner if they are in good standing in the community. Dinner is at 5:30, and evening study hall is from 7:30 to 9:30. All study halls are proctored by faculty members who monitor academic productivity and can offer assistance.

The Student Center is open on weekdays from 11:30 a.m. to 1:30 p.m., all day Saturday, and at other times depending on scheduled special activities.

WEEKEND LIFE

Weekend activities are planned by the Director of Student Life and the Coordinator of Weekend Activities, with student and faculty input. Students choose from an array of on- and off-campus activities, including sporting events, concerts, movies, plays, hayrides, open gymnasium, bicycle riding, skiing, attending performances by special guests on campus, dances, skating, festivals and fairs, hiking, and shopping. Visits to nearby cities and other places of interest are also offered. Boarders may leave for the weekend, with parental permission, either to go home or to visit a day student's family. Each weekend, approximately 75 percent of the boarding community remains on campus.

COSTS AND FINANCIAL AID

Tuition for a boarder in 2013–14 is $49,500; for an international boarder, it is $50,025; for a day student, it is $32,800. Additional costs for the Resource and Focus Programs is $10,200. The yearly book fee is about $650. Parents of a boarding student should plan to set up an account in the on-campus bank for weekly allowance needs. The amount varies from family to family and student to student.

Approximately 51 percent of students received financial aid for the 2013–14 academic year, with more than $2.5 million offered in grants and loans. Financial aid is based solely on need. St. Andrew's School is affiliated with School and Student Services by the National Association of Independent Schools (NAIS) in Randolph, Massachusetts for financial aid and works in conjunction with this organization to provide an objective and fair basis for awarding financial aid. All required information is due to the School by February 12. Final awards are determined by the School's Financial Aid Committee.

ADMISSIONS INFORMATION

In order to assess the match between student and school and to plan an appropriate academic program, the School requires a tour, a personal interview, an application with a fee of $50 ($100 for international students), a school transcript covering the last three years, three teacher recommendations, and standardized test scores. For applicants to the Resource Program, an educational evaluation and a psychological evaluation (both within eighteen months of potential enrollment) and a current Individualized Education Plan (if applicable) are required. A student applying to the Focus Program must establish a history of attention difficulties and supply the School with a medical diagnosis from a physician and appropriate testing results. International students must also submit results from a TOEFL or TOEFL Junior and the SSAT.

APPLICATION TIMETABLE

Parents and prospective students are encouraged to contact the Admissions Office for information during the fall semester. Because the School considers a visit to the campus and a personal interview with the candidate to be such a critical part of the admissions process, it asks that all families call for an appointment. It is best to visit the School during the fall if considering enrollment for the following September, although the School welcomes campus visitors throughout the year.

St. Andrew's School does not discriminate on the basis of race, creed, gender, or handicap in the administration of policies, practices, and procedures.

Applications are due by January 30. Students are notified of acceptance by March 10. Depending on available space, rolling admission may be offered thereafter. A nonrefundable deposit of $1,000 ($5,000 for international students) is due when students agree to attend and is credited toward tuition.

ADMISSIONS CORRESPONDENCE

R. Scott Telford
Director of Admissions
St. Andrew's School
63 Federal Road
Barrington, Rhode Island 02806
Phone: 401-246-1230
Fax: 401-246-0510
E-mail: inquiry@standrews-ri.org
Website: http://www.standrews-ri.org

SOUNDVIEW PREPARATORY SCHOOL

Yorktown Heights, New York

Type: Coeducational day college-preparatory school
Grades: Middle School, 6–8; Upper School, 9–12
Enrollment: Total, 68; Middle School, 12; Upper School, 56
Head of School: W. Glyn Hearn, Head of School

THE SCHOOL

Soundview Preparatory School, a coeducational, college-preparatory school for grades 6 through 12, was founded in 1989 on the belief that the best environment for students is one where classes are small, teachers know the learning style and interests of each student, and an atmosphere of mutual trust prevails. At Soundview, students and teachers work in close collaboration in classes with an average size of 7 students.

The School's mission is to provide a college-preparatory education in a supportive and noncompetitive environment that requires rigorous application to academics, instills respect for ethical values, and fosters self-confidence by helping each student feel recognized and valued. Soundview empowers students to develop their potential and reach their own goals in a setting that promotes respect for others and a sense of community.

Soundview Prep opened its doors with 13 students in the spring of 1989. In the spring of 1998, having outgrown its original quarters in Pocantico Hills, New York, the School moved to a larger facility in Mount Kisco, New York. On January 14, 2008, Soundview moved to its first permanent home, a 13.8-acre campus in Yorktown Heights, New York. New York City, only an hour away, provides a wealth of cultural opportunities for Soundview students to explore on class trips.

The School is governed by a 7-member Board of Trustees. The current operating budget is $1.82 million. In 2012–13, Soundview raised a gross total amount of $298,461 through the Annual Fund, a major gift appeal, and fund-raising events. Donations were made by parents, alumni families, grandparents, friends, foundations, and corporations.

Soundview is chartered by the New York State Board of Regents and is accredited by the New York State Association of Independent Schools. The School is a member of the National Association of Independent Schools, the Education Records Bureau, and the Council for Advancement and Support of Education.

ACADEMIC PROGRAM

Soundview provides a rigorous academic program to ensure that students not only develop the skills and acquire the knowledge needed for college work but also have the opportunity to pursue their own personal goals and interests.

The academic day is carefully structured but informal, with nurture a crucial ingredient. Soundview's student-teacher ratio of 5:1 guarantees that students are monitored closely and receive the support they need. At the same time, the School provides advanced courses for students who wish to go beyond the high school level or take a subject that is not usually offered, allowing students to soar academically and truly develop their potential.

The Middle School curriculum is designed to establish a foundation of knowledge and skills in each academic discipline, strong comprehension and communication skills, good work habits and study skills, confidence in using technology, and creativity in the arts.

The Upper School curriculum provides a traditional college-preparatory education in academics and the arts. In addition to the core subjects—English, history, math, and science—Soundview offers four languages (Latin, French, Spanish, and Italian); studio art; music; and electives that vary from year to year (recent offerings have included history of philosophy, drama, computer science, astronomy, journalism, environmental science, and human anatomy and physiology).

AP courses are made available according to students' abilities and interests. Recently, AP courses have been offered in calculus, biology, physics, U.S. history, European history, government, and art. This year, the School is adding AP computer science, AP English, and AP psychology.

Academic requirements for graduation are 4 years each of English and history, 3 years each of math and science, 3 years of one foreign language or 2 years each of two different languages, 1 year of art or music, and ½ year of health.

Computer technology at Soundview is integrated into the curriculum. Teachers post assignments on the School's website, and students upload completed work into teachers' folders. The School is wired for wireless technology and has a well-equipped computer lab.

The School's annual two-week trips abroad (to Russia, China, England, Wales and Ireland, Spain, and Italy over the last few years) offer students experience with other cultures. Last year, Soundview hosted two students from China for a two-week international exchange. The School's academic curriculum is supplemented throughout the year by a variety of trips within the New York metropolitan area, to museums, nature centers, science labs, and other educational venues.

The school year is divided into two semesters, with letter grades sent out at the end of each. Individual conferences with parents, students, faculty members, and the Head of School are arranged throughout the year.

FACULTY AND ADVISERS

The faculty consists of 14 teachers (11 women and 3 men); the majority hold advanced degrees. Three teachers are part-time; the rest, full-time. Turnover is low, with an average of one replacement or addition per year.

Each teacher serves as adviser to up to 5 students. Most faculty members supervise a club or publication or coach an athletic team.

W. Glyn Hearn has served as Head of School since Soundview was founded in 1989. He obtained his B.A. in English at the University of Texas at Austin and his M.A. in American literature at Texas Tech University. He spent twelve years at the Awty International School of Houston, Texas, where he served as Principal of the Lower, Middle, and Upper Schools and Head of the American Section, before becoming Assistant Headmaster and then Headmaster of the American Renaissance School in Westchester County in 1987. Mr. Hearn also teaches an English class at Soundview.

COLLEGE ADMISSION COUNSELING

College placement at Soundview is directed by Carol Gill, president of Carol Gill Associates and one of the nation's leading college counseling experts. The process starts early on, when eighth, ninth, and tenth graders plan and refine a course sequence that is appropriate for a competitive college. In the junior year, students and their parents begin meeting with Ms. Gill to discuss the college application process, develop lists of colleges, and plan college visits. The meetings continue through the senior year to complete applications. Representatives from approximately twenty colleges visit Soundview every year to speak with students.

Because of the School's small size, the faculty and staff members know each student well and are able to assist students in selecting colleges that are the right match for them. The Head of School writes a personal recommendation for each senior.

College acceptances in recent years include Bard, Barnard, Bates, Brown, Carnegie Mellon, Clark, Columbia, Dickinson, Duke, Emerson, Franklin & Marshall, Gettysburg, Hampshire, Hartwick, High Point, Hobart, Ithaca, Manhattanville, Maryland Institute College of Art, Muhlenberg, Northeastern, NYU, Oberlin, Reed, Rensselaer, Rhode Island School of Design, R.I.T., Roger Williams, Sarah Lawrence, St. John's (Santa Fe), Skidmore, SUNY, Susquehanna, Vassar, Williams, and the Universities of Maine and Vermont.

STUDENT BODY AND CONDUCT

Soundview reflects the diversity—ethnic, religious, and economic—of American society. The 33 boys and 35 girls come from Westchester, Fairfield, and Putnam Counties and New York City. Approximately 12 percent of the student body are members of minority groups.

Respect for ethical values such as kindness, honesty, and respect for others are paramount at Soundview, where individual responsibility and a sense of community are stressed.

The School's disciplinary structure is informal, since it is based on the assumption that students attending the School desire to be there and are therefore willing to adhere to a code of conduct that demonstrates awareness that the community is based upon a shared sense of purpose and commitment. Despite the cordiality of its atmosphere, Soundview has high expectations of personal conduct. The result of this policy is a remarkably cooperative, considerate group of students who value each other and who appreciate their teachers.

Attire appropriate for a school is expected of all students, although there is no formal dress code.

ACADEMIC FACILITIES

Soundview's campus consists of 13.8 rustic acres with a historic main house, numerous outbuildings, a large pond, meadows, and woods, all in the heart of the village of Yorktown Heights, New York. The main house, the former Underhill mansion built by Yorktown's leading family in the nineteenth century, contains classrooms, administrative offices, the computer lab, and meeting rooms.

A large barn houses the science lab, art studios, additional classrooms, and a meeting hall, while a third building is home to the Middle School. A fourth building provides another meeting and performance space, while a former chapel is used for the music program. Woodland paths and footbridges lead across streams and around the property. The campus is woven into the academic program in a variety of ways: students test pond water as part of environmental science, draw from nature in art, or enjoy a class outdoors on an especially fine day.

ATHLETICS

Physical education and sports at Soundview offer students the opportunity to develop leadership and teamwork skills as well as to excel in individual sports. Students participate on coed soccer, coed basketball, and Ultimate Frisbee teams that compete against other independent schools in the Hudson Valley region. Depending upon student interest in a given year, other sports, such as tennis, softball, and baseball may also be offered. Any student who wishes to play is accepted, regardless of ability.

The Ski and Snowboard and Bicycling Clubs offer opportunities for noncompetitive sports. For physical education, students play intramural sports, work out on exercise equipment, and participate in the Outdoors Club, clearing trails and planting gardens on school property.

Soundview's home gym is the Solaris Sports Club in Yorktown Heights, a state-of-the-art multisport center just blocks from the School. The facility includes tennis courts, a large indoor basketball court, and exercise equipment.

EXTRACURRICULAR OPPORTUNITIES

Soundview offers a wide range of clubs and activities, with additional choices added each year by students themselves. Current clubs include yearbook; literary magazine; the Westchester County Mock Trial program;

and clubs for math, foreign language, politics, music, technology, drama, outdoors, and community service.

The School sponsors activities to expose students to other cultures and experiences, such as trips to art exhibitions, dance performances, concerts, and plays. Students have the opportunity to perform music and drama at the annual talent show and at more informal coffeehouses throughout the year.

Major annual events at Soundview include the Back-to-School Picnic; Back-to-School Night, when parents learn about their student's classes; the Maple Syrup project, when students and faculty tap trees, boil sap into syrup, and serve a pancake breakfast; Texas Day, a lighthearted event featuring a barbecue, games, and spoofs on the Headmaster's home state; and the Graduation Dinner, an evening for Soundview parents to honor the graduating class. A parent-run Spring Gala and Auction fundraiser is held every other year.

DAILY LIFE

The school day begins at 8:10 with Morning Meeting, when the entire student body, faculty, and staff assemble to hear announcements about ongoing activities, listen to presentations by clubs, and discuss the day's national and international news. The Head of School encourages students to express their views and helps them to assess events that are unfolding in the world around them.

Classes begin at 8:25 and end at 3:25. There are eight academic periods plus lunch.

SUMMER PROGRAMS

Occasionally, Soundview offers a small summer school on an as-needed basis, with classes that vary each year. A typical offering includes English, writing, math, history, a science, and a language. Students have the opportunity to work one-on-one with a teacher or in small classes to skip ahead in a given subject or fulfill a requirement.

COSTS AND FINANCIAL AID

Tuition and fees for 2013–14 are $37,800 for Middle School and $39,000 for Upper School. Fees include gym, books, art and lab fees, ERB exams, and literary publications.

In 2012–13, the School provided a total of $420,000 in financial aid to 28 percent of the student body.

ADMISSIONS INFORMATION

Soundview operates on a rolling admissions policy, with students accepted throughout the year in all grades except twelfth. Families of prospective students meet with the Admissions Director, after which the student spends a day at the School. The SSAT is not required, but portions of the ERB standardized examination are administered (unless the applicant provides the School with sufficient, current test data).

Students of all backgrounds are welcomed. The academic program is demanding, but the School's small size allows it to work with each individual student in order to develop strategies for success.

APPLICATION TIMETABLE

Soundview accepts applications on a rolling basis throughout the year. The application fee is $50.

ADMISSIONS CORRESPONDENCE

Mary E. Ivanyi
Director of Admissions and Assistant Head
Soundview Preparatory School
370 Underhill Road
Yorktown Heights, New York 10598
United States
Phone: 914-962-2780
E-mail: info@soundviewprep.org
Website: http://www.soundviewprep.org

SOUTHWESTERN ACADEMY

Beaver Creek Ranch, Arizona

Type: Coeducational boarding and day college-preparatory and general academic school
Grades: 9–12, postgraduate year
Enrollment: 17
Head of School: Kenneth R. Veronda, Headmaster

THE SCHOOL

Southwestern Academy offers achievement-based, departmentalized, and supportively structured classes limited to 9 to 12 students. Small classes allow for individualized attention in a noncompetitive environment. Southwestern was founded by Maurice Veronda in 1924 as a college-preparatory program "for capable students who could do better" in small, supportive classes. While maintaining that commitment, Southwestern Academy includes U.S. and international students with strong academic abilities who are eager to learn and strengthen English-language skills as well as pursue a general scholastic program in a small, supportive school structure. Southwestern Academy is accredited by the Western Association of Schools and Colleges (WASC).

Southwestern Academy offers students the opportunity to study at either of two distinctly different and beautiful campuses. The Arizona campus, which is known as Beaver Creek Ranch, is located deep in a red-rock canyon in northern Arizona. The San Marino, California, campus is situated in a historic orange grove area near Pasadena. Students may attend either campus and, if space permits, may divide the academic year between the two.

The Beaver Creek campus is a 185-acre ranch located 100 miles north of Phoenix, 12 miles from the resort community of Sedona, and 45 miles south of Flagstaff. The San Marino campus occupies 8 acres in a residential suburb 10 miles from downtown Los Angeles and immediately south of Pasadena, home to the renowned Tournament of Roses Parade. Although the program and philosophies are the same at both campuses, each offers a very different learning environment. Students studying at the Beaver Creek Ranch campus enjoy a living and learning environment that takes full advantage of the rich cultural, scenic, and environmentally significant region. Students at the California campus draw on the offerings of the urban setting.

A mix of U.S. and international students from several countries offers a unique blend of cultural, social, and educational opportunities for all. Every effort is made to enroll a well-balanced student body that represents the rich ethnic diversity of U.S. citizens and students from around the world. The student body consists of college-bound students who prefer a small, personalized education; above-average students who have the potential to become excellent academic achievers in the right learning environment; and average students who, with a supportive structure, can achieve academic success.

Southwestern Academy is incorporated as a not-for-profit organization. Operating expenses are approximately $4.5 million per annum and are met by tuition (93 percent) and grants and annual giving (7 percent). The Academy has no indebtedness.

ACADEMIC PROGRAM

High school classes are divided by grade level, and students are assigned based on ability and achievement.

High school graduation requirements are based on University of California requirements and include completion of a minimum of 200 academic credits plus 40 credit hours of physical education. The academic term is mid-September through mid-June, with a summer quarter offered at both campuses. Requirements include 4 years of English, 3 years of mathematics, 2 years of a foreign language, 2 years of laboratory sciences, and 1 year each of U.S. history and world cultures, plus one semester of U.S. government and economics and 2 years of visual/performing arts. Proficiency exams in English, mathematics, and computer literacy, as well as community service hours, are also required for graduation.

A typical semester of course work includes six classes plus physical education. Advanced Placement classes are available in English, history, language, math, and science. Review and remedial classes are made available to students who need additional instruction. International students are offered three levels of classes in English as a second language (ESL), including an introductory class, to prepare them to enter and succeed in other academic areas.

Teachers are available daily during a midafternoon study period to work individually with students and meet with parents. There is no extra charge for this tutoring. Boarding students are required to attend a monitored evening study hall, where additional teacher assistance is available.

Student achievement is recognized with a grading system that ranges from A to F. Progress letters are sent monthly to parents and report cards are sent quarterly. The minimum college-recommending grade upon completion of academic requirements is C.

Students studying at the Beaver Creek Ranch campus attend classes on a block schedule, Monday through Thursday. Each Friday, students participate in educational, project-oriented, and assignment-based field trips. Experiential learning allows students to apply knowledge from the classroom. It also supports an integrated academic element that links core subject areas in a practical, applied manner, promoting understanding and retention of key concepts.

FACULTY AND ADVISERS

Headmaster Kenneth Veronda was born at the San Marino campus that his father founded. Mr. Veronda attended classes at Southwestern, graduated, and completed undergraduate and graduate work in American history and foreign relations at Stanford University. The majority of 32 faculty members, 10 in Arizona and 22 in California, hold advanced degrees in their subject areas. Each teacher serves as a faculty adviser to a few students and meets with them individually throughout the school year. On-campus college and career counselors are also available to meet with and assist students in making post–high school graduation plans.

COLLEGE ADMISSION COUNSELING

The college counselors closely monitor the advisement and placement needs of each student. Beginning in the ninth grade, every effort is made to assist students in researching a variety of colleges and universities that match their interests and academic achievement levels. Students are provided a college planning handbook that offers helpful hints and suggestions regarding college application processes. A variety of college representatives are invited annually to visit each campus and meet with students.

Approximately 35 students graduate each year from Southwestern Academy. All enter a U.S. college or university. Some choose to attend a local two-year community college before transferring to a four-year college or university. In recent years, Southwestern Academy graduates have been accepted to the following schools: American University; Arizona State; Art Center College of Design; Azusa Pacific; Boston College; Boston University; Brown; Butler; California State, Fullerton; Monterey Bay, and Northridge; California State Polytechnic, Pomona; Columbia; Hampton; Howard; Loyola; Marymount; Menlo College; Mills; Occidental; Oregon State; Parsons; Penn State; Pepperdine; Pitzer; Temple; USC; Whittier; Woodbury; Wooster; Xavier; the Universities of California Irvine, La Verne, and Los Angeles; and the Universities of Nevada, New Orleans, the Pacific, San Diego, San Francisco, St. Louis, Virginia, and Washington (Seattle).

ACADEMIC FACILITIES

At the Beaver Creek Ranch campus, newly renovated classrooms, a learning resource center, and the dormitories blend into the picturesque setting. The campus also includes recreation rooms, a gymnasium, several large activity fields, and an indoor, solar-heated swimming pool.

The San Marino campus includes seven buildings encircling a large multisport athletic field. Lincoln Hall, the main academic building, houses morning assembly and study hall, ten classrooms, science and computer labs, and the library. Pioneer Hall includes several classrooms, a kitchen, dining rooms, and business offices. A separate building is home to large music and art studios and an additional science classroom and laboratory.

BOARDING AND GENERAL FACILITIES

The Beaver Creek Ranch Campus offers dorm rooms that accommodate 1 to 4 people. Meals are served in the dining room and sometimes in the charming courtyard. Picnics are also popular. A lounge with a huge fireplace is a favorite spot for students to watch movies and DirectTV®.

Seven stone cottages are home to faculty and staff members and sometimes upperclassmen and are set along the trout-filled Beaver Creek. Two fishing ponds, pastures, prehistoric Indian caves, and a favorite swimming hole in the creek are found on campus. Even in this remote, rugged environment, students can e-mail friends and surf the Internet, thanks to the T-1 wireless connectivity.

Four dormitory halls are located on the San Marino campus. Each is designed to accommodate up to 20 boys in double and single rooms. Two off-campus dormitories (located within a mile) house a total of 32 girls. Dorm parents live in apartments adjoining each hall.

ATHLETICS

Gyms and playing fields are available to all students at both campuses, where sports opportunities exist for physical education requirements and recreation. As a member of federated leagues in Arizona and California, Southwestern Academy fields teams at both campuses in all major sports except tackle football. Athletic events are held in late afternoon following the regular school day.

EXTRACURRICULAR OPPORTUNITIES

At the Beaver Creek Ranch campus, students can learn to ride and care for horses or swing on a rope over the creek—and drop in for a swim! The indoor pool is heated for those who prefer warmer water. The campus offers a full program of sports, including golf, and a full range of art classes. Wildlife, including mule deer, bighorn sheep, and javelin, can be seen on hikes. Other recreation opportunities include camping, hiking, mountain biking, fishing, and backpacking.

Southwestern offers a wide range of co-curricular and extracurricular activities and opportunities, including art, drama, music, journalism, student government, and student clubs. Current clubs include chess, Interact, International, the Southwestern Arts Society, Southwestern Environmental Associates, and tennis. Frequent class trips to southern California and northern Arizona places of interest, such as tide pools, museums, archaeological sites, art galleries, and live theater, are great learning experiences for students at both campuses.

DAILY LIFE

Boarding students begin each school day with a breakfast buffet at 7:30 a.m. Following breakfast, day and boarding students meet for a required assembly at 8:10 a.m., with classes following from 8:30 a.m. to 2:45 p.m. Required study halls and optional clubs and athletic events are held between 2:50 and 4:30 p.m. Dinner is served at 6 p.m. and is followed by a monitored study hall lasting until 8 p.m. Lights out is at 10:30 p.m. for middle school students and 11 p.m. for those in high school.

SUMMER PROGRAMS

Summer school sessions are offered at both campuses. Both offer intensive yet enjoyable individualized classes in English and other subjects, plus educational and recreational trips to interesting places in northern Arizona and southern California.

Summer sessions at Beaver Creek Ranch combine review and enrichment courses with experiential learning and high-adventure activities in classwork, camp-type activities, and travel in northern Arizona. ESL is offered at the Beaver Creek campus during the summer.

The summer program in San Marino is an excellent opportunity for domestic students to catch up, if needed, or to move ahead academically in order to take more advanced courses before graduation. For non-English-speaking international students, the summer session can provide an entire semester of the appropriate ESL level necessary to successfully complete a college-preparatory curriculum.

COSTS AND FINANCIAL AID

Tuition for a 2013–14 U.S. boarding student is $33,750. International student tuition was $41,000. The cost for a day student (U.S. citizens) was $16,500. An incidental account containing $2,000 for boarding students or $1,000 for day students is required of all students to cover expenses such as books, school supplies, physical education uniforms, and discretionary spending money. Payment is due in advance unless other arrangements are made with the business office.

Financial aid is awarded based on financial need. More than $440,000 was awarded in 2013–14.

ADMISSIONS INFORMATION

Southwestern Academy admits students of any race, color, national and ethnic origin, creed, or sex. A completed application packet is required, followed by a personal on-campus interview with students and parents. A daylong visit to classes (and an overnight for prospective boarding students) is strongly encouraged for prospective students already living in the United States. Interviews with prospective international students and parents are scheduled by the international admissions director and do not require a campus visit.

Each campus offers exceptional learning opportunities. Prospective students are encouraged to seriously consider both campuses and apply to the one that seems better suited to them.

Admission materials and other information can be downloaded from the Southwestern Academy website. It can also be obtained by contacting the Office of Admissions.

APPLICATION TIMETABLE

Admission offers are made throughout the year, as space permits. Appointments are required for interviews and campus tours at both locations. The admissions office for both campus locations is located in San Marino. Students should write or call the San Marino office for information on either campus.

ADMISSIONS CORRESPONDENCE

Office of Admissions
Southwestern Academy
2800 Monterey Road
San Marino, California 91108
United States
Phone: 626-799-5010 Ext. 203
Fax: 626-799-0407
E-mail: jblake@southwesternacademy.edu
Website:
    http://www.southwesternacademy.edu

SOUTHWESTERN ACADEMY

San Marino, California

Type: Coeducational boarding and day college-preparatory and general academic school
Grades: 6–12, postgraduate year
Enrollment: 140
Head of School: Kenneth R. Veronda, Headmaster

THE SCHOOL

Southwestern Academy offers achievement-based, departmentalized, and supportively structured classes limited to 9 to 12 students. Small classes allow for individualized attention in a noncompetitive environment. Southwestern was founded by Maurice Veronda in 1924 as a college-preparatory program "for capable students who could do better" in small, supportive classes. While maintaining that commitment, Southwestern Academy includes U.S. and international students with strong academic abilities who are eager to learn and strengthen English-language skills as well as pursue a general scholastic program in a small, supportive school structure. Southwestern Academy is accredited by the Western Association of Schools and Colleges (WASC).

Southwestern Academy offers students the opportunity to study at either of two distinctly different and beautiful campuses. The San Marino, California, campus is situated in a historic orange grove area near Pasadena. The Arizona campus, which is known as Beaver Creek Ranch, is located deep in a red-rock canyon in northern Arizona. Students may attend either campus and, if space permits, may divide the academic year between the two.

The San Marino campus occupies 8 acres in a residential suburb 10 miles from downtown Los Angeles and immediately south of Pasadena, home to the renowned Tournament of Roses Parade. The Beaver Creek campus is a 185-acre ranch located 100 miles north of Phoenix, 12 miles from the resort community of Sedona, and 45 miles south of Flagstaff. Although the program and philosophies are the same at both campuses, each offers a very different learning environment. Students at the California campus draw on the offerings of the urban setting. Students studying at the Beaver Creek Ranch campus enjoy a living and learning environment that takes full advantage of the rich cultural, scenic, and environmentally significant region.

A mix of U.S. and international students from several countries offers a unique blend of cultural, social, and educational opportunities for all. Every effort is made to enroll a well-balanced student body that represents the rich ethnic diversity of U.S. citizens and students from around the world. The student body consists of college-bound students who prefer a small, personalized education; above-average students who have the potential to become excellent academic achievers in the right learning environment; and average students who, with a supportive structure, can achieve academic success.

Southwestern Academy is incorporated as a not-for-profit organization. Operating expenses are approximately $4.5 million per annum and are met by tuition (93 percent) and grants and annual giving (7 percent). The Academy has no indebtedness.

ACADEMIC PROGRAM

Middle school students are placed in classes based on individual achievement levels. High school classes are divided by grade level, and students are assigned based on ability and achievement.

High school graduation requirements are based on University of California requirements and include completion of a minimum of 200 academic credits plus 40 credit hours of physical education. The academic term is mid-September through mid-June, with a summer quarter offered at both campuses. Requirements include 4 years of English, 3 years of mathematics, 2 years of a foreign language, 2 years of laboratory sciences, and 1 year each of U.S. history and world cultures, plus one semester of U.S. government and economics and 2 years of visual/performing arts. Proficiency exams in English, mathematics, and computer literacy, as well as community service hours, are also required for graduation.

A typical semester of course work includes six classes plus physical education. Advanced Placement classes are available in English, history, language, math, and science. Review and remedial classes are made available to students who need additional instruction. International students are offered three levels of classes in English as a second language (ESL), including an introductory class, to prepare them to enter and succeed in other academic areas.

Teachers are available daily during a midafternoon study period to work individually with students and meet with parents. There is no extra charge for this tutoring. Boarding students are required to attend a monitored evening study hall, where additional teacher assistance is available.

Student achievement is recognized with a grading system that ranges from A to F. Progress letters are sent monthly to parents and report cards are sent quarterly. The minimum college-recommending grade upon completion of academic requirements is a "C."

While studying at the Beaver Creek Ranch campus, students attend classes on a block schedule, Monday through Thursday. Each Friday, students participate in educational, project-oriented, and assignment-based field trips. Experiential learning allows students to apply knowledge from the classroom. It also supports an integrated academic element that links core subject areas in a practical, applied manner, promoting understanding and retention of key concepts.

FACULTY AND ADVISERS

Headmaster Kenneth Veronda was born at the San Marino campus that his father founded. Mr. Veronda attended classes at Southwestern, graduated, and completed undergraduate and graduate work in American history and foreign relations at Stanford University. The majority of 32 faculty members, 22 in California and 10 in Arizona, hold advanced degrees in their subject areas. Each teacher serves as a faculty adviser to a few students and meets with them individually throughout the school year. On-campus college and career counselors are also available to meet with and assist students in making post–high school graduation plans.

COLLEGE ADMISSION COUNSELING

The college counselors closely monitor the advisement and placement needs of each student. Beginning in the ninth grade, every effort is made to assist students in researching a variety of colleges and universities that match their interests and academic achievement levels. Students are provided a college planning handbook that offers helpful hints and suggestions regarding college application processes. A variety of college representatives are invited annually to visit each campus and meet with students.

Approximately 35 students graduate each year from Southwestern Academy. All enter a U.S. college or university. Some choose to attend a local two-year community college before transferring to a four-year college or university. In recent years, Southwestern Academy graduates have been accepted to the following schools: American University; Arizona State; Art Center College of Design; Azusa Pacific; Boston College; Boston University; Brown; Butler; California State, Fullerton, Monterey Bay, and Northridge; California State Polytechnic, Pomona; Columbia; Hampton; Howard; Loyola; Marymount; Menlo College; Mills; Occidental; Oregon State; Parsons; Penn State; Pepperdine; Pitzer; Temple; USC, Whittier; Woodbury; Wooster; Xavier; the Universities of California La Verne and Los Angeles; and the Universities of Nevada, New Orleans, the Pacific, San Diego, San Francisco, St. Louis, Virginia, and Washington (Seattle).

ACADEMIC FACILITIES

The San Marino campus includes seven buildings encircling a large multisport athletic field. Lincoln Hall, the main academic building, houses morning assembly and study hall, ten classrooms, science and computer labs, and the library. Pioneer Hall includes several classrooms, a kitchen, dining rooms, and business offices. A separate building is home to large music and art studios and an additional science classroom and lab.

Newly renovated classrooms, a learning resource center, and the dormitories blend into the picturesque setting along Beaver Creek.

BOARDING AND GENERAL FACILITIES

Four dormitory halls are located on the San Marino campus. Each is designed to accommodate up to 20 boys in double and single rooms. Two off-campus dormitories (located within a mile) house a total of 34 girls. Dorm parents live in apartments adjoining each hall.

At Beaver Creek, seven stone cottages encircle the main campus area and provide faculty/staff housing. Four recently renovated residence halls accommodate up to 56 students. The Beaver Creek Ranch campus includes recreation rooms, a gymnasium, several large activity fields, and an indoor, solar-heated swimming pool.

ATHLETICS

Gyms and playing fields are available to all students at both campuses, where sports opportunities exist for physical education requirements and recreation. As a member of federated leagues in California and Arizona, Southwestern Academy fields teams at both campuses in all major sports except tackle football. Athletic events are held in late afternoon, following the regular school day.

EXTRACURRICULAR OPPORTUNITIES

Southwestern offers a wide range of co-curricular and extracurricular activities and opportunities, including art, drama, music, journalism, student government, and student clubs. Current clubs include chess, Interact, International, the Southwestern Arts Society, Southwestern Environmental Associates, and tennis. Frequent class trips to southern California and northern Arizona places of interest, such as tide pools, museums, archaeological sites, art galleries, and live theater, are great learning experiences for students at both campuses.

DAILY LIFE

Boarding students begin each school day with a breakfast buffet at 7:30 a.m. Following breakfast, day and boarding students meet for a required assembly at 8:10 a.m., with classes following from 8:30 a.m. to 2:45 p.m. Required study halls and optional clubs and athletic events are held between 2:50 and 4:30 p.m. Dinner is served at 6 p.m. and is followed by a monitored study hall lasting until 8 p.m. Lights out is at 10:30 p.m. for middle school students and 11 p.m. for high school students.

WEEKEND LIFE

Students in good standing may leave the campus, with permission, during any weekend. Many students take advantage of the planned activities that are arranged for them, including theater performances, shopping at the malls and Old Town Pasadena, barbecues, beach parties, and movies. Visits are planned to Disneyland, Magic Mountain, and Big Surf, and the other attractions of the two-state areas are a part of the social program at Southwestern Academy. Day students are welcome to attend all weekend activities if space permits.

SUMMER PROGRAMS

Summer school sessions are offered at both campuses. Both offer intensive yet enjoyable individualized classes in English and other subjects, plus educational and recreational trips to interesting places in southern California and northern Arizona.

The summer program in San Marino is an excellent opportunity for domestic students to catch up, if needed, or to move ahead academically in order to take more advanced courses before graduation. For non-English-speaking international students, the summer session can provide an entire semester of the appropriate ESL level necessary to successfully complete a college-preparatory curriculum.

Summer sessions at Beaver Creek Ranch combine review and enrichment courses with experiential learning and high-adventure activities in classwork, camp-type activities, and travel in northern Arizona. ESL is offered at the Beaver Creek campus during the summer.

COSTS AND FINANCIAL AID

Tuition for the 2013–14 U.S. boarding student is $33,750. International student tuition is $41,000. The cost for a day student (U.S. citizens) is $16,500. An incidental account containing $2,000 for boarding students or $1,000 for day students is required of all students to cover expenses such as books, school supplies, physical education uniforms, and discretionary spending money. Payment is due in advance unless other arrangements are made with the business office.

Financial aid is awarded based on financial need. More than $440,000 was awarded in the 2013–14 school year.

ADMISSIONS INFORMATION

Southwestern Academy admits students of any race, color, national and ethnic origin, creed, or sex. A completed application packet is required, followed by a personal on-campus interview with students and parents. A daylong visit to classes (and an overnight for prospective boarding students) is strongly encouraged for prospective students already living in the United States. Interviews with prospective international students and parents are scheduled by the international admissions director and do not require a campus visit, although a visit, tour, and interview are encouraged.

Each campus offers exceptional learning opportunities. Prospective students are encouraged to seriously consider both campuses and apply to the one that seems better suited to them.

Admission materials and other information may be downloaded from the Southwestern Academy website. It can also be obtained by contacting the Office of Admissions.

APPLICATION TIMETABLE

Admission offers are made throughout the year, as space permits. Appointments are required for interviews and campus tours at both locations. The admissions office for both campus locations is located in San Marino. Students should write or call the San Marino office for information on either campus.

ADMISSIONS CORRESPONDENCE

Office of Admissions
Southwestern Academy
2800 Monterey Road
San Marino, California 91108
United States
Phone: 626-799-5010 Ext. 203
Fax: 626-799-0407
E-mail: jblake@southwesternacademy.edu
Website:
    http://www.southwesternacademy.edu

Type: Coeducational boarding and day college-preparatory school
Grades: Nursery–12: Lower School, Nursery–4; Middle School, 5–8; Upper School, 9–12
Enrollment: Total: 750; Lower School: 160; Middle School: 200; Upper School: 390
Head of School: Mr. Michael McBrien, Headmaster

THE SCHOOL

TASIS The American School in England was founded in 1976 by Mrs. M. Crist Fleming and is a sister school of The American School in Switzerland (TASIS), which she established in 1956. In fulfillment of its mission statement, the School seeks to balance the pursuit of knowledge with the love of wisdom, and promotes the skills of lifelong learning, an appreciation for beauty, and the development of character.

TASIS England offers a challenging and traditional college-preparatory program. While academics are emphasized, a wide variety of sports, extracurricular activities, cultural excursions, and weekend trips ensure a balanced education.

The School's Strategic Plan includes the following goals:

· Prepare students with the knowledge and skills to be successful at the next stage of their education.
· Foster the full potential of each student through individualized educational and extracurricular opportunities.
· Cultivate the well-being of the entire community by offering support and educational programs that promote good judgment, healthy habits, and life balance.

The 46-acre campus is set in the village of Thorpe in the heart of the beautiful Thames valley, only 18 miles from central London and 6 miles from Heathrow Airport. The School takes full advantage of its location and the opportunities that England and Europe offer as extensions to classroom learning.

The TASIS Schools and Summer Programs are owned and controlled by the TASIS Foundation, a Swiss, independent, not-for-profit educational foundation, registered in Delémont, Switzerland. The Board of Directors of each school is responsible for providing its governance structure, determining its policies and strategies, providing trusteeship over its financial position, and appointing and evaluating its headmaster.

TASIS England is an International Baccalaureate (IB) World School, is accredited by the Council of International Schools (CIS) and the New England Association of Schools and Colleges (NEASC), and is a member of the National Association of Independent Schools (NAIS) and The Association of Boarding Schools (TABS).

ACADEMIC PROGRAM

The Upper School comprises grades 9 to 12. The minimum requirements for graduation from the Upper School are 4 years of English, 3 years of history (including U.S. history at the eleventh- or twelfth-grade level), a third-level proficiency in a foreign language, 3 years of mathematics (through algebra II), three laboratory sciences (including a biological and a physical science), and 1 year of fine arts. All seniors are required to take a full-year humanities course. Students who have attended TASIS England for three years or more are expected to complete 19 credits. A normal course load consists of six courses per year. Advanced Placement courses are offered for qualified students and include art history, biology, calculus, chemistry, computer science, economics, English, environmental science, European history, French, music theory, physics, Spanish, statistics, U.S. government, and U.S. history.

TASIS also offers the International Baccalaureate (IB) diploma. Students may apply to this program for their final two years at TASIS, and successful IB diploma candidates can earn both the IB diploma and the TASIS England high school diploma. Entry into the IB Program is made in consultation between the School, student, and family and is open to highly motivated students with strong academic, time management, and study skills.

With an average class size of 15, and a teacher-student ratio of 1:7, the School provides an intimate learning environment that challenges a young person to realize his or her full potential. The Advisory Program enhances this aspect of a TASIS education, as the advisors are charged with the social and academic well-being of each advisee.

A student's day is fully structured. Participation in supervised evening study hall for boarding students is a requirement for all but those who have earned the privilege of independent study in their rooms. Students have access to the extensive printed and online resources maintained by the Upper School Library. Laboratory work takes place during supervised classes in the modern and well-equipped Science Center, which opened in 2011.

The academic year is divided into two semesters, ending in January and June, respectively. Grades and comments are e-mailed home to parents four times a year at mid-semester and end-of-semester breaks, together with a summary report from the advisor. The grading system uses A to F, indicating achievement levels, and 1 to 5 as a measure of a student's attitude, effort, and application to his or her work.

An educational travel program during the October break is mandatory for all boarding students and is included in the tuition. Past trips have included such destinations as Austria, France, Germany, Greece, Hungary, Italy, Poland, Romania, Russia, Spain, and Switzerland. These school trips are also an option for day students.

FACULTY AND ADVISORS

Mr. Michael McBrien was appointed as headmaster of TASIS England in 2010. He holds a master's degree in education and a Bachelor of Arts in counseling, psychology, and communication. He has twenty-four years of experience in education and has worked as an administrator at the University of California, Berkeley, and at Babson College and Frontier Academy, in Colorado. Mr. McBrien was previously Head of Baylor School in Tennessee, an independent, coeducational college preparatory, day, and boarding school.

The faculty represents one of the School's strongest assets. Its members are dedicated professionals with a true sense of vocation. Duties are not limited to teaching but encompass the responsibilities of advisors, sports coaches, dorm parents, community service aides, and trip chaperones. There are 115 full-time faculty members and 22 part-time teachers—51 men and 86 women. Approximately 62 percent of them have advanced degrees, and 21 live on campus. In addition, music specialists visit the School for private instruction by arrangement.

COLLEGE ADMISSION COUNSELING

TASIS England employs a team of full-time college counselors who provide guidance about university choices and assist in managing the details of the search/application process at every stage of an upper school student's academic career. They meet with students in small groups in the freshman and sophomore years, and individually with students in their junior and senior years to discuss academic programs, careers, and college plans. Support programs include student seminars, essay-writing workshops, U.S. and U.K. case studies, and informational events for parents. The counselors have a welcoming University and College Counseling Center that maintains a reference library of college catalogs, provides access to computer software, and familiarizes students with the range of opportunities available to them.

The counselors coordinate visits to the School by college admissions officers from universities in the United States and around the world, and administer the college admissions testing programs. TASIS England is a test center for the Plan, Explore, ACT, PSAT, and SAT, as well as the Advanced Placement and International Baccalaureate examinations. The mid-range of SAT scores achieved by TASIS students graduating in 2013 (32 percent of whom speak English-as-an-additional language) were: math 560–680, critical reading 490–660, and writing 540–660. The mid-range composite score achieved by those taking the ACT (9 percent of whom speak English-as-an-additional language) was 23–29.

TASIS graduates are accepted by universities around the world and have recently attended such schools as Boston University, Bowdoin, Cornell, Duke, NYU, Rhode Island School of Design, Stanford, Tufts, and the United States Air Force Academy (U.S.); Bath, Bristol, Durham, Imperial College, King's College London, London School of Economics, St. George's Medical School, University College London, and York (U.K.); Trinity College Dublin (Ireland); and McGill, Queen's, and the University of British Columbia (Canada). TASIS believes that students should be encouraged to think deeply about the purposes of higher education, about the intangible benefits of genuine intellectual activity, and about the range of philosophical options offered by educational institutions. The major responsibility for college choices lies with each student, but the School provides as much advice and support as possible.

STUDENT BODY AND CONDUCT

For the 2013–14 academic year, there are 390 students in the Upper School (grades 9–12), including 185 boarding students. Year groups include: 110 seniors, 120 juniors, 95 sophomores, and 65 freshmen. The ratio of boys to girls in each grade level is close to 1:1. In some cases, boarding students' parents are expatriates undertaking assignments overseas, such as in Saudi Arabia, Africa, Europe, and various parts of the British Isles. The student body is culturally diverse, with about half of the students in the Upper School representing approximately fifty countries other than the United States. In the Lower School (nursery–grade 4), there are 160 children, and the Middle School (grades 5–8) has 200 students.

TASIS England promotes a purposeful environment for learning and growing, including demonstrating respect for one's self and for others. The *Student Handbook* clearly identifies the accepted codes of conduct within the School community. A uniform is required for upper school students. Lower and middle school students wear white and navy blue. An infraction of a major school rule is dealt with by the upper school administration with the Disciplinary Advisory Board. TASIS England reserves the right to dismiss at any time a student who has proved to be an unsatisfactory member of the school community, even though there may have been no infraction of a specific rule.

In the Upper School, the Student Council is made up of representatives from all grade levels and is the vehicle of student government. Prefects, as student leaders, carry special responsibilities in dormitory and general school life.

ACADEMIC FACILITIES

Two large Georgian mansions and purpose-built classrooms are the focal points of the campus. There are computer centers and a library for each school division, with the Upper School Library alone holding over 12,000 volumes. Additional facilities include art studios, a darkroom, an art gallery, music rooms, a language laboratory, a 24-hour health center, two multipurpose gymnasiums, a fitness center, two drama/dance studios, and a 350-seat theater. TASIS England is in the final phases of implementing a master plan to enhance all campus facilities. The most recent development, a state-of-the-art Science Center with three floors of classrooms and well-equipped laboratories, opened in 2011 and augments the School's vibrant science program. Wi-Fi is available throughout the campus.

BOARDING AND GENERAL FACILITIES

Approximately 185 boarding students (grades 9–12) are accommodated in single-sex dormitories supervised by a faculty resident dorm parent, assisted by prefects. Each unit holds 13–16 students, usually in 2- or 3-person rooms, which are located in the top floors of the main buildings as well as in the adjacent cottages, such as Tudor House, Orchard, Shepherd's Cottage, and Vicarage Mews. Construction of a new dormitory is underway. The Boarding Program is coordinated by two staff members, both of whom are experienced in providing boarding care and serving the needs of young people. All meals are provided, and the campus Health Center has an experienced 24-hour nursing staff, and a school doctor on call. A new student center, opened in 2012, provides an innovative and relaxed café-style space for both boarding and day students to meet friends and relax.

ATHLETICS

An awareness of physical fitness, the discipline of training the body as well as the mind, and the spirit of competition are viewed as important elements in a student's education at TASIS England. All upper school students participate in the afternoon sports/activities program, which operates on a three-term basis, reflecting seasonal sports. The minimum requirement is participation for two afternoons a week.

Varsity sports include basketball, cross-country, dance, golf, lacrosse, soccer, tennis, and volleyball as well as boys' teams in rugby and baseball and girls' teams in cheering and softball. Recreational sports include badminton, basketball, golf, horse riding, lacrosse, running, soccer, squash, swimming, tennis, yoga, and a conditioning program.

There are four large playing fields on campus, six all-weather tennis courts, two gymnasiums, and a fitness center that offers a complete weight-training circuit and a wide variety of cardiovascular machines. The nearby Egham Sports Center offers fine supplementary facilities.

Besides participating in local sports events, the School competes in International Schools Sports Tournaments (ISSTs) with other international schools throughout Europe and North Africa.

EXTRACURRICULAR OPPORTUNITIES

Proximity to London, only 18 miles away, provides an unrivaled opportunity for students to enjoy such pleasures as theater, opera, concerts, art galleries, and museums. Through course-related study or School-chaperoned trips, in the evenings and on weekends, students are regularly encouraged to participate in as many enriching and fun educational experiences as possible.

On-campus activities include drama productions; musical groups; choir; the School newspaper; Model UN; the Duke of Edinburgh Award Program; the Global Issues Network; art, debate, and drama clubs; and the yearbook committee, as well as School dances and movies.

A committee of students and teachers coordinates and plans on-campus and off-campus recreational activities, including day trips and weekends away. Traditionally, the International Festival, Spring Prom, and May Fair are the highlights of the year.

The Community Service Program aims to help each student to develop skills leading to a sense of involvement and greater responsibility for others. The minimum commitment involves approximately 1 hour a week. Students may serve the School community in a variety of ways, e.g., by helping in the library or tutoring younger children. They may serve the local community by visiting homes for the elderly, working with the disabled, participating in conservation projects, and raising funds for local charities. Special summer projects are also available.

DAILY LIFE

Classes commence at 8:15 (9:10 on Wednesdays) and end at 3:15. Each upper school class meets four times a week, allowing a structured advisory and tutorial period during the day. Sports/activities time is between 3:30 and 5 p.m. each day, except Fridays. An upper school meeting is regularly scheduled for Wednesdays. No classes are held on Saturday or Sunday.

WEEKEND LIFE

Day students as well as boarders participate freely in organized social events on the weekends. The Activities Coordinator and Student Council members collaborate to develop a wide variety of activities. These can include on-campus activities such as dances and bonfire night as well as trips to the theater and concerts, the ballet, and professional sports events.

Students are encouraged to initiate weekend day trips to destinations in the UK such as Stratford-upon-Avon, Salisbury, Cambridge, Oxford, Canterbury, and Bath. Organized excursions are chaperoned by members of the faculty.

SUMMER PROGRAMS

Three-week enrichment courses include the ShakespeareXperience, London Through a Lens, Television Production, Fashion and Textile Design, International Business, Creative Drawing & 3-D Design, and SAT Review. Six-week credit-based academic courses are offered in such subjects as Algebra II and Geometry. Some 550 students regularly participate from schools in the United States and from international schools all over the world. Qualified teachers and counselors from the United States and around the world make up the summer programs administration and faculty. Weekend travel to a variety of destinations in England, theater trips, and other excursions are included in the program.

In addition to the courses in England, TASIS offers intensive study of painting, photography, and architecture at Les Tapies in the Ardèche, France, and the TASIS Dorado Spanish Summer Program, which incorporates learning Spanish and environmental and marine discovery in Dorado Beach, Puerto Rico. All TASIS summer courses enrich the talents, skills, and interests of its participants.

COSTS AND FINANCIAL AID

In 2013–14, tuition and fees for day students are £6350–£20,600 per annum. Fees include lunches, loan of textbooks, IT and laboratory fees, some classroom materials, and the cost of most curriculum-related activities and field trips. Optional expenses, including costs for music lessons, are by private arrangement. Boarding fees are £35,110 and include tuition, room, full board, loan of textbooks, most IT and laboratory fees, annual laptop maintenance, some classroom materials, most curriculum-related activities and field trips, weekly laundry service for bed linen and towels, and travel insurance for school-sponsored trips. Costs for the October Travel Week are also included in the boarding fees. A recommended personal allowance is £50 per week.

There is a one-time-only Development Fund Fee of £750 per student for on-campus building projects and an enrollment deposit of £1000 for day students and £2000 for boarders. The balance of fees becomes payable for each semester by June 1 and November 15.

Students are invited to apply for financial aid, which is granted on the basis of merit, need, and available funds. In 2012–13, 27 students, including 15 in the Upper School, were awarded aid. Early application for financial help is recommended, and students who have been awarded financial aid must reapply for continued assistance each academic year. Each year the School awards approximately £150,000–£200,000 in financial aid.

ADMISSIONS INFORMATION

Applications for admission are considered by the Admissions Committee upon receipt of a completed application form together with the £125 application fee, three teachers' recommendations, and a transcript. Standardized test scores are requested, and a student questionnaire is required. A School visit is recommended unless distance is a prohibiting factor. A decision is reached on the basis of a student's academic and behavioral acceptability to the TASIS England School community. A student's nationality, religion, ethnic background, and gender play no part in the committee's decision, although availability of space in the dormitories (all are grouped by gender) is sometimes a limiting factor.

APPLICATION TIMETABLE

Applications are processed throughout the year. Visitors are welcome on campus at any time of the year other than the period between Christmas and New Year, when the School is closed. An interview by prior arrangement, even on very short notice, is recommended. It is preferable for visitors to choose days when school is in session in order to appreciate the working atmosphere of the community.

While early applications are encouraged, there is no final deadline, since a rolling admissions policy exists. Acceptances are made with the provision that students complete their current year in good standing.

ADMISSIONS CORRESPONDENCE

Karen House, Director of Admissions
TASIS The American School in England
Coldharbour Lane
Thorpe, Nr Egham
Surrey TW20 8TE
England
Phone: +44-1932-582316
Fax: +44-1932-564644
E-mail: ukadmissions@tasisengland.org
Website: http://www.tasisengland.org

TASIS Schools and Summer Programs in Europe
112 South Royal Street
Alexandria, Virginia 22314
United States
Phone: 703-299-8150
800-442-6005 (toll-free)
Fax: 703-299-8157
E-mail: usadmissions@tasis.com
Website: http://www.tasis.com

TASIS THE AMERICAN SCHOOL IN SWITZERLAND

Montagnola-Lugano, Switzerland

Type: Coeducational boarding and day college-preparatory school
Grades: Pre-K–12, PG: Elementary School, pre-K–5; Middle School, 6–8; High School, 9–12, postgraduate year
Enrollment: School total: 650; High School: 450; Middle School: 95; Elementary School: 105
Head of School: Dr. Charles Skipper

THE SCHOOL

TASIS The American School in Switzerland was founded in 1956 by Mrs. M. Crist Fleming to offer a strong American college-preparatory education in a European setting. TASIS was the first American boarding school established in Europe. Over time, it has become a school for students from more than fifty countries seeking an American independent school experience. The International Baccalaureate (I.B.) Program is also offered within this setting.

The objective of the School is to foster both a vital enthusiasm for learning and habits that are essential to a full realization of each student's moral and intellectual potential. The curriculum gives special emphasis to the achievements of the Western heritage, many elements of which are easily accessible from the School's location. By providing an international dimension to education, the School stresses the need for young people to mature with confidence and competence in an increasingly interrelated world.

The beautiful campus is in the village of Montagnola, overlooking the city and the lake of Lugano, nestled among the southernmost of the Swiss Alps in the Italian-speaking canton of Ticino. Ideally situated in the heart of Europe, the School makes the most of its location by introducing students to European cultures and languages through extensive travel programs.

The TASIS Foundation, a not-for-profit foundation, owns the School. The TASIS Foundation also has a school near London and offers summer programs in England, Spain, and Italy as well as Switzerland. Alumni provide enthusiastic support for the School's activities and participate in annual reunions and other special events.

TASIS is accredited by the Council of International Schools (CIS) and the New England Association of Schools and Colleges (NEASC) and is a member of the National Association of Independent Schools and the Swiss Group of International Schools.

ACADEMIC PROGRAM

The minimum requirements for graduation from the high school college-preparatory program are 4 years of English, 3 years of history (including European and U.S. history), a third-year proficiency in a modern foreign language, 3 years of mathematics (through algebra II), 3 years of laboratory science (including physical and biological sciences), and 1 year of fine arts, plus senior humanities, sports/physical education, and community service requirements. Students must satisfactorily complete a minimum of 19 credits. Students are required to enroll in a minimum of five full-credit courses per year or the equivalent. A normal course load for students consists of six courses.

TASIS offers an extensive English as an additional language program that focuses on oral and written academic English skills and competence in a high school curriculum leading to the TASIS college-preparatory diploma.

TASIS offers a diverse and challenging curriculum, including the Advanced Placement Program (AP), the International Baccalaureate (I.B.) Diploma Program, and a wide range of required and elective courses. In 2012, 40 students took sixty-eight AP exams in eleven subject areas; 44 percent of the scores were 4 or above and 13 percent earned the top score of 5. Students may also select I.B. courses and can earn subject-specific certificates or the full diploma.

The average class size is 12; the teacher-student ratio is 1:6. The student's day is fully structured, including time for academics, sports and activities, meals and socializing, and supervised evening study hours. The grading system uses A to F for performance and assigns effort grades of 1 to 5, reflecting students' attitudes and application to their work. The academic year is divided into two semesters and grades and comment reports are e-mailed to parents five times a year.

The postgraduate year presents an additional opportunity to high school graduates who wish to spend an interim year in Europe before going on to college. Each postgraduate student can design a tailor-made course of study with the assistance and approval of the Academic Dean that enables him or her to explore and develop new interests, strengthen academic weaknesses, or concentrate in areas of strength or particular interest. It includes a course-related Academic Travel program.

FACULTY AND ADVISORS

The faculty represents one of the School's strongest assets. Its members are a group of dedicated professionals who are enthusiastic about working with young people. The TASIS faculty includes 108 full-time teaching administrators and faculty members, of whom 57 are women and 51 are men. Seventy-one percent of the faculty members have advanced degrees. Thirty-two faculty members live on campus; the rest live nearby and participate in most campus activities. In addition to teaching, faculty members act as advisors, sports coaches, trip chaperones, and dormitory residents and help to create a warm, family-like atmosphere.

COLLEGE ADMISSION COUNSELING

The School employs 3 full-time college counselors, who meet with students individually and in groups during their junior and senior years. The college counseling office maintains a reference library of university catalogs from around the world so that students can familiarize themselves with the wide variety of opportunities that are open to them. As a counseling resource, the School provides a small computer lab for college research. Many college admissions officers from universities in the U.S. and Europe visit the School and speak to students. TASIS is an official testing center for the PSAT, SAT, SAT Subject Tests, ACT, PLAN, and all AP and I.B. examinations.

Recent graduates attend such institutions as Oxford, Edinburgh, Reading, and Nottingham Universities in the U.K. and Boston University, Colorado College, George Washington, Middlebury, Notre Dame, Northwestern, Stanford, and Tufts in the United States.

STUDENT BODY AND CONDUCT

Each student is honor bound to abide by the rules, as defined in the TASIS *Student Handbook*. The School employs a variety of counseling, disciplinary, and administrative responses to rules violations, determined on a case-by-case basis. The School administration and Conduct Review Board handle more serious offenses. All responses take into account the seriousness of the offense, the number of previous offenses, any mitigating circumstances, and the student's record as a member of the TASIS community.

Students at TASIS bear a serious responsibility to conduct themselves not only in a way that does credit to them, to their School, and to their country of origin, but also in a way that is consistent with the high standards set by the citizens of the European countries they visit. For this reason, TASIS has established reasonable but definitive standards of behavior, attitude, and appearance for all of its students. The School reserves the right to ask any student to withdraw for failure to maintain these standards.

ACADEMIC FACILITIES

The campus comprises twenty-three buildings; a combination of historical villas restored for school use and new, purpose-built facilities. The seventeenth-century Villa De Nobili was the School's original building and houses the dining hall, dormitories, administrative offices, and science laboratories. Hadsall House contains classrooms and dormitories. Villa Monticello contains modern classrooms, a computer center, a computer-based language lab, and dormitories. Next to Villa Monticello is the 22,000-volume M. Crist Fleming Library. Villa Aurora provides new classrooms for the Middle School. Classes are also held in the Belvedere and Villa Del Sole dormitories. The Palestra houses a sports complex with a gymnasium, fitness center, dance studio, locker rooms, student lounge with café, and music rooms. The School recently completed the John E. Palmer Cultural Center, which includes a state-of-the-art theater, and Fiammetta, which houses classrooms. Lanterna is the newest building, which includes classrooms and the health center. The newly renovated Casa Al Focolare houses Elementary School students from prekindergarten to first grade. A second gymnasium and new arts center opened in September 2012. The new Ferit Sahenk ('83) Arts Center houses spaces for art studios, architecture and design, painting and drawing, ceramics and sculpture, and photography.

BOARDING AND GENERAL FACILITIES

The campus includes ten dormitories, each of which houses from 6 to 43 students. Dormitories are located in the Villa De Nobili, Villa Monticello, Hadsall House, Villa Del Sole, Balmelli, Giani, Belvedere, and Lanterna buildings. All dormitories are supervised, and some faculty members live in the dormitories. Rooms accommodate from 2 to 4 students each. Although School facilities are closed during the winter and spring vacations, optional faculty-chaperoned trips are offered for students who are unable to return home.

Two recreation centers and a snack bar serve as focal points for student social activities. Three fully qualified nurses are in residence.

ATHLETICS

Students are required to participate in either a varsity sport three days a week or recreational sports after classes. Sports available include soccer, basketball, fitness training, mountain biking, volleyball, rugby, tennis, track and field, squash, swimming, rock climbing, and aerobics. Horseback riding and tennis are available at an extra cost. On weekends, students often go on hiking and mountain climbing trips in the Swiss Alps during the fall and spring and go skiing during the winter. During Ski Week in Crans-Montana (High School) or Verbier (Middle School), every student takes lessons in downhill or cross-country skiing or snowboarding. The Fleming Cup ski race and a faculty versus student hockey game are held during the Crans-Montana week.

Varsity sports give students the opportunity to compete against many schools in Switzerland and other countries and to take part in tournaments sponsored by the Swiss Group of International Schools. Varsity sports include soccer, volleyball, basketball, tennis, and track and field. Students also have the opportunity to enroll in the AC Milan soccer program, run by the coaches of the renowned Italian soccer team AC Milan.

Facilities include a playing field, a gym, and an outdoor basketball/volleyball area. The newly constructed Palestra sports complex includes a gymnasium with seating for up to 400 spectators, a dance studio, a fitness center, changing rooms, and a student lounge with a café.

EXTRACURRICULAR OPPORTUNITIES

The School's location in central Europe offers an enviable range of cultural opportunities. Trips to concerts, art galleries, and museums in Lugano, Locarno, and Milan extend education beyond the classroom. All students participate in the Academic Travel program, a four-day, faculty-chaperoned trip in the fall and a seven-day, faculty-chaperoned trip in the spring to such cities as Athens, Barcelona, Florence, Madrid, Munich, Nice, Paris, Prague, Rome, Venice, and Vienna.

On-campus activities include drama productions, choral and instrumental music, Model Congress, Environmental Club, Student Council, yearbook, and the Student Weekend Activities Team (SWAT). The Service Learning program focuses on the TASIS community, the local community, the interschool community, and the global community. Opportunities include peer tutoring, volunteering at a local domestic violence shelter, participating in Model UN, and work with Habitat for Humanity. TASIS also offers an annual summer service trip to Africa. Special annual social events include Family Weekend, dinner dances at the beginning of the academic year and at Christmas, prom, and the spring arts festival, along with a special graduation banquet and ceremony for seniors.

DAILY LIFE

Classes start at 8 a.m. and follow a rotating schedule. Classes meet from 50 to 65 minutes. There are weekly all-School assemblies, and students meet with their advisers every day. Sports and activities take place after school until 5:30 p.m. Meals are served buffet-style except for Wednesday evenings, when students share a formal dinner with their adviser group. Evening study is from 7 until 10.

WEEKEND LIFE

Both day and boarding students are encouraged to participate in organized events on weekends, including mountain-climbing and camping trips to scenic areas in Switzerland, shopping trips to open-air markets in northern Italy, and sightseeing excursions to Zurich, Milan, Venice, or Florence. On-campus events include talent shows, open-mic coffeehouse afternoons, films, and discotheque dances.

On weekends, students have Lugano town privileges if they have no School commitments and are in good academic and social standing. All excursions beyond Lugano are chaperoned by a member of the faculty, except those for seniors and some juniors, who, with parental permission, enjoy the privilege of independent travel in groups of 2 or more.

COSTS AND FINANCIAL AID

The all-inclusive tuition fee for boarding students is CHF 71,800 for the 2013–14 academic year, with an enrollment deposit of CHF 3000. This includes all fees that are necessary for attendance: room, board, tuition, eleven days of academic travel, Ski Week, all textbooks, laundry, activities, and most lab fees. A monthly personal allowance of CHF 250–300 is recommended. Seventy percent of the tuition is due by July 1 and the remainder by November 15.

Students may apply for financial assistance, which is granted on the basis of merit, need, and the student's ability to contribute to the School community.

ADMISSIONS INFORMATION

All applicants are considered on the basis of previous academic records, three teachers' evaluations, a personal statement, and a parental statement. The SSAT is recommended, and the SLEP test is required for students whose native language is not English. TASIS does not discriminate on the basis of race, color, nationality, or ethnic origin in its admissions policies and practices.

Application for entrance is recommended only for those students with sufficient academic interest and motivation to benefit from the program. The School accepts students from prekindergarten to grade 12 and at the postgraduate level.

APPLICATION TIMETABLE

TASIS has a rolling admissions policy and considers applications throughout the year. Applicants are encouraged to make an appointment to visit the campus. Within ten days of receipt of a completed application, the CHF 300 application fee, an official transcript from the previous school, and three teachers' evaluations, the Admissions Committee notifies the parents of its decision.

ADMISSIONS CORRESPONDENCE

Mr. William E. Eichner, Director of Admissions
TASIS The American School in Switzerland
CH-6926 Montagnola-Lugano
Switzerland
Phone: 41-91-960-5151
Fax: 41-91-993-2979
E-mail: admissions@tasis.ch
Website: http://www.tasis.com

or

The TASIS Schools
112 South Royal Street
Alexandria, Virginia 22314
United States
Phone: 703-299-8150
Fax: 703-299-8157
E-mail: usadmissions@tasis.com

THOMAS JEFFERSON SCHOOL

St. Louis, Missouri

Type: Coeducational boarding and day college-preparatory school
Grades: 7–12
Enrollment: 90
Head of School: Elizabeth L. Holekamp, Ph.D

THE SCHOOL

Thomas Jefferson School (TJ) was founded in 1946. It is known for its academic excellence and its commitment to enrolling students from all over the world since its inception. The School became coeducational in 1971. The campus is a 20-acre estate in Sunset Hills, a suburb 15 miles southwest of downtown St. Louis.

The School's mission is to give its students the strongest possible academic background through a classical education. Within a nurturing community, students develop a responsibility for their own learning and a desire to lift up the world with beauty and intellect. Many of the School's distinctive features, such as its size, its program, and even its daily schedule, are outgrowths of this mission.

The School has an active parent organization as well as an alumni association that bridges generations and continents and maintains a link with current students in an effort to ready them for life after TJ.

Thomas Jefferson School is a member of the National Association of Independent Schools, the Association of Boarding Schools, the Independent Schools Association of the Central States, Midwest Boarding Schools, the School and Student Service for Financial Aid, and the Educational Records Bureau.

ACADEMIC PROGRAM

Thomas Jefferson offers a challenging approach to learning, with the emphasis on the student's own efforts. Classes periods are short, and the teachers seldom lecture; instead, all students are called on to answer questions and generate discussion. During afternoon and evening study time, the students have a good deal of freedom in choosing when and where to do their homework, with help readily available from faculty members.

Seventh and eighth graders take English, mathematics, science, social studies, and Latin. In the ninth through twelfth grades, students take 4 years of English; 4 years of mathematics through calculus; 2 years of Ancient Greek (ninth and tenth grades); 2 years of Italian or French (tenth and eleventh); at least 3 years of science, including an AP course; and at least 2 years of history, including AP U.S. History. Electives include additional language, science, and history courses. Advanced Placement exams are a standard part of the courses in the social sciences, calculus, biology, physics, chemistry, advanced languages, and junior and senior English. Faculty members also help students work toward AP exams in other subject areas.

The English curriculum gives students intensive training in grammar, vocabulary, and writing skills. They also read and discuss a great deal of literature, including recognized classics (Shakespeare, the Bible, and epics), time-tested authors (Austen, Dickens, Dostoyevsky, Fitzgerald, Manzoni, Melville, and Shaw), and more contemporary major authors, such as Amy Tan, Ralph Ellison, and Chaim Potok.

A special feature is the study of classical Greek, which contributes to intellectual development (including concrete benefits such as enhanced vocabulary) and cultural knowledge. A number of graduates continue to study Greek in college; others do so independently or later in life.

The typical class size is 15, and the overall student-teacher ratio is 7:1. During the day, teachers are accessible to everyone and are ready to help; a teacher is on duty each evening and is available to assist with homework. Younger new students and those having academic difficulty are placed in supervised afternoon or evening study halls for additional support.

The grading system uses letter grades of A, B, C, D, and E. An average of B– is Honors; an average of A– is High Honors. To remain in good standing, a student must have no more than one D in any marking period; students in their first year, however, are allowed extra time to adjust. One-hour examinations are given at the end of the first and third quarters (October and April), and 2- to 3-hour examinations are given at midyear and at the end of the year. Following each exam period, a student's adviser sends the parents a letter discussing the student's progress and giving the latest grades and teachers' comments.

The unusually long winter and spring vacations (about one month each) give students an opportunity to unwind, spend time with their families, and do independent work.

FACULTY AND ADVISERS

The faculty, including the Head of School, consists of 22 full-time and part-time adjunct members, 13 women and 9 men. Faculty members hold twenty-two baccalaureate degrees, nine master's degrees, one law degree, and four Ph.D.'s.

Dr. Elizabeth Holekamp became the fourth Head of School in the summer of 2011. Dr. Holekamp attended the University of Missouri and holds a Ph.D. from Indiana University.

All faculty members are expected to continue educating themselves through a variety of professional development activities, including regular reading, both within and outside the subject areas they teach.

Currently, 5 faculty members live on the campus, along with 3 resident assistants and one staff member. Each teacher, whether resident or not, has several duties besides teaching, such as athletics supervision, evening study help, and advising students. Teachers meet with each of their advisees regularly to check the student's grades and to keep in touch with his or her personal development.

COLLEGE ADMISSION COUNSELING

Excellent preparation for college is the School's primary objective. Two experienced faculty members serve as college advisers, guiding the seniors through the process (including a College Boot Camp at the beginning of the senior year), helping them develop a realistic list of choices, and offering advice on writing personal essays. They also spend many hours following up with colleges by phone and e-mail. College admissions recruiters come to campus to talk with students virtually every week during each fall semester.

In sixty-seven years, the School has had 628 graduates; all have gone to college—most to well-known, selective institutions. Among the colleges and universities attended by recent Thomas Jefferson graduates are Beloit, Boston University, Brown, Caltech, Carnegie Mellon, Carleton, Claremont-McKenna, Columbia, Cornell, Duke, Emory, Harvard, Haverford, Johns Hopkins, Lawrence College, New York University–Stern, Northwestern, Penn State, Pitzer, Pomona, Reed, Rensselaer, Rhodes, Smith, Stanford, Swarthmore, Vanderbilt, Washington (St. Louis), Wesleyan, the University of Chicago, The University of Delaware, the University of Missouri, and the University of Pennsylvania.

The School consistently maintains first-tier SAT scores among U.S. boarding schools as listed by Boarding School Review.com.

STUDENT BODY AND CONDUCT

In 2013–14, the School has 89 students (58 boarding, 31 day). Domestic students come primarily from the region between the Appalachians and the Great Plains. Approximately one third of all students are international students from various countries (ESL instruction is available, although good English proficiency is required for admission). Most grades have girls and boys in about equal numbers.

A Student Council, whose members are elected twice a year, brings student concerns before the faculty and helps maintain a healthy, studious atmosphere. Collectively, the council has one vote in faculty meetings on many decisions concerning student life. A student prefect system gives students an additional layer of peer support.

Demerits are given for misconduct, lateness, and other routine matters; a student who receives too many demerits in one week has to do chores around the campus on Saturday. Students may appeal any demerits, even those given by the Head of School, before a Student Appeals Court.

ACADEMIC FACILITIES

The Charles E. Merrill, Jr. Main Building, built as a gracious family home on the original estate, provides a comfortable setting for classes and meals; it also contains faculty and administrative offices, the library collections, and an art gallery. The adjoining Sayers Hall provides science laboratories and classrooms. A five-year old art facility provides classroom and studio space for the fine arts, including a print-making shop. The recent addition to the gymnasium provides weight-training and yoga facilities.

BOARDING AND GENERAL FACILITIES

Boarders live in the Gables—a brick outbuilding from the original estate—and in six cottages constructed as living quarters for boarders. Each cottage has four double rooms; each room has an outside entrance, a private bath, large windows, wall-to-wall carpeting, air conditioning, and wireless Internet access. The cottages were designed to provide quiet, privacy, and independence. Normally, 2 or 3 boarding students share a room with 1 or 2 day students.

ATHLETICS

Thomas Jefferson School athletics are designed to support the physical and mental well-being of students. Outdoor sports include intramural tennis (five courts), varsity soccer, and fitness; indoor sports are volleyball and basketball (both varsity and JV), yoga, and general fitness. Athletics are required on Monday, Tuesday, Thursday, and Friday afternoons. Teams compete with other local schools in basketball, soccer, and volleyball. Some students with specialized interests fulfill this requirement off campus. Rowing is a current example of this practice.

EXTRACURRICULAR OPPORTUNITIES

The St. Louis area has a wealth of resources in art, music, and theater, as well as an excellent zoo, a science museum, and a world-renowned botanical garden. The School keeps the students informed about opportunities around town and helps with transportation and tickets whenever possible. Teachers often take groups of students on informal weekend field trips. In recent years, groups have gone to the Ozarks for camping, to the Mississippi River to see bald eagles, and to many symphony concerts, ballets, and plays. Students also attend movies, sports events, and concerts.

Service learning is an integral part of the program, and the School helps students find opportunities for volunteering. All students must plan and complete a required amount of voluntary community service before they graduate. Students are encouraged to pursue their own interests, such as music lessons or studying a language that is not part of the curriculum, and the School helps make arrangements. A piano is available for anyone to use for lessons or for personal enjoyment. Over the years, students have initiated and sustained major activities, such as the School yearbook, a student newspaper, mock trial, and the all-school play. Clubs include Robotics, Equality, Green, Chess, Dungeons and Dragons, and Pandora.

DAILY LIFE

A school day begins with breakfast at 7:45. Eight 35-minute class periods (and lunch) take place between 8:30 and 1:10. In grades 11 and 12, students take four classes and in grades 7 through 10, they take five. Classes meet daily, but AP classes, which have longer assignments, may meet only four days a week. After lunch, a student may have a science lab, a language lab, or other supplementary academic work. Then students have an hour of athletics, perhaps a meeting with their adviser or study help from another teacher, and some independent time in which they are expected to start their homework for the next day. Day students generally leave around 5:00. Dinner is at 6:00, and evenings are devoted to study. On Wednesday and Friday afternoons, there are fine-arts classes in such subjects as drawing, photography, ceramics, digital art, and art and music appreciation, and students may leave the campus for nearby shopping centers.

WEEKEND LIFE

Weekends are loosely structured. As long as students are in good standing academically, they have considerable freedom and may leave the campus for movies, shopping, and the like. A driver is employed on the weekends to provide student transportation. Older students may keep cars on campus at the discretion of the School. The sports facilities are available for weekend use. Events and outings are organized almost every weekend by the Student Council, the Student Activities Committee, and the on-campus staff.

SUMMER PROGRAMS

The School organizes both domestic and international study trips during school breaks or the summer, often led by faculty members. Trips may augment a particular field of study or present a new challenge. Some students choose to attend college classes during the summer months, work at internships, or volunteer over an extended period of time in their home community.

COSTS AND FINANCIAL AID

Charges for 2013–14 are $42,500 for full boarding international students, $41,500 for full boarding U.S. students, $39,250 for weekday boarding, and $23,550 for day students. This includes room plus all meals for boarders and all lunches for day students. An additional $1,800 should cover the cost of books, supplies, activity and technology fees, and other school expenses. This figure does not include travel expenses, weekly allowances, or College Board and Advanced Placement examinations for juniors. In addition, international students will be charged approximately $1,200 for health insurance.

A $2,000 deposit, nonrefundable but credited to tuition, is required when a student enrolls. The balance of the tuition is paid through various payment plans.

Financial aid is available, based on a family's need. Thirty-three percent of the student body currently receives some financial aid; the total amount awarded is more than $592,000. An applicant's family must file a statement with the School and Student Service, and this information is used in judging need. Many middle-income families receive some assistance.

ADMISSIONS INFORMATION

The School looks for evidence of strong intellect, liveliness, energy, ambition, and curiosity. Strong grades and test scores are important considerations but not always the deciding ones. A candidate should submit the results of the Secondary School Admission Test (SSAT); international students submit the results of the TOEFL. About 60 percent of those who complete the application process are accepted.

APPLICATION TIMETABLE

Inquiries and applications are welcome at any time, but the School has three rounds of admissions: early decision applicants submit their materials by mid-December and receive an answer in early January; regular decision applicants submit their materials by mid-February and receive an answer in early March; after April, applications for any remaining openings are considered as they are received. As part of the application process, prospective students usually spend a day at the School visiting classes, having lunch, and spending time with the admissions staff to ask questions and have an interview. Skype interviews are conducted with out-of-town applicants. There is a $40 fee for domestic applications, and a $100 fee for international applications.

ADMISSIONS CORRESPONDENCE

Anne Barenkamp, Director of Admissions
Thomas Jefferson School
4100 South Lindbergh Boulevard
St. Louis, Missouri 63127
United States
Phone: 314-843-4151
Fax: 314-843-3527
E-mail: admissions@tjs.org
Website: http://www.tjs.org

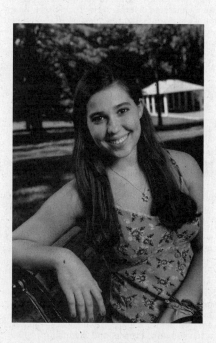

TRINITY–PAWLING SCHOOL

Pawling, New York

Type: Boys', boarding (9–PG) and day (7–PG) college-preparatory school
Grades: 7–12, postgraduate year
Enrollment: 310
Head of School: Archibald A. Smith III, Headmaster

THE SCHOOL

The Pawling School was founded in 1907 by Dr. Frederick Gamage. In 1946, it was renamed Trinity-Pawling School in recognition of its ties with Trinity School of New York City. In 1978, Trinity-Pawling School became a separate educational and corporate entity. Trinity-Pawling's Episcopal background is reflected in daily chapel services and course offerings in religion, ethics, and psychology.

The School is located 68 miles north of New York City along the Connecticut border; regular train service is available from Grand Central Station to Pawling (population 5,000). The campus, set on 140 acres of rolling hills, is just over an hour's drive from New York's major airports. On vacations, the School transports students to and from the airports and train stations.

It is Trinity-Pawling's belief that an appreciation of one's own worth can best be discovered by experiencing the worth of others, by understanding the value of one's relationship with others, and by acquiring a sense of self-confidence that comes through living and working competently at the level of one's own potential. Trinity-Pawling respects and recognizes the differences in individuals and the different processes required to achieve their educational potential.

The School is governed by a self-perpetuating 26-member Board of Trustees. The School raises more than $1 million in annual giving, in part from its more than 5,000 alumni. The School's endowment exceeds $33 million, and its operating budget for 2013–14 is more than $10 million.

Trinity-Pawling is accredited by the New York State Association of Independent Schools and chartered by the New York State Board of Regents. It is a member of the National Association of Independent Schools, the Secondary School Admission Test Board, the New York State Association of Independent Schools (NYSAIS), and the National Association of Episcopal Schools.

ACADEMIC PROGRAM

To graduate from Trinity-Pawling, a student must obtain a minimum of 112 credits in eight disciplines to earn a diploma. A full-year course is worth 6 credits, and a term course (trimester) is worth 2 credits. If a student enters after grade 9, his school record is evaluated and translated into Trinity-Pawling's system.

Students are required to complete 90 credits in the following subjects: 24 credits in English; 18 credits in mathematics; 18 credits in a laboratory science; 18 credits in history; 12 credits in a foreign language (excluding Language Program students); 6 credits in fine, performing, or studio arts (music, art, drafting, or drama); 4 credits in religion or philosophy; and 2 credits in health. Additionally, students must take 22 credits of elective courses. Advanced Placement courses are offered in English, U.S. history, European history, economics, chemistry, physics, biology, environmental science, mathematics, computer science, Latin, French, and Spanish.

Students carry a minimum of five courses per term. Evening study periods, held in student residences, are supervised by dorm masters. Students with academic difficulty have a formally supervised study hall. Teachers are available to give students extra help at any time that is agreeable to both. Reports are posted online for parents three times per term. Trinity-Pawling uses a number grading system (0–100) in which 60 is passing, 80 qualifies for honors, and 85 qualifies for high honors.

In addition to academic grades, the School utilizes a unique effort system to rank students based on overall effort in many aspects of School life, including academics, athletics, clubs, and dormitory life. A student's privileges are then tied to his overall effort ranking. This program is designed to work in conjunction with the School's philosophy of encouraging each student to work toward his own personal potential.

The Language Program, open to a maximum of 40 students, is initiated in the ninth and tenth grades. A modification of the Orton-Gillingham method, it strives to retrain students with developmental dyslexia. First-year students work in pairs with tutors. In addition, they take a skills-oriented language arts course. Phonetics, sequencing ideas, handwriting, memorization, and other language skills are emphasized. The second-year student is placed in an analytical writing class in addition to a skills-level English class. All students in the program also take basic science, mathematics, and history courses. The program's goal is to enable students to complete Trinity-Pawling's regular college-preparatory curriculum. Students in the program are not required to take a foreign language but may elect to do so.

FACULTY AND ADVISERS

There are 60 full-time members of the faculty, all of whom reside on the campus. Members of the teaching faculty hold sixty-one baccalaureate and thirty-two graduate degrees. All participate in counseling and advising students. The School actively supports advanced study for its teachers during summers and other holidays.

Archibald A. Smith III was appointed Headmaster in 1990, after having served at Trinity-Pawling as a chemistry teacher, Director of College Placement, and Assistant Headmaster at various times since 1975. He is a graduate of St. John's School in Houston, Texas; Trinity College (Hartford) (B.S., 1972); and Wesleyan University (M.S., 1980). His career also includes teaching at the Northwood School in Lake Placid, New York. Mr. Smith is the past president of the New York State Association of Independent Schools and a member of the Accreditation Council of NYSAIS. He is a trustee of Dutchess Day School, a trustee of the International Boys School Coalition, a trustee of the Parents' League of New York, and is a member of the Headmasters Association.

COLLEGE ADMISSION COUNSELING

Trinity-Pawling's Director of College Counseling works closely with other administrators and faculty members to advise and aid students and their families with college placement.

Individual meetings and group workshops are held on a regular basis, and more than 100 college representatives visit the campus each fall for presentations and interviews. More than 95 percent of the class of 2012 gained admission to their first- or second-choice college.

All of the 2012 graduates earned college or university acceptances. Among those they attend are Berkeley, Carnegie Mellon, Columbia, Cornell, George Washington, Northwestern, Occidental, Princeton, Purdue, Skidmore, Syracuse, Trinity, USC, U.S. Military Academy at West Point, and U.S. Naval Academy at Annapolis.

STUDENT BODY AND CONDUCT

Boarding students number 240, and day students number 60. Students come from twenty-nine states and thirteen countries. Students from minority groups make up 10 percent of the total enrollment. Students who choose Trinity-Pawling tend to desire a reasonably structured community that is dedicated to individual growth. A strong academic program in harmony with fine athletics and activities programs brings the School together. The School seeks students who want to actively pursue their academic and social development in a caring atmosphere.

Major violations of community rules are handled by a Faculty-Student Disciplinary Committee, which makes recommendations to the Headmaster. Less serious breaches are handled by the Dean of Students and others.

The Student-Faculty Senate is composed of School prefects and elected student and faculty representatives. The senate works to develop self-government, plans School activities, and fosters a bond between the students and the faculty. It consists of six committees, each with a responsibility for specific areas of School life.

ACADEMIC FACILITIES

The Dann Building (1964) and the Science and Technology Center (2002) house classrooms and science and computer labs. The Art Building, completed in 2004, houses the fine arts, theater, and music programs. This building contains a theater that is used for student productions, lectures, and visiting professional performances. The library features an online catalog, more than 28,000 volumes, and available computers. It is located in the historic Cluett Building, which also contains administrative offices and the student center.

BOARDING AND GENERAL FACILITIES

Students reside in single or double rooms in eighteen dormitory units located in eight buildings, including Starr Hall (1984), Starr East (1987), and Cluett (renovated 1995). Each is under the supervision of 1 or more faculty members aided by senior proctors. Students are allowed to choose roommates, and, whenever possible, housing choice is granted. Students are grouped in housing units according to grade level. A student's dorm master is usually his adviser, so a strong personal relationship often develops. Trinity-Pawling stresses the value of close student-faculty relationships.

Students enjoy a School store and snack bar that are open daily. The Scully Dining Hall was completed in 2009. Medical services are provided by the Health Center, staffed by a resident nurse and a doctor who makes daily visits. Several hospitals serve the area. Trinity-Pawling is within walking distance of the village of Pawling.

ATHLETICS

Trinity-Pawling is a member of the New England Private School Athletic Conference and the Founders League, which affords it the opportunity to play schools in New England, such as Avon, Choate, Hotchkiss, Kent, Loomis Chaffee, Salisbury, Taft, and Westminster. Because the School believes that athletics and physical development are key ingredients in a student's growth, all students are required to participate in the program during the school year. Three or four levels of teams are formed in each interscholastic sport, including baseball, basketball, cross-country, football, golf, hockey, lacrosse, soccer, squash, tennis, track and field, and wrestling. Also offered at both the interscholastic and intramural levels are running, skiing, and weight training.

The Carleton Gymnasium contains a 50-foot by 90-foot basketball court with two cross courts for practice. The lower floor and wing contain weight-training rooms, five international squash courts, and locker rooms. Adjacent to the gymnasium complex is a new turf football field which was completed for the opening of school in 2013. There are also six soccer fields, an additional football field, baseball diamonds, an all-weather track, nine brand-new tennis courts completed in summer 2013, three lacrosse fields, ponds for skating and fishing, the McGraw wrestling pavilion, and the enclosed Tirrell Hockey Rink, which underwent a $1 million renovation in 2007.

EXTRACURRICULAR OPPORTUNITIES

Each student is encouraged to participate in one or more of the twenty-four activities offered on the campus. These activities are often initiated and directed by the students with the guidance of an interested faculty adviser. Among the offerings are the student newspaper, Model United Nations, the Minority Student Union, the yearbook, the choir, the photography club, the dramatic club, the chess club, the computer club, the fishing club, foreign language clubs, jazz groups, and the outing club.

Trinity-Pawling encourages student initiative in starting new activities.

The School sponsors regular trips to nearby areas of educational and cultural interest, including museums and theaters in New York City. Annual events include Parents' Weekend, Junior Parents' Weekend, and several alumni functions. The concert series, offering five concerts annually, brings a rich variety of musical talent to the campus during the school year.

Each student participates in the work program that emphasizes the School's policy of self-responsibility and economy of operation. Boys assist with parts of the routine maintenance work throughout the buildings and on the grounds.

DAILY LIFE

At 8 a.m., three mornings a week, a brief community chapel service is held for all students. A more formal Episcopal service is held for the entire school mid-morning on Tuesdays. Classes are scheduled from 8:20 until 2:40 four days a week and until noon on Wednesdays and Saturdays. Wednesday and Saturday afternoons are reserved for interscholastic sports events. Athletic practices take place in the afternoon, while most extracurricular activities are scheduled in the evening. Lunches are generally served cafeteria-style, dinners sit-down family-style. Students are required to study from 8:00 to 9:30 in their rooms, the library, or the study hall, depending upon their academic status.

WEEKEND LIFE

Dances, plays, concerts, trips to New York City, and informal activities are planned for weekends. The Student-Faculty Senate organizes and plans many of the weekend activities. Social activities are also arranged with girls' schools in the area. Weekend leaves from the School are based upon a group rating, which encompasses a student's record in academic effort and achievement, general citizenship, and dormitory life. In general, as the group rating increases, so do the amount and nature of privileges. Students are evaluated twice per term.

COSTS AND FINANCIAL AID

Charges for 2013–14 are $51,000 for boarding students, $36,250 for day students in ninth through twelfth grade, and $24,750 for day students in seventh and eighth grade. Extra

expenses total approximately $2,000 per year. The Language Program is an additional $5,300–$7,600 per year, depending on the grade. A tuition payment plan and tuition insurance are available.

Thirty-five percent of the students receive a total of over $3.3 million in financial aid each year. Trinity-Pawling subscribes to the School and Student Service for Financial Aid and grants aid on the basis of need.

ADMISSIONS INFORMATION

Trinity-Pawling seeks the well-rounded student who will both gain from and give to the School. New students are accepted in all grades; a limited number are accepted for the postgraduate year. Selection is based upon all-around qualifications without regard to race, color, creed, or national origin. Candidates must submit a complete transcript plus two or three teachers' recommendations, have a personal interview at the School, and take the SSAT. Candidates for the Language Program are asked to have completed a Wechsler Test (WISC-R). International students are required to sit for the TOEFL test.

In 2012, there were 350 applicants, of whom 250 were accepted and 110 enrolled.

APPLICATION TIMETABLE

Initial inquiries are welcome at any time. Campus tours and interviews (allow 1½–2 hours) can be arranged by appointment, Monday through Friday, 8:30–1:30, and on Saturday, 8:30–11. All candidates must have an interview. The completed forms must be submitted by the February 1 deadline and must be accompanied by a nonrefundable fee of $50 ($100 for international students).

Fall is the usual time for applying, and notification of acceptance begins in early March. Parents are expected to reply to acceptances one month after notification.

ADMISSIONS CORRESPONDENCE

MacGregor Robinson
Assistant Headmaster for External Affairs
Trinity-Pawling School
Pawling, New York 12564
United States
Phone: 845-855-4825
Fax: 845-855-4827
E-mail: denisepalmer@trinitypawling.org
Website: http://www.trinitypawling.org

THE UNIVERSITY OF CHICAGO LABORATORY SCHOOLS

Chicago, Illinois

Type: Coeducational, day, college-preparatory school
Grades: N–12
Enrollment: Approximately 1,850
Head of School: Dr. David W. Magill

THE SCHOOL

The University of Chicago Laboratory Schools (Lab) is an independent, coeducational day school enrolling approximately 1,850 students from nursery school through twelfth grade. Founded in 1896 by John Dewey, Lab's progressive education is broad and deep, with an emphasis on the arts, humanities, math, and science. Lab is a division of the University of Chicago, and Lab students benefit from access to University professors, classes, and facilities. Lab prepares students to be critical thinkers who are equipped to handle the rigors of a complex and changing world. Each year, Lab graduates matriculate at top four-year colleges throughout the United States and abroad.

Lab is approved or accredited by the Independent Schools Association of the Central States, North Central Association of Colleges and Schools, and the Illinois Department of Education. Lab is a member of the National Association of Independent Schools.

ACADEMIC PROGRAM

The Laboratory Schools do not specialize in a particular academic area. Rather, Lab prepares students to be creative, in-depth thinkers who are lifelong learners, ready to face the challenges of an increasingly complex global society.

All students are required to take math, science, English, history, a world language (French, German, Spanish, Latin, and Mandarin), computer science, physical education, music, community learning, and fine arts. In addition, high school students may enroll in University of Chicago classes, utilize University libraries, and intern with University of Chicago faculty members. Lab graduates enter a variety of fields, including education, law, medicine, and others.

Students at University High (U-High) pursue a comprehensive liberal arts program that emphasizes analytical reading, writing, research, and strong math and science skills. Through discussion, hands-on lab work, research, and other school work, Lab students learn to read closely, form independent ideas, and write analytically. Approximately 90 percent enroll in at least one of the eight Advanced Placement or ten advanced topics courses.

FACULTY AND ADVISERS

Approximately 234 teachers, counselors, librarians, and assistant teachers comprise the faculty at the Laboratory Schools. Most

have higher education degrees and many have doctoral degrees.

A total of 9 current or former teachers throughout the Laboratory Schools have won the coveted Golden Apple Award for excellence in teaching, awarded by Illinois' Golden Apple Foundation, more than any other school.

COLLEGE ADMISSION COUNSELING

Three full-time college placement counselors provide step-by-step guidance to juniors, seniors, and their parents as they navigate the college admission and selection process. This includes conducting workshops on various college topics and directing families to appropriate information at each stage of the process. In 2007, the *Wall Street Journal* named the Laboratory Schools' college placement office the fourth best in the nation.

STUDENT BODY AND CONDUCT

Lab enrolls approximately 1,850 students from nursery school through twelfth grade, with a largely equal number of boys and girls. Lab students speak more than forty languages at home, and identify themselves as having fifty-nine different nationalities. The Nursery/Kindergarten program enrolls approximately 400 students, the Primary School (grades 1 and 2) enrolls approximately 230 students, the Lower School (grades 3–5) enrolls approximately 350 students, and the Middle School (grades 6–8) enrolls approximately 380 students. Lab's high school, University High (U-High), enrolls approximately 500 students. Lab students live throughout the greater Chicago area, with approximately half coming from the Hyde Park/Kenwood area. Approximately 50 percent of Lab students have parents who are affiliated with the University of Chicago.

ACADEMIC FACILITIES

The Laboratory Schools consist of Earl Shapiro Hall (Nursery 3 through grade 2) and the Historic Campus (grades 3–12). The Historic Campus consists of the Lower School (grades 3–5), the Middle School (grades 6–8), and the High School (grades 9–12). The lower, middle, and high school libraries together contain more than 100,000 volumes. Lab has art studios, a darkroom, music classrooms and practice rooms, a state-of-the-art language lab, a dance studio, and a theater. Wireless Internet access is available for students and faculty throughout the school.

Earl Shapiro Hall (ESH), Lab's newest building, opened in fall 2013 and is a significant addition to the Laboratory Schools. The ESH is a state-of-the-art facility that is uniquely designed for the academic and social needs of the youngest learners in Nursery/Kindergarten and Primary School.

Athletic facilities are located in Sunny and Kovler Gymnasium, steps away from the Historic Campus. Earl Shapiro Hall also has its own gymnasium, which is specifically designed to meet the needs of younger children. In addition, Lab students have access to the academic and athletic facilities at the University of Chicago.

ATHLETICS

The 2013–14 school year marks the 110th year that the Laboratory Schools have offered students interscholastic athletic competition. During the previous year, approximately 660 students from middle through high school competed in the athletic program on one or more of Lab's forty-four different teams. Over the last four years Lab's varsity teams have won seven sectional and sixteen regional championships in nine different varsity sports. Lab's no-cut policy ensures that all students may participate in any sport they choose. The Laboratory Schools are part of the Illinois High School Association (IHSA).

EXTRACURRICULAR OPPORTUNITIES

In the high school, students run more than forty school-sponsored organizations, ranging from religious and ethnic clubs to activities in the arts, culture, academics, philanthropy, and social activism. University High students devote significant time to many different extracurricular activities: joining sports, math, science, debate, or Model UN teams; writing and publishing the School's newspaper or yearbook; serving in student government or community service roles; and participating in theater productions or musical performances. Many of these extracurricular activities begin in the Middle School.

DAILY LIFE

Because Lab begins with children who are 3 years old, and slightly over half continue at Lab until they graduate from U-High in twelfth grade, there are enormous variances in the students' daily schedules and activities.

The nursery and kindergarten classrooms at Lab are busy, with many different activities going on at one time. This is Lab's negotiated curriculum in action: teachers prepare an environment filled with possibilities and encourage choice, initiative, exploration, and collaboration.

Lab's Primary and Lower School curricula (first through fifth grades) are designed to help children master the skills that will serve as the foundation to their intellectual life. Children entering the Middle School years (sixth through eighth grade) begin an intense period of social, emotional, physical, moral, and intellectual growth.

U-Highers are an independent group whose high expectations go hand in hand with a demanding workload and a great deal of personal freedom. Each year, Lab students are better able to think for themselves, challenge assumptions, and, most importantly, take on increasing levels of responsibility for their own education.

SUMMER PROGRAMS

Summer Lab is a six-week program that includes Summer School, Adventure Kids Day Camp, Sports Camps, Fun in the Sun, and Summer Lab on Stage. Summer Lab Field Study stages domestic and international summer travel. Summer Lab embodies the notion that love of learning never goes on vacation. Approximately 1,000 students, from ages 3 to 18, participated last summer in the rich and diverse program, mixing Labbies with children from all around the city of Chicago, the United States, and the world.

COSTS AND FINANCIAL AID

Tuition costs for the 2013–14 academic year are as follows: $17,832 for the nursery school half-day program; $25,296 for the nursery and kindergarten full-day program; $25,296 for grades 1–5; $27,096 for grades 6–8; and $28,290 for grades 9–12.

Each year, Lab provides financial assistance to help meet the needs of students and their families. Lab does not have a specific income threshold for financial aid. Rather, the Financial Aid Committee reviews a family's entire financial picture, including income, expenses, and other circumstances. Financial aid awards are not automatically renewed; families are required to reapply for aid each year. Awards are recalculated annually based on the most recent financial data.

ADMISSIONS INFORMATION

Every applicant family receives personal attention, including a meeting with an admissions officer, a tour of the schools, and an opportunity to interact with other students and faculty. Lab believes that each applicant is unique and possesses special qualities that cannot always be captured by test scores and applications alone. Lab learns about its applicants through playgroups, classroom visits, interviews, shadow days, and tours. Applicant families also learn more about Lab's special character through this process.

APPLICATION TIMETABLE

Historically, most students enter Lab at either Nursery 3 (3 years old) or ninth grade and begin the application process in August or September of the year prior to enrollment. Admissions deadlines and details on the application process for all grades are available on Lab's website at www.ucls. uchicago.edu.

ADMISSIONS CORRESPONDENCE

Irene M. Reed, Executive Director
Admissions and Financial Aid
University of Chicago Laboratory Schools
1362 East 59th Street
Chicago, Illinois 60637
United States
Phone: 773-702-9451
Fax: 773-702-1520
E-mail: admissions@ucls.uchicago.edu
Website: http://www.ucls.uchicago.edu

THE WILLISTON NORTHAMPTON SCHOOL

Easthampton, Massachusetts

Type: Coeducational boarding and day college-preparatory school
Grades: 7–PG: Middle School, 7–8; Upper School, 9–12, postgraduate year
Enrollment: School total: 530; Upper School: 450
Head of School: Robert W. Hill III, Head of School

THE SCHOOL

Founded through the merger agreement between Williston Academy (1841) and Northampton School for Girls (1924), the Williston Northampton School is a student-centered coeducational institution of 450 boarding and day students in grades 9 through postgraduate from twenty-five states and twenty-seven countries. The school's students are 65 percent boarding boys and girls and 35 percent day students. Its mission is to inspire students to live with purpose, passion, and integrity.

The school is located in the Pioneer Valley of Western Massachusetts on 125 acres near the base of Mount Tom, 90 miles west of Boston, and 150 miles north of New York. Within a 15-mile radius are the Five Colleges: Smith, Mount Holyoke, Hampshire, and Amherst Colleges, and the University of Massachusetts Amherst. Williston's location has led the school to form an academic collaboration with the five colleges to enrich the educational experience of its students. The school's distinctive Williston+ program brings the resources and faculty of the local Five College consortium to the curriculum, and the Williston Scholars program enables students to pursue a specific area of study through course work and independent projects.

The current endowment is estimated at $40 million. The school's alumni, families, and friends contributed more than $1.5 million to the Annual Fund last year.

Williston is accredited by the New England Association of Schools and Colleges and is affiliated with the National Association of Independent Schools, the Association of Independent Schools of New England, the College Board, the School and College Conference on English, the Art Association of New England Preparatory Schools, and the Council for Advancement and Support of Education.

ACADEMIC PROGRAM

Williston's outstanding facilities and the exceptional recreational and cultural offerings nearby provide the setting for an outstanding education. Through its unique Williston+ Program, the school provides superior college preparation by bringing the rich resources of the nearby Five Colleges into the classroom to enrich the school's curriculum.

At the heart of the school is a strong and varied academic program that seeks to strengthen, expand, and encourage students' skills and interests in the essential disciplines. Care is taken to place each student in the courses and sections most appropriate to his or her abilities. An average class size of 13 students enables faculty members to learn each student's abilities, and the flexibility of the program makes it possible for the school to structure programs that can best meet every individual student's needs. In addition, Williston offers numerous opportunities in competitive athletics, the arts, and leadership.

The school believes that each student should experience as many academic and creative disciplines as possible while they are at Williston. Therefore, Williston expects each of its students not only to satisfy the minimum basic requirements of 4 years of English, 3 years of math, 2 of science, 2 of a foreign language, and 2 in the social sciences, but also to select two trimester courses from the area of fine and performing arts. Students may also choose a 1-credit directed studies course on a special topic not included in the regular curriculum. Students generally take five courses per trimester.

Williston also offers 37 Advanced Placement (AP) and honors classes. Qualified students may elect to complete extra work in consultation with the teacher to prepare to take the AP exam in two additional subject areas. Of the 169 Williston students who took the AP exams in 2012, which is required of all AP students at the school, 78 percent received scores of 3 or higher, earning college credit at participating institutions. Students attaining honor grades are recognized at the end of each term. The highest honor is election to the Cum Laude Society and Williston's Cum Laude chapter—founded in 1906—is one of the oldest in the nation.

The Writing Center plays a central part in Williston's academic program. Located in the library, the Writing Center is staffed by members of the English department, as well as by highly qualified student writers who provide support for students at all levels, on any writing assignment. The goal is for students to build critical thinking skills and clarity of expression, both crucial tools that will be used again, in college and beyond. The Writing Center has over 1,000 visits annually.

Williston also offers the Writers' Workshop Series every fall. Founded by Williston parents and accomplished authors Madeleine Blais and Elinor Lipman, the Writers' Workshop Series has hosted a variety of distinguished writers who give a public reading and then work with students enrolled in the Writers' Workshop course on the craft of writing. Authors who have participated include Augusten Burroughs, Gregory Maguire, Sue Miller, Richard Russo, and Curtis Sittenfeld.

During the winter and spring trimesters, Williston hosts the Photographers' Lecture Series. Started in 2000, this lecture series features internationally acclaimed photojournalists, filmmakers, and commercial photographers who share their work and ideas with the community and Williston's advanced photography students. Past distinguished visiting photographers have included John Willis, Sean Kerman, Lori Grinker, Nina Berman, and David Burnett.

Students can participate in the Williston Scholars program, in which they work closely with a faculty member in a small-group, immersive exploration of a topic, cumulating in independent study projects. All courses take maximum advantage of Williston+ resources, and new courses become available each year. Recent Williston Scholars offerings include Colonial History of the Pioneer Valley, Contemporary Arts and Culture, and Sports Studies.

FACULTY AND ADVISERS

There are 70 full-time faculty members, and 61 percent hold advanced degrees (master's and doctorates). Almost half of the faculty lives in the school's dormitories. The school has established programs to support students with academic work, personal growth, and future educational goals and opportunities. Students each have a faculty adviser with whom they meet regularly and may also consult with the Dean of Students and Academic Dean. The school also employs the services of professional counselors in its Health and Wellness Services.

Williston's Ninth Grade Program is a unique program, designed to ease the transition for students from middle school to secondary school. The program includes an overnight orientation, special advisers, assemblies, and academic mentoring. The cornerstone of the program is C.O.R.E. (curiosity, organizations, reflection, and empathy). Each of these concepts is the focus of a special ninth grade–only assembly, where Williston adults and upperclass students address the ninth graders and discuss how these principles have helped them succeed. In addition, at the end of each trimester, the program holds assessment preparation clinics, where advisers outline for students the expectations for assessment periods and help the ninth graders fill out an hour-by-hour study schedule.

On July 1, 2010, Robert W. Hill III became Williston's nineteenth head of school. Mr. Hill came to Williston from the Carolina Day School in Asheville, North Carolina, where he served as Associate Head of School and Principal of the Upper School since 2007. Prior to 2007, he served for nine years at St. Paul's School (Concord, New Hampshire) in a variety of roles, including Academic Dean, Director of College Advising, and Associate Dean of Faculty. His tenure there also included responsibilities as an English teacher, varsity girls' squash coach, and dorm resident. Hill started his teaching career at Westminster School (Simsbury, Connecticut), where he taught for fifteen years. He received his B.A. cum laude from Middlebury College and earned his M.A. in English literature from Middlebury's Bread Loaf School of English.

COLLEGE COUNSELING

Williston provides a thorough and personalized college counseling program for every student, beginning in their junior year. Three full-time counselors work with the junior and senior classes. From the beginning, the counselors collaborate with both parents and students to establish a dialogue between the school and the family. During the junior year, counselors and faculty members meet with students to acquaint them with standardized test-taking, financial aid, roles and functions of college officials, and campus lifestyles. In addition, all juniors visit the Five Colleges and participate in mock interviews at the different campuses.

The 122 members of the Class of 2013 were accepted at over 450 colleges and universities, including Carleton, Cornell, Connecticut College, Kenyon, NYU, Stanford, Williams College, and the University of Pennsylvania.

STUDENT BODY AND CONDUCT

Most students enter Williston during the freshman or sophomore year. In 2013–14, grade 9 has 79 members (36 boys, 43 girls), of whom 37 are day students. Grade 10 has 111 members (60 boys, 51 girls), of whom 45 are day students. Grade 11 has 130 members (60 boys, 70 girls), of whom 40 are day students. Grade 12 has 136 members (61 boys, 75 girls), of whom 44 are day students. There are 14 postgraduate students. Eighteen percent of the students are members of minority groups. Students come from twenty-five states and twenty-seven countries.

The rules and regulations of the school provide clear guidelines for everyone living in the Williston community. It is expected that students will follow both the spirit and the letter of these regulations as described in the *Student Handbook*, which is provided to all enrolling students.

Students who are reported to have violated school rules and regulations meet with the Discipline Committee, made up of faculty and student representatives. The committee's decisions and recommendations are reviewed by the head of school, who makes the final decision in disciplinary matters.

ACADEMIC FACILITIES

The campus is located on approximately 125 acres. Its facilities include the Reed Campus Center, Scott Hall, the Boardman Theater, the Robert A. Ward Schoolhouse, the Robert Clapp Library, the Phillips Stevens Chapel, and the Whitaker-Bement Middle School Building.

BOARDING AND GENERAL FACILITIES

The buildings on campus include the Head's House, the Zachs Admission Center at the Homestead, the Chapel, the Birch Dining Commons, five dormitories with facilities for 25 to 50 students, five residence houses with boarding facilities for 8 to 12 students, and faculty homes. Ford Hall and Memorial Dorm each house 50 students. All dorm rooms allow wireless access to the campus computer network. A new ninth grade boys' dorm with housing for 32 students and three faculty families opened in 2008. The dorm, which is heated and cooled via seventeen geothermal wells, is the centerpiece of a planned residential quad.

Each dormitory or house is supervised by resident faculty houseparents to create an environment conducive to academic achievement and a warm and pleasant home atmosphere.

ATHLETICS

Sports are an integral part of student life at Williston, whether interscholastic or recreational. The school requires that each student be involved in the Afternoon Program in each of the three sports seasons or enrolled in an arts alternative. The athletics department instills the principles of fair play, good sportsmanship, teamwork, and respect for rules and authority. Most of the academic faculty members also coach competitive teams, and the Director of Athletics oversees the program.

Interscholastic teams for girls include crew, cross-country, field hockey, soccer, and volleyball in the fall; basketball, ice hockey, skiing, squash, swimming and diving, and wrestling in the winter; and crew, golf, lacrosse, softball, tennis, track, and water polo in the spring. Boys may elect crew, cross-country, football, soccer, or water polo; basketball, ice hockey, skiing, squash, swimming and diving, or wrestling; and baseball, crew, golf, lacrosse, tennis, or track. Horseback riding at a nearby stable and modern dance are available every season. Fitness training, aerobics, yoga, and self-defense are choices open to upperclass students.

The Athletic Center houses two basketball courts, a six-lane pool with a diving well, five international squash courts, a weight room and fitness center, a wrestling room, and a trainers' room staffed by two certified athletic trainers. Other facilities include a lighted, synthetic-surface football/lacrosse field with stadium seating; a dance studio; facility renovated hockey rink; twelve tennis courts; an all-weather running track that surrounds a synthetic surface field for field hockey, soccer, and lacrosse; more than 30 acres of playing fields; and a 3.4-mile cross-country course. In addition, the school's golf teams play on several golf courses in the Easthampton area, and the ski team competes on the slopes in the eastern Berkshires.

EXTRACURRICULAR OPPORTUNITIES

The countryside offers excellent climbing, biking, and skiing opportunities, and the proximity of the Five Colleges provides a culturally rich environment of fine museums, libraries, and theater programs as well. The cities of Northampton and Springfield, Massachusetts, and Hartford, Connecticut, are near enough so that concerts and activities there are as readily available, as are those at the local colleges.

DAILY LIFE

The academic day runs from 8:30 a.m. until 2:40 p.m. on Monday, Tuesday, Thursday, and Friday and until 12:25 p.m. on Wednesday. Classes are held every other Saturday morning as well. Students take five courses in a seven-period schedule, with classes lasting 60 minutes. All-school assemblies for announcements and special presentations are held once each week. Athletics are scheduled from the end of the class day until dinnertime. Except for theme-based formal dinners, most meals are served buffet-style. A free period immediately after classes end is frequently used for meetings of extracurricular organizations, library work, theater or music rehearsals, visiting between dormitories, or simply relaxing. Supervised evening study hours run from 8:00 to 10:00 p.m. All students are checked into the dorms at 8:00 p.m. by the dorm faculty.

WEEKEND LIFE

While the vast majority of students remain on campus, weekends at home or at the home of a friend are permitted with parental approval after all school obligations have been met. The Student Activities Director and students on the Activity Committee organize a variety of weekly activities, and students may take advantage of the events listed in the Five College calendar. Students travel off campus for college and professional athletic events, films, plays, dance performances, and concerts and to go skiing in Vermont. The many on-campus activities include dances and coffeehouse entertainment, talent shows, lectures by invited speakers, and a film series.

SUMMER PROGRAMS

Throughout the year, students have the opportunity to take part in several international excursions that enrich their studies. Trips to Canada and France during school vacations offer real-life practice for French language skills. A trip to Costa Rica allows students to perform community service while honing their Spanish. In the summer, the school also hosts many outside camps, offering theater, music, and athletics.

COSTS AND FINANCIAL AID

Tuition for boarders for 2013–14 is $50,900; for day students, it is $34,800. Additional expenses include a technology fee (which includes a device as part of the school's Curricular Technology Initiative), books, insurance, laundry, and other incidental expenses. Tuition payment and insurance plans are recommended upon request.

Financial aid is awarded on the basis of need. The grants totaled $5.7 million for 2013–14.

ADMISSIONS INFORMATION

Williston seeks students who are interested in a challenging academic program, who can demonstrate solid academic achievement and outstanding personal character. Students should also be involved and caring contributors to life beyond the classroom. Admission is based upon an evaluation of these traits, a personal interview, and satisfactory scores on the SSAT or TOEFL. In 2013–14, 160 new students were enrolled in the Upper School.

APPLICATION TIMETABLE

The fall or winter prior to a candidate's prospective admission is usually the best time for a visit, which includes a faculty and student-guided tour of the school and an interview. The Admission Office is open Monday through Friday, from 8:30 a.m. to 4:30 p.m. during the academic year and 8:00 a.m. to 4:00 p.m. in the summer months, and on alternate Saturday mornings during the academic year.

An application for admission should be submitted by January 15 along with a nonrefundable fee of $50. The school abides by the March 10 notification date. After that date, a rolling admission plan is in effect.

ADMISSIONS CORRESPONDENCE

Christopher J. Dietrich, Director of Admission and Financial Aid
The Williston Northampton School
19 Payson Avenue
Easthampton, Massachusetts 01027
United States
Phone: 413-529-3241
Fax: 413-527-9494
E-mail: admissions@williston.com
Website: http://www.williston.com

YORK PREPARATORY SCHOOL

New York, New York

Type: Coeducational day college-preparatory school
Grades: 6–12: Middle School, 6–8; Upper School, 9–12
Enrollment: 355
Head of School: Ronald P. Stewart, Headmaster

THE SCHOOL

York Prep is a college-preparatory school where contemporary methods enliven a strong, academically challenging, traditional curriculum. In a city known for its diversity of private schools, York Prep has developed a unique program that leads students to their highest potential. The School's approach emphasizes independent thought, builds confidence, and sends graduates on to the finest colleges and universities. At York, every student finds opportunities to flourish. York Prep believes that success breeds success, and excellence in academics, arts, or sports creates self-confidence that enhances all aspects of life, both in and out of the classroom.

York Prep was established in 1969 by its current Headmaster, Ronald P. Stewart, and his wife, Jayme Stewart, Director of College Guidance. Situated on West 68th Street between Columbus Avenue and Central Park West, the School is well served by public transportation. Consequently, it attracts students from all over the metropolitan area. York Prep takes full advantage of the prime location, with regular visits to museums, parks, and theaters, all of which are easily accessible.

York Prep is approved by the New York State Board of Regents and accredited by the Middle States Association of Colleges and Schools.

ACADEMIC PROGRAM

The curriculum is designed to develop the superior academic skills necessary for future success. Close attention to each student's needs ensures that progress toward personal excellence is carefully guided.

Students must complete 21 credits for graduation: 4 in English, 4 in math, 4 in science, 4 in history, a minimum of 3 in foreign language, 1 in art or music, and ½ in health.

Eleventh and twelfth graders choose from a number of course offerings in every subject area. In addition to selecting one course from each required category, a student must choose an elective from a variety of options that range from the creative and performing arts to the analytical sciences. Students are required to carry at least five major subjects a year plus physical education.

York Prep is proud of its commitment to community service. Student volunteer work benefits others, helps students realize their full potential, builds a well-rounded individual, and establishes a closer relationship between the school and community. Colleges expect students to have volunteer experience and York Prep College

Guidance strongly urges students to perform 25 hours of community service per year during high school as a mark of integrity, responsibility, and citizenship.

Classes at York are small—the average class has 15 students. There are close student-teacher relations and all students begin their day with a morning "house" period. Each student's academic and social progress is carefully monitored by the teachers, advisers, and deans of the Upper and Middle Schools. The deans, in turn, keep the Headmaster and the Principal informed at weekly meetings. In addition, the Headmaster and Principal maintain close relationships with the students. All of York's administrators, including the Headmaster and Principal, teach courses and are readily available to students and parents alike. At the close of each day, there is a period when students may go to faculty members or advisers for help.

Parents are kept informed of a student's progress through individual reports posted on "Edline," a component of the York Prep website, every Friday. Each family signs in with a unique password to see their child's progress in all academic subjects. The annual Curriculum Night, in which parents become students for an evening by attending their child's truncated classes, provides a good overview of the course work and the faculty members. Parent involvement is encouraged, and there is an active Parents' Association.

FACULTY AND ADVISERS

York Prep is proud of having maintained a stable faculty of outstanding and dedicated individuals. New teachers join the staff periodically, creating a nice balance between youth and experience.

There are 64 full-time faculty members, including 2 college guidance counselors, 15 reading and learning specialists, 2 computer specialists, and a librarian.

Mr. Ronald P. Stewart, the founding Headmaster, is a graduate of Oxford University (B.A., 1965; M.A., 1966; B.C.L., 1968), where he also taught.

COLLEGE ADMISSION COUNSELING

York Prep has a notable college guidance program. Mrs. Jayme Stewart, the Director of College Guidance, is well known for her expertise, experience, and authorship of *How to Get into the College of Your Choice.* She meets with all tenth graders to outline the program and then meets individually with eleventh graders and their parents. Extensive meetings continue through the twelfth grade

on an individual basis. In addition, the eleventh and twelfth graders take college guidance as a course where they write their essays, research colleges, and complete their applications during school hours.

One hundred percent of York Prep's graduating students attend college. The ultimate aim of the college guidance program is the placement of each student in the college best suited to him or her. More than 85 percent of York Prep graduates are accepted to, attend, and finish at their first- or second-choice college. Graduates are currently attending schools that include Barnard, Berkeley, Bowdoin, Colgate, Columbia, Cornell, Franklin and Marshall, Hamilton, Harvard, Hobart, Johns Hopkins, MIT, Oberlin, Pennsylvania, Skidmore, Vassar, Wesley, and the University of Michigan. Numerous college representatives visit the School regularly to meet with interested students.

STUDENT BODY AND CONDUCT

There are 355 students enrolled at York Prep. York Prep students reside in all five boroughs of New York City as well as Long Island, northern New Jersey, and Westchester County. The School has a student code of conduct and a dress code. The elected student council is also an integral part of life at York Prep.

ACADEMIC FACILITIES

Located steps from Central Park at 40 West 68th Street, York Prep is a seven-story granite building housing two modern science laboratories, state-of-the-art computer equipment, performance and art studios, and a sprung hardwood gymnasium with weight and locker room facilities. The classrooms are spacious and airy, carpeted, and climate controlled. All classrooms have computers, audiovisual (AV) projectors, and interactive white boards. High-speed Internet access is available for the entire School and enables students to e-mail their teachers and review homework assignments. The building is wheelchair accessible and is located near Lincoln Center on a safe and lovely tree-lined street.

ATHLETICS

All students are required to take courses in physical education and health each year. A varied and extensive program and after-school selection offer students the opportunity to participate in competitive, noncompetitive, team, and individual sports.

York Prep is a playing member of several athletics leagues.

EXTRACURRICULAR OPPORTUNITIES

The Student Council organizes regular social events and trips. The School provides a wide range of extracurricular activities, including Model UN, golf, electric blues band, beekeeping, and a drama club.

DAILY LIFE

The School day begins at 8:40 with a 10-minute house period. Academic classes of 42-minute duration begin at 8:56. There is a midmorning break at 10:24. Lunch period is from 12:08 to 12:50, Mondays through Thursdays, and classes end at 3:12. Following dismissal, teachers are available for extra help. During this time, clubs and sports teams also meet. On Fridays the school day ends at 1:35.

SUMMER PROGRAMS

The School provides workshops during the summer, both in study skills and in academic courses, most of which are set up on an individual tutorial basis. In addition, the athletic department provides summer sports camps.

COSTS AND FINANCIAL AID

Tuition for the 2013–14 academic year ranged from $40,500 to $41,200. More than 30 percent of the student body receives some financial assistance. During the previous year, $1 million was offered in scholarship assistance.

ADMISSIONS INFORMATION

York Prep seeks to enroll students of above-average intelligence with the will and ability to complete college-preparatory work. Students are accepted on the basis of their applications, ISEE or SSAT test scores, writing samples, and interviews.

APPLICATION TIMETABLE

York conforms to the notification guidelines established by the Independent Schools Admissions Association of Greater New York. Subsequent applications are processed on a rolling admissions basis. Requests for financial aid should be made at the time of application for entrance.

ADMISSIONS CORRESPONDENCE

Elizabeth Norton, Director of Enrollment
Cathy Minaudo, Director of Admissions
York Preparatory School
40 West 68th Street
New York, New York 10023
United States
Phone: 212-362-0400
Fax: 212-362-7424
E-mail: enorton@yorkprep.org
         cminaudo@yorkprep.org
Website: http://www.yorkprep.org

Special Needs Schools

ACACIA ACADEMY

6425 South Willow Springs Road
Lagrange Highlands, Illinois 60525
Head of School: Kathryn Fouks
General Information Coeducational day college-preparatory, general academic, arts, business, vocational, technology, and Transition Programs Ages 18-22 school; primarily serves underachievers, students with learning disabilities, individuals with Attention Deficit Disorder, individuals with emotional and behavioral problems, dyslexic students, and Autism Spectrum. Grades 1–12. Founded: 1970. Setting: suburban. Nearest major city is Chicago. 2 buildings on campus. Approved or accredited by Illinois Department of Education. Total enrollment: 100. Upper school average class size: 8. Upper school faculty-student ratio: 1:3. Upper School students typically attend 5 days per week. The average school day consists of 6 hours.
Faculty In upper school: 2 men, 8 women; 10 have advanced degrees.
Special Academic Programs Academic accommodation for the gifted; special instructional classes for deaf students, blind students.
College Admission Counseling 15 students graduated in 2013.
Student Life Upper grades have uniform requirement. Discipline rests primarily with faculty.
Summer Programs Remediation, enrichment, advancement, sports, art/fine arts, computer instruction programs offered; session focuses on academic and/or vocational development; held both on and off campus; held at Off site Vocational locations; accepts boys and girls; open to students from other schools. 60 students usually enrolled. 2014 schedule: June 19 to July 31.
Admissions Deadline for receipt of application materials: none. No application fee required. On-campus interview required.
Athletics Coed Interscholastic: baseball, flag football, softball, volleyball.
Computers Computer resources include Internet access, wireless campus network, Internet filtering or blocking technology. Campus intranet, student e-mail accounts, and computer access in designated common areas are available to students. Students grades are available online. The school has a published electronic and media policy.
Contact 708-579-9040. Fax: 708-579-5872. Website: www.acaciaacademy.com/

AMERICAN ACADEMY

12200 West Broward Boulevard
Plantation, Florida 33325
Head of School: William R. Laurie
General Information Coeducational day college-preparatory, arts, and technology school; primarily serves underachievers, students with learning disabilities, individuals with Attention Deficit Disorder, dyslexic students, and slow learners, and those with lowered self-esteem and confidence. Grades 1–12. Founded: 1965. Setting: suburban. Nearest major city is Fort Lauderdale. 40-acre campus. 11 buildings on campus. Approved or accredited by Association of Independent Schools of Florida, Southern Association of Colleges and Schools, and Florida Department of Education. Total enrollment: 297. Upper school average class size: 14. Upper school faculty-student ratio: 1:12. There are 175 required school days per year for Upper School students. Upper School students typically attend 5 days per week. The average school day consists of 7 hours and 15 minutes.
Upper School Student Profile Grade 9: 34 students (22 boys, 12 girls); Grade 10: 39 students (29 boys, 10 girls); Grade 11: 44 students (32 boys, 12 girls); Grade 12: 33 students (18 boys, 15 girls).
Faculty School total: 32. In upper school: 3 men, 18 women; 19 have advanced degrees.
Subjects Offered Algebra, American history, American literature, anatomy, art, band, biology, business mathematics, ceramics, chemistry, chorus, computer graphics, computer science, creative writing, drafting, drama, drawing, earth science, English, English literature, environmental science, fine arts, French, geometry, health, jazz, mathematics, music appreciation, oceanography, orchestra, photography, physical education, physical science, science, sculpture, Spanish, theater, vocal music, weight training, word processing, world geography, world history, world literature, writing, yearbook.
Graduation Requirements 20th century history, arts and fine arts (art, music, dance, drama), computer science, English, mathematics, physical education (includes health), science, social studies (includes history), must be accepted to a college, 120 community service hours over 4 years of high school. Community service is required.
Special Academic Programs Honors section; independent study; academic accommodation for the gifted, the musically talented, and the artistically talented; remedial reading and/or remedial writing; remedial math; programs in English, mathematics, general development for dyslexic students; ESL (2 students enrolled).
College Admission Counseling 35 students graduated in 2012; all went to college, including Broward College; Florida Atlantic University; Lynn University; Nova Southeastern University; Palm Beach State College.
Student Life Upper grades have uniform requirement, student council. Discipline rests primarily with faculty.
Tuition and Aid Day student tuition: $25,418–$29,399. Tuition installment plan (monthly payment plans, semester payment plan, annual payment plan). Tuition reduction for siblings, need-based scholarship grants available.

Admissions Traditional secondary-level entrance grade is 9. Psychoeducational evaluation, SAT and Slosson Intelligence required. Deadline for receipt of application materials: none. Application fee required: $100. On-campus interview required.
Athletics Interscholastic: baseball (boys), basketball (b,g), cheering (g), cross-country running (b,g), dance (g), dance squad (g), diving (b,g), football (b), golf (b,g), lacrosse (b,g), roller hockey (b), soccer (b,g), softball (g), swimming and diving (b,g), tennis (b,g), track and field (b,g), volleyball (b,g), weight lifting (b), weight training (b,g), winter soccer (b,g), wrestling (b). 7 PE instructors, 4 coaches, 1 athletic trainer.
Computers Computers are regularly used in graphic arts, literary magazine, newspaper, Web site design, word processing, writing, yearbook classes. Computer network features include on-campus library services, online commercial services, Internet access, Internet filtering or blocking technology, Questia. Student e-mail accounts and computer access in designated common areas are available to students. Students grades are available online. The school has a published electronic and media policy.
Contact William R. Laurie, President. 954-472-0022. Fax: 954-472-3088. Website: www.ahschool.com

ARROWSMITH SCHOOL

245 St. Clair Avenue West
Toronto, Ontario M4V 1R3, Canada
Head of School: Ms. Barbara Arrowsmith Young
General Information Coeducational day school; primarily serves underachievers, students with learning disabilities, and dyslexic students. Ungraded, ages 6–20. Founded: 1980. Setting: urban. 1 building on campus. Approved or accredited by Ontario Ministry of Education and Ontario Department of Education. Language of instruction: English. Total enrollment: 75. Upper school average class size: 20. Upper school faculty-student ratio: 1:10. Upper School students typically attend 5 days per week. The average school day consists of 7 hours and 30 minutes.
Faculty School total: 9. In upper school: 2 men, 2 women.
Special Academic Programs Remedial reading and/or remedial writing; remedial math; programs in English, mathematics for dyslexic students.
College Admission Counseling 10 students graduated in 2012; 8 went to college, including University of Toronto; York University. Other: 2 went to work.
Student Life Upper grades have specified standards of dress. Discipline rests primarily with faculty.
Tuition and Aid Day student tuition: CAN$22,000. Tuition installment plan (monthly payment plans).
Admissions Traditional secondary-level entrance age is 14. For fall 2012, 20 students applied for upper-level admission, 20 were accepted, 20 enrolled. Achievement tests, Cognitive Abilities Test, Differential Aptitude Test, Oral and Written Language Scales, Otis-Lennon Mental Ability Test, Raven (Aptitude Test); school's own exam, Reading for Understanding, school's own test, Wide Range Achievement Test, WISC/Woodcock-Johnson or writing sample required. Deadline for receipt of application materials: none. No application fee required. Interview required.
Computers Computer resources include Internet access.
Contact Ms. Daina Luszczek, Receptionist. 416-963-4962. Fax: 416-963-5017. E-mail: dluzchek@arrowsmithprogram.ca. Website: www.arrowsmithschool.org

ASSETS SCHOOL

One Ohana Nui Way
Honolulu, Hawaii 96818
Head of School: Mr. Paul Singer
General Information Coeducational day college-preparatory, arts, and technology school; primarily serves students with learning disabilities, individuals with Attention Deficit Disorder, dyslexic students, and gifted/talented students. Grades K–12. Founded: 1955. Setting: urban. 3-acre campus. 5 buildings on campus. Approved or accredited by Headmasters' Conference, The Hawaii Council of Private Schools, Western Association of Schools and Colleges, and Hawaii Department of Education. Member of National Association of Independent Schools. Endowment: $607,632. Total enrollment: 339. Upper school average class size: 7. Upper school faculty-student ratio: 1:8. There are 169 required school days per year for Upper School students. Upper School students typically attend 5 days per week. The average school day consists of 5 hours and 58 minutes.
Upper School Student Profile Grade 9: 24 students (19 boys, 5 girls); Grade 10: 30 students (20 boys, 10 girls); Grade 11: 34 students (21 boys, 13 girls); Grade 12: 29 students (20 boys, 9 girls).
Faculty School total: 68. In upper school: 9 men, 17 women; 18 have advanced degrees.
Subjects Offered 1 1/2 elective credits, algebra, American history, art, biology, business skills, calculus, chemistry, computer science, consumer education, creative writing, current events, earth science, economics, English, fine arts, fitness, general science, geometry, government/civics, health, humanities, independent study, integrated science, keyboarding, literature, marine biology, marine science, mathematics, music, music appreciation, philosophy, physical education, physics, pre-calculus, psychology,

sign language, social studies, Spanish, statistics, theater, trigonometry, women's health, woodworking, word processing, world history, world literature.

Graduation Requirements Arts and fine arts (art, music, dance, drama), biology, business skills (includes word processing), computer science, English, foreign language, mathematics, physical education (includes health), science, social studies (includes history), study skills, participation in mentorship program in 10th-12th grades.

Special Academic Programs Academic accommodation for the gifted; remedial reading and/or remedial writing; remedial math; programs in English, mathematics, general development for dyslexic students.

College Admission Counseling 24 students graduated in 2012; 23 went to college, including Chaminade University of Honolulu; Hawai'i Pacific University; McMaster University; Oregon State University; University of Hawaii at Manoa. Other: 1 went to work.

Student Life Upper grades have specified standards of dress, student council, honor system. Discipline rests primarily with faculty.

Tuition and Aid Day student tuition: $21,730. Tuition installment plan (monthly payment plans, individually arranged payment plans, semester payment plan). Need-based scholarship grants, partial tuition remission for children of staff available. In 2012–13, 37% of upper-school students received aid. Total amount of financial aid awarded in 2012–13: $170,000.

Admissions Traditional secondary-level entrance grade is 9. For fall 2012, 23 students applied for upper-level admission, 11 were accepted, 8 enrolled. WISC III or other aptitude measures; standardized achievement test required. Deadline for receipt of application materials: none. Application fee required: $75. On-campus interview required.

Athletics Interscholastic: baseball (boys), basketball (b,g), bowling (b,g), canoeing/kayaking (b,g), cheering (g), cross-country running (b,g), diving (b,g), football (b), golf (b,g), gymnastics (g), judo (b,g), kayaking (b,g), sailing (b,g), soccer (b,g), softball (g), swimming and diving (b,g), tennis (b,g), track and field (b,g), volleyball (b,g), water polo (b,g), wrestling (b,g); intramural: basketball (b,g), volleyball (b,g); coed intramural: basketball, dance, flag football, kickball, Newcombe ball, soccer, softball, tai chi, touch football, ultimate Frisbee, volleyball, whiffle ball, yoga. 2 PE instructors, 4 coaches.

Computers Computers are regularly used in English, mathematics, photography, science classes. Computer network features include on-campus library services, Internet access, wireless campus network, Internet filtering or blocking technology, assistive technology for learning differences. Computer access in designated common areas is available to students. The school has a published electronic and media policy.

Contact Ms. Sandi Tadaki, Director of Admissions. 808-423-1356. Fax: 808-422-1920. E-mail: stadaki@assets-school.net. Website: www.assets-school.net

BACHMAN ACADEMY

414 Brymer Creek Road
McDonald, Tennessee 37353

Head of School: Mr. Mark A. Frizzell, M.Ed.

General Information Coeducational boarding and day college-preparatory, general academic, arts, vocational, bilingual studies, and technology school; primarily serves underachievers, students with learning disabilities, individuals with Attention Deficit Disorder, dyslexic students, Non-verbal Learning Disorder, and Pervasive Developmental Disorder-Not Otherwise Specified. Grades 6–PG. Founded: 1999. Setting: suburban. Nearest major city is Chattanooga. Students are housed in single-sex dormitories. 200-acre campus. 6 buildings on campus. Approved or accredited by Southern Association of Colleges and Schools, Southern Association of Independent Schools, and Tennessee Department of Education. Total enrollment: 39. Upper school average class size: 5. Upper school faculty-student ratio: 1:3. There are 153 required school days per year for Upper School students. Upper School students typically attend 5 days per week. The average school day consists of 7 hours and 30 minutes.

Upper School Student Profile Grade 9: 4 students (3 boys, 1 girl); Grade 10: 6 students (4 boys, 2 girls); Grade 11: 10 students (7 boys, 3 girls); Grade 12: 7 students (4 boys, 3 girls); Postgraduate: 1 student (1 boy). 69% of students are boarding students. 50% are state residents. 10 states are represented in upper school student body. 11% are international students. International students from Bermuda, China, India, and Nigeria.

Faculty School total: 12. In upper school: 6 men, 6 women; 3 have advanced degrees; 1 resides on campus.

Subjects Offered ACT preparation, agriculture, art, biology, calculus, career exploration, career/college preparation, carpentry, chemistry, English, equine management, equitation, leadership and service, mathematics, mechanics, personal finance, physics, pre-algebra, SAT preparation, social studies, Spanish, wellness, woodworking.

Graduation Requirements All courses as required by the State of TN Department of Education.

Special Academic Programs Honors section; accelerated programs; independent study; academic accommodation for the gifted; remedial reading and/or remedial writing; remedial math; programs in English, mathematics, general development for dyslexic students.

College Admission Counseling 7 students graduated in 2013; 3 went to college, including Chattanooga State Community College; The University of Tennessee at Chattanooga. Other: 2 went to work, 2 entered military service.

Student Life Upper grades have uniform requirement, student council, honor system. Discipline rests primarily with faculty.

Summer Programs Remediation, enrichment, sports, art/fine arts programs offered; session focuses on learning disabilities; held on campus; accepts boys and girls; open to students from other schools. 150 students usually enrolled. 2014 schedule: July 1 to July 31. Application deadline: April 1.

Tuition and Aid Day student tuition: $20,500; 5-day tuition and room/board: $42,000; 7-day tuition and room/board: $49,750. Tuition installment plan (monthly payment plans, biannual payment plan, Your Tuition Solution). Need-based scholarship grants available. In 2013–14, 37% of upper-school students received aid. Total amount of financial aid awarded in 2013–14: $100,000.

Admissions Traditional secondary-level entrance grade is 9. For fall 2013, 52 students applied for upper-level admission, 19 were accepted, 10 enrolled. Any standardized test, Individual IQ, Achievement and behavior rating scale or WISC III or other aptitude measures; standardized achievement test required. Deadline for receipt of application materials: none. Application fee required: $100. Interview required.

Athletics Coed Intramural: archery, backpacking, basketball, billiards, bocce, bowling, canoeing/kayaking, dressage, drill team, equestrian sports, fishing, fitness, fitness walking, golf, hiking/backpacking, horseback riding, JROTC drill, kickball, outdoor activities, outdoor education, outdoor recreation, outdoor skills, outdoors, physical fitness, physical training, rafting, rappelling, rock climbing, ropes courses, strength & conditioning, swimming and diving, table tennis, tennis, volleyball, walking, wall climbing, weight training, wilderness, winter walking, yoga.

Computers Computers are regularly used in all academic classes. Computer network features include Internet access, wireless campus network. Student e-mail accounts and computer access in designated common areas are available to students. The school has a published electronic and media policy.

Contact Mrs. Bridgette Owen, Director of Admissions. 423-479-4523 Ext. 41. Fax: 423-472-2718. E-mail: admissions@bachmanacademy.org. Website: www.bachmanacademy.org/

BREHM PREPARATORY SCHOOL

1245 East Grand Avenue
Carbondale, Illinois 62901

Head of School: Mr. Brian P. Brown, PhD

General Information Coeducational boarding and day college-preparatory, general academic, and arts school; primarily serves students with learning disabilities, individuals with Attention Deficit Disorder, dyslexic students, and language-based learning differences. Grades 6–PG. Founded: 1982. Setting: small town. Nearest major city is St. Louis, MO. Students are housed in single-sex dormitories. 100-acre campus. 13 buildings on campus. Approved or accredited by Independent Schools Association of the Central States, North Central Association of Colleges and Schools, and Illinois Department of Education. Member of National Association of Independent Schools. Endowment: $900,000. Total enrollment: 85. Upper school average class size: 8. Upper school faculty-student ratio: 1:4. There are 185 required school days per year for Upper School students. Upper School students typically attend 5 days per week. The average school day consists of 7 hours and 30 minutes.

Upper School Student Profile Grade 9: 13 students (12 boys, 1 girl); Grade 10: 15 students (12 boys, 3 girls); Grade 11: 19 students (14 boys, 5 girls); Grade 12: 20 students (15 boys, 5 girls); Postgraduate: 8 students (8 boys). 86% of students are boarding students. 23% are state residents. 24 states are represented in upper school student body. 8% are international students. International students from Cameroon, Canada, India, Latvia, and Nigeria.

Faculty School total: 24. In upper school: 8 men, 16 women; 15 have advanced degrees.

Subjects Offered 20th century American writers, 20th century history, ACT preparation, algebra, American history, American literature, anatomy and physiology, art, biology, British literature, calculus, career exploration, chemistry, communication skills, composition, computer graphics, computer programming, computer science, computer skills, consumer education, creative writing, current events, current history, desktop publishing, digital imaging, digital photography, earth science, economics, English, English literature, environmental science, geometry, government/civics, health, keyboarding, language, learning cognition, mathematics, photography, physical education, pragmatics, pre-algebra, pre-calculus, psychology, reading/study skills, science, Shakespeare, social studies, sociology, Spanish, speech, trigonometry, video and animation, weight training, world history, writing.

Graduation Requirements ACT preparation, computer science, consumer education, English, government, learning cognition, mathematics, physical education (includes health), science, social studies (includes history).

Special Academic Programs Study at local college for college credit; academic accommodation for the gifted; remedial reading and/or remedial writing; remedial math; programs in English, mathematics, general development for dyslexic students.

College Admission Counseling 24 students graduated in 2013; they went to John A. Logan College; Marshall University; Southern Illinois University

Edwardsville. Other: 8 entered a postgraduate year. Median composite ACT: 17. 7% scored over 26 on composite ACT.

Student Life Upper grades have specified standards of dress, student council, honor system. Discipline rests equally with students and faculty.

Summer Programs Remediation, enrichment, art/fine arts programs offered; session focuses on Experiential Learning/PBL; held both on and off campus; held at Southern IL and Southern MO; accepts boys and girls; open to students from other schools. 32 students usually enrolled. 2014 schedule: June 29 to July 26. Application deadline: May 1.

Tuition and Aid Day student tuition: $42,400; 7-day tuition and room/board: $68,900. Tuition installment plan (individually arranged payment plans, Tuition Solution). Need-based scholarship grants available. In 2013–14, 8% of upper-school students received aid. Total amount of financial aid awarded in 2013–14: $99,300.

Admissions Traditional secondary-level entrance grade is 9. For fall 2013, 33 students applied for upper-level admission, 30 were accepted, 24 enrolled. Wechsler Individual Achievement Test, WISC or WAIS and Woodcock-Johnson required. Deadline for receipt of application materials: none. Application fee required: $75. On-campus interview required.

Athletics Interscholastic: basketball (boys, girls); coed interscholastic: soccer; coed intramural: aerobics, aerobics/dance, archery, basketball, billiards, bowling, dance, fishing, flag football, Frisbee, golf, hiking/backpacking, horseback riding, outdoor skills, paint ball, physical fitness, soccer, softball, strength & conditioning. 1 PE instructor, 1 coach.

Computers Computers are regularly used in all academic, career exploration, college planning, creative writing, design, desktop publishing, graphic arts, graphic design, keyboarding, learning cognition, photography, reading, remedial study skills, research skills, study skills, typing, word processing, writing, writing, yearbook classes. Computer network features include Internet access, wireless campus network, Internet filtering or blocking technology. Student e-mail accounts are available to students. Students grades are available online. The school has a published electronic and media policy.

Contact Mr. Brian Taylor, Associate Director of Admissions. 618-457-0371 Ext. 1305. Fax: 618-529-1248. E-mail: brian.taylor@brehm.org. Website: www.brehm.org

BRIDGES ACADEMY

3921 Laurel Canyon Boulevard
Studio City, California 91604

Head of School: Carl Sabatino

General Information Coeducational day college-preparatory, arts, technology, and music, drama, talent development school; primarily serves gifted students with non-verbal learning differences. Grades 5–12. Founded: 1994. Setting: suburban. Nearest major city is Los Angeles. 4-acre campus. 3 buildings on campus. Approved or accredited by Western Association of Schools and Colleges and California Department of Education. Total enrollment: 138. Upper school average class size: 9. Upper school faculty-student ratio: 1:8. There are 174 required school days per year for Upper School students. Upper School students typically attend 5 days per week. The average school day consists of 5 hours and 15 minutes.

Upper School Student Profile Grade 9: 14 students (13 boys, 1 girl); Grade 10: 22 students (17 boys, 5 girls); Grade 11: 22 students (20 boys, 2 girls); Grade 12: 16 students (12 boys, 4 girls).

Faculty School total: 25. In upper school: 17 men, 8 women; 10 have advanced degrees.

Subjects Offered 20th century history, algebra, American government, American literature, anatomy and physiology, art, biology, calculus, chemistry, drama, economics, European history, European literature, film, genetics, geometry, Japanese, modern European history, music, non-Western literature, photography, physics, pre-calculus, robotics, senior project, Spanish, statistics, study skills, technology, U.S. history, world history.

Graduation Requirements Economics, English, foreign language, government, history, mathematics, performing arts, science, senior seminar, visual arts.

Special Academic Programs Honors section; academic accommodation for the gifted.

College Admission Counseling 16 students graduated in 2013; 14 went to college, including California State University, Northridge. Other: 2 had other specific plans. 56% scored over 600 on SAT critical reading, 24% scored over 600 on SAT math.

Student Life Discipline rests primarily with faculty.

Summer Programs Enrichment, sports, art/fine arts, computer instruction programs offered; session focuses on enrichment; held on campus; accepts boys and girls; open to students from other schools. 2014 schedule: June 1 to June 30. Application deadline: none.

Tuition and Aid Day student tuition: $34,742. Tuition installment plan (Insured Tuition Payment Plan, monthly payment plans). Need-based scholarship grants available. In 2013–14, 15% of upper-school students received aid.

Admissions Traditional secondary-level entrance grade is 9. For fall 2013, 11 students applied for upper-level admission, 7 were accepted, 5 enrolled. Deadline for receipt of application materials: March 1. Application fee required: $150. On-campus interview required.

Athletics Coed Interscholastic: basketball, cross-country running, track and field. 2 PE instructors, 1 coach.

Computers Computers are regularly used in all classes. Computer network features include Internet access, wireless campus network, Internet filtering or blocking technology. Campus intranet and student e-mail accounts are available to students. Students grades are available online.

Contact Doug Lenzini, Director of Admissions. 818-506-1091. Fax: 818-506-8094. E-mail: doug@bridges.edu. Website: www.bridges.edu

CAMPHILL SPECIAL SCHOOL

1784 Fairview Road
Glenmoore, Pennsylvania 19343

Head of School: Mr. Bernard Wolf

General Information Coeducational boarding and day general academic, arts, and vocational school; primarily serves underachievers, intellectual and developmental disabilities, and mental retardation. Grades K–13. Founded: 1963. Setting: rural. Nearest major city is Philadelphia. Students are housed in on-campus single family homes. 82-acre campus. 1 building on campus. Approved or accredited by Association of Waldorf Schools of North America, Middle States Association of Colleges and Schools, National Council for Private School Accreditation, and Pennsylvania Department of Education. Total enrollment: 118. Upper school average class size: 9. Upper school faculty-student ratio: 1:5. There are 180 required school days per year for Upper School students. Upper School students typically attend 5 days per week. The average school day consists of 9 hours.

Upper School Student Profile Grade 9: 6 students (6 boys); Grade 10: 10 students (6 boys, 4 girls); Grade 11: 10 students (5 boys, 5 girls); Grade 12: 10 students (7 boys, 3 girls); Grade 13: 23 students (22 boys, 1 girl). 85% of students are boarding students. 72% are state residents. 13 states are represented in upper school student body. 3% are international students. International students from Jamaica; 1 other country represented in student body.

Faculty In upper school: 2 men, 2 women; 70 reside on campus.

Subjects Offered 20th century American writers, 20th century history, 20th century physics, 20th century world history, acting, agriculture, American Civil War, American culture, American democracy, American history, Ancient Greek, ancient history, ancient world history, animal husbandry, art, art and culture, art appreciation, astronomy, bell choir, biology, body human, botany, chemistry, choir, drama, drama performance, ecology, environmental education, eurythmy, gardening, geography, geometry, government, handbells, health and wellness, history, instruments, life skills, mathematics, medieval history, medieval literature, medieval/Renaissance history, meteorology, music, mythology, natural history, painting, physics, poetry, pottery, reading, science, Shakespeare, woodworking, zoology.

Special Academic Programs Remedial reading and/or remedial writing; remedial math.

Student Life Upper grades have student council. Discipline rests primarily with faculty.

Summer Programs Enrichment programs offered; session focuses on Extended School Year (ESY); held on campus; accepts boys and girls; not open to students from other schools. 45 students usually enrolled. 2014 schedule: June 28 to July 26.

Tuition and Aid Need-based scholarship grants available.

Admissions Traditional secondary-level entrance grade is 9. Deadline for receipt of application materials: none. No application fee required. On-campus interview required.

Contact 610-469-9236. Website: www.camphillspecialschool.org

CHELSEA SCHOOL

2970 Belcrest Center Drive, Suite 300
Hyattsville, Maryland 20782

Head of School: Katherine Fedalen

General Information Coeducational day college-preparatory, general academic, arts, and technology school; primarily serves students with learning disabilities, individuals with Attention Deficit Disorder, and dyslexic students. Grades 5–12. Founded: 1976. Setting: suburban. 1 building on campus. Approved or accredited by Maryland Department of Education. Total enrollment: 61. Upper school average class size: 8. Upper school faculty-student ratio: 1:8. There are 180 required school days per year for Upper School students. Upper School students typically attend 5 days per week. The average school day consists of 6 hours and 30 minutes.

Upper School Student Profile Grade 6: 5 students (1 boy, 4 girls); Grade 7: 5 students (3 boys, 2 girls); Grade 8: 7 students (7 boys); Grade 9: 4 students (4 boys); Grade 10: 16 students (13 boys, 3 girls); Grade 11: 10 students (9 boys, 1 girl); Grade 12: 14 students (13 boys, 1 girl).

Faculty School total: 21. In upper school: 6 men, 15 women.

Subjects Offered Algebra, American history, American literature, art, biology, calculus, career/college preparation, chemistry, community service, composition, computer graphics, computer technologies, computers, earth and space science, earth science, English, English literature, environmental science, foreign language, geometry, health, health and wellness, independent study, information technology, math review, music, personal fitness, physical education, physics, pre-algebra, pre-calculus, reading,

reading/study skills, remedial study skills, science, social skills, Spanish, state government, U.S. government, U.S. history, U.S. literature, wellness.

Graduation Requirements 20th century world history, algebra, American government, American history, art, biology, career/college preparation, chemistry, earth science, electives, English, English composition, English literature, general math, geometry, health and wellness, physical education (includes health), pre-algebra, Spanish, U.S. history.

Special Academic Programs Advanced Placement exam preparation; remedial reading and/or remedial writing; remedial math; programs in English, mathematics, general development for dyslexic students.

College Admission Counseling 14 students graduated in 2013; 12 went to college, including Eastern Connecticut State University. Other: 1 went to work.

Student Life Upper grades have student council. Discipline rests primarily with faculty.

Summer Programs Remediation, enrichment, computer instruction programs offered; session focuses on remediation; held on campus; accepts boys and girls; not open to students from other schools. 30 students usually enrolled. 2014 schedule: July to August. Application deadline: none.

Tuition and Aid Day student tuition: $35,610. Tuition installment plan (individually arranged payment plans). Need-based scholarship grants available.

Admissions Academic Profile Tests, Wechsler Individual Achievement Test, Wide Range Achievement Test, WISC III or other aptitude measures; standardized achievement test, WISC or WAIS, WISC-R or Woodcock-Johnson required. Deadline for receipt of application materials: none. Application fee required: $50. On-campus interview required.

Athletics Interscholastic: basketball (boys, girls); coed interscholastic: soccer, softball, track and field. 1 PE instructor.

Computers Computer network features include on-campus library services, Internet access, wireless campus network, Internet filtering or blocking technology. Campus intranet, student e-mail accounts, and computer access in designated common areas are available to students. The school has a published electronic and media policy.

Contact Debbie Lourie, Director of Admissions. 240-467-2100 Ext. 303. Fax: 240-467-2120. E-mail: dlourie@chelseaschool.edu. Website: www.chelseaschool.edu

COPPER CANYON ACADEMY

PO Box 230
Rimrock, Arizona 86335

Head of School: Paul Taylor

General Information Girls' boarding college-preparatory and general academic school; primarily serves students with learning disabilities, individuals with Attention Deficit Disorder, and individuals with emotional and behavioral problems. Grades 9–12. Founded: 1998. Setting: rural. Nearest major city is Sedona. Students are housed in single-sex dormitories. 29-acre campus. 8 buildings on campus. Approved or accredited by CITA (Commission on International and Trans-Regional Accreditation), North Central Association of Colleges and Schools, and Arizona Department of Education. Total enrollment: 90. Upper school average class size: 10. Upper school faculty-student ratio: 1:10. Upper School students typically attend 5 days per week. The average school day consists of 6 hours.

Upper School Student Profile Grade 9: 20 students (20 girls); Grade 10: 20 students (20 girls); Grade 11: 25 students (25 girls); Grade 12: 25 students (25 girls). 100% of students are boarding students. 20% are state residents. 22 states are represented in upper school student body. 5% are international students.

Faculty School total: 12. In upper school: 5 men, 7 women; 3 have advanced degrees; 2 reside on campus.

Subjects Offered ACT preparation, acting, adolescent issues, advanced math, algebra, American Civil War, American government, American history, American literature, ancient history, ancient world history, applied arts, applied music, art, art and culture, art appreciation, art education, art history, arts, athletic training, athletics, ballet, ballet technique, basketball, biology, botany, British literature, business, business communications, business mathematics, calculus, career planning, character education, chemistry, child development, choir, chorus, civics, Civil War, civil war history, college admission preparation, college awareness, college counseling, college placement, college planning, college writing, communication skills, communications, community garden, community service, comparative civilizations, composition, computer applications, computer education, computer graphics, computer literacy, computer math, computer science, computer skills, computers, consumer mathematics, contemporary art, contemporary history, contemporary issues, creative arts, creative dance, creative writing, current events, dance, dance performance, decision making skills, drama, drama performance, drama workshop, dramatic arts, drawing, drawing and design, earth science, economics, economics and history, electives, English, English composition, English literature, equality and freedom, equestrian sports, equine management, equine science, ethical decision making, European history, European literature, experiential education, female experience in America, film appreciation, fine arts, fitness, food and nutrition, foreign language, foreign policy, French, gender issues, general science, geography, geology, geometry, global studies, government, government/civics, grammar, graphic arts, health, health and safety, health and wellness, health education, health science, heritage of American Women, history, history of dance, history of drama, home economics, human biology, human

development, human sexuality, independent living, international studies, intro to computers, jazz dance, journalism, lab/keyboard, language, language and composition, language arts, leadership, leadership education training, learning strategies, library, life issues, life management skills, life skills, linear algebra, literature, literature by women, math applications, mathematics, modern dance, modern languages, moral and social development, music, music appreciation, music composition, music history, music performance, musical productions, musical theater, nature study, news writing, newspaper, non-Western literature, nutrition, oil painting, parenting, participation in sports, peer counseling, performing arts, personal development, personal growth, physical education, physics, play production, poetry, political science, political systems, portfolio art, pre-calculus, psychology, SAT preparation, SAT/ACT preparation, science, sex education, sexuality, Shakespeare, Shakespearean histories, social issues, sociology, softball, Spanish, Spanish literature, speech, speech and debate, sports, sports conditioning, stage and body movement, state history, statistics, student government, student publications, studio art, study skills, tap dance, theater, theater arts, theater history, theater production, trigonometry, U.S. government, U.S. government and politics, U.S. history, U.S. literature, visual and performing arts, visual arts, vocal music, volleyball, water color painting, weight fitness, weightlifting, wellness, Western literature, women in literature, women's health, women's literature, world civilizations, world cultures, world geography, world history, world studies, writing, writing, yoga.

Graduation Requirements Option of traditional academic graduation as well as graduation from the therapeutic side of school.

Special Academic Programs Accelerated programs; independent study; study at local college for college credit; academic accommodation for the gifted, the musically talented, and the artistically talented; programs in English, mathematics for dyslexic students.

Student Life Upper grades have uniform requirement, student council, honor system. Discipline rests primarily with faculty.

Tuition and Aid 7-day tuition and room/board: $6800. Middle-income loans, Keybank, prepGATE and Sallie Mae loans available. In 2012–13, 80% of upper-school students received aid. Total amount of financial aid awarded in 2012–13: $81,600.

Admissions Traditional secondary-level entrance grade is 10. For fall 2012, 400 students applied for upper-level admission, 150 were accepted, 90 enrolled. SAT required. Deadline for receipt of application materials: none. No application fee required.

Athletics Interscholastic: basketball, soccer, softball, volleyball; intramural: aerobics, aerobics/dance, badminton, ballet, basketball, cross-country running, dance, fitness, fitness walking, horseback riding, jogging, modern dance, physical fitness, physical training, soccer, softball, track and field, walking, yoga. 2 PE instructors, 1 coach, 1 athletic trainer.

Computers Computers are regularly used in all academic classes. Computer network features include Internet access, Internet filtering or blocking technology. Student e-mail accounts are available to students. Students grades are available online. The school has a published electronic and media policy.

Contact Stephanie Coleman, Admissions Counselor. 877-617-1222 Ext. 116. Fax: 928-567-1323. E-mail: stephaniecoleman@coppercanyonacademy.com. Website: www.coppercanyonacademy.com

DENVER ACADEMY

4400 East Iliff Avenue
Denver, Colorado 80222

Head of School: Mark Twarogowski

General Information Coeducational day college-preparatory, general academic, arts, vocational, and technology school; primarily serves underachievers, students with learning disabilities, individuals with Attention Deficit Disorder, dyslexic students, and unique learning styles. Grades 1–12. Founded: 1972. Setting: urban. 22-acre campus. 19 buildings on campus. Approved or accredited by Association of Colorado Independent Schools and Colorado Department of Education. Member of National Association of Independent Schools. Endowment: $3 million. Total enrollment: 331. Upper school average class size: 14. Upper school faculty-student ratio: 1:8. There are 169 required school days per year for Upper School students. Upper School students typically attend 5 days per week. The average school day consists of 6 hours and 15 minutes.

Upper School Student Profile Grade 9: 36 students (23 boys, 13 girls); Grade 10: 44 students (30 boys, 14 girls); Grade 11: 51 students (39 boys, 12 girls); Grade 12: 44 students (33 boys, 11 girls).

Faculty School total: 63. In upper school: 26 men, 23 women; 18 have advanced degrees.

Subjects Offered ACT preparation, adolescent issues, algebra, American history, American literature, anatomy, art, art history, arts, baseball, basic skills, basketball, biology, botany, business, calculus, ceramics, chemistry, comparative cultures, computer applications, computer graphics, computer math, computer processing, computer programming, computer science, computer skills, creative writing, drama, dramatic arts, earth science, English, English literature, environmental science, ethics, European history, film, filmmaking, fine arts, geography, geometry, government/civics, grammar, health, history, life skills, mathematics, music, philosophy, photography, physical education, physics, physiology, psychology, science, social sciences, social studies, Spanish, speech, theater, trigonometry, values and decisions, world history, world literature, writing, yearbook.

Graduation Requirements Arts and fine arts (art, music, dance, drama), English, mathematics, physical education (includes health), science, social sciences, social studies (includes history).

Special Academic Programs Independent study; academic accommodation for the gifted; remedial reading and/or remedial writing; remedial math; programs in English, mathematics, general development for dyslexic students.

College Admission Counseling 66 students graduated in 2013; 56 went to college, including Colorado State University; Metropolitan State University of Denver; University of Denver; University of Northern Colorado. Other: 2 went to work, 5 entered a postgraduate year, 3 had other specific plans.

Student Life Upper grades have specified standards of dress, student council, honor system. Discipline rests primarily with faculty.

Summer Programs Remediation, enrichment, advancement, art/fine arts, rigorous outdoor training, computer instruction programs offered; session focuses on academics, remediation, and summer fun camp; held both on and off campus; held at various locations around the city and the Rocky Mountains; accepts boys and girls; open to students from other schools. 150 students usually enrolled. 2014 schedule: June to July. Application deadline: June.

Tuition and Aid Day student tuition: $25,650. Tuition installment plan (monthly payment plans). Tuition reduction for siblings, need-based scholarship grants available. In 2013–14, 30% of upper-school students received aid.

Admissions For fall 2013, 35 students applied for upper-level admission, 31 were accepted, 24 enrolled. WISC or WAIS and Woodcock-Johnson Revised Achievement Test required. Deadline for receipt of application materials: none. Application fee required: $75. On-campus interview required.

Athletics Interscholastic: baseball (boys), basketball (b,g), cross-country running (b,g), golf (b), soccer (b,g), volleyball (g); intramural: volleyball (g); coed interscholastic: cheering, physical fitness, physical training; coed intramural: backpacking, basketball, boxing, canoeing/kayaking, climbing, cooperative games, fishing, flag football, golf, indoor hockey, indoor soccer, indoor track, jump rope, mountaineering, outdoor activities, rafting, rock climbing, skiing (downhill), soccer, swimming and diving, track and field, wall climbing. 4 PE instructors, 4 coaches.

Computers Computers are regularly used in basic skills, career exploration, career technology, college planning, drawing and design, English, foreign language, independent study, introduction to technology, mathematics, media arts, media production, media services, multimedia, music, occupational education, SAT preparation, science, writing, yearbook classes. Computer network features include on-campus library services, online commercial services, Internet access, wireless campus network, Internet filtering or blocking technology. Student e-mail accounts and computer access in designated common areas are available to students. Students grades are available online. The school has a published electronic and media policy.

Contact Janet Woolley, Director of Admissions. 303-777-5161. Fax: 303-777-5893. E-mail: jwoolley@denveracademy.org. Website: www.denveracademy.org

EAGLE HILL SCHOOL

45 Glenville Road
Greenwich, Connecticut 06831

Head of School: Dr. Marjorie E. Castro

General Information Coeducational boarding and day college-preparatory, arts, and technology school; primarily serves students with learning disabilities, dyslexic students, and language-based learning disabilities. Boarding grades 5–9, day grades 1–9. Founded: 1975. Setting: suburban. Nearest major city is New York, NY. Students are housed in single-sex by floor dormitories. 20-acre campus. 21 buildings on campus. Approved or accredited by Connecticut Department of Education. Member of Secondary School Admission Test Board. Endowment: $18 million. Total enrollment: 255. Upper school average class size: 6. Upper school faculty-student ratio: 1:4. There are 180 required school days per year for Upper School students. Upper School students typically attend 5 days per week. The average school day consists of 7 hours and 40 minutes.

Upper School Student Profile 30% of students are boarding students. 50% are state residents. 4 states are represented in upper school student body.

Faculty School total: 65. In upper school: 15 men, 20 women; 33 have advanced degrees; 28 reside on campus.

Subjects Offered Art, English, health, history, mathematics, music, physical education, science, technology.

Graduation Requirements Arts and fine arts (art, music, dance, drama), computer science, English, mathematics, physical education (includes health), science, social sciences, social studies (includes history), study skills.

Special Academic Programs Remedial reading and/or remedial writing; remedial math; programs in English, mathematics, general development for dyslexic students.

College Admission Counseling 69 students graduated in 2013.

Student Life Upper grades have specified standards of dress, student council, honor system. Discipline rests primarily with faculty.

Tuition and Aid Day student tuition: $60,750; 5-day tuition and room/board: $80,225. Tuition installment plan (monthly payment plans). Need-based scholarship grants available.

Admissions For fall 2013, 179 students applied for upper-level admission, 90 were accepted, 70 enrolled. Psychoeducational evaluation and Wechsler Intelligence Scale for Children III required. Deadline for receipt of application materials: none. Application fee required: $100. On-campus interview required.

Athletics Interscholastic: baseball (boys), basketball (b,g), cheering (g), field hockey (g), lacrosse (b,g); intramural: aerobics (g), aerobics/dance (g), aerobics/Nautilus (b), flag football (b), football (b), lacrosse (g); coed interscholastic: basketball, cross-country running, ice hockey; coed intramural: basketball, bicycling, billiards, canoeing/kayaking, dance, fitness, fitness walking, floor hockey, Frisbee, golf, gymnastics, ice skating, jogging, judo, lacrosse, martial arts, outdoor activities, outdoor education, outdoor recreation, physical fitness, physical training, volleyball, yoga. 1 PE instructor, 1 athletic trainer.

Computers Computers are regularly used in English, history, mathematics, science classes. Computer network features include on-campus library services, online commercial services, Internet access, wireless campus network, Internet filtering or blocking technology, digital lab, iMovie, Active Boards, Intranet. The school has a published electronic and media policy.

Contact Mr. Thomas Cone, Director of Admissions and Placement. 203-622-9240 Ext. 648. Fax: 203-622-0914. E-mail: t.cone@eaglehill.org. Website: www.eaglehillschool.org

EAGLE HILL SCHOOL

PO Box 116
242 Old Petersham Road
Hardwick, Massachusetts 01037

Head of School: Peter J. McDonald

General Information Coeducational boarding and day college-preparatory and arts school; primarily serves students with learning disabilities, individuals with Attention Deficit Disorder, dyslexic students, and non-verbal learning disabilities. Grades 8–12. Founded: 1967. Setting: small town. Nearest major city is Worcester. Students are housed in single-sex dormitories. 225-acre campus. 16 buildings on campus. Approved or accredited by Association of Independent Schools in New England, Massachusetts Office of Child Care Services, New England Association of Schools and Colleges, and The Association of Boarding Schools. Member of National Association of Independent Schools and Secondary School Admission Test Board. Endowment: $5 million. Total enrollment: 205. Upper school average class size: 5. Upper school faculty-student ratio: 1:4. There are 165 required school days per year for Upper School students. Upper School students typically attend 5 days per week. The average school day consists of 6 hours and 20 minutes.

Upper School Student Profile Grade 9: 49 students (31 boys, 18 girls); Grade 10: 48 students (32 boys, 16 girls); Grade 11: 48 students (21 boys, 27 girls); Grade 12: 51 students (31 boys, 20 girls). 90% of students are boarding students. 33% are state residents. 29 states are represented in upper school student body. 5% are international students. International students from Bermuda, Canada, Mexico, New Zealand, Norway, and United Kingdom; 2 other countries represented in student body.

Faculty School total: 54. In upper school: 23 men, 27 women; 35 have advanced degrees; 21 reside on campus.

Subjects Offered 1968, 20th century history, acting, advanced math, algebra, American foreign policy, American government, American history, American literature, anatomy and physiology, art, arts and crafts, athletics, biology, botany, British literature, calculus, career/college preparation, cell biology, ceramics, chemistry, chorus, civil war history, college admission preparation, college counseling, college planning, college writing, communication skills, composition, computer graphics, conceptual physics, contemporary issues, creative writing, critical writing, culinary arts, current events, desktop publishing, drama, dramatic arts, drawing, earth science, English, English composition, English literature, environmental science, expository writing, film appreciation, film studies, filmmaking, food and nutrition, foreign policy, forensics, French, French as a second language, gender issues, general science, geography, geometry, government, government/civics, graphic arts, graphics, guidance, health, history of music, history of rock and roll, Holocaust studies, illustration, Internet research, interpersonal skills, keyboarding, lab science, language arts, language development, Latin, leadership, life management skills, literacy, literary magazine, marine biology, mathematics, mentorship program, multicultural literature, music appreciation, music composition, music history, music performance, music theory, newspaper, outdoor education, Pacific Island studies, participation in sports, peer counseling, personal finance, personal fitness, philosophy, photo shop, photography, physical education, physical science, physics, poetry, pragmatics, pre-algebra, pre-calculus, printmaking, psychology, publishing, reading, reading/study skills, relationships, SAT/ACT preparation, science, sculpture, set design, Shakespeare, short story, silk screening, social sciences, social skills, social studies, Spanish, speech therapy, studio art, technical theater, technology, theater arts, trigonometry, U.S. government, U.S. history, video and animation, video film production, visual and performing arts, visual arts, Web site design, women in literature, women's literature, woodworking, work-study, world history, world literature, world wide web design, writing, writing, writing workshop, yearbook, zoology.

Graduation Requirements Art, college counseling, computer science, electives, history, literature, mathematics, physical education (includes health), science, writing. Community service is required.

Special Academic Programs Honors section; academic accommodation for the gifted, the musically talented, and the artistically talented; remedial reading and/or remedial writing; remedial math; programs in English, mathematics, general development for dyslexic students.

College Admission Counseling 42 students graduated in 2012; 41 went to college, including American University; Brandeis University; Curry College; Suffolk University; Syracuse University; University of Denver. Other: 1 entered a postgraduate year. Mean composite ACT: 30.

Student Life Upper grades have specified standards of dress, student council, honor system. Discipline rests primarily with faculty.

Tuition and Aid Day student tuition: $46,249; 7-day tuition and room/board: $65,346. Tuition installment plan (Key Tuition Payment Plan). Need-based scholarship grants available. In 2012–13, 4% of upper-school students received aid. Total amount of financial aid awarded in 2012–13: $125,000.

Admissions Traditional secondary-level entrance grade is 9. For fall 2012, 252 students applied for upper-level admission, 64 were accepted, 57 enrolled. Achievement tests, WISC/Woodcock-Johnson and writing sample required. Deadline for receipt of application materials: none. Application fee required: $100. On-campus interview required.

Athletics Interscholastic: basketball (boys, girls), softball (b,g); intramural: dance (g), yoga (g); coed interscholastic: cross-country running, Frisbee, golf, lacrosse, running, soccer, tennis, ultimate Frisbee, wrestling; coed intramural: aerobics, aerobics/dance, aerobics/Nautilus, alpine skiing, badminton, basketball, bicycling, fencing, fitness, fitness walking, floor hockey, ice skating, jogging, mountain biking, Nautilus, outdoor adventure, paint ball, physical training, roller blading, roller skating, skiing (cross-country), skiing (downhill), snowboarding, snowshoeing, swimming and diving, touch football, weight lifting. 1 PE instructor.

Computers Computers are regularly used in college planning, creative writing, desktop publishing, English, foreign language, graphic arts, keyboarding, mathematics, music, music technology, newspaper, photojournalism, programming, research skills, theater arts, video film production, Web site design, writing, yearbook classes. Computer network features include on-campus library services, Internet access, wireless campus network, Internet filtering or blocking technology. Student e-mail accounts are available to students. Students grades are available online.

Contact Dana M. Harbert, Director of Admission. 413-477-6000. Fax: 413-477-6837. E-mail: admission@ehs1.org. Website: www.ehs1.org

FAIRHILL SCHOOL

16150 Preston Road
Dallas, Texas 75248

Head of School: Ms. Jane Sego

General Information Coeducational day college-preparatory, arts, and technology school; primarily serves students with learning disabilities, individuals with Attention Deficit Disorder, and dyslexic students. Grades 1–12. Founded: 1971. Setting: suburban. 16-acre campus. 2 buildings on campus. Approved or accredited by Southern Association of Colleges and Schools and Texas Department of Education. Endowment: $4 million. Total enrollment: 220. Upper school average class size: 12. Upper school faculty-student ratio: 1:12. There are 175 required school days per year for Upper School students. Upper School students typically attend 5 days per week. The average school day consists of 7 hours and 30 minutes.

Upper School Student Profile Grade 9: 22 students (12 boys, 10 girls); Grade 10: 23 students (17 boys, 6 girls); Grade 11: 25 students (17 boys, 8 girls); Grade 12: 20 students (12 boys, 8 girls).

Faculty School total: 32. In upper school: 6 men, 10 women; 4 have advanced degrees.

Subjects Offered American history, American literature, art, biology, British literature, chemistry, computer science, economics, English, government, health, journalism, mathematics, music, performing arts, physical education, physical science, physics, psychology, reading, Spanish, speech, study skills, world geography.

Graduation Requirements Arts and fine arts (art, music, dance, drama), computer science, English, mathematics, physical education (includes health), science, social studies (includes history), 60 hours of volunteer service for seniors.

Special Academic Programs Remedial reading and/or remedial writing; remedial math; programs in English, mathematics, general development for dyslexic students.

College Admission Counseling 22 students graduated in 2012; 20 went to college, including Collin County Community College District; Southern Methodist University; St. Edward's University; Texas Tech University; University of Oklahoma. Other: 1 went to work, 1 entered military service.

Student Life Upper grades have uniform requirement, student council. Discipline rests primarily with faculty.

Tuition and Aid Day student tuition: $15,500. Need-based scholarship grants available. In 2012–13, 6% of upper-school students received aid. Total amount of financial aid awarded in 2012–13: $50,000.

Admissions Traditional secondary-level entrance grade is 9. For fall 2012, 7 students applied for upper-level admission, 5 were accepted, 5 enrolled. Psychoeducational evaluation required. Deadline for receipt of application materials: none. Application fee required: $1500. Interview required.

Athletics Interscholastic: baseball (boys), basketball (b,g), cheering (b,g), golf (b,g), soccer (b,g), tennis (b,g), volleyball (g); intramural: cheering (b,g); coed interscholastic: cheering, golf, soccer, tennis. 3 coaches.

Computers Computers are regularly used in college planning, English, technology, yearbook classes. Computer network features include on-campus library services, Internet access, wireless campus network, Internet filtering or blocking technology. Student e-mail accounts are available to students. Students grades are available online. The school has a published electronic and media policy.

Contact Mrs. Melinda Cameron, Head of Upper School. 972-233-1026. Fax: 972-233-8205. E-mail: mcameron@fairhill.org. Website: www.fairhill.org

FOOTHILLS ACADEMY

745 37th Street NW
Calgary, Alberta T2N 4T1, Canada

Head of School: Mr. G.M. Bullivant

General Information Coeducational day college-preparatory, general academic, and technology school; primarily serves underachievers, students with learning disabilities, individuals with Attention Deficit Disorder, dyslexic students, and Asperger's Syndrome. Grades 3–12. Founded: 1979. Setting: urban. 7-acre campus. 1 building on campus. Approved or accredited by Association of Independent Schools and Colleges of Alberta and Alberta Department of Education. Affiliate member of National Association of Independent Schools. Language of instruction: English. Endowment: CAN$3 million. Total enrollment: 200. Upper school average class size: 12. Upper school faculty-student ratio: 1:12. There are 177 required school days per year for Upper School students. Upper School students typically attend 5 days per week. The average school day consists of 6 hours and 10 minutes.

Upper School Student Profile Grade 9: 36 students (20 boys, 16 girls); Grade 10: 26 students (10 boys, 16 girls); Grade 11: 24 students (18 boys, 6 girls); Grade 12: 29 students (19 boys, 10 girls).

Faculty School total: 40. In upper school: 10 men, 15 women; 7 have advanced degrees.

Subjects Offered Algebra, art, athletics, basic skills, biology, career and personal planning, career education, chemistry, college admission preparation, college awareness, college planning, community service, computer animation, computer applications, computer education, computer literacy, computer multimedia, computer skills, conflict resolution, consumer mathematics, decision making skills, digital photography, drama, drama performance, dramatic arts, electives, English composition, English literature, environmental studies, expository writing, food and nutrition, grammar, health education, information processing, Internet research, interpersonal skills, keyboarding, language arts, leadership, leadership and service, learning strategies, library research, library skills, mathematics, mechanics of writing, oral communications, painting, personal and social education, photography, physical fitness, poetry, reading, reading/study skills, remedial study skills, research and reference, research skills, science, Shakespeare, short story, social skills, social studies, speech therapy, study skills, technological applications, track and field, writing.

Graduation Requirements Athletics, career and personal planning, English, English composition, English literature, expository writing, grammar, keyboarding, language arts, learning strategies, mathematics, mechanics of writing, physical fitness, reading/study skills, research skills, science, social studies (includes history), study skills, Alberta education standards.

Special Academic Programs Remedial reading and/or remedial writing; remedial math; programs in English, mathematics, general development for dyslexic students.

College Admission Counseling 26 students graduated in 2012; 24 went to college, including Mount Allison University; Mount Royal University; University of Calgary; University of Victoria. Other: 2 went to work.

Student Life Upper grades have specified standards of dress, student council, honor system. Discipline rests primarily with faculty.

Tuition and Aid Day student tuition: CAN$13,500–CAN$26,500. Tuition installment plan (The Tuition Plan, monthly payment plans, individually arranged payment plans). Bursaries, need-based scholarship grants available. In 2012–13, 60% of upper-school students received aid. Total amount of financial aid awarded in 2012–13: CAN$500,000.

Admissions Traditional secondary-level entrance grade is 9. For fall 2012, 30 students applied for upper-level admission, 10 were accepted, 10 enrolled. Achievement tests, CTBS, Stanford Achievement Test, any other standardized test, math, reading, and mental ability tests, Wechsler Intelligence Scale for Children or writing sample required. Deadline for receipt of application materials: none. Application fee required: CAN$50. On-campus interview required.

Athletics Interscholastic: badminton (boys, girls), basketball (b,g); intramural: badminton (b,g), basketball (b,g), football (b); coed interscholastic: cross-country running, golf, indoor track & field, tennis, track and field, volleyball; coed intramural: badminton, ball hockey, baseball, climbing, cooperative games, cross-country running, curling, fitness, flag football, floor hockey, golf, gymnastics, handball, hiking/backpacking, in-line skating, indoor soccer, indoor track & field, jogging, kickball, life saving, outdoor activities, outdoor adventure, outdoor education, outdoor recreation, outdoor skills, physical fitness, physical training, roller blading, running, skiing (downhill), snowboarding, snowshoeing, soccer, softball, strength & conditioning, tennis, touch football, track and field, volleyball, walking, weight training, wilderness, wilderness survival, wrestling. 1 PE instructor, 10 coaches, 2 athletic trainers.

Computers Computers are regularly used in all academic, animation, basic skills, career education, career exploration, computer applications, creative writing, desktop publishing, keyboarding, library skills, mentorship program, research skills, social studies, Web site design, word processing, writing, yearbook classes. Computer network features include on-campus library services, online commercial services, Internet access, wireless campus network, Internet filtering or blocking technology. Computer access in designated common areas is available to students. The school has a published electronic and media policy.

Contact Ms. A. Rose, Student Applications. 403-270-9400. Fax: 403-270-9438. E-mail: arose@foothillsacademy.org. Website: www.foothillsacademy.org

THE FROSTIG SCHOOL

971 North Altadena Drive
Pasadena, California 91107

Head of School: Dr. Chris Schnieders

General Information Coeducational day arts, vocational, and technology school; primarily serves underachievers, students with learning disabilities, individuals with Attention Deficit Disorder, and dyslexic students. Grades 1–12. Founded: 1951. Setting: suburban. Nearest major city is Los Angeles. 2-acre campus. 1 building on campus. Approved or accredited by Western Association of Schools and Colleges and California Department of Education. Endowment: $3 million. Total enrollment: 90. Upper school average class size: 12. Upper school faculty-student ratio: 1:6. There are 180 required school days per year for Upper School students. Upper School students typically attend 5 days per week. The average school day consists of 6 hours and 10 minutes.

Upper School Student Profile Grade 6: 8 students (6 boys, 2 girls); Grade 7: 11 students (9 boys, 2 girls); Grade 8: 3 students (3 boys); Grade 9: 16 students (13 boys, 3 girls); Grade 10: 15 students (13 boys, 2 girls); Grade 11: 11 students (7 boys, 4 girls); Grade 12: 10 students (6 boys, 4 girls).

Faculty School total: 25. In upper school: 6 men, 7 women; 2 have advanced degrees.

Subjects Offered Algebra, American government, American history, art, athletics, basic skills, career and personal planning, career education, computer animation, computer applications, consumer economics, creative drama, economics, English, filmmaking, geometry, government, health education, music, physical education, physics, U.S. history.

Special Academic Programs Remedial reading and/or remedial writing; remedial math; programs in English, mathematics, general development for dyslexic students.

College Admission Counseling 10 students graduated in 2013; 7 went to college, including Glendale Community College; Pasadena City College. Other: 1 went to work.

Student Life Upper grades have specified standards of dress, student council. Discipline rests equally with students and faculty.

Summer Programs Remediation, sports, art/fine arts programs offered; session focuses on maintaining skills obtained during the regular term, work experience for high school students; held on campus; accepts boys and girls; not open to students from other schools. 48 students usually enrolled. 2014 schedule: July 1 to July 29.

Tuition and Aid Day student tuition: $28,928. Tuition installment plan (monthly payment plans, individually arranged payment plans). Need-based scholarship grants available. In 2013–14, 5% of upper-school students received aid. Total amount of financial aid awarded in 2013–14: $50,000.

Admissions Traditional secondary-level entrance grade is 9. For fall 2013, 15 students applied for upper-level admission, 11 were accepted, 11 enrolled. Admissions testing required. Deadline for receipt of application materials: none. Application fee required: $100. On-campus interview required.

Athletics Coed Interscholastic: basketball, flag football, softball, touch football. 1 PE instructor, 2 coaches.

Computers Computers are regularly used in art, basic skills, career education, career exploration, college planning, computer applications, creative writing, current events, English, geography, health, history, keyboarding, lab/keyboard, library, library skills, life skills, mathematics, media, music, occupational education, photography, psychology, reading, remedial study skills, research skills, science, social sciences, social studies, study skills, technology, video film production, Web site design, word processing, writing, writing, yearbook classes. Computer network features include on-campus library services, Internet access, wireless campus network, Internet filtering or blocking technology, assistive technology services, laptops.

Contact Ms. Jacquie Knight, IEP and Admissions Administrator. 626-791-1255. Fax: 626-798-1801. E-mail: admissions@frostig.org. Website: www.frostig.org

GATEWAY SCHOOL

2570 NW Green Oaks Boulevard
Arlington, Texas 76012

Head of School: Mrs. Harriet R. Walber

General Information Coeducational day college-preparatory, general academic, arts, and technology school; primarily serves underachievers, students with learning disabilities, individuals with Attention Deficit Disorder, and dyslexic students. Grades 5–12. Founded: 1980. Setting: urban. 7-acre campus. 1 building on campus. Approved or accredited by Southern Association of Colleges and Schools, Southern Association of Independent Schools, and Texas Department of Education. Upper school average class size: 10. Upper school faculty-student ratio: 1:5. There are 176 required school days per year for Upper School students. Upper School students typically attend 5 days per week. The average school day consists of 8 hours.

Faculty School total: 5. In upper school: 5 women; 3 have advanced degrees.

Subjects Offered Algebra, American literature, art, biology, British literature, career planning, chemistry, college awareness, college counseling, community service, composition, computer education, computer literacy, computer science, computer skills, developmental math, drama, earth science, economics, English, English composition, English literature, environmental science, geometry, government, government/civics, grammar, health, health education, history, intro to computers, introduction to theater, journalism, keyboarding, language arts, literature, mathematics, music, music performance, music theater, newspaper, physical education, pre-algebra, reading, reading/study skills, science, social studies, Spanish, speech, state history, theater, U.S. government, U.S. history, word processing, world history, world literature, writing, writing workshop, yearbook.

Graduation Requirements Computer science, English, foreign language, mathematics, physical education (includes health), science, social studies (includes history). Community service is required.

Special Academic Programs Independent study; study at local college for college credit; remedial reading and/or remedial writing; remedial math; programs in English, mathematics, general development for dyslexic students.

College Admission Counseling 1 student graduated in 2013 and went to Tarrant County College District.

Student Life Upper grades have uniform requirement, student council. Discipline rests primarily with faculty.

Summer Programs Remediation, enrichment programs offered; held on campus; accepts boys and girls; open to students from other schools.

Tuition and Aid Day student tuition: $13,500. Guaranteed tuition plan. Tuition installment plan (monthly payment plans, individually arranged payment plans, Payment by the Semester).

Admissions Traditional secondary-level entrance grade is 9. School's own test, Wechsler Intelligence Scale for Children and Woodcock-Johnson required. Deadline for receipt of application materials: none. Application fee required: $250. On-campus interview required.

Athletics Interscholastic: basketball (boys, girls), golf (g); intramural: basketball (b,g), bowling (b,g), golf (b,g), jogging (b,g); coed interscholastic: fitness walking, golf, jogging, scuba diving; coed intramural: bowling. 1 PE instructor.

Computers Computers are regularly used in basic skills, English, history, mathematics, science classes. Computer network features include Internet access. The school has a published electronic and media policy.

Contact Harriet R. Walber, Executive Director. 817-226-6222. Fax: 817-226-6225. E-mail: walberhr@aol.com. Website: www.gatewayschool.com

THE GLENHOLME SCHOOL, DEVEREUX CONNECTICUT

81 Sabbaday Lane
Washington, Connecticut 06793

Head of School: Maryann Campbell

General Information Coeducational boarding and day college-preparatory, arts, vocational, technology, social coaching and motivational management, and self-discipline strategies and character development school; primarily serves underachievers, students with learning disabilities, individuals with Attention Deficit Disorder, individuals with emotional and behavioral problems, Asperger's Syndrome, ADHD, PDD, OCD, and anxiety disorders. Founded: 1968. Setting: small town. Nearest major city is Hartford. Students are housed in single-sex dormitories. 105-acre campus. 30 buildings on campus. Approved or accredited by Association of Independent Schools in New England, Connecticut Department of Children and Families, Council of Accreditation and School Improvement, Massachusetts Department of Education, National Association of Private Schools for Exceptional Children, New England Association of Schools and Colleges, New Jersey Department of Education, New York Department of Education, US Department of State, and Connecticut Department of Education. Member of National Association of Independent Schools. Total enrollment: 95. Upper school average class size: 10. Upper school faculty-student ratio: 1:10. There are 215 required school days per year for Upper School students. Upper School students typically attend 5 days per week. The average school day consists of 5 hours and 45 minutes.

Upper School Student Profile Grade 6: 6 students (6 boys); Grade 7: 3 students (3 boys); Grade 8: 10 students (7 boys, 3 girls); Grade 9: 7 students (3 boys, 4 girls); Grade 10: 15 students (10 boys, 5 girls); Grade 11: 17 students (11 boys, 6 girls); Grade 12: 25 students (16 boys, 9 girls); Grade 13: 6 students (2 boys, 4 girls); Postgraduate: 6 students (4 boys, 2 girls). 92% of students are boarding students. 20% are state residents. 11 states are represented in upper school student body. 9% are international students. International students from China, Egypt, Hong Kong, Russian Federation, and Saudi Arabia; 4 other countries represented in student body.

Faculty School total: 21. In upper school: 4 men, 17 women; 12 have advanced degrees; 3 reside on campus.

Subjects Offered ADL skills, adolescent issues, aerobics, algebra, art, basketball, biology, career and personal planning, career education, career exploration, career/college preparation, character education, chemistry, choral music, chorus, college admission preparation, college planning, communication skills, community service, computer animation, computer applications, computer art, computer education, computer graphics, computer literacy, computer skills, creative arts, creative dance, creative drama, creative thinking, creative writing, culinary arts, dance, decision making skills, digital photography, drama, drama performance, earth science, English, equine management, fine arts, geometry, graphic arts, guidance, health, health and wellness, health education, Internet research, interpersonal skills, keyboarding, library, life skills, mathematics, media arts, moral and social development, music, participation in sports, performing arts, personal fitness, photography, physical education, piano, play production, radio broadcasting, SAT preparation, science, social sciences, Spanish, theater, U.S. history, video and animation, world history, writing, yearbook.

Graduation Requirements Art, electives, English, language, mathematics, physical education (includes health), science, social studies (includes history), students must meet either Glenholme graduation requirements or the requirements of their home state, depending on the funding source.

Special Academic Programs Academic accommodation for the gifted; remedial reading and/or remedial writing; remedial math; programs in English, mathematics, general development for dyslexic students.

College Admission Counseling 18 students graduated in 2013; 12 went to college. Other: 4 went to work, 2 entered a postgraduate year.

Student Life Upper grades have uniform requirement, student council, honor system. Discipline rests primarily with faculty.

Summer Programs Remediation, enrichment, sports, art/fine arts, computer instruction programs offered; session focuses on strengthening social skills and boosting academic proficiency; held on campus; accepts boys and girls; open to students from other schools. 90 students usually enrolled. 2014 schedule: July 7 to August 22.

Admissions Individual IQ, Achievement and behavior rating scale or psychoeducational evaluation required. Deadline for receipt of application materials: none. Application fee required: $150. On-campus interview required.

Athletics Intramural: aerobics (boys, girls), aerobics/dance (b,g), aquatics (b,g), archery (b,g), artistic gym (b,g), basketball (b,g), cheering (b,g), combined training (b,g), cooperative games (b,g), cross-country running (b,g), dance (b,g), dance squad (b,g), dance team (b,g), equestrian sports (b,g), figure skating (b,g), fishing (b,g), fitness (b,g), fitness walking (b,g), flag football (b,g), Frisbee (b,g), golf (b,g), hiking/backpacking (b,g), horseback riding (b,g), ice skating (b,g), jogging (b,g), jump rope (b,g), kickball (b,g), modern dance (b,g), outdoor activities (b,g), outdoor recreation (b,g), paddle tennis (b,g), physical fitness (b,g), physical training (b,g), roller blading (b,g), ropes courses (b,g), soccer (b,g), softball (b,g), strength & conditioning (b,g), tennis (b,g), ultimate Frisbee (b,g), volleyball (b,g), walking (b,g), weight training (b,g), yoga (b,g); coed interscholastic: basketball, cross-country running, soccer, softball, tennis; coed intramural: aerobics, aerobics/dance, aquatics, archery, artistic gym, basketball, cheering, combined training, cooperative games, cross-country running, dance, dance squad, dance team, equestrian sports, figure skating, fishing, fitness, fitness walking, flag football, Frisbee, golf, hiking/backpacking, horseback riding, ice skating, jogging, jump rope, kickball, modern dance, outdoor activities, outdoor recreation, paddle tennis, physical fitness, physical training, roller blading, ropes courses, soccer, softball, strength & conditioning, tennis, ultimate Frisbee, volleyball, walking, weight training, yoga. 1 PE instructor, 2 coaches, 1 athletic trainer.

Computers Computers are regularly used in all academic, technology classes. Computer network features include on-campus library services, Internet access, wireless campus network, Internet filtering or blocking technology, online learning, Web cam parent communications. Campus intranet, student e-mail accounts, and computer access in designated common areas are available to students. Students grades are available online. The school has a published electronic and media policy.

Contact David Dunleavy, Admissions. 860-868-7377 Ext. 285. Fax: 860-868-7413. E-mail: ddunleav@devereux.org. Website: www.theglenholmeschool.org

THE HILL TOP PREPARATORY SCHOOL

737 South Ithan Avenue
Rosemont, Pennsylvania 19010

Head of School: Mr. Thomas W. Needham

General Information Coeducational day college-preparatory, arts, and technology school; primarily serves students with learning disabilities, individuals with Attention Deficit Disorder, and Asperger's Syndrome, PDDNOS, LDNOS. Grades 5–12. Founded: 1971. Setting: suburban. Nearest major city is Philadelphia. 25-acre campus. 4 buildings on campus. Approved or accredited by Middle States Association of Colleges and Schools and Pennsylvania Department of Education. Member of National Association of Independent Schools. Total enrollment: 73. Upper school average class size: 8. Upper school faculty-student ratio: 1:6. There are 180 required school days per year for Upper School students. Upper School students typically attend 5 days per week.

Upper School Student Profile Grade 10: 14 students (12 boys, 2 girls); Grade 11: 14 students (10 boys, 4 girls); Grade 12: 8 students (7 boys, 1 girl).

Faculty School total: 29. In upper school: 10 men, 9 women.

Subjects Offered Algebra, American history, American literature, art, biology, ceramics, chemistry, civics, college counseling, computer math, computer science, computers, creative writing, drama, earth science, electives, English, English literature, environmental science, European history, geography, geometry, government/civics, grammar, health, history, keyboarding, mathematics, media studies, music appreciation, photography, physical education, physics, psychology, public speaking, science, senior project, social studies, study skills, theater, U.S. history, world cultures, world history, writing.

Graduation Requirements English, mathematics, physical education (includes health), science, senior project, social sciences, social studies (includes history), study skills.

Special Academic Programs Independent study; study at local college for college credit; academic accommodation for the gifted and the artistically talented; programs in English, mathematics, general development for dyslexic students.

College Admission Counseling 16 students graduated in 2013; 13 went to college, including Penn State University Park. Other: 1 entered a postgraduate year, 2 had other specific plans. Median SAT critical reading: 550, median SAT math: 510, median SAT writing: 500, median combined SAT: 1640, median composite ACT: 23. 42% scored over 600 on SAT critical reading, 33% scored over 600 on SAT math, 25% scored over 600 on SAT writing, 25% scored over 1800 on combined SAT.

Student Life Upper grades have specified standards of dress, student council, honor system. Discipline rests primarily with faculty.

Summer Programs Remediation, enrichment programs offered; session focuses on remediation, enrichment, recreation, teaching independence; held both on and off campus; held at Pathways to Independence 2013: One week at Eastern University and Hill Top Summer trip to Ireland; accepts boys and girls; open to students from other schools. 9 students usually enrolled. 2014 schedule: July 1 to July 30. Application deadline: none.

Tuition and Aid Day student tuition: $39,190. Tuition installment plan (monthly payment plans, payment in full, 60% due June 1 and 40% due December 1, monthly payments over 10 months). Tuition reduction for siblings, need-based scholarship grants available. In 2013–14, 15% of upper-school students received aid.

Admissions Traditional secondary-level entrance grade is 10. For fall 2013, 7 students applied for upper-level admission, 5 were accepted, 2 enrolled. Achievement tests, psychoeducational evaluation, WISC or WAIS and WISC/Woodcock-Johnson required. Deadline for receipt of application materials: none. Application fee required: $100. On-campus interview required.

Athletics Interscholastic: wrestling (boys); coed interscholastic: basketball, golf, soccer, tennis; coed intramural: aerobics/Nautilus, basketball, bicycling, climbing, combined training, cooperative games, cross-country running, fitness, golf, indoor soccer, martial arts, Newcombe ball, outdoor activities, outdoor adventure, outdoor recreation, outdoor skills, physical fitness, physical training, running, skiing (downhill), snowboarding, soccer, strength & conditioning, tennis, wall climbing, yoga. 2 PE instructors, 5 coaches.

Computers Computers are regularly used in English, mathematics, science, study skills, writing classes. Computer network features include on-campus library services, Internet access, wireless campus network, Internet filtering or blocking technology, one-to-one student and faculty laptop initiative, online student information system, ACTIVBoards, projectors, and audio in all classrooms. Campus intranet, student e-mail accounts, and computer access in designated common areas are available to students. Students grades are available online. The school has a published electronic and media policy.

Contact Ms. Cindy Falcone, Assistant Headmaster. 610-527-3230 Ext. 697. Fax: 610-527-7683. E-mail: cfalcone@hilltopprep.org. Website: www.hilltopprep.org

THE HOWARD SCHOOL

1192 Foster Street
Atlanta, Georgia 30318

Head of School: Ms. Marifred Cilella

General Information Coeducational day college-preparatory, general academic, arts, and technology school; primarily serves students with learning disabilities, individuals with Attention Deficit Disorder, dyslexic students, and students with language learning disabilities and differences. Grades K–12. Founded: 1950. Setting: urban. 15-acre campus. 2 buildings on campus. Approved or accredited by Georgia Independent School Association, Southern Association of Colleges and Schools, Southern Association of Independent Schools, and Georgia Department of Education. Member of National Association of Independent Schools. Total enrollment: 256. Upper school average class size: 9. Upper school faculty-student ratio: 1:8. There are 173 required school days per year for Upper School students. Upper School students typically attend 5 days per week. The average school day consists of 6 hours and 30 minutes.

Upper School Student Profile Grade 9: 24 students (16 boys, 8 girls); Grade 10: 21 students (14 boys, 7 girls); Grade 11: 10 students (7 boys, 3 girls); Grade 12: 25 students (12 boys, 13 girls).

Faculty School total: 63. In upper school: 7 men, 15 women; 13 have advanced degrees.

Subjects Offered Algebra, American history, American literature, art, biology, communications, computer science, creative writing, drama, ecology, economics, English, English literature, European history, film studies, geography, geometry, government/civics, grammar, history, journalism, mathematics, music, physical education, physical science, psychology, reading, science, service learning/internship, social studies, Spanish, study skills, trigonometry, world history, world literature, writing.

Graduation Requirements English, foreign language, health, mathematics, physical education (includes health), science, social studies (includes history).

Special Academic Programs Independent study; academic accommodation for the artistically talented; remedial reading and/or remedial writing; remedial math; programs in English, mathematics, general development for dyslexic students.

College Admission Counseling 15 students graduated in 2013; 14 went to college, including Georgia Southern University; Kennesaw State University; Lynn University; Reinhardt University; Savannah College of Art and Design; Young Harris College. Other: 1 had other specific plans.

Student Life Upper grades have specified standards of dress, student council, honor system. Discipline rests equally with students and faculty.

Summer Programs Remediation, advancement programs offered; session focuses on make-up of academic courses; held on campus; accepts boys and girls; open to students from other schools. 19 students usually enrolled. 2014 schedule: June 10 to July 26. Application deadline: April 1.

Tuition and Aid Day student tuition: $27,820. Tuition installment plan (SMART Tuition Payment Plan, 1-, 2-, 3- and 8-payment plans). Need-based scholarship grants available. In 2013–14, 30% of upper-school students received aid.

Admissions Psychoeducational evaluation required. Deadline for receipt of application materials: none. Application fee required: $150. On-campus interview required.

Athletics Interscholastic: basketball (boys, girls), soccer (b), track and field (b,g), volleyball (g), weight training (b,g); coed interscholastic: golf, soccer, track and field. 3 PE instructors, 6 coaches.

Computers Computers are regularly used in all classes. Computer network features include online commercial services, Internet access, wireless campus network. Student e-mail accounts are available to students. Students grades are available online. The school has a published electronic and media policy.

Contact Ms. Dawn Splinter, Assistant to the Director of Admissions and Registrar. 404-377-7436 Ext. 259. Fax: 404-377-0884. E-mail: dsplinter@howardschool.org. Website: www.howardschool.org

HUMANEX ACADEMY

2700 South Zuni Street
Englewood, Colorado 80110

Head of School: Mr. Daniel R. Toomey

General Information Coeducational day college-preparatory, general academic, and arts school; primarily serves underachievers, students with learning disabilities, individuals with Attention Deficit Disorder, individuals with emotional and behavioral problems, dyslexic students, and Asperger's Syndrome, Autism Spectrum Disorder. Grades 6–12. Founded: 1983. Setting: suburban. Nearest major city is Denver. 1-acre campus. 1 building on campus. Approved or accredited by North Central Association of Colleges and Schools and Colorado Department of Education. Total enrollment: 30. Upper school average class size: 8. Upper school faculty-student ratio: 1:8. There are 170 required school days per year for Upper School students. Upper School students typically attend 5 days per week. The average school day consists of 6 hours and 30 minutes.

Upper School Student Profile Grade 6: 4 students (4 boys); Grade 7: 4 students (2 boys, 2 girls); Grade 8: 4 students (4 boys); Grade 9: 4 students (4 girls); Grade 10: 4 students (1 boy, 3 girls); Grade 11: 2 students (2 boys); Grade 12: 8 students (7 boys, 1 girl).

Faculty School total: 8. In upper school: 4 men, 4 women; all have advanced degrees.

Subjects Offered 1 1/2 elective credits, 1968, 20th century American writers, 20th century history, 20th century physics, 20th century world history, 3-dimensional art, 3-dimensional design, ACT preparation, addiction, ADL skills, adolescent issues, advanced biology, advanced math, advanced studio art-AP, advanced TOEFL/grammar, aerobics, American Civil War, American culture, American democracy, American foreign policy, American government, American history, American legal systems, American literature, American politics in film, anatomy, anatomy and physiology, ancient world history, animal behavior, animation, anthropology, art, art appreciation, art history, arts and crafts, athletic training, athletics, biology, British literature, calculus, career and personal planning, career exploration, cartooning/animation, chemistry, civics, civics/free enterprise, Civil War, civil war history, college counseling,

college placement, comedy, composition, computer art, computer graphics, conflict resolution, consumer mathematics, creative writing, critical thinking, current events, drawing, English, English literature, epic literature, evolution, existentialism, expository writing, film, film and literature, fitness, foreign language, general, general math, general science, geography, geology, geometry, government, government/civics, grammar, graphic arts, graphic design, great books, Greek drama, guitar, Harlem Renaissance, health, health education, history, Holocaust, honors algebra, honors English, honors geometry, honors U.S. history, honors world history, human anatomy, human biology, human sexuality, illustration, independent living, keyboarding, language, language arts, language structure, languages, literacy, literary genres, literary magazine, literature, mathematics, media literacy, military history, newspaper, non-Western literature, North American literature, novels, nutrition, peer counseling, philosophy, physical fitness, physics, physiology, play/screen writing, poetry, politics, pottery, pre-algebra, pre-calculus, psychology, public speaking, reading, reading/study skills, remedial study skills, remedial/makeup course work, research, research skills, SAT preparation, SAT/ACT preparation, science, science fiction, sculpture, sexuality, Shakespeare, short story, speech, speech and debate, sports, statistics, U.S. government, U.S. government and politics, U.S. history, U.S. literature, Vietnam history, Vietnam War, weight fitness, weight training, weightlifting, Western civilization, Western literature, world geography, world governments, world history.

Graduation Requirements Career exploration, career/college preparation, research, speech. Community service is required.

Special Academic Programs Honors section; academic accommodation for the gifted; remedial reading and/or remedial writing; remedial math; programs in English, mathematics, general development for dyslexic students; special instructional classes for deaf students, blind students.

College Admission Counseling 11 students graduated in 2013; 5 went to college, including Arapahoe Community College; Colorado School of Mines; Colorado State University; Fort Lewis College; Metropolitan State University of Denver; University of Colorado Denver. Other: 4 went to work, 2 entered a postgraduate year. Median composite ACT: 24. 33% scored over 26 on composite ACT.

Student Life Upper grades have specified standards of dress, student council. Discipline rests primarily with faculty.

Summer Programs Remediation, advancement, sports, art/fine arts programs offered; session focuses on academics, credit recovery, outdoor educ/recreation; held both on and off campus; held at Colorado Natl Parks, CO rec centers; accepts boys and girls; open to students from other schools. 30 students usually enrolled. 2014 schedule: June 2 to June 27. Application deadline: May 16.

Tuition and Aid Day student tuition: $19,400. Tuition installment plan (FACTS Tuition Payment Plan). Tuition reduction for siblings, need-based scholarship grants, Sallie Mae loans available. In 2013–14, 25% of upper-school students received aid. Total amount of financial aid awarded in 2013–14: $6000.

Admissions Traditional secondary-level entrance grade is 9. For fall 2013, 16 students applied for upper-level admission, 14 were accepted, 14 enrolled. Wechsler Individual Achievement Test, Wechsler Intelligence Scale for Children III, WISC III or other aptitude measures; standardized achievement test, WISC or WAIS, WISC-III and Woodcock-Johnson, WISC-R, WISC-R or WISC-III and WISC/Woodcock-Johnson required. Deadline for receipt of application materials: none. Application fee required: $50. On-campus interview required.

Athletics Coed Intramural: aerobics, ball hockey, basketball, bocce, bowling, cooperative games, fitness, fitness walking, flag football, Frisbee, handball, jogging, kickball, outdoor activities, outdoor recreation, physical fitness, physical training, power lifting, ultimate Frisbee, weight lifting, weight training. 1 PE instructor.

Computers Computers are regularly used in art, English, health, history, literacy, mathematics, philosophy, psychology, reading, research skills, social studies, Spanish, speech, study skills, writing, writing classes. Computer resources include on-campus library services, online commercial services, Internet access, Internet filtering or blocking technology. Campus intranet and computer access in designated common areas are available to students. Students grades are available online. The school has a published electronic and media policy.

Contact Brenda Newton, Director of Admissions. 303-783-0187 Ext. 5006. Fax: 303-783-9159. E-mail: bnewton@humanexacademy.com. Website: www.humanexacademy.com

THE JUDGE ROTENBERG EDUCATIONAL CENTER

250 Turnpike Street
Canton, Massachusetts 02021-2341

Head of School: Glenda Crookes

General Information Coeducational boarding general academic and vocational school; primarily serves underachievers, students with learning disabilities, individuals with Attention Deficit Disorder, individuals with emotional and behavioral problems, dyslexic students, and autism and developmental disabilities. Founded: 1971. Setting: suburban. Nearest major city is Boston. Students are housed in group homes. 2 buildings on campus. Approved or accredited by Massachusetts Department of Education and Massachusetts Department of Education. Upper school average class size: 10. Upper School students typically attend 5 days per week. The average school day consists of 6 hours.

Special Academic Programs Remedial reading and/or remedial writing; remedial math; special instructional classes for deaf students, blind students.

Student Life Upper grades have specified standards of dress, honor system. Discipline rests primarily with faculty.

Admissions Deadline for receipt of application materials: none. No application fee required. Interview recommended.

Athletics Intramural: basketball (boys, girls); coed intramural: aerobics/dance, physical fitness. 2 PE instructors.

Computers Computers are regularly used in all academic classes. Computer network features include Internet access, Internet filtering or blocking technology. Student e-mail accounts are available to students.

Contact Julie Gomes, Director of Admissions. 781-828-2202 Ext. 4275. Fax: 781-828-2804. E-mail: j.gomes@judgerc.org. Website: www.judgerc.org

KILDONAN SCHOOL

425 Morse Hill Road
Amenia, New York 12501

Head of School: Kevin Pendergast

General Information Coeducational boarding and day college-preparatory, general academic, arts, and technology school; primarily serves students with learning disabilities, dyslexic students, and language-based learning differences. Boarding grades 7–PG, day grades 2–PG. Founded: 1969. Setting: rural. Nearest major city is New York. Students are housed in single-sex dormitories. 350-acre campus. 19 buildings on campus. Approved or accredited by Academy of Orton-Gillingham Practitioners and Educators, New York State Association of Independent Schools, and The Association of Boarding Schools. Member of National Association of Independent Schools and Secondary School Admission Test Board. Endowment: $579,300. Total enrollment: 91. Upper school average class size: 8. Upper school faculty-student ratio: 1:2. The average school day consists of 7 hours.

Upper School Student Profile Grade 6: 5 students (1 boy, 4 girls); Grade 7: 8 students (5 boys, 3 girls); Grade 8: 7 students (3 boys, 4 girls); Grade 9: 12 students (10 boys, 2 girls); Grade 10: 12 students (9 boys, 3 girls); Grade 11: 9 students (7 boys, 2 girls); Grade 12: 16 students (11 boys, 5 girls). 68% of students are boarding students. 44% are state residents. 15 states are represented in upper school student body. 9% are international students. International students from Bermuda, Brazil, France, Mexico, Puerto Rico, and United Arab Emirates; 1 other country represented in student body.

Faculty School total: 56. In upper school: 26 men, 28 women; 11 have advanced degrees; 48 reside on campus.

Subjects Offered Algebra, American history, American literature, anthropology, art, art history, biology, botany, business skills, calculus, ceramics, chemistry, computer programming, computer science, creative writing, earth science, ecology, economics, English, English literature, environmental science, European history, expository writing, fine arts, geography, geology, geometry, government/civics, grammar, health, history, mathematics, photography, physical education, physics, science, social studies, trigonometry, typing, world history, world literature, zoology.

Graduation Requirements Arts and fine arts (art, music, dance, drama), English, mathematics, physical education (includes health), science, social studies (includes history).

Special Academic Programs Independent study; remedial reading and/or remedial writing; programs in English, mathematics, general development for dyslexic students.

College Admission Counseling 14 students graduated in 2013; 8 went to college, including Curry College; Landmark College; Mitchell College; Rhode Island School of Design; Xavier University.

Student Life Upper grades have uniform requirement, student council, honor system. Discipline rests primarily with faculty.

Summer Programs Remediation, enrichment, art/fine arts programs offered; session focuses on intensive academic tutoring for students with dyslexia; exciting, fun summer camp activities; held on campus; accepts boys and girls; open to students from other schools. 85 students usually enrolled. 2014 schedule: June 24 to August 5. Application deadline: none.

Tuition and Aid Day student tuition: $43,000; 5-day tuition and room/board: $57,500; 7-day tuition and room/board: $60,000. Tuition installment plan (Tuition Management Systems). Need-based scholarship grants available. In 2013–14, 46% of upper-school students received aid. Total amount of financial aid awarded in 2013–14: $300,000.

Admissions Traditional secondary-level entrance grade is 9. For fall 2013, 60 students applied for upper-level admission, 43 were accepted, 23 enrolled. Wechsler Individual Achievement Test, WISC or WAIS, WISC/Woodcock-Johnson or Woodcock-Johnson Revised Achievement Test required. Deadline for receipt of application materials: none. Application fee required: $50. On-campus interview required.

Athletics Interscholastic: basketball (boys, girls); intramural: aerobics (g), basketball (b,g), dance (g); coed interscholastic: alpine skiing, lacrosse, skiing (downhill), snowboarding, soccer, softball, tennis, yoga; coed intramural: archery, basketball, bicycling, canoeing/kayaking, cross-country running, dressage, equestrian sports, fitness, fitness walking, flag football, freestyle skiing, golf, hiking/backpacking,

horseback riding, ice skating, lacrosse, martial arts, mountain biking, outdoor activities, physical fitness, rock climbing, running, skiing (cross-country), skiing (downhill), snowboarding, soccer, strength & conditioning, table tennis, touch football, walking, water skiing, weight lifting, weight training.

Computers Computers are regularly used in English, mathematics, multimedia classes. Computer network features include on-campus library services, Internet access, wireless campus network. Student e-mail accounts and computer access in designated common areas are available to students. Students grades are available online. The school has a published electronic and media policy.

Contact Beth A. Rainey, Director of Admissions/Financial Aid. 845-373-2012. Fax: 845-373-2004. E-mail: admissions@kildonan.org. Website: www.kildonan.org/

THE LAB SCHOOL OF WASHINGTON

4759 Reservoir Road NW
Washington, District of Columbia 20007

Head of School: Katherine Schantz

General Information Coeducational day college-preparatory and arts school; primarily serves students with learning disabilities, individuals with Attention Deficit Disorder, and dyslexic students. Grades 1–12. Founded: 1967. Setting: urban. 4-acre campus. 6 buildings on campus. Approved or accredited by Middle States Association of Colleges and Schools and District of Columbia Department of Education. Member of National Association of Independent Schools. Endowment: $4 million. Total enrollment: 356. Upper school average class size: 8. Upper school faculty-student ratio: 1:8. There are 180 required school days per year for Upper School students. Upper School students typically attend 5 days per week. The average school day consists of 6 hours and 30 minutes.

Upper School Student Profile Grade 9: 43 students (19 boys, 24 girls); Grade 10: 36 students (13 boys, 23 girls); Grade 11: 24 students (12 boys, 12 girls); Grade 12: 22 students (7 boys, 15 girls).

Faculty School total: 91. In upper school: 10 men, 17 women; 22 have advanced degrees.

Subjects Offered Algebra, American history, American literature, architecture, art, art history, biology, business, business skills, calculus, career education internship, chemistry, community service, computer science, creative writing, digital art, drama, earth science, English, English literature, environmental science, expository writing, film, fine arts, geography, geometry, government, government/civics, grammar, health, internship, Latin, mathematics, music, music appreciation, physical education, physical science, physics, public policy, rhetoric, science, social sciences, social studies, Spanish, technology, theater, trigonometry, video and animation, word processing, world history, writing.

Graduation Requirements Arts and fine arts (art, music, dance, drama), career education internship, computer science, English, foreign language, mathematics, physical education (includes health), science, social sciences, social studies (includes history), Senior Thesis. Community service is required.

Special Academic Programs Study abroad; academic accommodation for the gifted, the musically talented, and the artistically talented; remedial reading and/or remedial writing; remedial math; programs in English, mathematics, general development for dyslexic students.

College Admission Counseling 27 students graduated in 2013; 22 went to college, including Curry College; Guilford College; Roanoke College; Savannah College of Art and Design; University of Mississippi. Other: 3 entered a postgraduate year, 2 had other specific plans.

Student Life Upper grades have specified standards of dress, student council. Discipline rests primarily with faculty.

Summer Programs Advancement programs offered; session focuses on environmental studies; held both on and off campus; held at Maine; accepts boys and girls; not open to students from other schools. 12 students usually enrolled.

Tuition and Aid Day student tuition: $39,900. Tuition installment plan (FACTS Tuition Payment Plan). Need-based scholarship grants, some funding by local public school systems available. In 2013–14, 18% of upper-school students received aid. Total amount of financial aid awarded in 2013–14: $231,100.

Admissions Traditional secondary-level entrance grade is 9. For fall 2013, 45 students applied for upper-level admission, 19 were accepted, 10 enrolled. Latest standardized score from previous school, psychoeducational evaluation, WISC or WAIS or WISC-III and Woodcock-Johnson required. Deadline for receipt of application materials: February 1. Application fee required: $100. On-campus interview required.

Athletics Interscholastic: basketball (boys, girls), cross-country running (b,g), lacrosse (b,g), soccer (b,g), swimming and diving (b,g), track and field (b,g), volleyball (g); coed interscholastic: cheering, golf, tennis. 6 PE instructors, 1 coach.

Computers Computers are regularly used in all classes. Computer network features include on-campus library services, Internet access, wireless campus network, iPads provided to all high school and eighth-grade students. Computer access in designated common areas is available to students. Students grades are available online. The school has a published electronic and media policy.

Contact Robert Lane, Director of Admissions. 202-944-2214. Fax: 202-454-2338. E-mail: robert.lane@labschool.org. Website: www.labschool.org

LA CHEIM SCHOOL

1413 F Street
Portable 1
Antioch, California 94509

Head of School: Ms. Sue Herrera

General Information Coeducational day general academic and vocational school; primarily serves underachievers, students with learning disabilities, individuals with Attention Deficit Disorder, individuals with emotional and behavioral problems, and bipolar. Grades 1–12. Founded: 1974. Setting: suburban. 5 buildings on campus. Approved or accredited by Western Association of Schools and Colleges and California Department of Education. Total enrollment: 15. Upper school average class size: 10. There are 180 required school days per year for Upper School students. Upper School students typically attend 5 days per week. The average school day consists of 6 hours.

Upper School Student Profile Grade 6: 1 student (1 boy); Grade 7: 2 students (1 boy, 1 girl); Grade 8: 1 student (1 boy); Grade 9: 1 student (1 girl); Grade 10: 2 students (2 boys); Grade 12: 2 students (1 boy, 1 girl).

Faculty School total: 3. In upper school: 2 men.

Subjects Offered Adolescent issues, American government, American history, art, basic skills, biology, economics, grammar, health, language arts, life science, life skills, mathematics, physical education, physical science, science, social studies, vocational skills, world history, writing.

Special Academic Programs Remedial reading and/or remedial writing; remedial math.

College Admission Counseling 1 student graduated in 2012. Other: 1 had other specific plans.

Student Life Upper grades have specified standards of dress. Discipline rests primarily with faculty.

Tuition and Aid Tuition installment plan (expenses covered by referring district and county agencies with no cost to parents).

Admissions Traditional secondary-level entrance grade is 9. Deadline for receipt of application materials: none. No application fee required. On-campus interview required.

Athletics Intramural: basketball (boys, girls), flag football (b,g).

Computers Computers are regularly used in all academic classes. Computer resources include Internet access.

Contact Ms. Sue Herrera, Director. 925-777-1133. Fax: 925-777-9933. E-mail: sue@lacheim.org. Website: www.lacheim.org/schools/index.htm

LANDMARK SCHOOL

PO Box 227
429 Hale Street
Prides Crossing, Massachusetts 01965-0227

Head of School: Robert J. Broudo

General Information Coeducational boarding and day college-preparatory, general academic, and language arts tutorial, skill-based curriculum school; primarily serves students with learning disabilities, dyslexic students, and language-based learning disabilities. Boarding grades 9–12, day grades 2–12. Founded: 1971. Setting: suburban. Nearest major city is Boston. Students are housed in single-sex dormitories. 50-acre campus. 22 buildings on campus. Approved or accredited by Association of Independent Schools in New England, Massachusetts Department of Education, Massachusetts Office of Child Care Services, National Association of Private Schools for Exceptional Children, New England Association of Schools and Colleges, and Massachusetts Department of Education. Member of National Association of Independent Schools. Endowment: $10 million. Total enrollment: 449. Upper school average class size: 8. Upper school faculty-student ratio: 1:9. There are 177 required school days per year for Upper School students. Upper School students typically attend 5 days per week. The average school day consists of 7 hours.

Upper School Student Profile Grade 9: 63 students (53 boys, 10 girls); Grade 10: 83 students (54 boys, 29 girls); Grade 11: 81 students (51 boys, 30 girls); Grade 12: 71 students (48 boys, 23 girls). 45% of students are boarding students. 49% are state residents. 21 states are represented in upper school student body. 3% are international students. International students from Colombia, Mexico, Saudi Arabia, and United Kingdom.

Faculty School total: 84. In upper school: 19 women, 12 men; 12 have advanced degrees; 22 reside on campus.

Subjects Offered Advanced math, algebra, American government, American history, American literature, anatomy and physiology, art, auto mechanics, basketball, biology, boat building, calculus, calculus-AP, chemistry, chorus, communications, composition, computer programming, computer science, consumer mathematics, creative writing, cultural geography, dance, drama, early childhood, environmental science, expressive arts, filmmaking, geometry, grammar, integrated mathematics, language and composition, language arts, literature, marine science, modern world history, multimedia design, newspaper, oral communications, oral expression, photography, physical education, physical science, portfolio art, pragmatics, pre-algebra, pre-calculus, reading, reading/study skills, senior thesis, sociology, study skills, technical theater, technology, U.S. history, woodworking, world history, yearbook.

Graduation Requirements English, mathematics, physical education (includes health), science, social studies (includes history), Landmark School competency tests, minimum grade equivalents on standardized tests in reading and reading comprehension.

Special Academic Programs Study at local college for college credit; remedial reading and/or remedial writing; remedial math; programs in English, mathematics, general development for dyslexic students; special instructional classes for deaf students.

College Admission Counseling 82 students graduated in 2013; all went to college, including Curry College; Lynn University; The University of Arizona; University of Denver; Westfield State University. Mean SAT critical reading: 448, mean SAT math: 430, mean SAT writing: 441.

Student Life Upper grades have specified standards of dress. Discipline rests primarily with faculty.

Summer Programs Remediation programs offered; session focuses on academic remediation and study skills; held on campus; accepts boys and girls; open to students from other schools. 140 students usually enrolled. 2014 schedule: July 6 to August 8. Application deadline: June 2.

Tuition and Aid Day student tuition: $41,600–$49,200; 7-day tuition and room/board: $58,000–$65,500. Tuition installment plan (Key Tuition Payment Plan). Need-based scholarship grants, community and staff grants available. In 2013–14, 5% of upper-school students received aid.

Admissions Traditional secondary-level entrance grade is 9. For fall 2013, 317 students applied for upper-level admission, 196 were accepted, 121 enrolled. Achievement tests, psychoeducational evaluation and WISC or WAIS required. Deadline for receipt of application materials: none. Application fee required: $150. On-campus interview required.

Athletics Interscholastic: baseball (boys), basketball (b,g), lacrosse (b,g), soccer (b,g), tennis (b,g), volleyball (g), wrestling (b); intramural: basketball (b,g), dance (g), floor hockey (b), weight lifting (b), weight training (b); coed interscholastic: cross-country running, golf, swimming and diving, track and field; coed intramural: ropes courses, sailing, skateboarding, skiing (downhill). 5 PE instructors, 1 athletic trainer.

Computers Computers are regularly used in all academic, programming, publishing, technology, yearbook classes. Computer network features include on-campus library services, Internet access, wireless campus network, Internet filtering or blocking technology. Student e-mail accounts are available to students. The school has a published electronic and media policy.

Contact Carol Bedrosian, Admission Liaison. 978-236-3420. Fax: 978-927-7268. E-mail: cbedrosian@landmarkschool.org. Website: www.landmarkschool.org

THE LAUREATE ACADEMY

100 Villa Maria Place
Winnipeg, Manitoba R3V 1A9, Canada

Head of School: Mr. Stino Siragusa

General Information Coeducational day college-preparatory school; primarily serves students with learning disabilities, individuals with Attention Deficit Disorder, and dyslexic students. Grades 1–12. Founded: 1987. Setting: suburban. 10-acre campus. 1 building on campus. Approved or accredited by Manitoba Department of Education. Language of instruction: English. Total enrollment: 80. Upper school average class size: 10. Upper school faculty-student ratio: 1:6. There are 184 required school days per year for Upper School students. Upper School students typically attend 5 days per week. The average school day consists of 6 hours and 15 minutes.

Faculty School total: 16. In upper school: 5 men, 2 women; 3 have advanced degrees.

Subjects Offered All academic.

Graduation Requirements Algebra, biology, Canadian geography, Canadian history, chemistry, communication skills, composition, computer skills, English, English literature, geometry, life issues, mathematics, physical education (includes health), physics, public speaking, science, social studies (includes history), writing, Department of Manitoba Education requirements, classical studies. Community service is required.

Special Academic Programs Academic accommodation for the gifted; remedial reading and/or remedial writing; remedial math; programs in English, mathematics for dyslexic students.

College Admission Counseling 6 students graduated in 2013; 4 went to college, including The University of Winnipeg; University of Manitoba. Other: 2 went to work.

Student Life Upper grades have specified standards of dress, student council, honor system. Discipline rests primarily with faculty.

Summer Programs Remediation programs offered; session focuses on remedial reading; held on campus; accepts boys and girls; open to students from other schools. 8 students usually enrolled. 2014 schedule: July 4 to August 19. Application deadline: June 1.

Tuition and Aid Day student tuition: CAN$18,400. Tuition installment plan (monthly payment plans, quarterly payment plan). Tuition reduction for siblings, bursaries available. In 2013–14, 12% of upper-school students received aid. Total amount of financial aid awarded in 2013–14: CAN$68,000.

Admissions Traditional secondary-level entrance grade is 9. For fall 2013, 9 students applied for upper-level admission, 3 were accepted, 3 enrolled. WISC or WAIS, WISC-III and Woodcock-Johnson and writing sample required. Deadline for receipt of application materials: none. Application fee required: CAN$75. Interview required.

Athletics Interscholastic: basketball (boys), volleyball (b); intramural: badminton (b), ball hockey (b), basketball (b); coed interscholastic: badminton, cross-country running, soccer, track and field, volleyball; coed intramural: aerobics, alpine skiing, badminton, ball hockey, basketball, broomball, combined training, cooperative games, fitness, flag football, floor hockey, Frisbee, jogging, martial arts, outdoor activities, outdoor adventure, outdoor education, outdoor recreation, paddle tennis, physical fitness, physical training, running, self defense, skiing (downhill), snowboarding, soccer, softball, strength & conditioning, table tennis, touch football, track and field, ultimate Frisbee, volleyball, weight lifting, weight training. 2 PE instructors, 4 coaches.

Computers Computers are regularly used in career education, career exploration, computer applications, creative writing, English, mathematics, research skills, science, social studies, writing, yearbook classes. Computer network features include Internet access, wireless campus network, Internet filtering or blocking technology. Campus intranet, student e-mail accounts, and computer access in designated common areas are available to students. The school has a published electronic and media policy.

Contact Mrs. Dora Lawrie, Admissions Coordinator. 204-831-7107. Fax: 204-885-3217. E-mail: dlawrie@laureateacademy.com. Website: www.laureateacademy.com

LAWRENCE SCHOOL

Upper School
10036 Olde Eight Road
Sagamore Hills, Ohio 44067

Head of School: Mr. Lou Salza

General Information Coeducational day college-preparatory school; primarily serves students with learning disabilities, individuals with Attention Deficit Disorder, and dyslexic students. Grades K–12. Founded: 1969. Setting: suburban. Nearest major city is Cleveland. 47-acre campus. 1 building on campus. Approved or accredited by Independent Schools Association of the Central States, North Central Association of Colleges and Schools, and Ohio Department of Education. Endowment: $2 million. Total enrollment: 280. Upper school average class size: 11. Upper school faculty-student ratio: 1:11. There are 185 required school days per year for Upper School students. Upper School students typically attend 5 days per week. The average school day consists of 6 hours.

Faculty School total: 34. In upper school: 12 men, 18 women; 10 have advanced degrees.

Subjects Offered 20th century history, accounting, Advanced Placement courses, algebra, American history, American sign language, anatomy, art, astronomy, biology, calculus, choir, chorus, college counseling, computer applications, consumer economics, creative writing, debate, drama, earth science, economics, English, English composition, forensics, geography, geometry, global studies, government, graphic arts, graphic design, health, integrated mathematics, journalism, keyboarding, language arts, Latin, law, life science, life skills, mathematics, meteorology, military history, music, mythology, painting, physical education, physical science, physics, physics-AP, poetry, pre-algebra, psychology, research skills, sign language, society, politics and law, sociology, Spanish, speech, speech communications, The 20th Century, U.S. history, U.S. history-AP, video, video communication, Web site design, weight training, world geography, world history, yearbook.

Graduation Requirements Independent study project for seniors, community service project.

Special Academic Programs Honors section; independent study; remedial reading and/or remedial writing; remedial math; programs in English, mathematics, general development for dyslexic students.

College Admission Counseling 30 students graduated in 2013; 27 went to college, including Kent State University; Ohio University; Rochester Institute of Technology; The University of Akron; University of Utah; Xavier University. Other: 1 entered military service, 2 entered a postgraduate year.

Student Life Upper grades have specified standards of dress, student council, honor system. Discipline rests equally with students and faculty.

Tuition and Aid Day student tuition: $16,900–$20,750. Tuition installment plan (FACTS Tuition Payment Plan, monthly payment plans, individually arranged payment plans). Need-based scholarship grants available. In 2013–14, 31% of upper-school students received aid. Total amount of financial aid awarded in 2013–14: $800,000.

Admissions Traditional secondary-level entrance grade is 9. Admissions testing required. Deadline for receipt of application materials: none. Application fee required: $100. Interview required.

Athletics Interscholastic: baseball (boys), basketball (b,g), cross-country running (b,g); coed interscholastic: golf; coed intramural: badminton, bowling, cooperative games, fishing, flag football, floor hockey, outdoor activities. 1 PE instructor.

Computers Computers are regularly used in all academic classes. Computer network features include on-campus library services, Internet access, wireless campus network, Internet filtering or blocking technology, one-to-one notebook laptop program for grades 9 to 12, laptop program for grades 7-8, school-wide social networking through Saywire. Student e-mail accounts are available to students. Students grades are available online. The school has a published electronic and media policy.

Contact Mrs. Janet Robinson, Admissions Assistant. 440-526-0717. Fax: 440-526-0595. E-mail: jrobinson@lawrenceschool.org. Website: www.lawrenceschool.org

THE LEELANAU SCHOOL

One Old Homestead Road
Glen Arbor, Michigan 49636

Head of School: Mr. Matthew B. Ralston

General Information Coeducational boarding and day college-preparatory, arts, and experiential program school; primarily serves students with learning disabilities, individuals with Attention Deficit Disorder, dyslexic students, Attention Deficit Hyperactivity Disorder, language-based learning differences, and non-verbal learning disabilities. Grades 9–12. Founded: 1929. Setting: rural. Nearest major city is Traverse City. Students are housed in single-sex dormitories. 50-acre campus. 12 buildings on campus. Approved or accredited by Independent Schools Association of the Central States, Midwest Association of Boarding Schools, National Independent Private Schools Association, The Association of Boarding Schools, The College Board, and Michigan Department of Education. Member of National Association of Independent Schools and Secondary School Admission Test Board. Endowment: $435,200. Total enrollment: 50. Upper school average class size: 6. Upper school faculty-student ratio: 1:5. There are 165 required school days per year for Upper School students. Upper School students typically attend 5 days per week. The average school day consists of 5 hours and 50 minutes.

Upper School Student Profile Grade 9: 5 students (4 boys, 1 girl); Grade 10: 6 students (5 boys, 1 girl); Grade 11: 18 students (13 boys, 5 girls); Grade 12: 21 students (18 boys, 3 girls). 93% of students are boarding students. 25% are state residents. 9 states are represented in upper school student body. 18% are international students. International students from Angola, China, Turkey, and United Kingdom; 3 other countries represented in student body.

Faculty School total: 18. In upper school: 10 men, 5 women; 9 have advanced degrees; 11 reside on campus.

Subjects Offered 20th century history, acting, Advanced Placement courses, advanced TOEFL/grammar, algebra, American Civil War, American government, American history, American literature, anatomy and physiology, ancient history, ancient world history, animation, applied arts, applied music, art, art appreciation, arts, arts and crafts, arts appreciation, astronomy, athletics, audio visual/media, backpacking, basic language skills, biology, biotechnology, boat building, botany, British literature, business studies, calculus, calculus-AP, calligraphy, career and personal planning, career exploration, career/college preparation, cartooning/animation, ceramics, character education, chemistry, civil war history, classical civilization, clayworking, college admission preparation, college awareness, college counseling, college placement, college planning, college writing, comedy, computer animation, computer science, conflict resolution, conservation, constitutional history of U.S., CPR, critical thinking, critical writing, decision making skills, developmental language skills, digital art, digital imaging, digital music, digital photography, drama, drama performance, dramatic arts, drawing, drawing and design, earth science, ecology, electives, English, English as a foreign language, English composition, English literature, entrepreneurship, environmental education, environmental science, environmental studies, environmental systems, epic literature, equestrian sports, equine management, ESL, European history, experiential education, experimental science, expository writing, family living, fiction, field ecology, film and new technologies, filmmaking, fine arts, foreign language, general science, geography, geology, geometry, golf, government/civics, grammar, great books, guitar, history, honors English, human anatomy, human biology, human relations, illustration, improvisation, independent living, independent study, instruments, integrated arts, integrated science, interpersonal skills, jazz band, jazz ensemble, jewelry making, journalism, Korean culture, language, language and composition, language arts, languages, leadership, leadership education training, learning cognition, learning lab, learning strategies, life issues, life management skills, life science, life skills, literacy, literature, literature by women, marine biology, marine ecology, marine science, marine studies, mathematics, mentorship program, modern European history, modern history, modern world history, moral and social development, moral reasoning, multicultural literature, music, music appreciation, Native American history, Native American studies, nature study, nature writers, oil painting, organizational studies, outdoor education, painting, participation in sports, photography, physics, poetry, pottery, pre-calculus, printmaking, psychology, reading/study skills, relationships, religious studies, remedial study skills, remedial/makeup course work, SAT preparation, SAT/ACT preparation, science, science and technology, science project, science research, senior thesis, Shakespeare, silk screening, social studies, Spanish, speech, sports, statistics-AP, student government, studio art, study skills, theater, TOEFL preparation, travel, trigonometry, U.S. government, U.S. government and politics, visual arts, weight training, weightlifting, wellness, wilderness education, wilderness experience, world history, writing, yearbook.

Graduation Requirements Arts and fine arts (art, music, dance, drama), CPR, English, foreign language, mathematics, science, senior thesis, social studies (includes history), senior leadership orientation.

Special Academic Programs 5 Advanced Placement exams for which test preparation is offered; honors section; independent study; term-away projects; remedial reading and/or remedial writing; remedial math; ESL (5 students enrolled).

College Admission Counseling 28 students graduated in 2013; 27 went to college, including Curry College; Michigan Technological University; The College of Wooster; The Evergreen State College. Other: 1 had other specific plans.

Student Life Upper grades have specified standards of dress, student council. Discipline rests primarily with faculty.

Summer Programs Remediation, enrichment, advancement, ESL programs offered; session focuses on remediation and advancement for students with learning differences; held on campus; accepts boys and girls; open to students from other schools. 20 students usually enrolled. 2014 schedule: July 8 to August 5. Application deadline: none.

Tuition and Aid Day student tuition: $24,368; 5-day tuition and room/board: $42,572; 7-day tuition and room/board: $49,853. Tuition installment plan (individually arranged payment plans). Tuition reduction for siblings, need-based scholarship grants, Beals Scholarship for legacy families available. In 2013–14, 25% of upper-school students received aid. Total amount of financial aid awarded in 2013–14: $200,000.

Admissions Traditional secondary-level entrance grade is 10. For fall 2013, 25 students applied for upper-level admission, 25 were accepted, 15 enrolled. Individual IQ, Achievement and behavior rating scale, psychoeducational evaluation, Stanford Test of Academic Skills, TOEFL or SLEP, Wechsler Intelligence Scale for Children, Wechsler Intelligence Scale for Children III, Woodcock-Johnson or writing sample required. Deadline for receipt of application materials: none. Application fee required: $50. On-campus interview required.

Athletics Interscholastic: basketball (boys), volleyball (g); coed interscholastic: dressage, equestrian sports, golf, soccer, tennis; coed intramural: alpine skiing, backpacking, bicycling, broomball, canoeing/kayaking, climbing, combined training, cross-country running, dance team, fishing, fitness, flag football, fly fishing, freestyle skiing, Frisbee, hiking/backpacking, horseback riding, independent competitive sports, jogging, kayaking, mountain biking, outdoor activities, outdoor adventure, outdoor education, outdoor recreation, outdoor skills, outdoors, paddling, paint ball, physical fitness, physical training, rock climbing, ropes courses, running, skiing (cross-country), skiing (downhill), snowboarding, snowshoeing, table tennis, triathlon, wall climbing, yoga. 1 PE instructor, 6 coaches, 1 athletic trainer.

Computers Computers are regularly used in all academic, animation, creative writing classes. Computer resources include on-campus library services, Internet access, wireless campus network, Internet filtering or blocking technology. Students grades are available online.

Contact Ms. Maleah R. Gluck, Director of Admission. 231-334-5824. Fax: 231-334-5898. E-mail: admissions@leelanau.org. Website: www.leelanau.org

LITTLE KESWICK SCHOOL

PO Box 24
Keswick, Virginia 22947

Head of School: Marc J. Columbus

General Information Boys' boarding arts school; primarily serves underachievers, students with learning disabilities, individuals with Attention Deficit Disorder, individuals with emotional and behavioral problems, and dyslexic students. Founded: 1963. Setting: small town. Nearest major city is Washington, DC. Students are housed in single-sex dormitories. 25-acre campus. 10 buildings on campus. Approved or accredited by Virginia Association of Independent Specialized Education Facilities and Virginia Department of Education. Total enrollment: 34. Upper school average class size: 7. Upper school faculty-student ratio: 1:3. There are 205 required school days per year for Upper School students. The average school day consists of 5 hours and 30 minutes.

Upper School Student Profile 100% of students are boarding students. 16 states are represented in upper school student body. 10% are international students. International students from China; 1 other country represented in student body.

Faculty School total: 6. In upper school: 3 men, 3 women; 5 have advanced degrees.

Subjects Offered Algebra, American history, biology, computer applications, earth science, English, geography, government/civics, health, industrial arts, mathematics, physical education, practical arts, social studies, world history.

Special Academic Programs Academic accommodation for the gifted; remedial math; programs in English, mathematics, general development for dyslexic students.

Student Life Upper grades have specified standards of dress. Discipline rests primarily with faculty.

Tuition and Aid 7-day tuition and room/board: $106,294. Need-based scholarship grants available. In 2013–14, 2% of upper-school students received aid. Total amount of financial aid awarded in 2013–14: $20,000.

Admissions WISC/Woodcock-Johnson required. Deadline for receipt of application materials: none. Application fee required: $350. On-campus interview required.

Athletics Interscholastic: basketball (boys), combined training (b); intramural: basketball (b), bicycling (b), climbing (b), cross-country running (b), equestrian sports (b), fishing (b), fitness (b), gymnastics (b), hiking/backpacking (b), horseback riding (b), lacrosse (b), outdoor activities (b). 1 PE instructor, 2 coaches.

Computers Computer resources include Internet access. Computer access in designated common areas is available to students.

Contact Ms. Terry Columbus, Director. 434-295-0457 Ext. 14. Fax: 434-977-1892. E-mail: tcolumbus@littlekeswickschool.net. Website: www.littlekeswickschool.net

MAPLEBROOK SCHOOL

5142 Route 22
Amenia, New York 12501

Head of School: Donna M. Konkolics

General Information Coeducational boarding and day general academic, vocational, technology, and iPad Program school; primarily serves underachievers, students with learning disabilities, individuals with Attention Deficit Disorder, and low average cognitive ability (minimum I.Q. of 70). Ungraded, ages 11–18. Founded: 1945. Setting: small town. Nearest major city is Poughkeepsie. Students are housed in single-sex dormitories. 100-acre campus. 25 buildings on campus. Approved or accredited by Middle States Association of Colleges and Schools, National Association of Private Schools for Exceptional Children, New York Department of Education, New York State Board of Regents, US Department of State, United Private Schools Association of Pennsylvania, and New York Department of Education. Member of National Association of Independent Schools. Endowment: $500,000. Total enrollment: 75. Upper school average class size: 6. Upper school faculty-student ratio: 1:8. There are 180 required school days per year for Upper School students. Upper School students typically attend 7 days per week. The average school day consists of 6 hours and 5 minutes.

Upper School Student Profile 98% of students are boarding students. 16% are state residents. 18 states are represented in upper school student body. 25% are international students. International students from Egypt, Hong Kong, Morocco, Nigeria, South Africa, and United Kingdom; 8 other countries represented in student body.

Faculty School total: 55. In upper school: 12 men, 14 women; 26 have advanced degrees; 50 reside on campus.

Subjects Offered Algebra, American history, art, biology, business skills, computer science, consumer mathematics, creative writing, drama, driver education, earth science, English, geography, global studies, government/civics, health, home economics, industrial arts, integrated mathematics, keyboarding, mathematics, music, occupational education, performing arts, photography, physical education, physical science, science, social skills, speech, theater, world history, writing.

Graduation Requirements Career and personal planning, computer science, English, mathematics, physical education (includes health), science, social sciences, social skills, social studies (includes history), attendance at Maplebrook School for a minimum of 2 years.

Special Academic Programs Study at local college for college credit; remedial reading and/or remedial writing; remedial math; programs in English, mathematics, general development for dyslexic students; ESL (3 students enrolled).

College Admission Counseling 20 students graduated in 2013; 6 went to college, including Dutchess Community College; Mitchell College. Other: 14 entered a postgraduate year.

Student Life Upper grades have specified standards of dress, student council, honor system. Discipline rests primarily with faculty.

Summer Programs Remediation, enrichment, sports, art/fine arts, computer instruction programs offered; session focuses on preventing regression of skills; held both on and off campus; held at various locations for New York City day and overnight trips; accepts boys and girls; open to students from other schools. 45 students usually enrolled. 2014 schedule: June 29 to August 9. Application deadline: none.

Tuition and Aid Day student tuition: $32,000; 5-day tuition and room/board: $55,000; 7-day tuition and room/board: $59,900. Tuition installment plan (Key Tuition Payment Plan, individually arranged payment plans, Tuition Management Systems Plan, Sallie Mae loans). Merit scholarship grants, need-based scholarship grants, need-based loans, middle-income loans, paying campus jobs, minority and cultural diversity scholarships, day student scholarships, merit scholarships available. In 2013–14, 20% of upper-school students received aid; total upper-school merit-scholarship money awarded: $10,000. Total amount of financial aid awarded in 2013–14: $100,000.

Admissions Traditional secondary-level entrance age is 15. For fall 2013, 184 students applied for upper-level admission, 63 were accepted, 30 enrolled. Achievement tests, Bender Gestalt, TerraNova, Test of Achievement and Proficiency or WISC or WAIS required. Deadline for receipt of application materials: none. No application fee required. Interview required.

Athletics Interscholastic: basketball (boys, girls), cheering (g), field hockey (g); coed interscholastic: cooperative games, cross-country running, equestrian sports, fitness, freestyle skiing, horseback riding, running, skiing (cross-country), skiing (downhill), soccer, softball, swimming and diving, tennis, track and field, weight lifting, weight training; coed intramural: aerobics/dance, alpine skiing, basketball, bicycling, bowling, cooperative games, cricket, dance, figure skating, fitness, fitness walking, flag football, floor hockey, freestyle skiing, golf, hiking/backpacking, horseback riding, ice skating, indoor hockey, martial arts, outdoor education, outdoor recreation, roller blading, skiing (cross-country), skiing (downhill), soccer, softball, Special Olympics, swimming and diving, table tennis, tennis, volleyball, weight lifting, weight training, wrestling. 1 PE instructor, 12 coaches.

Computers Computers are regularly used in all academic classes. Computer network features include on-campus library services, Internet access, wireless campus network, Internet filtering or blocking technology. Campus intranet, student e-mail accounts, and computer access in designated common areas are available to students. Students grades are available online. The school has a published electronic and media policy.

Contact Jennifer L. Scully, Dean of Admissions. 845-373-8191. Fax: 845-373-7029. E-mail: admissions@maplebrookschool.org. Website: www.maplebrookschool.org

MILL SPRINGS ACADEMY

13660 New Providence Road
Alpharetta, Georgia 30004

Head of School: Mr. Robert W. Moore

General Information Coeducational day college-preparatory and arts school; primarily serves students with learning disabilities, individuals with Attention Deficit Disorder, and dyslexic students. Grades 1–12. Founded: 1981. Setting: suburban. Nearest major city is Atlanta. 85-acre campus. 5 buildings on campus. Approved or accredited by Georgia Association of Private Schools for Exceptional Children, Georgia Independent School Association, Southern Association of Colleges and Schools, and Southern Association of Independent Schools. Member of National Association of Independent Schools. Endowment: $140,000. Total enrollment: 321. Upper school average class size: 10. Upper school faculty-student ratio: 1:4. There are 180 required school days per year for Upper School students. Upper School students typically attend 5 days per week. The average school day consists of 7 hours.

Upper School Student Profile Grade 9: 49 students (38 boys, 11 girls); Grade 10: 33 students (28 boys, 5 girls); Grade 11: 38 students (23 boys, 15 girls); Grade 12: 25 students (18 boys, 7 girls).

Faculty School total: 49. In upper school: 11 men, 10 women; 15 have advanced degrees.

Subjects Offered Algebra, American history, American literature, anatomy and physiology, art, band, biology, British literature, British literature (honors), calculus, career/college preparation, chemistry, chorus, composition, creative writing, diversity studies, drama, ecology, economics, film, geometry, government, health, history, honors algebra, honors English, honors geometry, honors U.S. history, honors world history, journalism, literature, media, music theater, performing arts, physical education, physics, play production, play/screen writing, playwriting and directing, political science, pre-algebra, pre-calculus, psychology, sculpture, senior project, set design, Spanish, state government, studio art, symphonic band, technology, theater, theater design and production, trigonometry, U.S. history, values and decisions, visual and performing arts, voice, world literature, yearbook.

Graduation Requirements Algebra, American history, American literature, anatomy and physiology, biology, British literature, British literature (honors), calculus, chemistry, civics, ecology, economics, geometry, physical education (includes health), physics, Spanish, trigonometry, world history, world literature, senior English, 6 units of electives.

Special Academic Programs Honors section; study at local college for college credit; academic accommodation for the gifted, the musically talented, and the artistically talented; programs in English, mathematics, general development for dyslexic students.

College Admission Counseling 12 students graduated in 2012; 9 went to college, including Andrew College; Georgia College & State University; Georgia Perimeter College; Reinhardt University; Valdosta State University; Young Harris College. Other: 1 went to work, 1 entered military service, 1 had other specific plans. Mean SAT critical reading: 459, mean SAT math: 436, mean SAT writing: 426, mean composite ACT: 18. 4% scored over 600 on SAT critical reading, 3% scored over 600 on SAT math, 1% scored over 600 on SAT writing, 1% scored over 26 on composite ACT.

Student Life Upper grades have uniform requirement, student council, honor system. Discipline rests equally with students and faculty.

Tuition and Aid Day student tuition: $20,570. Tuition installment plan (FACTS Tuition Payment Plan). Tuition reduction for siblings, need-based scholarship grants available. In 2012–13, 14% of upper-school students received aid. Total amount of financial aid awarded in 2012–13: $77,000.

Admissions Traditional secondary-level entrance grade is 9. For fall 2012, 34 students applied for upper-level admission, 26 were accepted, 24 enrolled. Psychoeducational evaluation required. Deadline for receipt of application materials: none. Application fee required: $100. On-campus interview required.

Athletics Interscholastic: baseball (boys), basketball (b,g), golf (b), lacrosse (b), tennis (b,g), volleyball (g), wrestling (b); intramural: cheering (g), strength & conditioning (b), weight lifting (b); coed interscholastic: cross-country running, soccer, swimming and diving, track and field; coed intramural: archery, dance, fencing, fishing, golf, mountain biking, outdoor activities, physical fitness, scuba diving, yoga. 2 coaches.

Computers Computers are regularly used in all academic classes. Computer network features include on-campus library services, Internet access, wireless campus network, Internet filtering or blocking technology, all students 4-12th grades have laptops, electronic textbooks/literature books, assignments online. Student e-mail accounts are available to students. Students grades are available online. The school has a published electronic and media policy.

Contact Mrs. Sheila FitzGerald, Admissions Director. 770-360-1336 Ext. 1707. Fax: 770-360-1341. E-mail: sfitzgerald@millsprings.org. Website: www.millsprings.org

NOBLE ACADEMY

3310 Horse Pen Creek Road
Greensboro, North Carolina 27410

Head of School: Linda Hale

General Information Coeducational day college-preparatory, arts, and technology school; primarily serves students with learning disabilities, individuals with Attention Deficit Disorder, and dyslexic students. Grades K–12. Founded: 1987. Setting: suburban. Nearest major city is Greensboro/Winston-Salem. 40-acre campus. 3 buildings on campus. Approved or accredited by North Carolina Department of Exceptional Children, Southern Association of Colleges and Schools, Southern Association of Independent Schools, and North Carolina Department of Education. Endowment: $2.1 million. Total enrollment: 163. Upper school average class size: 9. Upper school faculty-student ratio: 1:9. There are 180 required school days per year for Upper School students. Upper School students typically attend 5 days per week. The average school day consists of 6 hours and 45 minutes.

Upper School Student Profile Grade 10: 19 students (15 boys, 4 girls); Grade 11: 14 students (11 boys, 3 girls); Grade 12: 6 students (6 boys).

Faculty School total: 34. In upper school: 3 men, 11 women; 5 have advanced degrees.

Subjects Offered Algebra, American history, art, basic skills, biology, career and personal planning, career exploration, chemistry, civics, college counseling, drama, earth science, economics, English, environmental science, geometry, health, journalism, life management skills, political systems, pre-algebra, pre-calculus, reading, reading/study skills, Spanish, world history, world history-AP, yearbook.

Graduation Requirements Algebra, American history, biology, earth science, economics, English, environmental science, geometry, physical education (includes health), Spanish, world history, 8th grade end-of-grade test, 20th percentile score on standardized reading test, North Carolina Computer Competency Test.

Special Academic Programs Study at local college for college credit; remedial reading and/or remedial writing; remedial math; programs in English, mathematics, general development for dyslexic students.

College Admission Counseling 14 students graduated in 2012; 10 went to college, including Brevard College; Elon University; Guilford College; St. Andrews University; The University of North Carolina at Greensboro; William Peace University. Other: 3 went to work, 1 had other specific plans. Median SAT critical reading: 510, median SAT math: 420, median SAT writing: 480. Mean combined SAT: 1458. 12% scored over 600 on SAT critical reading, 12% scored over 600 on SAT math, 12% scored over 600 on SAT writing.

Student Life Upper grades have student council, honor system. Discipline rests primarily with faculty.

Tuition and Aid Day student tuition: $15,850. Tuition installment plan (monthly payment plans, individually arranged payment plans). Need-based scholarship grants available. In 2012–13, 8% of upper-school students received aid. Total amount of financial aid awarded in 2012–13: $52,700.

Admissions Traditional secondary-level entrance grade is 10. For fall 2012, 12 students applied for upper-level admission, 7 were accepted, 7 enrolled. WISC/Woodcock-Johnson required. Deadline for receipt of application materials: none. Application fee required: $75. On-campus interview required.

Athletics Interscholastic: cheering (girls); coed interscholastic: basketball, cross-country running, flag football, golf, soccer, tennis, volleyball; coed intramural: tennis. 1 PE instructor, 7 coaches.

Computers Computers are regularly used in art, career education, career exploration, career technology, college planning, computer applications, current events, graphic arts, graphic design, history, information technology, introduction to technology, journalism, keyboarding, lab/keyboard, photography, social studies, Spanish, study skills, word processing, writing, writing, yearbook classes. Computer network features include Internet access, wireless campus network, Internet filtering or blocking technology. Student e-mail accounts are available to students. Students grades are available online. The school has a published electronic and media policy.

Contact Tim Montgomery, Assistant Head and Director of Admissions. 336-282-7044. Fax: 336-282-2048. E-mail: tmontgomery@nobleknights.org. Website: www.nobleknights.org

NORMAN HOWARD SCHOOL

275 Pinnacle Road
Rochester, New York 14623

Head of School: Linda Lawrence

General Information Coeducational day college-preparatory, general academic, and arts school; primarily serves students with learning disabilities, individuals with Attention Deficit Disorder, dyslexic students, and Autism (high functioning), anxiety. Boys grades 4–12, girls grades 5–12. Founded: 1980. Setting: suburban. 2-acre campus. 1 building on campus. Approved or accredited by New York State Board of Regents and New York Department of Education. Total enrollment: 123. Upper school average class size: 10. Upper school faculty-student ratio: 1:3. There are 180 required school days per year for Upper School students. Upper School students typically attend 5 days per week. The average school day consists of 6 hours and 30 minutes.

Upper School Student Profile Grade 9: 17 students (12 boys, 5 girls); Grade 10: 22 students (16 boys, 6 girls); Grade 11: 22 students (14 boys, 8 girls); Grade 12: 21 students (16 boys, 5 girls).

Faculty School total: 42. In upper school: 14 men, 11 women; 18 have advanced degrees.

Subjects Offered Algebra, American history, American literature, art, athletics, biology, career/college preparation, chemistry, creative writing, drama, earth science, ecology, economics, English, English literature, environmental science, European history, expository writing, geography, geometry, government/civics, history, keyboarding, life science, mathematics, photography, physical education, reading, reading/study skills, science, social studies, world history, writing.

Graduation Requirements Arts and fine arts (art, music, dance, drama), English, mathematics, physical education (includes health), science, social studies (includes history).

Special Academic Programs Independent study; study at local college for college credit; remedial reading and/or remedial writing; remedial math; programs in English, mathematics, general development for dyslexic students; special instructional classes for deaf students.

College Admission Counseling 20 students graduated in 2013; 13 went to college, including Monroe Community College. Other: 2 entered military service, 2 entered a postgraduate year, 3 had other specific plans.

Student Life Upper grades have uniform requirement, student council, honor system. Discipline rests equally with students and faculty.

Tuition and Aid Day student tuition: $26,000. Tuition installment plan (monthly payment plans, 60/40 Payment Option Plan). Need-based scholarship grants, substantial financial aid to families who qualify available.

Admissions Traditional secondary-level entrance grade is 9. Deadline for receipt of application materials: none. Application fee required: $50. On-campus interview required.

Athletics Coed Intramural: basketball, fitness, outdoor adventure, outdoor education, physical fitness, skiing (cross-country), skiing (downhill). 2 PE instructors.

Computers Computers are regularly used in creative writing, English, history, library skills, mathematics, photography, reading, science, social studies, writing, yearbook classes. Computer network features include on-campus library services, Internet access, wireless campus network, Internet filtering or blocking technology. Campus intranet and computer access in designated common areas are available to students. Students grades are available online. The school has a published electronic and media policy.

Contact Julie Murray, Admissions and Marketing Manager. 585-334-8010 Ext. 302. Fax: 585-334-8073. E-mail: jmurray@normanhoward.org. Website: www.normanhoward.org

OAKLAND SCHOOL

Boyd Tavern
Keswick, Virginia 22947

Head of School: Ms. Carol Williams

General Information Coeducational boarding and day general academic school; primarily serves underachievers, students with learning disabilities, individuals with Attention Deficit Disorder, dyslexic students, processing difficulties, and organizational challenges. Boarding grades 2–8, day grades 1–8. Founded: 1950. Setting: rural. Nearest major city is Richmond. Students are housed in single-sex dormitories. 450-acre campus. 25 buildings on campus. Approved or accredited by Virginia Association of Independent Specialized Education Facilities and Virginia Department of Education. Upper school average class size: 5. Upper school faculty-student ratio: 1:5. There are 180 required school days per year for Upper School students. Upper School students typically attend 5 days per week. The average school day consists of 6 hours and 45 minutes.

Upper School Student Profile 43% of students are boarding students. 55% are state residents. 9 states are represented in upper school student body. 22% are international students. International students from Colombia, United Arab Emirates, and Zimbabwe.

Faculty School total: 12. In upper school: 3 men, 8 women; 9 have advanced degrees; 2 reside on campus.

Subjects Offered Algebra, American history, art, art and culture, art appreciation, art history, computer literacy, computer skills, consumer mathematics, drama, drama performance, earth science, English, English composition, expository writing, geometry, grammar, health, health and wellness, health education, history of the Americas, keyboarding, life science, mathematics, physical education, physical science, remedial study skills, study skills, U.S. and Virginia history, world history.

Graduation Requirements Skills must be at or above grade/ability level.

Special Academic Programs Remedial reading and/or remedial writing; remedial math; programs in English, mathematics for dyslexic students.

College Admission Counseling 12 students graduated in 2013. Other: 12 had other specific plans.

Student Life Upper grades have specified standards of dress, student council, honor system. Discipline rests primarily with faculty.

Summer Programs Remediation, sports, art/fine arts, computer instruction programs offered; session focuses on academics; held on campus; accepts boys and girls; open to students from other schools. 135 students usually enrolled. 2014 schedule: June 29 to August 1.

Tuition and Aid Day student tuition: $27,500; 7-day tuition and room/board: $46,500. Tuition installment plan (SMART Tuition Payment Plan, individually arranged payment plans). Need-based scholarship grants available.

Admissions Wechsler Intelligence Scale for Children III required. Deadline for receipt of application materials: none. No application fee required. Interview required.

Athletics Interscholastic: basketball (boys, girls), cheering (g), cross-country running (b,g), equestrian sports (b,g), fishing (b,g), fitness (b,g), handball (b,g), horseback riding (b,g), outdoor activities (b,g), outdoor adventure (b,g), outdoor education (b,g), outdoor recreation (b,g), outdoor skills (b,g), outdoors (b,g), physical fitness (b,g), physical training (b,g), roller skating (b,g), running (b,g), soccer (b,g), softball (b,g), table tennis (b,g), tennis (b,g), volleyball (b,g), weight training (b,g), wilderness (b,g), wildernessways (b,g); intramural: soccer (b,g), yoga (g); coed interscholastic: aerobics/dance, archery, basketball, bicycling, cross-country running, equestrian sports, fishing, fitness, handball, horseback riding, kickball, outdoor activities, outdoor adventure, outdoor education, outdoor skills, outdoors, physical training, roller skating, running, soccer, softball, table tennis, tennis, volleyball, weight training, wilderness, wildernessways; coed intramural: archery, basketball, bicycling, billiards, cooperative games, cross-country running, equestrian sports, fishing, fitness, Frisbee, hiking/backpacking, horseback riding, in-line skating, indoor soccer, kickball, lacrosse, mountain biking, outdoor activities, outdoor recreation, outdoors, paddle tennis, physical fitness, roller blading, roller skating, running, skateboarding, soccer, softball, swimming and diving, table tennis, tennis. 1 PE instructor, 4 coaches.

Computers Computers are regularly used in English, word processing, writing classes. Computer resources include Internet access. The school has a published electronic and media policy.

Contact Mrs. Jamie Cato, Admissions Director. 434-293-9059. Fax: 434-296-8930. E-mail: admissions@oaklandschool.net. Website: www.oaklandschool.net

THE PATHWAY SCHOOL

162 Egypt Road
Norristown, Pennsylvania 19403

Head of School: Dr. Edmond Watters

General Information Coeducational day general academic, life skills/functional academics, and pre-vocational/career education school; primarily serves underachievers, students with learning disabilities, individuals with Attention Deficit Disorder, individuals with emotional and behavioral problems, neurologically impaired students, students with neuropsychiatric disorders, Asperger's Syndrome, Emotional Disturbance, and students needing speech/language therapy and occupational therapy. Ungraded, ages 7–21. Founded: 1961. Setting: suburban. Nearest major city is Philadelphia. 12-acre campus. 12 buildings on campus. Approved or accredited by Pennsylvania Department of Education. Endowment: $1 million. Total enrollment: 120. Upper school average class size: 9. Upper school faculty-student ratio: 1:6. There are 181 required school days per year for Upper School students. Upper School students typically attend 5 days per week. The average school day consists of 5 hours and 30 minutes.

Faculty School total: 22. In upper school: 2 men, 6 women; 4 have advanced degrees.

Subjects Offered Algebra, art, biology, career education, career experience, career/college preparation, computer skills, consumer mathematics, creative arts, drama, earth science, electives, English, environmental science, general math, geometry, health education, history, horticulture, interpersonal skills, language arts, mathematics, money management, physical education, pre-vocational education, senior seminar, social skills, social studies, work experience, world history.

Graduation Requirements Graduation requirements are as specified by the sending school district.

Special Academic Programs Study at local college for college credit; remedial reading and/or remedial writing; remedial math; programs in general development for dyslexic students; special instructional classes for emotional support program.

College Admission Counseling 24 students graduated in 2013; 4 went to college. Other: 16 went to work, 4 entered a postgraduate year.

Student Life Upper grades have student council. Discipline rests equally with students and faculty.

Summer Programs Remediation programs offered; session focuses on providing consistency for the entire calendar year; held on campus; accepts boys and girls; open to students from other schools. 85 students usually enrolled. 2014 schedule: July 7 to August 15.

Tuition and Aid Day student tuition: $46,790. Tuition installment plan (individually arranged payment plans).

Admissions Traditional secondary-level entrance age is 15. For fall 2013, 4 students applied for upper-level admission, 2 were accepted, 1 enrolled. Deadline for receipt of application materials: none. No application fee required. On-campus interview required.

Athletics Interscholastic: basketball (boys, girls), softball (b,g), Special Olympics (b,g); coed interscholastic: soccer, Special Olympics; coed intramural: basketball, flag football, soccer. 2 PE instructors, 2 coaches.

Computers Computers are regularly used in basic skills, business education, business skills, career education, data processing, newspaper, typing classes. Computer network features include Internet access, Internet filtering or blocking technology,

computer access in classroom. Computer access in designated common areas is available to students. The school has a published electronic and media policy.
Contact Diana Phifer, Director of Admissions. 610-277-0660 Ext. 289. Fax: 610-539-1493. E-mail: dphifer@pathwayschool.org. Website: www.pathwayschool.org

PINEHURST SCHOOL

10 Seymour Avenue
St. Catharines, Ontario L2P 1A4, Canada
Head of School: Mr. Dave Bird

General Information Coeducational boarding college-preparatory, arts, business, and technology school; primarily serves students with learning disabilities, individuals with Attention Deficit Disorder, and individuals with emotional and behavioral problems. Grades 7–12. Founded: 2000. Setting: urban. Students are housed in single-sex by floor dormitories. 5-acre campus. 1 building on campus. Approved or accredited by Ontario Ministry of Education and Ontario Department of Education. Language of instruction: English. Total enrollment: 22. Upper school average class size: 10. Upper school faculty-student ratio: 1:10. There are 165 required school days per year for Upper School students. Upper School students typically attend 5 days per week. The average school day consists of 5 hours and 50 minutes.
Upper School Student Profile Grade 11: 5 students (2 boys, 3 girls); Grade 12: 8 students (6 boys, 2 girls). 100% of students are boarding students. 90% are province residents. 2 provinces are represented in upper school student body. 10% are international students. International students from United States and Venezuela.
Faculty School total: 5. In upper school: 3 men, 2 women; 2 have advanced degrees.
Subjects Offered Science.
Graduation Requirements 20th century world history, art, business applications, Canadian geography, English, French, geography, health education, history, math applications, mathematics, science, outdoor education.
Special Academic Programs Honors section; accelerated programs; independent study; remedial reading and/or remedial writing; remedial math.
College Admission Counseling 8 students graduated in 2012; 1 went to college. Other: 7 entered a postgraduate year.
Student Life Upper grades have uniform requirement, student council, honor system. Discipline rests primarily with faculty.
Tuition and Aid 7-day tuition and room/board: CAN$35,000. Tuition installment plan (monthly payment plans).
Admissions Traditional secondary-level entrance grade is 11. For fall 2012, 5 students applied for upper-level admission, 5 were accepted, 5 enrolled. Deadline for receipt of application materials: none. No application fee required. On-campus interview required.
Athletics Coed Intramural: alpine skiing, aquatics, archery, backpacking, badminton, ball hockey, baseball, basketball, bicycling, billiards, blading, bocce, bowling, canoeing/kayaking, climbing, cooperative games, cricket, croquet, curling, field hockey, fishing, fitness, fitness walking, flag football, floor hockey, football, golf, hiking/backpacking, hockey, ice hockey, ice skating, in-line skating, indoor hockey, indoor soccer, kayaking, mountain biking, outdoor activities, outdoor adventure, outdoor education, outdoor skills, paddling, physical fitness, physical training, rock climbing, roller blading, ropes courses, running, scuba diving, skateboarding, skiing (cross-country), skiing (downhill), snowboarding, snowshoeing, soccer, softball, street hockey, strength & conditioning, swimming and diving, table tennis, touch football, volleyball, walking, wall climbing, weight lifting, weight training, wilderness, wilderness survival, wildernessways, winter soccer, winter walking, yoga. 1 PE instructor, 1 coach, 1 athletic trainer.
Computers Computers are regularly used in all classes. Computer network features include on-campus library services, Internet access, wireless campus network, Internet filtering or blocking technology. Student e-mail accounts are available to students.
Contact Mrs. Donna MacDonald, Admissions/Office Coordinator. 905-641-0993. Fax: 905-641-0399. E-mail: pinedonna@sympatico.ca. Website: www.pinehurst.on.ca

SHELTON SCHOOL AND EVALUATION CENTER

15720 Hillcrest Road
Dallas, Texas 75248
Head of School: Linda Kneese

General Information Coeducational day college-preparatory and general academic school; primarily serves students with learning disabilities, individuals with Attention Deficit Disorder, and dyslexic students. Grades PS–12. Founded: 1976. Setting: suburban. 1-acre campus. 1 building on campus. Approved or accredited by Independent Schools Association of the Southwest and Southern Association of Independent Schools. Endowment: $4.6 million. Total enrollment: 827. Upper school average class size: 8. Upper school faculty-student ratio: 1:8. There are 170 required school days per year for Upper School students. Upper School students typically attend 5 days per week. The average school day consists of 6 hours.
Upper School Student Profile Grade 9: 72 students (46 boys, 26 girls); Grade 10: 65 students (36 boys, 29 girls); Grade 11: 59 students (33 boys, 26 girls); Grade 12: 66 students (44 boys, 22 girls).

Faculty School total: 147. In upper school: 13 men, 28 women; 26 have advanced degrees.
Subjects Offered All academic, American sign language, ethics, Spanish, theater arts.
Graduation Requirements Arts and fine arts (art, music, dance, drama), computers, English, ethics, foreign language, mathematics, physical education (includes health), reading, science, social studies (includes history), speech.
Special Academic Programs Programs in English, mathematics, general development for dyslexic students.
College Admission Counseling 63 students graduated in 2013; 61 went to college, including Hendrix College; Stephen F. Austin State University; Texas A&M University; Texas State University–San Marcos; Texas Tech University; University of Arkansas. Other: 2 had other specific plans.
Student Life Upper grades have uniform requirement, student council, honor system. Discipline rests primarily with faculty.
Summer Programs Enrichment programs offered; session focuses on enrichment; held on campus; accepts boys and girls; open to students from other schools. 39 students usually enrolled. 2014 schedule: June 30 to July 25. Application deadline: May 9.
Tuition and Aid Day student tuition: $22,000. Tuition installment plan (SMART Tuition Payment Plan, Sallie Mae). Need-based scholarship grants available. In 2013–14, 16% of upper-school students received aid. Total amount of financial aid awarded in 2013–14: $225,950.
Admissions Traditional secondary-level entrance grade is 9. For fall 2013, 42 students applied for upper-level admission, 16 were accepted, 11 enrolled. WISC/Woodcock-Johnson required. Deadline for receipt of application materials: none. No application fee required. Interview required.
Athletics Interscholastic: baseball (boys), basketball (b,g), cheering (g), cross-country running (b,g), dance squad (g), drill team (g), football (b), tennis (b,g), track and field (b,g), volleyball (g); coed interscholastic: golf, soccer. 4 PE instructors, 2 coaches, 1 athletic trainer.
Computers Computers are regularly used in all academic, English, foreign language, information technology, lab/keyboard, library, research skills, SAT preparation, video film production classes. Computer network features include on-campus library services, Internet access, wireless campus network, Internet filtering or blocking technology. Campus intranet and student e-mail accounts are available to students. Students grades are available online. The school has a published electronic and media policy.
Contact Diann Slaton, Director of Admission. 972-774-1772. Fax: 972-991-3977. E-mail: dslaton@shelton.org. Website: www.shelton.org

SHOORE CENTRE FOR LEARNING

801 Eglinton Avenue West
Suite 201
Toronto, Ontario M5N 1E3, Canada
Head of School: Mr. Michael I. Shoore

General Information Coeducational day general academic and literacy, study skills, high school credit courses school; primarily serves underachievers, students with learning disabilities, individuals with Attention Deficit Disorder, individuals with emotional and behavioral problems, dyslexic students, and Autism Spectrum Disorder and Acquired Brain Injury. Grades 8–12. Founded: 1975. Setting: urban. 1 building on campus. Approved or accredited by Ontario Department of Education. Language of instruction: English. Total enrollment: 30. Upper school average class size: 6. Upper school faculty-student ratio: 1:6. There are 200 required school days per year for Upper School students. Upper School students typically attend 5 days per week. The average school day consists of 5 hours.
Faculty School total: 8. In upper school: 5 men, 2 women; 3 have advanced degrees.
Subjects Offered Advanced math, anthropology, art, business studies, calculus, Canadian geography, Canadian history, Canadian law, career education, chemistry, civics, drama, dramatic arts, earth science, English, general science, health and safety, history, independent study, law, mathematics, media arts, parenting, physical education, physics, science, science and technology, technology, visual arts, writing.
Special Academic Programs Remedial reading and/or remedial writing; remedial math; programs in English, mathematics; general development for dyslexic students; special instructional classes for high school credits, skill building.
College Admission Counseling 6 students graduated in 2012. Other: 4 entered a postgraduate year.
Student Life Upper grades have specified standards of dress. Discipline rests primarily with faculty.
Tuition and Aid Day student tuition: CAN$27,500. Tuition installment plan (monthly payment plans, individually arranged payment plans). Financial aid available to upper-school students. In 2012–13, 10% of upper-school students received aid.
Admissions Deadline for receipt of application materials: none. No application fee required. Interview required.
Computers Computers are regularly used in aerospace science classes. Computer resources include Internet access.
Contact Mr. Michael I. Shoore, Director. 416-781-4754. Fax: 416-781 0163. E-mail: info@shoorecentre.com. Website: www.shoorecentre.com

SMITH SCHOOL

131 West 86 Street
New York, New York 10024

Head of School: Karen Smith

General Information Coeducational day college-preparatory and art, music and technology programs school; primarily serves students with learning disabilities, individuals with Attention Deficit Disorder, and depression or anxiety disorders; emotional and/or motivational issues. Grades 7–12. Founded: 1990. Setting: urban. 1 building on campus. Approved or accredited by Middle States Association of Colleges and Schools, New York State Board of Regents, Rhode Island State Certified Resource Progam, Western Catholic Education Association, and New York Department of Education. Total enrollment: 57. Upper school average class size: 4. Upper school faculty-student ratio: 1:4. There are 160 required school days per year for Upper School students. Upper School students typically attend 5 days per week. The average school day consists of 6 hours and 30 minutes.

Upper School Student Profile Grade 9: 10 students (4 boys, 6 girls); Grade 10: 11 students (4 boys, 7 girls); Grade 11: 9 students (4 boys, 5 girls); Grade 12: 12 students (5 boys, 7 girls).

Faculty School total: 14. In upper school: 6 men, 8 women; all have advanced degrees.

Subjects Offered Algebra, American history, art, biology, chemistry, computer skills, earth science, English, environmental science, European history, film, French, geometry, lab science, life science, physical science, physics, pre-calculus, Spanish, trigonometry, U.S. government, U.S. history, world history.

Graduation Requirements Algebra, American history, art, biology, chemistry, conceptual physics, earth science, English, environmental science, European history, geometry, government, health education, languages, physical education (includes health), physical science, pre-algebra, pre-calculus, trigonometry, world history, community service/20 hours per year.

Special Academic Programs Accelerated programs; independent study; study at local college for college credit; remedial reading and/or remedial writing; remedial math; special instructional classes for peer mediation, socialization, and motivational issues.

College Admission Counseling 12 students graduated in 2013; all went to college, including American University; Fordham University; Purchase College, State University of New York; State University of New York at New Paltz; Syracuse University; Tulane University. Median SAT critical reading: 600, median SAT math: 620, median SAT writing: 620, median combined SAT: 600. 50% scored over 600 on SAT critical reading, 40% scored over 600 on SAT math, 50% scored over 600 on SAT writing, 45% scored over 1800 on combined SAT, 60% scored over 26 on composite ACT.

Student Life Upper grades have student council, honor system. Discipline rests primarily with faculty.

Summer Programs Remediation, enrichment, advancement, computer instruction programs offered; session focuses on academic courses for enrichment, remediation, or credit; held both on and off campus; held at local colleges; accepts boys and girls; open to students from other schools. 25 students usually enrolled. 2014 schedule: June 12 to August 15. Application deadline: June 1.

Tuition and Aid Day student tuition: $36,500–$52,500. Tuition installment plan (monthly payment plans, individually arranged payment plans, quarterly payment plan). Tuition reduction for siblings available. In 2013–14, 10% of upper-school students received aid. Total amount of financial aid awarded in 2013–14: $30,000.

Admissions Traditional secondary-level entrance grade is 9. For fall 2013, 47 students applied for upper-level admission, 26 were accepted, 21 enrolled. Comprehensive educational evaluation, psychoeducational evaluation, school placement exam, Wide Range Achievement Test or writing sample required. Deadline for receipt of application materials: none. Application fee required: $50. On-campus interview required.

Athletics Coed Interscholastic: basketball, dance, martial arts, physical fitness, running, volleyball, yoga. 2 PE instructors, 2 coaches.

Computers Computers are regularly used in creative writing, English, history, research skills, writing, yearbook classes. Computer network features include Internet access, wireless campus network, Internet filtering or blocking technology, yearbook and monthly newsletter. Computer access in designated common areas is available to students. The school has a published electronic and media policy.

Contact Jennifer Sudary-Narine, Executive Assistant. 212-879-6317. Fax: 212-879-0962. E-mail: jsudary@smithschool.org. Website: www.smithschool.org

SUMMIT PREPARATORY SCHOOL

1605 Danielson Road
Kalispell, Montana 59901

Head of School: Todd Fiske, M.Ed

General Information Coeducational boarding college-preparatory and arts school; primarily serves students with learning disabilities, individuals with Attention Deficit Disorder, individuals with emotional and behavioral problems, dyslexic students, college-bound students with depression, anxiety, family conflict, and substance abuse, adoption issues, trauma, ADHD, mild learning disabilities. Grades 9–12. Founded: 2003. Setting: rural. Students are housed in single-sex dormitories. 540-acre campus. 4 buildings on campus. Approved or accredited by Association for Experiential Education, Northwest Accreditation Commission, Northwest Association of Independent Schools, and Montana Department of Education. Total enrollment: 46. Upper school average class size: 8. Upper school faculty-student ratio: 1:5. The average school day consists of 5 hours.

Upper School Student Profile 100% of students are boarding students. 1% are state residents. 25 states are represented in upper school student body. 2% are international students. International students from Belgium, Honduras, and Mexico.

Faculty School total: 8. In upper school: 3 men, 5 women; 5 have advanced degrees.

Subjects Offered Accounting, algebra, American history, American literature, anatomy and physiology, art, astronomy, basketball, biology, British literature, calculus, ceramics, chemistry, choral music, composition, computer applications, drama, drawing, earth science, fitness, geometry, global studies, government, guitar, healthful living, interpersonal skills, journalism, painting, physical education, physics, poetry, portfolio art, pre-algebra, pre-calculus, SAT/ACT preparation, science fiction, sculpture, Shakespeare, Spanish, speech and debate, studio art, substance abuse, swimming, trigonometry, U.S. government, weight training, wilderness experience, world history, wrestling.

Graduation Requirements Electives, English, government, history, mathematics, physical fitness, science, completion of therapeutic program, which includes individual, group, and family therapy, and follows the student through a series of four therapeutic stages.

Special Academic Programs Advanced Placement exam preparation; accelerated programs; independent study; study at local college for college credit; academic accommodation for the gifted; remedial reading and/or remedial writing; remedial math.

College Admission Counseling 20 students graduated in 2013; 19 went to college, including Mississippi State University; New York University; Savannah College of Art and Design; The Ohio State University; The University of Montana; University of California, Berkeley.

Student Life Upper grades have specified standards of dress, student council. Discipline rests primarily with faculty.

Tuition and Aid 7-day tuition and room/board: $84,000. Tuition installment plan (monthly payment plans, individually arranged payment plans). Need-based scholarship grants available. In 2013–14, 30% of upper-school students received aid. Total amount of financial aid awarded in 2013–14: $100,000.

Admissions Individual IQ, Achievement and behavior rating scale, psychoeducational evaluation, Rorschach or Thematic Apperception Test or WISC or WAIS required. Deadline for receipt of application materials: none. No application fee required. Interview required.

Athletics Interscholastic: basketball (boys, girls), indoor soccer (b,g), martial arts (b,g), soccer (b,g), tennis (b,g); intramural: aerobics (b,g), alpine skiing (b,g), aquatics (b,g), backpacking (b,g), basketball (b,g), billiards (b,g), blading (b,g), bowling (b,g), broomball (b,g), canoeing/kayaking (b,g), climbing (b,g), cooperative games (b,g), cross-country running (b,g), fishing (b,g), fitness (b,g), floor hockey (b,g), fly fishing (b,g), Frisbee (b,g), golf (b,g), hiking/backpacking (b,g), horseback riding (b,g), ice skating (b,g), indoor soccer (b,g), indoor track (b,g), jogging (b,g), kayaking (b,g), lacrosse (b,g), martial arts (b,g), mountaineering (b,g), nordic skiing (b,g), outdoor activities (b,g), outdoor skills (b,g), physical fitness (b,g), physical training (b,g), rafting (b,g), rock climbing (b,g), roller blading (b,g), ropes courses (b,g), running (b,g), skateboarding (b,g), skiing (cross-country) (b,g), skiing (downhill) (b,g), snowboarding (b,g), snowshoeing (b,g), soccer (b,g), softball (b,g), strength & conditioning (b,g), swimming and diving (b,g), tennis (b,g), ultimate Frisbee (b,g), volleyball (b,g), walking (b,g), wall climbing (b,g), water polo (b,g), weight lifting (b,g), weight training (b,g), winter walking (b,g), wrestling (b), yoga (b,g); coed interscholastic: indoor soccer, mountain biking, tennis; coed intramural: bicycling, bowling, cooperative games, cross-country running, indoor soccer, mountain biking, outdoor activities, outdoor skills, rock climbing, tennis. 1 PE instructor, 3 coaches.

Computers Computers are regularly used in all academic, business, computer applications, creative writing, word processing, writing classes. Computer network features include on-campus library services, Internet filtering or blocking technology, supervised access only to Internet. Students grades are available online.

Contact Judy Heleva, M.A., Director of Admissions. 406-758-8113. Fax: 406-758-8150. E-mail: jheleva@summitprepschool.org. Website: www.summitprepschool.org

TEMPLE GRANDIN SCHOOL

6446 Jay Road
Boulder, Colorado 80301

Head of School: Ms. Jennifer Wilger

General Information Coeducational day college-preparatory and Social Communications school; primarily serves underachievers, individuals with Attention Deficit Disorder, individuals with emotional and behavioral problems, and Autism (Asperger's Syndrome). Grades 6–12. Founded: 1994. Setting: rural. Nearest major city is Denver. 1-acre campus. 1 building on campus. Approved or accredited by Colorado Department of Education. Total enrollment: 24. Upper school average class size: 7. Upper school faculty-student ratio: 1:3. There are 180 required school days per year for

Upper School students. Upper School students typically attend 5 days per week. The average school day consists of 6 hours and 15 minutes.

Upper School Student Profile Grade 6: 3 students (1 boy, 2 girls); Grade 7: 4 students (3 boys, 1 girl); Grade 8: 4 students (4 boys); Grade 9: 3 students (3 boys); Grade 10: 3 students (3 boys); Grade 11: 4 students (3 boys, 1 girl); Grade 12: 3 students (2 boys, 1 girl).

Faculty School total: 8. In upper school: 2 men, 6 women; 6 have advanced degrees.

Subjects Offered 1 1/2 elective credits, acting, advanced math, algebra, alternative physical education, American history, American literature, analysis and differential calculus, analytic geometry, applied skills, biology, calculus, career and personal planning, career education, career education internship, career exploration, career planning, career/college preparation, cell biology, chemistry, civics, civil rights, college planning, communication skills, composition, computer literacy, conceptual physics, consumer economics, consumer mathematics, contemporary history, contemporary issues, contemporary math, decision making skills, drama, earth science, economics, English, English composition, English literature, general math, general science, genetics, geometry, government, human biology, humanities, independent study, inquiry into relationship, integrated physics, interpersonal skills, Japanese, lab science, lab/keyboard, language arts, learning cognition, literature, mathematics, media literacy, participation in sports, personal and social education, personal development, personal fitness, physical science, physics, practical living, pre-algebra, pre-calculus, public speaking, reading, research, science, senior internship, senior project, sexuality, social education, social psychology, social skills, vocational skills.

Graduation Requirements Electives, English, mathematics, science, social studies (includes history), participation in college course, Internship, individualized criteria for success in next life phase.

Special Academic Programs Honors section; accelerated programs; independent study; study at local college for college credit; academic accommodation for the gifted, the musically talented, and the artistically talented; remedial reading and/or remedial writing; remedial math; special instructional classes for deaf students.

College Admission Counseling 3 students graduated in 2013; all went to college, including Colorado School of Mines; Knox College.

Student Life Discipline rests equally with students and faculty.

Summer Programs Session focuses on perspective taking (social communication); held both on and off campus; held at local radio station; accepts boys and girls; open to students from other schools. 7 students usually enrolled. 2014 schedule: June 10 to June 30. Application deadline: June 1.

Tuition and Aid Day student tuition: $25,000. Tuition installment plan (FACTS Tuition Payment Plan, monthly payment plans, individually arranged payment plans). Need-based scholarship grants available. In 2013–14, 25% of upper-school students received aid. Total amount of financial aid awarded in 2013–14: $65,000.

Admissions Traditional secondary-level entrance grade is 8. For fall 2013, 11 students applied for upper-level admission, 6 were accepted, 6 enrolled. Admissions testing, Cognitive Abilities Test, psychoeducational evaluation, WISC/Woodcock-Johnson and Woodcock-Johnson required. Deadline for receipt of application materials: none. Application fee required: $100. Interview required.

Computers Computers are regularly used in all classes. Computer network features include Internet access, wireless campus network, Internet filtering or blocking technology. Campus intranet, student e-mail accounts, and computer access in designated common areas are available to students. Students grades are available online. The school has a published electronic and media policy.

Contact Mr. Mark Inglis, Director of Admissions and Marketing. 303-554-7363. Fax: 303-554-7558. E-mail: info@templegrandinschool.org. Website: www.templegrandinschool.org/

TURNING WINDS ACADEMIC INSTITUTE

6885 Bauman Street
Bonners Ferry, Idaho 83805

Head of School: David Warren

General Information Coeducational boarding college-preparatory, religious studies, bilingual studies, and technology school, affiliated with Christian faith; primarily serves individuals with Attention Deficit Disorder and individuals with emotional and behavioral problems. Grades 7–12. Founded: 2002. Setting: rural. Nearest major city is Troy, MT. Students are housed in single-sex dormitories. 149-acre campus. 4 buildings on campus. Approved or accredited by Christian Schools International, National Independent Private Schools Association, and Northwest Accreditation Commission. Upper school average class size: 12. Upper school faculty-student ratio: 1:7. There are 260 required school days per year for Upper School students. Upper School students typically attend 5 days per week. The average school day consists of 6 hours.

Upper School Student Profile Grade 7: 2 students (1 boy, 1 girl); Grade 8: 4 students (2 boys, 2 girls); Grade 9: 4 students (3 boys, 1 girl); Grade 10: 14 students (8 boys, 6 girls); Grade 11: 10 students (5 boys, 5 girls); Grade 12: 8 students (4 boys, 4 girls). 70% of students are Christian.

Faculty School total: 5. In upper school: 3 men, 2 women; 2 have advanced degrees.

Subjects Offered ACT preparation, advanced biology, advanced chemistry, advanced math, Advanced Placement courses, algebra, art and culture, biology, calculus, chemistry, Christian scripture, classical studies, college planning, computer

science, fitness, gardening, geography, geology, geometry, health, history, honors English, mathematics, music appreciation, nutrition, physics, poetry, political science, pre-algebra, pre-calculus, pre-college orientation, psychology, radio broadcasting, Russian, SAT/ACT preparation, stock market, theater.

College Admission Counseling Median composite ACT: 19.

Student Life Upper grades have specified standards of dress, honor system. Discipline rests primarily with faculty.

Tuition and Aid Guaranteed tuition plan. Tuition installment plan (individually arranged payment plans, quarterly payments are required). Need-based scholarship grants available. In 2012–13, 10% of upper-school students received aid. Total amount of financial aid awarded in 2012–13: $100,000.

Admissions Deadline for receipt of application materials: none. Application fee required: $598. Interview required.

Athletics Intramural: backpacking (boys, girls), baseball (b,g), basketball (b,g), bicycling (b,g), bowling (b,g), canoeing/kayaking (b,g), cross-country running (b,g), flag football (b,g), fly fishing (b,g), football (b,g), Frisbee (b,g), hiking/backpacking (b,g), jogging (b,g), kayaking (b,g), kickball (b,g), mountain biking (b,g), outdoor activities (b,g), outdoor adventure (b,g), outdoor education (b,g), outdoor recreation (b,g), outdoor skills (b,g), outdoors (b,g), physical fitness (b,g), physical training (b,g), snowshoeing (b,g), volleyball (b,g), wilderness (b,g); coed intramural: backpacking, physical fitness, physical training, snowshoeing, volleyball, wilderness. 4 PE instructors.

Computers Computer network features include on-campus library services, Internet access. Campus intranet is available to students. Students grades are available online.

Contact Melanie Shreiner, Office Manager. 208-267-1500. Fax: 208-267-1600. E-mail: melanie@turningwinds.com. Website: www.turningwinds.com

VALLEY VIEW SCHOOL

91 Oakham Road
PO Box 338
North Brookfield, Massachusetts 01535

Head of School: Dr. Philip G. Spiva

General Information Boys' boarding college-preparatory, general academic, arts, and vocational school; primarily serves underachievers, students with learning disabilities, individuals with Attention Deficit Disorder, individuals with emotional and behavioral problems, and difficulty socially adjusting to family and surroundings. Grades 5–12. Founded: 1970. Setting: rural. Nearest major city is Worcester. Students are housed in single-sex dormitories. 215-acre campus. 9 buildings on campus. Approved or accredited by Massachusetts Office of Child Care Services. Endowment: $600,000. Total enrollment: 56. Upper school average class size: 6. Upper school faculty-student ratio: 1:6. Upper School students typically attend 5 days per week.

Upper School Student Profile 100% of students are boarding students. 10% are state residents. 25 states are represented in upper school student body. 15% are international students. International students from Canada, France, Kenya, Mexico, and United Arab Emirates; 3 other countries represented in student body.

Faculty School total: 11. In upper school: 6 men, 4 women; 4 have advanced degrees; 3 reside on campus.

Subjects Offered Algebra, American literature, anatomy, art, biology, chemistry, civics, composition, computer math, computer science, creative writing, drama, drama performance, drama workshop, dramatic arts, drawing, drawing and design, driver education, earth and space science, earth science, Eastern world civilizations, ecology, environmental systems, economics, economics and history, economics-AP, electronics, English, English composition, English language and composition-AP, English language-AP, English literature, English literature and composition-AP, English literature-AP, English-AP, English/composition-AP, environmental education, environmental geography, environmental science, environmental science-AP, epic literature, ethics and responsibility, ethnic studies, European history, European history-AP, general science, geography, geometry, government, grammar, health, history, life science, literature, mathematics, music, physical education, physical science, science, social studies, Spanish, study skills, theater, U.S. history, Western civilization, world history, world literature, writing, zoology.

Graduation Requirements English, mathematics, physical education (includes health), science, social studies (includes history).

Special Academic Programs Remedial reading and/or remedial writing; remedial math.

College Admission Counseling 1 student graduated in 2013.

Student Life Upper grades have specified standards of dress, student council, honor system. Discipline rests primarily with faculty.

Summer Programs Held on campus; accepts boys; not open to students from other schools. 45 students usually enrolled. 2014 schedule: July 10 to August 16. Application deadline: none.

Tuition and Aid 7-day tuition and room/board: $71,500. Tuition installment plan (quarterly payment plan).

Admissions Academic Profile Tests required. Deadline for receipt of application materials: none. No application fee required. On-campus interview required.

Athletics Interscholastic: basketball, cross-country running, golf, lacrosse, running, soccer, softball, tennis, ultimate Frisbee; intramural: alpine skiing, archery, backpacking, baseball, basketball, bicycling, billiards, blading, bocce, bowling, canoeing/kayaking, climbing, cross-country running, fishing, fitness, flag football, floor hockey, Frisbee, golf, hiking/backpacking, ice hockey, ice skating, in-line skating, indoor hockey, martial arts, mountain biking, outdoor recreation, outdoors, physical fitness, riflery, rock climbing, roller blading, running, skateboarding, skiing (cross-country), skiing (downhill), snowboarding, softball, street hockey, swimming and diving, table tennis, touch football, ultimate Frisbee, volleyball, wall climbing, weight lifting, whiffle ball. 2 PE instructors.

Computers Computers are regularly used in art, English, mathematics, science classes. Computer network features include Internet access. Student e-mail accounts are available to students.

Contact Dr. Philip G. Spiva, Director. 508-867-6505. Fax: 508-867-3300. E-mail: valview@aol.com. Website: www.valleyviewschool.org

THE VANGUARD SCHOOL

22000 Highway 27
Lake Wales, Florida 33859-6858

Head of School: Dr. Cathy Wooley-Brown

General Information Coeducational boarding and day and distance learning college-preparatory, general academic, arts, and vocational school; primarily serves underachievers, students with learning disabilities, individuals with Attention Deficit Disorder, dyslexic students, non-verbal learning disabilities, and higher functioning Asperger's Syndrome. Grades 5–PG. Distance learning grades 9–PG. Founded: 1966. Setting: small town. Nearest major city is Orlando. Students are housed in single-sex dormitories. 77-acre campus. 15 buildings on campus. Approved or accredited by Southern Association of Colleges and Schools, The Association of Boarding Schools, and Florida Department of Education. Member of National Association of Independent Schools and Secondary School Admission Test Board. Endowment: $3.8 million. Total enrollment: 109. Upper school average class size: 6. Upper school faculty-student ratio: 1:7. There are 180 required school days per year for Upper School students. Upper School students typically attend 5 days per week. The average school day consists of 7 hours and 15 minutes.

Upper School Student Profile Grade 9: 13 students (7 boys, 6 girls); Grade 10: 25 students (18 boys, 7 girls); Grade 11: 31 students (24 boys, 7 girls); Grade 12: 25 students (17 boys, 8 girls); Grade 13: 4 students (2 boys, 2 girls). 76% of students are boarding students. 34% are state residents. 22 states are represented in upper school student body. 38% are international students. International students from Bahamas, Bermuda, Guadeloupe, Jamaica, Portugal, and Switzerland; 18 other countries represented in student body.

Faculty School total: 20. In upper school: 6 men, 12 women; 6 have advanced degrees; 3 reside on campus.

Subjects Offered Algebra, American history, American legal systems, American literature, art, basic skills, biology, British literature, business mathematics, chemistry, creative writing, culinary arts, driver education, economics, economics and history, English, English literature, environmental science, environmental studies, film and literature, fine arts, geometry, government, government/civics, grammar, history, industrial arts, journalism, language arts, life management skills, mathematics, music, photography, physical education, physical science, physics, pre-calculus, reading, science, sign language, social studies, Spanish, speech, study skills, television, world history, world literature, yearbook.

Graduation Requirements Arts and fine arts (art, music, dance, drama), biology, economics, English, government, life management skills, literature, mathematics, physical education (includes health), reading, science, social studies (includes history).

Special Academic Programs Honors section; accelerated programs; independent study; study at local college for college credit; academic accommodation for the gifted; remedial reading and/or remedial writing; remedial math; programs in English, mathematics, general development for dyslexic students; special instructional classes for deaf students, blind students.

College Admission Counseling 42 students graduated in 2013; 29 went to college, including Florida Gulf Coast University; Johnson & Wales University; Lynn University; Nova Southeastern University; Santa Fe College; Warren Wilson College. Other: 4 went to work, 1 entered military service, 3 entered a postgraduate year, 5 had other specific plans.

Student Life Upper grades have specified standards of dress, student council, honor system. Discipline rests equally with students and faculty.

Summer Programs Remediation, enrichment, advancement programs offered; session focuses on academic enhancement and remediation; held both on and off campus; held at via distance learning; accepts boys and girls; open to students from other schools. 20 students usually enrolled. 2014 schedule: June to July.

Tuition and Aid Day student tuition: $22,500; 7-day tuition and room/board: $44,000. Tuition installment plan (monthly payment plans, individually arranged payment plans, Your Tuition Solution). Tuition reduction for siblings, merit scholarship grants, need-based scholarship grants, Presidential Scholarship (one per year) available. In 2013–14, 42% of upper-school students received aid; total upper-school merit-scholarship money awarded: $5000. Total amount of financial aid awarded in 2013–14: $500,800.

Admissions Traditional secondary-level entrance grade is 9. For fall 2013, 76 students applied for upper-level admission, 45 were accepted, 37 enrolled. Wechsler Intelligence Scale for Children required. Deadline for receipt of application materials: none. Application fee required: $100. Interview required.

Athletics Interscholastic: basketball (boys, girls), football (b), golf (b), running (b,g), soccer (b), tennis (b), track and field (b,g), volleyball (g), weight lifting (b); intramural: basketball (b,g), flag football (b,g); coed interscholastic: cheering, cross-country running, golf, soccer, tennis; coed intramural: archery, basketball, billiards, canoeing/kayaking, fishing, fitness, fitness walking, golf, horseback riding, paint ball, physical fitness, scuba diving, skateboarding, soccer, walking, weight lifting, weight training, yoga. 5 coaches.

Computers Computers are regularly used in all classes. Computer resources include on-campus library services, online commercial services, Internet access, wireless campus network, Internet filtering or blocking technology. Computer access in designated common areas is available to students. Students grades are available online. The school has a published electronic and media policy.

Contact Candi Medeiros, Admissions and Marketing Specialist. 863-676-6091 Ext. 1025. Fax: 863-676-8297. E-mail: candi.medeiros@vanguardschool.org. Website: www.vanguardschool.org

WELLSPRING FOUNDATION

21 Arch Bridge Road
PO Box 370
Bethlehem, Connecticut 06751

Head of School: Dan Murray

General Information Coeducational boarding and day college-preparatory and general academic school; primarily serves students with learning disabilities, individuals with Attention Deficit Disorder, individuals with emotional and behavioral problems, and depression, mood disorders, eating disorders, and bipolar disorder. Boarding boys grades 1–6, boarding girls grades 1–12, day boys grades 1–12, day girls grades 1–12. Founded: 1977. Setting: rural. Nearest major city is Hartford. Students are housed in single-sex dormitories. 13-acre campus. 6 buildings on campus. Approved or accredited by Connecticut Department of Children and Families and Connecticut Department of Education. Candidate for accreditation by New England Association of Schools and Colleges. Total enrollment: 51. Upper school average class size: 6. There are 189 required school days per year for Upper School students.

Faculty School total: 20.

Special Academic Programs Independent study; academic accommodation for the gifted; remedial reading and/or remedial writing; remedial math.

Student Life Upper grades have specified standards of dress.

Summer Programs Enrichment programs offered; held on campus; accepts boys and girls; open to students from other schools. 36 students usually enrolled.

Admissions Deadline for receipt of application materials: none. No application fee required. On-campus interview required.

Computers Computer network features include Internet access, Internet filtering or blocking technology. Campus intranet is available to students. The school has a published electronic and media policy.

Contact Nancy Thurston. 203-266-8002. Fax: 203-266-8030. E-mail: nancy.thurston@wellspring.org. Website: www.wellspring.org

WESTVIEW SCHOOL

11801 Mississippi Avenue
Los Angeles, California 90025

Head of School: Ms. Jackie Strumwasser

General Information Coeducational day college-preparatory, general academic, and arts school; primarily serves underachievers, students with learning disabilities, individuals with Attention Deficit Disorder, individuals with emotional and behavioral problems, and Autism Spectrum Disorder. Grades 5–12. Founded: 1990. Setting: urban. 1 building on campus. Approved or accredited by Western Association of Schools and Colleges and California Department of Education. Total enrollment: 134. Upper school average class size: 12. Upper school faculty-student ratio: 1:8. There are 180 required school days per year for Upper School students. Upper School students typically attend 5 days per week. The average school day consists of 6 hours and 35 minutes.

Upper School Student Profile Grade 9: 22 students (12 boys, 10 girls); Grade 10: 20 students (18 boys, 2 girls); Grade 11: 25 students (11 boys, 14 girls); Grade 12: 34 students (20 boys, 14 girls).

Faculty School total: 19. In upper school: 11 men, 4 women; 5 have advanced degrees.

Subjects Offered Acting, advanced computer applications, advanced math, algebra, American government, American history, American literature, analytic geometry, applied music, art, arts, arts and crafts, athletics, baseball, biology, calculus, career planning, career/college preparation, chemistry, civics, college admission preparation, college awareness, college counseling, college placement, college planning, community service, composition, computer applications, computer art, computer literacy, computer processing, computer skills, computer technologies, conflict resolution, contemporary art, creative arts, creative drama, critical writing, culinary arts, current events, dance, data processing, desktop publishing, digital applications, drama, drama performance, drama workshop, dramatic arts, drawing, drawing and design, driver education, economics, economics and history, English, English composition, English literature, environmental science, experimental science, expository writing, expressive arts, filmmaking, fine arts, general science, geometry, golf, government, grammar, guidance, health, health education, history, independent study, information processing, instrumental music, intro to computers, introduction to theater, keyboarding, lab science, language arts, languages, leadership and service, literature, math review, mathematics, music, music performance, musicianship, painting, participation in sports, performing arts, physical education, physical science, physics, play production, pre-algebra, pre-calculus, reading/study skills, remedial study skills, remedial/makeup course work, science, Shakespeare, social sciences, social studies, Spanish, sports, statistics, student government, study skills, trigonometry, U.S. government, U.S. history, visual arts, voice, Web site design, word processing, world history, world literature, writing, writing, yearbook, yoga.

Graduation Requirements Algebra, arts and fine arts (art, music, dance, drama), biology, career/college preparation, chemistry, composition, computer skills, economics, English, foreign language, geometry, health, life skills, mathematics, performing arts, physical education (includes health); science; social sciences, social studies (includes history), Spanish, U.S. government. Community service is required.

Special Academic Programs Independent study; study at local college for college credit; remedial reading and/or remedial writing; remedial math; programs in English, mathematics, general development for dyslexic students.

College Admission Counseling 18 students graduated in 2013; all went to college, including California State University, Long Beach; Santa Monica College; University of California, Davis; University of California, Irvine; University of Redlands; West Los Angeles College. Median SAT critical reading: 560, median SAT math: 540, median SAT writing: 510, median combined SAT: 1610. 33% scored over 600 on SAT critical reading, 16% scored over 600 on SAT math, 16% scored over 1800 on combined SAT.

Student Life Upper grades have specified standards of dress, student council. Discipline rests primarily with faculty.

Summer Programs Remediation, enrichment, advancement, sports, art/fine arts, computer instruction programs offered; session focuses on general academics; held on campus; accepts boys and girls; open to students from other schools. 60 students usually enrolled. 2014 schedule: July 7 to August 1. Application deadline: none.

Tuition and Aid Tuition installment plan (monthly payment plans, individually arranged payment plans).

Admissions Kaufman Test of Educational Achievement or Wechsler Individual Achievement Test required. Deadline for receipt of application materials: none. No application fee required. On-campus interview required.

Athletics Coed Interscholastic: baseball, basketball, golf, soccer.

Computers Computers are regularly used in career exploration, college planning, computer applications, data processing, desktop publishing, keyboarding, typing, video film production, Web site design, word processing, yearbook classes. Computer resources include Internet access, Internet filtering or blocking technology. The school has a published electronic and media policy.

Contact Ms. Bonnie Aharoni, Director of Admissions. 310-478-5544 Ext. 221. Fax: 310-473-5235. E-mail: baharoni@westviewschool.com. Website: www.westviewschool.com

WINSTON PREPARATORY SCHOOL

126 West 17th Street
New York, New York 10011

Head of School: Mr. William DeHaven

General Information Coeducational day college-preparatory, general academic, and arts school; primarily serves underachievers, students with learning disabilities, individuals with Attention Deficit Disorder, dyslexic students, and non-verbal learning difficulties. Grades 4–12. Founded: 1981. Setting: urban. 2 buildings on campus. Approved or accredited by New York State Association of Independent Schools. Member of National Association of Independent Schools. Total enrollment: 180. Upper school average class size: 10. Upper school faculty-student ratio: 1:3. There are 172 required school days per year for Upper School students. Upper School students typically attend 5 days per week. The average school day consists of 6 hours and 45 minutes.

Faculty School total: 66. In upper school: 21 men, 45 women; 55 have advanced degrees.

Subjects Offered 3-dimensional art, acting, algebra, American Civil War, American history, American literature, art, athletic training, athletics, biology, community service, creative writing, drama, English, English literature, expository writing, geography, geometry, grammar, health, history, mathematics, music, physical education, science, social skills, speech, theater, trigonometry, U.S. history, writing.

Graduation Requirements Art, English, history, mathematics, physical education (includes health), science.

Special Academic Programs Remedial reading and/or remedial writing; remedial math; programs in English, mathematics, general development for dyslexic students.

College Admission Counseling 45 students graduated in 2013; 35 went to college, including Adelphi University; Fashion Institute of Technology; Hofstra

University; Manhattanville College; Pace University. Other: 2 went to work, 3 entered a postgraduate year, 3 had other specific plans.

Student Life Upper grades have specified standards of dress, student council. Discipline rests primarily with faculty.

Summer Programs Remediation, enrichment, art/fine arts programs offered; session focuses on reading, writing, and math skill development as well as study skills; held on campus; accepts boys and girls; open to students from other schools. 35 students usually enrolled. 2014 schedule: June 30 to August 20. Application deadline: June.

Tuition and Aid Day student tuition: $52,550. Tuition installment plan (SMART Tuition Payment Plan, individually arranged payment plans). Need-based scholarship grants, Financial aid is available. Please contact the business office available. In 2013–14, 20% of upper-school students received aid. Total amount of financial aid awarded in 2013–14: $500,000.

Admissions Achievement tests, admissions testing, battery of testing done through outside agency, WISC or WAIS and writing sample required. Deadline for receipt of application materials: none. Application fee required: $70. On-campus interview required.

Athletics Interscholastic: basketball (boys, girls); coed interscholastic: cross-country running, golf, soccer, softball, track and field; coed intramural: fencing, outdoor education, physical fitness, physical training, sailing, strength & conditioning, weight training, yoga. 2 PE instructors, 3 coaches.

Computers Computers are regularly used in art, English, history, science, writing classes. Computer network features include Internet access, wireless campus network, Internet filtering or blocking technology, online discussion group and course information, integrated technology—iPads, SmartBoards, etc. Student e-mail accounts and computer access in designated common areas are available to students. The school has a published electronic and media policy.

Contact Ms. Medry Rodriguez, Assistant to Director of Admissions. 646-638-2705 Ext. 619. Fax: 646-839-5457. E-mail: mrodriguez@winstonprep.edu. Website: www.winstonprep.edu

THE WINSTON SCHOOL

5707 Royal Lane
Dallas, Texas 75229

Head of School: Dr. Polly Peterson

General Information Coeducational day college-preparatory, arts, technology, and science school; primarily serves students with learning disabilities, individuals with Attention Deficit Disorder, and dyslexic students. Grades 1–12. Founded: 1975. Setting: suburban. 4-acre campus. 1 building on campus. Approved or accredited by Independent Schools Association of the Southwest and Texas Department of Education. Member of National Association of Independent Schools. Endowment: $4.8 million. Total enrollment: 166. Upper school average class size: 9. Upper school faculty-student ratio: 1:5. The average school day consists of 6 hours and 10 minutes.

Upper School Student Profile Grade 9: 16 students (13 boys, 3 girls); Grade 10: 23 students (20 boys, 3 girls); Grade 11: 19 students (11 boys, 8 girls); Grade 12: 22 students (16 boys, 6 girls).

Faculty School total: 36. In upper school: 8 men, 12 women; 12 have advanced degrees.

Subjects Offered 3-dimensional art, algebra, American history, American literature, astronomy, athletics, biology, ceramics, cheerleading, chemistry, computer science, drama, economics, English, English literature, film, fine arts, foreign language, geometry, government/civics, grammar, health, keyboarding, photography, physical education, physics, SAT/ACT preparation, Spanish, speech, student government, technical theater, theater, trigonometry, world history, world literature, writing.

Graduation Requirements Computer science, English, foreign language, mathematics, physical education (includes health), science, social sciences, social studies (includes history), 30 service hours per year (120 total).

Special Academic Programs Accelerated programs; independent study; study at local college for college credit; remedial reading and/or remedial writing; remedial math; programs in English, mathematics, general development for dyslexic students.

College Admission Counseling 19 students graduated in 2013; 18 went to college, including Lynn University; Savannah College of Art and Design; Stephen F. Austin State University; Texas A&M University; Texas Tech University; University of North Texas. Other: 1 had other specific plans. Mean SAT critical reading: 547, mean SAT math: 510, mean SAT writing: 530, mean combined SAT: 1587, mean composite ACT: 22.

Student Life Upper grades have uniform requirement, student council, honor system. Discipline rests primarily with faculty.

Summer Programs Remediation, enrichment, advancement, sports, art/fine arts, computer instruction programs offered; session focuses on earning academic credit; held on campus; accepts boys and girls; open to students from other schools. 80 students usually enrolled. 2014 schedule: June 2 to July 3. Application deadline: June 1.

Tuition and Aid Day student tuition: $23,500–$24,000. Tuition installment plan (Insured Tuition Payment Plan, FACTS Tuition Payment Plan, monthly payment plans). Need-based scholarship grants available. In 2013–14, 67% of upper-school students received aid. Total amount of financial aid awarded in 2013–14: $290,500.

Admissions Traditional secondary-level entrance grade is 9. For fall 2013, 28 students applied for upper-level admission, 17 were accepted, 15 enrolled. Psychoeducational evaluation required. Deadline for receipt of application materials: none. Application fee required: $195. On-campus interview required.

Athletics Interscholastic: baseball (boys), basketball (b,g), cheering (g), fitness (b,g), flag football (b), football (b), indoor soccer (g), softball (g), volleyball (g), winter soccer (b,g); coed interscholastic: bowling, cross-country running, fitness, golf, independent competitive sports, outdoor education, physical fitness, running, soccer, strength & conditioning, tennis, weight training. 2 PE instructors, 2 coaches.

Computers Computers are regularly used in all academic classes. Computer resources include on-campus library services, online commercial services, Internet access, wireless campus network, Internet filtering or blocking technology. Students grades are available online. The school has a published electronic and media policy.

Contact Sara Collins, Director of Admission and Financial Aid. 214-691-6950. Fax: 214-691-1509. E-mail: sara_collins@winston-school.org. Website: www.winston-school.org

THE WINSTON SCHOOL SAN ANTONIO

8565 Ewing Halsell Drive
San Antonio, Texas 78229

Head of School: Dr. Charles J. Karulak

General Information Coeducational day college-preparatory, general academic, arts, and technology school; primarily serves students with learning disabilities, individuals with Attention Deficit Disorder, and dyslexic students. Grades K–12. Founded: 1985. Setting: urban. 16-acre campus. 2 buildings on campus. Approved or accredited by Independent Schools Association of the Southwest and Texas Education Agency. Total enrollment: 206. Upper school average class size: 10. Upper school faculty-student ratio: 1:8. There are 171 required school days per year for Upper School students. Upper School students typically attend 5 days per week. The average school day consists of 7 hours and 5 minutes.

Upper School Student Profile Grade 9: 25 students (19 boys, 6 girls); Grade 10: 21 students (16 boys, 5 girls); Grade 11: 25 students (17 boys, 8 girls); Grade 12: 24 students (17 boys, 7 girls).

Faculty School total: 29. In upper school: 7 men, 9 women; 9 have advanced degrees.

Subjects Offered Algebra, American history, American literature, anatomy and physiology, art, athletics, basketball, biology, calculus, cheerleading, chemistry, college counseling, college planning, community service, computer graphics, computer literacy, computer multimedia, drama, economics, English, English composition, English literature, environmental science, geography, geometry, government, graphic design, health, health education, journalism, mathematical modeling, multimedia, music, photography, physical education, physical science, physics, pre-calculus, reading, Spanish, speech, student publications, world geography, world history, yearbook.

Graduation Requirements Arts and fine arts (art, music, dance, drama), computer science, English, foreign language, history, mathematics, physical education (includes health), science, social sciences, 20 hours of community service per year, Transition Course, Job Shadowing Program.

Special Academic Programs Independent study; study at local college for college credit; remedial reading and/or remedial writing; programs in English, mathematics, general development for dyslexic students.

College Admission Counseling 27 students graduated in 2013; 23 went to college, including San Antonio College; Schreiner University; St. Mary's University; The University of Texas at Austin; The University of Texas at San Antonio; University of the Incarnate Word. Other: 4 went to work.

Student Life Upper grades have uniform requirement, student council, honor system. Discipline rests primarily with faculty.

Summer Programs Remediation, advancement, sports, art/fine arts, computer instruction programs offered; session focuses on high school classes for credit; held on campus; accepts boys and girls; open to students from other schools. 110 students usually enrolled. 2014 schedule: June 16 to July 11. Application deadline: May 31.

Tuition and Aid Day student tuition: $17,000. Tuition installment plan (monthly payment plans, individually arranged payment plans). Need-based scholarship grants available. In 2013–14, 25% of upper-school students received aid.

Admissions Traditional secondary-level entrance grade is 9. For fall 2013, 18 students applied for upper-level admission, 17 were accepted, 17 enrolled. Achievement tests, battery of testing done through outside agency, comprehensive educational evaluation, Individual IQ, Individual IQ, Achievement and behavior rating scale, psychoeducational evaluation, Wechsler Individual Achievement Test, Wechsler Intelligence Scale for Children, Wide Range Achievement Test or WISC or WAIS required. Deadline for receipt of application materials: none. Application fee required: $100. On-campus interview required.

Athletics Interscholastic: baseball (boys), basketball (b,g), football (b), volleyball (g); intramural: strength & conditioning (b); coed interscholastic: cheering, cross-country running, golf, outdoor education, physical fitness, strength & conditioning, track and field; coed intramural: cheering, golf, martial arts, outdoor education, physical fitness, physical training, tennis, track and field. 2 PE instructors.

Computers Computers are regularly used in all academic classes. Computer network features include on-campus library services, online commercial services, Internet access, wireless campus network, Internet filtering or blocking technology. Campus intranet is available to students. Students grades are available online. The school has a published electronic and media policy.

Contact Ms. Julie A. Saboe, Director of Admissions. 210-615-6544. Fax: 210-615-6627. E-mail: saboe@winston-sa.org. Website: www.winston-sa.org

Junior Boarding Schools

THE AMERICAN BOYCHOIR SCHOOL

75 Mapleton Road
Unit 4
Princeton, New Jersey 08540

Head of School: Mr. Rob D'Avanzo

General Information Boys' boarding and day college-preparatory, general academic, arts, choral music, and music theory and literacy school. Grades 4–8. Founded: 1937. Setting: small town. Students are housed in single-sex dormitories. 17-acre campus. 5 buildings on campus. Approved or accredited by Middle States Association of Colleges and Schools, National Independent Private Schools Association, and New Jersey Association of Independent Schools. Member of Secondary School Admission Test Board. Endowment: $4 million. Total enrollment: 51. Upper school average class size: 11. Upper school faculty-student ratio: 1:5. Upper School students typically attend 5 days per week. The average school day consists of 8 hours.

Student Profile 70% of students are boarding students. 60% are state residents. 13 states are represented in upper school student body. 8% are international students. International students from Republic of Korea.

Faculty School total: 13. In upper school: 5 men, 7 women; 6 have advanced degrees; 4 reside on campus.

Subjects Offered Computer music, computer skills, English, general science, health, mathematics, music, music performance, music theory, music theory-AP, physical education, physical fitness, social studies, Spanish.

Graduation Requirements Algebra, applied music, character education, choir, choral music, concert choir, English, eurythmics (guard), eurythmy, general science, geography, mathematics, music, music appreciation, music composition, music performance, music technology, music theory, musicianship, physical education (includes health), piano, pre-algebra, social studies (includes history), Spanish, values and decisions, vocal music, voice, participation in the concert choir.

Special Academic Programs Academic accommodation for the musically talented.

Secondary School Placement 16 students graduated in 2013; they went to St. Paul's School; The Hotchkiss School; The Lawrenceville School; The Pennington School.

Student Life Uniform requirement, student council, honor system. Discipline rests equally with students and faculty.

Summer Programs Enrichment, advancement, art/fine arts programs offered; held on campus; accepts boys; open to students from other schools.

Tuition and Aid Day student tuition: $24,700; 7-day tuition and room/board: $31,950. Tuition installment plan (individually arranged payment plans). Tuition reduction for siblings, need-based scholarship grants available. In 2013–14, 70% of students received aid. Total amount of financial aid awarded in 2013–14: $38,000.

Admissions For fall 2013, 26 students applied for admission, 22 were accepted, 13 enrolled. Audition or standardized test scores required. Deadline for receipt of application materials: none. No application fee required. On-campus interview required.

Athletics Intramural: baseball, basketball. 1 PE instructor.

Computers Computers are regularly used in English, history, mathematics, music, science classes. Computer resources include Internet access, wireless campus network, Internet filtering or blocking technology. Computer access in designated common areas is available to students. The school has a published electronic and media policy.

Contact Mrs. KP Weseloh, Director of Admissions. 609-924-5858 Ext. 633. Fax: 609-924-5812. E-mail: kpweseloh@americanboychoir.org. Website: www.americanboychoir.org

ARTHUR MORGAN SCHOOL

60 AMS Circle
Burnsville, North Carolina 28714

Head of School: Michelle Rehfield

General Information Coeducational boarding and day college-preparatory, general academic, arts, service learning, and outdoor experiential learning school. Grades 7–9. Founded: 1962. Setting: rural. Nearest major city is Asheville. Students are housed in coed boarding homes. 100-acre campus. 7 buildings on campus. Approved or accredited by North Carolina Department of Non-Public Schools and North Carolina Department of Education. Member of Small Boarding School Association. Endowment: $1 million. Total enrollment: 27. Upper school average class size: 9. Upper school faculty-student ratio: 1:2. There are 180 required school days per year for Upper School students. Upper School students typically attend 5 days per week. The average school day consists of 8 hours.

Student Profile 75% of students are boarding students. 75% are state residents. 6 states are represented in upper school student body.

Faculty School total: 15. In upper school: 7 men, 8 women; 1 has an advanced degree; 14 reside on campus.

Subjects Offered 3-dimensional art, 3-dimensional design, acting, ADL skills, adolescent issues, African American history, African American studies, African history, agriculture, agroecology, algebra, alternative physical education, American culture, American government, American history, American literature, American minority experience, American studies, anatomy, ancient/medieval philosophy, animal behavior, animal husbandry, anthropology, art, arts and crafts, astronomy, athletics, audio visual/media, audition methods, auto mechanics, backpacking, baseball, biology, bookbinding, botany, career education, career education internship, carpentry, ceramics, character education, chemistry, civics, civil rights, clayworking, communication skills, community garden, community service, comparative cultures, comparative politics, composition, computer skills, computers, conflict resolution, conservation, constitutional history of U.S., consumer education, crafts, creative arts, creative dance, creative drama, creative thinking, creative writing, critical thinking, culinary arts, current events, dance, debate, decision making skills, democracy in America, design, drama, drama performance, dramatic arts, drawing, earth science, ecology, English, English composition, English literature, entrepreneurship, ethical decision making, ethics, ethics and responsibility, evolution, experiential education, expressive arts, fabric arts, family and consumer science, family living, family studies, fiber arts, first aid, fitness, food and nutrition, foreign language, forestry, gardening, gender issues, general science, geography, geology, geometry, global issues, global studies, grammar, guitar, health and wellness, health education, high adventure outdoor program, history, horticulture, human rights, human sexuality, humanities, independent living, integrated mathematics, interpersonal skills, jewelry making, journalism, language arts, leadership, leadership and service, life issues, mathematics, media studies, medieval/Renaissance history, meditation, mentorship program, metalworking, music, mythology, Native American studies, natural history, natural resources management, nature study, North Carolina history, oil painting, organic gardening, outdoor education, painting, peace and justice, peace education, peace studies, peer counseling, permaculture, personal growth, photo shop, photography, physical education, physics, piano, playwriting, poetry, politics, pottery, practical living, printmaking, probability and statistics, reading/study skills, relationships, sex education, shop, social justice, social sciences, social skills, social studies, socioeconomic problems, Spanish, sports, stained glass, study skills, swimming, travel, values and decisions, Vietnam War, visual and performing arts, visual arts, weaving, wilderness education, woodworking, work experience, writing, yearbook, yoga.

Graduation Requirements Annual 18-day field service learning trip, annual 3-, 6- and 8-day outdoor education trips.

Secondary School Placement 6 students graduated in 2013; they went to Carolina Friends School; George School; The Meeting School; Westtown School.

Student Life Honor system. Discipline rests primarily with faculty.

Tuition and Aid Day student tuition: $11,495; 7-day tuition and room/board: $21,945. Tuition installment plan (40% by 8/15, 60% by Dec. 15; monthly payment 10% interest; full payment by 8/15- 2% discount). Need-based scholarship grants, individually negotiated barter arrangements may be made available. In 2013–14, 90% of students received aid. Total amount of financial aid awarded in 2013–14: $93,000.

Admissions Traditional entrance grade is 7. For fall 2013, 18 students applied for admission, 16 were accepted, 13 enrolled. Deadline for receipt of application materials: none. Application fee required: $35. On-campus interview required.

Athletics Coed Interscholastic: soccer; coed intramural: aquatics, backpacking, bicycling, billiards, blading, canoeing/kayaking, climbing, cooperative games, cross-country running, dance, fishing, Frisbee, hiking/backpacking, jogging, mountain biking, outdoor activities, rafting, running, skateboarding, soccer, swimming and diving, ultimate Frisbee, wilderness, winter walking, wrestling, yoga.

Computers Computers are regularly used in writing classes. Computer resources include supervised student access to computers for Web research, word processing, spreadsheet. Computer access in designated common areas is available to students.

Contact Bridget O'Hara, Admissions Coordinator. 828-675-4262. Fax: 828-675-0003. E-mail: admissions@arthurmorganschool.org. Website: www.arthurmorganschool.org

CARDIGAN MOUNTAIN SCHOOL

62 Alumni Drive
Canaan, New Hampshire 03741-9307

Head of School: Mr. David J. McCusker Jr.

General Information Boys' boarding and day college-preparatory, arts, and technology school. Grades 6–9. Founded: 1945. Setting: rural. Nearest major city is Manchester. Students are housed in single-sex dormitories. 525-acre campus. 18 buildings on campus. Approved or accredited by Association of Independent Schools in New England, Independent Schools of Northern New England, Junior Boarding Schools Association, New England Association of Schools and Colleges, The Association of Boarding Schools, and New Hampshire Department of Education. Member of National Association of Independent Schools and Secondary School Admission Test Board. Total enrollment: 215. Upper school average class size: 12. Upper school faculty-student ratio: 1:4. There are 165 required school days per year for Upper School students. Upper School students typically attend 6 days per week. The average school day consists of 4 hours.

Student Profile Grade 6: 23 students (23 boys); Grade 7: 33 students (33 boys); Grade 8: 91 students (91 boys); Grade 9: 68 students (68 boys). 89% of students are boarding students. 16% are state residents. 21 states are represented in upper school student body. 41% are international students. International students from Canada, China, Hong Kong, Japan, Mexico, and Republic of Korea; 9 other countries represented in student body.

Faculty School total: 46. In upper school: 35 men, 10 women; 20 have advanced degrees; 39 reside on campus.

Subjects Offered Algebra, American history, American literature, art, biology, ceramics, computer math, computer science, creative writing, drama, earth science, ecology, English, English literature, environmental science, ethics, European history, expository writing, fine arts, French, geography, geology, geometry, grammar, health, history, industrial arts, Latin, life skills, mathematics, music, physical science, reading, science, social studies, Spanish, speech, study skills, theater, trigonometry, typing, world history, world literature, writing.

Graduation Requirements Arts and fine arts (art, music, dance, drama), computer science, English, foreign language, mathematics, reading, science, social studies (includes history), study skills.

Special Academic Programs Honors section; independent study; academic accommodation for the gifted; remedial reading and/or remedial writing; remedial math; ESL (12 students enrolled).

Secondary School Placement 70 students graduated in 2012; they went to Avon Old Farms School; Berkshire School; Kent School; Salisbury School; St. Paul's School.

Student Life Specified standards of dress, student council, honor system. Discipline rests primarily with faculty.

Tuition and Aid Day student tuition: $27,690; 7-day tuition and room/board: $47,700. Tuition installment plan (The Tuition Plan, Insured Tuition Payment Plan, Academic Management Services Plan, Key Tuition Payment Plan, monthly payment plans). Need-based scholarship grants, need-based loans, prepGATE loans available. In 2012–13, 25% of students received aid. Total amount of financial aid awarded in 2012–13: $1,000,000.

Admissions For fall 2012, 220 students applied for admission, 155 were accepted, 80 enrolled. ISEE, SSAT, TOEFL or Wechsler Intelligence Scale for Children III required. Deadline for receipt of application materials: none. Application fee required: $50. Interview required.

Athletics Interscholastic: alpine skiing, baseball, basketball, climbing, cross-country running, football, freestyle skiing, ice hockey, independent competitive sports, lacrosse, mountain biking, nordic skiing, outdoor activities, physical training, rock climbing, running, sailing, skiing (cross-country), skiing (downhill), snowboarding, soccer, strength & conditioning, tennis, track and field, wall climbing, weight training, wrestling; intramural: archery, bicycling, bowling, boxing, climbing, equestrian sports, fitness, golf, ice hockey, martial arts, mountain biking, outdoor activities, physical training, riflery, rock climbing, ropes courses, sailing, skiing (downhill), snowboarding, swimming and diving, tennis, trap and skeet, weight lifting, whiffle ball. 1 coach, 1 athletic trainer.

Computers Computers are regularly used in English, history, mathematics, science, writing classes. Computer network features include on-campus library services, online commercial services, Internet access, wireless campus network, Internet filtering or blocking technology. Campus intranet, student e-mail accounts, and computer access in designated common areas are available to students. Students grades are available online. The school has a published electronic and media policy.

Contact Mrs. Karen Colburn, Administrative Assistant. 603-523-3748. Fax: 603-523-3565. E-mail: kcolburn@cardigan.orh. Website: www.cardigan.org

See Display below and Close-Up on page 620.

EAGLEBROOK SCHOOL

271 Pine Nook Road
P.O. Box #7
Deerfield, Massachusetts 01342

Head of School: Mr. Andrew C. Chase

General Information Boys' boarding and day college-preparatory, arts, and technology school. Grades 6–9. Founded: 1922. Setting: rural. Nearest major city is Springfield. Students are housed in single-sex dormitories. 750-acre campus. 26 buildings on campus. Approved or accredited by Association of Independent Schools in New England, Junior Boarding Schools Association, and The Association of Boarding Schools. Member of National Association of Independent Schools and Secondary School Admission Test Board. Endowment: $75 million. Total enrollment: 254. Upper school average class size: 10. Upper school faculty-student ratio: 1:4.

Student Profile 80% of students are boarding students. 35% are state residents. 28 states are represented in upper student body. 35% are international students. International students from China, Hong Kong, Mexico, Republic of Korea, Taiwan, and Venezuela; 22 other countries represented in student body.

Faculty School total: 84. In upper school: 48 men, 36 women; 34 have advanced degrees; 55 reside on campus.

Subjects Offered Acting, African-American history, algebra, American studies, anthropology, architectural drawing, architecture, art, astronomy, band, batik, biology, ceramics, Chinese, Chinese history, chorus, Civil War, civil war history, community service, computer art, computer science, computer-aided design, concert band, CPR, creative writing, current events, desktop publishing, digital music, digital photography, drafting, drama, drawing, drawing and design, earth science, ecology, English, English literature, environmental science, ESL, European history, expository writing, fine arts, first aid, French, general science, geography, geometry, grammar, health, history, industrial arts, instrumental music, journalism, keyboarding, Latin, mathematics, medieval history, music, newspaper, photography, physical education, pottery, pre-algebra, public speaking, publications, Russian history, science, sex education, social sciences, social studies, Spanish, study skills, swimming, theater, typing, U.S. history, Web site design, woodworking, world history, writing.

Graduation Requirements Arts and fine arts (art, music, dance, drama), English, foreign language, mathematics, physical education (includes health), science, social sciences, social studies (includes history). Community service is required.

Special Academic Programs Honors section; academic accommodation for the gifted, the musically talented, and the artistically talented; ESL (30 students enrolled).

Secondary School Placement 82 students graduated in 2013; they went to Choate Rosemary Hall; Deerfield Academy; Northfield Mount Hermon School; Phillips Exeter Academy; The Hotchkiss School; The Taft School.

Student Life Specified standards of dress, student council. Discipline rests primarily with faculty.

Summer Programs Enrichment, advancement, ESL, sports, art/fine arts, rigorous outdoor training, computer instruction programs offered; session focuses on enrichment; held on campus; accepts boys and girls; open to students from other schools. 60 students usually enrolled. 2014 schedule: July 7 to August 3. Application deadline: none.

Tuition and Aid Day student tuition: $33,700. Tuition installment plan (individually arranged payment plans). Need-based scholarship grants available. In 2013–14, 30% of students received aid. Total amount of financial aid awarded in 2013–14: $1,650,000.

Admissions SSAT and Wechsler Intelligence Scale for Children required. Deadline for receipt of application materials: none. Application fee required: $50. On-campus interview required.

Athletics Interscholastic: alpine skiing, aquatics, baseball, basketball, cross-country running, diving, football, Frisbee, golf, hiking/backpacking, hockey, ice hockey, ice skating, in-line hockey, indoor hockey, indoor soccer, lacrosse, mountain biking, outdoor activities, outdoor recreation, ski jumping, skiing (downhill), snowboarding, soccer, squash, strength & conditioning, swimming and diving, tennis, track and field, triathlon, ultimate Frisbee, water polo, wrestling; intramural: backpacking, bicycling, broomball, canoeing/kayaking, climbing, fishing, fitness, floor hockey, fly fishing, hiking/backpacking, hockey, ice hockey, ice skating, in-line hockey, in-line skating, indoor hockey, indoor soccer, juggling, kayaking, life saving, mountain biking, nordic skiing, outdoor activities, physical training, rafting, riflery, rock climbing, roller blading, roller hockey, roller skating, ropes courses, scuba diving, ski jumping, skiing (cross-country), street hockey, table tennis, volleyball, wallyball, weight lifting, weight training, wilderness survival. 1 athletic trainer.

Computers Computer network features include on-campus library services, Internet access, wireless campus network, Internet filtering or blocking technology. Student e-mail accounts are available to students. The school has a published electronic and media policy.

Contact Mr. Theodore J. Low, Director of Admission. 413-774-9111. Fax: 413-774-9119. E-mail: tlow@eaglebrook.org. Website: www.eaglebrook.org

See Display on this page and Close-Up on page 622.

FAY SCHOOL

48 Main Street
Southborough, Massachusetts 01772-9106

Head of School: Robert J. Gustavson

General Information Coeducational boarding and day college-preparatory, general academic, arts, bilingual studies, and technology school. Boarding grades 7–9, day grades PK–9. Founded: 1866. Setting: small town. Nearest major city is Boston. Students are housed in single-sex dormitories. 66-acre campus. 26 buildings on campus. Approved or accredited by Association of Independent Schools in New England, Junior Boarding Schools Association, The Association of Boarding Schools, and Massachusetts Department of Education. Member of National Association of Independent Schools and Secondary School Admission Test Board. Endowment: $41 million. Total enrollment: 473. Upper school average class size: 12. Upper school faculty-student ratio: 1:8. There are 166 required school days per year for Upper School students. Upper School students typically attend 5 days per week. The average school day consists of 7 hours.

Student Profile Grade 7: 71 students (35 boys, 36 girls); Grade 8: 96 students (50 boys, 46 girls); Grade 9: 56 students (32 boys, 24 girls). 50% of students are boarding students. 55% are state residents. 13 states are represented in upper school student body. 32% are international students. International students from China, Mexico, Mexico, Republic of Korea, Russian Federation, and Thailand; 14 other countries represented in student body.

Faculty School total: 82. In upper school: 15 men, 18 women; 21 have advanced degrees; 42 reside on campus.

Subjects Offered Algebra, American history, American literature, art, astronomy, biology, ceramics, computer science, creative writing, drama, English, English literature, environmental science, European history, expository writing, fine arts, French, geography, geometry, government/civics, grammar, Latin, Mandarin, mathematics, music, photography, physical education, science, social studies, Spanish, world history, writing.

Graduation Requirements Art, English, history, mathematics, music, science.

Special Academic Programs ESL (35 students enrolled).

Founded in 1922, Eaglebrook School is a leading boarding and day school for boys in grades 6 through 9.

For More Information, Please Contact:

Admissions Office
Eaglebrook School
Pine Nook Road
Deerfield, Massachusetts 01342
TEL: (413) 774-9111
FAX: (413) 774-9119
admissions@eaglebrook.org

w w w . e a g l e b r o o k . o r g

Secondary School Placement 55 students graduated in 2013; they went to Choate Rosemary Hall; Middlesex School; Phillips Exeter Academy; Saint Mark's School; St. George's School.

Student Life Specified standards of dress, student council, honor system. Discipline rests primarily with faculty.

Summer Programs Enrichment, ESL, sports, art/fine arts, computer instruction programs offered; session focuses on ESL and enrichment; held on campus; accepts boys and girls; open to students from other schools. 50 students usually enrolled. 2014 schedule: June 30 to August 8. Application deadline: April 1.

Tuition and Aid Day student tuition: $33,630–$34,070; 5-day tuition and room/board: $50,730–$53,800; 7-day tuition and room/board: $56,730–$59,800. Tuition installment plan (monthly payment plans, individually arranged payment plans). Need-based scholarship grants available. In 2013–14, 17% of students received aid. Total amount of financial aid awarded in 2013–14: $1,228,665.

Admissions Traditional entrance grade is 7. For fall 2013, 281 students applied for admission, 95 were accepted, 61 enrolled. ISEE, SSAT or TOEFL required. Deadline for receipt of application materials: none. Application fee required: $50. Interview required.

Athletics Interscholastic: baseball (boys), basketball (b,g), cross-country running (b,g), field hockey (g), football (b), ice hockey (b,g), independent competitive sports (b,g), lacrosse (b,g), soccer (b,g), softball (g), squash (b,g), tennis (b,g), track and field (b,g), volleyball (g), wrestling (b); coed intramural: fitness, golf, outdoor adventure, skiing (downhill), snowboarding, swimming and diving, tennis. 2 PE instructors, 2 athletic trainers.

Computers Computers are regularly used in art, English, foreign language, history, mathematics, music, science classes. Computer network features include on-campus library services, Internet access, wireless campus network, Internet filtering or blocking technology. Campus intranet, student e-mail accounts, and computer access in designated common areas are available to students. Students grades are available online. The school has a published electronic and media policy.

Contact Anique Seldon, Assistant to the Director of Admission. 508-490-8201. Fax: 508-481-7872. E-mail: aseldon@fayschool.org. Website: www.fayschool.org

See Display below, Close-Up on page 624, and Summer Program Close-Up on page 630.

THE GREENWOOD SCHOOL

14 Greenwood Lane
Putney, Vermont 05346

Head of School: Mr. Stewart Miller

General Information Boys' boarding and day arts, woodshop, and music school; primarily serves underachievers, students with learning disabilities, individuals with Attention Deficit Disorder, dyslexic students, and Executive Functioning Difficulties. Grades 6–12. Founded: 1978. Setting: rural. Nearest major city is Boston, MA. Students are housed in single-sex dormitories. 100-acre campus. 13 buildings on campus. Approved or accredited by Association of Independent Schools in New England, Independent Schools of Northern New England, Junior Boarding Schools Association, National Association of Private Schools for Exceptional Children, New England Association of Schools and Colleges, The Association of Boarding Schools, and Vermont Department of Education. Member of National Association of Independent Schools. Endowment: $840,000. Total enrollment: 45. Upper school average class size: 4. Upper school faculty-student ratio: 1:2. There are 199 required school days per year for Upper School students. Upper School students typically attend 7 days per week. The average school day consists of 7 hours and 30 minutes.

Student Profile Grade 6: 3 students (3 boys); Grade 7: 6 students (6 boys); Grade 8: 10 students (10 boys); Grade 9: 18 students (18 boys); Grade 10: 8 students (8 boys). 93% of students are boarding students. 16% are state residents. 16 states are represented in upper school student body. 9% are international students. International students from Canada, Hong Kong, and Panama; 2 other countries represented in student body.

Faculty School total: 33. In upper school: 15 men, 14 women; 20 have advanced degrees; 15 reside on campus.

Subjects Offered American history, American literature, art, athletics, biology, crafts, creative writing, drama, earth science, ecology, English, geography, grammar, history, mathematics, music, physical education, pragmatics, speech, theater, woodworking, writing.

Special Academic Programs Academic accommodation for the gifted, the musically talented, and the artistically talented; remedial reading and/or remedial writing; remedial math; programs in English, mathematics, general development for dyslexic students; ESL.

Secondary School Placement 12 students graduated in 2012; they went to Dublin School; The Gow School.

Student Life Specified standards of dress, student council, honor system. Discipline rests primarily with faculty.

Tuition and Aid Day student tuition: $52,000; 7-day tuition and room/board: $65,870. Tuition installment plan (individually arranged payment plans). Need-based scholarship grants available. In 2012–13, 12% of students received aid. Total amount of financial aid awarded in 2012–13: $249,290.

Admissions Traditional entrance grade is 9. For fall 2012, 30 students applied for admission, 15 were accepted, 12 enrolled. Wechsler Intelligence Scale for Children III or Woodcock-Johnson Revised Achievement Test required. Deadline for receipt of application materials: none. Application fee required: $75. On-campus interview required.

Athletics Interscholastic: baseball, basketball, cross-country running, soccer, wrestling; intramural: alpine skiing, archery, backpacking, badminton, ball hockey, basketball, bicycling, billiards, canoeing/kayaking, climbing, cooperative games, cricket, equestrian sports, fishing, fitness, flag football, floor hockey, fly fishing, football, freestyle skiing, Frisbee, golf, hiking/backpacking, hockey, horseback riding, horseshoes, ice hockey, ice skating, in-line skating, indoor hockey, indoor soccer, jogging, judo, juggling, jump rope, kayaking, kickball, lacrosse, mountain biking, mountaineering, nordic skiing, outdoor activities, outdoor adventure, outdoor education, outdoor recreation, outdoor skills, outdoors, physical fitness, rock climbing, roller blading, ropes courses, running, skateboarding, skiing (cross-country), skiing (downhill), snowboarding, snowshoeing, telemark skiing, tennis, ultimate Frisbee, volleyball, walking, wilderness, winter soccer. 1 PE instructor, 6 coaches.

Computers Computers are regularly used in English, mathematics, science, social studies, writing classes. Computer network features include Internet access, wireless campus network, Internet filtering or blocking technology, individual laptop for each student. Campus intranet and student e-mail accounts are available to students. Students grades are available online. The school has a published electronic and media policy.

Contact Mrs. Melanie Miller, Director of Admissions. 802-387-4545 Ext. 199. Fax: 802-387-5396. E-mail: mmiller@greenwood.org. Website: www.greenwood.org

HAMPSHIRE COUNTRY SCHOOL

28 Patey Circle
Rindge, New Hampshire 03461

Head of School: Bernd Foecking

General Information Boys' boarding college-preparatory and general academic school; primarily serves underachievers, individuals with Attention Deficit Disorder, Unusually high intellectual ability, and non-verbal learning disabilities and Asperger's Syndrome. Grades 3–12. Founded: 1948. Setting: rural. Nearest major city is Boston, MA. Students are housed in single-sex dormitories. 1,700-acre campus. 8 buildings on campus. Approved or accredited by New England Association of Schools and Colleges and New Hampshire Department of Education. Member of National Association of Independent Schools. Endowment: $1 million. Total enrollment: 21. Upper school average class size: 4. Upper school faculty-student ratio: 1:2. There are 180 required school days per year for Upper School students. Upper School students typically attend 5 days per week. The average school day consists of 5 hours and 30 minutes.

Student Profile Grade 7: 2 students (2 boys); Grade 8: 11 students (11 boys); Grade 9: 2 students (2 boys); Grade 11: 1 student (1 boy). 100% of students are boarding students. 5% are state residents. 13 states are represented in upper school student body. 10% are international students. International students from Mexico and Saudi Arabia.

Faculty School total: 14. In upper school: 7 men, 7 women; 3 have advanced degrees; 13 reside on campus.

Subjects Offered Algebra, civics, English, environmental science, geometry, German, history, life science, mathematics, pre-algebra, science, world history.

Graduation Requirements English, foreign language, mathematics, science, social studies (includes history).

Special Academic Programs Academic accommodation for the gifted; remedial reading and/or remedial writing; remedial math.

Secondary School Placement 1 student graduated in 2013 and went to Landmark College.

Student Life Specified standards of dress. Discipline rests primarily with faculty.

Summer Programs Session focuses on general recreation and play; held on campus; accepts boys; open to students from other schools. 14 students usually enrolled.

Tuition and Aid 7-day tuition and room/board: $51,500.

Admissions Traditional entrance grade is 7. Academic Profile Tests, any standardized test or Individual IQ required. Deadline for receipt of application materials: none. No application fee required. On-campus interview required.

Athletics Intramural: alpine skiing, backpacking, basketball, bicycling, canoeing/kayaking, fishing, flag football, floor hockey, hiking/backpacking, ice skating, kickball, outdoor activities, outdoor recreation, skiing (downhill), snowshoeing, soccer, softball, table tennis, tennis, touch football, walking, wall climbing, winter walking.

Computers Computers are regularly used in writing classes.

Contact William Dickerman, Admissions Director. 603-899-3325. Fax: 603-899-6521. E-mail: admissions@hampshirecountryschool.net. Website: www.hampshirecountryschool.org

HILLSIDE SCHOOL

404 Robin Hill Street
Marlborough, Massachusetts 01752

Head of School: David Z. Beecher

General Information Boys' boarding and day college-preparatory and leadership school; primarily serves individuals with Attention Deficit Disorder and dyslexic students. Grades 5–9. Founded: 1901. Setting: small town. Nearest major city is Boston. Students are housed in single-sex dormitories. 150-acre campus. 15 buildings on campus. Approved or accredited by Association of Independent Schools in New England, Junior Boarding Schools Association, New England Association of Schools and Colleges, The Association of Boarding Schools, and Massachusetts Department of Education. Member of National Association of Independent Schools and Secondary School Admission Test Board. Endowment: $4 million. Total enrollment: 135. Upper school average class size: 10. Upper school faculty-student ratio: 1:7. There are 160 required school days per year for Upper School students. Upper School students typically attend 5 days per week. The average school day consists of 9 hours.

Student Profile 70% of students are boarding students. 53% are state residents. 12 states are represented in upper school student body. 37% are international students. International students from China, Hong Kong, Japan, Mexico, Republic of Korea, and Singapore.

Faculty School total: 32. In upper school: 19 men, 13 women; 12 have advanced degrees; 27 reside on campus.

Subjects Offered Algebra, American government, American history, ancient history, art, earth science, economics, English, English literature, environmental science, ESL, French, geography, geometry, international relations, leadership, life science, mathematics, music, physical education, science, social skills, social studies, Spanish, woodworking, writing.

Graduation Requirements Art, English, foreign language, leadership, mathematics, music, science, social studies (includes history).

Special Academic Programs Honors section; academic accommodation for the gifted; remedial reading and/or remedial writing; remedial math; programs in general development for dyslexic students; special instructional classes for students with Attention Deficit Disorder, Attention Deficit Hyperactivity Disorder, and slight dyslexia; ESL (10 students enrolled).

Secondary School Placement 30 students graduated in 2013; they went to Berkshire School; Brewster Academy; Dublin School; Phillips Exeter Academy; St. Paul's School; The Williston Northampton School.

Student Life Specified standards of dress, student council, honor system. Discipline rests primarily with faculty.

Summer Programs ESL programs offered; session focuses on English as a second language; held on campus; accepts boys; open to students from other schools. 40 students usually enrolled. 2014 schedule: August 25 to September 8. Application deadline: none.

Tuition and Aid Day student tuition: $30,550; 5-day tuition and room/board: $46,155; 7-day tuition and room/board: $51,995. Tuition installment plan (SMART Tuition Payment Plan, monthly payment plans). Need-based scholarship grants available. In 2013–14, 36% of students received aid. Total amount of financial aid awarded in 2013–14: $1,103,300.

Admissions For fall 2013, 85 students applied for admission, 64 were accepted, 57 enrolled. Any standardized test, ISEE, SSAT, SSAT or WISC III, WISC III or other aptitude measures; standardized achievement test or WISC-III and Woodcock-Johnson required. Deadline for receipt of application materials: none. Application fee required: $50. Interview required.

Athletics Interscholastic: baseball, basketball, cross-country running, hockey, ice hockey, lacrosse, running, soccer, track and field, wrestling; intramural: alpine skiing, bicycling, canoeing/kayaking, climbing, crew, fishing, fitness, flag football, floor hockey, football, Frisbee, golf, hiking/backpacking, ice skating, indoor hockey, indoor soccer, mountain biking, outdoor activities, outdoor adventure, outdoor education, outdoor recreation, outdoor skills, physical training, rock climbing, ropes courses, rowing, running, sailing, skiing (downhill), snowboarding, soccer, swimming and diving, table tennis, tennis, touch football, ultimate Frisbee, volleyball, walking, weight training, whiffle ball.

Computers Computers are regularly used in all academic, art, music classes. Computer network features include on-campus library services, Internet access, Internet filtering or blocking technology. Student e-mail accounts and computer access in designated common areas are available to students.

Contact William J. Newman, Director of Admission and Financial Aid. 508-485-2824. Fax: 508-485-4420. E-mail: admissions@hillsideschool.net. Website: www.hillsideschool.net

THE RECTORY SCHOOL

528 Pomfret Street
Pomfret, Connecticut 06258

Head of School: Fred Williams

General Information Coeducational boarding and day college-preparatory, general academic, arts, bilingual studies, technology, and music school, affiliated with Episcopal Church; primarily serves underachievers, individuals with Attention Deficit

Disorder, dyslexic students, and OCD. Boarding grades 5–9, day grades K–9. Founded: 1920. Setting: rural. Nearest major city is Hartford. Students are housed in single-sex dormitories. 138-acre campus. 24 buildings on campus. Approved or accredited by International Baccalaureate Organization, Junior Boarding Schools Association, National Independent Private Schools Association, The Association of Boarding Schools, and Connecticut Department of Education. Member of National Association of Independent Schools and Secondary School Admission Test Board. Endowment: $8.3 million. Total enrollment: 251. Upper school average class size: 10. Upper school faculty-student ratio: 1:4. There are 175 required school days per year for Upper School students. Upper School students typically attend 5 days per week. The average school day consists of 7 hours and 45 minutes.

Student Profile 69% of students are boarding students. 30% are state residents. 13 states are represented in upper school student body. 48% are international students. International students from Bermuda, China, Japan, Mexico, Nigeria, and Republic of Korea; 4 other countries represented in student body. 11% of students are members of Episcopal Church.

Faculty School total: 65. In upper school: 27 men, 38 women; 25 have advanced degrees; 26 reside on campus.

Subjects Offered Algebra, American Civil War, American history, American literature, ancient world history, art, biology, chorus, creative arts, creative writing, drama, earth science, ecology, English, English as a foreign language, English literature, environmental science, European history, expository writing, fine arts, foreign language, French, general science, geography, geometry, grammar, history, journalism, Latin, life science, mathematics, medieval history, medieval/Renaissance history, music, photography, physical education, physical science, reading, science, social studies, Spanish, study skills, theater, vocal music, world history, world literature, writing.

Graduation Requirements Arts and fine arts (art, music, dance, drama), literature, mathematics, physical education (includes health), science, social studies (includes history).

Special Academic Programs Honors section; academic accommodation for the gifted, the musically talented, and the artistically talented; remedial reading and/or remedial writing; remedial math; programs in English, mathematics, general development for dyslexic students; special instructional classes for students with learning disabilities, Attention Deficit Disorder, and dyslexia; ESL (25 students enrolled).

Secondary School Placement 60 students graduated in 2013; they went to Northfield Mount Hermon School; Pomfret School; St. George's School; Suffield Academy; The Ethel Walker School; The Hotchkiss School.

Student Life Specified standards of dress, student council, honor system. Discipline rests primarily with faculty.

Tuition and Aid Day student tuition: $23,650; 5-day tuition and room/board: $48,300; 7-day tuition and room/board: $48,300. Tuition installment plan (SMART Tuition Payment Plan). Need-based scholarship grants available. In 2013–14, 37% of students received aid. Total amount of financial aid awarded in 2013–14: $1,500,000.

Admissions Traditional entrance grade is 8. For fall 2013, 192 students applied for admission, 138 were accepted, 78 enrolled. SSAT or TOEFL or SLEP required. Deadline for receipt of application materials: none. Application fee required: $50. Interview required.

Athletics Interscholastic: baseball (boys), basketball (b,g), cross-country running (b,g), football (b), golf (b,g), soccer (b,g), softball (g), wrestling (b); intramural: basketball (b,g), dance (g), soccer (b); coed interscholastic: cross-country running, equestrian sports, fencing, golf, horseback riding, ice hockey, lacrosse, running, soccer, tennis, track and field; coed intramural: basketball, bowling, climbing, cooperative games, cross-country running, equestrian sports, fencing, fitness, flag football, golf, ice hockey, lacrosse, life saving, outdoor adventure, ropes courses, skiing (downhill), snowboarding, snowshoeing, soccer, softball, squash, street hockey, strength & conditioning, table tennis, tennis, touch football, ultimate Frisbee, volleyball, weight training, whiffle ball, yoga. 2 coaches, 1 athletic trainer.

Computers Computers are regularly used in English, French, history, mathematics, multimedia, music, science, writing, yearbook classes. Computer network features include on-campus library services, online commercial services, Internet access, wireless campus network, Internet filtering or blocking technology. Campus intranet and student e-mail accounts are available to students. Students grades are available online. The school has a published electronic and media policy.

Contact Mark Blackman, Director of Enrollment. 860-928-1328. Fax: 860-928-4961. E-mail: admissions@rectoryschool.org. Website: www.rectoryschool.org

RUMSEY HALL SCHOOL
201 Romford Road
Washington Depot, Connecticut 06794
Head of School: Thomas W. Farmen
General Information Coeducational boarding and day college-preparatory, general academic, and arts school. Boarding grades 5–9, day grades K–9. Founded: 1900. Setting: rural. Nearest major city is Hartford. Students are housed in single-sex dormitories. 147-acre campus. 29 buildings on campus. Approved or accredited by Connecticut Association of Independent Schools, National Independent Private Schools Association, The Association of Boarding Schools, and Connecticut Department of Education. Member of National Association of Independent Schools and Secondary School Admission Test Board. Endowment: $8.5 million. Total enrollment: 333. Upper school average class size: 14. Upper school faculty-student ratio: 1:8. There are 180 required school days per year for Upper School students. Upper School students typically attend 6 days per week. The average school day consists of 6 hours and 40 minutes.

Student Profile Grade 6: 32 students (19 boys, 13 girls); Grade 7: 55 students (27 boys, 28 girls); Grade 8: 89 students (46 boys, 43 girls); Grade 9: 77 students (49 boys, 28 girls). 54% of students are boarding students. 21% are state residents. 16 states are represented in upper school student body. 20% are international students. International students from Bermuda, China, Japan, Mexico, Republic of Korea, and Russian Federation; 4 other countries represented in student body.

Faculty School total: 60. In upper school: 29 men, 31 women; 25 have advanced degrees; 42 reside on campus.

Subjects Offered Algebra, American history, American literature, art, art history, biology, computer science, creative writing, drama, earth science, English, English literature, environmental science, ESL, European history, fine arts, French, geography, geometry, government/civics, grammar, health, history, Japanese history, Latin, mathematics, music, physical education, science, social studies, Spanish, theater, world history, writing.

Graduation Requirements Arts and fine arts (art, music, dance, drama), computer science, English, foreign language, mathematics, physical education (includes health), science, social studies (includes history).

Special Academic Programs Academic accommodation for the gifted; remedial reading and/or remedial writing; programs in English for dyslexic students; special instructional classes for students with learning disabilities and Attention Deficit Disorder; ESL (23 students enrolled).

Secondary School Placement 72 students graduated in 2012; they went to Avon Old Farms School; Berkshire School; Kent School; St. George's School; The Gunnery; The Taft School.

Student Life Specified standards of dress, student council, honor system. Discipline rests primarily with faculty.

Tuition and Aid Day student tuition: $22,470; 7-day tuition and room/board: $47,355. Tuition installment plan (monthly payment plans, individually arranged payment plans). Need-based scholarship grants available. In 2012–13, 24% of students received aid. Total amount of financial aid awarded in 2012–13: $819,000.

Admissions Traditional entrance grade is 8. For fall 2012, 152 students applied for admission, 85 were accepted, 60 enrolled. Psychoeducational evaluation, SLEP, SSAT, Wechsler Intelligence Scale for Children III or writing sample required. Deadline for receipt of application materials: none. Application fee required: $100. On-campus interview required.

Athletics Interscholastic: baseball (boys), basketball (b,g), crew (b,g), field hockey (g), football (b), ice hockey (b,g), lacrosse (b), soccer (b), softball (g), volleyball (g), wrestling (b); coed interscholastic: alpine skiing, cross-country running, horseback riding, skiing (downhill), soccer, tennis; coed intramural: alpine skiing, archery, backpacking, bicycling, broomball, canoeing/kayaking, climbing, cooperative games, equestrian sports, fishing, fly fishing, Frisbee, hiking/backpacking, ice skating, mountain biking, outdoor activities, outdoors, physical fitness, physical training, project adventure, roller blading, ropes courses, running, skateboarding, skiing (downhill), snowboarding, strength & conditioning, table tennis, tennis, track and field, ultimate Frisbee, wall climbing, weight lifting, weight training, whiffle ball. 1 PE instructor, 28 coaches, 1 athletic trainer.

Computers Computers are regularly used in all academic, English, history, mathematics, science classes. Computer network features include on-campus library services, Internet access, wireless campus network, Internet filtering or blocking technology. Student e-mail accounts and computer access in designated common areas are available to students.

Contact Matthew S. Hoeniger, Assistant Headmaster. 860-868-0535. Fax: 860-868-7907. E-mail: admiss@rumseyhall.org. Website: www.rumseyhall.org

See Display on next page and Close-Up on page 626.

ST. CATHERINE'S ACADEMY
215 North Harbor Boulevard
Anaheim, California 92805
Head of School: Sr. Johnellen Turner, OP
General Information Boys' boarding and day college-preparatory, general academic, religious studies, leadership/military tradition, ESL, and military school, affiliated with Roman Catholic Church. Boarding grades 4–8, day grades K–8. Founded: 1889. Setting: suburban. Nearest major city is Los Angeles. Students are housed in single-sex dormitories. 8-acre campus. 8 buildings on campus. Approved or accredited by Military High School and College Association, National Catholic Education Association, The Association of Boarding Schools, Western Association of Schools and Colleges, Western Catholic Education Association, and California Department of Education. Total enrollment: 157. Upper school average class size: 16. Upper school faculty-student ratio: 1:14. There are 180 required school days per year for Upper School students. Upper School students typically attend 5 days per week. The average school day consists of 7 hours and 45 minutes.

Student Profile 74% of students are boarding students. 48% are state residents. 3 states are represented in upper school student body. 46% are international students. International students from China and Mexico. 58% of students are Roman Catholic.

Faculty School total: 21. In upper school: 2 men, 13 women; 10 have advanced degrees; 7 reside on campus.

Subjects Offered Art, band, Catholic belief and practice, character education, choir, Civil War, computer applications, computer literacy, computer skills, conflict resolution, decision making skills, English, environmental systems, ESL, ethical decision making, ethics and responsibility, fine arts, fitness, grammar, guidance, guitar, health and wellness, health education, healthful living, history, instrumental music, instruments, interpersonal skills, keyboarding, lab/keyboard, leadership, leadership education training, life skills, marching band, mathematics, military history, military science, moral and social development, music, music appreciation, music history, music performance, participation in sports, personal development, personal fitness, personal growth, physical education, physical fitness, piano, pre-algebra, reading/study skills, religion, religious education, science, service learning/internship, single survival, social studies, Spanish, sports, survival training, swimming, volleyball, wind instruments, word processing, yearbook.

Special Academic Programs Special instructional classes for students with Attention Deficit Disorder and learning disabilities; ESL (14 students enrolled).

Secondary School Placement 46 students graduated in 2013; they went to Army and Navy Academy; Mater Dei High School; New Mexico Military Institute; Servite High School.

Student Life Uniform requirement, honor system. Discipline rests equally with students and faculty. Attendance at religious services is required.

Summer Programs Remediation, enrichment, ESL, sports, art/fine arts programs offered; session focuses on academics and outdoor activities; held both on and off campus; held at local attractions, (e.g., beach, aquarium, water park); accepts boys; open to students from other schools. 120 students usually enrolled. 2014 schedule: July 1 to July 31. Application deadline: none.

Tuition and Aid Day student tuition: $12,100; 5-day tuition and room/board: $32,150; 7-day tuition and room/board: $42,835. Tuition installment plan (FACTS Tuition Payment Plan, monthly payment plans, individually arranged payment plans, 4 payments). Tuition reduction for siblings, need-based scholarship grants available. In 2013–14, 48% of students received aid. Total amount of financial aid awarded in 2013–14: $400,000.

Admissions Any standardized test required. Deadline for receipt of application materials: none. Application fee required: $100. Interview required.

Athletics Interscholastic: basketball, flag football, volleyball; intramural: ball hockey, baseball, basketball, bowling, cooperative games, cross-country running, drill team, equestrian sports, field hockey, fitness, flag football, golf, handball, life saving, physical fitness, physical training, soccer, softball, swimming and diving, touch football, track and field, volleyball, water volleyball, weight lifting. 1 PE instructor, 7 coaches.

Computers Computers are regularly used in English, history, science, social studies classes. Computer network features include Internet access, Internet filtering or blocking technology. Students grades are available online.

Contact Graciela Salvador, Director of Admissions. 714-772-1363 Ext. 103. Fax: 714-772-3004. E-mail: admissions@stcatherinesacademy.org. Website: www.StCatherinesAcademy.org

Junior Boarding Schools
Close-Ups

CARDIGAN MOUNTAIN SCHOOL

Canaan, New Hampshire

Type: Boys' day and boarding junior high school
Grades: 6–9
Enrollment: 216
Head of School: David J. McCusker Jr. '80, Head of School

THE SCHOOL
Cardigan Mountain School was founded in 1945 to serve the specific educational and developmental needs of boys during their formative middle school years. Two men whose vision and belief in their goal were unshakable—Harold P. Hinman, a Dartmouth College graduate, and William R. Brewster, then Headmaster of Kimball Union Academy—joined forces with legendary Dartmouth President Ernest M. Hopkins to obtain the land that is now the site of Cardigan Mountain's campus. Cardigan Mountain School opened with 24 boys, and, in 1954, upon merging with the Clark School of Hanover, New Hampshire, the School as it is known today began to emerge. Since that time, the School has grown to its current enrollment of more than 200 boys in grades 6 through 9, while the philosophy and objectives set forth by the founders have remained unchanged.

Cardigan was built upon an educational experience that emphasized rigorous academics and study habits, as well as spiritual guidance, physical training, and social orientation. In order to accomplish this purpose, Cardigan's program was tailored to each boy so that he made the best possible use of his potential in these areas. Thus, every boy had a balanced and well-rounded life: physically, mentally, and spiritually. This philosophy is the same today as it was in 1945.

The 425-acre campus, located on Canaan Street Lake, is 18 miles from Dartmouth College. Driving time from Boston is approximately 2½ hours. Some of the finest skiing in New England is only one hour away.

The self-perpetuating Board of Trustees is instrumental in guiding the School. The School's endowment is valued at more than $23 million. In 2012–13, Annual Giving was just over $1 million.

Cardigan Mountain School is accredited by the New England Association of Schools and Colleges. Its memberships include the National Association of Independent Schools (NAIS), the Junior Boarding Schools Association (JBSA), the Independent Schools Association of Northern New England (ISANNE), the Association of Independent Schools of New England (AISNE), the Secondary School Admission Test Board (SSATB), the International Boys' School Coalition (IBSC), and The Association of Boarding Schools (TABS).

ACADEMIC PROGRAM
Cardigan's curriculum is designed to both support and challenge the student as he prepares for the academic programs characteristic of most independent secondary schools most graduates attend. In all disciplines, emphasis is placed upon the mastery of fundamental skills, content, and study skills needed to become academically self-sufficient.

The curriculum provides each student with thorough instruction in all the major courses and substantial exposure to a number of other subject areas that round out a boy's education at this age. Cardigan requires all students to take yearlong courses in English, mathematics, social studies, and science. In addition, a foreign language (French, Latin, or Spanish) is required of boys not enrolled in English as a second language. The average class size ranges from 4 to 16 students, and there is ability tracking within each grade. Assignments and examinations are designed to challenge but not overwhelm students. The sixth grade is grouped heterogeneously and follows a self-contained classroom model.

Beyond these major courses, the School also requires each boy to broaden his horizons and strengthen his scholastic preparation through additional course work in music, life skills, leadership, art, inventing, and/or woodworking.

Cardigan students also take a course called Personalized Education for the Acquisition of Knowledge and Skills (PEAKS®), which helps them become stronger learners and self-advocates. The PEAKS program provides students with guided self-development and helps each student, no matter his skill level, become a better learner and self-advocate.

PEAKS facilitates collaboration among the members of the Cardigan Mountain School community to respond to the evolving needs of each student by focusing on the process of learning through the acquisition of developmentally appropriate knowledge and skills.

Cardigan believes that every student learns differently. Through the PEAKS program, each boy comes to understand how he learns best, and becomes equipped with tools to use as he goes forward, enabling him to find success as a lifelong learner. The PEAKS program also offers additional support for students in and out of the classroom.

PEAKS coaches are available for one-on-one assistance in the afternoons and evenings. Recognizing that some students require regular extra help, while others may need less-frequent support, the program is designed to maximize the accessibility of the coaches for their students.

FACULTY AND ADVISERS
The faculty consists of nearly 70 full-and part-time members, the majority of whom reside on campus. More than one quarter of the faculty members are women. More than half of the faculty members have earned advanced academic degrees. All faculty members teach, coach, supervise dormitories, and serve as advisers for the students. Cardigan has a 4:1 student-faculty ratio. Of the greatest importance to Cardigan are the faculty members who, by setting and attaining personal goals, serve as positive role models for the boys. Cardigan faculty members bring with them a love for learning and a variety of skills, experiences, and talents that broaden and enrich the educational experience and inject warmth and enthusiasm into campus life.

SECONDARY SCHOOL PLACEMENT
Cardigan offers extensive assistance to the students and their parents in selecting and then applying to independent secondary schools. The Secondary School Placement Office begins the counseling process in the spring of the eighth grade and continues to guide the student and his family throughout the application experience. The Placement Office offers workshops on interviewing techniques, SSAT preparation, and essay writing.

Over the past few years, a number of Cardigan graduates have matriculated to schools such as Avon Old Farms, Brooks, Deerfield, Holderness, Hotchkiss, Lawrence, Phillips Andover, Phillips Exeter, Pomfret, Salisbury, St. Mark's, St. Paul's, Tabor, Taft, and Westminster.

STUDENT BODY AND CONDUCT
For 2012–13, 216 boys enrolled at Cardigan. There were 67 boys in the ninth grade, 92 in the eighth, 35 in the seventh, and 22 in the sixth. Almost 90 percent of the Cardigan students were boarders. In 2012–13, students came to Cardigan from twenty-one states and nine countries.

Cardigan has a two-tiered disciplinary status system in order to inform students, their advisers, and parents when School expectations are not being met. This disciplinary system is used to correct patterns of misbehavior and to discipline those students who commit serious offenses. The Discipline Committee meets to hear cases deemed appropriate by the assistant headmaster and the dean of student life. Student leaders and faculty members are selected to participate in this committee which hears cases and makes a recommendation for consequences to the headmaster.

Cardigan has a clearly stated Honor Code, and all students are expected to abide by the spirit of that code.

ACADEMIC FACILITIES
The numerous buildings that house academic facilities are highlighted by the Bronfman Center. Completed in 1996, Bronfman Center features, among other things, the three Freda R. Caspersen state-of-the-art science laboratories, an art studio, the Bhirombhakdi Computer Center, and a large classroom for the sixth-grade class. Stoddard Center is the home of both the

Kirk Library and the Humann Theatre. Opened in 1982, the Kirk Library is a three-tiered, well-equipped multimedia resource center that offers students and faculty members computer software and audio-visual resources, in addition to more than 10,000 printed volumes and numerous journals and periodicals. Thousands of newspaper and magazine articles are available through online resources provided by the library. Computers with Internet access are available in both the Kirk Library and the adjacent PEAKS department. Affiliation with the New Hampshire State Library's Automated Information Access System enables users at the School to obtain materials through the interlibrary loan process. The library is supported by both a librarian and a technology integration specialist. A flexible access plan allows students and faculty members to work in groups, as well as individually, throughout the day and five evenings each week. Humann, the 250-seat theater, is the site of weekly All-School Meetings, lectures, films, concerts, and drama performances.

Cardigan emphasizes the visual arts. The Williams Woodshop and the Needham Gallery and art center are focal points for this important aspect of a boy's education. Opportunities for vocal and instrumental instruction are available, with the Humann Theatre and Cardigan chapel providing performance venues for individual performers, instrumental ensembles, and choral groups.

All dormitory rooms and many classrooms are wired for access to the Internet.

BOARDING AND GENERAL FACILITIES
Eleven dormitories house from 8 to 16 students each. Each dormitory houses faculty members and their families. Students reside in double rooms, with some singles provided. Two dormitories, referred to as "houses," were completed in fall 2000 and each houses 3 faculty members, their families, and 12 students.

Cardigan's newest facility, the Cardigan Commons, opened in May 2013 and includes a new kitchen and dining facility, a student center, a student store, and educational space—and is the hub of campus life.

The School operates the on-campus Hamilton Family Foundation Student Health Center, where most of the students' medical needs can be met. For extended services, Cardigan students benefit from the Alice Peck Day Hospital and Dartmouth-Hitchcock Medical Center, both of which are located in Lebanon, New Hampshire. The campus health center has a resident nurse, several full- and part-time staff members, and a visiting physician.

ATHLETICS
The objectives of the activities program at Cardigan are to provide the boys with opportunities to experience success, to offer healthy and enjoyable activities for the boys' free-time periods and weekends, to promote the physical and athletic development of each boy, to teach cooperation with and reliance on teammates, to allow the boys to experience sports and activities that may be new or unfamiliar to them, and to encourage good sportsmanship.

Over the years, Cardigan has been fortunate to acquire extensive athletics facilities, fields, and equipment. These include five fields for soccer, football, and lacrosse; fourteen outdoor tennis courts; two baseball diamonds; a state-of-the-art hockey rink that can be converted to a multipurpose arena in the fall and spring; an on-campus, lighted ski slope; mountain biking, cross-country running, and cross-country ski trails; ski team rooms; a wrestling room; an indoor climbing cave; a fully-equipped fitness room; and indoor and outdoor basketball courts.

As the School is situated on the shores of Canaan Street Lake, students and faculty members take full advantage of water-related activities. Sailing is pursued in the School's fleet of competition sailboats. Motorboats, rowboats, canoes, kayaks, and paddle boards provide additional opportunities for students to enjoy the water. The waterfront area is well supervised, and instruction is available in all activities.

The Sunapee Mountain ski area is close to the School and is used on weekdays by the Alpine ski team, recreational skiers, and snowboarders. On Sundays, there are day-long ski trips to major ski areas in New Hampshire and Vermont.

As in the classroom, the focus of interscholastic sports and individual activities is on learning the fundamentals. Teams are fielded on several levels in most sports, and they compete against local independent and public schools. Recreational sports are offered for the student who does not wish to compete interscholastically.

EXTRACURRICULAR OPPORTUNITIES

Many students and faculty members bring to Cardigan skills and interests that, though not included in the usual program of studies, may be pursued and developed in the informal setting of the Club Program. Clubs meet every Thursday afternoon in lieu of athletics, with the opportunity for additional meetings if the members and adviser so desire. Recent clubs have participated in community service, a rock band, technical rock-climbing, Rube Goldberg, Lego Robotics, ice fishing, kite surfing, chess, photography, SSAT prep, stained glass, Whiffleball, broomball, and team handball.

A boy may participate in the optional drama program in each of the three seasons. The department mounts four productions a year: a series of one-act plays, the annual Christmas pageant, a full-length play/musical, and scenes from plays during the spring term talent show. Boys are given opportunities to act, serve backstage, learn to work lights and sound, build and decorate sets, produce, and, in some cases, direct. During the nights of performance, the student stage managers and student technical staff run the entire show. The audition process gives boys an excellent opportunity to learn the skills required to get a part.

DAILY LIFE

The typical academic day begins six days per week with a required family-style breakfast. After room inspection in the dormitories, classes begin at 7:45 a.m. Six class periods precede a family-style lunch. On Monday, Tuesday, Thursday, and Friday, lunch is followed by an advisory/conference period. On Wednesday and Saturday, the academic day ends with lunch and is followed by a full slate of athletics and recreational activities. Dinner is a family-style meal every evening except Wednesday and Saturday, when a buffet is scheduled. A study period occurs each school night. Lights-out ranges from 9:20 to 10 p.m., depending on the evening and the age of the student.

Cardigan is nondenominational, yet the School seeks to strengthen each boy's spiritual development within his own religious heritage. All boys are required to attend the weekly Thursday afternoon Chapel service. Arrangements are made for students of different faiths to attend their own weekly services in the immediate area.

WEEKEND LIFE

In addition to the regularly scheduled vacations, all boys may take weekends away from the campus and parents are invited to the campus to share in their son's experience at any time. The majority of Cardigan students are on campus on weekends, and the School provides an exciting array of options for them. A typical Saturday night's schedule might include a movie, a trip off campus, various other on-campus activities and programs, or an excursion to Dartmouth College to watch a hockey game.

SUMMER PROGRAMS

The Cardigan Mountain Summer Session, a coeducational experience for 170 girls and boys, was instituted in 1951 to meet the needs of four groups of students: those who may be seeking admission to Cardigan in the fall, those who desire advanced academic work and enrichment, those who require intensive work in basic academic skills, and those who require review. The Summer Session also serves a limited number of international students for whom English is not the first language. Cardigan's outstanding range of sports and activities, along with its academic offerings, makes the Summer Session a special blend of camp and school.

Academic enrichment offerings in the sciences are a focal point for the more able students. Courses in environmental sciences were designed to better prepare youngsters for the changing world. The visual and performing arts, long a part of the Summer Session's afternoon program, achieved curricular status, allowing students to pursue drama, ceramics, and photography as part of their morning academic program of study.

The six-week program is still known for its individualized instruction, close supervision of daily study time, and general emphasis on improving study skills. Academic offerings include English, advanced English composition, pre-algebra, algebra I and II, geometry, study skills, French, Spanish, and Mandarin Chinese.

The Summer Session is open to students who have completed third through ninth grade. Need-based aid is available for tuition assistance.

COSTS AND FINANCIAL AID

In 2012–13, charges for boarding students were $49,725 and for day students, $28,865. There are additional charges for items such as textbooks, laundry service, and athletic equipment.

Financial aid is available to families of qualified students who complete the School and Student Service for Financial Aid forms and demonstrate need. Information about loans and payment plans is available from the Cardigan Admissions Office.

ADMISSIONS INFORMATION

Cardigan seeks to enroll students of good character and academic promise who will contribute to and benefit from the broad range of academic and extracurricular opportunities available. The Admissions Committee reviews applications on a rolling admissions basis for students wishing to enter the sixth through the ninth grades. Students in grades 3–9 are considered for the Summer Session. Decisions are based upon previous school records, teacher recommendations, aptitude testing, and a campus interview. Cardigan admits students of any race, color, nationality, or ethnic origin to all the rights, privileges, programs, and activities generally accorded or made available to students at the School.

APPLICATION TIMETABLE

Initial inquiries are welcome at any time. Office hours are 8:00 a.m. to 4:00 p.m., Monday through Friday, and 8:00 a.m. to noon on Saturday. School catalogs and applications can be obtained through the Admissions Office. The application fee is $50 for domestic applicants and $125 for international applicants.

ADMISSIONS CORRESPONDENCE

Chip Audett, Director of Admissions and Financial Aid
Cardigan Mountain School
62 Alumni Drive
Canaan, New Hampshire 03741
United States
Phone: 603-523-3510
Fax: 603-523-3565
E-mail: caudett@cardigan.org
Website: http://www.cardigan.org

Devin Clifford, Director of the Summer Session
Cardigan Mountain School
62 Alumni Drive
Canaan, New Hampshire 03741
United States
Phone: 603-523-3526
Fax: 603-523-3565
E-mail: dclifford@cardigan.org

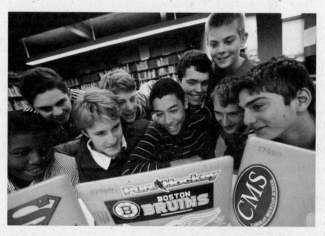

EAGLEBROOK SCHOOL

Deerfield, Massachusetts

Type: Boys' day and boarding school
Grades: 6–9
Enrollment: 254
Head of School: Andrew C. Chase, Headmaster

THE SCHOOL

Eaglebrook School was opened in 1922 by its Headmaster and founder, Howard B. Gibbs, a former faculty member of Deerfield Academy. One of the earliest members of his faculty was C. Thurston Chase. When Mr. Gibbs died in 1928, Mr. Chase became Headmaster, a position he held for thirty-eight years. From 1966 to 2002, Stuart and Monie Chase assumed leadership of the School. While continuing to foster the School's traditional commitment to excellence, the Chases have encouraged and developed many components of a vital school: expansion of both academic and recreational facilities, emphasis on the arts, increased endowment and financial aid, student and faculty diversity, and a balanced, healthful diet. Stuart and Monie's son, Andrew C. Chase, now assumes leadership duties as Headmaster. Eaglebrook's goals are simple—to help each boy come into full and confident possession of his innate talents, to improve the skills needed for the challenges of secondary school, and to establish values that will allow him to be a person who acts with thoughtfulness and humanity.

The School owns more than 750 acres on Mt. Pocumtuck, overlooking the Deerfield Valley and the historic town of Deerfield. It is located 100 miles west of Boston and 175 miles north of New York City.

The Allen-Chase Foundation was chartered in 1937 as a charitable, educational trust. It is directed by a 40-member self-perpetuating Board of Trustees, representing alumni, parents, and outside professionals in many fields.

Eaglebrook is a member of the National Association of Independent Schools, the Association of Independent Schools of New England, the Valley Independent School Association, the Junior Boarding School Association, and the Secondary School Admissions Test Board.

ACADEMIC PROGRAM

Sixth graders are taught primarily in a self-contained setting. Subjects include English, mathematics, reading, Latin, history, science, and trimester-length courses in studio art, computers, music, and woodworking. Required classes for grades 7 through 9 each year include foreign language study in Latin, French, Mandarin Chinese, or Spanish; a full year of mathematics; a full year of Colonial history in seventh grade, followed by a self-selected history the next two years; a full year of English; two trimesters of geography; two trimesters of science in seventh grade, followed by a full-year laboratory course; one trimester of human sexuality in eighth grade; and one trimester

of ethics in the ninth grade. The School offers extensive trimester electives, including band and instrumental instruction, computer skills, word processing, current events, conditioning, chess, film classics, drama, public speaking, industrial field trips, music appreciation, first aid, publications, and an extensive variety of studio arts. Drug and alcohol education is required of all students in every grade.

Class enrollment averages 8 to 12 students. Teachers report directly to a student's adviser any time the student's work is noteworthy, either for excellence or deficiency. This allows the adviser to communicate praise or concern effectively and initiate appropriate follow-up. Midway through each trimester, teachers submit brief written evaluations to the advisers of each of their students. Advisers stay in close touch with the parents of their advisees. Grades, along with full academic reports from each of the student's teachers, are given to advisers each trimester and then sent home. The reports are accompanied by a letter from the adviser discussing the student's social adjustment progress, athletic and activity accomplishments, and academic progress and study habits.

FACULTY AND ADVISERS

Andrew C. Chase, the current Headmaster, is a graduate of Deerfield Academy and Williams College. Along with his wife, Rachel Blain, a graduate of Phillips Andover Academy and Amherst College, Andrew succeeded his father as Headmaster in 2002.

Eaglebrook's full- and part-time faculty consists of 72 men and women, 46 of whom live on campus, many with families of their own. Seventy hold undergraduate degrees, and 30 also hold graduate degrees. Leaves of absence, sabbaticals, and financial assistance for graduate study are available. The ratio of students to faculty members is 4.9:1.

Teachers endeavor to make learning an adventure and watch over each boy's personal growth. They set the academic tone, coach the teams, serve as dorm parents, and are available for a boy when he needs a friend. They help each individual establish lifelong study habits and set standards for quality. Eaglebrook's teachers have the skill not only to challenge the very able but also to make learning happen for those who need close supervision. Faculty members are chosen primarily for their appreciation of boys this age, their character and integrity as role models, and competence in their subject areas. The fact that many are married and have children of their own helps to create a warm, experienced family atmosphere.

SECONDARY SCHOOL PLACEMENT

The Director of Placement assists families in selecting, visiting, and applying to secondary schools. He meets with parents and students in the spring of a boy's eighth-grade year to discuss which schools might be appropriate based on each boy's aptitude, interests, achievements, and talent. He arranges visits from secondary schools and helps with applications. Parents and the Director of Placement work together until the boy has decided upon his secondary school in April of his ninth-grade year.

Schools frequently attended by Eaglebrook School graduates include Deerfield Academy, Choate Rosemary Hall, the Hotchkiss School, Loomis Chaffee, Northfield Mount Hermon School, Phillips Andover Academy, Phillips Exeter Academy, Pomfret School, St. George's School, St. Paul's School, Taft School, and Westminster School.

STUDENT BODY AND CONDUCT

In the 2013–14 school year, of the 200 boarding students and 54 day students, 23 are in grade 6, 62 in grade 7, 87 in grade 8, and 82 in grade 9. Twenty-four states and seventeen countries are represented.

There are specified standards of dress, which are neat and informal most of the time. Discipline is handled on an individual basis by those faculty members who are closely involved with the student.

ACADEMIC FACILITIES

The C. Thurston Chase Learning Center contains classrooms, an audiovisual center, and an assembly area. It also houses the Copley Library, which contains 18,000 volumes and subscriptions to eighty-five publications, books on tape, newspapers, DVDs, and Internet access. The computer room is equipped with state-of-the-art computers, color printers, scanners, digital cameras, and a projection board. The Bartlett Assembly Room is an all-purpose area with seats for the entire School. The Jean Flagler Matthews Science Building houses three laboratories, classrooms, a project room, a library, an online computerized weather station, and teachers' offices. The Bryant Arts Building houses studios for drawing, painting, stained glass, architectural design, computer-aided design, stone carving, ceramics, silk-screening, printmaking, and computer art; a darkroom for photography; a woodworking shop; a band rehearsal room; a publications office; a piano studio; piano practice rooms; and a drama rehearsal room. The campus has a high-speed fiber-optic network with e-mail and access to the Internet for research.

BOARDING AND GENERAL FACILITIES

Dormitories are relatively small; the five dormitories house between 18 and 36 students each, with at least one faculty family to every 8 to 10 boys.

Most students live in double rooms. A limited number of single rooms are available. After the first year, a boy may request a certain dormitory and adviser.

ATHLETICS

The athletics program is suitable for boys of all sizes and abilities. Teams are small enough to allow each boy a chance to play in the games, master skills, and develop a good sense of sportsmanship. The School's Athletic Director arranges a competitive schedule to ensure games with teams of equal ability. Fall sports include cross-country, tennis, hiking, football, water polo, and soccer. Winter sports include ice hockey, basketball, recreational and competitive skiing, swimming and diving, snowboarding, squash, and wrestling. The School maintains the Easton Ski Area, consisting of several ski trails, the Macomber Chair Lift, and snowmaking equipment. Spring sports are baseball, track and field, golf, Ultimate Disc, lacrosse, triathlon, mountain and road biking, and tennis. The School plays host to numerous students throughout the year in seasonal tournaments in ice hockey, soccer, skiing, basketball, Ultimate Disc, swimming, and wrestling. The Schwab Family Pool is a six-lane facility for both competitive and recreational swimming. The McFadden Rink at Alfond Arena features a state-of-the-art NHL-dimensioned 200-foot by 85-foot indoor ice surface. A multisport indoor surface is installed in the arena in the off-season to enable use of the facility for in-line skating, in-line hockey, soccer, lacrosse, and tennis. The Lewis Track and Field was dedicated in 2002.

EXTRACURRICULAR OPPORTUNITIES

Service and leadership opportunities build a sense of pride in the School and camaraderie in the student body. Elected Student Council representatives meet with the Headmaster as an advisory group and discuss School issues. Boys act as admissions guides, help with recycling, organize dances, serve as proctors in the dormitories and the dining room, act as headwaiters, and give the morning assemblies. Boys also assume responsibility, with faculty guidance, for the School newspaper, yearbook, and literary magazine.

Many of the students participate in numerous outdoor activities that are sponsored by the Mountain Club. They maintain an active weekend schedule that includes camping, hiking, backpacking, canoeing, kayaking, white-water rafting, fishing, rock climbing, and snowshoeing.

DAILY LIFE

On weekdays, students rise at 7:20 a.m.; breakfast is at 8. Academic class periods, including assembly, begin at 8:30. Lunch is at noon, and classes resume at 12:33. Study hall and special appointments begin at 2:15; athletics begin at 3:15, and tutorial periods and other activities begin at 5. Dinner is at 6, and evening activities are scheduled between 6:45 and 7:30; study hall is then held until 9:15 p.m. or later, according to the grade.

WEEKEND LIFE

A wide variety of weekend activities are available at Eaglebrook, both on campus and off, including community service, riflery, museum visits, dances, field trips, tournaments, movies, plays, concerts, town trips, Deerfield Academy games, bicycle trips, ski trips, hiking, camping, and mountain climbing. On Sunday, the Coordinator of Religion supervises a nondenominational and nonsectarian meeting for the student body. Attendance is required for boarding students. The aim is to share different beliefs and ways of worship. Transportation is provided for boys who wish to maintain their own religious commitment by attending local places of worship. Students with permission may leave the School for the weekend; 5–10 percent of the student body normally do so on a given weekend.

COSTS AND FINANCIAL AID

Eaglebrook School's tuition for the 2013–14 school year is $54,700 for boarding students and $33,700 for day students. Eaglebrook seeks to enroll boys from different backgrounds from this country and abroad, regardless of their ability to pay. Approximately 30 percent of the students receive financial aid. To apply for tuition assistance, a candidate must complete the School Scholarship Service's Parents' Financial Statement, which is obtainable from the Financial Aid Office.

ADMISSIONS INFORMATION

Most students enter in either the seventh or eighth grade, although students can be admitted to any grade. Information regarding required testing and transcripts can be obtained from the Admissions Office. A School visit and interview are required.

Eaglebrook welcomes boys of any race, color, religion, nation, or creed, and all share the same privileges and duties.

APPLICATION TIMETABLE

The School accepts applications throughout the year, but it is to the candidate's advantage to make application as early as possible. Decisions and notifications are made whenever a boy's file is complete. There is a $50 application fee ($100 for international students).

ADMISSIONS CORRESPONDENCE

Theodore J. Low
Director of Admissions
Eaglebrook School
271 Pine Nook Road, P.O. Box #7
Deerfield, Massachusetts 01342
United States
Phone: 413-774-9111 (admissions)
413-774-7411 (main)
Fax: 413-774-9119 (admissions)
413-772-2394 (main)
E-mail: admissions@eaglebrook.org
Website: http://www.eaglebrook.org

FAY SCHOOL
Southborough, Massachusetts

Type: Coeducational school for grades pre-K–9; boarding available for grades 7–9
Grades: Primary School (pre-K–2), Lower School (3–6), Upper School (7–9)
Enrollment: School total: 450; Boarding 110
Head of School: Robert J. Gustavson Jr., Head of School; David Liebmann, Assistant Head of School; Ann Wardwell, Director of
    Advancement; Matt Heard, Head of Upper School; Lainie Schuster, Head of Lower School; Anne Bishop, Head of Primary School

THE SCHOOL

A dynamic learning environment since 1866, Fay School exemplifies a coeducational tradition of academic excellence coupled with a dedication to maximize the potential of each individual child. With a structured environment that recognizes both effort and achievement, Fay School offers both breadth and depth in academic, artistic, and athletic programs. Multilevel course offerings and the availability of tutorial support ensure each student an appropriate level of academic challenge. In small advisory groups, students receive extensive individualized attention. Relationships between students and teachers mirror those of parent and child. At Fay, faculty members and parents work as partners during the critically important childhood and adolescent years. Fay's comprehensive secondary school placement program not only provides guidance in identifying and applying to model secondary schools but also assists students and their parents in selecting the best environment for continuing their education at the next level. Exceptional facilities and a faculty committed to ongoing professional development create an environment where living and learning thrive.

Established in 1866 by two sisters, Eliza Burnett Fay and Harriet Burnett, the School is situated on 66 acres in semirural surroundings 25 miles west of Boston. Fay School's day students come from various surrounding communities, and boarding students are drawn from across the United States and numerous countries. Fay's graduates go on to thrive at independent secondary schools and area public high schools.

At Fay, each child's voice matters. Through its leadership opportunities, cultural program, comprehensive academic program, community service, arts, and sports offerings, the School caters to a wide range of interests and abilities. Students' endeavors are encouraged and supported by a dedicated and highly qualified faculty and monitored by an effort system that measures the level of engagement each student demonstrates in all aspects of campus life. Particular attention is given to the needs of boarding students and to making life in dormitories a "home away from home."

Fay School is a nonprofit institution and is governed by a self-perpetuating board of trustees. Its endowment stands at $35 million and is supplemented by an annual fund of more than $1 million in total gifts, bridging the gap between tuition and the operating budget. Through its development efforts, the School annually receives support from more than 1,000 alumni, parents, and friends.

ACADEMIC PROGRAM

Fay's program seeks to achieve far more than a sound foundation in course work; the emphasis is on fostering positive attitudes toward learning and living in the world beyond the campus. By limiting class size to an average of 12 Upper School students, Fay provides an environment in which children are active participants in their own education. Each student's specific needs and academic background are carefully considered when scheduling classes. A rotating block schedule and more than 200 class offerings ensure maximum flexibility in designing programs of study.

The School offers different levels in most subject areas. In the Primary and Lower Schools, the program emphasizes individual growth and the development of sound fundamental skills. From the seventh grade onward, students experience increasingly demanding academic requirements. The School challenges students to do their best, and actively supports their efforts. Every student works closely with an adult adviser who serves as a counselor and role model. Students are prepared for the next step in their education, so they are ready to succeed academically, socially, and emotionally in secondary school. Fay also provides leadership training in grades 1–9 through a full-year program that stresses the leadership skills of conflict management, social responsibility, team building, communication, and positive role modeling.

Fay School offers a comprehensive technology education program. Technology is integrated across the curriculum and throughout the grades. The School also offers technology classes to Upper and Lower School students that are designed to help students use technology to enhance their studies and to become safe, ethical, and effective computer users. Technology offerings range from Lower School introductory courses to information literacy, digital video production, and website design in the upper grades.

To facilitate success in a student's academic endeavors, deliberate attention is paid to the development of study skills through a study skills curriculum administered by Learning Center staff members and reinforced in the classroom. In particular, research skills, note-taking, time management, and test-taking strategies are taught at the appropriate grade levels. In the academic and athletics programs, the School also monitors each student's progress by means of biweekly effort evaluations and by trimester reports at the middle and end of terms. Specialized help is available through the Learning Services Department for children who need support in following their regular course of study.

The International Student Program (ISP) offers English courses for students whose native language is not English. Three levels and small classes afford opportunities to tailor ISP courses to individual needs in the areas of speaking, listening, writing, reading, and skill building. As students' proficiency in English increases, they are integrated into mainstream courses. Full participation in art, music, technology classes, and sports activities helps students adapt quickly to life in their new community.

FACULTY AND ADVISERS

Children entering Fay School are welcomed into a family whose heart is the faculty. Faculty members are selected for their empathy and enthusiasm for working with students at the elementary and junior level, as well as for their expertise in a particular discipline. Students and teachers work, learn, play, and have meals together. In the boarding community they also spend weekends together, sharing many vibrant experiences both on and off campus.

Advisers are teachers and administrators who form the nuclei of small groups of 4 to 6 students, both day and boarding. Advisory groups meet at least three times a week. This peer support, combined with the guidance of a concerned and involved adult, makes advisory groups an important source of nurturing for youngsters at Fay. A major responsibility for advisers is communicating with parents.

SECONDARY SCHOOL PLACEMENT

Ensuring a good match between each graduating student and a secondary school is the primary objective in placement. The Director of Secondary School Placement and a second placement counselor work closely with American students, their families, their advisers, coaches, and teachers in identifying the students' needs, strengths, and talents. The Director of the International Student Program provides the same service for Fay's international students. Throughout the application process, the Placement Office provides counsel in selecting and applying to appropriate schools. Schools currently attended by Fay graduates include Berkshire School, Brooks School, Cate School, Choate Rosemary Hall, Concord Academy, Cushing Academy, Deerfield Academy, Emma Willard, Episcopal High School, Governor Dummer Academy, Groton School, Kent School, Lawrence Academy, Lawrenceville School, Loomis Chaffee School, Middlesex School, Milton Academy, Noble and Greenough School, Phillips Andover Academy, Phillips Exeter Academy, Pomfret School, Proctor Academy, Rivers School, St. George's School, St. Mark's School, St. Paul's School, Salisbury School, Suffield Academy, Tabor Academy, Thacher School, Westminster School, and Worcester Academy.

STUDENT BODY AND CONDUCT

At Fay, every effort is made to establish a balance between freedom and responsibility for the young people in its care. Through small advisory groups and the Leadership Program, unstated School rules such as ethical behavior and respect for others are reinforced. Minor misconduct is dealt with by advisers or by the Head of the Primary, Lower, or Upper Schools, depending on the child's grade. Where infractions of major School rules are involved, the Discipline Committee, composed of the appropriate Head and 5 faculty members, may convene.

ACADEMIC FACILITIES

The Root Academic Center (1984) houses most of the Upper and Lower School classrooms. The Primary School (2010) is LEED certified and contains classrooms, a multipurpose room, a music room, and a dining area for pre-K to grade 2. The Mars Wing (2001) includes the Learning Center, the media lab, four state-of-the-art science labs, a writing lab, and a multimedia lab. The Reinke Building (1971) contains a large auditorium and houses the Fay Extended Day Program, band room, and innovation lab. The Picardi Art Center (1987) provides outstanding facilities for art classes, including a darkroom and ceramics studio. The Harris Events Center (1995) is home to Fay's Performing Arts Program and includes five music practice rooms, two music classrooms, a dance studio, and a 400-seat theater.

The School is completely networked and runs on PC and Mac technology in each classroom, in the library, the Learning Center, and in three computer labs. In addition, five multimedia carts are outfitted with the equipment necessary to create multimedia presentations, and three mobile laptop labs provide wireless Web connection for full class lessons. The library offers 18,000 volumes and nine computers for student use. The library webpage provides access to a fully automated catalog of Fay holdings, a connection to holdings outside of Fay via the Internet or the CD-ROM Catalogue of Independent Schools in Eastern Massachusetts, a subscription to 10 different databases to support teachers designing lessons and students accomplishing research, and links to many useful websites organized by subject and index. The library functions as a key point in the learning experience at Fay, providing students and faculty members with resources for study, research, and pleasure reading. The library program encourages a love of reading and an appreciation of quality literature, equips students with the knowledge and skills to become lifelong learners, and helps ensure that students are effective and responsible users of information and ideas.

BOARDING AND GENERAL FACILITIES

Boarding boys are housed in the Boys Village Dorm (2008) or Steward Dorm (1978), while girls live on the upper floors of the Girls Village Dorms (2008) and the Dining Room Building (1924), in Webster House (1880) and in East House (circa 1895). Family-style meals are served in the dining room. The Wellness Center, which opened in 2009, is situated in the lower level of the Steward Dorm and serves as the campus medical facility. Additional campus buildings include Brackett House (1860), home of advancement offices; Fay House (1860), the location for the Admission Office; and the Upjohn Building (1895), currently serving as a multiuse space.

ATHLETICS

Characterized by diversity, spirit, and sportsmanship, Fay's competitive athletics program involves all students and offers a wide range of sports and ability levels each term. Fay's interscholastic teams are noted for the high degree of pride and team spirit they bring with them. Fay's ten athletics fields and eight tennis courts are in constant use for practices and games during the fall and spring terms, while in warmer weather the pool becomes a popular place to cool off. In snowy weather, the Harlow Gymnasium and the Mars Wrestling Room become the centers of activity, with the ice rinks at the nearby New England Sports Center providing facilities for Fay's hockey teams. Participants in the skiing program enjoy the slopes of SkiWard, a local ski area. Fay hosts annual basketball, wrestling, and tennis tournaments, and many individual athletes and teams participate in tournaments hosted by other schools. The following sports and activities are offered: fall—cross-country, field hockey, football, golf, soccer, tennis, and volleyball; winter—basketball, dance, drama, fitness, ice hockey, skiing, and wrestling; and spring—baseball, fitness, golf, lacrosse, softball, squash, tennis, and track.

The School's athletics facilities were greatly enhanced with the completion of the Fay School Athletic Campus in 2009. The campus comprises 30 acres of dedicated regulation-sized outdoor fields for soccer, field hockey, baseball, softball, and lacrosse. The campus also features a cross-country course and four batting cages—two for baseball and two for softball. Additional facilities include the Harlow Gymnasium (1993), a facility that incorporates four basketball courts, expanded locker room space, team rooms, a wrestling room, a weight room, and a training room.

EXTRACURRICULAR OPPORTUNITIES

Fay's academic program is augmented by a wide choice of extracurricular activities. Dramatic productions and musical groups such as band, bell ringers, and chorus offer performance opportunities; aspiring journalists, photographers, and artists work on the yearbook and student newspaper; and activities such as videotaping, woodworking, community service, chess, and computers offer something for everyone. In addition, an 800-square-foot textured rock-climbing wall has been added to the state-of-the-art gymnasium. The rock wall, 26 feet in height, provides an ideal setting for climbing, bouldering, and rappelling. Full advantage is taken of the School's proximity to Boston, and visits to museums, sports events, and historic sites take place throughout the year.

DAILY LIFE

Classes are held Monday through Friday in flexible blocks, starting at 8:00 and ending at 2:30 for all students. Grades pre-K–4 are dismissed at 3:00. All other students go on to sports, which continue until 4:30 for grades 5–9. Boarders have free time after sports until a family-style dinner at 6:00, followed by free time until 7:30 and a study period until 9:00. Lights-out is between 9:30 and 10:00, depending on the student's age.

WEEKEND LIFE

Due to the geographic diversity of Fay's boarding community, few boarding students return home on weekends. Boarders look forward to weekends, when the Weekend Coordinator schedules a wide range of activities, including daylong and weekend-long skiing, white-water rafting, and hiking trips; athletics contests; nature trips; attendance at a wide range of cultural events and performances; and visits to amusement and recreational parks, movies, Boston shops, and community service projects.

Families of day students are warmly supportive of the boarders, opening their homes to youngsters for weekends and some holidays. The number of off-campus weekends is not limited, with the exception of a few closed weekends, but permission must be granted by advisers and teachers.

SUMMER PROGRAMS

Fay School offers a safe, fun-filled co-ed camp for children ages 3 through 15, called Fay Discovery. Campers use the Fay campus and extensive facilities to participate in a variety of summertime activities, including swimming instruction. Eight 1-week sessions run Monday through Friday from 9 a.m. to 4 p.m., with extended care available. The School's highly qualified staff members and low camper-to-counselor ratio ensure individualized attention in all activities.

The Summer Session of Fay's International Student Program is designed to enrich international students' use of English and to provide an academic and cultural introduction to Fay School and the United States.

This is a six-week boarding program for students ages 10–15, running from late June to early August each year. The program provides a structured schedule throughout the day, beginning with academic classes in the morning and ending with sports and activities in the afternoon and evening. The weekends include exciting excursions to Boston and surrounding areas.

COSTS AND FINANCIAL AID

Tuition for 2013–14 ranged from $23,325 for day students in pre-K to $31,660 for fifth graders and $34,070 for ninth graders. Tuition for domestic boarding students in grades 7–9 ranged from $56,730 to $57,170; for mainstream international boarding students in grades 7–9 ranged from $59,360 to $59,800; and for international boarding students with ESL ranged from $62,360 to $62,800. The School offers several creative payment plans.

Financial aid is awarded on the basis of need to 14 percent of the student body. Amounts, based upon demonstrated need and procedures established by the School and Student Service for Financial Aid, range from $1,000 to nearly full tuition.

ADMISSIONS INFORMATION

Fay School accepts day students for pre-K to grade 9 and boarding students for grades 7–9. The personal requirements for admission include satisfactory evidence of good character, an acceptable record of previous academic work, and the ability and motivation to successfully complete the work at Fay. All applicants must complete the application form and return it to the Director of Admission with the application fee, a transcript, and teacher recommendations. Applicants must visit the School for a personal interview and tour; interested students should call the Admission Office to arrange a time. If a student cannot visit the school a remote interview may be arranged via Skype. Candidates for grades 7–9 must take the SSAT or ISEE. International applicants whose native language is not English must take the TOEFL or TOEFL, Junior tests.

APPLICATION TIMETABLE

Applications for day students are due on February 1, 2014. Decisions on day student candidates whose folders are complete are announced on March 10, 2014. Fay continues to accept qualified candidates after this date until the grades are filled. Wait lists are often established. Boarding applicants are considered on a rolling basis beginning December 2, 2013. International applicants who would like to be considered in the first round of decisions should complete their applications by December 13, 2013. To hold a place for a child, a deposit and enrollment contract must be submitted. Information regarding dress code, course selection, and other pertinent items is sent upon enrollment.

ADMISSIONS CORRESPONDENCE

Beth Whitney, Director of Admission
Fay School
48 Main Street
Southborough, Massachusetts 01772-9106
United States
Phone: 508-490-8201
Fax: 508-481-7872
E-mail: admission@fayschool.org
Website: http://www.fayschool.org

RUMSEY HALL SCHOOL

Washington Depot, Connecticut

Type: Coeducational Junior Boarding (grades 5–9) and Day Preparatory School
Grades: K–9: Lower School, K–5; Upper School, 6–9
Enrollment: School total: 333
Head of School: Thomas W. Farmen, Headmaster

THE SCHOOL

Rumsey Hall School was founded in 1900 by Mrs. Lillias Rumsey Sanford. Since its inception, Rumsey Hall School has retained its original philosophy: to help each child develop to his or her maximum stature as an individual, as a member of a family, and as a contributing member of society. The curriculum emphasizes basic academic skills, a complete athletic program, fine arts, computer literacy, and numerous extracurricular offerings, which are all designed to encourage individual responsibility for academic achievement, accomplishment in team sports, and service to the School community. The School believes that "effort is the key to success."

The 147-acre campus on the Bantam River provides landscaped and wooded areas in a rural environment located outside of Washington, Connecticut. Rumsey Hall School is 90 miles from New York City and within an hour of the major Connecticut cities of Hartford and New Haven. The School's location enables students to take advantage of major cultural and athletic events in New York City and Boston throughout the school year.

A nonprofit institution, Rumsey Hall School is governed by a 21-member Board of Trustees that meets quarterly. The 2013–14 operating budget totaled $8.5 million. Revenues include tuition and fees and contributions from alumni, parents, corporations, foundations, and friends of the School. The School's endowment is approximately $9.5 million. Annual fund giving was $1.9 million in 2012.

Rumsey Hall School is a member of the National Association of Independent Schools, the Connecticut Association of Independent Schools, the Junior Boarding Schools Association, the Educational Records Bureau, Western Connecticut Boarding Schools, and the Educational Testing Service, and is a voting member of the Secondary School Admission Test Board.

ACADEMIC PROGRAM

At Rumsey Hall, effort is as important as academic achievement. Effort as a criterion for success opens a new world to the students. Effort does not start and end with the student. It is a shared responsibility between the student and each faculty member. Just as the faculty members expect maximum effort from each student, they promise in return to give each student their very best effort.

Students in the Upper School (sixth through ninth grades) carry at least five major subjects. There are eight 40-minute periods in each day, including lunch. Extra help is available each day for students who need additional instruction or extra challenges. All classes are departmentalized.

Final examinations are given in all subjects twice a year. Report cards, with numerical grades, are sent home every other week throughout the school year. Anecdotal comments and individualized teacher, adviser, and Headmaster comments are sent home three times each academic year.

A supplementary feature of the academic program is the Language Skills Department, which is directed toward intellectually able students with dyslexia or learning differences. Students in this program carry a regular academic course load, with the exception of a foreign language. In 2013–14, 15 percent of the student body was involved in this program.

English as a Second Language (ESL) is offered to international students and is comprised of two levels with three courses in each level. The courses are designed to help students develop their conversational and academic English, reading comprehension, awareness of social and cultural differences, and to introduce them to American history.

The school year, divided into trimesters, begins in September and runs until the first weekend in June. Vacations are scheduled at Thanksgiving and Christmas and in the spring.

Class size averages 12 students. Honors courses are offered to exceptional ninth grade students who demonstrate talent and whose scholarship indicates a strong sense of responsibility and motivation.

Students have a study hall built into their daily schedules, and there is an evening study hall for all boarding students. Study halls are supervised by faculty members, and there is ample opportunity for assistance. The library and computer facilities adjoin the formal study hall and are available at all study times.

In the Lower School (K through fifth grade), the nine daily academic periods begin at 8 a.m. after class meetings. English, reading, mathematics, science, and social studies are taught by the classroom teachers. Classes in foreign languages, language skills, health, music, art, and physical education vary the students' schedules by requiring them to move to different classrooms with specialized teachers. Normal class size is between 12 and 14 students, which makes for a dynamic learning environment where everyone's voice is heard and encouraged.

FACULTY AND ADVISERS

All 59 full- and part-time faculty members (30 men and 29 women) hold baccalaureate degrees, and half have master's degrees. Forty-two faculty members live on campus, many with their families. This enables Rumsey to provide the close supervision and warm family atmosphere that is an essential part of the School's culture.

Thomas W. Farmen was appointed Headmaster of Rumsey Hall School in 1985. He holds a Bachelor of Arts degree from New England College and a master's in school administration from Western Connecticut State University. He has served as President of the Association of Boarding Schools for the National Association of Independent Schools, President of the Junior Boarding Schools Association, and as a director of the Connecticut Association of Independent Schools.

The Dean of Students supervises and coordinates the advisory program. Each faculty member has 7 or 8 student advisees. Advisors meet with their advisees individually and in a weekly group setting. The advisor is the first link in the line of communication between school and home.

Faculty members at Rumsey Hall are encouraged to continue their professional development by taking postgraduate courses and attending seminars and conferences throughout the year. The School generously funds these programs.

SECONDARY SCHOOL PLACEMENT

The Director of Secondary School Placement supervises all facets of the secondary school search. Beginning in the eighth grade, a process of testing and interviewing with students and parents takes place that enables the placement director to highlight certain schools that seem appropriate. After visits and interviews with the schools, the list is pared down to those to which the student wishes to apply. Members of the 2012–13 class matriculated to 38 secondary schools: Albuquerque Academy, NM; Avon Old Farms, CT (2); Berkshire School, MA (4); Brewster Academy, NH (3); Canterbury School, CT (5); Choate Rosemary Hall School, CT; Cheshire Academy, CT; Darlington School, GA; Deerfield Academy, MA; Episcopal High School, VA; Ethel Walker School, CT; Forman School, CT; Friends Select School, PA; The Greenwood School, VT; The Gunnery, CT (5); Hebron Academy, ME; Holy Cross High School, CT; Hotchkiss School, CT; Kents Hill School, ME; Kimball Union Academy, NH; Lawrenceville School, NJ; Loomis Chaffee School, CT (2); The Madeira School, VA; Mercersburg Academy, PA; Miss Hall's School, MA; Northfield Mt. Hermon School, MA; Peddie School, NJ (2); Phillips Academy Andover, MA; Proctor Academy, NH; St. Andrew's School, RI; St. George's School, RI; St. Joseph's High School, CT; Salisbury School, CT; Springside Chestnut Hill Academy, PA; South Kent School, CT (2); Suffield Academy, CT; The Taft School, CT (2); Thomas Jefferson School, MO; Tilton School, NH; Trinity-Pawling School, NY; Vermont Academy, VT; Webb Schools, CA; and Williston Northampton School, MA.

STUDENT BODY AND CONDUCT

In 2013–14, Rumsey Hall enrolled 326 students. The Lower School (grades K–5) enrolled 73 day students. The Upper School (grades 6–9) enrolled 251 students: 116 day students and 135 boarders. The School population was 61 percent boys and 39 percent girls.

In 2012–13, Rumsey students came from sixteen states, eleven countries, and thirty local communities. International students enrolled in the ESL program composed 8 percent of the community.

The dress code requires jackets, collared shirts, and ties for boys and dresses or skirts and collared shirts or blouses for girls. In the winter term, boys may wear turtlenecks and sweaters and girls may wear slacks.

The School values of honesty, kindness, and respect comprise the yardstick by which Rumsey measures a student's thoughts and actions. Students living outside the spirit of the community are asked to meet with the Disciplinary and Senior Committees. These committees represent a cross section of administrators, faculty members, and students.

ACADEMIC FACILITIES

Situated alongside the Bantam River on a 147-acre campus, the School is housed in thirty buildings, most of which have been constructed since 1950. Nine structures house a total of thirty classrooms, including the Dane W. Dicke Family Math and Science Buildings. Other buildings include the Dicke Family Library; the Sanford House, which houses the study and meeting hall; the J. Seward Johnson Sr. Fine Arts Center, with spacious art and music rooms; and the Satyvati Science Center. Students and faculty members meet as a community for meals in the D. G. Barr Dining Hall.

The Garassino Building is home to three lower school classrooms including an all-day kindergarten. The Maxwell A. Sarofim '05 Performing Arts Center (the MAX) is the setting for student performances, visiting artists, and school assemblies; students' art and exhibits of Rumsey community interest are displayed in the adjacent Allen Finkelson Gallery.

Rumsey has three fully interactive computer labs on campus and more than 120 wireless networked computers throughout the School. The schoolwide intranet system enhances communication within the community.

BOARDING AND GENERAL FACILITIES

The close relationship between teachers and students is a special part of Rumsey Hall School. Students live in dormitories with supportive dorm parents, and students become a part of their dorm parents' families.

Rumsey's boarding students live in one of eight dormitories. Dormitories are assigned by age, and most students have roommates, although single rooms are available in most dorms. Each dormitory has its own common room that is the shared living space for the dorm. A snack bar and store are open every afternoon. Laundry and dry cleaning are sent out on a weekly basis. Four registered nurses staff the School's infirmary, and the School doctor, a local pediatrician, is available on a daily basis. Emergency facilities are available at New Milford Hospital, which is 10 miles away. There are telephones in all dormitories, and every student has an e-mail account.

ATHLETICS

Athletics are a healthy and essential part of the Rumsey experience. On the playing field, lifelong attitudes, values, and habits are born. All students participate at their own level in athletics. Effort is rewarded through athletic letters and certificates at the end of the season.

Rumsey Hall fields thirty-nine interscholastic teams throughout the year. Most sports are offered on different levels so that students are able to compete with children of their own size and skill level. Over three seasons, 403 interscholastic teams are fielded in baseball, basketball, crew, cross-country, field hockey, football, boys' ice hockey, girls' ice hockey, lacrosse, skiing, soccer, softball, tennis, volleyball, and wrestling. Other activities available include horseback riding, Outdoor Club, Lower School games and activities, recreational skiing and snowboarding, biking, and ice-skating.

The John F. Schereschewsky, Sr. Memorial Center houses the Magnoli and Blue Dog Gymnasiums where basketball, volleyball, and wrestling activities are held. Recent renovations to the indoor athletic facilities include an indoor climbing wall, boys' and girls' locker rooms, and three new and improved tennis courts. The Cornell Common Room serves as the weight-training room and offers other training machines, as well as housing the athletic director and athletic training staff. Lufkin Rink is the newest of Rumsey Hall's athletic facilities. Opened in late 2008, the rink provides home ice for the boys' and girls' hockey teams. Intramural and recreational activities make the space available to skaters of all abilities.

There are several athletic fields on campus including the Pavek Athletic Field, in honor of Veronica D. and Charles H. Pavek; Scott Evans Seibert '92 Memorial Field; Paul Lincoln Cornell Athletic Field, and Roy Field. There are also three outdoor tennis courts and two ponds for outdoor recreation and winter skating.

Holt Beach at Lake Waramaug is the site for spring crew training. Off-season training is available for rowers in the state-of-the-art indoor rowing facility. Students who ski and snowboard in the winter term travel to Mohawk Mountain in nearby Cornwall, Connecticut on weekday afternoons.

EXTRACURRICULAR OPPORTUNITIES

Throughout the year, Upper School students may participate in many activities and clubs. The choices include fishing, computers, chorus, art club, bicycling, fly fishing, School newspaper, yearbook, art, swimming, hiking, rocketry, baking, community service, intramural sports, and participation in School dramatic and musical productions. The Rumsey Chamber Orchestra, Clef Club, and the a cappella singing group, Passing Notes, practice weekly and perform at various events throughout the year.

The Lower School features an exciting afternoon enrichment program for all students in kindergarten through fifth grade after their daily academic curriculum is complete. In keeping with Rumsey Hall's mission to educate the whole child, the varied activities offered each afternoon are organized to cultivate interests that can be nurtured as the children grow. Most activities are led by Rumsey teachers while others enlist the skills of specialists from surrounding communities. Activities include but are not limited to the arts (ceramics, printmaking, theater, crafts), athletics (field/gymnasium sports, martial arts), and recreational and outdoor games.

Traditional annual events for the School community include a Winter Concert, Parents' Day, Grandparents' Day, and Headmaster's Weekend and ski trip to Bromley Mountain, Vermont. Service to the School and to the greater community is encouraged throughout the year by the community service/service learning program. During the 2011–12 academic year the students amassed 903 total hours of volunteer service.

The student body is divided into red and blue color teams. These teams enjoy friendly competition throughout the school year in areas of community service, academic achievement, and athletics.

DAILY LIFE

The school day begins at 8 a.m. with an all-School meeting. All administrators, faculty members, and students are in attendance. It is a time to share the news of the School and the world as well as important information and announcements with the whole community. The rest of the academic day consists of eight 40-minute periods and supervised study halls, with a 20-minute recess in the middle of the morning. Extra help is available every day after lunch. Athletic practices or contests take place from 3 to 4:30 p.m. Dinner is served family style at 6 and is followed by study hall from 7 to 8:30. Free time follows, with bedtimes varying depending on the grade of the child.

WEEKEND LIFE

Weekends for boarding students include a variety of activities on and off campus. There are School dances, special theme weekends, off-campus trips, and intramural activities on campus. Rumsey's proximity to four major cities—New York, Boston, Hartford, and New Haven—allows for a wide variety of cultural events, sports events (collegiate and professional), and shopping excursions. All trips are fully supervised, and an appropriate student-teacher ratio is maintained. Day students are encouraged to participate in weekend activities and are also allowed to invite boarding students home with them for the weekend.

SUMMER PROGRAMS

The five-week Rumsey Hall summer session is open to students in the third through ninth grades. The program is designed for students who desire enrichment or need additional work in a subject area in order to move on to the next grade with confidence.

Special emphasis is placed on English, mathematics, study skills, and computer skills. Normal class size ranges from 6 to 10 students with individual attention and help available. Students who need support in language skills or developmental reading work daily with trained specialists. ESL is offered to international students. In the afternoon, students enjoy recreational activities such as swimming, hiking, tennis, fishing, horseback riding, baseball, soccer, lacrosse, and basketball. Off-campus trips to museums, movies, concerts, amusement parks, and sporting events occur each week. Considerable effort is made to cultivate students' interests and to expose them to new experiences. For the 2013 summer session, tuition, room, and board was $7,385 for boarding students, $2,640 for day students, and $1,715 for half-day students. There are additional fees for individual tutoring in language skills and enrollment in ESL.

COSTS AND FINANCIAL AID

In 2013–14, full-year tuition was $19,000 for kindergarten and day students in grades 1 and 2, $23,370 for day students in grades 3–9, and $49,485 for boarding students. Additional fees included books, athletic fees, school supplies, and laundry and dry cleaning. A nonrefundable deposit of $2,000 serves as the boarding student's drawing account for the year. The annual fee for language skills was $5,480. The annual fee for ESL was $7,350. Two thirds of the total tuition is due July 15 and the balance by December 15. A ten-installment payment agreement is available.

Rumsey Hall is a member of the School and Student Service for Financial Aid. In the 2011–12 academic year just over $1 million in tuition assistance was awarded to one third of the students.

ADMISSIONS INFORMATION

Rumsey Hall welcomes students of average to above-average intelligence and achievement. Students must show evidence of good citizenship and the willingness to live in a boarding community. Acceptance is based on past school performance, scores on standardized achievement tests, and a personal interview. Rumsey is able to accept a limited number of students with learning differences if their learning profile is compatible with the School's Orton-Gillingham–based language skills program. Rumsey Hall School admits students of any race, color, religion, or national or ethnic origin.

APPLICATION TIMETABLE

Inquiries are welcome at any time of the year, with most families beginning the admission process in the fall or winter in anticipation of September enrollment. Admission interviews and tours are scheduled throughout the year. Boarding student applications are accepted on a rolling basis. Day student applicants should complete the application process by February 15. Applicants are notified of acceptance by March 1.

ADMISSION CORRESPONDENCE

Matthew S. Hoeniger '81, Director of Admission
Rumsey Hall School
201 Romford Road
Washington Depot, Connecticut 06794
United States
Phone: 860-868-0535
Fax: 860-868-7907
E-mail: admiss@rumseyhall.org
Website: http://www.rumseyhall.org

Summer Programs
Close-Ups

FAY SCHOOL

Fay
School

▼▲▼▲▼▲▼▲▼▲▼▲▼▲▼▲▼▲▼▲▼▲▼▲▼▲▼▲▼▲▼▲▼▲▼

INTERNATIONAL STUDENT PROGRAM

SOUTHBOROUGH, MASSACHUSETTS

Type of Program: International families who want their children to be educated in the United States have a unique opportunity at Fay School each summer. The International Student Program (ISP) offers academic programs in the morning and day camp activities in the afternoon, providing English language immersion and contact with domestic students of a comparable age.

Participants: Coeducational, international boarding students, ages 10–15

Enrollment: 45

Program Dates: Six weeks, from early July through mid-August

Head of Program: Courtney Sargent, Director of the Summer International Student Program

LOCATION

Fay School is situated on 66 beautiful acres in semirural surroundings in Southborough, Massachusetts, 25 miles west of Boston.

BACKGROUND AND PHILOSOPHY

Fay's summer boarding program makes it possible for international students ages 10–15 to participate in the Fay experience regardless of their level of English proficiency. It provides a meaningful introduction to Fay for students enrolling full-time in the upcoming academic year as well as a stand-alone program for international students who wish to focus on developing their English skills during the summer months, with the appropriate level of challenge and support.

The International Student Program is integrated into the entire summer Fay experience. In addition to their daily academic program, international students spend part of each day with U.S. students of similar age who are enrolled in Fay's summer day camp, choosing from a variety of fun and enriching activities that includes sports, games, swimming, art classes, day trips, woodworking, science, robotics, and computers. Each afternoon, students are immersed in English and put their language skills to work, all while participating in engaging activities with other campers.

PROGRAM OFFERINGS

Each morning, Summer ISP students take academic classes designed to improve their English writing, reading, and speaking skills. The program is engaging and innovative, and classes offer a range of activities and experiences designed to match each student's skill level and prior language experiences.

Upon entering the summer International Student Program, teachers assess each student's skill level and place him or her into one of three levels: Beginner, Intermediate, and Advanced. At each level, students focus on improving fluency and developing the necessary skills to become a successful language learner. In addition to daily coursework, students are expected to complete approximately one hour of homework each night. Throughout the summer, teachers continually assess student progress and send home regular program updates. Teachers also provide an end-of-summer written report on the performance of each student.

Each afternoon, ISP students participate in afternoon activities, which include sports, games, arts, and enrichment. These engaging, hands-on experiences provide ISP students the opportunity to enjoy afternoons full of activities they choose, as well as meeting American friends their age. All afternoon activities are included in the summer ISP tuition.

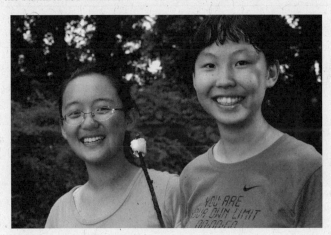

ENROLLMENT

During the summer of 2013, 45 students enrolled in Fay's Summer ISP program.

DAILY SCHEDULE

8:15 a.m.	Breakfast in the Dining Room
9:00 a.m.	Classes begin
12:00 p.m.	Lunch in the Dining Room
12:30 p.m.	Afternoon camp activities
4:00 p.m.	Back to dorms for supervised downtime
6:00 p.m.	Family-style dinner in the Dining Room
7:00 p.m.	Study hall
8:30 p.m.	Evening activity
9:30 p.m.	Back to dorm, lights out for bedtime

EXTRA OPPORTUNITIES AND ACTIVITIES

Summer weekends at Fay are a valuable time for students to put their language skills to use. They participate in academic and social activities on campus, explore Boston and the surrounding areas on field trips, and bond with other students and dorm parents. Students are also required to attend study hall each weekend in order to complete assignments for classes. The combination of trips and on-campus activities ensures that students remain engaged in the American experience while allowing them time to foster lasting relationships with students from all over the world.

FACILITIES

The Fay Discovery Summer International Student Program takes place on Fay School's 66-acre campus, and students have access to its state-of-the-art facilities, including classrooms with updated technology; comfortable dormitories; a dining room for family-style meals; a swimming pool; athletic fields; six tennis courts; gymnasiums; an indoor rock-climbing wall; an outdoor adventure course; a theater; a dance studio; and an art center that includes a painting studio, a printmaking room, and pottery wheels.

STAFF

The foundation of this high-quality summer program is its high-quality counselors and specialists. The team is composed of Fay School's faculty and staff, teachers from the local community, professionals in their fields, and college students who have experience working with children. The staff's experience, professional skills, and passion for working with young people create a summer full of meaningful and enriching experiences.

MEDICAL CARE

At Fay Discovery, safety is of primary importance. The staff participates in extensive training in preparation for their work with students. Low camper-to-staff ratios reflect a commitment to quality supervision. Swimming instructors are lifeguard certified, and staff are trained in first aid and CPR. Fay School's health staff members are on campus each day to provide routine and emergency care.

COSTS

Tuition for Fay Discovery's Summer International Student Program was $9,400 in 2013. Tuition covers all course costs, boarding, health insurance, food, and activities. There is an incidental fee of $800 to cover the student's additional expenses, with the remainder to be refunded at the end of the session.

FINANCIAL AID

Prospective families should contact Courtney Sargent, Director of the Summer International Student Program, to discuss the possible availability of financial aid.

TRANSPORTATION

Fay School will make ground transportation arrangements from and to the airport.

APPLICATION TIMETABLE

Student registration is conducted on a rolling basis throughout the 2013–14 school year.

FOR MORE INFORMATION, CONTACT:

Courtney Sargent, Director of the Summer International Student
    Program
Fay School
48 Main Street
Southborough, Massachusetts 01772
United States
Phone: 508-490-8299
E-mail: csargent@fayschool.org
Website: http://www.fayschool.org/summer/isp

GRIER SCHOOL

GRIER SUMMER

GRIER SUMMER CAMP

TYRONE, PENNSYLVANIA

Type of Program: All-girls visual and performing arts, horseback riding
Participants: Girls, 7–17
Enrollment: 85 per session
Program Dates: June 15–August 2, 2014
Head of Program: Katie Kingera and Jennifer Pepperman, Co-Directors

LOCATION
Grier Summer Camp is located in the Allegheny Mountains of central Pennsylvania and uses the facilities of the Grier School, an historic girls boarding school.

BACKGROUND AND PHILOSOPHY
Founded in 1975, Grier Summer is an all-girls camp with strong traditions in intensive programs in the visual and performing arts and horseback riding.

PROGRAM OFFERINGS
Grier Summer offers programming for students who range in ability from beginner to advanced in horseback riding, musical theater, art, or dance. Students may also choose to specialize in any of these areas.

Art: Campers can further develop existing art skills and explore new creative modalities. Campers choose four different elective activities from a variety of creative and recreational options. Creative activities may include pottery, digital art, drawing and painting, mythology, creative writing, sidewalk art, photography, and fun arts and crafts. In pottery classes, campers receive instruction on the potter's wheel. Campers interested in photography help document the adventures and activities that go on throughout the session. Art activities provide opportunities for creative expression with instructional guidance. Activities are taught by Grier School teachers, professionals hired for the summer, and students majoring in the arts at reputable colleges and universities. Art classes are open to all campers, even those participating in Grier's intensive programs. An end-of-camp art exhibit is held for parents and friends to view their camper's work.

Dance: Dancers of all abilities and style interests will improve their skills and expand their dancing repertoire by attending Grier Summer. Campers interested in dance are placed in classes according to their ability levels. Classes offered include stretch and strength, ballet and jazz technique, modern and contemporary, as well as choreography. Summer dance classes focus on preparing each dancer to perform in choreographed routines, which are performed at a show held at the end of camp. Campers learn small- and large-group numbers, which combine elements from a variety of styles.

Depending on a dancer's experience, they may participate in more than one 90-minute class per day. Intermediate dancers participate in two dance activity periods for a total of 3 hours per day, five days per week. A dance intensive program is offered for serious intermediate to advanced dancers age 12–17. Dancers interested in the intensive must audition upon their arrival at Grier Summer for proper placement. Dancers in the intensive receive instruction from Jocelyn Hrzic, head of the Grier School's Dance Department, choreographer, and coach of the school's award-winning dance

team. Members of the dance intensive program spend three activity periods dancing for a total of 4½ hours a day, five days per week. Intensive classes emphasize students' strengths, technique, musicality, and performance qualities.

When dancers are not in the dance studio, they may participate in all the other camp activities. Dancers can choose to explore other interests such as pottery, mixed media, aquatics, creative writing, yoga, or musical theater.

Equestrian: Students at the Grier Summer Riding Program have abundant opportunity to expand their equestrian horizons. Grier provides a personalized experience for every camper interested in riding. Lessons are tailored for beginners as well as for the seasoned competitive rider. Campers have morning, late afternoon, and evening opportunities to ride up to six days per week. All instructors and camp horses are hand selected to ensure a quality learning environment for each rider. Riders are assigned to a horse for the entire session to enhance continuity and ease while facilitating growth and rider confidence. Small classes promote one-to-one interactions between student and instructors in multiple indoor and outdoor lesson facilities. Private horses are welcome but are not required. On-site shows are hosted throughout the summer to provide all students with competition opportunities. There is also an end-of-camp on-site exhibition for friends and family to attend. More advanced and competitive riders have the opportunity to travel to local show series. Grier Summer Riding teaches girls to realize their potential though horsemanship, friendship, and respect for animals.

Musical Theater: Grier Summer offers girls who love to sing, dance, and/or act opportunities to enhance and showcase their talents. Whether she wants to join an ensemble group in a Broadway show tune number or hopes to acquire a small or large speaking part in a dramatic production, the Grier Summer musical theater program has a role for everyone. All interested actresses, regardless of their native language or nationality, are able to join in the fun of Grier's musical theater program.

There are musical theater experiences offered during both Grier Summer's one-week and three-week camp sessions. Girls who attend the one-week Early Camp program will perform in a Cabaret-style show. Girls who attend the musical theater intensive will be cast into a full-length show. Musical theater classes are offered three out of the four activity periods held each weekday. Campers, depending upon their interests and their role in the summer production, will spend portions of their day blocking scenes, reading and learning scripts, practicing choreography, and/or preparing music. Campers experience all aspects of a show's production since costuming, set design, and tech preparations are all done during the single camp session. Each daily activity period serves as a formal rehearsal. The entire production is brought to life using just 13 day's worth of rehearsal periods!

ENROLLMENT

Grier Summer averages 85 participants per session. Sixty-five percent of those are from the greater tri-state area of New York, New Jersey, and Pennsylvania; 25 percent are international students; and 10 percent of participants come from other areas throughout the United States.

DAILY SCHEDULE

Campers have four 90-minute activity periods each day which may include a combination of art, dance, musical theater, and/or horseback riding. Afternoon and evening programs feature both camp-wide events, such as camp fires, talent shows, color wars, scavenger hunts, and small-group adventure activities, including pool parties, spa nights, and geocaching.

EXTRA OPPORTUNITIES AND ACTIVITIES

Weekends may include themed days or adventure days, with day-long activities centered around a theme. The evening program may also be themed and often includes professional performers. During a regular session may be a camp-wide, off-campus field trip. Additional activities may include rails-to-trails hikes, small trips to local caverns and caves, or geocaching. Other recreational activities offered may include yoga, dance (in styles such as modern, hip hop, and ballet), Zumba, stagecraft, costume design, dramatic and comedic skits, as well as instrumental and singing performances.

FACILITIES

Equestrian facilities include two indoor arenas, an outdoor arena, and stables for 55+ horses. The Dance and Musical Theater programs share Grier's 9,600-square-foot Performing Arts Center equipped with a state-of-the-art floor and sound system—the perfect environment for spending the summer practicing and performing. Visual arts is housed in the Grier School art building which provides bright, open space perfect for creative expression. An outdoor swimming pool is available; pool games are among the afternoon activities. Campers sleep in the dorm rooms of the Grier School and use the dining room for meals.

STAFF

Katie Kingera and Jennifer Pepperman, Co-Directors of Grier Summer, have a combined 35 years of experience with children and adolescents in a variety of settings. Both have academic backgrounds in child development and mental health. Katie Kingera has a B.S. in family and child development and a M.A.Ed. in counselor education from Virginia Tech. Jennifer Pepperman has a B.A. in psychology and human development from Penn State and an M.S.W. from Temple University. They enjoy spending time with their families, pets, and crafting.

The dance, musical theater, and equestrian intensives are taught by Grier School teachers. The counselor to camper ratio is 1:4 for older campers and 1:3 for younger campers, with two counselors for every unit. Campers are assigned to a unit of 6 to 10 girls in the same age group. At least two staff members are assigned to each unit.

MEDICAL CARE

The health center is staffed with registered nurses. Seasonal camp staff is certified in first aid and CPR, and the nearest emergency facility is about 10 minutes away. Health forms are in compliance with the standards of the American Camp Association.

RELIGIOUS LIFE

There are opportunities for participants to attend religious services.

COSTS

Early Camp, 1-week session, June 15–21, 2014: $1,300 ($1,100)*
First Session, 3 weeks, June 22–July 12, 2014: $3,800 ($3,600)*
Second Session, 3 weeks, July 13–August 2, 2014: $3,800 ($3,600)*
Combined Sessions:
Early Camp, First and Second Sessions: $8,500 ($8,200)
Early Camp, First Session: $4,900 ($8,700)
First and Second Sessions: $7,200 ($7,000)
*Prices in parentheses are Early Bird Specials valid only until January 14, 2014.

FINANCIAL AID

Financial assistance is determined on an individual basis.

TRANSPORTATION

Grier Summer staff will meet campers for arrival or accompany campers for departure at five designated airports: State College (45 minutes away), Pittsburgh International Airport (3 hours away), Baltimore/Washington International Airport (3 hours away), Reagan National Airport (3 hours away), and Dulles International Airport (4 hours away). Fees for airport transfers may apply.

APPLICATION TIMETABLE

Grier Summer uses a rolling admission plan. More information is available on the camp website at www.griersummer.org.

FOR MORE INFORMATION, CONTACT

Katie Kingera, Co-Director
Jennifer Pepperman, Co-Director
Grier Summer Camp
2522 Grier School Road
Tyrone, Pennsylvania 16686
United States
Phone: 814-684-3000, ext. 113
Fax: 814-684-2177
E-mail: griersummer@grier.org
Website: www.griersummer.org

PARTICIPANT/FAMILY COMMENTS

Our daughter had a wonderful time at Grier Summer camp. While there, she discovered a talent in dance that we didn't know she had and was able to deepen her love of art. She had experiences at camp that she will carry for a lifetime.

Best camp ever. My daughter loves it!

We could not be happier with the camp, the counselors, and the friends that she made. We will happily sign her up next year for even longer.

PHILLIPS EXETER ACADEMY

▼▲▼▲▼▲▼▲▼▲▼▲▼▲▼▲▼▲▼▲▼▲▼▲▼▲▼▲▼

SUMMER SCHOOL

EXETER, NEW HAMPSHIRE

Type of Program: Academic enrichment
Participants: Coeducational, grades 8–12 and postgraduate year
Enrollment: 780
Program Dates: Five-week program; July 6–August 9, 2014
Head of Program: Ethan W. Shapiro, Director

LOCATION

The 400-acre Phillips Exeter Academy campus is located in the town of Exeter, the Colonial capital of New Hampshire, which is in the heart of the state's seacoast area. Boston, Newburyport, Portsmouth, and the White Mountains are all within easy access for excursions.

BACKGROUND AND PHILOSOPHY

Every summer, Phillips Exeter Academy welcomes to the campus more than 780 students for five weeks of academic study, athletics, and exploration that carry participants far beyond the classrooms and the playing fields. Typically, students come from more than forty states; Puerto Rico; Washington, D.C.; and several dozen foreign nations. Summer School students come from a variety of schools. Most reside in campus dormitories; others travel daily from their homes in the New Hampshire seacoast area. Together they embody a rich diversity of language, culture, religion, and race. They come to Exeter with that particular mix of intellectual curiosity and adventurous spirit that holds the promise of glimpsing new horizons and making new discoveries.

PROGRAM OFFERINGS

The UPPER SCHOOL offers a challenging academic experience for students who have completed grades 9, 10, 11, or 12. UPPER SCHOOL students are part of a richly international community in which students design their own programs of study by selecting courses from the more than 100 offered by the Academy. In shaping their own academic programs, students have the opportunity to expand their intellectual horizons. For instance, they might choose courses in math, art, and English, such as *Advanced Problem-Solving, Drawing,* and *Great Books/Great Reading.* Or they might sample offerings from science, history, and languages, like *Introduction to Biology, Great Issues in American History,* and *Introduction to Arabic.* Whatever their academic choices, students find themselves working in small classes with highly experienced, dedicated teachers. As students select their three classes, they are encouraged to venture into worlds rich in their personal appeal, worlds that may allow them to glimpse new horizons.

ACCESS EXETER offers students who have completed grades 7 or 8 access to a wide range of resources available at Phillips Exeter Academy. Participants will share in a partnership of cooperative learning and sharpen their skills of observation and expression. Students and their teachers will work together within the classroom and beyond. The ACCESS EXETER curriculum consists of six academic clusters. Each cluster has three courses organized around a central theme. Each cluster will include a two-night/three-day, off-campus excursion related to their topic of study midway through the session. Students choose to participate in one of six clusters: *Project*

Exeter: A Greener Earth; The Land and the Sea; Problem-Solving: An Odyssey of the Mind; A Global Community; The Creative Arts: Let Your Spirit Soar; and *Exeter C.S.I.: Crime Scene Investigation.*

Physical education, an important component of the Summer School, promotes fitness, cooperation, sportsmanship, and learning new skills. The offerings are designed to introduce fundamental rules and skills, provide some competition and recreation, and stimulate long-term participation in athletics. Each class meets four times per week for an hour each day. In the past, physical education offerings have included tennis, soccer, basketball, yoga, weight training, water polo, and many other options.

The Summer School also offers an opportunity for students to enjoy more intensive athletic experiences. UPPER SCHOOL students can sign up to participate in the crew program for the entire five weeks of Summer School. In addition, the Summer School and Seacoast United Soccer Club offer a special intensive instruction program for UPPER SCHOOL and ACCESS EXETER students. This program is for players who have a passion for soccer, have played at a competitive level, and want to continue a high level of training while at Summer School.

ENROLLMENT

Students come to the Summer School from forty-five countries and more than forty states. The UPPER SCHOOL is made up of approximately 500 students while ACCESS EXETER can accommodate about 280 participants. Students of all racial, religious, and socioeconomic backgrounds are welcome.

DAILY SCHEDULE

Students attend classes six days a week, Monday through Saturday. On Wednesday and Saturday afternoons students may participate in off-campus excursions, on-campus activities, do homework, or simply relax. Twice a week the entire student body gathers for special assemblies where speakers and performers share their talents. Students have their meals in the dining hall, located in the center of campus. Here they have time to catch up with new friends or chat with faculty members and their families. Dormitory check-in is at 9 p.m. for UPPER SCHOOL students and 8 p.m. for ACCESS

EXETER students (11 p.m. on Saturday). The dorm is expected to be conducive to study after check-in time.

EXTRA OPPORTUNITIES AND ACTIVITIES

Educational and recreational excursions are a regular feature of Wednesday afternoons and weekends, when there are no required appointments. Such excursions are optional and may consist of hikes in the White Mountains, tours of New England colleges, Boston museum visits, or whale watches. Extracurricular activities include theater, music, and various sports. Students are encouraged to enjoy the cultural and ethnic diversity that is at the heart of the Exeter Summer School experience.

FACILITIES

Exeter is proud of its outstanding academic and athletic facilities. The centerpiece of the campus is Louis Kahn's architectural landmark, The Class of 1945 Library, which has a capacity of 250,000 volumes and can seat approximately 400 students. The collection currently consists of 160,000 volumes in addition to an extensive collection of periodicals, DVDs, and CDs. Equally impressive is the Love Gymnasium, with its five basketball floors, Olympic pool, ten squash courts, and exercise and weight rooms. Outside there are acres of baseball diamonds, soccer fields, tennis courts, an all-weather 400-meter track, and a cross-country course through the nature preserve.

The Forrestal-Bowld Music Center has more than 24,000 square feet of space dedicated to the study of music. In addition to three large rehearsal rooms, there are eleven teacher studios, eight of them equipped with grand pianos, and sixteen practice rooms. The state-of-the-art Phelps Science Center offers students and teachers outstanding facilities for scientific investigation and study. Other highlights of the campus are the two-stage Fisher Theater, the Frederick R. Mayer Art Center and Lamont Gallery, and the Grainger Observatory.

STAFF

Many of the Summer School's instructors are Phillips Exeter Academy faculty members. Additional qualified instructors are recruited from other schools and universities from around the world, and many have made long-term commitments to teaching at Phillips Exeter Academy Summer School.

MEDICAL CARE

The Lamont Health and Wellness Center is staffed 24 hours a day. Exeter Hospital, which is just minutes away, offers emergency medical services. Enrollment in the Summer School Group Insurance Plan is included in the tuition.

RELIGIOUS LIFE

The Summer School is nondenominational; students may attend religious services at nearby churches and synagogues if they wish.

COSTS

The 2013 tuition for UPPER SCHOOL boarding students was $7,600. UPPER SCHOOL day students paid $1,150 per course. UPPER SCHOOL students can also register for SAT or ACT Prep

for an additional fee. The ACCESS EXETER boarding student tuition for 2013 was $7,995 and day students paid $4,900. ACCESS EXETER students can also register for SSAT Prep for an additional fee. A nonrefundable fee of $1,500 is due at the time of enrollment. Specific information about tuition for 2014 will be available on the Summer School website.

FINANCIAL AID

Limited financial aid is available and awards are determined by demonstrated need. The deadline for financial aid applications is March 1.

APPLICATION TIMETABLE

Admission to the Phillips Exeter Academy Summer School is competitive and is based on academic achievement. The Summer School seeks students who are motivated to learn and prepared to contribute fully to classroom work and the community. There is a rolling admissions procedure, and only completed applications will be considered. Since many courses fill quickly, it is in the candidate's best interest to complete the application as early as possible. Application information and the course catalog can be found on the Summer School Web site at www.exeter.edu/summer.

FOR MORE INFORMATION, CONTACT:

Ethan W. Shapiro, Director
Phillips Exeter Academy
Summer School
20 Main Street
Exeter, New Hampshire 03833-2460
United States
Phone: 603-777-3488
800-828-4325 Ext. 3488 (toll-free)
Fax: 603-777-4385
E-mail: summer@exeter.edu
Website: http://www.exeter.edu/summer
Facebook: www.facebook.com/ExeterSummerSchool

SOUTHWESTERN ACADEMY

```
▼▲▼▲▼▲▼▲▼▲▼▲▼▲▼▲▼▲▼▲▼▲▼▲▼▲▼▲▼▲▼▲▼▲
```

SUMMER ADVENTURES

RIMROCK, ARIZONA

Type of Program: Academic enrichment, ESL courses, outdoor recreation, environmental education, field trips, and academic credit courses

Participants: Coeducational, ages 12–19

Enrollment: 40

Program Dates: Full- and half-summer, four-, six-, and eight-week sessions, from June 23 to August 15

Head of Program: Mr. Jack Leyden, Head of Campus

LOCATION

Southwestern Academy's Beaver Creek Ranch Campus is in a secluded red sandstone canyon that was carved by the creek around it. The Coconino National Forest surrounds the 180-acre campus. The campus rests at an elevation of 4,000 feet and is located 15 miles from Sedona, 45 miles south of Flagstaff, and 100 miles north of Phoenix, Arizona. Surrounded by large sycamores and cottonwoods, two ponds and a trout stream are located on campus, making this a perfect location for high school students to board, study, and enjoy the summer.

BACKGROUND AND PHILOSOPHY

Southwestern Academy offers a warm, friendly, safe, and supportive environment for boys and girls to grow toward success. Founded in 1924, Southwestern is an accredited, not-for-profit, independent school for students from across the United States and around the world. Southwestern offers classes for grade 6 through high school. Small classes promote individual interaction with teachers and encourage the pursuit of interests beyond course requirements. Southwestern Academy's vision is to offer American and international students personalized, stimulating classes and supportive, nurturing care that allow individual student success and an understanding of diverse cultures. Summer Adventures at Southwestern Academy offers students entering high school full/half-summer and four-, six-, and eight-week programs that uniquely combine college-preparatory, academic enrichment, and language skills with the fun and exciting activities that the season presents.

PROGRAM OFFERINGS

Students enroll in classes that provide opportunities to link academics with some of the most popular hot spots of the area. Students also discover that the Summer Adventures program enables them to develop self-reliance and confidence while making new friendships with other students from around the world. The low teacher-student ratio provides a nurturing and supportive environment, establishing a sense of community and trust that embraces the school's core values. Field trips and scholastics are designed to be achievement based, with individual attention made available to each student as needed—all surrounded by an energetic and spirited atmosphere.

The Summer Adventures program includes a core curriculum with comprehensive courses in English, history, science, mathematics, Spanish, and art. Courses are selected individually to meet each student's academic needs. English as a second language is offered to international students who need to improve their skills in reading, writing, and speaking. Afternoons are left open for study time, enrichment through arts and crafts, elective course work, and travel. Electives also include outdoor and wilderness skills.

High school course credit and letters of achievement can be earned to make up credits for deficiencies, or students can gain a head start on the coming school year. Southwestern Academy, a college-preparatory school with a noncompetitive program, is accredited by the Western Association of Schools and Colleges.

ENROLLMENT

Campers and counselors generally come from the Southwest and are joined by other students from the U.S. and around the world. Southwestern Academy's programs are open to all qualified students without regard to race, creed, or national origin.

EXTRA OPPORTUNITIES AND ACTIVITIES

The canyon setting of the Beaver Creek Ranch Campus provides creek and pool swimming, archaeological and geological field trips, backpacking, rock climbing, and the exploration of nearby caves containing prehistoric remains. There is trout fishing in the creek as well as bass fishing in the campus ponds. The nights are clear for stargazing.

Recreational activities include basketball, softball, swimming, volleyball, horseback riding, hiking, billiards, table tennis, horseshoes, mountain biking, weight training, camping, and indoor games. A golf course is also nearby.

Weekend activities include overnight travel to Sunset Crater, the Grand Canyon, Lake Powell, Navajo and Hopi reservations, the Petrified Forest, and Canyon de Chelly. Camping skills are learned and applied during these trips. In addition, there are organized studies at each site that provide hands-on learning in history, geology, ecology, economics, and geography.

FACILITIES

Campus buildings include classic dorms with double and triple rooms; river-stone cottages for faculty members; classrooms and study assembly; a science lab; recreation halls; natural and man-made swimming pools; indoor tennis, basketball, and volleyball courts; weight and fitness rooms; an art building; and sports fields. There is a full gymnasium on campus. Computers and computer instruction are available to all students.

STAFF

The Beaver Creek Ranch Campus staff consists of the Head of School, teachers, and support staff members. Teachers from the school's regular term instruct the summer program classes. Resident teachers supervise all afternoon and evening travel and activities.

MEDICAL CARE

The application includes authorization for the school to coordinate any medical procedures that may be necessary during the program.

COSTS

Tuition, room, and board total $5,500 for the four-week session, $6,875 for the five-week session, $8,250 for the six-week session, and $13,920 for the eight-week session. A deposit of $500 is required for the student's personal expenses. Updated costs and program dates are available online at **http://www.southwesternacademy.edu**.

FINANCIAL AID

Limited financial aid is available. Special grants are based on financial need.

TRANSPORTATION

Beaver Creek Ranch Campus is 7 hours from Los Angeles by car and 1½ hours from Phoenix. A private airstrip is nearby. Unless other arrangements are made, students fly into Phoenix Sky Harbor Airport and take a shuttle to Camp Verde, where they are greeted by a Southwestern Academy staff or faculty member and escorted to the campus.

APPLICATION TIMETABLE

The completed application includes an application form, an emergency medical form, and a health statement. There is no application fee for the summer program. The school accepts applications throughout the year and accepts students as long as space is available. On acceptance, the contract reserves space in the school. Southwestern's year-round campuses are always open for tours, interviews, and/or admission information. Summer applications are due by May 30.

FOR MORE INFORMATION, CONTACT

Director of Admissions
San Marino Campus
Southwestern Academy
2800 Monterey Road
San Marino, California 91108
United States
Phone: 626-799-5010 Ext. 203
Fax: 626-799-0407
E-mail: jblake@southwesternacademy.edu
Website: http://www.southwesternacademy.edu

Beaver Creek Ranch Campus
Southwestern Academy
Rimrock, Arizona 86335
United States
Phone: 928-567-4581

PARTICIPANT/FAMILY COMMENTS

"Summer Adventures at Southwestern Academy is a place where everyone can find success."

"It was a good summer—the best of my life. The studying was difficult, but I'm so glad my parents sent me, or I never would have had this experience. You work for the teachers and counselors, and they work for you. There's not anything in the world they wouldn't do for us. They're just fantastic."

"Everybody works together as a unit. You know the teachers personally and respect their knowledge. But they're more than teachers, they're people who care. They teach you more than lessons—they teach you about life."

SOUTHWESTERN ACADEMY

SUMMER ADVENTURES

SAN MARINO, CALIFORNIA

Type of Program: Academic enrichment, credit, and English as a second language

Participants: Boys and girls in grades 6–12

Enrollment: 80

Program Dates: Full- and half-summer, four-, six-, and eight-week sessions, from June 9 to September 12

Head of Program: Kenneth Veronda, Headmaster

LOCATION

The San Marino campus is located in one of the most beautiful neighborhoods in Southern California, minutes from Pasadena and Los Angeles. The campus sprawls over more than 8 acres in a quiet and serene community, making this a perfect location for middle school and high school students to board, study, and enjoy the summer.

BACKGROUND AND PHILOSOPHY

Southwestern Academy offers a warm, friendly, safe, and supportive environment for boys and girls to grow toward success. Founded in 1924, Southwestern is an accredited, not-for-profit independent school for students from across the United States and around the world. Southwestern offers classes for grade 6 through high school. Small classes promote individual interaction with teachers and encourage the pursuit of interests beyond course requirements. Southwestern Academy's vision is to offer American and international students personalized, stimulating classes and supportive, nurturing care that allow individual student success and an understanding of diverse cultures. Summer Adventures at Southwestern Academy offers students entering high school full/half-summer and four-, six-, and eight-week programs that uniquely combine college-preparatory, academic enrichment, and language skills with the fun and exciting activities that the season presents.

PROGRAM OFFERINGS

The Southwestern Summer Adventures program consists of two components: an Intensive English as a Second Language (ESL)/American Culture Program and traditional college-prep classes. Courses range from four weeks to a full semester and are offered on the campuses in San Marino, California, and Beaver Creek, Arizona. Depending on the length of the program, students can earn academic credit.

The San Marino campus offers two English language programs. The **Intensive ESL Program** is designed to help students improve their English skills. There are three ability levels: beginning, intermediate, and advanced. Students improve their skills through listening and conversation, writing and grammar, and reading and vocabulary. There is also an SAT/TOEFL-preparation component. Students who enroll in the seven-week or fourteen-week program can earn half- or full-semester credit. The **American Culture Program** teaches English-speaking skills, but it also incorporates field trips in the region. Course work includes 20 hours of English per week, developing reading, vocabulary, and conversation skills. Students receive a certificate at the end of the program.

Students who do not need ESL can select from a wide range of core courses, such as math, science, history, and English.

Southwestern Academy is an accredited college-preparatory school with a noncompetitive program.

ENROLLMENT

Each program enrolls an average of 10 to 12 students, ages 12 through 19, who wish to improve their English skills and/or participate in a number of recreational and cultural activities in the region. Students are exposed to a multicultural learning atmosphere and gain a fresh perspective on academics. Students may commute to the program, or they can live in a dormitory at the school. Southwestern Academy's programs are open to all qualified students without regard to race, creed, or national origin.

EXTRA OPPORTUNITIES AND ACTIVITIES

Weekly educational and entertaining field trips are offered to a variety of popular attractions throughout Southern California. Such trips include Disneyland, Griffith Park, Huntington Library, the Los Angeles County Museum of Art, and the Getty Museum. For boarding students, there are three additional trips offered each weekend.

FACILITIES

All dorms are of modern masonry construction and have TVs, DVDs, and computers with Internet and e-mail access. Each dormitory is supervised by a resident counselor, who has an apartment adjacent to the dormitory. Boarding students are provided with a buffet-style cooked breakfast and a family-style lunch and dinner. Commuting students have a hot lunch with the whole school group at no additional charge. Teachers and staff members eat with the students.

STAFF

The San Marino campus staff consists of the school's Headmaster, Dean of Academics, Dean of Students, Director of ESL, Director of Admissions, and approximately 22 teachers and dorm counselors. Counseling, testing, and crisis-intervention services are provided by the school psychologist.

MEDICAL CARE

The application includes authorization for the school to coordinate any medical procedures that may be necessary during the program.

COSTS

Tuition, room, and board total $5,500 for the four-week program, $8,250 for the six-week program, $11,000 for the eight-week program, $9,625 for the half-summer program, and $18,550 for the full-summer program. A deposit of $500 is required for the student's personal expenses. Updated costs and program dates are available online at http://www.southwesternacademy.edu.

FINANCIAL AID

Limited financial aid is available. Special grants are based on financial need.

TRANSPORTATION

Southwestern Academy is approximately 25 miles from Los Angeles International Airport (LAX).

APPLICATION TIMETABLE

The completed application for the regular school year includes an application form, an emergency medical form, and a health statement. There is no application fee for the summer program; please submit the completed application. The school accepts applications for the regular school year program throughout the year and students are accepted as space is available. On acceptance, the contract reserves space in the school. Southwestern's year-round campuses are always open for tours, interviews, and/or admission information. Applications are welcome all summer, though early submission is requested due to demand and to assure availability.

FOR MORE INFORMATION, CONTACT

Director of Admissions
Southwest Academy
2800 Monterey Road
San Marino, California 91108
United States
Phone: 626-799-5010 Ext. 203
Fax: 626-799-0407
E-mail: admissions@southwesternacademy.edu
Website: http://www.southwesternacademy.edu

TASIS–THE AMERICAN SCHOOL IN SWITZERLAND

TASIS

▼▲▼▲▼▲▼▲▼▲▼▲▼▲▼▲▼▲▼▲▼▲▼▲▼▲▼▲▼▲▼▲▼▲▼▲▼▲

LANGUAGES, PERFORMING AND VISUAL ARTS, SPORTS, AND CULTURAL EXCURSIONS IN EUROPE

LUGANO AND CHÂTEAU D'OEX, SWITZERLAND

Type of Program: *Lugano:* Intensive foreign language study, performing and visual arts; *Château d'Oex:* Intensive French language instruction, English as an Additional Language (EAL), TASIS Ecological Leadership Action Program (TELAP, ages 14–18, 5 weeks)

Participants: Coeducational, *Lugano:* ages 4+–18; *Château d'Oex:* ages 11–18

Enrollment: *Lugano:* 300; *Château d'Oex:* 65

Program Dates: *Lugano:* Four weeks, 28 June–24 July; three weeks, 27 July–16 August; *Château d'Oex:* Four weeks, 28 June–1 August.

Heads of Programs: Betsy Newell, Marc Pierre Jansen, Jim Haley, Marie-Josée Breton, and Tom Lill

LOCATION

Lugano, Switzerland: Nestled in the foothills of the southern Swiss Alps, with spectacular views, the TASIS campus is a compact cluster of historic buildings and new facilities. It overlooks the attractive resort town of Lugano and is 2 miles from Agno International Airport and less than an hour's drive from Milan (Malpensa) International Airport in Italy. The idyllic setting allows for a wide range of enjoyable activities, including windsurfing, pleasure cruises to lakeside hamlets, picnics, and hiking to picturesque villages.

Château d'Oex, Switzerland: Located in the French-speaking canton of Vaud, the area offers outstanding opportunities for French language learning and an appreciation of the area's natural beauty.

BACKGROUND AND PHILOSOPHY

Founded in 1956 by Mrs. M. Crist Fleming, TASIS is a coed college-preparatory American boarding school for students in grades 6–12 and postgraduates.

The Summer Programs began thirty-six years ago and were designed to offer American and international students an opportunity to study abroad and a chance to live in a truly international environment. The programs in Château d'Oex, were founded seventeen years ago.

PROGRAM OFFERINGS

TASIS Summer Program (TSP): This program combines languages, arts, and outdoor pursuits, and is based on the campus of The American School in Switzerland in Lugano. Offerings include intensive language courses in English as an additional language, French, and Italian for 14- to 18-year-olds. The program includes artistic activities, a wide choice of sports, alpine activities, and weekend excursions in Switzerland and Italy. Both four- and three-week sessions are available. Besides language courses, the program offers courses in digital photography, architecture and design, fashion and textile design, and musical theater.

Middle School Program (MSP): This program, on the Lugano campus, is designed for students aged 11 to 13 to study English

as an additional language, French, Italian, or musical theater. The program provides appropriate academic challenges and recreational activities for this transitional age group within a warm and caring community. Students choose special workshops to attend two afternoons a week, including music and drama, art, special sports, or tennis. During the remaining afternoons, students participate in afternoon and weekend activities, sports, and excursions.

Optional intensive afternoon sports activities are offered in both MSP and TSP. TSP students can attend the AC Milan Junior Camp or Armani Junior Basketball Club four afternoons per week, while MSP offers four different special sports tracks that meet three afternoons per week. Students with proven previous experience can also choose the Golf Club or Tennis Academy.

Le Château des Enfants (CDE): This summer program offers learning and fun for 4+ to 10 year olds. Sharing the Lugano campus with TSP and MSP, but with its own separate living and dining facilities, the program teaches English, Italian, or French through lessons, games, activities, sports, and art in a close-knit, caring, family-style community specifically tailored to younger children.

Picnics, excursions, and camping trips are also offered. Both four- and three-week sessions are available. Children from 4+ to 6 years of age can attend the Minnows program as day students only.

The Summer Language Program (TSLP, ages 14–17) in Château-d'Oex: This program offers English- or French-language learning in an intimate alpine setting. Intensive outdoor sports options, arts and crafts workshops, excursions such as climbing and rafting, and special weekend activities make this program ideal for more adventurous students.

The Middle School Program (MSPCD, ages 11–13) in Château-d'Oex: This program is for students willing to improve or learn either English or French in this alpine setting of the Pays d'Enhaut. The study of the language is combined with mountain sports, cultural excursions, and a variety of activities which take advantage of the beautiful location.

TASIS Ecological Leadership Action Program (TELAP, ages 14–18) in Château-d'Oex: An exciting five-week program for students aged 14 to 18, TELAP is organized in collaboration with a team of experts in environmental studies, ecology, outdoor adventure, team building, stewardship, and wilderness survival skills. Students in this program must demonstrate that they are physically fit and have a keen interest in the preservation of the environment. The fifth week will be devoted to an eco-action project in a European country.

ENROLLMENT

In Lugano, more than 300 students represent as many as forty different countries. In Château d'Oex, approximately 65 students in the language-based programs and a maximum of 14 for the TELAP program, enroll from all over the world, including the Americas, Europe, and Asia.

EXTRA OPPORTUNITIES AND ACTIVITIES

Lugano: All students participate in afternoon sports and activities. Students choose from a variety of sports, including swimming, aerobic dance, basketball, cross-country running, soccer, softball, tennis, and volleyball. The afternoon activities include art, photography, and computer club. Weekend excursions provide ample opportunity for students to explore local areas of interest. Full-day excursions to Como and Milan, Lucerne, and Valley Verzasca and half-day excursions to nearby places of interest, such as Swiss Miniature in Melide and the antique street markets in Como, are organized. Optional weekend travel destinations (at an extra cost) include such cities as Florence, Nice, Paris, Venice, and Verona. Students ages 11–18 may also choose to attend special sports afternoon tracks such as the AC Milan Junior Camp or the Armani Basketball Club, under the supervision of trained coaches. Middle school students can also participate in the Golf Club or Tennis Academy if they have previous experience in these sports.

Château d'Oex: Hiking, rock climbing, tennis, swimming, basketball, and soccer are offered. Weekend destinations include Geneva, Interlaken, Zermatt, and Gstaad. The TELAP program will focus on environmental issues, wellness and nutrition, outdoor adventures and team-building activities, and basic sailing instruction on Lake Geneva.

FACILITIES

Lugano: The program uses all of the boarding school facilities of the American School in Switzerland. The historic Villa de Nobili houses the administrative offices, dining rooms/terraces, classrooms, and dormitory areas. Villa Monticello contains classrooms, a computer center, and dormitories. Hadsall House houses an audiovisual lab, a recreation center, and a snack bar, as well as dormitory accommodations. The M. Crist Fleming Library holds 20,000 volumes. In the brand-new Sahenk Arts Center, students of all ages will attend classes and workshops in the visual and creative arts. On-campus sports facilities include a gymnasium, an outdoor pool, a fitness center, and two multipurpose hard courts.

Château d'Oex: The historic wood-carved chalets, set in the heart of the village, are home to TASIS students. They house dormitories, classrooms, a dining room, and recreation areas. There are a tennis/basketball court and Ping-Pong tables in the garden of the main chalet. Nearby facilities include a swimming pool, soccer field, and beach volley. Tennis players of intermediate and advanced ability can enroll in the intensive tennis offering to improve their skills under the guidance of certified tennis instructors.

STAFF

There are 60 full-time summer staff members (the staff-student ratio is 1:5). Qualified classroom teachers also undertake supervisory responsibilities, including coaching sports, chaperoning trips, dormitory coverage, and the in loco parentis role. Counselors work alongside teachers in the dorms, on excursions, on the sports fields, and in recreational activities to help provide a caring environment for students.

Many of the staff members are current or former TASIS faculty members, and counselors are alumni from all TASIS programs.

COSTS

For Lugano and Château d'Oex, Switzerland, the all-inclusive cost for a four-week session in 2014 is CHF 7400. The cost for the three-week session is CHF 5950. The TASIS Summer Programs in Château-d'Oex, are four-week sessions only, and the boarding fee is CHF 7400. Students in the TSLP program can attend the optional fifth week to Paris, France, for an additional CHF 1600. The 5-week TELAP program is CHF 8800. There are no additional fees, with the exception of long-haul airfare, the optional European weekend travel costs, personal spending money, and medical expenses not covered by TASIS health insurance.

FOR MORE INFORMATION, CONTACT

TASIS U.S. Representative
The TASIS Schools
112 South Royal Street
Alexandria, Virginia 22314
United States
Phone: 703-299-8150
Fax: 703-299-8157
E-mail: usadmissions@tasis.com
Website: http://www.tasis.com

Specialized Directories

COEDUCATIONAL DAY SCHOOLS

Acacia Academy, IL
The Academy at Charlemont, MA
Academy at the Lakes, FL
The Academy for Gifted Children (PACE), ON, Canada
Albuquerque Academy, NM
Allendale Columbia School, NY
Alma Heights Christian High School, CA
Alpha Omega Academy, IA
American Community Schools of Athens, Greece
American Heritage School, Delray Beach, FL
American Heritage School, Plantation, FL
The American School Foundation, Mexico
The American School of Madrid, Spain
Annie Wright School, WA
Archbishop Alter High School, OH
Archbishop Hoban High School, OH
Archbishop Mitty High School, CA
Archbishop Thomas J. Murphy High School, WA
Arthur Morgan School, NC
The Athenian School, CA
Athens Academy, GA
Augusta Christian School, GA
Augusta Preparatory Day School, GA
Bachman Academy, TN
Baldwin School of Puerto Rico, PR
Bangor Christian School, ME
Barnstable Academy, NJ
Battle Ground Academy, TN
Bay Ridge Preparatory School, NY
The Bay School of San Francisco, CA
The Beekman School, NY
Benet Academy, IL
The Benjamin School, FL
Berkeley Carroll School, NY
Berkeley Preparatory School, FL
Berkshire School, MA
Besant Hill School, CA
Beth Haven Christian School, KY
The Birch Wathen Lenox School, NY
Bishop Brady High School, NH
Bishop Connolly High School, MA
Bishop Denis J. O'Connell High School, VA
Bishop Eustace Preparatory School, NJ
Bishop Guertin High School, NH
Bishop Ireton High School, VA
Bishop John J. Snyder High School, FL
Bishop Kelly High School, ID
Bishop McGuinness Catholic High School, OK
Bishop Montgomery High School, CA
Bishop O'Dowd High School, CA
Bishop Shanahan High School, PA
Bishop Stang High School, MA
Blanchet School, OR
Blessed Trinity High School, GA
The Bolles School, FL
Boston University Academy, MA
Bourgade Catholic High School, AZ
Boylan Central Catholic High School, IL
Brehm Preparatory School, IL
Brentwood School, CA
Briarcrest Christian High School, TN
Briarwood Christian High School, AL
Bridges Academy, CA
Brimmer and May School, MA
The British School of Boston, MA
Brookhaven Academy, MS
The Brook Hill School, TX

Brooks School, MA
Burr and Burton Academy, VT
Butte Central Catholic High School, MT
Buxton School, MA
Campbell Hall (Episcopal), CA
Camphill Special School, PA
Canterbury School, FL
The Canterbury School of Florida, FL
Cape Cod Academy, MA
Cape Fear Academy, NC
Cape Henry Collegiate School, VA
Capistrano Valley Christian Schools, CA
Cardinal Gibbons High School, NC
Cardinal Mooney Catholic High School, FL
Cardinal Newman High School, FL
Cardinal O'Hara High School, PA
Carlisle School, VA
Carmel High School, IL
Carrollton Christian Academy, TX
Cascadilla School, NY
Catholic Central High School, NY
Catholic Central High School, WI
The Catlin Gabel School, OR
Central Alberta Christian High School, AB, Canada
Central Catholic High School, CA
Central Catholic High School, MA
Chadwick School, CA
Chaminade College Preparatory, CA
Chaminade-Madonna College Preparatory, FL
Charlotte Country Day School, NC
Charlotte Latin School, NC
Chase Collegiate School, CT
Chattanooga Christian School, TN
Chelsea School, MD
The Chicago Academy for the Arts, IL
Children's Creative and Performing Arts Academy of
    San Diego, CA
Chinese Christian Schools, CA
Christ Church Episcopal School, SC
Christian Brothers Academy, NY
Christian Central Academy, NY
Christopher Dock Mennonite High School, PA
Chrysalis School, WA
Clarksville Academy, TN
Clearwater Central Catholic High School, FL
Colegio Bolivar, Colombia
Cole Valley Christian High School, ID
Columbia Academy, TN
Columbia International College of Canada, ON, Canada
The Columbus Academy, OH
Commonwealth School, MA
Community Hebrew Academy, ON, Canada
The Community School of Naples, FL
The Concept School, PA
Concord Academy, MA
Concordia Lutheran High School, IN
Cotter Schools, MN
The Country Day School, ON, Canada
Covenant Canadian Reformed School, AB, Canada
Crawford Adventist Academy, ON, Canada
The Crenshaw School, FL
Cretin-Derham Hall, MN
Crossroads School for Arts & Sciences, CA
Crystal Springs Uplands School, CA
The Culver Academies, IN
Currey Ingram Academy, TN
Darrow School, NY
Davidson Academy, TN

Deerfield Academy, MA
De La Salle College, ON, Canada
DeLaSalle High School, MN
De La Salle North Catholic High School, OR
Delphi Academy of Los Angeles, CA
Denver Academy, CO
Denver Christian High School, CO
DePaul Catholic High School, NJ
The Derryfield School, NH
Detroit Country Day School, MI
The Dr. Miriam and Sheldon G. Adelson Educational Campus,
    The Adelson Upper School, NV
Donelson Christian Academy, TN
The Donoho School, AL
Dowling Catholic High School, IA
Durham Academy, NC
Eagle Hill School, CT
Eastern Mennonite High School, VA
Eaton Academy, GA
Edgewood Academy, AL
Eldorado Emerson Private School, CA
Elgin Academy, IL
The Emery/Weiner School, TX
The Episcopal Academy, PA
Episcopal Collegiate School, AR
Episcopal High School, TX
Ezell-Harding Christian School, TN
Faith Christian High School, CA
Faith Lutheran High School, NV
Falmouth Academy, MA
Father Lopez High School, FL
Father Ryan High School, TN
Fayetteville Academy, NC
Fay School, MA
The First Academy, FL
First Baptist Academy, TX
First Presbyterian Day School, GA
Flintridge Preparatory School, CA
Fort Worth Christian School, TX
Foundation Academy, FL
Fountain Valley School of Colorado, CO
Fowlers Academy, PR
Franklin Road Academy, TN
Fredericksburg Academy, VA
Freeman Academy, SD
French-American School of New York, NY
Fresno Christian Schools, CA
Friends Academy, NY
Friends' Central School, PA
Front Range Christian High School, CO
The Frostig School, CA
Fryeburg Academy, ME
Fuqua School, VA
Gabriel Richard Catholic High School, MI
The Galloway School, GA
Gann Academy (The New Jewish High School of
    Greater Boston), MA
Gaston Day School, NC
Gateway School, TX
George School, PA
Georgetown Day School, DC
Germantown Friends School, PA
Glades Day School, FL
The Glenholme School, Devereux Connecticut, CT
Glenlyon Norfolk School, BC, Canada
Good Hope Country Day School, VI
Gould Academy, ME

The Governor French Academy, IL
Grace Baptist Academy, TN
Grace Brethren School, CA
Grace Christian School, AK
The Grauer School, CA
Great Lakes Christian High School, ON, Canada
Greenhill School, TX
Greenhills School, MI
Guamani Private School, PR
Gulliver Preparatory School, FL
The Gunnery, CT
Hampton Roads Academy, VA
Hanalani Schools, HI
Hank Haney International Junior Golf Academy, SC
The Harley School, NY
Harrells Christian Academy, NC
Harvard-Westlake School, CA
Hawaii Baptist Academy, HI
Hawai`i Preparatory Academy, HI
Hawthorne Christian Academy, NJ
Head-Royce School, CA
Hebrew Academy, CA
Hebrew Academy of the Five Towns & Rockaway, NY
Heritage Christian School, CA
Heritage Christian School, ON, Canada
The Heritage School, GA
Highland Hall Waldorf School, CA
High Mowing School, NH
Highroad Academy, BC, Canada
The Hill Top Preparatory School, PA
Holy Cross High School, CT
Holy Savior Menard Catholic High School, LA
Holy Trinity School, ON, Canada
Hopkins School, CT
Houghton Academy, NY
The Howard School, GA
The Hudson School, NJ
Humanex Academy, CO
The Hun School of Princeton, NJ
Huntington-Surrey School, TX
Hyde Park Baptist School, TX
Hyman Brand Hebrew Academy of Greater Kansas City, KS
IC Catholic Prep, IL
Immaculata-La Salle High School, FL
Independent School, KS
Institut Monte Rosa, Switzerland
Intermountain Christian School, UT
International High School, CA
International School Bangkok, Thailand
International School Manila, Philippines
International School of Indiana, IN
Istanbul International Community School, Turkey
Jean and Samuel Frankel Jewish Academy of Metropolitan
    Detroit, MI
John Burroughs School, MO
John T. Morgan Academy, AL
Kalamazoo Christian High School, MI
Kansas City Academy, MO
Kent Denver School, CO
The Kew-Forest School, NY
The Key School, MD
Keystone School, TX
Kildonan School, NY
Kimball Union Academy, NH
King Low Heywood Thomas, CT
Kings Christian School, CA
King's-Edgehill School, NS, Canada

Kingsway College, ON, Canada
Kingswood-Oxford School, CT
The Lab School of Washington, DC
La Jolla Country Day School, CA
Lakehill Preparatory School, TX
Lancaster Country Day School, PA
Lancaster Mennonite High School, PA
Landmark Christian Academy, KY
Landmark Christian School, GA
Landmark School, MA
Lansdale Catholic High School, PA
La Scuola D'Italia Guglielmo Marconi, NY
The Latin School of Chicago, IL
The Laureate Academy, MB, Canada
Lawrence Academy, MA
Lawrence School, OH
The Lawrenceville School, NJ
Lee Academy, ME
The Leelanau School, MI
Lehigh Valley Christian High School, PA
Lexington Catholic High School, KY
Lick-Wilmerding High School, CA
Linfield Christian School, CA
The Linsly School, WV
Lipscomb Academy, TN
Little Red School House and Elisabeth Irwin High School, NY
Lodi Academy, CA
Long Island Lutheran Middle and High School, NY
Long Trail School, VT
The Lovett School, GA
The Lowell Whiteman School, CO
Loyola School, NY
Lustre Christian High School, MT
Lutheran High School North, MO
Lutheran High School Northwest, MI
Lutheran High School of Hawaii, HI
Luther College High School, SK, Canada
Lycee International de Los Angeles, CA
Madison Academy, AL
Madison Country Day School, WI
Maharishi School of the Age of Enlightenment, IA
Maine Central Institute, ME
Manhattan Christian High School, MT
Maplebrook School, NY
Maranatha High School, CA
Maret School, DC
Marian Catholic High School, PA
Marian Central Catholic High School, IL
Marin Academy, CA
Marist School, GA
Marshall School, MN
Mars Hill Bible School, AL
Mary Institute and St. Louis Country Day School (MICDS), MO
The Masters School, NY
Matignon High School, MA
Maur Hill-Mount Academy, KS
McDonogh School, MD
McGill-Toolen Catholic High School, AL
Meadowridge School, BC, Canada
The Meadows School, NV
Mennonite Collegiate Institute, MB, Canada
Mercersburg Academy, PA
Mesa Grande Seventh-Day Academy, CA
Middlesex School, MA
Middle Tennessee Christian School, TN
Mid-Pacific Institute, HI
Mid-Peninsula High School, CA

Millbrook School, NY
MMI Preparatory School, PA
Modesto Christian School, CA
Mont'Kiara International School, Malaysia
Montverde Academy, FL
Moorestown Friends School, NJ
Mooseheart High School, IL
Moravian Academy, PA
Mt. De Sales Academy, GA
Mount Paran Christian School, GA
Mount Saint Charles Academy, RI
Mount Vernon Presbyterian School, GA
MU High School, MO
Nazareth Academy, IL
Nebraska Christian Schools, NE
Newark Academy, NJ
New Covenant Academy, MO
Newton's Grove School, ON, Canada
Niagara Christian Community of Schools, ON, Canada
Noble and Greenough School, MA
The Nora School, MD
Norfolk Academy, VA
Norman Howard School, NY
The North Broward Preparatory Upper School, FL
Northfield Mount Hermon School, MA
North Shore Country Day School, IL
North Toronto Christian School, ON, Canada
Northwest Academy, OR
Northwest Catholic High School, CT
The Norwich Free Academy, CT
Notre Dame Junior/Senior High School, PA
Oak Grove School, CA
The Oakland School, PA
Oakland School, VA
Oldenburg Academy, IN
The O'Neal School, NC
Oneida Baptist Institute, KY
Oregon Episcopal School, OR
Orinda Academy, CA
The Orme School, AZ
Our Lady of Mount Carmel High School, MD
Out-Of-Door-Academy, FL
The Overlake School, WA
Pacific Crest Community School, OR
Padua Franciscan High School, OH
The Paideia School, GA
Palo Alto Preparatory School, CA
Paradise Adventist Academy, CA
Parish Episcopal School, TX
The Park School of Baltimore, MD
The Park School of Buffalo, NY
The Pathway School, PA
The Pennington School, NJ
Pensacola Catholic High School, FL
Philadelphia-Montgomery Christian Academy, PA
Phoenix Christian Unified Schools, AZ
Piedmont Academy, GA
Pinecrest Academy, GA
The Pingree School, MA
The Pingry School, NJ
Pioneer Valley Christian School, MA
Pope John XXIII Regional High School, NJ
Porter-Gaud School, SC
Portsmouth Christian Academy, NH
The Potomac School, VA
Poughkeepsie Day School, NY
Powers Catholic High School, MI

Proctor Academy, NH
Professional Children's School, NY
Providence Academy, MN
Providence Country Day School, RI
Providence Day School, NC
Providence High School, CA
Punahou School, HI
Pusch Ridge Christian Academy, AZ
Queen Margaret's School, BC, Canada
Rabun Gap-Nacoochee School, GA
Randolph-Macon Academy, VA
Ranney School, NJ
Ransom Everglades School, FL
Realms of Inquiry, UT
The Rectory School, CT
Redeemer Christian High School, ON, Canada
Redwood Christian Schools, CA
Ridley College, ON, Canada
Riverdale Country School, NY
The Rivers School, MA
Riverstone International School, ID
Rolling Hills Preparatory School, CA
Rosseau Lake College, ON, Canada
Ross School, NY
Rowland Hall, UT
Royal Canadian College, BC, Canada
Rumsey Hall School, CT
Sacramento Country Day School, CA
Sacred Heart School of Halifax, NS, Canada
Saddlebrook Preparatory School, FL
Sage Hill School, CA
St. Andrew's Episcopal School, MD
St. Andrew's Regional High School, BC, Canada
St. Andrew's School, RI
Saint Anthony High School, IL
St. Benedict at Auburndale, TN
St. Croix Schools, MN
Saint Dominic Academy, ME
Saint Edward's School, FL
Saint Elizabeth High School, CA
Saint Francis High School, CA
St. Francis High School, KY
St. George's Independent School, TN
St. George's School, RI
St. George's School of Montreal, QC, Canada
Saint John's Preparatory School, MN
St. Joseph Academy, FL
St. Joseph High School, CT
Saint Joseph High School, IL
St. Joseph's Catholic School, SC
Saint Lawrence Academy, CA
St. Martin's Episcopal School, LA
Saint Mary's Hall, TX
Saint Mary's High School, AZ
Saint Mary's High School, MD
St. Mary's School, OR
Saint Maur International School, Japan
St. Patrick's Regional Secondary, BC, Canada
St. Paul Academy and Summit School, MN
St. Paul Preparatory School, MN
St. Pius X Catholic High School, GA
St. Pius X High School, TX
St. Stephen's & St. Agnes School, VA
St. Stephen's Episcopal School, TX
St. Stephen's School, Rome, Italy
St. Thomas Aquinas High School, FL
Saint Thomas Aquinas High School, KS

St. Thomas Aquinas High School, NH
Saint Thomas More Catholic High School, LA
Saint Viator High School, IL
Salem Academy, OR
Salpointe Catholic High School, AZ
Sandia Preparatory School, NM
San Diego Jewish Academy, CA
San Domenico School, CA
Sandy Spring Friends School, MD
San Marcos Baptist Academy, TX
Scattergood Friends School, IA
Scottsdale Christian Academy, AZ
Scotus Central Catholic High School, NE
Seattle Academy of Arts and Sciences, WA
Seton Catholic High School, AZ
The Seven Hills School, OH
Sewickley Academy, PA
Shady Side Academy, PA
Shanley High School, ND
The Sharon Academy, VT
Shattuck-St. Mary's School, MN
Shawe Memorial Junior/Senior High School, IN
Shawnigan Lake School, BC, Canada
Shelton School and Evaluation Center, TX
The Shipley School, PA
Shoreline Christian, WA
Signet Christian School, ON, Canada
Smith School, NY
Sonoma Academy, CA
Soundview Preparatory School, NY
Southfield Christian High School, MI
Southwestern Academy, AZ
Southwestern Academy, CA
Springside Chestnut Hill Academy, PA
Squaw Valley Academy, CA
Stevenson School, CA
The Storm King School, NY
The Sudbury Valley School, MA
Summerfield Waldorf School, CA
The Summit Country Day School, OH
Sunshine Bible Academy, SD
The Taft School, CT
Tampa Preparatory School, FL
Telluride Mountain School, CO
Temple Grandin School, CO
The Tenney School, TX
Teurlings Catholic High School, LA
The Thacher School, CA
Thomas Jefferson School, MO
Thornton Academy, ME
Tilton School, NH
Timothy Christian High School, IL
TMI - The Episcopal School of Texas, TX
Tower Hill School, DE
Trevor Day School, NY
Tri-City Christian Academy, AZ
Trinity Christian Academy, TN
Trinity College School, ON, Canada
Trinity High School, NH
Trinity High School, OH
Trinity Preparatory School, FL
Trinity School of Texas, TX
Trinity Valley School, TX
Tyler Street Christian Academy, TX
United Mennonite Educational Institute, ON, Canada
University Liggett School, MI
University of Chicago Laboratory Schools, IL

University School of Jackson, TN
University School of Milwaukee, WI
University School of Nova Southeastern University, FL
Valle Catholic High School, MO
Valley Christian High School, CA
The Valley School, MI
Vandebilt Catholic High School, LA
Venta Preparatory School, ON, Canada
Vicksburg Catholic School, MS
Victor Valley Christian School, CA
Viewpoint School, CA
Villa Angela-St. Joseph High School, OH
Villa Madonna Academy, KY
Wakefield School, VA
Waldorf High School of Massachusetts Bay, MA
The Waldorf School of Garden City, NY
The Waldorf School of Saratoga Springs, NY
Wasatch Academy, UT
Washington International School, DC
The Waterford School, UT
Watkinson School, CT
Waynflete School, ME
Webb School of Knoxville, TN
The Webb Schools, CA
Wellspring Foundation, CT
Wellsprings Friends School, OR
Wesleyan Academy, PR
Westbury Christian School, TX
Westchester Country Day School, NC
Westminster Christian Academy, LA
Westminster Christian School, FL
Westminster School, CT
West Sound Academy, WA
Westtown School, PA
Westview School, CA
Wheaton Academy, IL
The Wheeler School, RI
Whitefield Academy, KY
The White Mountain School, NH
Whitfield School, MO
Whitinsville Christian School, MA
Wilbraham & Monson Academy, MA
William Penn Charter School, PA
The Williston Northampton School, MA
Wilmington Christian School, DE
Wilmington Friends School, DE
Wilson Hall, SC
Windermere Preparatory School, FL
The Windsor School, NY
Winston Preparatory School, NY
The Winston School, TX
The Winston School San Antonio, TX
Woodlynde School, PA
Woodward Academy, GA
Worcester Academy, MA
Worcester Preparatory School, MD
York Preparatory School, NY
The York School, ON, Canada

BOYS' DAY SCHOOLS

Academy of the New Church Boys' School, PA
All Hallows High School, NY
The American Boychoir School, NJ
Archbishop Curley High School, MD
Archbishop Shaw High School, LA

Army and Navy Academy, CA
Belen Jesuit Preparatory School, FL
Bishop Hendricken High School, RI
Brophy College Preparatory, AZ
Brunswick School, CT
Calvert Hall College High School, MD
Cardigan Mountain School, NH
Central Catholic High School, TX
Christian Brothers Academy, NJ
Cistercian Preparatory School, TX
Colegio San Jose, PR
Collegiate School, NY
Crespi Carmelite High School, CA
Damien High School, CA
De La Salle High School, CA
Delbarton School, NJ
DeMatha Catholic High School, MD
Devon Preparatory School, PA
Dexter Southfield, MA
Eaglebrook School, MA
Fairfield College Preparatory School, CT
Father Judge High School, PA
Fishburne Military School, VA
Fordham Preparatory School, NY
Georgetown Preparatory School, MD
Gilman School, MD
Gonzaga College High School, DC
Hargrave Military Academy, VA
The Heights School, MD
Hillside School, MA
Holy Cross School, LA
Jesuit College Preparatory School, TX
Jesuit High School of Tampa, FL
Junipero Serra High School, CA
Landon School, MD
Loyola-Blakefield, MD
Merchiston Castle School, United Kingdom
Missouri Military Academy, MO
Montgomery Bell Academy, TN
Mount Michael Benedictine School, NE
Notre Dame College Prep, IL
Palma School, CA
The Phelps School, PA
Regis High School, NY
Rockhurst High School, MO
The Roxbury Latin School, MA
St. Albans School, DC
St. Andrew's College, ON, Canada
St. Augustine High School, CA
Saint Augustine Preparatory School, NJ
St. Catherine's Academy, CA
St. Francis de Sales High School, OH
Saint Francis High School, CA
St. George's School, BC, Canada
St. John's Preparatory School, MA
St. Joseph's Preparatory School, PA
St. Mark's School of Texas, TX
St. Michael's College School, ON, Canada
St. Paul's High School, MB, Canada
St. Stanislaus College, MS
Subiaco Academy, AR
Trinity High School, KY
Trinity-Pawling School, NY
Upper Canada College, ON, Canada
The Woodhall School, CT
Yeshiva High School, IL

* Coeducational in lower grades

GIRLS' DAY SCHOOLS

Academy of Our Lady of Guam, GU
Academy of Our Lady of Peace, CA
Academy of the Holy Cross, MD
Academy of the New Church Girls' School, PA
Academy of the Sacred Heart, LA
The Agnes Irwin School, PA
Balmoral Hall School, MB, Canada
Branksome Hall, ON, Canada
Carondelet High School, CA
Castilleja School, CA
Cathedral High School, NY
The Catholic High School of Baltimore, MD
Columbus School for Girls, OH
Convent of the Sacred Heart, NY
Country Day School of the Sacred Heart, PA
Dexter Southfield, MA
Dominican Academy, NY
Duchesne Academy of the Sacred Heart, TX
Elizabeth Seton High School, MD
Foxcroft School, VA
Garrison Forest School, MD*
Georgetown Visitation Preparatory School, DC
Girls Preparatory School, TN
Grier School, PA
The Harpeth Hall School, TN
Holy Names Academy, WA
Immaculate Heart High School and Middle School, CA
Institute of Notre Dame, MD
Josephinum Academy, IL
Lauralton Hall, CT
Louisville High School, CA
The Madeira School, VA
The Mary Louis Academy, NY
Marymount High School, CA
Mercy High School College Preparatory, CA
Miss Edgar's and Miss Cramp's School, QC, Canada
Miss Hall's School, MA
Miss Porter's School, CT
Mother McAuley High School, IL
National Cathedral School, DC
Nazareth Academy High School for Girls, PA
Nerinx Hall, MO
Notre Dame Academy, CA
Notre Dame Academy, MA
Notre Dame High School, CA
Our Lady of Mercy Academy, NJ
Preston High School, NY
Providence Catholic School, The College Preparatory School for Girls Grades 6-12, TX
St. Agnes Academy, TX
Saint Francis Girls High School, CA
Saint Gertrude High School, VA
St. Joseph's Academy, LA
St. Mary's Episcopal School, TN
Saint Teresa's Academy, MO
St. Timothy's School, MD
Saint Ursula Academy, OH
Salem Academy, NC
Santa Catalina School, CA
The Spence School, NY
The Study, QC, Canada
Trafalgar Castle School, ON, Canada
The Ursuline Academy of Dallas, TX
Villa Joseph Marie High School, PA
Villa Victoria Academy, NJ
Villa Walsh Academy, NJ

Westover School, CT
Westridge School, CA
The Woodward School, MA
Xavier College Preparatory, AZ

SCHOOLS ACCEPTING BOARDING BOYS AND GIRLS

Arthur Morgan School, NC†
The Athenian School, CA†
Bachman Academy, TN†
Berkshire School, MA†
Besant Hill School, CA†
The Bolles School, FL†
Brehm Preparatory School, IL†
The Brook Hill School, TX†
Brooks School, MA†
Burr and Burton Academy, VT†
Buxton School, MA†
Camphill Special School, PA†
Carlisle School, VA†
Cascadilla School, NY†
Children's Creative and Performing Arts Academy of San Diego, CA†
Chinese Christian Schools, CA†
Christopher Dock Mennonite High School, PA†
Columbia International College of Canada, ON, Canada†
Concord Academy, MA†
Cotter Schools, MN†
The Culver Academies, IN†
Darrow School, NY†
Deerfield Academy, MA†
Eagle Hill School, CT†
Episcopal High School, VA
Fay School, MA†
Forest Lake Academy, FL
Fountain Valley School of Colorado, CO†
Freeman Academy, SD†
Fryeburg Academy, ME†
George School, PA†
Girard College, PA
The Glenholme School, Devereux Connecticut, CT
Gould Academy, ME†
The Governor French Academy, IL†
Great Lakes Christian High School, ON, Canada†
The Gunnery, CT†
Hank Haney International Junior Golf Academy, SC†
Hawai`i Preparatory Academy, HI†
High Mowing School, NH†
Houghton Academy, NY†
The Hun School of Princeton, NJ†
Institut Monte Rosa, Switzerland†
The Judge Rotenberg Educational Center, MA
Kildonan School, NY†
Kimball Union Academy, NH†
King's-Edgehill School, NS, Canada†
Kingsway College, ON, Canada†
Lakefield College School, ON, Canada
Lake Mary Preparatory School, FL
Lancaster Mennonite High School, PA†
Landmark School, MA†
Lawrence Academy, MA†
The Lawrenceville School, NJ†
Lee Academy, ME†
The Leelanau School, MI†
The Linsly School, WV†

Coeducational in lower grades

The Lowell Whiteman School, CO†
Lustre Christian High School, MT†
Luther College High School, SK, Canada†
Maharishi School of the Age of Enlightenment, IA†
Maine Central Institute, ME†
Maplebrook School, NY
The Masters School, NY†
Maur Hill-Mount Academy, KS†
McDonogh School, MD†
Mennonite Collegiate Institute, MB, Canada†
Mercersburg Academy, PA†
Middlesex School, MA†
Midland School, CA
Millbrook School, NY†
Montverde Academy, FL†
Mooseheart High School, IL†
Nebraska Christian Schools, NE†
Niagara Christian Community of Schools, ON, Canada†
Noble and Greenough School, MA†
The North Broward Preparatory Upper School, FL†
North Central Texas Academy, TX
Northfield Mount Hermon School, MA†
Oak Grove School, CA†
Oakland School, VA†
Oneida Baptist Institute, KY†
Oregon Episcopal School, OR†
The Orme School, AZ†
The Park School of Buffalo, NY†
The Pennington School, NJ†
Presbyterian Pan American School, TX
Proctor Academy, NH†
Rabun Gap-Nacoochee School, GA†
Randolph-Macon Academy, VA†
The Rectory School, CT†
Ridley College, ON, Canada†
Rosseau Lake College, ON, Canada†
Ross School, NY†
Rumsey Hall School, CT†
Saddlebrook Preparatory School, FL†
St. Andrew's School, RI†
St. Croix Schools, MN†
St. George's School, RI†
Saint John's Preparatory School, MN†
St. Mary's School, OR†
St. Stephen's Episcopal School, TX†
St. Stephen's School, Rome, Italy†
Sandy Spring Friends School, MD†
San Marcos Baptist Academy, TX†
Scattergood Friends School, IA†
Shady Side Academy, PA†
Shattuck-St. Mary's School, MN†
Shawnigan Lake School, BC, Canada†
Southwestern Academy, AZ†
Southwestern Academy, CA†
Squaw Valley Academy, CA†
Stevenson School, CA†
The Storm King School, NY†
Summit Preparatory School, MT
Sunshine Bible Academy, SD†
The Taft School, CT†
The Thacher School, CA†
Thomas Jefferson School, MO†
Thornton Academy, ME†
Tilton School, NH†
TMI - The Episcopal School of Texas, TX†
Trinity College School, ON, Canada†
The Vanguard School, FL

Venta Preparatory School, ON, Canada†
Wasatch Academy, UT†
The Webb Schools, CA†
Wellspring Foundation, CT†
Westminster School, CT†
West Sound Academy, WA†
Westtown School, PA†
The White Mountain School, NH†
Wilbraham & Monson Academy, MA†
The Williston Northampton School, MA†
Worcester Academy, MA†

SCHOOLS ACCEPTING BOARDING BOYS
Academy of the New Church Boys' School, PA†
The American Boychoir School, NJ†
Army and Navy Academy, CA†
Butte Central Catholic High School, MT†
Cardigan Mountain School, NH†
Eaglebrook School, MA†
Fishburne Military School, VA†
Georgetown Preparatory School, MD†
The Grand River Academy, OH
Hampshire Country School, NH
Hargrave Military Academy, VA†
Hillside School, MA†
Little Keswick School, VA
Marine Military Academy, TX
Merchiston Castle School, United Kingdom
Missouri Military Academy, MO†
Mount Michael Benedictine School, NE†
The Phelps School, PA†
St. Albans School, DC†
St. Andrew's College, ON, Canada†
St. Catherine's Academy, CA†
St. George's School, BC, Canada†
St. Lawrence Seminary High School, WI
St. Michael's Preparatory School of the Norbertine Fathers, CA
St. Stanislaus College, MS†
Subiaco Academy, AR†
Trinity-Pawling School, NY†
Upper Canada College, ON, Canada†
Valley View School, MA
Windermere Preparatory School, FL†
The Woodhall School, CT†
Yeshiva High School, IL†

SCHOOLS ACCEPTING BOARDING GIRLS
Academy of the New Church Girls' School, PA†
Annie Wright School, WA†
Balmoral Hall School, MB, Canada†
Branksome Hall, ON, Canada†
Foxcroft School, VA†
Garrison Forest School, MD†
Grier School, PA†
Hebrew Academy, CA†
The Hockaday School, TX
The Madeira School, VA†
Miss Hall's School, MA†
Miss Porter's School, CT†
Queen Margaret's School, BC, Canada†
St. Timothy's School, MD†
Salem Academy, NC†
San Domenico School, CA†

† Accepts day students

Santa Catalina School, CA†
Trafalgar Castle School, ON, Canada†
Westover School, CT†

MILITARY SCHOOLS

Army and Navy Academy, CA
Fishburne Military School, VA
Hargrave Military Academy, VA
Marine Military Academy, TX
Missouri Military Academy, MO
Randolph-Macon Academy, VA
St. Catherine's Academy, CA
TMI - The Episcopal School of Texas, TX

SCHOOLS WITH A RELIGIOUS AFFILIATION

Anglican Church of Canada
Holy Trinity School, ON, Canada
Queen Margaret's School, BC, Canada

Assemblies of God
Victor Valley Christian School, CA

Assembly of God Church
Modesto Christian School, CA

Baptist Church
Bangor Christian School, ME
Beth Haven Christian School, KY
First Baptist Academy, TX
Foundation Academy, FL
Grace Baptist Academy, TN
Hyde Park Baptist School, TX
Landmark Christian Academy, KY
Tri-City Christian Academy, AZ
Whitefield Academy, KY

Baptist General Association of Virginia
Hargrave Military Academy, VA

Baptist General Conference
San Marcos Baptist Academy, TX

Bible Fellowship Church
Chinese Christian Schools, CA

Brethren Church
Grace Brethren School, CA

Brethren in Christ Church
Niagara Christian Community of Schools, ON, Canada

Christian
Academy of the New Church Girls' School, PA
Alma Heights Christian High School, CA
Briarcrest Christian High School, TN
Christopher Dock Mennonite High School, PA
Cole Valley Christian High School, ID
Faith Christian High School, CA
The First Academy, FL
First Presbyterian Day School, GA
Fort Worth Christian School, TX
Fowlers Academy, PR

Grace Brethren School, CA
Harrells Christian Academy, NC
Hawthorne Christian Academy, NJ
Highroad Academy, BC, Canada
Intermountain Christian School, UT
Mennonite Collegiate Institute, MB, Canada
Mesa Grande Seventh-Day Academy, CA
New Covenant Academy, MO
North Central Texas Academy, TX
Philadelphia-Montgomery Christian Academy, PA
Porter-Gaud School, SC
Redwood Christian Schools, CA
St. Croix Schools, MN
Scottsdale Christian Academy, AZ
Signet Christian School, ON, Canada
Timothy Christian High School, IL
TMI - The Episcopal School of Texas, TX
Valley Christian High School, CA
Westminster Christian School, FL

Christian Nondenominational
Alpha Omega Academy, IA
Brookhaven Academy, MS
The Brook Hill School, TX
Capistrano Valley Christian Schools, CA
Chattanooga Christian School, TN
Christian Central Academy, NY
Davidson Academy, TN
Donelson Christian Academy, TN
Fort Worth Christian School, TX
Front Range Christian High School, CO
Grace Christian School, AK
Hanalani Schools, HI
Hawthorne Christian Academy, NJ
Heritage Christian School, CA
Landmark Christian School, GA
Linfield Christian School, CA
Lustre Christian High School, MT
Manhattan Christian High School, MT
Maranatha High School, CA
Merchiston Castle School, United Kingdom
Missouri Military Academy, MO
Mount Paran Christian School, GA
Phoenix Christian Unified Schools, AZ
Portsmouth Christian Academy, NH
Redeemer Christian High School, ON, Canada
St. George's Independent School, TN
Shoreline Christian, WA
Southfield Christian High School, MI
Sunshine Bible Academy, SD
Tyler Street Christian Academy, TX
Westminster Christian Academy, LA
Wheaton Academy, IL

Christian Reformed Church
Central Alberta Christian High School, AB, Canada
Denver Christian High School, CO
Kalamazoo Christian High School, MI
Manhattan Christian High School, MT
Whitinsville Christian School, MA

Church of Christ
Columbia Academy, TN
Ezell-Harding Christian School, TN
Great Lakes Christian High School, ON, Canada
Lipscomb Academy, TN
Madison Academy, AL

Mars Hill Bible School, AL
Middle Tennessee Christian School, TN
Westbury Christian School, TX

Church of England (Anglican)
Lakefield College School, ON, Canada
Ridley College, ON, Canada
Trinity College School, ON, Canada

Church of the New Jerusalem
Academy of the New Church Boys' School, PA
Academy of the New Church Girls' School, PA

Episcopal Church
Annie Wright School, WA
Berkeley Preparatory School, FL
Brooks School, MA
Campbell Hall (Episcopal), CA
The Canterbury School of Florida, FL
Christ Church Episcopal School, SC
The Episcopal Academy, PA
Episcopal Collegiate School, AR
Episcopal High School, TX
Episcopal High School, VA
Harvard-Westlake School, CA
National Cathedral School, DC
Oregon Episcopal School, OR
Parish Episcopal School, TX
Porter-Gaud School, SC
The Rectory School, CT
St. Albans School, DC
St. Andrew's Episcopal School, MD
Saint Edward's School, FL
St. George's School, RI
St. Martin's Episcopal School, LA
St. Mary's Episcopal School, TN
St. Stephen's & St. Agnes School, VA
St. Stephen's Episcopal School, TX
St. Timothy's School, MD
Shattuck-St. Mary's School, MN
TMI - The Episcopal School of Texas, TX
Trinity-Pawling School, NY
Trinity Preparatory School, FL
Trinity School of Texas, TX
The White Mountain School, NH

Evangelical
Pioneer Valley Christian School, MA
Southfield Christian High School, MI

Evangelical Free Church of America
Intermountain Christian School, UT

Evangelical/Fundamental
Chinese Christian Schools, CA

Evangelical Lutheran Church in America
Faith Lutheran High School, NV

Jewish
Community Hebrew Academy, ON, Canada
The Dr. Miriam and Sheldon G. Adelson Educational Campus, The Adelson Upper School, NV
The Emery/Weiner School, TX
Gann Academy (The New Jewish High School of Greater Boston), MA
Hebrew Academy, CA

Hebrew Academy of the Five Towns & Rockaway, NY
Hyman Brand Hebrew Academy of Greater Kansas City, KS
Jean and Samuel Frankel Jewish Academy of Metropolitan Detroit, MI
San Diego Jewish Academy, CA
Yeshiva High School, IL

Lutheran Church
Long Island Lutheran Middle and High School, NY
Lutheran High School North, MO
Luther College High School, SK, Canada

Lutheran Church–Missouri Synod
Concordia Lutheran High School, IN
Faith Lutheran High School, NV
Lutheran High School Northwest, MI
Lutheran High School of Hawaii, HI
Walther Christian Academy, IL

Mennonite Brethren Church
Lustre Christian High School, MT

Mennonite Church
Christopher Dock Mennonite High School, PA
Eastern Mennonite High School, VA
Freeman Academy, SD
Lancaster Mennonite High School, PA
Mennonite Collegiate Institute, MB, Canada

Mennonite Church USA
United Mennonite Educational Institute, ON, Canada

Methodist Church
The Pennington School, NJ
Randolph-Macon Academy, VA

Moravian Church
Moravian Academy, PA
Salem Academy, NC

Presbyterian Church
Mount Vernon Presbyterian School, GA
Rabun Gap-Nacoochee School, GA

Presbyterian Church (U.S.A.)
Presbyterian Pan American School, TX

Presbyterian Church in America
Briarwood Christian High School, AL
First Presbyterian Day School, GA
Pusch Ridge Christian Academy, AZ

Protestant
Landmark Christian School, GA
Mooseheart High School, IL
Piedmont Academy, GA
Pioneer Valley Christian School, MA
Wilmington Christian School, DE

Protestant Church
Salem Academy, OR

Protestant-Evangelical
Fresno Christian Schools, CA
Kings Christian School, CA
Lehigh Valley Christian High School, PA
Nebraska Christian Schools, NE

North Toronto Christian School, ON, Canada
Westminster Christian Academy, LA

Reformed Church
Covenant Canadian Reformed School, AB, Canada
Heritage Christian School, ON, Canada

Reformed Church in America
Kalamazoo Christian High School, MI

Roman Catholic Church
Academy of Our Lady of Guam, GU
Academy of Our Lady of Peace, CA
Academy of the Holy Cross, MD
Academy of the Sacred Heart, LA
Alleman High School, IL
All Hallows High School, NY
Archbishop Alter High School, OH
Archbishop Curley High School, MD
Archbishop Hoban High School, OH
Archbishop Mitty High School, CA
Archbishop Shaw High School, LA
Archbishop Thomas J. Murphy High School, WA
Belen Jesuit Preparatory School, FL
Benet Academy, IL
Bishop Brady High School, NH
Bishop Connolly High School, MA
Bishop Denis J. O'Connell High School, VA
Bishop Eustace Preparatory School, NJ
Bishop Guertin High School, NH
Bishop Hendricken High School, RI
Bishop Ireton High School, VA
Bishop John J. Snyder High School, FL
Bishop Kelly High School, ID
Bishop McGuinness Catholic High School, OK
Bishop Montgomery High School, CA
Bishop O'Dowd High School, CA
Bishop Shanahan High School, PA
Bishop Stang High School, MA
Blanchet School, OR
Blessed Trinity High School, GA
Bourgade Catholic High School, AZ
Boylan Central Catholic High School, IL
Butte Central Catholic High School, MT
Calvert Hall College High School, MD
Cardinal Gibbons High School, NC
Cardinal Mooney Catholic High School, FL
Cardinal Newman High School, FL
Cardinal O'Hara High School, PA
Carmel High School, IL
Carondelet High School, CA
Cathedral High School, NY
Catholic Central High School, NY
Catholic Central High School, WI
The Catholic High School of Baltimore, MD
Central Catholic High School, CA
Central Catholic High School, MA
Central Catholic High School, TX
Chaminade College Preparatory, CA
Chaminade-Madonna College Preparatory, FL
Christian Brothers Academy, NJ
Christian Brothers Academy, NY
Cistercian Preparatory School, TX
Clearwater Central Catholic High School, FL
Colegio San Jose, PR
Convent of the Sacred Heart, CT
Convent of the Sacred Heart, NY

Cotter Schools, MN
Country Day School of the Sacred Heart, PA
Crespi Carmelite High School, CA
Cretin-Derham Hall, MN
Damien High School, CA
De La Salle College, ON, Canada
De La Salle High School, CA
DeLaSalle High School, MN
De La Salle North Catholic High School, OR
Delbarton School, NJ
DeMatha Catholic High School, MD
DePaul Catholic High School, NJ
Devon Preparatory School, PA
Dominican Academy, NY
Dowling Catholic High School, IA
Duchesne Academy of the Sacred Heart, TX
Elizabeth Seton High School, MD
Fairfield College Preparatory School, CT
Father Judge High School, PA
Father Lopez High School, FL
Father Ryan High School, TN
Fordham Preparatory School, NY
Gabriel Richard Catholic High School, MI
Georgetown Preparatory School, MD
Georgetown Visitation Preparatory School, DC
Gonzaga College High School, DC
The Heights School, MD
Holy Cross High School, CT
Holy Cross School, LA
Holy Names Academy, WA
Holy Savior Menard Catholic High School, LA
IC Catholic Prep, IL
Immaculata-La Salle High School, FL
Immaculate Heart High School and Middle School, CA
Institute of Notre Dame, MD
Jesuit High School of Tampa, FL
Josephinum Academy, IL
Junipero Serra High School, CA
Lansdale Catholic High School, PA
Lauralton Hall, CT
Lexington Catholic High School, KY
Louisville High School, CA
Loyola-Blakefield, MD
Marian Catholic High School, PA
Marian Central Catholic High School, IL
Marist School, GA
The Mary Louis Academy, NY
Marymount High School, CA
Matignon High School, MA
Maur Hill-Mount Academy, KS
McGill-Toolen Catholic High School, AL
Mercy High School College Preparatory, CA
Mooseheart High School, IL
Mother McAuley High School, IL
Mt. De Sales Academy, GA
Mount Michael Benedictine School, NE
Mount Saint Charles Academy, RI
Nazareth Academy, IL
Nazareth Academy High School for Girls, PA
Nerinx Hall, MO
Northwest Catholic High School, CT
Notre Dame Academy, CA
Notre Dame Academy, MA
Notre Dame College Prep, IL
Notre Dame High School, CA
Notre Dame Junior/Senior High School, PA
Oldenburg Academy, IN

Our Lady of Mercy Academy, NJ
Our Lady of Mount Carmel High School, MD
Padua Franciscan High School, OH
Palma School, CA
Pensacola Catholic High School, FL
Pinecrest Academy, GA
Pope John XXIII Regional High School, NJ
Powers Catholic High School, MI
Preston High School, NY
Providence Academy, MN
Providence Catholic School, The College Preparatory School for Girls Grades 6-12, TX
Providence High School, CA
Regina Junior-Senior High School, IA
Regis High School, NY
Rockhurst High School, MO
Sacred Heart School of Halifax, NS, Canada
St. Agnes Academy, TX
Saint Albert Junior-Senior High School, IA
St. Andrew's Regional High School, BC, Canada
Saint Anthony High School, IL
St. Augustine High School, CA
Saint Augustine Preparatory School, NJ
St. Benedict at Auburndale, TN
St. Catherine's Academy, CA
Saint Dominic Academy, ME
Saint Elizabeth High School, CA
St. Francis de Sales High School, OH
Saint Francis Girls High School, CA
Saint Francis High School, CA
Saint Francis High School, CA
Saint Gertrude High School, VA
St. John's Preparatory School, MA
Saint John's Preparatory School, MN
St. Joseph Academy, FL
St. Joseph High School, CT
Saint Joseph High School, IL
St. Joseph's Academy, LA
St. Joseph's Catholic School, SC
St. Joseph's Preparatory School, PA
Saint Lawrence Academy, CA
St. Lawrence Seminary High School, WI
Saint Mary's High School, AZ
Saint Mary's High School, MD
St. Mary's School, OR
Saint Maur International School, Japan
St. Michael's College School, ON, Canada
St. Michael's Preparatory School of the Norbertine Fathers, CA
St. Patrick's Regional Secondary, BC, Canada
St. Paul's High School, MB, Canada
St. Pius X Catholic High School, GA
St. Pius X High School, TX
St. Stanislaus College, MS
Saint Teresa's Academy, MO
St. Thomas Aquinas High School, FL
Saint Thomas Aquinas High School, KS
St. Thomas Aquinas High School, NH
Saint Thomas More Catholic High School, LA
Saint Ursula Academy, OH
Saint Viator High School, IL
Salpointe Catholic High School, AZ
San Domenico School, CA
Santa Catalina School, CA
Scotus Central Catholic High School, NE
Seisen International School, Japan
Seton Catholic High School, AZ

Shanley High School, ND
Shawe Memorial Junior/Senior High School, IN
Subiaco Academy, AR
The Summit Country Day School, OH
Teurlings Catholic High School, LA
Trinity High School, KY
Trinity High School, NH
Trinity High School, OH
The Ursuline Academy of Dallas, TX
Valle Catholic High School, MO
Vandebilt Catholic High School, LA
Vicksburg Catholic School, MS
Villa Angela-St. Joseph High School, OH
Villa Joseph Marie High School, PA
Villa Madonna Academy, KY
Villa Victoria Academy, NJ
Villa Walsh Academy, NJ
Visitation Academy, MO
Xavier College Preparatory, AZ

Roman Catholic Church (Jesuit Order)
Brophy College Preparatory, AZ
Jesuit College Preparatory School, TX
Loyola School, NY

Seventh-day Adventist Church
Crawford Adventist Academy, ON, Canada
Lodi Academy, CA

Seventh-day Adventists
Forest Lake Academy, FL
Kingsway College, ON, Canada
Mesa Grande Seventh-Day Academy, CA
Paradise Adventist Academy, CA

Society of Friends
Friends Academy, NY
Friends' Central School, PA
George School, PA
Germantown Friends School, PA
Moorestown Friends School, NJ
Sandy Spring Friends School, MD
Scattergood Friends School, IA
Wellsprings Friends School, OR
Westtown School, PA
William Penn Charter School, PA
Wilmington Friends School, DE

Southern Baptist Convention
First Baptist Academy, TX
Hawaii Baptist Academy, HI
Oneida Baptist Institute, KY

United Church of Christ
Mid-Pacific Institute, HI

United Methodist Church
Carrollton Christian Academy, TX

Wesleyan Church
Houghton Academy, NY
Wesleyan Academy, PR

Wisconsin Evangelical Lutheran Synod
St. Croix Schools, MN

SCHOOLS WITH ELEMENTARY DIVISIONS

The Academy at Charlemont, MA
Academy at the Lakes, FL
Academy of the Sacred Heart, LA
The Agnes Irwin School, PA
Albuquerque Academy, NM
Allendale Columbia School, NY
American Community Schools of Athens, Greece
American Heritage School, FL
The American School Foundation, Mexico
The American School of Madrid, Spain
Annie Wright School, WA
Army and Navy Academy, CA
Ashley Hall, SC
The Athenian School, CA
Athens Academy, GA
Augusta Preparatory Day School, GA
Baldwin School of Puerto Rico, PR
Balmoral Hall School, MB, Canada
Battle Ground Academy, TN
Bay Ridge Preparatory School, NY
The Benjamin School, FL
Berkeley Carroll School, NY
Berkeley Preparatory School, FL
The Birch Wathen Lenox School, NY
The Bolles School, FL
Branksome Hall, ON, Canada
Brehm Preparatory School, IL
Brentwood School, CA
Brimmer and May School, MA
The British School of Boston, MA
The Brook Hill School, TX
Brunswick School, CT
The Bryn Mawr School for Girls, MD
Campbell Hall (Episcopal), CA
Canterbury School, FL
The Canterbury School of Florida, FL
Cape Cod Academy, MA
Cape Fear Academy, NC
Cape Henry Collegiate School, VA
Cardigan Mountain School, NH
Carlisle School, VA
Castilleja School, CA
The Catlin Gabel School, OR
Chadwick School, CA
Charlotte Country Day School, NC
Charlotte Latin School, NC
Chase Collegiate School, CT
Christ Church Episcopal School, SC
Cistercian Preparatory School, TX
Clarksville Academy, TN
Collegiate School, NY
The Columbus Academy, OH
Columbus School for Girls, OH
The Community School of Naples, FL
Convent of the Sacred Heart, CT
Convent of the Sacred Heart, NY
The Country Day School, ON, Canada
Country Day School of the Sacred Heart, PA
Crossroads School for Arts & Sciences, CA
Crystal Springs Uplands School, CA
Currey Ingram Academy, TN
Delbarton School, NJ
Denver Academy, CO
The Derryfield School, NH
Detroit Country Day School, MI
Devon Preparatory School, PA

Dexter Southfield, MA
The Dr. Miriam and Sheldon G. Adelson Educational Campus, The Adelson Upper School, NV
The Donoho School, AL
Durham Academy, NC
Eaglebrook School, MA
Eastern Mennonite High School, VA
Elgin Academy, IL
The Episcopal Academy, PA
Episcopal Collegiate School, AR
Falmouth Academy, MA
Fayetteville Academy, NC
Fay School, MA
Flintridge Preparatory School, CA
Franklin Road Academy, TN
Fredericksburg Academy, VA
French-American School of New York, NY
Friends Academy, NY
Friends' Central School, PA
Fuqua School, VA
The Galloway School, GA
Garrison Forest School, MD
Gaston Day School, NC
Georgetown Day School, DC
Germantown Friends School, PA
Gilman School, MD
Girard College, PA
Girls Preparatory School, TN
Glenlyon Norfolk School, BC, Canada
Good Hope Country Day School, VI
Greenhill School, TX
Greenhills School, MI
Grier School, PA
Hampshire Country School, NH
Hampton Roads Academy, VA
Hanalani Schools, HI
Hargrave Military Academy, VA
The Harley School, NY
The Harpeth Hall School, TN
Harvard-Westlake School, CA
Hawaii Baptist Academy, HI
Hawai`i Preparatory Academy, HI
Head-Royce School, CA
The Heights School, MD
The Heritage School, GA
Hillside School, MA
The Hill Top Preparatory School, PA
The Hockaday School, TX
Hopkins School, CT
Houghton Academy, NY
The Howard School, GA
The Hudson School, NJ
The Hun School of Princeton, NJ
International High School, CA
International School Bangkok, Thailand
International School Manila, Philippines
International School of Indiana, IN
Istanbul International Community School, Turkey
John Burroughs School, MO
Kent Denver School, CO
Kent Place School, NJ
The Kew-Forest School, NY
The Key School, MD
Keystone School, TX
Kildonan School, NY
King Low Heywood Thomas, CT
Kingswood-Oxford School, CT

The Lab School of Washington, DC
La Jolla Country Day School, CA
Lakehill Preparatory School, TX
Lake Mary Preparatory School, FL
Lancaster Country Day School, PA
Landmark School, MA
Landon School, MD
The Latin School of Chicago, IL
The Linsly School, WV
Little Red School House and Elisabeth Irwin High School, NY
Long Island Lutheran Middle and High School, NY
Long Trail School, VT
The Lovett School, GA
Madison Country Day School, WI
Maharishi School of the Age of Enlightenment, IA
Maret School, DC
Marist School, GA
Marshall School, MN
Mary Institute and St. Louis Country Day School (MICDS), MO
The Masters School, NY
McDonogh School, MD
The Meadows School, NV
Middle Tennessee Christian School, TN
Mid-Pacific Institute, HI
Miss Edgar's and Miss Cramp's School, QC, Canada
Missouri Military Academy, MO
MMI Preparatory School, PA
Montgomery Bell Academy, TN
Montverde Academy, FL
Moorestown Friends School, NJ
Moravian Academy, PA
Mt. De Sales Academy, GA
Mount Vernon Presbyterian School, GA
National Cathedral School, DC
Newark Academy, NJ
Noble and Greenough School, MA
Norfolk Academy, VA
North Central Texas Academy, TX
North Shore Country Day School, IL
Northwest Academy, OR
Oak Grove School, CA
Oregon Episcopal School, OR
The Orme School, AZ
Out-Of-Door-Academy, FL
The Overlake School, WA
The Paideia School, GA
Parish Episcopal School, TX
The Park School of Baltimore, MD
The Park School of Buffalo, NY
The Pennington School, NJ
The Phelps School, PA
The Pingry School, NJ
Porter-Gaud School, SC
The Potomac School, VA
Poughkeepsie Day School, NY
Professional Children's School, NY
Providence Academy, MN
Providence Country Day School, RI
Providence Day School, NC
Punahou School, HI
Queen Margaret's School, BC, Canada
Rabun Gap-Nacoochee School, GA
Randolph-Macon Academy, VA
Ranney School, NJ
Ransom Everglades School, FL
The Rectory School, CT
Ridley College, ON, Canada

Riverdale Country School, NY
The Rivers School, MA
Riverstone International School, ID
Roland Park Country School, MD
Rolling Hills Preparatory School, CA
Ross School, NY
Rowland Hall, UT
The Roxbury Latin School, MA
Rumsey Hall School, CT
Sacramento Country Day School, CA
St. Albans School, DC
St. Andrew's College, ON, Canada
St. Andrew's Episcopal School, MD
St. Andrew's School, RI
Saint Edward's School, FL
St. George's Independent School, TN
St. George's School, BC, Canada
St. George's School of Montreal, QC, Canada
Saint John's Preparatory School, MN
St. Mark's School of Texas, TX
St. Martin's Episcopal School, LA
St. Mary's Episcopal School, TN
Saint Mary's Hall, TX
St. Mary's School, OR
St. Paul Academy and Summit School, MN
St. Stanislaus College, MS
St. Stephen's & St. Agnes School, VA
St. Stephen's Episcopal School, TX
Sandia Preparatory School, NM
San Domenico School, CA
Sandy Spring Friends School, MD
San Marcos Baptist Academy, TX
Seattle Academy of Arts and Sciences, WA
The Seven Hills School, OH
Sewickley Academy, PA
Shady Side Academy, PA
The Sharon Academy, VT
Shattuck-St. Mary's School, MN
Shawnigan Lake School, BC, Canada
The Shipley School, PA
Soundview Preparatory School, NY
The Spence School, NY
Springside Chestnut Hill Academy, PA
Stevenson School, CA
The Storm King School, NY
The Study, QC, Canada
Subiaco Academy, AR
The Summit Country Day School, OH
Tampa Preparatory School, FL
Telluride Mountain School, CO
Thomas Jefferson School, MO
Thornton Academy, ME
TMI - The Episcopal School of Texas, TX
Tower Hill School, DE
Trafalgar Castle School, ON, Canada
Trevor Day School, NY
Trinity College School, ON, Canada
Trinity-Pawling School, NY
Trinity Preparatory School, FL
Trinity Valley School, TX
University Liggett School, MI
University of Chicago Laboratory Schools, IL
University School of Jackson, TN
University School of Milwaukee, WI
University School of Nova Southeastern University, FL
Upper Canada College, ON, Canada
The Vanguard School, FL

Viewpoint School, CA
Villa Victoria Academy, NJ
Visitation Academy, MO
Wakefield School, VA
The Waldorf School of Garden City, NY
Wasatch Academy, UT
Washington International School, DC
The Waterford School, UT
Watkinson School, CT
Waynflete School, ME
Webb School of Knoxville, TN
Westchester Country Day School, NC
Westridge School, CA
Westtown School, PA
The Wheeler School, RI
Whitfield School, MO
Wilbraham & Monson Academy, MA
William Penn Charter School, PA
The Williston Northampton School, MA
Wilmington Friends School, DE
Winston Preparatory School, NY
The Winston School, TX
Woodlynde School, PA
Woodward Academy, GA
Worcester Academy, MA
Worcester Preparatory School, MD
York Preparatory School, NY

SCHOOLS REPORTING ACADEMIC ACCOMMODATIONS FOR THE GIFTED AND TALENTED

Acacia Academy, IL	G
The Academy for Gifted Children (PACE), ON, Canada	G
Academy of the Holy Cross, MD	G,A
Academy of the New Church Boys' School, PA	G,M,A
Academy of the New Church Girls' School, PA	G,M,A
The Agnes Irwin School, PA	G
The American Boychoir School, NJ	M
American Community Schools of Athens, Greece	G
American Heritage School, FL	G,M,A
American Heritage School, FL	G,M,A
Archbishop Hoban High School, OH	G
Archbishop Mitty High School, CA	G,M,A
Ashley Hall, SC	G,M,A
Augusta Preparatory Day School, GA	G
Bachman Academy, TN	G
Balmoral Hall School, MB, Canada	G
Barnstable Academy, NJ	G,M,A
Bay Ridge Preparatory School, NY	G,M,A
The Beekman School, NY	G,M,A
Benet Academy, IL	G
The Benjamin School, FL	G,M,A
Besant Hill School, CA	M,A
The Birch Wathen Lenox School, NY	G,M,A
Bishop Brady High School, NH	G
Bishop Denis J. O'Connell High School, VA	G
Bishop Eustace Preparatory School, NJ	G,M
Bishop Guertin High School, NH	G
Bishop Ireton High School, VA	M
Bishop McGuinness Catholic High School, OK	G,A
Bishop O'Dowd High School, CA	G,M,A
Blueprint Education, AZ	M,A
Boston University Academy, MA	G
Boylan Central Catholic High School, IL	G,M,A
Branksome Hall, ON, Canada	G,M,A

Brehm Preparatory School, IL	G
Brentwood School, CA	G,A
Briarcrest Christian High School, TN	G,M,A
Briarwood Christian High School, AL	G
Bridges Academy, CA	G
The British School of Boston, MA	G
Brunswick School, CT	G,M,A
The Bryn Mawr School for Girls, MD	G,M,A
Buxton School, MA	G,M,A
Calvert Hall College High School, MD	G,M,A
Cape Henry Collegiate School, VA	G,M,A
Cardigan Mountain School, NH	G
Cardinal Newman High School, FL	G
Cardinal O'Hara High School, PA	M
Carondelet High School, CA	G
Cascadilla School, NY	G,M,A
Castilleja School, CA	G
Catholic Central High School, WI	G,A
The Catlin Gabel School, OR	G,M,A
Chadwick School, CA	G,M,A
Chaminade-Madonna College Preparatory, FL	G,M,A
Charlotte Country Day School, NC	G
Charlotte Latin School, NC	G
Chase Collegiate School, CT	G
Chattanooga Christian School, TN	G,A
The Chicago Academy for the Arts, IL	M,A
Children's Creative and Performing Arts Academy of San Diego, CA	G,M,A
Chinese Christian Schools, CA	G
Christ Church Episcopal School, SC	G
Chrysalis School, WA	G
Columbia International College of Canada, ON, Canada	G
The Columbus Academy, OH	G
Commonwealth School, MA	G,M,A
Concord Academy, MA	G,M,A
Convent of the Sacred Heart, CT	G,A
Cotter Schools, MN	G,M,A
Country Day School of the Sacred Heart, PA	M
Cretin-Derham Hall, MN	G
Crossroads School for Arts & Sciences, CA	G,M,A
The Culver Academies, IN	G,M,A
Currey Ingram Academy, TN	G,M,A
Darrow School, NY	M,A
Deerfield Academy, MA	G,M,A
Delphi Academy of Los Angeles, CA	G
DeMatha Catholic High School, MD	G,M,A
Denver Academy, CO	G
Detroit Country Day School, MI	G,M,A
The Dr. Miriam and Sheldon G. Adelson Educational Campus, The Adelson Upper School, NV	G
Donelson Christian Academy, TN	G
Dowling Catholic High School, IA	G,M,A
Duchesne Academy of the Sacred Heart, TX	M,A
Eaglebrook School, MA	G,M,A
Eastern Mennonite High School, VA	G
Eaton Academy, GA	G,M,A
Eldorado Emerson Private School, CA	G,M,A
Elizabeth Seton High School, MD	G,M,A
The Ellis Academy, AL	G
The Emery/Weiner School, TX	G
Episcopal High School, VA	G,M,A
Explorations Academy, WA	G
Faith Lutheran High School, NV	M
Father Ryan High School, TN	G,M,A
Foxcroft School, VA	G,M,A
Franklin Road Academy, TN	G,M,A
Freeman Academy, SD	M,A

G — gifted; M — musically talented; A — artistically talented

Front Range Christian High School, CO	G
Fryeburg Academy, ME	M
The Galloway School, GA	G,M,A
Garrison Forest School, MD	G,M,A
Gaston Day School, NC	G
Georgetown Preparatory School, MD	G
Germantown Friends School, PA	G,M,A
Gilman School, MD	G,M,A
The Glenholme School, Devereux Connecticut, CT	G
Gould Academy, ME	G,M,A
The Governor French Academy, IL	G,A
The Grand River Academy, OH	G
The Grauer School, CA	G,M,A
Grier School, PA	G,M,A
Gulliver Preparatory School, FL	G,M,A
The Gunnery, CT	G,M,A
Hampshire Country School, NH	G
The Harpeth Hall School, TN	G,M,A
Harvard-Westlake School, CA	G,M,A
Head-Royce School, CA	G,M,A
Hebrew Academy of the Five Towns & Rockaway, NY	A
The Heights School, MD	G
High Mowing School, NH	M,A
Hillside School, MA	G
The Hill Top Preparatory School, PA	G,A
Ho'Ala School, HI	G,A
Holy Cross School, LA	G,M,A
The Howard School, GA	A
The Hudson School, NJ	G,M,A
Humanex Academy, CO	G
The Hun School of Princeton, NJ	G
Huntington-Surrey School, TX	G
Hyman Brand Hebrew Academy of Greater Kansas City, KS	G
Independent School, KS	G,M,A
Institute of Notre Dame, MD	G
International High School, CA	G,M,A
International School Manila, Philippines	G,M,A
Jean and Samuel Frankel Jewish Academy of Metropolitan Detroit, MI	G
The Kew-Forest School, NY	G
The Key School, MD	G
Keystone School, TX	G
King Low Heywood Thomas, CT	G,M,A
King's-Edgehill School, NS, Canada	G
The Lab School of Washington, DC	G,M,A
Lancaster Country Day School, PA	G,M,A
Lancaster Mennonite High School, PA	M
The Latin School of Chicago, IL	G
The Laureate Academy, MB, Canada	G
Lawrence Academy, MA	M,A
Lehigh Valley Christian High School, PA	G
The Linsly School, WV	G
Little Keswick School, VA	G
The Lovett School, GA	G,M,A
The Lowell Whiteman School, CO	G
Loyola-Blakefield, MD	G,M,A
Lutheran High School of Hawaii, HI	M,A
Luther College High School, SK, Canada	G
Maharishi School of the Age of Enlightenment, IA	G,M,A
Maine Central Institute, ME	G,M
Maranatha High School, CA	A
Maret School, DC	G,M,A
Marin Academy, CA	G,M,A
Marine Military Academy, TX	G
Marshall School, MN	G
Mary Institute and St. Louis Country Day School (MICDS), MO	G
The Mary Louis Academy, NY	G,M,A
The Masters School, NY	G,M,A
Maur Hill-Mount Academy, KS	G
The Meadows School, NV	G,M,A
Mennonite Collegiate Institute, MB, Canada	M
Mercersburg Academy, PA	G,M,A
Merchiston Castle School, United Kingdom	G,M,A
Middlesex School, MA	G
Mid-Pacific Institute, HI	G,A
Miss Hall's School, MA	G,M,A
Missouri Military Academy, MO	G,M,A
MMI Preparatory School, PA	G
Mount Paran Christian School, GA	G,M,A
MU High School, MO	G,M,A
National Cathedral School, DC	G
Nazareth Academy High School for Girls, PA	G,M,A
Newark Academy, NJ	G,M,A
Noble and Greenough School, MA	G,M,A
The Nora School, MD	G,A
Norfolk Academy, VA	G,M,A
The North Broward Preparatory Upper School, FL	G,M,A
North Central Texas Academy, TX	G,M,A
Northfield Mount Hermon School, MA	G,M,A
Northwest Academy, OR	G,M,A
Notre Dame College Prep, IL	G
The Oakland School, PA	G,A
Oregon Episcopal School, OR	G
Orinda Academy, CA	G
Pacific Crest Community School, OR	G
The Park School of Baltimore, MD	G,M,A
The Park School of Buffalo, NY	G
The Pennington School, NJ	G
Pensacola Catholic High School, FL	G
The Phelps School, PA	G
Philadelphia-Montgomery Christian Academy, PA	G,M,A
The Pingry School, NJ	G
Portsmouth Christian Academy, NH	G,M
Poughkeepsie Day School, NY	G,M,A
Proctor Academy, NH	G
Providence Country Day School, RI	G,M,A
Providence Day School, NC	G,M,A
Providence High School, CA	M,A
Queen Margaret's School, BC, Canada	G,M,A
Randolph-Macon Academy, VA	G
Realms of Inquiry, UT	G,M,A
The Rectory School, CT	G,M,A
Ridley College, ON, Canada	M,A
Riverdale Country School, NY	G,M,A
Rolling Hills Preparatory School, CA	G
Rosseau Lake College, ON, Canada	G
The Roxbury Latin School, MA	G,M,A
Rumsey Hall School, CT	G
Sage Hill School, CA	G,M,A
Saint Albert Junior-Senior High School, IA	G
St. Augustine High School, CA	G
St. Benedict at Auburndale, TN	G,M,A
St. Croix Schools, MN	G,M,A
Saint Edward's School, FL	G,M,A
St. Francis High School, KY	G,A
St. George's School, RI	G,M,A
St. George's School of Montreal, QC, Canada	G,M,A
St. John's Preparatory School, MA	G,M,A
St. Joseph Academy, FL	G,A
St. Joseph High School, CT	G
St. Joseph's Preparatory School, PA	G,M,A
St. Mark's School of Texas, TX	G
St. Mary's Episcopal School, TN	G,M,A

G — gifted; M — musically talented; A — artistically talented

Saint Mary's High School, MD	G
St. Mary's School, OR	G,M,A
Saint Maur International School, Japan	G,M,A
St. Paul Preparatory School, MN	G,M,A
St. Stephen's & St. Agnes School, VA	G,M,A
Saint Thomas Aquinas High School, KS	G
Saint Thomas More Catholic High School, LA	G
Salem Academy, OR	M,A
Sandia Preparatory School, NM	G,M,A
San Domenico School, CA	M
Sandy Spring Friends School, MD	G,M,A
San Marcos Baptist Academy, TX	G,M,A
Santa Catalina School, CA	G,M,A
Seattle Academy of Arts and Sciences, WA	G,M,A
The Seven Hills School, OH	G
Shady Side Academy, PA	G,M,A
Shattuck-St. Mary's School, MN	G,M,A
Shawe Memorial Junior/Senior High School, IN	G
Shawnigan Lake School, BC, Canada	G
The Shipley School, PA	G
Soundview Preparatory School, NY	G,M,A
Southwestern Academy, CA	M,A
Squaw Valley Academy, CA	G,M,A
The Storm King School, NY	G,M,A
Subiaco Academy, AR	G,M,A
The Summit Country Day School, OH	G,A
Summit Preparatory School, MT	G
Sunshine Bible Academy, SD	M
The Taft School, CT	G,M,A
Tampa Preparatory School, FL	G,M,A
Temple Grandin School, CO	G,M,A
The Tenney School, TX	G,M,A
The Thacher School, CA	G,M,A
Thomas Jefferson School, MO	G
Thornton Academy, ME	G,M,A
Tower Hill School, DE	G,M,A
Trinity High School, KY	G,M,A
Trinity High School, OH	G,A
Trinity Preparatory School, FL	G,M,A
Trinity School of Texas, TX	G,M,A
Trinity Valley School, TX	G,M,A
University Liggett School, MI	G,M,A
University School of Jackson, TN	G,M,A
University School of Nova Southeastern University, FL	G,M,A
Valle Catholic High School, MO	G,M,A
Valley Christian High School, CA	M,A
The Valley School, MI	G,A
The Vanguard School, FL	G
Venta Preparatory School, ON, Canada	G
Victor Valley Christian School, CA	G
Villa Joseph Marie High School, PA	G
Villa Victoria Academy, NJ	G,M,A
Villa Walsh Academy, NJ	G,M,A
The Waldorf School of Garden City, NY	M,A
Walther Christian Academy, IL	G,M,A
The Waterford School, UT	G,M,A
Watkinson School, CT	G,M,A
The Webb Schools, CA	G
Wellspring Foundation, CT	G
Westminster Christian School, FL	G,M,A
Westover School, CT	G,M,A
West Sound Academy, WA	G,M,A
Westtown School, PA	G,M,A
Wheaton Academy, IL	G,M,A
The Wheeler School, RI	G
Whitefield Academy, KY	G
The White Mountain School, NH	G,M,A

Whitfield School, MO	G,M,A
Wilbraham & Monson Academy, MA	M,A
William Penn Charter School, PA	G,M,A
The Williston Northampton School, MA	G,M,A
Wilmington Friends School, DE	G,M,A
Windermere Preparatory School, FL	M,A
The Windsor School, NY	G,M,A
Worcester Preparatory School, MD	G
Xavier College Preparatory, AZ	G,A
Yeshiva High School, IL	G
York Preparatory School, NY	G,M,A
The York School, ON, Canada	G,M,A

SCHOOLS WITH ADVANCED PLACEMENT PREPARATION

Academy at the Lakes, FL
The Academy for Gifted Children (PACE), ON, Canada
Academy of Our Lady of Guam, GU
Academy of Our Lady of Peace, CA
Academy of the Holy Cross, MD
Academy of the New Church Boys' School, PA
Academy of the New Church Girls' School, PA
Academy of the Sacred Heart, LA
The Agnes Irwin School, PA
Albuquerque Academy, NM
Allendale Columbia School, NY
Alma Heights Christian High School, CA
American Community Schools of Athens, Greece
American Heritage School, FL
American Heritage School, FL
The American School Foundation, Mexico
Archbishop Alter High School, OH
Archbishop Curley High School, MD
Archbishop Hoban High School, OH
Archbishop Mitty High School, CA
Archbishop Shaw High School, LA
Archbishop Thomas J. Murphy High School, WA
Army and Navy Academy, CA
Ashley Hall, SC
The Athenian School, CA
Athens Academy, GA
Augusta Christian School, GA
Baldwin School of Puerto Rico, PR
Balmoral Hall School, MB, Canada
Barnstable Academy, NJ
Battle Ground Academy, TN
Bay Ridge Preparatory School, NY
The Beekman School, NY
Belen Jesuit Preparatory School, FL
Benet Academy, IL
The Benjamin School, FL
Berkeley Preparatory School, FL
Berkshire School, MA
Besant Hill School, CA
The Birch Wathen Lenox School, NY
Bishop Brady High School, NH
Bishop Connolly High School, MA
Bishop Denis J. O'Connell High School, VA
Bishop Eustace Preparatory School, NJ
Bishop Guertin High School, NH
Bishop Hendricken High School, RI
Bishop Ireton High School, VA
Bishop John J. Snyder High School, FL
Bishop Kelly High School, ID
Bishop McGuinness Catholic High School, OK

Bishop Montgomery High School, CA
Bishop O'Dowd High School, CA
Bishop Shanahan High School, PA
Bishop Stang High School, MA
Blanchet School, OR
Blessed Trinity High School, GA
The Bolles School, FL
Bourgade Catholic High School, AZ
Boylan Central Catholic High School, IL
Brentwood School, CA
Briarcrest Christian High School, TN
Briarwood Christian High School, AL
Brimmer and May School, MA
The Brook Hill School, TX
Brooks School, MA
Brophy College Preparatory, AZ
Brunswick School, CT
The Bryn Mawr School for Girls, MD
Burr and Burton Academy, VT
Butte Central Catholic High School, MT
Calvert Hall College High School, MD
Campbell Hall (Episcopal), CA
Canterbury School, FL
The Canterbury School of Florida, FL
Cape Cod Academy, MA
Cape Fear Academy, NC
Cape Henry Collegiate School, VA
Capistrano Valley Christian Schools, CA
Cardinal Gibbons High School, NC
Cardinal Mooney Catholic High School, FL
Cardinal Newman High School, FL
Cardinal O'Hara High School, PA
Carlisle School, VA
Carmel High School, IL
Carondelet High School, CA
Cascadilla School, NY
Castilleja School, CA
Cathedral High School, NY
Catholic Central High School, NY
Catholic Central High School, WI
The Catholic High School of Baltimore, MD
Central Catholic High School, CA
Central Catholic High School, MA
Central Catholic High School, TX
Chadwick School, CA
Chaminade College Preparatory, CA
Chaminade-Madonna College Preparatory, FL
Charlotte Latin School, NC
Chase Collegiate School, CT
Chattanooga Christian School, TN
Chelsea School, MD
The Chicago Academy for the Arts, IL
Children's Creative and Performing Arts Academy of
    San Diego, CA
Chinese Christian Schools, CA
Christian Brothers Academy, NJ
Christian Brothers Academy, NY
Christian Central Academy, NY
Christopher Dock Mennonite High School, PA
Cistercian Preparatory School, TX
Clarksville Academy, TN
Clearwater Central Catholic High School, FL
Colegio Bolivar, Colombia
Colegio San Jose, PR
Cole Valley Christian High School, ID
Collegiate School, NY
Columbia Academy, TN

Columbia International College of Canada, ON, Canada
The Columbus Academy, OH
Columbus School for Girls, OH
Commonwealth School, MA
The Community School of Naples, FL
Concordia Lutheran High School, IN
Convent of the Sacred Heart, CT
Convent of the Sacred Heart, NY
Cotter Schools, MN
The Country Day School, ON, Canada
Country Day School of the Sacred Heart, PA
Crawford Adventist Academy, ON, Canada
Crespi Carmelite High School, CA
Cretin-Derham Hall, MN
The Culver Academies, IN
Damien High School, CA
Darrow School, NY
Davidson Academy, TN
Deerfield Academy, MA
De La Salle College, ON, Canada
De La Salle High School, CA
DeLaSalle High School, MN
De La Salle North Catholic High School, OR
Delbarton School, NJ
DeMatha Catholic High School, MD
DePaul Catholic High School, NJ
The Derryfield School, NH
Detroit Country Day School, MI
Devon Preparatory School, PA
Dexter Southfield, MA
Dexter Southfield, MA
The Dr. Miriam and Sheldon G. Adelson Educational Campus,
    The Adelson Upper School, NV
Dominican Academy, NY
Donelson Christian Academy, TN
The Donoho School, AL
Dowling Catholic High School, IA
Duchesne Academy of the Sacred Heart, TX
Durham Academy, NC
Eastern Mennonite High School, VA
Edgewood Academy, AL
Eldorado Emerson Private School, CA
Elgin Academy, IL
Elizabeth Seton High School, MD
The Ellis Academy, AL
The Emery/Weiner School, TX
The Episcopal Academy, PA
Episcopal Collegiate School, AR
Episcopal High School, TX
Episcopal High School, VA
Explorations Academy, WA
Ezell-Harding Christian School, TN
Fairfield College Preparatory School, CT
Faith Christian High School, CA
Faith Lutheran High School, NV
Falmouth Academy, MA
Father Judge High School, PA
Father Lopez High School, FL
Father Ryan High School, TN
Fayetteville Academy, NC
The First Academy, FL
First Baptist Academy, TX
First Presbyterian Day School, GA
Fishburne Military School, VA
Flintridge Preparatory School, CA
Fordham Preparatory School, NY
Fort Worth Christian School, TX

Foundation Academy, FL
Fountain Valley School of Colorado, CO
Foxcroft School, VA
Franklin Road Academy, TN
Fredericksburg Academy, VA
French-American School of New York, NY
Fresno Christian Schools, CA
Friends Academy, NY
Front Range Christian High School, CO
Fryeburg Academy, ME
Fuqua School, VA
Gabriel Richard Catholic High School, MI
The Galloway School, GA
Gann Academy (The New Jewish High School of
    Greater Boston), MA
Garrison Forest School, MD
Gaston Day School, NC
George School, PA
Georgetown Day School, DC
Georgetown Preparatory School, MD
Georgetown Visitation Preparatory School, DC
Gilman School, MD
Girard College, PA
Girls Preparatory School, TN
Glades Day School, FL
Gonzaga College High School, DC
Good Hope Country Day School, VI
Gould Academy, ME
The Governor French Academy, IL
Grace Baptist Academy, TN
Grace Brethren School, CA
Grace Christian School, AK
The Grand River Academy, OH
The Grauer School, CA
Greenhill School, TX
Greenhills School, MI
Grier School, PA
Guamani Private School, PR
Gulliver Preparatory School, FL
The Gunnery, CT
Hampton Roads Academy, VA
Hanalani Schools, HI
Hank Haney International Junior Golf Academy, SC
Hargrave Military Academy, VA
The Harley School, NY
The Harpeth Hall School, TN
Harrells Christian Academy, NC
Harvard-Westlake School, CA
Hawaii Baptist Academy, HI
Hawai`i Preparatory Academy, HI
Hawthorne Christian Academy, NJ
Head-Royce School, CA
Hebrew Academy, CA
Hebrew Academy of the Five Towns & Rockaway, NY
The Heights School, MD
Heritage Christian School, CA
The Heritage School, GA
High Mowing School, NH
Ho'Ala School, HI
The Hockaday School, TX
Holy Cross High School, CT
Holy Cross School, LA
Holy Savior Menard Catholic High School, LA
Holy Trinity School, ON, Canada
Hopkins School, CT
Houghton Academy, NY
The Hudson School, NJ

The Hun School of Princeton, NJ
Hyde Park Baptist School, TX
Hyman Brand Hebrew Academy of Greater Kansas City, KS
IC Catholic Prep, IL
Immaculata-La Salle High School, FL
Immaculate Heart High School and Middle School, CA
Independent School, KS
Indian Creek School, MD
Institute of Notre Dame, MD
Institut Monte Rosa, Switzerland
Intermountain Christian School, UT
International School Bangkok, Thailand
International School Manila, Philippines
Jean and Samuel Frankel Jewish Academy of Metropolitan
    Detroit, MI
Jesuit College Preparatory School, TX
Jesuit High School of Tampa, FL
John Burroughs School, MO
Josephinum Academy, IL
Junipero Serra High School, CA
Kalamazoo Christian High School, MI
Kent Denver School, CO
Kent Place School, NJ
The Kew-Forest School, NY
The Key School, MD
Keystone School, TX
Kimball Union Academy, NH
King Low Heywood Thomas, CT
Kings Christian School, CA
Kingswood-Oxford School, CT
La Jolla Country Day School, CA
Lakefield College School, ON, Canada
Lakehill Preparatory School, TX
Lake Mary Preparatory School, FL
Lancaster Country Day School, PA
Lancaster Mennonite High School, PA
Landmark Christian School, GA
Landon School, MD
Lansdale Catholic High School, PA
La Scuola D'Italia Guglielmo Marconi, NY
The Latin School of Chicago, IL
Lawrence Academy, MA
Lee Academy, ME
The Leelanau School, MI
Lehigh Valley Christian High School, PA
Lexington Catholic High School, KY
Lick-Wilmerding High School, CA
Linfield Christian School, CA
The Linsly School, WV
Lipscomb Academy, TN
Lodi Academy, CA
Long Island Lutheran Middle and High School, NY
Louisville High School, CA
The Lovett School, GA
The Lowell Whiteman School, CO
Loyola-Blakefield, MD
Lutheran High School North, MO
Lutheran High School Northwest, MI
Lutheran High School of Hawaii, HI
Lycee International de Los Angeles, CA
The Madeira School, VA
Maine Central Institute, ME
Manhattan Christian High School, MT
Maranatha High School, CA
Maret School, DC
Marian Catholic High School, PA
Marian Central Catholic High School, IL

Marin Academy, CA
Marine Military Academy, TX
Marist School, GA
Marshall School, MN
Mars Hill Bible School, AL
Mary Institute and St. Louis Country Day School (MICDS), MO
The Mary Louis Academy, NY
Marymount High School, CA
The Masters School, NY
Matignon High School, MA
Maur Hill-Mount Academy, KS
McDonogh School, MD
McGill-Toolen Catholic High School, AL
The Meadows School, NV
Mennonite Collegiate Institute, MB, Canada
Mercersburg Academy, PA
Mercy High School College Preparatory, CA
Middlesex School, MA
Middle Tennessee Christian School, TN
Midland School, CA
Mid-Pacific Institute, HI
Millbrook School, NY
Miss Edgar's and Miss Cramp's School, QC, Canada
Miss Hall's School, MA
Missouri Military Academy, MO
Miss Porter's School, CT
MMI Preparatory School, PA
Modesto Christian School, CA
Montgomery Bell Academy, TN
Montverde Academy, FL
Moorestown Friends School, NJ
Moravian Academy, PA
Mother McAuley High School, IL
Mount Michael Benedictine School, NE
Mount Paran Christian School, GA
Mount Saint Charles Academy, RI
MU High School, MO
National Cathedral School, DC
Nazareth Academy, IL
Nazareth Academy High School for Girls, PA
Nerinx Hall, MO
Newark Academy, NJ
Noble and Greenough School, MA
Norfolk Academy, VA
The North Broward Preparatory Upper School, FL
Northfield Mount Hermon School, MA
North Shore Country Day School, IL
Northwest Catholic High School, CT
The Norwich Free Academy, CT
Notre Dame Academy, CA
Notre Dame Academy, MA
Notre Dame College Prep, IL
Notre Dame High School, CA
Notre Dame Junior/Senior High School, PA
Oak Grove School, CA
Oldenburg Academy, IN
The O'Neal School, NC
Oneida Baptist Institute, KY
Oregon Episcopal School, OR
Orinda Academy, CA
The Orme School, AZ
Our Lady of Mount Carmel High School, MD
Out-Of-Door-Academy, FL
The Overlake School, WA
Padua Franciscan High School, OH
The Paideia School, GA
Palma School, CA

Palo Alto Preparatory School, CA
The Park School of Baltimore, MD
The Park School of Buffalo, NY
The Pennington School, NJ
Pensacola Catholic High School, FL
The Phelps School, PA
Philadelphia-Montgomery Christian Academy, PA
Phoenix Christian Unified Schools, AZ
Pinecrest Academy, GA
The Pingree School, MA
The Pingry School, NJ
Pioneer Valley Christian School, MA
Pope John XXIII Regional High School, NJ
Porter-Gaud School, SC
Portsmouth Christian Academy, NH
The Potomac School, VA
Poughkeepsie Day School, NY
Powers Catholic High School, MI
Preston High School, NY
Proctor Academy, NH
Providence Academy, MN
Providence Catholic School, The College Preparatory School for
    Girls Grades 6-12, TX
Providence Country Day School, RI
Providence Day School, NC
Providence High School, CA
Punahou School, HI
Pusch Ridge Christian Academy, AZ
Queen Margaret's School, BC, Canada
Rabun Gap-Nacoochee School, GA
Randolph-Macon Academy, VA
Ranney School, NJ
Ransom Everglades School, FL
Redwood Christian Schools, CA
Regina Junior-Senior High School, IA
Regis High School, NY
The Rivers School, MA
Rockhurst High School, MO
Roland Park Country School, MD
Rolling Hills Preparatory School, CA
Ross School, NY
Rowland Hall, UT
The Roxbury Latin School, MA
Sacramento Country Day School, CA
Sacred Heart School of Halifax, NS, Canada
Sage Hill School, CA
St. Agnes Academy, TX
St. Albans School, DC
Saint Albert Junior-Senior High School, IA
St. Andrew's College, ON, Canada
St. Andrew's Episcopal School, MD
St. Andrew's School, RI
Saint Anthony High School, IL
St. Augustine High School, CA
Saint Augustine Preparatory School, NJ
St. Benedict at Auburndale, TN
St. Croix Schools, MN
Saint Dominic Academy, ME
Saint Edward's School, FL
Saint Elizabeth High School, CA
St. Francis de Sales High School, OH
Saint Francis Girls High School, CA
Saint Francis High School, CA
Saint Francis High School, CA
St. Francis High School, KY
St. George's Independent School, TN
St. George's School, RI

St. George's School, BC, Canada
St. George's School of Montreal, QC, Canada
Saint Gertrude High School, VA
St. John's Preparatory School, MA
Saint John's Preparatory School, MN
St. Joseph Academy, FL
St. Joseph High School, CT
Saint Joseph High School, IL
St. Joseph's Academy, LA
St. Joseph's Catholic School, SC
St. Joseph's Preparatory School, PA
St. Mark's School of Texas, TX
St. Martin's Episcopal School, LA
St. Mary's Episcopal School, TN
Saint Mary's Hall, TX
Saint Mary's High School, AZ
Saint Mary's High School, MD
St. Mary's School, OR
Saint Maur International School, Japan
St. Michael's College School, ON, Canada
St. Michael's Preparatory School of the Norbertine Fathers, CA
St. Patrick's Regional Secondary, BC, Canada
St. Paul Preparatory School, MN
St. Paul's High School, MB, Canada
St. Pius X Catholic High School, GA
St. Pius X High School, TX
St. Stanislaus College, MS
St. Stephen's & St. Agnes School, VA
St. Stephen's Episcopal School, TX
St. Stephen's School, Rome, Italy
Saint Teresa's Academy, MO
St. Thomas Aquinas High School, FL
Saint Thomas Aquinas High School, KS
St. Thomas Aquinas High School, NH
Saint Thomas More Catholic High School, LA
Saint Ursula Academy, OH
Salem Academy, NC
Salem Academy, OR
Salpointe Catholic High School, AZ
San Diego Jewish Academy, CA
San Domenico School, CA
Sandy Spring Friends School, MD
San Marcos Baptist Academy, TX
Santa Catalina School, CA
Scottsdale Christian Academy, AZ
Scotus Central Catholic High School, NE
Seton Catholic High School, AZ
The Seven Hills School, OH
Sewickley Academy, PA
Shady Side Academy, PA
Shanley High School, ND
Shattuck-St. Mary's School, MN
Shawe Memorial Junior/Senior High School, IN
Shawnigan Lake School, BC, Canada
The Shipley School, PA
Sonoma Academy, CA
Soundview Preparatory School, NY
Southfield Christian High School, MI
Southwestern Academy, CA
The Spence School, NY
Springside Chestnut Hill Academy, PA
Squaw Valley Academy, CA
Stevenson School, CA
The Storm King School, NY
The Study, QC, Canada
Subiaco Academy, AR
The Summit Country Day School, OH

Summit Preparatory School, MT
The Taft School, CT
Tampa Preparatory School, FL
The Tenney School, TX
The Thacher School, CA
Thomas Jefferson School, MO
Thornton Academy, ME
Tilton School, NH
Timothy Christian High School, IL
TMI - The Episcopal School of Texas, TX
Tower Hill School, DE
Trafalgar Castle School, ON, Canada
Trevor Day School, NY
Trinity College School, ON, Canada
Trinity High School, KY
Trinity High School, NH
Trinity High School, OH
Trinity-Pawling School, NY
Trinity Preparatory School, FL
Trinity School of Texas, TX
Trinity Valley School, TX
Tyler Street Christian Academy, TX
University of Chicago Laboratory Schools, IL
University School of Jackson, TN
University School of Milwaukee, WI
University School of Nova Southeastern University, FL
The Ursuline Academy of Dallas, TX
Valley Christian High School, CA
Vicksburg Catholic School, MS
Victor Valley Christian School, CA
Viewpoint School, CA
Villa Angela-St. Joseph High School, OH
Villa Joseph Marie High School, PA
Villa Victoria Academy, NJ
Villa Walsh Academy, NJ
Visitation Academy, MO
Wakefield School, VA
Walther Christian Academy, IL
Wasatch Academy, UT
The Waterford School, UT
Webb School of Knoxville, TN
The Webb Schools, CA
Wesleyan Academy, PR
Westbury Christian School, TX
Westchester Country Day School, NC
Westminster Christian Academy, LA
Westminster Christian School, FL
Westminster School, CT
Westover School, CT
Westridge School, CA
West Sound Academy, WA
Westtown School, PA
Wheaton Academy, IL
The Wheeler School, RI
Whitefield Academy, KY
The White Mountain School, NH
Whitfield School, MO
Whitinsville Christian School, MA
Wilbraham & Monson Academy, MA
William Penn Charter School, PA
The Williston Northampton School, MA
Wilmington Christian School, DE
Wilmington Friends School, DE
Wilson Hall, SC
Windermere Preparatory School, FL
The Windsor School, NY
The Woodhall School, CT

Woodlynde School, PA
Woodward Academy, GA
The Woodward School, MA
Worcester Academy, MA
Worcester Preparatory School, MD
Xavier College Preparatory, AZ
Yeshiva High School, IL
York Preparatory School, NY

SCHOOLS REPORTING A POSTGRADUATE YEAR

The Academy at Charlemont, MA
Bachman Academy, TN
The Beekman School, NY
Berkshire School, MA
The Bolles School, FL
Brehm Preparatory School, IL
Cascadilla School, NY
The Culver Academies, IN
Deerfield Academy, MA
The Ellis Academy, AL
Fishburne Military School, VA
Fryeburg Academy, ME
Gould Academy, ME
The Grand River Academy, OH
Grier School, PA
The Gunnery, CT
Hank Haney International Junior Golf Academy, SC
Hargrave Military Academy, VA
Hawai`i Preparatory Academy, HI
Houghton Academy, NY
The Hun School of Princeton, NJ
Kildonan School, NY
Kimball Union Academy, NH
The Lawrenceville School, NJ
Lee Academy, ME
Maine Central Institute, ME
Marine Military Academy, TX
Mercersburg Academy, PA
Miss Hall's School, MA
Missouri Military Academy, MO
Montverde Academy, FL
Northfield Mount Hermon School, MA
The Orme School, AZ
The Phelps School, PA
Randolph-Macon Academy, VA
Ridley College, ON, Canada
Saint John's Preparatory School, MN
St. Stephen's School, Rome, Italy
Scattergood Friends School, IA
Shattuck-St. Mary's School, MN
Soundview Preparatory School, NY
Southwestern Academy, AZ
Southwestern Academy, CA
The Taft School, CT
Thomas Jefferson School, MO
Tilton School, NH
Trinity-Pawling School, NY
The Vanguard School, FL
Wasatch Academy, UT
Watkinson School, CT
Westminster School, CT
The White Mountain School, NH
Wilbraham & Monson Academy, MA
The Williston Northampton School, MA
The Windsor School, NY

The Woodhall School, CT
Worcester Academy, MA

SCHOOLS OFFERING THE INTERNATIONAL BACCALAUREATE PROGRAM

Academy of the Holy Cross, MD
Alma Heights Christian High School, CA
American Community Schools of Athens, Greece
The American School Foundation, Mexico
The American School of Madrid, Spain
Annie Wright School, WA
Branksome Hall, ON, Canada
The British School of Boston, MA
Cardinal Newman High School, FL
Carlisle School, VA
Central Catholic High School, MA
Charlotte Country Day School, NC
Christ Church Episcopal School, SC
Clearwater Central Catholic High School, FL
Colegio San Jose, PR
DePaul Catholic High School, NJ
Detroit Country Day School, MI
George School, PA
Glenlyon Norfolk School, BC, Canada
Gulliver Preparatory School, FL
Hebrew Academy, CA
Indian Creek School, MD
International High School, CA
International School Bangkok, Thailand
International School Manila, Philippines
International School of Indiana, IN
Istanbul International Community School, Turkey
King's-Edgehill School, NS, Canada
La Scuola D'Italia Guglielmo Marconi, NY
Long Trail School, VT
Luther College High School, SK, Canada
Lycee International de Los Angeles, CA
Madison Country Day School, WI
Meadowridge School, BC, Canada
Mid-Pacific Institute, HI
Mont'Kiara International School, Malaysia
Newark Academy, NJ
The North Broward Preparatory Upper School, FL
Palo Alto Preparatory School, CA
Providence Catholic School, The College Preparatory School for Girls Grades 6-12, TX
Ridley College, ON, Canada
Riverstone International School, ID
Saint Anthony High School, IL
Saint Dominic Academy, ME
Saint John's Preparatory School, MN
St. Joseph's Preparatory School, PA
Saint Maur International School, Japan
St. Stephen's School, Rome, Italy
St. Timothy's School, MD
Seisen International School, Japan
Shawe Memorial Junior/Senior High School, IN
Tyler Street Christian Academy, TX
Upper Canada College, ON, Canada
Washington International School, DC
West Sound Academy, WA
Wilmington Friends School, DE
Windermere Preparatory School, FL
The York School, ON, Canada

SCHOOLS REPORTING THAT THEY AWARD MERIT SCHOLARSHIPS

Academy of the Holy Cross, MD
Academy of the Sacred Heart, LA
All Hallows High School, NY
Alma Heights Christian High School, CA
American Heritage School, FL
American Heritage School, FL
Annie Wright School, WA
Archbishop Alter High School, OH
Archbishop Curley High School, MD
Archbishop Hoban High School, OH
Archbishop Shaw High School, LA
Balmoral Hall School, MB, Canada
Barnstable Academy, NJ
Battle Ground Academy, TN
Bay Ridge Preparatory School, NY
The Beekman School, NY
The Benjamin School, FL
Berkeley Preparatory School, FL
The Birch Wathen Lenox School, NY
Bishop Brady High School, NH
Bishop Connolly High School, MA
Bishop Denis J. O'Connell High School, VA
Bishop Eustace Preparatory School, NJ
Bishop Guertin High School, NH
Bishop Hendricken High School, RI
Bishop Ireton High School, VA
Bishop Montgomery High School, CA
Bishop O'Dowd High School, CA
Bishop Stang High School, MA
Blanchet School, OR
Bourgade Catholic High School, AZ
Branksome Hall, ON, Canada
The British School of Boston, MA
Calvert Hall College High School, MD
Canterbury School, FL
Cape Fear Academy, NC
Cape Henry Collegiate School, VA
Cardinal Mooney Catholic High School, FL
Carmel High School, IL
Cascadilla School, NY
Cathedral High School, NY
The Catholic High School of Baltimore, MD
The Catlin Gabel School, OR
Central Catholic High School, CA
Central Catholic High School, MA
Central Catholic High School, TX
Chaminade College Preparatory, CA
Chaminade-Madonna College Preparatory, FL
Charlotte Latin School, NC
Chase Collegiate School, CT
The Chicago Academy for the Arts, IL
Children's Creative and Performing Arts Academy of
    San Diego, CA
Chinese Christian Schools, CA
Christ Church Episcopal School, SC
Christian Brothers Academy, NJ
Christian Brothers Academy, NY
Christian Central Academy, NY
Clearwater Central Catholic High School, FL
Columbia International College of Canada, ON, Canada
The Columbus Academy, OH
The Community School of Naples, FL
Concordia Lutheran High School, IN
Cotter Schools, MN
Country Day School of the Sacred Heart, PA

Crespi Carmelite High School, CA
The Culver Academies, IN
Damien High School, CA
De La Salle College, ON, Canada
DeLaSalle High School, MN
DeMatha Catholic High School, MD
Denver Christian High School, CO
DePaul Catholic High School, NJ
The Derryfield School, NH
Devon Preparatory School, PA
Dominican Academy, NY
Duchesne Academy of the Sacred Heart, TX
Elgin Academy, IL
Elizabeth Seton High School, MD
The Ellis Academy, AL
Episcopal High School, VA
Explorations Academy, WA
Falmouth Academy, MA
Father Judge High School, PA
Father Lopez High School, FL
First Presbyterian Day School, GA
Fishburne Military School, VA
Fordham Preparatory School, NY
Forest Lake Academy, FL
Fountain Valley School of Colorado, CO
Foxcroft School, VA
Fredericksburg Academy, VA
Freeman Academy, SD
Fresno Christian Schools, CA
Front Range Christian High School, CO
Fuqua School, VA
Gabriel Richard Catholic High School, MI
Garrison Forest School, MD
Gaston Day School, NC
George School, PA
Georgetown Visitation Preparatory School, DC
Girls Preparatory School, TN
Glenlyon Norfolk School, BC, Canada
Gonzaga College High School, DC
Good Hope Country Day School, VI
Great Lakes Christian High School, ON, Canada
Grier School, PA
The Gunnery, CT
Hargrave Military Academy, VA
Hawthorne Christian Academy, NJ
The Heights School, MD
Ho'Ala School, HI
Holy Cross High School, CT
Holy Cross School, LA
Holy Savior Menard Catholic High School, LA
The Hun School of Princeton, NJ
Hyde Park Baptist School, TX
IC Catholic Prep, IL
Immaculata-La Salle High School, FL
Immaculate Heart High School and Middle School, CA
Indian Creek School, MD
Institute of Notre Dame, MD
International School of Indiana, IN
Jesuit College Preparatory School, TX
Josephinum Academy, IL
Junipero Serra High School, CA
Kimball Union Academy, NH
King's-Edgehill School, NS, Canada
Kingsway College, ON, Canada
Kingswood-Oxford School, CT
Lakefield College School, ON, Canada
Lake Mary Preparatory School, FL

Lancaster Country Day School, PA
Lancaster Mennonite High School, PA
Lansdale Catholic High School, PA
La Scuola D'Italia Guglielmo Marconi, NY
Lauralton Hall, CT
Lexington Catholic High School, KY
Lodi Academy, CA
Long Island Lutheran Middle and High School, NY
Long Trail School, VT
Louisville High School, CA
The Lowell Whiteman School, CO
Loyola-Blakefield, MD
Loyola School, NY
Lutheran High School North, MO
Lutheran High School Northwest, MI
Lutheran High School of Hawaii, HI
Luther College High School, SK, Canada
The Madeira School, VA
Madison Country Day School, WI
Maine Central Institute, ME
Maplebrook School, NY
Maranatha High School, CA
Marian Catholic High School, PA
Marine Military Academy, TX
Mary Institute and St. Louis Country Day School (MICDS), MO
The Mary Louis Academy, NY
Marymount High School, CA
Matignon High School, MA
Maur Hill-Mount Academy, KS
Meadowridge School, BC, Canada
Mennonite Collegiate Institute, MB, Canada
Mercersburg Academy, PA
Mercy High School College Preparatory, CA
Mid-Pacific Institute, HI
Miss Edgar's and Miss Cramp's School, QC, Canada
Miss Hall's School, MA
Missouri Military Academy, MO
Miss Porter's School, CT
MMI Preparatory School, PA
Modesto Christian School, CA
Mother McAuley High School, IL
Mt. De Sales Academy, GA
Mount Michael Benedictine School, NE
Nazareth Academy, IL
Nazareth Academy High School for Girls, PA
Nebraska Christian Schools, NE
Niagara Christian Community of Schools, ON, Canada
The North Broward Preparatory Upper School, FL
North Shore Country Day School, IL
Northwest Catholic High School, CT
Notre Dame Academy, CA
Notre Dame Academy, MA
Notre Dame College Prep, IL
Notre Dame High School, CA
The Oakland School, PA
Oldenburg Academy, IN
The O'Neal School, NC
Our Lady of Mercy Academy, NJ
Our Lady of Mount Carmel High School, MD
Padua Franciscan High School, OH
Palma School, CA
Paradise Adventist Academy, CA
The Park School of Buffalo, NY
The Phelps School, PA
Phoenix Christian Unified Schools, AZ
The Pingree School, MA
Presbyterian Pan American School, TX

Preston High School, NY
Providence Academy, MN
Providence Catholic School, The College Preparatory School for
 Girls Grades 6-12, TX
Providence Country Day School, RI
Providence High School, CA
Punahou School, HI
Queen Margaret's School, BC, Canada
Rabun Gap-Nacoochee School, GA
Randolph-Macon Academy, VA
Redwood Christian Schools, CA
Ridley College, ON, Canada
Rockhurst High School, MO
Rolling Hills Preparatory School, CA
Rosseau Lake College, ON, Canada
Rowland Hall, UT
Royal Canadian College, BC, Canada
Sacred Heart School of Halifax, NS, Canada
St. Agnes Academy, TX
Saint Albert Junior-Senior High School, IA
St. Andrew's College, ON, Canada
St. Augustine High School, CA
Saint Augustine Preparatory School, NJ
St. Benedict at Auburndale, TN
St. Croix Schools, MN
Saint Dominic Academy, ME
Saint Elizabeth High School, CA
St. Francis de Sales High School, OH
Saint Francis High School, CA
St. Francis High School, KY
St. George's School, BC, Canada
Saint Gertrude High School, VA
St. John's Preparatory School, MA
Saint John's Preparatory School, MN
St. Joseph High School, CT
Saint Joseph High School, IL
St. Joseph's Catholic School, SC
St. Joseph's Preparatory School, PA
Saint Lawrence Academy, CA
St. Martin's Episcopal School, LA
Saint Mary's Hall, TX
Saint Mary's High School, MD
St. Michael's College School, ON, Canada
St. Paul Preparatory School, MN
St. Pius X High School, TX
St. Stephen's Episcopal School, TX
St. Stephen's School, Rome, Italy
Saint Teresa's Academy, MO
Saint Thomas More Catholic High School, LA
St. Timothy's School, MD
Saint Ursula Academy, OH
Salem Academy, NC
Salpointe Catholic High School, AZ
San Diego Jewish Academy, CA
Santa Catalina School, CA
Scattergood Friends School, IA
Seton Catholic High School, AZ
The Seven Hills School, OH
Shady Side Academy, PA
Shanley High School, ND
Shattuck-St. Mary's School, MN
Shawnigan Lake School, BC, Canada
Springside Chestnut Hill Academy, PA
Squaw Valley Academy, CA
The Storm King School, NY
The Study, QC, Canada
The Summit Country Day School, OH

Tampa Preparatory School, FL
Telluride Mountain School, CO
Thomas Jefferson School, MO
Thornton Academy, ME
Tilton School, NH
TMI - The Episcopal School of Texas, TX
Tower Hill School, DE
Trafalgar Castle School, ON, Canada
Trinity High School, KY
Trinity School of Texas, TX
Tyler Street Christian Academy, TX
University Liggett School, MI
University School of Milwaukee, WI
Upper Canada College, ON, Canada
The Ursuline Academy of Dallas, TX
Valle Catholic High School, MO
The Valley School, MI
Vandebilt Catholic High School, LA
The Vanguard School, FL
Villa Angela-St. Joseph High School, OH
Villa Joseph Marie High School, PA
Villa Madonna Academy, KY
Villa Victoria Academy, NJ
Villa Walsh Academy, NJ
Waldorf High School of Massachusetts Bay, MA
The Waldorf School of Garden City, NY
Walther Christian Academy, IL
Wasatch Academy, UT
Westbury Christian School, TX
Westchester Country Day School, NC
West Sound Academy, WA
Westtown School, PA
Wheaton Academy, IL
The White Mountain School, NH
The Williston Northampton School, MA
Windermere Preparatory School, FL
The Woodward School, MA
York Preparatory School, NY
The York School, ON, Canada

SCHOOLS REPORTING A GUARANTEED TUITION PLAN

Academy of Our Lady of Guam, GU
Baldwin School of Puerto Rico, PR
Bangor Christian School, ME
Butte Central Catholic High School, MT
The Catholic High School of Baltimore, MD
Damien High School, CA
Gateway School, TX
Glenlyon Norfolk School, BC, Canada
Grace Brethren School, CA
Hank Haney International Junior Golf Academy, SC
Hargrave Military Academy, VA
Hawaii Baptist Academy, HI
Hebrew Academy, CA
Middlesex School, MA
Missouri Military Academy, MO
Mount Michael Benedictine School, NE
Nebraska Christian Schools, NE
New Covenant Academy, MO
Parish Episcopal School, TX
Piedmont Academy, GA
Pope John XXIII Regional High School, NJ
Presbyterian Pan American School, TX
St. George's School of Montreal, QC, Canada

San Marcos Baptist Academy, TX
Tampa Preparatory School, FL
Trinity Christian Academy, TN
Trinity High School, KY
Trinity High School, OH
Wesleyan Academy, PR
Westchester Country Day School, NC

SCHOOLS REPORTING A TUITION INSTALLMENT PLAN

The Academy at Charlemont, MA
Academy at the Lakes, FL
The Academy for Gifted Children (PACE), ON, Canada
Academy of Our Lady of Guam, GU
Academy of Our Lady of Peace, CA
Academy of the Holy Cross, MD
Academy of the New Church Boys' School, PA
Academy of the New Church Girls' School, PA
Academy of the Sacred Heart, LA
The Agnes Irwin School, PA
Albuquerque Academy, NM
Allendale Columbia School, NY
Alma Heights Christian High School, CA
Alpha Omega Academy, IA
The American Boychoir School, NJ
American Community Schools of Athens, Greece
American Heritage School, FL
American Heritage School, FL
The American School Foundation, Mexico
The American School of Madrid, Spain
Annie Wright School, WA
Archbishop Alter High School, OH
Archbishop Curley High School, MD
Archbishop Hoban High School, OH
Archbishop Mitty High School, CA
Archbishop Shaw High School, LA
Archbishop Thomas J. Murphy High School, WA
Army and Navy Academy, CA
Arthur Morgan School, NC
Ashley Hall, SC
The Athenian School, CA
Athens Academy, GA
Augusta Christian School, GA
Augusta Preparatory Day School, GA
Bachman Academy, TN
Baldwin School of Puerto Rico, PR
Balmoral Hall School, MB, Canada
Bangor Christian School, ME
Barnstable Academy, NJ
Battle Ground Academy, TN
Bay Ridge Preparatory School, NY
The Bay School of San Francisco, CA
The Beekman School, NY
Belen Jesuit Preparatory School, FL
Benet Academy, IL
The Benjamin School, FL
Berkeley Carroll School, NY
Berkeley Preparatory School, FL
Berkshire School, MA
Besant Hill School, CA
Beth Haven Christian School, KY
The Birch Wathen Lenox School, NY
Bishop Brady High School, NH
Bishop Connolly High School, MA
Bishop Denis J. O'Connell High School, VA

Bishop Eustace Preparatory School, NJ
Bishop Guertin High School, NH
Bishop Hendricken High School, RI
Bishop Ireton High School, VA
Bishop John J. Snyder High School, FL
Bishop Kelly High School, ID
Bishop McGuinness Catholic High School, OK
Bishop Montgomery High School, CA
Bishop O'Dowd High School, CA
Bishop Shanahan High School, PA
Bishop Stang High School, MA
Blanchet School, OR
Blessed Trinity High School, GA
The Bolles School, FL
Boston University Academy, MA
Bourgade Catholic High School, AZ
Boylan Central Catholic High School, IL
Branksome Hall, ON, Canada
Brehm Preparatory School, IL
Brentwood School, CA
Briarcrest Christian High School, TN
Briarwood Christian High School, AL
Bridges Academy, CA
Brimmer and May School, MA
Brookhaven Academy, MS
The Brook Hill School, TX
Brooks School, MA
Brophy College Preparatory, AZ
Brunswick School, CT
The Bryn Mawr School for Girls, MD
Burr and Burton Academy, VT
Butte Central Catholic High School, MT
Buxton School, MA
Calvert Hall College High School, MD
Campbell Hall (Episcopal), CA
Canterbury School, FL
The Canterbury School of Florida, FL
Cape Cod Academy, MA
Cape Fear Academy, NC
Cape Henry Collegiate School, VA
Capistrano Valley Christian Schools, CA
Cardigan Mountain School, NH
Cardinal Gibbons High School, NC
Cardinal Mooney Catholic High School, FL
Cardinal Newman High School, FL
Cardinal O'Hara High School, PA
Carlisle School, VA
Carmel High School, IL
Carondelet High School, CA
Carrollton Christian Academy, TX
Cascadilla School, NY
Castilleja School, CA
Cathedral High School, NY
Catholic Central High School, NY
Catholic Central High School, WI
The Catholic High School of Baltimore, MD
The Catlin Gabel School, OR
Central Alberta Christian High School, AB, Canada
Central Catholic High School, CA
Central Catholic High School, MA
Central Catholic High School, TX
Chadwick School, CA
Chaminade College Preparatory, CA
Chaminade-Madonna College Preparatory, FL
Charlotte Country Day School, NC
Charlotte Latin School, NC
Chase Collegiate School, CT

Chattanooga Christian School, TN
Chelsea School, MD
The Chicago Academy for the Arts, IL
Children's Creative and Performing Arts Academy of
    San Diego, CA
Chinese Christian Schools, CA
Christ Church Episcopal School, SC
Christian Brothers Academy, NJ
Christian Brothers Academy, NY
Christian Central Academy, NY
Christopher Dock Mennonite High School, PA
Chrysalis School, WA
Cistercian Preparatory School, TX
Clarksville Academy, TN
Clearwater Central Catholic High School, FL
Colegio Bolivar, Colombia
Colegio San Jose, PR
Cole Valley Christian High School, ID
Collegiate School, NY
Columbia Academy, TN
The Columbus Academy, OH
Columbus School for Girls, OH
Commonwealth School, MA
Community Hebrew Academy, ON, Canada
The Community School of Naples, FL
The Concept School, PA
Concord Academy, MA
Concordia Lutheran High School, IN
Convent of the Sacred Heart, CT
Convent of the Sacred Heart, NY
Cotter Schools, MN
Country Day School of the Sacred Heart, PA
Covenant Canadian Reformed School, AB, Canada
Crawford Adventist Academy, ON, Canada
Crespi Carmelite High School, CA
Cretin-Derham Hall, MN
Crossroads School for Arts & Sciences, CA
Crystal Springs Uplands School, CA
The Culver Academies, IN
Currey Ingram Academy, TN
Damien High School, CA
Darrow School, NY
Davidson Academy, TN
Deerfield Academy, MA
De La Salle College, ON, Canada
De La Salle High School, CA
DeLaSalle High School, MN
De La Salle North Catholic High School, OR
Delbarton School, NJ
Delphi Academy of Los Angeles, CA
DeMatha Catholic High School, MD
Denver Academy, CO
Denver Christian High School, CO
DePaul Catholic High School, NJ
The Derryfield School, NH
Detroit Country Day School, MI
Devon Preparatory School, PA
Dexter Southfield, MA
Dexter Southfield, MA
The Dr. Miriam and Sheldon G. Adelson Educational Campus,
    The Adelson Upper School, NV
Dominican Academy, NY
Donelson Christian Academy, TN
The Donoho School, AL
Dowling Catholic High School, IA
Duchesne Academy of the Sacred Heart, TX
Durham Academy, NC

Eaglebrook School, MA
Eagle Hill School, CT
Eastern Mennonite High School, VA
Edgewood Academy, AL
Eldorado Emerson Private School, CA
Elgin Academy, IL
Elizabeth Seton High School, MD
The Ellis Academy, AL
The Emery/Weiner School, TX
The Episcopal Academy, PA
Episcopal Collegiate School, AR
Episcopal High School, TX
Episcopal High School, VA
Explorations Academy, WA
Ezell-Harding Christian School, TN
Fairfield College Preparatory School, CT
Faith Christian High School, CA
Faith Lutheran High School, NV
Father Judge High School, PA
Father Lopez High School, FL
Father Ryan High School, TN
Fayetteville Academy, NC
Fay School, MA
The First Academy, FL
First Baptist Academy, TX
First Presbyterian Day School, GA
Fishburne Military School, VA
Flintridge Preparatory School, CA
Fordham Preparatory School, NY
Forest Lake Academy, FL
Fort Worth Christian School, TX
Foundation Academy, FL
Fountain Valley School of Colorado, CO
Fowlers Academy, PR
Foxcroft School, VA
Franklin Road Academy, TN
Fredericksburg Academy, VA
Freeman Academy, SD
French-American School of New York, NY
Fresno Christian Schools, CA
Friends Academy, NY
Friends' Central School, PA
Front Range Christian High School, CO
The Frostig School, CA
Fryeburg Academy, ME
Fuqua School, VA
Gabriel Richard Catholic High School, MI
The Galloway School, GA
Gann Academy (The New Jewish High School of
    Greater Boston), MA
Garrison Forest School, MD
Gaston Day School, NC
Gateway School, TX
George School, PA
Georgetown Day School, DC
Georgetown Preparatory School, MD
Georgetown Visitation Preparatory School, DC
Germantown Friends School, PA
Gilman School, MD
Girls Preparatory School, TN
Glades Day School, FL
Glenlyon Norfolk School, BC, Canada
Gonzaga College High School, DC
Good Hope Country Day School, VI
Gould Academy, ME
The Governor French Academy, IL
Grace Baptist Academy, TN

Grace Brethren School, CA
Grace Christian School, AK
The Grauer School, CA
Great Lakes Christian High School, ON, Canada
Greenhills School, MI
Grier School, PA
Gulliver Preparatory School, FL
The Gunnery, CT
Hampton Roads Academy, VA
Hanalani Schools, HI
Hank Haney International Junior Golf Academy, SC
Hargrave Military Academy, VA
The Harley School, NY
The Harpeth Hall School, TN
Harrells Christian Academy, NC
Harvard-Westlake School, CA
Hawaii Baptist Academy, HI
Hawai`i Preparatory Academy, HI
Hawthorne Christian Academy, NJ
Head-Royce School, CA
Hebrew Academy, CA
Hebrew Academy of the Five Towns & Rockaway, NY
The Heights School, MD
Heritage Christian School, CA
Heritage Christian School, ON, Canada
The Heritage School, GA
Highland Hall Waldorf School, CA
High Mowing School, NH
Hillside School, MA
The Hill Top Preparatory School, PA
Ho'Ala School, HI
Holy Cross High School, CT
Holy Cross School, LA
Holy Savior Menard Catholic High School, LA
Hopkins School, CT
Houghton Academy, NY
The Howard School, GA
The Hudson School, NJ
Humanex Academy, CO
The Hun School of Princeton, NJ
Huntington-Surrey School, TX
Hyde Park Baptist School, TX
Hyman Brand Hebrew Academy of Greater Kansas City, KS
IC Catholic Prep, IL
Immaculata-La Salle High School, FL
Immaculate Heart High School and Middle School, CA
Independent School, KS
Indian Creek School, MD.
Institute of Notre Dame, MD
Intermountain Christian School, UT
International High School, CA
International School Bangkok, Thailand
International School Manila, Philippines
International School of Indiana, IN
Jesuit College Preparatory School, TX
Jesuit High School of Tampa, FL
John Burroughs School, MO
John T. Morgan Academy, AL
Josephinum Academy, IL
Junipero Serra High School, CA
Kalamazoo Christian High School, MI
Kansas City Academy, MO
Kent Denver School, CO
Kent Place School, NJ
The Kew-Forest School, NY
The Key School, MD
Keystone School, TX

Kildonan School, NY
Kimball Union Academy, NH
King Low Heywood Thomas, CT
Kings Christian School, CA
King's-Edgehill School, NS, Canada
Kingsway College, ON, Canada
Kingswood-Oxford School, CT
The Lab School of Washington, DC
La Jolla Country Day School, CA
Lakefield College School, ON, Canada
Lakehill Preparatory School, TX
Lake Mary Preparatory School, FL
Lancaster Country Day School, PA
Lancaster Mennonite High School, PA
Landmark Christian Academy, KY
Landmark Christian School, GA
Landmark School, MA
Landon School, MD
Lansdale Catholic High School, PA
La Scuola D'Italia Guglielmo Marconi, NY
The Latin School of Chicago, IL
Lauralton Hall, CT
The Laureate Academy, MB, Canada
Lawrence Academy, MA
Lawrence School, OH
The Lawrenceville School, NJ
Lee Academy, ME
The Leelanau School, MI
Lehigh Valley Christian High School, PA
Lexington Catholic High School, KY
Lick-Wilmerding High School, CA
Linfield Christian School, CA
Lipscomb Academy, TN
Little Red School House and Elisabeth Irwin High School, NY
Lodi Academy, CA
Long Island Lutheran Middle and High School, NY
Long Trail School, VT
Louisville High School, CA
The Lovett School, GA
The Lowell Whiteman School, CO
Loyola-Blakefield, MD
Loyola School, NY
Lustre Christian High School, MT
Lutheran High School North, MO
Lutheran High School Northwest, MI
Lutheran High School of Hawaii, HI
Luther College High School, SK, Canada
Lycee International de Los Angeles, CA
The Madeira School, VA
Madison Academy, AL
Madison Country Day School, WI
Maharishi School of the Age of Enlightenment, IA
Maine Central Institute, ME
Manhattan Christian High School, MT
Maplebrook School, NY
Maranatha High School, CA
Maret School, DC
Marian Catholic High School, PA
Marian Central Catholic High School, IL
Marin Academy, CA
Marine Military Academy, TX
Marist School, GA
Marshall School, MN
Mars Hill Bible School, AL
Mary Institute and St. Louis Country Day School (MICDS), MO
The Mary Louis Academy, NY
Marymount High School, CA

The Masters School, NY
Matignon High School, MA
Maur Hill-Mount Academy, KS
McDonogh School, MD
McGill-Toolen Catholic High School, AL
Meadowridge School, BC, Canada
The Meadows School, NV
Mennonite Collegiate Institute, MB, Canada
Mercersburg Academy, PA
Mercy High School College Preparatory, CA
Mesa Grande Seventh-Day Academy, CA
Middlesex School, MA
Middle Tennessee Christian School, TN
Midland School, CA
Mid-Pacific Institute, HI
Mid-Peninsula High School, CA
Millbrook School, NY
Miss Edgar's and Miss Cramp's School, QC, Canada
Miss Hall's School, MA
Missouri Military Academy, MO
Miss Porter's School, CT
MMI Preparatory School, PA
Modesto Christian School, CA
Montgomery Bell Academy, TN
Montverde Academy, FL
Moorestown Friends School, NJ
Moravian Academy, PA
Mother McAuley High School, IL
Mt. De Sales Academy, GA
Mount Michael Benedictine School, NE
Mount Paran Christian School, GA
Mount Saint Charles Academy, RI
National Cathedral School, DC
Nazareth Academy, IL
Nazareth Academy High School for Girls, PA
Nebraska Christian Schools, NE
Nerinx Hall, MO
Newark Academy, NJ
New Covenant Academy, MO
Newton's Grove School, ON, Canada
Niagara Christian Community of Schools, ON, Canada
Noble and Greenough School, MA
The Nora School, MD
Norfolk Academy, VA
Norman Howard School, NY
The North Broward Preparatory Upper School, FL
North Central Texas Academy, TX
Northfield Mount Hermon School, MA
North Shore Country Day School, IL
North Toronto Christian School, ON, Canada
Northwest Academy, OR
Northwest Catholic High School, CT
Notre Dame Academy, CA
Notre Dame Academy, MA
Notre Dame College Prep, IL
Notre Dame High School, CA
Notre Dame Junior/Senior High School, PA
Oak Grove School, CA
The Oakland School, PA
Oakland School, VA
Oldenburg Academy, IN
The O'Neal School, NC
Oneida Baptist Institute, KY
Oregon Episcopal School, OR
Orinda Academy, CA
The Orme School, AZ
Our Lady of Mercy Academy, NJ

Our Lady of Mount Carmel High School, MD
Out-Of-Door-Academy, FL
The Overlake School, WA
Pacific Crest Community School, OR
Padua Franciscan High School, OH
The Paideia School, GA
Palma School, CA
Palo Alto Preparatory School, CA
Paradise Adventist Academy, CA
Parish Episcopal School, TX
The Park School of Baltimore, MD
The Park School of Buffalo, NY
The Pathway School, PA
The Pennington School, NJ
Pensacola Catholic High School, FL
The Phelps School, PA
Philadelphia-Montgomery Christian Academy, PA
Phoenix Christian Unified Schools, AZ
Piedmont Academy, GA
Pinecrest Academy, GA
The Pingree School, MA
The Pingry School, NJ
Pioneer Valley Christian School, MA
Pope John XXIII Regional High School, NJ
Porter-Gaud School, SC
Portsmouth Christian Academy, NH
The Potomac School, VA
Poughkeepsie Day School, NY
Powers Catholic High School, MI
Presbyterian Pan American School, TX
Preston High School, NY
Proctor Academy, NH
Professional Children's School, NY
Providence Academy, MN
Providence Catholic School, The College Preparatory School for
    Girls Grades 6-12, TX
Providence Country Day School, RI
Providence Day School, NC
Providence High School, CA
Punahou School, HI
Pusch Ridge Christian Academy, AZ
Queen Margaret's School, BC, Canada
Rabun Gap-Nacoochee School, GA
Randolph-Macon Academy, VA
Ranney School, NJ
Ransom Everglades School, FL
Realms of Inquiry, UT
The Rectory School, CT
Redwood Christian Schools, CA
Regina Junior-Senior High School, IA
Ridley College, ON, Canada
Riverdale Country School, NY
The Rivers School, MA
Riverstone International School, ID
Rockhurst High School, MO
Roland Park Country School, MD
Rolling Hills Preparatory School, CA
Rosseau Lake College, ON, Canada
Ross School, NY
Rowland Hall, UT
The Roxbury Latin School, MA
Rumsey Hall School, CT
Sacramento Country Day School, CA
Sacred Heart School of Halifax, NS, Canada
Saddlebrook Preparatory School, FL
Sage Hill School, CA
St. Agnes Academy, TX

St. Albans School, DC
Saint Albert Junior-Senior High School, IA
St. Andrew's College, ON, Canada
St. Andrew's Episcopal School, MD
St. Andrew's School, RI
Saint Anthony High School, IL
St. Augustine High School, CA
Saint Augustine Preparatory School, NJ
St. Benedict at Auburndale, TN
St. Catherine's Academy, CA
St. Croix Schools, MN
Saint Dominic Academy, ME
Saint Edward's School, FL
Saint Elizabeth High School, CA
St. Francis de Sales High School, OH
Saint Francis Girls High School, CA
Saint Francis High School, CA
Saint Francis High School, CA
St. Francis High School, KY
St. George's Independent School, TN
St. George's School, RI
St. George's School, BC, Canada
St. George's School of Montreal, QC, Canada
Saint Gertrude High School, VA
St. John's Preparatory School, MA
Saint John's Preparatory School, MN
St. Joseph Academy, FL
St. Joseph High School, CT
Saint Joseph High School, IL
St. Joseph's Academy, LA
St. Joseph's Catholic School, SC
St. Joseph's Preparatory School, PA
Saint Lawrence Academy, CA
St. Lawrence Seminary High School, WI
St. Mark's School of Texas, TX
St. Martin's Episcopal School, LA
St. Mary's Episcopal School, TN
Saint Mary's Hall, TX
Saint Mary's High School, AZ
Saint Mary's High School, MD
St. Mary's School, OR
St. Michael's College School, ON, Canada
St. Michael's Preparatory School of the Norbertine Fathers, CA
St. Patrick's Regional Secondary, BC, Canada
St. Paul Academy and Summit School, MN
St. Paul Preparatory School, MN
St. Paul's High School, MB, Canada
St. Pius X Catholic High School, GA
St. Pius X High School, TX
St. Stanislaus College, MS
St. Stephen's & St. Agnes School, VA
St. Stephen's Episcopal School, TX
St. Stephen's School, Rome, Italy
Saint Teresa's Academy, MO
St. Thomas Aquinas High School, FL
Saint Thomas Aquinas High School, KS
St. Thomas Aquinas High School, NH
Saint Thomas More Catholic High School, LA
St. Timothy's School, MD
Saint Ursula Academy, OH
Saint Viator High School, IL
Salem Academy, NC
Salem Academy, OR
Salpointe Catholic High School, AZ
Sandia Preparatory School, NM
San Diego Jewish Academy, CA
San Domenico School, CA

Sandy Spring Friends School, MD
San Marcos Baptist Academy, TX
Santa Catalina School, CA
Scattergood Friends School, IA
Scottsdale Christian Academy, AZ
Scotus Central Catholic High School, NE
Seattle Academy of Arts and Sciences, WA
Seisen International School, Japan
Seton Catholic High School, AZ
The Seven Hills School, OH
Sewickley Academy, PA
Shady Side Academy, PA
Shanley High School, ND
Shattuck-St. Mary's School, MN
Shawe Memorial Junior/Senior High School, IN
Shelton School and Evaluation Center, TX
The Shipley School, PA
Shoreline Christian, WA
Signet Christian School, ON, Canada
Smith School, NY
Sonoma Academy, CA
Southfield Christian High School, MI
Southwestern Academy, AZ
Southwestern Academy, CA
The Spence School, NY
Springside Chestnut Hill Academy, PA
Squaw Valley Academy, CA
Stevenson School, CA
The Storm King School, NY
The Study, QC, Canada
Subiaco Academy, AR
Summerfield Waldorf School, CA
The Summit Country Day School, OH
Summit Preparatory School, MT
Sunshine Bible Academy, SD
The Taft School, CT
Tampa Preparatory School, FL
Telluride Mountain School, CO
Temple Grandin School, CO
Teurlings Catholic High School, LA
The Thacher School, CA
Thomas Jefferson School, MO
Thornton Academy, ME
Tilton School, NH
Timothy Christian High School, IL
TMI - The Episcopal School of Texas, TX
Tower Hill School, DE
Trafalgar Castle School, ON, Canada
Trevor Day School, NY
Tri-City Christian Academy, AZ
Trinity Christian Academy, TN
Trinity College School, ON, Canada
Trinity High School, KY
Trinity High School, NH
Trinity High School, OH
Trinity-Pawling School, NY
Trinity Preparatory School, FL
Trinity School of Texas, TX
Trinity Valley School, TX
Tyler Street Christian Academy, TX
United Mennonite Educational Institute, ON, Canada
University Liggett School, MI
University of Chicago Laboratory Schools, IL
University School of Jackson, TN
University School of Milwaukee, WI
University School of Nova Southeastern University, FL
Upper Canada College, ON, Canada

The Ursuline Academy of Dallas, TX
Valle Catholic High School, MO
Valley Christian High School, CA
The Valley School, MI
Valley View School, MA
Vandebilt Catholic High School, LA
The Vanguard School, FL
Venta Preparatory School, ON, Canada
Vicksburg Catholic School, MS
Victor Valley Christian School, CA
Viewpoint School, CA
Villa Angela-St. Joseph High School, OH
Villa Joseph Marie High School, PA
Villa Madonna Academy, KY
Villa Victoria Academy, NJ
Villa Walsh Academy, NJ
Visitation Academy, MO
Wakefield School, VA
Waldorf High School of Massachusetts Bay, MA
The Waldorf School of Garden City, NY
The Waldorf School of Saratoga Springs, NY
Walther Christian Academy, IL
Wasatch Academy, UT
Washington International School, DC
The Waterford School, UT
Watkinson School, CT
Waynflete School, ME
Webb School of Knoxville, TN
The Webb Schools, CA
Wellsprings Friends School, OR
Wesleyan Academy, PR
Westbury Christian School, TX
Westchester Country Day School, NC
Westminster Christian Academy, LA
Westminster Christian School, FL
Westminster School, CT
Westover School, CT
Westridge School, CA
West Sound Academy, WA
Westtown School, PA
Westview School, CA
Wheaton Academy, IL
The Wheeler School, RI
Whitefield Academy, KY
The White Mountain School, NH
Whitfield School, MO
Wilbraham & Monson Academy, MA
William Penn Charter School, PA
The Williston Northampton School, MA
Wilmington Christian School, DE
Wilmington Friends School, DE
Wilson Hall, SC
Windermere Preparatory School, FL
The Windsor School, NY
Winston Preparatory School, NY
The Winston School, TX
The Winston School San Antonio, TX
The Woodhall School, CT
Woodlynde School, PA
Woodward Academy, GA
The Woodward School, MA
Worcester Academy, MA
Worcester Preparatory School, MD
Xavier College Preparatory, AZ
Yeshiva High School, IL
York Preparatory School, NY
The York School, ON, Canada

SCHOOLS REPORTING THAT THEY OFFER LOANS

Academy of the New Church Girls' School, PA	M,N
The Benjamin School, FL	N
The Bryn Mawr School for Girls, MD	M,N
Cardigan Mountain School, NH	N
Chaminade-Madonna College Preparatory, FL	N
Commonwealth School, MA	N
Community Hebrew Academy, ON, Canada	N
Concord Academy, MA	N
The Ellis Academy, AL	N
Episcopal High School, TX	M
Explorations Academy, WA	N
Falmouth Academy, MA	N
Georgetown Preparatory School, MD	M
Gilman School, MD	N
Gould Academy, ME	N
Great Lakes Christian High School, ON, Canada	M,N
Grier School, PA	N
The Gunnery, CT	N
Hargrave Military Academy, VA	N
John Burroughs School, MO	N
La Scuola D'Italia Guglielmo Marconi, NY	N
The Latin School of Chicago, IL	M,N
Lawrence Academy, MA	N
The Madeira School, VA	M,N
Maplebrook School, NY	M,N
Maur Hill-Mount Academy, KS	N
McDonogh School, MD	M,N
The Meadows School, NV	N
Mennonite Collegiate Institute, MB, Canada	M
Mercersburg Academy, PA	N
Mesa Grande Seventh-Day Academy, CA	M,N
Middlesex School, MA	N
Millbrook School, NY	N
Missouri Military Academy, MO	N
Moorestown Friends School, NJ	N
Mount Michael Benedictine School, NE	N
Noble and Greenough School, MA	N
Northfield Mount Hermon School, MA	N
North Shore Country Day School, IL	M,N
The Pingree School, MA	N
Ridley College, ON, Canada	N
St. Albans School, DC	N
St. Andrew's School, RI	N
St. George's School, RI	M,N
St. Joseph's Preparatory School, PA	M,N
St. Paul's High School, MB, Canada	N
St. Timothy's School, MD	N
The Taft School, CT	N
Tilton School, NH	N
Trinity High School, OH	M
Trinity-Pawling School, NY	N
United Mennonite Educational Institute, ON, Canada	N
Vandebilt Catholic High School, LA	M
Walther Christian Academy, IL	M,N
Wasatch Academy, UT	N
Westover School, CT	M,N
Wilbraham & Monson Academy, MA	N
Yeshiva High School, IL	N

TOTAL AMOUNT OF UPPER SCHOOL FINANCIAL AID AWARDED FOR 2013–14

The Academy at Charlemont, MA	$593,000
Academy of Our Lady of Guam, GU	$63,705
Academy of Our Lady of Peace, CA	$2,500,000
Academy of the New Church Boys' School, PA	$750,000
Academy of the New Church Girls' School, PA	$750,000
Academy of the Sacred Heart, LA	$265,000
The Agnes Irwin School, PA	$1,457,924
Albuquerque Academy, NM	$3,526,266
Allendale Columbia School, NY	$873,130
The American Boychoir School, NJ	$38,000
American Community Schools of Athens, Greece	€60,000
American Heritage School, FL	$4,623,928
American Heritage School, FL	$3,800,000
The American School Foundation, Mexico	8,300,000 Mexican pesos
Annie Wright School, WA	$1,093,935
Archbishop Alter High School, OH	$150,000
Archbishop Hoban High School, OH	$2,200,000
Archbishop Mitty High School, CA	$3,300,000
Archbishop Thomas J. Murphy High School, WA	$800,000
Army and Navy Academy, CA	$329,175
Arthur Morgan School, NC	$93,000
Ashley Hall, SC	$1,215,000
The Athenian School, CA	$2,100,000
Athens Academy, GA	$400,000
Augusta Preparatory Day School, GA	$250,000
Bachman Academy, TN	$100,000
Baldwin School of Puerto Rico, PR	$50,000
Balmoral Hall School, MB, Canada	CAN$253,096
Barnstable Academy, NJ	$200,000
Battle Ground Academy, TN	$530,941
Belen Jesuit Preparatory School, FL	$400,000
Benet Academy, IL	$150,000
The Benjamin School, FL	$1,388,838
Berkeley Carroll School, NY	$2,513,655
Besant Hill School, CA	$450,000
Beth Haven Christian School, KY	$8000
The Birch Wathen Lenox School, NY	$1,200,000
Bishop Denis J. O'Connell High School, VA	$1,800,000
Bishop Eustace Preparatory School, NJ	$800,000
Bishop Guertin High School, NH	$600,000
Bishop Hendricken High School, RI	$1,600,000
Bishop Ireton High School, VA	$592,000
Bishop John J. Snyder High School, FL	$300,000
Bishop Kelly High School, ID	$1,166,804
Bishop McGuinness Catholic High School, OK	$163,200
Bishop Montgomery High School, CA	$68,000
Bishop O'Dowd High School, CA	$2,300,000
Bishop Stang High School, MA	$500,000
Blanchet School, OR	$250,000
Boston University Academy, MA	$1,243,223
Bourgade Catholic High School, AZ	$1,600,000
Boylan Central Catholic High School, IL	$583,264
Branksome Hall, ON, Canada	CAN$675,000
Brehm Preparatory School, IL	$99,300
Brentwood School, CA	$3,500,000
Briarwood Christian High School, AL	$5000
Brimmer and May School, MA	$1,118,270
Brookhaven Academy, MS	$13,000
The Brook Hill School, TX	$850,000
Brooks School, MA	$3,300,000
Brophy College Preparatory, AZ	$2,098,895
Brunswick School, CT	$1,250,000
The Bryn Mawr School for Girls, MD	$1,359,941
Butte Central Catholic High School, MT	$68,000
Buxton School, MA	$1,600,000
Calvert Hall College High School, MD	$2,582,782
Campbell Hall (Episcopal), CA	$4,000,000
Canterbury School, FL	$782,050

M — middle-income loans; N — need-based loans

Cape Cod Academy, MA	$1,600,000
Cape Fear Academy, NC	$223,729
Capistrano Valley Christian Schools, CA	$250,000
Cardinal Mooney Catholic High School, FL	$200,000
Carlisle School, VA	$250,000
Carmel High School, IL	$1,300,000
Carondelet High School, CA	$1,300,000
Cascadilla School, NY	$60,000
Castilleja School, CA	$2,200,000
Catholic Central High School, NY	$240,000
Catholic Central High School, WI	$120,000
The Catholic High School of Baltimore, MD	$589,525
The Catlin Gabel School, OR	$1,323,000
Central Catholic High School, CA	$488,434
Central Catholic High School, MA	$1,460,044
Central Catholic High School, TX	$285,000
Chadwick School, CA	$1,841,675
Chaminade College Preparatory, CA	$2,290,865
Chaminade-Madonna College Preparatory, FL	$400,000
Charlotte Country Day School, NC	$1,250,457
Charlotte Latin School, NC	$887,525
Chase Collegiate School, CT	$2,716,560
Chattanooga Christian School, TN	$500,000
The Chicago Academy for the Arts, IL	$765,690
Children's Creative and Performing Arts Academy of San Diego, CA	$25,000
Chinese Christian Schools, CA	$120,000
Christ Church Episcopal School, SC	$519,018
Christian Brothers Academy, NJ	$1,152,500
Christian Central Academy, NY	$108,875
Christopher Dock Mennonite High School, PA	$500,000
Cistercian Preparatory School, TX	$319,485
Colegio San Jose, PR	$293,000
Collegiate School, NY	$150,000
Columbia Academy, TN	$55,000
The Columbus Academy, OH	$99,190
Columbus School for Girls, OH	$669,770
Commonwealth School, MA	$1,146,990
Community Hebrew Academy, ON, Canada	2,000,000
The Community School of Naples, FL	$1,042,686
Concord Academy, MA	$3,830,370
Convent of the Sacred Heart, CT	$2,500,000
Convent of the Sacred Heart, NY	$2,300,000
Country Day School of the Sacred Heart, PA	$424,500
Crawford Adventist Academy, ON, Canada	CAN$40,000
Cretin-Derham Hall, MN	$2,500,000
Crossroads School for Arts & Sciences, CA	$2,896,320
Crystal Springs Uplands School, CA	$2,200,000
The Culver Academies, IN	$8,900,000
Currey Ingram Academy, TN	$1,500,000
Damien High School, CA	$600,000
Darrow School, NY	$1,100,000
Deerfield Academy, MA	$7,800,000
De La Salle High School, CA	$2,250,000
DeLaSalle High School, MN	$2,530,000
Delbarton School, NJ	$1,700,000
Delphi Academy of Los Angeles, CA	$50,000
DeMatha Catholic High School, MD	$1,454,688
Denver Christian High School, CO	$35,000
The Derryfield School, NH	$1,595,407
Devon Preparatory School, PA	$1,030,000
Dexter Southfield, MA	$3,000,000
Dexter Southfield, MA	$3,000,000
The Dr. Miriam and Sheldon G. Adelson Educational Campus, The Adelson Upper School, NV	$1,000,000
Donelson Christian Academy, TN	$142,580
Dowling Catholic High School, IA	$1,000,000
Duchesne Academy of the Sacred Heart, TX	$641,530
Durham Academy, NC	$896,508
Eaglebrook School, MA	$1,650,000
Eastern Mennonite High School, VA	$150,000
Eldorado Emerson Private School, CA	$50,000
Elgin Academy, IL	$600,000
Elizabeth Seton High School, MD	$500,000
The Emery/Weiner School, TX	$1,200,000
The Episcopal Academy, PA	$3,456,893
Episcopal Collegiate School, AR	$482,000
Episcopal High School, TX	$1,700,000
Episcopal High School, VA	$5,000,000
Explorations Academy, WA	$200,000
Fairfield College Preparatory School, CT	$2,163,000
Faith Christian High School, CA	$50,000
Faith Lutheran High School, NV	$512,000
Falmouth Academy, MA	$928,000
Father Judge High School, PA	$740,000
Father Lopez High School, FL	$1,023,796
Father Ryan High School, TN	$550,000
Fayetteville Academy, NC	$465,212
Fay School, MA	$1,228,665
First Presbyterian Day School, GA	$874,000
Flintridge Preparatory School, CA	$2,047,000
Fordham Preparatory School, NY	$2,600,000
Forest Lake Academy, FL	$347,000
Fort Worth Christian School, TX	$111,000
Foundation Academy, FL	$300,000
Fountain Valley School of Colorado, CO	$2,387,900
Fowlers Academy, PR	$27,000
Foxcroft School, VA	$1,200,000
Franklin Road Academy, TN	$500,000
Fredericksburg Academy, VA	$750,000
Freeman Academy, SD	$32,000
French-American School of New York, NY	$223,276
Fresno Christian Schools, CA	$163,537
Friends Academy, NY	$1,699,000
Friends' Central School, PA	$2,928,646
Front Range Christian High School, CO	$176,880
The Frostig School, CA	$50,000
Fryeburg Academy, ME	$2,100,000
Fuqua School, VA	$44,000
The Galloway School, GA	$1,033,485
Gann Academy (The New Jewish High School of Greater Boston), MA	$2,200,000
Garrison Forest School, MD	$3,174,485
Gaston Day School, NC	$199,200
George School, PA	$8,364,060
Georgetown Day School, DC	$1,000,000
Georgetown Preparatory School, MD	$2,000,000
Georgetown Visitation Preparatory School, DC	$1,700,000
Germantown Friends School, PA	$1,879,209
Gilman School, MD	$1,839,100
Girls Preparatory School, TN	$1,419,908
Glenlyon Norfolk School, BC, Canada	CAN$130,000
Gonzaga College High School, DC	$2,400,000
Good Hope Country Day School, VI	$306,553
Gould Academy, ME	$1,355,000
Grace Christian School, AK	$200,000
The Grand River Academy, OH	$205,000
The Grauer School, CA	$156,977
Great Lakes Christian High School, ON, Canada	CAN$150,000
Greenhill School, TX	$1,755,310
Greenhills School, MI	$1,000,000
Grier School, PA	$1,900,000
The Gunnery, CT	$3,800,000
Hampton Roads Academy, VA	$900,000

Hargrave Military Academy, VA	$525,000	Little Keswick School, VA	$20,000
The Harpeth Hall School, TN	$911,425	Lodi Academy, CA	$38,000
Harrells Christian Academy, NC	$62,000	Long Island Lutheran Middle and High School, NY	$420,000
Harvard-Westlake School, CA	$8,069,000	Long Trail School, VT	$99,599
Hawaii Baptist Academy, HI	$367,247	Louisville High School, CA	$682,000
Hawai`i Preparatory Academy, HI	$1,500,000	The Lovett School, GA	$1,230,000
Hawthorne Christian Academy, NJ	$74,440	The Lowell Whiteman School, CO	$440,000
Head-Royce School, CA	$2,296,400	Loyola-Blakefield, MD	$2,500,000
Hebrew Academy, CA	$30,000	Loyola School, NY	$1,194,000
The Heights School, MD	$710,000	Lutheran High School North, MO	$750,000
Heritage Christian School, CA	$500,000	Lutheran High School Northwest, MI	$20,000
The Heritage School, GA	$367,651	Lutheran High School of Hawaii, HI	$500,000
Highland Hall Waldorf School, CA	$204,600	Luther College High School, SK, Canada	CAN$165,000
High Mowing School, NH	$600,000	Lycee International de Los Angeles, CA	$563,569
Hillside School, MA	$1,103,300	The Madeira School, VA	$2,776,071
Ho'Ala School, HI	$10,000	Madison Academy, AL	$100,000
Holy Cross High School, CT	$550,000	Maine Central Institute, ME	$384,000
Holy Savior Menard Catholic High School, LA	$150,000	Manhattan Christian High School, MT	$297,100
Holy Trinity School, ON, Canada	40,000	Maplebrook School, NY	$100,000
Hopkins School, CT	$3,130,350	Maret School, DC	$1,660,000
Houghton Academy, NY	$95,000	Marian Catholic High School, PA	$102,000
The Hudson School, NJ	$363,025	Marian Central Catholic High School, IL	$301,400
Humanex Academy, CO	$6000	Marin Academy, CA	$2,500,000
The Hun School of Princeton, NJ	$4,000,000	Marist School, GA	$2,000,000
Hyde Park Baptist School, TX	$145,250	Marshall School, MN	$1,400,000
Hyman Brand Hebrew Academy of Greater Kansas City, KS	$41,800	Mars Hill Bible School, AL	$150,000
IC Catholic Prep, IL	$175,000	Mary Institute and St. Louis Country Day School (MICDS), MO	$2,321,365
Immaculata-La Salle High School, FL	$351,257	The Mary Louis Academy, NY	$528,811
Institute of Notre Dame, MD	$843,000	Marymount High School, CA	$1,300,000
Intermountain Christian School, UT	$24,904	The Masters School, NY	$5,000,000
International High School, CA	$748,000	Matignon High School, MA	$315,000
Jesuit College Preparatory School, TX	$1,233,850	Maur Hill-Mount Academy, KS	$280,000
Jesuit High School of Tampa, FL	$1,342,290	McDonogh School, MD	$3,247,700
John Burroughs School, MO	$2,051,000	McGill-Toolen Catholic High School, AL	$958,000
Junipero Serra High School, CA	$2,100,000	The Meadows School, NV	$555,121
Kansas City Academy, MO	$121,000	Mennonite Collegiate Institute, MB, Canada	CAN$40,000
Kent Denver School, CO	$2,000,000	Mercy High School College Preparatory, CA	$1,200,000
Kent Place School, NJ	$1,299,061	Mesa Grande Seventh-Day Academy, CA	$35,000
The Kew-Forest School, NY	$1,129,100	Middlesex School, MA	$4,300,000
The Key School, MD	$439,397	Midland School, CA	$1,000,000
Kildonan School, NY	$300,000	Mid-Pacific Institute, HI	$2,900,000
Kimball Union Academy, NH	$3,201,052	Millbrook School, NY	$2,700,000
King Low Heywood Thomas, CT	$1,414,115	Miss Edgar's and Miss Cramp's School, QC, Canada	CAN$135,000
Kings Christian School, CA	$61,750	Miss Hall's School, MA	$3,000,000
King's-Edgehill School, NS, Canada	CAN$900,000	Missouri Military Academy, MO	$875,000
Kingsway College, ON, Canada	CAN$200,000	Miss Porter's School, CT	$3,100,000
Kingswood-Oxford School, CT	$2,300,000	MMI Preparatory School, PA	$841,200
The Lab School of Washington, DC	$231,100	Montgomery Bell Academy, TN	$1,300,000
La Jolla Country Day School, CA	$2,748,943	Montverde Academy, FL	$2,000,000
Lakefield College School, ON, Canada	CAN$160,000	Moorestown Friends School, NJ	$1,816,550
Lancaster Country Day School, PA	$1,026,312	Moravian Academy, PA	$1,305,425
Lancaster Mennonite High School, PA	$2,000,000	Mother McAuley High School, IL	$1,000,000
Landmark Christian School, GA	$250,000	Mt. De Sales Academy, GA	$813,771
Landon School, MD	$1,535,509	Mount Michael Benedictine School, NE	$595,000
Lansdale Catholic High School, PA	$106,000	Mount Saint Charles Academy, RI	$700,000
The Latin School of Chicago, IL	$2,300,000	National Cathedral School, DC	$917,760
Lauralton Hall, CT	$450,000	Nazareth Academy, IL	$300,000
The Laureate Academy, MB, Canada	CAN$68,000	Nebraska Christian Schools, NE	$133,000
Lawrence Academy, MA	$3,450,000	Nerinx Hall, MO	$695,529
Lawrence School, OH	$800,000	Newark Academy, NJ	$1,776,490
The Leelanau School, MI	$200,000	Niagara Christian Community of Schools, ON, Canada	CAN$400,000
Lehigh Valley Christian High School, PA	$270,684	Noble and Greenough School, MA	$3,796,650
Lexington Catholic High School, KY	$495,000	The Nora School, MD	$167,000
Lick-Wilmerding High School, CA	$4,300,000	The North Broward Preparatory Upper School, FL	$2,400,000
The Linsly School, WV	$2,345,000		
Lipscomb Academy, TN	$183,000		

Northfield Mount Hermon School, MA	$6,300,000
North Shore Country Day School, IL	$1,500,000
Northwest Academy, OR	$457,300
Northwest Catholic High School, CT	$1,300,000
Notre Dame Academy, MA	$600,000
Notre Dame High School, CA	$767,000
Oak Grove School, CA	$60,000
The Oakland School, PA	$26,000
Oldenburg Academy, IN	$65,000
The O'Neal School, NC	$465,050
Oregon Episcopal School, OR	$801,155
Orinda Academy, CA	$400,000
The Orme School, AZ	$1,200,000
Our Lady of Mercy Academy, NJ	$35,000
Out-Of-Door-Academy, FL	$869,850
The Overlake School, WA	$675,904
Pacific Crest Community School, OR	$60,000
Padua Franciscan High School, OH	$452,650
The Paideia School, GA	$1,255,760
Palma School, CA	$229,000
Paradise Adventist Academy, CA	$50,000
The Park School of Baltimore, MD	$1,270,175
The Park School of Buffalo, NY	$518,154
The Pennington School, NJ	$3,000,000
The Phelps School, PA	$850,000
Philadelphia-Montgomery Christian Academy, PA	$500,000
Piedmont Academy, GA	$25,000
The Pingree School, MA	$2,500,000
The Pingry School, NJ	$4,657,269
Pioneer Valley Christian School, MA	$80,300
Porter-Gaud School, SC	$467,620
Portsmouth Christian Academy, NH	$180,000
Poughkeepsie Day School, NY	$551,160
Powers Catholic High School, MI	$450,300
Presbyterian Pan American School, TX	$1,161,400
Preston High School, NY	$808,360
Proctor Academy, NH	$3,200,000
Professional Children's School, NY	$862,000
Providence Academy, MN	$941,948
Providence Catholic School, The College Preparatory School for Girls Grades 6-12, TX	$200,000
Providence Country Day School, RI	$1,500,000
Providence Day School, NC	$1,056,585
Providence High School, CA	$459,500
Punahou School, HI	$2,687,980
Pusch Ridge Christian Academy, AZ	$2,000,000
Queen Margaret's School, BC, Canada	CAN$150,000
Rabun Gap-Nacoochee School, GA	$5,000,000
Randolph-Macon Academy, VA	$304,242
Ranney School, NJ	$362,000
Ransom Everglades School, FL	$2,309,780
Realms of Inquiry, UT	$40,000
The Rectory School, CT	$1,500,000
Redwood Christian Schools, CA	$400,000
Ridley College, ON, Canada	CAN$3,000,000
The Rivers School, MA	$3,065,050
Rockhurst High School, MO	$1,800,000
Roland Park Country School, MD	$1,346,750
Rolling Hills Preparatory School, CA	$660,000
Rosseau Lake College, ON, Canada	CAN$160,000
Rowland Hall, UT	$591,190
The Roxbury Latin School, MA	$2,087,325
Royal Canadian College, BC, Canada	CAN$18,000
Sacramento Country Day School, CA	$429,050
Sacred Heart School of Halifax, NS, Canada	CAN$138,000
Sage Hill School, CA	$1,862,760
St. Agnes Academy, TX	$983,000
St. Albans School, DC	$2,541,164
Saint Albert Junior-Senior High School, IA	$380,000
St. Andrew's College, ON, Canada	CAN$1,877,530
St. Andrew's Episcopal School, MD	$2,193,800
St. Andrew's School, RI	$2,117,710
Saint Augustine Preparatory School, NJ	$1,100,000
St. Benedict at Auburndale, TN	$35,000
St. Catherine's Academy, CA	$400,000
St. Croix Schools, MN	$600,000
Saint Edward's School, FL	$1,750,000
Saint Elizabeth High School, CA	$990,000
St. Francis de Sales High School, OH	$1,665,000
Saint Francis Girls High School, CA	$1,200,000
Saint Francis High School, CA	$700,000
Saint Francis High School, CA	$2,100,000
St. George's Independent School, TN	$389,652
St. George's School, RI	$3,700,000
St. George's School, BC, Canada	CAN$800,000
St. John's Preparatory School, MA	$2,900,000
Saint John's Preparatory School, MN	$750,000
St. Joseph Academy, FL	$120,000
St. Joseph High School, CT	$235,000
Saint Joseph High School, IL	$1,000,000
St. Joseph's Academy, LA	$411,306
St. Joseph's Catholic School, SC	$454,986
St. Joseph's Preparatory School, PA	$3,250,000
St. Lawrence Seminary High School, WI	$778,110
St. Mark's School of Texas, TX	$1,013,991
St. Martin's Episcopal School, LA	$583,060
St. Mary's Episcopal School, TN	$352,800
Saint Mary's Hall, TX	$621,990
Saint Mary's High School, AZ	$2,200,000
Saint Mary's High School, MD	$250,000
St. Mary's School, OR	$850,000
St. Michael's College School, ON, Canada	CAN$1,800,000
St. Michael's Preparatory School of the Norbertine Fathers, CA	$500,000
St. Paul Academy and Summit School, MN	$1,810,480
St. Paul Preparatory School, MN	$764,650
St. Paul's High School, MB, Canada	CAN$340,000
St. Pius X Catholic High School, GA	$400,000
St. Pius X High School, TX	$711,000
St. Stephen's & St. Agnes School, VA	$2,327,954
St. Stephen's Episcopal School, TX	$2,800,000
St. Stephen's School, Rome, Italy	€405,150
Saint Teresa's Academy, MO	$150,000
Saint Thomas More Catholic High School, LA	$100,000
St. Timothy's School, MD	$2,500,000
Saint Ursula Academy, OH	$1,299,000
Saint Viator High School, IL	$1,300,000
Salem Academy, NC	$1,033,794
Salpointe Catholic High School, AZ	$1,678,295
Sandia Preparatory School, NM	$950,000
San Diego Jewish Academy, CA	$553,000
San Domenico School, CA	$2,000,000
Sandy Spring Friends School, MD	$3,035,000
San Marcos Baptist Academy, TX	$439,180
Santa Catalina School, CA	$2,100,000
Scattergood Friends School, IA	$500,000
Scotus Central Catholic High School, NE	$110,000
Seisen International School, Japan	¥1,170,000
Seton Catholic High School, AZ	$705,000
The Seven Hills School, OH	$530,000
Sewickley Academy, PA	$600,000
Shady Side Academy, PA	$2,012,350
Shattuck-St. Mary's School, MN	$3,900,000
Shawe Memorial Junior/Senior High School, IN	$161,537

Shawnigan Lake School, BC, Canada	CAN$1,000,000
Shelton School and Evaluation Center, TX	$225,950
The Shipley School, PA	$2,504,090
Shoreline Christian, WA	$170,000
Smith School, NY	$30,000
Sonoma Academy, CA	$2,600,000
Soundview Preparatory School, NY	$420,000
Southwestern Academy, AZ	$600,000
Southwestern Academy, CA	$600,000
The Spence School, NY	$1,911,707
Springside Chestnut Hill Academy, PA	$3,379,780
Squaw Valley Academy, CA	$175,000
Stevenson School, CA	$3,100,000
The Storm King School, NY	$405,575
The Study, QC, Canada	CAN$405,857
Subiaco Academy, AR	$449,540
Summit Preparatory School, MT	$100,000
Sunshine Bible Academy, SD	$38,520
The Taft School, CT	$7,300,000
Tampa Preparatory School, FL	$650,000
Telluride Mountain School, CO	$181,243
Temple Grandin School, CO	$65,000
Teurlings Catholic High School, LA	$84,000
The Thacher School, CA	$2,351,000
Tilton School, NH	$2,338,710
TMI - The Episcopal School of Texas, TX	$555,500
Tower Hill School, DE	$1,091,005
Trafalgar Castle School, ON, Canada	CAN$43,000
Trevor Day School, NY	$4,700,000
Tri-City Christian Academy, AZ	$25,000
Trinity College School, ON, Canada	CAN$1,750,000
Trinity High School, KY	$2,500,000
Trinity High School, OH	$138,000
Trinity-Pawling School, NY	$3,300,000
Trinity Preparatory School, FL	$1,972,600
Trinity Valley School, TX	$764,080
Tyler Street Christian Academy, TX	$92,200
United Mennonite Educational Institute, ON, Canada	CAN$20,000
University Liggett School, MI	$2,600,000
University of Chicago Laboratory Schools, IL	$1,182,716
University School of Jackson, TN	$150,000
University School of Milwaukee, WI	$1,025,310
University School of Nova Southeastern University, FL	$1,500,000
Upper Canada College, ON, Canada	CAN$3,700,000
The Ursuline Academy of Dallas, TX	$898,100
Valle Catholic High School, MO	$165,000
Valley Christian High School, CA	$1,300,000
The Valley School, MI	$51,376
Vandebilt Catholic High School, LA	$125,000
The Vanguard School, FL	$500,800
Vicksburg Catholic School, MS	$75,000
Viewpoint School, CA	$2,645,439
Villa Walsh Academy, NJ	$110,000
Wakefield School, VA	$1,500,000
Waldorf High School of Massachusetts Bay, MA	$357,455
The Waldorf School of Garden City, NY	$180,000
Wasatch Academy, UT	$2,650,000
The Waterford School, UT	$1,700,000
Watkinson School, CT	$1,689,180
Waynflete School, ME	$1,509,056
Webb School of Knoxville, TN	$722,480
The Webb Schools, CA	$3,600,000
Wesleyan Academy, PR	$1000
Westbury Christian School, TX	$182,294
Westchester Country Day School, NC	$450,000
Westminster Christian Academy, LA	$70,000
Westminster Christian School, FL	$750,000
Westminster School, CT	$4,459,000
Westridge School, CA	$1,742,800
West Sound Academy, WA	$251,931
Wheaton Academy, IL	$600,000
The Wheeler School, RI	$1,601,835
Whitefield Academy, KY	$42,175
The White Mountain School, NH	$1,412,000
Whitfield School, MO	$1,350,000
William Penn Charter School, PA	$2,321,390
The Williston Northampton School, MA	$6,169,500
Wilmington Christian School, DE	$292,720
Wilmington Friends School, DE	$1,088,338
Wilson Hall, SC	$135,000
Windermere Preparatory School, FL	$411,445
The Windsor School, NY	$20,000
Winston Preparatory School, NY	$500,000
The Winston School, TX	$290,500
Woodlynde School, PA	$525,475
The Woodward School, MA	$200,298
Worcester Academy, MA	$4,400,000
Xavier College Preparatory, AZ	$1,500,000

SCHOOLS REPORTING THAT THEY OFFER ENGLISH AS A SECOND LANGUAGE

Academy at the Lakes, FL
Academy of Our Lady of Guam, GU
Academy of the New Church Boys' School, PA
Academy of the New Church Girls' School, PA
Alma Heights Christian High School, CA
American Community Schools of Athens, Greece
American Heritage School, FL
American Heritage School, FL
The American School of Madrid, Spain
Annie Wright School, WA
Archbishop Thomas J. Murphy High School, WA
Army and Navy Academy, CA
The Athenian School, CA
Augusta Christian School, GA
Balmoral Hall School, MB, Canada
Bangor Christian School, ME
Barnstable Academy, NJ
The Beekman School, NY
Berkshire School, MA
Besant Hill School, CA
Bishop Brady High School, NH
Bishop Denis J. O'Connell High School, VA
Blanchet School, OR
The Bolles School, FL
Bourgade Catholic High School, AZ
Branksome Hall, ON, Canada
Brimmer and May School, MA
The British School of Boston, MA
The Brook Hill School, TX
Burr and Burton Academy, VT
Buxton School, MA
The Canterbury School of Florida, FL
Cape Henry Collegiate School, VA
Capistrano Valley Christian Schools, CA
Cardigan Mountain School, NH
Carlisle School, VA
Catholic Central High School, NY
Charlotte Country Day School, NC

Children's Creative and Performing Arts Academy of
   San Diego, CA
Chinese Christian Schools, CA
Christ Church Episcopal School, SC
Colegio Bolivar, Colombia
Columbia International College of Canada, ON, Canada
Community Hebrew Academy, ON, Canada
Cotter Schools, MN
Crawford Adventist Academy, ON, Canada
The Crenshaw School, FL
The Culver Academies, IN
Damien High School, CA
Darrow School, NY
Davidson Academy, TN
Deerfield Academy, MA
The Dr. Miriam and Sheldon G. Adelson Educational Campus,
   The Adelson Upper School, NV
Donelson Christian Academy, TN
The Donoho School, AL
Eaglebrook School, MA
Eastern Mennonite High School, VA
Eldorado Emerson Private School, CA
The Ellis Academy, AL
Falmouth Academy, MA
Father Lopez High School, FL
Fay School, MA
First Presbyterian Day School, GA
Forest Lake Academy, FL
Fountain Valley School of Colorado, CO
Foxcroft School, VA
French-American School of New York, NY
Fryeburg Academy, ME
Fuqua School, VA
Garrison Forest School, MD
Gaston Day School, NC
George School, PA
Georgetown Preparatory School, MD
Germantown Friends School, PA
Glenlyon Norfolk School, BC, Canada
Gould Academy, ME
The Governor French Academy, IL
The Grand River Academy, OH
The Grauer School, CA
Great Lakes Christian High School, ON, Canada
Grier School, PA
The Gunnery, CT
Hank Haney International Junior Golf Academy, SC
Hargrave Military Academy, VA
Hawai`i Preparatory Academy, HI
Heritage Christian School, CA
High Mowing School, NH
Highroad Academy, BC, Canada
Hillside School, MA
The Hockaday School, TX
Houghton Academy, NY
The Hudson School, NJ
The Hun School of Princeton, NJ
Hyde Park Baptist School, TX
Institut Monte Rosa, Switzerland
International High School, CA
International School Bangkok, Thailand
International School Manila, Philippines
International School of Indiana, IN
Istanbul International Community School, Turkey
Josephinum Academy, IL
The Kew-Forest School, NY
King's-Edgehill School, NS, Canada

Kingsway College, ON, Canada
Lake Mary Preparatory School, FL
Lancaster Country Day School, PA
Lancaster Mennonite High School, PA
La Scuola D'Italia Guglielmo Marconi, NY
Lawrence Academy, MA
Lee Academy, ME
The Leelanau School, MI
Lehigh Valley Christian High School, PA
Long Island Lutheran Middle and High School, NY
Long Trail School, VT
Luther College High School, SK, Canada
Lycee International de Los Angeles, CA
The Madeira School, VA
Maharishi School of the Age of Enlightenment, IA
Maine Central Institute, ME
Maplebrook School, NY
Marine Military Academy, TX
The Masters School, NY
Matignon High School, MA
Maur Hill-Mount Academy, KS
Mennonite Collegiate Institute, MB, Canada
Merchiston Castle School, United Kingdom
Mesa Grande Seventh-Day Academy, CA
Mid-Pacific Institute, HI
Miss Hall's School, MA
Missouri Military Academy, MO
Miss Porter's School, CT
Mont'Kiara International School, Malaysia
Montverde Academy, FL
Mooseheart High School, IL
Mount Vernon Presbyterian School, GA
Nebraska Christian Schools, NE
Newton's Grove School, ON, Canada
Niagara Christian Community of Schools, ON, Canada
The North Broward Preparatory Upper School, FL
North Central Texas Academy, TX
Northfield Mount Hermon School, MA
North Toronto Christian School, ON, Canada
The Norwich Free Academy, CT
Notre Dame Academy, MA
Notre Dame College Prep, IL
Oak Grove School, CA
The Oakland School, PA
Oldenburg Academy, IN
Oneida Baptist Institute, KY
Oregon Episcopal School, OR
Orinda Academy, CA
The Orme School, AZ
The Park School of Buffalo, NY
The Pennington School, NJ
The Phelps School, PA
Philadelphia-Montgomery Christian Academy, PA
Phoenix Christian Unified Schools, AZ
Pinecrest Academy, GA
Pope John XXIII Regional High School, NJ
Portsmouth Christian Academy, NH
Poughkeepsie Day School, NY
Presbyterian Pan American School, TX
Professional Children's School, NY
Queen Margaret's School, BC, Canada
Rabun Gap-Nacoochee School, GA
Randolph-Macon Academy, VA
The Rectory School, CT
Redwood Christian Schools, CA
Ridley College, ON, Canada
Riverstone International School, ID

Rolling Hills Preparatory School, CA
Rosseau Lake College, ON, Canada
Ross School, NY
Royal Canadian College, BC, Canada
Rumsey Hall School, CT
Sacred Heart School of Halifax, NS, Canada
Saddlebrook Preparatory School, FL
St. Andrew's College, ON, Canada
St. Andrew's Episcopal School, MD
St. Andrew's School, RI
St. Catherine's Academy, CA
St. Croix Schools, MN
Saint Edward's School, FL
St. Francis de Sales High School, OH
St. George's School of Montreal, QC, Canada
Saint John's Preparatory School, MN
St. Joseph High School, CT
St. Mary's School, OR
Saint Maur International School, Japan
St. Michael's Preparatory School of the Norbertine Fathers, CA
St. Patrick's Regional Secondary, BC, Canada
St. Paul Preparatory School, MN
St. Stanislaus College, MS
St. Stephen's Episcopal School, TX
St. Stephen's School, Rome, Italy
St. Timothy's School, MD
Salem Academy, NC
Salem Academy, OR
San Domenico School, CA
Sandy Spring Friends School, MD
San Marcos Baptist Academy, TX
Scattergood Friends School, IA
Seisen International School, Japan
Shattuck-St. Mary's School, MN
Shawnigan Lake School, BC, Canada
Signet Christian School, ON, Canada
Southwestern Academy, AZ
Southwestern Academy, CA
Squaw Valley Academy, CA
The Storm King School, NY
Subiaco Academy, AR
The Tenney School, TX
Thomas Jefferson School, MO
Tilton School, NH
TMI - The Episcopal School of Texas, TX
Trafalgar Castle School, ON, Canada
Tri-City Christian Academy, AZ
Trinity College School, ON, Canada
Trinity-Pawling School, NY
University School of Jackson, TN
University School of Nova Southeastern University, FL
Victor Valley Christian School, CA
Wasatch Academy, UT
Westover School, CT
West Sound Academy, WA
Westtown School, PA
Wheaton Academy, IL
The White Mountain School, NH
Whitinsville Christian School, MA
Wilbraham & Monson Academy, MA
The Williston Northampton School, MA
Wilmington Christian School, DE
Windermere Preparatory School, FL
The Windsor School, NY
The Woodhall School, CT
The Woodward School, MA
Worcester Academy, MA

SCHOOLS REPORTING A COMMUNITY SERVICE REQUIREMENT

The Academy for Gifted Children (PACE), ON, Canada
Academy of Our Lady of Peace, CA
Academy of the Sacred Heart, LA
The Agnes Irwin School, PA
All Hallows High School, NY
American Heritage School, FL
American Heritage School, FL
Archbishop Curley High School, MD
Archbishop Thomas J. Murphy High School, WA
The Athenian School, CA
Battle Ground Academy, TN
Belen Jesuit Preparatory School, FL
Berkeley Carroll School, NY
Berkeley Preparatory School, FL
Berkshire School, MA
The Birch Wathen Lenox School, NY
Bishop Brady High School, NH
Bishop Connolly High School, MA
Bishop Denis J. O'Connell High School, VA
Bishop Eustace Preparatory School, NJ
Bishop Ireton High School, VA
Bishop Kelly High School, ID
Bishop Stang High School, MA
Blanchet School, OR
Boston University Academy, MA
Boylan Central Catholic High School, IL
Brentwood School, CA
Briarwood Christian High School, AL
Brimmer and May School, MA
Brookhaven Academy, MS
The Brook Hill School, TX
Brooks School, MA
Brophy College Preparatory, AZ
Brunswick School, CT
The Bryn Mawr School for Girls, MD
Burr and Burton Academy, VT
Butte Central Catholic High School, MT
Campbell Hall (Episcopal), CA
Canterbury School, FL
The Canterbury School of Florida, FL
Cape Cod Academy, MA
Cape Fear Academy, NC
Cape Henry Collegiate School, VA
Cardinal Mooney Catholic High School, FL
Cardinal Newman High School, FL
Cascadilla School, NY
The Catholic High School of Baltimore, MD
The Catlin Gabel School, OR
Central Catholic High School, TX
Chaminade College Preparatory, CA
Chaminade-Madonna College Preparatory, FL
Charlotte Country Day School, NC
Chattanooga Christian School, TN
Children's Creative and Performing Arts Academy of San Diego, CA
Christian Brothers Academy, NY
Christian Central Academy, NY
Colegio San Jose, PR
Collegiate School, NY
The Columbus Academy, OH
Commonwealth School, MA
Community Hebrew Academy, ON, Canada
The Community School of Naples, FL
Concordia Lutheran High School, IN
Convent of the Sacred Heart, CT

Cotter Schools, MN
Country Day School of the Sacred Heart, PA
Crespi Carmelite High School, CA
Crossroads School for Arts & Sciences, CA
The Culver Academies, IN
Currey Ingram Academy, TN
Devon Preparatory School, PA
Donelson Christian Academy, TN
Dowling Catholic High School, IA
Duchesne Academy of the Sacred Heart, TX
Durham Academy, NC
Eaglebrook School, MA
Edgewood Academy, AL
Eldorado Emerson Private School, CA
Elizabeth Seton High School, MD
The Emery/Weiner School, TX
Explorations Academy, WA
Fairfield College Preparatory School, CT
Father Lopez High School, FL
First Baptist Academy, TX
Flintridge Preparatory School, CA
Forest Lake Academy, FL
Fort Worth Christian School, TX
Fountain Valley School of Colorado, CO
Franklin Road Academy, TN
French-American School of New York, NY
Friends Academy, NY
Fryeburg Academy, ME
Fuqua School, VA
Gaston Day School, NC
Gateway School, TX
George School, PA
Georgetown Day School, DC
Georgetown Preparatory School, MD
Georgetown Visitation Preparatory School, DC
Girard College, PA
Glenlyon Norfolk School, BC, Canada
Gonzaga College High School, DC
Good Hope Country Day School, VI
The Grand River Academy, OH
The Grauer School, CA
Greenhill School, TX
Greenhills School, MI
Guamani Private School, PR
Gulliver Preparatory School, FL
The Gunnery, CT
Hampton Roads Academy, VA
Hanalani Schools, HI
The Harley School, NY
Harvard-Westlake School, CA
Head-Royce School, CA
Hebrew Academy of the Five Towns & Rockaway, NY
Highland Hall Waldorf School, CA
High Mowing School, NH
The Hockaday School, TX
Holy Cross School, LA
Hopkins School, CT
The Hudson School, NJ
Humanex Academy, CO
The Hun School of Princeton, NJ
Hyde Park Baptist School, TX
Hyman Brand Hebrew Academy of Greater Kansas City, KS
Immaculata-La Salle High School, FL
Independent School, KS
Institute of Notre Dame, MD
Intermountain Christian School, UT
International School Bangkok, Thailand

Jesuit College Preparatory School, TX
Jesuit High School of Tampa, FL
Josephinum Academy, IL
Junipero Serra High School, CA
Kalamazoo Christian High School, MI
Kent Denver School, CO
The Kew-Forest School, NY
Keystone School, TX
Kingswood-Oxford School, CT
The Lab School of Washington, DC
La Jolla Country Day School, CA
The Latin School of Chicago, IL
Lauralton Hall, CT
The Laureate Academy, MB, Canada
Lawrence School, OH
The Lawrenceville School, NJ
Linfield Christian School, CA
Lipscomb Academy, TN
Little Red School House and Elisabeth Irwin High School, NY
Lodi Academy, CA
Long Trail School, VT
Louisville High School, CA
Lutheran High School North, MO
Lutheran High School Northwest, MI
The Madeira School, VA
Manhattan Christian High School, MT
Maranatha High School, CA
Maret School, DC
Marin Academy, CA
Marist School, GA
Marshall School, MN
Mars Hill Bible School, AL
Mary Institute and St. Louis Country Day School (MICDS), MO
The Mary Louis Academy, NY
Matignon High School, MA
McDonogh School, MD
The Meadows School, NV
Mercy High School College Preparatory, CA
Mesa Grande Seventh-Day Academy, CA
Mid-Peninsula High School, CA
Miss Hall's School, MA
Missouri Military Academy, MO
Miss Porter's School, CT
Moorestown Friends School, NJ
Mount Michael Benedictine School, NE
National Cathedral School, DC
Nerinx Hall, MO
Newark Academy, NJ
Noble and Greenough School, MA
The Nora School, MD
Norfolk Academy, VA
The North Broward Preparatory Upper School, FL
North Shore Country Day School, IL
North Toronto Christian School, ON, Canada
Northwest Academy, OR
Northwest Catholic High School, CT
Notre Dame Academy, CA
Notre Dame College Prep, IL
Notre Dame High School, CA
Oak Grove School, CA
The Oakland School, PA
Oldenburg Academy, IN
The O'Neal School, NC
Orinda Academy, CA
The Orme School, AZ
Out-Of-Door-Academy, FL
The Overlake School, WA

The Paideia School, GA
Palma School, CA
Paradise Adventist Academy, CA
The Park School of Buffalo, NY
The Phelps School, PA
The Pingry School, NJ
Pioneer Valley Christian School, MA
Pope John XXIII Regional High School, NJ
Poughkeepsie Day School, NY
Powers Catholic High School, MI
Providence Catholic School, The College Preparatory School for
    Girls Grades 6-12, TX
Providence Country Day School, RI
Punahou School, HI
Queen Margaret's School, BC, Canada
Riverdale Country School, NY
The Rivers School, MA
Rockhurst High School, MO
Roland Park Country School, MD
Ross School, NY
Sacramento Country Day School, CA
Sacred Heart School of Halifax, NS, Canada
St. Agnes Academy, TX
St. Albans School, DC
St. Andrew's College, ON, Canada
St. Andrew's Episcopal School, MD
St. Andrew's School, RI
Saint Edward's School, FL
Saint Elizabeth High School, CA
St. Francis de Sales High School, OH
Saint Francis High School, CA
St. Francis High School, KY
Saint Gertrude High School, VA
St. Joseph High School, CT
Saint Joseph High School, IL
St. Joseph's Catholic School, SC
Saint Lawrence Academy, CA
St. Mark's School of Texas, TX
St. Martin's Episcopal School, LA
Saint Mary's Hall, TX
Saint Mary's High School, AZ
St. Mary's School, OR
St. Michael's College School, ON, Canada
St. Pius X High School, TX
St. Stephen's & St. Agnes School, VA
St. Stephen's Episcopal School, TX
Saint Teresa's Academy, MO
St. Thomas Aquinas High School, NH
St. Timothy's School, MD
Saint Ursula Academy, OH
Salem Academy, OR
San Domenico School, CA
Sandy Spring Friends School, MD
Scattergood Friends School, IA
Seattle Academy of Arts and Sciences, WA
The Seven Hills School, OH
Sewickley Academy, PA
The Sharon Academy, VT
Shattuck-St. Mary's School, MN
The Shipley School, PA
Smith School, NY
Southwestern Academy, AZ
Southwestern Academy, CA
The Storm King School, NY
The Study, QC, Canada
Subiaco Academy, AR
The Summit Country Day School, OH

Thomas Jefferson School, MO
Tilton School, NH
TMI - The Episcopal School of Texas, TX
Tower Hill School, DE
Trevor Day School, NY
Trinity Christian Academy, TN
Trinity College School, ON, Canada
Trinity High School, KY
Trinity Valley School, TX
University Liggett School, MI
University of Chicago Laboratory Schools, IL
University School of Jackson, TN
University School of Milwaukee, WI
University School of Nova Southeastern University, FL
Upper Canada College, ON, Canada
The Ursuline Academy of Dallas, TX
Valle Catholic High School, MO
Victor Valley Christian School, CA
Viewpoint School, CA
Villa Victoria Academy, NJ
Visitation Academy, MO
Waldorf High School of Massachusetts Bay, MA
Wasatch Academy, UT
Washington International School, DC
Waynflete School, ME
Webb School of Knoxville, TN
Wellsprings Friends School, OR
Wesleyan Academy, PR
Westbury Christian School, TX
Westchester Country Day School, NC
Westminster Christian School, FL
Westover School, CT
Westridge School, CA
Westview School, CA
The Wheeler School, RI
The White Mountain School, NH
Wilmington Christian School, DE
Wilmington Friends School, DE
Wilson Hall, SC
Windermere Preparatory School, FL
The Winston School San Antonio, TX
Woodlynde School, PA
The Woodward School, MA
Worcester Academy, MA
Xavier College Preparatory, AZ
York Preparatory School, NY

SCHOOLS REPORTING EXCHANGE PROGRAMS WITH OTHER U.S. SCHOOLS

Academy of the Sacred Heart, LA
The Athenian School, CA
Convent of the Sacred Heart, CT
Convent of the Sacred Heart, NY
Country Day School of the Sacred Heart, PA
Crystal Springs Uplands School, CA
Duchesne Academy of the Sacred Heart, TX
Germantown Friends School, PA
Josephinum Academy, IL
La Scuola D'Italia Guglielmo Marconi, NY
Providence Day School, NC
Sacred Heart School of Halifax, NS, Canada
St. Stephen's School, Rome, Italy
Trafalgar Castle School, ON, Canada

SCHOOLS REPORTING PROGRAMS FOR STUDY ABROAD

The Academy at Charlemont, MA
The Agnes Irwin School, PA
Albuquerque Academy, NM
Annie Wright School, WA
Ashley Hall, SC
The Athenian School, CA
Berkeley Carroll School, NY
Berkeley Preparatory School, FL
Berkshire School, MA
The Birch Wathen Lenox School, NY
Brooks School, MA
Brophy College Preparatory, AZ
The Bryn Mawr School for Girls, MD
Burr and Burton Academy, VT
The Canterbury School of Florida, FL
Cape Cod Academy, MA
Cape Fear Academy, NC
Catholic Central High School, WI
The Catlin Gabel School, OR
Chadwick School, CA
Charlotte Country Day School, NC
Charlotte Latin School, NC
Chase Collegiate School, CT
Chinese Christian Schools, CA
Collegiate School, NY
Commonwealth School, MA
The Community School of Naples, FL
Concord Academy, MA
Convent of the Sacred Heart, CT
Convent of the Sacred Heart, NY
Cotter Schools, MN
The Country Day School, ON, Canada
Country Day School of the Sacred Heart, PA
Crystal Springs Uplands School, CA
The Culver Academies, IN
Deerfield Academy, MA
Eastern Mennonite High School, VA
The Episcopal Academy, PA
Episcopal High School, VA
Falmouth Academy, MA
Flintridge Preparatory School, CA
Foxcroft School, VA
Gann Academy (The New Jewish High School of
    Greater Boston), MA
Georgetown Preparatory School, MD
Germantown Friends School, PA
The Grauer School, CA
Grier School, PA
The Gunnery, CT
The Harpeth Hall School, TN
Harvard-Westlake School, CA
Head-Royce School, CA
Hebrew Academy of the Five Towns & Rockaway, NY
Highland Hall Waldorf School, CA
High Mowing School, NH
The Hockaday School, TX
Hopkins School, CT
The Hudson School, NJ
International High School, CA
International School of Indiana, IN
Jean and Samuel Frankel Jewish Academy of Metropolitan
    Detroit, MI
Josephinum Academy, IL
Kimball Union Academy, NH
King's-Edgehill School, NS, Canada

Kingswood-Oxford School, CT
The Lab School of Washington, DC
La Jolla Country Day School, CA
Lakefield College School, ON, Canada
Lakehill Preparatory School, TX
Lake Mary Preparatory School, FL
Landon School, MD
La Scuola D'Italia Guglielmo Marconi, NY
The Latin School of Chicago, IL
Lawrence Academy, MA
The Lawrenceville School, NJ
Lee Academy, ME
Little Red School House and Elisabeth Irwin High School, NY
The Lovett School, GA
The Lowell Whiteman School, CO
Loyola School, NY
Luther College High School, SK, Canada
Lycee International de Los Angeles, CA
Madison Country Day School, WI
Maret School, DC
Marin Academy, CA
Marshall School, MN
Mary Institute and St. Louis Country Day School (MICDS), MO
The Masters School, NY
Matignon High School, MA
Mercersburg Academy, PA
Merchiston Castle School, United Kingdom
Millbrook School, NY
Miss Porter's School, CT
Montgomery Bell Academy, TN
Moorestown Friends School, NJ
Mount Paran Christian School, GA
National Cathedral School, DC
Newark Academy, NJ
Noble and Greenough School, MA
Norfolk Academy, VA
Northfield Mount Hermon School, MA
North Shore Country Day School, IL
Oregon Episcopal School, OR
Padua Franciscan High School, OH
Palo Alto Preparatory School, CA
The Park School of Baltimore, MD
The Park School of Buffalo, NY
The Pennington School, NJ
The Pingry School, NJ
Proctor Academy, NH
Providence Academy, MN
Providence Day School, NC
Punahou School, HI
Rabun Gap-Nacoochee School, GA
Randolph-Macon Academy, VA
Realms of Inquiry, UT
Regis High School, NY
Ridley College, ON, Canada
Riverdale Country School, NY
Riverstone International School, ID
Roland Park Country School, MD
Rosseau Lake College, ON, Canada
Sacred Heart School of Halifax, NS, Canada
St. Albans School, DC
St. Andrew's College, ON, Canada
St. Augustine High School, CA
Saint Augustine Preparatory School, NJ
Saint Edward's School, FL
St. Francis High School, KY
St. George's School, RI
St. John's Preparatory School, MA

Saint John's Preparatory School, MN
St. Joseph's Preparatory School, PA
St. Mark's School of Texas, TX
Saint Mary's Hall, TX
Saint Mary's High School, MD
St. Paul Academy and Summit School, MN
St. Paul Preparatory School, MN
St. Stephen's & St. Agnes School, VA
St. Stephen's Episcopal School, TX
Salem Academy, NC
Sandia Preparatory School, NM
Scattergood Friends School, IA
Seattle Academy of Arts and Sciences, WA
The Seven Hills School, OH
Sewickley Academy, PA
Shady Side Academy, PA
The Sharon Academy, VT
The Shipley School, PA
Sonoma Academy, CA
The Spence School, NY
Stevenson School, CA
Summerfield Waldorf School, CA
The Summit Country Day School, OH
The Taft School, CT
Tampa Preparatory School, FL
Telluride Mountain School, CO
The Thacher School, CA
Trevor Day School, NY
Trinity College School, ON, Canada
Trinity High School, KY
Trinity Preparatory School, FL
Trinity School of Texas, TX
University Liggett School, MI
Upper Canada College, ON, Canada
Viewpoint School, CA
Waldorf High School of Massachusetts Bay, MA
The Waldorf School of Garden City, NY
The Waldorf School of Saratoga Springs, NY
Waynflete School, ME
Webb School of Knoxville, TN
Westminster School, CT
Westover School, CT
Westtown School, PA
The Wheeler School, RI
The Williston Northampton School, MA
Wilmington Friends School, DE
Xavier College Preparatory, AZ
The York School, ON, Canada

SCHOOLS REPORTING SUMMER SESSIONS OPEN TO STUDENTS FROM OTHER SCHOOLS

Acacia Academy, IL — A,C,F,S
The Academy at Charlemont, MA — F,S
Academy at the Lakes, FL — A,C,F,S
Academy of Our Lady of Peace, CA — A
Academy of the Holy Cross, MD — A,C,F,S
Academy of the New Church Boys' School, PA — S
Academy of the New Church Girls' School, PA — S
The Agnes Irwin School, PA — A,C,F,S
Albuquerque Academy, NM — A,C,F,S
Allendale Columbia School, NY — A,C,F,S
Alma Heights Christian High School, CA — F,R,S
Alpha Omega Academy, IA — A
The American Boychoir School, NJ — A,F
American Community Schools of Athens, Greece — A,C,F,S

American Heritage School, FL — A
American Heritage School, FL — A,C,F
The American School of Madrid, Spain — A,C,F,S
Archbishop Curley High School, MD — A,C,F,S
Archbishop Mitty High School, CA — A,C,F,S
Army and Navy Academy, CA — A,C,F,R,S
Ashley Hall, SC — A,C,F,S
The Athenian School, CA — A,C,F,S
Athens Academy, GA — A,C
Augusta Christian School, GA — A
Augusta Preparatory Day School, GA — A,F,S
Bachman Academy, TN — A,F,S
Baldwin School of Puerto Rico, PR — A
Barnstable Academy, NJ — A
Battle Ground Academy, TN — A,C,F,S
The Beekman School, NY — A
The Benjamin School, FL — A,C,S
Berkeley Carroll School, NY — A,F,S
Besant Hill School, CA — A
Bishop Brady High School, NH — A,S
Bishop Denis J. O'Connell High School, VA — A,C,F,S
Bishop Eustace Preparatory School, NJ — A,S
Bishop Hendricken High School, RI — A,C,F,S
Bishop Ireton High School, VA — A,C,F
Bishop O'Dowd High School, CA — A,C
Bishop Stang High School, MA — A,C,F,S
Blanchet School, OR — A,S
Blueprint Education, AZ — A
The Bolles School, FL — A,C,F
Boylan Central Catholic High School, IL — A,F,R,S
Branksome Hall, ON, Canada — A
Brehm Preparatory School, IL — A,F
Brentwood School, CA — A,C,F,S
Bridges Academy, CA — A,C,F,S
Brookhaven Academy, MS — A,S
The Brook Hill School, TX — A,F,S
Brooks School, MA — A,C,S
Brophy College Preparatory, AZ — A,C,F,S
Brunswick School, CT — A
The Bryn Mawr School for Girls, MD — A,F,S
Calvert Hall College High School, MD — A,C,F,S
Campbell Hall (Episcopal), CA — A,C,F,S
Canterbury School, FL — A,F,S
The Canterbury School of Florida, FL — A,C,F,S
Cape Fear Academy, NC — A,C,F,S
Cape Henry Collegiate School, VA — A,C,F,S
Capistrano Valley Christian Schools, CA — A,F,S
Cardinal Gibbons High School, NC — F,S
Carlisle School, VA — A,C,F,S
Cascadilla School, NY — A,F
Cathedral High School, NY — A
Catholic Central High School, WI — S
The Catlin Gabel School, OR — A,C,F,S
Central Catholic High School, CA — A
Chadwick School, CA — C,F,S
Chaminade College Preparatory, CA — A,C,F,S
Charlotte Country Day School, NC — A,C,F,S
Charlotte Latin School, NC — A,C,F,S
Chase Collegiate School, CT — A,C,F,S
Chattanooga Christian School, TN — A,F,S
Children's Creative and Performing Arts Academy of San Diego, CA — A,C,F
Chinese Christian Schools, CA — A,S
Christ Church Episcopal School, SC — A,S
Christian Central Academy, NY — S
Chrysalis School, WA — A,C
Cistercian Preparatory School, TX — A,C,F,S

A — academic; C — computer instruction; F — art/fine arts; R — rigorous outdoor training; S — sports; O — other

Clarksville Academy, TN	A,C,F,S	Gilman School, MD	A,F,R,S
Clearwater Central Catholic High School, FL	A,C,S	Girard College, PA	A,C,F,S
Colegio San Jose, PR	A	Girls Preparatory School, TN	A,C,F,S
Columbia International College of Canada, ON, Canada	A,C,F,S	The Glenholme School, Devereux Connecticut, CT	A,C,F,S
The Columbus Academy, OH	A,C,F	Gonzaga College High School, DC	A
Columbus School for Girls, OH	A,C,F,R,S	The Governor French Academy, IL	A
The Community School of Naples, FL	A	Grace Baptist Academy, TN	A
Concordia Lutheran High School, IN	A,C,F,S	Grace Brethren School, CA	A
Convent of the Sacred Heart, NY	C,F,S	Grace Christian School, AK	A
Cotter Schools, MN	A,F,S	The Grand River Academy, OH	A,C,F,S
The Country Day School, ON, Canada	A,F,S	The Grauer School, CA	A,C,F,R,S
Crespi Carmelite High School, CA	A,F,S	Greenhill School, TX	A,C,F,S
Cretin-Derham Hall, MN	A,C,F,R,S	Greenhills School, MI	A,F,R,S
Crossroads School for Arts & Sciences, CA	A,C,F,S	Grier School, PA	A,F,S
The Culver Academies, IN	A,C,F,R,S	Guamani Private School, PR	A
Currey Ingram Academy, TN	A,F	Hampshire Country School, NH	O
Damien High School, CA	A,C,F,S	Hampton Roads Academy, VA	A,C,F,R,S
Davidson Academy, TN	A,F,S	Hanalani Schools, HI	A,C,F,S
De La Salle College, ON, Canada	A	Hank Haney International Junior Golf Academy, SC	A,F,S
DeLaSalle High School, MN	A	Hargrave Military Academy, VA	A,C,R,S
Delbarton School, NJ	A,C,S	The Harley School, NY	A,C,F,S
Delphi Academy of Los Angeles, CA	A,C,F,S	The Harpeth Hall School, TN	A,C,F,S
DeMatha Catholic High School, MD	A,C,F,S	Harvard-Westlake School, CA	A,C,F,R,S
Denver Academy, CO	A,C,F,R	Hawaii Baptist Academy, HI	A,C,F,S
DePaul Catholic High School, NJ	A,C,S	Hawai`i Preparatory Academy, HI	A
The Derryfield School, NH	A,F	Head-Royce School, CA	A
Detroit Country Day School, MI	A,C,F,S	The Heights School, MD	A,S
Dominican Academy, NY	A	Heritage Christian School, CA	A,C,S
The Donoho School, AL	A	Hillside School, MA	A
Duchesne Academy of the Sacred Heart, TX	A,C,F	The Hill Top Preparatory School, PA	A
Durham Academy, NC	A,C,F,S	Holy Cross High School, CT	F,S
Eaglebrook School, MA	A,C,F,R,S	Holy Trinity School, ON, Canada	A,S
Eaton Academy, GA	A,C,F,S	Hopkins School, CT	A,S
Edgewood Academy, AL	O	The Howard School, GA	A
Elgin Academy, IL	A,F,S	The Hudson School, NJ	F
Elizabeth Seton High School, MD	A,C,F,S	Humanex Academy, CO	A,F,S
The Ellis Academy, AL	A,C,F,S	The Hun School of Princeton, NJ	A,C,F,S
The Episcopal Academy, PA	A,C,F	Huntington-Surrey School, TX	A
Episcopal Collegiate School, AR	A,C,F,S	Immaculata-La Salle High School, FL	A
Episcopal High School, TX	A,F	Immaculate Heart High School and Middle School, CA	A,F,S
Episcopal High School, VA	A,F,S	Independent School, KS	A,C,F,S
Explorations Academy, WA	A,F,R	Institute of Notre Dame, MD	A,C,F,R,S
Fairfield College Preparatory School, CT	A,C,S	Institut Monte Rosa, Switzerland	A,S
Falmouth Academy, MA	A,F,S	International High School, CA	A
Father Ryan High School, TN	A,C,F,S	International School Bangkok, Thailand	A,F
Fayetteville Academy, NC	A,C,F,S	International School Manila, Philippines	A,S
Fay School, MA	A,C,F,S	International School of Indiana, IN	A,F,S
The First Academy, FL	A,F,S	Jesuit College Preparatory School, TX	A,C,F,S
First Presbyterian Day School, GA	A,F,S	Josephinum Academy, IL	A,C,F,S
Fishburne Military School, VA	A,S	Junipero Serra High School, CA	A,C,F,S
Flintridge Preparatory School, CA	A,C,F,R,S	Kent Denver School, CO	A,C,F,S
Foundation Academy, FL	A,F,S	Kent Place School, NJ	O
Fowlers Academy, PR	A	The Kew-Forest School, NY	A
Foxcroft School, VA	F,S	The Key School, MD	A,F,R,S
Franklin Road Academy, TN	A,C,F,S	Keystone School, TX	S
Fredericksburg Academy, VA	A	Kildonan School, NY	A,F
Friends Academy, NY	F	Kimball Union Academy, NH	A,F,S
Friends' Central School, PA	A	King Low Heywood Thomas, CT	A,F,S
Front Range Christian High School, CO	A,F,S	Kingsway College, ON, Canada	A
Fuqua School, VA	A,F,S	Kingswood-Oxford School, CT	A,F,S
The Galloway School, GA	A,F,S	La Jolla Country Day School, CA	A,C,F,S
Garrison Forest School, MD	F,S	Lakefield College School, ON, Canada	A
Gaston Day School, NC	A,C,F,S	Lakehill Preparatory School, TX	A,C,F,S
Gateway School, TX	A	Lake Mary Preparatory School, FL	A,C,F,R
Georgetown Day School, DC	A	Lancaster Mennonite High School, PA	A,F,S
Georgetown Preparatory School, MD	A,S	Landmark School, MA	A
Germantown Friends School, PA	A,C,F,S	Landon School, MD	A,F,S

A — academic; C — computer instruction; F — art/fine arts; R — rigorous outdoor training; S — sports; O — other

Lansdale Catholic High School, PA	A,F,S
The Latin School of Chicago, IL	A,C,F,R,S
The Laureate Academy, MB, Canada	A
Lee Academy, ME	A
The Leelanau School, MI	A
Linfield Christian School, CA	F
The Linsly School, WV	A,C
Lipscomb Academy, TN	A,F,S
Long Island Lutheran Middle and High School, NY	C,F,S
Louisville High School, CA	S
The Lovett School, GA	A
Loyola-Blakefield, MD	A,C,F,S
Lutheran High School of Hawaii, HI	A,C,F,S
Luther College High School, SK, Canada	A
The Madeira School, VA	A,F,S
Maine Central Institute, ME	A,F
Maplebrook School, NY	A,C,F,S
Maranatha High School, CA	A,F,S
Maret School, DC	A,F,S
Marian Catholic High School, PA	S
Marian Central Catholic High School, IL	A,S
Marin Academy, CA	F
Marist School, GA	A,F,S
Marshall School, MN	A,C,F,S
Mars Hill Bible School, AL	A,F,S
Mary Institute and St. Louis Country Day School (MICDS), MO	A,C,F,R,S
The Mary Louis Academy, NY	A,F,S
Marymount High School, CA	A,C,F,S
Matignon High School, MA	A
Maur Hill-Mount Academy, KS	A
McDonogh School, MD	A,C,F,S
The Meadows School, NV	A,F,S
Mercersburg Academy, PA	A,F,R,S
Merchiston Castle School, United Kingdom	A,S
Mercy High School College Preparatory, CA	A
Mesa Grande Seventh-Day Academy, CA	S
Mid-Pacific Institute, HI	A,C,F
Mid-Peninsula High School, CA	A,F
Missouri Military Academy, MO	A,R,S
Miss Porter's School, CT	A
Modesto Christian School, CA	A
Montgomery Bell Academy, TN	A,C,F,R,S
Montverde Academy, FL	A
Moorestown Friends School, NJ	A
Moravian Academy, PA	A,F,S
Mother McAuley High School, IL	A,C,F,S
Mount Michael Benedictine School, NE	S
Mount Saint Charles Academy, RI	F,S
Mount Vernon Presbyterian School, GA	A,F,S
MU High School, MO	A
National Cathedral School, DC	A,F,S
Nazareth Academy, IL	A,F,S
Nazareth Academy High School for Girls, PA	A,F,S
Newark Academy, NJ	A,C,F,S
Newton's Grove School, ON, Canada	A,C,F,S
Norfolk Academy, VA	A,F,S
The North Broward Preparatory Upper School, FL	A,C,F,S
Northfield Mount Hermon School, MA	A,F
Northwest Catholic High School, CT	S
Notre Dame Academy, CA	A,C,F,S
Notre Dame College Prep, IL	A,C,F,S
Notre Dame High School, CA	A
Oak Grove School, CA	A
Oakland School, VA	A,C,F,S
Oneida Baptist Institute, KY	A
Oregon Episcopal School, OR	A,C,F,S
Orinda Academy, CA	A
The Orme School, AZ	A
Our Lady of Mount Carmel High School, MD	A,S
Out-Of-Door-Academy, FL	A,F,S
Padua Franciscan High School, OH	A,C,F,S
Palma School, CA	A,F,S
Palo Alto Preparatory School, CA	A,R
Paradise Adventist Academy, CA	S
Parish Episcopal School, TX	A,C,F,S
The Park School of Buffalo, NY	A,F,S
The Pathway School, PA	A
The Phelps School, PA	S
Phoenix Christian Unified Schools, AZ	A,S
The Pingry School, NJ	A,S
Pope John XXIII Regional High School, NJ	A,S
Porter-Gaud School, SC	A
Portsmouth Christian Academy, NH	A,S
The Potomac School, VA	A,F,S
Poughkeepsie Day School, NY	F
Providence Academy, MN	A,F,S
Providence Catholic School, The College Preparatory School for Girls Grades 6-12, TX	A,C,F,S
Providence Day School, NC	A,C,F,S
Providence High School, CA	A,C,F,S
Queen Margaret's School, BC, Canada	A,S
Randolph-Macon Academy, VA	A,C,F
Ranney School, NJ	A,C,F,S
Ransom Everglades School, FL	A,C
Realms of Inquiry, UT	R
Regina Junior-Senior High School, IA	S
Riverstone International School, ID	A,F,R,S
Rockhurst High School, MO	A,C,F,S
Roland Park Country School, MD	A,F,S
Rolling Hills Preparatory School, CA	A,F
Rosseau Lake College, ON, Canada	A
Ross School, NY	A,F,S
Rowland Hall, UT	A,C,F,S
The Roxbury Latin School, MA	A,C,S
Royal Canadian College, BC, Canada	A
Sacred Heart School of Halifax, NS, Canada	A
Saddlebrook Preparatory School, FL	A,F,S
Sage Hill School, CA	A,F,S
St. Albans School, DC	A,C,F,R,S
St. Andrew's College, ON, Canada	A,F,S
St. Andrew's Episcopal School, MD	A,F,S
St. Andrew's School, RI	A,C,F,R,S
St. Augustine High School, CA	A,R,S
Saint Augustine Preparatory School, NJ	A,F,R,S
St. Catherine's Academy, CA	A,F,S
St. Croix Schools, MN	A,S
Saint Dominic Academy, ME	A,F,S
Saint Edward's School, FL	A,C,F,S
Saint Francis Girls High School, CA	A,F,S
Saint Francis High School, CA	A,S
Saint Francis High School, CA	A,C,F,S
St. Francis High School, KY	A,S
St. George's Independent School, TN	A,C,F,S
St. George's School, BC, Canada	A,C,F,S
St. John's Preparatory School, MA	A,C,F,S
Saint John's Preparatory School, MN	A,F
Saint Joseph High School, IL	A,S
St. Joseph's Catholic School, SC	F,S
St. Joseph's Preparatory School, PA	A,C,F,S
St. Martin's Episcopal School, LA	A,C,F,S
St. Mary's Episcopal School, TN	A,F,S
Saint Mary's Hall, TX	A,C,F,S
Saint Mary's High School, AZ	A,F,S

A — academic; C — computer instruction; F — art/fine arts; R — rigorous outdoor training; S — sports; O — other

St. Mary's School, OR — A,S
Saint Maur International School, Japan — A,C,F,S
St. Paul Academy and Summit School, MN — A
St. Paul Preparatory School, MN — A
St. Paul's High School, MB, Canada — S
St. Pius X Catholic High School, GA — A,F,S
St. Stanislaus College, MS — A
St. Stephen's & St. Agnes School, VA — A,C,F,S
St. Stephen's Episcopal School, TX — F,S
St. Stephen's School, Rome, Italy — A,F
Saint Teresa's Academy, MO — A,C,F,S
St. Thomas Aquinas High School, FL — A,C,F
Saint Thomas Aquinas High School, KS — A,C,S
St. Timothy's School, MD — A
Saint Ursula Academy, OH — A,C,F,S
Salpointe Catholic High School, AZ — A,C,S
Sandia Preparatory School, NM — A,C,F,S
San Diego Jewish Academy, CA — R,S
Sandy Spring Friends School, MD — A,F,S
Santa Catalina School, CA — A,F,S
Scottsdale Christian Academy, AZ — F,S
Seattle Academy of Arts and Sciences, WA — A,F,S
Seton Catholic High School, AZ — A,F,S
The Seven Hills School, OH — A
Sewickley Academy, PA — A,F,S
Shady Side Academy, PA — A,C,F,S
Shattuck-St. Mary's School, MN — A,F,S
Shawnigan Lake School, BC, Canada — S
Shelton School and Evaluation Center, TX — A
Smith School, NY — A,C
Southwestern Academy, AZ — A,F,R
Southwestern Academy, CA — A,C,F
Springside Chestnut Hill Academy, PA — A,C,F,S
Squaw Valley Academy, CA — A,F,S
Stevenson School, CA — A,F,S
The Summit Country Day School, OH — A,C,F,S
The Taft School, CT — A,F,S
Tampa Preparatory School, FL — A,C
Temple Grandin School, CO — O
The Tenney School, TX — A
Thornton Academy, ME — A,C,F,S
Tilton School, NH — A,C,F,S
Timothy Christian High School, IL — F,S
TMI - The Episcopal School of Texas, TX — A,S
Tower Hill School, DE — A,S
Trinity High School, OH — A,F,S
Trinity Preparatory School, FL — A,C,F,S
Trinity School of Texas, TX — A
Trinity Valley School, TX — A,C,F,R,S
Tyler Street Christian Academy, TX — O
University Liggett School, MI — A,S
University of Chicago Laboratory Schools, IL — A,S
University School of Jackson, TN — A,C,F,S
University School of Milwaukee, WI — A,C,F,S
University School of Nova Southeastern University, FL — A,F,S
Upper Canada College, ON, Canada — A,C,F
Valley Christian High School, CA — A,C,F,S
The Vanguard School, FL — A
Victor Valley Christian School, CA — A
Viewpoint School, CA — A,C,F,S
Villa Angela-St. Joseph High School, OH — A,F,S
Villa Joseph Marie High School, PA — A,F,S
Visitation Academy, MO — S
Wakefield School, VA — A,C,F,S
The Waldorf School of Garden City, NY — A
Walther Christian Academy, IL — A
Wasatch Academy, UT — A

Washington International School, DC — A
Watkinson School, CT — A
Waynflete School, ME — A,F,S
Webb School of Knoxville, TN — A,F,S
The Webb Schools, CA — A,C,F,S
Wellspring Foundation, CT — A
Wesleyan Academy, PR — A
Westbury Christian School, TX — A,F,S
Westchester Country Day School, NC — A,C,F,S
Westminster Christian School, FL — A,C
Westminster School, CT — A,S
West Sound Academy, WA — A
Westview School, CA — A,C,F,S
Wheaton Academy, IL — A,C,F,S
The Wheeler School, RI — A,F,S
Whitefield Academy, KY — A,F,S
The White Mountain School, NH — S
Whitfield School, MO — A,C,F,S
Wilbraham & Monson Academy, MA — A
William Penn Charter School, PA — A,F,S
Wilmington Christian School, DE — A
Windermere Preparatory School, FL — A,C,F,S
The Windsor School, NY — A
Winston Preparatory School, NY — A,F
The Winston School, TX — A,C,F,S
The Winston School San Antonio, TX — A,C,F,S
Woodward Academy, GA — A,C,F,S
Worcester Academy, MA — A

SCHOOLS REPORTING THAT THEY ACCOMMODATE UNDERACHIEVERS

Acacia Academy, IL
Bachman Academy, TN
Camphill Special School, PA
Denver Academy, CO
Fowlers Academy, PR
The Frostig School, CA
Gateway School, TX
The Glenholme School, Devereux Connecticut, CT
The Grand River Academy, OH
Hampshire Country School, NH
Humanex Academy, CO
The Judge Rotenberg Educational Center, MA
Little Keswick School, VA
Maplebrook School, NY
Marine Military Academy, TX
Mid-Peninsula High School, CA
Mooseheart High School, IL
Oakland School, VA
The Pathway School, PA
The Rectory School, CT
Temple Grandin School, CO
Valley View School, MA
The Vanguard School, FL
Wellsprings Friends School, OR
Westview School, CA
Winston Preparatory School, NY

SCHOOLS REPORTING PROGRAMS FOR STUDENTS WITH SPECIAL NEEDS

Remedial Reading and/or Writing

Academy of the New Church Boys' School, PA

Academy of the New Church Girls' School, PA
All Hallows High School, NY
American Community Schools of Athens, Greece
American Heritage School, FL
The American School Foundation, Mexico
Archbishop Curley High School, MD
Archbishop Hoban High School, OH
Bachman Academy, TN
Barnstable Academy, NJ
Bay Ridge Preparatory School, NY
The Beekman School, NY
Bishop O'Dowd High School, CA
Bishop Stang High School, MA
Blueprint Education, AZ
Boylan Central Catholic High School, IL
Brehm Preparatory School, IL
Burr and Burton Academy, VT
Butte Central Catholic High School, MT
Camphill Special School, PA
Cardigan Mountain School, NH
Cardinal Mooney Catholic High School, FL
Cardinal Newman High School, FL
Cascadilla School, NY
Catholic Central High School, NY
The Catholic High School of Baltimore, MD
Central Catholic High School, CA
Chaminade-Madonna College Preparatory, FL
Chattanooga Christian School, TN
Chelsea School, MD
Children's Creative and Performing Arts Academy of
    San Diego, CA
Chinese Christian Schools, CA
Christ Church Episcopal School, SC
Christopher Dock Mennonite High School, PA
Colegio Bolivar, Colombia
The Concept School, PA
Cotter Schools, MN
Covenant Canadian Reformed School, AB, Canada
Crawford Adventist Academy, ON, Canada
Cretin-Derham Hall, MN
Currey Ingram Academy, TN
Damien High School, CA
De La Salle North Catholic High School, OR
Delphi Academy of Los Angeles, CA
DeMatha Catholic High School, MD
Denver Academy, CO
DePaul Catholic High School, NJ
Dowling Catholic High School, IA
Eagle Hill School, CT
Eastern Mennonite High School, VA
Eaton Academy, GA
Fishburne Military School, VA
Foundation Academy, FL
Fresno Christian Schools, CA
Friends Academy, NY
Front Range Christian High School, CO
The Frostig School, CA
Fryeburg Academy, ME
Gateway School, TX
Girard College, PA
The Glenholme School, Devereux Connecticut, CT
The Grand River Academy, OH
Grier School, PA
Hampshire Country School, NH
Hanalani Schools, HI
Hargrave Military Academy, VA
Hebrew Academy, CA

Heritage Christian School, ON, Canada
Hillside School, MA
Ho'Ala School, HI
The Howard School, GA
The Hudson School, NJ
Humanex Academy, CO
Institute of Notre Dame, MD
International School Manila, Philippines
Jean and Samuel Frankel Jewish Academy of Metropolitan
    Detroit, MI
Josephinum Academy, IL
The Judge Rotenberg Educational Center, MA
Kildonan School, NY
Kings Christian School, CA
The Lab School of Washington, DC
Lancaster Mennonite High School, PA
Landmark School, MA
La Scuola D'Italia Guglielmo Marconi, NY
The Latin School of Chicago, IL
The Laureate Academy, MB, Canada
Lawrence School, OH
The Leelanau School, MI
Maharishi School of the Age of Enlightenment, IA
Maine Central Institute, ME
Manhattan Christian High School, MT
Maplebrook School, NY
Maranatha High School, CA
Maret School, DC
Marian Central Catholic High School, IL
Marine Military Academy, TX
Marshall School, MN
McGill-Toolen Catholic High School, AL
Mennonite Collegiate Institute, MB, Canada
Merchiston Castle School, United Kingdom
Mid-Peninsula High School, CA
Missouri Military Academy, MO
Modesto Christian School, CA
Mooseheart High School, IL
Mount Paran Christian School, GA
MU High School, MO
The Nora School, MD
Norman Howard School, NY
The North Broward Preparatory Upper School, FL
The Norwich Free Academy, CT
Notre Dame College Prep, IL
The Oakland School, PA
Oakland School, VA
Oneida Baptist Institute, KY
Padua Franciscan High School, OH
The Pathway School, PA
Pensacola Catholic High School, FL
The Phelps School, PA
Pioneer Valley Christian School, MA
Powers Catholic High School, MI
The Rectory School, CT
Redwood Christian Schools, CA
Rosseau Lake College, ON, Canada
Rumsey Hall School, CT
Saint Albert Junior-Senior High School, IA
St. Andrew's School, RI
St. Augustine High School, CA
St. Benedict at Auburndale, TN
St. Croix Schools, MN
Saint Elizabeth High School, CA
St. George's School, BC, Canada
St. George's School of Montreal, QC, Canada
Saint Joseph High School, IL

Saint Mary's High School, AZ
St. Paul Preparatory School, MN
St. Pius X High School, TX
St. Stanislaus College, MS
St. Thomas Aquinas High School, FL
Saint Thomas Aquinas High School, KS
Saint Thomas More Catholic High School, LA
Salpointe Catholic High School, AZ
San Marcos Baptist Academy, TX
Seattle Academy of Arts and Sciences, WA
Seisen International School, Japan
Shattuck-St. Mary's School, MN
Shawe Memorial Junior/Senior High School, IN
Shawnigan Lake School, BC, Canada
Shoreline Christian, WA
Smith School, NY
The Storm King School, NY
Summit Preparatory School, MT
Temple Grandin School, CO
The Tenney School, TX
Thornton Academy, ME
Timothy Christian High School, IL
Trinity High School, KY
Trinity-Pawling School, NY
University School of Nova Southeastern University, FL
Valle Catholic High School, MO
Valley View School, MA
The Vanguard School, FL
Venta Preparatory School, ON, Canada
Villa Angela-St. Joseph High School, OH
The Waldorf School of Saratoga Springs, NY
Walther Christian Academy, IL
Webb School of Knoxville, TN
Wellspring Foundation, CT
Wellsprings Friends School, OR
Westview School, CA
Wheaton Academy, IL
Wilmington Christian School, DE
The Windsor School, NY
Winston Preparatory School, NY
The Winston School, TX
The Winston School San Antonio, TX
Woodlynde School, PA
Yeshiva High School, IL

Remedial Math

Academy of the New Church Boys' School, PA
Academy of the New Church Girls' School, PA
All Hallows High School, NY
Alpha Omega Academy, IA
American Community Schools of Athens, Greece
American Heritage School, FL
Archbishop Curley High School, MD
Archbishop Hoban High School, OH
Bachman Academy, TN
Barnstable Academy, NJ
Bay Ridge Preparatory School, NY
The Beekman School, NY
Bishop Denis J. O'Connell High School, VA
Bishop O'Dowd High School, CA
Bishop Stang High School, MA
Blueprint Education, AZ
Boylan Central Catholic High School, IL
Brehm Preparatory School, IL
Burr and Burton Academy, VT
Butte Central Catholic High School, MT
Camphill Special School, PA

Cardigan Mountain School, NH
Cardinal Mooney Catholic High School, FL
Cardinal Newman High School, FL
Cascadilla School, NY
Catholic Central High School, NY
The Catholic High School of Baltimore, MD
Central Catholic High School, CA
Chaminade-Madonna College Preparatory, FL
Chattanooga Christian School, TN
Chelsea School, MD
Children's Creative and Performing Arts Academy of
    San Diego, CA
Christ Church Episcopal School, SC
Colegio Bolivar, Colombia
The Concept School, PA
Cotter Schools, MN
Covenant Canadian Reformed School, AB, Canada
Cretin-Derham Hall, MN
Damien High School, CA
De La Salle High School, CA
De La Salle North Catholic High School, OR
Delphi Academy of Los Angeles, CA
Denver Academy, CO
DePaul Catholic High School, NJ
Dowling Catholic High School, IA
Eagle Hill School, CT
Eastern Mennonite High School, VA
Eaton Academy, GA
Ezell-Harding Christian School, TN
Fishburne Military School, VA
Foundation Academy, FL
Fresno Christian Schools, CA
Friends Academy, NY
Front Range Christian High School, CO
The Frostig School, CA
Fryeburg Academy, ME
Gateway School, TX
Girard College, PA
The Glenholme School, Devereux Connecticut, CT
Grace Brethren School, CA
Grier School, PA
Hampshire Country School, NH
Hanalani Schools, HI
Hargrave Military Academy, VA
Hebrew Academy, CA
Heritage Christian School, ON, Canada
High Mowing School, NH
Hillside School, MA
Ho'Ala School, HI
The Howard School, GA
The Hudson School, NJ
Humanex Academy, CO
Institute of Notre Dame, MD
International School Manila, Philippines
Jean and Samuel Frankel Jewish Academy of Metropolitan
    Detroit, MI
Josephinum Academy, IL
The Judge Rotenberg Educational Center, MA
Kings Christian School, CA
The Lab School of Washington, DC
Lancaster Mennonite High School, PA
Landmark School, MA
La Scuola D'Italia Guglielmo Marconi, NY
The Latin School of Chicago, IL
The Laureate Academy, MB, Canada
Lawrence School, OH
The Leelanau School, MI

Little Keswick School, VA
Maharishi School of the Age of Enlightenment, IA
Maine Central Institute, ME
Manhattan Christian High School, MT
Maplebrook School, NY
Maranatha High School, CA
Maret School, DC
Marian Central Catholic High School, IL
Marine Military Academy, TX
Marshall School, MN
McGill-Toolen Catholic High School, AL
Mennonite Collegiate Institute, MB, Canada
Merchiston Castle School, United Kingdom
Mid-Peninsula High School, CA
Missouri Military Academy, MO
Modesto Christian School, CA
Mooseheart High School, IL
Mount Paran Christian School, GA
The Nora School, MD
Norman Howard School, NY
The North Broward Preparatory Upper School, FL
The Norwich Free Academy, CT
Notre Dame College Prep, IL
The Oakland School, PA
Oakland School, VA
Oneida Baptist Institute, KY
Padua Franciscan High School, OH
Paradise Adventist Academy, CA
The Pathway School, PA
Pensacola Catholic High School, FL
The Phelps School, PA
Pioneer Valley Christian School, MA
Powers Catholic High School, MI
The Rectory School, CT
Redwood Christian Schools, CA
Rosseau Lake College, ON, Canada
Saint Albert Junior-Senior High School, IA
Saint Anthony High School, IL
St. Augustine High School, CA
St. Benedict at Auburndale, TN
St. Croix Schools, MN
Saint Elizabeth High School, CA
St. George's School of Montreal, QC, Canada
Saint Joseph High School, IL
Saint Mary's High School, AZ
St. Paul Preparatory School, MN
St. Paul's High School, MB, Canada
St. Pius X High School, TX
St. Stanislaus College, MS
St. Thomas Aquinas High School, FL
Saint Thomas Aquinas High School, KS
Saint Thomas More Catholic High School, LA
Salpointe Catholic High School, AZ
San Marcos Baptist Academy, TX
Seattle Academy of Arts and Sciences, WA
Seisen International School, Japan
Shattuck-St. Mary's School, MN
Shawnigan Lake School, BC, Canada
Smith School, NY
Summit Preparatory School, MT
Sunshine Bible Academy, SD
Temple Grandin School, CO
The Tenney School, TX
Thornton Academy, ME
Trinity High School, KY
Trinity High School, OH
Valle Catholic High School, MO

Valley View School, MA
The Vanguard School, FL
Venta Preparatory School, ON, Canada
Villa Angela-St. Joseph High School, OH
The Waldorf School of Saratoga Springs, NY
Walther Christian Academy, IL
Webb School of Knoxville, TN
Wellspring Foundation, CT
Wellsprings Friends School, OR
Westtown School, PA
Westview School, CA
Wheaton Academy, IL
Wilmington Christian School, DE
The Windsor School, NY
Winston Preparatory School, NY
The Winston School, TX
Woodlynde School, PA
Yeshiva High School, IL

Deaf Students

Acacia Academy, IL
American Community Schools of Athens, Greece
American Heritage School, FL
The American School Foundation, Mexico
Bishop Hendricken High School, RI
Blanchet School, OR
Boylan Central Catholic High School, IL
Burr and Burton Academy, VT
Carmel High School, IL
The Catlin Gabel School, OR
Cretin-Derham Hall, MN
Denver Christian High School, CO
DePaul Catholic High School, NJ
Eaton Academy, GA
Foundation Academy, FL
Front Range Christian High School, CO
The Grauer School, CA
Humanex Academy, CO
International School Manila, Philippines
Jean and Samuel Frankel Jewish Academy of Metropolitan
    Detroit, MI
The Judge Rotenberg Educational Center, MA
Kansas City Academy, MO
Lancaster Mennonite High School, PA
Landmark School, MA
Lawrence Academy, MA
Marshall School, MN
Merchiston Castle School, United Kingdom
Norman Howard School, NY
Pensacola Catholic High School, FL
Saint Albert Junior-Senior High School, IA
St. Andrew's Episcopal School, MD
St. Andrew's School, RI
Saint Anthony High School, IL
Saint Joseph High School, IL
San Marcos Baptist Academy, TX
Shawe Memorial Junior/Senior High School, IN
Temple Grandin School, CO
The Tenney School, TX
Trinity High School, KY
University Liggett School, MI
The Vanguard School, FL
Walther Christian Academy, IL
Watkinson School, CT
Westover School, CT
The Williston Northampton School, MA

Blind Students

Acacia Academy, IL
American Community Schools of Athens, Greece
American Heritage School, FL
The American School Foundation, Mexico
Bishop Hendricken High School, RI
Boylan Central Catholic High School, IL
Burr and Burton Academy, VT
Carmel High School, IL
Cretin-Derham Hall, MN
DePaul Catholic High School, NJ
Dowling Catholic High School, IA
Front Range Christian High School, CO
Greenhills School, MI
Humanex Academy, CO

Jean and Samuel Frankel Jewish Academy of Metropolitan Detroit, MI
The Judge Rotenberg Educational Center, MA
Kansas City Academy, MO
Lancaster Mennonite High School, PA
Lawrence Academy, MA
Mennonite Collegiate Institute, MB, Canada
Merchiston Castle School, United Kingdom
MMI Preparatory School, PA
Pensacola Catholic High School, FL
St. Andrew's School, RI
St. Augustine High School, CA
Saint Joseph High School, IL
Trinity High School, KY
The Vanguard School, FL
Walther Christian Academy, IL

Index

Alphabetical Listing of Schools

In the index that follows, page numbers for school profiles are shown in regular type, page numbers for Close-Ups are shown in **boldface** type, and page numbers for Displays are shown in *italics*.

NOTES

NOTES

NOTES

NOTES

NOTES

NOTES

NOTES

NOTES